Text
Orig. Und.
Structure
Historical Practice
Tradition
Moral
Consequential
Preceden (S Ct.)

CONSTITUTIONAL LAW

THIRTEENTH EDITION

by

GERALD GUNTHER
William Nelson Cromwell Professor of Law Emeritus,
Stanford University

KATHLEEN M. SULLIVAN
Stanley Morrison Professor of Law,
Stanford University

WESTBURY, NEW YORK
THE FOUNDATION PRESS, INC.
1997

COPYRIGHT © 1937,1941, 1946, 1950, 1954, 1959, 1965, 1970, 1975,
1980, 1985, 1991 THE FOUNDATION PRESS, INC.
COPYRIGHT © 1997 By THE FOUNDATION PRESS, INC.

> 615 Merrick Ave.
> Westbury, N.Y. 11590–6607
> (516) 832–6950

Library of Congress Cataloging-in-Publication Data
Gunther, Gerald, 1927–
    Constitutional law / by Gerald Gunther, Kathleen Sullivan. — 13th
ed.
      p.   cm. — (University casebook series)
    Includes index.
    ISBN 1–56662–453–3 (hardcover)
    1. Constitutional law—United States—Cases. I. Sullivan,
Kathleen, 1955–   . II. Title. III. Series.
KF4549.G85 1997
342.73—dc21   97–9362

To our families

*

PREFACE TO THE THIRTEENTH EDITION

This book is a major revision of the prior edition. The structure of the book remains largely unchanged; the substantial rethinking and rewriting are reflected in the contents of the chapters. We have modified the overall structure in only one respect: chapter 15, on the proper conditions for constitutional adjudication, has been folded into earlier chapters—mainly into chapter 1, on the judicial function in constitutional cases, and partly into chapter 9, on equal protection. The move of most of old chapter 15 into chapter 1 was prompted by the impossibility of teaching about the federal judicial power without touching on such questions as the scope of standing to sue and the political question doctrine. The move of the final section of old chapter 15 into chapter 9 was prompted by the growing significance of the concept of vote dilution: Reynolds v. Sims and its progeny—formerly in chapter 15—originated that concept and therefore provide essential background for the consideration of the vote dilution and racial gerrymandering cases in the equal protection chapter.

In revising this book, our primary aim has been to preserve the comprehensive scope, professional focus and sensitive editing that marked its predecessors. As in the past, this edition emphasizes constitutional law as a species of *law*, not mainly as a philosophical inquiry. This feature, we believe, will assure that the book will remain the best teaching tool to provide students with the skills needed for advocacy.

This edition seeks to preserve the strengths of its ancestors, from the earliest editions, launched by Noel T. Dowling in 1937, to the major reshapings in the 1960s by Gerald Gunther, with the advice of Herbert Wechsler. We owe a considerable debt to our predecessors. Constitutional law has of course seen dramatic changes since the 1930s—ever more so in recent years, with the large number of new Justices and the significant changes in doctrine.

Writing a constitutional law book of manageable size has been a challenge more formidable than ever. We are gratified that we have been able to produce a book that is over 100 pages shorter than the previous edition. We have done so even though we had had to include the important recent developments in the most recent, more-than-500 page 1996 Supplement; and we have done so without compromising our standards of careful editing.[1] We have refused to permit editing of cases to degenerate into a potpourri of

[1] This book covers decisions through the 1995-96 Supreme Court Term. Decisions after the close of that Term will be included in a supplement to be published in the summer of 1997 and in annual supplements thereafter.

skeletal segments of opinions. And as in the past, we have sought to compile the kind of volume we would most enjoy using in class.[2]

Acknowledgments. We have benefited greatly from the suggestions (and criticisms) we received from the many users—law school and college students as well as teachers—of this book. Our special thanks to Dan T. Coenen, Murray Dry, Kenneth L. Karst, Michael L. Smith, and James Weinstein for their careful comments.

Deepest thanks go to those whose help and devotion in recent months was essential to the timely completion of this book: our superb Stanford assistants, Pat Sheeler and Arline Wyler, and our research assistants, Lydia Fillingham, Liza Weiman Hanks, Elizabeth K. MacDonald, Erin Sawyer, Matthew Shors, and Jay Wexler. Our thanks, too, to Frederick Schauer, whose Supplements over nearly two decades kept the earlier editions up-to-date and provided stimulation to us.

Gerald Gunther
Kathleen M. Sullivan

———

The preparation of this edition carries a special significance for me. After more than four decades of law school teaching, this edition is my first venture into co-authorship. After a professional lifetime of solo writing, I genuinely feared the risks of the differences and disagreements that I thought were inevitable in collaborations and that too often reduce the substance of a book to its lowest common denominator. Kathleen Sullivan's agreement to join this enterprise assured that these fears would not materialize. In my view, this collaboration was truly made in heaven. We see eye-to-eye on the basic issues and on the desirable shape and content of a teaching book in constitutional law. We have collaborated productively and in complete harmony. Kathleen's well-known analytical skills have enhanced the content in numerous respects; and her gift for lucid, concise expression are in large part accountable for the reduced length of this book. Future editions and supplements will be in her enormously capable hands. Had I had access to Aladdin's lamp, I could not have wished for a better co-author or a more talented guardian of the future of this book.

Gerald Gunther

———

Few books change one's life, but this one did mine. I first studied constitutional law at Harvard Law School in a superb class taught by Laurence H. Tribe from the Ninth Edition of Gerald Gunther's casebook. Little did I imagine then that I would be fortunate enough to have a career practicing, teaching and writing about constitutional law, or to have each of these remarkable men as colleagues. Still less did I imagine that I would one day become co-author of this casebook. Gerry's invitation to me to work with

[2] In the editing of the materials, deletions are indicated by the use of brackets rather than ellipses. Most footnotes in opinions have been omitted; those retained have been renumbered consecutively.

him was an extraordinary professional honor; collaborating with him on this edition has been an extraordinary professional pleasure. I am deeply grateful to him for both, and for the wise and architectonic sense of constitutional law he has given me, beginning long before we ever met.

KATHLEEN M. SULLIVAN

Stanford, California
May, 1997

*

SUMMARY OF CONTENTS

PREFACE TO THE THIRTEENTH EDITION --- v

TABLE OF CASES --- lix

TABLE OF AUTHORITIES -- lxxiii

PART I. THE JUDICIAL FUNCTION IN CONSTITUTIONAL CASES --- 1

CHAPTER 1. The Nature and Sources of the Supreme Court's Authority --- 2

Section

1. Judicial Review: The Bases and Implications of Marbury v. Madison   3
2. Constitutional and Prudential Limits on Constitutional Adjudication -- 27
3. Supreme Court Authority to Review State Court Judgments ---------- 60
4. Political Restraints on the Supreme Court: May Congress Strip the Court of Its Jurisdiction? --- 74

PART II. THE STRUCTURE OF GOVERNMENT: NATION AND STATES IN THE FEDERAL SYSTEMS ----------------------- 87

CHAPTER 2. National Powers and Local Activities: Origins and Recurrent Themes --- 88

CHAPTER 3. The Commerce Power -------------------------------------- 141

Section

1. Introduction --- 141
2. The Development of Commerce Power Doctrine From 1824 to 1936 159
3. The Decline of Limits on the Commerce Power: The Era Beginning in 1937 --- 185
4. External Limits on the Commerce Power: The State Autonomy and Sovereignty Concerns Reflected in the Tenth and Eleventh Amendments --- 206

CHAPTER 4 Federalism-Based Restraints on Other National Powers in the 1787 Constitution -------------------------------- 228

Section

1. The Taxing Power as a Regulatory Tool ----------------------------- 229
2. The Spending Power as a Regulatory Device ----------------------------- 235
3. War, Foreign Affairs, and Federalism -------------------------------- 249

CHAPTER 5.   Federal Limits on State Power to Regulate the National Economy -- 258

Section
1. State Regulation and the Dormant Commerce Clause-------------------- 259
2. The Privileges and Immunities Clause of Article IV ---------------------- 328
3. Congressional Ordering of Federal-State Relationships By Preemption and Consent --- 337
4. Some Other Aspects of Federalism: A Brief Survey ---------------------- 350

CHAPTER 6.   Separation of Powers--- 354

Section
1. The Authority to Make National Policy: The Conflict Between Executive Authority and Legislative Powers------------------------------- 355
2. Separation of Powers: Congressional Encroachments on the Executive's Domain--- 375
3. Executive Privilege and Immunities --------------------------------------- 404

PART III.   INDIVIDUAL RIGHTS --------------------------------------- 415

CHAPTER 7.   The Bill of Rights and the Post-Civil War Amendments: "Fundamental" Procedural Rights and the "Incorporation" Dispute --------------------------------------- 417

Section
1. The Pre-Civil War Situation --- 418
2. The Purpose and Impact of the Post-Civil War Amendments---------- 420
3. The Meaning of Due Process: Criminal Procedure and the "Incorporation" Controversy--- 432

CHAPTER 8.   Substantive Due Process: Rise, Decline, Revival --- 453

Section
1. Substantive Due Process and Economic Regulation: The Rise and
2. Other Constitutional Safeguards of Economic Rights: The "Taking-Regulation" Distinction; The Contracts Clause ------------------------- 486
3. The Revival of Substantive Due Process, for Noneconomic Rights: Privacy; Autonomy; Family Relations; Sexuality; The Right to Die 516
4. The Scope of "Liberty" and "Property": The Right To Hearing Cases --- 615

CHAPTER 9.   Equal Protection--- 628

Section
1. An Overview --- 628
2. Scrutiny of Means in Economic Regulations: The Rationality Requirement --- 635
3. Suspect Classifications and the Problems of Forbidden Discrimination --- 662
4. The "Fundamental Interests" Strand of Equal Protection Strict Scrutiny --- 840

CHAPTER 10. The Post-Civil War Amendments and Civil Rights Legislation: Constitutional Restraints on Private Conduct; Congressional Power to Implement the Amendment ---- 917

Section
1. The Statutory Framework ---- 919
2. The Problem of State Action ---- 921
3. Congressional Power to Reach Private Interferences with Constitutional Rights: Modern Scope and Problems ---- 962
4. Congressional Power to Change the Content of Constitutional Rights?—"Remedial" and "Substantive" Power Under § 5 of the 14th Amendment ---- 984

CHAPTER 11. Freedom of Speech—Why Government Restricts Speech—Unprotected and Less Protected Expression -1022

Section
1. Free Speech: An Overview ----1022
2. Incitement ----1034
3. Fighting Words and Hostile Audiences----1076
4. Injury to Reputation and Sensibility----1091
5. Sexually Explicit Expression ----1125
6. Commercial Speech----1175

CHAPTER 12. Freedom of Speech—How Government Restricts Speech—Modes of Abridgment and Standards of Review ----1203

Section
1. The Distinction Between Content-Based and Content-Neutral Regulations----1203
2. Government's Power to Limit Speech in Its Capacity as Proprietor, Educator, Employer and Patron----1234
3. Impermissible Forms of Speech-Restrictive Law: Overbreadth, Vagueness and Prior Restraint ----1325

CHAPTER 13. Rights Ancillary to Freedom of Speech ----1361

Section
1. Compelled Speech: The Right *Not* to Speak ----1361
2. Freedom of Association----1374
3. Money and Political Campaigns ----1400
4. Freedom of the Press ----1420

CHAPTER 14. The Religion Clauses: Free Exercise and Establishment ----1461

Section
1. An Overview of the Religion Clauses----1462
2. The Free Exercise of Religion ----1471
3. The Establishment Clause ----1500

APPENDICES

App.
A. The Constitution of the United States --- A–1
B. Table of Justices --- B–1

INDEX --- I–1

TABLE OF CONTENTS

PREFACE TO THE THIRTEENTH EDITION --- v

TABLE OF CASES -- lix

TABLE OF AUTHORITIES --- lxxiii

PART I. THE JUDICIAL FUNCTION IN CONSTITUTIONAL CASES --- 1

CHAPTER 1. The Nature and Sources of the Supreme Court's Authority --- 2

Introduction --- 2

Section

1. Judicial Review: The Bases and Implications of Marbury v. Madison --- 3

Marbury v. Madison --- 3

The Historical Setting of the Marbury Case ----------------------------- 11

The political environment: Judicial "reform"; Impeachment --------- 11

Were there alternative grounds of decision? ------------------------ 12

The Legitimacy of Judicial Review ------------------------------------- 13

Introduction --- 13

Historical anteccdents-- 14

The Constitutional Convention------------------------------------ 15

The Federalist Papers -- 16

The Hand-Wechsler debate --------------------------------------- 17

Judicial review and democracy ----------------------------------- 18

Judicial review abroad-- 19

The Authoritativeness of Supreme Court Decisions: Binding on All Public Officials? --- 20

Introduction --- 20

Thomas Jefferson --- 20

Andrew Jackson --- 21

Abraham Lincoln-- 22

Franklin D. Roosevelt -- 22

The autonomy of the coordinate branches ----------------------- 23

Some comments on the presidential statements ------------------ 23

Legitimate disagreement and improper defiance ----------------- 24

Is the Court "the ultimate interpreter of the Constitution"?—Some modern assertions--- 25

Cooper v. Aaron --- 25

The legal consequences of judicial "invalidation"-------------------- 26

2. Constitutional and Prudential Limits on Constitutional Adjudication-- 27

Introduction --- 27

Section

2. **Constitutional and Prudential Limits on Constitutional Adjudication**—Continued

Advisory opinions -- 28

Rescue Army v. Municipal Court of Los Angeles -------------------- 28

Standing To Litigate --- 30

The requisite personal interest -- 30

Standing to sue in traditional contexts-------------------------------------- 30

Warth v. Seldin--- 30

Allen v. Wright -- 36

Standing in "public actions": Suits by federal taxpayers and citizens; congressional power to confer standing------------------ 37

Lujan v. Defenders of Wildlife -------------------------------------- 38

Additional barriers to adjudication: Questions of timing—Mootness and lack of ripeness of the issues --------------------------- 43

Mootness --- 44

Ripeness --- 44

The Nonjusticiability of Political Questions--------------------------------- 45

Introduction --- 45

The situation before Baker v. Carr-- 46

Baker v. Carr--- 47

Some efforts to invoke the political question doctrine since Baker v. Carr --- 53

Powell v. McCormack--- 53

Goldwater v. Carter --- 53

Nixon v. United States -- 54

3. **Supreme Court Authority to Review State Court Judgments** -- 60

Martin v. Hunter's Lessee --- 60

The background of the Martin litigation ------------------------------- 61

The contending positions in Martin------------------------------------- 62

Cohens v. Virginia: Supreme Court review of state criminal cases 63

State challenges to Supreme Court authority—19th century variants and 20th century emulations --------------------------- 64

Modern Court Jurisdiction and Practice ------------------------------------- 65

Introduction --- 65

The modern statutory framework—The growth and triumph of discretionary review -- 66

The 1988 reforms-- 66

Assuring supremacy and uniformity----------------------------------- 67

The exercise of the Court's discretionary jurisdiction --------------- 68

The certiorari petition --- 68

The Court's workload -- 69

The "adequate and independent state grounds" barrier to Supreme Court review of state court decisions -------------------- 69

State substantive law--- 70

Michigan v. Long --- 71

State procedural law--- 73

Section

4. **Political Restraints on the Supreme Court: May Congress Strip the Court of Its Jurisdiction?** ---------------------------------- 74
   Introduction --- 74
   Ex parte McCardle-- 76
   The scope of the jurisdiction-stripping power of Congress-------------- 77
   McCardle --- 78
   The vitality of McCardle and the Klein case--------------------------- 79
   United States v. Klein --- 79
   Plaut v. Spendthrift Farm, Inc. ----------------------------------- 80
   The search for constitutional limits on congressional power over
   appellate jurisdiction --- 81
   "Internal" restraints: Limits on congressional power arguably
   inherent in Art. III itself--- 81
   "External" restraints: Restraints drawn from constitutional
   sources other than Art. III --- 82
   Practical considerations --- 83
   Congressional control of appellate jurisdiction: Modern efforts-- 83
   The Jenner-Butler attack --- 83
   The 1968 crime control bill --- 84
   The Helms Amendment and other modern efforts to curb ap-
   pellate jurisdiction --- 84
   Congressional control of lower federal court jurisdiction: Argu-
   able modern limitations?--- 84

PART II. THE STRUCTURE OF GOVERNMENT: NATION AND STATES IN THE FEDERAL SYSTEMS ----------------------- 87

   Introduction --- 87

CHAPTER 2. National Powers and Local Activities: Origins and Recurrent Themes--- 88

   Introduction: Federalism—Antiquarian Relic? Contemporary Value? 88
   McCulloch v. Maryland -- 89
   Implied National Powers and the Necessary and Proper Clause—
   The Historical Context--- 98
   Introduction --- 98
   The allocation of powers in the Articles of Confederation and the
   Constitution --- 99
   The Confederation --- 99
   The Constitutional Convention -- 100
   The Jefferson-Hamilton debate on the Bank in 1791--------------- 100
   Broad and narrow construction: The Jeffersonian positions and
   the 1805 Marshall reply -- 101
   National powers after the War of 1812---------------------------------- 102
   The Bank controversy --- 104
   The constitutional contentions and John Marshall's pseudony-
   mous defense--- 105
   The national bank—A "private" or "public" institution? ---------- 106
   Congressional Power, the Judicial Function, and Political Restraints 107

Restraints on congressional power: Some general questions about judicially-imposed limits ------------------------------------- 107

Necessary and proper means to achieve enumerated ends: Judicial scrutiny of means-ends relationships ------------------- 107

"Pretext": Judicial inquiry into congressional purposes and abuses of power --- 108

Some additional questions on the Marshall opinion in McCulloch: Methods of constitutional interpretation------------------------ 109

Restraints on congressional power: The Political Safeguards of Federalism --- 110

Wechsler-- 110

Choper --- 112

The Term Limits Case and the Modern Antifederalist Revival ------- 113

U.S. Term Limits, Inc. v. Thornton ----------------------------------- 115

Possible implications of the Term Limits dissent--------------------- 139

CHAPTER 3.   The Commerce Power ------------------------------------- 141

Section

1. **Introduction**--- 141

United States v. Lopez --- 142

2. **The Development of Commerce Power Doctrine from 1824 to 1936**-- 159

Gibbons v. Ogden -- 159

Early commerce power legislation -- 162

Emerging doctrinal difficulties—a transitional note: Regulation of national economic problems vs. regulation of "police" problems 162

Regulating intrastate activities because of their relationship to interstate commerce --- 162

"Police" regulations—morality, crime, and the commerce power 162

Justifying national regulation of local activities on the basis of their relationship to interstate commerce: The requisite "local" –"interstate" connection—Knight and Shreveport as sources of contending approaches-- 163

The Knight approach and its sources --------------------------------- 164

United States v. E.C. Knight Co. ------------------------------------- 164

The limited impact of Knight on antitrust enforcement------------ 165

The Shreveport Rate case and the origins of the "substantial economic effects" approach -- 166

The Shreveport Rate case -- 166

Houston E. & W. Texas Ry. Co. v. United States (The Shreveport Rate Case) --- 166

Other examples of local railroad matters with an adequate impact on interstate commerce --------------------------------------- 167

The "stream of commerce" theory----------------------------------- 168

Stafford v. Wallace -- 169

National "police" regulation: Prohibition of interstate commerce as a tool-- 169

Champion v. Ames [The Lottery Case]---------------------------------- 169

The ghost of Marshall -- 171

Section
2. **The Development of Commerce Power Doctrine from 1824 to 1936**—Continued
The impact on Congress --- 171
Exclusion of allegedly "harmful" goods and persons --- 172
Impure foods --- 172
Hipolite Egg Co. v. United States --- 172
The Mann Act --- 172
Hoke v. United States --- 172
Caminetti v. United States --- 173
Hammer v. Dagenhart [The Child Labor Case] --- 173
Effective limits on the commerce power and the Holmes dissent --- 175
The Court threatens the New Deal --- 176
Introduction --- 176
Railroad Retirement Board v. Alton Railroad Co. --- 177
The Schechter case and its aftermath --- 178
The Carter case --- 180
Carter v. Carter Coal Co. --- 180
FDR's Court-packing Plan: Background and fate --- 183
The President's Message to Congress, Feb. 5, 1937 --- 183
The proposed bill --- 183
Letter of Chief Justice Charles Evans Hughes to Senator Burton K. Wheeler, March 21, 1937 --- 184
Radio Address by President Roosevelt, March 9, 1937 --- 184
Conclusion of Adverse Report of Senate Judiciary Committee, June 14, 1937 --- 184
The impact of the plan --- 184
3. **The Decline of Limits on the Commerce Power: The Era Beginning in 1937** --- 185
NLRB v. Jones & Laughlin Steel Corp. --- 185
Transitional Note --- 188
Wickard v. Filburn --- 189
The scope of the Wickard rationale --- 191
United States v. Darby --- 191
The commerce power in the post-Darby years --- 195
The commerce-prohibiting technique as a regulatory tool after Darby --- 195
Imposing the prohibition sanction at the state border --- 195
The commerce-prohibiting technique as the basis for direct sanctions on intrastate activities: The superbootstrap suggestion of Darby --- 195
The commerce power and crime --- 196
Perez v. United States --- 196
The implications of Perez --- 197
The "implications of the federal system" as a restraint on statutory interpretation --- 198
United States v. Bass --- 198
The "affecting commerce" rationale at the end of the Wickard v. Filburn era --- 198

Section

3. **The Decline of Limits on the Commerce Power: The Era Beginning in 1937**—Continued

Congressional reliance on the "affecting commerce" rationale and the role of congressional findings ---------------------------- 198

Potential limits on the commerce power in pre-1990s cases: "Trivial" economic impacts? --------------------------------------- 199

Maryland v. Wirtz -- 199

Hodel v. Virginia Surface Min. & Recl. Ass'n --------------------- 200

Using the commerce power for social ends: The ban on discrimination in public accommodations in the Civil Rights Act of 1964- 201

Heart of Atlanta Motel v. United States --------------------------- 203

Katzenbach v. McClung --- 203

4. **External Limits on the Commerce Power: The State Autonomy and Sovereignty Concerns Reflected in the Tenth and Eleventh Amendments** ------------------------------------- 206

The Tenth Amendment limit on congressional authority -------------- 207

United States v. California --------------------------------------- 207

Maryland v. Wirtz -- 207

Fry v. United States --- 207

National League of Cities v. Usery -------------------------------- 207

Hodel v. Virginia Surface Min. & Recl. --------------------------- 208

United Transportation Union v. Long Island Railroad Co. ----------- 208

EEOC v. Wyoming --- 208

Garcia v. San Antonio Metropolitan Transit Authority ------------- 209

The protection of state autonomy after Garcia --------------------- 211

South Carolina v. Baker --- 212

New York v. United States --------------------------------------- 212

Some comments and questions on New York v. United States -------- 224

The Eleventh Amendment as a protector of state sovereignty and a curb on congressional powers------------------------------------- 225

Seminole Tribe of Florida v. Florida ----------------------------- 225

CHAPTER 4. Federalism-Based Restraints on Other National Powers in the 1787 Constitution ------------------------------- 228

Scope Note --- 228

Section

1. **The Taxing Power as a Regulatory Tool** ------------------------- 229

Introduction --- 229

Child Labor Tax Case [Bailey v. Drexel Furniture Co.] ------------ 229

The scope of the taxing power: Doctrinal developments-------------- 231

The prior decisions -- 231

Early 20th century commerce and tax cases: Parallels and contrasts --- 231

From the Child Labor Tax Case to Kahriger ---------------------- 232

United States v. Kahriger --------------------------------------- 232

The taxing and commerce powers: Modern parallels and contrasts - 234

Divergent paths -- 234

Judicial competence to ascertain primary congressional purposes 234

Section

2 . The Spending Power as a Regulatory Device ---------------------- 235
  Introduction -- 235
  United States v. Butler --- 235
  Conditional spending: The Butler case and its aftermath-------------- 240
    The majority opinion-- 240
    The dissent--- 240
  The 1937 Social Security cases -- 241
  Charles C. Steward Machine Co. v. Davis------------------------------- 241
  Helvering v. Davis -- 243
  Conditional federal grants to states: Some modern problems --------- 243
    The practical dimensions of federal grants to states---------------- 243
  State autonomy as a limit on conditional spending?---------------------- 244
  South Dakota v. Dole --- 244
  Any modern constitutional restraints on conditional spending?------ 249

3. War, Foreign Affairs, and Federalism ------------------------------- 249
  Introduction -- 249
  A. The War Power -- 250
    Woods v. Cloyd W. Miller Co. --- 250
    Domestic regulation through the war power -------------------------- 252
  B. Treaties, Foreign Affairs, and Federalism------------------------- 252
    Introduction -- 252
    Missouri v. Holland -- 252
    The scope and limits of the treaty power ------------------------------ 254
      The supremacy of treaties over state law --------------------------- 254
      Limits on the treaty power?—The subject-matter of treaties-- 254
      The Bricker Amendment controversy-------------------------------- 254
    The reassurance of Reid v. Covert-- 255
      Reid v. Covert -- 255
    The foreign affairs power of Congress--------------------------------- 256

**CHAPTER 5. Federal Limits on State Power to Regulate the
  National Economy**-- 258

  Introduction -- 258

Section
1. State Regulation and the Dormant Commerce Clause --------- 259
  Introduction -- 259
    The sources of the "dormant" commerce clause --------------------- 259
    The constitutional history-- 259
    The values served by the "dormant" commerce clause ------------- 260
  A. Early Developments--- 261
    The Marshall Court --- 261
    Gibbons v. Ogden --- 261
    Willson v. Black Bird Creek Marsh Co. ------------------------------ 263
    From Marshall to the Early Taney Court ------------------------------ 264
      The Marshall legacy and the "commerce"–"police" distinction 264
      The early Taney Court--- 264
    Cooley v. Board of Wardens--- 265
    The Aftermath of Cooley -- 267

Section

1. State Regulation and the Dormant Commerce Clause— Continued

Cooley's "national"–"local" distinction ------------------------- 267

The effect of congressional consent ----------------------------- 268

Applications of Cooley --- 268

The rise and decline of the "direct"–"indirect" distinction ----- 268

Di Santo v. Pennsylvania ------------------------------------- 269

The licensing cases -- 269

Buck v. Kuykendall --- 269

Bradley v. Public Utilities Comm'n --------------------------- 269

B. The Modern Court's Approach ----------------------------- 270

Introduction --- 270

Pike v. Bruce Church, Inc. ----------------------------------- 270

Facial Discrimination Against Out-of-State Commerce ------------ 271

Facial Discrimination By States -------------------------------- 271

Introduction --- 271

Philadelphia v. New Jersey ----------------------------------- 271

The harm of interstate discrimination -------------------------- 274

Protectionist purpose -- 274

Social welfare --- 275

Representation reinforcement ----------------------------------- 275

Overcoming the presumption against facial discrimination ---- 276

Facially discriminatory taxes and fees ------------------------- 277

Chemical Waste Management, Inc. v. Hunt ---------------------- 277

Oregon Waste Systems, Inc. v. Department of Environmental Quality -- 277

West Lynn Creamery, Inc. v. Healy ---------------------------- 278

Home processing requirements ----------------------------------- 279

Foster-Fountain Packing Co. v. Haydel ------------------------ 280

Other facially discriminatory state laws ----------------------- 280

Facial Discrimination By Localities ---------------------------- 281

Dean Milk Co. v. Madison ------------------------------------- 281

Interstate and intrastate discrimination ----------------------- 283

Judicial inquiry into "reasonable nondiscriminatory alternatives" -- 283

Other examples of invalid local discrimination against non-local competitors -------------------------------------- 284

Fort Gratiot Sanitary Landfill, Inc. v. Michigan Department of Natural Resources --------------------------------------- 284

C & A Carbone, Inc. v. Clarkstown ---------------------------- 284

Protectionist Purpose and Effect ------------------------------- 286

Introduction --- 286

State Barriers to Out-of-State Sellers ------------------------- 287

Baldwin v. Seelig -- 287

Baldwin v. G.A.F. Seelig, Inc. ------------------------------- 287

The limits of Baldwin: compensating use taxes ------------------ 288

Henneford v. Silas Mason Co. --------------------------------- 288

De facto discrimination -- 289

Bacchus Imports, Ltd. v. Dias -------------------------------- 289

Section

1. State Regulation and the Dormant Commerce Clause—
Continued

   Hunt v. Washington State Apple Advertising Comm'n -------- 289
   The limits of inferring protectionism from discriminatory
    effect -- 290
   Breard v. Alexandria --- 290
  State Barriers to Out-of-State Buyers ------------------------------ 291
  Introduction --- 291
  Milk Control Board v. Eisenberg Farm Products Co. ------------- 291
  H. P. Hood & Sons v. DuMond ----------------------------------- 292
  Implications of Hood --- 294
   Cities Service Gas Co. v. Peerless Oil & Gas Co. ---------------- 295
  State restraints on exports of natural resources ------------------ 295
  Hughes v. Oklahoma --- 295
  New England Power Co. v. New Hampshire ----------------------- 296
  Sporhase v. Nebraska -- 297
  The Modern Balancing Test --- 297
  Introduction --- 297
  Pike v. Bruce Church, Inc. -- 297
  State Burdens on Transportation ------------------------------------- 299
  South Carolina State Highway Department v. Barnwell Bros. 299
  Southern Pacific Co. v. Arizona ----------------------------------- 300
  The contrast between Southern Pacific and Barnwell ----------- 304
  The changing criteria of judicial scrutiny ------------------------- 304
  The Bibb case -- 305
  Bibb v. Navajo Freight Lines, Inc. -------------------------------- 305
  Kassel v. Consolidated Freightways Corp. ------------------------ 306
  State Burdens on Trade -- 314
  Exxon Corp. v. Governor of Maryland --------------------------- 314
  Minnesota v. Clover Leaf Creamery Co. ------------------------- 315
  State Burdens on Business Entry ------------------------------------ 317
  Lewis v. BT Investment Managers, Inc. ------------------------- 317
  Edgar v. Mite Corp. --- 317
  CTS Corp. v. Dynamics Corp. of America ----------------------- 318
  Final observations on balancing ------------------------------------- 321
 C. **The "Market Participant" Exception to the Dormant Commerce Clause** --- 322
  Introduction --- 322
  South-Central Timber Development, Inc. v. Wunnicke ----------- 323
2. The Privileges and Immunities Clause of Article IV ------------- 328
 Introduction -- 328
  United Building & Construction Trades Council v. Mayor and Council of Camden -- 329
  The practice of law by nonresidents as an Art. IV "privilege" ---- 334
  Supreme Court of New Hampshire v. Piper ------------------------ 334
  A right of personal mobility: What constitutional sources? -------- 335
  Edwards v. California -- 336

Section
3. **Congressional Ordering of Federal-State Relationships By**
   Preemption and Consent --- 337
   Introduction --- 337
   A. **Preemption of State Authority** ----------------------------------- 337
      Introduction -- 337
      Pacific Gas & Elec. Co. v. State Energy Resources Conservation
         & Development Comm'n -------------------------------------- 338
      Types of preemption --- 342
      Field preemption --- 342
         Rice v. Santa Fe Elevator Corp. ---------------------------- 342
      Conflict preemption -- 343
         Hines v. Davidowitz --------------------------------------- 343
         Florida Lime & Avocado Growners, Inc. v. Paul ------------- 343
         Gade v. National Solid Wastes Management Ass'n ----------- 344
      The impact of unexercised federal authority ----------------------- 344
   B. **Consent to State Laws** --- 344
      Introduction -- 344
      The Wilson Act and the Rahrer case ------------------------------- 345
      Leisy v. Hardin --- 345
      Wilkerson v. Rahrer -- 345
      The Webb-Kenyon Act --- 345
      The McCarran Act and the Prudential case ------------------------- 346
         The Act --- 346
         Prudential Insurance Co. v. Benjamin --------------------- 346
      Equal protection as a limit on state protectionism ------------------ 348
         Metropolitan Life Ins. Co. v. Ward ------------------------- 348
      Other devices for congressional ordering of federal-state relation-
         ships --- 349
4. **Some Other Aspects of Federalism: A Brief Survey** ------------- 350
   A. **State Taxation and Free Trade** ------------------------------- 350
   B. **Intergovernmental Tax Immunities** --------------------------- 351
   C. **Intergovernmental Regulatory Immunities** ------------------- 352
   D. **Interstate Relationships** ----------------------------------- 353

CHAPTER 6. **Separation of Powers** ------------------------------- 354

   Introduction --- 354

Section
1. **The Authority to Make National Policy: The Conflict Be-**
   tween Executive Authority and Legislative Powers ---------- 355
   A. **Domestic Affairs** ---
      Presidential leadership and congressional lawmaking -------------- 355
      Youngstown Sheet & Tube Co. v. Sawyer [The Steel Seizure Case] 356
      The Steel Seizure Case and the Jackson Analysis ------------------- 364
         Dicta, holding, and competing analyses --------------------- 364
         The Jackson distinctions and their applicability ------------- 364
         Domestic affairs --- 364
         External affairs --- 365

Section

1. The Authority to Make National Policy: The Conflict Between Executive Authority and Legislative Powers—
Continued

Presidential Authority to Set Policy on Foreign Relations
through Executive Agreements ------------------------------------ 365
Introduction--- 365
Sources of authority for executive agreements --------------------- 366
Dames & Moore v. Regan -- 367
Some questions on Dames & Moore --------------------------------- 370
President, Congress, and the Use of Armed Forces ------------------ 371
The War Powers Resolution: Constitutional problems? --------- 373
Practical impacts -- 374

**2. Separation of Powers: Congressional Encroachments on
the Executive's Domain**--- 375
INS v. Chadha --- 375
Chadha and the Legislative Veto Controversy----------------------- 382
The Impoundment Controversy--------------------------------------- 383
Introduction -- 383
The Impounding Control Act of 1974------------------------------- 384
Constitutional problems?-- 384
Legislation to promote a balanced budget------------------------- 384
Bowsher v. Synar-- 385
Congress and the presidential power to appoint and remove subordinates: The background -- 389
Congress and the President's power to appoint "Officers of the
United States"--- 390
Congress and the President's power to remove subordinates - 390
Myers v. United States --- 391
Humphrey's Executor v. United States------------------------------- 391
Wiener v. United States --- 391
Morrison v. Olson--- 391
Metropolitan Wash. Airports Authority v. Citizens for Abatement of Aircraft Noise-- 398
Delegation of Legislative Powers by Congress----------------------- 399
Domestic sphere--- 399
Delegation of legislative power to the executive branch--------- 399
Delegation of legislative powers to the judiciary----------------- 400
Mistretta v. United States -- 400
Foreign affairs --- 403
United States v. Curtiss-Wright Export Corp.----------------------- 403

3. Executive Privilege and Immunities ---------------------------------- 404
United States v. Nixon--- 404
Presidential and other executive officials' amenability to judicial
process --- 408
The Nixon case -- 408
Absolute immunity from civil liability----------------------------------- 408
Executive privilege --- 410
The Nixon case -- 410
The proper scope of executive privilege ----------------------------- 410

Section
3. **Executive Privilege and Immunities**—Continued
    Congressional power over presidential papers -------------------- 411
    Nixon v. Administrator of General Services --------------------- 411
    Impeaching the president --------------------------------------- 411
    Legislative immunity and the Speech and Debate Clause------------- 413

PART III. INDIVIDUAL RIGHTS ---------------------------------- 415

    Scope Note -- 415

CHAPTER 7. The Bill of Rights and the Post-Civil War
Amendments: "Fundamental" Procedural Rights and the
"Incorporation" Dispute --------------------------------------- 417

    Introduction -- 417

Section
1. **The Pre-Civil War Situation** -------------------------------- 418
    The 1787 document --- 418
    The Bill of Rights -- 418
    Barron v. Mayor and City Council of Baltimore ----------------- 418
    The Marshall Court's Position------------------------------------ 419
2. **The Purpose and Impact of the Post-Civil War Amendments**   420
    Slaughter-House Cases-- 421
    The Aftermath of the Slaughter-House Cases: Privileges and Im-
        munities; Due Process -------------------------------------- 429
        Privileges and immunities of national citizenship ---------- 429
        Due process -- 431
3. **The Meaning of Due Process: Criminal Procedure and the**
    "Incorporation" Controversy---------------------------------- 432
    Introduction -- 432
    Due process and procedure before the Civil War------------------- 433
    The inadequacy of English history ------------------------------- 433
    A. **The Palko-Adamson Dispute: Do the Bill of Rights**
        Guarantees Apply to State Criminal Proceedings? -------- 434
        The Battle Between "Selective" and "Total" Incorporation ------- 434
            Introduction -- 434
            "Selective" incorporation: Cardozo in Palko ------------- 435
            Palko v. Connecticut----------------------------------- 435
            "Total" incorporation: Black's argument in Adamson, and
                Frankfurter's response ----------------------------- 436
            Adamson v. California --------------------------------- 436
            Examining the Black-Frankfurter debate: "Specific" rights;
                vague guarantees; impersonal, predictable standards ---- 439
            Due process methodology in search of impersonal standards 439
            Avoiding subjectivity: The problems of Justice Black's ap-
                proach-- 440
            Federalism and the Palko-Adamson approach------------------ 441
            The reign and modifications of the Palko-Adamson approach 441
    B. **The Modern Approach and Its Problems**----------------------- 442

Section
3. **The Meaning of Due Process: Criminal Procedure and the "Incorporation" Controversy**—Continued
     Duncan v. Louisiana -- 442
     Problems of the Modern Approach: The Contours of "Incorporated" Rights --- 449
       Incorporating Bill of Rights guarantees "jot-for-jot" ------------- 449
       The jury trial guarantee after Duncan: Dilution of federal rights as an escape from the incorporationist "straitjacket"? -- 450
         The Williams case--- 450
         Williams v. Florida-- 450
         The Apodaca case -- 451
         Apodaca v. Oregon --- 451

CHAPTER 8. Substantive Due Process: Rise, Decline, Revival --- 453

     Introduction --- 453

Section
1. **Substantive Due Process and Economic Regulation: The Rise and Decline of Judicial Intervention** ------------------------- 454
     A. Antecedents -- 454
       Introduction -- 454
         Calder v. Bull --- 455
       The early Marshall Court -- 456
       Due process before the Civil War ------------------------------- 457
       The movement toward substantive due process in the generation after the Slaughter-House Cases ------------------------ 457
         Rate regulation and the Munn case ------------------------------ 458
         Munn v. Illinois --- 458
         Mugler v. Kansas --- 459
         The Allgeyer case and liberty of contract------------------------- 460
         Allgeyer v. Louisiana -- 460
     B. The Lochner Era: Judicial Intervention and Economic Regulation --- 460
       Lochner v. New York --- 460
       The Discredited Period of Judicial Intervention: What Was Wrong With Lochner? --- 465
       Introduction -- 465
       Lochner and the language of the 14th Amendment -------------- 466
         "Liberty" and economic rights----------------------------------- 466
         "Liberty" and noneconomic rights ------------------------------- 467
         "Property" and "due process" ----------------------------------- 467
       Lochner and legislative ends ------------------------------------- 468
       Lochner and means-ends relationships --------------------------- 469
         Minimum rationality -- 469
         Stricter scrutiny--- 469
       Judicial Scrutiny of Economic Regulations During the Lochner Era—Some Examples --- 470

Section

1. **Substantive Due Process and Economic Regulation: The Rise and Decline of Judicial Intervention**—Continued

   Maximum hours—Muller and Bunting ------------------------------ 470
      Muller v. Oregon -- 470
      Bunting v. Oregon -- 471
   "Yellow dog" contracts, Coppage, and Adair ----------------------- 471
      Coppage v. Kansas --- 471
      Adair v. United States --- 472
   Minimum wages and the Adkins case ------------------------------ 472
      Adkins v. Children's Hospital ---------------------------------- 472
   Price regulations --- 473
   Restrictions on business entry and other economic regulations 473
      Business entry --- 473
      New State Ice Co. v. Liebmann --------------------------------- 473
      Adams v. Tanner --- 473
      Scrutiny of means --- 473
      Weaver v. Palmer Bros. Co. ------------------------------------ 473

C. **The Modern Era: The Decline—and Disappearance?—of Judicial Scrutiny of Economic Regulation** ------------------- 474
   Nebbia v. New York --- 474
   West Coast Hotel Co. v. Parrish -------------------------------- 476
   The Impact of Nebbia and West Coast Hotel ------------------------ 477
      The standards of the mid-1930s ---------------------------------- 477
      The political context of Nebbia and West Coast Hotel ---------- 477
   The Modern Era: Reduced Judicial Scrutiny or Abdication? ------ 478
   Economic regulation and the Carolene Products case ------------- 478
      United States v. Carolene Products Co. -------------------------- 478
      Total withdrawal from review? ----------------------------------- 479
      Olsen v. Nebraska -- 479
      Lincoln Federal Labor Union v. Northwestern Iron & Metal Co. -- 480
      Ferguson v. Skrupa -- 480
   Williamson v. Lee Optical Co. ----------------------------------- 481
   The "Hands Off" Approach to Economic Legislation: Excessive Withdrawal? Justifiable Double Standard? -------------------- 482
   Introduction --- 482
   The possibility of more substantial scrutiny of economic regulation -- 483
   The new interventionism: The Carolene Products footnote --- 484
      United States v. Carolene Products Co. -------------------------- 484
   Property and economic rights and the contrast with fundamental personal liberties ------------------------------------- 485
   Economic rights and the contrast with First Amendment liberties -- 485
   The contrast with non-"specific," noneconomic fundamental rights and interests --- 485
   Transitional Note -- 486

Section

2. **Other Constitutional Safeguards of Economic Rights: The "Taking-Regulation" Distinction; The Contracts Clause** --- 486
   A. **Eminent Domain and the "Taking-Regulation" Distinction** -------- 486
      Introduction --- 486
      Pennsylvania Coal Co. v. Mahon ------------------------------------- 487
      Miller v. Schoene --- 490
      Keystone Bituminous Coal Ass'n v. DeBenedictis -------------------- 491
      The "Taking-Regulation" Distinction and the Modern Court ---- 491
         Zoning and other regulations of the environment----------------- 491
         Goldblatt v. Hempstead -------------------------------------- 492
         Remedies for "regulatory" takings: Damage actions for inverse condemnation --- 492
         First English Evangelical Lutheran Church v. Los Angeles County --- 492
         Historic landmarks protection and the "taking-regulation" distinction --- 492
         Penn Central Transportation Co. v. New York City ------------ 492
         "Taking" problems in the most recent decades -------------------- 494
            A per se rule (rather than balancing) for "permanent physical occupations"--- 494
            Loretto v. Teleprompter Manhattan CATV Corp. --------------- 494
            Heightened scrutiny for takings claims: Conditions on permits to develop property ------------------------------- 494
            Nollan v. California Coastal Comm'n ------------------------ 495
            Dolan v. City of Tigard----------------------------------- 496
         Regulations prohibiting all economically beneficial uses of land -- 499
         Lucas v. South Carolina Coastal Council --------------------- 499
      A Note on "Public Use" -- 504
         Hawaii Housing Authority v. Midkiff-------------------------- 504
   B. **The Contracts Clause** -- 505
      Introduction --- 505
      The contracts clause in the 19th Century ----------------------------- 506
      Home Building & Loan Ass'n v. Blaisdell ---------------------------- 507
      Contracts clause cases between Blaisdell and the late 1970s------ 510
         El Paso v. Simmons--- 510
      How Far Has the Modern Court Revitalized the Contracts Clause?--- 510
         State obligations --- 510
         United States Trust Co. v. New Jersey -------------------------- 510
         Private obligations --- 513
         Allied Structural Steel Co. v. Spannaus ----------------------- 513
         A partial return to greater deference? --------------------------- 514
         Energy Reserves Group v. Kansas Power & Light Co.------------ 514
         Exxon Corp. v. Eagerton -- 515
         Retroactivity and regulatory laws ------------------------------- 515

Section

3. **The Revival of Substantive Due Process, for Noneconomic Rights: Privacy; Autonomy; Family Relations; Sexuality; The Right to Die** --- 516

Introduction -- 516

    Meyer v. Nebraska -- 516

    Pierce v. Society of Sisters --- 517

    Skinner v. Oklahoma --- 517

Griswold v. Connecticut --- 518

    Poe v. Ullman -- 522

Griswold, Penumbras, and Double Standards ----------------------------- 527

    The constitutional basis of Griswold---------------------------------- 527

    The scope of "privacy" in Griswold----------------------------------- 528

    Eisenstadt v. Baird --- 528

    Griswold and the double standard------------------------------------ 529

Roe v. Wade -- 530

    Doe v. Bolton -- 537

Roe v. Wade and the Legitimate Sources of Constitutional Values -- 538

    The protected personal interest: "Privacy," "autonomy," and Roe -- 538

    "Balancing" the competing interests --------------------------------- 538

    Is Roe distinguishable from Lochner? -------------------------------- 539

    The difference between Roe and Griswold (and other Warren Court decisions) -- 540

    Roe and "noninterpretive" modes of adjudication ------------------- 541

    The implications of Roe and Griswold: Private autonomy and public morality --- 543

      The individual interest in autonomy --------------------------- 543

      The state interest in morality ----------------------------------- 544

    The political reaction to Roe: Proposed constitutional amendments; legislative efforts --- 545

From Roe to Casey: Efforts to Overturn Roe; Regulations of Abortion Procedures--- 546

    Introduction--- 546

    Pre-Casey challenges to Roe v. Wade in the Court --------------- 546

      Akron v. Akron Center for Reproductive Health ----------------- 546

      Thornburgh v. American Coll. of Obst. & Gyn. ------------------ 547

    State regulations of abortions (and contraceptives) in the wake of Roe --- 548

      Spousal and parental consent requirements --------------------- 548

      Regulations of medical practices; protection of viable fetuses -- 549

      Governmental refusals to fund abortions ------------------------ 550

      Maher v. Roe -- 550

      Harris v. McRae-- 551

      Rust v. Sullivan -- 553

    Access of minors to contraceptives after Griswold and Roe ---- 554

      Carey v. Population Services International ----------------------- 554

      Webster v. Reproductive Health Services-------------------------- 555

Planned Parenthood of Southeastern Pa. v. Casey------------------------- 557

Section
3. **The Revival of Substantive Due Process, for Noneconomic Rights: Privacy; Autonomy; Family Relations; Sexuality; The Right to Die**—Continued
    Some Thoughts on Casey --- 583
        The force of precedent -- 583
        Abortion as sex discrimination ----------------------------- 583
        The "undue burden" standard ----------------------------- 583
Family Relationships and the Role of Tradition -------------------------- 584
Introduction -- 584
Protected family relationships: Zoning restrictions and the "extended family" -- 584
    Moore v. East Cleveland -- 584
The "fundamental right to marry": "Critical examination" of "significant" interferences with the right ------------------------------ 587
    Zablocki v. Redhail -- 587
Substantive due process methodology in light of the family relations cases: The role of tradition --- 589
    The utility of the tradition-oriented approach ----------------------- 589
    Tradition and the appropriate level of generality -------------------- 590
    Michael H. v. Gerald D. -- 590
Consensual Sexual Behavior -- 593
Bowers v. Hardwick --- 593
    Some comments on Hardwick------------------------------------- 599
Other Efforts to Assert Privacy and Autonomy Interests-------------- 599
    Personal appearance: Hair style------------------------------------ 599
    Kelley v. Johnson--- 599
    Substantive due process and the mentally retarded --------------- 600
    Youngberg v. Romeo-- 600
    Computerized data banks and "privacy" ------------------------- 601
    Whalen v. Roe --- 601
    A general right of intimate association as an aspect of liberty? -- 601
    Roberts v. United States Jaycees----------------------------------- 601
A Right to Die? --- 602
    The right to refuse unwanted medical treatment and nourishment -- 602
    Cruzan v. Director, Missouri Dept. of Health ------------------- 602
    A right to physician-assisted suicide?-------------------------------- 610
        The Ninth Circuit and due process------------------------------ 610
        Compassion in Dying v. Washington ------------------------- 610
        The Second Circuit: Quill v. Vacco --------------------------- 613
        Quill v. Vacco -- 613
        Some comments-- 614
4. **The Scope of "Liberty" and "Property": The Right To Hearing Cases** -- 615
Introduction -- 615
The Background of the Modern Developments: The Procedural Due Process Revolution of the Early 1970s--------------------------------- 616
    Goldberg v. Kelly --- 616
    Board of Regents v. Roth --- 618

Section

4. The Scope of "Liberty" and "Property": The Right To Hearing Cases—Continued

"Property," "Liberty," and Hearing Rights of Public Employees in
    Light of Roth--- 619
    The Roth approach: Property and state law----------------------------- 619
    The Arnett case: The "bitter with the sweet"-------------------------- 620
    Arnett v. Kennedy -- 620
    The Bishop case --- 621
    Bishop v. Wood -- 621
    The Loudermill case --- 621
    Cleveland Board of Education v. Loudermill-------------------------- 621
The Shrinking Scope of "Liberty" in the Procedural Due Process
    Cases --- 622
    Paul v. Davis and its problems--- 622
    Paul v. Davis --- 622
    The impact of the Paul v. Davis approach------------------------------- 624
    State law as a source of "liberty" interests in the modern cases - 625
    Vitek v. Jones-- 625
    Procedural due process in other contexts -------------------------------- 626
    What process is "due"?-- 626
    Mathews v. Eldridge -- 626

CHAPTER 9. Equal Protection--- 628

Section

1. An Overview-- 628
Introduction --- 628
Modest origins: The "old equal protection" in the pre-Warren
    Court years --- 629
From marginal intervention to major cutting edge: The Warren
    Court's "new equal protection" and the two-tier approach ----- 630
The post-Warren Court years and equal protection---------------------- 631
    Blocking the expansion of the "new" equal protection-------------- 631
    The unsettled state of modern equal protection doctrine: The
        discontent with two-tier formulations and the groping for
        new standards -- 631
Modern equal protection: Summary and challenge ----------------------- 632
Does equal protection protect core values of its own? -------------------- 633
A note on organization --- 634

2. Scrutiny of Means in Economic Regulations: The Rationality Requirement --- 635
The Rationality Requirement: When Are Classifications Excessively "Underinclusive" or "Overinclusive"?------------------------------ 635
    Introduction --- 635
    Classifications and adequate congruence: The Tussman-tenBroek
        analysis --- 636
    Some preliminary observations on the requirements of congru-
        ence -- 638
    Railway Express Agency v. New York ----------------------------------- 639

Section

2. **Scrutiny of Means in Economic Regulations: The Rationality Requirement**—Continued

The Warren Court's Approach in Operation -------------------------------- 641

    Some introductory questions --- 641

    Williamson v. Lee Optical Co. --- 642

    McGowan and McDonald: The Warren Court's deferential approach at its extreme --- 642

        McGowan v. Maryland --- 642

        McDonald v. Board of Election Commissioners ------------------- 642

    The "one step at a time" justification ------------------------------- 643

Possibilities of Greater Scrutiny Within the Rationality Framework? --- 643

    Introduction --- 643

    "Selective intervention" on behalf of minorities (including economic minorities?): The relevance of the Carolene Products footnote --- 644

    Civil republicanism: Equal protection as a safeguard against "naked preferences" --- 645

    Rationality review "with bite": The "newer equal protection" argument --- 646

Rationality Review in the Post-Warren Era ------------------------------- 648

    The early 1970s --- 648

    U.S. Dept. of Agriculture v. Moreno ------------------------------- 648

    The late 1970s --- 649

    New Orleans v. Dukes --- 649

    Massachusetts Bd. of Retirement v. Murgia --------------------------- 649

    New York City Transit Auth. v. Beazer ----------------------------- 651

    Rationality review since the 1980s ------------------------------------ 652

    U.S. Railroad Retirement Bd. v. Fritz ------------------------------- 653

    Schweiker v. Wilson --- 657

    Logan v. Zimmerman Brush Co. --- 658

    Allegheny Pittsburgh Coal v. Webster County --------------------------- 659

    Nordlinger v. Hahn --- 660

    FCC v. Beach Communications, Inc. ------------------------------------- 661

3. **Suspect Classifications and the Problems of Forbidden Discrimination** --- 662

Introduction -- 662

A. **Race** --- 663

    1. **The Intensive Scrutiny of Disadvantaging Racial and Ethnic Classifications** --- 663

        The Strauder case --- 663

        Strauder v. West Virginia --- 663

        Race as a "suspect" classification triggering "the most rigid scrutiny": The Korematsu case ----------------------------------- 664

        Korematsu v. United States --- 664

        Loving v. Virginia --- 667

        McLaughlin v. Florida --- 669

        Palmore v. Sidoti --- 669

Section
3. **Suspect Classifications and the Problems of Forbidden Discrimination**—Continued

Scrutinizing Racial Classifications: Some Examples and Questions --- 670

2. **The Unconstitutionality of Racial Segregation**---------- 671

The "separate but equal" era -- 671

The Plessy case--- 671

Plessy v. Ferguson --- 671

The 20th century attack on de jure segregation------------------ 673

Brown v. Board of Education [Brown I—The Constitutional Ruling] --- 673

Bolling v. Sharpe -- 677

Segregation and the Brown Principle ------------------------------ 678

Legally mandated segregation in other public facilities------- 678

The Brown rationale--- 678

History --- 678

Impact on educational and psychological development ------- 678

The scope of the holding--- 680

Brown v. Board of Education [Brown II—The Implementation Decision] -- 680

B. **Gender**-- 681

Introduction: Bases for expanding the categories of "suspect" classifications--- 681

The changing attitude toward gender classifications----------- 683

The deferential old equal protection in action --------------------- 683

Goesaert v. Cleary--- 683

Heightened scrutiny under a deferential, old equal protection guise -- 683

Reed v. Reed -- 683

Frontiero v. Richardson-- 684

Craig v. Boren-- 686

"Real" Differences or Archaic Generalizations?---------------------- 690

Michael M. v. Superior Court --- 690

Some comments--- 692

Rostker v. Goldberg -- 693

Discrimination against fathers (and preference for mothers) of nonmarital children--- 695

More on the problem of sex-specific traits: What constitutes sex discrimination? --- 697

Geduldig v. Aiello--- 697

Scrutiny of Gender Classifications on the Modern Court: Requiring an "Exceedingly Persuasive Justification"? ---------- 698

Mississippi University for Women v. Hogan ----------------------- 698

A note on the proposed Equal Rights Amendment--------------- 701

Los Angeles Dept. of Water & Power v. Manhart---------------- 701

J.E.B. v. Alabama --- 702

United States v. Virginia -- 704

Some questions on Hogan, J.E.B., and Virginia---------------- 715

The Benign, Compensatory Use of Gender Classifications -------- 716

Section

3. **Suspect Classifications and the Problems of Forbidden Discrimination**—Continued

Introduction --- 716

The early approach --------------------------------------- 716

Kahn v. Shevin -- 716

Benignness in alimony laws --------------------------- 717

Orr v. Orr --- 717

Benefits programs --------------------------------------- 717

Weinberger v. Wiesenfeld ---------------------------- 717

Califano v. Goldfarb ----------------------------------- 718

Schlesinger v. Ballard --------------------------------- 718

Califano v. Webster ------------------------------------ 718

Discrimination against whom? --------------------- 719

Wengler v. Druggists Mutual Ins. Co. -------------- 719

C. **Other Classifications Arguably Warranting Heightened Scrutiny** --- 720

1. **Alienage** --- 720

Introduction -- 720

The rise of strict scrutiny of alienage classifications ------------ 720

Graham v. Richardson and welfare benefits -------------------- 720

Graham v. Richardson --------------------------------- 720

Bar admission and public employment --------------------- 721

In re Griffiths --- 721

Sugarman v. Dougall ---------------------------------- 721

The impairment of strict scrutiny: Deferential review under the "governmental function" exception --------------------- 722

Foley v. Connelie -- 722

Ambach v. Norwick ------------------------------------ 722

Bernal v. Fainter --------------------------------------- 723

Alienage restrictions and federal preemption: A more appropriate analysis? -- 723

Federal restrictions on aliens ------------------------- 724

Public employment -------------------------------------- 724

Hampton v. Mow Sun Wong -------------------------- 724

Medical benefits --- 725

Mathews v. Diaz -- 725

2. **Nonmarital Children** -- 725

Introduction -- 725

The origin -- 725

Levy v. Louisiana --------------------------------------- 725

The wavering aftermath in the early 1970s ----------------------- 726

The late 1970s -- 726

Trimble v. Gordon -------------------------------------- 726

Lalli v. Lalli --- 727

The 1980s -- 727

3. **Disabilities: Mental Retardation; Age; Poverty** ---------- 728

Mental retardation -------------------------------------- 728

Cleburne v. Cleburne Living Center, Inc. --------------- 728

Age classifications -------------------------------------- 734

Section

3. **Suspect Classifications and the Problems of Forbidden Discrimination**—Continued
    Massachusetts Bd. of Retirement v. Murgia ---------------------- 734
    Poverty and wealth classifications----------------------------------- 735
    James v. Valtierra --- 736
4. **Sexual Orientation** --- 737
    Romer v. Evans--- 737
    Some Notes and Comments on Romer v. Evans ------------------ 746
    The Romer opinions-- 746
    Alternative justifications for Romer ----------------------------- 747
    The implications of Romer--- 748
D. **The "Purposeful Discrimination" Requirement and the "Purpose"–"Impact" Distinction** --------------------------------- 749
    1. **Types of Discrimination** ------------------------------------- 749
        Introduction --- 749
        Discrimination in the administration of law --------------------- 750
        Yick Wo v. Hopkins--- 750
        Proof of purposeful discrimination ----------------------------- 750
        Discriminatory motivation-------------------------------------- 751
        Palmer v. Thompson --- 751
        De facto discrimination: Should differential effect be suffi-cient?--- 753
        Griggs v. Duke Power Co. -------------------------------------- 753
        Jefferson v. Hackney -- 754
    2. **Proving Purposeful Discrimination: The Modern Court's Position**--- 754
        Introduction --- 754
        Washington v. Davis-- 755
        Arlington Heights v. Metropolitan Housing Corp. ------------- 759
        Personnel Administrator of Mass. v. Feeney ------------------ 761
        Rogers v. Lodge--- 764
        Hunter v. Underwood-- 770
        Discriminatory purpose and the 13th Amendment ------------ 771
        Memphis v. Greene -- 771
    3. **The De Jure-De Facto Distinction in the School De-segregation Context**-- 771
        The Implementation of Brown: From Desegregation to Inte-gration -- 771
        Introduction --- 771
        "Freedom of choice" --- 773
        Green v. County School Board --------------------------------- 773
        Swann v. Charlotte-Mecklenburg Board of Education--------- 775
        Desegregation in the North-------------------------------------- 775
        Broad intradistrict remedies for de jure segregation ----------- 776
        Keyes v. School District --------------------------------------- 776
        Demonstrating "discriminatory purpose" and imposing intradistrict systemwide remedies in 1979: Reaffirma-tion of Keyes, or drastic expansion? --------------------------- 777
        Columbus Board of Education v. Penick---------------------- 777

Section

3. **Suspect Classifications and the Problems of Forbidden Discrimination**—Continued

    Dayton Board of Education v. Brinkman -------------------------- 777

    How much vitality does the de jure-de facto distinction retain in school desegregation cases? --------------------------------- 781

    Keyes v. School District ------------------------------------- 781

    Limits on judicial power to remedy de jure segregation -------- 783

    Interdistrict remedies -- 783

    Milliken v. Bradley -- 783

    Enforcing compliance with court orders: The extent of the federal courts' remedial powers -------------------------------- 785

    Missouri v. Jenkins -- 785

    Measuring compliance with long-standing decrees: The 1990s Court's unwillingness to support continuing judicial involvement --- 786

    Board of Ed. v. Dowell --------------------------------------- 786

    Freeman v. Pitts --- 789

    United States v. Fordice ------------------------------------- 789

    Missouri v. Jenkins -- 789

    Restructuring the Political Process (and Repealing Remedies) that Disadvantage Minorities --------------------------------- 789

    Introduction -- 789

    Hunter v. Erickson --- 790

    Washington v. Seattle School Dist. --------------------------- 790

    Crawford v. Los Angeles Board of Education ------------------- 792

    Some more questions about the restructuring cases ----------- 793

  E. **The Benign Use of Racial Criteria: Affirmative Action and Related Programs** ------------------------------------- 793

    Introduction -- 793

    Color consciousness to remedy purposeful discrimination: The school desegregation context ----------------------------- 794

    Preferential admissions programs ------------------------------ 794

    DeFunis v. Odegaard -- 794

    Benign programs and objecting members of minority groups - 795

    Regents of Univ. of California v. Bakke ---------------------- 795

    The vitality of Bakke --- 809

    Hopwood v. Texas --- 809

    Benign Uses of Racial Criteria in Employment, Contracting, and Licensing Programs Since the 1980s ---------------------------- 810

    Employment discrimination ------------------------------------- 810

    Wygant v. Jackson Board of Education ------------------------- 810

    Some comments --- 811

    Contracting and licensing programs ---------------------------- 812

    Fullilove v. Klutznick --------------------------------------- 812

    Richmond v. J.A. Croson Co. ---------------------------------- 814

    Metro Broadcasting, Inc. v. FCC ------------------------------ 828

    Adarand Constructors, Inc. v. Pena --------------------------- 830

    Race-Conscious Voting Districts: A Transitional Note ---------- 839

Section

4. **The "Fundamental Interests" Strand of Equal Protection Strict Scrutiny** --- 840

   Introduction --- 840

   A. **The Modern Court's General Stance: Rodriguez and Plyler** -- 842

   San Antonio Independent School Dist. v. Rodriguez ---------------- 842

   Plyler v. Doe -- 850

   The limits of Plyler -- 857

   B. **Denial and "Dilution" of Voting Rights** ------------------------ 858

   Introduction --- 858

   1. **Denials of the Franchise** --------------------------------------- 858

   Harper v. Virginia State Board of Elections ----------------------- 858

   The bases and impact of Harper ------------------------------------ 860

   Kramer v. Union Free School District No. 15 ---------------------- 860

   Additional Restrictions on the Franchise---------------------------- 862

   Introduction -- 862

   Efforts to limit the franchise in the contexts of limited purpose elections and special purpose governmental units -- 862

   Cipriano v. Houma --- 862

   Phoenix v. Kolodziejski -- 862

   *Salyer Land Co. v. Tulare Lake Basin Water Storage Dis-
   trict* --- 862

   Ball v. James --- 863

   Quinn v. Millsap -- 863

   Durational residence requirements -------------------------------- 863

   Dunn v. Blumstein -- 863

   Disenfranchisement of felons ------------------------------------- 864

   Richardson v. Ramirez --- 864

   Anti-"raiding" cutoff requirements for voting in primaries:
   The appropriate level of scrutiny------------------------------ 864

   Rosario v. Rockefeller --- 864

   Kusper v. Pontikes --- 864

   Tashjian v. Republican Party ----------------------------------- 865

   Eu v. San Francisco Democratic Central Comm. --------------- 865

   2. **Vote "Dilution": The Reapportionment Cases, Gerrymandering, and Race-Conscious Districitng** ------------ 865

   Colegrove v. Green --- 865

   Reynolds v. Sims --- 866

   Lucas v. Forty-Fourth Gen. Assembly --------------------------- 869

   The Progeny of Reynolds v. Sims: Some Elaborations of the
   "One Person-One Vote" Theme--------------------------------- 871

   Introduction--- 871

   Application of Reynolds to local government --------------------- 871

   Avery v. Midland County --------------------------------------- 871

   Hadley v. Junior College Dist. ---------------------------------- 872

   Mathematical inequalities: Permissible deviations from "one
   person-one vote"--- 872

   Congressional districting --------------------------------------- 872

   Kirkpatrick v. Preisler --- 872

Section

4. The "Fundamental Interests" Strand of Equal Protection Strict Scrutiny—Continued

White v. Weiser ---- 872
Karcher v. Daggett ---- 872
State districting ---- 872
Abate v. Mundt ---- 873
Mahan v. Howell ---- 873
Gaffney v. Cummings ---- 873
White v. Regester ---- 873
Brown v. Thomson ---- 873
Board of Estimate v. Morris ---- 873
Supermajorities ---- 874
Gordon v. Lance ---- 874
The initial judicial reluctance to scrutinize political gerrymanders ---- 874
Gaffney v. Cummings ---- 874
Davis v. Bandemer ---- 875
Political gerrymandering: Some comments ---- 879
Race-Conscious Districting ---- 880
Shaw v. Reno [Shaw I] ---- 880
The Aftermath of Shaw I ---- 887
Miller v. Johnson ---- 887
Shaw II ---- 889
Shaw v. Hunt ---- 889
Bush v. Vera ---- 889

3. Access to the Ballot: Restrictions on Candidates and Parties ---- 890

Introduction ---- 890
Williams v. Rhodes ---- 890
Jenness v. Fortson ---- 891
The 1974 decisions ---- 892
Storer v. Brown ---- 892
American Party of Texas v. White ---- 892
Financial barriers to ballot access ---- 892
Bullock v. Carter ---- 892
Lubin v. Panish ---- 892
More deferential scrutiny in ballot access cases: Public officials' candidacies ---- 892
Clements v. Fashing ---- 892
A new approach? Emphasizing the First Amendment rather than equal protection in ballot access cases ---- 893
Anderson v. Celebrezze ---- 893
Write-in voting ---- 894
Burdick v. Takushi ---- 894

C. Access to Courts ---- 895

Introduction ---- 895
Griffin v. Illinois ---- 896
Douglas v. California ---- 897

Section

4. **The "Fundamental Interests" Strand of Equal Protection Strict Scrutiny**—Continued

Economic Differentiations and the Criminal Process: The Reach of the Griffin-Douglas Principles -------------------------------- 989

Counsel -- 898

Ross v. Moffitt -- 898

Jail sentences to "work off" fines -------------------------------- 898

Noneconomic distinctions and the criminal process -------------- 899

Economic Barriers and Civil Litigation: The Bases (and Limits) of Boddie --- 899

Boddie v. Connecticut --------------------------------------- 899

United States v. Kras -------------------------------------- 900

Ortwein v. Schwab -- 900

Little v. Streater --- 901

D. **Durational Residence Requirements That "Penalize" the Right of Interstate Migration** ----------------------------- 901

Shapiro v. Thompson -- 901

Durational Residence Requirements -------------------------------- 905

Introduction --- 905

Medical care for indigents -------------------------------------- 906

Memorial Hospital v. Maricopa County ------------------------ 906

Divorce laws -- 907

Sosna v. Iowa --- 907

Zobel v. Williams --- 908

E. **Refusals to Expand Fundamental Interests Analysis to Redress of Economic Inequalities** ----------------------------- 910

Introduction -- 910

The potentials and problems at the end of the Warren era ----- 911

Welfare benefits --- 912

Dandridge v. Williams --- 912

Housing -- 913

Lindsey v. Normet -- 913

Do Any Bases Remain for Heightened Scrutiny of Welfare Laws? --- 914

A review -- 914

The brief and troubled life of "irrebuttable presumptions" analysis -- 914

Weinberger v. Salfi -- 915

CHAPTER 10. The Post-Civil War Amendments and Civil Rights Legislation: Constitutional Restraints on Private Conduct; Congressional Power to Implement the Amendment --- 917

Introductory Overview --- 917

"State action" limits and private actors -------------------------- 917

Congress and the Amendments ------------------------------------- 917

Court-Congress interactions -------------------------------------- 918

A note on organization -- 918

Section

1. **The Statutory Framework**--- 919
   The Laws of the Reconstruction Era -- 919
      Introduction: The historical background and the Slaughter-
         House Cases--- 919
      The 1866 Act --- 919
      The 1870 Act --- 919
      The 1871 and 1875 Acts -- 919
   The Surviving Remnants of the Post-Civil War Laws: The Modern
      Counterparts--- 920
      Criminal provisions -- 920
      Civil provisions --- 920
      A brief note on modern civil rights legislation ---------------------- 921
2. **The Problem of State Action**--- 921
   A. State Action in the 19th Century: The Collapse of Early Congres-
      sional Efforts to Reach Private Conduct ---------------------------- 921
      Civil Rights Cases --- 921
      Cruikshank and the Legacy of the Civil Rights Cases-------------- 925
         Cruikshank, the 14th Amendment limitation to state action
            —and the recognition of rights against private action
            outside the 14th Amendment-- 925
         United States v. Cruikshank --- 925
         The legacy of the Civil Rights Cases: A transitional note ------ 925
   B. **Court Elaborations of the State Action Concept in the**
      20th Century-- 926
      Introduction -- 926
      The "Public Function" Strand of State Action Analysis------------ 928
         Marsh v. Alabama and modern "public function" analysis ----- 928
         Marsh v. Alabama --- 928
         Some questions --- 929
         The refusal to extend Marsh: The modern shopping center
            cases -- 929
         The reach of the "public function" rationale: The parks con-
            text -- 930
         Evans v. Newton-- 930
         Public function and private power------------------------------------- 931
         The modern Court's curtailment of public function analysis:
            The limitation to powers "exclusively reserved to the
            State" --- 931
         Jackson v. Metropolitan Edison Co. --------------------------------- 931
         Flagg Bros., Inc. v. Brooks --- 932
      The White Primary Cases --- 934
         Smith v. Allwright --- 935
         Terry v. Adams --- 935
      State Action Through State "Involvement": The "Nexus" Strand
         of State Action Analysis --- 936
      Shelley v. Kraemer--- 936
      Shelley v. Kraemer: The Applications and the Search for Limits 938
         Introduction --- 938
         Restrictive covenants and damage actions-------------------------- 939

Section

2. The Problem of State Action—Continued

Barrows v. Jackson -- 939
Reverter provisions in deeds ---------------------------------- 939
Evans v. Abney --- 939
Other testamentary provisions: The Girard College litigation 940
Pennsylvania v. Board of Directors of Trusts ---------------------- 940
Trespass actions and the sit-in cases ---------------------------- 941
Bell v. Maryland --- 941
Transitional note -- 942
Burton v. Wilmington Parking Authority -------------------------- 942
State Involvement in Private Action—"To Some Significant Extent" -- 945
Leases and sales of public property ----------------------------- 945
Use of public property by private groups------------------------- 945
Gilmore v. Montgomery --- 945
Governmental involvement through licensing -------------------- 946
Moose Lodge No. 107 v. Irvis ------------------------------------- 947
CBS, Inc. v. Democratic Nat. Comm. -------------------------------- 948
Transitional Note: The relevance of governmental licensing, regulation, and benefits -------------------------------------- 948
State Action Through State "Encouragement" and "Authorization" -- 948
Reitman v. Mulkey -- 948
State "encouragement" -- 950
"Authorization" of racial discrimination ------------------------ 951
Transitional Note-- 951
Jackson v. Metropolitan Edison Co. -------------------------------- 952
Flagg Bros., Inc. v. Brooks ------------------------------------- 954
State Action Doctrine Since the 1980s -------------------------------- 955
Blum v. Yaretsky-- 956
Rendell-Baker v. Kohn --- 956
Lugar v. Edmondson Oil Co. ------------------------------------- 957
NCAA v. Tarkanian-- 958
San Fran. Arts & Athletics v. U.S.O.C. -------------------------- 959
Edmonson v. Leesville Concrete Co. ------------------------------ 959
DeShaney v. Winnebago Cty. Soc. Servs. Dept. -------------------- 960

3. Congressional Power to Reach Private Interferences with Constitutional Rights: Modern Scope and Problems -------- 962
The Ingredients of the Problem: An Introductory Sketch -------------- 962
The sources of constitutional rights------------------------------ 962
Specificity and vagueness-- 963
Statutory interpretation -- 963
A. Private Interferences With Federal Rights: Criminal Sanctions-- 964
United States v. Guest --- 964
Some Problems of Applying Criminal Sanctions to State-Involved Defendants Interfering with 14th Amendment Rights ------ 968
Introduction --- 968
United States v. Price-- 968

Section

3. Congressional Power to Reach Private Interferences with Constitutional Rights: Modern Scope and Problems—
Continued
    Williams v. United States -- 969
    United States v. Williams -- 969
    The Screws case: Vagueness and civil rights laws ----------------- 969
    Screws v. United States --- 969
    Congressional Power to Reach Private Behavior, the Guest Case, and the 1968 Law-- 970
    Congressional power to reach private actors under § 5 of the 14th Amendment-- 970
    Criminal sanctions against private conduct: Sources outside the 14th Amendment -- 972

B. Private Interferences With Federal Rights: Civil Sanctions -- 973
Introduction -- 973
Civil remedies against private conspiracies -- 974
    The Griffin interpretations of § (1985(c) -------------------------- 974
    Griffin v. Breckenridge-- 974
    The potential reach of § 1985(3) and the Carpenters case ------ 975
    United Brotherhood of Carpenters v. Scott-------------------------- 975
    Section 1985(3), abortion, and the Bray case --------------------- 976
    Bray v. Alexandria Women's Health Clinic----------------------- 976
Civil remedies against actions "under color" of state law --------- 977

C. Congressional Power to Reach Private Conduct Under the 13th Amendment -- 978
Jones v. Alfred H. Mayer Co. --- 978
13th Amendment Powers and the 1866 Act --------------------------- 981
    The scope of congressional power after the Jones case --------- 981
    Modern interpretations of the 1866 Act ---------------------------- 982
    Sullivan v. Little Hunting Park, Inc. ------------------------------- 982
    Runyon v. McCrary -- 982

4. Congressional Power to Change the Content of Constitutional Rights?—"Remedial" and "Substantive" Power Under § 5 of the 14th Amendment -------------------------------- 984
Introduction -- 984
Congressional Protection of Voting Rights: The Background and the South Carolina Case -- 985
Chief Justice Warren's summary of the background --------------- 985
The constitutional status of literacy tests before the 1965 Act --- 986
Lassiter v. Northampton County Election Bd. ------------------------- 987
The South Carolina case-- 987
South Carolina v. Katzenbach-- 987
The nationwide suspension of literacy tests in the 1970 Act and later extensions of the Voting Rights Act ----------------------- 989
Some questions about "remedial" legislation and the "remedial" –"substantive" distinction -- 991
Rome v. United States -- 991
Katzenbach v. Morgan-- 998

Section

4. Congressional Power to Change the Content of Constitutional Rights?—"Remedial" and "Substantive" Power Under § 5 of the 14th Amendment—Continued

Cardona v. Power --1001
Congressional Power and the Morgan Case --------------------------1003
Oregon v. Mitchell --1004
Congressional Power After the Morgan, Oregon, and Rome Cases --1011
  Introduction --1011
  Some pervasive problems--1011
  Limiting congressional power to "dilute" constitutional rights: Justice Brennan's footnotes-----------------------------------1012
  Potential applications of the Morgan rationale------------------1012
  Limits on (and justifications for) congressional power to "interpret" constitutional rights: Some alternative views ----------1015
  "Line-drawing" capacities and congressional power "around the edges" of Court doctrine—consistent with judicial "value preferences"---1016
  Fact-finding capacities and the Morgan power-------------------1017
  A distinction between "federalism" and "liberty" issues? ------1018
  The state of the Morgan "substantive" rationale in the 1980s ---1018
  Rome v. United States--1020
  Mississippi University for Women v. Hogan-------------------1020

CHAPTER 11. Freedom of Speech—Why Government Restricts Speech—Unprotected and Less Protected Expression 1022

Section

1. Free Speech: An Overview -------------------------------------1022
  Introduction --1022
  A. First Amendment History ----------------------------------1023
    Prior restraints ---1023
    Seditious libel --1024
    Later history---1025
  B. First Amendment Theory-----------------------------------1025
    Truth ---1025
    Self-government---1027
    Autonomy --1028
    Negative theories ---1028
    Eclectic theories ---1029
  C. First Amendment Jurisprudence ---------------------------1029
    Justifying special protection for speech----------------------1030
    Absolutes versus balancing ---------------------------------1031
    Categorization versus balancing -----------------------------1032
2. Incitement --1034
  A. The World War I Cases: "Clear and Present Danger" ------1034
    Introduction ---1034
    Schenck v. United States----------------------------------1036
    Frohwerk v. United States---------------------------------1037
    Debs v. United States -------------------------------------1038

Section

2. **Incitement**—Continued

    Abrams v. United States --1040

    Subversive Advocacy From Schenck to Abrams----------------------1044

        Comparing the Schenck-Frohwerk-Debs approach ---------------1044

        The evolution of Holmes' Abrams dissent -------------------------1045

        The impact of the Abrams dissent-------------------------------------1045

        An alternative approach: Learned Hand and the Masses case

    Masses Publishing Co. v. Patten--1046

    Comparing the Holmes and Hand Approaches ------------------------1049

        The strengths and weaknesses of Hand's "incitement" ap-

          proach--1049

        The differences between Hand and Holmes: Some historical

          data ---1049

  B. **The "Red Scare" Cases** --1050

    Gitlow v. New York --1050

    Whitney v. California --1054

    The Gitlow-Whitney Problem--1059

        Legislative presumptions of harm from speech --------------------1059

        An alternative approach: the Masses test----------------------------1059

        Comparing the Holmes and Brandeis approaches-----------------1059

        Retreat from Gitlow-Whitney: Fiske, DeJonge and Herndon--1059

        Fiske v. Kansas---1059

        DeJonge v. Oregon ---1060

        Herndon v. Lowry --1060

  C. **The Smith Act Prosecutions**--1060

    Dennis v. United States ---1061

    "Clear and Present Danger" After Dennis-----------------------------1066

        The Dennis formulation ---1066

        Clear and present danger and Learned Hand ---------------------1067

        Free speech theory and the advocacy of totalitarian govern-

          ment--1067

        Retreat from Dennis: Yates, Scales and Noto----------------------1068

        Yates v. United States ---1068

        Scales v. United States --1068

        Noto v. United States ---1069

        The impact of Yates, Scales and Noto -------------------------------1069

        Other federal anti-Communist legislation of the 1950s----------1069

        Communist Party v. SACB---1070

        Aptheker v. Secretary of State --------------------------------------1070

        United States v. Robel --1070

        Lamont v. Postmaster General--1070

        Vietnam era cases --1070

        Bond v. Floyd --1070

        Watts v. United States --1071

  D. **The Modern Incitement Test**--------------------------------------1071

    Brandenburg v. Ohio--1071

    The Impact of Brandenburg ---1074

        The best of Hand and Holmes?---1074

        Later applications of Brandenburg------------------------------------1074

Section

2. Incitement—Continued

Hess v. Indiana---1074

NAACP v. Claiborne Hardware Co.-------------------------------1074

The scope of Brandenburg---1075

Deference to legislative determinations of the dangerousness
of speech --1075

Landmark Communications, Inc. v. Virginia-------------------1075

3. Fighting Words and Hostile Audiences--------------------------1076

Introduction ---1076

A. Fighting Words --1076

Cantwell v. Connecticut--1076

Chaplinsky v. New Hampshire -------------------------------1077

The Court's methodology in excluding "fighting words" from
First Amendment protection --------------------------------1078

The contemporary vitality of the "fighting words" exception -1078

Gooding v. Wilson --1079

Rosenfeld v. New Jersey ------------------------------------1079

Lewis v. New Orleans --1079

Brown v. Oklahoma--1079

The limitation of the "fighting words" exception to words that
"tend to incite an immediate breach of the peace"---------1080

Texas v. Johnson--1080

Cohen v. California --1081

The Court's methodology in Cohen -----------------------------1085

B. Hostile Audiences ---1085

Terminiello and "provocative" speech which "invites dispute" --1085

Terminiello v. Chicago--1085

The Feiner problem: Focus on protected words or on audience
context?--1086

Feiner v. New York --1086

Distinguishing Feiner in later cases ----------------------------1088

Street Demonstrations--1088

Edwards v. South Carolina-----------------------------------1088

Cox v. Louisiana ---1088

Gregory v. Chicago ---1089

Permit requirements as an alternative approach --------------------1089

Kunz v. New York---1090

Permit fees--1090

Forsyth County, Georgia v. Nationalist Movement --------------1090

The right to heckle ---1090

4. Injury to Reputation and Sensibility--------------------------1091

Introduction --1091

A. Beauharnais and Group Libel --------------------------------1092

Beauharnais v. Illinois--1092

Debate over Beauharnais--1093

The vitality of Beauharnais--------------------------------------1093

B. Libel --1094

New York Times Co. v. Sullivan----------------------------------1094

The Meaning of New York Times----------------------------------1097

Section

4. Injury to Reputation and Sensibility—Continued

The immediate impact of the decision --------------------------------1097
The First Amendment interest in false statements of fact -----1097
The Court's methodology in New York Times----------------------1098
Criticism of New York Times --1098
Procedural developments after New York Times------------------1099
Extension of New York Times to other settings----------------------1099
Public Figures --1100
Curtis Publishing Co. v. Butts ---------------------------------------1100
Associated Press v. Walker--1100
Private Figures--1101
Rosenbloom v. Metromedia, Inc. -------------------------------------1101
Gertz v. Robert Welch, Inc. ---1102
Speech on Matters of Private Concern----------------------------1103
Dun & Bradstreet, Inc. v. Greenmoss Builders --------------------1103
Defamation law: a summary --1104

C. Non-Defamation Torts --1105
Intentional infliction of emotional distress ---------------------------1105
Hustler Magazine v. Falwell--1105
Invasion of Privacy --1107
"False light" invasion of privacy --1107
Time, Inc. v. Hill --1107
Disclosure of rape victims' names -------------------------------------1108
Cox Broadcasting Corp. v. Cohn--1108
Florida Star v. B.J.F. --1108
Appropriation torts--1109
Zacchini v. Scripps-Howard Broadcasting Co. ----------------------1109

D. Hate Speech--1109
Arguments for regulation of hate speech -----------------------------1109
Arguments against regulation of hate speech------------------------1111
Restraining Nazi demonstrations: the Skokie controversy --------1112
National Socialist Party v. Skokie ------------------------------------1112
Smith v. Collin--1113
Regulating racist and other bigoted speech on campus ------------1114
R.A.V. v. City of St. Paul---1115
The Implications of R.A.V. ---1123
Distinguishing the regulation of hate speech from the regula-
   tion of hate crimes --1123
Wisconsin v. Mitchell --1123
The limits of the distinction between R.A.V. and Mitchell -----1124
Hostile environment sexual or racial harassment----------------1125

5. Sexually Explicit Expression--1125
Introduction ---1125
A. Obscenity--1126
Roth v. United States ---1126
Alberts v. California---1126
The Struggle to Define Obscenity Between Roth and Miller---1128
Overview --1128
Kingsley Int'l Pictures Corp. v. Regents ------------------------------1129

Section

5. Sexually Explicit Expression—Continued

Stanley v. Georgia --1130

United States v. Reidel ---1131

The 1970 Obscenity Commission Report--------------------1132

The Burger Court's new judicial definition of obscenity --------1132

Miller v. California --1132

Paris Adult Theatre I v. Slaton --1135

Obscenity Law After Miller and Paris------------------------------------1140

Justifications for obscenity regulation ---------------------------1140

Debasement of individual character ---------------------------1140

Offense to unwilling onlookers ----------------------------------1140

Inducement of criminal conduct --------------------------------1140

Eroding moral standards ---1141

Harming the social fabric --1141

The value of obscenity as "speech"? ------------------------------1141

Non-political--1141

Non-cognitive --1141

Not susceptible to counterspeech -------------------------------1142

Critiques of obscenity law after Miller-------------------------------1142

Post-Miller decisions---1142

Jenkins v. Georgia--1142

Community standards---1143

Hamling v. United States --1143

Smith v. United States --1143

Serious value--1144

The Attorney General's Commission on Pornography, 1986 --1144

B. Child Pornography --1145

New York v. Ferber---1145

The Court's methodology in Ferber ------------------------------1148

Possession of child pornography ---------------------------------1148

Osborne v. Ohio ---1148

C. Pornography as Subordination of Women----------------------1149

Feminist anti-pornography theory --------------------------------1149

Feminist arguments against pornography regulation --------------1149

Gay pornography ---1150

The invalidation of the MacKinnon-Dworkin ordinance --------1150

American Booksellers Ass'n v. Hudnut ----------------------------1151

D. Sexually Explicit But Non-Obscene Expression -------------1155

Introduction --1155

1. Nudity Bans--1156

Nudity on drive-in movie screens-------------------------------------1156

Erznoznik v. Jacksonville ---------------------------------------1156

Live nude dancing ---1158

Schad v. Mount Ephraim--1158

2. "Erogenous Zoning" ---1159

Low value speech? --1159

Young v. American Mini Theatres --------------------------------1159

"Secondary effects" --1162

Renton v. Playtime Theatres, Inc. --------------------------------1162

Section

5. Sexually Explicit Expression—Continued

    3. Indecency Bans on the Communications Media----------1164

        FCC v. Pacifica Foundation --1164

        The Limits of Pacifica--1169

          Captive audiences: Pacifica's privacy invasion rationale -----1169

          Rowan v. U.S. Post Office Department ----------------------------1169

          Consolidated Edison v. Public Service Comm'n ----------------1170

          Bolger v. Youngs Drug Products Corp. --------------------------1170

          Total indecency bans --1171

          Sable Communications, Inc. v. FCC------------------------------1171

          Authorizing cable operators to regulate indecent program-
            ming --1171

          *Denver Area Educational Telecommunications Consortium
            v. FCC*--1171

          Indecency on the Internet--1174

          American Civil Liberties Union v. Reno --------------------------1174

6. Commercial Speech --1175

    Introduction --1175

      Valentine v. Chrestensen --1175

      Pittsburgh Press Co. v. Pittsburgh Human Relations Comm'n ---1175

      Bigelow v. Virginia --1176

  Virginia Pharmacy Board v. Virginia Citizens Consumer Council ---1176

  Commercial Speech and First Amendment Theory ---------------------1181

    Advertising as "speech"--1181

    Advertising and the rationales for freedom of speech --------------1182

      Self-government --1182

      Truth --1182

      Autonomy --1182

      Negative First Amendment theory----------------------------------1183

    "Commonsense differences" between commercial and other
      speech --1183

      Hardiness --1184

      Verifiability--1184

    Defining commercial speech --1184

    Bolger v. Youngs Drug Products Corp. ----------------------------1184

    Board of Trustees, State Univ. of New York v. Fox -------------------1184

  Commercial Speech After Virginia Pharmacy ----------------------------1185

    Real estate "For Sale" signs as protected speech --------------------1185

    Linmark Associates, Inc. v. Willingboro ----------------------------1185

    Contraceptive advertising --1185

    Carey v. Population Services Int'l----------------------------------1185

    Regulating the legal profession and other professions -------------1185

    Bates v. State Bar of Arizona --------------------------------------1186

    Ohralik v. Ohio State Bar Association-------------------------------1186

    Zauderer v. Office of Disciplinary Counsel ------------------------1186

    Shapero v. Kentucky Bar Ass'n ------------------------------------1187

    Peel v. Attorney Registration and Disciplinary Comm'n of Ill.----1187

    Edenfield v. Fane --1187

    Ibanez v. Florida --1188

Section

6. Commercial Speech—Continued

Florida Bar v. Went For It, Inc.--1188

What Standard of Scrutiny for Commercial Speech? --------------------1189

Central Hudson Gas v. Public Service Comm'n --------------------------1189

Commercial Speech Regulation After Central Hudson -----------------1192

    Commercial speech and "least restrictive alternative" analysis--1192

    Board of Trustees, State Univ. of New York v. Fox -------------------1192

    Billboards and newsracks: may commercial speech be treated

        differently?--1193

    Metromedia, Inc. v. San Diego --1193

    City of Cincinnati v. Discovery Network, Inc. ---------------------1193

    The rise and fall of the "vice" exception: restrictions on adver-

        tising harmful products and services --------------------------1195

    *Posadas De Puerto Rico Assocs. v. Tourism Company of Puerto

        Rico* --1195

    United States v. Edge Broadcasting Co. -------------------------1196

    Rubin v. Coors Brewing Co. --------------------------------------1197

44 Liquormart, Inc. v. Rhode Island--------------------------------------1198

Commercial Speech Regulation After Liquormart ----------------------1201

    What standard of scrutiny? ---1201

    Paternalism and commercial speech ----------------------------------1202

CHAPTER 12. Freedom of Speech—How Government Restricts Speech—Modes of Abridgment and Standards of Review --1203

Section

1. The Distinction Between Content-Based and Content-Neutral Regulations--1203

Introduction --1203

  A. Content-Based Restrictions --------------------------------------1204

    Viewpoint restrictions --1204

    Subject matter restrictions---1204

    Police Dept. v. Mosley ---1205

    Carey v. Brown---1205

    *Simon & Schuster, Inc. v. Members of New York State Crime

        Victims Board*---1206

    Burson v. Freeman --1207

    Speaker restrictions--1208

    Communicative impact on the audience -----------------------------1208

    Boos v. Barry --1208

    Content-neutral laws --1209

    Reasons for differential treatment of content-based and content-

        neutral laws --1210

      Purpose ---1210

      Effect --1210

      Political safeguards ---1211

    Total medium bans---1211

  B. Content-Neutral Laws and Symbolic Conduct ---------------1212

Section

1. **The Distinction Between Content-Based and Content-Neutral Regulations**—Continued

  Introduction--1212
  United States v. O'Brien --1213
  The Significance of O'Brien -----------------------------------1216
    Expression and action--1216
    Legislative motivation---1217
    The O'Brien test and the content-based/content-neutral distinction ---1217
    "Incidental" restrictions on expression---------------------1218
    Arcara v. Cloud Books, Inc.-----------------------------------1218
  Flag Desecration --1219
    Street v. New York--1219
    Smith v. Goguen --1219
    Spence v. Washington --1220
  Texas v. Johnson --1220
  The Aftermath of Texas v. Johnson----------------------------1228
    Congressional response to Johnson ------------------------1228
    United States v. Eichman ------------------------------------1228
    Statute versus amendment ------------------------------------1230
  Nude Dancing---1230
  Barnes v. Glen Theatre, Inc. ----------------------------------1230

2. **Government's Power to Limit Speech in Its Capacity as Proprietor, Educator, Employer and Patron** --------------------1234

  A. **Speech in Public Forums and Other Government Property**--1234
  Introduction --1234

  1. **Early Public Forum Cases** ------------------------------------1235
    The First Amendment "right" to a public forum ------------------1235
    Guaranteed access versus equal access: is the issue distribution or discrimination? -------------------------------1236
    Early cases: standardless licensing and the problem of discrimination--1237
    Saia v. New York ---1237
    Staub v. Baxley --1237
    Hynes v. Mayor of Oradell -----------------------------------1237
    Lakewood v. Plain Dealer Publishing Co. ------------------1238
    Cox v. New Hampshire--1238
    Early cases: total medium bans and the problem of distribution--1239
    Schneider v. State ---1239
    Martin v. Struthers--1240
    Kovacs v. Cooper --1241
    City of Ladue v. Gilleo--------------------------------------1243

  2. **The Modern "Time, Place and Manner" Test** ---------------1244
    Introduction--1244
    Public Order and Safety ---------------------------------------1245
    Cox v. Louisiana ---1245
    Heffron v. International Society for Krishna Consciousness ---1245

Section

2. Government's Power to Limit Speech in Its Capacity as Proprietor, Educator, Employer and Patron—Continued

Aesthetics --1248
Metromedia, Inc. v. San Diego ------------------------------1248
Members of City Council v. Taxpayers for Vincent ----------------1249
Clark v. Community for Creative Non-Violence --------------------1254
Tranquility, Privacy and Repose------------------------------------1260
Noise regulations --1260
Ward v. Rock Against Racism ------------------------------------1260
Protecting "captive audiences"--------------------------------------1261
Targeted residential picketing--------------------------------------1261
Frisby v. Schultz --1261
Abortion clinic protests --1263
Madsen v. Women's Health Center, Inc. ---------------------------1263
Is a Time, Place or Manner Regulation Ever Invalid? -----------1266
United States v. Grace--1266

3. Speaker Access to Public Places Other Than Streets and Parks ---1267
Introduction--1267
Libraries, Jails and Schools ---------------------------------------1268
Brown v. Louisiana ---1268
Adderley v. Florida--1269
Grayned v. Rockford --1271
Buses, Theaters, and Military Bases--------------------------------1272
Lehman v. Shaker Heights--1272
Southeastern Promotions, Ltd. v. Conrad --------------------------1273
Greer v. Spock --1274
United States v. Albertini --1276
The Modern Trichotomy of Traditional, Designated and Non-public Forums ---1276
Mailboxes --1276
U.S. Postal Service v. Council of Greenburgh Civic Assns. -----1276
Teachers' mailboxes --1277
Perry Education Assn. v. Perry Local Educators' Assn. ---------1277
Charitable campaigns in federal offices-----------------------------1279
Cornelius v. NAACP Legal Defense and Ed. Fund ----------------1279
Post Office sidewalks ---1281
United States v. Kokinda--1281
Airport terminals --1283
International Society for Krishna Consciousness v. Lee ---------1283
The Court's trichotomy of public places-----------------------------1287
The special problem of solicitation --------------------------------1287

4. Religious Speech on Public Property----------------------------1289
Widmar v. Vincent---1289
Lamb's Chapel v. Center Moriches Union Free School Dist.----1290
Capitol Square Review Board v. Pinette --------------------------1291

5. First Amendment Access Rights to Private Property? -1292
Introduction--1292

Section

2. **Government's Power to Limit Speech in Its Capacity as Proprietor, Educator, Employer and Patron**—Continued

  Amalgamated Food Employees v. Logan Valley Plaza ----------- 1292
  Lloyd Corp. v. Tanner --- 1292
  Hudgens v. NLRB -- 1293

 B. **Speech in Public Schools** --- 1293
  Introduction --- 1293
  Tinker v. Des Moines Independent Community School District - 1293
  Board of Education v. Pico --- 1295
  Bethel School Dist. No. 403 v. Fraser --------------------------------- 1299
  Hazelwood School District v. Kuhlmeier ----------------------------- 1300

 C. **Speech and Association by Public Employees and Contractors** -- 1302
  Introduction --- 1302
  McAuliffe v. Mayor of New Bedford ------------------------------------ 1302
  Public Employee Speech --- 1303
  Pickering v. Board of Education --- 1303
  Connick v. Myers --- 1304
  Rankin v. McPherson -- 1308
  Waters v. Churchill -- 1309
  United States v. National Treasury Employees Union ------------ 1309
  Public Employee Party Affiliation -- 1311
  Prohibitions of political activities by public employees: The Hatch Act cases --- 1311
  United Public Workers v. Mitchell -------------------------------------- 1311
  United States Civil Service Comm'n v. National Ass'n of Letter Carriers -- 1312
  Patronage dismissals of public employees ------------------------------ 1312
  Elrod v. Burns -- 1312
  Branti v. Finkel -- 1313
  Rutan v. Republican Party of Illinois ---------------------------------- 1314
  Speech and Party Affiliation of Independent Contractors --------- 1316
  Board of Commissioners, Wabaunsee Co. v. Umbehr ------------- 1316
  O'Hare Truck Service, Inc. v. City of Northlake ------------------- 1316

 D. **Speech Subsidized by Public Funds** ------------------------------ 1318
  Speiser v. Randall --- 1318
  Regan v. Taxation with Representation of Washington ---------- 1319
  FCC v. League of Women Voters --- 1320
  Rust v. Sullivan -- 1321
  Rosenberger v. Rector and Visitors of the University of Virginia -- 1324

3. **Impermissible Forms of Speech-Restrictive Law: Overbreadth, Vagueness and Prior Restraint** -------------------------- 1325
 A. **Overbreadth** --- 1326
  Introduction --- 1326
  Gooding v. Wilson --- 1326
  The distinctive features of overbreadth ------------------------------- 1326
  The attractiveness of overbreadth analysis --------------------------- 1327
  Criticisms of overbreadth analysis -------------------------------------- 1328

Section
3. Impermissible Forms of Speech-Restrictive Law: Over-breadth, Vagueness and Prior Restraint—Continued

Limits on overbreadth analysis: the requirement of "substantial" overbreadth --1328
Broadrick v. Oklahoma --1329
New York v. Ferber --1331
Limits on overbreadth analysis: requiring that a statute be incapable of a narrowing construction ------------------------------1332
Brockett v. Spokane Arcades, Inc. --------------------------------1332
Schaumburg v. Citizens for Better Environment ----------------1332
Secretary of State v. Joseph H. Munson Co. -----------------------1334
Overbreadth and due process --1334
Massachusetts v. Oakes ---1334
Osborne v. Ohio ---1335
The Court's continued reliance on overbreadth invalidation --1335
Houston v. Hill ---1335
Board of Airport Commissioners v. Jews for Jesus--------------1336
"Less restrictive means" analysis and its relation to over-breadth --1337
B. Vagueness ---1337
Coates v. Cincinnati ---1338
C. Prior Restraint --1339
Introduction --1339
1. Licensing --1339
The concern with administrative discretion----------------------1339
Lovell v. Griffin ---1340
Lakewood v. Plain Dealer Publishing Co. -----------------------1340
Procedural safeguards ---1342
Freedman v. Maryland ---1342
FW/PBS, Inc. v. Dallas---1343
Standing to challenge licensing schemes -------------------------1343
Poulos v. New Hampshire---1343
Does the prior restraint-subsequent punishment distinction make sense? --1344
Kingsley Books, Inc. v. Brown -------------------------------------1344
2. Injunctions ---1345
Near v. Minnesota ---1345
Walker v. Birmingham--1348
Carroll v. President & Comm'rs of Princess Anne--------------1348
Prior Restraint and National Security ----------------------------1349
New York Times Co. v. United States [The Pentagon Papers Case]--1349
United States v. Progressive, Inc. --------------------------------1355
Snepp v. United States ---1357
Prior Restraint and Fair Trial--------------------------------------1357
Nebraska Press Ass'n v. Stuart-----------------------------------1357

CHAPTER 13. Rights Ancillary to Freedom of Speech -----------1361

Introduction --1361

Section
1. **Compelled Speech: The Right *Not* to Speak** ------------------------1361
    A. **Compelled Individual Speech** -------------------------------------1361
        Citizens as mouthpieces --1361
        Minersville School Dist. v. Gobitis-----------------------------1362
        West Virginia State Bd. of Educ. v. Barnette -------------------1362
        Citizens as mobile billboards-------------------------------------1363
        Wooley v. Maynard --1363
        Compelled disclosure of speaker identity--------------------------1363
        Talley v. California ---1363
        McIntyre v. Ohio Elections Commission --------------------------1364
    B. **Compelled Access for the Speech of Others** ---------------------1364
        Compelled rights of reply --1366
        Red Lion Broadcasting Co. v. FCC--------------------------------1366
        Miami Herald Pub. Co. v. Tornillo-------------------------------1366
        Compelled access by speakers to private property-----------------1366
        PruneYard Shopping Center v. Robins-----------------------------1366
        Pacific Gas & Elec. Co. v. Public Util. Comm'n -----------------1367
        Turner Broadcasting System, Inc. v. FCC (Turner I)-------------1369
        Turner Broadcasting System, Inc. v. FCC (Turner II) -----------1371
        Compelled access to a parade -------------------------------------1372
        *Hurley v. Irish-American Gay, Lesbian and Bisexual Group of
            Boston*---1372
        The Court's methodology in compelled speech cases --------------1374
        Constitutional compelled speech----------------------------------1374
2. **Freedom of Association**---1374
    Introduction ---1374
    A. **Compelled Disclosure of Membership** ----------------------------1375
        NAACP v. Alabama ---1376
        Shelton v. Tucker---1377
        Gibson v. Florida Legislative Investigation Comm. --------------1379
        Compelled Disclosure of Political Campaign Contributions -------1381
        Buckley v. Valeo ---1381
        Brown v. Socialist Workers '74 Campaign Committee -----------1383
    B. **Restrictions on Organizational Activity**------------------------1383
        1. **Litigation** --1383
        NAACP v. Button --1383
        Brotherhood of Railroad Trainmen v. Virginia -------------------1386
        United Mine Workers v. Illinois State Bar Ass'n-----------------1386
        United Transportation Union v. State Bar of Michigan ---------1386
        2. **Boycotts**---1387
        NAACP v. Claiborne Hardware Co. --------------------------------1387
        *International Longshoremen's Ass'n v. Allied International,
            Inc.* --1389
    C. **Denial of Government Benefits Because of Association** --1390
        The Cold War period --1390
        Konigsberg v. State Bar of California---------------------------1390
        The Warren Court ---1392
        Cramp v. Board of Public Instruction----------------------------1392
        Baggett v. Bullitt ---1392

Section

2. Freedom of Association—Continued

     Elfbrandt v. Russell --1393

     Keyishian v. Board of Regents ---------------------------------------1394

     Loyalty Requirements and the Modern Court -----------------------1395

        Loyalty oaths---1395

        Cole v. Richardson --1395

        Bar admission cases--1396

        Baird v. State Bar of Arizona ----------------------------------1396

        Application of Stolar--1396

        Law Students Civil Rights Research Council v. Wadmond-----1397

    D. The Right *Not* to Associate ------------------------------------1397

        Compulsory fees--1397

        Abood v. Detroit Board of Educ.---------------------------------1397

        Compulsory membership--1399

        Roberts v. United States Jaycees -----------------------------1399

        Board of Directors of Rotary International v. Rotary Club------1400

        New York State Club Ass'n v. City of New York -------------------1400

3. Money and Political Campaigns-----------------------------------1400

     Buckley v. Valeo --1400

     The Problems and Progeny of Buckley---------------------------------1409

        The Court's methodology in Buckley --------------------------------1409

        Equalization of speaking power --------------------------------------1410

        Public funding of political campaigns-------------------------------1410

        Other government interests in campaign finance limits------------1411

        Post-Buckley decisions: political action committees ----------------1411

        California Medical Ass'n v. FEC----------------------------------1411

        FEC v. National Conservative PAC-----------------------------1412

        Post-Buckley decisions: political parties ---------------------------1412

        Colorado Republican Federal Campaign Committee v. FEC ------1412

        Post-Buckley decisions: corporations and political campaigns----1413

        First National Bank of Boston v. Bellotti -------------------------1413

        FEC v. National Right to Work Committee -----------------------1416

        FEC v. Massachusetts Citizens for Life---------------------------1416

        Austin v. Michigan Chamber of Commerce -----------------------1417

        Post-Buckley decisions: referenda --------------------------------1418

        Citizens Against Rent Control v. Berkeley ----------------------1418

        Meyer v. Grant --1419

        The limits of Buckley's anticorruption rationale: candidates'

           promises in election campaigns ----------------------------------1419

        Brown v. Hartlage ---1419

4. Freedom of the Press ---1420

     Introduction --1420

     The press as a "fourth branch" of government----------------------1420

     The press as just another speaker --------------------------------------1421

     First National Bank of Boston v. Bellotti----------------------------1421

    A. Press Access to Newsworthy Governmental Information-1422

        Introduction---1422

    1. Press Access to Jails---1423

        Pell v. Procunier ---1423

Section

4. Freedom of the Press—Continued

Saxbe v. Washington Post Co. --1424

Houchins v. KQED, Inc. ---1424

2. Press Access to Judicial Proceedings ---------------------------1425

Pretrial hearings---1425

Gannett Co. v. DePasquale---1425

Criminal trials ---1426

Richmond Newspapers, Inc. v. Virginia ---------------------------1426

The scope of Richmond Newspapers--------------------------------------1429

Globe Newspaper Co. v. Superior Court-------------------------------1429

Press-Enterprise Co. v. Superior Court-------------------------------1430

Press interference with judicial proceedings -------------------------1431

Landmark Communications, Inc. v. Virginia----------------------1431

Bridges v. California --1432

Pennekamp v. Florida---1432

Craig v. Harney ---1432

Wood v. Georgia---1433

B. Governmental Demands for Information From the Press 1433

Introduction --1433

Branzburg v. Hayes--1434

Journalistic Privilege After Branzburg ---------------------------------1438

The judicial and legislative response to Branzburg---------------1438

Searches of newsrooms pursuant to ex parte warrants---------1439

Zurcher v. Stanford Daily--1439

C. Laws Discriminating Against the Press -----------------------------1440

Minneapolis Star & Tribune Co. v. Minnesota Comm'r of Revenue --1440

The Implications and Limits of Minneapolis Star -------------------1444

Is the press special? --1444

Slippery slopes---1444

Antimedia, intramedium and intermedia discrimination -------1445

Arkansas Writers' Project, Inc. v. Ragland ----------------------------1445

Leathers v. Medlock ---1445

Turner Broadcasting v. FCC--1446

Laws of general applicability---1447

Cohen v. Cowles Media Co. ---1447

D. Differential Regulation of the Broadcast Media -------------1449

Introduction --1449

Scarcity, Access and the Broadcasting Media ------------------------1450

Right-of-reply obligations on the broadcasting media-----------1450

Red Lion Broadcasting Co. v. FCC---1450

The limits of Red Lion: technological versus economic scarcity-1452

Repeal of the fairness doctrine ---1452

A constitutional right of access to the broadcasting media for editorial advertisements? -- 1453

Columbia Broadcasting, Inc. v. Democratic National Comm. -1453

A statutory right of access to the broadcasting media for candidates seeking federal elective office ---------------------------1454

CBS, Inc. v. FCC---1454

Section

4. Freedom of the Press—Continued

The standard of review in broadcasting cases --------------------1454

FCC v. League of Women Voters------------------------------------1454

New Media: Cable Television and the Internet----------------------1455

Cable television and the First Amendment-------------------------1455

Turner Broadcasting v. FCC -------------------------------------1455

Denver Area Educational Telecommunications Consortium v. FCC---1456

The Internet and the First Amendment-----------------------------1458

ACLU v. Reno---1459

CHAPTER 14. The Religion Clauses: Free Exercise and Establishment--1461

Introduction --1461

Section

1. An Overview of the Religion Clauses-------------------------------1462

History of the religion clauses ---1462

The dominant view: voluntarism and separatism --------------------1462

Everson v. Board of Education--1462

A minority view: nonpreferentialism ---------------------------------1463

Wallace v. Jaffree ---1464

Rosenberger v. Rector ---1464

Reply to the minority view---1464

Lee v. Weisman ---1465

The relevance of original history---1466

The incorporation of the religion clauses against the states -----------1466

Reconciling the religion clauses --1467

Sherbert v. Verner---1467

The definition of "religion" ---1468

United States v. Seeger ---1468

Welsh v. United States---1468

Gillette v. United States ---1468

The limits of judicial inquiry into religious content--------------------1470

United States v. Ballard ---1470

2. The Free Exercise of Religion ---------------------------------------1471

Introduction ---1471

A. Laws Discriminating Against Religion-----------------------------1471

Torcaso v. Watkins ---1471

McDaniel v. Paty---1472

Church of the Lukumi Babalu Aye v. City of Hialeah----------------1472

Lukumi and Religious Gerrymanders -------------------------------1476

Larson v. Valente ---1476

B. Neutral Laws Adversely Affecting Religion: Are Religious Exemptions Constitutionally Compelled?------------1477

Reynolds v. United States ---1477

Cantwell v. Connecticut ---1478

Prince v. Massachusetts---1478

Braunfeld v. Brown ---1478

Section

2. **The Free Exercise of Religion**—Continued

 Sherbert v. Verner---1479

 Free Exercise Exemptions From Sherbert to Smith----------------1481

  Unemployment compensation cases after Sherbert--------------1481

  Thomas v. Review Board---------------------------------------1481

  Hobbie v. Unemployment Appeals Comm'n----------------------1482

  Frazee v. Illinois Employment Security Dept.----------------------1482

  Compulsory education laws------------------------------------1482

  Wisconsin v. Yoder--1482

  Denials of free exercise claims between Sherbert and Smith--1484

   United States v. Lee--------------------------------------1484

   Bob Jones University v. United States----------------------1484

   Goldman v. Weinberger-------------------------------------1485

   O'Lone v. Estate of Shabazz--------------------------------1486

   Bowen v. Roy--1486

   Lyng v. Northwest Indian Cemetery Protective Ass'n---------1487

  The Court's methodology in the era between Sherbert and

   Smith---1488

 Employment Division, Dept. of Human Resources v. Smith-------1489

  Smith and Religious Exemptions--------------------------------1496

  The history of religious exemptions----------------------------1496

  The political theory of religious exemptions--------------------1497

  Smith and constitutional jurisprudence-------------------------1498

  Religious exemptions and anarchy------------------------------1499

  The aftermath of Smith: The Religious Freedom Restoration

   Act of 1993--1499

3. **The Establishment Clause**--1500

 Introduction--1500

 Lemon v. Kurtzman--1500

 A. **Enshrining Official Beliefs**--------------------------------1501

  1. **"Released Time" Programs in Public Schools**-------------1501

   McCollum v. Board of Education----------------------------1501

   Zorach v. Clauson---1502

  2. **The School Prayer Cases**-----------------------------------1504

   Teacher-led prayers, Bible readings, and moments of silence-1504

   Engel v. Vitale---1504

   Abington School Dist. v. Schempp--------------------------1505

   Wallace v. Jaffree--1506

   School prayer and "coercion"--------------------------------1506

   Lee v. Weisman--1507

  3. **Religion in the Public School Curriculum**------------------1513

   The Ten Commandments--------------------------------------1513

   Stone v. Graham--1513

   Teaching evolution and creationism--------------------------1514

   Epperson v. Arkansas-------------------------------------1514

   Edwards v. Aguillard-------------------------------------1515

  4. **Religious Symbolism Outside the School Context**------------1519

   Sunday closing law--1519

   McGowan v. Maryland-------------------------------------1519

Section

3. The Establishment Clause—Continued
    Legislative prayer --1519
    Marsh v. Chambers --1519
    Public religious displays --1520
    Lynch v. Donnelly---1521
    Allegheny County v. American Civil Liberties Union ------------1526
    Capitol Square Review Board v. Pinette --------------------------1528
B. Financial Aid to Religious Institutions ----------------------------1531
    Introduction --1531
    1. Everson: "No Tax Large or Small"-------------------------------1532
    Everson v. Board of Education --------------------------------------1532
    2. Aid to Parochial Education Since Everson ------------------1534
    The "wall of separation" --1534
    Forms of aid: texts, tests, teachers, teaching aids and tuition-1534
    Mueller v. Allen --1535
    Grand Rapids School District v. Ball -----------------------------1541
    Aguilar v. Felton---1541
    Aid to higher education: Is a different standard appropriate?-1542
    Tilton v. Richardson---1542
    Roemer v. Maryland Public Works Bd. ----------------------------1542
    3. From Separationism to Assimilationism on Financial
        Aid--1543
    Walz v. Tax Comm'n--1543
    Widmar v. Vincent---1543
    Witters v. Washington Dept. of Services for Blind ----------------1544
    Bowen v. Kendrick--1544
    Zobrest v. Catalina Foothills School Dist. ----------------------------1545
    Rosenberger v. Rector and Visitors of the Univ. of Virginia ----1546
C. Legislative Accommodations of Religion ------------------------1548
    Introduction --1548
    Accommodation versus delegation ----------------------------------1548
    Larkin v. Grendel's Den, Inc. ---------------------------------------1548
    Permissible statutory accommodations and their limits --------1548
    Estate of Thornton v. Caldor, Inc. ---------------------------------1548
    Corporation of Presiding Bishop v. Amos ---------------------------1549
    Texas Monthly, Inc. v. Bullock--------------------------------------1550
    Board of Education v. Mergens--------------------------------------1551
    Accommodation and religious gerrymandering -------------------1551
    Board of Educ. of Kiryas Joel v. Grumet --------------------------1551

APPENDICES

App.
A. THE CONSTITUTION OF THE UNITED STATES -------------------- A–1
B. TABLE OF JUSTICES--- B–1
INDEX --- I–1

TABLE OF CASES

Principal and other major cases are in bold type. Non-principal cases are in roman type. References are to Pages.

Abate v. Mundt, 873
Abington School Dist. v. Schempp, 1466, 1505
Able v. United States, 748
Abood v. Detroit Bd. of Ed., 1397
Abrams v. United States, 1026, 1030, 1040
Action v. Gannon, 975
Adair v. United States, 469, 472
Adams v. Tanner, 473
Adamson v. California, 436
Adarand Constructors, Inc. v. Pena, 809, 830
Adderley v. State of Fla., 1269
Addyston Pipe & Steel Co. v. United States, 165
Adickes v. S. H. Kress & Co., 978
Adkins v. Children's Hospital of the District of Columbia, 472
Adler v. Board of Education of City of New York, 1390
Aguilar v. Felton, 1541
Akron, City of v. Akron Center for Reproductive Health, Inc., 546, 549
Alamo Foundation v. Secretary of Labor, 1499
Alberts v. California, 1126
Albertini, United States v., 1276
Albertson v. Subversive Activities Control Bd., 1070
Allegheny, County of v. American Civil Liberties Union Greater Pittsburgh Chapter, 1526
Allegheny Pittsburgh Coal Co. v. Webster County, W. Va., 659
Allen v. State Bd. of Elections, 989
Allen v. Wright, 36
Allgeyer v. State of La., 400
Allied Structural Steel Co. v. Spannaus, 513
Allied Tube & Conduit Corp. v. Indian Head, Inc., 1389
Amalgamated Food Emp. Union Local 590 v. Logan Valley Plaza, Inc., 1292
Ambach v. Norwick, 720, 722
American Booksellers Ass'n, Inc. v. Hudnut, 1151, 1204
American Civil Liberties Union v. Reno, 1174, 1459
American Party of Texas v. White, 892
American Textile Mfrs. Institute, Inc. v. Donovan, 400
Anastaplo, In re, 1392
Anderson v. Celebrezze, 893

Anderson v. Liberty Lobby, Inc., 1099
Anderson v. Martin, 670
Apodaca v. Oregon, 451
Application of (see name of party)
Aptheker v. Secretary of State, 517, 1070, 1392
Arcara v. Cloud Books, Inc., 1209, 1218
Arkansas Elec. Co-op. Corp. v. Arkansas Public Service Com'n, 344
Arkansas Writers' Project, Inc. v. Ragland, 1445
Arlington Heights, Village of v. Metropolitan Housing Development Corp., 35, 759
Arnett v. Kennedy, 620
Ashwander v. Tennessee Valley Authority, 29
Associated Press v. Walter, 1100
Atlantic Coast Line R. Co. v. City of Goldsboro, 507
Attorney General of New York v. Soto–Lopez, 910
Austin v. Michigan Chamber of Commerce, 1417
Avery v. Midland County, Tex., 871
Avery v. State of Ga., 750

Bacchus Imports, Ltd. v. Dias, 289, 346
Baggett v. Bullitt, 1338, 1392
Baird v. State Bar of Ariz., 1396
Baker v. Carr, 46, 47, 53, 54, 866, 867
Baker, United States v., 1456, 1459
Baldwin v. Fish and Game Commission of Montana, 330
Baldwin v. G.A.F. Seelig, Inc., 260, 271, 272, 287, 292
Ball v. James, 863
Ballard, United States v., 1470
Ballew v. Georgia, 451
Bankers Life and Cas. Co. v. Crenshaw, 914
Bankers' Trust Co., United States v., 177, 250
Bantam Books, Inc. v. Sullivan, 1339
Barenblatt v. United States, 1379
Barnes v. Glen Theatre, Inc., 1158, 1231
Barron v. City of Baltimore, 418, 420
Barrows v. Jackson, 939
Bass, United States v., 198
Bates v. City of Little Rock, 521, 1375, 1379
Bates v. State Bar of Arizona, 1186
Batson v. Kentucky, 750, 959
Beal v. Doe, 551
Bearden v. Georgia, 899

Beauharnais v. Illinois, **1092,** 1110, 1113

Beer v. United States, 989

Bell v. State of Md., 941

Bell v. Wolfish, 624

Bellamy v. Mason's Stores, Inc. (Richmond), 975

Belle Terre, Village of v. Boraas, 587

Bellotti v. Baird, 99 S.Ct. 3035, p. 549

Bellotti v. Baird, 96 S.Ct. 2857, p. 548

Belmont, United States v., 366

Bendix Autolite Corp. v. Midwesco Enterprises, Inc., 270, 321

Benton v. Maryland, 436

Berman v. Parker, 504

Bernal v. Fainter, 723

Bethel School Dist. No. 403 v. Fraser, 1299

Betts v. Brady, 441

Bibb v. Navajo Freight Lines, Inc., 305

Bigelow v. Virginia, 1176

Bishop v. Wood, 621

Blum v. Yaretsky, 956

Board of Airport Com'rs of City of Los Angeles v. Jews for Jesus, Inc., 1336

Board of County Com'rs, Wabaunsee County, Kan. v. Umbehr, 1316

Board of Curators of University of Missouri v. Horowitz, 626

Board of Ed. of Central School Dist. No. 1 v. Allen, 1534

Board of Educ., Island Trees Union Free School Dist. No. 26 v. Pico, 1295

Board of Educ. of Kiryas Joel Village School Dist. v. Grumet, 1551

Board of Educ. of Oklahoma City Public Schools v. Dowell, 786

Board of Educ. of Westside Community Schools v. Mergens, 1551

Board of Estimate of City of New York v. Morris, 873

Board of Regents of State Colleges v. Roth, 618

Board of Trustees of State University of New York v. Fox, 1184, 1192

Bob Jones University v. United States, 1484

Boddie v. Connecticut, 899

Bolger v. Youngs Drug Products Corp., 1170, **1184,** 1185, **1261**

Bolling v. Sharpe, 677, 938

Bond v. Floyd, 1070

Boos v. Barry, 1164, 1208, 1235

Bors v. Preston, 13

Bose Corp. v. Consumers Union of United States, Inc., 1099

Bowen v. Kendrick, 1544

Bowen v. Roy, 1486

Bowers v. Hardwick, 543, 593, 746

Bowsher v. Synar, 356, 385, 390

Bradfield v. Roberts, 1531

Bradley v. Public Utilities Commission of Ohio, 269

Bradwell v. People of State of Illinois, 683, 684

Brandenburg v. Ohio, 1071, 1113, 1204, 1216

Branti v. Finkel, 1313

Branzburg v. Hayes, 1434

Braunfeld v. Brown, 1478

Bray v. Alexandria Women's Health Clinic, 976

Breard v. City of Alexandria, La., 290, 1288

Breedlove v. Suttles, 858, 859

Brewer v. Hoxie School Dist., 971

Brewster, United States v., 413

Bridges v. State of Cal., 1432

Broadrick v. Oklahoma, 1329

Brockett v. Spokane Arcades, Inc., 1332

Bronson v. Kinzie, 507

Brotherhood of R. R. Trainmen v. Virginia, 1386

Brotherhood of Ry. and S. S. Clerks, Freight Handlers, Exp. and Station Emp. v. Allen, 1397

Brown v. Board of Ed. of Topeka, 65, **673,** 680, 843, 938

Brown v. Glines, 1276

Brown v. Hartlage, 1419

Brown v. Oklahoma, 1079

Brown v. Socialist Workers '74 Campaign Committee (Ohio), 1383

Brown v. State of La., 1212, 1268

Brown v. Thomson, 873

Brown, United States v., 1390

Brown–Forman Distillers Corp. v. New York State Liquor Authority, 269

Buck v. Bell, 518, 532, 629

Buck v. Kuykendall, 269, 271

Buckley v. Valeo, 220, 243, **390, 1381, 1400**

Budd v. New York, 458

Bullock v. Carter, 892

Bunting v. State of Oregon, 471

Burch v. Louisiana, 452

Burdick v. Takushi, 891, 894

Burlington Northern R. Co. v. Ford, 652

Burns v. Fortson, 864

Burnside v. Byars, 1295

Burson v. Freeman, 1207, 1243

Burton v. Wilmington Parking Authority, 942

Bush v. Vera, 889

Butler v. State of Mich., 1167

Butler, United States v., 17, **235**

Caban v. Mohammed, 695

C & A Carbone, Inc. v. Town of Clarkstown, N.Y., 280, **284**

Calder v. Bull, 455, 457

Caldwell v. Mississippi, 74

Califano v. Goldfarb, 656, 718

Califano v. Webster, 699, **718**

California Med. Ass'n v. Federal Elec. Com'n, 1411

California, United States v., 207

Caminetti v. United States, 173

Cammermeyer v. Aspin, 748

Cantwell v. State of Connecticut, 1076, 1237, 1471, **1478**

Capitol Square Review and Advisory Bd. v. Pinette, 1291, 1528

Cardona v. Power, 984, 1001

Carey v. Brown, 1205, 1243, 1261

Carey v. Population Services, Intern., 554, 1185

Carolene Products Co., United States v., 478, 484, 1030

Carroll v. President and Com'rs of Princess Anne, 1348

Carter v. Carter Coal Co., 23, 180, 187

Carter v. Jury Commission of Greene County, 750

Castaneda v. Partida, 750

Castle v. Hayes Freight Lines, 344

Causby, United States v., 494

CBS, Inc. v. F. C. C., 1454

Central Hudson Gas & Elec. Corp. v. Public Service Commission of New York, 1189

Champion v. Ames (The Lottery Case), 163, 169, 252

Chaplinsky v. State of New Hampshire, 1033, 1077

Charles River Bridge v. Warren Bridge, 507

Chemical Waste Management, Inc. v. Hunt, 277

Chicago, B. & Q.R. Co. v. City of Chicago, 486

Chicago, M. & St. P. Ry. Co. v. Minnesota, 459

Chicago & Southern Air Lines v. Waterman S. S. Corp., 1354

Chicago Teachers Union, Local No. 1, AFT, AFL–CIO v. Hudson, 1398

Child Labor Tax Case (Bailey v. Drexel Furniture Co.), 142, 229

Chisholm v. Georgia, 225

Church of the Lukumi Babalu Aye, Inc. v. City of Hialeah, 1472

Cincinnati, City of v. Discovery Network, Inc., 1193

Cipriano v. City of Houma, 862

Cities Service Gas Co. v. Peerless Oil & Gas Co., 295

Citizen Pub. Co. v. United States, 1492

Citizens Against Rent Control v. City of Berkeley, Cal., 1418

City of (see name of city)

Civil Rights Cases, 921

Clark v. Community for Creative Non-Violence, 1210, 1212, 1254

Clark v. Jeter, 725, 728

Cleburne, Tex., City of v. Cleburne Living Center, 728

Clements v. Fashing, 892

Cleveland Bd. of Educ. v. LaFleur, 915

Cleveland Bd. of Educ. v. Loudermill, 621

Coates v. City of Cincinnati, 1338

Cohen v. California, 1032, 1080, 1081, 1113, 1261

Cohen v. Cowles Media Co., 1447

Cohens v. State of Virginia, 13, 63

Colautti v. Franklin, 501

Cole v. Richardson, 1395

Colegrove v. Green, 46, 865

Coleman v. Miller, 48

Colgate v. Harvey, 429

Collector v. Day, 351

Collin v. Smith, 578 F.2d 197, pp. 1093, 1113

Collin v. Smith, 447 F.Supp. 676, p. 1113

Collins v. Hardyman, 920, 974

Colorado Republican Federal Campaign Committee v. Federal Election Com'n, 1412

Columbia Broadcasting System, Inc. v. Democratic Nat. Committee, 948, 1453

Columbus Bd. of Ed. v. Penick, 777

Committee For Public Ed. and Religious Liberty v. Nyquist, 1535

Committee for Public Ed. and Religious Liberty v. Regan, 1535

Commonwealth v. _____ (see opposing party)

Commonwealth of (see name of Commonwealth)

Communist Party of United States v. Subversive Activities Control Bd., 1070

Communist Party v. Catherwood, 1070

Communist Party of United States v. United States, 1070

Compassion in Dying v. State of Wash., 610

Connally v. General Const. Co., 1337

Connecticut Bd. of Pardons v. Dumschat, 624

Connecticut General Life Ins. Co. v. Johnson, 459

Connick v. Myers, 1304

Connolly v. Pension Ben. Guar. Corp., 494

Consolidated Edison Co. of New York, Inc. v. Public Service Commission of New York, 1170, 1261

Constantine, United States v., 232

Cooley v. Board of Wardens, 265, 300, 301

Cooper v. Aaron, 25, 410, 772

Coppage v. State of Kansas, 467, 468, 471

Corfield v. Coryell, 328, 425, 428

Cornelius v. NAACP Legal Defense and Educational Fund, Inc., 1208, 1279

Corporation of Presiding Bishop of Church of Jesus Christ of Latter-Day Saints v. Amos, 1549

County of (see name of county)

Cox v. State of Louisiana, 1088, 1245, 1433

Cox v. State of New Hampshire, 1238, 1244, 1274, 1342

Cox Broadcasting Corp. v. Cohn, 1108

Craig v. Boren, 631, 632, 683, 684, 686, 698, 725

Craig v. Harney, 1432

Cramp v. Board of Public Instruction of Orange County, Fla., 1392

Crandall v. State of Nevada, 336, 426

Crawford v. Board of Educ. of City of Los Angeles, 792

Cruikshank, United States v., 925

Cruzan v. Director, Missouri Dept. of Health, 602

CTS Corp. v. Dynamics Corp. of America, 318

Cubby, Inc. v. CompuServe, Inc., 1456, 1458

Cumming v. Board of Ed. of Richmond County, 675

Cummings v. Missouri, 1390

Curtis Pub. Co. v. Butts, 1100

Curtiss–Wright Export Corporation, United States v., 256, 359, 403

Dallas, City of v. Stanglin, 1375
Dames & Moore v. Regan, 367
Dandridge v. Williams, 551, 649, 844, 845, 847, 849, **912**
Daniel v. Family Sec. Life Ins. Co., 641
Darby, United States v., 189, **191,** 213
Dartmouth College v. Woodward, 506
Davidson v. City of New Orleans, 458
Davis v. Bandemer, 53, **875,** 879, 880
Davis v. Beason, 740, 745
Davis, Commonwealth v., 1235
Davis, Helvering v., 241, **243**
Davis v. Schnell, 987
Dayton Bd. of Ed. v. Brinkman, 777
Dean Milk Co. v. City of Madison, Wis., 281
Debs, In re, 1353
Debs v. United States, 1038
DeCanas v. Bica, 343
DeFunis v. Odegaard, 44, **794**
De Geofroy v. Riggs, 254, 257
De Jonge v. State of Oregon, 1060, 1374
Dellums v. Bush, 374
Dennis v. United States, 1032, **1061**
Denver Area Educational Telecommunications Consortium, Inc. v. F.C.C., 1171, 1456
Derrington v. Plummer, 945
DeShaney v. Winnebago County Dept. of Social Services, 601, 960
Di Santo v. Commonwealth of Pennsylvania, 269
Doe v. Bolton, 530, 536, **537,** 537
Doe v. Commonwealth's Attorney for City of Richmond, 96 S.Ct. 1489, p. 593
Doe v. Commonwealth's Attorney for City of Richmond, 403 F.Supp. 1199, p. 593
Doe v. University of Michigan, 1114
Dolan v. City of Tigard, 496
Dombrowski v. Pfister, 1326
Douglas v. People of State of Cal., 897
Dr. Bonham's Case, 14
Dred Scott v. Sandford, 13, 22, 424
Dun & Bradstreet, Inc. v. Greenmoss Builders, Inc., 1103
Duncan v. State of La., 442
Dunn v. Blumstein, 844, **863,** 906

E. C. Knight Co., United States v., 163, **164**
Edelman v. Jordan, 225
Edenfield v. Fane, 1187
Edgar v. MITE Corp., 317, 322
Edge Broadcasting Co., United States v., 1196
Edmonson v. Leesville Concrete Co., Inc., 959
Edwards v. Aguillard, 1498, **1515**
Edwards v. California, 336, 429
Edwards v. South Carolina, 1088
E.E.O.C. v. Wyoming, 1020
Eichman, United States v., 1228
Eisenstadt v. Baird, 528, 844
Elfbrandt v. Russell, 1393
Elkins v. Moreno, 915
Ellis v. Railway Clerks, 1398

El Paso, City of v. Simmons, 510
Elrod v. Burns, 1312, 1398
Employment Div., Dept. of Human Resources of Oregon v. Smith, 1014, 1476, **1489**
Employment Div., Dept. of Human Resources of State of Or. v. Smith, 108 S.Ct. 1444, p. 1014
Energy Reserves Group, Inc. v. Kansas Power and Light Co., 514
Engel v. Vitale, 1504
Enmons, United States v., 198
Epperson v. State of Ark., 1514
Erznoznik v. City of Jacksonville, 1156, 1205, 1326
Estate of (see name of party)
Eu v. San Francisco County Democratic Cent. Committee, 865
Euclid, Ohio, Village of v. Ambler Realty Co., 492
Evans v. Abney, 939
Evans v. Newton, 930, 931
Everson v. Board of Ed. of Ewing Tp., 1462, 1531, **1532**
Ex parte (see name of party)
Exxon Corp. v. Eagerton, 515, 652
Exxon Corp. v. Governor of Maryland, 314

Fairfax's Devisee v. Hunter's Lessee, 61
F.C.C. v. Beach Communications, Inc., 661
F.C.C. v. Florida Power Corp., 494
F.C.C. v. League of Women Voters of California, 1320, 1322, **1454**
F. C. C. v. Pacifica Foundation, 1164, 1261
Federal Base Ball Club of Baltimore v. National League of Professional Base Ball Clubs, 166
Federal Election Com'n v. Massachusetts Citizens for Life, Inc., 1416, 1417
Federal Election Com'n v. National Conservative Political Action Committee, 1412
Federal Election Com'n v. National Right to Work Committee, 1416
Federal Power Commission v. Hope Natural Gas Co., 459
Feiner v. New York, 1086
Felker v. Turpin, 78
F. E. R. C. v. Mississippi, 208, **209,** 212, 215, 222
Ferguson v. Skrupa, 480
Fiallo v. Bell, 727
First Agr. Nat. Bank of Berkshire County v. State Tax Commission, 351
First English Evangelical Lutheran Church of Glendale v. Los Angeles County, Cal., 492
First Nat. Bank of Boston v. Bellotti, 1413, 1421
Fiske v. State of Kansas, 1059
Fitzpatrick v. Bitzer, 225
Flagg Bros., Inc. v. Brooks, 932, 954
Flast v. Cohen, 37

Flemming v. Nestor, 654
Fletcher v. Peck, 13, 456, 506
Flood v. Kuhn, 166
Flores v. City of Boerne, 1015
Florida Bar v. Went for It, Inc., 1188
Florida Lime & Avocado Growers, Inc. v. Paul, 343
Florida Star v. B.J.F., 1108
Flower v. United States, 1274
Foley v. Connelie, 720, 722
Fordice, United States v., 788
Forsyth County, Ga. v. Nationalist Movement, 1090, 1208
Fort Gratiot Sanitary Landfill, Inc. v. Michigan Dept. of Natural Resources, 284
44 Liquormart, Inc. v. Rhode Island, 1197, **1198**
Foster–Fountain Packing Co. v. Haydel, 272, **280**
Franks v. Bowman Transp. Co., Inc., 798
Frazee v. Illinois Dept. of Employment Sec., 1482
Freedman v. State of Md., 1273, **1342**
Freeman v. Pitts, 788
Frisby v. Schultz, 1261
Frohwerk v. United States, 1037
Frontiero v. Richardson, 684
Frothingham v. Mellon, 37
Fry v. United States, 207
F.T.C. v. Superior Court Trial Lawyers Ass'n, 1389
Fullilove v. Klutznick, 248, **812**
Furman v. Georgia, 441
FW/PBS, Inc. v. City of Dallas, 1343

Gade v. National Solid Wastes Management Ass'n, 344
Gaffney v. Cummings, 873, 874
Gannett Co., Inc. v. DePasquale, 1425
Garcia v. San Antonio Metropolitan Transit Authority, 209, 222
Gardner v. Broderick, 1391
Garland, Ex parte, 1390
Garner v. Board of Public Works of City of Los Angeles, 1390
Garner v. State of La., 946
Garrison v. State of La., 1106
Garrity v. State of N. J., 1391
Gaston County, N. C. v. United States, 989
Gayle v. Browder, 678
G. D. Searle & Co. v. Cohn, 652
Geduldig v. Aiello, 697
Geer v. State of Conn., 295
General Bldg. Contractors Ass'n, Inc. v. Pennsylvania, 983
Georgia, State of v. Stanton, 78
Gerhardt, Helvering v., 351
Gertz v. Robert Welch, Inc., 1097, 1102
Gibbons v. Ogden, 113, 159, 190, 192, **261,** 264, 301
Giboney v. Empire Storage & Ice Co., 1387
Gibson v. Florida Legislative Investigation Committee, 1379
Gideon v. Wainwright, 441
Gillette v. United States, 1469, 1491

Gilmore v. City of Montgomery, Ala., 945
Ginsberg v. State of N. Y., 1166
Gitlow v. New York, 467, **1050**
Givhan v. Western Line Consol. School Dist., 1303
Glidden Co. v. Zdanok, 79
Globe Newspaper Co. v. Superior Court for Norfolk County, 1429
Goesaert v. Cleary, 641, **683**
Gold v. Dicarlo, 473
Goldberg v. Kelly, 616, 624
Goldblatt v. Town of Hempstead, N. Y., 492
Goldman v. Weinberger, 1276, **1485**
Goldstein v. California, 258
Goldwater v. Carter, 53
Gomillion v. Lightfoot, 752
Gong Lum v. Rice, 675
Gooding v. Wilson, 1079, 1113, 1326, 1328, 1329
Gordon v. Gordon, 940
Gordon v. Lance, 874
Goss v. Board of Ed. of City of Knoxville, Tenn., 772
Goss v. Lopez, 626
Grace, United States v., 1266
Graham v. Richardson, 683, **720**
Grand Rapids v. Ball, 1541
Graves v. People of State of New York ex rel. O'Keefe, 351
Gray v. Sanders, 866, 867, 868
Grayned v. City of Rockford, 1271, 1338
Great Atlantic & Pac. Tea Co., Inc. v. Cottrell, 281
Green v. County School Bd. of New Kent County, Va., 773
Greenholtz v. Inmates of Nebraska Penal and Correctional Complex, 624
Greer v. Spock, 1274
Gregory v. City of Chicago, 1089
Griffin v. Breckenridge, 974
Griffin v. California, 439
Griffin v. County School Bd. of Prince Edward County, 752
Griffin v. Illinois, 847, **896**
Griffiths, Application of, 645, 683, **721**
Griggs v. Allegheny County, Pa., 494
Griggs v. Duke Power Co., 753
Griswold v. Connecticut, 453, **518,** 591
Grosjean v. American Press Co., 1441
Grovey v. Townsend, 934
Guest, United States v., 962, **964**
Gulf, C. & S.F. Ry. Co. v. Ellis, 629

Hadley v. Junior College Dist. of Metropolitan Kansas City, Mo., 872
Hague v. Committee for Indus. Organization, 430, **1236,** 1237, 1267, 1270
Hamling v. United States, 1143
Hamm v. City of Rock Hill, 942
Hammer v. Dagenhart (Child Labor Case), 142, 163, 166, 172, **173,** 176, 189, 195, 229, 231, 232, 234
Hampton v. Mow Sun Wong, 724, 814
Hans v. Louisiana, 225
Harlow v. Fitzgerald, 410

Harper v. Virginia State Bd. of Elections, 858
Harper & Row Publishers, Inc. v. Nation Enterprises, 1109
Harris v. McRae, 249, 551, 736
Hauenstein v. Lynham, 254
Hawaii Housing Authority v. Midkiff, 504
Hazelwood School Dist. v. Kuhlmeier, 1300
Healy v. James, 1383
Heart of Atlanta Motel, Inc. v. United States, 203
Heffron v. International Soc. for Krishna Consciousness, Inc., 1243, 1245, 1288
Helvering v. _____ (see opposing party)
Henneford v. Silas Mason Co., 288
Henry v. State of Miss., 74
Herb v. Pitcairn, 69
Herbert v. Lando, 1099
Hernandez v. State of Tex., 664, 750
Herndon v. Lowry, 1060, 1073
Hess v. Indiana, 1074
Hewitt v. Helms, 625
Hicklin v. Orbeck, 328, 331, 909
Hines v. Davidowitz, 343
Hipolite Egg Co. v. United States, 172
Hirabayashi v. United States, 638
Hishon v. King & Spalding, 1400
H. L. v. Matheson, 549
Hobbie v. Unemployment Appeals Com'n of Florida, 1482
Hodel v. Virginia Surface Min. and Reclamation Ass'n, Inc., 200, 208, 215, 217, 218, 222
Hodgson v. Minnesota, 549
Hoke v. United States, 172
Holden v. Hardy, 461
Hollenbaugh v. Carnegie Free Library, 599
Holmes v. City of Atlanta, 678
Home Bldg. & Loan Ass'n v. Blaisdell, 177, 507
Hooper v. Bernalillo County Assessor, 910
Hopwood v. State of Tex., 809
Hostetter v. Idlewild Bon Voyage Liquor Corp., 346
Houchins v. KQED, Inc., 1423
Houston, Tex., City of v. Hill, 1335
H. P. Hood & Sons v. Du Mond, 260, 271, 292
Hudgens v. N. L. R. B., 930, 1293
Hudson County Water Co. v. McCarter, 295
Hughes v. Alexandria Scrap Corp., 323
Hughes v. Oklahoma, 280, 295, 297
Humphrey's Ex'r v. United States, 391
Hunt v. McNair, 1542
Hunt v. Washington State Apple Advertising Commission, 289
Hunter v. Erickson, 746, 790, 949
Hunter v. Underwood, 770
Hurd v. Hodge, 938
Hurley v. Irish–American Gay, Lesbian and Bisexual Group of Boston, 1212, 1371
Hurtado v. People of State of Cal., 434
Hustler Magazine v. Falwell, 1105
Hutchinson v. Proxmire, 413, 1101

Hynes v. Mayor and Council of Borough of Oradell, 1237, 1287

Ibanez v. Florida Dept. of Business and Professional Regulation, Bd. of Accountancy, 1188
Ingraham v. Wright, 626
In re (see name of party)
I.N.S. v. Chadha, 220, 375
International Ass'n of Machinists v. Street, 1397
International Boxing Club of N.Y., United States v., 166
International Broth. of Teamsters, Local 695, A.F.L. v. Vogt, Inc., 1387
International Longshoremen's Ass'n, AFL–CIO v. Allied Intern., Inc., 1389
International Soc. for Krishna Consciousness, Inc. v. Lee, 1283
Itel Containers Intern. Corp. v. Huddleston, 322
Ives v. South Buffalo Ry. Co., 67

Jackson v. Indiana, 899
Jackson v. Metropolitan Edison Co., 931, 952
Jacobs, In re, 458
Jacobson v. Commonwealth of Massachusetts, 465
James v. Valtierra, 736
James Clark Distilling Co. v. Western Maryland R. Co., 346
J.E.B. v. Alabama ex rel. T.B., 664, 702, 751
Jefferson v. Hackney, 737, 754, 756, 844, 913
Jenkins v. Georgia, 1142
Jenness v. Fortson, 891
Jimenez v. Weinberger, 649, 914
Johnson v. Haydel, 280
Johnson v. Robison, 647, 655, 656
Johnson v. State of Maryland, 352
Johnson v. State of Va., 678
Jones v. Alfred H. Mayer Co., 978
Jones v. Clinton, 410
Jones v. Wolf, 1471
Jordan v. De George, 1337
Joseph Burstyn, Inc. v. Wilson, 1342
Joseph S. Finch & Co. v. McKittrick, 346

Kadrmas v. Dickinson Public Schools, 857
Kahn v. Shevin, 716
Kahriger, United States v., 232
Karcher v. Daggett, 872
Kassel v. Consolidated Freightways Corp. of Delaware, 306
Katzenbach v. McClung, 203, 214
Katzenbach v. Morgan, 228, 348, 643, 876, 918, 971, 984, 998
Kay, In re, 1091
Keller v. State Bar of California, 1398
Kelley v. Johnson, 543, 599
Kentucky, Com. of v. Dennison, 353
Kewanee Oil Co. v. Bicron Corp., 258

Keyes v. School Dist. No. 1, Denver, Colo., 776, 781

Keyishian v. Board of Regents of University of State of N. Y., 1394

Keystone Bituminous Coal Ass'n v. DeBenedictis, 490, 491

Kidd v. Pearson, 164, 187

Kingsley Books, Inc. v. Brown, 1344

Kingsley Intern. Pictures Corp. v. Regents of University of State of N.Y., 1129, 1204

Kirchberg v. Feenstra, 699

Kirkpatrick v. Preisler, 872

Klein, United States v., 79

Kleindienst v. Mandel, 1070

Kokinda, United States v., 1281

Kolender v. Lawson, 1337

Konigsberg v. State Bar of Cal., 81 S.Ct. 997, pp. 1031, 1391

Konigsberg v. State Bar of Cal., 77 S.Ct. 722, p. 1391

Korematsu v. United States, 252, 664

Kotch v. Board of River Port Pilot Com'rs for Port of New Orleans, 641

Kovacs v. Cooper, 1031, 1241, 1260, 1402

Kramer v. Union Free School Dist. No. 15, p. 860

Kras, United States v., 900

Kunz v. New York, 1090

Kusper v. Pontikes, 864

Labine v. Vincent, 726

Ladue, City of v. Gilleo, 1212, 1243, 1249

Laird v. Tatum, 45

Lakewood, City of v. Plain Dealer Pub. Co., 1238, 1249, 1340

Lalli v. Lalli, 727

Lamb's Chapel v. Center Moriches Union Free School Dist., 1290, 1543

Lamont v. Postmaster General of United States, 1070

Landmark Communications, Inc. v. Virginia, 1075, 1431

Larkin v. Grendel's Den, Inc., 1548

Larson v. Valente, 1476, 1497

Lassiter v. Department of Social Services of Durham County, N. C., 901

Lassiter v. Northampton County Bd. of Elections, 987

Lathrop v. Donohue, 1397

Lauf v. E.G. Shinner & Co., 85

Law Students Civil Rights Research Council, Inc. v. Wadmond, 1397

Leathers v. Medlock, 1445

Lee v. International Soc. for Krishna Consciousness, Inc., 1283

Lee, United States v., 1484, 1491

Lee v. Washington, 671

Lee v. Weisman, 1465, 1507

Lefkowitz v. Turley, 1391

Lehman v. City of Shaker Heights, 1272

Lehnert v. Ferris Faculty Ass'n, 1398

Lehr v. Robertson, 696

Leisy v. Hardin, 345

Lemon v. Kurtzman, 1501, 1534

Lerner v. Casey, 1391

Leslie Miller, Inc. v. State of Ark., 352

Levitt v. Committee for Public Ed. and Religious Liberty, 1534

Levy v. Louisiana, 725

Lewis v. BT Inv. Managers, Inc., 317

Lewis v. City of New Orleans, 1079

License Cses (Thurlow v. Com. of Mass.), 265

Liggett Co. v. Baldridge, 474

Lincoln Federal Labor Union No. 19129, A.F. of L. v. Northwestern Iron & Metal Co., 480

Lindsey v. Normet, 844, 849, **913**

Lindsley v. Natural Carbonic Gas Co., 636

Linkletter v. Walker, 445

Linmark Associates, Inc. v. Willingboro Tp., 1185

Little v. Streater, 901

Lloyd Corp., Limited v. Tanner, 930, **1292**

Local 2677, Am. Federation of Government Emp. v. Phillips, 384

Lochner v. New York, 453, 460, 1030

Lockport, New York, Town of v. Citizens for Community Action at Local Level, Inc., 749

Logan v. Zimmerman Brush Co., 658

Lombard v. State of La., 941

Lopez, United States v., 114, 141, **142**

Loretto v. Teleprompter Manhattan CATV Corp., 494

Los Angeles, City of v. Preferred Communications, Inc., 1455

Los Angeles, City Council of v. Taxpayers for Vincent, 1212, 1243, **1249**

Los Angeles, Dept. of Water and Power, City of v. Manhart, 701

Louisiana ex rel. Gremillion v. National Ass'n for the Advancement of Colored People, 1375

Louisiana, State of, United States v., 65

Lovell v. City of Griffin, Ga., 1237, **1340,** 1471

Loving v. Virginia, 667

Lubin v. Panish, 892

Lucas v. Forty–Fourth General Assembly of State of Colo., 869, 869

Lucas v. South Carolina Coastal Council, 499

Lugar v. Edmondson Oil Co., Inc., 957

Lujan v. Defenders of Wildlife, 38

Luke Records, Inc. v. Navarro, 1144

Luther v. Borden, 49

Lynch v. Donnelly, 1507, **1521,** 1534

Lynch v. Household Finance Corp., 485

Lynch v. United States, 515

Lyng v. Castillo, 648, 914

Lyng v. International Union, United Auto., Aerospace and Agr. Implement Workers of America, UAW, 648

Lyng v. Northwest Indian Cemetery Protective Ass'n, 1487

Madden v. Commonwealth of Kentucky, 429

Madsen v. Women's Health Center, Inc., 1208, **1263**

Mahan v. Howell, 873

Maher v. Roe, 550

Maine v. Taylor, 276
Malloy v. Hogan, 439, 1391
Manigault v. Springs, 507
Mapp v. Ohio, 450
Marbury v. Madison, 3, 12, 27, 66, 406, 408, 456, 541, 919, 985
Marigold, United States v., 162
Marsh v. Chambers, 1519
Marsh v. State of Ala., 928, 959, 1293
Marston v. Lewis, 864
Martin v. City of Struthers, Ohio, 1212, 1240, 1259, 1471
Martin v. Hunter's Lessee, 11, 13, 60, 66
Martinez v. Bynum, 857
Maryland v. Wirtz, 191, 199, 207
Maryland, State of v. Baltimore Radio Show, 68
Massachusetts v. Oakes, 1334
Massachusetts v. United States, 351
Massachusetts Bd. of Retirement v. Murgia, 649, 734
Masses Pub. Co. v. Patten, 1046, 1049
Mathews v. Diaz, 725, 727
Mathews v. Eldridge, 615, 626
Mathews v. Lucas, 655, 726
Mayor, Aldermen and Commonalty of City of New York v. Miln, 265
Mayor and City Council of Baltimore City v. Dawson, 678
McAuliffe v. Mayor of New Bedford, 1302
McCardle, Ex parte, 76
McCarroll v. Dixie Greyhound Lines, 350
McCarthy v. Philadelphia Civil Service Commission, 331
McCollum v. Board of Ed. of School Dist. No. 71, Champaign County, Ill., 1501
McDaniel v. Paty, 1471, 1472, 1474
McDonald v. Board of Election Com'rs of Chicago, 642
McDonald v. Santa Fe Trail Transp. Co., 981
McGinnis v. Royster, 647, 899
McGowan v. State of Md., 642, 1478, 1519
McIntyre v. Ohio Elections Com'n, 1364
McLaughlin v. State of Fla., 668, 669
McLaurin v. Oklahoma State Regents for Higher Ed., 675
M'Culloch v. Maryland, 21, 89, 103, 171, 230, 248, 351, 352, 963, 1192
Meachum v. Fano, 624
Meek v. Pittenger, 1534
Meinhold v. United States Dept. of Defense, 748
Meltzer v. C. Buck LeCraw & Co., 900
Members of City Council of City of Los Angeles v. Taxpayers for Vincent, 1212, 1243, 1249
Memorial Hospital v. Maricopa County, 906
Memphis, City of v. Greene, 771, 983
Metro Broadcasting, Inc. v. F.C.C., 828
Metromedia, Inc. v. City of San Diego, 1193, 1248
Metropolitan Life Ins. Co. v. Ward, 347, 348

Metropolitan Washington Airports Authority v. Citizens for Abatement of Aircraft Noise, Inc., 398
Meyer v. Grant, 1419
Meyer v. State of Nebraska, 467, 516
Miami Herald Pub. Co. v. Tornillo, 1366
Michael H. v. Gerald D., 590
Michael M. v. Superior Court of Sonoma County, 690, 697
Michelin Tire Corp. v. Wages, 327
Michigan v. Long, 71
Milk Control Board of Pennsylvania v. Eisenberg Farm Products, 291
Milkovich v. Lorain Journal Co., 1098
Miller v. California, 1132
Miller v. Johnson, 839, 887
Miller v. Schoene, 490
Milligan, Ex parte, 78
Milliken v. Bradley, 783
Mills v. Habluetzel, 727
Mills v. State of Ala., 1027
Milnot Co. v. Richardson, 478
Minersville School Dist. v. Gobitis, 1362
Minneapolis Star and Tribune Co. v. Minnesota Com'r of Revenue, 1440
Minnesota v. Clover Leaf Creamery Co., 315
Minnesota, State of v. Barber, 280
Miranda v. Arizona, 84, 1017
Mississippi, State of v. Johnson, 78, 408
Mississippi University for Women v. Hogan, 698, 1020
Missouri v. Jenkins, 115 S.Ct. 2038, p. 789
Missouri v. Jenkins, 110 S.Ct. 1651, p. 785
Missouri ex rel. Gaines, State of v. Canada, 673
Missouri Pac. Ry. Co. v. State of Nebraska, 486
Missouri, State of v. Holland, 252, 365
Mistretta v. United States, 400
Mitchell v. Forsyth, 410
Mobile, Ala., City of v. Bolden, 754, 765, 876, 990
Monell v. Department of Social Services of City of New York, 977
Monroe v. Pape, 977
Moore v. City of East Cleveland, Ohio, 584, 649
Moose Lodge No. 107 v. Irvis, 947
Mora v. McNamara, 371
Morehead v. New York ex rel. Tipaldo, 183, 478
Morey v. Doud, 483, 636
Morrison v. Olson, 356, 390, 391, 397, 398
Mourning v. Family Publications Service, Inc., 915
Mt. Healthy City School Dist. Bd. of Educ. v. Doyle, 759
Mueller v. Allen, 1535, 1543, 1544
Mugler v. Kansas, 459
Muller v. State of Oregon, 466, 470
Munn v. People of State of Illinois, 458
Murdock v. Pennsylvania, 1287
Murray's Lessee v. Hoboken Land & Imp. Co., 433
Myers v. United States, 354, 391

N. A. A. C. P. v. Claiborne Hardware Co., **1074, 1387,** 1389

Napier v. Atlantic Coast Line R. Co., 344

National Ass'n for Advancement of Colored People v. Button, 1383

National Ass'n for Advancement of Colored People v. State of Ala., ex rel. Patterson, 1326, 1375, **1376,** 1381, 1382, 1397, 1403, 1436, 1438

National Broadcasting Co. v. United States, 1450

National Collegiate Athletic Ass'n v. Tarkanian, 958

National League of Cities v. Usery, 206, 207

National R.R. Passenger Corp. v. Atchison Topeka and Santa Fe Ry. Co., 516

National Socialist Party of America v. Village of Skokie, 1112

National Treasury Employees Union, United States v., 1309

Near v. State of Minnesota ex rel. Olson, 1345

Nebbia v. New York, 177, 287, **474**

Nebraska Press Ass'n v. Stuart, 1357

Nectow v. City of Cambridge, 492

New Energy Co. of Indiana v. Limbach, 280

New England Power Co. v. New Hampshire, 280, **296**

New Mexico, United States v., 352

New Orleans, City of v. Dukes, 636, **649**

New Orleans City Park Improvement Association v. Detiege, 678

New State Ice Co. v. Liebmann, **473**

New York v. Ferber, 1145, 1331

New York v. O'Neill, 353

New York v. United States, 114, 139, 207, 208, **212,** 224, 235

New York City Transit Authority v. Beazer, 651

New York ex rel. Bryant v. Zimmerman, 1377

New York State Club Ass'n, Inc. v. City of New York, 1400

New York Times Co. v. Sullivan, 1027, 1092, **1094,** 1122

New York Times Co. v. United States (The Pentagon Papers Cases), 1349

Nixon v. Administrator of General Services, 411

Nixon v. Condon, 934

Nixon v. Fitzgerald, 408, 410

Nixon v. Herndon, 934

Nixon v. United States, 54

Nixon, United States v., 24, 54, **404,** 412

N.L.R.B. v. Jones & Laughlin Steel Corp., 185

Nollan v. California Coastal Com'n, 495

Nordlinger v. Hahn, 660

North Carolina State Bd. of Ed. v. Swann, 794

North Dakota v. United States, 352

North Dakota State Bd. of Pharmacy v. Snyder's Drug Stores, Inc., 473

Northeast Bancorp, Inc. v. Board of Governors of Federal Reserve System, 349

Northern Securities Co. v. United States, 165

Northwest Central Pipeline Corp. v. State Corp. Com'n of Kansas, 322

Northwestern States Portland Cement Co. v. State of Minn., 350

Norton v. Shelby County, 27

Noto v. United States, 1069

O'Brien, United States v., 1081, **1209,** 1213

Ogden v. Saunders, 506

O'Hare Truck Service, Inc. v. City of Northlake, 1316

Ohio v. Akron Center for Reproductive Health, 549

Ohralik v. Ohio State Bar Ass'n, 1186

Oklahoma v. United States Civil Service Com'n, 248

Olim v. Wakinekona, 625

O'Lone v. Estate of Shabazz, 1486

Olsen v. State of Nebraska, 473, **480**

Oregon v. Mitchell, 984, 985, 989, **1004**

Oregon, United States v., 199

Oregon Waste Systems, Inc. v. Department of Environmental Quality of State of Or., 277

Orr v. Orr, 717

Ortwein v. Schwab, 900

Osborne v. Ohio, 1148, 1335

Owen v. City of Independence, Mo., 977

Ownbey v. Morgan, 433

Pacific Gas and Elec. Co. v. Public Utilities Com'n of California, 1367

Pacific Gas and Elec. Co. v. State Energy Resources Conservation & Development Com'n, 338

Pacific States Telephone & Telegraph Co. v. State of Oregon, 50

Palko v. State of Connecticut, 435

Palmer v. Thompson, 751

Palmore v. Sidoti, 669

Panama Refining Co. v. Ryan, 177, 400

Papachristou v. City of Jacksonville, 1337

Parham v. Hughes, 696

Parham v. J. R., 584

Paris Adult Theatre I v. Slaton, 596, 1128, **1135**

Passenger Cases (Smith v. Turner), 265

Patterson v. Colorado, 1024, 1037

Paul v. Davis, **622,** 624, 625

Paul v. State of Virginia, 328

Payton v. New York, 445

Peel v. Attorney Registration and Disciplinary Com'n of Illinois, 1187

Pell v. Procunier, 1423

Penn Cent. Transp. Co. v. City of New York, 492

Pennekamp v. State of Fla., 1432

Pennhurst State School and Hospital v. Halderman, 244, 1019

Pennsylvania v. State of West Virginia, 295

Pennsylvania v. Union Gas Co., 225

Pennsylvania, Com. of v. Board of Directors of City Trusts of City of Philadelphia, 940

Pennsylvania, Com. of v. Brown, 940

Pennsylvania Coal Co. v. Mahon, 487

Pension Ben. Guar. Corp. v. R.A. Gray & Co., 515
People v. _____ (see opposing party)
Perez v. Brownell, 256
Perez v. Campbell, 258
Perez v. United States, 196
Perry v. Sindermann, 618
Perry v. United States, 23
Perry Educ. Ass'n v. Perry Local Educators' Ass'n, 1208, 1268, **1277**
Personnel Adm'r of Massachusetts v. Feeney, 761
Peters v. Kiff, 664
Peterson v. City of Greenville, S. C., 941
Phalen v. Commonwealth of Virginia, 169
Philadelphia, City of v. New Jersey, 270, **271,** 274, 275, 286, 296, 297
Philadelphia Newspapers, Inc. v. Hepps, 1099, 1104
Philips v. Perry, 748
Phoenix, Ariz., City of v. Kolodziejski, 862
Pickering v. Board of Ed. of Tp. High School Dist. 205, Will County, Illinois, 1303
Pickett v. Brown, 727
Pierce v. Society of the Sisters of the Holy Names of Jesus and Mary, 517
Pike v. Bruce Church, Inc., 270, 280, **297**
Pink, United States v., 366, 369
Pittsburgh Press Co. v. Pittsburgh Commission on Human Relations, 1175, 1445
Planned Parenthood Ass'n of Kansas City, Mo., Inc. v. Ashcroft, 549
Planned Parenthood of Central Missouri v. Danforth, 548
Planned Parenthood of Southeastern Pennsylvania v. Casey, 557
Plaut v. Spendthrift Farm, Inc., 80
Plessy v. Ferguson, 583, 670, **671**
Plyler v. Doe, 683, 728, 841, 843, 844, **850**
Poe v. Ullman, 522, 585
Poelker v. Doe, 551
Police Dept. of City of Chicago v. Mosley, 844, **1205,** 1235, 1243
Pollock v. Farmers' Loan & Trust Co., 351
Pope v. Illinois, 1143
Posadas de Puerto Rico Associates v. Tourism Co. of Puerto Rico, 1195
Poulos v. State of N.H., 1343
Powe v. Miles, 948
Powell v. McCormack, 53, 115, 405
Powell v. State of Ala., 433, 441
Presbyterian Church in United States v. Hull Memorial Presbyterian Church, 1471
Press–Enterprise Co. v. Superior Court of California for Riverside County, 106 S.Ct. 2735, p. **1431**
Press–Enterprise Co. v. Superior Court of California, Riverside County, 104 S.Ct. 829, p. **1430**
Price, United States v., 958, **968**
Primus, In re, 1186
Prince v. Massachusetts, 531, **1478**
Progressive, Inc., United States v., 1355
Providence Bank v. Billings, 507
Prudential Ins. Co. v. Benjamin, 217, **346**

PruneYard Shopping Center v. Robins, 930, **1366**
Public Utilities Commission of District of Columbia v. Pollak, 952, 1273

Quill v. Vacco, 613
Quill Corp. v. North Dakota, 350
Quinn v. Millsap, 863

Radovich v. National Football League, 166
Railroad Commission Cases, 459
Railroad Commission of Wisconsin v. Chicago, B. & Q. R. Co., 167
Railroad Retirement Board v. Alton R. Co., 177
Railway Emp. Dept. v. Hanson, 1397
Railway Exp. Agency v. New York, 252, 629, **639**
Ramirez, People v., 624
Rankin v. McPherson, 1308
R.A.V. v. City of St. Paul, Minn., 1112, 1114, **1115,** 1204, 1208, 1212, 1326, 1334
Ravara, United States v., 13
Raymond Motor Transp., Inc. v. Rice, 307
Red Lion Broadcasting Co. v. F. C. C., 1320, **1366, 1450**
Reed v. Reed, 683, 728
Reeves, Inc. v. Stake, 323
Regan v. Taxation With Representation of Washington, 1208, **1319**
Regents of University of California v. Bakke, 795
Reid v. Covert, 255
Reidel, United States v., 1131
Reitman v. Mulkey, 948
Rendell–Baker v. Kohn, 956
Renton, City of v. Playtime Theatres, Inc., 1162, 1209, 1230
Rescue Army v. Municipal Court of City of Los Angeles, 28
Reuben Quick Bear v. Leupp, 1531
Reynolds v. Sims, 47, 847, 858, **866,** 869
Reynolds v. United States, 1477
Ribnik v. McBride, 473
Rice v. Elmore, 935
Rice v. Santa Fe Elevator Corp., 342
Rice v. Sioux City Memorial Park Cemetery, 939
Richardson v. Belcher, 844, 913
Richardson v. Ramirez, 864
Richardson, United States v., 37
Richmond, City of v. J.A. Croson Co., 814
Richmond Newspapers, Inc. v. Virginia, 1426
Riley v. National Federation of the Blind of North Carolina, Inc., 1334
R. M. J., In re, 1186
Robel, United States v., 1070, 1327, 1392
Roberts v. United States Jaycees, 543, **601,** 1374, **1399**
Robinson v. California, 747
Rochin v. California, 440
Roe v. Wade, 44, 453, 468, **530,** 535, 536, 539, 541, 841, 844

Roemer v. Board of Public Works of Maryland, 1542
Rogers v. Lodge, 102 S.Ct. 3272, pp. 754, 764, 772, 839, 880, 884
Rogers v. Lodge, 102 S.Ct. 86, p. 990
Rohr Aircraft Corp. v. San Diego County, 351
Rome, City of v. United States, 918, 985, 991, 1018
Romer v. Evans, 543, 599, 631, 634, 648, 737, 748, 790, 949
Rosario v. Rockefeller, 864
Rosenberger v. Rector and Visitors of University of Virginia, 1291, 1324, 1464, 1466, 1546
Rosenbloom v. Metromedia, Inc., 1101
Rosenfeld v. New Jersey, 1079
Ross v. Moffitt, 898
Rostker v. Goldberg, 693, 1276
Rotary Intern. v. Rotary Club of Duarte, 1400
Roth v. United States, 1126
Rowan v. United States Post Office Dept., 1169
Royster Guano Co. v. Virginia, 636
Rubin v. Coors Brewing Co., 1197
Runyon v. McCrary, 981, 982
Rust v. Sullivan, 553, 1321
Rutan v. Republican Party of Illinois, 1314
Rutherford, United States v., 543

Sable Communications of California, Inc. v. F.C.C., 1171
Saia v. People of State of New York, 1237
Saint Francis College v. Al-Khazraji, 981
Salyer Land Co. v. Tulare Lake Basin Water Storage Dist., 862
San Antonio Independent School Dist. v. Rodriguez, 842
Sandin v. Conner, 625, 627
San Francisco Arts & Athletics, Inc. v. United States Olympic Committee, 956, 959
Santa Clara County v. Southern Pac. R. Co., 459
Saxbe v. Washington Post Co., 1423
Scales v. United States, 1068
Scarborough v. United States, 198
Schad v. Borough of Mount Ephraim, 1158, 1230, 1326
Schaumburg, Village of v. Citizens for a Better Environment, 1287, 1332
Schechter Poultry Corporation v. United States, 22, 178, 187
Schenck v. United States, 1036
Schlesinger v. Ballard, 647, 699, 718
Schlesinger v. Reservists Committee to Stop the War, 37
Schneider v. New Jersey, 1212, 1239
Schware v. Board of Bar Exam. of State of N.M., 1391
Schweiker v. Wilson, 653, 657, 728
Screws v. United States, 969
Seaboard Air Line Ry. Co. v. Blackwell, 268

Secretary of State of Md. v. Joseph H. Munson Co., Inc., 1334
Seeger, United States v., 1468
Sei Fujii v. State, 255
Seminole Tribe of Florida v. Florida, 114, 225
Senate Select Committee on Presidential Campaign Activities v. Nixon, 411
Serrano v. Priest, 70
Shaare Tefila Congregation v. Cobb, 981
Shapero v. Kentucky Bar Ass'n, 1187
Shapiro v. Thompson, 335, 630, 844, 901, 905, 911
Sharpnack, United States v., 349
Shaw v. Hunt, 889
Shaw v. Reno, 753, 755, 756, 839, 880, 889
Shelley v. Kraemer, 936, 959
Shelton v. Tucker, 1377, 1382, 1393
Shepherd v. City of Wheeling, 27
Sheppard v. Maxwell, 1358
Sherbert v. Verner, 1467, 1479
Shreveport Rate Case (Houston, E. & W.T.R. Co. v. United States), 166
Shuttlesworth v. City of Birmingham, Ala., 1343
Siegert v. Gilley, 624
Simon & Schuster, Inc. v. Members of New York State Crime Victims Bd., 1206
Skinner v. Oklahoma, 517, 844
Slaughter–House Cases, 125, 328, 421, 457, 628, 663, 919
Slochower v. Board of Higher Ed. of City of New York, 1391
Smith v. Allwright, 935, 936
Smith v. Collin, 99 S.Ct. 291, p. 1113
Smith v. Collin, 98 S.Ct. 3085, pp. 1093, 1113
Smith v. Goguen, 1220, 1337, 1338
Smith v. State of Alabama, 268
Smith v. United States, 1143
Smyth v. Ames, 459
Snowden v. Hughes, 751
Sonzinsky v. United States, 232
Sosna v. Iowa, 907
South Carolina v. Baker, 212
South Carolina State Highway Department v. Barnwell Bros., 299
South Carolina, State of v. Katzenbach, 984, 985, 987
South–Central Timber Development, Inc. v. Wunnicke, 280, 323
South Dakota v. Dole, 244, 249
Southeastern Promotions, Ltd. v. Conrad, 1273
South-Eastern Underwriters Ass'n, United States v., 166, 346
Southern Pac. Co. v. Arizona, 276, 300
Southern R. Co. v. United States, 167
Southern Ry. Co. v. King, 268
Speiser v. Randall, 1318, 1342
Spence v. State of Wash., 1221
Spevack v. Klein, 1391
Sporhase v. Nebraska, ex rel. Douglas, 297
Stafford v. Wallace, 169, 187
Stanley v. Georgia, 1130
Stanley v. Illinois, 915
Stanton v. Stanton, 684
Starns v. Malkerson, 908

Starrett City Associates, United States v., 795
State of (see name of state)
Staub v. City of Baxley, 1237
Steffan v. Perry, 748
Stell v. Savannah–Chatham County Bd. of Ed., 678
Steward Mach. Co. v. Davis, 241, 293
Stolar, Application of, 1396
Stone v. Graham, 1513
Stone v. State of Mississippi, 507
Storer v. Brown, 892
Stratton Oakmont, Inc. v. Prodigy Services Co., 1456, 1459
Strauder v. West Virginia, 663, 750
Street v. New York, 1220
Stromberg v. California, 1212
Stuart v. Laird, 12
Sturges v. Crowninshield, 258, 506
Sugarman v. Dougall, 721
Sullivan v. Little Hunting Park, Inc., 982
Supreme Court of New Hampshire v. Piper, 334
Swain v. Alabama, 750
Swann v. Adams, 872
Swann v. Charlotte–Mecklenburg Bd. of Ed., 775
Sweatt v. Painter, 675
Swift & Co. v. United States, 168

Takahashi v. Fish and Game Commission, 721
Talley v. California, 1363
Tancil v. Woolls, 670
Tashjian v. Republican Party of Connecticut, 865
Tate v. Short, 899
Taylor v. Louisiana, 664, 703
Teague v. Lane, 445
Terminiello v. City of Chicago, 1080, 1085
Terry v. Adams, 935, 959
Testa v. Katt, 219, 223, 224
Texas v. Johnson, 1080, 1221
Texas Monthly, Inc. v. Bullock, 1550
Thomas v. Review Bd. of Indiana Employment Sec. Division, 1481
Thomas, United States v., 1456, 1460
Thornburg v. Gingles, 990
Thornburgh v. American College of Obstetricians and Gynecologists, 547, 550
Thornhill v. State of Alabama, 1387
Thornton, Estate of v. Caldor, Inc., 1548
Tilton v. Richardson, 1542
Time, Inc. v. Firestone, 1101
Time, Inc. v. Hill, 1107
Times Film Corp. v. City of Chicago, 1342
Tinker v. Des Moines Independent Community School Dist., 1212, 1293
Toll v. Moreno, 723
Toolson v. New York Yankees, Inc., 166
Toomer v. Witsell, 271, 280, 330
Torcaso v. Watkins, 1471
Touby v. United States, 399
Town of (see name of town)

Train v. City of New York, 384
Trans World Airlines, Inc. v. Hardison, 1548
Trimble v. Gordon, 646, 664, 726
Turner v. City of Memphis, Tenn., 678
Turner Broadcasting System, Inc. v. F.C.C., 117 S.Ct. 1174, pp. 1369, 1371
Turner Broadcasting System, Inc. v. F.C.C., 114 S.Ct. 2445, pp. 1208, 1369, 1446, 1455
Twining v. New Jersey, 430, 434
Tyson & Bro.–United Theatre Ticket Offices v. Banton, 473

United Bldg. and Const. Trades Council of Camden County and Vicinity v. Mayor and Council of City of Camden, 283, 329
United Broth. of Carpenters and Joiners of America, Local 610, AFL–CIO v. Scott, 975
United Jewish Organizations of Williamsburgh, Inc. v. Carey, 799
United Mine Workers of America, Dist. 12 v. Illinois State Bar Ass'n, 1386
United Public Workers of America (C.I.O.) v. Mitchell, 45, 1311
United States v. _____ (see opposing party)
United States Civil Service Commission v. National Ass'n of Letter Carriers, AFL–CIO, 1312
United States Dept. of Agriculture v. Moreno, 648, 914
United States Dept. of Agriculture v. Murry, 915
United States Postal Service v. Council of Greenburgh Civic Associations, 1276
United States R.R. Retirement Bd. v. Fritz, 653
United States Senate v. F.T.C. 382
United States Steel Corp. v. Multistate Tax Commission, 353
United States Term Limits, Inc. v. Thornton, 115, 224
United States Trust Co. of New York v. New Jersey, 510
United Steelworkers of America, AFL–CIO–CLC v. Weber, 811
United Transp. Union v. Long Island R. Co., 208
United Transp. Union v. State Bar of Mich., 1386
Uphaus v. Wyman, 1380

Valentine v. Chrestensen, 1175
Valley Forge Christian College v. Americans United for Separation of Church and State, Inc., 37
Vance v. Bradley, 632, 651
Village of (see name of village)
Virginia, Com. of v. State of Tenn., 353
Virginia, United States v., 698, 704

Virginia State Bd. of Pharmacy v. Virginia Citizens Consumer Council, Inc., 1176
Vitek v. Jones, 625, 626
Vlandis v. Kline, 908, 914
Vorchheimer v. School District of Philadelphia, 715

Wabash, St. L. & P. Ry. Co. v. State of Illinois, 268
Walker v. City of Birmingham, 1348
Wallace v. Jaffree, 1464, 1506
Walz v. Tax Commission of City of New York, 1543
Ward v. Rock Against Racism, 1193, 1260
Ware v. Hylton, 254, 255
Warth v. Seldin, 30, 35
Washington v. Davis, 749, 754, 755
Washington v. Seattle School Dist. No. 1, pp. 746, 790
Waters v. Churchill, 1309
Watkins v. United States, 83
Watkins v. United States Army, 748
Watts v. United States, 1071
W.B. Worthen Co. v. Thomas, 510
W.B. Worthen Co. v. Kavanaugh, 507
Weaver v. Palmer Bros. Co., 473
Weber v. Aetna Cas. & Sur. Co., 726
Webster v. Reproductive Health Services, 548, 555
Weinberger v. Salfi, 915
Weinberger v. Wiesenfeld, 629, 647, 699, 716, 717
Welsh v. United States, 1468
Welton v. State of Missouri, 271
Wengler v. Druggists Mut. Ins. Co., 719
Wesberry v. Sanders, 866, 867, 868
West Coast Hotel Co. v. Parrish, 476
Western and Southern Life Ins. Co. v. State Bd. of Equalization of California, 348
Westfall v. United States, 197
West Lynn Creamery, Inc. v. Healy, 278
West River Bridge Co. v. Dix, 507
West Virginia State Board of Education v. Barnette, 1029, 1212, 1362
Whalen v. Roe, 528, 601
Wheeling Steel Corp. v. Glander, 459
White v. Massachusetts Council of Const. Employers, Inc., 323
White v. Regester, 753, 873, 880
White v. Weiser, 872
Whitney v. California, 467, 1026, 1054
Wickard v. Filburn, 113, 188, 189, 191, 198, 214
Widmar v. Vincent, 1289, 1543
Wieman v. Updegraff, 1390
Wiener v. United States, 391
Wilkerson v. Rahrer, 345

Williams v. Florida, 450
Williams v. Illinois, 898
Williams v. Rhodes, 891
Williams v. Standard Oil Co. of Louisiana, 473
Williams v. State of Georgia, 74
Williams v. United States, 969
Williams, United States v., 969
Williams v. Vermont, 910
Williamson v. Lee Optical of Okl., 481, 559, 636, 642
Willson v. Black-bird Creek Marsh Co., 263
Winship, In re, 438
Wisconsin v. Constantineau, 622
Wisconsin v. Mitchell, 1112, 1123
Wisconsin v. Yoder, 1481, 1482
Witters v. Washington Dept. of Services for the Blind, 1544
Wolf v. Colorado, 450
Wolman v. Walter, 1534
Wolston v. Reader's Digest Ass'n, Inc., 1101
Wood v. Georgia, 1433
Woods v. Cloyd W. Miller Co., 250
Wooley v. Maynard, 1363, 1471, 1490
Worcester v. State of Ga., 24
Wright v. Rockefeller, 752
Wyatt v. Cole, 410
Wygant v. Jackson Bd. of Educ., 810
Wynehamer v. People, 457
Wyoming v. Oklahoma, 280

Yakus v. United States, 80, 400
Yates v. United States, 1068
Yerger, Ex parte, 78
Yick Wo v. Hopkins, 664, 750
Young, Ex parte, 225
Young v. American Mini Theatres, Inc., 1159, 1230, 1339
Youngberg v. Romeo, 600, 961
Younger v. Harris, 1328
Youngstown Sheet & Tube Co. v. Sawyer (The Steel Seizure Case), 356, 1352

Zablocki v. Redhail, 587
Zacchini v. Scripps–Howard Broadcasting Co., 1109
Zauderer v. Office of Disciplinary Counsel of Supreme Court of Ohio, 1186
Zimmer v. McKeithen, 766
Zobel v. Williams, 328, 908
Zobrest v. Catalina Foothills School Dist., 1545
Zorach v. Clauson, 1502
Zschernig v. Miller, 257, 258
Zurcher v. Stanford Daily, 1439

*

TABLE OF AUTHORITIES

References are to Pages.

Abascal & Kramer, "Presidential Impoundment, Part II: Judicial and Legislative Responses," 63 Geo.L.J. 149 (1974), 384

Abraham, Justices and Presidents (3d ed. 1992), 75

Ackerman, "Integration for Subsidized Housing and the Question of Racial Occupancy Controls," 26 Stan.L.Rev. 245 (1975), 795

Ackerman, Private Property and the Constitution (1977), 487

Adler, "Note, Post–Modern Art and the Death of Obscenity Law," 99 Yale L.J. 1359 (1990), 1144

Aleinikoff, "Constitutional Law in the Age of Balancing," 96 Yale L.J. 943 (1987), 1034, 1098

Aleinikoff & Issacharoff, "Race and [Redistricting]," 92 Mich.L.Rev. 588 (1993), 890

Alexander, "Speech in the Local [Marketplace]," 14 San Diego L.Rev. 357 (1977), 1184

Alexander, "Trouble on Track Two: Incidental Regulations of Speech and Free Speech Theory," 44 Hastings L.J. 921 (1993), 1219

Alfange, "Free Speech and Symbolic Content: The Draft–Card Burning Case," 1968 Sup. Ct.Rev. 1, 1216

Alfange, "The Relevance of Legislative Facts in Constitutional Law," 114 U.Pa.L.Rev. 637 (1966), 471

Alfange, "The Supreme Court and the Separation of Powers: A Welcome Return to Normalcy?" 58 Geo.Wash.L.Rev. 668 (1990), 398

Alsop & Catledge, The 168 Days (1938), 185

Amar, "A Neo–Federalist View of Article III: Separating the Two Tiers of Federal Jurisdiction," 65 B.U.L.Rev. 205 (1985), 82

Amar, "Attainder and Amendment 2: Romer's Rightness," 95 Mich.L.Rev. 203 (1996), 747

Amar, "The Two–Tiered Structure of the Judiciary Act of 1789," 138 U.Pa.L.Rev. 1569 (1990), 82

Amsterdam, "The Void-for-Vagueness Doctrine in the Supreme Court," 109 U.Pa. L.Rev. 67 (1960), 1337

Anderson, "Libel and Press Self–Censorship," 53 Tex.L.Rev. 422 (1975), 1098

Anderson, "The Origins of the Press Clause," 30 UCLA L.Rev. 455 (1983), 1421

Appleton, "Professor Michelman's Quest for a Constitutional Welfare Right," 1979 Wash.U.L.Q. 715, p. 912

Ariens, "A Thrice–Told Tale, or Felix the Cat," 107 Harv.L.Rev. 620 (1994), 185, 478

Audi, "The Separation of Church and State and the Obligations of Citizenship," 18 Phil. & Pub. Affairs 259 (1989), 1498

Auerbach, "The Communist Control Act of 1954: A Proposed Legal–Political Theory of Free Speech," 23 U.Chi.L.Rev. 173 (1956), 1067

Auerbach, "The Reapportionment Cases: One Person, One Vote—One Vote, One Value," 1964 Sup.Ct.Rev. 1, p. 871

Bailyn, The Ideological Origins of the American Revolution (1967), 14

Baker, Back to Back—The Duel Between FDR and the Supreme Court (1967), 185

Baker, "Commercial [Speech]," 62 Iowa L.Rev. 1 (1976), 1183

Baker, Human Liberty and Freedom of Speech (1989), 1028, 1183

Baker, The Justice from Beacon Hill (1991), 1045

Baker, "Neutrality, Process, and Rationality: Flawed Interpretations of Equal Protection," 58 Tex.L.Rev. 1029 (1980), 634, 635

Baker, "Press Rights and Government Power to Structure the Press," 34 U.Miami L.Rev. 819 (1980), 1422

Baker, "Scope of the First Amendment Freedom of Speech," 25 UCLA L.Rev. 964 (1978), 1026, 1028, 1217

Baker, "Turner Broadcasting: Content–Based Regulation of Persons and Presses," 1994 Sup.Ct. Rev. 57, pp. 1210, 1369

Balkin, "Some Realism about Pluralism: Legal Realist Approaches to the First Amendment," 1990 Duke L.J. 375, p. 1031

Barnett, "The Puzzle of Prior Restraint," 29 Stan.L.Rev. 539 (1977), 1360

Barrett, "Judicial Supervision of Legislative Classifications—A More Modest Role for Equal Protection?" 1976 B.Y.U.L.Rev. 89, p. 633

Barron, "Access to the Press—A New First Amendment Right," 80 Harv.L.Rev. 1641 (1967), 1026, 1452

Barton, "The General–Election Ballot: More Nominees or More Representative Nominees?" 22 Stan.L.Rev. 165 (1970), 891

Bator, "Congressional Power Over Federal Courts," 27 Vill.L.Rev. 1032 (1982), 82, 85

Baucus & Kay, "The Court Stripping Bills: Their Impact on the Constitution, the Courts, and Congress," 27 Vill.L.Rev. 988 (1982), 84

Beard, The Supreme Court and the Constitution (1912), 15

Bell, "In Defense of Minority [Admissions Programs]," 119 U.Pa.L.Rev. 364 (1970), 795

Bennett, " 'Mere' Rationality in [Constitutional Law]," 67 Calif.L.Rev. 1049 (1979), 635, 639

Bennett, "Objectivity in Constitutional Law," 132 U.Pa.L.Rev. 445 (1984), 542

Berg, "What Hath Congress Wrought? An Interpretive Guide to [RFRA]," 39 Vill. L.Rev. 1 (1994), 1015

Berger, Congress v. The Supreme Court (1969), 13

Berger, Executive Privilege: A Constitutional Myth (1974), 410

Berger, "The Ninth Amendment," 66 Cornell L.Rev. 1 (1980), 528

Berger, "A Policy Analysis of the Taking Problem," 49 N.Y.U.L. Rev. 165 (1974), 487

Berle, "Constitutional Limitations on Corporate Activity—Protection of Personal Rights from Invasion through Economic Power," 100 U.Pa.L.Rev. 933 (1952), 931

Berns, The First Amendment and the Future of American Democracy (1976), 1085

Berns, "Freedom of the Press and the Alien and Sedition Laws: A Reappraisal," 1970 Sup.Ct.Rev. 109, p. 1025

Bernstein, "Power, Prejudice, and the Right to Speak: Litigating 'Outness' Under the Equal Protection Clause," 47 Stan.L.Rev. 269 (1995), 749

Beschle, "The Conservative as Liberal: The Religion Clauses, Liberal Neutrality, and the Approach of Justice O'Connor," 62 Notre Dame L.Rev. 151 (1987), 1531

Beth, "Group Libel and Free Speech," 39 Minn. L.Rev. 167 (1955), 1093

Beveridge, The Life of John Marshall (1919), 12

BeVier, "Campaign Finance Reform: Specious Arguments, Intractable Dilemmas," 94 Colum.L.Rev. 1258 (1994), 1410

BeVier, "The First Amendment and Political Speech: An Inquiry Into the Substance and Limits of Principle," 30 Stan.L.Rev. 299 (1978), 1027

BeVier, "An Informed Public, An Informing Press: The Search for a Constitutional Principle," 68 Calif.L.Rev. 482 (1980), 1422

BeVier, "Money and Politics: A Perspective on the First Amendment and Campaign Finance Reform," 73 Calif.L.Rev. 1045 (1985), 1410

BeVier, "Rehabilitating Public Forum Doctrine: In Defense of Categories," 1993 Sup.Ct.Rev. 79, p. 1287

Beytagh, "Ten Years of Non–Retroactivity: A Critique and a Proposal," 61 Va.L.Rev. 1557 (1975), 445

Bezanson, "Institutional Speech," 80 Iowa L.Rev. 735 (1995), 1369

Bezanson, "The New Free Press Guarantee," 63 Va.L.Rev. 731 (1977), 1421

Bhagwat, "Of Markets and Media: The First Amendment, the New Mass Media, and the Political Components of Culture," 74 N.Car.L.Rev. 141 (1995), 1455

Bice, "Rationality Analysis in Constitutional Law," 65 Minn.L.Rev. 1 (1980), 635

Bice, "Standards of Judicial Review under the Equal Protection and Due Process Clauses," 50 S.Cal.L.Rev. 689 (1977), 633

Bickel, "A Decade of School Desegregation," 64 Colum.L.Rev. 193 (1964), 773

Bickel, The Least Dangerous Branch (1962), 18, 26, 1328

Bickel, The Morality of Consent (1975), 670, 678, 1085

Bickel, "The Original Understanding and the Segregation Decision," 69 Harv.L.Rev. 1 (1955), 678

Bickel, The Supreme Court and the Idea of Progress (1970), 774, 871

Biklé, "Judicial Determination of Questions of Fact Affecting the Constitutional Validity of Legislative Action," 38 Harv.L.Rev. 6 (1924), 471

Bittker, "The Case of The Checker–Board [Ordinance]," 71 Yale L.J. 1387 (1962), 795

Bittker & Kaufman, "Taxes and Civil Rights: 'Constitutionalizing' the Internal Revenue Code," 82 Yale L.J. 51 (1972), 946

Black, "Amending the Constitution," 82 Yale L.J. 189 (1972), 250

Black, "The Bill of Rights," 35 N.Y.U.L.Rev. 865 (1960), 1031

Black, A Constitutional Faith (1968), 1031

Black, "Foreword: 'State Action,' Equal Protection and California's Proposition 14," 81 Harv.L.Rev. 69 (1967), 926, 951

Black, Impeachment: A Handbook (1974), 412

Black, "The Lawfulness of Segregation the Decisions," 69 Yale L.J. 421 (1960), 678, 679

Black, The People and the Court: Judicial Review in a Democracy (1960), 18

Black, "The Presidency and the Congress," 32 Wash. & Lee L.Rev. 841 (1975), 83

Black, Structure and Relationship in Constitutional Law (1969), 19, 109, 110, 431

Blasi, "The Checking Value in First Amendment Theory," 1977 A.B.F.Res.J. 521, p. 1027

Blasi, "The First Amendment and the Ideal of Civic Courage: The Brandeis Opinion in Whitney v. California," 29 Wm. & Mary L.Rev. 653 (1988), 1059

Blasi, "Free Speech and the Widening Gyre of Fund–Raising: Why Campaign Spending Limits May Not Violate the First Amendment After All," 94 Colum.L.Rev. 1281 (1994), 1411

Blasi, "The Pathological Perspective and the First Amendment," 85 Colum.L.Rev. 449 (1985), 1029

Blasi, "Prior Restrains on Demonstrations," 68 Mich.l.Rev. 1481 (1970), 1089, 1239, 1345, 1348

Blasi, "Six Conservatives in Search of the First Amendment: The Revealing Case of Nude Dancing," 33 Wm. & Mary L.Rev. 611 (1992), 1234

Blasi, "Toward a Theory of Prior Restraint: The Central Linkage," 66 Minn.L.Rev. 11 (1981), 1345

Blasi & Monaghan, "The First Amendment and Cigarette Advertising," 250 JAMA 502 (1986), 1202

Bloustein, "The Origin, Validity, and Interrelationships of the Political Values Served by Freedom of Expression," 33 Rutgers L.Rev. 372 (1981), 1029

Blumstein, "Defining and Proving Race Discrimination: Perspectives on the Purpose vs. Results Approach from the Voting Rights Act," 69 Va.L.Rev. 633 (1983), 990

Bobbitt, Constitutional Fate: Theory of the Constitution (1982), 542

Bogen, "First Amendment Ancillary Doctrines," 37 Md.L.Rev. 679 (1978), 1343

Bogen, "The Free Speech Metamorphosis of Mr. Justice Holmes," 11 Hofstra L.Rev. 97 (1982), 1045

Bollinger, "Freedom of the Press and Public Access: Toward a Theory of Partial Regulation of Mass Media," 75 Mich.L.Rev. 1 (1976), 1452

Bork, "The Impossibility of Finding Welfare Rights in the Constitution," 1979 Wash. U.L.Q. 695, pp. 735, 910

Bork, "Neutral Principles and Some First Amendment Problems," 47 Ind.L.J. 1 (1971), 541, 1027, 1034, 1067

Bork, The Tempting of America: The Political Seduction of the Law (1990), 75, 546

Boskey and Gressman, "The Supreme Court's New Rules—Model 1995," 116 S.Ct. vi (1995), 68

Boudin, Government by Judiciary (1932), 13

Bowman, "Street Harassment and the Informal Ghettoization of Women," 106 Harv. L.Rev. 517 (1993), 1080

Bradley, "The Right Not to Endorse Gay Rights: A Reply to Sunstein," 70 Ind.L.J. 29 (1994), 749

Braeman, Bremner and Walter, Change and Continuity in Twentieth Century America (1964), 172

Brameld, Educational Costs, in Discrimination and National Welfare (McIver, ed., 1949), 676

Brennan, "State Constitutions and the Protection of Individual Rights," 90 Harv. L.Rev. 489 (1977), 70

Brest, "The Conscientious Legislator's Guide to Constitutional Interpretation," 27 Stan.L.Rev. 585 (1975), 24

Brest, "The Federal Government's Power to Protect Negroes and Civil Rights Workers Against Privately Inflicted Harm," 1 Harv.C.R.-C.L.L.Rev. 1 (1966), 972

Brest, "Foreword: In Defense of the Antidiscrimination Principle," 90 Harv.L.Rev. 1 (1976), 754

Brest, "The Fundamental Rights [Controversy]," 90 Yale L.J. 1063 (1981), 542

Brest, "The Misconceived Quest for the Original Understanding," 60 B.U.L.Rev. 204 (1980), 19, 541

Brest, "Palmer v. Thompson: An Approach to the Problem of Unconstitutional Legislative Motive," 1971 Sup.Ct.Rev. 95, pp. 108, 751, 1217

Brest, Processes of Constitutional Decisionmaking (1975), 545

Brest, "State Action and Liberal [Theory]," 130 U.Pa.L.Rev. 1296 (1982), 934

Brest & Oshige, "Affirmative Action for Whom?," 47 Stan.L.Rev. 855 (1995), 809

Brest, et al., "Constitutional Scholars' Statement on Affirmative Action After [Croson]," 98 Yale L.J. 1711 (1989), 828

Brest, et al., "Scholars' Reply to Professor Fried," 99 Yale L.J. 163 (1989), 828

Breyer, "The Legislative Veto After Chadha," 72 Geo.L.J. 785 (1984), 383

Bronner, Battle for Justice: How the Bork Nomination Shook America (1989), 546

Brown, Emerson, Falk & Freedman, "The Equal Rights Amendment: A Constitutional Basis for Equal Rights for Women," 80 Yale L.J. 871 (1971), 701

Brown, Loyalty and Security: Employment Tests in the United States (1958), 1390

Browne, "Title VII as Censorship: Hostile-Environment Harassment and the First Amendment," 52 Ohio State L.J. 481 (1991), 1125

Brownstein, "How Rights Are Infringed: The Role of Undue Burden Analysis in Constitutional Doctrine," 45 Hast.L.J. 867 (1994), 584

Brudney, "Association, Advocacy and the First Amendment," 4 Wm. & Mary Bill of Rts.J. 3 (1995), 1418

Bryden, "Brandeis' Facts," 1 Constitutional Commentary 281 (1984), 471

Buchanan, "The Right of Privacy: Past, Present and Future," 16 Ohio No.L.Rev. 403 (1989), 599

Burke, "The Cherokee Cases: A Study in Law, Politics, and Morality," 21 Stan. L.Rev. 500 (1969), 24

Burns, Roosevelt: The Lion and the Fox (1956), 185

Burt, "The Constitution of the Family," 1979 Sup.Ct.Rev. 329, pp. 584, 586

Burt, "Constitutional Law and the Teaching of the Parables," 93 Yale L.J. 455 (1984), 543

Burt, "Miranda and Title II: A Morganatic Marriage," 1969 Sup.Ct.Rev. 81, pp. 1003, 1016

Bybee, "Taking Liberties With the First Amendment: Congress, Section 5 and

[RFRA]," 48 Vand.L.Rev. 1539 (1995), 1015

Cahn, "Jurisprudence," 30 N.Y.U.L.Rev. 150 (1955), 678, 679, 680
Calhoun, The Calhoun Papers, The Library of Congress (1827), 64
Calhoun, The Papers of John C. Calhoun (Meriwether ed. 1959), 103
Calhoun, "The 13th and 14th Amendments: Constitutional Authority for Federal Legislation Against Private Sex Discrimination," 61 Minn.L.Rev. 313 (1977), 981
Calleros, "Paternalism, Counter–Speech, and Campus Hate–Speech [Codes]," 27 Ariz. St.L.J. 1249 (1995), 1111
Cantor, "Forced Payments to Service Institutions and Constitutional Interests in Ideological Non–Association," 36 Rutgers L.Rev. 3 (1984), 1398
Caplan, "The History and Meaning of the Ninth Amendment," 69 Va.L.Rev. 223 (1983), 528
Cappelletti & Cohen, Comparative Constitutional Law (1979), 20
Carr, Federal Protection of Civil Rights (1947), 920
Carter, The Culture of Disbelief: How American Law and Politics Trivialize Religious Devotion (1993), 1497
Carter, Franklin & Wright, The First Amendment and the Fifth Estate—Regulation of Electronic Mass Media (1989), 1450
Carter, "The Independent Counsel Mess," 102 Harv.L.Rev. 105 (1988), 398
Carter, Reflections of an Affirmative Action Baby (1991), 795
Casper, "Jones v. Mayer: Clio, Bemused and Confused Muse," 1968 Sup.Ct.Rev. 89, p. 982
Casper, "[Williams v. Rhodes]," 1969 Sup.Ct. Rev. 271, p. 891
Cass, "Commercial Speech, Constitutionalism, Collective Choice," 56 U.Cinn.L.Rev. 1317 (1988), 1182
Cass, "First Amendment Access to Government Facilities," 65 Va.L.Rev. 1287 (1979), 1236
Catterall, The Second Bank of the United States (1902), 105
Chafee, "Book Review," 62 Harv.L.Rev. 891 (1949), 1027, 1934
Chafee, Free Speech in the United States (1941) (revising Freedom of Speech (1920)), 1024
Chemerinsky, "Controlling Inherent Presidential Power: Providing a Framework for Judicial Review," 56 S.Cal.L.Rev. 863 (1983), 365
Chemerinsky, "In Defense of [Equality]," 81 Mich.L.Rev. 575 (1983), 633
Chemerinsky, "Making the Right Case for Constitutional Entitlements," 44 Mercer L.Rev. 525 (1993), 911
Choper, "Congressional Power to Expand Judicial Definitions of the Substantive Terms of the Civil War Amendments," 67 Minn.L.Rev. 299 (1982), 1016
Choper, "Defining 'Religion' in the First Amendment," 1982 U.Ill.L.Rev. 579, p. 1469
Choper, Judicial Review and the National Political Process (1980), 112
Choper, "Religion in the Schools," 47 Minn. L.Rev. 329 (1963), 1507
Choper, "The Religion Clauses of the First Amendment: Reconciling the Conflict," 41 U.Pitt.L.Rev. 673 (1980), 1467
Choper, "Thoughts on State [Action]," 1979 Wash.U.L.Q. 757, p. 926
Christie, "Why the First Amendment Should Not Be Interpreted From the Pathological [Perspective]," 1986 Duke L.J. 683, p. 1029
Clark, "Charitable Trusts, the 14th Amendment, and the Will of Stephen Girard," 66 Yale.L.J. 979 (1957), 940
Clark, "The Desegregation Cases," 5 Vill. L.Rev. 224 (1959), 678
Clark, Effect of Prejudice and Discrimination on Personality Development (Midcentury White House Conference on Children and Youth, 1950), 676
Clark, "The Social Scientists, the Brown Decision, and Contemporary Confusion," Argument (Friedman ed. 1969), 678
Clinton, Marbury v. Madison and Judicial Review (1989)
Clor, Obscenity and Public Morality (1969), 1142
Clor, "Science, Eros and [the Law]," 10 Duq. L.Rev. 63 (1971), 1132
Clune, "The Supreme Court's Treatment of [Wealth Discriminations]," 1975 Sup.Ct. Rev. 289, p. 735
Coase, "Advertising and Free Speech," 6 J.Legal Studies 1 (1977), 1182
Coase, "The Economics of the First Amendment: The Market for Goods and the Market for Ideas," 64 Am.Econ.Rev.Proc. 384 (1974), 1031
Coase, "The Federal Communications Commission," 2 J.L. & Econ. 1 (1959), 1450
Coenen, "Untangling the Market–Participant Exemption to the Dormant Commerce Clause," 88 Mich.L.Rev. 395 (1989), 323
Cohen, "Congressional Power to Define State Power to Regulate Commerce," in 2 Courts and Free Markets (Sandalow & Stein, eds., 1982), 348, 629
Cohen, "Congressional Power to Interpret Due Process and Equal Protection," 27 Stan.L.Rev. 603 (1975), 1012, 1018
Cohen, "Congressional Power to Validate Unconstitutional Laws: A Forgotten Solution to an Old Enigma," 35 Stan.L.Rev. 387 (1983), 348, 1018
Cohen, "Federalism in Equality [Clothing]," 38 Stan.L.Rev. (1985), 349
Cohen, "Is Equal Protection Like Oakland? Equality as a Surrogate for Other Rights," 59 Tul.L.Rev. 884 (1985), 589
Cohen, "A Look Back at Cohen v. California," 34 UCLA L.Rev. 1595 (1987), 1085

Cohen, "State Law in Equality Clothing: A Comment on [Allegheny]." 38 UCLA L.Rev. 87 (1990), 660

Cole, "Beyond Unconstitutional Conditions: Charting Spheres of Neutrality in Government–Funded Speech," 67 N.Y.U. L. Rev. 675 (1992), 1323

Cole, "Playing by Pornography's Rules: The Regulation of Sexual Expression," 143 U.Pa.L.Rev. 111 (1994), 1142

Collins, "Economic Union as a Constitutional Value," 63 N.Y.U.L.Rev. 43 (1988), 271

Commager, Majority Rule and Minority Rights (1943), 18

Comment, "The California Marijuana Possession [Statute]," 19 Hast.L.J. 758 (1968), 543

Comment, "The Courts, HEW, and Southern School Desegregation," 77 Yale L.J. 321 (1967), 773

Comment, "Lemon [Reconstituted]," 1986 B.Y.U.L.Rev. 465, p. 1531

Comment, " 'Newer' Equal Protection: The Impact of the Means–Focused Model," 23 Buffalo L.Rev. 665 (1974), 646

Comment, "State Economic Due Process: A Proposed Approach," 88 Yale L.J. 1487 (1979), 483

Commission on Wartime Relocation and Internment of Civilians, Personal Justice Denied (1982), 665

Conkle, "[RFRA]: The Constitutional Significance of an Unconstitutional Statute," 56 Mont.L.Rev. 39 (1995), 1015

Conkle, "The Second Death of Substantive Due Process," 62 Ind.L.J. 215 (1987), 599

Corwin, "The Basic Doctrine of American Constitutional Law," 12 Mich.L.Rev. 247 (1914), 455

Corwin, "The 'Higher Law' Background of American Constitutional Law," 42 Harv. L.Rev. 149, 365 (1928–29), 455

Corwin, Liberty Against Government (1948), 455, 457

Corwin, "The Passing of Dual Federalism," 36 Va.L.Rev. 1 (1950), 165

Corwin, "The Steel Seizure Case: A Judicial Brick Without Straw," 53 Colum.L.Rev. 53 (1953), 364

Cover, "Federalism and Administrative Structure," 92 Yale L.J. 1342 (1983), 244

Cover, "Foreword: Nomos and Narrative," 97 Harv.L.Rev. 4 (1983), 543

Cover, "The Left, the Right, and the First Amendment: 1918–1928," 40 Md.L.Rev. 349 (1981), 1045

Cox, "Foreword: Constitutional Adjudication and the Promotion of Human Rights," 80 Harv.L.Rev. 91 (1966), 911, 971, 1015, 1017

Cox, "Foreword: Freedom of Expression in the Burger Court," 94 Harv.L.Rev. 1 (1980), 1357, 1429

Cox, "The Role of Congress in Constitutional Determinations," 40 U.Cinn.L.Rev. 199 (1971), 1017

Cox, The Role of the Supreme Court in American Government (1976), 1085

Cox, The Warren Court (1968), 1328

Crosskey, "Charles Fairman, 'Legislative History' and the Constitutional Limitations on State Authority," 22 U.Chi. L.Rev. 1 (1954), 437

Crosskey, Politics and the Constitution in the History of the United States (1953), 420

Cushman, "The National Police Power Under the Commerce Clause of the Constitution," 3 Minn.L.Rev. 289 (1919), 172

Cushman, "Social and Economic Control through Federal Taxation," 18 Minn. L.Rev. 759 (1934), 232

Dabbs, "Constitutional [Considerations] in Mandatory Sickle Cell Anemia Testing," 7 U.C.D.L.Rev. 509 (1974), 671

D'Amato, "Is Equality a Totally Empty Idea?" 81 Mich.L.Rev. 600 (1983), 633

Delgado, "Words that Wound: A Tort Action for Racial Insults, Epithets, and Name–Calling," 17 Harv.C.R.-C.L.L.Rev. 133 (1982), 1110

Delgado & Yun, "The Speech We Hate: First Amendment Totalism, The ACLU and the Principle of Dialogic Politics," 27 Ariz.St. L.J. 1281 (1995), 1112

Dellinger, "The Recurring Question of a 'Limited' Constitutional Convention," 88 Yale L.J. 1623 (1979), 250

Deutscher and Chein, "The Psychological Effects of Enforced Segregation: A Survey of Social Science Opinion," 26 J.Psychol. 259 (1948), 676

Deutscher & Chein, "What Are the Psychological Effects of Segregation Under Conditions of Equal Facilities?" 3 Int.J.Opinion and Attitudes Res. 229 (1949), 676

Developments, "The Constitution and the Family," 93 Harv.L.Rev. 1156 (1980), 584, 589

Developments, 82 Harv.L.Rev. 1065 (1969), 794, 911

Developments in the Law—Religion and the State," 100 Harv.L.Rev. 1606 (1987), 1531

Diamond, "The First Amendment and Public Schools: The Case Against Judicial Intervention," 59 Tex.L.Rev. 477 (1981), 1301

Dorf, "Facial Challenges to State and Federal Statutes," 46 Stan.L.Rev. 235 (1994), 1332

Dorf, "Incidental Burdens on Fundamental Rights," 109 Harv.L.Rev. 1175 (1996), 1219

Dorsen & Shattuck, "Executive Privilege, the Congress and the Courts," 35 Ohio St.L.J. 1 (1974), 411

Dowling, "Interstate Commerce and State Power," 27 Va.L.Rev. 1 (1940), 304, 348

Dowling, "Interstate Commerce and State Power—Revised Version," 47 Colum.L.Rev. 547 (1947), 348

Dunham, "[Thirty] Years of Supreme Court Expropriation Law," 1962 Sup.Ct.Rev. 63, p. 487

Dworkin, "Against the Male Flood: Censorship, Pornography, and Equality," 8 Harv. Women's L.J. 1 (1985), 1149

Dworkin, "The Curse of American Politics," N.Y.Rev. of Books (Oct. 17, 1996), 1410

Dworkin, Life's Dominion: An Argument About Abortion, Euthanasia, and Individual Freedom (1993), 614

Dyk, "Newsgathering, Press Access, and the First Amendment," 44 Stan.L.Rev. 927 (1992), 1422

Easterbrook, "Abstraction and Authority," 59 U.Chi.L.Rev. 349, 305 (1992), 599

Easterbrook, "Insider Trading, Secret Agents, Evidentiary Privileges, and the Production of Information," 1981 Sup.Ct. Rev. 309, p. 1357

Edelman, "Free Press v. Privacy: Haunted by the Ghost of Justice Black," 68 Tex.L.Rev. 1195 (1990), 1107

Eisenberg, "Congressional Authority to Restrict Lower Federal Court Jurisdiction," 83 Yale L.J. 498 (1974), 84

Eisenberg, "Disproportionate Impact and Illicit Motive: Theories of Constitutional Adjudication," 52 N.Y.U. L.Rev. 36 (1977), 760

Eisgruber & Sager, "Why the Religious Freedom Restoration Act is Unconstitutional," 69 N.Y.U.L.Rev. 437 (1994), 1015, 1500

Elazar, The American Partnership: Intergovernmental Co-operation in the Nineteenth Century United States (1962), 244

Ellickson, "Controlling Chronic Misconduct in City Spaces: Of Panhandlers, Skid Rows, and Public Space Zoning," 105 Yale L.J. 1165 (1996), 1288

Ellis, The Jeffersonian Crisis: Courts and Politics in the Young Republic (1971), 12

Ely, "The American War in Indochina, Part I: The (Troubled) Constitutionality of the War They Told Us About," 42 Stan.L.Rev. 877 (1990), 371

Ely, "The American War in Indochina, Part II: The Unconstitutionality of the War They Didn't Tell Us About," 42 Stan. L.Rev. 1093 (1990), 371

Ely, "Another Spin on [Allegheny]," 38 UCLA L.Rev. 107 (1990), 660

Ely, "Choice of Law and the State's Interest in Protecting its Own," 23 Wm. & Mary L.Rev. 173 (1981), 328

Ely, "The Constitutionality of Reverse Racial Discrimination," 41 U.Chi.L.Rev. 723 (1974), 794

Ely, Democracy and Distrust (1980), 275, 416, 430, 431, 457, 484, 539, 633, 645, 682, 817, 858, 1027, 1209

Ely, "Flag Desecration: A Case Study in the Roles of Categorization and Balancing in First Amendment Analysis," 88 Harv. L.Rev. 1482 (1975), 1032, 1034, 1085, 1209, 1216, 1217, 1218, 1221

Ely, "Foreword: On Discovering Fundamental Values," 92 Harv.L.Rev. 5 (1978), 539, 543

Ely, "Legislative and Administrative Motivation in Constitutional Law," 79 Yale L.J. 1205 (1970), 108, 751, 1217

Ely, "Suppose Congress Wanted a War Powers Act That Worked," 88 Colum.L.Rev. 1379 (1988), 375

Ely, "The Wages of Crying Wolf: A Comment on Roe v. Wade," 82 Yale L.J. 920 (1973), 537 539, 682

Ely & Tribe, "Let There Be Life," The New York Times (March 17, 1981), 1014

Emerson, "The Doctrine of Prior Restraint'," 20 Law & Contemp.Probs. 648 (1955), 1344

Emerson, "First Amendment Doctrine and the Burger Court," 68 Calif.L.Rev. 422 (1980), 1211

Emerson, The System of Freedom of Expression (1970), 1025, 1027

Emerson, "Toward a General Theory of the First Amendment," 72 Yale L.J. 877 (1963), 1098

Epstein, "Caste and the Civil Rights Law: From Jim Crow to Same–Sex Marriages," 92 Mich.L.Rev. 2456 (1994), 749

Epstein, "Foreword: Unconstitutional Conditions, State Power, and the Limits of Consent," 102 Harv.L.Rev. 4 (1988), 249, 1302, 1318

Epstein, "The Proper Scope of the Commerce Power," 73 Va.L.Rev. 1387 (1987), 200

Epstein, "Property, Speech, and the Politics of Distrust," 59 U.Chi.L.Rev. 41 (1992), 1031

Epstein, "Substantive Due Process by Any Other Name: The Abortion Cases," 1973 Sup.Ct.Rev. 159, p. 537

Epstein, Takings: Private Property and Eminent Domain (1985), 487

Epstein, "Toward a Revitalization of the Contract Clause," 51 U.Chi.L.Rev. 703 (1984), 509

Epstein, "Was New York Times v. Sullivan Wrong?," 53 U.Chi.L.Rev. 782 (1986), 1099

Estreicher, "Congressional Power and Constitutional Rights: Reflections on Proposed 'Human Life' Legislation," 68 Va. L.Rev. 333 (1982), 1014

Eule, "Laying the Dormant Commerce Clause to Rest," 91 Yale L.J. 425 (1982), 270, 335

Fairman, "Does the Fourteenth Amendment Incorporate the Bill of Rights? The Original Understanding," 2 Stan.L.Rev. 5 (1949), 429, 437

Fairman, Reconstruction and Reunion: 1864–1888, Part One (6 History of the Supreme Court of the United States) (1971), 981, 982

Fallon, "Individual Rights and the Powers of Government," 27 Ga.L.Rev. 343 (1993), 911

Fallon, "Making Sense of Overbreadth," 100 Yale L.J. 853 (1991), 1327, 1331

Fallon, "Sexual Harassment, Content–Neutrality, and the First Amendment Dog That Didn't Bark," 1994 S.Ct.Rev. 1, p. 1125

Fallon, "Two Senses of Autonomy," 46 Stan. L.Rev. 875 (1994), 1183

Fallon & Meltzer, "New Law, Non–Retroactivity, and Constitutional Remedies," 104 Harv.L.Rev. 1731 (1991), 446

Farber, "Civilizing Public Discourse: [The] Enduring Significance of Cohen v. California," 1980 Duke L.J. 283, p. 1085

Farber, "Commercial Speech and First Amendment Theory," 74 Nw.L.Rev. 372 (1979), 1181

Farber, "Content Regulation and the First Amendment: A Revisionist View," 68 Geo. L.J. 727 (1980), 1211

Farber, "State Regulation and the Dormant Commerce Clause," 3 Const.Comm. 395 (1986), 270

Farber, "The Supreme Court and the Rule of Law: Cooper v. Aaron Revisited," 1983 U.Ill.L.Rev. 387, p. 26

Farber & Nowak, "The Misleading Nature of Public Forum Analysis: Content and Context in First Amendment Adjudication," 70 Va.L.Rev. 1219 (1984), 1236, 1287

Farber & Sherry, "The Pariah Principle," 13 Constitutional Commentary 257 (1996), 747, 748

Farrand, The Records of the Federal Convention of 1787 (1911), 15, 100

Feuerstein, "Civil Rights [Crimes]," 19 Vand. L.Rev. 641 (1966), 971

Field, "Abortion Law Today," 14 J.Legal.Med. 3 (1993), 584

Fisch, "Frankenstein's Monster Hits the Campaign Trail: An Approach to Regulation of Corporate Political Expenditures," 32 Wm. & Mary L.Rev. 587 (1991), 1418

Fiss, "The Charlotte–Mecklenburg Case—Its Significance for Northern School Desegregation," 38 U.Chi.L.Rev. 697 (1971), 776

Fiss, The Civil Rights Injunction (1978), 1345

Fiss, "The Fate of an Idea Whose Time Has [Come]," 41 U.Chi.L.Rev. 742 (1974), 754

Fiss, "Free Speech and Social Structure," 71 Iowa L.Rev. 1405 (1986), 1028, 1452

Fiss, "Groups and the Equal Protection Clause," 5 Phil. & Publ. Affairs 107 (1976), 754

Fiss, "State Activism and State Censorship," Yale L.J. 2087 (1991), 1323

Foley, "Equal–Dollars–Per–Voter: A Constitutional Principle of Campaign Finance," 94 Colum.L.Rev. 1204 (1994), 1410

Foote, "The Proper Role of the [Supreme Court] in Civil Liberties Cases," 10 Wayne L.Rev. 457 (1964), 518

Frank & Munro, "The Original Understanding of 'Equal Protection of the Laws,'" 1972 Wash.U.L.Q. 421, p. 923

Frankfurter, "John Marshall and the Judicial Function," 69 Harv.L.Rev. 217 (1955), 109

Frankfurter, "Mr. Justice Roberts," 104 U.Pa.L.Rev. 311 (1955), 185

Franklin, "A Declaratory Judgment Alternative to Current Libel Law," 74 Calif.L.Rev. 809 (1986), 1099

Frantz, "The First Amendment in the Balance," 71 Yale L.J. 1424 (1962), 1032

Frantz, "Is the First Amendment Law? A Reply to Professor Mendelson," 51 Cal. L.Rev. 729 (1963), 1032

Frazier, The Negro in the United States (1949), 677

Freedman, "Sex Equality, Sex Differences, and the Supreme Court," 92 Yale L.J. 913 (1983), 692

Freeman, "The Misguided Search for the Constitutional Definition of Religion," 71 Geo.L.J. 1519 (1983), 1469, 1470

Freidel, Roosevelt: A Rendezvous with Destiny (1990), 185

Freund, "The Debs Case and Freedom of Speech," The New Republic, May 3, 1919, reprinted at 40 U.Chi.L.Rev. 239 (1973), 1044

Freund, On Understanding the Supreme Court (1949), 471

Frickey, "The Fool on the Hill: Congressional Findings, Constitutional Adjudication, and United States v. Lopez," 46 Case W.Res. L.Rev. 695 (1996), 199

Fried, "Constitutional Doctrine," 107 Harv. L.Rev. 1140, 1143 (1994), 583

Fried, "A New First Amendment Jurisprudence: A Threat to Liberty," 59 U.Chi. L.Rev. 225 (1992), 1111

Fried, Order and Law (1991), 529, 599

Fried, "[A] Response to the Scholars' Statement," 99 Yale L.J. 155 (1989), 828

Friedman, "A Reaffirmation: The Authenticity of the Roberts Memorandum, or Felix the Non–Forger," 142 U.Pa.L.Rev. 1985 (1994), 185, 478

Friedman, "Switching Time and Other Thought Experiments: The Hughes Court and Constitutional Transformation," 142 U.Pa.L.Rev. 1091 (1994), 185

Friendly, "The Bill of Rights as a Code of Criminal Procedure," 53 Calif.L.Rev. 929 (1965), 437

Friendly, The Good Guys, The Bad Guys and the First Amendment (1976), 1452

Friendly, "Some Kind of Hearing," 123 U.Pa. L.Rev. 1267 (1975), 627

Frug, "Progressive Feminist Legal Scholarship: Can We Claim 'A Different Voice'?," 15 Harv. Women's L.J. 37 (1992), 716

Galebach, "A Human Life Statute," Human Life Review 5 (1981) [reprinted in 127 Cong.Rec. S 288], 1014

Gard, "Fighting Words as Free Speech," 58 Wash.U.L.Q. 531 (1980), 1078

Garvey & Aleinikoff, Modern Constitutional Theory: A Reader (1989), 19

Gates, "Let Them Talk," The New Republic, Sept. 20, 1993 at 37, p. 1111

Gellhorn, Individual Freedom and Government Restraints (1956), 485, 1390

Gellman, "Sticks and Stones Can Put You in Jail, But Can Words Increase Your Sentence?," 39 U.C.L.A. L.Rev. 333 (1991), 1123

Gergen, "The Selfish State and the Market," 66 Tex.L.Rev. 1097 (1988), 323

Gey, "The Apologetics of Suppression: The Regulation of Pornography as Act and Idea," 86 Mich.L.Rev. 1564 (1988), 1142

Gianella, "The Religious Liberty Guarantee," 80 Harv.L.Rev. 1381 (1967), 1498

Gilligan, In a Different Voice (1982), 716

Ginsburg, "Afterword to Ernst Freund and the First Amendment Tradition," 40 U.Chi.L.Rev. 243 (1973), 1045

Ginsburg, "Some Thoughts on Autonomy and Equality in Relation to Roe v. Wade," 63 N.C.L.Rev. 375 (1985), 540

Glennon, Constitutional Diplomacy (1990), 375

Glennon, "Taxation and Equal Protection," 58 Geo.Wash.L.Rev. 261 (1990), 660

Glennon & Nowak, "A Functional Analysis of the Fourteenth Amendment's 'State Action' Requirement," 1976 Sup.Ct.Rev. 221, pp. 926, 927

Goebel, Antecedents and Beginnings to 1801 (1 History of the Supreme Court of the United States) (1971), 14

Goldberger, "Judicial Scrutiny in Public Forum Cases: Misplaced Trust in the Judgment of Public Officials," 32 Buffalo L.Rev. 175 (1983), 1236

Goldberger, "A Reconsideration of Cox v. New Hampshire: Can Demonstrators Be Required to Pay the Costs of Using America's Public Forums?," 62 Tex.L.Rev. 403 (1983), 1239

Goodman, "De Facto School Segregation: A Constitutional and Empirical Analysis," 70 Calif.L.Rev. 275 (1972), 679, 783

Goodman, "Professor Brest on State Action and Liberal [Theory]," 130 U.Pa.L.Rev. 1331 (1982), 934

Goodpaster, "The Integration of Equal Protection, Due Process Standards, and the Indigent's Right of Free Access to the Courts," 56 Iowa L.Rev. 223 (1970), 895

Gordon, "The Nature and Uses of Congressional Power under Section Five of the 14th Amendment to Overcome Decisions of the Supreme Court," 72 Nw.U.L.Rev. 656 (1977), 1016

Graglia, Disaster by [Decree] (1976), 774

Graglia, "Special Admission of the 'Culturally Deprived' to Law School," 119 U.Pa. L.Rev. 351 (1970), 795

Graham, "The 'Conspiracy Theory' of the Fourteenth Amendment," 47 Yale L.J. 371 & 48 Yale L.J. 171 (1938), 459

Greenawalt, "The Enduring Significance of Neutral Principles," 78 Colum.L.Rev. 982 (1978), 18

Greenawalt, "How Empty is the Idea of Equality?" 83 Colum.L.Rev. 1167 (1983), 633

Greenawalt, "Insults and Epithets, Are They Protected Free Speech?" 42 Rutgers L.Rev. 287 (1990), 1078

Greenawalt, "Judicial Scrutiny of 'Benign' Racial Preference in Law School Admissions," 75 Colum.L.Rev. 559 (1975), 670, 795

Greenawalt, "Religion as a Concept in Constitutional Law," 72 Cal.L.Rev. 753 (1984), 1470

Greenawalt, Religious Convictions and Political Choice (1988), 1497

Greenawalt, "Religious Expression in the Public Square," 29 Loyola L.Rev. 1411 (1996), 1497

Greenawalt, "Speech and Crime," 1980 A.B.F.Res.J. 647, p. 1061

Greene, "The Political Balance of the Religion Clauses," 102 Yale L.J. 1611 (1993), 1497

Gressman, "The Unhappy History of Civil Rights Legislation," 50 Mich.L.Rev. 1323 (1952), 920

Grey, "Civil Rights vs. Civil Liberties: The Case of Discriminatory Verbal Harassment," 8 Soc.Phil. & Pol. 81 (1991), 1110

Grey, "The Constitution as Scripture," 37 Stan.L.Rev. 1 (1985), 541

Grey, "Do We Have an Unwritten Constitution?," 27 Stan.L.Rev. 703 (1975), 19, 455, 541

Grey, "Eros, Civilization and the Burger Court," 43 Law & Contemp.Prob. 83 (1980), 544

Grey, "How to Write a Speech Code Without Really Trying: Reflections on the Stanford Experience," 29 U.C. Davis L.Rev. 891 (1996), 1115

Grey, "Origins of the Unwritten [Constitution]," 30 Stan.L.Rev. 843 (1978), 455

Grodzins, Americans Betrayed: Politics and the Japanese Evacuation (1949), 665

Guinier, "[E]racing Democracy: The Voting Rights Cases," 108 Harv.L.Rev. 109 (1994), 890

Guinier, "Groups, Representation and Race–Conscious Districting: A Case of the Emperor's Clothes," 71 Tex.L.Rev. 1589 (1993), 880

Gunther, "Commentary," 71 Chi.-Kent L.Rev. 813 (1996), 646

Gunther, "Congressional Power to Curtail Federal Court Jurisdiction: An Opinionated Guide to the Ongoing Debate," 36 Stan.L.Rev. 895 (1984), 81

Gunther, "The Convention Method of Amending the United States Constitution," 14 Ga.L.Rev. 1 (1979), 250

Gunther, "Foreword: In Search of Evolving Doctrine on a Changing Court: A Model for a Newer Equal Protection," 86 Harv.

L.Rev. 1 (1972), 468, 483, 529, 630, 631, 646, 647, 650, 651, 684, 849, 910

Gunther, "Good Speech, Bad Speech—Should Universities Restrict Expression That is Racist or Otherwise Denigrating? No," 42 Stanford Lawyer 7 (Spring 1990), 1114

Gunther, "The Highest Court,The Toughest Issues," Stanford Magazine (Fall Winter 1978), 34, 1170

Gunther, "In Search of Judicial Quality on a Changing Court: The Case of Justice Powell," 24 Stan.L.Rev. 1001 (1972), 1032, 1085

Gunther (ed.), John Marshall's Defense of McCulloch v. Maryland (1969), 106, 108

Gunther, "Judicial Hegemony and Legislative Autonomy: The Nixon Case and the Impeachment Process," 22 UCLA L.Rev. 30 (1974), 405, 412

Gunther, Learned Hand: The Man and the Judge (1994), 466, 1044, 1045, 1046, 1049, 1067

Gunther, "Learned Hand and the Origins of Modern First Amendment Doctrine: Some Fragments of History," 27 Stan.L.Rev. 719 (1975), 176, 232, 1044, 1050, 1069, 1074

Gunther, "Of Rights and Remedies, Legitimacy and Competence," 1979 Wash. U.L.Q. 815, p. 773

Gunther, "Reflections on Kobel," 20 Stan. L.Rev. 1140 (1968), 1328

Gunther, "The Subtle Vices of the 'Passive Virtues'—A Comment on Principle and Expediency in Judicial Review," 64 Colum.L.Rev. 1 (1964), 26

Gunther, "Toward 'A More Perfect Union': Framing and Implementing the Distinctive Nation–Building Elements of the Constitution," in Aspects of American Liberty—Philosophical, Historical, and Political (Corner ed. 1977), 99

Hafen, "Hazelwood School District and the Role of the First Amendment Institutions," 1988 Duke L.J. 685, p. 1301

Hale, "Force and the [State]," 35 Colum.L.Rev. 149 (1935), 927

Hale, "The Supreme Court and the Contract Clause: III," 57 Harv.L.Rev. 852 (1944), 505

Hale, "Unconstitutional Conditions and Constitutional Rights," 25 Colum.L.Rev. 321 (1935), 249, 1318

Halley, "The Politics of the Closet: Towards Equal Protection for Gay, Lesbian, and Bisexual Identity," 36 UCLA L.Rev. 915 (1989), 749

Hamburger, "A Constitutional Right of Religious Exemption: An Historical Perspective," 60 Geo.Wash.L.Rev. 915 (1992), 1497

Hamburger, "The Development of the Law of Seditious Libel and the Control of the Press," 37 Stan.L.Rev. 661 (1985), 1024

Hamilton, "[RFRA]: Letting the Fox Into the Henhouse Under Cover of [§ 5 of the Fourteenth Amendment]," 16 Cardozo L.Rev. 357 (1995), 1015

Hammond, Banks and Politics in America—From the Revolution to the Civil War (1957), 105

Hand, The Bill of Rights (1958), 17, 526, 527, 1067

Hand, "Chief Justice Stone's Concept of the Judicial Function," in The Spirit of Liberty (3d ed. Dillard 1969), 1067

Hand, "Due Process of Law and the Eight–Hour Day," 21 Harv.L.Rev. 495 (1908), 466

Hart, "The Power of Congress to Limit the Jurisdiction of Federal Courts: An Exercise in Dialectic," 66 Harv.L.Rev. 1362 (1953), 81

Hart, "The Relations Between State and Federal Law," 54 Colum.L.Rev. 489 (1954), 349

Hart & Wechsler, Federal Courts (4th ed. 1996), 69, 83

Hart & Wechsler, The Federal Courts and the Federal System (3d ed. 1988), 15, 27, 28, 80

Hawkins & Zimring, Pornography in a Free Society (1988), 1145

Heatherington, "State Economic Regulation and Substantive Due Process of Law," 53 Nw.U.L. Rev. 13 (1958), 483

Heinzerling, "The Commercial Constitution," 1995 Sup.Ct.Rev. 217, p. 276

Hellerstein, "Hughes v. Oklahoma: The Court, the Commerce Clause, and State Control of Natural Resources," 1979 Sup. Ct.Rev. 51, p. 296

Henkin, Foreign Affairs and the Constitution (2d ed. 1996), 257

Henkin, "Foreword: On Drawing Lines," 82 Harv.L.Rev. 63 (1968), 1216

Henkin, "Is There a 'Political Question' Doctrine?" 85 Yale L.J. 597 (1976), 46

Henkin, "Morals and the Constitution: The Sin of Obscenity," 63 Colum.L.Rev. 391 (1963), 1130, 1140

Henkin, "On Drawing Lines," 82 Harv. L.Rev. 63 (1968), 983

Henkin, "Privacy and Autonomy," 74 Colum.L.Rev. 1410 (1974), 528, 543

Henkin, " 'Selective Incorporation' in the Fourteenth Amendment," 73 Yale L.J. 74 (1963), 437

Henkin, "Shelley v. Kraemer: Notes for a Revised Opinion," 100 U.Pa.L.Rev. 473 (1962), 926, 939

Henkin, "The Treaty Makers and the Law Makers: The Law of the Land and Foreign Relations," 107 U.Pa.L.Rev. 903 (1959), 257

Henkin & Rosenthal, Constitutionalism and Rights: The Influence of the American Constitution Abroad (1989), 20

Hershkoff & Cohen, "Begging to Differ: The First Amendment and the Right to Beg," 104 Harv.L.Rev. 896 (1991), 1288

Heymann & Barzelay, "The Forest and the Trees: Roe v. Wade and Its Critics," 53 B.U.L. Rev. 765 (1973), 537

Hills, "A Defense of State Constitutional Limits on Federal Congressional Term Limits," 53 U.Pitt.L.Rev. 97 (1991), 133

Hochman, "The Supreme Court and the Constitutionality of Retroactive Legislation," 73 Harv.L.Rev. 692 (1960), 515

Holmes, Collected Legal Papers (1920), 65, 88

Horowitz, "The Misleading Search for ['State Action']," 30 S.Cal.L.Rev. 208 (1957), 926

Horowitz & Karst, Law, Lawyers and Social Change (1969), 25

Howard & Howard, "The Dilemma of the Voting Rights Act—Recognizing the Emerging Political Equality Norm," 83 Colum.L.Rev. 1615 (1983), 880, 990

Hunter & Law, "Brief Amici Curiae of Feminist Anti–Censorship Task Force," 21 U.Mich.J.L.Ref. 69 (1987–88), 1150

Hutchinson, "More Substantive Equal Protection?" 1982 Sup.Ct.Rev. 167, p. 857

Idelman, "[RFRA]: Pushing the Limits of Legislative Power," 73 Tex.L.Rev. 247 (1994), 1015, 1500

Ingber, "The Marketplace of Ideas: A Legitimizing Myth," 1984 Duke L.J. 1, p. 1026

Irons, Justice at War (1983), 665

Irons, The New Deal Lawyers (1982), 178

Israel, "Gideon v. Wainwright: The 'Art' of Overruling," 1963 Sup.Ct.Rev. 211, p. 441

Israel, "Selective Incorporation Revisited," 71 Geo.L.J. 253 (1982), 445

Issacharoff, "The Constitutional Contours of Race and Politics," 1995 Sup.Ct. Rev. 45, p. 890

Issacharoff, "Judging Politics: The Elusive Quest for Judicial Review of Political Fairness," 71 Tex.L.Rev. 1643 (1993), 866

Issacharoff, "Polarized Voting in the Political Process: The Transformation of Voting Rights Jurisprudence," 90 Mich.L.Rev. 1833 (1992), 866

Jackson, The Struggle for Judicial Supremacy (1941), 185

Jackson, "The Supreme Court, the Eleventh Amendment, and State Sovereign Immunity," 98 Yale L.J. 1 (1988), 225

Jackson & Jeffries, "Commercial Speech: Economic Due Process and the First Amendment," 65 Va.L.Rev. 1 (1979), 1182

Jaffe, "Impromptu Remarks," 76 Harv. L.Rev. 1111 (1963), 25

Jefferson, The Writings of Thomas Jefferson (Ford ed. 1897), 20, 102

Jeffries, Justice Lewis F. Powell, Jr. (1994), 596

Jeffries, "Legality, Vagueness and the Construction of Statutes," 71 Va.L.Rev. 189 (1985), 1338

Jeffries, "Rethinking Prior Restraint," 92 Yale L.J. 409 (1983), 1345, 1348

Kaden, "Politics, Money, and State Sovereignty: The Judicial Role," 79 Colum.L.Rev. 847 (1979), 209, 216, 244

Kadish, "Methodology and Criteria in Due Process Adjudication—A Survey and Criticism," 66 Yale L.J. 319 (1957), 440

Kagan, "Regulation of Hate Speech and Pornography After R.A.V.," 60 U.Chi.L.Rev. 873 (1993), 1151

Kalven, "The Concept of the Public Forum: Cox v. Louisiana," 1965 Sup.Ct.Rev. 1, pp. 1235, 1236, 1240, 1267

Kalven, "The Metaphysics of the Law of Obscenity," 1960 Sup.Ct.Rev. 1, pp. 1033, 1141

Kalven, The Negro and the First Amendment (1965), 1376

Kalven, "The New York Times Case: A Note on 'The Central Meaning of the First Amendment,' "1964 Sup.Ct.Rev. 191, p. 1098

Kalven, "Privacy in Tort Law—Were Warren and Brandeis Wrong?," 31 Law & Contemp.Prob. 326 (1966), 1107

Kalven, "Professor Ernst Freund and Debs v. United States," 40 U.Chi.L.Rev. 235 (1973), 1045

Kalven, "The Reasonable Man and the First Amendment: Hill, Butts, and Walker," 1967 Sup.Ct.Rev. 267, p. 1108

Kalven, "Upon Rereading Mr. Justice Black on the First Amendment," 14 UCLA L.Rev. 428 (1967), 1032, 1269

Kalven & Zeisel, The American Jury (1966), 449

Kamenshine, "The First Amendment's Implied Political Establishment Clause," 67 Calif.L.Rev. 1104 (1979), 1302

Kamisar, "Against Suicide—Even a Very Limited Form," 72 U.Det. Mercy L.Rev. 735 (1995), 615

Kamisar, "Physician–Assisted Suicide: A Bad Idea," [Michigan] Law Quadrangle Notes, vol. 39, no. 3, Fall/Winter 1996, pp. 82, 615

Kamisar, "The Reasons So Many People Support [PAS]," 12 Issues in Law & Medicine 113 (1996), 615

Kamisar, "The 'Right to Die': Green Lights and Yellow Lights," [Michigan] Law Quadrangle Notes, Fall 1990, pp. 3, 609

Kaplan, "Equal Justice in an Unequal World," 61 Nw.U.L.Rev. 363 (1966), 671, 794

Kaplan, "Segregation Litigation in the Schools—Part II: The General Northern Problem," 58 Nw.U.L.Rev. 157 (1963), 776

Karlan, "All Over the [Map]," 1993 Sup.Ct. Rev. 254, p. 890

Karlan, "Still Hazy After All These Years: Voting Rights in the Post–Shaw Era," 26 Cumb.L.Rev. 287 (1995), 890

Karst, "Book Review," 89 Harv.L.Rev. 1028 (1976), 540

Karst, "Boundaries and Reasons: Freedom of Expression and the Subordination of Groups," 1990 Ill.L.Rev. 95, p. 1111

Karst, "Equality as a Central Principle in the First Amendment," 43 U.Chi.L.Rev.20 (1975), 1211, 1327

Karst, "Foreword: Equal Citizenship Under the Fourteenth Amendment," 91 Harv. L.Rev. 1 (1977), 431, 540, 941

Karst, "The Freedom of Intimate Association," 89 Yale L.J. 624 (1980), 543, 597, 602

Karst, "Invidious Discrimination: Justice Douglas and the Return to the 'Natural–Law–Due–Process Formula,'"16 UCLA L.Rev. 716 (1969), 631, 644, 911

Karst, "Legislative Facts in Constitutional Litigation," 1960 Sup.Ct.Rev. 75, p. 471

Karst, "Not One Law at Rome and Another at Athens: The Fourteenth Amendment in Nationwide Application," 1972 Wash. U.L.Q. 383, p. 783

Karst, "Serrano v. Priest: A State Court's Responsibilities and Opportunities in the Development of Federal Constitutional Law," 60 Calif.L.Rev. 720 (1972), 70

Karst, "Why Equality Matters," 17 Ga.L.Rev. 245 (1983), 633

Karst, "Women's Constitution," 1984 Duke L.J. 447, p. 692

Karst & Horowitz, "Reitman v. Mulkey: A Telophase of Substantive Equal Protection," 1967 Sup.Ct.Rev. 39, pp. 539, 631, 840

Kauper, "Penumbras, Peripheries, Emanations, Things Fundamental and Things Forgotten: The Griswold Case," 64 Mich. L.Rev. 235 (1965), 528

Kauper, "The Steel Seizure Case: Congress, the President, and the Supreme Court," 51 Mich.L.Rev. 141 (1952), 364

Kay, "Adherence to the Original Intentions in Constitutional Adjudication: Three Objections and Responses," 82 Nw.L.Rev. 226 (1988), 19

Kevles, In the Name of Eugenics: Genetics and the Uses of Human Heredity (1985), 518

Kitch, "The Return of Color–Consciousness to the Constitution: Weber, Dayton, and Columbus," 1979 Sup.Ct.Rev. 1, p. 780

Klarman, "An Interpretive History of Modern Equal Protection," 70 Mich.L.Rev. 213 (1991), 641

Klarman, "Brown, Originalism and Constitutional Theory," 81 Va.L.Rev. 1881

Klitgaard, "The Civil Rights Acts and Mr. Monroe," 49 Calif.L.Rev. 144 (1961), 977

Kluger, Simple Justice: The History of Brown v. Board of Education and Black America's Struggle for Equality (1976), 673

Koh, The National Security Constitution: Sharing Power After the Iran–Contra Affair (1990), 370, 375

Koppelman, "Why Discrimination Against Lesbians and Gay Men is Sex Discrimination," 69 NYU.L.Rev. 197 (1994), 749

Kozinski & Banner, "Who's Afraid of Commercial Speech?," 76 Va.L.Rev. 627 (1990), 1184

Krattenmaker & Powe, "The Fairness Doctrine Today: A Constitutional Curiosity and An Impossible Dream," 1985 Duke L.J. 151, p. 1452

Kreimer, "Allocational Sanctions: The Problem of Negative Rights in a Positive State," 132 U.Pa.L.Rev. 1293 (1984), 1302, 1318

Kreimer, "Does Pro–Choice Mean Pro–Kevorkian? An Essay on Roe, Casey and the Right to Die," 44 Am.U.L.Rev. 803 (1995), 609, 614

Krislov, "The OEO Lawyers Fail to Constitutionalize a Right to [Welfare]," 58 Minn. L.Rev. 211 (1973), 910

Kurland, " 'Brown v. Board of Education Was the Beginning': The School Desegregation Cases in the United States Supreme Court, 1954–1979," 1979 Wash.U.L.Q. 309, p. 773

Kurland, "Of Church and State and the Supreme Court," 29 U.Chi.L.Rev. 1 (1961), 1467, 1481

Kurland, "The Privileges or Immunities Clause: 'Its Hour Come Round at Last'?" 1972 Wash.U.L.Q. 405, p. 430

Kurland, "The Religion Clauses and the Burger Court," 34 Cath.U.L.Rev. 1 (1984), 1530

Kutler, Privilege and Creative Destruction: The Charles River Bridge Case (1971), 507

La Pierre, "Political Accountability in the National Political Process—The Alternative to Judicial Review of Federalism Issues," 80 Nw.L.Rev. 577 (1985), 216

Lahav, "Holmes and Brandeis: Libertarian and Republican Justifications for Free Speech," 4 J.Law & Pol. 451 (1987), 1059

Lange, "The Role of the Access Doctrine in the Regulation of the Mass Media," 52 N.Car.L.Rev. 1 (1973), 1452

Lange, "The Speech and Press Clauses," 23 UCLA L.Rev. 77 (1975), 1421

Law, "Addiction, Autonomy and Advertising," 46 Stan.L.Rev. 875 (1994), 1183

Law, "Rethinking Sex and the Constitution," 132 U.Pa.L.Rev. 955 (1984), 540, 692

Lawrence, "The Id, the Ego, and Equal Protection: Reckoning With Unconscious Racism," 39 Stan.L.Rev. 317 (1987), 753

Laycock, "Formal, Substantive, and Disaggregated Neutrality Toward Religion," 39 DePaul L.Rev. 993 (1990), 1543

Laycock, " 'Nonpreferential' Aid to Religion: A False Claim About Original Intent," 27 Wm. & Mary L.Rev. 875 (1986), 1465

Laycock, "The Religious Freedom Restoration Act," 1993 B.Y.U.L.Rev. 221, p. 1500

Laycock, "RFRA, Congress, and the Ratchet," 56 Mont.L.Rev. 145 (1995), 1015

Laycock & Thomas, "Interpreting the Religious Freedom Restoration Act," 73 Tex. L.Rev. 209 (1994), 1500

LeBel, "Reforming the Tort of Defamation [Within] the Current Constitutional Framework," 66 Neb.L.Rev. 249 (1987), 1099

Leedes, "The Rationality Requirement of the Equal Protection Clause," 42 Ohio St.L.J. 639 (1981), 636

Leedes, "State Action Limitations on Courts and Congressional Power," 60 N.C.L.Rev. 747 (1982), 1013

Leuchtenburg, "The Origins of Franklin D. Roosevelt's Court–Packing Plan," 1966 Sup.Ct. Rev. 347, p. 185

Leuchtenburg, The Supreme Court Reborn: The Constitutional Revolution in the Age of Roosevelt (1995), 185

Leval, "The No–Money, No–Fault Libel Suit: Keeping Sullivan in Its Proper Place," 101 Harv.L.Rev. 1287 (1988), 1099

Levi, "Dangerous Liaisons: Seduction and Betrayal in Confidential Press–Source Relations," 43 Rutgers L.Rev. 609 (1991), 1449

Levi, "The FCC, Indecency, and Anti–Abortion Political Advertising," III Villanova Sports & Ent.L.J. 85 (1996), 1170

Levinson, "Book Review," 26 Stan.L.Rev. 461 (1974), 982

Levinson, " 'The Constitution' in American Civil Religion," 1979 Sup.Ct.Review 123, p. 542

Levinson, "Law as Literature," 60 Tex. L.Rev. 373 (1982), 19

Levitas & Branch, "Congressional Review of Executive and Agency Actions After Chadha; 'The Son of Legislative Veto' Lives On," 72 Geo.L.J. 801 (1984), 383

Levy, Jefferson and Civil Liberties—The Darker Side (1963), 102, 1025

Levy, Judicial Review and the Supreme Court (1967), 16, 18

Levy, "The Legacy Reexamined," 37 Stan. L.Rev. 767 (1985), 1024

Levy, Legacy of Suppression: Freedom of Speech and Press in Early American History (1960), 1024, 1421

Lewis, "Burton v. Wilmington Parking Authority—A Case Without Precedent," 61 Colum.L.Rev. 1458 (1961), 945

Lewis, Make No Law (1991), 1097

Lewis, "The Meaning of State Action," 60 Colum.L.Rev. 1083 (1960), 926

Lewis, "New York Times v. Sullivan [Reconsidered]," 83 Colum.L.Rev. 602 (1983), 1098

Lewis, "A Preferred Position for Journalism?," 7 Hofstra L.Rev. 595 (1979), 1439

Lewis, "A Public Right to Know About Public Institutions: The First Amendment as Sword," 1980 Sup.Ct.Rev. 1, p. 1429

Lewis & Rosenberg, "Legal Analysis of Congress' Authority to Enact a Human Life Statute" (Congressional Research Service, The Library of Congress, Feb. 20, 1981), 1014

Lincoln, The Collected Works of Abraham Lincoln (Basler ed. 1953), 22

Linde, " 'Clear and Present Danger' Reexamined: Dissonance in the Brandenberg Concerto," 22 Stan.L.Rev. 1163 (1970), 1059, 1067

Linde, "Due Process of Lawmaking," 55 Nebr.L.Rev. 197 (1976), 481, 635

Linde, "First Things First: Rediscovering the States' Bill of Rights," 9 U.Balt.L.Rev. 379 (1980), 70

Linde, "Judge, Critics, and the Realist Tradition," 82 Yale L.J. 227 (1972), 541

Linde, "Justice Douglas on Freedom in the Welfare State," 39 Wash.L.Rev. 4 (1964), 246

Linde, "Without ['Due Process']," 49 Ore. L.Rev. 125 (1970), 481

Linder, "Freedom of Association after [Roberts]," 82 Mich.L.Rev. 1878 (1984), 1400

Linzer, "The Meaning of Certiorari Denials," 79 Colum.L.Rev. 1227 (1979), 69

Locke, Of Civil Government, 485

Lockhart & McClure, "Literature, the Law of Obscenity, and the Constitution," 38 Minn.L.Rev. 295 (1954), 1141

Lofgren, "United States v. Curtiss–Wright Corporation: An Historical Reassessment," 83 Yale L.J. 1 (1973), 257

Lowenstein, "A Patternless Mosaic: Campaign Finance and the First Amendment after Austin," 21 Cap.U.L.Rev. 381 (1992), 1418

Lowenstein & Steinberg, "The Quest for Legislative Districting in the Public Interest: Elusive or Illusory?," 33 UCLA L.Rev. 1 (1985), 880

Luker, Abortion and the Politics of Motherhood (1984), 540

Lupu, "Constitutional Theory and the Search for the Workable Premise," 8 U.Dayton L.Rev. 579 (1983), 541

Lupu, "The Lingering Death of Separationism," 62 Geo.Wash.L.Rev. 230 (1994), 1544

Lupu, "Of Time and the RFRA: A Lawyer's Guide to the Religious Freedom Restoration Act," 56 Mont.L.Rev. 171 (1995), 1015, 1500

Lupu, "Statutes Revolving in Constitutional Law Orbits," 79 Va.L.Rev. 1 (1993), 1015, 1016

Lupu, "Untangling the Strands of the Fourteenth Amendment," 77 Mich.L.Rev. 981 (1979), 518, 589, 634, 900

Lupu, "Where Rights Begin: The Problem of Burdens on the Free Exercise of Religion," 102 Harv.L.Rev. 933 (1988), 1489

Lusky, "Footnote Redux: A Carolene Products Reminiscence," 82 Colum.L.Rev. 1093 (1982), 484

MacKinnon, Feminism Unmodified: Discourses on Life and Law (1987), 1149

MacKinnon, "Not a Moral Issue," 2 Yale L. & Pol.Rev. 321 (1984), 1149

MacKinnon, Only Words (1993), 1149

MacKinnon, "Pornography, Civil Rights, and Speech," 20 Harv.C.R.-C.L.L.Rev. 1 (1985), 1149

MacKinnon, "Roe v. Wade: A Study in Male Ideology," in Abortion: Moral and Legal Perspectives 45 (Garfield & Hennessey eds. 1984), 540

Magrath, Yazoo, Law and Politics in the New Republic (1966), 506

Manheim, "Smoke and Mirrors: Providing Only An Illusion of Neutrality, Prop. 209 Violates [Equal Protection]," San Francisco Daily Journal, Dec. 9, 1996, pp. 4, 793

Marcus, "[Applying] Standards Under the Free Exercise Clause," 1973 Duke L.J. 1217, p. 1498

Marcus, Truman and the Steel Seizure Case: The Limits of Presidential Power (1977), 364

Marcuse, "Repressive Tolerance," in A Critique of Pure Tolerance (Robert Wolff et al. 1965), 1026

Marshall, "In Defense of Smith and Free Exercise Revisionism," 58 U.Chi.L.Rev. 1109 (1990), 1498

Marshall, "The Religious Freedom Restoration Act: Establishment, Equal Protection and Free Speech Concerns," 56 Mont. L.Rev. 227 (1995), 1500

Marshall, " 'We Know It When We See It': The Supreme Court and Establishment," 59 S.Cal.L.Rev. 495 (1986), 1531

Marzen et al., "Suicide: A Constitutional Right?" 24 Duq.L.Rev. 1 (1985), 614

Mashaw, Due Process in the Administrative State (1985), 627

Mashaw, "The Supreme Court's Due Process Calculus for Administrative Adjudication in Matthews v. Eldridge: Three Factors in Search of a Theory of Value," 44 U.Chi. L.Rev. 28 (1976), 627

Matheson, "Procedure in Public Person Defamation Cases: The Impact of the First Amendment," 66 Tex.L.Rev. 215 (1987), 1099

Matsuda, "Public Response to Racist Speech: Considering the Victim's Story," 87 Mich. L.Rev. 2320 (1989), 1110

Mayo, "Constitutionalizing the 'Right to Die,' "49 Md.L.Rev. 103 (1990), 609

Mayton, "Seditious Libel and the Lost Guarantee of a Freedom of Expression," 84 Colum.L.Rev. 91 (1984), 1024

Mayton, "Toward a Theory of First Amendment Process: Injunctions of Speech, Subsequent Punishment, and the Costs of the Prior Restraint Doctrine," 67 Cornell L.Rev. 245 (1982), 1345

McAffee, "The Original Meaning of the Ninth Amendment," 90 Colum.L.Rev. 1215 (1990), 528

McCloskey, The American Supreme Court (2d ed., Levinson, 1994), 12

McCloskey, "Economic Due Process and the Supreme Court: An Exhumation and Reburial," 1962 Sup.Ct.Rev. 34, p. 483

McCloskey, "Foreword: The Reapportionment Case," 76 Harv.L.Rev. 54 (1962), 871

McConnell, "Coercion: The Lost Element of Establishment," 27 Wm. & Mary L.Rev. 933 (1986), 1510

McConnell, "Federalism: Evaluating the Founders' Design," 54 U.Chi.L.Rev. 1484 (1987), 214

McConnell, "Free Exercise Revisionism and the Smith Decision," 57 U.Chi.L.Rev. 1109 (1990), 1497, 1498

McConnell, "How Not to Promote Serious Deliberation about Abortion," 58 U.Chi. L.Rev. 1181 (1991), 557

McConnell, "Originalism and the Desegregation Decision," 81 Va.L.Rev. 947 (1995), 678

McConnell, "The Origins and Historical Understanding of Free Exercise of Religion," 103 Harv.L.Rev. 1409 (1990), 1496

McConnell, "Religious Freedom at a Crossroads," 59 U.Chi.L.Rev. 115 (1992), 1499, 1543

McKay, "Reapportionment: Success Story of the Warren Court," 67 Mich.L.Rev. 223 (1968), 871

McKay, "With All Deliberate Speed," 31 N.Y.U.L.Rev. 991 (1956) and 43 Va.L.Rev. 1205 (1957), 773

Medow, "The First Amendment and the Secrecy State," 130 U.Pa.L.Rev. 775 (1982), 1357

Meiklejohn, "The First Amendment Is An Absolute," 1961 Sup.Ct.Rev. 245, 1027, 1141

Meiklejohn, Free Speech and Its Relation to Self-Government (1948), 1027, 1068

Meisel, The Right to Die (2d ed. 1995), 614

Mendelson, "The First Amendment and the Judicial Process: A Reply to Mr. Frantz," 17 Va.L.Rev. 479 (1964), 1032

Merritt, "The Guarantee Clause and State Autonomy: Federalism for a Third Century," 68 Colum.L.Rev. 1 (1988), 214

Michelman, "Foreword: On Protecting the Poor Through the Fourteenth Amendment," 83 Harv.L.Rev. 7 (1969), 735, 711

Michelman, "Liberties, Fair Values, and Constitutional Method," 59 U.Chi.L.Rev. 91 (1992), 1031

Michelman, "Politics and Values, or What's Really Wrong with Rationality Review," 13 Creighton L.Rev. 487 (1979), 635, 646

Michelman, "Property, Utility, and Fairness: Comments on the Ethical Foundations of 'Just Compensation' Law," 80 Harv. L.Rev. 1165 (1967), 487

Michelman, "Saving Old Glory: On Constitutional Iconography," 42 Stan.L.Rev. 1337 (1990), 1230

Michelman, "The Supreme Court and Litigation Access [Fees]," 1973 Duke L.J. 1153 and 1974 Duke L.J. 527, pp. 895, 900

Michelman, "Welfare Rights in a Constitutional Democracy," 1979 Wash.U.L.Q. 659, p. 910

Michigan Commission on Death and Dying, Final Report (1994), 614

Mikva & Hertz, "Impoundment of Funds—The Courts, The Congress and The Presidency: A Constitutional Triangle," 69 Nw. L.Rev. 335 (1974), 384

Mill, On Liberty (1959), 545, 1025, 1034

Miller, "The True Story of Carolene Products," 1988 Sup.Ct.Rev. 397, p. 478

Milton, Areopagitica—A Speech for the Liberty of Unlicensed Printing (1664), 1023, 1025

Mishkin, "Foreword: The High Court, The Great Writ, and the Due Process of Time and Law," 79 Harv.L.Rev. 56 (1965), 445

Mnookin, In the Interest of Children (1985), 549

Monaghan, "Constitutional Adjudication: The Who and When," 82 Yale L.J. 1363 (1973), 28

Monaghan, "Constitutional Common Law," 89 Harv.L.Rev. 1 (1975), 1016

Monaghan, "First Amendment 'Due Process,' "83 Harv.L.Rev. 518 (1970), 1343

Monaghan, "Of 'Liberty' and 'Property'," 62 Cornell L.Rev. 405 (1977), 616, 622, 1098

Monaghan, "Overbreadth," 1981 Sup.Ct.Rev. 1, pp. 1327, 1334, 1337

Monaghan, "Our Perfect Constitution," 56 N.Y.U.L.Rev. 353 (1981), 19, 542

Monaghan, "Third–Party Standing," 84 Colum.L.Rev. 277 (1984), 1327

Morgan, Congress and the Constitution (1966), 24

Munzer, "A Theory of Retroactive Legislation," 61 Tex.L.Rev. 425 (1982), 515

Murasky, "The Journalist's Privilege: Branzburg and Its Aftermath," 52 Tex.L.Rev. 829 (1974), 1438

Murphy, Congress and the Court (1962), 83

Myrdal, An American Dilemma (1944), 677

Nagel, "Equal Treatment and Compensatory Discrimination," 2 Phil. & Pub.Affrs. 348 (1973), 806

Nagel, "How Useful is Judicial Review in Free Speech Cases?" 69 Corenll L.Rev. 302 (1984), 1098

Nahmod, "Artistic Expression and Aesthetic Theory: The Beautiful, the Sublime and the First Amendment," 1987 Wis.L.Rev. 221, p. 1141

Navasky, "The Benevolent Housing Quota," 6 Howard L.J. 30 (1960), 795

Neeley, "[The] Mounting Urgency in the Call for Judicial Recognition of a Constitutional Right to Self–Directed Death," 26 U.Tol.L.Rev. 81 (1994), 614

Neisser, "Charging for Free Speech: User Fees and Insurance in the Marketplace of Ideas," 74 Geo.L.J. 257 (1985), 1239

Nelson, "The Impact of the Antislavery Movement upon Styles of Judicial Reasoning in Nineteenth Century America," 87 Harv.L.Rev. 513 (1974), 457

Neuborne, "The First Amendment and Government Regulation of Capital Markets," 55 Brooklyn L.Rev. 5 (1989), 1183

Neuborne, "The Myth of Parity," 90 Harv. L.Rev. 1105 (1977), 64

New York State Task Force on Life and the Law, When Death is Sought: Assisted Suicide and Euthanasia in the Medical Context (1994), 614

Nimmer, "The Meaning of Symbolic Speech Under the First Amendment," 21 UCLA L.Rev. 29 (1973), 1217

Nimmer, "The Right to Speak from Times to Time: The First Amendment Theory Applied to Libel and Misapplied to Privacy," 56 Cal.L.Rev. 935 (1968), 1033, 1098, 1108

Note, "Benign Steering and Benign [Quotas]," 93 Harv.L.Rev. 938 (1980), 795

Note, "Boys Muscling in on Girls' Sports," 53 Ohio St.L.J. 891 (1992), 715

Note, "The Chilling Effect in Constitutional Law," 69 Colum.L.Rev. 808 (1969), 1327

Note, "The Constitutional Imperative of Proportional Representation," 94 Yale L.J. 163 (1984), 880

Note, "Developments in the Law—The National Security Interest and Civil Liberties," 85 Harv.L.Rev. 1130 (1972), 1390

Note, "The Equal Treatment of Aliens: Preemption or Equal Protection?" 31 Stan. L.Rev. 1069 (1979), 723

Note, "Federal Power to Regulate Private [Discrimination]," 74 Colum.L.Rev. 451 (1974), 972

Note, "The First Amendment Overbreadth Doctrine," 83 Harv.L.Rev. 844 (1970), 1327

Note, "First Amendment Protection of Ambiguous Conduct," 84 Colum.L.Rev. 467 (1984), 1221

Note, "Fornication, Cohabitation, and the Constitution," 77 Mich.L.Rev. 252 (1978), 599

Note, "Inner–City Single–Sex Schools: Educational Reform or Invidious Discrimination?" 105 Harv.L.Rev. 1741 (1992), 715

Note, "Irrebuttable Presumptions: An Illusory Analysis," 27 Stan.L.Rev. 449 (1975), 915

Note, "The Irrebuttable Presumption Doctine in the Supreme Court," 87 Harv. L.Rev. 1534 (1974), 915

Note, "Legislative Purpose, Rationality, and Equal Protection," 82 Yale L.J. 123 (1972), 646

Note, "The Mootness Doctrine in the Supreme Court," 88 Harv.L.Rev. 373 (1974), 44

Note: "Motorcycle Helmets and the Constitutionality of Self–Protective Legislation," 30 Ohio St.L.J. 355 (1969), 543

Note, "The 'New' 13th [Amendment]," 82 Harv.L.Rev. 1294 (1969), 981

Note, "Physician–Assisted Suicide and the Right to Die with Assistance," 105 Harv. L.Rev. 2021 (1992), 614

Note, "A Process–Oriented Approach to the Contract Clause," 89 Yale L.J. 1623 (1980), 514

Note, "The Proper Scope of the Civil Rights Acts," 66 Harv.L.Rev. 1285 (1953), 977

Note, "Rediscovering the Contract Clause," 97 Harv.L.Rev. 1414 (1984), 514

Note, "Reforming the One Step at a Time Justification in Equal Protection Cases," 90 Yale L.J. 1777 (1981), 643

Note, "Roe and Paris: Does Privacy Have a Principle?" 26 Stan.L.Rev. 1161 (1974), 528

Note, "Sex Discrimination and [Equal Protection]," 84 Harv.L.Rev. 1499 (1971), 685

Note, "Standing to Assert Constitutional Jus Tertii," 88 Harv.L.Rev. 423 (1974), 1327

Note, "The Supreme Court, 1991 Term," 106 Harv.L.Rev. 163, (1992), 206, 584

Note, "Toward a Constitutional Definition of Religion," 91 Harv.L.Rev. 1056 (1978), 1470

Note, "When the Supreme Court Restricts Constitutional Rights, Can Congress Save Us? An Examination of [§ 5 of the 14th Amendment]," 141 U.Pa.L.Rev. 1029 (1993), 1015

Note, 69 Colum.L.Rev. 1019 (1969), 981

Note, 83 Harv.L.Rev. 96 (1969), 891

Novick, Honorable Justice: The Life of Oliver Wendell Holmes (1989), 1045

Novick, "The Unrevised Holmes and Freedom of Expression," 1991 Sup.Ct.Rev. 303, p. 1945

Nozick, Anarchy, State, and Utopia (1975), 912

Oakes, "The 'Original' Writ of Habeas Corpus in the Supreme Court," 1962 Sup.Ct. Rev. 153, p. 79

Olsen, "Statutory Rape: A Feminist Critique of Rights Analysis," 63 Tex.L.Rev. 387 (1984), 692

O'Fallon, "Adjudication and Contested Concepts: The Case of Equal Protection," 54 N.Y.Y.L.Rev. 19 (1979), 633, 634

O'Fallon & Rogat, "Mr. Justice Holmes: A Dissenting Opinion," 36 Stan.L.Rev. 1349 (1984), 1045

O'Neil, "Preferential Admissions: Equalizing the Access of Minority Groups to Higher Education," 80 Yale L.J. 699 (1971), 795

O'Neil, "Racial Preference and Higher [Education]," 60 Va.L.Rev. 925 (1974), 807

O'Neil, "Unconstitutional Conditions: Welfare Benefits with Strings Attached," 54 Calif.L.Rev. 443 (1966), 249

Patterson, The Forgotten Ninth Amendment (1955), 520

Paul, Conservative Crisis and the Rule of Law: Attitudes of Bar and Bench 1887–1896 (1960), 458

Perry, "Abortion, the Public Morals, and the Police Power," 23 UCLA L.Rev. 689 (1976), 537

Perry, "The Authority of Text, Tradition, and Reason," 58 S. Cal.L.Rev. 551 (1985), 537

Perry, The Constitution, the Courts, and Human Rights (1982), 537

Perry, Deciding to Decide: Agenda Setting in [the] Supreme Court (1991), 69

Perry, "The Disproportionate Impact Theory of Racial Discrimination," 125 U.Pa. L.Rev. 540 (1977), 754

Perry, "Freedom of Expression: An Essay on Theory and Doctrine," 78 Nw.U.L.Rev. 1137 (1983), 1049

Perry, Love and Power: The Role of Religion and Morality in American Politics (1991), 1497

Perry, "Modern Equal Protection," 79 Colum.L.Rev. 1023 (1979), 633, 635

Perry, "Religious Arguments in Public Political Debate," 29 Loyola L.Rev. 1421 (1996), 1497

Peters, "Civil Rights and State Non–Action," 34 Notre Dame L.Rev. 303 (1959), 923

Pfeffer, "Religion–Blind Government," 15 Stan.L.Rev. 389 (1963), 1467

Pildes & Niemi, "Expressive Harms, 'Bizarre Districts,' and [Voting Rights]," 92 Mich. L.Rev. 483, p. 880

Plous & Baker, "McCulloch v. Maryland: Right Principle, Wrong Case," 9 Stan. L.Rev. 710 (1957), 107

Pollak, "Racial Discrimination and Judicial Integrity: A Reply to Professor Wechsler," 108 U.Pa.L.Rev. 1 (1959), 678, 926

Polsby, "Buckley v. Valeo: The Special Nature of Political Speech," 1976 Sup.Ct. Rev. 1, p. 1410

Polsby (ed.), Reapportionment in the 1970's (1971), 871

Pope, "The Three–Systems Ladder of First Amendment Values: Two Rungs and a Black Hole," 11 Hast.Con.L.Q. (1984), 1293

Posner, "Bork and Beethoven," 42 Stan. L.Rev. 1365 (1990), 546

Posner, "[The] Constitutionality of Preferential Treatment of Racial Minorities," 1974 Sup.Ct.Rev. 1, p. 646

Posner, Economic Analysis of Law (2d ed. 1977), 635

Posner, "Free Speech in an Economic Perspective," 20 Suffolk L.Rev. 1 (1986), 1181

Posner, "The Meaning of Judicial Self–Restraint," 59 Ind.L.J. 1 (1983), 542

Posner, "The Right to Privacy," 12 Ga.L.Rev. 393 (1978), 1107

Posner, Sex and Reason (1992), 599

Posner, "The Uncertain Protection of Privacy by the Supreme Court," 1979 Sup.Ct. Rev. 173, p. 529

Post, "Between Governance and Management: The History and Theory of the Public Forum," 34 UCLA L.Rev. 1713 (1987), 1236

Post, "The Constitutional Concept of Public Discourse: Outrageous Opinion, Democratic Deliberation, and Hustler Magazine v. Falwell," 103 Harv.L.Rev. 603 (1990), 1107

Post, Constitutional Domains: Democracy, Community, Management (1995), 1028

Post, "Recuperating First Amendment Doctrine," 47 Stan.L.Rev. 1249 (1995), 1221

Post, "The Social Foundations of Defamation Law: Reputation and the Constitution," 74 Calif.L.Rev. 691 (1986), 1098

Post, "Subsidized Speech," 106 Yale L.J. 151 (1996), 1323

Powe, "Mass Speech and the Newer First Amendment," 1982 Sup.Ct.Rev. 243, pp. 1026, 1411

Powe, "Or of The [Broadcast] Press," 55 Tex.L.Rev. 39 (1976), 1452

Powe, "Tornillo," 1987 Sup.Ct.Rev. 345, p. 1452

Powell, "Carolene Products Revisited," 82 Colum.L.Rev. 1087 (1982), 484

Prosser, "Privacy," 48 Calif.L.Rev. 383 (1960), 1107

Rabban, "An Ahistorical Historian: Leonard Levy on Freedom of Expression in Early American History," 37 Stan.L.Rev. 795 (1986)

Rabban, "The Emergence of Modern First Amendment Doctrine," 50 U.Chi.L.Rev. 1205 (1983), 1045

Rabban, "The First Amendment in Its Forgotten Years," 90 Yale L.J. 514 (1981), 1025

Rabban, "The Free Speech League, the ACLU, and Changing Conceptions of Free Speech in American History," 45 Stan. L.Rev. 47 (1992), 1025

Rabban, "The IWW Free Speech Fights and Popular Conceptions of Free Expression Before World War I," 80 Va.L.Rev. 1055 (1994), 1025

Rabin, "Job Security and Due Process: Monitoring Discretion Through a Reasons Requirement," U.Chi.L.Rev. 60 (1976), 621

Radin, Market Rhetoric and Reality: Commodification in Words and the World (1996), 1031

Ragan, "Justice Oliver Wendell Holmes, Jr., Zechariah Chafee, Jr., and the Clear and Present Danger Test for Free Speech: The First Year, 1919," 58 J.Am.Hist. 24 (1971), 1045

Rapaczynski, "From Sovereignty to Process: The Jurisprudence of Federalism after Garcia," 1985 Sup.Ct.Rev. 341, p. 212

Raskin & Bonifaz, "The Constitutional Imperative and Practical Superiority of Democratically Financed Elections," 94 Colum.L.Rev. 1160 (1994), 1411

Rawls, A Theory of Justice (1971), 912

Read, "Judicial Evolution of the Law of School Integration Since [Brown]," 39 Law & Contemp.Probs. 7 (1975), 773

Redish, "Congressional Power to Regulate Supreme Court Jurisdiction Under the Exceptions Clause: An Internal and External Examination," 27 Vill.L.Rev. 900 (1982), 82

Redish, "Constitutional Limitations on Congressional Power to Control Federal Jurisdiction: A Reaction to Professor Sager," 77 Nw.L.Rev. 143 (1982), 85

Redish, "The Content Distinction in the First Amendment Analysis," 34 Stan.L.Rev. 113 (1981), 1211

Redish, "Federal Judicial Independence: Constitutional and Political Perspectives," 46 Mercer L.Rev. 697 (1995), 81

Redish, "The First Amendment in the Marketplace: Commercial Speech and the Values of Free Expression," 39 Geo. Wash.L.Rev. 429 (1971), 1183

Redish, "The Proper Role of the Prior Restraint Doctrine in First Amendment Theory," 70 Va.L.Rev. 53 (1984), 1344, 1347

Redish, "The Role of Pathology in First Amendment Theory: A Skeptical Examination," 38 Case W.Res.L.Rev. 618 (1988), 1029

Redish, "Tobacco Advertising and the First Amendment," 81 Iowa L.Rev. 589 (1996), 1202

Redish, "The Value of Free Speech," 130 U.Pa.L.Rev. 591 (1982), 1028, 1184

Redish, "The Warren Court, the Burger Court, and the First Amendment Overbreadth Doctrine," 78 Nw.L.Rev. 1031 (1983), 1327

Redish & Kessler, "Government Subsidies and Free Expression," 80 Minn.L.Rev. 543 (1995), 1323

Regan, "The Supreme Court and State Protectionism: Making Sense of the Dormant Commerce Clause," 84 Mich.L.Rev. 1091 (1986), 270, 274, 323

Reich, The Greening of America (1970), 617

Reich, "The New Property," 73 Yale L.J. 733 (1964), 617

Rendleman, "The New Due Process: Rights and Remedies," 63 Ky.L.J. 531 (1975), 617

Rhode, "Moral Character as a Professional Credential," 94 Yale L.J. 491 (1985), 1397

Richards, "Free Speech and Obscenity Law: Toward a Moral Theory of the First Amendment," 123 U.Pa.L.Rev. 45 (1974), 1142

Richardson (ed.), Messages and Papers of the Presidents (1896), 21

Roberts, "Heightened Scrutiny Under the Equal Protection Clause: A Remedy to Discrimination Based on Sexual Orientation," 42 Drake L.Rev. 485 (1993), 749

Roberts, "Rust v. Sullivan and Control of Knowledge," 61 Geo.Wash.L.Rev. 587 (1993), 1323

Robin–Vergeer, "Disposing of the Red Herrings: A Defense of [RFRA]," 69 So.Cal. L.Rev. 589 (1996), 1015

Rogat, "The Judge as Spectator," 31 U. Chi. L.Rev. 213 (1964), 518

Roosevelt, F.D.R.—His Personal Letters, 1928–1945 (Elliot Roosevelt ed. 1950), 23

Roosevelt, The Public Papers and Addresses of Franklin D. Roosevelt (1938), 22

Rose–Ackerman, "Cooperative Federalism and Co-optation," 92 Yale L.J. 1344 (1983), 244

Rosenberg, The Hollow Hope (1993), 871

Rosenthal, "Conditional Federal Spending and the Constitution," 39 Stan.L.Rev. 1103 (1987), 244

Rostow, "The Democratic Character of Judicial Review," 66 Harv.L.Rev. 193 (1952), 18

Rostow, "The Japanese American Cases—A Disaster," 54 Yale L.J. 489 (1945), 665

Rubenfeld, "On the Legal Status of the Proposition That 'Life Begins at Conception,' "43 Stan.L.Rev. 559 (1991), 557

Rubenfeld, "The Right to Privacy," 102 Harv.L.Rev. 737 (1989), 528, 599

Rutzick, "Offensive Language and the Evolution of First Amendment Protection," 9 Harv.C.R.-C.L. L.Rev. 1 (1974), 1085

Sabrin, "Thinking About Content: Can It Play an Appropriate Role in Government Funding of the Arts?," 102 Yale L.J. 1209 (1993), 1323

Sack, "Reflections on the Wrong Question: Special Constitutional Privilege for the Institutional Press," 7 Hofstra L.Rev. 629 (1979), 1439

Sager, "Fair Measure: The Legal Status of Underenforced Constitutional Norms," 91 Harv.L.Rev. 1212 (1978), 72

Sager, "Foreword: Constitutional Limits on Congress' Ability to Regulate the Jurisdiction of the Federal Courts," 95 Harv. L.Rev. 17 (1981), 85

Sager, "Tight Little Islands: Exclusionary Zoning, Equal Protection, and the Indigent," 21 Stan.L.Rev. 767 (1969), 911

Sandalow, "Racial Preferences in Higher [Education]," 42 U.Chi.L.Rev. 653 (1975), 795

Sax, "Takings and the Police Power," 74 Yale L.J. 36 (1964), 487

Sax, "Takings, Private Property, and Public Rights," 81 Yale L.J. 149 (1971), 487

Scalia, "The Rule of Law as a Law of Rules," 56 U.Chi.L.Rev. 1175 (1989), 1498

Scanlon, "Freedom of Expression and Categories of Expression," 40 U.Pitt.L.Rev. 519 (1979), 1028, 1034, 1049, 1183

Scanlon, "A Theory of Freedom of Expression," 1 Phil. & Pub.Aff. 204 (1972), 1028, 1049

Schaefer, "Federalism and State Criminal Procedures," 70 Harv.L.Rev. 1 (1956), 437

Schauer, "Categories and the First Amendment: A Play in Three Acts," 34 Vand. L.Rev. 265 (1981), 1034, 1155

Schauer, "Causation Theory and the Causes of Sexual Violence," 1987 A.B.F.REs.J. 737, p. 1145

Schauer, "Codifying the First Amendment: New York v. Ferber," 1982 Sup.Ct.Rev. 285, pp. 1034, 1148

Schauer, "Easy Cases," 58 S.Cal.L.Rev. 399 (1985), 19

Schauer, Free Speech: A Philosophical Enquiry (1982), 1028, 1029, 1344

Schauer, " 'Private' Speech and the 'Private' Forum," 1979 Sup.Ct.Rev. 217, p. 1304

Schauer, "The Second–Best First Amendment," 31 Wm. & Mary L.Rev. 1 (1989), 1929

Schauer, "Slippery Slopes," 99 Harv.L.Rev. 361 (1985), 1445

Schauer, "Speech and 'Speech'—Obscenity and 'Obscenity': An Exercise in the Interpretation of Constitutional Language," 67 Geo.L.J. 899 (1979), 1034, 1142

Schauer, "Uncoupling Free Speech," 64 U.Colo.L.Rev. 935 (1993), 1031, 1091

Schmidt, Freedom of the Press vs. Public Access (1976), 1452

Schuck, "The Thickest Thicket: Partisan Gerrymandering and Judicial Regulation of Politics," 87 Colum.L.Rev. 1325 (1987), 880

Scordato, "Distinction Without a Difference: A Reappraisal of the Doctrine of Prior Restraint," 68 N.C.L.Rev. 1 (1989), 1345

Sedler, "The Assertion of Constitutional Jus Tertii: A Substantive Approach," 70 Calif.L.Rev. 1308 (1982), 1327

Sedler, "The Legitimacy Debate in Constitutional [Adjudication]," 44 Ohio St.L.J. 93 (1983), 542

Sedler, "Metropolitan Desegregation in the Wake of Milliken," 1975 Wash.U.L.Q. 535, p. 784

Sedler, "The Negative Commerce Clause as a Restriction on State Regulation," 31 Wayne L.Rev. 885 (1985), 270

Seidman, "Confusion at the Border: Cruzan, 'The Right to Die,' and the Public/Private Distinction," 1992 Sup.Ct.Rev. 47, p. 609

Selected Essays on Constitutional Law, Vol. 1 (1938), 14

Senate Committee on the Judiciary, Subcommittee on the Constitution, Federal Civil Rights Laws: A Sourcebook (1984), 920

Shaman, "Constitutional Fact: The Perception of Reality by the Supreme Court," 35 U.Fla.L. Rev. 236 (1983), 471

Shapiro, "Fathers and Sons," in The Burger Court 216 (Blasi ed., 1983), 530

Shapiro, Federalism—A Dialogue (1995), 89

Sherman, "Love Speech: The Social Utility of Pornography," 47 Stan.L.Rev. 661 (1995), 1150

Shiffrin, "Defamatory Non–Media Speech and First Amendment Methodology," 25 UCLA L.Rev. 915 (1978), 1100

Shiffrin, "The First Amendment and Economic Regulation: Away From a General Theory of the First Amendment," 78 Nw. U.L.Rev. 1212 (1983), 1029, 1182

Shiffrin, "Government Speech," 27 UCLA L.Rev. 565 (1980), 1302

Siebert, Freedom of the Press in England, 1476–1776 (1952), 1024

Siegan, Economic Liberties and the Constitution (1980), 469, 484

Siegel, "Understanding the Lochner Era: Lessons from the Controversy over Railroad and Utility Rate Regulation," 70 Va. L.Rev. 187 (1984), 459

Simon, "Equality as a Comparative Right," 65 B.U.L.Rev. 387 (1985), 633

Simon, "Liberty and Property in the Supreme Court: A Defense of Roth and Perry," 71 Calif.L.Rev. 146 (1983), 619

Simson, "Discrimination Against Nonresidents and the Privileges and Immunities Clause of Article IV," 128 U.Pa.L.Rev. 279 (1979), 328

Smith, "Symbols, Perceptions, and Doctrinal Illusions: Establishment Neutrality and the 'No Endorsement' Test," 86 Mich. L.Rev. 266 (1987), 1531

Smolla, "The Displacement of Federal Due Process Claims by State Tort Remedies," 1982 U.Ill.L.F. 831, p. 625

Smolla, "[The] Rejuvenation of the American Law of Libel," 132 U.Pa.L.Rev. 1 (1984), 1098

Sofaer, "The Presidency, War, and Foreign Affairs ...," 40 Law & Contemp.Probs. 12 (1976), 371

Sorauf, "Politics, Experience, and the First Amendment: The Case of American Campaign Finance," 94 Colum.L.Rev. 1348 (1994), 1411

Spitzer, "The Constitutionality of Licensing Broadcasters," 64 N.Y.U.L.Rev. 990 (1989), 1450

St. Clair et al., An Analysis of the Constitutional Standard for Presidential Impeachment (1974), 412

Steinbeck, The Grapes of Wrath (1939), 336

Stephan, "The First Amendment and Content Discrimination," 68 Va.L.Rev. 203 (1982), 1211

Sterk, "The Continuity of Legislatures: Of Contracts and the Contracts Clause," 88 Colum.L.Rev. 647 (1988), 515

Stern, "The Commerce Clause and the National Economy, 1933–1946," 59 Harv. L.Rev. 645 (1946), 177, 178

Stern, "The Commerce Clause Revisited— The Federalization of Intrastate Crime," 15 Ariz.L.Rev. 271 (1973), 197

Stewart, "Or of the Press," 26 Hast.L.J. 631 (1975), 1421

Stone, "Anti-Pornography Legislation as Viewpoint Discrimination," 9 Harv.J.L. & Pub.Pol. 701 (1986), 1151

Stone, "Content–Neutral Restrictions," 54 U.Chi.L.Rev. 46 (1987), 1244

Stone, "Content Regulation and the First Amendment," 25 Wm. & Mary L.Rev. 189 (1983), 1209, 1210, 1218

Stone, "Flag Burning and the Constitution," 75 Iowa L.Rev. 111 (1989), 1228

Stone, "Fora Americana: Speech in Public Places," 1974 Sup.Ct.Rev. 233, pp. 1236, 1268

Stone, "Retrictions of Speech Because of Its Content: The Peculiar Case of Subject Matter Restrictions," 46 U.Chi.L.Rev. 81 (1976), 1211

Storing, The Complete Anti–Federalist (1981), 99

Strauss, "Abortion, Toleration, and Moral Uncertainty," 1993 Sup.Ct.Rev. 1, p. 583

Strauss, "Corruption, Equality, and Campaign Finance," 94 Colum.L.Rev. 1369 (1994), 1410

Strauss, "Formal and Functional Approaches to Separation of Powers Questions—A Foolish Inconsistency?" 72 Cor.L.Rev. 488 (1987), 356

Strauss, "Persuasion, Autonomy, and Freedom of Expression," 91 Colum.L.Rev. 334 (1991), 1028, 1183

Strauss, "Was There a Baby in the Bathwater? A Comment on the Supreme Court's Legislative Veto Decision," 1983 Duke L.J. 789, p. 383

Strickman, "School Desegregation at the Crossroads," 70 Nw.U.L.Rev. 725 (1975), 784

Strong, "A Post–Script to Carolene Products," 5 Const.Commentary 185 (1988), 478

Strong, Substantive Due Process: A Dichotomy of Sense and Nonsense (1986), 478

Strossen, Defending Pornography: Free Speech, Sex and the Fight for Women's Rights (1995), 1150

Strossen, "Regulating Racist Speech on Campus: A Modest Proposal?," 1990 Duke L.J. 484, p. 1111

Strossen, "Regulating Workplace Sexual Harassment and Upholding the First Amendment—Avoiding a Collision," 37 Vill.L.Rev. 757 (1992), 1125

Struve, "The Less–Restrictive Alternative Principle and Economic Due Process," 80 Harv.L.Rev. 1463 (1967), 474, 483

Sullivan, "Cheap Spirits, Cigarettes and Free Speech," 1996 Sup.Ct.Rev. 123, p. 1202

Sullivan, "Dueling Sovereignties: U.S. Term Limits v. Thorton," 109 Harv.L.Rev. 78 (1995), 114

Sullivan, "Free Speech and Unfree Markets," 42 UCLA L.Rev. 949 (1995), 1031

Sullivan, "Post–Liberal Judging: The Roles of Categorization and Balancing," 63 U.Colo. L.Rev. 293 (1992), 1033

Sullivan, "Religion and Liberal Democracy," 59 U.Chi.L.Rev. 195 (1992), 1499, 1543

Sullivan, "The Supreme Court 1991 Term— Foreword: The Justices of Rules and Standards," 106 Harv.L.Rev. 22 (1992), 583, 1033

Sullivan, "Unconstitutional Conditions," 102 Harv.L.Rev. 1413 (1989), 249, 496, 1302, 1318

Sullivan & Estrich, "Abortion Politics: Writing for an Audience of One," 138 U.Pa. L.Rev. 119 (1989), 557

Sunderland, Obscenity: The Court, the Congress and the President's Commission (1975), 1132

Sunstein, "Constitutionalism After the New Deal," 101 Harv.L.Rev. 421 (1987), 356

Sunstein, Democracy and the Problem of Free Speech (1993), 1027, 1028, 1031, 1034, 1182, 1210

Sunstein, "Foreword: Leaving Things Undecided," 110 Harv.L.Rev. 4 (1996), 747

Sunstein, "Free Speech Now," 59 U.Chi.L.Rev. 255 (1992), 1027, 1028, 1410

Sunstein, "Government Control of Information," 74 Calif.L.Rev. 889 (1986), 1357

Sunstein, "Homosexuality and the Constitution," 70 Ind.L.J. 1 (1994), 749

Sunstein, "Interest Groups in American Public Law," 38 Stan.L.Rev. 29 (1985), 645

Sunstein, "Lochner's Legacy," 87 Colum.L.Rev. 873 (1987), 469

Sunstein, "Naked Preferences and the Constitution," 84 Colum.L.Rev. 1689 (1984), 469, 645, 647

Sunstein, The Partial Constitution (1993), 469, 583

Sunstein, "Pornography and the First Amendment," 1986 Duke L.J. 589 (1986), 1150

Sunstein, "Public Values, Private Interests, and the Equal Protection Clause," 1982 Sup.Ct.Rev. 127, pp. 645, 793

Sunstein, "Sexual Orientation and the Constitution: A Note in the Relationship between Due Process and Equal Protection," 55 U.Chi.L.Rev. 1161 (1988), 747, 749

Sunstein, "Words, Conduct, Caste," 60 U.Chi.L.Rev. 795 (1993), 1142

Symposium, "The Courts, Social Science, and School Desegregation," Law & Contemp.Prob. (1975), 678

Symposium, "Defamation and the First Amendment: New Perspectives," 25 Wm. & Mary L.Rev. 743 (1984), 1098

Symposium, "Emerging Media Technology and the First Amendment," 104 Yale L.J. 1611 (1995), 1455

Symposium, "Equal Rights for Women: . . . the Proposed Constitutional Amendment," 6 Harv.Civ.Rts.-Civ.Libs.L.Rev. 125 (1971), 701

Symposium on Interpreting the Ninth Amendment, 64 Chi.-Kent L.Rev. 37 (1988), 528

Symposium, "Legislative Motivation," 15 San Diego L.Rev. 925 (1978), 751

Symposium on Lucas, 45 Stan.L.Rev. 1369 (1993), 502

Symposium, "National Security and the First Amendment," 26 Wm. & Mary L.Rev. 715 (1985), 1357

Symposium, "School Desegregation: Lessons of the First Twenty-Five Years," Law & Contemp. Prob. (1978), 678

Tanenhaus, "Group Libel," 35 Cornell L.Q. 261 (1950), 1093

Teitel, "A Critique of Religion as Politics in the Public Sphere," 78 Cornell L.Rev. 747 (1993), 1497, 1498

tenBroek, "Thirteenth [Amendment]—Consummation to Abolition and Key to the Fourteenth Amendment," 39 Calif.L.Rev. 171 (1951), 423

Thayer, "The Origin and Scope of the American Doctrine of Constitutional Law," 7 Harv.L.Rev. 129 (1983), 18

Tribe, Abortion: The Clash of Absolutes (1990), 557

Tribe, American Constitutional Law (2d Ed. 1988), 276, 469, 518, 539, 614, 1029, 1156, 1209, 1470, 1535

Tribe, "Childhood, Suspect Classifications, and Conclusive Presumptions," 39 Law & Contemp.Prob. 8 (1975), 539

Tribe, "Foreword: Toward a Model of Roles in the Due Process of Life and Law," 87 Harv.L.Rev. 1 (1973), 539

Tribe, God Save this Honorable Court (1985), 75

Tribe, "Jurisdictional Gerrymandering: Zoning Disfavored Rights Out of the Federal Courts," 16 Harv.C.R.-C.L.L.Rev. 129 (1981), 82

Tribe, "The Mystery of Motive, Private and [Public]," 1993 Sup.Ct.Rev. 1, p. 1125

Tribe, "Structural Due Process," 10 Harv. Civ.Rts.-Civ.Lib.L.Rev. 269 91975), 539

Tribe & Dorf, "Levels of Generality in the Definition of Rights," 57 U.Chi.L.Rev. 1057 (1990), 599

Truman, Memoirs: Years of Trial and Hope (1956), 364

Turner, "The Impeachment of John Pickering," 54 Am.Hist.Rev. 485 (1949), 12

Tushnet, "The Constitution of Religion," 18 Conn.L.Rev. 701 (1986), 1530

Tushnet, "Following the Rules Laid Down: A Critique of Interpretivisim and Neutral Principles," 96 Harv.L.Rev. 781 (1983), 542

Tushnet, "Justice Lewis F. Powell and the Jurisprudence of Centrism," 93 Mich. L.Rev. 1854 (1995), 650, 651

Tushnet, The NAACP's Legal Strategy Against Segregated Education, 1925–1950 (1987), 673

Tushnet, "The Newer Property: Suggestions for the Revival of Substantive Due Process," 1975 Sup.Ct.Rev. 261, p. 617

Tushnet, "The Optimist's Tale," 132 U.Pa. L.Rev. 1257 (1984), 857

Tushnet, "Rethinking the Dormant Commerce Clause," 1979 Wisc.L.Rev. 125, p. 271

Tussman & tenBroek, "The Equal Protection of the Laws," 37 Calif.L.Rev. 341 (1949), 636, 637

Twiss, Lawyers and the Constitution: How Laissez Faire Came to the Supreme Court (1942), 458

Van Alstyne, "Cracks in 'The New Property': Adjudicative Due Process in the Administrative State," 62 Cornell L.Rev. 445 (1977), 617, 624

Van Alstyne, "A Critical Guide to Ex Parte McCardle," 15 Ariz.L.Rev. 229 (1973), 78

Van Alstyne, "A Critical Guide to Marbury v. Madison," 1969 Duke L.J., 13

Van Alstyne, "The Demise of the Right–Privilege Distinction in Constitutional Law," 81 Harv.L.Rev. 1439 (1968), 617, 1302, 1318

Van Alstyne, "Does Article V Restrict the States to Calling Unlimited Conventions Only?" 1978 Duke L.J. 1295 (1979), 250

Van Alstyne, "A Graphic Review of the Free Speech Clause," 70 Calif.L.Rev. 107 (1982), 1067

Van Alstyne, "Interpreting *This* Constitution: The Unhelpful Contributions of Special Theories of Judicial Review," 35 U.Fla.L.Rev. 209 (1983), 541, 542

Van Alstyne, "The Mobius Strip of the First Amendment: Perspectives on Red Lion," 29 S.C.L.Rev. 539 (1978), 1452

Van Alstyne, "The Role of Congress in Determining Incidental Powers of the President and of the Federal Courts: A Comment on the Horizontal Effect of the Sweeping Clause," 40 Law & Contemp.Probs. 102 (1976), 365

Van Alstyne, "The Third Impeachment Article: Congressional Bootstrapping," 60 A.B.A.J. 1199 (1974)

Van Alstyne, "Trends in the Supreme Court: Mr. Jefferson's Crumbling Wall—A Comment on Lynch v. Donnelly," 1984 Duke L.J. 770, pp. 1463, 1530

Van Alstyne & Karst, "State Action," 14 Stan.L.Rev. 3 (1961), 926, 927

Varat, "State 'Citizenship' and Interstate Equality," 48 U.Chi.L.Rev. 487 (1981), 323, 328

Velvel, "Freedom of Speech and the Draft Card Burning Cases," 16 U.Kan.L.Rev. 149 (1968), 1216

Volokh, "Freedom of Speech and Workplace Harassment," 39 UCLA L.Rev. 1791 (1992), 1125

Warren, "Legislative and Judicial Attacks on the Supreme Court of the United States—A History of the Twenty–Fifth Section of the Judiciary Act," 47 Am.L.Rev. 1 (1913), 64

Warren, "The New 'Liberty' under the Fourteenth Amendment," 39 Harv.L.Rev. 431 (1926), 466

Warren, The Supreme Court in United States History (Rev. Ed. 1926), 12, 103

Warren & Brandeis, "The Right to Privacy," 4 Harv.L.Rev. 193 (1890), 525, 1107

Washburn, "Land Use Control, the Individual and Society," 52 Md.L.Rev. 162 (1993), 502

Wechsler, "The Courts and the Constitution," 65 Colum.L.Rev. 1001 (1965), 24, 81

Wechsler, "The Political Safeguards of Federalism—The Role of the States in the Composition and Selection of the National Government," 54 Colum.L.Rev. 543 (1954), 111, 185

Wechsler, "Toward Neutral Principles of Constitutional Law," 73 Harv.L.Rev. 1 (1959), 17, 178, 678, 679, 680, 926

Weinberg, "Broadcasting and Speech," 81 Calif.L.Rev. 1101 (1993), 1450

Weinstein, "A Constitutional Roadmap to the Regulation of Campus Hate Speech," 38 Wayne L.Rev. 163 (1991), 1111

Weisberg, "A Great Writ While It Lasted," 81 J.Crim.L. & Criminology 9 (1990), 445

Wellington, "Common Law Rules and Constitutional Double Standards," 83 Yale L.J. 221 (1973), 529

Wellington, "History and Morals in Constitutional Adjudication," 97 Harv.L.Rev. 326 (1983), 542

Wellington, "On Freedom of Expression," 88 Yale L.J. 1105 (1979), 1026

Wells & Hellerstein, "The Government–Proprietary Distinction in Constitutional Law," 66 Va.L.Rev. 1073 (1980), 323, 1273

West, "The Feminist–Conservative Anti–Pornography [Alliance]," 1987 A.B.F.Res.J. 681, p. 1149

Westin, The Anatomy of a Constitutional Law Case (1958), 364

Westen, "The Empty Idea of Equality," 95 Harv.L.Rev. 537 (1982), 629, 633

Westen, "To Lure the Tarantula from Its Hole: A Response," 83 Colum.L.Rev. 1186 (1983), 633

Westen, "The Meaning of Equality in Law, Science, Math, and Morals: A Reply," 81 Mich.L.Rev. 604 (1983), 633

Westen, "On 'Confusing Ideas': A Reply," 91 Yale L.J. 1153 (1982), 633

White, "Justice Holmes and the Modernization of Free Speech Jurisprudence: The Human Dimension," 80 Cal.L.Rev. 391 (1992), 1045

Wigmore, "Abrams v. United States: Freedom of Speech and Freedom of Thuggery in War-time and Peace–Time," 14 Ill. L.Rev. 539 (1920), 1045

Wilkinson, From Brown to Bakke—The Supreme Court and School Integration: 1954–1978 (1979), 772

Wilkinson, "The Supreme Court, the Equal Protection Clause, and the Three Faces of Constitutional Equality," 61 Va.L.Rev. 945 (1975), 633

Williams, "Content Discrimination and the First Amendment," 139 U.Pa.L.Rev. 615 (1991), 1211

Williams, "The Equality Crisis: Some Reflections on Culture, Courts and Feminism," 7 Women's Rts.L.Rep. 175 (1982), 692

Williams, "The Twilight of State Action," 41 Texas L.Rev. 347 (1963), 926

Williams & Williams, "Volitionalism and Religious Liberty," 76 Cornell L.Rev. 769 (1991), 1488

Winter, "Changing Concepts of Equality: From Equality Before the Law to the Welfare State," 1979 Wash.U.L.Q. 741, p. 911

Winter, "Poverty, Economic Equality, and the Equal Protection Clause," 1972 Sup. Ct.Rev. 41, p. 735

Wiseman, "The New Supreme Court Commentators: The Principled, the Political and the Philosophical," 10 Hastings Const.L.Q. 315 (1983), 542

Witmer & Kotinsky, Personality in the Making (1952), 676

Wood, Constitutional Politics in the Progressive Era (1968), 172

Wood, The Creation of the American Republic, 1776–1787 (1969), 14

Wright, "The Constitution on Campus," 22 Vand. L.Rev. 1027 91969), 1301

Wright, The Contract Clause of the Constitution (1938), 506

Wright, The Growth of American Constitutional Law (1942), 465

Wright, "Money and the Pollution of Politics: Is the First Amendment an Obstacle to Political Equality?," 82 Colum.L.Rev. 609 (1982), 1410

Wright, "Politics and the Constitution: Is Money Speech?" 85 Yale L.J. 1001 (1976), 1410

Young, "Congressional Regulation of Federal Courts' Jurisdiction and Processes: United States v. Klein Revisited," 1981 Wisc. L.Rev. 1189, p. 80

Yudof, "Equal Protection, Class Legislation, and Sex Discrimination: One Small Cheer for Mr. Herbert Spencer's Social Statics," 88 Mich.L.Rev. 1366 (1990), 472

Yudof, "Library Book Selection and the Public Schools: The Quest for the Archimedean Point," 59 Ind.L.J. 527 (1984), 1298

Yudof, When Government Speaks: Politics, Law, and Government Expression in America (1983), 1302

Ziegler, "Government Speech and the Constitution: The Limits of Official Partisanship," 21 B.C.L.Rev. 578 (1980), 1302

Zimmerman, "Requiem for a Heavyweight: A Farewell to Warren and Brandeis's Privacy Tort," 68 Cornell L.Rev. 291 (1983), 1107

*

CONSTITUTIONAL LAW

*

PART I

The Judicial Function in Constitutional Cases

CHAPTER 1

THE NATURE AND SOURCES OF THE SUPREME COURT'S AUTHORITY

———

Introduction. Constitutional law courses and materials emphasize Supreme Court decisions. But the Supreme Court is not the only court authorized to examine constitutional claims, and courts are not the only forums for significant constitutional debates. In the cases that follow, only a very few passages of the constitutional text get extensive scrutiny: the few words about judicial power in Art. III; the allocations of legislative powers found especially in Art. I, § 8; the individual rights guarantees in the Bill of Rights and the post-Civil War Amendments. Yet many of the other provisions significantly affect the operations of constitutional government: those dealing with selection and structure of Presidency and Congress are obvious illustrations. And some provisions (that on impeachment, for instance) have given rise to major constitutional controversies that have not been adjudicated.

More than pedagogical tradition supports the emphasis on the Supreme Court. On those questions that do get to court, the Supreme Court's last word makes it obviously the most important judicial voice. And a remarkable range of constitutional questions *has* reached the Court: the over 500 volumes of reports of a court increasingly preoccupied with constitutional questions are no doubt the richest source of constitutional law. It is traditional, too, to begin the examination of constitutional law problems with opinions from the Court presided over by Chief Justice John Marshall early in the 19th century. Thus, Part I begins with Marbury v. Madison; Part II, with McCulloch v. Maryland and Gibbons v. Ogden. Attention to Marshall Court cases is more than a ritualistic bow to historical landmarks: the reason is not simply that those cases were important in the development of judicial authority and federal power allocations; it is also that those cases of the early 1800s—much more so than many of the decisions of intervening years—are important *today.*

So it is with Marbury v. Madison, which follows. Some attention to it would be justified if it represented no more than the historical fact of the Court's first elaborate justification of its judicial review power. But the extensive concern with Marbury here would not be warranted if it were a closed book. Instead, Marbury is very much alive: it rests on reasoning significant for the contemporary exercise of judicial power.

To what extent, for example, is the authority asserted in Marbury simply an incidental byproduct of the ordinary judicial function in deciding lawsuits: to look to the governing law, to consider the Constitution as one relevant source of law—and, in cases of conflicting legal statements, to give priority to the Constitution and to refuse enforcement of any contravening legal norm? To what extent does the Marbury authority rest instead on a claim that the Constitution thrust a more extraordinary mission upon the Supreme Court: that the Court was endowed with a roving commission to police the other branches, as the central guardian of constitutional principles and the special enforcer of constitutional norms? In the proper reading of Marbury may lie answers to many of the questions raised in this chapter: May Congress curtail the Court's jurisdiction? May or must the Court intervene in all constitutional disputes? When is resort to the Court permissible? Who may obtain answers to constitutional questions from the Court? When? As to what questions?

Understanding the core reasoning of Marbury, then, is essential to thinking about Court power today. And appreciation of the Marbury reasoning in turn requires some attention to historical antecedents and context. The assertions of the power of judicial review, and the justifications for it, did not spring fullblown in 1803: they reflected a variety of earlier developments. The purpose of the materials that follow the case is to develop these themes of intellectual and political history, as well as to explore a number of legal issues opened up by Marbury.

SECTION 1.   JUDICIAL REVIEW: THE BASES AND IMPLICATIONS OF MARBURY V. MADISON

Marbury v. Madison   FIRST S.C. JUSTIFICATION FOR JUDICIAL REVIEW

1 Cranch* (5 U.S.) 137, 2 L.Ed. 60 (1803).

[William Marbury was one of those named a justice of the peace for the District of Columbia at the very close of the Federalist Administration of President John Adams, during a rash of last-minute judicial appointments in March 1801 (described in the historical note which follows this case). The incoming Jefferson Administration chose to disregard those appointments for which formal commissions had not been delivered before the end of Adams' term. Marbury and some disappointed colleagues then decided to go directly to the Supreme Court, in the December Term 1801, to compel Jefferson's Secretary of State, James Madison, to deliver their commissions. The Court did not announce a decision on this 1801 request until February 1803. Before printing the opinion, the reporter summarized the earlier proceedings. His paragraph is reprinted here both to clarify the technical posture of the case and to dramatize (by adding some proper names in brackets) the involvement of John Marshall in the underlying dispute.]

At the last term, viz., December term, 1801, William Marbury, Dennis Ramsay, Robert Townsend Hooe, and William Harper, by their counsel, Charles Lee, Esq., late attorney general of the United States, severally moved the court for a rule to James Madison, Secretary of State of the United States, to show cause why a mandamus should not issue commanding him to cause to be

* 1 Cranch was the first volume devoted wholly to the reports of cases in the Supreme Court. It was not published until 1804. The 1790s cases were reported by A. J. Dallas in volumes which also covered Pennsylvania decisions. Not until 1816 did Congress provide for an official reporter. Henry Wheaton of New York was the first incumbent. In 1884, the Court announced (108 U.S. vi) that it "is the custom of the Court to cite decisions reported since Wallace only by the number in the official series, as '91 U.S.,' '92 U.S.,' & c." Up to 91 U.S., the reporters, and number of volumes for each, were as follows: Dallas, 4; Cranch, 9; Wheaton, 12; Peters, 16; Howard, 24; Black, 2; Wallace, 23.

Most of the cases in this volume are decisions of the U.S. Supreme Court. Accordingly, the tribunal is not named unless it is a court other than the Supreme Court.

delivered to them respectively their several commissions as justices of the peace in the District of Columbia. This motion was supported by affidavits [including one by John Marshall's brother, James] of the following facts: that notice of this motion had been given to Mr. Madison; that Mr. Adams, the late President of the United States, nominated the applicants to the senate for their advice and consent to be appointed justices of the peace of the District of Columbia; that the senate advised and consented to the appointments; that commissions in due form were signed by the said President appointing them justices, & c.; and that the seal of the United States was in due form affixed to the said commissions by the Secretary of State [John Marshall]; that the applicants have requested Mr. Madison to deliver them their said commissions, who has not complied with that request; and that said commissions are withheld from them. [Whereupon] a rule was laid to [show cause].

Afterwards, on the 24th of February [1803], the following opinion of the Court was delivered by the Chief Justice [MARSHALL]:

At the last term on the affidavits then read and filed with the clerk, a rule was granted in this case, requiring the Secretary of State to show cause why a mandamus should not issue, directing him to deliver to William Marbury his commission as a justice of the peace for the county of Washington, in the district of Columbia.

No cause has been shown, and the present motion is for a mandamus. The peculiar delicacy of this case, the novelty of some of its circumstances, and the real difficulty attending the points which occur in it, require a complete exposition of the principles on which the opinion to be given by the court is [founded].

In the order in which the court has viewed this subject, the following questions have been considered and decided:

1st. Has the applicant a right to the commission he demands?

2d. If he has a right, and that right has been violated, do the laws of this country afford him a remedy?

3d. If they do afford him a remedy, is it a mandamus issuing from this court?

The first object of inquiry is—1st. Has the applicant a right to the commission he demands?

[It is] decidedly the opinion of the court, that when a commission has been signed by the president, the appointment is made; and that the commission is complete, when the seal of the United States has been affixed to it by the [secretary of state].

[To] withhold [Marbury's] commission, therefore, is an act deemed by the court not warranted by law, but violative of a vested legal right.

This brings us to the second inquiry; which is: If he has a right, and that right has been violated, do the laws of his country afford him a remedy?

The very essence of civil liberty certainly consists in the right of every individual to claim the protection of the laws, whenever he receives an injury. One of the first duties of government is to afford that protection. [The] government of the United States has been emphatically termed a government of laws, and not of men. It will certainly cease to deserve this high appellation, if the laws furnish no remedy for the violation of a vested legal right. If this obloquy is to be cast on the jurisprudence of our country, it must arise from the peculiar character of the case.

It behooves us then to enquire whether there be in its composition any ingredient which shall exempt it from legal investigation, or exclude the injured party from [legal redress].

Is it in the nature of the transaction? Is the act of delivering or withholding a commission to be considered as a mere political act, belonging to the executive department alone, for the performance of which entire confidence is placed by our constitution in the supreme executive; and for any misconduct respecting which, the injured individual has no remedy. That there may be such cases is not to be questioned; but that every act of duty, to be performed in any of the great departments of government, constitutes such a case, is not to be [admitted].

It follows, then, that the question, whether the legality of an act of the head of a department be examinable in a court of justice or not, must always depend on the nature of that [act].

By the constitution of the United States, the President is invested with certain important political powers, in the exercise of which he is to use his own discretion, and is accountable only to his country in his political character, and to his own conscience. To aid him in the performance of these duties, he is authorized to appoint certain officers, who act by his authority and in conformity with his orders. In such cases, their acts are his acts; and whatever opinion may be entertained of the manner in which executive discretion may be used, still there exists, and can exist, no power to control that discretion. The subjects are political. They respect the nation, not individual rights, and being entrusted to the executive, the decision of the executive is conclusive. The application of this remark will be perceived by adverting to the act of congress for establishing the department of foreign affairs. This officer, as his duties were prescribed by that act, is to conform precisely to the will of the President. He is the mere organ by whom that will is communicated. The acts of such an officer, as an officer, can never be examinable by the courts. But when the legislature proceeds to impose on that officer other duties; when he is directed peremptorily to perform certain acts; when the rights of individuals are dependent on the performance of those acts; he is so far the officer of the law; is amenable to the laws for his conduct; and cannot at his discretion sport away the vested rights of others.

The conclusion from this reasoning is, that where the heads of departments are the political or confidential agents of the executive, merely to execute the will of the President, or rather to act in cases in which the executive possesses a constitutional or legal discretion, nothing can be more perfectly clear than that their acts are only politically examinable. But where a specific duty is assigned by law, and individual rights depend upon the performance of that duty, it seems equally clear, that the individual who considers himself injured, has a right to resort to the laws of his country for a [remedy].

It is, then, the opinion of the Court [that Marbury has a] right to the commission; a refusal to deliver which is a plain violation of that right, for which the laws of his country afford him a remedy.

It remains to be inquired whether [he] is entitled to the remedy for which he applies. This depends on—1st. The nature of the writ applied for; and 2d. The power of this court.

1st. The nature of the writ. [This] writ, if awarded, would be directed to an officer of government, and its mandate to him would be, to use the words of Blackstone, "to do a particular thing therein specified, which appertains to his office and duty and which the court has previously determined, or at least supposes, to be consonant to right and justice." Or, in the words of Lord Mansfield, the applicant, in this case, has a right to execute an office of public concern, and is kept out of possession of that right. These circumstances certainly concur in this case.

Still, to render the mandamus a proper remedy, the officer to whom it is to be directed, must be one to whom, on legal principles, such writ may be directed; and the person applying for it must be without any other specific and legal remedy.

1st. With respect to the officer to whom it would be directed. The intimate political relation, subsisting between the president of the United States and the heads of departments, necessarily renders any legal investigation of the acts of one of those high officers peculiarly irksome, as well as delicate; and excites some hesitation with respect to the propriety of entering into such investigation. Impressions are often received without much reflection or examination, and it is not wonderful, that in such a case as this, the assertion, by an individual, of his legal claims in a court of justice, to which claims it is the duty of that court to attend, should at first view be considered by some, as an attempt to intrude into the cabinet, and to intermeddle with the prerogatives of the executive.

It is scarcely necessary for the court to disclaim all pretensions to such a jurisdiction. An extravagance, so absurd and excessive, could not have been entertained for a moment. The province of the court is, solely, to decide on the rights of individuals, not to enquire how the executive, or executive officers, perform duties in which they have a discretion. Questions, in their nature political, or which are, by the constitution and laws, submitted to the executive, can never be made in this court.

But, if this be not such a question; if so far from being an intrusion into the secrets of the cabinet, it respects a paper, which, according to law, is upon record, and to a copy of which the law gives a right, on the payment of ten cents; if it be no intermeddling with a subject, over which the executive can be considered as having exercised any control; what is there in the exalted station of the officer, which shall bar a citizen from asserting, in a court of justice, his legal rights, or shall forbid a court to listen to the claim; or to issue a mandamus, directing the performance of a duty, not depending on executive discretion, but on particular acts of congress and the general principles of law?

[Where the head of a department] is directed by law to do a certain act affecting the absolute rights of individuals, [it] is not perceived on what ground the courts of the country are further excused from the duty of giving [judgment].

This, then, is a plain case for a mandamus, either to deliver the commission, or a copy of it from the record; and it only remains to be enquired,

Whether it can issue from this court.

The act to establish the judicial courts of the United States authorizes the Supreme Court "to issue writs of mandamus in cases warranted by the principles and usages of law, to any courts appointed, or persons holding office, under the authority of the United States."*

* The full text of Section 13 of the Judiciary Act of 1789, 1 Stat. 73: "*And be it further enacted,* That the Supreme Court shall have exclusive jurisdiction of all controversies of a civil nature, where a state is a party, except between a state and its citizens; and except also between a state and citizens of other states, or aliens, in which latter case it shall have original but not exclusive jurisdiction. And shall have exclusively all such

The secretary of state, being a person holding an office under the authority of the United States, is precisely within the letter of the description; and if this court is not authorized to issue a writ of mandamus to such an officer, it must be because the law is unconstitutional, and therefore absolutely incapable of conferring the authority, and assigning the duties which its words purport to confer and assign.

The constitution vests the whole judicial power of the United States in one Supreme Court, and such inferior courts as congress shall, from time to time, ordain and establish. This power is expressly extended to all cases arising under the laws of the United States; and, consequently, in some form, may be exercised over the present case; because the right claimed is given by a law of the United States.

In the distribution of this power it is declared that "the Supreme Court shall have original jurisdiction in all cases affecting ambassadors, other public ministers and consuls, and those in which a state shall be a party. In all other cases, the Supreme Court shall have appellate jurisdiction."

It has been insisted, at the bar, that as the original grant of jurisdiction, to the supreme and inferior courts, is general, and the clause, assigning original jurisdiction to the Supreme Court, contains no negative or restrictive words, the power remains to the legislature, to assign original jurisdiction to that court in other cases than those specified in the article which has been recited; provided those cases belong to the judicial power of the United States.

If it had been intended to leave it in the discretion of the legislature to apportion the judicial power between the supreme and inferior courts according to the will of that body, it would certainly have been useless to have proceeded further than to have defined the judicial power, and the tribunals in which it should be vested. The subsequent part of the section is mere surplusage, is entirely without meaning, if such is to be the construction. If congress remains at liberty to give this court appellate jurisdiction, where the constitution has declared their jurisdiction shall be original; and original jurisdiction where the constitution has declared it shall be appellate; the distribution of jurisdiction, made in the constitution, is form without substance.

Affirmative words are often, in their operation, negative of other objects than those affirmed; and in this case, a negative or exclusive sense must be given to them or they have no operation at all.

It cannot be presumed that any clause in the constitution is intended to be without effect; and, therefore, such a construction is inadmissible, unless the words [require].

When an instrument organizing fundamentally a judicial system, divides it into one supreme, and so many inferior courts as the legislature may ordain

jurisdiction of suits or proceedings against ambassadors, or other public ministers, or their domestics, or domestic servants, as a court of law can have or exercise consistently with the law of nations; and original, but not exclusive jurisdiction of all suits brought by ambassadors, or other public ministers, or in which a consul, or vice consul, shall be a party. And the trial of issues of fact in the Supreme Court, in all actions at law against citizens of the United States, shall be by jury. *The Supreme Court shall also have appellate*

jurisdiction from the circuit courts and courts of the several states, in the cases herein after specially provided for; and shall have power to issue writs of prohibition to the district courts, when proceeding as courts of admiralty and maritime jurisdiction, and writs of mandamus, in cases warranted by the principles and usages of law, to any courts appointed, or persons holding office, under the authority of the United States." [Emphasis added.]

Marshall:
org. juris — mandamus
power from
this language

& counter intuitive
don't read statutes this way

& Art III

and establish; then enumerates its powers, and proceeds so far to distribute them, as to define the jurisdiction of the supreme court by declaring the cases in which it shall take original jurisdiction, and that in others it shall take appellate jurisdiction; the plain import of the words seems to be, that in one class of cases its jurisdiction is original, and not appellate; in the other it is appellate, and not original. If any other construction would render the clause inoperative, that is an additional reason for rejecting such other construction, and for adhering to their obvious meaning.

To enable this court, then, to issue a mandamus, it must be shown to be an exercise of appellate jurisdiction, or to be necessary to enable them to exercise appellate jurisdiction.

It has been stated at the bar that the appellate jurisdiction may be exercised in a variety of forms, and that if it be the will of the legislature that a mandamus should be used for that purpose, that will must be obeyed. This is true, yet the jurisdiction must be appellate, not original.

It is the essential criterion of appellate jurisdiction, that it revises and corrects the proceedings in a cause already instituted, and does not create that cause. Although, therefore, a mandamus may be directed to courts, yet to issue such a writ to an officer for the delivery of a paper, is in effect the same as to sustain an original action for that paper, and, therefore, seems not to belong to appellate, but to original jurisdiction. Neither is it necessary in such a case as this, to enable the court to exercise its appellate jurisdiction.

The authority, therefore, given to the Supreme Court, by the act establishing the judicial courts of the United States, to issue writs of mandamus to public officers, appears not to be warranted by the constitution; and it becomes necessary to enquire whether a jurisdiction, so conferred, can be exercised.

The question, whether an act, repugnant to the constitution, can become the law of the land, is a question deeply interesting to the United States; but, happily, not of an intricacy proportioned to its interest. It seems only necessary to recognize certain principles, supposed to have been long and well established, to decide it.

That the people have an original right to establish, for their future government, such principles as, in their opinion, shall most conduce to their own happiness, is the basis on which the whole American fabric has been erected. The exercise of this original right is a very great exertion; nor can it, nor ought it, to be frequently repeated. The principles, therefore, so established, are deemed fundamental. And as the authority from which they proceed is supreme, and can seldom act, they are designed to be permanent.

This original and supreme will organizes the government, and assigns to different departments their respective powers. It may either stop here, or establish certain limits not to be transcended by those departments. The government of the United States is of the latter description. The powers of the legislature are defined and limited; and that those limits may not be mistaken, or forgotten, the constitution is written. To what purpose are powers limited, and to what purpose is that limitation committed to writing, if these limits may, at any time, be passed by those intended to be restrained? The distinction between a government with limited and unlimited powers is abolished, if those limits do not confine the persons on whom they are imposed, and if acts prohibited and acts allowed, are of equal obligation. It is a proposition too plain to be contested, that the constitution controls any legislative act repugnant to it; or, that the legislature may alter the constitution by an ordinary act.

Between these alternatives there is no middle ground. The constitution is either a superior, paramount law, unchangeable by ordinary means, or it is on a level with ordinary legislative acts, and, like other acts, is alterable when the legislature shall please to alter it.

If the former part of the alternative be true, then a legislative act contrary to the constitution is not law: if the latter part be true, then written constitutions are absurd attempts, on the part of the people, to limit a power in its own nature illimitable.

Certainly all those who have framed written constitutions contemplate them as forming the fundamental and paramount law of the nation, and consequently, the theory of every such government must be, that an act of the legislature, repugnant to the constitution, is void.

This theory is essentially attached to a written constitution, and is, consequently, to be considered, by this court, as one of the fundamental principles of our society. It is not therefore to be lost sight of in the further consideration of this subject.

If an act of the legislature, repugnant to the constitution, is void, does it, notwithstanding its invalidity, bind the courts, and oblige them to give it effect? Or, in other words, though it be not law, does it constitute a rule as operative as if it was a law? This would be to overthrow in fact what was established in theory; and would seem, at first view, an absurdity too gross to be insisted on. It shall, however, receive a more attentive consideration.

It is emphatically the province and duty of the judicial department to say what the law is. Those who apply the rule to particular cases, must of necessity expound and interpret that rule. If two laws conflict with each other, the courts must decide on the operation of each.

So if a law be in opposition to the constitution; if both the law and the constitution apply to a particular case, so that the court must either decide that case conformably to the law, disregarding the constitution; or conformably to the constitution, disregarding the law; the court must determine which of these conflicting rules governs the case. This is of the very essence of judicial duty.

If, then, the courts are to regard the constitution, and the constitution is superior to any ordinary act of the legislature, the constitution, and not such ordinary act, must govern the case to which they both apply.

Those then who controvert the principle that the constitution is to be considered, in court, as a paramount law, are reduced to the necessity of maintaining that courts must close their eyes on the constitution, and see only the law.

This doctrine would subvert the very foundation of all written constitutions. It would declare that an act which, according to the principles and theory of our government, is entirely void, is yet, in practice, completely obligatory. It would declare that if the legislature shall do what is expressly forbidden, such act, notwithstanding the express prohibition, is in reality effectual. It would be giving to the legislature a practical and real omnipotence, with the same breath which professes to restrict their powers within narrow limits. It is prescribing limits, and declaring that those limits may be passed at pleasure.

That it thus reduces to nothing what we have deemed the greatest improvement on political institutions—a written constitution—would of itself be sufficient, in America, where written constitutions have been viewed with so much reverence, for rejecting the construction. But the peculiar expressions of the constitution of the United States furnish additional arguments in favour of its rejection.

The judicial power of the United States is extended to all cases arising under the constitution. Could it be the intention of those who gave this power, to say that in using it the constitution should not be looked into? That a case arising under the constitution should be decided without examining the instrument under which it arises? This is too extravagant to be maintained.

In some cases, then, the constitution must be looked into by the judges. And if they can open it at all, what part of it are they forbidden to read or to obey?

There are many other parts of the constitution which serve to illustrate this subject. It is declared that "no tax or duty shall be laid on articles exported from any state." Suppose a duty on the export of cotton, of tobacco, or of flour; and a suit instituted to recover it. Ought judgment to be rendered in such a case? Ought the judges to close their eyes on the constitution, and only see the law?

The constitution declares that "no bill of attainder or ex post facto law shall be passed." If, however, such a bill should be passed, and a person should be prosecuted under it; must the court condemn to death those victims whom the constitution endeavors to preserve?

"No person," says the constitution, "shall be convicted of treason unless on the testimony of two witnesses to the same overt act, or on confession in open court." Here the language of the constitution is addressed especially to the courts. It prescribes, directly for them, a rule of evidence not to be departed from. If the legislature should change that rule, and declare *one* witness, or a confession *out* of court, sufficient for conviction, must the constitutional principle yield to the legislative act?

From these, and many other selections which might be made, it is apparent, that the framers of the constitution contemplated that instrument as a rule for the government of *courts,* as well as of the legislature.

Why otherwise does it direct the judges to take an oath to support it? This oath certainly applies, in an especial manner, to their conduct in their official character. How immoral to impose it on them, if they were to be used as the instruments, and the knowing instruments, for violating what they swear to support!

The oath of office, too, imposed by the legislature, is completely demonstrative of the legislative opinion on this subject. It is in these words: "I do solemnly swear that I will administer justice without respect to persons, and do equal right to the poor and to the rich; and that I will faithfully and impartially discharge all the duties incumbent on me as _____, according to the best of my abilities and understanding, agreeably to *the constitution,* and laws of the United States."

Why does a judge swear to discharge his duties agreeably to the constitution of the United States, if that constitution forms no rule for his government? If it is closed upon him, and cannot be inspected by him? If such be the real state of things, this is worse than solemn mockery. To prescribe, or to take this oath, becomes equally a crime.

It is also not entirely unworthy of observation that in declaring what shall be the *supreme* law of the land, the *constitution* itself is first mentioned; and not the laws of the United States generally, but those only which shall be made in *pursuance* of the constitution, have that rank. Thus, the particular phraseology of the constitution of the United States confirms and strengthens the principle, supposed to be essential to all written constitutions, that a law repugnant to the constitution is void; and that *courts,* as well as other departments, are bound by that instrument.

The rule must be discharged.

———

THE HISTORICAL SETTING OF THE MARBURY CASE

1. *The political environment.* a. *Judicial "reform."* The Marbury case was an early manifestation of the clashes between the Jeffersonian Republicans and the Marshall Court. John Marshall, Secretary of State in the Cabinet of lame-duck Federalist President John Adams, was nominated Chief Justice in January 1801 and took his oath of office on February 4, 1801. On February 17, the House of Representatives elected Thomas Jefferson as President. Marshall continued to act as Secretary of State through March 3, 1801, the end of Adams's term. Indeed, he may have stayed on somewhat longer: on March 4, 1801—the day Marshall as Chief Justice administered the oath of office to new President Jefferson—he agreed to comply with Jefferson's request "to perform the duties of Secretary of State until a successor be appointed." (James Madison, the defendant in Marbury, was Marshall's successor.)

Four days before Jefferson's election, the Federalist Congress began its efforts to maintain control of the federal judiciary. The Circuit Court Act of February 13, 1801, created sixteen Circuit Court judgeships. As expected, the new judgeships went to Federalists, for Adams hastily nominated his "midnight judges" during the last two weeks of his term. Marbury and his co-petitioners, however, were not among the "midnight judges" named pursuant to the Circuit Court Act. Their positions had been created even later: the Organic Act of the District of Columbia was passed on February 27, 1801, less than a week before the end of Adams's term. The Act authorized the President to name justices of the peace for the District. Adams named 42 justices on March 2, 1801, and the Senate confirmations came on March 3, Adams's last day in office. The commissions of the petitioners in the Marbury case had been signed by Adams—as well as signed and sealed by Secretary of State Marshall—but not all of them had been delivered by the end of the day; and the new President chose to treat them as a "nullity." As John Marshall wrote two weeks later, "I should [have] sent out the commissions which had been signed & sealed but for the extreme hurry of the time."

Marshall was therefore intimately acquainted with the facts of the Marbury controversy. Yet the issue of the existence of the commissions was extensively considered in the Court hearing in Marbury. For example, an affidavit by James Marshall—John Marshall's brother—was introduced to prove the existence of some of the commissions. (James Marshall stated that he was to deliver a number of the commissions but that, "finding he could not conveniently carry the whole," he returned "several of them" to his brother's office.) In view of his involvement in the controversy, should Marshall have disqualified himself from participation in the decision? Compare Martin v. Hunter's Lessee, p. 60 below, where Marshall did not sit because he and his brother James were interested property owners.

The Jeffersonians soon demonstrated that they would not complacently accept Federalist entrenchment in the judiciary: they made repeal of the Circuit Court Act of 1801 an early item of business in the new Congress. The 1801 Act was repealed on March 31, 1802, while the Marbury case was pending in the Supreme Court. During these congressional debates, a few Jeffersonians for the first time questioned the Court's authority to consider the constitutionality of congressional acts. There was still another sign of the mounting hostility to the Court: Congress abolished the June and December Terms of the Supreme Court created by the 1801 Act and provided that there would be only one Term, in February.[1] Accordingly, there was no Court session in 1802; the Court that had received Marbury's petition in December 1801 could not reconvene until February 1803.

    b. *Impeachment.* The Jeffersonians soon unsheathed a still more potent weapon. Early in 1802, the House voted to impeach Federalist District Judge John Pickering of New Hampshire, and many feared that impeachment of Supreme Court Justices would follow. The choice of Pickering as the first target was a "tragic blunder," however. Pickering, an insane drunkard, was plainly incompetent to serve as a judge, but it took some stretching to convert this into "Treason, Bribery, or other high Crimes and Misdemeanors" as required by Art. II, § 4, of the Constitution.[2] Nevertheless, the Senate voted to remove Pickering from office in March 1804.[3]

    On the day after Pickering's removal, Congress moved on to bigger game: the House impeached Supreme Court Justice Samuel Chase. To the Jeffersonians, Chase was a glaring example of Federalist abuse of judicial office: he had made electioneering statements from the bench in 1800, and he had conducted several vindictive sedition trials. A few months after the Marbury decision, he provided the immediate provocation for his impeachment: in May 1803, in a partisan charge to the federal grand jury in Baltimore, he criticized the Jeffersonians' repeal of the 1801 Circuit Court Act. The Senate tried Chase early in 1805. Were judges impeachable for conduct that did not constitute an indictable offense? The debate was lengthy and important: if the case against Chase succeeded, it was widely expected, John Marshall and other federal judges would be next. But the Senate vote did not produce the constitutional majority necessary to convict Chase. The impeachment weapon was deflated—it was a "farce," "not even a scare-crow," as Jefferson reluctantly concluded. The Jefferson–Marshall dispute continued, but the Court had survived the most critical stage.[4]

    2. *Were there alternative grounds of decision?* Most contemporary commentary on the Marbury decision ignored the passages on the authority of the courts to consider the constitutionality of congressional acts. Instead, Jeffersonians criticized the Court's assertion of the right to examine some executive acts. Was Marshall's opinion a reflection of a "masterful sense of strategy," as is often alleged? Was it a shrewd scheme in which the denial of mandamus avoided an immediate confrontation with the executive and provided a shield for the Court's criticism of Jefferson's behavior—and for its assertion and exercise of judicial review over statutes? See, e.g., McCloskey, The American

---

    1. Congress acted mainly to delay a constitutional challenge to the repeal of the 1801 Circuit Court Act. A few days after Marbury v. Madison was decided, the Court upheld the repeal. Stuart v. Laird, 1 Cranch (5 U.S.) 299 (1803).

    2. The problem of dealing with incompetent federal judges persists. See the Judicial Conduct and Disability Act of 1980, 94 Stat. 2035.

    3. See Turner, "The Impeachment of John Pickering," 54 Am.Hist.Rev. 485 (1949).

    4. See generally 1 Warren, The Supreme Court in United States History (rev. ed. 1926); III Beveridge, The Life of John Marshall (1919), and Ellis, The Jeffersonian Crisis: Courts and Politics in the Young Republic (1971).

Supreme Court (2d ed., Levinson, 1994), 25: "The decision is a masterwork of indirection, a brilliant example of Marshall's capacity to sidestep danger while seeming to court it, to advance in one direction while his opponents are looking in another." This conclusion needs to be taken with a grain of salt.

Some critics of Marbury insist that, given Marshall's conclusion, the Court had no business saying any more than that it lacked jurisdiction. Were the opening parts of the opinion, on remedies against executive illegality, inappropriate? Jefferson insisted until the end of his life that most of the opinion was "merely an *obiter* dissertation of the Chief Justice."[5] But note that the Court will ordinarily avoid constitutional questions where a narrower ground of decision is available. Other critics have insisted that Marshall could and should have made those important final pages on judicial review unnecessary by resolving the preliminary issues differently. For example, more than the signing and sealing might have been held necessary to complete the appointment, or greater presidential authority regarding appointees might have been recognized. See the materials on the presidential removal power, p. 390 below. And a position that mandamus was not available against Cabinet officers was possible.

Moreover, the Court's interpretations of § 13 and Art. III have been attacked. Marshall's underlying conception of mutually exclusive categories of original and appellate jurisdiction has not prevailed. Congress still may not add to the Court's original jurisdiction, and so the specific holding of Marbury stands. But Congress may grant lower courts jurisdiction over cases within the constitutional delineation of Supreme Court original jurisdiction—and cases of that description may then come to the Supreme Court on review. For example, § 13 itself recognized concurrent original jurisdiction in the lower courts, and several Supreme Court Justices on circuit had sustained lower court jurisdiction in foreign consul cases as early as 1793, United States v. Ravara, 2 Dall. (2 U.S.) 297. Years later, the Supreme Court agreed. Bors v. Preston, 111 U.S. 252 (1884). And Marshall himself, in a rare admission of error, called some of his statements about Art. III in Marbury unduly broad when he rejected Virginia's arguments against the Supreme Court's exercise of appellate jurisdiction in a case involving a state, in Cohens v. Virginia, 6 Wheat. (19 U.S.) 264 (1821), p. 63 below.[6]

THE LEGITIMACY OF JUDICIAL REVIEW

Introduction. Was the judicial review authority asserted in Marbury v. Madison a usurpation? That question has long sparked controversy.[1] The

5. Jefferson to Justice William Johnson, June 12, 1823, 1 S.Car.His. & Gen.Mag. 1, 9–10 (1900).

6. See generally Van Alstyne, "A Critical Guide to Marbury v. Madison," 1969 Duke L.J. See also Clinton, Marbury v. Madison and Judicial Review (1989).

A few years after Marbury, the Marshall Court also exercised the power to hold a state statute unconstitutional. In Fletcher v. Peck, 6 Cranch (10 U.S.) 87 (1810), a case from a lower federal court, a statute of Georgia was held to be in violation of the Contracts Clause. Authority to review state court decisions was sustained in Martin v. Hunter's Lessee, p. 60 below. After Marbury, the Court did not hold another major federal law unconstitutional until the controversial and ill-fated decision in Dred Scott v. Sandford, 19 How. (60 U.S.) 393 (1857).

1. See, e.g., the extensive attack on judicial review in Boudin, Government by Judiciary (1932). And the debate lives. See, e.g., the elaborate defense of legitimacy in Berger, Congress v. The Supreme Court (1969).

attackers say that Marshall's opinion is question-begging and weak; that the Constitution does not explicitly authorize judicial review; that the Framers did not clearly intend to grant that extraordinary power; and that the pre-Convention theories and practices were not sufficiently clear and widespread to provide legitimation. The materials that follow reflect that ongoing debate. After a brief review of the historical roots of the authority and of the Convention debates, a longer excerpt contains the most important anticipation of that reasoning, Hamilton's No. 78 of The Federalist. Professor Herbert Wechsler's debate with Judge Learned Hand illustrates the continuing controversy regarding the constitutional justification for Marbury—a controversy that bears directly on contemporary evaluations of the Court's exercises of power.

1. *Historical antecedents.* Though Marshall's opinion in Marbury relied on general principles and constitutional text, not historical data, efforts to justify judicial review have often provoked explorations of historical roots. Some of these searches have taken rather remote and tangential byways. For example, there has been frequent mention of Lord Coke's famous statement in Dr. Bonham's Case, at 8 Rep. 118a (C.P. 1610), that "the common law will controul acts of Parliament, [and] adjudge them to be utterly void," when the acts are "against common right and reason." But that was not truly descriptive of British practice in the seventeenth century; by the eighteenth, it was not even respectable dictum. More in point was the appellate jurisdiction of the Privy Council over colonial courts; but invalidation of legislation through that route was rare and unpopular. The practice of state courts in the years immediately following independence holds the greatest promise as a source of relevant information. But here, too, the examples are few and controversial; and there is doubt that many people at the Convention or in the early national period knew about the scattered actual or alleged examples of judicial invalidation of state legislation.[2]

The spread of general ideas conducive to the acceptance of judicial review was in any event probably more important than the existence of specific precedents.[3] A pervasive theme, and one reflected in Marshall's reasoning, was the development of written constitutions, with the assurance of limited government as a major purpose. Constitutionalism was hardly an American invention, but Americans had an unusually extensive experience with basic documents of government, from royal charters to state constitutions and the Articles of Confederation. Yet the constitutional historians who justify judicial review as a natural outgrowth of constitutionalism make an argument that is incomplete. It *is* possible to have a constitution without judicial review. There is accordingly a large question-begging element in deriving judicial enforceability simply from

2. For an extensive selection of articles examining the antecedents of judicial review, see vol. 1 of Selected Essays on Constitutional Law (1938). Compare also the discussion of antecedents in Goebel, Antecedents and Beginnings to 1801 (1 History of the Supreme Court of the United States) (1971), with Nelson, "Changing Conceptions of Judicial Review: The Evolution of Constitutional Theory in the States, 1790–1860," 120 U.Pa.L.Rev. 1166 (1972). On Goebel's conclusion that the doctrine of judicial review was "preached [during the 1780s] apparently without protest," Nelson comments that "Goebel somewhat overstates his case."

3. See generally Bailyn, The Ideological Origins of the American Revolution (1967), and Wood, The Creation of the American Republic, 1776–1787 (1969). Wood's influential book finds an especially hospitable climate for the development of judicial review in the evolving theories of the 1780s, particularly the replacement of traditional notions of legislative sovereignty by emphasis on popular sovereignty. Note Hamilton's argument in No. 78 of the Federalist, below, that courts "were designed to be an intermediate body between the people and the legislature," and the echoes of that theme in the Marbury opinion.

the existence of written constitutions: to say that a government cannot exceed its constitutional powers does not demonstrate *who* is to decide whether a law conflicts with the constitution. Viewing a constitution as a species of "law," then, becomes the vital link between constitutionalism and *judicial* competence to decide constitutional issues. That link, hardly a prominent feature in the political theory of the Revolutionary era, is central in the Marbury opinion.

As this background of ideas and practices indicates, Marshall's assertion of judicial review authority in Marbury was no sudden innovation or single-handed achievement. But the pre-Constitutional Convention heritage hardly made the 1803 result inevitable. Nor does that heritage clearly tell us what view of judicial authority in constitutional interpretation was central to Marshall when he wrote Marbury. Was the Marbury opinion merely concerned with establishing judicial *competence* to interpret the Constitution? Or was Marshall chiefly concerned with carving out for courts a role as *special*—supreme, perhaps even exclusive—guardians of constitutional norms? The Marbury opinion does not yield an entirely clear answer to these questions. Marbury can be read as emphasizing a narrow, incidental role of courts in constitutional cases; but there are also passages suggesting a broader, more central role for courts. As later materials in this book demonstrate, the debate about the proper reading of Marbury continues to this day. And as those materials also indicate, the answers to the questions raised in this paragraph may govern attitudes about the proper timing, scope, and content of constitutional decisions.

2. *The Constitutional Convention.* The U.S. Constitution (unlike most 20th century constitutions in other nations) does not explicitly grant the judicial review power asserted in Marbury. That silence has made the legitimacy debate possible. Did the Framers intend to grant the power? Some efforts to demonstrate such an original understanding have relied heavily on Framers' statements not made in Philadelphia in 1787. See Beard, The Supreme Court and the Constitution (1912). But the most persuasive data regarding the Framers' intent are of course the Convention debates themselves. See Farrand, The Records of the Federal Convention of 1787 (1911).

The Convention context in which the most important statements regarding judicial power were made was the discussion of a Council of Revision proposal— a proposal that the Justices join with the President in the veto process. That provision was rejected, partly on grounds supporting the legitimacy of judicial review. According to Madison's Notes, Anti-Federalist Luther Martin, for example, thought "the association of the Judges with the Executive" a "dangerous innovation": "A knowledge of mankind, and of Legislative Affairs, cannot be presumed to belong in a higher degree to the Judges than to the Legislature. And as to the Constitutionality of laws, that point will come before the Judges in their proper official character. In this character they have a negative on the laws. Join them with the Executive in the Revision and they will have a double negative. It is necessary that the Supreme Judiciary should have the confidence of the people. This will soon be lost, if they are employed in the task of remonstrating agst. popular measures of the Legislature." An incisive brief survey of the debates concludes: "The grant of judicial power was to include the power, where necessary in the decision of cases, to disregard state or federal statutes found to be unconstitutional. Despite the curiously persisting myth of usurpation, the Convention's understanding on this point emerges from its records with singular clarity."[4] Compare the survey of the

---

4. Bator, Meltzer, Mishkin & Shapiro, Hart & Wechsler's The Federal Courts and the Federal System (3d ed. 1988), 8. [This volume is cited hereinafter as Hart & Wechsler, Federal Courts.]

legitimacy debate in Leonard Levy's excellent introduction to a paperback volume of selected essays edited by him, *Judicial Review and the Supreme Court* (1967).[5]

3. *The Federalist Papers.* Support for judicial review far more explicit than anything found in the Convention debates appears in The Federalist. Hamilton, Jay and Madison wrote these newspaper essays in defense of the proposed Constitution as campaign documents in the ratification battle in New York. They have become classic commentaries on the Constitution. The papers most directly concerned with the judiciary were five written by Alexander Hamilton, Nos. 78 through 82 of The Federalist. The most famous, No. 78, contains some striking parallels to—as well as some provocative variations on— the Marbury v. Madison theme.

Hamilton, Federalist No. 78

[Whoever] attentively considers the different departments of power must perceive, that in a government in which they are separated from each other, the judiciary, from the nature of its functions, will always be the least dangerous to the political rights of the constitution; because it will be least in a capacity to annoy or injure them. The judiciary [has] no influence over either the sword or the purse, no direction either of the strength or of the wealth of the society, and can take no active resolution whatever. It may truly be said to have neither Force nor Will, but merely judgment. . . .

Some perplexity respecting the right of the courts to pronounce legislative acts void, because contrary to the constitution, has arisen from an imagination that the doctrine would imply a superiority of the judiciary to the legislative power. It is urged that the authority which can declare the acts of another void, must necessarily be superior to the one whose acts may be declared [void].

There is no position which depends on clearer principles, than that every act of a delegated authority, contrary to the tenor of the commission under which it is exercised, is void. No legislative act therefore contrary to the constitution can be valid. To deny this would be to affirm that the deputy is greater than his principal; that the servant is above his master; that the representatives of the people are superior to the people themselves; that men acting by virtue of powers may do not only what their powers do not authorise, but what they forbid.

If it be said that the legislative body are themselves the constitutional judges of their own powers, and that the construction they put upon them is conclusive upon the other departments, it may be answered, that this cannot be the natural presumption, where it is not to be collected from any particular provisions in the constitution. It is not otherwise to be supposed that the constitution could intend to enable the representatives of the people to substitute their *will* to that of their constituents. It is far more rational to suppose that the courts were designed to be an intermediate body between the people and the legislature, in order, among other things, to keep the latter within the limits assigned to their authority. The interpretation of the laws is the proper and peculiar province of the courts. A constitution is in fact, and must be,

---

5. Levy quotes Edward S. Corwin's testimony on the 1937 Court–Packing Plan: "[I]n blunt language he declared, 'The people who say the framers intended [judicial review] are talking nonsense'—to which he hastily added, 'and the people who say they did not intend it are talking nonsense.'" Levy adds: "A close textual and contextual examination of the evidence will not result in an improvement on these propositions."

regarded by the judges as a fundamental law. It therefore belongs to them to ascertain its meaning as well as the meaning of any particular act proceeding from the legislative body. If there should happen to be an irreconcilable variance between the two, that which has the superior obligation and validity ought of course to be preferred; or in other words, the constitution ought to be preferred to the statute, the intention of the people to the intention of their agents.

Nor does this conclusion by any means suppose a superiority of the judicial to the legislative power. It only supposes that the power of the people is superior to both; and that where the will of the legislature declared in its statutes, stands in opposition to that of the people declared in the constitution, the judges ought to be governed by the latter, rather than the former. They ought to regulate their decisions by the fundamental laws, rather than by those which are not fundamental. . . .

It can be of no weight to say that the courts, on the pretence of a repugnancy, may substitute their own pleasure to the constitutional intentions of the legislature. This might as well happen in the case of two contradictory statutes; or it might as well happen in every adjudication upon any single statute. The courts must declare the sense of the law; and if they should be disposed to exercise WILL instead of JUDGMENT, the consequence would equally be the substitution of their pleasure to that of the legislative body. The observation, if it prove any thing, would prove that there ought to be no judges distinct from that body.[6]

4. *The Hand–Wechsler debate.* For an illuminating revival of the legitimacy debate, and a sharp disagreement about the basis for judicial review in the constitutional text, see Hand, The Bill of Rights (1958), 1–30, and Wechsler, "Toward Neutral Principles of Constitutional Law," in his Principles, Politics, and Fundamental Law (1961), 4–10. Judge Learned Hand insisted that there was "nothing in the United States Constitution that gave courts any authority to review the decisions of Congress." He claimed that "it was a plausible— indeed to my mind an unanswerable—argument" that such an authority was inconsistent with separation of powers. He asserted that "when the Constitution emerged from the Convention in September 1787, the structure of the proposed government, if one looked to the text, gave no ground for inferring that the decisions of the Supreme Court [were] to be authoritative upon the Executive and the Legislature." Judge Hand found justification for the Supreme Court's assumption of judicial review authority solely in the practical need "to prevent the defeat of the venture at hand"—to keep the government from foundering. Professor Wechsler, relying on the Art. VI Supremacy Clause and on Art. III, replied: "I believe the power of the courts is grounded in the language of the Constitution and is not a mere interpolation."

The Hand–Wechsler debate of the mid–20th century illustrates how the legitimacy issue may influence views regarding the contemporary exercise of

6. To what extent does Hamilton's justification for judicial review differ from Marshall's? Is Hamilton's distinction between "will" and "judgment" persuasive? Does Hamilton's view of "judgment" assume that the task of constitutional interpretation involved in judicial review is an essentially mechanical one (as the Court suggested in United States v. Butler, 297 U.S. 1 (1936), p. 235 below)? That view of interpretation may describe the judgment called for in determining whether a citizen meets the age qualification for being President, Art. II, Sec. 1. But does it also describe interpretation of a far more vague, open-ended provision such as "due process" or "equal protection"? Do these provisions invite far more "will" and discretion than the kind of "judgment" Hamilton apparently had in mind?

the power. Thus, Judge Hand concluded that "since this power is not a logical deduction from the structure of the Constitution but only a practical condition upon its successful operation, it need not be exercised whenever a court sees, or thinks that it sees, an invasion of the Constitution. It is always a preliminary question how importantely the occasion demands an answer." Professor Wechsler objected to so broad a discretion to decline to adjudicate a constitutional objection in a case properly before a court: "For me, as for anyone who finds the judicial power anchored in the Constitution, there is no such escape from the judicial obligation; the duty cannot be attenuated in this way." (The "duty," he added, was "not that of policing or advising legislatures or executives," but rather simply "to decide the litigated case and to decide it in accordance with the law.")

The Hand–Wechsler debate illustrates, too, that evaluations of the content as well as the timing of contemporary court decisions may evolve from discussions beginning with concern over legitimacy. Since Wechsler's defense of legitimacy is so closely tied to implications of the judicial function, he insisted that Constitution-interpreting courts must above all *act* like courts. Accordingly, he warned against "ad hoc evaluation" as "the deepest problem of our constitutionalism" and insisted that decisions must rest on "neutral principles": "the main constituent of the judicial process is precisely that it must be genuinely principled, resting with respect to every step that is involved in reaching judgment on analysis and reasons quite transcending the immediate result that is achieved."[7] To Judge Hand, judicial review of legislative choices inevitably turned courts into "a third, legislative, chamber." He added: "For myself it would be most irksome to be ruled by a bevy of Platonic Guardians, even if I knew how to choose them, which I assuredly do not."

5. *Judicial review and democracy.* As the Hand–Wechsler debate illustrates, concern with the bases of judicial review in constitutional history and text is often closely connected with explorations of the consistency between judicial review and democratic government. Views on that issue, too, may profoundly affect exercises and evaluations of the judicial power, as is amply revealed in many of the opinions in this volume. Anxiety about the undemocratic, countermajoritarian aspects of judicial review often underlies the advocacy of judicial self-restraint—the position that courts should be reluctant to set aside the decisions of other organs of government.

Leonard Levy's paperback, Judicial Review and the Supreme Court (1967), includes a critical analysis of the major contending arguments regarding the propriety of judicial invalidation of legislative decisions. Classic statements viewing judicial review as undemocratic and as undercutting popular responsibility are Thayer, "The Origin and Scope of the American Doctrine of Constitutional Law," 7 Harv.L.Rev. 129 (1893), and Commager, Majority Rule and Minority Rights (1943). Important defenses of judicial intervention are Rostow, "The Democratic Character of Judicial Review," 66 Harv.L.Rev. 193 (1952), and C.L. Black, Jr., The People and the Court: Judicial Review in a Democracy (1960). For an especially provocative and sophisticated effort to justify judicial intervention while recognizing that it is countermajoritarian, see Bickel, The Least Dangerous Branch (1962). As noted, the issues in this debate permeate

7. See also Greenawalt, "The Enduring Significance of Neutral Principles," 78 Co- lum.L.Rev. 982 (1978).

constitutional law courses. The problems are best explored in the specific contexts of the cases below.

Closely related to this debate about the propriety and scope of judicial intervention are several other themes that recur throughout this book. For example, views about the legitimacy of judicial review may influence attitudes about the appropriate sources of constitutional interpretation. To what extent must the Court confine itself to the text and history of the relevant constitutional provision?[8] To what extent can and should courts limit themselves to the "original intent" of those who adopted the Constitution?[9] To what extent may courts rely on inferences from the structures and relationships established by the basic document? See C. L. Black, Jr., Structure and Relationship in Constitutional Law (1969). To what extent is the Court authorized to implement values derived from sources outside the written document—e.g., the society's political and moral values, or the Justices' personal ones?[10] Moreover, views about the legitimacy of judicial review and its consistency with democracy may influence positions about the appropriate deference the Court owes to legislative judgments. When should a legislative judgment be accorded a strong "presumption of constitutionality" and be sustained so long as it is merely "reasonable"? When may the Court properly apply stricter scrutiny and demand that more than "mere rationality" be shown in support of a legislative judgment? These themes surface in a variety of contexts, in every chapter of Parts II and III. Note, e.g., the intense controversies about appropriate standards of review in the interpretations of the frequently litigated due process and equal protection clauses of the 14th Amendment.

6. *Judicial review abroad.* After World War II, while Americans continued to agonize over the proper scope of judicial review, more and more other nations looked to courts to enforce constitutional norms. Judicial review became especially important in Germany and Italy. Most judicial review mechanisms in civil law countries differ from the American model in form: for example, creation of special Constitutional Courts has been common. Beginning in the late 1980s, the political changes in Eastern Europe provoked an explosion of interest in new constitutional safeguards; and in Western Europe, the growing importance of the European Court of Justice prompted heightened attention to the judicial enforceability of constitutional provisions in the

8. On the utility of the text in constitutional interpretation, see, e.g., Schauer, "Easy Cases," 58 S.Cal.L.Rev. 399 (1985), Monaghan, "Our Perfect Constitution," 56 N.Y.U.L.Rev. 353 (1981), and Levinson, "Law as Literature," 60 Tex.L.Rev. 373 (1982).

9. See Brest, "The Misconceived Quest for the Original Understanding," 60 B.U.L.Rev. 204 (1980), and Kay, "Adherence to the Original Intentions in Constitutional Adjudication: Three Objections and Responses," 82 Nw.U.L.Rev. 226 (1988).

10. The last in this series of questions has sparked an especially vigorous scholarly debate. Most often, that debate has been couched as a battle between "interpretivism" and "noninterpretivism"—between the view that judges can only enforce norms stated or clearly implicit in the Constitution and the position that courts can legitimately go be-

yond those sources. Examples of "noninterpretivist" positions include the claim that the Court has the obligation to articulate the changing content of the nation's fundamental values and that it is charged with evolving and applying the society's fundamental principles. For contemporary arguments that noninterpretive review is legitimate, see, e.g., Grey, "Do We Have An Unwritten Constitution?" 27 Stan.L.Rev. 703 (1975). Excerpts from many of the leading works in the debate are collected in Garvey & Aleinikoff, Modern Constitutional Theory: A Reader (1989), chap. II. The contending positions involved in the "interpretivist"-"noninterpretivist" debate surface frequently throughout this book. See especially chap. 8, sec. 3, on modern substantive due process, below. It is wise to reserve judgment for now on the relative merits of the contending positions.

countries of the region.[11]

―――――

THE AUTHORITATIVENESS OF SUPREME COURT DECISIONS: BINDING ON ALL PUBLIC OFFICIALS?

Introduction. To what extent are other departments of government obligated to follow judicial interpretations of the Constitution? Must, or may, the President and Congress give independent consideration to questions of constitutionality in the exercise of their official functions? Are the courts the ultimate, even the exclusive, interpreters of the Constitution, or do other organs of government share in that authority? Questions such as these raise the issue of the true scope of the power of judicial review. Is judicial review simply a byproduct of a court's duty to decide cases within its jurisdiction in accordance with law, including the Constitution; or do courts have special competence to interpret law, including the Constitution, so that they are the ultimate, supreme interpreters of the Constitution? Even Marshall's reasoning in Marbury v. Madison, though leaning to the former, more modest view, is not free from ambiguity. And later developments—not only popular understandings but also Court assertions such as those in the 1958 decision in Cooper v. Aaron, note 6 below—suggest a broader, binding effect for judicial interpretations.

To promote examination of these questions, notes 1 to 4 below present a series of presidential statements claiming varying degrees of autonomy vis-à-vis judicial interpretations, in a variety of contexts. Consider, with regard to each statement, whether anything in the President's position is inconsistent with Marshall's justification for judicial review in Marbury. Consider, moreover, whether any of the presidential statements is inconsistent with the modern Court's claims in Cooper v. Aaron (note 6 below)—claims which include the assertion that a Supreme Court interpretation of the Constitution "is the supreme law of the land." (See also the additional comments about the presidential assertions in note 5.)

Recall that much of Marshall's argument in Marbury was directed against contentions that courts lacked *competence* or *authority* to consider issues of constitutionality. Can it be argued on the basis of that Marshall argument that a judicial interpretation is the *ultimate, final* one? That it is *binding* on those not parties to the litigation? That the judiciary is the *exclusive* source of constitutional interpretations? Recall Marshall's quite modest, defensive statement that the Constitution is "a rule for the government of *courts* as well as the legislature" and his conclusion that "*courts,* as well as other departments, are bound by that instrument." Yet Marshall also stated: "It is emphatically the province and duty of the judicial department to say what the law is." Does that sentence support a *special* judicial competence, a *superior* role, in constitutional interpretation? Contrast Hamilton's stronger statement in No. 78 of The Federalist, above: "The interpretation of the laws is the proper and *peculiar* province of the courts." (Emphasis added.)

1. *Thomas Jefferson.* a. *Letter to Abigail Adams, Sept. 11, 1804* (8 The Writings of Thomas Jefferson (Ford ed. 1897), 310):

11. See generally Cappelletti & Cohen, Comparative Constitutional Law (1979), and Henkin & Rosenthal (eds.), Constitutionalism and Rights: The Influence of the United States Constitution Abroad (1989).

"You seem to think it devolved on the judges to decide on the validity of the sedition law. But nothing in the Constitution has given them a right to decide for the Executive, more than to the Executive to decide for them. Both magistracies are equally independent in the sphere of action assigned to them. The judges, believing the law constitutional, had a right to pass a sentence of fine and imprisonment; because that power was placed in their hands by the Constitution. But the Executive, believing the law to be unconstitutional, was bound to remit the execution of it; because that power has been confided to him by the Constitution. That instrument meant that its co-ordinate branches should be checks on each other. But the opinion which gives to the judges the right to decide what laws are constitutional, and what not, not only for themselves in their own sphere of action, but for the Legislature & Executive also, in their spheres, would make the judiciary a despotic branch."

b. *Letter to William C. Jarvis, Sept. 28, 1820* (10 The Writings of Thomas Jefferson (Ford ed. 1899), 160):

"You seem [to] consider the judges as the ultimate arbiters of all constitutional questions; a very dangerous doctrine indeed, and one which would place us under the despotism of an oligarchy. [The] constitution has erected no such single tribunal, knowing that to whatever hands confided, with the corruptions of time and party, its members would become despots. It has more wisely made all the departments co-equal and co-sovereign within themselves. If the legislature fails to pass laws for a census, for paying the judges and other officers of government, for establishing a militia, for naturalization as prescribed by the constitution, or if they fail to meet in congress, the judges cannot issue their mandamus to them; if the President fails to supply the place of a judge, to appoint other civil or military officers, to issue requisite commissions, the judges cannot force him. [The] judges certainly have more frequent occasion to act on constitutional questions, because the laws of *meum* and *tuum* and of criminal action, forming the great mass of the system of law, constitute their particular department."

2. *Andrew Jackson—Veto Message (on bill to recharter the Bank of the United States), July 10, 1832* (2 Messages and Papers of the Presidents (Richardson ed. 1896), 576, 581–583):

"It is maintained by the advocates of the bank that its constitutionality in all its features ought to be considered as settled by precedent and by the decision of the Supreme Court. [McCulloch v. Maryland (1819), p. 89 below.] To this conclusion I can not assent. Mere precedent is a dangerous source of authority, and should not be regarded as deciding questions of constitutional power except where the acquiescence of the people and the States can be considered as well settled. [Even if] the opinion of the Supreme Court covered the whole ground of this act, it ought not to control the coordinate authorities of this Government. [It] is as much the duty of the House of Representatives, of the Senate, and of the President to decide upon the constitutionality of any bill or resolution which may be presented to them for passage or approval as it is of the supreme judges when it may be brought before them for judicial decision. The opinion of the judges has no more authority over Congress than the opinion of Congress has over the judges, and on that point the President is independent of both. The authority of the Supreme Court must not, therefore, be permitted to control the Congress or the Executive when acting in their legislative capacities, but to have only such influence as the force of their reasoning may deserve.

"But in the case relied upon the Supreme Court have not decided that all the features of this corporation are compatible with the Constitution. [Under] the decision of the Supreme Court, [it] is the exclusive province of Congress and the President to decide whether the particular features of this act are *necessary* and *proper* in order to enable the bank to perform conveniently and efficiently the public duties assigned to it as a fiscal agent, and therefore constitutional, or *unnecessary* and *improper,* and therefore unconstitutional. Without commenting on the general principle affirmed by the Supreme Court, let us examine the details of this act in accordance with the rule of legislative action which they have laid down. It will be found that many of the powers and privileges conferred on it can not be supposed necessary for the purpose for which it is proposed to be created, and are not, therefore, means necessary to attain the end in view, and consequently not justified by the Constitution."

3. *Abraham Lincoln.* a. *Speech during the Lincoln–Douglas Senatorial Campaign, October 1858* (3 The Collected Works of Abraham Lincoln (Basler ed. 1953), 255):

"We oppose the Dred Scott decision [Dred Scott v. Sandford, 19 How. (60 U.S.) 393 (1857)] in a certain way. [We] do not propose that when Dred Scott has been decided to be a slave by the court, we, as a mob, will decide him to be free. We do not propose that, when any other one, or one thousand, shall be decided by that court to be slaves, we will in any violent way disturb the rights of property thus settled; but we nevertheless do oppose that decision as a political rule which shall be binding on the voter, to vote for nobody who thinks it wrong, which shall be binding on the members of Congress or the President to favor no measure that does not actually concur with the principles of that decision. [We] propose so resisting it as to have it reversed if we can, and a new judicial rule established upon this subject."

b. *First Inaugural Address, March 4, 1861* (6 Messages and Papers of the Presidents (Richardson ed. 1897), 5, 9–10):

"I do not forget the position assumed by some that constitutional questions are to be decided by the Supreme Court, nor do I deny that such decisions must be binding in any case upon the parties to a suit as to the object of that suit, while they are also entitled to very high respect and consideration in all parallel cases by all other departments of the Government. And while it is obviously possible that such decision may be erroneous in any given case, still the evil effect following it, being limited to that particular case, with the chance that it may be overruled and never become a precedent for other cases, can better be borne than could the evils of a different practice. At the same time, the candid citizen must confess that if the policy of the Government upon vital questions affecting the whole people is to be irrevocably fixed by decisions of the Supreme Court, the instant they are made in ordinary litigation between parties in personal actions, the people will have ceased to be their own rulers, having to that extent practically resigned their Government into the hands of that eminent tribunal."

4. *Franklin D. Roosevelt.* a. *Letter to Congressman Hill, July 6, 1935* (4 The Public Papers and Addresses of Franklin D. Roosevelt (1938), 297–98): [The letter was written after the Supreme Court's 1935 decision in A.L.A. Schechter Poultry Corp. v. United States, 295 U.S. 495 (1935), the "sick chicken" case narrowly construing national regulatory powers and invalidating an important segment of New Deal emergency legislation, the National Industrial Recovery Act. President Roosevelt nevertheless urged Congress to enact a law establishing an NIRA-like regulatory scheme for the bituminous coal industry. The President's letter explained the need for the law, noted that its constitutionality depended on "whether production conditions directly affect, promote or obstruct interstate commerce," and added:] "Manifestly, no one is

in a position to give assurance that the proposed act will withstand constitutional tests. [But] the situation is so urgent and the benefits of the legislation so evident that all doubts should be resolved in favor of the bill, leaving to the courts, in an orderly fashion, the ultimate question of constitutionality. A decision by the Supreme Court relative to this measure would be helpful as indicating [the] constitutional limits within which this Government must operate. [I] hope your committee will not permit doubts as to constitutionality, however reasonable, to block the suggested legislation."[1]

b. *Proposed speech on the Gold Clause Cases, Feb. 1935* (1 F.D.R.—His Personal Letters, 1928–1945 (Elliott Roosevelt ed. 1950), 459–60): [This was a draft of a speech President Roosevelt planned to deliver in the event the Court decided against the Government on the constitutionality of abrogating "gold clauses" in federal obligations. In fact, the Court decided for the Roosevelt Administration, and the speech was not delivered. See Perry v. United States, 294 U.S. 330 (1935).] "I do not seek to enter into any controversy with the distinguished members of the Supreme Court of the United States who have participated in this [decision]. They have decided these cases in accordance with the letter of the law as they read it. But it is appropriate to quote a sentence from the First Inaugural Address of President Lincoln: [quoting the "At the same time" sentence in note 3b, above].

"[It] is the duty of the Congress and the President to protect the people of the United States to the best of their ability. It is necessary to protect them from the unintended construction of voluntary acts, as well as from intolerable burdens involuntarily imposed. To stand idly by and to permit the decision of the Supreme Court to be carried through to its logical, inescapable conclusion would so imperil the economic and political security of this nation that the legislative and executive officers of the Government must look beyond the narrow letter of contractual obligations, so that they may sustain the substance of the promise originally made in accord with the actual intention of the parties. [I] shall immediately take such steps as may be necessary, by proclamation and by message to [Congress]."

5. *The autonomy of the coordinate branches. a. Some comments on the presidential statements.* If constitutional interpretation were a special or exclusive judicial function, most of the quoted presidential statements would be indefensible. Yet are not most of them consistent with the major thrust of Marshall's rationale in Marbury—the rationale that rests judicial review not on any special judicial guardianship of constitutional norms, but simply on the courts' duty to decide cases before them in accordance with the relevant law?

The presidential statements suggest, too, that attention to context is essential if uncritical condemnation is to be avoided whenever other branches claim some autonomy in constitutional judgments. In the Jackson bank veto situation (note 2 above), the Supreme Court had indeed spoken. But Jackson emphasized the autonomy of "the Congress or the Executive when acting in their legislative capacities": though bank recharter legislation would be constitutional under McCulloch v. Maryland, Congress or the President could refuse to enact new legislation because of constitutional doubts. Would the broader view of judicial authority in Cooper v. Aaron (note 6b below) deny that a member of Congress may (indeed, must) vote against legislation he or she believes to be unconstitutional, even though the law would be constitutional

---

1. Congress promptly enacted the legislation urged by the President; but the Court, less than a year later, invalidated the Bituminous Coal Conservation Act of 1935, in Carter v. Carter Coal Co., 298 U.S. 238 (1936). On the Court-packing crisis provoked by such invalidations of New Deal laws, see p. 183 below.

under the standards of prior Court decisions? Is there any greater difficulty as a matter of constitutional principle with the variety of legislative autonomy President Roosevelt urged upon Congressman Hill (note 4a above)?

Jefferson (note 1a) and Lincoln (note 3) were faced with prior judicial decisions that spoke with special immediacy to the problems that confronted them. Yet Jefferson was defending the exercise of the pardoning power, a power specifically vested in the President with broad discretion; he simply insisted on autonomy in his "own sphere of action." And Lincoln was careful to distinguish between direct interference with the Court decision in Dred Scott's case and acceptance of the constitutional interpretation of that case "as a political rule." All of these positions fell short of direct conflict with a court order; each recognized judicial authority to adjudicate constitutionality with respect to the case before the court and simply insisted on autonomy within the President's "own sphere of action."

Only President Roosevelt's proposed speech on the "gold clause" issue (note 4b above) contemplated direct defiance of a court order, direct contravention of the narrow justification of Marbury. And serious presidential considerations of direct defiance have been very rare indeed. There is a legend that President Jackson, shortly before his veto of the bank recharter bill, said of a Supreme Court decision: "John Marshall has made his decision. Now let him enforce it." The decision was Worcester v. Georgia, 6 Pet. (31 U.S.) 515 (1832), where the Marshall Court held that Georgia had no legislative authority over Cherokee Nation lands. In fact, Jackson's support for enforcement of the decision was never put to a test: though he was no doubt unhappy about it, the litigation was abandoned before any call for presidential assistance arose. See Burke, "The Cherokee Cases: A Study in Law, Politics, and Morality," 21 Stan.L.Rev. 500 (1969). In this century, while the Special Prosecutor's effort to gain access to Watergate tapes was pending before the courts, President Nixon and his counsel hinted that the President might not comply with an order to turn over the tapes. Yet on the day in 1974 that the Supreme Court decision against the President was handed down, in United States v. Nixon, 418 U.S. 683 (1974), President Nixon announced that he had instructed his counsel "to take whatever measures are necessary to comply with that decision in all respects."

If the Marbury rationale leaves to legislators and the President considerable autonomy even in the face of Supreme Court interpretations quite closely in point, their authority to consider constitutionality is surely even greater when they are writing on a relatively blank slate. Yet even in those situations, legislators sometimes suggest that problems of constitutionality are solely the courts' business. Is such a stance defensible under Marbury? Under Cooper v. Aaron, which follows?[2]

b. *Legitimate disagreement and improper defiance.* Is never-ending, chaotic questioning of Court interpretations inevitable if one takes a narrow view of the authoritativeness of judicial decisions? Consider the solution advanced in Wechsler, "The Courts and the Constitution," 65 Colum.L.Rev. 1001, 1008 (1965), which draws on aspects of President Lincoln's position quoted in note 3b above. Lincoln spoke of the "chance" that the ruling "may be overruled and never become a precedent for other cases." Wechsler comments: "When that chance has been exploited and has run its course, with reaffirmation rather than reversal of decision, has not the time arrived when its acceptance is

2. See Morgan, Congress and the Constitution (1966), and Brest, "The Conscientious Legislator's Guide to Constitutional Interpretation," 27 Stan.L.Rev. 585 (1975).

demanded, without insisting on repeated litigation? The answer here, it seems to me, must be affirmative, both as the necessary implication of our constitutional tradition and to avoid the greater evils that will otherwise ensue."

Does this position permit too broad a range of challenges to Court rulings, in theory and in practice? And is such criticism acceptable only so long as it is calm and rational? Note Professor Jaffe's observation that intense criticism is especially appropriate as well as likely in the area of constitutional adjudication: "There will be and there should be popular response to the Supreme Court's decision; not just the 'informed' criticism of law professors but the deep-felt, emotion-laden, unsophisticated reaction of the laity. This is so because more than any court in the modern world the Supreme Court 'makes policy,' and is at the same time so little subject to formal democratic control. [Yet] those who urge the Court on to political innovation are outraged when its decisions arouse, as they must, resentment and political attack." Jaffe, "Impromptu Remarks," 76 Harv.L.Rev. 1111 (1963).

6. *Is the Court "the ultimate interpreter of the Constitution"?—Some modern assertions. a. Cooper v. Aaron: Are Court interpretations "the supreme law of the land"?* The opinion in COOPER v. AARON, 358 U.S. 1 (1958), provides the major judicial support for a view widely held by the public, that the Court *is* the ultimate or supreme interpreter of the Constitution. Cooper v. Aaron arose against a background of opposition by Governor Faubus and other Arkansas officials against public school desegregation in Little Rock. The state officials claimed that they were not "bound" by the Supreme Court's basic school desegregation ruling, the 1954 decision in Brown v. Board of Education (p. 673 below). Arkansas was not a party to the Brown case; but a later lower court, relying on Brown, directed desegregation by the Little Rock school board, and the state officials tried to prevent the school board from complying with that desegregation decree.[3] In that context, the Supreme Court could have limited itself to its reminder that state officials lacked "power to nullify a federal court order." But the Court's response—signed by each of the nine Justices—went considerably beyond. Instead of confining itself to implementing the Little Rock lower federal court decree, it spoke broadly about the impact of Brown on the Arkansas officials.[4] In that dictum in Cooper, the Justices asserted:

3. To sketch the context of Cooper v. Aaron more fully: The Little Rock school board, seeking to desegregate the public schools pursuant to a plan approved by the lower federal court, was blocked in its efforts by Governor Faubus's action in calling out the National Guard in September 1957. The Governor placed Little Rock's Central High School "off limits" to black students. After a trial court injunction against the Governor, the troops were withdrawn. Thereafter, black students were able to attend school under the protection of federally-commanded troops. In February 1958, the school board sought a long postponement of the desegregation program. The U.S. District Court granted that relief, after noting the existence of "chaos, bedlam and turmoil" and finding the situation "intolerable." The Court of Appeals reversed; and that decision was affirmed by the Supreme Court. The Supreme Court found that the school officials had acted in "entire good faith" but concluded that "the actions of the other state agencies responsible for those conditions compel us to reject the Board's legal position. [The] constitutional rights of respondents are not to be sacrificed or yielded to the violence and disorder which have followed upon the actions of the Governor and Legislature."

4. Note the suggestion of a "crucial difference" between Governor Faubus's stated opposition to the Brown decision and his efforts to block school board implementation of a desegregation plan approved by the federal court in Arkansas, in Horowitz & Karst, Law, Lawyers and Social Change (1969), 253. Are the authors persuasive in their analogy— "it is the difference between arguing with the umpire and refusing to leave the base when you are called out"?

"[W]e should answer the premise of the actions of the Governor and Legislature that they are not bound by our holding in the Brown case. It is necessary only to recall some basic constitutional propositions which are settled doctrine. Article VI of the Constitution makes the Constitution the 'supreme Law of the Land.' In 1803, Chief Justice Marshall, speaking for a unanimous Court, referring to the Constitution as 'the fundamental and paramount law of the nation,' declared in the notable case of Marbury v. Madison that 'It is emphatically the province and duty of the judicial department to say what the law is.' This decision declared the basic principle that the federal judiciary is supreme in the exposition of the law of the Constitution, and that principle has ever since been respected by this Court and the Country as a permanent and indispensable feature of our constitutional system. It follows that the interpretation of the Fourteenth Amendment enunciated by this Court in the Brown case is the supreme law of the land, and Art. VI of the Constitution makes it of binding effect on the States 'any Thing in the Constitution or Laws of any State to the Contrary notwithstanding.' Every state legislator and executive and judicial officer is solemnly committed by oath taken pursuant to Art. VI, ¶ 3, 'to support this Constitution.' "

Was that Court view of its own powers truly a statement of "settled doctrine"? Was it merely a restatement of Marbury v. Madison—or was it a substantial expansion of the authority asserted by Chief Justice Marshall? Assuming that most of the presidential views noted earlier are consistent with Marbury, can they also be reconciled with Cooper v. Aaron?[5] Would the Court's opinion in Cooper, in support of the importance of its own decisions, have been more persuasive if it had reasoned along the following lines: Although the Brown decision was not technically binding on Arkansas because that state had not been a party to the case, the unanimous ruling in Brown would presumably be followed in the future by the Court, given the force of precedent and the Court's normal adherence to its own decisions. Hence, state officials in Arkansas would have been better advised, on the basis of prudence and in the interest of avoiding chaos in the legal system, to "obey" rather than resist Brown, because of the strong prospect of Supreme Court adherence to its views in Brown. Moreover, the Court might have noted, congressional action (rather than the Brown case itself) makes state officials civilly and criminally liable for deprivations of federal constitutional rights (see the post-Civil War civil rights laws noted at the beginning of chapter 10, sec. 1, below). The congressional civil rights laws do not delineate the contents of the rights and privileges "secured by the Constitution"; instead, Congress left the elaboration of these rights to judicial decisionmaking and thereby in effect made Court interpretations "binding" on State officials.

7. *The legal consequences of judicial "invalidation."* Under the classic Marbury theory, a court confronted with an unconstitutional statute simply refuses enforcement to that law in the case before it. In civil law countries, by contrast, a court exercising judicial review issues a ruling of general invalidity binding on all, not just on the parties before it. But in this respect, civil law and

---

5. Note Gunther, "The Subtle Vices of the 'Passive Virtues'—A Comment on Principle and Expediency in Judicial Review," 64 Colum.L.Rev. 1, 25 (1964): "[Bickel, The Least Dangerous Branch (1962),] draws from Marbury v. Madison [the] notion that the Court's 'doctrines are not to be questioned,' by citizens or by other departments of government. [That] confuses Marshall's assertion of judicial authority to interpret the Constitution with judicial exclusiveness; that confuses Marbury v. Madison with statements in the Little Rock case, Cooper v. Aaron." For a defense of the Cooper v. Aaron approach, see Farber, "The Supreme Court and the Rule of Law: Cooper v. Aaron Revisited," 1983 U.Ill.L.Rev. 387.

American law are closer in practice than in theory. Thus, it does not tell the whole story to say, as an American court once said, that a decision upon constitutionality "affects the parties only, and there is no judgment against the statute." Shepherd v. Wheeling, 4 S.E. 635 (W.Va.1887). For example, some practical reach of a court ruling beyond the immediate parties is assured by the usual judicial adherence to stare decisis.

Yet to say that an invalidity ruling affects more than the parties is not to say that it is the same as wiping a statute off the books: it is as inaccurate to claim too broad an impact for a ruling as it is to state it too narrowly. The best-known example of overstatement is an assertion in Norton v. Shelby County, 118 U.S. 425 (1886), a statement that has required some important qualifications: "An unconstitutional act is not a law; it confers no rights; it imposes no duties; it affords no protection; it creates no office; it is [as] inoperative as though it had never been passed." But a law held unconstitutional in an American court is by no means so wholly a nullity, as the Attorney General advised President Roosevelt in 1937. The Supreme Court had held the District of Columbia minimum wage law unconstitutional in 1923, in the Adkins case; but in 1937, in sustaining a similar Washington law in the West Coast Hotel Co. case, the Court formally overruled Adkins. (The cases are in chap. 8, sec. 1, below.) The Attorney General advised that the 1923 ruling had simply "suspend[ed]" enforcement, and that the act was valid and enforceable after the 1937 decision, explaining: "The decisions are practically in accord in holding that the courts have no power to repeal or abolish a statute, and that notwithstanding a decision holding it unconstitutional a statute continues to remain on the statute books." 39 Ops.Atty.Gen. 22 (1937).

SECTION 2.   CONSTITUTIONAL AND PRUDENTIAL LIMITS ON CONSTITUTIONAL ADJUDICATION

1. *Introduction.* A basic premise of Marbury v. Madison is that the Supreme Court plays a role in constitutional elaboration only because it is a *court*, a judicial body deciding *cases*. This theme has prompted recurrent Court efforts to delineate the elements of what constitutes a "case" appropriate for judicial resolution. *Who* may go to court? That question, relating to what a litigant must show in order to invoke judicial power, involves the problem of standing to sue, the question of the personal interest necessary to trigger a judicial response. How much of a personal stake in the outcome must an individual show in order to obtain a judicial ruling? *When*—at what stage in the evolution of a dispute? How far advanced must a dispute be, how fully developed and concrete must the issues be, to elicit a judicial resolution? This involves the question of ripeness. As to *what* constitutional issues? This question is most often encountered with regard to the political question doctrine, the doctrine that some constitutional questions are not justiciable— i.e., not suitable for judicial decision.

The purpose of this section is to provide a general overview of the who, when, and what of constitutional adjudication.[1] These problems are not mere

---

1. The themes of this section are more fully explored in federal jurisdiction case-books and courses. See, e.g., Hart & Wechsler, Federal Courts (4th ed., 1996). For an

technicalities; they go to the heart of the Court's place in the governmental structure. Two related problems recur frequently with respect to each of the limits considered in this chapter. First, where does the limit come from? To what extent does each derive from the Constitution, especially Art. III, § 2, which spells out the "cases" and "controversies" within the judicial power? To what extent does it derive from congressional action regarding jurisdiction and remedies? To what extent do these limits stem from the Court's own prudential discretionary elaborations, reflecting its views of the appropriate scope of judicial authority and the optimum conditions for its exercise?

2. *Advisory opinions.* The earliest of all nonjusticiability doctrines, predating even Marbury, stems from the Court's refusal to issue "advisory opinions"—opinions on the legality of executive or legislative action that did not involve an actual "case." In 1793, President Washington sought the advice of the Justices on some legal questions involving America's neutrality toward the ongoing war between England and France. Secretary of State Jefferson, on behalf of the President, wrote to the Justices: "These questions depend for their solution on the construction of our treaties, on the laws of nature and nations, and on the laws of the land, and are often presented under circumstances which do not give a cognizance of them to the tribunals of the country. Yet their decision is so little analogous to the ordinary functions of the executive, as to occasion much embarrassment and difficulty to them. The President therefore would be much relieved if he found himself free to refer questions of this description to the opinions of the judges of the [Court], whose knowledge of the subject would secure us against errors dangerous to the peace of the United States, and their authority insure the respect of all parties."

A few weeks later, the Justices firmly rejected that invitation: "[T]he three departments of the government [being] in certain respects checks upon each other, and our being judges of a court in the last resort, are considerations which afford strong arguments against the propriety of our extrajudicially deciding the questions alluded to, especially as the power given by the Constitution to the President, of calling on the heads of departments for opinions, seems to have been *purposely* as well as expressly united to the executive departments. We exceedingly regret every event that may cause embarrassment to your administration, but we derive consolation from the reflection that your judgment will discern what is [right]."[2]

Are there persuasive constitutional or policy arguments against advisory opinions? Early, authoritative resolution of constitutional doubts would often be desirable for legislative and executive officials. Note that some state supreme courts are authorized to issue advisory opinions. Note also that, just before the Court-packing crisis in 1937, President Roosevelt briefly considered a plan that would require the Court to give advisory opinions, "to say in advance of the passing of a law whether it was unconstitutional." See The Secret Diary of Harold L. Ickes—The First Thousand Days, 1933–1936 (1953), 529.

For a Court effort to articulate some of the policy reasons, especially of judicial restraint, underlying the refusal to issue advisory opinions as well as other limitations on the exercise of judicial power (considered in the notes that follow), consider Justice Rutledge's opinion in RESCUE ARMY v. MUNICIPAL COURT OF LOS ANGELES, 331 U.S. 549 (1947). Justice RUTLEDGE empha-

especially useful commentary on the "who" and "when," see Monaghan, "Constitutional Adjudication: The Who and When," 82 Yale L.J. 1363 (1973).

2. The exchange of letters is reprinted in Hart & Wechsler, Federal Courts (4th ed., 1996), 92–93.

sized the overarching theme of "strict necessity": the Court's unwillingness to adjudicate constitutional issues unless such rulings are unavoidable. He stated: "The earliest exemplifications [of the "strict necessity" theme arose] in the Court's refusal to render advisory opinions. [The] policy [has] not been limited to jurisdictional determination. For, in addition, 'the court [has] developed, for its own governance in the cases confessedly within its jurisdiction, a series of rules under which it has avoided passing upon a large part of all the constitutional questions pressed upon it for decision.' [Justice Brandeis, concurring in Ashwander v. TVA, 297 U.S. 288, 346 (1936).] Thus, constitutional issues affecting legislation will not be determined in friendly, nonadversary proceedings; in advance of the necessity of deciding them; in broader terms than are required by the precise facts to which the ruling is to be applied; [at] the instance of one who fails to show that he is injured by the statute's operation; [or] if a construction of the statute is fairly possible by which the question may be avoided. [Every] application [of these rules] has been an instance of reluctance, indeed, of refusal, to undertake the most important and the most delicate of the Court's functions [until] necessity compels it. [The] policy [is] one of substance grounded in considerations which transcend all such particular limitations. Like the case and controversy limitation itself and the policy against entertaining political questions, it is one of the rules basic to the federal system and this Court's appropriate place within that structure. [The] policy's ultimate foundations [lie] in all that goes to make up the unique place and character, in our scheme, of judicial review of governmental action for constitutionality. They are found in the delicacy of that function, particularly in view of possible consequences for others stemming also from constitutional roots; [the] necessity, if government is to function constitutionally, for each [branch of government] to keep within its power, including the courts; the inherent limitations of the judicial process, arising especially from its largely negative character and limited resources of enforcement. [The execution of this policy] has involved a continuous choice between the obvious advantages it produces [and] the very real disadvantage, for the assurance of rights, which deferring decision very often entails. On the other hand it is not altogether speculative that a contrary policy, of accelerated decision, might do equal or greater harm for the security of private rights. [For] premature and relatively abstract decisions, which such a policy would be most likely to promote, have their part too in rendering rights uncertain and insecure. [Time] and experience [have] verified [that] the choice [of the "strict necessity" policy] was wisely made. Any other indeed might have put an end to or seriously impaired the distinctively American institution of judicial review."

integrity of the Court.

A.   STANDING TO LITIGATE

1. *The requisite personal interest.* a. *Standing to sue in traditional contexts.* Traditionally, standing questions related to parties—to the sufficiency of the litigant's concern with the subject matter of the lawsuit—rather than to the fitness for adjudication of the legal issues presented for decision. More recently, however, the Court has tended to blur these separable themes, so that fitness of the issue for adjudication has become intertwined with the question of the litigant's interest, as the next principal case and the notes illustrate. Ordinarily, the question of standing presents no barrier to adjudication where, for example, the government takes coercive action against an individual: e.g., the defendant in a criminal case can challenge the constitutionality of the statute. The more troublesome standing issues arise when the challenger seeks anticipatory relief—for example, when a challenger seeks to obtain a constitutional ruling without assuming the risk of civil or criminal liability by acting in disregard of a law. Suits seeking injunctive or declaratory relief against the enforcement of a statute are the most common contexts raising standing problems, as the materials that follow illustrate.

———

Warth v. Seldin

422 U.S. 490, 95 S.Ct. 2197, 45 L.Ed.2d 343 (1975).

Justice POWELL delivered the opinion of the Court.

Petitioners, various organizations and individuals resident in the Rochester, N.Y., metropolitan area, brought this action [against] the town of Penfield and against members of Penfield's Zoning, Planning, and Town Boards. Petitioners claimed that the town's zoning ordinance effectively excluded persons of low and moderate income from living in the town, in contravention of petitioners' [constitutional and statutory rights]. The [lower federal courts held] that none of the plaintiffs [had] standing. [W]e affirm.

[II. In] essence the question of standing is whether the litigant is entitled to have the court decide the merits of the dispute or of particular issues. This inquiry involves both constitutional limitations on federal court jurisdiction and prudential limitations on its exercise. In both dimensions it is founded in concern about the proper—and properly limited—role of the courts in a democratic society. In its constitutional dimension, standing imports justiciability: whether the plaintiff has made out a "case or controversy" between himself and the defendant within the meaning of Art. III. [The] Art. III judicial power exists only to redress or otherwise to protect against injury to the complaining party, even though the court's judgment may benefit others collaterally. A federal court's jurisdiction therefore can be invoked only when the plaintiff himself has suffered "some threatened or actual injury resulting from the putatively illegal action."[1] Apart from this minimum constitutional mandate,

---

1. The standing question [bears] close affinity to questions of ripeness—whether the harm asserted has matured sufficiently to warrant judicial intervention—and of moot-

this Court has recognized other limits on the class of persons who may invoke the courts' decisional and remedial powers. First, the Court has held that when the asserted harm is a "generalized grievance" shared in substantially equal measure by all or a large class of citizens, that harm alone normally does not warrant exercise of jurisdiction. Second, even when the plaintiff has alleged injury sufficient to meet the "case or controversy" requirement, this Court has held that the plaintiff generally must assert his own legal rights and interests, and cannot rest his claim to relief on the legal rights or interests of third parties. Without such limitations—closely related to Art. III concerns but essentially matters of judicial self-governance—the courts would be called upon to decide abstract questions of wide public significance even though other governmental institutions may be more competent to address the questions and even though judicial intervention may be unnecessary to protect individual rights.

Although standing in no way depends on the merits of the plaintiff's contention that particular conduct is illegal, it often turns on the nature and source of the claim asserted. The actual or threatened injury required by Art. III may exist solely by virtue of "statutes creating legal rights, the invasion of which creates standing." Moreover, the source of the plaintiff's claim to relief assumes critical importance with respect to the prudential rules of standing that, apart from Art. III's minimum requirements, serve to limit the role of the courts in resolving public disputes. Essentially, the standing question in such cases is whether the constitutional or statutory provision on which the claim rests properly can be understood as granting persons in the plaintiff's position a right to judicial relief. [Moreover,] Congress may grant an express right of action to persons who otherwise would be barred by prudential standing rules. Of course, Art. III's requirement remains: the plaintiff still must allege a distinct and palpable injury to himself, even if it is an injury shared by a large class of other possible litigants. But so long as this requirement is satisfied, persons to whom Congress has granted a right of action, either expressly or by clear implication, may have standing to seek relief on the basis of the legal rights and interests of others, and, indeed, may invoke the general public interest in support of their [claim].

III.   With these general considerations in mind, we turn first to the claims of petitioners Ortiz, Reyes, Sinkler, and Broadnax, each of whom asserts standing as a person of low or moderate income and, coincidentally, as a member of a minority racial or ethnic group. We must assume, taking the allegations of the complaint as true, that Penfield's zoning ordinance and the pattern of enforcement by respondent officials have had the purpose and effect of excluding persons of low and moderate income, many of whom are members of racial or ethnic minority groups. We also assume [that] such intentional exclusionary practices, if proved in a proper case, would be adjudged violative of the constitutional and statutory rights of the persons excluded. But the fact that these petitioners share attributes common to persons who may have been excluded from residence in the town is an insufficient predicate for the conclusion that petitioners themselves have been excluded, or that the respondents' assertedly illegal actions have violated their rights. Petitioners must allege and show that they personally have been injured, not that injury has been suffered by other, unidentified members of the class to which they belong and which they purport to [represent].

ness—whether the occasion for judicial intervention persists. [Footnote by Justice Powell.]

In their complaint, petitioners Ortiz, Reyes, Sinkler, and Broadnax alleged in conclusory terms that they are among the persons excluded by respondents' actions. None of them has ever resided in Penfield; each claims at least implicitly that he desires, or has desired, to do so. Each asserts, moreover, that he made some effort, at some time, to locate housing in Penfield that was at once within his means and adequate for his family's needs. Each claims that his efforts proved fruitless. We may assume [that] respondents' actions have [contributed] to the cost of housing in Penfield. But there remains the question whether petitioners' inability to locate suitable housing in Penfield reasonably can be said to have resulted, in any concretely demonstrable way, from respondents' alleged constitutional and statutory infractions. Petitioners must allege facts from which it reasonably could be inferred that, absent the respondents' restrictive zoning practices, there is a substantial probability that they would have been able to purchase or lease in Penfield and that, if the court affords the relief requested, the asserted inability of petitioners will be removed.

We find the record devoid of the necessary allegations. [N]one of these petitioners has a present interest in any Penfield property; none is himself subject to the ordinance's strictures; and none has ever been denied a variance or permit by respondent officials. Instead, petitioners claim that respondents' enforcement of the ordinance against third parties—developers, builders, and the like—has had the consequence of precluding the construction of housing suitable to their needs at prices they might be able to afford. The fact that the harm to petitioners may have resulted indirectly does not in itself preclude standing. When a governmental prohibition or restriction imposed on one party causes specific harm to a third party, harm that a constitutional provision or statute was intended to prevent, the indirectness of the injury does not necessarily deprive the person harmed of standing to vindicate his rights. But it may make it substantially more difficult to meet the minimum requirement of Art. III: to establish that, in fact, the asserted injury was the consequence of the defendants' actions, or that prospective relief will remove the harm.

Here, by their own admission, realization of petitioners' desire to live in Penfield always has depended on the efforts and willingness of third parties to build low-and moderate-cost housing. The record specifically refers to only two such efforts: that of Penfield Better Homes Corp., in late 1969, to obtain the rezoning of certain land in Penfield to allow the construction of subsidized cooperative townhouses that could be purchased by persons of moderate income; and a similar effort by O'Brien Homes, Inc., in late 1971. But the record is devoid of any indication that these projects, or other like projects, would have satisfied petitioners' needs at prices they could afford, or that, were the court to remove the obstructions attributable to respondents, such relief would benefit petitioners. Indeed, petitioners' descriptions of their individual financial situations and housing needs suggest precisely the contrary—that their inability to reside in Penfield is the consequence of the economics of the area housing market, rather than of respondents' assertedly illegal acts. In short, the facts alleged fail to support an actionable causal relationship between Penfield's zoning practices and petitioners' asserted injury. [We] hold only that a plaintiff who seeks to challenge exclusionary zoning practices must allege specific, concrete facts demonstrating that the challenged practices harm *him,* and that he personally would benefit in a tangible way from the courts' intervention. Absent the necessary allegations of demonstrable, particularized injury, there can be no confidence of "a real need to exercise the power of judicial review" or that relief can be framed "no broader than required by the precise facts to which the court's ruling would be applied."

IV.   The petitioners who assert standing on the basis of their status as taxpayers of the city of Rochester [claim] that Penfield's persistent refusal to allow or to facilitate construction of low-and moderate-cost housing forces the city of Rochester to provide more such housing than it otherwise would do; that to provide such housing, Rochester must allow certain tax abatements; and that as the amount of tax-abated property increases, Rochester taxpayers are forced to assume an increased tax burden in order to finance essential public services. [Apart] from the conjectural nature of [this] asserted injury, the line of causation between Penfield's actions and such injury is not apparent from the complaint. Whatever may occur in Penfield, the injury complained of—increases in taxation—results only from decisions made by the appropriate Rochester authorities who are not parties to this case. But even if we assume that the taxpayer-petitioners could establish that Penfield's zoning practices harm them, their complaint nonetheless was properly dismissed. Petitioners do not, even if they could, assert any personal right under the Constitution or any statute [but only] that Penfield's zoning ordinance and practices violate the constitutional and statutory rights of third parties, namely, persons of low and moderate income who are said to be excluded from Penfield. In short the claim of these petitioners falls squarely within the prudential standing rule that normally bars litigants from asserting the rights or legal interests of others in order to obtain relief from injury to [themselves].

V.   We turn next to the standing problems presented by the petitioner associations. [There] is no question that an association may have standing in its own right to seek judicial relief from injury to itself and to vindicate whatever rights and immunities the association itself may enjoy. Moreover, in attempting to secure relief from injury to itself the association may assert the rights of its members, at least so long as the challenged infractions adversely affect its members' associational ties. [Even] in the absence of injury to itself, an association may have standing solely as the representative of its members. The possibility of such representational standing, however, does not eliminate or attenuate the constitutional requirement of a case or controversy. The association must allege that its members, or any one of them, are suffering immediate or threatened injury as a result of the challenged action of the sort that would make out a justiciable case had the members themselves brought suit. So long as this can be established, and so long as the nature of the claim and of the relief sought does not make the individual participation of each injured party indispensable to proper resolution of the cause, the association may be an appropriate representative of its members, entitled to invoke the court's jurisdiction.

A.   Petitioner Metro–Act's claims to standing on its own behalf as a Rochester taxpayer, and on behalf of its members who are Rochester taxpayers or persons of low or moderate income, are precluded by our holdings in Parts [III and IV]. Metro–Act [a civic action group] also alleges, however, that 9% of its membership is composed of present residents of Penfield. It claims that, as a result of the persistent pattern of exclusionary zoning, [its] members who are Penfield residents are deprived of the benefits of living in a racially and ethnically integrated community. [Metro–Act] does not assert on behalf of its members any right of action under the 1968 Civil Rights Act. [Even] if we assume, arguendo, that apart from any statutorily created right the asserted harm to Metro–Act's Penfield members is sufficiently direct and personal to satisfy the case-or-controversy requirement of Art. III, prudential considerations strongly counsel against according them or Metro–Act standing to prosecute this action. We do not understand Metro–Act to argue that Penfield residents themselves have been denied any constitutional rights. [Instead], their complaint is that they have been harmed indirectly by the exclusion of others. This is an attempt to raise putative rights of third parties, and none of the exceptions that allow such claims is present [here].

B. Petitioner Home Builders [asserted] standing to represent its member firms engaged in the development and construction of residential housing in the Rochester area, including Penfield. Home Builders alleged that the Penfield zoning restrictions [had] deprived some of its members of "substantial business opportunities and profits." [Home Builders] can have standing as the representative of its members only if it has alleged facts sufficient to make out a case or controversy had the members themselves brought suit. No such allegations were made. The complaint refers to no specific project of any of its members that is currently precluded either by the ordinance or by respondents' action in enforcing it. [A] like problem is presented with respect to petitioner Housing Council [which] includes in its membership "at least seventeen" groups that have been, are, or will be involved in the development of low-and moderate-cost housing. But, with one exception, the complaint does not suggest that any of these groups has focused its efforts on Penfield or has any specific plan to do so. [The] exception is the Penfield Better Homes Corp. [It] applied to respondents in late 1969 for a zoning variance to allow construction of a housing project designed for persons of moderate income. It is therefore possible that in 1969, or within a reasonable time thereafter, Better Homes itself and possibly Housing Council as its representative would have had standing to seek review of respondents' action. The complaint, however, does not allege that the Penfield Better Homes project remained viable in 1972 when this complaint was filed, or that respondents' actions continued to block a then-current construction project. In short, neither the complaint nor the record supplies any basis from which to infer that the controversy between respondents and Better Homes, however vigorous it may once have been, remained a live, concrete dispute when this complaint was filed.

VI. The rules of standing, whether as aspects of the Art. III case-or-controversy requirement or as reflections of prudential considerations defining and limiting the role of the courts, are threshold determinants of the propriety of judicial intervention. It is the responsibility of the complainant clearly to allege facts demonstrating that he is a proper party to invoke judicial resolution of the dispute and the exercise of the court's remedial powers. [N]one of the petitioners here has met this threshold requirement.

Affirmed.

Justice BRENNAN, with whom Justice WHITE and Justice MARSHALL, join, dissenting.

In this case, a wide range of plaintiffs [claimed] to have been affected by the Penfield zoning ordinance. [The] Court today, in an opinion that purports to be a "standing" opinion but that actually [has] overtones of outmoded motions of pleading and justiciability, refuses to find that any of the [plaintiffs] can clear numerous hurdles [necessary] to establish "standing." While the Court gives lip service to the principle, oft repeated, [that] "standing in no way depends on the merits of the plaintiff's contention that the conduct is illegal," in fact, the opinion can be explained only by an indefensible hostility to the claim on the merits. [It] is quite clear, when the record is viewed with dispassion, that at least three of the groups of plaintiffs have made allegations [sufficient] to survive a motion to dismiss for lack of standing.

Low-income and Minority Plaintiffs. [The] Court's real holding is not that these petitioners have not *alleged* an injury resulting from respondents' action, but that they are not to be allowed to prove one, because "realization of petitioners' desire to live in Penfield always has depended on the efforts [of] third parties to build low-and moderate-cost housing," and "the record is devoid of any indication that [any] projects would have satisfied petitioners' needs at prices they could afford." Certainly, this is not the sort of demonstration that can or should be required of petitioners' at this preliminary stage. [Here], the very fact [that] these petitioners' claim rests in part upon proving the intentions and capabilities of third parties to build in Penfield suitable housing which they can afford, coupled with the exclusionary character of the claim on the merits, makes it particularly inappropriate to assume that these petitioners' lack of specificity reflects a fatal weakness in their theory of causation. Obviously they cannot be expected, prior to discovery and trial, to know the future plans of building companies, the precise details of the housing market in Penfield, or everything which has transpired in 15 years of application of the Penfield zoning ordinance, including every housing plan suggested and refused. To require them to allege such facts is to require them to prove their case on paper in order to get into court [at all].

Associations Including Building Concerns. [Again,] the Court ignores the thrust of the complaints and asks petitioners to allege the impossible. According to the allegations, the building concerns' experience in the past with Penfield officials has shown any plans for low-and moderate-income housing to be futile for, again according to the allegations, the respondents are engaged in a purposeful, conscious scheme to exclude such housing. Particularly with regard to a low-or moderate-income project, the cost of litigating, with respect to any particular project, the legality of a refusal to approve it may well be prohibitive. And the merits of the exclusion of this or that project is not at the heart of the complaint; the claim is that respondents will not approve *any* project which will provide residences for low-and moderate-income people. When this sort of pattern-and-practice claim is at the heart of the controversy, allegations of past injury, which members of both of these organizations have clearly made, and of a future intent, if the barriers are cleared, again to develop suitable housing for Penfield, should be more than sufficient. The past experiences, if proved at trial, will give credibility and substance to the claim of interest in future building activity in Penfield. These parties, if their allegations are proved, certainly have the requisite personal stake in the outcome of *this* controversy, and the Court's conclusion otherwise is only a conclusion that *this* controversy may not be litigated in a [federal court].*

---

* Justice DOUGLAS also submitted a dissent.

Contrast, with the majority's refusal to find standing in Warth v. Seldin, the Court's recognition of standing in Arlington Heights v. Metropolitan Housing Corp. (1977; ruling on the merits in chap. 9, p. 759 below)—a case which, like Warth, presented a racial discrimination claim in a zoning context. In Arlington Heights, the challenge was to a Chicago suburb's refusal to rezone a tract from a single-family to a multi-family classification. The prevailing opinion, as in Warth, was written by Justice Powell. The Court found that the developer had standing to challenge the allegedly discriminatory denial of rezoning, even though the developer's construction project was contingent not only on

Since *Warth*, the Court has repeatedly relied upon it to elaborate standing barriers to access to federal courts, emphasizing the importance of demonstrating adequate causation by requiring that the allegedly unlawful conduct caused plaintiff's "injury in fact" and that the injury was likely to be redressed by a favorable decision. Note, for example, ALLEN v. WRIGHT, 468 U.S. 737 (1984). The plaintiffs were parents of black public school children then attending school in districts that were in the process of desegregation; allegedly racially discriminatory private schools receiving tax exemptions were located in these districts. The parents claimed that the Internal Revenue Service had "not adopted sufficient standards and procedures to fulfill its obligation to deny tax-exempt status to the racially discriminatory private schools," thus effectively providing subsidies to unlawful segregation. Justice O'CONNOR rejected the parents' claims of two different injuries as their basis for demonstrating standing. The first was that they were, as blacks, stigmatized by the granting of tax exemptions to racially discriminatory schools. The second claimed injury was the denial of their rights to have their children attend a desegregated school. They alleged that, by providing a subsidized alternative of segregated private schools, the IRS made the task of desegregating the public schools more difficult. Justice O'Connor treated the first claim as an excessively generalized one. She rejected the second claim "because the injury alleged is not fairly traceable to the Government conduct [plaintiffs] challenge as unlawful." She noted that it was uncertain how many racially discriminatory private schools were in fact receiving tax exemptions and added that it was "entirely speculative" whether withdrawal of tax exemption from any particular school would lead the school to change its policies. She added that it was "just as speculative" when any given parent of a child attending such a private school would decide to transfer the child to public school as a result of any changes in financial policy made by the private school once it was threatened with loss of tax-exempt status. Finally, she noted, it was "also pure speculation whether, in a particular community, a large enough number of the numerous relevant school officials and parents would reach decisions that collectively would have a significant impact on the racial composition on the public schools." Justice O'Connor concluded, relying on *Warth* and referring to the separation of powers, that "the links in the chain of causation between the challenged Government conduct and the asserted injury [was far] too weak for the chain as a whole to sustain [plaintiffs'] standing." Justices BRENNAN and STEVENS,

its ability to procure rezoning but also on its capacity to obtain financing and qualify for federal subsidies. Justice Powell noted that "all housing developments are subject to some extent to similar uncertainties. When a project is as detailed and specific as [this one], a court is not required to engage in undue speculation as a predicate for finding that the plaintiff has the requisite personal stake in the controversy." The Court noted, moreover, that "economic injury is not the only kind of injury that can support a plaintiff's standing." The concern of the developer, a nonprofit corporation interested in providing low-cost housing, was "not a mere abstract concern about a problem of general interest"; instead, its involvement in a specific project provided "that 'essential dimension

of specificity' that informs judicial decision-making." The Court also found that an individual black plaintiff had standing to assert the racial discrimination claim. That plaintiff had alleged that he would qualify for the proposed housing and would probably move there if it were built, since it was closer to his job. Justice Powell stated: "His is not a generalized grievance. Instead, as we suggested in *Warth*, it focuses on a particular project and is not dependent on speculation about the possible actions of third parties not before the court. Unlike the individual plaintiffs in *Warth*, [this plaintiff] has adequately averred an 'actionable causal relationship' between Arlington Heights' zoning practices and his asserted injury."

joined by Justice Blackmun, dissented, accusing the majority of using the standing determination as a reflection of its view of the merits.

2. *Standing in "public actions": Suits by federal taxpayers and citizens; congressional power to confer standing.* The Court has long insisted that it will not adjudicate constitutional claims at the behest of a plaintiff who is merely one of millions of taxpayers or citizens interested in resolving constitutional doubts about governmental action. In rejecting these claims, the Court has repeatedly relied on standing concerns, insisting that it does not sit to resolve "generalized grievances," and that it will only adjudicate legal questions arising in a concrete factual context. As long ago as 1923, in Frothingham v. Mellon, 262 U.S. 447, the Court refused to entertain a taxpayer's action to enjoin the Secretary of the Treasury from making expenditures under the Maternity Act of 1921, which provided for conditional grants to state programs "to reduce maternal and infant mortality." The Court held unanimously that the plaintiff had "no such interest in the subject-matter, [nor] is any such injury inflicted or threatened, as would enable her to sue." The opinion stated that the interest of a federal taxpayer in the monies of the Treasury is "shared with millions of others; is comparatively minute and indeterminable; and the effect upon future taxation, of any payment out of the funds, so remote, fluctuating and uncertain," that no ground for access to the federal courts existed. The Frothingham Court relied on a mixture of constitutional and prudential grounds.

In 1968, the Court made an exception to the general barrier announced in Frothingham by upholding standing by taxpayers to challenge aid to religious schools under the Elementary and Secondary Education Act of 1965. Flast v. Cohen, 392 U.S. 83. The Court concluded that "the Frothingham barrier should be lowered when a taxpayer attacks a federal statute on the ground that it violates the Establishment and Free Exercise Clauses of the First Amendment." Subsequent cases showed that this exception was a narrow one and that the general hostility to taxpayers' and citizens' suits persists. Thus, in United States v. Richardson, 418 U.S. 166 (1974), the Court held that a taxpayer did not have standing to claim that a law providing that CIA expenditures not be made public violated Article I, § 9, cl. 7, of the Constitution, requiring that "a regular Statement of Account of the Receipts and Expenditures of all public Money shall be published from time to time." Chief Justice Burger's majority opinion emphasized that the plaintiff was "seeking 'to employ a federal court as a forum in which to air his generalized grievances about the conduct of government.'" Similarly, in a companion case, Schlesinger v. Reservists Committee to Stop the War, 418 U.S. 208 (1974) the Court rejected a claim of standing by plaintiffs who were past and present members of the Reserves and who sought to challenge the Reserve membership of certain Members of Congress as being in violation of the Incompatibility Clause, the clause in Article I, § 6, cl. 2, stating that "no Person holding any Office under the United States shall be a Member of either House during his continuance in the Office." Chief Justice Burger's majority opinion concluded that the plaintiffs lacked standing either as taxpayers or as citizens. In the course of his opinion, he explained why a "generalized citizen interest" is not a sufficient basis for access to the federal courts. He noted: "Concrete injury, whether actual or threatened, is that indispensable element of a dispute which serves in part to cast it in a form traditionally capable of judicial resolution. It adds the essential dimension of specificity to the dispute. [Only] concrete injury presents the factual context within which a court [is] capable of making decisions." Nearly a decade later, in Valley Forge Christian College v. Americans United, 454 U.S. 464 (1982), the Court rejected a taxpayer's suit claiming that the federal government had transferred property in violation of the Establishment Clause.

In reviewing the standing barrier, Justice Rehnquist sought to disentangle the constitutional and prudential ingredients of the standing limit and emphasized that the constitutional barrier arose from separation of powers concerns and from the Art. III case and controversy requirement.

What is the significance of this line of cases for congressional efforts to authorize "public actions" by "private Attorneys General" in citizens' and taxpayers' suits to challenge the legality and constitutionality of governmental action? Presumably, to the extent that the standing barrier is rooted in constitutional concerns, Congress may not remove it, but to the extent that it rests merely on prudential considerations, Congress may have a greater role to play. Although opinions in Flast and Richardson suggested a generous stance toward congressional grants of remedies, later opinions, from Warth to Valley Forge, suggest an increased emphasis on constitutional sources of standing rules and accordingly indicate a greater reluctance to permit Congress to expand access to federal courts. Is that reluctance justified? By the need for adverseness and an adequate record? By considerations of judicial self-restraint? Do judicial self-restraint considerations suffice to support judicial barriers to standing where Congress has asked the courts to resolve disputes? If Congress authorized "any taxpayer" or "any citizen" to bring suit against allegedly illegal action, would that be tantamount to directing advisory opinions in violation of Art. III? Consider in this connection the Court's position in Lujan, which follows. The case provides a useful depiction of the Court's attitude toward standing in the 1990s: it continues the modern trend to rely primarily on constitutional rather than prudential themes in standing cases, and it casts added doubt on the authority of Congress to lower the barriers to access to courts through explicit grants of standing.

Lujan v. Defenders of Wildlife
504 U.S. 555, 112 S.Ct. 2130, 119 L.Ed.2d 351 (1992).

JUSTICE SCALIA delivered the opinion of the Court with respect to Parts I, II, III–A, and IV, and an opinion with respect to Part III–B in which The Chief Justice [REHNQUIST], Justice WHITE, and Justice THOMAS join.

This case involves a challenge to a rule promulgated by the Secretary of the Interior interpreting § 7 of the Endangered Species Act of 1973 (ESA) in such fashion as to render it applicable only to actions within the United States or on the high seas. The preliminary issue, and the only one we reach, is whether the respondents here, plaintiffs below, have standing to seek judicial review of the rule.

I.   The ESA seeks to protect species of animals against threats to their continuing existence caused by man. The ESA instructs the Secretary of the Interior to promulgate by regulation a list of those species which are either endangered or threatened under enumerated criteria, and to define the critical habitat of these species. Section 7(a)(2) of the Act then provides, in pertinent part: "Each Federal agency shall, in consultation with and with the assistance of the Secretary [of the Interior], insure that any action authorized, funded, or carried out by such agency [is] not likely to jeopardize the continued existence of any endangered species or threatened species or result in the destruction or adverse modification of habitat of such species which is determined by the Secretary, after consultation as appropriate with affected States, to be critical." In 1978, the Fish and Wildlife Service (FWS) and the National Marine Fisheries Service (NMFS), on behalf of the Secretary of the Interior and the Secretary of Commerce respectively, promulgated a joint regulation stating that the obligations imposed by § 7(a)(2) extend to actions taken in foreign nations. The next year, however, the Interior Department began to reexamine its position. A revised joint regulation, reinterpreting § 7(a)(2) to require consultation only for actions taken in the United States or on the high seas, [was] promulgated in 1986. Shortly thereafter, [the plaintiffs], organizations dedicated to wildlife conservation and other environmental causes, filed this action against the Secretary of the Interior, seeking a declaratory judgment that the new regulation is in error as to the geographic scope of § 7(a)(2), and an injunction requiring the Secretary to promulgate a new regulation restoring the initial [interpretation]. [T]he Secretary moved for summary judgment on the standing issue, and [plaintiffs] moved for summary judgment on the merits. The District Court denied the Secretary's motion; it granted plaintiffs' merits motion, and ordered the Secretary to publish a revised regulation. The [Court of Appeals] affirmed.

P, H.

(extend to acts in foreign nations)

II.   Though some of [the] elements [of the doctrine of standing] express merely prudential considerations that are part of judicial self-government, the core component of standing is an essential and unchanging part of the case-or-controversy requirement of Article III. Over the years, our cases have established that the irreducible constitutional minimum of standing contains three elements: First, the plaintiff must have suffered an "injury in fact"—an invasion of a legally-protected interest which is (a) concrete and particularized, and (b) "actual or imminent, not 'conjectural' or 'hypothetical.'" Second, there must be a causal connection between the injury and the conduct complained of—the injury has to be "fairly [traceable] to the challenged action of the defendant, and [not] the result [of] the independent action of some third party not before the court." Third, it must be "likely," as opposed to merely "speculative," that the injury will be "redressed by a favorable decision."

"Standing" ELEMENTS

III.   [Plaintiffs have] not made the requisite demonstration of (at least) injury and redressability. [A.] [Plaintiffs'] claim to injury is that the lack of consultation with respect to certain funded activities abroad "increases the rate of extinction of endangered and threatened species." Of course, the desire to use or observe an animal species, even for purely aesthetic purposes, is undeniably a cognizable interest for purpose of standing. "But the 'injury in fact' test requires more than an injury to a cognizable interest. It requires that the party seeking review be himself among the injured." [With] respect to this aspect of the case, the Court of Appeals focused on the affidavits of two Defenders' members—Joyce Kelly and Amy Skilbred. Ms. Kelly stated that she traveled to Egypt in 1986 and "observed the traditional habitat of the endangered nile crocodile there and intends to do so again, and hopes to observe the crocodile directly," and that she "will suffer harm in fact as a result of [the] American [role] in overseeing the rehabilitation of the Aswan High Dam on the Nile [and in] developing [Egypt's] Master Water Plan." Ms. Skilbred averred that she traveled to Sri Lanka in 1981 and "observed the habitat" of "endangered species such as the Asian elephant and the leopard" at what is now the site of the Mahaweli Project funded by the Agency for International Development (AID), although she "was unable to see any of the endangered species"; "this development project," she continued, "will seriously reduce endangered, threatened, and endemic species habitat including areas that I visited, [which] may severely shorten the future of these species"; that threat, she concluded, harmed her because she "intends to return to Sri Lanka in the future and hopes to be more fortunate in spotting at least the endangered elephant and leopard." When Ms. Skilbred was asked at a subsequent deposition if and when she had any plans to return to Sri Lanka, she reiterated that "I intend to go back to Sri Lanka," but confessed that she had no current plans: "I don't know

π argues injury

when. There is a civil war going on right now. I don't know. Not next year, I will say. In the future."

We shall assume for the sake of argument that these affidavits contain facts showing that certain agency-funded projects threaten listed species— though that is questionable. They plainly contain no facts, however, showing how damage to the species will produce "imminent" injury to Mss. Kelly and Skilbred. That the women "had visited" the areas of the projects before the projects commenced proves nothing. And the affiants' profession of an "intent" to return to the places they had visited before [is] simply not enough. Such "some day" intentions—without any description of concrete plans, or indeed even any specification of when the some day will be—do not support a finding of the "actual or imminent" injury that our cases require.

[Plaintiffs, besides relying on the Kelly and Skilbred affidavits,] propose a series of novel standing themes. [Among these are theories] called, alas, the "animal nexus" approach, whereby anyone who has an interest in studying or seeing the endangered animals anywhere on the globe has standing; and the "vocational nexus" approach, under which anyone with a professional interest in such animals can sue. Under these theories, anyone who goes to see Asian elephants in the Bronx Zoo, and anyone who is a keeper of Asian elephants in the Bronx Zoo, has standing to sue because the Director of AID did not consult with the Secretary regarding the AID-funded project in Sri Lanka. This is beyond all reason. Standing is not "an ingenious academic exercise in the conceivable," but as we have said requires, at the summary judgment stage, a factual showing of perceptible harm. It is clear that the person who observes or works with a particular animal threatened by a federal decision is facing perceptible harm, since the very subject of his interest will no longer exist. It is even plausible—though it goes to the outermost limit of plausibility—to think that a person who observes or works with animals of a particular species in the very area of the world where that species is threatened by a federal decision is facing such harm, since some animals that might have been the subject of his interest will no longer exist. It goes beyond the limit, however, and into pure speculation and fantasy, to say that anyone who observes or works with an endangered species, anywhere in the world, is appreciably harmed by a single project affecting some portion of that species with which he has no more specific connection.

B. Besides failing to show injury, [plaintiffs] failed to demonstrate redressability. [Since] the agencies funding the projects were not parties to the case, the District Court could accord relief only against the Secretary. [Moreover, there is no assurance that the threat of withdrawing U.S. funding—a fraction of the total funding needed by foreign projects—would cause projects to be terminated.] But this would not remedy [plaintiffs'] alleged injury unless the funding agencies were bound by the Secretary's regulation, which is very much an open question.

IV. The Court of Appeals found that respondents had standing for an additional reason: because they had suffered a "procedural injury." The so-called "citizen-suit" provision of the ESA provides, in pertinent part, that "any person may commence a civil suit on his own behalf (A) to enjoin any person, including the United States and any other governmental instrumentality or agency, [who] is alleged to be in violation of any provision of this chapter." The court held that, because § 7(a)(2) requires interagency consultation, the citizen-suit provision creates a "procedural right" to consultation in all "persons"—so that anyone can file suit in federal court to challenge the Secretary's (or presumably any other official's) failure to follow the assertedly correct consultative procedure, notwithstanding their inability to allege any discrete injury flowing from that failure. To understand the remarkable nature of this holding one must be clear about what it does not rest upon: This is not a case where plaintiffs are seeking to enforce a procedural requirement the disregard of which could impair a separate concrete interest of theirs (e.g., the procedural requirement for a hearing prior to denial of their license application, or the procedural requirement for an environmental impact statement before a federal facility is constructed next door to them). Nor is it simply a case where concrete injury has been suffered by many persons, as in mass fraud or mass tort situations. Nor, finally, is it the unusual case in which Congress has created a concrete private interest in the outcome of a suit against a private party for the government's benefit, by providing a cash bounty for the victorious plaintiff. Rather, the court held that the injury-in-fact requirement had been satisfied by congressional conferral upon all persons of an abstract, self-contained, noninstrumental "right" to have the Executive observe the procedures required by law. We reject this view.

We have consistently held that a plaintiff raising only a generally available grievance about government—claiming only harm to his and every citizen's interest in proper application of the Constitution and laws, and seeking relief that no more directly and tangibly benefits him than it does the public at large—does not state an Article III case or controversy. [E.g.,] Frothingham v. Mellon; U.S. v. Richardson. To be sure, our generalized-grievance cases have typically involved Government violation of procedures assertedly ordained by the Constitution rather than the Congress. But there is absolutely no basis for making the Article III inquiry turn on the source of the asserted right. Whether the courts were to act on their own, or at the invitation of Congress, in ignoring the concrete injury requirement described in our cases, they would be discarding a principle fundamental to the separate and distinct constitutional role of the Third Branch—one of the essential elements that identifies those "Cases" and "Controversies" that are the business of the courts rather than of the political branches. "The province of the court," as Chief Justice Marshall said in Marbury v. Madison, "is, solely, to decide on the rights of individuals." Vindicating the public interest (including the public interest in government observance of the Constitution and laws) is the function of Congress and the Chief Executive. The question presented here is whether the public interest in proper administration of the laws (specifically, in agencies' observance of a particular, statutorily prescribed procedure) can be converted into an individual right by a statute that denominates it as such, and that permits all citizens (or, for that matter, a subclass of citizens who suffer no distinctive concrete harm) to sue. If the concrete injury requirement has the separation-of-powers significance we have always said, the answer must be obvious: To permit Congress to convert the undifferentiated public interest in executive officers' compliance with the law into an "individual right" vindicable in the courts is to permit Congress to transfer from the President to the courts the Chief Executive's most important constitutional duty, to "take Care that the Laws be faithfully executed." It would enable the courts, with the permission of Congress, "to assume a position of authority over the governmental acts of another and co-equal department," and to become " 'virtually continuing monitors of the wisdom and soundness of Executive action.' " We have always rejected that vision of our role: "[U]nder Article III, Congress established courts to adjudicate cases and controversies as to claims of infringement of individual rights whether by unlawful action of private persons or by the exertion of unauthorized administrative power." "Individual rights," within the meaning of this passage, do not mean public rights that have been legislatively pronounced to belong to each individual who forms part of the public. Nothing in this contradicts the principle that "[the] injury required by Art. III may exist solely by virtue of 'statutes creating legal rights, the invasion of which creates standing.' " [Warth v. Seldin.] [I]t is clear that in suits against the government, at least, the concrete injury requirement must remain. [We] hold that respondents lack standing to bring this action.

[Reversed.]

Justice KENNEDY, with whom Justice SOUTER joins, concurring in part and concurring in the judgment.

Although I agree with the essential parts of the Court's analysis, I write separately to make several observations. [I] join Part IV of the Court's opinion with the following observations. As government programs and policies become more complex and far-reaching, we must be sensitive to the articulation of new rights of action that do not have clear analogs in our common-law tradition. Modern litigation has progressed far from the paradigm of Marbury suing Madison to get his commission. [In] my view, Congress has the power to define injuries and articulate chains of causation that will give rise to a case or controversy where none existed before, and I do not read the Court's opinion to suggest a contrary view. See Warth v. Seldin. In exercising this power, however, Congress must at the very least identify the injury it seeks to vindicate and relate the injury to the class of persons entitled to bring suit. The citizen-suit provision of the Endangered Species Act does not meet these minimal requirements, because while the statute purports to confer a right on "any person [to] enjoin [the] United States and any other governmental instrumentality or agency [who] is alleged to be in violation of any provision of this chapter," it does not of its own force establish that there is an injury in "any person" by virtue of any "violation."

The Court's holding that there is an outer limit to the power of Congress to confer rights of action is a direct and necessary consequence of the case and controversy limitations found in Article III. I agree that it would exceed those limitations if, at the behest of Congress and in the absence of any showing of concrete injury, we were to entertain citizen-suits to vindicate the public's nonconcrete interest in the proper administration of the laws. [The] party bringing suit must show that the action injures him in a concrete and personal way. This requirement is not just an empty formality. It preserves the vitality of the adversarial process by assuring both that the parties before the court have an actual, as opposed to professed, stake in the outcome, and that "the legal questions presented [will] be resolved [in] a concrete factual context conducive to a realistic appreciation of the consequences of judicial action." In addition, the requirement of concrete injury confines the Judicial Branch to its proper, limited role in the constitutional framework of [government].

JUSTICE STEVENS, concurring in the judgment.

Because I am not persuaded that Congress intended the consultation requirement in § 7(a)(2) [to] apply to activities in foreign countries, I concur in the judgment of reversal. I do not, however, agree with the Court's conclusion that [plaintiffs] lack standing because the threatened injury to their interest [is] not "imminent." Nor do I agree with the plurality's additional conclusion that respondents' injury is not "redressable" in this [litigation].

Justice BLACKMUN, with whom Justice O'CONNOR joins, dissenting.

I part company with the Court in this case in two respects. First, I believe that [plaintiffs] have raised genuine issues of fact—sufficient to survive summary judgment—both as to injury and as to redressability. Second, I question the Court's breadth of language in rejecting standing for "procedural" injuries. I fear the Court seeks to impose fresh limitations on the constitutional authority of Congress to allow citizen-suits in the federal courts for injuries deemed "procedural" in nature. I dissent. The Court concludes that any "procedural injury" suffered by respondents is insufficient to confer standing. It rejects the view that the "injury-in-fact requirement [is] satisfied by congressional conferral upon all person of an abstract, self-contained, noninstrumental 'right' to have the Executive observe the procedures required by law." Whatever the Court might mean with that very broad language, it cannot be saying that "procedural injuries" as a class are necessarily insufficient for purposes of Article III standing. Congress legislates in procedural shades of gray not to aggrandize its own power but to allow maximum Executive discretion in the attainment of Congress' legislative goals. Congress could simply impose a substantive prohibition on executive conduct; it could say that no agency action shall result in the loss of more than 5% of any listed species. Instead, Congress sets forth substantive guidelines and allows the Executive, within certain procedural constraints, to decide how best to effectuate the ultimate goal. The Court never has questioned Congress' authority to impose such procedural constraints on executive power. Just as Congress does not violate separation of powers by structuring the procedural manner in which the Executive shall carry out the laws, surely the federal courts do not violate separation of powers when, at the very instruction and command of Congress, they enforce these procedures.

[To] prevent Congress from conferring standing for "procedural injuries" is another way of saying that Congress may not delegate to the courts authority deemed "executive" in nature. Here Congress seeks not to delegate "executive" power but only to strengthen the procedures it has legislatively mandated. [Ironically,] this Court has previously justified a relaxed review of congressional delegation to the Executive on grounds that Congress, in turn, has subjected the exercise of that power to judicial review. The Court's intimation today that procedural injuries are not constitutionally cognizable threatens this understanding upon which Congress has undoubtedly relied. In no sense is the Court's suggestion compelled by our "common understanding of what activities are appropriate to legislatures, to executives, and to courts." In my view, it reflects an unseemly solicitude for an expansion of power of the Executive Branch. [There] is no room for a per se rule or presumption excluding injuries labeled "procedural" in nature. [I] cannot join the Court on what amounts to a slash-and-burn expedition through the law of environmental standing. In my view, "the very essence of civil liberty certainly consists in the right of every individual to claim the protection of the laws, whenever he receives an injury." [Marbury v. Madison.]

---

3. *Additional barriers to adjudication: Questions of timing—Mootness and lack of ripeness of the issues.* The mootness and ripeness limits on adjudication pertain to the timing of lawsuits. The mootness cases involve litigants who clearly had standing to sue at the outset of the litigation; the problems arise from events occurring after the lawsuit has gotten under way—changes in the facts or in the law—that allegedly deprive the litigants of the necessary stake in the outcome. The ripeness doctrine seeks to prevent premature adjudication; it involves situations where the dispute is insufficiently developed and is instead too remote or speculative to warrant judicial action. In short, a case is not ripe when it is brought too soon, when the parties have not yet reached an eyeball-

to-eyeball confrontation; a case is moot when changing circumstances developing after the initiation of the lawsuit have ended the controversy, so that the court no longer confronts a live dispute.

a. *Mootness.* The mootness doctrine requires that "an actual controversy must be extant at all stages of review, not merely at the time the complaint is filed." The Court has repeatedly insisted that the doctrine is an aspect of the Art. III case or controversy requirement. Yet, despite that constitutional basis, the Court has recurrently relaxed the mootness barrier, found a number of exceptions to it, and has, in some commentators' views, applied them erratically. Note an attempt to summarize "the different kinds of harm which may prevent a case from being held moot: a continuing harm to the plaintiff; the likelihood of future recurrence of past harm, either to the plaintiff personally or to the group he represents; and the probability that some of the cases arising in the future will evade judicial review." Note, "The Mootness Doctrine in the Supreme Court," 88 Harv.L.Rev. 373, 378 (1974).

For examples of the Court's flexibility and arguably erratic rulings regarding mootness, contrast the first abortion decision, Roe v. Wade, 410 U.S. 113 (1973), with the first preferential minority admissions case, DeFunis vs. Odegaard, 416 U.S. 312 (1974). In the abortion case, Ms. Roe's suit, brought in 1970, was not decided by the Court until 1973, when she obviously was no longer pregnant; yet the Court refused to dismiss the case as moot. Justice Blackmun explained: "[T]he normal 266–day human gestation period is so short that the pregnancy will come to term before the usual appellate process is complete. If that termination makes a case moot, pregnancy litigation seldom will survive much beyond the trial stage, and appellate review will be effectively denied. Our laws should not be that rigid. Pregnancy produces a classic justification for a conclusion of non-mootness. It truly could be 'capable of repetition, yet evading review.' " (The "capable of repetition, yet evading review" exception to the mootness barrier is one of the most commonly invoked ones.) However, the majority did find mootness a year later, in DeFunis. DeFunis had challenged the University of Washington's admissions program as racially discriminatory, but had attended the school a result of a lower court decision while the case was on appeal. By the time his case reached the Court, he was in his third year of law school. The majority of the Court held his challenge moot, noting his "recent registration for the last quarter of his final law school year, and the Law School's assurance that his registration is fully effective." DeFunis had not brought a class action and the Court did not find in his case the "exceptional situation" of an issue "capable of repetition, yet evading review": "[T]here is no reason to suppose that a subsequent case attacking [admissions] procedures will not come with relative speed to this Court." Justice Brennan's dissent insisted the case was not moot and argued that the dismissal disserved the public interest, since the issues "must inevitably return to the federal courts and ultimately again to this Court." (The issues did in fact return to the Court within four years, in Bakke, p. 795 below.)

b. *Ripeness.* How ripe must a controversy be to present appropriate circumstances for adjudication? At one end of the spectrum lies the much-reiterated premise that federal courts will not render advisory opinions even though the litigants have intense curiosity about the answer. At the other end of the scale is the common situation of the defendant resisting enforcement of the criminal law; in that situation, the relevant facts occurred in the past and are on the record; in that context, accordingly, courts normally adjudicate legal challenges. The typical problem of ripeness arises from situations in between these extremes. It arises most characteristically with requests for anticipatory relief, where plaintiffs seek injunctive or declaratory relief regarding the

ripeness
grounds
Art III
Discretionary
Remedial
Prudential

legality of actions that they fear may be taken against them. In such situations, the problems of contingencies and uncertainties as to the facts are most prominent, and the courts are most likely to insist on a clearly defined record to assure informed and narrow decisionmaking. While a ripeness ruling may rest on Art. III case or controversy grounds, they are sometimes based on discretionary, remedial or prudential, grounds.

For a sampling of the Court's handling of ripeness issues, contrast United Public Workers v. Mitchell, 330 U.S. 75 (1947), with Adler v. Board of Educ., 342 U.S. 485 (1952). Both involved First Amendment challenges to restrictions on the associations and speech of public employees. In Mitchell, the Court found most of the claims nonjusticiable; in Adler, by contrast, the Court reached the merits. Mitchell was an attack on a section of the Hatch Act of 1940 which prohibited federal executive branch employees from taking "any active part in political management or in political campaigns." The challengers sought a declaratory judgment that the provision was unconstitutional. The complaints of most of the challengers stated only that they desired to act contrary to the rule against political activity but not that the rule had been violated. Moreover, the threats that menaced most of the challengers were "closer to a general threat by officials to enforce those laws which they are charged to administer, than they [were] to the direct threat of punishment [for] a completed act." The Court thought such complaints premature: in its view, most of the challengers seemed "clearly to seek advisory opinions upon broad claims of constitutional rights," and this did not make "a justiciable case or controversy." In the Court's view, the challenger's "generality of objection [was] really an attack on the political expediency of the [law], not the presentation of legal issues. It is beyond the competence of courts to render such a decision." While the majority relied on constitutional grounds in reaching its ripeness conclusion, an opinion by Justice Rutledge stated that he did not rule on most of the constitutional questions presented "for the reason that he feels the controversy [is] not yet appropriate for the discretionary exercise of declaratory judgment jurisdiction." By contrast, in the Adler case, a challenge to a New York law designed to eliminate "subversive persons from the public school system," the Supreme Court affirmed a ruling on the merits without ever discussing justiciability. Only Justice Frankfurter's dissent argued that this case, like Mitchell, was nonjusticiable. Are these cases reconcilable because Adler, unlike Mitchell, originated in the state courts and arguably was not so unripe as to fall short of being an Art. III case or controversy? For a notable later dismissal for lack of ripeness, see Laird v. Tatum, 408 U.S. 1 (1972), a lawsuit seeking redress against allegedly unlawful "surveillance of lawful citizen political activity" by the U.S. Army. The majority, relying on Mitchell, held that the plaintiffs' claim did not present "a case for resolution by the courts because it rested mainly on the challengers' fear of future, punitive action"—action based on the results of the surveillance. According to the majority, the complaint rested largely on "speculative apprehensiveness that the Army might at some future date misuse the information in some way that would cause harm" to the plaintiffs, and such fears did not amount to "specific present objective harm" or "threat of specific future harm."

B.   THE NONJUSTICIABILITY OF POLITICAL QUESTIONS

1. *Introduction.* Particularly in the twentieth century, the Court has developed a somewhat amorphous political questions doctrine, the doctrine that so-called political questions are inappropriate for judicial resolution and are therefore nonjusticiable. The political question doctrine rests on a blend of

themes, in part reflecting normal constitutional interpretation and in part resting on prudential considerations that counsel against rulings that might generate excessive conflicts with the other branches. The basic doctrine that some constitutional issues are "political" and thus nonjusticiable is well-established; what the proper ingredients of that concept are has produced considerable uncertainty and controversy. A widely invoked strand of the political question doctrine, and the strand that seems the most confined and legitimate one, emphasizes "a textually demonstrable constitutional commitment of the issue to a coordinate political department." See Baker v. Carr, which follows. Another widely invoked element is the perception of "a lack of judicially discoverable and manageable standards for resolving an issue," a strand which may be partly an aspect of constitutional interpretation and partly a reliance on prudential considerations. Still another, even more open-ended and most clearly prudential strand suggests that resolution of issues ought to be avoided where they are too controversial or could produce enforcement problems or other institutional difficulties.

If Marbury v. Madison were viewed as establishing the Court as the "ultimate" interpreter of all constitutional questions, the political question doctrine would seem inconsistent with that ruling. But if a major theme of Marshall's opinion in Marbury was to establish the *competence* of federal courts to adjudicate constitutional issues, the tension between the political question doctrine and Marbury would be considerably reduced. Indeed, in Marbury itself, the early parts of Marshall's opinion disavowed the Court's authority to intervene with presidential decisions on "political" subjects—i.e., questions in which the President possessed "a Constitutional or legal discretion": "Questions, in their nature political, or which are, by the Constitution and laws, submitted to the executive can never be made in this court."

Some commentators doubt the very existence of any general discretionary political question doctrine. For example, Henkin, "Is There a Political Question Doctrine," 85 Yale L.J. 597 (1976), argues that all so-called political question cases involve the Court's either "accept[ing] decisions by the political branches [as being] within their constitutional authority" or "refus[ing] some (or all) remedies for reasons of equity." In examining the cases that follow, consider whether Henkin's theory adequately explains the Court's invoking of the political question doctrine.[1] This general overview of the political question doctrine begins with a frequently relied on 1962 case, Baker v. Carr, which summarizes the strands of the doctrine and some of its applications, and which also reviews one of the rare nineteenth century examples of it, in Luther v. Borden in 1849.

2. *The situation before Baker v. Carr.* In Baker, the Court rejected the claim that equal protection challenges to districting plans presented a nonjusticiable political question. That was a sharp departure from the Court's prior aversion to adjudicating such disputes. The pre-Baker attitude regarding the justiciability of districting plans is illustrated by Justice Frankfurter's opinion in Colegrove v. Green, 328 U.S. 549 (1946). There, the majority of the Court

---

1. Note also Henkin's suggestion that "there may be no doctrine requiring abstention from judicial review of 'political questions.' The cases which are supposed to have established the political question doctrine required no such extra-ordinary abstention from judicial review; they called only for the ordinary respect by the courts for the politi- cal domain. Having reviewed, the Court refused to invalidate the challenged actions because they were within the constitutional authority of President or Congress. In no case did the Court have to use the phrase 'political question.'" Henkin, "Is There a 'Political Question' Doctrine?" 85 Yale L.J. 597 (1976).

(only seven Justices participated) refused to reach the merits of a challenge to the congressional districting scheme in Illinois. The challengers contended that the Illinois districting scheme was unconstitutional because the districts were not approximately equal in population. Justice Frankfurter stated: "[T]he petitioners ask of this Court what is beyond its competence to grant. [This] controversy concerns matters that bring courts into immediate and active relations with party contests. From the determination of such issues this Court has traditionally remained aloof. [T]he Constitution has conferred upon Congress exclusive authority to secure fair representation by the States in the popular [House of Representatives]. [Art. I, § 4.] Courts ought not to enter this political thicket." With Baker, the aversion to entering that thicket came to an end. Two years after Baker, with Reynolds v. Sims, 377 U.S. 533 (1964) (p. 866 below), the Court launched its extensive involvement with redistricting controversies. Chief Justice Warren's majority opinion in that case laid down the "one person-one vote" standard, a standard that seemed sufficiently clear and relatively simple enough to provide a "judicially manageable standard." 2

Baker v. Carr

369 U.S. 186, 82 S.Ct. 691, 7 L.Ed.2d 663 (1962)

Justice BRENNAN delivered the opinion of the [Court].

[Voters in Tennessee claimed that the apportionment of the Tennessee General Assembly violated their equal protection rights "by virtue of the debasement of their votes." They alleged that, although the state constitution allocated representation on a population basis, the Assembly had not been reapportioned since 1901, even though there had been substantial growth and redistribution of the population since then. They also claimed that, because of the malapportioned legislature, redress through changes in state law was difficult or impossible. They sought an injunction against further elections under the 1901 system and asked the federal trial court either to direct elections at large or to decree a reapportionment "by mathematical application of the Tennessee constitutional formulae to the most recent Federal Census figures." The lower court denied relief.]

[We] hold that this challenge to an apportionment presents no nonjusticiable "political question." [Of course] the mere fact that the suit seeks protection of a political right does not mean it presents a political question. Such an objection "is little more than a play upon words." Rather, it is argued that apportionment cases [can] involve no federal constitutional right except one resting on the guaranty of a republican form of government [Art. IV, § 4] and that complaints based on that clause have been held to present political questions which are nonjusticiable. We hold that the claim pleaded here neither rests upon nor implicates the Guaranty Clause. [To] show why we reject the argument based on the Guaranty Clause, we must examine the authorities under it. But because there appears to be some uncertainty as to why those cases did present political questions, and specifically as to whether this apportionment case is like those cases, we deem it necessary first to consider the contours of the "political question" doctrine.

Our discussion [requires] review of a number of political question cases, in order to expose the attributes of the doctrine—attributes which, in various settings, diverge, combine, appear, and disappear in seeming disorderliness. [That] review reveals that in the Guaranty Clause cases and in the other "political question" cases, it is the relationship between the judiciary and the coordinate branches of the Federal Government, and not the federal judiciary's relationship to the States, which gives rise to the "political question." We have said that "In determining whether a question falls within [the political question] category, the appropriateness under our system of government of attributing finality to the action of the political departments and also the lack of satisfactory criteria for a judicial determination are dominant considerations." The nonjusticiability of a political question is primarily a function of the separation of powers. Much confusion results from the capacity of the "political question" label to obscure the need for case-by-case inquiry. Deciding whether a matter has in any measure been committed by the Constitution to another branch of government, or whether the action of that branch exceeds whatever authority has been committed, is itself a delicate exercise in constitutional interpretation, and is a responsibility of this Court as ultimate interpreter of the [Constitution].

Foreign relations: There are sweeping statements to the effect that all questions touching foreign relations are political questions. Not only does resolution of such issues frequently turn on standards that defy judicial application, or involve the exercise of a discretion demonstrably committed to the executive or legislature; but many such questions uniquely demand single-voiced statement of the Government's views. Yet it is error to suppose that every case or controversy which touches foreign relations lies beyond judicial cognizance. Our cases in this field seem invariably to show a discriminating analysis of the particular question posed, in terms of the history of its management by the political branches, of its susceptibility to judicial handling in the light of its nature and posture in the specific case, and of the possible consequences of judicial [action].

Validity of enactments: In Coleman v. Miller, [307 U.S. 433 (1939)], this Court held that the questions of how long a proposed amendment to the Federal Constitution remained open to ratification, and what effect a prior rejection had on a subsequent ratification, were committed to congressional resolution and involved criteria of decision that necessarily escaped the judicial grasp. Similar considerations apply to the enacting process: "The respect due to coequal and independent departments," and the need for finality and certainty about the status of a statute contribute to judicial reluctance to inquire whether, as passed, it complied with all requisite [formalities].

It is apparent that several formulations which vary slightly according to the settings in which the questions arise may describe a political question, although each has one or more elements which identify it as essentially a function of the separation of powers. Prominent on the surface of any case held to involve a political question is found a textually demonstrable constitutional commitment of the issue to a coordinate political department; or a lack of judicially discoverable and manageable standards for resolving it; or the impossibility of deciding without an initial policy determination of a kind clearly for nonjudicial discretion; or the impossibility of a court's undertaking independent resolution without expressing lack of the respect due coordinate branches of government; or an unusual need for unquestioning adherence to a political decision already made; or the potentiality of embarrassment from multifarious pronouncements by various departments on one question. Unless one of these formulations is inextricable from the case at bar, there should be no dismissal for nonjusticiability on the ground of a political question's presence. The doctrine of which we treat is one of "political questions," not one of "political cases."

[But] it is argued that this case shares the characteristics of decisions that constitute a category not yet considered, cases concerning the Constitution's guaranty [of] a republican form of government. A conclusion as to whether the case at bar does present a political question cannot be confidently reached until we have considered those cases with special care. We shall discover that Guaranty Clause claims involve those elements which define a "political question," and for that reason and no other, they are nonjusticiable. In particular, [the] nonjusticiability of such claims has nothing to do with their touching upon matters of state governmental organization.

Republican form of government: Luther v. Borden, 7 How. 1 [1849], though in form simply an action for damages for trespass was, as Daniel Webster said in opening the argument for the defense, "an unusual case." The defendants, admitting an otherwise tortious breaking and entering, sought to justify their action on the ground that they were agents of the established lawful government of Rhode Island, which State was then under martial law to defend itself from active insurrection; that the plaintiff was engaged in that insurrection; and that they entered under orders to arrest the plaintiff. The case arose "out of the unfortunate political differences which agitated the people of Rhode Island in 1841 and 1842," and which had resulted in a situation wherein two groups laid competing claims to recognition as the lawful government. The plaintiff's right to recover depended upon which of the two groups was entitled to such recognition; but the lower court's refusal to receive evidence or hear argument on that issue, its charge to the jury that the earlier established or "charter" government was lawful, and the verdict for the defendants, were affirmed upon appeal to this Court.

Chief Justice Taney's opinion for the Court reasoned as follows: (1) If a court were to hold the defendants' acts unjustified because the charter government had no legal existence during the period in question, it would follow that all of that government's actions—laws enacted, taxes collected, salaries paid, accounts settled, sentences passed—were of no effect; and that "the officers who carried their decisions into operation [were] answerable as trespassers, if not in some cases as criminals." [A] decision for the plaintiff would inevitably have produced some significant measure of chaos, a consequence to be avoided if it could be done without abnegation of the judicial duty to uphold the Constitution. (2) No state court had recognized as a judicial responsibility settlement of the issue of the locus of state governmental [authority]. (3) Since "the question relates, altogether, to the constitution and laws of [the] State," the courts of the United States had to follow the state courts' decisions unless there was a federal constitutional ground for overturning them. (4) No provision of the Constitution could be or had been invoked for this purpose except Art. IV, § 4, the Guaranty Clause. Having already noted the absence of standards whereby the choice between governments could be made by a court acting independently, Chief Justice Taney now found further textual and practical reasons for concluding that, if any department of the United States was empowered by the Guaranty Clause to resolve the issue, it was not the judiciary: "Under this article of the Constitution it rests with Congress to decide what government is the established one in a State. For as the United States guarantee to each State a republican government, Congress must necessarily decide what government is established in the State before it can determine whether it is republican or not. And when the senators and representatives of a State are admitted into the councils of the Union, the authority of the government under which they are appointed, as well as its republican character, is recognized by the proper constitutional authority. And its decision is binding on every other department of the government, and could not be questioned in a judicial tribunal. It is true that the contest in this case did not last long enough to bring the matter to this issue; and ... Congress was not called upon to decide the controversy. Yet the right to decide is placed there, and not in the courts. So, too, as relates to the clause in the [Constitution, Art. IV, § 2] providing for cases of domestic violence. It rested with Congress, too, to determine upon the means proper to be adopted to fulfill this guarantee. [By] the act of February 28, 1795, [Congress] provided, that, 'in case of an insurrection in any State against the government thereof, it shall be lawful for the President of the United States, on application of the legislature of such State or of the executive (when the legislature cannot be convened), to call forth such number of the militia of any other State or States, as may be applied for, as he may judge sufficient to suppress such insurrection.' [It] is true that in this case the militia were not called out by the President. But upon the application of the governor under the charter government, the President recognized him as the executive power of the State, and took measures to call out the militia to support his authority if it should be found necessary for the general government to [interfere.]"

Clearly, several factors were thought by the Court in Luther to make the question there "political": the commitment to the other branches of the decision as to which is the lawful state government; the unambiguous action by the President, in recognizing the charter government as the lawful authority; the need for finality in the executive's decision; and the lack of criteria by which a court could determine which form of government was republican. But the only significance that Luther could have for our immediate purposes is in its holding that the Guaranty Clause is not a repository of judicially manageable standards which a court could utilize independently in order to identify a State's lawful government. The Court has since refused to resort to the Guaranty Clause—which alone had been invoked for the purpose—as the source of a constitutional standard for invalidating state action. See, [e.g.,] Pacific States Tel. & Telegraph Co. v. Oregon, 223 U.S. 118 [1912] (claim that initiative and referendum negated republican government held nonjusticiable).

[We] come, finally, to the ultimate inquiry whether our precedents as to what constitutes a nonjusticiable "political question" bring the case before us under the umbrella of that doctrine. A natural beginning is to note whether any of the common characteristics which we have been able to identify and label descriptively are present. We find none: The question here is the consistency of state action with the Federal Constitution. We have no question decided, or to be decided, by a political branch of government coequal with this Court. Nor do we risk embarrassment of our government abroad, or grave disturbance at home, if we take issue with Tennessee as to the constitutionality of her action here challenged. Nor need the appellants, in order to succeed in this action, ask the Court to enter upon policy determinations for which judicially manageable standards are lacking. Judicial standards under the Equal Protection Clause are well developed and familiar, and it has been open to courts since the enactment of the Fourteenth Amendment to determine, if on the particular facts they must, that a discrimination reflects no policy, but simply arbitrary and capricious action. This case does, in one sense, involve the allocation of political power within a State, and the appellants might conceivably have added a claim under the Guaranty Clause. Of course, as we have seen, any reliance on that clause would be futile. But because any reliance on the Guaranty Clause could not have succeeded it does not follow that appellants may not be heard on the equal protection claim which in fact they tender. True, it must be clear that the Fourteenth Amendment claim is not so enmeshed with those political question elements which render Guaranty Clause claims nonjusticiable as actually to present a political question itself. But we have found that not to be the case [here].

Reversed and remanded.

Justice FRANKFURTER, whom Justice HARLAN joins, [dissenting].

[From] its earliest opinions this Court has consistently recognized a class of controversies which do not lend themselves to judicial standards and judicial remedies. To classify the various instances as "political questions" is rather a form of stating this conclusion than revealing of analysis. Some of the cases so labeled have no relevance here. But from others emerge unifying considerations that are compelling.

1. The cases concerning war or foreign affairs, for example, are usually explained by the necessity of the country's speaking with one voice in such matters. While this concern alone undoubtedly accounts for many of the decisions, others do not fit the pattern. It would hardly embarrass the conduct of war were this Court to determine, in connection with private transactions between litigants, the date upon which war is to be deemed terminated. But the Court has refused to do so. [A] controlling factor in such cases is that, decision respecting these kinds of complex matters of policy being traditionally committed not to courts but to the political agencies of government for determination by criteria of political expediency, there exists no standard ascertainable by settled judicial experience or process by reference to which a political decision affecting the question at issue between the parties can be [judged].

2. The Court has been particularly unwilling to intervene in matters concerning the structure and organization of the political institutions of the States. The abstention from judicial entry into such areas has been greater even than that which marks the Court's ordinary approach to issues of state power challenged under broad federal guarantees. [Where], however, state law has made particular federal questions determinative of relations within the structure of state government, not in challenge of it, the Court has resolved such narrow, legally defined questions in proper proceedings. In such instances there is no conflict between state policy and the exercise of federal judicial [power].

3. The cases involving Negro disfranchisement are no exception to the principle of avoiding federal judicial intervention into matters of state government in the absence of an explicit and clear constitutional imperative. For here the controlling command of Supreme Law is plain and unequivocal. An end of discrimination against the Negro was the compelling motive of the Civil War [Amendments].

4. The Court has refused to exercise its jurisdiction to pass on "abstract questions of political power, of sovereignty, of government." The "political question" doctrine, in this aspect, reflects the policies underlying the requirement of "standing": that the litigant who would challenge official action must claim infringement of an interest particular and personal to himself, as distinguished from a cause of dissatisfaction with the general frame and functioning of government—a complaint that the political institutions are awry. What renders cases of this kind non-justiciable is not necessarily the nature of the parties to them, for the Court has resolved other issues between similar parties; nor is it the nature of the legal question involved, for the same type of question has been adjudicated when presented in other forms of controversy. The crux of the matter is that courts are not fit instruments of decision where what is essentially at stake is the composition of those large contests of policy tradition-

ally fought out in non-judicial forums, by which governments and the actions of governments are made and [unmade].

5. The influence of these converging considerations—the caution not to undertake decision where standards meet for judicial judgment are lacking, the reluctance to interfere with matters of state government in the absence of an unquestionable and effectively enforceable mandate, the unwillingness to make courts arbiters of the broad issues of political organization historically committed to other institutions and for whose adjustment the judicial process is ill-adapted—has been decisive of the settled line of cases, reaching back more than a century, which holds that Art. IV, § 4, of the Constitution, guaranteeing to the States "a Republican Form of Government," is not enforceable through the [courts].

The present case involves all of the elements that have made the Guarantee Clause cases non-justiciable. It is, in effect, a Guarantee Clause claim masquerading under a different label. But it cannot make the case more fit for judicial action that appellants invoke the Fourteenth Amendment rather than Art. IV, § 4, where, in fact, the gist of their complaint is the same—unless it can be found that the Fourteenth Amendment speaks with greater particularity to their situation. We have been admonished to avoid "the tyranny of labels." Art. IV, § 4, is not committed by express constitutional terms to Congress. It is the nature of the controversies arising under it, nothing else, which has made it judicially unenforceable. [W]here judicial competence is wanting, it cannot be created by invoking one clause of the Constitution rather than another.

What, then, is this question of legislative apportionment? Appellants invoke the right to vote and to have their votes counted. But they are permitted to vote and their votes are counted. [Their] complaint is simply that the representatives are not sufficiently numerous or powerful—in short, that Tennessee has adopted a basis of representation with which they are dissatisfied. Talk of "debasement" or "dilution" is circular talk. One cannot speak of "debasement" or "dilution" of the value of a vote until there is first defined a standard of reference as to what a vote should be worth. What is actually asked of the Court in this case is to choose among competing bases of representation—ultimately, really, among competing theories of political philosophy—in order to establish an appropriate frame of government for the State of Tennessee and thereby for all the States of the Union.

Once the electoral apportionment process is recognized for what it is—the product of legislative give-and-take and of compromise among policies that often conflict—the relevant constitutional principles at once put these appellants out of the federal courts. [Manifestly], the Equal Protection Clause supplies no clearer guide for judicial examination of apportionment methods than would the Guarantee Clause itself. Apportionment, by its character, is a subject of extraordinary complexity, involving—even after the fundamental theoretical issues concerning what is to be represented in a representative legislature have been fought out or compromised—considerations of geography, demography, electoral convenience, economic and social cohesions or divergences among particular local groups, communications, the practical effects of political institutions, ancient [traditions], respect for proven [incumbents], mathematical mechanics, [and] a host of others. [T]hese are not factors that lend themselves to evaluations of a nature that are the staple of judicial determinations or for which judges are equipped to adjudicate by legal training or experience or native wit. And this is the more so true because in every strand of this complicated, intricate web of values meet the contending forces of partisan politics. [Apportionment] battles are overwhelmingly party or intraparty contests. It will add a virulent source of friction and tension in federal-state relations to embroil the federal judiciary in them.

[Justices DOUGLAS, CLARK, and STEWART each submitted separate concurring opinions, omitted here. A separate dissent by Justice HARLAN is also omitted.]

———

Some efforts to invoke the political question doctrine since Baker v. Carr. After Baker suggested a relatively narrow range for the political question concept, several additional efforts were made to invoke the doctrine to support a claim of nonjusticiability. Most, but not all, failed. Consider the following cases: POWELL v. McCORMACK, 395 U.S. 486 (1969), was a challenge to the refusal of the House of Representatives in 1967 to seat Representative Adam Clayton Powell, Jr., based upon House committee's finding that he had "wrongfully diverted House funds for the use of others and himself" and had made "false reports on expenditures of foreign currency" to a committee of the House. Powell argued that he had met all the formal requirements of Art. I, § 2, cl. 2 [i.e., age, citizenship, and residence]. McCormack, the Speaker of the House, argued in response that Art. I, § 5, cl. 1 (stating that "each House shall be the Judge of [the] Qualifications of its own Members") constituted a textual commitment of the issue to another branch and that the controversy was therefore nonjusticiable. McCormack also claimed that judicial resolution of the issue would yield a "potentially embarrassing confrontation between coordinate branches." The Court found the controversy justiciable. Chief Justice WARREN's majority opinion concluded that Art. I, § 5, was "at most a 'textually demonstrable commitment' to Congress to judge only the qualifications expressly set forth in the Constitution." Therefore, this strand of the political question doctrine did not bar adjudication of Powell's claim. Nor could the Court find "other considerations" to justify a finding of nonjusticiability. In rejecting McCormack's "potentially embarrassing confrontation between coordinate branches" argument, the Court stated: "Our system of government requires that federal courts on occasion interpret the Constitution in a manner at variance with the construction given the document by another branch. The alleged conflict that such an adjudication may cause cannot justify the courts' avoiding their constitutional [responsibility]. Nor are any other formulations of a political question 'inextricable from the case at bar.' [Powell seeks] a determination that the House was without power to exclude [him], [which] requires an interpretation of the Constitution—a determination for which clearly there are 'judicially manageable standards.' Finally, judicial resolution of [Powell's] claim will not result in 'multifarious pronouncements by various departments on one question.' For, as we noted in [Baker], it is the responsibility of this Court to act as the ultimate interpreter of the Constitution. Marbury v. Madison." (Note also Davis v. Bandemer, 478 U.S. 109 (1986) (p. __ below), where the majority, relying in part on Baker, held that the justiciability of an equal protection challenge to political gerrymandering was not barred by the political question doctrine.)

Contrast with Powell v. McCormack the ruling in GOLDWATER v. CARTER, 444 U.S. 996 (1979), where the Court (without hearing argument) set aside lower court decisions on the merits of the question whether the President has authority to terminate a treaty without the participation of the Senate. Justice REHNQUIST's plurality opinion, joined by Chief Justice Burger and Justices Stewart and Stevens, insisted that the case presented a nonjusticiable political question. He claimed the issue was political because "it involves the authority of the President and the conduct of our country's foreign relations,'' arguing that the controversy ''should be left for resolution by the Executive and Legislative Branches'' since the Constitution ''is silent as to [the Senate's] participation in the abrogation of a Treaty.'' Claiming that the question ''must surely be controlled by political standards,'' he noted that this was ''a dispute between coequal branches of our government, each of which has resources available to protect and assert its interests, resources not available to private litigants outside the judicial forum.'' Justice POWELL concurred in the judgment solely because he thought the dispute was not ripe for decision. He strongly disagreed with Justice Rehnquist's nonjusticiability view, however, insisting that the issue was not political under the Baker v. Carr criteria. There was no ''textually demonstrable constitutional commitment'' of the treaty termination power to the President, nor was there any ''lack of judicially discoverable and manageable standards: 'Resolution of the question may not be easy, but it only requires us to apply normal principles of [constitutional] interpretation. [The case] involves neither review of the President's activities as Commander-in-Chief nor impermissible interference in the field of foreign affairs.' '' Justice Powell acknowledged that the political question doctrine does rest in part on ''prudential concerns,'' but those inhibitions were not appropriate here: ''Interpretation of the Constitution does not imply a lack of respect for a coordinate [branch]. The spectre of [the] Government brought to a halt because of the mutual intransigences of the President and the Congress would require this Court to provide a resolution pursuant to our duty 'to say what the law is.' [Marbury.]'' Only Justice BRENNAN, the author of Baker v. Carr, dissented, insisting that Justice Rehnquist's approach ''profoundly misrepresents the political-question principle as it applies to matters of foreign relations.'' He would have found the case justiciable, but on the merits ruled that ''the Constitution commits to the President alone the power to recognize, and withdraw recognition from, foreign regimes.''

Note the recurrent reliance by some of the Justices on the view that Marbury v. Madison establishes the Court as ''the ultimate interpreter of the Constitution.'' Repeatedly, beginning with Baker v. Carr, that view was invoked to reject political question claims. See, in addition to Powell and Goldwater above, the Watergate Tapes case, United States v. [Richard] Nixon, 418 U.S. 683 (1974), sustaining the issuance of a subpoena to the President. Note Gunther's comment, in ''Judicial Hegemony and Legislative Autonomy: The Nixon Case and the Impeachment Process,'' 22 UCLA L.Rev. 30 (1974), that ''there is nothing in Marbury v. Madison that precludes a constitutional interpretation which gives final authority to another branch. I do not believe that the Court intended to announce that every constitutional issue requires final adjudication on the merits by the judiciary. [For example,] I would think (and hope) that a [Senate] conviction on impeachment would be found unreviewable in the courts.'' The issue of the reviewability of impeachment proceedings reached the Court in 1993, in Nixon v. United States, which follows. Consider especially what added light that ruling throws on the extent to which the political-question doctrine rests on constitutional interpretation and to what extent it reflects more discretionary, prudential concerns.

Nixon v. United States

506 U.S. 224, 113 S.Ct. 732, 122 L.Ed.2d 1 (1993).

Chief Justice REHNQUIST delivered the opinion of the Court.

Petitioner Walter L. Nixon, Jr., asks this court to decide whether Senate Rule XI, which allows a committee of Senators to hear evidence against an individual who has been impeached and to report that evidence to the full Senate, violates the Impeachment Trial Clause, Art. I, § 3, cl. 6. That Clause provides that the "Senate shall have the sole Power to try all Impeachments." But before we reach the merits of such a claim, we must decide whether it is "justiciable," that is, whether it is a claim that may be resolved by the courts. We conclude that it is not.

Nixon, a former Chief Judge of the United States District Court for the Southern District of Mississippi, was convicted by a jury of two counts of making false statements before a federal grand jury and sentenced to prison. The grand jury investigation stemmed from reports that Nixon had accepted a gratuity from a Mississippi businessman in exchange for asking a local district attorney to halt the prosecution of the businessman's son. [In May 1989,] the House of Representatives adopted three articles of impeachment for high crimes and misdemeanors. [After] the House presented the articles to the Senate, the Senate voted to invoke its own Impeachment Rule XI, under which the presiding officer appoints a committee of Senators to "receive evidence and take testimony." The Senate committee held four days of hearings. [The] committee presented the full Senate with a complete transcript of the proceeding and a report stating the uncontested facts and summarizing the evidence on the contested facts. Nixon and the House impeachment managers submitted extensive final briefs to the full Senate and delivered arguments from the Senate floor during the three hours set aside for oral argument in front of that body. Nixon himself gave a personal appeal, and several Senators posed questions directly to both parties. The Senate voted by more than the constitutionally required two-thirds majority to convict Nixon on the first two articles. The presiding officer then entered judgment removing Nixon from his office. [Nixon] thereafter commenced the present suit, arguing that Senate Rule XI violates the constitutional grant of authority to the Senate to "try" all impeachments because it prohibits the whole Senate from taking part in the evidentiary hearings. [The] District Court held that his claim was nonjusticiable, and the [Court of Appeals] agreed.

A controversy is nonjusticiable—i.e., involves a political question—where there is "a textually demonstrable constitutional commitment of the issue to a coordinate political department, or a lack of judicially discoverable and manageable standards for resolving it...." [Baker v. Carr.] But the courts must, in the first instance, interpret the text in question and determine whether and to what extent the issue is textually committed. As the discussion that follows makes clear, the concept of a textual commitment to a coordinate political department is not completely separate from the concept of a lack of judicially discoverable and manageable standards for resolving it; the lack of judicially manageable standards may strengthen the conclusion that there is a textually demonstrable commitment to a coordinate branch.

In this case, we must examine Art. I, § 3, cl. 6, to determine the scope of authority conferred upon the Senate by the Framers regarding impeachment. It provides: "The Senate shall have the sole Power to try all Impeachments. When sitting for that Purpose, they shall be on Oath or Affirmation. When the President of the United States is tried, the Chief Justice shall preside: And no Person shall be convicted without the Concurrence of two thirds of the Members present." Petitioner argues that the word "try" in the first sentence imposes by implication [a] requirement that the proceedings must be in the nature of a judicial trial. From there petitioner goes on to argue that this limitation precludes the Senate from delegating to a select committee the task of hearing the testimony of witnesses. " '[Try]' means more than simply 'vote on' or 'review' or 'judge.' In 1787 and today, trying a case means hearing the evidence, not scanning a cold record." Petitioner concludes from this that courts may review whether or not the Senate "tried" him before convicting him.

There are several difficulties with this position which lead us ultimately to reject it. The word "try," both in 1787 and later, has considerably broader meanings than those to which petitioner would limit it. [Based] on the variety of definitions, [we] cannot say that the Framers used the word "try" as an implied limitation on the method by which the Senate might proceed in trying impeachments. The conclusion that the use of the word "try" in the first sentence [lacks] sufficient precision to afford any judicially manageable standard of review of the Senate's actions is fortified by the existence of the three very specific requirements that the Constitution does impose on the Senate when trying impeachments: the members must be under oath, a two-thirds vote is required to convict, and the Chief Justice presides when the President is tried. These limitations are quite precise, and their nature suggests that the Framers did not intend to impose additional limitations on the form of the Senate proceedings by the use of the word "try" in the first sentence.

Petitioner devotes only two pages in his brief to negating the significance of the word "sole" in the first sentence of Clause 6. [T]hat sentence provides that "the Senate shall have the sole Power to try all Impeachments." We think that the word "sole" is of considerable significance. Indeed, the word "sole" appears only one other time in the Constitution—with respect to the House of Representatives' "sole Power of Impeachment." Art. I, § 2, cl. 5. The common sense meaning of the word "sole" is that the Senate alone shall have authority to determine whether an individual should be acquitted or convicted. The dictionary definition bears this out. [Nixon] argues that even if significance be attributed to the word "sole," [the] authority granted is to the Senate, and this means that "the Senate—not the courts, not a lay jury, not a Senate Committee—shall try impeachments." It would be possible to read [the] Clause this way, but it is not a natural reading. Petitioner's interpretation would bring into judicial purview not merely the sort of claim made by petitioner, but other similar claims based on the conclusion that the word "Senate" has imposed by implication limitations on procedures which the Senate might adopt. Such limitations would be inconsistent with the construction of the Clause as a whole, which, as we have noted, sets out three express limitations in separate sentences.

The history and contemporary understanding of the impeachment provisions support our reading of the constitutional language. The parties do not offer evidence of a single word in the history of the Constitutional Convention or in contemporary commentary that even alludes to the possibility of judicial review in the context of the impeachment powers. This silence is quite meaningful in light of the several explicit references to the availability of judicial review as a check on the Legislature's power with respect to bills of attainder, ex post facto laws, and statutes. The Framers labored over the question of where the impeachment power should lie. Significantly, in at least two considered scenarios the power was placed with the Federal Judiciary. Indeed, Madison and the Committee of Detail proposed that the Supreme Court should have the power to determine impeachments. Despite these proposals, the Convention ultimately decided that the Senate would have "the sole Power to Try all Impeachments." According to [Hamilton], the Senate was the "most fit depositary of this important trust" because its members are representatives of the people. See Federalist No. 65.

[There] are two additional reasons why the Judiciary, and the Supreme Court in particular, were not chosen to have any role in impeachments. First, the Framers recognized that most likely there would be two sets of proceedings for individuals who commit impeachable offenses—the impeachment trial and a separate criminal trial. In fact, the Constitution explicitly provides for two separate proceedings. See Art. I, 3, cl. 7. The Framers deliberately separated the two forums to avoid raising the specter of bias and to ensure independent judgments. [Certainly] judicial review of the Senate's "trial" would introduce the same risk of bias as would participation in the trial itself. Second, judicial review would be inconsistent with the Framers' insistence that our system be one of checks and balances. In our constitutional system, impeachment was designed to be the only check on the Judicial Branch by the Legislature. [Judicial] involvement in impeachment proceedings, even if only for purposes of judicial review, is counterintuitive because it would eviscerate the "important constitutional check" placed on the Judiciary by the Framers. Nixon's argument would place final reviewing authority with respect to impeachments in the hands of the same body that the impeachment process is meant to regulate. [Nevertheless,] Nixon argues that judicial review is necessary in order to place a check on the Legislature. Nixon fears that if the Senate is given unreviewable authority to interpret the Impeachment Trial Clause, there is a grave risk that the Senate will usurp judicial power. The Framers anticipated this objection and created two constitutional safeguards to keep the Senate in check. The first safeguard is that the whole of the impeachment power is divided between the two legislative bodies, with the House given the right to accuse and the Senate given the right to judge. [The] second safeguard is the two-thirds supermajority vote requirement.

[In] addition to the textual commitment argument, we are persuaded that the lack of finality and the difficulty of fashioning relief counsel against justiciability. [Opening] the door of judicial review to the procedures used by the Senate in trying impeachments would "expose the political life of the country to months, or perhaps years, of chaos." This lack of finality would manifest itself most dramatically if the President were impeached. The legitimacy of any successor, and hence his effectiveness, would be impaired severely, not merely while the judicial process was running its course, but during any retrial that a differently constituted Senate might conduct if its first judgment of conviction were invalidated. Equally uncertain is the question of what relief a court may give other than simply setting aside the judgment of conviction. Could it order the reinstatement of a convicted federal judge, or order Congress to create an additional judgeship if the seat had been filled in the interim?

Petitioner finally contends that a holding of nonjusticiability cannot be reconciled with [Powell]. [Our] conclusion in Powell was based on the fixed meaning of "qualifications" set forth in Art. I, § 2. [The] decision as to whether a member satisfied these qualifications was placed with the House, but the decision as to what these qualifications consisted of was not. In the case before us, there is no separate provision of the Constitution which could be defeated by allowing the Senate final authority to determine the meaning of the word "try" in the Impeachment Trial Clause. We agree with Nixon that courts possess power to review either legislative or executive action that transgresses identifiable textual limits. [But] we conclude [that] the word "try" in the Impeachment Clause does not provide an identifiable textual limit on the authority which is committed to the Senate.

[Affirmed.]

Justice STEVENS, concurring.

For me, the debate about the strength of the inferences to be drawn from the use of the words "sole" and "try" is far less significant than the central fact that the Framers decided to assign the impeachment power to the Legislative Branch. The disposition of the impeachment of Samuel Chase in 1805 demonstrated that the Senate is fully conscious of the profound importance of that assignment, and nothing in the subsequent history of the Senate's exercise of this extraordinary power suggests otherwise. See Beveridge, The Life of John Marshall (1919); W. Rehnquist, Grand Inquests (1992). Respect for a coordinate Branch of the Government forecloses any assumption that improbable hypotheticals like those mentioned by Justice White and Justice Souter will ever occur. Accordingly, the wise policy of judicial restraint, coupled with the potential anomalies associated with a contrary view, provide a sufficient justification for my agreement with the views of the Chief Justice.

Justice WHITE, with whom Justice BLACKMUN joins, concurring in the judgment.

Petitioner contends that the method by which the Senate convicted him [violates] the Constitution. [The] Court is of the view that the Constitution forbids us even to consider his contention. I find no such prohibition and would therefore reach the merits of the claim. I concur in the judgment because the Senate fulfilled its constitutional obligation to "try" petitioner.

I.   [A]s a practical matter, it will likely make little difference whether the Court's or my view controls this case. This is so because the Senate has very wide discretion in specifying impeachment trial procedures and because it is extremely unlikely that the Senate would abuse its discretion and insist on a procedure that could not be deemed a trial by reasonable judges. Even taking a wholly practical approach, I would prefer not to announce an unreviewable discretion in the Senate to ignore completely the constitutional direction to "try" impeachment cases. When asked at oral argument whether that direction would be satisfied if, after a House vote to impeach, the Senate, without any procedure whatsoever, unanimously found the accused guilty of being "a bad guy," counsel for the United States answered that the Government's theory "leads me to answer that question yes." Especially in light of this advice from the Solicitor General, I would not issue an invitation to the Senate to find an excuse, in the name of other pressing business, to be dismissive of its critical role in the impeachment process. Practicalities aside, however, since the meaning of a constitutional provision is at issue, my disagreement with the Court should be stated.

II.   [Of] course the issue in the political question doctrine is not whether the Constitutional text commits exclusive responsibility for a particular governmental function to one of the political branches. There are numerous instances of this sort of textual commitment, e. g., Art. I, § 8, and it is not thought that disputes implicating these provisions are nonjusticiable. Rather, the issue is whether the Constitution has given one of the political branches final responsibility for interpreting the scope and nature of such a power.

The majority finds a clear textual commitment in the Constitution's use of the word "sole" in the phrase "the Senate shall have the sole Power to try all impeachments." [In] disagreeing with the Court, I note that the Solicitor General stated at oral argument that "we don't rest our submission on sole power to try." The Government was well advised in this respect. The significance of the Constitution's use of the term "sole" lies not in the infrequency with which the term appears, but in the fact that it appears exactly twice, in parallel provisions concerning impeachment. That the word "sole" is found only in the House and Senate Impeachment Clauses demonstrates that its purpose is to emphasize the distinct role of each in the impeachment process. [While] the majority is thus right to interpret the term "sole" to indicate that the Senate ought to " 'function independently and without assistance or interference,' " it wrongly identifies the judiciary, rather than the House, as the source of potential interference with which the Framers were concerned when they employed the term "sole." [The] majority's review of the historical record [explains] why the power to try impeachments properly resides with the Senate. It does not explain, however, the sweeping statement that the judiciary was "not chosen to have any role in impeachments." Not a single word in the historical materials cited by the majority addresses judicial review of the Impeachment Trial Clause. And a glance at the arguments surrounding the Impeachment Clauses negates the majority's attempt to infer nonjusticiability from the Framers' arguments in support of the Senate's power to try impeachments.

[The] historical evidence reveals above all else that the Framers were deeply concerned about placing in any branch the "awful discretion, which a court of impeachments must necessarily have." Viewed against this history, the discord between the majority's position and the basic principles of checks and balances underlying the Constitution's separation of powers is clear. In essence, the majority suggests that the Framers conferred upon Congress a potential tool of legislative dominance yet at the same time rendered Congress' exercise of that power one of the very few areas of legislative authority immune from any judicial review. While the majority rejects petitioner's justiciability argument as espousing a view "inconsistent with the Framers' insistence that our system be one of checks and balances," it is the Court's finding of nonjusticiability that truly upsets the Framers' careful design. In a truly balanced system, impeachments tried by the Senate would serve as a means of controlling the largely unaccountable judiciary, even as judicial review would ensure that the Senate adhered to a minimal set of procedural standards in conducting impeachment trials.

The majority concludes that the term ["try"] provides no "identifiable textual limit." Yet [the] term "try" is hardly so elusive as the majority would have it. Were the Senate, for example, to adopt the practice of automatically entering a judgment of conviction whenever articles of impeachment were delivered from the House, it is quite clear that the Senate will have failed to "try" impeachments. Indeed in this respect, "try" presents no greater, and perhaps fewer, interpretive difficulties than some other constitutional standards that have been found amenable to familiar techniques of judicial construction, including, for example, "Commerce [among] the several States" and "due process of law."[1]

III. The majority's conclusion that "try" is incapable of meaningful judicial construction is not without irony. One might think that if any class of

1. The majority's in terrorem argument against justiciability—that judicial review of impeachments might cause national disruption and that the courts would be unable to fashion effective relief—merits only brief attention. In the typical instance, court review of impeachments would no more render the political system dysfunctional than has this litigation. [The] relief granted for unconstitutional impeachment trials would presumably be similar to the relief granted to other unfairly tried public employee-litigants. Finally, as applied to the special case of the President, the majority's argument merely points out that, were the Senate to convict the President without any kind of a trial, a constitutional crisis might well result. It hardly follows that the Court ought to refrain from upholding the Constitution in all impeachment cases. Nor does it follow that, in cases of Presidential impeachment, the Justices ought to abandon their Constitutional responsibilities because the Senate has precipitated a crisis. [Footnote by Justice White.]

concepts would fall within the definitional abilities of the judiciary, it would be that class having to do with procedural [justice].

Justice SOUTER, concurring in the judgment.

I agree with the Court that this case presents a nonjusticiable political question. Because my analysis differs somewhat from the Court's, however, I concur in its judgment by this separate opinion. As we cautioned in Baker v. Carr, "the 'political question' label" tends "to obscure the need for case-by-case inquiry." The need for such close examination is nevertheless clear from our precedents, which demonstrate that the functional nature of the political question doctrine requires analysis of "the precise facts and posture of the particular case," [precluding] "resolution by any semantic cataloguing." [Whatever] considerations feature most prominently in a particular case, the political question doctrine is "essentially a function of the separation of powers," existing to restrain courts "from inappropriate interference in the business of the other branches of Government," and deriving in large part from prudential concerns about the respect we owe the political departments. Not all interference is inappropriate or disrespectful, however, and application of the doctrine ultimately turns, as Learned Hand put it, on "how importunately the occasion demands an answer." L. Hand, The Bill of Rights (1958). This occasion does not demand an answer. [It] seems fair to conclude that the [Impeachment Trial] Clause contemplates that the Senate may determine, within broad boundaries, such subsidiary issues as the procedures for receipt and consideration of evidence necessary to satisfy its duty to "try" impeachments. Other significant considerations confirm a conclusion that this case presents a nonjusticiable political question. [As] the Court observes, judicial review of an impeachment trial would under the best of circumstances entail significant disruption of government.

One can, nevertheless, envision different and unusual circumstances that might justify a more searching review of impeachment proceedings. If the Senate were to act in a manner seriously threatening the integrity of its results, convicting, say, upon a coin-toss, or upon a summary determination that an officer of the United States was simply " 'a bad guy,' " judicial interference might well be appropriate. In such circumstances, the Senate's action might be so far beyond the scope of its constitutional authority, and the consequent impact on the Republic so great, as to merit a judicial response despite the prudential concerns that would ordinarily counsel [silence].

SECTION 3. SUPREME COURT AUTHORITY TO REVIEW STATE COURT JUDGMENTS

MARTIN v. HUNTER'S LESSEE, 1 Wheat. (14 U.S.) 304 (1816), ranks second only to Marbury v. Madison among the Marshall era decisions articulating the contours of federal judicial authority. The Martin decision defended the legitimacy of Supreme Court review of state court judgments resting on interpretations of federal law and rejected the highest Virginia court's challenge to the constitutionality of § 25 of the Judiciary Act of 1789. Sec. 25 essentially provided for Supreme Court review of final decisions of the highest state courts *rejecting* claims based on federal law—including federal constitutional law. (The full text of § 25 is printed—together with its broader modern counterpart, 28 U.S.C. § 1257—at p. 67 below.)

In many respects, the textual and historical support for the Supreme Court authority asserted in Martin is stronger than can be mustered for Marbury v. Madison. The Court had sporadically exercised § 25 authority for years prior to the Virginia challenge in Martin, and some support for the authority can be drawn from the language of Articles III and VI of the Constitution. Moreover, an expectation of Supreme Court review of state court judgments runs through the Constitutional Convention debates. At the Convention, the question of establishing lower, "inferior" federal courts provoked a major controversy. The relevant provisions of Art. III reflect a compromise between opposing views: one insisting on the mandatory creation of lower federal courts; the other leaving initial application of federal law entirely to the state courts. The compromise left the creation and jurisdiction of lower federal courts to the discretion of Congress. This compromise, as well as the supremacy clause of Art. VI, contemplated that federal questions could initially arise in state as well as federal courts and assumed that Supreme Court review would assure any necessary uniformity and federal supremacy.

Despite this strong support for the Supreme Court decision in Martin, some attention to the Martin controversy is warranted, because of contemporary as well as historical concerns. The excerpts below delineate the core of the contending positions of the Virginia judges and of Justice Story of the Supreme Court. They throw light on the question of what the fighting in the early 19th century was all about: for example, did the Virginians advocate a hopelessly unworkable, anarchical scheme of allocation of authority among state and federal courts? Beyond that, the Martin materials also introduce themes of continuing importance: the existence of state as well as federal courts as interpreters of federal law; the obligation as well as authority of state courts to heed the "supreme" law; the complex interrelations between state and federal judiciaries in a system which apportions the function of interpreting federal (including constitutional) law among the judicial structures of separate, state and federal, governments.

1. *The background of the Martin litigation.* The immediate provocation for the Supreme Court's decision in Martin was the refusal by the Virginia Court of Appeals to obey the Supreme Court mandate in Fairfax's Devisee v. Hunter's Lessee, 7 Cranch (11 U.S.) 603 (1813). That Fairfax ruling in turn was the culmination of land litigation that had been instituted many years earlier, in 1791. The dispute concerned the vast land holdings of Lord Fairfax. Virginia claimed that it had properly seized the Fairfax properties prior to 1783 as lands belonging to British loyalists during the Revolution. Virginia parceled out some of the land to its own citizens; and Hunter claimed the land at issue under such a grant from the State of Virginia. Martin claimed title under a devise from Fairfax: he insisted that the Fairfax lands were protected against seizure because of the Peace Treaty of 1783 and the Jay Treaty of 1794. In short, Hunter's claim rested on a series of Virginia statutes relating to the forfeiture to the State of lands owned by British subjects; Martin's position, by contrast, was that title to the land acquired under the Fairfax will in 1781 had not vested in Virginia prior to 1783, and that it was thereafter protected by the treaty provisions.

Although Hunter had instituted his action to establish his right to the land as early as 1791, the litigation was in abeyance for almost two decades. In the interim, there were complicated negotiations—negotiations which involved John Marshall, for the future Chief Justice and his brother James had contracted for the purchase of a large part of the Fairfax estate from the Fairfax heirs. (Because of this involvement, John Marshall did not participate in the 1813 and 1816 cases. The opinions were written by Justice Joseph Story, a Jeffersonian Republican from Massachusetts.) It was not until 1810 that the Virginia Court of Appeals first ruled on the case—and decided for Hunter and the effectiveness of Virginia's seizure of the Fairfax lands. It was that decision that the Supreme Court reversed in 1813, siding with Martin. Pursuant to that 1813 decision, the Supreme Court mandate, in strong language, "instructed" and "commanded" the Virginia judges to enter judgment for Martin.

The issue of compliance with that mandate stirred considerable controversy in Virginia. It was a somewhat surprising time for states' rights agitation to reemerge in Virginia. A divided nation was at war with England; James Madison, the President from Virginia, was trying to unite the nation against vociferous states' rights criticisms from anti-war forces centered in New England; and yet the Virginia judges, with their ruling on § 25, initiated new waves of states' rights attacks that were to engulf the Marshall Court for years. The Virginia court's decision was not announced until 1815, more than a year after argument; apparently, the Virginia judges delayed publication in order to avoid encouraging the secessionist feelings mounting in New England near the close of the War of 1812.

2. *The contending positions in Martin.* The Virginia judges concluded that "the appellate power of the Supreme Court of the United States does not extend to this court, under a sound construction of the constitution of the United States, 'and that § 25 was therefore unconstitutional.'" This conclusion rested on several premises. The Virginia judges claimed that the Constitution did not authorize federal courts to act directly upon, and reverse, state court rulings. "It must have been foreseen," they argued, "that controversies would sometimes arise, [yet] the constitution has provided no umpire, has erected no tribunal by which they shall be settled. The omission proceeded, probably, from the belief that such a tribunal would produce evils greater than those of the occasional collisions which it would be designed to remedy." Moreover, they insisted that other methods (such as removal of cases to federal courts before final judgments in state courts) were available to minimize the risk of conflicts and to facilitate uniformity in interpretation of federal law. Note that the Virginia judges did *not* deny the supremacy of valid federal law under Art. VI of the Constitution. Nor did the Virginia judges deny the legitimacy of a federal judicial enforcement machinery. Indeed, their response to nationalistic needs was to point to the congressional authority under Art. III to expand the number and jurisdiction of the lower federal courts. In short, the Virginia position, rather than totally flouting federal supremacy or advocating direct resistance to federal court orders, was a more moderate assertion of limited state judicial autonomy: to the extent judiciary legislation left federal questions to arise and make their way through the state courts, final adjudication had to be by that judicial system; if that channeling of cases proved unsatisfactory, the federal government's recourse was to route federal issues into lower federal courts at an earlier point. In this view, only Supreme Court review of final state court decisions constituted an impermissible trampling upon state judicial autonomy.

The Virginia court's challenge to § 25 stirred Justice STORY into an elaborate response. At the outset of his detailed examination of Art. III, Story inserted several paragraphs suggesting that its provisions were "mandatory upon the legislature." But he soon abandoned that theme and rested most of his analysis on the assumption that Art. III left considerable discretion to Congress with respect to the allocation of jurisdiction to federal courts. He contended: "The appellate power is not limited by the terms of the third article [of the Constitution] to any particular courts. It is the *case,* [and] not the *court,* that gives the jurisdiction. If the judicial power extends to the case, it will be in vain to search in the letter of the constitution for any qualification as to the tribunal where it depends. [It] has been argued that such an appellate jurisdiction over state courts is inconsistent with the genius of our governments, and the spirit of the constitution. That the latter was never designed to act upon state sovereignties, but only upon the people, and that if the power exists, it will materially impair the sovereignty of the states, and the independence of their courts. We cannot yield to the force of this reasoning; it assumes principles which we cannot admit, and draws conclusions to which we do not yield our assent. It is a mistake [to believe] that the constitution was not designed to operate upon states, in their corporate capacities. It is crowded with provisions which restrain or annul the sovereignty of the states in some of the highest branches of their prerogatives."

Justice Story continued: "[Nor] can [this] be deemed to impair the independence of state judges. It is assuming the very ground in controversy to assert that they possess an absolute independence of the United States. In respect to the powers granted to the United States, they are not independent; they are expressly bound to obedience, by the letter of the [constitution]. [The] argument urged from the possibility of the abuse of the revising power, is equally unsatisfactory. It is always a doubtful course, to argue against the use or existence of a power, from the possibility of its abuse. [From] the very nature of things, the absolute right of decision, in the last resort, must rest somewhere—wherever it may be vested, it is susceptible of abuse. [It] is further argued, that no great public mischief can result from a construction which shall limit the appellate power of the United States to cases in their own courts: first, because state judges are bound by an oath to support the constitution of the United States and must be presumed to be men of learning and integrity. [A]dmitting that the judges of the state courts are, and always will be, of as much learning, integrity and wisdom, [it] does not aid the argument. It is manifest that the constitution has proceeded upon a theory of its own, and given or withheld powers according to the judgment of the American people, by whom it was adopted. [The] constitution has presumed [that] state attachments, state prejudices, state jealousies, and state interests, might sometimes obstruct, or control, or be supposed to obstruct or control, the regular administration of justice. [This] is not all. A motive of another kind, perfectly compatible with the most sincere respect for state tribunals, might induce the grant of appellate power over their decisions. That motive is the importance, and even necessity of *uniformity* of decisions throughout the whole United States, upon all subjects within the purview of the constitution. Judges of equal learning and integrity, in different states, might differently interpret a statute, or a treaty of the United States, or even the constitution itself: if there were no revising authority to control these jarring and discordant judgments, and harmonize them into uniformity, the laws, the treaties and the constitution of the United States would be different in different states. [The] public mischiefs that would attend such a state of things would be truly [deplorable]."

3. *Cohens v. Virginia: Supreme Court review of state criminal cases.* The Martin dispute was only the beginning of several waves of states' rights attacks. Sec. 25 was a common, though by no means the only, target of these attacks. Most often, the hostility to § 25 manifested itself in efforts to obtain congressional repeal of the provision. But there was one important post-Martin occasion for the Supreme Court to address the issue again. It came in COHENS v. VIRGINIA, 6 Wheat. (19 U.S.) 264 (1821), where the Court sustained its

jurisdiction to review the validity of state laws in criminal proceedings. That case arose from the conviction of the Cohen brothers in a Norfolk court for selling District of Columbia lottery tickets in violation of Virginia laws. The Cohens claimed that, under the supremacy clause, they were immune from state laws in selling congressionally authorized lottery tickets. The Supreme Court ultimately decided against them on the merits, reading the congressional statute as conferring no such immunity. But the major issue was jurisdictional: did the Supreme Court have constitutional authority to review such state judgments? Virginia's counsel not only reiterated the arguments advanced in Martin, but raised new ones. They emphasized that here, unlike in Martin, the State was a named party in the case, and they argued especially that the grant of original jurisdiction to the Supreme Court of cases "in which a state shall be a party" precluded the exercise of appellate jurisdiction. The Cohens case at last gave Chief Justice MARSHALL the chance to have his say on the § 25 issue officially. Marshall's opinion reaffirmed and extended Story's defense of the constitutionality of § 25 and answered Virginia's new contentions by concluding "that the judicial [power] extends to all cases arising under the constitution or a law of the United States, whoever may be the parties." Marshall's opinion, no doubt reflecting the mounting anxieties about states' rights attacks, took a harsher view of the reliability of state judges than Story had expressed in Martin. For example, he commented: "In many States, the judges are dependent for office and for salary on the will of the legislature. [When] we observe the importance which [the Constitution] attaches to the independence of judges, we are the less inclined to suppose that it can have intended to leave these constitutional questions to tribunals where this independence may not exist." Marshall's doubts about the capacity of state judges to interpret and enforce federal law adequately have echoed through the years. See, e.g., Neuborne, "The Myth of Parity," 90 Harv.L.Rev. 1105 (1977), emphasizing that federal judges are "as insulated from majoritarian pressures as is functionally possible" but that state judges "generally are elected for a fixed term, rendering them vulnerable to majoritarian pressure when deciding constitutional cases."

4. *State challenges to Supreme Court authority—19th century variants and 20th century emulations.* A number of states other than Virginia challenged the right of the Supreme Court to review state court decisions in the years before the Civil War—often on grounds far broader than those advanced by Virginia in the Martin and Cohens cases. See generally Warren, "Legislative and Judicial Attacks on the Supreme Court of the United States—A History of the Twenty–Fifth Section of the Judiciary Act," 47 Am.L.Rev. 1, 161 (1913). The courts of seven states issued challenges. And in Congress, there were several attempts to repeal § 25—the first major one in 1821, immediately after Cohens; the most serious one in 1831. The critical significance of § 25 was appreciated, for example, by John C. Calhoun, long before he emerged as the chief public spokesman for nullification (the claimed power of a state to block— at least temporarily, until the Constitution could be amended—enforcement of "unconstitutional" federal laws within the state). Months before he privately drafted the South Carolina Exposition of 1828, Calhoun suggested that, if § 25 could be repealed, more drastic remedies (such as nullification and, years later, secession) would be unnecessary. See John C. Calhoun to Senator Littleton W. Tazewell of Virginia, August 25, 1827 (in the Calhoun Papers, The Library of Congress).

The position of Virginia in Martin and Cohens should be distinguished from the more extreme positions that denied the general authoritativeness— and occasionally the specific enforceability—of federal court decisions, on the ground of the states' right to "interpose" their own interpretations of the Constitution against federal action. These "interposition" statements ranged from the general protest of the Virginia and Kentucky Resolutions of 1798 to South Carolina's nullification in 1832 and the later secession effort. Though these more extreme contentions tended to share common premises (e.g., the compact theory of the Union) and common language (e.g., "null and void" declarations), they varied widely in operative consequences. In considering the pre-Civil War state contentions, it is important to read the broad assertions in light of the specific remedial, operative portions of the state resolutions. As with the presidential statements in the notes following Marbury v. Madison, it is useful to distinguish between statements (a) denying that constitutional interpretations are *exclusively* the function of the federal courts or that federal court interpretations bind the nation, and (b) asserting that specific federal court orders may be directly disobeyed. Compare, for example, Madison's 1800 Report on the Virginia Resolutions [denying that "the judicial authority is to be regarded as the sole expositor of the Constitution in the last resort," in the context of urging *congressional* repeal of the Alien and Sedition Laws], with direct state defiance of federal court authority [e.g., the South Carolina Nullification Ordinance of 1832, making punishable as contempt the taking of certain appeals to the Supreme Court].

For modern echoes of state "interposition" resolutions, reviving the pre-Civil War tradition, see, e.g., 1 Race Rel.L.Rep. 437–447 (1956) (1956 legislative resolutions of Alabama, Georgia, Mississippi, South Carolina, and Virginia, in the wake of Brown v. Board of Education). For Supreme Court replies, see Bush v. Orleans Parish School Board, 364 U.S. 500 (1960), where the Court, per curiam, denied motions for a stay of a three-judge District Court order enjoining the enforcement of Louisiana interposition laws directed at school desegregation. The Court quoted from the District Court decision: "The conclusion is clear that interposition is not a *constitutional* doctrine. If taken seriously, it is illegal defiance of constitutional authority." The Supreme Court added: "The main basis for challenging this ruling is that the State of Louisiana 'has interposed itself in the field of public education over which it has exclusive control.' This objection is without substance, as we held, upon full consideration, in Cooper v. Aaron." On the importance of Supreme Court review of cases challenging state laws, see Justice Holmes' well-known statement: "I do not think the United States would come to an end if we lost our power to declare an Act of Congress void. I do think the Union would be imperiled if we could not make that declaration as to the laws of the several States." Holmes, Collected Legal Papers (1920), 295.

———

MODERN COURT JURISDICTION AND PRACTICE

1. *Introduction.* What are the contemporary jurisdictional and procedural groundrules that govern the exercise of Supreme Court authority? How does the Court conduct its business? The purpose of this section is to give an overview of the main features and problems of the modern framework. Art. III of the Constitution provides the foundation. But on the few words of that Article has been built a complex superstructure, of congressional statutes and Supreme Court Rules and practices.

Art. III, § 1, for example, provides for "one supreme Court." But it is for Congress to set the size of the Court. The number of Justices has been set at nine since 1869. But earlier in the 19th century, the number fluctuated quite frequently: at the time of Marbury v. Madison, for example, it was six; and at the time of Martin v. Hunter's Lessee, it was seven. Most of the increases in the early years came because the number of federal judicial circuits grew with the expansion of the country, and sitting on circuit was a major part of a Supreme Court Justice's duties until well into the 19th century. But the congressional power over size is also a potential source of political checks on the Court. President Franklin D. Roosevelt's proposed Court-curbing weapon in 1937 was to expand the size of the Court. (See the materials on the Court-packing Plan, p. 183 below.) Even such relatively routine legislation as that setting the time at which the Court shall convene can be made to serve political ends: recall the Jeffersonian legislation which caused the decision in Marbury to be postponed until 1803, as noted above. Under present law (28 U.S.C. § 2), the Court is directed to convene for "a term of court commencing on the first Monday in October of each year." Because of that provision, a typical session—from the fall to the following summer—is referred to as the "October Term."

The more complex Art. III ingredients of the judicial framework are the provisions of Art. III, § 2, stating that the Judicial Power shall extend to certain specified "Cases" and "Controversies." What constitutes a "case" or "controversy" suitable for federal judicial resolution is a complex and much-litigated question, as noted in the preceding section. After listing those categories of "Cases" and "Controversies" within the federal judicial power, Art. III, § 2, proceeds to address the Supreme Court's jurisdiction specifically: "In all Cases affecting Ambassadors, other public Ministers and Consuls, and those in which a State shall be a Party, the supreme Court shall have original Jurisdiction. In all the other Cases before mentioned, the supreme Court shall have appellate Jurisdiction, both as to Law and Fact, with such Exceptions, and under such Regulations as the Congress shall make." Some of the problems inherent in those words have already surfaced, in cases such as Marbury and Martin. What concerns us now is the fleshing out of those jurisdictional categories. The original jurisdiction need not detain us: it is rarely invoked; and it is even more rarely the source of significant constitutional interpretations. The present contours of the Court's appellate jurisdiction—the avenues to review in the Supreme Court from state and lower federal courts—are the major concerns of the materials that follow. After sketching the contemporary jurisdictional provisions (and some of their problems) the materials look at the Supreme Court's Rules and its practices governing the exercise of review. The section concludes with an examination of the contemporary concerns about the Supreme Court's workload.

2. *The modern statutory framework—The growth and triumph of discretionary review.* a. *The 1988 reforms.* During the 19th century, the Supreme Court lacked all discretion in selecting the state court decisions it would review. Instead, the Court was compelled to hear all cases within the jurisdictional statutes. Beginning in the early 20th century, and culminating in a major reform of 1925, Congress, even while expanding the types of state court decisions the Court was empowered to hear, granted the Court the discretion to decide whether to review certain state court judgments deciding federal issues. Under the scheme in effect until 1988, the laws distinguished between obligatory, mandatory review (review by "appeal") and discretionary review (review by "certiorari"): Congress delineated two different review routes to the Supreme Court from state courts: review as a matter of the appellant's right, in "appeals"; review if the Court chose to exercise its discretion, in "certiorari"

situations. The "appeal"-"certiorari" distinction came under mounting attack beginning in the late 1970s. The critics of the "appeal" provision, concerned about the Court's mounting workload, urged that the Court be given complete discretion to determine what cases it would decide on the merits. All nine Justices supported the virtual elimination of obligatory review. Prior to 1988, obligatory review on "appeal" was available in two situations: when a state court held a state law constitutional in the face of a federal challenge, and when a state court held a federal law or treaty unconstitutional.

After a decade of legislative discussions, the statutory elimination of almost all of the Supreme Court's mandatory jurisdiction ("appeals") finally took place in 1988. The new law, 102 Stat. 662, recast § 1257 of Title 28 of the U.S. Code. As a result of the 1988 revision, § 1257 in effect provides for discretionary Supreme Court review of all state court decisions turning on questions of federal law. The core of § 1257 now reads as follows: "Final judgments or decrees rendered by the highest court of a State in which a decision could be had, may be reviewed by the Supreme Court by writ of certiorari where the validity of a treaty or statute of the United States is drawn in question or where the validity of a statute of any State is drawn in question on the ground of its being repugnant to the Constitution, treaties, or laws of the United States, or where any title, right, privilege, or immunity is specially set up or claimed under the Constitution or the treaties or statutes of, or any commission held or authority exercised under, the United States."

b. *Assuring supremacy and uniformity.* Note the similarities and differences between the modern jurisdictional statute, 28 U.S.C. § 1257, and its earliest antecedent, § 25 of the Judiciary Act of 1789, considered in Martin and Cohens, above.[1] Note that under § 25 (and indeed well into the 20th century), Supreme Court review was available only if the state court *denied* federal claims—e.g., by sustaining a state law against federal objections or by striking down a federal law. Jurisdiction was broadened in 1914, when Supreme Court review was for the first time extended to cases in which the state court had *sustained* rather than rejected the federal claim. With that change, assurance of greater uniformity in interpretation of federal law, rather than mere assurance of federal supremacy, became a major goal of the review statute.

Is the uniformity need adequately met today? Not even the 1914 extension provided for the correction of *all* errors in state court interpretations of federal law. The decision which provoked the 1914 change illustrates the point. In Ives v. South Buffalo Ry. Co., 201 N.Y. 271, 94 N.E. 431 (1911), the state court had held New York's workmen's compensation law unconstitutional under the due process clauses of the state as well as the federal constitution. The New York court's interpretation of the federal due process clause was thought to be more restrictive than the Supreme Court's position, yet no review was possible under the old jurisdictional statute. But, ironically, not even the 1914 expansion

---

1. The text of § 25 of the 1789 Judiciary Act: "That a final judgment or decree in any suit, in the highest court of law or equity of a State in which a decision in the suit could be had, where is drawn in question the validity of a treaty or statute of, or an authority exercised under the United States, and the decision is against their validity; or where is drawn in question the validity of a statute of, or an authority exercised under any State, on the ground of their being repugnant to the constitution, treaties or laws of the United States, and the decision is in favour of such their validity, or where is drawn in question the construction of any clause of the constitution, or of a treaty, or statute of, or commission held under the United States, and the decision is against the title, right, privilege or exemption specially set up or claimed by either party, under such clause of the said constitution, treaty, statute or commission, may be re-examined and reversed or affirmed in the Supreme Court of the United States upon a [writ of error]."

would have permitted review in the Ives case—because of the "adequate state grounds" barrier to Supreme Court review.

3. *The exercise of the Court's discretionary jurisdiction.* a. *The certiorari petition.* The Court's discretionary jurisdiction is invoked by filing a petition for a writ of certiorari. Supreme Court Rule 10 prescribes the contents of the petition.[2] The major purpose of the petition is to demonstrate that the case is "certworthy"—that it is of sufficient general significance, and not simply of importance to the parties in the case, to warrant review. The votes of four Justices are needed to grant certiorari. The Court's Rule 10 is an attempt to state in general terms the "Considerations Governing Review on Certiorari." It provides: "A review on writ of certiorari is not a matter of right, but of judicial discretion. A petition for a writ of certiorari will be granted only for compelling reasons. The following, while neither controlling nor fully measuring the Court's discretion, indicate the character of reasons the Court considers:

"(a) a United States court of appeals has entered a decision in conflict with the decision of another United States court of appeals on the same important matter; has decided an important federal question in a way that conflicts with a decision by a state court of last resort; or has so far departed from the accepted and usual course of judicial proceedings, or so far sanctioned such a departure by a lower court, as to call for an exercise of this Court's supervisory power;

"(b) a state court of last resort has decided an important federal question in a way that conflicts with the decision of another state court of last resort or of a United States court of appeals.

"(c) a state court or a United States court of appeals has decided an important question of federal law which has not been, but should be, settled by this Court, or has decided an important federal question in a way that conflicts with relevant decisions of this Court.

"A petition for a writ of certiorari is rarely granted when the asserted error consists of erroneous factual findings or the misapplication of a properly stated rule of law."

Over the years, as the number of certiorari petitions has increased and the consequent Court workload has grown, Justices have repeatedly urged lawyers to use greater self-restraint in filing petitions. Some have suggested that the Court could help by providing guidelines more specific than those in Rule 10 or by giving reasons when it denies a certiorari petition. (For arguments against the latter route, see the next paragraph.)

A denial of a petition for certiorari is not a decision on the merits. Justice Frankfurter explained the significance that should be (and usually is) given a denial of certiorari in a separate opinion in Maryland v. Baltimore Radio Show, 338 U.S. 912 (1950): "[A] denial simply means that fewer than four members of the Court deemed it desirable to review a decision of the lower court as a matter 'of sound judicial discretion.' [A] variety of considerations underlie denials of the writ, and as to the same petition different reasons may lead different Justices to the same result. This is especially true of petitions for review on writ of certiorari to a State court. Narrowly technical reasons may lead to denials. [A] decision may satisfy all [the] technical requirements and yet may commend itself for review to fewer than four members of the Court. Pertinent considerations of judicial policy here come into play. A case may raise

---

2. The most recently revised Rules went into effect on Oct. 2, 1995. See generally Boskey and Gressman, "The Supreme Court's New Rules—Model 1995," 116 S.Ct. vi (1995).

an important question but the record may be cloudy. It may be desirable to have different aspects of an issue further illumined by the lower courts. Wise adjudication has its own time for ripening. Since there are these conflicting and, to the uninformed, even confusing reasons for denying petitions for certiorari, it has been suggested from time to time that the Court indicate its reasons for denial. Practical considerations preclude. [If] the Court is to do its work it would not be feasible to give reasons, however brief, for refusing to take these cases. The time that would be required is prohibitive, apart from the fact as already indicated that different reasons not infrequently move different members of the Court in concluding that a particular case at a particular time makes review undesirable. [Accordingly], this Court has rigorously insisted that [a denial] carries with it no implication whatever regarding the Court's views on the merits of a case which it has declined to review." See generally Linzer, "The Meaning of Certiorari Denials," 79 Colum.L.Rev. 1227 (1979), and Perry, Deciding to Decide: Agenda Setting in [the] Supreme Court (1991).

b. *The Court's workload.* For most years during recent decades, the Court confronted a striking increase in the annual number of cases presented for review. In the October 1983 Term, for example, it disposed of 4,162 cases, granting review in 194 and writing 163 opinions. Compare this high number of cases disposed of in 1983 with the data for earlier Terms: 3,943 in the 1978 Term, 3,117 in the 1968 Term, 1,763 in the 1958 Term, and 1,426 in the 1948 Term. Beginning in the mid–1980s, however, the dramatic annual increases ended and the caseload remained relatively constant—and in some years, indeed, declined. Moreover, the number of cases decided with full opinions has not varied significantly over the years. As an indication of the end of the rapid increases in annual caseload, note that the Court disposed of 4,401 cases during the October 1987 Term. In very recent years, moreover, the Court has cut back substantially on the number of cases given full consideration. Although the Court decided an average of 150 cases per Term in the 1980s, the number has dropped considerably in more recent years. In the 1994 Term, the Court issued opinions in only 86 cases; in the 1995 Term, the number was only 75, the lowest since the early 1950s. The New York Times, July 3, 1996.

4. *The "adequate and independent state grounds" barrier to Supreme Court review of state court decisions.* The Court has long held that it lacks power to review state court decisions that rest on "adequate and independent state grounds." Efforts to obtain review of such decisions are dismissed for lack of jurisdiction. Thus, where a state court has addressed both state and federal questions in deciding a case, its decision is not reviewable if the state ground alone is sufficient to support its judgment: In such situations, an error in the state court's interpretation of federal law would not affect the result in the case. Determining whether a state court's reliance on a state law ground bars Supreme Court review is a frequently encountered and complex problem. State grounds of decision may be substantive or procedural: a state court ruling may rest on a mixture of state and federal substantive grounds; or a state court may fail to reach a federal issue because of an allegedly dispositive state procedural barrier. In either situation, assessing the "adequacy" and "independence" of the state ground may be difficult. The intricacies of these problems are beyond the scope of a constitutional law course; they are pursued in federal jurisdiction courses. See, e.g., Hart & Wechsler, Federal Courts (4th ed. 1996), chap. 5. But the theoretical underpinnings and a few of the practical consequences of the adequate state grounds barrier are worth noting here.

Justice Jackson, in Herb v. Pitcairn, 324 U.S. 117 (1945), summarized the theoretical bases of the doctrine as follows: "This Court [has always] adhered to the principle that it will not review judgments of state courts that rest on

adequate and independent state grounds. [The reason] is found in the partition-
ing of power between the state and federal judicial systems and in the
limitations of our own jurisdiction. Our only power over state judgments is to
correct them to the extent that they incorrectly adjudge federal rights. And our
power is to correct wrong judgments, not to revise opinions. We are not
permitted to render an advisory opinion, and if the same judgment would be
rendered by the state court after we corrected its views of federal laws, our
review could amount to nothing more than an advisory opinion." Justice
Jackson found the rule a constitutional mandate, in view of the Art. III
preclusion of advisory opinions by federal courts. Others have suggested that,
whether or not the rule is constitutionally required, it is mandated by the
jurisdictional statute.

a. *State substantive law.* In constitutional litigation, the most common
example of an independent and adequate state substantive ground is a state
court ruling that a state law violates both the federal constitution and an
identical or similar provision in the state constitution. In principle, it is clear
that even though the state court opinion may include an elaborate discussion of
the meaning of the federal guarantee—an interpretation that may be wrong—
the Supreme Court will not review if the state judges rest their decision on
their own constitutional provision as well. In such a situation, correction of the
state court's interpretation would not change the outcome of the case; Court
correction of the state court's error would accordingly be an unpermitted
advisory opinion, even though the erroneous state court ruling would produce a
nonuniform interpretation of federal law.

Interrelated developments in recent years have made applications of the
adequate state grounds principle controversial. These developments are products of the modern Court's occasional proclivity to cut back on federal constitutional guarantees announced by the Warren Court, especially in the area of
criminal defendants' rights. One consequence was that a number of state courts
began to invalidate state laws in opinions which, while primarily discussing the
federal Constitution (although arguably out of line with narrower modern
Court rulings), were nevertheless allegedly immune from Court review because
of an additional, brief statement by the state court that a similar state
constitutional provision had been violated as well. While that pattern was
developing, some Justices of the Supreme Court were probably increasingly
frustrated by the existence of such "erroneous" yet unreviewable federal
constitutional rulings in the state court reports. [Should such traditionally
unreviewable state court ventures into federal constitutional law be praised as
creative, or criticized as irresponsible? For an admiring evaluation, see Karst,
"Serrano v. Priest: A State Court's Responsibilities and Opportunities in the
Development of Federal Constitutional Law," 60 Calif.L.Rev. 720 (1972). See
generally Brennan, "State Constitutions and the Protection of Individual
Rights," 90 Harv.L.Rev. 489 (1977). For an especially principled examination of
state court interpretations of *state* constitutional provisions, see Linde, "First
Things First: Rediscovering the States' Bills of Rights," 9 U.Balt.L.Rev. 379
(1980). Quite often, nonreviewable statements about federal law by state courts
have had considerable impact on other courts. See, e.g., Serrano v. Priest, 5
Cal.3d 584, 487 P.2d 1241 (1971), sustaining a challenge to interdistrict
inequalities in school financing in an opinion discussing federal law at length,
yet immune from Court review. In Serrano, the California court's extensive
discussion of federal law was followed by several other state and federal courts
before the Supreme Court announced a different view of the federal equal
protection clause in the Rodriguez case in 1973, p. 842 below.]

These developments may have helped prompt the Court's 1983 decision in MICHIGAN v. LONG, 463 U.S. 1032. That decision purports not to disturb the traditional view that an independent and adequate state ground bars Supreme Court jurisdiction. But the ruling does a virtual about-face regarding the guidelines for determining the reviewability of state court decisions in situations where the state court opinion is not absolutely clear about its bases. The traditional presumption was that the Court lacked jurisdiction unless its authority to review was clear on the face of the state court opinion. When faced with uncertainty, the Court in the past occasionally remanded such cases to the state court for clarification. But more commonly, the Court would deny jurisdiction where there was uncertainty. Under the new approach, by contrast, the Court will no longer remand for clarification or dismiss for lack of jurisdiction, but will instead treat as reviewable any state ruling that is less than crystal-clear. However, the state court can still preclude Supreme Court review if it clearly states that it was relying on an independent state ground.

In Michigan v. Long, the state court had held that Long's search and seizure rights had been violated. The Michigan court's opinion discussed primarily Fourth Amendment principles as elaborated by the Supreme Court. However, the state court opinion also made two references to the search and seizure guarantee in the Michigan Constitution. Most important was a statement at the conclusion of its opinion, for it was the kind of statement that in recent years had been recurrently put forth by state courts as a way of barring Court review: "We hold, therefore, that the deputies' search of the vehicle was proscribed by the Fourth Amendment to the United States Constitution, *and* art. 1 § 11 of the Michigan Constitution." (Emphasis added.) Nevertheless, Justice O'CONNOR'S majority opinion asserted jurisdiction and reversed on the merits.

Justice O'Connor insisted that there was need to "reexamine" the application of the adequate state grounds principle because "we have thus far not developed a satisfying and consistent approach for resolving [the] vexing issue [of determining] whether various forms of references to state law constitute adequate and independent state grounds." She stated the new approach as follows: "If the state court decision indicates clearly and expressly that it is alternatively based on bona fide separate, adequate, and independent grounds, we, of course, will not undertake to review the decision. [Our] requirement of a 'plain statement' that a decision rests upon adequate and independent state grounds does not in any way authorize the rendering of advisory opinions. Rather, in determining, as we must, whether we have jurisdiction to review a case that is alleged to rest on adequate and independent state grounds, we merely assume that there are no such grounds when it is not clear from the opinion itself that the state court relied upon an adequate and independent state ground and when it fairly appears that the state court rested its decision primarily on federal law." Applying that standard here, she stated: "Our review of the decision below [leaves] us unconvinced that it rests upon an independent state ground. [It] fairly appears in this case the Michigan Supreme Court rested its decision primarily on federal law. [It] appears to us that the state court 'felt compelled by what it understood to be federal constitutional considerations to construe [its] own law in the manner it did.'" Hence, the state ground was not a truly "independent" one. Justice O'Connor elaborated: "Respect for the independence of state courts, as well as avoidance of rendering advisory opinions, have been the cornerstones of this Court's refusal to decide cases where there is an adequate and independent state ground. [If] a state court chooses merely to rely on federal precedents as it would on the precedents of all other jurisdictions, then it need only make clear by a plain statement in its judgment or opinion that the federal cases are being used only for the purpose of guidance, and do not themselves compel the result that the court has reached. In this way, both justice and judicial administration will be greatly improved. [We] believe that such an approach will provide state judges with a clearer opportunity to develop state jurisprudence unimpeded by federal interference, and yet will preserve the integrity of federal law." She added that "outright dismissal of cases [that are unclear about their state grounds bases] is clearly not a panacea because it cannot be doubted that there is an important need for uniformity in federal law, and that this need goes unsatisfied when we fail to review an opinion that rests primarily upon federal grounds and where the *independence* of an alleged state ground is not apparent from the four corners of the opinion."

Justice STEVENS's dissent took sharp issue with the majority's approach: "The state law ground is clearly adequate to support the judgment, but the question whether it is independent of the [state court's] understanding of federal law is more difficult. Four possible ways of resolving that question present themselves: (1) asking [the state court] directly, (2) attempting to infer from all possible sources of state law what the [state court] meant, (3) presuming that adequate state grounds are independent unless it clearly appears otherwise, or (4) presuming that adequate state grounds are *not* independent unless it clearly appears otherwise. This Court has, on different occasions, employed each of the first three approaches; never until today has it even hinted at the fourth. [I] cannot accept the Court's decision to choose the fourth approach over the third—to presume that adequate state grounds are intended to be dependent on federal law unless the record plainly shows otherwise. If we reject the intermediate approaches, we are left with a choice between two presumptions: one in favor of our taking jurisdiction, and one against it. Historically, the latter presumption has always prevailed. [Since approaches (1) and (2)] are now to be rejected, however, I would think that stare decisis would call for a return to historical principle. Instead, the Court seems to conclude that because some precedents ought to be rejected, we must overrule them all." He stated that, even if he agreed that the Court was free to assert "presumptive jurisdiction over the decisions of sovereign states," he would not agree that an "expansive attitude makes good sense." He insisted that respect for state courts, avoidance of advisory opinions, and the interest in managing scarce federal judicial resources all counseled "against the exercise of federal jurisdiction." He argued, too, that "a policy of judicial restraint—one that allows other decisional bodies to have the last word in legal interpretation until it is truly necessary for this Court to intervene—enables this Court to makes its most effective contribution to our federal [system]."

Justice Stevens insisted that a case such as Long's "hardly compels a departure from tradition." He noted that cases such as this did not involve deprivation of federal rights. "Rather, they are cases in which a state court has upheld a citizen's assertion of a right, finding the citizen to be protected under both federal and state law. The complaining party is an officer of the state itself, who asks us to rule that the state court interpreted federal rights too broadly and 'overprotected' the citizen. Such cases should not be of inherent concern to this Court. [Michigan] simply provided greater protection to one of its citizens than some other State might provide or, indeed, than this Court might require throughout the country." He added: "I believe that in reviewing the decisions of state courts, the primary role of this Court is to make sure that persons who seek to *vindicate* federal rights have been fairly heard." [A similar approach was advocated by several commentators in the years immediately preceding Michigan v. Long. See, e.g., Sager, "Fair Measure: The Legal Status of Underenforced Constitutional Norms," 91 Harv.L.Rev. 1212, 1248 (1978) (arguing that the Court should at times decline to set aside state court decisions "based upon a broader reading of the pertinent federal constitutional norm than that which the Court would itself adopt").] The majority had offered "only one reason" for asserting jurisdiction over cases such as this: the "need for uniformity in federal law." Justice Stevens responded: "Of course, the supposed need to 'review an opinion' clashes directly with our oft-repeated reminder that 'our power is to correct wrong judgments, not to revise opinions.' Herb v. Pitcairn. The clash is not merely one of form: the 'need for uniformity in federal law' is truly an ungovernable engine. That same need is no less present when it is perfectly clear that a state ground is both independent and adequate. In fact it is equally present if a state prosecutor announces that he believes a certain policy of nonenforcement is commanded by federal law. Yet we have never claimed jurisdiction to correct such errors, no matter how egregious they may be. [We] do not sit to expound our understanding of the Constitution to interested listeners in the legal community; we sit to resolve disputes. If it is not apparent that our views would affect the outcome of a particular case, we cannot presume to interfere." In a closing passage, Justice Stevens stated that he was "thoroughly baffled by the Court's suggestion that it must stretch its jurisdiction" in order to show respect for the independence of state courts. He asked: "Would we show respect for the Republic of Finland by convening a special sitting for the sole purpose of declaring that its decision to release an American citizen was based upon a misunderstanding of American law?" Justice BRENNAN's dissent, joined by Justice Marshall, dealt almost entirely with the merits of the search and seizure issue. Twelve years after Long, Chief Justice Rehnquist's majority opinion reaffirmed that ruling in Arizona v. Evans, 514 U.S. 1 (1995), in the face of a dissent by Justice Ginsburg, joined by Justice Stevens, urging that Michigan v. Long be overruled. She urged, "[Long] is out of sync with the principle that this Court will avoid constitutional questions when an alternative basis of decision presents itself. Most critically, [the] Long presumption interferes prematurely with state-court endeavors to explore different solutions to new problems facing modern society."

b. *State procedural law.* As noted above, an allegedly adequate and independent state ground may be procedural rather than substantive. The typical state procedural ground case differs from the state substantive ground situation. In the substantive ground model, the state court discusses federal as well as state issues; the problem on Supreme Court review is to assess the importance and independence of the state ground in the state-federal mix. In the usual procedural ground case, by contrast, the state court does not get to the federal claim at all. Rather, the state decision relies solely on state law and holds that noncompliance with a state procedural requirement precludes adjudication of the federal issue. Suppose, for example, a state criminal defendant objects to introduction of evidence on the ground that it was illegally seized, or to a confession on the ground that it was coerced. Suppose, moreover, the state court refuses to rule on the merits of those objections on the ground that they were not raised in accordance with state procedural groundrules—e.g., "with fair precision" or "in due time." May the Supreme Court on review nevertheless reach the federal objection? Or is the state procedural ground "adequate" to support the conviction?

That problem arises from the fact that state courts have from the beginning been a significant initial forum for the adjudication of federal claims. And from the beginning, a state's control of its own judicial machinery has implied considerable autonomy in prescribing the processes for the raising of all claims (federal as well as state) in the state courts. Ordinarily, then, compliance with state procedural requirements as to the time and manner of raising and preserving federal questions is necessary in order to invoke Court review. Yet deference to state procedures has never been total: precluding all Court review upon a state court's mere recital of a state procedural ground would endanger vindication of federal rights. What, then, are the governing considerations in determining whether the asserted state procedural ground is "adequate" to preclude review? The Court has often said that a state court's refusal to decide a federal question must rest on "fair" and "substantial" grounds.

This is not the place to explore in depth what is necessary to establish "unfairness" or "insubstantiality." But a statement from Justice Clark's dissent in Williams v. Georgia, 349 U.S. 375, 399 (1955), summarizes some typical avenues of Supreme Court inquiry: "A purported state ground is not independent and adequate in two instances. *First*, where the circumstances give rise to an inference that the state court is guilty of an evasion—an interpretation of state law with the specific intent to deprive a litigant of a federal right. [A footnote at this point added: "This charge upon the integrity of a State Supreme Court is so serious that this Court has restricted such findings to cases where the state court decision lacked 'fair support' in the state law."] *Second*, where the state law, honestly applied though it may be, and even dictated by the precedents, throws such obstacles in the way of enforcement of federal rights that it must be struck down as unreasonably interfering with the vindication of such rights." For a somewhat greater Court willingness to reexamine procedural grounds, see Henry v. Mississippi, 379 U.S. 443 (1965), where the majority—in examining an asserted state ground of "waiver"—suggested that state procedural grounds are subject to broader Court reexamination than state substantive grounds. Note that the Court has held the Michigan v. Long "plain statement" rule applicable to procedural matters as well as to substantive ones. Caldwell v. Mississippi, 472 U.S. 320 (1985).

SECTION 4.   POLITICAL RESTRAINTS ON THE SUPREME COURT: MAY CONGRESS STRIP THE COURT OF ITS JURISDICTION?

Introduction. Supreme Court decisions frequently stir opposition in the political branches of government. Rulings on school desegregation, school prayer, abortion, and flag burning are major examples from recent decades. What weapons are available to the executive and legislative branches in reacting to rulings with which they disagree, other than voicing their disapproval through the vehement criticism that is an accepted part of the national scene? Theoretically, the judicial branch, with its life tenure, was established to be independent, free from public pressures and political restraints. Yet, while the Court does not literally follow the election returns, the Justices are not likely to be wholly oblivious to the recurrent surfacing of constitutional issues in political discourse.

But the constitutional scheme does not provide for many routes through which the political branches can effectively vent their dissatisfactions with the directions of the judiciary. True, Art. V provides for amendments to the Constitution, and that route has been used at times to overturn specific Supreme Court decisions. See Amendments XI, XIV, XVI, and XXVI. Yet achieving amendments through Art. V is a difficult task, requiring the support of supermajorities in Congress as well as the states. Moreover, the presumptive life-time tenure of Supreme Court Justices can be ended through the impeachment route, authorizing removal from office for "Treason, Bribery, or other High Crimes and Misdemeanors." No Supreme Court Justice has ever been removed under that provision. Federalist Justice Samuel Chase was impeached by the House, but the Jeffersonians were unable to achieve the requisite majority in the Senate to convict him, as noted in sec. 1 of this chapter. An ideological disagreement with a sitting Justice has not been viewed as a proper ground for impeachment since Chase's day. A more solid basis for political reprisal against the Justices lies in the fact that Congress sets the size of the Court. That the congressional power over size is a potential source of political checks on the Court is illustrated by President Franklin D. Roosevelt's proposed Court-curbing Plan in 1937 to increase the size of the Court and thereby assure a majority of pro-New Deal Justices. Even such relatively routine legislation as that of setting the time at which the Court meets can be used to serve political ends: recall the Jeffersonian legislation which caused the decision in Marbury to be postponed until 1803.

A far more effective political tool to influence the direction of the Court lies in the selection process. The President nominates Justices to the Supreme Court, but Art. II, § 2, cl. 2, provides that the appointment will not be effective unless the President obtains the "Advice and Consent of the Senate." It has long been accepted that the President may choose nominees who share his ideological views. But the proper role of the Senate in exercising its power to confirm or reject has been the subject of much dispute. The Senate rejected about twenty percent of presidential nominations for the Court in the nineteenth century, but most rejections were not based on ideological grounds. In the several decades beginning the the New Deal era of the 1930s, the general view was that the Senate could reject a nominee only on grounds of incompetence or defects in character or temperament—or, as a wag put it, only if the nominee was an idiot, a drunkard, or a crook. That attitude changed dramatically with the nomination of Judge Robert Bork in 1987. The committee and floor debates were extensive and heated, much of the debate turned on ideological considerations, and the Bork nomination was rejected by a 42–58 vote. Ever since, the Judiciary Committee has felt free to probe a nominee's constitutional views. Is so active a senatorial role in the confirmation process appropriate and desirable? See generally Abraham, "Justices and Presidents" (3d ed., 1992); Tribe, "God Save This Honorable Court" (1985); and Bork, "The Tempting of America: The Political Seduction of the Law" (1990).

The role of the political branches in the selection process for the Court exerts an obvious influence on the direction of the Court. While it helps to assure that the Court will not depart too sharply from the views of the political mainstream, the influence of the President and the Senate should not be overstated. Thus, a President's foresight is likely to be limited to those constitutional issues central to his political agenda at the time of the nomination. Franklin D. Roosevelt, for example, had the opportunity to nominate eight new Justices after his Court-packing Plan failed in 1937, and he selected individuals who could be counted to uphold his New Deal program by taking a generous attitude toward regulation of the economy. That hope was vindicated, but his appointees soon divided sharply about the appropriate degree of judicial activism in the protection of individual rights, an issue not dominant in FDR's thinking. Similarly, President Nixon, who ran on a platform urging a more restrained Court and emphasizing law-and-order issues, named Chief Justice Burger and Justices Blackmun, Powell and Rehnquist. Observers assumed that this would assure a more conservative Court and a solid Nixon–Burger bloc, but the new Justices' voting record soon showed that they were not peas out of the same pod, so that the Court proved far less conservative than Nixon presumably hoped. See Blasi, "The Burger Court: The Counter–Revolution That Wasn't" (1983). President Reagan, whose campaigns similarly emphasized constitutional issues, found his selections not nearly as conservative as he may have hoped: Chief Justice Rehnquist and Justice Scalia are fairly regular members of the conservative wing, but Justices O'Connor and Kennedy have proved to be far more centrist. The President and the Senate, in short, tend to undervalue the independence that accompanies ascending the bench and attaining lifetime tenure. President Bush's appointment of Justice Souter, for example, produced a more liberal member of the Court than many anticipated at the time of nomination.

(b) A final route that may be available to Congress for retaliating against unpalatable Court decisions is the power, in Art. III, to make "Exceptions" to the Supreme Court's appellate jurisdiction. The next principal case and the notes following it consider the scope of and limits on that power.

Ex Parte McCardle

7 Wall. (74 U.S.) 506, 19 L.Ed. 264 (1869).

[Under the post-Civil War Reconstruction Acts, Congress imposed military government on a large number of former Confederate States. McCardle was a Mississippi newspaper editor in military custody on charges of publishing "incendiary and libelous articles." He brought this habeas corpus proceeding under the Act of Congress of February 5, 1867, which authorized federal courts to grant habeas corpus to anyone restrained "in violation of the Constitution" and also authorized appeals to the Supreme Court. He claimed that the Reconstruction Acts were beyond the constitutional power of Congress. After the lower court denied McCardle's habeas petition, he appealed to the Supreme Court. After the Supreme Court sustained jurisdiction of that appeal, 6 Wall. (73 U.S.) 318 (1868), and after argument was heard on the merits, Congress passed the Act of March 27, 1868. That law stated that so much of the 1867 Act "as authorized an appeal from the judgment of the Circuit Court to the Supreme Court of the United States, or the exercise of any such jurisdiction by said Supreme Court, on appeals which have been, or may hereafter be taken, be, and the same is, hereby repealed." The historical context is described further in note 1a following the opinion dismissing the appeal.]

The Chief Justice [CHASE] delivered the opinion of the Court.

The first question necessarily is that of jurisdiction; for, if the act of March, 1868, takes away the jurisdiction defined by the act of February, 1867, it is useless, if not improper, to enter into any discussion of other questions.

It is quite true, as was argued by the counsel for the petitioner, that the appellate jurisdiction of this Court is not derived from acts of Congress. It is, strictly speaking, conferred by the Constitution. But it is conferred "with such exceptions and under such regulations as Congress shall make." It is unnecessary to consider whether, if Congress had made no exceptions and no regulations, this court might not have exercised general appellate jurisdiction under rules prescribed by itself. For among the earliest acts of the first Congress, at its first session, was the act of September 24th, 1789, to establish the judicial courts of the United States. That act provided for the organization of this court, and prescribed regulations for the exercise of its jurisdiction.

The source of that jurisdiction, and the limitations of it by the Constitution and by statute, have been on several occasions subjects of consideration here. In the case of Durousseau v. The United States, 6 Cranch (10 U.S.) 307 (Marshall, C.J.; 1810) particularly, the whole matter was carefully examined, and the court held, that while "the appellate powers of this court are not given by the judicial act, but are given by the Constitution," they are, nevertheless, "limited and regulated by that act, and by such other acts as have been passed on the subject." The court said, further, that the judicial act was an exercise of the power given by the Constitution to Congress "of making exceptions to the appellate jurisdiction of the Supreme Court." "They have described affirmatively," said the court, "its jurisdiction, and this affirmative description has been understood to imply a negation of the exercise of such appellate power as is not comprehended within it." The principle that the affirmation of appellate jurisdiction implies the negation of all such jurisdiction not affirmed having been thus established, it was an almost necessary consequence that acts of Congress, providing for the exercise of jurisdiction, should come to be spoken of as acts granting jurisdiction, and not as acts making exceptions to the constitutional grant of it.

The exception to appellate jurisdiction in the case before us, however, is not an inference from the affirmation of other appellate jurisdiction. It is made in terms. The provision of the act of 1867 affirming the appellate jurisdiction of this court in cases of habeas corpus is expressly repealed. It is hardly possible to imagine a plainer instance of positive exception.

We are not at liberty to inquire into the motives of the legislature. We can only examine into its power under the Constitution; and the power to make exceptions to the appellate jurisdiction of this court is given by express words. What, then, is the effect of the repealing act upon the case before us? We cannot doubt as to this. Without jurisdiction the court cannot proceed at all in any cause. Jurisdiction is power to declare the law, and when it ceases to exist, the only function remaining to the court is that of announcing the fact and dismissing the cause. And this is not less clear upon authority than upon principle. [It] is quite clear, therefore, that this court cannot proceed to pronounce judgment in this case, for it has no longer jurisdiction of the appeal; and judicial duty is not less fitly performed by declining ungranted jurisdiction than in exercising firmly that which the Constitution and the laws confer.

Counsel seem to have supposed, if effect be given to the repealing act in question, that the whole appellate power of the court, in cases of habeas corpus, is denied. But this is an error. The act of 1868 does not except from that jurisdiction any cases but appeals from Circuit Courts under the act of 1867. It does not affect the jurisdiction which was previously exercised.

[Appeal dismissed for lack of jurisdiction.]

————

1. *The scope of the jurisdiction-stripping power of Congress.* Consider, in examining the principal case and the following notes: How far-reaching is the congressional power sustained in McCardle? Does the historical context of that case weaken its force as precedent? Is it possible to state principled limits on the power of Congress to enact "Exceptions" to the Supreme Court's appellate jurisdiction? Does Art. III impose significant limits? Do other provisions of the Constitution—for example, the Fifth Amendment? Is the Court truly vulnerable to serious political reprisals from Congress unless limiting principles on

McCardle can be stated? Or are there significant practical restraints on the jurisdiction-curbing weapon?

a. *McCardle in historical context.* Congressional policies after the Civil War produced sharp conflicts with the other branches. President Andrew Johnson opposed the Reconstruction Acts, for example; and there were repeated efforts to test their constitutionality in the courts. The McCardle case moved to a climax at the height of the tension between Congress and President and after two efforts to elicit Court rulings had failed.

Soon after the basic provisions of reconstruction legislation had been passed over the President's veto, challenges in the courts were launched. Prospects for success seemed good if the Court reached the merits: the military government features looked vulnerable in view of a case decided by the Supreme Court just before the reconstruction laws were passed. Ex parte Milligan, 4 Wall. (71 U.S.) 2 (1867). But the first two major challenges failed because of nonjusticiability objections. See Mississippi v. Johnson, 4 Wall. (71 U.S.) 475 (1867) (Court lacks power to enjoin President); Georgia v. Stanton, 6 Wall. (73 U.S.) 50 (1868) (suit by State raises nonjusticiable political question). But then, while Congress was considering measures to avert the judicial threat to reconstruction, the Court took jurisdiction of McCardle's appeal. With that constitutional challenge formally before the Court and with argument on the merits already concluded (but, as the official report noted, "before conference in regard to the decision proper to be made"), Congress passed the 1868 law withdrawing appellate jurisdiction. By then, impeachment proceedings against President Johnson had begun. Nevertheless, he vetoed the law. With the Court standing by and withholding action on the case before it pending the outcome of the political battle, Congress overrode the veto. Argument on the jurisdiction-curtailing law was then sought in the Court. And, as one more manifestation of the political crisis hovering over the case, that argument was postponed because of "the Chief Justice being detained from his place here, by his duties in the Court of Impeachment."

There was one post-McCardle effort to elicit a ruling on reconstruction. In Ex parte Yerger, 8 Wall. (75 U.S.) 85 (1869), the Court took jurisdiction of a proceeding by another petitioner in military detention in Mississippi. Yerger, like McCardle, had unsuccessfully sought habeas in a lower federal court. But Yerger came to the Supreme Court by a route different from McCardle's: he did not invoke the appeal provision of the 1867 Act and instead sought relief under a preexisting law authorizing "original" jurisdiction in the Court for habeas petitions; accordingly, the Court found, the 1868 repeal did not apply. (Recall the final paragraph of McCardle.) Yet a decision on the constitutionality of the Reconstruction Acts was once again averted: before the Court could rule on the merits, Yerger was released from military custody. See generally Van Alstyne, "A Critical Guide to Ex Parte McCardle," 15 Ariz.L.Rev. 229 (1973).

Ex parte Yerger played an important role 127 years later when the Court considered whether provisions of the 1996 Antiterrorism and Effective Death Penalty Act unconstitutionally curtailed the Supreme Court's appellate jurisdiction. FELKER v. TURPIN, 116 S.Ct. 2333 (1996). The Act included provisions curtailing state prisoners' second or successive applications for federal habeas corpus relief. Among these was one precluding the Supreme Court review of any decision by a court of appeals granting or denying authorization for a state prisoner to file a second or successive application. (The courts of appeals were given a "gatekeeping" function requiring their permission for the consideration of prisoners' second or successive applications by the district courts.) Chief Justice REHNQUIST's majority opinion concluded that the availability of relief in the Supreme Court by filing an "original" habeas petition "obviates any claim by petitioner under the Exceptions Clause of Art. III, § 2." The Court had noted that route in the final paragraph of Ex parte McCardle, above, and, as noted, that route was utilized when Yerger filed a habeas petition soon after McCardle. The Felker opinion discussed Yerger at some length and found that, as in Yerger, there was no reason to find that the new, 1996 law intended to repeal by implication the Court's habeas power in "original" jurisdiction cases. (Note that this jurisdiction is "original" only because it is filed in the first instance in the Supreme Court. For constitutional purposes, such an "original" petition is an exercise of the Court's appellate (rather than original) jurisdiction. See Oakes, "The 'Original' Writ of Habeas Corpus in the Supreme Court," 1962 Sup. Ct. Rev. 153.) The Felker Court noted that the 1996 law had "not repealed our authority to entertain original habeas petitions, for reasons similar to those stated in Yerger"; since the law did not "repeal our authority to entertain a petition for habeas corpus, there can be no plausible argument that the Act has deprived this Court of appellate jurisdiction in violation of Article III, § 2." A concurrence by Justice SOUTER, joined by Justices Stevens and Breyer, pointed out that "if it should later turn out that statutory avenues other than certiorari for reviewing a gatekeeping determination were closed, the question whether the statute exceeded Congress's Exceptions Clause power would be open. The question could arise if the Court of Appeals adopted divergent interpretations of the gatekeeper standard."

b. *The vitality of McCardle and the Klein case.* Congress has not given the Court cause to reexamine McCardle directly, but Justice Douglas found occasion to call it into question in a footnote to a dissent some years ago. "There is a serious question whether the McCardle case could command a majority view today," he said in an opinion joined by Justice Black in Glidden Co. v. Zdanok, 370 U.S. 530, 605 (1962). The Glidden case, with a plurality opinion by Justice Harlan, dealt mainly with the distinction between Art. I "legislative courts" and Art. III courts. The context of Justice Douglas' remark about McCardle was as follows: "The opinion of my Brother Harlan stirs a host of problems that need not be opened. What is done will, I fear, plague us for years. First, that opinion cites with approval Ex parte McCardle [1869], in which Congress withdrew jurisdiction of this Court to review a habeas corpus case that was *sub judice* and then apparently draws a distinction between that case and United States v. Klein [1872], where such withdrawal was not permitted in a property claim. There is a serious question whether the McCardle case could command a majority view today. Certainly the distinction between liberty and property (which emanates from this portion of my Brother Harlan's opinion) has no vitality even in terms of the Due Process Clause."

Is that all there is to the distinction between McCardle and UNITED STATES v. KLEIN, 13 Wall. (80 U.S.) 128 (1872)? Consider the fuller statement of Klein which follows. It suggests that the Klein–McCardle difference may not reflect simply a preference of property over liberty; instead, Klein may rest on a principle more acceptable today, a principle of continuing utility as a limit on congressional power over jurisdiction. Justice Harlan's reference to Klein came in the following passage in Glidden: "The authority [of Congress to curb the jurisdiction of Art. III courts] is not, of course, unlimited. In 1870, Congress purported to withdraw jurisdiction from the Court of Claims and from this Court on appeal over cases seeking indemnification for property captured during the Civil War, so far as eligibility therefor might be predicated upon an amnesty awarded by the President, as both courts had previously held that it might. Despite Ex parte McCardle, the Court refused to apply the statute to a case in which the claimant had already been adjudged entitled to recover by the

Court of Claims, calling it an unconstitutional attempt to invade the judicial province by prescribing a rule of decision in a pending case. United States v. Klein."

In the Klein controversy, earlier rulings had held that a presidential pardon satisfied the statutory requirement that a property claimant was not a supporter of the "rebellion." The new statute enacted while Klein's appeal was pending provided that a pardon was to be taken as showing quite the opposite, that the claimant *had* aided the rebellion, and went on to provide that the courts were to dismiss such claims for want of jurisdiction. The opinion holding the law unconstitutional stated that the Court would have upheld it as an exercise of the "exceptions" power if "it simply denied the right of appeal in a particular class of cases." But here the jurisdictional language was only "a means to an end": "to deny to pardons granted by the President the effect which this court had adjudged them to have." The Court concluded that dismissing the appeal would allow Congress to "prescribe rules of decision to the Judicial Department of the government in cases pending before it," and this was a violation of separation of powers principles. In short, the Court found the statute unconstitutional on two separation of powers grounds: the law prescribed how a court should decide an issue and hence interfered with judicial autonomy; and it denied effect to a presidential pardon, thus interfering with executive autonomy.

Note also Hart & Wechsler, Federal Courts (3d ed. 1988), 369, viewing Klein as holding that it is "an unconstitutional invasion of the judicial function when Congress purports, not to withdraw appellate jurisdiction completely, but to bind the Court to decide a case in accordance with a rule of law independently unconstitutional on other grounds." Note also the reiteration of the Klein principle in Justice Rutledge's dissent in Yakus v. United States, 321 U.S. 414, 468 (1944): "It is one thing for Congress to withhold jurisdiction. It is entirely another to confer it and direct that it be exercised in a manner inconsistent with constitutional requirements or, what in some instances may be the same thing, without regard to them. [W]henever the judicial power is called into play it is responsible directly to the fundamental law and no other authority can intervene to force or authorize the judicial body to disregard it." See generally Young, "Congressional Regulation of Federal Courts' Jurisdiction and Processes: United States v. Klein Revisited," 1981 Wis.L.Rev. 1189. Consider the modern Court-curbing proposals in note 3 below: Which are legitimate jurisdictional controls and which are efforts to dictate the outcome of a case on the merits? Which are withdrawals of categories of cases, and which are simply efforts to withdraw particular issues from judicial consideration in cases otherwise left to the courts for decision on the merits? If Klein is read to bar withdrawal of particular issues where that is tantamount to directing the outcome of a case, does that draw into question as well the legitimacy of congressional withdrawal of jurisdiction of an entire class of cases, when that withdrawal of jurisdiction is prompted by a desire to affect the outcome?

Contrast with Klein the decision in PLAUT v. SPENDTHRIFT FARM, INC., 514 U.S. 211 (1995). There, the Court held that Congress violated separation of powers principles by impermissibly intruding upon the judicial role. Congress had enacted a law that required Art. III courts to reopen final judgments dismissing suits by one private party against another. The case involved § 27A of the Securities Exchange Act of 1934, added on December 19, 1991, which not only specified the statute of limitations to be applied in certain securities actions, but also provided for the "reinstate[ment]" of causes of action that had been dismissed on statute-of-limitations grounds prior to December 19, 1991, but subsequent to June 19, 1991. The relevance of the latter date was that it was one day after a Supreme Court decision on statutes of limitations that § 27A sought to change. Writing for the Court, Justice SCALIA concluded that the attempt by Congress to reopen litigation that had already been dismissed by an Art. III court violated separation of powers. He distinguished Klein by noting that "later decisions have made clear that its prohibition does not take hold when Congress 'amend[s] applicable law.' [§ 27A] indisputably does set out substantive legal standards for the Judiciary to apply, and in that sense changes the law (even if solely retroactively)." Nevertheless, he concluded that the provision offended "a postulate of Article III just as deeply rooted in our law" as those involved in Klein and other cases: "The record of history shows that the Framers crafted this charter of the judicial department with an expressed understanding that it gives the Federal Judiciary the power, not merely to rule on cases, but to decide them, subject to review only by superior courts in the Article III hierarchy—with an understanding, in short, that 'a judgment conclusively resolves the case' because a '"Judicial power" is one to render dispositive judgments.' By retroactively commanding the federal courts to reopen final judgments, Congress has violated this fundamental principle." Justice BREYER submitted a narrower concurring opinion; Justice STEVENS, joined by Justice Ginsburg, dissented. See generally Redish, "Federal Judicial Independence: Constitutional and Political Perspectives," 46 Mercer L.Rev. 697 (1995).

2. *The search for constitutional limits on congressional power over appellate jurisdiction.* Assertions of broad congressional power to make exceptions to appellate jurisdiction, as in McCardle, understandably have proved tempting to some critics of modern Court decisions—as they have to critics since Marshall's days. As described in note 3 below, controversial decisions of the modern Court—abortion, school busing, school prayer, and so forth—have prompted recurrent congressional efforts to curb the Court's jurisdiction. And these efforts have in turn spurred searches for principles to blunt that congressional weapon. How persuasive are the limiting principles articulated in recent years? For a review of the controversy, see Gunther, "Congressional Power to Curtail Federal Court Jurisdiction: An Opinionated Guide to the Ongoing Debate," 36 Stan.L.Rev. 895 (1984).

a. *"Internal" restraints: Limits on congressional power arguably inherent in Art. III itself.* In examining the arguable limits on congressional power, it is useful to distinguish between "internal" restraints (those traceable to Art. III itself) and "external" ones (those derived from constitutional provisions other than Art. III). One Art. III limit on congressional power, initially urged by Professor Henry M. Hart, Jr., has been widely invoked by Court defenders in and out of Congress. This restraining principle argues that the "exceptions" power of Congress cannot be exercised in a way that would interfere with the "essential" or "core" functions of the Court. Hart urged that "the exceptions must not be such as will destroy the essential role of the Supreme Court in the constitutional plan." See Hart, "The Power of Congress to Limit the Jurisdiction of Federal Courts: An Exercise in Dialectic," 66 Harv.L.Rev. 1362, 1365 (1953).

What *is* the "essential" or "core" role of the Court? Compare with Hart's argument the position of Herbert Wechsler in "The Courts and the Constitution," 65 Colum.L.Rev. 1001 (1965), rejecting constitutional arguments that would prohibit any alterations of appellate jurisdiction "motivated by hostility to the decisions of the Court": "I see no basis for this view and think it antithetical to the plan of the Constitution for the courts—which was quite simply that the Congress would decide from time to time how far the federal judicial institutions should be used within the limits of the federal judicial power." See also Bator, "Congressional Power Over the Federal Courts," 27 Vill.L.Rev. 1032 (1982), Redish, "Congressional Power to Regulate Supreme Court Appellate Jurisdiction Under the Exceptions Clause: An Internal and External Examination," 27 Vill.L.Rev. 900 (1982), and Gunther, above. For an argument that there *are* significant "internal" restraints, see the writings by Akhil Amar, especially "A Neo–Federalist View of Article III: Separating the Two Tiers of Federal Jurisdiction," 65 B.U.L.Rev. 205 (1985), and "The Two–Tiered Structure of the Judiciary Act of 1789," 138 U.Pa.L.Rev. 1499 (1990). Amar emphasizes the word "all" in the first three categories of cases listed in Art. III and concludes that the federal judicial power "must, as an absolute minimum, comprehend the subject matter jurisdiction to decide finally all cases involving federal questions, admiralty, or public ambassadors" and "may—but need not—extend to cases in the six other, party-defined, jurisdictional categories." For a view critical of Amar's, see Meltzer, "The History and Structure of Article III," 138 U.Pa.L.Rev. 1569 (1990).

b. *"External" restraints: Restraints drawn from constitutional sources other than Art. III.* Even if Art. III cannot be persuasively read to curtail congressional power over appellate jurisdiction, other limitations in the Constitution, as in the Bill of Rights, apply. For example, Congress could not bar Supreme Court review by excluding certain litigants on the basis of race or political beliefs. Indeed, recent efforts to articulate constitutional limits on congressional power increasingly rely on such "external" restraints rather than on Art. III itself. Note the review of recent "external" restraints arguments in Gunther, above: "It is widely agreed that legislation singling out particular classes of *litigants* on the basis of their race or other 'suspect' classifications, or injuring them in the exercise of fundamental federal rights, triggers a strict scrutiny inquiry and is [presumptively] invalid, justifiable only after a frequently impossible demonstration that the legislation serves a compelling governmental interest and utilizes the least burdensome means to achieve that interest. Hence, the argument goes, singling out classes of *issues* for primary or exclusive adjudication in state rather than federal courts is similarly vulnerable to constitutional challenge. [See, e.g., Tribe, "Jurisdictional Gerrymandering: Zoning Disfavored Rights Out of the Federal Courts," 16 Harv.C.R.–C.L.L.Rev. 129 (1981).] [The] central question raised by such invocations of the equal protection-strict scrutiny lines of cases is whether they can properly be read to condemn jurisdiction-channeling laws by Congress—laws which prescribe primary reliance on state courts for some subjects of federal question litigation and allow access to federal courts for others. [This] is not a frivolous argument; but I do not think it is in the end persuasive. Rather, it strikes me as ultimately circular and question-begging. The central problem [is] that it too readily expands the reasons for the obvious flaw in laws which distinguish among *litigants* on the basis of race or other forbidden criteria and extends the constitutional attack to jurisdictional statutes which differentiate on the basis of *subject matter*. The basic difficulty is that there simply is no principle requiring all classes of federal question litigation to be handled in the same way. If one pays adequate heed to the Art. III compromise giving Congress the power to make decisions about appropriate channeling of federal issues as between federal and state courts, assigning some classes of cases to the state courts does not 'discriminate against' or 'burden' or 'prejudice' the rights involved in those cases."

c. *Practical considerations.* There *are* practical limits on congressional resort to the power to curb federal court jurisdiction. If access to the Supreme Court were barred, for example, decision would be left to lower courts, with inconsistent results and a threat to the uniformity need articulated by Justice Story in Martin v. Hunter's Lessee. Moreover, the unpopular Supreme Court decisions that prompted congressional response would remain on the books. Indeed, it can be argued that the congressional power over appellate jurisdiction is ultimately a source of strength rather than weakness for the Court. Thus, Hart & Wechsler suggest [Federal Courts (4th ed. 1996), 370] that it may be "politically healthy" that "the limits of congressional power have never been completely clarified": "In some circumstances, may not attempts to restrict jurisdiction be an appropriate and important way for the political branches to register disagreement with the Court? And is it not enormously significant that, ever since McCardle, such 'attempts' have, in the main, been just that— that Congress has not significantly cut back the Supreme Court's jurisdiction in a vindictive manner despite the great unpopularity of some of its rulings?" Note also Charles Black's argument that the existence of congressional power over federal court jurisdiction (and the traditional forbearance of Congress in using it) is "the rock on which rests the legitimacy of the judicial work in a democracy." Black, "the Presidency and Congress," 32 Wash. & Lee L.Rev. 841, 846 (1975).

3. *Congressional control of appellate jurisdiction: Modern efforts. a. The Jenner–Butler attack.* The most important modern congressional attack on Court jurisdiction occurred in the late 1950s, in response to decisions allegedly too soft on "subversiveness." See, e.g., Senator Jenner's bill—provoked by several Warren Court decisions—eliminating appellate jurisdiction in cases involving, for example, the federal employees' security program, state subversive legislation, and state bar admissions. S. 2646, 85th Cong., 1st Sess. (1957). The Jenner–Butler bill [S. 3386, 85th Cong., 2d Sess.(1958)] would have included the following provision, prompted by the 1957 decisions in Konigsberg and Schware (p. 1391 below): "[The] Supreme Court shall have no jurisdiction to review, either by appeal, writ of certiorari, or otherwise, any case where there is drawn into question the validity of any law, rule, or regulation of any State, or of any board of bar examiners, or similar body, or of any action or proceeding taken pursuant to any such law, rule, or regulation pertaining to the admission of persons to the practice of law within such State." Was that Jenner–Butler provision constitutional? The Jenner–Butler bill was narrowly defeated. For the political struggle, see Murphy, Congress and the Court (1962), and Hearings on S. 2646, 85th Cong., Limitation of the Appellate Jurisdiction of the Supreme Court (1957–58).[33]

33. Another provision in the Jenner–Butler omnibus proposal—in reaction to such cases as Watkins v. United States (1957)–would have amended 2 U.S.C. § 192, the congressional contempt statute. That law states that anyone "who having been summoned as a witness" by any congressional committee and who wilfully "refuses to answer any question pertinent to the question under inquiry" shall be guilty of a misdemeanor. The Jenner–Butler bill would have added: "Provided, That for the purposes of this section any question shall be deemed pertinent unless timely objection is made thereto on the ground that such question lacks pertinency, or when such objection is made, if such question is ruled pertinent by the body conducting the hearing." Note that the basic provision made "pertinency" an element of the statutory crime, and that the Jenner–Butler bill would have deprived the courts of power to adjudicate that element. Would that provision have been subject to valid constitutional doubts under Klein?

b. *The 1968 crime control bill.* The Senate Judiciary Committee's version of the 1968 crime control bill included a provision—provoked by decisions such as Miranda v. Arizona, 384 U.S. 436 (1966)—which stated that neither the Supreme Court nor any other Art. III court "shall have jurisdiction to review or to reverse, vacate, modify, or disturb in any way, a ruling of any trial court of any State in any criminal prosecution admitting in evidence as voluntarily made an admission or confession of any accused." That Report contained an elaborate defense of congressional power over jurisdiction, but all anti-Miranda provisions couched in jurisdictional terms were eliminated on the floor of the Senate. Would such legislation have raised constitutional doubts? Under McCardle? Under Klein? Under Marbury?

c. *The Helms Amendment and other recent efforts to curb appellate jurisdiction.* The most recent wave of efforts to curb the Court's appellate jurisdiction crested in the early 1980s. Senator Jesse Helms of North Carolina was frequently at the center of those efforts, and one of his proposals, a bill to curb federal court jurisdiction in cases involving "voluntary" school prayers, received the most continuous attention in Congress. The Helms effort began in 1979. The Helms Amendment to S. 210, 96th Cong., 1st Sess., would have removed jurisdiction over such cases from all federal courts—lower ones as well as the Supreme Court. Senator Kennedy attacked that proposal on the Senate floor as an evisceration of the principle of Martin v. Hunter's Lessee. Senator Helms responded by referring to "the acknowledged power of Congress to make exceptions and prescribe regulations to the appellate power." Was Senator Kennedy's reliance on Martin persuasive? Was the Helms Amendment consistent with McCardle and Klein? Marbury?

During the early 1980s, proposals to curb the Court's appellate jurisdiction in specified categories of cases went well beyond the school prayer issue and attracted more attention than they had in years. During 1981 and 1982, some 30 jurisdiction-stripping bills were introduced in Congress, with some eliciting extensive committee hearings. See the collection of proposals in Baucus & Kay, "The Court Stripping Bills: Their Impact on the Constitution, the Courts, and Congress," 27 Vill.L.Rev. 988 (1982). The most comprehensive hearings are printed in Constitutional Restraints upon the Judiciary: Hearings Before the Subcomm. on the Constitution of the Senate Comm. on the Judiciary, 97th Cong., 1st Sess. (1981). The proposals would have eliminated the Court's appellate jurisdiction in such controversial areas as busing and abortion as well as school prayers. All these proposals failed. By the mid–1980s, the momentum behind these efforts waned considerably, largely because many opponents of the challenged Court ruling shifted their energies to an attempt to amend the Constitution to permit voluntary school prayers. During the early 1990s, the decline of congressional attention to jurisdiction-stripping devices continued, though a few—e.g., bills to bar review of decisions pertaining to abortion—did surface.

4. *Congressional control of lower federal court jurisdiction: Arguable modern limitations?* The Constitution and recurrent statements in Court opinions suggest a broad congressional authority over lower federal court jurisdiction. Are there nevertheless limits inherent in Art. III on what Congress may do? For example, is there an "essential" role for lower federal courts analogous to that claimed regarding the Supreme Court's appellate jurisdiction? Note Eisenberg, "Congressional Authority to Restrict Lower Federal Court Jurisdiction," 83 Yale L.J. 498 (1974), concluding: "It can now be asserted that the [existence of lower federal courts] in some form is constitutionally required." (Eisenberg relied on the "need" for lower federal courts to enforce "innovative" Supreme Court decisions in areas such as desegregation and

reapportionment, and on the impossibility, given the modern Court's workload, of Supreme Court review of all state court cases involving federal issues.) Contrast Bator, "Congressional Power Over the Jurisdiction of the Federal Courts," 27 Vill.L.Rev. 1030 (1982): "If the Congress decides that a certain category of case arising under a federal law should be litigated in a state court, subject to Supreme Court review, neither the letter nor the spirit of the Constitution has been violated. What has happened is that Congress has taken up one of the precise options which the Constitutional Framers specifically envisaged." Can it at least be argued that Congress may not impose limits on lower federal courts when it is motivated by hostility to unpopular decisions? Note that the Supreme Court had no difficulty in sustaining the Norris–LaGuardia Act of 1932, depriving federal courts of "jurisdiction" to issue injunctions in labor disputes—a jurisdictional curb largely motivated by congressional hostility to excessive intervention by federal courts in labor disputes. Lauf v. E.G. Shinner & Co., 303 U.S. 323 (1938).

Even if asserted constitutional restraints on congressional power are not persuasive with respect to curbs on Supreme Court or lower court jurisdiction, can a stronger case be made for restraints when Congress seeks to strip jurisdiction from *all* federal courts—the Supreme Court as well as the lower courts—in a specified class of cases? Some of the modern jurisdiction-stripping proposals, such as the Helms Amendment, took just such a form. Lawrence Sager has argued that Art. III requires that there must be *some* federal judicial forum for the enforcement of federal constitutional rights—either an "inferior" court or the Supreme Court. Sager, "Foreword: Constitutional Limitations on Congress' Authority to Regulate the Jurisdiction of the Federal Courts," 95 Harv.L.Rev. 17 (1981). Sager relies primarily on an "internal" limitation: the guarantee of federal judicial independence in Art. III (the tenure and salary provisions governing federal judges). He notes that many state judges are not afforded such protections and argues that some Art. III forum is constitutionally mandated for the enforcement of federal constitutional rights. Compare Martin Redish's reply, commenting that Sager "effectively adopts a 'floating' essential functions thesis." See Redish, "Constitutional Limitations on Congressional Power to Control Federal Jurisdiction: A Reaction to Professor Sager," 77 Nw.U.L.Rev. 143 (1982). Redish argues that the tenure and salary provisions relied on by Sager were simply designed "to preserve the integrity of the federal courts when they actually were used," not to assure that federal courts *must* be used.

Alternate argument

*

Art III v. Art I cts?
How far does Congress constitutional pwr of exceptiongo, wrt classes of cases?/subject matter

PART II

THE STRUCTURE OF GOVERNMENT: NATION AND STATES IN THE FEDERAL SYSTEM

Introduction. Stronger government was necessary, but the national government must not become too powerful: these were dominant concerns to the Framers. The Constitution reflects their effort to accommodate these needs and risks. That document granted greater powers to the central government to cure some of the weaknesses under the Articles of Confederation; yet the Constitution also assured restraints on governmental power. To the drafters of 1787, protection against excessive concentrations of power lay less in explicit limits such as the "shall nots" of the Bill of Rights than in diffusions of power among a variety of governmental units. Thus, the Constitution allocated powers among nation and states: a federal division of powers was achieved by specifying (most notably in Art. I, § 8) those powers Congress might exercise and by emphasizing (in the Tenth Amendment) that undelegated powers were "reserved to the States respectively, or to the people." Moreover, the less-than-total powers given to the national government were diffused among three separate branches, separately delineated in the first three Articles of the Constitution.

Part II of this book considers these grants and dispersals of power. These chapters explore not only the governmental actions these grants justify but also the limits these grants imply. How can the scope of national authority be articulated with an adequate regard for the interest in local autonomy? That is the focus of chapters 2 through 4: they examine the extent and limits of authority when national power seeks to reach arguably local affairs. (See also chapter 10, exploring the scope of congressional power under the Civil War Amendments.) Chapter 5 focuses on the states rather than on national authority—and especially on the limits on state power imposed by national concerns, particularly as reflected in the grant to Congress of the power to regulate interstate commerce. And chapter 6, finally, turns from the vertical nation-state dimension to examine the horizontal restraints imposed by the separation of powers within the national government—by the distribution of national powers among executive, legislative, and judicial branches.

CHAPTER 2

NATIONAL POWERS AND LOCAL ACTIVITIES: ORIGINS AND RECURRENT THEMES

———

Introduction: Federalism—Antiquarian Relic? Contemporary Value? Federalism is the major concern of Part II of this book. The first three chapters of Part II, on the scope of the powers granted to Congress by the Constitutional Convention, consider the most controversial impacts of federalism on American history. Again and again in these pages, legislation enacted with wide popular support is held unconstitutional by the Supreme Court, particularly in the early decades of this century. And in a larger number of instances, states' rights arguments—some principled, some disingenuous—have delayed or defeated action by Congress. The materials that follow focus on federalism-related limits on national power: limits developed in the interest of curtailing national intrusion into local affairs, as distinguished from restraints stemming from individual rights guarantees (considered in Part III of this book).

The controversial impacts of federalism-related limits suggest questions relevant to much of what follows: What were the historical justifications for American federalism? How successfully has the Court applied those values to changing circumstances? These questions in turn raise even more basic ones: Does federalism retain substantial value in the 20th century, or is it an obsolete obstruction to be dismissed with minimal lip service? And should the Court rather than Congress be the predominant custodian of federalism? Are significant Court-imposed limits on congressional power unnecessary because local interests are adequately safeguarded by the political process? Even if judicial checks on Congress are inappropriate, is the Court nevertheless compelled to act as the interventionist umpire of the federal system vis-à-vis the states, by blocking state impingements on national interests?*

The appropriate role of the Court in the evolution of federalism is an issue apparent on the face of many of the materials that follow. Related, equally pervasive questions typically lurk beneath the surface: What are the values, historical and contemporary, of federalism? Can it still be said that federalism enhances liberty, encourages diversity, promotes creative experimentation and responsive self-government? Or is it a legalistic obstruction, a harmful brake on governmental responses to pressing social issues, a shield for selfish vested interests? Is federalism a theme that constitutional law must grapple with simply because it is *there,* in the Constitution? In confronting federalism issues, should the Court seek primarily to minimize the obstacles that the complexities

———

* Recall Justice Holmes' famous remark: "I do not think the United States would come to an end if we lost our power to declare an Act of Congress void. I do think the Union would be imperiled if we could not make that declaration as to the laws of the several States." Holmes, Collected Legal Papers (1920), 295.

of the federal structure put in the way of meeting modern needs? Or does federalism embody more appealing values that deserve some of the imaginative enthusiasm with which modern constitutional law embraces the promotion of such values as equality and freedom of speech? See generally Shapiro, Federalism—A Dialogue (1995).

The United States has not been the only nation to resort to federalism for the purpose of governing large geographical areas with diverse local needs. The federal model has also provided a mechanism for governments of other nations, as well as for international cooperation. The frictions and accommodations during nearly two centuries of American experience—the concerns of the materials that follow—deserve consideration not only for their own sake but also for the light they shed on federalism's capacity to adapt to future needs, here and elsewhere.

[handwritten margin note: LIMITS ON FED INTRUSION INTO LOCAL AFFAIRS]

[handwritten margin note: review: means & ends]

McCulloch v. Maryland

4 Wheat. (17 U.S.) 316, 4 L.Ed. 579 (1819).

[Congress chartered the Second Bank of the United States in 1816. The Bank soon established branches in many states. Its branch in Baltimore quickly became the most active of all. In April 1818, the Maryland legislature adopted "An Act to impose a Tax on all Banks or Branches thereof in the State of Maryland, not chartered by the Legislature." The law provided that any banks operating in Maryland "without authority from the State" could issue bank notes only on stamped paper, furnished by the State upon payment of a fee varying with the denomination of each note; but any bank subject to that requirement could "relieve itself" from it "by paying annually, in advance, [the] sum of fifteen thousand dollars." The statute also provided for penalties for violators: for example, the president, cashier and all other officers of the bank were to "forfeit" five hundred dollars "for each and every offense." The penalties were enforceable by indictment or by "action of debt, in the County Court," "one half to the informer, and the other half to the use of the State."

[This action for the statutory penalty was brought in the County Court of Baltimore County by one John James, suing for himself and the State, against James McCulloch, the Cashier of the Baltimore branch of the Bank of the United States. McCulloch admitted that the Bank was doing business without authority from the State and that he had issued bank notes without complying with the Maryland law. The case was decided against McCulloch on the basis of an agreed statement of facts, and the decision was affirmed by the Maryland Court of Appeals From there, the case was taken by writ of error to the Supreme Court.[1] For the historical context of the dispute, see the materials following the Court's opinion.]

[handwritten margin note: measure of necessity]

Chief Justice MARSHALL delivered the opinion of the Court.

In the case now to be determined, the defendant [in error], a sovereign state, denies the obligation of a law enacted by the legislature of the Union, and

---

1. Court Reporter Henry Wheaton noted that, because of the great importance of the case, "the Court dispensed with its general rule, permitting only two counsel to argue for each party." Six counsel (United States Attorney General William Wirt, Daniel Web- ster and William Pinkney for the Bank; State Attorney General Luther Martin, Joseph Hopkinson and Walter Jones for Maryland) argued the case over a period of nine days. The opinion was delivered only three days after the arguments concluded.

the plaintiff [in error], on his part, contests the validity of an act which has been passed by the legislature of that state. The constitution of our country, in its most interesting and vital parts, is to be considered; the conflicting powers of the government of the Union and of its members, as marked in that constitution, are to be discussed; and an opinion given, which may essentially influence the great operations of the government. No tribunal can approach such a question without a deep sense of its importance, and of the awful responsibility involved in its decision. But it must be decided peacefully, or remain a source of hostile legislation, perhaps of hostility of a still more serious nature; and if it is to be so decided, by this tribunal alone can the decision be made. On the Supreme Court of the United States has the constitution of our country devolved this important duty.

The first question made in the cause is, has Congress power to incorporate a bank? It has been truly said that this can scarcely be considered as an open question, entirely unprejudiced by the former proceedings of the nation respecting it. The principle now contested was introduced at a very early period of our history, has been recognized by many successive legislatures, and has been acted upon by the judicial department, in cases of peculiar delicacy, as a law of undoubted obligation. [The] power now contested was exercised by the first Congress elected under the present constitution. The bill for incorporating the bank of the United States did not steal upon an unsuspecting legislature, and pass unobserved. Its principle was completely understood, and was opposed with equal zeal and ability. After being resisted, first in the fair and open field of debate, and afterwards in the executive cabinet, with as much persevering talent as any measure has ever experienced, and being supported by arguments which convinced minds as pure and as intelligent as this country can boast, it became a law. The original act was permitted to expire; but a short experience of the embarrassments to which the refusal to revive it exposed the government, convinced those who were most prejudiced against the measure of its necessity, and induced the passage of the present law. It would require no ordinary share of intrepidity to assert that a measure adopted under these circumstances was a bold and plain usurpation, to which the constitution gave no countenance. These observations belong to the cause; but they are not made under the impression that, were the question entirely new, the law would be found irreconcilable with the constitution.

In discussing this question, the counsel for the State of Maryland have deemed it of some importance, in the construction of the constitution, to consider that instrument not as emanating from the people, but as the act of sovereign and independent states. The powers of the general government, it has been said, are delegated by the states, who alone are truly sovereign; and must be exercised in subordination to the states, who alone possess supreme dominion.

It would be difficult to sustain this proposition. The Convention which framed the constitution was indeed elected by the state legislatures. But the instrument, when it came from their hands, was a mere proposal, without obligation, or pretensions to it. It was reported to the then existing Congress of the United States, with a request that it might "be submitted to a convention of delegates, chosen in each State by the people thereof, under the recommendation of its legislature, for their assent and ratification." This mode of proceeding was adopted; and by the convention, by Congress, and by the state legislatures, the instrument was submitted to the people. They acted upon it in the only manner in which they can act safely, effectively, and wisely, on such a subject, by assembling in convention. It is true, they assembled in their several states—and where else should they have assembled? No political dreamer was ever wild enough to think of breaking down the lines which separate the states, and of compounding the American people into one common mass. Of consequence, when they act, they act in their states. But the measures they adopt do not, on that account, cease to be the measures of the people themselves, or become the measures of the state governments.

From these conventions the constitution derives its whole authority. The government proceeds directly from the people; is "ordained and established" in the name of the people; and is declared to be ordained, "in order to form a more perfect union, establish justice, ensure domestic tranquility, and secure the blessings of liberty to themselves and to their posterity." The assent of the states, in their sovereign capacity, is implied in calling a convention, and thus submitting that instrument to the people. But the people were at perfect liberty to accept or reject it; and their act was final. It required not the affirmance, and could not be negatived, by the state governments. The constitution, when thus adopted, was of complete obligation, and bound the State sovereignties. [The] government of the Union, then (whatever may be the influence of this fact on the case), is, emphatically, and truly, a government of the people. In form and in substance it emanates from them. Its powers are granted by them, and are to be exercised directly on them, and for their benefit.

This government is acknowledged by all to be one of enumerated powers. The principle, that it can exercise only the powers granted to it, [is] now universally admitted. But the question respecting the extent of the powers actually granted, is perpetually arising, and will probably continue to arise, as long as our system shall exist. [If] any one proposition could command the universal assent of mankind, we might expect it would be this—that the government of the Union, though limited in its powers, is supreme within its sphere of action.

[Among] the enumerated powers, we do not find that of establishing a bank or creating a corporation. But there is no phrase in the instrument which, like the articles of confederation, excludes incidental or implied powers; and which requires that everything granted shall be expressly and minutely described. [The Articles of Confederation had provided that each state "retains" every power not "expressly delegated."] Even the 10th amendment, which was framed for the purpose of quieting the excessive jealousies which had been excited, omits the word "expressly," and declares only that the powers "not delegated to the United States, nor prohibited to the States, are reserved to the States or to the people"; thus leaving the question, whether the particular power which may become the subject of contest has been delegated to the one government, or prohibited to the other, to depend on a fair construction of the whole instrument. The men who drew and adopted this amendment had experienced the embarrassments resulting from the insertion of this word in the articles of confederation, and probably omitted it to avoid those embarrassments. A constitution, to contain an accurate detail of all the subdivisions of which its great powers will admit, and of all the means by which they may be carried into execution, would partake of the prolixity of a legal code, and could scarcely be embraced by the human mind. It would probably never be understood by the public. Its nature, therefore, requires, that only its great outlines should be marked, its important objects designated, and the minor ingredients which compose those objects be deduced from the nature of the objects themselves. That this idea was entertained by the framers of the American constitution, is not only to be inferred from the nature of the instrument, but from the language. Why else were some of the limitations, found in the ninth section of the 1st article, introduced? It is also, in some degree, warranted by their having omitted to use any restrictive term which might prevent its receiving a fair and just interpretation. In considering this question, then, we must never forget that it is *a constitution* we are expounding.

Although, among the enumerated powers of government, we do not find the word "bank," or "incorporation," we find the great powers to lay and collect taxes; to borrow money; to regulate commerce; to declare and conduct a war; and to raise and support armies and navies. The sword and the purse, all the external relations, and no inconsiderable portion of the industry of the nation, are entrusted to its government. It can never be pretended that these vast powers draw after them others of inferior importance, merely because they are inferior. [But] it may with great reason be contended, that a government, entrusted with such ample powers, on the due execution of which the happiness and prosperity of the nation so vitally depends, must also be entrusted with ample means for their execution. The power being given, it is the interest of the nation to facilitate its execution. It can never be their interest, and cannot be presumed to have been their intention, to clog and embarrass its execution by withholding the most appropriate means. Throughout this vast republic, from the St. Croix to the Gulf of Mexico, from the Atlantic to the Pacific, revenue is to be collected and expended, armies are to be marched and supported. The exigencies of the nation may require that the treasure raised in the north should be transported to the south, that raised in the east conveyed to the west, or that this order should be reversed. Is that construction of the constitution to be preferred which would render these operations difficult, hazardous, and expensive? Can we adopt that construction (unless the words imperiously require it) which would impute to the framers of that instrument, when granting these powers for the public good, the intention of impeding their exercise by withholding a choice of means? If, indeed, such be the mandate of the constitution, we have only to obey; but that instrument does not profess to enumerate the means by which the powers it confers may be executed; nor does it prohibit the creation of a corporation, if the existence of such a being be essential to the beneficial exercise of those powers. It is, then, the subject of fair inquiry, how far such means may be employed.

[The] government which has a right to do an act, and has imposed on it the duty of performing that act, must, according to the dictates of reason, be allowed to select the means; and those who contend that it may not select any appropriate means, that one particular mode of effecting the object is excepted, take upon themselves the burden of establishing that exception. [The] power of creating a corporation, though appertaining to sovereignty, is not, like the power of making war, or levying taxes, or of regulating commerce, a great substantive and independent power, which cannot be implied as incidental to other powers, or used as a means of executing them. It is never the end for which other powers are exercised, but a means by which other objects are accomplished. [The] power of creating a corporation is never used for its own sake, but for the purpose of effecting something else. No sufficient reason is, therefore, perceived, why it may not pass as incidental to those powers which are expressly given, if it be a direct mode of executing them.

But the constitution of the United States has not left the right of Congress to employ the necessary means, for the execution of the powers conferred on the government, to general reasoning. To its enumeration of powers is added that of making "all laws which shall be necessary and proper for carrying into execution the foregoing powers, and all other powers vested by this constitution, in the government of the United States, or in any department thereof." The counsel for the State of Maryland have urged various arguments, to prove that this clause, though in terms a grant of power, is not so in effect; but is really restrictive of the general right, which might otherwise be implied, of selecting means for executing the enumerated powers.

[The] argument on which most reliance is placed, is drawn from the peculiar language of this clause. Congress is not empowered by it to make all laws, which may have relation to the powers conferred on the government, but such only as may be *"necessary and proper"* for carrying them into execution. The word *"necessary"* is considered as controlling the whole sentence, and as limiting the right to pass laws for the execution of the granted powers, to such as are indispensable, and without which the power would be nugatory. That it excludes the choice of means, and leaves to Congress, in each case, that only which is most direct and simple.

Is it true, that this is the sense in which the word "necessary" is always used? Does it always import an absolute physical necessity, so strong, that one thing, to which another may be termed necessary, cannot exist without that other? We think it does not. If reference be had to its use, in the common affairs of the world, or in approved authors, we find that it frequently imports no more than that one thing is convenient, or useful, or essential to another. To employ the means necessary to an end, is generally understood as employing any means calculated to produce the end, and not as being confined to those single means, without which the end would be entirely unattainable. [It] is essential to just construction, that many words which import something excessive should be understood in a more mitigated sense—in that sense which common usage justifies. The word "necessary" is of this description. It has not a fixed character peculiar to itself. It admits of all degrees of comparison. [A] thing may be necessary, very necessary, absolutely or indispensably necessary. To no mind would the same idea be conveyed by these several phrases. This comment on the word is well illustrated by the passage cited at the bar, from the 10th section of the 1st article of the constitution. It is, we think, impossible to compare the sentence which prohibits a state from laying "imposts, or duties on imports or exports, except what may be *absolutely* necessary for executing its inspection laws," with that which authorizes Congress "to make all laws which shall be necessary and proper for carrying into execution" the powers of the general government, without feeling a conviction that the convention understood itself to change materially the meaning of the word "necessary," by prefixing the word "absolutely." This word, then, like others, is used in various senses; and, in its construction, the subject, the context, the intention of the person using them, are all to be taken into view.

Let this be done in the case under consideration. The subject is the execution of those great powers on which the welfare of a nation essentially depends. It must have been the intention of those who gave these powers, to insure, as far as human prudence could insure, their beneficial execution. This could not be done by confining the choice of means to such narrow limits as not to leave it in the power of Congress to adopt any which might be appropriate, and which were conducive to the end. This provision is made in a constitution intended to endure for ages to come, and, consequently, to be adapted to the various *crises* of human affairs. To have prescribed the means by which government should, in all future time, execute its powers, would have been to change, entirely, the character of the instrument, and give it the properties of a legal code. It would have been an unwise attempt to provide, by immutable rules, for exigencies which, if foreseen at all, must have been seen dimly, and which can be best provided for as they occur. To have declared that the best means shall not be used, but those alone without which the power given would be nugatory, would have been to deprive the legislature of the capacity to avail itself of experience, to exercise its reason, and to accommodate its legislation to circumstances. If we apply this principle of construction to any of the powers of the government, we shall find it so pernicious in its operation that we shall be compelled to discard it.

[Take], for example, the power "to establish post offices and post roads." This power is executed by the single act of making the establishment. But, from this has been inferred the power and duty of carrying the mail along the post road, from one post office to another. And, from this implied power, has again been inferred the right to punish those who steal letters from the post office, or rob the mail. It may be said, with some plausibility, that the right to carry the mail, and to punish those who rob it, is not indispensably necessary to the establishment of a post office and post road. This right is indeed essential to the beneficial exercise of the power, but not indispensably necessary to its existence. So, of the punishment of the crimes of stealing or falsifying a record or process of a Court of the United States, or of perjury in such Court. To punish these offences is certainly conducive to the due administration of justice. But courts may exist, and may decide the causes brought before them, though such crimes escape punishment.

[If a] limited construction of the word "necessary" must be abandoned in order to punish, whence is derived the rule which would reinstate it, when the government would carry its powers into execution by means not vindictive in their nature? If the word "necessary" means "needful," "requisite," "essential," "conducive to," in order to let in the power of punishment for the infraction of law; why is it not equally comprehensive when required to authorize the use of means which facilitate the execution of the powers of government without the infliction of punishment?

In ascertaining the sense in which the word "necessary" is used in this clause of the constitution, we may derive some aid from that with which it is associated. Congress shall have power "to make all laws which shall be necessary and *proper* to carry into execution" the powers of the government. If the word "necessary" was used in that strict and rigorous sense for which the counsel for the State of Maryland contend, it would be an extraordinary departure from the usual course of the human mind, as exhibited in composition, to add a word, the only possible effect of which is to qualify that strict and rigorous meaning; to present to the mind the idea of some choice of means of legislation not straitened and compressed within the narrow limits for which gentlemen contend.

But the argument which most conclusively demonstrates the error of the construction contended for by the counsel for the State of Maryland, is founded on the intention of the Convention, as manifested in the whole clause. To waste time and argument in proving that, without it, Congress might carry its powers into execution, would be not much less idle than to hold a lighted taper to the sun. As little can it be required to prove, that in the absence of this clause, Congress would have some choice of means. That it might employ those which, in its judgment, would most advantageously effect the object to be accomplished. That any means adapted to the end, any means which tended directly to the execution of the constitutional powers of the government, were in themselves constitutional. This clause, as construed by the State of Maryland, would abridge, and almost annihilate this useful and necessary right of the legislature to select its means. That this could not be intended, is, we should think, had it not been already controverted, too apparent for controversy. We think so for the following reasons: 1st. The clause is placed among the powers of Congress, not among the limitations on those powers. 2nd. Its terms purport to enlarge, not to diminish the powers vested in the government. It purports to be an additional power, not a restriction on those already granted. No reason has been, or can be assigned for thus concealing an intention to narrow the discretion of the national legislature under words which purport to enlarge it.

[The] result of the most careful and attentive consideration bestowed upon this clause is, that if it does not enlarge, it cannot be construed to restrain the powers of Congress, or to impair the right of the legislature to exercise its best judgment in the selection of measures to carry into execution the constitutional powers of the government. If no other motive for its insertion can be suggested, a sufficient one is found in the desire to remove all doubts respecting the right to legislate on that vast mass of incidental powers which must be involved in the constitution, if that instrument be not a splendid bauble.

We admit, as all must admit, that the powers of the government are limited, and that its limits are not to be transcended. But we think the sound construction of the constitution must allow to the national legislature that discretion, with respect to the means by which the powers it confers are to be carried into execution, which will enable that body to perform the high duties assigned to it, in the manner most beneficial to the people. Let the end be legitimate, let it be within the scope of the constitution, and all means which are appropriate, which are plainly adapted to that end, which are not prohibited, but consist with the letter and spirit of the constitution, are constitutional.

[If] a corporation may be employed indiscriminately with other means to carry into execution the powers of the government, no particular reason can be assigned for excluding the use of a bank, if required for its fiscal operations. To use one, must be within the discretion of Congress, if it be an appropriate mode of executing the powers of government. That it is a convenient, a useful, and essential instrument in the prosecution of its fiscal operations, is not now a subject of controversy. All those who have been concerned in the administration of our finances, have concurred in representing its importance and necessity; and so strongly have they been felt, that statesmen of the first class, whose previous opinions against it had been confirmed by every circumstance which can fix the human judgment, have yielded those opinions to the exigencies of the nation. [But], were its necessity less apparent, none can deny its being an appropriate measure; and if it is, the degree of its necessity, as has been very justly observed, is to be discussed in another place. Should Congress, in the execution of its powers, adopt measures which are prohibited by the constitution; or should Congress, under the pretext of executing its powers, pass laws for the accomplishment of objects not entrusted to the government; it would become the painful duty of this tribunal, should a case requiring such a decision come before it, to say that such an act was not the law of the land. But where the law is not prohibited, and is really calculated to effect any of the objects entrusted to the government, to undertake here to inquire into the degree of its necessity, would be to pass the line which circumscribes the judicial department, and to tread on legislative ground. This court disclaims all pretensions to such a power.

After this declaration, it can scarcely be necessary to say that the existence of state banks can have no possible influence on the question. No trace is to be found in the constitution of an intention to create a dependence of the government of the Union on those of the states, for the execution of the great powers assigned to it. Its means are adequate to its ends; and on those means alone was it expected to rely for the accomplishment of its ends. To impose on it the necessity of resorting to means which it cannot control, which another government may furnish or withhold, would render its course precarious, the result of its measures uncertain, and create a dependence on other governments, which might disappoint its most important designs, and is incompatible with the language of the constitution. But were it otherwise, the choice of means implies a right to choose a national bank in preference to state banks, and Congress alone can make the election. [It] being the opinion of the Court, that the act incorporating the bank is constitutional; and that the power of establishing a branch in the State of Maryland might be properly exercised by the bank itself, we proceed to inquire—

2.   Whether the State of Maryland may, without violating the constitution, tax that branch? That the power of taxation is one of vital importance; that it is retained by the states; that it is not abridged by the grant of a similar power to the government of the Union; that it is to be concurrently exercised by the two governments: are truths which have never been denied. But, such is the paramount character of the constitution, that its capacity to withdraw any subject from the action of even this power, is admitted. The states are expressly forbidden to lay any duties on imports or exports, except what may be absolutely necessary for executing their inspection laws. If the obligation of this prohibition must be conceded, [the] same paramount character would seem to restrain, as it certainly may restrain, a state from such other exercise of this power, as is in its nature incompatible with, and repugnant to, the constitutional laws of the Union. A law, absolutely repugnant to another, as entirely repeals that other as if express terms of repeals were used. On this ground the counsel for the bank place its claim to be exempted from the power of a State to tax its operations. There is no express provision for the case, but the claim has been sustained on a principle which so entirely pervades the constitution, is so intermixed with the materials which compose it, so interwoven with its web, so blended with its texture, as to be incapable of being separated from it, without rending it into shreds. This great principle is, that the constitution and the laws made in pursuance thereof are supreme; that they control the constitution and laws of the respective States, and cannot be controlled by them. From this, which may be almost termed an axiom, other propositions are deduced as corollaries, on the truth or error of which, and on their application to this case, the cause has been supposed to depend. These are, 1st. That a power to create implies a power to preserve. 2d. That a power to destroy, if wielded by a different hand, is hostile to, and incompatible with these powers to create and to preserve. 3d. That where this repugnancy exists, that authority which is supreme must control, not yield to that over which it is supreme.

[That] the power of taxing [the bank] by the states may be exercised so as to destroy it, is too obvious to be denied. But taxation is said to be an absolute power, which acknowledges no other limits than those expressly prescribed in the constitution, and like sovereign power of every other description, is trusted to the discretion of those who use it. But the very terms of this argument admit, that the sovereignty of the state, in the article of taxation itself, is subordinate to, and may be controlled by the constitution of the United States. How far it has been controlled by that instrument must be a question of construction. In making this construction, no principle, not declared, can be admissible, which would defeat the legitimate operations of a supreme government. It is of the very essence of supremacy, to remove all obstacles to its action within its own sphere, and so to modify every power vested in subordinate governments, as to exempt its own operations from their own influence. This effect need not be stated in terms. It is so involved in the declaration of supremacy, so necessarily implied in it, that the expression of it could not make it more certain. We must, therefore, keep it in view, while construing the constitution.

The argument on the part of the State of Maryland is, not that the states may directly resist a law of Congress, but that they may exercise their acknowledged powers upon it, and that the constitution leaves them this right in the confidence that they will not abuse it. Before we proceed to examine this argument, and to subject it to the test of the constitution, we must be permitted to bestow a few considerations on the nature and extent of this original right of taxation, which is acknowledged to remain with the states. It is admitted that the power of taxing the people and their property is essential to the very existence of government, and may be legitimately exercised on the objects to which it is applicable, to the utmost extent to which the government may choose to carry it. The only security against the abuse of this power, is found in the structure of the government itself. In imposing a tax the legislature acts upon its constituents. This is in general a sufficient security against erroneous and oppressive taxation. [But] the means employed by the government of the Union have no such security, nor is the right of a state to tax them sustained by the same theory. Those means are not given by the people of a particular state, [but] by the people of all the states. They are given by all, for the benefit of all—and upon theory, should be subjected to that government only which belongs to all.

[We] find, then, on just theory, a total failure of this original right to tax the means employed by the government of the Union, for the execution of its powers. The right never existed, and the question whether it has been surrendered, cannot arise. But, waiving this theory for the present, let us resume the inquiry, whether this power can be exercised by the respective states, consistently with a fair construction of the constitution?

That the power to tax involves the power to destroy; that the power to destroy may defeat and render useless the power to create; that there is a plain repugnance, in conferring on one government a power to control the constitutional measures of another, which other, with respect to those very measures, is declared to be supreme over that which exerts the control, are propositions not to be denied. But all inconsistencies are to be reconciled by the magic of the word CONFIDENCE. Taxation, it is said, does not necessarily and unavoidably destroy. To carry it to the excess of destruction would be an abuse, to presume which, would banish that confidence which is essential to all government.

But is this a case of confidence? Would the people of any one state trust those of another with a power to control the most insignificant operations of their state government? We know they would not. Why, then, should we suppose that the people of any one state should be willing to trust those of another with a power to control the operations of a government to which they have confided their most important and most valuable interests? In the legislature of the Union alone, are all represented. The legislature of the Union alone, therefore, can be trusted by the people with the power of controlling measures which concern all, in the confidence that it will not be abused. This, then, is not a case of confidence, and we must consider it as it really is.

[If] we apply the principle for which the State of Maryland contends, to the constitution generally, we shall find it capable of changing totally the character of that instrument. We shall find it capable of arresting all the measures of the government, and of prostrating it at the foot of the states. [If] the states may tax one instrument, employed by the government in the execution of its powers, they may tax any and every other instrument. They may tax the mail; they may tax the mint; they may tax patent rights; they may tax the papers of the custom-house; they may tax judicial process; they may tax all the means employed by the government, to an excess which would defeat all the ends of government. [The American people] did not design to make their government dependent on the states.

[It] has also been insisted, that, as the power of taxation in the general and state governments is acknowledged to be concurrent, every argument which would sustain the right of the general government to tax banks chartered by the states, will equally sustain the right of the states to tax banks chartered by the general government. But the two cases are not on the same reason. The people of all the states have created the general government, and have conferred upon it the general power of taxation. The people of all the states, and the states themselves, are represented in Congress, and, by their representatives, exercise this power. When they tax the chartered institutions of the states, they tax their constituents; and these taxes must be uniform. But, when a state taxes the operations of the government of the United States, it acts upon institutions created, not by their own constituents, but by people over whom they claim no control. It acts upon the measures of a government created by others as well as themselves, for the benefit of others in common with themselves. The difference is that which always exists, and always must exist, between the action of the whole on a part, and the action of a part on the whole—between the laws of a government declared to be supreme, and those of a government which, when in opposition to those laws, is not supreme. But if the full application of this argument could be admitted, it might bring into question the right of Congress to tax the State banks, and could not prove the right of the States to tax the Bank of the United States.

[We conclude] that the states have no power, by taxation or otherwise, to retard, impede, burden, or in any manner control, the operations of the constitutional laws enacted by Congress to carry into execution the powers vested in the general government. [We] are unanimously of opinion, that the law passed by the legislature of Maryland, imposing a tax on the Bank of the United States, is unconstitutional and void. This opinion does not deprive the states of any resources which they originally possessed. It does not extend to a tax paid by the real property of the bank, in common with the other real property within the state, nor to a tax imposed on the interest which the citizens of Maryland may hold in this institution, in common with other property of the same description throughout the state. But this is a tax on the operations of the bank, and is, consequently, a tax on the operation of an instrument employed by the government of the Union to carry its powers into execution. Such a tax must be unconstitutional.

[Reversed.]

———

IMPLIED NATIONAL POWERS AND THE NECESSARY AND PROPER CLAUSE—THE HISTORICAL CONTEXT

Introduction. The nation was 30 years old when the Bank case came to the Supreme Court. The issues presented were not novel ones in 1819: both the specific question of the constitutionality of the Bank and the general one regarding the scope of national powers had been repeatedly debated since the beginning. These notes focus on the highlights of the contentions before 1819 and during the following decade. The McCulloch decision, important as it is, was no more the end than the beginning of the debate. The scope of the national legislature's authority to reach local affairs is a characteristic, never-ending problem of our federal system. It continues to breed conflicts and to generate searches for new accommodations; and the next two chapters will trace these conflicts and accommodations from Marshall's day to ours.

1. *The allocation of powers in the Articles of Confederation and the Constitution. a. The Confederation.* The American federal structure allocates powers between nation and states by enumerating the powers delegated to the national government and acknowledging the retention by the states of the remainder. That allocation technique did not originate at the 1787 Constitutional Convention. The Articles of Confederation followed a similar scheme. What the Convention contributed was an expansion of enumerated national powers to remedy perceived weaknesses under the Articles. Thus, the most important enumeration of congressional powers in the Constitution, Art. I, § 8, had a counterpart quite similar in form if not in scope in one of the Articles of Confederation, Art. IX.[1]

Art. II of the Articles emphasized the limited nature of national powers by stating that each state retained "every Power, Jurisdiction and right, which is not by this confederation expressly delegated to the United States." That provision is analogous to the Tenth Amendment of the Constitution, which omits the adverb "expressly" in assuring that the "powers not delegated to the United States" nor prohibited to the States "are reserved to the States respectively, or to the people." [Recall Marshall's reference to this change in McCulloch.] The move from the Articles to the Constitution was not, then, one from a central government of no powers to one with all powers; rather, it was a shift from one with fewer powers to one with more powers (and with improved machinery to enforce those powers, through a separate national executive and judiciary[2]). And the Tenth Amendment was designed to allay fears that were an understandable concomitant of greater powers, fears frequently expressed in the ratification debates: the fears of an excessively powerful, excessively centralized national government.[3] Note the differences between the congressional power grants in the two documents. The most important new specifications were the grants of the powers to levy taxes and to regulate interstate and foreign commerce. It was the lack of those powers (the Confederation's funds,

---

1. Art. IX provided: "The United States in Congress assembled, shall have the sole and exclusive right and power of determining on peace and war—[of] sending and receiving ambassadors—entering into treaties and alliances, provided that no treaty of commerce shall be made whereby the legislative power of the respective States shall be restrained from imposing such imposts and duties on foreigners, as their own people are subjected to, or from prohibiting the exportation or importation of any species of goods or commodities whatsoever—[of] granting letters of marque and reprisal in times of peace—appointing courts for the trial of piracies and felonies committed on the high seas and establishing courts for receiving and determining finally appeals in all cases of captures.

"[The] United States in Congress assembled shall also have the sole and exclusive right and power of regulating the alloy and value of coin struck by their own authority, or by that of the respective States—fixing the standard of weights and measures throughout the United States—regulating the trade and managing all affairs with the Indians, not members of any of the States, provided that the legislative right of any State within its own limits be not infringed or violated—establishing or regulating post-offices from one State to another, throughout all the [United States]—making rules for the government and regulation of [the] land and naval forces, and directing their [operations]."

2. See Gunther, "Toward 'A More Perfect Union': Framing and Implementing the Distinctive Nation–Building Elements of the Constitution," in Aspects of American Liberty—Philosophical, Historical, and Political (Corner, ed., 1977).

3. See generally Storing's seven-volume collection, The Complete Anti–Federalist (1981)—especially his first volume, What the Anti-Federalists Were *For* (1981).

for example, came from the states, who had the sole power to impose taxes)
that had been widely blamed for the failures of the Articles.

b. *The Constitutional Convention.* Consensus that the new Constitution
should strengthen national powers did not inevitably mean that a fuller
enumeration of powers would be the chosen technique. Rather than building on
the enumeration format of the Articles, a simpler, more general, more inclusive
statement of congressional powers was conceivable. That, indeed, was the
approach the Convention adopted initially. Is it significant in determining the
breadth of the granted powers that the specification route was ultimately
followed in Art. I? At the Convention, the Virginia plan proposed "[t]hat the
National Legislature ought to be empowered to enjoy the Legislative Rights
vested in Congress by the Confederation; and moreover to legislate in all cases,
to which the separate States are incompetent, or in which the harmony of the
United States may be interrupted by exercise of individual legislation." Indeed,
the Convention delegates twice voted for formulations in similarly general
terms.[4] The ultimate scheme of Art. I, § 8—specifying the granted powers and
ending with the Necessary and Proper Clause in paragraph 18—originated in
the Convention's Committee of Detail.

There was virtually no discussion of the Necessary and Proper Clause at
the Convention. During the ratification debates, however, many of the fears of
a powerful central government focused on that Clause. Defenders of the
Constitution—e.g., Hamilton and Madison—insisted that the Clause was
"harmless" and that objections to it were a "pretext." As Madison explained in
Federalist No. 44: "Had the Constitution been silent on this head, there can be
no doubt that all the particular powers requisite as means of executing the
general powers would have resulted to the government, by unavoidable implication." (Note the similarity to McCulloch.)

2. *The Jefferson–Hamilton debate on the Bank in 1791.* With the establishment of the new government, agreement among the supporters of the new
Constitution on general formulations soon gave way to conflicts on applications.
The best known dispute in Washington's Administration warrants special
attention: it was characteristic of the emerging conflicts between broad and
narrow constructionists; and it focused on the very issue that ultimately came
to the Court in McCulloch—and provided some of the ideological legacy that
found its way into Marshall's opinion.

In December 1790, Alexander Hamilton, Washington's Secretary of the
Treasury, sent to the House of Representatives a lengthy Report urging the
incorporation of a national bank. He listed as among its principal advantages
"[t]he augmentation of the active or productive capital," a greater "facility as
to the government in obtaining pecuniary aids, especially in sudden emergencies," and the "facilitating of the payment of taxes." Less than two months
later, Congress enacted a law creating the First Bank of the United States—a
law much like the one passed in 1816 and sustained in McCulloch. While the
bill was on Washington's desk, the President requested opinions on its constitutionality from several of his Cabinet members. Secretary of State Jefferson
thought it unconstitutional; Secretary of the Treasury Hamilton considered it
constitutional. The President followed Hamilton's advice.

Jefferson, after invoking the Tenth Amendment, insisted that the Necessary and Proper Clause did not justify the creation of the Bank: a bank was

4. See 1 Farrand, The Records of the   and 2 Farrand, 21.
Federal Convention of 1787 (1911), 47, 53

"not *necessary,* and consequently not authorized by this phrase." He added: "If such a latitude of construction be allowed to this phrase as to give any non-enumerated power, it will go to every one, for there is not one which ingenuity may not torture into a *convenience* in some instance *or other,* to *some one* of so long a list of enumerated powers. It would swallow up all the delegated powers. [Therefore] it was that the Constitution restrained them to the *necessary* means, that is to say, to those means without which the grant of power would be nugatory. [Can] it be thought that the Constitution intended that for a shade or two of *convenience,* more or less, Congress should be authorized to break down the most ancient and fundamental laws of the several States; such as [the] rules of descent, the acts of distribution, [etc.]?"

In response, Hamilton strongly defended the constitutionality of the Bank. Taking specific issue with Jefferson's view of the Necessary and Proper Clause, he argued: "[N]either the grammatical nor popular sense of the term ["necessary"] requires [Jefferson's] construction. According to both, *necessary* often means no more than *needful, requisite, incidental, useful* or *conducive to.* [The] whole turn of the [clause] indicates, that it was the intent of the Convention [to] give a liberal latitude to the exercise of the specified powers. [Jefferson's] construction would beget endless uncertainty and embarrassment. The cases must be palpable and extreme, in which it could be pronounced, with certainty, that a measure was absolutely necessary, or one, without which the exercise of a given power would be nugatory. There are few measures of any government which would stand so severe a test." Hamilton added: "[W]hile on the one hand [Jefferson's construction] is deemed inadmissible, it will not be contended, on the other, that the clause in question gives any *new* or *independent* power. But it gives an explicit sanction to the doctrine of *implied powers.* [The] criterion is the *end,* to which the measure relates as a *means.* If the *end* be clearly comprehended within any of the specified powers, and if the measure have an obvious relation to that *end,* and is not forbidden by any particular provision of the Constitution, it may safely be deemed to come within the compass of the national authority. There is also this further criterion, which may materially assist the decision: Does the proposed measure abridge a pre-existing right of any State or of any individual? If it does not, there is a strong presumption in favor of its constitutionality." Hamilton concluded that the creation of the Bank "has a relation, more or less direct, to the power of collecting taxes, to that of borrowing money, to that of regulating trade between the States, and to those of raising and maintaining fleets and armies." Compare Hamilton's argument with Marshall's opinion in McCulloch. Are their differences significant?

3. *Broad and narrow construction: The Jeffersonian positions and the 1805 Marshall reply.* The fear of "consolidation" of powers in the national government did not end with the 1791 Bank controversy. Indeed, strict construction of congressional authority became a central plank in the opposition platform of the Jeffersonian Republicans later in the decade. In 1798, when Jefferson drafted the Kentucky Resolutions and Madison those of Virginia, their protests against the Federalists' Alien and Sedition Acts were not simply defenses of First Amendment freedoms. The Resolutions also reflected an insistence on states' rights: Madison protested against the tendency of "the Federal Government to enlarge its powers by forced constructions" (Virginia Resolutions); Jefferson protested against the "construction applied by the general government" to such provisions as the Necessary and Proper Clause and asserted that "words meant by [the Constitution] to be subsidiary [ought] not to be so construed as themselves to give unlimited powers" (Kentucky Resolutions).

After the Republicans assumed power in 1801, the responsibilities of their offices induced Jefferson and Madison to depart from consistent adherence to the strict construction position. At times, it was left to a few orthodox Republicans such as Spencer Roane to defend the traditional Jeffersonian creed. Yet, from a number of sources—and for a variety of motives, from philosophical conviction to temporary self-interest—the opposing positions on national powers were kept alive until and beyond the year McCulloch was decided.

The purity of Jefferson's constitutional principles was more apparent in the years before and after his presidential terms than while he was in office (1801–1809). President Jefferson found it possible, for example, to overcome his constitutional scruples regarding the purchase of Louisiana: though at first he thought it "important, in the present case, to set an example against broad construction," he ultimately dropped his plan to seek a constitutional amendment to ratify his actions: "[If] our friends shall think differently, certainly I shall acquiesce with satisfaction; confiding, that the good sense of our country will correct the evil of construction when it shall produce ill effects."[5] Compare Jefferson's colorful articulation of strict constructionists' fears when he commented, just before he was elected President, on a bill to grant a federal charter to a mining company: "Congress are authorized to defend the nation. Ships are necessary for defense; copper is necessary for ships; mines, necessary for copper; a company necessary to work the mines; and who can doubt this reasoning who has ever played at 'This is the House that Jack Built'? Under such a process of filiation of necessities the sweeping clause makes clean work."[6] While Jefferson was in the White House, supporters of national legislation continued to maintain that congressional powers should be broadly construed. And an early opinion by Chief Justice Marshall, United States v. Fisher, 2 Cranch (6 U.S.) 358 (1805), gave support to that position and anticipated his more elaborate discussion in McCulloch.[7]

4. *National powers after the War of 1812.* The controversy over the scope of congressional powers intensified in the years immediately before the McCulloch decision. Before and during the War, New England Federalists hostile to the Republican Administrations began to embrace strict construction theories. By the end of the War, the Federalist Party was in its death throes. But proposals for ambitious congressional programs now came from a new generation of Republicans, especially in the short period of nationalistic optimism that followed the end of the War of 1812.

The drive to charter the Second Bank of the United States was only a small part of this wave of nationalism. In 1816, for example, John C. Calhoun was still more than a decade away from his role as chief theoretician of the

---

5. See 8 The Writings of Thomas Jefferson (Ford ed.), 247, 248, and generally Levy, Jefferson and Civil Liberties—The Darker Side (1963).

6. See 7 id. 443, 444. Note the recurrent manifestations of "House That Jack Built" arguments in the cases in the next chapter.

7. The Fisher case sustained a law giving priority, in insolvency cases, to debts owed to the United States. Marshall said: "In construing [the Necessary and Proper Clause] it would be incorrect and would pro-duce endless difficulties, if the opinion should be maintained that no law was authorized which was not indispensably necessary to give effect to a specified power. Where various systems might be adopted for that purpose, it might be said with respect to each, that it was not necessary, because the end might be obtained by other means. Congress must possess the choice of means, and must be empowered to use any means which are in fact conducive to the exercise of a power granted by the constitution."

Nullifiers; in 1816, he was the legislative leader who successfully steered the Bank bill through the House, supported the tariff, and proposed a national system of roads and canals. So with Henry Clay: as Speaker of the House early in 1817, he praised Calhoun's roads and canals bill and defended his American System—particularly those "most worthy" subjects, "Internal Improvements and Domestic Manufactures."[8] Yet these nationalistic proposals provoked opposition arguments—arguments frequently couched in constitutional terms. President Madison, for example, vetoed Calhoun's bill establishing an internal improvements fund from the bonus paid to the United States under the Bank charter. He found "insuperable difficulty [in] reconciling the bill with the Constitution," for authority for the congressional action was not "among the enumerated powers" and did not fall "by any just interpretation" within the Necessary and Proper Clause.

McCulloch, then, was not an abstract or novel exercise in constitutional interpretation. The scope of congressional powers had been a continuous and controversial issue in American debates from the start. McCulloch added a weighty ingredient to the debate—but the debate continued. President Monroe, for example, vetoed the Cumberland Road Bill in 1822—though the Justices, unofficially (and despite the barrier to advisory opinions), did not agree with his position.[9] With President John Quincy Adams' election in 1825, a strong supporter of broad congressional powers came into office at last. Adams' proposals included not only internal improvements but also national action in aid of education and science. But by now Congress was reluctant, and the Adams Administration faced increasingly hostile criticism.

Many of the constitutional criticisms in the 1820s came from the state legislatures. The resolutions adopted illustrate both the pervasiveness of the criticism and the challenges to McCulloch inherent in the attacks. See generally Ames, State Documents on Federal Relations (1906). Late in 1825, for example, the South Carolina legislature—still years away from Nullification but increasingly discontented with national actions—asked a special committee to report on "the decisions of the federal judiciary and the acts of Congress contravening the letter and spirit of the Constitution." There was little doubt about the prime judicial target: as a similar committee reported two years later "with great pain," the "reasoning of the Court in the case of McCulloch" was "founded on a misconstruction" of the Constitution. This was the premise that underlay the action of the South Carolina legislature in December 1825, when it adopted the special committee's recommended Resolutions attacking a range of assertions of power in Congress. The Resolutions challenged congressional powers to promote internal improvements, lay duties to protect domestic manufacturers, and exercise powers "granted for particular objects to effect other [unenumerated] objects." 1 Statutes at Large of South Carolina (1836), 229, 231.

The impact of McCulloch v. Maryland extended far beyond the immediate issues of the case and far beyond its own day—not only to South Carolina in the 1820s, but also to the recurrent disputes about the scope of congressional power leading to the Civil War and recurrently erupting ever since. But it is not

---

8. On Calhoun, see 1 The Papers of John C. Calhoun (Meriwether ed. 1959). On Clay, see especially 2 The Papers of Henry Clay (Hopkins ed. 1961), 308.

9. See letter of Justice William Johnson (purporting to report on behalf of his "Brother Judges" as well) to President James Monroe in 1822, ending with the suggestion that "it would not be unproductive of good, if the Secretary of State were to have the opinion of this Court on the Bank question, printed and dispersed through the Union." See 1 Warren, The Supreme Court in United States History (rev. ed. 1926), 597.

enough to view McCulloch in its larger setting; a word about its immediate context accordingly follows.

5. *The Bank controversy: Politics and economics.* The expiration of the charter of the First Bank of the United States in 1811 coincided with—and to some extent contributed to—increasing national fiscal difficulties. Financial problems were aggravated during the War of 1812, and demands for a new national bank proliferated. By the end of the War, even President Madison—who had earlier echoed Jefferson's argument that the first Bank was unconstitutional—urged consideration of a successor institution: in his Annual Message of December 1815, he advised Congress that "the probable operation of a national bank will merit consideration."

The Republicans in Congress did not need that reminder. They had approved a new bank charter almost a year earlier, but the President had vetoed it in January 1815. But the Veto Message demonstrated that the Administration's constitutional position had shifted: while disapproving the details of the bill, President Madison had "waive[d]" the question of congressional power to incorporate a bank, "as being precluded in my judgment by repeated recognitions under varied circumstances of the validity of such an institution in acts of the legislative, executive, and judicial branches of the Government." In 1816, Congress established a Second Bank acceptable to Madison; and Marshall's 1819 opinion sustaining its constitutionality took pains to remind the nation of Madison's "waiver."

The Bank got off to a flourishing start. In 1817 and for most of 1818, few questions about constitutionality were raised: the country was in a postwar economic boom, trade was active, prices were rising. And the Bank, which could have exercised some of the regulatory functions of a modern central bank by controlling credit expansion, chose instead to be "liberal" and to encourage the speculative boom. The harsh morning-after was not far off, however: by the fall of 1818, a financial panic and depression shook the economy. The Bank, short of specie reserves, called in its excessive loans—and the debtors (state banks as well as private individuals) reacted with understandable anger toward the central "monied power," the "monster" Bank. In October 1818, a congressional investigation of the Bank began, and there was considerable support for repeal of its charter. The January 1819 report of the investigating committee found that the Bank had indeed suffered from loose management under its first president, William Jones. But the charter-repeal move failed in February 1819; instead, Jones resigned and was succeeded by the more competent Langdon Cheves.

When the McCulloch case came before the Court, then, the Bank issue was the most heated one of the congressional session. Moreover, by early 1819, the Baltimore branch of the Bank—one of 18 branches in existence at the time—was the most controversial of the Bank's operations, for reasons going quite beyond Maryland's tax. As cashier, James McCulloch was no minor functionary in the Bank's structure: the branch cashiers were the chief local agents of the national management. And during the congressional investigation, McCulloch was the Bank's main legislative lobbyist in Washington. He was even more busy at home: the Baltimore branch was the most active of all, and McCulloch and his accomplices were systematically looting the Bank by instigating unsecured loans and sanctioning unreported overdrafts. Reports of Baltimore misconduct were circulating in Washington by late 1818; by the time the case was argued in March 1819, there were rumors that McCulloch was heavily implicated. But there were also indignant denials of the rumors. Official charges of McCulloch's misconduct did not come until a month after the Court decision;

and in May, he was removed from office. Criminal proceedings against McCulloch and his associates were brought by Maryland and continued for several years. But Maryland had no embezzlement statute as yet, and the difficult effort to obtain a common law conspiracy conviction failed.

Thus, the banner of national power in the McCulloch case was carried by a most unsavory figure, a scoundrel whose schemes cost the Bank more than a million dollars. But the Bank controversy litigated in the McCulloch case was not merely a Baltimore matter. The hard times, and the antipathy of state banks under pressure from the Bank of the United States, produced anti-Bank measures in a number of states—some antedating the Maryland tax law. Indiana and Illinois flatly prohibited banks not chartered by the state. Tennessee, Georgia, North Carolina, Kentucky and Ohio—like Maryland—imposed taxes on "foreign" bank operations, taxes that were typically even more burdensome than Maryland's. Similar efforts in several other state legislatures failed by narrow margins. The Court's decision did not silence all of the attacks: in the face of the McCulloch decision in March 1819, Ohio in September chose to collect its $50,000 per branch tax by force. Ohio officials seized more than $100,000 from the vaults of the Bank's Chillicothe branch, in part to stimulate a relitigation of the McCulloch issues. The Ohio leaders insisted that the issues had not been adequately aired in the Maryland litigation. It took another Court decision—Osborn v. Bank of the United States, 9 Wheat. (22 U.S.) 738 (1824)—to settle the Ohio dispute, reaffirm McCulloch, and validate the Bank's statutory authority to sue in the federal courts. By that time the Bank's difficulties had eased: it was managed more competently, and the nation had recovered from the depression. Not until the Jackson Administration did the Bank face another severe attack. And the Jackson challenge was fatal: the McCulloch decision was not an adequate shield against President Jackson's veto of the 1832 Bank recharter, and the Bank went out of existence in 1836.[10]

6. *The Bank controversy: The constitutional contentions and John Marshall's pseudonymous defense.* By contrast with the often bitter and sometimes bizarre political controversies that engulfed the Bank, the constitutional submissions in the McCulloch case were calm and largely predictable. The lawyers' arguments were primarily conduits for constitutional contentions that had become routine in debates during the preceding three decades. Though Daniel Webster's reputation was enhanced by his Court arguments in 1819, it was William Pinkney who was the major orator in the McCulloch case. And neither Webster nor Pinkney considered the McCulloch argument the chief challenge of the 1819 Term: they were preoccupied with other cases, especially their possible encounter if the Dartmouth College Case (p. 506 below) were to be reargued. As Pinkney wrote Webster in December 1818, a preargument "interchange of Ideas" among co-counsel for the Bank seemed unnecessary, since the argument probably would involve "little else than the threadbare topics connected with the constitutionality of the establishment of the Bank."

The constitutional arguments were not novel, and the pro-Bank holding was no surprise. But to the far-sighted, the case signified more than the immediate result. For John Marshall and his Virginia states' rights critics, especially, what was truly at stake was McCulloch's impact on national programs other than the Bank and, above all, on the general scope of national powers. General principles of constitutional interpretation really did matter the most in the long run. And general principles were central in a fierce ideological

10. For additional background on the Bank controversy, see Catterall, The Second Bank of the United States (1902), and Hammond, Banks and Politics in America—From the Revolution to the Civil War (1957).

newspaper debate that ensued—with Judge Spencer Roane of Virginia as the chief pseudonymous critic in the Richmond Enquirer, and John Marshall himself, for the only time in his career, as chief pseudonymous newspaper defender of the Court.

Within weeks of the McCulloch decision, the Richmond Enquirer, the organ of Virginia states' rights leaders, began publishing elaborate attacks. Marshall saw in them a revival of the feared strict constructionist principles of 1798: if they prevailed, "the constitution would be converted into the old confederation." The Chief Justice, afraid that no one else would make an adequate defense, took to the newspapers himself. In April 1819, he wrote two essays for a Philadelphia paper. But then Virginia Judge Spencer Roane sharply attacked McCulloch in a series of essays signed "Hampden." Marshall, his letters disclose, found himself "more stimulated on this subject than on any other because I believe the design to be to injure the Judges & impair the constitution." Anxious and intense, he hastily wrote nine elaborate essays that were published in the Alexandria Gazette over the pseudonym "A Friend of the Constitution."[11]

The Bank aspects of the case were hardly mentioned in this newspaper battle, either by the attackers or by Marshall. As Marshall realized, it was doctrine, not result, that troubled the Virginians: they would have preferred "an obsequious, silent opinion without reasons"; it was "our heretical reasoning" that was "pronounced most damnable." And it was that reasoning that concerned Marshall most: he defended it against charges that it legitimated unlimited congressional powers; he denied that McCulloch endorsed consolidation; he insisted that the decision struck a moderate balance between excessively broad and unduly narrow conceptions of national powers. (His elaborations are considered further in the next group of notes.)

7. *The national bank—A "private" or "public" institution?* Note that Marshall in McCulloch said very little about the organization and actual operations of the Bank. Nor did he explain in any detail how the creation of the Bank was "necessary and proper" to the exercise of any specific enumerated power of Congress. Should he have said more? Recall also that the Bank's success was considerably greater during its prosperous first year than in the depression months immediately preceding the decision. Could the 1819 circumstances have been relied on to challenge the constitutionality of the Bank, if the 1816 context provided substantial basis for the congressional judgment to charter the Bank? (See also the further questions about Marshall's opinion in the next group of notes.)

The Bank was manifestly not a purely governmental operation—not like a mint or an army fort. As early as 1790, Hamilton had argued, in proposing a national bank: "To attach full confidence to an institution of this nature, it appears to be an essential ingredient in its structure, that it shall be under a *private* not a *public* direction—under the guidance of *individual interest,* not of *public policy.*" Any suspicion that the nationally chartered bank was "too much influenced by *public necessity,*" he asserted, would "be a canker that would continually corrode the vitals of the credit of the bank." He added: "The keen, steady, and, as it were, magnetic sense of their own interest as proprietors, in the directors of a bank, pointing invariably to its true pole—the prosperity of the institution,—is the only security that can always be relied upon for a careful and prudent administration" and for "permanent confidence" in the

11. For these essays (unearthed in the 1960s) and their background, see Gunther (ed.), John Marshall's Defense of McCulloch v. Maryland (1969).

bank. Obviously, Hamilton and, later, the proponents of the Second Bank expected substantial governmental benefits from a congressionally chartered bank, as a source of loans, as a depository and fiscal agent, and as a stabilizer of currency. But these benefits were to be by-products of the bank's operations as a largely private, profit-making, commercial institution. The charter of the Second Bank accordingly provided that 80% of the stock ownership and of the directors were to be private. Walter Jones and Joseph Hopkinson mentioned the "private" nature of the Bank in the course of their argument in McCulloch, though mainly on the question of the Bank's immunity from state taxation rather than of its constitutionality under Art. I. Were the "private" features relevant, on either question? Should Marshall have discussed them? See Plous & Baker, "McCulloch v. Maryland: Right Principle, Wrong Case," 9 Stan.L.Rev. 710 (1957).

CONGRESSIONAL POWER, THE JUDICIAL FUNCTION, AND POLITICAL RESTRAINTS

1. *Restraints on congressional power: Some general questions about judicially-imposed limits.* Consider, in examining the McCulloch opinion and the cases in the next two chapters, what principled limits courts can and should impose to guard against excessive intrusion of national authority into local affairs. Are courts capable of articulating effective federalism-related limits (as distinguished from limits designed to protect individual rights, considered in Part III below)? Or is the imposition of restraints best left largely or wholly to the political process, in view of the representation of local interest in the national government? (See note 3 below.) Did Marshall's McCulloch opinion legitimate an unlimited congressional discretion? In intent? In language? In effect?[1]

a. *Necessary and proper means to achieve enumerated ends: Judicial scrutiny of means-ends relationships.* One way in which Marshall suggested judicially enforceable limits on congressional powers was to articulate criteria to determine whether the means chosen by Congress were adequately related to legitimate ends. Marshall spoke of means "which tended directly to the execution" of delegated powers, means which were "appropriate" and "plainly adapted" to achieving legitimate ends. Ever since McCulloch, the Supreme Court has been engaged in efforts, often unsuccessful, to put teeth into those limits. Implementing this "means"-"ends" requirement has raised a host of puzzling subsidiary questions. For example, how attenuated a chain of inferences will suffice to justify a law as a "necessary and proper" means to effectuate a granted power? (Recall the "House That Jack Built," slippery slope argument that Jefferson feared.) Must the proffered "means"-"ends" justification be one that was in fact considered by the enacting Congress, or may it be supplied subsequent to enactment, by counsel's argument or by the Justices' speculations about the justifications the legislature *might* have relied upon? Does the required "reasonable relation" nexus between means and ends turn on standards of logic? Of empiric observations? Is the required nexus "uniform and invariable, the same today as tomorrow," as Hamilton argued, or does it

1. It bears emphasizing that general, preliminary questions such as these— here and elsewhere in this book—are not designed to elicit immediate answers. Instead, they are intended to serve as guideposts in examining the materials that follow, and they are included for the purpose of calling attention to recurrent problems in the judicial enforcement of constitutional norms.

depend on "circumstances" "at a particular time"? What "time": Date of enactment? Date of adjudication?[2]

Marshall wrote his pseudonymous "Friend of the Constitution" essays of 1819 to counter Roane's charge that in McCulloch "the court had granted to congress unlimited powers under the pretext of a discretion in selecting means." Marshall insisted that the required means-ends relationship *was* a judicially enforceable one, and some of his essays tried to elaborate the requirement. For example, "neither a feigned convenience nor a strict necessity; but a reasonable convenience, and a qualified necessity," had to be shown to demonstrate that the means were constitutional; means must have "a plain relation to the end," they must be "direct, natural and appropriate." McCulloch, he insisted, denied "the unlimited power of congress to adopt any means whatever." Despite Marshall's insistence that the means-ends inquiry assured a significant judicial restraint on Congress, it can be argued that Roane was right after all about the effective scope of congressional discretion after McCulloch, given the broad exercises of national power sustained by the Court in many of the cases that follow. Nearly two centuries later, it is possible to claim that Roane was ultimately right about the "consolidating" effect of McCulloch, if not about Marshall's purpose. Was that because Marshall did not seriously look for limits? Because the McCulloch limits were inadequate? Could better limits have been stated?[3]

b. *"Pretext": Judicial inquiry into congressional purposes and abuses of power.* In articulating limits on congressional choices, Marshall spoke not only of the required means-ends relationships, but also of inquiry into congressional purposes. Can courts effectively assure legislative good faith in exercising powers? Can and should courts scrutinize the nature and purity of legislative motives?[4] Marshall asserted in McCulloch—and reiterated in his newspaper replies to Roane—that the Court *would* invalidate laws "for the accomplishment of objects, not entrusted to the government," laws enacted "under the pretext" of exercising granted powers.[5] Is the "pretext" limitation really

PRETEXT

2. The problem of judicial scrutiny of means-ends relationships arises not only in the context of federalism limits on congressional power. It recurs throughout this volume, and may well be the most frequently invoked technique in the judicial review of the validity of federal and state legislation. See, e.g., the discussion of a "means-oriented" scrutiny under the due process clause in chap. 8 and under the equal protection clause in chap. 9.

3. Consider Gunther (ed.), John Marshall's Defense of McCulloch v. Maryland (1969), at 20: "The degree of centralization that has taken place [since McCulloch] may well have come about in the face of Marshall's intent rather than in accord with his expectations. That centralization may be the inevitable consequence of economic and social changes. And this development may suggest the impossibility of articulating general constitutional standards capable of limiting those centralizing forces, particularly through judicial action. But to say this is very

different from saying that Marshall knew he was engaging in a hopeless task."

4. What *are* the institutional and practical difficulties inhibiting such inquiries? That problem will recur in later materials in this volume. See, e.g., chaps. 4 and 9, below, and generally Ely, "Legislative and Administrative Motivation in Constitutional Law," 79 Yale L.J. 1205 (1970) and Brest, "Palmer v. Thompson: An Approach to the Problem of Unconstitutional Legislative Motive," 1971 Sup.Ct.Rev. 95.

5. See, e.g., Gunther (ed.), above, at 187; see also Marshall's newspaper statement, id. at 173: "It is not pretended that this right of selection [of means] may be fraudulently used to the destruction of the fair land marks of the constitution. Congress certainly may not, under the pretext of collecting taxes, or of guaranteeing to each state a republican form of government, alter the law of descents; but if the means have a plain relation to the end—if they be direct, natural and appropriate," they are constitutional.

capable of judicial enforcement? Does it require a judicial determination of the "true" object of the law—of congressional purposes and motives? Are otherwise constitutional laws invalidated by impermissible "pretext" statements by Congress? More basically, should the Art. I, § 8, powers of Congress be read as specifying the permissible *aims* (or ends or purposes) of legislation, or simply the permissible, objectively determinable *areas* of national regulation? Does the commerce clause, for example, authorize legislative control for any purpose so long as the *field* regulated is that of "interstate commerce"? (Such a view would authorize Congress to seek "morality," "police" objectives—e.g., to legislate against prostitution or for racial justice or against rioters—so long as the sanction of the law took hold on some commerce-connected activity.) Or must the regulation rest on a primarily commercial purpose? Must the *evil* being regulated at least have commercial dimensions? [For further pursuit of these problems in the context of the commerce power, see chap. 3.]

2. *Some additional questions on the Marshall opinion in McCulloch: Methods of constitutional interpretation.* a. How useful is Marshall's emphasis on the theme that "it is *a constitution* we are expounding"?[6] Is this more than a truism? Was anyone denying that? Does the emphasis on *constitutional* interpretation aid in the delineation of implied powers? Is a broad construction of national powers an inevitable consequence of interpreting *"a constitution"*? Would not that approach also justify a broad construction of *limits* on national power? Could not Spencer Roane and other states' righters have argued that their views, too, had in mind *"a constitution"*—that the Constitution as they interpreted it was no less *"a constitution"* because it provided for tighter controls on national power and greater protection of state authority in a federal scheme of divided sovereignty?

b. How significant was the Necessary and Proper Clause to Marshall's result? The opinion suggests that he had established his conclusion—that the Constitution legitimated implied powers—even before he turned to the consideration of that Clause in Art. I, § 8, cl. 18. How persuasive is Marshall's textual and contextual reading of the Necessary and Proper Clause once he reaches it? More broadly, consider the sources of Marshall's interpretation: to some extent he relies on text; to some extent, on history. Consider also the relevance of Marshall's comment about "a constitution intended to endure for ages to come, and, consequently, to be adapted to the various *crises* of human affairs." McCulloch also includes considerable emphasis on "inference from the structures and relationships created by the constitution." See C.L. Black, Jr., Structure and Relationship in Constitutional Law (1969). Note the way Marshall relies heavily upon considerations of structure and relationship, not only to justify his views on congressional powers but also to defend his position on the Bank's immunity from state taxation. Professor Black's book advocates a greater emphasis on structural interpretation, as against often "manipulative" textual exegesis. Inferences from structures and relationships are often defensible; but are they more immune from the risk of manipulation than resort to other sources of constitutional interpretation?[7]

6. Justice Frankfurter once called this statement "the single most important utterance in the literature of constitutional law—most important because most comprehensive and comprehending." Frankfurter, "John Marshall and the Judicial Function," 69 Harv.L.Rev. 217 (1955).

7. Note that the Necessary and Proper Clause, by its own terms, is *not* limited to implementing the allocations of power in Art. I, § 8. Rather, it applies as well to "all other Powers vested by this Constitution in the Government of the United States." See, e.g., the reliance on McCulloch in interpreting the scope of congressional enforcement powers

c. What, in Marshall's view, was the source of the Bank's immunity from the state tax: Text? History? Structures and relationships?[8] The nationalist value preferences of a portion of early 19th century society? Marshall's personal nationalist views? Should Marshall have considered more fully, on the question of state taxing power, the practical operations of the Bank, including its largely private ownership? Should he have considered a narrower rule more responsive to Maryland's discriminatory tax—a tax not applicable to all banks but only to those not chartered by the State? How far-reaching are Marshall's implications as to governmental immunity? How can his principles justify what he suggests in the last paragraph of his opinion: a valid tax on the Bank's real property, or on Maryland citizens' holdings of Bank stock? (See the additional materials on intergovernmental tax immunities below.)

In finding an implicit bar to state taxation of a national instrumentality, the Bank, Marshall relies less on text and history than on the structure and operation of representative government. When a legislature taxes its constituents, he points out, the constituents' right to vote for or against their representatives is usually "a sufficient security against erroneous and oppressive taxation." But only in the national legislature "are all represented." He argues that this political check, the power to elect representatives, will not work when a state taxes a national organ, because most voters in the nation are not represented in the state legislature. In suggesting that judicial intervention is justified in such circumstances, Marshall may have been the first to articulate a position increasingly important in modern constitutional law: the notion that "representation-reinforcement" serves as a justification for judicial action. Under that view, developed at length in Ely, Democracy and Distrust (1980), a central role of the courts is to make up for flaws in the operation of representative government. In Ely's view, a breakdown in the political processes justifies judicial action. This theme of representation-reinforcement is developed more fully below, especially in chap. 9. Was this representation-reinforcing theme aptly applied in McCulloch? If Americans throughout the nation were truly oppressed by state taxation of the Bank, did not Congress have ample power to enact a law to bar state taxation? Especially in view of the powerful Washington lobby of the Bank of the United States, was this truly an appropriate case for judicial rather than congressional intervention on behalf of the Bank?

3. *Restraints on congressional power: The Political Safeguards of Federalism.* a. *Wechsler.* Consider, in examining the Court's efforts to formulate limits on national powers in the cases that follow, whether the need for judicial efforts to safeguard federalism values is minimal in view of the representation of local interests in the political structure of the national government. Do these "political safeguards" operate with equal effectiveness with regard to all kinds of congressional action? As effectively in cases of regulations of morals and crime as in cases of economic regulation? As effectively when the spending power is invoked (see chap. 4, sec. 2) as with proposals for direct regulation of local affairs? These questions are raised by the following excerpts from Wech-

under the Civil War Amendments, in chap. 10 below.

8. See Black, Structure and Relationship in Constitutional Law (1969), 15: "Marshall's reasoning on this branch of the case is, as I read it, essentially structural. It has to do in great part with what he conceives to be the warranted relational proprieties between the national government and the government of the states, with the structural corollaries of national supremacy—and, at one point, of the mode of formation of the Union. [In] this, perhaps the greatest of our constitutional cases, judgment is reached not fundamentally on the basis of that kind of textual exegesis which we tend to regard as normal, but on the basis of reasoning from the total structure which the text has created."

sler, "The Political Safeguards of Federalism—The Role of the States in the Composition and Selection of the National Government," in Principles, Politics, and Fundamental Law (1961), 49–82:[9]

"The actual extent of central intervention in the governance of our affairs is determined far less by the formal power distribution than by the sheer existence of the states and their political power to influence the action of the national authority. [National action has] always been regarded as exceptional in our polity, an intrusion to be justified by some necessity, the special rather than the ordinary case. This point of view cuts even deeper than the concept of the central government as one of granted, limited authority, articulated in the tenth amendment. National power may be quite unquestioned in a given situation; those who would advocate its exercise must none the less answer the preliminary question why the matter should not be left to the states. Even when Congress acts, its tendency has been to frame enactments on an ad hoc basis to accomplish limited objectives, supplanting state-created norms only so far as may be necessary for the purpose. Indeed, with all the centralizing growth throughout the years, federal law is still a largely interstitial product, rarely occupying any field completely, building normally upon legal relationships established by the states. [As] a state legislature views the common law as something to be left alone unless a need for change has been established, so Congress has traditionally viewed the governance of matters by the states. [The] tradition plainly serves the values of our federalism in so far as it maintains a burden of persuasion on those favoring national intervention.

"If I have drawn too much significance from the mere fact of the existence of the states, the error surely will be rectified by pointing also to their crucial role in the selection and the composition of the national authority. Representatives no less than Senators are allotted by the Constitution to the states, although their number varies with state population as determined by the census. [And] with the President, as with Congress, the crucial instrument of the selection—whether through electors, or, in the event of failure of majority, by the House voting as state units—is again the states. The consequence, of course, is that the states are the strategic yardsticks for the measurement of interest and opinion, the special centers of political activity, the separate geographical determinants of national as well as local politics.

"[To] the extent that federalist values have real significance they must give rise to local sensitivity to central intervention; to the extent that such a local sensitivity exists, it cannot fail to find reflection in the Congress. [The] President must be [the] main repository of 'national spirit' in the central government. But both the mode of his selection and the future of his party require that he also be responsive to local values that have large support within the states. And since his programs must, in any case, achieve support in Congress, [he] must surmount the greater local sensitivity of Congress before anything is done.

"If this analysis is correct, the national political process in the United States—and especially the role of the states in the composition and selection of the central government—is intrinsically well adapted to retarding or restraining new intrusions by the center on the domain of the states. Far from a national authority that is expansionist by nature, the inherent tendency in our system is precisely the reverse, necessitating the widest support before intru-

9. These excerpts are reprinted here with the permission of the publisher, © copyright 1961 by the President and Fellows of Harvard College. The essay also appears in 54 Colum.L.Rev. 543 (1954), and in Selected Essays on Constitutional Law 1938–62 (1963), 185.

sive measures of importance can receive significant consideration, reacting readily to opposition grounded in resistance within the states. Nor is this tendency effectively denied by pointing to the size or scope of the existing national establishment. However useful it may be to explore possible contractions in specific areas, such evidence points mainly to the magnitude of unavoidable responsibility under the circumstances of our time.

"It is in light of this inherent tendency, reflected most importantly in Congress, that the governmental power distribution clauses of the Constitution gain their largest meaning as an instrument for the protection of the states. Those clauses, as is well known, have served far more to qualify or stop intrusive legislative measures in the Congress than to invalidate enacted legislation in the Supreme Court. [This] does not differ from the expectation of the framers quite as markedly as might be thought. For the containment of the national authority Madison did not emphasize the function of the Court; he pointed to the composition of the Congress and to the political [processes].

"The prime function envisaged for judicial review—in relation to federalism—was the maintenance of national supremacy against nullification or usurpation by the individual states, the national government having no part in their composition or their councils. [Except] for the brief interlude that ended with the crisis of the thirties, it is mainly in the realm of such policing of the states that the Supreme Court has in fact participated in determining the balances of federalism.[10] This is not to say that the Court can decline to measure national enactments by the Constitution when it is called upon to face the question in the course of ordinary litigation; the supremacy clause governs there as well. It is rather to say that the Court is on weakest ground when it opposes its interpretation of the Constitution to that of Congress in the interest of the states, whose representatives control the legislative process and, by hypothesis, have broadly acquiesced in sanctioning the challenged Act of Congress."

b. *Choper.* More than two decades after the publication of the Wechsler position, Dean Jesse Choper relied on somewhat similar premises to support a more extreme conclusion. In Judicial Review and the National Political Process (1980), Choper argues that the Court should "abstain from deciding constitutional questions of national power versus states' rights," largely in order "to ease the commendable and crucial task of judicial review in cases of individual constitutional liberties."[11] Like Wechsler, Choper claims that "[n]umerous

---

10. "Of the great controversies with respect to national power before the Civil War, only the Bank and slavery within the territories were carried to the Court and its participation with respect to slavery was probably its greatest failure. The question of internal improvements, for example, which raised the most acute problem of constitutional construction, was fought out politically and in Congress. After the War only the Civil Rights Cases and income tax decisions were important in setting limits on national power—until the Child Labor Case and the New Deal decisions. The recasting of constitutional positions since the crisis acknowledges much broader power in the Congress—as against the states—than it is likely soon or ever to employ." [Footnote by Professor Wechsler.]

[Wechsler's views were first set forth in 1954 and published in book form in 1961. Do the expansive invocations of congressional power in the years since then undermine any part of the Wechsler thesis? In recent decades, congressional exercises of its powers have grown considerably in frequency and scope, as the next two chapters illustrate. Can it still be said as confidently as Wechsler was able to say that "the national political process [is] intrinsically well adapted to retarding or restraining new intrusions by the center on the domain of the states"?]

11. Toward that same end, Choper also argues that the Court should "abstain from deciding ultimate issues of constitutional authority between Congress and the President." See chap. 6 below.

structural aspects of the national political system serve to assure that states' rights will not be trampled, and the lesson of practice is that they have not been." In arguing that "constitutional questions that concern the scope of national power vis-a-vis the states" should be held "nonjusticiable," Choper claims that federalism issues, unlike individual liberties ones, are issues of "practicality" rather than "issues of principle." Moreover, he finds a greater likelihood of "fair resolution [of federalism issues] within the national political chambers." Accordingly, "the thoroughly effective voice of the states in the national lawmaking system allows the Court to forgo review of that class of issues."

Choper claims that his approach would promote the Court's institutional strength in defending individual liberties by removing from the judicial arena a group of decisions that sometimes "result in a hostile public attitude toward the Court." He insists, too, that judicial review is unnecessary even in situations of "Congress and the President joining forces and ignoring clear constitutional mandate," for in such cases "it is probably futile to rely on the Court to right the matter." In any event, "as a general matter, Congresses and Presidents have been extremely solicitous of the sovereign prerogatives of the states." Thus, although Choper concedes that federalism values are clearly expressed in the Constitution, he concludes that, in order to "conserve the Court's precious capital for those cases in which it is really needed," the Court should "explicitly hold that it will not pass on constitutional questions concerning the reach of national authority versus states' rights."

Note that Choper's proposal goes well beyond Wechsler's. Wechsler had stated: "This is not to say that the Court can decline to measure national enactments by the Constitution when it is called upon to face the question in the course of ordinary litigation; the supremacy clause governs there as well." May the Court nevertheless decline to reach the merits in such cases, as Choper urges? Even if Court refusal to adjudicate can be reconciled with the principles of Marbury and the Supremacy Clause, are Choper's policy arguments persuasive? For example, would the Court's defense of individual liberties, which Choper would make the Court's virtually exclusive function, be tolerable to the public if the Court declined jurisdiction over most or all other constitutional issues? Recall the questions preceding the Wechsler excerpt. Do the political safeguards on which Choper, like Wechsler, relies operate with equal effectiveness with regard to all kinds of congressional action? As effectively in cases of morals and criminal regulation as in cases of economic regulation? Questions such as these are pursued in the next chapter.

STOP

THE TERM LIMITS CASE AND THE MODERN ANTIFEDERALIST REVIVAL

Marshall's opinion in McCulloch stated an approach that provided a foundation for expansive readings of national powers not only for the Marshall Court (e.g., Gibbons v. Ogden, p. 159 below) but also for the Court's articulation of a broad scope of national authority for decades beginning in the late 1930s (e.g., Wickard v. Filburn, p. 189 below). McCulloch relied heavily on implications from the constitutional structure to assure the immunity of federal operations from state challenges. The Term Limits case which follows (especially Justice Stevens's majority opinion) strikes down state-adopted term limits on federal officeholders for reasons somewhat similar to those given for invalidating Maryland's tax in McCulloch. But Justice Thomas's dissent for four

[handwritten margin note: GOOD SUMMARY OF JUSTICES' METHODS OF ANALYSIS]

Justices in Term Limits rests in essence on the flip-side of the McCulloch approach, emphasizing state rather than federal authority. In Term Limits, the opposing sides on the Court, in a context where neither text nor historical data clearly resolved the issue, relied instead on sharply contrasting structural default rules: the dissenters endorsed infinite state power except as clearly surrendered by the Constitution; constitutional silence was taken as barring federal but not state action. To Justice Stevens, by contrast, the lack of decisive data from text and history produced reliance on structural implications justifying judicially implied state disabilities to act in the federal sphere. In short, where text and history do not provide a clear answer, Justice Stevens's default rule was to read federal powers and immunities broadly, rather than to favor state powers and immunities. See generally Sullivan, "Dueling Sovereignties: U.S. Term Limits, Inc. v. Thornton," 109 Harv.L.Rev. 78 (1995).

[handwritten margin note: STATE RTS FEDERAL RTS]

The dissent in the Term Limits case also illustrates the modern antifederalist revival that has periodically surfaced and occasionally found majority support on the Court of the 1990s, as the next chapter demonstrates. In addition to the 1995 ruling in United States v. Lopez, finding federalism-based limits on the scope of the commerce power, note also Seminole Tribes of Florida v. Florida in 1996, holding that the congressional commerce power is not adequate to eliminate a state's Eleventh Amendment immunity, as well as New York v. United States in 1992, holding that the Tenth Amendment bars congressional power to direct the states to regulate "in a particular field or a particular way."

[handwritten margin note: BROAD NARROW]

[handwritten margin note: What is Thomas' default position?]

Consider as well the Justices' extensive reliance on historical materials in Term Limits, especially in the opinions of Justices Stevens and Thomas. Both explore the historical record more thoroughly than Marshall had in McCulloch (the Constitutional Convention records had not yet been published in 1819, the year of McCulloch). Whose explanation of the historical record is more persuasive in Term Limits? Ultimately, neither text nor history provided compelling conclusions, and both sides resorted to the default positions noted earlier. Sullivan concludes: "To the majority, judicial intervention is needed to protect the federal government from the states; to the dissent, it is needed to protect the states from the federal government. Justice Kennedy alone would intervene to protect each side from encroachment by the other." And, as she also points out, both the Stevens and Thomas opinions are largely formalist in their emphases on structural implications, and neither opinion takes the functionalist approach more common in the modern federalism-related cases discussed in chapters 3, 4, and 5 below.

[handwritten margin note: FUNCTIONALIST FORMALIST]

The sharpness of the contending positions advanced in Term Limits (with Justice Stevens echoing some of Marshall's approach in McCulloch and Justice Thomas providing a sharp counterargument reminiscent of antifederalist attacks on McCulloch) at least makes clear that the heated federal power/states' rights disputes that underlay the central constitutional issues during the pre-Civil War decades were not merely nineteenth century phenomena. In reflecting on the chapters that follow, consider the possible implications of Justice Thomas' dissent in Term Limits on the questions pursued there. The Stevens opinion at least bars state interference with the *procedures* of the federal government. To what extent may that ruling also preclude state efforts to regulate the *substance* of the federal legislative agenda? Consider, for example, modern proposals for block grants that would yield to the states broad discretion in deciding how to distribute federal revenues and administer federal programs.

U.S. Term Limits, Inc. v. Thornton 5|4 ?

514 U.S. 779, 115 S.Ct. 1842, 131 L.Ed.2d 881 (1995).

Justice STEVENS delivered the opinion of the Court.

The Constitution sets forth qualifications for membership in the Congress of the United States [—the age, citizenship, and residence requirements of Art. I, § 2, cl. 2, and Art I, § 3, cl. 3]. Today's cases present a challenge to an amendment to the Arkansas State Constitution that prohibits the name of an otherwise-eligible candidate for Congress from appearing on the general election ballot if that candidate has already served three terms in the House of Representatives or two terms in the Senate. The Arkansas Supreme Court held that the amendment violates the Federal Constitution. We agree with that holding. Such a state-imposed restriction is contrary to the "fundamental principle of our representative democracy," embodied in the Constitution, that "the people should choose whom they please to govern them." Powell v. McCormack [1969; p. 53 above.] Allowing individual States to adopt their own qualifications for congressional service would be inconsistent with the Framers' vision of a uniform National Legislature representing the people of the United States. If the qualifications set forth in the text of the Constitution are to be changed, that text must be amended.

I. At the general election on November 3, 1992, the voters of Arkansas adopted Amendment 73 to their State Constitution. Proposed as a "Term Limitation Amendment," its preamble stated: "The people of Arkansas find and declare that elected officials who remain in office too long become preoccupied with reelection and ignore their duties as representatives of the people. Entrenched incumbency has reduced voter participation and has led to an electoral system that is less free, less competitive, and less representative than the system established by the Founding Fathers. Therefore, the people of Arkansas, exercising their reserved powers, herein limit the terms of the [elected officials]."

II. [T]he constitutionality of Amendment 73 depends critically on the resolution of two distinct issues. The first is whether the Constitution forbids States from adding to or altering the qualifications specifically enumerated in the Constitution. The second is, if the Constitution does so forbid, whether the fact that Amendment 73 is formulated as a ballot access restriction rather than as an outright disqualification is of constitutional significance. Our resolution of these issues draws upon our prior resolution of a related but distinct issue: whether Congress has the power to add to or alter the qualifications of its Members. [I]n [Powell], the principal issue was whether the power granted to each House in Art. I, § 5, to judge the "Qualifications of its own Members" includes the power to impose qualifications other than those set forth in the text of the Constitution. [W]e held that it does not. Because of the obvious importance of the issue, the Court's review of the history and meaning of the relevant constitutional text was especially thorough. We therefore begin our analysis today with a full statement of what we decided in that case.

In November 1966, Adam Clayton Powell, Jr., was elected from a District in New York to serve in the United States House of Representatives for the 90th Congress. Allegations that he had engaged in serious misconduct while serving as a committee chairman during the 89th Congress led to the appointment of a Select Committee to determine his eligibility to take his seat. That Committee found that Powell met the age, citizenship, and residency requirements set forth in Art. I, § 2, cl. 2. The Committee also found, however, that Powell had wrongfully diverted House funds for the use of others and himself and had made false reports on expenditures of foreign currency. Based on those findings, the House after debate adopted House Resolution 278, excluding Powell from membership in the House, and declared his seat vacant.

Powell and several voters of the District from which he had been elected filed suit seeking a declaratory judgment that the House Resolution was invalid because Art. I, § 2, cl. 2, sets forth the exclusive qualifications for House membership. We ultimately accepted that contention, concluding that the House of Representatives has no "authority to exclude any person, duly elected by his constituents, who meets all the requirements for membership expressly prescribed in the Constitution." [In] reaching that conclusion, we undertook a detailed historical review to determine the intent of the Framers. Though recognizing that the Constitutional Convention debates themselves were inconclusive, we determined that the "relevant historical materials" reveal that Congress has no power to alter the qualifications in the text of the Constitution.

POWELL'S RELIANCE ON HISTORY. We started our analysis in Powell by examining the British experience with qualifications for membership in Parliament, focusing in particular on the experience of John Wilkes. While serving as a member of Parliament, Wilkes had published an attack on a peace treaty with France. This literary endeavor earned Wilkes a conviction for seditious libel and a 22–month prison sentence. In addition, Parliament declared Wilkes ineligible for membership and ordered him expelled. Despite (or perhaps because of) these difficulties, Wilkes was reelected several times. Parliament, however, persisted in its refusal to seat him. After several years of Wilkes' efforts, the House of Commons voted to expunge the resolutions that had expelled Wilkes and had declared him ineligible, labeling those prior actions " 'subversive of the rights of the whole body of electors of this kingdom.' " After reviewing Wilkes' "long and bitter struggle for the right of the British electorate to be represented by men of their own choice," we concluded in Powell that "on the eve of the Constitutional Convention, English precedent stood for the proposition that 'the law of the land had regulated the qualifications of members to serve in parliament' and those qualifications were 'not occasional but fixed.' " Against this historical background, we viewed the Convention debates as manifesting the Framers' intent that the qualifications in the Constitution be fixed and exclusive. We found particularly revealing the debate concerning a proposal made by the Committee of Detail that would have given Congress the power to add property qualifications. James Madison argued that such a power would vest " 'an improper & dangerous power in the Legislature.' " [We] also recognized in Powell that the post-Convention ratification debates confirmed that the Framers understood the qualifications in the Constitution to be fixed and unalterable by Congress. The exercise by Congress of its power to judge the qualifications of its Members further confirmed this understanding. We concluded that, during the first 100 years of its existence, "Congress strictly limited its power to judge the qualifications of its members to those enumerated in the Constitution." [As this] summary reveals, our historical analysis in Powell was both detailed and persuasive. We thus conclude now, as we did in Powell, that history shows that, with respect to Congress, the Framers intended the Constitution to establish fixed qualifications.[1]

---

1. The text of the Qualifications Clauses also supports the result we reached in Powell. John Dickinson of Delaware observed that the enumeration of a few qualifications "would by implication tie up the hands of the Legislature from supplying omissions." Justice Story made the same point: "It would seem but fair reasoning upon the plainest

POWELL'S RELIANCE ON DEMOCRATIC PRINCIPLES. In Powell, [w]e noted that allowing Congress to impose additional qualifications would violate that "fundamental principle of our representative [democracy] 'that the people should choose whom they please to govern them' " [quoting Alexander Hamilton]. [T]his broad principle incorporated at least two fundamental ideas. First, we emphasized the egalitarian concept that the opportunity to be elected was open to all. We noted in particular Madison's statement in The Federalist [No. 52] that " 'under these reasonable limitations [enumerated in the Constitution], the door of this part of the federal government is open to merit of every description, whether native or adoptive, whether young or old, and without regard to poverty or wealth, or to any particular profession of religious faith.' " [Second,] we recognized the critical postulate that sovereignty is vested in the people, and that sovereignty confers on the people the right to choose freely their representatives to the National Government. [Powell] thus establishes two important propositions: first, that the "relevant historical materials" compel the conclusion that, at least with respect to qualifications imposed by Congress, the Framers intended the qualifications listed in the Constitution to be exclusive; and second, that that conclusion is equally compelled by an understanding of the "fundamental principle of our [representative democracy] 'that the people should choose whom they please to govern them.' "

POWELL'S HOLDING. Petitioners argue somewhat half-heartedly that the narrow holding in Powell, which involved the power of the House to exclude a member pursuant to Art. I, § 5, does not control the more general question whether Congress has the power to add qualifications. Powell, however, is not susceptible to such a narrow reading. Our conclusion that Congress may not alter or add to the qualifications in the Constitution was integral to our analysis and [outcome].[2]

III. Our reaffirmation of Powell does not necessarily resolve the specific questions presented in these cases. For petitioners argue that whatever the

principles of interpretation, that when the constitution established certain qualifications, as necessary for office, it meant to exclude all others, as prerequisites. From the very nature of such a provision, the affirmation of these qualifications would seem to imply a negative of all others." 1 J. Story, Commentaries on the Constitution of the United States. As Dickinson's comment demonstrates, the Framers were well aware of the expressio unius argument that would result from their wording of the Qualifications Clauses; they adopted that wording nonetheless. There thus is no merit either to the dissent's suggestion that Story was the first to articulate the expressio unius argument, or to the dissent's assertion that that argument is completely without merit. [Footnote by Justice Stevens.]

2. Justice THOMAS's dissent purports to agree with the outcome of Powell, but rejects the reasoning in the opinion. The dissent treats Powell as simply an application of the "default rule" that if "the Constitution is silent about the exercise of a particular power—that is, where the Constitution does not

speak either expressly or by necessary implication—the Federal Government lacks that power and the States enjoy it." However, there is not a word in the Court's opinion in Powell suggesting that the decision rested on the "default rule" that undergirds the dissent's entire analysis. On the contrary, [our] conclusion in Powell was based on our understanding of the "fixed meaning of 'qualifications' set forth in Art. I, § 2."

[Moreover,] the Court has never treated the dissent's "default rule" as absolute. In McCulloch v. Maryland, for example, Chief Justice Marshall rejected the argument that the Constitution's silence on state power to tax federal instrumentalities requires that States have the power to do so. Under the dissent's unyielding approach, it would seem that McCulloch was wrongly decided. Similarly, the dissent's approach would invalidate our dormant Commerce Clause jurisprudence [chap. 5 below], because the Constitution is clearly silent on the subject of state legislation that discriminates against [interstate commerce]. [Footnote by Justice Stevens.]

constitutionality of additional qualifications for membership imposed by Congress, the historical and textual materials discussed in Powell do not support the conclusion that the Constitution prohibits additional qualifications imposed by States. In the absence of such a constitutional prohibition, petitioners argue, the Tenth Amendment and the principle of reserved powers require that States be allowed to add such qualifications. [We] disagree for two independent reasons. First, [the] power to add qualifications is not within the "original powers" of the States, and thus is not reserved to the States by the Tenth Amendment. Second, even if States possessed some original power in this area, we conclude that the Framers intended the Constitution to be the exclusive source of qualifications for members of Congress, and that the Framers thereby "divested" States of any power to add qualifications.

The "plan of the convention" [draws] a basic distinction between the powers of the newly created Federal Government and the powers retained by the pre-existing sovereign States. As Chief Justice Marshall explained, "it was neither necessary nor proper to define the powers retained by the States. These powers proceed, not from the people of America, but from the people of the several States; and remain, after the adoption of the constitution, what they were before, except so far as they may be abridged by that instrument." Sturges v. Crowninshield, 4 Wheat. (17 U.S.) 122 (1819). This classic statement by the Chief Justice endorsed Hamilton's reasoning in The Federalist No. 32 that the plan of the Constitutional Convention did not contemplate "an entire consolidation of the States into one complete national sovereignty," but only a partial consolidation in which "the State governments would clearly retain all the rights of sovereignty which they before had, and which were not, by that act, exclusively delegated to the United States." The text of the Tenth Amendment unambiguously confirms this [principle].

SOURCE OF THE POWER. [Petitioners'] Tenth Amendment argument misconceives the nature of the right at issue because that Amendment could only "reserve" that which existed before. As Justice Story recognized, "the states can exercise no powers whatsoever, which exclusively spring out of the existence of the national government, which the constitution does not delegate to them. [No] state can say, that it has reserved, what it never possessed." 1 Story § 627. Justice Story's position thus echoes that of Chief Justice Marshall in McCulloch, [which] rejected the argument that the Constitution's silence on the subject of state power to tax corporations chartered by Congress implies that the States have "reserved" power to tax such federal instrumentalities. As [Marshall] pointed out, an "original right to tax" such federal entities "never existed, and the question whether it has been surrendered, cannot arise."

[With] respect to setting qualifications for service in Congress, no such right existed before the Constitution was ratified. [T]he Framers envisioned a uniform national system, rejecting the notion that the Nation was a collection of States, and instead creating a direct link between the National Government and the people of the United States. In that National Government, representatives owe primary allegiance not to the people of a State, but to the people of the Nation. [See] 1 Story § 627. Representatives and Senators are as much officers of the entire union as is the [President]. States thus "have just as much right, and no more, to prescribe new qualifications for a representative, as they have for a president." [See 1 Story § 627.] We believe that the Constitution reflects the Framers' general agreement with the approach later articulated by Justice Story. For example, Art. I, § 5, cl. 1 provides: "Each House shall be the Judge of the Elections, Returns and Qualifications of its own Members." The text of the Constitution thus gives the representatives of all the people the final say in judging the qualifications of the representatives of any one State. For

[Handwritten margin notes:]
Pwr argues: Powell → Congress pwr to add quals, not state pwr (I'm not sure of the bases of these arguments)
where does + can state must have orig. pwr? (Can't not prohibited?)
Text: really?
History: did the right exist before the US govt? McC
Orig Kind: direct link between people + nat'l govt: representatives serve people not states & cannot be regulated by states
Text

this reason, the dissent falters when it states that "the people of Georgia have no say over whom the people of Massachusetts select to represent them in Congress." Two other sections of the Constitution further support our view of the Framers' vision. First, [the] salary provisions [Art. I, § 6] reflect the view that representatives owe their allegiance to the people, and not to States. Second, the provisions governing elections reveal [that] powers over the election of federal officers had to be delegated to, rather than reserved by, the States. It surely is no coincidence that the context of federal elections provides one of the few areas in which the Constitution expressly requires action by the States, namely that "the Times, Places and Manner of holding Elections for Senators and Representatives, shall be prescribed in each State by the legislature thereof." This duty parallels the duty under Article II that "Each State shall appoint, in such Manner as the Legislature thereof may direct, a Number of Electors." Art II., § 1, cl. 2. [Such] Clauses are express delegations of power to the States to act with respect to federal elections.

[Margin note: Textual support of orig. understand. Framer's vision: -Congress regulates US representative 1. Art I §5- 2. Art I §6 salary 3. election pwr delegated NOT reserved to states. (Art II §1 cl. 2)]

[In] short, as the Framers recognized, electing representatives to the National Legislature was a new right, arising from the Constitution itself. The Tenth Amendment thus provides no basis for concluding that the States possess reserved power to add qualifications to those that are fixed in the Constitution. Instead, any state power to set the qualifications for membership in Congress must derive not from the reserved powers of state sovereignty, but rather from the delegated powers of national sovereignty. In the absence of any constitutional delegation to the States of power to add qualifications to those enumerated in the Constitution, such a power does not exist.

THE PRECLUSION OF STATE POWER. Even if we believed that States possessed as part of their original powers some control over congressional qualifications, the text and structure of the Constitution, the relevant historical materials, and, most importantly, the "basic principles of our democratic system" all demonstrate that the Qualifications Clauses were intended to preclude the States from exercising any such power and to fix as exclusive the qualifications in the Constitution. Much of the historical analysis was undertaken by the Court in Powell. There is, however, additional historical evidence that pertains directly to the power of States. That [evidence] leads unavoidably to the conclusion that the States lack the power to add qualifications.

[Margin note: Text Structure; History]

The Convention and Ratification Debates. The [evidence] indicates the Framers' intent that States have no role in the setting of qualifications. In Federalist No. 52, [Madison] explicitly contrasted the state control over the qualifications of electors with the lack of state control over the qualifications of the elected: "The qualifications of the elected, being less carefully and properly defined by the State constitutions, and being at the same time more susceptible of uniformity, have been very properly considered and regulated by the convention. [Under] these reasonable [age, citizenship, and residence] limitations, the door of this part of the federal government is open to merit of every description, whether native or adoptive, whether young or old, and without regard to poverty or wealth, or to any particular profession of religious faith."[3]

[Margin note: Orig. UNDERSTANDING]

3. The dissent places a novel and implausible interpretation on this paragraph. Consistent with its entire analysis, the dissent reads Madison as saying that the sole purpose of the Qualifications Clause was to set minimum qualifications that would prevent the States from sending incompetent representatives to Congress; in other words, Madison viewed the Clause as preventing the States from opening the door to this part of the federal service too widely. [The] text of Federalist No. 52 belies the dissent's reading. First, Madison emphasized that "the qualifications of the elected [were] more susceptible of uniformity." His emphasis on uniformity would be quite anomalous if he envisioned

The provisions in the Constitution governing federal elections confirm the Framers' intent that States lack power to add qualifications. The Framers feared that the diverse interests of the States would undermine the National Legislature, and thus they adopted provisions intended to minimize the possibility of state interference with federal elections. For example, [the] Framers required in Art. I, § 2, cl. 1, that the qualifications for federal electors be the same as those for state electors. [Similarly,] in Art. I, § 4, cl. 1, though giving the States the freedom to regulate the "Times, Places and Manner of holding Elections," the Framers created a safeguard against state abuse by giving Congress the power to "by Law make or alter such Regulations." The Convention debates make clear that the Framers' overriding concern was the potential for States' abuse of the power to set the "Times, Places and Manner" of [elections].[4] The Framers' discussion of the salary of representatives reveals similar concerns. When the issue was first raised, Madison argued that congressional compensation should be fixed in the Constitution, rather than left to state legislatures, because otherwise "it would create an improper dependence." [The] Convention ultimately agreed to vest in Congress the power to set its own compensation. See Art. I, § 6. In light of the Framers' evident concern that States would try to undermine the National Government, they could not have intended States to have the power to set [qualifications].

We find further evidence of the Framers' intent in Art. 1, § 5, cl. 1, which provides: "Each House shall be the Judge of the Elections, Returns and Qualifications of its own Members." That Art. I, § 5 vests a federal tribunal with ultimate authority to judge a Member's qualifications is fully consistent with the understanding that those qualifications are fixed in the Federal Constitution, but not with the understanding that they can be altered by the States. If the States had the right to prescribe additional [qualifications], state law would provide the standard for judging a Member's eligibility. [Federal] questions are generally answered finally by federal tribunals. [The] judging of

that States would create for their representatives a patchwork of qualifications. Second, the idea that Madison was in fact concerned that States would open the doors to national service too widely is entirely inconsistent with Madison's emphasizing that the Constitution kept "the door [open] to merit of every description, whether native or adoptive, whether young or old, and without regard to poverty or wealth, or to any particular profession of religious faith." [Though] the dissent attempts to minimize the extensiveness of state-imposed qualifications by focusing on the qualifications that States imposed on delegates to Congress and the age restrictions that they imposed on state legislators, the dissent neglects to give appropriate attention to the abundance of property, religious, and other qualifications that States imposed on state elected officials. As we describe in some detail, nearly every State had property qualifications, and many States had religious qualifications, term limits, or other qualifications. As Madison surely recognized, without a constitutional prohibition, these qualifications could be applied to federal representatives. We cannot read Madison's comments on the

"open door" of the Federal Government as anything but a rejection of the "unduly high" barriers imposed by States. [Footnote by Justice Stevens.]

4. The dissent attacks our holding today by arguing that the Framers' distrust of the States extended only to measures adopted by "state legislatures," and not to measures adopted by "the people themselves." The novelty and expansiveness of the dissent's attack is quite astonishing. We are aware of no case that would even suggest that the validity of a state law under the Federal Constitution would depend at all on whether the state law was passed by the state legislature or by the people directly through amendment of the state constitution. Indeed, no party has so argued. Quite simply, in our view, the dissent's distinction between state legislation passed by the state legislature and legislation passed by state constitutional amendment is untenable. The qualifications in the Constitution are fixed, and may not be altered by either States or their legislatures. [Footnote by Justice Stevens.]

questions concerning rights which depend on state law is not, however, normally assigned to federal tribunals. The Constitution's provision for each House to be the judge of its own qualifications thus provides further evidence that the Framers believed that the primary source of those qualifications would be federal law. [We] also find compelling the complete absence in the ratification debates of any assertion that States had the power to add qualifications. In those debates, the question whether to require term limits, or "rotation," was a major source of controversy. The draft of the Constitution that was submitted for ratification contained no provision for rotation. In arguments that echo in the preamble to Arkansas' Amendment 73, opponents of ratification condemned the absence of a rotation requirement. [At] several ratification conventions, participants proposed amendments that would have required rotation. The Federalists' responses to those criticisms and proposals addressed the merits of the issue, arguing that rotation was incompatible with the people's right to choose. [Regardless] of which side has the better of the debate over rotation, it is most striking that nowhere in the extensive ratification debates have we found any statement [that] the draft constitution would permit States to require rotation for the representatives of their own citizens. If the participants in the debate had believed that the States retained the authority to impose term limits, it is inconceivable that the Federalists would not have made this obvious response to the arguments of the pro-rotation [forces].

Congressional Experience. Congress' subsequent experience with state-imposed qualifications provides further evidence of the general consensus on the lack of state power in this area. In Powell, we [noted] that during the first 100 years of its existence, "Congress strictly limited its power to judge the qualifications of its members to those enumerated in the Constitution." Congress first confronted the issue in 1807 when it faced a challenge to the qualifications of William McCreery, a Representative from Maryland who allegedly did not satisfy a residency requirement imposed by that State. In recommending that McCreery be seated, the Report of the House Committee on Elections noted: " 'The committee proceeded to examine the Constitution, with relation to the case submitted to them, and find that qualifications of members are therein determined, without reserving any authority to the State Legislatures to change, add to, or diminish those qualifications; and that, by that instrument, Congress is constituted the sole judge of the qualifications prescribed by it, and are obliged to decide agreeably to the Constitutional [rules].' " [Though] the House Debate may be inconclusive, commentators at the time apparently viewed the seating of McCreery as confirmation of the States' lack of power to add qualifications. [Similarly,] for over 150 years prior to Powell, commentators viewed the seating of McCreery as an expression of the view of the House that States could not add to the qualifications established in the Constitution. [We] recognize [that] "congressional practice has been erratic" and that the precedential value of congressional exclusion cases is "quite limited." Nevertheless, those incidents lend support to the result we reach today.

Democratic Principles. Our conclusion that States lack the power to impose qualifications vindicates the same "fundamental principle of our representative democracy" that we recognized in Powell, namely that "the people should choose whom they please to govern them." As we noted earlier, the Powell Court recognized that an egalitarian ideal—that election to the National Legislature should be open to all people of merit—provided a critical foundation for the Constitutional structure. This egalitarian theme echoes throughout the constitutional debates. [E.g., The Federalist No. 57 (Madison).] Similarly, we believe that state-imposed qualifications, as much as congressionally imposed qualifications, would undermine the second critical idea recognized in Powell: that an aspect of sovereignty is the right of the people to vote for whom they wish. Again, the source of the qualification is of little moment in assessing the qualification's restrictive impact. Finally, state-imposed restrictions, unlike the congressionally imposed restrictions at issue in Powell, violate a third idea central to this basic principle: that the right to choose representatives belongs not to the States, but to the people. [T]he Framers, in perhaps their most important contribution, conceived of a Federal Government directly responsible to the people, possessed of direct power over the people, and chosen directly, not by States, but by the people. [They] implemented this ideal most clearly in the provision [that] calls for the Members of the House of Representatives to be "chosen every second Year by the People of the several States." Art. I, § 2, cl. 1. Following the adoption of the 17th Amendment in 1913, this ideal was extended to elections for the Senate. The Congress of the United States, therefore, is not a confederation of nations in which separate sovereigns are represented by appointed delegates, but is instead a body composed of representatives of the people. [See] McCulloch v. Maryland. Ours is a "government of the people, by the people, for the people." A. Lincoln, Gettysburg Address (1863). Permitting individual States to formulate diverse qualifications for their representatives would result in a patchwork of state qualifications, undermining the uniformity and the national character that the Framers envisioned and sought to ensure. Cf. [McCulloch].

State Practice. Petitioners attempt to overcome this formidable array of evidence against the States' power to impose qualifications by arguing that the practice of the States immediately after the adoption of the Constitution demonstrates their understanding that they possessed such power. One may properly question the extent to which the States' own practice is a reliable indicator of the contours of restrictions that the Constitution imposed on States, especially when no court has ever upheld a state-imposed qualification of any sort. But petitioners' argument is unpersuasive even on its own terms. At the time of the Convention, "almost all the State Constitutions required members of their Legislatures to possess considerable property." Despite this near uniformity, only [Virginia] placed similar restrictions on members of Congress. [Moreover,] several States [revised] their Constitutions at around the time of the Federal Constitution. In the revised Constitutions, each State retained property qualifications for its own state elected officials yet placed no property qualification on its congressional representatives. The contemporaneous state practice with respect to term limits is similar. At the time of the Convention, States widely supported term limits in at least some circumstances. The Articles of Confederation contained a provision for term limits. [In] addition, many States imposed term limits on state officers, four placed limits on delegates to the Continental Congress, and several States voiced support for term limits for Members of Congress. Despite this widespread support, no State sought to impose any term limits on its own federal representatives. Thus, a proper assessment of contemporaneous state practice provides further persuasive evidence of a general understanding that the qualifications in the Constitution were unalterable by the States.[5] In sum, the available

---

5. Petitioners and the dissent also point out that [several States] added district residency requirements. [They] rely on these facts to show that the States believed they had the power to add qualifications. We again are unpersuaded. [I]t seems to us that States may simply have viewed district residency requirements as the necessary analog to state residency requirements. Thus state practice with respect to residency requirements does not necessarily indicate that States believed that they had a broad power to add restric-

historical and textual evidence, read in light of the basic principles of democracy, [reveal] the Framers' intent that neither Congress nor the States should possess the power to supplement the exclusive qualifications set forth in the text of the Constitution.

IV. Petitioners argue that, even if States may not add qualifications, Amendment 73 is constitutional because it is not such a qualification, and because Amendment 73 is a permissible exercise of state power to regulate the "Times, Places and Manner of Holding Elections." We reject these contentions.

Unlike §§ 1 and 2 of Amendment 73, which create absolute bars to service for long-term incumbents running for state office, § 3 merely provides that certain Senators and Representatives shall not be certified as candidates and shall not have their names appear on the ballot. They may run as write-in candidates and, if elected, they may serve. Petitioners contend that only a legal bar to service creates an impermissible qualification, and that Amendment 73 is therefore consistent with the Constitution. [We] need not decide whether petitioners' narrow understanding of qualifications is correct because, even if it is, Amendment 73 may not stand. [Amendment 73] is an indirect attempt to accomplish what the Constitution prohibits Arkansas from accomplishing directly. As the plurality opinion of the Arkansas Supreme Court recognized, Amendment 73 is an "effort to dress eligibility to stand for Congress in ballot access clothing," because the "intent and the effect of Amendment 73 are to disqualify congressional incumbents from further service." We must [accept] the State Court's view of the purpose of its own law: we are thus authoritatively informed that the sole purpose of § 3 of Amendment 73 was to attempt to achieve a result that is forbidden by the Federal Constitution. [The] preamble of Amendment 73 states explicitly: "The people of Arkansas [herein] limit the terms of elected officials." Sections 1 and 2 create absolute limits on the number of terms that may be served. There is no hint that § 3 was intended to have any other purpose.

[Petitioners] contest the Arkansas Supreme Court's conclusion that the Amendment has the same practical effect as an absolute bar. They argue that the possibility of a write-in campaign creates a real possibility for victory, especially for an entrenched incumbent. One may reasonably question the merits of that contention. [But] even if petitioners are correct that incumbents may occasionally win reelection as write-in candidates, there is no denying that the ballot restrictions will make it significantly more difficult for the barred candidate to win the election. In our view, an amendment with the avowed purpose and obvious effect of evading the requirements of the Qualifications Clauses by handicapping a class of candidates cannot stand.

---

tions. Finally, we consider the number of state-imposed qualifications to be remarkably small. Despite the array of property, religious, and other qualifications that were contained in State Constitutions, petitioners and the dissent can point to only one instance of a state-imposed property qualification on candidates for Congress, and five instances of district residency requirements. The state practice seems to us notable for its restraint, and thus supports the conclusion that States did not believe that they generally had the power to add qualifications. Nor are we persuaded by the more recent state practice involving qualifications such as those that bar

felons from being elected. As we have noted, the practice of States is a poor indicator of the effect of restraints on the States, and no court has ever upheld one of these restrictions. Moreover, as one moves away from 1789, it seems to us that state practice is even less indicative of the Framers' understanding of state power. Finally, it is important to reemphasize that the dissent simply has no credible explanation as to why almost every State imposed property qualifications on state representatives but not on [federal representatives]. [Footnote by Justice Stevens.]

[Petitioners] make the related argument that Amendment 73 merely regulates the "Manner" of elections, and that the Amendment is therefore a permissible exercise of state power under Article I, § 4, cl. 1 (the Elections Clause) to regulate the "Times, Places and Manner" of elections. We cannot agree. A necessary consequence of petitioners' argument is that Congress itself would have the power to "make or alter" a measure such as Amendment 73. That the Framers would have approved of such a result is unfathomable. [Moreover,] petitioners' broad construction of the Elections Clause is fundamentally inconsistent with the Framers' view of that Clause. The Framers intended the Elections Clause to grant States authority to create procedural regulations, not to provide States with license to exclude classes of candidates from [federal office].

V. The merits of term limits, or "rotation," have been the subject of debate since the formation of our Constitution. [The] cogent arguments on both sides of the question that were articulated during the process of ratification largely retain their force today. Over half the States have adopted measures that impose such limits on some offices either directly or indirectly, and the Nation as a whole, notably by constitutional amendment, has imposed a limit on the number of terms that the President may serve. Term limits, like any other qualification for office, unquestionably restrict the ability of voters to vote for whom they wish. On the other hand, such limits may provide for the infusion of fresh ideas and new perspectives, and may decrease the likelihood that representatives will lose touch with their constituents. It is not our province to resolve this longstanding debate. We are, however, firmly convinced that allowing the several States to adopt term limits for congressional service would effect a fundamental change in the constitutional framework. Any such change must come not by legislation adopted either by Congress or by an individual State, but rather—as have other important changes in the electoral process—through the Amendment procedures set forth in Article V. [Members] of Congress are chosen by separate constituencies, but [they] become, when elected, servants of the people of the United States. They are not merely delegates appointed by separate, sovereign States; they occupy offices that are integral and essential components of a single National Government. In the absence of a properly passed constitutional amendment, allowing individual States to craft their own qualifications for Congress would thus erode the structure envisioned by the Framers, a structure that was designed, in the words of the Preamble to our Constitution, to form a "more perfect Union."

[Affirmed.]

Justice KENNEDY, concurring.

I join the opinion of the Court. [I]t is well settled that the whole people of the United States asserted their political identity and unity of purpose when they created the federal system. The dissent's course of reasoning suggesting otherwise might be construed to disparage the republican character of the National Government, and it seems appropriate to add these few remarks to explain why that course of argumentation runs counter to fundamental principles of federalism. Federalism was our Nation's own discovery. The Framers split the atom of sovereignty. It was the genius of their idea that our citizens would have two political capacities, one state and one federal, each protected from incursion by the other. The resulting Constitution created a legal system unprecedented in form and design, establishing two orders of government, each with its own direct relationship, its own privity, its own set of mutual rights and obligations to the people who sustain it and are governed by it. It is appropriate to recall these [origins].

A distinctive character of the National Government, the mark of its legitimacy, is that it owes its existence to the act of the whole people who created it. It must be remembered that the National Government too is republican in essence and in theory. [Once] the National Government was formed under our Constitution, the same republican principles continued to guide its operation and practice. As James Madison explained, the House of Representatives "derives its powers from the people of America," and "the operation of the government on the people in their individual capacities" makes it "a national government," not merely a federal one. The Federalist No. 39. The Court confirmed this principle in [McCulloch]. [I]t is true that "the people of each State retained their separate political identities," for the Constitution takes care both to preserve the States and to make use of their identities and structures at various points in organizing the federal union. It does not at all follow from this that the sole political identity of an American is with the State of his or her residence. It denies the dual character of the Federal Government which is its very foundation to assert that the people of the United States do not have a political identity as well, one independent of, though consistent with, their identity as citizens of the State of their residence.

[It] might be objected that because the States ratified the Constitution, the people can delegate power only through the States or by acting in their capacities as citizens of particular States. But in [McCulloch], the Court set forth its authoritative rejection of this idea. The political identity of the entire people of the Union is reinforced by the proposition, which I take to be beyond dispute, that, though limited as to its objects, the National Government is and must be controlled by the people without collateral interference by the States. McCulloch affirmed this proposition as well, when the Court rejected the suggestion that States could interfere with federal powers. The States have no power, reserved or otherwise, over the exercise of federal authority within its proper sphere. That the States may not invade the sphere of federal sovereignty is as incontestable, in my view, as the corollary proposition that the Federal Government must be held within the boundaries of its own power when it intrudes upon matters reserved to the States. See United States v. Lopez [p. 142 below].

Of course, because the Framers recognized that state power and identity were essential parts of the federal balance, the Constitution is solicitous of the prerogatives of the States, even in an otherwise sovereign federal province. The Constitution uses state boundaries to fix the size of congressional delegations, ensures that each State shall have at least one representative, grants States certain powers over the times, places, and manner of federal elections (subject to congressional revision), requires that when the President is elected by the House of Representatives, the delegations from each State have one vote, and allows States to appoint electors for the President. Nothing in the Constitution or The Federalist Papers, however, supports the idea of state interference with the most basic relation between the National Government and its citizens, the selection of legislative representatives. The federal character of congressional elections flows from the political reality that our National Government is republican in form and that national citizenship has privileges and immunities protected from state abridgement by the force of the Constitution [itself]. [See the Slaughter–House Cases, p. 421 below.]

Not the least of the incongruities in the position advanced by Arkansas is the proposition, necessary to its case, that it can burden the rights of resident voters in federal elections by reason of the manner in which they earlier had exercised it. If the majority of the voters had been successful in selecting a candidate, they would be penalized from exercising that same right in the future. This observation serves to illustrate the extent of the State's attempted interference with the federal right to vote (and the derivative right to serve if elected by majority vote) in a congressional election, rights that do not derive from the state power in the first instance but that belong to the voter in his or her capacity as a citizen of the United States. It is maintained by our dissenting colleagues that the State of Arkansas seeks nothing more than to grant its people surer control over the National Government, a control, it is said, that will be enhanced by the law at issue here. The arguments for term limitations [are] not lacking in force; but the issue [is] not the efficacy of those measures but whether they have a legitimate source, given their origin in the enactments of a single State. There can be no doubt, if we are to respect the republican origins of the Nation and preserve its federal character, that there exists a federal right of citizenship, a relationship between the people of the Nation and their National Government, with which the States may not interfere. Because the Arkansas enactment intrudes upon this federal domain, it exceeds the boundaries of the Constitution.

JUSTICE THOMAS, with whom The Chief Justice [REHNQUIST], Justice O'CONNOR, and Justice SCALIA join, dissenting.

It is ironic that the Court [defends] the right of the people of Arkansas to "choose whom they please to govern them" by invalidating a provision that won nearly 60% of the votes cast in a direct election and that carried every congressional district in the State. I dissent. Nothing in the Constitution deprives the people of each State of the power to prescribe eligibility requirements for the candidates who seek to represent them in Congress. The Constitution is simply silent on this question. And where the Constitution is silent, it raises no bar to action by the States or the people.

I. Because the majority fundamentally misunderstands the notion of "reserved" powers, I start with some first principles. Contrary to the majority's suggestion, the people of the States need not point to any affirmative grant of power in the Constitution in order to prescribe qualifications for their representatives in Congress, or to authorize their elected state legislators to do so.

A. Our system of government rests on one overriding principle: all power stems from the consent of the people. To phrase the principle in this way, however, is to be imprecise about something important to the notion of "reserved" powers. The ultimate source of the Constitution's authority is the consent of the people of each individual State, not the consent of the undifferentiated people of the Nation as a whole. The ratification procedure erected by Article VII makes this point clear. The Constitution took effect once it had been ratified by the people gathered in convention in nine different States. But the Constitution went into effect only "between the States so ratifying the same." [In] Madison's words, the popular consent upon which the Constitution's authority rests was "given by the people, not as individuals composing one entire nation, but as composing the distinct and independent States to which they respectively belong." The Federalist No. 39.

When they adopted the Federal Constitution, of course, the people of each State surrendered some of their authority to the United States (and hence to entities accountable to the people of other States as well as to themselves). [Because] the people of the several States are the only true source of power, however, the Federal Government enjoys no authority beyond what the Constitution confers: the Federal Government's powers are limited and enumerated. [In] each State, the remainder of the people's powers—"the powers not delegated to the United States by the Constitution, nor prohibited by it to the States"—are either delegated to the state government (or) retained by the people. The Federal Constitution does not specify which of these two possibilities obtains; it is up to the various state constitutions to declare which powers the people of each State have delegated to their state government. As far as the Federal Constitution is concerned, then, the States can exercise all powers that the Constitution does not withhold from them. The Federal Government and the States thus face different default rules: where the Constitution is silent about the exercise of a particular power—that is, where the Constitution does not speak either expressly or by necessary implication—the Federal Government lacks that power and the States enjoy it. These basic principles are enshrined in the Tenth Amendment.

[To] be sure, when the Tenth Amendment uses the phrase "the people," it does not specify whether it is referring to the people of each State or the people of the Nation as a whole. But the latter interpretation would make the Amendment pointless: there would have been no reason to provide that where the Constitution is silent about whether a particular power resides at the state level, it might or might not do so. In addition, it would make no sense to speak of powers as being reserved to the undifferentiated people of the Nation as a whole, because the Constitution does not contemplate that those people will either exercise power or delegate it. The Constitution simply does not recognize any mechanism for action by the undifferentiated people of the Nation. In short, the notion of popular sovereignty that undergirds the Constitution does not erase state boundaries, but rather tracks them. The people of each State obviously did trust their fate to the people of the several States when they consented to the Constitution. At the same time, however, the people of each State retained their separate political identities. As Chief Justice Marshall put it, "no political dreamer was ever wild enough to think of breaking down the lines which separate the States, and of compounding the American people into one common mass." [McCulloch]. [I]f we are to invalidate Arkansas' Amendment 73, we must point to something in the Federal Constitution that deprives the people of Arkansas of the power to enact such measures.

B.   The majority disagrees that it bears this burden. But its arguments are unpersuasive. 1. The majority begins by announcing an enormous and untenable limitation on the principle expressed by the Tenth Amendment. According to the majority, the States possess only those powers that the Constitution affirmatively grants to them or that they enjoyed before the Constitution was adopted; the Tenth Amendment "could only 'reserve' that which existed before." From the fact that the States had not previously enjoyed any powers over the particular institutions of the Federal Government established by the Constitution, the majority derives a rule precisely opposite to the one that the Amendment actually prescribes: " 'The states can exercise no powers whatsoever, which exclusively spring out of the existence of the national government, which the constitution does not delegate to them' " [quoting 1 J. Story, Commentaries]. The majority's essential logic is that the state governments could not "reserve" any powers that they did not control at the time the Constitution was drafted. But it was not the state governments that were doing the reserving. The Constitution derives its authority instead from the consent of the people of the States. Given the fundamental principle that all governmental powers stem from the people of the States, it would simply be incoherent to assert that the people of the States could not reserve any powers that they had not previously controlled.

The majority [seeks] support for its view of the Tenth Amendment in [McCulloch]. But this effort is misplaced. McCulloch did make clear that a power need not be "expressly" delegated to the United States or prohibited to the States in order to fall outside the Tenth Amendment's reservation; delegations and prohibitions can also arise by necessary implication.[1] True to the text of the Tenth Amendment, however, McCulloch indicated that all powers as to which the Constitution does not speak (whether expressly or by necessary implication) are "reserved" to the state level. Thus, in its only discussion of the Tenth Amendment, McCulloch observed that the Amendment "leaves the question, whether the particular power which may become the subject of contest has been delegated to the one government, or prohibited to the other, to depend on a fair construction of the whole [Constitution]." McCulloch did not qualify this observation by indicating that the question also turned on whether the States had enjoyed the power before the framing. To the contrary, McCulloch seemed to assume that the people had "conferred on the general government the power contained in the constitution, and on the States the whole residuum of power." For the past 175 years, McCulloch has been understood to rest on the proposition that the Constitution affirmatively barred Maryland from imposing its tax on the Bank's operations. For the majority, however, McCulloch apparently turned on the fact that before the Constitution was adopted, the States had possessed no power to tax the instrumentalities of the governmental institutions that the Constitution created. This understanding of McCulloch makes most of Chief Justice Marshall's opinion irrelevant; according to the majority, there was no need to inquire into whether federal law deprived Maryland of the power in question, because the power could not fall into the category of "reserved" powers anyway.

[T]he only true support for [the majority's] view of the Tenth Amendment comes from Joseph Story's 1833 treatise on constitutional law. Justice Story was a brilliant and accomplished man, and one cannot casually dismiss his views. On the other hand, he was not a member of the Founding generation, and his Commentaries on the Constitution were written a half century after the framing. Rather than representing the original understanding of the Constitution, they represent only his own understanding. In a range of cases concerning the federal/state relation, moreover, this Court has deemed positions taken in Story's commentaries to be more nationalist than the Constitution warrants. In this case too, Story's position that the only powers reserved to the States are those that the States enjoyed before the framing conflicts with both the plain language of the Tenth Amendment and the underlying theory of the Constitution.

2. The majority also sketches out [an] alternative (and narrower) argument. Again citing Story, the majority suggests that it would be inconsistent with the notion of "national sovereignty" for the States or the people of the States, to have any reserved powers over the selection of Members of Congress. The majority apparently reaches this conclusion in two steps. First, it asserts that because Congress as a whole is an institution of the National Government, the individual Members of Congress "owe primary allegiance not to the people of a State, but to the people of the Nation." Second, it concludes that because each Member of Congress has a nationwide constituency once he takes office, it would be inconsistent with the Framers' scheme to let a single State prescribe qualifications for him.

Political scientists can debate about who commands the "primary allegiance" of Members of Congress once they reach Washington. From the framing to the present, however, the selection of the Representatives and Senators from each State has been left entirely to the people of that State or to their state legislature. The very name "congress" suggests a coming together of

---

1. Despite the majority's odd suggestion to the contrary, I fully agree with this sensible position. [Footnote by Justice Thomas.]

representatives from distinct entities. In keeping with the complexity of our federal system, once the representatives chosen by the people of each State assemble in Congress, they form a national body and are beyond the control of the individual States until the next election. But the selection of representatives in Congress is indisputably an act of the people of each State, not some abstract people of the Nation as a whole. [Although] the United States obviously is a Nation, and although it obviously has citizens, the Constitution does not call for Members of Congress to be elected by the undifferentiated national citizenry; indeed, it does not recognize any mechanism at all (such as a national referendum) for action by the undifferentiated people of the Nation as a whole. Even at the level of national politics, then, there always remains a meaningful distinction between someone who is a citizen of the United States and of Georgia and someone who is a citizen of the United States and of Massachusetts. The Georgia citizen who is unaware of this distinction will have it pointed out to him as soon as he tries to vote in a Massachusetts congressional election. In short, while the majority is correct that the Framers expected the selection process to create a "direct link" between members of the House of Representatives and the people, the link was between the Representatives from *people of states control elections* each State and the people of that State; the people of Georgia have no say over whom the people of Massachusetts select to represent them in Congress. This arrangement must baffle the majority, whose understanding of Congress would surely fit more comfortably within a system of nationwide elections. But the fact remains that when it comes to the selection of Members of Congress, the people of each State have retained their independent political identity. As a result, there is absolutely nothing strange about the notion that the people of the States or their state legislatures possess "reserved" powers in this [area].

The majority seeks support from [Art. I, § 6, cl. 1]. But the fact that Members of Congress draw a federal salary once they have assembled hardly means that the people of the States lack reserved powers over the selection of their representatives. [As] for the fact that a State has no reserved power to establish qualifications for the office of President, it surely need not follow that a State has no reserved power to establish qualifications for the Members of Congress who represent the people of that State. Because powers are reserved to the States "respectively," it is clear that no State may legislate for another [State]. In a final effort to deny that the people of the States enjoy "reserved" powers over the selection of their representatives in Congress, the majority suggests that the Constitution expressly delegates to the States certain powers over congressional elections. Such delegations of power, the majority argues, *Art I §4 — no delegation of auth. to states* would be superfluous if the people of the States enjoyed reserved powers in this area. Only one constitutional provision—the Times, Places and Manner Clause of Article I, § 4—even arguably supports the majority's suggestion. Contrary to the majority's assumption, however, this Clause does not delegate any authority to the States. Instead, it simply imposes a duty upon them. The majority gets it exactly right: by specifying that the state legislatures "shall" prescribe the details necessary to hold congressional elections, the Clause "expressly requires action by the States." This command meshes with one of the principal purposes of Congress' "make or alter" power: to ensure that the States hold congressional elections in the first place, so that Congress continues to exist. [Constitutional] provisions that impose affirmative duties on the States are hardly inconsistent with the notion of reserved powers. Of course, the second part of the Times, Places and Manner Clause does grant a power rather than impose a duty. As its contrasting uses of the words "shall" and "may" confirm, however, the Clause grants power exclusively to Congress, not to the States. If the Clause did not exist at all, the States would still be able to prescribe the times, *power v. duty* places, and manner of holding congressional elections; the deletion of the provision would simply deprive Congress of the power to override these state [regulations].

II.   I take it to be established, then, that the people of Arkansas do enjoy "reserved" powers over the selection of their representatives in Congress. Purporting to exercise those reserved powers, they have agreed among themselves that [those] whom they have already elected to three or more terms in the House of Representatives or to two or more terms in the Senate [should] not be eligible to appear on the ballot for reelection, but should nonetheless be returned to Congress if enough voters are sufficiently enthusiastic about their candidacy to write in their names. Whatever one might think of the wisdom of this arrangement, we may not override the decision of the people of Arkansas unless something in the Federal Constitution deprives them of the power to enact such measures.

The majority settles on "the Qualifications Clauses" as the constitutional provisions that Amendment 73 violates. Because I do not read those provisions to impose any unstated prohibitions on the States, it is unnecessary for me to decide whether the majority is correct to identify Arkansas' ballot-access restriction with laws fixing true term limits or otherwise prescribing "qualifications" for congressional office. As I discuss in Part A below, the Qualifications Clauses are merely straightforward recitations of the minimum eligibility requirements that the Framers thought it essential for every Member of Congress to meet. They restrict state power only in that they prevent the States from abolishing all eligibility requirements for membership in Congress. Because the text of the Qualifications Clauses does not support its position, the majority turns instead to its vision of the democratic principles that animated the Framers. But the majority's analysis goes to a question that is not before us: whether Congress has the power to prescribe qualifications for its own members. As I discuss in Part B, the democratic principles that contributed to the Framers' decision to withhold this power from Congress do not prove that the Framers also deprived the people of the States of their reserved authority to set eligibility requirements for their own representatives. In Part C, I review the majority's more specific historical evidence. To the extent that they bear on this case, the records of the Philadelphia Convention affirmatively support my unwillingness to find hidden meaning in the Qualifications Clauses, while the surviving records from the ratification debates help neither side. As for the postratification period, five States supplemented the constitutional disqualifications in their very first election laws. The historical evidence thus refutes any notion that the Qualifications Clauses were generally understood to be exclusive. Yet the majority must establish just such an understanding in order to justify its position that the Clauses impose unstated prohibitions on the States and the people. In my view, the historical evidence is simply inadequate to warrant the majority's conclusion that the Qualifications Clauses mean anything more than what they say.

A.   [The] majority is quite correct that the "negative phrasing" of these Clauses has little relevance. [Whether phrased in the negative or the affirmative, they merely establish *minimum* qualifications. They are quite different from *exclusive* formulations.] At least on their face, then, the Qualifications Clauses do nothing to prohibit the people of a State from establishing additional eligibility requirements for their own representatives. Joseph Story thought that such a prohibition was nonetheless implicit in the constitutional list of qualifications, because "from the very nature of such a provision, the affirmation of these qualifications would seem to imply a negative of all others." This argument rests on the maxim expressio unius est exclusio alterius. When the

Framers decided which qualifications to include in the Constitution, they also decided not to include any other qualifications in the Constitution. In Story's view, it would conflict with this latter decision for the people of the individual States to decide, as a matter of state law, that they would like their own representatives in Congress to meet additional eligibility requirements. To spell out the logic underlying this argument is to expose its weakness. Even if one were willing to ignore the distinction between requirements enshrined in the Constitution and other requirements that the Framers were content to leave within the reach of ordinary law, Story's application of the expressio unius maxim takes no account of federalism. At most, the specification of certain nationwide disqualifications in the Constitution implies the negation of other nationwide disqualifications; it does not imply that individual States or their people are barred from adopting their own disqualifications on a state-by-state basis.

[The] Qualifications Clauses do prevent the individual States from abolishing all eligibility requirements for Congress. This restriction on state power reflects the fact that when the people of one State send immature, disloyal, or unknowledgeable representatives to Congress, they jeopardize not only their own interests but also the interests of the people of other States. Because Congress wields power over all the States, the people of each State need some guarantee that the legislators elected by the people of other States will meet minimum standards of competence. The Qualifications Clauses provide that guarantee: they list the requirements that the Framers considered essential to protect the competence of the National Legislature. If the people of a State decide that they would like their representatives to possess additional qualifications, however, they have done nothing to frustrate the policy behind the Qualifications Clauses. Anyone who possesses all of the constitutional qualifications, plus some qualifications required by state law, still has all of the federal qualifications. Accordingly, the fact that the Constitution specifies certain qualifications that the Framers deemed necessary to protect the competence of the National Legislature does not imply that it strips the people of the individual States of the power to protect their own interests by adding other requirements for their own representatives. The people of other States could legitimately complain if the people of Arkansas decide, in a particular election, to send a 6–year-old to Congress. But the Constitution gives the people of other States no basis to complain if the people of Arkansas elect a freshman representative in preference to a long-term incumbent. That being the case, it is hard to see why the rights of the people of other States have been violated when the people of Arkansas decide to enact a more general disqualification of long-term incumbents. The majority responds that "a patchwork of state qualifications" would "undermine the uniformity and the national character that the Framers envisioned and sought to ensure." Yet the Framers thought it perfectly consistent with the "national character" of Congress for the Senators and Representatives from each State to be chosen by the legislature or the people of that State. The majority never explains why Congress' fundamental character permits this state-centered system, but nonetheless prohibits the people of the States and their state legislatures from setting any eligibility requirements for the candidates who seek to represent [them].

B. Although the Qualifications Clauses neither state nor imply the prohibition that it finds in them, the majority infers from the Framers' "democratic principles" that the Clauses must have been generally understood to preclude the people of the States and their state legislatures from prescribing any additional qualifications for their representatives in Congress. But the majority's evidence on this point establishes only two more modest propositions: (1)

the Framers did not want the Federal Constitution itself to impose a broad set of disqualifications for congressional office, and (2) the Framers did not want the Federal Congress to be able to supplement the few disqualifications that the Constitution does set forth. The logical conclusion is simply that the Framers did not want the people of the States and their state legislatures to be constrained by too many qualifications imposed at the national level. The evidence does not support the majority's more sweeping conclusion that the Framers intended to bar the people of the States and their state legislatures from adopting additional eligibility requirements to help narrow their own choices.

I agree with the majority that Congress has no power to prescribe qualifications for its own Members. This fact, however, does not show that the Qualifications Clauses contain a hidden exclusivity provision. The reason for Congress' incapacity is not that the Qualifications Clauses deprive Congress of the authority to set qualifications, but rather that nothing in the Constitution grants Congress this power. In the absence of such a grant, Congress may not act. But deciding whether the Constitution denies the qualification-setting power to the States and the people of the States requires a fundamentally different legal analysis. The majority appears to believe that restrictions on eligibility for office are inherently undemocratic. But the Qualifications Clauses themselves prove that the Framers did not share this view; eligibility requirements to which the people of the States consent are perfectly consistent with the Framers' scheme. [When] the people of a State themselves decide to restrict the field of candidates whom they are willing to send to Washington as their representatives, they simply have not violated the principle that "the people should choose whom they please to govern them." See [remarks of Alexander Hamilton at the New York convention].

[The] fact that the Framers did not grant a qualification-setting power to Congress does not imply that they wanted to bar its exercise at the state level. One reason why the Framers decided not to let Congress prescribe the qualifications of its own members was that incumbents could have used this power to perpetuate themselves or their ilk in office. As Madison pointed out, [Members of Congress] would have an obvious conflict of interest if they could determine who may run against them. But neither the people of the States nor the state legislatures would labor under the same conflict of interest when prescribing qualifications for Members of Congress, and so the Framers would have had to use a different calculus in determining whether to deprive them of this power. As the majority argues, democratic principles also contributed to the Framers' decision to withhold the qualification-setting power from Congress. But the majority is wrong to suggest that the same principles must also have led the Framers to deny this power to the people of the States and the state legislatures. In particular, it simply is not true that "the source of the qualification is of little moment in assessing the qualification's restrictive impact." There is a world of difference between a self-imposed constraint and a constraint imposed from above.

Congressional power over qualifications would have enabled the representatives from some States, acting collectively in the National Legislature, to prevent the people of another State from electing their preferred candidates. The John Wilkes episode in 18th-century England illustrates the problems that might result. [Americans] who remembered these events might well have wanted to prevent the National Legislature from fettering the choices of the people of any individual State (for the House of Representatives) or their state legislators (for the Senate). Yet this is simply to say that qualifications should not be set at the national level for offices whose occupants are selected at the state level. [The] majority does not explain why democratic principles forbid the people of a State from adopting additional eligibility requirements to help narrow their choices among candidates seeking to represent them in the House of Representatives. [The] majority appears to believe that restrictions on eligibility for office are inherently undemocratic. But the Qualifications Clauses themselves prove that the Framers did not share this view; eligibility requirements to which the people of the States consent are perfectly consistent with the Framers' scheme. [When] the people of a State themselves decide to restrict the field of candidates whom they are willing to send to Washington as their representatives, they simply have not violated the principle that "the people should choose whom they please to govern them." [In fact,] the authority to narrow the field of candidates [may] be part and parcel of the right to elect Members of Congress. That is, the right to choose may include the right to winnow. See Hills, A Defense of State Constitutional Limits on Federal Congressional Terms, 53 U. Pitt. L. Rev. 97, 107–109 (1991).

[I] see nothing in the Constitution that precludes the people of each State (if they so desire) from authorizing their elected state legislators to prescribe qualifications on their behalf. If the people of a State decide that they do not trust their state legislature with this power, they are free to amend their state constitution to withdraw it. This arrangement seems perfectly consistent with the Framers' scheme. [But] one need not agree with me that the people of each State may delegate their qualification-setting power in order to uphold Arkansas' Amendment 73. Amendment 73 is not the act of a state legislature; it is the act of the people of Arkansas, adopted at a direct election and inserted into the state constitution. The majority never explains why giving effect to the people's decision would violate the "democratic principles" that undergird the Constitution. Instead, the majority's discussion of democratic principles is directed entirely to attacking eligibility requirements imposed on the people of a State by an entity other than themselves. The majority protests that any distinction between the people of the States and the state legislatures is "untenable" and "astonishing." In the limited area of congressional elections, however, the Framers themselves drew this distinction: they specifically provided for Senators to be chosen by the state legislatures and for Representatives to be chosen by the people. In the context of congressional elections, the Framers obviously saw a meaningful difference between direct action by the people of each State and action by their [state legislatures].

C.   In addition to its arguments about democratic principles, the majority asserts that more specific historical evidence supports its view that the Framers did not intend to permit supplementation of the Qualifications Clauses. But when one focuses on the distinction between congressional power to add qualifications for congressional office and the power of the people or their state legislatures to add such qualifications, one realizes that this assertion has little basis. In particular, the detail with which the majority recites the historical evidence set forth in [Powell] should not obscure the fact that this evidence has no bearing on the question now before the Court. As the majority ultimately concedes, [if] anything, the solidity of the evidence supporting Powell's view that Congress lacks the power to supplement the constitutional disqualifications merely highlights the weakness of the majority's evidence that the States and the people of the States also lack this power.

1.   To the extent that the records from the Philadelphia Convention itself shed light on this case, they tend to hurt [the majority's case]. 2. Unable to glean from the Philadelphia Convention any direct evidence that helps its position, the majority seeks signs of the Framers' unstated intent in the Framers' comments about [other] constitutional provisions [—Art. I, § 2, cl. 1;

§ 4, cl. 1; § 5, cl. 1; and § 6, cl. 1]. The majority infers from these provisions that the Framers wanted "to minimize the possibility of state interference with federal elections." But even if the majority's reading of its evidence were correct, the most that one could infer is that the Framers did not want state legislatures to be able to prescribe qualifications that would narrow the people's choices. However wary the Framers might have been of permitting state legislatures to exercise such power, there is absolutely no reason to believe that the Framers feared letting the people themselves exercise this power. In any event, none of the provisions cited by the majority is inconsistent with state power to add qualifications for congressional office. [For example,] the majority cites the constitutional requirement that congressional salaries be "ascertained by Law, and paid out of the Treasury of the United States." Like the Qualifications Clauses themselves, however, the salary provision can be seen as simply another means of protecting the competence of the National Legislature. As reflected in the majority's own evidence, one of the recurring themes of the debate over this provision was that if congressional compensation were left up to the States, parsimonious States might reduce salaries so low that only incapable people would be willing to serve in Congress. As the majority stresses, some delegates to the Philadelphia Convention did argue that leaving congressional compensation up to the various States would give Members of Congress "an improper dependence" upon the States. The Framers may well have thought that state power over salary, like state power to recall, would be inconsistent with the notion that Congress was a national legislature once it assembled. But state power over initial eligibility requirements does not raise the same concerns: it was perfectly coherent for the Framers to leave selection matters to the state level while providing for Members of Congress to draw a federal salary once they took office. Thus, the Compensation Clause seems wholly irrelevant; contrary to the majority's suggestion, it does not address elections at all.

[T]he majority [also] emphasizes that "each House [of Congress] shall be the Judge of the Elections, Returns and Qualifications of its own Members." [Art. I, § 5.] According to the [majority], § 5 implies that the Framers could not have intended state law ever to "provide the standard for judging a Member's eligibility." My conclusion that States may prescribe eligibility requirements for their Members of Congress does not necessarily mean that the term "Qualifications," as used in Article I, § 5, includes such state-imposed requirements. One surely could read the term simply to refer back to the requirements that the Framers had just listed in the Qualifications Clauses, and not to encompass whatever requirements States might add on their own. The Framers had deemed the constitutional qualifications essential to protect the competence of Congress, and hence the national interest. It is quite plausible that the Framers would have wanted each House to make sure that its Members possessed these qualifications, but would have left it to the States to enforce whatever qualifications were imposed at the state level to protect state interests. But even if this [is] incorrect, I see nothing odd in the notion that a House of Congress might have to consider state law in judging the "Qualifications" of its Members. In fact, § 5 itself refutes the majority's argument. Because it generally is state law that determines what is necessary to win an election and whether any particular ballot is valid, each House of Congress clearly must look to state law in judging the "Elections" and "Returns" of its Members. It would hardly be strange if each House had to do precisely the same thing in judging "Qualifications." More generally, there is no basis for the majority's assertion that the Framers would not have charged "federal tribunals" with the task of "judging [questions] concerning rights which depend on state law." Cases involving questions of federal law hardly exhaust the categories of cases that the Framers authorized the federal courts to [decide].

3.   In discussing the ratification period, the majority stresses two principal data. One of these pieces of evidence is no evidence at all—literally. The majority devotes considerable space to the fact that the recorded ratification debates do not contain any affirmative statement that the States can supplement the constitutional qualifications. For the majority, this void is "compelling" evidence that "unquestionably reflects the Framers' common understanding that States lacked that power." The majority reasons that delegates at several of the ratifying conventions attacked the Constitution for failing to require Members of Congress to rotate out of office. If supporters of ratification had believed that the individual States could supplement the constitutional qualifications, the majority argues, they would have blunted these attacks by pointing out that rotation requirements could still be added State by State. But the majority's argument cuts both ways. The recorded ratification debates also contain no affirmative statement that the States cannot supplement the constitutional qualifications. While ratification was being debated, the existing rule in America was that the States could prescribe eligibility requirements for their delegates to Congress, even though the Articles of Confederation gave Congress itself no power to impose such qualifications. If the Federal Constitution had been understood to deprive the States of this significant power, one might well have expected its opponents to seize on this point in arguing against ratification. The fact is that arguments based on the absence of recorded debate at the ratification conventions are suspect, because the surviving records of those debates are fragmentary. We have no records at all of the debates in several of the conventions, and only spotty records from most of the others.

If one concedes that the absence of relevant records from the ratification debates is not strong evidence for either side, then the majority's only significant piece of evidence from the ratification period is Federalist No. 52. Contrary to the majority's assertion, however, this essay simply does not talk about "the lack of state control over the qualifications of the elected," whether "explicitly" or otherwise. It is true that Federalist No. 52 contrasts the Constitution's treatment of the qualifications of voters in elections for the House of Representatives with its treatment of the qualifications of the Representatives themselves. [But] while Madison did say that the qualifications of the elected were "more susceptible of uniformity" than the qualifications of electors, he did not say that the Constitution prescribes anything but uniform minimum qualifications for congressmen. That, after all, is more than it does for [congressional electors].

4.   [State] practice immediately after the ratification of the Constitution refutes the majority's suggestion that the Qualifications Clauses were commonly understood as being exclusive. Five States supplemented the constitutional disqualifications in their very first election laws, and the surviving records suggest that the legislatures of these States considered and rejected the interpretation of the Constitution that the majority adopts today. As the majority concedes, the first Virginia election law erected a property qualification for Virginia's contingent in the Federal House of Representatives. What is more, while the Constitution merely requires representatives to be inhabitants of their State, the legislatures of five of the seven States that divided themselves into districts for House elections added that representatives also had to be inhabitants of the district that elected them. Three of these States adopted durational residency requirements too, insisting that representatives have

resided within their districts for at least a year (or, in one case, three years) before being elected.

[The majority] points out that no State required its own federal representatives to rotate out of office after serving one or more terms. At the time of the framing, however, such requirements were increasingly disfavored on policy grounds. The advantages of incumbency were substantially fewer then than now, and turnover in office was naturally quite high. The perceived advantages of term limits were therefore smaller than they are today. But the perceived disadvantages were just as great: term limits prevented the States or the people of the States from keeping good legislators in office, even if they wanted to do so. It is true that under the Articles of Confederation, four States had imposed term limits on their delegates to Congress. But three of these provisions added nothing to the limits in the Articles themselves, and the other one contained only a minor variation on the provision in the Articles. Indeed, though the majority says that "many States imposed term limits on state officers," it appears that at the time of the framing only Pennsylvania imposed any restriction on the re-election of members of the state legislature, and Pennsylvania deleted this restriction when it adopted a new Constitution in 1790. It seems likely, then, that the failure of any State to impose term limits on its senators and representatives simply reflected policy-based decisions against such restrictions.

[W]e are left [with] state treatment of property qualifications. It is true that nine of the state constitutions in effect at the time of the framing required members of the lower house of the state legislature to possess some property, and that four of these constitutions were revised shortly after the framing but continued to impose such requirements. Only one State, by contrast, established a property qualification for the Federal House of Representatives. But the fact that more States did not adopt congressional property qualifications does not mean that the Qualifications Clauses were commonly understood to be exclusive; there are a host of other explanations for the relative liberality of state election laws. And whatever the explanation, the fact remains that five of the election laws enacted immediately after ratification of the Constitution imposed additional qualifications that would clearly be unconstitutional under today's holding. This history of state practice [refutes] the majority's position that the Qualifications Clauses were generally understood to include an unstated exclusivity provision.

5. The same is true of the final category of historical evidence discussed by the majority: controversies in the House and the Senate over seating candidates who were duly elected but who arguably failed to satisfy qualifications imposed by state law. As the majority concedes, " 'congressional practice has been erratic' " and is of limited relevance anyway. Actions taken by a single House of Congress in 1887 or in 1964 shed little light on the original understanding of the Constitution. Presumably for that reason, the majority puts its chief emphasis on the 1807 debate in the House of Representatives about whether to seat Maryland's William McCreery. I agree with the majority that this debate might lend some support to the majority's position if it had transpired as reported in [Powell]. But the Court's discussion—both in Powell and today—is misleading. A Maryland statute dating from 1802 had created a district entitled to send two representatives to the House, one of whom had to be a resident of Baltimore County and the other of whom had to be a resident of Baltimore City. McCreery was elected to the Ninth Congress as a resident of Baltimore City. After his reelection to the Tenth Congress, however, his qualifications were challenged on the ground that because he divided his time between his summer estate in Baltimore County and his residence in Washing-

ton, D. C., he was no longer a resident of Baltimore City at all. As the majority notes, a report of the House Committee of Elections recommended that McCreery be seated on the ground that state legislatures have no authority to add to the qualifications set forth in the Constitution. But the Committee's submission of this initial report sparked a heated debate that spanned four days, with many speeches on both sides of the issue. Finally, a large majority of the House voted to recommit the report to the Committee of Elections. The Committee thereupon deleted all references to the constitutional issue and issued a revised report that focused entirely on the factual question whether McCreery satisfied the state residency requirement. After receiving the new report, the House seated McCreery with a resolution simply saying: "Resolved, That William McCreery is entitled to his seat in this House." By overwhelming majorities, the House rejected both a proposal to specify that McCreery possessed "the qualifications required by the law of Maryland" and a proposal to declare only that he was "duly qualified, agreeably to the constitution of the United States." Far from supporting the majority's position, the McCreery episode merely demonstrates that the 10th House of Representatives was deeply divided over whether state legislatures may add to the qualifications set forth in the Constitution. The majority needs more than that. The prohibition that today's majority enforces is found nowhere in the text of the Qualifications Clauses. In the absence of evidence that the Clauses nonetheless were generally understood at the time of the framing to imply such a prohibition, we may not use the Clauses to invalidate the decisions of a State or its people.

III. It is radical enough for the majority to hold that the Constitution implicitly precludes the people of the States from prescribing any eligibility requirements for the congressional candidates who seek their votes. This holding, after all, does not stop with negating the term limits that many States have seen fit to impose on their Senators and Representatives. Today's decision also means that no State may disqualify congressional candidates whom a court has found to be mentally incompetent, who are currently in prison, or who have past vote-fraud convictions. Likewise, after today's decision, the people of each State must leave open the possibility that they will trust someone with their vote in Congress even though they do not trust him with a vote in the election for Congress. See, e.g., R. I. Gen. Laws (restricting candidacy to people "qualified to vote"). In order to invalidate § 3 of Amendment 73, however, the majority must go farther. The bulk of the majority's analysis—like Part II of my dissent—addresses the issues that would be raised if Arkansas had prescribed "genuine, unadulterated, undiluted term limits." But as the parties have agreed, Amendment 73 does not actually create this kind of disqualification. [I]t says only that if they are to win reelection, they must do so by write-in votes.

One might think that this is a distinction without a difference. As the majority notes, "the uncontested data submitted to the Arkansas Supreme Court" show that write-in candidates have won only six congressional elections in this century. But while the data's accuracy is indeed "uncontested," petitioners filed an equally uncontested affidavit [by a political science professor, James S. Fay] challenging the data's relevance. [According to Professor Fay's affidavit, the data] "demonstrate that when a write-in candidate is well-known and well-funded, it is quite possible for him or her to win an election." The majority responds that whether "the Arkansas amendment has the likely effect of creating a qualification" is "simply irrelevant to our holding today." But the majority—which, after all, bases its holding on the asserted exclusivity of the Qualifications Clauses—never adequately explains how it can take this position and still reach its conclusion.

[The] majority emphasizes [a] purported conclusion of the Arkansas Supreme Court, [where the plurality] asserted that "the intent" of Amendment 73 was "to disqualify congressional incumbents from further service." According to the majority, "we must, of course, accept the State Court's view of the purpose of its own law: we are thus authoritatively informed that the sole purpose of § 3 of Amendment 73 was to attempt to achieve a result that is forbidden by the Federal Constitution." I am not sure why the intent behind a law should affect our analysis under the Qualifications Clauses. If a law does not in fact add to the constitutional qualifications, the mistaken expectations of the people who enacted it would not seem to affect whether it violates the alleged exclusivity of those Clauses. But in any event, the majority is wrong about what "the State Court" has told us. Even the plurality below did not flatly assert that the desire to "disqualify" congressional incumbents was the sole purpose behind § 3 of Amendment 73. More important, neither of the Justices who concurred in the plurality's holding said anything at all about the intent behind Amendment 73. As a result, we cannot attribute any findings on this issue to the Arkansas Supreme Court.

The majority suggests that this does not matter, because Amendment 73 itself says that it has the purpose of "evading the requirements of the Qualifications Clauses." The majority bases this assertion on the Amendment's preamble, which speaks of "limiting the terms of elected officials." [But] inquiries into legislative intent are even more difficult than usual when the legislative body whose unified intent must be determined consists of 825,162 Arkansas voters. The majority nonetheless thinks it clear that the goal of § 3 is "to prevent the election of incumbents." [Petitioners] do not deny that § 3 of Amendment 73 intentionally handicaps a class of candidates, in the sense that it decreases their pre-existing electoral chances. But petitioners do deny that § 3 is intended to (or will in fact) "prevent" the covered candidates from winning reelection, or "disqualify" them from further service. One of petitioners' central arguments is that congressionally conferred advantages have artificially inflated the pre-existing electoral chances of the covered candidates, and that Amendment 73 is merely designed to level the playing field on which challengers compete with them.

To understand this argument requires some background. Current federal law [confers] numerous advantages on incumbents. [For instance,] federal law gives incumbents enormous advantages in building name recognition and good will in their home districts. At the same time [Congress] imposes spending and contribution limits in congressional campaigns that "can prevent challengers from spending more [to] overcome their disadvantage in name recognition." [At] the same time that incumbents enjoy the electoral advantages that they have conferred upon themselves, they also enjoy astonishingly high reelection rates. [Even] in the November 1994 elections, which are widely considered to have effected the most sweeping change in Congress in recent memory, 90 percent of the incumbents who sought reelection to the House were successful, and nearly half of the losers were completing only their first terms. [The] voters of Arkansas evidently believe that incumbents would not enjoy such overwhelming success if electoral contests were truly fair—that is, if the government did not put its thumb on either side of the scale. The majority offers no reason to question the accuracy of this belief. Given this context, petitioners portray § 3 of Amendment 73 as an effort at the state level to offset the electoral advantages that congressional incumbents have conferred upon themselves at the federal level. To be sure, the offset is only rough and approximate; no one knows exactly how large an electoral benefit comes with having been a long-term Member of Congress, and no one knows exactly how large an electoral disadvantage comes from forcing a well-funded candidate with high name recognition to run a write-in campaign. But the majority does not base its holding on the premise that Arkansas has struck the wrong balance. Instead, the majority holds that the Qualifications Clauses preclude Arkansas from trying to strike any balance at all. [T]he majority apparently would reach the same result even if one could demonstrate at trial that the electoral advantage conferred by Amendment 73 upon challengers precisely counterbalances the electoral advantages conferred by federal law upon long-term Members of Congress.

For me, this suggests only two possibilities. Either the majority's holding is wrong and Amendment 73 does not violate the Qualifications Clauses, or (assuming the accuracy of petitioners' factual claims) the electoral system that exists without Amendment 73 is no less unconstitutional than the electoral system that exists with Amendment 73. I do not mean to suggest that States have unbridled power to handicap particular classes of candidates, even when those candidates enjoy federally conferred advantages that may threaten to skew the electoral process. But laws that allegedly have the purpose and effect of handicapping a particular class of candidates traditionally are reviewed under the First and Fourteenth Amendments rather than the Qualifications Clauses. To analyze such laws under the Qualifications Clauses may open up whole new vistas for courts. If it is true that "the current congressional campaign finance system [has] created an electoral system so stacked against challengers that in many elections voters have no real choices," are the Federal Election Campaign Act Amendments of 1974 unconstitutional under (of all things) the Qualifications Clauses? If it can be shown that nonminorities are at a significant disadvantage when they seek election in districts dominated by minority voters, would the intentional creation of "majority-minority districts" violate the Qualifications Clauses even if it were to survive scrutiny under the Fourteenth Amendment? More generally, if "district lines are rarely neutral phenomena" and if "districting inevitably has and is intended to have substantial political consequences," will plausible Qualifications Clause challenges greet virtually every redistricting decision? The majority's opinion may not go so far, although it does not itself suggest any principled stopping point. No matter how narrowly construed, however, today's decision reads the Qualifications Clauses to impose substantial implicit prohibitions on the States and the people of the States. I would not draw such an expansive negative inference [from the Constitution's age, residence, and citizenship requirements]. Rather, I would read the Qualifications Clauses to do no more than what they say. I respectfully dissent.

———

Possible implications of the Term Limits dissent. In reflecting on the implications of the Term Limits dissent for the future, consider the extent to which Justice Thomas' approach might revive the Tenth Amendment limit on federal regulatory power announced in 1976 in the National League of Cities case, a ruling overturned in Garcia a decade later but to a limited extent revived in New York v. United States in 1992. See chap. 3 below. Sullivan, p. 114 above, suggests: "The dissent's choice of [its] structural default rule [supports] the continued expansion of judicially imposed external constraints on congressional power." Moreover, as Sullivan also points out, "[narrow] interpretation of Congress's commerce power is the flip side of imposing on Congress an external, federalism-based constraint: both protect the states from the reach of federal legislative power." Consider also, in the light of the next chapter, her suggestion that the Term Limits dissent "would appear to support further judicial restraint of congressional intrusions into traditional state domains such as criminal law." Consider as well whether the major theme underlying the many decades of dormant commerce clause restraints on states (preventing states from imposing undue burdens on or discriminating against interstate commerce—see chap. 5 below) are put at risk by the approach suggested in the Term Limits dissent. Is Sullivan persuasive in suggesting that, "under [the dissent's] formal structural default rule, [there] is no structural basis for judicially implied state disabilities to act in the federal sphere"?

CHAPTER 3

THE COMMERCE POWER

REFER TO PART II INTRO p. 87

SECTION 1. INTRODUCTION

The poor condition of American commerce and the proliferating trade rivalries among the states were the immediate provocations for the calling of the Constitutional Convention. One of the new Constitution's major innovations was a response to those concerns: Congress was granted the power "To Regulate Commerce with foreign Nations, and among the Several States." A central purpose of that grant was to suppress the "interfering and unneighborly regulations of some States"—regulations which, "if not restrained by a national control," would prove to be ever more "serious sources of animosity and discord." (Hamilton's No. 22 of The Federalist.) The national commerce power, it was hoped, would afford the means to end hostile state restrictions, retaliatory trade regulations, and protective tariffs on imports from other states.

That congressional power, designed to promote a national market and curb balkanization of the economy, has been a subject of extensive and continuous consideration by the Court since Marshall's day. The commerce power has had a two-fold impact: as a restraint on state action (considered in chap. 5), and as a source of congressional authority (the concern of this chapter). In the hundreds of cases in which *state* regulations and taxes have been challenged under the commerce clause, free trade—a value clearly rooted in the history of the clause—was the national interest that claimed protection. In cases in which the clause is invoked to justify *congressional* regulation, the nexus with historical purposes is often more tenuous. But the modern pressures for national action on an ever widening range of problems have prompted increasingly intense searches for constitutional justifications among the enumerated powers. And in these searches, the commerce clause has frequently proved to be an attractive and often hospitable basis for the assertion of regulatory authority.

This chapter examines in some detail the Court's efforts to articulate the scope and limits of the commerce power. That examination is worthwhile not only for its own sake—for the sake of tracing the contours of congressional authority over commerce—but also for its institutional aspects, for the light it sheds on the Court's general capacity to develop enforceable limits on governmental powers. Many of the doctrines articulated in these cases proved ineffective as restraints; some were explicitly abandoned by the Court. In the early decades of the twentieth century, the Court frequently struck down national regulatory laws. Beginning in 1937, the Court showed great deference to congressional action under the commerce power; indeed, no law was struck down as exceeding the reach of the commerce power for nearly six decades. But in 1995, in United States v. Lopez, below, the majority found reasons to invalidate a federal law. In examining the contemporary constitutional terrain, consider: Are the political restraints on Congress adequate to protect federalism-related values (recall the Wechsler and Choper arguments in chap. 2 above), or are there continuing justifications (and need) for judicially imposed

P. 110
P. 112

limits on Congress? Did the limits articulated by past Courts fail because they were unjustifiable in content? Because they were applied inconsistently and with result-oriented biases? What principled limits were possible? What limits remain? What are the implications for the future scope of the national commerce power in light of Lopez and other manifestations of the modern antifederalist revival (note the Seminole Indians case, p. 225 below, and the additional airing of state sovereignty and autonomy concerns at the end of this chapter). Does the history of commerce clause litigation suggest that judicially-developed doctrines limiting government tend to be facades for the personal preferences of the judges? Are restraints designed to protect individual rights (see Part III of this book) likely to be more principled and effective in the long run than the federalism-related limits considered in this chapter?

These problems underlie the recurrent questions of commerce power doctrine which surface throughout this chapter. Often, Congress has sought to deal with problems far removed from the evils that gave rise to the commerce clause. Should the purpose of Congress determine the legitimacy of resort to the commerce power? Can a standard of constitutionality distinguish between "commercial" or "economic" legislation on the one hand and "moral," "social," "police" regulation on the other? Between local affairs remote from commerce and intrastate activities with a sufficiently close connection to interstate commerce? Even if adequate judicially enforceable limits are beyond the *Court's* capacity (or proper institutional role), do the text and structure of the Constitution nevertheless establish federalism-related restraints that a *legislator* should heed in considering proposals for national action? This chapter singles out the commerce power to explore limits on national regulation because congressional resort to that power has been the most prolific source of litigation. But the general problem of localist restraints on national power is not confined to commerce power issues. There is some doctrinal, and an even closer historical, connection between the commerce cases in this chapter and the taxing and spending power materials in the next.[1]

This Introduction concludes with the decision in United States v. Lopez, the Court's 1995 decision which invalidated, for the first time in nearly sixty years, a congressional reliance on its commerce power. The case is printed at the outset of this chapter not only for its intrinsic potential significance for the scope of the commerce power, but also because its holding and its review of the evolution of commerce power doctrine offer useful vantage points from which to critically evaluate the evolution of the commerce clause doctrine, an evolution surveyed in the Lopez opinions and examined more fully in the rest of this chapter.

United States v. Lopez

514 U.S. 549, 115 S.Ct. 1624, 131 L.Ed.2d 626 (1995).

Chief Justice REHNQUIST delivered the opinion of the Court.

1. On the doctrinal relationship, compare, e.g., the problem of abuses of power—invoking a delegated power as a "pretext" to achieve ulterior ends—in the Child Labor Case, Hammer v. Dagenhart (p. 173 of this chapter), with the Child Labor Tax Case (p. 229 of the next chapter). On the historical relationship, compare the Court's efforts to curb exercises of the commerce power in the early decades of this century with similar efforts to restrain congressional uses of other Art. I, § 8, powers: e.g., the 1936 commerce power decision in the Carter case (p. 180 of this chapter) parallels the 1936 decision in a spending power case, United States v. Butler (p. 235 of the next chapter). These and other doctrinal and historical interrelations are developed in several notes below.

In the Gun–Free School Zones Act of 1990, Congress made it a federal offense "for any individual knowingly to possess a firearm at a place that the individual knows, or has reasonable cause to believe, is a school zone." 18 U.S.C. § 922 (q). The Act neither regulates a commercial activity nor contains a requirement that the possession be connected in any way to interstate commerce. We hold that the Act exceeds the authority of Congress "to regulate Commerce [among] the several [States]." [Lopez, a 12th grade student, was convicted for knowingly possessing a concealed handgun and bullets at his San Antonio high school. The Court of Appeals reversed, ruling that the law was beyond the reach of the commerce power.] [W]e now affirm.

We start with first principles. The Constitution creates a Federal Government of enumerated powers. As James Madison wrote, "the powers delegated by the proposed Constitution to the federal government are few and defined. Those which are to remain in the State governments are numerous and indefinite." The Federalist No. 45. The Constitution delegates to Congress the power [to regulate commerce]. The Court, through Chief Justice Marshall, first defined the nature of Congress' commerce power in Gibbons v. Ogden [1824; p. 159 below]: "Commerce, undoubtedly, is traffic, but it is something more: it is intercourse. It describes the commercial intercourse between nations, and parts of nations, in all its branches, and is regulated by prescribing rules for carrying on that intercourse." The commerce power "is the power to regulate; that is, to prescribe the rule by which commerce is to be governed. This power, like all others vested in Congress, is complete in itself, may be exercised to its utmost extent, and acknowledges no limitations, other than are prescribed in the constitution." The Gibbons Court, however, acknowledged that limitations on the commerce power are inherent in the very language of the Commerce Clause. "It is not intended to say that these words comprehend that commerce, which is completely internal, which is carried on between man and man in a State, or between different parts of the same State, and which does not extend to or affect other States. Such a power would be inconvenient, and is certainly unnecessary. Comprehensive as the word 'among' is, it may very properly be restricted to that commerce which concerns more States than one. [The] enumeration presupposes something not enumerated; and that something, if we regard the language or the subject of the sentence, must be the exclusively internal commerce of a State."

For nearly a century thereafter, the Court's Commerce Clause decisions dealt but rarely with the extent of Congress' power, and almost entirely with the Commerce Clause as a limit on state legislation that discriminated against interstate commerce. Under this line of precedent, the Court held that certain categories of activity such as "production," "manufacturing," and "mining" were within the province of state governments, and thus were beyond the power of Congress under the Commerce Clause. In 1887, Congress enacted the Interstate Commerce Act, and in 1890, Congress enacted the Sherman Antitrust Act. These laws ushered in a new era of federal regulation under the commerce power. When cases involving these laws first reached this Court, we imported from our negative Commerce Clause cases the approach that Congress could not regulate activities such as "production," "manufacturing," and "mining." See, e.g., United States v. E. C. Knight Co. [1895; p. 164 below]. ("Commerce succeeds to manufacture, and is not part of it"); Carter v. Carter Coal Co. [1936; p. 180 below] ("Mining brings the subject matter of commerce into existence. Commerce disposes of it."). Simultaneously, however, the Court held that, where the interstate and intrastate aspects of commerce were so mingled together that full regulation of interstate commerce required incidental regulation of intrastate commerce, the Commerce Clause authorized such regulation. See, e.g., Houston, E. & W. T. R. Co. v. United States, [1914; p. 166 below] (Shreveport Rate Cases). In A. L. A. Schechter Poultry Corp. v. United States, [1935; p. 178 below], the Court struck down regulations that fixed the hours and wages of individuals employed by an intrastate business because the activity being regulated related to interstate commerce only indirectly. In doing so, the Court characterized the distinction between direct and indirect effects of intrastate transactions upon interstate commerce as "a fundamental one, essential to the maintenance of our constitutional system." Activities that affected interstate commerce directly were within Congress' power; activities that affected interstate commerce indirectly were beyond Congress' reach. The justification for this formal distinction was rooted in the fear that otherwise "there would be virtually no limit to the federal power and for all practical purposes we should have a completely centralized government."

Two years later, in the watershed case of NLRB v. Jones & Laughlin Steel Corp. [1937; p. 185 below], the Court upheld the National Labor Relations Act against a Commerce Clause challenge, and in the process, departed from the distinction between "direct" and "indirect" effects on interstate commerce. ("The question [of the scope of Congress' power] is necessarily one of degree".) The Court held that intrastate activities that "have such a close and substantial relation to interstate commerce that their control is essential or appropriate to protect that commerce from burdens and obstructions" are within Congress' power to regulate. In United States v. Darby [1941; p. 191 below], the Court upheld the Fair Labor Standards Act, stating: "The power of Congress over interstate commerce is not confined to the regulation of commerce among the states. It extends to those activities intrastate which so affect interstate commerce or the exercise of the power of Congress over it as to make regulation of them appropriate means to the attainment of a legitimate end, the exercise of the granted power of Congress to regulate interstate commerce." In Wickard v. Filburn [1942; p. 189 below], the Court upheld the application of amendments to the Agricultural Adjustment Act of 1938 to the production and consumption of home-grown wheat. The Wickard Court explicitly rejected earlier distinctions between direct and indirect effects on interstate commerce, stating: "Even if appellee's activity be local and though it may not be regarded as commerce, it may still, whatever its nature, be reached by Congress if it exerts a substantial economic effect on interstate commerce, and this irrespective of whether such effect is what might at some earlier time have been defined as 'direct' or 'indirect.'" The Wickard Court emphasized that although Filburn's own contribution to the demand for wheat may have been trivial by itself, that was not "enough to remove him from the scope of federal regulation where, as here, his contribution, taken together with that of many others similarly situated, is far from trivial."

Jones & Laughlin Steel, Darby, and Wickard ushered in an era of Commerce Clause jurisprudence that greatly expanded the previously defined authority of Congress under that Clause. In part, this was a recognition of the great changes that had occurred in the way business was carried on in this country. Enterprises that had once been local or at most regional in nature had become national in scope. But the doctrinal change also reflected a view that earlier Commerce Clause cases artificially had constrained the authority of Congress to regulate interstate commerce. But even these modern-era precedents which have expanded congressional power under the Commerce Clause confirm that this power is subject to outer limits. In Jones & Laughlin Steel, the Court warned that the scope of the interstate commerce power "must be considered in the light of our dual system of government and may not be extended so as to embrace effects upon interstate commerce so indirect and remote that to embrace them, in view of our complex society, would effectually obliterate the distinction between what is national and what is local and create a completely centralized government." [S]ee also Darby; Wickard. Since that time, the Court has heeded that warning and undertaken to decide whether a rational basis existed for concluding that a regulated activity sufficiently affected interstate commerce. See, e.g., Heart of Atlanta Motel v. United States [1964; p. 203 below]. Similarly, in Maryland v. Wirtz [1968; p. 199 below], the Court reaffirmed that "the power to regulate commerce, though broad indeed, has limits" that "the Court has ample power" to enforce. In response to the dissent's warnings that the Court was powerless to enforce the limitations on Congress' commerce powers because "all activities affecting commerce, even in the minutest degree [Wickard], may be regulated and controlled by Congress," (Douglas, J., dissenting), the Wirtz Court replied that the dissent had misread precedent as "neither here nor in Wickard has the Court declared that Congress may use a relatively trivial impact on commerce as an excuse for broad general regulation of state or private activities," Rather, "the Court has said only that where a general regulatory statute bears a substantial relation to commerce, the de minimis character of individual instances arising under that statute is of no consequence."

Consistent with this structure, we have identified three broad categories of activity that Congress may regulate under its commerce power. First, Congress may regulate the use of the channels of interstate commerce. See, e.g., Darby; Heart of Atlanta Motel. Second, Congress is empowered to regulate and protect the instrumentalities of interstate commerce, or persons or things in interstate commerce, even though the threat may come only from intrastate activities. See, e.g., Shreveport Rate Cases. Finally, Congress' commerce authority includes the power to regulate those activities having a substantial relation to interstate commerce, Jones & Laughlin, those activities that substantially affect interstate commerce. Within this final category, admittedly, our case law has not been clear whether an activity must "affect" or "substantially affect" interstate commerce in order to be within Congress' power to regulate it under the Commerce Clause. We conclude, consistent with the great weight of our case law, that the proper test requires an analysis of whether the regulated activity "substantially affects" interstate commerce.

We now turn to consider the power of Congress, in the light of this framework, to enact § 922(q). The first two categories of authority may be quickly disposed of: § 922(q) is not a regulation of the use of the channels of interstate commerce, nor is it an attempt to prohibit the interstate transportation of a commodity through the channels of commerce; nor can § 922(q) be justified as a regulation by which Congress has sought to protect an instrumentality of interstate commerce or a thing in interstate commerce. Thus, if § 922(q) is to be sustained, it must be under the third category as a regulation of an activity that substantially affects interstate commerce.

First, we have upheld a wide variety of congressional Acts regulating intrastate economic activity where we have concluded that the activity substantially affected interstate commerce. Examples include the regulation of intrastate coal mining, intrastate extortionate credit transactions, restaurants utilizing substantial interstate supplies, inns and hotels catering to interstate guests, and production and consumption of home-grown wheat. These examples are by no means exhaustive, but the pattern is clear. Where economic activity substantially affects interstate commerce, legislation regulating that activity will be sustained. Even [Wickard], which is perhaps the most far reaching example of Commerce Clause authority over intrastate activity, involved economic activity in a way that the possession of a gun in a school zone does not. Section 922(q) is a criminal statute that by its terms has nothing to do with "commerce" or any sort of economic enterprise, however broadly one might define those terms.[1] Section 922(q) is not an essential part of a larger regulation of economic activity, in which the regulatory scheme could be undercut unless the intrastate activity were regulated. It cannot, therefore, be sustained under our cases upholding regulations of activities that arise out of or are connected with a commercial transaction, which, viewed in the aggregate, substantially affects interstate commerce.

Second, § 922(q) contains no jurisdictional element which would ensure, through case-by-case inquiry, that the firearm possession in question affects interstate commerce. For example, in United States v. Bass, 404 U.S. 336 (1971), the Court interpreted former 18 U.S.C. § 1202(a), which made it a crime for a felon to "receive, possess, or transport in commerce or affecting commerce [any] firearm." The Court interpreted the possession component of § 1202(a) to require an additional nexus to interstate commerce both because the statute was ambiguous and because "unless Congress conveys its purpose clearly, it will not be deemed to have significantly changed the federal-state balance." [The] Court set aside the conviction because although the Government had demonstrated that Bass had possessed a firearm, it had failed "to show the requisite nexus with interstate commerce." Unlike the statute in Bass, § 922(q) has no express jurisdictional element which might limit its reach to a discrete set of firearm possessions that additionally have an explicit connection with or effect on interstate commerce. Although as part of our independent evaluation of constitutionality under the Commerce Clause we of course consider legislative findings, and indeed even congressional committee findings, regarding effect on interstate commerce, the Government concedes that "neither the statute nor its legislative history contains express congressional findings regarding the effects upon interstate commerce of gun possession in a school zone." We agree with the Government that Congress normally is not required to make formal findings as to the substantial burdens that an activity has on interstate commerce. But to the extent that congressional findings would enable us to evaluate the legislative judgment that the activity in question substantially affected interstate commerce, even though no such substantial effect was visible to the naked eye, they are lacking [here].

The Government's essential contention, in fine, is that we may determine here that § 922(q) is valid because possession of a firearm in a local school zone does indeed substantially affect interstate commerce. The Government argues that possession of a firearm in a school zone may result in violent crime and that violent crime can be expected to affect the functioning of the national economy in two ways. First, the costs of violent crime are substantial, and, through the mechanism of insurance, those costs are spread throughout the population. Second, violent crime reduces the willingness of individuals to travel to areas within the country that are perceived to be unsafe. The Government also argues that the presence of guns in schools poses a substantial threat to the educational process by threatening the learning environment. A handicapped educational process, in turn, will result in a less productive citizenry. That, in turn, would have an adverse effect on the Nation's economic well-being. As a result, the Government argues that Congress could rationally have concluded that § 922(q) substantially affects interstate commerce. We

1. Under our federal system, the " 'States possess primary authority for defining and enforcing the criminal law.' " The Government acknowledges that § 922(q) "displaces state policy choices [in] that its prohibitions apply even in States that have chosen not to outlaw the conduct in question." [Footnote by Chief Justice Rehnquist.]

pause to consider the implications of the Government's arguments. The Government admits, under its "costs of crime" reasoning, that Congress could regulate not only all violent crime, but all activities that might lead to violent crime, regardless of how tenuously they relate to interstate commerce. Similarly, under the Government's "national productivity" reasoning, Congress could regulate any activity that it found was related to the economic productivity of individual citizens: family law (including marriage, divorce, and child custody), for example. Under the theories that the Government presents in support of § 922(q), it is difficult to perceive any limitation on federal power, even in areas such as criminal law enforcement or education where States historically have been sovereign. Thus, if we were to accept the Government's arguments, we are hard-pressed to posit any activity by an individual that Congress is without power to regulate.

Although Justice Breyer argues that acceptance of the Government's rationales would not authorize a general federal police power, he is unable to identify any activity that the States may regulate but Congress may not. Justice Breyer posits that there might be some limitations on Congress' commerce power such as family law or certain aspects of education. These suggested limitations, when viewed in light of the dissent's expansive analysis, are devoid of substance. Justice Breyer focuses, for the most part, on the threat that firearm possession in and near schools poses to the educational process and the potential economic consequences flowing from that threat. Specifically, the dissent reasons that (1) gun-related violence is a serious problem; (2) that problem, in turn, has an adverse effect on classroom learning; and (3) that adverse effect on classroom learning, in turn, represents a substantial threat to trade and commerce. This analysis would be equally applicable, if not more so, to subjects such as family law and direct regulation of education. For instance, if Congress can, pursuant to its Commerce Clause power, regulate activities that adversely affect the learning environment, then, a fortiori, it also can regulate the educational process directly. Congress could determine that a school's curriculum has a "significant" effect on the extent of classroom learning. As a result, Congress could mandate a federal curriculum for local elementary and secondary schools because what is taught in local schools has a significant "effect on classroom learning," and that, in turn, has a substantial effect on interstate commerce. Justice Breyer rejects our reading of precedent and argues that "Congress [could] rationally conclude that schools fall on the commercial side of the line." Again, Justice Breyer's rationale lacks any real limits because, depending on the level of generality, any activity can be looked upon as commercial. Under the dissent's rationale, Congress could just as easily look at child rearing as "falling on the commercial side of the line" because it provides a "valuable service—namely, to equip [children] with the skills they need to survive in life and, more specifically, in the workplace." We do not doubt that Congress has authority under the Commerce Clause to regulate numerous commercial activities that substantially affect interstate commerce and also affect the educational process. That authority, though broad, does not include the authority to regulate each and every aspect of local schools.

Admittedly, a determination whether an intrastate activity is commercial or noncommercial may in some cases result in legal uncertainty. But, so long as Congress' authority is limited to those powers enumerated in the Constitution, and so long as those enumerated powers are interpreted as having judicially enforceable outer limits, congressional legislation under the Commerce Clause always will engender "legal uncertainty." [See McCulloch.] The Constitution mandates this uncertainty by withholding from Congress a plenary police power that would authorize enactment of every type of legislation. Congress has operated within this framework of legal uncertainty ever since this Court determined that it was the judiciary's duty "to say what the law is" [Marbury]. Any possible benefit from eliminating this "legal uncertainty" would be at the expense of the Constitution's system of enumerated powers. In Jones & Laughlin, we held that the question of congressional power under the Commerce Clause "is necessarily one of degree." To the same effect is the concurring opinion of Justice Cardozo in Schechter Poultry: "There is a view of causation that would obliterate the distinction of what is national and what is local in the activities of commerce. Motion at the outer rim is communicated perceptibly, though minutely, to recording instruments at the center. A society such as ours 'is an elastic medium which transmits all tremors throughout its territory; the only question is of their size.' " (quoting [Second Circuit decision in Schechter], (L. Hand, J., concurring)). These are not precise formulations, and in the nature of things they cannot be. But we think they point the way to a correct decision of this case. The possession of a gun in a local school zone is in no sense an economic activity that might, through repetition elsewhere, substantially affect any sort of interstate commerce. [Lopez] was a local student at a local school; there is no indication that he had recently moved in interstate commerce, and there is no requirement that his possession of the firearm have any concrete tie to interstate commerce.

To uphold the Government's contentions here, we would have to pile inference upon inference in a manner that would bid fair to convert congressional authority under the Commerce Clause to a general police power of the sort retained by the States. Admittedly, some of our prior cases have taken long steps down that road, giving great deference to congressional action. The broad language in these opinions has suggested the possibility of additional expansion, but we decline here to proceed any further. To do so would require us to conclude that the Constitution's enumeration of powers does not presuppose something not enumerated, cf. Gibbons v. Ogden, and that there never will be a distinction between what is truly national and what is truly local, cf. Jones & Laughlin Steel. This we are unwilling to do.

Affirmed.

Justice KENNEDY, with whom Justice O'CONNOR joins, concurring.

The history of the judicial struggle to interpret the Commerce Clause during the transition from the economic system the Founders knew to the single, national market still emergent in our own era counsels great restraint before the Court determines that the Clause is insufficient to support an exercise of the national power. That history gives me some pause about today's decision, but I join the Court's opinion with these observations on what I conceive to be its necessary though limited holding. [The] progression of our Commerce Clause cases from Gibbons to the present was not marked [by] a coherent or consistent course of interpretation; for neither the course of technological advance nor the foundational principles for the jurisprudence itself were self-evident to the courts that sought to resolve contemporary disputes by enduring principles. Furthermore, for almost a century after the adoption of the Constitution, the Court's Commerce Clause decisions did not concern the authority of Congress to legislate. Rather, the Court faced the related but quite distinct question of the authority of the States to regulate matters that would be within the commerce power had Congress chosen to act.

The history of our Commerce Clause decisions contains at least two lessons of relevance to this case. The first [is] the imprecision of content-based boundaries [such as the manufacture-commerce distinction] used without more to define the limits of the Commerce Clause. The second, related to the first but of even greater consequence, is that the Court as an institution and the legal system as a whole have an immense stake in the stability of our Commerce Clause jurisprudence as it has evolved to this point. [That] fundamental restraint on our power forecloses us from reverting to an understanding of commerce that would serve only an 18th-century [economy]; it also mandates against returning to the time when congressional authority to regulate undoubted commercial activities was limited by a judicial determination that those matters had an insufficient connection to an interstate system. Congress can regulate in the commercial sphere on the assumption that we have a single market and a unified purpose to build a stable national economy. [It] does not follow, however, that in every instance the Court lacks the authority and responsibility to review congressional attempts to alter the federal balance. This case requires us to consider our place in the design of the Government and to appreciate the significance of federalism in the whole structure of the Constitution.

Of the various structural elements in the Constitution, separation of powers, checks and balances, judicial review, and federalism, only concerning the last does there seem to be much uncertainty respecting the existence, and the content, of standards that allow the judiciary to play a significant role in maintaining the design contemplated by the Framers. [There] is irony in this, because of the four structural elements in the Constitution just mentioned, federalism was the unique contribution of the Framers to political science and political theory. Though on the surface the idea may seem counterintuitive, it was the insight of the Framers that freedom was enhanced by the creation of two governments, not one. The theory that two governments accord more liberty than one requires for its realization two distinct and discernable lines of political accountability: one between the citizens and the Federal Government; the second between the citizens and the States. If, as Madison expected, the federal and state governments are [to] hold each other in check by competing for the affections of the people, those citizens must have some means of knowing which of the two governments to hold accountable for the failure to perform a given function. Were the Federal Government to take over the regulation of entire areas of traditional state concern, areas having nothing to do with the regulation of commercial activities, the boundaries between the spheres of federal and state authority would blur and political responsibility would become illusory. The resultant inability to hold either branch of the government answerable to the citizens is more dangerous even than devolving too much authority to the remote central power.

To be sure, one conclusion that could be drawn from The Federalist Papers is that the balance between national and state power is entrusted in its entirety to the political process. Madison's observation that "the people ought not surely to be precluded from giving most of their confidence where they may discover it to be most due" can be interpreted to say that the essence of responsibility for a shift in power from the State to the Federal Government rests upon a political judgment, though he added assurance that "the State governments could have little to apprehend, because it is only within a certain sphere that the federal power can, in the nature of things, be advantageously administered." Whatever the judicial role, it is axiomatic that Congress does have substantial discretion and control over the federal balance. For these reasons, it would be mistaken and mischievous for the political branches to forget that the sworn obligation to preserve and protect the Constitution in maintaining the federal balance is their own in the first and primary instance. [S]ome Congresses have accepted responsibility to confront the great questions of the proper federal balance in terms of lasting consequences for the constitu-

[handwritten margin note: judicial power to interfere w/ Congress action under C.C.]

tional design. The political branches of the Government must fulfill this grave constitutional obligation if democratic liberty and the federalism that secures it are to endure. At the same time, the absence of structural mechanisms to require those officials to undertake this principled task, and the momentary political convenience often attendant upon their failure to do so, argue against a complete renunciation of the judicial role. Although it is the obligation of all officers of the Government to respect the constitutional design, the federal balance is too essential a part of our constitutional structure and plays too vital a role in securing freedom for us to admit inability to intervene when one or the other level of Government has tipped the scales too far. [T]he substantial element of political judgment in Commerce Clause matters leaves our institutional capacity to intervene more in doubt than when we decide cases, for instance, under the Bill of Rights even though clear and bright lines are often absent in the latter class of disputes. But our cases do not teach that we have no role at all in determining the meaning of the Commerce Clause.

Our position in enforcing the dormant Commerce Clause is instructive. [I]n contrast to the prevailing skepticism that surrounds our ability to give meaning to the explicit text of the Commerce Clause, there is widespread acceptance of our authority to enforce the dormant Commerce Clause, which we have but inferred from the constitutional structure as a limitation on the power of the [States]. True, if we invalidate a state law, Congress can in effect overturn our judgment, whereas in a case announcing that Congress has transgressed its authority, the decision is more consequential, for its stands unless Congress can revise its law to demonstrate its commercial character. This difference no doubt informs the circumspection with which we invalidate an Act of Congress, but it does not mitigate our duty to recognize meaningful limits on the [commerce power]. The statute before us upsets the federal balance to a degree that renders it an unconstitutional assertion of the commerce power, and our intervention is required. As the Chief Justice explains, unlike the earlier cases to come before the Court here neither the actors nor their conduct have a commercial character, and neither the purposes nor the design of the statute have an evident commercial nexus. [In] a sense any conduct in this interdependent world of ours has an ultimate commercial origin or consequence, but we have not yet said the commerce power may reach so far. If Congress attempts that extension, then at the least we must inquire whether the exercise of national power seeks to intrude upon an area of traditional state concern. An interference of these dimensions occurs here, for it is well established that education is a traditional concern of the States. The proximity to schools [is] the very premise for making the conduct criminal. In these circumstances, we have a particular duty to insure that the federal-state balance is not destroyed.

The statute now before us forecloses the States from experimenting and exercising their own judgment in an area to which States lay claim by right of history and expertise, and it does so by regulating an activity beyond the realm of commerce in the ordinary and usual sense of that term. The tendency of this statute to displace state regulation in areas of traditional state concern is evident from its territorial operation. There are over 100,000 elementary and secondary schools in the United States. Each of these now has an invisible federal zone extending 1,000 feet beyond the (often irregular) boundaries of the school property. In some communities no doubt it would be difficult to navigate without infringing on those zones. Yet throughout these areas, school officials would find their own programs for the prohibition of guns in danger of displacement by the federal authority unless the State chooses to enact a parallel rule. This is not a case where the etiquette of federalism has been violated by a formal command from the National Government directing the

State to enact a certain policy, cf. New York v. United States [1992; p. 212 below], or to organize its governmental functions in a certain way, cf. FERC v. Mississippi [1982 (O'Connor separate opinion); p. 209 below]. While the intrusion on state sovereignty may not be as severe in this instance as in some of our recent Tenth Amendment cases, the intrusion is nonetheless significant. Absent a stronger connection or identification with commercial concerns that are central to the Commerce Clause, that interference contradicts the federal balance the Framers designed and that this Court is obliged to [enforce].

Justice THOMAS, concurring.

[Although] I join the majority, I write separately to observe that our case law has drifted far from the original understanding of the Commerce Clause. In a future case, we ought to temper our Commerce Clause jurisprudence in a manner that both makes sense of our more recent case law and is more faithful to the original understanding of that Clause. We have said that Congress may regulate not only "Commerce [among] the several states," but also anything that has a "substantial effect" on such commerce. This test, if taken to its logical extreme, would give Congress a "police power" over all aspects of American life. Unfortunately, we have never come to grips with this implication of our substantial effects formula. [In] an appropriate case, I believe that we must further reconsider our "substantial effects" test with an eye toward constructing a standard that reflects the text and history of the Commerce Clause without totally rejecting our more recent Commerce Clause jurisprudence. Today, however, I merely support the Court's conclusion with a discussion of the text, structure, and history of the Commerce Clause and an analysis of our early case law. My goal is simply to show how far we have departed from the original understanding and to demonstrate that the result we reach today is by no means "radical," see [Stevens, J., dissenting]. I also want to point out the necessity of refashioning a coherent test that does not tend to "obliterate the distinction between what is national and what is local and create a completely centralized government."

I. At the time the original Constitution was ratified, "commerce" consisted of selling, buying, and bartering, as well as transporting for these purposes. As one would expect, the term "commerce" was used in contradistinction to productive activities such as manufacturing and agriculture. [The] Constitution not only uses the word "commerce" in a narrower sense than our case law might suggest, it also does not support the proposition that Congress has authority over all activities that "substantially affect" interstate commerce. [After all,] if Congress may regulate all matters that substantially affect commerce, there is no need for the Constitution to specify that Congress may enact bankruptcy laws, cl. 4, or coin money and fix the standard of weights and measures, cl. 5, or punish counterfeiters of United States coin and securities, cl. 6. Likewise, Congress would not need the separate authority to establish post offices and post roads, cl. 7, or to grant patents and copyrights, cl. 8, or to "punish Piracies and Felonies committed on the high Seas," cl. 10. It might not even need the power to raise and support an Army and Navy, cls. 12 and 13, for fewer people would engage in commercial shipping if they thought that a foreign power could expropriate their property with ease. Indeed, if Congress could regulate matters that substantially affect interstate commerce, there would have been no need to specify that Congress can regulate international trade and commerce with the Indians. As the Framers surely understood, these other branches of trade substantially affect interstate commerce. Put simply, much if not all of Art. I, § 8 (including portions of the Commerce Clause itself) would be surplusage if Congress had been given authority over matters that substantially affect interstate commerce. An interpretation of cl. 3 that makes the rest of § 8 superfluous simply cannot be correct. Yet this Court's Commerce Clause jurisprudence has endorsed just such an interpretation: the power we have accorded Congress has swallowed Art. I, § 8. Indeed, if a "substantial effects" test can be appended to the Commerce Clause, why not to every other power of the Federal Government? There is no reason for singling out the Commerce Clause for special treatment. Accordingly, Congress could regulate all matters that "substantially affect" the Army and Navy, bankruptcies, tax collection, expenditures, and so on. In that case, the clauses of § 8 all mutually overlap, something we can assume the Founding Fathers never intended. Our construction of the scope of congressional authority has the additional problem of coming close to turning the Tenth Amendment on its head. Our case law could be read to reserve to the United States all powers not expressly prohibited by the Constitution. Taken together, these fundamental textual problems should, at the very least, convince us that the "substantial effects" test should be reexamined.

II.   The exchanges during the ratification campaign reveal the relatively limited reach of the Commerce Clause and of federal power generally. The Founding Fathers confirmed that most areas of life (even many matters that would have substantial effects on commerce) would remain outside the reach of the Federal Government. Such affairs would continue to be under the exclusive control of the States. [D]espite being well aware that agriculture, manufacturing, and other matters substantially affected commerce, the founding generation did not cede authority over all these activities to Congress. [In] short, the Founding Fathers were well aware of what the principal dissent [of Breyer, J.] calls " 'economic . . . realities.' " Even though the boundary between commerce and other matters may ignore "economic reality" and thus seem arbitrary or artificial to some, we must nevertheless respect a constitutional line that does not grant Congress power over all that substantially affects interstate commerce.

III.   If the principal dissent's understanding of our early case law were correct, there might be some reason to doubt this view of the original understanding of the Constitution. According to that dissent, Chief Justice Marshall's opinion in Gibbons v. Ogden established that Congress may control all local activities that "significantly affect interstate commerce." In my view, the dissent is wrong about the holding and reasoning of Gibbons. Because this error leads the dissent to characterize the first 150 years of this Court's case law as a "wrong turn," I feel compelled to put the last 50 years in proper perspective.

A.   [First,] the Court [in Gibbons] made the uncontroversial claim that federal power does not encompass "commerce" that "does not extend to or affect other States." From this statement, the principal dissent infers that whenever an activity affects interstate commerce, it necessarily follows that Congress can regulate such activities. Of course, Chief Justice Marshall said no such thing and the inference the dissent makes cannot be drawn. There is a much better interpretation of the "affects" language: because the Court had earlier noted that the commerce power did not extend to wholly intrastate commerce, the Court was acknowledging that although the line between intrastate and interstate/foreign commerce would be difficult to draw, federal authority could not be construed to cover purely intrastate commerce. Commerce that did not affect another State could never be said to be commerce "among the several States." But even if one were to adopt the dissent's reading, the "affects" language, at most, permits Congress to regulate only intrastate commerce that substantially affects interstate and foreign commerce.

There is no reason to believe that Chief Justice Marshall was asserting that Congress could regulate all activities that affect [interstate commerce].

B.   I am aware of no cases prior to the New Deal that characterized the power flowing from the Commerce Clause as sweepingly as does our substantial effects test. My review of the case law indicates that the substantial effects test is but an innovation of the 20th century. [These] cases all establish a simple point: from the time of the ratification of the Constitution to the mid–1930's, it was widely understood that the Constitution granted Congress only limited powers, notwithstanding the Commerce Clause. Moreover, there was no question that activities wholly separated from business, such as gun possession, were beyond the reach of the commerce power. If anything, the "wrong turn" was the Court's dramatic departure in the 1930's from a century and a half of precedent.

IV.   Apart from its recent vintage and its corresponding lack of any grounding in the original understanding of the Constitution, the substantial effects test suffers from the further flaw that it appears to grant Congress a police power over the Nation. When asked at oral argument if there were any limits to the Commerce Clause, the Government was at a loss for words. Likewise, the principal dissent insists that there are limits, but it cannot muster even one example. Indeed, the dissent implicitly concedes that its reading has no limits when it criticizes the Court for "threatening legal uncertainty in an area of law [that] seemed reasonably well settled." The one advantage of the dissent's standard is certainty: it is certain that under its analysis everything may be regulated under the guise of the Commerce Clause. The substantial effects test suffers from this flaw, in part, because of its "aggregation principle." Under so-called "class of activities" statutes, Congress can regulate whole categories of activities that are not themselves either "interstate" or "commerce." In applying the effects test, we ask whether the class of activities as a whole substantially affects interstate commerce, not whether any specific activity within the class has such effects when considered in isolation. The aggregation principle is clever, but has no stopping point. Suppose all would agree that gun possession within 1,000 feet of a school does not substantially affect commerce, but that possession of weapons generally (knives, brass knuckles, nunchakus, etc.) does. Under our substantial effects doctrine, even though Congress cannot single out gun possession, it can prohibit weapon possession generally. But one always can draw the circle broadly enough to cover an activity that, when taken in isolation, would not have substantial effects on commerce. Under our jurisprudence, if Congress passed an omnibus "substantially affects interstate commerce" statute, purporting to regulate every aspect of human existence, the Act apparently would be constitutional. Even though particular sections may govern only trivial activities, the statute in the aggregate regulates matters that substantially affect commerce.

V.   This extended discussion of the original understanding and our first century and a half of case law does not necessarily require a wholesale abandonment of our more recent opinions.[1] It simply reveals that our substantial effects test is far removed from both the Constitution and from our early case law and that the Court's opinion should not be viewed as "radical" or

---

1.   Although I might be willing to return to the original understanding, I recognize that many believe that it is too late in the day to undertake a fundamental reexamination of the past 60 years. Consideration of stare decisis and reliance interests may convince us that we cannot wipe the slate clean. [Footnote by Justice Thomas.]

another "wrong turn" that must be corrected in the future.[2] The analysis also suggests that we ought to temper our Commerce Clause jurisprudence. Unless the dissenting Justices are willing to repudiate our long-held understanding of the limited nature of federal power, I would think that they too must be willing to reconsider the substantial effects test in a future case. If we wish to be true to a Constitution that does not cede a police power to the Federal Government, our Commerce Clause's boundaries simply cannot be "defined" as being " 'commensurate with the national needs' " or self-consciously intended to let the Federal Government " 'defend itself against economic forces that Congress decrees inimical or destructive of the national economy.' " See Breyer, J., dissenting. Such a formulation of federal power is no test at all: it is a blank check. At an appropriate juncture, I think we must modify our Commerce Clause jurisprudence. Today, it is easy enough to say that the Clause certainly does not empower Congress to ban gun possession within 1,000 feet of a school.

Justice BREYER, with whom Justice STEVENS, Justice SOUTER, and Justice GINSBURG join, dissenting.

I. [First,] the power to "regulate Commerce [among] the several States" encompasses the power to regulate local activities insofar as they significantly affect interstate commerce. See, e.g., Gibbons v. Ogden; Wickard v. Filburn. [I] use the word "significant" because the word "substantial" implies a somewhat narrower power than recent precedent suggests. But, to speak of "substantial" effect" rather than "significant effect" would make no difference in this case. Second, in determining whether a local activity will likely have a significant effect upon interstate commerce, a court must consider, not the effect of an individual act (a single instance of gun possession), but rather the cumulative effect of all similar instances (i.e., the effect of all guns possessed in or near schools). See, e.g., Wickard. [Third,] the Constitution requires us to judge the connection between a regulated activity and interstate commerce, not directly, but at one remove. Courts must give Congress a degree of leeway in determining the existence of a significant factual connection between the regulated activity and interstate commerce—both because the Constitution delegates the commerce power directly to Congress and because the determination requires an empirical judgment of a kind that a legislature is more likely than a court to make with accuracy. The traditional words "rational basis" capture this leeway. Thus, the specific question before us, as the Court recognizes, is not whether the "regulated activity sufficiently affected interstate commerce," but, rather, whether Congress could have had "a rational basis" for so concluding. I recognize that we must judge this matter independently. [I] also recognize that Congress did not write specific "interstate commerce" findings into the law under which Lopez was convicted. Nonetheless, [the] matter that we review independently (i.e., whether there is a "rational basis") already has considerable leeway built into it. And, the absence of findings, at most, deprives a statute of the benefit of some extra leeway. This extra deference, in principle, might change the result in a close case, though, in practice, it has not made a critical legal difference.

2. Nor can the majority's opinion fairly be compared to Lochner v. New York [1905; p. 460 below]. Unlike Lochner and our more recent "substantive due process" cases, today's decision enforces only the Constitution and not "judicial policy judgments." Notwithstanding Justice Souter's discussion, " 'commercial character' " is not only a natural but an inevitable "ground of Commerce Clause distinction." Our invalidation of the Gun–Free School Zones Act therefore falls comfortably within our proper role in reviewing federal legislation to determine if it exceeds congressional authority as defined by the Constitution [itself]. [Footnote by Justice Thomas.]

II. Applying these principles to the case at hand, we must ask whether Congress could have had a rational basis for finding a significant (or substantial) connection between gun-related school violence and interstate commerce. Or, to put the question in the language of the explicit finding that Congress made when it amended this law in 1994 [after Lopez's conviction]: Could Congress rationally have found that "violent crime in school zones," through its effect on the "quality of education," significantly (or substantially) affects "interstate" or "foreign commerce"? As long as one views the commerce connection, not as a "technical legal conception," but as "a practical one," Swift & Co. v. United States [1905; p. 168 below], the answer to this question must be yes. Numerous reports and studies—generated both inside and outside government—make clear that Congress could reasonably have found the empirical connection that its law, implicitly or explicitly, asserts. (See Appendix for a sample of the [documentation].) [Justice Breyer's Appendix, omitted here, listed 163 government documents and private studies.] For one thing, reports, hearings, and other readily available literature make clear that the problem of guns in and around schools is widespread and extremely serious. [Based on such reports, Congress] obviously could have thought that guns and learning are mutually exclusive. And, Congress could therefore have found a substantial educational problem—teachers unable to teach, students unable to learn—and concluded that guns near schools contribute substantially to the size and scope of that problem. Having found that guns in schools significantly undermine the quality of education in our Nation's classrooms, Congress could also have found, given the effect of education upon interstate and foreign commerce, that gun-related violence in and around schools is a commercial, as well as a human, problem. Education, although far more than a matter of economics, has long been inextricably intertwined with the Nation's economy. [The] economic links I [have] sketched seem fairly obvious. Why then is it not equally obvious, in light of those links, that a widespread, serious, and substantial physical threat to teaching and learning also substantially threatens the commerce to which that teaching and learning is inextricably tied? That is to say, guns in the hands of six percent of inner-city high school students and gun-related violence throughout a city's schools must threaten the trade and commerce that those schools support. The only question, then, is whether the latter threat is (to use the majority's terminology) "substantial." And, the evidence of (1) the extent of the gun-related violence problem, (2) the extent of the resulting negative effect on classroom learning, and (3) the extent of the consequent negative commercial effects, when taken together, indicate a threat to trade and commerce that is "substantial." At the very least, Congress could rationally have concluded that the links are "substantial."

Specifically, Congress could have found that gun-related violence near the classroom poses a serious economic threat (1) to consequently inadequately educated workers who must endure low paying jobs, and (2) to communities and businesses that might (in today's "information society") otherwise gain, from a well-educated work force, an important commercial advantage, of a kind that location near a railhead or harbor provided in the past. Congress might also have found these threats to be no different in kind from other threats that this Court has found within the commerce power. As I have pointed out, Congress has written that "the occurrence of violent crime in school zones" has brought about a "decline in the quality of education" that "has an adverse impact on interstate commerce and the foreign commerce of the United States." The violence-related facts, the educational facts, and the economic facts, taken together, make this conclusion rational. And, because under our case law, the sufficiency of the constitutionally necessary Commerce Clause link between a crime of violence and interstate commerce turns simply upon size or degree, those same facts make the statute constitutional.

To hold this statute constitutional is not to "obliterate" the "distinction of what is national and what is local"; nor is it to hold that the Commerce Clause permits the Federal Government to "regulate any activity that it found was related to the economic productivity of individual citizens," to regulate "marriage, divorce, and child custody," or to regulate any and all aspects of education. For one thing, this statute is aimed at curbing a particularly acute threat to the educational process—the possession (and use) of life-threatening firearms in, or near, the classroom. [For] another thing, the immediacy of the connection between education and the national economic well-being is documented by scholars and accepted by society at large in a way and to a degree that may not hold true for other social institutions. It must surely be the rare case, then, that a statute strikes at conduct that (when considered in the abstract) seems so removed from commerce, but which (practically speaking) has so significant an impact upon commerce. In sum, a holding that the particular statute before us falls within the commerce power would not expand the scope of that Clause. Rather, it simply would apply pre-existing law to changing economic circumstances. It would recognize that, in today's economic world, gun-related violence near the classroom makes a significant difference to our economic, as well as our social, well-being. In accordance with well-accepted precedent, such a holding would permit Congress "to act in terms of [economic] realities," would interpret the commerce power as "an affirmative power commensurate with the national needs," and would acknowledge that the "commerce clause does not operate so as to render the nation powerless to defend itself against economic forces that Congress decrees inimical or destructive of the national economy."

III.   The majority's [holding] creates three serious legal problems. First, the majority's holding runs contrary to modern Supreme Court cases that have upheld congressional actions despite connections to interstate or foreign commerce that are less significant than the effect of school violence. The second legal problem the Court creates comes from its apparent belief that it can reconcile its holding with earlier cases by making a critical distinction between "commercial" and noncommercial "transactions." That is to say, the Court believes the Constitution would distinguish between two local activities, each of which has an identical effect upon interstate commerce, if one, but not the other, is "commercial" in nature. As a general matter, this approach fails to heed this Court's earlier warning not to turn "questions of the power of Congress" upon "formulas" that would give "controlling force to nomenclature such as 'production' and 'indirect' and foreclose consideration of the actual effects of the activity in question upon interstate commerce." Wickard. Moreover, the majority's test is not consistent with what the Court saw as the point of the cases that the majority now characterizes. Although the majority today attempts to categorize [several cases] as involving intrastate "economic activity," the Courts that decided each of those cases did not focus upon the economic nature of the activity regulated. Rather, they focused upon whether that activity affected interstate or foreign commerce. In fact, the Wickard Court expressly held that Wickard's consumption of home grown wheat, "though it may not be regarded as commerce," could nevertheless be regulated—"whatever its nature"—so long as "it exerts a substantial economic effect on interstate commerce."

More importantly, if a distinction between commercial and noncommercial activities is to be made, this is not the case in which to make it. The majority clearly cannot intend such a distinction to focus narrowly on an act of gun possession standing by itself, for such a reading could not be reconciled with either the civil rights cases [e.g., McClung, p. 203 below] [or] Perez [p. 196 below]—in each of those cases the specific transaction (the race-based exclusion, the use of force) was not itself "commercial." And, if the majority instead means to distinguish generally among broad categories of activities, differentiating what is educational from what is commercial, then, as a practical matter, the line becomes almost impossible to draw. Schools that teach reading, writing, mathematics, and related basic skills serve both social and commercial purposes, and one cannot easily separate the one from the other. American industry itself has been, and is again, involved in teaching. When, and to what extent, does its involvement make education commercial? Does the number of vocational classes that train students directly for jobs make a difference? Does it matter if the school is public or private, nonprofit or profit-seeking? Does it matter if a city or State adopts a voucher plan that pays private firms to run a school? Even if one were to ignore these practical questions, why should there be a theoretical distinction between education, when it significantly benefits commerce, and environmental pollution, when it causes economic harm?

Regardless, if there is a principled distinction that could work both here and in future cases, Congress (even in the absence of vocational classes, industry involvement, and private management) could rationally conclude that schools fall on the commercial side of the line. In 1990, the year Congress enacted the statute before us, primary and secondary schools spent $230 billion—that is, nearly a quarter of a trillion dollars—which accounts for a significant portion of our $5.5 trillion Gross Domestic Product for that year. The business of schooling requires expenditure of these funds on student transportation, food and custodial services, books, and teachers' salaries. And, these expenditures enable schools to provide a valuable service—namely, to equip students with the skills they need to survive in life and, more specifically, in the workplace. Certainly, Congress has often analyzed school expenditure as if it were a commercial investment, closely analyzing whether schools are efficient, whether they justify the significant resources they spend, and whether they can be restructured to achieve greater returns. Why could Congress, for Commerce Clause purposes, not consider schools as roughly analogous to commercial investments from which the Nation derives the benefit of an educated work force?

The third legal problem created by the Court's holding is that it threatens legal uncertainty in an area of law that, until this case, seemed reasonably well settled. Congress has enacted many statutes (more than 100 sections of the United States Code), including criminal statutes (at least 25 sections), that use the words "affecting commerce" to define their scope, and other statutes that contain no jurisdictional language at all. Do these, or similar, statutes regulate noncommercial activities? If so, would that alter the meaning of "affecting commerce" in a jurisdictional element? More importantly, in the absence of a jurisdictional element, are the courts nevertheless to take Wickard (and later similar cases) as inapplicable, and to judge the effect of a single noncommercial activity on interstate commerce without considering similar instances of the forbidden conduct? However these questions are eventually resolved, the legal uncertainty now created will restrict Congress' ability to enact criminal laws aimed at criminal behavior that, considered problem by problem rather than instance by instance, seriously threatens the economic, as well as social, well-being of [Americans].

Justice SOUTER, dissenting.

deferring to rational legislation is a form of judicial restraint

In reviewing congressional legislation under the Commerce Clause, we defer to what is often a merely implicit congressional judgment that its regulation addresses a subject substantially affecting interstate commerce "if there is any rational basis for such a finding." The practice of deferring to rationally based legislative judgments "is a paradigm of judicial restraint." In judicial review under the Commerce Clause, it reflects our respect for the institutional competence of the Congress on a subject expressly assigned to it by the Constitution and our appreciation of the legitimacy that comes from Congress's political accountability in dealing with matters open to a wide range of possible choices. It was not ever thus, however, as even a brief overview of Commerce Clause history during the past century reminds us. The modern respect for the competence and primacy of Congress in matters affecting commerce developed only after one of this Court's most chastening experiences, when it perforce repudiated an earlier and untenably expansive conception of judicial review in derogation of congressional commerce power. A look at history's sequence will serve to show how today's decision tugs the Court off course, leading it to suggest opportunities for further developments that would be at odds with the rule of restraint to which the Court still wisely states adherence. [T]he period from the turn of the century to 1937 [is] noted for a series of cases applying highly formalistic notions of "commerce" to invalidate federal social and economic legislation. [See, e.g., Carter, Schechter, Hammer v. Dagenhart.] [D]uring this same period the Court routinely invalidated state social and economic legislation under an expansive conception of Fourteenth Amendment substantive due process. [See chap. 8, sec. 1, below.] The fulcrums of judicial review in these cases were the notions of liberty and property characteristic of laissez-faire economics, whereas the Commerce Clause cases turned on what was ostensibly a structural limit of federal power, but under each conception of judicial review the Court's character for the first third of the century showed itself in exacting judicial scrutiny of a legislature's choice of economic ends and of the legislative means selected to reach them. It was not merely coincidental, then, that sea changes in the Court's conceptions of its authority under the Due Process and Commerce Clauses occurred virtually together, in 1937, with West Coast Hotel Co. v. Parrish [p. 476 below] and Jones & Laughlin. In the years following these decisions, deference to legislative policy judgments on commercial regulation became the powerful theme under both the Due Process and Commerce Clauses and in due course that deference became articulate in the standard of rationality review.

substantive economic review test

There is today, however, a backward glance at both the old pitfalls, as the Court treats deference under the rationality rule as subject to gradation according to the commercial or noncommercial nature of the immediate subject of the challenged regulation. The distinction between what is patently commercial and what is not looks much like the old distinction between what directly affects commerce and what touches it only indirectly. And the act of calibrating the level of deference by drawing a line between what is patently commercial and what is less purely so will probably resemble the process of deciding how much interference with contractual freedom was fatal. Thus, it seems fair to ask whether the step taken by the Court today does anything but portend a return to the untenable jurisprudence from which the Court extricated itself almost 60 years ago. The answer is not reassuring. To be sure, the occasion for today's decision reflects the century's end, not its beginning. But if it seems anomalous that the Congress of the United States has taken to regulating school yards, the act in question is still probably no more remarkable than state regulation of bake shops 90 years ago [in Lochner v. New York, p. 460 below]. In any event, there is no reason to hope that the Court's qualification of rational basis review will be any more successful than the efforts at substantive economic review made by our predecessors as the century began. Taking the Court's opinion on its own terms, Justice Breyer has explained both the hopeless porosity of "commercial" character as a ground of Commerce Clause distinction in America's highly connected economy, and the inconsistency of this categorization with our rational basis precedents from the last 50 years. Further glosses on rationality review, moreover, may be in the offing. Although this case turns on commercial character, the Court gestures toward two other considerations that it might sometime entertain in applying rational basis scrutiny (apart from a statutory obligation to supply independent proof of a jurisdictional element): does the congressional statute deal with subjects of traditional state regulation, and does the statute contain explicit factual findings supporting the otherwise implicit determination that the regulated activity substantially affects interstate commerce? Once again, any appeal these considerations may have depends on ignoring the painful lesson learned in 1937, for neither of the Court's suggestions would square with rational basis scrutiny.

Justice STEVENS, dissenting.

The welfare of our future is vitally dependent on the character of the education of our children. I therefore agree entirely with Justice Breyer's explanation of why Congress has ample power to prohibit the possession of firearms in or near schools—just as it may protect the school environment from harms posed by controlled substances such as asbestos or alcohol. I also agree with Justice Souter's exposition of the radical character of the Court's holding and its kinship with the discredited, pre-Depression version of substantive due process. I believe, however, that the Court's extraordinary decision merits this additional comment. Guns are both articles of commerce and articles that can be used to restrain commerce. Their possession is the consequence, either directly or indirectly, of commercial activity. In my judgment, Congress' power to regulate commerce in firearms includes the power to prohibit possession of guns at any location because of their potentially harmful use; it necessarily follows that Congress may also prohibit their possession in particular markets. The market for the possession of handguns by school-age children is, distressingly, substantial. Whether or not the national interest in eliminating that market would have justified federal legislation in 1789, it surely does today.

times change.

SKIP top. 206

Section 2. The Development of Commerce Power Doctrine From 1824 to 1936

1. GIBBONS v. OGDEN, 9 Wheat. (22 U.S.) 1 (1824): Gibbons v. Ogden was the Marshall Court's major contribution to the interpretation of the commerce power. Nearly 120 years later, Justice Jackson's opinion for the Court in Wickard v. Filburn [1942; p. 189 below] stated, during the New Deal: "At the beginning Chief Justice Marshall described the federal commerce power with a breadth never yet exceeded. Gibbons v. Ogden. He made emphatic the embracing and penetrating nature of this power by warning that effective restraints on its exercise must proceed from political rather than judicial processes." And the Court's decisions from 1937 to the early 1990s seemed to validate Justice Jackson's dictum. Yet the 1995 Lopez ruling, above, indicates that the Court has not yet withdrawn from imposing judicial restraints upon congressional exercises of the power, and Justice Thomas's opinion in Lopez takes issue with expansive readings of Gibbons. The meaning of Gibbons, in short, remains in controversy.

The Gibbons case arose when the New York legislature granted to Robert Livingston and Robert Fulton the exclusive right to operate steamboats in New York waters, in order to encourage the development of steamboat technology. Livingston and Fulton licensed Aaron Ogden to operate a ferry between New York City and Elizabethtown, New Jersey. Thomas Gibbons, once Ogden's partner, began operating a competing steamboat service in violation of Ogden's monopoly. Gibbons's ferries were licensed as "vessels to be employed in the coasting trade" under a federal law of 1793. Ogden obtained an injunction from the New York courts that ordered Gibbons to stop operating his ferries in New York waters. Although the central question before the Court in Gibbons was whether the New York monopoly law was invalid in view of the congressional commerce power and the Supremacy Clause (as conflicting with the federal statute enacted in 1793), an issue pursued further in chap. 5 below, Chief Justice Marshall began his opinion with an examination of the scope of the commerce power. In delineating the meaning of the commerce clause, he stated: "The subject to be regulated is commerce; and [to] ascertain the extent of the power, it becomes necessary to settle the meaning of the word. The counsel for the appellee would limit it to traffic, to buying and selling, or the interchange of commodities, and do not admit that it comprehends navigation. This would restrict a general term, applicable to many objects, to one of its significations. Commerce, undoubtedly, is traffic, but it is something more—it is intercourse. It describes the commercial intercourse between nations, and parts of nations, in all its branches, and is regulated by prescribing rules for carrying on that intercourse. [All] America understands, and has uniformly understood, the word 'commerce' to comprehend navigation."

Marshall continued: "The subject to which the power [is] applied [is] commerce 'among the several states.' The word 'among' means intermingled with. A thing which is among others, is intermingled with them. Commerce among the states cannot stop at the external boundary line of each state, but may be introduced into the interior. It is not intended to say that these words comprehend that commerce which is completely internal, which is carried on between man and man in a state, or between different parts of the same state, and which does not extend to or affect other states. Such a power would be inconvenient, and is certainly unnecessary. Comprehensive as the word 'among' is, it may very properly be restricted to that commerce which concerns more states than one. The phrase is not one which would probably have been selected to indicate the completely interior traffic of a state, because it is not an apt phrase for that purpose; and the enumeration of the particular classes of commerce to which the power was to be extended, would not have been made, had the intention been to extend the power to every description. The enumeration presupposes something not enumerated; and that something, if we regard the language or the subject of the sentence, must be the exclusively internal commerce of a state. The genius and character of the whole government seem to be, that its action is to be applied to all the external concerns of the nation, and to those internal concerns which affect the states generally; but not to those which are completely within a particular state, which do not affect other states, and with which it is not necessary to interfere, for the purpose of executing some of the general powers of the government. The completely internal commerce of a state, then, may be considered as reserved for the state itself."

After focusing on the meaning of the phrase "among the several states," the Chief Justice turned to exploring the limits on the exercises of that power. He stated that the congressional power was a "power to regulate; that is, to prescribe the rule by which commerce is to be governed. This power, like all others vested in congress, is complete in itself, may be exercised to its utmost extent, and acknowledges no limitations, other than are prescribed in the constitution. [If], as has always been understood, the sovereignty of congress, though limited to specified objects, is plenary as to those objects, the power over [commerce] is vested in congress as absolutely as it would be in a single government, having in its constitution the same restrictions on the exercise of the power as are found in the constitution of the United States. The wisdom and the discretion of congress, their identity with the people, and the influence which their constituents possess at elections, are, in this, as in many other instances, as that, for example, of declaring war, the sole restraints on which they have relied, to secure them from its abuse. They are the restraints on which the people must often rely solely, in all representative governments."

In the course of examining the validity of the New York monopoly law, Marshall considered but did not ultimately decide Gibbons's claim that the grant of the commerce power to Congress was an exclusive power, barring all state laws regulating commerce. Instead, he ultimately ruled that Ogden's claim under New York's monopoly law was barred because of the federal statute under which Gibbons was authorized to engage in the coastal trade. In the course of discussing the possible restraints that the unexercised, "dormant" congressional commerce power imposed on state regulations, he noted the state laws requiring the inspection of goods shipped into interstate commerce: "[T]he inspection laws are said to be regulations of commerce, and are certainly recognized in the Constitution, as being passed in the exercise of the power remaining with the states. That inspection laws may have a remote and considerable influence on commerce, will not be denied; but that a power to regulate commerce is a source from which the right to pass them is derived, cannot be admitted. The object of inspection laws, is to improve the quality of articles produced by the labour of countries; to fit them for exploitation; or, it may be, for domestic use. They act upon the subject before it becomes an article of foreign commerce, or of commerce among the states, and prepare it for that purpose. They form a portion of that immense mass of legislation, which embraces everything within the territory of a state, not surrendered to the general government: all of which can be most advantageously exercised by the states themselves. Inspection laws, quarantine laws, health laws of every description, as well as laws for regulating the internal commerce of the state, and those which respect turnpike roads, ferries, etc., & c., are component parts of this mass. No direct general power over these objects is granted to congress; and consequently, they remain subject to state legislation. If the legislative power of the Union can reach them, it must be for national purposes; it must be where the power is expressly given for a special purpose, or is clearly incidental to some power which is expressly given."

Marshall's opinion ended with the following passage: "Powerful and ingenious minds, taking, as postulates, that the powers expressly granted to the government of the Union, are to be contracted, by construction, into the narrowest possible compass, and that the original powers of the states are retained, if any possible construction will retain them, may, by a course of well digested, but refined and metaphysical reasoning, founded on these premises, explain away the constitution of our country, and leave it, a magnificent structure, indeed, to look at, but totally unfit for use. They may so entangle and perplex the understanding, as to obscure principles, which were before thought quite plain, and induce doubts where, if the mind were to pursue its own course, none would be perceived. In such a case, it is peculiarly necessary to recur to safe and fundamental [principles]."

2. *Early commerce power legislation.* During the nation's first century most of the Court's discussions of the scope of the commerce power arose—as did Gibbons—in cases dealing with limits on state action affecting interstate commerce. And in most of those cases (unlike Gibbons), Congress had not exercised its power at all. Rather, the commerce clause came into play only because state laws were challenged as infringing the freedom of interstate commerce allegedly guaranteed by Art. I, § 8, even though Congress's authority under that clause was unexercised and "dormant." (Those limits on state regulation are developed in chap. 5, below.) Nevertheless, the concepts of interstate commerce developed in those state regulation cases served as a source of limits on national action when Congress turned to major uses of the commerce power in later years. See, e.g., the Knight case, p. 164 below.

Large-scale regulatory action by Congress did not begin until the Interstate Commerce Act of 1887 and the Sherman Anti–Trust Act of 1890. Challenges to those statutes initiated the major modern confrontations between the Court and congressional authority over commerce. But there were occasional exercises of the national commerce power even before 1887. For example, Congress enacted laws to improve water and land transportation. And there was also some commerce legislation of a "police" character, as in United States v. Marigold, 9 How. (50 U.S.) 560 (1850) (prohibiting the importation of counterfeit money). But the most troublesome problems about the reach of the national power did not emerge until Congress turned to weightier legislative efforts. The rapid 19th century developments in industrialization, transportation and communication produced national economic problems and demands for congressional regulation. Regulations of railroad rates and restraints on competition were the early congressional responses to these demands and yielded the Knight and Shreveport cases, below.

3. *Emerging doctrinal difficulties—a transitional note: Regulation of national economic problems vs. regulation of "police" problems. a. Regulating intrastate activities because of their relationship to interstate commerce.* It was in cases such as Shreveport and Knight, below, that the Court tried to state the extent to which Congress may regulate local activities because of their relationship to interstate commerce. The doctrinal problems of those cases foreshadow the difficulties encountered in subsequent efforts at national economic regulation—especially the New Deal attempts considered in the cases from Schechter to Wickard, below. How far, and with what justifications, may Congress reach intrastate activities related to national economic concerns? Can the local production of goods be regulated because it "affects" interstate commerce? Or is the production of goods not reachable by the commerce power, because production is neither commerce nor has a "direct" effect on commerce?

b. *"Police" regulations—morality, crime, and the commerce power.* Efforts to deal with the emerging problems of the national economy were not the only examples of expanded congressional resort to the commerce power starting with the turn of the 19th century. Congress also manifested an increased interest in problems of morality and criminality—gambling, prostitution, theft. Those congressional "police" regulations came to the Court contemporaneously with the new national economic regulations. Did the Court handle those two types of laws differently? Should they have been handled differently? Are laws directed at police problems less justifiable invocations of the commerce power than regulations of economic problems? Is it useful, or possible, to distinguish national legislation dealing with police problems—directed ultimately at "bad" local activities—from laws concerned with national economic problems? Is it constitutionally significant that police legislation typically relied, as the regulatory technique, on prohibition of interstate transportation rather than direct control of local activities? (See, e.g., the Lottery Case and Hammer v. Dagen-hart, below.) Did these police regulations invoke the commerce power as a "pretext"? Should the Court consider the ulterior purpose of legislation, if the law's immediate sanction falls on the movement of commerce across state lines?

The distinctions suggested in the preceding paragraph, even if valid, are more difficult to apply than to state. What if economic and "police" objectives both underlie legislation? Can a distinction between economic and "police" purposes be applied, for example, to regulations of working conditions and to prohibitions of racial discrimination? Can and should the Court make such a distinction on the basis of the primary purposes of the legislators? Even if the Court, for institutional reasons, finds it impossible to curb questionable invocations of the power, should a legislator be troubled by attempts to use the commerce clause for social or moral—predominantly noneconomic—objectives? Questions such as these should be borne in mind in examining the ensuing notes.

4. *Justifying national regulation of local activities on the basis of their relationship to interstate commerce: The requisite "local"-"interstate" connection—Knight and Shreveport as sources of contending approaches.* The two earliest examples of major modern regulatory legislation—the Sherman Act and the Interstate Commerce Act—produced important Court efforts to formulate commerce clause doctrine. The Sherman Act came before the Court in 1895, in the Sugar Trust case, United States v. E.C. Knight Co. (1895). The most important early Court encounter with the Interstate Commerce Act came two decades later, in the Shreveport Rate case (1914). The doctrinal approaches of these cases cast significant, and often contradictory, shadows over subsequent litigation. Thus, when New Deal laws came before the Court in the 1930s, the differing progeny of the Knight and Shreveport cases offered the Justices a choice of standards. Until 1936, the Court drew mainly on the Knight heritage and invalidated major national laws; beginning with 1937, the Shreveport approach, more receptive to expansive congressional uses of the commerce power, became central.

The Knight and Shreveport cases presented similar problems. In a sense, the Court struggled with the "means-ends" theme addressed by Marshall in McCulloch. Typically, the Government argued that local activities could be reached as a "means" of implementing the "end" of regulating interstate commerce. What were the standards to be applied when Congress sought to invoke the commerce power to reach arguably "local" economic activities? What constituted an adequate connection between the "local" and the "interstate"? Was the required relationship one of formal, logical nexus or one of realistic, practical impact? The Knight case symbolizes the former approach; the Shreveport case, the latter. Knight suggested that the local activity was not reachable unless it had a "direct" rather than an "indirect" effect on interstate commerce: an attempt to monopolize sugar refining, though of significant interstate economic consequences, was not controllable through federal legislation because the relationship between "manufacturing" and "commerce" was "indirect." In the Shreveport case, by contrast, "local" railroad rates were reachable because of their practical, economic impact on interstate transportation.

The next group of notes deals with the Knight case and its immediate consequences for antitrust enforcement. That group is followed by notes focusing on the Shreveport case and related problems. The logical nexus, "direct"-"indirect" emphasis of Knight, it turned out, did not prove a significant barrier to application of the antitrust laws. But it did leave a legacy of doctrine capable of being invoked in other contexts; and that legacy proved decisive in the early New Deal cases. When the Court struck down national economic regulations in the 1930s, the "direct"-"indirect" distinction of Knight proved fatal to congressional efforts in cases such as Carter (1936; p. 180 below). But then, just a year later, in the wake of Franklin D. Roosevelt's Court-packing plan of 1937, the Court became more receptive to national economic regulation: the Shreveport heritage was invoked to provide support for that new constitutional direction, and an emphasis on the substantial economic effect of the local activity on interstate commerce played a central role in such cases as Wickard (p. 189 below).

a. *The Knight approach and its sources.* In the Sugar Trust Case, UNIT-ED STATES v. E.C. KNIGHT CO., 156 U.S. 1 (1895), the Court affirmed the dismissal of a Government civil action to set aside, under the Sherman Act, the acquisition by the American Sugar Refining Company of the stock of four other sugar refineries.[1] The Government alleged that the acquired companies had produced about 33% of all sugar refined in the United States, and that American's acquisition gave it control of 98% of the nation's sugar refining capacity. The Court's decision rested on statutory construction; but that interpretation was premised on confining constitutional doctrines, especially the view that Congress could not under the commerce clause reach a monopoly in "manufacture."

Chief Justice FULLER's majority opinion indicated that, even conceding "the existence of a monopoly in manufacture," the monopoly could not be "directly suppressed." He stated: "Doubtless the power to control the manufacture of a given thing involves in a certain sense the control of its disposition, but this is a secondary and not the primary sense; and although the exercise of that power may result in bringing the operation of commerce into play, it does not control it, and affects it only incidentally and indirectly. Commerce succeeds to manufacture, and is not a part of it." Monopolies might sometimes be regulated under the commerce power, but only when "the transaction is itself a monopoly of commerce." In elaborating the distinction between "manufacture" and "commerce," Fuller relied heavily on decisions which had not involved congressional exercises of commerce power at all but rather questions of state authority in the face of the "dormant" commerce clause. (What weight *should* have been given to those opinions stemming from a state rather than a national regulatory context?) He relied particularly on Kidd v. Pearson, 128 U.S. 1 (1888), sustaining an Iowa prohibition of the manufacture of intoxicating liquors intended for export to other states. Chief Justice Fuller quoted from the Court's opinion in Kidd: "No distinction is more popular to the common mind, or more clearly expressed in economic and political literature, than that between manufacture and commerce. Manufacture is transformation—the fashioning of raw materials into a change of form for use. The functions of commerce are different. The buying and selling and the transportation incidental thereto constitute commerce. [If] it be held that [regulation of commerce] includes the regulation of all such manufactures as are intended to be the subject of commercial transactions in the future, it is impossible to deny that it would also include all productive industries that contemplate the same thing. The result would be that Congress would be invested, to the exclusion of the States, with the power to regulate, not only manufactures, but also agriculture,

---

1. Sec. 1 of the Sherman Act prohibited any contract, combination or conspiracy "in restraint of trade or commerce among the several states." Sec. 2 provided penalties for any person "who shall monopolize, or combine or conspire [to] monopolize any part of the trade or commerce among the several states."

horticulture, stock raising, domestic fisheries, mining—in short every branch of human industry. For is there one of them that does not contemplate, more or less clearly, an interstate or foreign market? [The] power being vested in Congress and denied to the States, it would follow as an inevitable result that the duty would devolve on Congress to regulate all of these delicate, multiform and vital interests—interests which in their nature are and must be local."

This approach of the Kidd case governed the Court's Knight analysis and led it to insist that the nexus between the local and the interstate was a formal, qualitative one of logical relationships, rather than an empiric, practical one of economic impacts. As the Chief Justice put it: "Contracts, combinations, or conspiracies to control domestic enterprise in manufacture, agriculture, mining, production in all its forms, or to raise or lower prices or wages, might unquestionably tend to restrain external as well as domestic trade, but the restraint would be an indirect result, however inevitable and whatever its extent, and such result would not necessarily determine the object of the contract, combination, or conspiracy." He added: "Slight reflection will show that if the national power extends to all contracts and combinations in manufacture, agriculture, mining, and other productive industries, whose ultimate result may affect external commerce, comparatively little of business operations and affairs would be left for state control."[2] Those standards barred the suit against the Sugar Trust: the challenged actions "related exclusively to the acquisition of the Philadelphia refineries" and "bore no direct relation to commerce between the States." The first Justice HARLAN submitted a strong dissent.

b. *The limited impact of Knight on antitrust enforcement.* Though the Knight approach became a major obstacle to national economic regulation in the early 1930s, it did not paralyze antitrust enforcement. In a number of cases soon after Knight, the Court perceived a range of justifications for applying the Sherman and Clayton Acts. Thus, in Addyston Pipe & Steel Co. v. United States, 175 U.S. 211 (1899), the Court sustained an action against six companies manufacturing iron pipe who had made agreements in restraint of competition. The Court found that the aim of the agreement was not only to restrain manufacturing but also "to directly and by means of such combination increase the prices." This was held to be a "direct restraint upon interstate commerce." And in Northern Securities Co. v. United States, 193 U.S. 197 (1904), the 5-4 decision sustained an action to set aside the control acquired by Northern over two companies operating parallel railroad lines. Justice Holmes urged in dissent that the statute be construed in such a way as "not to raise grave doubts" about its constitutionality. Recalling the "indirect effect" theme of Knight, he added: "Commerce depends upon population, but Congress could not, on that ground, undertake to regulate marriage and divorce. If the act before us is to be carried out according to what seems to be the logic of the argument for the

2. Passages such as this reflect the much-criticized concept of "dual federalism" characteristic of Court opinions of the pre–1937 era—the notion that the powers reserved to the states operated as an independent limitation on the scope of congressional powers, that state and national legislative domains were mutually exclusive areas. When Justice Stone remarked in Darby in 1941 (p. 191 below) that the Tenth Amendment is "but a truism that all is retained which has not been surrendered," the state-

ment was widely hailed as a reminder of the death of "dual federalism" after 1937. See Corwin, "The Passing of Dual Federalism," 36 Va.L.Rev. 1 (1950). But should the abandonment of rigid, mutually exclusive categories of state and federal competence carry with it abandonment of all concern with federalism-related structural limits on the exercise of national powers? Recall the majority opinions in Lopez, above, and note the other recent manifestations suggesting a revival of antifederalism. (See sec. 3 below.)

Government, which I do not believe that it will be, I can see no part of the conduct of life with which on similar principles Congress might not interfere." Could marriage and divorce nevertheless be regulated under the theory of Justice Holmes' dissent in Hammer v. Dagenhart, p. 173 below (a dissent that became the majority view a generation later)? More recently, the Court has said that "Congress wanted to go to the utmost extent of its Constitutional power in restraining trust and monopoly agreements." United States v. South–Eastern Underwriters Association, 322 U.S. 533, 558 (1944) (holding the business of insurance to be covered by the antitrust laws despite older rulings stating that insurance was not commerce). Nevertheless, some modern decisions find businesses outside antitrust coverage as a matter of statutory construction, though presumably within the reach of the commerce power.[3]

5. *The Shreveport Rate case and the origins of the "substantial economic effects" approach.* Even while the Knight approach and its emphasis on the formal "direct"-"indirect" distinction remained on the books, the Court began to develop a quite different analysis of the nexus necessary to justify regulation of "local" matters under the commerce power. The railroad context was the most prolific source of this alternate approach—an alternative emphasizing the practical, empirical rather than the formal, logical relationship between the "local" and the "interstate." Most of the early congressional attempts to regulate the railroad industry withstood constitutional attack: the Court repeatedly sustained the laws under the commerce power because of the physical or economic effects of the regulated intrastate activities on interstate commerce. The Shreveport case, below, is the best example of this approach, and the analyses of Shreveport and other railroad cases were to provide useful constitutional underpinnings for the Court's increasingly benign attitude toward national economic regulation that began in 1937. (Moreover, the Shreveport approach was not the only route toward expanded national regulatory power opened by the cases of the early 20th century. There was also an occasional willingness to reach arguably "local" matters by viewing them as being "in" interstate commerce: in those cases, considered in note 5c below.)

a. *The Shreveport Rate case.* In HOUSTON E. & W. TEXAS RY. CO. v. UNITED STATES (THE SHREVEPORT RATE CASE), 234 U.S. 342 (1914), Justice HUGHES's majority opinion sustained congressional authority to reach intrastate rail rates that discriminated against interstate railroad traffic. The Interstate Commerce Commission, after setting rates for transportation of goods between Shreveport, Louisiana, and points within Texas, ordered several railroads to end their practice of setting rates for hauls between points within

---

3. The best-known example is professional baseball. In Toolson v. New York Yankees, 346 U.S. 356 (1953), the Court found reserve clauses in players' contracts outside the antitrust laws. The Court pointed to a decision in 1922 in which Justice Holmes had stated for the Court that "personal effort, not related to production, is not a subject of commerce." Federal Baseball Club v. National League, 259 U.S. 200. In Toolson, the Court stated: "The business [has] been left for thirty years to develop on the understanding that it was not subject to existing antitrust [laws]. Without reexamination of the underlying issues, the judgments below are affirmed on the authority of Federal Baseball Club, [so] far as that decision determines that Congress had no intention of including the business of baseball within the scope of the federal antitrust laws." The Court has adhered to Federal Baseball and Toolson: in a 5-3 decision in Flood v. Kuhn, 407 U.S. 258 (1972), Justice Blackmun's majority opinion, while recognizing that the exemption of baseball from the antitrust laws was "an anomaly" and "an aberration," refused "to overturn those cases judicially when Congress, by its positive inaction, has allowed those decisions to stand for so long." Other professional sports, however, *have* been held subject to the antitrust laws. See United States v. International Boxing Club, 348 U.S. 236 (1955), and Radovich v. National Football League, 352 U.S. 445 (1957).

Texas which were proportionately lower than their rates for transportation from Texas points to Shreveport, Louisiana. (For example, the rate to carry wagons from Marshall in East Texas to Dallas, a distance of 147.7 miles, was 36.8 cents; the rate from Marshall to Shreveport, Louisiana, only 42 miles away, was 56 cents. Shreveport competed with Texas cities for shipments from East Texas.) The ICC found that this rate structure "unjustly discriminated in favor of traffic within the state of Texas, and against similar traffic between Louisiana and Texas," and ordered the railroads to end the discrimination, thereby effectively controlling the intrastate Marshall–Dallas rates. In challenging that ICC order, the railroads argued that "Congress is impotent to control the intrastate charges of an interstate carrier."

Justice Hughes rejected that challenge. He insisted that congressional authority, "extending to these interstate carriers as instruments of interstate commerce, necessarily embraces the right to control their operations in all matters having such a close and substantial relation to interstate traffic that the control is essential or appropriate to the security of that traffic, to the efficiency of the interstate service, and to the maintenance of conditions under which interstate commerce may be conducted upon fair terms and without molestation or hindrance. As it is competent for Congress to legislate to these ends, unquestionably it may seek their attainment by requiring that the agencies of interstate commerce shall not be used in such manner as to cripple, retard, or destroy it. The fact that carriers are instruments of intrastate commerce, as well as of interstate commerce, does not derogate from the complete and paramount authority of Congress over the latter, or preclude the Federal power from being exerted to prevent the intrastate operations of such carriers from being made a means of injury to that which has been confided to Federal care. Whenever the interstate and intrastate transactions of carriers are so related that the government of the one involves the control of the other, it is Congress, and not the State, that is entitled to prescribe the final and dominant rule, for otherwise Congress would be denied the exercise of its constitutional authority and the State, and not the Nation, would be supreme within the national field. [This] is not to say that Congress possesses the authority to regulate the internal commerce of a State, as such, but that it does possess the power to foster and protect interstate commerce, and to take all measures necessary or appropriate to that end, although intrastate transactions of interstate carriers may thereby be controlled." (Justices LURTON and PITNEY noted their dissents.)

b. *Other examples of local railroad matters with an adequate impact on interstate commerce.* The Shreveport case was only one of a series justifying the regulation of local rate structures because of the economic burdens imposed by the intrastate situation on interstate activities. See, e.g., Railroad Commission of Wisconsin v. Chicago, Burlington & Quincy Railroad, 257 U.S. 563 (1922), where the Court sustained an ICC order requiring a blanket increase in all intrastate rates, even though state law prescribed a lower maximum. In upholding such economic regulations, the Court drew on earlier decisions sustaining national regulation of local matters where the local activity imposed a *physical* rather than an economic burden on interstate transportation. Safety regulations understandably were the easiest to sustain under this rationale, for they presented the most readily observable manifestations of local activities burdening interstate commerce: the obstruction to interstate movement caused by local accidents was a visible, physical one. See, e.g., the approach in SOUTHERN RAILWAY CO. v. UNITED STATES, 222 U.S. 20 (1911), where the court sustained a penalty judgment under the Federal Safety Appliance Act, imposed for operating railroad cars equipped with defective couplers. Three of the cars were used in moving solely intrastate traffic. The act covered all cars "used on any railroad engaged in interstate commerce"; the court found that this provision was satisfied because the intrastate cars were used "on a railroad which is a highway of interstate commerce." The application of the law to intrastate vehicles was found constitutional, "not because congress possesses any power to regulate intrastate commerce as such, but because its power to regulate interstate commerce [may] be exerted to secure the safety of the persons and property transported therein and of those who are employed in such transportation no matter what may be the source of the dangers which threaten it." The court emphasized "practical considerations" that "are of common knowledge," including the fact that "the absence of appropriate safety appliances from any part of any train is a menace not only to that train, but to others." (Note the reliance on a similar rationale in sustaining national regulation of labor relations—to avert obstructions of commerce inherent in strikes—in the Jones & Laughlin case, p. 185 below.)

c. *The "stream of commerce" theory.* While the Court's emphasis on "practical considerations" was providing one type of rationale for demonstrating the impact of the local on the interstate (as in Southern Railway), several other decisions were sketching an alternate basis for arguing that an intrastate activity could be reachable under the commerce power. The "current of commerce" rationale suggested that some local activities were controllable not because of their effects on commerce, but because they could themselves be viewed as "in" commerce or as an integral part of the "current of commerce." Justice Holmes's opinion in Swift & Co. v. United States, 196 U.S. 375 (1905), provided the impetus. In sustaining a Sherman Act injunction against price fixing by meat dealers, Justice Holmes stated: "When cattle are sent for sale from a place in one State, with the expectation that they will end their transit, after purchase in another, and when in effect they do so, with only the interruption necessary to find a purchaser at the stockyard, and when this is a typical, constantly recurring course, the current thus existing is a current of commerce among the States, and the purchase of the cattle is a part and incident of such commerce." He commented: "[C]ommerce among the States is not a technical legal conception, but a practical one, drawn from the course of business."

Congress successfully drew on this "stream of commerce" concept in drafting subsequent regulation of stockyard practices. The Packers and Stockyards Act of 1921 was aimed primarily at preventing "unfair, discriminatory, or deceptive practices" by meat packers in interstate commerce. One of the provisions of the Act stated that a "transaction in respect to any article shall be considered to be in commerce if such article is part of that current of commerce usual in the livestock and meat packing industries, whereby livestock [and its products] are sent from one State with the expectation that they will end their transit, after purchase, in [another]. Articles normally in such current of commerce shall not be considered out of such current through resort being had to any means or device intended to remove transactions in respect thereto from the provisions of this Act." Commission men and dealers in stockyards, subject to Secretary of Agriculture regulation of their charges and practices under the 1921 Act, challenged its constitutionality. The court rejected the attack in STAFFORD v. WALLACE, 258 U.S. 495 (1922). Chief Justice TAFT's majority opinion stated that the central question was "whether the business done in the stockyards between the receipt of the livestock in the yards and the shipments of them therefrom is a part of interstate commerce. [The] stockyards are but a throat through which the current flows, and the transactions which occur therein are only incident to this current from the West to the East, and from one State to another. [The] commission men are essential in making the sales without which the flow of the current would be obstructed, and this, whether they are made to packers or dealers. The dealers are essential to the sales to the stock farmers and feeders. The sales are not in this aspect merely local transactions. They create a local change of title, it is true, but they do not stop the flow; they merely change the private interests in the subject of the current, not interfering with, but, on the contrary, being indispensable to its continuity. [The] stockyards and the sales are necessary factors in the middle of this current of commerce." Justice McREYNOLDS dissented. (How useful is the "stream of commerce" concept? Why couldn't the stockyards situation equally be viewed as two streams rather than one—as streams to and from the stockyards?)

6. *National "police" regulation: Prohibition of interstate commerce as a tool.* In the cases in preceding notes, the Court confronted congressional efforts to impose direct regulations on local activities—regulations allegedly justified by the nexus between the local activity and interstate commerce. When that technique of regulation was used, the Court pursued a wavering course, from the restrictive interpretation of Knight to the more generous one of Shreveport. Yet in the same era, the Court rendered a series of decisions remarkably receptive to congressional action. The cases which follow differ from the preceding ones in two respects. First, the objective of the legislation seemed to be primarily moral, as with efforts to control gambling and prostitution; the primary aim was typically quite far removed from the economic concerns that presumably had prompted the commerce clause. Second, the technique of regulation differed: the congressional sanction was imposed at the state line, though the "harm" sought to be alleviated was primarily local; the form of regulation was to prohibit certain types of interstate movements. That commerce-prohibiting technique gave the Court far less trouble than efforts by Congress to impose sanctions directly upon intrastate activity. But when legislators sought to apply the technique to a problem with more significant economic as well as moral dimensions, that of child labor, the Court called a halt, at least for a generation. In examining the materials in this group of notes, consider whether there was any justification for the differing Court responses to the problems and techniques in the materials that follow and those considered earlier. Which variety of legislation was closer to the original purposes of the commerce clause? Which technique of regulation was more susceptible to effective judicial scrutiny?

a. CHAMPION v. AMES [THE LOTTERY CASE], 188 U.S. 321 (1903): This landmark case arose when Champion was indicted for shipping a box of Paraguayan lottery tickets from Texas to California in violation of the Federal Lottery Act of 1895. The Act prohibited importing, mailing, or interstate transporting of lottery tickets. Champion challenged the constitutionality of the Act, but the lower court rejected his challenge. The Court affirmed in a 5-4 ruling. Justice HARLAN's majority opinion, after holding that "lottery tickets are subjects of traffic and therefore are subjects of commerce" and that the prohibition of commerce lay within the regulatory power of Congress, continued: "In Phalen v. Virginia [8 How. (49 U.S.) 163 (1850) (involving a state regulation)], the Court observed that the suppression of nuisances injurious to public health or morality is among the most important duties of Government. [If] a State, when considering legislation for the suppression of lotteries within its own limits, may properly take into view the evils that inhere in the raising of money, in that mode, why may not Congress, invested with the power to regulate commerce among the several States, provide that such commerce shall not be polluted by the carrying of lottery tickets from one State to another? [What clause] can be cited which [countenances] the suggestion that one may, of right, carry [from] one State to another that which will harm the public morals? [As] a State may, for the purpose of guarding the morals of its own people, forbid all sales of lottery tickets within its limits, so Congress, for the purpose of guarding the people of the United States against the 'widespread pestilence of lotteries' and to protect the commerce which concerns all the States, may prohibit the carrying of lottery tickets from one State to another. In legislating upon the subject of the traffic in lottery tickets, as carried on through interstate commerce, Congress only supplemented the action of those States—perhaps all of them—which, for the protection of the public morals, prohibit the drawing of lotteries, as well as the sale or circulation of lottery tickets, within their respective limits. [We] should hesitate long before adjudging that an evil of such appalling character, carried on through interstate commerce, cannot be met and crushed by the only power competent to that end.''

Justice Harlan added: "It is said, however, that if, in order to suppress lotteries carried on through interstate commerce, Congress may exclude lottery tickets from such commerce, that principle leads necessarily to the conclusion that Congress may arbitrarily exclude from commerce among the States any article, commodity or thing, of whatever kind or nature, or however useful or valuable, which it may choose, no matter with what motive. [It] will be time enough to consider the constitutionality of such legislation when we must do so. [It] would not be difficult to imagine legislation that [would be] hostile to the objects for the accomplishment of which Congress was invested with the general power to regulate commerce among the several States. But [the] possible abuse of a power is not an argument against its existence. If what is done by Congress is manifestly in excess of the powers granted to it, then upon the courts will rest the duty of adjudging that its action is neither legal nor binding upon the people. But if what Congress does is within the limits of its power, and is simply unwise or injurious, the remedy is that suggested by Chief Justice Marshall in [Gibbons].'' [The Court then quoted the "wisdom [and] discretion of Congress'' passage from Gibbons.]

Chief Justice FULLER's dissent, joined by Justices Brewer, Shiras, and Peckham, responded: "That the purpose of Congress in this enactment was the suppression of lotteries cannot reasonably be denied. [D]oubtless an act prohibiting the carriage of lottery matter would be necessary and proper to the execution of a power to suppress lotteries; but that power belongs to the States and not to Congress. To hold that Congress has general police power would be to hold that it may accomplish objects not entrusted to the General Government, and to defeat the operation of the 10th Amendment. But apart from the question of *bona fides,* this act cannot be brought within the power to regulate commerce among the several States, unless lottery tickets are articles of commerce, and, therefore, when carried across state lines, of interstate commerce; or unless the power to regulate interstate commerce includes the absolute and exclusive power to prohibit the transportation of any thing or anybody from one State to another. [Is] the carriage of lottery tickets from one

State to another commercial intercourse? [The dissent concluded that it was not "commercial intercourse."]

"If a lottery ticket is not an article of commerce, how can it become so when placed in an envelope or box or other covering, and transported by an express company? [That] is to transform a non-commercial article into a commercial one simply because it is transported. I cannot conceive that any such result can properly follow. It would be to say that everything is an article of commerce the moment it is taken to be transported from place to place, and of interstate commerce if from State to State. [An] invitation to dine, or to take a drive, or a note of introduction, all become articles of commerce under the ruling in this case, by being deposited with an express company for transportation. [The] necessary consequence is to take from the States all jurisdiction over the subject so far as interstate communication is concerned. It is a long step in the direction of wiping out all traces of state lines, and the creation of a centralized Government. [It] will not do to say [that] state laws have been found to be ineffective for the suppression of lotteries, and therefore Congress should interfere. The scope of the commerce clause of the Constitution cannot be enlarged because of present views of [public interest]. [At this point, the dissent quoted Marshall's "pretext" statement in McCulloch, at p. 89 above.]

"The power to prohibit the transportation of diseased animals and infected goods over railroads or on steamboats is an entirely different thing, for they would be in themselves injurious to the transaction of interstate commerce, and, moreover, are essentially commercial in their nature. And the exclusion of diseased persons rests on different ground, for nobody would pretend that persons could be kept off the trains because they were going from one State to another to engage in the lottery business. However enticing that business may be, we do not understand these pieces of paper themselves can communicate bad principles by contact. [I] regard this decision as inconsistent with the views of the framers of the Constitution, and of Marshall, its great expounder. Our form of government may remain notwithstanding legislation or decision, but, as long ago observed, it is with governments, as with religions, the form may survive the substance of the faith."

b. *The ghost of Marshall.* Note the competing uses of Marshall statements in the Harlan and Fuller opinions. Was the "wisdom [and] discretion of Congress" quotation from Gibbons v. Ogden, used by Harlan, apposite to the problem of the Lottery Case? Did that make it unnecessary to consider Fuller's reliance on the "pretext" statement in McCulloch v. Maryland—the statement that, "should Congress, under the pretext of executing its powers, pass laws for the accomplishment of objects not entrusted to the government," the Court would have to strike down the congressional enactment? Should, or must, the Court consider the dominant purpose of Congress (here, concededly a moral objective)? Should the Court scrutinize congressional legislation to determine whether it rested on a pretextual invocation of an enumerated power? Would it have been possible to sustain the statute on the assumption that its true "object" was the control of a local "harm"—intrastate lottery-promoting activities? On the theory that gambling "affected" or "burdened" commerce? On the basis of the "current of commerce" theory? Should the Court have insisted on an adequate economic justification for reaching intrastate activities? Was the failure to require such a justification (and the acceptance of the rationale that this was merely a regulation of interstate commerce) fatal to the development of commerce power doctrine of adequate integrity during the pre–1937 era?

c. *The impact on Congress.* Early-twentieth century reformers seeking a constitutional basis for broader federal "police" measures quickly seized on the encouragement provided by the majority position in the Lottery Case. In 1906, for example, Senator Albert J. Beveridge successfully proposed a Meat Inspection Amendment to an appropriations bill. The Amendment became law: it prohibited interstate shipment of meats that had not been federally inspected. In the same session, Congress enacted the Pure Food and Drugs Act. Later that year, Senator Beveridge suggested a law excluding from commerce goods produced by child labor. He was confident that the Lottery Case "absolutely settled" the constitutionality of his proposal. But passage of a child labor law was still a decade away—and the Court found the 1916 Child Labor Act unconstitutional after all, in Hammer v. Dagenhart, below. See "The Square Deal in Action: A Case Study in the Growth of the 'National Police Power,' " in Braeman, Bremner and Walter, Change and Continuity in Twentieth Century America (1964), 35–80, and Wood, Constitutional Politics in the Progressive Era (1968).

d. *Exclusion of allegedly "harmful" goods and persons.* The Lottery Case precedent was, however, adequate to sustain a wide variety of early-twentieth century laws excluding from interstate commerce objects or persons claimed to be harmful. Decisions sustaining the Pure Food and Drugs Act and the Mann (White Slave) Act were especially important in building the hopes that were crushed by Hammer v. Dagenhart. See Cushman, "The National Police Power under the Commerce Clause of the Constitution," 3 Minn.L.Rev. 289, 381 (1919).

(i) *Impure foods.* In HIPOLITE EGG CO. v. UNITED STATES, 220 U.S. 45 (1911), a shipment of preserved eggs had been confiscated under the Pure Food and Drugs Act of 1906 because the label failed to disclose that they contained a "deleterious" ingredient. The action was challenged on the ground that "the shipment had passed out of interstate commerce before the seizure of the eggs." A unanimous Court rejected the attack. Justice McKENNA insisted: "The question here is whether articles which are outlaws of commerce may be seized wherever found. [Can] they escape the consequences of their illegal transportation by being mingled at the place of destination with other property? To give them such immunity would defeat, in many cases, the provision for their confiscation, and their confiscation or destruction is the especial concern of the law. The power to do so is certainly appropriate to the right to bar them from interstate commerce, and completes its purpose, which is not to prevent merely the physical movement of adulterated articles, but the use of them, or rather to prevent trade in them between the States by denying to them the facilities of interstate commerce. And appropriate means to that end, which we have seen is legitimate, are the seizure and condemnation of the articles at their point of destination. [McCulloch]." How far-reaching is this application of McCulloch? Does it justify a direct ban on producing adulterated goods as a "means appropriate to the right to bar them from interstate commerce"? Only if the goods are intended for interstate shipment? Does it justify national marriage and divorce standards as an "appropriate means" to implement a ban on interstate movement of persons married or divorced in violation of national standards? Only if the persons getting married or divorced intend to travel interstate? Does it offer a bootstrap technique for reaching local affairs via the prohibition route: in order to regulate a local matter, simply prohibit interstate movements connected with it and then reach the local matter as an incidental means to implement the interstate prohibition? Note the elaboration of this justification of local control as an incident of interstate commerce prohibition in Darby, p. 191 below.

(ii) *The Mann Act.* The Mann Act, prohibiting the transportation of women in interstate commerce for immoral purposes, was upheld in HOKE v. UNITED

STATES, 227 U.S. 308 (1913). Again, Justice McKENNA wrote for a unanimous Court. The opinion in Hoke contained one of the broadest early statements of the commerce-prohibiting power: "[Surely] if the facility of interstate transportation can be taken away from the demoralization of lotteries, the debasement of obscene literature, the contagion of diseased cattle or persons, the impurity of food and drugs, the like facility can be taken away from the systematic enticement to and the enslavement in prostitution and debauchery of women, and, more insistently, of girls. [The] principle established by the cases is the simple one, [that] Congress has power over transportation 'among the several States'; that the power is complete in itself, and that Congress, as an incident to it, may adopt not only means necessary but convenient to its exercise, and the means may have the quality of police regulations." Justice McKENNA dissented, however, when the Court, in a 5-3 decision, found the Mann Act applicable to activities not constituting "commercialized vice." CAMINETTI v. UNITED STATES, 242 U.S. 470 (1917). Justice DAY wrote for the majority. The dissent argued that "everybody knows that there is a difference between the occasional immoralities of men and women and that systematized and mercenary immorality epitomized in the statute's graphic phrase 'White-slave traffic.' And it was such immorality that was in the legislative mind and not the other. The other is occasional, not habitual—inconspicuous—does not offensively obtrude upon public notice. Interstate commerce is not its instrument as it is of the other, nor is prostitution its object or its end. It may, indeed, in instances, find a convenience in crossing state lines, but this is its accident, not its aid." Could this objection to the interpretation of the Act be the basis of a valid constitutional objection? One year after Caminetti, the Court held the Child Labor Law unconstitutional, in the case that follows. Note that Justice Day once again wrote the majority opinion in that case—and that Justice McKenna was once again with the dissenters.

7.   a. HAMMER v. DAGENHART [THE CHILD LABOR CASE], 247 U.S. 251 (1918): This case, too, was a landmark one—it refused to uphold the commerce-prohibiting technique of the Lottery Case and struck down a congressional law of 1916 that excluded the products of child labor from interstate commerce. The law barred the transportation in interstate commerce of goods produced in factories employing children under the age of fourteen or employing those between the ages of fourteen and sixteen for more than eight hours a day, or six days a week, or at night. The father of two children employed in a cotton mill in North Carolina obtained an injunction barring enforcement of the law on constitutional grounds. Justice DAY's majority opinion stated: "[The commerce power] is one to control the means by which commerce is carried on, which is directly the contrary of the assumed right to forbid commerce from moving and thus destroying it as to particular commodities. But it is insisted that adjudged cases in this court establish the doctrine that the power to regulate given to Congress incidentally includes the authority to prohibit the movement of ordinary commodities. [The] cases demonstrate the contrary. They rest upon the character of the particular subjects dealt with and the fact that the scope of governmental authority, state or national, possessed over them is such that the authority to prohibit is as to them but the exertion of the power to regulate."

After discussing such rulings as the Lottery Case, Hipolite Egg, and Hoke, Justice Day continued: "In each of these instances the use of interstate transportation was necessary to the accomplishment of harmful results. In other words, although the power over interstate transportation was to regulate, that could only be accomplished by prohibiting the use of the facilities of interstate commerce to effect the evil intended. This element is wanting in the present case. [The] act in its effect does not regulate transportation among the states, but aims to standardize the ages at which children may be employed in mining and manufacturing within the states. The goods shipped are of themselves harmless. [When] offered for shipment, and before transportation begins, the labor of their production is over, and the mere fact that they were intended for interstate commerce transportation does not make their production subject to federal control. [Over] interstate transportation, or its incidents, the regulatory power of Congress is ample, but the production of articles, intended for interstate commerce, is a matter of local regulation. [If] it were otherwise, all manufacture intended for interstate shipment would be brought under federal control to the practical exclusion of the authority of the States.

"It is further contended that the authority of Congress may be exerted to control interstate commerce in the shipment of child-made goods because of the effect of the circulation of such goods in other States where the evil of this class of labor has been recognized by local legislation, and the right to thus employ child labor has been more rigorously restrained than in the State of production. In other words, that the unfair competition, thus engendered, may be controlled by closing the channels of interstate commerce to manufacturers in those States where the local laws do not meet what Congress deems to be the more just standard of other States. There is no power vested in Congress to require the States to exercise their police power so as to prevent possible unfair competition. Many causes may coöperate to give one State, by reason of local laws or conditions, an economic advantage over others. The Commerce Clause was not intended to give to Congress a general authority to equalize such conditions." Justice Day concluded: "[We] have neither authority nor disposition to question the motives of Congress in enacting this legislation. [T]he necessary effect of this act [is] to regulate the hours of labor of children in factories and mines within the States, a purely state authority. Thus the act in a two-fold sense is repugnant to the Constitution. It not only transcends the authority delegated to Congress over commerce but also exerts a power as to a purely local matter to which the federal authority does not extend. The far reaching result of upholding the act cannot be more plainly indicated than by pointing out that if Congress can thus regulate matters entrusted to local authority by prohibition of the movement of commodities in interstate commerce, all freedom of commerce will be at an end, and the power of the States over local matters may be eliminated, and thus our system of government be practically destroyed."

Justice HOLMES, joined by Justices McKenna, Brandeis, and Clarke, dissented: "[If] an act is within the powers specifically conferred upon Congress, it seems to me that it is not made any less constitutional because of the indirect effects that it may have, however obvious it may be that it will have those [effects]. The first step in my argument is to make plain what no one is likely to dispute—that the statute in question is within the power expressly given to Congress if considered only as to its immediate effects and that if invalid it is so only upon some collateral ground. The statute confines itself to prohibiting the carriage of certain goods in interstate or foreign commerce. Congress is given power to regulate such commerce in unqualified terms. It would not be argued today that the power to regulate does not include the power to prohibit. [The] question then is narrowed to whether the exercise of its otherwise constitutional power by Congress can be pronounced unconstitutional because of its possible reaction upon the conduct of the States in a matter upon which I have admitted that they are free from direct control. [I] should have thought that the most conspicuous decisions of this Court had made it clear that the power to regulate commerce [could] not be cut down or qualified by the fact that it might interfere with the carrying out of the domestic policy of any State. [The] manufacture of oleomargarine is as much a matter of state regulation as the manufacture of cotton cloth. Congress levied a tax upon the compound when colored so as to resemble butter that was so great as obviously to prohibit the manufacture and sale. In a very elaborate discussion the present Chief Justice excluded any inquiry into the purpose of an act which apart from that purpose was within the power of Congress. McCray v. United States, [1904; p. 231 below. Justice Holmes also pointed to the decisions upholding the Pure Food and Drugs Act and the Mann Act].

"The notion that prohibition is any less prohibition when applied to things now thought evil I do not understand. But if there is any matter upon which civilized countries have agreed [it] is the evil of premature and excessive child labor. I should have thought that if we were to introduce our own moral conceptions where in my opinion they do not belong, this was preeminently a case for upholding the exercise of all its powers by the United States. But I had thought that the propriety of the exercise of a power admitted to exist in some cases was for the consideration of Congress alone and that this Court always had disavowed the right to intrude its judgment upon questions of policy or morals. It is not for this Court to pronounce when prohibition is necessary to regulation if it ever may be necessary—to say that it is permissible as against strong drink but not as against the product of ruined lives. The act does not meddle with anything belonging to the States. They may regulate their internal affairs and their domestic commerce as they like. But when they seek to send their products across the state line they are no longer within their rights. [Congress] may carry out its views of public policy whatever indirect effect they may have upon the activities of the States. [The] public policy of the United States is shaped with a view to the benefit of the nation as a whole. [If] a State should take a different view of the propriety of sustaining a lottery from that which generally prevails, I cannot believe that the fact would require a different decision from that reached in Champion v. Ames. Yet in that case it would be said with quite as much force as in this that Congress was attempting to intermeddle with the State's domestic affairs. The national welfare as understood by Congress may require a different attitude within its sphere from that of some self-seeking State. It seems to me entirely constitutional for Congress to enforce its understanding by all the means at its command."

b. *Effective limits on the commerce power and the Holmes dissent.* Justice Day's distinction of earlier cases involving the commerce-prohibiting power has been widely criticized as unpersuasive. But it may also be argued that the Holmes dissent (which the Court adopted as a majority position a generation later) was needlessly broad. The point of the questions that follow is to suggest that a narrower view of the commerce power (a view that would have sustained the Child Labor Law without embracing so far reaching a view of congressional power) was possible.

Should Justice Holmes have paid greater attention to the "unfair competition" effects of interstate shipment of the goods? Are the evils produced by child labor-made goods more closely related to "commercial" concerns than the evils involved in the Mann Act cases and the Lottery Case? It is possible to argue that the Child Labor Act was more "economic," "commercial" in purpose than most of the "police" regulations sustained in the cases between the Lottery Case and Hammer. Should the dominant purpose of a law be decisive in determining the constitutionality of an exercise of the commerce power? Recall that, in his Northern Securities dissent (p. 165 above), Justice Holmes could see "no part of the conduct of life with which on similar principles Congress might not interfere," if the "logic of the argument for the Government" were accepted. Is this criticism also appropriate for the "logic of the argument" of the Holmes dissent in Hammer? Was Justice Holmes simply ceasing to argue for restrictions on the commerce-prohibiting power because the majority had abandoned the opportunity to adhere to principled limitations in the rulings beginning with the Lottery Case? Was it necessary to ignore the "collateral" effects of the law and to limit judicial vision to the "immediate effects" of the statute in order to justify the Child Labor Law? Would it not have been possible to concede that the law in effect regulated local production for interstate commerce, and yet sustain it because the activities regulated "affected" commerce? Note that Holmes' dissent suggests that the states "are free from direct control" regarding child labor. If that is so, is his position not an endorsement of the "pretext" usage of power condemned by Marshall in McCulloch? Or is the "pretext" concern inapt here, because Congress, in prohibiting interstate commerce, is exercising an "explicitly authorized" power (even though for an arguably *un*authorized purpose)? Compare the restrictions on the commerce power articulated by the majority in the Lopez case, sec. 1 above.

Holmes's "hands-off" policy ultimately prevailed in 1941, in Darby (p. 191 below), when the Court explicitly overruled Hammer v. Dagenhart. If the Holmesian position is justifiable in view of institutional limitations on the Court—e.g., the difficulties of identifying congressional "purpose" and "pretextual" abuses of power—does it follow that a legislator is wholly free to vote for commerce power regulations with primarily moral rather than commercial objectives? Even when judicial unwillingness to invalidate is predictable, is not a legislator nevertheless compelled—given the lawmaker's constitutional oath— to examine his or her purposes in supporting legislation and to determine whether those purposes are consistent with the constitutional allocations of power? Justice Holmes himself did perceive such a difference between a judge's and a legislator's approaches to constitutional questions. In a letter of April 3, 1919, Holmes wrote to then District Judge Learned Hand, on problems such as those presented by the Child Labor Case: "In my opinion Congress may have what ulterior motives they please if the act passed in the immediate aspect is within its powers—though personally, were I a legislator I might think it dishonest to use powers in that way." (The letter is printed in Gunther, "Learned Hand and the Origins of Modern First Amendment Doctrine: Some Fragments of History," 27 Stan.L.Rev. 719 (1975).)[4]

8. *The Court threatens the New Deal.* a. *Introduction.* President Franklin D. Roosevelt took office in 1933 in the midst of a grave economic crisis and with a call for "action, and action now." Symptoms of the Great Depression were everywhere: sharp drops in employment, production, income; widespread business failures and home mortgage foreclosures. The response was swift: an unprecedented flow of far-reaching measures came from Congress—torrentially during the dramatic "First Hundred Days," with more deliberate speed thereafter. Many New Deal measures were based on the commerce power, for the "problems were economic, and the Commerce Clause was the enumerated power most directly concerned with business and economic, or commercial matters." And the regulatory justification typically invoked to reach those economic problems was the "affecting commerce" rationale considered above.

4. In the wake of Hammer v. Dagenhart, Congress sought to regulate child labor through the taxing power. That law was invalidated in the Child Labor Tax Case in 1922 (p. 229 below); Justice Holmes was with the majority there. After the unsuccessful legislative efforts, Congress submitted to the states a proposed constitutional amendment authorizing national child labor laws. The amendment was never ratified; but the need for ratification disappeared in view of the Darby decision (1941; p. 191 below), which overruled Hammer.

The commerce-prohibiting technique, after all, appeared blocked by the Child Labor Case, and prohibitions of interstate movements seemed in any event an awkward approach to New Deal era problems. Practically as well as legally, then, efforts to regulate intrastate affairs based upon their relationship to interstate commerce seemed the more attractive approach. Cases such as Shreveport were encouraging; yet cases like Knight looked the other way. Would the New Deal measures survive judicial scrutiny? There could be no certainty, for "there was ample authority in the Supreme Court opinions looking both ways." Stern, "The Commerce Clause and the National Economy, 1933–1946," 59 Harv.L.Rev. 645, 646 (1946).

The first signs from the Court were encouraging. Early in 1934, decisions sustained state laws in the face of attacks that were clearly substantial under prior interpretations of the due process and contracts clauses.[5] A few months later, however, in the first Court test of a major New Deal law, the National Industrial Recovery Act of 1933 was wounded, though the reach of the commerce power was not discussed: in the "hot oil" case, the petroleum code under the NIRA was invalidated on the ground of excessive delegation of legislative power to the executive. Panama Refining Co. v. Ryan, 293 U.S. 388 (1935) (chap. 6 below). But an important early New Deal measure—a 1933 Joint Resolution declaring "gold clauses" in private contracts to be "against public policy"—was sustained, Norman v. Baltimore & Ohio Railroad Co., 294 U.S. 240 (1935), though the Government won only a narrow victory in its attempt to avoid payment under gold clauses in public obligations, Perry v. United States, 294 U.S. 330 (1935).

There was still no ruling on major New Deal regulation under the commerce power, however; that did not come until later in 1935. In the first test, the Court invalidated a measure not central to the New Deal program, the Railroad Retirement Act of 1934. RAILROAD RETIREMENT BOARD v. ALTON RAILROAD CO., 295 U.S. 330 (1935). That decision seemed an especially gloomy omen because Congress had long regulated railroad matters and had seldom encountered constitutional obstacles. Nevertheless, the 5-4 decision in Alton invalidated a law establishing a compulsory retirement and pension plan for all carriers subject to the Interstate Commerce Act. Justice ROBERTS's majority opinion concluded that the law was "not in purpose or effect a regulation of interstate commerce within the meaning of the Constitution." He rejected the argument that pensions were "related to efficiency of transportation." Was it not "apparent," he asked, that such regulations "are really and essentially related solely to the social welfare of the worker, and therefore remote from any regulation of commerce as such?" The Alton decision proved to be an accurate omen. Attempts to justify more important New Deal laws under the commerce power soon failed: three weeks after Alton, the Government lost the Schechter case challenging the National Industrial Recovery Act—a decision that seemed to President Roosevelt a return to "the horse-and-buggy age." In the following year, the commerce clause basis once again failed when the Bituminous Coal Conservation Act of 1935 was held unconstitutional in the Carter case. And the New Deal's failures were not limited to commerce power cases: in the same year, for example, an effort to resort to the spending power as justification for national regulation of agricultural production was rejected by the Court, in the Butler case (p. 235 below). The Schechter and Carter cases follow. Consider whether the majority positions were consistent

---

5. See Home Building & Loan Association v. Blaisdell, 290 U.S. 398 (1934) (mortgage moratorium law); Nebbia v. New York, 291 U.S. 502 (1934) (milk price regulation), both in chap. 8.

with earlier commerce clause rulings. Can any of the decisions be justified as "principled"—as a decision that rests on "reasons that in their generality and their neutrality transcend any immediate result that is involved"?[6] Or were those decisions simply willful fiats by a Court majority hostile to reform, as many New Deal critics charged?

b. *The Schechter case and its aftermath.* The most dramatic and most controversial New Deal effort to combat the Depression and revive the economy was the enactment of the National Industrial Recovery Act of 1933. The NIRA authorized the President—ordinarily upon application by trade associations—to promulgate "codes of fair competition for the trade or industry." Several hundred codes were soon adopted. The typical code contained provisions regarding unfair trade practices, minimum wages and prices, maximum hours, and collective bargaining. Violation of any code provision "in any transaction in or affecting interstate commerce" was made punishable as a misdemeanor. The law was held unconstitutional in the "sick chicken" case, A.L.A. SCHECHTER POULTRY CORP. v. UNITED STATES, 295 U.S. 495 (1935). By then, the regime of the NIRA was near an end in any event: the scheme had worked well at the outset, but by the time of Schechter, its regulatory structure was disintegrating in the face of waning enthusiasm, administrative difficulties, and lower court injunctions. The Court test of the Act was not sought by the Government: the record in the Schechter case contained few data to show the nexus between the slaughterer and the interstate poultry business; and application of the law to a relatively small segment of the national economy—a wholesale poultry market in Brooklyn—was not an ideal context in which to seek validation of the law. But after the Second Circuit struck down the application of the wage and hour requirements to Schechter, the Government decided not to oppose review. The decision came on May 27, 1935, just before the Act would have expired.[7] The Schechter case stemmed from convictions for violating the wage, hour, and trade practice provisions of the "Code of Fair Competition for the Live Poultry Industry of the Metropolitan [New York City] Area." Ninety-six percent of the poultry marketed in New York came from other states; but Schechter sold only to local poultry dealers. Poultry was ordinarily purchased from commission men in New York City, trucked to Schechter's Brooklyn slaughterhouses, and sold there to retailers. Schechter's challenge had two prongs: first, that the Act unconstitutionally delegated legislative power [see chap. 6 below]; second, that the application of the Act to intrastate activities exceeded the commerce power. The Court agreed with both grounds and held that the wages and hours of Schechter's employees were not subject to federal control.

The Government's defense of the Act tried to rely on two strains in prior doctrine: the "stream of commerce" rationale of Swift and Stafford v. Wallace, and the "affecting commerce" legacy of Shreveport. Chief Justice HUGHES's opinion for the Court rejected both analogies. These were not "transactions '*in*' interstate commerce," he insisted: the interstate transactions regarding poultry ended when the shipments reached the Brooklyn slaughterhouses. Moreover, the Chief Justice refused to find that Schechter's transactions "directly '*affect*' interstate commerce." In applying the "affecting commerce" rationale, he insisted, "there is a necessary and well-established distinction between direct

6. Wechsler, "Toward Neutral Principles of Constitutional Law," 73 Harv.L.Rev. 1, 19 (1959).

7. On the Government's litigation strategy regarding the NIRA and the

Schechter case, see Stern, "The Commerce Clause and the National Economy, 1933–1946," 59 Harv.L.Rev. 645 (1946). See also Irons, The New Deal Lawyers (1982).

and indirect effects." Applying this principle to Schechter's operations, Hughes insisted that the hours and wages of Schechter employees had "no direct relation to interstate commerce." He rejected the Government argument "that hours and wages affect prices; that slaughterhouse men sell at a small margin above operating costs; that labor represents 50 to 60 per cent. of these costs; that a slaughterhouse operator paying lower wages or reducing his costs by exacting long hours of work, translates his saving into lower prices; that this results in demands for a cheaper grade of goods; and that the cutting of prices brings about a demoralization of the price structure." That argument, Hughes found, "proves too much": "If the federal government may determine the wages and hours of employees in the internal commerce of a State, because of their relation to cost and prices and their indirect effect upon interstate commerce, it would seem that a similar control might be exerted over other elements of cost, also affecting prices, such as the number of employees, rent, advertising, methods of doing business, etc. All the processes of production and distribution that enter into costs could likewise be controlled. If the cost of doing an intrastate business is in itself the permitted object of federal control, the extent of the regulation of cost would be a question of discretion and not of power." Finally, Hughes rejected an even broader argument "based upon the serious economic situation which led to the passage of the Recovery Act,—the fall in prices, the decline in wages and employment, and the curtailment of the market for commodities." He found no constitutional justification in "the great importance of maintaining wage distributions which would provide the necessary stimulus in starting 'the cumulative forces making for expanding commercial activity.'" To that argument[8] he replied: "Without in any way disparaging this motive, it is enough to say that the recuperative efforts of the federal government must be made in a manner consistent with the authority granted by the Constitution." In a similar vein, he had said, at the outset of his opinion: "Extraordinary conditions do not create or enlarge constitutional power."

Justice CARDOZO, joined by Justice Stone, submitted a brief concurring opinion—one particularly notable because they were among the Justices who typically dissented from decisions invalidating New Deal legislation. Justice Cardozo agreed with the Chief Justice on both grounds: not only was there "unlawful delegation"—"This is delegation running riot"—; there was also the "far-reaching and incurable" commerce power objection. On the latter, he elaborated: "There is a view of causation that would obliterate the distinction between what is national and what is local in the activities of commerce. Motion at the outer rim is communicated perceptibly, though minutely, to

8. Note a similar argument paraphrased in the Stern article, footnote 4 above, emphasizing "that depressed business conditions had catastrophically affected all commerce" and "that a possible remedy was to increase the purchasing power of all wage earners through wage and hour regulation, thereby increasing the demand for products to be shipped in commerce." Such an argument, Stern notes, would apply to all workers, "irrespective of whether they themselves were in activities related to interstate activities." Wage and hour regulation of employees such as Schechter's would thus be "a reasonable means of improving the nation's business and the commerce—interstate or intrastate—of which that business consisted. The

argument treats the whole national economy as inseparable into interstate and intrastate segments, insofar as the fluctuations of the business cycle are concerned." Stern notes that Government counsel realized in 1935 that such an argument had "little chance of success in the judicial climate of the period." Was that argument a more plausible one factually than the "demoralization of the price structure" theme pressed by the Government and rejected by Chief Justice Hughes? Would a better record or more substantial economic arguments have persuaded the Court? Or would the "direct"-"indirect" distinction have proved an immovable obstacle in any event?

recording instruments at the center. A society such as ours 'is an elastic medium which transmits all tremors throughout its territory; the only question is of their size.' Per Learned Hand, J., in the court below. The law is not indifferent to considerations of degree. Activities local in their immediacy do not become interstate and national because of distant repercussions. What is near and what is distant may at times be uncertain. [There] is no penumbra of uncertainty obscuring judgment here. To find immediacy or directness here is to find it almost everywhere. If centripetal forces are to be isolated to the exclusion of the forces that oppose and counteract them, there will be an end to our federal system.''

c. *The aftermath of Schechter.* In a press conference soon after Schechter, President Roosevelt articulated the Administration's concerns about the decision. According to him, the case raised "the big issue in the country": "Does this decision mean that the United States Government has no control over any national economic problem?" He added that the decision "—if you accept the obiter dicta and all the phraseology of it—seems to be squarely on the side of restoring to the States forty-eight different controls over national economic problems. [In] some ways it may be the best thing that has happened to the country for a long time that such a decision has come from the Supreme Court, because it clarifies the issue." But the Schechter language was not necessarily fatal to the New Deal cause. As to doctrine, the "very weakness of the Schechter case, from the Government's viewpoint, was its saving grace." The Court had not yet passed on congressional power "to control trade practices or labor relations [in] any major industry, such as petroleum, lumber, coal or steel." In future litigation, "the case—and perhaps its language—could clearly be distinguished, when and if such regulation was attempted." Stern, above, at 662. The attempt to move the New Deal forward despite the Schechter language came immediately. For example, the right of collective bargaining, recognized in the NIRA, was guaranteed in a more permanent statute: the National Labor Relations Act (Wagner Act) became law on July 5, 1935. And President Roosevelt quickly urged Congress to enact a law establishing an NIRA-like regulatory scheme for the bituminous coal industry. While that bill was pending in a House subcommittee, President Roosevelt wrote his controversial letter to Congressman Hill—the letter ending with the statement: "I hope your committee will not permit doubts as to constitutionality, however reasonable, to block the suggested legislation." (Recall the excerpt at p. 22 above.) The bill became law soon after, and a court challenge was filed the next day. That test case produced the Carter ruling, which follows.

9. *The Carter case.* CARTER v. CARTER COAL CO., 298 U.S. 238 (1936), a year after Schechter, invalidated the Bituminous Coal Conservation Act of 1935. Among the objectives of the law was the regulation of maximum hours and minimum wages in coal mines. Producers were to comply with a national bituminous coal code. The minimum wage and maximum hour provisions of the code, binding on all code members, were negotiated by a specified percentage of producers' and workers' representatives. The sanction imposed to make the provisions effective was, in effect, to levy a tax of 13.5% on all producers who did not accept the code. Carter brought a stockholder's suit against his company to enjoin it from paying the tax and complying with the code. The lower court sustained the Act. The Court reversed, with Justice SUTHERLAND writing the majority opinion.[9]

---

9. The Government conceded, in light of the Child Labor Tax Case (p. 229 below), that the Act could not be sustained under the taxing power: the "tax" was a "penalty"; to be valid, it had to be justified under the commerce power. In addition to the wage,

Justice Sutherland stated: "Certain recitals [in] the act plainly suggest that its makers were of the opinion that its constitutionality could be sustained under some general federal power, thought to exist, apart from the specific grants of the Constitution. [The recitals] are to the effect that the distribution of bituminous coal is of national interest, affecting the health and comfort of the people and the general welfare of the nation. [The] proposition, often advanced and as often discredited, that the power of the federal government inherently extends to purposes affecting the nation as a whole with which the states severally [cannot] adequately deal, and the related notion that Congress, entirely apart from those powers delegated by the Constitution, may enact laws to promote the general welfare, have always definitely [been] rejected by this court. [The] general purposes which the act recites [are] beyond the power of Congress except so far, and only so far, as they may be realized by an exercise of some specific power granted by the Constitution. [W]e find no grant of power which authorizes Congress to legislate in respect of these general purposes unless it be found in the commerce clause—and this we now [consider].

"[T]he effect of the labor provisions of the [act] primarily falls upon production and not upon commerce. [P]roduction is a purely local activity. It follows that none of these essential antecedents of production constitutes a transaction in or forms any part of interstate commerce. [Schechter.] [T]he local character of mining, of manufacturing and of crop growing is a fact, and remains a fact, whatever may be done with the products. [That] the production of every commodity intended for interstate sale and transportation has some effect upon interstate commerce may [be] freely granted; and we are brought to the final and decisive inquiry, whether here that effect is direct, as the 'preamble' recites, or indirect. The distinction is not formal, but substantial in the highest degree, as we pointed out in [Schechter].

"Whether the effect of a given activity or condition is direct or indirect is not always easy to determine. The word 'direct' implies that the activity or condition invoked or blamed shall operate proximately—not mediately, remotely, or collaterally—to produce the effect. It connotes the absence of an efficient intervening agency or condition. And the extent of the effect bears no logical relation to its character. The distinction between a direct and an indirect effect turns, not upon the magnitude of either the cause or the effect, but entirely upon the manner in which the effect has been brought about. If the production by one man of a single ton of coal intended for interstate sale and shipment, and actually so sold and shipped, affects interstate commerce indirectly, the effect does not become direct by multiplying the tonnage, or increasing the number of men employed, or adding to the expense or complexities of the business, or by all combined. It is quite true that rules of law are sometimes qualified by considerations of degree, as the government argues. But the matter of degree has no bearing upon the question here, since that question is not— What is the *extent* of the local activity or condition, or the *extent* of the effect produced upon interstate commerce? but—What is the *relation* between the activity or condition and the effect?

hour and other labor provisions, the code also provided for minimum and maximum prices for sales of bituminous coal. However, the majority opinion spoke mainly of the validity of the labor provisions under the commerce power. The price provisions were found inseparable from the labor provisions; hence, the entire Act fell without separate consideration of the constitutionality of the price regulations. By contrast, Justice Cardozo's dissent found the price provisions constitutional under the commerce power and argued that the suit was premature with respect to the labor provisions.

"Much stress is put upon the evils which come from the struggle between employers and employees over the matter of wages, working conditions, the right of collective bargaining, etc., and the resulting strikes, curtailment and irregularity of production and effect on prices; and it is insisted that interstate commerce is *greatly* affected thereby. But, [the] conclusive answer is that the evils are all local evils over which the federal government has no legislative control. [Such] effect as they may have upon commerce, however extensive it may be, is secondary and indirect. An increase in the greatness of the effect adds to its importance. It does not alter its character. [A] reading of the entire opinion [in Schechter] makes clear, what we now declare, that the want of power on the part of the federal government is the same whether the wages, hours of service, and working conditions, and the bargaining about them, are related to production before interstate commerce has begun, or to sale and distribution after it has [ended]."

Justice CARDOZO's dissent, joined by Justices Brandeis and Stone insisted: "[I] am satisfied that the Act is within the power of the central government in so far as it provides for minimum and maximum prices. [Whether] it is valid also in other provisions that have been considered and condemned in the opinion of the court, I do not find it necessary to determine [now]. Regulation of prices being an exercise of the commerce power in respect of interstate transactions, the question remains whether it comes within that power as applied to intrastate sales where interstate prices are directly or intimately affected. Mining and agriculture and manufacture are not interstate commerce considered by themselves, yet their relation to that commerce may be such that for the protection of the one there is need to regulate the other. [Schechter.] Sometimes it is said that the relation must be 'direct' to bring that power into play. In many circumstances such a description will be sufficiently precise to meet the needs of the occasion. But a great principle of constitutional law is not susceptible of comprehensive statement in an adjective. The underlying thought is merely this, that 'the law is not indifferent to considerations of degree.' [Schechter, concurring opinion.] It cannot be indifferent to them without an expansion of the commerce clause that would absorb or imperil the reserved powers of the states. At times, as in the case cited, the waves of causation will have radiated so far that their undulatory motion, if discernible at all, will be too faint or obscure, too broken by cross-currents, to be heeded by the law. In such circumstances the holding is not directed at prices or wages considered in the abstract, but at prices or wages in particular conditions. The relation may be tenuous or the opposite according to the facts. Always the setting of the facts is to be viewed if one would know the closeness of the tie. Perhaps, if one group of adjectives is to be chosen in preference to another, 'intimate' and 'remote' will be found to be as good as any. At all events, 'direct' and 'indirect,' even if accepted as sufficient, must not be read too narrowly. [A] survey of the cases shows that the words have been interpreted with suppleness of adaptation and flexibility of meaning. The power is as broad as the need that evokes it. [What the railroad cases such as Shreveport] really mean is that the causal relation in such circumstances is so close and intimate and obvious as to permit it to be called direct without subjecting the word to an unfair or excessive strain. There is a like immediacy here. Within rulings the most orthodox, the prices for intrastate sales of coal have so inescapable a relation to those for interstate sales that a system of regulation for transactions of the one class is necessary to give adequate protection to the system of regulation adopted for the other. The argument is strongly pressed [that] this may not be true in all communities or in exceptional conditions. If so, the operators unlawfully affected may show that the Act to that extent is invalid as to them." (In a separate opinion, Chief

Justice HUGHES agreed that the labor provisions were invalid, but thought the price provisions were constitutional and separable from the invalid labor ones. In finding the labor provisions constitutionally flawed, he conceded that the commerce power "embraces the power to protect [commerce] from injury, whatever may be the source of the dangers which threaten it," but insisted that "Congress may not use this protective authority as a pretext for the exertion of power to regulate activities and relations within the States which affect interstate commerce only indirectly."]

10. *FDR's Court–packing Plan: Background and fate.* The 1935 and 1936 decisions persuaded the Roosevelt Administration that strong measures were needed to save the New Deal from judicial invalidation. Several major New Deal laws had already been held unconstitutional; others—the National Labor Relations Act and the Social Security Act among them—might well meet a similar fate. The Carter decision confirmed the worst anticipations generated by Schechter. And there were others as well. (E.g., the Butler cases (1936; p. 235 below; spending power) and Morehead v. New York ex rel. Tipaldo (1936; p. 478 below; due process restraints).) As a result, convictions hardened within the Administration that something had to be done about the Court. But President Roosevelt did not make Court reform an issue en route to his landslide 1936 reelection. Rather, he waited until February 1937 to propose changes, giving reasons that seemed disingenuous to many. A month later, in a radio address, he challenged the Court more directly and defended his plan more forthrightly. But the content of the plan, and its initial method of presentation, provoked widespread opposition—including that of a number of New Deal supporters. After extensive hearings, the Senate Judiciary Committee rejected the proposal in June 1937. While the controversy was raging, the Court seemed to change direction in a number of decisions sustaining regulatory statutes, and Justice Van Devanter retired. The final Senate debate was almost anti-climactic. Proposed amendments by the proponents failed to save the heart of the plan, and in late July it was in effect killed. The following excerpts illustrating highlights of the battle are from documents in Sen.Rep.No. 711, 75th Cong., 1st Sess. (1937) (Reorganization of the Federal Judiciary—Adverse Report of the Committee on the Judiciary).

a. *The President's Message to Congress, Feb. 5, 1937:* [It is] one of the definite duties of the Congress constantly to maintain the effective functioning of the Federal judiciary. [A]t the present time the Supreme Court is laboring under a heavy burden. [P]art of the problem of obtaining a sufficient number of judges to dispose of cases is the capacity of the judges themselves. This brings forward the question of aged or infirm judges—a subject of delicacy and yet one which requires frank discussion. [Modern] complexities call also for a constant infusion of new blood in the courts, just as it is needed in executive functions of the Government and in private business. [I], therefore, earnestly recommend that the necessity of an increase in the number of judges be supplied by legislation providing for the appointment of additional judges in all Federal courts, without exception, where there are incumbent judges of retirement age who do not choose to retire or to resign.

b. *The proposed bill:* When any judge of a court of the United States, appointed to hold his office during good behavior, has heretofore or hereafter attained the age of seventy years and has held a commission or commissions as judge of any such court or courts at least ten years, continuously or otherwise, and within six months thereafter has neither resigned nor retired, the President, for each such judge who has not so resigned or retired, shall nominate, and by and with the advice and consent of the Senate, shall appoint one additional judge to the court to which the former is commissioned. [No judge shall] be so appointed if such appointment would result [in] more than fifteen members of the Supreme Court of the United States. [Six Justices were over seventy in 1937: Butler (71), Hughes (75), Sutherland (75), McReynolds (75), Van Devanter (78), and Brandeis (81).]

c. *Letter of Chief Justice Charles Evans Hughes to Senator Burton K. Wheeler, March 21, 1937:* In response to your inquiries, I have the honor to present the following statement with respect to the work of the Supreme Court: 1. The Supreme Court is fully abreast of its work. [7.] An increase in the number of Justices of the Supreme Court, apart from any question of policy, which I do not discuss, would not promote the efficiency of the Court. It is believed that it would impair that efficiency so long as the Court acts as a unit. There would be more judges to hear, more judges to confer, more judges to discuss, more judges to be convinced and to decide. The present number of Justices is thought to be large enough so far as the prompt, adequate, and efficient conduct of [our work] is concerned.

d. *Radio Address by President Roosevelt, March 9, 1937:* I want to talk with you very simply about the need for present action in this crisis—the need to meet the unanswered challenge of one-third of a nation ill-nourished, ill-clad, ill-housed. [When] the Congress has sought to stabilize national agriculture, to improve the conditions of labor, to safeguard business against unfair competition, to protect our national resources, and in many other ways to serve our clearly national needs, the majority of the Court has been assuming the power to pass on the wisdom of these acts of the Congress—and to approve or disapprove the public policy written into these laws. This is not only my accusation, it is the accusation of most distinguished Justices of the present Supreme Court. [See especially Justice Stone's vigorous dissent in the Butler case in 1936, p. 238 below.]

[We] have, therefore, reached the point as a Nation where we must take action to save the Constitution from the Court and the Court from itself. We must find a way to take an appeal from the Supreme Court to the Constitution itself. We want a Supreme Court which will do justice under the Constitution—not over it. [My] plan has two chief purposes: By bringing into the judicial system a steady and continuing stream of new and younger blood, I hope, first, to make the administration of all Federal justice speedier and therefore less costly; secondly, to bring to the decision of social and economic problems younger men who have had personal experience and contact with modern facts and circumstances under which average men have to live and work. This plan will save our [Constitution] from hardening of the judicial arteries. We cannot rely on an amendment as the immediate or only answer to our present difficulties. [An] amendment like the rest of the Constitution is what the Justices say it is rather than what its framers or you might hope it is.

e. *Conclusion of Adverse Report of Senate Judiciary Committee, June 14, 1937:* We recommend the rejection of this bill as a needless, futile, and utterly dangerous abandonment of constitutional principle. [Under] the form of the Constitution it seeks to do that which is unconstitutional. [I]ts practical operation would be to make the Constitution what the executive or legislative branches of the Government choose to say it is—an interpretation to be changed with each change of administration. It is a measure which should be so emphatically rejected that its parallel will never again be presented to the free representatives of the free people of America.

f. *The impact of the plan.* Two years after his Court-packing plan was rejected, President Roosevelt claimed that he had lost the battle but won the war. Do the decisions since 1937 support that assertion? The Jones & Laughlin case, which follows, was decided on April 12, 1937, while the debate was still raging. Could any of the cases from 1937 to 1991 have been decided the same way if the "direct"-"indirect" standard of the Knight–Schechter–Carter line of cases standard had prevailed? Note the reliance on the Shreveport legacy of "practical effects" in the post–1937 cases. Note also that, in several major decisions, the majority proved itself willing to go further than the Government's narrower, more hesitant arguments. And note the fuller economic record submitted by the Government in the cases that follow: contrast, e.g., the economic data in Jones & Laughlin with those in Schechter.[10]

Section 3. The Decline of Limits on the Commerce Power: The Era Beginning in 1937

NLRB v. Jones & Laughlin Steel Corp.
301 U.S. 1, 57 S.Ct. 615, 81 L.Ed. 893 (1937).

[This was the major case testing the constitutionality of the National Labor Relations Act of 1935. Unlike Schechter, this test arose in a context desired by the Government: labor practices in a major industry. The NLRB found that the company had engaged in "unfair labor practices" by discriminatory discharges of employees for union activity. The Board ordered the company to end discrimination and coercion. When the company failed to comply, the NLRB sought judicial enforcement of its order, but the Court of Appeals denied the Board's petition on the ground that "the order lay beyond the range of federal power."]

10. The commerce power decisions were not the only indications of a changing judicial response. Two weeks before Jones & Laughlin, for example, the Court overruled prior decisions invalidating minimum wage laws as violative of due process. West Coast Hotel Co. v. Parrish, p. 476 below. West Coast Hotel, in particular, provoked the charge that Justice Roberts had changed his position in the face of the Roosevelt challenge—the "switch in time" that supposedly "saved the Nine." But, as a memorandum left by the Justice demonstrates, the Court voted in West Coast Hotel weeks before the judicial reorganization plan was announced See Frankfurter, "Mr Justice Roberts," 104 U.Pa.L.Rev. 311 (1955). Compare Justice Roberts's votes in Alton, Schechter and Carter, above, with those in the commerce clause decisions which follow; and compare his position in United States v. Butler with that in Steward Machine Co. v. Davis (pp. 235 and 241 below). Note the changes in Court personnel from 1937 through 1941· President Roosevelt made seven appointments—Justices Black, Reed, Frankfurter, Douglas, Murphy, Byrnes and Jackson. For contrasting evaluations of the alleged "switch" by Rob-

erts, see Ariens, "A Thrice-Told Tale, or Felix the Cat," 107 Harv.L.Rev. 620 (1994), Friedman, "A Reaffirmation: The Authenticity of the Roberts Memorandum, or Felix the Non-Forger," 142 U.Pa.L.Rev. 1985 (1994), and Friedman, "Switching Time and Other Thought Experiments: The Hughes Court and Constitutional Transformation," 142 U.Pa.L.Rev. 1091 (1994).

The background and consequences of the Court-packing plan are discussed in Jackson, The Struggle for Judicial Supremacy (1941). For the political aspects of the controversy, see the useful contemporary account in Alsop & Catledge, The 168 Days (1938); the colorful modern review in Baker, Back to Back—The Duel Between FDR and the Supreme Court (1967); Freidel, Roosevelt: A Rendezvous with Destiny (1990); and the astute retrospective analysis in Chapter 15, "Court Packing: The Miscalculated Risk," Burns, Roosevelt: The Lion and the Fox (1956). See also Leuchtenburg, "The Origins of Franklin D. Roosevelt's 'Court Packing Plan,'" 1966 Sup.Ct.Rev. 347, and Leuchtenburg, The Supreme Court Reborn: The Constitutional Revolution in the Age of Roosevelt (1995).

Chief Justice HUGHES delivered the opinion of the Court.

[The NLRB] has found: The corporation [is] engaged in the business of manufacturing iron and steel in plants situated in Pittsburgh and nearby Aliquippa, Pennsylvania. It manufactures and distributes a widely diversified line of steel and pig iron, being the fourth largest producer of steel in the United States. With its subsidiaries—nineteen in number—it is a completely integrated enterprise, owning and operating ore, coal and limestone properties, lake and river transportation facilities and terminal railroads located at its manufacturing plants. It owns or controls mines in Michigan and Minnesota. It operates four ore steamships on the Great Lakes. It owns coal mines in Pennsylvania. It operates towboats and steam barges used in carrying coal to its factories. [It owns two railroads which connect its plants to major lines.] Much of its product is shipped to its warehouses in Chicago, Detroit, Cincinnati and Memphis,—to the last two places by means of its own barges and transportation equipment. In Long Island City, New York, and in New Orleans it operates structural steel fabricating shops in connection with the warehousing of semi-finished materials sent from its works. Through one of its wholly-owned subsidiaries it owns, leases and operates stores, warehouses and yards for the distribution of equipment and supplies for drilling and operating oil and gas wells and for pipe lines, refineries and pumping stations. It has sales offices in twenty cities in the United States and a wholly-owned subsidiary which is devoted exclusively to distributing its product in Canada. Approximately 75 per cent. of its product is shipped out of Pennsylvania.

Summarizing these operations, the Labor Board concluded that the works in Pittsburgh and Aliquippa "might be likened to the heart of a self-contained, highly integrated body. They draw in the raw materials from Michigan, Minnesota, West Virginia, Pennsylvania in part through arteries and by means controlled by the respondent; they transform the materials and then pump them out to all parts of the nation through the vast mechanism which the respondent has elaborated." To carry on the activities of the entire steel industry, 33,000 men mine ore, 44,000 men mine coal, 4,000 men quarry limestone, 16,000 men manufacture coke, 343,000 men manufacture steel, and 83,000 men transport its product. Respondent has about 10,000 employees in its Aliquippa plant, which is located in a community of about [30,000 persons].

First. The scope of the Act.—The Act is challenged in its entirety as an attempt to regulate all industry, thus invading the reserved powers of the States over their local concerns. It is asserted [that] the Act is not a true regulation [of] commerce or of matters which directly affect it but on the contrary has the fundamental object of placing under the compulsory supervision of the federal government all industrial labor relations within the nation. [We] think it clear that [the] Act may be construed so as to operate within the sphere of constitutional authority. The jurisdiction conferred upon the Board, and invoked in this instance, is found in § 10(a), which [provides]: "The Board is empowered [to] prevent any person from engaging in any [unfair labor practice] affecting commerce." [The Act] purports to reach only what may be deemed to burden or obstruct that commerce and, thus qualified, it must be construed as contemplating the exercise of control within constitutional bounds. It is a familiar principle that acts which directly burden or obstruct interstate or foreign commerce, or its free flow, are within the reach of the congressional power. Acts having that effect are not rendered immune because they grow out of labor disputes. [It] is the effect upon commerce, not the source of the injury, which is the criterion. [Whether] or not particular action does affect commerce in such a close and intimate fashion as to be subject to federal control [is] left by the statute to be determined as individual cases arise. We are thus to inquire whether in the instant case the constitutional boundary has been [passed].

Third. The application of the Act to employees engaged in production.—The principle involved.—Respondent says that whatever may be said of employees engaged in interstate commerce, the industrial relations and activities in the manufacturing department of respondent's enterprise are not subject to federal regulation. The argument rests upon the proposition that manufacturing in itself is not commerce. [Kidd v. Pearson; Schechter; Carter.] The Government distinguishes these cases, [urging] that these activities constitute a "stream" or "flow" of commerce, of which the Aliquippa manufacturing plant is the focal point, and that industrial strife at that point would cripple the entire movement. [Stafford v. Wallace.] [Respondent] contends that the instant case presents material distinctions. The raw materials which are brought to the plant are delayed for long periods and, after being subjected to manufacturing processes, "are changed substantially as to character, utility and value." The finished products which emerge "are to a large extent manufactured without reference to pre-existing orders and contracts and are entirely different from the raw materials which enter at the other end." [We] do not find it necessary to determine whether these features of defendant's business dispose of the asserted analogy to the "stream of commerce" cases. The instances in which that metaphor has been used are but particular, and not exclusive, illustrations of the protective power which the Government invokes in support of the present Act. The congressional authority to protect interstate commerce from burdens and obstructions is not limited to transactions which can be deemed to be an essential part of a "flow" of interstate or foreign commerce. Burdens and obstructions may be due to injurious action springing from other sources. The fundamental principle is that the power to regulate commerce is the power to enact "all appropriate legislation" for "its protection and advancement"; to adopt measures "to promote its growth and insure its safety"; "to foster, protect, control and restrain." That power is plenary and may be exerted to protect interstate commerce "no matter what the source of the dangers which threaten it." Although activities may be intrastate in character when separately considered, if they have such a close and substantial relation to interstate commerce that their control is essential or appropriate to protect that commerce from burdens and obstructions, Congress cannot be denied the power to exercise that control. [Schechter.] Undoubtedly the scope of this power must be considered in the light of our dual system of government and may not be extended so as to embrace effects upon interstate commerce so indirect and remote that to embrace them, in view of our complex society, would effectually obliterate the distinction between what is national and what is local and create a completely centralized government. Id. The question is necessarily one of degree. [That] intrastate activities, by reason of close and intimate relation to interstate commerce, may fall within federal control is demonstrated in the case of carriers who are engaged in both interstate and intrastate transportation. [The] close and intimate effect which brings the subject within the reach of federal power may be due to activities in relation to productive industry although the industry when separately viewed is local. [T]he fact that the employees here concerned were engaged in production is not determinative. The question remains as to the effect upon interstate commerce of the labor practice involved. [In Schechter], we found that the effect there was so remote as to be beyond the federal power. [In Carter], the Court was of the opinion that the provisions of the statute relating to production were invalid upon several grounds. [These] cases are not controlling here.

Fourth. Effects of the unfair labor practice in respondent's enterprise.—[I]t is idle to say that the effect [of labor strife at respondent's manufacturing operations on interstate commerce] would be indirect or remote. It is obvious that it would be immediate and might be catastrophic. We are asked to shut our eyes to the plainest facts of our national life and to deal with the question of direct and indirect effects in an intellectual vacuum. Because there may be but indirect and remote effects upon interstate commerce in connection with a host of local enterprises throughout the country, it does not follow that other industrial activities do not have such a close and intimate relation to interstate commerce as to make the presence of industrial strife a matter of the most urgent national concern. When industries organize themselves on a national scale, making their relation to interstate commerce the dominant factor in their activities, how can it be maintained that their industrial labor relations constitute a forbidden field into which Congress may not enter when it is necessary to protect interstate commerce from the paralyzing consequences of industrial war? We have often said that interstate commerce itself is a practical conception. It is equally true that interferences with that commerce must be appraised by a judgment that does not ignore actual experience. Experience has abundantly demonstrated that the recognition of the right of employees to self-organization and to have representatives of their own choosing for the purpose of collective bargaining is often an essential condition of industrial [peace].

Reversed.

Justice McREYNOLDS [dissented].[1]

Any effect on interstate commerce by the discharge of employees shown here would be indirect and remote in the highest degree, as consideration of the facts will show. In [Jones & Laughlin] ten men out of ten thousand were discharged; in the other cases only a few. The immediate effect in the factory may be to create discontent among all those employed and a strike may follow, which, in turn, may result in reducing production, which ultimately may reduce the volume of goods moving in interstate commerce. By this chain of indirect and progressively remote events we finally reach the evil with which it is said the legislation under consideration undertakes to deal. A more remote and indirect interference with interstate commerce or a more definite invasion of the powers reserved to the states is difficult, if not impossible, to imagine. [Whatever] effect any cause of [labor] discontent may ultimately have upon commerce is far too indirect to justify Congressional regulation. Almost anything—marriage, birth, death—may in some fashion affect [commerce].

––––––––––

Transitional Note. Jones & Laughlin gave new life to the "affecting commerce" rationale—the rationale justifying national regulation of intrastate activities because of their practical effect on interstate commerce. Five years later, in Wickard v. Filburn (1942), the Court elaborated and expanded that rationale. Wickard is printed immediately below, to permit tracing the development of that "affecting commerce" doctrinal strand at this point. But in between Jones & Laughlin and Wickard, the Court made another major contribution to an expansive reading of the commerce power, in United States

1. The dissent in this 5-4 decision was joined by Justices Van Devanter, Sutherland, and Butler. Justice McReynolds's dissent was also applicable to two companion cases: NLRB v. Fruehauf Trailer Co., 301 U.S. 49 (1937), involving the largest trailer manufacturer in the nation, with sales offices in 12 states; and NLRB v. Friedman–Harry Marks Clothing Co., 301 U.S. 58 (1937), involving a Virginia clothing manufacturer.

v. Darby in 1941. Consideration of Darby is postponed until after Wickard, because Darby deals with the "commerce-prohibiting" device as well as the "affecting commerce" technique of regulation; printing Darby after Wickard accordingly aids separate focus on the modern aspects of the commerce-prohibiting problems first encountered in the Lottery Case and in Hammer v. Dagenhart, above.[2]

Wickard v. Filburn

317 U.S. 111, 63 S.Ct. 82, 87 L.Ed. 122 (1942).

[Filburn, a farmer in Ohio, sued Wickard, the Secretary of Agriculture, to enjoin enforcement of a marketing penalty imposed under the Agricultural Adjustment Act of 1938 "upon that part of his 1941 wheat crop which was available for market in excess of the market quota established for his farm." Filburn operated a dairy farm on which he also raised a small acreage of wheat, to feed his livestock, to use for seed, to make flour for home consumption, and to sell. The 1941 quota was approved, as required by the law, in a referendum of wheat growers. Filburn's quota for 1941 was 223 bushels, but he harvested an excess of 239 bushels beyond his quota. As a result, he faced a penalty of $117 for the excess grown. Filburn attacked the marketing quota provisions of the Act as, inter alia, beyond the commerce power. The lower court enjoined enforcement on other grounds, and Wickard appealed.]

Justice JACKSON delivered the opinion of the Court.

[It] is urged that under the Commerce [Clause], Congress does not possess the power it has in this instance sought to exercise. The question would merit little consideration since our decision in [Darby], except for the fact that this Act extends federal regulation to production not intended in any part for commerce but wholly for consumption on the farm. [M]arketing quotas not only embrace all that may be sold without penalty but also what may be consumed on the premises. [Appellee] says that this is a regulation of production and consumption of wheat. Such activities are, he urges, beyond the reach of Congressional power under the Commerce Clause, since they are local in character, and their effects upon interstate commerce are at most "indirect." In answer the Government argues that the statute regulates neither production nor consumption, but only marketing; and, in the alternative, that if the Act does go beyond the regulation of marketing it is sustainable as a "necessary and proper" implementation of the power of Congress over interstate commerce. The Government's concern lest the Act be held to be a regulation of production or consumption, rather than of marketing, is attributable to a few dicta and decisions of this Court which might be understood to lay it down that activities such as "production," "manufacturing," and "mining" are strictly "local" and, except in special [circumstances], cannot be regulated under the commerce power because their effects upon interstate commerce are, as matter of law, only "indirect." [But] questions of the power of Congress are not to be decided by reference to any formula which would give controlling force to

---

2. The decisions sustaining national power in Wickard and Darby, unlike that in Jones & Laughlin, were unanimous. There were rapid changes in the composition of the Court after Jones & Laughlin: by the time of the Darby decision, all of the four dissenters in Jones & Laughlin had left. Justice McReynolds was the last to go: he retired just a few days before Darby was announced.

nomenclature such as "production" and "indirect" and foreclose consideration of the actual effects of the activity in question upon interstate commerce.

At the beginning Chief Justice Marshall described the federal commerce power with a breadth never yet exceeded. [Gibbons.] He made emphatic the embracing and penetrating nature of this power by warning that effective restraints on its exercise must proceed from political rather than from judicial processes [Justice Jackson proceeded to review commerce power decisions from Knight through Shreveport. He continued:] The Court's recognition of the relevance of the economic effects in the application of the Commerce Clause [has] made the mechanical application of legal formulas no longer feasible. Once an economic measure of the reach of the power granted to Congress in the Commerce Clause is accepted, questions of federal power cannot be decided simply by finding the activity in question to be "production" nor can consideration of its economic effects be foreclosed by calling them "indirect." [E]ven if appellee's activity be local and though it may not be regarded as commerce, it may still, whatever its nature, be reached by Congress if it exerts a substantial economic effect on interstate commerce, and this irrespective of whether such effect is what might at some earlier time have been defined as "direct" or "indirect."

[The] parties have stipulated a summary of the economics of the wheat industry. Commerce among the states in wheat is large and important. Although wheat is raised in every state but one, production in most states is not equal to consumption. [The] wheat industry has been a problem industry for some years. Largely as a result of increased foreign production and import restrictions, annual exports of wheat and flour from the United States during the ten-year period ending in 1940 averaged less than 10 per cent of total production, while during the 1920's they averaged more than 25 per cent. The decline in the export trade has left a large surplus in production which, in connection with an abnormally large supply of wheat and other grains in recent years, caused congestion in a number of markets; tied up railroad cars; and caused elevators in some instances to turn away grains, and railroads to institute embargoes to prevent further congestion. [In] the absence of regulation the price of wheat in the United States would be much affected by world conditions. During 1941, producers who cooperated with the Agricultural Adjustment program received an average price on the farm of about $1.16 a bushel, as compared with the world market price of 40 cents a bushel. [The] effect of consumption of homegrown wheat on interstate commerce is due to the fact that it constitutes the most variable factor in the disappearance of the wheat crop. Consumption on the farm where grown appears to vary in an amount greater than 20 per cent of average production. The total amount of wheat consumed as food varies but relatively little, and use as seed is relatively constant. The maintenance by government regulation of a price for wheat undoubtedly can be accomplished as effectively by sustaining or increasing the demand as by limiting the supply. The effect of the statute before us is to restrict the amount which may be produced for market and the extent as well to which one may forestall resort to the market by producing to meet his own needs. That appellee's own contribution to the demand for wheat may be trivial by itself is not enough to remove him from the scope of federal regulation where, as here, his contribution, taken together with that of many others similarly situated, is far from trivial.

[One] of the primary purposes of the Act in question was to increase the market price of wheat, and to that end to limit the volume thereof that could affect the market. It can hardly be denied that a factor of such volume and variability as home-consumed wheat would have a substantial influence on price and market conditions. This may arise because being in marketable condition such [homegrown] wheat overhangs the market and, if induced by rising prices, tends to flow into the market and check price increases. But if we assume that it is never marketed, it supplies a need of the man who grew it which would otherwise be reflected by purchases in the open market. Home-grown wheat in this sense competes with wheat in commerce. The stimulation of commerce is a use of the regulatory function quite as definitely as prohibitions or restrictions thereon. This record leaves us in no doubt that Congress may properly have considered that wheat consumed on the farm where grown, if wholly outside the scheme of regulation, would have a substantial effect in defeating and obstructing its purpose to stimulate trade therein at increased [prices].

Reversed.

The scope of the Wickard rationale. Was the "national market" theory essential to sustain the sanction imposed in Wickard v. Filburn? Could Congress have imposed a limit on farm production directly, without the superstructure of the market control scheme, by simply invoking the "affecting commerce" argument? Note that Justice Jackson in Wickard still required a showing of "substantial economic effect on interstate commerce." But was any real substance left to that notion if the requirement was satisfied whenever the activity regulated, "taken together with that of many others similarly situated, is far from trivial"? Did this "aggregation" approach leave any local activities so minimal as to be unreachable? Did Wickard, then, in effect abandon all judicial concern with federalism-related limits on congressional power? Was the scope of Wickard limited by Justice Jackson's emphasis on the economic magnitude of the wheat production problem? Was aggregation allowable only when the resultant commercial problem was of truly substantial dimensions? Is the scope of Wickard limited by the fact that Congress was dealing with a genuine economic problem? Or is the aggregation theory also usable for national "police" regulations? (Cf. the Perez case, p. 196 below.) Compare with Justice Jackson's broad statements Justice Harlan's comment in Maryland v. Wirtz in 1968 (p. 199 below), suggesting that Wickard did *not* mean "that Congress may use a relatively trivial impact on commerce as an excuse for broad general regulation of state or private activities." Compare also the differing treatments of Wickard in the opinions of the majority and the dissenters, in Lopez, sec. 1 above.

United States v. Darby

312 U.S. 100, 61 S.Ct. 451, 85 L.Ed. 609 (1941).

[Darby, a Georgia lumber manufacturer, challenged an indictment charging him with violating the Fair Labor Standards Act of 1938. The District Court quashed the indictment, holding that the Act was unconstitutional because it sought to regulate hours and wages of employees in local manufacturing activities.]

Justice STONE delivered the opinion of the Court.

[The] two principal questions [in] this case are, *first,* whether Congress has constitutional power to prohibit the shipment in interstate commerce of lumber manufactured by employees whose wages are less than a prescribed minimum or whose weekly hours of labor at that wage are greater than a prescribed maximum, and, *second,* whether it has power to prohibit the employment of workmen in the production of goods "for interstate commerce" at other than prescribed wages and hours. [The Act's purpose is] to exclude from interstate commerce goods produced for the commerce and to prevent their production for interstate commerce, under conditions detrimental to the maintenance of the minimum standards of living necessary for health and general well-being; and to prevent the use of interstate commerce as the means of competition in the distribution of goods so produced, and as the means of spreading and perpetuating such substandard labor conditions among the workers of the several [states].

The prohibition of shipment of the proscribed goods in interstate commerce. [While] manufacture is not of itself interstate commerce the shipment of manufactured goods interstate is such commerce and the prohibition of such shipment by Congress is indubitably a regulation of the commerce. The power to regulate commerce is the power "to prescribe the rule by which commerce is governed." [Gibbons.] It extends not only to those regulations which aid, foster and protect the commerce, but embraces those which prohibit it. It is conceded that the power of Congress to prohibit transportation in interstate commerce includes noxious articles, stolen articles, kidnapped persons, and articles such as intoxicating liquor or convict-made goods, traffic in which is forbidden or restricted by the laws of the state of destination. [But] it is said that the present prohibition falls within the scope of none of these categories; that while the prohibition is nominally a regulation of the commerce its motive or purpose is regulation of wages and hours of persons engaged in manufacture, the control of which has been reserved to the states and upon which Georgia and some of the states of destination have placed no [restriction]. The power of Congress over interstate commerce [can] neither be enlarged nor diminished by the exercise or non-exercise of state power. Congress, following its own conception of public policy concerning the restrictions which may appropriately be imposed on interstate commerce, is free to exclude from the commerce articles whose use in the states for which they are destined it may conceive to be injurious to the public health, morals or welfare, even though the state has not sought to regulate their use [Lottery Case]. Such regulation is not a forbidden invasion of state power merely because either its motive or its consequence is to restrict the use of articles of commerce within the states of destination; and is not prohibited unless by other Constitutional provisions. It is no objection to the assertion of the power to regulate interstate commerce that its exercise is attended by the same incidents which attend the exercise of the police power of the states.

[The] motive and purpose of the present regulation are plainly to make effective the Congressional conception of public policy that interstate commerce should not be made the instrument of competition in the distribution of goods produced under substandard labor conditions, which competition is injurious to the commerce and to the states from and to which the commerce flows. The motive and purpose of a regulation of interstate commerce are matters for the legislative judgment upon the exercise of which the Constitution places no restriction and over which the courts are given no control. "The judicial cannot prescribe to the legislative department of the government limitations upon the exercise of its acknowledged power."[1] Whatever their motive and purpose,

---

1. In support of the preceding two sentences, the Court cited a number of cases involving the taxing power (and rejecting claims that Congress had abused its power to

regulations of commerce which do not infringe some constitutional prohibition are within the plenary power conferred on Congress by the Commerce Clause. Subject only to that limitation, [we] conclude that the prohibition of the shipment interstate of goods produced under the forbidden substandard labor conditions is within the constitutional authority of Congress. [T]hese principles of constitutional interpretation have been so long and repeatedly recognized by this Court as applicable to the Commerce Clause, that there would be little occasion for repeating them now were it not for the decision of this Court twenty-two years ago in Hammer v. Dagenhart. In that case it was held by a bare majority of the Court over the powerful and now classic dissent of Mr. Justice Holmes [that] Congress was without power to exclude the products of child labor from interstate commerce. The reasoning and conclusion of the Court's opinion there cannot be reconciled with the conclusion which we have [reached]. Hammer v. Dagenhart has not been followed. The distinction on which the decision was rested that Congressional power to prohibit interstate commerce is limited to articles which in themselves have some harmful or deleterious property—a distinction which was novel when made and unsupported by any provision of the Constitution—has long since been abandoned. The thesis of the opinion that the motive of the prohibition or its effect to control in some measure the use or production within the states of the article thus excluded from the commerce can operate to deprive the regulation of its constitutional authority has long since ceased to have force. [The] conclusion is inescapable that Hammer v. Dagenhart was a departure from the principles which have prevailed in the interpretation of the Commerce Clause both before and since the decision and that such vitality, as a precedent, as it then had has long since been exhausted. It should be and now is overruled.

Validity of the wage and hour requirements. Section 15(a)(2) and §§ 6 and 7 require employers to conform to the wage and hour provisions with respect to all employees engaged in the production of goods for interstate commerce. As appellees' employees are not alleged to be "engaged in interstate commerce" the validity of the prohibition turns on the question whether the employment, under other than the prescribed labor standards, of employees engaged in the production of goods for interstate commerce is so related to the commerce and so affects it as to be within the reach of the power of Congress to regulate it.

[The] power of Congress [over] interstate commerce extends [to] activities intrastate which have a substantial effect on the commerce or the exercise of the Congressional power over it. [Congress,] having by the present Act adopted the policy of excluding from interstate commerce all goods produced for the commerce which do not conform to the specified labor standards, [may] choose the means reasonably adapted to the attainment of the permitted end, even though they involve control of intrastate activities. Such legislation has often been sustained with respect to powers, other than the commerce power, [when] the means chosen, although not themselves within the granted power, were nevertheless deemed appropriate aids to the accomplishment of some purpose within an admitted power of the national government. [A] familiar like exercise of power is the regulation of intrastate transactions which are so commingled with or related to interstate commerce that all must be regulated if the interstate commerce is to be effectively controlled. Shreveport Case. Similarly Congress may require inspection and preventive treatment of all cattle in a disease infected area in order to prevent shipment in interstate commerce of

tax by seeking regulatory objectives through taxation): McCray v. United States, Sonzinsky v. United States, and Veazie Bank v. Fenno. These cases are noted in chap. 4, below.

some of the cattle without the treatment. It may prohibit the removal, at destination, of labels required by the Pure Food & Drugs Act to be affixed to articles transported in interstate commerce. McDermott v. Wisconsin, 228 U.S. 115 (1913).

[We] think also that § 15(a)(2), now under consideration, is sustainable independently of § 15(a)(1), which prohibits shipment or transportation of the proscribed goods. [T]he evils aimed at by the Act are the spread of substandard labor conditions through the use of the facilities of interstate commerce for competition by the goods so produced with those produced under the prescribed or better labor conditions; and the consequent dislocation of the commerce itself caused by the impairment or destruction of local businesses by competition made effective through interstate commerce. The Act is thus directed at the suppression of a method or kind of competition in interstate commerce which it has in effect condemned as "unfair," as the Clayton Act has condemned other "unfair methods of competition" made effective through interstate commerce. [The] means adopted by § 15(a)(2) for the protection of interstate commerce by the suppression of the production of the condemned goods for interstate commerce is so related to the commerce and so affects it as to be within the reach of the commerce power. Congress, to attain its objective in the suppression of nationwide competition in interstate commerce by goods produced under substandard labor conditions, has made no distinction as to the volume or amount of shipments in the commerce or of production for commerce by any particular shipper or producer. It recognized that in present day industry, competition by a small part may affect the whole and that the total effect of the competition of many small producers may be great. [So] far as [Carter] is inconsistent with this conclusion, its doctrine is limited in principle by the decisions under the Sherman Act and the National Labor Relations Act, which [we] follow. [Our] conclusion is unaffected by the Tenth Amendment, which [states] but a truism that all is retained which has not been surrendered.[2] There is nothing in the history of its adoption to suggest that it was more than declaratory of the relationship between the national and state governments as it had been established by the Constitution before the amendment or that its purpose was other than to allay fears that the new national

---

2. In the generation after Darby, this "truism" passage was widely quoted in Court opinions endorsing broad exercises of congressional power. Many commentators assumed that the Court was unlikely ever to strike down another law of Congress on the ground that it exceeded the commerce power. But a footnote in Justice Marshall's majority opinion in Fry v. United States, 421 U.S. 542 (1975), warned that the reports of the death of federalism-related limitations might be premature. Although sustaining the application of temporary federal wage controls to state employees in a narrow opinion, Justice Marshall commented: "While the Tenth Amendment has been characterized as a 'truism,' stating merely that 'all is retained which has not been surrendered,' United States v. Darby, it is not without significance.

The Amendment expressly declares the constitutional policy that Congress may not exercise power in a fashion that impairs the States' integrity or their ability to function effectively in a federal system." A year later, that observation blossomed into a prevailing opinion in National League of Cities v. Usery in 1976, where the majority held a federal law unconstitutional on federalism-related, state autonomy grounds resting on the Tenth Amendment for the first time in four decades. National League of Cities is considered at p. 207 below. National League of Cities was overruled nine years later, in the 1985 ruling in Garcia, p. 209 below. And in Lopez (1992; sec. 1 above), the Court, for the first time in nearly six decades, found that a congressional law exceeded the reach of the commerce power.

government might seek to exercise powers not granted, and that the states might not be able to exercise fully their [reserved powers].

Reversed.

———

1. *The commerce power in the post–Darby years.* a. *The commerce–prohibiting technique as a regulatory tool after Darby.* (i) *Imposing the prohibition sanction at the state border.* Do the "prohibition of shipment" aspects of Darby leave any "local" private sector activities outside of congressional power—at least so long as the commerce-prohibiting technique is used? Consider again the questions raised earlier, after Hammer v. Dagenhart. Now, Hammer is overruled. Now, with Darby, the Court disavows all control over the "motive and purpose" of such regulation. Was such a broad disavowal of judicial scrutiny necessary or justified? Consider, in examining the materials in sec. 1 of the next chapter (involving the taxing power as a regulatory device), whether the Court has in fact disavowed all "motive and purpose" inquiries in the tax area. Did the disavowal in Darby signify a final rejection of the "pretext" limitation in McCulloch? Would and should the Darby Court have sustained, as commerce power legislation, prohibitions of interstate movement of persons not educated, or married, or divorced, in accordance with national standards? Under Darby, could Congress at least prohibit interstate shipment of goods produced by such persons? What "objects" *are* "entrusted" to Congress by the commerce clause? Should the Court restrict Congress to "commercial," "economic" objects? Did the opportunity to impose such a limit end with the Lottery Case and its progeny? Did Lopez, sec. 1 above, revive such a limit? What explains the Darby Court's failure to impose effective restraints on the "commerce-prohibiting" technique? The earlier Court's doctrinal chaos and inconsistency as to scrutiny of congressional purposes—the inconsistency that prompted Holmes's dissent in Hammer? Modern perceptions of interrelationships within the economy? Felt institutional constraints, reflecting the Court's concern about its competence to ascertain congressional purposes?

(ii) *The commerce-prohibiting technique as the basis for direct sanctions on intrastate activities: The superbootstrap suggestion of Darby.* The preceding comments suggest that judicial noninterference is at its greatest when Congress prohibits the crossing of state lines. Recall, however, that when Congress has sought to impose sanctions directly on the intrastate activity, justifications have typically relied on the "affecting commerce" rationale, as the series of cases culminating in Wickard indicate. But there are passages in Darby suggesting that resort to the "affecting commerce" rationale may no longer be necessary to justify sanctions directed at activities within a state. Those passages, read most broadly, suggest that Darby offers an end run around the "affecting commerce" rationale. Consider the portion of the opinion beginning with the heading "Validity of the wage and hour requirements." These requirements were applicable directly to employees engaged in the production of goods for interstate commerce. Yet the first rationale Justice Stone offers for the constitutionality of the requirements does *not* speak about the impact of that local activity on interstate commerce. Rather, the "end" which is invoked in this passage to justify the local "means" is the relationship of the local sanction to the *ban* on interstate shipments (not the relationship between the regulated local activity and a national commercial problem). Does that mean that regulation of local activities can now be justified *without* any showing of the impact of the local activity on commerce, simply by having the regulatory scheme include a ban on interstate shipments, and then justifying the "local" regulation as a means to effectuate that "commerce-prohibiting" sanction? Are the "political safeguards of federalism" adequate protection against abuses of such a power, even in areas of regulation without major economic dimensions? (These questions rest, as noted, on a literal reading of the Darby Court's first ground for sustaining the production regulations. But perhaps such a reading is unwarranted. After all, it was merely an alternative holding: the Court did go on to justify the production regulations in the traditional "affecting commerce" manner. And there may be political inhibitions in Congress against excessive invocation of the "prohibition" technique.)

2. *The commerce power and crime.* Expansion of federal criminal jurisdiction raises some of the most sensitive problems of potential congressional impingement upon the values of federalism. Criminal laws are often among the clearest examples of federal regulation of "traditionally local" concerns. Moreover, the substantial economic (rather than moral or social) dimensions of the "evils" regulated are often far less evident in federal criminal legislation than, for example, in the regulatory laws of the New Deal era. The risks of abuse of national power in national criminal laws were evident as early as the measures directed at gambling and prostitution at the turn of the century. And the risks persist in the mounting modern resort to the commerce power as the basis for new federal criminal laws, relying both on the "commerce-prohibiting" and "affecting commerce" techniques.

This group of notes examines some of the modern uses of the power in the criminal context. Do they raise serious constitutional problems? Do they risk violating the "spirit" of the Constitution that Marshall spoke of in the McCulloch case? If the broad dicta of Darby and Wickard were taken at face value, few if any uses of the commerce power should give any real difficulty to the Court. And there is some evidence that the modern Court's "hands-off" attitude carries over to commerce power-based criminal laws. Yet, even in the Wickard–Darby era, there were occasional countersignals as well: in the context of statutory interpretation, at least, the Justices sometimes voiced misgivings about the expansion of federal criminal jurisdiction. And in Lopez, sec. 1 above, with its emphasis on "commercial" objectives, the Court found a commerce power-based federal criminal statute unconstitutional for the first time in nearly six decades.

a. PEREZ v. UNITED STATES, 402 U.S. 146 (1971): This ruling upheld a federal criminal law prohibiting "extortionate credit transactions"—loan-sharking enforced by threats of violence. Perez had loaned money to the owner of a butcher shop and threatened violence when the butcher insisted that he could not repay the loan in the amount of the agreed-upon weekly installments. In upholding Perez's conviction, Justice DOUGLAS's opinion cited the findings made by Congress (after hearings), including: "Even where extortionate credit transactions are purely intrastate in character, they nevertheless directly affect interstate and foreign commerce." Justice Douglas found the constitutional question "a substantial one," but thought the law justified under the "affecting commerce" rationale. He noted that, in Darby, "*a class of activities* was held properly regulated by Congress without proof that the particular intrastate activity against which a sanction was laid had an effect on commerce. [Perez] is clearly *a member of the class* which engages in 'extortionate credit transactions' as defined by Congress." A similar approach had been invoked in sustaining the ban on racial discrimination in public accommodations in the Civil Rights Act of 1964, in the Heart of Atlanta and McClung cases [1964; p. 203 below]. Justice Douglas added: "Extortionate credit transactions, though purely intrastate, may in the judgment of Congress affect interstate commerce. [The] findings of Congress are quite adequate on that ground. [The hearings] supplied Congress with the knowledge that the loan shark racket provides organized crime with its second most lucrative source of revenue, exacts millions from the pockets of people, coerces its victims into the commission of crimes against property, and causes the takeover by racketeers of legitimate businesses. We have mentioned [the] economic, financial, and social setting of the problem as revealed to Congress. We do so not to infer that Congress need make particularized findings in order to legislate. We relate the history of the Act [to] answer the impassioned plea of [Perez] that all that is involved in loan sharking is a traditionally local activity. It appears, instead, that loan sharking in its national setting is one way organized interstate crime holds its guns to the heads of the poor and the rich alike and syphons funds from numerous localities to finance its national operations."

Justice STEWART was the lone dissenter, stating: "In order to sustain this law we would, in my view, have to be able at the least to say that Congress could rationally have concluded that loan sharking is an activity with interstate attributes that distinguish it in some substantial respect from other local crime. But it is not enough to say that loan sharking is a national problem, for all crime is a national problem. It is not enough to say that some loan sharking has interstate characteristics, for any crime may have an interstate setting. And the circumstance that loan sharking has an adverse impact on interstate business is not a distinguishing attribute, for interstate business suffers from almost all criminal activity, be it shoplifting or violence in the streets. Because I am unable to discern any rational distinction between loan sharking and other local crime, I cannot escape the conclusion that this statute was beyond the power of Congress to enact. The definition and prosecution of local, intrastate crime are reserved to the States under the Ninth and Tenth Amendments."

b. *The implications of Perez.* Is the majority's statement of the commerce power justification in Perez adequate? Consider the comment on Perez by Robert L. Stern, formerly of the Solicitor General's Office and a participant in many Government efforts to apply the commerce power to national economic problems in the 1930s: "Even a lawyer who fought for a realistic interpretation which would recognize that in commercial matters the United States was one nation finds himself surprised at where we are now—and at how readily the recent expansion is accepted. [The] ease with which the public and the judiciary now swallow the federal regulation of what were once deemed exclusively local matters undoubtedly reflects the general integration of the nation, in disregard of state lines." Stern, "The Commerce Clause Revisited—The Federalization of Intrastate Crime," 15 Ariz.L.Rev. 271 (1973). Note also Stern's suggestion that the "key to [Perez] may be found in the difficulty of proving in each individual case that the loan shark had an interstate connection even when it existed." Stern quotes from Westfall v. United States, 274 U.S. 256, 259 (1927): "[W]hen it is necessary in order to prevent an evil to make the law embrace more than the precise thing to be prevented, it may do so." Is that concept adequate to overcome federalism-related objections and to authorize all-embracing national regulation of even the local elements of a problem whenever it is "difficult" to distinguish between "local" and interstate commerce-related activities? How far-reaching is the Perez rationale? Stern asks: "Can Congress forbid the possession or transfer of all pills, or all white pills, because of the difficulty of distinguishing dangerous pills from others and because some might move interstate?" If that question is answered in the affirmative, does the answer rest on another limitless "bootstrap" principle, subject only to the practical restraint that "Congress is unlikely to interject the federal government into local transactions without good reason"? (Stern draws from Perez the principle that "Congress may regulate local acts which in themselves have no interstate nexus or effect if as a practical matter it is difficult to distinguish such transactions from others which may have some relation to interstate commerce.'')

3. *The "implications of the federal system" as a restraint on statutory interpretation.* The Court has repeatedly rejected federal prosecutors' efforts to read less than clear statutes as reaching deeply into traditionally local domains. Should the federalism-related concerns voiced by the Court in these statutory interpretation contexts find their way into constitutional interpretation as well? In Wickard, the Court indicated that federalism concerns might affect the construction of statutes: "That an activity is of local character may help in a doubtful case to determine whether Congress meant to reach it." What is a "doubtful" case? Note, for example, UNITED STATES v. BASS, 404 U.S. 336 (1971), where Justice MARSHALL's majority opinion reversed a conviction for possession of firearms in violation of a provision of the Omnibus Crime Control and Safe Streets Act of 1968, which applies to any person convicted of a felony "who receives, possesses, or transports in interstate commerce or affecting commerce [any] firearm." There had been no showing that defendant's firearms were commerce-related. The prosecution claimed that the commerce limitations in the law applied only to "transports" and that possession and receipt were punishable without showing a connection with commerce. The Court disagreed: "Because its sanctions are criminal, and because, under the Government's broader reading, the statute would mark a major inroad into a domain traditionally left to the States, we refuse to adopt the broad reading in the absence of a clearer direction from Congress. [U]nless Congress conveys its purpose clearly, it will not be deemed to have significantly changed the federal-state balance." See also United States v. Enmons, 410 U.S. 396 (1973); but see Scarborough v. United States, 431 U.S. 563 (1977).

4. *The "affecting commerce" rationale at the end of the Wickard v. Filburn era.* In the wake of Wickard v. Filburn (and before Lopez) it was difficult indeed to articulate *any* limits on the reach of the commerce power. Congress typically regulated for primarily economic purposes, usually resorting to the "affecting commerce" rationale. Note 4a provides an illustrative example of recent congressional uses of the power and asks whether it approaches the constitutional boundaries. The concluding materials return once more to the problem of judicially imposed limitations: e.g., can proffered "affecting commerce" rationales be rejected as resting on too insubstantial a nexus between the local and the interstate? (Note also the related issues raised by the Civil Rights Act of 1964, in the next group of notes.)

a. *Congressional reliance on the "affecting commerce" rationale and the role of congressional findings.* Do the following provisions in 21 U.S.C. press "affecting commerce" justifications too far? § 347: *"Intrastate sales of colored oleomargarine—Law governing.* (a) Colored oleomargarine or colored margarine which is sold in the same State or Territory in which it is produced shall be subject in the same manner and to the same extent to the provisions of this chapter as if it had been introduced in [interstate commerce]." [The law required any public eating place to display, "prominently and conspicuously," a sign that colored margarine was being served.] § 347a: *"Congressional declaration of policy regarding oleomargarine sales.* The Congress finds and declares that the sale, or the serving in public eating places, of colored oleomargarine or colored margarine without clear identification as such [depresses] the market in interstate commerce for butter and for oleomargarine or margarine clearly identified and constitutes a burden on interstate commerce in such articles. Such burden exists, irrespective of whether such oleomargarine or margarine originates from an interstate source or from the State in which it is sold."

What is the significance of such congressional findings? Recall the differences, on the *lack* of findings, between Chief Justice Rehnquist's majority opinion and Justice Souter's dissent in Lopez, sec. 1 above. Consider also the comments in Frickey, "The Fool on the Hill: Congressional Findings, Constitutional Adjudication, and United States v. Lopez," 46 Case W.Res.L.Rev. 695 (1996). Frickey, while skeptical of the value of boilerplate formal findings, supports greater judicial emphasis on congressional procedures and factfinding processes and suggests that "the quality of legislative procedures should make a difference in assessing constitutionality." He notes that "explicit legislative findings based on a well-developed legislative history would be very helpful to the government in defending [a] statute." He argues that, at least in noneconomic cases, "heightened concern about congressional fact-development and fact-finding suggested by Lopez could be a possible technique for curbing legislative excess" and "would promote a meaningful dialogue between judiciary and legislature concerning just where the difficult-to-draw lines should exist concerning important constitutional values [such as] federalism." He urges, moreover, that the arguably implicit Lopez approach regarding the lack of legislative findings should be extended "to analogous situations, such as some equal protection cases" (see chap. 9, sec. 2, below), lest Lopez be seen as promoting "formalist" values and " 'reflect[ing] an overall constitutional vision that is strikingly old-fashioned.' " *Should* congressional factfinding be significant in Court adjudication?

b. *Potential limits on the commerce power in pre–1990s cases: "Trivial" economic impacts?* Coverage of the Fair Labor Standards Act (recall Darby) was extended by two amendments in the 1960s. Constitutional challenges to these 1961 and 1966 amendments first came to the Court in MARYLAND v. WIRTZ, 392 U.S. 183 (1968). The Court sustained both amendments. The case cast important light on the availability of both the "trivial impacts" and the Tenth Amendment, "state autonomy" defenses to applications of commerce clause regulations.[3] Maryland v. Wirtz continues to be good law with respect to the "trivial impacts" defense. But the aftermath of the rejection of the "state autonomy" defense in Maryland v. Wirtz proved more ambivalent, as is explored sec. 4 below.

The 1961 amendment considered in Wirtz dealt with a major traditional concern of the FLSA, employees in *private* industry. Prior to the amendment, coverage was limited to employees "engaged in commerce or in the production of goods for commerce." The 1961 extension included every employee who "is employed in an enterprise engaged in commerce or in the production of goods for commerce." In effect, that amendment extended protection "to the fellow employees of any employee who would have been protected by the original Act." Justice HARLAN's majority opinion found this "enterprise concept" constitutionally justified on alternative grounds: either under the "unfair competition" theory of Darby or on the Jones & Laughlin "labor dispute" theory. However, Justice Harlan also asserted continuing limits on "affecting

---

3. Note also, as another potential limit, the occasional advocacy of special judicial scrutiny when Congress seeks to regulate a "historically local" field. Recall that Hamilton suggested such a limit as early as 1791 (p. 100 above). Similar arguments have surfaced recurrently since. Note, e.g., United States v. Oregon, 366 U.S. 643 (1961), where the majority sustained a law providing for the vesting in the United States of the property of an intestate veteran. Justice Douglas, joined by Justice Whittaker, dissented: "[W]hen the Federal Government enters a field as historically local as the administration of decedents' estates, some clear relation of the asserted power to one of the delegated powers should be shown. [Today's] decision does not square with our conception of federalism."

commerce" rationales by stating: "We uphold the enterprise concept on the explicit premise that an 'enterprise' is a set of operations whose activities in commerce would all be expected to be affected by the wages and hours of any group of [employees]. So defined, the term is quite cognizant of limitations on the commerce power. Neither here nor in Wickard has the Court declared that Congress may use a relatively trivial impact on commerce as an excuse for broad general regulation of state or private activities. The Court has said only that where a general regulatory statute bears a substantial relation to commerce, the de minimis character of individual instances arising under that statute is of no consequence."

More recently, the Court upheld the constitutionality of the Surface Mining Control and Reclamation Act of 1977 regulating strip mining, in HODEL v. VIRGINIA SURFACE MIN. & RECL. ASS'N, 452 U.S. 264 (1981). One of the challengers' arguments was that the Act regulated "the use of private lands within the borders of the States" and was hence not justified by the commerce power. In rejecting that argument, Justice MARSHALL found the commerce power "broad enough to permit congressional regulation of activities causing air or water pollution, or other environmental hazards that may have effects in more than one State." He added: "[W]hen Congress has determined that an activity affects interstate commerce, the courts need inquire only whether the finding is rational." He emphasized congressional findings that "many surface mining operations [burden] and adversely affect commerce and the public welfare by destroying [the] utility of land, [by] causing erosion and landslides, by contributing to floods, by polluting the water, by destroying fish and wildlife habitats, by impairing [natural beauty]." He concluded that the legislative record provided ample support for these findings, and therefore "we cannot say that Congress did not have a rational basis for concluding that surface coal mining has substantial effects on interstate commerce."

Consider the suggestions for a more limited view of the commerce power in Justice REHNQUIST's opinion concurring in the judgment, an opinion that foreshadowed his majority opinion in 1995 in Lopez. He noted that "one of the greatest 'fictions' of our federal system is that the Congress exercises only those powers delegated to it. [The] manner in which this Court has construed the Commerce Clause amply illustrates the extent of this fiction. [One] could easily get the sense from this Court's opinions that the federal system exists only at the sufferance of Congress." After reviewing the cases, he emphasized that, despite their holdings and broad dicta, "there *are* constitutional limits" and that "it would be a mistake to conclude that Congress' power [is] unlimited": "Some activities may be so private or local in nature that they simply may not be *in* commerce. Nor is it sufficient that the person or activity reached have *some* nexus with interstate commerce. Our cases have consistently held that the regulated activity must have a *substantial* effect on interstate commerce. [Jones & Laughlin.] Moreover, simply because Congress may conclude that a particular activity substantially affects interstate commerce does not necessarily make it so. Congress' findings must be supported by a 'rational basis' and are reviewable by the courts. [Perez (Stewart dissent).]" He nevertheless concluded that, although the challenged Act stretched congressional authority "to the 'nth degree,'" the precedents compelled him to concur. (Chief Justice BURGER's concurrence stated that he agreed with Justice Rehnquist's remarks but thought that the Court's opinion adequately reaffirmed the "*substantial* effect" limitation.) [For a critique of the modern expansions of the commerce power, see Epstein, "The Proper Scope of the Commerce Power," 73 Va.L.Rev. 1387 (1987).]

5. *Using the commerce power for social ends: The ban on discrimination in public accommodations in the Civil Rights Act of 1964.* The congressional consideration and judicial scrutiny of Title II of the Civil Rights Act of 1964 provides a useful case history of the state of commerce power doctrine in the 1960s. It also illustrates a relatively rare exercise of the legislators' independent obligation to consider constitutional norms, not only policy questions. As drafted, Title II prohibited discrimination "on the ground of race, color, religion, or national origin" in certain places of public accommodation. Under the law, a facility was covered "if its operations affect commerce, or if discrimination [is] supported by State action." The latter ground invoked congressional power under § 5 of the Fourteenth Amendment (discussed at length in chap. 10 below). But most of the congressional concerns—like those of the Court in the cases challenging the constitutionality of the law—focused on the reach of the commerce power. As the central coverage provisions of the law showed, the Fourteenth Amendment rationale was a congressional after-thought. The covered facilities included "any inn, hotel, motel [etc.]," "any restaurant, cafeteria, lunch room, lunch counter [etc.]," and any "theater, concert hall, sports arena [etc.]." The law defined establishments "affect[ing] commerce" as including any establishment that "offers to serve interstate travelers or a substantial portion of the food which it serves has moved in commerce."

The 1964 Act, passed in the wake of President Kennedy's assassination in 1963, produced unusually extensive congressional consideration. One of the recurrent issues in the debates was whether a national antidiscrimination law should rest on the commerce power or on congressional power under the Fourteenth Amendment. Even though the law was spurred primarily by the nation's moral outrage at the evils of racial discrimination, the Administration's arguments relied centrally on the "affecting commerce" rationale. While critics of the proposals urged that Fourteenth Amendment reliance was more appropriate for a law dealing with racial equality, the Administration chose to press the commerce power ground because of feared legal obstacles: while the Court had treated commerce power-based legislation leniently for decades, the Fourteenth Amendment was in terms limited to actions of a "state" and its reach to seemingly private action remained uncertain.

Congressional consideration of the proposed law began in the summer of 1963. While the Administration bill was being drafted, the press reported that the Administration would rely solely on the commerce power. Contending positions about use of the commerce power are reflected in two letters by law professors. The first, by Gerald Gunther, was sent to the Justice Department two weeks before the Administration bill was submitted to Congress. (Was there substance to the concerns expressed? Were all grounds of concern removed by the testimony presented to Congress, as reflected in the opinions in the Heart of Atlanta Motel and McClung, below?) Gunther wrote: "I hope [that] the Justice Department [will] reexamine its reported decision to rely exclusively on the commerce clause. [If] a federal ban on discrimination [is] to be enacted, it should rest on the obviously most relevant source of national power, the Fourteenth Amendment, rather than the tenuously related commerce clause. [I] know of course that the commerce power is a temptingly broad one. [But the] substantive content of the commerce clause would have to be drained beyond any point yet reached to justify the simplistic argument that all intrastate activity may be subjected to any kind of national regulation merely because some formal crossing of an interstate boundary once took place, without regard to the relationship between the aim of the regulation and interstate trade. [I] would much prefer to see the Government channel its resources of ingenuity and advocacy into the development of a viable interpretation of the Fourteenth Amendment, the provision with a natural linkage to the race problem. That would seem to me a considerably less demeaning task than the construction of an artificial commerce facade." Compare a passage from a letter six weeks later by Professor Herbert Wechsler to the Chairman of the Senate Commerce Committee: "[I] see nothing fictive in the proposition that the practices to which the measure is directed may occur in or affect 'the commerce that concerns more States than one.' [There] are, in fact, effects upon such matters as the free movement of individuals and goods across State lines, the level of demand for products of the national market and the freedom of enterprises engaged in interstate commerce to abandon the restrictions that some of their local competitors may impose. To legislate within the area of such effects on commerce seems to me to fall within the great tradition of the Congress in the exercise of this explicit power."

The decision to rely mainly on the commerce power raised concerns in Congress about the *reach* of that power. The Senate Commerce Committee's hearings in the summer of 1963 were the most important ones on that issue. There, Attorney General Robert F. Kennedy defended the Administration's constitutional argument. Under that power, Kennedy claimed, the law would be "clearly constitutional"; reliance on the Fourteenth Amendment would carry the risk that the Court might find that Congress lacked the power to act here. Kennedy encountered sharp questioning from Senators, especially Democratic ones sympathetic to the policy of the law. Thus, Senator Monroney was "worried about the use" of the commerce clause "on matters which have been for more than 170 years thought to be within the realm of local control": "[If] we pass this bill, even though the end we seek is good, I wonder how far we are stretching the Constitution." He thought it "difficult to stretch the clause to cover an eating place simply because some of the [food it serves] moves from one state into another." Senator Monroney finally asked Kennedy whether his argument meant that Congress could use the commerce power to regulate any business "no matter how intrastate in nature." The Attorney General responded: "If the establishment is covered by the commerce clause, then you can regulate; that is correct." Assistant Attorney General Burke Marshall, the Chief of the Justice Department's Civil Rights Division, took pains to modify Kennedy's broad arguments in later testimony and in a subsequent memorandum. (The memorandum stated, for example: "Of course there are limits in congressional power under the Commerce Clause. It may be conceded that Congress does not hold the power to regulate all of man's conduct solely because he has [a] relationship with interstate commerce. What is required is that there be a relationship between the interstate commerce and the evil to be regulated.") Marshall's testimony focused on the second pervasive theme raised by the bill: assuming that the commerce power were invoked, how close a nexus between the regulated activity and interstate commerce had to be shown? Marshall testified: "We do not propose to regulate the businesses covered merely because they are engaged in some phase of interstate commerce. Discrimination by the establishment [should] be prohibited because it is that discrimination itself which adversely affects interstate commerce." This narrower submission did not satisfy all the Senators. Democratic Senator Pastore, for example, said: "[I] believe in this bill, because I believe in the dignity of man, not because it impedes our [commerce]. [I] like to feel that what we are talking about is a moral issue. [And] that morality, it seems to me, comes under the 14th Amendment [about] equal protection of the law. [I] am saying we are being a little too careful, cagey, and cautious." Ultimately, the bill was enacted with primary reliance on the commerce power. Test cases were quickly brought, and the Court sustained the law in the cases that follow.

HEART OF ATLANTA MOTEL v. UNITED STATES, 379 U.S. 241 (1964): In this case, a motel located in downtown Atlanta challenged the constitutionality of the public accommodations provisions because it wanted to continue its practice of refusing to rent rooms to African Americans. The Court, in a unanimous opinion by Justice CLARK, rejected the challenge and stated: "While the Act as adopted carried no congressional findings, the record of its passage through each house is replete with evidence of the burdens that discrimination by race or color places upon interstate commerce. [This] testimony included the fact that our people have become increasingly mobile with millions of all races traveling from State to State; that Negroes in particular have been the subject of discrimination in transient accommodations, having to travel great distances to secure the same; that often they have been unable to obtain accommodations and have had to call upon friends to put them up overnight, [and] that these conditions had become so acute as to require the listing of available lodging for Negroes in a special guidebook which was itself 'dramatic testimony of the difficulties' Negroes encounter in travel. [We] shall not burden this opinion with further details since the voluminous testimony presents overwhelming evidence that discrimination by hotels and motels impedes interstate travel [both in impairing "the Negro traveler's pleasure and convenience" and in "discouraging travel on the part of a substantial portion of the Negro community"].

"[T]he determinative test of the exercise of power by the Congress under the Commerce Clause is simply whether the activity sought to be regulated is 'commerce which concerns more States than one' and has a real and substantial relation to the national interest. [The] same interest in protecting interstate commerce which led Congress to deal with segregation in interstate carriers and the white slave traffic has prompted it to extend the exercise of its power to gambling [and] to racial discrimination by owners and managers of terminal restaurants. That Congress was legislating against moral wrongs in many of these areas rendered its enactments no less valid. In framing [Title II] Congress was also dealing with what it considered a moral problem. But that fact does not detract from the overwhelming evidence of the disruptive effect that racial discrimination has had on commercial intercourse. It was this burden which empowered Congress to enact appropriate legislation, and given this basis for the exercise of its power, Congress was not restricted by the fact that the particular obstruction to interstate commerce with which it was dealing was also deemed a moral and social wrong. It is said that the operation of the motel here is of a purely local character. [But] the power of Congress to promote interstate commerce also includes the power to regulate the local incidents thereof, including local activities in both the States of origin and destination, which might have a substantial and harmful effect upon that commerce. One need only examine the evidence which we have discussed above to see that Congress may—as it has—prohibit racial discrimination by motels serving travelers, however 'local' their operations may appear." (Concurring opinions by Justices Black, Douglas and Goldberg, applicable to this case as well as McClung, which follows, are summarized below, with McClung.)

KATZENBACH v. McCLUNG, 379 U.S. 294 (1964): A companion case to Heart of Atlanta, this ruling involved Ollie's Barbecue, a family restaurant in Birmingham, Alabama, with a seating capacity of 220 customers and located 11 blocks from an interstate highway. The barbecue catered to a family and white-collar trade with a take-out service for African Americans. During the preceding year, the restaurant had purchased about $150,000 worth of food, 46% of which was meat bought from a local supplier who had purchased it out of state. The lower court, after conceding that a substantial portion of the food served had moved in interstate commerce, enjoined enforcement of Title II against the restaurant, holding that Congress had "legislated a conclusive presumption that a restaurant affects interstate commerce [if]a substantial portion of the food which it serves has moved in commerce. This [it] could not do because there was no demonstrable connection between food purchased in interstate commerce and sold in a restaurant and the conclusion of Congress that discrimination at the restaurant would affect that commerce." The Court reversed. In his prevailing opinion, Justice CLARK relied on the evidence put forth in the congressional hearings. He stated: "The sole [question] narrows down to whether Title II, as applied to a restaurant receiving about $70,000 worth of food which has moved in commerce, is a valid exercise of the power of Congress. [Congress] conducted prolonged hearings on the Act. [W]hile no formal findings were made, which of course is not necessary, it is well that we make mention of the testimony to determine whether the Act is a reasonable and appropriate means [to regulate commerce]. The record is replete with testimony of the burdens placed on interstate commerce by racial discrimination in restaurants. A comparison of per capita spending by Negroes in restaurants, theaters, and like establishments indicated less spending, after discounting income differences, in areas where discrimination is widely practiced. This condition, which was especially aggravated in the South, was attributed in the testimony [to] racial segregation. [This] diminutive spending springing from a refusal to serve Negroes and their total loss as customers has, regardless of the absence of direct evidence, a close connection to interstate commerce. [Moreover] there was an impressive array of testimony that discrimination in restaurants had a direct and highly restrictive effect upon interstate travel by Negroes. This resulted, it was said, because discriminatory practices prevent Negroes from buying prepared food served on the premises while on a trip, except in isolated and unkempt restaurants and under most unsatisfactory and often unpleasant conditions. This obviously discourages travel and obstructs interstate commerce for one can hardly travel without eating. Likewise, it was said that discrimination deterred professional, as well as skilled, people from moving into areas where such practices occurred and thereby caused industry to be reluctant to establish there. [We] believe that this testimony afforded ample basis for the conclusion that established restaurants in such areas sold less interstate goods because of the discrimination, that interstate travel was obstructed directly by it, that business in general suffered and that many new businesses refrained from establishing there as a result of it. Hence the District Court was in error in concluding that there was no connection between discrimination and the movement of interstate commerce."

Justice Clark continued: "It goes without saying that, viewed in isolation, the volume of food purchased by Ollie's Barbecue from sources supplied from out of state was insignificant when compared with the total foodstuffs moving in commerce. But, as our late Brother Jackson said [in] Wickard: [quoting Justice Jackson's "aggregation" passage]. [We] noted in Heart of Atlanta that a number of witnesses attested to the fact that racial discrimination was not merely a state or regional problem but was one of nationwide scope. Against this background, we must conclude that while the focus of the legislation was on the individual restaurant's relation to interstate commerce, Congress appropriately considered the importance of that connection with the knowledge that the discrimination was but 'representative of many others throughout the country, the total incidence of which if left unchecked may well become far-reaching in its harm to commerce.' The appellees contend that Congress has arbitrarily created a conclusive presumption that all restaurants meeting the criteria set out in the Act 'affect commerce.' Stated another way, they object to the omission of a provision for a case-by-case determination—judicial or administrative—that racial discrimination in a particular restaurant affects commerce. But Congress' action in framing this Act was not unprecedented. [See Darby.] Confronted as we are with the facts laid before Congress, we must conclude that it had a rational basis for finding that racial discrimination in restaurants had a direct and adverse effect on the free flow of interstate commerce. [We think] that Congress acted well within its power to protect and foster commerce in extending the coverage of Title II only to those restaurants offering to serve interstate travelers or serving food, a substantial portion of which has moved in interstate commerce. The absence of direct evidence connecting discriminatory restaurant service with the flow of interstate food, a factor on which the appellees place much reliance, is not, given the evidence as to the effect of such practices on other aspects of commerce, a crucial matter."

Justice BLACK's concurring opinion stated that not "every remote, possible, speculative effect on commerce" should be accepted "as an adequate constitutional ground to uproot and throw into the discard all our traditional distinctions between what is purely local [and] what affects the national interest." He insisted, moreover, that "some isolated and remote lunchroom which sells only to local people and buys almost all its supplies in the locality may possibly be beyond the reach of the [commerce] power of Congress." But here, "we do not consider the effect on interstate commerce of only one isolated, individual, local event, without regard to the fact that this single local event when added to many others of a similar nature may impose a burden on interstate commerce by reducing its volume or distorting its flow." Relying on the "aggregation" theory of Wickard, he found the application of the Act valid under the commerce power and therefore found it unnecessary to consider whether it was also "constitutionally supportable under Section 5 of the Fourteenth Amendment." [But five years later, in Daniel v. Paul, 395 U.S. 298 (1969), Justice Black was the sole dissenter when the Court upheld the Act as applied to the Lake Nixon Club near Little Rock, Arkansas. The club was a "232–acre amusement area with swimming, boating, sun bathing, picnicking, miniature golf, dancing facilities and a snack bar." Justice Brennan's majority opinion found the entire establishment covered by the Act because the snack bar was covered (under the rationale of McClung). Justice Black's dissent stated that he would have agreed with the result if the 1964 Act had been based on § 5 of the Fourteenth Amendment. But, since Congress had "tied the Act and limited its protection" to the commerce power, a finding was required that the Club's operation "affect commerce" within the meaning of the law; and to him, the lower courts' fact findings did not support application of the Act here. He objected to extending coverage of the Act to "this country people's recreation center, lying in what may be, so far as we know, a little 'sleepy hollow' between Arkansas hills miles away from any interstate highway. This would be stretching the Commerce Clause so as to give the Federal Government complete control over every little remote country place of recreation in every nook and cranny of every precinct and county in every one of the 50 States. This goes too far for me."]

Justice DOUGLAS's concurrence in McClung stated that he was "somewhat reluctant [to] rest solely on the Commerce Clause," because of his belief that the right to be free from discriminatory state action occupied a more protected constitutional position than the movement of goods across state lines. He explained: "The result reached by the Court is for me much more obvious as a protective measure under the Fourteenth Amendment than under the

Commerce Clause. [A] decision based on the Fourteenth Amendment would have a more settling effect, making unnecessary litigation over whether a particular restaurant [is] within the definitions of the Act or whether a particular customer is an interstate traveler. [Our] decision should be based on the [Fourteenth Amendment]." In his concurrence, Justice Goldberg also joined the Court's opinions in both Heart of Atlanta and McClung but emphasized that the primary purpose of the Act was "the vindication of human dignity and not mere economics." In his view, Congress "clearly had authority under both § 5 of the Fourteenth Amendment and the Commerce Clause" to enact the law.

Did the application of Title II to Ollie's Barbecue rest on persuasive commerce power justifications? Did the statutory coverage formula adequately mesh with the constitutional rationale? Did McClung persuasively link restaurant discrimination with the interstate flow of food? Was it more persuasive in viewing restaurant discrimination as an obstruction of interstate travel? Were more persuasive commerce power rationales available? Recall Perez, above: Could the McClung decision be justified on the ground that regulation of intrastate discrimination was necessary because of the difficulty of distinguishing discrimination which affects interstate commerce from that which does not? Could Congress have relied on the "superbootstrap" commerce-prohibiting technique? Recall the comments after Darby, p. 195 above.

The preceding cases, from Jones & Laughlin, Wickard v. Filburn, and Darby to McClung, suggested very few limits on congressional resorts to the commerce power. But the Lopez decision in 1995 (printed at p. 142 above and worth revisiting here) revealed a less lenient Court attitude toward congressional action. Are the limits articulated in Lopez consistent with the prior cases? What does Lopez portend for the future?

SECTION 4.   EXTERNAL LIMITS ON THE COMMERCE POWER: THE STATE AUTONOMY AND SOVEREIGNTY CONCERNS REFLECTED IN THE TENTH AND ELEVENTH AMENDMENTS

As the preceding materials illustrate, the reach of the commerce power, virtually unrestrained for the six decades after Jones & Laughlin in 1937, was curbed by the Lopez decision in 1995. Nevertheless, the congressional regulatory power regarding private activity remains broad, under rationales finding the activity either "in" or "affecting" interstate commerce. The central question in this section is whether a *state's* activities, even though they otherwise relate to commerce, are nevertheless immune from federal regulation, because of external limits stemming from the Tenth Amendment, the Eleventh Amendment, or other structural considerations drawn from the federal scheme.

During the four decades preceding 1976, the "state autonomy" barrier to congressional regulation found little receptivity on the Court. But in 1976, the Court for the first time in 40 years held that a federal law based on the commerce power but infringing on state autonomy was unconstitutional, in National League of Cities v. Usery, below. In a number of rulings of the early 1980s, the Court tried to clarify the standards of National League of Cities; in each case, the challenged federal law was upheld. Then, in 1985, in Garcia v. San Antonio Metropolitan Transit Authority, below, National League of Cities was overruled and the Court, for the time being, abandoned judicial efforts to impose a state autonomy restraint on Congress. But elements of the progeny of National League of Cities survived Garcia, as New York v. United States, below, illustrates. And more recently, the antifederalists revival on the Court that produced Lopez and New York v. United States also found expression in an interpretation of the Eleventh Amendment, which bars certain lawsuits against states, as Seminole Tribe of Florida v. Florida, below, indicates.

for national govt [or] for state rights ?????

1. *The Tenth Amendment limit on congressional authority.* The modern history of claims of state immunity from federal regulation begins with UNITED STATES v. CALIFORNIA, 297 U.S. 175 (1936). There, the Court upheld a penalty imposed on a state-owned railroad for violation of the Federal Safety Appliance Act. Justice STONE's opinion found it unnecessary to rule upon California's argument that its operation of a railroad involved the exercise of "a public function in its sovereign capacity." "The sovereign power of the states," he insisted, "is necessarily diminished to the extent of the grants of power to the federal government in the Constitution." He also rejected California's argument that the State could claim immunity from federal regulation for "activities in which the States have traditionally engaged," as it could in resisting federal taxation: "[T]here is no such limitation upon the plenary power to regulate commerce. The state can no more deny the power if its exercise has been authorized by Congress than can an individual." (Justice Rehnquist's majority opinion in National League of Cities sharply repudiated the thrust of that last sentence: "We think the dicta from United States v. California simply wrong.")

state not immune fm federal law
× not sovereign over pwrs (expressly) given to fed. govt in Const.
× no "traditional" basis argument

Until 1976, the Court consistently rejected challenges to federal regulations allegedly interfering with state autonomy. A significant dissent from that dismissive view of the state autonomy defense first surfaced in MARYLAND v. WIRTZ, (1968; p. 199 above). There, a 1966 amendment to the Fair Labor Standards Act, applying the law to employees of state-operated schools and hospitals, was upheld against a challenge that it interfered with the operations of state government. Justice DOUGLAS's dissent, joined by Justice Stewart, insisted that "what is done here [is] such a serious invasion of state sovereignty protected by the Tenth Amendment that it is in my belief not consistent with our constitutional federalism." In FRY v. UNITED STATES, 421 U.S. 542 (1975), the Court sustained the application of the Economic Stabilization Act to wage increases of public employees. Justice MARSHALL's majority opinion was a narrow one, emphasizing that the federal law was an emergency measure of limited scope. However, his opinion, in the first evidence of the Court's growing sensitivity to Tenth Amendment limits, acknowledged that the Amendment, though characterized as merely a "truism" in the Darby case, was "not without significance": "The Amendment expressly declares the constitutional policy that Congress may not exercise power in a fashion that impairs the States' integrity or their ability to function effectively in a federal system."

Darby case?

The state autonomy defense reached its modern zenith in NATIONAL LEAGUE OF CITIES v. USERY, 426 U.S. 833 (1976). That case involved still another amendment of the Fair Labor Standards Act. It extended the Act's maximum hour and minimum wage provisions to all employees of state and local governments. The 5-4 decision overruled the state autonomy aspect of Maryland v. Wirtz and held the extension unconstitutional. Justice REHNQUIST's majority opinion concluded that the law could not be applied to state employees performing traditional governmental functions. He argued that the law, which applied directly to "States *qua* States," would "impermissibly interfere [with] integral governmental functions": it would "significantly alter or displace the States' abilities to structure employer-employee relationships in such areas as fire prevention, police protection, sanitation, public health, and parks and recreation." Justice BLACKMUN joined Justice Rehnquist's opinion, even though he was "not untroubled by certain possible implications of the Court's opinion." He viewed the prevailing opinion as adopting "a balancing approach" that permitted federal regulation "in areas such as environmental protection, where the federal interest is demonstrably greater and where state facility compliance with imposed federal standards would be essential." Justice BRENNAN's dissent, joined by Justices White and Marshall, began with the emotional charge that the prevailing opinion repudiated "principles governing judicial interpretation of our Constitution settled since the time of Chief Justice John Marshall, discarding his postulate that the Constitution contemplates that restraints upon exercise by Congress of its plenary commerce power lie in the political process and not in the judicial process." Do you agree with Justice Brennan's charge that the Court had "turn[ed] aside longstanding constitutional jurisprudence"? Justice Brennan urged "[j]udicial restraint" by recognizing the fact that "the political branches of our Government are structured to protect the interests of the States as well as the Nation as a whole, and that the States are fully able to protect their own interests." Hence, he could not accept this "catastrophic judicial body blow at Congress' power under the Commerce Clause." (Justice STEVENS also submitted a dissent.)

In the early 1980s, however, the Court sustained applications of several federal laws, regularly rejecting challenges based on National League of Cities. HODEL v. VIRGINIA SURFACE MIN. & RECL. ASS'N, 452 U.S. 264 (1981), upheld a federal law regulating strip mining against a state autonomy challenge. Justice MARSHALL's opinion for the Court restated the National League of Cities standard as a three-part test. A challenger had to meet each of three criteria: "First, there must be a showing that the challenged statute regulates the 'States as States.' Second, the federal regulation must address matters that are indisputably 'attributes of state sovereignty.' And third, it must be apparent that the States' compliance with the federal law would directly impair their ability 'to structure integral operations in areas of traditional governmental functions.'" In a footnote, the Court suggested a fourth factor: even if a Tenth Amendment challenge satisfied this three-part test, it might not succeed because "the federal interest advanced may be such that it justifies state submission" (the footnote cited the balancing test in Justice Blackmun's National League of Cities concurrence). Justice Marshall's opinion rejecting the challenge in Hodel contained an aside that was to prove important in later cases. He noted that the law here did not "commandeer[ ] the legislative processes of the States by directly compelling them to enact and enforce a federal regulatory program." (Compare Justice O'Connor's opinions in FERC v. Mississippi and New York v. United States, both below.) In UNITED TRANSPORTATION UNION v. LONG ISLAND RAILROAD CO., 455 U.S. 678 (1982), the Court unanimously rejected a state autonomy challenge to the application of the Railway Labor Act to the state-owned Long Island Railroad. The Court found the third part of the Hodel test not satisfied because there was no interference with "traditional [state] functions": operation of railroads had "traditionally been a function of private industry." In EEOC v. WYOMING, 460 U.S. 226 (1983), the Court upheld a 1974 amendment to the Age Discrimination in Employment Act extending the law to state employees. Justice Blackmun joined the four dissenters in National League of Cities to form the majority. Justice BRENNAN's majority opinion concluded that "the degree of federal intrusion in this case is sufficiently less serious than it was in National League of Cities" and that there was no showing of a "potential impact of the [federal scheme] on the States' ability to structure operations and set priorities over a wide range of decisions."

One additional case decided under the regime of National League of Cities, FERC v. MISSISSIPPI, 456 U.S. 742 (1982), is worth noting. The FERC ruling rejected a constitutional challenge to portions of the Public Utility Regulatory Policies Act of 1978 (PURPA). The Act, designed to combat a nationwide energy crisis, sought to encourage conservation of oil and natural gas by utilities in order to lessen the nation's dependence on foreign oil. Portions of the law directed state utilities commissions to "consider" the adoption of specific federal "rate design" and regulatory standards. The state agencies were not required to follow the federal standards, but they were required to "consider" them. Moreover, they were compelled to adopt certain procedures in proceedings held to consider the adoption of federal standards. Justice BLACKMUN's majority opinion upheld the mandatory consideration requirement on the ground that Congress "could have pre-empted the field" entirely; accordingly, "PURPA should not be invalid simply because, out of deference to state authority, Congress adopted a less intrusive scheme and allowed the states to continue regulating in the area on the condition that they *consider* the suggested federal standards."

Justice O'CONNOR's dissent, joined by Chief Justice Burger and Justice Rehnquist, objected that the challenged provisions "conscript state utility commissions into the national bureaucratic army," an objection similar to the "commandeering" concern noted in passing in Hodel, above. In her view, the mandatory consideration provisions interfered with the State's sovereign authority to set its own agenda for consideration of issues of public policy. She called the "choice" left to the States for escaping PURPA—"simply by ceasing regulation of public utilities"—"an absurdity. [T]here is nothing 'cooperative' about a federal program that compels state agencies either to function as bureaucratic puppets of the Federal Government or to abandon regulation of an entire field traditionally reserved to state authority." She argued, moreover, that PURPA was not "less intrusive than pre-emption";[1] indeed, the States "might well prefer that Congress simply impose the standards described in PURPA; this, at least, would leave them free to exercise their power in other areas." (Justice POWELL also dissented in part.)

GARCIA v. SAN ANTONIO METROPOLITAN TRANSIT AUTHORITY, 469 U.S. 528 (1985): In Garcia, Justice BLACKMUN, who had concurred in National League of Cities in 1976, wrote the majority opinion overruling that decision. The case involved the subjection of the Transit Authority to the minimum-wage and overtime requirements of the Fair Labor Standards Act. In holding that application constitutional, Justice Blackmun found that the aftermath of National League of Cities demonstrated that the effort to articulate the boundaries of state regulatory immunity in terms of "traditional governmental functions" was "unworkable." After reviewing the rulings that showed that "this Court itself has made little headway in defining the scope of the governmental functions being protected under National League of Cities,"

---

1. Justice O'Connor added: "In 1975, then Attorney General Edward H. Levi responded to a similar argument that the 'greater' power of preemption includes the 'lesser' power of demanding affirmative action from state governments. Attorney General Levi remarked that 'it is an insidious point to say that there is more federalism by compelling a State instrumentality to work for the Federal Government.'" Levi's comments came while he announced the Justice Department's opposition to a proposed federal no-fault insurance law that would have compelled the states to enact and implement no-fault laws. For an endorsement of the Justice Department's position, see Kaden, "Politics, Money, and State Sovereignty: The Judicial Role," 79 Colum.L.Rev. 847 (1979). (On preemption of state power by commerce clause regulation and the Supremacy Clause, see chap. 5 below.)

Justice Blackmun turned to "a more fundamental problem": "[The] problem is that [no distinction] that purports to separate out important governmental functions can be faithful to the role of federalism in a democratic society. [Any] rule of state immunity that looks to the 'traditional,' 'integral,' or 'necessary' nature of governmental functions inevitably invites an unelected federal judiciary to make decisions about which state policies it favors and which one it dislikes. [We] therefore now reject, as unsound in principle and unworkable in practice, a rule of state immunity from federal regulation that turns on a judicial appraisal of whether a particular governmental function is 'integral' or 'traditional.' "

Although Justice Blackmun recognized that there are "limits on the Federal Government's power to interfere with state functions," he insisted that, ordinarily, imposing such limits was not the business of the Court: "Apart from the limitation of federal authority inherent in the delegated nature of Congress' Article I powers, the principal means chosen by the Framers to insure the role of the States in the federal system lies in the structure of the federal government itself." Citing Choper and Wechsler (recall chap. 2 above), he added: "It is no novelty to observe that the composition of the Federal Government was designed in large part to protect the States from overreaching by Congress." He added: "States' sovereign interests [are] more properly protected by procedural safeguards inherent in the structure of the federal system than by judicially created limitations on federal power. [Any] substantive restraint on the exercise of Commerce Clause powers [must] be tailored to compensate for possible failings in the national political process rather than to dictate a 'sacred province of state autonomy.' [The] principal and basic limit on the federal commerce power is that inherent in all congressional action—the built-in restraints that our system provides through state participation in federal governmental action. The political process insures that laws that unduly burden the States will not be promulgated."

Justice POWELL, joined by Chief Justice Burger and Justices Rehnquist and O'Connor, dissented. In the course of concluding that the majority's position "reject[ed] the basic precepts of our federal system and limit[ed] the constitutional role of judicial review," he challenged the majority's claim that the National League of Cities standard "disserves principles of democratic self government." He claimed that "the Court looks myopically only to persons elected to positions in the federal government. It disregards entirely the far more effective role of democratic self-government at the state and local levels. [Federal] legislation is drafted primarily by the staffs of the congressional committees. In view of the hundreds of bills introduced at each session of Congress and the complexity of many of them, it is virtually impossible for even the most conscientious legislators to be truly familiar with many of the statutes enacted. Federal departments and agencies customarily are authorized to write regulations. [As] is true of the original legislation, these are drafted largely by staff personnel. The administration and enforcement of federal laws and regulations necessarily are largely in the hands of staff and civil service employees. These employees may have little or no knowledge of the States and localities that will be affected by the statutes and regulations for which they are responsible. In any case, they hardly are as accessible and responsive as those who occupy analogous positions in State and local governments. In drawing this contrast, I imply no criticism of these federal employees or the officials who are ultimately in charge. [My] point is simply that members of the immense federal bureaucracy are not elected, know less about the services traditionally rendered by States and localities, and are inevitably less responsive to recipients of such services, than are state legislatures, city councils, boards of supervisors, and state and local commissions, boards, and agencies. It is at these state and local levels—not in Washington as the Court so mistakenly thinks—that 'democratic self-government' is best exemplified."[2]

Justice O'CONNOR's dissent, joined by Justices Powell and Rehnquist stated: "In my view, federalism cannot be reduced to the weak 'essence' distilled by the majority today. [The] true 'essence' of federalism is that the States *as States* have legitimate interests which the National Government is bound to respect even though its laws are supreme. If federalism so conceived [is] to remain meaningful, this Court cannot abdicate its constitutional responsibility to oversee the Federal Government's compliance with its duty to respect the legitimate interests of the States." She added: "The last two decades have seen an unprecedented growth of federal regulatory activity, as the majority itself acknowledges. In 1954, one could still speak of a 'burden of persuasion on those favoring national intervention.' [Wechsler.] Today, as federal legislation and coercive grant programs have expanded to embrace innumerable activities that were once viewed as local, the burden of persuasion has surely shifted, and the extraordinary has become ordinary. The political process has not protected against these encroachments on state activities [as in the EEOC and FERC cases], even though they directly impinge on a State's ability to make and enforce its laws. With the abandonment of National League of Cities, all that stands between the remaining essentials of state sovereignty and Congress is the latter's underdeveloped capacity for self-restraint. The problems of federalism in an integrated national economy are capable of more responsible resolution than holding that the States as States retain no status apart from that which Congress chooses to let them retain. The proper resolution, I suggest, lies in weighing state autonomy as a factor in the balance when interpreting the means by which Congress can exercise its authority on the States as States. It is insufficient, in assessing the validity of congressional regulation of a State pursuant to the commerce power, to ask only whether the same regulation would be valid if enforced against a private party. That reasoning, embodied in the majority opinion, is inconsistent with the spirit of our Constitution. It remains relevant that a *State* is being regulated. [If] state autonomy is ignored in assessing the means by which Congress regulates matters affecting commerce, then federalism becomes irrelevant simply because the set of activities remaining beyond the reach of such a commerce power 'may well be negligible.'" Justice REHNQUIST's very brief dissent stated: "I do not think it incumbent on those of us in dissent to spell out further the fine points of principle that will, I am confident, in time again command the support of the majority of this Court." (Justice O'Connor's dissent stated that she shared Justice Rehnquist's belief.)

2. *The protection of state autonomy after Garcia.* a. The Garcia majority indicated that the only remaining state autonomy limit on the commerce power is "one of process rather than one of result." Any "substantive restraint" on the commerce power "must find its justification in the procedural nature of this basic limitation, and it must be tailored to compensate for possible failings in

2. In a footnote elsewhere in the opinion, Justice Powell noted: "The Court [does not] identify the circumstances in which the 'political process' may fail and 'affirmative limits' are to be imposed. Presumably, such limits are to be determined by the Judicial Branch even though it is 'unelected.' Today's opinion, however, has rejected the balancing standard and suggests no other standard that would enable a court to determine when there has been a malfunction of the 'political process.' The Court's failure to specify the 'affirmative limits' on federal power, or when and how these limits are to be determined, may well be explained by the transparent fact that any such attempt would be subject to precisely the same objections on which it relies to overrule National League of Cities."

the national political process." Is this likely to be an effective, judicially enforceable limit? The Court has considered such a "failings in the political process" limit only once since Garcia. In SOUTH CAROLINA v. BAKER, 485 U.S. 505 (1988), the Court held that the federal income tax could be imposed on interest from bearer bonds issued by the states. The effect of this removal of the tax exemption was to bar states from issuing bearer bonds and to require them to issue registered bonds (which remained tax-exempt) in order to raise debt capital. Nevertheless, the Court rejected the State's argument that this was one of those situations in which state interests were impaired because of "extraordinary defects in the national political process." Justice BRENNAN's majority opinion noted the possibility of such a limit under Garcia, but recalled that Garcia itself "had no occasion to identify or define the defects that might lead to such invalidation." He added: "Nor do we attempt any definitive articulation here. It suffices to observe that South Carolina has not even alleged that it was deprived of any right to participate in the national political process or that it was singled out in a way that left it politically isolated and powerless. Rather, South Carolina argues that the political process failed here because [the law repealing some tax exemptions] was 'imposed by a vote of an uninformed Congress relying upon incomplete information.' But nothing in Garcia or the Tenth Amendment authorizes courts to second-guess the substantive basis for congressional legislation. Where, as here, the national political *process* did not operate in a defective manner, the Tenth Amendment is not implicated." In the course of his opinion, Justice Brennan also voiced doubts that the "commandeering" concern voiced in FERC v. Mississippi survived Garcia. But see New York v. United States, below. (Justice O'CONNOR dissented; Chief Justice REHNQUIST and Justice SCALIA submitted separate concurring opinions.)

For the suggestion that the "procedural" limit of Garcia may indeed prove fruitful, see Rapaczynski, "From Sovereignty to Process: The Jurisprudence of Federalism After Garcia," 1985 Sup.Ct.Rev. 341. He suggests that "the process-oriented analysis of the constitutional functions of federalism, endorsed but not really carried out in the Garcia decision, leads to a more affirmative procedural role of the States within the federal system than suggested on the face of [Garcia]." He notes that two important functions of the States ("tyranny prevention" and "the provision of a space for participatory politics") "are likely to be endangered by the national government and warrant a close judicial scrutiny of federal interference with state and local governmental operations." In the course of developing the doctrinal implications of his process-oriented approach to federalism, he notes that "there are some state governmental functions so directly related to the federalist concern with preventing tyranny" that they "present rather easy cases for judicial intervention": "for example, federal interference with the agenda of the highest state legislative [and] executive organs." With respect to the "state's function of enhancing participation," moreover, he notes that, "given the special participatory mode in which school boards operate in most states, a federal education law that would attempt to transform those boards into an extension of the federal bureaucratic machinery would strike at the very core of participatory politics."

New York v. United States

505 U.S. 144, 112 S.Ct. 2408, 120 L.Ed.2d 120 (1992).

Justice O'CONNOR delivered the opinion of the Court.

This case implicates one of our Nation's newest problems of public policy and perhaps our oldest question of constitutional law. The public policy issue involves the disposal of radioactive waste: In this case, we address the constitutionality of three provisions of the Low–Level Radioactive Waste Policy Amendments Act of 1985. The constitutional question is as old as the Constitution: It consists of discerning the proper division of authority between the Federal Government and the States. We conclude that while Congress has substantial power under the Constitution to encourage the States to provide for the disposal of the radioactive waste generated within their borders, the Constitution does not confer upon Congress the ability simply to compel the States to do so. We therefore find that only two of the Act's three provisions at issue are [constitutional].

[The challenged law was enacted when Congress confronted an impending shortage, in 31 states, of disposal sites for low level radioactive waste. The law imposed upon states the obligation to provide for the disposal of waste generated within their borders and contained three provisions providing "incentives" to states to comply with that obligation. (1) The first set of incentives—the monetary incentives—involved three steps: (a) states with disposal sites are authorized to impose a surcharge on radioactive waste received from other states; (b) the Secretary of Energy collects a portion of this surcharge in places it in a trust account; and (c) states achieving a series of milestones in developing sites receive a portion of this fund. The second set of incentives—the access incentives—authorizes sited states and regional contracts gradually to increase the cost of access to their sites and then to deny access altogether to waste generated in states that do not meet federal deadlines. The third incentive—the "take title" provision—provides that a state that fails to provide for the disposal of all internally generated waste by a particular date must in most cases take title to and possession of the waste and become liable for all damages suffered by the waste's generator or owner as a result of the state's failure to promptly take possession. This suit arose when New York and two of its counties sought a declaratory judgment that the three incentive provisions were unconstitutional as, inter alia, exceeding the delegated powers of Congress and as violating the Tenth Amendment. The lower courts dismissed the complaint, but the Court held the third incentive—the "take title" provision— unconstitutional (while upholding the first two incentives).]

II. A. [T]he task of ascertaining the constitutional line between federal and state power has given rise to many of the Court's most difficult and celebrated cases. [Federalism] questions can be viewed in either of two ways. In some cases the Court has inquired whether an Act of Congress is authorized by one of the powers delegated to Congress in Article I of the Constitution. In other cases the Court has sought to determine whether an Act of Congress invades the province of state sovereignty reserved by the Tenth Amendment. In a case like this one, [the] two inquiries are mirror images of each other. If a power is delegated to Congress in the Constitution, the Tenth Amendment expressly disclaims any reservation of that power to the States; if a power is an attribute of state sovereignty reserved by the Tenth Amendment, it is necessarily a power the Constitution has not conferred on Congress. It is in this sense that the Tenth Amendment "states but a truism that all is retained which has not been surrendered." [Darby.]

Congress exercises its conferred powers subject to the limitations contained in the Constitution. Thus, [under] the Commerce Clause Congress may regulate publishers engaged in interstate commerce, but Congress is constrained in the exercise of that power by the First Amendment. The Tenth Amendment likewise restrains the power of Congress, but this limit is not derived from the text of the Tenth Amendment itself, which [is] essentially a tautology. Instead, the Tenth Amendment confirms that the power of the Federal Government is subject to limits that may, in a given instance, reserve power to the States. The Tenth Amendment thus directs us to determine, as in this case, whether an incident of state sovereignty is protected by a limitation on an Article I power.

The benefits of this federal structure have been extensively catalogued elsewhere, see, e.g., Merritt, The Guarantee Clause and State Autonomy: Federalism for a Third Century, 88 Colum.L. Rev. 1 (1988); McConnell, Federalism: Evaluating the Founders' Design, 54 U. Chi. L. Rev. 1484 (1987), but they need not concern us here. Our task consists not of devising our preferred system of government, but of understanding and applying the framework set forth in the Constitution. [This] framework has been sufficiently flexible over the past two centuries to allow for enormous changes in the nature of government. The Federal Government undertakes activities today that would have been unimaginable to the Framers in two senses; first, because the Framers would not have conceived that any government would conduct such activities; and second, because the Framers would not have believed that the Federal Government, rather than the States, would assume such responsibilities. Yet the powers conferred upon the Federal Government by the Constitution were phrased in language broad enough to allow for the expansion of the Federal Government's role. Among the provisions of the Constitution that have been particularly important in this regard, three concern us here. First, the Constitution allocates to Congress the power "to regulate Commerce [among] the several States." [The] volume of interstate commerce and the range of commonly accepted objects of government regulation [have] expanded considerably in the last 200 years, and the regulatory authority of Congress has expanded along with them. As interstate commerce has become ubiquitous, activities once considered purely local have come to have effects on the national economy, and have accordingly come within the scope of Congress' commerce power. See [McClung; Wickard.] Second, the Constitution authorizes Congress "to pay the Debts and provide for [the] general Welfare of the United States." Art. I, § 8, cl. 1. As conventional notions of the proper objects of government spending have changed over the years, so has the ability of Congress to "fix the terms on which it shall disburse federal money to the States." Compare, e.g., United States v. Butler [1936; p. 235 below] with South Dakota v. Dole [1987; p. 244 below] (spending power permits Congress to condition highway funds on States' adoption of minimum drinking age). While the spending power is "subject to several general restrictions articulated in our cases," these restrictions have not been so severe as to prevent the regulatory authority of Congress from generally keeping up with the growth of the federal budget. [Finally,] the Constitution provides [the Supremacy Clause]. As the Federal Government's willingness to exercise power within the confines of the Constitution has grown, the authority of the States has correspondingly diminished to the extent that federal and state policies have conflicted. [The] actual scope of the Federal Government's authority with respect to the States has changed over the years, therefore, but the constitutional structure underlying and limiting that authority [has not].

B. Petitioners do not contend that Congress lacks the power to regulate the disposal of low level radioactive waste. Regulation of [the] resulting interstate market in waste disposal [is] well within Congress' authority under the Commerce Clause. Petitioners likewise do not dispute that under the Supremacy Clause Congress could, if it wished, pre-empt state radioactive waste regulation. Petitioners contend only that the Tenth Amendment limits the power of Congress to regulate in the way it has chosen. Rather than addressing the problem of waste disposal by directly regulating the generators and disposers of waste, petitioners argue, Congress has impermissibly directed the States to regulate in this field.

Most of our recent cases interpreting the Tenth Amendment have concerned the authority of Congress to subject state governments to generally applicable laws. This case presents no occasion to apply or revisit the holdings of any of these cases, as this is not a case in which Congress has subjected a State to the same legislation applicable to private parties. Cf. [FERC v. Mississippi]. This case instead concerns the circumstances under which Congress may use the States as implements of regulation; that is, whether Congress may direct or otherwise motivate the States to regulate in a particular field or a particular way. Our cases have established a few principles that guide our resolution of the issue.

1. As an initial matter, Congress may not simply "commandeer the legislative processes of the States by directly compelling them to enact and enforce a federal regulatory program." [Hodel; see also FERC]. [T]he Constitution has never been understood to confer upon Congress the ability to require the States to govern according to Congress' instructions. Indeed, the question whether the Constitution should permit Congress to employ state governments as regulatory agencies was a topic of lively debate among the Framers. Under the Articles of Confederation, Congress lacked the authority in most respects to govern the people directly. [The] inadequacy of this governmental structure was responsible in part for the Constitutional Convention. Alexander Hamilton observed: "The great and radical vice in the construction of the existing Confederation is in the principle of LEGISLATION for STATES or GOVERNMENTS, in their CORPORATE or COLLECTIVE CAPACITIES, and as contra-distinguished from the INDIVIDUALS of whom they consist." The Federalist No. 15. As Hamilton saw it, "[we] must extend the authority of the Union to the persons of the citizens—the only proper objects of government." [The] Convention generated a great number of proposals for the structure of the new Government, but two quickly took center stage. Under the Virginia Plan, [Congress] would exercise legislative authority directly upon individuals, without employing the States as intermediaries. Under the New Jersey Plan, [Congress] would continue to require the approval of the States before legislating, as [under] the Articles of Confederation. These two plans [remained] the two primary options discussed by the delegates. One frequently expressed objection to the New Jersey Plan was that it might require the Federal Government to coerce the States into implementing legislation. [Under] one preliminary draft of what would become the New Jersey Plan, state governments would occupy a position relative to Congress similar to that contemplated by the Act at issue in this case: "The laws of the United States ought, as far as may be consistent with the common interests of the Union, to be carried into execution by the judiciary and executive officers of the respective states, wherein the execution thereof is required." This idea apparently never even progressed so far as to be debated by the [delegates]. In the end, the Convention opted for a Constitution in which Congress would exercise its legislative authority directly over individuals rather than [over States]. This choice was made clear to the subsequent state ratifying conventions. In providing for a stronger central government, therefore, the Framers explicitly chose a Constitution that confers upon Congress the power to regulate individuals, not States. [We] have always understood that even where Congress has the authority under the Constitution to pass laws requiring or prohibiting certain acts, it lacks the power directly to compel the States to require or prohibit those acts. E.g., [FERC v. Mississippi; Hodel]. The allocation of power contained in the

Commerce Clause, for example, authorizes Congress to regulate interstate commerce directly; it does not authorize Congress to regulate state governments' regulation of interstate commerce.

2.   This is not to say that Congress lacks the ability to encourage a State to regulate in a particular way, or that Congress may not hold out incentives to the States as a method of influencing a State's policy choices. Our cases have identified a variety of methods, short of outright coercion, by which Congress may urge a State to adopt a legislative program consistent with federal interests. Two of these methods are of particular relevance here. First, under Congress' spending power, "Congress may attach conditions on the receipt of federal funds." South Dakota v. Dole. Such conditions must (among other requirements) bear some relationship to the purpose of the federal spending; otherwise, [the] spending power could render academic the Constitution's other grants and limits of federal authority. Where the recipient of federal funds is a State, as is not unusual today, the conditions attached to the funds by Congress may influence a State's legislative choices. See Kaden, Politics, Money, and State Sovereignty: The Judicial Role, 79 Colum. L. Rev. 847 (1979). Dole was one such [case]. [Second,] where Congress has the authority to regulate private activity under the Commerce Clause, we have recognized Congress' power to offer States the choice of regulating that activity according to federal standards or having state law pre-empted by federal regulation. [Hodel.] By either of these two methods, [the] residents of the State retain the ultimate decision as to whether or not the State will comply. If a State's citizens view federal policy as sufficiently contrary to local interests, they may elect to decline a federal grant. If state residents would prefer their government to devote its attention and resources to problems other than those deemed important by Congress, they may choose to have the Federal Government rather than the State bear the expense of a federally mandated regulatory program, and they may continue to supplement that program to the extent state law is not preempted. Where Congress encourages state regulation rather than compelling it, state governments remain responsive to the local electorate's preferences; state officials remain accountable to the people. By contrast, where the Federal Government compels States to regulate, the accountability of both state and federal officials is diminished. If the citizens of New York, for example, do not consider that making provision for the disposal of radioactive waste is in their best interest, they may elect state officials who share their view. That view can always be preempted under the Supremacy Clause if is contrary to the national view, but in such a case it is the Federal Government that makes the decision in full view of the public, and it will be federal officials that suffer the consequences if the decision turns out to be detrimental or unpopular. But where the Federal Government directs the States to regulate, it may be state officials who will bear the brunt of public disapproval, while the federal officials who devised the regulatory program may remain insulated from the electoral ramifications of their decision. Accountability is thus diminished when, due to federal coercion, elected state officials cannot regulate in accordance with the views of the local electorate in matters not pre-empted by federal regulation. [See, e.g., La Pierre, Political Accountability in the National Political Process—The Alternative to Judicial Review of Federalism Issues, 80 Nw. U. L. Rev. 577 (1985).]

III.   A. [The] first set of incentives works in three steps. First, Congress has authorized States with disposal sites to impose a surcharge on radioactive waste received from other States. Second, the Secretary of Energy collects a portion of this surcharge and places the money in an escrow account. Third, States achieving a series of milestones receive portions of this fund. The first of these steps is an unexceptionable exercise of Congress' power to authorize the

States to burden interstate commerce. While the Commerce Clause has long been understood to limit the States' ability to discriminate against interstate commerce, that limit may be lifted [by] an expression of the "unambiguous intent" of Congress. [E.g., Prudential Ins. Co. v. Benjamin (1946); chap. 5 below.] The second step, the Secretary's collection of a percentage of the surcharge, is no more than a federal tax on interstate commerce, which petitioners do not claim to be an invalid exercise of either Congress' commerce or taxing power. The third step is a conditional exercise of Congress' authority under the Spending Clause: Congress has placed conditions—the achievement of the milestones—on the receipt of federal funds. Petitioners do not contend that Congress has exceeded its authority in any of the four respects our cases have identified. See generally [Dole]. [Because] the first set of incentives is supported by affirmative constitutional grants of power to Congress, it is not inconsistent with the Tenth Amendment.

B. In the second set of incentives, Congress has authorized States and regional compacts with disposal sites gradually to increase the cost of access to the sites, and then to deny access altogether, to radioactive waste generated in States that do not meet federal deadlines. As a simple regulation, this provision would be within the power of Congress to authorize the States to discriminate against interstate commerce. Where federal regulation of private activity is within the scope of the Commerce Clause, we have recognized the ability of Congress to offer states the choice of regulating that activity according to federal standards or having state law pre-empted by federal regulation. See [Hodel]. This is the choice presented to non-sited States by the Act's second set of incentives: States may either regulate the disposal of radioactive waste according to federal standards by attaining local or regional self-sufficiency, or their residents who produce radioactive waste will be subject to federal regulation authorizing sited States and regions to deny access to their disposal sites. The affected States are not compelled by Congress to regulate, because any burden caused by a State's refusal to regulate will fall on those who generate waste and find no outlet for its disposal, rather than on the State as a sovereign. A State whose citizens do not wish it to attain the Act's milestones may devote its attention and its resources to issues its citizens deem more worthy; the choice remains at all times with the residents of the State, not with Congress. The State need not expend any funds, or participate in any federal program, if local residents do not view such expenditures or participation as worthwhile. Nor must the State abandon the field if it does not accede to federal direction; the State may continue to regulate the generation and disposal of radioactive waste in any manner its citizens see fit. The Act's second set of incentives thus represents a conditional exercise of Congress' commerce power, along the lines of those we have held to be within Congress' [authority].

C. The take title provision is of a different character. This third so-called "incentive" offers States, as an alternative to regulating pursuant to Congress' direction, the option of taking title to and possession of the low level radioactive waste generated within their borders and becoming liable for all damages waste generators suffer as a result of the States' failure to do so promptly. In this provision, Congress has crossed the line distinguishing encouragement from coercion. [The] take title provision offers state governments a "choice" of either accepting ownership of waste or regulating according to the instructions of Congress. Respondents do not claim that the Constitution would authorize Congress to impose either option as a freestanding requirement. On one hand, the Constitution would not permit Congress simply to transfer radioactive waste from generators to state governments. Such a forced transfer, standing alone, would in principle be no different than a congressionally compelled subsidy from state governments to radioactive waste producers. The same is true of the provision requiring the States to become liable for the generators' damages. Standing alone, this provision would be indistinguishable from an Act of Congress directing the States to assume the liabilities of certain state residents. Either type of federal action would "commandeer" state governments into the service of federal regulatory purposes, and would for this reason be inconsistent with the Constitution's division of authority between federal and state governments. On the other hand, the second alternative held out to state governments—regulating pursuant to Congress' direction—would, standing alone, present a simple command to state governments to implement legislation enacted by Congress. As we have seen, the Constitution does not empower Congress to subject state governments to this type of instruction.

Because an instruction to state governments to take title to waste, standing alone, would be beyond the authority of Congress, and because a direct order to regulate, standing alone, would also be beyond the authority of Congress, it follows that Congress lacks the power to offer the States a choice between the two. Unlike the first two sets of incentives, the take title incentive does not represent the conditional exercise of any congressional power enumerated in the Constitution. In this provision, Congress has not held out the threat of exercising its spending power or its commerce power; it has instead held out the threat, should the States not regulate according to one federal instruction, of simply forcing the States to submit to another federal instruction. A choice between two unconstitutionally coercive regulatory techniques is no choice at all. Either way, "the Act commandeers the legislative processes of the States by directly compelling them to enact and enforce a federal regulatory program" [Hodel], an outcome that has never been understood to lie within the authority conferred upon Congress by the Constitution. Respondents emphasize the latitude given to the States to implement Congress' plan. The Act enables the States to regulate pursuant to Congress' instructions in any number of different ways. States may avoid taking title by contracting with sited regional compacts, by building a disposal site alone or as part of a compact, or by permitting private parties to build a disposal site. States that host sites may employ a wide range of designs and disposal methods, subject only to broad federal regulatory limits. This line of reasoning, however, only underscores the critical alternative a State lacks: A State may not decline to administer the federal program. No matter which path the State chooses, it must follow the direction of Congress. The take title provision appears to be unique. No other federal statute has been cited which offers a state government no option other than that of implementing legislation enacted by Congress. Whether one views the take title provision as lying outside Congress' enumerated powers, or as infringing upon the core of state sovereignty reserved by the Tenth Amendment, the provision is inconsistent with the federal structure of our Government established by the Constitution.

IV. Respondents raise a number of objections to this understanding of the limits of Congress' power. A. [First,] the United States argues that the Constitution's prohibition of congressional directives to state governments can be overcome where the federal interest is sufficiently important to justify state submission. This argument contains a kernel of truth: In determining whether the Tenth Amendment limits the ability of Congress to subject state governments to generally applicable laws, the Court has in some cases stated that it will evaluate the strength of federal interests in light of the degree to which such laws would prevent the State from functioning as a sovereign; that is, the extent to which such generally applicable laws would impede a state government's responsibility to represent and be accountable to the citizens of the

State. But whether or not a particularly strong federal interest enables Congress to bring state governments within the orbit of generally applicable federal regulation, no Member of the Court has ever suggested that such a federal interest would enable Congress to command a state government to enact state regulation. No matter how powerful the federal interest involved, the Constitution simply does not give Congress the authority to require the States to regulate. The Constitution instead gives Congress the authority to regulate matters directly and to pre-empt contrary state regulation. Where a federal interest is sufficiently strong to cause Congress to legislate, it must do so directly; it may not conscript state governments as its agents. Second, the United States argues that the Constitution does, in some circumstances, permit federal directives to state governments. Various cases are cited for this proposition, but none support it. Some of these cases discuss the well established power of Congress to pass laws enforceable in state courts. See Testa v. Katt, 330 U.S. 386 (1947). These cases involve no more than an application of the Supremacy Clause's provision that federal law "shall be the supreme Law of the Land," enforceable in every State. More to the point, all involve congressional regulation of individuals, not congressional requirements that States regulate. Federal statutes enforceable in state courts do, in a sense, direct state judges to enforce them, but this sort of federal "direction" of state judges is mandated by the text of the Supremacy Clause. No comparable constitutional provision authorizes Congress to command state legislatures to legislate.

Third, the United States [argues] that the Constitution envisions a role for Congress as an arbiter of interstate disputes. The United States observes that federal courts [have] frequently resolved conflicts among States. Many of these disputes have involved the allocation of shared resources among the States, a category perhaps broad enough to encompass the allocation of scarce disposal space for radioactive waste. The United States suggests that if the Court may resolve such interstate disputes, Congress can surely do the same under the Commerce Clause. [While] the Framers no doubt endowed Congress with the power to regulate interstate commerce in order to avoid further instances of the interstate trade disputes that were common under the Articles of Confederation, the Framers did not intend that Congress should exercise that power through the mechanism of mandating state regulation. The Constitution established Congress as "a superintending authority over the reciprocal trade" among the States, The Federalist No. 42, by empowering Congress to regulate that trade directly, not by authorizing Congress to issue trade-related orders to state governments. As Madison and Hamilton explained, "a sovereignty over sovereigns, a government over governments, a legislation for communities, as contradistinguished from individuals, as it is a solecism in theory, so in practice it is subversive of the order and ends of civil polity." Id., No. 20.

B. The sited State respondents focus their attention on the process by which the Act was formulated. They correctly observe that public officials representing [New York] lent their support to the Act's enactment. Respondents note that the Act embodies a bargain among the sited and unsited States, a compromise to which New York was a willing participant and from which New York has reaped much benefit. Respondents then pose what appears at first to be a troubling question: How can a federal statute be found an unconstitutional infringement of State sovereignty when state officials consented to the statute's enactment? The answer follows from an understanding of the fundamental purpose served by our Government's federal structure. The Constitution does not protect the sovereignty of States for the benefit of the States or state governments as abstract political entities, or even for the benefit of the public officials governing the States. To the contrary, the Constitution

power of the people

State sovereignty is the means to an end

(recall Advisory opinions)

divides authority between federal and state governments for the protection of individuals. State sovereignty is not just an end in itself: "Rather, federalism secures to citizens the liberties that derive from the diffusion of sovereign power." Where Congress exceeds its authority relative to the States, therefore, the departure from the constitutional plan cannot be ratified by the "consent" of state officials. An analogy to the separation of powers among the Branches of the Federal Government clarifies this point. The Constitution's division of power among the three Branches is violated where one Branch invades the territory of another, whether or not the encroached-upon Branch approves the encroachment. [The Court cited Buckley v. Valeo (1976) and INS v. Chadha (1983), both in chap. 6 below.] The constitutional authority of Congress cannot be expanded by the "consent" of the governmental unit whose domain is thereby narrowed, whether that unit is the Executive Branch or the States. State officials thus cannot consent to the enlargement of the powers of Congress beyond those enumerated in the Constitution. Indeed, the facts of this case raise the possibility that powerful incentives might lead both federal and state officials to view departures from the federal structure to be in their personal interests. Most citizens recognize the need for radioactive waste disposal sites, but few want sites near their homes. As a result, while it would be well within the authority of either federal or state officials to choose where the disposal sites will be, it is likely to be in the political interest of each individual official to avoid being held accountable to the voters for the choice of location. If a federal official is faced with the alternatives of choosing a location or directing the States to do it, the official may well prefer the latter, as a means of shifting responsibility for the eventual decision. If a state official is faced with the same set of alternatives—choosing a location or having Congress direct the choice of a location—the state official may also prefer the latter, as it may permit the avoidance of personal responsibility. The interests of public officials thus may not coincide with the Constitution's intergovernmental allocation of authority. Where state officials purport to submit to the direction of Congress in this manner, federalism is hardly being [advanced].

Guarantee Clause:

V. Petitioners also contend that the Act is inconsistent with the Constitution's Guarantee Clause [Art. IV, § 4]. Because we have found the take title provision [unconstitutional], we need only address the applicability of the Guarantee Clause to the Act's other two challenged provisions. We approach the issue with some trepidation, because the Guarantee Clause has been an infrequent basis for litigation throughout our history. In most of the cases in which the Court has been asked to apply the Clause, the Court has [usually] found the claims presented to be nonjusticiable under the "political question" doctrine. [Recall chap. 1 above.] [Contemporary] commentators [have] suggested that courts should address the merits of such claims, at least in some circumstances. We need not resolve this difficult question today. Even if we assume that petitioners' claim is justiciable, neither the monetary incentives provided by the Act nor the possibility that a State's waste producers may find themselves excluded from the disposal sites of another State can reasonably be said to deny any State a republican form of government.

VII. [After finding the take title provision severable, so that "we may leave the remainder of the Act in force," the Court continued:] Some truths are so basic that, like the air around us, they are easily overlooked. Much of the Constitution is concerned with setting forth the form of our government, and the courts have traditionally invalidated measures deviating from that form. The result may appear "formalistic" in a given case to partisans of the measure at issue, because such measures are typically the product of the era's perceived necessity. But the Constitution protects us from our own best intentions: It divides power among sovereigns and among branches of government precisely so that we may resist the temptation to concentrate power in one location as an expedient solution to the crisis of the day. The shortage of disposal sites for radioactive waste is a pressing national problem, but a judiciary that licensed extraconstitutional government with each issue of comparable gravity would, in the long run, be far worse. States are not mere political subdivisions of the United States. State governments are neither regional offices nor administrative agencies of the Federal Government. The positions occupied by state officials appear nowhere on the Federal Government's most detailed organizational chart. The Constitution instead "leaves to the several States a residuary and inviolable sovereignty," The Federalist No. 39, reserved explicitly to the States by the Tenth Amendment. Whatever the outer limits of that sovereignty may be, one thing is clear: The Federal Government may not compel the States to enact or administer a federal regulatory program. The Constitution permits both the Federal Government and the States to enact legislation regarding the disposal of low level radioactive waste. The Constitution enables the Federal Government to pre-empt state regulation contrary to federal interests, and it permits the Federal Government to hold out incentives to the States as a means of encouraging them to adopt suggested regulatory schemes. It does not, however, authorize Congress simply to direct the States to provide for the disposal of the radioactive waste generated within their borders. While there may be many constitutional methods of achieving regional self-sufficiency in radioactive waste disposal, the method Congress has chosen is not one of them.

[Affirmed in part and reversed in part.]

Justice WHITE, with whom Justice BLACKMUN and Justice STEVENS join, dissenting [with respect to the holding that the take title provision is unconstitutional].

I.   My disagreement with the Court's analysis begins at the basic descriptive level of how the legislation at issue in this case came to be enacted. [The Act] resulted from the efforts of state leaders to achieve a state-based set of remedies to the waste problem. They sought not federal pre-emption or intervention, but rather congressional sanction of interstate compromises they had reached. [The] 1985 Act was very much the product of cooperative federalism, in which the States bargained among themselves to achieve compromises for Congress to sanction. [Unlike] legislation that directs action from the Federal Government to the States, the [congressional action] reflected hard-fought agreements among States as refereed by Congress. The distinction is key, and the Court's failure properly to characterize this legislation ultimately affects its analysis of the take title provision's constitutionality.

II.   [I] am unmoved by the Court's vehemence in taking away Congress' authority to sanction a recalcitrant unsited State now that New York has reaped the benefits of the sited States' concessions. A. In my view, New York's actions subsequent to enactment of the [laws] fairly indicate its approval of the interstate agreement process embodied in those laws within the meaning of Art. I, § 10, cl. 3. [B. I] am convinced that, seen as a term of an agreement entered into between the several States, this measure proves to be less constitutionally odious than the Court opines. First, the practical effect of New York's position is that because it is unwilling to honor its obligations to provide in-state storage facilities for its low-level radioactive waste, other States with such plants must accept New York's waste, whether they wish to or not. Otherwise, the many economically and socially-beneficial producers of such waste in the State would have to cease their operations. The Court's refusal to force New York to accept responsibility for its own problem inevitably means that some other State's sovereignty will be impinged by it being forced, for public health reasons, to accept New York's low-level radioactive waste. I do not understand the principle of federalism to impede the National Government from acting as referee among the States to prohibit one from bullying another. Moreover, it is utterly reasonable that, in crafting a delicate compromise between the three overburdened States that provided low-level radioactive waste disposal facilities and the rest of the States, Congress would have to ratify some punitive measure as the ultimate sanction for noncompliance. The take title provision, though surely onerous, does not take effect if the generator of the waste does not request such action, or if the State lives up to its bargain of providing a waste disposal facility either within the State or in another State pursuant to a regional compact arrangement or a separate contract.

     III.   The Court announces that it has no occasion to revisit such decisions as [Garcia and National League of Cities] because "this is not a case in which Congress has subjected a State to the same legislation applicable to private parties." Although this statement sends the welcome signal that the Court does not intend to cut a wide swath through our recent Tenth Amendment precedents, it nevertheless is unpersuasive. I have several difficulties with the Court's analysis in this respect: it builds its rule around an insupportable and illogical distinction in the types of alleged incursions on state sovereignty; it derives its rule from cases that do not support its analysis; it fails to apply the appropriate tests from the cases on which it purports to base its rule; and it omits any discussion of the most recent and pertinent test for determining the take title provision's constitutionality.

     The Court's distinction between a federal statute's regulation of States and private parties for general purposes, as opposed to a regulation solely on the activities of States, is unsupported by our recent Tenth Amendment cases. In no case has the Court rested its holding on such a distinction. [An] incursion on state sovereignty hardly seems more constitutionally acceptable if the federal statute that "commands" specific action also applies to private parties. The alleged diminution in state authority over its own affairs is not any less because the federal mandate restricts the activities of private parties. Even were such a distinction to be logically sound, the Court's "anti-commandeering" principle cannot persuasively be read as springing from the two cases cited for the proposition. [In Hodel,] the language about "commandeering" States was classic dicta. [The] Court also claims support for its rule from our decision in [FERC]. The phrase highlighted by the Court merely means that we have not had the occasion to address whether Congress may "command" the States to enact a certain law, [and] this case does not raise that issue. Moreover, it should go without saying that the absence of any on-point precedent from this Court has no bearing on the question whether Congress has properly exercised its constitutional authority under Article I. Silence by this Court on a subject is not authority for anything. [T]he more appropriate analysis should flow from Garcia. [T]he Court tacitly concedes that a failing of the political process cannot be shown in this case because it refuses to rebut the unassailable arguments that the States were well able to look after themselves in the legislative process that culminated in the 1985 Act's passage. The Court rejects this process-based argument by resorting to generalities and platitudes about the purpose of federalism being to protect individual rights. Ultimately, I suppose, the entire structure of our federal constitutional government can be traced to an interest in establishing checks and balances to prevent the exercise of tyranny against individuals. But these fears seem extremely far distant to me in a situation such as this. We face a crisis of national proportions in the disposal of low-level radioactive waste, and Congress has acceded to the wishes of the States by permitting local decisionmaking rather than imposing a solution from Washington. New York itself participated and supported passage of this legislation at both the gubernatorial and federal representative levels, and then enacted state laws specifically to comply with the deadlines and timetables agreed upon by the States in the 1985 Act. For me, the Court's civics lecture has a decidedly hollow ring at a time when action, rather than rhetoric, is needed to solve a national problem.[1]

IV.   Though I disagree with the Court's conclusion that the take title provision is unconstitutional, I do not read its opinion to preclude Congress from adopting a similar measure through its powers under the Spending or Commerce Clauses. [Congress could] condition the payment of funds on the State's willingness to take title if it has not already provided a waste disposal facility. Similarly, should a State fail to establish a waste disposal facility by the appointed deadline, [Congress] has the power pursuant to the Commerce Clause to regulate directly the producers of the waste. Thus, as I read it, Congress could amend the statute to say that if a State fails to meet the January 1, 1996 deadline for achieving a means of waste disposal, and has not taken title to the waste, no low-level radioactive waste may be shipped out of the State of New York. [T]he threat of federal pre-emption may suffice to induce States to accept responsibility for failing to meet critical time deadlines for solving their low-level radioactive waste disposal problems. [And] of course, should Congress amend the statute to meet the Court's objection and a State refuse to act, the National Legislature will have ensured at least a federal solution to the waste management problem. Finally, our precedents leave open the possibility that Congress may create federal rights of action in the generators of low-level radioactive waste against persons acting under color of state law for their failure to meet certain functions designated in federal-state programs. [In] addition to compensating injured parties for the State's failure

---

1. With selective quotations from the era in which the Constitution was adopted, the majority attempts to bolster its holding that the take title provision is tantamount to federal "commandeering" of the States. In view of the many Tenth Amendment cases decided over the past two decades in which resort to the kind of historical analysis generated in the majority opinion was not deemed necessary, I do not read the majority's many invocations of history to be anything other than elaborate window-dressing. Certainly nowhere does the majority announce that its rule is compelled by an understanding of what the Framers may have thought about statutes of the type at issue here. Moreover, I would observe that, while its quotations add a certain flavor to the opinion, the majority's historical analysis has a distinctly wooden quality. One would not know from reading the majority's account, for instance, that the nature of federal-state relations changed fundamentally after the Civil War. That conflict produced in its wake a tremendous expansion in the scope of the Federal Government's law-making authority, so much so that the persons who helped to found the Republic would scarcely have recognized the many added rules the National Government assumed for itself. Moreover, the majority fails to mention the New Deal era, in which the Court recognized the enormous growth in Congress' power under the Commerce Clause. While I believe we should not be blind to history, neither should we read it so selectively as to restrict the proper scope of Congress' powers under Article I, especially when the history not mentioned by the majority fully supports a more expansive understanding of the legislature's authority than may have existed in the late 18th-century. Given the scanty textual support for the majority's position, it would be far more sensible to defer to a coordinate branch of government in its decision to devise a solution to a national problem of this kind. Certainly in other contexts, principles of federalism have not insulated States from mandates by the National Government. The Court has upheld congressional statutes that impose clear directives on state officials, including laws that require state courts to hear certain actions, see, e.g., Testa v. Katt. [Footnote by Justice White.]

to act, the exposure to liability established by such suits also potentially serves as an inducement to compliance with the program mandate.

V.   The ultimate irony of the decision today is that in its formalistically rigid obeisance to "federalism," the Court gives Congress fewer incentives to defer to the wishes of state officials in achieving local solutions to local problems. This legislation was a classic example of Congress acting as arbiter among the States in their attempts to accept responsibility for managing a problem of grave import.

Justice STEVENS, concurring in part and dissenting in part.

Under the Articles of Confederation, the Federal Government had the power to issue commands to the States. Because that indirect exercise of federal power proved ineffective, the Framers of the Constitution empowered the Federal Government to exercise legislative authority directly over individuals within the States, even though that direct authority constituted a greater intrusion on State sovereignty. Nothing in that history suggests that the Federal Government may not also impose its will upon the several States as it did under the Articles. The Constitution enhanced, rather than diminished, the power of the Federal Government. The notion that Congress does not have the power to issue "a simple command to state governments to implement legislation enacted by Congress" is incorrect and unsound. There is no such limitation in the Constitution. The Tenth Amendment surely does not impose any limit on Congress' exercise of the powers delegated to it by Article I. Nor does the structure of the constitutional order or the values of federalism mandate such a formal rule. To the contrary, the Federal Government directs state governments in many realms. The Government regulates state-operated railroads, state school systems, state prisons, state elections, and a host of other state functions. Similarly, there can be no doubt that, in time of war, Congress could either draft soldiers itself or command the States to supply their quotas of troops. I see no reason why Congress may not also command the States to enforce federal water and air quality standards or federal standards for the disposition of low-level radioactive [wastes].

―――――

Some comments and questions on New York v. United States. a. New York v. United States makes clear that the anticommandeering principle that first surfaced in the cases preceding Garcia retains vitality. New York v. United States can best be seen as part of the antifederalism revival of the 1990s, akin to cases such as Lopez, U.S. Term Limits v. Thornton (chap. 2 above), and the Seminole Tribe case (in the note that follows). To what extent does New York v. United States vindicate the prediction of Justices Rehnquist's and O'Connor's dissents in Garcia that their views would "in time again command the support of a majority"? Is the majority in New York v. United States persuasive in arguing, on the basis of history, that the Framers intended to end the national power to regulate the states directly? Or are the dissenters correct in claiming that the Framers wanted merely to supplement that power with authority to regulate individuals directly? Are the congressional spending and preemption routes supported by the majority in New York v. United States truly less intrusive upon state autonomy than the take title provision held unconstitutional? Note that the majority in New York v. United States continues to accept Testa v. Katt, which usually requires state courts to enforce national laws. Is Justice O'Connor persuasive in arguing that such "commandeering" of state judges is constitutional, even though state legislatures are immune under the anticommandeering principle? What are the implications of New York v. United States? In its wake, a number of federal laws have been challenged as violating the anticommandeering principle.

The Eleventh Amendment as a protector of state sovereignty and a curb on congressional powers. The Eleventh Amendment states: "The judicial power of the United States shall not be construed to extend to any [suit] commenced or prosecuted against one of the United States by Citizens of another State, or by Citizens or Subjects of any Foreign States." It was adopted because of the uproar created by Chisholm v. Georgia, 2 U.S. (2 Dall.) 419 (1793), where the Court took original jurisdiction of a suit against Georgia by a South Carolina creditor seeking payment for goods purchased by Georgia during the Revolution. The interpretation of the Amendment has produced a welter of rulings. Most are beyond the scope of this course; they are considered in courses on federal jurisdiction. But one aspect bears upon this chapter's consideration of external limits on congressional power, especially because a 1996 decision infused new force into the restraining capacity of the Amendment.

In 1890, in Hans v. Louisiana, 134 U.S. 1, a much criticized ruling held that the Eleventh Amendment applied not only to cases within the diversity jurisdiction but also to cases within the federal question jurisdiction of the federal courts. Subsequent cases made considerable inroads on the state sovereign immunity provided by the Amendment. In Ex parte Young, 209 U.S. 123 (1908), the Court held that a federal court could issue an injunction against state officials enforcing an unconstitutional state law, on the ground that the state was not really the defendant (instead, the defendant was the official, acting beyond his constitutional authority). Moreover, in Edelman v. Jordan, 415 U.S. 651 (1974), the Court ruled that the Eleventh Amendment permitted lawsuits for prospective injunctive relief against state officers, but not lawsuits for retrospective relief via a judgment for damages. In Fitzpatrick v. Bitzer, 427 U.S. 445 (1976), the Court held that Congress could abrogate the state's Eleventh Amendment immunity and allow states to be sued directly for retrospective damages, pursuant to its enforcement power under the Fourteenth Amendment, an amendment adopted well after the Eleventh. See generally Jackson, "The Supreme Court, the Eleventh Amendment, and State Sovereign Immunity," 98 Yale L.J. 1 (1988). Fitzpatrick left open the question whether Congress could also abrogate state immunity under its Art. I, § 8, powers, such as the commerce power. In Pennsylvania v. Union Gas Co., 491 U.S. 1 (1989), a divided Court held that a congressional environmental law constitutionally permitted suits for monetary damages against states in federal court; the Court held that "Congress has the authority to create such a course of action when legislating pursuant to the Commerce Clause." The majority in that case could not agree on a rationale for its holding. Seven years later, in SEMINOLE TRIBE OF FLORIDA v. FLORIDA, ___ U.S. ___, 116 S.Ct. 1114 (1996), the majority overruled Union Gas and rejected the claim that the commerce power could abrogate a state's Eleventh Amendment immunity (thus adding to the decisions above another example of the antifederalist revival of the 1990s).

The Seminole Tribe case arose under the Indian Gaming Regulatory Act, which provided that an Indian tribe may conduct certain gaming activities only in conformance with a valid compact between the tribe and the state in which the gaming activities are located. The Act, passed under the Indian commerce aspect of the commerce clause, imposed upon the states a duty to negotiate in good faith with an Indian tribe toward the formation of a compact and authorized a tribe to sue the state in a federal court in order to compel performance of that duty. Justice REHNQUIST's majority opinion held that "notwithstanding Congress' clear attempt to abrogate the States' sovereign immunity, the Indian Commerce Clause does not grant Congress that power, and therefore [the law] cannot grant jurisdiction over a state that does not consent to be sued." The Court rejected the argument that a power to abrogate sovereign immunity should be recognized here because the Act authorized only prospective injunctive relief rather than retroactive monetary relief. The Chief Justice added: "[W]e have often made it clear that the relief sought by a plaintiff suing a State is irrelevant to the question whether the suit is barred by the Eleventh Amendment." He rejected the claim that the abrogation power was properly invoked here "because the Act grants the States a power that they would not otherwise have, viz., some measure of authority over gaming on Indian lands": "The Eleventh Amendment may not be lifted by Congress unilaterally deciding that it will be replaced by grant of some other authority." Although reaffirming Fitzpatrick v. Bitzer, he concluded that Pennsylvania v. Union Gas Co., the only other case sustaining congressional abrogation of the states' immunity, could not stand. The Chief Justice explained: "[T]he plurality opinion in Union Gas allows no principled distinction in favor of the States to be drawn between the Indian Commerce Clause and the Interstate Commerce Clause." In his view, the principle of stare decisis was not binding here. He claimed that the plurality's rationale in Union Gas had "deviated sharply from our established federalism jurisprudence and essentially eviscerated our decision in Hans." The plurality's reliance on Fitzpatrick v. Bitzer in Union Gas was "misplaced," for that ruling was wholly inapplicable to the commerce clause, since "the Fourteenth Amendment, adopted well after the adoption of the Eleventh Amendment and the ratification of the Constitution, operated to alter the preexisting balance between state and federal power achieved by Article III and the Eleventh Amendment. [Reconsidering] the decision in Union Gas, we conclude that none of the policies underlying stare decisis require our continuing adherence to its holding. [In] overruling Union Gas today, we can reconfirm that the background principle of state sovereign immunity embodied in the Eleventh Amendment is not so ephemeral as to dissipate when the subject of the suit is an area, like the regulation of Indian commerce, that is under the exclusive control of the Federal Government. [The] Eleventh Amendment restricts the judicial power under Article III, and Article I cannot be used to circumvent the constitutional limitations placed upon federal jurisdiction." (The majority also held that Ex parte Young did not justify the lawsuit: "The situation presented here [is] sufficiently different from that giving rise to the traditional Ex parte Young actions so as to preclude the availability of that doctrine.")

Justice STEVENS's dissent stated: "This case is about power—the power of [Congress] to create a private federal cause of action against a State, or its Governor, for the violation of a federal right. [In] a sharp break with the past, today the Court holds that, with the narrow and illogical exception of statutes enacted pursuant to [the Fourteenth Amendment], Congress has no such power." He added that the importance of overruling Union Gas "cannot be overstated. The majority's opinion does not simply preclude Congress from establishing the rather curious statutory scheme under which the Indian tribes may seek the aid of a federal court to secure a State's good faith negotiations over gaming regulations. Rather, it prevents Congress from providing a federal forum for a broad range of actions against States, from those sounding in copyright and patent law to those concerning bankruptcy, environmental law, and the regulation of our vast national economy." In a separate dissent, Justice SOUTER, joined by Justices Ginsburg and Breyer, objected primarily because he was "convinced" that the decision was "fundamentally mistaken." He explained: "In the past, we have assumed that a plain statement requirement [requiring that Congress clearly intended to abrogate state immunity] is sufficient to protect the States from undue federal encroachment upon their traditional immunity from suit." Since "the political safeguards of federalism are working [see Garcia], a plain statement rule is an adequate check on congressional overreaching, [and] today's abandonment of that approach is wholly unwarranted."

CHAPTER 4

FEDERALISM–BASED RESTRAINTS ON OTHER NATIONAL POWERS IN THE 1787 CONSTITUTION

Scope Note. Because of the central role of the commerce power as a source of national authority to regulate local activities, that power was the focus of the preceding chapter. This chapter turns more briefly to several other national powers granted at the Constitutional Convention that have also had significant impacts on the allocation of authority within the federal system. The taxing and spending powers are of special interest because of their close functional and doctrinal ties to the commerce power. The Constitutional Convention delegated the taxing and spending powers in the opening clause of Art. I, § 8: "The Congress shall have power To lay and collect Taxes, Duties, Imposts, and Excises, to pay the Debts and provide for the common Defense and general Welfare of the United States." The manner in which taxes are imposed and the way in which revenues are spent often have significant regulatory impacts. As with the commerce power, the taxing and spending powers have been invoked to regulate "police" as well as economic problems. Not surprisingly, regulations through taxing and spending have been resorted to in periods, as in the early 20th century, when the need for legislation seemed great and direct regulation through the commerce power was under constitutional clouds. To what extent are the limits pertaining to taxing and spending regulations similar to, and to what extent are they different from, those considered in connection with the commerce power? Are courts more capable of imposing effective limits on the former? Those are the primary themes of secs. 1 and 2. Sec. 3 briefly considers two other sources of national authority that are significant to the federal scheme, though even less frequently litigated: it deals with national powers relating to war and foreign relations.[1]

1. For a more comprehensive view of national powers with significant impact on the federal system, one other important basis for congressional action should be noted. That additional source lies not in the 1787 document but in the post-Civil War changes. The 13th, 14th, and 15th Amendments each specifies that Congress may "enforce this article by appropriate legislation." This authority long lay dormant because of congressional inaction and restrictive judicial interpreta- tions. But modern congressional efforts and new Court approaches have dramatized the vast impact of those Amendments on the federal system. The effect of the post-Civil War Amendments on congressional authority is examined in chap. 10 below; see especially Katzenbach v. Morgan, p. 998 below. (Consideration is postponed to chap. 10 because these issues are best examined after exploring the *judicial* interpretations of the self-executing impacts of those Amendments.)

SECTION 1. THE TAXING POWER AS A REGULATORY TOOL

Introduction. To what extent may the congressional taxing power be used as a means of national regulation of arguably local affairs? The materials in this section examine the Court's handling of that problem, and they are offered primarily for critical comparison with the preceding commerce power cases. A number of relationships between the two lines of cases has already been noted. For example, tax cases were relied on in the Hammer v. Dagenhart dissent and in Darby; and Congress has repeatedly invoked the taxing power when the commerce power seemed unusable. Consider, in examining these cases, the similarities and the differences in the development of limits on the commerce and taxing powers. Do the differences in doctrine reflect differences in the nature of the problems? Has the Court been more successful in curbing "abuses" of the taxing power than of the commerce power? Is it easier to detect pretextual uses of the taxing power?

————

Child Labor Tax Case [Bailey v. Drexel Furniture Co.]

259 U.S. 20, 42 S.Ct. 449, 66 L.Ed. 817 (1922).

[A few months after the Court had held regulation of child labor through the commerce power unconstitutional in Hammer v. Dagenhart (p. 173 above), Congress enacted the Child Labor Tax Law of 1919. That law imposed a federal excise tax of 10% of annual net profits on every employer of child labor in the covered businesses. The coverage provisions were similar to those in the law invalidated in Hammer v. Dagenhart. After paying a tax of over $6000, the Company successfully brought a refund suit in the District Court.]

Mr. Chief Justice TAFT delivered the opinion of the Court.

[The] law is attacked on the ground that it is a regulation of the employment of child labor in the States—an exclusively state function under the Federal Constitution and within the reservations of the Tenth Amendment. It is defended on the ground that it is a mere excise tax levied by the Congress of the United States under its broad power of taxation. [We] must construe the law and interpret the intent and meaning of Congress from the language of the act. [Does] this law impose a tax with only that incidental restraint and regulation which a tax must inevitably involve? Or does it regulate by the use of the so-called tax as a penalty? If a tax, it is clearly an excise. If it were an excise on a commodity or other thing of value we might not be permitted under previous decisions of this court to infer solely from its heavy burden that the act intends a prohibition instead of a tax. But this act is more. It provides a heavy exaction for a departure from a detailed and specified course of conduct in business. The course of business is that employers shall employ in mines and quarries, children of an age greater than 16 years; in mills and factories, children of an age greater than 14 years, and shall prevent children of less than 16 years in mills and factories from working more than 8 hours a day or 6 days in a week. If an employer departs from its prescribed course of business, he is to pay the government one-tenth of his entire net income in the business for a full year. The amount is not to be proportioned in any degree to the extent or frequency of the departures, but is to be paid by the employer in full measure whether he employs five hundred children for a year, or employs only one for a day. Moreover, [it] is only where he knowingly departs from the prescribed course that payment is to be exacted. Scienter is associated with penalties, not with taxes. The employer's factory is to be subject to inspection at any time not only by the taxing officers of the Treasury, the Department normally charged with the collection of taxes, but also by the Secretary of Labor and his subordinates whose normal function is the advancement and protection of the welfare of the workers. In the light of these features of the act, a court must be blind not to see that the so-called tax is imposed to stop the employment of children within the age limits prescribed. Its prohibitory and regulatory effect and purpose are palpable. All others can see and understand this. How can we properly shut our minds to it?

[Out of] a proper respect for the acts of a coordinate branch of the Government, this court has gone far to sustain taxing acts as such, even though there has been ground for suspecting from the weight of the tax it was intended to destroy its subject. But [here], the presumption of validity cannot prevail, because the proof of the contrary is found on the very face of the provisions. Grant the validity of this law, and all that Congress would need to do, hereafter, in seeking to take over to its control any one of the great number of subjects of public interest [reserved to the States] would be to enact a detailed measure of complete regulation of the subject and enforce it by a so-called tax upon departures from it. To give such magic to the word "tax" would be to break down all constitutional limitation of the powers of Congress and completely wipe out the sovereignty of the States. The difference between a tax and a penalty is sometimes difficult to define and yet the consequences of the distinction in the required method of their collection often are important. Where the sovereign enacting the law has power to impose both tax and penalty the difference between revenue production and mere regulation may be immaterial, but not so when one sovereign can impose a tax only, and the power of regulation rests in another. Taxes are occasionally imposed in the discretion of the legislature on proper subjects with the primary motive of obtaining revenue from them and with the incidental motive of discouraging them by making their continuance onerous. They do not lose their character as taxes because of the incidental motive. But there comes a time in the extension of the penalizing features of the so-called tax when it loses its character as such and becomes a mere penalty with the characteristics of regulation and punishment. Such is the case [here]. The case before us can not be distinguished from that of Hammer v. Dagenhart. [This] case requires [the] application of the principle announced by Chief Justice Marshall in [McCulloch], in a much quoted passage [—the "pretext" passage].

But it is pressed upon us that this court has gone so far in sustaining taxing measures the effect or tendency of which was to accomplish purposes not directly within congressional power that we are bound by authority to maintain this law. The first of these is Veazie Bank v. Fenno, 8 Wall. 533 [1869]. In that case, [a] law which increased a tax on the circulating notes of persons and state banks from one per centum to ten per centum was [upheld]. It will be observed that the sole objection to the tax there was its excessive character. [There] were no elaborate specifications on the face of the act, as here, indicating the purpose to regulate matters of state concern and jurisdiction through an exaction so applied as to give it the qualities of a penalty for violation of law rather than a tax. [But] more than this, what was charged to be the object of the excessive tax was within the congressional [authority]. After having pointed out the legitimate means taken by Congress to secure a national medium or currency, the court said: "Having thus, in the exercise of undisputed constitutional powers, undertaken to provide a currency for the whole country, it cannot be questioned that Congress may, constitutionally, secure the benefit of it to the people by appropriate legislation. To this end, [Congress] may restrain, by suitable enactments, the circulation as money of any notes not issued under its own authority."

[The] next case is that of McCray v. United States, 195 U.S. 27 [1904]. That, like [Veazie], was the increase of an excise tax upon a subject properly taxable in which the taxpayers claimed that the tax had become invalid because the increase was excessive. It was a tax on oleomargarine, a substitute for butter. The tax on the white oleomargarine was one-quarter of a cent a pound, and on the yellow oleomargarine [was] ten cents per pound. This court [upheld the tax, applying] the same principle as that applied in [Veazie]. It was that Congress, in selecting its subjects for taxation, might impose the burden where and as it would and that a motive disclosed in its selection to discourage sale or manufacture of an article by a higher tax than on some other did not invalidate the tax. [Finally], United States v. Doremus, 249 U.S. 86 [1919], involved the validity of the Narcotic Drug Act, which imposed a special tax on the manufacture, importation and sale or gift of opium or coca leaves or their compounds or derivatives. It required every person subject to the special tax to register with the Collector of Internal Revenue his name and place of business and forbade him to sell except upon the written order of the person to whom the sale was made on a form prescribed by the Commissioner of Internal Revenue. [The] validity of a special tax in the nature of an excise tax on the manufacture, importation and sale of such drugs was, of course, unquestioned. The provisions for subjecting the sale and distribution of the drugs to official supervision and inspection were held to have a reasonable relation to the enforcement of the tax and were therefore held valid. The court said that the act could not be declared invalid just because another motive than taxation, not shown on the face of the act, might have contributed to its [passage].

[Affirmed.][1]

----

1. *The scope of the taxing power: Doctrinal developments.* a. *The prior decisions.* The important regulatory tax cases before the Child Labor Tax Case—Veazie, McCray, and Doremus—are described in Chief Justice Taft's opinion. Are the prior decisions distinguishable, or did the principal case manifest a significant shift in approach? Is the distinction between a "tax" and a "penalty"—between "revenue production" and "mere regulation"—persuasive? Judicially manageable?

b. *Early 20th century commerce and tax cases: Parallels and contrasts.* i. Note that Justice Holmes was in the majority in the Child Labor Tax Case, just four years after his dissent in Hammer v. Dagenhart. In the principal case, he joined in looking beyond the congressional label to invalidate because of forbidden purpose; in his dissent in Hammer v. Dagenhart, he had insisted that the Court could *not* look to purposes and obvious collateral effects and must sustain a law using the commerce-prohibiting technique. Are Holmes's positions in the two cases reconcilable? Moreover, in Hammer v. Dagenhart, Holmes had relied on McCray, the oleomargarine tax case, to show that judicial inquiry into congressional purpose was improper. And the McCray tax decision of 1904, in turn, had relied on the commerce power Lottery Case of 1903 in rejecting the notion "that the judiciary may restrain the exercise of lawful

---

1. Only Justice CLARKE dissented.

power on the assumption that a wrongful purpose or motive has caused the power to be exerted." At the time of Hammer v. Dagenhart in 1918, in short, Holmes was opposing judicial invalidation because of improper purpose in tax (McCray) as well as commerce (Lottery, Child Labor) cases. By 1922, in the principal case, had Holmes abandoned that position? In commerce as well as in tax cases? Because he was in the minority in Hammer? Only in tax cases? Only in some tax cases—because bad purpose was clearer in the principal case than in McCray?[2]

ii. Shortly after the Narcotics Act decision in Doremus in 1919, Justice Holmes wrote to Judge Learned Hand: "As to the [Drug Act case], *(between ourselves)* I am tickled at every case of that sort as they seem to me to confirm the ground of my dissent in the Child Labor case last term. Hammer v. Dagenhart. Also, I think the drug act cases rightly decided. In my opinion Congress may have what ulterior motives they please if the act passed in the immediate aspect is within their powers—though personally, were I a legislator I might think it dishonest to use powers in that way."[3] Are Justice Holmes's positions in Doremus and the Child Labor Tax Case reconcilable? Are the cases distinguishable because the tax sanction in the child labor situation (10% of net profits for noncompliance) was more substantial than that in the narcotics situation ($1 a year)? Which scheme was more justifiable as a regulatory device incidental to a revenue raising measure?[4]

c. *From the Child Labor Tax Case to Kahriger.* In United States v. Constantine, 296 U.S. 287 (1935), defendant was convicted of conducting the business of retail dealer in malt liquor contrary to the laws of Alabama without having paid a special excise tax of $1000 imposed by Congress. He had paid the normal tax of $25 for conducting the business, and the question presented was "whether the exaction of $1000 in addition, by reason solely of his violation of state law, is a tax or penalty." Justice Roberts's opinion for the Court concluded that "the indicia which the section exhibits of an intent to prohibit and to punish violations of state law as such are too strong to be disregarded, remove all semblance of a revenue act and stamp the sum it exacts as a penalty. [T]he statute is a clear invasion of the police power, inherent in the [states]."[5] But Sonzinsky v. United States, 300 U.S. 506 (1937), sustained the National Firearms Act of 1934, which imposed a $200 annual license tax on dealers in firearms. Noting that the tax "is productive of some revenue," the Court said "we are not free to speculate as to the motives which moved Congress to impose it, or as to the extent to which it may operate to restrict the activities taxed. As it is not attended by an offensive regulation, and since it operates as a tax, it is within the national taxing power."

d. UNITED STATES v. KAHRIGER, 345 U.S. 22, (1953): This case—a rare modern example of Court consideration of a claim that a tax was unconstitutional because it was a regulatory penalty—sustained the constitutionality of an occupational tax imposed by the 1951 Revenue Act, which levied a tax on

---

2. Compare Justice Frankfurter's "purpose" emphasis in Kahriger, note 1d below, and note the additional questions on tax-commerce parallels and contrasts after Kahriger.

3. Oliver Wendell Holmes to Learned Hand, April 3, 1919, quoted in Gunther, "Learned Hand and the Origins of Modern First Amendment Doctrine," 27 Stan.L.Rev. 719 (1975).

4. See generally Cushman, "Social and Economic Control through Federal Taxation," 18 Minn.L.Rev. 759 (1934).

5. Justice Cardozo, joined by Justices Brandeis and Stone, dissented: "Thus the process of psychoanalysis has spread to unaccustomed fields."

persons engaged in the business of accepting wagers and required such persons to register with the Collector of Internal Revenue.[1] The challenger claimed, inter alia, that Congress, "under the pretense of exercising its power to tax, has attempted to penalize illegal intrastate gambling through the regulatory features of the Act" and thus infringed "the police power which is reserved to the states." Justice REED's majority opinion rejected the challenge. He did not think that it was determinative that the legislative history suggested a congressional motive to suppress wagering.[2] He responded: "[An] intent to curtail and hinder, as well as tax, was also manifest in the series of cases beginning with [Veazie], and in each of them the tax was [upheld]. [A] federal excise tax does not cease to be valid merely because it discourages or deters the activities taxed. Nor is the tax invalid because the revenue obtained is negligible. [The] instant tax has a regulatory effect. But regardless of [that], the wagering tax produces revenue. As such it surpasses both the narcotics and firearms taxes which we have found valid."[3] He added: "Without specific differentiation between the power to tax, and other federal powers, the indirect results from the exercise of the power to tax have raised more doubts [than, especially, use of the commerce power]. It is hard to understand why the power to tax should raise more doubts because of indirect effects than other federal powers. Unless there are [penalty] provisions extraneous to any tax need, courts are without authority to limit the exercise of the taxing power. All of the provisions of this [tax] are adapted to the collection of a valid tax. Nor do we find the registration requirements of the wagering tax offensive. [The] registration provisions make the tax simpler to collect."

Justice JACKSON's concurrence joined the majority opinion, "but with such doubts that if the minority agreed upon an opinion which did not impair legitimate use of the taxing power I probably would join it. [One] cannot formulate a revenue-raising plan that would not have economic and social

1. In a footnote, Justice Reed quoted the provisions of the Act imposing on covered persons an annual excise tax of 10% on all wagers, a special tax of fifty dollars per year, and a requirement that name, residence, place of business, and name and residence of each employee, be registered with the Collector of Internal Revenue. Justice Reed did not quote a number of other provisions of the law, including one requiring the Collector to "place and keep conspicuously in his office, for public inspection, an alphabetical list of the names" of all taxpayers under these provisions, and to furnish certified copies of those lists "upon application of any prosecuting officer of any State, county, or municipality." Should Justice Reed have quoted those provisions as well? Is there a significant difference between (a) regulatory effects challenged because of the direct impact of the tax in deterring the taxed activity, and (b) regulatory effects challenged because of the impact of collateral enforcement features of the tax (such as registration), as in Doremus, above, and arguably in Kahriger as well?

2. There are suggestions in the debates that Congress sought to hinder, if not prevent, the type of gambling taxed. See [e.g.] "If the local official does not want to enforce the law and no one catches him winking at the law, he may keep on winking at it, but when the Federal Government identifies a law violator, and the local newspaper gets hold of it, and the local church organizations get hold of it, and the people who do want the law enforced get hold of it, they say, Mr. Sheriff, what about it? We understand that there is a place down here licensed to sell liquor.' He says, 'Is that so? I will put him out of business.'" [Footnote by Justice Reed.]

3. One of the indicia which appellee offers to support his contention that the wagering tax is not a proper revenue measure is that the tax amount collected under it was $4,371,869, as compared with an expected amount of $400,000,00 a year. The figure of $4,371,869, however, is relatively large when it is compared with the $3,501 collected under the tax on adulterated and processed or renovated butter and filled cheese, the $914,910 collected under the tax on narcotics, [and] the $28,911 collected under the tax on [firearms]. [Footnote by Justice Reed.]

consequences." But here the purported tax law imposed tax and reporting obligations only on certain gamblers whose activities in most states were illegal. "This is difficult to regard as a rational or good-faith revenue measure. [On] the contrary, it seems to be a plan to tax out of existence a professional gambler whom it has been found impossible to prosecute out of existence. [The] evil that can come from this statute will probably soon make itself manifest to Congress. The evil of a judicial decision impairing the legitimate taxing power by extreme constitutional interpretations might not be transient. Even though this statute approaches the fair limits of constitutionality, I join the [decision]."

Justice FRANKFURTER, joined in large part by Justice Douglas, dissented: "[When] oblique use is made of the taxing power as to matters which substantively are not within the powers delegated to Congress, the Court cannot shut its eyes to orders obviously, because designedly, an attempt to control conduct which the Constitution left to the responsibility of the States, merely because Congress wrapped the legislation in the verbal cellophane of a revenue measure." (He pointed out that Justice Holmes had joined the ruling in the Child Labor Tax Case and added: "What is relevant to judgment here is that, even the history of the legislation as it went through Congress did not give one the libretto to the song, the context of the circumstances which brought forth this enactment [including "sensationally exploited disclosures regarding gambling"], emphatically supports what was revealed on the floor of Congress, namely, that what was formally a means of raising revenue [was] essentially an effort to check if not to stamp out professional gambling. A nominal taxing measure must be found an inadmissable intrusion [into the domain of the states] not merely when Congress requires that such a measure is to be enforced through a detailed scheme of administration beyond the obvious fiscal needs, as in the Child Labor Tax Case. [Another] basis for deeming such a formal revenue measure inadmissible is presented by this case. In addition to the fact that Congress was concerned with activity beyond the authority [of Congress], the enforcing provision [is] designed for the systematic confession of crimes with a view to prosecution for such crimes under State law. [The] motive of congressional legislation is not for our scrutiny, provided only that the ulterior purpose is not expressed in ways which negative what the revenue words on their face express and which do not seek enforcement of the formal revenue purpose through means that offend those standards of decency [barred by due process]."

e. *The taxing and commerce powers: Modern parallels and contrasts.* i. *Divergent paths.* With respect to judicial inquiry into the purposes and collateral effects of the commerce-prohibiting technique, the majority view in Hammer v. Dagenhart was overruled in Darby. Has there been a parallel development regarding the taxing power? Is the majority approach in the Child Labor Tax Case (1922) more respectable today than the discredited Hammer v. Dagenhart (1918) position? Note that Justice Stone's opinion in Darby relied on McCray and Veazie (the early taxing power cases discussed in the Child Labor Tax Case) in support of his refusal to inquire into the motive and purpose of commerce regulation. In the commerce area, in short, the modern Court has apparently abandoned all "pretext" control. Yet as to taxing, Kahriger produced several opinions on that abuse of power issue from members of the post–1937 Court. Is the difference justifiable?

ii. *Judicial competence to ascertain primary congressional purposes.* Justice Reed in Kahriger thought it "hard to understand why the power to tax should raise more doubts because of indirect effects than other federal powers." What *is* the explanation of the difference? Is it because "ordinary," revenue-raising taxes are less likely to have "indirect effects" than "ordinary" commerce regulations? But see Justice Jackson's concurrence: "[One] cannot formulate a revenue-raising plan that would not have economic and social consequences." Is this because the statutory scheme conveys clearer implications about the primary purpose of tax than of commerce legislation? But is there no historical guidance about the proper primary purpose of commerce regulations? And if some Justices are willing to distinguish between primary and ancillary objectives with respect to the taxing power, why are they unwilling—or view themselves as incompetent—to do so with respect to the commerce power? Are the kinds of data Justice Frankfurter relies on to identify an unconstitutional "ulterior purpose" in Kahriger the kinds the Court *should* rely on? In taxing cases? In commerce power cases as well?

SECTION 2.   THE SPENDING POWER AS A REGULATORY DEVICE

Introduction. The national spending power is probably the most important of all Art. I, § 8, powers in its impact on the actual functioning of the federal system. Whether in the context of payments to individuals for particular purposes (as with old age support under Social Security) or of conditional grants to states (as with education or welfare) or of direct financing of federal entrepreneurial operations (as with the TVA), national decisions about spending involve pervasive policy choices and have significant regulatory consequences. Litigation about the scope of the power has been rare, for restrictive doctrines regarding standing to sue have traditionally barred taxpayer challenges to federal spending programs. But the constitutional questions are no less real for the sparsity of judicial decisions. The scope of the spending power has been a recurrent source of controversy ever since the early 19th century. What *are* the legitimate purposes of national spending? What is the proper role of courts in assessing legitimacy? What conditions may Congress impose on spending programs? What is constitutionally required with respect to the relationship between the condition, the particular program, and the "general welfare"? To what extent may Congress "coerce" state or individual behavior when it resorts to the carrot of federal funds rather than the stick of civil and criminal sanctions? These are the questions for major attention in examining the materials in this section. (Recall the opinions in New York v. United States in 1992, p. 212 above, summarizing the modern spending power options open to Congress, and note also South Carolina v. Dole, the 1987 decision at the end of this section.)

United States v. Butler

297 U.S. 1, 56 S.Ct. 312, 80 L.Ed. 477 (1936).

Justice ROBERTS delivered the opinion of the Court.

[This decision invalidated one of the major New Deal measures, the Agricultural Adjustment Act of 1933. The Act sought to stabilize farm prices by curtailing agricultural production. It authorized the Secretary of Agriculture to make contracts with farmers to reduce their productive acreage in exchange for benefit payments. The payments were to be made out of funds payable by the processor: a processing tax was imposed "upon the first domestic processing" of the particular commodity. A processing tax on cotton was imposed upon the Hoosac Mills Corporation. Butler and his co-receivers for the company successfully attacked the tax, claiming that it was an integral part of an unconstitutional program to control agricultural production. The Court held that the Act was not a valid exercise of the power to spend for the general welfare.]

The Government asserts that even if the respondents may question the propriety of the appropriation embodied in the statute their attack must fail because Article I, § 8 of the Constitution authorizes the contemplated expenditure of the funds raised by the tax. This contention presents the great and the controlling question in the case. [There] should be no misunderstanding as to the function of this court in such a case. It is sometimes said that the court assumes a power to overrule or control the action of the people's representatives. This is a misconception. [When] an act of Congress is appropriately challenged in the courts as not conforming to the constitutional mandate the judicial branch of the Government has only one duty,—to lay the article of the Constitution which is invoked beside the statute which is challenged and to decide whether the latter squares with the former. [This] court neither approves nor condemns any legislative policy. Its delicate and difficult office is to ascertain and declare whether the legislation is in accordance with, or in contravention of, the provisions of the Constitution; and, having done that, its duty ends. [After noting that the Government had not sought to justify the Act on the basis of the commerce power, Justice Roberts continued:] The clause thought to authorize the [Act] confers upon the Congress power "to lay and collect Taxes, Duties, Imposts and Excises, to pay the Debts and provide for the common Defense and general Welfare of the United States." [It] is not contended that this provision grants power to regulate agricultural production upon the theory that such legislation would promote the general welfare. The Government concedes that the phrase "to provide for the general welfare" qualifies the power "to lay and collect taxes." The view that the clause grants power to provide for the general welfare, independently of the taxing power, has never been authoritatively accepted. Mr. Justice Story points out that if it were adopted "it is obvious that under color of the generality of the words, to 'provide for the common defense and general welfare,' the government of the United States is in reality, a government of general and unlimited powers, notwithstanding the subsequent enumeration of specific powers." The true construction undoubtedly is that the only thing granted is the power to tax for the purpose of providing funds for payment of the nation's debts and making provision for the general welfare. Nevertheless, the Government asserts that warrant is found in this clause for the adoption of the [Act]. The argument is that Congress may appropriate and authorize the spending of moneys for the "general welfare"; that the phrase should be liberally construed to cover anything conducive to national welfare; that decision as to what will promote such welfare rests with Congress alone, and the courts may not review its determination; and finally that the appropriation under attack was in fact for the general welfare of the United States.

[Since] the foundation of the Nation, sharp differences of opinion have persisted as to the true interpretation of the phrase. Madison asserted it amounted to no more than a reference to the other powers enumerated in the subsequent clauses of the same section; that, as the United States is a government of limited and enumerated powers, the grant of power to tax and spend for the general national welfare must be confined to the enumerated legislative fields committed to the Congress. In this view the phrase is mere tautology, for taxation and appropriation are or may be necessary incidents of the exercise of any of the enumerated legislative powers. Hamilton, on the other hand, maintained the clause confers a power separate and distinct from those later enumerated, is not restricted in meaning by the grant of them, and

Congress consequently has a substantive power to tax and to appropriate, limited only by the requirement that it shall be exercised to provide for the general welfare of the United States. [We] conclude that the reading advocated by [Hamilton and followed by Story] is the correct one. While, therefore, the power to tax is not unlimited, its confines are set in the clause which confers it, and not in those of § 8 which bestow and define the legislative powers of the Congress. It results that the power of Congress to authorize expenditure of public moneys for public purposes is not limited by the direct grants of legislative power found in the Constitution. But the adoption of the broader construction leaves the power to spend subject to limitations. [We] are not now required to ascertain the scope of the phrase "general welfare of the United States" or to determine whether an appropriation in aid of agriculture falls within it. Wholly apart from that question, another principle embedded in our Constitution prohibits the enforcement of the [act]. The act invades the reserved rights of the states. It is a statutory plan to regulate and control agricultural production, a matter beyond the powers delegated to the federal government. The tax, the appropriation of the funds raised, and the direction for their disbursement, are but parts of the plan. They are but means to an unconstitutional end. [It] is an established principle that the attainment of a prohibited end may not be accomplished under the pretext of the exertion of powers which are granted [quoting Marshall's "pretext" statement in McCulloch].

[If] the taxing power may not be used as the instrument to enforce a regulation of matters of state concern with respect to which the Congress has no authority to interfere [e.g., Child Labor Tax Case], may it, as in the present case, be employed to raise the money necessary to purchase a compliance which the Congress is powerless to command? The Government asserts that whatever might be said against the validity of the plan if compulsory, it is constitutionally sound because the end is accomplished by voluntary co-operation. There are two sufficient answers to the contention. The regulation is not in fact voluntary. The farmer, of course, may refuse to comply, but the price of such refusal is the loss of benefits. The amount offered is intended to be sufficient to exert pressure on him to agree to the proposed regulation. The power to confer or withhold unlimited benefits is the power to coerce or destroy. If the cotton grower elects not to accept the benefits, he will receive less for his crops. [The] result may well be financial ruin. [This] is coercion by economic pressure. The asserted power of choice is illusory. [But] if the plan were one for purely voluntary co-operation it would stand no better so far as federal power is concerned. At best, it is a scheme for purchasing with federal funds submission to federal regulation of a subject reserved to the states. It is said that Congress has the undoubted right to appropriate money to executive officers for expenditure under contracts between the government and individuals. [But] appropriations and expenditures under contracts for proper governmental purposes cannot justify contracts which are not within federal power. And contracts for the reduction of acreage and the control of production are outside the range of that power. An appropriation to be expended by the United States under contracts calling for violation of a state law clearly would offend the Constitution. Is a statute less objectionable which authorizes expenditure of federal moneys to induce action in a field in which the United States has no power to intermeddle? The Congress cannot invade state jurisdiction to compel individual action; no more can it purchase such action.

[We] are not here concerned with a conditional appropriation of money, nor with a provision that if certain conditions are not complied with the appropriation shall no longer be available. By the [Act] the amount of the tax is appropriated to be expended only in payment under contracts whereby the parties bind themselves to regulation by the Federal Government. There is an obvious difference between a statute stating the conditions upon which moneys shall be expended and one effective only upon assumption of a contractual obligation to submit to a regulation which otherwise could not be enforced. Many examples pointing the distinction might be cited. We are referred to appropriations in aid of education, and it is said that no one has doubted the power of Congress to stipulate the sort of education for which money shall be expended. But an appropriation to an educational institution which by its terms is to become available only if the beneficiary enters into a contract to teach doctrines subversive of the Constitution is clearly bad. An affirmance of the authority of Congress so to condition the expenditure of an appropriation would tend to nullify all constitutional limitations upon legislative power. [Congress] has no power to enforce its commands on the farmer to the ends sought by the [Act]. It must follow that it may not indirectly accomplish those ends by taxing and spending to purchase compliance. The Constitution and the entire plan of our government negative any such use of the power to tax and to spend as the act undertakes to authorize. It does not help to declare that local conditions throughout the nation have created a situation of national concern; for this is but to say that whenever there is a widespread similarity of local conditions, Congress may ignore constitutional limitations upon its own powers and usurp those reserved to the states. [If the Act is] a proper exercise of the federal taxing power, evidently the regulation of all industry throughout the United States may be accomplished by similar exercises of the same power. [The] sole premise [of the Government's argument] is that, though the makers of the Constitution, in erecting the federal government, intended sedulously to limit [its powers], they nevertheless by a single clause gave power to the Congress to tear down the barriers, to invade the states' jurisdiction, and to become a parliament of the whole people, subject to no restrictions save such as are self-imposed. The argument when seen in its true character and in the light of its inevitable results must be [rejected].

Affirmed.

Justice STONE, dissenting.[1]

The power of courts to declare a statute unconstitutional is subject to two guiding principles of decision which ought never to be absent from judicial consciousness. One is that courts are concerned only with the power to enact statutes, not with their wisdom. The other is that while unconstitutional exercise of power by the executive and legislative branches of the government is subject to judicial restraint, the only check upon our own exercise of power is our own sense of self-restraint. For the removal of unwise laws from the statute books appeal lies not to the courts but to the ballot and to the processes of democratic government. [As] the present depressed state of agriculture is nation wide in its extent and effects, there is no basis for saying that the expenditure of public money in aid of farmers is not within the specifically granted power of Congress to levy taxes to "provide for [the] general welfare." The opinion of the Court does not declare otherwise. [The majority's] sugges-

---

1. The opening and closing passages in this dissent—a dissent joined by Justices Brandeis and Cardozo—are of special historical interest: it was passages like these that President Roosevelt relied on in his attacks on the Court at the time of the Court-packing plan. See, e.g., his radio address of March 9, 1937, quoted at p. 184 above: "[T]he Court has been assuming the power to pass on the wisdom of these acts of the Congress. [That] is not only my accusation. It is the accusation of most distinguished Justices of the present Supreme Court."

tion of coercion finds no support in the record or in any data showing the actual operation of the act. Threat of loss, not hope of gain, is the essence of economic coercion.

[It] is upon the contention that state power is infringed by purchased regulation of agricultural production that chief reliance is placed. [But the] Constitution requires that public funds shall be spent for a defined purpose, the promotion of the general welfare. Their expenditure usually involves payment on terms which will insure use by the selected recipients within the limits of the constitutional purpose. Expenditures would fail of their purpose and thus lose their constitutional sanction if the terms of payment were not such that by their influence on the action of the recipients the permitted end would be attained. The power of Congress to spend is inseparable from persuasion to action over which Congress has no legislative control. Congress may not command that the science of agriculture be taught in state universities. But if it would aid the teaching of that science by grants to state institutions, it is appropriate, if not necessary, that the grant be on the condition, incorporated in the Morrill Act, that it be used for the intended purpose. Similarly it would seem to be compliance with the Constitution, not violation of it, for the government to take and the university to give a contract that the grant would be so used. It makes no difference that there is a promise to do an act which the condition is calculated to induce. Condition and promise are alike valid since both are in furtherance of the national purpose for which the money is appropriated. [It] is a contradiction in terms to say that there is power to spend for the national welfare, while rejecting any power to impose conditions reasonably adapted to the attainment of the end which alone would justify the expenditure.

The limitation now sanctioned must lead to absurd consequences. The government may give seeds to farmers, but may not condition the gift upon their being planted in places where they are most needed or even planted at all. The government may give money to the unemployed, but may not ask that those who get it shall give labor in return, or even use it to support their families. [It] may support rural schools, [but] may not condition its grant by the requirement that certain standards be maintained. [Do] all its activities collapse because, in order to effect the permissible purpose, in myriad ways the money is paid out upon terms and conditions which influence action of the recipients within the states, which Congress cannot command? The answer would seem plain. If the expenditure is for a national public purpose, that purpose will not be thwarted because payment is on condition which will advance that purpose. The action which Congress induces by payments of money to promote the general welfare, but which it does not command or coerce, is but an incident to a specifically granted power, but a permissible means to a legitimate end. If appropriation in aid of a program of curtailment of agricultural production is constitutional, and it is not denied that it is, payment to farmers on condition that they reduce their crop acreage is constitutional. It is not any the less so because the farmer at his own option promises to fulfill the condition.

That the governmental power of the purse is a great one is not now for the first time announced. [The] suggestion that it must now be curtailed by judicial fiat because it may be abused by unwise use hardly rises to the dignity of argument. So may judicial power be abused. [The] power to tax and spend is not without constitutional restraints. One restriction is that the purpose must be truly national. Another is that it may not be used to coerce action left to state control. Another is the conscience and patriotism of Congress and the Executive. [A] tortured construction of the Constitution is not to be justified by recourse to extreme examples of reckless congressional spending which might occur if courts could not prevent—expenditures which, even if they could be thought to effect any national purpose, would be possible only by action of a legislature lost to all sense of public responsibility. Such suppositions are addressed to the mind accustomed to believe that it is the business of courts to sit in judgment on the wisdom of legislative action. Courts are not the only agency of government that must be assumed to have capacity to govern. Congress and the courts both unhappily may falter or be mistaken in the performance of their constitutional duty. But interpretation of our great charter of government which proceeds on any assumption that the responsibility for the preservation of our institutions is the exclusive concern of any one of the three branches of government, or that it alone can save them from destruction is far more likely, in the long run, "to obliterate the constituent members" of "an indestructible union of indestructible states" than the frank recognition that language, even of a constitution, may mean what it says: that the power to tax and spend includes the power to relieve a nationwide economic maladjustment by conditional gifts of money.

———

1. *Conditional spending: The Butler case and its aftermath.* a. *The majority opinion.* Was the Butler majority's endorsement of the Hamilton position on the spending power consistent with the result? Did the majority in effect adopt the Madison position after all? If the power to spend for the "general Welfare" is not limited by the other grants of power in Art. I, § 8, why was it unconstitutional to spend for the purpose of reducing agricultural production, even though that production was not (in 1936) directly reachable under the other powers? If, as the majority apparently concedes, "conditional appropriation of money," including to education, is permissible, why is conditional aid to farmers unconstitutional? Was the problem of agricultural production less "general" than that of education? Could the Government have given money to farmers who voluntarily cut agricultural production, with provisions that grants would not be renewed if productive acreage were not reduced? What constitutional difference should it make that the Act involved contractual arrangements? Can the result in Butler be reconciled with the 1937 Social Security cases, below?

2. *The dissent.* Was Justice Stone persuasive in asserting in his dissent: "Threat of loss, not hope of gain, is the essence of economic coercion"? What restrictions on the spending power would the dissenters recognize? Justice Stone states that "the purpose must be truly national." Is the Court competent to identify "non-national" purposes in the face of a judgment by the national legislature that a spending program serves the national interest? Justice Stone also asserts that the spending power "may not be used to coerce action left to state control." Does he not effectively sustain economic coercion of farmers? Would there nevertheless be a barrier in Justice Stone's view if the national program sought to compel state governments rather than individuals to take affirmative action?[1] What constitutional standards must conditions on spending meet under Justice Stone's view? Is it enough that the conditions are relevant to the general welfare? Is there a more focused requirement that the conditions be related to the purpose of the particular spending program?[2]

1. Recall the modern state autonomy cases in chap. 3 (especially New York v. United States) and compare the Steward Machine and South Dakota v. Dole cases, which follow.

2. Note Justice Stone's comment: "If

3. *The 1937 Social Security cases.* After the Butler case, New Dealers feared that the Social Security Act of 1935 was at risk. But in companion cases in 1937, the Court sustained the unemployment compensation and old age benefits schemes of the Social Security Act. The first of these cases, Steward Machine, probably raised the more difficult issue, for it involved a federal taxing structure designed to induce states to adopt laws complying with federal standards (and accordingly encountered a state autonomy claim). The second case, Helvering v. Davis, did not try to enlist state legislatures but instead involved merely an exclusively federal spending scheme. It accordingly raised anew questions of the scope of the direct federal spending power.

a. The 5–4 decision in CHARLES C. STEWARD MACHINE CO. v. DAVIS, 301 U.S. 548 (1937), sustained the unemployment compensation provisions of the Social Security Act. Title IX of the Act imposed a payroll tax on employers of eight or more. Unlike the tax in the Butler case, this tax was not earmarked but went into general funds. But a credit provision in the tax sought to induce the enactment of state laws that complied with federal standards. Under the scheme an employer was entitled to a credit of up to 90% of the federal tax for any contributions to a state unemployment fund certified by a federal agency as meeting the requirements of the Act. The company sought a refund of taxes paid under Title IX.

Justice CARDOZO's majority opinion concluded that the scheme was "not void as involving the coercion of the States in contravention of the Tenth Amendment or of restrictions implicit in our federal form of government." He insisted that it had not been shown that "the tax and the credit in combination are weapons of coercion, destroying or impairing the autonomy of the states." He explained: "To draw the line intelligently between duress and inducement there is no need to remind ourselves of facts as to the problem of unemployment that are now matters of common knowledge." After reviewing the data regarding widespread unemployment during the Great Depression, Justice Cardozo noted: "The fact developed quickly that the states were unable to give the requisite relief. [There] was need of help from the nation if the people were not to starve." He continued: "[The] question is to be answered whether the [law] adopted has overleapt the bounds of power. The assailants of the statute say that its dominant end [is] to drive the state legislatures under the whip of economic pressure into the enactment of unemployment compensation laws at the bidding of the central government. Supporters of the statute say that its operation is not constraint, but the creation of a larger freedom, the states and the nation joining in a cooperative endeavor to avert a common evil. Before Congress acted, unemployment compensation insurance was still, for the most part, a project and no more. [Many states] held back through alarm lest, in laying such a toll upon their industries, they would place themselves in a position of economic disadvantage as compared with neighbors or competitors. [Two] consequences ensued. One was that the freedom of a state to contribute its fair share to the solution of a national problem was paralyzed by fear. The other was that in so far as there was failure by the states to contribute relief

the expenditure is for a national public purpose, that purpose will not be thwarted because payment is on condition which will advance that purpose." Note also his earlier reference to "conditions reasonably adapted to the attainment of the end which alone would justify the expenditure." What "purpose," what "end," did Justice Stone have in mind? Merely a relationship to the "general welfare"? Or a relationship to the purpose of the particular spending program? What criteria for judicial scrutiny of conditional spending remained after the 1937 Social Security cases, which follow? After the subsequent decisions?

according to the measure of their capacity, a disproportionate burden, [was] laid upon the resources of the Government of the nation.

"The [Act] is an attempt to find a method by which all these public agencies may work together to a common end. Every dollar of the new taxes will continue in all likelihood to be used and needed by the nation as long as states are unwilling, whether through timidity or for other motives, to do what can be done at home. At least the inference is permissible that Congress so believed, though retaining undiminished freedom to spend the money as it pleased. On the other hand fulfillment of the home duty will be lightened and encouraged by crediting the [federal] taxpayer [to] the extent that his contributions under the laws of the locality have simplified or diminished the problem of relief and the probable demand upon the resources of the fisc. [Who] then is coerced through the operation of this statute? Not the taxpayer. He pays in fulfillment of the mandate of the local legislature. Not the state. Even now [Alabama] does not offer a suggestion that in passing the unemployment law she was affected by duress. [The] difficulty with petitioner's contention is that it confuses motive with coercion. [E]very rebate from a tax when conditioned upon conduct is in some measure a temptation. But to hold that motive or temptation is equivalent to coercion is to plunge the law in endless difficulties. The outcome of such a doctrine is the acceptance of a philosophical determinism by which choice becomes impossible. Till now the law has been guided by a robust common sense which assumes the freedom of the will as a working hypothesis in the solution of its problems. The wisdom of the hypothesis has illustration in this case. There would be a strange irony, indeed, if [Alabama's] choice were now to be annulled on the basis of an assumed duress in the enactment of a statute which her courts have accepted as a true expression of her will.

"[In] ruling as we do, we leave many questions open. We do not say that a tax is valid, when imposed by act of Congress, if it is laid upon the condition that a state may escape its operation through the adoption of a statute unrelated in subject matter to activities fairly within the scope of national policy and power. No such question is before us. The purpose of [Congress's] intervention, as we have shown, is to safeguard its own treasury and as an incident to that protection to place the states upon a footing of equal opportunity. [It] is one thing to impose a tax dependent upon the conduct of the taxpayers, or of the state in which they live, where the conduct to be stimulated or discouraged is unrelated to the fiscal need subserved by the tax in its normal operation, or to any other end legitimately national. The Child Labor Tax Case [was] decided in the belief that the [law] there condemned [was] exposed to that reproach. It is quite another thing to say that a tax will be abated upon the doing of an act that will satisfy the fiscal need, the tax and the alternative being approximate equivalents. In such circumstances, if in no others, inducement or persuasion does not go beyond the bounds of power. We do not fix the outermost line. Enough for present purposes that wherever the line may be, this statute is within it. Definition more precise must abide the wisdom of the future. The statute does not call for a surrender by the states of powers essential to their quasi-sovereign existence. [A] credit to taxpayers for payments made to a state under a state unemployment law will be manifestly futile in the absence of some assurance that the law leading to the credit is in truth what it professes to be. An unemployment law framed in such a way that the unemployed who look to it will be deprived of reasonable protection is one in name and nothing more. What is basic and essential may be assured by suitable conditions. The terms embodied in these sections are directed to that end. A wide range of judgment is given to the several states as to the particular type of statute to be spread upon their books. [What] they may not do, if they would earn the credit, is to depart from those standards which in the judgment of Congress are to be ranked as fundamental."[1]

b. In a companion case to Steward Machine, HELVERING v. DAVIS, 301 U.S. 619 (1937), Justice CARDOZO again wrote for the majority, with only Justices McReynolds and Butler dissenting. Helvering v. Davis upheld the old age benefits provisions in Titles VIII and II of the Social Security Act of 1935. Those provisions established an entirely federal program: they laid special taxes on covered employers and employees and provided for the payment of federal old age benefits. Justice Cardozo's opinion rejected the Tenth Amendment challenge by relying on the endorsement of the Hamilton position on the spending power in Butler. He noted that "difficulties" remain even when a broad view of the power to spend is accepted: "The line must still be drawn between one welfare and another, between particular and general. Where this shall be placed cannot be known through a formula in advance of the event. There is a middle ground or certainly a penumbra in which discretion is at large. The discretion, however, is not confided to the courts. The discretion belongs to Congress, unless the choice is clearly wrong, a display of arbitrary power, not an exercise of judgment." Here, it was clear, "Congress did not improvise a judgment when it was found that the award of old age benefits would be conducive to the general welfare." Justice Cardozo explained: "The problem is plainly national in area and dimensions. Moreover, laws of the separate states cannot deal with it effectively. Congress, at least, had a basis for that belief. [Apart] from the failure of resources, states and local governments are at times reluctant to increase so heavily the burden of taxation to be borne by their residents for fear of placing themselves in a position of economic disadvantage. A system of old age pensions has special dangers of its own, if put in force in one state and rejected in another. The existence of such a system is a bait to the needy and dependent elsewhere, encouraging them to migrate and seek a haven of repose. Only a power that is national can serve the interests of all." He concluded: "When money is spent to promote the general welfare, the concept of welfare or the opposite is shaped by Congress, not the states. So the concept be not arbitrary, the locality must yield." (In later cases, the Court has repeatedly endorsed a broad congressional discretion regarding the scope of the spending power. See, e.g., Buckley v. Valeo, 424 U.S. 1 (1976) (p. 1400 below). In rejecting a claim that the provisions for public financing of presidential election campaigns in the Federal Election Campaign Act exceeded the spending power, the Court stated: "It is for Congress to decide which expenditures will promote the general welfare.")

4. *Conditional federal grants to states: Some modern problems. 1. The practical dimensions of federal grants to states.* The traditional and pervasive nature of federal spending programs was recognized in Butler. Federal policy guidance (and control) via the spending power, especially through conditional

---

1. Justice Cardozo found the Butler decision distinguishable: "None of [the objections there] is applicable to the situation here developed. (a) The proceeds of the tax in controversy are not earmarked for a special group. (b) The unemployment compensation law which is a condition of the credit has had the approval of the state and could not be a law without it. (c) The condition is not linked to an irrevocable agreement, for the state at its pleasure may repeal its [law], terminate the credit, and place itself where it was before the credit was accepted. (d) The condition is not directed to the attainment of an unlawful end, but to an end, the relief of unemployment, for which nation and state may lawfully cooperate." (Justices McREYNOLDS, SUTHERLAND, VAN DEVANTER and BUTLER dissented.) Is Justice Cardozo's distinction of Butler persuasive? Did not Steward Machine, unlike Butler, involve an arguably greater "coercion" of states?

grants-in-aid to state and local governments, go back to the 19th century. The size and range of the programs have increased considerably over the years, and detailed federal conditions have proliferated.[1] During the 1960s, there was growing opposition to narrow categorical grants-in-aid and widespread advocacy of broader, less restricted block grants to states and local governments. The drive for "no strings money" instead of "strings money" bore fruit in the State and Local Fiscal Assistance Act of 1972. But the battle between advocates of block grants and categorical grants continues. Note the criticism of conditional federal grants to states in Cover, "Federalism and Administrative Structure," 92 Yale L.J. 1342 (1983): "By debilitating, if not disarming, the alternative sources of political power in our federal structure, 'cooperative federalism' undermines the only viable restraint on the congressional exercise of enumerated powers: the political process. Thus, cooperative ventures should be considered of dubious constitutionality." Compare the criticisms of Cover in Rose–Ackerman, "Cooperative Federalism and Co-optation," 92 Yale L.J. 1344 (1983).

5. *State autonomy as a limit on conditional spending?* Recall that in Steward Machine, Justice Cardozo asked whether the Social Security Act involved "the coercion of the States in contravention of the Tenth Amendment or of restrictions implicit in our federal form of government." He found no constitutional violation then. But in the years since, federal conditions on assistance to states have multiplied. When, if ever, do such conditions run counter to "restrictions implicit in our federal form of government"? So far, the Court has shown little receptivity to challenges to federal spending conditions on state autonomy grounds. Is greater receptivity warranted? Should the modern concerns about state autonomy limits on the commerce power, see sec. 4 of the preceding chapter, also be applicable to the spending power?[2] Justice Rehnquist left that question open in National League of Cities. But five years later, he stated in dictum in Pennhurst State School v. Halderman, 451 U.S. 1 (1981): "There are limits on the power of Congress to impose conditions on the States pursuant to its spending power [e.g., Steward Machine; see National League of Cities]. Even the [plaintiffs] recognize the 'constitutional difficulties' with imposing affirmative obligations on the States pursuant to the spending power. That issue, however, is not now before us." Contrast the Rehnquist majority opinion in South Dakota v. Dole, the next principal case. What constitutional limits on the spending power remain after that case? Do they adequately safeguard federalism-related concerns?

South Dakota v. Dole

483 U.S. 203, 107 S.Ct. 2793, 97 L.Ed.2d 171 (1987).

[In 1984, Congress enacted 20 U.S.C. § 158, which directs the Secretary of Transportation to withhold 5% of the federal highway funds otherwise payable to states from any State which permits purchase or public possession of any

---

1. For a discussion of early practices, see Elazar, The American Partnership: Intergovernmental Co-operation in the Nineteenth Century United States (1962). For a modern survey, see Rosenthal, "Conditional Federal Spending and the Constitution," 39 Stan. L.Rev. 1103 (1987).

2. For a strong argument that they should be (written in the years between National League of Cities and Garcia), see Kaden, "Politics, Money, and State Sovereignty: The Judicial Role," 79 Colum.L.Rev. 847 (1979).

alcoholic beverage by a person less than 21 years old. South Dakota, which permitted persons 19 years of age or older to purchase 3.2% beer, sought a declaratory judgment that § 158 violated constitutional limits on the congressional spending power and also violate the Twenty-first Amendment. The lower federal courts rejected these claims.]

Chief Justice REHNQUIST delivered the opinion of the Court.

[We] need not decide in this case whether [the Twenty-first Amendment] would prohibit an attempt by Congress to legislate directly a national minimum drinking age. Here, Congress has acted indirectly under its spending power to encourage uniformity in the States' drinking ages. [We] find this legislative effort within constitutional bounds even if Congress may not regulate drinking ages directly. [Incident to the spending power], Congress may attach conditions on the receipt of federal funds, and has repeatedly employed the power "to further broad policy objectives by conditioning receipt of federal moneys upon compliance by the recipient with [federal] directives." Fullilove v. Klutznick [1980; p. 812 below (opinion of Burger, C.J.)]. The breadth of this power was made clear in [Butler]. Thus, objectives not thought to be within Article I's "enumerated legislative fields" may nevertheless be attained through the use of the spending power and the conditional grant of federal funds. The spending power is of course not unlimited. [The] first of these limitations is derived from the language of the Constitution itself: the exercise of the spending power must be in pursuit of "the general welfare." In considering whether a particular expenditure is intended to serve general public purposes, courts should defer substantially to the judgment of Congress. Second, we have required that if Congress desires to condition the States' receipt of federal funds, it "must do so unambiguously ..., enabl[ing] the States to exercise their choice knowingly, cognizant of the consequences of their participation." Third, our cases have suggested (without significant elaboration) that conditions on federal grants might be illegitimate if they are unrelated "to the federal interest in particular national projects or programs." Finally, we have noted that other constitutional provisions may provide an independent bar to the conditional grant of federal funds.

South Dakota does not seriously claim that § 158 is inconsistent with any of the first three restrictions mentioned above. [The] State itself [admits] that it "has never contended that the congressional action [was] unrelated to a national concern in the absence of the Twenty-first Amendment." Indeed, the condition imposed by Congress is directly related to one of the main purposes for which highway funds are expended—safe interstate travel.[1] This goal of the interstate highway system had been frustrated by varying drinking ages among the States. A Presidential commission appointed to study alcohol-related accidents and fatalities on the Nation's highways concluded that the lack of uniformity in the States' drinking ages created "an incentive to drink and drive" because "young persons commut[e] to border States where the drinking

---

1. Our cases have not required that we define the outer bounds of the "germaneness" or "relatedness" limitation on the imposition of conditions under the spending power. Amici urge that we take this occasion to establish that a condition on federal funds is legitimate only if it relates directly to the purpose of the expenditure to which it is attached. See Brief for National Conference of State Legislatures et al. as Amici Curiae. Because petitioner has not sought such a restriction, and because we find any such limitation on conditional federal grants satisfied in this case in any event, we do not address whether conditions less directly related to the particular purpose of the expenditure might be outside the bounds of the spending power. [Footnote by Chief Justice Rehnquist.]

age is lower." By enacting § 158, Congress conditioned the receipt of federal funds in a way reasonably calculated to address this particular impediment to a purpose for which the funds are expended.

The remaining question about the validity of § 158—and the basic point of disagreement between the parties—is whether the Twenty-first Amendment constitutes an "independent constitutional bar" to the conditional grant of federal funds. Petitioner, relying on its view that the Twenty-first Amendment prohibits *direct* regulation of drinking ages by Congress, asserts that "Congress may not use the spending power to regulate that which it is prohibited from regulating directly under the Twenty-first Amendment." But our cases show that this "independent constitutional bar" limitation on the spending power is not of the kind petitioner suggests. [Butler], for example, established that the constitutional limitations on Congress when exercising its spending power are less exacting than those on its authority to regulate directly. We have also held that a perceived Tenth Amendment limitation on congressional regulation of state affairs did not concomitantly limit the range of conditions legitimately placed on federal grants. In Oklahoma v. Civil Service Comm'n, 330 U.S. 127 (1947), the Court considered the validity of the Hatch Act insofar as it was applied to political activities of state officials whose employment was financed in whole or in part with federal funds. The State contended that an order under this provision to withhold certain federal funds unless a state official was removed invaded its sovereignty in violation of the Tenth Amendment. [The Court held] that the Federal Government "does have power to fix the terms upon which its money allotments to states shall be disbursed." The Court found no violation of the State's sovereignty because the State could, and did, adopt "the 'simple expedient' of not yielding to what she urges is federal coercion. The offer of benefits to a state by the United States dependent upon cooperation by the state with federal plans, assumedly for the general welfare, is not unusual."[2]

These cases establish that the "independent constitutional bar" limitation on the spending power is not, as petitioner suggests, a prohibition on the indirect achievement of objectives which Congress is not empowered to achieve directly. Instead, we think that the language in our earlier opinions stands for the unexceptionable proposition that the power may not be used to induce the States to engage in activities that would themselves be unconstitutional. Thus, for example, a grant of federal funds conditioned on invidiously discriminatory state action or the infliction of cruel and unusual punishment would be an illegitimate exercise of the Congress' broad spending power. But no such claim can be or is made [here]. Our decisions have recognized that in some circumstances the financial inducement offered by Congress might be so coercive as to pass the point at which "pressure turns into compulsion." [Steward Machine.] Here, however, Congress has directed only that a State desiring to establish a minimum drinking age lower than 21 lose a relatively small percentage of certain federal highway funds. Petitioner contends that the coercive nature of this program is evident from the degree of success it has achieved. We cannot conclude, however, that a conditional grant of federal money of this sort is unconstitutional simply by reason of its success in achieving the congressional objective. When we consider, for a moment, that all South Dakota would lose if she adheres to her chosen course as to a suitable minimum drinking age is 5%

2. For a sharp criticism of the Court's dismissive treatment of the Tenth Amendment claim in the Oklahoma case, see Linde, "Justice Douglas on Freedom in the Welfare State," 39 Wash.L.Rev. 4 (1964) (criticizing the majority's "easy generalizations about conditioned federal spending").

of the funds otherwise obtainable under specified highway grant programs, the argument as to coercion is shown to be more rhetoric than [fact]. Here Congress has offered relatively mild encouragement to the States to enact higher minimum drinking ages than they would otherwise choose. But the enactment of such laws remains the prerogative of the States not merely in theory but in fact. Even if Congress might lack the power to impose a national minimum drinking age directly, we conclude that encouragement to state action found in § 158 is a valid use of the spending power.

[Affirmed.]

Justice O'CONNOR, dissenting.

[Sec. 158] is not a condition on spending reasonably related to the expenditure of federal funds and cannot be justified on that ground. Rather, it is an attempt to regulate the sale of liquor, an attempt that lies outside Congress' power to regulate commerce because it falls within the ambit of § 2 of the Twenty-first Amendment.[1] My disagreement with the Court is relatively narrow on the spending power issue: it is a disagreement about the application of a principle rather than a disagreement on the principle itself. [T]he Court's application of the requirement that the condition imposed be reasonably related to the purpose for which the funds are expended is cursory and unconvincing. We have repeatedly said that Congress may condition grants under the spending power only in ways reasonably related to the purpose of the federal program. In my view, establishment of a minimum drinking age of 21 is not sufficiently related to interstate highway construction to justify so conditioning funds appropriated for that purpose. [The] Court asserts the reasonableness of the relationship between the supposed purpose of the expenditure—"safe interstate travel"—and the drinking age condition. The Court reasons that Congress wishes that the roads it builds may be used safely, that drunken drivers threaten highway safety, and that young people are more likely to drive while under the influence of alcohol under existing law than would be the case if there were a uniform national drinking age of 21. It hardly needs saying, however, that if the purpose of § 158 is to deter drunken driving, it is far too over- and under-inclusive. It is over-inclusive because it stops teenagers from drinking even when they are not about to drive on interstate highways. It is under-inclusive because teenagers pose only a small part of the drunken driving problem in this Nation.

When Congress appropriates money to build a highway, it is entitled to insist that the highway be a safe one. But it is not entitled to insist as a condition of the use of highway funds that the State impose or change regulations in other areas of the State's social and economic life because of an attenuated or tangential relationship to highway use or safety. Indeed, if the rules were otherwise, the Congress could effectively regulate almost any area of a State's social, political, or economic life on the theory that use of the interstate transportation system is somehow enhanced. If, for example, the United States were to condition highway moneys upon moving the state capital, I suppose it might argue that interstate transportation is facilitated by locating local governments in places easily accessible to interstate highways—or, conversely, that highways might become overburdened if they had to carry traffic

---

1. Justice BRENNAN submitted a separate dissent agreeing with Justice O'Connor on this issue.

to and from the state capital. In my mind, such a relationship is hardly more attenuated than the one which the Court finds supports § 158.

There is a clear place at which the Court can draw the line between permissible and impermissible conditions on federal grants. It is the line identified in the Brief for the National Conference of State Legislatures et al. as Amici Curiae: "Congress has the power to *spend* for the general welfare, it has the power to *legislate* only for delegated [purposes]. The appropriate inquiry, then, is whether the spending requirement or prohibition is a condition on a grant or whether it is regulation. The difference turns on whether the requirement specifies in some way how the money should be spent, so that Congress' intent in making the grant will be effectuated. Congress has no power under the Spending Clause to impose requirements on a grant that go beyond specifying how the money should be spent. A requirement that is not such a specification is not a condition, but a regulation, which is valid only if it falls within one of Congress' delegated regulatory powers." This approach harks back to United States v. Butler. The Butler Court saw the Agricultural Adjustment Act for what it was—an exercise of regulatory, not spending, power. The error in Butler was not the Court's conclusion that the Act was essentially regulatory, but rather its crabbed view of the extent of Congress' regulatory power under the Commerce Clause. The Agricultural Adjustment Act was regulatory but it was regulation that today would likely be considered within Congress' commerce power. While Butler's authority is questionable insofar as it assumes that Congress has no regulatory power over farm production, its discussion of the spending power and its description of both the power's breadth and its limitations remain sound. The Court's decision in Butler also properly recognizes the gravity of the task of appropriately limiting the spending power. If the spending power is to be limited only by Congress' notion of the general welfare, the reality, given the vast financial resources of the Federal Government, is that the Spending Clause gives "power to the Congress to tear down the barriers, to invade the states' jurisdiction, and to become a parliament of the whole people, subject to no restrictions save such as are self-imposed." [Butler.] This, of course, as Butler held, was not the Framers' plan and it is not the meaning of the Spending Clause.

Our later cases are consistent with the notion that, under the spending power, the Congress may only condition grants in ways that can fairly be said to be related to the expenditure of federal funds. [E.g., Oklahoma v. CSC.] [Other] conditions that have been upheld by the Court may be viewed as independently justified under some regulatory power of the Congress. [E.g., Fullilove.] This case, however, falls into neither class. As discussed above, a condition that a State will raise its drinking age to 21 cannot fairly be said to be reasonably related to the expenditure of funds for highway construction. The only possible connection, highway safety, has nothing to do with how the funds Congress has appropriated are expended. Rather, it is a regulation determining who shall be able to drink liquor. As such it is not justified by the spending power. Of the other possible sources of congressional authority for regulating the sale of liquor only the commerce power comes to mind. But in my view, the regulation of the age of the purchasers of liquor, just as the regulation of the price at which liquor may be sold, falls squarely within the scope of those powers reserved to the States by the Twenty-first Amendment. Accordingly, Congress simply lacks power under the Commerce Clause to displace state regulation of this kind. The immense size and power of the Government of the United States ought not obscure its fundamental character. It remains a Government of enumerated powers. [McCulloch.] Because § 158 cannot be justified as an exercise of any power delegated to the Congress, it is not authorized by the [Constitution].[2]

————

Any modern constitutional restraints on conditional spending? Although South Dakota v. Dole illustrates the modern Court's diminished concerns with federalism-related restraints on spending programs, other constitutional problems remain with respect to the validity of the conditions. Chief Justice Rehnquist's opinion in the South Dakota case notes some of the continuing constraints. For example, conditions on federal grants are illegitimate if they are "unrelated" to the spending program, and "other constitutional provisions may provide an independent bar to the conditional grant of federal funds." The reasonable relationship requirement harks back to the earliest cases in this section; the "independent bar" requirement looks forward to problems that arise in later materials in this book, when conditions on spending raise issues, for example, under the First Amendment and the due process and equal protection guarantees. Note, for example, the controversies about abortion funding, as in, e.g., Harris v. McRae, p. 551 below. Note also the extensive modern literature on the problem of arguably "unconstitutional conditions"— e.g., O'Neil, "Unconstitutional Conditions: Welfare Benefits with Strings Attached," 54 Calif.L.Rev. 443 (1966); Sullivan, "Unconstitutional Conditions," 102 Harv.L.Rev. 1413 (1989); and Epstein, "Foreword: Unconstitutional Conditions, State Power, and the Limits of Consent," 102 Harv.L.Rev. 4 (1988). The classic early study is Hale, "Unconstitutional Conditions and Constitutional Rights," 35 Colum.L.Rev. 321 (1935).

SECTION 3. WAR, FOREIGN AFFAIRS, AND FEDERALISM

Introduction. The commerce, taxing, and spending powers considered in the preceding materials are by far the most important national powers with an impact on federalism-related concerns, but they are by no means the only ones. The limited purpose of this section is to examine briefly what, if any, federalism-based constraints may exist on two other potentially broad sources of authority: the war power, and the national government's powers to make treaties and deal with foreign affairs. With respect to each of these powers, consider whether the scope of the power is narrower or broader than that of the commerce power; and consider as well whether the political restraints on Congress, so heavily relied on in many modern commerce power cases, are likely to be less effective with respect to these powers, thus arguably justifying greater Court concern with imposing federalism-related constraints. [The powers considered in this section frequently risk impingement on constitutional concerns other than federalism: both the war power and the foreign affairs power often generate controversies involving separation of powers and individual rights issues. Consideration of the powers in the context of those countervailing interests is postponed to later chapters (see, e.g., chap. 6, on separation of powers); here, the limited sampling of additional national powers focuses on

2. Contrast Justice O'Connor's expansive view of the spending power in her majority opinion in New York v. United States, chap. 3, sec. 4. Does the New York case demonstrate a retreat from her dissenting position in the principal case?

their impacts on federalism.[1]]

_____

A.   The War Power

Woods v. Cloyd W. Miller Co.

333 U.S. 138, 68 S.Ct. 421, 92 L.Ed. 596 (1948).

Justice DOUGLAS delivered the opinion of the Court.

The case is here on a direct appeal [from] a judgment of the District Court holding unconstitutional Title II of the Housing and Rent Act of 1947. The District Court was of the view that the authority of Congress to regulate rents by virtue of the war power ended with the Presidential Proclamation terminating hostilities on December 31, 1946, since that proclamation inaugurated "peace-in-fact" though it did not mark termination of the war. It also concluded that, even if the war power continues, Congress did not act under it because it did not say [so]. [In our view, the] war power sustains this legislation. The Court said in Hamilton v. Kentucky Distilleries Co., 251 U.S. 146, 161 [1919], that the war power includes the power "to remedy the evils which have arisen

---

1. *Other congressional powers.* As the text of the Necessary and Proper Clause shows, the Clause grants Congress not only the authority to implement the powers enumerated in Art. I, but also the authority to enforce "all other Powers" granted to the national government. Among the Art. I, § 8 powers not considered in detail here is the power to "coin money" and "regulate the Value thereof," see, e.g., one of the "gold clause" cases, Norman v. Baltimore & Ohio Railroad Co., 294 U.S. 240 (1935).

The constitutional amendment process. Article V, on amending the Constitution, also contains important, though rarely discussed, powers of Congress that may have an important impact on the federal-state balance. Art. V specifies two methods for initiating the amendment process: Congress, by a two-thirds vote, may propose amendments for ratification by three-fourths of the states; or two-thirds of the states may apply to Congress for the calling of a constitutional convention "for proposing Amendments." The first, congressionally-initiated method is the traditionally used one, and it may produce significant shifts in the allocation of power between nation and states, as with the post-Civil War Amendments. Congressional action relating to that amendment route can be controversial. Note, e.g., the congressional decision in 1978 to extend the period for ratification of the proposed Equal Rights Amendment until 1982, and to refuse permis-

sion to states to rescind prior votes for ratification. There is even greater potential for controversy in the untried second, state-initiated amendment route. For example, by the mid–1980s, 32 states had applied for a constitutional convention to add a balanced budget amendment to the Constitution. There is no doubt that Congress is under a duty to call such a convention when 34 valid state applications are at hand. But in most other respects, the convention route is clouded by uncertainty. The most widely debated question has been whether Congress may limit the scope of deliberations at a convention (e.g., to the balanced budget issue), or whether a convention is entitled to set its own agenda. For the view that Congress can limit the convention agenda in accordance with the purpose reflected in the state applications, see, e.g., ABA Special Constitutional Convention Study Comm., Amendment of the Constitution by the Convention Method under Article V (1974), and Van Alstyne, "Does Article V Restrict the States to Calling Unlimited Conventions Only?" 1978 Duke L.J. 1295 (1979). For arguments that Congress cannot effectively limit the scope of the convention, see, e.g., Black, "Amending the Constitution," 82 Yale L.J. 189 (1972), Dellinger, "The Recurring Question of the 'Limited' Constitutional Convention," 88 Yale L.J. 1623 (1979), and Gunther, "The Convention Method of Amending the United States Constitution," 14 Ga.L.Rev. 1 (1979).

from its rise and progress" and continues for the duration of that emergency. Whatever may be the consequences when war is officially terminated, the war power does not necessarily end with the cessation of hostilities. [In Hamilton] and Ruppert v. Caffey, 251 U.S. 264 [1920], prohibition laws which were enacted after the Armistice in World War I were sustained as exercises of the war power because they conserved manpower and increased efficiency of production in the critical days during the period of demobilization, and helped to husband the supply of grains and cereals depleted by the war effort. [The] constitutional validity of the present legislation follows a fortiori from those cases. The legislative history of the present Act makes abundantly clear that there has not yet been eliminated the deficit in housing which in considerable measure was caused by the heavy demobilization of veterans and by the cessation or reduction in residential construction during the period of hostilities due to the allocation of building materials to military projects. Since the war effort contributed heavily to that deficit, Congress has the power even after the cessation of hostilities to act to control the forces that a short supply of the needed article created. If that were not true, the Necessary and Proper Clause would be drastically limited in its application to the several war powers.

[We] recognize the force of the argument that the effects of war under modern conditions may be felt in the economy for years and years, and that if the war power can be used in days of peace to treat all the wounds which war inflicts on our society, it may not only swallow up all other powers of Congress but largely obliterate the Ninth and the Tenth Amendments as well. There are no such implications in today's decision. We deal here with the consequences of a housing deficit greatly intensified during the period of hostilities. [Any] power, of course, can be abused. But we cannot assume that Congress is not alert to its constitutional responsibilities. [The] question of the constitutionality of action taken by Congress does not depend on recitals of the power which it undertakes to exercise. Here it is plain from the legislative history that Congress was invoking its war power to cope with a current condition of which the war was a direct and immediate [cause].

Reversed.

Justice JACKSON, concurring.

I agree with the result in this case, but the arguments that have been addressed to us lead me to utter more explicit misgivings about war powers than the Court has done. The Government asserts no constitutional basis for this legislation other than this vague, undefined and undefinable "war power." No one will question that this power is the most dangerous one to free government in the whole catalogue of powers. It usually is invoked in haste and excitement when calm legislative consideration of constitutional limitation is difficult. It is executed in a time of patriotic fervor that makes moderation unpopular. And, worst of all, it is interpreted by judges under the influence of the same passions and pressures. Always, as in this case, the Government urges hasty decision to forestall some emergency or serve some purpose and pleads that paralysis will result if its claims to power are denied or their confirmation delayed. Particularly when the war power is invoked to do things to the liberties of people, or to their property or economy that only indirectly affect conduct of the war and do not relate to the management of the war itself, the constitutional basis should be scrutinized with care.

I think we can hardly deny that the war power is as valid a ground for federal rent control now as it has been at any time. We still are technically in a state of war. I would not be willing to hold that war powers may be indefinitely prolonged merely by keeping legally alive a state of war that had in fact ended.

I cannot accept the argument that war powers last as long as the effects and consequences of war, for if so they are permanent—as permanent as the war debts. But I find no reason to conclude that we could find fairly that the present state of war is merely technical. We have armies abroad exercising our war power and have made no peace terms with our allies, not to mention our principal enemies. I think the conclusion that the war power has been applicable during the lifetime of this legislation is unavoidable.[1]

Domestic regulation through the war power. As Woods illustrates, the war power is available for national regulation of a wide range of problems, of the "police" as well as the economic variety. Note, for example, the rationale for sustaining the post-World War I prohibition law as described in Woods. Was there adequate judicial scrutiny in the Hamilton and Ruppert cases in 1919–20? Or are those decisions additional illustrations of the early 20th century Court's insensitivity to federalism values when Congress moved against such "evils" as immorality and crime? (Recall the Lottery Case, p. 169 above.) Are there judicially enforceable limits on war power-based regulation, either of the economic or the "police" variety?

B.   TREATIES, FOREIGN AFFAIRS, AND FEDERALISM

Introduction. To what extent does the national government's authority over foreign affairs authorize national regulation of an otherwise local area? That is the central concern of this section. [Other constitutional problems pertaining to international affairs are left to later chapters—especially chap. 6.] Most of the materials in this section involve domestic regulatory consequences of national action resting on the treaty power. The final note considers whether there is a foreign affairs power of Congress independent of authority derived from treaties—and what the source of that power is. The central question in this section is: To what extent may a treaty authorize national regulation of local affairs not reachable under other grants of power?

Missouri v. Holland

252 U.S. 416, 40 S.Ct. 382, 64 L.Ed. 641 (1920).

Justice HOLMES delivered the opinion of the court.

This is a bill in equity brought by the State of Missouri to prevent a game warden of the United States from attempting to enforce the [1918] Migratory Bird Treaty Act [on the ground] that the statute is an unconstitutional interference with the rights reserved to the States by the Tenth Amendment and that the [threatened] acts of the defendant [contravened] its will manifest-

----

1. Another concurring opinion, by Justice FRANKFURTER, is omitted. [Justice Jackson's stance of noting misgivings, often in concurring opinions, was one he took in a variety of contexts. Recall, for example, his doubts about the taxing power in the Kahriger case, p. 232 above. There are similar examples in later chapters: e.g., on the war power and individual rights, in Korematsu v. United States, p. 664 below, and on equal protection restraints on economic regulation, in Railway Express Agency v. New York, p. 639 below.]

ed in statutes. [The District Court held the Act constitutional.] On December 8, 1916, a treaty between the United States and Great Britain was proclaimed by the President. It recited that many species of birds in their annual migrations traversed certain parts of the United States and of Canada, that they were of great value as a source of food and in destroying insects injurious to vegetation, but were in danger of extermination through lack of adequate protection. It therefore provided for specified closed seasons and protection in other forms, and agreed that the two powers would take or propose to their law making bodies the necessary measures for carrying the treaty out. The [1918 Act] prohibited the killing, capturing or selling any of the migratory birds included in the terms of the treaty except as permitted by [federal] regulations compatible with those [terms].

To answer this question it is not enough to refer to the Tenth Amendment [because] by Article II, § 2, the power to make treaties is delegated expressly, and by Article VI treaties made under the authority of the United States [are] declared the supreme law of the land. If the treaty is valid there can be no dispute about the validity of the statute under Article I, § 8, as a necessary and proper means to execute the powers of the Government. It is said that a treaty cannot be valid if it infringes the Constitution, that there are limits, therefore, to the treaty-making power, and that one such limit is that what an act of Congress could not do unaided, in derogation of the powers reserved to the States, a treaty cannot do. [The fact that an] earlier act of Congress that attempted by itself and not in pursuance of a treaty to regulate the killing of migratory birds within the States had been held bad [in two lower court decisions] cannot be accepted as a test of the treaty power.[1] Acts of Congress are the supreme law of the land only when made in pursuance of the Constitution, while treaties are declared to be so when made under the authority of the United States. It is open to question whether the authority of the United States means more than the formal acts prescribed to make the convention. We do not mean to imply that there are no qualifications to the treaty-making power; but they must be ascertained in a different way. It is obvious that there may be matters of the sharpest exigency for the national well being that an act of Congress could not deal with but that a treaty followed by such an act could, and it is not lightly to be assumed that, in matters requiring national action, "a power which must belong to and somewhere reside in every civilized government" is not to be found. [W]hen we are dealing with words that also are a constituent act, like the [Constitution], we must realize that they have called into life a being the development of which could not have been foreseen completely by the most gifted of its begetters. It was enough for them to realize or to hope that they had created an organism; it has taken a century and has cost their successors much sweat and blood to prove that they created a nation. The case before us must be considered in the light of our whole experience and not merely in that of what was said a hundred years ago. The treaty in question does not contravene any prohibitory words to be found in the Constitution. The only question is whether it is forbidden by some invisible radiation from the general terms of the Tenth Amendment. We must consider what this country has become in deciding what that Amendment has reserved. [Here] a national interest of very nearly the first magnitude is involved. It can be protected only by national action in concert with that of another power. The subject matter is only transitorily within the State and has no permanent habitat therein. But for the treaty and the statute there soon

---

1. Under modern commerce clause doctrine, would a law such as the "earlier act of Congress" be constitutional?

might be no birds for any powers to deal with. We see nothing in the Constitution that compels the Government to sit by while a food supply is cut off and the protectors of our forests and our crops are destroyed. It is not sufficient to rely upon the States. The reliance is vain, and were it otherwise, the question is whether the United States is forbidden to act. We are of opinion that the treaty and statute must be upheld.

[Affirmed.][2]

———

1. *The scope and limits of the treaty power.* a. *The supremacy of treaties over state law.* As Missouri v. Holland reminds, a treaty made by the President with the required concurrence of two-thirds of the Senate is, under the Supremacy Clause of Art. VI, § 2, part of "the supreme Law of the Land," which takes precedence over contrary state laws. Even before the days of the Marshall Court, the Court began to implement the principle that a valid treaty overrides a state law on matters otherwise within state control. For example, in Ware v. Hylton, 3 Dall. (3 U.S.) 199 (1796), a treaty was held to have overridden a Virginia confiscation law. Similarly, in Hauenstein v. Lynham, 100 U.S. 483 (1880), a Virginia law providing for the escheat to the state of real estate of aliens dying intestate had to give way to a treaty, with the Court quoting from a treatise stating that "all questions which may arise between us and other powers, be the subject-matter what it may, fall within the treaty-making power."

b. *Limits on the treaty power?—The subject-matter of treaties.* Are there any judicially enforceable limits on the permissible subject-matter of a treaty? Whenever Art. I powers prove insufficient to reach a local problem, may the national government overcome that obstacle simply by making a treaty with a cooperating foreign government? Are there any traditionally local questions that cannot be "properly the subject of negotiation with a foreign country"?[1] Does not the fact that a treaty exists, that a treaty about a particular matter *has* been negotiated, demonstrate that the matter *is* a proper subject for negotiation? Can the courts scrutinize the good faith of President and Senate in entering into treaties?

c. *The Bricker Amendment controversy.* In the early 1950s, widely voiced concerns that the treaty power was the Achilles heel of the Constitution—that any and all constitutional limitations could be overridden via the international agreement route—spurred efforts to amend the Constitution. Justice Holmes's broad statements in Missouri v. Holland were frequently cited sources for those anxious to demonstrate the substantiality of the threat to constitutional restrictions. Moreover, the fears that generated popular support for the Bricker Amendment were fed by occasional arguments made in American courts that relied on United Nations provisions.[2] These anxieties produced Senator Brick-

---

2. Justices VAN DEVANTER and PITNEY dissented.

1. The "properly the subject of negotiation" phrase comes from DeGeofroy v. Riggs, 133 U.S. 258 (1890). Compare comment b to ALI, Restatement (Second) Foreign Relations Law of the United States § 117 (1965): "An international agreement of the United States must relate to the external concerns of the nation as distinguished from matters of a purely internal nature." Is this an effective limit on the treaty power? Fear about a potentially unlimited treaty power spawned the Bricker Amendment controversy of the 1950s, considered in the next note.

2. The concern was that the UN Charter or resolutions by UN agencies (e.g., the Draft Covenant on Civil and Political Rights) might undercut American constitutional

er's constitutional amendment proposal. The version recommended by the Senate Judiciary Committee in 1953 included the statement, as Sec. 1: "A provision of a treaty which conflicts with this Constitution shall not be of any force or effect." And Sec. 2 added: "A treaty shall become effective as internal law in the United States only through legislation which would be valid in the absence of treaty." That second section was directed against the doctrine of enlargement of congressional powers through treaties, as in Missouri v. Holland, as well as against the principle that treaties can be self-executing, as had been true since Ware v. Hylton. After extensive debates in the Senate in 1954, various modifications were offered. A substitute by Senator George of Georgia attracted a majority vote of 60–31 in February 1954—just short of the required two-thirds. The George substitute included the statement: "A provision of a treaty or other international agreement which conflicts with this Constitution shall not be of any force or effect." Similar proposals during the ensuing years also failed.

d.   *The reassurance of Reid v. Covert.* While the Bricker Amendment debate was still alive, the Supreme Court handed down REID v. COVERT, 354 U.S. 1 (1957); and Justice BLACK's plurality opinion contained a passage directly responsive to some of the concerns voiced by the supporters of the Bricker Amendment. Did it give adequate reassurance on all of their concerns? Reid v. Covert dealt mainly with congressional power under Art. 1, § 8, to provide for military jurisdiction over civilian dependents of American servicemen overseas. But in a passage relevant to the Bricker issue, the Court also rejected an argument that the law might be independently supportable because of the existence of an international agreement. Executive agreements had been entered into with other countries permitting American military courts to exercise exclusive jurisdiction over offenses by American servicemen or their dependents overseas. (On the distinction between executive agreements and treaties, see chap. 6.) The Government argued that the challenged statute could be sustained "as legislation which is necessary and proper to carry out the United States' obligations under the international agreements." Justice Black replied: "The obvious and decisive answer to this, of course, is that no agreement with a foreign nation can confer power on the Congress, or on any other branch of Government, which is free from the restraints of the Constitution." He found nothing in the history or language of the Supremacy Clause, Art. VI, § 2, "which intimates that treaties and laws enacted pursuant to them do not have to comply with the provisions of the Constitution." Rather, he thought it "clear that the reason treaties were not limited to those made in 'pursuance' of the Constitution [see the text of Art. VI] was so that agreements made by the United States under the Articles of Confederation [would] remain in effect." He added: "It would be manifestly contrary to the objectives of those who created the Constitution, as well as those who were responsible for the Bill of Rights—let alone alien to our entire constitutional history and tradition—to construe Article VI as permitting the United States to exercise power under an international agreement without observing constitutional prohibitions." Moreover, he found nothing to the contrary in Missouri v. Holland. Justice Black explained: "There the Court carefully noted that the

guarantees. For example, Art. 55 of the UN Charter states that the UN shall promote "universal respect for, and observance of, human rights and fundamental freedoms without distinction as to race, sex, language, or religion." In Sei Fujii v. State, 217 P.2d 481 (1950), a California District Court of

Appeal held an alien land law invalid on the ground that the UN Charter was self-executing. The California Supreme Court, however, rested its affirmance of the result on the 14th Amendment, 242 P.2d 617 (1952), after finding that the UN Charter provision was "not self-executing."

treaty involved was not inconsistent with any specific provision of the Constitution." Noting that Missouri v. Holland had been solely concerned with the Tenth Amendment, he added: "To the extent that the United States can validly make treaties, the people and the States have delegated their power to the National Government and the Tenth Amendment is no barrier." Justice Black's comments contributed greatly to putting to rest the concerns that treaties might be the basis for domestic action affecting individual rights beyond the limits governing other national powers.

2. *The foreign affairs power of Congress.* The national government's treaty power is explicitly granted in the Constitution. Is there also a foreign affairs power of Congress independent of authority to implement validly adopted treaties? Where in the Constitution is it found? Is it an inference from granted power? Or does it derive from extraconstitutional sources, as the Court has sometimes suggested? Is the notion of extraconstitutional sources of power consistent with the premises of constitutional government?

a. That there is a power in Congress to regulate foreign affairs has been repeatedly recognized by the Court. The source of the power remains unclear, however. For a modern statement of the power, see Perez v. Brownell, 356 U.S. 44, 57 (1958), sustaining a statutory provision regarding loss of citizenship: "Although there is in the Constitution no specific grant to Congress of power to enact legislation for the effective regulation of foreign affairs, there can be no doubt of the existence of this power in the law-making organ of the Nation. See, [e.g., United States v. Curtiss–Wright Export Corp., 299 U.S. 304, 318 (1936)]. The States that joined together to form a single Nation and to create, through the Constitution, a Federal Government to conduct the affairs of that Nation must be held to have granted that Government the powers indispensable to its functioning effectively in the company of sovereign nations. The Government must be able not only to deal affirmatively with foreign nations, as it does through the maintenance of diplomatic relations with them and the protection of American citizens sojourning within their territories. It must also be able to reduce to a minimum the frictions that are unavoidable in a world of sovereigns sensitive in matters touching their dignity and interests."

b. In the Curtiss–Wright passage cited in Perez, Justice Sutherland's majority opinion had discussed the supposedly "fundamental" differences "between the powers of the federal government in respect to foreign or external affairs and those in respect of domestic or internal affairs." He insisted that the "two classes of power are different, both in respect of their origin and their nature. The broad statement that the federal government can exercise no powers except those specifically enumerated in the Constitution, and such implied powers as are necessary and proper to carry into effect the enumerated powers, is categorically true only in respect of our internal affairs. In that field, the primary purpose of the Constitution was to carve from the general mass of legislative powers *then possessed by the states* such portions as it was thought desirable to vest in the federal government, leaving those not included in the enumeration still in the states. [That] this doctrine applies only to powers which the states had, is self-evident. And since the states severally never possessed international powers, such powers could not have been carved from the mass of state powers but obviously were transmitted to the United States from some other source." His review of history led him to conclude that "the investment of the federal government with the powers of external sovereignty did not depend upon the affirmative grants of the Constitution. The powers to declare and wage war, to conclude peace, to make treaties, to maintain diplomatic relations with other sovereignties, if they had never been mentioned in the Constitution, would have vested in the federal government as necessary concomitants of nationality." Justice Sutherland's Curtiss–Wright dictum is questionable historically[1] and certainly represents an approach to national powers notably different from that applied to other powers since the days of McCulloch. Nevertheless, as Perez illustrates, it represents a pervasive thread in Court discussions of foreign affairs matters.[2]

c. How extensive is the congressional power "to enact legislation for the effective regulation of foreign affairs"? Is it limited to matters that are generally the subject matter of foreign relations? Can the Court reexamine the good faith of—or factual basis for—a congressional assertion that a problem *is* a foreign affairs concern? Is this congressional power subject to any greater federalism-related limits than the DeGeofroy v. Riggs "properly the subject of negotiation" criterion regarding treaties?[3]

d. The national concern with foreign affairs is a powerful one, even though its bases are not fully spelled out in the Constitution. It supports not only congressional action; its mere existence, though unexercised, may preclude state action as well. The impact of the national power as a restraint on state authority is illustrated by Zschernig v. Miller, 389 U.S. 429 (1968), where the Court barred application of a state alien inheritance law because it intruded "into the field of foreign affairs which the Constitution entrusts to the President and the Congress."

1. See Lofgren, "United States v. Curtiss–Wright Corporation: An Historical Reassessment," 83 Yale L.J. 1 (1973).

2. See generally Henkin, Foreign Affairs and the Constitution (2d ed., 1996). (The Curtiss–Wright case is considered further in chap. 6, at p. 403.)

3. See generally Henkin, "The Treaty Makers and the Law Makers: The Law of the Land and Foreign Relations," 107 U.Pa. L.Rev. 903 (1959).

CHAPTER 5

FEDERAL LIMITS ON STATE POWER TO REGULATE THE NATIONAL ECONOMY

Introduction. The preceding three chapters examined the scope of *national* powers as limited by state concerns; this chapter focuses on the limits on *state* powers that flow from national concerns. On what basis, and to what extent, do the grants of enumerated powers to the national government, and the exercises of those powers, curtail state authority? Do the constraints arise from text? From history? From inferences based on the structure of the Constitution? From society's values—or those of the Justices? This chapter explores those problems mainly in the context of the commerce power; but similar restrictions on state authority arise in connection with other national powers as well.[1]

The commerce barrier to state action arises in two situations. In the first, Congress is silent: it has taken no action, express or implied, indicating its own policy on a given subject matter. In that situation, the objection to state authority rests entirely on the negative implications of the commerce clause of Art. I, § 8—on the unexercised commerce power itself, and on the free trade value it symbolizes. This situation is typically referred to as the operation of the "dormant" commerce clause. In the second situation, Congress *has* exercised the commerce power, and the challenge to inconsistent state action rests on both the exercise of the commerce power under Art. I, § 8 and the preemptive effect of the federal legislation under the supremacy clause of Art. VI. These materials explore the appropriate roles of Court and Congress in furthering commerce clause values; the source and scope of commerce power-based barriers to state action; and the extent of congressional authority to overturn Court-discovered obstacles to state action.

In recent years, the Court has revitalized another constitutional barrier to state action with purposes that somewhat overlap those of the commerce clause: the privileges and immunities clause of Art. IV, § 2, which guarantees to the "Citizens of each State [all] Privileges and Immunities of Citizens in the several States." Like the commerce clause, the Art. IV provision can be seen as directed against state legislation that *discriminates* against out-of-state economic interests. Interstate privileges and immunities decisions are considered later in this chapter together with related commerce clause developments and invocations of the equal protection guarantee of the 14th Amendment as a tool against economic protectionism. This chapter concludes with a brief survey of other interstate obligations in Art. IV, and with further materials on the

---

1. See, e.g., as to bankruptcy, Sturges v. Crowninshield, 4 Wheat. (17 U.S.) 122 (1819), and Perez v. Campbell, 402 U.S. 637 (1971); as to foreign affairs, Zschernig v. Mil-ler, 389 U.S. 429 (1968); as to copyright, Goldstein v. California, 412 U.S. 546 (1973); as to patents, Kewanee Oil Co. v. Bicron Corp., 416 U.S. 470 (1974).

intergovernmental immunities problem first raised in McCulloch, chap. 2 above.

SECTION 1. STATE REGULATION AND THE DORMANT COMMERCE CLAUSE

———

Introduction. 1. The sources of the "dormant" commerce clause. Under the "dormant" commerce clause, the Court invalidates some "protectionist" state legislation, even in the absence of congressional preemption. The Constitution nowhere explicitly gives the Court this task. Article I, § 10 bars states from imposing duties on imports or exports in foreign commerce without the consent of Congress. But the text of the Constitution nowhere expressly limits state power to regulate *interstate* commerce, nor imposes any explicit barrier to state protectionism or discrimination against trade. For such limitations, the Court has drawn on the negative implications of the grant of power to Congress to regulate interstate commerce. Article I, § 8, provides that "The Congress shall have Power [to] regulate Commerce [among] the several States." Into that affirmative grant the Court has read judicially enforceable limits on state legislation when Congress has not acted. To justify these implications from the commerce clause, the Court has relied largely on history and on inferences from the federal structure.

2. *The constitutional history.* The framers of the Constitution centralized the power to regulate interstate commerce in the Congress because they viewed destructive trade wars among the states as a major problem under the Articles of Confederation. Justice JACKSON reviewed this history in his opinion for the Court in H.P. HOOD & SONS v. DU MOND, 336 U.S. 525 (1949), which held that a state may not deny a milk processing license to an out-of-state distributor in order to stabilize in-state milk supply (see p. 292, below): "When victory relieved the Colonies from the pressure for solidarity that war had exerted, a drift toward anarchy and commercial warfare between states began. '[Each] State would legislate according to its estimate of its own interests, the importance of its own products, and the local advantages or disadvantages of its position in a political or commercial view.' This came 'to threaten at once the peace and safety of the Union.' The sole purpose for which Virginia initiated the movement which ultimately produced the Constitution was 'to take into consideration the trade of the United States; to examine the relative situations and trade of the said States; to consider how far a uniform system in their commercial regulations may be necessary to their common interest and their permanent harmony' and for that purpose the General Assembly of Virginia in January of 1786 named commissioners and proposed their meeting with those from other states. The desire of the Forefathers to federalize regulation of foreign and interstate commerce stands in sharp contrast to their jealous preservation of the state's power over its internal affairs. No other federal power was so universally assumed to be necessary, no other state power was so readily relinquished. [As Madison] indicated, 'want of a general power over Commerce led to an exercise of this power separately, by the States, wch [sic] not only proved abortive, but engendered rival, conflicting and angry regulations.' The necessity of centralized regulation of commerce among the states was so obvious and so fully recognized that the few words of the Commerce Clause were little illuminated by debate."

3. *The values served by the "dormant" commerce clause.* State laws that protect local economic interests at the expense of out-of-state interests are said to impair both the political and the economic vision of the framers. The political vision was one of national unity. As Justice Cardozo wrote for the Court in Baldwin v. G.A.F. Seelig, Inc. (1935; p. 287 below), "The Constitution was framed upon the theory that the peoples of the several states must sink or swim together, and that in the long run prosperity and salvation are in union and not division." The economic vision was one of free trade, in order that goods, labor and investments might be allocated efficiently by flowing to the place where they are most highly valued. As Justice Jackson's opinion in H.P. Hood & Sons v. DuMond elaborated, the dormant commerce clause thus advances national "prosperity" as well as "solidarity":

"The Commerce Clause is one of the most prolific sources of national power and an equally prolific source of conflict with legislation of the state. While the Constitution vests in Congress the power to regulate commerce among the states, it does not say what the states may or may not do in the absence of congressional action. [Perhaps] even more than by interpretation of its written word, this Court has advanced the solidarity and prosperity of this Nation by the meaning it has given to these great silences of the Constitution. [The] principle that our economic unit is the Nation, which alone has the gamut of powers necessary to control of the economy, including the vital power of erecting customs barriers against foreign competition, has as its corollary that the states are not separable economic units. [The] material success that has come to inhabitants of the states which make up this federal free trade unit has been the most impressive in the history of commerce, but the established interdependence of the states only emphasizes the necessity of protecting interstate movement of goods against local burdens. [The] distinction between the power of the State to shelter its people from menaces to their health or safety and from fraud, even when those dangers emanate from interstate commerce, and its lack of power to retard, burden or constrict the flow of such commerce for their economic advantage, is one deeply rooted in both our history and our law. [This] Court consistently has rebuffed attempts of states to advance their own commercial interests by curtailing the movement of articles of commerce, either into or out of the state, while generally supporting their right to impose even burdensome regulations in the interest of local health and safety. [Our] system, fostered by the Commerce Clause, is that every farmer and every craftsman shall be encouraged to produce by the certainty that he will have free access to every market in the Nation, that no home embargoes will withhold his exports, and no foreign state will by customs duties or regulations exclude them. Likewise, every consumer may look to the free competition from every producing area in the Nation to protect him from exploitation by any. Such was the vision of the Founders; such has been the doctrine of this Court which has given it [reality]."

Assuming that the history and structure of the Constitution place some limits on state power to discriminate against out-of-state economic interests, how strict should those limits be, and who should enforce them? Should Congress be understood to have exclusive power to regulate interstate commerce? Should Congress and the states be understood to have concurrent and overlapping powers in this area, subject only to congressional override through preemptive legislation? Or may the courts invalidate some exercises of concurrent state power even in the absence of congressional preemption? The early cases grappled with these questions.

A. EARLY DEVELOPMENTS

THE MARSHALL COURT

Gibbons v. Ogden

9 Wheat. (22 U.S.) 1, 6 L.Ed. 23 (1824).

[In the first part of his opinion in this case challenging New York's steamboat monopoly grant, Chief Justice MARSHALL considered the reach of the congressional commerce power into local affairs. (See p. 159, above.) In the portion printed here, Marshall discussed the impact of the commerce clause, and of national legislation based upon it, on state authority.]

[I]t has been urged, with great earnestness, that although the power of congress to regulate commerce with foreign nations, and among the several states, be co-extensive with the subject itself, and have no other limits than are prescribed in the constitution, yet the states may severally exercise the same power, within their respective jurisdictions. In support of this argument, it is said, that they possessed it as an inseparable attribute of sovereignty, before the formation of the constitution, and still retain it, except so far as they have surrendered it by that instrument; that this principle results from the nature of the government, and is secured by the tenth amendment; that an affirmative grant of power is not exclusive, unless in its own nature it be such that the continued exercise of it by the former possessor is inconsistent with the grant, and that this is not of that description. The appellant, conceding these postulates, except the last, contends that full power to regulate a particular subject, implies the whole power, and leaves no residuum; that a grant of the whole is incompatible with the existence of a right in another to any part of it.

[The] grant of the power to lay and collect taxes is, like the power to regulate commerce, made in general terms, and has never been understood to interfere with the exercise of the same power by the states; and hence has been drawn an argument which has been applied to the question under consideration. But the two grants are not, it is conceived, similar in their terms or their nature. [The] state governments remain, and constitute a most important part of our system. The power of taxation is indispensable to their existence, and is a power which, in its own nature, is capable of residing in, and being exercised by, different authorities at the same time. [When] each government exercises the power of taxation, neither is exercising the power of the other. But, when a state proceeds to regulate [interstate or foreign] commerce, it is exercising the very power that is granted to congress, and is doing the very thing which congress is authorized to do. There is no analogy, then, between the power of taxation and the power of regulating commerce.

[But] the inspection laws are said to be regulations of commerce, and are certainly recognised in the constitution, as being passed in the exercise of a power remaining with the states. That inspection laws may have a remote and considerable influence on commerce, will not be denied; but that a power to regulate commerce is the source from which the right to pass them is derived, cannot be admitted. The object of inspection laws, is to improve the quality of articles produced by the labour of a country; to fit them for exportation; or, it may be, for domestic use. They act upon the subject, before it becomes an article of [commerce], and prepare it for that purpose. They form a portion of that immense mass of legislation, which embraces every thing within the territory of a state, not surrendered to the general government; all which can be most advantageously exercised by the states themselves. Inspection laws, quarantine laws, health laws of every description, as well as laws for regulating the internal commerce of a state, and those which respect turnpike roads, ferries, & c., are component parts of this mass.

No direct general power over these objects is granted to congress; and, consequently, they remain subject to state legislation. If the legislative power of the Union can reach them, it must be for national purposes; it must be where the power is expressly given for a special purpose, or is clearly incidental to some power which is expressly given. It is obvious, that the government of the Union, in the exercise of its express powers, that, for example, of regulating [interstate commerce], may use means that may also be employed by a state, in the exercise of its acknowledged powers; that, for example, of regulating commerce within the state. [If] a state, in passing laws on subjects acknowledged to be within its control, and with a view to those subjects, shall adopt a measure of the same character with one which congress may adopt, it does not derive its authority from the particular power which has been granted, but from some other, which remains with the state, and may be executed by the same means. All experience shows, that the same measures, or measures scarcely distinguishable from each other, may flow from distinct powers; but this does not prove that the powers themselves are identical. Although the means used in their execution may sometimes approach each other so nearly as to be confounded, there are other situations in which they are sufficiently distinct, to establish their individuality. In our complex system, presenting the rare and difficult scheme of one general government, whose action extends over the whole, but which possesses only certain enumerated powers; and of numerous state governments, which retain and exercise all powers not delegated to the Union, contests respecting power must arise. Were it even otherwise, the measures taken by the respective governments to execute their acknowledged powers, would often be of the same description, and might, sometimes, interfere. This, however, does not prove that the one is exercising, or has a right to exercise, the powers of the other.

[It] has been contended by counsel for the appellant, that, as the word "to regulate" implies in its nature, full power over the thing to be regulated, it excludes, necessarily, the action of all others that would perform the same operation on the same thing. That regulation is designed for the entire result, applying in those parts which remain as they were, as well as to those which are altered. It produces a uniform whole, which is as much disturbed and deranged by changing what the regulating power designs to leave untouched, as that on which it has operated. There is great force in this argument, and the court is not satisfied that it has been refuted.

Since, however, in exercising the power of regulating their own purely internal affairs, whether of trading or police, the states may sometimes enact laws, the validity of which depends on their interfering with, and being contrary to, an act of congress passed in pursuance of the constitution, the court will enter upon the inquiry, whether the laws of New York [have], in their application to this case, come into collision with an act of congress, and deprived a citizen of a right to which that act entitles him. Should this collision exist, it will be immaterial, whether those laws were passed in virtue of a concurrent power "to regulate commerce with foreign nations and among the several states," or, in virtue of a power to regulate their domestic trade and police. In one case and the other, the acts of New York must yield to the law of congress; and the decision sustaining the privilege they confer, against a right given by a law of the Union, must be erroneous.

[Chief Justice Marshall found the New York steamboat monopoly grant to be in conflict with the federal laws licensing those engaged in the coastal trade. Accordingly, the state law was invalid under the supremacy clause of Art. VI of the Constitution. He thus disagreed with Chancellor Kent's view in the state court that the coasting license was merely intended to immunize American ships from the burdens imposed on foreign shipping. The Supreme Court decree accordingly reversed the decision below. As a result, Gibbons, the federal licensee, prevailed, and the injunction proceeding brought by Ogden, the holder of the New York monopoly, was dismissed.]

Reversed.

[Justice JOHNSON—a Jeffersonian Republican from South Carolina and President Jefferson's first appointee to the Court—concurred separately. Instead of joining Marshall's reliance on the preemptive effect of the federal licensing law, he rested on the ground suggested but not embraced by Marshall: the federal commerce power "must be exclusive." But for Johnson, as for Marshall, denial of a state power to regulate commerce did not mean total state inability to enact laws with some *effect* on commerce. Rather, the "purpose" of the state legislation was a critical criterion in distinguishing between permissible and impermissible state law: "It is no objection to the existence of distinct, substantive powers, that, in their application, they bear upon the same subject. [E.g., the same goods imported may be the subject of commercial regulation, yet also of state health regulation, because the goods may be 'the vehicle of disease.'] [The] different purposes [of the federal and state laws] mark the distinction between the powers brought into action. [Wherever] the powers of the respective governments are frankly exercised, with a distinct view to the ends of such powers, they may act upon the same object, or use the same means, and yet the powers be kept perfectly distinct."]

Willson v. Black Bird Creek Marsh Co.

2 Pet. (27 U.S.) 245, 7 L.Ed. 412 (1829).

[The Company was authorized by a Delaware law to build a dam in Black Bird Creek—which flowed into the Delaware River—and also to "bank" the adjoining "marsh and low ground." The dam obstructed navigation of the creek. Willson and others were owners of a sloop licensed under the federal navigation laws. The sloop "broke and injured" the Company's dam in order to pass through the creek. The Company successfully sued for damages; the state courts rejected Willson's defense that the law authorizing the dam violated the commerce clause.]

Chief Justice MARSHALL delivered the opinion of the Court.

The act of assembly by which the plaintiffs were authorized to construct their dam, shows plainly that this is one of those many creeks, passing through a deep level marsh adjoining the Delaware, up which the tide flows for some distance. The value of the property on its banks must be enhanced by excluding the water from the marsh, and the health of the inhabitants probably improved. Measures calculated to produce these objects, provided they do not come into collision with the powers of the general government, are undoubtedly within those which are reserved to the states. But the measure authorized by this act stops a navigable creek, and must be supposed to abridge the rights of those who have been accustomed to use it.

[The] counsel for the plaintiffs in error insist that it comes in conflict with the power of the United States "to regulate commerce with foreign nations and among the several states." If congress had passed any act which bore upon the case; any act in execution of the power to regulate commerce, the object of which was to control state legislation over those small navigable creeks into which the tide flows, and which abound throughout the lower country of the middle and southern states; we should feel not much difficulty in saying that a state law coming in conflict with such act would be void. But congress has passed no such act. The repugnancy of the law of Delaware to the constitution is placed entirely on its repugnancy to the power to regulate commerce with foreign nations and among the several states; a power which has not been so exercised as to affect the question. We do not think that the act empowering the [Company] to place a dam across the creek, can, under all the circumstances of the case, be considered as repugnant to the power to regulate commerce in its dormant state, or as being in conflict with any law passed on the subject.

[Affirmed.]

FROM MARSHALL TO THE EARLY TANEY COURT

1. *The Marshall legacy and the "commerce"-"police" distinction.* Gibbons v. Ogden and the Black Bird case were Marshall's only opportunities to write about the impact of the commerce clause on state regulatory authority. It is sometimes said that Marshall viewed the commerce power as exclusive. Is that borne out by his opinions? To be sure, Marshall in Gibbons did note the "great force" in the argument for exclusiveness and said that he was "not satisfied that it has been refuted." But this was dictum, as he rested ultimately on the supremacy clause. Moreover, in Gibbons, Marshall emphasized the purpose of state regulation in distinguishing permissible "police" regulations from impermissible "commerce" regulations. His suggestion of a possibly exclusive national commerce power coexisted with a recognition of state power to enact legislation which might affect commerce—"[i]nspection laws, quarantine laws, health laws of every description."

What explains Marshall's brief opinion in Black Bird? Was it a retreat from exclusiveness? Was it based on the notion that the Delaware law was a "health" law rather than a "commercial" regulation? See Frankfurter, The Commerce Clause Under Marshall, Taney and Waite (1937) (suggesting that Marshall in Black Bird "plainly implies that the Delaware statute falls outside the ban of the 'dormant' commerce clause, because it is not a regulation of commerce, but of 'police' "). Was it an unarticulated move toward a variety of "balancing" of state and national interests—a sustaining of the state law because the need for it was great and the burden it imposed on interstate commerce was small?

2. *The early Taney Court.* After Marshall's death in 1835, the Court, under his successor, Roger Brooke Taney, searched for formulations of the negative implications of the commerce clause with little clarity or agreement. Some of the Justices sought to follow what they perceived to be Marshall's guidance: state regulations of "commerce" were prohibited because of the "exclusive" commerce power, but "police" regulations were constitutional. Chief Justice Taney himself took a position at the polar extreme from the exclusiveness of the commerce power. To Taney, *no* implied prohibitions from

the dormant commerce clause were acceptable: state regulations of commerce were valid "unless they come in conflict with a law of Congress."

Thus, in Mayor of the City of New York v. Miln, 11 Pet. (36 U.S.) 102 (1837), the Court sustained a New York statute requiring the master of a vessel arriving in the port of New York from any point out of the state to report the names, residences, etc., of the passengers. The Court found the law to be "not a regulation of commerce, but of police," and accordingly found it unnecessary to decide whether the power to regulate commerce "be or be not exclusive of the States." Justice Story dissented, arguing that the commerce power belonged exclusively to Congress and that the state law unconstitutionally usurped it. In the Passenger Cases, 7 How. (48 U.S.) 283 (1849), however, the Court invalidated two other state laws: a New York statute imposing on the masters of ships coming from foreign or other state ports a tax for each passenger, the revenue to be used to defray the costs of examination of passengers for contagious diseases and to maintain a hospital for the treatment of those found to be diseased; and a similar Massachusetts tax applicable to aliens, with the further requirement that the master should post a bond in the amount of $1000 for each alien likely to become a public charge. Five Justices concurred in the result and four (including Chief Justice Taney) dissented. There was no opinion by the Court, but a series of individual opinions.

Finally, in The License Cases, 5 How. (46 U.S.) 504 (1847), the Court sustained state laws requiring licenses for the sale of intoxicating liquors. In rejecting challenges by sellers who had brought liquor from outside the state, the Court was unanimous on the result, but could not agree on a majority view; instead, the Justices produced six opinions. Chief Justice Taney stated: "It is well known that upon this subject a difference of opinion [exists] among the members of this court. But [it] appears to me to be very clear, that the mere grant of power to the general government cannot [be] construed to be an absolute prohibition to the exercise of any power over the same subject by the States. The controlling and supreme power over commerce with foreign nations and the several States is undoubtedly conferred upon Congress. Yet, in my judgment, the State may nevertheless, for the safety or convenience of trade, or for the protection of the health of its citizens, make regulations of commerce for its own ports and harbours, and for its own territory; and such regulations are valid unless they come in conflict with a law of Congress." A majority finally converged on a single standard in Cooley, which follows.

———

Cooley v. Board of Wardens

12 How. (53 U.S.) 299, 13 L.Ed. 996 (1851).

[A Pennsylvania law of 1803 required ships entering or leaving the port of Philadelphia to engage a local pilot to guide them through the harbor. For failure to comply, the law imposed a penalty of half the pilotage fee, payable to the Board for a fund for retired pilots and their dependents. The state courts held Cooley liable for the penalty. In addition to the 1803 Pennsylvania law, the case involved a 1789 congressional statute which provided that "all pilots in the bays, inlets, rivers, harbors, and ports in the United States shall continue to be regulated in conformity with the existing laws of the states, respectively, wherein such pilots may be, or with such laws as the states may respectively hereafter enact for the purpose, until further legislative provision shall be made by Congress."]

Justice CURTIS delivered the opinion of the Court.

[Regulations of pilots do] constitute regulations of navigation, and consequently of commerce, within the just meaning of [the commerce clause]. [It] becomes necessary, therefore, to consider whether this law of Pennsylvania, being a regulation of commerce, is valid [in view of the grant of the commerce power to Congress]. If the law of Pennsylvania, now in question, had been in existence at the date of this act of Congress, we might hold it to have been adopted by Congress, and thus made a law of the United States, and so valid. [But] the law on which these actions were founded was not enacted till 1803. What effect then can be attributed to so much of the act of 1789, as declares, that pilots shall continue to be regulated in conformity, "with such laws as the States may respectively hereafter enact for the purpose, until further legislative provision shall be made by Congress"?

If the States were divested of the power to legislate on this subject by the grant of the commercial power to Congress, it is plain this act could not confer upon them power thus to legislate. If the Constitution excluded the States from making any law regulating commerce, certainly Congress cannot regrant, or in any manner reconvey to the States that power. And yet this act of 1789 gives its sanction only to laws enacted by the States. This necessarily implies a constitutional power [in the States] to legislate. [Holding] these views we are brought directly and unavoidably to the consideration of the question, whether the grant of the commercial power to Congress, did per se deprive the States of all power to regulate pilots. This question has never been decided by this court, nor, in our judgment, has any case depending upon all the considerations which must govern this one, come before this court.

[The] diversities of opinion, [which] have existed on this subject, have arisen from the different views taken of the nature of this power. But when the nature of a power like this is spoken of, when it is said that the nature of the power requires that it should be exercised exclusively by Congress, it must be intended to refer to the subjects of that power, and to say they are of such a nature as to require exclusive legislation by Congress. Now the power to regulate commerce, embraces a vast field, containing not only many, but exceedingly various subjects, quite unlike in their nature; some imperatively demanding a single uniform rule, operating equally on the commerce of the United States in every port; and some, like the subject now in question, as imperatively demanding that diversity, which alone can meet the local necessities of navigation.

Either absolutely to affirm, or deny that the nature of this power requires exclusive legislation by Congress, is to lose sight of the nature of the subjects of this power, and to assert concerning all of them, what is really applicable but to a part. Whatever subjects of this power are in their nature national, or admit only of one uniform system, or plan of regulation, may justly be said to be of such a nature as to require exclusive legislation by Congress. That this cannot be affirmed of laws for the regulation of pilots and pilotage is plain. The act of 1789 contains a clear and authoritative declaration by the first Congress, that the nature of this subject is such, that until Congress should find it necessary to exert its power, it should be left to the legislation of the States; that it is local and not national; that it is likely to be the best provided for, not by one system, or plan of regulations, but by as many as the legislative discretion of the several States should deem applicable to the local peculiarities of the ports within their limits.

Viewed in this light, so much of this act of 1789 as declares that pilots shall continue to be regulated "by such laws as the States may respectively hereafter enact for that purpose," instead of being held to be inoperative, as an attempt to confer on the States a power to legislate, of which the Constitution had deprived them, is allowed an appropriate and important signification. It manifests the understanding of Congress, at the outset of the government, that the nature of this subject is not such as to require its exclusive legislation. The practice of the States, and of the national government, has been in conformity with this declaration, from the origin of the national government to this time; and the nature of the subject when examined, is such as to leave no doubt of the superior fitness and propriety, not to say the absolute necessity, of different systems of regulation, drawn from local knowledge and experience, and conformed to local wants. How then can we say, that by the mere grant of power to regulate commerce, the States are deprived of all the power to legislate on this subject, because from the nature of the power the legislation of Congress must be exclusive?

[It] is the opinion of a majority of the court that the mere grant to Congress of the power to regulate commerce, did not deprive the States of power to regulate pilots, and that although Congress has legislated on this subject, its legislation manifests an intention, with a single exception, not to regulate this subject, but to leave its regulation to the several states. To these precise questions, which are all we are called on to decide, this opinion must be understood to be confined. It does not extend to the question what other subjects, under the commercial power, are within the exclusive control of Congress, or may be regulated by the States in absence of all congressional legislation; nor to the general question, how far any regulation on a subject by Congress may be deemed to operate as an exclusion of all legislation by the States upon the same [subject].

Affirmed. [Justices McLean and Wayne dissented; Justice Daniel concurred on other grounds.]

THE AFTERMATH OF COOLEY

1. *Cooley's "national" "local" distinction.* Cooley steered a middle course between the polar positions that had clashed in the earlier Taney Court cases. It rejected the view that the congressional commerce power was exclusive and that the states therefore lacked *all* power to regulate commerce. But it also rejected the view that the commerce clause, in the absence of national legislation, imposed *no* limits on the states at all. Cooley recognized *some* concurrent state regulatory power over commerce and adopted a position that has sometimes been called one of selective exclusiveness. The Court's continuously dominant position since Cooley has been that the commerce clause by its own force bars some, but not all, state regulation.

Cooley identified as the determinative factor the "subject" of regulation; it appeared to abandon the "purpose" inquiry. According to Cooley, some subjects are "of such a nature" as to require "a single uniform rule" by Congress; others are local, "imperatively demanding that diversity which alone can meet the local necessities." But Cooley left unanswered questions about how the "subjects" were to be identified and distinguished. For example, what was the "subject" found to be "local and not national" in Cooley itself? All pilotage regulation? Pilotage regulation with a certain purpose? (Presumably, the Cooley Court assumed that the pilotage rule was directed at the safety of local harbor traffic. Could it have been argued that an additional purpose was to assure the economic support of local pilots? Would the Cooley formula have permitted such an argument to be taken into account?) Pilotage regulation with a certain effect? Pilotage regulation recognized by Congress to be "local"? And once a subject is recognized as "local" under the Cooley doctrine, does every variety of state regulation become permissible? Or are there still limitations? For example, may a state give preference to local businesses when it regulates a "local" subject? Nor do these questions exhaust the uncertainties left in the wake of Cooley. For example, Cooley does not clarify the proper level of generalization when a "national subject"-"local subject" distinction is invoked. Thus, does Cooley require that an entire field—e.g., the field of railroad regulation—be categorized as either "local" or "national"? Or may some state regulations of railroads be permissible while others are invalid? Questions such as these were left for the decades to come.

2. *The effect of congressional consent.* The Cooley Court gave only a limited effect to the congressional law of 1789 authorizing state pilotage laws. Justice Curtis did find one "appropriate and important signification" for it: he viewed it simply as guidance to the Court in determining whether pilotage was a "local" or "national" subject. But the Court emphatically refused to consider the congressional declaration as binding: "If the Constitution excluded the States from making any law regulating commerce, certainly Congress cannot regrant or in any manner reconvey to the States that power." To the Cooley Court, once the Court found a commerce clause restriction, Congress could not remove it. That aspect of Cooley clearly has been overruled: Congress is now viewed as having authority to consent to state regulations of commerce that would otherwise be barred by the dormant commerce power. See Prudential Insurance Co. v. Benjamin (1946; p. 346 below).

3. *Applications of Cooley.* The Cooley test continued to be cited in the increasing number of state regulation cases that came to the Court at the end of the 19th century and in the early decades of the 20th. In the late 19th century, the growth of a nationwide railroad system spurred demands for more extensive legislative controls. The early railroad regulation cases frequently cited Cooley, but it was difficult to square the course of the decisions with any simplistic application of the "national"-"local" distinction. For example, the Court held unconstitutional an early state ban on freight rate discrimination by railroads in Wabash, St. Louis & P. Ry. Co. v. Illinois, 118 U.S. 557 (1886), reasoning that regulations of interstate shipments were of a "national," not "local," character. But, whatever the national "subject" in Wabash was, it was not all that broad: the Court soon made it clear that the Wabash ruling did not cover *all* incidents of transportation "to which the word 'regulation' can be applied."

4. *The rise and decline of the "direct"-"indirect" distinction.* Just two years after Wabash, the Court sustained a state examination requirement applied to engineers on interstate trains. Smith v. Alabama, 124 U.S. 465 (1888), justified the state regulation of railroad engineers on the ground that the law rested on safety considerations and that its impact on commerce was merely "indirect," not "direct." This "direct"-"indirect" distinction was increasingly invoked. Application of this test often turned as a practical matter, however, on an empirical showing of the burden on interstate commerce. Compare Southern Railway Co. v. King, 217 U.S. 524 (1910) (upholding, as imposing no "direct" burden on interstate commerce, a Georgia safety law requiring railroad trains to slow down and blow their whistles at set intervals) with Seaboard Air Line Ry. v. Blackwell, 244 U.S. 310 (1917) (invalidating as a "direct" burden on commerce the same law upon a showing that compliance with the law would have required a train to stop 124 times in 123 miles and thus more than doubled the duration of an Atlanta to South Carolina trip).

Justice (later Chief Justice) Stone, who joined the Court in 1926, soon took the lead in urging more useful and realistic criteria. In Di SANTO v. PENNSYLVANIA, 273 U.S. 34 (1927), the Court held unconstitutional, on "direct burden" grounds, a state law imposing a license fee of $50 on travel agents selling steamship tickets for foreign travel. The license was granted only on proof of good character and fitness and was revocable for misbehavior. The majority found the law to be a "direct burden" on commerce and insisted that the "purpose" of a "direct" regulation was irrelevant. In dissent, Justice Stone, joined by Justices Holmes and Brandeis, found the direct-indirect distinction "too mechanical, too uncertain in its application, and too remote from actualities, to be of value." He added: "[We] are doing little more than using labels to describe a result rather than any trustworthy formula by which it is reached. [It] seems clear that those interferences [with commerce that are] not deemed forbidden are to be sustained, not because the effect on commerce is nominally indirect, but because a consideration of all the facts and circumstances, such as the nature of the regulation, its function, the character of the business involved and the actual effect on the flow of commerce, lead to the conclusion that the regulation concerns interests peculiarly local and does not infringe the national interest in maintaining the freedom of commerce across state lines." Justice Stone's balancing formula anticipated the later Court's approach. For a modern use of the direct-indirect distinction, see Brown–Forman Distillers Corp. v. New York State Liquor Auth., 476 U.S. 573 (1986) (holding a state price floor on out-of-state liquor sales an impermissibly "direct" burden).

5. *The licensing cases.* Inquiries into the "purposes" of state regulations seemed to be irrelevant in the usual formulations of both the Cooley "national"-"local" distinction and the "direct"-"indirect" distinction. Yet judicial perceptions of the law's purpose often seemed in fact determinative. For example, in BUCK v. KUYKENDALL, 267 U.S. 307 (1925), Justice BRANDEIS, writing for the Court, held unconstitutional Washington's denial of a certificate of convenience and necessity to an applicant seeking to operate an "auto stage line" to carry passengers and freight between Portland and Seattle. The denial relied on the ground that the territory was "already being adequately served by other carriers." Justice Brandeis noted that state regulations "adopted primarily to promote safety upon the highways and conservation in their use are not obnoxious to the Commerce Clause," but held that here the state's purpose was not safety but rather "the prohibition of competition." In contrast, in BRADLEY v. PUBLIC UTILITIES COMM'N, 289 U.S. 92 (1933), Justice BRANDEIS again wrote for the Court, this time sustaining Ohio's denial of a certificate to operate between Cleveland, Ohio, and Flint, Michigan. The stated reason for denial was that the highway to be used was "so badly congested by established motor vehicle operations, that the addition of the applicant's proposed service would create and maintain an excessive and undue hazard to the safety and security of the traveling public, and the property upon such highway." Justice Brandeis noted that here, unlike in Buck, "the purpose of the denial was to promote safety; and the test employed was congestion of the highway. The effect of the denial upon interstate commerce was merely an incident." (The licensing of interstate motor carriers has since become largely federalized as a result of congressional regulation, especially the Motor Carrier Act of 1935.)

B.   THE MODERN COURT'S APPROACH

Introduction. Like earlier decisions, modern dormant commerce clause decisions hold unconstitutional some but not all state regulations that burden interstate commerce. Unlike earlier decisions, however, they have generally abandoned any attempt to apply categorical distinctions between exercises of "police" and "commerce" powers, between "local" and "national" subject matters, or between "indirect" and "direct" effects. Such distinctions continue to play at most a background role.

The modern cases are organized into three groups in the materials that follow. *First*, the Court has shown clear antipathy to overt "discrimination" against out-of-state interests. A state law that on its face discriminates against out-of-state commerce is subject to an extraordinarily strong presumption of invalidity, and will virtually always be struck down. *Second*, the Court has likewise invalidated laws that favor local economic interests at the expense of out-of-state competitors even when they do not take the form of overtly discriminatory statutes. Overtly discriminatory laws are rare. But the Court has been willing to look behind state laws that are facially neutral toward outsiders in order to assess whether they have a forbidden, protectionist purpose. It has also looked to a law's protectionist effect, sometimes as evidence of protectionist purpose. A finding of "protectionism" is generally fatal to a state regulation; as the Court summarized its previous holdings in Philadelphia v. New Jersey, which follows, "where simple economic protectionism is effected by state legislation, a virtually per se rule of invalidity has been erected." In a *third* category of cases, the Court has also struck down facially neutral laws that "unduly burden" interstate commerce, applying a "balancing" approach. A widely invoked formulation of that approach was set forth in PIKE v. BRUCE CHURCH, INC., 397 U.S. 137 (1970), see p. 297 below, where a unanimous Court stated: "Where the statute regulates evenhandedly to effectuate a legitimate local public interest, and its effects on interstate commerce are only incidental, it will be upheld unless the burden imposed on such commerce is clearly excessive in relation to the putative local benefits. [If] a legitimate local purpose is found, then the question becomes one of degree. And the extent of the burden that will be tolerated will of course depend on the nature of the local interest involved, and on whether it could be promoted as well with a lesser impact in interstate activities."

The third approach has been more controversial than the first two. Condemnation of state discrimination against interstate commerce has evoked a widespread consensus on the Court. But Justices Scalia and Thomas, who would not find any dormant commerce clause implicit in the Constitution as an original matter, have argued that, as a matter of stare decisis, "discrimination" is the *only* acceptable basis for judicial invalidation of state laws and that the Court's resort to "balancing" usurps a task that more properly belongs to Congress. As Justice Scalia wrote, concurring in the judgment in Bendix Autolite Corp. v. Midwesco Enterprises, Inc., 486 U.S. 888 (1988): "I [would] abandon the 'balancing' approach to these negative commerce clause cases [and] leave essentially legislative judgments to the Congress. [In] my view, a state statute is invalid under the Commerce Clause if, and only if, it accords discriminatory treatment to interstate commerce in a respect not required to achieve a lawful state purpose." Some commentators have also criticized resort to judicial balancing in this area. See, e.g., Regan, "The Supreme Court and State Protectionism: Making Sense of the Dormant Commerce Clause," 84 Mich.L.Rev. 1091 (1986); Farber, "State Regulation and the Dormant Commerce Clause," 3 Const.Comm. 395 (1986); Sedler, "The Negative Commerce Clause as a Restriction on State Regulation," 31 Wayne L.Rev. 885 (1985);

Eule, "Laying the Dormant Commerce Clause to Rest," 91 Yale L.J. 425 (1982); and Tushnet, "Rethinking the Dormant Commerce Clause," 1979 Wis.L.Rev. 125. Contrast the general defense of the Court's approach, including balancing, in Collins, "Economic Union as a Constitutional Value," 63 N.Y.U.L.Rev. 43 (1988).

FACIAL DISCRIMINATION AGAINST OUT–OF–STATE COMMERCE

FACIAL DISCRIMINATION BY STATES

Introduction. A law that overtly blocked the flow of interstate commerce at a state's borders plainly would amount to forbidden protectionism. For a paradigm example, imagine a state's imposition of a tariff on incoming goods from out of state. The Court has treated as likewise barred by the dormant commerce clause other laws that, by their terms, treat out-of-state economic interests differently than their local competitors. Welton v. Missouri, 1 Otto (91 U.S.) 275 (1876), is one of the earliest and most widely cited condemnations of state laws discriminatory on their face. Welton invalidated a Missouri license requirement for peddlers (itinerant sellers). The law applied only to peddlers of merchandise "not the growth, produce, or manufacture of the State"; peddlers of Missouri goods did not need a license. Justice Field stated for the Court that the "very object" of the commerce clause was to protect "against discriminating State legislation." For a modern example of the Court's invalidation of a facially discriminatory law, consider the following case.

Philadelphia v. New Jersey

437 U.S. 617, 98 S.Ct. 2531, 57 L.Ed.2d 475 (1978).

Justice STEWART delivered the opinion of the Court.

[The Court held unconstitutional a 1973 New Jersey law which prohibited the importation of most "solid or liquid waste which originated or was collected outside the territorial limits of this State." The ban was challenged by operators of private landfills in New Jersey and by several cities in other states that had agreements with these operators for waste disposal. A state trial judge declared the law unconstitutional because it discriminated against interstate commerce. The highest state court reversed, holding that the law advanced vital health and environmental objectives with no economic discrimination against, and with little burden upon, interstate commerce. In holding the law unconstitutional, Justice Stewart's majority opinion found that it had not been preempted by federal legislation and rejected suggestions that interstate movement of waste was not "commerce" within the commerce clause. Turning to the central issues, he proceeded as follows:]

The opinions of the Court through the years have reflected an alertness to the evils of "economic isolation" and protectionism, while at the same time recognizing that incidental burdens on interstate commerce may be unavoidable when a State legislates to safeguard the health and safety of its people. Thus, where simple economic protectionism is effected by state legislation, a virtually per se rule of invalidity has been erected. See, e.g., [Hood, p. 292 below; Toomer v. Witsell, p. 280 below; Baldwin v. Seelig, p. 287 below; Buck, p. 269 above]. The clearest example of such legislation is a law that overtly blocks the flow of interstate commerce at a State's borders. Cf. Welton v. Missouri.

But where other legislative objectives are credibly advanced and there is no patent discrimination against interstate trade, the Court has adopted a much more flexible approach, the general contours of which were outlined in [the Pike "balancing" formulation, above.] The crucial inquiry, therefore, must be directed to determining whether [the law] is basically a protectionist measure, or whether it can fairly be viewed as a law directed to legitimate local concerns, with effects upon interstate commerce that are only incidental.

[Justice Stewart noted the contending positions of the state and the challengers regarding the actual purpose of the law, but found it unnecessary to resolve the conflict. The highest state court had concluded that the law was "designed to protect, not the State's economy, but its environment." The challengers claimed that the law, "while outwardly cloaked 'in the currently fashionable garb of environmental protection,' [is] actually no more than a legislative effort to suppress competition and stabilize the cost of solid waste disposal for New Jersey residents." In response, the state denied that the law "was motivated by financial concerns or economic protectionism," insisting that the "complaint is not that New Jersey has forged an economic preference for its own commercial interests, but rather that it has denied a small group of its entrepreneurs [i.e., its private landfill operators] an economic opportunity to traffic in waste in order to protect the health, safety and welfare of the citizenry at large." He continued:]

This dispute about ultimate legislative purpose need not be resolved, because its resolution would not be relevant to the constitutional issue to be decided in this case. Contrary to the evident assumption of the [state] and the parties, the evil of protectionism can reside in legislative means as well as legislative ends. Thus, it does not matter whether the ultimate aim of [the law] is to reduce the waste disposal costs of New Jersey residents or to save remaining open lands from pollution, for we assume New Jersey has every right to protect its residents' pocketbooks as well as their environment. And it may be assumed as well that New Jersey may pursue those ends by slowing the flow of *all* waste into the State's remaining landfills, even though interstate commerce may incidentally be affected. But whatever New Jersey's ultimate purpose, it may not be accomplished by discriminating against articles of commerce coming from outside the State unless there is some reason, apart from their origin, to treat them differently. Both on its face and in its plain effect, [the law] violates this principle of nondiscrimination.

The Court has consistently found parochial legislation of this kind to be constitutionally invalid, whether the ultimate aim of the legislation was to assure a steady supply of milk by erecting barriers to allegedly ruinous outside competition [Baldwin v. Seelig]; or to create jobs by keeping industry within the State [e.g., Foster–Fountain Packing]; or to preserve the State's financial resources from depletion by fencing out indigent immigrants, Edwards v. California. In each of these cases, a presumably legitimate goal was sought to be achieved by the illegitimate means of isolating the State from the national economy. Also relevant here are the Court's decisions holding that a State may not accord its own inhabitants a preferred right of access over consumers in other States to natural resources located within its borders. [E.g.,] Pennsylvania v. West Virginia. These cases stand for the basic principle that a "State is without power to prevent privately owned articles of trade from being shipped and sold in interstate commerce on the ground that they are required to satisfy local demands or because they are needed by the people of the State." [Foster–Fountain.]

The New Jersey law at issue in this case falls squarely within the area that the Commerce Clause puts off limits to state regulation. On its face, it imposes on out-of-state commercial interests the full burden of conserving the State's remaining landfill space. It is true that in our previous cases the scarce natural resource was itself the article of commerce, whereas here the scarce resource and the article of commerce are distinct. But that difference is without consequence. In both instances, the State has overtly moved to slow or freeze the flow of commerce for protectionist reasons. It does not matter that the State has shut the article of commerce inside the State in one case and outside the State in the other. What is crucial is the attempt by one State to isolate itself from a problem common to many by erecting a barrier against the movement of interstate trade.

The appellees argue that not all laws which facially discriminate against out-of-state commerce are forbidden protectionist regulations. In particular, they point to quarantine laws, which this Court has repeatedly upheld even though they appear to single out interstate commerce for special treatment. In the appellees' view, [this law] is analogous to such health-protective measures, since it reduces the exposure of New Jersey residents to the allegedly harmful effects of landfill sites. It is true that certain quarantine laws have not been considered forbidden protectionist measures, even though they were directed against out-of-state commerce. But those quarantine laws banned the importation of articles such as diseased livestock that required destruction as soon as possible because their very movement risked contagion and other evils. Those laws thus did not discriminate against interstate commerce as such, but simply prevented traffic in noxious articles, whatever their origin.

The New Jersey statute is not such a quarantine law. There has been no claim here that the very movement of waste into or through New Jersey endangers health, or that waste must be disposed of as soon and as close to its point of generation as possible. The harms caused by waste are said to arise after its disposal in landfill sites, and at that point, as New Jersey concedes, there is no basis to distinguish out-of-state waste from domestic waste. If one is inherently harmful, so is the other. Yet New Jersey has banned the former while leaving its landfill sites open to the latter. The New Jersey law blocks the importation of waste in an obvious effort to saddle those outside the State with the entire burden of slowing the flow of refuse into New Jersey's remaining landfill sites. That legislative effort is clearly impermissible under the [commerce clause]. Today, cities in Pennsylvania and New York find it expedient or necessary to send their waste into New Jersey for disposal, and New Jersey claims the right to close its borders to such traffic. Tomorrow, cities in New Jersey may find it expedient or necessary to send their waste into Pennsylvania or New York for disposal, and those States might then claim the right to close their borders. The Commerce Clause will protect New Jersey in the future, just as it protects her neighbors now, from efforts by one State to isolate itself in the stream of interstate commerce from a problem shared by all.

[Reversed.]

Justice REHNQUIST, with whom Chief Justice BURGER joins, dissenting.

[The cases sustaining quarantine laws] are dispositive of the present one. Under them, New Jersey may require germ-infected rags or diseased meat to be disposed of as best as possible within the State, but at the same time prohibit the *importation* of such items for disposal at the facilities that are set up within New Jersey for disposal of such material generated *within* the State. The physical fact of life that New Jersey must somehow dispose of its own noxious items does not mean that it must serve as a depository for those of every other

State. Similarly, New Jersey should be free under our past precedents to prohibit the importation of solid waste because of the health and safety problems that such waste poses to its citizens. The fact that New Jersey continues to, and indeed must continue to, dispose of its own solid waste does not mean that New Jersey may not prohibit the importation of even more solid waste into the State. I simply see no way to distinguish solid waste, on the record of this case, from germ-infected rags, diseased meat, and other noxious items. [I] do not see why a State may ban the importation of items whose movement risks contagion, but cannot ban the importation of items which, although they may be transported into the State without undue hazard, will then simply pile up in an ever increasing danger to the public's health and safety. The Commerce Clause was not drawn with a view to having the validity of state laws turn on such pointless distinctions.

[The] Court implies that the challenged laws must be invalidated because New Jersey has left its landfills open to domestic waste. But, as the Court notes, this Court has repeatedly upheld quarantine laws "even though they appear to single out interstate commerce for special treatment." The fact that New Jersey has left its landfill sites open for domestic waste does not, of course, mean that solid waste is not innately harmful. Nor does it mean that New Jersey prohibits importation of solid waste for reasons other than the health and safety of its population. New Jersey must out of sheer necessity treat and dispose of its solid waste in some fashion, just as it must treat New Jersey cattle suffering from hoof-and-mouth disease. It does not follow that New Jersey must, under the Commerce Clause, accept solid waste or diseased cattle from outside its borders and thereby exacerbate its problems. [Because] I find no basis for distinguishing the [health] laws under challenge here from our past cases upholding state laws that prohibit the importation of items that could endanger the population of the State, I dissent.

———

1. *The harm of interstate discrimination.* The Court suggests in Philadelphia v. New Jersey that state laws that facially discriminate against outsiders are nearly always invalid. Why? What values are served by the "principle of nondiscrimination" referred to by the Court? Consider the following possibilities:

a. *Protectionist purpose.* Perhaps the structure of the federal government makes protectionism an illegitimate government purpose, just as hostility to ideas is an illegitimate purpose under the First Amendment and racial animus is an illegitimate purpose under the equal protection clause. For the view that the dormant commerce clause aims centrally at protectionist purpose, defined as "the purpose of improving the competitive position of local economic actors, just because they are local, vis-a-vis their foreign competitors," see Regan, "The Supreme Court and State Protectionism: Making Sense of the Dormant Commerce Clause," 84 Mich. L. Rev. 1091 (1986).

But, as the Court noted in Philadelphia v. New Jersey, the purpose of the New Jersey ban on out-of-state waste was not clearly protectionist: New Jersey claimed it was motivated by health, safety and aesthetic considerations, not economic favoritism, and the Court declined to second-guess the good faith of that assertion. Should facial discrimination against outsiders give rise to a conclusive presumption of protectionist motive, regardless of actual legislative motivation? Is that because actual protectionist motive will rarely be made explicit, and will be difficult to smoke out? Does such a presumption give adequate weight to state autonomy?

b. *Social welfare.* The Court often suggests that free trade across state boundaries is more likely to bring about national "prosperity" or aggregate social welfare than is trade among a patchwork of mutually protectionist states. Each state will have an incentive to hoard benefits and export costs. On this view, state laws that produce local benefits that exceed local costs may nonetheless contribute to a situation in which national costs exceed national benefits. National social welfare will thus be maximized by inhibiting each state's incentives to maximize its own welfare.

On this economic theory of the dormant commerce clause, the Court should invalidate laws whose net effect is to export costs to other states. Did the law invalidated in Philadelphia v. New Jersey have such an effect? The Court suggested that it did, stating that New Jersey has "saddle[d] those outside the State with the entire burden of slowing the flow of refuse into New Jersey's remaining landfill sites." But note that the plaintiffs challenging the law included *New Jersey landfill operators* as well as non-New Jersey waste producers. The law imposed costs on in-state landfill operators by limiting demand for their services and thus driving down the prices they could charge. It benefitted in-state landfill users correlatively. But what costs did New Jersey export to outsiders? By increasing demand for non-New Jersey landfill space, it increased prices and profits for out-of-state landfill operators. But while New Jersey exported benefits to out-of-state landfill operators, it exported costs to out-of-state waste landfill users, who faced higher prices for waste disposal in their own states or elsewhere. Whether New Jersey has on balance exported costs to out-of-state interests depends on whether the benefits to out-of-state landfill operators exceed the costs to out-of-state landfill users. And whether the law increases or decreases total social welfare depends on which is greater: aggregate benefits to in-state landfill users and out-of-state landfill operators, or aggregate costs to in-state landfill operators and out-of-state landfill users. The Court ignored both these questions, focusing solely on New Jersey's export of costs to out-of-state landfill users.

Are courts competent to assess the comparative costs and benefits of discriminatory state laws on a case-by-case basis? Would the economic predictions involved be susceptible to manageable judicial standards? If not, should courts be free to presume that facially discriminatory laws on balance export costs out-of state? Even if some facially discriminatory laws actually increase total social welfare? Consider in this regard the relevance of the Court's closing remarks about the possibility of mutual retaliation among the states. Even if net social welfare is not decreased by one state's barriers to trade, it might well be decreased by many state's mutual barriers to trade in the aggregate. Thus, the above analysis is arguably too static, and a presumption against facial discrimination represents the best protection for net social welfare over time.

c. *Representation reinforcement.* One prominent theory of the justification for judicial review is that courts are needed to protect interests that will be systematically disadvantaged in the political process. Such representation-reinforcement arguably justifies judicial intervention on behalf of racial minorities under the equal protection clause or religious or political dissidents under the First Amendment. See the discussion of footnote 4 of the Carolene Products decision, p. 484 below; see generally J. Ely, Democracy and Distrust (1980).

The dormant commerce clause likewise might be understood as a representation-reinforcement device. Out-of-state interests are, by definition, formally unrepresented in a state's political process. State lawmakers may be expected to advance the interests of in-staters who are their constituents at the expense of out-of-staters who cannot penalize them at the polls. Thus discrimination against outsiders may be expected predictably to result from the normal operation of in-state politics. Chief Justice Stone captured this point in his opinion for the Court in Southern Pacific Co. v. Arizona (1945; p. 300 below): "The court has often recognized that to the extent [the] burden of state regulation falls on interests outside the state it is unlikely to be alleviated by the operation of those political restraints normally exerted when interests within the state are affected." On this view, a court need not decide whether outsiders are actually harmed, on balance, by a particular discriminatory state law; a state's incentives to harm outsiders alone are sufficient to render a discriminatory law suspect. For elaboration of this approach, see L. Tribe, American Constitutional Law § 6–5 (2d ed. 1988).

Are outsiders wholly without political influence in a state's political processes, as the representation-reinforcement theory suggests? In-state interests may provide surrogate representation to the extent they share economic interests with out-of-staters. For example, the New Jersey landfill operators arguably provided virtual representation in New Jersey's political process for out-of-state waste producers whose business they wanted. Should a court be permitted to invalidate the law on the theory that such representation by proxy is inadequate? Moreover, out-of-state interests are generally free to lobby and donate campaign funds to in-state political representatives. Do these opportunities for political speech offset the absence of formal political representation?

Note that none of the above justifications for dormant commerce clause intervention is limited to facial discrimination. Each of these theories plays a role in other aspects of the Court's modern approach, as discussed below. For criticism of these justifications for the "nondiscrimination" principle in the dormant commerce clause cases, see Heinzerling, "The Commercial Constitution," 1995 Sup. Ct. Rev. 217 (arguing that dormant commerce clause decisions do not serve national unity because they leave states free to prefer insiders in various ways; fail to take into account all the costs and benefits relevant to economic efficiency; and overprotect out-of-staters who can represent themselves through in-state allies and lobbying).

2. *Overcoming the presumption against facial discrimination.* Are state laws that facially discriminate against outsiders always invalid? Philadelphia v. New Jersey stated a strong presumption against overtly discriminatory statutes (even when the motive was not clearly protectionist). Justice Stewart found only very limited exceptions to the principle that "all laws which facially discriminate against out-of-state commerce are forbidden protectionist regulations": "certain quarantine laws" are permissible, but New Jersey's law was "not such a quarantine law." MAINE v. TAYLOR, 477 U.S. 131 (1986), is another notable exception to the rule of "virtually per se invalidity." The 8–1 decision in Taylor upheld a law banning the importation of out-of-state baitfish. Justice BLACKMUN's majority opinion, affording great deference to the findings of the district court, held that the ban had a legitimate environmental purpose stemming from "uncertainty about possible ecological effects on the possible presence of parasites and nonnative species" in shipments of out-of-state baitfish, and that that purpose could not be adequately served in nondiscriminatory ways.

Nevertheless, Justice Blackmun reiterated the Court's commitment to special scrutiny of discriminatory laws. He stated: "This Court has distinguished between state statutes that burden interstate transactions only incidentally, and those that affirmatively discriminate against such transactions.

While statutes in the first group violate the Commerce Clause only if the burdens they impose on interstate trade are 'clearly excessive in relation to the putative local benefits' [Pike], statutes in the second group are subject to more demanding scrutiny." Discriminatory laws may be upheld only if they serve "'a legitimate local purpose,' [that] could not be served as well by available nondiscriminatory means." Here, he concluded, the State had met this burden for sustaining discriminatory laws. Only Justice STEVENS dissented: "If Maine wishes to rely on its interest in ecological preservation, it must show that interest, and the infeasibility of other alternatives, with far greater specificity. [The] State has not carried its substantial burden of proving why it cannot meet its environmental concerns in the same manner as other States with the same interest in the health of their fish and ecology."

3. *Facially discriminatory taxes and fees.* In CHEMICAL WASTE MANAGEMENT, INC. v. HUNT, 504 U.S. 334 (1992), the Court invalidated on dormant commerce clause grounds an Alabama law imposing a hazardous waste disposal fee upon hazardous wastes generated outside Alabama and disposed of at a commercial facility in Alabama, but not upon identical wastes having a source in Alabama. Justice WHITE's opinion for the Court found the differential fee indistinguishable from the outright prohibition invalidated in Philadelphia v. New Jersey. Applying strictest scrutiny, he found that the state had available "less discriminatory alternatives" for reducing the volume of hazardous waste disposal, such as higher fees or quantity limits applicable to all waste disposed of in Alabama, regardless of its origin. He also found that out-of-state waste posed no greater cost to Alabama than in-state waste, distinguishing Maine v. Taylor on the ground that "Maine there demonstrated that the out-of-state baitfish were subject to parasites foreign to in-state baitfish." Chief Justice REHNQUIST was the lone dissenter. He argued that the Court's decision would give Alabama a "perverse regulatory incentive" to ban hazardous waste disposal altogether: "the Court today gets it exactly backward when it suggests that Alabama is attempting to 'isolate itself from a problem common to the several States.' To the contrary, it is the 34 States that have no hazardous waste facility whatsoever [that] have isolated themselves."

Chemical Waste left open the possibility that a differential fee for out-of-state waste disposal might be valid. But in OREGON WASTE SYSTEMS, INC. v. DEPARTMENT OF ENVIRONMENTAL QUALITY, 511 U.S. 93 (1994), the Court invalidated such a discriminatory fee. Oregon imposed a $2.25 per ton surcharge on the disposal of out-of-state solid waste and a $0.85 surcharge on the disposal of identical solid waste generated in-state. Writing for the 7–2 majority, Justice THOMAS found the differential surcharge facially discriminatory and thus subject to the "strictest scrutiny" or a "virtually per se rule of invalidity." He went on to reject the state's argument that the higher fee for out-of-state waste merely compensated for costs charged in other ways, such as by general taxation, to in-state waste producers: "[I]nterstate commerce may be made to 'pay its way.' [A] facially discriminatory tax that imposes on interstate commerce the rough equivalent of an identifiable and 'substantially similar' tax on intrastate commerce does not offend the negative Commerce Clause. [Although] it is often no mean feat to determine whether a challenged tax is a compensatory tax, we have little difficulty concluding that the Oregon surcharge is not such a tax. Oregon does not impose a specific charge of at least $2.25 per ton on shippers of waste generated in Oregon, for which the out-of-state surcharge might be considered compensatory." Nor did in-state producers' payment of general taxes justify the higher fee to out-of-state waste, for the two forms of taxation did not pertain to substantially equivalent economic events. Chief Justice REHNQUIST, joined by Justice Blackmun, dissented, arguing that "the Court's analysis turns the Commerce Clause on its head. Oregon's neighbors will operate under a competitive advantage against their Oregon counterparts as they can now produce solid waste with reckless abandon and avoid paying concomitant state taxes to develop new landfills and clean up retired landfill sites. [Oregon] businesses [alone] will have to pay the 'nondisposal' fees associated with solid waste: landfill siting, landfill clean-up, insurance to cover environmental accidents, and transportation improvement costs associated with out-of-state waste being shipped into the State."

WEST LYNN CREAMERY, INC. v. HEALY, 512 U.S. 186 (1994), treated as an impermissibly discriminatory tax a Massachusetts law that imposed an assessment on all sales of milk to Massachusetts retailers, but rebated all proceeds from this assessment to Massachusetts dairy farmers. (Two thirds of Massachusetts milk sales involved milk from out of state.) Justice STEVENS, writing for the Court, stated: "The paradigmatic example of a law discriminating against interstate commerce is the protective tariff or customs duty, which taxes goods imported from other States, but does not tax similar products produced in State. A tariff is an attractive measure because it simultaneously raises revenue and benefits local producers by burdening their out-of-state competitors. Nevertheless, it violates the principle of the unitary national market by handicapping out-of-state competitors, thus artificially encouraging in-state production even when the same goods could be produced at lower cost in other States. Because of their distorting effects on the geography of production, tariffs have long been recognized as violative of the Commerce Clause. In fact, tariffs against the products of other States are so patently unconstitutional that our cases reveal not a single attempt by any State to enact one. Instead, the cases are filled with state laws that aspire to reap some of the benefits of tariffs by other means. [Massachusetts'] pricing order is clearly unconstitutional. Its avowed purpose and its undisputed effect are to enable higher cost Massachusetts dairy farmers to compete with lower cost dairy farmers in other States. The 'premium payments' are effectively a tax which makes milk produced out of State more expensive. Although the tax also applies to milk produced in Massachusetts, its effect on Massachusetts producers is entirely (indeed more than) offset by the subsidy provide exclusively to Massachusetts dairy farmers. Like an ordinary tariff, the tax is thus effectively imposed only on out-of-state products."

Justice Stevens rejected the state's argument that, because a nondiscriminatory tax is constitutional, and subsidies to in-state interests are generally constitutional, the program's combination of the two was constitutional: "A pure subsidy funded out of general revenue ordinarily imposes no burden on interstate commerce, but merely assists local business. The pricing order in this case, however, is funded principally from taxes on the sale of milk produced in other States. [The] pricing order thus violates the cardinal principle that a State may not 'benefit in-state economic interests by burdening out-of-state competitors.' [Moreover,] when a nondiscriminatory tax is coupled with a subsidy to one of the groups hurt by the tax, a state's political processes can no longer be relied upon to prevent legislative abuse, because one of the in-state interests which would otherwise lobby against the tax has been mollified by the subsidy. [Massachusetts] dairy farmers, instead of exerting their influence against the tax, were in fact its primary supporters." Nor did the fact that increased retail milk prices would be borne by Massachusetts consumers neutralize the protectionist character of the law: "This argument, if accepted, would undermine almost every discriminatory tax case. State taxes are ordinarily paid by in-state businesses and consumers, yet if they discriminate against out-of-state products, they are unconstitutional. [The] cost of a tariff is also borne primarily by local consumers, yet a tariff is the paradigmatic Commerce Clause violation."

Justice SCALIA, joined by Justice Thomas, concurred in the judgment. He reiterated that he found in the Constitution no self-executing commerce clause limitations on the states but was willing, on stare decisis grounds, to invalidate state laws that facially discriminated against interstate commerce and laws that could not be distinguished from those previously invalidated by the Court. In this case, he found that the law functioned analogously to a discriminatory tax of the kind previously struck down: "There at least four possible devices that would enable a State to produce the economic effect that Massachusetts has produced here: (1) a discriminatory tax upon the industry, imposing a higher liability on out-of-state members than on their in-state competitors; (2) a tax upon the industry that is nondiscriminatory in its assessment, but that has an 'exemption' or 'credit' for in-state members; (3) a nondiscriminatory tax upon the industry, the revenues from which are placed into a segregated fund, which fund is disbursed as 'rebates' or 'subsidies' to in-state members of the industry (the situation at issue in this case); and (4) with or without nondiscriminatory taxation of the industry, a subsidy for the in-state members of the industry, funded from the State's general revenues. It is long settled that the first of these methodologies is unconstitutional under the negative Commerce Clause. The second of them, 'exemption' from or 'credit' against a 'neutral' tax, is no different in principle from the first, and has likewise been held invalid. The fourth methodology, application of a state subsidy from general revenues, is so far removed from what we have hitherto held to be unconstitutional, that prohibiting it must be regarded as an extension of our negative-Commerce– Clause jurisprudence and therefore, to me, unacceptable.

"[The] issue before us in the present case is whether the third of these methodologies must fall. Although the question is close, I conclude it would not be a principled point at which to disembark from the negative-Commerce– Clause train. The only difference between methodology (2) (discriminatory 'exemption' from nondiscriminatory tax) and methodology (3) (discriminatory refund of nondiscriminatory tax) is that the money is taken and returned rather than simply left with the favored in-state taxpayer in the first place. The difference between (3) and (4), on the other hand, is the difference between assisting in-state industry through discriminatory taxation, and assisting in-state industry by other means." Justice Scalia insisted that subsidies of a local industry from *general* tax revenues would not offend the negative commerce clause, and thus objected to the majority's broad language suggesting that the clause always barred "artificially encouraging in-state production even when the same goods could be produced at lower cost in other States."

Chief Justice REHNQUIST, joined by Justice Blackmun, dissented, arguing that the law provided merely for a permissible subsidy. He disagreed with the majority that the law "distorts the 'State's political process," noting that, even if dairy farmers were "mollified by the subsidy, [there] are still at least two strong interest groups opposed to the milk order—consumers and milk dealers." He concluded: "The wisdom of a messianic insistence on a grim sink-or-swim policy of laissez-faire economics would be debatable had Congress chosen to enact it; but Congress has done nothing of the kind. It is the Court which has imposed the policy under the dormant Commerce Clause, a policy which bodes ill for the values of federalism which have long animated our constitutional jurisprudence."

4. *Home processing requirements.* The Court has repeatedly invalidated state requirements that products be processed in-state before they may be

shipped out-of-state. Such statutes generally single out by their terms in-state businesses and by definition give them an advantage over potential out-of-state competitors. In C & A Carbone, Inc. v. Clarkstown (1994; p. 284 below), Justice Kennedy's opinion for the Court summarized this line of cases, citing a series of "local processing requirements that we long have held invalid. See Minnesota v. Barber, 136 U.S. 313 (1890) (striking down a Minnesota statute that required any meat sold within the state, whether originating within or without the State, to be examined by an inspector within the State); Foster–Fountain Packing Co. v. Haydel, 278 U.S. 1 (1928) (striking down a Louisiana statute that forbade shrimp to be exported unless the heads and hulls had first been removed within the State); Johnson v. Haydel, 278 U.S. 16 (1928) (striking down analogous Louisiana statute for oysters); Toomer v. Witsell, 334 U.S. 385 (1948) (striking down South Carolina statute that required shrimp fishermen to unload, pack, and stamp their catch before shipping it to another State); Pike v. Bruce Church, Inc., 397 U.S. 137 (1970) (striking down Arizona statute that required all Arizona-grown cantaloupes to be packaged within the State prior to export); South–Central Timber Development, Inc. v. Wunnicke, 467 U.S. 82 (1984) (striking down an Alaska regulation that required all Alaska timber to be processed within the State prior to export). The essential vice in laws of this sort is that they bar the import of the processing service. Out-of-state meat inspectors, or shrimp hullers, [are] deprived of access to local demand for their services. Put another way, the offending local laws hoard a local resource [for] the benefit of local businesses that treat it."

Are such laws best understood as facially discriminatory? Justice Souter, dissenting in Carbone, placed the "local processing cases squarely within the larger class of cases in which this Court has invalidated facially discriminatory legislation." Or are they better understood, as Justice O'Connor described them in her Carbone concurrence, as "protectionist either in purpose or practical effect"? Either way, they are subject to the Court's "virtually per se rule of invalidity," as opposed to a balancing test. Each of these laws plainly draws a geographic boundary around permitted economic activities, but does a finding of discrimination require a further finding that the boundary has been drawn for the *purpose* of advantaging local businesses over out-of-state competitors? In FOSTER–FOUNTAIN PACKING CO. v. HAYDEL, 278 U.S. 1 (1928), Justice Butler looked behind the face of the law banning export of unhulled shrimp, and its asserted purpose (to keep shrimp hulls and heads in-state for use as fertilizer), to conclude: "The purpose [of the law] is not to retain the shrimp for the use of the people of Louisiana; it is to favor the canning of the meat and the manufacture of bran in Louisiana by withholding raw or un-shelled shrimp from [Mississippi] plants. [The] practical operation and effect of the provisions complained of will be directly to obstruct and burden interstate commerce." Was the finding of purpose necessary to the determination of invalidity here?

5. *Other facially discriminatory state laws.* The Court has invalidated as facially discriminatory a variety of other laws that differentiate by their terms between in-state and out-of-state businesses. See, e.g., Wyoming v. Oklahoma, 502 U.S. 437 (1992) (Oklahoma statute requiring power plants to burn at least 10 percent Oklahoma-mined coal); New Energy Co. of Indiana v. Limbach, 486 U.S. 269 (1988) (Ohio statute awarding tax credit for sales of ethanol only if it is produced in Ohio or in a State that awards similar tax breaks for Ohio-produced ethanol); New England Power Co. v. New Hampshire, 455 U.S. 331 (1982) (New Hampshire statute prohibiting hydroelectric power from being sold out of State without permission from the State's Public Utilities Commission); Hughes v. Oklahoma, 441 U.S. 322 (1979) (Oklahoma law forbidding out-of-

state sale of natural minnows); Great A. & P. Tea Co., Inc. v. Cottrell, 424 U.S. 366 (1976) (Mississippi statute providing that milk from another state could be sold in Mississippi only if the other state accepted Mississippi milk on a reciprocal basis). For discussion of express state restraints on the export of natural resources, see p. 295 below.

FACIAL DISCRIMINATION BY LOCALITIES

Should the strong presumption against discrimination against outsiders by a *state* extend to discrimination against outside interests by a town, city or county? The following cases consider whether facial discrimination by a *local* jurisdiction in favor of its own or against nonlocal interests violates the dormant commerce clause.

Dean Milk Co. v. Madison

340 U.S. 349, 71 S.Ct. 295, 95 L.Ed. 329 (1951).

Justice CLARK delivered the opinion of the Court.

[A Madison, Wisconsin, ordinance barred the sale of pasteurized milk unless it had been processed and bottled at an approved pasteurization plant within five miles of the central square of Madison. Within that five-mile area were five processing plants, only three of which did business in Madison. Within the county in which Madison is located were 5,600 dairy farms. Justice Clark stated that the total raw milk production of these farms was more than ten times the requirements of Madison. Madison officials inspected the plants and farms every 30 days. Dean Milk, which challenged the ordinance, was based in Illinois, bought its milk from farms in northern Illinois and southern Wisconsin, and pasteurized it at its two Illinois plants, 65 and 85 miles from Madison. Dean Milk was denied a license to sell its products in Madison solely because its plants were more than five miles away. Dean Milk's farms and plants were licensed and inspected by Chicago public health authorities, and its milk was labeled "Grade A" under a Chicago ordinance which had adopted rating standards recommended by the U.S. Public Health Service. The Chicago ordinance, like that of Madison, was patterned on the Model Milk Ordinance of the U.S. Public Health Service. Justice Clark noted, however, that "Madison contends and we assume that in some particulars its ordinance is more rigorous than that of Chicago." The highest state court rejected the commerce clause attack. Justice Clark concluded that "the ordinance imposes an undue burden on interstate commerce." He explained:]

[There can be no] objection to the avowed purpose of this enactment. We assume that difficulties in sanitary regulation of milk and milk products originating in remote areas may present a situation in which "it appears that the matter is one which may appropriately be regulated in the interest of the safety, health and well-being of local communities." [But] this regulation [in] practical effect excludes from distribution in Madison wholesome milk produced and pasteurized in Illinois. [In] thus erecting an economic barrier protecting a major local industry against competition from without the State, Madison plainly discriminates against interstate commerce.[1] This it cannot do, even in

---

1. It is immaterial that Wisconsin milk from outside the Madison area is subjected to the same proscription as that moving in interstate [commerce]. [Footnote by Justice Clark.]

the exercise of its unquestioned power to protect the health and safety of its people, if reasonable nondiscriminatory alternatives, adequate to conserve legitimate local interests, are available. A different view, that the ordinance is valid simply because it professes to be a health measure, would mean that the Commerce Clause of itself imposes no limitations on state action other than those laid down by the Due Process Clause, save for the rare instance where a state artlessly discloses an avowed purpose to discriminate against interstate goods. Our issue then is whether the discrimination inherent in the Madison ordinance can be justified in view of the character of the local interests and the available methods of protecting them.

[It] appears that reasonable and adequate alternatives are available. If [Madison] prefers to rely upon its own officials for inspection of distant milk sources, such inspection is readily open to it without hardship for it could charge the actual and reasonable cost of such inspection to the importing producers and processors. Moreover, appellee Health Commissioner of Madison testified that as proponent of the local milk ordinance he had submitted the provisions here in controversy and an alternative proposal based on § 11 of the Model Milk Ordinance recommended by the [U.S.] Public Health Service. The model provision imposes no geographical limitation on location of milk sources and processing plants but excludes from the municipality milk not produced and pasteurized conformably to standards as high as those enforced by the receiving city. In implementing such an ordinance, the importing city obtains milk ratings based on uniform standards and established by health authorities in the jurisdiction where production and processing occur. The receiving city may determine the extent of enforcement of sanitary standards in the exporting area by verifying the accuracy of safety ratings of specific plants or of the milkshed in the distant jurisdiction through the [U.S.] Public Health Service. The Commissioner testified that Madison consumers "would be safeguarded adequately" under either proposal and that he had expressed no preference. [The Commissioner and a state official] agreed that a local health officer would be justified in relying upon the evaluation by the Public Health Service of enforcement conditions in remote producing areas.

To permit Madison to adopt a regulation not essential for the protection of local health interests and placing a discriminatory burden on interstate commerce would invite a multiplication of preferential trade areas destructive of the very purpose of the Commerce Clause. Under the circumstances here presented, the regulation must yield to the principle that "one state in its dealings with another may not place itself in a position of economic isolation." Baldwin v. Seelig.

[Reversed.]

Justice BLACK, with whom Justices DOUGLAS and MINTON concur, dissenting.

[I] disagree with the Court's premises, reasoning, and judgment. (1) This ordinance does not exclude wholesome milk coming from Illinois or anywhere else. It does require that all milk sold in Madison must be pasteurized within five miles of the center of the city. But there was no finding in the state courts [that Dean] is unable to have its milk pasteurized within the defined geographical [area]. (2) Characterization of [the law] as a "discriminatory burden" on interstate commerce is merely a statement of the Court's result, which I think incorrect. [B]oth state courts below found that [the law] represents a good-faith attempt to safeguard public health by making adequate sanitation inspections possible. [The] fact that [the law], like all health regulations, imposes some burden on trade, does not mean that it "discriminates" against interstate commerce. (3) This health regulation should not be invalidated merely because the Court believes that alternative milk-inspection methods might insure the cleanliness and healthfulness of Dean's Illinois milk. [If] the principle announced today is to be followed, the Court should not strike down local health regulations unless satisfied beyond a reasonable doubt that the substitutes it proposes would not lower health standards. [I] do not think that either of the alternatives suggested by the Court would assure the people of Madison as pure a supply of milk as they receive under their own ordinance. On this record I would uphold the Madison law. At the very least, however, I would not invalidate it without giving the parties a chance to present evidence and get findings on the ultimate issues the Court thinks crucial—namely, the relative merits of the Madison ordinance and the alternatives suggested by the Court today.

————

1. *Interstate and intrastate discrimination.* The majority in Dean Milk asserts that "Madison plainly discriminates against interstate commerce," stating in footnote 1 that it is "immaterial" that intrastate milk from outside the Madison area was subject to the same prohibition as that moving in interstate commerce. Should it be relevant that a local regulation burdens some intrastate as well as out-of-state producers? Arguably, the impact on intrastate businesses assures political restraints upon potential abuses. Intrastate interests also burdened by the law might be thought to virtually represent out-of-state interests that are adversely affected. Yet there may be the counterargument that at least some burdens on intrastate interests in addition to interstate ones should be considered "immaterial" because otherwise protectionist lawmakers might escape condemnation simply by making some of their rules applicable to some intrastate businesses as well. Moreover, other Wisconsin residents might tolerate Madison's protectionism if the state allows them to do the same, in which case they will not have any incentive to protect out-of-state interests. For similar observations in the context of a local regulation challenged under the Privileges and Immunities Clause of Article IV, see United Bldg. & Constr. Trades v. Camden (1984; p. 329).

2. *Judicial inquiry into "reasonable nondiscriminatory alternatives."* Dean Milk is frequently cited for requiring judicial inquiry into "reasonable nondiscriminatory alternatives." When a "rationality" standard of scrutiny prevails, courts do *not* speculate about alternatives; instead, they defer to the legislative choice if it is *a* reasonable method of promoting the state interest. (See, e.g., the modern economic regulation-due process cases in chap. 8 and recall the wide congressional authority to choose means under McCulloch.) Yet the Court has developed a more intensive scrutiny, including consideration of "alternatives," in order to protect commerce clause values. (The Court has likewise employed close scrutiny of regulatory "alternatives" in the context of First Amendment, equal protection and substantive due process challenges.) Is judicial inquiry into less burdensome alternative methods of regulation appropriate? Feasible? Does it amount to haphazard, uninformed judicial intrusion into the legislative sphere? Or is it a neutral means by which the court can determine whether the asserted, legitimate purpose is a pretext for an illicit underlying purpose? In this regard, note that, in Dean Milk, while the majority did not charge that the Madison ordinance was enacted in bad faith, it did mention that milk production is a "major local industry" in the Madison area,

hinting at possible protectionist motives. Did the availability to Madison of nondiscriminatory alternatives amount to evidence that its motives were more likely protecting local dairy farmers than ensuring healthful milk?

3. *Other examples of invalid local discrimination against nonlocal competitors.* In FORT GRATIOT SANITARY LANDFILL, INC. v. MICHIGAN DEPARTMENT OF NATURAL RESOURCES, 504 U.S. 353 (1992), the Court invalidated a Michigan law that prohibited private landfill operators from accepting solid waste that originated outside the county in which their facilities were located. The Court found the law indistinguishable for dormant commerce clause purposes from the waste import ban struck down in Philadelphia v. New Jersey. Following Dean Milk, the Court also found that the law could not be saved by the fact that it drew the line at the county rather than the state border, and thus discriminated against in-state as well as out-of-state interests. Writing for the Court, Justice STEVENS explained: "[O]ur prior cases teach that a State (or one of its political subdivisions) may not avoid the strictures of the Commerce Clause by curtailing the movement of articles of commerce through subdivisions of the State, rather than through the State itself." Citing Dean Milk, he noted that "[t]he fact that the [Madison] ordinance also discriminated against all Wisconsin producers whose facilities were more than five miles from the center of the city did not mitigate its burden on interstate commerce." Chief Justice REHNQUIST, joined by Justice Blackmun, dissented, arguing that the restriction, unlike that in Dean Milk, was based on legitimate environmental and health concerns rather than economic protectionism.

In C & A CARBONE, INC. v. CLARKSTOWN, 511 U.S. 383 (1994), the Court relied on Dean Milk to invalidate a town's local processing requirement for solid waste. The town of Clarkstown, New York, authorized a private company to build and operate a solid waste transfer facility, with an agreement that it would be sold to the town for $1 after five years. In order to guarantee a minimum supply of waste to the transfer station in order to finance its cost, the town adopted a "flow control ordinance," requiring all nonrecyclable, nonhazardous solid waste within the town to be deposited at the transfer station, which charged fees exceeding prevailing market rates. Carbone, a private recycler with a sorting facility in Clarkstown, sought to ship its nonrecyclable waste to cheaper processors outside the state. The town sought to enjoin Carbone and Carbone raised the unconstitutionality of the flow control ordinance as a defense.

Justice KENNEDY, writing for the Court, rejected the argument that the ordinance was saved by having intrastate as well as interstate effect: "While the immediate effect of the ordinance is to direct local transport of solid waste to a designated site within the local jurisdiction, its economic effects are interstate in reach. [By] prevent[ing] everyone except the favored local operator from performing the initial processing step, [the]ordinance [deprives] out-of-state businesses of access to a local market." Citing Dean Milk and Fort Gratiot, he wrote: "The ordinance is no less discriminatory because in-state or in-town processors are also covered by the prohibition." Having found state and local discrimination equally suspect, Justice Kennedy found the ordinance indistinguishable from other in-state processing requirements the Court had long held invalid (see p. 280 above). Thus, the flow control ordinance had "[t]he essential vice [of] bar[ring] the import of the processing service. [It] hoards solid waste, and the demand to get rid of it, for the benefit of the preferred processing facility. The only conceivable distinction [is] that the flow control ordinance favors a single local proprietor. But this difference just makes the protectionist effect of the ordinance more acute. In Dean Milk, the local processing requirement at least permitted pasteurizers within five miles of the city to compete. An out-of-state pasteurizer who wanted access to that market might have built a pasteurizing facility within the radius. The flow control ordinance at issue here squelches competition in the waste-processing service altogether, leaving no room for investment from outside."

Justice Kennedy continued: "Discrimination against interstate commerce in favor of local business or investment is per se invalid, save in a narrow class of cases in which the municipality can demonstrate, under rigorous scrutiny, that it has no other means to advance a legitimate local interest." He rejected the town's argument that the ordinance was necessary to ensure safe waste handling: "Clarkstown has any number of nondiscriminatory alternatives for addressing the health and environmental problems alleged to justify the ordinance in question. The most obvious would be uniform safety regulations enacted without the object to discriminate." And he found impermissibly protectionist the justification that the ordinance helped finance the waste transfer facility: "[R]evenue generation is not a local interest that can justify discrimination against interstate commerce. Otherwise States could impose discriminatory taxes against solid waste originating outside the State." He concluded that, while the town was free to subsidize the facility from general taxes or bonds, "[s]tate and local governments may not use their regulatory power to favor local enterprise by prohibiting patronage of out-of-state competitors or their facilities."

Justice O'CONNOR concurred in the judgment. She found that the ordinance did not discriminate against interstate commerce. Cases such as Dean Milk and Fort Gratiot, she noted, involved "discrimination on the basis of geographic origin": "the challenged enactment gave a competitive advantage to local business as a group vis-a-vis their out-of-state or nonlocal competitors as a group. In effect, the regulating jurisdiction [drew] a line around itself and treated those inside the line more favorably than those outside the line." Unlike such regulations, she found, the flow control ordinance "does not give more favorable treatment to local interests as a group as compared to out-of-state or out-of-town economic interests. Rather, the garbage sorting monopoly is achieved at the expense of all competitors, be they local or nonlocal. The law 'discriminates' evenhandedly against all potential participants in the waste processing business, while benefiting only the chosen operator of the transfer facility." Nonetheless, she found that the ordinance did impose an undue burden on interstate commerce under the Pike balancing test.

Justice SOUTER, joined by Chief Justice Rehnquist and Justice Blackmun, dissented: "The law does not differentiate between all local and all out-of-town providers of a service, but instead between the one entity responsible for ensuring that the job gets done and all other enterprises, regardless of their location. The ordinance thus falls outside that class of tariff or protectionist measures that the Commerce Clause has traditionally been thought to bar States from enacting against each other." The ordinance's "exclusion of outside capital is part of a broader exclusion of private capital, not a discrimination against out-of-state investors as such." It was thus "anticompetitive" but not "protectionist." The costs of the ordinance would be borne principally by local residents, not out-of-state businesses, he wrote, and "[t]he Commerce Clause was not passed to save the citizens of Clarkstown from themselves. It should not be wielded to prevent them from attacking their local garbage problems with an ordinance that does not discriminate between local and out-of-town participants in the private market for trash disposal services and that is not protectionist in its purpose or effect."

Would the discrimination in Carbone have been permissible if the town of Clarkstown itself had owned and operated the facility? Justice Souter, in dissent, suggested that the waste transfer station was essentially a "municipal facility," and that concerns about economic protectionism generally do not apply to public sector monopolies. Why not? Such questions are explored below in materials on the "market participant" exception to the dormant commerce clause at p. 322.

———

PROTECTIONIST PURPOSE AND EFFECT

Introduction. Facial discrimination against interstate commerce may be expected to be relatively rare, given the Court's strong condemnation of it. Recall Justice Stevens' observation in West Lynn Creamery: "[T]ariffs against the products of other States are so patently unconstitutional that our cases reveal not a single attempt by any State to enact one. Instead, the cases are filled with state laws that aspire to reap some of the benefits of tariffs by other means." Yet the Court has treated as "protectionist" or "discriminatory"—and thus as "virtually per se invalid"—some laws beyond those explicitly discriminating against outside commerce. What laws deserve such treatment? One possible view is that the "discrimination" label should be reserved for those situations where a discriminatory *purpose* can be demonstrated. Should forbidden "discrimination" also include regulations whose "effect" is to favor local interests and disadvantage out-of-state ones?

The Court has invalidated some facially discriminatory laws, such as the New Jersey waste import ban struck down in Philadelphia v. New Jersey or the milk processing requirement struck down in Dean Milk, without openly ascribing improper purposes or motivations to the lawmakers who enacted them. But where a law is not facially discriminatory, the Court sometimes seeks to smoke out a discriminatory purpose before subjecting it to the "virtually per se rule of invalidity." What are the difficulties of such purposive analysis? One is evidentiary: a purpose may be difficult to discern from the text and history of a statute. The purpose to discriminate is often hidden rather than overt. But this difficulty may be overcome to the extent that proof of a forbidden purpose may be inferred from the effects of a state rule. Another difficulty is analytical: a law with a benign purpose may have an unduly discriminatory effect, while a law motivated wholly by protectionist intent might fail to produce significant discriminatory effects. Thus an inquiry into purpose without an inquiry into effect may be insufficient. These difficulties arise in other areas of constitutional law as well, especially equal protection. See Ch. 9 below.

Alternatively, courts might seek to identify protectionist legislation by reference to its effects, finding discriminatory effects suspect apart from providing evidence of purpose. When the Court uses the term "discrimination" to describe effects rather than to attribute purposes, however, is it doing anything that could not be done as well by balancing legitimate local justifications such as health against the burdens on commerce, with the anticompetitive aspects of the burden playing a role in the analysis? In reading the cases that follow, consider which is more desirable: deciding whether a law is "discriminatory" by reference to its protectionist purpose and/or effects, or engaging in open-ended balancing of local benefits against interstate burdens, as under the Pike balancing test explored in the next subsection. For clarity of exposition, the cases that follow are organized according to the type of economic discrimination involved, although nothing doctrinal turns on the distinctions between imports and exports or purchases and sales or on the type of businesses at issue.

———

STATE BARRIERS TO OUT–OF–STATE SELLERS

1. *Baldwin v. Seelig.* BALDWIN v. G.A.F. SEELIG, INC., 294 U.S. 511 (1935), is the leading case holding that states may not protect local economic interests by limiting access to local markets by out-of-state sellers—even in the absence of facial discrimination. The case involved a state effort, prompted by the Depression of the 1930s, to stabilize milk prices. The New York Milk Control Act of 1933 set the minimum prices to be paid to milk producers by New York dealers. A year before Baldwin, the Court had recognized that the law did not violate due process limits on the state's police power so far as its wholly intrastate impact was concerned. (Nebbia v. New York, p. 474 below.) But Baldwin held that the commerce clause did bar the application of the law to out-of-state milk producers. Seelig, a New York milk dealer, bought milk in Vermont at prices lower than the New York minimum. The law prohibited New York sales of out-of-state milk if the milk had been purchased below the price for similar purchases within New York. The State refused to license Seelig to sell milk in New York unless it agreed to conform to the state's price regulation regarding the sale of imported milk. The Court unanimously held unconstitutional that application of the law.

Justice CARDOZO stated that New York's regulation "set a barrier to traffic between one state and another as effective as if customs duties, equal to the price differential, had been laid upon the [goods]. Nice distinctions have been made at times between direct and indirect burdens. They are irrelevant when the avowed purpose of the obstruction, as well as its necessary tendency, is to suppress or mitigate the consequences of competition between the states. Such an obstruction is direct by the very terms of the hypothesis. We are reminded in the opinion below that a chief occasion of the commerce clause was 'the mutual jealousies and aggressions of the States, taking form in customs barriers and other economic retaliation.' [If] New York, in order to promote the economic welfare of her farmers, may guard them against competition with the cheaper prices of Vermont, the door has been opened to rivalries and reprisals that were meant to be averted by subjecting commerce between the states to the power of the nation."

The Court rejected the argument that the Act was justified by the state's aim to assure "a regular and adequate supply of pure and wholesome milk." Supply was jeopardized, New York claimed, when farmers could not earn a living income: "the economic motive is secondary and subordinate; the state intervenes to make its inhabitants healthy, and not to make them rich." Justice Cardozo replied that this could not validate the Act as a "police" measure with only "incidental" impact on commerce: "This would be to eat up the rule under the guise of an exception. Economic welfare is always related to health. Let such an exception be admitted, and all that a state will have to do in times of stress and strain is to say that its farmers and merchants and workmen must be protected against competition from without, lest they go upon the poor relief lists or perish altogether. To give entrance to that excuse would be to invite a speedy end of our national solidarity. The Constitution was framed under the dominion of a political philosophy less parochial in range. It was framed upon the theory that the peoples of the several states must sink or swim together, and that in the long run prosperity and salvation are in union and not division. [The] line of division between direct and indirect restraints of commerce involves in its marking a reference to considerations of degree. Even so, the borderland is wide between the restraints upheld as incidental and those attempted here. [None of the valid laws]—inspection laws, game laws, laws intended to curb fraud or exterminate disease—approaches in drastic quality the statute here in controversy which would neutralize the economic consequences of free trade among the states."

Justice Cardozo added: "What is ultimate is the principle that one state in its dealings with another may not place itself in a position of economic isolation. Formulas and catchwords are subordinate to this overmastering requirement. [The] police power [may] not be used by the state of destination with the aim and effect of establishing an economic barrier against competition with the products of another [state]. Restrictions so contrived are an unreasonable clog on the mobility of commerce. They set up what is the equivalent of a rampart of customs duties designed to neutralize advantages belonging to the place of origin. They are thus hostile in conception as well as burdensome in result."

2. *The limits of Baldwin: compensating use taxes.* States with sales taxes often seek to avoid the loss of revenue by imposing a "use" tax, equal to the sales tax, on in-state use of products purchased out of state. Does such a "use" tax amount to the equivalent of the "customs rampart" struck down in Baldwin? Justice Cardozo, the author of Baldwin, found that it did not, in HENNEFORD v. SILAS MASON CO., 300 U.S. 577 (1937). That decision upheld a Washington use tax on goods bought in other states. Washington law placed a 2% tax on retail sales within Washington; another section imposed a "compensating tax" on the price of goods (including transportation costs) for the "privilege of using" in Washington goods bought at retail out of the state. (The use tax was inapplicable to any article which had already been subjected to a sales or use tax of at least 2%; for articles previously taxed at less than 2% there was a prorated exemption from the use tax.) The point of that scheme was clear to the Court: as Justice CARDOZO put it in his opinion for a unanimous Court, local retail sellers "will be helped to compete upon terms of equality with retail dealers in other states who are exempt from a sales tax"; local buyers will "no longer [be] tempted to place their orders in other states" to escape the local sales tax.

Nevertheless, this was not a forbidden economic barrier. Justice Cardozo wrote: "Equality is the theme that runs through all sections of the statute. [When] the account is made up, the stranger from afar is subject to no greater burdens as a consequence of ownership than the dweller within the gates. [In] each situation the burden borne by the owner is balanced by an equal burden where the sale is strictly local." Nor were the reasons for the use tax fatal. The challengers attacked it as "equivalent to a protective tariff." Justice Cardozo was not impressed: "[M]otives alone will seldom, if ever, invalidate a tax that apart from its motives would be recognized as [lawful]. Least of all will they be permitted to accomplish that result when equality and not preference is the end to be achieved. Catch words and labels, such as the words 'protective tariff,' are subject to the dangers that lurk in metaphors and symbols, and must be watched with circumspection lest they put us off our guard. [A] tax upon use [unlike a tariff] is not a clog on the process of importation at all." Distinguishing Baldwin v. Seelig, he wrote: "[New York] was attempting to project its legislation within the borders of another state by regulating the price to be paid in that state for milk acquired there. She said in effect to farmers in Vermont: your milk cannot be sold by dealers to whom you ship it in New York unless you sell it to them in Vermont at a price determined here. What Washington is saying to sellers beyond her borders is something very different. In substance what she says is this: You may ship your goods in such amounts and at such prices as you please, but the goods when used in Washington after the transit is completed, will share an equal burden with goods that have been purchased here.''

Is Justice Cardozo's distinction persuasive? Both cases involved some ''extraterritorial'' impacts of the state laws: in Baldwin, the New York distributor subject to New York's law was discouraged from buying from Vermont farmers; similarly, the Washington tax discouraged buying from out-of-state sellers. But Washington's use tax cancelled only the out-of-state seller's *tax* advantage, while New York's scheme cancelled the advantages the Vermont producer had arguably earned because of lower costs of production. Washington's plan still permitted some price competition; New York's did not. Is the free trade ideal described by Justice Cardozo in Baldwin adequately achieved by a finding that at least *some* price competition remains in the consumer market? Would the Court have been clearer if it had held invalid the state *purpose* of eliminating *all* price competition? If it had resorted to an open balancing analysis? For the Court's reluctance to find taxation on out-of-state sellers permissibly compensatory outside the sales-and-use-tax context, see Oregon Waste Systems (1994; p. 277 above).

3. *De facto discrimination.* The Court has invalidated facially neutral statutes that actually appear to exist solely in order to protect a particular in-state interest or target a particular out-of-state interest. In such cases, the facial neutrality of the statute is no defense against a finding of impermissible protectionism. Sometimes the Court rests on the underlying protectionist motive of such statutes. For example, in BACCHUS IMPORTS, LTD. v. DIAS, 468 U.S. 263 (1984), the Court invalidated a Hawaii statute that exempted from the State's liquor tax a brandy distilled from the root of a shrub indigenous to Hawaii. Because this was a local product, the tax exemption did not need to be drafted explicitly along state lines to demonstrate its discriminatory design. Bacchus Imports also involved a tax exemption for fruit wine. Although this exemption was general in nature and did not specify an indigenous product, there was evidence that it was enacted to promote the local pineapple-wine industry. Thus, because the exemption was motivated by an intent to confer a benefit upon local industry not granted to out-of-state industry, the exemption was held invalid.

In other cases, the Court has concluded that a law was impermissibly discriminatory or protectionist while expressly avoiding attributing a protectionist motive to the legislature. In HUNT v. WASHINGTON STATE APPLE ADVERTISING COMM'N, 432 U.S. 333 (1977), for example, the Court unanimously (by a vote of 8–0; Justice Rehnquist did not participate) invalidated a North Carolina law requiring that closed containers of apples offered for sale or shipped into the State bear ''no grade other than the applicable U.S. grade or standard.'' Washington State, the nation's largest producer of apples, was the source of half of all apples shipped in closed containers in interstate commerce. Washington had adopted strict inspection programs and required all apples shipped from the state to be graded in accordance with its quality standards. The Washington State grades were equivalent or superior to the comparable grades adopted by the U.S. Department of Agriculture (USDA). The North Carolina ban, which required the display of either the USDA grade or a ''not graded'' label, explicitly prohibited the display of any state grades. The Washington Commission, confronted with a serious obstacle to the marketing of its apples in North Carolina, prevailed in the district court, which found that the

North Carolina law, while neutral on its face, discriminated against Washington growers in favor of their local counterparts and concluded that this discrimination was not justified by the asserted local interest in eliminating deception and confusion in the marketplace.

In affirming that result, the Court, while finding some aspects of the North Carolina law "somewhat suspect," found it unnecessary to "ascribe an economic protection motive to the North Carolina Legislature to resolve this case." Instead, Chief Justice BURGER concluded that the law could not stand "even if enacted for the declared purpose of protecting consumers." Instead of finding the law flawed because of any protectionist motive, the Court relied mainly on discriminatory *effect*. The Court noted that "a finding that state legislation furthers matters of legitimate local concern, even in health and consumer protection areas, does not end the inquiry. [Dean Milk.] Rather, when such state legislation comes into conflict with the Commerce Clause's overriding requirement of a national 'common market,' we are confronted with the task of effecting an accommodation of the competing national and local interests."

Here, the Court found, the law had "the practical effect of not only burdening interstate sales of Washington apples, but also discriminating against them. This discrimination takes various forms. The first, and most obvious, is the statute's consequence of raising the costs of doing business in the North Carolina market for Washington apple growers and dealers, while leaving those of their North Carolina counterparts unaffected. [This] disparate effect results from the fact that North Carolina apple producers, unlike their Washington competitors, were not forced to alter their marketing practices in order to comply with the statute." The increased costs thus imposed tended "to shield the local apple industry from the competition of Washington apple growers and dealers." Second, the law had the effect of "stripping away from the Washington apple industry the competitive and economic advantages it has earned for itself through its expensive inspection and grading system." Third, the law had "a leveling affect which insidiously operates to the advantage of local apple producers," because "Washington apples which would otherwise qualify for and be sold under the superior Washington grades will now have to be marketed under their inferior USDA counterparts. Such 'downgrading' offers the North Carolina apple industry the very sort of protection against competing out-of-state products that the Commerce Clause was designed to prohibit."

Chief Justice Burger added: "When discrimination against commerce of the type we have found is demonstrated, the burden falls on the State to justify it both in terms of the local benefits flowing from the statute and the unavailability of nondiscriminatory alternatives adequate to preserve the local interests at stake. [Dean Milk.] North Carolina has failed to sustain that burden on both scores. [Since] Washington grades are in all cases equal or superior to their USDA counterparts, they could only 'deceive' or 'confuse' a consumer to his benefit, hardly a harmful result." Moreover, nondiscriminatory alternatives were "readily available"—for example, North Carolina "could effectuate its goal by permitting out-of-state growers to utilize state grades only if they also marked their shipments with the applicable USDA label."

4. *The limits of inferring protectionism from discriminatory effect.* The Court does not always infer discrimination against out-of-state interests from practical burdens upon them. For example, in BREARD v. ALEXANDRIA, 341 U.S. 622 (1951), the Court sustained the application of an Alexandria, La., ordinance prohibiting door-to-door solicitation of orders to sell goods except by consent of the occupants. Breard, a Texan, led a crew of salespersons who

solicited subscriptions for national magazines on behalf of a Pennsylvania corporation. Justice REED's majority opinion rejected Breard's claim that the "practical operation of the ordinance" imposed "an undue and discriminatory burden" on commerce. Breard argued that Dean Milk demonstrated that "this Court will not permit local interests to protect themselves against out-of-state competition by curtailing interstate business." But Justice Reed was not persuaded: "It was partly because the regulation [in Dean Milk] discriminated against interstate commerce that it was struck down. [Nor] does the clause as to alternatives [in Dean Milk] apply to the Alexandria ordinance. Interstate commerce itself knocks on the local door. It is only by regulating that knock that the interests of the home may be protected by public as distinct from private action." Chief Justice VINSON's dissent, joined by Justice Douglas, objected: "Lack of discrimination on its face has not heretofore been regarded as sufficient to sustain an ordinance without inquiry into its practical effects upon interstate commerce. [I] think it plain that a 'blanket prohibition' upon appellant's solicitation discriminates against and unduly burdens interstate commerce in favoring local retail merchants. 'Whether or not it was so intended, those are its necessary effects.' "

STATE BARRIERS TO OUT–OF–STATE BUYERS

Introduction. In the preceding section, state restrictions were attacked as efforts to hamper out-of-state *sellers* from reaching the local market. The cases in this subsection involve state barriers hampering out-of-state *buyers* seeking access to a state's products and resources, including natural resources. In the cases below the challenged state is typically charged with engaging in hoarding. As before, the state laws are attacked as discriminatory or protectionist; as before, the attackers typically claim that the state is pursuing impermissible "economic" purposes. The pervasive question is the extent to which a state may impose embargoes, production and price controls or other restraints on outgoing trade. Facial discrimination against out-of-state purchasers of in-state supplies or services is plainly impermissible, as illustrated, for example, by Philadelphia v. New Jersey, above. The harder question presented in the following cases is whether laws that effect such discrimination without singling out interstate commerce by their terms should be presumed impermissible.

The Court has upheld application to out-of-state buyers of local price and production controls when it finds their effects on interstate commerce merely "incidental" to regulation of a local market. For example, in MILK CONTROL BOARD v. EISENBERG FARM PRODUCTS CO., 306 U.S. 346 (1939), the Court sustained the application of a Pennsylvania minimum price regulation to a New York milk dealer who bought milk from Pennsylvania producers for shipment out of state. Justice Roberts' majority opinion explained: "The purpose of the [law] obviously is to reach a domestic situation in the interests of the welfare of the producers and consumers of milk in Pennsylvania." He emphasized that the activity affected was "essentially local in Pennsylvania": "If dealers conducting receiving stations in [Pennsylvania] were free to ignore the requirements of the statute on the ground that all or a part of the milk they purchase is destined to another state the uniform operation of the statute locally would be crippled and might be impracticable. Only a small fraction of the milk produced by farmers in Pennsylvania is shipped out of the Commonwealth. There is, therefore, a comparatively large field remotely affecting and wholly unrelated to interstate commerce within which the statute operates." Contrast the Court's holding in the following case.

————

H.P. Hood & Sons v. Du Mond

336 U.S. 525, 69 S.Ct. 657, 93 L.Ed. 865 (1949).

Justice JACKSON delivered the opinion of the Court.

[Hood was a Boston milk distributor. The Boston area obtained 90% of its milk supply from outside of Massachusetts. Hood had long obtained milk from New York producers and had maintained three receiving depots there. Hood sought a New York license to establish a fourth depot, a few miles away from two of its existing depots. The N.Y. Commissioner of Agriculture and Markets denied a license for the depot on the basis of a state law stating that licenses for new plants could not be issued unless the Commissioner was satisfied that "issuance of the license will not tend to a destructive competition in a market already adequately served, and that the issuance of the license is in the public interest." The state courts rejected Hood's commerce clause challenge to the license denial.]

This case concerns the power of [New York] to deny additional facilities to acquire and ship milk in interstate commerce where the grounds of denial are that such limitation upon interstate business will protect and advance local economic interests. The Commissioner found that Hood, if licensed at Greenwich, would permit its present suppliers, at their option, to deliver at the new plant rather than the old ones and for a substantial number this would mean shorter hauls and savings in delivery costs. The new plant also would attract twenty to thirty producers, some of whose milk Hood anticipates will or may be diverted from other buyers. Other large milk distributors have plants within the general area and dealers serving Troy obtain milk in the locality. He found that Troy was inadequately supplied during the preceding short season.

[The] present controversy begins where the Eisenberg decision left off. New York's regulations, designed to assure producers a fair price and a responsible purchaser, and consumers a sanitary and modernly equipped handler, are not challenged here but have been complied with. It is only additional restrictions, imposed for the avowed purpose and with the practical effect of curtailing the volume of interstate commerce to aid local economic interests, that are in question here, and no such measures were attempted or such ends sought to be served in the Act before the Court in the Eisenberg case. Our decision in a milk litigation most relevant to the present controversy deals with the converse of the present situation. [Justice Jackson quoted from Baldwin v. Seelig.]

This distinction between the power of the State to shelter its people from menaces to their health or safety and from fraud, even when those dangers emanate from interstate commerce, and its lack of power to retard, burden or constrict the flow of such commerce for their economic advantage, is one deeply rooted in both our history and our law. [Justice Jackson's statements on commerce clause history and interpretation are quoted at p. 259 above.] [Baldwin v. Seelig] is an explicit, impressive, [and] unanimous condemnation by this Court of economic restraints on interstate commerce for local economic advantage, but it does not stand alone. This Court consistently has rebuffed attempts of states to advance their own commercial interests by curtailing the movement of articles of commerce, either into or out of the state, while generally supporting their right to impose even burdensome regulations in the interest of local health and safety. As most states serve their own interests best by sending their produce to market, the cases in which this Court has been obliged to deal with prohibitions or limitations by states upon exports of articles of commerce are not numerous.

[The] principle that our economic unit is the Nation, which alone has the gamut of powers necessary to control of the economy, including the vital power of erecting customs barriers against foreign competition, has as its corollary that the states are not separable economic units. [In Baldwin v. Seelig, the Court] but followed the principle that the state may not use its admitted powers to protect the health and safety of its people as a basis for suppressing competition. [This] Court has not only recognized this disability of the state to isolate its own economy as a basis for striking down parochial legislative policies designed to do so, but it has recognized the incapacity of the state to protect its own inhabitants from competition as a reason for sustaining particular exercises of the commerce power of Congress to reach matters in which states were so disabled. Cf. [Steward Machine Co., p. 241 above].

The material success that has come to inhabitants of the states which make up this federal free trade unit has been the most impressive in the history of commerce, but the established interdependence of the states only emphasizes the necessity of protecting interstate movement of goods against local burdens and repressions. We need only consider the consequences if each of the few states that produce copper, lead, high-grade iron ore, timber, cotton, oil or gas should decree that industries located in that state shall have priority. What fantastic rivalries and dislocations and reprisals would ensue if such practices were begun! Or suppose that the field of discrimination and retaliation be industry. May Michigan provide that automobiles cannot be taken out of that State until local dealers' demands are fully met? Would she not have every argument in the favor of such a statute that can be offered in support of New York's limiting sales of milk for out-of-state shipment to protect the economic interests of her competing dealers and local consumers? Could Ohio then pounce upon the rubber-tire industry, on which she has a substantial grip, to retaliate for Michigan's auto monopoly?

The State, however, insists that denial of the license for a new plant does not restrict or obstruct interstate commerce, because petitioner has been licensed at its other plants without condition or limitation as to the quantities it may purchase. [In] the face of affirmative findings that the proposed plant would increase petitioner's supply, we can hardly be asked to assume that denial of the license will not deny petitioner access to such added supplies. While the state power is applied in this case to limit expansion by a handler of milk who already has been allowed some purchasing facilities, the argument for doing so, if sustained, would be equally effective to exclude an entirely new foreign handler from coming into the State to purchase. [Since] the statute as applied violates the Commerce Clause and is not authorized by federal legislation pursuant to that Clause, it cannot stand.

[Reversed and remanded.]

Justice BLACK, joined by Justice MURPHY, dissenting.

Had a dealer supplying New York customers applied for a license to operate a new plant, the commissioner would have been compelled under the Act to protect petitioner's plants supplying Boston consumers in the same manner that this order would have protected New York consumers. [T]he Court cannot attribute to the commissioner an invidious purpose to [discriminate]. The language of this state Act is not discriminatory, the legislative

history shows it was not so intended, and the commissioner has not administered it with a hostile eye. The Act must stand or fall on this basis notwithstanding the overtones of the Court's opinion. If petitioner [is] to be placed
above and beyond this law, it must be done solely on this Court's new
constitutional formula which bars a state from protecting itself against local
destructive competitive practices so far as they are indulged in by dealers who
ship their milk into other states. [The] basic question here is not the greatness
of the commerce clause concept, but whether all local phases of interstate
business are to be judicially immunized from state laws against destructive
competitive business practices such as those prohibited by New York's law.
[While] I have doubt about the wisdom of this New York law, I do not conceive
it to be the function of this Court to revise that state's economic [judgments].

Justice FRANKFURTER, joined by Justice RUTLEDGE, dissenting.

[The effect of the Court's opinion] is to hold that no matter how important
to the internal economy of a State may be the prevention of destructive
competition, and no matter how unimportant the interstate commerce affected,
a State cannot as a means of preventing such competition deny an applicant
access to a market within the State if that applicant happens to intend the out-
of-state shipment of the product that he buys. [I] dissent because I cannot
agree in treating what is essentially a problem of striking a balance between
competing interests as an exercise in absolutes. Nor does it seem to me that
such a problem should be disposed of on a record from which we cannot tell
what weights to put in which side of the scales.

[As] matters now stand, [it] is impossible to say whether or not the
restriction of competition among dealers in milk does in fact contribute to their
economic well-being and, through them, to that of the entire industry. And if
we assume that some contribution is made, we cannot guess how much. [E.g., is
the State] concerned with protecting consumers from excessive prices? Or is it
concerned with seeing that marginal dealers, forced by competition to pay more
and charge less, are not driven either to cut corners in the maintenance of their
plants or to close them down entirely? [C]ould Hood's potential competitors in
the Greenwich area maintain efficient and sanitary standards of operation on a
lower margin of profit? [How] much of a strain would be put on the price
structure maintained by the State by a holding that it cannot regulate the
competition of dealers buying for an out-of-state market? [We] should, I submit,
have answers at least to some of these questions before we can say either how
seriously interstate commerce is burdened by New York's licensing power or
how necessary to New York is that power. [My] conclusion [is] that the case
should be [remanded].

———————

1. *Implications of Hood.* Was Justice Jackson persuasive in characterizing
the Hood restraint as forbidden economic discrimination? Does Hood reject a
balancing approach in favor of a per se rule when the state interest is economic
rather than health or safety? Or does Hood balance state and national interests
but hold that economic objectives tend to tip the scale against the state
regulation? Arguably, the major flaw in Hood was the reason given by the state
for denying Hood's license (and the fact that the applicant whose license was
denied happened to be from out of state). Arguably, the licensing scheme in its
application created too much of a risk of economic protectionism. Does Hood,
taken together with Eisenberg, stand for no more than that out-of-staters

cannot be subjected to laws excluding new competitors in order to protect existing businesses?

Consider the light shed on Hood in a case decided a year later, CITIES SERVICE GAS CO. v. PEERLESS OIL & GAS CO., 340 U.S. 179 (1950). There, the Court rejected a commerce clause attack on a state regulation of natural gas prices designed to conserve an important local resource. An Oklahoma agency fixed a minimum wellhead price on all natural gas taken from a field, requiring a pipeline company to pay more than the prevailing rates. Most of the gas from the field was destined for consumers outside of Oklahoma. Justice Clark's opinion emphasized Oklahoma's justifiable concern with "preventing rapid and uneconomic dissipation of one of its chief natural resources" by inferior uses of the gas at bargain rates. Citing Eisenberg, he stated that, "in a field of this complexity with such diverse interests involved, we cannot say that there is a clear national interest so harmed that the state price-fixing orders here employed" are barred by the commerce clause. He distinguished Hood by saying: "The vice in the regulation invalidated [there] was solely that it denied facilities to a company in interstate commerce on the articulated ground that such facilities would divert milk supplies needed by local consumers; in other words, the regulation discriminated against interstate commerce. There is no such problem here. The price regulation applies to all gas taken from the field, whether destined for interstate or intrastate consumers." Was this a persuasive distinction? Or was it in effect a narrowing of Hood?

2. *State restraints on exports of natural resources.* Hood raised the broad problem of to what extent a state may prefer domestic needs in curtailing the export of local products. Justice Jackson emphasized the commerce clause policy against "home embargoes." The scope of that anti-embargo principle has troubled the Court various contexts. State embargoes on natural resources have been an especially litigated subject. A number of early cases sustained state preferences for local users of natural resources. Often, those cases rested on notions of state property interests. More recently, however, the Court has barred most state efforts to give preference to local interests.

In the early cases the Court often endorsed local preferences in broad terms. For example, Geer v. Connecticut, 161 U.S. 519 (1896), upheld a law that prevented the killing of certain game birds for the purpose of shipment out of the state, even though intrastate commerce in game birds was permitted. The Court emphasized property rights: the birds were collectively owned by the people of the state. Hudson County Water Co. v. McCarter, 209 U.S. 349 (1908), sustained a law prohibiting the transportation of water from the state's rivers and lakes to any other state. The Court noted that the state, as "guardian of the public welfare," had a strong interest in maintaining local rivers "substantially undiminished." But even in earlier decades, some local barriers were invalidated. Thus, in Pennsylvania v. West Virginia, 262 U.S. 553 (1923), West Virginia had required that all local needs for natural gas be met before any gas could be exported. The majority found that requirement a "prohibited interference" with interstate commerce. But in a dissent Justice Holmes insisted that he could "see nothing in the commerce clause to prevent a State from giving a preference to its inhabitants in the enjoyment of its natural advantages."

HUGHES v. OKLAHOMA, 441 U.S. 322 (1979), overruled Geer v. Connecticut and held invalid under the commerce clause an Oklahoma law forbidding any person to "transport or ship minnows for sale outside the state which were seined or procured within the waters of this state." Hughes was a Texan engaged in the commercial minnow business who was charged with violating the law for transporting from Oklahoma to Texas a load of natural minnows purchased from an Oklahoma minnow dealer. After expressly overruling Geer and abandoning the "19th century legal fiction of state ownership" of even those wild animals "that had been lawfully reduced to possession," Justice BRENNAN's majority opinion found that the statute could not survive scrutiny under modern commerce clause standards. He stated that the Oklahoma law "on its face discriminates against interstate commerce. [E.g., Philadelphia v. New Jersey.] [Such] facial discrimination by itself may be a fatal defect, regardless of the State's purpose, because 'the evil of protectionism can reside in legislative means as well as legislative ends.' At a minimum such facial discrimination invokes the strictest scrutiny of any purported legitimate local purpose and of the absence of nondiscriminatory alternatives." Here, that scrutiny was fatal. Oklahoma had failed to resort to nondiscriminatory alternatives: "The State places no limits on the number of minnows that can be taken by licensed minnow dealers; nor does it limit in any way how these minnows may be disposed of within the State. Yet it forbids the transportation of any commercially significant number of natural minnows out of the State for sale. [The law] is certainly not a 'last ditch' attempt at conservation after nondiscriminatory alternatives have proved unfeasible. It is rather a choice of the most discriminatory means even though nondiscriminatory alternatives would seem likely to fulfill the State's purported legitimate local purpose more effectively." Overruling Geer did not mean that the states were powerless to conserve wildlife within their borders. But "States may promote this legitimate purpose only in ways consistent with the basic principle that 'our economic unit is the Nation' [Hood], and that when a wild animal 'becomes an article of commerce, [its] use cannot be limited to the citizens of one State to the exclusion of citizens of another State'."

Justice REHNQUIST, joined by Chief Justice Burger, dissented, arguing that the ownership language of cases such as Geer was "simply a shorthand way of describing a State's substantial interest in preserving and regulating the exploitation of [natural resources] within its boundaries for the benefit of its citizens. [The] range of regulations that a State may adopt under these circumstances is extremely broad, particularly where, as here, the burden on interstate commerce is, at most, minimal." He emphasized that there was no showing here that "requiring appellant to purchase his minnows from hatcheries [not subject to the statute] instead of from persons licensed to seine minnows from the State's waters in any way increases appellant's costs of doing business." Moreover, hatchery minnows and naturally seined minnows apparently were fungible. Hence, any minimal burden on petitioner was "more than outweighed by Oklahoma's substantial interest in conserving and regulating exploitation of its natural minnow population."

For commentary, see Hellerstein, "Hughes v. Oklahoma: The Court, the Commerce Clause, and State Control of Natural Resources," 1979 Sup.Ct.Rev. 51.

In NEW ENGLAND POWER CO. v. NEW HAMPSHIRE, 455 U.S. 331 (1982), a unanimous Court strongly condemned state restrictions on the export of natural resources. For many years, the Company had exported most of the hydroelectric energy generated at its federally licensed power stations on the Connecticut River in New Hampshire. In 1980, a New Hampshire agency withdrew the Company's authority to export the locally generated power. The agency acted pursuant to a state law banning the exportation of energy whenever the agency determined that the energy "is reasonably required for use within this state and that the public good requires that it be delivered for such use." The major issue in the case turned on New Hampshire's unsuccessful claim that Congress, in the Federal Power Act, had expressly consented to the export restriction; Chief Justice BURGER's discussion of the commerce clause challenge was brief:

"Our cases consistently have held that the Commerce Clause [precludes] a state from mandating that its residents be given a preferred right of access, over out-of-state consumers, to natural resources located within its borders or to the products derived therefrom. E.g., [Hughes; Philadelphia v. New Jersey.] [The order challenged here] is precisely the sort of protectionist regulation that the Commerce Clause declares off-limits to the states. The [state agency] has made clear that its order is designed to gain an economic advantage for New Hampshire citizens at the expense of [the Company's] customers in neighboring states. Moreover, it cannot be disputed that [the agency's] 'exportation ban' places direct and substantial burdens on transactions in interstate commerce. Such state-imposed burdens cannot be squared with the Commerce Clause when they serve only to advance 'simple economic protectionism.' Philadelphia v. New Jersey." Chief Justice Burger rejected any argument that New Hampshire "owned" the Connecticut River, finding that the federal government had primary authority over the flow of navigable waters and that the relevant commodity was "electric energy, a product entirely distinct from the river waters used to produce it."

The Court reiterated its skepticism about state export controls on natural resources in SPORHASE v. NEBRASKA, 458 U.S. 941 (1982), which involved a state restriction on the export of ground water. Because of the traditional recognition of the predominance of state law in the delineation of water rights, advocates of state restraints in the interest of "conservation" had long maintained that the regulation of water resources enjoyed a special, broad immunity from commerce clause restrictions on export bans. But the Court's 7–2 decision, while acknowledging some state authority to restrict export of water, refused to accept the State's broadest claims. Accordingly, the Court held unconstitutional a portion of a statutory restriction on the withdrawal of ground water from any well within Nebraska intended for use in an adjoining state. Justice STEVENS' majority opinion rejected, inter alia, the state court's reliance on such cases as Geer which had rested on the "fiction" of state ownership of its water. Invoking Hood, he found that some of the State's restrictions constituted an "explicit barrier to commerce." Justice Rehnquist, joined by Justice O'Connor, dissented.

THE MODERN BALANCING TEST

Introduction. As the preceding two subsections have shown, the Court treats laws that facially discriminate against interstate commerce and laws that are "protectionist" in purpose or practical effect as "virtually per se invalid." A law that is neither discriminatory nor protectionist, however, may still be reviewed and possibly struck down under the Court's residual balancing test. The balancing test asks whether the burden on interstate commerce outweighs benefit to the regulating state. In many cases, plaintiffs claim first that a law is discriminatory or protectionist, and also, in the alternative, that it is unduly burdensome upon interstate commerce. This subsection turns to the Court's decisions using this balancing approach.

The Court's current formulation of the balancing test, as mentioned earlier, was set forth in PIKE v. BRUCE CHURCH, INC., 397 U.S. 137 (1970). That case involved a home-state processing requirement. An Arizona statute required that Arizona-grown cantaloupes advertise their State of origin on each package. Church was an Arizona grower of high quality cantaloupes. Instead of packing them in Arizona, it transported them to nearby California facilities; when packed in California, they were not identified as Arizona-grown. Arizona issued an order prohibiting Church from shipping uncrated cantaloupes from the company's Arizona ranch, and requiring that the cantaloupes be packed in Arizona and identified as coming from an Arizona packer. Compliance with the requirement would have required a capital outlay of $200,000 to pack Church's $700,000 cantaloupe crop. In invalidating the requirement, Justice STEWART's opinion for a unanimous Court began with the restatement of the balancing test: "Where the statute regulates even-handedly to effectuate a legitimate local public interest, and its effects on interstate commerce are only incidental, it will be upheld unless the burden imposed on such commerce is clearly excessive in relation to the putative local benefits. [If] a legitimate local purpose is found, then the question becomes one of degree. And the extent of the burden that will be tolerated will of course depend on the nature of the local interest involved, and on whether it could be promoted as well with a lesser impact on interstate activities."

Turning to the Arizona requirement in light of this balancing formula, he noted that law was not one to promote safety or to protect consumers from unfit goods. Rather, its "purpose and design are simply to protect and enhance the reputation of growers within the State. These are surely legitimate state interests. [But] application of the Act [to Church] has a far different impact, and quite a different purpose. [Arizona] is not complaining because the company is putting the good name of Arizona on an inferior or deceptively packaged product, but because it is not putting that name on a product that is superior and well packaged. [Although] it is not easy to see why the other growers of Arizona are entitled to benefit at the company's expense from the fact that it produces superior crops, we may assume that the asserted state interest is a legitimate one. But the State's tenuous interest in having the company's cantaloupes identified as originating in Arizona cannot constitutionally justify the requirement that the company build and operate an unneeded $200,000 packing plant in the State."

It is debatable whether Pike, having announced the influential balancing test, seriously applied it; portions of the opinion suggest that Arizona's order was invalid because, like other home-processing requirements, it was facially discriminatory: "The nature of [the] burden [on Church] is, constitutionally, more significant than its extent. For the Court has viewed with particular suspicion state statutes requiring business operations to be performed in the home State that could more efficiently be performed elsewhere. Even where the State is pursuing a clearly legitimate local interest, this particular burden on commerce has been declared to be virtually per se illegal. [E.g., Foster–Fountain.]" Nonetheless, Pike remains the canonical source for the balancing test used in the modern cases discussed below. The antecedents of the Pike test are the transportation cases in which the Court first began to employ dormant commerce clause balancing weighing the strength of state interests against the burdens on interstate commerce.

STATE BURDENS ON TRANSPORTATION

Today, standards for interstate transportation operations are largely set by Congress through its affirmative exercise of the commerce power.[1] But for much of this century, interstate carriers sought to use the dormant commerce clause to alter aspects of a patchwork of state transportation regulations. After deferring to the state in the 1938 Barnwell case, which follows, the Court began to develop the modern balancing test beginning with the 1945 Southern Pacific case.

In SOUTH CAROLINA STATE HIGHWAY DEPARTMENT v. BARNWELL BROS., 303 U.S. 177 (1938), the Court upheld a 1933 South Carolina law prohibiting the use on state highways of trucks that were over 90 inches wide or that had a gross weight over 20,000 pounds. About 85 to 90% of the nation's trucks exceeded these limits. The trial court, noting the substantial burdens on commerce, found the law an unreasonable means of preserving highways, because wheel or axle weight was a more accurate measure than gross weight of the risk that trucks might damage the highways. Moreover, the trial court found that trucks weighing over 20,000 pounds would not damage the highways. In reversing this ruling, Justice STONE, writing for the Court, applied a deferential standard of review despite his earlier advocacy of balancing in DiSanto (p. 269 above):

"While the constitutional grant to Congress of power to regulate interstate commerce has been held to operate of its own force to curtail state power in some measure, it did not forestall all state action affecting interstate commerce. Ever since [Black Bird and Cooley], it has been recognized that there are matters of local concern, the regulation of which unavoidably involves some regulation of interstate commerce but which, because of their local character and their number and diversity, may never be fully dealt with by Congress. Notwithstanding the commerce clause, such regulation in the absence of Congressional action has for the most part been left to the [states]. The commerce clause, by its own force, prohibits discrimination against interstate commerce, whatever its form or method, and the decisions of this Court have recognized that there is scope for its like operation when state legislation nominally of local concern is in point of fact aimed at interstate commerce, or by its necessary operation is a means of gaining a local benefit by throwing the attendant burdens on those without the state. [It] was to end these practices that the commerce clause was adopted.

"[But] the present case affords no occasion for saying that the bare possession of power by Congress to regulate the interstate traffic forces the states to conform to standards which Congress might, but has not adopted, or curtails their power to take measures to insure the safety and conservation of

1. Federal laws enacted in the 1980s prescribe uniform weight and width requirements as well as maximum length requirements for the trucks using the Interstate Highway System and other "qualifying" Federal-aid highways. For the first time, trailer lengths are federally regulated. Under the laws, states must modify their laws to comply with the federal standards, and both injunctive relief and withholding of federal funds are available as remedies against non-complying states. See the Surface Transportation Assistance Act of 1982 (Pub.L. 97–424, 96 Stat. 2097) and the Department of Transportation Appropriations Act, 1983 (Pub.L. 97–369, 96 Stat. 1765).

In the legislative history accompanying the new federal uniform weight requirements, Congress indicated that the existence of differing weight laws in the states imposed an "undue burden on interstate commerce." Does this congressional determination suggest that *all* remaining state highway regulations should receive close judicial scrutiny? Or does this evidence of congressional willingness to deal with the problem of state burdens on interstate commerce in the highway area indicate that Congress is fully able to protect its own prerogatives and the interests of interstate commerce *without* the active assistance of the courts?

their highways which may be applied to like traffic moving intrastate. Few subjects of state regulation are so peculiarly of local concern as is the use of state highways. There are few, local regulation of which is so inseparable from a substantial effect on interstate commerce. Unlike the railroads, local highways are built, owned and maintained by the state or its municipal subdivisions. The state has a primary and immediate concern in their safe and economical administration. The present regulations, or any others of like purpose, if they are to accomplish their end, must be applied alike to interstate and intrastate traffic, both moving in large volume over the highways. The fact that they affect alike shippers in interstate and intrastate commerce in large number within as well as without the state is a safeguard against their abuse. [With] respect to the extent and nature of the local interests to be protected and the unavoidable effect upon interstate and intrastate commerce alike, regulations of the use of the highways are akin to local regulation of rivers, harbors, piers and docks, quarantine regulations, and game laws, which, Congress not acting, have been sustained even though they materially interfere with interstate commerce. [This] Court has often sustained the exercise of [state power over state highways] although it has burdened or impeded interstate commerce. [So] long as the state action does not discriminate, the burden is one which the Constitution permits because it is an inseparable incident of the exercise of a legislative authority, which, under the Constitution, has been left to the states.

"Congress, in the exercise of its plenary power to regulate interstate commerce, may determine whether the burdens imposed on it by state regulation, otherwise permissible, are too great, and may, by legislation designed to secure uniformity or in other respects to protect the national interest in the commerce, curtail to some extent the state's regulatory power. But that is a legislative, not a judicial function. [In] the absence of such legislation the judicial function, under the commerce clause as well as the Fourteenth Amendment, stops with the inquiry whether the state Legislature in adopting regulations such as the present has acted within its province, and whether the means of regulation chosen are reasonably adapted to the end sought. [Since] the adoption of one weight or width regulation, rather than another, is a legislative not a judicial choice, its constitutionality is not to be determined by weighing in the judicial scales the merits of the legislative choice and rejecting it if the weight of evidence presented in court appears to favor a different standard. [Hence], in reviewing the present determination we examine the record, not to see whether the findings of the court below are supported by evidence, but to ascertain upon the whole record whether it is possible to say that the legislative choice is without rational basis. [Not] only does the record fail to exclude that possibility, but it shows affirmatively that there is adequate support for the legislative judgment."

Southern Pacific Co. v. Arizona

325 U.S. 761, 65 S.Ct. 1515, 89 L.Ed. 1915 (1945).

[The Arizona Train Limit Law of 1912 prohibited operating railroad trains of more than 14 passenger or 70 freight cars. In 1940, the State sued the Company to recover the statutory penalties for violating the law. After an extended trial, the trial court found the law to be an unconstitutional burden on commerce. The Arizona Supreme Court reversed, concluding that a state law enacted in the exercise of the police power, with some reasonable relation to health and safety, could not be overturned despite its adverse affect on interstate commerce. The U.S. Supreme Court reversed. After rejecting a contention that Congress, by authorizing the ICC to regulate train lengths, had superseded state power, the Court turned to the commerce clause challenge.]

Chief Justice STONE delivered the opinion of the Court.

[Ever since Gibbons v. Ogden], the states have not been deemed to have authority to impede substantially the free flow of commerce from state to state, or to regulate those phases of the national commerce which, because of the need of national uniformity, demand that their regulation, if any, be prescribed by a single authority.[1] [Cooley.] Whether or not this long-recognized distribution of power between the national and the state governments is predicated upon the implications of the commerce clause itself, [or] upon the presumed intention of Congress, where Congress has not spoken, Dowling, Interstate Commerce and State Power, 27 Va.Law Rev. 1 [1940], the result is the same. In the application of these principles some enactments may be found to be plainly within and others plainly without state power. But between these extremes lies the infinite variety of cases, in which regulation of local matters may also operate as a regulation of commerce, in which reconciliation of the conflicting claims of state and national power is to be attained only by some appraisal and accommodation of the competing demands of the state and national interests involved. [For] a hundred years it has been accepted constitutional doctrine that the commerce clause, without the aid of Congressional legislation, [affords] some protection from state legislation inimical to the national commerce, and that in such cases, where Congress has not acted, this Court, and not the state legislature, is under the commerce clause the final arbiter of the competing demands of state and national interests. [Cooley.]

Congress has undoubted power to redefine the distribution of power over interstate commerce. It may either permit the states to regulate the commerce in a manner which would otherwise not be permissible, [or] exclude state regulation even of matters of peculiarly local concern which nevertheless affect interstate commerce. But in general Congress has left it to the courts to formulate the rules thus interpreting the commerce clause in its application, doubtless because it has appreciated the destructive consequences to the commerce of the nation if their protection were withdrawn, and has been aware that in their application state laws will not be invalidated without the support of relevant factual material which will "afford a sure basis" for an informed judgment. Meanwhile, Congress has accommodated its legislation, as have the states, to these rules as an established feature of our constitutional [system].

Hence the matters for ultimate determination here are the nature and extent of the burden which the state regulation of interstate trains, adopted as a safety measure, imposes on interstate commerce, and whether the relative weights of the state and national interests involved are such as to make inapplicable the rule, generally observed, that the free flow of interstate commerce and its freedom from local restraints in matters requiring uniformity of regulation are interests safeguarded by the commerce clause from state interference. [The] findings show that the operation of long trains [is] standard practice over the main lines of the railroads of the United States, and that, if the length of trains is to be regulated at all, national uniformity in the regulation adopted, such as only Congress can prescribe, is practically indis-

---

1. In applying this rule the Court has often recognized that to the extent that the burden of state regulation falls on interests outside the state, it is unlikely to be alleviated by the operation of those political restraints normally exerted when interests within the state are [affected]. [Footnote by Chief Justice Stone.]

pensable to the operation of an efficient and economical national railway [system].

[The] unchallenged findings leave no doubt that the Arizona Train Limit Law imposes a serious burden on the interstate commerce conducted by [appellant]. Enforcement of the law in Arizona, while train lengths remain unregulated or are regulated by varying standards in other states, must inevitably result in an impairment of uniformity of efficient railroad [operation]. Compliance with a state statute limiting train lengths requires interstate trains of a length lawful in other states to be broken up and reconstituted as they enter each state according as it may impose varying limitations upon train lengths. The alternative is for the carrier to conform to the lowest train limit restriction of any of the states through which its trains pass, whose laws thus control the carriers' operations both within and without the regulating state.[2] [If] one state may regulate train lengths, so may all the others, and they need not prescribe the same maximum limitation. The practical effect of such regulation is to control train operations beyond the boundaries of the state exacting it because of the necessity of breaking up and reassembling long trains at the nearest terminal points before entering and after leaving the regulating state. The serious impediment to the free flow of commerce by the local regulation of train lengths and the practical necessity that such regulation, if any, must be prescribed by a single body having a nation-wide authority are apparent.

The trial court found that the Arizona law had no reasonable relation to safety, and made train operation more dangerous. [This] conclusion was rested on facts found which indicate that such increased danger of accident and personal injury as may result from the greater length of trains is more than offset by the increase in the number of accidents resulting from the larger number of trains when train lengths are reduced. In considering the effect of the statute as a safety measure, therefore, the factor of controlling significance for present purposes is not whether there is basis for the conclusion of the Arizona Supreme Court that the increase in length of trains beyond the statutory maximum has an adverse effect upon safety of operation. The decisive question is whether in the circumstances the total effect of the law as a safety measure in reducing accidents and casualties is so slight or problematical as not to outweigh the national interest in keeping interstate commerce free from interferences which seriously impede it and subject it to local regulation which does not have a uniform effect on the interstate train journey which it interrupts.[3]

2. Chief Justice Stone noted that nearly 95% of rail traffic in Arizona was interstate. The state law required appellant to haul over 30% more trains in Arizona. The financial impact of the added cost of train operations was about $1,000,000 a year. Moreover, reduction in train lengths caused delays because of the need to break up and remake long trains. He noted, too, that Arizona was the only state with a 14 passenger car limit, and one of only two states with a 70 freight car limit. He commented, moreover, that it was frequently not feasible to reassemble trains near the Arizona border, "with the result that the Arizona limitation governs the flow of traffic as far east as El Paso, Texas," and as far west as Los Angeles.

3. In engaging in this inquiry, Chief Justice Stone stated: "The principal source of danger of accident from increased length of trains is the resulting increase of 'slack action' of the train. Slack action is the amount of free movement of one car before it transmits its motion to an adjoining coupled car. [On] comparison of the number of slack action accidents in Arizona with those in Nevada, where the length of trains is now unregulated, the trial court found that with substantially the same amount of traffic in each state the number of accidents was relatively the same in long as in short train

[We] think, as the trial court found, that the Arizona Train Limit Law, viewed as a safety measure, affords at most slight and dubious advantage, if any, over unregulated train lengths, because it results in an increase in the number of trains and train operations and the consequent increase in train accidents of a character generally more severe than those due to slack action. Its undoubted effect on the commerce is the regulation, without securing uniformity, of the length of trains operated in interstate commerce, which lack is itself a primary cause of preventing the free flow of commerce by delaying it and by substantially increasing its cost and impairing its efficiency. In these respects the case differs from those where a state, by regulatory measures affecting the commerce, has removed or reduced safety hazards without substantial interference with the interstate movement of trains. Such are measures abolishing the car stove; requiring locomotives to be supplied with electric headlights; providing for full train crews; and for the equipment of freight trains with cabooses. The principle that, without controlling Congressional action, a state may not regulate interstate commerce so as substantially to affect its flow or deprive it of needed uniformity in its regulation is not to be avoided by "simply invoking the convenient apologetics of the police power." [Here] we conclude that the state does go too far. Its regulation of train lengths, admittedly obstructive to interstate train operation, and having a seriously adverse effect on transportation efficiency and economy, passes beyond what is plainly essential for safety since it does not appear that it will lessen rather than increase the danger of accident. Its attempted regulation of the operation of interstate trains cannot establish nation-wide control such as is essential to the maintenance of an efficient transportation system, which Congress alone can prescribe.

[Barnwell involved state regulation of] highways, a legislative field over which the state has a far more extensive control than over interstate railroads. [There], we were at pains to point out that there are few subjects of state regulation affecting interstate commerce which are so peculiarly of local concern as is the use of the state's highways. Unlike the railroads, local highways are built, owned and maintained by the [state]. [The] fact that [state safety regulations] affect alike shippers in interstate and intrastate commerce in great numbers, within as well as without the state, is a safeguard against regulatory abuses. The contrast between the present regulation and [the] highway safety regulations, in point of the nature of the subject of regulation and the state's interest in it, illustrate and emphasize the considerations which enter into a determination of the relative weights of state and national [interests]. Here examination of all the relevant factors makes it plain that the state interest is outweighed by the interest of the nation in an adequate economical and efficient railway transportation service, which must prevail.

Reversed.

Justice BLACK, dissenting.

[In] the state court a rather extraordinary "trial" took place. [Before] the state trial court finally determined that the dangers found by the legislature in 1912 no longer existed, it heard evidence over a period of 5½ months which appears in about 3,000 pages of the printed record before us. It then adopted findings of fact submitted to it by the railroad, which cover 148 printed pages, and conclusions of law which cover 5 pages. [This] new pattern of trial

operations. [Reduction] of the length of trains also tends to increase the number of accidents because of the increase in the number of trains. [The] record lends support to the trial court's conclusion that the train length limitation increased rather than diminished the number of accidents."

procedure makes it necessary for a judge to hear all the evidence offered as to why a legislature passed a law and to make findings of fact as to the validity of those reasons. If under today's ruling a court does make findings as to a danger contrary to the findings of the legislature, and the evidence heard "lends support" to those findings, a court can then invalidate the law. In this respect, the [trial court] acted, and this Court today is acting, as a "super-legislature." Even if this method of invalidating legislative acts is a correct one, I still think that the "findings" of the state court do not authorize today's decision. [When] we finally get down to the gist of what the Court today actually decides, it is this: [that] running shorter trains would increase the cost of railroad operations. [This] record in its entirety leaves me with no doubt whatever that many employees have been seriously injured and killed in the past, and that many more are likely to be so in the future, because of "slack movement" in trains. [It] may be that offsetting dangers are possible in the operation of short trains. The balancing of these probabilities, however, is not in my judgment a matter for judicial determination, but one which calls for legislative [consideration].

Justice DOUGLAS, dissenting.

[My] view has been that the courts should intervene only where the state legislation discriminated against interstate commerce or was out of harmony with laws which Congress had enacted. It seems to me particularly appropriate that that course be followed here. For Congress has given the [ICC] broad powers of regulation over interstate carriers. [W]e are dealing here with state legislation in the field of safety where the propriety of local regulation has long been recognized. Whether the question arises under the Commerce Clause or the Fourteenth Amendment, [the] legislation is entitled to a presumption of [validity].

———

1. *The contrast between Southern Pacific and Barnwell.* Clearly, Southern Pacific reflected greater judicial scrutiny than Barnwell had. Arising in 1938, shortly after the Court-packing controversy, Barnwell might have reflected some hesitance about judicial intervention in this area. By 1945, the Court's "hands off" attitude in national power and due process cases might have allowed greater latitude for some judicial intervention, especially in areas where the political process could not be relied upon to protect all relevant interests.

Were Chief Justice Stone's reasons for distinguishing Barnwell in Southern Pacific persuasive? Are highways "peculiarly local" in nature? In later trucking cases, the Court displayed a steadily growing interest in safeguarding interstate trucking from excessive state burdens. What explains the changes in scrutiny? Arguably, the Court was influenced by the changes in the relative degree of state and federal financing of highways after 1938. Similarly, the growth in importance of the trucking industry since 1938, and the changes in the relative economic conditions of the trucking and railroad industries in more recent decades, may have had an impact.

2. *The changing criteria of judicial scrutiny.* The Southern Pacific opinion, unlike Barnwell, engaged in an extensive balancing process. The evolution of Chief Justice Stone's position between Barnwell and Southern Pacific may have been influenced by an article by Professor Noel T. Dowling, an article (cited by Stone) that appeared between the two decisions, "Interstate Commerce and State Power," 27 Va.L.Rev. 1 (1940). After criticizing the "direct"-"indirect" test as "far from satisfying," Dowling drew a different doctrine from the cases: that, in the absence of congressional consent, "a Congressional

negative will be presumed" where state regulation produces an "unreasonable interference" with commerce. Adoption of that "unreasonable interference" standard, he explained, would "involve an avowal that the Court is deliberately balancing national and local interests and making a choice as to which of the two *should* prevail." That, he conceded, would involve "a policy judgment." He emphasized, moreover, that "the test of reasonableness in interstate commerce cases" was "not the same" as in due process cases: "In a sense, a state law must take the hurdle of due process before it comes to the interstate barrier."

Contrast Chief Justice Stone's endorsement of balancing in Southern Pacific with his objections to quasi-legislative judgments in Barnwell—and with Justice Black's objections to elaborate trials on the benefits and burdens of state laws in his Southern Pacific dissent. This contrast once again raises the issue of the appropriate judicial role and competence in commerce clause cases. Are courts institutionally equipped to undertake balancing inquiries? Are such inquiries worthwhile investments of the courts' energies? Is balancing the appropriate approach not only in transportation cases but also in *all* situations involving allegations of excessive burdens on interstate commerce? Would balancing by Congress be a preferable solution?

3. *The Bibb case.* BIBB v. NAVAJO FREIGHT LINES, INC., 359 U.S. 520 (1959), was the Court's first indication that, even in trucking cases, the Justices might be willing to exercise greater scrutiny than that in Barnwell. Notably, Justice Douglas wrote for the majority in Bibb, even though he had been one of those who had earlier opposed any significant judicial role in commerce clause cases going beyond safeguarding against discrimination. Bibb held invalid an Illinois law requiring the use of contour mudguards on trucks and trailers operating on Illinois highways. That requirement conflicted with an Arkansas rule requiring straight mudguards and forbidding contoured ones. Moreover, at least 45 states authorized the use of straight mudguards.

Justice DOUGLAS' opinion began by echoing the tenor of (and citing) Barnwell: "The power of the State to regulate the use of its highways is broad and pervasive. [Safety] measures carry a strong presumption of validity. [If] there are alternative ways of solving a problem, we do not sit to determine which of them is best suited to achieve a valid state objective. Policy decisions are for the state legislature, absent federal entry into the field." But he quickly moved on to indicate that Barnwell did not wholly reflect the proper commerce clause limit on state safety regulations of highways: "Unless we can conclude on the whole record that 'the total effect of the law as a safety measure in reducing accidents and casualties is so slight or problematical as not to outweigh the national interest in keeping interstate commerce free from interferences which seriously impede it' [Southern Pacific], we must uphold the statute." Justice Douglas proceeded to examine the evidence regarding the "substantial" cost of equipping interstate trucks with contour mudguards and the relative safety advantages of contour mudguards over the conventional or straight mudguards. He concluded that examination by stating: "If we had here only a question whether the cost of adjusting an interstate operation to these new local safety [regulations] unduly burdened interstate commerce, we would have to sustain the law." But this case, he added, presented "a different issue." Here, the Illinois requirement made it necessary for a trucker "to shift its cargo to differently designed vehicles once another state line was reached." The Illinois law seriously interfered with the "interline" operations of motor carriers—"the interchanging of trailers between an originating carrier and another carrier when the latter serves an area not served by the former." Considerations such as these persuaded him that there was a "rather massive showing of burden on interstate commerce."

The State countered with the argument that a federal court was "precluded from weighing the relative merits of the contour mudguard against any other kind of mudguard and must sustain the validity of the statute notwithstanding the extent of the burden it imposes on commerce." Understandably, the State placed its major reliance on Barnwell. Justice Douglas conceded that there was "language in [Barnwell] which read in isolation from such later decisions as [Southern Pacific], would suggest that no showing of burden on interstate commerce is sufficient to invalidate local safety regulations in the absence of some element of discrimination against interstate commerce." But he proceeded: "The various exercises by the States of their police power stand [on] an equal footing. All are entitled to the same presumption of validity when challenged under the Due Process Clause of the Fourteenth Amendment. [Similarly] the various state regulatory statutes are of equal dignity when measured against the Commerce Clause. Local regulations which would pass muster under the Due Process Clause might nonetheless fail to survive other challenges to constitutionality that bring the Supremacy Clause into play. Like any local law that conflicts with federal regulatory measures, [state] regulations that run afoul of the policy of free trade reflected in the Commerce Clause must also bow. This is one of those cases—few in number—where local safety measures that are nondiscriminatory place an unconstitutional burden on interstate commerce. [The] heavy burden which the Illinois mudguard law places on the interstate movement of trucks and trailers seems to us to pass the permissible limits even for safety regulations." Justice Harlan, joined by Justice Stewart, concurred in the judgment.

Kassel v. Consolidated Freightways Corp.

450 U.S. 662, 101 S.Ct. 1309, 67 L.Ed.2d 580 (1981).

Justice POWELL announced the judgment of the Court and delivered an opinion in which Justice WHITE, Justice BLACKMUN, and Justice STEVENS joined.

The question is whether an Iowa statute that prohibits the use of certain large trucks within the State unconstitutionally burdens interstate commerce.

I. [Consolidated Freightways] is one of the largest common carriers in the country. [Among] other routes, Consolidated carries commodities through Iowa on Interstate 80, the principal east-west route linking New York, Chicago, and the West Coast, and on Interstate 35, a major north-south route. Consolidated mainly uses two kinds of trucks. One consists of a three-axle tractor pulling a 40–foot two-axle trailer. This unit, commonly called a single, or "semi," is 55 feet in length overall. Such trucks have long been used on the Nation's highways. Consolidated also uses a two-axle tractor pulling a single-axle trailer which, in turn, pulls a single-axle dolly and a second single-axle trailer. This combination, known as a double, or twin, is 65 feet long overall. Many trucking companies, including Consolidated, increasingly prefer to use doubles to ship certain kinds of commodities. Doubles have larger capacities, and the trailers can be detached and routed separately if necessary. Consolidated would like to use 65–foot doubles on many of its trips through Iowa.

[Iowa], however, by statute restricts the length of vehicles that may use its highways. Unlike all other States in the West and Midwest, Iowa generally prohibits the use of 65–foot doubles within its borders. Instead, most truck combinations are restricted to 55 feet in length. Doubles, mobile homes, trucks carrying vehicles such as tractors and other farm equipment, and singles hauling livestock, are permitted to be as long as 60 feet. Notwithstanding these restrictions, Iowa's statute permits cities abutting the state line by local ordinance to adopt the length limitations of the adjoining State.[1]

Because of Iowa's statutory scheme, Consolidated cannot use its 65–foot doubles to move commodities through the State. Instead, the company must do one of four things: (i) use 55–foot singles, (ii) use 60–foot doubles; (iii) detach the trailers of a 65–foot double and shuttle each through the State separately; or (iv) divert 65–foot doubles around Iowa. Dissatisfied with these options, Consolidated filed this suit in the District Court averring that Iowa's statutory scheme unconstitutionally burdens interstate commerce. Iowa defended the law as a reasonable safety measure enacted pursuant to its police power. The State asserted that 65–foot doubles are more dangerous than 55–foot singles and, in any event, that the law promotes safety and reduces road wear within the State by diverting much truck traffic to other States. In a 14–day trial, both sides adduced evidence on safety, and on the burden on interstate commerce imposed by Iowa's law. On the question of safety, the District Court found that the "evidence clearly establishes that the twin is as safe as the semi." [It] applied the standard we enunciated in Raymond Motor Transportation, Inc. v. Rice [434 U.S. 429 (1978)], and concluded that the state law impermissibly burdened interstate commerce: "[The] *total effect* of the law as a safety measure in reducing accidents and casualties is so slight and problematical that it does not outweigh the national interest in keeping interstate commerce free from interferences that seriously impede it." [The] Court of Appeals agreed. [We] affirm.

II. [A] state's power to regulate commerce is never greater than in matters traditionally of local concern. For example, regulations that touch upon safety—especially highway safety—are those that "the Court has been most reluctant to invalidate." Raymond. Indeed, "if safety justifications are not illusory, the court will not second guess legislative judgment about their importance in comparison with related burdens on interstate commerce." Raymond (Blackmun, J., concurring). Those who would challenge such bona fide safety regulations must overcome a "strong presumption of validity." [Bibb.] But the incantation of a purpose to promote the public health or safety does not insulate a state law from Commerce Clause attack. Regulations designed for that salutary purpose nevertheless may further the purpose so marginally, and interfere with commerce so substantially, as to be invalid under the Commerce Clause. In [Raymond], we declined to "accept the State's contention that the inquiry under the Commerce Clause is ended without a weighing of the asserted safety purpose against the degree of interference with interstate commerce." This "weighing" by a court requires—and indeed the constitutionality of the state regulation depends on—"a sensitive consideration of the weight and nature of the state regulatory concern in light of the extent of

---

1. Justice Powell also noted two other relevant Iowa exemptions. First, an Iowa truck manufacturer could obtain a permit to ship trucks as long as 70 feet. Second, permits were available to move oversized mobile homes if the unit was to be moved from a point within Iowa or delivered to an Iowa resident. In commenting on the second exemption, Justice Powell stated: "The parochial restrictions in the mobile home provision were enacted after Governor Ray vetoed a bill that would have permitted the interstate shipment of all mobile homes through Iowa. Governor Ray commented, in his [1972] veto message: 'This bill [would] make Iowa a bridge state as these oversized units are moved into Iowa after being manufactured in another state and sold in a third. None of the activity would be of particular economic benefit to Iowa.'"

the burden imposed on the course of interstate commerce." Id.; accord, [Pike; Bibb; Southern Pacific].[2]

III.   Applying these general principles, we conclude that the Iowa truck-length limitations unconstitutionally burden interstate commerce. [This] case is Raymond revisited. Here, as in Raymond, the State failed to present any persuasive evidence that 65–foot doubles are less safe than 55–foot singles. Moreover, Iowa's law is now out of step with the laws of all other midwestern and western States. Iowa thus substantially burdens the interstate flow of goods by truck. In the absence of congressional action to set uniform standards, some burdens associated with state safety regulations must be tolerated. But where, as here, the State's safety interest has been found to be illusory, and its regulations impair significantly the federal interest in efficient and safe inter-state transportation, the state law cannot be harmonized with the Commerce Clause.

A.   The District Court found that the "evidence clearly establishes that the twin is as safe as the semi." The record supports this finding. The trial focused on a comparison of the performance of the two kinds of trucks in various safety categories. [The] District Court found [that] the 65–foot double was at least the equal of the 55–foot single in the ability to brake, turn, and maneuver. The double, because of its axle placement, produces less splash and spray in wet weather. And, because of its articulation in the middle, the double is less susceptible to dangerous "off-tracking,"[3] and to wind. None of these findings is seriously disputed by Iowa. [Although] Iowa introduced more evidence on the question of safety than did Wisconsin in Raymond, the record as a whole was not more favorable to the State.[4]

B.   Consolidated, meanwhile, demonstrated that Iowa's law substantially burdens interstate commerce. Trucking companies that wish to continue to use 65–foot doubles must route them around Iowa or detach the trailers of the doubles and ship them through separately. Alternatively, trucking companies must use the smaller 55–foot singles or 60–foot doubles permitted under Iowa law. Each of these options engenders inefficiency and added expense. The record shows that Iowa's law added about $12.6 million each year to the costs of trucking companies. Consolidated alone incurred about $2 million per year in increased costs. In addition to increasing the costs of the trucking companies (and, indirectly, of the service to consumers), Iowa's law may aggravate, rather than ameliorate, the problem of highway accidents. Fifty-five foot singles carry less freight than 65–foot doubles. Either more small trucks must be used to carry the same quantity of goods through Iowa, or the same number of larger trucks must drive longer distances to bypass Iowa. In either case, [the]

---

2. It is highly relevant that here, as in Raymond, the state statute contains exemptions that weaken the deference traditionally accorded to a state safety regulation. [Footnote by Justice Powell.]

3. "Off-tracking" refers to the extent to which the rear wheels of a truck deviate from the path of the front wheels while turning. [Footnote by Justice Powell.]

4. In suggesting that Iowa's law actually promotes safety, the dissenting opinion ignores the findings of the courts below and relies on largely discredited statistical evidence. The dissent implies that a statistical study identified doubles as more dangerous

than singles. At trial, however, the author of that study—Iowa's own statistician—conceded that his calculations were statistically biased, and therefore "not very meaningful."

The dissenting opinion also suggests that its conclusions are bolstered by the fact that the American Association of State Highway and Transportation Officials (AASHTO) recommends that States limit truck lengths. The dissent fails to point out, however, that AASHTO specifically recommends that States permit 65–foot doubles. [Footnote by Justice Powell.]

restriction requires more highway miles to be driven to transport the same quantity of goods. Other things being equal, accidents are proportional to distance traveled. Thus, if 65–foot doubles are as safe as 55–foot singles, Iowa's law tends to *increase* the number of accidents, and to shift the incidence of them from Iowa to other States.

IV. Perhaps recognizing the weakness of the evidence supporting its safety argument, and the substantial burden on commerce that its regulations create, Iowa urges the Court simply to "defer" to the safety judgment of the State. It argues that the length of trucks is generally, although perhaps imprecisely, related to safety. The task of drawing a line is one that Iowa contends should be left to its legislature. The Court normally does accord "special deference" to state highway safety regulations. [Less] deference to the legislative judgment is due, however, where the local regulation bears disproportionately on out-of-state residents and businesses. Such a disproportionate burden is apparent here. Iowa's scheme, although generally banning large doubles from the State, nevertheless has several exemptions that secure to Iowans many of the benefits of large trucks while shunting to neighboring States many of the costs associated with their use.

At the time of trial there were two particularly significant exemptions. First, singles hauling livestock or farm vehicles were permitted to be as long as 60 feet. [T]his provision undoubtedly was helpful to local interests. Second, cities abutting other States were permitted to enact local ordinances adopting the larger length limitation of the neighboring State. This exemption offered the benefits of longer trucks to individuals and businesses in important border cities without burdening Iowa's highways with interstate through traffic. The origin of the "border cities exemption" also suggests that Iowa's statute may not have been designed to ban dangerous trucks, but rather to discourage interstate truck traffic. In 1974, the legislature passed a bill that would have permitted 65–foot doubles in the State. Governor Ray vetoed the bill. He said: "I find sympathy with those who are doing business in our state and whose enterprises could gain from increased cargo carrying ability by trucks. However, with this bill, the Legislature has pursued a course that would benefit only a few Iowa-based companies while providing a great advantage for out-of-state trucking firms and competitors at the expense of our Iowa citizens."[5] After the veto, the "border cities exemption" was immediately enacted and signed by the Governor.

It is thus far from clear that Iowa was motivated primarily by a judgment that 65–foot doubles are less safe than 55–foot singles. Rather, Iowa seems to have hoped to limit the use of its highways by deflecting some through traffic. In the [lower courts], the State explicitly attempted to justify the law by its claimed interest in keeping trucks out of Iowa. The Court of Appeals correctly concluded that a State cannot constitutionally promote its own parochial interests by requiring safe vehicles to detour around it.

V. In sum, the statutory exemptions, their history, and the arguments Iowa has advanced in support of its law in this litigation, all suggest that the deference traditionally accorded a State's safety judgment is not warranted. The controlling factors thus are the findings of the District Court, accepted by the Court of Appeals, with respect to the relative safety of the types of trucks at issue, and the substantiality of the burden on interstate commerce. Because

---

5. [E]xceptions also are available to benefit Iowa truck makers and Iowa mobile home manufacturers or purchasers. Although these exemptions are not directly relevant to the controversy over the safety of 65–foot doubles, they do contribute to the pattern of parochialism apparent in Iowa's statute. [Footnote by Justice Powell.]

Iowa has imposed this burden without any significant countervailing safety interest[6] its statute violates the [Commerce Clause].

Affirmed.

Justice BRENNAN, with whom Justice MARSHALL joins, concurring in the judgment.

Iowa's truck length regulation challenged in this case is nearly identical to the Wisconsin regulation struck down in [Raymond]. In my view the same Commerce Clause restrictions that dictated that holding also require invalidation of Iowa's regulation insofar as it prohibits 65–foot doubles. The reasoning bringing me to that conclusion does not require, however, that I engage in the debate between [Justices] Powell and Rehnquist over what the District Court record shows on the question whether 65–foot doubles are more dangerous than shorter trucks. With all respect, [they] ask and answer the wrong question. For me, analysis of Commerce Clause challenges to state regulations must take into account three principles: (1) The courts are not empowered to second-guess the empirical judgments of lawmakers concerning the utility of legislation. (2) The burdens imposed on commerce must be balanced against the local benefits actually sought to be achieved by the State's lawmakers, and not against those suggested after the fact by counsel. (3) Protectionist legislation is unconstitutional under the Commerce Clause, even if the burdens and benefits are related to safety rather than economics.

I. [The Powell and Rehnquist opinions are both] predicated upon the supposition that the constitutionality of a state regulation is determined by the factual record created by the State's lawyers in trial court. But that supposition cannot be correct, for it would make the constitutionality of state laws and regulations depend on the vagaries of litigation rather than on the judgments made by the State's lawmakers. In considering a Commerce Clause challenge to a state regulation, the judicial task is to balance the burden imposed on commerce against the local benefits sought to be achieved by the State's *lawmakers*. In determining those benefits, a court should focus ultimately on the regulatory purposes identified by the lawmakers and on the evidence before or available to them that might have supported their judgment. See generally Clover Leaf Creamery [1981; p. 315 below]. Since the court must confine its analysis to the purposes the lawmakers had for maintaining the regulation, the only relevant evidence concerns whether the lawmakers could rationally have believed that the challenged regulation would foster those purposes. It is not the function of the court to decide whether *in fact* the regulation promotes its intended purpose, so long as an examination of the evidence before or available to the lawmaker indicates that the regulation is not wholly irrational in light of its purposes.[1]

---

6. [The District Court] found that the statute did not discriminate against such commerce. Because the record fully supports the decision below with respect to the burden on interstate commerce, we need not consider whether the statute also operated to discriminate against that commerce. The latter theory was neither briefed nor argued in this Court. [Footnote by Justice Powell.]

1. Moreover, I would emphasize that in the field of safety—and perhaps in other fields where the decisions of State lawmakers are deserving of a heightened degree of defer-

ence—the role of the courts is not to balance asserted burdens against intended benefits as it is in other fields. Compare Raymond (Blackmun, J., concurring) (safety regulation) with [Pike] (regulation intended "to protect and enhance the reputation of growers within the State"). In the field of safety, once the court has established that the intended safety benefit is not illusory, insubstantial, or non-existent, it must defer to the State's lawmakers on the appropriate balance to be struck against other interests. I therefore disagree with my Brother Powell when he asserts that

II. [Justices] Powell and Rehnquist make the mistake of disregarding the intention of Iowa's lawmakers and assuming that resolution of the case must hinge upon the argument offered by Iowa's attorneys: that 65–foot doubles are more dangerous than shorter trucks. They then [reach] opposite conclusions as to whether the evidence adequately supports that empirical judgment. I repeat: [Justices] Powell and Rehnquist have asked and answered the wrong question. For although Iowa's lawyers in this litigation have defended the truck length regulation on the basis of the safety advantages of 55–foot singles and 60–foot doubles over 65–foot doubles, Iowa's actual rationale for maintaining the regulation had nothing to do with these purported differences. Rather, Iowa sought to discourage interstate truck traffic on Iowa's highways. Thus, the safety advantages and disadvantages of the types and lengths of trucks involved in this case are irrelevant to the [decision].[2]

III. Though [Justice] Powell recognizes that the State's actual purpose in maintaining the truck length regulation was "to limit the use of its highways by deflecting some through traffic," he fails to recognize that this purpose, being *protectionist* in nature, is *impermissible* under the Commerce Clause. The Governor admitted that he blocked legislative efforts to raise the length of trucks because the change "would benefit only a few Iowa-based companies while providing a great advantage for out-of-state trucking firms and competitors at the expense of our Iowa citizens." Appellant [Kassel], Director of the Iowa Department of Transportation, while admitting that the greater 65–foot length standard would be *safer* overall, defended the more restrictive regula-

the degree of interference with interstate commerce may in the first instance be "weighed" against the State's safety [interests]. [Footnote by Justice Brennan.]

2. [Justice] Rehnquist claims that the "argument" that a Court should defer to the actual purposes of the lawmakers rather than to the post hoc justifications of counsel "has been consistently rejected by the Court in other [contexts]." The extent to which we may rely upon post hoc justifications of counsel depends on the circumstances surrounding passage of the legislation. Where there is no evidence bearing on the actual purpose for a legislative classification, our analysis necessarily focuses on the suggestions of counsel. Even then, "marginally more demanding scrutiny" is appropriate to "test the plausibility of the tendered purpose." Schweiker v. Wilson [1981; p. 657 below] (Powell, J., dissenting). But where the lawmakers' purposes in enacting a statute are explicitly set forth, or are clearly discernible from the legislative history, this Court should not take—and, with the possible exception of United States Railroad Retirement Board v. Fritz [1980; p. 653 below] (Brennan, J., dissenting), has not taken—the extraordinary step of disregarding the *actual* purpose in favor of some "imaginary basis or purpose." McGinnis v. Royster [p. 647 below]. The principle of separation of powers requires, after all, that we defer to the elected lawmakers' judgment as to the

appropriate means to accomplish an end, not that we defer to the arguments of lawyers.

If, as here, the only purpose ever articulated by the State's lawmakers for maintaining a regulation is illegitimate, I consider it contrary to precedent as well as to sound principles of constitutional adjudication for the courts to base their analysis on purposes never conceived by the lawmakers. This is especially true where, as the dissent's strained analysis of the relative safety of 65–foot doubles to shorter trucks amply demonstrates, the post hoc justifications are implausible as well as imaginary. I would emphasize that, although my Brother Powell's plurality opinion does not give as much weight to the illegitimacy of Iowa's actual purpose as I do, both that opinion and this concurrence have found the actual motivation of the Iowa lawmakers in maintaining the truck length regulation highly relevant to, if not dispositive of, the case. [Footnote by Justice Brennan. The cases relied on by Justice Brennan in this footnote are equal protection, not commerce clause, cases. The Court's division about the relevance of "actual purpose" recurs frequently in modern equal protection and due process cases, especially those reviewing economic regulations under the widely applied "rationality" standard. The debate on that issue is more fully considered below, in chapters 8 and 9.]

tions because of their benefits *within Iowa*. [Iowa] may not shunt off its fair share of the burden of maintaining interstate truck routes, nor may it create increased hazards on the highways of neighboring States in order to decrease the hazards on Iowa highways. Such an attempt has all the hallmarks of the "[simple] protectionism" this Court has condemned in the economic area. Philadelphia v. New Jersey. Just as a State's attempt to avoid interstate competition in economic goods may damage the prosperity of the Nation as a whole, so Iowa's attempt to deflect interstate truck traffic has been found to make the Nation's highways as a whole more hazardous. That attempt should therefore be subject to "a virtually per se rule of invalidity." Ibid. This Court's heightened deference to the judgments of state lawmakers in the field of safety is largely attributable to a judicial disinclination to weigh the interests of safety against other societal interests, such as the economic interest in the free flow of commerce. [Here,] the decision of Iowa's lawmakers to promote *Iowa's* safety and other interests at the direct expense of the safety and other interests of neighboring States merits no such deference. No special judicial acuity is demanded to perceive that this sort of parochial legislation violates the Commerce Clause. [Baldwin v. Seelig.]

Justice REHNQUIST, with whom Chief Justice BURGER and Justice STEWART join, dissenting.

The result in this case suggests, to paraphrase Justice Jackson, that the only state truck length limit "that is valid is one which this court has not been able to get its hands on." [Although] the plurality and concurring opinions strike down Iowa's law by different routes, I believe the analysis in both opinions oversteps our "limited authority to review state legislation under the commerce clause" and seriously intrudes upon the fundamental right of the States to pass laws to secure the safety of their [citizens].

I.   It is necessary to elaborate somewhat on the facts as presented in the plurality opinion to appreciate fully what the Court does today. Iowa's action in limiting the length of trucks which may travel on its highways is in no sense unusual. Every [state] regulates the length of vehicles permitted to use the public roads. Nor is Iowa a renegade in having length limits which operate to exclude the 65–foot doubles favored by Consolidated. These trucks are prohibited in other areas of the country as well, some 17 States and the District of Columbia, including all of New England and most of the Southeast. [In short], the persistent effort in the plurality opinion to paint Iowa as an oddity standing alone to block commerce carried in 65–foot doubles is simply not supported [by the facts].

II.   [A] determination that a state law is a rational safety measure does not end the Commerce Clause inquiry. A "sensitive consideration" of the safety purpose in relation to the burden on commerce is required. When engaging in such a consideration the Court does not directly compare safety benefits to commerce costs and strike down the legislation if the latter can be said in some vague sense to "outweigh" the former. Such an approach would make an empty gesture of the strong presumption of validity accorded state safety measures, particularly those governing highways. It would also arrogate to this Court functions of forming public policy, functions which, in the absence of congressional action, were left by the [Framers] to state legislatures. [The] purpose of the "sensitive consideration" referred to above is rather to determine if the asserted safety justification, although rational, is merely a pretext for discrimination against interstate commerce. We will conclude that it is if the safety benefits from the regulation are demonstrably trivial while the burden on commerce is great. [See Southern Pacific; Bibb.] [The cases] demonstrate that the safety benefits of a state law must be slight indeed before it will be struck down under the dormant Commerce Clause.

III. [There] can be no doubt that the challenged statute is a valid highway safety regulation and thus entitled to the strongest presumption of validity against Commerce Clause challenges. [There] can also be no question that the particular limit chosen by Iowa [is] rationally related to Iowa's safety objective. [Iowa] adduced evidence supporting the relation between vehicle length and highway safety. [In sum], there was sufficient evidence presented at trial to support the legislative determination that length is related to safety, and nothing in Consolidated's evidence undermines this conclusion.

The District Court approached the case as if the question were whether Consolidated's 65–foot trucks were as safe as others permitted on Iowa highways. [The] question, however, is whether the Iowa Legislature has acted rationally in regulating vehicle lengths and whether the safety benefits from this regulation are more than slight or problematical. [See, e.g., Barnwell.] The answering of the relevant question is not appreciably advanced by comparing trucks slightly over the length limit with those at the length limit. It is emphatically not our task to balance any incremental safety benefits from prohibiting 65–foot doubles as opposed to 60–foot doubles against the burden on interstate commerce. Lines drawn for safety purposes will rarely pass muster if the question is whether a slight increment can be permitted without sacrificing safety. The question is rather whether it can be said that the benefits flowing to Iowa from a rational truck length limitation are "slight or problematical." See Bibb. The particular line chosen by Iowa—60 feet—is relevant only to the question whether the limit is a rational one. Once a court determines that it is, it considers the overall safety benefits *from the regulation* against burdens on interstate commerce, and not any marginal benefits from the scheme the State established as opposed to that the plaintiffs desire. See [Southern Pacific; Barnwell]. The difficulties with the contrary approach are patent. While it may be clear that there are substantial safety benefits from a 55–foot truck as compared to a 105–foot truck, these benefits may not be discernible in 5–foot jumps. Appellee's approach would permit what could not be accomplished in one lawsuit to be done in ten separate suits, each challenging an additional five feet. Any direct balancing of marginal safety benefits against burdens on commerce would make the burdens on commerce the sole significant factor, and make likely the odd result that similar state laws enacted for identical safety reasons might violate the Commerce Clause in one part of the country but not [another].

[Striking] down Iowa's law because Consolidated has made a voluntary business decision to employ 65–foot doubles, a decision based on the actions of other state legislatures, would essentially be compelling Iowa to yield to the policy choices of neighboring States. Under our Constitutional scheme, however, there is only one legislative body which can pre-empt the rational policy determination of the Iowa Legislature and that is Congress. Forcing Iowa to yield to the policy choices of neighboring States perverts the primary purpose of the Commerce Clause, that of vesting power to regulate interstate commerce in Congress, where all the States are [represented].

[Justice] Brennan argues that the Court should consider only *the* purpose the Iowa legislators *actually* sought to achieve by the length limit, and not the purposes advanced by Iowa's lawyers in defense of the statute. This argument calls to mind what was said of the Roman Legions: that they may have lost battles, but they never lost a war, since they never let a war end until they had won it. The argument has been consistently rejected by the Court in other [i.e., equal protection] contexts, and Justice Brennan can cite no authority for the proposition that possible legislative purposes suggested by a state's lawyers should not be considered in Commerce Clause cases. The problems with a view such as that advanced in the concurring opinion are apparent. To name just a few, it assumes that individual legislators are motivated by one discernible "actual" purpose, and ignores the fact that different legislators may vote for a single piece of legislation for widely different reasons. How, for example, would a court adhering to the views expressed in the concurring opinion approach a statute, the legislative history of which indicated that 10 votes were based on safety considerations, 10 votes were based on protectionism, and the statute passed by a vote of 40–20? What would the *actual* purpose of the *legislature* have been in that [case]?

[The] effort in both the plurality and concurring opinions to portray the legislation involved here as protectionist is in error. Whenever a State enacts more stringent safety measures than its neighbors, in an area which affects commerce, the safety law will have the incidental effect of deflecting interstate commerce to the neighboring States. Indeed, the safety and protectionist motives cannot be separated: The whole purpose of safety regulation of vehicles is to *protect* the State from unsafe vehicles. If a neighboring State chooses *not* to protect its citizens from the danger discerned by the enacting State, that is its business, but the enacting State should not be penalized when the vehicles it considers unsafe travel through the neighboring State. The other States with truck length limits that exclude Consolidated's 65–foot doubles would not at all be paranoid in assuming that they might be next on Consolidated's "hit list." The true problem with today's decision is that it gives no guidance whatsoever to these States as to whether their laws are valid or how to defend them. For that matter, the decision gives no guidance to Consolidated or other trucking firms either. Perhaps, after all is said and done, the Court today neither says nor does very much at all. We know only that Iowa's law is invalid and that the jurisprudence of the "negative side" of the Commerce Clause remains hopelessly confused.

STATE BURDENS ON TRADE

In EXXON CORP. v. GOVERNOR OF MARYLAND, 437 U.S. 117 (1978), the Court sustained a law prohibiting producers or refiners of petroleum products from operating retail service stations in Maryland. (No gasoline was produced or refined in the state.) Maryland acted in response to evidence that stations operated by producers and refiners (about 5% of Maryland's service stations) had received preferential treatment during the 1973 petroleum shortage. The challengers claimed that the law discriminated against and imposed an undue burden on interstate commerce. Justice STEVENS' majority opinion rejected both attacks.

On the former claim, Justice Stevens stated: "Plainly, the [law] does not discriminate against interstate goods, nor does it favor local producers and refiners. Since Maryland's entire gasoline supply flows in interstate commerce and since there are no local producers or refiners, such claims of disparate treatment between interstate and local commerce would be meritless. Appellants, however, focus on the retail market, arguing that the effect of the statute is to protect in-state independent dealers from out-of-state competition. [They] rely on the fact that [the] divestiture requirements [fall] solely on interstate companies. But this fact does not lead, either logically or as a practical matter, to a conclusion that the State is discriminating against interstate commerce at the retail level. [There] are several major interstate marketers of petroleum that own and operate their own retail gasoline stations. [E.g., Sears Roebuck.] These interstate dealers, who compete directly with the Maryland independent dealers, are not affected by the Act because they do not refine or produce gasoline. In fact, the Act creates no barriers whatsoever against interstate independent dealers: it does not prohibit the flow of interstate goods, place added costs upon them, or distinguish between in-state and out-of-state companies in the retail market. The absence of any of these factors fully distinguishes this case from those in which a State has been found to have discriminated against interstate commerce. See, e.g., [Hunt; Dean Milk]."[1]

Turning to the claim that the law "impermissibly *burdens* interstate commerce," Justice Stevens found it no more persuasive, even though some refiners might be driven from the Maryland market: "[Even if that happens], there is no reason to assume that their share of the entire supply will not be promptly replaced by other interstate refiners. The source of the consumers' supply may switch from company-operated stations to independent dealers, but interstate commerce is not subjected to an impermissible burden simply because an otherwise valid regulation causes some business to shift from one interstate supplier to another." The challengers also claimed that the law interfered with "the natural functioning of the interstate market" and would "surely change the market structure by weakening the independent refiners." Justice Stevens replied: "We [cannot] accept appellants' underlying notion that the Commerce Clause protects the particular structure or methods of operation in a retail market. See [Breard]. [The] Clause protects the interstate market, not particular interstate firms, from prohibitive or burdensome regulations. It may be true that the consuming public will be injured by the loss of the high-volume, low-priced stations operated by the independent refiners, but again that argument relates to the wisdom of the statute, not to its burden on commerce."

Justice BLACKMUN was the sole dissenter. He insisted that the Maryland law was discriminatory: "[It] is true that merely demonstrating a burden on some out-of-state actors does not prove unconstitutional discrimination. But when the burden is significant, when it falls on the most numerous and effective group of out-of-state competitors, when a similar burden does not fall on the class of protected in-state businessmen, and when the State cannot justify the resulting disparity by showing that its legislative interests cannot be vindicated by more evenhanded regulation, unconstitutional discrimination exists."

In MINNESOTA v. CLOVER LEAF CREAMERY CO., 449 U.S. 456 (1981), the Court, by a vote of 6–2, upheld a state law that banned the retail sale of milk products in plastic nonreturnable containers but permitted sales in nonreturnable containers—mainly containers made of pulpwood. In enacting the law, the legislature found that the use of nonreturnable containers "presents a solid waste management problem, [promotes] energy waste, and depletes

---

1. "If the effect of a state regulation is to cause local goods to constitute a larger share, and goods with an out-of-state source to constitute a smaller share, of the total sales in the market—as in Hunt and Dean Milk—the regulation may have a discriminatory effect on interstate commerce. But the Maryland statute has no impact on the rela- tive proportions of local and out-of-state goods sold in Maryland and, indeed, no demonstrable effect whatsoever on the interstate flow of goods. The sales by independent retailers are just as much a part of the flow of [commerce] as the sales made by the refiner-operated stations." [Footnote by Justice Stevens.]

natural resources." The plastic containers originated out of state; pulpwood was a major instate product.

Justice BRENNAN's majority opinion rejected challenges based both on the anti-protectionism principle and on the Pike balancing formula. He explained: "If a state law purporting to promote environmental purposes is in reality 'simple economic protectionism,' we have applied a 'virtually per se rule of invalidity.' Philadelphia v. New Jersey. Even if a statute regulates 'even-handedly,' and imposes only 'incidental' burdens on interstate commerce, the courts must nevertheless strike it down if 'the burden imposed on such commerce is clearly excessive in relation to the putative local benefits.' [Pike.] [The law here] does not effect 'simple protectionism,' but 'regulates evenhandedly' by prohibiting all milk retailers from selling their products in plastic, nonreturnable milk containers, without regard to whether the containers, or the sellers are from outside the State. [Since] the statute does not discriminate between interstate and intrastate commerce, the controlling question is whether the incidental burden imposed on interstate commerce by the Minnesota Act is 'clearly excessive in relation to the putative local benefits.' [Pike]. We conclude that it is not. The burden imposed on interstate commerce by the statute is relatively minor. Milk products may continue to move freely across the Minnesota border, and since most dairies package their products in more than one type of containers, the inconvenience of having to conform to different packaging requirements in Minnesota and the surrounding States should be slight. Within Minnesota, business will presumably shift from manufacturers of plastic nonreturnable containers to producers of paperboard cartons, refillable bottles, and plastic pouches, but there is no reason to suspect that the gainers will be Minnesota firms, or the losers out-of-state firms. Indeed, two of the three dairies, the sole milk retailer, and the sole milk container producer challenging the statute in this litigation are Minnesota firms.[1]

"Pulpwood producers are the only Minnesota industry likely to benefit significantly from the Act at the expense of out-of-state firms. Respondents point out that plastic resin, the raw material used for making plastic nonreturnable milk jugs, is produced entirely by non-Minnesota firms, while pulpwood, used for making paperboard, is a major Minnesota product. Nevertheless, it is clear that respondents exaggerate the degree of burden on out-of-state interests, both because plastics will continue to be used in the production of plastic pouches, plastic returnable bottles, and paperboard itself, and because out-of-state pulpwood producers will presumably absorb some of the business generated by the Act. Even granting that the out-of-state plastics industry is burdened relatively more heavily than the Minnesota pulpwood industry, we find that this burden is not 'clearly excessive' in light of the substantial state interest in promoting conservation of energy and other natural resources and easing solid waste disposal problems. [We] find these local benefits ample to support Minnesota's decision under the Commerce Clause. Moreover, we find that no approach with 'a lesser impact on interstate activities' [Pike] is available. Respondents have suggested several alternative statutory schemes, but these alternatives are either more burdensome on commerce than the Act

---

1. [The] existence of major in-state interests adversely affected by the Act is a powerful safeguard against legislative abuse. [Barnwell.] [Footnote by Justice Brennan.] [The challengers included not merely in-state interests, but also a non-Minnesota company that manufactured equipment for producing plastic nonreturnable milk jugs, a non-Minnesota dairy that sold milk products in Minnesota in plastic nonreturnable milk jugs, a non-Minnesota manufacturer of polyethylene resin that sold such resin in many states, including Minnesota, and a plastics industry trade association.]

(as, for example, banning all nonreturnables) or less likely to be effective (as, for example, providing incentives for recycling).

"In [Exxon], we upheld a Maryland statute barring producers and refiners of petroleum products—all of which were out-of-state businesses—from retailing gasoline in the State. We stressed that the Commerce Clause 'protects the interstate market, not particular interstate firms, from prohibitive or burdensome regulations.' A nondiscriminatory regulation serving substantial state purposes is not invalid simply because it causes some business to shift from a predominantly out-of-state industry to a predominantly in-state industry. Only if the burden on interstate commerce clearly outweighs the State's legitimate purposes does such a regulation violate the Commerce Clause." Justice POWELL dissented, urging that the case be remanded for consideration by the highest state court, to "consider specifically whether the statute discriminated impermissibly against interstate commerce." (The state trial court had struck down the law under equal protection after finding that the statutes rested on a discriminatory purpose. The highest state court had overturned that equal protection ruling but had not reached the commerce clause claim. Justice Powell thought the trial court findings were "highly relevant" to the question of discrimination against commerce and urged that they be considered on remand.) Justice Stevens also dissented. Justice Rehnquist did not participate.

STATE BURDENS ON BUSINESS ENTRY

The Pike balancing formula has also surfaced in decisions involving limits on business entry and regulations of corporate affairs (such as anti-takeover statutes). An early example was LEWIS v. BT INVESTMENT MANAGERS, INC., 447 U.S. 27 (1980). There, Justice BLACKMUN's opinion for a unanimous Court struck down a Florida law prohibiting ownership of local investment advisory businesses by out-of-state banks, bank holding companies and trust companies. (The law barred only some, not all, investment advisory companies owned by out-of-state interests.) The Court noted that the law "prevents competition in local markets by out-of-state firms with the kinds of resources and business interests that make them likely to attempt de novo entry" and found the law "parochial" in the sense that "it overtly prevents foreign enterprises from competing in local markets." Although Justice Blackmun noted that "on its face and in actual effect," the law displayed "a local favoritism or protectionism" that made it suspect under the commerce clause, he found it unnecessary to decide whether this was sufficient to render the law "per se invalid, for we are convinced that the disparate treatment of out-of-state bank holding companies cannot be justified as an incidental burden necessitated by legitimate local concerns." He invoked "the general principle that the Commerce Clause prohibits a State from using its regulatory power to protect its own citizens from outside competition. See [e.g., Hood]."

The Court's attention shifted from barriers on business entry to restraints on takeover efforts in EDGAR v. MITE CORP., 457 U.S. 624 (1982). There, a sharply divided Court held unconstitutional the interstate commerce impacts of the Illinois Business Take–Over Act, designed to regulate tender offers made to target companies that had certain specified business contacts with Illinois. Under the Act, takeover offers had to be registered with the Illinois Secretary of State 20 days before the offer became effective. During this 20–day period, the offeror could not communicate with shareholders, although the target company was free to disseminate information to them. The Secretary of State could refuse registration for lack of full and fair disclosure or where the offer was deemed inequitable or fraudulent. The only ground on which the majority could agree was the Pike balancing formula: the majority concluded that the Act imposed "a substantial burden on interstate commerce which outweighs its putative local benefits."

CTS CORP. v. DYNAMICS CORP. OF AMERICA, 481 U.S. 69 (1987), involved a dormant commerce clause challenge to an Indiana law providing that a purchaser who acquired "control shares" in an Indiana corporation could acquire voting rights only to the extent approved by a majority vote of the prior disinterested stockholders. In addition to rejecting the argument that the Indiana law was preempted by the federal anti-takeover Williams Act, the Court rejected the commerce clause claim. Justice POWELL's majority opinion stated: "The principal objects of dormant Commerce Clause scrutiny are statutes that discriminate against interstate commerce. See, e.g., [Lewis; Philadelphia v. New Jersey]. The Indiana Act is not such a statute. It has the same effects on tender offers whether or not the offeror is a domiciliary or resident of Indiana. Thus, it 'visits its effects equally upon both interstate and local business.' Lewis. [Because] nothing in the Indiana Act imposes a greater burden on out-of-state offerors than it does on similarly situated Indiana offerors, we reject the contention that the Act discriminates against interstate commerce.

"This Court's recent Commerce Clause cases also have invalidated statutes that may adversely affect interstate commerce by subjecting activities to inconsistent regulations. E.g., [Kassel (plurality opinion of Powell, J.). See Southern Pacific; Cooley]. The Indiana Act poses no such problem. So long as each State regulates voting rights only in the corporations it has created, each corporation will be subject to the law of only one State. No principle of corporation law and practice is more firmly established than a State's authority to regulate domestic corporations, including the authority to define the voting rights of shareholders. [Accordingly], we conclude that the Indiana Act does not create an impermissible risk of inconsistent regulation by different States."

But the lower court had not held the law unconstitutional for "either of these threshold reasons. Rather, its decision rested on its view of the Act's potential to hinder tender offers." Justice Powell rejected this argument because it failed "to appreciate the significance for Commerce Clause analysis of the fact that state regulation of corporate governance is regulation of entities whose very existence and attributes are a product of state law. [Every State] has enacted laws regulating corporate governance. By prohibiting certain transactions, and regulating others, such laws necessarily affect certain aspects of interstate commerce. [Large] corporations that are listed on national exchanges [will] have shareholders in many States and shares that are traded frequently. The markets that facilitate this national and international participation in ownership of corporations are essential for providing capital not only for new enterprises but also for established companies that need to expand their businesses. This beneficial free market system depends at its core upon the fact that a corporation—except in the rarest situations—is organized under, and governed by, the law of a single jurisdiction, traditionally the corporate law of the State of its incorporation.

"These regulatory laws may affect directly a variety of corporate transactions. Mergers are a typical example. In view of the substantial effect that a merger may have on the shareholders' interests in a corporation, many States require supermajority votes to approve mergers. By requiring a greater vote for mergers than is required for other transactions, these laws make it more difficult for corporations to merge. [It] thus is an accepted part of the business landscape in this country for States to create corporations, to prescribe their powers, and to define the rights that are acquired by purchasing their shares. A State has an interest in promoting stable relationships among parties involved in the corporations it charters, as well as in ensuring that investors in such corporations have an effective voice in corporate affairs.

"There can be no doubt that the Act reflects these concerns. The primary purpose of the Act is to protect the shareholders of Indiana corporations. It does this by affording shareholders, when a takeover offer is made, an opportunity to decide collectively whether the resulting change in voting control of the corporation, as they perceive it, would be desirable. A change of management may have important effects on the shareholders' interests; it is well within the State's role as overseer of corporate governance to offer this opportunity. The autonomy provided by allowing shareholders collectively to determine whether the takeover is advantageous to their interests may be especially beneficial where a hostile tender offer may coerce shareholders into tendering their shares.

"Appellee Dynamics responds to this concern by arguing that the prospect of coercive tender offers is illusory, and that tender offers generally should be favored because they reallocate corporate assets into the hands of management who can use them most effectively. [Indiana's] concern with tender offers is not groundless. Indeed, the potentially coercive aspects of tender offers have been recognized by the SEC and by a number of scholarly commentators. The Constitution does not require the States to subscribe to any particular economic theory. We are not inclined "to second-guess the empirical judgments of lawmakers concerning the utility of legislation" [Kassel (Brennan, J., concurring).] In our view, the possibility of coercion in some takeover bids offers additional justification for Indiana's decision to promote the autonomy of independent shareholders.

"Dynamics argues in any event that the State has 'no legitimate interest in protecting the nonresident shareholders.' Dynamics relies heavily on the statement by the MITE Court that '[i]nsofar as [the] law burdens out-of-state transactions, there is nothing to be weighed in the balance to sustain the law.' But that comment was made in reference to an Illinois law that applied as well to out-of-state corporations as to in-state corporations. We agree that Indiana has no interest in protecting nonresident shareholders *of nonresident corporations*. But this Act applies only to corporations incorporated in Indiana. We reject the contention that Indiana has no interest in providing for the shareholders of its corporations the voting autonomy granted by the Act. Indiana has a substantial interest in preventing the corporate form from becoming a shield for unfair business dealing. Moreover, unlike the Illinois statute invalidated in MITE, the Indiana Act applies only to corporations that have a substantial number of shareholders in Indiana. Thus, every application of the Indiana Act will affect a substantial number of Indiana residents, whom Indiana indisputably has an interest in protecting.

"[Dynamics'] argument that the Act is unconstitutional ultimately rests on its contention that the Act will limit the number of successful tender offers. There is little evidence that this will occur. But even if true, this result would not substantially affect our Commerce Clause analysis. We reiterate that this Act does not prohibit any entity—resident or nonresident—from offering to purchase, or from purchasing, shares in Indiana corporations, or from attempting thereby to gain control. It only provides regulatory procedures designed for the better protection of the corporations' shareholders. We have rejected the 'notion that the Commerce Clause protects the particular structure or methods of operation in [a] market.' [Exxon.] The very commodity that is traded in the securities market is one whose characteristics are defined by state law. Similarly, the very commodity that is traded in the 'market for corporate control'—the corporation—is one that owes its existence and attributes to state law. Indiana need not define these commodities as other States do; it need only provide that residents and nonresidents have equal access to them. This Indiana has done. Accordingly, even if the Act should decrease the number of successful tender offers for Indiana corporations, this would not offend the Commerce Clause." Justice Powell concluded: "On its face, the Indiana [Act] evenhandedly determines the voting rights of shares of Indiana corporations. [To] the limited extent that the Act affects interstate commerce, this is justified by the State's interests in defining the attributes of shares in its corporations and in protecting shareholders."

Justice SCALIA, who concurred in part and in the judgment, strenuously rejected the Pike balancing approach and suggested that the Court limit itself to determining whether a state law "discriminates against interstate commerce" or "create[s] an impermissible risk of inconsistent regulation by different States." He explained: "While it has become standard practice at least since [Pike] to consider, in addition to these factors, whether the burden on commerce imposed by a state statute 'is clearly excessive in relation to the putative local benefits,' such an inquiry is ill suited to the judicial function and should be undertaken rarely if at all. This case is a good illustration of the point. Whether the control shares statute 'protects shareholders of Indiana corporations' or protects incumbent management seems to me a highly debatable question, but it is extraordinary to think that the constitutionality of the Act should depend on the answer. Nothing in the Constitution says that the protection of entrenched management is any less important a 'putative local benefit' than the protection of entrenched shareholders, and I do not know what qualifies us to make that judgment—or the related judgment as to how effective the present statute is in achieving one or the other objective—or the ultimate (and most ineffable) judgment as to whether, given importance-level x, and effectiveness-level y, the worth of the statute is 'outweighed' by impact-on-commerce z.

"One commentator has suggested that, at least much of the time, we do not in fact mean what we say when we declare that statutes which neither discriminate against commerce nor present a threat of multiple and inconsistent burdens might nonetheless be unconstitutional under a 'balancing' test. See Regan, 'The Supreme Court and State Protectionism: Making Sense of the Dormant Commerce Clause,' 84 Mich.L.Rev. 1091 (1986). If he is not correct, he ought to be. As long as a State's corporation law governs only its own corporations and does not discriminate against out-of-state interests, it should survive this Court's scrutiny under the Commerce Clause, whether it promotes shareholder welfare or industrial stagnation. Beyond that, it is for Congress to prescribe its invalidity. [I] do not share the Court's apparent high estimation of the beneficence of the state statute at issue here. But a law can be both economic folly and constitutional. The Indiana [Act] is at least the latter. I therefore concur in the judgment of the Court."

Justice WHITE's dissent, joined by Justices Blackmun and Stevens, concluded in part that the Act "directly inhibits interstate commerce, the very economic consequences the Commerce Clause was intended to prevent." He elaborated: "Given the impact of the [Act], it is clear that Indiana is directly regulating the purchase and sale of shares of stock in interstate commerce. Appellant CTS' stock is traded on the New York Stock Exchange, and people from all over the country buy and sell CTS' shares daily. Yet, under Indiana's scheme, any prospective purchaser will be effectively precluded from purchasing CTS' shares if the purchaser crosses one of the Chapter's threshold ownership levels and a majority of CTS' shareholders refuse to give the purchaser voting rights. This Court should not countenance such a restraint on interstate trade.

"The United States, as amicus curiae, argues that Indiana's Control Share Acquisitions Chapter 'is written as a restraint on the *transferability* of voting rights in specified transactions, and it could not be written in any other way without changing its meaning. Since the restraint on the transfer of voting rights is a restraint on the transfer of shares, the Indiana Chapter, like the Illinois Act [in MITE], restrains "transfers of stock by stockholders to a third party." ' I agree. The majority ignores the practical impact of the Chapter in concluding that the Chapter does not violate the Commerce Clause. The Chapter is characterized as merely defining 'the attributes of shares in its corporations.' The majority sees the trees but not the forest.

"The Commerce Clause was included in our Constitution by the Framers to prevent the very type of economic protectionism Indiana's [Act] represents: [A] state law which permits a majority of an Indiana corporation's stockholders to prevent individual investors, including out-of-state stockholders, from selling their stock to an out-of-state tender offeror and thereby frustrate any transfer of corporate control, is the archetype of the kind of state law that the Commerce Clause forbids. Unlike state blue sky laws, Indiana's [Act] regulates the purchase and sale of stock of Indiana corporations in interstate commerce. Indeed, [the Act] will inevitably be used to block interstate transactions in such stock. Because the Commerce Clause protects the [interstate market] in such securities [Exxon], and because the [Act] substantially interferes with this interstate market, [the Act] clearly conflicts with the Commerce Clause."

Final observations on balancing. Is balancing of state and national interests within the institutional competence of the courts? Are the relevant factual determinations within their administrative competence? Are the relevant judgments within their judicial competence? Or does balancing inevitably involve findings and judgments more suited to political resolution? Consider Justice Scalia's attack on balancing in Bendix Autolite Corp. v. Midwesco Enterprises, Inc., 486 U.S. 888 (1988). In Bendix, the majority struck down an Ohio law providing for unlimited tolling of the statute of limitations with respect to entities located outside of Ohio that had not designated an Ohio agent for service of process. Justice Kennedy's majority opinion relied on both discrimination and balancing grounds. Justice Scalia's concurrence objected to the balancing aspects of the majority's opinion. In "balancing," he noted, "the scale analogy is not really appropriate, since the interests on both sides are incommensurate. It is more like judging whether a particular line is longer than a particular rock is heavy. [Weighing] the governmental interests of a State against the needs of interstate commerce is [a] task squarely within the responsibility of Congress. [I] would therefore abandon the 'balancing approach' to these negative commerce clause cases [Pike] and leave essentially legislative judgments to Congress."

Is the problem with balancing that its results are uncertain and difficult to predict? Consider Powell, Vagaries and Varieties in Constitutional Interpretation (1956), recalling that, "after my students had searched in vain for a formula, I suggested that one might safely say that the states may regulate commerce some, but not too much." That was a variant of an earlier quip by Professor Thomas Reed Powell in his mock Restatement of Constitutional Law, which suggested that Congress may regulate commerce, that the states may also regulate commerce but not too much, and that how much was too much was beyond the scope of his Restatement. See also Itel Containers Int'l Corp. v. Huddleston, 507 U.S. 60 (1993) (Scalia, J., concurring in part and in the judgment) (stating a willingness to adhere to prior dormant commerce clause precedents in discrimination cases as a matter of stare decisis, in order "to protect reliance interests and to foster stability in the law" but stating that "I do not believe [that] either of those purposes is significantly furthered by continuing to apply vague and open-ended tests [such as] the 'balancing' approach of Pike v. Bruce Church.").

Does the CTS case represent a deemphasis on balancing? Does it forecast victory for the Justice Scalia's position? Once again, the case raises the question of whether, absent protectionist purpose, the dormant commerce clause should impose any scrutiny at all on state regulations of commerce. After CTS and Minnesota v. Clover Leaf, above, is there any genuine bite left to such scrutiny, at least where the burden does not involve instrumentalities of interstate commerce? Or does Edgar v. MITE Corp., which applied the Pike balancing formula to a wholly nondiscriminatory state law, suggest that balancing still plays an important role even in the absence of hostile economic purposes? Even after CTS, the Pike balancing formula has continued to be invoked by the Court. See, e.g., Northwest Central Pipeline Corp. v. State Corporation Comm'n of Kansas, 489 U.S. 493 (1989).

C. THE "MARKET PARTICIPANT" EXCEPTION TO THE DORMANT COMMERCE CLAUSE

Introduction. In a series of modern cases, a divided Court carved out a significant exception from the usual commerce clause scrutiny: the Court's concern about detecting parochialism was found inappropriate when the state functioned not as a "regulator" of the market but rather as a "market participant." The impact of that exception was felt particularly in situations where the state itself produced goods for commerce or where it engaged in a program of subsidies or other economic incentives to aid in-state businesses. The justifications for and applications of the "market participant" exception are controversial, and the Court has limited the exception, as the plurality opinion in South–Central Timber, the next principal case, illustrates. Justice White's opinion in that case provides a useful review of the modern cases establishing the exception, cases beginning with Alexandria Scrap in 1976.

In examining the exception and its limits, consider whether the exception makes sense. Is there good reason to leave the states alone in these situations, by not applying the usual commerce clause restraints? Why may a state hoard the benefits of its market participation if it may not hoard its natural resources (see Hughes; p. 295 above)? Is the reason for the exemption textual—subsidies are not "regulation" within the meaning of the commerce clause? Donald Regan suggests that preferential state expenditures pose less harm to commerce clause values than do discriminatory regulation or taxes because they are less coercive, appear less hostile to other states, may benefit national welfare although they would not exist at all if the local preference were not allowed, are self-limiting because they require the expenditure of general public funds, and are less likely to cause resentment and retaliation. Regan, "The Supreme Court and State Protectionism: Making Sense of the Dormant Commerce Clause," 84 Mich.L.Rev. 1091 (1986). Are these distinctions persuasive? For additional commentary, see Wells & Hellerstein, "The Governmental–Proprietary Distinction in Constitutional Law," 66 Va.L.Rev. 1073, 1121–41 (1980); Varat, "State 'Citizenship' and Interstate Equality," 48 U. Chi. L. Rev. 487 (1981); Gergen, "The Selfish State and the Market," 66 Tex. L. Rev. 1097 (1988); Coenen, "Untangling the Market–Participant Exemption to the Dormant Commerce Clause," 88 Mich.L.Rev. 395 (1989).

South–Central Timber Development, Inc. v. Wunnicke

467 U.S. 82, 104 S.Ct. 2237, 81 L.Ed.2d 71 (1984).

[Alaska proposed to sell a large amount of timber owned by the State. It included a special provision in all of its timber sale contracts requiring that the purchaser would partially process the timber in Alaska before it was shipped out of the state. The Alaska requirement was designed to protect existing timber-processing industries, promote new industries, and derive revenue from the State's timber resources. South–Central is an Alaska corporation that purchases and logs timber and then ships it elsewhere (primarily to Japan) for processing. The Company claimed that the in-state processing requirement violated the commerce clause. Alaska replied that its restriction on export of unprocessed timber was exempt from the commerce clause because of the "market participant" doctrine.

[The Court of Appeals found Congress had implicitly authorized Alaska's processing requirement. In the first part of his opinion, Justice White, joined by six members of the Court, found that Congress had not authorized the State requirement, insisting that the congressional consent "must be unmistakably clear" in interest of avoiding economic Balkanization. In the portion of his opinion printed here, Justice White turned to the commerce clause issue and the applicability of the "market participant" exception. This part of his opinion was joined by only three other Justices.[1]]

Opinion of Justice WHITE.

[Our] cases make clear that if a State is acting as a market participant, rather than as a market regulator, the dormant Commerce Clause places no limitation on its activities. See White v. Massachusetts Council of Construction Employers, Inc., 460 U.S. 204 (1983); Reeves, Inc. v. Stake, 447 U.S. 429 (1980); Hughes v. Alexandria Scrap Corp., 426 U.S. 794 (1976). The precise contours of the market-participant doctrine have yet to be established, however, the doctrine having been applied in only three cases of this Court to date.

---

1. Justice Powell and Chief Justice Burger urged that the case be remanded for consideration of the commerce clause challenge. Justice Marshall took no part in the decision of the case. Justice Brennan, who concurred in all of Justice White's opinion, noted that Justice White's "treatment of the market-participant doctrine and the response of Justice Rehnquist point up the inherent weakness of the doctrine." The only dissenters from Justice White's plurality opinion on the applicability of the market participant doctrine were Justices Rehnquist and O'Connor, as noted below.

The first of the cases, Hughes v. Alexandria Scrap Corp.,[2] involved a Maryland program designed to reduce the number of junked automobiles in the State. A "bounty" was established on Maryland-licensed junk cars, and the State imposed more stringent documentation requirements on out-of-state scrap processors than on in-state ones. The Court rejected a Commerce Clause attack on the program, although it noted that under traditional Commerce Clause analysis the program might well be invalid because it had the effect of reducing the flow of goods in interstate commerce. The Court concluded that Maryland's action was not "the kind of action with which the Commerce Clause is concerned," because "[n]othing in the purposes animating the Commerce Clause prohibits a State, in the absence of congressional action, from participating in the market and exercising the right to favor its own citizens over others."

In Reeves, Inc. v. Stake,[3] the Court upheld a South Dakota policy of restricting the sale of cement from a state-owned plant to state residents, declaring that "[t]he basic distinction drawn in Alexandria Scrap between States as market participants and States as market regulators makes good sense and sound law." The Court relied upon " 'the long recognized right of trader or manufacturer, engaged in an entirely private business, freely to exercise his own independent discretion as to parties with whom he will deal.' " In essence, the Court recognized the principle that the Commerce Clause places no limitations on a State's refusal to deal with particular parties when it is participating in the interstate market in goods.

The most recent of this Court's cases developing the market-participant doctrine is White v. Massachusetts Council of Construction Employers, Inc.,[4] in which the Court sustained against a Commerce Clause challenge an executive order of the Mayor of Boston that required all construction projects funded in whole or in part by city funds or city-administered funds to be performed by a work force of at least 50% city residents. The Court rejected the argument that the city was not entitled to the protection of the doctrine because the order had the effect of regulating employment contracts between public contractors and their employees. Recognizing that "there are some limits on a state or local government's ability to impose restrictions that reach beyond the immediate parties with which the government transacts business," the Court found it unnecessary to define those limits because "[e]veryone affected by the order [was], in a substantial if informal sense, 'working for the city.' " The fact that the employees were "working for the city" was "crucial" to the market-participant analysis in White.

The State of Alaska contends that its primary-manufacture requirement fits squarely within the market-participant doctrine, arguing that "Alaska's entry into the market may be viewed as precisely the same type of subsidy to local interests that the Court found unobjectionable in Alexandria Scrap." However, when Maryland became involved in the scrap market it was as a purchaser of scrap; Alaska, on the other hand, participates in the timber market, but imposes conditions downstream in the timber-processing market. Alaska is not merely subsidizing local timber processing in an amount "roughly

---

2. In Alexandria Scrap, the majority opinion was by Justice Powell. Justice Stevens concurred in a separate opinion. Justice Brennan, joined by Justices White and Marshall, dissented.

3. In Reeves, Justice Blackmun wrote the majority opinion. Justice Powell, joined

by Justices Brennan, White and Stevens, dissented.

4. In White, Justice Rehnquist wrote the majority opinion. Justice Blackmun, joined by Justice White, dissented.

equal to the difference between the price the timber would fetch in the absence of such a requirement and the amount the state actually receives." If the State directly subsidized the timber-processing industry by such an amount, the purchaser would retain the option of taking advantage of the subsidy by processing timber in the State or forgoing the benefits of the subsidy and exporting unprocessed timber. Under the Alaska requirement, however, the choice is made for him: if he buys timber from the State he is not free to take the timber out of state prior to processing.

The State also would have us find Reeves controlling. It states that "Reeves made it clear that the Commerce Clause imposes no limitation on Alaska's power to choose the terms on which it will sell its timber." Such an unrestrained reading of Reeves is unwarranted. Although the Court in Reeves did strongly endorse the right of a State to deal with whomever it chooses when it participates in the market, it did not—and did not purport to—sanction the imposition of any terms that the State might desire. For example, the Court expressly noted in Reeves that "Commerce Clause scrutiny may well be more rigorous when a restraint on foreign commerce is alleged"; that a natural resource "like coal, timber, wild game, or minerals," was not involved, but instead the cement was "the end product of a complex process whereby a costly physical plant and human labor act on raw materials;" and that South Dakota did not bar resale of South Dakota cement to out-of-state purchasers. In this case, all three of the elements that were not present in Reeves—foreign commerce, a natural resource, and restrictions on resale—are present.

Finally, Alaska argues that since the Court in White upheld a requirement that reached beyond "the boundary of formal privity of contract," then, a fortiori, the primary-manufacture requirement is permissible, because the State is not regulating contracts for resale of timber or regulating the buying and selling of timber, but is instead "a seller of timber, pure and simple." Yet it is clear that the State is more than merely a seller of timber. In the commercial context, the seller usually has no say over, and no interest in, how the product is to be used after sale; in this case, however, payment for the timber does not end the obligations of the purchaser, for, despite the fact that the purchaser has taken delivery of the timber and has paid for it, he cannot do with it as he pleases. Instead, he is obligated to deal with a stranger to the contract after completion of the sale.[5]

That privity of contract is not always the outer boundary of permissible state activity does not necessarily mean that the Commerce Clause has no application within the boundary of formal privity. The market-participant doctrine permits a State to influence "a discrete, identifiable class of economic activity in which [it] is a major participant." [White.] Contrary to the State's contention, the doctrine is not *carte blanche* to impose any conditions that the

---

5. The facts of the present case resemble closely the facts of Foster–Fountain Packing Co. v. Haydel, 278 U.S. 1 (1928), in which the Court struck down a Louisiana law prohibiting export from the State of any shrimp from which the heads and hulls had not been removed. The Court rejected the claim that the fact that the shrimp were owned by the State authorized the State to impose such limitations. Although not directly controlling here, because of the Court's recognition that "the State owns, or has power to control, the game and fish within its borders not abso-lutely or as proprietor or for its own use or benefit but in its sovereign capacity as representative of the people," the Court's reasoning is relevant. The Court noted that the State might have retained the shrimp for consumption and use within its borders, but "by permitting its shrimp to be taken and all the products thereof to be shipped and sold in interstate commerce, the State necessarily releases its hold and, as to the shrimp so taken, definitely terminates its control." [Footnote by Justice White.]

State has the economic power to dictate, and does not validate any requirement merely because the State imposes it upon someone with whom it is in contractual privity.

The limit of the market-participant doctrine must be that it allows a State to impose burdens on commerce within the market in which it is a participant, but allows it to go no further. The State may not impose conditions, whether by statute, regulation, or contract, that have a substantial regulatory effect outside of that particular market.[6] Unless the "market" is relatively narrowly defined, the doctrine has the potential of swallowing up the rule that States may not impose substantial burdens on interstate commerce even if they act with the permissible state purpose of fostering local industry.

At the heart of the dispute in this case is disagreement over the definition of the market. Alaska contends that it is participating in the processed timber market, although it acknowledges that it participates in no way in the actual processing. South–Central argues, on the other hand, that although the State may be a participant in the timber market, it is using its leverage in that market to exert a regulatory effect in the processing market, in which it is not a participant. We agree with the latter position.

There are sound reasons for distinguishing between a State's preferring its own residents in the initial disposition of goods when it is a market participant and a State's attachment of restrictions on dispositions subsequent to the goods coming to rest in private hands. First, simply as a matter of intuition a state market participant has a greater interest as a "private trader" in the immediate transaction than it has in what its purchaser does with the goods after the State no longer has an interest in them. The common law recognized such a notion in the doctrine of restraints on alienation. Similarly, the antitrust laws place limits on vertical restraints. It is no defense in an action charging vertical trade restraints that the same end could be achieved through vertical integration; if it were, there would be virtually no antitrust scrutiny of vertical arrangements. We reject the contention that a State's action as a market regulator may be upheld against Commerce Clause challenge on the ground that the State could achieve the same end as a market participant. We therefore find it unimportant for present purposes that the State could support its processing industry by selling only to Alaska processors, by vertical integration, or by direct subsidy.

Second, downstream restrictions have a greater regulatory effect than do limitations on the immediate transaction. Instead of merely choosing its own trading partners, the State is attempting to govern the private, separate economic relationships of its trading partners; that is, it restricts the post-purchase activity of the purchaser, rather than merely the purchasing activity. In contrast to the situation in White, this restriction on private economic activity takes place after the completion of the parties' direct commercial obligations, rather than during the course of an ongoing commercial relationship in which the city retained a continuing proprietary interest in the subject

---

6. The view of the market-participant doctrine expressed by Justice Rehnquist would validate under the Commerce Clause any contractual condition that the State had the economic power to impose, without regard to the relationship of the subject matter of the contract and the condition imposed. If that were the law, it would have been irrele-vant that the employees in White were in effect "working for the city." If the only question were whether the condition is imposed by contract, a residency requirement could have been imposed with respect to the work force on all projects of any employer doing business with the city. [Footnote by Justice White.]

of the contract.[7] In sum, the State may not avail itself of the market-participant doctrine to immunize its downstream regulation of the timber-processing market in which it is not a participant.

Finally, the State argues that even if we find that Congress did not authorize the processing restriction, and even if we conclude that its actions do not qualify for the market-participant exception, the restriction does not substantially burden interstate or foreign commerce under ordinary Commerce Clause principles. We need not labor long over that contention.

Viewed as a naked restraint on export of unprocessed logs, there is little question that the processing requirement cannot survive scrutiny under the precedents of the Court. [E.g., Pike.] [Because] of the protectionist nature of Alaska's local-processing requirement and the burden on commerce resulting therefrom, we conclude that it falls within the rule of virtual per se invalidity of laws that "bloc[k] the flow of interstate commerce at a State's borders." [Philadelphia v. New Jersey.]

We are buttressed in our conclusion that the restriction is invalid by the fact that foreign commerce is burdened by the restriction. It is a well-accepted rule that state restrictions burdening foreign commerce are subjected to a more rigorous and searching scrutiny. It is crucial to the efficient execution of the Nation's foreign policy that "the Federal Government [speak] with one voice when regulating commercial relations with foreign governments." Michelin Tire Corp. v. Wages, 423 U.S. 276, 285 (1976). In light of the substantial attention given by Congress to the subject of export restrictions on unprocessed timber, it would be peculiarly inappropriate to permit state regulation of the subject.

[Reversed and remanded.]

Justice REHNQUIST, with whom Justice O'CONNOR joins, dissenting.

In my view, the line of distinction drawn in the plurality opinion between the State as market participant and the State as market regulator is both artificial and unconvincing. The plurality draws this line "simply as a matter of intuition," but then seeks to bolster its intuition through a series of remarks more appropriate to antitrust law than to the Commerce Clause.[1]

The contractual term at issue here no more transforms Alaska's sale of timber into "regulation" of the processing industry than the resident-hiring preference imposed by the city of Boston in [White] constituted regulation of the construction industry. Alaska is merely paying the buyer of the timber indirectly, by means of a reduced price, to hire Alaska residents to process the timber. Under existing precedent, the State could accomplish that same result

7. This is not to say that the State could evade the reasoning of this opinion by merely including a provision in its contract that title does not pass until the processing is complete. It is the substance of the transaction, rather than the label attached to it, that governs Commerce Clause analysis. [Footnote by Justice White.]

1. The plurality does offer one other reason for its demarcation of the boundary between these two concepts. "[D]ownstream restrictions have a greater regulatory effect than do limitations on the immediate transaction. Instead of merely choosing its own trading partners, the State is attempting to govern the private, separate economic relationships of its trading partners; that is, it restricts the post-purchase activity of the purchaser, rather than merely the purchasing activity." But, of course, this is not a "reason" at all, but merely a restatement of the conclusion. The line between participation and regulation is what we are trying to determine. To invoke that very distinction in support of the line drawn is merely to fall back again on intuition. [Footnote by Justice Rehnquist.]

in any number of ways. For example, the State could choose to sell its timber only to those companies that maintain active primary-processing plants in Alaska. [Reeves.] Or the State could directly subsidize the primary-processing industry within the State. [Alexandria Scrap.] The State could even pay to have the logs processed and then enter the market only to sell processed logs. It seems to me unduly formalistic to conclude that the one path chosen by the State as best suited to promote its concerns is the path forbidden it by the Commerce Clause. For these reasons, I would affirm the judgment of the Court of Appeals.

SECTION 2.   THE PRIVILEGES AND IMMUNITIES CLAUSE OF ARTICLE IV

Introduction. The Privileges and Immunities Clause of Art. IV, § 2 states: "The Citizens of each State shall be entitled to all Privileges and Immunities of Citizens in the several States." Its function overlaps those of several other provisions of the Constitution. Like the commerce clause, it serves as a restraint on state efforts to bar out-of-staters from access to local resources. As the Court noted in Hicklin v. Orbeck, 437 U.S. 518 (1978), there is a "mutually reinforcing relationship between the Privileges and Immunities Clause of Art. IV, § 2, and the Commerce Clause—a relationship that stems [in part from] their shared vision of federalism." And like the Fourteenth Amendment equal protection clause, it protects citizens against discrimination—in this context, on the basis of state residency. For the overlap of these two clauses, see Justice O'Connor's concurrence in Zobel v. Williams (1982; p. 908 below). See generally Varat, "State 'Citizenship' and Interstate Equality," 48 U.Chi.L.Rev. 487 (1981); Simson, "Discrimination Against Nonresidents and the Privileges and Immunities Clause of Article IV," 128 U.Pa.L.Rev. 379 (1979); Ely, "Choice of Law and the State's Interest in Protecting Its Own," 23 Wm. & Mary L.Rev. 173 (1981).

But the close relationship between Art. IV, § 2 and the commerce clause does not mean that they are wholly synonymous. There are several significant differences. First, corporations enjoy no protection under the Privileges and Immunities clause. Paul v. Virginia, 75 U.S. (8 Wall.) 168 (1869). Second, while Congress may consent to state practices that would otherwise be impermissible under the commerce clause, the Privileges and Immunities clause is a rights provision, not a grant of authority to Congress, and so is arguably nonwaivable by Congress. Third, the standard of review for privileges and immunities denials is arguably stricter than the balancing test used in dormant commerce clause analysis, though not as strict as that for discriminatory legislation challenged as a commerce violation. Fourth, the Privileges and Immunities clause extends not to all commercial activity but only to "fundamental rights." See Corfield v. Coryell, 4 Wash.C.C. 371, 6 F.Cas. 546 (C.C.E.D.Pa.1823), discussed in the Slaughter–House Cases (1873; p. 421 below). And fifth, the Court has recognized no "market participant" exception to privileges and immunities violations as it has to commerce clause scrutiny, as the next case illustrates.

United Building & Construction Trades Council v. Mayor and Council of Camden

465 U.S. 208, 104 S.Ct. 1020, 79 L.Ed.2d 249 (1984).

[This case involved a challenge to a Camden, N.J. ordinance requiring that at least 40% of the employees of contractors and subcontractors working on city construction projects be Camden residents. The ordinance was adopted in 1980 pursuant to a statewide affirmative action plan for public work programs. The local-residents preference that was added to the ordinance provided: "The developer/contractor, in hiring for jobs, shall make every effort to employ persons residing within the City of Camden but, in no event, shall less than forty percent (40%) of the entire labor force be residents of the City of Camden." The contractor was also obliged to ensure that any subcontractors working on such projects adhered to the same requirement. The United Building and Construction Trades Council of Camden and Vicinity (the Council), challenged the ordinance as a violation of the Privileges and Immunities Clause of Art. IV and the dormant commerce clause. After the case was filed, the Supreme Court rejected the commerce clause challenge to the substantially identical local jobs preference order in White v. Mass. Construction Council, p. 324 above, but specifically declined to reach the merits of a privileges and immunities challenge to the Boston program because the Massachusetts court had not reached that issue. Accordingly, the Camden Council dropped its commerce clause challenge but pressed its privileges and immunities challenge.]

Justice REHNQUIST delivered the opinion of the Court.

The Supreme Court of New Jersey rejected [the Council's privileges and immunities] attack on the ground that the ordinance discriminates on the basis of *municipal,* not state, residency. The court "decline[d] to apply the Privileges and Immunities Clause in the context of a municipal ordinance that has identical effects upon out-of-state citizens and New Jersey citizens not residing in the locality." We conclude that the challenged ordinance is properly subject to the strictures of the Clause. We therefore reverse the [judgment] and remand the case for a determination of the validity of the ordinance under the appropriate constitutional standard.

[We] first address the argument [that] the Clause does not even apply to a *municipal* ordinance such as this. Two separate contentions are advanced in support of this position: first, that the Clause only applies to laws passed by a *State* and, second, that the Clause only applies to laws that discriminate on the basis of *state* citizenship. The first argument can be quickly rejected. [It] is as true of the Privileges and Immunities Clause as of the Equal Protection Clause that what would be unconstitutional if done directly by the State can no more readily be accomplished by a city deriving its authority from the State. Thus, even if the ordinance had been adopted solely by Camden, and not pursuant to a state program or with state approval, the hiring preference would still have to comport with the [Clause].

The second argument merits more consideration. The New Jersey Supreme Court concluded that the [Clause] does not apply to an ordinance that discriminates solely on the basis of *municipal* residency. The Clause is phrased in terms of *state* [citizenship]. "The primary purpose of this clause like the clauses between which it is located—those relating to full faith and credit and to interstate extradition of fugitives from justice—was to help fuse into one Nation a collection of independent, sovereign States. It was designed to insure to a citizen of State A who ventures into State B the same privileges which the citizens of State B enjoy. For protection of such equality the citizen of State A was not to be restricted to the uncertain remedies afforded by diplomatic processes and official retaliation." Toomer v. Witsell.[1] Municipal residency classifications, it is argued, simply do not give rise to the same concerns.

We cannot accept this argument. We have never read the Clause so literally as to apply it only to distinctions based on state citizenship. [Despite] some initial uncertainty, it is now established that the terms "citizen" and "resident" are "essentially interchangeable" for purposes of analysis of most cases under the [clause]. A person who is not residing in a given State is ipso facto not residing in a city within that State. Thus, whether the exercise of a privilege is conditioned on state residency or on municipal residency, he will just as surely be excluded.

Given the Camden ordinance, an out-of-state citizen who ventures into New Jersey will not enjoy the same privileges as the New Jersey citizen residing in Camden. It is true that New Jersey citizens not residing in Camden will be affected by the ordinance as well as out-of-state citizens. And it is true that the disadvantaged New Jersey residents have no claim under the Privileges and Immunities Clause. But New Jersey residents at least have a chance to remedy at the polls any discrimination against them. Out-of-state citizens have no similar opportunity, and they must "not be restricted to the uncertain remedies afforded by diplomatic processes and official retaliation."[2] We conclude that Camden's ordinance is not immune from constitutional review at the behest of out-of-state residents merely because some in-state residents are similarly disadvantaged. Cf. [Zobel v. Williams (O'Connor, J., concurring), p. 908 below].

Application of the [Clause] to a particular instance of discrimination against out-of-state residents entails a two-step inquiry. As an initial matter, the court must decide whether the ordinance burdens one of those privileges and immunities protected by the Clause. [Baldwin].[3] Not all forms of discrimi-

---

1. Toomer v. Witsell, 334 U.S. 385 (1948), relied on Art. IV to invalidate South Carolina's discriminatory license fee on residents trawling for shrimp in its waters. Note the similarity to the commerce clause cases restricting out-of-staters' access to local resources.

2. The dissent suggests that New Jersey citizens not residing in Camden will adequately protect the interests of out-of-state residents and that the scope of the [Clause] should be measured in light of this political reality. What the dissent fails to appreciate is that the Camden ordinance at issue in this case was adopted pursuant to a comprehensive, state-wide program applicable in all New Jersey cities. The Camden resident-preference ordinance has already received state sanction and approval, and every New Jersey city is free to adopt a similar protectionist measure. Some have already done so. Thus, it is hard to see how New Jersey residents living outside Camden will protect the interests of out-of-state citizens.

More fundamentally, the dissent's proposed blanket exemption for all classifications that are less than state-wide would

provide States with a simple means for evading the strictures of the [Clause]. Suppose, for example, that California wanted to guarantee that all employees of contractors and subcontractors working on construction projects funded in whole or in part by state funds are state residents. Under the dissent's analysis, the California legislature need merely divide the State in half, providing one resident-hiring preference for Northern Californians on all such projects taking place in Northern California, and one for Southern Californians on all projects taking place in Southern California. State residents generally would benefit from the law at the expense of out-of-state residents; yet, the law would be immune from scrutiny under the Clause simply because it was not phrased in terms of *state* citizenship or residency. Such a formalistic construction would effectively write the Clause out of the Constitution. [Footnote by Justice Rehnquist.]

3. Baldwin v. Montana Fish and Game Comm'n, 436 U.S. 371 (1978), rejected an Art. IV attack on a Montana elk-hunting license scheme imposing substantially higher fees on nonresidents than on residents. The

nation against citizens of other States are constitutionally suspect. "Some distinctions between residents and nonresidents merely reflect the fact that this is a Nation composed of individual States, and are permitted; other distinctions are prohibited because they hinder the formation, the purpose, or the development of a single Union of those States. Only with respect to those 'privileges' and 'immunities' bearing upon the vitality of the Nation as a single entity must the State treat all citizens, resident and nonresident, equally." Ibid. As a threshold matter, then, we must determine whether an out-of-state resident's interest in employment on public works contracts in another State is sufficiently "fundamental" to the promotion of interstate harmony so as to "fall within the purview of the [Clause]." Id.

Certainly, the pursuit of a common calling is one of the most fundamental of those privileges protected by the Clause. [Public] employment, however, is qualitatively different from employment in the private sector; it is a subspecies of the broader opportunity to pursue a common calling. We have held that there is no fundamental right to government employment for purposes of the Equal Protection Clause. Massachusetts v. Murgia [1976; p. 649 below]. Cf. McCarthy v. Philadelphia Civil Service Comm'n, 424 U.S. 645 (1976) (per curiam) (rejecting equal protection challenge to municipal residency requirement for municipal workers). And in White we held that for purposes of the Commerce Clause everyone employed on a city public works project is, "in a substantial if informal sense, 'working for the city.'"

It can certainly be argued that for purposes of the Privileges and Immunities Clause everyone affected by the Camden ordinance is also "working for the city" and, therefore, has no grounds for complaint when the city favors its own residents. But we decline to transfer mechanically into this context an analysis fashioned to fit the Commerce Clause. Our decision in White turned on a distinction between the city acting as a market participant and the city acting as a market regulator. The question whether employees of contractors and subcontractors on public works projects were or were not, in some sense, working for the city was crucial to that analysis. [But] the distinction between market participant and market regulator relied upon in White to dispose of the Commerce Clause challenge is not dispositive in this context. The two Clauses have different aims and set different standards for state conduct.

The Commerce Clause acts as an implied restraint upon state regulatory powers. Such powers must give way before the superior authority of Congress to legislate on (or leave unregulated) matters involving interstate commerce. When the State acts solely as a market participant, no conflict between state *regulation* and federal regulatory authority can arise. The Privileges and Immunities Clause, on the other hand, imposes a direct restraint on state action in the interests of interstate harmony. Hicklin v. Orbeck.[4] This concern

---

majority opinion by Justice Blackmun (the dissenter in the Camden case) insisted that the precedents could best be understood in terms of the "fundamental rights" approach of Corfield v. Coryell, and concluded that, "[w]hatever rights or activities may be 'fundamental'" under Art. IV, "elk hunting by nonresidents in Montana is not one of them."

4. Hicklin v. Orbeck, 437 U.S. 518 (1978), was a unanimous decision invalidating an Alaska law requiring that residents be preferred over nonresidents in certain jobs.

The "Alaska Hire" law was "an attempt to force virtually all businesses that benefit in some way from the economic ripple effect of Alaska's decision to develop its oil and gas resources to bias their employment practices in favor of the State's residents." Justice Brennan's opinion stated that Alaska had not demonstrated "that nonresidents were 'a peculiar source of the evil' [the law] was enacted to remedy, namely Alaska's 'uniquely high unemployment.'" He accordingly concluded that Alaska's discrimination against nonresi-

with comity cuts across the market regulator-market participant distinction that is crucial under the Commerce Clause. It is discrimination against out-of-state residents on matters of fundamental concern which triggers the Clause, not regulation affecting interstate commerce. Thus, the fact that Camden is merely setting conditions on its expenditures for goods and services in the marketplace does not preclude the possibility that those conditions violate the Privileges and Immunities Clause. [Much] the same analysis [as in Hicklin] is appropriate to a city's efforts to bias private employment decisions in favor of its residents on construction projects funded with public monies. The fact that Camden is expending its own funds or funds it administers in accordance with the terms of a grant is certainly a factor—perhaps the crucial factor—to be considered in evaluating whether the statute's discrimination violates the [Clause]. But it does not remove the Camden ordinance completely from the purview of the Clause.

In sum, Camden may, without fear of violating the Commerce Clause, pressure private employers engaged in public works projects funded in whole or in part by the city to hire city residents. But that same exercise of power to bias the employment decisions of [contractors] against out-of-state residents may be called to account under the Privileges and Immunities Clause. A determination of whether a privilege is "fundamental" for purposes of that Clause does not depend on whether the employees of private contractors and subcontractors engaged in public works projects can or cannot be said to be "working for the city." The opportunity to seek employment with such private employers is "sufficiently basic to the livelihood of the Nation" [Baldwin] as to fall within the purview of the [Clause] even though the contractors and subcontractors are themselves engaged in projects funded in whole or part by the city.

The conclusion that Camden's ordinance discriminates against a protected privilege does not, of course, end the inquiry. We have stressed in prior cases that "[l]ike many other constitutional provisions, the privileges and immunities clause is not an absolute." [Toomer.] It does not preclude discrimination against citizens of other States where there is a "substantial reason" for the difference in treatment. "[T]he inquiry in each case must be concerned with whether such reasons do exist and whether the degree of discrimination bears a close relation to them." Id. As part of any justification offered for the discriminatory law, nonresidents must somehow be shown to "constitute a peculiar source of the evil at which the statute is aimed." Id.

[Camden] contends that its ordinance is necessary to counteract grave economic and social ills. Spiralling unemployment, a sharp decline in population, and a dramatic reduction in the number of businesses located in the city have eroded property values and depleted the city's tax base. The resident hiring preference is designed, the city contends, to increase the number of employed persons living in Camden and to arrest the "middle class flight" currently plaguing the city. The city also argues that all non-Camden residents employed on city public works projects, whether they reside in New Jersey or Pennsylvania, constitute a "source of the evil at which the statute is aimed." That is, they "live off" Camden without "living in" Camden. Camden contends that the scope of the discrimination practiced in the ordinance, with its municipal residency requirement, is carefully tailored to alleviate this evil without unreasonably harming nonresidents, who still have access to 60% of the available positions.

dents did not "bear a substantial relationship to the particular 'evil' they [were] said to present." (Justice Brennan's opinion found additional support for the result in commerce clause cases pertaining to a state's control over its natural resources.)

Every inquiry under the Privileges and Immunities Clause "must [be] conducted with due regard for the principle that the states should have considerable leeway in analyzing local evils and in prescribing appropriate cures." [Toomer.] This caution is particularly appropriate when a government body is merely setting conditions on the expenditure of funds it controls. The Alaska Hire statute at issue in Hicklin v. Orbeck swept within its strictures not only contractors and subcontractors dealing directly with the State's oil and gas; it also covered suppliers who provided goods and services to those contractors and subcontractors. We invalidated the Act as "an attempt to force virtually all businesses that benefit in some way from the economic ripple effect of Alaska's decision to develop its oil and gas resources to bias their employment practices in favor of the State's residents." No similar "ripple effect" appears to infect the Camden ordinance. It is limited in scope to employees working directly on city public works projects. Nonetheless, we find it impossible to evaluate Camden's justification on the record as it now stands. No trial has ever been held in the case. No findings of fact have been made. The Supreme Court of New Jersey certified the case for direct appeal after the brief administrative proceedings that led to approval of the ordinance by the State Treasurer. It would not be appropriate for this Court either to make factual determinations as an initial matter or to take judicial notice of Camden's decay. We, therefore, deem it wise to remand the case to the [New Jersey Supreme Court to make the necessary findings].

[Reversed and remanded.]

Justice BLACKMUN, dissenting.

For over a century the underlying meaning of the Privileges and Immunities Clause [has] been regarded as settled: at least absent some substantial noninvidious justification, a State may not discriminate between its own residents and residents of other States on the basis of state citizenship. Today, however, the Court casually extends the scope of the Clause by holding that it applies to laws that discriminate *among* state residents on the basis of *municipal* residence, simply because discrimination on the basis of municipal residence disadvantages citizens of other States "ipso facto." This novel interpretation arrives accompanied by little practical justification and no historical or textual support whatsoever. Because I believe that the [Clause] was not intended to apply to the kind of municipal discrimination presented by this case, I would affirm the judgment [below].

The historical underpinnings of the [Clause] are not in serious dispute. The Clause was derived from the fourth Article of Confederation[1] and was designed to carry forward that provision's prescription of interstate comity. Both the text of the Clause and the historical record confirm that the Framers meant to foreclose any one State from denying citizens of other States the same "privileges and immunities" accorded its own citizens. [While] the Framers [conceived of the Clause] as an instrument for frustrating discrimination based on state citizenship, there is no evidence of any sort that they were concerned by intrastate discrimination based on municipal residence. The most obvious

---

1.   "The better to secure and perpetuate mutual friendship and intercourse among the people of the different States in this Union, the free inhabitants of each of these States, paupers, vagabonds and fugitives from justice excepted, shall be entitled to all privileges and immunities of free citizens in the several States; and the people of each State shall have free ingress and regress to and from any other State, and shall enjoy therein all the privileges of trade and commerce, subject to the same duties, impositions and restrictions as the inhabitants thereof [respectively.]." Articles of Confederation, Art. IV (1777). [Footnote by Justice Blackmun.]

reason for this is also the most simple one: by the time the Constitution was enacted, such discrimination was rarely practiced and even more rarely successful.

[Finally,] the Court fails to attend to the functional considerations that underlie the [Clause]. The Clause has been a necessary limitation on state autonomy not simply because of the self-interest of individual States, but because state parochialism is likely to go unchecked by state political processes when those who are disadvantaged are by definition disenfranchised as well. The Clause remedies this breakdown in the representative process by requiring state residents to bear the same burdens that they choose to place on nonresidents; "by constitutionally tying the fate of outsiders to the fate of those possessing political power, the framers insured that their interests would be well looked after." J. Ely, Democracy and Distrust 83 (1980). As a practical matter, therefore, the scope of the Clause may be measured by asking whether failure to link the interests of those who are disadvantaged with the interests of those who are preferred will consign the former group to "the uncertain remedies afforded by diplomatic processes and official retaliation." [Toomer.]

Contrary to the Court's tacit assumption, discrimination on the basis of municipal residence is substantially different in this regard from discrimination on the basis of state citizenship. The distinction is simple but fundamental: discrimination on the basis of municipal residence penalizes persons within the State's political community as well as those without. The Court itself points out that while New Jersey citizens who reside outside Camden are not protected by the [Clause], they may resort to the State's political processes to protect themselves. What the Court fails to appreciate is that this avenue of relief for New Jersey residents works to protect residents of other States as well; disadvantaged state residents who turn to the state legislature to displace ordinances like Camden's further the interests of nonresidents as well as their own. Nor is this mechanism for relief merely a theoretical one: in the past decade, several States [have] repealed or forbidden protectionist ordinances like the one at issue here. The Court [has] applied the [Clause] without regard for the political ills [that] it was designed to cure.[2]

The practice of law by nonresidents as an Art. IV "privilege." In SUPREME COURT OF NEW HAMPSHIRE v. PIPER, 470 U.S. 274 (1985), the Court held that a state rule limiting bar admission to state residents violated the Privileges and Immunities Clause. The challenge was brought by a woman who lived in Vermont, 400 yards from the New Hampshire border, took and passed the New Hampshire bar examination, but was denied admission to the bar because she

---

2. The Court raises the alternative prospect that a State might evade the [Clause] by dividing itself in half and granting the residents in each half of the State employment preferences over residents in the other half of the State. The Clause exists to protect against those classifications that a State's political process cannot be relied on to prevent, however, not those that it can, and there is no reason to believe that state residents will be willing to forgo access to employment in one half of a State merely to obtain privileged access to jobs in the other half. The fact that no State has attempted anything resembling the Court's proposed maneuver in the two centuries since the adoption of the Clause, despite the fact that none of this Court's precedents has foreclosed the option, strongly suggests that state political processes can be trusted to prevent this kind of Balkanization. The Court cannot justify deforming the Constitution's response to real problems by invoking imaginary and unrealistic ones. [Footnote by Justice Blackmun.]

was a nonresident. Justice POWELL's majority opinion found that her claim involved a "privilege" under the Clause because, "[l]ike the occupations considered in our earlier cases, the practice of law is important to the national economy." He noted, moreover, the legal profession's role in representing "persons who raise unpopular federal claims." He found none of the state's asserted justifications for the discrimination sufficient under the standard of the Camden case. He pointed out: "The Clause does not preclude discrimination against nonresidents where: (i) there is a substantial reason for the difference in treatment; and (ii) the discrimination practiced against nonresidents bears a substantial relationship to the State's objective. [In] deciding whether the discrimination bears a close or substantial relationship to the State's objective, the Court has considered the availability of less restrictive means." Here, the State argued that nonresident members of the bar would be less likely "to become, and remain, familiar with local rules and procedures," to "behave ethically," to "be available for court proceedings," and to "do pro bono and other volunteer work in the State." Justice Powell concluded: "We find that none of these reasons meets the test of 'substantiality,' and that the means chosen do not bear the necessary relationship to the State's objectives."

Justice REHNQUIST's dissent argued that "the practice of law [is] fundamentally different from those other occupations that are practiced across state lines without significant deviation from State to State." He especially stressed the State's interest "in maximizing the number of resident lawyers, so as to increase the quality of the pool from which its lawmakers can be drawn." Moreover, he found the Court's "less restrictive means" analysis "both ill-advised and potentially unmanageable." He insisted that "such an analysis, when carried too far, will ultimately lead to striking down almost any statute on the ground that the Court could think of another 'less restrictive' way to write it," and that "the less-restrictive-means analysis, which is borrowed from our First Amendment jurisprudence," was "out of place in the context" of Art. IV.[1]

Under the tests set forth in Camden and Piper, should Camden's jobs preference program have survived privileges and immunities scrutiny upon remand? What facts would be relevant to this analysis? (The actual case was settled.) Would the barrier in Piper survive commerce clause scrutiny? Given the focus of Art. IV on discrimination, does it provide an adequate basis for judicially created rather than congressionally enacted restraints on state burdens on interstate commerce? See Eule, "Laying the Dormant Commerce Clause to Rest," 91 Yale L.J. 425 (1982).

––––––––

A Right of Personal Mobility: What Constitutional Sources? The Court has long recognized a constitutionally protected individual interest in migrating from state to state. But the Justices have been clearer about the existence of a protected right to interstate mobility than about its constitutional sources. While the Court has relied largely on the equal protection clause in invalidating durational residency requirements that deter exercise of this right, see Shapiro

1. Since Piper, the Court has relied on it several times to strike down other barriers to nonresident lawyers. See, e.g., Supreme Court of Virginia v. Friedman, 487 U.S. 59 (1988), striking down a Virginia rule limiting admission to the Bar on motion, as opposed to admission after passing the bar examination. (Justice Scalia joined Chief Justice Rehnquist's dissent in that case.) See also Barnard v. Thorstenn, 489 U.S. 546 (1989); cf. Frazier v. Heebe, 482 U.S. 641 (1987).

v. Thompson (1969; p. 901 below), it has also drawn on both the commerce clause and Art. IV, Sec. 2 in limiting restraints on personal mobility.

The best known commerce clause case is EDWARDS v. CALIFORNIA, 314 U.S. 160 (1941), where the Court invalidated a law making it a misdemeanor to bring into California "any indigent person who is not a resident of the State, knowing him to be an indigent person." The so-called "anti-Okie law" became especially controversial during the Great Depression. California argued, as the Court put it, "that the huge influx of migrants into California in recent years has resulted in problems of health, morals, and especially finance, the proportions of which are staggering."[1] The Court was unanimous in striking down the law, but the Justices differed about the proper reasoning. Justice BYRNES' majority opinion relied solely on the commerce clause. He cited Baldwin v. Seelig and reiterated the commerce clause "prohibition against attempts on the part of any single State to isolate itself from difficulties common to all of them by restraining the transportation of persons and property across its borders." In addition, invoking the Cooley approach, he stated that "the social phenomenon of large-scale interstate migration is [certainly] a matter of national concern [and] does not admit of diverse treatment by the several States."

Justice DOUGLAS' concurrence, joined by Justices Black and Murphy, found the commerce clause ground inappropriate here: "I am of the opinion that the right of persons to move freely from State to State occupies a more protected position in our constitutional system than does the movement of cattle, fruit, steel and coal across state lines." He insisted that the right was a "fundamental" one, an "incident of *national* citizenship protected by the privileges and immunities clause of the Fourteenth Amendment against state interference"—a provision invoked only very rarely by the Court. Another concurrence, by Justice JACKSON, also relied on the Fourteenth Amendment provision and also thought the commerce clause inappropriate: "[The] migrations of a human being [do] not fit easily into my notions as to what is commerce." Justice Douglas also noted that "there are expressions in the cases that this right of free movement of persons is an incident of *state* citizenship protected against discriminatory state action by Art. IV, § 2 of the Constitution." Recall that protection of interstate mobility in effect underlies a number of the modern Art. IV decisions reviewed above. Still other cases have drawn the protection of interstate mobility from even more general sources, especially inferences drawn from the structure of the Constitution. See, e.g., Justice Stewart's majority opinion in United States v. Guest (1966; federal civil rights violence law; p. 964 below): "Although the Articles of Confederation provided that 'the people of each State shall have free ingress and regress to and from any other State,' that right finds no explicit mention in the Constitution. The reason, it has been suggested, is that a right so elementary was conceived from the beginning to be a necessary concomitant of the stronger Union the Constitution created. In any event, freedom to travel throughout the United States has long been recognized as a basic right under the Constitution."[2]

1. Counsel for California had stated to the Court: "A social problem in the South and Southwest for over half a century, the 'poor white' tenants and share croppers, following reduction of cotton planting, droughts and adverse conditions for small-scale farming, swarmed into California. [The "ordinary routine" of the indigent newcomers allegedly had been to go on relief as soon as possible.] Naturally, when these people can live on relief in California better than they can by working in Mississippi, Arkansas, Texas or Oklahoma, they will continue to come to this State." Cf. Steinbeck, The Grapes of Wrath (1939).

2. See also Crandall v. Nevada, 6 Wall. (73 U.S.) 35 (1867), which invalidated a tax on passengers leaving the state via common carriers and emphasized the citizen's basic

SECTION 3. CONGRESSIONAL ORDERING OF FEDERAL–STATE RELATIONSHIPS BY PREEMPTION AND CONSENT

Introduction. The "dormant" commerce clause limits state regulatory power in the absence of congressional action. The commerce clause is not "dormant" when Congress acts in an affirmative *exercise* of the power. Objections to state action may rest on either or both grounds. That, indeed, was so as early as Gibbons v. Ogden; it is even more common in the modern context of proliferating national legislation. This section briefly examines the impact of congressional exercises of power.

The major concern is with two types of congressional action: (1) laws allegedly imposing new limits on state authority (sec. 3A); and (2) laws allegedly removing preexisting barriers to state regulation (sec. 3B). Much of the material deals with national laws pertaining to commerce, but congressional action is of course significant with regard to a wide range of other delegated powers as well, as the next principal case illustrates. This section highlights what has been a pervasive but occasionally obscured phenomenon in the earlier materials: that the Court in fact operates as an important yet only a limited partner of Congress in articulating federalism limits on state power; that Congress often plays a decisive role in determining the relations between state and federal power; and that the interrelationships between state and federal law present subtle and complex problems for Congress and Court.

A. PREEMPTION OF STATE AUTHORITY

Introduction. When Congress exercises a granted power, the federal law may supersede state laws and preempt state authority, because of the operation of the supremacy clause of Art. VI. In these cases, it is ultimately Art. VI, not the commerce clause or some other grant of delegated power, that overrides the state law. When a valid federal statute explicitly bars certain types of state action, there are no difficulties. But problems arise when the federal legislation does not clearly disclose its intended impact on state laws. In those situations, the claim is nevertheless often made that congressional action "preempts" state authority regarding the same subject matter. The Court's preemption rulings often turn on a determination of congressional intent in the setting of the particular text, history and purposes of the federal legislation involved. This section does not deal with the details of the various statutory contexts in which preemption problems arise. Instead, these materials attempt to identify some

"right to come to the seat of [the national] government." That decision, which has since been read as implying a right to move freely throughout the nation, presumably rested on structural inferences, since it was rendered before the ratification of the Fourteenth Amendment and did not rest on any specific provision of the original Constitution. Crandall is discussed in the Slaughter–House Cases (p. 421 below).

recurrent themes in cases that seek to determine whether congressional action has preempted state authority.

Pacific Gas & Elec. Co. v. State Energy Resources Conservation & Development Comm'n
461 U.S. 190, 103 S.Ct. 1713, 75 L.Ed.2d 752 (1983).

Justice WHITE delivered the opinion of the Court.

[This decision sustained a California law dealing with the problem of finding a long-term solution for disposing of nuclear waste. Sec. 25524.2 of the law, adopted in 1976, imposes a moratorium on the certification of nuclear energy plants until the State Energy Resources Conservation & Development Commission "finds that there has been developed and that the United States through its authorized agency has approved and there exists a demonstrated technology or means for the disposal of high-level nuclear waste." "Disposal" is defined as a "method for the permanent and terminal disposition" of such waste. P.G.&E. sought a declaratory judgment that this provision was preempted by the federal Atomic Energy Act of 1954 as amended and therefore invalid under the supremacy clause. The district court granted that relief, but the court of appeals reversed. The Supreme Court agreed with the court of appeals' result.]

The turning of swords into plowshares has symbolized the transformation of atomic power into a source of energy in American society. To facilitate this development the federal government relaxed its monopoly over fissionable materials and nuclear technology, and in its place, erected a complex scheme to promote the civilian development of nuclear energy, while seeking to safeguard the public and the environment from the unpredictable risks of a new technology. Early on, it was decided that the states would continue their traditional role in the regulation of electricity production. The interrelationship of federal and state authority in the nuclear energy field has not been simple. [This] case emerges from the intersection of the federal government's efforts to ensure that nuclear power is safe with the exercise of the historic state authority over the generation and sale of electricity.

[A] nuclear reactor must be periodically refueled and the "spent fuel" removed. This spent fuel is intensely radioactive and must be carefully stored. The general practice is to store the fuel in a water-filled pool at the reactor site. For many years, it was assumed that this fuel would be reprocessed; accordingly, the storage pools were designed as short-term holding facilities with limited storage capacities. As expectations for reprocessing remained unfulfilled, the spent fuel accumulated in the storage pools, creating the risk that nuclear reactors would have to be shutdown. This could occur if there were insufficient room in the pool to store spent fuel and also if there were not enough space to hold the entire fuel core when certain inspections or emergencies required unloading of the reactor. In recent years, the problem has taken on special urgency. [Government] studies indicate that a number of reactors could be forced to shut down in the near future due to the inability to store spent fuel.

There is a second dimension to the problem. Even with water-pools adequate to store safely all the spent fuel produced during the working lifetime of the reactor, permanent disposal is needed because the wastes will remain radioactive for thousands of years. A number of long-term nuclear waste management strategies have been extensively examined. These range from sinking the wastes in stable deep seabeds, to placing the wastes beneath ice sheets in Greenland and Antarctica, to ejecting the wastes into space by rocket. The greatest attention has been focused on disposing of the wastes in subsurface geologic repositories such as salt deposits. Problems of how and where to store nuclear wastes [have] engendered considerable scientific, political, and public debate. There are both safety and economic aspects to the nuclear waste issue: first, if not properly stored, nuclear wastes might leak and endanger both the environment and human health; second, the lack of a long-term disposal option increases the risk that the insufficiency of interim storage space for spent fuel will lead to reactor-shutdowns, rendering nuclear energy an unpredictable and uneconomical adventure. The California [laws] at issue here are responses to these [concerns].

It is well-established that within Constitutional limits Congress may preempt state authority by so stating in express terms. Absent explicit preemptive language, Congress' intent to supersede state law altogether may be found from a "scheme of federal regulation so pervasive as to make reasonable the inference that Congress left no room to supplement it," "because the Act of Congress may touch a field in which the federal interest is so dominant that the federal system will be assumed to preclude enforcement of state laws on the same subject," or because "the object sought to be obtained by the federal law and the character of obligations imposed by it may reveal the same purpose." [E.g., Rice; p. 342 below.] Even where Congress has not entirely displaced state regulation in a specific area, state law is preempted to the extent that it actually conflicts with federal law. Such a conflict arises when "compliance with both federal and state regulations is a physical impossibility" [Florida Lime; p. 343 below], or where state law "stands as an obstacle to the accomplishment and execution of the full purposes and objectives of Congress." Hines v. Davidowitz [p. 343 below].

Petitioners [present] three major lines of argument as to why § 25524.2 is preempted. First, they submit that the statute—because it regulates construction of nuclear plants and because it is allegedly predicated on safety concerns—ignores the division between federal and state authority created by the Atomic Energy Act, and falls within the field that the federal government has preserved for its own exclusive control. Second, the statute, and the judgments that underlie it, conflict with decisions concerning the nuclear waste disposal issue made by Congress and the [federal] Nuclear Regulatory Commission. Third, the California statute frustrates the federal goal of developing nuclear technology as a source of energy. We consider each of these contentions in turn.

A.   Even a brief perusal of the Atomic Energy Act reveals that, despite its comprehensiveness, it does not at any point expressly require the States to construct or authorize nuclear power plants or prohibit the States from deciding [not] to permit the construction of any further reactors. Instead, petitioners argue that the Act is intended to preserve the federal government as the sole regulator of all matters nuclear, and that § 25524.2 falls within the scope of this impliedly preempted field. But as we view the issue, Congress, in passing the 1954 Act and in subsequently amending it, intended that the federal government should regulate the radiological safety aspects involved in the construction and operation of a nuclear plant, but that the States retain their traditional responsibility in the field of regulating electrical utilities for determining questions of need, reliability, cost and other related state concerns. Need for new power facilities, their economic feasibility, and rates and services, are areas that have been characteristically governed by the States. [Thus], "Congress legislated here in a field which the States have traditionally occupied [so] we start with the assumption that the historic police powers of the States were not to be superseded by the Federal Act unless that was the clear and manifest purpose of Congress." [Rice.]

The Atomic Energy Act must be read, however, against another background. [Until 1954] the use, control and ownership of nuclear technology remained a federal monopoly. The Atomic Energy Act of 1954 grew out of Congress' determination that the national interest would be best served if the Government encouraged the private sector to become involved in the development of atomic energy for peaceful purposes under a program of federal regulation and licensing. The Act implemented this policy decision by providing for licensing of private construction, ownership, and operation of commercial nuclear power reactors. The AEC, however, was given exclusive jurisdiction to license the transfer, delivery, receipt, acquisition, possession and use of nuclear materials. Upon these subjects, no role was left for the states.

The Commission, however, was not given authority over the generation of electricity itself, or over the economic question whether a particular plant should be built. [The] Nuclear Regulatory Commission (NRC), which now exercises the AEC's regulatory authority, does not purport to exercise its authority based on economic considerations, [and] utility financial qualifications are only of concern to the NRC if related to the public health and safety. It is almost inconceivable that Congress would have left a regulatory vacuum; the only reasonable inference is that Congress intended the states to continue to make these judgments. Any doubt that ratemaking and plant-need questions were to remain in state hands was removed by § 271, which provided: "Nothing in this chapter shall be construed to affect the authority or regulations of any Federal, State or local agency with respect to the generation, sale, or transmission of electric power produced through the use of nuclear facilities licensed by the [Commission]." [This] account indicates that from the passage of the Atomic Energy Act in 1954 [to] the present day, Congress has preserved the dual regulation of nuclear-powered electricity generation: the federal government maintains complete control of the safety and "nuclear" aspects of energy generation; the states exercise their traditional authority over the need for additional generating capacity, the type of generating facilities to be licensed, land use, ratemaking, and the like.

The above is not particularly controversial. But deciding how § 25524.2 is to be construed and classified is a more difficult proposition. At the outset, we emphasize that the statute does not seek to regulate the construction or operation of a nuclear powerplant. It would clearly be impermissible for California to attempt to do so, for such regulation, even if enacted out of non-safety concerns, would nevertheless directly conflict with the NRC's exclusive authority over plant construction and operation. Respondents appear to concede as much. Respondents do broadly argue, however, that although safety regulation of nuclear plants by states is forbidden, a state may completely prohibit new construction until its safety concerns are satisfied by the federal government. We reject this line of reasoning. State safety regulation is not preempted only when it conflicts with federal law. Rather, the federal government has occupied the entire field of nuclear safety concerns, except the limited powers expressly ceded to the states. When the federal government completely occupies a given field or an identifiable portion of it, as it has done here, the test of preemption is whether "the matter on which the state asserts the right to act is in any way regulated by the federal government." [Rice.] A state moratorium on nuclear construction grounded in safety concerns falls squarely within the prohibited field. Moreover, a state judgment that nuclear power is not safe enough to be further developed would conflict directly with the countervailing judgment of the NRC that nuclear construction may proceed notwithstanding extant uncertainties as to waste disposal. A state prohibition on nuclear construction for safety reasons would also be in the teeth of the Atomic Energy Act's objective to insure that nuclear technology be safe enough for widespread development and use—and would be preempted for that reason.

That being the case, it is necessary to determine whether there is a nonsafety rationale for § 25524.2. [The California Assembly Committee which proposed the bill] reported that the waste disposal problem was "largely economic or the result of poor planning, *not* safety related." The Committee explained that the lack of a federally approved method of waste disposal created a "clog" in the nuclear fuel cycle. Storage space was limited while more nuclear wastes were continuously produced. Without a permanent means of disposal, the nuclear waste problem could become critical leading to unpredictably high costs to contain the problem or, worse, shutdowns in reactors. "Waste disposal *safety*," the [Committee] notes, "is not directly addressed by the bills, which ask only that a method [of waste disposal] be chosen and accepted by the federal government." [Although specific] indicia of California's intent in enacting § 25524.2 are subject to varying interpretation, [we] should not become embroiled in attempting to ascertain California's true motive. First, inquiry into legislative motive is often an unsatisfactory venture. [Second], it would be particularly pointless for us to engage in such inquiry here when it is clear that the states have been allowed to retain authority over the need for electrical generating facilities easily sufficient to permit a state so inclined to halt the construction of new nuclear plants by refusing on economic grounds to issue certificates of public convenience in individual proceedings. In these circumstances, it should be up to Congress to determine whether a state has misused the authority left in its hands. Therefore, we accept California's avowed economic purpose as the rationale for enacting § 25524.2. Accordingly, the statute lies outside the occupied field of nuclear safety regulation.

B. Petitioners' second major argument concerns federal regulation aimed at the nuclear waste disposal problem itself. It is contended that § 25524.2 conflicts with federal regulation of nuclear waste disposal, with the NRC's decision that it is permissible to continue to license reactors, notwithstanding uncertainty surrounding the waste disposal problem, and with Congress' recent passage of legislation directed at that problem.

[The NRC has promulgated extensive and detailed regulations concerning the operation of nuclear facilities and the handling of nuclear materials. The regulations specify design and control requirements for fuel storage and handling of radioactive waste, both at the reactor site and away from the reactor. But no federal agency has yet licensed any permanent disposal facilities, and there is continued authorization of storage of spent fuel at reactor sites in pools of water. In 1977, the NRC refused to halt reactor licensing until a method of permanent disposal was certified.] The NRC's imprimatur, however, indicates only that it is safe to proceed with such plants, not that it is economically wise to do so. Because the NRC order does not and could not compel a utility to develop a nuclear plant, compliance with both it and § 25524.2 are possible. Moreover, because the NRC's regulations are aimed at insuring that plants are safe, not necessarily that they are economical, § 25524.2 does not interfere with the objective of the federal regulation. Nor has California sought through § 25524.2 to impose its own standards on nuclear waste disposal. The statute accepts that it is the federal responsibility to develop and license such technology. As there is no attempt on California's part to enter this field, one which is occupied by the federal government, we do not find § 25524.2 preempted any more by the NRC's obligations in the waste disposal field than by its licensing power over the plants [themselves].

C. Finally, it is strongly contended that § 25524.2 frustrates the Atomic Energy Act's purpose to develop the commercial use of nuclear power. It is well established that state law is preempted if it "stands as an obstacle to the accomplishment of the full purposes and objectives of Congress." [E.g., Hines; Florida Lime]. There is little doubt that a primary purpose of the Atomic Energy Act was, and continues to be, the promotion of nuclear power. [The] Court of Appeals is right, however, that the promotion of nuclear power is not to be accomplished "at all costs." The elaborate licensing and safety provisions and the continued preservation of state regulation in traditional areas belie that. Moreover, Congress has allowed the States to determine—as a matter of economics—whether a nuclear plant vis-a-vis a fossil fuel plant should be built. The decision of California to exercise that authority does not, in itself, constitute a basis for preemption. Therefore, while the argument of petitioners and the United States has considerable force, the legal reality remains that Congress has left sufficient authority in the states to allow the development of nuclear power to be slowed or even stopped for economic reasons. Given this statutory scheme, it is for Congress to rethink the division of regulatory authority in light of its possible exercise by the states to undercut a federal objective. The courts should not assume the role which our system assigns to Congress.

[Affirmed.]

Justice BLACKMUN, with whom Justice STEVENS joins, concurring in part and concurring in the judgment.

I join the Court's opinion, except to the extent it suggests that a State may not prohibit the construction of nuclear power plants if the State is motivated by concerns about the safety of such plants. Since the Court finds that California was not so motivated, this suggestion is unnecessary to the Court's holding.

———

1. *Types of preemption.* As the Court acknowledged in P.G. & E., Congress may preempt state power to regulate in three ways: (1) by express statement, (2) by implied occupation of a regulatory field, or (3) by implied preclusion of conflicting state regulations. When preemption is *express*, the only issue is whether a state statute falls within the area preempted. The two types of implied preemption, however, require further analysis.

2. *Field preemption.* The Court requires a clear showing that Congress meant to occupy a field. In RICE v. SANTA FE ELEVATOR CORP., 331 U.S. 218 (1947), Justice DOUGLAS' majority opinion stated: "The question in each case is what the purpose of Congress was. Congress legislated here in a field which the States have traditionally occupied [grain warehousing practices]. So we start with the assumption that the historic police powers of the States were not to be superseded by the Federal Act unless that was the clear and manifest purpose of Congress. Such a purpose may be evidenced in several ways. The scheme of federal regulation may be so pervasive as to make reasonable the inference that Congress left no room for the States to supplement it. Or the Act of Congress may touch a field in which the federal interest is so dominant that the federal system will be assumed to preclude enforcement of state laws on the same subject." Are such findings similar to findings of inherent national interest in the dormant commerce clause context under Cooley? Why should the Court apply a strong presumption against field regulation in areas of

traditionally local concern? Because field preemption creates at least a temporary regulatory vacuum, in which neither the states nor Congress are acting?

3. *Conflict preemption.* In HINES v. DAVIDOWITZ, 312 U.S. 52 (1941),[1] Justice BLACK's majority opinion stated: "[Where] the federal government, in the exercise of its superior authority in this field, has enacted a complete scheme of regulation and has therein provided a standard for the registration of aliens, states cannot, inconsistently with the purpose of Congress, conflict or interfere with, curtail or complement, the federal law, or enforce additional or auxiliary regulations. There is not—and from the very nature of the problem there cannot be—any rigid formula or rule which can be used as a universal pattern to determine the meaning and purpose of every act of Congress. This Court, in considering the validity of state laws in the light [of] federal laws touching the same subject, has made use of the following expressions: conflicting; contrary to; occupying the field; repugnance; difference; irreconcilability; inconsistency; violation; curtailment; and interference. But none of these expressions provides an infallible constitutional test or an exclusive constitutional yardstick. In the final analysis, there can be no one crystal clear distinctly marked formula. Our primary function is to determine whether, under the circumstances of [this] case, Pennsylvania's law stands as an obstacle to the accomplishment and execution of the full purposes and objectives of Congress."

In FLORIDA LIME & AVOCADO GROWERS, INC. v. PAUL, 373 U.S. 132 (1963), the Court described conflict preemption as a situation where "compliance with both federal and state regulations is a physical impossibility." Florida Lime involved avocados certified as mature under the federal regulations but containing less than the minimum California oil content. Justice BRENNAN's majority opinion concluded that "there is neither such actual conflict between the two schemes of regulation that both cannot stand in the same area, nor evidence of a congressional design to pre-empt the field." He noted that there was no "physical impossibility" of complying with both standards and that the "maturity of avocados seems to be an inherently unlikely candidate for exclusive federal regulation. [Federal] regulation by means of minimum standards [of] agricultural commodities, however comprehensive *for those purposes* [of marketing] that regulation may be, does not of itself import displacement of state control over the distribution and retail sale of those commodities in the interests of the *consumers* of the commodities within the State." Nor could the Court find "an unambiguous congressional mandate" to exclude state regulation. The federal law here involved concerned "minimum" rather than "uniform" standards. The statutory scheme was "one of maturity regulations drafted and administered locally by the growers' own representatives, and designed to do no more than promote orderly competition among the South Florida growers."

Justice WHITE's dissent, joined by Justices Black, Douglas and Clark, concluded that the supremacy clause barred the application of California's "inconsistent and conflicting" legislation. The dissenters saw the federal scheme as a "comprehensive regulatory program" and insisted that California's interest was identical to the federal one. "There is no health interest here. The

---

1. Hines barred enforcement of Pennsylvania's Alien Registration Act of 1939 because of the federal Alien Registration Act of 1940. Much of the opinion dealt with the broad national power over immigration and aliens rather than its specific exercise. But even in this traditionally federal area, not all state regulation is barred. Thus, Hines was distinguished in DeCanas v. Bica, 424 U.S. 351 (1976), sustaining a California law which prohibited the knowing employment of aliens not entitled to lawful residence in the United States if such employment would have an adverse effect on lawful resident workers.

question is [a] purely economic one. [Despite] the repeated suggestions to this effect in the Court's opinion, there is no indication that the state regulatory scheme has any purpose other than protecting the good will of the avocado industry—such as protecting health or preventing deception of the public— unless as a purely incidental byproduct."

In GADE v. NATIONAL SOLID WASTES MANAGEMENT ASS'N, 505 U.S. 88 (1992), the Court found several Illinois provisions for licensing workers who handle hazardous waste preempted by federal Occupational Safety and Health Administration regulations, even though the federal regulations aimed only at worker safety and the state regulations aimed both at worker safety and public health. A plurality opinion by Justice O'CONNOR found conflict preemption, reading the federal scheme to forbid duplicative regulation. Both Justice KENNEDY, concurring in part and in the judgment because he found express preemption, and Justice SOUTER, dissenting along with Justices Blackmun, Stevens and Thomas, objected to the plurality's departure from the presumption that historic state powers may not be superseded without a clear showing of congressional intent.

Do these decisions rest more on balancing national and local interests as in the dormant commerce clause cases than they do on pure statutory construction? Note, e.g., the emphasis in the Florida Lime dissent on the state interest: "no health interest"; "a purely economic one." Do differing perceptions about the true state purpose, a central factor in commerce clause cases, explain the division on the Court in the Florida Lime case? See generally Note, "Preemption as a Preferential Ground: a New Canon of Construction," 12 Stan. L. Rev. 208 (1959).

4. *The impact of unexercised federal authority.* A recurrent issue in preemption cases is the meaning to be attributed to the federal authorities' failure to exercise power to regulate a particular area. Should such unexercised authority be taken to leave regulation to the states, or to bar state regulation as an expression of a federal intent to bar *any* regulation? The Court has sometimes, but not always, relied on the existence of unexercised federal administrative authority to justify a preemption finding. Compare Napier v. Atlantic Coast Line, 272 U.S. 605 (1926) (railroad safety equipment), and Castle v. Hayes Freight Lines, 348 U.S. 61 (1954) (suspension of right to use highways for violation of state truck weight limits), with Southern Pacific, p. 300 above (railroads) and Bibb, p. 305 above (trucks). The first pair of cases produced preemption findings in part on the basis of unexercised ICC authority; the second pair did not. For the view that the existence of unexercised authority indicates a congressional determination that such authority should not be exercised by anyone, see Arkansas Electric Co-op. v. Arkansas Public Service Comm'n, 461 U.S. 375 (1983): "[A] federal decision to forgo regulation in a given area may imply an authoritative federal determination that the area is best left *un*regulated, and in that event would have as much pre-emptive force as a decision *to* regulate."

B.   CONSENT TO STATE LAWS

Introduction. May Congress, instead of precluding state action through preemption, validate state laws that, in the absence of such federal consent, would violate the dormant commerce clause? In the Cooley case, the Court indicated that Congress could not validate laws which were "unconstitutional" under the commerce clause; yet a century later, it seemed clear to Justice Stone in the Southern Pacific case that the "undoubted" congressional "power to redefine the distribution of power over interstate commerce" included the authority "to permit the states to regulate the commerce in a manner which would otherwise not be permissible." What is the justification for that congressional authority? What is its scope? The examples of congressional "consent" in this section explore these problems. On the general problems of congressional "consent," see generally Bikle, "The Silence of Congress," 41 Harv.L.Rev. 200 (1927); Dowling, "Interstate Commerce and State Power," 27 Va.L.Rev. 1 (1940), and "Interstate Commerce and State Power—Revised Version," 47 Colum.L.Rev. 547 (1947).

1. *The Wilson Act and the Rahrer case.* a. In LEISY v. HARDIN, 135 U.S. 100 (1890), the Court invalidated an Iowa law prohibiting the sale of intoxicating liquors as applied to beer brewed in Illinois and offered for sale in the "original package" in Iowa. Chief Justice Fuller, after reviewing the Cooley doctrine, tied it to congressional intent and stated that "inasmuch as interstate commerce [is] national in its character, and must be governed by a uniform system, so long as Congress does not pass any law to regulate it, or allowing the States so to do, it thereby indicates its will that such commerce shall be free and untrammeled." He insisted that Peirce v. New Hampshire (one of the License Cases, p. 265 above), "in so far as it rests on the view that the law of New Hampshire was valid because Congress had made no regulation on the subject, must be regarded as having been distinctly overthrown by numerous cases." Accordingly, he concluded that Leisy "had the right to import this beer into that State, [and] had the right to sell it, by which act alone it would become mingled in the common mass of property within the State. Up to that point of time, we hold that, *in the absence of congressional permission to do so,* the State had no power to interfere by seizure." [Emphasis added.]

b. In August, 1890, only a few months after the decision in Leisy v. Hardin, Congress passed the Wilson Act which provided that all intoxicating liquors "transported into any state or territory, or remaining therein, for use, consumption, sale, or storage therein, shall upon arrival in such state or territory be subject to the operation and effect of the laws of such state or territory enacted in the exercise of its police powers, to the same extent and in the same manner as though [such] liquors had been produced in such state or territory, and shall not be exempt therefrom by reason of being introduced therein in original packages or otherwise." Soon after, the Court held that by virtue of this Act a state may apply its prohibition laws to sales of intoxicating liquors in the original packages. WILKERSON v. RAHRER, 140 U.S. 545 (1891). According to Rahrer, "Congress has not attempted to delegate the power to regulate commerce, or to exercise any power reserved to the States, or to grant a power not possessed by the States, or to adopt state laws. [It] imparted no power to the State not then possessed, but allowed imported property to fall at once upon arrival within the local jurisdiction." The Court added: "No reason is perceived why, if Congress chooses to provide that certain designated subjects of interstate commerce shall be governed by a rule which divests them of that character at an earlier period of time than would otherwise be the case, it is not within its competency to do so."

2. *The Webb–Kenyon Act.* In 1913, Congress passed the Webb–Kenyon Act, an "Act divesting intoxicating liquors of their interstate character in certain cases"—a reliance on the "divesting" language of Rahrer, above. The law prohibited the shipment of liquor into a state if the liquor was to be "in

any manner used in violation of any law of such State." In an action to compel a railroad to accept a consignment of liquor for shipment to West Virginia, the defendant argued that such shipment was illegal under the Webb–Kenyon Act because West Virginia law barred shipment of liquor into the State. The plaintiff countered that the federal law was unconstitutional. James Clark Distilling Co. v. Western Maryland R. Co., 242 U.S. 311 (1917), upheld the federal law, finding that the Act was "but a larger degree of exertion of the identical power which was brought into play in the [Wilson Act]."[1]

3. *The McCarran Act and the Prudential case.* a. *The Act.* In 1944, the Supreme Court found that the Sherman Anti–Trust Act of 1890 applied to the insurance business, even though the Court had held in 1868 that insurance was not commerce. United States v. South–Eastern Underwriters Ass'n, 322 U.S. 533 (1944). The Court concluded that "a nationwide business" such as insurance "is not deprived of its interstate character merely because it is built [upon] contracts which are local in nature." In response, Congress enacted the McCarran Act of 1945, which not only limited the applicability of antitrust laws to the business, but also sought to assure continued state authority over insurance. The Act contained a declaration "that the continued regulation and taxation by the several States of the business of insurance is in the public interest, and that silence on the part of the Congress shall not be construed to impose any barrier to the regulation or taxation of such business by the several States." And sec. 2 of the law provided: "(a) The business of insurance [shall] be subject to the laws of the several States which relate to the regulation or taxation of such business. (b) No Act of Congress shall be construed to invalidate, impair, or supersede any law enacted by any State for the purpose of regulating the business of insurance, or which imposes a fee or tax upon such business, unless such Act specifically relates to the business of insurance."

b. PRUDENTIAL INSURANCE CO. v. BENJAMIN, 328 U.S. 408 (1946): The Company, a New Jersey corporation, objected to the continued collection of a long-standing tax of 3% of the premiums received from all business done in South Carolina. No similar tax was required of South Carolina corporations. The Court assumed that the tax was "discriminatory" and hence invalid under commerce clause decisions. Nevertheless, the Court held that the McCarran Act validated the tax. Justice RUTLEDGE disagreed with the Company's contention that "Congress' declaration of policy adds nothing to the validity of what the states have done within the area covered by the declaration." To accept that claim "would ignore the very basis on which [the] Clark Distilling case

---

1. The substance and much of the language of the Webb–Kenyon Act was written into the Twenty-first Amendment, which also repealed the Eighteenth. Does the broad recognition of state power over liquor in the Twenty-first Amendment make commerce clause concerns wholly inapplicable in that area? Justice Brandeis once so suggested for a unanimous Court: "Since that amendment, the right of a State to prohibit or regulate the importation of intoxicating liquor is not limited by the commerce clause." Joseph S. Finch Co. v. McKittrick, 305 U.S. 395 (1939). In more recent decades, however, the Court has made it clear that the Amendment does *not* bar all commerce clause challenges and does *not* leave absolute control of liquor traffic to the states. See, e.g., Hostetter v. Idlewild Bon Voyage Liquor Corp., 377 U.S. 324 (1964), holding that New York could not prohibit the sale of tax-free liquor to departing international airline passengers for delivery upon arrival at foreign destinations. See also Bacchus Imports, Ltd. v. Dias, 468 U.S. 263 (1984) (p. 289 above), barring Hawaii's discriminatory excise tax on wholesale liquor sales despite the existence of the Twenty-first Amendment. Three dissenters insisted that the Amendment made permissible what would otherwise be a violation of the commerce clause.

[has] set the pattern of the law for governing situations like that now present-ed." He stated:

"Not yet has this Court held such a disclaimer [of a commerce clause prohibition] invalid. [On] the contrary, in each instance it has given effect to the congressional judgment contradicting its own previous one. It is true that rationalizations have differed concerning those decisions. [But] the results have been lasting and are at least as important, for the direction given to the process of accommodating federal and state authority, as the reasons stated for reaching them. [Apart from the] function of defining the outer boundary of its power, whenever Congress' judgment has been uttered affirmatively to contradict the Court's previously expressed view that specific action taken by the states in Congress' silence was forbidden by the commerce clause, this body has accommodated its previous judgment to Congress' expressed approval. Some part of this readjustment may be explained in ways acceptable on any theory of the commerce clause and the relations of Congress and the courts toward its functioning. Such explanations, however, hardly go to the root of the matter. For the fact remains that, in these instances, the sustaining of Congress' overriding action has involved something beyond correction of erroneous factual judgment in deference to Congress' presumably better-informed view of the facts, and also beyond giving due deference to its conception of the scope of its powers, when it repudiates, just as when its silence is thought to support, the inference that it has forbidden state action.

"[W]e would be going very far to rule that South Carolina no longer may collect her tax. To do so would flout the expressly declared policies of both Congress and the state. Moreover it would establish a ruling never heretofore made and in doing this would depart from the whole trend of decision in a great variety of situations most analogous to the one now presented. [The] power of Congress over commerce exercised entirely without reference to coordinated action of the states is not restricted, except as the Constitution expressly provides, by any limitation which forbids it to discriminate against interstate commerce and in favor of local trade. [This] broad authority Congress may exercise alone, subject to those limitations, or in conjunction with coordinated action by the states, in which case limitations imposed for the preservation of their powers become inoperative and only those designed to forbid action altogether by any power or combination of powers in our governmental system remain effective. Here both Congress and South Carolina have acted, and in complete co-ordination, to sustain the tax. It is therefore reinforced by the exercise of all the power of government residing in our scheme. Clear and gross must be the evil which would nullify such an exertion, one which could arise only by exceeding beyond cavil some explicit and compelling limitation imposed by a constitutional [provision] designed and intended to outlaw the action taken entirely from our constitutional framework."[2]

c. Justice Rutledge's conclusion regarding very broad congressional "consent" power is clearer than his reasoning. Congress can "consent" to any variety of state legislation impinging on commerce: in the exercise of the national commerce power, it can permit state laws the Court would otherwise consider "unconstitutional" under the dormant commerce clause. To the Cooley Court, congressional "consent" authority was questionable; to Justice

---

2. The McCarran Act, despite its apparent breadth, is limited in scope: it has been construed as exempting the insurance industry from commerce clause constrictions only, *not* from other constitutional restraints such as equal protection. See Metropolitan Life Ins. Co. v. Ward, 470 U.S. 869 (1985), considered more fully in the final note in this subsection.

Rutledge a century later, the authority was clear. Why? What explanations *do* go "to the root of the matter," in Justice Rutledge's phrase? What "something beyond" justifies congressional authority today?

After examining the Rutledge opinion, Noel Dowling confessed that "I was still not sure that my vision had caught the 'something beyond.'" Dowling, "Interstate Commerce and State Power—Revised Version," 47 Colum.L.Rev. 547 (1947). In his earlier "State Power" article, 27 Va.L.Rev. 1 (1940), Dowling had suggested rationalizing congressional "consent" by viewing commerce clause restraints as resting on implied congressional policy: "[I]n the absence of affirmative consent a Congressional negative will be presumed [against] state action [unreasonably interfering with interstate commerce], the presumption being rebuttable at the pleasure of Congress." Is that explanation preferable to Justice Rutledge's effort to explain the "consent" power?

William Cohen finds Justice Rutledge's explanation clearer and more persuasive than Noel Dowling did. After examining the line of cases culminating in Prudential Insurance, Cohen discerned "a rather bright line for determining when congressional consent to otherwise unconstitutional state laws will be effective." In his view, "Congress can validly consent to state laws when [the] constitutional limitation on state power is not matched by a similar or identical limitation on federal power." See Cohen, "Congressional Power to Define State Power to Regulate Commerce," in 2 Courts and Free Markets (Sandalow & Stein, eds., 1982), 523, and Cohen, "Congressional Power to Validate Unconstitutional State Laws: A Forgotten Solution to an Old Enigma," 35 Stan.L.Rev. 387 (1983).

Does this congressional power to consent to otherwise "unconstitutional" state laws support arguments for a similar congressional power to modify constitutional restraints on state authority *outside* the commerce area? Does congressional power under § 5 of the Fourteenth Amendment, for example, authorize Congress to validate state laws otherwise unconstitutional under the due process and equal protection clauses of § 1 of that Amendment? Congress has not traditionally attempted to authorize actions that would otherwise violate equal protection, and there is in fact doubt that it has the constitutional power to do so. See Katzenbach v. Morgan (1966; p. 998 below).

4. *Equal protection as a limit on state protectionism.* In addition to the commerce clause and the Privileges and Immunities Clause of Art. IV, the Equal Protection Clause of the Fourteenth Amendment can also serve as a bar to state discrimination in favor of local business. As the Court stated in Western & Southern L.I. Co. v. State Board of Equalization, 451 U.S. 648 (1981), "the Equal Protection Clause imposes limits upon a State's power to condition the right of a foreign corporation to do business within its borders." "[Whatever] the extent of a State's authority to exclude foreign corporations from doing business within its boundaries, that authority does not justify imposition of more onerous taxes or other burdens on foreign corporations than those imposed on domestic corporations, unless the discrimination between foreign and domestic corporations bears a rationale relation to a legitimate purpose." (For a full examination of equal protection principles, see chap. 9 below.)

This equal protection limitation was applied to strike down an Alabama law in METROPOLITAN LIFE INS. CO. v. WARD, 470 U.S. 869 (1985). Justice POWELL's majority opinion rejected the State's justifications for a tax preference for local insurance companies: "[Alabama] asks us to approve its purpose of promoting the business of its domestic insurers in Alabama by penalizing foreign insurers who also want to do business in the State. [Alabama's] aim to promote domestic industry is purely and completely discriminatory, designed only to favor domestic industry within the State, no matter what the cost to foreign corporations also seeking to do business there. Alabama's purpose [constitutes] the very sort of parochial discrimination that the Equal Protection Clause was intended to prevent." Justice Powell noted that a state's burden of meeting an equal protection challenge was ordinarily lighter than a commerce clause one, but here "discriminating against non-resident competitors [was] not a legitimate state purpose."

Because of the equal protection flaw in the law, the Court refused to apply the McCarran Act, sustained in the Prudential Insurance case, note above. Justice Powell explained: "Although the [Act] exempts the insurance industry from Commerce Clause restrictions, it does not purport to limit in any way the applicability of the Equal Protection Clause." Justice O'CONNOR's dissent, joined by Justices Brennan, Marshall, and Rehnquist, argued: "[The Court] supplants a legislative policy endorsed by both Congress and the individual States that explicitly sanctioned the very parochialism in regulation and taxation of insurance that the Court's decision holds illegitimate. [In the McCarran Act], Congress expressly sanctioned such economic parochialism in the context of state regulation and taxation of insurance. The doctrine adopted by the majority threatens the freedom not only of the States but also of the Federal Government to formulate economic policy."

The implications of Metropolitan Life remain uncertain. Thus, Northeast Bancorp v. Board of Governors, 472 U.S. 159 (1985), upheld regional limitations on banks contained in Massachusetts and Connecticut statutes. There was no question there of dormant commerce clause limits, because Congress had specifically authorized this kind of regional protectionism in the banking industry. Justice Rehnquist's majority opinion refused to find any equal protection violation either, distinguishing between discrimination against all out-of-state corporations and discrimination that favors only some out-of-state corporations over others. For critical analysis of Metropolitan Life and Northeast Bancorp, see Cohen, "Federalism in Equality [Clothing]," 38 Stan.L.Rev. 1 (1985).

5. *Other devices for congressional ordering of federal-state relationships.* Congressional consent and preemption are two examples of a wide range of techniques Congress may employ in the ordering of the complex relations between nation and state. Additional examples illustrating the devices Congress may employ include: the congressional role in determining the scope of intergovernmental immunities, p. 351 below; federal incorporation or adoption of state law—either expressly (as in the Federal Tort Claims Act or in the Federal Assimilative Crimes Act, see United States v. Sharpnack, 355 U.S. 286 (1958)) or by implication, as in many areas of tax, copyright and bankruptcy law; and state administration of federal law, as in the unemployment compensation scheme of the Social Security Act, or in the varied exercises of the federal spending power through conditional grants-in-aid to the states, or in the utilization of state courts and agencies for federal law enforcement. See generally Hart, "The Relations Between State and Federal Law," 54 Colum.L.Rev. 489 (1954).

SECTION 4.   SOME OTHER ASPECTS OF FEDERALISM: A BRIEF SURVEY

A.   STATE TAXATION AND FREE TRADE

Sec. 1 of this chapter examined problems of state regulations challenged under the commerce clause. But regulation is not the only variety of state legislative activity subject to commerce clause restraints. A similarly prolific source of litigation has been state taxation challenged as impinging upon interstate commerce. States need tax revenues, and the Court has recognized that state tax bases would be unjustifiably curtailed if *all* interstate business were immunized from tax obligations: "Even interstate business must pay its way, by bearing its share of local tax burdens." Yet, with respect to taxes as with regulations, the commerce clause "by its own force" creates "an area of trade free from interference by the State." States may not impose discriminatory or unduly burdensome taxes, for the Court has feared that, without commerce clause restraints, interstate business would be subject to the risk of multiple taxation, with most or all of its property or income being subjected to the tax scheme of each state in which it does business. From the beginning, the Court has sought to draw lines distinguishing between the permissible and the impermissible state tax. As in the regulatory area, it has sought to accommodate legitimate local needs and the interest in a national economy.

As the Court itself has said, in an understatement: "The decisions have been 'not always [clear], consistent or reconcilable.'" Northwestern States Portland Cement Co. v. Minnesota, 358 U.S. 450 (1959). The cases have been what Justices have called a "tangled underbrush" and a "quagmire" because in the area of state taxation the variables are even more numerous and complex and the tools of analysis even more uncertain than in the field of state regulation of commerce. Types of taxes and types of taxed activities vary widely. The most commonly litigated taxes have been property taxes, sales and use taxes, net and gross receipts taxes, and license and franchise taxes. The typical subjects of taxation have been interstate transportation and interstate sales, and various segments thereof. Moreover, far more than in the state regulatory area, the Court has had great difficulty in assessing the validity of particular tax schemes: in the search for legitimate interests, the need for revenue can always be set forth.

The special complexity of state tax problems has prompted some Justices to voice perceptions of judicial incompetence. Advocacy of a substantial Court withdrawal from the tax area has been more common than in the regulatory area. A well-known statement appeared in a 1940 dissent by Justice Black: "Spasmodic and unrelated instances of litigation cannot afford an adequate basis for the creation of integrated national rules. [The problem raised by the challenged tax should accordingly be left] for consideration of Congress in a nation-wide survey of the constantly increasing barriers to trade among the States." McCarroll v. Dixie Greyhound Lines, 309 U.S. 176 (1940) (Black, J., dissenting, joined by Justices Frankfurter and Douglas).

Yet, assuming that Congress *is* more competent to solve the problem, what should the Court do in the absence of congressional guidance: let the challenged tax stand, or invalidate it? The characteristic majority stance has been to exercise some continued commerce clause scrutiny even while urging legislative assistance. But congressional responses have been sparse and narrow of range. Accordingly, the problems of judicially enforced restraints on state taxes in the interest of the national economy continue to be of considerable importance. Although many of the old barriers to state taxes have been discarded, state taxes continue to generate substantial litigation. See, e.g., Quill Corp. v. North Dakota, 504 U.S. 298 (1992) (holding it permissible under the due process clause but impermissible under the dormant commerce clause for a state to attempt to tax out-of-state mail-order businesses with neither outlets nor representatives in the state, and whose only contacts with the state were by common carrier or the mails). However, pursuit of the intricacies of state taxation in a book on the basics of constitutional law would require more time and space than the undertaking warrants. Detailed consideration of commerce clause limits on state taxes is accordingly not attempted here.

B. INTERGOVERNMENTAL TAX IMMUNITIES

As McCulloch v. Maryland (p. 89 above) has already illustrated, one of the constitutional principles that governs relations between state and nation is that neither may destroy the autonomy of the other. In McCulloch itself, John Marshall struck down Maryland's tax on the operations of a federal instrumentality, the Bank of the United States. For over a century after McCulloch, constitutional tax immunities expanded in a number of directions. Marshall in McCulloch had indicated that his views of federal immunity from state taxation did not imply a reciprocal immunity of state operations from federal taxes. Nevertheless, the post-Civil War Court held that state activities did enjoy a reciprocal immunity from federal taxation. Collector v. Day, 11 Wall. (78 U.S.) 113 (1871).[1] Moreover, the Court steadily expanded the circle of immunities, from the primary immunity of the government itself to the derivative immunity of third persons—employees, lessees, patentees—in some ways related to governmental activities. In the late 1930s, that circle began to contract. For example, Helvering v. Gerhardt, 304 U.S. 405 (1938), and Graves v. New York ex rel. O'Keefe, 306 U.S. 466 (1939), held that the salaries of the employees of one government are not immune from income taxes imposed by the other. In recent years, intergovernmental tax immunities have continued to wane, although the Court continues to enforce a few constitutional tax immunities, as when states impose property taxes directly on federal property. See Rohr Aircraft Corp. v. San Diego County, 362 U.S. 628 (1960); see generally Massachusetts v. United States, 435 U.S. 444 (1978).

Increasingly, however, the modern scope of federal immunities turns on congressional statements recognizing or waiving immunities. Thus, when the specific McCulloch issue resurfaced in the Court a century and a half later, in First Agric. Nat. Bank v. State Tax Comm'n, 392 U.S. 339 (1968), the Court emphasized the dimensions of the *statutory* grant of immunity. Justice Marshall's dissent, joined by Justices Harlan and Stewart, argued that, in light of the "present functions and role of national banks," they should not be considered "constitutionally immune from nondiscriminatory state taxation." He suggested that McCulloch and other "hoary cases" could "and perhaps

----

1. See also Pollock v. Farmers' Loan & Trust Co., 157 U.S. 429 (1895), holding that the interest earned on state bonds was constitutionally immune from federal taxation. Pollock was overruled in South Carolina v. Baker, 485 U.S. 505 (1988), p. 212 above. The Court reaffirmed there that the sources of federal and state tax immunities are different: "[T]he state immunity arises from the constitutional structure and a concern for protecting state sovereignty whereas the federal immunity arises from the Supremacy Clause."

should" be read as banning only discriminatory taxes. That would "require a re-evaluation of the validity of the doctrine of intergovernmental tax immunities—a doctrine which does not rest upon any specific provisions of the Constitution, but rather upon this Court's concepts of federalism." Since Congress is able to provide statutory immunities, "there is little reason for this Court to cling to the view that the Constitution itself makes federal instrumentalities immune from state taxation in the absence of authorizing legislation."

For an effort to articulate "a narrow approach to governmental tax immunity," see United States v. New Mexico, 455 U.S. 720 (1982). There Justice Blackmun stated the basic principles as follows: "The one constant [is] simple enough to express: a State may not, consistent with the Supremacy Clause, lay a tax 'directly upon the United States.' [But] the limits on the immunity doctrine are [as] significant as the rule itself. [What] the Court's cases leave room for, then, is the conclusion that tax immunity is appropriate in only one circumstance: when the levy falls on the United States itself, or on an agency or instrumentality so closely connected to the Government that the two cannot realistically be viewed as separate entities. [This] view, we believe, comports with the principal purpose of the immunity doctrine, that of forestalling 'clashing sovereignty' [McCulloch], by preventing the States from laying demands directly on the Federal Government." But even under this "narrow approach," the Court continues to scrutinize closely those taxes alleged to discriminate against the federal government. See, e.g., Davis v. Michigan Dept. of Treasury, 489 U.S. 803 (1989).

C. INTERGOVERNMENTAL REGULATORY IMMUNITIES

As with intergovernmental tax immunities, intergovernmental regulatory immunities have already surfaced in the earlier materials. Structural considerations reinforced by the Tenth Amendment arguably give some protection against federal laws enacted under the Art. I powers of Congress that threaten to undermine state autonomy. The dimensions of that state autonomy limit have divided the Court in a number of cases over the last decade. (Recall the overruling of National League of Cities in Garcia, p. 207 above.) To what extent is there an immunity of federal operations from state regulation? The immunity principle of McCulloch v. Maryland applies here as well. A leading case is Johnson v. Maryland, 254 U.S. 51 (1920), relying on McCulloch in reversing the conviction of a post office employee for driving a truck without a state license. Justice Holmes' opinion for the Court concluded: "It seems to us that the immunity of the instruments of the United States from state control in the performance of their duties extends to a requirement that they desist from performance until they satisfy a state officer upon examination that they are competent for a necessary part of them and pay a fee for permission to go on." But he left the scope of the immunity somewhat unclear: "Of course an employee of the United States does not secure a general immunity from state law while acting in the course of his employment. [It] very well may be that, when the United States has not spoken, the subjection to local law would extend to general rules that might affect incidentally the mode of carrying out the employment—as, for instance, a [statute] regulating the mode of turning at the corners of streets." The federal immunity from state regulation may at times be claimed by those in a close relationship with the government; and the scope of the immunity, as in the state tax area, turns largely on congressional policy. See, for example, Leslie Miller, Inc. v. Arkansas, 352 U.S. 187 (1956), barring application of a state licensing scheme to a federal contractor because of a "conflict" between the state requirement and federal regulations designed to ensure the reliability of contractors. As in the state tax area, moreover, the Court is particularly alert to state regulations based on hostility to federal law. For example, in North Dakota v. United States, 460 U.S. 300 (1983), several state laws were evidently enacted to slow down or control federal acquisition of easements pursuant to the Migratory Bird Conservation Act. Applying a standard of whether the state laws were "hostile to federal interests," Justice Blackmun's opinion found that standard met here.

D. INTERSTATE RELATIONSHIPS

A number of constitutional provisions impose interstate obligations or facilitate interstate relationships. The major constitutional source of interstate obligations, Art. IV, § 2, contains two important restraints: the interstate privileges and immunities clause (explored above), and the obligation regarding rendition of fugitives from justice. The rendition clause of Art. IV, § 2 speaks in mandatory terms: a fugitive from justice "shall [be] delivered up" on "Demand of the executive Authority of the State from which he fled." Until recently, the mandatory duty of the rendition clause (also called the Extradition Clause) was held not to be enforceable by the federal courts, in the interest of avoiding confrontations between state and federal sovereignties. Kentucky v. Dennison, 24 How. (65 U.S.) 66 (1861). However, Dennison was overruled in Puerto Rico v. Branstad, 483 U.S. 219 (1987), and thus failure by a state to comply with its obligations under the rendition clause *can* be remedied by mandamus or injunctive relief in the federal courts. Congress has enacted legislation to deal with interstate fugitives from justice. Moreover, many states have adopted the Uniform Law to Secure the Attendance of Witnesses from Within or Without a State in Criminal Proceedings. In New York v. O'Neill, 359 U.S. 1 (1959), the Court sustained the Act as adopted by Florida.

The major device for interstate collaboration recognized in the Constitution is the interstate compact. Art. I, § 10 states that no state "shall, without the Consent of the Congress, [enter into] any Agreement or Compact with another State." Interstate compacts have been used to deal with a wide variety of interstate and regional problems, including boundaries, natural resources regulation and allocation, flood control, transportation, taxation, and crime control. Congress has at times encouraged compacts by giving advance consent, as with crime and flood control. But not all interstate agreements require congressional consent. Virginia v. Tennessee, 148 U.S. 503 (1893), stated that the compact clause is directed at the formation of any combination "which may tend to increase [the] political influence of the contracting States" so as to "impair the supremacy of the United States," and that there are "many matters upon which different States may agree that can in no respect concern the United States." The application of these criteria divided the Court in U.S. Steel Corp. v. Multistate Tax Commission, 434 U.S. 452 (1978), finding that the Multistate Tax Compact drafted in 1966 was not invalid for lack of congressional consent.

CHAPTER 6

SEPARATION OF POWERS

———

Introduction. This final chapter of Part II, like the four preceding ones, deals with problems of structure and relationships among units of government. The Framers limited power by diffusing authority on a horizontal as well as a vertical plane. The preceding chapters focused on the vertical allocations of power, between nation and states; this chapter turns to the horizontal allocation of power, among the branches of the national government.

The makers of the Constitution, influenced not only by their own experiences but also by theorists such as Montesquieu, consciously provided for allocation of national authority among the executive, legislative, and judicial branches. This separation is symbolized by the discrete treatment of each branch, in Articles I, II, and III of the Constitution. By insisting upon separation of powers, the Framers sought to promote such aims as safeguarding against tyranny and promoting efficiency—although the tripartite scheme often produces more inefficiencies than, for example, a parliamentary system. Justice Brandeis recognized the inherent conflict between preventing tyranny and assuring efficiency in a well-known passage in his dissent in Myers v. United States, 272 U.S. 52 (1926) (p. 391 below), noting that "the doctrine of the separation of powers was adopted [not] to promote efficiency but to preclude the exercise of arbitrary power. The purpose was, not to avoid friction, but, by means of the inevitable friction incident to the distribution of the governmental powers among three departments, to save the people from autocracy."

The constitutional provisions themselves reveal, however, that separation was not intended to be airtight. Repeatedly, powers are intermixed, as with the participation of the President in the legislative process through the veto power. And repeatedly, restraints by one branch upon another are authorized as aspects of the system of checks and balances, which coexists (and is often in tension with) any pure separation of powers scheme. See, e.g., the check of the congressional impeachment power on both the executive and the judicial branches. Beyond the explicit restraints and overlaps, moreover, lie boundary lines indistinct in the original document and blurred by historical practice. These areas of uncertainty have left ample room for competitions among the branches—conflicts that have historically most often been resolved by tests of political strength. These conflict-producing ambiguities may themselves have contributed to furthering the Framers' purpose of combating excessive concentration of power; yet they also yield an area of constitutional law with special disappointments for those yearning for clear lines. In the area of separation of powers, far more so than with problems of federalism and individual rights, judicial resolutions have been relatively sparse and political accommodations have predominated. As Justice Jackson commented in his concurring opinion in the Steel Seizure Case, below: "A century and a half of partisan debate and scholarly speculation yields no net result but only supplies more or less apt quotations from respected sources on each side of any question." Yet sparsity of Court decisions does not make separation of powers any less important and challenging an area of constitutional interpretation. The raw materials for study here, more than in other areas, lie in executive documents and legislative assertions as well as in Court opinions. But as in other areas, text and history and inferences from structure and relationships warrant searches for appropriate guidelines.

The sampling of separation of powers problems here begins with some examples of competition between President and Congress over the authority to make policy governing national affairs. To what extent does the constitutional grant of executive powers authorize the President to fashion policy in the absence of, or in the face of, congressional decisionmaking? In what manner may Congress impose restraints on executive discretion? Sec. 1 examines the boundaries between executive powers and legislative authority not only in the domestic sphere but also with regard to external affairs, with particular emphasis on conflicts regarding the making of foreign policy and the use of military force. Sec. 2 turns to problems concerning the autonomy of each branch vis-á-vis interferences by the others. To what extent does the separation of powers protect each branch against intervention in performing its functions? Sec. 3, finally, examines the degree to which the executive and legislative branches are immune from judicial processes.

SECTION 1.   THE AUTHORITY TO MAKE NATIONAL POLICY: THE CONFLICT BETWEEN EXECUTIVE AUTHORITY AND LEGISLATIVE POWERS

Presidential leadership and congressional lawmaking. Because the President is the only elected official with a national constituency and the party leader, the actual influence of the Presidency on national policy is obviously great. What of the President's constitutional authority to devise policy to deal with domestic problems? Are the President's policy-making powers justifiably greater in the sphere of foreign affairs? Does the Chief Executive have residual emergency powers? Do the specified executive powers in Art. II or any inherent powers of the Presidency authorize the President to act when Congress has been silent? Are there any circumstances in which the President's powers take precedence even over conflicting congressional directives? Or is the President limited to the specific tasks assigned by Art. II and to the execution of laws Congress enacts?

Claims of power to make "law" have evoked frequent and intense battles, most commonly over abstractions, with Presidents and commentators often on opposing sides. But the most helpful answers may lie less in embracive absolutes than in discriminating distinctions and practical adjustments. This problem has reached the Court with growing frequency in recent years. A battle has raged between those Justices who embrace a rigid, formalistic approach tending to categorize and rigidly separate legislative, executive and judicial functions and those who adopt a more flexible, functional approach attuned to historical developments and practical needs. Compare, for example, the compartmentalized, formalistic analysis of Justice Black with the more flexible, functional approach of some Justices who joined the majority in the Steel Seizure Case in 1952; consider Chief Justice Burger's quite rigid majority opinion with Justice White's dissent in Chadha, the legislative veto case of 1983; and note the reflection of similar conflicts in cases of the late 1980s,

Bowsher v. Synar and Morrison v. Olson, all printed below. [Much of the modern scholarly commentary has criticized the formalistic approach and endorsed the functional one. See, e.g., Strauss, "Formal and Functional Approaches to Separation of Powers Questions—A Foolish Inconsistency?," 72 Corn.L.Rev. 488 (1987), and Sunstein, "Constitutionalism After the New Deal," 101 Harv.L.Rev. 421 (1987).]

Youngstown Sheet & Tube Co. v. Sawyer [The Steel Seizure Case]

343 U.S. 579, 72 S.Ct. 863, 96 L.Ed. 1153 (1952).

Justice BLACK delivered the opinion of the Court.

[We] are asked to decide whether [President Truman] was acting within his constitutional power when he issued an order directing the Secretary of Commerce [Sawyer] to take possession of and operate most of the Nation's steel mills. The mill owners argue that the President's order amounts to lawmaking, a legislative function which the Constitution has expressly confided to the Congress and not to the President. The Government's position is that the order was made on findings of the President that his action was necessary to avert a national catastrophe which would inevitably result from a stoppage of steel production, and that in meeting this grave emergency the President was acting within the aggregate of his constitutional powers as the Nation's Chief Executive and the Commander in Chief of the [Armed Forces]. The issue emerges here from the following series of events:

In the latter part of 1951 [during the Korean War], a dispute arose between the steel companies and their employees over terms and conditions [for] new collective bargaining agreements. [Efforts to settle the dispute—including reference to the Federal Wage Stabilization Board—failed.] On April 4, 1952, the [Steelworkers'] Union gave notice of a nation-wide strike called to begin [on] April 9. The indispensability of steel as a component of substantially all weapons and other war materials led the President to believe that the proposed work stoppage would immediately jeopardize our national defense and that governmental seizure of the steel mills was necessary in order to assure the continued availability of steel. [Accordingly,] the President, a few hours before the strike was to begin, issued Executive Order 10340 [directing] the Secretary of Commerce to take possession of most of the steel mills and keep them running. The Secretary immediately issued his own possessory orders, calling upon the presidents of the various seized companies to serve as operating managers for the United States. [The] next morning the President sent a message to Congress reporting his [action]. Congress has taken no action. Obeying the Secretary's orders under protest, the companies brought proceedings against him in the District Court, [which] on April 30 issued a preliminary injunction restraining the Secretary from "continuing the seizure and possession of the plants [and] from acting under the purported authority of Executive Order No. 10340." On the same day the Court of Appeals stayed the District Court's injunction. Deeming it best that the issues raised be promptly decided by this Court, we granted certiorari on May 3 and set the cause for argument on May 12. [This decision was announced soon after, on June 2, 1952.]

The President's power, if any, to issue the order must stem either from an act of Congress or from the Constitution itself. There is no statute that expressly authorizes the President to take possession of property as he did here. Nor is there any act of Congress to which our attention has been directed from which such a power can fairly be implied. [There] are two statutes which do authorize the President to take both personal and real property under certain conditions, [the Selective Service Act of 1948 and the Defense Production Act of 1950]. However, the Government admits that these conditions were not met and that the President's order was not rooted in either of the statutes. The Government refers to the seizure provisions of one of these statutes [the 1950 Act] as "much too cumbersome, involved, and time-consuming for the crisis which was at hand." Moreover, the use of the seizure technique to solve labor disputes in order to prevent work stoppages was not only unauthorized by any congressional enactment; prior to this controversy, Congress had refused to adopt that method of settling labor disputes. When the Taft–Hartley Act was under consideration in 1947, Congress rejected an amendment which would have authorized such governmental seizures in cases of emergency.

It is clear that if the President had authority to issue the order he did, it must be found in some provision of the Constitution. And it is not claimed that express constitutional language grants this [power]. The contention is that presidential power should be implied from the aggregate of his powers under the Constitution. Particular reliance is placed on provisions in Article II which say that "The executive Power shall be vested in a President"; that "he shall take Care that the Laws be faithfully executed"; and that he "shall be Commander in Chief of the [Army and Navy]." The order cannot properly be sustained as an exercise of the President's military power as Commander in Chief of the Armed Forces. The Government attempts to do so by citing [cases] upholding broad powers in military commanders engaged in day-to-day fighting in a theater of war. Such cases need not concern us here. Even though "theater of war" be an expanding concept, we cannot with faithfulness to our constitutional system hold that the [Commander in Chief] has the ultimate power as such to take possession of private property in order to keep labor disputes from stopping production. This is a job for the Nation's lawmakers, not for its military authorities. Nor can the seizure order be sustained because of the several constitutional provisions that grant executive power to the President. In the framework of our Constitution, the President's power to see that the laws are faithfully executed refutes the idea that he is to be a lawmaker. The Constitution limits his functions in the law-making process to the recommending of laws he thinks wise and the vetoing of laws he thinks bad. And the Constitution is neither silent nor equivocal about who shall make laws which the President is to execute [quoting Art. I, § 1, and Art. I, § 8, cl. 18].

The President's order does not direct that a congressional policy be executed in a manner prescribed by Congress—it directs that a presidential policy be executed in a manner prescribed by the President. The preamble of the order itself, like that of many statutes, sets out reasons why the President believes certain policies should be adopted, proclaims these policies as rules of conduct to be followed, and again, like a statute, authorizes a government official to promulgate additional [regulations] consistent with the policy proclaimed and needed to carry that policy into execution. The power of Congress to adopt such public policies as those proclaimed by the order is beyond question. It can authorize the taking of private property for public use. It can make laws, [e.g.], those regulating the relationships between employers and [employees]. The Constitution does not subject this lawmaking power of Congress to presidential or military supervision or control.

It is said that other Presidents without congressional authority have taken possession of private business enterprises in order to settle labor disputes. But even if this be true, Congress has not thereby lost its exclusive constitutional authority to make laws necessary and proper to carry out the powers vested by the Constitution "in the Government of the United States, or any Department or Officer thereof." The Founders of this Nation entrusted the lawmaking power to the Congress alone in both good and bad times. It would do no good to recall the historical events, the fears of power and the hopes for freedom that lay behind their choice. Such a review would but confirm our holding that this seizure order cannot stand.

[Affirmed.][1]

Justice FRANKFURTER [concurring].

Although the considerations relevant to the legal enforcement of the principle of separation of powers seem to me more complicated and flexible than may appear from what Mr. Justice Black has written, I join his opinion because I thoroughly agree with the application of the principle to the circumstances of this case. [The Framers] rested the structure of our central government on the system of checks and balances. [Not] so long ago it was fashionable to find [that system] obstructive to effective government. It was easy to ridicule that system as outmoded—too easy. The experience for which the world has passed in our own day has made vivid the realization that the [Framers] were not inexperienced doctrinaires. These long-headed statesmen had no illusion that our people enjoyed biological or psychological or sociological immunities from the hazards of concentrated power. [Marshall's admonition in McCulloch] that "it is *a constitution* we are expounding" is especially relevant when the Court is required to give legal sanction to an underlying principle of the Constitution—that of separation of powers. "The great ordinances of the Constitution do not establish and divide fields of black and white." The issue before us can be met, and therefore should be, without attempting to define the President's powers comprehensively. [We must] put to one side considerations of what powers a President would have had if there had been no legislation whatever bearing on the authority asserted by the seizure or if the seizure had been only for a short, explicitly temporary period, to be terminated automatically unless Congressional approval [were given].

It cannot be contended that the President would have had power to issue this order had Congress explicitly negated such authority in formal legislation. [In view of the Taft–Hartley Act of 1947], Congress has expressed its will to withhold this power from the President as though it had said so in so many words. [In effect], Congress said to the President, "You may not seize. Please report to us and ask for seizure power if you think it is needed in a specific situation." [The] content of the three authorities of government is not to be derived from an abstract analysis. The areas are partly interacting, not wholly disjointed. The Constitution is a framework for government. Therefore the way the framework has consistently operated fairly establishes that it has operated according to its true nature. Deeply embedded traditional ways of conducting government cannot supplant the Constitution or legislation, but they give meaning to the words of a text or supply them. It is an inadmissibly narrow conception of American constitutional law to confine it to the words of the Constitution and to disregard the gloss which life has written upon them. In short, a systematic, unbroken, executive practice, long pursued to the knowledge of the Congress and never before questioned, engaged in by Presidents who have also sworn to uphold the Constitution, making as it were such

---

1. The Court divided 6–3. Although all but one of the concurring Justices—Justice Clark—joined the opinion as well as the judgment announced by Justice Black, the separate opinions included important variations on Justice Black's approach.

exercise of power part of the structure of our government, may be treated as a gloss on "executive Power" vested in the [President]. [Justice Frankfurter added an elaborate historical appendix to his opinion.] [But the] list of executive assertions of the power of seizure in circumstances comparable to the present reduces to three in the six-month period from June to December of 1941. [These] three isolated instances do not add up, either in number, scope, duration or contemporaneous legal justification, to the kind of executive construction of the Constitution [necessary to justify the action here]. Nor do they come to us sanctioned by long-continued acquiescence of Congress giving decisive weight to a construction by the Executive of its [powers].

Justice JACKSON, concurring in the judgment and opinion of the Court.

[A] judge, like an executive advisor, may be surprised at the poverty of really useful and unambiguous authority applicable to concrete problems of executive power as they actually present themselves. Just what our forefathers did envision, or would have envisioned had they foreseen modern conditions, must be divined from materials almost as enigmatic as the dreams Joseph was called upon to interpret for Pharaoh. A century and a half of partisan debate and scholarly speculation yields no net result but only supplies more or less apt quotations from respected resources on each side of any question. They largely cancel each other. And court decisions are indecisive because of the judicial practice of dealing with the largest questions in the most narrow way. The actual art of governing under our Constitution does not and cannot conform to judicial definitions of the power of any of its branches based on isolated clauses or even single Articles torn from context. While the Constitution diffuses power the better to secure liberty, it also contemplates that practice will integrate the dispersed powers into a workable government. It enjoins upon its branches separateness but interdependence, autonomy but reciprocity. Presidential powers are not fixed but fluctuate, depending upon their disjunction or conjunction with those of Congress. We may well begin by a somewhat over-simplified grouping of practical situations in which a President may doubt, or others may challenge, his powers, and by distinguishing roughly the legal consequences of this factor of relativity.

1. When the President acts pursuant to an express or implied authorization of Congress, his authority is at its maximum, for it includes all that he possesses in his own right plus all that Congress can delegate.[1] In these circumstances, and in these only, may he be said (for what it may be worth) to personify the federal sovereignty. If his act is held unconstitutional under these circumstances, it usually means that the Federal Government as an undivided whole lacks power. A seizure executed by the President pursuant to an Act of Congress would be supported by the strongest of presumptions and the widest latitude of judicial interpretation, and the burden of persuasion would rest heavily upon any who might attack it.

---

1. It is in this class of cases that we find the broadest recent statements of presidential power, including those relied on here. [Curtiss–Wright (1936; p. 403 below)] involved, not the question of the President's power to act without congressional authority, but the question of his right to act under and in accord with an Act of Congress. The constitutionality of the Act under which the President had proceeded was assailed on the ground that it delegated legislative powers to the President. Much of the Court's opinion is [dictum]. That case does not solve the present controversy. It recognized internal and external affairs as being in separate categories, and held that the strict limitation upon congressional delegations of power to the President over internal affairs does not apply with respect to delegations of power in external affairs. It was intimated that the President might act in external affairs without congressional authority, but not that he might act contrary to an [Act of Congress]. [Footnote by Justice Jackson.]

2. When the President acts in absence of either a congressional grant or denial of authority, he can only rely upon his own independent powers, but there is a zone of twilight in which he and Congress may have concurrent authority, or in which its distribution is uncertain. Therefore, congressional inertia, indifference or quiescence may sometimes, at least as a practical matter, enable, if not invite, measures on independent presidential responsibility. In this area, any actual test of power is likely to depend on the imperatives of events and contemporary imponderables rather than on abstract theories of law.

3. When the President takes measures incompatible with the expressed or implied will of Congress, his power is at its lowest ebb, for then he can rely only upon his own constitutional powers minus any constitutional powers of Congress over the matter. Courts can sustain exclusive presidential control in such a case only by disabling the Congress from acting upon the subject. Presidential claim to a power at once so conclusive and preclusive must be scrutinized with caution, for what is at stake is the equilibrium established by our constitutional system.

Into which of these classifications does this executive seizure of the steel industry fit? It is eliminated from the first by admission, for it is conceded that no congressional authorization exists for this seizure. [Can] it then be defended under flexible tests available to the second category? It seems clearly eliminated from that class because Congress has not left seizure of private property an open field but has covered it by three statutory policies inconsistent with this seizure. [This] leaves the current seizure to be justified only by the severe tests under the third grouping, where it can be supported only by any remainder of executive power after subtraction of such powers as Congress may have over the subject. In short, we can sustain the President only by holding that seizure of such strike-bound industries is within his domain and beyond control by [Congress].

The Solicitor General seeks the power of seizure in three clauses of the Executive Article, the first reading, "The executive Power shall be vested in a [President]." [The Government argues:] "In our view, this clause constitutes a grant of all the executive powers of which the Government is capable." If that be true, it is difficult to see why the forefathers bothered to add several specific items, including some trifling ones. [I] cannot accept the view that this clause is a grant in bulk of all conceivable executive power but regard it as an allocation to the presidential office of the generic powers thereafter stated. The clause on which the Government next relies is that "The President shall be Commander in Chief of the Army and Navy of the United States." [T]his loose appellation is sometimes advanced as support for any presidential action, internal or external, involving use of force, the idea being that it vests power to do anything, anywhere, that can be done with an army or navy. That seems to be the logic of an argument tendered at our bar—that the President having, on his own responsibility, sent American troops abroad derives from that act "affirmative power" to seize the means of producing a supply of steel for them. [No] doctrine that the Court could promulgate would seem to me more sinister and alarming than that a President whose conduct of foreign affairs is so largely uncontrolled, and often even is unknown, can vastly enlarge his mastery over the internal affairs of the country by his own commitment of the Nation's armed forces to some foreign venture. I do not, however, find it necessary or appropriate to consider the legal status of the Korean enterprise to discountenance argument based on it.

[The] Constitution expressly places in Congress power "to raise and *support* Armies" and "to *provide* and *maintain* a Navy." (Emphasis supplied.) This certainly lays upon Congress primary responsibility for supplying the armed forces. Congress alone controls the raising of revenues and their appropriation and may determine in what manner and by what means they shall be spent for military and naval procurement. [There] are indications that the Constitution did not contemplate that the title Commander in Chief *of the Army and Navy* will constitute him also Commander in Chief of the country, its industries and its inhabitants. He has no monopoly of "war powers," whatever they are. [That] military powers of the Commander in Chief were not to supersede representative government of internal affairs seems obvious from the Constitution and from elementary American history. The third clause in which the Solicitor General finds seizure powers is that "he shall take Care that the Laws be faithfully executed." That authority must be matched against [the due process clause of the Fifth Amendment]. One gives a governmental authority that reaches so far as there is law, the other gives a private right that authority shall go no farther. These signify about all there is of the principle that ours is a government of laws, not of men, and that we submit ourselves to rulers only if under rules.

The Solicitor General lastly grounds support of the seizure upon nebulous, inherent powers never expressly granted but said to have accrued to the office from the customs and claims of preceding administrations. The plea is for a resulting power to deal with a crisis or an emergency according to the necessities of the case, the unarticulated assumption being that necessity knows no law. Loose and irresponsible use of adjectives colors all nonlegal and much legal discussion of presidential powers. "Inherent" powers, "implied" powers, "incidental" powers, "plenary" powers, "war" powers and "emergency" powers are used, often interchangeably and without fixed or ascertainable meanings. The vagueness and generality of the clauses that set forth presidential powers afford a plausible basis for pressures within and without an administration for presidential action beyond that supported by those whose responsibility it is to defend his actions in court. The claim of inherent and unrestricted presidential powers has long been a persuasive dialectical weapon in political controversy. While it is not surprising that counsel should grasp support from such unadjudicated claims of power, a judge cannot accept self-serving press statements of the attorney for one of the interested parties as authority in answering a constitutional question, even if the advocate was himself.[2] But prudence has counseled that actual reliance on such nebulous claims stop short of provoking a judicial [test].

In view of the ease, expedition and safety with which Congress can grant and has granted large emergency powers, certainly ample to embrace this crisis, I am quite unimpressed with the argument that we should affirm possession of them without statute. Such power either has no beginning or it has no end. If it exists, it need submit to no legal restraint. I am not alarmed that it would plunge us straightway into dictatorship, but it is at least a step in that wrong direction. As to whether there is imperative necessity for such powers, it is relevant to note the gap that exists between the President's paper powers and his real powers. The Constitution does not disclose the measure of the actual controls wielded by the modern presidential [office]. Vast accretions of federal

2. Justice Jackson was the U.S. Attor-   Court in 1941.
ney General when he was named to the

power, eroded from that reserved by the States, have magnified the scope of presidential [activity].

Executive power has the advantage of concentration in a single head in whose choice the whole Nation has a part, making him the focus of public hopes and expectations. No other personality in public life can begin to compete with him in access to the public mind through modern methods of communications. By his prestige as head of state and his influence upon public opinion he exerts a leverage upon those who are supposed to check and balance his power which often cancels their effectiveness. Moreover, rise of the party system has made a significant extra constitutional supplement to real executive power. [I] have no illusion that any decision by this Court can keep power in the hands of Congress if it is not wise and timely in meeting its problems. A crisis that challenges the President equally, or perhaps primarily, challenges Congress. If not good law, there was worldly wisdom in the maxim attributed to Napoleon that "The tools belong to the man who can use them." We may say that power to legislate for emergencies belongs in the hands of Congress, but only Congress itself can prevent power from slipping through its [fingers]. With all its defects, delays and inconveniences, men have discovered no technique for long preserving free government except that the Executive be under the law, and that the law be made by parliamentary deliberations. Such institutions may be destined to pass away. But it is the duty of the Court to be last, not first, to give them up.[3]

Chief Justice VINSON, with whom Justice REED and Justice MINTON join, dissenting.

[Chief Justice Vinson's 43–page dissent, the longest of the opinions, emphasized that in deciding "the question of Presidential powers in this case, we must first consider the context in which those powers were exercised." He began with a review of "our responsibilities in the world community" in the post-World War II years. After reciting congressional actions assuring financial support for the Korean War, he continued:] The President has the duty to execute the foregoing legislative programs. Their successful execution depends upon continued production of steel and stabilized prices for steel. Accordingly, [when] a strike shutting down the entire basic steel industry was threatened, the President acted to avert a complete shutdown of steel production. [One] is not here called upon even to consider the possibility of executive seizure of a farm, a corner grocery store or even a single industrial plant. Such considerations arise only when one ignores the central fact of this case—that the Nation's entire basic steel production would have shut down completely if there had been no Government seizure. [Accordingly], if the President has any power under the Constitution to meet a critical situation in the absence of express

3. Each of the other Justices in the majority also wrote separate opinions. Justice Douglas' was a broad one; Justices Burton and Clark wrote more narrowly. Justice DOUGLAS concluded that the presidential seizure was legislative in nature; that it constituted "taking" in the constitutional sense, requiring just compensation under the Fifth Amendment; that the President has no power to raise revenues; and that the "branch of government that has the power to pay compensation for a seizure is the only one able to authorize a seizure." Justice BURTON concluded that the President's order "invaded the jurisdiction of Congress" because Congress had "prescribed for the President specific procedures, exclusive of seizure, for his use in meeting the present type of emergency." Justice CLARK, the only Justice in the majority who did not join Justice Black's opinion, similarly emphasized that Congress had prescribed methods to be followed by the President for emergencies such as this. He added, however, "that in the absence of such action by Congress, the President's independent power to act depends upon the gravity of the situation confronting the nation."

statutory authorization, there is no basis whatever for criticizing the exercise of such power in this [case]. We are not called upon today to expand the Constitution to meet a new situation. For, in this case, we need only look to history and time-honored principles of constitutional law. [A] review of executive action demonstrates that our Presidents have on many occasions exhibited the leadership contemplated by the Framers when they made the President Commander in Chief, and imposed upon him the trust to "take Care that the Laws be faithfully executed." With or without explicit statutory authorization, Presidents have at such times dealt with national emergencies by acting promptly and resolutely to enforce legislative programs, at least to save those programs until Congress could act. Congress and the courts have responded to such executive initiative with consistent approval. [Chief Justice Vinson undertook a lengthy examination of historical episodes from George Washington to Franklin D. Roosevelt, including:]

history

Beginning with the Bank Holiday Proclamation and continuing through World War II, executive leadership and initiative were characteristic of President Franklin D. Roosevelt's administration. [Six] months before Pearl Harbor, a dispute at a single aviation plant at Inglewood, California, interrupted a segment of the production of military [aircraft]. President Roosevelt ordered the seizure of the plant "pursuant to the powers vested in [him] by the Constitution and laws of the United States, as President [and] Commander in [Chief]." The Attorney General [Jackson] vigorously proclaimed that the President had the moral duty to keep this Nation's defense effort a "going concern." [Before and after Pearl Harbor], industrial concerns were seized to avert interruption of needed production. During the same period, the President directed seizure of the Nation's coal mines to remove an obstruction to the effective prosecution of the war. [This] is but a cursory summary of executive leadership. But it amply demonstrates that Presidents have taken prompt action to enforce the laws and protect the country whether or not Congress happened to provide in advance for the particular method of execution. [T]he fact that Congress and the courts have consistently recognized and given their support to such executive action indicates that such a power of seizure has been accepted throughout our [history].

example

moral duty
see p. 361 fn 2

Much of the argument in this case has been directed at straw men. We do not now have before us the case of a President acting solely on the basis of his own notions of the public welfare. Nor is there any question of unlimited executive power in this case. The President himself closed the door to any such claim when he sent his Message to Congress stating his purpose to abide by any action of Congress, whether approving or disapproving his seizure action. [The] absence of a specific statute authorizing seizure of the steel mills as a mode of executing the laws—both the military procurement program and the anti-inflation program—has not until today been thought to prevent the President from executing the laws. [Here], there is no statute prohibiting the action taken by the [President]. Executive inaction in [this] situation, courting national disaster, is foreign to the concept of energy and initiative in the Executive as created by the Founding Fathers. [The] broad executive power granted by Article II to an officer on duty 365 days a year cannot, it is said, be invoked to avert disaster. Instead, the President must confine himself to sending a message to Congress recommending action. Under this messenger-boy concept of the Office, the President cannot even act to preserve legislative programs from destruction so that Congress will have something left to act upon. [There is no question here that the possession] was other than temporary in character and subject to congressional direction—either approving, disapproving or regulating the manner in which the mills were to be administered and returned to

majority says there are 3!

practicality

the owners. [No] basis for claims of arbitrary action, unlimited powers or dictatorial usurpation of congressional power appears from the facts of this case. On the contrary, judicial, legislative and executive precedents throughout our history demonstrate that in this case the President acted in full conformity with his duties under the [Constitution].

THE STEEL SEIZURE CASE AND THE JACKSON ANALYSIS

1. *Dicta, holding, and competing analyses.* Does Justice Black recognize *any* "emergency powers" of the President? Does the majority of the Court? Is Justice Black's opinion, somewhat mechanically classifying all relevant governmental action into "legislative" or "executive" categories, unduly rigid and formalistic?[1] Are the problems "more complicated" than that, as Justice Frankfurter suggests? What holding does the majority truly agree upon? Does it go beyond the third category described by Justice Jackson? Does the case stand for any principle other than that the President may not establish domestic policy "incompatible with the expressed or implied will of Congress"?[2]

2. *The Jackson distinctions and their applicability.* a. *Domestic affairs.* Does Justice Jackson's distinction among three types of situations provide a useful general framework for the analysis of presidential power problems? To what extent do the other opinions accept that framework? To what extent do the various opinions accept Justice Frankfurter's view that unquestioned and continuous "executive practice" "may be treated as a gloss on 'Executive power'" granted by Art. II? How persuasive should such "practice" be in constitutional interpretation? Are the Jackson and Frankfurter analyses too open-ended to be useful?

Justice Jackson's first category—presidential action pursuant to congressional authority—refers to the most common variety of executive action. Justice Jackson's second category—presidential action in the context of congressional silence—presents greater difficulty. Justice Jackson suggests "a zone of twilight" in which President and Congress "may have concurrent authority." Note that Justice Jackson found that this case did not fall into this second category. Instead, he construed congressional silence—and refusals to grant the President statutory seizure authority—as a significant restraint on executive power;

1. Arguably, Justice Black's categorical statements were in part provoked by the broad arguments of the Government. Note, e.g., the arguments at the District Court hearing, printed in Westin, The Anatomy of a Constitutional Law Case (1958), 56–65. Consider the exchange between District Judge Pine and Assistant Attorney General Baldridge: *"The Court:* So [the Constitution] limited the powers of the Congress and limited the powers of the judiciary, but did not limit the powers of the Executive. Is that what you say? *Mr. Baldridge:* That is the way we read Article II of the Constitution. *The Court:* I see." A few days after the argument, President Truman issued a statement: "The powers of the President are derived from the Constitution, and they are limited, of course, by the provisions of the Constitution." For President Truman's subsequent reflections, see Truman, II Memoirs: Years of Trial and Hope (1956), 475–78, concluding: "Whatever the six justices of the Supreme Court meant by their differing opinions, [the President] must always act in a national emergency."

2. The Steel Seizure decision provoked extensive commentary. See, e.g., Kauper, "The Steel Seizure Case: Congress, the President, and the Supreme Court," 51 Mich. L.Rev. 141 (1952), and Corwin, "The Steel Seizure Case: A Judicial Brick Without Straw," 53 Colum.L.Rev. 53 (1953). For a useful historical study, see Marcus, Truman and the Steel Seizure Case: The Limits of Presidential Power (1977).

hence, the case fell into his third category. Was that a plausible reading of congressional silence? Contrast the apparently different inference drawn from congressional silence in the Dames & Moore case in 1981, p. 367 below. Congressional authority in the twilight zone typically stems from Art. I, § 8, powers.[3] But what is the source of executive power in that twilight zone? What are the "flexible tests" appropriate for that twilight zone? Is it in any event a presidential authority subject to being overridden by congressional action? Are there any situations in the domestic sphere that fall within Justice Jackson's third category: a presidential power to act even in the face of contrary congressional directions?[4] Are any such powers in fact granted by Art. II?

   b. *External affairs.* Can and should Justice Jackson's tripartite analysis be applied outside the domestic sphere? Are there more explicit constitutional grants of autonomous presidential authority as to external affairs? Note especially the controversy over the War Powers Resolution of 1973, a congressional effort to delineate guidelines for the use of armed forces in hostilities. Is that Resolution an exercise of congressional authority in Justice Jackson's second category—a congressional effort to speak where there long had been congressional silence in "a zone of twilight"? Or is it an exercise of congressional power in Justice Jackson's third category, an exercise that may improperly tread upon autonomous executive power? For an example of a challenge to presidential power to set foreign policy by making executive agreements (without the requirement of Senatorial consent to treaties), consider the next principal case, Dames & Moore.

PRESIDENTIAL AUTHORITY TO SET POLICY ON FOREIGN RELATIONS THROUGH EXECUTIVE AGREEMENTS

   Introduction. Over the years, the executive branch has frequently resorted to executive agreements rather than treaties in its foreign relations activities. Concerns have recurrently been voiced that the executive agreements route may unduly intrude upon the Senate's role by bypassing treaty-making. (Fears have also been voiced that executive agreements may be on a par with treaties and may thus be able to supersede prior legislation. Recall Missouri v. Holland, p. 252 above.) To a large extent, the magnitude of these risks turns on when such agreements are constitutionally justified. Are they supportable simply on

   3. Note that congressional power under the necessary and proper clause, Art. I, § 8, cl. 18, is not limited to implementation of powers specifically granted to Congress. Instead, it enables Congress to make all laws "necessary and proper for carrying into Execution the foregoing Powers, and *all other Powers* vested by this Constitution in the Government of the United States, or in any Department or Officer thereof." (Emphasis added.) Should this congressional implementation power be read as giving priority to congressional resolutions of conflicts between the legislative and executive branches in the "zone of twilight"? See generally Van Alstyne, "The Role of Congress in Determining Incidental Powers of the President and of the Federal Courts: A Comment on the Horizontal Effect of The Sweeping Clause," 40 Law & Contemp.Probs. 102 (1976).

   4. Of all the opinions in the Steel Seizure Case, Justice Jackson's has been the mostly widely relied on in judicial decisions and most praised in academic commentary. For an example of analyses akin to that of Justice Jackson, note several of the concurring opinions in the Pentagon Papers case (1971; p. 404 below). Note also Justice Rehnquist's prevailing opinion in the Iranian assets case, Dames & Moore v. Regan in 1981, below. See generally Chemerinsky, "Controlling Inherent Presidential Power: Providing a Framework for Judicial Review," 56 S.Cal. L.Rev. 863 (1983).

the basis of an inherent presidential authority? To what extent can executive agreements be justified as incidental to specified Art. II powers? Must all executive agreements be made in pursuance of a statute? The following materials sample the range of problems raised by the executive agreements device.

In an important consideration of executive agreements, United States v. Belmont, 301 U.S. 324 (1937), the Court sustained the validity of an executive agreement and held that it took precedence over conflicting state policy. Justice Sutherland, who had written Curtiss–Wright (p. 403 below) a year earlier, wrote for the majority. The agreement arose out of the American diplomatic recognition of the Soviet Union in 1933. At the same time as President Roosevelt recognized the U.S.S.R., an exchange of diplomatic correspondence between the President and Maxim Litvinov effected an assignment to the United States of all Soviet claims against Americans who held funds of Russian companies seized after the Revolution. The Belmont suit was brought by the United States in reliance upon that assignment, in order to recover funds deposited by a Russian corporation with a private New York banker. The lower courts dismissed the action on the ground that implementing the U.S.S.R.'s confiscation would violate the public policy of New York. Justice Sutherland's majority opinion emphasized that recognition, the establishment of diplomatic relations, and the assignment "were all parts of one transaction, resulting in an international compact between the two governments." He had no doubt that the negotiations and the agreements "were within the competence of the President": "in respect of what was done here, the Executive had authority to speak as the sole organ." And the assignment and agreement, unlike treaties, did not require the Senate's participation. He stated that "an international compact, as this was, is not always a treaty which requires the participation of the Senate. There are many such compacts, of which a protocol, a modus vivendi, a postal convention, and agreements like that now under consideration are illustrations." And the supremacy clause required that contrary state policies must give way. (The Litvinov Assignment resurfaced in the Court in United States v. Pink, 315 U.S. 203 (1942). Justice Douglas's opinion for the Court stated that the President "has the power to determine the policy [to] govern the question of recognition" and that, under the supremacy clause, such "international compacts and agreements as the Litvinov Assignment have a similar dignity" as treaties.)

2. *Sources of authority for executive agreements.* Does Belmont, against the background of Curtiss–Wright, support a broad autonomous presidential authority to enter into executive agreements? Or is it important to distinguish among constitutional sources for particular agreements? Is it useful to invoke the three-pronged analysis of Justice Jackson's opinion in the Steel Seizure Case? Many executive agreements fall within his first category: they are adopted pursuant to statutory authority, as in trade agreements legislation, authorizing modification of tariffs through presidential agreements. The Litvinov agreement involved in Belmont, by contrast, rested on the specifically delegated presidential authority regarding diplomatic recognition, in Art. II, § 3 (stating that the President "shall receive Ambassadors and other public Ministers"). As to such agreements, it is arguable that Congress possesses *no* authority to interfere with executive power. Could Congress, under the necessary and proper clause, enact guidelines for the negotiation of executive agreements? Is there a broader inherent executive power such as that suggested in Curtiss–Wright which may justify executive agreements? Consider the scope of the modern Court's endorsement of an executive agreement in the Dames & Moore case, which follows.

Dames & Moore v. Regan

453 U.S. 654, 101 S.Ct. 2972, 69 L.Ed.2d 918 (1981).

Justice REHNQUIST delivered the opinion of the Court.

[This] dispute involves various Executive Orders and regulations by which the President nullified attachments and liens on Iranian assets in the United States, directed that these assets be transferred to Iran, and suspended claims against Iran that may be presented to an International Claims Tribunal. This action was taken in an effort to comply with an Executive Agreement between the United States and Iran. [On] November 4, 1979, the American Embassy in Tehran was seized and our diplomatic personnel were captured and held hostage. In response to that crisis, President Carter, acting pursuant to the International Emergency Economic Powers Act [IEEPA], declared a national emergency on November 14, 1979, and blocked the removal or transfer of "all property and interests in property of the Government of Iran, its instrumentalities and controlled entities and the Central Bank of Iran which are or become subject to the jurisdiction of the [United States]." [On] November 15, 1979, the Treasury Department's Office of Foreign Assets Control issued a regulation providing that "[unless] licensed or authorized [any] attachment, judgment, decree, lien, execution, garnishment, or other judicial process is null and void with respect to any property in which on or since [November 14, 1979,] there existed an interest of Iran."

On December 19, 1979, petitioner Dames & Moore filed suit in the United States District Court [against] the Government of Iran, the Atomic Energy Organization of Iran, and a number of Iranian banks. In its complaint, petitioner alleged that its wholly owned subsidiary, Dames & Moore International, S. R. L., was a party to a written contract with the Atomic Energy Organization, and that the subsidiary's entire interest in the contract had been assigned to petitioner. [Petitioner] contended [that] it was owed $3,436,694.30 plus interest for services performed under the contract prior to the date of termination. The District Court issued orders of attachment directed against property of the defendants, and the property of certain Iranian banks was then attached to secure any judgment that might be entered against them.

On January 20, 1981, the Americans held hostage were released by Iran pursuant to an [Executive Agreement] entered into the day before. The Agreement stated that "[it] is the purpose of [the United States and Iran] [to] terminate all litigation as between the Government of each party and the nationals of the other, and to bring about the settlement and termination of all such claims through binding arbitration." In furtherance of this goal, the Agreement called for the establishment of an Iran–United States Claims Tribunal which would arbitrate any claims not settled within six months. Awards of the Claims Tribunal are to be "final and binding" and "enforceable [in] the courts of any nation in accordance with its laws." Under the Agreement, the United States is obligated "to terminate all legal proceedings in United States courts involving claims of United States persons and institutions against Iran and its state enterprises, to nullify all attachments and judgments obtained therein, to prohibit all further litigation based on such claims, and to bring about the termination of such claims through binding arbitration." In addition, the United States must "act to bring about the transfer" by July 19, 1981, of all Iranian assets held in this country by American banks. One billion dollars of these assets will be deposited in a security account in the Bank of England, to the account of the Algerian Central Bank, and used to satisfy awards rendered against Iran by the Claims Tribunal. On January 19, 1981, President Carter issued a series of Executive Orders implementing the terms of the agreement. [On] February 24, 1981, President Reagan issued an Executive Order in which he "ratified" the January 19th Executive Orders. Moreover, he "suspended" all "claims which may be presented to [the] Tribunal" and provided that such claims "shall have no legal effect in any action now pending in any court of the United States." The suspension of any particular claim terminates if the Claims Tribunal determines that it has no jurisdiction over that claim; claims are discharged for all purposes when the Claims Tribunal either awards some recovery and that amount is paid, or determines that no recovery is [due].

[The] parties and the lower courts [have] all agreed that much relevant analysis is contained in [Youngstown]. Although we have in the past found and do today find Justice Jackson's classification of executive actions into three general categories analytically useful, [Jackson] himself recognized that his three categories represented "a somewhat over-simplified grouping," and it is doubtless the case that executive action in any particular instance falls, not neatly in one of three pigeonholes, but rather at some point along a spectrum running from explicit congressional authorization to explicit congressional prohibition. This is particularly true as respects cases such as the one before us, involving responses to international crises the nature of which Congress can hardly have been expected to anticipate in any detail.

[The Government] has principally relied on § 203 of the IEEPA as authorization for these actions. Section 1702 (a)(1) provides in part: "[T]he President may [nullify], void, prevent or prohibit, any acquisition, holding, withholding, use, transfer, withdrawal, transportation, importation or exportation of, or dealing in, or exercising any right, power, or privilege with respect to, or transactions involving, any property in which any foreign country or a national thereof has any interest; by any person, or with respect to any property, subject to the jurisdiction of the United States." The Government contends that the acts of "nullifying" the attachments and ordering the "transfer" of the frozen assets are specifically authorized by the plain language of the above [statute]. Because the President's action in nullifying the attachments and ordering the transfer of the assets was taken pursuant to specific congressional authorization, it is "supported by the strongest of presumptions and the widest latitude of judicial interpretation, and the burden of persuasion would rest heavily upon any who might attack it." Youngstown (Jackson, J., concurring). Under the circumstances of this case, we cannot say that petitioner has sustained that heavy burden. A contrary ruling would mean that the Federal Government as a whole lacked the power exercised by the President and that we are not prepared to say.

[T]here remains the question of the President's authority to suspend claims pending in American courts. Such claims have, of course, an existence apart from the attachments which accompanied them. In terminating these claims, [the] President purported to act under authority of both the IEEPA and the so-called "Hostage Act" [of 1868]. [We conclude] that neither the IEEPA nor the Hostage Act constitutes specific authorization of the President's [action]. [However, this] is not to say that these statutory provisions are entirely irrelevant to the question of the validity of the President's action. We think both statutes highly relevant in the looser sense of indicating congressional acceptance of a broad scope for executive action in circumstances such as those presented in this case. [T]he IEEPA delegates broad authority to the President to act in times of national emergency with respect to property of a foreign country. The Hostage Act similarly indicates congressional willingness that the President have broad discretion when responding to the hostile acts of foreign sovereigns. [We] cannot ignore the general tenor of Congress' legislation in this area in trying to determine whether the President is acting alone or at least with the acceptance of Congress. [Congress] cannot anticipate and legislate with regard to every possible action the President may find it necessary to take or every possible situation in which he might act. Such failure of Congress specifically to delegate authority does not, "especially [in] the areas of foreign policy and national security," imply "congressional disapproval" of action taken by the Executive. On the contrary, the enactment of legislation closely related to the question of the President's authority in a particular case which evinces legislative intent to accord the President broad discretion may be considered to "invite" "measures on independent presidential responsibility," Youngstown (Jackson, J., concurring). At least this is so where there is no contrary indication of legislative intent and when, as here, there is a history of congressional acquiescence in conduct of the sort engaged in by the President. It is to that history which we now turn.

Not infrequently in affairs between nations, outstanding claims by nationals of one country against the government of another country are "sources of friction" between the two sovereigns. [United States v. Pink.] To resolve these difficulties, nations have often entered into agreements settling the claims of their respective nationals. As one treatise writer puts it, international agreements settling claims by nationals of one state against the government of another "are established international practice reflecting traditional international theory." L. Henkin, Foreign Affairs and the Constitution 262 (1972). Consistent with that principle, the United States has repeatedly exercised its sovereign authority to settle the claims of its nationals against foreign countries. Though those settlements have sometimes been made by treaty, there has also been a longstanding practice of settling such claims by executive agreement without the advice and consent of the Senate. Under such agreements, the President has agreed to renounce or extinguish claims of United States nationals against foreign governments in return for lump-sum payments or the establishment of arbitration procedures. [It] is clear that the practice of settling claims continues today. Since 1952, the President has entered into at least 10 binding settlements with foreign nations, including an $80 million settlement with the People's Republic of China.

Crucial to our decision today is the conclusion that Congress has implicitly approved the practice of claim settlement by executive agreement. This is best demonstrated by Congress' enactment of the International Claims Settlement Act of 1949. [Over] the years Congress has frequently amended the International Claims Settlement Act to provide for particular problems arising out of settlement agreements, thus demonstrating Congress' continuing acceptance of the President's claim settlement authority. [Finally,] the legislative history of the IEEPA further reveals that Congress has accepted the authority of the Executive to enter into settlement agreements. Though the IEEPA was enacted to provide for some limitation on the President's emergency powers, Congress stressed that "[nothing] in this act is intended [to] interfere with the authority of the President to [block assets], or to impede the settlement of claims of U.S. citizens against foreign countries."[1] In addition to congressional acquiescence in the President's power to settle claims, prior cases of this Court have also recognized that the President does have some measure of power to enter into

---

1. Indeed, Congress has consistently failed to object to this longstanding practice of claim settlement by executive agreement, even when it has had an opportunity to do so. In 1972, Congress entertained legislation relating to congressional oversight of such agreements. But Congress took only limited [action]. [Footnote by Justice Rehnquist.]

executive agreements without obtaining the advice and consent of the Senate. [United States v. Pink.]

[In] light of all of the foregoing—the inferences to be drawn from the character of the legislation Congress has enacted in the area, such as the IEEPA and the Hostage Act, and from the history of acquiescence in executive claims settlement—we conclude that the President was authorized to suspend pending [claims]. As Justice Frankfurter pointed out in Youngstown, "a systematic, unbroken, executive practice, long pursued to the knowledge of the Congress and never before questioned [may] be treated as a gloss on 'Executive Power' vested in the President by § 1 of Art. II." Past practice does not, by itself, create power, but "long-continued practice, known to and acquiesced in by Congress, would raise a presumption that the [action] had been [taken] in pursuance of its [consent]." [In] light of the fact that Congress may be considered to have consented to the President's action in suspending claims, we cannot say that action exceeded the President's powers. Our conclusion is buttressed by the fact that the means chosen by the President to settle the claims of American nationals provided an alternative forum, the Claims Tribunal, which is capable of providing meaningful [relief]. [Just] as importantly, Congress has not disapproved of the action taken here. Though Congress has held hearings on the Iranian Agreement itself, Congress has not enacted legislation, or even passed a resolution, indicating its displeasure with the Agreement. Quite the contrary, the relevant Senate Committee has stated that the establishment of the Tribunal is "of vital importance to the United States." We are thus clearly not confronted with a situation in which Congress has in some way resisted the exercise of Presidential authority. Finally, we re-emphasize the narrowness of our decision. We do not decide that the President possesses plenary power to settle claims, even as against foreign governmental entities. [But] where, as here, the settlement of claims has been determined to be a necessary incident to the resolution of a major foreign policy dispute between our country and another, and where, as here, we can conclude that Congress acquiesced in the President's action, we are not prepared to say that the President lacks the power to settle such claims.[2]

———

Some questions on Dames & Moore. Is the approach of Dames & Moore reconcilable with that of Justice Black's opinion in Youngstown? Justice Rehnquist in Dames & Moore seemingly followed the Youngstown approaches of Justices Jackson and Frankfurter more closely than Justice Black's. Was Justice Rehnquist's view that Congress had given legislative approval to the executive agreement consistent with the implications drawn from congressional silence in Youngstown? Is Koh, The National Security Constitution: Sharing Power after the Iran–Contra Affair (1990), 140, persuasive in arguing that Dames & Moore "not only inverted the Steel Seizure holding" (construing failure of Congress to approve the Presidential Act as legislative disapproval), "but also condoned legislative inactivity at a time that demanded interbranch dialogue and bipartisan consensus"? Koh notes, however, that the Dames & Moore ruling is understandable in view of the crisis atmosphere at the time and the national support for the hostage agreement. But Koh adds that the "Court should have demanded more specific legislative approval for the President's far-reaching measures."

2. Opinions concurring in part, by Justices POWELL and STEVENS, are omitted.

Does Dames & Moore (as well as the Court's upholding of every executive agreement it has confronted) suggest that presidential policy-making in the foreign affairs area stands on much stronger footing than that in the domestic sphere? Is there adequate constitutional justification for that difference?

PRESIDENT, CONGRESS, AND THE USE OF ARMED FORCES

The respective roles of President and Congress in decisions to commit military forces overseas are among the most contentious issues in American history. The divisive national debate begun in the late 1960s about American military involvement in Southeast Asia launched the modern concern with the problem. Usually, the White House claimed autonomous authority under the constitutional powers of the President, especially as Commander in Chief. Sometimes, Congress sought to interpose its judgment, relying especially on its power over spending, to "declare War," and to "raise and support Armies."

The Supreme Court has not undertaken to resolve this separation of powers dispute. True, a number of lawsuits were brought to challenge the legality the American engagement in Vietnam. Some lower courts denied justiciability; others rejected attacks on the war on the merits. The Court denied certiorari in all the cases, albeit sometimes with dissents. See e.g., Mora v. McNamara, 389 U.S. 934 (1967). The lack of authoritative Court pronouncements, however, does not make the issue any less a constitutional one. During the Vietnam era, the major forum for constitutional debates was the Senate Committee on Foreign Relations under the chairmanship of Senator J. William Fulbright. In 1967, the Committee produced a lengthy Report, "National Commitments." The Committee examined with special care the twentieth century expansions of executive power, noting that recent Presidents had "all asserted unrestricted executive authority to commit the armed forces without the consent of Congress, and Congress, for the most part, has acquiesced in the transfer of its war power to the [executive branch]. Claims to unlimited executive authority over the use of armed force are made on grounds of both legitimacy and necessity. The committee finds both sets of contentions unsound, rejects the contention that the war powers as spelled out in the Constitution are obsolete, and strongly recommends that the Congress reassert its constitutional authority over the use of the armed forces."[1] In the wake of the Vietnam War[2] (and the Watergate controversy), Congress sought at last to provide guidelines for the future use of armed forces. It adopted (overriding President Nixon's veto) a joint resolution, the War Powers Resolution of 1973, an unusual, structural, quasi-constitutional variety of congressional action,

1. For a different emphasis, see Sofaer, "The Presidency, War, and Foreign Affairs ...," 40 Law & Contemp. Probs. 12 (1976), warning against attributing "the evils produced by our recent Presidents and Congresses to the violation of imagined norms allegedly established by the leaders of our constitutional period."

2. For an incisive assessment of the American military efforts in Indochina, see two 1990 articles and a book by John Hart Ely, "The American War in Indochina, Part I: The (Troubled) Constitutionality of the War They Told Us About," 42 Stan.L.Rev. 877 (1990), "The American War In Indochina, Part II: The Unconstitutionality of the War They Didn't Tell Us About," 42 Stan. L.Rev. 1093 (1990), and War and Responsibility: Constitutional Lessons of Vietnam and Its Aftermath (1993). Ely contends that American engagement in Vietnam "was constitutional under currently prevailing notions of congressional authorization [including appropriations bills]," but that "the rest of the American war in Indochina [in Laos and Cambodia] was unconstitutional."

focusing not on substantive policy but on processes and relationships. Excerpts from the War Powers Resolution follow.

PURPOSE AND POLICY

Sec. 2. (a) It is the purpose of this joint resolution to fulfill the intent of the framers of the Constitution of the United States and insure that the collective judgment of both the Congress and the President will apply to the introduction of United States Armed Forces into hostilities, or into situations where imminent involvement in hostilities is clearly indicated by the circumstances, and to the continued use of such forces in hostilities or in such situations.

(b) Under article I, section 8, of the Constitution, it is specifically provided that the Congress shall have the power to make all laws necessary and proper for carrying into execution, not only its own powers but also all other powers vested by the Constitution in the Government of the United States, or in any department or officer thereof.

(c) The constitutional powers of the President as Commander-in-Chief to introduce United States Armed Forces into hostilities, or into situations where imminent involvement in hostilities is clearly indicated by the circumstances, are exercised only pursuant to (1) a declaration of war, (2) specific statutory authorization, or (3) a national emergency created by attack upon the United States, its territories or possessions, or its armed forces.

CONSULTATION

Sec. 3. The President in every possible instance shall consult with Congress before introducing United States Armed Forces into hostilities or into situations where imminent involvement in hostilities is clearly indicated by the circumstances, and after every such introduction shall consult regularly with the Congress until United States Armed Forces are no longer engaged in hostilities or have been removed from such situations.

REPORTING

Sec. 4. (a) In the absence of a declaration of war, in any case in which United States Armed Forces are introduced—

(1) into hostilities or into situations where imminent involvement in hostilities is clearly indicated by the circumstances;

(2) into the territory, airspace or waters of a foreign nation, while equipped for combat, except for deployments which relate solely to supply, replacement, repair, or training of such forces; or

(3) in numbers which substantially enlarge United States Armed Forces equipped for combat already located in a foreign nation; the President shall submit within 48 hours to the Speaker of the House of Representatives and to the President pro tempore of the Senate a report, in writing, setting forth [the circumstances necessitating the introduction of "[armed forces]," "the constitutional and legislative authority for such introductions," and "such other information as the Congress may request."]

CONGRESSIONAL ACTION

Sec. 5. [(b)] Within sixty calendar days after a report is submitted or is required to be submitted pursuant to section 4(a)(1), whichever is earlier, the President shall terminate any use of United States Armed Forces with respect to which such report was submitted (or required to be submitted), unless the Congress (1) has declared war or has enacted a specific authorization for such use of United States Armed Forces, (2) has extended by law such sixty-day period, or (3) is physically unable to meet as a result of an armed attack upon the United States. Such sixty-day period shall be extended for not more than an additional thirty days if the President determines and certifies to the Congress in writing that unavoidable military necessity respecting the safety of United States Armed Forces requires the continued use of such armed forces in the course of bringing about a prompt removal of such forces.

(c) Notwithstanding subsection (b), at any time that United States Armed Forces are engaged in hostilities outside the territory of the United States, [without] a declaration of war or specific statutory authorization, such forces shall be removed by the President if the Congress so directs by concurrent [resolution].

INTERPRETATION OF JOINT RESOLUTION

Sec. 8. (a) Authority to introduce United States Armed Forces into hostilities or into situations wherein involvement in hostilities is clearly indicated by the circumstances shall not be inferred—

(1) from any provision of law (whether or not in effect before the date of the enactment of this joint resolution), including any provision contained in any appropriation Act, unless such provision specifically authorizes the introduction of United States Armed Forces into hostilities or into such situations and states that it is intended to constitute specific statutory authorization within the meaning of this joint resolution; or

(2) from any treaty heretofore or hereafter ratified unless such treaty is implemented by legislation specifically authorizing the introduction of United States Armed Forces into hostilities or into such situations and stating that it is intended to constitute specific statutory authorization within the meaning of this joint [resolution].

(d) Nothing in this joint resolution—

(1) is intended to alter the constitutional authority of the Congress or of the President, or the provisions of existing treaties; or

(2) shall be construed as granting any authority to the President with respect to the introduction of United States Armed Forces into hostilities or into situations wherein involvement in hostilities is clearly indicated by the circumstances which authority he would not have had in the absence of this joint [resolution].

———

1. *The War Powers Resolution: Constitutional problems?* The presidential veto that Congress overrode in adopting the War Powers Resolution in 1973 rested heavily on alleged constitutional defects. President Nixon especially objected to provisions which "would attempt to take away, by a mere legislative act, authorities which the President has properly exercised under the Constitution for almost 200 years." He singled out § 5(b), requiring the President to withdraw American forces from foreign hostilities within 60 days unless Congress grants authorization, and § 5(c), requiring immediate withdrawal of forces if Congress so directs by concurrent resolution—a resolution not subject to presidential veto. President Nixon was "particularly disturbed by the fact that certain of the President's constitutional powers as Commander-in-Chief of the Armed Forces would terminate automatically" without "overt congressional action." He insisted that Congress was in effect "attempting to increase its

policy-making role through a provision which requires it to take absolutely no action at all. [O]ne cannot become a responsible partner unless one is prepared to take responsible action." Can the legislative veto aspects of the Resolution, in Sec. 5(c), survive constitutional scrutiny in light of the analysis in Chadha, p. 375 below?

In addition to the issues raised in the President Nixon's veto message, does the Resolution present other constitutional difficulties? Note that the Resolution does not limit the use of armed forces to formal declarations of war; it also mentions "specific statutory authorization," though it excludes mere congressional appropriations. Are the congressional "authorization[s]" recognized by the Resolution constitutionally adequate alternatives for formal declarations of war? Can a measure such as the Resolution, designed to provide a legal framework for the resolution of executive-legislative conflicts in this area, adequately deal with the varying circumstances arising in foreign relations? Or must resolution of conflicts between the branches inevitably turn upon the political processes of negotiation and accommodation?

2. *Practical impacts.* Most observers agree that the War Powers Resolution has not effectively restrained executive discretion. Presidents have quite regularly ignored it, usually claiming its inapplicability or unconstitutionality, and Congress has never taken formal action under the Resolution. The reasons for the Resolution's ineffectiveness include the fact that it does not cover short-term military involvements. To the extent these can be completed quickly and in light of the 60–day time limit of Sec. 5(b), President Ford in the 1970s used troops in Vietnam to evacuate American citizens and President Carter launched an unsuccessful military rescue of American hostages in Iran in April 1980. President Reagan used armed forces in Grenada in 1983, and a surgical air strike against Libya in 1986. Moreover, the Resolution had no practical effect in curbing "brief" military interventions that might escalate into longer involvements. Thus, President Reagan's use of troops in Lebanon in 1982 lasted until early 1984. When, in response to Iraq's invasion of Kuwait, President Bush sent massive American forces to Saudi Arabia in August 1990, he relied on his constitutional powers as Commander in Chief; like earlier Presidents, he denied the efficacy of the 1973 Resolution. When he increased the number of American troops in the Persian Gulf in November 1990, Bush acted in order to assure that the nation would have an "adequate offensive option." This decision set off a major constitutional debate. Near the end of November, the U.N. Security Council voted to authorize "all means necessary" to remove Iraq from Kuwait if it did not withdraw by Jan. 15, 1991. In the same month, 54 Members of Congress brought suit to prevent the President from initiating an offensive attack against Iraq without explicit congressional authorization. The trial court dismissed the suit for lack of "ripeness," but agreed with the major contentions in a memorandum submitted by a group of law professors: the Court stated that it had "no hesitation in concluding that an offensive entry into Iraq by several-hundred-thousand United States servicemen could be described as a 'war' within the meaning of the [Constitution]. To put it another way: the Court is not prepared to read out of the Constitution the clause granting to the Congress, and to it alone, the authority 'to declare War.'" Dellums v. Bush, 752 F.Supp. 1141 (D.D.C.1990). In the ensuing weeks, the constitutional debates intensified and, when the issue reached the floor of Congress, there was widespread agreement that congressional authorization *was* necessary if the nation was to embark on offensive warfare. On January 12, 1991, Congress, by a relatively narrow margin, adopted a Joint Resolution authorizing the President "to use United States Armed Forces" pursuant to the U.N. Resolution.

American aerial warfare against Iraq commenced soon after; the ground war against Iraq began on Feb. 24, 1991, and ended 100 hours later.

The general ineffectiveness of the War Powers Resolution has produced considerable discussion about possible revisions of the Resolution. See, e.g., Ely, "Suppose Congress Wanted a War Powers Act That Worked," 88 Colum.L.Rev. 1379 (1988), stating: "*No* statute in this area is likely to prove effective so long as the President continues to protect his turf by condemning attempts at congressional 'intervention' as illegitimate. [Thus] the most important need is probably for socialization—an acceptance on all sides of the constitutional norm that wars must be authorized by Congress." He states as well: "In large measure the tale of the [Resolution] has been a tale of congressional spineless-ness." He suggests that the general idea of Congress committing itself to accountability for future wars is not "unthinkable." The 1973 effort, he adds, "did not sufficiently plan for presidential defiance. However, [this] defect can be repaired, if Congress still has the will to be held accountable." See also Glennon, Constitutional Diplomacy (1990), and Koh, The National Security Constitution (1990). Should Congress adopt a Resolution to authorize courts to resolve questions of whether the Resolution's withdrawal deadlines have been violated, as Ely suggests? Should courts view such questions as justiciable? Note that Choper, in Judicial Review and the National Political Process (1980), argues that courts should decline to resolve any separation of powers dispute, much as he claimed that courts should not adjudicate claims that Congress has exceeded federalism-based bounds on its delegated powers. Recall chap. 2 above, at p. 112.

SECTION 2. SEPARATION OF POWERS: CONGRESSIONAL ENCROACHMENTS ON THE EXECUTIVE'S DOMAIN

In most of the materials that follow, the recurrent claim is that congressional action interferes unduly with presidential functions. Consider especially whether the Court of the 1980s tended to follow Justice Black's quite sweeping, formalistic approach in Youngstown, or whether it was more inclined to the more discriminating, functional approach of Justice Jackson in that case.

sweeping/formal
v
discriminating/functional

INS v. Chadha

462 U.S. 919, 103 S.Ct. 2764, 77 L.Ed.2d 317 (1983).

Chief Justice BURGER delivered the opinion of the Court.

[These consolidated cases present] a challenge to the constitutionality of the provision in § 244(c)(2) of the Immigration and Nationality Act authorizing one House of Congress, by resolution, to invalidate the decision of the Executive Branch, pursuant to authority delegated by Congress to the Attorney General of the United States, to allow a particular deportable alien to remain in the United States. [The 1952 Act authorized the Attorney General to suspend deportation of a deportable alien if the alien met specified conditions and would suffer "extreme hardship" if deported. The Attorney General was required to report to Congress on each such suspension. Sec. 244(c)(2), the provision challenged here, provided that one House of Congress could veto the Attorney

grant/take away

General's determination that an alien should not be deported. Chadha was an East Indian born in Kenya who had overstayed his student visa and was thus deportable. The Attorney General suspended his deportation pursuant to the Act and notified Congress of his action. A year and a half after Chadha's deportation was suspended, the House of Representatives passed a resolution under § 244(c)(2) that the deportation "should not be suspended," after a House Committee indicated that Chadha and others did not meet the statutory requirements, particularly with regard to "hardship." The House resolution was not submitted to the Senate or presented to the President. The Court of Appeals held the House action unconstitutional as a violation of separation of powers. In affirming that decision, Chief Justice Burger's majority opinion rejected several challenges to the authority of the Court to resolve the issue raised. He found, for example, that the one-House veto provision was severable from the rest of § 244 and that Chadha had standing to challenge the constitutionality of the one-House veto. He also rejected the argument that the veto issue presented a "nonjusticiable political question." The Chief Justice then turned to the merits of the separation of powers challenge:]

A. [The] fact that a given law or procedure is efficient, convenient, and useful in facilitating functions of government, standing alone, will not save it if it is contrary to the Constitution. Convenience and efficiency are not the primary objectives—or the hallmarks—of democratic government and our inquiry is sharpened rather than blunted by the fact that Congressional veto provisions are appearing with increasing frequency in statutes which delegate authority to executive and independent agencies. [Justice White] undertakes to make a case for the proposition that the one-House veto is a useful "political invention," and we need not challenge that assertion. [But] policy arguments supporting even useful "political inventions" are subject to the demands of the Constitution which defines powers and, with respect to this subject, sets out just how those powers are to be exercised. Explicit and unambiguous provisions of the Constitution prescribe and define the respective functions of the Congress and of the Executive in the legislative process. Since the precise terms of those familiar provisions are critical to the resolution of this case, we set them out verbatim.[1] [These] provisions of Art. I are integral parts of the constitutional design for the separation of powers. [We] find that the purposes underlying the Presentment Clauses, Art. I, § 7, cls. 2, 3, and the bicameral requirement of Art. I, § 1 and § 7, cl. 2, guide our resolution of the important question presented [here].

The Presentment Clauses. The records of the Constitutional Convention reveal that the requirement that all legislation be presented to the President before becoming law was uniformly accepted by the Framers. [During] the final debate on Art. I, § 7, cl. 2, James Madison expressed concern that it might easily be evaded by the simple expedient of calling a proposed law a "resolu-

---

1. The Chief Justice quoted the following provisions of Art. I: "All legislative Powers herein granted shall be vested in a Congress of the United States, which shall consist of a Senate *and* a House of Representatives." Art. I, § 1; "Every Bill which shall have passed the House of Representatives *and* the Senate, *shall*, before it become a Law, be presented to the [President]." Art. I, § 7, cl. 2 [one of the Presentment Clauses]; "*Every* Order, Resolution, or Vote to which the Concurrence of the Senate and House of Representatives may be necessary (except on a question of Adjournment) *shall be* presented to the President of the United States; and before the Same shall take Effect, *shall be* approved by him, or being disapproved by him, *shall be* repassed by two thirds of the Senate and House of Representatives, according to the Rules and Limitations prescribed in the Case of a Bill." Art. I, § 7, cl. 3 [another Presentment Clause]. [Emphases by the Chief Justice.]

tion" or "vote" rather than a "bill." As a consequence, Art. I, § 7, cl. 3 was added. [The] decision to provide the President with a limited and qualified power to nullify proposed legislation by veto was based on the profound conviction of the Framers that the powers conferred on Congress were the powers to be most carefully circumscribed. It is beyond doubt that lawmaking was a power to be shared by both Houses and the [President].

Bicameralism. The bicameral requirement of Art. I, §§ 1, 7 was of scarcely less concern to the Framers than was the Presidential veto and indeed the two concepts are interdependent. By providing that no law could take effect without the concurrence of the prescribed majority of the Members of both Houses, the Framers reemphasized their belief [that] legislation should not be enacted unless it has been carefully and fully considered by the Nation's elected officials. [After quoting from James Wilson, Alexander Hamilton, and Joseph Story, the Chief Justice continued:] We see therefore that the Framers were acutely conscious that the bicameral requirement and the Presentment Clauses would serve essential constitutional functions. The President's participation in the legislative process was to protect the Executive Branch from Congress and to protect the whole people from improvident laws. The division of the Congress into two distinctive bodies assures that the legislative power would be exercised only after opportunity for full study and debate in separate settings. The President's unilateral veto power, in turn, was limited by the power of two thirds of both Houses of Congress to overrule a veto thereby precluding final arbitrary action of one person. It emerges clearly that the prescription for legislative action in Art. I, §§ 1, 7 represents the Framers' decision that the legislative power of the Federal government be exercised in accord with a single, finely wrought and exhaustively considered, procedure.

[Although] not "hermetically" sealed from one another, the powers delegated to the three Branches are functionally identifiable. [When] the Executive acts, he presumptively acts in an executive or administrative capacity as defined in Art. II. And when, as here, one House of Congress purports to act, it is presumptively acting within its assigned sphere. Beginning with this presumption, we must nevertheless establish that the challenged action under [the law] is of the kind to which the procedural requirements of Art. I, § 7 apply. Not every action taken by either House is subject to the bicameralism and presentment requirements of Art. I. Whether actions taken by either House are, in law and fact, an exercise of legislative power depends not on their form but upon "whether they contain matter which is properly to be regarded as legislative in its character and effect." Examination of the action taken here by one House [reveals] that it was essentially legislative in purpose and effect. In purporting to exercise power defined in Art. I, § 8, cl. 4 to "establish an uniform Rule of Naturalization," the House took action that had the purpose and effect of altering the legal rights, duties and relations of persons, including the Attorney General, Executive Branch officials and Chadha, all outside the legislative branch. [The] one-House veto operated in this case to overrule the Attorney General and mandate Chadha's deportation; absent the House action, Chadha would remain in the United States. Congress has *acted* and its action has altered Chadha's status.

The legislative character of the one-House veto in this case is confirmed by the character of the Congressional action it supplants. Neither the House of Representatives nor the Senate contends that, absent the veto [provision] either of them, or both of them acting together, could effectively require the Attorney General to deport an alien once the Attorney General, in the exercise of legislatively delegated authority,[2] had determined the alien should remain in the United States. Without the challenged [provision], this could have been achieved, if at all, only by legislation requiring deportation.

[The] nature of the decision implemented by the one-House veto in this case further manifests its legislative character. After long experience with the clumsy, time consuming private bill procedure, Congress made a deliberate choice to delegate to the Executive Branch [the] authority to allow deportable aliens to remain in this country in certain specified circumstances. It is not disputed that this choice to delegate authority is precisely the kind of decision that can be implemented only in accordance with the procedures set out in Art. I. Disagreement with the Attorney General's decision on Chadha's deportation--that is, Congress' decision to deport Chadha—no less than Congress' original choice to delegate to the Attorney General the authority to make that decision, involves determinations of policy that Congress can implement in only one way: bicameral passage followed by presentment to the President. Congress must abide by its delegation of authority until that delegation is legislatively altered or revoked.

Finally, we see that when the Framers intended to authorize either House of Congress to act alone and outside of its prescribed bicameral legislative role, they narrowly and precisely defined the procedure for such action. There are but four provisions in the Constitution, explicit and unambiguous, by which one House may act alone with the unreviewable force of law, not subject to the President's veto: [The Chief Justice referred to the power of the House to initiate impeachments, the Senate's power to conduct trials on impeachment charges, the Senate's power over Presidential appointments, and the Senate's power to ratify treaties.] These carefully defined exceptions from presentment and bicameralism [provide] further support for the conclusion that Congressional authority is not to be [implied]. Since it is clear that the action by the House under § 244(c)(2) was not within any of the express constitutional exceptions authorizing one House to act alone, and equally clear that it was an exercise of legislative power, that action was subject to the standards prescribed in Article I.[3]

2. Congress protests that affirming the Court of Appeals in this case will sanction "lawmaking by the [Attorney General]." [To] be sure, some administrative agency action—rule making, for example—may resemble "lawmaking." [But when] the Attorney General performs his duties pursuant to § 244, he does not exercise "legislative" power. The bicameral process is not necessary as a check on the Executive's administration of the laws because his administrative activity cannot reach beyond the limits of the statute that created [it]. The constitutionality of the Attorney General's execution of the authority delegated to him by § 244 involves only a question of delegation doctrine [see p. 399 below]. [A] one-House veto is clearly legislative in both character and effect and is [not checked in the manner administrative actions are]; the need for the check provided by Art. I, §§ 1, 7 is therefore clear. Congress' authority to delegate portions of its power to administrative agencies provides no support for the argument that Congress can constitutionally control administration of the laws by way of a Congressional veto. [Footnote by the Chief Justice.]

3. Justice Powell's position is that the one-House veto in this case is a *judicial* act and therefore unconstitutional as beyond the authority vested in Congress by the Constitution. We agree that there is a sense in which one-House action pursuant to [this law] has a judicial cast, since it purports to "review" Executive action. [But] the attempted analogy between judicial action and the one-House veto is less than perfect. Federal courts do not enjoy a roving mandate to correct alleged excesses of administrative agencies; we are limited by Art. III [and] no justiciable case or controversy was presented by the Attorney General's decision to allow Chadha to remain in this country. We are aware of no decision [where] a federal court has reviewed a decision of the Attorney General suspending de-

The choices we discern as having been made in the Constitutional Convention impose burdens on governmental processes that often seem clumsy, inefficient, even unworkable, but those hard choices were consciously made by men who had lived under a form of government that permitted arbitrary governmental acts to go unchecked. There is no support in the Constitution or decisions of this Court for the proposition that the cumbersomeness and delays often encountered in complying with explicit Constitutional standards may be avoided, either by the Congress or by the President. [Youngstown.] With all the obvious flaws of delay, untidiness, and potential for abuse, we have not yet found a better way to preserve freedom than by making the exercise of power subject to the carefully crafted restraints spelled out in the Constitution. We hold that the Congressional Veto [challenged here is unconstitutional].

[Affirmed.]

Justice POWELL, concurring in the judgment.

[This] case may be decided on a narrower ground. When Congress finds that a particular person does not satisfy the statutory criteria for permanent residence in this country it has assumed a judicial function in violation of the principle of separation of powers. [The Framers were concerned] that trial by a legislature lacks the safeguards necessary to prevent the abuse of power. [On] its face, the House's action appears clearly adjudicatory. The House did not enact a general rule; rather it made its own determination that six specific persons did not comply with certain statutory criteria. It thus undertook the type of decision that traditionally has been left to other branches. [The] impropriety of the House's assumption of this function is confirmed by the fact that its action raises the very danger the Framers sought to avoid—the exercise of unchecked [power].

Justice WHITE, dissenting.

Today the Court not only invalidates § 244(c)(2) of the [Act], but also sounds the death knell for nearly 200 other statutory provisions in which Congress has reserved a "legislative veto." For this reason, the Court's decision is of surpassing importance. And it is for this reason that the Court would have been well-advised to decide the case, if possible, on the narrower grounds of separation of powers, leaving for full consideration the constitutionality of other congressional review statutes operating on such varied matters as war powers and agency rulemaking, some of which concern the independent regulatory agencies. The prominence of the legislative veto mechanism in our contemporary political system and its importance to Congress can hardly be overstated. It has become a central means by which Congress secures the accountability of executive and independent agencies. Without the legislative veto, Congress is faced with a Hobson's choice: either to refrain from delegating the necessary authority, leaving itself with a hopeless task of writing laws with the requisite specificity to cover endless special circumstances across the entire policy landscape, or in the alternative, to abdicate its lawmaking function to the executive branch and independent agencies. To choose the former leaves major national problems unresolved; to opt for the latter risks unac-

portation [pursuant to the statute]. This is not surprising, given that no party to such action has either the motivation or the right to appeal from it. [Thus], Justice Powell's statement that the one-House veto in this case is "clearly adjudicatory" simply is not supported by his accompanying assertion that the House has "assumed a function ordinarily entrusted to the federal courts." We are satisfied that the one-House veto is legislative in purpose and effect and subject to the procedures set out in Art. I. [Footnote by the Chief Justice.]

countable policymaking by those not elected to fill that role. Accordingly, over the past five decades, the legislative veto has been placed in nearly 200 statutes. The device is known in every field of governmental concern: reorganization, budgets, foreign affairs, war powers, and regulation of trade, safety, energy, the environment and the economy.

I. [Justice White reviewed the history of the legislative veto. He noted that it began as a "response to the problems of reorganizing the sprawling government structure" created after the Depression, that it "balanced delegations of statutory authority in new areas," and that it had been "important in resolving a series of major constitutional disputes between the President and Congress over claims of the President to broad impoundment, war, and national emergency powers." He continued:] Even this brief review [demonstrates] that the legislative veto [is] an important if not indispensable political invention that allows the President and Congress to resolve major constitutional and policy differences, assures the accountability of independent regulatory agencies, and preserves Congress' control over lawmaking. Perhaps there are other means of accommodation and accountability, but the increasing reliance of Congress upon the legislative veto suggests that the alternatives to which Congress must now turn are not entirely satisfactory.[1] [The] history of the legislative veto also makes clear that it has not been a sword with which Congress has struck out to aggrandize itself at the expense of the other branches—the concerns of Madison and Hamilton. Rather, the veto has been a means of defense, a reservation of ultimate authority necessary if Congress is to fulfill its designated role [as] the nation's lawmaker. [The] Executive has [often] agreed to legislative review as the price for a broad delegation of authority. To be sure, the President may have preferred unrestricted power, but that could be precisely why Congress thought it essential to retain a check on the exercise of delegated authority.

II. For all these reasons, the apparent sweep of the Court's decision today is regrettable. The Court's Article I analysis appears to invalidate all legislative vetoes irrespective of form or subject. Because the legislative veto is commonly found as a check upon rulemaking by administrative agencies and upon broad-based policy decisions of the Executive Branch, it is particularly unfortunate that the Court reaches its decision in a case involving the exercise of a veto over deportation decisions regarding particular individuals. [The] Constitution does not directly authorize or prohibit the legislative veto. Thus, our task should be to determine whether the legislative veto is consistent with the purposes of Art. I and the principles of Separation of [Powers]. We should not find the lack of a specific constitutional authorization for the legislative veto surprising, and I would not infer disapproval of the mechanism from its absence. From the summer of 1787 to the present the government of the United States has become an endeavor far beyond the contemplation of the Framers. Only within the last half century has the complexity and size of the Federal Government's responsibilities grown so greatly that the Congress must rely on the legislative veto as the most effective if not the only means to insure their role as the nation's lawmakers. But the wisdom of the Framers was to anticipate that the nation would grow and new problems of governance would require different

---

1. While Congress could write certain statutes with greater specificity, it is unlikely that this is a realistic or even desirable substitute for the legislative veto. [Oversight] hearings and congressional investigations have their purpose, but unless Congress is to be rendered a think tank or debating society, they are no substitute for the exercise of actual authority. [Finally], the passage of corrective legislation after agency regulations take effect or Executive Branch officials have acted entail the drawbacks endemic to a retroactive [response]. [Footnote by Justice White.]

solutions. Accordingly, our Federal Government was intentionally chartered with the flexibility to respond to contemporary needs without losing sight of fundamental democratic [principles].

III. [The bicameralism and presentment provisions of Art. I. do not answer] the constitutional question before us. The power to exercise a legislative veto is not the power to write new law without bicameral approval or presidential consideration. The veto must be authorized by statute and may only negative what an Executive department or independent agency has proposed. On its face, the legislative veto no more allows one House of Congress to make law than does the presidential veto confer such power upon the President. [The] historical background of the Presentation Clause itself [reveals] only that the Framers were concerned with limiting the methods for enacting new legislation. [There] is no record that the Convention contemplated, let alone intended, that [the] Article I requirements would someday be invoked to restrain the scope of Congressional authority pursuant to duly-enacted law. When the Convention did turn its attention to the scope of Congress' lawmaking power, the Framers were expansive. [McCulloch.] The Court heeded this counsel in approving the modern administrative state. The Court's holding today that all legislative-type action must be enacted through the lawmaking process ignores that legislative authority is routinely delegated to the Executive branch, to the independent regulatory agencies, and to private individuals and groups. [This] Court's decisions sanctioning such delegations make clear that Article I does not require all action with the effect of legislation to be passed as a law. Theoretically, agencies and officials were asked only to "fill up the details," and the rule was that "Congress cannot delegate any part of its legislative power except under a limitation of a prescribed standard." [In] practice, however, restrictions on the scope of the power that could be delegated diminished and all but disappeared. [The] wisdom and the constitutionality of these broad delegations are matters that still have not been put to rest. But for present purposes, [the] cases establish that by virtue of congressional delegation, legislative power can be exercised by independent agencies and Executive departments without the passage of new legislation. For some time, the sheer amount of law—the substantive rules that regulate private conduct and direct the operation of government—made by the agencies has far outnumbered the lawmaking engaged in by Congress through the traditional process. There is no question but that agency rulemaking is lawmaking in any functional or realistic sense of the term. [If] Congress may delegate lawmaking power to independent and executive agencies, it is most difficult to understand Article I as forbidding Congress from also reserving a check on legislative power for itself. Absent the veto, the agencies receiving delegations of legislative or quasi-legislative power may issue regulations having the force of law without bicameral approval and without the President's signature. It is thus not apparent why the reservation of a veto over the exercise of that legislative power must be subject to a more exacting test. In both cases, it is enough that the initial statutory authorizations comply with the Article I requirements. [Under] the Court's analysis, the Executive Branch and the independent agencies may make rules with the effect of law while Congress, in whom the Framers confided the legislative power, may not exercise a veto which precludes such rules from having operative [force].

The Court also takes no account of perhaps the most relevant consideration: However resolutions of disapproval under [the law] are formally characterized, in reality, a departure from the status quo occurs only upon the concurrence of opinion among the House, Senate, and President. Reservations of legislative authority to be exercised by Congress should be upheld if the exercise of such reserved authority is consistent with the distribution of and limits upon legislative power that Article I provides. [The law] did not alter the division of actual authority between Congress and the Executive. At all times, whether through private bills, or through affirmative concurrent resolutions, or through the present one-House veto, a permanent change in a deportable alien's status could be accomplished only with the agreement of the Attorney General, the House, and the Senate. The central concern of the presentation and bicameralism requirements of Article I [is] fully satisfied by the operation of [this law].

IV.   [The] history of the separation of powers doctrine is also a history of accommodation and practicality. Apprehensions of an overly powerful branch have not led to undue prophylactic measures that handicap the effective working of the national government as a whole. The Constitution does not contemplate total separation of the three branches of Government. [Our] decisions reflect this judgment. [The] veto provision does not "preven[t] the Executive Branch from accomplishing its constitutionally assigned functions." [Moreover], the Court believes that [this] legislative veto [is] best characterized as an exercise of legislative or quasi-legislative authority. Under this characterization, the practice does not, even on the surface, constitute an infringement of executive or judicial prerogative. [Nor] does § 244 infringe on the judicial power, as Justice Powell would [hold]. [I] do not suggest that all legislative vetoes are necessarily consistent with separation of powers principles. A legislative check on an inherently executive function, for example that of initiating prosecutions, poses an entirely different question. But the legislative veto device here—and in many other settings—is far from an instance of legislative tyranny over the Executive. It is a necessary check on the unavoidably expanding power of the agencies, both executive and independent, as they engage in exercising authority delegated by Congress.

V.   [I] regret the destructive scope of the Court's holding. It reflects a profoundly different conception of the Constitution than that held by the Courts which sanctioned the modern administrative state. Today's decision strikes down in one fell swoop provisions in more laws enacted by Congress than the Court has cumulatively invalidated in its history. I fear it will now be more difficult "to insure that the fundamental policy decisions in our society will be made not by an appointed official but by the body immediately responsible to the people," Arizona v. California, 373 U.S. 546, 626 (1963) (Harlan, J., dissenting). I must dissent. [Justice REHNQUIST, joined by Justice White, submitted a separate dissent, believing that the legislative veto provision was not severable.]

CHADHA AND THE LEGISLATIVE VETO CONTROVERSY

The Chadha ruling was the Court's first full encounter with the problem which had pervaded political and academic debates for years: the constitutionality of legislative vetoes. Chadha attempts to resolve most of the controversy in sweeping terms. Does it try to decide too much? Decisions in the wake of Chadha demonstrated its broad impact. For example, summary decisions by the Supreme Court soon after Chadha struck down not only one-House veto provisions in regulatory statutes involving independent agencies but also two-House vetoes as in the Federal Trade Commission Improvements Act of 1980. See, e.g., U.S. Senate v. FTC, 463 U.S. 1216 (1983), and Process Gas Consumers Group v. Consumer Energy Council, 463 U.S. 1216 (1983). Both rulings struck down legislative veto provisions regarding rulemaking by independent agencies, unlike the individualized context of Chadha. Justice White dissented: "When the veto is placed as a check upon the agencies, [the] analysis relied on in Chadha has a particularly hollow ring." ("Two–House vetoes" require the agreement of both Houses before a legislative veto becomes effective.) Did Chadha leave room for distinguishing two-house vetoes from one-house ones? Should they have been distinguished? See generally Strauss, "Was There a Baby in the Bathwater? A Comment on the Supreme Court's Legislative Veto Decision," 1983 Duke L.J. 789. Despite Chadha, Congress continued to enact legislative veto provisions in a number of statutes. Congress apparently assumed that fear of budgetary retaliation would assure that the executive branch would honor these provisions.

Consider the persuasiveness of the various opinions in Chadha. Was Justice Powell's concurrence, viewing the case as one involving an "adjudicatory" proceeding, a plausible way of narrowing the reach of the decision? What questions remain open after Chadha? Consider whether Chadha leaves open the possibility of arguments that legislative veto provisions are still permissible in contexts where congressional power may be especially strong, as with the appropriation of funds and the waging of war. For example, can the legislative veto provisions in the Impounding Control Act of 1974, below, and the War Powers Resolution of 1973, above, survive constitutional challenge after Chadha? The rise of the modern administrative state and the congressional power to delegate considerable policymaking authority to the executive branch clearly raise the question of what congressional checks on administrators *are* permissible under the separation of powers scheme. If all or most legislative vetoes are barred by Chadha, what alternative techniques are left to Congress for controlling executive and administrative implementations of federal laws? See, e.g., Breyer, "The Legislative Veto After Chadha," 72 Geo.L.J. 785 (1984), and Levitas & Branch, "Congressional Review of Executive and Agency Actions After Chadha, 'The Son of Legislative Veto' Lives On," 72 Geo.L.J. 801 (1984).

THE IMPOUNDMENT CONTROVERSY

Introduction. Does the President have inherent constitutional power to refuse to spend funds appropriated by Congress—even when Congress *mandates* such spending? A claimed executive authority to impound was one of the executive-legislative conflicts which reached new levels of intensity and scope beginning in the 1970s. The "power of the purse" is traditionally associated with Congress and is reflected in several provisions of Art. I. Yet Presidents have repeatedly refused to spend money appropriated by Congress. Most of those refusals rested on express or implied grants of executive discretion in the legislation. Exercise of executive power in that situation readily falls within the first of Justice Jackson's three categories in the Steel Seizure case. In 1973, in the face of mounting congressional criticism and court challenges to executive impoundments, President Nixon turned to constitutional justifications, asserting an inherent discretion to impound even in the face of a mandatory spending directive from Congress: he claimed that there was an "absolutely clear" "constitutional right" of the President to "impound" funds when the spending "would mean either increasing prices or increasing taxes for all the people." That position moved the central issue in the impoundment controversy from

Justice Jackson's first category to his third category.[1]

1. *The Impounding Control Act of 1974.* Increasingly broad executive claims were matched by increasingly insistent proposals for congressional countermeasures. Efforts initiated by Senator Ervin culminated in the enactment of the Congressional Budget and Impounding Control Act of 1974. That Act—like the War Powers Resolution of 1973, p. 372 above—represents congressional action of an unusual and especially important nature. Instead of congressional directives regarding substantive governmental policies, it delineates structures and processes. It is legislation that can be viewed as quasi-constitutional in nature, for it seeks to clarify and define basic relationships among the branches of government. The 1974 Act attempts to impose substantial restraints on presidential authority to impound, requiring legislative approval of executive decisions to reduce or end programs for which funds are authorized. The Act distinguishes between two types of impoundments. Where the President proposes simply to *defer* the expenditure of appropriated funds, the initiative to curb falls on Congress: either house may disapprove the deferral by adopting a simple resolution. But for proposed presidential impoundments to *terminate* a particular spending authority, or to withhold funds beyond the end of the fiscal year, the executive action is permissible only with the affirmative concurrence of both houses of Congress. In such instances the presidential recommendations do not take effect unless, within 45 days after transmittal of the President's proposal, "the Congress has completed action on a rescission bill rescinding all or part of the amount proposed to be rescinded." To enable Congress to exercise these controls, the Act requires the President to report all proposed impoundment actions.

2. *Constitutional problems?* Do the impoundment control provisions in the 1974 Act raise any constitutional problems? As applied to domestic spending programs? As applied to foreign programs? Can any plausible constitutional arguments be made that executive discretion to impound is an inherent power untouchable by Congress? Does the congressional spending power in Art. I, § 8 resolve any conflicts in favor of the legislative branch in contexts such as Justice Jackson's third category? Can the legislative veto aspects of the 1974 Act be justified in the wake of the Chadha case, above?

3. *Legislation to promote a balanced budget.* Partly in response to dissatisfactions with the efficacy of the Impounding Control Act of 1974, Congress adopted the Balanced Budget and Emergency Deficit Control Act in 1985 to establish maximum annual permissible deficits with the aim of reducing the federal deficit to zero by fiscal year 1991. The 1985 Act's procedures for budget-cutting were successfully challenged on separation of powers grounds in Bowsher v. Synar, which follows. (Congress has also continued to seek other means to deal with balanced budget problems. Congressional efforts to propose a balanced budget constitutional amendment failed to garner the requisite superma-

---

1. In the only modern Court case on the impoundment issue, the executive branch raised only a statutory claim that the President was authorized to impound funds. The Court unanimously rejected that claim in Train v. New York, 420 U.S. 35 (1975). However, several federal trial courts considered (and rejected) presidential claims to impound based on inherent constitutional powers. See, e.g., Local 2677 v. Phillips, 358 F.Supp. 60 (D.D.C.1973). (For a sampling of the extensive literature produced by the controversy, see Abascal & Kramer, "Presidential Impoundment Part II: Judicial and Legislative Responses," 63 Geo.L.J. 149 (1974), and Mikva & Hertz, "Impoundment of Funds—The Courts, The Congress and The President: A Constitutional Triangle," 69 Nw. U.L.Rev. 335 (1974).)

jority in the Senate by a narrow margin in March 1995. But in April 1995, the Line Item Veto Act became law, to become effective in 1997.)

Bowsher v. Synar

478 U.S. 714, 106 S.Ct. 3181, 92 L.Ed.2d 583 (1986).

Chief Justice BURGER delivered the opinion of the Court.

The question presented by these appeals is whether the assignment by Congress to the Comptroller General of the United States of certain functions under the Balanced Budget and Emergency Deficit Control Act of 1985 [the Gramm–Rudman–Hollings Act] violates the doctrine of separation of powers. [The Act established maximum annual permissible deficits designed to reduce the federal deficit to zero by fiscal year 1991. If needed to keep the deficit within the maximum, the Act required across-the-board cuts, half in defense programs, half elsewhere. Sec. 251 of the Act set out the procedure to be followed: First, each year the Directors of the Office of Management and Budget (OMB) and the Congressional Budget Office (CBO) were required to estimate independently the amount of the federal budget deficit for the next fiscal year. If the estimated deficit exceeded the target, the Directors were to calculate independently, on a program-by-program basis, the budget reductions required to meet the target and to submit a joint report of their calculations to the Comptroller General. Second, the Comptroller General, after exercising independent judgment in evaluating the estimates submitted to him, was to report his conclusions about the required budget reductions to the President. Third, the President was required to issue an order putting into effect the reductions submitted by the Comptroller General, unless Congress, within a specified time, met the deficit goal in other ways. The constitutional challenge focused on the participation of the Comptroller General in this process. The office of the Comptroller General, the head of the General Accounting Office, was created by the Budget and Accounting Act of 1921. The Comptroller General is nominated by the President from a list of three persons recommended by the presiding officers of the House and the Senate; the Comptroller General is removable only by impeachment or by a Joint Resolution of Congress (which is subject to presidential veto) on the basis of reasons specified in the 1921 Act. The Act was challenged by Congressman Synar and by the National Treasury Employees Union. A three-judge district court held the Act unconstitutional on the ground that the Act imposed executive functions on the Comptroller General—functions that could not be constitutionally exercised by an officer removable by Congress. (The case is printed here because of its importance to general separation of powers principles. The President's power to appoint and remove executive personnel is further discussed in the notes following this case.)]

[The] Constitution does not contemplate an active role for Congress in the supervision of officers charged with the execution of the laws it enacts. The President appoints "Officers of the United States" with the "Advice and Consent of the [Senate]." Article II, § 2. Once the appointment has been made and confirmed, however, the Constitution explicitly provides for removal of Officers of the United States by Congress only upon impeachment by the House of Representatives and conviction by the Senate. [After reviewing the Myers and Humphrey's Executor cases on the Presidential removal power, p. 391 below, the Court continued:] In light of these precedents, we conclude that Congress cannot reserve for itself the power of removal of an officer charged

telling Pres.
what to do

with the execution of the laws except by impeachment. To permit the execution of the laws to be vested in an officer answerable only to Congress would, in practical terms, reserve in Congress control over the execution of the laws. [The] structure of the Constitution does not permit Congress to execute the laws; it follows that Congress cannot grant to an officer under its control what it does not possess.[1] Our decision in [Chadha] supports this conclusion. [To] permit an officer controlled by Congress to execute the laws would be, in essence, to permit a congressional veto. Congress could simply remove, or threaten to remove, an officer for executing the laws in any fashion found to be unsatisfactory to Congress. This kind of congressional control over the execution of the laws, Chadha makes clear, is constitutionally impermissible.

[Appellants] urge that the Comptroller General performs his duties independently and is not subservient to Congress. We agree with the District Court that this contention does not bear close scrutiny. The critical factor lies in the provisions of the statute defining the Comptroller General's office relating to removability. [The 1921 Act] permits removal for "inefficiency," "neglect of duty," or "malfeasance." These terms are very broad and, as interpreted by Congress, could sustain removal of a Comptroller General for any number of actual or perceived transgressions of the legislative will. The Constitutional Convention chose to permit impeachment of executive officers only for "Treason, Bribery, or other high Crimes and Misdemeanors." It rejected language that would have permitted impeachment for "maladministration," with Madison arguing that "[s]o vague a term will be equivalent to a tenure during pleasure of the Senate." We need not decide whether "inefficiency" or "malfeasance" are terms as broad as "maladministration" in order to reject the dissent's position that removing the Comptroller General requires "a feat of bipartisanship more difficult than that required to impeach and convict." [Justice] White, however, assures us that "[r]ealistic consideration" of the "practical result of the removal provision" reveals that the Comptroller General is unlikely to be removed by Congress. The separated powers of our government can not be permitted to turn on judicial assessment of whether an officer exercising executive power is on good terms with Congress. The Framers recognized that, in the long term, structural protections against abuse of power were critical to preserving liberty. In constitutional terms, the removal powers over the Comptroller General's office dictate that he will be subservient to Congress. [The] dissent is simply in error to suggest that the political realities reveal that the Comptroller General is free from influence by [Congress].

It is clear that Congress has consistently viewed the Comptroller General as an officer of the Legislative Branch. The Reorganization Acts of 1945 and 1949, for example, both stated that the Comptroller General and the GAO are "a part of the legislative branch of the Government." [Over] the years, the Comptrollers General have also viewed themselves as part of the Legislative Branch. [Against] this background, we see no escape from the conclusion that, because Congress had retained removal authority over the Comptroller General, he may not be entrusted with executive powers. The remaining question is whether the Comptroller General has been assigned such powers in the [1985 Act]. [Appellants] suggest that the duties assigned to the Comptroller General

---

1. Appellants [are] wide of the mark in arguing that an affirmance in this case requires casting doubt on the status of "independent" agencies, because no issues involving such agencies are presented here. [This] case involves [a] statute that provides for direct congressional involvement over the decision to remove the Comptroller General. Appellants have referred us to no independent agency whose members are removable by the Congress for certain causes short of impeachable offenses, as is the Comptroller General. [Footnote by the Chief Justice.]

in the Act are essentially ministerial and mechanical so that their performance does not constitute "execution of the law" in a meaningful sense. On the contrary, we view these functions as plainly entailing execution of the law in constitutional terms. Interpreting a law enacted by Congress to implement the legislative mandate is the very essence of "execution" of the law. Under [the Act], the Comptroller General must exercise judgment concerning facts that affect the application of the Act. He must also interpret the provisions of the Act to determine precisely what budgetary calculations are required. Decisions of that kind are typically made by officers charged with executing a statute.

The executive nature of the Comptroller General's functions under the Act is revealed in § 252(a)(3) which gives the Comptroller General the ultimate authority to determine the budget cuts to be made. Indeed, the Comptroller General commands the President himself to carry out, without the slightest variation (with exceptions not relevant to the constitutional issues presented), the directive of the Comptroller General as to [budget reductions]. Congress of course initially determined the content of the [Act]; and undoubtedly the content of the Act determines the nature of the executive duty. However, as Chadha makes clear, once Congress makes its choice in enacting legislation, its participation ends. Congress can thereafter control the execution of its enactment only indirectly—by passing new legislation. By placing the responsibility for execution of the [Act] in the hands of an officer who is subject to removal only by itself, Congress in effect has retained control over the execution of the Act and has intruded into the executive function. The Constitution does not permit such [intrusion]. [No one] can doubt that Congress and the President are confronted with fiscal and economic problems of unprecedented magnitude, [but] "[c]onvenience and efficiency are not the primary objectives—or the hallmarks—of democratic [government]." [Chadha.]

[Affirmed.][2]

Justice WHITE, dissenting.

The Court, acting in the name of separation of powers, takes upon itself to strike down the Gramm–Rudman–Hollings Act, one of the most novel and far-reaching legislative responses to a national crisis since the New Deal. The basis of the Court's action is a solitary provision of another statute that was passed over sixty years ago and has lain dormant since that time. I cannot concur in the Court's action. [I will] address the wisdom of the Court's willingness to interpose its distressingly formalistic view of separation of powers as a bar to the attainment of governmental objectives through the means chosen by the Congress and the President in the legislative process established by the Constitution. [The] Court's decision rests on a feature of the legislative scheme that is of minimal practical significance and that presents no substantial threat to the basic scheme of separation of powers. In attaching dispositive significance to what should be regarded as a triviality, the Court neglects what has in the past been recognized as a fundamental principle governing consideration of

practical effects analysis

2. Justice STEVENS, joined by Justice Marshall, submitted an opinion concurring in the judgment but disagreeing with the majority's grounds: "It is not the dormant, carefully circumscribed congressional removal power that represents the primary constitutional evil. Nor do I agree [that] the analysis depends on a labeling of the functions assigned to the Comptroller General as 'executive powers.' Rather, I am convinced that the Comptroller General must be characterized as an agent of Congress [and] that the powers assigned to him under the [Act] require him to make policy that will bind the Nation." He concluded: "Congress may not exercise [its] power to formulate national policy by delegating that power [to] an individual agent of the Congress such as [the] Comptroller General."

disputes over separation of powers: "The actual art of governing under our Constitution does not and cannot conform to judicial definitions of the power of any of its branches based on isolated clauses or even single Articles torn from context. While the Constitution diffuses power the better to secure liberty, it also contemplates that practice will integrate the dispersed powers into a workable government." [Youngstown] (Jackson, J. concurring).

[Before] examining the merits of the Court's argument, I wish to emphasize what it is that the Court quite pointedly and correctly does *not* hold: namely, that "executive" powers of the sort granted the Comptroller by the Act may only be exercised by officers removable at will by the President. [The] Court's recognition of the legitimacy of legislation vesting "executive" authority in officers independent of the President does not imply derogation of the President's own constitutional [duty], for any such duty is necessarily limited to a great extent by the content of the laws enacted by the Congress. [There] are undoubtedly executive functions that, regardless of the enactments of Congress, must be performed by officers subject to removal at will by the President. Whether a particular function falls within this class or within the far larger class that may be relegated to independent officers "will depend upon the character of the office." [Humphrey's Executor.] It is evident (and nothing in the Court's opinion is to the contrary) that the powers exercised by the Comptroller General under [the] Act are not such that vesting them in an officer not subject to removal at will by the President would in itself improperly interfere with Presidential powers. Determining the level of spending by the Federal Government is not by nature a function central either to the exercise of the President's enumerated powers or to his general duty to ensure execution of the laws; rather, appropriating funds is a peculiarly legislative [function].

[The] question remains whether, as the Court concludes, the fact that the officer to whom Congress has delegated the authority to implement the Act is removable by a joint resolution of Congress should require invalidation of the Act. [I] have no quarrel with the proposition that the powers exercised by the Comptroller under the Act may be characterized as "executive" in that they involve the interpretation and carrying out of the Act's mandate. I can also accept the general proposition that although Congress has considerable authority in designating the officers who are to execute legislation, the constitutional scheme of separated powers does prevent Congress from reserving an executive role for itself or for its "agents." I cannot accept, however, that the exercise of authority by an officer removable for cause by a joint resolution of Congress is analogous to the impermissible execution of the law by Congress itself, nor would I hold that the congressional role in the removal process renders the Comptroller an "agent" of the Congress, incapable of receiving "executive" power. [Because] the Comptroller is not an appointee of Congress but an officer of the United States appointed by the President with the advice and consent of the Senate, Buckley [p. 390 below] neither requires that he be characterized as an agent of the Congress nor in any other way calls into question his capacity to exercise "executive" authority. [However,] the Court's decision in [Chadha] recognizes additional limits on the ability of Congress to participate in or influence the execution of the laws. As interpreted in Chadha, the Constitution prevents Congress from interfering with the actions of officers of the United States through means short of legislation satisfying the demands of bicameral passage and presentment to the President for approval or disapproval. Today's majority concludes that the same concerns that underlay Chadha indicate the invalidity of a statutory provision allowing the removal by joint resolution for specified cause of any officer performing executive functions [because it] constitutes a "congressional veto" analogous to that struck down in [Chadha].

[T]he Court baldly mischaracterizes the removal provision when it suggests that it allows Congress to remove the Comptroller for "executing the laws in any fashion found to be unsatisfactory"; in fact, Congress may remove the Comptroller only for one or more of five specified [reasons]. Second, [the] Court overlooks or deliberately ignores the decisive difference between the congressional removal provision and the legislative veto struck down in Chadha: [Congress] may remove the Comptroller only through a joint resolution, which by definition must be passed by both Houses and signed by the President. In other words, a removal of the Comptroller under the statute *satisfies the requirements of bicameralism and presentment laid down in* Chadha.

[That] a joint resolution removing the Comptroller General would satisfy the requirements for legitimate legislative action laid down in Chadha does not fully answer the separation of powers argument, for it is apparent that even the results of the constitutional legislative process may be unconstitutional if those results are in fact destructive of the scheme of separation of powers. The question to be answered [is] whether there is a genuine threat of "encroachment or aggrandizement of one branch at the expense of the other." Common sense indicates that the existence of the removal provision poses no such threat to the principle of separation of powers. [Action] taken in accordance with the "single, finely wrought, and exhaustively considered, procedure" established by Art. I [Chadha], should be presumptively viewed as a legitimate exercise of legislative power. That such action may represent a more or less successful attempt by Congress to "control" the actions of an officer of the United States surely does not in itself indicate that it is unconstitutional, for no one would dispute that Congress has the power to "control" administration through legislation imposing duties or substantive restraints on executive officers, through legislation increasing or decreasing the funds made available to such officers, or through legislation actually abolishing a particular office. [The] practical result of the removal provision is not to render the Comptroller unduly dependent upon or subservient to Congress, but to render him one of the most independent officers in the entire federal establishment. Those who have studied the office agree that the procedural and substantive limits on the power of Congress and the President to remove the Comptroller make dislodging him against his will practically impossible. [Realistic] consideration of the nature of the Comptroller General's relation to Congress thus reveals that the threat to separation of powers conjured up by the majority is wholly chimerical. [The] majority's contrary conclusion rests on the rigid dogma that, outside of the impeachment process, any "direct congressional role in the removal of officers charged with the execution of the laws [is] inconsistent with separation of powers." Reliance on such an unyielding principle to strike down a statute posing no real danger of aggrandizement of congressional power is extremely misguided and insensitive to our constitutional [role]. I dissent.[1]

----

1. *Congress and the presidential power to appoint and remove subordinates: The background.* Congressional efforts to curb presidential control of

1. In a separate dissent, Justice BLACKMUN argued that any constitutional problems "should be cured by refusing to allow congressional removal—if it ever is attempted—and not by striking down the central provisions of the [1985] Act. [I] cannot see the sense of invalidating legislation of this magnitude in order to preserve a cumbersome, 65–year–old removal power that has never been exercised and appears to have been all but forgotten until this litigation."

officials engaged in enforcing the law have produced recurrent constitutional disputes. Bowsher v. Synar, the preceding case, indirectly involved one such dispute. Morrison v. Olson, the next principal case, involved another, particularly focusing on the method of appointment of an "independent counsel" to investigate and, if appropriate, prosecute certain high-ranking governmental officials. The notes which follow sketch the Court's considerations (prior to the major rulings of the late 1980s) of alleged interferences with presidential powers regarding personnel.

a. *Congress and the President's power to appoint "Officers of the United States."* Art. II, § 2, cl. 2, the Appointments Clause, reinforces separation of powers principles by providing that the President "shall nominate, and by and with the Advice and Consent of the Senate, shall appoint [Ambassadors], Judges of the Supreme Court, and all other Officers of the United States, whose Appointments are not herein otherwise provided for, and which shall be established by Law: but the Congress may by Law vest the Appointment of such inferior Officers, as they think proper, in the President alone, in the Courts of Law, or in the Heads of Departments." In BUCKLEY v. VALEO, 424 U.S. 1 (1976), the Court's per curiam opinion relied on the Appointments Clause in holding unconstitutional, for most purposes, the composition of the Federal Election Commission [FEC] established by the Federal Election Campaign Act. Under the law, a majority of the FEC members was appointed by the President pro tempore of the Senate and the Speaker of the House. The FEC was given "direct and wide-ranging" enforcement power such as instituting civil actions against violations of the Act as well as "extensive rulemaking and adjudicative powers." The Court held that such powers could be exercised only by "Officers of the United States" appointed in accordance with the Appointments Clause. According to the Court, an agency with a majority of congressionally named personnel could only exercise those powers that Congress might delegate to one of its own committees—e.g., investigatory and informative powers; since only "Officers" appointed in the constitutionally prescribed manner could undertake executive or quasi-judicial tasks, the FEC could not exercise such functions. The Buckley opinion insisted that "any appointee exercising significant authority pursuant to the laws of the United States is an Officer of the United States, and must, therefore, be appointed in the manner prescribed by [the Appointments Clause]." Although Congress could vest appointment of "inferior Officers" in "Courts of Law" or "Heads of Departments" instead of the President, providing for the appointment of most FEC members by congressional officials was impermissible, since they could not be considered "Heads of Departments." The Court rejected the argument that, because of "the extraordinary authority reposed in Congress to regulate elections, this case stands on a different footing than if Congress had exercised its legislative authority in another field." The defenders of the FEC structure also argued that "Congress had good reason for not vesting in a Commission composed wholly of Presidential appointees the authority to administer the Act, since the administration of the Act would undoubtedly have a bearing on any incumbent President's campaign for reelection." To that argument, the Court responded that "such fears, however rational, do not by themselves warrant a distortion of the Framers' work." (Soon after the Buckley decision, Congress cured the constitutional flaw by reconstituting the FEC with a membership consisting entirely of presidential appointees.)

b. *Congress and the President's power to remove subordinates.* The only explicit constitutional reference to the removal of executive personnel lies in the impeachment provisions. But from the outset, a power to remove subordinate executive officials by routes other than impeachment has been assumed.

Is that power solely in the President? Or may Congress limit presidential removal authority? The first modern judicial answer was a broad endorsement of executive autonomy, but subsequent decisions have found considerable room for congressional participation and for restraints on the President's removal power, in cases such as Humphrey's Executor (involving a member of an independent regulatory agency), below. How does the Court's recognition of "independent" agencies square with separation of powers? Are "independent" agencies a fourth branch? Are they quasi-legislative or quasi-judicial? See generally Symposium, "The Independence of Independent Agencies," 1988 Duke L.J. 215; Strauss, "The Place of Agencies in Government: Separation of Powers and the Fourth Branch," 84 Colum.L.Rev. 573 (1984); and Lessig & Sunstein, "The President and the Administration," 94 Colum.L.Rev. 1 (1994).

In MYERS v. UNITED STATES, 272 U.S. 52 (1926) the Court held unconstitutional a legislative provision that certain groups of postmasters could not be removed by the President without the consent of the Senate. Chief Justice TAFT's opinion rested on an expansive reading of executive powers under Art. II and found the statute an unconstitutional restriction on the President's control over executive personnel. The Chief Justice found that it was a "reasonable implication" from the President's power to execute the laws that "he should select those who were to act for him under his direction in the execution of the laws." And it was an additional plausible implication that "as his selection of administrative officers is essential to the execution of the laws by him, so must be his power of removing those for whom he can not continue to be responsible." Less than a decade after Myers, however, the Court curtailed some of its implications and distinguished Myers in holding that the President could *not* remove a member of an independent regulatory agency in defiance of restrictions in the statutory framework. HUMPHREY'S EXECU-TOR v. UNITED STATES, 295 U.S. 602 (1935). Justice SUTHERLAND's opinion found that the Federal Trade Commission Act specified the causes for removal of Commissioners and held that, in view of the functions of the agency, Congress *could* limit the President's power of removal; the Court found the Myers principle limited to "purely executive officers." The FTC, by contrast, "cannot in any proper sense be characterized as an arm or an eye of the executive": under the statute, its duties were to be "free from executive control." Rather, it acted "in part quasi-legislatively and in part quasi-judicially." The Myers rule, then, stands simply for "the unrestrictable power of the President to remove purely executive officers." More recently, the Court applied the Humphrey's rather than the Myers rule in WIENER v. UNITED STATES, 357 U.S. 349 (1958), involving the removal of a member of the War Claims Commission. The statute establishing that Commission, unlike the one in Humphrey's Executor, did not specify permissible grounds to remove. But the Court emphasized that the Commission's function was of an "intrinsic judicial character" and held the removal illegal. As to officers who were not purely executive, power to remove existed "only if Congress may fairly be said to have conferred it." The Court noted: "This sharp differentiation derives from the difference in functions between those who are part of the Executive establishment and those whose tasks require absolute freedom from Executive interference."

Morrison v. Olson
487 U.S. 654, 108 S.Ct. 2597, 101 L.Ed.2d 569 (1988).

Chief Justice REHNQUIST delivered the opinion of the Court.

This case presents us with a challenge to the independent counsel provisions of the Ethics in Government Act of 1978. [We] hold today that these provisions of the Act do not violate the Appointments Clause [or] the limitations of Article III, nor do they impermissibly interfere with the President's authority under Article II in violation of the constitutional principle of separation of powers. [The 1978 Act authorized the appointment of an independent counsel to investigate and, if appropriate, prosecute certain high-ranking government officials for violations of federal criminal laws. The Act required the Attorney General, upon receipt of information that she considered "sufficient grounds" to investigate possible official violations of federal criminal law, to conduct a preliminary investigation. The Attorney General then reports to the Special Division[1] of the U.S. Court of Appeals for the District of Columbia Circuit as to whether there are "reasonable grounds to believe that further investigation is warranted." If the Attorney General finds such "reasonable grounds," she must apply to the Special Division for the appointment of an independent counsel, and the Special Division then appoints an appropriate independent counsel and defines that counsel's prosecutorial jurisdiction. The Act granted the independent counsel "full power and independent authority to exercise all investigative and prosecutorial functions and powers" of the Justice Department. Moreover, the Justice Department, upon appointment of an independent counsel, was required to suspend all investigations and proceedings regarding the matter.

[The immediate case arose after an independent counsel was appointed and a grand jury issued subpoenas to the appellees, who moved to quash the subpoenas on the ground that the Act was unconstitutional. The District Court upheld the Act, but the Court of Appeals reversed. The appellant, independent counsel Alexia Morrison, brought the case to the Supreme Court. Chief Justice Rehnquist's majority opinion first rejected the claim that vesting the appointment of the independent counsel in the Special Division violated the Appointments Clause. He found the independent counsel to be an "inferior" officer for purposes of the Clause: although she was not wholly "subordinate" to the Attorney General because she did exercise considerable discretion, the fact that the Act authorized her removal by the Attorney General for "good cause" indicated that she was to some degree "inferior" in rank and authority. Moreover, her duties were limited under the Act, under the terms of her appointment by the Special Division. In addition, her tenure of office was "temporary" because an independent counsel is appointed to accomplish only a single task. These factors regarding tenure, duration and duties of her office were "sufficient to establish that [Morrison] is an 'inferior' officer in the constitutional sense." Under the Constitution, then, she was not a "principal officer" who, under the Appointments Clause, could only be named by the President. The appellees nevertheless argued that, even if she was an "inferior" officer, the Appointments Clause did not permit Congress to place the power to appoint outside the Executive Branch. They claimed that the Clause did not "contemplate congressional authorization of 'interbranch appointments,' in which an officer of one branch is appointed by officers of another branch." In rejecting this challenge, the Court relied on the concluding words of the Appointments Clause—"but the Congress may by Law vest the Appointment of such inferior Officers, as they think proper, in the President alone, in the courts of Law, or in the Heads of Departments." This language did not limit interbranch appointments; indeed, it seemed to give Congress "significant

---

1. The Special Division created by the Act consisted of three Circuit Judges appointed by the Chief Justice for two-year terms.

discretion" to determine whether it was "proper" to vest the appointment of executive officials in the "courts of Law." The Court recognized that the congressional power to provide for interbranch appointments was not unlimited. For example, congressional vesting of the appointment power in the courts "would be improper if there was some 'incongruity' between the functions normally performed by the courts and the performance of their duty to appoint." But here, the Court concluded, "we do not think that appointment of the independent counsels by the Court runs afoul of the constitutional limitation on 'incongruous' interbranch appointments."

[Chief Justice Rehnquist next rejected the claim that the powers vested in the Special Division (including the judges' power to define the independent counsel's jurisdiction) conflicted with Art. III of the Constitution: "Particularly when, as here, Congress creates a temporary 'office' the nature and duties of which will by necessity vary with the factual circumstances giving rise to the need for an appointment in the first place, it may vest the power to define the scope of the office in the Court as an incident to the appointment of the officer pursuant to the Appointments Clause. [The] Act simply does not give the Division the power to 'supervise' the independent counsel in the exercise of his or her investigative or prosecutorial authority." Finally, the Court turned to broader challenges resting on separation of powers principles. The Chief Justice stated:]

V. [Two] related issues must be addressed: The first is whether the provision of the Act restricting the Attorney General's power to remove the independent counsel to only those instances in which he can show "good cause," taken by itself, impermissibly interferes with the President's exercise of his constitutionally appointed functions. The second is whether, taken as a whole, the Act violates the separation of powers by reducing the President's ability to control the prosecutorial powers wielded by the independent counsel. A. [Unlike] both Bowsher and Myers, this case does not involve an attempt by Congress itself to gain a role in the removal of executive officials other than its established powers of impeachment and conviction. The Act instead puts the removal power squarely in the hands of the Executive Branch; an independent counsel may be removed from office "only by the personal action of the Attorney General, and only for good cause." There is no requirement of congressional approval of the Attorney General's removal decision, though the decision is subject to judicial review. In our view, the removal provisions of the Act make this case more analogous to [Humphrey's Executor] and [Wiener] than to Myers or Bowsher.

[Appellees] contend that Humphrey's Executor and Wiener are distinguishable from this case because they did not involve officials who performed a "core executive function." They argue that our decision in Humphrey's Executor rests on a distinction between "purely executive" officials and officials who exercise "quasi-legislative" and "quasi-judicial" powers. [We] undoubtedly did rely on the terms "quasi-legislative" and "quasi-judicial" to distinguish the officials involved in Humphrey's Executor and Wiener from those in Myers, but our present considered view is that the determination of whether the Constitution allows Congress to impose a "good cause"-type restriction on the President's power to remove an official cannot be made to turn on whether or not that official is classified as "purely executive." The analysis contained in our removal cases is designed not to define rigid categories of those officials who may or may not be removed at will by the President, but to ensure that Congress does not interfere with the President's exercise of the "executive power" and his constitutionally appointed duty to "take care that the laws be faithfully executed" under Article II. [We] do not mean to suggest that an

FUNCTIONALIST
TEST

removal restrictions

analysis of the functions served by the officials at issue is irrelevant. But the real question is whether the removal restrictions are of such a nature that they impede the President's ability to perform his constitutional duty, and the functions of the officials in question must be analyzed in that light.

Considering for the moment the "good cause" removal provision in isolation from the other parts of the Act at issue in this case, we cannot say that the imposition of a "good cause" standard for removal by itself unduly trammels on executive authority. There is no real dispute that the functions performed by the independent counsel are "executive" in the sense that they are law enforcement functions that typically have been undertaken by officials within the Executive Branch. As we noted above, however, the independent counsel is an inferior officer under the Appointments Clause, with limited jurisdiction and tenure and lacking policymaking or significant administrative authority. Although the counsel exercises no small amount of discretion and judgment in deciding how to carry out his or her duties under the Act, we simply do not see how the President's need to control the exercise of that discretion is so central to the functioning of the Executive Branch as to require as a matter of constitutional law that the counsel be terminable at will by the President. Nor do we think that the "good cause" removal provision at issue here impermissibly burdens the President's power to control or supervise the independent counsel, as an executive official, in the execution of his or her duties under the Act. This is not a case in which the power to remove an executive official has been completely stripped from the [President]. Rather, because the independent counsel may be terminated for "good cause," the Executive, through the Attorney General, retains ample authority to assure that the counsel is competently performing his or her statutory responsibilities in a manner that comports with the provisions of the Act. Although we need not decide in this case exactly what is encompassed within the term "good cause" under the Act, the legislative history of the removal provision also makes clear that the Attorney General may remove an independent counsel for "misconduct." Here, [the] congressional determination to limit the removal power of the Attorney General was essential, in the view of Congress, to establish the necessary independence of the office. We do not think that this limitation as it presently stands sufficiently deprives the President of control over the independent counsel to interfere impermissibly with his constitutional obligation to ensure the faithful execution of the laws.

why?

B.   The final question to be addressed is whether the Act, taken as a whole, violates the principle of separation of powers by unduly interfering with the role of the Executive Branch. [We] observe first that this case does not involve an attempt by Congress to increase its own powers at the expense of the Executive Branch. Unlike some of our previous cases, most recently [Bowsher], this case simply does not pose a "dange[r] of congressional usurpation of Executive Branch functions." [See also Chadha.] [Congress's] role under the Act is [largely] limited to receiving reports or other information and oversight of the independent counsel's activities, functions that we have recognized generally as being incidental to the legislative function of Congress. Similarly, we do not think that the Act works any *judicial* usurpation of properly executive functions. [Once] the court has appointed a counsel and defined his or her jurisdiction, it has no power to supervise or control the activities of the counsel. [T]he various powers delegated by the statute to the [Special] Division are not supervisory or administrative, nor are they functions that the Constitution requires be performed by officials within the Executive Branch. [Finally,] we do not think that the Act "impermissibly undermine[s]" the powers of the Executive Branch or "disrupts the proper balance between the coordinate

TREND

Act

branches [by] prevent[ing] the Executive Branch from accomplishing its constitutionally assigned functions." It is undeniable that the Act reduces the amount of control or supervision that the Attorney General and, through him, the President exercises over the investigation and prosecution of a certain class of alleged criminal activity. [Nonetheless], the Act does give the Attorney General several means of supervising or controlling the prosecutorial powers that may be wielded by an independent counsel. Most importantly, the Attorney General retains the power to remove the counsel for "good cause." [Notwithstanding] the fact that the counsel is to some degree "independent" and free from Executive supervision to a greater extent than other federal prosecutors, in our view [the] Act give the Executive Branch sufficient control over the independent counsel to ensure that the President is able to perform his constitutionally assigned [duties].

[Reversed.][2]

Justice SCALIA, dissenting.

[Justice Scalia's lengthy dissent began with a review of the Framers' commitment to the principle of separation of powers and proceeded to review the history of the case, concluding that what it was about was "Power": "The allocation of power among Congress, the President and the courts in such fashion as to preserve the equilibrium the Constitution sought to establish—so that 'a gradual concentration of the several powers in the same department,' Federalist No. 51, can effectively be resisted. Frequently an issue of this sort will come before the Court clad, so to speak, in sheep's clothing; the potential of the asserted principle to effect important change in the equilibrium of power is not immediately evident, and must be discerned by a careful and perceptive analysis. But this wolf comes as a wolf." By the application of the Act here, he insisted, Congress had "effectively compelled a criminal investigation of a high-level appointee of the President in connection with his actions arising out of a bitter power dispute between the President and the Legislative Branch." He continued:]

If to describe this case is not to decide it, the concept of a government of separate and coordinate powers no longer has meaning. [Art. II, § 1, cl. 1] of the Constitution provides: "The executive Power shall be vested in a President of the United States." [This] does not mean *some of* the executive power, but *all of* the executive power. It seems to me, therefore, that the decision [below] invalidating the present statute must be upheld on fundamental separation-of-powers principles if the following two questions are answered affirmatively: (1) Is the conduct of a criminal prosecution (and of an investigation to decide whether to prosecute) the exercise of purely executive power? (2) Does the statute deprive the President of the United States of exclusive control over the exercise of that power? Surprising to say, the Court appears to concede an affirmative answer to both questions, but seeks to avoid the inevitable conclusion that since the statute vests some purely executive power in a person who is not the President of the United States it is void. The Court concedes that "(t)here is no real dispute that the functions performed by the independent counsel are 'executive'." [Governmental] investigation and prosecution of crimes is a quintessentially executive function. As for the second question, whether the statute before us deprives the President of exclusive control over that quintessentially executive activity: The Court does not, and could not possibly, assert that it does not. That is indeed the whole object of the statute. Instead, the Court points out that the President, through his Attorney General,

2. Justice KENNEDY did not participate in the case.

has at least *some* control. That concession is alone enough to invalidate the statute, but I cannot refrain from pointing out that the Court greatly exaggerates the extent of that "some" presidential [control]. [It] is ultimately irrelevant *how much* the statute reduces Presidential control. [It] is not for us to determine [how] much of the purely executive powers of government must be within the full control of the President. The Constitution prescribes that they *all* are.

The utter incompatibility of the Court's approach with our constitutional traditions can be made more clear, perhaps, by applying it to the powers of the other two Branches. Is it conceivable that if Congress passed a statute depriving itself of less than full and entire control over some insignificant area of legislation, we would inquire whether the matter was "*so central* to the functioning of the Legislative Branch" as really to require complete control, or whether the statute gives Congress "*sufficient* control over the surrogate legislator to ensure that Congress is able to perform its constitutionally assigned duties"? Of course we would have none of that. Once we determined that a purely legislative power was at issue we would require it to be exercised, wholly and entirely, by Congress. [We] should say here that the President's constitutionally assigned duties include *complete* control over investigation and prosecution of violations of the law, and that the inexorable command of Article II is clear and definite: the executive power must be vested in the President of the United States. Is it unthinkable that the President should have such exclusive power, even when alleged crimes by him or his close associates are at issue? No more so than that Congress should have the exclusive power of legislation, even when what is at issue is its own exemption from the burdens of certain laws. No more so than that this Court should have the exclusive power to pronounce the final decision on justiciable cases and controversies, even those pertaining to the constitutionality of a statute reducing the salaries of the Justices. A system of separate and coordinate powers necessarily involves an acceptance of exclusive power that can theoretically be abused. [The] Court has, nonetheless, replaced the clear constitutional prescription that the executive power belongs to the President with a "balancing test." What are the standards to determine how the balance is to be struck, that is, how much removal of presidential power is too much? Once we depart from the text of the Constitution, just where short of that do we stop? The most amazing feature of the Court's opinion is that it does not even purport to give an answer. It simply *announces*, with no analysis, that the ability to control the decision whether to investigate and prosecute the President's closest advisors, and indeed the President himself, is not "so central to the functioning of the Executive Branch" as to be constitutionally required to be within the President's control.

[Justice Scalia discussed at length his objections to the Court's conclusion that the independent counsel is an "inferior" officer. He concluded: "Because appellant is not subordinate to another officer, she is not an 'inferior' officer and her appointment other than by the President with the advice and consent of the Senate is unconstitutional." Justice Scalia then turned to demonstrating "why the restrictions upon the removal of the independent counsel also violate our established precedent in dealing with that specific subject." He explained:] [Before] the present decision it was [established] (1) that the President's power to remove principal officers who exercise purely executive powers could not be restricted [Myers], and (2) that his power to remove inferior officers who exercise purely executive powers, and whose appointment Congress had removed from the usual procedure of presidential appointment with Senate consent, could be restricted, at least where the appointment had been made by an officer of the Executive Branch. Since our 1935 decision in [Humphrey's

Executor]—which was considered by many at the time the product of an activist, anti-New Deal court bent on reducing the power of President Franklin Roosevelt—it has been established that the line of permissible restriction upon removal of principal officers lies at the point at which the powers exercised by those officers are no longer purely executive. Thus, removal restrictions have been generally regarded as lawful for so-called "independent regulatory agencies." [It] has often been observed, correctly in my view, that the line between "purely executive" functions and "quasi-legislative" or "quasi-judicial" functions is not a clear one or even a rational one. But at least it permitted the identification of certain officers, and certain agencies, whose functions were entirely within the control of the President. [Today,] however, Humphrey's Executor is swept into the dustbin of repudiated constitutional principles. [As] far as I can discern from the Court's opinion, it is now open season upon the President's removal power for all executive officers, with not even the superficially principled restriction of Humphrey's Executor as cover. The Court essentially says to the President "Trust us. We will make sure that you are able to accomplish your constitutional role." I think the Constitution gives the President—and the people—more protection than that.

The purpose of the separation and equilibration of powers in general, and of the unitary Executive in particular, was not merely to assure effective government but to preserve individual freedom. Those who hold or have held offices covered by the Ethics in Government Act are entitled to that protection as much as the rest of us, and I conclude my discussion by considering the effect of the Act upon the fairness of the process they receive. [Under] our system of government, the primary check against prosecutorial abuse is a political one. The prosecutors who exercise this awesome discretion are selected and can be removed by a President, whom the people have trusted enough to elect. Moreover, when crimes are not investigated and prosecuted fairly, nonselectively, with a reasonable sense of proportion, the President pays the cost in political damage to his administration. [That] is the system of justice the rest of us are entitled to, but what of that select class consisting of present or former high-level executive-branch officials? If an allegation is made against them of any violation of any federal criminal law, [the] Attorney General must give it his attention. That in itself is not objectionable. But if, after a 90-day investigation without the benefit of normal investigatory tools, the Attorney General is unable to say that there are "no reasonable grounds to believe" that further investigation is warranted, a process is set in motion that is *not* in the full control of persons "dependent on the people," and whose flaws cannot be blamed on the President. An independent counsel is selected, and the scope of his or her authority prescribed, by a panel of judges. What if they are politically partisan, as judges have been known to be, and select a prosecutor antagonistic to the [administration]? There is no remedy for that, not even a political one.

[The] ad hoc approach to constitutional adjudication has real attraction, even apart from its work-saving potential. It is guaranteed to produce a result, in every case, that will make a majority of the Court happy with the law. The law is, by definition, precisely what the majority thinks, taking all things into account, it *ought* to be. I prefer to rely upon the judgment of the wise men who constructed our system, and of the people who approved it, and of two centuries of history that have shown it to be sound. Like it or not, that judgment says, quite plainly, that "[t]he executive Power shall be vested in a President of the United States."[1]

---

1. For a commentary on Morrison v. Olson, see Carter, "The Independent Counsel Mess," 102 Harv.L.Rev. 105 (1988). (For the successor to the statute upheld in Morrison v. Olson, see the Independent Counsel Reauthorization Act of 1987, P.L. 100–191.)

METROPOLITAN WASII. AIRPORTS AUTHORITY v. CITIZENS FOR ABATEMENT OF AIRCRAFT NOISE, INC., 501 U.S. 252 (1991): In the wake of the late 1980s cases—Morrison v. Olson as well as Mistretta (p. 400 below)—, a commentator found reasons to hope that the Court had abandoned its "rigid and formal conception" of separation of powers (illustrated by Chadha and Bowsher) and had returned instead to "a functional standard" applying the "traditional flexible approach" under which "innovative solutions to governmental problems, seeking attainment of Justice Jackson's goal of 'a workable government,'" would be sustained in the absence of evidence of "danger to liberty or sacrifice of government efficiency." Alfange, "The Supreme Court and the Separation of Powers: A Welcome Return to Normalcy?," 58 Geo.Wash.L.Rev. 668 (1990). But the Court's 6–3 decision in Washington Airports in 1991, with its reliance on Chadha and Bowsher, suggested that the majority continues to insist on a quite stringent, rigid review under separation of powers principles. The majority upheld a challenge to an Act of Congress that conditioned the transfer of Dulles and National airports near Washington, D.C., from the federal government to the Metropolitan Washington Airports Authority upon the creation by the Authority of a Board of Review composed of nine members of Congress and having veto power over Authority decisions. The Transfer Act provided that the Board of Review's congressional members would serve "in their individual capacities, as representative of users" of the airports. The nine congressional members were to be appointed by the Authority's board of directors from lists provided by the Speaker of the House and the President Pro Tem of the Senate.

Justice STEVENS's majority opinion held that Congress's conditioning of the airport's transfer on the creation of the Board of Review violated the separation of powers. Justice Stevens began his analysis by rejecting the claim that separation of powers principles were inapplicable because the Board was created by state law and was not an arm of Congress: "We [confront] an entity created at the initiative of Congress, the powers of which Congress has delineated, the purpose of which is to protect and acknowledge federal interests, and membership in which is restricted to congressional officials. Such an entity necessarily exercises sufficient federal power as an agent of Congress to mandate separation-of-powers scrutiny." Justice Stevens stated in developing constitutional principles: "To forestall the danger of encroachment 'beyond the legislative sphere,' the Constitution imposes two basic and related constraints on the Congress." The first of these was illustrated by Bowsher; the second, by Chadha. Justice Stevens found it unnecessary to choose between two alternative grounds for the decision, for either ground resulted in a holding of unconstitutionality: "If the power [of the Board] is executive, the Constitution does not permit an agent of Congress to exercise it. If the power is legislative, Congress must exercise it in conformity with the bicameralism and presentment requirements" set forth in Chadha. Justice Stevens, ended with a warning of the implications of a contrary ruling. Although the establishment of the Board might be seen as a "practical accommodation" that "should be permitted in a 'workable government,'" "the statutory scheme challenged today provides a blueprint for extensive expansion of the legislative power beyond its constitutionally confined role. Given the scope of federal power to dispense benefits to the States in a variety of forms and subject to a host of statutory conditions, Congress could, if this [Board] were valid, use similar expedients to enable its Members or its Agents to retain control, outside the ordinary legislative process, of the activities of State grant recipients charged with executing virtually every aspect of national policy." He added in a footnote that this invalidation under "basic separation-of-powers principles" made it unnecessary to address the challengers' claim that service on the Board by Members of Congress violated the Incompatibility and Ineligibility Clauses, Art. I, § 6. He also thought it unnecessary to consider the relevance of the Appointments Clause of the Constitution. [Were Justice Stevens' concerns justifiable? Were there good reasons for the Court to rely on general principles rather than on specific constitutional clauses in deciding this case? Recall the heavy reliance on the text in the majority opinion in Chadha.]

Justice WHITE, joined by Chief Justice Rehnquist and Justice Marshall, dissented. He began: "Today the Court strikes down yet another innovative and otherwise lawful governmental experiment in the name of separation of powers." He noted that both Congress and the Executive Branch had supported the constitutionality of the challenged law, and he insisted that the Court had "strain[ed]" to reach a result that was "untenable" because prior decisions "in no way compel[led] the decision." After noting that, for the first time, the Court had used "separation-of-powers doctrine to invalidate a body created under state law," he insisted at length that neither Bowsher nor Chadha supported the result. He noted that this century had "witnessed a vast increase in the power that Congress has transferred to the Executive. Given this shift in the constitutional balance, the Framers' fears of legislative tyranny ring hollow when invoked to portray a body like the Board as a serious encroachment on the powers of the Executive." In any event, he thought, Bowsher was inapplicable because there, a critical factor in determining whether an official was under congressional control was "the degree to which Congress maintains the power of removal." Here, unlike Bowsher, the Act contained no provision authorizing Congress to discharge anyone from the Board. Nor was the majority persuasive, in his view, in alternatively suggesting that the Board wielded an unconstitutional legislative veto contrary to Chadha. In Justice White's view, the Chadha theory was clearly inapplicable: "if the Board is exercising federal power, its power is not legislative" but rather executive. He noted that, before the Transfer Act, the federal agencies running the airports "exercised paradigmatic executive power"; "the transfer of the airports [to the Board] in no way altered that power." Justice White took issue as well with the Court's fear that the statutory structure in this case provided a "blueprint for extensive expansion of the legislative power beyond its constitutionally confined role." This "utterly ignore[d] the Executive's ability to protect itself through [the] veto. Should Congress ever undertake such improbable projects as transferring national parklands to the States on the condition that its agents control their oversight, there is little doubt that the President would be equal to the task of safeguarding his or her interests."

[margin annotation: focus on whether Congress keeps or gives away pwr?]

DELEGATION OF LEGISLATIVE POWERS BY CONGRESS

1. *Domestic sphere.* a. *Delegation of legislative power to the executive branch.* In principle, the constitutional grant of all legislative powers to Congress has spawned the nondelegation doctrine—the theory that Congress may not constitutionally delegate its legislative power to another branch of government. But in practice, that doctrine has had very little bite. As the Court put it in Touby v. United States, 500 U.S. 160 (1991), the doctrine "does not prevent Congress from seeking assistance, within proper limits, from the coordinate Branches. [Thus,] Congress does not violate the Constitution merely

because it legislates in broad terms, leaving a certain degree of discretion to executive or judicial actors. So long as Congress 'lay[s] down by legislative act an intelligible principle to which the person or body authorized to [act] is directed to conform, such legislative action is not a forbidden delegation of legislative power.' " The rise of the modern state has made such broad delegations well-nigh unavoidable.

There are only two cases, both in the early 1930s, in which the Court found a violation of the nondelegation doctrine. In the Schechter case (1935; p. 178 above), the Court unanimously struck down the provision of the National Industrial Recovery Act that authorized the President to approve "codes of fair competition." (Recall that Justice Cardozo's separate opinion in that case commented: "This is delegation run riot.") And in Panama Ref. Co. v. Ryan, 293 U.S. 388 (1935), the "hot oil" case, the Court struck down another provision of the NIRA on delegation grounds. But right before and after those cases, involving domestic economic regulation, the Court found no substantial delegation barriers. See, e.g., Yakus v. United States, 321 U.S. 414 (1944; World War II price controls). Only rarely have dissenters urged that the nondelegation doctrine be given sharper teeth. See, e.g., Justice Rehnquist's opinion in American Textile Mfr. Inst. v. Donovan, 452 U.S. 490 (1981).

Note that the nondelegation doctrine cases, unlike the preceding cases in this section, involve no conflicts between President and Congress. Instead, the charge is in a sense one of excessive harmony between Congress and the President: not that Congress has usurped presidential powers, but that Congress has given to the executive branch too much of its own legislative powers. Does the recurrent surfacing of quite formalistic, rigid notions of separation of powers in cases from Youngstown to some of the 1980s rulings suggest a basis for a renewed effort to put more force into the nondelegation doctrine? Is there a constitutional basis to support some of the political charges that administrative agencies and executive departments have been granted too much discretion?

b. *Delegation of legislative powers to the judiciary.* In MISTRETTA v. UNITED STATES, 488 U.S. 361 (1989), the Court entertained a rare claim that Congress had improperly delegated its powers not to the executive branch but to an agency composed in part of federal judges. In rejecting the delegation and general separation-of-powers attacks, the 8–1 ruling followed the flexible, functional approach of Morrison v. Olson rather than the more formalistic analysis of Bowsher and Chadha. The suit was a challenge to the creation and powers of the U.S. Sentencing Commission, established by the Sentencing Reform Act of 1984. The Commission was set up "as an independent commission in the judicial branch," consisting of seven voting members appointed by the President with the advice and consent of the Senate, at least three of whom must be federal judges selected from a list of six recommended to the President by the U.S. Judicial Conference. The members were removable from the Commission by the President for "good cause." The Act was a response to concern about "the great variation among sentences imposed by different judges upon similarly situated offenders" and "the uncertainty as to the time the offender would spend in prison." The law provided instead that the Commission would establish mandatory guidelines that federal judges would have to apply in sentencing. The guidelines specify fairly narrow ranges of permissible sentences for different offenses, with some leeway for the differing circumstances in which criminal defendants act.

Justice BLACKMUN's majority opinion began by rejecting the claim that Congress had granted the Commission "excessive legislative discretion in violation of the constitutionally based nondelegation doctrine." Applying the principle that Congress must lay down an "intelligible principle" to guide the agency exercising the congressionally delegated power, the Court noted that "our jurisprudence has been driven by a practical understanding that in our increasingly complex society, [Congress] simply cannot do its job absent an ability to delegate power under broad general directives." On this issue, he concluded that "we harbor no doubt that Congress' delegation of authority to the Sentencing Commission is sufficiently specific and detailed to meet constitutional requirements." He acknowledged that the Commission enjoyed "significant discretion in formulating guidelines," but added that "our cases do not at all suggest that delegations of this type may not carry with them the need to exercise judgment on matters of policy."

nondelegation doctrine (is this a subset of sep/pwrs?)

Justice Blackmun then turned to the broader claim that the Act violated separation of powers principles. He stated: "[T]he Framers did not require—and indeed rejected—the notion that the three Branches must be entirely separate and [distinct]. In adopting [a] flexible understanding of separation of powers [see Justice Jackson's opinion in Youngstown], we simply have recognized Madison's teaching that the greatest security against tyranny [lies] not in a hermetic division between the Branches, but in a carefully crafted system of checked and balanced power within each Branch. [The] Framers 'built into the tripartite Federal Government [a] self-executing safeguard against the encroachment or aggrandizement of one branch at the expense of the other.' It is this concern of encroachment and aggrandizement that has animated our separation-of-powers jurisprudence and aroused our vigilance against the 'hydraulic pressure inherent within each of the separate Branches to exceed the outer limits of its power.' Accordingly, we have not hesitated to strike down provisions of law that either accrete to a single branch powers more appropriately diffused among separate branches or that undermine the authority and independence of one or another coordinate branch. For example, [we have] invalidated attempts by Congress to exercise the responsibilities of other Branches or to reassign powers vested by the Constitution in either the Judicial Branch or the Executive Branch. [Bowsher; Chadha.] By the same token, we have upheld statutory provisions that to some degree commingle the functions of the Branches, but that pose no danger of either aggrandizement or encroachment. [Morrison.] [In] cases specifically involving the Judicial Branch, we have expressed our vigilance against two dangers: first, that the Judicial Branch neither be assigned nor allowed 'tasks that are more appropriately accomplished by [other] branches,' Morrison, and, second, that no provision of law 'impermissibly threatens the institutional integrity of the Judicial Branch.'

Separation of Powers

orig. and structure

Unconstitutional

"[Petitioner] argues that the Act suffers from each of these constitutional infirmities. He argues that Congress [effected] an unconstitutional accumulation of power within the Judicial Branch while at the same time undermining the Judiciary's independence and integrity. Specifically, petitioner claims [that] Congress unconstitutionally has required the [Judicial] Branch, and individual Article III judges, to exercise not only their judicial authority, but legislative authority—the making of sentencing policy—as well. At the same time, petitioner asserts, Congress unconstitutionally eroded the integrity and independence of the Judiciary by requiring Article III judges to sit on the Commission, by requiring that those judges share their rulemaking authority with nonjudges, and by subjecting the Commission's members to appointment and removal by the President. [Although] the unique composition and responsibilities of the Sentencing Commission give rise to serious concerns about a disruption of the appropriate balance of governmental power among the coordinate Branches, we conclude [that] petitioner's fears for the fundamental structural protections of

too much pwr judicial infringeon independence

sentencing policy = legislative policy

the Constitution prove, at least in this case, to be 'more smoke than fire,' and do not compel us to invalidate Congress' considered scheme for resolving the seemingly intractable dilemma of excessive disparity in criminal sentencing.

"[The] Sentencing Commission unquestionably is a peculiar institution within the framework of our Government. Our constitutional principles of separated powers are not violated, however, by mere anomaly or innovation. [Congress's] decision to create an independent rulemaking body to promulgate sentencing guidelines and to locate that body within the Judicial Branch is not unconstitutional unless Congress has vested in the Commission powers that are more appropriately performed by the other Branches or that undermine the integrity of the Judiciary. [As] a general principle, we stated [that] 'executive or administrative duties of a nonjudicial nature may not be imposed on judges holding office under Article III of the Constitution.' [Morrison.] Nonetheless, we have recognized significant exceptions to this general rule and have approved the assumption of some nonadjudicatory activities by the Judicial Branch. [That] judicial rulemaking, at least with respect to some subjects, falls within [a] twilight area is no longer an issue for dispute. None of our cases indicate that rulemaking per se is a function that may not be performed by an entity within the [Judicial Branch]. In light of this precedent and practice, we can discern no separation-of-powers impediment to the placement of the Sentencing Commission within the Judicial Branch. [That] Congress should vest such rulemaking in the Judicial Branch [simply] acknowledges the role that the Judiciary always has played, and continues to play, in sentencing. [In] sum, since substantive judgment in the field of sentencing has been and remains appropriate to the Judicial Branch, and the methodology of rulemaking has been and remains appropriate to that Branch, Congress' considered decision to combine these functions in an independent Sentencing Commission and to locate that Commission within the Judicial Branch does not violate the principle of separation of powers.

"[Petitioner also] urges us to strike down the Act on the ground that its requirement of judicial participation on the Commission unconstitutionally conscripts individual federal judges for political service and thereby undermines the essential impartiality of the Judicial Branch. We find Congress' requirement of judicial service somewhat troublesome, but we do not believe that the Act impermissibly interferes with the functioning of the Judiciary. [The] principle of separation of powers does not absolutely prohibit Article III judges from serving on commissions such as that created by the Act. The judges serve on the Sentencing Commission not pursuant to their status and authority as Article III judges, but solely because of their appointment by the President as the Act directs. Such power as these judges wield as Commissioners is not judicial power; it is administrative power derived from the enabling legislation. [The] Constitution, at least as a per se matter, does not forbid judges from wearing two hats; it merely forbids them from wearing both hats at the same time. [That] the Constitution does not absolutely prohibit a federal judge from assuming extrajudicial duties does not mean that every extrajudicial service would be compatible with, or appropriate to, continuing service on the bench; nor does it mean that Congress may require a federal judge to assume extrajudicial duties as long as the judge is assigned those duties in an individual, not judicial, capacity. The ultimate inquiry remains whether a particular extrajudicial assignment undermines the integrity of the Judicial Branch. [We] cannot see how the service of federal judges on the Commission will have a constitutionally significant practical effect on the operation of the Judicial Branch. [While] in the abstract a proliferation of commissions with congressionally mandated judiciary participation might threaten judicial independence by exhausting the resources of the Judicial Branch, that danger is far too remote for consideration here.

"We are somewhat more troubled by petitioner's argument that the Judiciary's entanglement in the political work of the Commission undermines public confidence in the disinterestedness of the Judicial Branch. [Although] it is a judgment that is not without difficulty, we conclude that the participation of federal judges on the Sentencing Commission does not threaten, either in fact or in appearance, the impartiality of the Judicial Branch. We are drawn to this conclusion by one paramount consideration: that the Sentencing Commission is devoted exclusively to the development of rules to rationalize a process that has been and will continue to be performed exclusively by the Judicial Branch. In our view, this is an essentially neutral endeavor and one in which judicial participation is peculiarly appropriate. [Moreover, we] do not believe that the President's appointment and removal powers over the Commission afford him influence over the functions of the Judicial Branch or undue sway over its members. [We] simply cannot imagine that federal judges will comport their actions to the wishes of the President for the purpose of receiving an appointment to the Sentencing Commission."

impartiality

← *This is crazy!*

In a lengthy dissent, Justice SCALIA insisted that "I can find no place within our constitutional system for an agency created by Congress to exercise no governmental power other than the making of laws." Although he agreed with the Courts' rejection of the unconstitutional delegation attack, he added: "Precisely because the scope of delegation is largely uncontrollable by the courts, we must be particularly rigorous in preserving the Constitution's structural restrictions that deter excessive delegation. The major one [is] that the power to make law cannot be exercised by anyone other than Congress, except in conjunction with the lawful exercise of executive or judicial power. [A] pure delegation of legislative power is precisely what we have before us. It is irrelevant whether the standards are adequate, because they are not standards related to the exercise of executive or judicial powers; they are, plainly and simply, standards for further legislation. [Today's] decision may aptly be described as the Humphrey's Executor of the Judicial Branch, and I think we will live to regret it." He concluded with a more general criticism of "the regrettable tendency of our recent separation-of-powers jurisprudence to treat the Constitution as though it were no more than a generalized prescription that the functions of the Branches should not be commingled too much—how much is too much to be determined, case-by-case, by this Court. The Constitution is not that. Rather, [it] is a prescribed structure, a framework, for the conduct of government. [I] think the Court errs [not] so much because it mistakes the degree of commingling, but because it fails to recognize that this case is not about commingling, but about the creation of a new branch altogether, a sort of junior-varsity Congress. [In] the long run the improvisation of a constitutional structure on the basis of currently perceived utility will be disastrous."

pure delegation of leg. power

2. *Foreign affairs.* The nondelegation doctrine, very weak in the domestic sphere, is an even more toothless barrier in the context of foreign affairs. In UNITED STATES v. CURTISS–WRIGHT EXPORT CORP., 299 U.S. 304 (1936), (already noted with respect to broad national authority regarding foreign affairs at p. 256 above), Justice SUTHERLAND's opinion ended with an emphasis on "the unwisdom of requiring Congress in this field of governmental power to lay down narrowly definite standards by which the President is to be governed." That sentence is especially noteworthy because the decision came just a year after the strong (and rare) invocation of the nondelegation principle in the Schechter case, above.

In the aspect most immediately relevant here, Curtiss–Wright was a case about delegation of congressional powers. The case involved a Joint Resolution of Congress in 1934 authorizing the President to prohibit the sale of arms and munitions to Bolivia and Paraguay, which were involved in armed conflict. President Roosevelt immediately proclaimed an embargo. Curtiss–Wright was indicted for conspiracy to sell arms to Bolivia and challenged the Joint Resolution as an unconstitutional delegation of legislative power to the President. Justice Sutherland, after uttering his broad statements on the national foreign affairs power, noted earlier, added equally broad claims about the special role of the President in that sphere: "In this vast external realm, with its important, complicated, delicate and manifold problems, the President alone has the power to speak or listen as a representative of a nation." (Recall Justice Jackson's footnote in his Youngstown opinion, at p. 356 above, stating that "[m]uch of the Court's opinion [in Curtiss–Wright] is dictum" and that Curtiss-Wright involved "not the question of the President's power to act without congressional authority, but the question of his right to act under and in accord with an Act of Congress.")

SECTION 3.   EXECUTIVE PRIVILEGE AND IMMUNITIES

United States v. Nixon

418 U.S. 683, 94 S.Ct. 3090, 41 L.Ed.2d 1039 (1974).

Chief Justice BURGER delivered the opinion of the Court.

This litigation presents for review the denial of a motion, filed [on] behalf of the [President] in the case of United States v. Mitchell et al., to quash a third-party subpoena duces tecum issued by the [District Court] pursuant to Fed.R.Crim.Proc. 17(c). The subpoena directed the President to produce certain tape recordings and documents relating to his conversations with aides and advisers. The court rejected the President's claims of absolute executive privilege, of lack of jurisdiction, and of failure to satisfy the requirements of [Rule 17(c)].

[This case is an important segment of the Watergate controversy—the controversy that grew out of a burglary at Democratic National Headquarters in Washington's Watergate Hotel during the 1972 presidential campaign, by employees of President Nixon's re-election committee. After investigations by a Senate Select Committee disclosed White House involvements in the planning and cover-up of the burglary, President Nixon authorized the appointment of a Special Prosecutor. In this case, the Court upheld a subpoena requiring President Nixon to produce specified tapes and documents relating to his actions and discussions as President; the Court rejected the President's claim of executive privilege and immunity. The case arose from a federal grand jury indictment on March 1, 1974, of seven associates of President Nixon for conspiracy to obstruct justice and other offenses relating to the Watergate burglary. The President was named as an unindicted co-conspirator. On April 18, 1974, the District Court, upon motion of the Special Prosecutor, issued a subpoena duces tecum to the President requiring him to produce, before the September 8 trial date, certain tapes and documents relating to precisely identified meetings between the President and others. On April 30, the President released edited transcripts of 43 conversations, including portions of 20 conversations subject to subpoena in the present case. On May 1, the President's counsel filed a "special appearance" and moved to quash the subpoena. This motion was accompanied by a formal claim of executive privilege. On May 20, the District Court denied the motion. The President appealed to the Court of Appeals, but, before a decision in that court, the Supreme Court granted certiorari before judgment.[1] Before turning to the major issues in the case, the Court held that (1) the District Court order was an appealable order and that the case was properly "in" the Court of Appeals when the Supreme Court granted certiorari; (2) the Special Prosecutor's subpoena satisfied the requirements of Fed.R.Crim.Proc. 17(c)—i.e., the requisite relevancy, admissibility, and specificity were shown; and (3) that the case was not a nonjusticiable intrabranch dispute between the President and the Special Prosecutor. The Chief Justice then turned to the central portion of the opinion, entitled "The Claim of Privilege," and proceeded as follows:]

A. [W]e turn to the claim that the subpoena should be quashed because it demands "confidential conversations between a President and his close advisors that it would be inconsistent with the public interest to produce." The first contention is a broad claim that the separation of powers doctrine precludes judicial review of a President's claim of privilege. The second contention is that if he does not prevail on the claim of absolute privilege, the court should hold as a matter of constitutional law that the privilege prevails over the subpoena duces tecum. In the performance of assigned constitutional duties each branch of the Government must initially interpret the Constitution, and the interpretation of its powers by any branch is due great respect from the others. The President's counsel [reads] the Constitution as providing an absolute privilege of confidentiality for all Presidential communications. Many decisions of this Court, however, have unequivocally reaffirmed the holding of [Marbury v. Madison] that "it is emphatically the province and duty of the judicial department to say what the law is."

No holding of the Court has defined the scope of judicial power specifically relating to the enforcement of a subpoena for confidential Presidential communications for use in a criminal prosecution, but other exercises of powers by the Executive Branch and the Legislative Branch have been found invalid as in conflict with the Constitution. [Powell v. McCormack, Youngstown.] In a series of cases, the Court interpreted the explicit immunity conferred by express provisions of the Constitution on Members of the House and Senate by the Speech or Debate Clause. [See p. 413 below.] Since this Court has consistently exercised the power to construe and delineate claims arising under express powers, it must follow that the Court has authority to interpret claims with respect to powers alleged to derive from enumerated powers. [Notwithstanding] the deference each branch must accord the others, the "judicial Power of the United States" vested in the federal courts by [Art. III] can no more be shared with the Executive Branch than the Chief Executive, for example, can share with the Judiciary the veto [power]. Any other conclusion would be contrary to

---

1. The Court granted certiorari on May 31, heard argument on July 8, and decided the case on July 24, 1974, while the House Judiciary Committee was considering the Articles of Impeachment noted at p. 411 below. For a criticism of the Court's decision to bypass full consideration in the Court of Appeals and to grant extraordinarily speedy review in the case—a criticism noting that the Court's timing of its judgment aborted completion of the impeachment process—see Gunther, "Judicial Hegemony and Legislative Autonomy: The Nixon Case and the Impeachment Process," 22 UCLA L.Rev. 30 (1974).

the basic concept of separation of powers and the checks and balances that flow from the scheme of a tripartite government. We therefore reaffirm that it is the province and the duty of this Court "to say what the law is" with respect to the claim of privilege presented in this case. [Marbury v. Madison.]

B.   In support of his claim of absolute privilege, the President's counsel urges two [grounds]: the need to protect the confidentiality of executive communications, and the implications of the separation of powers structure. [After noting the importance of confidentiality, the Chief Justice continued:] [I]t is argued that the independence of the Executive Branch within its own sphere insulates a President from a judicial subpoena in an ongoing criminal prosecution, and thereby protects confidential Presidential communications. However, neither the doctrine of separation of powers, nor the need for confidentiality of high level communications, without more, can sustain an absolute, unqualified Presidential privilege of immunity from judicial process under all circumstances. The President's need for complete candor and objectivity from advisers calls for great deference from the courts. However, when the privilege depends solely on the broad, undifferentiated claim of public interest in the confidentiality of such conversations, a confrontation with other values arises. Absent a claim of need to protect military, diplomatic, or sensitive national security secrets, we find it difficult to accept the argument that even the very important interest in confidentiality of Presidential communications is significantly diminished by production of such material for in camera inspection with all the protection that a district court will be obliged to provide. The impediment that an absolute, unqualified privilege would place in the way of the primary constitutional duty of the Judicial Branch to do justice in criminal prosecutions would plainly conflict with the function of the courts under Art. III. In designing the structure of our Government and dividing and allocating the sovereign power among three co-equal branches, the [Framers] sought to provide a comprehensive system, but the separate powers were not intended to operate with absolute independence. [To] read the Art. II powers of the President as providing an absolute privilege as against a subpoena essential to enforcement of criminal statutes on no more than a generalized claim of the public interest in confidentiality of non-military and nondiplomatic discussions would upset the constitutional balance of "a workable government" and gravely impair the role of the courts under Art. III.

C.   [After articulating justifications for a "presumptive privilege for Presidential communications," a privilege "inextricably rooted in the separation of powers," the Chief Justice continued:] But this presumptive privilege must be considered in light of our historic commitment to the rule of law. This is nowhere more profoundly manifest than in our view that "the twofold aim [of criminal justice] is that guilt shall not escape or innocence suffer." [The] need to develop all relevant facts in the adversary system is both fundamental and comprehensive. [To] ensure that justice is done, it is imperative to the function of courts that compulsory process be available for the production of evidence needed either by the prosecution or by the defense. [Evidentiary privileges] are designed to protect weighty and legitimate competing interests [e.g., self-incrimination, attorney, and priest privileges] [and] are not lightly created nor expansively construed, for they are in derogation of the search for truth. In this case the President challenges a subpoena served on him as a third party requiring the production of materials for use in a criminal prosecution; he does so on the claim that he has a privilege against disclosure of confidential communications. He does not place his claim of privilege on the ground they are military or diplomatic secrets. As to these areas of Art. II duties the courts have traditionally shown the utmost deference to presidential responsibilities. [No] case of the Court, however, has extended this high degree of deference to a

President's generalized interest in confidentiality. Nowhere in the Constitution [is] there any explicit reference to a privilege of confidentiality, yet to the extent this interest relates to the effective discharge of a President's powers, it is constitutionally based. The right to the production of all evidence at a criminal trial similarly has constitutional [dimensions].

In this case we must weigh the importance of the general privilege of confidentiality of Presidential communications in performance of his responsibilities against the inroads of such a privilege on the fair administration of criminal justice.[2] The interest in preserving confidentiality is weighty indeed and entitled to great respect. However, we cannot conclude that advisers will be moved to temper the candor of their remarks by the infrequent occasions of disclosure because of the possibility that such conversations will be called for in the context of a criminal prosecution. On the other hand, the allowance of the privilege to withhold evidence that is demonstrably relevant in a criminal trial would cut deeply into the guarantee of due process of law and gravely impair the basic function of the courts. A President's acknowledged need for confidentiality in the communications of his office is general in nature, whereas the constitutional need for production of relevant evidence in a criminal proceeding is specific and central to the fair adjudication of a particular criminal [case]. Without access to specific facts a criminal prosecution may be totally frustrated. The President's broad interest in confidentiality of communications will not be vitiated by disclosure of a limited number of conversations preliminarily shown to have some bearing on the pending criminal cases. We conclude that when the ground for asserting privilege as to subpoenaed materials sought for use in a criminal trial is based only on the generalized interest in confidentiality, it cannot prevail over the fundamental demands of due process of law in the fair administration of [criminal justice].

D. If a President concludes that compliance with a subpoena would be injurious to the public interest he may properly, as was done here, invoke a claim of privilege on the return of the subpoena. Upon receiving a claim of privilege from the Chief Executive, it became the further duty of the District Court to treat the subpoenaed material as presumptively privileged and to require the Special Prosecutor to demonstrate that the Presidential material was "essential to the justice of the [pending criminal] case."[3] [We] affirm the order of the District Court that subpoenaed materials be transmitted to that court. We now turn to the important question of the District Court's responsibilities in conducting the in camera examination of Presidential materials or communications delivered under the compulsion of the subpoena duces tecum.

E. [The Court proceeded to offer guidelines to the District Court in implementing the decision:] Statements that meet the test of admissibility and relevance must be isolated; all other material must be excised. [The] District Court has a very heavy responsibility to see to it that Presidential conversations, which are either not relevant or not admissible, are accorded that high

---

2. We are not here concerned with the balance between the President's generalized interest in confidentiality and the need for relevant evidence in civil litigation, nor with that between the confidentiality interest and congressional demands for information, nor with the President's interest in preserving state secrets. We address only the conflict between the President's assertion of a generalized privilege of confidentiality against the constitutional need for relevant evidence in criminal trials. [Footnote by Chief Justice Burger.]

3. Here and elsewhere in the opinion, Chief Justice Burger cited and quoted from the Aaron Burr treason trial in the early 19th century (in which John Marshall, sitting on the Circuit Court, issued a subpoena to President Thomas Jefferson). See United States v. Burr, 25 Fed.Cas. 187 (No. 14,694) (1807).

degree of respect due the [President]. Mr. Chief Justice Marshall sitting as a trial judge in [Burr] was extraordinarily careful to point out that: "[I]n no case of this kind would a Court be required to proceed against the president as against an ordinary individual." Marshall's statement cannot be read to mean in any sense that a President is above the law, but relates to the singularly unique role under Art. II of a President's communications and activities, related to the performance of duties under that Article. Moreover, a President's communications and activities encompass a vastly wider range of sensitive material than would be true of any "ordinary individual." It is therefore necessary in the public interest to afford Presidential confidentiality the greatest protection consistent with the fair administration of justice. The need for confidentiality even as to idle conversations with associates in which casual reference might be made concerning political leaders within the country or foreign statesmen is too obvious to call for further treatment. We have no doubt that the District Judge will at all times accord to Presidential records that high degree of deference suggested in [Burr].

Affirmed.[4] [Justice REHNQUIST did not participate.]

———

1. *Presidential and other executive officials' amenability to judicial process*. a. *The Nixon case*. One of the claims of the President in the Nixon case was that the President was not amenable to judicial process and that impeachment and removal were preconditions to judicial proceedings against him. The President offered two other claims as well: first, the question of executive privilege was an issue committed to the executive branch for final decision and thus was not justiciable when it was not reviewable by the courts, second, on the merits of the executive privilege issue, the President could not be subpoenaed, as here—i.e., even if the Court could adjudicate the scope of executive privilege, it should find the subpoenaed materials within the appropriate scope of the privilege, in view of the need for confidentiality. Did the Court adequately distinguish among and respond to each of these contentions—presidential immunity; presidential autonomy and finality; and the scope of executive privilege? Or did the Court unduly blur the three differing questions before it? The decision clearly rejected Nixon's claim that he was immune from judicial process while in office. That question had long been in doubt, especially because of the Court's ruling in Mississippi v. Johnson, 71 U.S. (4 Wall.) 475 (1867), where the Court refused to entertain a suit attempting to enjoin President Andrew Johnson's enforcement of the Reconstruction Act. The Court emphasized the difficulties of enforcement and the availability of the impeachment route. Were the Court's references in U.S. v. Nixon to the lower court proceedings in the Burr case as well as to Marbury v. Madison truly helpful on the amenability issue?

b. *Absolute immunity from civil liability*. Eight years after the Nixon case, the Court announced an absolute presidential immunity from *civil* liability. The 5–4 decision in NIXON v. FITZGERALD, 457 U.S. 731 (1982), held that "the

___

4. Before the July 24, 1974, decision in this case, the President and his counsel had left it unclear whether Nixon would obey an adverse Court decision. But eight hours after the Court decision was announced, President Nixon's office issued a statement reporting that he would comply. Among the 64 tape recordings covered by the decision was a particularly damaging one of conversations on June 23, 1972, six days after the Watergate burglary. On August 5, President Nixon released transcripts of those conversations. On August 8, President Nixon announced that he would resign on the next day.

President is absolutely [rather than qualifiedly] immune from civil damages liability for his official acts"—at least "in the absence of explicit affirmative action by Congress."[1] Fitzgerald, a widely publicized "whistle blower" of the late 1960s, lost his position with the Department of the Air Force in 1970. He was fired, he claimed, because of his widely publicized testimony before a congressional subcommittee. Fitzgerald's damage action claimed violation of his First Amendment and statutory rights, and the named defendants included former President Nixon as well as other officials. In finding absolute civil damages immunity, Justice POWELL's majority opinion emphasized the President's "unique position in the constitutional scheme." He elaborated: "Because of the singular importance of the President's duties, diversion of his energies by concern with private lawsuits would raise unique risks to the effective functioning of government. As is the case with prosecutors and judges—for whom absolute immunity now is established—a President must concern himself with matters likely to 'arouse the most intense feelings.' [In] view of the visibility of his office and the effect of his actions on countless people, the President would be an easily identifiable target for suits for civil damages. Cognizance of this personal vulnerability frequently could distract a President from his public duties, to the detriment not only of the President and his office but also the [Nation]." Justice Powell added: "A rule of absolute immunity for the President will not leave the nation without sufficient protection against misconduct on the part of the chief executive. There remains the constitutional remedy of impeachment. In addition, there are formal and informal checks on Presidential action that do not apply with equal force to other executive officials. The President is subjected to constant scrutiny by the press. Vigilant oversight by Congress also may serve to deter Presidential abuses of [office]. Other incentives to avoid misconduct may include a desire to earn re-election, the need to maintain prestige as an element of Presidential influence, and a President's traditional concern for his historical stature. The existence of alternative remedies and deterrents establishes that absolute immunity will not place the President 'above the law.'" Justice WHITE, joined by Justices Brennan, Marshall and Blackmun, submitted a long and vehement dissent: "Attaching absolute immunity to the office of the President, rather than to particular activities that the President might perform, places the President above the law. It is a reversion to the old notion that the King can do no wrong." He charged that the majority's abandonment of "basic principles" tracing back to Marbury v. Madison rested on a judgment that had "few, if any, indicia of a judicial decision; it is almost wholly a policy choice," and "very poor policy" to boot. He summarized the appropriate "functional" immunity approach he would apply as follows: "The scope of immunity is determined by function, not office. [The] *functional* only question that must be answered here is whether the dismissal of employees falls within a constitutionally assigned executive function, the performance of which would be substantially impaired by the possibility of a private action

1. Could Congress change the absolute immunity established by this case? Justice Powell's majority opinion left that question open. Contrast Chief Justice BURGER'S position: although he joined Justice Powell's opinion, he argued in a concurrence that presidential immunity was mandated by the constitutional separation of powers and insisted: "Nothing in the Court's opinion is to be read as suggesting that a Constitutional holding of this Court can be legislatively overruled or modified. Marbury v. Madison."

Justice WHITE, while dissenting from the majority's holding, in effect agreed with the Chief Justice on the issue of congressional power to alter the immunity: "We are never told [how] or why Congressional action could make a difference. It is not apparent that any of the propositions relied upon by the majority to immunize the President would not apply equally to such a statutory cause of action; nor does the majority indicate what new principles would operate to undercut those propositions."

does not extend to other exec. officials

for damages. I believe it does not." (In a companion ruling, the Court refused to extend the absolute presidential immunity to the President's senior aides, although such persons are entitled to qualified immunity. Harlow v. Fitzgerald, 457 U.S. 800 (1982). See also Mitchell v. Forsyth, 472 U.S. 511 (1985), and Wyatt v. Cole, 504 U.S. 158 (1992).)

To what extent does any of the rationale of Nixon v. Fitzgerald justify an immunity of a President in office to lawsuits for alleged misconduct prior to his or her election? See Jones v. Clinton, 879 F.Supp. 86 (E.D.Ark.1995), a suit by Paula Corbin Jones against President Clinton based on alleged sexual harassment that occurred prior to President Clinton's election to office. The trial court held that the action should be delayed until after Clinton's service as President, but saw no reason to delay discovery proceedings. The Eighth Circuit reversed that ruling in part, 72 F.3d 1354 (1996), finding no justification to delay pretrial proceedings. The Court granted review, and the case was argued during the October 1996 Term. See generally Amar & Katyal, "Executive Privileges and Immunities: The Nixon and Clinton Cases," 108 Harv. L.Rev. 701 (1994).

2. *Executive privilege.* a. *The Nixon case.* In the Nixon case, the Court ruled both that the President was subject to court orders issued in the course of a criminal proceeding and that his presumptive executive privilege did not bar compliance with the subpoena. Did the Court jump too quickly from its view that the President was amenable to judicial process to its conclusions that it was for the *courts* to decide the content of executive privilege? Note Gunther, "Judicial Hegenomy and Legislative Autonomy: The Nixon Case and the Impeachment Process," 22 UCLA L.Rev. 30 (1974), arguing that "it was possible to decide against President Nixon's claim as to amenability and yet support his argument as to autonomy" i.e., that it was possible to conclude that the President, as a matter of constitutional interpretation of Article II, had absolute discretion to determine the scope of executive privilege. "Marbury v. Madison is an extremely relevant source in deciding the [amenability to judicial powers] issue. It is far more tenuously related to the second. Respectable arguments after all have been made [that] absolute executive immunity is a legitimate constitutional [interpretation]. The opinion in United States v. Nixon tended to merge and blur those separate issues. And the linchpin in intertwining them was the excessive use of Marbury v. Madison." Gunther argued that "there is nothing in [Marbury] that precludes a constitutional interpretation which gives final authority to another branch." He claimed that the Chief Justice's invocation of Marbury conveyed "a misleadingly broad view of judicial competence, exclusivity and supremacy," with the Court suggesting "that recognizing absolute executive privilege as a matter of constitutional interpretation [would] somehow be contrary to Marbury v. Madison's view of the proper judicial role." Recall the materials in chapter 1 on presidential claims to autonomy in the face of some Supreme Court decisions. Did the views of Jefferson, Jackson, and Lincoln support Nixon's position, or were those situations distinguishable? Does Cooper v. Aaron, p. 25 above, weaken Nixon's position? Should the Court have mentioned it?

b. *The proper scope of executive privilege.* Administrations since George Washington's have claimed that they can refuse to turn over information to the legislative branch, and Congress has repeatedly denied the constitutional justifications for such a privilege. In that sense, the Nixon case, although rejecting the President's claim to an absolute privilege, can be seen as a triumph for the executive branch, for the Court did recognize a qualified, "presumptive" privilege. Note Berger, "Executive Privilege: A Constitutional Myth" (1974); see also Dorsen & Shattuck, "Executive Privilege, the Congress and the

Courts," 35 Ohio St.L.J. 1 (1974). Is the broad congressional power to investigate sufficiently weighty to trump the executive's privilege claim in the balancing process, as the interest in the "fair administration of criminal justice" outweighed the privilege claimed in the Nixon case? Note that the Court in Nixon did not pass on the balance "between the confidentiality interest and congressional demands for information." Note also the ruling in Senate Select Committee on Presidential Campaign Activities v. Nixon, 370 F.Supp. 521 (D.D.C. 1974), rejecting enforcement of a subpoena for tapes by the Senate Committee investigating the Watergate matter. The court held that the Committee's need to know did not outweigh the interest in executive confidentiality.

3. *Congressional power over presidential papers.* In NIXON v. ADMINISTRATOR OF GENERAL SERVICES, 433 U.S. 425 (1977), the Court upheld the "facial validity" of the Presidential Recordings and Materials Preservation Act of 1974, adopted by Congress a few months after President Nixon's resignation. The Act directed the Administrator of General Services, an executive official, to take custody of the Nixon materials, to screen them, and to return to Nixon those materials that are personal and private in nature. Nixon challenged the law on several grounds, including the claimed violation of separation of powers. The 7–2 decision by the Court sustained the Act. Justice BRENNAN's majority opinion stated that only the custody and screening provisions were properly before the Court and emphasized the narrowness of the decision, stressing the uniqueness of the Nixon resignation and its aftermath. Nixon's basic contention was that the "Act encroache[d] upon the Presidential prerogatives to control internal operations of the Presidential office." Justice Brennan found Nixon's view "inconsistent with the origins of [the separation of powers] doctrine, recent decisions of the Court, and the contemporary realities of our political system." In his view, the touchstone for determining whether those principles had been violated was whether one branch's action vis-à-vis another constituted undue "disruption" on another. The "disruption" inquiry, he elaborated, "focuses on the extent to which [the Act] prevents the executive branch from accomplishing its constitutionally *functional* assigned functions"; he concluded that there was nothing "unduly disruptive of the Executive Branch" here. Justice Brennan found adequate justification for the "limited intrusion into executive confidentiality" here in the "substantial public interest" reflected in Congress's "desire to restore public confidence in our political processes by preserving the materials as a source for facilitating a full airing of the events leading to [Nixon's] resignation" and its "need to understand how those political processes had in fact operated in order to gauge the necessity for remedial legislation." He emphasized, moreover, that "control of the material remains in the Executive Branch." Chief Justice BURGER's dissent gave three reasons for finding a violation of separation of powers principles: the Act constituted a congressional coercion of the President; the Act was "an exercise of executive—not legislative—power by the Legislative Branch"; and the Act worked "a sweeping modification of the constitutional privilege and historical practice of confidentiality of every Chief Executive since 1789." Justice REHNQUIST submitted a separate dissent, largely agreeing with the Chief Justice's separation of powers analysis.

4. *Impeaching the president.* Many of the arguments for presidential immunity from court proceedings have relied on the argument that impeachment is the exclusive route to reach the President's misbehavior in office. American experience with presidential impeachments has been sparse. Andrew Johnson is the only President who was impeached, escaping conviction and removal by the Senate by only one vote; most impeachments voted by the

House have involved federal judges. Recall Nixon v. United States (1993; p. 404 above.) The proceedings in the House Judiciary Committee during the spring and summer of 1974, considering the impeachment of President Richard M. Nixon, provoked the most intense national attention to problems of impeachment in more than a century. Art. II, § 4, states: "The President, Vice President are all civil Officers of the United States, shall be removed from Office on Impeachment for, and Conviction of, Treason, Bribery, or other high Crimes and Misdemeanors." The meaning of the "high Crimes and Misdemeanors" provision has been a central source of controversy. What is the scope of that phrase? What presidential misconduct is properly the subject of impeachment proceedings? Must the conduct constitute a criminal offense? If the scope of impeachable offenses is not coextensive with criminality, what acceptable criteria can be stated? The modern debate about impeachable offenses focused on two contending views: President Nixon's counsel claimed that "other high Crimes and Misdemeanors" is limited to serious acts which would be indictable as criminal offenses; the staff of the Judiciary Committee insisted that the scope of impeachable offenses and of criminality are not synonymous, and that the impeachment route may reach serious abuses of office or breaches of trust even when they do not constitute criminal acts. The main support for the President's position rested on the text of the Constitution, though the language is not unambiguous. The main reliance of the defenders of the broader position was on history—both English historical background and evidence regarding the intent of the Framers. Moreover, both sides marshaled policy arguments on their behalf.[1]

The three Articles of Impeachment adopted by the House Judiciary Committee in late July 1974 followed the approach of the impeachment inquiry staff. The more general Articles, I and II, dealt with a Watergate cover-up and related abuses of power. Article III charged that the President had "willfully disobeyed" (relying on executive privilege) a series of subpoenas issued by the Impeachment Committee. The support for Article III in the Committee was weaker than that for the first two Articles, with several Representatives suggesting that, in light of United States v. Nixon, that issue should be left to the Court as the "ultimate interpreter of the Constitution." Did Article III state an impeachable offense? The Committee ultimately voted to impeach on all three Articles.[2] Article I, focusing on the Watergate cover-up, concluded that, "[in] all of this, Richard M. Nixon has acted in a manner contrary to his trust as President and subversive of constitutional government." Article II charged, with a similar conclusion, that Nixon had "repeatedly engaged in conduct violating the constitutional rights of citizens, impairing the due and proper administration of justice [or] contravening the laws governing the agencies of the executive branch." Among the specific acts alleged was an attempt to obtain confidential information in income tax returns, misusing the FBI to obtain information and using it for purposes unrelated to national security, and maintaining a secret investigative unit within the Office of the President. (Although all three Articles were adopted by the House Committee, further proceedings in the process—including a vote by the full House and a

1. See St. Clair et al., "An Analysis of the Constitutional Standard for Presidential Impeachment" (1974), and Staff Report, "Constitutional Grounds for Presidential Impeachment" (1974). See also Black, "Impeachment: A Handbook" (1974).

2. For a defense of Article III, and a criticism for the Court for overbroad statements casting a shadow over the congressional debate on that Article, see Gunther, "Judicial Hegemony and Legislative Autonomy: The Nixon Case and the Impeachment Process," 22 UCLA L.Rev. 30 (1974). For criticism of Article III, see Van Alstyne, "The Third Impeachment Article: Congressional Bootstrapping," 60 A.B.A.J. 1199 (1974).

trial by the Senate—were abandoned when President Nixon resigned on August 9, 1974, after the release of the most incriminating Watergate tapes in the wake of the Court's ruling in United States v. Nixon.)

5. *Legislative immunity and the Speech and Debate Clause.* The claims for executive immunities in the preceding notes have had to rely on general separation of powers implications, for Art. II of the Constitution is silent on the issue. Members of Congress, by contrast, can rely on Art. I, § 6, which states that Senators and Representatives "shall not be questioned in any other Place" for "any Speech or Debate in either House." The purpose of the Clause is to assure that legislators will not be hauled into court to defend their behavior in exercising their legislative functions and to safeguard against the risk that open debate in Congress will be inhibited by judicial scrutiny. Moreover, the Clause safeguards legislators against politically motivated prosecutions. In recent years, the Court has had repeated occasion to interpret the Clause. The decisions have limited the immunity to suits based on "legislative acts." Thus, the Clause did not bar conviction of a former Senator for accepting, while in Congress, a bribe relating to his actions on pending legislation. United States v. Brewster, 408 U.S. 501 (1972). Chief Justice Burger concluded that the Clause did not protect all conduct "*relating* to the legislative process," but only "protects against inquiry into acts which occur in the regular course of the legislative process and the motivation for those acts." Here, he explained, the prosecution could succeed simply by showing acceptance of the bribe, without getting into the question whether the illegal promise was performed. The Court has also had several occasions to interpret the Clause in the context of civil actions against legislators or their staff. See, e.g., Hutchinson v. Proxmire, 443 U.S. 111 (1979), holding that Senator Proxmire could not claim immunity from a defamation suit based on statements he made in press releases and newsletters.

*

PART III

INDIVIDUAL RIGHTS

Scope Note. Part III focuses on the Constitution's protections of individual freedoms. Like most of Part II, this Part explores limitations on governmental power. In the preceding chapters, the argued limits stemmed from the allocations of power among governmental units—the division of powers between nation and states, and the separation of powers among the three branches of the national government. In the remaining chapters, the sources of the argued limits are the constitutional guarantees of individual rights. As with the earlier materials, the concern here goes well beyond the delineation of the past and present contours of constitutional doctrines. It extends to the recurrent problems regarding the process of constitutional interpretation. How can one give content to the constitutional guarantees? Are there legitimate sources of interpretation beyond text and history and structural inferences? Interpreting the relatively "specific" guarantees such as the First Amendment protections of freedom of speech and of religion is difficult enough. But the challenge is especially acute when the task is that of pouring content into the vague assurances of due process and equal protection in the 14th Amendment. Are those broad phrases appropriate vessels for judicial infusion of values drawn from sources other than constitutional text, history and structure? Do those phrases tempt judges to read contemporary social, moral, and personal values into constitutional law?

In order to examine both the development of doctrine and the nature of the interpretive process, chap. 7, which follows, begins with a sketch of the constitutional framework and an initial venture into the problems of interpretation in a relatively uncomplicated context—the nationalizing impact on state criminal procedures of the 14th Amendment's guarantees. It contrasts the scope of constitutional guarantees in the original Constitution and in the post-Civil War Amendments, and it begins the exploration of the judicial function in the delineation of individual rights. A review of the "incorporation" controversy provides the vehicle for that initial exploration. Did the 14th Amendment's due process clause make the Bill of Rights—originally adopted as limits addressed solely to the federal government—applicable to the states as well? Or does the due process clause assign to the Court the more open-ended task of ascertaining what is "fundamental" to a fair trial? Are the Justices limited to enforcement of rights specified in the Constitution, or does that document authorize a broader Court function?[1]

1. This dispute about the proper range of the Court's role pervades this Part of this book. Are the Justices limited to enforcing rights explicitly guaranteed in the Constitu-

The tension reflected in the "incorporation" controversy echoes throughout the remaining materials. It emerges most controversially in chap. 8, on "substantive due process." The procedures by which personal rights and duties are delineated are the most obvious concerns of the due process provision; and the Court's preoccupation with criminal procedure problems in chap. 7 is accordingly a readily understandable impact of the due *process* clause. But the Court has not limited itself to a consideration of the *methods* of governmental action; since the late 19th century, the Court has found in due process constitutional restraints on the *content* of governmental action as well. The Court of an earlier generation found in substantive due process special protection of economic and property rights, and the rise and decline of that emphasis is traced in sec. 1 of chap. 8. The modern Court, even while repudiating that economic thrust of substantive due process, has elaborated a variation of its own: a constitutional protection of individual rights that are not explicit in the basic document—especially the personal rights of privacy and autonomy. That development is the focus of sec. 3 of chap. 8.

Chap. 9 turns to the developments in the interpretation of the equal protection clause of the 14th Amendment—developments occasionally parallel to those under the due process clause. From an initial concern with racial discrimination and a limited early impact on the means of governmental regulation, that clause came to have a far broader sweep during the Warren era. The "new" equal protection found constitutional safeguards for a variety of "fundamental interests," as in the area of voting. That value-laden process of equal protection interpretation bears considerable resemblance to the substantive due process mode noted above; indeed, some have referred to it as "substantive equal protection." Chap. 10 turns to two problems of 14th Amendment reach that have been most commonly raised in equal protection contexts: the applicability of the 14th Amendment's guarantees to "private" rather than "state" action; and the authority of Congress, under the enforcement power granted by § 5 of the Amendment, to enact its own interpretations of the scope of 14th Amendment guarantees—interpretations differing from the Court's delineation of the self-executing first section of the Amendment.[2] Chaps. 11, 12, and 13 examine the guarantees of freedom of expression in the First Amendment, made applicable to the states as a result of interpretations of the 14th Amendment. Chap. 14, finally, turns to another controversial aspect of First Amendment interpretation, the religion clauses, which purport to assure the "free exercise" of religion and to safeguard against the "establishment" of religion.

tion, or may they articulate and enforce unenumerated, "fundamental" rights as well? The dispute is often characterized as one between "interpretivism" and "noninterpretivism" (although today, most commentators—even those advocating broad judicial searches for "fundamental values"—insist that they are "interpreting" the Constitution). The former position holds that "judges deciding constitutional issues should confine themselves to enforcing norms that are stated or clearly implicit in the written Constitution"; the latter argues that "courts should go beyond that set of references and enforce norms that cannot be discovered within the four corners of the document." Ely, Democracy and Distrust (1980). Fuller exploration of this important debate is postponed until chap. 8, sec. 3, although these issues surface even earlier, as in chap. 7, sec. 3, on the "incorporation" controversy.

2. Somewhat similar problems about congressional powers are raised by the other post-Civil War Amendments as well, since each of those Amendments, the 13th and 15th as well as the 14th, concludes with a section granting power to Congress to "enforce" the Amendment "by appropriate legislation."

THE BILL OF RIGHTS AND THE POST–CIVIL WAR AMENDMENTS: "FUNDAMENTAL" PROCEDURAL RIGHTS AND THE "INCORPORATION" DISPUTE

Introduction. The major theme of this chapter is the way in which the 14th Amendment's due process clause has been read to make applicable to state criminal proceedings virtually all of the procedural requirements that govern federal criminal law enforcement as a result of the Bill of Rights. This process of "incorporating" Bill of Rights guarantees into the 14th Amendment illustrates two larger themes. First, it provides a reminder that federalism themes pervade individual rights concerns. State constitutions typically contain bills of rights of their own; but the concern here is with the restraints imposed on the states by the *federal* Constitution. Those restraints were very few prior to the Civil War. The post-Civil War Amendments signified a major escalation in the national concern with the protection of individual rights from state governmental action. It was the 14th Amendment's due process clause that became the major vehicle for that nationalization of individual rights. Federalism and constitutional protection of individual rights are thus frequently intertwined in the process of interpreting the scope of those new guarantees. Second, this exploration of the *procedures* that due process requires of the states introduces the larger problems of the appropriate ingredients of due process interpretation.* It is easier to find a procedural content in the due process clause than to derive substantive due process principles from it; but even the procedural due process materials reflect the tensions that permeate all due process litigation— the tensions between "objective" standards and judicial subjectivity; between the specific and the vague; between the fixed and the flexible; between historical meaning and contemporary values; between ingredients readily traceable to constitutional text and structure and those resting ultimately on extraconstitutional values. To provide the backdrop for the nationalizing impact of the post-Civil War Amendments, this chapter begins with a brief sketch

---

* The examination of procedural due process in this chapter is largely limited to the procedures constitutionally required in the administration of *criminal* law. (Procedural due process also plays a large role in delineating the process required in *civil* litigation and in administrative law. The discussion of the modern contours of procedural due process in the civil and administrative contexts is post- poned until the final section of the next chapter, sec. 4 of chap. 8. The reason for that postponement is that the non-criminal procedural due process cases are of greatest interest in this book for the light they cast on the Court's interpretations of the "liberty" and "property" protected by the due process clauses of the Fifth and 14th Amendments.)

of the pre-Civil War situation (sec. 1) and reviews the Court's earliest interpretation of the Amendments (sec. 2) before turning to the details of the "incorporation" dispute (sec. 3).

SECTION 1.   THE PRE-CIVIL WAR SITUATION

———

The 1787 document. There were relatively few explicit references to individual rights in the original Constitution: its major concern was with governmental structures. The most litigated limitation on state power protective of individual rights was the contracts clause, considered in chap. 8. Moreover, prohibitions of state bills of attainder and ex post facto laws were coupled with the contracts clause in Art. I, § 10; and Art. IV, § 4, announced that the "Citizens of each State shall be entitled to all Privileges and Immunities of Citizens in the several States." Nor was there a significantly broader spectrum of individual rights restrictions on the national government. Art. I, § 9, stated that the "privilege of the Writ of Habeas Corpus" could not be "suspended" and, paralleling restrictions on states, prohibited ex post facto laws and bills of attainder. And Art. III defined treason narrowly and assured jury trials in criminal cases.

The Bill of Rights. The ratification debates soon revealed that there was a widespread demand for additional constitutional protection of individual—as well as states'—rights. In response to these pressures, Madison introduced proposals for constitutional amendments at the first session of Congress, and the first ten amendments were ratified in 1791. In the Barron case, which follows, the Marshall Court held that the Bill of Rights restricted only the national government and did not limit state authority. There was relatively little occasion for Court interpretation of the Bill of Rights before the Civil War—in part because federal criminal decisions were not ordinarily reviewable by the Supreme Court during those years.

———

Barron v. Mayor and City Council of Baltimore
7 Pet. (32 U.S.) 243, 8 L.Ed. 672 (1833).

[Barron sued the City for ruining the use of his wharf in Baltimore harbor. He claimed that the City had diverted the flow of streams in the course of street construction work; that this diversion had deposited "large masses of sand and earth" near the wharf; and that the water had therefore become too shallow for most vessels. The trial court awarded Barron $45,000, but the state appellate court reversed. Barron claimed that the state's action violated the Fifth Amendment guarantee that private property shall not be "taken for public use, without just compensation." The Court rejected Barron's argument that this provision, "being in favour of the liberty of the citizen, ought to be so construed as to restrain the legislative power of a state, as well as that of the United States."]

Chief Justice MARSHALL delivered the opinion of the Court.

[The question is] of great importance, but not of much difficulty. The constitution was ordained and established by the people of the United States for themselves, for their own government, and not for the government of the individual states. Each state established a constitution for itself, and, in that constitution, provided such limitations and restrictions on the powers of its particular government as its judgment dictated. The people of the United States framed such a government for the United States as they supposed best adapted to their situation, and best calculated to promote their interests. The powers they conferred on this government were to be exercised by itself; and the limitations on power, if expressed in general terms, are naturally, and, we think, necessarily applicable to the government created by the instrument. They are limitations of power, granted in the instrument itself; not of distinct governments, framed by different persons and for different purposes. [If] these propositions be correct, the fifth amendment must be understood as restraining the power of the general government, not as applicable to the [states].

The ninth section [of Art. I] having enumerated, in the nature of a bill of rights, the limitations intended to be imposed on the powers of the general government, the tenth proceeds to enumerate those which were to operate on the state legislatures. [If] the original constitution, in the ninth and tenth sections of the first article, draws this plain and marked line of discrimination between the limitations it imposes on the powers of the general government, and on those of the states; if in every inhibition intended to act on state power, words are employed which directly express that intent; some strong reason must be assigned for departing from this safe and judicious course in framing the amendments, before that departure can be assumed. We search in vain for that [reason]. Had the framers of these amendments intended them to be limitations on the powers of the state governments, they would have imitated the framers of the original constitution, and have expressed that [intention].

But it is universally understood, it is a part of the history of the day, that the great revolution which established the constitution of the United States, was not effected without immense opposition. Serious fears were extensively entertained that those powers which the patriot statesmen, who then watched over the interests of our country, deemed essential to union, and to the attainment of those invaluable objects for which union was sought, might be exercised in a manner dangerous to liberty. In almost every convention by which the constitution was adopted, amendments to guard against the abuse of power were recommended. These amendments demanded security against the apprehended encroachments of the general government—not against those of the local governments. In compliance with a sentiment thus generally expressed, to quiet fears thus extensively entertained, amendments were proposed by the required majority in congress, and adopted by the states. These amendments contain no expression indicating an intention to apply them to the state governments. This court cannot so apply them. We are of opinion that the [just compensation] provision in the fifth amendment [is] intended solely as a limitation on the exercise of power by the government of the United States, and is not applicable to the legislation of the states. We are therefore of opinion that there is no repugnancy between the [state's action] and the constitution of the United States. This court, therefore, has no jurisdiction of the cause; and it is dismissed.

THE MARSHALL COURT'S POSITION

The Marshall Court's position that the Bill of Rights guarantees applied only to the national government and not to the states seemed a self-evident proposition to the Justices in 1833. Marshall described the question as "not of much difficulty"; indeed, counsel for the Baltimore officials—including soon-to-become Chief Justice Roger Brooke Taney—were "stopped by the Court" before they could complete their oral argument. But was the question all that easy? Note that a different inference might be drawn from the text of the Bill of Rights: the First Amendment explicitly inhibits "Congress" (but has been read to apply to the entire national government); the Seventh Amendment is explicitly addressed to "any Court of the United States"; all of the other Bill of Rights provisions speak in general terms. And a few courts, before Barron, thought those provisions generally applicable.[1] Yet Marshall—ordinarily not averse to nationalistic interpretations—refused to find the amendments applicable to the states; and his position prevailed. Note the bases of Marshall's reasoning, including his reliance on the structure of the Constitution and on "the history of the day."

SECTION 2.   THE PURPOSE AND IMPACT OF THE POST-CIVIL WAR AMENDMENTS

Before the Civil War, as Barron v. Baltimore illustrates, the Constitution afforded individuals very limited protection against state action. The 13th, 14th and 15th Amendments, adopted soon after the Civil War, dramatically changed that picture. With the hindsight of more than a century, it is clear that those Amendments, and particularly the 14th, have spawned national protection of a wide range of individual rights, procedural and substantive. But that far-reaching impact was not immediately apparent. The immediate provocation for the Amendments was the Civil War concern with problems of slavery and emancipation. And the Court's first interpretation of the Amendments, in the Slaughter–House Cases below, rejected the effort to give the Amendments a content extending beyond the problems which prompted them. Justice Miller's majority opinion, like Marshall's in Barron, relied strongly on historical memory: paralleling Marshall's reference to "the history of the day," Miller spoke of the history "fresh within the memory of us all"—the "history of the times" which showed the "one pervading purpose" of the Amendments to be "the freedom of the slave race, the security and firm establishment of that freedom, and the protection of the newly-made freeman and citizen from the oppressions of those who had formerly exercised unlimited dominion over him." To Miller and his colleagues in the majority, the Amendments were not to be given a reading which "radically changes the whole theory of the relations of the State and Federal governments to each other and of both these governments to the people"; they were not to be read to "constitute this court a perpetual censor upon all legislation of the States, on the civil rights of their own citizens." But Miller's position did not endure. Within a generation, the essence of the position of the dissenters prevailed, and a vast expansion of national power resulted.

The Slaughter–House Cases were immediately concerned with an effort to read substantive rather than procedural content into the Amendments: the

---

1.   See 2 Crosskey, Politics and the Constitution in the History of the United States   (1953), 1049–82.

effort was to use the Amendments as a weapon in support of free enterprise and against state monopoly legislation. The ultimate vindication of the dissenting position in the Slaughter–House Cases appears in the next chapter, in the materials tracing the rise of substantive due process. But the Slaughter–House Cases warrant attention here as well, for the decision implicitly speaks to the issue of the applicability to the states of the procedural guarantees of the Bill of Rights. The Slaughter–House majority's narrow reading of the Amendments meant temporary defeat for any claim that the Amendments amounted to a de facto overturning of Barron v. Baltimore. That narrow reading of the Amendments, tying them closely to the immediate historical background, meant that, for the time being, the procedural guarantees of the Bill of Rights would not be nationally enforceable safeguards in state criminal proceedings. It would be left to later generations and their broader readings of the Amendments to realize the full nationalizing potential of the post-Civil War changes. One realization came through the growth of substantive due process, traced in the next chapter. The other came in the selective (but by now virtually total) incorporation of Bill of Rights guarantees into the 14th, traced in sec. 3 of this chapter.

The Slaughter–House Cases also provide a useful, nearly contemporaneous perception of the historical background of the post-Civil War Amendments. As Justice Miller develops more fully, in 1865 the 13th Amendment gave constitutional sanction to President Lincoln's wartime Emancipation Proclamation. But that anti-slavery amendment did not end the problems of ex-slaves: their rights continued to be severely limited by the "black codes" of several states. Congress accordingly adopted the Civil Rights Act of 1866—over President Andrew Johnson's veto, based on constitutional grounds—and immediately set the amendment process in motion to assure the constitutional validity of that law.[1] The 14th Amendment was ratified in 1868. The 14th Amendment used even more sweeping, general terms than the Act it was designed to sustain: the Amendment's language was not limited to the problems of race, color, or previous condition of servitude. The last of the post-Civil War Amendments came two years later, in 1870; and that 15th Amendment did speak explicitly about racial discrimination, in voting. For generations, delineation of the scope of the Amendments was left almost entirely to the Court. But each of the three post-Civil War Amendments ended with a section authorizing Congress to enact legislation to enforce its provisions. Those congressional enforcement provisions, too, contained a vast nationalizing potential—a potential not realized until the abandonment of restrictive judicial interpretations and the revival of legislative interest in the 1960s, as the materials in chap. 10 illustrate.

Slaughter–House Cases

16 Wall. (83 U.S.) 36, 21 L.Ed. 394 (1873).

[A Louisiana law of 1869 chartered a corporation—the Crescent City Live–Stock Landing and Slaughter–House Company—and granted to it a 25–year monopoly "to maintain slaughterhouses, landings for cattle and stockyards" in an area which included the city of New Orleans. All competing facilities were required to close, but the corporation was required to permit independent butchers to slaughter cattle in its slaughterhouses at charges fixed by statute. Butchers not included in the monopoly claimed that the law deprived them of

---

1. For the provisions of the post-Civil War Civil Rights Acts and their interrelation- ships with the Amendments and with modern civil rights laws, see chap. 10.

their right "to exercise their trade" and challenged it under the 13th and 14th Amendments. The highest state court sustained the law.]

Justice MILLER delivered the opinion of the Court.

[The] regulation of the place and manner of conducting the slaughtering of animals [is] among the most necessary and frequent exercises of [the states' police] power. [The 1869 law] is aptly framed to remove from the more densely populated part of the city, the noxious slaughter-houses, and large and offensive collections of animals necessarily incident to [them], and to locate them where the convenience, health, and comfort of the people require they shall be located. [The] means adopted by the act for this purpose are appropriate, are stringent, and effectual. But it is said that in creating a corporation for this purpose, and conferring upon it exclusive privileges—privileges which it is said constitute a monopoly—the legislature has exceeded its power. [The only arguable constraints are those arising from the Federal Constitution. The challengers claim that the law created an "involuntary servitude" in violation of the 13th Amendment, and that it violated the 14th Amendment by abridging the "privileges and immunities" of citizens of the United States, denying the challengers "the equal protection of the laws," and depriving them "of their property without due process of law."] This Court is thus called upon for the first time to give construction to these [Amendments].

The most cursory glance at [the three post-Civil War Amendments] discloses a unity of purpose, when taken in connection with the history of the times, which cannot fail to have an important bearing on any question of doubt concerning their true meaning. Nor can such doubts [be] safely and rationally solved without a reference to that [history]. Fortunately that history is fresh within the memory of us all, and its leading features, as they bear upon the matter before us, free from doubt. [Undoubtedly] the overshadowing and efficient cause [of "the war of the rebellion"] was African slavery. In that struggle slavery, as a legalized social relation, perished. It perished as a necessity of the bitterness and force of the conflict. [Lincoln's Emancipation Proclamation] expressed an accomplished fact as to a large portion of the insurrectionary districts, when he declared slavery abolished in them all. But the war being over, those who had succeeded in re-establishing the authority of the Federal government were not content to permit this great act of emancipation to rest on the actual results of the contest or the proclamation of the Executive, both of which might have been questioned in after times, and they determined to place this main and most valuable result in the Constitution of the restored Union as one of its fundamental articles. Hence the [13th Amendment].

To withdraw the mind from the contemplation of this grand yet simple declaration of the personal freedom of all the human race within the jurisdiction of this government—a declaration designed to establish the freedom of four millions of slaves—and with a microscopic search endeavor to find in it a reference to servitudes, which may have been attached to property in certain localities, requires an effort, to say the least of it. That a personal servitude was meant is proved by the use of the word "involuntary," which can only apply to human beings. [The] word servitude is of larger meaning than slavery, as the latter is popularly understood in this country, and the obvious purpose was to forbid all shades and conditions of African slavery. It was very well understood that in the form of apprenticeship for long terms, as it had been practiced in the West India Islands, on the abolition of slavery by the English government, or by reducing the slaves to the condition of serfs attached to the plantation, the purpose of the article might have been evaded, if only the word slavery had been used. [And] it is all that we deem necessary to say [about the 13th Amendment].[1]

The process of restoring to their proper relations with the Federal government and with the other States those which had sided with the [rebellion] developed the fact that, notwithstanding the formal recognition by those States of the abolition of slavery, the condition of the slave race would, without further protection of the Federal government, be almost as bad as it was before. Among the first acts of legislation adopted by several of the States [were] laws which imposed upon the colored race onerous disabilities and burdens, and curtailed their rights in the pursuit of life, liberty, and property to such an extent that their freedom was of little value, while they had lost the protection which they had received from their former owners from motives both of interest and humanity. They were in some States forbidden to appear in the towns in any other character than menial servants. They were required to reside on and cultivate the soil without the right to purchase or own it. They were excluded from many occupations of gain, and were not permitted to give testimony in the courts in any case where a white man was a party. It was said that their lives were at the mercy of bad men, either because the laws for their protection were insufficient or were not enforced. These circumstances [forced] upon the statesmen who had conducted the Federal government in safety through the crisis of the rebellion, and who supposed that by [the 13th Amendment] they had secured the result of their labors, the conviction that something more was necessary in the way of constitutional protection to the unfortunate race who had suffered so much. They accordingly [proposed the 14th Amendment]. A few years' experience satisfied the thoughtful men who had been the authors of the other two amendments that [these] were inadequate for the protection of life, liberty, and property, without which freedom to the slave was no boon. They were in all those States denied the right of suffrage. The laws were administered by the white man alone. It was urged that a race of men distinctively marked as was the negro, living in the midst of another and dominant race, could never be fully secured in their person and the property without the right of suffrage. Hence [the 15th Amendment].

We repeat, then, in the light of this recapitulation of events, almost too recent to be called history, but which are familiar to us all; and on the most casual examination of the language of these amendments, no one can fail to be impressed with the one pervading purpose found in them all, lying at the foundation of each, and without which none of them would have been even suggested; we mean the freedom of the slave race, the security and firm establishment of that freedom, and the protection of the newly-made freeman and citizen from the oppressions of those who had formerly exercised unlimited dominion over him. It is true that only the fifteenth amendment, in terms, mentions the negro by speaking of his color and his slavery. But it is just as true that each of the other articles was addressed to the grievances of that race, and designed to remedy them as the fifteenth. We do not say that no one else

[handwritten margin note: DISREGARDS EXPLICIT RACE TERMS IN XV BUT NO XIII, XIV.]

---

1. The scope of the 13th Amendment—especially as a source of congressional power "rationally to determine what are the badges and the incidents of slavery" and to enact laws limiting private as well as state discrimination—is examined in chap. 10, sec. 3. (For a Court encounter with an application of the 13th Amendment to a problem other than racial discrimination, see Bailey v. Alabama, 219 U.S. 219 (1911), invalidating state laws which sought to compel "service of labor" under contracts "by making it a crime to refuse or fail to perform." But the Amendment does not ban all compulsory service—e.g., by military draftees, Selective Service Draft Law Cases, 245 U.S. 366 (1918). See generally tenBroek, "Thirteenth [Amendment]—Consummation to Abolition and Key to the Fourteenth Amendment," 39 Calif.L.Rev. 171 (1951).)

but the negro can share in this protection. Both the language and spirit of these articles are to have their fair and just weight in any question of construction. Undoubtedly while negro slavery alone was in the mind of the Congress which proposed the thirteenth article, it forbids any other kind of slavery, now or hereafter. If Mexican peonage or the Chinese coolie labor system shall develop slavery of the Mexican or Chinese race within our territory, this amendment may safely be trusted to make it void. And so if other rights are assailed by the States which properly and necessarily fall within the protection of these articles, that protection will apply, though the party interested may not be of African descent. But what we do say [is] that in any fair and just construction of any section or phrase of these amendments, it is necessary to look to the purpose which [was] the pervading spirit of them all, the evil which they were designed [to remedy].

The first section of the [14th Amendment], to which our attention is more specially invited, opens with a definition of citizenship. [I]t overturns the Dred Scott decision by making *all persons* born within the United States and subject to its jurisdiction citizens of the United States.[2] That its main purpose was to establish the citizenship of the negro can admit [of no doubt]. The next observation is more important in view of the arguments of counsel in the present case. It is, that the distinction between citizenship of the United States and citizenship of a State is clearly recognized and established. Not only may a man be a citizen of the United States without being a citizen of a State, but an important element is necessary to convert the former into the latter. He must reside within the State to make him a citizen of it, but it is only necessary that he should be born or naturalized in the United States to be a citizen of the Union. It is quite clear, then, that there is a citizenship of the United States, and a citizenship of a State, which are distinct from each other, and which depend upon different characteristics or circumstances in the individual.

We think this distinction and its explicit recognition in this amendment of great weight in this argument, because the next paragraph of this same section, which is the one mainly relied on by the plaintiffs in error, speaks only of privileges and immunities of citizens of the United States, and does not speak of those of citizens of the several States. The argument, however, in favor of the plaintiffs rests wholly on the assumption that the citizenship is the same, and the privileges and immunities guaranteed by the clause are the same. The language is, "No State shall make or enforce any law which shall abridge the privileges or immunities of citizens of *the United States.*" It is a little remarkable, if this clause was intended as a protection to the citizen of a State against the legislative power of his own State, that the word citizen of the State should be left out when it is so carefully used, and used in contradistinction to citizens of the United States, in the very sentence which precedes it. It is too clear for argument that the change in phraseology was adopted understandingly and with a purpose. Of the privileges and immunities of the citizen of the United States, and of the privileges and immunities of the citizen of the State, and what they respectively are, we will presently consider; but we wish to state here that it is only the former which are placed by this clause under the protection of the Federal Constitution, and that the latter, whatever they may be, are not intended to have any additional protection by this paragraph of the amendment. If, then, there is a difference between the privileges and immunities belonging to a citizen of the United States as such, and those belonging to the

---

2. Dred Scott v. Sandford, 19 How. (60 U.S.) 393 (1857), held unconstitutional (in part on Fifth Amendment due process grounds) the Missouri Compromise of 1820, a congressional law that excluded slavery from specified portions of American territory.

citizen of the State as such, the latter must rest for their security and protection where they have heretofore rested; for they are not embraced by this paragraph of the amendment.

[In] the Constitution, [Art. IV, § 2, states]: "The citizens of each State shall be entitled to all the privileges and immunities of citizens of the several States." [W]e are not without judicial construction of this clause of the Constitution. The first and the leading case on the subject is that of Corfield v. Coryell, decided by Mr. Justice Washington in the Circuit Court [in] 1823. "The inquiry," he says, "is, what are the privileges and immunities of citizens of the several States? We feel no hesitation in confining these expressions to those privileges and immunities which are *fundamental,* which belong of right to the citizens of all free governments, and which have at all times been enjoyed by citizens of the several States which compose this Union, from the time of their becoming free, independent, and sovereign. What these fundamental principles are, it would be more tedious than difficult to enumerate. They may all, however, be comprehended under the following general heads: protection by the government, with the right to acquire and possess property of every kind, and to pursue and obtain happiness and safety, subject, nevertheless, to such restraints as the government may prescribe for the general good of the whole." [This] description, when taken to include others not named, but which are of the same general character, embraces nearly every civil right for the establishment and protection of which organized government is instituted. They are, in the language of Judge Washington, those rights which are fundamental. [T]hey have always been held to be the class of rights which the State governments were created to establish and secure. [Art. IV] did not create those rights, which it called privileges and immunities of citizens of the States. It threw around them in that clause no security for the citizen of the State in which they were claimed or exercised. Nor did it profess to control the power of the State governments over the rights of its own citizens. Its sole purpose was to declare to the several States, that whatever those rights, as you grant or establish them to your own citizens, or as you limit or qualify, or impose restrictions on their exercise, the same, neither more nor less, shall be the measure of the rights of citizens of other States within your jurisdiction.

[U]p to the adoption of the recent amendments, no claim or pretense was set up that those rights depended on the Federal government for their existence or protection, beyond the very few express limitations which the Federal Constitution imposed upon the [States]. But with the exception of these and a few other restrictions, the entire domain of the privileges and immunities of citizens of the [States] lay within the constitutional and legislative power of the States, and without that of the Federal government. Was it the purpose of the fourteenth amendment, by the simple declaration that no State should make or enforce any law which shall abridge the privileges and immunities of *citizens of the United States,* to transfer the security and protection of all the civil rights which we have mentioned, from the States to the Federal government? And where it is declared that Congress shall have the power to enforce that article, was it intended to bring within the power of Congress the entire domain of civil rights heretofore belonging exclusively to the States?

All this and more must follow, if the proposition of the plaintiffs in error be sound. For not only are these rights subject to the control of Congress whenever in its discretion any of them are supposed to be abridged by State legislation, but that body may also pass laws in advance, limiting and restricting the exercise of legislative power by the States, in their most ordinary and usual functions, as in its judgment it may think proper on all such subjects. And still further, such a construction followed by a reversal of the judgments of the Supreme Court of Louisiana in these cases, would constitute this court a perpetual censor upon all legislation of the States, on the civil rights of their own citizens, with authority to nullify such as it did not approve as consistent with those rights, as they existed at the time of the adoption of this amendment. The argument we admit is not always the most conclusive which is drawn from the consequences urged against the adoption of a particular construction of an instrument. But when, as in the case before us, these consequences are so serious, so far-reaching and pervading, so great a departure from the structure and spirit of our institutions; when the effect is to fetter and degrade the State governments by subjecting them to the control of Congress, in the exercise of powers heretofore universally conceded to them of the most ordinary and fundamental character; when in fact it radically changes the whole theory of the relations of the State and Federal governments to each other and of both these governments to the people; the argument has a force that is irresistible, in the absence of language which expresses such a purpose too clearly to admit of doubt. We are convinced that no such results were intended by the Congress which proposed these amendments, nor by the legislatures of the States which ratified them.

Having shown that the privileges and immunities relied on in the argument are those which belong to citizens of the States as such, and that they are left to the State governments for security and protection, and not by this article placed under the special care of the Federal government, we may hold ourselves excused from defining the privileges and immunities of citizens of the United States which no State can abridge, until some case involving those privileges may make it necessary to do so. But lest it should be said that no such privileges and immunities are to be found if those we have been considering are excluded, we venture to suggest some which owe their existence to the Federal government, its National character, its Constitution, or its laws. One of these is well described in the case of Crandall v. Nevada [6 Wall. (73 U.S.) 35 (1868)]. It is said to be the right of the citizen of this great country, protected by implied guarantees of its Constitution, "to come to the seat of government to assert any claim he may have upon that government, to transact any business he may have with it, to seek its protection, to share its offices, to engage in administering its functions. He has the right of free access to its seaports, through which all operations of foreign commerce are conducted, to the subtreasuries, land offices, and courts of justice in the several States." Another privilege of a citizen of the United States is to demand the care and protection of the Federal government over his life, liberty, and property when on the high seas or within the jurisdiction of a foreign government. [The] right to peaceably assemble and petition for redress of grievances, the privilege of the writ of habeas corpus, are rights of the citizen guaranteed by the Federal Constitution. The right to use the navigable waters of the United States, however they may penetrate the territory of the several States, all rights secured to our citizens by treaties with foreign nations, are dependent upon citizenship of the United States, and not citizenship of a State. [To] these may be added the rights secured by the thirteenth and fifteenth articles of amendment, and by the other clause of the fourteenth, next to be considered. [But] it is useless to pursue this branch of the inquiry, since we are of opinion that the rights claimed by these plaintiffs in error, if they have any existence, are not privileges and immunities of citizens of the United States within the meaning of the [clause under consideration].

The argument has not been much pressed in these cases that the defendant's character deprives the plaintiffs of their property without due process of law, or that it denies to them the equal protection of the law. The first of these paragraphs has been in the Constitution since the adoption of the fifth amendment, as a restraint upon the Federal power. It is also to be found in some form of expression in the constitutions of nearly all the States, as a restraint upon the power of the States. [We] are not without judicial interpretation, therefore, both State and National, of the meaning of this clause. And it is sufficient to say that under no construction of that provision that we have ever seen, or any that we deem admissible, can the restraint imposed by [Louisiana] upon the exercise of their trade by the butchers of New Orleans be held to be a deprivation of property within the meaning of that provision.

"Nor shall any State deny to any person within its jurisdiction the equal protection of the laws." In the light of the history of these amendments, and the pervading purpose of them, [it] is not difficult to give a meaning to this clause. The existence of laws in the States where the newly emancipated negroes resided, which discriminated with gross injustice and hardship against them as a class, was the evil to be remedied by this clause, and by it such laws are forbidden. If, however, the States did not conform their laws to its requirements, then by the fifth section of the [Amendment] Congress was authorized to enforce it by suitable legislation. We doubt very much whether any action of a State not directed by way of discrimination against the negroes as a class, or on account of their race, will ever be held to come within the purview of this provision. It is so clearly a provision for that race and that emergency, that a strong case would be necessary for its application to any [other]. Unquestionably [the "late civil war"] added largely to the number of those who believe in the necessity of a strong National government. But, however pervading this sentiment, and however it may have contributed to the adoption of the amendments we have been considering, we do not see in those amendments any purpose to destroy the main features of the general system. Under the pressure of all the excited feeling growing out of the war, our statesmen have still believed that the existence of the States with powers for domestic and local government, including the regulation of civil rights—the rights of person and of property—was essential to the perfect working of our complex form of government, though they have thought proper to impose additional limitations on the States, and to confer additional power on that of the [Nation].

[Affirmed.]

Justice FIELD [joined by Chief Justice CHASE and Justices SWAYNE and BRADLEY], dissenting:

[The] question presented [is] one of the gravest [importance]. It is nothing less than the question whether the recent [Amendments] protect the citizens of the United States against the deprivation of their common rights by State legislation. In my judgment the fourteenth amendment does afford such [protection]. The amendment does not attempt to confer any new privileges or immunities upon citizens, or to enumerate or define those already existing. It assumes that there are such privileges and immunities which belong of right to citizens as such, and ordains that they shall not be abridged by State legislation. If this inhibition has no reference to privileges and immunities of this character, but only refers, as held by [the majority], to such privileges and immunities as were before its adoption specifically designated in the Constitution or necessarily implied as belonging to citizens of the United States, it was a vain and idle enactment, which accomplished [nothing]. With privileges and immunities thus designated or implied no State could ever have interfered by its laws, and no new constitutional provision was required to inhibit such interference. [But] if the amendment refers to the natural and inalienable rights which belong to all citizens, the inhibition has a profound [significance].

The terms, privileges and immunities, are not new in the amendment; they were in the Constitution before the amendment was adopted. [Justice Field, as had Justice Miller, quoted Justice Bushrod Washington's elaboration of Art. IV, § 2, in Corfield v. Coryell.] The privileges and immunities designated are those *which of right belong to the citizens of all free governments.* Clearly among these must be placed the right to pursue a lawful employment in a lawful manner, without other restraint than such as equally affects all persons. [What Art. IV, § 2] did for the protection of the citizens of one State against hostile and discriminating legislation of other States, the fourteenth amendment does for the protection of every citizen of the United States against hostile and discriminating legislation against him in favor of others, whether they reside in the same or in different States. If under the fourth article of the Constitution equality of privileges and immunities is secured between citizens of different States, under the fourteenth amendment the same equality is secured between citizens of the [United States].

This equality of right, with exemption from all disparaging and partial enactments, in the lawful pursuits of life, throughout the whole country, is the distinguishing privilege of citizens of the United States. To them, everywhere, all pursuits, all professions, all avocations are open without other restrictions than such as are imposed equally upon all others of the same age, sex, and condition. The State may prescribe such regulations for every pursuit and calling of life as will promote the public health, secure the good order and advance the general prosperity of society, but when once prescribed, the pursuit or calling must be free to be followed by every citizen who is within the conditions designated, and will conform to the regulations. This is the fundamental idea upon which our institutions rest, and unless adhered to in the legislation of the country our government will be a republic only in name. The fourteenth amendment, in my judgment, makes it essential to the validity of the legislation of every State that this equality of right should be respected. [I]t is to me a matter of profound regret that [the] validity [of the Louisiana law] is recognized by a majority of this court, for by it the right of free labor, one of the most sacred and imprescriptible rights of man, is violated.[1] [Grants] of exclusive privileges [are] opposed to the whole theory of free government, and it requires no aid from any bill of rights to render them void. That only is a free government, in the American sense of the term, under which the inalienable right of every citizen to pursue his happiness is unrestrained, except by just, equal, and impartial laws.[2]

Justice BRADLEY, also dissenting:

[In] my judgment, it was the intention of the people of this country in adopting [the 14th] amendment to provide National security against violation

---

1. "The property which every man has in his own labor," says Adam Smith, "as it is the original foundation of all other property, so it is the most sacred and invoidable. The patrimony of the poor man lies in the strength and dexterity of his own hands; and to hinder him from employing this strength and dexterity in what manner he thinks proper, without injury to his neighbor, is a plain violation of this most sacred property. It is a manifest encroachment upon the just liberty both of the workman and of those who might be disposed to employ him. As it hinders the one from working at what he thinks proper, so it hinders the others from employing whom they think proper." (Smith's Wealth of Nations, b. 1, ch. 10, part 2.) [Footnote by Justice Field.]

2. "Civil liberty, the great end of all human society and government, is that state in which each individual has the power to pursue his own happiness according to his own views of his interest, and the dictates of his conscience, unrestrained, except by equal, just, and impartial laws." (1 Sharswood's Blackstone, 127, note 8.) [Footnote by Justice Field.]

by the States of the fundamental rights of the citizen. [Any] law which establishes a sheer monopoly, depriving a large class of citizens of the privilege of pursuing a lawful employment, does abridge the privileges of those citizens. [In] my view, a law which prohibits a large class of citizens from adopting a lawful employment, or from following a lawful employment previously adopted, does deprive them of liberty as well as property, without due process of law. Their right of choice is a portion of their liberty; their occupation is their property. Such a law also deprives those citizens of the equal protection of the laws, contrary to the last clause of the section. [It] is futile to argue that none but persons of the African race are intended to be benefited by this amendment. They may have been the primary cause of the amendment, but its language is general, embracing all citizens, and I think it was purposely so [expressed].

But great fears are expressed that this construction of the amendment will lead to enactments by Congress interfering with the internal affairs of the [States]; or else, that it will lead the Federal courts to draw to their cognizance the supervision of State tribunals on every subject of judicial inquiry. [In] my judgment no such practical inconveniences would arise. Very little, if any, legislation on the part of Congress would be required to carry the amendment into effect. Like the prohibition against passing a law impairing the obligation of a contract, it would execute itself. [Even] if the business of the National courts should be increased, Congress could easily supply the remedy by increasing their number and efficiency. The great question is, What is the true construction of the amendment? When once we find that, we shall find the means of giving it effect. The argument from inconvenience ought not to have a very controlling influence in questions of this sort. The National will and National interest are of far greater [importance].[3]

THE AFTERMATH OF THE SLAUGHTER–HOUSE CASES: PRIVILEGES AND IMMUNITIES; DUE PROCESS

1. *Privileges and immunities of national citizenship.* The framers of the 14th Amendment had great difficulty in articulating a specific content for its broad phrases—"due process," "equal protection," "privileges and immunities." In no part of the congressional debates on the Amendment is there greater evidence of vagueness and inconsistencies than in the discussions of "privileges and immunities."[1] The Court has not been able to be much more concrete since. There have been only sporadic attempts to give the clause a more expansive scope than that found by Justice Miller in 1873. His majority position in the Slaughter–House Cases has so far prevailed: the clause is limited to a few rights of national (as distinct from state) citizenship.[2] Does this

3. Justice SWAYNE also submitted a dissent.

1. Note a contemporary recollection that the clause "came from [Congressman] Bingham of Ohio. Its euphony and indefiniteness of meaning were a charm to him." See Fairman, "Does the Fourteenth Amendment Incorporate the Bill of Rights? The Original Understanding," 2 Stan.L.Rev. 5 (1949). Contrast Graham, "Our 'Declaratory' Fourteenth Amendment," 7 Stan.L.Rev. 3 (1954).

2. The privileges and immunities clause has been relied on only once for a majority invalidation of a state law, in Colgate v. Harvey, 296 U.S. 404 (1935), striking down a Vermont tax provision. But that interpretation of the clause was short-lived: Colgate was overruled in Madden v. Kentucky, 309 U.S. 83 (1940), where the Court reiterated Justice Miller's position. For examples of reliance on the clause by individual Justices, see Edwards v. California, 314 U.S. 160 (1941),

interpretation render the clause superfluous and "redundant"? See Tribe, American Constitutional Law (2d ed., 1988), 558. Even though the language of the clause speaks to substantive matters more explicitly than do the companion clauses in the first section of the 14th Amendment, the development of privileges and immunities has been overshadowed by expanding views of due process and equal protection, as the remaining chapters show.

For an early 20th century effort to catalogue national privileges and immunities, see Twining v. New Jersey, 211 U.S. 78 (1908), which lists the right to travel from state to state, to petition Congress, to vote for national offices, to enter the public lands, the right to be "protected against violence while in the lawful custody of a United States marshal," and "the right to inform the United States authorities of violation of its laws." Consider this list, and recall also Justice Miller's potpourri of rights "which owe their existence to the Federal government, its National character, its Constitution, or its laws." Was the privileges and immunities clause necessary to give constitutional protection to any of these? Were they not already protected, by the structural limitations implied under the McCulloch approach? And did not Congress accordingly have power to safeguard all of them even without the 14th Amendment?[3]

What explains the Court's reluctance to give a broader content to the 14th Amendment's privileges and immunities clause? Arguably, a striving for the broad reading rejected in the Slaughter–House Cases became no longer necessary when later Courts read the due process and equal protection clauses expansively. Perhaps the Court was reluctant to expand the privileges and immunities clause because it is limited to the "citizen," while the due process and equal protection clauses apply to any "person" (and "persons" include corporations). Is it nevertheless possible that the moribund privileges and immunities clause may yet be revived, as a last resort basis for expansive judicial interpretations when the elastic capacities of due process and equal protection come to be perceived as exhausted? Note the "prognosis" regarding "the existent and potential needs that the privileges or immunities clause may be able to meet," in Kurland, "The Privileges or Immunities Clause: 'Its Hour Come Round at Last'?" 1972 Wash.U.L.Q. 405: "With government in control of so many essentials of our life, where in the Constitution can we turn for haven against the impositions of *1984*? [I]f the legislative and executive discretion is to be limited by the Constitution on such matters as public education, public welfare, and public housing; police, fire, and sanitation; ecology; [and], most importantly, with reference to the right of privacy, I expect it will come as an attempt to define the privileges or immunities of American citizenship."[4] See also Ely, Democracy and Distrust (1980), arguing that "the most plausible interpretation of the [Clause] is the one suggested by its language—that it was

(Justice Douglas concurring—the "right to move freely from State to State"); Hague v. CIO (1939; p. 1236 below), (Justice Roberts, concurring—right to assemble and "discuss national legislation"). Note also Justice Black's concurrence in Duncan v. Louisiana, below (right to jury trial).

3. The power of Congress to enforce individual rights stemming from sources other than the 14th Amendment is pursued in chap. 10.

4. Note also the comments on this "potentially robust" clause in Tribe, above, stating that "one should not rule out the possibility that courts and lawyers [might] yet turn to the still shadowy [clause] for a fresh source of distinctly personal rights." If the view of the dissenters in Slaughter–House had prevailed, how would the Court go about delineating the content of protected "privileges and immunities?" If a modern Court were to follow this path, could its discretion be adequately confined in "interpreting" such an open-ended provision?

a delegation to future constitutional decision-makers to protect certain rights that the document neither lists, at least not exhaustively, nor even in any specific way gives directions for finding."[5]

2. *Due process.* Though the efforts to turn the privileges and immunities clause into a significant instrument for protection of individual rights have failed so far, many of the arguments of the dissenters in the Slaughter–House Cases have found their way into majority opinions through the channels of the due process and equal protection clauses. Thus, the insistence of dissenting Justice Bradley that the due process clause imposed substantive limits on state economic regulation was echoed by other dissenters for the next generation. By the end of the 19th century, a majority of the Court embraced substantive due process; and in the first three decades of the 20th century, the Court applied that doctrine frequently. Since the mid–1930s, the Court has repudiated most substantive limits on state regulation of economic affairs. Yet a substantive due process approach has reemerged more recently, on behalf of personal rights such as privacy, as discussed in the next chapter. Moreover, a range of fundamental interests have found protection in the modern emergence of the "new" equal protection.[6]

Among the broad positions implicitly rejected by the Slaughter–House Cases was the position that all the Bill of Rights guarantees were made applicable to the states by the post-Civil War constitutional changes.[7] What criminal procedure protections *were* made available in state cases as a result of the 14th Amendment's due process clause? The majority's narrow reading in the Slaughter–House Cases did not mark the end of the development of procedural due process any more than it signified a permanent halt to the evolution of substantive guarantees. But the course of development of procedural rights has differed from that respecting substantive ones. Wholesale incorporation of Bill of Rights guarantees into the 14th Amendment continues to be rejected by the Court; but the modern Court's technique of "selective incorporation" has achieved virtually the same result—nearly all of the procedural protections in the first eight Amendments now apply to the states in the same way in which they restrict federal criminal proceedings. The next section traces this development.

5. Note also the efforts by some commentators to find justifications for broad readings in still another neglected provision of the 14th Amendment—the first sentence, conferring citizenship. For example, Professor Charles L. Black, Jr. has argued that the citizenship conferral could serve as an alternative basis for modern Court expansions of due process and equal protection, especially in the race area. Black, Structure and Relationship in Constitutional Law (1969). Note, moreover, Professor Kenneth L. Karst's imaginative argument that the "substantive core" of the 14th Amendment is "a principle of equal citizenship, which presumptively guarantees to each individual a right to be treated by the organized society as a respected, responsible, and participating member." Karst, "Foreword: Equal Citizenship under the Fourteenth Amendment," 91 Harv.L.Rev.

1 (1977), and the stimulating book-length elaboration in Karst, Belonging to America: Equal Citizenship and the Constitution (1989).

6. These developments are traced in chaps. 8 and 9.

7. Compare Ely, Democracy and Distrust (1980), 196–97, questioning this sentence in the text and arguing that "a close reading of the various opinions [suggests] at least the possibility that all nine justices meant to take exactly that position!" In Ely's view, all nine Justices "appear" to have endorsed, "with varying degrees of clarity," the proposition that "whatever else it did, the Privileges or Immunities Clause at least applied to the states the constitutionally stated prohibitions that had previously applied only to the federal government."

SECTION 3.   THE MEANING OF DUE PROCESS: CRIMINAL PROCEDURE AND THE "INCORPORATION" CONTROVERSY

Introduction. On its face, the due *process* clause most obviously addresses problems of procedure. But what are the aspects of criminal procedure that the due process guarantee of the 14th Amendment requires the states to provide?[1] That question has provoked heated debates on the Court; and pursuit of that problem provides a useful introductory vehicle for exploring the difficulties of defining the meaning of due process. The Court's battles over issues of state criminal procedure have taken place in the larger arena of the "incorporation" controversy: Did the 14th Amendment "incorporate" or "absorb" all of the Bill of Rights guarantees and make them applicable to the states? For decades after the Slaughter–House Cases, the Court was very reluctant to impose federal constitutional requirements on state procedures; but it clothed that reluctance in formulas which proved ultimately expansive after all.

The traditional Court position was that only "fundamental" matters—rights essential to "fundamental principles of liberty and justice," rights "essential to a fair trial"—were constitutionally required in state proceedings. Those broad formulations, which have their origins in late 19th century cases, have been most articulately elaborated in the 20th century by Justices Cardozo, Frankfurter, Harlan and Powell. Beginning in the 1940s, however, a forceful counterposition began to be voiced, especially by Justice Black. He insisted that the 14th Amendment *did* incorporate the "specific" guarantees of the Bill of Rights; he objected to the vague, "natural law" formulations of the majority that spoke in terms of "fundamentals." That battle over the meaning of due process is traced in the series of decisions beginning with Palko and Adamson, below. Are at least some of the guarantees of the Bill of Rights applicable to the states as a result of the 14th Amendment? If so, do those guarantees limit the states in precisely the same way that they restrain the national government?

As the concluding cases in this chapter illustrate, the outcome of the incorporation battle is fairly well settled: as to doctrine, the majority has adhered to the "fundamental rights" approach and has refused to accept Justice Black's wholesale incorporation notion; in practice, most of the procedural guarantees of the Bill of Rights *have* been incorporated into the 14th Amendment, and the incorporated guarantees apply to the states in precisely the same way that they restrain the national government. Nevertheless, that battle is worth examining, especially for the light it throws on due process methodology. The controversy over procedural due process echoes as well as anticipates some of the continuing concerns about the judicial subjectivity long associated with substantive due process. What *are* the guidelines available to the Court in giving content to due process? Consider first the potential guidance available from text, early interpretations, and English history.

1. This section's emphasis on criminal procedure is not intended as an exhaustive survey of all constitutional aspects of the criminal process; that task is left to other courses. The purpose of this section is simply to illustrate recurrent controversies about giving content to the procedural aspects of 14th Amendment due process.

1. *Due process and procedure before the Civil War.* The procedural aspects of due process were not a wholly blank slate when the clause was put into the 14th Amendment. The Court had already had occasion to speak about the history and scope of due process in the course of interpreting the due process clause of the Fifth Amendment. The best known statement was that by Justice Curtis in the course of considering the constitutionality of a distress warrant procedure in Murray's Lessee v. Hoboken Land & Improvement Co., 59 U.S. 272, 18 How. 272 (1856): "The words, 'due process of law,' were undoubtedly intended to convey the same meaning as the words, 'by the law of the land,' in Magna Charta. [The] constitution contains no description of those processes which it was intended to allow or forbid. It does not even declare what principles are to be applied to ascertain whether it be due process. [To] what principles, then, are we to resort to ascertain whether this process, enacted by congress, is due process? To this the answer must be twofold. We must examine the constitution itself, to see whether this process be in conflict with any of its provisions. If not found to be so, we must look to those settled usages and modes of proceeding existing in the common and statute law of England, before the emigration of our ancestors, and which are shown not to have been unsuited to their civil and political condition by having been acted on by them after the settlement of this country. [T]hough 'due process of law' generally implies and includes actor, reus, judex, regular allegations, opportunity to answer and a trial according to some settled course of judicial proceedings, [this] is not universally true." As Justice Curtis's last sentence suggests, concepts of notice and hearing have been at the core of due process from the beginning; and adaptation of those concepts to varied circumstances has contributed greatly to the flexibility of procedural due process. (See, e.g., Powell v. Alabama, note 2 below.) But Justice Curtis's major emphasis is not on flexibility but on a more confining, static reference, to English history. That history has indeed proved useful, but the Court has not limited itself to that source.

2. *The inadequacy of English history.* English history has been decisive in some cases,[2] but that history may at times be silent; and even where it speaks, the Court has not always felt compelled to listen. A good example is Powell v. Alabama, 287 U.S. 45 (1932), where the Court for the first time found a limited right to counsel essential to due process in some criminal cases, despite the lack of a corresponding guarantee in the English practice of the late 18th century. In England, a full right to representation by counsel in felony cases was not granted until 1836, almost 50 years after the adoption of the U.S. Constitution. But this did not inhibit the Court in requiring the appointment of counsel in a capital case such as Powell. The Court relied on the "unanimous accord" in the American states regarding appointment of counsel in capital cases: it was that American practice that lent "convincing support to the conclusion we have reached as to the fundamental nature of that right." And in deriving that right, the Court reached back to the core meaning of due process articulated by Justice Curtis: the Powell Court emphasized that "notice and hearing" were "basic elements of the constitutional requirement of due process of law"; and the concept of a "hearing," in turn, was the basis for inferences as to legal representation: "The right to be heard would be, in many cases, of little avail if it did not comprehend the right to be heard by counsel."

2. See, e.g., Ownbey v. Morgan, 256 U.S. 94 (1921), where the Court sustained the validity of a Delaware statute under which, in foreign attachment proceedings, special bail was required of defendant as a condition of being heard on the merits. The statute in question had been modeled on the Custom of London and had been on the statute books of Delaware from early colonial days.

Thus, the Court has not attempted to tie American lawmakers to the English tradition. For example, Hurtado v. California, 110 U.S. 516 (1884), sustained a California statute which permitted criminal proceedings to be instituted by information rather than by grand jury indictment. In explaining that conclusion, the Court used a phrase—"principles of liberty and justice"—characteristic of the flexible, open-ended majority view during much of the 20th century incorporation controversy. The Hurtado opinion stated: "There is nothing in Magna Charta [that] ought to exclude the best ideas of all systems and of every age. [Any] legal proceeding enforced by public authority, whether sanctioned by age and custom, or newly devised in the discretion of the legislative power, in furtherance of the general public good, which regards and [preserves] principles of liberty and justice, must be held to be due process of law." Not the details of English practice, but "principles of liberty and justice," became the dominant ingredients of due process. As used in cases such as Hurtado, that broad formula tended to minimize federal intervention in state criminal procedures. That, too, was the thrust of later variations on the Hurtado theme in cases such as Palko and Adamson. But, as the more recent cases show, references to vague standards such as "fundamental justice" also provided the Court with the bases for an increasing nationalization of standards of state criminal procedure.

A.   THE PALKO–ADAMSON DISPUTE: DO THE BILL OF RIGHTS GUARANTEES APPLY TO STATE CRIMINAL PROCEEDINGS?

THE BATTLE BETWEEN "SELECTIVE" AND "TOTAL" INCORPORATION

Introduction. The majority of the Court has never accepted the view that the 14th Amendment in effect "incorporated" all the provisions of the Bill of Rights. Instead, the dominant position has been that due process merely requires "fundamental fairness" in state proceedings. But for decades the majority has also recognized that "fundamental fairness" may afford the defendant rights that correspond to some of the guarantees in the Bill of Rights. As the Court recognized as early as 1908, in Twining v. New Jersey, 211 U.S. 78: "It is possible that some of the personal rights safeguarded by the first eight Amendments against National action may also be safeguarded against state action, because a denial of them would be a denial of due process of law. If this is so, it is not because those rights are enumerated in the first eight Amendments, but because they are of such a nature that they are included in the conception of due process." That "selective" incorporation position was expounded by Justice Cardozo in Palko in 1937 and was reiterated by Justice Frankfurter in Adamson in 1947. But in a strong dissent in Adamson, Justice Black insisted that the 14th Amendment, rather than signifying vague notions of "fundamental fairness," meant that *all* of the individual guarantees in the Bill of Rights applied to the states. In theory, "selective" incorporation continues to be the majority view; in result, virtually all of Justice Black's ends have been achieved: the Court *has* found most Bill of Rights guarantees pertaining to the criminal process applicable to the states, but the Court has achieved that result by finding the Bill of Rights guarantees to be "fundamental" one by one, rather than by incorporating them in one fell swoop, as Justice Black would have done.[1]

Two themes predominate in the Palko–Adamson debate between the Cardozo–Frankfurter position and that of Black. One concerns questions of federalism; the other, problems of "objective" standards and judicial subjectivity. Cardozo and Frankfurter defended their refusal to incorporate all of the Bill of Rights into the 14th Amendment by arguing that such a position would unduly limit state autonomy in the enforcement of criminal law. Black's recurrent rejoinder was that the majority's "fundamental fairness"-"essence of a scheme of ordered liberty" approach was too vague and open-ended and left too much room for subjective views. Black insisted that his "total" incorporation view would curb excessive judicial discretion by relying on the allegedly clearer standards of the "specific" guarantees of the Bill of Rights.

1. *"Selective" incorporation: Cardozo in Palko.* In PALKO v. CONNECTICUT, 302 U.S. 319 (1937), Justice CARDOZO provided the best known articulation of the "selective" incorporation approach. Connecticut permitted the State to take appeals in criminal cases. Palko's second degree murder conviction had been set aside by the highest state court on an appeal taken by the State. On retrial, he was convicted of first degree murder. He claimed that such a retrial in the federal courts would have violated the Fifth Amendment's double jeopardy guarantee, and insisted that "whatever is forbidden by the Fifth Amendment is forbidden by the Fourteenth also." Moreover, he argued more broadly that whatever would be "a violation of the original bill of rights [if] done by the federal government is now equally unlawful by force of the 14th Amendment if done by a state." Justice Cardozo replied: "There is no such general rule." He noted that the Court had refused to apply some Bill of Rights guarantees to the states (e.g., the grand jury indictment requirement and the protection against self-incrimination) even though other limits—such as free speech and aspects of the right to counsel—had been imposed on the states via the 14th Amendment. Explaining the criteria that determined which Bill of Rights safeguards were applicable to the states and which were not, he stated:

"The line of division may seem to be wavering and broken if there is a hasty catalogue of the cases on the one side and the other. Reflection and analysis will induce a different view. There emerges the perception of a rationalizing principle which gives to discrete instances a proper order and coherence. The right to trial by jury and the immunity from prosecution except as the result of an indictment may have value and importance. Even so, they are not of the very essence of a scheme of ordered liberty. To abolish them is not to violate a 'principle of justice so rooted in the traditions and conscience of our people as to be ranked as fundamental.' Snyder v. Massachusetts, [291 U.S. 97 (1934)]. Few would be so narrow or provincial as to maintain that a fair and enlightened system of justice would be impossible without them. What is true of jury trials and indictments is true also [of] the immunity from compulsory self-incrimination. This too might be lost, and justice still be [done]. We reach a different plane of social and moral values when we pass to [those guarantees of the Bill of Rights] brought within the [14th Amendment] by a process of

---

1. The range of rights "selectively" incorporated is reflected in Duncan v. Louisiana (1968; p. 442 below). However, as Duncan also indicates, the content of the Court's "selective" incorporation approach has changed since the days of Palko and Adamson. Instead of asking whether a particular guarantee is "implicit in the concept of ordered liberty," the modern Court asks whether the guarantee found in the Bill of Rights is "fundamental to the American scheme of justice" or "fundamental in the context of the criminal processes maintained by the American states."

absorption. These in their origin were effective against the federal government alone. If the [14th Amendment] has absorbed them, the process of absorption has had its source in the belief that neither liberty nor justice would exist if they were sacrificed. This is true, for illustration, of freedom of thought, and speech. Of that freedom one may say that it is the matrix, the indispensable condition, of nearly every other form of [freedom]. Fundamental too in the concept of due process, and so in that of liberty, is the thought that condemnation shall be rendered only after trial. [The] hearing, moreover, must be a real one, not a sham or a pretense. Moore v. Dempsey, 261 U.S. 86 [1923]. For that reason, ignorant defendants in a capital case were held to have been condemned unlawfully when in truth, though not in form, they were refused the aid of counsel. [Powell v. Alabama, above.] The decision did not turn upon the fact that the benefit of counsel would have been guaranteed to the defendants by [the] Sixth Amendment if they had been prosecuted in a federal court. The decision turned upon the fact that in the particular situation laid before us in the evidence the benefit of counsel was essential to the substance of a hearing. Our survey of the cases serves, we think, to justify the statement that the dividing line between them, if not unfaltering throughout its course, has been true for the most part to a unifying principle. On which side of the line the case made out by the appellant has appropriate location must be the next inquiry and the final one. Is that kind of double jeopardy to which the statute has subjected him a hardship so acute and shocking that our polity will not endure it? Does it violate those 'fundamental principles of liberty and justice which lie at the base of all our civil and political institutions'? Hebert v. Louisiana [272 U.S. 312 (1926)]. The answer surely must be 'no.' What the answer would have to be if the state were permitted after a trial free from error to try the accused over again or to bring another case against him, we have no occasion to consider. [The] state is not attempting to wear the accused out by a multitude of cases with accumulated trials. It asks no more than this, that the case against him shall go on until there shall be a trial free from the corrosion of substantial legal error. [This] is not cruelty at all, nor even vexation in any immoderate [degree]."[1]

2. *"Total" incorporation: Black's argument in Adamson, and Frankfurter's response.* Ten years after Palko, a 5-4 majority adhered to Justice Cardozo's approach and rejected a strong challenge by Justice Black. In ADAMSON v. CALIFORNIA, 332 U.S. 46 (1947), Adamson claimed that his murder conviction violated the 14th Amendment because the prosecution had been permitted to comment on his failure to take the stand at his trial. Justice REED's majority opinion assumed that such a comment would violate the 5th Amendment's self-incrimination privilege in a federal proceeding. He conceded, moreover, that the 14th Amendment's due process clause guaranteed a right to a "fair trial." But, under Palko, not all Bill of Rights guarantees were protected by the 14th Amendment, and he found no ground to make the self-incrimination privilege applicable to the states.

Justice BLACK's dissent, joined by Justice Douglas, contains the most famous exposition of his "total" incorporation position. He insisted that full incorporation of all Bill of Rights guarantees was the "original purpose" of the 14th Amendment and accordingly concluded that "the full protection of the Fifth Amendment's proscription against compelled testimony must be afford-

---

1. In Benton v. Maryland, 395 U.S. 784 (1969), the Court held that the Fifth Amendment's double jeopardy guarantee "should apply to the States through the Fourteenth." The Court added: "Insofar as it is inconsistent with this holding, Palko v. Connecticut is overruled."

ed" to Adamson. He explained: "This decision reasserts a constitutional theory spelled out in [Twining], that this Court is endowed by the Constitution with boundless power under 'natural law' periodically to expand and contract constitutional standards to conform to the Court's conception of what at a particular time constitutes 'civilized decency' and 'fundamental liberty and justice.' [I] would not reaffirm [Twining]. I think that decision and the 'natural law' theory of the Constitution upon which it relies degrade the constitutional safeguards of the Bill of Rights and simultaneously appropriate for this Court a broad power which we are not authorized by the Constitution to exercise. My reasons for believing that [Twining] should not be revitalized can best be understood by reference to the constitutional, judicial and general history that preceded and followed the [case]. I am attaching to this dissent an appendix which contains a resumé, by no means complete, of the Amendment's history.[2] In my judgment that history conclusively demonstrates that the language of the first section of the Fourteenth Amendment, taken as a whole, was thought by those responsible for its submission to the people, and by those who opposed its submission, sufficiently explicit to guarantee that thereafter no state could deprive its citizens of the privileges and protections of the Bill of Rights. Whether this Court ever will, or whether it now should, in the light of past decisions, give full effect to what the Amendment was intended to accomplish is not necessarily essential to a decision here. However that may be, our prior decisions, including Twining, do not prevent our carrying out that purpose, at least to the extent of making applicable to the states, not a mere part, as the Court has, but the full protection of the Fifth Amendment's provision against compelling evidence from an accused to convict him of crime. And I further contend that the 'natural law' formula which the Court uses to reach its conclusion in this case should be abandoned as an incongruous excrescence on our Constitution. [I] fear to see the consequences of the Court's practice of substituting its own concepts of decency and fundamental justice for the language of the Bill of Rights as its point of departure in interpreting and enforcing that Bill of Rights. If the choice must be between the selective process of the Palko decision applying some of the Bill of Rights to the States, or the Twining rule applying none of them, I would choose the Palko selective process. But rather than accept either of these choices, I would follow what I believe was the original purpose of the Fourteenth Amendment—to extend to all the people of the nation the complete protection of the [Bill of Rights].

"It is an illusory apprehension that literal application of some or all of the provisions of the Bill of Rights to the States would unwisely increase the sum total of the powers of this Court to invalidate state legislation. [It] must be conceded, of course, that the natural-law-due-process formula, which the Court today reaffirms, has been interpreted to limit substantially this Court's power to prevent state violations of the individual civil liberties guaranteed by the Bill

---

2. The appendix is omitted. For an historical examination disagreeing with Justice Black's position, see Fairman, "Does the Fourteenth Amendment Incorporate the Bill of Rights? The Original Understanding," 2 Stan.L.Rev. 5 (1949). Justice Black reviewed the historical dispute and replied to Fairman in the 1968 decision in Duncan, below. Searches in the origins of the 14th Amendment have been inconclusive. Compare Fairman's criticism of the Black position with Crosskey, "Charles Fairman, 'Legislative History,' and the Constitutional Limitations on State Authority," 22 U.Chi.L.Rev. 1 (1954). The implications of the "incorporation" controversy have engendered an even wider range of commentary than the historical debate. See, e.g., Schaefer, "Federalism and State Criminal Procedures," 70 Harv. L.Rev. 1 (1956); Henkin, " 'Selective Incorporation' in the 14th Amendment," 73 Yale L.J. 74 (1963); and Friendly, "The Bill of Rights as a Code of Criminal Procedure," 53 Calif.L.Rev. 929 (1965).

of Rights. But this formula also has been used in the past, and can be used in the future, to license this Court, in considering regulatory legislation, to roam at large in the broad expanses of policy and morals and to trespass, all too freely, on the legislative domain of the States as well as the Federal Government. [See chap. 8, sec. 1, below.] Since [Marbury], the practice has been firmly established [that] courts can strike down legislative enactments which violate the Constitution. This process, of course, involves interpretation, and since words can have many meanings, interpretation obviously may result in contraction or extension of the original purpose of a constitutional provision thereby affecting policy. But to pass upon the constitutionality of statutes by looking to the particular standards enumerated in the Bill of Rights and other parts of the Constitution is one thing; to invalidate statutes because of application of 'natural law' deemed to be above and undefined by the Constitution is another. 'In the one instance, courts proceeding within clearly marked constitutional boundaries seek to execute policies written into the Constitution; in the other, they roam at will in the limitless area of their own beliefs as to reasonableness and actually select policies, a responsibility which the Constitution entrusts to the legislative representatives of the people.' "[3]

   In a concurring opinion, Justice FRANKFURTER mounted an extensive attack on Justice Black's "total" incorporation position. He insisted that the 14th Amendment's due process clause has "independent potency" and an "independent function": it "neither comprehends the specific provisions by which the founders deemed it appropriate to restrict the federal government nor is it confined to them." Rejecting the view that the 14th Amendment is "a shorthand summary of the first eight amendments," he argued that to draw support for Adamson's claim "out of 'due process' in its protection of ultimate decency in a civilized society is to suggest that the Due Process Clause fastened fetters of unreason upon the States." He commented: "[It] would be extraordinarily strange for a Constitution to convey such specific commands in such a roundabout and inexplicit way [as the phrase 'due process of law']." He added: "Those reading the English language with the meaning which it ordinarily conveys, those conversant with the political and legal history of the concept of due process, those sensitive to the relations of the States to the central government as well as the relation of some of the provisions of the Bill of Rights to the process of justice, would hardly recognize the [14th Amendment] as a cover for the various explicit provisions of the first [eight]. [Indeed], the suggestion that the Fourteenth Amendment incorporates the first eight Amendments as such is not unambiguously urged. [There] is suggested merely a selective incorporation of the first eight Amendments into the [14th] Amendment. Some are in and some are out, but we are left in the dark as to which are in and which are out. [If] the basis of selection is merely that those provisions

---

3. In a separate dissent, Justice MURPHY, joined by Justice Rutledge, announced something of a "having your cake and eating it too" position. He agreed with Justice Black that "the specific guarantees of the Bill of Rights should be carried over intact into the first section of the [14th] Amendment," but added: "I am not prepared to say that the latter is entirely and necessarily limited by the Bill of Rights. Occasions may arise where a proceeding falls so far short of conforming to fundamental standards of procedure as to warrant constitutional condemnation in terms of a lack of due process despite the absence of a specific provision in the Bill of Rights." [For an example of such a situation (relying on due process as a reservoir for added limits on state proceedings when no relevant "specific" provision in the Bill of Rights is available), see In re Winship, 397 U.S. 358 (1970), holding that "proof beyond a reasonable doubt is among the 'essentials of due process and fair treatment.' " Justice Black, consistent with his view in Adamson, dissented, emphasizing that "nowhere in the [Constitution] is there any statement that conviction of crime requires proof of guilt beyond a reasonable doubt."]

of the first eight Amendments are incorporated which commend themselves to individual justices as indispensable to the dignity and happiness of a free man, we are thrown back to a merely subjective test. [In] the history of thought 'natural law' has a much longer and much better founded meaning and justification than such subjective selection of the first eight Amendments for incorporation into the [14th]. If all that is meant is that due process contains within itself certain minimal standards which are 'of the very essence of a scheme of ordered liberty' [Palko], putting upon this Court the duty of applying these standards from time to time, then we have merely arrived at the insight which our predecessors long ago expressed. [It] ought not to require argument to reject the notion that due process of law meant one thing in the Fifth Amendment and another in the [14th].

"A construction which gives to due process no independent function but turns it into a summary of the specific provisions of the Bill of Rights [would] deprive the States of opportunity for reforms in legal process designed for extending the area of freedom. It would assume that no other abuses would reveal themselves in the course of time than those which had become manifest in 1791. Such a view not only disregards the historic meaning of 'due process.' It leads inevitably to a warped construction of specific provisions of the Bill of Rights to bring within their scope conduct clearly condemned by due process but not easily fitting into the pigeon-holes of the specific [provisions]. And so, [the issue in a case such as this] is not whether an infraction of one of the specific provisions of the first eight Amendments is disclosed by the record. The relevant question is whether the criminal proceedings which resulted in conviction deprived the accused of the due process of [law]. Judicial review of that [guaranty] inescapably imposes upon this Court an exercise of judgment upon the whole course of the proceedings in order to ascertain whether they offend those canons of decency and fairness which express the notions of justice of English-speaking peoples even toward those charged with the most heinous offenses. These standards of justice are not authoritatively formulated anywhere as though they were prescriptions in a pharmacopoeia. But neither does the application of the Due Process Clause imply that judges are wholly at large. The judicial judgment in applying the [Clause] must move within the limits of accepted notions of justice and is not to be based upon the idiosyncrasies of a merely personal judgment. The fact that judges among themselves may differ whether in a particular case a trial offends accepted notions of justice is not disproof that general rather than idiosyncratic standards are applied. An important safeguard against such merely individual judgment is an alert deference to the judgment of the State court under review."[4]

3. *Examining the Black–Frankfurter debate: "Specific" rights; vague guarantees; impersonal, predictable standards. a. Due process methodology in search of impersonal standards.* Justice Frankfurter's flexible due process approach in Adamson insists that due process interpretation "is not based on the idiosyncrasies of merely personal judgment." Yet can that approach be truly impersonal? What external criteria are available to give content to procedural due process? As Justice Black commented a few years after Adamson, if "canons of decency and fairness which express the notions of justice of English-speaking peoples" are to govern, "one may well ask what avenues of

4. In Malloy v. Hogan, 378 U.S. 1 (1964), the Court held that the Fifth Amendment's privilege against self-incrimination *was* applicable to the states under the 14th: "Decisions of the Court since Twining and Adamson have departed from the contrary view expressed in those cases." A year later, the Court overruled the specific holding in Adamson and found unconstitutional the California rule permitting comment on the defendant's failure to testify. Griffin v. California, 380 U.S. 609 (1965).

investigation are open to discover 'canons' of conduct so universally favored that this Court should write them into the Constitution."[5] What *are* the appropriate sources for giving content to the Palko–Adamson approach? Note the comments by Sanford Kadish.[6] Kadish traces the two main routes by which the majority in the post-Adamson years sought "to eliminate the purely personal preference from flexible due process decision making": the first was "a respectful deference to the judgment of the state court or the act of the legislature under review"; the second was to rely on four types of external evidence of judgments already made by others: "the opinions of the progenitors and architects of American institutions"; "the implicit opinions of the policy-making organs of state governments"; "the explicit opinions of other American courts that have evaluated the fundamentality of a given mode of procedure"; and "the opinions of other countries in the Anglo–Saxon tradition." Kadish views due process as ultimately "more a moral command than a strictly jural precept," but suggests that there are "possibilities of reason and pragmatic inquiry" in such morally-centered due process decisionmaking. He also explores the primary values underlying procedural due process decisions: "insuring the reliability of the guilt-determining process," and "insuring respect for the dignity of the individual."

b. *Avoiding subjectivity: The problems of Justice Black's approach.* In Justice Black's view, the Palko–Adamson technique could not avoid judicial subjectivity. Did Justice Black's position avoid that difficulty any more effectively? Does incorporation of a "specific" Bill of Rights provision significantly curtail the range of judicial judgment? How specific are those guarantees? Contrast the guarantee of jury trial in civil cases involving more than $20 with the considerably more open-ended dimensions of the protection against "unreasonable" searches and seizures and the assurance of "the Assistance of Counsel." There have been recurrent disputes, for example, about whether the exclusionary rule is part of the Fourth Amendment guarantees, whether compulsory blood samples violate the Fifth Amendment's self-incrimination provision, and whether the Sixth Amendment right to counsel extends to pretrial proceedings. Does emphasis on "specific" Bill of Rights guarantees breed warped constructions of these rights in order "to bring within their scope conduct clearly condemned by due process but not easily fitting into the pigeonholes of the specific provisions," as Justice Frankfurter argued? May that emphasis on "specifics" also have a restrictive rather than an expansive impact: may it breed a dilution of Bill of Rights guarantees in order to escape

---

5. Justice Black's comment came in Rochin v. California, 342 U.S. 165 (1952), one of several occasions on which Justices Frankfurter and Black renewed their Adamson debate. Justice Frankfurter stated: "[To] practice the requisite detachment and to achieve sufficient objectivity [demands] of judges the habit of self-discipline and self-criticism, incertitude that one's own views are incontestable, and alert tolerance towards views not shared. [The] Due Process Clause may be indefinite and vague, but the mode [of] ascertainment is not self-willed. In each case 'due process of law' requires an evaluation based on a disinterested inquiry pursued in the spirit of science, on a balanced order of facts exactly and fairly stated, on the detached consideration of conflicting claims, on a judgment not ad hoc and episodic but duly mindful of reconciling the needs both of continuity and change in a progressive society." Justice Black retorted by attacking the "nebulous standards" stated by the majority: "[I] long ago concluded that the accordion-like qualities of the ['evanescent standards of the majority's philosophy'] must inevitably imperil all the individual liberties safeguards specifically enumerated in the Bill of Rights."

6. Kadish, "Methodology and Criteria in Due Process Adjudication—A Survey and Criticism," 66 Yale L.J. 319 (1957).

from the incorporationist "strait-jacket," as Justice Harlan was to charge?[7]

c. *Federalism and the Palko–Adamson approach.* Respect for state policy-makers permeates the majority positions of the Palko–Adamson tradition. There are elements in that tradition, however, that contravene state interests. The unpredictability of the flexible due process approach is arguably more harmful to state concerns than a more rigid—possibly more interventionist, yet also more certain—due process interpretation. In the right to counsel area, even Justice Harlan, an adherent of the Cardozo–Frankfurter position, ultimately came to support fixed rather than flexible rules. Powell v. Alabama in 1932 had required appointment of counsel in capital cases; but for years it was the Court's position in non-capital cases that appointment of counsel was required only if lack of counsel produced unfairness in a particular case—the "special circumstances" rule of Betts v. Brady, 316 U.S. 455 (1942). In the two decades of experience under that rule, many state convictions were reversed by applying that case-by-case approach. Finally, in Gideon v. Wainwright, 372 U.S. 335 (1963), Betts was overruled and a flat requirement of counsel in *all* felony cases was substituted. In a concurring opinion in Gideon, Justice Harlan commented that, in application, "the Betts v. Brady rule is no longer a reality," for the Court for years had found "special circumstances" justifying reversal for lack of counsel in virtually every case decided by it on the merits. He added: "This evolution, however, appears not to have been fully recognized by many state courts. [To] continue a rule which is honored by this Court only with lip service is not a healthy thing and in the long run will do disservice to the federal system."[8]

d. *The reign and modifications of the Palko–Adamson approach.* For a decade and a half after Adamson, the Court persisted in applying the flexible due process analysis articulated in Palko and Adamson. Beginning in the early 1960s, however, the Warren Court—without ever formally abandoning the "fundamental fairness" standard—began to look ever more to the Bill of Rights for guidance and began to apply ever more of those guarantees to the states via the 14th Amendment. In effect, that development has made all of the criminal procedure guarantees of the Bill of Rights, except for the grand jury indictment provision of the Fifth Amendment, applicable to the states. Moreover, perceived essentials of fairness have been found in due process even though they are not specified in the Bill of Rights—as with the holding, noted earlier, that proof beyond a reasonable doubt is a constitutional requirement in criminal cases.

Duncan, the 1968 decision below, reviews the rapid expansion of the list of incorporated guarantees in the 1960s and illustrates the modern Court's manner of applying the modified incorporation approach. Under Palko–Adamson, the Court looked at the facts in the case before it and asked whether the challenged state action violated the "fair trial," "fundamental fairness" requirement implicit in due process; and, sometimes, the claim found essential to

---

7. See, e.g., the Black–Harlan 1968 debate in Duncan, below. The degree to which "vague" standards akin to due process can continue to plague the Court even when "specific" guarantees are incorporated is illustrated by the interpretations of the Eighth Amendment's prohibition of "cruel and unusual punishments." Note especially the first Death Penalty Case, Furman v. Georgia, 408 U.S. 238 (1972). Though in form the nine opinions in that case focused on the "specific" Eighth Amendment provision, the issues

considered were very similar to those encountered in giving content to the "vague contours" of due process. Indeed, several of the opinions in Furman explicitly recognized the kinship between the Palko–Adamson due process approach and Eighth Amendment analysis.

8. See Israel, "Gideon v. Wainwright: The 'Art' of Overruling," 1963 Sup.Ct.Rev. 211.

a fair trial corresponded to aspects of a right specified in the Bill of Rights. In the modern modification of that approach, as illustrated by Duncan, the Court proceeds on a more wholesale basis: typically, it looks to the facts in the case before it simply to ascertain whether they raise issues of the sort covered by the Bill of Rights; having identified the relevant Bill of Rights provision, the Court pays little further attention to the facts and asks instead whether the particular Bill of Rights guarantee is essential to "fundamental fairness" and should be made applicable to the states. The Duncan approach raises problems of its own. The most pervasive one has been the question of the *contours* of a Bill of Rights guarantee incorporated into the 14th Amendment and made applicable to the states. When a Bill of Rights guarantee is incorporated into the 14th Amendment, does it apply to the states in precisely the same manner as it applies to the federal criminal process? Is every detail of the "incorporated" Bill of Rights provisions applicable "jot-for-jot" to the states? That problem is pursued in the notes after Duncan.

B.   THE MODERN APPROACH AND ITS PROBLEMS

Duncan v. Louisiana

391 U.S. 145, 88 S.Ct. 1444, 20 L.Ed.2d 491 (1968).

Justice WHITE delivered the opinion of the Court.

Appellant, Gary Duncan, was convicted of simple battery, [a misdemeanor] punishable by a maximum of two years' imprisonment and a $300 fine. Appellant sought trial by jury, but because the Louisiana Constitution grants jury trials only in cases in which capital punishment or imprisonment at hard labor may be imposed, the trial judge denied the request. Appellant was convicted and sentenced to serve 60 days in the parish prison and pay a fine of $150. Appellant [alleges] that the Sixth and [14th Amendments] secure the right to jury trial in state criminal prosecutions where a sentence as long as two years may be [imposed].

[In] resolving conflicting claims concerning the meaning of this spacious language [of due process], the Court has looked increasingly to the Bill of Rights for guidance; many of the rights guaranteed by the first eight Amendments to the Constitution have been held to be protected against state action by the Due Process Clause of the [14th] Amendment. That clause now protects the right to compensation for property taken by the State;[1] the rights of speech, press, and religion covered by the First Amendment;[2] the Fourth Amendment rights to be free from unreasonable searches and seizures and to have excluded from criminal trials any evidence illegally seized;[3] the right guaranteed by the Fifth Amendment to be free of compelled self-incrimination;[4] and the Sixth

---

1. Chicago, Burlington & Quincy Railway Co. v. Chicago, 166 U.S. 226 (1897). [All non-bracketed materials in the numbered footnotes to this opinion are by Justice White.]

2. See, e.g., Fiske v. Kansas, 274 U.S. 380 (1927).

3. See Mapp v. Ohio, 367 U.S. 643 (1961). [On the current vitality of Mapp, see footnote 2 to the post-Duncan notes, below.]

4. Malloy v. Hogan, 378 U.S. 1 (1964).

Amendment rights to counsel,[5] to a speedy[6] and public[7] trial, to confrontation of opposing witnesses,[8] and to compulsory process for obtaining witnesses.[9]

The test for determining whether a right extended by the Fifth and Sixth Amendments with respect to federal criminal proceedings is also protected against state action by the [14th Amendment] has been phrased in a variety of ways in the opinions of this Court. The question has been asked whether a right is among those " 'fundamental principles of liberty and justice which lie at the base of all our civil and political institutions,' " Powell v. Alabama;[10] whether it is "basic in our system of jurisprudence," In re Oliver; and whether it is "a fundamental right, essential to a fair trial," Gideon v. Wainwright; Malloy v. Hogan; Pointer v. Texas [380 U.S. 400, 403 (1965)]. The claim before us is that the right to trial by jury guaranteed by the Sixth Amendment meets these tests. The position of Louisiana, on the other hand, is that the Constitution imposes upon the States no duty to give a jury trial in any criminal case, regardless of the seriousness of the crime or the size of the punishment which may be imposed. Because we believe that trial by jury in criminal cases is fundamental to the American scheme of justice, we hold that the [14th] Amendment guarantees a right of jury trial in all criminal cases which—were they to be tried in a federal court—would come within the Sixth Amendment's guarantee.[11] Since we consider the appeal before us to be such a case, we hold

---

5. Gideon v. Wainwright, 372 U.S. 335 (1963).

6. Klopfer v. North Carolina, 386 U.S. 213 (1967).

7. In re Oliver, 333 U.S. 257 (1948).

8. Pointer v. Texas, 380 U.S. 400 (1965).

9. Washington v. Texas, 388 U.S. 14 (1967).

10. Quoting from Hebert v. Louisiana, 272 U.S. 312, 316 (1926).

11. In one sense recent cases applying provisions of the first eight Amendments to the States represent a new approach to the "incorporation" debate. Earlier the Court can be seen as having asked, when inquiring into whether some particular procedural safeguard was required of a State, if a civilized system could be imagined that would not accord the particular protection. [Palko.] The recent cases, on the other hand, have proceeded upon the valid assumption that state criminal processes are not imaginary and theoretical schemes but actual systems bearing virtually every characteristic of the common-law system that has been developing contemporaneously in England and in this country. The question thus is whether given this kind of system a particular procedure is fundamental—whether, that is, a procedure is necessary to an Anglo–American regime of ordered liberty. It is this sort of inquiry that can justify the conclusions that state courts must exclude evidence seized in violation of the Fourth Amendment, Mapp v. Ohio; that state prosecutors may not comment on a defendant's failure to testify, Griffin v. California; and that criminal punishment may not be imposed for the status of narcotics addiction, Robinson v. California [370 U.S. 660 (1962)]. Of immediate relevance for this case are the Court's holdings that the States must comply with certain provisions of the Sixth Amendment, specifically that the States may not refuse a speedy trial, confrontation of witnesses, and the assistance, at state expense if necessary, of counsel. See cases cited in nn. [5–9], above. Of each of these determinations that a constitutional provision originally written to bind the Federal Government should bind the States as well it might be said that the limitation in question is not necessarily fundamental to fairness in every criminal system that might be imagined but is fundamental in the context of the criminal processes maintained by the American States. When the inquiry is approached in this way the question whether the States can impose criminal punishment without granting a jury trial appears quite different from the way it appeared in the older cases opining that States might abolish jury trial. See, e.g., Maxwell v. Dow, 176 U.S. 581 (1900). A criminal process which was fair and equitable but used no juries is easy to imagine. It would make use of alternative guarantees and protections which would serve the purposes that the jury serves in the English and American systems. Yet no American State has undertaken to construct such a system. Instead, every American State, in-that the Constitution was violated when appellant's demand for jury trial was refused.

The history of trial by jury in criminal cases has been frequently told. [That history] is impressive support for considering the right to jury trial in criminal cases to be fundamental to our system of justice. [Jury] trial continues to receive strong support. The laws of every State guarantee a right to jury trial in serious criminal [cases]. We are aware of prior cases in this Court in which the prevailing opinion contains statements contrary to our holding today that the right to jury trial in serious criminal cases is a fundamental right and hence must be recognized by the States as part of their obligation to extend due process of law to all persons within their jurisdiction. [None] of these cases, however, dealt with a State which had purported to dispense entirely with a jury trial in serious criminal cases. [We] reject the prior dicta regarding jury trial in criminal cases. The guarantees of jury trial in the Federal and State Constitutions reflect a profound judgment about the way in which law should be enforced and justice administered. A right to jury trial is granted to criminal defendants in order to prevent oppression by the Government. [The] deep commitment of the Nation to the right of jury trial in serious criminal cases as a defense against arbitrary law enforcement qualifies for protection under the Due Process Clause of the [14th] Amendment, and must therefore be respected by the States.

Of course jury trial has "its weaknesses and the potential for misuse." We are aware of the long debate, especially in this century, [as] to the wisdom of permitting untrained laymen to determine the facts in civil and criminal proceedings. [Most] of the controversy has centered on the jury in civil cases. [Louisiana] urges that holding that the [14th] Amendment assures a right to jury trial will cast doubt on the integrity of every trial conducted without a jury. Plainly, this is not the import of our holding. Our conclusion is that in the American States, as in the federal judicial system, a general grant of jury trial for serious offenses is a fundamental right, essential for preventing miscarriages of justice and for assuring that fair trials are provided for all defendants. We would not assert, however, that every criminal trial—or any particular trial—held before a judge alone is unfair or that a defendant may never be as fairly treated by a judge as he would be by a jury. Thus we hold no constitutional doubts about the practices, common in both federal and state courts, of accepting waivers of jury trial and prosecuting petty crimes without extending a right to [jury trial].[12]

cluding Louisiana, uses the jury extensively, and imposes very serious punishments only after a trial at which the defendant has a right to a jury's verdict. In every State, including Louisiana, the structure and style of the criminal process—the supporting framework and the subsidiary procedures—are of the sort that naturally complement jury trial, and have developed in connection with and in reliance upon jury trial.

12. Louisiana also asserts that if due process is deemed to include the right to jury trial, States will be obligated to comply with all past interpretations of the Sixth Amendment, an amendment which in its inception was designed to control only the federal courts and which throughout its history has operated in this limited environment where uniformity is a more obvious and immediate consideration. In particular, Louisiana objects to application of the decisions of this Court interpreting the Sixth Amendment as guaranteeing a 12–man jury in serious criminal cases, Thompson v. Utah, 170 U.S. 343 (1898); as requiring a unanimous verdict before guilt can be found, Maxwell v. Dow, 176 U.S. 581, 586 (1900); and as barring procedures by which crimes subject to the Sixth Amendment jury trial provision are tried in the first instance without a jury but at the first appellate stage by de novo trial with a jury, Callan v. Wilson, 127 U.S. 540, 557 (1888). It seems very unlikely to us that our decision today will require widespread

Louisiana's final contention is that even if it must grant jury trials in serious criminal cases, the conviction before us [is] constitutional because here the petitioner was tried for simple battery and was sentenced to only 60 days in the parish prison. We are not persuaded. It is doubtless true that there is a category of petty crimes or offenses which is not subject to the Sixth Amendment [and] should not be subject to the [14th Amendment]. Crimes carrying possible penalties up to six months do not require a jury trial if they otherwise qualify as petty offenses. [But here, the state] has made simple battery a criminal offense punishable by imprisonment for two years and a fine. The question [is] whether a crime carrying such a penalty is an offense which Louisiana may insist on trying without a jury. We think [not].

Reversed and remanded.*

changes in state criminal processes. First, our decisions interpreting the Sixth Amendment are always subject to reconsideration, a fact amply demonstrated by the instant decision. In addition, most of the States have provisions for jury trials equal in breadth to the Sixth Amendment, if that amendment is construed, as it has been, to permit the trial of petty crimes and offenses without a [jury]. [For the Court's post-Duncan struggles with the problems raised in this footnote, see the notes following this case.]

* *Incorporation since Duncan.* The process of incorporation has continued since Duncan. In Benton v. Maryland, 395 U.S. 784 (1969), the majority held "that the double jeopardy prohibition of the Fifth Amendment represents a fundamental ideal in our constitutional heritage, and that it should apply to the [States]." As a result of the selective incorporation technique illustrated by Duncan, all of the criminal process guarantees of the Bill of Rights are now applicable to the states, with the exception of the grand jury indictment provision of the Fifth Amendment and, arguably, the "excessive bail" provision of the Eighth Amendment (but see Schilb v. Kuebel, 404 U.S. 357 (1971)). Moreover, incorporation is not the sole source of 14th Amendment restraints on state procedures. Recall In re Winship (1970; p. 417 above). For a useful survey, see Israel, "Selective Incorporation Revisited," 71 Geo.L.J. 253 (1982).

Incorporation and the retroactivity problem. Traditionally, newly announced doctrines have been given fully retroactive effect by American courts, with the new standard applicable to all cases pending in the judicial system. But amid the pressure to expand the list of incorporated rights in the 1960s, that traditional retroactivity principle was perceived as a substantial brake on the incorporation of new constitutional rights into the due process clause. Given the availability of

collateral challenges to convictions via habeas corpus, the concern was that a rapid pace in incorporating new Bill of Rights guarantees would flood the federal courts and open the prison gates by permitting reliance on the newly recognized rights by prisoners whose convictions had long become final for direct review purposes. Those pragmatic considerations no doubt played a role in inducing the Warren Court to develop major exceptions to the normal retroactivity rule in the midst of the rapid expansion of selective incorporation during the 1960s. The legitimacy of those exceptions, and the appropriate contours of permissible prospectivity, have produced sharp divisions on and off the Court. See, e.g., Linkletter v. Walker, 381 U.S. 618 (1965), and Payton v. New York, 445 U.S. 573 (1980). Do the Court's frequent denials of retroactivity expose it to the charge of acting more like a legislative than a judicial body? Are the differing treatments of defendants under the varying cut-off rules arbitrary and discriminatory? (Justices Black and Douglas so argued in dissent in several of the Linkletter line of cases.) See generally Mishkin, "Foreword: The High Court, The Great Writ, and the Due Process of Time and Law," 79 Harv.L.Rev. 56 (1965), and Beytagh, "Ten Years of Non–Retroactivity: A Critique and a Proposal," 61 Va.L.Rev. 1557 (1975). The Court's latest grappling with the retroactivity standard commenced in a series of cases beginning with Teague v. Lane, 489 U.S. 288 (1989). There, a majority of the Court rejected the Linkletter approach and adopted instead an analysis under which "new" constitutional rules would be applied to all cases on direct review that were not yet final, but would ordinarily not be applied to final judgments attacked on collateral review, except in extraordinary cases in which "fundamental fairness" would be denied by not applying the "new" rule. For a criticism of Teague and its progeny, see Weisberg, "A Great Writ

Justice BLACK, with whom Justice DOUGLAS joins, concurring.

[I agree with the holding] for reasons given by the Court. I also agree because of reasons given in my dissent in [Adamson]. I am very happy to support this selective process through which our Court has since the Adamson case held most of the specific Bill of Rights' protections applicable to the States to the same extent they are applicable to the [Federal Government]. All of these holdings making Bill of Rights' provisions applicable as such to the States mark, of course, a departure from the Twining doctrine. [The] dissent in this case, however, makes a spirited and forceful defense of that now discredited doctrine. My Brother Harlan's objections to my Adamson dissent history, like that of most of the objectors, relies most heavily on a criticism written by Professor Charles Fairman and published in the Stanford Law Review. 2 Stan.L.Rev. 5 (1949). I have read and studied this article extensively, including the historical references, but am compelled to add that in my view it has completely failed to refute the inferences and arguments that I suggested in my Adamson [dissent].

[The dissent also] states that "the great words of the four clauses of the first section of the Fourteenth Amendment would have been an exceedingly peculiar way to say that 'The rights heretofore guaranteed against federal intrusion by the first eight Amendments are henceforth guaranteed against state intrusion as well.' "In response to this I can say only that the words "No State shall make or enforce any law which shall abridge the privileges or immunities of citizens of the United States" seem to me an eminently reasonable way of expressing the idea that henceforth the Bill of Rights shall apply to the States.[1] What more precious "privilege" of American citizenship could there be than that privilege to claim the protections of our great Bill of Rights? I suggest that any reading of "privileges or immunities of citizens of the United States" which excludes the Bill of Rights' safeguards renders the words of this section of the [14th] Amendment meaningless. [If] anything, it is "exceedingly peculiar" to read the [14th] Amendment differently from the way I do.

While I do not wish at this time to discuss at length my disagreement with Brother Harlan's forthright and frank restatement of the now discredited Twining doctrine, I do want to point out what appears to me to be the basic difference between us. [D]ue process, according to my Brother Harlan, is to be a phrase with no permanent meaning, but one which is found to shift from time to time in accordance with judges' predilections and understandings of what is best for the country. [It] is impossible for me to believe that such unconfined power is given to judges in our Constitution that is a written one in order to limit governmental power. Another tenet of the Twining doctrine as restated by my Brother Harlan is that "due process of law requires only fundamental fairness." But the "fundamental fairness" test is one on a par with that of shocking the conscience of the Court. Each of such tests depends entirely on the particular judge's idea of ethics and morals instead of requiring him to depend on the boundaries fixed by the written words of the Constitution. [I] am not bothered by the argument that applying the Bill of Rights to the States [may] prevent States from trying novel social and economic experiments. I have

While It Lasted," 81 J.Crim.L. & Criminology 9 (1990). See also Fallon & Meltzer, "New Law, Non–Retroactivity, and Constitutional Remedies," 104 Harv.L.Rev. 1731 (1991), and the thrust resembling Teague reflected in the Anti-Terrorism and Habeas Corpus Reform Act of 1996.

1. My view has been and is that the Fourteenth Amendment, *as a whole,* makes the Bill of Rights applicable to the States. This would certainly include the language of the Privileges and Immunities Clause, as well as the Due Process Clause. [Footnote by Justice Black.]

never believed that under the guise of federalism the States should be able to experiment with the protections afforded [by] the [Bill of Rights]. I believe as strongly as ever that the [14th] Amendment was intended to make the Bill of Rights applicable to the States. I have been willing to support the selective incorporation doctrine, however, as an alternative, although perhaps less historically supportable than complete incorporation. The selective incorporation process, if used properly, does limit the [Court in the 14th Amendment] field to specific Bill of Rights' protections only and keeps judges from roaming at will in their own notions of what policies outside the Bill of Rights are desirable and what are not. And, most importantly for me, the selective incorporation process has the virtue of having already worked to make most of the Bill of Rights' protections applicable to the States.

Justice FORTAS, concurring.

[A]lthough I agree with the decision of the Court, I cannot agree with the implication that the tail must go with the hide: that when we hold, influenced by the Sixth Amendment, that "due process" requires that the States accord the right of jury trial for all but petty offenses, we automatically import all of the ancillary rules which have been or may hereafter be developed incidental to the right to jury trial in the federal courts. I see no reason whatever, for example, to assume that our decision today should require us to impose federal requirements such as unanimous verdicts or a jury of 12 upon the States. We may well conclude that these and other features of federal jury practice are by no means fundamental [and] that they are not obligatory on the States. [There] is no reason whatever for us [to be] bound slavishly to follow not only the Sixth Amendment but all of its bag and baggage. To take this course [would] be not only unnecessary but mischievous because it would inflict a serious blow upon the principle of [federalism].

Justice HARLAN, whom Justice STEWART joins, dissenting.

[The] Due Process Clause of the [14th] Amendment requires that [state] procedures be fundamentally fair in all respects. It does not, in my view, impose or encourage nationwide uniformity for its own sake; it does not command adherence to forms that happen to be old; and it does not impose on the States the rules that may be in force in the federal courts except where such rules are also found to be essential to basic fairness. The Court's approach to this case is an uneasy and illogical compromise among the views of various Justices on how the Due Process Clause should be interpreted. The Court does not say that those who framed the [14th] Amendment intended to make the Sixth Amendment applicable to the States. And the Court concedes that it finds nothing unfair about the procedure by which the present appellant was tried. Nevertheless, the Court reverses his conviction: it holds, for some reason not apparent to me, that the Due Process Clause incorporates the particular clause of the Sixth Amendment that requires trial by jury in federal criminal cases—including, as I read its opinion, the sometimes trivial accompanying baggage of judicial interpretation in federal contexts. I have raised my voice many times before against the Court's continuing undiscriminating insistence upon fastening on the States federal notions of criminal justice, and I must do so again in this instance. With all respect, the Court's approach and its reading of history are altogether topsy-turvy.

[The] first section of the [14th] Amendment was meant neither to incorporate, nor to be limited to, the specific guarantees of the first eight Amendments. The overwhelming historical evidence marshalled by Professor Fairman demonstrates, to me conclusively, that the Congressmen and state legislators who wrote, debated, and ratified the [14th] Amendment did not think they were "incorporating" the Bill of Rights. [N]either history, nor sense, supports using the [14th] Amendment to put the States in a constitutional straitjacket with respect to their own development in the administration of criminal or civil law. Although [I] fundamentally disagree with the total incorporation view of the [14th] Amendment, it seems to me that such a position does at least have the virtue, lacking in the Court's selective incorporation approach, of internal consistency: we look to the Bill of Rights, word for word, clause for clause, precedent for precedent because, it is said, the men who wrote the Amendment wanted it that way. [Apart] from the approach taken by the absolute incorporationists, I can see only one method of analysis that has any internal logic. That is to start with the words "liberty" and "due process of law" and attempt to define them in a way that accords with American traditions and our system of government. This approach, involving a much more discriminating process of adjudication than does "incorporation," is, albeit difficult, the one that was followed throughout the 19th and most of the present century. It entails a "gradual process of judicial inclusion and exclusion," seeking, with due recognition of constitutional tolerance for state experimentation and disparity, to ascertain those "immutable principles [of] free government which no member of the Union may disregard." Due process was not restricted to rules fixed in the past. [Nor] did it impose nationwide uniformity in details. The relationship of the Bill of Rights to this "gradual process" seems to me to be twofold. In the first place it has long been clear that the Due Process Clause imposes some restrictions on state action that parallel Bill of Rights restrictions on federal action. Second, and more important than this accidental overlap, is the fact that the Bill of Rights is evidence, at various points, of the content Americans find in the term "liberty" and of American standards of [fundamental fairness].

Today's Court still remains unwilling to accept the total incorporationists' view of the history of the [14th] Amendment. [The] Court is also, apparently, unwilling to face the task of determining whether denial of trial by jury in the situation before us, or in other situations, is fundamentally unfair. Consequently, the Court has compromised on the ease of the incorporationist position, without its internal logic. It has simply assumed that the question before us is whether the Jury Trial Clause of the Sixth Amendment should be incorporated into the Fourteenth, jot-for-jot and case-for-case, or ignored. Then the Court merely declares that the clause in question is "in" rather than "out." The Court has justified neither its starting place nor its conclusion. If the problem is to discover and articulate the rules of fundamental fairness in criminal proceedings, there is no reason to assume that the whole body of rules developed in this Court constituting Sixth Amendment jury trial must be regarded as a unit. The requirement of trial by jury in federal criminal cases has given rise to numerous subsidiary questions respecting the exact scope and content of the right. It surely cannot be that every answer the Court has given, or will give, to such a question is attributable to the Founders; or even that every rule announced carries equal conviction of this Court; still less can it be that every such subprinciple is equally fundamental to ordered liberty. Examples abound. I should suppose it obviously fundamental to fairness that a "jury" means an "impartial jury." I should think it equally obvious that the rule, imposed long ago in the federal courts, that "jury" means "jury of exactly twelve," is not fundamental to anything: there is no significance except to mystics in the number 12. Again, trial by jury has been held to require a unanimous verdict of jurors in the federal courts, although unanimity has not been found essential to liberty in Britain, where the requirement has been [abandoned].

Even if I could agree that the question before us is whether Sixth Amendment jury trial is totally "in" or totally "out," I can find in the Court's opinion no real reasons for concluding that it should be "in." The basis for differentiating among clauses in the Bill of Rights cannot be that only some clauses are in the Bill of Rights, or that only some are old and much praised, or that only some have played an important role in the development of federal law. These things are true of all. The Court says that some clauses are more "fundamental" than others, but it turns out to be using this word in a sense that would have astonished Mr. Justice Cardozo and which, in addition, is of no help. The word does not mean "analytically critical to procedural fairness" for no real analysis of the role of the jury in making procedures fair is even attempted. Instead, the word turns out to mean "old," "much praised," and "found in the Bill of Rights." The definition of "fundamental" thus turns out to be circular. [The] argument that jury trial is not a requisite of due process is quite simple. [If] due process of law requires only fundamental fairness, then the inquiry in each case must be whether a state trial process was a fair one. The Court has held, properly I think, that in an adversary process it is a requisite of fairness, for which there is no adequate substitute, that a criminal defendant be afforded a right to counsel and to cross-examine opposing witnesses. But it simply has not been demonstrated, nor, I think, can it be demonstrated, that trial by jury is the only fair means of resolving issues of fact. The jury is of course not without virtues. [The] jury system can also be said to have some inherent defects. [That] trial by jury is not the only fair way of adjudicating criminal guilt is well attested by the fact that it is not the prevailing way, either in England or in this country. In the United States, [two] experts have estimated that, of all prosecutions for crimes triable to a jury, 75% are settled by guilty plea and 40% of the remainder are tried to the court.[1] [I] see no reason why this Court should reverse the conviction of appellant, absent any suggestion that his particular trial was in fact unfair, or compel [Louisiana] to afford jury trial in an as yet unbounded category of cases that can, without unfairness, be tried to a court. [The] Court has chosen to impose upon every State one means of trying criminal cases; it is a good means, but it is not the only fair means, and it is not demonstrably better than the alternatives States might [devise].

PROBLEMS OF THE MODERN APPROACH: THE CONTOURS OF "INCORPORATED" RIGHTS

1. *Incorporating Bill of Rights guarantees "jot-for-jot."* By the end of the 1960s, it was clear that virtually all Bill of Rights guarantees pertaining to criminal proceedings were applicable to the states via the 14th Amendment. But the embracive scope of modern "selective" incorporation has not solved all of the problems debated in earlier decades. In the Palko–Adamson era, advocates of the total incorporation of "specific" Bill of Rights guarantees had urged that technique as a cure for the vices of unpredictability and judicial subjectivity. During the heyday of the unmodified Palko–Adamson regime, there was indeed ample ground for the charges of uncertainty and subjectivity. Under the Cardozo–Frankfurter approach, a finding that a right reflected in one of the Bill of Rights provisions was essential to "fundamental fairness" did not mean that all of the detailed interpretations of the relevant Bill of Rights provision were applicable to the states. The treatment of the Fourth Amendment's

---

1. Kalven & Zeisel, [The American Jury (1966)]. [Footnote by Justice Harlan.]

guarantee against unreasonable searches and seizures illustrates the resulting difficulties. In 1949, in Wolf v. Colorado, 338 U.S. 25, Justice Frankfurter's opinion for the Court held that the "core" of the Fourth Amendment guarantee was an ingredient of due process, but went on to find that the exclusionary rule applied in federal courts (barring the use of evidence obtained in violation of the Fourth Amendment) was not constitutionally required of the states. After more than a decade of controversy and confusion in the aftermath of Wolf, the Court changed its mind. In Mapp v. Ohio, 367 U.S. 643 (1961), Justice Clark's majority opinion found the exclusionary rule to be "an essential part of the right to privacy" recognized in Wolf: henceforth, states could no longer admit evidence obtained in violation of Fourth Amendment standards. Incorporation thereafter meant not merely incorporating the "core" of the Bill of Rights guarantee, but applying to the states every detail of the contours of the guarantee.

From the beginning of that new era of applying the Bill of Rights provisions to the states to exactly the same extent as they applied to the federal government, some Justices objected. The objections were essentially those voiced by Justices Harlan and Fortas in Duncan, claiming that "bag and baggage," "jot-for-jot and case-for-case" incorporation would impose needlessly detailed constraints on the states. Moreover, as Justice Frankfurter had warned as long ago as Adamson, incorporation of specific Bill of Rights guarantees risked a "warped construction"—and possible dilution—of those provisions. The post-Duncan cases that follow illustrate those problems. Duncan for the first time found the Sixth Amendment jury trial provision applicable to the states. As Justice Harlan's dissent noted, that Bill of Rights guarantee had, in its applications to federal proceedings in the past, apparently mandated a 12–person, unanimous jury verdict for federal criminal convictions. But in the aftermath of Duncan, the Court found that the Sixth Amendment did *not* require 12–person or unanimous juries after all—in federal *or* state courts. In examining the post-Duncan decisions, consider whether the modern incorporation approach affords adequate defenses against the charges of subjectivity and unpredictability so long levied against the earlier Palko–Adamson technique. Have the recent decisions vindicated the warnings that incorporation of "specific" rights would produce distortion and dilution of those rights? What goals are furthered, and what costs are incurred, by making all interpretations of specific guarantees applicable to the states, "bag and baggage," "jot-for-jot"?

2. *The jury trial guarantee after Duncan: Dilution of federal rights as an escape from the incorporationist "straitjacket"?* a. *The Williams case.* In WILLIAMS v. FLORIDA, 399 U.S. 78 (1970), the petitioner seeking reversal of a robbery conviction claimed that he should have been tried by a 12–person jury rather than the six-person panel provided by Florida law in all but capital cases. Justice WHITE's majority opinion concluded, however, that "the twelve-man panel is not a necessary ingredient of 'trial by jury.' "Though earlier interpretations of the Sixth Amendment had "assumed" the 12–person panel to be constitutionally necessary, Justice White explained, "that particular feature of the jury system appears to have been a historical accident, unrelated to the great purposes which gave rise to the jury in the first place." He conceded that a 12–person jury might well have been "the usual expectation" of the Framers, but argued that the constitutionally required features of a jury turned on "other than purely historical considerations": "The relevant inquiry [must] be the function that the particular feature performs and its relation to the purposes of the jury trial." Justice White found a critical purpose of a jury to be "the interposition between the accused and his accuser of the common sense judgment of a group of laymen"; and that did not require any particular

number on the jury. Moreover, "neither currently available evidence nor theory suggests that the twelve-man jury is necessarily more advantageous to the defendant than a jury composed of fewer members." Do you agree?

In an extensive opinion concurring in the result, Justice HARLAN reiterated his adherence to the Palko–Adamson approach, restated his opposition to Duncan, and objected to the majority's "dilution" of Sixth Amendment guarantees: "The necessary consequence of this decision is that twelve-member juries are not constitutionally required in *federal* criminal trials either. [The] decision evinces, I think, a recognition that the 'incorporationist' view must be tempered to allow the States more elbow room in ordering their own criminal systems. With that much I agree. But to accomplish this by diluting constitutional protections within the federal system itself is something to which I cannot possibly subscribe. Tempering the rigor of Duncan should be done forthrightly, by facing up to the fact that at least in this area the 'incorporation' doctrine does not fit well with our federal structure." He claimed: "I consider that before today it would have been unthinkable to suggest that the Sixth Amendment's right to a trial by jury is satisfied by a jury of six, or less, [or] by less than a unanimous verdict. [The] Court's elaboration of what is required provides no standard and vexes the meaning of the right to a jury trial in federal courts, as well as state courts, by uncertainty. Can it be doubted that a unanimous jury of 12 provides a greater safeguard than a majority vote of six?" He added: "These decisions demonstrate that the difference between a [Palko] 'due process' approach [and] 'selective incorporation' is not an abstract [one]. The 'backlash' in Williams exposes the malaise, for there the Court dilutes a federal guarantee in order to reconcile the logic of 'incorporation,' the 'jot-for-jot and case-for-case' application of the federal right to the States, with the reality of federalism. Can one doubt that had Congress tried to undermine the common-law right to trial by jury before Duncan came on the books the history today recited would have barred such action? Can we expect repeat performances when this Court is called upon to give definition and meaning to other federal guarantees that have been 'incorporated'?"[2]

b. *The Apodaca case.* Another issue left open by Duncan—the question whether a *unanimous* jury verdict is required in state courts after the incorporation of the Sixth Amendment—came before the Court in APODACA v. OREGON, 406 U.S. 404 (1972). As in Williams, the Court ruled that what had formerly been thought to be an ingredient of the Sixth Amendment guarantee was not constitutionally required after all and accordingly sustained the constitutionality of a state nonunanimous jury verdict. This time, however, the division on the Court was particularly sharp and unusual. The nonunanimous jury verdict was approved though eight of the Justices adhered to the Duncan position that each element of the Sixth Amendment jury trial guarantee is fully

2. Justice STEWART joined most of Justice Harlan's objections to the "mechanistic 'incorporation' approach." Justice MARSHALL's dissent stated that he was "convinced that the requirement of 12 should be applied to the States." In contrast, a separate opinion by Justice BLACK, joined by Justice Douglas, supported the majority view on jury size and disagreed with some of Justice Harlan's assertions: "Today's decision is in no way attributable to any desire to dilute the Sixth Amendment in order more easily to apply it to the States, but follows solely as a necessary consequence of our duty to reexamine prior decisions to reach the correct constitutional meaning in each case." He claimed that, had the question been presented to the Court in a federal case before Duncan, "this Court would still, in my view, have reached the result announced today." [Eight years after Williams had found a six-person criminal jury permissible, the Court found that six was the minimum constitutional size and held that a five-member jury in serious criminal cases was unconstitutional. Ballew v. Georgia, 435 U.S. 223 (1978).]

applicable to the states via the 14th, and even though five of the Justices read the Sixth Amendment as requiring unanimous jury verdicts in federal trials. The result nevertheless sustaining the nonunanimous verdict in state trials was made possible by the decisive concurring position of Justice Powell. Following in the footsteps of Justice Harlan's argument in Duncan and Williams, Justice Powell found that the Sixth Amendment required the traditional jury unanimity in federal trials, but did not think that all of the elements of the federal guarantee should be imposed on the states as a requirement of due process.

The Oregon system sustained in Apodaca requires the vote of at least ten out of twelve jurors for conviction in noncapital cases. Justice WHITE's plurality opinion, joined by Chief Justice Burger and Justices Blackmun and Rehnquist, adhered to the Williams approach: unanimity was not constitutionally required because it "does not materially contribute to" the central function "served by the jury in contemporary society"—to interpose "the common sense judgment of a group of laymen" between accused and accuser.[3] Justice POWELL's opinion explaining his decisive vote for the result rejected the plurality's "major premise" that "the concept of jury trial, as applicable to the States under the [14th] Amendment, must be identical in every detail to the concept required in federal courts by the Sixth Amendment." In federal proceedings, he explained, he would require unanimity, "not because unanimity is necessarily fundamental to the function performed by the jury, but because that result is mandated by history." But as to state proceedings, due process simply required that states adhere to "what is fundamental in jury trial"; and the Oregon system adequately respected the fundamentals. To impose upon the state every detail of incorporated federal guarantees would deprive the states of "freedom to experiment with adjudicatory processes different from the federal model." Moreover, under the prevailing approach, the Court ended up, here as in Williams, with "the dilution of federal rights which were, until these decisions, never seriously questioned."[4]

---

3. Justices DOUGLAS, BRENNAN, STEWART, and MARSHALL each submitted a dissenting opinion.

4. In Burch v. Louisiana, 441 U.S. 130 (1979), the Court confronted a problem it described as lying at "the intersection of our decisions concerning jury size and unanimity"—i.e., Williams and Apodaca. The Court held that "conviction by a nonunanimous six-member jury in a state criminal trial for a nonpetty offense deprives an accused of his constitutional right to trial by jury." Setting aside a conviction obtained by a 5–1 jury vote, Justice Rehnquist found the issue a "close" one and commented: "[H]aving already departed from the strictly historical requirements of jury trial, it is inevitable that lines must be drawn somewhere if the substance of a jury trial right is to be preserved."

CHAPTER 8

SUBSTANTIVE DUE PROCESS: RISE, DECLINE, REVIVAL

Introduction. In no part of constitutional law has the search for legitimate ingredients of constitutional interpretation been more difficult and controversial than in the turbulent history of substantive due process. To what extent does the due process clause concern itself not simply with the methods of governmental action but also with its substance? To what extent does the due process clause authorize the Court to articulate fundamental values—values not explicitly designated for special protection by the Constitution, yet values which government may not impinge upon without meeting an unusually high standard of justification? That the due process clause *can* serve as a springboard for judicial articulation of "fundamentals" has already been demonstrated in the preceding materials on the incorporation controversy. But that course of decisions led the Court to search merely for the fundamentals of *procedure.* In its first interpretation of the 14th Amendment, in the Slaughter–House Cases, the majority rejected any notion of *substantive* due process. But the dissenters' plea for the protection of fundamental values prevailed by the end of the 19th century.

The 1905 decision in Lochner v. New York (p. 460), striking down New York's maximum hours law for bakers, symbolizes the rise of substantive due process as a protection of economic and property rights. For three decades thereafter, the Court engaged in "Lochnerizing"—scrutinizing economic regulations with care and frequently striking them down. In the mid–1930s, judicial intervention in economic legislation began to decline. Today, the use of substantive due process to assure special protection of economic and property rights is discredited. Yet in recent years, substantive due process has flourished once again, as a haven for fundamental values other than economic ones; and that development is illustrated by modern decisions that, to protect autonomy and privacy, strike down laws restricting abortions and the use of contraceptives.

These substantive due process cases, old and new, raise some common issues: Are these decisions, from Lochner v. New York to Griswold v. Connecticut (p. 518), Roe v. Wade (p. 530), Casey (p. 557) and beyond, justifiable as interpretations of the Constitution? Are the fundamental values identified in such cases plausible extrapolations from constitutional text, history, or structure? Or are they ultimately extraconstitutional, noninterpretive judicial infusions? What fundamental values, if any, *may* the Court properly impose? Are there basic values—moral, social, or economic—that truly reflect a national consensus? Even if there are such values, does the existence of a consensus authorize the Justices to read them into the Constitution? Are fundamental value adjudications unacceptable if the Court cannot demonstrate an adequate link to constitutional text, history, or structure? Is it possible to state a principled "fundamental values" approach that safeguards adequately against merely subjective judicial lawmaking?

There is reason to examine the early 20th century cases of the Lochner era even though substantive due process does not impose serious constraints on economic regulation today. The economic rights cases bear directly on the judicial function in the protection of those individual liberties that receive greater attention from the modern Court. Are the abortion and contraception decisions essentially modern examples of Lochnerizing, or are those recent judicial interventions more justifiable than the earlier ones? The resemblances between Lochner and the Griswold–Roe line of cases are most evident, but there are additional linkages between the Lochner era and modern Court developments. For example, the textual source of the Court's interventions in the Lochner era was most commonly the "liberty" protected by the due process clauses: "liberty of contract" and its role as a constitutional support for a laissez faire economy were major preoccupations of the Justices of the Lochner years; and the term "liberty" is also the major basis of the Court's active enforcement of personal rights today—not only "fundamental" rights not explicitly listed in the Constitution (such as privacy), but also the "specific" First Amendment guarantees of freedom of speech, press and religion long "incorporated" into the 14th Amendment. Is there justification for the sharp decline in judicial protection of some varieties of "liberty" and the dramatic rise in judicial intervention on behalf of other kinds of "liberty"? That problem of a "double standard" pervades the rest of this book, but it is raised with special force by the contrast between the old and new varieties of substantive due process in secs. 1 and 3 of this chapter.

The Court's encounters with substantive due process in the economic sphere in sec. 1 provide essential background for a critical assessment of the modern responses. Substantive due process is the major vehicle for the protection of economic interests examined in sec. 1, but it has not been the only vehicle. Sec. 1A examines some historical antecedents of economic due process developments; sec. 2 surveys two themes tangential to the development of substantive due process as a protection of economic rights: the role of the contracts clause; and the protection of property against "taking" without just compensation.

SECTION 1. SUBSTANTIVE DUE PROCESS AND ECONOMIC REGULATION: THE RISE AND DECLINE OF JUDICIAL INTERVENTION

———

A. ANTECEDENTS

Introduction. Substantive due process as a protection of fundamental economic rights did not receive wholehearted support from a Court majority until the end of the 19th century. But arguments that property and economic rights were basic had long been in the air: the notion that there *were* fundamental rights, and that they were entitled to judicial protection, had considerable earlier support. Some of that support was voiced by the dissenters in the Slaughter–House Cases. And the fundamental values those dissenters sought to enshrine in the post-Civil War Amendments were values in turn rooted in the thinking of earlier generations: the legacy of Magna Carta, Blackstone and Adam Smith is explicit in those dissents. There was thus a respectable natural law tradition which, drawing on English antecedents, viewed a written constitution not as the initial source but as a reaffirmation of a social compact preserving preexisting fundamental rights—rights entitled to protection whether or not they were explicitly stated in the basic document.[1]

1. *Calder v. Bull.* Some of these natural law ideas surfaced sporadically in early Court opinions: during the pre-Marshall years, some Justices were tempted to read the Constitution as a whole as a guarantor of fundamental rights— rights that stemmed from the social compact and did not need explicit textual support. The prime example is Justice CHASE's opinion in 1798, in CALDER v. BULL, 3 Dall. (3 U.S.) 386. There, the Court rejected an attack on a Connecticut legislative act setting aside a probate court decree that had refused to approve a will. The legislation required a new hearing; and at that second hearing, the will was approved. The challenge to the law came from the heirs who would have taken the property if the will had been ineffective. The Court rejected their claim that the ex post facto clause barred the Connecticut act: that clause was construed as being limited to criminal legislation. But more important for present purposes is the willingness of some Justices to entertain arguments based on natural law. Calder v. Bull was handed down in the years before John Marshall persuaded his colleagues to abandon *seriatim* opinions. And of the several opinions, Justice Chase's dicta most elaborately announced an early inclination to invalidate legislation quite apart from explicit constitutional limitations. Justice Chase stated (with the emphases—but not the typeface that made s's look like f's—as they appear in the original Reports):

"I cannot subscribe to the *omnipotence* of a *State Legislature,* or that it is *absolute* and *without control;* although its authority should not be *expressly* restrained by the *Constitution,* or *fundamental law,* of the State. The people of the *United States* erected their Constitutions, or forms of governments, to establish justice, to promote the general welfare, to secure the blessings of liberty; and to protect their *persons* and *property* from violence. The purposes for which men enter into society will determine the *nature* and *terms* of the *social* compact; and as *they* are the foundation of the *legislative* power, *they* will decide what are the *proper* objects of it: The *nature,* and *ends* of *legislative* power will limit the *exercise* of it. This *fundamental* principle flows from the very nature of our free *Republican* governments, that no man should be compelled to do what the laws do *not* require; *nor to refrain from acts which the laws permit.* There are acts which the *Federal,* or *State,* Legislature cannot do, *without exceeding their authority.* There are certain *vital* principles in our *free Republican governments,* which will determine and over-rule an *apparent and flagrant* abuse of *legislative* power; as to authorize *manifest injustice by positive law;* or to take away that security for *personal liberty,* or *private property,* for the protection whereof the government was established. An ACT of the Legislature (for I cannot call it a *law*) contrary to the *great first principles* of the *social* compact, cannot be considered a *rightful exercise* of *legislative authority.* The obligation of a law in governments established on *express compact, and on republican principles,* must be determined by the *nature* of the *power,* on which it is founded. A few instances will suffice to explain what I mean. A law that punished a citizen for an *innocent* action, or, in other words, for an act, which, when done, was in violation of no *existing* law; a law that destroys, or impairs, the *lawful private* contracts of citizens; a law that makes a man *a Judge in his*

---

1. See generally Corwin, "The Basic Doctrine of American Constitutional Law," 12 Mich.L.Rev. 247 (1914); Corwin, "The 'Higher Law' Background of American Constitutional Law," 42 Harv.L.Rev. 149, 365 (1928–29); Corwin, Liberty Against Government (1948). See also Grey, "Do We Have an Unwritten Constitution?" 27 Stan.L.Rev. 703 (1975), and Grey, "Origins of the Unwritten [Constitution]," 30 Stan.L.Rev. 843 (1978).

own cause; or a law that takes *property* from A. and gives it to B. It is against all reason and justice, for a people to entrust a Legislature with SUCH powers; and, therefore, it cannot be presumed that they have done it. The *genius,* the *nature,* and the *spirit,* of our State Governments, amount to a prohibition of *such acts of legislation;* and the *general principles of law and reason* forbid them. The Legislature [cannot] change *innocence* into *guilt;* [or] violate the right of an *antecedent lawful private contract;* or the *right of private property.* To maintain that our Federal, or State, Legislature possesses *such powers,* if they had not been *expressly* restrained; would, in my opinion, be a *political heresy,* altogether inadmissible in our *free republican governments.''*²*

Justice IREDELL's dicta challenged Justice Chase's natural law-social compact-vested rights approach. He stated: "[S]ome speculative jurists have held, that a legislative act against natural justice must, in itself, be void; but I cannot think that, under [a constitutional scheme allocating powers without explicit limitations], any Court of Justice would possess a power to declare it so. Sir *William Blackstone,* having put the strong case of an act of Parliament, which should authorize a man to try his own cause, explicitly adds, that even in that case, 'there is no court that has power to defeat the intent of the Legislature.' In order, therefore, to guard against so great an evil, it has been the policy of all the *American* states, which have, individually, framed their state constitutions since the revolution, and of the people of the *United States,* when they framed the Federal Constitution, to define with precision the objects of the legislative power, and to restrain its exercise within marked and settled boundaries. If any act of Congress, or of the Legislature of a state, violates those constitutional provisions, it is unquestionably [void]. If, on the other hand, the Legislature of the Union, or the Legislature of any member of the Union, shall pass a law, within the general scope of their constitutional power, the Court cannot pronounce it to be void, merely because it is, in their judgment, contrary to the principles of natural justice. The ideas of natural justice are regulated by no fixed standard: the ablest and the purest men have differed upon the subject; and all that the Court could properly say, in such an event, would be, that the Legislature (possessed of an equal right of opinion) had passed an act which, in the opinion of the judges, was inconsistent with the abstract principles of natural justice."

2. *The early Marshall Court.* In the early years of the Marshall Court, there were occasional echoes of Chase's natural law-vested rights approach. For example, in Fletcher v. Peck, 6 Cranch (10 U.S.) 87 (1810), Marshall flirted with such a notion as an alternative ground for invalidating a Georgia effort to revoke a land grant. He thought the result justified "either by general principles which are common to our free institutions, or by the particular provisions of the constitution of the United States." Justice Johnson's concurrence went even further in that direction. He repudiated any reliance on the contracts clause of the Constitution; instead, he relied on "general principle, on the reason and nature of things." But passages such as these vanished from the opinions in the later Marshall Court years. Instead, the Court linked all of its protections of economic rights to specific constitutional provisions—most often, the contracts clause. (See sec. 2B.) In short, Justice Iredell's insistence that only explicit constitutional limits on legislative power were judicially enforceable ultimately prevailed, at least in form. Marshall's rationale for judicial authority in Marbury v. Madison helped assure that Iredell's position, not

2. Justice Chase concluded that the Connecticut law had not exceeded legislative powers: since the initial invalidation of the will had not created any "vested" property rights in the heirs, the law was consistent with "natural justice."

Chase's, would emerge as the dominant one: a justification for judicial review that relied so heavily on the implications of a written constitution probably found it more congenial to justify any invalidations on the bases of explicit constitutional restraints. Nevertheless, notions of natural law and vested rights remained useful and influential, not as an adequate formal basis for invalidation, but as a source of values for giving content to the guarantees such as the contracts clause and, later, substantive due process.

3. Due process before the Civil War. Though most pre-Civil War discussion of due process clauses in state constitutions and in the Fifth Amendment spoke of the more obvious procedural implications of due process, there were some intimations that due process might also impose substantive restraints on legislation. Thus, in the infamous Dred Scott decision, Chief Justice Taney's opinion commented, without elaboration: "An Act of Congress which deprives a citizen of the United States of his liberty or property, merely because he came himself or brought his property into a particular Territory of the United States, and who had committed no offense against the laws, could hardly be dignified with the name of due process of law."[3]

4. The movement toward substantive due process in the generation after the Slaughter–House Cases. The Slaughter–House Cases (p. 421 above) temporarily blocked the utilization of the 14th Amendment as a substantive restraint on state legislation. But a generation later, a new majority embraced substantive due process, including its novel "liberty of contract" argument. It was not a sudden change: a variety of pressures, on and off the Court, contributed to the gradual conversion of due process into a more interventionist tool. For one, lawyers kept pressing the Court to restrain economic regulation despite the rebuff of the Slaughter–House Cases. As Justice Miller noted five years later, "the docket of this court is crowded with cases in which we are asked to hold that state courts and state legislatures have deprived their own citizens of life, liberty, or property without due process of law. There is here abundant evidence that there exists some strange misconception of the scope of this

---

3. On the state level, the best-known pre-Civil War suggestion of a substantive ingredient in due process came in Wynehamer v. People, 13 N.Y. 378 (1856), invalidating a liquor prohibition law. As the most prolific student of due process wrote, Wynehamer read due process to "prohibit, regardless of the matter of procedure, a certain kind or degree of exertion of legislative power altogether" : due process, rather than merely protecting the "mode of procedure," was made to reach "the substantive content of legislation." Corwin, Liberty Against Government (1948). [Other substantive due process arguments before the Civil War came from anti-slavery lawyers, who argued that slavery was a deprivation of liberty without a proper basis in law (such as conviction for crime). But the influence of this type of argument on 14th Amendment developments has been discounted by some because it was identified almost totally with abolitionists and played no significant role in court decisions or widely accepted legal commentary. See generally Nelson, "The Impact of the Antislavery

Movement upon Styles of Judicial Reasoning in Nineteenth Century America," 87 Harv. L.Rev. 513 (1974).]

The usual modern position, then, is that substantive due process had very little pre-Civil War basis. See, e.g., Ely, Democracy and Distrust (1980), 18: "[We] apparently need periodic reminding that 'substantive due process' is a contradiction in terms—sort of like 'green pastel redness.' " But some research regarding the "prehistory" of substantive due process challenges that position. Grey concedes that the "liberty"-emphasizing aspect of substantive due process—as with the "liberty of contract" of Lochner—is indeed a late–19th century invention. But he insists that, in the decades preceding the 14th Amendment, some state courts read state due process clauses as affording substantive protection to property from arbitrary legislative interferences. He views those state court rulings as propounding a variety of vested rights theories and protections against "takings" somewhat akin to Justice Chase's dicta in Calder v. Bull.

provision as found in the 14th Amendment. In fact, it would seem [that] the clause under consideration is looked upon as a means of bringing to the test of the decision of this court the abstract opinions of every unsuccessful litigant in a State court of the justice of the decision against him, and of the merits of the legislation on which such a decision may be founded." Davidson v. New Orleans, 96 U.S. 97 (1877). The lawyers' arguments that seemed a "misconception" of due process to Justice Miller reflected deeper social and economic developments and ideological movements.[4] The growth of industrialization and corporate power in the post-Civil War years stirred popular demands and legislative responses. The new regulatory laws, opponents argued, contravened not only the economic laissez faire theories of Adam Smith but also the social views of 19th century writers such as Herbert Spencer. (In his Lochner dissent in 1905, Justice Holmes insisted that the 14th Amendment "does not enact Mr. Herbert Spencer's Social Statics.") But Spencer's emphasis on the survival of the fittest in his 1850 volume, and the echoes of Social Darwinism in the writings of American defenders of governmental hands-off policies regarding economic inequalities, found their way into legal treatises and briefs. And, increasingly, there were responsive listeners on the bench. As Justice Brewer stated in dissent in Budd v. New York, 143 U.S. 517 (1892): "The paternal theory of government is to me odious. The utmost possible liberty to the individual, and the fullest possible protection to him and his property, is both the limitation and duty of government."[5] Soon, the seeds of substantive due process began to surface in majority opinions.

a. *Rate regulation and the Munn case.* A leading case of the 1870s, for example, is commonly viewed as a symbol of judicial deference to legislative judgments; yet at the same time it suggested potential limits on legislative power. In MUNN v. ILLINOIS, 94 U.S. 113 (1877), the Court rejected an attack on a state law regulating the rates of grain elevators. Chief Justice WAITE's majority opinion emphasized that the police power included regulation of individual use of property "when such regulation becomes necessary for the public good." He relied in part on 17th century English writings to conclude that private property may be regulated when it is "affected with a public interest" and that property becomes "clothed with a public interest when used in a manner to make it of public consequence, and affect the community at large." The business owners regulated here easily fell within that category: they had a near monopoly on grain storage; regulation of their rates was similar to traditional price regulation of utilities and monopolies. The majority refused to scrutinize the reasonableness of the rates: since there was power to regulate, the legislative right to establish maximum rates was implied. Chief Justice Waite added: "We know that this is a power which may be abused; but that is no argument against its existence." Yet the Chief Justice prefaced that passage with a statement which was relied on later to justify judicial control of rate regulation: "Undoubtedly, in mere private contracts, relating to matters in

---

4. See generally Paul, Conservative Crisis and the Rule of Law: Attitudes of Bar and Bench 1887–1896 (1960), and Twiss, Lawyers and the Constitution: How Laissez Faire Came to the Supreme Court (1942). The lawyers' advocacy of substantive due process frequently relied on an influential treatise published in the same year the 14th Amendment was adopted, Cooley, Constitutional Limitations (1868).

5. Substantive due process flourished in some state courts before it found majority support in the Supreme Court. The leading late 19th century case was In the Matter of Jacobs, 98 N.Y. 98 (1885), holding unconstitutional a law prohibiting the manufacture of cigars in tenement houses. To the state court, the public health justification was unpersuasive, and the law interfered not only with "the profitable and free use" of property but also with "personal liberty."

which the public has no interest, what is reasonable must be ascertained judicially."[6]

Chief Justice Waite took a similar noninterventionist stance in The Railroad Commission Cases, 116 U.S. 307 (1886), sustaining state regulation of railroad rates. But, again, the deference to legislative judgments was joined with a passage which left the door open for greater judicial control in the future. He warned that "it is not to be inferred that this power [of] regulation [is] without limit. This power to regulate is not a power to destroy. Under pretense of regulating fares and freights, the State cannot require a railroad corporation to carry persons or property without reward; neither can it do that which in law amounts to a taking of private property for public use without just compensation, or without due process of law."[7] In the same year, in Santa Clara County v. Southern Pac. Railroad, 118 U.S. 394 (1886), the Court held, without discussion, that corporations were "persons" within the meaning of the 14th Amendment.[8] The early resistance to judicial intervention was weakening; dicta even in noninterventionist cases were leaving the door slightly ajar; and soon it swung wide open.

b. *Mugler v. Kansas.* Before long, substantive due process review, ranging well beyond rate regulation and encompassing a wide variety of police power exercises as well, was fully launched. MUGLER v. KANSAS, 123 U.S. 623 (1887), signaled the impending receptivity of the Court. Mugler sustained a law prohibiting intoxicating beverages, but the Court announced that it was prepared to examine the substantive reasonableness of state legislation. The first Justice HARLAN spoke for a Court whose composition had changed almost totally since the Slaughter–House Cases. He stated that not "every statute enacted ostensibly for the promotion" of "the public morals, the public health, or the public safety" would be accepted "as a legitimate exertion of the police powers of the State." The courts would not be "misled by mere pretenses": they were obligated "to look at the substance of things." Accordingly, if a purported exercise of the police powers "has no real or substantial relation to those objects, or is a palpable invasion of rights secured by the fundamental law, it is the duty of the courts to so adjudge." And facts "within the knowledge of all" would be relied on in making that determination.

6. Note the reexamination of the Munn legacy in Nebbia (1934; p. 474 below).

7. In the further development of judicial control of rate making, Chicago, M. & St. P. Ry. Co. v. Minnesota, 134 U.S. 418 (1890), was a significant turning point. That decision invalidated a state law authorizing administrative ratemaking without providing for judicial review. The immediate vice of the statute was the lack of adequate procedural protection for the railroads—the lack of judicial review. But the majority explanation suggested Court concern with substance as well as procedure: reasonableness of rates was found to be "eminently a question for judicial investigation"; depriving the railroad of the power to charge reasonable rates by administrative order would be, "in substance and effect," a deprivation of property without due process of law. By the end of the decade, the Court was wholeheartedly in the business of scrutinizing the reasonableness of rates. Smyth v. Ames, 169 U.S. 466 (1898), provided the governing ratemaking formulas for decades. For a review of rate regulation developments after the 1890s (and the repudiation of the reign of Smyth v. Ames), see FPC v. Hope Natural Gas Co., 320 U.S. 591 (1944). See also Siegel, "Understanding the Lochner Era: Lessons from the Controversy over Railroad and Utility Rate Regulation," 70 Va.L.Rev. 187 (1984).

8. See Graham, "The 'Conspiracy Theory' of the Fourteenth Amendment," 47 Yale L.J. 371 and 48 Yale L.J. 171 (1938). Justices Black and Douglas objected to this interpretation. See their dissents in Connecticut General Life Ins. Co. v. Johnson, 303 U.S. 77 (1938), and Wheeling Steel Corp. v. Glander, 337 U.S. 562 (1949).

c. *The Allgeyer case and liberty of contract.* Ten years later, in ALLGEYER v. LOUISIANA, 165 U.S. 578 (1897), the slow movement to substantive due process was completed: for the first time, the Court invalidated a state law on substantive due process grounds. Allgeyer involved a Louisiana law that prohibited obtaining insurance on Louisiana property "from any marine insurance company which has not complied in all respects" with Louisiana law. Allgeyer was convicted for mailing a letter advising an insurance company in New York of the shipment of goods, in accordance with a marine policy. The company was not licensed to do business in Louisiana. The Court reversed, holding the statute in violation of the 14th Amendment "in that it deprives the defendants of their liberty without due process of law." Although Justice PECKHAM's opinion for a unanimous Court focused on state power over foreign corporations, it was his broad articulation of the "liberty of contract" that gave the case its special significance in the development of substantive due process: "The liberty mentioned in that amendment means not only the right of the citizen to be free from the mere physical restraint of his person, as by incarceration, but the term is deemed to embrace the right of the citizen to be free in the enjoyment of all his faculties; to be free to use them in all lawful ways; to live and work where he will; to earn his livelihood by any lawful calling; to pursue any livelihood or avocation, and for that purpose to enter into all contracts which may be proper, necessary and essential to his carrying out to a successful conclusion the purposes above mentioned." Soon after the turn of the century, this expansive conception of "liberty" bore fruit in more controversial contexts, as exemplified by the Lochner case, which follows. When the modern Court looks back to the discredited "Allgeyer–Lochner–Adair–Coppage constitutional doctrine" (the phrase is from the Lincoln Federal Labor Union case in 1949, p. 480 below), the Allgeyer reference is not to its specific insurance setting but to its significance in opening the door to the substitution of the Justices' notions of public policy and fundamental values for legislative choices involving economic and social regulation, as assertedly took place in Lochner. Is that what happened in Lochner and its progeny? Has that due process philosophy been wholly rejected by the modern Court?

B. THE LOCHNER ERA: JUDICIAL INTERVENTION AND ECONOMIC REGULATION

Lochner v. New York

198 U.S. 45, 25 S.Ct. 539, 49 L.Ed. 937 (1905).

Justice PECKHAM [delivered] the opinion of the court.

[A New York law prohibited the employment of bakery employees for more than 10 hours a day or 60 hours a week. Lochner was convicted and fined for permitting an employee to work in his Utica, N.Y., bakery for more than 60 hours in one week, or more than 10 hours in one day.]

[The] statute necessarily interferes with the right of contract between the employer and [employés]. The general right to make a contract in relation to his business is part of the liberty of the individual protected by the 14th Amendment. [Allgeyer.] The right to purchase or to sell labor is part of the liberty protected by this amendment, unless there are circumstances which exclude the right. There are, however, [state police] powers [relating] to the safety, health, morals and general welfare of the public. [When] the [state legislature], in the assumed exercise of its police powers, has passed an act which seriously limits the right to labor or the right of contract in regard to their means of livelihood between persons who are sui juris (both employer and employé), it becomes of great importance to determine which shall prevail—the right of the individual to labor for such time as he may choose, or the right of the State to prevent the individual from laboring [beyond] a certain time prescribed by the State. This court [has] upheld the exercise of the police powers of the States in many cases which might fairly be considered as border ones, and it [has] been guided by rules of a very liberal nature, the application of which has resulted, in numerous instances, in upholding the validity of state statutes thus assailed. Among the later cases where the state law has been upheld [is] that of Holden v. Hardy.[1] [I]t was held that the kind of employment, mining, smelting, etc., and the character of the employés in such kinds of labor, were such as to make it reasonable and proper for the State to interfere to prevent the employés from being constrained by the rules laid down by the proprietors in regard to labor. [There] is nothing in Holden v. Hardy which covers the case now before [us].

It must, of course, be conceded that there is a limit to the valid exercise of the [police power]. Otherwise the 14th Amendment would have no efficacy and the legislatures of the States would have unbounded power, and it would be enough to say that any piece of legislation was enacted to conserve the morals, the health or the safety of the [people]. The claim of the police power would be a mere [pretext]. In every case that comes before this court, therefore, [the] question necessarily arises: Is this a fair, reasonable and appropriate exercise of the [police power], or is it an unreasonable, unnecessary and arbitrary interference with the right of the individual to his personal liberty or to enter into those contracts in relation to labor which may seem to him appropriate or necessary for the support of himself and his family? Of course the liberty of contract relating to labor includes both parties to it. The one has as much right to purchase as the other to sell labor. This is not a question of substituting the judgment of the court for that of the legislature. If the act be within the power of the State it is valid, although the judgment of the court might be totally opposed to the enactment of such a law. But the question would still remain: Is it within the police power of the State? and that question must be answered by the court.

The question whether this act is valid as a labor law, pure and simple, may be dismissed in a few words. There is no reasonable ground for interfering with the liberty of person or the right of free contract, by determining the hours of labor, in the occupation of a baker. There is no contention that bakers as a class are not equal in intelligence and capacity to men in other trades or manual occupations, or that they are not able to assert their rights and care for themselves without the protecting arm of the State, interfering with their independence of judgment and of action. They are in no sense wards of the State. Viewed in the light of a purely labor law, with no reference whatever to the question of health, we think that a law like the one before us involves neither the safety, the morals nor the welfare of the public, and that the interest of the public is not in the slightest degree affected by such an act. The law must be upheld, if at all, as a law pertaining to the health of the individual engaged in the occupation of a baker. [Clean] and wholesome bread does not

---

1. Holden v. Hardy, 169 U.S. 366 (1898), sustained a Utah law limiting the employment of workers in underground mines to eight hours a day. The case was decided in the period between Allgeyer and Lochner.

depend upon whether the baker works but ten hours per day or only sixty hours a week. [The] mere assertion that the subject relates though but in a remote degree to the public health does not necessarily render the enactment valid. The act must have a more direct relation, as a means to an end, and the end itself must be appropriate and legitimate, before an act can be held to be valid which interferes with the general right of an individual to be free in his person and in his power to contract in relation to his own [labor].

We think the limit of the police power has been reached and passed in this case. There is, in our judgment, no reasonable foundation for holding this to be necessary or appropriate as a health law to safeguard the public health or the health of the individuals who are following the trade of a baker. If this statute be valid, [there] would seem to be no length to which legislation of this nature might not go. [We] think that there can be no fair doubt that the trade of a baker, in and of itself, is not an unhealthy one to that degree which would authorize the legislature to interfere with the right to labor, and with the right of free contract on the part of the individual, either as employer or employé. In looking through statistics regarding all trades and occupations, it may be true that the trade of a baker does not appear to be as healthy as some other trades, and is also vastly more healthy than still others. To the common understanding the trade of a baker has never been regarded as an unhealthy one. [It] might be safely affirmed that almost all occupations more or less affect the health. There must be more than the mere fact of the possible existence of some small amount of unhealthiness to warrant legislative interference with liberty. It is unfortunately true that labor, even in any department, may possibly carry with it the seeds of unhealthiness. But are we all, on that account, at the mercy of legislative majorities?

[It] is also urged [that] it is to the interest of the State that its population should be strong and robust, and therefore any legislation which may be said to tend to make people healthy must be valid as health laws, enacted under the police power. If this be a valid argument and a justification for this kind of legislation, it follows that the protection of the Federal Constitution from undue interference with liberty of person and freedom of contract is visionary, wherever the law is sought to be justified as a valid exercise of the police power. Scarcely any law but might find shelter under such [assumptions]. Not only the hours of employés, but the hours of employers, could be regulated, and doctors, lawyers, scientists, all professional men, as well as athletes and artisans, could be forbidden to fatigue their brains and bodies by prolonged hours of exercise, lest the fighting strength of the State be impaired. We mention these extreme cases because the contention is extreme. We do not believe in the soundness of the views which uphold this law. [The] act is not, within any fair meaning of the term, a health law, but is an illegal interference with the rights of individuals, both employers and employés, to make contracts regarding labor upon such terms as they may think best, or which they may agree upon with the other parties to such contracts. Statutes of the nature of that under review, limiting the hours in which grown and intelligent men may labor to earn their living, are mere meddlesome interferences with the rights of the individual, and they are not saved from condemnation by the claim that they are passed in the exercise of the police power and upon the subject of the health of the individual whose rights are interfered with, unless there be some fair ground, reasonable in and of itself, to say that there is material danger to the public health or to the health of the employés, if the hours of labor are not curtailed. [All that the State] could properly do has been done by it with regard to the conduct of bakeries, as provided for in the other sections of the act, [which] provide for the inspection of the premises where the bakery is carried on, with regard to furnishing proper wash-rooms and water-closets, [also] with regard to providing proper drainage, plumbing and painting [and] for other things of that [nature].

It was further urged [that] restricting the hours of labor in the case of bakers was valid because it tended to cleanliness on the part of the workers, as a man was more apt to be cleanly when not overworked, and if cleanly then his "output" was also more likely to be so. In our judgment it is not possible in fact to discover the connection between the number of hours a baker may work in the bakery and the healthful quality of the bread made by the workman. The connection, if any exists, is too shadowy and thin to build any argument for the interference of the legislature. If the man works ten hours a day it is all right, but if ten and a half or eleven his health is in danger and his bread may be unhealthful, and, therefore, he shall not be permitted to do it. This, we think, is unreasonable and entirely arbitrary. When assertions such as we have adverted to become necessary in order to give, if possible, a plausible foundation for the contention that the law is a "health law," it gives rise to at least a suspicion that there was some other motive dominating the legislature than the purpose to subserve the public health or welfare. This interference on the part of the legislatures of the several States with the ordinary trades and occupations of the people seems to be on the increase. [It] is impossible for us to shut our eyes to the fact that many of the laws of this character, while passed under what is claimed to be the police power for the purpose of protecting the public health or welfare, are, in reality, passed from other motives. We are justified in saying so when, from the character of the law and the subject upon which it legislates, it is apparent that the public health or welfare bears but the most remote relation to the law. The purpose of a statute must be determined from the natural and legal effect of the language employed; and whether it is or is not repugnant to the Constitution [must] be determined from the natural effect of such statutes when put into operation, and not from their proclaimed purpose.

[It] is manifest to us that the [law here] has no such direct relation to and no such substantial effect upon the health of the employé as to justify us in regarding the section as really a health law. It seems to us that the real object and purpose were simply to regulate the hours of labor between the master and his employés (all being men, sui juris), in a private business, not dangerous in any degree to morals or in any real and substantial degree, to the health of the employés. Under such circumstances the freedom of master and employé to contract with each other in relation to their [employment] cannot be prohibited or interfered with, without violating the Federal Constitution.

[Reversed.]

Justice HARLAN, with whom Justice WHITE and Justice DAY concurred, [dissenting].

[There] is a liberty of contract which cannot be violated, [but] is subject to [reasonable police regulations]. It is plain that this statute was enacted in order to protect the physical well-being of those who work in [bakery] establishments. It may be that the statute had its origin in part, in the belief that employers and employés in such establishments were not upon an equal footing, and that the necessities of the latter often compelled them to submit to such exactions as unduly taxed their strength. Be this as it may, the statute must be taken as expressing the belief of the people of New York that, as a general rule, and in the case of the average man, labor in excess of sixty hours during a week in such establishments may endanger the health of those who thus labor. Whether or not this be wise legislation, it is not the province of the court to inquire. [The] courts are not concerned with the wisdom or policy of legislation. So that in determining the question of power to interfere with liberty of contract, the court may inquire whether the means devised by the State are germane to an end which may be lawfully accomplished and have a real or substantial relation to the protection of health, as involved in the daily work of the persons, male and female, engaged in [bakery] establishments. But when this inquiry is entered upon I find it impossible, in view of common experience, to say that there is here no real or substantial relation between the means employed by the State and the ends sought to be accomplished by its legislation. [Still] less can I say that the statute is, beyond question, a plain, palpable invasion of rights secured by the fundamental [law].

Professor Hirt in his treatise on the "Diseases of the Workers" has said: "The labor of the bakers is among the hardest and most laborious imaginable, because it has to be performed under conditions injurious to the health of those engaged in it. It is hard, very hard work, not only because it requires a great deal of physical exertion in an overheated workshop and during unreasonably long hours, but more so because of the erratic demands of the public, compelling the baker to perform the greater part of his work at [night]." Another writer says: "The constant inhaling of flour dust causes inflammation of the lungs and of the bronchial tubes. The eyes also suffer through this [dust]. The long hours of toil to which all bakers are subjected produce rheumatism, cramps and swollen legs. [Nearly] all bakers are pale-faced and of more delicate health than the workers of other crafts, which is chiefly due to their hard work and their irregular and unnatural mode of living. [The] average age of a baker is below that of other workmen; they seldom live over their fiftieth [year]." [Additional data are omitted.]

We judicially know that the question of the number of hours during which a workman should continuously labor has been, for a long period, and is yet, a subject of serious consideration among civilized peoples, and by those having special knowledge of the laws of health. [We] also judicially know that the number of hours that should constitute a day's labor in particular occupations involving the physical strength and safety of workmen has been the subject of enactments by Congress and by nearly all of the States. Many, if not most, of those enactments fix eight hours as the proper basis of a day's labor. I do not stop to consider whether any particular view of this economic question presents the sounder theory. [It] is enough for the determination of this case [that] the question is one about which there is room for debate and for an honest difference of opinion. There are many reasons of a weighty, substantial character, based upon the experience of mankind, in support of the theory that, all things considered, more than ten hours' steady work each day, from week to week, in a bakery or confectionery establishment, may endanger the health, and shorten the lives of the workmen, thereby diminishing their physical and mental capacity to serve the State, and to provide for those dependent upon them. If such reasons exist that ought to be the end of this case, for the State is not amenable to the judiciary, in respect of its legislative enactments, unless such enactments are plainly, palpably, beyond all question, inconsistent with the [Constitution]. A decision that the New York statute is void under the 14th Amendment will, in my opinion, involve consequences of a far-reaching and mischievous character; for such a decision would seriously cripple the inherent power of the States to care for the lives, health and well-being of their [citizens].

Justice HOLMES, dissenting.

[This] case is decided upon an economic theory which a large part of the country does not entertain. If it were a question whether I agreed with that theory, I should desire to study it further and long before making up my mind.

But I do not conceive that to be my duty, because I strongly believe that my agreement or disagreement has nothing to do with the right of a majority to embody their opinions in law. It is settled by various decisions of this court that [state laws] may regulate life in many ways which we as legislators might think as injudicious or if you like as tyrannical as this, and which equally with this interfere with the liberty to contract. Sunday laws and usury laws are ancient examples. A more modern one is the prohibition of lotteries. The liberty of the citizen to do as he likes so long as he does not interfere with the liberty of others to do the same, which has been a shibboleth for some well-known writers, is interfered with by school laws, by the Post Office, by every state or municipal institution which takes his money for purposes thought desirable, whether he likes it or not. The 14th Amendment does not enact Mr. Herbert Spencer's Social Statics. The other day we sustained the Massachusetts vaccination law. Jacobson v. Massachusetts, 197 U.S. 11 [1905]. United States and state statutes and decisions cutting down the liberty to contract by way of combination are familiar to this court. [The] decision sustaining an eight hour law for miners is still recent. Some of these laws embody convictions or prejudices which judges are likely to share. Some may not. But a constitution is not intended to embody a particular economic theory, whether of paternalism and the organic relation of the citizen to the State or of laissez faire. It is made for people of fundamentally differing views, and the accident of our finding certain opinions natural and familiar or novel and even shocking ought not to conclude our judgment upon the question whether statutes embodying them conflict with the [Constitution].

General propositions do not decide concrete cases. The decision will depend on a judgment or intuition more subtle than any articulate major premise. But I think that the proposition just stated, if it is accepted, will carry us far toward the end. Every opinion tends to become a law. I think that the word liberty in the 14th Amendment is perverted when it is held to prevent the natural outcome of a dominant opinion, unless it can be said that a rational and fair man necessarily would admit that the statute proposed would infringe fundamental principles as they have been understood by the traditions of our people and our law. It does not need research to show that no such sweeping condemnation can be passed upon the statute before us. A reasonable man might think it a proper measure on the score of health. Men whom I certainly could not pronounce unreasonable would uphold it as a first instalment of a general regulation of the hours of work. Whether in the latter aspect it would be open to the charge of inequality I think it unnecessary to discuss.

THE DISCREDITED PERIOD OF JUDICIAL INTERVENTION: WHAT WAS WRONG WITH LOCHNER?

Introduction. From the Lochner decision in 1905 to the mid–1930s, the Court invalidated a considerable number of laws on substantive due process grounds.[1] Regulations of prices, labor relations (including wages and hours), and conditions for entry into business were especially vulnerable. Typically, as in Lochner, the invalidations provoked dissents, most often by Holmes and,

---

1. For a comprehensive summary of the decisions of the period, see The Constitution of the United States (Gov't Printing Office, 1987 ed.). See also Wright, The Growth of American Constitutional Law (1942).

later, Brandeis, Stone and Cardozo.[2] But even during the Lochner era, while nearly 200 regulations were struck down, most challenged laws withstood attack. Thus, the Court sustained a maximum hours law for women only three years after Lochner, in Muller v. Oregon, below; and it upheld a 10–hour day for factory workers in Bunting v. Oregon in 1917, below. Yet the extent of judicial intervention during the Lochner era was clearly substantial; and the modern Court has repeatedly insisted that it has turned its back on the evils of the Lochner philosophy. What *were* those evils? The giving of substantive content to due process? The expansive view of "liberty" and "property" to include values not explicitly stated in the Constitution? The selection of the "wrong" fundamental values for special judicial protection? The failure to state adequate general standards? The failure to apply the standards with adequate consistency? The failure to apply the standards with adequate receptiveness to factual data? Excessive preoccupation with the permissibility of legislative ends? Excessive preoccupation with the "reasonableness" of legislative means—the extent to which the means contributed to the achievement of permissible ends?

Examining the cases of the Lochner era in light of questions such as these is of more than historical interest. Rejection of the Lochner heritage is a common starting point for modern Justices: reaction against the excessive intervention of the "Old Men" of the pre–1937 Court strongly influenced the judicial philosophies of their successors. Yet the modern Court has *not* drawn from Lochner the lesson that *all* judicial intervention via substantive due process is improper. Rather, it has withdrawn from careful scrutiny in most economic areas but has increased intervention regarding a range of noneconomic personal interests not explicitly protected by the Constitution. Identifying the evils of the Lochner era is especially relevant, then, to determine (a) whether the modern Court's interventions avoid those evils, and (b) whether those evils warranted as substantial a withdrawal from the economic area as has taken place.

1. *Lochner and the language of the 14th Amendment.* a. *"Liberty" and economic rights.* Did the basic vice of Lochner lie in its expansive reading of "liberty"? Justice Peckham read "liberty" broadly to include freedom of contract. Some critics identify that as the basic flaw of the Lochner philosophy: they claim liberty at common law meant only freedom from physical restraint, and that it was not intended to mean any more in the due process clause.[3] But even if that view of common law is correct, should it govern the constitutional meaning of "liberty"? Instead of criticizing Lochner for its generous reading of "liberty," is the approach of the case more vulnerable because of its selection of

2. Among the many critics not on the Court was Learned Hand. See Hand, "Due Process of Law and the Eight–Hour Day," 21 Harv.L.Rev. 495 (1908), and Gunther, Learned Hand: The Man and the Judge (1994), 118–23. Moreover, the Lochner era decisions became political issues well before the New Deal attacks of the mid–1930s—e.g., in the third party campaigns of Teddy Roosevelt in 1912 (in which Learned Hand participated) and in the Robert LaFollette campaign in 1924. (Substantive due process was far and away the most important judicial tool, but it was not the only basis for restraints on economic regulation during this period. On the role of the 14th Amendment's equal protection clause as a source of limits on economic regulation—a role which paralleled but was less significant than that of substantive due process—see chap. 9, sec. 2, below. Recall also the restrictive interpretations of national regulatory powers considered in earlier chapters; and note the continued reliances on the contracts and "taking" clauses even after the advent of substantive due process, sec. 2B below.)

3. See, e.g., Warren, "The New 'Liberty' under the Fourteenth Amendment," 39 Harv.L.Rev. 431 (1926).

some aspects of liberty for *special* protection? Simply reading "liberty" broadly is not likely to produce frequent Court invalidations of laws: if a "mere rationality" standard is used—if legislative restraints on liberty are permissible so long as reasonable persons might think that the restraints plausibly promote broadly conceived legislative objectives—an expansive reading of liberty does not support frequent judicial vetoes. It is only when the "liberty" allegedly infringed is thought to be "*fundamental*," deserving of special protection, and thus eliciting heightened scrutiny from the Court and imposing on the state especially high burdens of justification, that due process review often proves fatal to the challenged legislation. As sec. 1C shows, retreat from interventionism in the economic area on the modern Court has typically not taken place via a shrinking of "liberty"; instead, it has taken the form of extremely deferential scrutiny, a "minimum rationality" standard in testing whether alleged infringements of economic liberties are justifiable.

b. *"Liberty" and noneconomic rights.* Note, too, that it is the reading of "liberty" beyond the narrowest common law confines that has made possible the protection of a wide range of noneconomic interests under the 14th Amendment. Not only economic regulations fell victim to substantive due process attacks in the three decades beginning with Lochner. That period also saw the early development of 14th Amendment protections of civil liberties and of the rights of the accused. The Allgeyer–Lochner philosophy formed the basis for absorbing rights such as those in the First Amendment into the 14th Amendment's concept of liberty, as chap. 11 shows.[4] Moreover, the Allgeyer–Lochner view that liberty should not be limited to its narrowest reading helped justify intervention on behalf of personal, noneconomic rights other than those that had counterparts in the First Amendment. Note, for example, the noneconomic personal liberties recognized in Meyer v. Nebraska (1923; p. 516 below), reversing a conviction of a parochial school teacher under a law prohibiting teaching "in any language other than" English. Justice McReynolds's majority opinion, squarely within the Lochner tradition, contained a broad reading of liberty that has attained renewed significance in the modern revival of substantive due process on behalf of noneconomic fundamental rights such as privacy. He stated that "liberty" denotes "not merely freedom from bodily restraint but also the right of the individual to contract, to engage in any of the common occupations of life, to acquire useful knowledge, to marry, to establish a home and bring up children, to worship God according to the dictates of his own conscience, and generally to enjoy those privileges long recognized at common law as essential to the orderly pursuit of happiness by free men."

c. *"Property" and "due process".* Does criticism of the broad readings of "property" and "due process" get any closer to the roots of the Court's difficulties in the Lochner era than the questioning of the expansive view of "liberty"? A good many of the cases of the Lochner era involved restrictions on the use of property even under the narrowest reading of that term. But the Court's penchant for broad interpretations extended to "property" as well: the much-invoked right to contract, for example, was not traced solely to "liberty," as in Lochner, but was also viewed as a derivation from notions of "property." See, e.g., Coppage v. Kansas (1915; p. 471 below). The strongest textual

---

4. Justice Brandeis' eloquent defense of free speech in Whitney v. California (1927; p. 1054 below) included a reluctant acceptance of the triumph of substantive due process—a triumph that supported the speech protection he advocated there. Indeed, Charles Warren's article cited above—attacking the reading of "liberty" beyond common law confines—had as its main target Gitlow v. New York (1925; p. 1050 below), where the Court for the first time assumed that the First Amendment freedoms of speech and press were "among the fundamental personal rights and liberties" protected by the 14th Amendment.

criticism of the Court's substantive due process developments, however, focuses not on "liberty" or "property" but on the phrase "due process:" How does a legitimate method of interpretation draw from a phrase with procedural connotations a basis for scrutiny of the substance of legislation? What, if any, "process" is the Court concerned with in substantive due process cases?

2. *Lochner and legislative ends.* Justice Peckham's opinion in Lochner did not consider liberty of contract an absolute. He recognized that liberty of contract is subject to restraints under the police power. But what governmental objectives *are* legitimately within the police power? Does the real vice of the Lochner philosophy lie in its unduly narrow conception of those objectives? Justice Peckham recognized that "health" is a legitimate end of the police power, and most of his opinion considered whether New York's regulation could be justified as a health law—as a law to promote the health of bakers or of the consuming public. He was not satisfied that the means adequately promoted a "health" end. But there was another arguable end of the law—one that received short shrift from Justice Peckham. That justification stressed the unequal bargaining position of bakery workers and argued that a state may, under its police power, redress perceived economic inequalities. That is what Justice Peckham called "a labor law, pure and simple"; and to him, a "purely labor law" was not within the objectives contemplated by the police power: "There is no contention that bakers as a class are not equal in intelligence and capacity to men in other trades or manual occupations. [They] are in no sense wards of the State."[5] This refusal of the Court to accept the redressing of inequalities as a legitimate ingredient of the police power lay at the base of many of the Lochner era invalidations. Coppage v. Kansas (1915; p. 471 below) makes the point very clearly: in striking down a law designed to protect labor organizing efforts, the majority stated that the police power may not be invoked to remove "those inequalities that are but the normal and inevitable result" of the exercise of rights of contract and property. Justice Holmes' dissent in Coppage, as in Lochner, was squarely directed at that narrow view of legislative ends: the police power, he insisted in Coppage, may be used "to establish the equality of position between the parties in which liberty of contract begins." And, as he said in the Lochner dissent, a constitution "is not intended to embody a particular economic theory, whether of paternalism and the organic relation of the citizen to the State or of laissez faire."[6]

It is difficult to perceive a basis for the Lochner majority's view of impermissible ends other than an improper reading of a particular (economic) philosophy into the Constitution. Is there a more persuasive basis for the modern Court's new assertions of impermissible ends? Or do the modern cases, analogously to Lochner, simply read a particular (social) philosophy into the Constitution? (See the notes following Roe v. Wade, at p. 538 below.) Even if the Lochner Court's view of impermissible ends is justifiable, were the applications of that position defensible? Can Lochner be squared with the cases

5. Mine workers and women, by contrast, *were* among those perceived by the Lochner era Court to be "unequal" and hence, presumably, legitimate "wards." See Holden v. Hardy, above, and Muller v. Oregon, below.

6. Consider the comment in Gunther, "Foreword: [A] Model for a Newer Equal Protection," 86 Harv.L.Rev. 1, 42 (1972): "[T]he primary evil of the discredited [Lochner] doctrine was the dogmatic judicial intervention regarding ends, not means. [T]he majority's devotion to liberty of contract typically led it to deny the legitimacy of paternalistic legislation. [Justice Holmes's] classic dis-

involving miners and working women?[7]

3. *Lochner and means-ends relationships.* a. *Minimum rationality.* The Lochner majority's objection to the New York law goes not merely to ends but also to means. Viewed as a "labor law," a law designed to protect bakery workers in an unequal bargaining position, the Lochner majority rejected the legitimacy of the legislative end out of hand. But the majority conceded the validity of health objectives. In its scrutiny of the legislation as a health law, the Court purported to be concerned only with the means invoked to promote this legitimate objective. Justice Peckham conceded that a valid health law *could* restrict liberty of contract: his test was that there must be "some fair ground, reasonable in and of itself, to say that there is material danger to [health]." Why was that test not satisfied in Lochner? Justice Harlan's dissent, unlike that of Justice Holmes, was directed at the means rather than the ends analysis in the majority opinion.[8] Did the majority's articulated standard as to means-ends relationships differ from Justice Harlan's insistence that there be a "real or substantial relation between the means employed by the State and the end sought to be accomplished by its legislation"? Was the difference between the majority and Justice Harlan one in application rather than in statement of the rule? Note Justice Harlan's recital of data regarding the health of bakers. Did the majority disagree with those data? Note Justice Harlan's statement that it is enough that "the question is one about which there is room for debate and for an honest difference of opinion." Did the majority demand more than that? Note the majority's statement that the bakers' trade "is not an unhealthy one to that degree which would authorize the legislature to interfere." Arguably, the majority in effect imposed a greater burden of justification than "minimum rationality" on the defenders of the law; apparently, it demanded more than a showing that reasonable persons might think that the means would promote the end. If so, the majority in fact applied a stricter, heightened scrutiny than its own articulated, seemingly deferential, standard suggested.

b. *Stricter scrutiny.* Is it defensible to impose a burden of justification higher than the minimum scrutiny of the "mere rationality" standard? Usually, heightened judicial scrutiny is appropriate only when particularly cherished constitutional rights are threatened. The Lochner majority's approach apparently rested on an implicit assumption that liberty of contract *was* a fundamental value warranting special judicial protection. If so, that may constitute one of the genuine "evils" of Lochner: not the recognition that liberty of contract can be viewed as an aspect of "liberty," but rather that it is such a *fundamental* aspect of liberty that "mere reasonableness" in means-ends relationships will not justify restraints. In short, it may be one of the "evils" that the Lochner Court paid only lip service to a reasonableness standard and applied stricter scrutiny of the means in fact. When such stricter scrutiny is applied, does it inevitably rest on a value judgment: not only a judgment selecting some values for special judicial protection, but also implementing that protection by "balancing" the competing public and private interests?

sents properly identified the dominant evil of that approach."

7. On impermissible "ends" and Lochner generally, see Sunstein, "Naked Preferences and the Constitution," 84 Colum.L.Rev. 1689 (1984), Tribe, American Constitutional Law (2d ed. 1988), and Siegan, Economic Liberties and the Constitution (1980). See also Sunstein, "Lochner's Legacy," 87 Colum.L.Rev. 873 (1987), and his The Partial Constitution (1993).

8. Apparently, Justice Harlan would have agreed with the majority on the illegitimacy of the "labor law" end, to judge by his majority opinion three years later in Adair v. United States (1908; p. 472 below).

Court insistence on scrutiny stricter than "mere rationality" has become a commonplace modern technique in areas other than economic regulation. One way of stating a pervasive problem in the exercise of judicial review is to ask what—in constitutional text, history, structure or justifiable value choices— legitimates judicial applications of heightened scrutiny. As chap. 5 shows, the Court has frequently exercised greater than minimal scrutiny by "balancing" when it examines state regulations of commerce. Higher standards of justification and stricter degrees of scrutiny also surface in later materials: e.g., with respect to the "fundamental right" of privacy, sec. 3 below, and "fundamental" First Amendment rights, chaps. 11 to 13 below. Arguably, it was a major "evil" of Lochner that the majority imposed a scrutiny stricter than "mere rationality" without adequately justifying that special protection of liberty of contract. Why, if at all, was that special scrutiny less justified than some of the currently accepted areas of stricter scrutiny?

If the de facto heightened scrutiny of Lochner is rejected as an evil of that discredited era, does it follow that even "mere rationality" scrutiny of means— means scrutiny according to the standard stated but not followed by Justice Peckham, or that stated and followed by Justice Harlan—should be abandoned? Has the modern Court abandoned even "mere rationality" scrutiny of means in the economic area? See sec. 1C below. Is abandonment of means scrutiny in the economic area a justifiable response to the evils of Lochner? The conferral of an especially high value on liberty of contract without adequate justifications for that cherished status permeated the Lochner era, both in the narrow conception of legislative goals and the stricter scrutiny applied to legislative means. But concern with means may not be as questionable a judicial intervention as a narrow view of police power objectives. Hence, repudiation of the "evils" of the Lochner philosophy may not warrant judicial withdrawal from means scrutiny as well as from ends scrutiny. Can a genuine means scrutiny "with bite" avoid the problems of adjudication based on extraconstitutional values?[9] Arguably, the Court is better equipped to scrutinize means than ends. If the Court were to exercise greater means scrutiny, it would have to address a number of unsettled problems, including those pertaining to the relevant data for determining whether the requisite means-ends relationship exists. For example, the Court might restrict itself to data considered by the legislature or subject to judicial notice, or it might also examine data put forth by the litigants. Problems such as these are considered further below.

JUDICIAL SCRUTINY OF ECONOMIC REGULATIONS DURING THE LOCHNER ERA—SOME EXAMPLES

1. *Maximum hours—Muller and Bunting.* MULLER v. OREGON, 208 U.S. 412 (1908), sustained an Oregon law that provided that "no female" shall

9. These questions are pursued briefly in sec. 1C and more fully in the next chapter, on equal protection. Note the advocacy of a "rational means" scrutiny "with bite" in the context of equal protection in the 1972 Gunther article cited in footnote 6 (and pursued further in chap. 9). That means-focused inquiry would have the Court "assess the means in terms of legislative purposes that have substantial basis in actuality, not mere-ly in conjecture," and "would have the Justices gauge the reasonableness of questionable means on the basis of materials that are offered to the Court, rather than resorting to rationalizations created by perfunctory judicial hypothesizing." Though that article speaks of the equal protection context, the means-oriented analysis is relevant to due process as well.

be employed in any factory or laundry for "more than ten hours during any one day." The conviction of Muller, a laundry operator, was affirmed by the Court, supposedly "without questioning in any respect the decision" in Lochner. Justice BREWER stated that it was obvious that "woman's physical structure" placed her "at a disadvantage in the struggle for subsistence," and that, "as healthy mothers are essential to vigorous offspring, the physical well-being of woman becomes an object of public interest." Moreover, "woman has always been dependent upon man." Legislation to protect women "seems necessary to secure a real equality of right"; and such protective legislation is valid, "even when like legislation is not necessary for men and could not be sustained." The "inherent difference between the two sexes" justified "a difference in legislation" and "upholds that which is designed to compensate for some of the burdens which rest upon her."[1] Nine years later, however, in BUNTING v. OREGON, 243 U.S. 426 (1917), a divided Court upheld a law establishing a maximum 10–hour day for factory workers (female as well as male), but permitting up to three hours a day overtime at a time-and-a-half rate. The conviction was for not paying the overtime rate. Although the Court did not mention Lochner, the ruling in effect overturned its specific holding. But the Lochner philosophy survived for another two decades.

2. *"Yellow dog" contracts, Coppage, and Adair.* The modern Court has referred to the discredited line of cases of the Lochner era as "the Allgeyer–Lochner–Adair–Coppage constitutional doctrine." The first two cases are noted above. Coppage and Adair involved laws protecting the right to organize unions. In COPPAGE v. KANSAS, 236 U.S. 1 (1915), Coppage had been convicted under a Kansas law directed against "yellow dog" contracts: it prohibited employers from requiring that employees agree as a condition of employment "not to join or become or remain a member of any labor organization." The Court, in an opinion by Justice PITNEY, held that the law violated due process: "Included in the right of personal liberty and the right of private property [is] the right to make contracts. [An] interference with this liberty so serious as that now under consideration, and so disturbing of equality of right, must be deemed to be arbitrary, unless it be supportable as a reasonable exercise of the police power of the State. [I]t is said by the [state court] to be a matter of common knowledge that 'employés, as a rule, are not financially able to be as

---

1. Muller was the first major case to resort to a fact-filled brief that came to be known as a "Brandeis brief," submitted by the defenders of the legislation. At the outset of its opinion, the Court noted: "In the brief filed by Mr. Louis D. Brandeis a very copious collection of [expressions of opinion from other than judicial sources]. [The] legislation and opinions referred [to] may not be, technically speaking, authorities, [yet] they are significant of a widespread belief that woman's physical structure, and the functions she performs in consequence thereof, justify special legislation. [Constitutional] questions, it is true, are not settled by even a consensus of present public opinion. [At] the same time, when a question of fact is debated and debatable, and the extent to which a special constitutional limitation goes is affected by the truth in respect to that fact, a widespread and long continued belief concerning it is

worthy of consideration. We take judicial cognizance of all matters of general knowledge." Is the "Brandeis brief" technique as useful in attacking legislation as in sustaining it? See Freund, On Understanding the Supreme Court (1949), 86–91, and Karst, "Legislative Facts in Constitutional Litigation," 1960 Sup.Ct.Rev. 75. On the utility of the "Brandeis brief" and the presentation of "constitutional facts," see also Biklé, "Judicial Determination of Questions of Fact Affecting the Constitutional Validity of Legislative Action," 38 Harv.L.Rev. 6 (1924). For more recent comments on the problem, see Alfange, "The Relevance of Legislative Facts in Constitutional Law," 114 U.Pa.L.Rev. 637 (1966), Shaman, "Constitutional Fact: The Perception of Reality by the Supreme Court," 35 U.Fla.L.Rev. 236 (1983), and Bryden, "Brandeis's Facts," 1 Constitutional Commentary 281 (1984).

independent in making contracts for the sale of their labor as are employers in making contracts of purchase thereof.' No doubt, wherever the right of private property exists, there must and will be inequalities of fortune; and thus it naturally happens that parties negotiating about a contract are not equally unhampered by circumstances. [But it] is from the nature of things impossible to uphold freedom of contract and the right of private property without at the same time recognizing as legitimate those inequalities of fortune that are the necessary result of the exercise of those rights. [And since] a State may not strike them down directly it is clear that it may not do so indirectly, as by declaring in effect that the public good requires the removal of those inequalities that are but the normal and inevitable result of their exercise, and then invoking the police power in order to remove the inequalities, without other object in view." Justice HOLMES stated in dissent: "In present conditions a workman not unnaturally may believe that only by belonging to a union can he secure a contract that shall be fair to him. [If] that belief, whether right or wrong, may be held by a reasonable man, it seems to me that it may be enforced by law in order to establish the equality of position between the parties in which liberty of contract begins. Whether in the long run it is wise for the workingmen to enact legislation of this sort is not my concern, but I am strongly of opinion that there is nothing in the [Constitution] to prevent it." Justice DAY, joined by Justice Hughes, also dissented. The Court in Coppage relied on ADAIR v. UNITED STATES, 208 U.S. 161 (1908), which had held unconstitutional, under the due process clause of the Fifth Amendment, a federal law barring "yellow dog" contracts on interstate railroads. The opinion in Adair was written by Justice HARLAN, one of the dissenters in Lochner. Justice Harlan stated that the "right of a person to sell his labor upon such terms as he deems proper [is] the same as the right of the purchaser of labor to prescribe the conditions. [T]he employer and the employé have equality of right, and any legislation that disturbs that equality is an arbitrary interference with the liberty of contract."[2]

3. *Minimum wages and the Adkins case.* Though Bunting in 1917 had sustained regulation of *hours*—including a requirement of overtime wages—(and though Muller in 1908 had sustained regulation of women's working hours), the Court held in 1923 that a District of Columbia law prescribing minimum *wages* for women violated due process. ADKINS v. CHILDREN'S HOSPITAL, 261 U.S. 525 (1923). Justice SUTHERLAND noted that since Muller, the 19th Amendment had been adopted, and the civil inferiority of women was thus almost at a "vanishing point." Hence, the liberty of contract could not be subjected to greater restriction in the case of women than of men. His chief objection was that the law compelled payment of wages without regard to the employment contract, the business involved, or the work done; this was "a naked, arbitrary exercise" of legislative power. Justice HOLMES stated in dissent: "I confess that I do not understand the principle on which the power to fix a minimum for the wages of women can be denied by those who admit the power to fix a maximum for their hours of work. [The] bargain is equally affected whichever half you regulate. [It] will need more than the 19th Amendment to convince me that there are no differences between men and women, or that legislation cannot take those differences into account."[3]

2. What about the "disturbing of equality" in Muller v. Oregon (note 1 above), decided in the same year as Adair? See Yudof, "Equal Protection, Class Legislation, and Sex Discrimination: One Small Cheer for Mr.

Herbert Spencer's Social Statics," 88 Mich. L.Rev. 1366, 1401–02 (1990). (Justices Holmes and McKenna dissented in Adair.)

3. Chief Justice Taft and Justice Sanford also dissented. Justice Brandeis did not

4. *Price regulations*. The Court of the Lochner era imposed a variety of restraints on laws that interfered with the free market by controlling prices. The noninterventionist decision in Munn v. Illinois (p. 458 above) was read narrowly to mean that rate regulation was permissible only for businesses "affected with a public interest." In the private sector areas not so "affected," price regulation was barred altogether. The Court stated the general rule applied during this period to price (as well as wage) regulations as follows: "[A] state legislature is without constitutional power to fix prices at which commodities may be sold, services rendered, or property used, unless the business or property involved is 'affected with a public interest.'" Williams v. Standard Oil Co., 278 U.S. 235 (1929).[4] Note the more generous view of price regulation in Nebbia (1934; p. 474 below).

5. *Restrictions on business entry and other economic regulations*. a. *Business entry*. In a number of cases, the Court invalidated restraints on competition that curtailed entry into a particular line of business. For example, in NEW STATE ICE CO. v. LIEBMANN, 285 U.S. 262 (1932), the Court invalidated an Oklahoma law which treated the manufacture of ice like a public utility, requiring a certificate of convenience and necessity as a prerequisite to entry into the business. See also ADAMS v. TANNER, 244 U.S. 590 (1917), striking down a law prohibiting employment agencies from collecting fees from workers. Justice BRANDEIS submitted extensive, data-laden dissents in both cases to demonstrate why reasonable legislators might think the restraints necessary. Note, moreover, Liggett Co. v. Baldridge, 278 U.S. 105 (1928), striking down a law generally barring corporate ownership of pharmacies. Decisions such as these have been undermined if not explicitly overruled by the developments since the 1930s.[5]

b. *Scrutiny of means*. During the Lochner era, the Court did recognize the validity of the state interest in curtailing business practices that might defraud consumers or injure their health. When statutes of that variety were invalidated, the Court criticized the means rather than the ends of the legislation. An example is WEAVER v. PALMER BROS. CO., 270 U.S. 402 (1926). There, the majority invalidated a total prohibition of the use, in the manufacture of bedding materials such as mattresses and quilts, of shoddy (cut up or torn up fabrics). Other secondhand materials could be used so long as they were sterilized and the finished product carried a label showing the materials used.

participate. Was the 19th Amendment sufficient to explain the difference between Muller and Adkins? Or was regulation of hours more acceptable than regulation of wages because (despite the Lochner result) control of the hours worked could be seen as promoting health, a legitimate legislative end, while control of wages looked more like redressing inequalities in bargaining power in the market, a generally impermissible objective? Does that laissez faire attitude toward "equalizing" legislation help to explain the majority's hostility to price regulations, in the next note? (The Court adhered to the Adkins decision in the Morehead case in 1936, but overruled Adkins in West Coast Hotel in 1937. See p. 476 below.)

4. The Williams case involved gasoline prices; see also Tyson & Brother v. Banton, 273 U.S. 418 (1927) (resale price of theatre tickets); Ribnik v. McBride, 277 U.S. 350 (1928) (employment agency fees). [The Tyson decision was explicitly overruled (in a per curiam decision) in Gold v. Dicarlo, 380 U.S. 520 (1965). Ribnik had been overruled earlier, in Olsen v. Nebraska (1941; p. 479 below).]

5. See sec. 1C below and, e.g., North Dakota Bd. of Pharmacy v. Snyder's Drug Stores, 414 U.S. 156 (1973), reversing a state court decision relying on Liggett in invalidating a similar law. Justice Douglas, speaking for a unanimous Court, called Liggett "a derelict in the stream of law" and stated that it "belongs to that vintage of decisions which exalted substantive due process by striking down state legislation which a majority of the Court deemed unwise."

The Court found the absolute prohibition of shoddy "purely arbitrary": protection of health and against consumer deception did not justify so drastic a remedy. As to health, the Court emphasized that the parties had agreed that "shoddy may be rendered harmless by disinfection or sterilization," even where the shoddy had been made from "filthy rags." As to public deception, the Court noted the inspection requirements applicable to other bedding and stated: "Obviously, such regulations [are] adequate [and] may be effectively applied to shoddy-filled articles." Justice Holmes's dissent, joined by Justices Brandeis and Stone, argued that the lawmakers "may have been of opinion" that "the actual practice of filling comfortables with unsterilized shoddy gathered from filthy floors was wide spread"—an opinion "we must assume to be true." Moreover, it was impossible "to distinguish the innocent from the infected [product] in any practicable way." Thus, the total ban was justifiable for health reasons, for the legislature might have "regarded the danger as very great and inspection and tagging as inadequate remedies." Would such a means-oriented inquiry be appropriate in Weaver under the principles of the more recent decisions, below? Would there be any scrutiny of the means in fact by the modern Court, in view of the summary manner in which the Court applies those principles? Should there be? The degree of scrutiny exercised by the majority in Weaver seems more intense than that justified by the "mere reasonableness" standard.[6] If the majority's scrutiny was too strict for a rationality standard, was Justice Holmes's too deferential?

C. THE MODERN ERA: THE DECLINE—AND DISAPPEARANCE?—OF JUDICIAL SCRUTINY OF ECONOMIC REGULATION

Nebbia v. New York

291 U.S. 502, 54 S.Ct. 505, 78 L.Ed. 940 (1934).

Justice ROBERTS delivered the opinion of the Court.

The Legislature of New York established [in 1933] a Milk Control Board with power [to] "fix minimum and maximum [retail] prices to be charged [by] stores to consumers for consumption off the premises where sold." The Board fixed nine cents as the price to be charged by a store for a quart of milk. Nebbia, the proprietor of a grocery store in Rochester, sold two quarts and a five cent loaf of bread for eighteen cents, and was convicted [of selling milk below the minimum price]. [The] question for decision is whether the [Constitution] prohibits a state from so fixing the selling price of milk. We first inquire as to the occasion for the legislation and its history. During 1932 the prices received by farmers for milk were much below the cost of production. [The] situation of the families of dairy producers had become desperate and called for state aid similar to that afforded the unemployed, if conditions should not improve. [The Court summarized the conclusions reached after an extensive study by a legislative committee:] Milk is an essential item of diet. Failure of producers to receive a reasonable return [threatens] a relaxation of vigilance

6. Cf. Struve, "The Less–Restrictive–Alternative Principle and Economic Due Pro-   cess," 80 Harv.L.Rev. 1463 (1967).

against contamination. The production and distribution of milk is a paramount industry of the state, and largely affects the health and prosperity of its people. [The] fluid milk industry is affected by factors of [price] instability peculiar to itself which call for special methods of control. [The] legislature adopted [this law] as a method of correcting the evils, which the report of the committee showed could not be expected to right themselves through the ordinary play of the forces of supply and demand, owing to the peculiar and uncontrollable factors affecting the industry.

[Under] our form of government the use of property and the making of contracts are normally matters of private and not a public concern. The general rule is that both shall be free of governmental interference. But neither property rights nor contract rights are absolute; for government cannot exist if the citizen may at will use his property to the detriment of his fellows, or exercise his freedom of contract to work them harm. Equally fundamental with the private right is that of the public to regulate it in the common interest. [The] guaranty of due process [demands] only that the law shall not be unreasonable, arbitrary or capricious, and that the means selected shall have a real and substantial relation to the object sought to be attained. [But] we are told that because the law essays to control prices it denies due process. [The] argument runs that the public control of rates or prices is per se unreasonable and unconstitutional, save as applied to business affected with a public interest; that a business so affected is [one] such as is commonly called a public utility; or a business in its nature a monopoly. The milk industry, it is said, possesses none of these [characteristics]. [The Court acknowledged that the dairy industry was not, "in the accepted sense of the phrase, a public utility," nor a "monopoly."] But if, as must be conceded, the industry is subject to regulation in the public interest, what constitutional principle bars the state from correcting existing maladjustments by legislation touching prices? We think there is no such principle. The due process clause makes no mention of sales or of prices any more than it speaks of business or contracts or buildings or other incidents of property. The thought seems nevertheless to have persisted that there is something peculiarly sacrosanct about the price one may charge for what he makes or sells, and that, however able to regulate other elements of manufacture or trade, with incidental effect upon price, the state is incapable of directly controlling the price itself. This view was negatived many years ago. Munn v. Illinois. "[Affected] with a public interest" is the equivalent of "subject to the exercise of the police power" and it is plain that nothing more was intended by the expression. [It] is clear that there is no closed class or category of businesses affected with a [public interest]. The phrase "affected with a public interest" can, in the nature of things, mean no more than that an industry, for adequate reason, is subject to control for the public good. [There] can be no doubt that upon proper occasion and by appropriate measures the state may regulate a business in any of its aspects, including the prices to be charged for the products or commodities it sells.

So far as the requirement of due process is concerned, [a] state is free to adopt whatever economic policy may reasonably be deemed to promote public welfare, and to enforce that policy by legislation adapted to its purpose. The courts are without authority either to declare such policy, or, when it is declared by the legislature, to override it. If the laws passed are seen to have a reasonable relation to a proper legislative purpose, and are neither arbitrary nor discriminatory, the requirements of due process are [satisfied]. With the wisdom of the policy adopted, with the adequacy or practicability of the law enacted to forward it, the courts are both incompetent and unauthorized to deal. [Price] control, like any other form of regulation, is unconstitutional only if arbitrary, discriminatory, or demonstrably irrelevant to the policy the legislature is free to adopt, and hence an unnecessary and unwarranted interference with individual liberty. Tested by these considerations we find no basis [for] condemning the provisions of the [law] here drawn into question.

[Affirmed.]

Separate opinion of Justice McREYNOLDS [dissenting].[1]

[Regulation] to prevent recognized evils in business has long been upheld as permissible legislative action. But fixation of the price at which "A," engaged in an ordinary business, may sell, in order to enable "B," a producer, to improve his condition, has not been regarded as within legislative power. This is not regulation, but management, control, dictation—it amounts to the deprivation of the fundamental right which one has to conduct his own affairs honestly and along customary lines. [Plainly,] I think, this Court must have regard to the wisdom of the enactment. At least, we must inquire concerning its purpose and decide whether the means proposed have reasonable relation to something within legislative power—whether the end is legitimate, and the means appropriate. [Here,] we find direct interference with guaranteed rights defended upon the ground that the purpose was to promote the public welfare by increasing milk prices at the farm. [The court below has not] attempted to indicate how higher charges at stores to impoverished customers when the output is excessive and sale prices of producers are unrestrained, can possibly increase receipts at the farm. The Legislative Committee pointed out as the obvious cause of decreased consumption notwithstanding low prices, the consumers' reduced buying power. Higher store prices will not enlarge this power; nor will they decrease production. [It] is not true as stated that "the State seeks to protect the producer by fixing a minimum price for his milk." She carefully refrained from doing this; but did undertake to fix the price after the milk had passed to other owners. [It] appears to me wholly unreasonable to expect this legislation to accomplish the proposed end—increase of prices at the farm. [Not] only does the statute interfere arbitrarily with the rights of the little grocer to conduct his business according to standards long accepted; [it] takes away the liberty of twelve million consumers to buy a necessity of life in an [open market].

———

WEST COAST HOTEL CO. v. PARRISH, 300 U.S. 379 (1937): This 5-4 decision overruled Adkins (p. 472 above) and upheld a state minimum wage law for women. Chief Justice HUGHES's majority opinion included the following passages: "[T]he violation [of due process] alleged by those attacking minimum wage regulation for women is deprivation of freedom of contract. What is this freedom? The Constitution does not speak of freedom of contract. It speaks of liberty and prohibits the deprivation of liberty without due process of law. In prohibiting that deprivation the Constitution does not recognize an absolute and uncontrollable liberty. [Liberty] under the Constitution [is] necessarily subject to the restraints of due process, and regulation which is reasonable in relation to its subject and is adopted in the interests of the community is due process. [We] think that [the Adkins decision] was a departure from the true application of the principles governing the regulation by the State of the relation of employer and employed. [What] can be closer to the public interest than the health of women and their protection from unscrupulous and over-

1. Justices Van Devanter, Sutherland and Butler joined this dissent.

reaching employers? [The] legislature [was] clearly entitled to consider that [women] are in the class receiving the least pay, that their bargaining power is relatively weak, and that they are the ready victims of those who would take advantage of their necessitous circumstances. The legislature was entitled to adopt measures to reduce the evils of the 'sweating system,' the exploiting of workers at wages so low as to be insufficient to meet the bare cost of living, thus making their very helplessness the occasion of a most injurious competition. The legislature had the right to consider that its minimum wage requirements would be an important aid in carrying out its policy of protection. The adoption of similar requirements by many States evidences a deep-seated conviction both as to the presence of the evil and as to the means adapted to check it. Legislative response to that conviction cannot be regarded as arbitrary or capricious, and that is all we have to decide. [There] is an additional and compelling consideration which recent economic experience has brought into a strong light. The exploitation of a class of workers who are in an unequal position with respect to bargaining power and are thus relatively defenseless against the denial of a living wage is not only detrimental to their health and well being but casts a direct burden for their support upon the community. What these workers lose in wages the taxpayers are called upon to pay. [We] may take judicial notice of the unparalleled demands for relief which arose during the recent period of depression. [The] community is not bound to provide what is in effect a subsidy for unconscionable employers. The community may direct its law-making power to correct the abuse which springs from their selfish disregard of the public interest. [Adkins is] overruled.''*

THE IMPACT OF NEBBIA AND WEST COAST HOTEL

1. *The standards of the mid–1930s.* The Nebbia and West Coast decisions obviously marked a significant shift from the Lochner era. But how far did they reduce judicial intervention? Do the decisions that follow simply apply the Nebbia and West Coast Hotel approaches? Or do they carry the rejection of the Lochner philosophy even further, to an even greater "hands off" position? Nebbia and West Coast Hotel obviously mark a sharp retreat from the Lochner era's preoccupation with impermissible legislative ends. Is there a similarly great retreat with respect to scrutiny of means-ends relationships? Note that Nebbia insists that the means must have "a real and substantial relation to the object sought to be attained." And note that both majority opinions contain explanations of the rationales for the challenged laws. Compare the curt statements (or assumptions) about legislative justifications in the later decisions, below. Were the relations between means and ends so evident there that no fuller explanation was warranted?

2. *The political context of Nebbia and West Coast Hotel.* Note that Nebbia's deference to the legislature came in 1934, just before the Court rendered

---

* Justice SUTHERLAND, joined by Justices Van Devanter, McReynolds and Butler, dissented, insisting that "the meaning of the Constitution does not change with the ebb and flow of economic events" and that the law had not "the slightest relation to the capacity or earning power of the employee, to the number of hours which constitute the day's work, the character of the place where the work is to be done, or the circumstances [of] the employment." To the extent that the minimum wage exceeded the fair value of the services rendered, the law amounted to "a compulsory exaction from the employer for the support of a partially indigent person, [and] therefore [arbitrarily] shifts to his shoulders a burden which, if it belongs to anybody, belongs to society as a whole."

its major decisions striking down a variety of New Deal laws as exceeding national powers. (Recall chap. 3.) The course of relaxation of due process restraints was not smooth: Court critics thought that due process restraints were hardening when—two years after Nebbia—the Court adhered to Adkins in Morehead v. New York ex rel. Tipaldo, 298 U.S. 587 (1936), invalidating New York's minimum wage law for women. A few months after Morehead, President Roosevelt announced his Court-packing Plan. While that controversy was raging, West Coast Hotel came down. Justice Roberts was with the majority in each case. Some viewed Justice Roberts's vote in West Coast Hotel as "the switch in time that saved the Nine" from the Court-packing Plan that failed in the Senate soon after. But recall Justice Roberts's own explanation of his votes in Morehead and West Coast Hotel, in a memorandum noted at p. 185 above.** It is nevertheless clear that constitutional doctrine changed significantly during this period. But arguing that the shift was a response to the Court-packing Plan is easiest with respect to national powers doctrines; with respect to due process, West Coast Hotel is certainly of a deferential piece with the pre-Court-packing decision in Nebbia (written by Justice Roberts).

THE MODERN ERA: REDUCED JUDICIAL SCRUTINY OR ABDICATION?

Nebbia suggested a continuing, though reduced, judicial role in scrutinizing the means employed in economic regulations—both in its announced standard that "the means selected shall have a real and substantial relation to the object sought to be attained" and in its examination of the background of the legislation. Have the due process decisions since the mid–1930s shrunk the judicial role beyond that? Have they, in formulation or in exercise, eliminated it altogether?

1. *Economic regulation and the Carolene Products case.* In 1938, in UNITED STATES v. CAROLENE PRODUCTS CO., 304 U.S. 144, the Court rejected a due process challenge to a federal prohibition of the interstate shipment of "filled milk"—skimmed milk mixed with non-milk fats.[1] In enact-

** Justice Roberts's memorandum made it clear that the Court's conference vote in West Coast Hotel came weeks *before* the Court-packing Plan was announced; he claimed that he was *not* responding directly to that threat. Moreover, he stated that his Morehead vote to adhere to Adkins rested on the fact that the Court in Morehead, unlike West Coast Hotel, was not explicitly asked to overrule Adkins. (The genuineness and persuasiveness of the Roberts memorandum have provoked academic controversy in recent years. See Ariens, "A Thrice-Told Tale, or Felix the Cat," 107 Harv.L.Rev. 620 (1994), and Friedman, "A Reaffirmation: The Authenticity of the Roberts Memorandum, or Felix the Non-Forger," 142 U.Pa. L.Rev. 1985 (1994).)

1. The sustaining of the Filled Milk Act in the Carolene Products case has not with-stood the test of time. In 1972, a federal District Court held the ban on shipments of filled milk in violation of due process. Milnot Co. v. Richardson, 350 F.Supp. 221 (S.D.Ill. 1972). The Government withdrew its appeal from that decision, and the Food and Drug Administration announced soon after that "the Filled Milk Act will no longer be enforced." See Strong, "A Post–Script to Carolene Products," 5 Const. Commentary 185 (1988). (See also his Substantive Due Process: A Dichotomy of Sense and Nonsense (1986).) For a careful study of the Carolene Products problem, see Miller, "The True Story of Carolene Products," 1988 Sup.Ct.Rev. 397, arguing that the law upheld in the case was an "utterly unprincipled 'example of special interest legislation'" and that the claimed justifications for the ban were "patently bogus." If these claims were justified, should the law have been struck down?

ing the law, Congress relied on committee findings that the use of filled milk rather than pure milk resulted in "undernourishment" and that filled milk was an "adulterated article of food" whose sale constituted a "fraud upon the public." Justice STONE's majority opinion stated: "We may assume for present purposes [that] a statute would deny due process which precluded the disproof in judicial proceedings of all facts which would show [that] a statute depriving the suitor of life, liberty, or property had a rational basis." Here, the congressional declarations that filled milk was injurious to health and a fraud upon the public did not bar such "disproof"; but challenging the "rational basis" of economic legislation, he made clear, would be a difficult task. The legislative findings, like reports of legislative committees, were simply aids to "informed judicial review," "by revealing the rationale of the legislation." But they were not essential: "Even in the absence of such aids, the existence of facts supporting the legislative judgment is to be presumed, for regulatory legislation affecting ordinary commercial transactions is not to be pronounced unconstitutional unless in the light of the facts made known or generally assumed it is of such a character as to preclude the assumption that it rests upon some rational basis within the knowledge and experience of the legislators."[2] He added:

"Where the existence of a rational basis for legislation whose constitutionality is attacked depends upon facts beyond the sphere of judicial notice, such facts may properly be made the subject of judicial inquiry, and the constitutionality of a statute predicated upon the existence of a particular state of facts may be challenged by showing to the court that those facts have ceased to exist. Similarly we recognize that the constitutionality of a statute, valid on its face, may be assailed by proof of facts tending to show that the statute as applied to a particular article is without support in reason because the article, although within the prohibited class, is so different from others of the class as to be without the reason for the prohibition, though the effect of such proof depends on the relevant circumstances of each case, as for example the administrative difficulty of excluding the article from the regulated class. [But] by their very nature such inquiries, where the legislative judgment is drawn in question, must be restricted to the issue whether any state of facts either known or which could reasonably be assumed, affords support for it. Here the demurrer challenges the validity of the statute on its face and it is evident from all the considerations presented to Congress, and those of which we may take judicial notice, that the question is at least debatable whether commerce in filled milk should be left unregulated, or in some measure restricted, or wholly prohibited. [That] decision was for Congress, [and] neither the finding of a court derived by weighing the evidence nor the verdict of a jury can be substituted for it."

2. *Total withdrawal from review?* Carolene Products indicated some continued willingness to consider the "rational basis" of economic legislation. In the cases in this note, the Court rejected due process attacks even more summarily. Do these "hands off" decisions indicate an even greater withdrawal from judicial scrutiny than that suggested by the standards of the 1930s decisions? Or are these cases explainable on the ground that their central concerns were the legitimacy of legislative objectives, not the reasonableness of the means? An early example of the extreme "hands off" attitude was OLSEN

---

2. At this point, Justice Stone added his famous footnote 4, suggesting that there may be a stronger case for judicial intervention in regulation of matters other than "commercial transactions." That footnote 4 has been widely relied on to explain the Court's growing interventionism regarding "legislation which [restricts] political processes," even while it has retreated from review of economic regulation. The footnote is printed at p. 484 below; and the question whether that footnote adequately justifies the "double standard" of judicial review recurs frequently in this and the next chapters.

v. NEBRASKA, 313 U.S. 236 (1941), where the state courts had held unconstitutional a law fixing maximum employment agency fees, in reliance on the 1928 decision in Ribnik (p. 473 above). The Court unanimously reversed, in an opinion by Justice DOUGLAS: "We are not concerned [with] the wisdom, need, or appropriateness of the legislation. [There] is no necessity for the state to demonstrate before us that evils persist despite the competition which attends the bargaining in this field. [T]he only restraints which respondents have suggested for the invalidation of this legislation are those notions of public policy embedded in earlier decisions of this Court but which, as Mr. Justice Holmes long admonished, should not be read into the Constitution. [Since] they do not find expression in the Constitution, we cannot give them continuing validity as standards by which the constitutionality of the economic and social programs of the states is to be determined." In LINCOLN FEDERAL LABOR UNION v. NORTHWESTERN IRON & METAL CO., 335 U.S. 525 (1949), the Court was again unanimous in sustaining state "right to work" laws requiring that employment decisions not be based on union membership. Justice BLACK's opinion recalled the Lochner era, when the Adair and Coppage decisions had struck down pro-union laws banning "yellow-dog contracts," and emphasized the change in doctrine since then. The "Allgeyer–Lochner–Adair–Coppage constitutional doctrine" had been repudiated, and in doing so the Court had "consciously returned closer and closer to the earlier constitutional principle that states have power to legislate against what are found to be injurious practices in their internal commercial and business affairs, so long as their laws do not run afoul of some specific federal constitutional prohibition, or of some valid federal law." He concluded: "Just as we have held that the due process clause erects no obstacle to block legislative protection of union members, we now hold that legislative protection can be afforded non-union workers."

A more recent example of broad deference to legislative judgments is FERGUSON v. SKRUPA, 372 U.S. 726 (1963), sustaining a Kansas law prohibiting anyone from engaging "in the business of debt adjusting" except as an incident to "the lawful practice of law." Justice BLACK's opinion concluded that Kansas "was free to decide for itself that legislation was needed to deal with the business of debt adjusting." He reiterated that the Court had abandoned "the use of the 'vague contours' of the Due Process Clause to nullify laws which a majority of the Court believed to be economically unwise." And he added: "Unquestionably, there are arguments showing that the business of debt adjusting has social utility, but such arguments are properly addressed to the legislature, not to us. We refuse to sit as a 'super legislature to weigh the wisdom of legislation.' [Whether] the legislature takes for its textbook Adam Smith, Herbert Spencer, Lord Keynes or some other is no concern of ours." (Note the list of economists mentioned by Justice Black. Suppose the legislature instead took for its textbook Karl Marx? What if the legislature, affording the "just compensation" required for confiscations by the Constitution, sought to promote Marxist purposes through condemnation and redistribution of property? Would there be any principled constitutional reasons to invalidate such judgments?)

Justice HARLAN concurred in a brief separate notation, "on the ground that this state measure bears a rational relation to a constitutionally permissible objective. See [Lee Optical, below]." What is the significance of Justice Harlan's separate notation? Does his "rational relation" standard indicate greater judicial scrutiny than Justice Black's approach? Recall Justice Black's statement in the Lincoln case rejecting any judicial intervention in "commercial and business" regulation so long as state laws "do not run afoul of some specific federal constitutional prohibition." Does that suggest the total inapplicability of due process? Has the majority of the Court committed itself to so complete a withdrawal from review? Or does Lee Optical, cited by Justice Harlan, suggest that some judicial scrutiny remains? Does the variety of scrutiny exercised in Lee Optical have any teeth in fact, or is it the functional equivalent of total withdrawal, with only lip service to a judicially enforceable "rational relation" standard as to scrutiny of means? Is Justice Black correct in suggesting that there is no constitutional basis for requiring more of legislatures than compliance with specific constitutional prohibitions?[3] Or can the due process clause properly be read to impose a judicially enforceable requirement that legislatures show a "real and substantial" relationship between means and ends even in the economic area?

———

Williamson v. Lee Optical Co.

348 U.S. 483, 75 S.Ct. 461, 99 L.Ed. 563 (1955).

Justice DOUGLAS delivered the opinion of the Court.

[The] District Court held unconstitutional [several sections of an Oklahoma law of 1953]. First, it held invalid under the Due Process Clause [the] portions of § 2 which make it unlawful for any person not a licensed optometrist or ophthalmologist to fit lenses to a face or to duplicate or replace into frames lenses or other optical appliances, except upon written prescriptive authority of an Oklahoma licensed ophthalmologist or optometrist. An ophthalmologist is a duly licensed physician who specializes in the care of the eyes. An optometrist examines eyes for refractive error, recognizes (but does not treat) diseases of the eye, and fills prescriptions for eyeglasses. The optician is an artisan qualified to grind lenses, fill prescriptions, and fit frames. The effect of § 2 is to forbid the optician from fitting or duplicating lenses without a prescription from an ophthalmologist or optometrist. In practical effect, it means that no optician can fit old glasses into new frames or supply a lens, whether it be a new lens or one to duplicate a lost or broken lens, without a prescription. The [District Court] rebelled at the notion that a State could require a prescription [to] "take old lenses and place them in new frames and then fit the completed spectacles to the *face* of the eyeglass wearer." [The] court found that through mechanical devices and ordinary skills the optician could take a broken lens or a fragment thereof, measure its power, and reduce it to prescriptive terms. The court held that "Although [the legislature] was dealing with a matter of public interest, the particular means chosen are neither reasonably necessary nor reasonably related to the end sought to be achieved."

[The] Oklahoma law may exact a needless, wasteful requirement in many cases. But it is for the legislature, not the courts, to balance the advantages and disadvantages of the new requirement. It appears that in many cases the optician can easily supply the new frames or new lenses without reference to the old written prescription. It also appears that many written prescriptions contain no directive data in regard to fitting spectacles to the face. But in some cases the directions contained in the prescription are essential, if the glasses are to be fitted so as to correct the particular defects of vision or alleviate the eye condition. The legislature might have concluded that the frequency of occasions when a prescription is necessary was sufficient to justify this regulation of the fitting of eyeglasses. Likewise, when it is necessary to duplicate a

3. See Linde, "Without ['Due Process']," 49 Ore.L.Rev. 125 (1970), and Linde, "Due Process of Lawmaking," 55 Nebr. L.Rev. 197 (1976).

lens, a written prescription may or may not be necessary. But the legislature might have concluded that one was needed often enough to require one in every case. Or the legislature may have concluded that eye examinations were so critical, not only for correction of vision but also for detection of latent ailments or diseases, that every change in frames and every duplication of a lens should be accompanied by a prescription from a medical expert. To be sure, the present law does not require a new examination of the eyes every time the frames are changed or the lenses duplicated. For if the old prescription is on file with the optician, he can go ahead and make the new fitting or duplicate the lenses. But the law need not be in every respect logically consistent with its aims to be constitutional. It is enough that there is an evil at hand for correction, and that it might be thought that the particular legislative measure was a rational way to correct it. The day is gone when this Court uses the Due Process Clause [to] strike down state laws, regulatory of business and industrial conditions, because they may be unwise, improvident, or out of harmony with a particular school of [thought].[1]

[The] District Court [also held that] portion of § 3 which makes it unlawful "to solicit the sale [of] frames, mountings, [or] any other optical appliances" [violative of due process]. [R]egulation of the advertising of eyeglass frames was said to intrude "into a mercantile field only casually related to the visual care of the public" and restrict "an activity which in no way can detrimentally affect the people." [An] eyeglass frame, considered in isolation, is only a piece of merchandise. But an eyeglass frame is not used in isolation; [it] is used with lenses; and lenses, pertaining as they do to the human eye, enter the field of health. Therefore, the legislature might conclude that to regulate one effectively it would have to regulate the other. Or it might conclude that both the sellers of frames and the sellers of lenses were in a business where advertising should be limited or even abolished in the public interest. [The] advertiser of frames may be using his ads to bring in customers who will buy lenses. If the advertisement of lenses is to be abolished or controlled, the advertising of frames must come under the same restraints; or so the legislature might think. We see no constitutional reason why a State may not treat all who deal with the human eye as members of a profession who should use no merchandising methods for obtaining [customers].[2]

[Reversed.]

THE "HANDS OFF" APPROACH TO ECONOMIC LEGISLATION: EXCESSIVE WITHDRAWAL? JUSTIFIABLE DOUBLE STANDARD?

Introduction. The modern Court has turned away due process challenges to economic regulation with a broad "hands off" approach. No such law has been

1. Another section of the law, subjecting opticians to the regulatory scheme but exempting all sellers of ready-to-wear glasses, was held violative of equal protection by the lower court. The Court's rejection of that equal protection attack is noted in chap. 9, at p. 642 below. [Most modern challenges to economic regulations involve equal protection as well as due process claims. In the equal protection area, the withdrawal from scrutiny of economic regulations has generally (but not wholly) paralleled that under due process. The equal protection developments are pursued in chap. 9, sec. 2.]

2. Two decades after Lee Optical, the Court began to include "commercial speech"—i.e., most advertising—within the protection of the First Amendment. Critics have claimed that the "commercial speech" cases represent a resurrection of the Lochner philosophy. The cases are discussed below.

invalidated on substantive due process grounds since 1937.[1] Indeed, opinions from the Court are rare, and argument is ordinarily heard only when a lower court has struck down a law. Only on a few occasions have some Justices expressed doubts about the Court's stance of extreme deference to economic regulation. This Court withdrawal from serious scrutiny raises two basic questions. First, has the Court gone too far in its withdrawal? Would it be possible, and justifiable, to exercise a level of review which would have more content than the modern "hands off" attitude and yet avoid the vices of the Lochner era? Second, is the substantial withdrawal from review in the economic area reconcilable with the modern Court's considerable intensity of review when non-economic interests are affected? Is there justification for such a "double standard," for a two-tier level of scrutiny, strict in some areas, minimal or virtually nonexistent in others? And the two problems are related: Even if some double standard is justifiable, is the wide gap between levels of review justifiable?

1.   *The possibility of more substantial scrutiny of economic regulation.* Are the summary dispositions of the Court in many modern due process cases consistent with the Court's own articulated requirements? Can the theoretically still operative Nebbia standard—"that the means selected shall have a real and substantial relation to the object sought to be attained"—be translated into genuine practice? Note the suggestions about more intense means-oriented scrutiny, p. 646 below: Can the minimal rationality standard be applied with greater "bite"? By a reduced willingness of the Court to hypothesize legislative objectives—by testing the reasonableness of the means in terms of purposes put forth by the defenders of the law, rather than the Court's attribution of purposes a legislature *might* have had? And by requiring the defenders of the law to come forth with some data to show how the means promote the legislative purposes? Can such means scrutiny avoid the dangers of judicial value infusions of the Lochner era?[2]

1. The Court's response to equal protection challenges before the 1970s was very similar. Only one law was struck down on equal protection grounds during the post–1930s generation, Morey v. Doud, 354 U.S. 457 (1957); and that decision was overruled in New Orleans v. Dukes (1976; p. 649 below). Economic equal protection, like economic due process, typically meant "minimal scrutiny in theory and virtually none in fact." Gunther, "[A] Model for a Newer Equal Protection," 86 Harv.L.Rev. 1, 8 (1972). However, some state courts, applying state constitutional provisions similar to due process and equal protection, continued throughout this period to scrutinize legislation with greater care and to invalidate laws more frequently. See Hetherington, "State Economic Regulation and Substantive Due Process of Law," 53 Nw.U.L.Rev. 13, 226 (1958), and Comment, "State Economic Due Process: A Proposal Approach," 88 Yale L.J. 1487 (1979); cf. Struve, "The Less–Restrictive–Alternative Principle and Economic Due Process," 80 Harv.L.Rev. 1463 (1967).

2. The possibility of more genuine means scrutiny is more fully explored below,

in the context of equal protection, in chap. 9, sec. 2. Note preliminarily the comment in McCloskey, "Economic Due Process and the Supreme Court: An Exhumation and Reburial," 1962 Sup.Ct.Rev. 34: "Why did the Court move all the way from the inflexible negativism of the old majority to the all-out tolerance of the new? Why did it not establish a halfway house between the extremes, retaining a measure of control over economic legislation but exercising that control with discrimination and self-restraint?" McCloskey suggested as one explanation that the "intransigence" of the majority of the Lochner era "tended to discredit the whole concept of judicial supervision"—that "extremism had bred extremism." Would an intensified means scrutiny represent such a halfway house? And may the time now be ripe to move in that direction, under the banner of equal protection if not due process? Note McCloskey's suggested "halfway house": the Court would "not strike down an arguably rational law, but it would require some showing by the State that there was a basis for believing it to be rational and would consider evidence to the contrary presented by the

2. *The new interventionism: The Carolene Products footnote.* Is the withdrawal from review of economic regulations consistent with the increased scrutiny that has marked the Court's activities in other areas? That the Court would not abandon interventionism across the board when it turned its back on Lochner was suggested in a famous footnote by Justice Stone in the Carolene Products case in 1938. While describing in the text of his opinion some guidelines for the deferential "rational basis" review of economic legislation challenged under due process (p. 478 above), Justice STONE added a footnote 4 [UNITED STATES v. CAROLENE PRODUCTS CO., 304 U.S. 144 (1938)]:

"There may be narrower scope for operation of the presumption of constitutionality when legislation appears on its face to be within a specific prohibition of the Constitution, such as those of the first ten Amendments, which are deemed equally specific when held to be embraced within the 14th. See Stromberg v. California, 283 U.S. 359, 369–370; Lovell v. Griffin, 303 U.S. 444, 452.

"It is unnecessary to consider now whether legislation which restricts those political processes which can ordinarily be expected to bring about repeal of undesirable legislation, is to be subjected to more exacting judicial scrutiny under the general prohibitions of the 14th Amendment than are most other types of legislation. On restrictions upon the right to vote, see Nixon v. Herndon, 273 U.S. 536; Nixon v. Condon, 286 U.S. 73; on restraints upon the dissemination of information, see Near v. Minnesota, 283 U.S. 697, 713–714, 718–720, 722; Grosjean v. American Press Co., 297 U.S. 233; Lovell v. Griffin, supra; on interferences with political organizations, see Stromberg v. California, supra, 369; Fiske v. Kansas, 274 U.S. 380; Whitney v. California, 274 U.S. 357, 373–378; Herndon v. Lowry, 301 U.S. 242; and see Holmes, J., in Gitlow v. New York, 268 U.S. 652, 673; as to prohibition of peaceable assembly, see De Jonge v. Oregon, 299 U.S. 353, 365.

"Nor need we enquire whether similar considerations enter into the review of statutes directed at particular religious, Pierce v. Society of Sisters, 268 U.S. 510, or national, Meyer v. Nebraska, 262 U.S. 390; Bartels v. Iowa, 262 U.S. 404; Farrington v. Tokushige, 273 U.S. 284, or racial minorities, Nixon v. Herndon, supra; Nixon v. Condon, supra; whether prejudice against discrete and insular minorities may be a special condition, which tends seriously to curtail the operation of those political processes ordinarily to be relied upon to protect minorities, and which may call for a correspondingly more searching judicial inquiry. Compare McCulloch v. Maryland, 4 Wheat. 316, 428; South Carolina v. Barnwell Bros., 303 U.S. 177, 184, n. 2, and cases cited."[3]

The "double standard" suggested by this footnote—an interventionist stance in some areas, a deferential one in others—has had a pervasive influ-

---

affected business. Laws like those involved in [Lee Optical might] be invalidated, or at any rate more sharply queried." In 1962 McCloskey did not expect such a change to come about. Is there greater basis to anticipate such a change today? (For a book-length advocacy of a return to intensive economic due process review, akin to that of the Lochner era's emphasis on liberty of contract, see Siegan, Economic Liberties and the Constitution (1980).)

3. Justice Stone's "political process" rationale in the Carolene Products case footnote reverberates in much of the modern literature seeking to justify the Court's interventionism in selected areas. For an especially influential variant on the "political process" theme, see Ely, Democracy and Distrust (1980). On the origins of the footnote, see Lusky, "Footnote Redux: A Carolene Products Reminiscence," 82 Colum.L.Rev. 1093 (1982). See also Powell, "Carolene Products Revisited," 82 Colum.L.Rev. 1087 (1982). [Most of the cases cited in the Carolene Products footnote are considered in the chapters that follow.]

ence. As a justification for the varieties of scrutiny by the modern Court at levels higher than minimal rationality, the footnote raises a number of difficulties. (See, e.g., the modern substantive due process cases, sec. 3 below.) But there can be no doubt that the modern Court has been characterized by a notable activism on behalf of fundamental rights and interests outside the economic sphere. Should, and can, judicial scrutiny in the economic due process sphere remain deferential, given the sharp intensification of review in so many other areas?

3. *Property and economic rights and the contrast with fundamental personal liberties.* Can the different standards of review be justified because of an inherent difference in the "fundamentalness" of economic rights and other personal rights? In the modern due process cases, the Court repeatedly states its determination to keep hands off the economic sphere. Does protection of property and economic interest have less textual and historical basis than protection of other interests? Compare the repudiation of the frequent modern efforts to explain the "double standard" of judicial intervention in terms of an allegedly sharp difference between property and noneconomic rights stated by Justice Stewart in Lynch v. Household Finance Corp., 405 U.S. 538 (1972): "[T]he dichotomy between personal liberties and property rights is a false one. Property does not have rights. People have rights. The right to enjoy property without unlawful deprivation, no less than the right to speak or the right to travel, is, in truth, a 'personal' right, whether the 'property' in question be a welfare check, a home or a savings account. In fact, a fundamental interdependence exists between the personal right to liberty and the personal right in property. Neither could have meaning without the other. That rights in property are basic civil rights has long been recognized. J. Locke, Of Civil Government; J. Adams, A Defense of the Constitutions of the Government of the United States of America; 1 W. Blackstone Commentaries *138–140."[4]

4. *Economic rights and the contrast with First Amendment liberties.* In the area of First Amendment liberties, the modern Court has imposed very substantial restraints on state action.[5] Is the distinction between "economic" and "civil liberties" cases sufficiently clear to justify the vast differences in the levels of judicial scrutiny? Is the "liberty" of the individual who is denied a master electrician's license under a guild-type state law all that different from the kind of "liberty" protected in the free speech cases?[6]

5. *The contrast with non-"specific," noneconomic fundamental rights and interests.* Is the Court's "hands-off" stance in the economic regulation cases made substantially more untenable by the modern protection of a range of fundamental values no more explicit in the Constitution than such economic rights as freedom of contract? During the 1960s, the Court's "new" equal protection exercised strict scrutiny under the equal protection clause when a variety of "fundamental interests" were affected—fundamental interests such as voting and the fair administration of justice. Do those developments signify a breakdown of the economic-personal rights double standard in the equal protection area? But the questions raised by the virtual demise of economic due process scrutiny are most acute when contrasted with the recent invigorations of the due process clause itself. In the cases in sec. 3 below, "fundamental

---

4. Justice Stewart's opinion in this 4-3 decision was joined by Justices Douglas, Brennan and Marshall, viewed at the time as the most "liberal," interventionist Justices.

5. On the First Amendment, see chaps. 11 to 14.

6. See, e.g., chap. 3, "The Right to Make a Living," in Gellhorn, Individual Freedom and Governmental Restraints (1956), 105–151, on "the significant interference with the traditional freedom to work" by "the occupational license."

rights" of "privacy" and "autonomy" were enforced in such contexts as contraception and abortion. Does a broad right of "privacy" have any stronger textual or historical basis than economic rights? Does the revival of substantive due process in those cases cast added doubt on the virtual abandonment of scrutiny in the economic area? Even if the Court may enforce extraconstitutional values, is the present hierarchy justifiable? Perhaps economic liberties should rank lower than speech and privacy on such a scale; but should they rank so low as to justify the decline of judicial scrutiny to the level manifested in the modern economic due process cases?

6. *Transitional note.* The comparison between the Lochner era and the modern revival of substantive due process is pursued in sec. 3 below. Those materials can usefully be considered at this point. But before turning to them, the next section completes the coverage of constitutional protections of property and economic rights with a review of (a) the "taking-regulation" distinction and (b) the role of the contracts clause.

SECTION 2. OTHER CONSTITUTIONAL SAFEGUARDS OF ECONOMIC RIGHTS: THE "TAKING–REGULATION" DISTINCTION; THE CONTRACTS CLAUSE

A. EMINENT DOMAIN AND THE "TAKING–REGULATION" DISTINCTION

Introduction. Among the earliest "specific" Bill of Rights guarantees absorbed into the 14th Amendment's due process guarantee was the Fifth Amendment's command that private property shall not "be taken for public use, without just compensation."[1] State and federal resorts to the power of eminent domain are common, and a prolific source of constitutional litigation: when government seeks to "take" private land for a new schoolhouse or a park or an airport or an urban redevelopment project, the property is "taken" through condemnation, and the owner is entitled to "just compensation." The specialized bodies of doctrine as to the meaning of "just compensation" and "public use" are largely beyond the scope of this book. But one area of condemnation law touches so closely on economic due process that it warrants some mention here, though its details, too, are left to other courses. Suppose government, rather than condemning property and formally transferring title to itself, merely "regulates" its use and substantially diminishes its value (thus engaging in what is often called "inverse condemnation")? Can such governmental action give rise to an obligation to afford the property owner "just compensation" for the loss? The answer is clear: it can. What has been unclear and remains perplexing is the question of when. Justice Holmes, in the Pennsylvania Coal case, which follows, stated the "general rule": "[W]hile property may be regulated to a certain extent, if regulation goes too far it will be recognized as a taking." Government need *not* compensate the property owner for losses that are incidental consequences of valid regulation; it *must* compensate when regulation is tantamount to taking. When does governmental

---

1. See Chicago, B. & Q. R. R. Co. v. Chicago, 166 U.S. 226 (1897) (just compensation), and Missouri Pac. Ry. v. Nebraska, 164 U.S. 403 (1896) (property may not be taken for "private" rather than "public" use).

action give rise to a duty to compensate? When may government impose property losses without paying compensation, through "the petty larceny of the police power"?[2]

With the modern Court's expansive reading of the police power and its retreat from careful scrutiny of economic regulations, successful "taking" challenges to regulatory schemes were rare for several decades after the late 1930s. Even during these quite deferential years, however, the Court recognized the possibility of compensation in some circumstances, and the taking-regulation problems were typically addressed by the Justices in a less summary manner than those of economic due process. By the late 1980s, moreover, the Court turned to more serious enforcement of the "just compensation" requirement, as cases such as Nollan, below, illustrate. Throughout these years, considerable uncertainty has prevailed regarding the appropriate criteria to distinguish between compensable and noncompensable impositions of property losses by government. In examining these materials, consider what criteria might best serve to draw the taking-regulation distinction: The magnitude of the harm to the private interest? The manner of imposing the harm? The degree to which the imposition interferes with legitimate private expectations? The nature and magnitude of the public interest? This survey begins with two well-known decisions of the 1920s that raise these problems. Can the Court do better than Justice Holmes's effort in the Pennsylvania Coal case, which follows?[3]

Pennsylvania Coal Co. v. Mahon

260 U.S. 393, 43 S.Ct. 158, 67 L.Ed. 322 (1922).

Justice HOLMES delivered the opinion of the court.

This is a bill in equity [to] prevent the Pennsylvania Coal Company from mining under [the plaintiffs'] property in such way as to remove the supports and cause a subsidence of the surface and of their house. [The plaintiffs claim under] a deed executed by the Coal Company in 1878 [which] conveys the surface, but in express terms reserves the right to remove all the coal under the same, and the grantee takes the premises with the risk, and waives all claim for damages that may arise from mining out the coal. But the plaintiffs say that whatever may have been the Coal Company's rights, they were taken away by an Act of Pennsylvania commonly known there as the Kohler Act. [This 1921 law, upheld by the state court,] forbids the mining of anthracite coal in such way as to cause the subsidence of, among other things, any structure used as a human habitation, with certain exceptions. [As] applied to this case the statute

2. This subsection focuses mainly on the question of what constitutes a "taking," and the related taking-regulation distinction. It also briefly considers the Fifth Amendment's requirement that the eminent domain power can only be exercised for "public use."

3. For valiant efforts to articulate a general approach, see, e.g., Michelman, "Property, Utility, and Fairness: Comments on the Ethical Foundations of 'Just Compensation' Law," 80 Harv.L.Rev. 1165 (1967),

Epstein, Takings: Private Property and Eminent Domain (1985), Sax, "Takings and the Police Power," 74 Yale L.J. 36 (1964), Sax, "Takings, Private Property and Public Rights," 81 Yale L.J. 149 (1971), Berger, "A Policy Analysis of the Taking Problem," 49 N.Y.U.L.Rev. 165 (1974), Dunham, "[Thirty] Years of Supreme Court Expropriation Law," 1962 Sup.Ct.Rev. 63, and Ackerman, Private Property and the Constitution (1977).

is admitted to destroy previously existing rights of property and contract. The question is whether the police power can be stretched so far.

Government hardly could go on if to some extent values incident to property could not be diminished without paying for every such change in the general law. As long recognized, some values are enjoyed under an implied limitation and must yield to the police power. But obviously the implied limitation must have its limits, or the contract and due process clauses are gone. One fact for consideration in determining such limits is the extent of the diminution. When it reaches a certain magnitude, in most if not in all cases there must be an exercise of eminent domain and compensation to sustain the act. So the question depends upon the particular facts. [This] is the case of a single private house. No doubt there is a public interest even in this. [But] usually in ordinary private affairs the public interest does not warrant much of this kind of interference. A source of damage to such a house is not a public nuisance even if similar damage is inflicted on others in different places. The damage is not common or public. [The law] is not justified as a protection of personal safety. That could be provided for by notice. Indeed the very foundation of this bill is that the defendant gave timely notice of its intent to mine under the house. On the other hand the extent of the taking is great. It purports to abolish what is recognized in Pennsylvania as [a "very valuable" estate in land]. If we were called upon to deal with the plaintiffs' position alone, we should think it clear that the statute does not disclose a public interest sufficient to warrant so extensive a destruction of the defendant's constitutionally protected rights.

But the case has been treated as one in which the general validity of the act should be discussed. [It] is our opinion that the act cannot be sustained as an exercise of the police power, so far as it affects the mining of coal under streets or cities in places where the right to mine such coal has been reserved. [What] makes the right to mine coal valuable is that it can be exercised with profit. To make it commercially impracticable to mine certain coal has very nearly the same effect for constitutional purposes as appropriating or destroying it. This we think that we are warranted in assuming that the statute [does]. The rights of the public in a street purchased or laid out by eminent domain are those that it has paid for. If in any case its representatives have been so short sighted as to acquire only surface rights without the right of support, we see no more authority for supplying the latter without compensation than there was for taking the right of way in the first place and refusing to pay for it because the public wanted it very much. The protection of private property in the Fifth Amendment presupposes that it is wanted for public use, but provides that it shall not be taken for such use without compensation. [When] this seemingly absolute protection is found to be qualified by the police power, the natural tendency of human nature is to extend the qualification more and more until at last private property disappears. But that cannot be accomplished in this way under the [Constitution]. The general rule at least is, that while property may be regulated to a certain extent, if regulation goes too far it will be recognized as a taking. [In] general it is not plain that a man's misfortunes or necessities will justify his shifting the damages to his neighbor's shoulders. [We] are in danger of forgetting that a strong public desire to improve the public condition is not enough to warrant achieving the desire by a shorter cut than the constitutional way of paying for the change. [It] is a question of degree. [This goes beyond] any of the cases decided by this [Court]. We assume, of course, that the statute was passed upon the conviction that an exigency existed that would warrant it, and we assumed that an exigency exists that would warrant the exercise of eminent domain. But the question at bottom is upon whom the loss of the changes desired should fall. So far as private persons or communities have seen fit to take the risk of acquiring only surface rights, we cannot see that the fact that their risk has become a danger warrants the giving to them greater rights than they bought.

[Reversed.]

Justice BRANDEIS, dissenting.

[Every] restriction upon the use of property imposed in the exercise of the police power deprives the owner of some right theretofore enjoyed, and is, in that sense, an abridgment by the State of rights in property without making compensation. But a restriction imposed to protect the public health, safety or morals from dangers threatened is not a taking. The restriction here in question is merely the prohibition of a noxious use. The property so restricted remains in the possession of its owner. The State does not appropriate it or make any use of it. The State merely prevents the owner from making a use which interferes with paramount rights of the [public]. The restriction upon the use of this property can not, of course, be lawfully imposed, unless its purpose is to protect the public. But the purpose of a restriction does not cease to be public, because incidentally some private persons may thereby receive gratuitously valuable special benefits. Thus, owners of low buildings may obtain, through statutory restrictions upon the height of neighboring structures, benefits equivalent to an easement of light and air. [Furthermore], a restriction, though imposed for a public purpose, will not be lawful, unless the restriction is an appropriate means to the public end. But to keep coal in place is surely an appropriate means of preventing subsidence of the surface; and ordinarily it is the only available means. Restriction upon use does not become inappropriate as a means, merely because it deprives the owner of the only use to which the property can then be profitably put. [Nor] is a restriction imposed through exercise of the police power inappropriate as a means, merely because the same end might be effected through exercise of the power of eminent domain, or otherwise at public expense. Every restriction upon the height of buildings might be secured through acquiring by eminent domain the right of each owner to build above the limiting height; but it is settled that the state need not resort to that power. If by mining anthracite coal the owner would necessarily unloose poisonous gases, I suppose no one would doubt the power of the state to prevent the mining, without buying his coal fields. And why may not the state, likewise, without paying compensation, prohibit one from digging so deep or excavating so near the surface, as to expose the community to like dangers?

[It] is said that one fact for consideration in determining whether the limits of the police power have been exceeded is the extent of the resulting diminution in value, and that here the restriction destroys existing rights of property and contract. But values are relative. If we are to consider the value of the coal kept in place by the restriction, we should compare it with the value of all other parts of the land. [The law was] obviously enacted for a public purpose; and it seems, likewise, clear that mere notice of intention to mine would [not] secure the public safety. Yet it is said that [the law] cannot be sustained as an exercise of the police power where the right to mine such coal has been reserved. The conclusion seems to rest upon the assumption that in order to justify such exercise of the police power there must be "an average reciprocity of advantage" as between the owner of the property restricted and the rest of the community; and that here such reciprocity is absent. Reciprocity of advantage is an important consideration, and may even be essential, where the State's power is exercised for the purpose of conferring benefits upon the property of a neighborhood, as in drainage projects [or] upon adjoining owners, as by party wall provisions. But where the police power is exercised, not to confer benefits upon property owners but to protect the public from detriment and danger, there is in my opinion, no room for considering reciprocity of advantage. There was no reciprocal advantage to the owner prohibited [by a number of prior decisions] from using his oil tanks, his brickyard, his livery stable, his billiard hall, his oleomargarine factory, [or] his brewery; unless it be the advantage of living and doing business in a civilized community. That reciprocal advantage is given by the act to the coal operators.[1]

———

MILLER v. SCHOENE, 276 U.S. 272 (1928): A Virginia law provided for the destruction as a public nuisance of all ornamental red cedar trees that were or might be the source of a communicable plant disease known as cedar rust and that were growing within a prescribed radius of any apple orchard. Under the law, owners of the cedars were paid only the cost of removing their trees; they were not compensated for loss of the value of the standing cedars or the decrease in the value of their land caused by the destruction of the trees. The state courts upheld the state entomologist's order that a large number of cedars be cut down to protect nearby apple orchards. In affirming that decision and concluding that the cedars could be destroyed without paying compensation to their owners, Justice STONE's opinion for the unanimous Court stated:

"[Cedar rust] is an infectious plant disease in the form of a fungoid organism which is destructive of the fruit and foliage of the apple, but without effect on the value of the cedar. [The] only practicable method of controlling the disease and protecting apple trees [is] the destruction of all red cedar trees, subject to the infection, located within two miles of apple orchards. The red cedar, aside from its ornamental use, has occasional use and value as lumber. It is indigenous to Virginia, is not cultivated or dealt in commercially on any substantial scale, and its value throughout the state is shown to be small as compared with that of the apple orchards of the state. Apple growing is one of the principal agricultural pursuits in Virginia. The apple is used there and exported in large quantities. Many millions of dollars are invested in the orchards, which furnish employment for a large portion of the population. [On] the evidence we may accept the conclusion of the [state court] that the state was under the necessity of making a choice between the preservation of one class of property and that of the other wherever both existed in dangerous proximity. It would have been none the less a choice if, instead of enacting the present statute, the state, by doing nothing, had permitted serious injury to the apple orchards within its borders to go on unchecked. When forced to such a choice the state does not exceed its constitutional powers by deciding upon the destruction of one class of property in order to save another which, in the judgment of the legislature, is of greater value to the public. It will not do to say that the case is merely one of a conflict of two private interests and that the misfortune of apple growers may not be shifted to cedar owners by ordering the destruction of their property; for it is obvious that there may be, and that here there is, a preponderant public concern in the preservation of the one interest over the other. [And] where the public interest is involved preferment of that interest over the property interest of the individual, to the extent even of its destruction, is one of the distinguishing characteristics of every exercise of the

———

1. In 1987, the Court refused to apply Pennsylvania Coal, in Keystone Bituminous Coal Assn. v. DeBenedictis. That decision is noted immediately after the next case.

police power which affects property. [Where], as here, the choice is unavoidable, we cannot say that its exercise, controlled by considerations of social policy which are not unreasonable, involves any denial of due process."

KEYSTONE BITUMINOUS COAL ASS'N v. DeBENEDICTIS, 480 U.S. 470 (1987): This 5-4 decision cast serious doubt on the continuing vitality of the Pennsylvania Coal case by upholding a modern day counterpart to the Kohler Act struck down in Pennsylvania Coal. At issue was a 1966 Pennsylvania law prohibiting coal mining that causes subsidence damage to preexisting public buildings, dwellings and cemeteries. Implementing administrative regulations require that 50% of the coal beneath such structures be kept in place as a means of providing surface support. Even though the problems addressed by the law were similar to those involved in Pennsylvania Coal, Justice STEVENS's majority opinion held that the restrictions in the 1966 law did *not* constitute a taking. He dismissed most of Justice Holmes's language in Pennsylvania Coal as an "uncharacteristic" "advisory opinion" in a case that needed to deal only with the particular facts and not with the general validity of the statute. But Justice Stevens also went on to note that even under the factors described by Justice Holmes, this case was distinguishable. First, this law did not merely involve a balancing of private interests, but rather the protecting of "the public interest in health, the environment, and the fiscal integrity of the area. That private individuals erred in taking a risk cannot estop the Commonwealth from exercising its police power to abate activity akin to a public nuisance." Second, there had been no showing here of a deprivation equivalent to that in Pennsylvania Coal, where certain mining was made "commercially impracticable" by the Kohler Act. As to the 27 million tons of coal that had to be left in place as a result of the law—less than 2% of the owners' total coal—this did "not constitute a separate segment of property for takings purposes. Many zoning ordinances place limits on the property owner's right to make reasonable use of some segments of his property. A requirement that a building occupy no more than a specified percentage of the lot on which it is located could be characterized as a taking of the vacant area as readily as the requirement that coal pillars be left in place. [There] is no basis for treating the less than 2% of petitioners' coal as a separate parcel of property." Chief Justice REHNQUIST, joined by Justices Powell, O'Connor and Scalia, dissented, insisting that both the language and the holding of Pennsylvania Coal dictated a similar "taking" finding here. He also objected to the majority's emphasis on the public purpose of the law: "[Public purpose] does not resolve the question of whether a taking has occurred; the existence of such a public purpose is merely a necessary prerequisite to the government's exercise of its taking power." The dissent also found the majority's reliance on the "public nuisance" theory misplaced, and its conclusion about the extent of the loss erroneous. With respect to the 27 million tons of coal to be left in place, "[t]here is no question that this coal is an identifiable and separate property interest. Unlike many property interests, the 'bundle' of rights in this coal is sparse. [From] the relevant perspective—that of the property owners—this interest has been destroyed every bit as much as if the government had proceeded to mine the coal for its own use."

THE "TAKING–REGULATION" DISTINCTION AND THE MODERN COURT

1. *Zoning and other regulations of the environment.* When can zoning laws be challenged as being compensable "takings"? Even during the heyday of

economic due process, a divided Court sustained a general zoning ordinance as a valid "police regulation," in Euclid v. Ambler Realty Co., 272 U.S. 365 (1926). But the Euclid Court emphasized that it was not passing on specific applications of zoning ordinances; and two years later, in Nectow v. Cambridge, 277 U.S. 183 (1928), an application of a zoning law was invalidated. Property owners' challenges to zoning and other environmental laws have produced much litigation in state and lower federal courts, but few came to the Warren Court. One example is GOLDBLATT v. HEMPSTEAD, 369 U.S. 590 (1962), where, after a state court had blocked an effort to deal with a local problem via zoning, the town resorted to a "safety regulation"—and prevailed in the Court. Goldblatt owned a sand and gravel pit in a suburban area; the town had expanded rapidly. In the last of a series of local regulations of excavations, the town banned some types of mining and imposed a duty to refill some pits. Goldblatt claimed that the latest ordinance was "not regulatory" but rather amounted to confiscation of property without compensation. Justice CLARK's opinion for the Court conceded that the regulation "completely prohibits a beneficial use to which the property has previously been devoted," but nevertheless found it justified as a "reasonable," noncompensable exercise of the police power.[1]

2. *Remedies for "regulatory" takings: Damage actions for inverse condemnation.* In FIRST ENGLISH EVANGELICAL LUTHERAN CHURCH v. LOS ANGELES COUNTY, 482 U.S. 304 (1987), the Court at last reached the question of the remedy the Constitution requires when government regulation proves sufficiently burdensome to constitute a "taking." Chief Justice REHNQUIST's majority opinion in the 6-3 decision concluded that mere invalidation of the regulation restricting the use of the property was a constitutionally insufficient remedy. The State was also required to pay damages for the temporary taking in effect during the period before the ordinance was struck down. The State could "elect to abandon its intrusion or discontinue regulations," yet it had to pay compensation "for the period of time during which regulations deny a landowner all use of his land": "where the government's activities have already worked a taking of all use of property, no subsequent action by the government can relieve it of the duty to provide compensation for the period during which the taking was effective." He recognized that this holding would "undoubtedly lessen" the flexibility of land-use planners, but "such consequences necessarily flow from any decision upholding a claim of constitutional right." Justice STEVENS, joined in part by Justice Blackmun and O'Connor, dissented.

3. *Historic landmarks protection and the "taking-regulation" distinction.* In 1978, in its closest look at the "taking-regulation" distinction in years, the divided Court held in PENN CENTRAL TRANSPORTATION CO. v. NEW YORK CITY, 438 U.S. 104, that the constitutional bounds of permissible regulation had not been exceeded. Under New York City's Landmarks Preservation Law, Grand Central Terminal was designated as a "landmark." The law requires the owner of a designated landmark to keep the building's exterior "in good repair" and to obtain approval from a commission before making exterior alterations. A request for approval to build a multistory office building atop Grand Central Terminal was denied by the commission because, in its view, the

---

1. Note the doubt cast on the continued vitality of Goldblatt by the 1987 ruling in Nollan (note 3b below), where Justice Scalia's majority opinion suggested that Goldblatt was incorrect in assuming that due process, equal protection and Takings Clause restrictions were "identical" with regard to judicial scrutiny of property regulations. See also the Dolan ruling in 1994, also in note 3b.

office tower would impair the aesthetic quality of the Terminal's "flamboyant Beaux Arts facade." The owner of the Terminal brought suit claiming that the application of the law constituted a "taking." The 6-3 decision rejected that claim.

Justice BRENNAN's majority opinion concluded that a city may, as part of a comprehensive historic landmarks preservation program, "place restrictions on the development of individual historic landmarks [without] effecting a 'taking.'" Though the majority undertook an extensive canvass of the "taking-regulation" precedents, it conceded once again that the application of the legal standards involved "essentially ad hoc factual inquiries" and acknowledged that the Court had been "unable to develop any 'set formula' for determining when 'justice and fairness' require that economic injuries caused by public action be compensated by the Government, rather than remain disproportionately concentrated on a few persons." Justice Brennan surveyed "several factors" that had been identified as having "particular significance." He noted that zoning laws were "classic" examples of ordinarily permissible impairments of real property interests for the sake of "the health, safety, morals or general welfare." Pennsylvania Coal, on the other hand, served as a warning that a law "that substantially furthers important public policies may so frustrate distinct investment-backed expectations as to amount to a 'taking.'" He found landmarks regulation more akin to the zoning precedents than to Pennsylvania Coal. He conceded that, unlike zoning laws and historic district legislation, "landmark laws apply only to selected parcels." But he insisted that "landmark laws are not like discriminatory, or 'reverse spot,' zoning: that is, a land use decision which arbitrarily singles out a particular parcel for different, less favorable treatment than the neighboring ones. In contrast to discriminatory zoning, [the law here] embodies a comprehensive plan to preserve structures of historic or aesthetic interest wherever they may be found in the city, [and] over 400 landmarks [have] been designated pursuant to this plan." Moreover, the interference with the owner's property was not so great as to fall within the Pennsylvania Coal principle. He emphasized that the owner's use of the air space had not been wholly banned and that the owner had exaggerated the economic effect of the law, since development rights on the restricted parcel were transferable to other nearby parcels. He concluded: "The restrictions imposed are substantially related to the promotion of the general welfare and not only permit reasonable beneficial use of the landmark site but afford [the owner] opportunities further to enhance not only the Terminal site proper but also other properties."

Justice REHNQUIST's dissent, joined by Chief Justice Burger and Justice Stevens, insisted that the severe impact of the law was not justified by either of the two exceptions to the normal rule that "destruction of property" constitutes a compensable taking. The permissible prohibition of "noxious uses" was not applicable here. And a second exception to the compensation rule did not apply either: "Even where the government prohibits a noninjurious use, the Court has ruled that a taking does not take place if the prohibition applies over a broad cross section of land and thereby 'secure[s] an average reciprocity of advantage.' Pennsylvania Coal. It is for this reason that zoning does not constitute a 'taking.' While zoning at times reduces *individual* property values, the burden is shared relatively evenly and it is reasonable to conclude that on the whole an individual who is harmed by one aspect of the zoning will be benefited by another. Here, however, a multimillion dollar loss has been imposed on [the owner]; it is uniquely felt and is not offset by any benefits flowing from the preservation of some 500 other 'Landmarks' in New York. [The City has] imposed a substantial cost on less than one-tenth of one percent of the buildings in New York for the general benefit of all its people. It is exactly this imposition of general costs on a few individuals at which the 'taking' protection is directed. [A] taking does not become a noncompensable exercise of police power simply because the government in its grace allows the owner to make some 'reasonable' use of his property."[2]

4. *"Taking" problems in the most recent decades.* Several decision of the 1980s indicate that the Court is once again prepared to view the Takings Clause quite seriously. In contrast to the usual results in cases of earlier decades, the Court in the Loretto and Nollan rulings of the 1980s found that compensable takings *had* occurred. And the serious concern regarding takings claims continued in Lucas and Dolan, the 1990s cases following this note.

a. *A per se rule (rather than balancing) for "permanent physical occupations."* The 6-3 decision in LORETTO v. TELEPROMPTER MANHATTAN CATV CORP., 458 U.S. 419 (1982), held that, when the government authorizes a "permanent physical occupation" (albeit a "minor" one) of an owner's property, there "is a taking without regard to the public interests that [the government action] may serve." The majority rejected as inappropriate here the balancing analysis typical in earlier takings cases. The Court's newly articulated per se rule led it to invalidate a New York law which provided that a landlord must permit a cable television company to install its cable facilities upon a landlord's rental property. In defending the majority's per se rule, applicable to all "permanent physical occupations," Justice MARSHALL insisted that the precedents confirmed a distinction "between a permanent physical occupation, a physical invasion short of an occupation, and a regulation that merely restricts the use of property." Even Penn Central and its balancing approach did not "repudiate the rule that a permanent physical occupation is a governmental action of such a unique character that it is a taking without regard to other factors that a court might ordinarily examine." Accordingly, "when the 'character of the governmental action' [Penn Central] is a permanent physical occupation of property, our cases uniformly have found a taking to the extent of the occupation, without regard to whether the action achieves an important public benefit or has only minimal economic impact on the owner."[3]

b. *Heightened scrutiny for takings claims: Conditions on permits to develop property.* i. *Nollan.* The Court's increased willingness to find certain govern-

---

2. For other confrontations with the "takings" problem by the post–1930s Court, see, e.g., the decisions sustaining compensation for "takings" by low-flying airplanes and rejecting arguments that the injuries were "merely incidental" consequences of authorized air navigation, United States v. Causby, 328 U.S. 256 (1946), and Griggs v. Allegheny County, 369 U.S. 84 (1962). Note also Connolly v. Pension Benefit Guaranty Corp., 475 U.S. 211 (1986), holding that no compensable taking was imposed by amendments to the Employee Retirement Income Security Act of 1974 (ERISA) that require employers withdrawing from the program to pay their pro rata share of unfunded pension obligations.

3. In dissenting, Justice BLACKMUN, joined by Justices Brennan and White, condemned the decision as unduly formalistic. In his view, "history teaches that takings claims are properly evaluated under a multifactor balancing test." He asserted, moreover, that the Court had not demonstrated how the law impaired private rights "in a manner *qualitatively* different from other garden-variety landlord-tenant legislation." (The unanimous Court distinguished Loretto in FCC v. Florida Power Corp., 480 U.S. 245 (1987), upholding a law authorizing the FCC to regulate the rates utility companies charge cable operators for the use of utility poles. Justice Marshall's opinion held that, for takings purposes, the distinction between a beneficiary of a government license and a commercial lessee was dispositive, so that rate control with respect to commercial leases did not constitute a taking.)

mental actions to be compensable takings became especially apparent in NOL-LAN v. CALIFORNIA COASTAL COMM'N, 483 U.S. 825 (1987). The Nollans were owners of beachfront property in California who sought permission to replace their small bungalow with a larger house. The Commission conditioned its grant of permission on the Nollans' agreement to allow the public to pass across their beach, which was located between two public beaches. The Nollans claimed that this requirement constituted a taking, and the Court agreed. Justice SCALIA's majority opinion in the 5-4 decision began by noting that there clearly would have been a taking if the state regulation had directly imposed such an easement, instead of conditioning the Nollans' permit to rebuild their house on their agreeing to an easement. Relying on cases such as Loretto, Justice Scalia pointed out that "a 'permanent physical occupation' has occurred [where] individuals are given a permanent and continuous right to pass to and fro, so that the real property may continuously be traversed, even though no particular individual is permitted to station himself permanently on the premises." He acknowledged, however, that California could have denied the permit entirely, or imposed any number of other restrictions without those restrictions being a taking—as long as the restrictions "substantially advanced" "the end advanced as the justification for the prohibition [the building restriction regarding houses near the beach]." Applying this heightened level of scrutiny, Justice Scalia examined the relationship between the State's professed interest in preserving sightlines to the beach and related goals, on the one hand, and the easement required of the Nollans, on the other, concluding that "the condition substituted for the [presumably permitted total] prohibition utterly fails to further the end advanced as the justification for the prohibition. [It] is quite impossible to understand how a requirement that people already on the public beaches be able to walk across the Nollans' property reduces any obstacles to viewing the beach created by the new house. [If California] wants an easement across the Nollans' property, it must pay for it." He thus found no adequate nexus between the condition and the original purpose of the building restriction. He emphasized: "In short, unless the permit condition serves the same governmental purpose as the development ban, the building restriction is not a valid regulation of land use but 'an out-and-out plan of extortion.' "

In the course of reaching his conclusion, Justice Scalia sought to clarify the appropriate level of scrutiny. He noted: "Our cases have not elaborated on the standards for determining what constitutes a 'legitimate state interest' or what type of connection between the regulation and the state interest satisfies the requirement that the former 'substantially advanced' the latter." Although he did not detail precisely the appropriate level of scrutiny, he did indicate that the standard is more rigorous than the deferential approach associated with determining minimum rationality in due process or equal protection contexts: "[O]ur verbal formulations in the takings field have generally been quite different. [There] is no reason to believe (and the language of our cases give some reason to disbelieve) that so long as the regulation of property is at issue the standards for takings challenges, due process challenges, and equal protection challenges are identical. Goldblatt v. Hempstead [above] does appear to assume that the inquiries are the same, but that assumption is inconsistent with the formulations of our later cases." Justice BRENNAN, joined by Justice Marshall, filed a lengthy dissent, objecting to the majority's imposition of "a standard of precision for the exercise of a State's police power that has been discredited for the better part of this century. [The] Court demands a degree of exactitude that is inconsistent with our standard for reviewing the rationality of a State's exercise of its police power for the welfare of its citizens. [The] Nollans' development blocks visual access, the Court tells us, while the Commission seeks to preserve lateral access along the coastline. Thus, it concludes, the State acted irrationally. Such a narrow conception of rationality, however, has long since been discredited as a judicial arrogation of legislative authority." (Justices BLACKMUN and STEVENS also submitted dissents.)

ii. *Dolan.* Two years after Nollan, the Court tightened the requirements regarding the relationship between permit conditions imposed by government and the governmental interests in mitigating the adverse effects of developments. In DOLAN v. CITY OF TIGARD, 512 U.S. 374 (1994), Dolan had sought a permit to increase the size of her plumbing and electrical supply store. The store was located on one side of her nearly two acre lot; on the other side of the lot lay the flood plain of Fanno Creek, which flowed along the west side of the property. The City conditioned the approval of a building permit on the dedication of a portion of her property for flood control and traffic improvements. With respect to flood control, the City's condition required her to dedicate the flood plain portion of her lot to permit improvement of the drainage system along the creek. With respect to traffic concerns, she was required to dedicate a 15–foot strip adjoining the flood plain for a public pedestrian/bicycle path. Dolan challenged the City's dedication conditions on the ground that they were not sufficiently related to the interest in curbing harmful effects of the development and that they therefore constituted an uncompensated taking of her property.

Chief Justice REHNQUIST's majority opinion held the conditions unconstitutional. He began by distinguishing land use regulations involved in cases such as Pennsylvania Coal and Dolan's situation. Earlier cases involved "essentially legislative determinations classifying entire areas of the City, whereas here the City made an adjudicative decision to condition petitioner's application for a building permit on an individual parcel. [Moreover,] the conditions imposed [here] were not simply a limitation on the use petitioner might make of her own parcel, but a requirement that she deed portions of the property to the City." Nollan, he reminded, held that the imposition of conditions was limited by the takings clause: "Under the well-settled doctrine of 'unconstitutional conditions,' the government may not require a person to give up a constitutional right—here the right to receive just compensation when property is taken for a public use—in exchange for a discretionary benefit conferred by the government where the property sought has little or no relationship to the benefit." [See generally Sullivan, "Unconstitutional Conditions," 102 Harv. L.Rev. 1415 (1989).] Here, Dolan argued that the City had identified "no special benefits" conferred on her, and had not identified any "special quantifiable burdens" created by her new store that "would justify the particular dedications required from her which are not required from the public at large." Responding to this challenge, the Chief Justice stated: "We must first determine whether the 'essential nexus' exists between the 'legitimate state interests' and the permit condition exacted by the City. Nollan. If we find that a nexus exists, we must then decide the required degree of connection between the exactions and the projected impact of the proposed development. We were not required to reach this question in Nollan, because we concluded that the connection did not meet even the loosest standard. Here, however, we must decide this question." Unlike Nollan, the "essential nexus" requirement was easily met here. But the conditions fell afoul of the second question, "whether the degree of the exactions demanded by the city's permit conditions bear the required relationship to the projected impact of petitioner's proposed development."

In analyzing this second question, the Court majority noted that the Oregon Supreme Court had deferred "to what it termed the 'city's unchallenged factual findings' supporting the dedication conditions and found them to be reasonably related to the impact of the expansion of petitioner's business." In determining whether these findings were constitutionally sufficient, the Court examined decisions of other state courts, which had been "dealing with this question a good deal longer than we have." The Chief Justice noted that some state courts accepted "very generalized statements as to the necessary connection between the required dedication and the proposed development." This approach, the Chief Justice concluded, was "too lax to adequately protect" the property owner. Other state courts required "a very exacting correspondence, described as the 'specifi[c] and uniquely attributable' test." This too was unacceptable to the majority: "We do not think the Federal Constitution requires such exacting scrutiny given the nature of the interests involved." The Chief Justice continued: "A number of state courts have taken an intermediate position, requiring the municipality to show a 'reasonable relationship' between the required dedication and the impact of the proposed development." But the Chief Justice did not accept the widely used "reasonable relationship" test without adding a significant, presumably more rigorous clause: "We think the 'reasonable relationship' test adopted by a majority of the state courts is closer to the federal constitutional norm than either of those previously discussed. But we do not adopt it as such, partly because the term 'reasonable relationship' seems confusingly similar to the term 'rational basis' which describes the minimal level of scrutiny under the Equal Protection [Clause]. We think a term such as 'rough proportionality' best encapsulates what we hold to be the requirement of the Fifth Amendment. No precise mathematical calculation is required, but the City must make some sort of individualized determination that the required dedication is related both in nature and extent to the impact of the proposed development." The Chief Justice discounted the argument of Justice Stevens, in dissent, that the imposition of conditions was "a species of business regulation that heretofore warranted a strong presumption of constitutional validity." He replied: "[S]imply denominating a governmental measure as a 'business regulation' does not immunize it from constitutional challenge on the grounds that it violates a provision of the Bill of Rights. [We] see no reason why the Takings Clause, [as] much a part of the Bill of Rights as the First Amendment or Fourth Amendment, should be relegated to the status of the poor relation."

Turning to the question of whether the findings in this case satisfied the newly enhanced requirements, the Chief Justice explained: "It is axiomatic that increasing the amount of impervious surface will increase the quantity and rate of storm-water flow from petitioner's property. Therefore, keeping the floodplain open and free from development would likely confine the pressures on Fanno Creek created by petitioner's development. [But] the city demanded more—it not only wanted petitioner not to build in the floodplain, but it also wanted petitioner's property along Fanno Creek for its greenway system. The city has never said why a public greenway, as opposed to a private one, was required in the interest of flood control. The difference to petitioner, of course, is the loss of her ability to exclude others. [This] right to exclude others is 'one of the most essential sticks in the bundle of rights that are commonly characterized as property.' [It] is difficult to see why a recreational visitor's trampling along petitioner's floodplain easement are sufficiently related to the city's legitimate interest in reducing flooding problems along Fanno Creek, and the city has not attempted to make any individualized determination to support this part of its request. [Moreover,] the city must make some effort to quantify its findings in support of the dedication for the pedestrian/bicycle pathway beyond the conclusory statement that it would offset some of the traffic demand generated." In a concluding passage, the Chief Justice stated: "Cities have long engaged in the commendable task of land use planning, made necessary by increasing urbanization particularly in metropolitan areas such as Portland. The city's goals of reducing flooding hazards and traffic congestion, and providing for public greenways, are laudable, but there are outer limits to how this may be done. 'A strong public desire to improve the public condition [will not] warrant achieving the desire by a shorter cut than the constitutional way of paying for the change.' Pennsylvania Coal."

Justice STEVENS, joined by Justices Blackmun and Ginsburg, submitted an extensive dissent. He began by criticizing the majority's reliance on state precedents, noting that, "although the state cases do lend support to the Court's reaffirmance of Nollan's reasonable nexus requirement, the role the Court accords them in the announcement of its newly minted second phase of the constitutional inquiry [the "rough proportionality" approach] is remarkably inventive." Taking direct issue with the majority's standard, he noted: "The Court's assurances that its 'rough proportionality' test leaves ample role for cities to pursue the 'commendable task of land use planning' [are] wanting given the result that test compels here. Under the Court's approach, a city must not only 'quantify its findings,' and make 'individualized determination[s]' with respect to the nature and extent of the relationship between the conditions and the impact, but also demonstrate 'proportionality.' The correct inquiry should instead concentrate on whether the required nexus is present and venture beyond considerations of a condition's nature or germaneness only if the developer establishes that a concededly germane condition is so grossly disproportionate to the proposed development's adverse effects that it manifests motives other than land use regulation on the part of the city."

Moreover, Justice Stevens charged the majority with Lochnerizing this area of law. He claimed that the Court had made "a serious error by abandoning the traditional presumption of constitutionality and imposing a novel burden of proof on a city implementing an admittedly valid comprehensive land use plan." He claimed that the majority had resurrected "a species of substantive due process analysis," illustrated by Lochner: "The so-called 'regulatory takings' doctrine that the Holmes dictum [in Pennsylvania Coal] kindled has an obvious kinship with the line of substantive due process cases that Lochner exemplified. Besides having similar ancestry, both doctrines are potentially open-ended sources of judicial power to invalidate state economic regulations that Members of this Court view as unwise or unfair." He also thought it inappropriate to apply the "unconstitutional conditions" doctrine to "a mutually beneficial transaction between a property owner and a city." He argued that "the Court's reliance on the 'unconstitutional conditions' doctrine is assuredly novel, and arguably incoherent." While the city's conditions were subject to constitutional scrutiny, the "level of scrutiny [does] not approximate the kind of review that would apply if the city had insisted on a surrender of Dolan's First Amendment rights in exchange for a building permit. One can only hope that the Court's reliance today on First Amendment cases, and its candid disavowal of the term 'rational basis' to describe its new standard of review, do not signify a reassertion of the kind of superlegislative power the Court exercised during the Lochner era." In a concluding passage, Justice Stevens added: "In our changing world one thing is certain: uncertainty will characterize predictions about the impact of new urban developments on the risks of floods, earthquakes, traffic congestion, or environmental harms. When there is doubt concerning the magnitude of those impacts, the public interest in averting them must outweigh the private interest of the commercial entrepreneur. If the government can demonstrate that the conditions it has imposed in a land-use permit are rational, impartial and conducive to fulfilling the aims of a valid land-use plan, a strong presumption of validity should attach to those conditions. The burden of demonstrating that those conditions have unreasonably impaired the economic value of the proposed improvement belongs squarely on the shoulders of the party challenging the state action's constitutionality. That allocation of burdens has served us well in the past. The Court has stumbled badly today by reversing it." [In a footnote, the Chief Justice replied to part of this passage by Justice Stevens as follows: "[The] dissent takes us to task for placing the burden on the city to justify the required dedication. He is correct in arguing that in evaluating most generally applicable zoning regulations, the burden properly rests on the party challenging the regulation to prove that it constitutes an arbitrary regulation of property rights. Here, by contrast, the city made an adjudicative decision to condition petitioner's application for a building permit on an individual parcel. In this situation, the burden properly rests on the city. Nollan."][4]

5. *Regulations prohibiting all economically beneficial uses of land.* LUCAS v. SOUTH CAROLINA COASTAL COUNCIL, 505 U.S. 1003 (1992), produced the most extensive consideration yet of the question whether denying all economically productive use of land constituted a taking. Lucas had paid nearly one million dollars for two lots on which he planned to build single family homes. In 1988, his plans were brought to "an abrupt end" with the enactment of South Carolina's Beachfront Management Act, an anti-erosion law, which had the effect of barring Lucas from erecting any permanent habitable structures on his two parcels. A state trial court found that this prohibition "deprive[d] Lucas of any reasonable economic use of the lots" and rendered his parcels "valueless." Finding a "taking," it ordered "just compensation" of more than one million dollars. The highest state court reversed, ruling that when a regulation was designed "to prevent serious public harm," no compensation was owed, regardless of the regulation's effect on the property's value. The Court granted review in order to decide whether the Act's dramatic effect on the economic value of Lucas's lots accomplished a taking of private property, and held that a taking had occurred.

Justice SCALIA's majority opinion stated that Pennsylvania Coal "offered little insight into when, and under what circumstances, a given regulation would be seen as going 'too far' for purposes of the Fifth Amendment. In 70–odd years of succeeding 'regulatory takings' jurisprudence, we have generally eschewed any 'set formula' for determining how far is too far, preferring to 'engag[e] [in] essentially ad hoc, factual inquiries.' Penn Central. We have, however, described at least two discrete categories of regulatory action as compensable without case-specific inquiry into the public interest advanced in support of the restraint. The first encompasses regulations that compel the property owner to suffer a physical 'invasion' of his property. In general (at least with regard to permanent invasions), no matter how minute the intrusion, and no matter how weighty the public purpose behind it, we have required compensation. [Loretto.] [The] second situation [is] where regulation denies all economically beneficial or productive use of land. As we have said on numerous occasions, the Fifth Amendment is violated when land-use regulation 'does not substantially advance legitimate state interests or denies an owner economically viable use of his land.'[5]

4. Justice SOUTER filed a brief, separate dissent.

5. "Regrettably, the rhetorical force of our 'deprivation of all economically feasible use' rule is greater than its precision, since the rule does not make clear the 'property interest' against which the loss of value is to be measured. When, for example, a regula-

"We have never set forth the justification for this rule. Perhaps it is simply [that] total deprivation of beneficial use is, from the landowner's point of view, the equivalent of a physical appropriation. [Surely,] at least, in the extraordinary circumstance when no productive or economically beneficial use of land is permitted, it is less realistic to indulge our usual assumption that the legislature is simply 'adjusting the benefits and burdens of economic life' [Penn Central] in a manner that secures an 'average reciprocity of advantage' to everyone concerned. [Pennsylvania Coal.] And the functional basis for permitting the government, by regulation, to affect property values without compensation—that 'Government hardly could go on if to some extent values incident to property could not be diminished without paying for every such change in the general law'—does not apply to the relatively rare situations where the government has deprived a landowner of all economically beneficial uses. On the other side of the balance, affirmatively supporting a compensation requirement, is the fact that regulations that leave the owner of land without economically beneficial or productive options for its use—typically, as here, by requiring land to be left substantially in its natural state—carry with them a heightened risk that private property is being pressed into some form of public service under the guise of mitigating serious public harm. [The] many statutes on the books, both state and federal, that provide for the use of eminent domain to impose servitudes on private scenic lands preventing developmental uses, or to acquire such lands altogether, suggest the practical equivalence in this setting of negative regulation and appropriation. We think, in short, that there are good reasons for our frequently expressed belief that when the owner of real property has been called upon to sacrifice all economically beneficial uses in the name of the common good, that is, to leave his property economically idle, he has suffered a taking.[6]

"[In the highest state court's view, the Act] involved an exercise of 'police powers' to mitigate the harm to the public interest that petitioner's use of his land might occasion. [It] is correct that many of our prior opinions have suggested that 'harmful or noxious uses' of property may be proscribed by government regulation without the requirement of compensation. Mugler v. Kansas [1887; p. 459 above]. The 'harmful or noxious uses' principle was the Court's early attempt to describe in theoretical terms why government may,

tion requires a developer to leave 90% of a rural tract in its natural state, it is unclear whether [the] situation [is] one in which the owner has been deprived of all economically beneficial use of the burdened portion of the tract, or [one] in which the owner has suffered a mere diminution in value of the tract as a whole. [The] answer to this difficult question may lie in how the owner's reasonable expectations have been shaped by the State's law of property—i.e., whether and to what degree the State's law has accorded legal recognition and protection to the particular interest in land with respect to which the takings claimant alleges a diminution in (or elimination of) value. In any event, we avoid this difficulty in the present case, since the 'interest in land' that Lucas has pleaded (a fee simple interest) is an estate with a rich tradition of protection at common law, and since [the trial court] found that the [Act]

left each of Lucas's [lots] without economic value." [Footnote by Justice Scalia.]

6. "Justice Stevens criticizes the 'deprivation of all economically beneficial use' rule as 'wholly arbitrary' in that 'the landowner whose property is diminished in value 95% recovers nothing' while the landowner who suffers a complete elimination of value 'recovers the land's full value.' This analysis errs in its assumption that the landowner whose deprivation is one step short of complete is not entitled to compensation. Such an owner might not be able to claim the benefit of our categorical formulation, but '[the] economic impact of the regulation on the claimant [and] the extent to which the regulation has interfered with distinct investment-backed expectations' are keenly relevant to takings analysis generally. [Penn Central.]" [Footnote by Justice Scalia.]

consistent with the Takings Clause, affect property values by regulation without incurring an obligation to [compensate]. [These] cases are better understood as resting not on any supposed 'noxious' quality of the prohibited uses but rather on the ground that the restrictions were reasonably related to the implementation of a policy—not unlike historic preservation—expected to produce a widespread public benefit and applicable to all similarly situated property. 'Harmful or noxious use' analysis was [simply] the progenitor of our more contemporary statements that 'land-use regulation does not effect a taking if it substantially advance[s] legitimate state interests.' [Nollan.] [When] it is understood that 'prevention of harmful use' was merely our early formulation of the police power justification necessary to sustain (without compensation) any regulatory diminution in value; and that the distinction between regulation that 'prevents harmful use' and that which 'confers benefits' is difficult, if not impossible, to discern on an objective, value-free basis; it becomes self-evident that noxious-use logic cannot serve as a touchstone to distinguish regulatory 'takings'—which require compensation—from regulatory deprivations that do not require compensation. A fortiori, the legislature's recitation of a noxious-use justification cannot be the basis for departing from our categorical rule that total regulatory takings must be compensated. If it were, departure would virtually always be allowed.

"[Where] the State seeks to sustain regulation that deprives land of all economically beneficial use, we think it may resist compensation only if the logically antecedent inquiry into the nature of the owner's estate shows that the proscribed use interests were not part of his title to begin with. This accords, we think, with our 'takings' jurisprudence, which has traditionally been guided by the understandings of our citizens, regarding the content of, and the State's power over, the 'bundle of rights' that they acquire when they obtain title to property. [A] property owner necessarily expects the uses of his property to be restricted, from time to time, by various measures newly enacted by the State in legitimate exercise of its police powers. [And] in the case of personal property, by reason of the State's traditionally high degree of control over commercial dealings, he ought to be aware of the possibility that new regulation might even render his property economically worthless (at least if the property's only economically productive use is sale or manufacture for sale), Andrus v. Allard, 444 U.S. 51 (1979) (prohibition on sale of eagle feathers). In the case of land, however, [the] notion pressed by the Council that title is somehow held subject to the 'implied limitation' that the State may subsequently eliminate all economically valuable use is inconsistent with the historical compact recorded in the Takings Clause that has become part of our constitutional culture.

"Where 'permanent physical occupation' of land is concerned, we have refused to allow the government to decree it anew (without compensation), no matter how weighty the asserted 'public interests' involved [Loretto], though we assuredly would permit the government to assert a permanent easement that was a pre-existing limitation upon the landowner's title. We believe similar treatment must be accorded confiscatory regulations, i.e., regulations that prohibit all economically beneficial use of land: Any limitation so severe cannot be newly legislated or decreed (without compensation), but must inhere in the title itself, in the restrictions that background principles of the State's law of property and nuisance already place upon land ownership. A law or decree with such an effect must, in other words, do no more than duplicate the result that could have been achieved in the courts—by adjacent landowners (or other uniquely affected persons) under the State's law of private nuisance, or by the State under its complementary power to abate nuisances that affect the public generally, or otherwise. On this analysis, the owner of a lake bed, for example, would not be entitled to compensation when he is denied the requisite permit to engage in a landfilling operation that would have the effect of flooding others' land. [Such] regulatory action may well have the effect of eliminating the land's only economically productive use, but it does not proscribe a productive use that was previously permissible under relevant property and nuisance principles. The use of these properties for what are now expressly prohibited purposes was always unlawful, and [it] was open to the State at any point to make the implication of those background principles of nuisance and property law explicit. [This] recognition that the Takings Clause does not require compensation when an owner is barred from putting land to a use that is proscribed by those 'existing rules or understandings' is surely unexceptional. When, however, a regulation that declares 'off-limits' all economically productive or beneficial uses of land goes beyond what the relevant background principles would dictate, compensation must be paid to sustain it.

"The 'total taking' inquiry we require today would ordinarily entail (as the application of state nuisance law ordinarily entails) analysis of, among other things, the degree of harm to public lands and resources, or adjacent private property, imposed by the claimant's proposed activities, the social value of the claimant's activities and their suitability to the locality in question, and the relative ease with which the alleged harm can be avoided through measures taken by the claimant and the government (or adjacent private landowners) alike [see Restatement Second of Torts, §§ 826–831.] The fact that a particular use has long been engaged in by similarly situated owners ordinarily imports a lack of any common-law prohibition (though changed circumstances and new knowledge may make what was previously permissible no longer so). So also does the fact that other landowners, similarly situated, are permitted to continue the use denied to the claimant. It seems unlikely that common-law principles would have prevented the erection of any habitable or productive improvements on petitioner's land; they rarely support prohibition of the 'essential use' of land. The question, however, is one of state law to be dealt with on remand. [To] win its case South Carolina must do more than proffer the legislature's declaration that the uses Lucas desires are inconsistent with the public interest. [Instead,] as it would be required to do if it sought to restrain Lucas in a common-law action for public nuisance, South Carolina must identify background principles of nuisance and property law that prohibit the uses he now intends in the circumstances in which the property is presently found. Only on this showing can the State fairly claim that, in proscribing all such beneficial uses, the [Act] is taking nothing."[7]

In an opinion concurring in the judgment, Justice KENNEDY took a somewhat broader view of state power: "In my view, reasonable expectations must be understood in light of the whole of our legal tradition. The common law of nuisance is too narrow a confine for the exercise of regulatory power in a complex and interdependent society. Goldblatt v. Hempstead. The State should not be prevented from enacting new regulatory initiatives in response to changing conditions, and courts must consider all reasonable expectations whatever their source. The Takings Clause does not require a static body of state property law; it protects private expectations to ensure private invest-

---

7. On remand, the state supreme court held that common law principles of property and nuisance would not prohibit the planned development. Therefore, Lucas was entitled to compensation. See Washburn, "Land Use Control, the Individual and Society ...," 52 Md.L.Rev. 162 (1993), and a symposium on Lucas (including articles by Epstein and Sax), 45 Stan.L.Rev. 1369 (1993).

ment. I agree with the Court that nuisance prevention accords with the most common expectations of property owners who face regulation, but I do not believe this can be the sole source of state authority to impose severe restrictions. Coastal property may present such unique concerns for a fragile land system that the State can go further in regulating its development and use than the common law of nuisance might otherwise permit."

In a sharp dissent, Justice BLACKMUN expressed his fear "that the Court's new policies will spread beyond the narrow confines of the present case." He criticized the majority's effort "to create a new scheme for regulations that eliminate all economic value. From now on, there is a categorical rule finding these regulations to be a taking unless the use they prohibit is a background common-law nuisance or property principle." He criticized the majority's adoption of a per se rule and its refusal to engage in a case-specific inquiry. He commented: "When the government regulation prevents the owner from any economically valuable use of his property, the private interest is unquestionably substantial, but we have never before held that no public interest can outweigh it. Instead, the Court's prior decisions 'uniformly reject the proposition that diminution in property value, standing alone, can establish a "taking." ' Penn Central." He added: "Even more perplexing, however, is the Court's reliance on common-law principles of nuisance in its quest for a value-free taking jurisprudence. In determining what is a nuisance at common law, state courts make exactly the decision that the Court finds so troubling when made by the General Assembly today: they determine whether the use is harmful. Common-law public and private nuisance law is simply a determination whether a particular use causes harm. [If] judges in the 18th and 19th centuries can distinguish a harm from a benefit, why not judges in the 20th century, and if judges can, why not legislators? There simply is no reason to believe that new interpretations of the hoary common law nuisance doctrine will be particularly 'objective' or 'value-free.' "

Another dissent, by Justice STEVENS, found the majority's ruling "an illogical expansion of the concept of 'regulatory takings.' " He thought that the "categorical rule the Court establishes [an] unsound and unwise addition to the law and the Court's formulation of the exception to that rule 'too rigid and too narrow.' " He added: "The Court's holding today effectively freezes the State's common-law, denying the legislature much of its traditional power to revise the law governing the rights and uses of property. Until today, I had thought that we had long abandoned this approach to constitutional law. More than a century ago we recognized that 'the great office of statutes is to remedy defects in the common law [and] to adapt it to the changes of time and circumstances.' Munn v. Illinois. As Justice Marshall observed about a position similar to that adopted by the Court today: 'If accepted, that claim would represent a return to the era of Lochner v. New York, when common-law rights were also found immune from revision by State or Federal Government. Such an approach would freeze the [common law]. It would allow no room for change and response to changes in circumstance. The Due Process Clause does not require such a result.' PruneYard Shopping Center v. Robins (1980; concurring opinion; p. 1366 below). Arresting the development of the common-law is not only a departure from our prior decisions, it is also profoundly unwise."[8]

---

8. In a brief separate statement, Justice SOUTER thought that certiorari should be dismissed as improperly granted. He noted that it was no longer clear that Lucas had

A NOTE ON "PUBLIC USE"

The Fifth Amendment not only requires "just compensation" for takings, but also bars takings unless they are for *"public use."* The modern Court, in a development paralleling the decline of economic due process scrutiny, tends to be extremely deferential toward legislative determinations of what constitutes "public use." (Recall the similarly deferential stance regarding what constitutes the "general Welfare" when Congress exercises its power to tax and spend for that purpose, in chap. 4 above.) The characteristic Court tenor is illustrated by Berman v. Parker, 348 U.S. 26 (1954). There, Justice Douglas' opinion for a unanimous Court stated: "The role of the judiciary in determining whether [the eminent domain power] is being exercised for a public purpose is an extremely narrow one."[1] This "extremely narrow" judicial role on public use issues was more recently demonstrated in the Court's unanimous decision in HAWAII HOUSING AUTHORITY v. MIDKIFF, 467 U.S. 229 (1984). The decision upheld Hawaii's use of eminent domain to solve the problem of concentrated land ownership, a problem traceable to Hawaii's early feudal land tenure system. In the 1960s, the legislature found that 72 private landowners owned 47% of the State's land and the state and federal governments 49%, leaving only 4% for other private owners. Moreover, on Oahu, the most urbanized island, 22 landowners owned 72.5% of the fee simple titles. The legislature concluded that "concentrated land ownership was responsible for skewing the State's residential fee simple market, inflating land prices, and injuring the public tranquility and welfare." The Hawaii Land Reform Act of 1967, designed to compel large landowners to break up their estates, created a mechanism to implement that purpose. Under the Act, tenants living on single-family residential lots were entitled to ask the State's Housing Authority to condemn the property on which they lived. After the state agency acquired the property by eminent domain, it could sell the land to tenants who had applied for fee simple ownership. Justice O'CONNOR rejected the claim that the purpose of the Hawaii scheme was redistribution for private rather than public benefit. After reviewing Berman, she noted that the "public use" requirement was "coterminous with the scope of a sovereign's police powers." She added: "[Where] the exercise of the eminent domain power is rationally related to a conceivable public purpose, the Court has never held a compensated taking to be proscribed by the Public Use Clause. On this basis, we have no trouble concluding that the Hawaii Act is constitutional. [When] the legislature's purpose is legitimate and its means are not irrational, our cases make clear

been deprived of his entire economic interest, in view of a later amendment to the South Carolina Act permitting some building on beachfront property after obtaining a special permit.

1. Berman was a challenge to a District of Columbia law authorizing the taking of private property for the purpose of redeveloping blighted areas. After condemnation, the government could lease or sell that property to private developers, who were required to conform to redevelopment plans adopted by a D.C. agency. In the course of sustaining that scheme, Justice Douglas made a much-quoted statement about the breadth of governmental power: "The concept of the public welfare is broad and inclusive. The values it represents are spiritual as well as physical, aesthetic as well as monetary. It is within the power of the legislature to determine that the community should be beautiful as well as healthy, spacious as well as clean, well-balanced as well as carefully patrolled. [If] those who govern the District of Columbia decide that the Nation's Capital should be beautiful as well as sanitary, there is nothing in the Fifth Amendment that stands in the way. [The] rights of these property owners are satisfied when they receive that just compensation which the Fifth Amendment exacts as the price of the taking." (In the course of his opinion, Justice Douglas repeatedly cited modern economic due process cases of the post–1937 era.)

that empirical debates over the wisdom of takings [are] not to be carried out in the federal courts. [The] mere fact that property taken outright by eminent domain is transferred in the first instance to private beneficiaries does not condemn that taking as having only a private purpose."

As the modern cases illustrate, the "public use" limitation relates closely to issues of economic due process. What is a public rather than a private use is often a function of both economic theory and political philosophy, akin to the questions raised in "ends" inquiries under economic due process. A narrow view of the role of the state, as in Lochner, would logically carry with it a narrow view of the contours of permissible public use. By contrast, a broad view, akin to that of the Holmes dissent in Lochner, would eschew invoking a particular conception of public use and would thereby avoid using the Constitution to enforce a particular economic or political theory. The recent cases suggest that the modern Court is almost as disinclined to second-guess "public use" determinations as it is to curtail police power ends in economic due process inquiries. Would a different result have been likely in Midkiff if Hawaii's professed purpose had rested on a perception that concentrated ownership was simply unjust? Or that private ownership of property was tantamount to theft? In short, is there anything in the constitutional restrictions on eminent domain, any more than in modern economic due process analyses, to bar a socialist governmental policy?

———

B. THE CONTRACTS CLAUSE

Introduction. During the first century of the Constitution, the prohibition of any state "Law impairing the Obligation of Contracts," Art. I, § 10, was the major restraint on state economic regulation. Since the late 19th century, when the Court began to develop substantive due process restraints on economic regulation, the contracts clause has played a less prominent role in constitutional litigation. And as economic due process restrictions waned beginning in the 1930s, contract clause barriers diminished as well. Until the 1970s, indeed, the widespread modern view was that interpretations of the contracts and due process clauses had merged to such an extent that the "results might be the same if the contract clause were dropped out of the Constitution, and the challenged statutes all judged as reasonable or unreasonable deprivations of property" under due process.[1] Yet the contracts clause deserves separate attention. It *was,* after all, the major textual basis for judicial protection of "fundamental" economic rights for many years. It *is,* unlike most of the fundamental values of the Lochner era, an explicit constitutional guarantee. And, most important, the modern Court has at times demonstrated that the contracts clause has a bite greater than that of due process. In short, the contracts clause has an importance of its own, in contemporary as well as historical terms. The opening note reviews the developments in the 19th century. The principal case that follows, Blaisdell, came in 1934, the same year as Nebbia (p. 474 above), and suggested a loosening of contracts clause restraints paralleling those regarding due process. The section concludes with some modern cases disclosing occasional revitalizations of the contracts clause.

1. Hale, "The Supreme Court and the Contract Clause: III," 57 Harv.L.Rev. 852, 890 (1944).

The contracts clause in the 19th century. The major purpose of the contracts clause was to restrain state laws affecting private contracts. It was aimed mainly at debtor relief laws—e.g., laws postponing payments of debts and laws authorizing payments in installments or in commodities. Yet the Court first interpreted the clause in cases involving public grants rather than private contracts. See, e.g., Fletcher v. Peck, 6 Cranch (10 U.S.) 87 (1810),[2] and Dartmouth College v. Woodward, 4 Wheat. (17 U.S.) 518 (1819).[3] As Marshall said in Dartmouth College: "It is more than possible that the preservation of rights of this description was not particularly in the view of the framers of the Constitution. [It] is probable that interferences of more frequent recurrence, [of] which the mischief was more extensive, constituted the great motive for imposing this restriction on the State legislatures." But that, he found, was no reason for limiting the scope of the clause to private contracts. A few weeks after Dartmouth College, the Marshall Court applied the contracts clause to a law closer to the "mischief" which had motivated the Framers: in Sturges v. Crowninshield, 4 Wheat. (17 U.S.) 122 (1819), the Court held unconstitutional a New York insolvency law discharging debtors of their obligations upon surrender of their property.

Historians have probably exaggerated the impact of the early contracts clause decisions on American economic and legal developments. The cases did indeed restrict; but they did *not* compel legislative paralysis, they were *not* the keystone of American corporate development, they did *not* establish an inflexible safeguard for all vested rights. (For an extreme example of the recurrent hyperbole in comments on the early cases, see Sir Henry Maine's statement that the contracts clause "is the bulwark of American individualism against democratic impatience and socialistic fantasy." Popular Government (1885), 247–48.) The lack of statutory restrictions on corporations in the 19th century, for example, was probably more attributable to the legislators' unwillingness to enact them than to any constitutionally imposed incapacities. Indeed, in Dartmouth College itself, Justice Story's concurring opinion had pointed out what state political leaders already knew well: "If the legislature mean to claim such an authority [to alter or amend corporate charters], it must be reserved in the grant." Yet many states failed to include adequate reservations of amending powers in corporate charters even after the Dartmouth decision. In short, the protected position of corporations later in the 19th century was due less to any shield supplied by the Court than to legislative unwillingness to impose restraints—an unwillingness reflecting the laissez faire philosophy of the day.

Moreover, from the beginning the Court's interpretations assured that, even in the absence of a reserved power to amend grants, the contracts clause would not be an inflexible barrier to public regulation. Only a few of the bases for sustaining state regulatory authority can be noted here. See generally Wright, The Contract Clause of the Constitution (1938). Thus, just a few years after Dartmouth College, a divided Court stated that the contracts clause did not prohibit *all* state insolvency laws: Ogden v. Saunders, 12 Wheat. (25 U.S.) 213 (1827), held that such laws could be validly applied to contracts made *after*

---

2. In 1795, several companies had obtained a huge grant of land from the Georgia legislature. There were charges of bribery, and a new legislature annulled the grant in 1796. The grantees had in the meanwhile sold their lands to investors. The Court held the 1796 law invalid: according to Marshall, the law was barred "either by general principles which are common to our free institutions, or by the particular provisions" of the Constitution. On the background of the controversy, see Magrath, Yazoo: Law and Politics in the New Republic (1966).

3. The Court struck down New Hampshire's effort to "pack" the College Board of Trustees by increasing its size, finding that the law violated the 1769 charter of the College that had given the trustees the power to fill all Board vacancies.

the law was enacted; the earlier decision in Sturges, the Court made clear, applied only to retroactive insolvency laws. Moreover, the Court soon elaborated a distinction stated in Sturges: that the constitutional ban on the impairment of contracts "obligations" did not prohibit legislative changes in "remedies." Thus, in Bronson v. Kinzie, 1 How. (42 U.S.) 311 (1843), the Court stated that the permissible scope of remedial changes depended on their "reasonableness," provided "no substantial right" was impaired.[4] The early Court also safeguarded against excessively broad interpretations of publicly granted privileges. In Providence Bank v. Billings, 4 Pet. (29 U.S.) 514 (1830), for example, Marshall refused to read an implied immunity from taxation into a bank's charter. Taney, Marshall's successor, quickly developed that approach, in the better-known Charles River Bridge Case in 1837. Charles River Bridge v. Warren Bridge, 11 Pet. (36 U.S.) 420 (1837). See Kutler, Privilege and Creative Destruction: The Charles River Bridge Case (1971). There, the company's charter to operate a toll bridge did not prevent the state from authorizing the construction of a competing, free bridge: "[Any] ambiguity in the terms of the contract must operate against the adventurers, and in favour of the public." Moreover, the states were not left entirely powerless even where the interpretation of granted privileges uncovered a corporate immunity. Certain powers of the state were held to be inalienable. No legislative assurance that the power of eminent domain would not be exercised could prevent subsequent action taking corporate property upon payment of just compensation. See, e.g., West River Bridge Co. v. Dix, 6 How. (47 U.S.) 507 (1848). So, still more important, with at least some exercises of the police power: a Mississippi grant of a charter to operate a lottery did not bar the enforcement of a later law prohibiting lotteries. Stone v. Mississippi, 101 U.S. 814 (1880). As a later Court put it broadly: "It is settled that neither the 'contract' clause nor the 'due process' clause has the effect of overriding the power of the State to establish all regulations that are reasonably necessary to secure the health, safety, good order, comfort, or general welfare of the community; that this power can neither be abdicated nor bargained away, and is inalienable even by express grant; and that all contract and property rights are held subject to its fair exercise." Atlantic Coast Line R. Co. v. Goldsboro, 232 U.S. 548 (1914). And so with private contracts: "[P]arties by entering into contracts may not estop the legislature from enacting laws intended for the public good." Manigault v. Springs, 199 U.S. 473 (1905). In the late 19th century, the Court used broad language of that sort primarily in cases involving prohibitions of matters widely regarded as "evil"—e.g., lotteries and intoxicating beverages. Would the Court also sustain legislation provoked by 20th century economic crises—the modern versions of the debtor relief laws that had motivated the adoption of the clause? Blaisdell, which follows, addresses that question.

Home Building & Loan Ass'n v. Blaisdell

290 U.S. 398, 54 S.Ct. 231, 78 L.Ed. 413 (1934).

[The Minnesota Mortgage Moratorium Law of 1933, enacted during the Depression, authorized relief from mortgage foreclosures and execution sales of

----

4. Justice Cardozo was guilty of something of an understatement when he said that the "dividing line" between remedy and obligation "is at times obscure." W. B. Worthen Co. v. Kavanaugh, 295 U.S. 56 (1935). Yet the permissibility of remedial changes provided some flexibility: it authorized extensions of time, for example, so long as extensions were not "so piled up as to make the remedy a shadow," as Cardozo put it.

real property. Local courts were permitted to extend the period of redemption from foreclosure sales "for such additional time as the court may deem just and equitable," but not beyond May 1, 1935. Extensions were to be conditioned upon an order requiring the mortgagor to "pay all or a reasonable part" of the fair income or rental value of the property toward the payment of taxes, insurance, interest and principal. No action for a deficiency judgment could be brought during such a court-extended period of redemption. The Blaisdells obtained a court order under the Act extending the period of redemption on condition that they pay the Association $40 per month. This extension clearly modified the lender's contractual right to foreclose. The highest state court sustained the law as an "emergency" measure.]

Chief Justice HUGHES delivered the opinion of the Court.

[In] determining whether the provision for this temporary and conditional relief exceeds the power of the State by reason of the [contracts clause], we must consider the relation of emergency to constitutional power, the historical setting of [the] clause, the development of the jurisprudence of this Court in the construction of that clause, and the principles of construction which we may consider to be established. Emergency does not create power. Emergency does not increase granted power [or] diminish the restrictions imposed upon power [granted]. While emergency does not create power, emergency may furnish the occasion for the exercise of power. [T]he reasons which led to the adoption of [the clause have] frequently been described. The widespread distress following the revolutionary period, and the plight of debtors, had called forth in the States an ignoble array of legislative schemes for the defeat of creditors and the invasion of contractual obligations. Legislative interferences had been so numerous and extreme that the confidence essential to prosperous trade had been undermined and the utter destruction of credit was threatened. [It] was necessary to interpose the restraining power of a central authority in order to secure the foundations even of "private faith." But full recognition of the occasion and general purposes of the clause does not suffice to fix its precise scope. [To] ascertain the scope of the [clause] we examine the course of judicial decisions in its application. These put it beyond question that the prohibition is not an absolute one and is not to be read with literal exactness like a mathematical formula. [The] inescapable problems of construction have been: What is a contract? What are the obligations of contracts? What constitutes impairment of these obligations? What residuum of power is there still in the States [to] protect the vital interests of the [community]?

Not only is the [contracts clause] qualified by the measure of control which the State retains over remedial processes, but the State also continues to possess authority to safeguard the vital interests of its people. [The] reservation of essential attributes of sovereign power [is] read into contracts as a postulate of the legal order. The policy of protecting contracts against impairment presupposes the maintenance of a government by virtue of which contractual relations are [worth while]. This principle of harmonizing the constitutional prohibition with the necessary residuum of state power has had progressive recognition in the decisions of this Court. [The] protective power of the State, its police power, may be exercised [in] directly preventing the immediate and literal enforcement of contractual obligations by a temporary and conditional restraint, where vital public interests would otherwise suffer. Undoubtedly, whatever is reserved of state power must be consistent with the fair intent of the constitutional limitation of that power. The reserved power cannot be construed so as to destroy the limitation, nor is the limitation to be construed to destroy the reserved power in its essential aspects. They must be construed in harmony with each other. This principle precludes a construction which would permit the State to adopt as its policy the repudiation of debts or the destruction of contracts or the denial of means to enforce them. But it does not follow that conditions may not arise in which a temporary restraint of enforcement may be consistent with the spirit and purpose of the constitutional [provision]. If state power exists to give temporary relief from the enforcement of contracts in the presence of disasters due to physical causes such as fire, flood, or earthquake, that power cannot be said to be nonexistent when the urgent public need demanding such relief is produced [by] economic causes. [It] is manifest from [our] decisions that there has been a growing appreciation of public needs and of the necessity of finding ground for a rational compromise between individual rights and public welfare. [The] question is no longer merely that of one party to a contract as against another, but of the use of reasonable means to safeguard the economic structure upon which the good of all depends.

It is no answer to say that this public need was not apprehended a century ago, or to insist that what the provision of the Constitution meant to the vision of that day it must mean to the vision of our time. If by the statement that what the Constitution meant at the time of its adoption it means today, it is intended to say that the great clauses of the Constitution must be confined to the interpretation which the framers, with the conditions and outlook of their time, would have placed upon them, the statement carries its own refutation. It was to guard against such a narrow conception that Chief Justice Marshall uttered the memorable warning—"We must never forget, that it is *a constitution* we are expounding" [McCulloch]. [When] we consider the contract clause and the decisions which have expounded it, [we] find no warrant for the conclusion that the clause has been warped by these decisions from its proper significance or that the founders of our government would have interpreted the clause differently had they had occasion to assume that responsibility in the conditions of the later day. [With] a growing recognition of public needs and the relation of individual right to public security, the Court has sought to prevent the perversion of the clause through its use as an instrument to throttle the capacity of the States to protect their fundamental [interests]. Applying the criteria established by our decisions, we conclude [inter alia]: [The] conditions upon which the period of redemption is extended do not appear to be unreasonable. [The] integrity of the mortgage indebtedness is not impaired; interest continues to run; the validity of the sale and the right of a mortgagee-purchaser to title or to obtain a deficiency judgment, if the mortgagor fails to redeem within the extended period, are maintained; and the conditions of redemption, if redemption there be, stand as they were under the prior law. If it be determined, as it must be, that the contract clause is not an absolute [restriction] of the State's protective power, this legislation is clearly so reasonable as to be within the legislative competency. [The] legislation is temporary in operation. It is limited to the exigency which called it forth. [T]he operation of the statute itself could not validly outlast the emergency or be so extended as virtually to destroy the contracts. We are of the opinion that the Minnesota statute as here applied does not violate the [contracts clause].

Judgment affirmed.[1]

Justice SUTHERLAND, dissenting.

If it be possible by resort to the testimony of history to put any question of constitutional intent beyond the domain of uncertainty, the [history reviewed

---

1. For a sharp criticism of the Court's broad reading of the police power and its alleged departure from original intent, see Epstein, "Toward a Revitalization of the Contract Clause," 51 U.Chi.L.Rev. 703 (1984).

earlier in the dissent] leaves no reasonable ground upon which to base a denial that the [contracts clause] was meant to foreclose state action impairing the obligation of contracts *primarily and especially* in respect of such action aimed at giving relief to debtors *in time of emergency*. [A] statute which materially delays enforcement of the mortgagee's contractual right of ownership and possession does not modify the remedy merely; it destroys, for the period of delay, *all* remedy so far as the enforcement of that right is concerned. The phrase "obligation of a contract" in the constitutional sense imports a legal duty to perform the specified obligation of *that* contract, not to substitute and perform, against the will of one of the parties, a different [obligation]. And a state [has] no more power to accomplish such a substitution than has one of the parties to the contract against the will of the other. [If] it could, the efficacy of the constitutional restriction would, in large measure, be made to [disappear]. [Justices Van Devanter, McReynolds and Butler joined this dissent.]

————

Contracts clause cases between Blaisdell and the late 1970s. Although most cases in the four decades after Blaisdell rejected contracts clause attacks on state laws, Blaisdell did not assure the validity of all state measures. Soon after Blaisdell, for example, Worthen Co. v. Thomas, 292 U.S. 426 (1934), struck down an Arkansas law exempting most payments under life insurance policies from garnishment. Nevertheless, by the late 1960s, the restraints imposed by the contracts clause seemed minor. EL PASO v. SIMMONS, 379 U.S. 497 (1965), symbolized the Warren Court's reluctance to invalidate. The 8-1 decision upheld a Texas effort to wipe out the rights of purchasers of certain public lands to reinstate their interests in the lands by payment of delinquent interest. Although Justice WHITE's majority opinion conceded that the Texas curtailment of reinstatement rights modified the State's contractual obligation, not merely the remedy, he found it justified because of the public interest. Emphasizing the importance of the State's purposes, he insisted that "not every modification of a contractual promise" violates the clause. Justice BLACK's dissent argued that "the Court through its balancing process states the case in a way inevitably destined to bypass the Contract Clause and let Texas break its solemn obligation."

————

HOW FAR HAS THE MODERN COURT REVITALIZED THE CONTRACTS CLAUSE?

1. *State obligations.* In 1977, for the first time in about 40 years, the Court invalidated a state law as violating the contracts clause, in UNITED STATES TRUST CO. v. NEW JERSEY, 431 U.S. 1. The prevailing opinion in the 4-3 decision was by Justice BLACKMUN.[1] He suggested that a law impairing a state's *own* obligations was entitled to less deference than legislation interfering with *private* contracts. Implementing that approach, he formulated a heightened standard of review: he insisted that a law impairing a *state* obligation must be "reasonable and necessary to serve an important public purpose" in order to pass muster under the contracts clause. The dissenters

——————

1. Justices Stewart and Powell did not participate. (They were both in the majority a   year later in Allied Structural Steel, note 2 below.)

sharply attacked this departure from the deferential stance typical of modern contracts clause decisions.

The suit was directed against the 1974 repeals of a statutory covenant made by New Jersey and New York in 1962—a covenant that had limited the ability of the Port Authority of New York and New Jersey to subsidize rail passenger transportation from revenues and reserves.[2] The covenant was designed in part to assure bondholders that bond revenues would not be used to any great extent to finance the predictably unprofitable rail operations. The New Jersey courts rejected the contracts clause challenge,[3] finding the 1974 repeal justified as "a reasonable exercise [of] police power." The Court reversed. Justice Blackmun insisted that modern interpretations of the contracts clause had not drained that provision of all force. He claimed that neither Blaisdell nor El Paso "indicated that the Contract Clause was without meaning in modern constitutional jurisprudence. [Whether] or not the protection of contract rights comports with current views of wise public policy, the Contract Clause remains a part of our written Constitution." Justice Blackmun had little difficulty finding that the 1974 repeal had "the effect of impairing a contractual obligation." But "a finding that there has been a technical impairment is merely a preliminary step in resolving the more difficult question whether that impairment is [unconstitutional]." It was in pursuing that question that Justice Blackmun set forth a standard of review more intensive than that customary in prior contracts clause cases. Where a state interference with *private* contracts is challenged, "courts properly defer to legislative judgment as to the necessity and reasonableness of a particular measure," as is "customary in reviewing economic and social regulation." (Cf. note 2 below.) But greater judicial scrutiny was warranted when a state was charged with impairing its *own* obligations: "As with laws impairing the obligations of private contracts, an impairment [of state obligations] may be constitutional if it is reasonable and necessary to serve an important public purpose. In applying this standard, however, complete deference to a legislative assessment of reasonableness and necessity is not appropriate because the State's self-interest is at stake. [If] a State could reduce its financial obligations whenever it wanted to spend the money for what it regarded as an important public purpose, the Contract Clause would provide no protection at all." Applying that "dual standard"— with heightened scrutiny for a *state's* impairment of its own obligations— Justice Blackmun rejected the state courts' view that the police power justified state repudiations so long as they fell short of "total destruction of the prior obligation." He accordingly proceeded to engage in an independent analysis of the "reasonableness" and "necessity" of the repeal in this case.

Justice Blackmun conceded the importance of "mass transportation, energy conservation, and environmental protection" as legislative goals. But he rejected New Jersey's contention that "these goals are so important that any harm to bondholders from repeal of the 1962 covenant is greatly outweighed by the public benefit": "We do not accept this invitation to engage in a utilitarian comparison of public benefit and private loss. Contrary to Mr. Justice Black's fear expressed in sole dissent in [El Paso], the Court has not 'balanced away' the limitation on state action imposed by the Contract Clause. Thus a State

2. The Port Authority was established by a bistate compact between New York and New Jersey; its activities (including the provision of transportation facilities) were largely financed by bonds sold to the public.

3. This suit was brought to challenge New Jersey's repeal of the 1962 covenant.

(The Company sued as both a trustee for and a holder of Port Authority bonds.) The New York legislature enacted a concurrent repeal of the covenant, and a separate suit was brought to challenge New York's action.

cannot refuse to meet its legitimate financial obligations simply because it would prefer to spend the money to promote the [public good]." And here, the repeal was neither "reasonable" nor "necessary." The States argued that the 1974 repeal was justified by "the States' plan for encouraging users of private automobiles to shift to public transportation" by raising bridge and tunnel tolls and using the extra revenue from those tolls to subsidize improved commuter rail service. Repeal of the 1962 covenant was supposedly necessary to implement this plan "because the new mass transit facilities could not possibly be self-supporting and the covenant's 'permitted deficits' level had already been exceeded." But that argument proved unpersuasive: "We reject this justification because the repeal was neither necessary to achievement of the plan nor reasonable in light of the circumstances." Justice Blackmun rejected the claim that "choosing among these alternatives is a matter for legislative discretion," replying that "a State is not completely free to consider impairing the obligations of its own contracts on a par with other policy alternatives. Similarly, a State is not free to impose a drastic impairment when an evident and more moderate course would serve its purpose equally well." (In a brief concurring notation, Chief Justice BURGER stated that, to avoid contracts clause invalidation, a state must demonstrate "that the impairment was essential to the achievement of an important state purpose.")

Justice BRENNAN's strongly worded dissent, joined by Justices White and Marshall, insisted that the decision rejected the "previous understanding" "that lawful exercises of a State's police power stand paramount to private rights held under contract" and "remolds the Contract Clause into a potent instrument for overseeing important policy determinations of the state legislature. At the same time, by creating a constitutional safe haven for property rights embodied in a contract, the decision substantially distorts modern constitutional jurisprudence governing regulation of private economic interests." He accused the Court of "dust[ing] off" the clause and "fundamentally misconceiv[ing]" its nature. Extending the clause to cover governmental as well as private contracts was itself an extension of the Framers' purpose, he recalled. Later decisions had sought to interpret the clause in situations such as this "consistently with the demands of our governing processes." For a century, he insisted, the "central principle" had been to accord "unusual deference to the lawmaking authority of state and local governments." But this decision, he claimed, imposed "severe substantive restraints on New Jersey's attempt to free itself from a contractual provision that it deems inconsistent with the broader interests of its citizens." The Court's "reasonable and necessary" standard of review, he objected, "stands the Contract Clause completely on its head and both formulates and strictly applies a novel standard for reviewing a State's attempt to relieve its citizens from unduly harsh contracts entered into by earlier legislators." Moreover, there was no justification for the Court's "multi-headed view of the scope of the Clause," applying "different standards for reviewing governmental interference with public and private contractual obligations." In his closing passages, Justice Brennan found reason for "broader concern." He noted: that, in economic due process adjudication, the Court had abandoned the Lochner view. But, he added: "If today's case signals return to substantive constitutional review of States' policies, [then] more than the citizens of New Jersey and New York will be the losers." He added that he was not suggesting that states "should blithely proceed down the path of repudiating their obligations, financial or otherwise." But their need for "credibility in the credit market" as well as the political processes were likely to be substantial safeguards against that. He concluded: "[T]his Court should have learned long ago that the Constitution—be it through the Contract or Due Process

Clause—can actively intrude into such economic and policy matters only if my Brethren are prepared to bear enormous institutional and social costs."

2. *Private obligations.* The Court continued the process of reinvigorating the contracts clause in ALLIED STRUCTURAL STEEL CO. v. SPANNAUS, 438 U.S. 234 (1978), a decision criticized by the dissent as "greatly expand[ing] the reach of the Clause." Unlike United States Trust, the 1978 case involved the application of the clause to private rather than state obligations. The 5-3 decision invalidated the application of Minnesota's Private Pension Benefits Protection Act.[4] Justice STEWART's majority opinion held that the Act's imposition of a new obligation on the employer violated the clause. He found the impact of the law both "substantial" and "severe," emphasizing that the law retroactively modified the payment obligations assumed by the company under its voluntarily established pension plan, and that the element of reliance was vital, since the state had intervened in a previously unregulated area. Justice Stewart conceded that the contracts clause had "receded into comparative desuetude" with the rise of due process jurisprudence. But, he insisted, "the Contract Clause [is] not a dead letter." He commented that "the severity of the impairment measures the height of the hurdle the state legislation must clear. Minimal alteration of contractual obligations may end the inquiry at its first stage. Severe impairment, on the other hand, will push the inquiry to a careful examination of the nature and purpose of the state legislation. [Here, the Company] had no reason to anticipate that its employees' pension rights could become vested except in accordance with the terms of the plan. It relied heavily, and reasonably, on this legitimate contractual expectation in calculating its annual contributions to the pension fund." The law nullified "express terms of the company's contractual obligations and impose[d] a completely unexpected liability in potentially disabling amounts." He added: "[This] law simply does not possess the attributes of those state laws that in the past have survived [challenge]. The law was not even purportedly enacted to deal with a broad, generalized economic or social problem. Cf. [Blaisdell]." Moreover, the law was not "enacted to protect a broad societal interest rather than a narrow class." In addition, it did not "operate in an area already subject to state regulation. [It] did not effect simply a temporary alteration of the contractual relationships of those within its coverage, but worked a severe, permanent, and immediate change in those relationships—irrevocably and retroactively. Cf. [United States Trust]. And its narrow aim was leveled not at every Minnesota employer, not even at every Minnesota employer who left the State, but only at those who had in the past been sufficiently enlightened as voluntarily to agree to establish pension plans for their employees."

Justice BRENNAN's dissent, joined by Justices White and Marshall, insisted that the clause was applicable only to laws which "diminished or nullified" private contractual obligations. Here, the law, "like all positive social legislation," simply imposed "new, additional obligations on a particular class of persons." The only relevant constitutional limitation in the case was due process, and that guarantee had not been violated. Enlarging the employer's obligations raised no contracts clause issue: the Court, the dissent insisted, had acted on the "mistaken" premise that the clause protects "all contract based

4. Under the Act, employers who had established an employee pension plan and who terminated the plan or closed a Minnesota office were required to pay a "pension funding charge" if their pension funds were insufficient to finance full pensions for all employees who had worked at least 10 years. When the Company closed its Minnesota office in 1975, it was subjected to a charge of about $185,000 because some discharged workers, who had no vested rights under the pension plan, had been employed for more than 10 years.

expectations from unjustifiable interference" and had "distort[ed]" the meaning of the clause by interpreting the ban against "impairing" obligations as "including laws which create new duties." The Court's broad reading of the clause, Justice Brennan argued, created "anomalies" and threatened "to undermine the jurisprudence of property rights developed over the last 40 years." He added: "Under the Court's opinion, any law that may be characterized as 'superimposing' new obligations on those provided for by contract is to be regarded as creating 'sudden, substantial, and unanticipated burdens' and then to be subjected to the most exacting scrutiny. The validity of such a law will turn upon whether judges see it as a law that deals with a generalized social problem, whether it is temporary (as few will be) or permanent, whether it operates in an area previously subject to regulation, and, finally, whether its duties apply to a broad class of persons. The necessary consequence of the extreme malleability of these rather vague criteria is to vest judges with broad subjective discretion to protect property interests that happen to appeal to them." [On the late 1970s cases, see Note, "A Process–Oriented Approach to the Contract Clause," 89 Yale L.J. 1623 (1980), and Note, "Rediscovering the Contract Clause," 97 Harv.L.Rev. 1414 (1984).]

3. *A partial return to greater deference?* Although the late 1970s decisions had suggested stricter scrutiny, two 1983 decisions seemed more deferential, for the Court unanimously rejected contracts clause attacks on alleged state impairments of private contracts. The first decision was ENERGY RESERVES GROUP v. KANSAS POWER & LIGHT CO., 459 U.S. 400 (1983). Kansas Power & Light (KPL) was a party to a 1975 contract with Energy Reserves Group (ERG), pursuant to which ERG supplied natural gas to KPL at a price that was set in the contract, but which, according to the contract, could be raised to match any governmentally fixed price that exceeded the contract price. When Congress passed the Natural Gas Policy Act of 1978, Kansas responded by enacting a law which in effect precluded ERG from using the price escalator clause in the contract to the full extent of the 1978 federal increase. ERG claimed that the 1975 contract allowed it to take advantage of subsequent changes in governmental price ceilings and that the Kansas limitation therefore violated the contracts clause by limiting a price increase that otherwise would have been permissible. In rejecting this challenge, Justice BLACKMUN announced a three-step inquiry supposedly derived from the Court's recent decisions. The first step was " 'whether the state law has, in fact, operated as a substantial impairment of a contractual relationship.' " If there was such a "substantial impairment," then, as a second step, "the State, in justification, must have a significant and legitimate public purpose behind the regulation [United States Trust], such as the remedying of a broad and general social or economic problem. [Allied Steel.]" The final step was to determine "whether the adjustment of 'the rights and responsibilities of contracting parties [is based] upon reasonable conditions and [is] of a character appropriate to the public purpose justifying [the legislation's] adoption.' [United States Trust.] Unless the State itself is a contracting party, '[a]s is customary in reviewing economic and social regulation,' [courts] properly defer to a legislative judgment as to the necessity and reasonableness of a particular measure." On the first step of the inquiry, Justice Blackmun noted that, because ERG knew at the time of the contracting that it was subject to both state and federal regulation of prices, a change in those very regulations would not constitute the "substantial impairment" required to trigger the contracts clause. "In short, ERG's reasonable expectations have not been impaired by the Kansas Act." Despite that conclusion, Justice Blackmun undertook the final two steps of the inquiry as well. He concluded that, even if there was an

impairment, it was justified by Kansas' "significant and legitimate" interest in protecting consumers from the escalation of natural gas prices. On the third step, he concluded that Kansas had chosen appropriate, reasonable means to achieve its purpose. [Justice POWELL's concurrence, joined by Chief Justice Burger and Justice Rehnquist, agreed that the threshold requirement of substantial impairment had not been satisfied, thought this conclusion "dispositive," and stated that "it is unnecessary for the Court" to address the other issues in its three-step analysis.]

A few months later, in EXXON CORP. v. EAGERTON, 462 U.S. 176 (1983), the Court was once again quite deferential in rejecting a contracts clause challenge. Moreover, Justice MARSHALL, for the unanimous Court, found it unnecessary to engage in any part of the three-step inquiry of the Energy Reserves Case. He emphasized that the alleged impairment of contractual obligations was merely the incidental by-product of "a generally applicable rule of conduct." At issue was an increase in the Alabama severance tax for oil and gas extracted from Alabama wells, coupled with a prohibition on passing on the increase from producers to purchasers. Rejecting that attack, Justice Marshall drew a sharp distinction between laws specifically directed at contractual obligations and those, like the one here, that merely had the *effect* of impairing contractual rights: "[T]he pass-through prohibition did not prescribe a rule limited in effect to contractual obligations or remedies, but instead imposed a generally applicable rule of conduct designed to advance 'a broad societal interest.'" Because the pass-through prohibition imposed a generally applicable rule of conduct, "it is sharply distinguishable from the measures struck down in [United States Trust and Allied Steel]," both of which involved laws whose "sole effect" was to alter contractual duties. [Do these 1983 decisions truly leave U.S. Trust and Allied Steel unimpaired? See generally Sterk, "The Continuity of Legislatures: Of Contracts and the Contracts Clause," 88 Colum.L.Rev. 647 (1988).]

4. *Retroactivity and regulatory laws.* Retroactivity is a pervasive concern in the preceding cases: the extent to which reasonable private expectations are defeated by governmental action is the focus of many of the opinions. That is so not only with respect to the contracts clause, which on its face purports to safeguard prior contractual arrangements, but also in such "taking" opinions as Pennsylvania Coal. But the contracts clause applies only to state, not federal, action; and retroactive legislation may affect private rights other than those based on a "contract." Moreover, despite occasional arguments to the contrary, the ex post facto clauses have long been held to apply only to criminal, not civil, legislation. Is there any other, more general, constitutional safeguard against retroactive legislation? Some additional restraint on retroactivity has been found in due process, particularly in challenges to federal legislation. But, like the contracts clause and "takings" barriers, this due process limit may not help if there is a sufficiently overriding public interest. See generally Hochman, "The Supreme Court and the Constitutionality of Retroactive Legislation," 73 Harv.L.Rev. 692 (1960); Munzer, "A Theory of Retroactive Legislation," 61 Tex.L.Rev. 425 (1982). With respect to federal legislation, the due process retroactivity barrier (like the contracts clause restraint on states) has been found greater when the government seeks to modify its own contractual obligations than when it regulates private contracts. For an example of the first situation, see Lynch v. United States, 292 U.S. 571 (1934), where the Court held that Congress could not cancel government war risk life insurance policies, as it had attempted to do in 1933 because of the Depression crisis. On the second situation, regarding alleged federal interference with private contracts, note the Court's deferential approach in Pension Benefit Guaranty Corp. v.

R.A. Gray & Co., 467 U.S. 717 (1984), commenting that it had never held that Fifth Amendment due process principles "are coextensive with prohibitions in [the contracts clause]," noting that retroactive legislation may offend due process if it is "particularly harsh and oppressive," but adding that "the strong deference accorded legislation in the field of national economic policy is no less applicable when that legislation is applied retroactively." See also National R. Passenger Corp. v. A.T. & S.F.R. Co., 470 U.S. 451 (1985), rejecting a due process challenge advanced as a federal analogue to contracts clause restraints and indicating that the Court, in reviewing federal economic legislation, applies a "less searching inquiry" than that appropriate in contracts clause cases.

SECTION 3.   THE REVIVAL OF SUBSTANTIVE DUE PROCESS, FOR NONECONOMIC RIGHTS: PRIVACY; AUTONOMY; FAMILY RELATIONS; SEXUALITY; THE RIGHT TO DIE

———

Introduction. We now return to substantive due process, the theme of sec. 1. The question here, as there, is whether due process authorizes the Court to resort to fairly open-ended modes of constitutional adjudication: to pour into the due process clause fundamental values not traceable to constitutional text or history or structure. The modern cases contain frequent assertions that the Lochner approach is discredited. But is it? This section focuses on modern decisions that critics have characterized as indistinguishable from the Lochner philosophy. The modern trend began with Griswold in 1965, striking down a ban on the use of contraceptives, and Roe v. Wade in 1973, invalidating most abortion-related laws. Do Griswold, Roe, and their progeny constitute "Lochnerizing," or are they distinguishable? Do they suggest that "Lochnerizing" is justifiable after all? Before turning to the decisions, a brief historical reminder is appropriate. Griswold and Roe were not sudden revivals of substantive due process: in one sense, they built on an aspect of the Lochner tradition that never wholly died. True, the applications of Lochner that curtailed economic regulation clearly waned in the 1930s. But the Lochner era's protection of "fundamental values" was not wholly limited to economic rights: to the Court of that era, there was no sharp distinction between economic and noneconomic, "personal" liberties; some of the Lochner era decisions did protect personal rights; and the modern Court had no qualms about citing those decisions.

MEYER v. NEBRASKA, 262 U.S. 390 (1923), is an outstanding example. Its broad reading of "liberty" came from the pen of Justice McREYNOLDS, supposedly one of the most reactionary of the "Old Men" of the majority that provoked the Court-packing crisis of the 1930s; and that "libertarian" Meyer decision came over the dissent of Justice Holmes. In Meyer, the Court reversed the conviction of a teacher for teaching German and thus violating a state law prohibiting the teaching of foreign languages to young children. Recall Justice McReynolds's broad view of "liberty" (noted earlier), a view encompassing the personal as well as the economic: "Without doubt, it denotes not merely freedom from bodily restraint but also the right of the individual to contract, to engage in any of the common occupations of life, to acquire useful knowledge, to marry, establish a home and bring up children, to worship God according to the dictates of his own conscience, and generally to enjoy those privileges long recognized at common law as essential to the orderly pursuit of happiness by free men." Justice McReynolds found that the Nebraska law "materially" interfered "with the calling of modern language teachers, with the opportunities of pupils to acquire knowledge, and with the power of parents to control the education of their own." A legislative interest "to foster a homogeneous people with American ideals" was understandable, particularly in view of the "[u]nfortunate experiences during the late war." But now it was a "time of peace and domestic tranquility," and there was accordingly "no adequate justification" for these restraints on liberty.

Justice McREYNOLDS wrote in a similar vein for a unanimous Court two years later, in PIERCE v. SOCIETY OF SISTERS, 268 U.S. 510 (1925), sustaining a challenge by parochial and private schools to an Oregon law requiring children to attend public schools. Again, he found "no peculiar circumstances or present emergencies which demand extraordinary measures relative to primary education." Under the Meyer view of fundamental rights, the law interfered "with the liberty of parents and guardians to direct the upbringing and education of children under their control." There was no "general power of the State to standardize its children by forcing them to accept instruction from public teachers only. The child is not the mere creature of the State; those who nurture him and direct his destiny have the right, coupled with the high duty, to recognize and prepare him for additional obligations." (In the years before Griswold, the Warren Court, too, occasionally protected aspects of liberty even though they were not explicitly designated in the Constitution. For example, Aptheker v. Secretary of State, 378 U.S. 500 (1964), invalidated a provision denying passports to Communist Party members because it "too broadly and indiscriminately restricts the right to travel and thereby abridges the liberty guaranteed by the Fifth Amendment.")

In light of modern First Amendment doctrine, those cases may be explainable on the bases of freedom of speech, association, and religion, though they did not rest on them explicitly. (Justice Douglas so explained some of them in Griswold, below.) But another decision only a few years after the supposed withdrawal from the Lochner philosophy is not readily explainable on the basis of specific constitutional guarantees. SKINNER v. OKLAHOMA, 316 U.S. 535 (1942), was a forerunner of the special protection of some "fundamental interests" under the "new" equal protection, traced in the next chapter. It was an equal protection case in part, but it rested ultimately on a view akin to substantive due process. Justice DOUGLAS's opinion invalidated Oklahoma's Habitual Criminal Sterilization Act, providing for compulsory sterilization after a third conviction for a felony involving "moral turpitude," but excluding such felonies as embezzlement. Although state classifications of crimes would not ordinarily be overturned, Justice Douglas explained, that usual deference to state police power legislation was not warranted here: "We are dealing here with legislation which involves one of the basic civil rights of man. Marriage and procreation are fundamental to the very existence and survival of the race. [There] is no redemption for the individual whom the law touches. Any experiment which the State conducts is to his irreparable injury. He is forever deprived of a basic liberty. We mention these matters not to reexamine the scope of the police power of the States. We advert to them merely in emphasis of our view that *strict scrutiny* of the classification which a State makes in a sterilization law is essential, lest unwittingly, or otherwise, invidious discriminations are made against groups or types of individuals in violation of the constitutional guaranty of just and equal laws. [Sterilization] of those who have thrice committed grand larceny, with immunity for those who are embezzlers, is a clear, pointed, unmistakable discrimination."[1] But the 1942 reference in Skinner to "fundamental," "basic" liberties was extraordinary: that decision, mixing due process and equal protection considerations, was virtually the only one in that period between the demise of Lochner and Griswold to exercise special scrutiny in favor of a "fundamental liberty" not tied to a specific constitutional guarantee.[2] In short, between the Lochner era and Griswold, the methodology of substantive due process review on behalf of judicially defined, extraconstitutional, noninterpretive "fundamental values" was largely dormant. With Griswold and Roe, below, it regained greater vitality than it had had in more than a generation. Do the modern cases suggest that the Court now believes that the problem with substantive due process was not its methodology but rather that it "generally selected the 'wrong' values for protection"? Lupu, "Untangling the Strands of the Fourteenth Amendment," 77 Mich.L.Rev. 981 (1979).

Griswold v. Connecticut

381 U.S. 479, 85 S.Ct. 1678, 14 L.Ed.2d 510 (1965).

Justice DOUGLAS delivered the opinion of the Court.

Appellant Griswold is Executive Director of the Planned Parenthood League of Connecticut. Appellant Buxton is a licensed physician and a professor at the Yale Medical School who served as Medical Director for the [League]. They gave information, instruction, and medical advice to *married persons* as to the means of preventing conception. [Fees] were usually charged, although some couples were serviced free. [The] constitutionality [of two Connecticut provisions] is involved. [One] provides: "Any person who uses any drug, medicinal article or instrument for the purpose of preventing conception shall be fined not less than fifty dollars or imprisoned not less than sixty days nor more than one year or [both]." [The other] provides: "Any person who assists, abets, counsels, causes, hires or commands another to commit any offense may be prosecuted and punished as if he were the principal offender." The appellants were found guilty as accessories and fined $100 each, against the claim that the accessory statute as so applied violated the 14th Amendment. [The state appellate courts affirmed.][1]

---

1. [Emphasis added.] Compare Buck v. Bell, 274 U.S. 200 (1927), sustaining a state law authorizing the sterilization of institutionalized mental defectives. Justice Holmes—in a much criticized opinion, though characteristic of his stance on substantive due process—rejected the due process claims summarily, saying that "three generations of imbeciles are enough." For a criticism of the Holmes stance, see Rogat, "The Judge as Spectator," 31 U.Chi.L.Rev. 213 (1964). For a criticism of the Skinner Court for relying on a narrow equal protection rather than a broad due process ground and thus failing to help "the thousands of institutional inmates [subject] to sterilization" at the time, see Foote, "The Proper Role of the [Supreme Court] in Civil Liberties Cases," 10 Wayne L. Rev. 457 (1964). For the background of the eugenics movement (and of Buck v. Bell), see Kevles, In the Name of Eugenics: Genetics and the Uses of Human Heredity (1985).

2. Consider Tribe, American Constitutional Law (2d ed. 1988), 1464: "[T]he Court's opinion [in Skinner] makes evident an even greater preoccupation with the notion that the state's classifications had been promulgated with their harshest effect against a relatively powerless minority, that of lower-class, as opposed to white-collar, criminals."

1. Earlier efforts to test the constitutionality of the Connecticut contraception law had been turned away by the majority of the Court on justiciability grounds. See, e.g., Tileston v. Ullman, 318 U.S. 44 (1943).

[We] are met with a wide range of questions that implicate the Due Process Clause of the 14th Amendment. Overtones of some arguments suggest that [Lochner] should be our guide. But we decline that invitation as we did in [the West Coast Hotel, Olsen v. Nebraska, Lincoln Union, and Lee Optical cases]. We do not sit as a super-legislature to determine the wisdom, need, and propriety of laws that touch economic problems, business affairs, or social conditions. This law, however, operates directly on an intimate relation of husband and wife and their physician's role in one aspect of that relation. The association of people is not mentioned in the Constitution nor in the Bill of Rights. The right to educate a child in a school of the parents' choice—whether public or private or parochial—is also not mentioned. Nor is the right to study any particular subject or any foreign language. Yet the First Amendment has been construed to include certain of those rights. By [Pierce v. Society of Sisters], the right to educate one's children as one chooses is made applicable to the States. [By Meyer v. Nebraska], the same dignity is given the right to study the German language in a private school. In other words, the State may not, consistently with the spirit of the First Amendment, contract the spectrum of available knowledge. The right of freedom of speech and press includes not only the right to utter or to print, but the right to distribute, the right to receive, the right to read [and] freedom of inquiry, freedom of thought, and freedom to [teach]. Without those peripheral rights the specific rights would be less secure. And so we reaffirm the principle of the Pierce and the Meyer cases. In NAACP v. Alabama [1958; p. 1376 below], we protected the "freedom to associate and privacy in one's association," noting that freedom of association was a peripheral First Amendment right. Disclosure of membership lists of a constitutionally valid association, we held, was invalid. In other words, the First Amendment has a penumbra where privacy is protected from governmental intrusion. In like context, we have protected forms of "association" that are not political in the customary sense but pertain to the social, legal, and economic benefit of the members [NAACP v. Button (1963; p. 1383 below)]. [The right of association], while it is not expressly included in the First Amendment, [is] necessary in making the express guarantees fully meaningful.

The foregoing cases suggest that specific guarantees in the Bill of Rights have penumbras, formed by emanations from those guarantees that help give them life and substance. Various guarantees create zones of privacy. The right of association contained in the penumbra of the First Amendment is one, as we have seen. The Third Amendment in its prohibition against the quartering of soldiers "in any house" in time of peace without the consent of the owner is another facet of that privacy. The Fourth Amendment explicitly affirms the "right of the people to be secure in their persons, houses, papers, and effects against unreasonable searches and seizures." The Fifth Amendment in its Self-Incrimination Clause enables the citizen to create a zone of privacy which government may not force him to surrender to his detriment. The Ninth Amendment provides: "The enumeration in the Constitution, of certain rights, shall not be construed to deny or disparage others retained by the people." The Fourth and Fifth Amendments were described in Boyd v. United States, 116 U.S. 616 [1886], as protection against all governmental invasions "of the sanctity of a man's home and the privacies of life." We recently referred [to] the Fourth Amendment as creating a "right to privacy, no less important than any other right carefully and particularly reserved to the people." We have had many controversies over these penumbral rights of "privacy and repose." [E.g., Skinner v. Oklahoma.] These cases bear witness that the right of privacy which presses for recognition here is a legitimate one.

The present case, then, concerns a relationship lying within the zone of privacy created by several fundamental constitutional guarantees. And it concerns a law which, in forbidding the *use* of contraceptives rather than regulating their manufacture or sale, seeks to achieve its goals by means having a maximum destructive impact upon that relationship. Such a law cannot stand in light of the familiar principle [that] a "governmental purpose to control or prevent activities constitutionally subject to state regulation may not be achieved by means which sweep unnecessarily broadly and thereby invade the area of protected freedoms." NAACP v. Alabama. Would we allow the police to search the sacred precincts of marital bedrooms for telltale signs of the use of contraceptives? The very idea is repulsive to the notions of privacy surrounding the marriage relationship. We deal with a right of privacy older than the [Bill of Rights]. Marriage is a coming together for better or for worse, hopefully enduring, and intimate to the degree of being sacred. The association promotes a way of life, not causes; a harmony in living, not political faiths; a bilateral loyalty, not commercial or social projects. Yet it is an association for as noble a purpose as any involved in our prior decisions.

Reversed.

Justice GOLDBERG, whom The Chief Justice [WARREN] and Justice BRENNAN join, concurring [in the Court's opinion].

[Although] I have not accepted the view that "due process" as used in the 14th Amendment incorporates all of the first eight Amendments, [I] do agree that the concept of liberty protects those personal rights that are fundamental, and is not confined to the specific terms of the Bill of Rights. My conclusion [that liberty] embraces the right of marital privacy though that right is not mentioned explicitly in the Constitution is supported both by numerous decisions [and] by the language and history of the Ninth Amendment, [which] reveal that the Framers [believed] that there are additional fundamental rights, protected from governmental infringement, which exist alongside those fundamental rights specifically mentioned in the first [eight] amendments. The Ninth Amendment reads, "The enumeration in the Constitution, of certain rights, shall not be construed to deny or disparage others retained by the people." [It] was proffered to quiet expressed fears that a bill of specifically enumerated rights could not be sufficiently broad to cover all essential rights and that the specific mention of certain rights would be interpreted as a denial that others were protected. [This] Court has had little occasion to interpret the Ninth Amendment,[1] [but to] hold that a right so basic and fundamental and so deep-rooted in our society as the right of privacy in marriage may be infringed because that right is not guaranteed in so many words by the first eight amendments [is] to ignore the Ninth Amendment and to give it no effect whatsoever. [I] do not mean to imply that the Ninth Amendment is applied against the States by the Fourteenth [nor] that the Ninth Amendment constitutes an independent source of rights protected from infringement by either the States or Federal Government. [Rather,] the Ninth Amendment simply lends strong support to the view that the "liberty" protected by the Fifth and [14th] Amendments [is] not restricted to rights specifically mentioned in the first eight amendments.

In determining which rights are fundamental, judges are not left at large to decide cases in light of their personal and private notions. Rather, they must look to the "traditions and [collective] conscience of our people" to determine

---

1. This Amendment has been referred to as "The Forgotten Ninth Amendment," in a book with that title by Bennet B. Patterson (1955). ...[Footnote by Justice Goldberg.]

whether a principle is "so rooted [there] as to be ranked as fundamental." [The] entire fabric of the Constitution and the purposes that clearly underlie its specific guarantees demonstrate that the rights to marital privacy and to marry and raise a family are of similar order and magnitude as the fundamental rights specifically protected. [The] logic of the dissents would sanction federal or state legislation that seems to me even more plainly unconstitutional than the statute before us. Surely the Government, absent a showing of a compelling subordinating state interest, could not decree that all husbands and wives must be sterilized after two children have been born to them. [If] upon a showing of a slender basis of rationality, a law outlawing voluntary birth control by married persons is valid, then, by the same reasoning, a law requiring compulsory birth control also would seem to be valid. In my view, however, both types of law would unjustifiably intrude upon rights of marital privacy which are constitutionally protected.

In a long series of cases this Court has held that where fundamental personal liberties are involved, they may not be abridged by the States simply on a showing that a regulatory statute has some rational relationship to the effectuation of a proper state purpose. "Where there is a significant encroachment upon personal liberty, the State may prevail only upon showing a subordinating interest which is compelling" [Bates v. Little Rock (1960; p. 1375)]. The law must be shown "necessary, and not merely rationally related, to the accomplishment of a permissible state policy." [McLaughlin v. Florida (1964; p. 669).] The State, at most, argues that there is some rational relation between this statute and what is admittedly a legitimate subject of state concern—the discouraging of extra-marital relations. It says that preventing the use of birth-control devices by married persons helps prevent the indulgence by some in such extra-marital relations. The rationality of this justification is dubious, particularly in light of the admitted widespread availability to all persons [in] Connecticut, unmarried as well as married, of birth-control devices for the prevention of disease, as distinguished from the prevention of conception. But, in any event, it is clear that the state interest in safeguarding marital fidelity can be served by a more discriminately tailored statute, which does not, like the present one, sweep unnecessarily broadly, reaching far beyond the evil sought to be dealt with and intruding upon the privacy of all married couples. [Connecticut] does have statutes, the constitutionality of which is beyond doubt, which prohibit adultery and fornication. These statutes demonstrate that means for achieving the same basic purpose of protecting marital fidelity are available to Connecticut without the need to "invade the area of protected freedoms." [In] sum, I believe that the right of privacy in the marital relation is fundamental and basic—a personal right "retained by the people" within the meaning of the Ninth Amendment, [a right] which is protected by the Fourteenth Amendment from infringement by the [States].

Justice HARLAN, concurring in the judgment.

[I] find myself unable to join the Court's opinion [because] it seems to me to evince an approach [that] the Due Process Clause of the 14th Amendment does not touch this Connecticut statute unless the enactment is found to violate some right assured by the letter or penumbra of the Bill of Rights. [In] my view, the proper constitutional inquiry in this case is whether this Connecticut statute infringes the Due Process Clause of the 14th Amendment because the enactment violates basic values "implicit in the concept of ordered liberty" [Palko]. For reasons stated at length in my dissenting opinion in Poe v. Ullman [see the excerpts which follow], I believe that it does. While the relevant inquiry may be aided by resort to one or more of the provisions of the Bill of Rights, it is not dependent on them or any of their radiations. The [Due Process Clause] stands, in my opinion, on its own bottom. [While] I could not more heartily agree that judicial "self restraint" is an indispensable ingredient of sound constitutional adjudication, I do submit that the formula suggested for achieving it is more hollow than real. "Specific" provisions of the Constitution, no less than "due process," lend themselves as readily to "personal" interpretations by judges whose constitutional outlook is simply to keep the Constitution in supposed "tune with the times." [Judicial self-restraint will be achieved] only by continual insistence upon respect for the teachings of history, solid recognition of the basic values that underlie our society, and wise application of the great roles that the doctrines of federalism and separation of powers have played [in] preserving American freedoms. Adherence to these principles will not, of course, obviate all constitutional differences of opinion among judges, nor should it. Their continued recognition will, however, go farther toward keeping most judges from roaming at large in the constitutional field than will the interpolation into the Constitution of an artificial and largely illusory restriction on the content of [due process].

[Justice Harlan relied on his dissent in POE v. ULLMAN, 367 U.S. 497, 523 (1961), where he had elaborated his due process approach and had found the application of the Connecticut law unconstitutional. The Poe majority had failed to reach the merits: it dismissed the appeal on justiciability grounds. Excerpts from Justice HARLAN's dissent in Poe follow:] [I] believe that a statute making it a criminal offense for *married couples* to use contraceptives is an intolerable and unjustifiable invasion of privacy in the conduct of the most intimate concerns of an individual's personal life. [I] feel it desirable at the outset to state the framework of Constitutional principles in which I think the issue must be [judged]. [Through] the course of this Court's decisions, [due process] has represented the balance which our Nation, built upon postulates of respect for the liberty of the individual, has struck between that liberty and the demands of organized society. [The] balance of which I speak is the balance struck by this country, having regard to what history teaches are the traditions from which it developed as well as the traditions from which it broke. That tradition is a living thing. [The] full scope of the liberty guaranteed by the Due Process Clause cannot be found in or limited by the precise terms of the specific guarantees elsewhere provided in the Constitution. This "liberty" is not a series of isolated points pricked out in terms of [such specific guarantees as speech and religion]. It is a rational continuum which, broadly speaking, includes a freedom from all substantial arbitrary impositions and purposeless restraints, see [e.g., Allgeyer; Nebbia], and which also recognizes [that] certain interests require particularly careful scrutiny of the state needs asserted to justify their abridgment. Cf. [e.g., Skinner].

It is argued by appellants that the judgment implicit in this statute—that the use of contraceptives by married couples is immoral—is an irrational one, that in effect it subjects them in a very important matter to the arbitrary whim of the legislature, and that it does so for no good purpose. [Yet] the very inclusion of the category of morality among state concerns indicates that society is not limited in its objects only to the physical well-being of the community, but has traditionally concerned itself with the moral soundness of its people as well. Indeed to attempt a line between public behavior and that which is purely consensual or solitary would be to withdraw from community concern a range of subjects with which every society in civilized times has found it necessary to deal. The laws regarding marriage which provide both when the sexual powers may be used and the legal and societal context in which children are born and brought up, as well as laws forbidding adultery, fornication and homosexual practices which express the negative of the proposi-

[handwritten: every modern case Griswold]

tion, confining sexuality to lawful marriage, form a pattern so deeply pressed into the substance of our social life that any Constitutional doctrine in this area must build upon that basis. It is in this area of sexual morality, which contains many proscriptions of consensual behavior having little or no direct impact on others, that [Connecticut] has expressed its moral judgment that all use of contraceptives is improper. [Certainly,] Connecticut's judgment is no more demonstrably correct or incorrect than are the varieties of judgment, expressed in law, on marriage and divorce, on adult consensual homosexuality, abortion, and sterilization, or euthanasia and suicide.)If we had a case before us which required us to decide simply, and in abstraction, whether the moral judgment implicit in the application of the present statute to married couples was a sound one, the very controversial nature of these questions would, I think, require us to hesitate long before concluding that the Constitution precluded Connecticut from choosing as it has among these various views. [But we] are not presented simply with this moral judgment to be passed on as an abstract proposition. The secular state is not an examiner of consciences: it must operate in the realm of behavior, of overt actions, and where it does so operate, not only the underlying, moral purpose of its operations, but also the *choice of means* becomes relevant to any Constitutional judgment on what is [done].

[handwritten right margin: sexual morality as a basis]

[handwritten right margin: not the judges place to comment on the wisdom of a law. /morality]

[handwritten: ★]

    Precisely what is involved here is this: the State is asserting the right to enforce its moral judgment by intruding upon the most intimate details of the marital relation with the full power of the criminal law. Potentially, this could allow the deployment of all the incidental machinery of the criminal law, arrests, searches and seizures; inevitably, it must mean at the very least the lodging of criminal charges, a public trial, and testimony as to the corpus delicti. Nor could any imaginable elaboration of presumptions, testimonial privileges, or other safeguards alleviate the necessity for testimony as to the mode and manner of the married couples' sexual relations, or at least the opportunity for the accused to make denial of the charges. In sum, the statute allows the State to enquire into, prove and punish married people for the private use of their marital intimacy. The statute must pass a more rigorous Constitutional test than that going merely to the plausibility of its underlying rationale. This enactment involves what, by common understanding throughout the English-speaking world, must be granted to be a most fundamental aspect of "liberty," the privacy of the home in its most basic sense, and it is this which requires that the statute be subjected to "strict scrutiny." [Skinner.] That aspect of liberty which embraces the concept of the privacy of the home receives explicit Constitutional protection at two places only [—the Third and Fourth Amendments]. [It] is clear, of course, that [this] statute does not invade the privacy of the home in the usual sense, since the invasion involved [here] doubtless usually would [be] accomplished without any physical intrusion whatever into the home. What the statute undertakes to do, however, is to create a crime which is grossly offensive to this privacy, while the Constitution refers only to methods of ferreting out substantive [wrongs]. But such an analysis forecloses any claim to Constitutional protection against this form of deprivation of privacy, only if due process in this respect is limited to what is explicitly provided in the Constitution, divorced from the rational purposes, historical roots, and subsequent developments of the relevant provisions. [If] the physical curtilage of the home is protected, it is surely as a result of solicitude to protect the privacies of the life within. [The] home derives its pre-eminence as the seat of family life. And the integrity of that life is something so fundamental that it has been found to draw to its protection the principles of more than one explicitly granted Constitutional right. [See, e.g., Meyer; Pierce.]

[handwritten right margin: intent of Const. prot- structure?]

Of [the] whole "private realm of family life" it is difficult to imagine what is more private or more intimate than a husband and wife's [marital relations].

Of course, [there] are countervailing considerations. [I]t would be an absurdity to suggest either that offenses may not be committed in the bosom of the family or that the home can be made a sanctuary for crime. The right of privacy [is] not an absolute. Thus, I would not suggest that adultery, homosexuality, fornication and incest are immune from criminal enquiry, however privately practiced. [But] not to discriminate between what is involved in this case and either the traditional offenses against good morals or crimes which, though they may be committed anywhere, happen to have been committed or concealed in the home, would entirely misconceive the argument that is being made. (Adultery, homosexuality and the like are sexual intimacies which the State forbids altogether, but the intimacy of husband and wife is necessarily an essential and accepted feature of the institution of marriage, an institution which the State not only must allow, but which always it has fostered and protected. It is one thing when the State exerts its power either to forbid extra-marital sexuality altogether, or to say who may marry, but it is quite another when, having acknowledged a marriage and the intimacies inherent in it, it undertakes to regulate by means of the criminal law the details of that intimacy. In sum, [the] intrusion of the whole machinery of the criminal law into the very heart of marital privacy, requiring husband and wife to render account before a criminal tribunal of their uses of that intimacy, is surely a very different thing indeed from punishing those who establish intimacies which the law has always forbidden and which can have no claim to social protection.) [Since the law] marks an abridgment of important fundamental liberties, [it] will not do to urge in justification [simply] that the statute is rationally related to the effectuation of a proper state purpose. A closer scrutiny and stronger justification than that are required. Though the State has argued the Constitutional permissibility of the moral judgment underlying this statute, [its arguments do not] even remotely [suggest] a justification for the obnoxiously intrusive means it has chosen to effectuate that policy. [But] conclusive, in my view, is the utter novelty of this enactment. [No other State] has made the *use* of contraceptives a crime. [Though] undoubtedly the States [should] be allowed broad scope in experimenting, [I] must agree with [Justice Jackson's concurrence in Skinner] that "There are limits to the extent to which a legislatively represented majority may [conduct] experiments at the expense of the dignity and personality" of the individual. In this instance these limits are, in my view, reached and [passed].

Justice WHITE, concurring in the judgment.

In my view this Connecticut law as applied to married couples deprives them of "liberty" without [due process]. Surely the right invoked in this case, to be free of regulation of the intimacies of the marriage relationship, "come[s] to this Court with a momentum for respect lacking when appeal is made to liberties which derive merely from shifting economic arrangements." Kovacs v. Cooper [1949; Frankfurter, J.; p. 1241 below]. The Connecticut [law] deals rather substantially with this relationship. [A] statute with these effects bears a substantial burden of justification when attacked under the 14th Amendment. [An] examination of the justification offered, however, cannot be avoided by saying that the Connecticut anti-use statute invades a protected area of privacy and association or that it demeans the marriage relationship. The nature of the right invaded is pertinent, to be sure, for statutes regulating sensitive areas of liberty [do] require "strict scrutiny" and "must be viewed in light of less drastic means for achieving the same basic purpose." [But] such statutes, if reasonably necessary for the effectuation of a legitimate and substantial state interest, and not arbitrary or capricious in application, are not [invalid].

There is no serious contention that Connecticut thinks the use of artificial or external methods of contraception immoral or unwise in itself, or that the anti-use statute is founded upon any policy of promoting population expansion. Rather, the statute is said to serve the State's policy against all forms of promiscuous or illicit sexual relationships, be they premarital or extramarital, concededly a permissible and legitimate legislative goal. [But I] wholly fail to see how the ban on the use of contraceptives by married couples in any way reinforces the State's ban on illicit sexual relationships. [Perhaps] the theory is that the flat ban on use prevents married people from possessing contraceptives and without the ready availability of such devices for use in the marital relationship, there will be no or less temptation to use them in extramarital ones. This reasoning rests on the premises that married people will comply with the anti-use ban in regard to their marital relationship, notwithstanding total nonenforcement in this context and apparent nonenforcibility, but will not comply with criminal statutes prohibiting extramarital affairs and the anti-use statute in respect to illicit sexual relationships, a premise whose validity has not been demonstrated and whose intrinsic validity is not very evident. At most the broad ban is of marginal utility to the declared objective. A statute limiting its prohibition on use to persons engaging in the prohibited relationship would serve the end posited by Connecticut in the same way, and with the same effectiveness, or ineffectiveness, as the broad anti-use statute under attack in this case. I find nothing in this record justifying the sweeping scope of this statute, with its telling effect on the freedoms of [married persons].

Justice BLACK [joined by Justice STEWART] dissenting.

[The] law is every bit as offensive to me as it is to my Brethren [who], reciting reasons why it is offensive to them, hold it unconstitutional. [But] I cannot [join] their conclusion. [The] Court talks about a constitutional ["right of privacy"]. There are, of course, guarantees in certain specific constitutional provisions which are designed in part to protect privacy at certain times and places with respect to certain activities. Such, for example, is the [Fourth Amendment]. But I think it belittles that Amendment to talk about it as though it protects nothing but "privacy." One of the most effective ways of diluting or expanding a constitutionally guaranteed right is to substitute for the crucial word or words of a constitutional guarantee another word or words, more or less flexible and more or less restricted in [meaning]. "Privacy" is a broad, abstract and ambiguous concept which can easily be shrunken in meaning but which can [also] easily be interpreted as a constitutional ban against many things other than searches and seizures. [I] get nowhere in this case by talk about a constitutional "right of privacy" as an emanation from one or more constitutional provisions.[1] I like my privacy as well as the next one, but I am nevertheless compelled to admit that government has a right to invade it unless prohibited by some specific constitutional [provision].

This brings me to the arguments made by my Brothers Harlan, White and Goldberg. [I] discuss the due process and Ninth Amendment arguments together because on analysis they turn out to be the same thing—merely using

1. The phrase "right to privacy" appears first to have gained currency from an article written by Messrs. Warren and (later Mr. Justice) Brandeis in 1890 which urged that States should give some form of tort relief to persons whose private affairs were exploited by others. The Right to Privacy, 4 Harv.L.Rev. 193. [Now, this Court exalts] a phrase which Warren and Brandeis used in discussing grounds for [common law] tort relief, to the level of a constitutional [rule]. [Footnote by Justice Black.]

different words to claim [the] power to invalidate any legislative act which the judges find irrational, unreasonable or offensive. [If] these formulas based on "natural justice" [are] to prevail, they require judges to determine what is or is not constitutional on the basis of their own appraisal of what laws are unwise or unnecessary.[2] The power to make such decisions is of course that of a legislative body. [I] do not believe that we are granted [this power.] [Of] the cases on which my Brothers White and Goldberg rely so heavily, undoubtedly the reasoning of two of them supports their result here—as would that of a number of others which they do not bother to name, e.g., [Lochner, Coppage and Adkins]. The two they do cite and quote from, [Meyer] and [Pierce], were both decided in opinions by Mr. Justice McReynolds which elaborated the same natural law due process philosophy found in [Lochner]. [That was a] philosophy which many later opinions repudiated, and which I cannot [accept].

My Brother Goldberg has adopted the recent discovery that the Ninth Amendment as well as the Due Process Clause can be used by this Court as authority to strike down all state legislation which this Court thinks violates "fundamental principles of liberty and justice," or is contrary to the "traditions and collective conscience of our people." He also states [that] in making decisions on this basis judges will not consider "their personal and private notions." One may ask how they can avoid considering them. [The Framers did not give this Court] veto powers over [lawmaking]. Nor does anything in the history of the Amendment offer any support for such a shocking doctrine. [That] Amendment was passed [to] assure the people that the [Constitution] was intended to limit the Federal Government to the powers granted expressly or by necessary implication. [This] fact is perhaps responsible for the peculiar phenomenon that for a period of a century and a half no serious suggestion was ever made that the Ninth Amendment, enacted to protect state powers against federal invasion, could be used as a weapon of federal power to prevent state legislatures from passing laws they consider appropriate to govern [local affairs].

I realize that many good and able men have eloquently spoken and written [about] the duty of this Court to keep the Constitution in tune with the times. [I] reject that philosophy. The Constitution makers knew the need for change and provided for it [through the amendment process]. [The] Due Process Clause with an "arbitrary and capricious" or "shocking to the conscience" formula was liberally used by this Court to strike down economic legislation in the early decades of this century, threatening, many people thought, the tranquility and stability of the Nation. See, e.g., [Lochner]. That formula, based on subjective considerations of "natural justice," is no less dangerous when used to enforce this Court's views about personal rights than those about economic rights. I had thought that we had laid that formula, as a means for striking down state legislation, to rest. [Apparently] my Brethren have less quarrel with state economic regulations than former Justices of their persuasion had. But any limitation upon their using the natural law due process philosophy to strike down any state law, dealing with any activity whatever, will obviously be only self-imposed. [The] late Judge Learned Hand, after

---

2. See Hand, The Bill of Rights (1958) 70: "[J]udges are seldom content merely to annul the particular solution before them; they do not, indeed they may not, say that taking all things into consideration, the legislators' solution is too strong for the judicial stomach. On the contrary they wrap up their veto in a protective veil of adjectives such as 'arbitrary,' 'artificial,' 'normal,' 'reasonable,' 'inherent,' 'fundamental,' or 'essential,' whose office usually, though quite innocently, is to disguise what they are doing and impute to it a derivation far more impressive than their personal preferences, which are all that in fact lie behind the [decision]." [Footnote by Justice Black.]

emphasizing his view that judges should not use the due process formula suggested in the concurring opinions today or any other formula like it to invalidate legislation offensive to their "personal preferences," made the statement, with which I fully agree, that: "For myself it would be most irksome to be ruled by a bevy of Platonic Guardians, even if I knew how to choose them, which I assuredly do not."[3] So far as I am concerned, Connecticut's law as applied here is not forbidden by any provision of the Federal Constitution as that Constitution was [written].

Justice STEWART, whom Justice BLACK joins, dissenting.

[I] think this is an uncommonly silly law. [But] we are not asked in this case to say whether we think this law is unwise, or even asinine. We are asked to hold that it violates [the] Constitution. And that I cannot do. In the course of its opinion the Court refers to no less than six Amendments to the Constitution [but] does not say which of these Amendments, if any, it thinks is infringed by this Connecticut law. We *are* told that the Due Process Clause of the 14th Amendment is not, as such, the "guide" in this case. With that much I agree. [As] to the First, Third, Fourth, and Fifth Amendments, I can find nothing in any of them to invalidate this Connecticut [law]. [And to] say that the Ninth Amendment has anything to do with this case is to turn somersaults with history. The Ninth Amendment, like its companion the Tenth, [was] simply to make clear that the adoption of the Bill of Rights did not alter the plan that the *Federal* Government was to be a government of express and limited powers. [What] provision of the Constitution, then, does make this state law invalid? The Court says it is the right of privacy "created by several fundamental constitutional guarantees." With all deference, I can find no such general right of privacy in the Bill of Rights, in any other part of the Constitution, or in any case ever before decided by this [Court].

GRISWOLD, PENUMBRAS, AND DOUBLE STANDARDS

1. *The constitutional basis of Griswold.* Consider the range of modes of constitutional adjudication disclosed by the opinions in Griswold. Is Justice Black right in charging that Griswold is of a piece with the free-wheeling, subjective variety of substantive due process adjudication long discredited in the economic regulation area? Or is Griswold distinguishable? How? Justice Douglas disavows Lochner as a guide. He relies instead on the "penumbras" and "emanations" of several specific guarantees in the Bill of Rights. Is the "right of privacy" he finds a legitimate derivation from the Constitution? Does that depend on what the content of that "right of privacy" is? (See note 2 below.) Does Justice Douglas's "penumbras"-"emanations" approach avoid subjective, idiosyncratic, extraconstitutional, "natural law" adjudication more effectively than the Lochner approach or the other opinions on the majority side in Griswold? Does Justice Douglas's approach channel judicial power more rigorously than do the analyses of the other opinions? Than Justice Harlan's

3. [Hand, The Bill of Rights (1958)], at 73. While Judge Hand condemned as unjustified the invalidation of state laws under the natural law due process formula, he also expressed the view that this Court in a number of cases had gone too far in holding legislation to be in violation of specific guarantees of the Bill of Rights. Although I agree with his criticism of use of the due process formula, I do not agree with all the views he expressed about construing the specific guarantees of the Bill of Rights. [Footnote by Justice Black.]

"basic values 'implicit in the concept of ordered liberty' " approach?[1] Than Justice Goldberg's Ninth Amendment-"fundamental rights" approach?[2] Does Justice Douglas's approach help distinguish "economic" and "personal" rights and justify a double standard? Are liberty of contract and the right to use property, the favored rights of the Lochner era, distinguishable because they are not specifically mentioned in the Constitution? But arguably liberty of contract could be seen as an emanation, or within the penumbra, of the contracts clause. And a general protection of property could be seen as within the penumbra of the specific mention of "property" in the condemnation clause of the Fifth Amendment—not to speak of the historical importance of property rights and the "specific" reference to property in the 14th Amendment itself.[3]

2. *The scope of "privacy" in Griswold.* What *is* the scope of the "right of privacy" recognized in Griswold? Is it the interest in preventing intrusions into the home? The interest in avoiding disclosure of personal information? The interest in the protection of the "intimacies of the marriage relationship"? A broader interest in personal autonomy—in freedom from governmental regulation of a range of personal activities that do not harm others? Consider the emphases of the various opinions in Griswold, and their implications for laws other than that banning the use of contraceptives in Griswold. And consider the distinction suggested in Note, "Roe and Paris: Does Privacy Have a Principle?" 26 Stan.L.Rev. 1161 (1974)—a distinction between two meanings of privacy: (1) a "right of selective disclosure," or interest in control of information; and (2) a private "autonomy" of choice about performing acts or undergoing experiences.[4]

3. *The Eisenstadt case.* Between Griswold and Roe, the Court decided one other case involving the control of contraceptives: EISENSTADT v. BAIRD, 405 U.S. 438 (1972). One important passage in Eisenstadt clarified (more accurately, expanded) the nature of the right of privacy. In fact, the superficially quite modest sounding Eisenstadt opinion is widely seen in retrospect as a critical stepping point from the arguably narrow ruling in Griswold to the unmistakably broad one in Roe. Griswold involved the *use* of contraceptives by

1. Compare Justice Stewart's comment on Griswold, eight years after his dissent in that case, when he concurred in Roe v. Wade, the abortion decision which follows: "Griswold stands as one in a long line of pre-Ferguson v. Skrupa cases decided under the doctrine of substantive due process, and I now accept it as such."

2. On the Ninth Amendment generally, see, e.g., Caplan, "The History and Meaning of the Ninth Amendment," 69 Va.L.Rev. 223 (1983), Berger, "The Ninth Amendment," 66 Cornell L.Rev. 1 (1980), and Symposium on Interpreting the Ninth Amendment, 64 Chi.-Kent L.Rev. 37 (1988). For a useful, critical overview of the voluminous literature on (and history of) the Ninth Amendment, see McAffee, "The Original Meaning of the Ninth Amendment," 90 Colum.L.Rev. 1215 (1990). McAffee concludes that "the affirmative rights reading of the ninth amendment cannot be firmly established as its original meaning. [The] more interesting question is the bearing of [the historical] materials on larger issues concerning the status of natural rights and notions of unwritten fundamental law in our constitutional system. The history of the ninth amendment strongly suggests that this provision articulates no such theory. Indeed, the ratification materials seem to cut against the view that at the time of the founding there was a clear consensus in favor of the concept of enforceable unwritten limitations."

3. See Kauper, "Penumbras, Peripheries, Emanations, Things Fundamental and Things Forgotten: The Griswold Case," 64 Mich.L.Rev. 235 (1965), and note generally Henkin, "Privacy and Autonomy," 74 Colum.L.Rev. 1410 (1974), and Rubenfeld, "The Right to Privacy," 102 Harv.L.Rev. 737 (1989).

4. Note the adoption of a similar distinction in Whalen v. Roe (1977; p. 601 below). Consider also what added light on the scope of constitutionally protected "privacy" and "autonomy" is shed by Roe v. Wade and Casey, which follow.

married persons; there, Justice Douglas had distinguished the regulation of the "manufacture or sale" of contraceptives from prohibitions of "use." But Eisenstadt overturned a conviction under a law banning the *distribution* of contraceptives; and, most significantly, marriage proved not to be a critical factor after all. Baird had distributed contraceptive foam, and the recipient was described by the state court as an *unmarried* person. The Court managed to avoid explicit decision of the questions of whether the fundamental right recognized in Griswold extended beyond use to distribution and beyond married couples to unmarried persons. Instead, it purported to decide the case on a minimum rationality-equal protection ground.[5] Yet, despite Justice BRENNAN's asserted care to avoid writing a "fundamental rights" opinion, he made some significant comments on Griswold in his Eisenstadt opinion: "It is true that in Griswold the right of privacy in question inhered in the marital relationship. Yet the marital couple is not an independent entity with a mind and heart of its own, but an association of two individuals each with a separate intellectual and emotional make-up. If the right of privacy means anything, it is the right of the *individual,* married or single, to be free from unwarranted governmental intrusion into matters so fundamentally affecting a person as the decision whether to bear or beget a child. See Stanley v. Georgia [1969; banning prosecution for possessing obscene materials in the home; p. 1130 below]. See also [Skinner]."[6] Justice Brennan's passing remarks in Eisenstadt proved important indeed. [See Fried, Order and Law (1991), 77, claiming that Justice Brennan's emphasis on childbearing in Eisenstadt planted the "seed [from] which Roe grew."] Not only was the decision relied on in Roe, but, little more than a decade after Griswold, Justice Brennan was also able to restate the holding of Griswold (in light of Eisenstadt and Roe) as follows: "Griswold may no longer be read as holding only that a State may not prohibit a married couple's use of contraceptives. Read in light of its progeny, the teaching of Griswold is that the Constitution protects individual decisions in matters of childbearing from unjustified intrusion by the State." After noting that "intrusion into 'the sacred precincts of marital bedrooms' made [the law in Griswold] particularly 'repulsive,'" he added that "subsequent decisions have made clear that the constitutional protection of individual autonomy in matters of childbearing is not dependent on that element."[7]

4. *Griswold and the double standard.* There is a common theme in all of the opinions supporting the majority result in Griswold: all agree that Griswold involves interests sufficiently special and cherished to warrant review at something beyond the deferential, minimum rationality stance of judicial scru-

---

5. In fact, however, the degree of equal protection rationality scrutiny exercised seemed a good deal stricter than the extremely deferential one of the post-Lochner era. See Gunther, "Foreword: [A] Model for a Newer Equal Protection," 86 Harv.L.Rev. 1 (1972).

6. For a comment that Eisenstadt decided ("by assertion, without a pretext of reasoning,") an issue left open by Griswold, the constitutionality of banning distribution of contraceptives to unmarried persons, see Wellington, "Common Law Rules and Constitutional Double Standards," 83 Yale L.J. 221 (1973). See also Posner, "The Uncertain Protection of Privacy by the Supreme Court,"

1979 Sup.Ct.Rev. 173, arguing that Eisenstadt, unlike the arguably narrow Griswold ruling, was "a pure essay in substantive due process" and that Eisenstadt "unmasks Griswold as based on the idea of sexual liberty rather than privacy." (On whether the modern cases truly protect anything as broad as "sexual liberty," see the materials following Roe v. Wade, below.)

7. This passage is from Carey (1977; p. 554 below). The Carey case involved state restrictions on the distribution and advertising of contraceptives. (The case is considered below because it reveals the impact of the later abortion decisions as well as well as the earlier contraception decisions.)

tiny. And once a heightened degree of scrutiny is justified and applied, invalidation of the law becomes much more probable. That common theme provokes once again the recurrent question: What justifies that "double standard"—of strict scrutiny in some situations, hands off in others? The frequently invoked justification suggested by Justice Stone's footnote in Carolene Products (p. 484 above) is not very helpful in a situation like Griswold. The value protected in Griswold does not fit Stone's descriptions: even the Justices to whom the core of the penumbra is most visible would not call privacy a "specific" guarantee, or one central to the "political processes." Justice Stone also suggested special judicial solicitude for some "discrete and insular minorities." Is there anything in the Griswold context that satisfies that criterion? Is it arguable, for example, that Griswold is best seen as a women's rights case? Or an equality case?[8] Or is there nothing more to be said for Griswold than could have been said for any of the Court's invalidations in the Lochner era?[9] What is clear in Griswold, then, is that all of the Justices in the majority found some ordering of constitutional values justified: *some* "fundamental values" *do* deserve special protection. That consensus poses a question common to all of the modern substantive due process cases: How does the Court determine the proper place of a particular right in the hierarchy of values? How does Justice White, for example, defend placing the right invoked in Griswold at a different place in the hierarchy from "mere" economic rights? Further consideration of this problem is postponed until after Roe v. Wade which follows. Roe raises even more acutely the twin pervasive issues: What justifies a double standard in degrees of scrutiny? What *are* the proper sources of "fundamental values"?

Roe v. Wade

410 U.S. 113, 93 S.Ct. 705, 35 L.Ed.2d 147 (1973).

[This was an attack on the Texas abortion laws—typical of those adopted by most states—making it a crime to "procure an abortion" except "by medical advice for the purpose of saving the life of the mother."[1] The challengers here

8. See Shapiro, "Fathers and Sons," in The Burger Court 216 (Blasi ed., 1983), arguing that "Griswold was an equality not a privacy decision," because the practical impact of the Connecticut law meant that middle-class women had access to birth control information and supplies, but poor women did not, since the law was enforced only against birth control clinics. See the sex discrimination materials in chap. 9 below.

9. Justice Black in his dissent obviously thought there was not. But ironically, he repeatedly quotes Judge Learned Hand. As Justice Black's footnote 3 suggests, Judge Hand repudiated any double standard and was profoundly skeptical of the judicial enforceability of the due process clause in any context, whether of civil liberties or of economic regulation: he disapproved of Justice Black's variety of "absolute" enforcement of free speech as he did of the Lochner case. As

he said of the shift in the Court after the 1937 Court crisis: "It began to seem as though, when 'personal rights' were in issue, something strangely akin to the discredited attitude toward the Bill of Rights of the old apostles of the institution of property was regaining recognition." Judge Hand thought that this was "an opportunistic reversion." To him, the principle of nonintervention via the due process clause of the 14th Amendment could not mean "that, when concerned with interests other than property, the Court should have a wider latitude for enforcing their own predilections." Do Griswold, Roe, and their progeny illustrate the validity of Hand's critique?

1. In a companion case, Doe v. Bolton, which follows, the Court also held unconstitutional most aspects of the Georgia abortion laws, less restrictive statutes with "a modern cast."

were a pregnant single woman (Jane Roe), a childless couple, with the wife not pregnant (John and Mary Doe), and a licensed physician (Dr. Hallford). The suits by Roe and the Does were class actions. The three-judge District Court ruled the Does' complaint nonjusticiable, but granted declaratory relief to Roe and Dr. Hallford, holding the law unconstitutional under the Ninth Amendment.]

Justice BLACKMUN delivered the opinion of the Court.

[We] forthwith acknowledge our awareness of the sensitive and emotional nature of the abortion controversy, of the vigorous opposing views, [and] of the deep and seemingly absolute convictions that the subject inspires. [Our] task, of course, is to resolve the issue by constitutional measurement, free of emotion and of predilection. We seek earnestly to do this, and, because we do, we have inquired into, and in this opinion place some emphasis upon, medical and medical-legal history and what that history reveals about man's attitudes toward the abortion procedure over the centuries. We bear in mind, too, Mr. Justice Holmes' admonition in his now-vindicated dissent in [Lochner]. [The] principal thrust of appellant's attack on the Texas statutes is that they improperly invade a right, said to be possessed by the pregnant woman, to choose to terminate her pregnancy. [Before] addressing this claim, we feel it desirable briefly to survey, in several aspects, the history of abortion, for such insight as that history may afford us. [Justice Blackmun's review of that history is omitted. His survey began with "ancient attitudes"—starting with "Persian Empire abortifacients"—and continued through "the Hippocratic Oath," "the common law," "English statutory law," and "American law," to the positions of the American Medical, Public Health and Bar Associations. After stating the possible state interests in restricting abortions (summarized below), he continued:]

The Constitution does not explicitly mention any right of privacy. [But] the Court has recognized that a right of personal privacy, or a guarantee of certain areas or zones of privacy, does exist under the Constitution. In varying contexts, the Court or individual Justices have, indeed, found at least the roots of that right in the First Amendment [Stanley v. Georgia (obscenity; p. 1130 below)]; in the Fourth and Fifth Amendments; in the penumbras of the Bill of Rights [Griswold]; in the Ninth Amendment [id.]; or in the concept of liberty guaranteed [by] the 14th Amendment, see [Meyer]. These decisions make it clear that only personal rights that can be deemed "fundamental" or "implicit in the concept of ordered liberty" [Palko] are included in this guarantee of personal privacy. They also make it clear that the right has some extension to activities relating to marriage [Loving v. Virginia], procreation [Skinner], contraception [Eisenstadt v. Baird], family relationships [Prince v. Massachusetts, 321 U.S. 158 (1944)], and child rearing and education [Pierce; Meyer].

This right of privacy, whether it be founded in the 14th Amendment's concept of personal liberty [as] we feel it is, or, as the District Court determined, in the [Ninth Amendment], is broad enough to encompass a woman's decision whether or not to terminate her pregnancy. The detriment that the State would impose upon the pregnant woman by denying this choice altogether is apparent. Specific and direct harm medically diagnosable even in early pregnancy may be involved. Maternity, or additional offspring, may force upon the woman a distressful life and future. Psychological harm may be imminent. Mental and physical health may be taxed by child care. There is also the distress, for all concerned, associated with the unwanted child, and there is the problem of bringing a child into a family already unable, psychologically and otherwise, to care for it. In other cases, as in this one, the additional difficulties

[handwritten margin notes:] calls the rights listed in the Bill of Rights a right of privacy as long as are personal, fundamental or implicit in the concept of ordered liberty (14th) → extensions

[handwritten margin note:] harm to woman in denying right to terminate

and continuing stigma of unwed motherhood may be involved. All these are factors the woman and her responsible physician necessarily will consider in consultation.

On the basis of elements such as these, appellants and some amici argue that the woman's right is absolute and that she is entitled to terminate her pregnancy at whatever time, in whatever way, and for whatever reason she alone chooses. With this we do not agree. [The] Court's decisions recognizing a right of privacy also acknowledge that some state regulation in areas protected by that right is appropriate. [A] state may properly assert important interests in safeguarding health, in maintaining medical standards, and in protecting potential life.[2] At some point in pregnancy, these respective interests become sufficiently compelling to sustain regulation of the factors that govern the abortion decision. The privacy right involved, therefore, cannot be said to be absolute. In fact, it is not clear to us that the claim asserted by some amici that one has an unlimited right to do with one's body as one pleases bears a close relationship to the right of privacy previously articulated in the Court's decisions. The Court has refused to recognize an unlimited right of this kind in the past. [Jacobson v. Massachusetts (1905)] (vaccination); [Buck v. Bell (1927)] (sterilization). We, therefore, conclude that the right of personal privacy includes the abortion decision, but that this right is not unqualified and must be considered against important state interests in regulation. [Where] certain "fundamental rights" are involved, the Court has held that regulation limiting these rights may be justified only by a "compelling state interest" [and] that legislative enactments must be narrowly drawn to express only the legitimate state interests at stake. [Appellant claims] an absolute right that bars any state imposition of criminal penalties in the area. Appellee argues that the State's determination to recognize and protect prenatal life from and after conception constitutes a compelling state interest. [We] do not agree fully with either formulation.

A. The appellee [argues] that the fetus is a "person" within the language and meaning of the 14th Amendment. [If so,] the appellant's case, of course, collapses, for the fetus' right to life is then guaranteed specifically by the Amendment. [The] Constitution does not define "person" in so many words. Section 1 of the 14th Amendment contains three references to "person." ["Person"] is used in other places in the Constitution.[3] [But] in nearly all these

2. In discussing these interests earlier in his opinion, Justice Blackmun had stated: "[The] State has a legitimate interest in seeing to it that abortion, like any other medical procedure, is performed under circumstances that ensure maximum safety for the patient. [The] State retains a definite interest in protecting the woman's own health and safety when an abortion is proposed at a late stage of pregnancy. [There is also] the State's interest [in] protecting prenatal life. Some of the argument for this justification rests on the theory that a new human life is present from the moment of conception. [Logically,] of course, a legitimate state interest in this area need not stand or fall on acceptance of the belief that life begins at conception or at some other point prior to live birth. In assessing the State's interest, recognition may be given to the less rigid claim that as long as at

least *potential* life is involved, the State may assert interests beyond the protection of the pregnant woman alone. [It] is with these interests, and the weight to be attached to them, that this case is concerned."

3. At this point, Justice Blackmun recited all the other constitutional references to "person": "in the listing of qualifications for Representatives and Senators, Art. I, § 2, cl. 2, and § 3, cl. 3; in the Apportionment Clause, Art. I, § 2, cl. 3; in the Migration and Importation provision, Art. I, § 9, cl. 1; in the Emolument Clause, Art. I, § 9, cl. 8; in the Electors provisions, Art. II, § 1, cl. 2, and the superseded cl. 3; in the provision outlining qualifications for the office of President, Art. II, § 1, cl. 5; in the Extradition provisions, Art. IV, § 2, cl. 2, and the superseded Fugitive Slave Clause 3; and in the Fifth, Twelfth

instances, the use of the word is such that it has application only postnatally. *text*
None indicates, with any assurance, that it has any possible prenatal applica- *social practices/9th amt.*
tion.[4] All this, together with our observation [that] throughout the major
portion of the 19th century prevailing legal abortion practices were far freer
than they are today, persuades us that the word "person," as used in the 14th
Amendment, does not include the unborn. [We] pass on to other considerations.

B. The pregnant woman cannot be isolated in her privacy. She carries an
embryo and, later, a [fetus]. The situation therefore is inherently different from
marital intimacy, or bedroom possession of obscene material, or marriage, or
procreation, or education, with which Eisenstadt, Griswold, Stanley, Loving,
Skinner, Pierce, and Meyer [were] concerned. [I]t is reasonable and appropriate
for a State to decide that at some point in time another interest, that of health
of the mother or that of potential human life, becomes significantly involved.
The woman's privacy is no longer sole and any right of privacy she possesses
must be measured accordingly.

Texas urges that, apart from the 14th Amendment, life begins at concep-
tion and is present throughout pregnancy, and that, therefore, the State has a *It is not the Court's*
compelling interest in protecting that life from and after conception. We need *place to decide whether*
not resolve the difficult question of when life begins. When those trained [in] *fetus = person.*
medicine, philosophy, and theology are unable to arrive at any consensus, the
judiciary, at this point in the development of man's knowledge, is not in a
position to speculate as to the answer. It should be sufficient to note [the] wide
divergence of thinking on this most sensitive and difficult question. [After
reviewing a range of philosophical and religious beliefs, Justice Blackmun
noted:] Physicians [have] tended to focus either upon conception, upon live
birth, or upon the interim point at which the fetus becomes "viable," that is,
potentially able to live outside the mother's womb, albeit with artificial aid.
Viability is usually placed at about seven months (28 weeks) but may occur
earlier, even at 24 weeks. [The modern official belief of the Catholic Church,
recognizing the existence of life from the moment of conception,] is a view
strongly held by many non-Catholics as well, and by many physicians. Substantial problems for precise definition of this view are posed, however, by new
embryological data that purport to indicate that conception is a "process" over *Technology*
time, rather than an event, and by new medical techniques such as menstrual
extraction, the "morning-after" pill, implantation of embryos, artificial insemi- *criminal abortion*
nation, and even artificial wombs. In areas other than criminal abortion, the *precedent* ⎱ *if the*
law has been reluctant to endorse any theory that life, as we recognize it, *historical* ⎰ *law*
begins before live birth or to accord legal rights to the unborn except in *practices*
narrowly defined situations and except when the rights are contingent upon
live birth. [Justice Blackmun noted illustrations in the law of torts and of
inheritance.] In short, the unborn have never been recognized in the law as
persons in the whole sense. In view of all this, we do not agree that, by
adopting one theory of life, Texas may override the rights of the pregnant
woman that are at stake. We repeat, however, that the State does have an
important and legitimate interest in preserving and protecting the health of the

and Twenty-second Amendments, as well as
in §§ 2 and 3 of the 14th Amendment."

4. When Texas urges that a fetus is
entitled to 14th Amendment protection as a
person, it faces a dilemma. Neither in Texas
nor in any other State are all abortions prohibited. Despite broad proscription, an exception always exists. The exception [in the
Texas law], for an abortion procured or attempted by medical advice for the purpose of
saving the life of the mother, is typical. But
if the fetus is a person who is not to be deprived of life without due process of law, and
if the mother's condition is the sole determinant, does not the Texas exception appear to
be out of line with the Amendment's [com-
mand]? [Footnote by Justice Blackmun.]

[margin note: Two State interests: 1. unborn {health —viable} 2. woman —1st trimester]

pregnant woman [and] that it has still *another* important and legitimate interest in protecting the potentiality of human life. These interests are separate and distinct. Each grows in substantiality as the woman approaches term and, at a point during pregnancy, each becomes "compelling."

[margin note: what kind of analysis is this?]

With respect to [the] interest in the health of the mother, the "compelling" point, in the light of present medical knowledge, is at approximately the end of the first trimester. This is so because of the now established medical fact [that] until the end of the first trimester mortality in abortion is less than mortality in normal childbirth. It follows that, from and after this point, a State may regulate the abortion procedure to the extent that the regulation reasonably relates to the preservation and protection of maternal health. Examples of permissible state regulation in this area are requirements as to the qualifications of the person who is to perform the abortion; [as] to the facility in which the procedure is to be performed; and the like. This means, on the other hand, that, for the period of pregnancy prior to this "compelling" point, the attending physician, in consultation with his patient, is free to determine, without regulation by the State, that, in his medical judgment, the patient's pregnancy should be terminated. If that decision is reached, the judgment may be effectuated by an abortion free of interference by the State. With respect to [the] interest in potential life, the "compelling" point is at viability. This is so because the fetus then presumably has the capability of meaningful life outside the mother's womb. State regulation protective of fetal life after viability thus has both logical and biological justifications. If the State is interested in protecting fetal life after viability, it may go so far as to proscribe abortion during that period, except when it is necessary to preserve the life or health of

[margin note: because the TX law is not justified by compelling State interest?]

the mother. Measured against these standards, [the Texas law] sweeps too broadly [and] cannot survive the constitutional attack made upon it here.

[margin note: Due process violation. (substantive?)]

To summarize and repeat: A state criminal abortion statute of the current Texas type, that excepts from criminality only a *life saving* procedure on behalf of the mother, without regard to pregnancy stage and without recognition of the other interests involved, is violative of [due process]. (a) For the stage prior to approximately the end of the first trimester, the abortion decision and its effectuation must be left to the medical judgment of the pregnant woman's attending physician. (b) For the stage subsequent to approximately the end of the first trimester, the State, in promoting its interest in the health of the mother, may, if it chooses, regulate the abortion procedure in ways that are reasonably related to maternal health. (c) For the stage subsequent to viability, the State in promoting its interest in the potentiality of human life may, if it chooses, regulate, and even proscribe, abortion except where it is necessary, in appropriate medical judgment, for the preservation of the life or health of the

[margin note: basis]

mother. [This] holding, we feel, is consistent with the relative weights of the respective interests involved, with the lessons and examples of medical and legal history, with the lenity of the common law, and with the demands of the profound problems of the present day. The decision leaves the State free to place increasing restrictions on abortion as the period of pregnancy lengthens, so long as those restrictions are tailored to the recognized state interests. The decision vindicates the right of the physician to administer medical treatment according to his professional judgment up to the points where important state interests provide compelling justifications for intervention. Up to those points, the abortion decision in all its aspects is inherently, and primarily, a medical decision, and basic responsibility for it must rest with the [physician].

It is so ordered.

Justice STEWART, concurring.

In 1963, this Court, in [Ferguson v. Skrupa], purported to sound the death knell for the doctrine of substantive due process. Barely two years later, in [Griswold], the Court held a Connecticut birth control law unconstitutional. In view of what had been so recently said in Skrupa, the Court's opinion in Griswold understandably did its best to avoid reliance on [due process]. [Yet] the Connecticut law did not violate [any] specific provision of the Constitution. So it was clear to me then, and it is equally clear to me now, that the Griswold decision can be rationally understood only as a holding that the Connecticut statute substantively invaded ["liberty"]. As so understood Griswold stands as one in a long line of pre-Skrupa cases decided under the doctrine of substantive due process, and I now accept it as such. [T]he "liberty" protected by [due process] covers more than those freedoms explicitly named in the Bill of Rights. [In Eisenstadt], we recognized "the right of the *individual,* married or single, to be free from unwarranted governmental intrusion into matters so fundamentally affecting a person as the decision whether to bear or beget a child." That right necessarily includes the right of a woman to decide whether or not to terminate her [pregnancy]. It is evident that the Texas abortion statute infringes that right directly. [The] question then becomes whether the state interests advanced to justify this abridgment can survive the "particularly careful scrutiny" that the 14th Amendment here requires. The asserted state interests [are] legitimate objectives [but as] the Court today [has] demonstrated [these] state interests cannot constitutionally support the broad abridgment of personal liberty worked by [the] Texas [law].

Justice **DOUGLAS** [joining the opinions in Doe v. Bolton, the Georgia case below, as well as in Roe v. Wade].[1]

[These cases] involve the right of privacy. [The] Ninth Amendment obviously does not create federally enforceable rights [but] a catalogue of [the rights acknowledged by it] includes customary, traditional and time-honored rights, amenities, privileges, and immunities that come within the sweep of "the Blessings of Liberty" mentioned in the preamble to the Constitution. Many of them in my view come within the meaning of the term "liberty" as used in the 14th Amendment. *First is the autonomous control over the development and expression of one's intellect, interests, tastes, and personality.* These are rights protected by the First Amendment and in my view they are [absolute]. *Second is freedom of choice in the basic decisions of one's life respecting marriage, divorce, procreation, contraception, and the education and upbringing of children.* These ["fundamental"] rights, unlike those protected by the First Amendment, are subject to some control by the [police power].[2] *Third is the freedom to care for one's health and person, freedom from bodily restraint or compulsion, freedom to walk, stroll, or loaf.* These rights, though fundamental, are likewise subject to regulation on a showing of ["compelling state interest"]. [A] woman is free to make the basic decision whether to bear an unwanted child. [Childbirth] may deprive a woman of her preferred life style and force upon her a radically different and undesired future. [Such] reasoning is, however, only the beginning of the problem. The State has interests to protect. [Voluntary] abortion at any time and place regardless of medical standards

1. Another concurring opinion applicable to both cases, by Chief Justice **BURGER,** is omitted.

2. My Brother Stewart [says] that our decision in Griswold reintroduced substantive due process that had been rejected in Ferguson v. Skrupa. [Decisions such as Griswold, Pierce and Meyer], with all respect, have nothing to do with substantive due process. One may think they are not peripheral to other rights that are expressed in the Bill of Rights. But that is not enough to bring into play the protection of [substantive due process]. [Footnote by Justice Douglas.]

would impinge on a rightful concern of society. The woman's health is part of that concern; as is the life of the fetus after quickening. These concerns justify the State in treating the procedure as [a medical one].

Justice WHITE, with whom Justice REHNQUIST joins, dissenting [in Doe v. Bolton as well as in Roe v. Wade].

[I] find nothing in the language or history of the Constitution to support the Court's judgment. The Court simply fashions and announces a new constitutional right for pregnant mothers and, with scarcely any reason or authority for its action, invests that right with sufficient substance to override most existing state abortion statutes. The upshot is that the people and the legislatures of the 50 States are constitutionally disentitled to weigh the relative importance of the continued existence and development of the fetus on the one hand against a spectrum of possible impacts on the mother on the other hand. As an exercise of raw judicial power, the Court perhaps has authority to do what it does today; but in my view its judgment is an improvident and extravagant exercise of the power of [judicial review]. In a sensitive area such as this, involving as it does issues over which reasonable men may easily and heatedly differ, I cannot accept the Court's exercise of its [power]. This issue [should] be left with the [people].

Justice REHNQUIST, dissenting.

[I] have difficulty in concluding [that] the right of "privacy" is involved in this case. [Texas] bars the performance of a medical abortion by a licensed physician on a plaintiff such as Roe. A transaction resulting in an operation such as this is not "private" in the ordinary usage of that word. Nor is the "privacy" which the Court finds here even a distant relative of the [Fourth Amendment freedom from searches and seizures]. If the Court means by the term "privacy" no more than that the claim of a person to be free from unwanted state regulation of consensual transactions may be a form of "liberty" protected by the 14th Amendment, there is no doubt that similar claims have been upheld in our earlier decisions on the basis of that liberty. I agree [that "liberty"] embraces more than the rights found in the Bill of Rights. But that liberty is not guaranteed absolutely against deprivation, but only against deprivation without due process of law. The test traditionally applied in the area of social and economic legislation is whether or not a law such as that challenged has a rational relation to a valid state objective. [Lee Optical.] [If] the Texas statute were to prohibit an abortion even where the mother's life is in jeopardy, I have little doubt that such a statute would lack a rational relation to a valid state objective under the test stated in [Lee Optical]. But the Court's sweeping invalidation of any restrictions on abortion during the first trimester is impossible to justify under that [standard]. While the Court's opinion quotes from the dissent of Mr. Justice Holmes in [Lochner], the result it reaches is more closely attuned to the majority opinion of Mr. Justice Peckham in that case. As in Lochner and similar cases applying substantive due process standards to economic and social welfare legislation, the adoption of the compelling state interest standard will inevitably require this Court to examine the legislative policies and pass on the wisdom of these policies in the very process of deciding whether a particular state interest put forward may or may not be "compelling." The decision here to break the term of pregnancy into three distinct terms and to outline the permissible restrictions the State may impose in each one, for example, partakes more of judicial legislation than it does of a determination of the intent of the drafters of the 14th Amendment. The fact that a majority of the [states] have had restrictions on abortions for at least a century is a strong indication, it seems to me, that the asserted right to an abortion is not "so rooted in the traditions and conscience of our people as to be ranked as fundamental." Even today, when society's views on abortion are changing, the very existence of the debate is evidence that the "right" to an abortion is not so universally accepted as the appellants would have us believe. [By] the time of the adoption of the 14th Amendment in 1868, there were at least 36 laws enacted by state or territorial legislatures limiting abortion. [The] only conclusion possible from this history is that the drafters did not intend to have the 14th Amendment withdraw from the States the power to legislate with respect to this [matter].[1]

history is to contrary "traditions+conscience" argument or's und.

DOE v. BOLTON, 410 U.S. 179 (1973), was the companion case to Roe v. Wade. The Georgia abortion law attacked in Doe—unlike the traditional ones invalidated in Roe—was a statute with "a modern cast," enacted in 1968, patterned after the American Law Institute's Model Penal Code, and similar to laws enacted by about one-fourth of the states. Nevertheless, the Court invalidated substantial portions of the Georgia statute. Georgia law made noncriminal an abortion performed by a licensed physician when, "based upon his best clinical judgment," an abortion was necessary because continued pregnancy would endanger the life or seriously injure the health of a pregnant woman; or the fetus would likely be born with serious defects; or if the pregnancy had resulted from rape. In addition to a requirement that the patient must be a Georgia resident, the scheme imposed procedural conditions regarding hospital accreditation and medical judgments beyond that of the performing physician. The three-judge District Court invalidated the statutory reference to the three situations in which the attending physician might undertake an abortion (leaving only the bare reference to "his best clinical judgment"), but sustained the procedural requirements regarding "manner of performance" of an abortion, relying partly on the state interest in the protection of a *potential of independent human existence.*" Justice BLACKMUN's majority opinion upheld the "best clinical judgment" provision but struck down the procedural conditions as well as the residence requirement, relying on the Privileges and Immunities Clause of Art. IV, Sec. 2. The Court rejected the argument that the lower court's interpretation of the provisions governing the physician's judgment had rendered the statute unconstitutionally vague. As the Court read the remaining reference to "best clinical judgment," it required the exercise of professional judgment "in the light of *all* the attendant circumstances"; judgment "may be exercised in light of all factors—physical, emotional, psychological, familial, and the woman's age—relevant to the well-being of the patient." The three challenged procedural requirements ran into a variety of constitutional obstacles. (1) In striking down the requirement that abortion be performed in a hospital accredited by JCAH (Joint Commission on Accreditation of Hospitals), the Court invoked the 1957 equal protection ruling in Morey v. Doud (p. 649 below), insisting that "the State must show more than it has in order to prove that only the full resources of a licensed hospital, rather than those of some other appropriately licensed institution, satisfy [the] health interests." (2) The second requirement, requiring prior approval for an abor-

rape

---

1. Roe v. Wade provoked extensive commentary. For a particularly strong criticism of the case, more elaborate than those in the dissenting opinions in Roe, see Ely, "The Wages of Crying Wolf: A Comment on Roe v. Wade," 82 Yale L.J. 920 (1973). For a defense of the decision, see Heymann & Barzelay, "The Forest and the Trees: Roe v. Wade and Its Critics," 53 B.U.L.Rev. 765 (1973). See also Perry, "Abortion, the Public Morals, and the Police Power," 23 UCLA L.Rev. 689 (1976) [but see the same author's The Constitution, the Courts, and Human Rights (1982), and "The Authority of Text, Tradition, and Reason," 58 S.Cal.L.Rev. 551 (1985)], and Epstein, "Substantive Due Process by Any Other Name: The Abortion Cases," 1973 Sup.Ct.Rev. 159.

tion by the hospital staff abortion committee, was also struck down: the Court could find "no constitutionally justifiable pertinence" for that requirement. (3) The final invalid procedural condition required "confirmation [of the abortion judgment] by two Georgia-licensed physicians in addition to the recommendation of the pregnant woman's own consultant (making under the statute, a total of six physicians involved, including the three on the hospital's abortion committee)." The Court concluded that the attending physician's "best clinical judgment" "should be sufficient."

ROE v. WADE AND THE LEGITIMATE SOURCES OF CONSTITUTIONAL VALUES

1. *The protected personal interest: "Privacy," "autonomy," and Roe.* What *is* the "privacy" right recognized in Roe? Justice Blackmun finds the right of privacy "broad enough to encompass a woman's decision whether or not to terminate her pregnancy." It is not an "absolute" right, but neither is it one that can be overridden simply by merely "rational" state legislation. Rather, it is a prima facie, specially protected, qualified right to have an abortion that is subject to regulation only on the showing of a "compelling" state interest. What aspect of "privacy" explains this powerful interest? The interests in protecting the home against intrusions or in the marital relationship or in avoiding disclosures of information seem inapplicable here: as the Court recognizes, the situation here "is inherently different from marital intimacy, or bedroom possession of obscene material, or marriage, or procreation, or education" with which the cases from Meyer to Eisenstadt were concerned. Is the relevant interest then that in personal "autonomy" of choice about performing acts or undergoing experiences? Yet Justice Blackmun expressed doubt that the claim "that one has an unlimited right to do with one's body as one pleases bears a close relationship to the right of privacy previously articulated in the Court's decisions." But surely the autonomy aspects of privacy gained additional force in the wake of Roe. Roe involved not only the interest of the woman but some concern for the fetus—what the Court calls the state's "important and legitimate interest in protecting the potentiality of human life." That suggested that an autonomy claim should be even stronger when no other competing personal interest, actual or potential, is involved—when only the claimant's body or life style, or only private consensual behavior, is involved. But see note 6 below.

2. *"Balancing" the competing interests.* The Court finds that the woman's prima facie right to abort her pregnancy can be defeated only by "compelling" state interests. Justice Blackmun notes two relevant state interests: protecting the woman's health; and "protecting the potentiality of human life." At differing points in the trimester scheme, those interests become sufficiently "compelling" to justify state restraints. Consider how the Court determines when these interests become "compelling." Is it helpful to discuss whether the fetus is a "person" within the 14th Amendment—or within any other provision of the Constitution? Is it accurate to say: "We need not resolve the difficult question of when life begins"? Must not the Court at least determine when "the potentiality of human life" represents a sufficiently strong moral claim to justify curtailment of the woman's interest in autonomy? Justice Blackmun states that Texas may not, "by adopting one theory of life," "override the rights of the pregnant woman that are at stake." Yet Justice Blackmun also notes that there is wide disagreement, in medicine and philosophy and law,

about when life begins. Why should not that lack of consensus lead the Court to defer to, rather than invalidate, the state's judgment?[1] Can the Court's judgment be supported by anything other than a judicial authority to infuse a particular set of moral values into the Constitution? Is it possible to articulate a more confining, disciplined approach to substantive due process?

3. *Is Roe distinguishable from Lochner?* Is Roe v. Wade more justifiable than the value-laden interventions of the Lochner era? Are the judicially articulated values of Roe more defensible? Can it be argued that Roe—rather than being more defensible than Lochner, or at least as defensible—is even *less* defensible? John Hart Ely made such an argument in "The Wages of Crying Wolf: A Comment on Roe v. Wade," 82 Yale L.J. 920 (1973). He insisted that the "general philosophy of constitutional adjudication" is the same in Roe as in Lochner. To argue that noneconomic rights such as the right to abort a pregnancy accord more closely with "this generation's idealization of America" (a phrase taken from Karst & Horowitz, "Reitman v. Mulkey: A Telophase of Substantive Equal Protection," 1967 Sup.Ct.Rev. 39) does not help to distinguish Lochner: it was precisely the point of the Lochner philosophy, Ely argued, to "grant unusual protection to those 'rights' that somehow *seem* most pressing, regardless of whether the Constitution suggests any special solicitude for them." Ely went on to argue, moreover, that Roe may be a "more dangerous precedent" than Lochner. At least the cases of the Lochner era "did us the favor of sowing the seeds of their destruction." Lochner era invalidations rested either on the illegitimacy of the legislative goal or the lack of a "plausible argument" that legislative means furthered the permissible end. By contrast, Roe's rejection of the legislative judgment "takes neither of these forms." The state interest in protecting potential life is not denied, and the efficacy of the means is not questioned. Instead, Roe simply announces that the "goal is not important enough to sustain the restriction." Unlike the Lochner era cases, "Roe's 'refutation' of the legislative judgment [is] *not* obviously wrong, for the substitution of one nonrational judgment for another [can] be labeled neither wrong nor right. The problem with Roe is not so much that it bungles the question it sets itself, but rather that it sets itself a question the Constitution has not made the Court's business." See also Ely, "Foreword: On Discovering Fundamental Values," 92 Harv.L.Rev. 5 (1978), and Ely, Democracy and Distrust, chap. 3 (1980). Is Ely's criticism persuasive?

[margin note: Roe more dangerous than Lochner]

1. Compare Laurence Tribe's suggestion that the result of Roe v. Wade may be supportable on other grounds. In "Foreword: Toward a Model of Roles in the Due Process of Life and Law," 87 Harv.L.Rev. 1 (1973), he argued that "some types of choices ought to be remanded, on principle, to private decision-makers unchecked by substantive governmental control." As he viewed Roe in this 1973 article, the Court was not choosing simply between abortion and continued pregnancy, but "instead *choosing among alternative allocations of decisionmaking authority.*" And he suggested that the religion clauses of the First Amendment barred legislators from making judgments about potential life because, given the nature of the problem, "views of organized religious groups have come to play a pervasive role" in legislative considerations of that issue. Does Tribe's general "role allocation" approach help justify substantive due process invalidations? Subsequently, Tribe said that he was not satisfied with his earlier explanation of Roe. He suggested another one: the right of the judiciary to intervene when moral consensus is in flux, to permit a new moral consensus to evolve. (See, e.g., "Structural Due Process," 10 Harv.Civ.Rts.-Civ.Lib.L.Rev. 269 (1975), and "Childhood, Suspect Classifications, and Conclusive Presumptions," 39 Law & Contemp.Prob. 8 (1975). Cf. Tribe, American Constitutional Law (2d ed., 1988).) Is principled justification for such judicial intervention possible? Can the existence of instability in society's consensus argue *for* rather than *against* judicial intervention? Recall Holmes's arguments for rejecting the interventionism of the Lochner era.

autonomy v. home privacy

4. *The difference between Roe and Griswold (and other Warren Court decisions).* Ely also argued that Roe is even *less* defensible than Griswold. Does that depend upon how Griswold is read? Ely read it as being a case "about likely invasions of the privacy of the bedroom," not one "directly enshrining a right to contraception." He found "a general right of privacy" a legitimate constitutional inference, *"so long as some care is taken in defining the sort of right the inference will support."* In Griswold, the contraceptives use law was invalid because its enforcement implied "prying into the privacy of the home." According to Ely, in short, a general right of privacy regarding "governmental snooping" is justifiable; a general right of autonomy is not, and was not asserted in Griswold. Does that reading of Griswold adequately take account of what Ely concedes to be "vague and openended" passages in Griswold?

Can Roe v. Wade be criticized without calling into question many of the interventionist decisions of the Warren Court? Ely insisted that, despite the problems of some Warren Court opinions, their results can all be justified more persuasively than Roe: "What is frightening about Roe is that this super-protected right is not inferable from the language of the Constitution, the framers' thinking respecting the specific problem in issue, any general value derivable from the provisions they included, or the nation's governmental structure. Nor is it explainable in terms of the unusual political impotence of the group judicially protected vis-à-vis the interest that legislatively prevailed over it.[2] And that, I believe, [is] a charge that can responsibly be leveled at no other decision of the past twenty years. At times the inferences the Court has drawn from the values the Constitution marks for special protection have been controversial, even shaky, but never before has its sense of an obligation to

2. The reference here was to the rationale of Stone's Carolene Products footnote, justifying special protection for "discrete and insular minorities" that do not receive adequate consideration in the political process. Ely argued that, "even assuming that that approach can be given principled content," it is only applicable to "those interests which, *as compared with the interest to which they have been subordinated,* constitute minorities unusually incapable of protecting themselves." He added: "Compared with men, women may constitute such a 'minority'; compared with the unborn, they do not." But see Karst, "Book Review," 89 Harv.L.Rev. 1028 (1976) (in the course of commenting on this section in a previous edition of this casebook): "[The] implicit message [is] that the issues of process and technique are *the* issues worth considering. [But what] is happening in these cases is a constitutional revolution comparable in scope and social importance to the Supreme Court's 1937 abdication from supervising economic regulation, and its intervention [to] secure the recognition of black Americans as fully participating members of the national community. Not merely the sex discrimination cases, but the cases on conception, abortion, and illegitimacy as well, present various faces of a single issue: the roles women are to play in our society. This is a *constitutional* issue, perhaps the most important of the 1970's. [It] is simply inconceivable that the majority Justices in Roe were indifferent to the question of 'woman's role.'" See also Karst, "Foreword: Equal Citizenship Under the Fourteenth Amendment," 91 Harv.L.Rev. 1 (1977), and Law, "Rethinking Sex and the Constitution," 132 U.Pa.L.Rev. 955 (1984) (emphasizing that "laws governing reproduction implicate equality concerns" and noting that "restrictions on access to abortion plainly oppress women"). Note, too, MacKinnon, "Roe v. Wade: A Study in Male Ideology," in Abortion: Moral and Legal Perspectives 45 (Garfield & Hennessey eds. 1984), and Luker, Abortion and the Politics of Motherhood (1984). See also Ruth Bader Ginsburg's lecture, "Some Thoughts on Autonomy and Equality in Relation to Roe v. Wade," 63 N.C.L.Rev. 375 (1985). These articles, like Karst's 1977 comment, are part of the growing body of literature tying the substantive due process issues raised in cases such as Roe to the sex discrimination ones considered in the next, equal protection chapter. Note also the references to sex discrimination in some of the opinions in the 1992 abortion case, Casey, p. 557 below.

draw one been so obviously lacking." Note also Ely's comment that Roe is "a very bad decision [because] it is *not* constitutional law and gives almost no sense of an obligation to try to be."

5. *Roe and "noninterpretive" modes of adjudication.* Ely's criteria in criticizing Roe and distinguishing it from interventionist Warren era decisions once again suggest a pervasive problem of judicial review—a problem most acutely raised by the substantive due process cases in this chapter. Are those criteria the right ones? Must constitutional decisionmaking be "interpretive" rather than "noninterpretive"? Must the Court limit itself to the sources of values Ely lists: is the Court's authority limited to values derived from text, history, structure, and perhaps, Stone's political process rationale? Or does this unduly confine the Court? Roe v. Wade calls attention to these problems with special force. Professor Lupu has noted that Roe uniquely attests to the Court's "willingness to reach results which no defensible interpretivist position could support. Although rhetorically tied to the meaning of 'liberty' [and] loosely aligned with the penumbral analysis [of Griswold], Roe cut fundamental rights adjudication loose from the constitutional text. The widely perceived inadequacies in the Court's opinion had predictable results. There followed in the constitutional literature a vast array of doctrinal, methodological, and theoretical inquiries into the outcome in Roe. [These] scholarly efforts offered a variety of justifications for noninterpretive review—natural law underpinnings of the 1787 Constitution [e.g., Grey, below], transplantation of common law method into constitutional adjudication [e.g., Brest, Wellington, below], the search for enduring or traditional unwritten norms, [and] judicial manifestation of consensus morality."[3]

For one of the earliest explicit arguments that "noninterpretive" modes of adjudication *are* legitimate, see Grey, "Do We Have an Unwritten Constitution?" 27 Stan.L.Rev. 703 (1975). Grey disagrees with Ely's criticism of Roe and with the Marbury v. Madison–Justice Black heritage of the "pure interpretive model" on which it rests.[4] Grey suggests that the Court is not limited to

3. Lupu, "Constitutional Theory and the Search for the Workable Premise," 8 U. Dayton L.Rev. 579, 583 (1983). Professor Lupu's essay expressed his worry about "the spread of 'intellectual hemophilia,' an ailment that accompanies excessive inbreeding of ideas. Constitutional scholars have, of late, talked mainly to each other. [Many] have been reluctant to tie their sophisticated intellectual insights to the concrete problems and day-to-day issues arising in constitutional adjudication." See also the 1983 Van Alstyne article, footnote 5 below.

4. Grey cited as other examples of "interpretive" criticism Bork, "Neutral Principles and Some First Amendment Problems," 47 Ind.L.J. 1 (1971) ("[T]he choice of 'fundamental values' by the Court cannot be justified. The judge must stick close to the text and the history, and their implications, and not construct new rights"), and Linde, "Judges, Critics, and the Realist Tradition," 82 Yale L.J. 227 (1972) ("The judicial responsibility begins and ends with determining the present scope and meaning of a decision that

the nation, at an earlier time, articulated and enacted into constitutional text"). The common denominator of all "unduly narrow," "purely interpretive" models, Grey finds, is the insistence "that the only norms used in constitutional adjudication must be those inferable from the text"; the interpretive model does not authorize courts "to articulate and apply contemporary norms not demonstrably expressed or implied by the Framers." More recently, Grey has recanted his "interpretive-noninterpretive" distinction, in "The Constitution as Scripture," 37 Stan.L.Rev. 1 (1985). He now believes that that distinction "distorts the debate": "If the current interest in interpretive theory, or hermeneutics, does nothing else, at least it makes evident that the concept of interpretation is broad enough to encompass any plausible mode of constitutional adjudication." (See Brest, "The Misconceived Quest for the Original Understanding," 60 B.U.L.Rev. 204 (1980).) Grey adds: "We are all interpretivists; and the real arguments are not over whether judges should stick to interpreting, but over what they

enforcing "norms derived from the written Constitution": it may "also enforce principles of liberty and justice when the normative content of those principles is not to be found within the four corners of our founding document." He argues that "there was an original understanding, both implicit and textually expressed [in the Ninth Amendment], that unwritten higher law principles had constitutional status," and he claims that the courts have "enforced unwritten constitutional principles" from the beginning. He recognizes a number of difficulties with the open avowal of the "noninterpretive" approach, especially: "Conceding the natural-rights origins of our Constitution, does not the erosion and abandonment of the 18th century ethics and epistemology on which the natural rights theory was founded require the abandonment of the mode of judicial review flowing from that theory? Is a 'fundamental law' judicially enforced in a climate of historical and cultural relativism the legitimate offspring of a fundamental law which its exponents felt expressed rationally demonstrable, universal and immutable human rights?" *Is* it possible to develop a "legitimate pedigree of noninterpretive judicial review"? *Can* a "higher law-natural rights" approach be reconciled with democratic theory? What guidance for judicial judgment can be articulated if a natural rights, noninterpretive fundamental values approach is openly adopted? As the post-Roe cases, below, indicate, the modern Court seems clearly committed to substantive due process, "fundamental values" adjudication—at least in selected areas. That development in turn has spurred the enormous flood of literature on the proper sources for "noninterpretive" decisionmaking. These questions, then, are of pressing contemporary relevance.[5]

should interpret and what interpretive attitudes they should adopt. Repenting past errors, I will therefore use the less misleading labels 'textualists' and 'supplementers' for, respectively, those who consider the text the sole legitimate source of operative norms in constitutional adjudication, and those who accept supplementary sources of constitutional law." Is that revision in terminology truly helpful? Pure "textualists" are in any event a very underpopulated subgroup these days; "interpretivists" rely on sources well beyond text. (See the next footnote.) Grey also identifies a recent development of a "third and fastgrowing group of constitutional theorists"—the "rejectionists," who argue that neither approach is satisfactory, since "the text if read with an appropriately generous notion of context provides as lively a constitution as the most activist judge might need." The rejectionist position, according to Grey, "summons sophisticated notions of the nature of interpretation in its support, and gains further appeal from the ennui that the standard debate has come to induce in all but its most obsessive practitioners." Grey himself argues that, "for reasons that are largely political, we should reject rejectionism." Grey lists, among the "rejectionists," Wellington, "History and Morals in Constitutional Adjudication," 97 Harv.L.Rev. 326 (1983).

5. For a useful summary of the modern range of noninterpretivist arguments, see, in addition to Lupu above, Wiseman, "The New Supreme Court Commentators: The Principled, the Political and the Philosophical," 10 Hastings Const.L.Q. 315 (1983). For strong critiques of noninterpretivism, see, e.g., Van Alstyne, "Interpreting *This* Constitution: The Unhelpful Contributions of Special Theories of Judicial Review," 35 U.Fla.L.Rev. 209 (1983), and Monaghan, "Our Perfect Constitution," 56 N.Y.U.L.Rev. 353 (1981). See generally Tushnet, "Following the Rules Laid Down: A Critique of Interpretivism and Neutral Principles," 96 Harv.L.Rev. 781 (1983), Bennett, "Objectivity in Constitutional Law," 132 U.Pa.L.Rev. 445 (1984), Posner, "The Meaning of Judicial Self–Restraint," 59 Ind. L.J. 1 (1983), Sedler, "The Legitimacy Debate in Constitutional [Adjudication]," 44 Ohio St.L.J. 93 (1983), Brest, "The Fundamental Rights [Controversy]," 90 Yale L.J. 1063 (1981), and Bobbitt, Constitutional Fate: Theory of the Constitution (1982). Note also the recent interest in literary theory as a guide to problems of interpretation in constitutional law, reflected in some of the articles cited above. By contrast to that approach, there have been a growing number of arguments that, as Grey puts it, "scripture is more likely than literature to be an illuminating analog to law." See, e.g., Levinson, " 'The Constitution' in American Civil Religion," 1979 Sup.Ct.Review 123. See also, on

6. *The implications of Roe and Griswold: Private autonomy and public morality*. a. *The individual interest in autonomy*. Has a basis for a broad fundamental interest in personal autonomy now been established? Griswold arguably involved less than that (especially if it had been limited to the intrusion-into-the-marital-home-rationale), but Roe involves more—not only the pregnant woman's interest, but also that of the potential life of the fetus. But do the Griswold and Roe opinions and their general statements suggest the basis for a constitutionally recognized right of private autonomy—of private choice in performing acts or undergoing experiences—so long as there is no demonstrable harm to others? What varieties of laws would be threatened by recognition of such a right? Claims to autonomy have been advanced not only in Roe but in a wide range of other contexts. For example, should such a right apply to regulations of all consensual sexual behavior? See Bowers v. Hardwick (1986; p. 593 below). Regulations of dress and hair style? Note the Court's rejection of such a claim in Kelley v. Johnson (1976; p. 599 below). The "right to die" and to physician-assisted suicide? See p. 602 below. Requirements that motorcyclists wear helmets, see Note, "Motorcycle Helmets and the Constitutionality of Self–Protective Legislation," 30 Ohio St.L.J. 355 (1969)? Prohibitions of the possession or use of marijuana, see Comment, "The California Marijuana Possession [Statute]," 19 Hast.L.J. 758 (1968)? Access to nontoxic but unproven drugs such as Laetrile by cancer patients? Cf. United States v. Rutherford, 442 U.S. 544 (1979), and, generally, Henkin, "Privacy and Autonomy," 74 Colum.L.Rev. 1410 (1974).

As the post-Roe decisions below indicate, the modern Court's considerable interventionism has in fact fallen far short of any general recognition of a "fundamental value" in individual autonomy. Instead, the Court has used the Roe methodology to protect a selected number of "fundamental values." It is often unclear what animates the Court's selection of some, and rejection of other, values as "fundamental." A process rationale does not explain the post-Roe developments: as Ely put it, "No Carolene Products Court this." And as he also commented, the modern Court's "value-imposition methodology" has been manifested "principally though not exclusively in the 'area' (at least the Court sees it as an area) of sex-marriage-childbearing-childrearing—complete with all the apparent inconsistency [to] which such a 'we'll protect it because it seems important' approach is unusually susceptible."[6] True, some areas have become quite regular occasions for heightened scrutiny. For example, extraordinary protection of individual rights in family contexts has become commonplace, as developed below. But if "sex" has become a part of the protected "area," it has certainly not encompassed all consensual sexual behavior, as the Bowers v. Hardwick ruling, p. 593 below, illustrates. But see Romer v. Evans (1996; p. 737 below).

the analogy to theology, Cover, "Foreword: Nomos and Narrative," 97 Harv.L.Rev. 4 (1983), and Burt, "Constitutional Law and the Teaching of the Parables," 93 Yale L.J. 455 (1984).

6. Ely, "Foreword: On Discovering Fundamental Values," 92 Harv.L.Rev. 5 (1978). For a stimulating response to Ely's question about what "makes all this a unit," see Karst, "The Freedom of Intimate Association," 89 Yale L.J. 624 (1980). Karst urges the Court to acknowledge a "presumptive freedom of intimate association," a freedom which Karst sees as lying behind many of the "recent decisions in the areas of marriage, procreation, and parent-child relationships." He defines "intimate association" as a "close and familiar personal relationship with another [comparable] to a marriage or family relationship." (Note the Court's recognition of an aspect of "freedom of intimate association" protected by due process in Roberts v. United States Jaycees (1984; p. 601 below).)

Consider the suggestion in Grey, "Eros, Civilization and the Burger Court," 43 Law & Contemp.Prob. 83 (1980), that the Court's decisions regarding sexuality do not endorse any "Millian" (see footnote 7) individual autonomy interest in sexual behavior. He states: "I believe that the contraception and abortion cases [are] dedicated to the cause of social stability through the reinforcement of traditional institutions, and have nothing to do with the sexual liberation of the individual. The contraception and abortion cases [represent] two standard conservative views: that social stability is threatened by excessive population growth; and that family stability is threatened by unwanted [pregnancies]. The conventions of constitutional adjudication of course demand that the decisions be justified, not on the basis of social stability, but in the language of individual rights. And so they were." True, Roe and Eisenstadt "stressed the importance of the choice to the individual; but [the] choice was not sexual but procreational. [The] Court has consistently protected traditional familial institutions [against] the centrifugal forces of an anomic modern society. Where less traditional values have been directly protected [e.g., as to contraception and abortion], the decisions reflect not any Millian glorification of diverse individuality, but the stability-centered concerns of moderate conservative family and population policy." Grey adds: "I expect that within a few years fornication and sodomy laws will be found unconstitutional, on something like the very dogma of the rights of consenting adults to control their own sex lives that the Court has until now so rigorously avoided. But the real reasons for the decisions will have little to do with any notion in the Justices' minds that sexual freedom is essential to the pursuit of happiness. Rather the decisions will respond to the same demands of order and social stability that have produced the contraception and abortion decisions. Thousands of couples are living together today outside of marriage. The fornication laws [stand] in the way of providing a stabilizing legal framework for these unions. [Therefore] those laws will be struck down. [Similarly], the homosexual community is becoming an increasingly public sector of our society. For that community to be governed effectively, it must be recognized as legitimate. [If legislatures do not change their laws, the Court will] step in and play its traditional role as enlightened conservator of the social interest in ordered stability, and will strike down those laws, in the glorious name of the individual." Consider an alternative explanation for the Court's decisions in the "sex" area, an alternative considered but rejected by Grey: "The alternative is to see the Court as engaged in the covert promotion of Mill's principle. The failure to carry the principle through, then, must represent a prudential guess that to place the protection of the Constitution behind what most people still reject as unnatural sexual practices would too much strain the Court's limited stock of public good will."

b. *The state interest in morality.* Is the regulation of morality a constitutionally legitimate state interest? Is it a compelling one? Recall Justice Harlan's discussion (at p. 522 above) of Connecticut's claim that use of contraceptives could be banned "to protect the moral welfare of its citizenry": though Justice Harlan found the means impermissible, he suggested that the "morality" end was legitimate. He noted that the police power traditionally included the "morality objective": "Indeed to attempt a line between public behavior and that which is purely consensual or solitary would be to withdraw from community concern a range of subjects with which every society in civilized times has found it necessary to deal. Connecticut's judgment is no more demonstrably correct or incorrect than are the varieties of judgment, expressed in law, on marriage and divorce, on adult consensual homosexuality, abortion, and sterilization, or euthanasia and suicide." Can and should the traditional state interest in private morality nevertheless be found noncompelling under the modes of adjudication reflected in Griswold and Roe? Consider the question in Brest, Processes of Constitutional Decisionmaking (1975), chap. 7: "If the Constitution does not enact Herbert Spencer's Social Statics, does it enact John Stuart Mill's On Liberty (1859)?"[7]

7. *The political reaction to Roe: Proposed constitutional amendments; legislative efforts.* In the wake of Roe, well-publicized efforts to amend the Constitution were launched. None proved successful. For one echoing Justice Rehnquist's position in his dissent, see the amendment introduced in the House in 1973, providing that nothing in the Constitution shall bar any State "from allowing, regulating, or prohibiting the practice of abortion." Contrast with this "neutral" provision two 1973 proposals in the Senate that are clearly anti-abortion in tendency. One, introduced by Senator Helms, sought to protect life "from the moment of conception." Another, introduced by Senator Buckley, protected unborn children "at every stage of their biological development," but was inapplicable "in an emergency when a reasonable medical certainty exists that continuation of the pregnancy will cause the death of the mother."[8] Subsequently, the focus of some of the political responses to Roe shifted from constitutional amendments to legislative action. One type of response was to bar the use of public funds for many types of abortions. In decisions in 1977 and 1980 (p. 550 below), the Court held that such state and federal efforts were constitutional. A second legislative response was unveiled in 1981, when some members of Congress proposed a Human Life Statute, relying on power under § 5 of the 14th Amendment. See chap. 10, sec. 4, below. But some "right to life" proponents doubted the constitutionality of such an approach and continued to attack Roe via the constitutional amendment route. By the time of the 2d session of the 104th Congress, in 1996, congressional interest in constitutional amendments had waned (though a call for an amendment was included in the 1996 Republican Platform) and the focus reverted to legislative measures. Congress enacted a law banning so-called "partial birth," late-term abortions, but this first congressional effort to ban an abortion procedure was blocked by President Clinton's veto.

More recently, the interpretivism/noninterpretivism dispute and the fate of Roe v. Wade became persistent subtexts in the Senate's consideration of nominations to the Supreme Court, most controversially in the case of President Reagan's 1987 nomination of Judge Robert H. Bork to succeed Justice Powell. Judge Bork's interpretivist views were attacked by those who saw both the Constitution and the Court's role in more flexible and dynamic terms. Judge Bork viewed Griswold and Roe as examples of the "judicial activism" he opposed. Although Judge Bork had harsh criticisms for Roe and Griswold and had in the past indicated that the role of precedent in constitutional adjudication was of limited importance, he expressed in his confirmation hearings a stronger "respect for precedent," without taking a stand on whether he would

7. Mill's well-known argument elaborated "one very simple principle": "That the sole end to which mankind are warranted, individually or collectively, in interfering with the liberty of action of any of their number is self-protection"; that government may control the individual only "to prevent harm to others"; "[h]is own good, either physical or moral, is not a sufficient warrant. [Over] himself, over his own body and mind, the individual is sovereign."

8. Abortion laws have produced controversial decisions around the world in recent years. Note, e.g., a decision by Germany's Federal Constitutional Court in 1975 reaching a result quite contrary to Roe v. Wade: the German court, relying on the protection of "life" in the German Constitution, struck down a law loosening restrictions on abortions.

vote to uphold or overrule Roe.[9] In the 1990 hearings on the confirmation of Justice David H. Souter, the nominee refused to commit himself on issues regarding abortion, but did indicate that he generally shared Justice Harlan's approach to due process and supported the enforcement of at least some aspects of "privacy" and of unenumerated rights generally. In the first part of the hearings on the nomination of Justice Clarence Thomas in 1991, the issue of noninterpretivism resurfaced: his pre-nomination statements sympathetic to "natural law" were viewed by some as support for noninterpretivism. But Justice Thomas insisted before the Senate Judiciary Committee that his interest in natural law was philosophical and political and did not relate to his view of proper constitutional adjudication.

FROM ROE TO CASEY: EFFORTS TO OVERTURN ROE; REGULATIONS OF ABORTION PROCEDURES

Introduction. The aftermath of Roe included not only the contentious political challenges surveyed in note 7 above, but also repeated efforts to persuade the Court itself to overturn Roe. In the 1992 ruling in Casey, p. 557 below, the Court reaffirmed "the essential holding of Roe." The notes that follow review the highlights of the Court's encounters with abortion-related issues—not only its refusals to accept the invitations to overturn the 1973 decision, but also its handling of regulations of abortion procedures. In short, these notes cover the nearly two decades of litigation from 1973 to 1992. The 1992 decision in Casey follows this group of notes. Its importance lies not only in its reaffirmation of the "essential holding of Roe" but also in the guidelines it seeks to articulate for challenges to abortion regulations in the future.

1. *Pre-Casey challenges to Roe v. Wade in the Court.* a. *Akron.* A decade after Roe v. Wade (after years of cases carefully scrutinizing and often striking down restrictions on access to abortions—(see note 2)), the Court rejected an invitation to overturn Roe and its trimester framework. AKRON v. AKRON CENTER FOR REPRODUCTIVE HEALTH (Akron I), 462 U.S. 416 (1983). The majority struck down a range of abortion regulations enacted by the City of Akron (see note 2). But a major thrust of Justice POWELL's majority opinion was to reject the argument that the Court had erred in Roe. He responded that "the doctrine of stare decisis, while perhaps never entirely persuasive on a constitutional question, is a doctrine that demands respect in a society governed by the rule of law. We respect it today, and reaffirm Roe v. Wade." He not only reaffirmed the "central" liberty found in Roe, but also reiterated Roe's basic trimester division. Justice O'CONNOR's dissent, joined by Justices White and Rehnquist, stopped short of embracing and overruling Roe, but advocated a substantial change in the Court's approach to abortion cases. She urged, as a substitute for the strict scrutiny-trimester approach of Roe, that an abortion regulation "is not unconstitutional unless it unduly burdens the right to seek an abortion." She sketched her influential approach as follows: "In my view, this 'unduly burdensome' standard should be applied to the challenged regulation throughout the entire pregnancy without reference to the particular 'stage' of pregnancy involved. If the particular regulation does

---

9. For Judge Bork's own views of his confirmation hearings, and an exposition of his originalist approach to constitutional interpretation, see Bork, The Tempting of America: The Political Seduction of the Law (1990). Cf. the critique of Bork's position in Posner, "Bork and Beethoven," 42 Stan. L.Rev. 1365 (1990). See also Bronner, Battle for Justice: How the Bork Nomination Shook America (1989).

not 'unduly burden' the fundamental right, then our evaluation of that regulation is limited to our determination that the regulation rationally relates to a legitimate state purpose." In justifying her opposition to continuation of the trimester approach, she stated: "The [Roe framework is] clearly on a collision course with itself. As the medical risks of various abortion procedures decrease, the point at which the State may regulate for reasons of maternal health is moved further forward to actual childbirth. As medical science becomes better able to provide for the separate existence of the fetus, the point of viability is moved further back toward conception." Elaborating her challenge to the Roe framework, she added that, in her view, the "point at which [the legitimate state interests] become compelling does not depend on the trimester of pregnancy. Rather, these interests are present *throughout* pregnancy."

b. *Thornburgh*. The challenges to Roe continued in THORNBURGH v. AMERICAN COLL. OF OBST. & GYN., 476 747 (1986). In this case, the solicitor general filed an amicus brief explicitly urging that Roe be overruled. But the narrowly divided court once again refused to retreat from Roe. The case involved provisions of a Pennsylvania law regulating the performance of abortions; several of them were struck down by the court of appeals. The divided supreme court upheld that ruling, with Justice Blackmun's majority opinion once again reaffirming that a majority adhered to Roe: "In the years since this court's decision in Roe, states and municipalities have adopted a number of measures seemingly designed to prevent a woman, with the advice of her physician, from exercising her freedom of choice. [But] the constitutional principles that led this court to its decision in 1973 still provide the compelling reason for recognizing the constitutional dimensions of a woman's right to decide whether to end her pregnancy." At the end of his opinion, Justice Blackmun was even more emphatic: "constitutional rights do not always have easily ascertainable boundaries. [As] Judges, however, we are sworn to uphold the law even when its content gives rise to bitter dispute. Cooper v. Aaron. We recognized [in] Roe that abortion raises moral and spiritual questions over which honorable persons can disagree sincerely and profoundly. But those disagreements did not then and do not now relieve us of our duty to apply the constitution faithfully. [Few] decisions are more personal and intimate, more properly private, or more basic to individual dignity and autonomy, than a woman's decision—with the guidance of her physician and within the limits of Roe—whether to end her pregnancy. A woman's right to make that choice freely is fundamental." Justice Stevens's concurring opinion emphasized the importance of stare decisis. Chief Justice Burger, who had concurred in Roe, dissented, claiming that the court's invalidation of various state regulations had undercut his agreement with Roe: "[E]very member of the Roe court rejected the idea of abortion on demand. The court's opinion today, however, plainly undermines that important principle, and I regretfully conclude that some of the concerns of the dissenting justices in Roe [have] now been realized."

Justice WHITE, joined by Justice Rehnquist, both of whom had dissented in Roe, also dissented here, but on more fundamental grounds: "[I] continue to believe that this venture has been fundamentally misguided since its inception." He acknowledged the importance of stare decisis, but felt that there were more important constraints on judicial decisions, especially that based on the view that "decisions that find in the Constitution principles or values that cannot fairly be read into that document usurp the people's authority, for such decisions represent choices that the people have never made and that they cannot disavow through corrective legislation." He detailed at length his belief that, although constitutional interpretation requires more than "mere textual analysis or a search for the specific intent of the Framers," it did not justify "unrestrained imposition of [the Court's] own, extraconstitutional value prefer- ences." He added: "As for the notion that choice in the matter of abortion is implicit in the concept of ordered liberty, it seems apparent to me that a free, egalitarian, and democratic society does not presuppose any particular rule or set of rules with respect to abortion. [The] fact that many men and women of good will [place] themselves on both sides of the abortion controversy strength- ens my own conviction that the values animating the Constitution do not compel recognition of the abortion liberty as fundamental." Justice O'CON- NOR, joined by Justice Rehnquist, also dissented, restating her "undue bur- den" standard in even more confining terms ("An undue burden will generally be found 'in situations involving absolute obstacles or severe limitations on the abortion [decision].' ")

c. *Webster*. The recurrent direct challenges to Roe (which began with Akron in 1983 and resurfaced regularly, on a three-year cycle) culminated in the 1980s with a sharply divided ruling in Webster v. Reproductive Health Services, 492 U.S. 490 (1989). Once again, the opponents of Roe on the Court failed to muster a clear-cut majority to overrule it. Instead, the Court upheld several provisions of a Missouri law regulating abortions, with only a plurality endorsing a significant "restatement" of Roe's trimester scheme. Further attention to Webster is postponed until after the next group of notes, which survey the judicial fate of a range of state regulations in the Court in the late 1970s and the early 1980s, in order to aid evaluation of the modifications of the Court's approaches in Webster and in Casey.

2. *State regulations of abortions (and contraceptives) in the wake of Roe.* For most of the 1970s and 1980s (before Webster and Casey), the Court's careful scrutiny of state efforts to limit access to abortions usually produced defeats for the challenged laws. The Court's intensive scrutiny during these years is illustrated by the stance it articulated for laws enacted to promote the interest in protecting the pregnant woman's health, in Akron I, above. The majority in Akron noted that some regulations, those justified "by important state health objectives," were permissible even in the first trimester; but "even these minor regulations [may] not interfere with physician-patient consultation or with the woman's choice between abortion and childbirth." And with respect to second trimester regulations, when the state's health interest did become "compelling," the Court insisted on strong demonstrations of justification: "The existence of a compelling state interest in health [is] only the beginning of the inquiry. The State's regulation may be upheld only if it is reasonably designed to further that state interest." As this group of notes illustrates, a number of regulations failed to survive the second step in that inquiry.

a. *Spousal and parental consent requirements.* In the first major post-Roe abortion decision, the Court struck down a requirement of *spousal* consent. Planned Parenthood of Central Missouri v. Danforth, 428 U.S. 52 (1976). Missouri required a husband's written consent for an abortion during the first 12 weeks of pregnancy. The 6-3 decision, with Justice Blackmun writing for the majority, insisted that "the State cannot delegate authority [even to the spouse] to prevent abortion during the first trimester," since the woman "is the more directly and immediately affected by the pregnancy." In the same case, the majority struck down another provision requiring an unmarried woman under eighteen to obtain the consent of a parent as a prerequisite to obtaining an abortion. After insisting that a state could not "give a third party an [absolute] veto" over the abortion decision, the Court added that this did not mean that "every minor, regardless of age or maturity, may give effective consent for termination of her pregnancy." Rather, as elaborated in a compan- ion case, Bellotti v. Baird (Bellotti I), 428 U.S. 132 (1976), a blanket "parental veto" is "fundamentally different" from one permitting "a mature minor [to] obtain [an] order permitting the abortion without parental consultation." In short, a parental consent requirement was unconstitutional only if "it unduly burdens the right to seek an abortion."

The Court clarified the extent to which parents could be involved in a minor's abortion decision in a series of subsequent cases beginning with Bellotti v. Baird (Bellotti II), 443 U.S. 622 (1979). There, Justice Powell's plurality opinion announced that a state could involve a parent in a minor's abortion decision only if it also provided an "alternative procedure" (normally a judicial one), in order that the parental involvement would not amount to an "absolute, and possibly arbitrary, veto." The plurality approach in Bellotti II quickly became the operative standard in the pre-Casey years, as illustrated by Planned Parenthood Assn. of Kansas City v. Ashcroft, 462 U.S. 476 (1983), where the Court upheld a requirement of parental consent or a judicial alternative, because the alternative comported with the Bellotti II requirement that "the State must provide an alternative procedure whereby a pregnant minor may demonstrate that she is sufficiently mature to make the abortion decision herself or that, despite her immaturity, an abortion would be in her best interests." (For a criticism suggesting that the individualized judicial bypass proceedings suggested an excessive confidence in judges' wisdom, see Mnookin, "In the Interest of Children" (1985), 262, commenting that the post-Bellotti II situation in Massachusetts showed that "the new judicial process does not involve a careful individualized assessment, but is instead a rubber-stamp, administrative operation.") One kind of parental involvement that was sustained by the Court was a parental *notice* (rather than consent) requirement. See H. L. v. Matheson, 450 U.S. 398 (1981), sustaining a Utah law requiring physicians in most cases to notify parents of any minor upon whom an abortion was to be performed. (After Webster but before Casey, in Hodgson v. Minnesota, 497 U.S. 417 (1990), a divided Court struck down a requirement that both parents of any minor be notified forty-eight hours before an abortion was performed on a minor, but found such a notification requirement permissible provided that a proper judicial bypass procedure was available. And in Ohio v. Akron Center for Reproductive Health, 497 U.S. 502 (1990) (Akron II), the Court upheld a one-parent notification requirement accompanied a judicial bypass procedure.)

b. *Regulations of medical practices; protection of viable fetuses.* In Akron v. Akron Center for Reproductive Health (Akron I), 462 U.S. 416 (1983), the Court, after reaffirming Roe (see note 1a), considered a number of specific restrictions on the abortion process. Perhaps the most important was Akron's requirement that abortions performed after the first trimester had to be performed in a hospital, thus preventing such abortions in outpatient facilities. The Court struck down that provision as "a significant obstacle in the path of women seeking an abortion." The Court also invalidated a provision mandating a set of detailed guidelines regarding information the attending physician had to convey to the woman, supposedly to insure that the "written consent of the pregnant woman" to an abortion would be "truly informed." The mandated information pertained to the development of the fetus, the date of possible viability, and the complications that might result from an abortion. Justice Powell's majority opinion found this information requirement unconstitutional, noting that much of the information required was "designed not to inform the woman's consent but rather to persuade her to withhold it altogether." Moreover, the mandated material intruded upon the discretion of the pregnant woman's physician. The Court also struck down a mandatory 24–hour waiting period after the pregnant woman signed a consent form, a provision that increased the cost of obtaining an abortion by requiring two separate trips to the abortion facility. And in Thornburgh v. American Coll. of Obst. & Gyn., 476 U.S. 747 (1986) (see note 1b), the Court struck down several reporting requirements regarding the identities of the physician and the pregnant woman. Moreover, the Court struck down the provisions requiring the use of the abortion technique that would provide the most protection for the life of the fetus in post-viability abortions and requiring a second physician for post-viability abortions. The majority found that all of the invalidated provisions would "chill" the freedom to have an abortion. See also Colautti v. Franklin, 439 U.S. 379 (1979), invalidating on vagueness grounds a law assertedly designed to further the state interest in protecting viable fetuses. The law imposed criminal liability for failure to follow a statutorily prescribed standard of care when the fetus was "viable" or when there was "sufficient reason to believe that the fetus may be viable."

   c. *Governmental refusals to fund abortions.* As the preceding notes indicate, the pre-Casey Court struck down most post-Roe efforts to restrict access to abortions. The most important exception to this generalization stems from decisions in 1977 and 1980 holding that, in structuring welfare programs, government may constitutionally choose *not* to fund abortions for financially needy pregnant women (even where it does pay for childbirth). The cases presented a clash between two themes of the modern Court: the broad protection of the woman's right to choose whether or not to have an abortion, recognized in the Roe line of due process cases, and the reluctance to impose affirmative financial obligations on government, developed in equal protection cases (see chap. 9 below). In the 1980 case, the Court summarized the principle at the heart of Roe (and explained its holding regarding funding) as follows: "[Although] government may not place obstacles in the path of a woman's exercise of a freedom of choice, it need not remove those not of its own creation." The 1977 cases sustained governmental refusals to fund nontherapeutic abortions; the 1980 decision extended that ruling to medically necessary abortions as well.

   (i). *Maher v. Roe.* The first major abortion funding case was MAHER v. ROE, 432 U.S. 464 (1977). This 6-3 decision sustained a Connecticut regulation granting Medicaid benefits for childbirth but denying them for nontherapeutic, medically unnecessary abortions. According to Justice POWELL's majority opinion, the challengers claimed that Connecticut "must accord equal treatment to both abortion and childbirth, and may not evidence a policy preference by funding only the medical expenses incident to childbirth." In rejecting this claim, Justice Powell used an equal protection mode of analysis; but determining whether strict scrutiny was warranted required deciding whether the scheme interfered with the fundamental right recognized in Roe. According to the majority, it did not; a more deferential "rationality" standard of review was therefore appropriate; and the law readily passed muster under that standard. In rejecting the argument that the Connecticut law interfered with a fundamental right, Justice Powell stated: "[The] right [in Roe and its progeny] protects the woman from unduly burdensome interference with her freedom to decide whether to terminate her pregnancy. It implies no limitation on the authority of a State to make a value judgment favoring childbirth over abortion, and to implement that judgment by the allocation of public funds." He insisted that the law attacked here was "different in kind from the laws invalidated in our previous abortion decisions": "The Connecticut regulation places no obstacles—absolute or otherwise—in the pregnant woman's path to an abortion. An indigent woman who desires an abortion suffers no disadvantage as a consequence of Connecticut's decision to fund childbirth; she continues as before to be dependent on private sources for the service she desires. The State may have made childbirth a more attractive alternative, thereby influencing the woman's decision, but it has imposed no restriction on access to abortions that was not already there. The indigency that may make it difficult—and in some cases, perhaps, impossible—for some women to have abortions is neither created nor in any way affected by the Connecticut regulation." He insisted that this signaled "no retreat from Roe or the cases applying it. There is a basic difference between direct state interference with a protected activity and state encouragement of an alternative [activity]. Constitutional concerns are greatest when the State attempts to impose its will by force of law; the State's power to encourage actions deemed to be in the public interest is necessarily far broader."[1]

Justice BRENNAN's dissent, joined by Justices Marshall and Blackmun, accused the majority of "a distressing insensitivity to the plight of impoverished pregnant women." Moreover, the distinction in state funding coerced "indigent pregnant women to bear children they would not otherwise choose to have." He insisted that the ruling "seriously erodes the principles that Roe and Doe announced to guide the determination of what constitutes an unconstitutional infringement of the fundamental right of pregnant women to be free to decide whether to have an abortion." Financial pressure on indigent women to bear children, in his view, "unconstitutionally impinges upon [the] claim of privacy." Justice Brennan was not persuaded by Justice Powell's efforts to distinguish the earlier abortion cases. Some of the post-Roe decisions, Justice Brennan noted, involved requirements which operated as less than "an absolute bar to elective abortions," yet the Court had struck them down. And in a wide range of situations outside the privacy area, the Court had found that "infringements of fundamental rights are not limited to outright denials of those rights." What was critical in those cases was that state law had "inhibited [the woman's] fundamental right to make [the] choice free from state interference." Nor did the funding context serve to distinguish this case: withholding financial benefits had been held to constitute invalid burdens on fundamental rights in other contexts. Justice MARSHALL's dissent argued that the regulations were "in reality intended to impose a moral viewpoint that no State may constitutionally enforce." He viewed the funding scheme as an attempt to circumvent Roe and its progeny, and he added: "I am appalled at the ethical bankruptcy of those who preach a 'right to life' that means [a] bare existence in utter misery for so many poor women and their children." He, too, was unpersuaded by the majority's efforts to avoid "any meaningful scrutiny": "[The] Court pulls from thin air a distinction between laws that absolutely prevent exercise of the fundamental right to abortion and those that 'merely' make its exercise difficult for some people." He argued for application of his "sliding scale" equal protection approach (see p. 632 below) and found the asserted state interest plainly inadequate in light of "the brutal effect" of the challenged law. (Justice BLACKMUN submitted a separate dissent, joined by Justices Brennan and Marshall.)

(ii). *Harris v. McRae.* Three years later, HARRIS v. McRAE, 448 U.S. 297 (1980), rejected constitutional challenges to federal funding limitations that barred payments for most medically necessary abortions, and thus went well

---

1. The deferential scrutiny, "rationality" requirement was readily met here: "The subsidizing of costs incident to childbirth is a rational means of encouraging childbirth. [Our] cases uniformly have accorded the States a wide latitude in choosing among competing demands for limited public funds. [Dandridge v. Williams (1970; p. 912 below).]" The majority also rejected attacks on similar funding provisions in two companion cases, Beal v. Doe, 432 U.S. 438 (1977), and Poelker v. Doe, 432 U.S. 519 (1977).

beyond the medically "unnecessary," nontherapeutic ones unfunded in Maher. Nevertheless, relying heavily on Maher, the Court's 5-4 decision sustained the Hyde Amendment.[2] In rejecting a substantive due process attack, Justice STEWART's majority opinion concluded that "it simply does not follow [from Roe] that a woman's freedom of choice carries with it a constitutional entitlement to the financial resources to avail herself of the full range of protected choices. The reason why was explained in Maher: although government may not place obstacles in the path of a woman's exercise of her freedom of choice, it need not remove those not of its own creation. Indigency falls in the latter category. The financial constraints that restrict an indigent woman's ability to enjoy the full range of constitutionally protected freedom of choice are the product not of governmental restrictions on access to abortions, but rather of her indigency. Although Congress has opted to subsidize medically necessary services generally [under Medicaid], but not certain medically necessary abortions, the fact remains that the Hyde Amendment leaves an indigent woman with at least the same range of choice in deciding whether to obtain a medically necessary abortion as she would have had if Congress had chosen to subsidize no health care costs at all." Justice Stewart added: "Although the liberty protected by the Due Process Clause affords protection against unwarranted governmental interference with freedom of choice in the context of certain personal decisions, it does not confer an entitlement to such funds as may be necessary to realize all the advantages of that freedom. To hold otherwise would mark a drastic change in our understanding of the Constitution. It cannot be that because government may not prohibit the use of contraceptives [Griswold] or prevent parents from sending their child to a private school [Pierce], government, therefore, has an affirmative constitutional obligation to ensure that all persons have the financial resources to obtain contraceptives or send their children to private schools. To translate the limitation on governmental power implicit in [due process] into an affirmative funding obligation would require Congress to subsidize the medically necessary abortion of an indigent woman even if Congress had not enacted a Medicaid program to subsidize other medically necessary services. Nothing in the Due Process Clause supports such an extraordinary result. Whether freedom of choice that is constitutionally protected warrants federal subsidization is a question for Congress to answer, not a matter of constitutional entitlement."[3]

Justice BRENNAN, joined by Justices Marshall and Blackmun—the dissenters in Maher as well—reiterated their criticism: "The proposition for which [Roe and its progeny stand] is not that the State is under an affirmative obligation to ensure access to abortions for all who may desire them; it is that the State must refrain from wielding its enormous power and influence in a

2. The Hyde Amendment refers to a series of funding restrictions adopted by Congress between 1976 and 1980 to bar, except under specified circumstances, the use of federal funds for the reimbursement of abortion costs under the Medicaid program. The provision applicable for fiscal year 1980 permitted public payment only "where the life of the mother would be endangered" and for "victims of rape or incest when such rape or incest has been reported promptly."

3. With respect to the equal protection challenge, Justice Stewart followed the traditional "two-tier" approach discussed in the next chapter. Here, only the deferential, "rationality" requirement applied, and that standard was readily satisfied. In rejecting an added claim based on the religion clauses, Justice Stewart reached only the Establishment Clause issue and concluded that "the fact that the funding restrictions [may] coincide with the religious tenets of the Roman Catholic Church does not, without more, contravene the Establishment Clause." (Justice WHITE, who agreed with Justice Stewart's "straightforward analysis," also submitted a separate opinion.)

manner that might burden the pregnant woman's freedom to choose whether to have an abortion." He accused the majority of failing to appreciate that "it is not simply the woman's indigency that interferes with her freedom of choice, but the combination of her own poverty and the government's unequal subsidization of abortion and childbirth." He added: "[The] fundamental flaw in the Court's due process analysis [is] its failure to acknowledge that the discriminatory distribution of the benefits of governmental largesse can discourage the exercise of fundamental liberties just as effectively as can an outright denial of those rights through criminal and regulatory sanctions." Justice STEVENS, a member of the Maher majority, dissented, insisting that this case was "fundamentally different" from Maher because medically necessary abortions were involved: "This case involve[s] a special exclusion of women who, by definition, are confronted with a choice between two serious harms: serious health damage to themselves on the one hand and abortion on the other. [Government may not] exclude a woman from medical benefits to which she would otherwise be entitled solely to further an interest in potential life when a physician [certifies] that an abortion is necessary 'for the preservation of the life or health of the mother.' Roe v. Wade. The Court totally fails to explain why this reasoning is not dispositive here." [Having] decided to alleviate some of the hardships of poverty by providing necessary medical care, the Government must use neutral criteria in distributing benefits. "[It] may not create exceptions for the sole purpose of furthering a governmental interest that is constitutionally subordinate to the individual interest that the entire program was designed to protect."

(iii). *Rust v. Sullivan.* In RUST v. SULLIVAN, 500 U.S. 173 (1991), the Court extended the reasoning of Maher and McRae to a restriction on abortion counseling by any project receiving federal family planning funds. At issue were three regulations promulgated by the Health and Human Services Department. The regulations provided that a family planning project funded under Title X of the Public Health Service Act (1) "may not provide counseling concerning the use of abortion as a method of family planning or provide referral for abortion as a method of family planning," (2) may not "encourage, promote or advocate abortion as a method of family planning," and (3) must be "physically and financially separate" from any abortion counseling or encouragement the recipient might otherwise conduct. The regulations permitted Title X projects to provide pregnant women with information about childbirth and prenatal care, but advised them to tell any pregnant woman who inquired about abortion that the project does not consider abortion an "appropriate method of family planning." Doctors and Title X grantees challenged the regulations under both the right of privacy implicit in the Fifth Amendment's due process clause and under the First Amendment. The Court rejected both challenges. (For the portions of the decision rejecting the First Amendment challenge, see p. 1321 below.)

Chief Justice REHNQUIST, writing for the majority in the 5–4 decision, reiterated that the due process clauses confer no affirmative right to governmental aid, even with respect to a liberty with which government may not otherwise interfere: "The Government has no constitutional duty to subsidize an activity merely because the activity is constitutionally protected and may validly choose to fund childbirth over abortion and 'implement that judgment by the allocation of public funds' for medical services relating to childbirth but not to those relating to abortion. [Government's] decision to fund childbirth but not abortion 'places no governmental obstacle in the path of a woman who chooses to terminate her pregnancy, but rather, by means of unequal subsidization of abortion and other medical services, encourages alternative activity deemed in the public interest.' [McRae.] [Just] as Congress' refusal to fund abortions in McRae left 'an indigent woman with at least the same range of choice in deciding whether to obtain a medically necessary abortion as she would have had if Congress had chosen to subsidize no health care costs at all, '[Congress's] refusal to fund abortion counseling and advocacy leaves a pregnant woman with the same choices as if the Government had chosen not to fund family-planning services at all. The difficulty that a woman encounters when a Title X project does not provide abortion counseling or referral leaves her in no different position than she would have been if the Government had not enacted Title X."

Nor did the regulations impermissibly infringe on the doctor-patient relationship, held Chief Justice Rehnquist. A law generally requiring all doctors within a jurisdiction to withhold information about abortion would be problematic, he conceded, but "[u]nder the Secretary's regulations, [a] doctor's ability to provide, and a woman's right to receive, information concerning abortion and abortion-related services outside the context of the Title X project remains unfettered. It would undoubtedly be easier for a woman seeking an abortion if she could receive information about abortion from a Title X project, but the Constitution does not require that the Government distort the scope of its mandated program in order to provide that information. [If] most Title X clients are effectively precluded by indigency and poverty from seeing a [private]health care provider who will provide abortion-related services, [they] are in no worse position than if Congress had never enacted Title X. [McRae.]"

Justice BLACKMUN dissented, joined on this point by Justices Marshall and Stevens: "By suppressing medically pertinent information and injecting a restrictive ideological message unrelated to considerations of maternal health, the Government places formidable obstacles in the path of Title X clients' freedom of choice and thereby violates their Fifth Amendment rights. [Although] her physician's words, in fact, are strictly controlled by the Government and wholly unrelated to her particular medical situation, the Title X client will reasonably construe them as professional advice to forgo her right to obtain an abortion. [In] view of the inevitable effect of the regulations, the majority's conclusion that [the regulations leave a woman in no worse a position than if the Government had not enacted Title X] is insensitive and contrary to common human experience. Both the purpose and result of the challenged regulations is to deny women the ability voluntarily to decide their procreative destiny. For these women, the Government will have obliterated the freedom to choose as surely as if it had banned abortions outright. The denial of this freedom is not a consequence of poverty but of the Government's ill-intentioned distortion of information it has chosen to provide." Justice Blackmun added that the obstacles imposed by the regulations were "doubly offensive" because they "manipulat[ed] the doctor-patient dialogue, [which] embodies a unique relationship of trust." Nor could the regulations be saved because they applied only to grantees, not to all physicians: "It cannot be that an otherwise unconstitutional infringement of choice is made lawful because it touches only some of the Nation's pregnant women and not all of them." Justice O'Connor dissented separately on the ground that the regulations exceeded statutory authority.

d. *Access of minors to contraceptives after Griswold and Roe.* In CAREY v. POPULATION SERVICES INTERNATIONAL, 431 U.S. 678 (1977), a divided Court struck down a New York prohibition of the sale or distribution of contraceptives to minors under 16. Justice BRENNAN's plurality opinion, joined by Justices Stewart, Marshall and Blackmun, stated that strict scrutiny was required for restrictions on access to contraceptives, "because such access is essential to exercise of the constitutionally protected right of decision in matters of childbearing that is the underlying foundation of the holdings in Griswold, Eisenstadt, and Roe." He rejected the argument that the ban on distribution to persons under 16 could be justified "as a regulation of the morality of minors." He noted that minors have some constitutional rights, but that state power over children is greater than over adults. Against that background, he was unpersuaded by the allegedly "significant" state interests in promoting its policy of discouraging sexual activity among the young. He also found "substantial reason for doubt [that] limiting access to contraceptives will in fact substantially discourage early sexual behavior." He added that, when a state "burdens the exercise of a fundamental right, its attempt to justify that burden as a rational means for the accomplishment of some significant state policy requires more than a bare assertion [that] the burden is connected to such a policy." Justice WHITE concurred only in the result, on the ground that "the State has not demonstrated that the prohibition against distribution of contraceptives to minors measurably contributes to the deterrent purpose which the State advances." Justice STEVENS, in another separate opinion, concurred because of the irrationality of the means employed. Justice POWELL's separate concurrence, while objecting to "extraordinary protection [of] all personal decisions in matters of sex," found the challenged restriction "defective" because it prohibited parents from distributing contraceptives to their children, "a restriction that unjustifiably interferes with parental interests in rearing their children." (Justice REHNQUIST submitted a brief dissent; Chief Justice BURGER dissented without opinion.)

WEBSTER v. REPRODUCTIVE HEALTH SERVICES, 492 U.S. 490 (1989): This case, upholding several provisions of a Missouri abortion law, was decided three years after Akron I, above, and three years before Casey, which follows. The state and the United States once again urged the court to overrule Roe v. Wade outright. The court once more refused that invitation, even though a plurality significantly modified Roe's trimester approach. The ruling attracted a great deal of public attention, with pro-choice forces deploring it as portending the imminent doom of Roe and pro-life forces hailing it for similar reasons. The court reversed the eighth circuit's ruling holding several provisions unconstitutional.

A majority found that the law's preamble, stating that "[t]he life of each human being begins at conception," did not conflict with Roe's statement that "a State may not adopt one theory of when life begins to justify its regulation of abortions." Chief Justice REHNQUIST's opinion found that the preamble could be read simply to express a value judgment and thought it therefore unnecessary to rule on its constitutionality. The law also contained a ban on state employees performing abortions and on the use of public facilities for abortions, even where the patient paid for the abortion herself. Once again, the majority held that provision constitutional especially in light of abortion-funding cases such as Harris v. McRae, noting that "our cases have recognized that the Due Process Clauses generally confer no affirmative right to governmental aid" [DeShaney (1989; p. 960 below)]. The Court concluded that "Missouri's refusal to allow public employees to perform abortions in public hospitals leaves a pregnant woman with the same choices as if the State had chosen not to operate any public hospitals at all." The Chief Justice added that the abortion-funding cases "all support the view that the State need not commit any resources to facilitating abortions, even if it can turn a profit by doing so."

The most controversial and divisive Missouri provision was a viability-testing requirement. Speaking only for a plurality on this issue, the Chief

Justice (joined by Justices White and Kennedy) adopted a controversial interpretation of the provision that required a physician, prior to performing an
abortion "on a woman he has reason to believe is carrying an unborn child of
twenty or more weeks gestational age," to determine "if the unborn child is
viable by using and exercising that degree of care, skill, and proficiency, be
exercised by the ordinarily skillful, careful, and prudent physician." Although
the provision went on to prescribe that the physician perform specified tests
necessary to a finding of the gestational age, weight, and lung maturity of the
unborn child, the plurality interpreted this by deemphasizing the prescribed
tests and reading the statute "to require only those tests that are useful to
making subsidiary findings as to viability." So read, the provision passed
muster; as construed, it did not require the physician to undertake the tests *in
all circumstances* and tests could be dispensed with "when the physician's
reasonable professional judgment indicates that the tests would be irrelevant to
determining viability or even dangerous to the mother and the fetus." Noting
that the trial court had found that "there may be a 4-week error in estimating
gestational age, which supports testing at 20 weeks," the Chief Justice, speaking for the plurality, stated that "the doubt cast upon this provision by earlier
cases was 'not so much a flaw in the statute' as it was 'a reflection of the fact
that the rigid trimester analysis of the course of a pregnancy enunciated in Roe
has resulted in subsequent cases like Colautti and Akron making constitutional
law in this area a virtual Procrustean bed.'" He proceeded to significantly
"modify and narrow Roe" and its progeny by substantially altering Roe's
approach.

The plurality elaborated by noting that "[s]tare decisis is a cornerstone of
our legal system, but it has less power in constitutional cases, where, save for
constitutional amendments, this Court is the only body able to make needed
changes." Quoting Garcia (chap. 3 above), the opinion noted that the Court had
been willing to reconsider prior constitutional interpretations that had proved
"unsound in principle and unworkable in practice" and added: "We think the
Roe trimester framework falls into that category." In justifying his modification
of Roe, the Chief Justice argued that Roe's framework was "hardly consistent
with a notion of a Constitution cast in general terms. [The] key elements of the
Roe framework—trimesters and viability—are not found in the text of the
Constitution or any place else one would expect to find a constitutional
principle. Since the bounds of the inquiry are essentially indeterminate, the
result has been a web of legal rules that have become increasingly intricate.
[Moreover,] we do not see why the State's interest in protecting potential
human life should come into existence only at the point of viability, and that
there should therefore be a rigid line allowing state regulation after viability
but prohibiting it before viability. [The] State here has chosen viability as the
point at which its interest in potential life must be safeguarded. [We] are
satisfied that the requirement of these tests permissibly furthers the State's
interest in protecting human [life]." The plurality rejected the charge in the
separate opinions that it had failed to join in a "great issues" debate regarding
the existence of an "unenumerated" general right to privacy, and also the
charge that it was failing to deal with "the most politically divisive domestic
legal issue of our time."

On the viability-testing provisions, Justice O'CONNOR insisted in her
separate concurrence that the law was constitutional even within the Roe
trimester framework. She explained: "No decision of this Court has held that
the State may not directly promote its interest in potential human life when
viability is possible. Quite the contrary. [Thornburgh.]" In short, there was "no
necessity" to reexamine Roe. "[When] the constitutional invalidity of a State's

abortion statute actually turns on the constitutional validity of Roe v. Wade, there will time enough to reexamine Roe. And to do so carefully." Justice BLACKMUN, joined by Justice Brennan and Marshall, charged that the plurality had "silently" overruled Roe and added that, in his memory, no plurality had ever "gone about its business in such a deceptive fashion." He, too, focused on the viability-testing requirement. He claimed that the plurality's perceived conflict between the statute and Roe's trimester framework was "a contrived conflict." He continued: "No one contests that under the Roe framework the State, in order to promote its interest in potential human life, may regulate and even proscribe non-therapeutic abortions once the fetus becomes viable. If, as the plurality appears to hold, the testing provision simply requires the physician to use [appropriate] tests to determine whether the fetus is actually viable, [then] I see little or no conflict with Roe. [In] short, the testing provision, as construed by the plurality, [could] be upheld effortlessly under current doctrine." Instead, the majority had "distort[ed]" the law, in order to rush headlong into the reconsideration of the Roe framework. He reiterated his support for the trimester framework, and continued: "Thus, 'not with a bang, but a whimper,' the plurality discards a landmark case [and] casts into darkness the hopes and visions of every woman in this country" who had believed that the Constitution guaranteed the right to choice in childbearing. He ended: "For today, at least, the law of abortion stands undisturbed. [But] the signs are evident and very ominous, and a chill wind blows." Justice STEVENS also dissented, supporting an invalidation of the testing requirement and a portion of the preamble as well. And in a long and intense separate opinion, Justice SCALIA urged that Roe v. Wade should be "explicitly" overruled. He added: "Since today we contrive to avoid doing it, [I] need not set forth my reasons. [The] outcome of today's case will doubtless be heralded as a triumph of judicial statesmanship. It is not that, unless it is statesmanlike needlessly to prolong this Court's self-awarded sovereignty over a field where it has little proper business since the answers to most of the cruel questions posed are political and not juridical—a sovereignty which therefore quite properly, but to the great damage of the Court, makes it the object of the sort of organized public pressure that political institutions in a democracy ought to receive."*

Planned Parenthood of Southeastern Pa. v. Casey

505 U.S. 833, 112 S.Ct. 2791, 120 L.Ed.2d 674 (1992).

Justice O'CONNOR, Justice KENNEDY, and Justice SOUTER announced the judgment of the Court and delivered the opinion of the Court with respect to Parts I, II, III, V–A, V–C, and VI, an opinion with respect to Part V–E, in

---

* Note the comment on Webster in Sullivan & Estrich, "Abortion Politics: Writing for an Audience of One," 138 U.Pa.L.Rev. 119 (1989): "[If] little was decided in Webster, a good deal was nonetheless said. The Chief Justice, writing for three members of the Court, made plain that it was ready to jettison [the] trimester approach of [Roe]. The genius of [his] approach, if you can call it that, is that it effectively overrules Roe with- out ever even suggesting that a woman lacks the privacy or autonomy interest in her own body." See also, generally, Tribe, Abortion: The Clash of Absolutes (1990), McConnell, "How Not to Promote Serious Deliberation About Abortion," 58 U.Chi.L.Rev. 1181 (1991), and Rubenfeld, "On the Legal Status of the Proposition That 'Life Begins at Conception,'" 43 Stan.L.Rev. 559 (1991).

which Justice STEVENS joins, and an opinion with respect to Parts IV, V–B, and V–D.

I.   Liberty finds no refuge in a jurisprudence of doubt. Yet 19 years after our holding that the Constitution protects a woman's right to terminate her pregnancy in its early stages, [Roe's] definition of liberty is still questioned. [T]he United States, as it has done in five other cases in the last decade, again asks us to overrule Roe. At issue in these cases are five provisions of the Pennsylvania Abortion Control Act of 1982 [as amended]. The Act requires that a woman seeking an abortion give her informed consent prior to the abortion procedure, and specifies that she be provided with certain information at least 24 hours before the abortion is performed. For a minor to obtain an abortion, the Act requires the informed consent of one of her parents, but provides for a judicial bypass option. [Another] provision [requires] that, unless certain exceptions apply, a married woman seeking an abortion must sign a statement indicating that she has notified her husband of her intended abortion. The Act exempts compliance with these requirements in the event of a "medical emergency." [In] addition, [the] Act imposes [reporting] requirements on facilities that provide abortion services. Before [these] provisions took effect, petitioners [brought] this suit seeking declaratory and injunctive relief. Each provision was challenged as unconstitutional on its face. The District Court [held] all the provisions at issue here [unconstitutional]. The Court of Appeals [upheld] all of the regulations except for the husband notification requirement.

[A]t oral argument, [the] attorney for the parties challenging the statute took the position that none of the enactments can be upheld without overruling [Roe]. We disagree with that analysis; but we acknowledge that our decisions after Roe cast doubt upon the meaning and reach of its holding. Further, the Chief Justice admits that he would overrule the central holding of Roe and adopt the rational relationship test as the sole criterion of constitutionality. State and federal courts as well as legislatures throughout the Union must have guidance as they seek to address this subject in conformance with the Constitution. Given these premises, we find it imperative to review once more the principles that define the rights of the woman and the legitimate authority of the State respecting the termination of pregnancies by abortion procedures. After considering the fundamental constitutional questions resolved by Roe, principles of institutional integrity, and the rule of stare decisis, we are led to conclude this: the essential holding of [Roe] should be retained and once again reaffirmed. [Roe's] essential holding, the holding we reaffirm, has three parts. First is a recognition of the right of the woman to choose to have an abortion before viability and to obtain it without undue interference from the State. Before viability, the State's interests are not strong enough to support a prohibition of abortion or the imposition of a substantial obstacle to the woman's effective right to elect the procedure. Second is a confirmation of the State's power to restrict abortions after fetal viability, if the law contains exceptions for pregnancies which endanger a woman's life or health. And third is the principle that the State has legitimate interests from the outset of the pregnancy in protecting the health of the woman and the life of the fetus that may become a child. These principles do not contradict one another; and we adhere to each.

II.   Constitutional protection of the woman's decision to terminate her pregnancy derives from the Due Process Clause. [The] controlling word [is] "liberty." Although a literal reading might suggest that [the Clause] governs only the procedures by which a State may deprive persons of liberty, for at least 105 years, at least since Mugler v. Kansas [1887; p. 459 above] the Clause has been understood to contain a substantive component as well, one "barring certain government actions regardless of the fairness of the procedures used to implement them." [It] is tempting, as a means of curbing the discretion of federal judges, to suppose that liberty encompasses no more than those rights already guaranteed to the individual against federal interference by the express provisions of the first eight amendments. [But] of course this Court has never accepted that view. It is also tempting, for the same reason, to suppose that the Due Process Clause protects only those practices, defined at the most specific level, that were protected against government interference by other rules of law when the Fourteenth Amendment was ratified. See Michael H. v. Gerald D. [1989; p. 590 below; opinion of Scalia, J.]. But such a view would be inconsistent with our law. It is a promise of the Constitution that there is a realm of personal liberty which the government may not enter. We have vindicated this principle before. Marriage is mentioned nowhere in the Bill of Rights and interracial marriage was illegal in most States in the 19th century, but the Court was no doubt correct in finding it to be an aspect of liberty protected [by substantive due process] in Loving v. Virginia [1988; p. 667 below]. [Neither] the Bill of Rights nor the specific practices of States at the time of the adoption of the Fourteenth Amendment marks the outer limits of the substantive sphere of liberty which the Fourteenth Amendment protects. See U.S. Const.Amend. 9. [After quoting from Justice Harlan's opinion in Poe v. Ullman, p. 522 above, the Justices continued:] [It] is settled now, as it was when the Court heard arguments in Roe, that the Constitution places limits on a State's right to interfere with a person's most basic decisions about family and parenthood, as well as bodily integrity. The inescapable fact is that adjudication of substantive due process claims may call upon the Court [to] exercise that same capacity which by tradition courts always have exercised: reasoned judgment. Its boundaries are not susceptible of expression as a simple rule. That does not mean we are free to invalidate state policy choices with which we disagree; yet neither does it permit us to shrink from the duties of our office. [Men] and women of good conscience can disagree, and we suppose some always shall disagree, about the profound moral and spiritual implications of terminating a pregnancy, even in its earliest stage. Some of us as individuals find abortion offensive to our most basic principles of morality, but that cannot control our decision. Our obligation is to define the liberty of all, not to mandate our own moral code. The underlying constitutional issue is whether the State can resolve these philosophic questions in such a definitive way that a woman lacks all choice in the matter, except perhaps in those rare circumstances in which the pregnancy is itself a danger to her own life or health, or is the result of rape or incest. It is conventional constitutional doctrine that where reasonable people disagree the government can adopt one position or the other. [E.g., Williamson v. Lee Optical.] That theorem, however, assumes a state of affairs in which the choice does not intrude upon a protected liberty. [Our] law affords constitutional protection to personal decisions relating to marriage, procreation, contraception, family relationships, child rearing, and education. [These] matters, involving the most intimate and personal choices a person may make in a lifetime, choices central to personal dignity and autonomy, are central to the liberty protected by the Fourteenth Amendment. At the heart of liberty is the right to define one's own concept of existence, of meaning, of the universe, and of the mystery of human life. Beliefs about these matters could not define the attributes of personhood were they formed under compulsion of the State.

These considerations begin our analysis of the woman's interest in terminating her pregnancy but cannot end it, for this reason: though the abortion decision may originate within the zone of conscience and belief, it is more than a philosophic exercise. Abortion is a unique act. It is an act fraught with consequences for others: for the woman who must live with the implications of her decision; for the persons who perform and assist in the procedure; for the spouse, family, and society which must confront the knowledge that these procedures exist, procedures some deem nothing short of an act of violence against innocent human life; and, depending on one's beliefs, for the life or potential life that is aborted. Though abortion is conduct, it does not follow that the State is entitled to proscribe it in all instances. That is because the liberty of the woman is at stake in a sense unique to the human condition and so unique to the law. The mother who carries a child to full term is subject to anxieties, to physical constraints, to pain that only she must bear. That these sacrifices have from the beginning of the human race been endured by woman with a pride that ennobles her in the eyes of others and gives to the infant a bond of love cannot alone be grounds for the State to insist she make the sacrifice. Her suffering is too intimate and personal for the State to insist, without more, upon its own vision of the woman's role, however dominant that vision has been in the course of our history and our culture. The destiny of the woman must be shaped to a large extent on her own conception of her spiritual imperatives and her place in society. [Moreover, in] some critical respects the abortion decision is of the same character as the decision to use contraception, to which Griswold, Eisenstadt, and Carey afford constitutional protection. We have no doubt as to the correctness of those decisions. They support the reasoning in Roe relating to the woman's liberty because they involve personal decisions concerning not only the meaning of procreation but also human responsibility and respect for it. Roe was, of course, an extension of those cases and, as the decision itself indicated, the separate States could act in some degree to further their own legitimate interests in protecting pre-natal life. [While] we appreciate the weight of the arguments made on behalf of the State in the case before us, arguments [which] conclude that Roe should be over-ruled, the reservations any of us may have in reaffirming the central holding of Roe are outweighed by the explication of individual liberty we have given combined with the force of stare decisis. We turn now to that doctrine.

III.   A. [W]hen this Court reexamines a prior holding, its judgment is customarily informed by a series of prudential and pragmatic considerations designed to test the consistency of overruling a prior decision with the ideal of the rule of law, and to gauge the respective costs of reaffirming and overruling a prior case. Thus, for example, we may ask whether the rule has proved to be intolerable simply in defying practical workability; whether the rule is subject to a kind of reliance that would lend a special hardship to the consequences of overruling and add inequity to the cost of repudiation; whether related principles of law have so far developed as to have left the old rule no more than a remnant of abandoned doctrine; or whether facts have so changed or come to be seen so differently, as to have robbed the old rule of significant application or justification. So in this case we may inquire whether Roe's central rule has been found unworkable; whether the rule's limitation on state power could be removed without serious inequity to those who have relied upon it or significant damage to the stability of the society governed by the rule in question; whether the law's growth in the intervening years has left Roe's central rule a doctrinal anachronism discounted by society; and whether Roe's premises of fact have so far changed in the ensuing two decades as to render its central holding somehow irrelevant or unjustifiable in dealing with the issue it addressed.

1. Although Roe has engendered opposition, it has in no sense proven "unworkable," see [Garcia], representing as it does a simple limitation beyond which a state law is unenforceable. While Roe has [required] judicial assess-

ment of [laws] affecting the exercise of the choice guaranteed against government infringement, and although the need for such review will remain as a
consequence of today's decision, [these] determinations fall within judicial
competence. (2) [Since] the classic case for weighing reliance heavily in favor of
following the earlier rule occurs in the commercial context, where advance
planning of great precision is most obviously a necessity, it is no cause for
surprise that some would find no reliance worthy of consideration in support of
Roe. [But] for two decades, [people] have organized intimate relationships and
made choices that define their views of themselves and their places in society,
in reliance on the availability of abortion in the event that contraception should
fail. The ability of women to participate equally in the economic and social life
of the Nation has been facilitated by their ability to control their reproductive
lives. [While] the effect of reliance on Roe cannot be exactly measured, neither
can the certain cost of overruling Roe for people who have ordered their
thinking and living around that case be dismissed.

3. No evolution of legal principle has left Roe's doctrinal footings weaker
than they were in 1973. No development of constitutional law since the case
was decided has [left] Roe behind as a mere survivor of obsolete constitutional
thinking. [Roe] itself placed its holding in the succession of cases most prominently exemplified by Griswold. When it is so seen, Roe is clearly in no
jeopardy, since subsequent [developments] have neither disturbed, nor do they
threaten to diminish, the scope of recognized protection accorded to the liberty
relating to intimate relationships, the family, and decisions about whether or
not to beget or bear a child. [And if Roe is seen] as a rule (whether or not
mistaken) of personal autonomy and bodily integrity, with doctrinal affinity to
cases recognizing limits on governmental power to mandate medical treatment
or to bar its rejection, [our] cases since Roe accord with Roe's view that a
State's interest in the protection of life falls short of justifying any plenary
override of individual liberty claims. Cruzan [1990; p. 602 below]. [Nor] will
courts building upon Roe be likely to hand down erroneous decisions as a
consequence. Even on the assumption that the central holding of Roe was in
error, that error would go only to the strength of the state interest in fetal
protection, not to the recognition afforded [the] woman's liberty. [The] soundness of this prong of [Roe] is apparent from a consideration of the alternative.
If indeed the woman's interest in deciding whether to bear and beget a child
had not been recognized as in Roe, the State might as readily restrict a
woman's right to choose to carry a pregnancy to term as to terminate it, to
further asserted state interests in population control, or eugenics, for example.
Yet Roe has been sensibly relied upon to counter any such [suggestions]. (4.)
[Time] has overtaken some of Roe's factual assumptions: advances in maternal
health care allow for abortions safe to the mother later in pregnancy than was
true in 1973, and advances in neonatal care have advanced viability to a point
somewhat earlier. But these facts go only to the scheme of time limits on the
realization of competing interests, and the divergences from the factual underpinnings of 1973 have no bearing on the validity of Roe's central holding that
viability marks the earliest point at which the State's interest in fetal life is
constitutionally adequate to justify a legislative ban on nontherapeutic abortions. [T]he attainment of viability may continue to serve as the critical fact,
just as it has done since Roe; [no] change in Roe's factual underpinning has left
its central holding obsolete, and none supports an argument for overruling it (5.)
The sum of the precedential inquiry to this point shows Roe's underpinnings
unweakened in any way affecting its central holding. [Within] the bounds of
normal stare decisis analysis, [the] stronger argument is for affirming Roe's

central holding, with whatever degree of personal reluctance any of us may have, not for overruling it.

B. In a less significant case, stare decisis analysis [would] stop at the point we have reached. But the sustained and widespread debate Roe has provoked calls for some comparison between that case and others of comparable dimension that have responded to national controversies and taken on the impress of the controversies addressed. Only two such decisional lines from the past century present themselves for examination, and in each instance the result reached by the Court accorded with the principles we apply today. The first example is that line of cases identified with [Lochner]. [West Coast Hotel] signaled the demise of Lochner by overruling Adkins. In the meantime, the Depression had come and, with it, the lesson that seemed unmistakable to most people by 1937, that the interpretation of contractual freedom protected in Adkins rested on fundamentally false factual assumptions about the capacity of a relatively unregulated market to satisfy minimal levels of human welfare. [The] facts upon which the earlier case had premised a constitutional resolution of social controversy had proved to be untrue, and history's demonstration of their untruth not only justified but required the new choice of constitutional principle that West Coast Hotel announced. Of course, it was true that the Court lost something by its misperception, or its lack of prescience, and the Court-packing crisis only magnified the loss; but the clear demonstration that the facts of economic life were different from those previously assumed warranted the repudiation of the old law.

The second comparison that 20th century history invites is with the cases employing the separate-but-equal rule. [They] began with Plessy v. Ferguson [1896; p. 671 below], holding that legislatively mandated racial segregation in public transportation works no denial of equal protection. [The] Plessy Court considered "the underlying fallacy of the plaintiff's argument to consist in the assumption that the enforced separation of the two races stamps the colored race with a badge of inferiority. If this be so, it is not by reason of anything found in the act, but solely because the colored race chooses to put that construction upon it." [T]his understanding of the facts and the rule it was stated to justify were repudiated in Brown v. Bd. of Educ. [1954; p. 673 below]. The Court in Brown [observed] that whatever may have been the understanding in Plessy's time of the power of segregation to stigmatize those who were segregated with a "badge of inferiority," it was clear by 1954 that legally sanctioned segregation had just such an effect, to the point that racially separate [facilities] were deemed inherently unequal. Society's understanding of the facts upon which a constitutional ruling was sought in 1954 was thus fundamentally different from the basis claimed for the decision in 1896. While we think Plessy was wrong the day it was decided, we must also recognize that the Plessy Court's explanation for its decision was so clearly at odds with the facts apparent to the Court in 1954 that the decision to reexamine Plessy was on this ground alone not only justified but required. West Coast Hotel and Brown each rested on facts, or an understanding of facts, changed from those which furnished the claimed justifications for the earlier constitutional resolutions. [In] constitutional adjudication as elsewhere in life, changed circumstances may impose new obligations, and the thoughtful part of the Nation could accept each decision to overrule a prior case as a response to the Court's constitutional duty. [Because] neither the factual underpinnings of Roe's central holding nor our understanding of it has changed, [the] Court could not pretend to be reexamining the prior law with any justification beyond a present doctrinal disposition to come out differently from the Court of 1973. To overrule prior law for no other reason than that would run counter to the view repeated in our cases that a decision to overrule should rest on some special reason over and above the belief that a prior case was wrongly decided.

C.   The examination of the conditions justifying the repudiation of Adkins by West Coast Hotel and Plessy by Brown is enough to suggest the terrible price that would have been paid if the Court had not overruled as it did. In the present case, however, [the] terrible price would be paid for overruling. Our analysis would not be complete, however, without explaining why overruling Roe's central holding would not only reach an unjustifiable result under principles of stare decisis, but would seriously weaken the Court's capacity to exercise the judicial power and to function as the Supreme Court of a Nation dedicated to the rule of law. To understand why this would be so it is necessary to understand the course of this Court's authority, the conditions necessary for its preservation, and its relationship to the country's understanding of itself as a constitutional Republic. [As] Americans of each succeeding generation are rightly told, the Court cannot buy support for its decisions by spending money and, except to a minor degree, it cannot independently coerce obedience to its decrees. The Court's power lies, rather, in its legitimacy, a product of substance and perception that shows itself in the people's acceptance of the Judiciary as fit to determine what the Nation's law means and to declare what it demands. The underlying substance of this legitimacy is of course the warrant for the Court's decisions in the [Constitution]. But even when justification is furnished by apposite legal principle, something more is required. Because not every conscientious claim of principled justification will be accepted as such, the justification claimed must be beyond dispute. The Court must take care to speak and act in ways that allow people to accept its decisions on the terms the Court claims for them, as grounded truly in principle, not as compromises with social and political pressures having, as such, no bearing on the principled choices that the Court is obliged to make. Thus, the Court's legitimacy depends on making legally principled decisions under circumstances in which their principled character is sufficiently plausible to be accepted by the Nation.

The need for principled action to be perceived as such is implicated to some degree whenever [any appellate court] overrules a prior case. [In] two circumstances, however, the Court would almost certainly fail to receive the benefit of the doubt in overruling prior cases. There is, first, a point beyond which frequent overruling would overtax the country's belief in the Court's good faith. [That] first circumstance can be described as hypothetical; the second is to the point here and now. Where, in the performance of its judicial duties, the Court decides a case in such a way as to resolve the sort of intensely divisive controversy reflected in Roe and those rare, comparable cases, its decision has a dimension that the resolution of the normal case does not carry. It is the dimension present whenever the Court's interpretation of the Constitution calls the contending sides of a national controversy to end their national division by accepting a common mandate rooted in the Constitution. The Court is not asked to do this very often, having thus addressed the Nation only twice in our lifetime, in [Brown] and Roe. But when the Court does act in this way, its decision requires an equally rare precedential force to counter the inevitable efforts to overturn it and to thwart its implementation. [T]o overrule under fire in the absence of the most compelling reason to reexamine a watershed decision would subvert the Court's legitimacy beyond any serious question. The country's loss of confidence in the judiciary would be underscored by an equally certain and equally reasonable condemnation for another failing in overruling unnecessarily and under pressure. Some cost will be paid by anyone who approves or implements a constitutional decision where it is [unpopular]. An extra price will be paid by those who themselves disapprove of the decision's results when viewed outside of constitutional terms, but who nevertheless struggle to accept it, because they respect the rule of law. To all those who will be so tested by following, the Court implicitly undertakes to remain steadfast, lest in the end a price be paid for nothing. The promise of constancy, once given, binds its maker for as long as the power to stand by the decision survives and the understanding of the issue has not changed so fundamentally as to render the commitment obsolete. [No] Court that broke its faith with the people could sensibly expect credit for principle in the decision by which it did that. [The] Court's duty in the present case is clear. In 1973, it confronted the already-divisive issue of governmental power to limit personal choice to undergo abortion, for which it provided a new [resolution]. Whether or not a new social consensus is developing on that issue, its divisiveness is no less today than in 1973, and pressure to overrule the decision, like pressure to retain it, has grown only more intense. A decision to overrule Roe's essential holding under the existing circumstances would address error, if error there was, at the cost of [profound] and unnecessary damage to the Court's legitimacy, and to the Nation's commitment to the rule of law. It is therefore imperative to adhere to the essence of Roe's original decision, and we do so today.

IV.   [We] conclude that the basic decision in Roe was based on a constitutional analysis which we cannot now repudiate. The woman's liberty is not so unlimited, however, that from the outset the State cannot show its concern for the life of the unborn, and at a later point in fetal development the State's interest in life has sufficient force so that the right of the woman to terminate the pregnancy can be restricted. That brings us [to] the point where much criticism has been directed at Roe, a criticism that always inheres when the Court draws a specific rule from what in the Constitution is but a general standard. But [l]iberty must not be extinguished for want of a line that is clear. We conclude the line should be drawn at viability, so that before that time the woman has a right to choose to terminate her pregnancy. We adhere to this principle for two reasons. First [is] stare decisis. [The] second reason is that the concept of viability [is] the time at which there is a realistic possibility of maintaining and nourishing a life outside the womb, so that the independent existence of the second life can [be] the object of state protection that now overrides the rights of the woman. [The] woman's right to terminate her pregnancy before viability is the most central principle of Roe. [On] the other side of the equation is the interest of the State in the protection of potential life. [The] weight to be given this state interest, not the strength of the woman's interest, was the difficult question faced in Roe. We do not need to say whether each of us, [as] an original matter, would have concluded [that] its weight is insufficient to justify a ban on abortions prior to viability even when it is subject to certain exceptions. [Yet] it must be remembered that Roe speaks with clarity in establishing not only the woman's liberty but also the State's "important and legitimate interest in potential life." That portion of [Roe] has been given too little acknowledgment [in] subsequent cases [holding] that any regulation touching upon the abortion decision must survive [strict scrutiny]. Not all of the cases decided under that formulation can be reconciled with the holding in Roe itself that the State has legitimate interests in the health of the woman and in protecting the potential life within her. In resolving this tension, we choose to rely upon Roe, as against the later cases. [The] trimester framework no doubt was erected to ensure that the woman's right to choose not become so subordinate to the State's interest in promoting fetal life that her choice exists in theory but not in fact. We do not agree, however, that the trimester approach is necessary to accomplish this objective. [Though] the woman has a right to choose to terminate or continue her pregnancy before viability, it does not [follow] that the State is prohibited from taking steps to ensure that this choice is thoughtful and informed.

[We] reject the trimester framework, which we do not consider to be part of the essential holding of Roe. Measures aimed at ensuring that a woman's choice contemplates the consequences for the fetus do not necessarily interfere with the right recognized in Roe, although those measures have been found to be inconsistent with the rigid trimester framework announced. [The] trimester framework suffers from these basic flaws: in its formulation it misconceives the nature of the pregnant woman's interest; and in practice it undervalues the State's interest in potential life. [The] fact that a law which serves a valid purpose, one not designed to strike at the right itself, has the incidental effect of making it more difficult or more expensive to procure an abortion cannot be enough to invalidate it. Only where state regulation imposes an undue burden on a woman's ability to make this decision does the power of the State reach into the heart of the [protected] liberty. [Roe] was express in its recognition of the State's "important and legitimate interest[s] in preserving and protecting the health of the pregnant woman [and] in protecting the potentiality of human life." The trimester framework, however, does not fulfill Roe's own promise that the State has an interest in protecting fetal life or potential life. Roe began the contradiction by using the trimester framework to forbid any regulation of abortion designed to advance that interest before viability. This [is incompatible] with the recognition that there is a substantial state interest in potential life throughout pregnancy. [Not] all burdens on the right to decide whether to terminate a pregnancy will be undue. In our view, the undue burden standard is the appropriate means of reconciling the State's interest with the woman's constitutionally protected liberty. [It] is important to clarify what is meant by an undue burden. A finding of an undue burden is a shorthand for the conclusion that a state regulation has the purpose or effect of placing a substantial obstacle in the path of a woman seeking an abortion of a nonviable fetus. A statute with this purpose is invalid because the means chosen by the State to further the interest in potential life must be calculated to inform the woman's free choice, not hinder it. And a statute which [has] the effect of placing a substantial obstacle in the path of a woman's choice cannot be considered a permissible means of serving its legitimate ends. [An] undue burden is an unconstitutional burden. [A] law designed to further the State's interest in fetal life which imposes an undue burden on the woman's decision before fetal viability [is unconstitutional]. Some guiding principles should emerge. What is at stake is the woman's right to make the ultimate decision, not a right to be insulated from all others in doing so. Regulations which do no more than create a structural mechanism by which the State, or the parent or guardian of a minor, may express profound respect for the life of the unborn are permitted, if they are not a substantial obstacle to the woman's exercise of the right to choose. Unless it has that effect on her right of choice, a state measure designed to persuade her to choose childbirth over abortion will be upheld if reasonably related to that goal. Regulations designed to foster the health of a woman seeking an abortion are valid if they do not constitute an undue burden.

Even when jurists reason from shared premises, some disagreement is inevitable. That is to be expected in the application of any legal standard which must accommodate life's complexity. We do not expect it to be otherwise with respect to the undue burden standard. We give this summary: (a) To protect the central right recognized by Roe while at the same time accommodating the State's profound interest in potential life, we will employ the undue burden analysis as explained in this opinion. An undue burden exists, and therefore a provision of law is invalid, if its purpose or effect is to place a substantial obstacle in the path of a woman seeking an abortion before the fetus attains viability. (b) We reject the rigid trimester framework of Roe. To promote the State's profound interest in potential life, throughout pregnancy the State may take measures to ensure that the woman's choice is informed, and measures designed to advance this interest will not be invalidated as long as their purpose is to persuade the woman to choose childbirth over abortion. These measures must not be an undue burden on the right. (c) As with any medical procedure, the State may enact regulations to further the health or safety of a woman seeking an abortion. Unnecessary health regulations that have the purpose or effect of presenting a substantial obstacle to a woman seeking an abortion impose an undue burden on the right. (d) Our adoption of the undue burden analysis does not disturb the central holding of Roe, and we reaffirm that holding. [A] State may not prohibit any woman from making the ultimate decision to terminate her pregnancy before viability. (e) We also reaffirm Roe's holding that "subsequent to viability, the State in promoting its interest in the potentiality of human life may, if it chooses, regulate, and even proscribe, abortion except where it is necessary, in appropriate medical judgment, for the preservation of the life or health of the mother." [We] now turn to [the] validity of [the] challenged provisions.

V.   A. Because it is central to the operation of various other requirements, we begin with the statute's definition of medical emergency, "[that] condition which, on the basis of the physician's good faith clinical judgment, so complicates the medical condition of a pregnant woman as to necessitate the immediate abortion of her pregnancy to avert her death or for which a delay will create serious risk of substantial and irreversible impairment of a major bodily function." Petitioners argue that the definition is too narrow, contending that it forecloses the possibility of an immediate abortion despite some health risks. [But] the Court of Appeals read "the medical emergency exception as intended by the legislature to assure that compliance with its abortion regulations would not in any way pose a significant threat to the life or health of a woman." [We conclude] that the medical emergency definition [as so construed] imposes no undue burden on a woman's abortion right.

B.   We next consider the informed consent requirement. Except in a medical emergency, the statute requires that at least 24 hours before performing an abortion a physician inform the woman of the nature of the procedure, the health risks of the abortion and of childbirth, and the "probable gestational age of the unborn child." The physician or a qualified nonphysician must inform the woman of the availability of printed materials published by the State describing the fetus and providing information about medical assistance for childbirth, information about child support from the father, and a list of agencies which provide adoption and other services as alternatives to abortion. An abortion may not be performed unless the woman certifies in writing that she has been informed of the availability of these printed materials and has been provided them if she chooses to view them. Our prior decisions establish that as with any medical procedure, the State may require a woman to give her written informed consent to an abortion. [To] the extent Akron I and Thornburgh find a constitutional violation when the government requires, as it does here, the giving of truthful, nonmisleading information about the nature of the procedure, the attendant health risks and those of childbirth, and the "probable gestational age" of the fetus, those cases go too far [and] are overruled. [Most] women considering an abortion would deem the impact on the fetus relevant, if not dispositive, to the decision. In attempting to ensure that a woman apprehend the full consequences of her decision, the State furthers the legitimate purpose of reducing the risk that a woman may elect an abortion, only to discover later, with devastating psychological consequences, that her decision was not fully informed. If the information the State requires to be made available to a woman is truthful and not misleading, the requirement may be permissible. We also see no reason why the State may not require doctors to inform a woman seeking an abortion of the availability of materials relating to the consequences to the fetus, even when those consequences have no direct relation to her health. [For example, we] would think it constitutional for the State to require that in order for there to be informed consent to a kidney transplant operation the recipient must be supplied with information about risks to the donor as well as risks to himself or herself. [Similarly, we] conclude [that] informed choice need not be defined in such narrow terms that all considerations of the effect on the fetus are made irrelevant. [We] depart from [Akron I] and Thornburgh to the extent that we permit a State to further its legitimate goal of protecting the life of the unborn by enacting legislation aimed at ensuring a decision that is mature and informed, even when in so doing the State expresses a preference for childbirth over abortion. [The] statute also requires us to reconsider the holding in Akron I that the State may not require that a physician, as opposed to a qualified assistant, provide information relevant to a woman's informed consent. Since there is no evidence on this record that requiring a doctor to give the information as provided by the statute would amount in practical terms to a substantial obstacle to a woman seeking an abortion, we conclude that it is not an undue burden.

[Our] analysis of Pennsylvania's 24–hour waiting period between the provision of the information deemed necessary to informed consent and the performance of an abortion under the undue burden standard requires us to reconsider the premise behind the decision in Akron I invalidating a parallel requirement. [We] consider [its] conclusion to be wrong. The idea that important decisions will be more informed and deliberate if they follow some period of reflection does not strike us as unreasonable, particularly where the statute directs that important information become part of the background of the decision. [Whether] the mandatory 24–hour waiting period is nonetheless invalid because in practice it is a substantial obstacle to a woman's choice to terminate her pregnancy is a closer question. The findings of fact [indicate] that because of the distances many women must travel to reach an abortion provider, the practical effect will often be a delay of much more than a day because the waiting period requires that a woman seeking an abortion make at least two visits to the doctor. The District Court also found that in many instances this will increase the exposure of women seeking abortions to "the harassment and hostility of anti-abortion protestors demonstrating outside a clinic." As a result, [for] those women who have the fewest financial resources, those who must travel long distances, and those who have difficulty explaining their whereabouts to husbands, employers, or others, the 24–hour waiting period will be "particularly burdensome." These findings are troubling in some respects, but they do not demonstrate that the waiting period constitutes an undue burden. We do not doubt that, as the District Court held, the waiting period has the effect of "increasing the cost and risk of delay of abortions," but the District Court did not conclude that the increased costs and potential delays amount to substantial obstacles. [As] we have stated, under the undue burden standard a State is permitted to enact persuasive measures which favor childbirth over abortion, even if those measures do not further a health interest. And while the waiting period does limit a physician's discretion, that is not, standing alone, a reason to invalidate it. In light of the construction given the statute's definition of medical emergency by the Court of Appeals, and the

District Court's findings, we cannot say that the waiting period imposes a real health risk. We also disagree with the District Court's conclusion that the "particularly burdensome" effects of the waiting period on some women require its invalidation. A particular burden is not of necessity a substantial obstacle. Whether a burden falls on a particular group is a distinct inquiry from whether it is a substantial obstacle even as to the women in that group. And the District Court did not conclude that the waiting period is such an obstacle even for the women who are most burdened by it. Hence, on the record before us, [we] are not convinced that the 24–hour waiting period constitutes an undue burden. We are left with the argument that the various aspects of the informed consent requirement are unconstitutional because they place barriers in the way of abortion on demand. Even the broadest reading of Roe, however, has not suggested that there is a constitutional right to abortion on demand. Rather, the right protected by Roe is a right to decide to terminate a pregnancy free of undue interference by the State. Because the informed consent requirement facilitates the wise exercise of that right it cannot be classified as an interference with the right Roe protects. The informed consent requirement is not an undue burden on that right.

C. [Pennsylvania's] abortion law provides, except in cases of medical emergency, that no physician shall perform an abortion on a married woman without receiving a signed statement from the woman that she has notified her spouse that she is about to undergo an abortion. The woman has the option of providing an alternative signed statement certifying that her husband is not the man who impregnated her; that her husband could not be located; that the pregnancy is the result of spousal sexual assault which she has reported; or that the woman believes that notifying her husband will cause him or someone else to inflict bodily injury upon [her].

The District Court [made] detailed findings of fact regarding the effect of this statute: "273. The vast majority of women consult their husbands prior to deciding to terminate their [pregnancy]. 279. The 'bodily injury' exception could not be invoked by a married woman whose husband, if notified, would, in her reasonable belief, threaten to (a) publicize her intent to have an abortion to family, friends or acquaintances; (b) retaliate against her in future child custody or divorce proceedings; (c) inflict psychological intimidation or emotional harm upon her, her children or other persons; (d) inflict bodily harm on other persons such as children, family members or other loved ones; or (e) use his control over finances to deprive of necessary monies for herself or her [children]. 281. Studies reveal that family violence occurs in two million families in the United States. This figure [substantially] understates (because battering is usually not reported until it reaches life-threatening proportions) the actual number of families affected by domestic violence. In fact, researchers estimate that one of every two women will be battered at some time in their [life]. [286]. Married women, victims of battering, have been killed in Pennsylvania and throughout the [United States]. 287. Battering can often involve a substantial amount of sexual abuse, including marital rape and sexual [mutilation]. 288. In a domestic abuse situation, it is common for the battering husband to also abuse the children in an attempt to coerce the [wife]. 289. Mere notification of pregnancy is frequently a flashpoint for battering and violence within the family. [The] battering husband may deny parentage and use the pregnancy as an excuse for [abuse]. 290. Secrecy typically shrouds abusive families. [Battering] husbands often threaten their wives or her children with further abuse if she tells an outsider of the violence and tells her that nobody will believe [her]. [294.] A woman in a shelter or a safe house unknown to her husband is not 'reasonably likely' to have bodily harm inflicted upon her by her batterer, however her attempt to notify her husband [could] accidentally disclose her whereabouts to her [husband]. 295. Marital rape is rarely discussed with others or reported to law enforcement authorities, and of those reported only few are [prosecuted]. 296. It is common for battered women to have sexual intercourse with their husbands to avoid being [battered]." These findings are supported by studies of domestic violence. The American Medical Association [indicates] that in an average 12–month period in this country, approximately two million women are the victims of severe assaults by their male partners. [Other] studies fill in the rest of this troubling picture. Physical violence is only the most visible form of abuse. Psychological abuse, particularly forced social and economic isolation of women, is also common. Many victims of domestic violence remain with their abusers, perhaps because they perceive no superior alternative. Many abused women who find temporary refuge in shelters return to their husbands, in large part because they have no other source of income. Returning to one's abuser can be dangerous. [Thirty] percent of female homicide victims are killed by their male partners. The limited research that has been conducted with respect to notifying one's husband about an abortion, although involving samples too small to be representative, also supports the [findings] of fact. The vast majority of women notify their male partners of their decision to obtain an abortion. In many cases in which married women do not notify their husbands, the pregnancy is the result of an extramarital affair. Where the husband is the father, the primary reason women do not notify their husbands is that the husband and wife are experiencing marital difficulties, often accompanied by incidents of violence. This information and the District Court's findings reinforce what common sense would suggest. In well-functioning marriages, spouses discuss important intimate decisions such as whether to bear a child. But there are millions of women in this country who are the victims of regular physical and psychological abuse at the hands of their husbands. Should these women become pregnant, they may have very good reasons for not wishing to inform their husbands of their decision to obtain an abortion. [The] spousal notification requirement is thus likely to prevent a significant number of women from obtaining an abortion. It does not merely make abortions a little more difficult or expensive to obtain; for many women, it will impose a substantial obstacle. [The] significant number of women who fear for their safety and the safety of their children are likely to be deterred from procuring an abortion as surely as if [Pennsylvania] had outlawed abortion in all cases.

Respondents [point] out that [the spousal notification requirement] imposes almost no burden at all for the vast majority of women seeking abortions. They begin by noting that only about 20 percent of the women who obtain abortions are married. They then note that of these women about 95 percent notify their husbands of their own volition. Thus, respondents argue, the effects of [the requirement] are felt by only one percent of the women who obtain abortions. [And] since some of these women will be able to notify their husbands without adverse consequences or will qualify for one of the exceptions, the statute affects fewer than one percent of women seeking abortions. For this reason, it is asserted, the statute cannot be invalid on its face. We [disagree]. The analysis does not end with the one percent of women upon whom the statute operates; it begins there. Legislation is measured [by] its impact on those whose conduct it affects. [The] proper focus of constitutional inquiry is the group for whom the law is a restriction, not the group for whom the law is irrelevant. [The provision's] real target is narrower even than the class of women seeking abortions identified by the State: it is married women seeking abortions who do not wish to notify their husbands of their intentions and who do not qualify for one of the statutory exceptions to the notice requirement. The unfortunate yet persisting conditions we document above will mean that in a large fraction of the cases in which [the provision] is relevant, it will operate as a substantial obstacle to a woman's choice to undergo an abortion. It is an undue burden, and therefore invalid. This conclusion [is] in no way inconsistent with our decisions upholding parental notification or consent requirements. Those enactments [are] based on the quite reasonable assumption that minors will benefit from consultation with their parents and that children will often not realize that their parents have their best interests at heart. We cannot adopt a parallel assumption about adult women. [If] this case concerned a State's ability to require the mother to notify the father before taking some action with respect to a living child raised by both, [it] would be reasonable to conclude [that] the father's interest in the welfare of the child and the mother's interest are equal. Before birth, however, the issue takes on a very different cast. It is an inescapable biological fact that state regulation with respect to the child a woman is carrying will have a far greater impact on the mother's liberty than on the father's.

[There] was a time, not so long ago, when a different understanding of the family and of the Constitution prevailed. In Bradwell v. Illinois [1873; p. 684 below] three Members of this Court reaffirmed the common-law principle that "a woman had no legal existence separate from her husband, who was regarded as her head and representative in the social state; and, notwithstanding some recent modifications of this civil status, many of the special rules of law flowing from and dependent upon this cardinal principle still exist in full force in most States." [These] views, of course, are no longer consistent with our understanding of the family, the individual, or the Constitution. [For] the great many women who are victims of abuse inflicted by their husbands, or whose children are the victims of such abuse, a spousal notice requirement enables the husband to wield an effective veto over his wife's decision. [The] husband's interest in the life of the child [does] not permit the State to empower him with this troubling degree of authority over his wife. The contrary view leads to consequences reminiscent of the common law. A husband has no enforceable right to require a wife to advise him before she exercises her personal choices. If a husband's interest in the potential life of the child outweighs a wife's liberty, the State could require a married woman to notify her husband before she uses a postfertilization contraceptive. Perhaps next in line would be a statute requiring pregnant married women to notify their husbands before engaging in conduct causing risks to the fetus. After all, if the husband's interest in the fetus' safety is a sufficient predicate for state regulation, the State could reasonably conclude that pregnant wives should notify their husbands before drinking alcohol or smoking. Perhaps married women should notify their husbands before using contraceptives or before undergoing any type of surgery that may have complications affecting the husband's interest in his wife's reproductive organs. And if a husband's interest justifies notice in any of these cases, one might reasonably argue that it justifies exactly what Danforth held it did not justify—a requirement of the husband's consent as well. A State may not give to a man the kind of dominion over his wife that parents exercise over their children. [The provision] embodies a view of marriage consonant with the common-law understanding of marriage but repugnant to our present understanding of marriage and of the nature of rights secured by the Constitution. Women do not lose their constitutionally protected liberty when they marry. The Constitution protects all individuals, male or female, married or unmarried, from the abuse of governmental power, even where that power is employed for the supposed benefit of a member of the individual's [family].

D.   We next consider the parental consent provision. Except in a medical emergency, an unemancipated young woman under 18 may not obtain an abortion unless she and one of her parents (or guardian) provides informed consent as defined above. If neither a parent nor a guardian provides consent, a court may authorize the performance of an abortion upon a determination that the young woman is mature and capable of giving informed consent and has in fact given her informed consent, or that an abortion would be in her best interests. We have been over most of this ground before. [We] reaffirm today that a State may require a minor seeking an abortion to obtain the consent of a parent or guardian, provided there is an adequate judicial bypass [procedure].

E.   [E]very facility which performs abortions is required to file a report stating its name and address as well as the name and address of any related entity, such as a controlling or subsidiary organization. In the case of state-funded institutions, the information becomes public. For each abortion performed, a report must be filed identifying: the physician; the facility; the referring physician or agency; the woman's age; the number of prior pregnancies and prior abortions she has had; gestational age; the type of abortion procedure; the date of the abortion; whether there were any pre-existing medical conditions which would complicate pregnancy; medical complications with the abortion; where applicable, the basis for the determination that the abortion was medically necessary; the weight of the aborted fetus; and whether the woman was married, and if so, whether notice was provided or the basis for the failure to give notice. Every abortion facility must also file quarterly reports showing the number of abortions performed broken down by trimester. In all events, the identity of each woman who has had an abortion remains confidential. [We] think [all these] provisions except that relating to spousal notice are constitutional. Although they do not relate to the State's interest in informing the woman's choice, they do relate to health. The collection of information with respect to actual patients is a vital element of medical research, and so it cannot be said that the requirements serve no purpose other than to make abortions more difficult. Nor do we find that the requirements impose a substantial obstacle to a woman's choice. At most they might increase the cost of some abortions by a slight amount. While at some point increased cost could become a substantial obstacle, there is no such showing [here].

VI.   Our Constitution is a covenant running from the first generation of Americans to us and then to future generations. It is a coherent succession. Each generation must learn anew that the Constitution's written terms embody ideas and aspirations that must survive more ages than one. We accept our responsibility not to retreat from interpreting the full meaning of the covenant in light of all of our precedents. We invoke it once again to define the freedom guaranteed by the Constitution's own promise, the promise of [liberty].

It is so ordered.

Justice STEVENS, concurring in part and dissenting in part.

The portions of the Court's opinion that I have joined are more important than those with which I [disagree]. I. The Court is unquestionably correct in concluding that the doctrine of stare decisis has controlling significance in a case of this [kind]. The societal costs of overruling Roe at this late date would be enormous. Roe is an integral part of a correct understanding of both the concept of liberty and the basic equality of men and [women]. II. My disagreement with the joint opinion begins with its understanding of the trimester framework. [It] is not a "contradiction" to recognize that the State may have a legitimate interest in potential human life and, at the same time, to conclude that that interest does not justify the regulation of abortion before viability (although other interests, such as maternal health, may). The fact that the State's interest is legitimate does not tell us when, if ever, that interest outweighs the [interest] in personal liberty. It is appropriate, therefore, to consider more carefully the nature of the interests at stake. First, [the] State's interest must be secular; consistent with the First Amendment the State may not promote a theological or sectarian interest. Moreover, [the] state interest in potential human life is not an interest in loco parentis, for the fetus is not a person. Identifying the State's interests—which the States rarely articulate with any precision—makes clear that the interest in protecting potential life is not grounded in the Constitution. It is, instead, an indirect interest supported by both humanitarian and pragmatic concerns. Many of our citizens believe that any abortion reflects an unacceptable disrespect for potential human life and that the performance of more than a million abortions each year is intolerable; many find third-trimester abortions performed when the fetus is approaching personhood particularly offensive. The State has a legitimate interest in minimizing such offense. The State may also have a broader interest in expanding the population, believing society would benefit from the services of additional productive citizens—or that the potential human lives might include the occasional Mozart or Curie. These [kinds] of concerns [comprise] the State's interest in potential human life. In counterpoise is the woman's constitutional interest in [liberty]. Weighing [these state interests], I agree with the joint opinion that the State may "expres[s] a preference for normal childbirth," that the State may take steps to ensure that a woman's choice "is thoughtful and informed," and that "States are free to enact laws to provide a reasonable framework for a woman to make a decision that has such profound and lasting meaning." Serious questions arise, however, when a State attempts to "persuade the woman to choose childbirth over abortion." Decisional autonomy must limit the State's power to inject into a woman's most personal deliberations its own views of what is best. The State may promote its preferences by funding childbirth, by creating and maintaining alternatives to abortion, and by espousing the virtues of family; but it must respect the individual's freedom to make such judgments. [The] principles established in [our previous] cases [should] govern our decision today. [Those] sections requir[ing] a physician or counselor to provide the woman with a range of materials clearly designed to persuade her to choose not to undergo the abortion [are unconstitutional.] While the State is free [to] produce and disseminate such material, the State may not inject such information into the woman's deliberations just as she is weighing such an important [choice].

III. The 24–hour waiting period [raises] even more serious concerns. Such a requirement arguably furthers the State's interests in two ways, neither of which is permissible. First, it may be argued that the 24–hour delay is justified by the mere fact that it is likely to reduce the number of abortions, thus furthering the State's interest in potential life. But [the] State cannot further its interests by simply wearing down the ability of the pregnant woman to exercise her constitutional right. Second, it can more reasonably be argued that the 24–hour delay furthers the State's interest in ensuring that the woman's decision is informed and thoughtful. But there is no evidence that the mandated delay benefits women or that it is necessary to enable the physician to convey any relevant information to the patient. The mandatory delay thus appears to rest on outmoded and unacceptable assumptions about the decision-making capacity of women. While there are [reasons] for the State to view with skepticism the ability of minors to make decisions, none [applies] to an adult woman's decisionmaking [ability]. IV. [A] correct application of the "undue burden" standard leads to the same conclusion. A state-imposed burden on the exercise of a constitutional right is measured both by its effects and by its character: A burden may be "undue" either because [it] is too severe or because it lacks a legitimate, rational justification. The 24–hour delay requirement fails both parts of this test. [The] counseling provisions are similarly infirm. Whenever government commands private citizens to speak or to listen, careful review [is] particularly appropriate. [Here] the statute requires that [the prescribed] information be given to all women seeking abortions, including those for whom such information is [of] little decisional value. [I] conclude that the information requirements do not serve a useful purpose and thus constitute an unnecessary—and therefore undue—burden on the woman's constitutional liberty to decide to terminate her [pregnancy].

Justice BLACKMUN, concurring in part, concurring in the judgment in part, and dissenting in part.

Three years ago, [in Webster,] four Members of this Court appeared poised to "cas[t] into darkness the hopes and visions of every woman in this country" who had come to believe that the Constitution guaranteed her the right to reproductive choice. All that remained between the promise of Roe and the darkness of the plurality was a single, flickering flame. [But] now, just when so many expected the darkness to fall, the flame has grown bright. I do not underestimate the significance of today's joint opinion. Yet I remain steadfast [that] the right to reproductive choice is entitled to the full protection afforded [before] Webster. And I fear for the darkness as four Justices anxiously await the single vote necessary to extinguish the [light].

Today, no less than yesterday, the Constitution [requires] that abortion restrictions be subjected to the strictest of judicial scrutiny. [State] restrictions on abortion violate a woman's right of privacy in two ways. First, compelled continuation of a pregnancy infringes upon a woman's right to bodily integrity by imposing substantial physical intrusions and significant risks of physical harm. [Further,] when the State restricts a woman's right to terminate her pregnancy, it deprives a woman of the right to make her own decision about reproduction and family planning—critical life choices that this Court long has deemed central to the right to privacy. [A] State's restrictions on a woman's right to terminate her pregnancy also implicate constitutional guarantees of gender equality. [By] restricting the right to terminate pregnancies, the State conscripts women's bodies into its service, forcing women to continue their pregnancies, suffer the pains of childbirth, and in most instances, provide years of maternal care. The State does not compensate women for their services; instead, it assumes that they owe this duty as a matter of course. This assumption—that women can simply be forced to accept the "natural" status and incidents of motherhood—appears to rest upon a conception of women's role that has triggered the protection of the Equal Protection Clause. The joint opinion recognizes that these assumptions about women's place in society are "no longer consistent with our understanding of the family, the individual, or the Constitution."

[Limitations] on the right of privacy are permissible only if they survive "strict" constitutional scrutiny—only if the governmental entity imposing the restriction can demonstrate that the limitation is both necessary and narrowly tailored to serve a compelling governmental interest. [No] majority of this Court has ever agreed upon an alternative approach [to Roe]. The factual premises of the trimester framework have not been undermined, and the Roe framework is far more administrable, and far less manipulable, than the "undue burden" standard. [Application] of [strict scrutiny] results in the invalidation of all the challenged provisions. Indeed, as this Court has invalidated virtually identical provisions in prior cases, stare decisis requires that we again strike them down.

[If] there is much reason to applaud the advances made by the joint opinion today, there is far more to fear from the Chief Justice's opinion. The Chief Justice's criticism of Roe follows from his stunted conception of individual liberty. While recognizing that Due Process protects more than simple physical liberty, he then goes on to construe [our] personal-liberty cases as establishing only a laundry list of particular rights, rather than a principled account of how these particular rights are grounded in a more general right of privacy. This constricted view is reinforced by the Chief Justice's exclusive reliance on tradition as a source of fundamental rights. [Even] more shocking than the Chief Justice's cramped notion of individual liberty is his complete omission of any discussion of the effects that compelled childbirth and motherhood have on women's lives. The only expression of concern with women's health is purely instrumental—for the Chief Justice only women's psychological health is a concern, and only to the extent that he assumes that every woman who decides to have an abortion does so without serious consideration of the moral implications of their decision. In short, the Chief Justice's view of the State's compelling interest in maternal health has less to do with health than it does with compelling women to be maternal. Nor does the Chief Justice give any serious consideration to [stare decisis]. The Chief Justice's narrow conception of individual liberty and stare decisis leads him to propose the same standard of review proposed by the plurality in [Webster]. But, we are reassured, there is always the protection of the democratic process. While there is much to be praised about our democracy, our country since its founding has recognized that there are certain fundamental liberties that are not to be left to the whims of an election. A woman's right to reproductive choice is one of those fundamental liberties. Accordingly, that liberty need not seek refuge at the ballot box. In one sense, the Court's approach is worlds apart from that of the Chief Justice and Justice Scalia. And yet, in another sense, the distance between the two approaches is short—the distance is but a single vote. I am 83 years old. I cannot remain on this Court forever, and when I do step down, the confirmation process for my successor well may focus on the issue before us today. That, I regret, may be exactly where the choice between the two worlds will be made.

Chief Justice REHNQUIST, with whom Justice WHITE, Justice SCALIA, and Justice THOMAS join, concurring in the judgment in part and dissenting in part.

The joint opinion, following its newly-minted variation on stare decisis, retains the outer shell of Roe, but beats a wholesale retreat from the substance of that case. We believe that Roe was wrongly decided, and that it can and should be overruled consistently with our traditional approach to stare decisis in constitutional cases. We would adopt the approach of the plurality in Webster, and uphold the challenged provisions in their entirety.

[I.] We are now of the view that, in terming [the pregnant woman's] right fundamental, the Court in Roe read the earlier opinions upon which it based its decision much too broadly. Unlike marriage, procreation and contraception, abortion "involves the purposeful termination of potential life." [One] cannot ignore the fact that a woman is not isolated in her pregnancy, and that the decision to abort necessarily involves the destruction of a fetus. Nor do the historical traditions of the American people support the view that the right to terminate one's pregnancy is "fundamental." The common law which we inherited from England made abortion after "quickening" an offense. At the time of the adoption of the Fourteenth Amendment, statutory prohibitions or restrictions on abortion were commonplace. [By] the turn of the century virtually every State had a law prohibiting or restricting abortion on its books. By the middle of the present century, a liberalization trend had set in. But 21 of the restrictive abortion laws in effect in 1868 were still in effect in 1973 when Roe was decided, and an overwhelming majority of the States prohibited abortion unless necessary to preserve the life or health of the mother. On this record, it can scarcely be said that any deeply rooted tradition of relatively unrestricted abortion in our history supported the classification of the right to abortion as ["fundamental"]. We think, therefore, both in view of this history and of our decided cases dealing with substantive liberty under the Due Process Clause, that the Court was mistaken in Roe when it classified a woman's decision to terminate her pregnancy as a "fundamental right" that could be abridged only in a manner which withstood ["strict scrutiny"].

II.   The joint opinion [cannot] bring itself to say that Roe was correct as an original matter, but the authors are of the view that "the immediate question is not the soundness of Roe's resolution of the issue, but the precedential force that must be accorded to its holding." Instead of claiming that Roe was correct as a matter of [original] interpretation, the opinion therefore contains an elaborate discussion of stare decisis. This discussion of the principle of stare decisis appears to be almost entirely dicta, because the joint opinion does not apply that principle in dealing with Roe. Roe decided that a woman had a fundamental right to an abortion. The joint opinion rejects that view. Roe decided that abortion regulations were to be subjected to "strict scrutiny." [The] joint opinion rejects that view. Roe analyzed abortion regulation under a rigid trimester framework. [The] joint opinion rejects that framework. [Decisions] following Roe, such as Akron [I; 1983] and Thornburgh [1986] are frankly overruled in part under the "undue burden" standard expounded in the joint opinion. [Authentic] principles of stare decisis do not require that any portion of [Roe] be kept intact. [Erroneous] decisions in [constitutional] cases are uniquely durable, because correction through legislative action, save for constitutional amendment, is impossible. [Our] constitutional watch does not cease merely because we have spoken before on an issue; when it becomes clear that a prior constitutional interpretation is unsound we are obliged to reexamine the question. The joint opinion discusses several stare decisis factors which, it asserts, point toward retaining a portion of Roe. Two of these factors are that the main "factual underpinning" of Roe has remained the same, and that its doctrinal foundation is no weaker now than it was in 1973. Of course, what might be called the basic facts which gave rise to Roe have remained the same—women become pregnant, there is a point somewhere, depending on medical technology, where a fetus becomes viable, and women give birth to children. But this is only to say that the same facts which gave rise to Roe will continue to give rise to similar cases. It is not a reason, in and of itself, why those cases must be decided in the same incorrect manner as was [Roe]. The joint opinion also points to reliance interests [to] explain why precedent must be followed for precedent's sake. But, as the joint opinion apparently agrees, any traditional notion of reliance is not applicable here. [In] the end, having failed to put forth any evidence to prove any true reliance, the joint opinion's argument is based solely on generalized assertions about the national psyche, on a belief that the people of this country have grown accustomed to the Roe decision over the last 19 years and have "ordered their thinking and living around" it. As an initial matter, one might inquire how the joint opinion can view the "central holding" of Roe as so deeply rooted in our constitutional culture, when it so casually uproots and disposes of that same decision's trimester framework. [However,] the simple fact that a generation or more had grown used to [Plessy and Lochner] did not prevent the Court from correcting its errors in those cases, nor should it prevent us [here].

Apparently realizing that conventional stare decisis principles do not support its position, the joint opinion advances a belief that retaining a portion of Roe is necessary to protect the "legitimacy" of this Court. Because the Court must take care to render decisions "grounded truly in principle," and not simply as political and social compromises, the joint opinion properly declares it to be this Court's duty to ignore the public criticism and protest that may arise as a result of a decision. [The] joint opinion goes on to state that when the Court "resolve[s] the sort of intensely divisive controversy reflected in Roe and those rare, comparable cases," its decision is exempt from reconsideration under established principles of stare decisis in constitutional cases. [This] is a truly novel principle, one which is contrary to both the Court's historical practice and to the Court's traditional willingness to tolerate criticism of its opinions. Under this principle, when the Court has ruled on a divisive issue, it is apparently prevented from overruling that decision for the sole reason that it was incorrect, unless opposition to the original decision has died away. The first difficulty with this principle lies in its assumption that cases which are "intensely divisive" can be readily distinguished from those that are not. The question of whether a particular issue is "intensely divisive" enough to qualify for special protection is entirely [subjective]. In addition, because the Court's duty is to ignore public opinion and criticism on issues that come before it, its members are in perhaps the worst position to judge whether a decision divides the Nation deeply enough to justify such uncommon protection. [The] joint opinion picks out and discusses two prior rulings it believes are of the "intensely divisive" variety, and concludes that they are of comparable dominion to Roe. It appears to us very odd indeed that the joint opinion chooses as benchmarks two cases in which the Court chose not to adhere to erroneous constitutional precedent, but instead enhanced its stature [by] correcting its error, apparently in violation of the joint opinion's "legitimacy" [principle].

Taking the joint opinion on its own terms, we doubt that its distinction between Roe, on the one hand, and Plessy and Lochner, on the other, withstands analysis. The joint opinion acknowledges that the Court improved its stature by overruling Plessy on a deeply divisive issue. And our decision in West Coast Hotel [was] rendered at a time when Congress was considering President Roosevelt's proposal to "reorganize" this Court and enable him to name six additional Justices in the event that any member of the Court over the age of 70 did not elect to retire. It is difficult to imagine a situation in which the Court would face more intense opposition to a prior ruling than it did at that time, and, under the general principle proclaimed in the joint opinion, the Court seemingly should have responded to this opposition by stubbornly refusing to reexamine the Lochner rationale, lest it lose legitimacy by appearing to "overrule under fire." The joint opinion agrees that the Court's stature would have been seriously damaged if in Brown and West Coast Hotel it had dug in its heels and refused to apply normal principles of stare decisis to the earlier decisions. But the opinion contends that the Court was entitled to overrule Plessy and Lochner in those cases, despite the existence of opposition to the original decisions, only because both the Nation and the Court had learned new lessons in the interim. This is at best a feebly supported, post hoc rationalization. For example, the opinion asserts that the Court could justifiably overrule [Lochner] only because the Depression had convinced "most people" that constitutional protection of contractual freedom contributed to an economy that failed to protect the welfare of all. Surely the joint opinion does not mean to suggest that people saw this Court's failure to uphold minimum wage statutes as the cause of the Great Depression! In any event, the Lochner Court did not base its rule upon the policy judgment that an unregulated market was fundamental to a stable economy; it simply believed, erroneously, that "liberty" under the Due Process Clause protected the "right to make a contract." Nor is it the case that the people of this Nation only discovered the dangers of extreme laissez faire economics because of the Depression. [When] the Court finally recognized its error in West Coast Hotel, it did not engage in the post hoc rationalization that the joint opinion attributes to it; it did not state that Lochner had been based on an economic view that had fallen into disfavor, and that it therefore should be overruled. [The] theme of the opinion is that the Court had been mistaken as a matter of constitutional law when it embraced "freedom of contract" 32 years previously.

The joint opinion also agrees that the Court acted properly in rejecting the doctrine of "separate but equal" in Brown. In fact, the opinion lauds Brown in comparing it to Roe. This is strange, in that under the opinion's "legitimacy" principle the Court would seemingly have been forced to adhere to its errone-ous decision in Plessy because of its "intensely divisive" character. To us, adherence to Roe today under the guise of "legitimacy" would seem to resemble more closely adherence to Plessy on the same ground. Fortunately, the Court did not choose that option in Brown, and instead frankly repudiated Plessy. The joint opinion concludes that such repudiation was justified only because of newly discovered evidence that segregation had the effect of treating one race as inferior to another. But it can hardly be argued that this was not urged upon those who decided Plessy, as Justice Harlan observed in his dissent that the law "puts the brand of servitude and degradation upon a large class of our fellow-citizens, our equals before the law." [The] same arguments made before the Court in Brown were made in Plessy as well. The Court in Brown simply recognized, as Justice Harlan had recognized beforehand, that the Fourteenth Amendment does not permit racial segregation. The rule of Brown is not tied to popular opinion about the evils of segregation; it is a judgment that the Equal Protection Clause does not permit racial segregation, no matter whether the public might come to believe that it is beneficial. [There] is also a suggestion in the joint opinion that the propriety of overruling a "divisive" decision depends in part on whether "most people" would now agree that it should be overruled. [How] such agreement would be ascertained, short of a public opinion poll, the joint opinion does not say. But surely even the suggestion is totally at war with the idea of "legitimacy" in whose name it is invoked. The Judicial Branch derives its legitimacy, not from following public opinion, but from deciding by its best lights whether legislative enactments [comport] with the Constitution.

The end result of the joint opinion's paeans of praise for legitimacy is the enunciation of a brand new standard for evaluating state regulation of a woman's right to abortion—the "undue burden" standard. While we disagree with [Roe's strict scrutiny] standard, it at least had a recognized basis [at] the time Roe was decided. The same cannot be said for the "undue burden" standard, created largely out of whole cloth by the authors of the joint opinion. [T]he undue burden standard presents nothing more workable than the trimes-ter framework. [The] sum of the joint opinion's labors in the name of stare decisis and "legitimacy" is this: Roe stands as a sort of judicial Potemkin Village, which may be pointed out to passers by as a monument to the importance of adhering to precedent. But behind the facade, an entirely new method of analysis [is] imported to decide the constitutionality of state laws regulating abortion. Neither stare decisis nor "legitimacy" are truly served by such an effort.

We have stated [our] belief that the Constitution does not subject state abortion regulations to heightened scrutiny. Accordingly, we think that the correct analysis is that set forth by the plurality opinion in Webster. A woman's interest in having an abortion is a form of liberty protected by [due process], but States may regulate abortion procedures in ways rationally related to a legitimate state interest. [Williamson v. Lee Optical.]

With this rule in mind, we examine each of the challenged provisions. [One of the questions before us is] whether the spousal notification requirement rationally furthers any legitimate state interests. We conclude that it does. First, a husband's interests in procreation within marriage and in the potential life of his unborn child are certainly substantial ones. The State [has] legitimate interests both in protecting these interests of the father and in protecting the potential life of the fetus, and the spousal notification requirement is reasonably related to advancing those state interests. By providing that a husband will usually know of his spouse's intent to have an abortion, the provision makes it more likely that the husband will participate in deciding the fate of his unborn child, a possibility that might otherwise have been denied him. This participation might in some cases result in a decision to proceed with the pregnancy. [It] is unrealistic to assume that every husband-wife relationship is either (1) so perfect that this type of truthful and important communication will take place as a matter of course, or (2) so imperfect that, upon notice, the husband will react selfishly, violently, or contrary to the best interests of his wife. The spousal notice provision will admittedly be unnecessary in some circumstances, and possibly harmful in others, but "the existence of particular cases in which a feature of a statute performs no function (or is even counterproductive) ordinarily does not render the statute unconstitutional or even constitutionally suspect." [Thornburgh; White, J., dissenting.] The Pennsylvania Legislature was in a position to weigh the likely benefits of the provision against its likely adverse effects, and presumably concluded, on balance, that the provision would be beneficial. Whether this was a wise decision or not, we cannot say that it was irrational. [We hold] that each of the challenged provisions [is] consistent with the Constitution. It bears emphasis that our conclusion in this regard does not carry with it any necessary approval of these regulations. Our task is, as always, to decide only whether the challenged provisions of a law comport with the [Constitution].

Justice SCALIA, with whom the Chief Justice [REHNQUIST], Justice WHITE, and Justice THOMAS join, concurring in the judgment in part and dissenting in part.

[A] State's choice between two positions on which reasonable people can disagree is constitutional even when (as is often the case) it intrudes upon a "liberty" in the absolute sense. Laws against bigamy, for example—which entire societies of reasonable people disagree with—intrude upon men and women's liberty to marry and live with one another. But bigamy happens not to be a liberty specially "protected" by the Constitution. That is, quite simply, the issue in this case: not whether the power of a woman to abort her unborn child is a "liberty" in the absolute sense; or even whether it is a liberty of great importance to many women. Of course it is both. The issue is whether it is a liberty protected by the Constitution. I am sure it is not. I reach that conclusion [for] the same reason I reach the conclusion that bigamy is not constitutionally protected—because of two simple facts: (1) the Constitution says absolutely nothing about it, and (2) the longstanding traditions of American society have permitted it to be legally proscribed.* The Court destroys the proposition, evidently meant to represent my position, that "liberty" includes "only those practices, defined at the most specific level, that were protected against government interference by other rules of law when the Fourteenth Amendment was ratified" (citing Michael H. v. Gerald D. [1989; p. 590 below]). That is not, however, what Michael H. says; it merely observes that, in defining "liberty," we may not disregard a specific, "relevant tradition protecting, or denying protection to, the asserted right." But the Court does not wish to be fettered by any such limitations on its preferences. The Court's statement that it is "tempting" to acknowledge the authoritativeness of tradition in order to "cur[b] the discretion of federal judges" is of course rhetoric rather than reality; no government official is "tempted" to place restraints upon his own freedom of action, which is why Lord Acton did not say "Power tends to purify." The Court's temptation is in the quite opposite and more natural direction—towards systematically eliminating checks upon its own power; and it succumbs. Beyond that brief summary of the essence of my position, I will not swell the United States Reports with repetition of what I have said before; and applying the rational basis test, I would uphold the Pennsylvania statute in its entirety. I must, however, respond to a few of the more outrageous arguments in today's opinion, which it is beyond human nature to leave unanswered. I shall discuss each of them under a quotation from the Court's opinion to which they pertain.

> "The inescapable fact is that adjudication of substantive due process claims may call upon the Court in interpreting the Constitution to exercise that same capacity which by tradition courts always have exercised: reasoned judgment."

The emptiness of the "reasoned judgment" that produced Roe is displayed in plain view by the fact that, after more than 19 years of effort by some of the brightest (and most determined) legal minds in the country, after more than 10 cases upholding abortion rights in this Court, and after dozens upon dozens of amicus briefs submitted in this and other cases, the best the Court can do to explain how it is that the word "liberty" must be thought to include the right to destroy human fetuses is to rattle off a collection of adjectives that simply decorate a value judgment and conceal a political choice. [It] is not reasoned judgment that supports the Court's decision; only personal [predilection].

> "Liberty finds no refuge in a jurisprudence of doubt."

One might have feared to encounter this august and sonorous phrase in an opinion defending the real Roe, rather than the revised version fabricated by the authors of the joint opinion. The shortcomings of Roe did not include lack

---

* The Court's suggestion that adherence to tradition would require us to uphold laws against interracial marriage is entirely wrong. Any tradition in that case was contradicted by a text—an Equal Protection Clause that explicitly establishes racial equality as a constitutional value. See Loving v. Virginia [1967; p. 667 below]. The enterprise launched in Roe, by contrast, sought to establish—in the teeth of a clear, contrary tradition—a value found nowhere in the constitutional text. There is, of course, no comparable tradition barring recognition of a "liberty interest" in carrying one's child to term free from state efforts to kill it. For that reason, it does not follow that the Constitution does not protect childbirth simply because it does not protect abortion. The Court's contention that the only way to protect childbirth is to protect abortion shows the utter bankruptcy of constitutional analysis deprived of tradition as a validating factor. It drives one to say that the only way to protect the right to eat is to acknowledge the constitutional right to starve oneself to death. [Footnote by Justice Scalia.]

of clarity: Virtually all regulation of abortion before the third trimester was invalid. But to come across this phrase in the joint opinion—which calls upon federal district judges to apply an "undue burden" standard as doubtful in application as it is unprincipled in origin—is really more than one should have to bear. [The joint opinion's] efforts at clarification make clear only that the standard is inherently manipulable. [I] do not [have] any objection to the notion that, in applying legal principles, one should rely only upon the facts contained in the record properly subject to judicial notice. But what is remarkable about the joint opinion's fact-intensive analysis is that it does not result in any measurable clarification of the "undue burden" standard. [The] inherently standardless nature of this inquiry invites [a] district judge to give effect to his personal preferences about abortion. By finding and relying upon the right facts, he can invalidate [almost] any abortion restriction that strikes him as "undue"—subject, of course, to the possibility of being reversed by a Circuit Court or Supreme Court that is as unconstrained in reviewing his decision as he was in making it. To the extent I can discern any meaningful content in the "undue burden" standard as applied in the joint opinion, it appears to be that a State may not regulate abortion in such a way as to reduce significantly its incidence. [As] Justice Blackmun recognizes (with evident hope), the "undue burden" standard may ultimately require the invalidation of each provision upheld today if it can be shown [that] the State is too effectively "express[ing] a preference for childbirth over abortion." Reason finds no refuge in this jurisprudence of confusion.

> "While we appreciate the weight of the arguments [that] Roe should be overruled, the reservations any of us may have in reaffirming the central holding of Roe are outweighed by the explication of individual liberty we have given combined with the force of stare decisis."

The Court's reliance upon stare decisis can best be described as contrived. [I] confess never to have heard of this new, keep-what-you-want-and-throw-away-the-rest version. [I] have always thought [that] the arbitrary trimester framework [was] quite as central to Roe as the arbitrary viability test which the Court today retains.

> "Where, in the performance of its judicial duties, the Court decides a case in such a way as to resolve the sort of intensely divisive controversy reflected in [Roe], its decision has a dimension that the resolution of the normal case does not carry. It is the dimension present whenever the Court's interpretation of the Constitution calls the contending sides of a national controversy to end their national division by accepting a common mandate rooted in the Constitution."

The Court's description of the place of Roe in the social history of the United States is unrecognizable. Not only did Roe not [resolve] the deeply divisive issue of abortion; it did more than anything else to nourish it, by elevating it to the national level where it is infinitely more difficult to resolve. National politics were not plagued by abortion protests [or] abortion marches on Congress before Roe was decided. Profound disagreement existed among our citizens over the issue [but] that disagreement was being worked out at the state level. As with many other issues, the division of sentiment within each State was not as closely balanced as it was among the population of the Nation as a whole, meaning not only that more people would be satisfied with the results of state-by-state resolution, but also that those results would be more stable. Pre–Roe, moreover, political compromise was possible. Roe's mandate for abortion-on-demand destroyed the compromises of the past, rendered compromise impossible for the future, and required the entire issue to be resolved uniformly, at the national level. At the same time, Roe created a vast new class of abortion consumers and abortion proponents by eliminating the moral opprobrium that had attached to the act. ("If the Constitution guarantees abortion, how can it be bad?"—not an accurate line of thought, but a natural one.) Many favor all of those developments, and it is not for me to say that they are wrong. But to portray Roe as the statesmanlike "settlement" of a divisive issue, a jurisprudential Peace of Westphalia that is worth preserving, is nothing less than Orwellian. Roe fanned into life an issue that has inflamed our national politics in general, and has obscured with its smoke the selection of Justices to this Court in particular, ever since. And by keeping us in the abortion-umpiring business, it is the perpetuation of that disruption [that] the Court's new majority decrees.

> "[T]o overrule under fire [would] subvert the Court's legitimacy. [To] all those who will [be] tested by following, the Court implicitly undertakes to remain steadfast. [The] promise of constancy, once given, binds its maker for as long as the power to stand by the decision survives and [the] commitment [is not] obsolete. [The American people's] belief in themselves as [a] people [who aspire to live according to the rule of law] is not readily separable from their understanding of the Court invested with the authority to decide their constitutional cases and speak before all others for their constitutional ideals. If the Court's legitimacy should be undermined, then, so would the country be in its very ability to see itself through its constitutional ideals."

The Imperial Judiciary lives. It is instructive to compare this Nietzschean vision of us unelected, life-tenured judges—leading a Volk who will be "tested by following," and whose very "belief in themselves" is mystically bound up in their "understanding" of a Court that "speak[s] before all others for their constitutional ideals"—with the somewhat more modest role envisioned for these lawyers by the Founders. "The judiciary [has] no direction either of the strength or of the wealth of the society, and can take no active resolution whatever. It may truly be said to have neither FORCE nor WILL but merely judgment." Federalist No. 78. [It] is particularly difficult, in the circumstances of the present decision, to sit still for the Court's lengthy lecture upon the virtues of "constancy," of "remain[ing] steadfast," of adhering to "principle." Among the five Justices who purportedly adhere to Roe, at most three agree upon the principle that constitutes adherence (the joint opinion's "undue burden" standard)—and that principle is inconsistent with Roe. To make matters worse, two of the three, in order thus to remain steadfast, had to abandon previously stated positions. It is beyond me how the Court expects these accommodations to be accepted "as grounded truly in principle, not as compromises with social and political [pressures]." The only principle the Court "adheres" to, it seems to me, is the principle that the Court must be seen as standing by Roe. That is not a principle of law (which is what I thought the Court was talking about), but a principle of Realpolitik—and a wrong one at that. I cannot agree with, indeed I am appalled by, the Court's suggestion that the decision whether to stand by an erroneous constitutional decision must be strongly influenced—against overruling, no less—by the substantial and continuing public opposition the decision has generated. The Court's judgment that any other course would "subvert the Court's legitimacy" must be another consequence of reading the error-filled history book that described the deeply divided country brought together by Roe. In my history-book, the Court was covered with dishonor and deprived of legitimacy by Dred Scott v. Sandford, an erroneous (and widely opposed) opinion that it did not abandon, rather than by West Coast Hotel, which produced the famous "switch in time" from the

Court's erroneous (and widely opposed) constitutional opposition to the social measures of the New Deal. But whether it would "subvert the Court's legitimacy" or not, the notion that we would decide a case differently from the way we otherwise would have in order to show that we can stand firm against public disapproval is frightening. [Instead] of engaging in the hopeless task of predicting public perception—a job not for lawyers but for political campaign managers—the Justices should do what is legally right by asking two questions: (1) Was Roe correctly decided? (2) Has Roe succeeded in producing a settled body of law? If the answer to both questions is no, Roe should undoubtedly be overruled.

In truth, I am as distressed as the Court [about] the "political pressure" directed to the Court: the marches, the mail, the protests aimed at inducing us to change our opinions. [The] Court would profit, I think, from giving less attention to the fact of this distressing phenomenon, and more attention to the cause of it. That cause permeates today's opinion: a new mode of constitutional adjudication that relies not upon text and traditional practice to determine the law, but upon what the Court calls "reasoned judgment," which turns out to be nothing but philosophical predilection and moral [intuition]. What makes all this relevant to the bothersome application of "political pressure" against the Court are the twin facts that the American people love democracy and the American people are not fools. As long as this Court thought (and the people thought) that we Justices were doing essentially lawyers' work up here—reading text and discerning our society's traditional understanding of that text—the public pretty much left us alone. Texts and traditions are facts to study, not convictions to demonstrate about. But if in reality our process of constitutional adjudication consists primarily of making value judgments, [then] a free and intelligent people's attitude towards us can be expected to be (ought to be) quite different. The people know that their value judgments are quite as good as those taught in any law school—maybe better. If [the] "liberties" protected by the Constitution are [undefined] and unbounded, then the people should demonstrate, to protest that we do not implement their values instead of ours. Not only that, but confirmation hearings for new Justices should deteriorate into question-and-answer sessions in which Senators go through a list of their constituents' most favored and most disfavored alleged constitutional rights, and seek the nominee's commitment to support or oppose them. Value judgments, after all, should be voted on, not dictated; and if our Constitution has somehow accidentally committed them to the Supreme Court, at least we can have a sort of plebiscite each time a new nominee to that body is put forward. Justice Blackmun not only regards this prospect with equanimity, he solicits it. [There] is a poignant aspect to today's opinion. Its length, and what might be called its epic tone, suggest that its authors believe they are bringing to an end a troublesome era in the history of our Nation and of our Court. [It] is no more realistic for us in this case, than it was for [Chief Justice Taney in the Dred Scott case] to think that an issue of the sort they both involved—an issue involving life and death, freedom and subjugation—can be "speedily and finally settled" by [this Court]. Quite to the contrary, by foreclosing all democratic outlet for the deep passions this issue arouses, by banishing the issue from the political forum that gives all participants, even the losers, the satisfaction of a fair hearing and an honest fight, by continuing the imposition of a rigid national rule instead of allowing for regional differences, the Court merely prolongs and intensifies the anguish. We should get out of this area, where we have no right to be, and where we do neither ourselves nor the country any good by remaining.

———

SOME THOUGHTS ON CASEY

The important opinions in Casey bear upon a number of recurrent issues in this book, from the proper role of the Supreme Court and the force of precedent to the meaning of liberty and equality.

1. *The force of precedent.* Was the joint opinion wise and persuasive in going beyond "normal stare decisis analysis" to examine, in part III.B., the relevance of controversial rulings "of comparable dimension" to the agitation over Roe? Do you agree with the view that the overrulings of the Lochner line of cases and of Plessy v. Ferguson were justifiably based on changed "facts, or [society's] understanding of facts"? Is there an important difference between a change in "facts" and in "understandings of facts"? Is it arguable that the more important changes that explain West Coast Hotel and Brown were changes in values rather than facts? Was the joint opinion wise to emphasize the risks of "overrul[ing] under fire," in part III.C.? Consider the questions raised in Chief Justice Rehnquist's dissent about this emphasis. Was the joint opinion persuasive in its preoccupation with the view that the Court's legitimacy turns in large part on avoiding the country's "loss of confidence in the judiciary"? Note the comment in Fried, "Constitutional Doctrine," 107 Harv. L.Rev. 1140, 1143 (1994), that "paradoxically [the authors of the joint opinion in Casey] seem to give [continuity and stability] undue prominence relative to their conviction of the rightness of the actual [Roe] decision—almost as if the decision could not stand on its own and needed an apology."

Consider especially the joint opinion's discussion of the Lochner and Plessy eras. Should the Justices have paid greater attention to the question of whether the specific constitutional provisions involved in those cases justified them? Is it arguable that Lochner, like Roe, involved an interventionist use of due process, while Plessy dealt with a central meaning of equal protection? Consider Sunstein, The Partial Constitution (1993), returning to the question of the "double standard" and conceding that, if Lochner is simply understood as a due process decision, Lochner and Roe might be "thought to stand or fall together," but claiming that this is "a crude and ahistorical approach to the Lochner period." He argues that "it is probably more fruitful to think of Roe, not as a rerun of Lochner, but as raising many of the same sorts of questions at issue in Brown."

2. *Abortion as sex discrimination.* Note that several of the opinions in Casey refer to the relationship between the right in Roe (and Casey) and gender equality. Recall Karst's comment at p. 540 above and consider Strauss, "Abortion, Toleration, and Moral Uncertainty," 1993 Sup.Ct.Rev. 1, noting that the Court in Casey addressed, "essentially for the first time," one of the issues central to the abortion debate, "the effect of abortion laws on the status of women." He states that the "Court adopted [a] plausible and coherent justification for a regime of toleration in the area of abortion. That justification is premised on, first, fundamental moral uncertainty about the status of fetal life; and, second, the danger that the political process will subordinate women," implicating the risk of gender discrimination.

3. *The "undue burden" standard.* Does the joint opinion's "undue burden" standard promise clarity and stability? What is its likely effect on restrictions on abortions of the sort litigated during the pre-Casey era but not considered in Casey? Note Sullivan's comment, "Foreword: The Justices of Rules and Standards," 106 Harv.L.Rev. 24 (1992): "Why didn't pro-choice activists celebrate when five justices reaffirmed 'the essential holding of Roe"? Because the Court stole their thunder by adopting a moderate, difference-splitting standard." She notes, too, that "Casey's undue burden test will be

applied principally by the lower federal courts [appointed by Presidents Reagan and Bush]" and adds: "No wonder lawyers for the pro-choice side predict that the undue burden test will be applied in practice to uphold more antiabortion measures than the test will strike down." Can the test be viewed more benignly than that, as mainly putting a heavier burden on challengers to produce factual data of the sort relied on by the joint opinion in invalidating the spousal notice provision? A number of commentators have criticized the joint opinion's alleged lack of consistency in striking down the spousal notification provision but upholding the parental consent and the 24–hour waiting period requirements. See [Supreme Court] Note, 106 Harv.L.Rev. 163, 206, and Field, "Abortion Law Today," 14 J.Legal.Med. 3 (1993). Cf. Brownstein, "How Rights Are Infringed: The Role of Undue Burden Analysis in Constitutional Doctrine," 45 Hast.L.J. 867 (1994).

FAMILY RELATIONSHIPS AND THE ROLE OF TRADITION

Introduction. A notable aspect of the Court's work since the late 1970s is the striking extent to which family relations have become a significant part of constitutional law. The Court has recognized a wide range of individual rights in the family context; and some of these rights exist even though they are not exercised in a traditional family unit. Repeatedly, the Court has been confronted with conflicts among the three potential centers of authority in the family context: the parents; the child; and the state. See, e.g., Parham v. J. R., 442 U.S. 584 (1979). The problems that have surfaced have covered a wide range of functional problems and constitutional sources. Functionally, litigation has involved such problems as parent-child relationships, rights involved in divorce and child custody cases, procreative rights, and regulations of the marriage relationship. Legally, the process of constitutionalizing family law has drawn on such diverse sources as the First Amendment's speech and religion clauses and equal protection scrutiny of discriminations on the basis of sex and illegitimacy, considered in the chapters that follow. But a central modern phenomenon, and the concern of these notes, is the increasingly commonplace reliance on substantive due process as the source of groundrules for constitutionalized family law.[1] These developments refocus attention on the pervasive problems of substantive due process methodology and "fundamental values" adjudication. The modern family law cases have produced sharp divisions on the Court and, to most observers, as yet no satisfactory and consistent resolutions of disputes among parents, children, and the state. These cases provide important added evidence of the modern Court's commitment to substantive due process. Moreover, they cast added light on the recurrent problems regarding the appropriate sources for judicial identification of "fundamental values."

1. *Protected family relationships: Zoning restrictions and the "extended family."* MOORE v. EAST CLEVELAND, 431 U.S. 494 (1977), elicited an unusually explicit confrontation with the substantive due process underpinnings of modern family law cases. Moore invalidated a zoning ordinance limiting occupancy of a dwelling to members of a single "family," narrowly

1. That substantive due process can contain ingredients for the resolution of family law problems is of course not a discovery of the modern Court. Recall the Meyer and Pierce cases of the Lochner era, above. For a useful review, largely supportive of the modern Court's actions, see Developments, "The Constitution and the Family," 93 Harv. L.Rev. 1156 (1980) (hereinafter cited as "Developments"). For a more critical commentary, see Burt, "The Constitution of the Family," 1979 Sup.Ct.Rev. 329.

defined as including only "a few categories of related individuals." Mrs. Moore was convicted because she shared her home with her two grandsons, who were first cousins. This relationship was not sufficiently close to constitute a "family" under the ordinance. (Under the "unusual and complicated definitional section," the ordinance would have permitted the living arrangement if the grandsons had been brothers.) According to the City's position, "any constitutional right to live together as a family extends only to the nuclear family— essentially a couple and their dependent children." Justice Powell's plurality opinion invalidated the application of the ordinance to Mrs. Moore on substantive due process grounds. Two of the dissenters, Justices Stewart and White, took sharp issue with his substantive due process methodology.

Justice POWELL insisted that a scrutiny stricter than deferential review was appropriate "[w]hen a city undertakes such intrusive regulation of the family": "[W]hen the government intrudes on choices concerning family living arrangements, this Court must examine carefully the importance of the governmental interests advanced and the extent to which they are served by the challenged regulation." The ordinance could not survive that scrutiny: though such articulated city interests as "preventing overcrowding" and "minimizing traffic and parking congestion" were "legitimate," the ordinance "serves them marginally, at best," and "has but a tenuous relation to them." The most difficult aspect of the case was presented by the city's argument that any "right to live together as a family" was limited to the situation of "the nuclear family—essentially a couple and its dependent children." Justice Powell held that the principles of the cases beginning with Meyer and Pierce covered "extended family" relationships such as Mrs. Moore's as well. In articulating his substantive due process methodology, Justice Powell stated: "To be sure, [the Meyer–Pierce line of cases] did not expressly consider the family relationship presented here. [But] unless we close our eyes to the basic reasons why certain rights associated with the family have been accorded shelter under [due process], we cannot avoid applying the force and rationale of these precedents to the family choice involved in this case. Understanding those reasons requires careful attention to this Court's function under the Due Process Clause. [Justice Harlan] described it eloquently." [He quoted at length from Justice Harlan's opinion in Poe v. Ullman, printed with Griswold, above, and continued:]

"Substantive due process has at times been a treacherous field for this Court. There *are* risks when the judicial branch gives enhanced protection to certain substantive liberties without the guidance of the more specific provisions of the Bill of Rights. As the history of the Lochner era demonstrates, there is reason for concern lest the only limits to such judicial intervention become the predilections of those who happen at the time to be Members of this Court. That history counsels caution and restraint. But it does not counsel abandonment, nor does it require what the city urges here: cutting off any protection of family rights at the first convenient, if arbitrary boundary—the boundary of the nuclear family." In suggesting limits to guard against judicial excesses in exercising substantive due process review, he took a position challenged by the dissents. He stated: "Appropriate limits on substantive due process come not from drawing arbitrary lines but rather from 'careful respect for the teachings of history [and] solid recognition of the basic values that underlie our society.' [Griswold; Harlan, J., concurring.] Our decisions establish that the Constitution protects the sanctity of the family precisely because the institution of the family is deeply rooted in this Nation's history and tradition. It is through the family that we inculcate and pass down many of our most cherished values, moral and cultural. Ours is by no means a tradition limited to respect for the bonds uniting the members of the nuclear family. The tradition of uncles, aunts, cousins, and especially grandparents sharing a household along with parents and children has roots equally venerable and equally deserving of constitutional recognition. Over the years millions of our citizens have grown up in just such an environment. [Even] if conditions of modern society have brought about a decline in extended family households, they have not erased the accumulated wisdom of civilization [that] supports a larger conception of the family. Out of choice, necessity, or a sense of family responsibility, it has been common for close relatives to draw together and participate in the duties and satisfactions of a common home. [Especially] in times of adversity, such as the death of a spouse or economic need, the broader family has tended to come together for mutual sustenance and to maintain or rebuild a secure home life. This is apparently what happened here. Whether or not such a household is established because of personal tragedy, the choice of relatives in this degree of kinship to live together may not lightly be denied by the State. [The] Constitution prevents East Cleveland from standardizing its children—and its adults—by forcing all to live in certain narrowly defined family patterns."

In a separate opinion supporting Justice Powell's result, Justice BRENNAN, joined by Justice Marshall, added that the ordinance reflected "cultural myopia" and displayed "a distressing insensitivity toward the economic and emotional needs of a very large part of our society." He noted, too, that the "extended" form was "especially familiar among black families." He concluded that the Constitution cannot "tolerate the imposition by government upon the rest of us of white suburbia's preference in patterns of family living." [Compare a comment in Justice Stewart's dissent: "In point of fact, East Cleveland is a predominantly Negro community, with a Negro City Manager and City Commission." And note Burt, "The Constitution of the Family," 1979 Sup.Ct.Rev. 329: "The plurality did not consider that the purpose of the ordinance was quite straightforward: to exclude from a middle-class, predominantly black [and nuclear family] community, that saw itself as socially and economically upwardly mobile, other black [extended] families most characteristic of lower-class ghetto life."] Justice WHITE's dissent argued that Justice Powell's emphasis on history and tradition would "broaden enormously the horizons" of substantive due process. He commented: "That the Court has ample precedent for the creation of new constitutional rights should not lead it to repeat the process at will." In his view, "the interest in residing with more than one set of grandchildren is [not] one that calls for any kind of heightened protection." He insisted that, under Palko, that interest was not a right "implicit in ordered liberty" or "one of which it could be said that 'neither liberty nor justice would exist if [it] were sacrificed.'" He added: "[Justice Powell] would apparently construe the Due Process Clause to protect from all but quite important state regulatory interests any right or privilege that in his estimate is deeply rooted in the country's traditions. For me, this suggests a far too expansive charter for this Court. [What] the deeply rooted traditions of the country are is arguable; which of them deserves the protection of the Due Process Clause is even more debatable. [If] the interest involved here is any measure of what the States would be forbidden to regulate, the courts would be substantively weighing and very likely invalidating a wide range of measures that Congress and state legislatures think appropriate to respond to a changing economic and social order." He recalled Justice Black's dissent in Griswold and urged the Court to be "extremely reluctant to breathe still further substantive content" into due process. Justice Powell responded by noting that "an approach grounded in history imposes limits on the judiciary that are more meaningful than any based on the abstract formula taken from [Palko]."[2]

Contrast with Moore the decision in Belle Terre v. Boraas, 416 U.S. 1 (1974), where Justice Douglas's majority opinion, over Justice Marshall's dissent, found no privacy rights involved in a family-oriented zoning restriction excluding most *unrelated* groups from a village. Justice Douglas insisted the ordinance represented "economic and social legislation" and invoked the deferential judicial stance characteristic of zoning cases. Justice Marshall argued that strict scrutiny was appropriate: "The choice of household companions—of whether a person's 'intellectual and emotional' needs are best met by living with family, friends, professional associates or others—involves deeply personal considerations as to the kind and quality of intimate relationships within the home. That decision surely falls within the ambit of the right to privacy protected by the Constitution." In Moore, Justice Powell distinguished Belle Terre because it had affected "only *unrelated* individuals."

2. *The "fundamental right to marry": "Critical examination" of "significant" interferences with the right.* ZABLOCKI v. REDHAIL, 434 U.S. 374 (1978), invalidated a Wisconsin law which provided that any resident "having minor issue not in his custody and which he is under an obligation to support by any court order" could not marry without obtaining court approval. Under the statute, court permission required proof that the applicant's support obligation had been met and that children covered by the support order "are not then and are not likely thereafter to become public charges." Redhail's application for a marriage license was denied because he had not obtained court permission. He had not petitioned for permission because he could not satisfy the two requirements: he had not been paying court-ordered support for an illegitimate daughter, and the child had been receiving benefits under the AFDC program since her birth. He brought a class action challenging the law under the equal protection and due process clauses. Though the majority ultimately analyzed the case in terms of the "fundamental rights" strand of the "new equal protection," it was strongly influenced by substantive due process precedents which had asserted that the "right to marry" was "fundamental." In short, determining what qualifies as a "fundamental right" for purposes of triggering strict equal protection scrutiny turned, as it does quite frequently (though often more obscurely), on whether substantive due process precedents support such a "fundamental right."

In articulating the majority's standard of review, Justice MARSHALL's opinion stated that, since "the right to marry is of fundamental importance, and since the classification at issue here significantly interferes with the exercise of that right, we believe that 'critical examination' of the state interests advanced [is] required." In explaining why "the right to marry is of fundamental importance for all individuals," he pointed to Loving v. Virginia, the 1967 miscegenation decision (p. 667 below). He noted that Griswold and other recent decisions had "established that the right to marry is part of the

---

2. Justice STEWART's dissent, joined by Justice Rehnquist, argued, like Justice White, that Mrs. Moore's interest could not be considered "implicit in the concept of ordered liberty." He added: "To equate this interest with the fundamental decisions to marry and to bear and raise children is to extend the limited substantive contours of the Due Process Clause beyond recognition."

Justice STEVENS, whose vote was necessary for the result in the 5-4 decision, concurred in the result, applying the "limited standard of review" generally applicable in zoning cases and finding an unjustifiable restriction on Mrs. Moore's "right to use her own property as she sees fit." Chief Justice BURGER dissented on procedural grounds.

fundamental 'right of privacy' implicit in [the] Due Process Clause." He elaborated: "It is not surprising that the decision to marry has been placed on the same level of importance as decisions relating to procreation, childbirth, child-rearing, and family relationships. [It] would make little sense to recognize a right of privacy with respect to other matters of family life and not with respect to the decision to enter the relationship that is the foundation of the family in our society. [If the] right to procreate means anything at all, it must imply some right to enter the only relationship in which [the State] allows sexual relations legally to take place." But, after "reaffirming the fundamental character of the right to marry," Justice Marshall made clear that not "every state regulation which relates in any way to the incidents of or prerequisites for marriage must be subjected to rigorous scrutiny. [Reasonable] regulations that do not significantly interfere with decisions to enter into the marital relationship may legitimately be imposed. See Califano v. Jobst."[3] Here, however, the law "interfere[d] directly and substantially with the right to marry." In engaging in his "critical examination" of the law, Justice Marshall stated that the classification in the law "cannot be upheld unless it is supported by sufficiently important state interests and is closely tailored to effectuate only those interests." He accepted, "for present purposes," that the asserted state interests were "legitimate and substantial," but found that "the means selected [for] achieving these interests unnecessarily impinge on the right to marry." One asserted state interest was "safeguarding the welfare of out-of-custody children," by providing an incentive to make support payments. Justice Marshall concluded that this "collection device" rationale could not justify the law's "broad infringement on the right to marry": he stated that the State had other, less intrusive means "for exacting compliance with support obligations," such as direct enforcement "via wage assignments, civil contempt proceedings, and criminal penalties." He noted, finally, that "the net result of preventing the marriage is simply more illegitimate children."

Justice POWELL's concurrence in the judgment insisted that the majority's rationale swept "too broadly in an area which traditionally has been subject to pervasive state regulation." He commented: "Since state regulation in this area typically takes the form of a prerequisite or barrier to marriage or divorce, the degree of 'direct' interference with the decision to marry or to divorce is unlikely to provide either guidance for state legislatures or a basis for judicial oversight." He added that "[a] 'compelling state purpose' inquiry would cast doubt on the network of restrictions that the States have fashioned to govern marriage and divorce," such as "bans on incest, bigamy, and homosexuality, as well as various preconditions to marriage, such as blood tests." Nevertheless, Justice Powell concluded that the law could not pass muster under either the due process or the equal protection standards he deemed appropriate, emphasizing especially the "intermediate level of scrutiny" he had articulated in Craig v. Boren, a 1976 sex discrimination-equal protection case (p. 686 below).

Justice STEVENS stated that the Constitution permits "direct and substantial" restraints on the right to marry, such as prohibitions on marriage to a child or close relative. But in this case, there was "deliberate discrimination against the poor." Under the Wisconsin law, "a person's economic status may

3.   Califano v. Jobst, 434 U.S. 47 (1977), sustained a Social Security Act provision which cuts off disabled children's benefits upon marriage to nonbeneficiaries but not upon marriage to beneficiaries, even if the nonbeneficiary is disabled. In Zablocki, Justice Marshall claimed that the "directness and substantiality of the interference with the freedom to marry" distinguished Zablocki from Jobst.

determine his eligibility to enter into a lawful marriage. A noncustodial parent whose children are 'public charges' may not marry even if he has met his court-ordered obligations. Thus, within the class of parents who have fulfilled their court-ordered obligations, the rich may marry and the poor may not." Accordingly, the law violated equal protection. Justice STEWART's opinion concurring in the judgment was the only one which found substantive due process the sole appropriate basis for decision. He added: "The Court is understandably reluctant to rely on substantive due process. But to embrace the essence of that doctrine under the guise of equal protection serves no purpose but obfuscation [and] invites mechanical or thoughtless application of misfocused doctrine. To bring it into the open forces a healthy and responsible recognition of the nature and purpose of the extreme power we wield." [See generally Cohen, "Is Equal Protection Like Oakland? Equality as a Surrogate for Other Rights," 59 Tul.L.Rev. 884 (1985).] He insisted that to rely on equal protection in a case such as this was "no more than substantive due process by another name." Instead, he found the law invalid "because it exceeds the bounds of permissible state regulation of marriage, and invades the sphere of liberty protected by [due process]." He relied especially on cases such as Boddie v. Connecticut (1971; p. 899 below), in stating that "a person's inability to pay money demanded by the State does not justify the total deprivation of a constitutionally protected liberty." (Boddie held that indigents could not be compelled to pay fees in order to institute divorce actions.) He added that the State "must stop short of telling people they may not marry because they are too poor or because they might persist in their financial irresponsibility. The invasion of constitutionally protected liberty and the chance of erroneous prediction are simply too great." Justice REHNQUIST, the sole dissenter, found no basis for applying any "heightened standard of review," insisting on "the traditional presumption of validity" as expressed in such cases as Lee Optical. (The unanimous Court relied on Zablocki in Turner v. Safley, 482 U.S. 78 (1987), striking down a prison regulation that severely restricted the inmates' right to marry.)[4]

3. *Substantive due process methodology in light of the family relations cases: The role of tradition.* a. *The utility of the tradition-oriented approach.* Recurrently, this chapter has raised the question whether the quest for "fundamental values" in modern substantive due process cases can be channeled in a manner that keeps it from becoming a wholly open-ended route for infusing subjective judicial values into the Constitution. Do the family law cases offer greater hope in this regard than Griswold, Roe, and their progeny? Note especially the heavy reliance in Moore, above, on Justice Harlan's tradition-oriented approach. And consider the approving comments on such an approach in "Developments," 93 Harv.L.Rev. 1156 (1980): "In the family cases, the Court has consistently turned to tradition as a source of previously unrecognized aspects of [liberty]. Recognition of a traditional value as fundamental, however, does not mean that individual cases can be decided solely by reference to historical notions about the right. [Once] a traditional value has been accepted, [the] Court must give that value a consistent and principled interpretation. [While] tradition offers guidance, [due process] is not merely a mandate

---

4. Consider Lupu, "Untangling the Strands of the Fourteenth Amendment," 77 Mich.L.Rev. 981 (1979), criticizing the Court's wavering course between substantive due process and equal protection rationales in identifying values warranting special protection. He views the due process and equal protection clauses as "complementary, not interchangeable" bases, argues that "judicial discoveries" of fundamental values outside the text should be grounded in due process, and urges that equal protection should "not bear a substantive content" but should instead "remain [rooted] in the pure anti-discrimination concerns that sparked" that clause.

for the perpetuation of tradition with all its fortuitous historical attributes. Once it has been found that a particular right is an element of [liberty], the Court no longer looks exclusively to tradition to ascertain its contours. Instead, [the Court may adopt] a functional approach to the right, letting its rationale dictate its scope. [Because] a functional approach extends the scope of a traditional right beyond its historical contours, it may be criticized as manipulation of the level of generality of the relevant tradition so that rights not historically regarded as important liberties are brought within the scope of protection. This criticism misses the point. A court which extends the right of procreative autonomy from a marital to a nonmarital context is not contending that the procreative rights of the unmarried are traditional. It is merely claiming that, given a longstanding cultural consensus that procreative activities comprise an area of human endeavor that should be regarded as within the realm of liberty, there must be some principled basis for treating the unmarried and married differently."

Does that approach adequately confine substantive due process adjudication? The "Developments" comment finds the "tradition-based approach" very appealing: "Recourse to traditional values enables the Court to afford protection to rights Americans traditionally have assumed to be part of our nation's scheme of liberty. [Not] all these rights would be preserved by exclusive resort to other theories, for example, one recognizing only rights essential to all possible systems of ordered liberty, or one concentrating on defects in the democratic process. Tradition ensures proper protection for important liberties that an abstract formula might overlook. The use of tradition [has] also appealed to the Court's need for a sense of impartiality. [Reference] to tradition does not involve the Court in the ambitious task of developing its own unified theory of political liberty; rather, the initial appeal is to a relatively objective history. While tradition is not always easy to ascertain, it is easier to tell that a value is deeply rooted in American tradition than to determine that it is a valid proposition of moral philosophy, or that it is supported by a convergence of contemporary views amounting to consensus." Does this position—essentially, an endorsement and elaboration of the Harlan–Powell methodology—adequately answer the charge of "Lochnerizing"?

b. *Tradition and the appropriate level of generality.* The problem of the appropriate level of generality in defining the relevant tradition for substantive due process purposes was one of the issues that divided the Court in MICHAEL H. v. GERALD D., 491 U.S. 110 (1989). As noted in the preceding paragraphs, if the tradition is defined too narrowly, the challenged legislation will presumably conform to the relevant "tradition" and substantive due process loses its bite; but if the tradition is defined too broadly, judges are encouraged to act as free-wheeling censors of state judgments. These competing views of "tradition" provoked sharp exchanges in the Michael H. case, a case that arose on facts that were simultaneously complex, sad, and amusing. At issue was a California law establishing a presumption that a child born to the wife is legitimately a child of the marriage, a presumption rebuttable only under limited circumstances. Michael H., claiming to be the father of the child of Carole D. and Gerald D., a married couple, sought visitation and other rights with respect to the child. The California courts, relying on the presumption, rejected Michael H.'s claim of paternity, even though blood tests established a 98.07% probability that he was the child's father. Although there was no majority opinion, the Court upheld the California judgment. Justice SCALIA, writing also for Chief Justice Rehnquist and in part for Justices O'Connor and Kennedy, concluded that none of Michael H.'s constitutional rights had been violated. He proceeded to analyze the case in substantive rather than procedural due process terms. In

Justice Scalia's view, due process protection required "not merely that the interest denominated as a 'liberty' be 'fundamental' (a concept that, in isolation, is hard to objectify), but also that it be an interest traditionally protected by our society." Central to him was "the historic respect—indeed, sanctity would not be too strong a term—traditionally accorded to the relationships that develop within the unitary family. [Thus,] the legal issue [here] reduces to whether the relationship between the persons in the situation of Michael and Victoria [the child] has been treated as a protected family unit under the historic practices of our society, or whether on any other basis it has been accorded special protection. We think it impossible to find that it has. In fact, quite to the contrary, our traditions have protected the marital family (Gerald, Carole, and the child they acknowledge to be theirs) against the sort of claim Michael asserts."

In a lengthy footnote, Justice Scalia defended his position that resort to "tradition" required emphasis on the "most specific" level of generality at which the history and tradition could be perceived. Justice Scalia stated: "Justice Brennan [in dissent] criticizes our methodology in using historical traditions specifically relating to the rights of an adulterous natural father, rather than inquiring more generally 'whether parenthood is an interest that historically has received our attention and protection.' [Though] the dissent has no basis for the level of generality it would select, we do: We refer to the most specific level at which a relevant tradition protecting, or denying protection to, the asserted right can be identified. If [there] were no societal tradition, either way, regarding the rights of the natural father of a child adulterously conceived, we would have to consult, and [if possible] reason from, the traditions regarding natural fathers in general. But there is such a more specific tradition, and it unqualifiedly denies protection to such a parent. [Because] general traditions provide such imprecise guidance, they permit judges to dictate rather than discern the society's views. [Although] assuredly having the virtue (if it be that) of leaving judges free to decide as they think best when the unanticipated occurs, a rule of law that binds neither by text nor by any particular, identifiable tradition, is no rule of law at all." Justice O'CONNOR, joined by Justice Kennedy, joined all of Justice Scalia's opinion *except* that footnote. Justice O'Connor commented: "This footnote sketches a mode of historical analysis [that] may be somewhat inconsistent with our past decisions in this area. See [Griswold; Eisenstadt]. On occasion the Court has characterized relevant traditions protecting asserted rights at levels of generality that might not be 'the most specific level' available. [See, e.g., Loving v. Virginia.] I would not foreclose the unanticipated by the prior imposition of a single mode of historical analysis. Poe v. Ullman [1961; Harlan, J., dissenting (a dissent printed with Griswold v. Connecticut above)]."

Justice BRENNAN's dissent, joined by Justices Marshall and Blackmun, included a strong objection to Justice Scalia's methodology: "Apparently oblivious to the fact that [the] concept [of tradition] can be as malleable and as elusive as 'liberty' itself, the plurality pretends that tradition places a discernible border around the Constitution. The pretense is seductive. [The] plurality has not found the objective boundary that it seeks. [If] we had looked to tradition with such specificity [as the plurality] in past cases, many a decision would have reached a different result. [E.g., Eisenstadt; Griswold.] The plurality's interpretive method [ignores] the good reasons for limiting the role of 'tradition' in interpreting the Constitution's deliberately capacious language. In the plurality's constitutional universe, we may not take notice of the fact that the original reasons for the conclusive presumption of paternity are out of place in a world in which blood tests can prove virtually beyond a shadow of a doubt who sired a particular child and in which the fact of illegitimacy no longer plays the burdensome and stigmatizing role it once did. [In] construing the Fourteenth Amendment to offer shelter only to those interests specifically protected by historical practice, moreover, the plurality ignores the kind of society in which our Constitution exists. We are not an assimilative, homogeneous society, but a facilitative, pluralistic one, in which we must be willing to abide someone else's unfamiliar or even repellent practice because the same tolerant impulse protects our own idiosyncracies. [In] a community such as ours, 'liberty' must include the freedom not to conform. [The] plurality today squashes this freedom by requiring specific approval from history before protecting anything in the name of liberty. The document that the plurality construes today is unfamiliar to me. It is not the living charter that I have taken to be our Constitution; it is instead a stagnant, archaic, hidebound document steeped in the prejudices and superstitions of a time long past. *This* Constitution does not recognize that times change. [I] cannot accept an interpretive method that does such violence to the charter that I am bound by oath to uphold." Accordingly objecting to the plurality's focus on the "unitary family," Justice Brennan went on to view the case primarily in procedural terms, stressing the distinction between the existence of a liberty interest, which he thought existed here, and the procedures that may be used to curtail it. To him, the fatal flaw was the unavailability of a hearing in which Michael H. could prove that he was Victoria's father, and the case was properly viewed as one of procedural rather substantive due process. (Justice STEVENS, who concurred only in the judgment, saw the case primarily in terms of visitation rights. He insisted that nothing in California law would have precluded the state courts from granting such rights, and that Michael H. was given a fair opportunity to show that he was Victoria's natural father. Justice WHITE, joined by Justice Brennan, also submitted a dissent, concluding that a putative natural father had a constitutional liberty interest, and that on the facts of this case, the unavailability of a hearing at which Michael could establish his paternity was constitutionally impermissible.)

The debate between Justices Scalia and Brennan about the appropriate sources of "tradition" in substantive due process cases continued in several later rulings. See, e.g., Burnham v. Superior Court, 495 U.S. 604 (1990), a personal jurisdiction case, where Justice Brennan argued that due process principles should turn on "contemporary notions of due process" and that history should not be "the only factor." Justice Scalia, by contrast, attacked this approach because of its "subjectivity, and hence inadequacy": "Justice Brennan's approach does not establish a rule of law at all, but only a 'totality of the circumstances' test. [The] difference between [Justice Brennan and me] has to do with whether the changes are to be adopted as progressive by the American people or decreed as progressive by the Justices of this Court."[5]

***

5. Note also the somewhat related divisions on the Court that have surfaced in a number of modern cases challenging punitive damage awards in civil cases as violating the due process requirement of fairness. (Those cases most often focus on the elements of procedural fairness, not on the derivation of "fundamental" rights under substantive due process.) See, e.g., Pacific Mutual Life Insurance Co. v. Haslip, 499 U.S. 1 (1991): Justice Blackmun's majority opinion upheld the award; a concurring opinion by Justice Scalia, suggested that "unbroken historical usage" can demonstrate a procedure's "compliance with the [general] guarantee of 'due process.'" A dissent by Justice O'Connor noted that the majority had "properly rejected" Justice Scalia's preoccupation with histo-

CONSENSUAL SEXUAL BEHAVIOR

Does the right recognized in the Griswold–Roe line of cases extend to consensual sexual behavior? That question first came to the Court in Doe v. Commonwealth's Attorney, 425 U.S. 901 (1976), where the majority summarily affirmed, without hearing argument, a three-judge federal court's dismissal of a challenge by male homosexuals to Virginia's sodomy law. The three-judge court had divided 2-1 in rejecting the challenge. 403 F.Supp. 1199 (E.D.Va.1975). The majority in the lower court insisted that the Supreme Court decisions were limited to restrictions on "the incidents of marriage, upon the sanctity of the home, or upon the nurture of family life." The dissenter emphasized that Eisenstadt had seriously impaired the "marital-nonmarital distinction" and argued that the "right to select consenting adults' sexual partners," "whether heterosexual or homosexual," could not be restricted in the absence of "compelling justification." Was the Supreme Court's summary affirmance, with its refusal even to hear argument in the case, properly criticizable as "irresponsible" and "lawless"? (Gunther so commented in The New York Times, April 3, 1976. Compare Grey's analysis of "sexual freedom" cases at p. 544 above.) The significance of the Doe ruling elicited several comments in the course of the opinions in Carey (1977; p. 552 above; distribution of contraceptives). Justice Brennan's opinion insisted that "the Court has not definitively answered the difficult question whether and to what extent the Constitution prohibits state statutes regulating [private consensual sexual] behavior among adults." Justice Rehnquist's dissent challenged that remark, citing the 1976 Doe ruling and stating: "[The] facial constitutional validity of criminal statutes prohibiting certain consensual acts has been 'definitively' established." A decade later, the Court confronted the issue in full at last, in the principal case that follows.

Bowers v. Hardwick

478 U.S. 186, 106 S.Ct. 2841, 92 L.Ed.2d 140 (1986).

Justice WHITE delivered the opinion of the Court.

[Respondent, an adult male, was charged with violating Georgia's sodomy law by committing a sexual act with another adult male in his own bedroom. The law defines sodomy as committing or submitting to "any sexual act involving the sex organs of one person and the mouth or anus of another." After the prosecutor chose not to present the case to a grand jury, the respondent sued in federal court to challenge the constitutionality of the law. The trial court rejected the claim, but the court of appeals reversed, relying on such cases as Griswold, Eisenstadt, and Roe. The Court of Appeals held that the law "violated respondent's fundamental rights because his homosexual activity is a private and intimate association that is beyond the reach of state regulation." The Court reversed.]

ry: "Due process is not a fixed notion. Although history creates a sharp presumption of continuing validity, [circumstances] today are different than they were 200 years ago, and nothing in the Fourteenth Amendment requires us to blind ourselves to this fact." The Court has continued to wrestle with the question of due process limits on punitive damages awards. See, e.g., TXO Production Corp. v. Alliance Resources Corp., 509 U.S. 443 (1993), Honda Motor Co., Ltd. v. Oberg, 512 U.S. 415 (1994), and BMW of North America, Inc. v. Gore, 523 U.S. ___ (1996).

This case does not require a judgment on whether laws against sodomy between consenting adults in general, or between homosexuals in particular, are wise or desirable. [The] issue presented is whether the Federal Constitution confers a fundamental right upon homosexuals to engage in sodomy[1] and hence invalidates the laws of the many States that still make such conduct illegal and have done so for a very long time. The case also calls for some judgment about the limits of the Court's role in carrying out its constitutional mandate. We first register our disagreement with the Court of Appeals [that] the Court's prior cases have construed the Constitution to confer a right of privacy that extends to homosexual sodomy and for all intents and purposes have decided this case. [Pierce and Meyer] were described as dealing with child rearing and education; [Skinner] with procreation; [Loving] with marriage; [Griswold and Eisenstadt] with contraception; and [Roe] with abortion. The latter three cases were interpreted as construing [due process] to confer a fundamental individual right to decide whether or not to beget or bear a child. Accepting the decisions in these cases and the above description of them, we think it evident that none of the rights announced in those cases bears any resemblance to the claimed constitutional right of homosexuals to engage in acts of sodomy, that is asserted in this case. No connection between family, marriage, or procreation on the one hand and homosexual activity on the other has been demonstrated. [Moreover,] any claim that these cases nevertheless stand for the proposition that any kind of private sexual conduct between consenting adults is constitutionally insulated from state proscription is [unsupportable]. Precedent aside, however, respondent would have us announce [a] fundamental right to engage in homosexual sodomy. This we are quite unwilling to do. It is true that despite the language of the [Due Process Clauses] which appears to focus only on the processes by which life, liberty, or property is taken, the cases are legion in which those Clauses have been interpreted to have substantive [content]. Among such cases are those recognizing rights that have little or no textual support in the constitutional language. [E.g., Meyer, Prince, Pierce, Griswold and Carey.] Striving to assure itself and the public that announcing rights not readily identifiable in the Constitution's text involves much more than the imposition of the Justices' own choice of [values], the Court has sought to identify the nature of the rights qualifying for heightened judicial protection. In [Palko] it was said that this category includes those fundamental liberties that are "implicit in the concept of ordered liberty," such that "neither liberty nor justice would exist if [they] were sacrificed." A different description of fundamental liberties appeared in [Moore], where they are characterized as those liberties that are "deeply rooted in this Nation's history and tradition."

It is obvious to us that neither of these formulations would extend a fundamental right to homosexuals to engage in acts of consensual sodomy. Proscriptions against that conduct have ancient roots. Sodomy was a criminal offense at common law and was forbidden by the laws of the original thirteen States when they ratified the Bill of Rights. In 1868, when the Fourteenth Amendment was ratified, all but 5 of the 37 States in the Union had criminal sodomy laws. In fact, until 1961, all States outlawed sodomy, and today, 24 States and the District of Columbia continue to provide criminal penalties for sodomy performed in private and between consenting adults. Against this background, to claim that a right to engage in such conduct is "deeply rooted in this Nation's history and tradition" or "implicit in the concept of ordered

---

1. [The] only claim properly before the Court [is] Hardwick's challenge to the Georgia statute as applied to consensual homosexual sodomy. We express no opinion on the constitutionality of the Georgia statute as applied to other acts of sodomy. [Footnote by Justice White, earlier in the opinion.]

liberty" is, at best, facetious. Nor are we inclined to take a more expansive view of our authority to discover new fundamental rights imbedded in the Due Process Clause. The Court is most vulnerable and comes nearest to illegitimacy when it deals with judge-made constitutional law having little or no cognizable roots in the language or design of the Constitution. That this is so was painfully demonstrated by the face-off between the Executive and the Court in the 1930's, which resulted in the repudiation of much of the substantive gloss that the Court had placed on [due process]. There should be, therefore, great resistance to expand the substantive reach of those Clauses, particularly if it requires redefining the category of rights deemed to be fundamental. Otherwise, the Judiciary necessarily takes to itself further authority to govern the country without express constitutional authority. The claimed right pressed on us today falls far short of overcoming this resistance.

Respondent, however, asserts that the result should be different where the homosexual conduct occurs in the privacy of the home. He relies on Stanley v. Georgia [1969, p. 1130 below], where the Court held that the First Amendment prevents conviction for possessing and reading obscene material in the privacy of his home. [Stanley] did protect conduct that would not have been protected outside the home, and it partially prevented the enforcement of state obscenity laws; but the decision was firmly grounded in the First Amendment. The right pressed upon us here has no similar support in the text of the Constitution, and it does not qualify for recognition under the prevailing principles for construing the Fourteenth Amendment. Its limits are also difficult to discern. Plainly enough, otherwise illegal conduct is not always immunized whenever it occurs in the home. Victimless crimes, such as the possession and use of illegal drugs, do not escape the law where they are committed at home. Stanley itself recognized that its holding offered no protection for the possession in the home of drugs, firearms, or stolen goods. And if respondent's submission is limited to the voluntary sexual conduct between consenting adults, it would be difficult, except by fiat, to limit the claimed right to homosexual conduct while leaving exposed to prosecution adultery, incest, and other sexual crimes even though they are committed in the home. We are unwilling to start down that road.

Even if the conduct at issue here is not a fundamental right, respondent asserts that there must be a rational basis for the law and that there is none in this case other than the presumed belief of a majority of the electorate in Georgia that homosexual sodomy is immoral and unacceptable. This is said to be an inadequate rationale to support the law. The law, however, is constantly based on notions of morality, and if all laws representing essentially moral choices are to be invalidated under the Due Process Clause, the courts will be very busy indeed. Even respondent makes no such claim, but insists that majority sentiments about the morality of homosexuality should be declared inadequate. We do not agree, and are unpersuaded that the sodomy laws of some 25 States should be invalidated on this basis.[2]

[Reversed.]

Chief Justice BURGER, concurring.

2. Respondent does not defend the judgment below based on the Ninth Amendment, the Equal Protection Clause, or the Eighth Amendment. [Footnote by Justice White.] After Hardwick, *could* a successful attack on sodomy laws be brought under equal protection? See chap. 9, sec. 3, below, and note Justice Stevens's dissent in this case. And see especially Romer v. Evans [1996; p. 737 below]. Does Romer undercut Bowers? Can the two cases be reconciled?

[As] the Court notes, the proscriptions against sodomy have very "ancient roots." [Condemnation of homosexual] practices is firmly rooted in [Judeo–Christian] moral and ethical standards. Homosexual sodomy was a capital crime under Roman law. [Blackstone] described "the infamous crime against nature" as an offense of "deeper malignity" than rape, an heinous act "the very mention of which is a disgrace to human nature," and "a crime not fit to be named." [To] hold that the act of homosexual sodomy is somehow protected as a fundamental right would be to cast aside millennia of moral teaching. [I] find nothing in the Constitution depriving a State of the power to enact the statute challenged here.

Justice POWELL, concurring.

[I] agree with the Court that there is no fundamental right—i.e., no substantive right under the Due Process Clause—such as that claimed by [respondent]. This is not to suggest, however, that respondent may not be protected by the Eighth Amendment of the Constitution. The Georgia statute at issue in this case authorizes a court to imprison a person for up to 20 years for a single private, consensual act of sodomy. In my view, a prison sentence for such conduct [would] create a serious Eighth Amendment [issue]. In this case however, respondent has not been tried, much less convicted and [sentenced.]*

Justice BLACKMUN, with whom Justice BRENNAN, Justice MARSHALL, and Justice STEVENS join, dissenting.

This case is no more about "a fundamental right to engage in homosexual sodomy" [than Stanley] was about a fundamental right to watch obscene movies. Rather, this case is about "the most comprehensive of rights and the right most valued by civilized men," namely, "the right to be let alone." [W]e must analyze respondent's claim in the light of the values that underlie the constitutional right to privacy. If that right means anything, it means that, before Georgia can prosecute its citizens for making choices about the most intimate aspects of their lives, it must do more than assert that the choice they have made is an " 'abominable crime not fit to be named among Christians.' " [The] Court concludes today that none of our prior cases dealing with various decisions that individuals are entitled to make free of governmental interference "bears any resemblance to the claimed constitutional right of homosexuals to engage in acts of sodomy that is asserted in this case." While it is true that these cases may be characterized by their connection to protection of the family, the Court's conclusion that they extend no further than this boundary ignores the warning in [Moore] against "clos[ing] our eyes to the basic reasons why certain rights associated with the family have been accorded shelter under [due process]." We protect those rights not because they contribute, in some direct and material way, to the general public welfare, but because they form so central a part of an individual's life. Only the most willful blindness could obscure the fact that sexual intimacy is "a sensitive, key relationship of human existence, central to family life, community welfare, and the development of human personality [Paris Adult Theatre (1973); p. 1135 below.]" [The] fact that individuals define themselves in a significant way through their intimate sexual relationships with others suggests, in a Nation as diverse as ours, that there may be many "right" ways of conducting those relationships, and that much of the richness of a relationship will come from the freedom an individual

---

* According to press reports, retired Justice Powell, who had cast the deciding vote in Bowers, stated on October 25, 1990, that he "probably made a mistake" in voting as he did. But he added that he still regarded the decision as "one of little or no importance" because no one had actually been prosecuted for homosexual conduct. The New York Times, Oct. 26, 1990. See also Jeffries, Justice Lewis F. Powell, Jr. (1994), 511–30.

has to *choose* the form and nature of these intensely personal bonds. See Karst, The Freedom of Intimate Association, 89 Yale L.J. 624 (1980). [The] Court claims that its decision today merely refuses to recognize a fundamental right to engage in homosexual sodomy; what the Court really has refused to recognize is the fundamental interest all individuals have in controlling the nature of their intimate associations with others. [Moreover, the] behavior for which Hardwick faces prosecution occurred in his own home, a place to which the Fourth Amendment attaches special significance. [The] Court's interpretation of the pivotal case of [Stanley] is entirely unconvincing. [Stanley did not rest entirely on the First Amendment.] Rather, the Stanley Court anchored its holding in the Fourth Amendment's special protection for the individual in his home. [Indeed,] the right of an individual to conduct intimate relationships in the intimacy of his or her own home seems to me to be the heart of the Constitution's protection of privacy.

own home

The Court's failure to comprehend the magnitude of the liberty interests at stake in this case leads it to slight the question whether [petitioner] has justified Georgia's infringement on these interests. I believe that neither of the two general justifications [that] petitioner has advanced warrants dismissing respondent's challenge for failure to state a claim. First, petitioner asserts that the acts made criminal by the statute may have serious adverse consequences for "the general public health and welfare," such as spreading communicable diseases or fostering other criminal activity. Inasmuch as this case was dismissed by the District Court on the pleadings, it is not surprising that the record before us is barren of any evidence to support petitioner's claim. In light of the state of the record, I see no justification for the Court's attempt to equate the private, consensual sexual activity at issue here with the 'possession in the home of drugs, firearms, or stolen goods,' to which Stanley refused to extend its protection. [The] core of petitioner's defense of [the law], however, is that respondent and others who engage in the [conduct] interfere with Georgia's exercise of the " 'right of the Nation and of the States to maintain a decent society.' " [The] assertion that "traditional Judeo–Christian values proscribe" the conduct involved cannot provide an adequate justification for [the law]. That certain, but by no means all, religious groups condemn the behavior at issue gives the State no license to impose their judgments on the entire citizenry. The legitimacy of secular legislation depends instead on whether the State can advance some justification for its law beyond its conformity to religious doctrine. [Certainly,] some private behavior can affect the fabric of society as a whole. [But the Court fails] to see the difference between laws that protect public sensibilities and those that enforce private morality. Statutes banning public sexual activity are entirely consistent with protecting the individual's liberty interest in decisions concerning sexual relations: the same recognition that those decisions are intensely private which justifies protecting them from governmental interference can justify protecting individuals from unwilling exposure to the sexual activities of others. But the mere fact that intimate behavior may be punished when it takes place in public cannot dictate how States can regulate intimate behavior that occurs in intimate places. [This] case involves no real interference with the rights of others, for the mere knowledge that other individuals do not adhere to one's value system cannot be a legally cognizable interest, let alone an interest that can justify invading the houses, hearts, and minds of citizens who choose to live their lives differently. [Depriving] individuals of the right to choose for themselves how to conduct these intimate relationships poses a far greater threat [to the Nation's historical values] than tolerance of nonconformity could ever [do].

mixing state + religion

Justice STEVENS, with whom Justice BRENNAN and Justice MAR-
SHALL join, dissenting.

Like the statute that is challenged in this case, the rationale of the Court's
opinion applies equally to the prohibited conduct regardless of whether the
parties who engage in it are married or unmarried, or are of the same or
different sexes. [Because] the Georgia statute expresses the traditional view
that sodomy is an immoral kind of conduct regardless of the identity of the
persons who engage in it, I believe that a proper analysis of its constitutionality
requires consideration of two questions: First, may a State totally prohibit the
described conduct by means of a neutral law applying without exception to all
persons subject to its jurisdiction? If not, may the State save the statute by
announcing that it will only enforce the law against homosexuals? The two
questions merit separate discussion.

I.   Our prior cases make two propositions abundantly clear. First, the fact
that the governing majority in a State has traditionally viewed a particular
practice as immoral is not a sufficient reason for upholding a law prohibiting
the practice; neither history nor tradition could save a law prohibiting miscegenation from constitutional attack. Second, individual decisions by married
persons, concerning the intimacies of their physical relationship, even when not
intended to produce offspring, are a form of "liberty" protected by [due process.
Griswold.] Moreover, this protection extends to intimate choices by unmarried
as well as married persons. [Carey; Eisenstadt.] [The] essential "liberty" that
animated the development of the law in cases like Griswold, Eisenstadt, and
Carey surely embraces the right to engage in nonreproductive sexual conduct
that others may consider offensive or immoral. Paradoxical as it may seem, our
prior cases thus establish that a State may not prohibit sodomy within "the
sacred precincts of marital bedrooms," Griswold, or, indeed, between unmarried heterosexual adults, Eisenstadt.

II.   If the Georgia statute cannot be enforced as it is written—if the
conduct it seeks to prohibit is a protected form of liberty for the vast majority
of Georgia's citizens—the State must assume the burden of justifying a selective application of its law. Either the persons to whom Georgia seeks to apply
its statute do not have the same interest in "liberty" that others have, or there
must be a reason why the State may be permitted to apply a generally
applicable law to certain persons that it does not apply to others. The first
possibility is plainly unacceptable. Although the meaning of the principle that
"all men are created equal" is not always clear, it surely must mean that every
free citizen has the same interest in "liberty" that the members of the majority
share. From the standpoint of the individual, the homosexual and the heterosexual have the same interest in deciding how he will live his own life, and,
more narrowly, how he will conduct himself in his personal and voluntary
associations with his companions. State intrusion into the private conduct of
either is equally burdensome. The second possibility is similarly unacceptable.
A policy of selective application must be supported by a neutral and legitimate
interest—something more substantial than a habitual dislike for, or ignorance
about, the disfavored group. Neither the State nor the Court has identified any
such interest in this case. The Court has posited as a justification for the
Georgia statute "the presumed belief of a majority of the electorate in Georgia
that homosexual sodomy is immoral and unacceptable." But the Georgia
electorate has expressed no such belief—instead, its representatives enacted a
law that presumably reflects the belief that *all sodomy* is immoral and unacceptable. Unless the Court is prepared to conclude that such a law is constitutional, it may not rely on the work product of the Georgia Legislature to support its
holding. For the Georgia statute does not single out homosexuals as a separate

class meriting special disfavored [treatment]. Both the Georgia statute and the Georgia prosecutor [because of nonenforcement of the law in this case and in earlier decades] completely fail to provide the Court with any support for the conclusion that homosexual sodomy, *simpliciter,* is considered unacceptable conduct in that State, and that the burden of justifying a selective application of the generally applicable law has been [met].

Some comments on Hardwick. The Hardwick ruling has been widely criticized, by conservative as well as liberal commentators. See, e.g., Fried (former Solicitor General), Order and Law (1991), 82 (criticizing Justice White's "stunningly harsh and dismissive opinion),'' and Posner, Sex and Reason (1992). Conkle, "The Second Death of Substantive Due Process," 62 Ind.L.J. 215 (1987), while criticizing the result in Hardwick, claims that it "represents the death of substantive due process as a principled doctrine of law." Do you agree? Does Hardwick represent a sharp departure from the principles of Eisenstadt and Roe, or does it merely illustrate the largely unprincipled, subjective nature of substantive due process throughout the decades? Note generally Rubenfeld, "The Right of Privacy," 102 Harv.L.Rev. 737 (1989) and Buchanan, "The Right of Privacy: Past, Present, and Future," 16 Ohio No.L.Rev. 403 (1989). Are Roe and Hardwick reconcilable? See Easterbrook, "Abstraction and Authority," 59 U.Chi.L.Rev. 349, 305 (1992), and Tribe & Dorf, "Levels of Generality in the Definition of Rights," 57 U.Chi. L.Rev. 1057 (1990). Would equal protection have been a preferable basis for the challenge in Hardwick? See Sunstein, "Sexual Orientation and the Constitution: A Note in the Relationship between Due Process and Equal Protection," 55 U.Chi.L.Rev. 1161 (1988), and note especially Romer v. Evans (1996; p. 737 below). Does Romer v. Evans undermine Hardwick, or are these cases reconcilable? [No other issues of private sexual behavior have been decided by the Court other than those involved in Roe, Hardwick, and Romer. Note, however, Hollenbaugh v. Carnegie Free Library, 439 U.S. 1052 (1978), where the Court denied certiorari from a decision upholding the discharge of two public library employees for adulterous cohabitation. Justice Marshall wrote a strong dissent from the denial of certiorari. (Justice Brennan also dissented, without opinion.) See Note, "Fornication, Cohabitation, and the Constitution," 77 Mich.L.Rev. 252 (1978).]

OTHER EFFORTS TO ASSERT PRIVACY AND AUTONOMY INTERESTS

1. *Personal appearance: Hair style.* An effort to rely on privacy and autonomy concerns to invalidate a local regulation of the length and style of policemen's hair failed in KELLEY v. JOHNSON, 425 U.S. 238 (1976). Justice REHNQUIST's majority opinion insisted that the deferential standard of review of Lee Optical applied, and the hair grooming regulation easily met that "mere rationality standard." He argued that the "liberty" interest claimed here was "distinguishable" from the interests involved in cases from Meyer through Roe: "[W]hether the citizenry at large has some sort of 'liberty' interest [in] matters of personal appearance is a question on which this Court's cases offer little, if any, guidance. We can, nevertheless, assume an affirmative answer for purposes of deciding this case, because we find that assumption

insufficient to carry the day." He emphasized that the claimant was a police-man, not "a member of the citizenry at large." Justice Rehnquist noted that most police forces were uniformed, and that similarity in appearance "may be based on a desire to make police officers readily recognizable to the members of the public, or a desire for the esprit de corps which such similarity is felt to inculcate within the police force itself." Justice MARSHALL's dissent, joined by Justice Brennan, claimed that the regulation could not even meet the "rational basis" standard, and went on to argue that personal appearance *is* an aspect of constitutionally protected liberty: "An individual's personal appearance may reflect, sustain, and nourish his personality and may well be used as a means of expressing his attitude and lifestyle. [To] say that the liberty guarantee of the 14th Amendment does not encompass matters of personal appearance would be fundamentally inconsistent with the values of privacy, self-identity, autonomy, and personal [integrity]."

2. *Substantive due process and the mentally retarded.* In YOUNGBERG v. ROMEO, 457 U.S. 307 (1982), the Court considered "for the first time the substantive [due process] rights of involuntarily-committed mentally retarded persons." Romeo, a "profoundly retarded" man with the mental capacity of an 18–month–old child, had been committed to a state institution at the behest of his mother. His mother became concerned about injuries he had suffered in the institution. She sued the officials of the institution, claiming that they had violated his constitutional rights by failing to take appropriate measures to protect him against injuries. That suit presented the Court with the question whether Romeo had "substantive [due process] rights [to] (i) safe conditions of confinement; (ii) freedom from bodily restraints; and (iii) training or 'habilitation.'" ("Habilitation," a term of art in programs for the mentally retarded, focuses upon "training and development of needed skills.")

Justice POWELL's opinion for the Court had no difficulty finding constitutional support for the first two substantive rights claimed by Romeo: he found constitutionally protected liberty interests in "safety" and in "freedom of movement." But he found Romeo's third claim more troubling. But that claim, too, was supportable to a limited extent. He explained: "As a general matter, a State is under no constitutional duty to provide substantive services for those within its border. [If], as seems the case, [Romeo] seeks only training related to safety and freedom from restraints, this case does not present the difficult question whether a mentally retarded person, involuntarily committed to a state institution, has some general constitutional right to training per se, even when no type or amount of training would lead to freedom. Here, we only conclude that [Romeo's] liberty interests require the State to provide minimally adequate or reasonable training to ensure safety and freedom from undue restraint." In determining what was "reasonable training," he emphasized that "courts must show deference to the judgment exercised by a qualified professional." A concurrence by Justice BLACKMUN, joined by Justices Brennan and O'Connor, noted "two difficult and important issues" which he thought properly left unresolved by the Court's opinion. The first was whether the State could accept Romeo for "care and treatment" and then "constitutionally refuse to provide him any 'treatment,' as that term is defined by state law." The second was "whether [Romeo] has an independent [due process]" claim "that 'habilitation' or training necessary to *preserve* those basic self-care skills he possessed when he first entered [the state institution]—for example, the ability to dress himself and care for his personal hygiene. In my view, it would be consistent with the Court's reasoning today to include within the 'minimally adequate training required by the Constitution' such training as is reasonably necessary to prevent a person's pre-existing self-care skills from *deteriorating* because of his commitment." Chief Justice BURGER, concurring only in the judgment, emphasized that he "would hold flatly that respondent has no constitutional right to training, or 'habilitation,' per se."[1]

3. *Computerized data banks and "privacy."* WHALEN v. ROE, 429 U.S. 589 (1977), was the Court's first major encounter with the constitutional risks generated by governmental storage of personal data in computers. Patients and physicians made an on-the-face attack on a New York law under which the State recorded in a centralized computer file the names and addresses of all patients obtaining prescriptions for certain dangerous but legitimate drugs—drugs such as opium derivatives and amphetamines. A lower court held the patient identification provisions of the law unconstitutional on the ground that they invaded constitutionally protected "zones of privacy" with "a needlessly broad sweep." The Court unanimously reversed. Justice STEVENS's opinion commented that prior "privacy" cases had "in fact involved at least two different kinds of interests. One is the individual interest in avoiding disclosure of personal matters [e.g., Griswold], and another is the interest in independence in making certain kinds of important decisions [e.g., Roe]." He concluded, however, "that the New York program does not, on its face, pose a sufficiently grievous threat to either interest to establish a constitutional violation." With respect to disclosure of personal matters, he emphasized the careful security provisions in the law (which barred the disclosure of the identity of patients). He was no more impressed with the claim of impingement on the "interest in making important decisions independently." The patients had argued that, even without unwarranted disclosures, "the knowledge that the information is readily available in a computerized file creates a genuine concern that causes some persons to decline needed medication." Justice Stevens responded that, despite the law, about 100,000 prescriptions for the covered drugs were being filled each month and insisted that the law did not significantly inhibit the patient-physician decision regarding needed medication.

4. *A general right of intimate association as an aspect of liberty?* Although most Court recognitions of fundamental privacy interests have occurred in marriage and family contexts, statements in a 1984 opinion suggest that the "freedom of association" protected by the due process clause may also extend to other relationships—relationships characterized by "relative smallness, a high degree of selectivity in decisions to begin and maintain the affiliation, and seclusion from others in critical aspects of the relationship." Those criteria were suggested by Justice BRENNAN writing for the Court in ROBERTS v. UNITED STATES JAYCEES, 468 U.S. 609 (1984), a case rejecting a freedom of association challenge by the U.S. Jaycees, a formerly male-only organization, to the applicability of a Minnesota civil rights law banning sex discrimination in "public accommodations." Freedom of association related to the exercise of First Amendment rights has long been recognized by the Court, as later materials illustrate. But the Jaycees opinion also commented at some length on a broader associational right: it distinguished between the Jaycees members' "freedom of intimate association" and their "freedom of expressive association"; and the former was derived from the general concept of liberty rather than First Amendment needs. Accordingly, Justice Brennan spoke not only of

---

1. The extent to which Youngberg supports a principle regarding a state's affirmative obligations on the basis of due process was central in DeShaney v. Winnebago County Dept. of Social Services, 489 U.S. 189 (1989). Because the DeShaney case raises basic questions about the nature of governmental affirmative constitutional obligations, it is set out at p. 960 below, with the materials on the "state action" requirement.

First Amendment adjuncts but also of the safeguarding of "choices to enter into and maintain certain intimate human relationships." On the latter, he stated:

"The Court has long recognized that, because the Bill of Rights is designed to secure individual liberty, it must afford the formation and preservation of certain kinds of highly personal relationships a substantial measure of sanctuary from unjustified interference by the State. E.g., [Pierce; Meyer]. [We] have noted that certain kinds of personal bonds have played a critical role in the culture and traditions of the Nation by cultivating and transmitting shared ideals and beliefs; they thereby foster diversity and act as critical buffers between the individual and the [State]. Moreover, the constitutional shelter afforded such relationships reflects the realization that individuals draw much of their emotional enrichment from close ties with others. Protecting these relationships from unwarranted state interference therefore safeguards the ability independently to define one's identity that is central to any concept of liberty. The personal affiliations that exemplify these considerations, and that therefore suggest some relevant limitations on the relationships that might be entitled to this sort of constitutional protection, are those that attend the creation and sustenance of a family—marriage; childbirth; the raising and education of children; and cohabitation with one's relatives. [Among] other things, [family relationships] are distinguished by such attributes as relative smallness, a high degree of selectivity in decisions to begin and maintain the affiliation, and seclusion from others in critical aspects of the relationship. As a general matter, only relationships with these sorts of qualities are likely to reflect the considerations that have led to an understanding of freedom of association as an intrinsic element of personal liberty. Conversely, an association lacking these qualities—such as a large business enterprise—seems remote from the concerns giving rise to this constitutional protection. [Between] these poles, of course, lies a broad range of human relationships that may make greater or lesser claims to constitutional protection from particular incursions by the State. Determining the limits of state authority over an individual's freedom to enter into a particular association therefore unavoidably entails a careful assessment of where that relationship's objective characteristics locate it on a spectrum from the most intimate to the most attenuated of personal attachments. We need not mark the potentially significant points on this terrain with any precision. We note only that factors that may be relevant include size, purpose, policies, selectivity, congeniality, and other characteristics that in a particular case may be pertinent." See generally Karst, "The Freedom of Intimate Association," 89 Yale L.J. 624 (1980), relied on by Justice Blackmun's dissent in Hardwick.

A RIGHT TO DIE?

1. *The right to refuse unwanted medical treatment and nourishment.* In CRUZAN v. DIRECTOR, MISSOURI DEPT. OF HEALTH, 497 U.S. 261 (1990), a widely publicized case, the Court for the first time considered the question of a constitutional "right to die." Although the 5–4 majority held that on the facts of the case, discontinuation of life sustaining procedures (here, artificial nutrition and hydration) was not constitutionally required, most of the Justices did seem to acknowledge or assume a constitutional "right to die" under certain circumstances. The case arose in the following context: Since 1983, when the then 25–year–old Nancy Beth Cruzan suffered severe injuries in

an automobile accident, she had been in a persistent vegetative state, a state in which she exhibited some motor reflexes but no indications of significant cognitive functions. (More than 10,000 patients are being maintained in a persistent vegetative state in this country, and the number is expected to grow significantly in the near future.) When it became apparent that Cruzan had virtually no chance of regaining her cognitive faculties, her parents sought to discontinue tubal feeding. (For a number of years, she had received all her nutrition and fluids through a gastrostomy tube, a feeding and hydration tube inserted into her stomach.) The Missouri trial court ordered the removal of the tube, finding that no state interest outweighed her "right to liberty." The trial court found that there was evidence suggesting that Cruzan "would not wish to continue on with her nutrition and hydration." However, she had neither executed a living will nor designated anyone to make health-care decisions for her in the event she became incompetent. The closely divided Missouri Supreme Court reversed the trial court ruling, finding Cruzan's remarks relied on by the trial judge so remote and general as to be "unreliable for the purposes of establishing her intent" and insisting that "clear and convincing evidence" of her wishes was lacking here.

Chief Justice REHNQUIST's opinion affirmed that ruling. He explained: "[As state cases] demonstrate, the common law doctrine of informed consent is viewed as generally encompassing the right of a competent individual to refuse medical treatment. Beyond that, [the] decisions demonstrate both similarity and diversity in their approach to decision of what all agree is a perplexing question with unusually strong moral and ethical overtones. State courts have available to them for decision a number of sources—state constitutions, statutes, and common law—which are not available to us. In this Court, the question is simply and starkly whether the [U.S.] Constitution prohibits Missouri from choosing the rule of decision which it did. [The] principle that a competent person has a constitutionally protected liberty interest in refusing unwanted medical treatment may be inferred from our prior decisions. [But] determining that a person has a 'liberty interest' under the Due Process Clause does not end the inquiry;[1] 'whether respondent's constitutional rights have been violated must be determined by balancing his liberty interests against the relevant state interests.' Youngberg v. Romeo.

"Petitioners insist that under the general holdings of our cases, the forced administration of life-sustaining medical treatment, and even of artificially-delivered food and water essential to life, would implicate a competent person's liberty interest. Although we think the logic of [our] cases [would] embrace such a liberty interest, the dramatic consequences involved in refusal of such treatment would inform the inquiry as to whether the deprivation of that interest is constitutionally permissible. But for purposes of this case, we assume that the [Constitution] would grant a competent person a constitutionally protected right to refuse lifesaving hydration and nutrition. Petitioners go on to assert that an incompetent person should possess the same right in this respect as is possessed by a competent person. [The] difficulty with petitioners' claim is that in a sense it begs the question: an incompetent person is not able to make an informed and voluntary choice to exercise a hypothetical right to refuse treatment or any other right. Such a 'right' must be exercised for her, if at all, by some sort of surrogate. Here, Missouri has in effect recognized that under

1. "Although many state courts have held that a right to refuse treatment is encompassed by a generalized constitutional right of privacy, we have never so held. We believe this issue is more properly analyzed in terms of a Fourteenth Amendment liberty interest. See [Hardwick]." [Footnote by Chief Justice Rehnquist.]

certain circumstances a surrogate may act for the patient in electing to have hydration and nutrition withdrawn in such a way as to cause death, but it has established a procedural safeguard to assure that the action of the surrogate conforms as best it may to the wishes expressed by the patient while competent. Missouri requires that evidence of the incompetent's wishes as to the withdrawal of treatment be proved by clear and convincing evidence. The question, then, is whether the United States Constitution forbids the establishment of this procedural requirement by the State. We hold that it does not.

"Whether or not Missouri's clear and convincing evidence requirement comports with the [Constitution] depends in part on what interests the State may properly seek to protect in this situation. Missouri relies on its interest in the protection and preservation of human life, and there can be no gainsaying this interest. [E.g.,] the majority of States [have] laws imposing criminal penalties on one who assists another to commit suicide. We do not think a State is required to remain neutral in the face of an informed and voluntary decision by a physically-able adult to starve to death. But in the context presented here, a State has more particular interests at stake. The choice between life and death is a deeply personal decision of obvious and overwhelming finality. We believe Missouri may legitimately seek to safeguard the personal element of this choice through the imposition of heightened evidentiary requirements. It cannot be disputed that the Due Process Clause protects an interest in life as well as an interest in refusing life-sustaining medical treatment. Not all incompetent patients will have loved ones available to serve as surrogate decisionmakers. And even where family members are present, '[t]here will, of course, be some unfortunate situations in which family members will not act to protect a patient.' A State is entitled to guard against potential abuses in such situations. [Finally,] we think a State may properly decline to make judgments about the 'quality' of life that a particular individual may enjoy, and simply assert an unqualified interest in the preservation of human life to be weighed against the constitutionally protected interests of the individual.

"In our view, Missouri has permissibly sought to advance these interests through the adoption of a 'clear and convincing' standard of proof to govern such proceedings. [The] more stringent the burden of proof a party must bear, the more that party bears the risk of an erroneous decision. We believe that Missouri may permissibly place an increased risk of an erroneous decision on those seeking to terminate an incompetent individual's life-sustaining treatment. An erroneous decision not to terminate results in a maintenance of the status quo; the possibility of subsequent developments such as advancements in medical science, the discovery of new evidence regarding the patient's intent, changes in the law, or simply the unexpected death of the patient despite the administration of life-sustaining treatment, at least create the potential that a wrong decision will eventually be corrected or its impact mitigated. An erroneous decision to withdraw life-sustaining treatment, however, is not susceptible of correction. [In] sum, we conclude that a State may apply a clear and convincing evidence standard in proceedings where a guardian seeks to discontinue nutrition and hydration of a person diagnosed to be in a persistent vegetative state.

"The Supreme Court of Missouri held that in this case the testimony adduced at trial did not amount to clear and convincing proof of the patient's desire to have hydration and nutrition withdrawn. [The] testimony adduced at trial consisted primarily of Nancy Cruzan's statements made to a housemate about a year before her accident that she would not want to live should she face life as a 'vegetable,' and other observations to the same effect. The observations did not deal in terms with withdrawal of medical treatment or of hydration and nutrition. We cannot say that the Supreme Court of Missouri committed constitutional error in reaching the conclusion that it did. Petitioners alternatively contend that Missouri must accept the 'substituted judgment' of close family members even in the absence of substantial proof that their views reflect the views of the patient. [But] we do not think [due process] requires the State to repose judgment on these matters with anyone but the patient herself. Close family members may have a strong feeling—a feeling not at all ignoble or unworthy, but not entirely disinterested, either—that they do not wish to witness the continuation of the life of a loved one which they regard as hopeless, meaningless, and even degrading. But there is no automatic assurance that the view of close family members will necessarily be the same as the patient's would have been had she been confronted with the prospect of her situation while [competent]."

Justice O'CONNOR's concurrence "agree[d] that a protected liberty interest in refusing unwanted medical treatment may be inferred from our prior decisions, and that the refusal of artificially delivered food and water is encompassed within that liberty interest." She elaborated: "Because our notions of liberty are inextricably entwined with our idea of physical freedom and self-determination, the Court has often deemed state incursions into the body repugnant to the interests protected by [due process]. [The] State's imposition of medical treatment on an unwilling competent adult necessarily involves some form of restraint and intrusion. [The] State's artificial provision of nutrition and hydration implicates identical concerns. [Requiring] a competent adult to endure such procedures against her will burdens the patient's liberty, dignity, and freedom to determine the course of her own treatment. Accordingly, the liberty guaranteed by [due process] must protect, if it protects anything, an individual's deeply personal decision to reject medical treatment, including the artificial delivery of food and water." She noted, moreover, that the Court had not decided "whether a State must also give effect to the decisions of a surrogate decisionmaker. In my view, such a duty may well be constitutionally required to protect the patient's liberty interest in refusing medical treatment. [Delegating] the authority to make medical decisions to a family member or friend is becoming a common method of planning for the future. Today's decision [does] not preclude a future determination that the Constitution requires the States to implement the decisions of a patient's duly appointed surrogate. [Today] we decide only that one State's practice does not violate the Constitution; the more challenging task of crafting appropriate procedures for safeguarding incompetents' liberty interests is entrusted to the 'laboratory' of the States in the first instance."

Justice SCALIA's concurrence argued that "the federal courts have no business in this field." He elaborated: "The various opinions in this case portray quite clearly the difficult, indeed agonizing, questions that are presented by the constantly increasing power of science to keep the human body alive for longer than any reasonable person would want to inhabit it. The States have begun to grapple with these problems through legislation. I am concerned, from the tenor of today's opinions, that we are poised to confuse that enterprise as successfully as we have confused the enterprise of legislating concerning abortion—requiring it to be conducted against a background of federal constitutional imperatives that are unknown because they are being newly crafted from Term to Term. That would be a great misfortune. While I agree with the Court's analysis today, and therefore join in its opinion, I would have preferred that we announce, clearly and promptly, that the federal courts have no business in this field; that American law has always accorded the State the power to prevent, by force if necessary, suicide—including suicide by refusing to take appropriate measures necessary to preserve one's life; that the point at which life becomes 'worthless,' and the point at which the means necessary to preserve it become 'extraordinary' or 'inappropriate,' are neither set forth in the Constitution nor known to the nine Justices of this Court any better than they are known to nine people picked at random from the Kansas City telephone directory; and hence, that even when it is demonstrated by clear and convincing evidence that a patient no longer wishes certain measures to be taken to preserve her life, it is up to the citizens of Missouri to decide, through their elected representatives, whether that wish will be honored. It is quite impossible (because the Constitution says nothing about the matter) that those citizens will decide upon a line less lawful than the one we would choose; and it is unlikely (because we know no more about 'life-and-death' than they do) that they will decide upon a line less reasonable. It is at least true that no 'substantive due process' claim can be maintained unless the claimant demonstrates that the State has deprived him of a right historically and traditionally protected against State interference. [Michael H.; Hardwick; Moore.] That cannot possibly be established here.

"[Suicide or attempted suicide are traditional criminal offenses.] Petitioners rely on three distinctions to separate Nancy Cruzan's case from ordinary suicide: (1) that she is permanently incapacitated and in pain; (2) that she would bring on her death not by any affirmative act but by merely declining treatment that provides nourishment; and (3) that preventing her from affectuating her presumed wish to die requires violation of her bodily integrity. None of these suffices. Suicide was not excused even when committed 'to avoid those ills which [persons] have not the fortitude to endure.' [The] second asserted distinction [relies] on the dichotomy between action and inaction. Suicide, it is said, consists of an affirmative act to end one's life; refusing treatment is not an affirmative act 'causing' death, but merely a passive acceptance of the natural process of dying. I readily acknowledge that the distinction between action and inaction has some bearing upon the legislative judgment of what ought to be prevented as suicide—though even there it would seem to me unreasonable to draw the line precisely between action and inaction, rather than between various forms of inaction. [As to the irrelevance of the action-inaction distinction:] Starving oneself to death is no different from putting a gun to one's temple so far as a common-law definition of suicide is concerned. [Of] course the common-law rejected the action-inaction distinction in other contexts involving the taking of human life as well. [E.g., a physician] could be criminally liable for failure to provide care that could have extended the patient's life, even if death was immediately caused by the underlying disease that the physician failed to treat. [The] third asserted basis of distinction—that frustrating Nancy Cruzan's wish to die in the present case requires interference with her bodily integrity—is likewise inadequate, because such interference is impermissible only if one begs the question whether her refusal to undergo the treatment on her own is suicide. It has always been lawful not only for the State, but even for private citizens, to interfere with bodily integrity to prevent a felony. That general rule has of course been applied to suicide.

"[The] dissents of Justices Brennan and Stevens make a plausible case for our intervention here only by embracing [a] political principle that the States are free to adopt, but that is demonstrably not imposed by the Constitution. [Insofar] as balancing the relative interests of the State and the individual is concerned, there is nothing distinctive about accepting death through the refusal of 'medical treatment,' as opposed to accepting it through the refusal of food, or through the failure to shut off the engine and get out of the car after parking in one's garage after work. [Justice Brennan's] position ultimately rests upon the proposition that it is none of the State's business if a person wants to commit suicide. Justice Stevens is explicit on the point. [This] is a view that some societies have held, and that our States are free to adopt if they wish. But it is not a view imposed by our constitutional traditions, in which the power of the State to prohibit suicide is unquestionable. [To] raise up a constitutional right here we would have to create out of nothing (for it exists neither in text nor tradition) some constitutional principle whereby, although the State may insist that an individual come in out of the cold and eat food, it may not insist that he take medicine; and although it may pump his stomach empty of poison he has ingested, it may not fill his stomach with food he has failed to ingest. Are there, then, no reasonable and humane limits that ought not to be exceeded in requiring an individual to preserve his own life? There obviously are, but they are not set forth in the Due Process Clause. What assures us that those limits will not be exceeded is the same constitutional guarantee that is the source of most of our [protection]. Our salvation is the Equal Protection Clause, which requires the democratic majority to accept for themselves and their loved ones what they impose on you and me. This Court need not, and has no authority to, inject itself into every field of human activity where irrationality and oppression may theoretically occur, and if it tries to do so it will destroy itself."

Justice BRENNAN's dissent, joined by Justices Marshall and Blackmun, stated: "Today the Court, while tentatively accepting that there is some degree of constitutionally protected liberty interest in avoiding unwanted medical treatment, [affirms] the decision of the Missouri Supreme Court. [Because] I believe that Nancy Cruzan has a fundamental right to be free of unwanted artificial nutrition and hydration, which right is not outweighed by any interests of the State, and because I find that the improperly biased procedural obstacles imposed by the Missouri Supreme Court impermissibly burden that right, I respectfully dissent. Nancy Cruzan is entitled to choose to die with dignity. [Today,] the Court concedes that our prior decisions 'support the recognition of a general liberty interest in refusing medical treatment.' The Court, however, avoids discussing either the measure of that liberty interest or its application by assuming, for purposes of this case only, that a competent person has a constitutionally protected liberty interest in being free of unwanted artificial nutrition and hydration. [But] if a competent person has a liberty interest to be free of unwanted medical treatment, as both the majority and Justice O'Connor concede, it must be fundamental. [The] right to be free from unwanted medical attention is a right to evaluate the potential benefit of treatment and its possible consequences according to one's own values and to make a personal decision whether to subject oneself through the intrusion. For a patient like Nancy Cruzan, the sole benefit of medical treatment is being kept metabolically alive. Neither artificial nutrition or any other form of medical treatment available today can cure or in any way ameliorate her condition. Irreversibly vegetative patients are devoid of thought, emotion, and sensation; they are permanently and completely unconscious. [Although] the right to be free of unwanted medical intervention, like other constitutionally protected interests, may not be absolute, no State interest could outweigh the rights of an individual in Nancy Cruzan's position. Whatever a State's possible interests in mandating life-support treatment under other circumstances, there is no good to be obtained here by Missouri's insistence that Nancy Cruzan remain on life-support systems if it is indeed her wish not to do so. Missouri does not claim, nor could it, that society as a whole will be benefited by Nancy's receiving medical treatment. No third party's situation will be improved and no harm to others will be averted. The only state interest asserted here is a general interest in the preservation of life. But the State has no legitimate general interest in someone's life, completely abstracted from the interest of the person living that life, that could outweigh the person's choice to avoid medical treatment. [Thus,] the State's general interest in life must accede to Nancy Cruzan's particularized and intense interest in self-determination in her choice of medical treatment. There is simply nothing legitimately within the State's purview to be gained by superseding her decision.

"[This] is not to say that the State has no legitimate interests to assert here. As the majority recognizes, Missouri has a parens patriae interest in providing Nancy Cruzan, now incompetent, with as accurate as possible a determination of how she would exercise her rights under these circumstances. [Accuracy,] therefore, must be our touchstone. [But Missouri] may constitutionally impose only those procedural requirements that serve to enhance the accuracy of a determination of Nancy Cruzan's wishes or are at least consistent with an accurate determination. The Missouri 'safeguard' that the Court upholds today does not meet that standard. [Missouri's] rule of decision imposes a markedly asymmetrical evidentiary burden. Only evidence of specific statements of treatment choice made by the patient when competent is admissible to support a finding that the patient, now in a persistent vegetative state, would wish to avoid further medical treatment. Moreover, this evidence must be clear and convincing. No proof is required to support a finding that the incompetent person would wish to continue treatment. [Even] more than its heightened evidentiary standard, the Missouri court's categorical exclusion of relevant evidence dispenses with any semblance of accurate factfinding. The court adverted to no evidence supporting its decision, but held that no clear and convincing, inherently reliable evidence had been presented to show that Nancy would want to avoid further treatment. In doing so, the court failed to consider statements Nancy had made to family members and a close friend. The court also failed to consider testimony from Nancy's mother and sister that they were certain that Nancy would want to discontinue artificial nutrition and hydration, even after the court found that Nancy's family was loving and without malignant motive. [The] court did not specifically define what kind of evidence it would consider clear and convincing, but its general discussion suggests that only a living will or equivalently formal directive from the patient when competent would meet this standard. Too few people execute living wills or equivalently formal directives for such an evidentiary rule to ensure adequately that the wishes of incompetent persons will be honored. While it might be a wise social policy to encourage people to furnish such instructions, no general conclusion about a patient's choice can be drawn from the absence of the [formalities]. [A] State may insure that the person who makes the decision on the patient's behalf is the one whom the patient himself would have selected to make that choice for him. And a State may exclude from consideration anyone having improper motives. But a State generally must either repose the choice with the person whom the patient himself would most likely have chosen as proxy or leave the decision to the patient's family. [Missouri] and this Court have displaced Nancy's own assessment of the processes associated with dying. They have discarded evidence of her will, ignored her values, and deprived her of the right to a decision as closely approximating her own choice as humanly possible. They have done so disingenuously in her name, and openly in Missouri's own. That Missouri and this Court may truly be motivated only by concern for incompetent patients makes no matter. As one of our most prominent jurists warned us decades ago: 'Experience should teach us to be most on our guard to protect liberty when the government's purposes are beneficent. [The] greatest dangers to liberty lurk in insidious encroachment by men of zeal, well meaning but without understanding.' Olmstead v. United States [1928; Brandeis, J., dissenting]."

Justice STEVENS's separate dissent argued that "the Constitution requires the State to care for Nancy Cruzan's life in a way that gives appropriate respect to her own best interests." He stated that the State's insistence on continuing her physical existence was to him "comprehensible only as an effort to define life's meaning, not as an attempt to preserve its sanctity." He elaborated: "[If] Nancy Cruzan has no interest in continued treatment, and if she has a liberty interest in being free from unwanted treatment, and if the cessation of treatment would have no adverse impact on third parties, and if no reason exists to doubt the good faith of Nancy's parents, then what possible basis could the State have for insisting upon continued medical treatment? [My] disagreement with the Court [is] unrelated to its endorsement of the clear and convincing standard of proof for cases of this kind. [The] critical question [is] not how to prove the controlling facts but rather what proven facts should be controlling. In my view, the constitutional answer is clear: the best interests of the individual, especially when buttressed by the interests of all related third parties, must prevail over any general state policy that simply ignores those interests. [The] failure of Missouri's policy to heed the interests of a dying individual with respect to matters so private is ample evidence of the policy's illegitimacy." He continued: "Only because Missouri has arrogated to itself the power to define life, and only because the Court permits this usurpation, are Nancy Cruzan's life and liberty put into disquieting conflict. If Nancy Cruzan's life were defined by reference to her own interests [then] her constitutionally protected interest in freedom from unwanted treatment would not come into conflict with her constitutionally protected interest in life. Conversely, if there were any evidence that Nancy Cruzan herself defined life to encompass every form of biological persistence by a human being, so that the continuation of treatment would serve Nancy's own liberty, then once again there would be no conflict between life and liberty. The opposition of life and liberty in this case are thus not the result of Nancy Cruzan's tragic accident, but are instead the artificial consequence of Missouri's effort, and this Court's willingness, to abstract Nancy Cruzan's life from Nancy Cruzan's person. [However] commendable may be the State's interest in human life, it cannot pursue that interest by appropriating Nancy Cruzan's life as a symbol for its own purposes. Lives do not exist in abstraction from persons, and to pretend otherwise is not to honor but to desecrate the State's responsibility for protecting life. A State that seeks to demonstrate its commitment to life may do so by aiding those who are actively struggling for life and health. In this endeavor, unfortunately, no State can lack for opportunities: there can be no need to make an example of tragic cases like that of Nancy Cruzan."*

---

* A few months after the Court's Cruzan decision, Nancy Cruzan's parents asked the state trial court for a new evidentiary hearing. In mid-December 1990, the court ruled that there *was* clear evidence that Cruzan's intent, "if mentally able, would be to terminate her nutrition and hydration." The Court promptly authorized the ending of nutrition and hydration. Less than two weeks later, Nancy Cruzan died. The Supreme Court's ruling in Cruzan stirred wide-ranging commentary. (Note the questions raised after the next group of notes.) See, e.g., Kreimer, "Does Pro–Choice Mean Pro–Kevorkian? An Essay on Roe, Casey and the Right to Die," 44 Am.U.L.Rev. 803 (1995); Mayo, "Constitutionalizing the 'Right to Die,' " 49 Md.L.Rev. 103 (1990), Seidman, "Confusion at the Border: Cruzan, 'the Right to Die,' and the Public/Private Distinction," 1992 Sup.Ct.Rev. 47; and Kamisar, "The 'Right to Die': Green Lights and Yellow Lights," [Michigan] Law Quadrangle Notes, Fall 1990, 3. The questions raised by Cruzan and in later cases that came before the Court during the Oct. 1996 Term (see the next group of notes) are pursued at the end of the following note.

2. *A right to physician-assisted suicide?* The ruling in Cruzan provoked intense attention to a more complex question indirectly involved in Cruzan: Does a physician risk criminal liability for aiding another person to commit suicide? In the spring of 1996, two federal courts of appeals, the Ninth Circuit and the Second Circuit, decided that issue. Both courts held state laws prohibiting such physician assistance unconstitutional in certain circumstances, but on different grounds. The Court soon granted certiorari in both cases, and a decision is expected during the Oct. 1996 Term. (The United States, in an amicus brief filed in Nov. 1996, urged the Court to uphold both laws. The brief sought to distinguish right-to-die cases from abortion rulings and opposed the recognition of a right to physician-assisted suicide, stating: "There is an important and common-sense distinction between withdrawing artificial supports so that a disease will progress to its incurable end, and providing chemicals to be used to kill someone.") This note summarizes the rationales of the court of appeals decisions. Are they persuasive? What reasons and precedents support such rulings?

a. *The Ninth Circuit and due process: Compassion in Dying v. Washington.* The "limited en banc" ruling of the Ninth Circuit (with 11 of 24 active judges sitting) struck down Washington's law that prohibited aiding another person to commit suicide. Relying on substantive due process grounds, the 8–3 majority held the law unconstitutional as applied to terminally ill patients who wished to hasten their own deaths with medication prescribed by their physicians. COMPASSION IN DYING v. WASHINGTON, 79 F.3d 790 (9th Cir. 1996). (The caption of this case in the Supreme Court is Washington v. Glucksberg.) Judge Reinhardt's majority opinion concluded that "there is a constitutionally-protected liberty interest in determining the time and manner of one's own death, an interest that must be weighed against the state's legitimate and countervailing interests, especially those that relate to the preservation of human life." After balancing these interests, he concluded that "insofar as the Washington statute prohibits physicians from prescribing life-ending medication for use by terminally ill, competent adults who wish to hasten their own deaths, it violates [due process]." He elaborated: "In examining whether a liberty interest exists in determining the time and manner of one's death, we begin with the compelling similarities between right-to-die cases and abortion cases. [Both] types of cases raise issues of life and death, and both arouse similar religious and moral concerns. Both also present basic questions about an individual's right to abortion. [In] deciding right-to-die cases, we are guided by the Court's approach to the abortion cases. Casey in particular provides a powerful precedent. [Although] Casey was influenced by the doctrine of stare decisis, [its fundamental message lies in statements such as]: 'These matters, involving the most intimate and personal choices a person may make in a lifetime, choices central to personal dignity and autonomy, are central to the liberty protected by the Fourteenth Amendment.'"

In defining the liberty interest involved here, the majority stated: "we do not ask simply whether there is a liberty interest in receiving 'aid in killing oneself' because such a narrow interest could not exist in the absence of a broader and more important underlying interest—the right to die. [We] believe that the broader terms 'the right to die,' 'controlling the time and manner of one's death,' and 'hastening one's death'—more accurately describe the liberty interest at issue here. [Moreover,] we have serious doubts that the terms 'suicide' and 'assisted suicide' are appropriate legal descriptions of the specific conduct at issue here." Reviewing prior decisions relevant to identifying important substantive due process interests, the majority noted that the Court had repeatedly stated "that the limits of the substantive reach of [due process] are not frozen at any point in time." The majority stated: "We believe that a careful examination of [decisions such as Loving v. Virginia, Skinner, Pierce, Griswold, Eisenstadt, and Roe] demonstrates that there is a strong liberty interest in determining how and when one's life shall end, and that an explicit recognition of that interest follows naturally, indeed inevitably, from their reasoning. [A] common thread running through these cases is that they involve decisions that are highly personal and intimate, as well as of great importance to the individual. [While those cases] lend general support to our conclusion, we believe that two relatively recent decisions, [Casey and Cruzan], are fully persuasive, and leave little doubt as to the proper result. [Both] provide persuasive evidence that the Constitution encompasses a due process liberty interest in controlling the time and manner of one's death—that there is, in short, a constitutionally recognized 'right to die.' Our conclusion is strongly influenced by, but not limited to, the plight of mentally competent, terminally ill adults. We are influenced as well by the plight of others, such as those whose existence is reduced to a vegetative state or a permanent and irreversible state of unconsciousness. Our conclusion that there is a liberty interest in determining the time and manner of one's death does not mean that there is a concomitant right to exercise that interest in all circumstances or to do so free from state regulation. To the contrary, we explicitly recognize that some prohibitory and regulatory state action is fully consistent with constitutional principles. In short, finding a liberty interest constitutes a critical first step toward answering the question before us. The determination that must now be made is whether the state's attempt to curtail the exercise of that interest is constitutionally justified."

In analyzing the importance of the relevant state interests, the court discussed six such interests: "1) the state's general interest in preserving life; 2) the state's more specific interest in preventing suicide; 3) the state's interest in avoiding the involvement of third parties and in precluding the use of arbitrary, unfair, or undue influence; 4) the state's interest in protecting family members and loved ones; 5) the state's interest in protecting the integrity of the medical profession; and, 6) the state's interest in avoiding adverse consequences that might ensue if the statutory provision at issue is declared unconstitutional." "Weighing and then balancing [the] constitutionally-protected interest against the state's countervailing interests," the majority concluded: "The liberty interest at issue here is an important one and, in the case of the terminally ill, is at its peak. Conversely, the state interests, while equally important in the abstract, are for the most part at a low point here. We recognize that in the case of life and death decisions the state has a particularly strong interest in avoiding undue influence and other forms of abuse. Here, that concern is ameliorated in large measure because of the mandatory involvement in the decision-making process of physicians [and] because the process itself can be carefully regulated and rigorous standards adopted. Under these circumstances, we believe that the possibility of abuse, even when considered along with the other state interests, does not outweigh the liberty interest at issue. The state has chosen to pursue its interests by means of what for terminally ill patients is effectively a total prohibition, even though its most important interests could be adequately served by a far less burdensome measure. The consequence of rejecting the as-applied challenge would be disastrous for the terminally ill, while the adverse consequences for the state would be of a far lesser order. This, too, weighs in favor of upholding the liberty interest. [The] state has wide power to regulate, but it may not *ban* the exercise of the liberty interest, and that is the practical effect of the program before us." In a concluding paragraph, the majority added: "There is one final point we must emphasize. Some argue strongly that decisions regarding matters affecting life or death should not be made by the courts. Essentially, we agree with that proposition. In this case, by permitting the *individual* to exercise the right to *choose* we are following the constitutional mandate to take such decisions out of the hands of the government [and] to put them where they rightly belong, in the hands of the people. We are allowing individuals to make the decisions that so profoundly affect their very existence—and precluding the state from intruding excessively into that critical realm. [Under] our constitutional system, neither the state nor the majority of the people in a state can impose its will upon the individual in a matter so highly 'central to personal dignity and autonomy,' Casey. Those who believe strongly that death must come without physician assistance are free to follow that creed, be they doctors or patients. They are not free, however, to force their views, their religious convictions, or their philosophies on all the other members of a democratic society, and to compel those whose values differ with theirs to die painful, protracted, and agonizing deaths.''

There were three separate dissents. Judge Beezer's dissent commented: ''Plaintiffs ask us to blur the line between withdrawal of life-sustaining treatment and physician-assisted suicide. At the same time, some proponents of physician-assisted suicide would maintain a conceptual distinction between physician-assisted suicide and euthanasia. Associating physician-assisted suicide with a relatively accepted procedure and dissociating it from an unpalatable one are rhetorically powerful devices, [but the] proper place to draw the line is between withdrawing life-sustaining treatment (which is based on the right to be free from unwanted intrusion) and physician-assisted suicide and euthanasia (which implicate the assistance of others in controlling the timing and manner of death). The former is constitutionally protected (under Cruzan); the latter are not.'' This Ninth Circuit case returned to the court a few months later on a motion for rehearing by the full court, not just the ''limited en banc'' panel convened earlier. This motion was denied (85 F.3d 1440), once again with three judges dissenting. Note some comments in Judge O'Scannlain's dissent: ''[I] am convinced that by misapplying language uniquely crafted by the Supreme Court for application in circumstances wholly inapposite to those presented here, the opinion usurps the state [legislative function]. The majority's method of constitutional interpretation lays the foundation for the discovery of an endless parade of protected liberty interests involving choices that could be cast as 'intimate' and 'personal.' If physician-assisted suicide is [protected], why aren't polygamy, consensual duels, prostitution, and, indeed, the use of illicit drugs? Furthermore, if assisted suicide is so clearly [protected] why immunize only the [physician]? Why wouldn't the Constitution also immunize family members or friends who profess compassion for the dying and act without consulting a physician? [The] majority goes on to err by concluding that there is no constitutionally permissible distinction between suicide and refusing medical treatment; such a conclusion ignores a long line of judicial decisions that recognize the distinction. [The] removal of life-support is not the actual cause of death; there, death results from natural causes. [The] hesitancy and narrowness of the Cruzan holding should have given the majority pause in its endeavor to recognize a new right under [due process]. [Moreover, the] Supreme Court has never recognized a substantive due process right without first finding that there is a tradition of protecting that particular interest. Here, there is absolutely no tradition of protecting assisted suicides. [No] state has ever accepted consent of the victim as a defense to a charge of homicide. These are the political judgments made by the democratic process; if they are no longer 'politically correct,' let the legislatures act to change them, not life-tenured judges immune from the voters' reach.''

b. *The Second Circuit: Quill v. Vacco.* Less than a month after the Ninth Circuit ruling, the Second Circuit struck down New York statutes criminalizing assistance in suicide, in QUILL v. VACCO, 80 F.3d 716 (2d Cir.1996). The laws were challenged by physicians claiming them invalid to the extent that they prohibited them from acceding to the requests of terminally-ill, mentally competent patients for help in hastening death. The court held that "physicians who are willing to do so may prescribe drugs to be self-administered by mentally competent patients who seek to end their lives during the final stages of the terminal illness." However, the Second Circuit, unlike the Ninth, did not base its decision on substantive due process grounds; it relied on equal protection instead. (The Ninth Circuit had found it unnecessary to reach an equal protection claim, stating: "Because we are convinced that [the due process ground] is correct, we need not consider [equal protection].")

Judge Miner wrote for the court; Judge Calabresi concurred only in the result. Judge Miner, in rejecting the substantive due process claim, noted that the "Court has been reluctant to further expand [its] list of federal rights [under due process], and it would be most speculative for a lower court to do so," concluding that it would not "identify a new fundamental right, in the absence of a clear direction from the Court whose precedents we are bound to follow." However, he found no obstacle to examining the laws under equal protection: finding laws to be species of "social welfare legislation," he purported to apply only deferential "rational basis" scrutiny in determining whether New York had treated "in a similar manner all individuals who are similarly situated." He stated: "New York law does not treat equally all competent persons who are in the final stages of fatal illness and wish to hasten their death; [the] distinctions made by New York law with regard to such persons do not further any legitimate state purpose; [and] accordingly, to the extent that the [laws] prohibit persons in the final stages of terminal illness from having assistance in ending their lives by the use of self-administered, prescribed drugs, the [laws] lack any rational basis" and thus violated equal protection. He elaborated: "[It] seems clear that New York does not treat similarly circumstanced persons alike: those in the final stages of terminal illness who are on life-support systems are allowed to hasten their deaths by directing the removal of such systems, but those who are similarly situated, except for the previous attachment of life-sustaining equipment, are not allowed to hasten death by self-administering prescribed drugs. [Justice Scalia,] for one, has remarked upon 'the irrelevance of the action-inaction distinction,' noting that 'the cause of death in both cases is the suicide's conscious decision to' 'pu[t] an end to his own existence.' Cruzan (Scalia, J., concurring). Indeed, there is nothing 'natural' about causing death by means other than the original illness or its complications." Moreover, he noted that "the writing of a prescription to hasten death, after consultation with a patient, involves a far less active role for the physician than is required in bringing about death through asphyxiation, starvation, and/or dehydration. Withdrawal of life support [is] nothing more nor less than assisted suicide." Judge Miner could find no rational reason for this dissimilar statutory treatment: "[What] interest can the state possibly have in requiring the prolongation of a life that is all but ended? [And] what business is it of the state to require the continuation of agony when the result is imminent and inevitable? What concern prompts the state to interfere with a mentally competent patient's 'right to define [his] own concept of existence, of meaning, of the universe, and of the mystery of human life,' Casey, when the patient seeks to have drugs prescribed to end life during the final stages of a terminal illness? The greatly reduced interest of the state in preserving life compels the answer to those questions: 'None.' "

Judge Calabresi's concurrence in the result, while agreeing that these laws could not stand, claimed there was no necessity "to make a final judgment under either [due process or equal protection] as to the validity" of the laws. He stated that he "would therefore leave open the question of whether, [if New York] were to enact new laws prohibiting assisted suicide, [such] laws would stand or fall." He urged a "constitutional remand": when a law is neither plainly unconstitutional or plainly constitutional, "the courts ought not to decide the ultimate validity of that law without current and clearly expressed statements, by the people or by their elected officials, of the state interests involved." He claimed that, "after such statements, the courts have frequently struck down such laws, while leaving open the possibility of reconsideration if appropriate statements were subsequently made." He explained: "[A] constitutional remand does no more than this: It tells [governments] that if they wish to regulate conduct that, if not protected by our Constitution, is very close to being protected, they must do so clearly and openly. They must, in other words, face the consequences of their decision before the people. Unless they do this, they cannot expect courts to tell them whether what they may or may not actually wish to enact is constitutionally permitted."[1] He suggested, moreover, that his "notion of a constitutional remand may respond to some of the concerns expressed by the dissenters in the Ninth Circuit case, Compassion in Dying." In the course of his opinion, Judge Calabresi noted that "neither Cruzan, nor Casey, nor the language of our Constitution, nor our constitutional tradition clearly makes these laws invalid." He added, however, that the rationale for the New York laws had "eroded with the passage of time. In the nineteenth century, both suicide and attempted suicide were crimes, [but] suicide and attempted suicide are no longer crimes. Nevertheless, the prohibitions on assisted suicide might serve other valid ends." He also noted that even if the action-inaction, "active" assisted suicide/"passive" behavior distinction were accepted, there was "no reason to believe that New York has consciously made such a judgment. Certainly New York has never enacted a law based on a reasoned defense of the difference."

c. *Some comments.* The question of whether there is a right to physician-assisted suicide (PAS) has generated an enormous literature (discussed at length in the Ninth Circuit and Second Circuit opinions, above). The most comprehensive studies of the background data are Marzen et al., "Suicide: A Constitutional Right?" 24 Duq.L.Rev. 1 (1985), and Meisel, The Right to Die (2d ed. 1995). See also New York State Task Force on Life and the Law, When Death is Sought: Assisted Suicide and Euthanasia in the Medical Context (1994), and Michigan Commission on Death and Dying, Final Report (1994). The New York Task Force recommended retaining the state's prohibition on assisted suicide; the Michigan Commission recommended decriminalizing PAS under some circumstances. For a sampling of the general literature (often supporting PAS) see Note, "Physician–Assisted Suicide and the Right to Die With Assistance," 105 Harv.L.Rev. 2021 (1992); Neeley, "[The] Mounting Urgency in the Call for Judicial Recognition of a Constitutional Right to Self–Directed Death," 26 U.Tol.L.Rev. 81 (1994); Tribe, "American Constitutional Law" (2d ed. 1988), § 15–11; Dworkin, Life's Dominion: An Argument About

---

1. Judge Calabresi had suggested judicial "remands" in his academic writing while on the Yale faculty (before becoming dean). See, e.g., Calabresi, A Common Law for the Age of Statutes (1982); see also Bickel & Wellington, "Legislative Purpose and the Judicial [Process]," 71 Harv.L.Rev. 1 (1957).

Abortion, Euthanasia, and Individual Freedom (1993), 179–217; and Kreimer, "Does Pro–Choice Mean Pro–Kevorkian? An Essay on Roe, Casey, and the Right to Die," 44 Am.U.L.Rev. 803 (1995) (claiming that a right to PAS does not follow plausibly from the abortion cases).

Professor Yale Kamisar, described by the Ninth Circuit as "a long-time, outspoken, and nationally-recognized opponent of assisted-suicide," has expressed his views in a flow of articles during recent decades. See, e.g., "Against Assisted Suicide—Even A Very Limited Form," 72 U.Det. Mercy L.Rev. 735 (1995). See also his "Physician–Assisted Suicide: A Bad Idea," [Michigan] Law Quadrangle Notes, vol. 39, no. 3, Fall/Winter 1996, 82, and "The Reasons So Many People Support [PAS]," 12 Issues in Law & Medicine 113 (1996). Kamisar recognizes that there is an "ever-growing support" for physician-assisted suicide for a number of reasons and explains why he does not "find any of them convincing." The reasons examined by Kamisar include "the compelling force of heartrending individual cases"; the claim that objections to legalizing PAS are limited to religious grounds; the view that PAS is a fact of modern life, "so we ought to legalize and regulate" it; and the argument that there is "little difference between ending life support and intervening to promote death." (Kamisar, while acknowledging that the distinction "is neither perfectly neat nor perfectly logical," argues that "the line between 'letting die' and actively intervening to bring about death represents a cultural and pragmatic compromise"; he emphasizes especially the "need to protect the weak and the vulnerable"); and the claim that a right to PAS "would only apply to the terminally ill." Kamisar concludes, citing Professor Robert Burt, that "at a time when tens of millions of Americans lack adequate healthcare, [it] would be most ironic if the judiciary were to select PAS as 'the one healthcare right that deserves constitutional status.' "

SECTION 4. THE SCOPE OF "LIBERTY" AND "PROPERTY": THE RIGHT TO HEARING CASES

Introduction. Since the 1970s, the Court has decided a large number of cases involving claims that due process requires some form of individualized hearing. In the typical situation, the claimant asserts a relationship or status vis-à-vis government—e.g., as employee or licensee or welfare recipient—and insists that it may not be terminated without a hearing. In deciding these cases, the Court has repeatedly confronted one of the central themes in the preceding sections: What constitutes constitutionally protected "liberty" and "property" under the due process clauses of the Fifth and 14th Amendments? True, the right to hearing cases deal with procedural due process, not substantive due process. But these procedural cases, like the substantive ones, ultimately involve resolution of the problem of identifying the appropriate sources for giving content to the meaning of "liberty" and "property."[1] What light does this sampling of cases throw on the proper ingredients of the meaning of "liberty" and "property"? To what extent do their sources lie in federal

---

1. Many of the procedural due process-right to hearing cases deal at length with the *kind* of hearing required when a hearing right is triggered because of an impingement upon liberty or property. The type of hearing required depends on a number of variables pertaining to the context of the problem.

Exploration of the contours of the constitutionally mandated kind of hearing is beyond the scope of this book. The general considerations deemed important by the Court are articulated in Mathews v. Eldridge (1976; p. 626 below).

constitutional law? To what extent are they determined instead by statutes or by common law? Consider, for example, the question of "liberty." In the substantive due process cases, the Court adopted a very embracive view of the individual interests encompassed by the term "liberty" and has exercised heightened scrutiny for those deemed "fundamental." In Lochner and Meyer, for example, the old Court extended "liberty" far beyond the freedom from physical restraint. And that approach has been embraced by the modern Court, as Griswold, Roe, and their progeny show. True, Justices have differed about what aspects of liberty are sufficiently "fundamental" to warrant special scrutiny by the Court. But those differences have been accompanied by a widespread consensus that the phrase "life, liberty or property" in the due process clauses is "a unitary concept embracing all interests valued by sensible men."[2] In the substantive due process area, in short, the typical Court focus has not been on whether a constitutionally protected interest has been impinged upon, but rather on what amount of justification the state must put forth to defend that impingement successfully. Starting in the early 1970s, the procedural due process-right to hearing cases diverged from that pattern. In a growing number of cases, the Court has found the claimed interest, albeit significant to the individual, not included within the constitutional notion of "liberty." Moreover, in delineating "liberty" (and, even more often, "property") in the procedural due process context, the Court has repeatedly drawn on state law or federal legislation. The Court's course has been a wavering one; but a sampling of the developments is warranted not only to inquire whether the modern Court's methodology in the right to hearing sphere justifiably departs from that familiar from the substantive due process area, but also to ask what impact the modern procedural due process analyses may have on future elaborations of substantive due process.

THE BACKGROUND OF THE MODERN DEVELOPMENTS: THE PROCEDURAL DUE PROCESS REVOLUTION OF THE EARLY 1970s

The major case launching the modern procedural due process revolution, a revolution that guaranteed hearing rights to those engaged in a variety of relations with government, was GOLDBERG v. KELLY, 397 U.S. 254 (1970). Justice BRENNAN's majority opinion held that due process required that a welfare recipient be afforded "an evidentiary hearing *before* the termination of benefits." He noted that the appellant, the Social Services Commissioner, had not claimed that "procedural due process is not applicable to the termination of welfare benefits" and added: "Such benefits are a matter of statutory entitlement for persons qualified to receive them." He commented, moreover, that welfare assistance is "not a mere charity" and added "that termination of aid pending resolution of the controversy over eligibility may deprive an *eligible* recipient of the very means by which to live while he waits." A series of post-Goldberg cases in the early 1970s extended procedural due process guarantees

---

2. Monaghan, "Of 'Liberty' and 'Property'," 62 Cornell L.Rev. 405 (1977). This article, an unusually penetrating one amidst the flow of modern commentary on the right to hearing cases, is cited hereinafter as Monaghan, "Of 'Liberty' and 'Property.'" See also the Van Alstyne and Tushnet articles cited below.

to a wide range of other claimants: employees, students, prisoners, parolees, debtors, automobile drivers, and so forth.[1]

In finding that a claim to welfare benefits could trigger procedural due process protection (even though there was no constitutional right to such benefits and the claim to them arose initially from legislative decisions), Justice Brennan quoted Charles Reich, the author of the influential article "The New Property," 73 Yale L.J. 733 (1964) (as well as of a widely sold 1970 book, The Greening of America). Reich's "new property" concept traced the emergence of government as a major source of wealth, noting that it was pouring forth "money, benefits, services, contracts, franchises and licenses [on] a vast, imperial scale." He argued that, in view of the broad functions of the modern state, "it must be recognized that we are becoming a society based upon relationship and status—status deriving primarily from source of livelihood. Status is so closely linked to personality that destruction of one may well destroy the other. Status must therefore be surrounded with the kind of safeguards once reserved for personality." His claim that deprivations of governmental largess warranted protection similar to that given traditional property rights formed an important part of the background for the procedural due process revolution that began with Goldberg v. Kelly. See Van Alstyne, "Cracks in 'The New Property': Adjudicative Due Process in the Administrative State," 62 Cornell L.Rev. 445 (1977); cf. Tushnet, "The Newer Property: Suggestion for the Revival of Substantive Due Process," 1975 Sup.Ct.Rev. 261. (Another important ingredient for the background of the early 1970s hearing cases was the effective abandonment, especially during the 1960s, of the traditional "right-privilege" distinction. The famous early expression of that distinction came from Justice Holmes in 1892, while he was still a state judge, in McAuliffe v. Mayor of New Bedford, rejecting any constitutional attack on the discharge of a public employee for political activities: "The petitioner may have the constitutional right to talk politics, but he has no constitutional right to be a policeman." The late 20th century cases make it clear that, even though an individual does not have a right to a public job or license or contract, he or she is protected by constitutional guarantees when government seeks to terminate the relationship. See generally Van Alstyne, "The Demise of the Right–Privilege Distinction in Constitutional Law," 81 Harv.L.Rev. 1439 (1968).)

The recognition of a wide range of individual interests in the early 1970s soon triggered a partial reaction on the Court. Some of the Justices were evidently concerned that the requirement of adjudicatory hearings in a large number of settings would excessively constitutionalize government's relations with licensees, employees and persons of similar status. There may have been fear as well that imposing hearing requirements in an ever wider range of settings would ultimately prove so inconvenient and expensive that it might inhibit the state from granting benefits it concededly was not obliged to provide. It is the methodology of that partial counterrevolution that has produced special doctrinal patterns regarding the meaning of "liberty" and "property." Instead of finding that in some settings procedural due process requirements could be satisfied with very informal or truncated hearings, or none at all, the main focus of the majority's limiting efforts shifted to asking initially whether there was any "liberty" or "property" at all involved that warranted a triggering of procedural due process concerns. That has become the first step in the inquiry; the question of what process is due is typically

---

1. See the review of the developments in Rendleman, "The New Due Process: Rights and Remedies," 63 Ky.L.J. 531 (1975). (Some of the major cases are further noted below).

reached only if the first step produces an affirmative answer. The most significant case delineating the new position was Roth, which follows.

BOARD OF REGENTS v. ROTH, 408 U.S. 564 (1972): Roth, hired to teach for one year at a campus of Wisconsin State University, was informed without explanation that he would not be rehired for the following year. He had no tenure rights under state law. He brought a federal lawsuit claiming that the failure to give him "any reason for nonretention and an opportunity for a hearing" violated procedural due process. The Court held that Roth had no constitutional right to a statement of reasons and a hearing. Justice STEWART's opinion for the Court stated:

"The requirements of procedural due process apply only to the deprivation of interests encompassed by the 14th Amendment's protection of liberty and property. When protected interests are implicated, the right to some kind of prior hearing is paramount. But the range of interests protected by procedural due process is not infinite. [Undeniably,] the respondent's re-employment prospects were of major concern to him—[a] concern that we surely cannot say was insignificant. [But to] determine whether due process requirements apply in the first place, we must look not to the 'weight' but to the *nature* of the interest at stake. ['Liberty'] and 'property' are broad and majestic terms. [The] Court has fully and finally rejected the wooden distinction between 'rights' and 'privileges' that once seemed to govern the applicability of procedural due process rights. The Court has also made clear that the property interests protected by procedural due process extend well beyond actual ownership of real estate, chattels, or money. By the same token, the Court has required due process protection for deprivations of liberty beyond the sort of formal constraints imposed by the criminal process. Yet, while the Court has eschewed rigid or formalistic limitations on the protection of procedural due process, it has at the same time observed certain boundaries.

"[The] 14th Amendment's procedural protection of property is a safeguard of the security of interests that a person has already acquired in specific benefits. These interests—property interests—may take many forms. [Thus,] the welfare recipients in Goldberg v. Kelly had a claim of entitlement to welfare payments that was grounded in the statute defining eligibility for them. [Similarly,] respondent's 'property' interest in employment at [the University] was created and defined by the terms of his appointment [which] specifically provided that the respondent's employment was to terminate on June 30. [There was] no provision for renewal whatsoever. Thus, the terms of the respondent's appointment secured absolutely no interest in re-employment for the next year. [Nor,] significantly, was there any state statute or University rule or policy that secured his interest in re-employment or that created any legitimate claim to it.[2] In these circumstances, the respondent surely had an

2. To be sure, the respondent does suggest that most teachers hired on a year-to-year basis by [the University] are, in fact, rehired. But the District Court has not found that there is anything approaching a 'common law' of re-employment, see Perry v. Sindermann [below], so strong as to require University officials to give the respondent a statement of reasons and a hearing on their decision not to rehire him. [Footnote by Justice Stewart.] [PERRY v. SINDERMANN, 408 U.S. 593 (1972), was a companion case to Roth. Like Roth, Sindermann involved a claim of a nontenured college teacher who asserted a procedural due process right to a hearing where he might be informed of the grounds for his nonretention and challenge their sufficiency. But Sindermann, unlike Roth, won his case. Justice STEWART's majority opinion held that Sindermann's lack of a formal "tenure right to re-employment, taken alone, [did not defeat] his claim that the non-renewal of his contract violated due process." On the issue closest to that discussed at length in Roth (the procedural due

abstract concern in being rehired, but he did not have a *property* interest sufficient to require the University authorities to give him a hearing when they declined to renew his [contract]."

Justice MARSHALL's dissent stated that he would go further than the Court in defining the terms "liberty" and "property": "In my view, every citizen who applies for a government job is entitled to it unless the government can establish some reason for denying the employment. This is the 'property' right that I believe is protected by the 14th Amendment and that cannot be denied 'without due process of law.' And it is also liberty—liberty to work—which is the 'very essence of the personal freedom and opportunity' secured by the 14th Amendment. [It] may be argued that to provide procedural due process to all public employees or prospective employees would [impose] an intolerable [burden]. The short answer [is] that it is not burdensome to give reasons when reasons exist. [It] is only where the government acts improperly that procedural due process is truly burdensome. And that is precisely when it is most [necessary]." Chief Justice BURGER submitted a concurring statement; Justice DOUGLAS submitted a dissent. In another dissent, Justice BRENNAN, joined by Justice Douglas, stated that he agreed with Justice Marshall's conclusion. Compare Cleveland Board of Education v. Loudermill (1985; p. 621 below).

"PROPERTY," "LIBERTY," AND HEARING RIGHTS OF PUBLIC EMPLOYEES IN LIGHT OF ROTH

1. *The Roth approach: Property and state law.* Monaghan, "Of 'Liberty' and 'Property,'" viewed Roth as working a "significant" analytical shift: the unitary, generous view of "life, liberty and property" was abandoned in the procedural due process area in favor of an approach examining each word of the phrase separately and reading "liberty" and "property" in a manner that did not include "the full range of state conduct having serious impact upon individual interests." Monaghan commented that "Roth's emphasis on the need for careful analysis of the 'nature of the interest at stake' [has] not proved to be an isolated event," and the cases that follow illustrate the accuracy of that observation. What is objectionable about emphasizing the "*nature* of the interest" rather than the severity and importance of the challenged deprivation to the individual? Consider especially the Court's emphasis on state law in determining the content of "property" in Roth. Is the central determinant the

process one), the question of Sindermann's job entitlement was central. The Court distinguished Roth. Although Sindermann could not claim (any more than Roth) that mere failure to rehire deprived him of liberty or property, Sindermann had alleged that his interest in continued employment, "though not secured by a formal contractual or tenure provision, was secured by a no less binding understanding fostered by the college administration": he claimed that "the college had a de facto tenure program, and that he had tenure under that program." Justice Stewart agreed that Sindermann was entitled to a hearing on this de facto tenure claim. He noted: "A person's interest in a benefit is a 'property' interest for due process purposes if there are such rules or mutually explicit understandings that support his claim of entitlement to the benefit and that he may invoke at a hearing." Reemphasizing that protected "property" interests were governed by state law, Justice Stewart concluded that Sindermann was entitled to an opportunity to prove "the existence of rules and understandings [that] may justify his legitimate claim of entitlement to continued employment absent 'sufficient cause.'" (See Simon, "Liberty and Property in the Supreme Court: A Defense of Roth and Perry," 71 Calif.L.Rev. 146 (1983).)]

complainant's legitimate expectation or reliance? Or is the central question the less subjective one of identifying a reasonable interpretation of the state's intentions with regard to creating entitlements? (Note the light thrown on these questions by Arnett and Bishop, below.) Monaghan notes that the role of state law in giving content to constitutionally protected "property" had been recognized before Roth, with the Court occasionally asking whether there was a "fair and substantial" basis in state law for the recognition of certain interests. But Monaghan adds an important comment: "The 'fair and substantial basis' rule [is] entirely consistent with the principle that there is a federal *content* to the word 'property.' To be sure, the *interests* must be initially created by state law," and state law is ordinarily determinative on that question. But the state court's *characterization* of those 'interests' is another matter altogether. The difference between the existence of an interest—a matter of state law—and its significance—a matter of federal law—is firmly established in other areas of law." To what extent does Roth adhere to that distinction? Did Arnett and Bishop, the post-Roth cases, erode it?

2.   *The Arnett case: The "bitter with the sweet."* To what extent should the underlying statutory or common law from which the term "property" derives at least part of its content govern the question of whether a claimant is entitled to a hearing? May state law or federal legislation, in the process of delineating the existence of the property interest, include binding provisions barring hearings? An affirmative answer to the latter question was suggested by Justice REHNQUIST's opinion in ARNETT v. KENNEDY, 416 U.S. 134 (1974), a decision rejecting a nonprobationary federal civil service employee's claim to a full hearing prior to dismissal. The governing federal law prescribed not only the grounds for removal but also set forth removal procedures. (The employee could be removed only for "cause"; but the procedures did not provide for an adversary hearing.) To Justice Rehnquist, those provisions were dispositive of the procedural due process claim. Although the law created a constitutionally protected property interest (an expectation of continued employment), "where the grant of a substantive right is inextricably intertwined with the limitations on the procedures which are to be employed in determining that right, a litigant [must] take the bitter with the sweet. [Here] the property interest which appellee had in his employment was itself conditioned by procedural limitations which had accompanied the grant of that interest." But Justice Rehnquist's approach was not shared by the majority: he spoke only for three Justices, with Chief Justice Burger and Justice Stewart joining his opinion. Although a majority rejected the procedural due process claim, the remaining Justices, in several opinions, dissociated themselves from the Rehnquist approach. Justice POWELL's concurrence, for example, found it incompatible with Roth and Sindermann and stated: "While the legislature may elect not to confer a property interest in federal employment, it may not constitutionally authorize the deprivation of such an interest, once conferred, without appropriate procedural safeguards." Did Justice Rehnquist's position become that of the majority *since* Arnett? That was the contention of the dissenters in Bishop v. Wood (which follows), a case involving state rather than federal employment. The majority in Bishop denied that it was following the Rehnquist–Arnett approach. In examining Bishop, then, consider whether it made state law determinative not only with respect to the initial creation of property interests but also with regard to the existence of hearing rights. Did Bishop obliterate the distinction suggested by Monaghan: Did it abandon any significant independent federal judicial role with regard to the "characterization" of state-created property interests? Compare the repudiation of Justice Rehnquist's Arnett

approach in Cleveland Board of Education v. Loudermill (1985; below), explicitly endorsing Justice Powell's approach in Arnett.

3. *The Bishop case.* In BISHOP v. WOOD, 426 U.S. 341 (1976), a 5–4
decision, a majority concluded that the dismissal of a policeman did not
implicate any "property" or "liberty" interests. Bishop lost his city job as a
policeman without a hearing to determine the sufficiency of the cause for his
discharge. His suit contended that, since a city ordinance classified him as a
"permanent employee," he had a constitutional right to a pretermination
hearing. During pretrial discovery, he was advised that his dismissal was based
on a failure to follow certain orders, poor attendance at training classes,
causing low morale, and conduct unsuited to an officer. Bishop denied these
charges and claimed a due process right to a hearing. In finding no constitutional "property" interest, Justice STEVENS's majority opinion emphasized
that Bishop's claim had to be decided "by reference to state law" and relied on
the lower courts' interpretation of the city ordinance and resultant finding that
Bishop "held his position at the will and pleasure of the city." As a result, state
law "necessarily establishe[d] that he had *no* property interest," in the majority's view. Nor was the majority persuaded by Bishop's claim that he had been
deprived of liberty because the reasons given for his discharge were "so serious
as to constitute a stigma" and that "those reasons were false." Justice Stevens
emphasized: "The federal court is not the appropriate forum in which to review
the multitude of personnel decisions that are made daily by public agencies.
[In] the absence of any claim that the public employer was motivated by a
desire to curtail or to penalize the exercise of an employee's constitutionally
protected rights, we must presume that official action was regular and, if
erroneous, can best be corrected in other ways. [Due process] is not a guarantee
against incorrect or ill-advised personnel decisions." Justice BRENNAN, joined
by Justice Marshall, dissented, protested reading out of the due process clauses
still another personal interest. A dissent by Justice WHITE, joined by Justice
Brennan, Marshall, and Blackmun, charged that the majority's approach to
property rights was "precisely the reasoning which was embraced by only three
and expressly rejected by six Members of this Court in [Arnett]." Since the city
ordinance "plainly grants petitioner a right to his job unless there is cause to
fire him," it was the Constitution, not state law, which determined the process
to be applied in connection with any state decision to deprive him of it. For
critical analysis of Bishop, see Rabin, "Job Security and Due Process: Monitoring Discretion Through a Reasons Requirement," 44 U.Chi.L.Rev. 60 (1976).

4. *The Loudermill case.* The uncertainty regarding the status of the
"bitter with the sweet" principle espoused by Justice Rehnquist in Arnett
finally ended with the decision in CLEVELAND BOARD OF EDUCATION v.
LOUDERMILL, 470 U.S. 532 (1985). With only Justice REHNQUIST dissenting on this issue, Justice WHITE for the other eight members of the Court
made clear that, although state law remains the primary focus for the determination of whether a property right exists, state procedures contained in the law
creating that property right are *not* the source of the constitutionally required
procedures upon termination of that property right: "[It] is settled that the
'bitter with the sweet' approach [of the plurality in Arnett] misconceives the
constitutional guarantee. If a clearer holding is needed, we provide it today.
The point is straightforward: the Due Process Clause provides that certain
substantive rights—life, liberty, and property—cannot be deprived except pursuant to constitutionally adequate procedures. The categories of substance and
procedure are distinct. Were the rule otherwise, the Clause would be reduced to
a mere tautology. 'Property' cannot be defined by the procedures provided for
its deprivation any more than can life or liberty. [Once] it is determined that

the Due Process Clause applies, 'the question remains what process is due.' The answer to that question is not to be found in [state law]." In looking to the Constitution for a determination of what procedures are required *prior* to termination of a state civil service employee, the Court noted that only in Goldberg v. Kelly had "the Court required a full adversarial evidentiary hearing prior to adverse governmental action." But the Court held that the considerations involved in the termination of public employment differ from those involved in the termination of welfare benefits. Because of the government's particularly strong interest "in quickly removing an unsatisfactory employee," a tenured public employee is only "entitled to oral or written notice of the charges against him, an explanation of the employer's evidence, and an opportunity to present his side of the story. To require more than this prior to termination would intrude to an unwarranted extent [on the government's interest]." Justice REHNQUIST's dissent recalled his opinion in Arnett. "While [the Court] does not impose a federal definition of property, [it] departs from the full breadth of the holding in Roth by its selective choice from among the sentences the Ohio legislature chooses to use in establishing and qualifying a right."

THE SHRINKING SCOPE OF "LIBERTY" IN THE PROCEDURAL DUE PROCESS CASES

The preceding right to hearing cases make clear that the Court has often deferred to state law in delineating constitutionally protected *property* rights. To what extent has there been a parallel development regarding hearing rights triggered by alleged infringements of *liberty*? Can the Court narrow the reading of liberty in the procedural due process context without casting doubt on its very broad interpretations of liberty in the substantive due process cases from Meyer to Roe and beyond?

1. *Paul v. Davis and its problems.* The most widely debated (and widely criticized) modern decision about the scope of "liberty" in procedural due process cases was PAUL v. DAVIS, 424 U.S. 693 (1976), where a sharply divided Court held, in a majority opinion by Justice REHNQUIST, that the plaintiff, whom the local police had named as an "active shoplifter" in flyers distributed to local merchants, had suffered no deprivation of liberty resulting from injury to his reputation. The plaintiff sued the local police under a federal civil rights law after the shoplifting charges were dismissed. Earlier cases had indicated that the personal interest in reputation is included within the constitutional protection of "liberty." (See, e.g., Wisconsin v. Constantineau, 400 U.S. 433 (1971).) Justice Rehnquist found such cases distinguishable. He insisted that reputation alone was not a constitutionally protected interest and sought to distinguish all earlier cases speaking of "stigma" and damage to reputation as involving situations where some "more tangible interests such as employment were also present."[1] Justice Rehnquist's explanation included the following passages: "The words 'liberty' and 'property' as used in the 14th Amendment do not in terms single out reputation as a candidate for special protection over and above other interests that may be protected by state law.

---

1. Note the comment in Monaghan, "Of 'Liberty' and 'Property,' " on this aspect of Paul v. Davis: "The Court's re-rationalization of the earlier cases is wholly startling to anyone familiar with [the] precedents. In many ways I find this Paul's most disturbing aspect. Fair treatment by the Court of its own precedents is an indispensable condition of judicial legitimacy."

While we have in a number of our prior cases pointed out the frequently drastic effect of the 'stigma' which may result from defamation by the government in a variety of contexts, this line of cases does not establish the proposition that reputation alone, apart from some more tangible interests such as employment, is either 'liberty' or 'property' by itself sufficient to invoke the procedural protection of the Due Process Clause. [There] exists a variety of interests which are difficult of definition but are nevertheless comprehended within the meaning of either 'liberty' or 'property' as meant in the Due Process Clause. These interests attain this constitutional status by virtue of the fact that they have been initially recognized and protected by state law, and we have repeatedly ruled that the procedural guarantees of the 14th Amendment apply whenever the State seeks to remove or significantly alter that protected status.[2] [In] each of these cases, as a result of the state action complained of, a right or status previously recognized by state law was distinctly altered or extinguished. It was this alteration, officially removing the interest from the recognition and protection previously afforded by the State, which we found sufficient to invoke the procedural guarantees contained in the [due process]. But the interest in reputation alone [is] quite different from the 'liberty' or 'property' recognized in those decisions. Kentucky law does not extend to respondent any legal guarantee of present enjoyment of reputation which has been altered as a result of petitioners' actions. Rather his interest in reputation is simply one of a number which the State may protect against injury by virtue of its tort law, providing a forum for vindication of those interests by means of damages actions. And any harm or injury to that interest [does not] result in a deprivation of any 'liberty' or 'property' recognized by state or federal law, nor has it worked any change of respondent's status as theretofore recognized under the State's [laws]."

Justice BRENNAN's dissent, joined by Justices Marshall and White, attacked the majority's alleged distortion of precedent, expressed the hope that the ruling would be but "a short-lived aberration," and stated: "The Court accomplishes [its] result by excluding a person's interest in his good name and reputation from all constitutional protection, regardless of the character of or necessity for the government's actions. The result [is] demonstrably inconsistent with our prior case law and unduly restrictive in its construction of our precious Bill of Rights. [The] Court by mere fiat and with no analysis wholly excludes personal interest in reputation from the ambit of 'life, liberty, or property,' [thus] rendering due process concerns *never* applicable to the official stigmatization, however arbitrary, of an individual. The logical and disturbing corollary of this holding is that no due process infirmities would inhere in a statute constituting a commission to conduct ex parte trials of individuals, so long as the only official judgment pronounced was limited to the public condemnation and branding of a person as a Communist, a traitor, an 'active murderer,' a homosexual, or any other mark that 'merely' carries social opprobrium. The potential of today's decision is [frightening]."[3]

2. See Bell v. Burson, 402 U.S. 535 (1971) (revoking driver's license); Morrissey v. Brewer, 408 U.S. 471 (1972) (altering status of parolee).

3. Consider Monaghan's criticisms of the Paul ruling in "Of 'Liberty' and 'Property,' ": "[Paul's] rationale would confine the *federal content* of 'liberty' to specific constitutional guarantees and the Roe right of privacy, and perhaps, to the Framers' under-

standing of liberty as freedom from personal restraint. [Paul's] difficulties are deep ones. Even if the Court was free to view the question before it as an open one, it was surely not compelled to reject freedom from defamation as a protected interest. [The] opinion does more than repudiate the long-standing tradition of an expansive reading of the word 'liberty' as a matter of federal law. [It] seems to have proceeded from the premise that if

2. *The impact of the Paul v. Davis approach.* Paul v. Davis is by no means the only modern case that has been criticized as adopting an unduly narrow reading of "liberty" in the procedural due process context. Similar criticisms have been directed at the Roth and Bishop cases, above, for example. Moreover, soon after Paul, the Court decided Meachum v. Fano, 427 U.S. 215 (1976), rejecting a challenge to the procedures afforded when a state prisoner was transferred to a more restrictive prison. The Court emphasized that traditional, broad "liberty" was not implicated, because the original decision to imprison was clearly valid, and that state law created no independent liberty interest. See also the dissent by Justice Marshall, joined by Justices Brennan and Stevens, in Greenholtz v. Nebraska Penal Inmates, 442 U.S. 1 (1979), protesting the majority's "unduly narrow view of the liberty protected by the 14th Amendment." (Greenholtz involved parole release proceedings.) Note the reliance on the preceding cases in Connecticut Board of Pardons v. Dumschat, 452 U.S. 458 (1981), holding that the Board's practice of granting about 75% of the applications for commutation of life sentences did *not* create a constitutionally protected "liberty interest" or "entitlement." Thus, the Board was not required to give reasons for denying an application. Compare, however, Justice Stevens's comment welcoming the majority's generous reading of "liberty" in the course of his dissent in Bell v. Wolfish, 441 U.S. 520 (1979). There, the majority recognized a "liberty" interest of pretrial detainees in the conditions of their confinements (though rejecting the claims on the merits). But see the application and reaffirmation of Paul v. Davis in Siegert v. Gilley, 500 U.S. 226 (1991), where Chief Justice Rehnquist relied heavily on Paul in rejecting a claim against federal agents for damages resulting from injury to reputation. The Chief Justice insisted that the Paul principle was fully applicable even when the plaintiff alleged tangible loss as a result of the reputational injury. The restrictive reading of "liberty" in Paul v. Davis and its progeny evidently stemmed from a range of institutional concerns, including the fear of excessive Court interference in the administration of state programs and Justice Rehnquist's related fear about reading the 14th Amendment as "a font of tort law to be superimposed upon whatever systems may already be administered by the States." But, assuming the substantiality of these concerns, were there no alternative routes to the result other than reading "liberty" more narrowly than its traditional broad reach? Would it have been possible to retain a more generous view of liberty and property and focus on the question of what procedural due process requires—and find that its requirements could be satisfied with informal hearings or no individualized hearings at all in many circumstances? Note also Van Alstyne's suggestion, in "Cracks in ['The New Property']," 62 Cornell L.Rev. 445, urging a shift away from the "new property" approach that underlay Goldberg v. Kelly and advocating recognition of a *"freedom from arbitrary adjudicative procedures* as a substantive element of one's liberty." Is there basis in the cases or in principle for avoiding the elaborate (if at times shaky) superstructure the Court has developed in the procedural due process cases and bluntly recognizing such an across-the-board "freedom from arbitrary adjudicative procedures"? (The California Supreme Court adopted Van Alstyne's view in People v. Ramirez, 25 Cal.3d 260 (1979).)

the challenged conduct would constitute a common-law tort by a private person, it cannot constitute an interference with the 'liberty' protected by the 14th Amendment. Thus, the more reprehensible and subject to legal redress the conduct, the freer the state is to engage in it—at least until that conduct bumps up against some specific constitutional guarantee or the hodge-podge right of privacy. [Recent cases such as Paul] have narrowed the content of 'liberty.'"

Cf. Smolla, "The Displacement of Federal Due Process Claims by State Tort Remedies," 1982 U.Ill.L.F. 831.

3. *State law as a source of "liberty" interests in the modern cases.* In thinking about the line of cases beginning with Paul v. Davis, consider the repeated assertions that state law is an important source in delineating constitutionally protected liberty. The 1980 decision in VITEK v. JONES, 445 U.S. 480, suggested that the court was somewhat ambivalent about these problems. Justice White's majority opinion, in finding a protected liberty interest, spoke not only of a state-created right, but also of the court's independent recognition of the "stigma" ingredient of liberty. Vitek held that "the involuntary transfer of a Nebraska state prisoner to a mental hospital implicates a liberty interest that is protected by the due process clause." Here, there was an " 'objective expectation, firmly fixed in state law and [official] practice,' that a prisoner would not be transferred unless he suffered from a mental disease or defect that could not be adequately treated in the prison"; that "objective expectation" gave the prisoner "a liberty interest that entitled him to the benefits of appropriate procedures in connection with determining the conditions that warranted his transfer to a mental hospital." Justice White went on to comment: "We have recognized that for the ordinary citizen, commitment to a mental hospital produces 'a massive curtailment of liberty' and in consequence 'requires due process protection.' The loss of liberty produced by an involuntary commitment is more than a loss of freedom from confinement. It is indisputable that commitment to a mental hospital 'can engender adverse social consequences to the individual' and that '[w]hether we label this phenomenon "stigma" or choose to call it something else [we] recognize that it can occur and that it can have a very significant impact on the individual.' Also, '[a]mong the historic liberties' protected by the due process clause is the 'right to be free from, and to obtain judicial relief for, unjustified intrusions on personal security.' Compelled treatment in the form of mandatory behavior modification programs, to which [the prisoner] was exposed in this case, was a proper factor to be weighed [here]. We conclude that a convicted felon [is] entitled to the benefit of procedures appropriate in the circumstances before he [is] transferred to a mental hospital."

The modern Court's tendency to narrow the range of liberty interests independently recognized by the Constitution and to look primarily to state law as determinative in many cases has not meant rejection of all claims of liberty triggering procedural due process protections. Rather, some of the modern cases have found that state-created rights and expectations created procedurally safeguarded liberty interests. Consider, for example, two 1983 decisions, Hewitt v. Helms, 459 U.S. 460, and Olim v. Wakinekona, 461 U.S. 238. In both cases, the Court found no liberty interest independently based on the Constitution, yet proceeded to examine quite carefully the possibility that state law had created interests in liberty triggering procedural protection. In Hewitt, the issue arose in the context of a transfer of a prisoner from the general prison population to administrative segregation, a more restrictive environment. Olim involved the transfer of a prisoner to an out-of-state prison. In both cases, the Court proceeded to an examination of state law to determine whether it had created a liberty interest. The Court found none in Olim, but did in Hewitt. In its Hewitt discussion, the majority reaffirmed that "liberty interests protected by the 14th Amendment may arise from two sources—the Due Process Clause itself and the laws of the States." The decision in Hewitt suggested that the latter source had potential for expansion, but Sandin v. Conner, 115 S.Ct. 2293 (1995), rejected the Hewitt approach, holding that procedural due process protections were triggered not merely by the fact of punitive action but only for "a dramatic departure from the basic conditions" of the sentence.

4. *Procedural due process in other contexts.* Most of the cases in this section have focused on hearing rights in the employment context. But, as the immediately preceding materials indicate, the Court has confronted the definition of "liberty" and "property" in a range of other contexts as well. Other areas that have prompted prolific litigation are the hearing rights of prisoners (e.g., Vitek v. Jones) and the procedural due process guarantees available in the school environment. A controversial example of the latter is Goss v. Lopez, 419 U.S. 565 (1975), where a divided Court afforded a right to an informal hearing to high school students threatened with brief disciplinary suspensions. Having created the public school system, the state had created an entitlement that it could not remove without due process. See also Ingraham v. Wright, 430 U.S. 651 (1977), holding that corporal punishment in public schools "implicates a constitutionally protected liberty interest," but that procedural due process does not require a hearing before beatings can be inflicted, since the traditional common law after-the-fact remedies satisfied due process. On the procedural safeguards necessary in the context of "academic" rather than "disciplinary" actions in the school context, see generally Board of Curators, Univ. of Mo. v. Horowitz, 435 U.S. 78 (1978), involving a student's dismissal from medical school because of her performance in the clinical program.

5. *What process is "due"?* The focus of this section has been on the question of delineating constitutionally protected "liberty" and "property" interests for procedural due process purposes. But another controversial question arises whenever the case involves an interest that *is* found protected by the due process clause and accordingly triggers the right to some sort of hearing. Exploring the details of the Court's methodology in delineating the nature of the hearing required in varied contexts is beyond the scope of this book. It is worth noting, however, that the modern Court has reached agreement on a general balancing formula, albeit not a wholly informative one—a formula governing the identification of the procedural guarantees appropriate to a particular context. The source of the widely invoked modern balancing approach is Justice POWELL's majority opinion in MATHEWS v. ELDRIDGE, 424 U.S. 319 (1976). There, the Court held that pretermination evidentiary hearings were not required in the context of disability benefits. In articulating the approach that has become the dominant one for determining what process is due, Justice Powell stated: "In recent years this Court increasingly has had occasion to consider the extent to which due process requires an evidentiary hearing prior to the deprivation of some type of property interest even if such a hearing is provided thereafter. In only one case, Goldberg v. Kelly, has the Court held that a hearing closely approximating a judicial trial is necessary. In other cases requiring some type of pretermination hearing as a matter of constitutional right, the Court has spoken sparingly about the requisite procedures. [Our] decisions underscore the truism that ' "[d]ue process," unlike some legal rules, is not a technical conception with a fixed content unrelated to time, place and circumstances.' '[Due process] is flexible and calls for such procedural protections as the particular situation demands.' Accordingly, resolution of the issue whether the administrative procedures provided here are constitutionally sufficient requires analysis of the governmental and private interests that are affected. More precisely, our prior decisions indicate that identification of the specific dictates of due process generally requires consideration of three distinct factors: First, the private interest that will be affected by the official action; second, the risk of an erroneous deprivation of such interest through the procedures used, and the probable value, if any, of additional or

substitute procedural safeguards; and finally, the Government's interest, including the function involved and the fiscal and administrative burdens that the additional or substitute procedural requirement would entail." Do Justice Powell's three factors provide adequate guidance? Moreover, is it proper for judges to second-guess the legislature in weighing factors that presumably went into the formulation of the benefits scheme in the first place? For a criticism of the Mathews balancing test, see Mashaw, "The Supreme Court's Due Process Calculus for Administrative Adjudication in Mathews v. Eldridge: Three Factors in Search of a Theory of Value," 44 U.Chi.L.Rev. 28 (1976); note also the same author's Due Process in the Administrative State (1985). See also Friendly, "Some Kind of Hearing," 123 U.Pa.L.Rev. 1267 (1975).

CHAPTER 9

EQUAL PROTECTION

SECTION 1. AN OVERVIEW

Introduction. We now turn to the range of complex problems raised by the simple-sounding command of the 14th Amendment that no state shall "deny to any person within its jurisdiction the equal protection of the laws." Presumably, that command cannot mean that laws must deal in the same way with everyone. Almost all laws classify (or "discriminate") by imposing special burdens or granting special benefits to some people and not to others. But if legislation almost by its nature classifies, what content can be given to the equal protection guarantee? In its efforts to divine meanings, the Court has constructed a morass of doctrines, tried to identify types of situations warranting different degrees of judicial scrutiny (from the most deferential to the strictest), and purported to find in equal protection a range of specially protected fundamental values. The purpose of this introductory overview is to provide a rough road map through the maze. It surveys the historical changes in the significance of the equal protection clause; it outlines the most commonly invoked doctrinal tools, particularly the Court's efforts to delineate the occasions for varying levels (or "tiers") of judicial scrutiny of governmental actions; and it calls attention to some recurrent problems regarding the central content of constitutionally protected equality.

It may be surprising that, more than a century after the adoption of the 14th Amendment, the question of the inherent content of equal protection continues to be a subject of intense debate. In fact, the issue is very much in controversy. The strongest consensus about the meaning of equal protection is drawn from its historical origins: at the very least it was directed at governmental racial discrimination against blacks. What, if anything, beyond that concern can equal protection be fairly read to include? In the earliest interpretation of the 14th Amendment, in the Slaughter–House Cases (1873; p. 421 above), the Court suggested that racial concerns exhausted the meaning of the clause. (Even in the area of race discrimination, controversies about the meaning and scope of the clause still abound, as sec. 3 demonstrates.) Beyond this widely agreed-upon core, the broadest agreement concerns the notion that equal protection imposes a variation of the "rationality" requirement already encountered in the examination of due process. A classification, the argument goes, must be reasonably related to the purpose of the legislation. But even that widely supported minimum is not universally accepted; and those who support the existence of the rationality requirement disagree sharply about what it should mean in terms of actual judicial scrutiny of legislative action.

Beyond these points of quite wide consensus, equal protection is an embattled terrain. Particularly controversial are the modern Court's efforts to find some fundamental values inherent in equal protection. Can equal protection be viewed as an independent source of fundamental rights, or must all fundamental rights be traceable to some other constitutional source, such as the First Amendment or substantive due process? One contemporary scholar has stirred a wide debate with his assertion that equality is an "empty idea."

Westen, "The Empty Idea of Equality," 95 Harv.L.Rev. 537 (1982). Another has asked whether equal protection is really like Oakland (borrowing Gertrude Stein's quip that the trouble with Oakland is that "there is no there there"). Cohen, "Is Equal Protection Like Oakland? Equality as a Surrogate for Other Rights," 59 Tul.L.Rev. 884 (1985). These opening notes are designed to introduce the pervasive questions. The complexity of the questions raised can best be appreciated in the context of the fuller exploration that follows, and a return to these introductory materials may be worthwhile after that exploration is concluded.[1]

1. *Modest origins: The "old equal protection" in the pre-Warren Court years.* Traditionally, equal protection supported only minimal judicial intervention in most contexts. Ordinarily, the command of equal protection was only that government must not impose differences in treatment "except upon some reasonable differentiation fairly related to the object of regulation," as Justice Jackson put it in the Railway Express case, p. 639 below. That "old" variety of equal protection scrutiny focused on the *means* used by the legislature: it insisted merely that the classification in the statute reasonably relate to a legitimate legislative purpose. Unlike substantive due process, equal protection scrutiny was not typically concerned with identifying "fundamental values" and restraining legislative ends. And usually that rational classification requirement was readily satisfied: the courts did not demand a tight fit between classification and purpose; perfect congruence between means and ends was not required; judges allowed legislators flexibility to act on the basis of broadly accurate generalizations and tolerated considerable overinclusiveness and underinclusiveness in classification schemes. Only in special, limited contexts was equal protection found to have a deeper bite during most of its history—most notably in racial discrimination cases.

During the early 20th century era of extensive Court interference with state economic legislation, it was usually due process, not equal protection, that provided the cutting edge. Thus, at the height of the Lochner era, Justice Holmes referred to equal protection as "the usual last resort of constitutional arguments."[2] Another comment, by Justice Jackson in the Railway Express case, also reflects the relatively narrow intrusion into the legislative domain traditionally associated with equal protection: "Invalidation of a statute or an ordinance on due process grounds leaves ungoverned and ungovernable conduct which many people find objectionable. Invocation of the equal protection clause, on the other hand, does not disable any governmental body from dealing with the subject at hand. It merely means that the prohibition or regulation must have a broader impact." What Justice Jackson there emphasized is that the "old" equal protection ordinarily focused solely on legislative means, on the rationality of classifications, not on legislative objectives. Although due process

---

1. Although the equal protection requirement of the 14th Amendment literally applies only to state action, judicial interpretation has made it applicable to the federal government as well, as an aspect of Fifth Amendment due process. The most notable case announcing that de facto process of reverse incorporation is Bolling v. Sharpe, the District of Columbia school desegregation case (1954; p. 677 below). Generally, the Court's "approach to Fifth Amendment equal protection claims [has] been precisely the same as to equal protection claims under the 14th Amendment." Weinberger v. Wiesenfeld (1975; p. 717 below).

2. Buck v. Bell, 274 U.S. 200 (1927). The fact that due process was the favorite interventionist tool of the Lochner years does not mean, however, that equal protection invalidations were wholly unknown. As early as 1897, in Gulf, C. & S. F. Ry. v. Ellis, 165 U.S. 150, for example, the Court relied on equal protection to strike down an economic regulation requiring railroads (but not other defendants) to pay attorneys' fees to successful plaintiffs in certain cases.

also has a "rational means" ingredient, it is more commonly associated with restraints on legislative ends, in the era of Roe as well as of Lochner.

2. *From marginal intervention to major cutting edge: The Warren Court's "new equal protection" and the two-tier approach.* From its traditional modest role, equal protection burgeoned into a major interventionist tool during the Warren era, especially in the 1960s. The Warren Court did not abandon the deferential ingredients of the old equal protection: in most areas of economic and social legislation, the demands imposed by equal protection remained minimal. (Indeed, the Warren Court's hands-off stance was even more lenient than that of its predecessors.) But the Court launched an equal protection revolution by finding large new areas for strict rather than deferential scrutiny. A sharply differentiated two-tier approach evolved by the late 1960s. In addition to the deferential "old" equal protection, a "new" equal protection, connoting strict scrutiny, arose: "The Warren Court embraced a rigid two-tier attitude. Some situations evoked the aggressive 'new' equal protection, with scrutiny that was 'strict' in theory and fatal in fact; in other contexts, the deferential 'old' equal protection reigned, with minimal scrutiny in theory and virtually none in fact."[3] The intensive review associated with the new equal protection imposed two demands—a demand not only as to means but also as to ends. Legislation qualifying for strict scrutiny required a far closer fit between classification and statutory purpose than the rough and ready flexibility traditionally tolerated by the old equal protection: means had to be shown "necessary" to achieve statutory ends, not merely "reasonably related." Moreover, equal protection became a source of ends scrutiny as well: legislation in the areas of the new equal protection had to be justified by "compelling" state interests, not merely the much broader spectrum of "legitimate" state ends. The Warren Court identified the areas appropriate for strict scrutiny by searching for two characteristics: the presence of a "suspect" classification; or an impact on "fundamental" rights or interests. In the category of "suspect classifications," the Warren Court's major contribution was to intensify the strict scrutiny in the traditionally interventionist area of racial classifications. But tantalizing statements also suggested that there might be other suspect categories as well: illegitimacy and wealth, for example. But it was the "fundamental interests" ingredient of the new equal protection that proved particularly dynamic, open-ended, and amorphous: "It was the element that bore the closest resemblance to freewheeling substantive due process, for it circumscribed legislative choices in the name of newly articulated values that lacked clear support in constitutional text and history. The list of interests identified as fundamental by the Warren Court was in fact quite modest: voting, criminal appeals, and the right of interstate travel were the prime examples. But in the extraordinary amount of commentary that followed, analysts searching for justifications for those enshrinements [were] tempted to ponder analogous spheres that might similarly qualify. Welfare benefits, exclusionary zoning, municipal services and school financing came to be the most inviting frontiers."[4]

3. Gunther, "Foreword: In Search of Evolving Doctrine on a Changing Court: A Model for a Newer Equal Protection," 86 Harv.L.Rev. 1 (1972) (hereinafter cited as Gunther, "Newer Equal Protection"). All quotations in this overview, unless otherwise attributed, are from that article. For a survey of the state of equal protection doctrine near the end of the Warren years, distinguishing the "restrained review" and "active review" spheres, see "Developments in the Law— Equal Protection," 82 Harv.L.Rev. 1065 (1969) (hereinafter cited as "Developments").

4. For a critical evaluation of new equal protection developments at the end of the Warren era, see Justice Harlan's dissent in Shapiro v. Thompson (1969; p. 904 below).

3. *The post-Warren Court years and equal protection.* In more recent decades, there has been neither undiminished carrying forward nor wholesale turning back of the Warren Court approach. The response has been more complex. In form, the two-tier distinction between new, strict scrutiny and old, deferential review equal protection persists. In fact, the modern exercises of review in equal protection cases do not conform to that simple, bifurcated pattern. A summary of the early years of the Burger era stated, in terms that continue largely valid: "(1) The Burger Court is reluctant to expand the scope of the new equal protection, although its best established ingredients retain vitality. (2) There is mounting discontent with the rigid two-tier formulations of the Warren Court's equal protection doctrine. (3) The Court is prepared to use the clause as an interventionist tool without resorting to the strict scrutiny language of the new equal protection."[5]

a. *Blocking the expansion of the "new" equal protection.* The Burger Court's "thus far and no further" approach to the "new" equal protection has been especially notable with respect to the most amorphous aspect of Warren Court doctrine: the use of strict scrutiny where "fundamental interests" were affected. Those inclined to read Warren Court decisions most broadly had perceived in equal protection a potential tool on a wide front: there were suggestions that all legislation impinging on "necessities" (welfare, housing, education, etc.) might be subjected to strict scrutiny. Those hopes (or fears) did not materialize, see, e.g., Rodriguez (1973; p. 842 below), perhaps in part because the Warren Court's doctrinal legacy was least well-fixed in those areas. But refusal to expand has not meant that the modern Court has scuttled the new equal protection. Its best established strands survive, as in the area of the fundamental interests in voting and access to the ballot. With respect to classifications, indeed, the post-Warren Court has not only maintained strict scrutiny of racial criteria but has added to the list of classifications triggering at least some heightened scrutiny those based on sex, alienage and illegitimacy.

b. *The unsettled state of modern equal protection doctrine: The discontent with two-tier formulations and the groping for new standards.* Even while the two-tier scheme has often been adhered to in form, there has also been an increasingly noticeable resistance to the sharp difference between deferential "old" and interventionist "new" equal protection. A number of Justices, from all segments of the Court, have sought formulations that would blur the sharp distinctions of the two-tiered approach or that would narrow the gap between strict scrutiny and deferential review. That mounting discontent with the two-tier scheme has sometimes been manifested in claims that a single standard applies to all equal protection cases.[6] But the most elaborate attacks on the

---

For a more sympathetic view, see Karst & Horowitz, "Reitman v. Mulkey: A Telophase of Substantive Equal Protection," 1967 Sup. Ct.Rev. 39, noting that "some classifications although far from irrational [are] nonetheless unconstitutional because they produce inequities that are unacceptable in this generation's idealization of America" and praising the "egalitarian revolution" launched by the Warren Court. Note also the comment by one of the authors of that article, in Karst, "Invidious Discrimination: Justice Douglas and the Return to the 'Natural–Law–Due–Process Formula,' " 16 U.C.L.A.L.Rev. 716 (1969), ac-

knowledging: "The doctrine of invidious discrimination [as used in the new equal protection cases] does not permit an escape from the problems associated with substantive due process."

5. Gunther, "Newer Equal Protection," at 12. (For a modern illustration of the third theme, see Romer v. Evans (1996; p. 737 below).)

6. Justice Stevens has been the most frequent advocate of that position. See, e.g., his concurring opinion in Craig v. Boren (1976; p. 686 below), beginning: "There is only one Equal Protection Clause."

two-tier notion came from Justice Marshall. His frequently stated position was developed most elaborately in his dissent in Rodriguez (1973; p. 842 below): "The Court apparently seeks to establish [that] equal protection cases fall into one of two neat categories which dictate the appropriate standard of review—strict scrutiny or mere rationality. But this Court's [decisions] defy such easy categorization. A principled reading of what this Court has done reveals that it has applied a spectrum of standards in reviewing discrimination allegedly violative of the Equal Protection Clause. This spectrum clearly comprehends variations in the degree of care with which the Court will scrutinize particular classifications, depending, I believe, on the constitutional and societal importance of the interest adversely affected and the recognized invidiousness of the basis upon which the particular classification is drawn." This "sliding scale" approach may describe many of the modern decisions, but it is a formulation that a majority has refused to embrace—at least in form. Yet the modern Court's results indicate at least two significant changes in equal protection law. *First,* invocation of the "old" equal protection formula no longer signals, as it did with the Warren Court, an extreme deference to legislative classifications and a virtually automatic validation of challenged statutes. Instead, several cases, even while voicing the "minimal rationality," "hands-off" standards of the old equal protection, proceeded to find the statute unconstitutional: for the first time in years, old equal protection standards occasionally trigger something more than perfunctory opinions sustaining the law under attack. See, for a modern example, Cleburne (1985; p. 728 below). Occasionally, moreover, reformulations of "mere rationality" standards hint at increased bite to the scrutiny. See sec. 2 below.

Second, in some areas the modern Court has put forth standards for equal protection review that, while clearly more intensive than the deference of the "old" equal protection, are less demanding than the strictness of the "new" equal protection. Sex discrimination is the best established example of this "intermediate" level of review. Thus, in Craig v. Boren (1976; p. 686 below), the majority was able to agree that "classifications by gender must serve *important* governmental objectives and must be *substantially related* to achievement of those objectives." That standard is "intermediate" with respect to both ends and means: where ends must be "compelling" to survive strict scrutiny and need be merely "legitimate" under the "old" mode, "important" objectives are required here; and where means must be "necessary" under the "new" equal protection, and merely "rationally related" under the "old" equal protection, they must be "substantially related" to survive the "intermediate" level of review. More recently, the Court has insisted that gender classifications require an "exceedingly persuasive justification." See United States v. Virginia (1996; p. 704 below). (There have been similar but far more erratic efforts to prescribe something in between the old and the new equal protection with respect to other classifications as well.)

4. *Modern equal protection: Summary and challenge.* Equal protection continues to be in flux. Clearly, it has come a long way from being the "last resort of constitutional arguments"; instead, it is a prolific source of modern constitutional litigation. The Warren Court created a relatively clear, if not always well explained and justified, two-tiered approach. The gropings for new formulations by all wings of the post-Warren Court made for less clear doctrine: two-tiered analyses were not formally abandoned, but the intensity of review under the lower tier was occasionally sharpened, and varieties of intermediate levels of scrutiny surfaced. At the end of the 1970s, the Court seemed to be retreating toward great deference for most varieties of economic and social legislation (e.g., Vance v. Bradley [1979; p. 651 below]), yet with the 1980s and

1990s, there remained ample bases for the widespread charge that the modern Court's exercise of equal protection review has been erratic. Is the modern Court's variety of equal protection simply an accumulation of ad hoc interventions? Is it most intelligible via Justice Marshall's sliding scale analysis? Does it offer promise for evolution toward a different variety of analysis, retaining the well established ingredients of the new equal protection and its strict scrutiny, but raising the level of scrutiny appropriate in the old equal protection sphere? The search for coherence in the volatile, sometimes chaotic field of equal protection law, then, is the challenge—not only for the Court, but also in the examination of the materials that follow. Those materials reveal a doctrinal landscape strewn with not always reconcilable fragments. The doctrinal strands touched on in this introduction are examined at greater length in a variety of settings below. The recurrent questions are: Do the individual strands make sense? Do they provide ingredients for a coherent whole? Or is equal protection doctrine simply the modern Justices' garb for judicially selected value infusions, for Lochnerizing without wearing the occasionally discredited mantle of substantive due process?[7]

5. *Does equal protection protect core values of its own?* Once one gets beyond the hostility to racial discrimination, is it possible to identify a value or a set of values that the constitutional equality principle is designed to implement? This question is a pervasive one in the materials that follow. The terms of the clause extend beyond the race background, and its applications similarly have gone well beyond. Value judgments underlie many of the decisions below, and not only those in the materials (in sec. 4) dealing with the "fundamental rights" strand of the new equal protection. Yet the legitimacy of fundamental values adjudication under the guise of equal protection is not at all clear. To say that persons who are alike must be treated alike does not tell us how to determine whether persons are alike or not with respect to the purposes of the legislation. Thus, in a series of articles in the early 1980s, Professor Westen asserted that equality is in fact an "empty idea." As a matter of formal logic, he insists, a statement such as "people who are alike should be treated alike" is "entirely 'circular.' "[8] Westen suggests that the emphasis on "equality" distorts the analysis of underlying substantive rights and that, because "equality" is an "empty [and confusing] vessel with no substantive moral content of its own," it "should be banished from moral and legal discourse as an explanatory norm." In response, a number of scholars have sprung to the defense of the utility of the equality concept.[9] The typical responses are two-fold. First, it is

7. Modern equal protection developments have spurred an extraordinary flood of commentary. In addition to the materials cited in the preceding footnotes, see, e.g., Ely, Democracy and Distrust (1980); Wilkinson, "The Supreme Court, the Equal Protection Clause, and the Three Faces of Constitutional Equality," 61 Va.L.Rev. 945 (1975); Barrett, "Judicial Supervision of Legislative Classifications—A More Modest Role for Equal Protection?" 1976 B.Y.U.L.Rev. 89; Perry, "Modern Equal Protection: A Conceptualization and Appraisal," 79 Colum.L.Rev. 1023 (1979); O'Fallon, "Adjudication and Contested Concepts: The Case of Equal Protection," 54 N.Y.U.L.Rev. 19 (1979); and Bice, "Standards of Judicial Review under

the Equal Protection and Due Process Clauses," 50 S.Cal.L.Rev. 689 (1977).

8. The major Westen article is "The Empty Idea of Equality," 95 Harv.L.Rev. 537 (1982). See also his elaborations in 91 Yale L.J. 1153 (1982), 81 Mich.L.Rev. 604 (1983), and 83 Colum.L.Rev. 1186 (1983).

9. See, e.g., Greenawalt, "How Empty is the Idea of Equality?" 83 Colum.L.Rev. 1167 (1983); Karst, "Why Equality Matters," 17 Ga.L.Rev. 245 (1983); Chemerinsky, "In Defense of [Equality]," 81 Mich.L.Rev. 575 (1983); and D'Amato, "Is Equality a Totally Empty Idea?" 81 Mich.L.Rev. 600 (1983). Note especially Simon, "Equality as a Comparative Right," 65 B.U.L.Rev. 387 (1985) ("A different conception of equality" than

argued that the equality notion at least creates a strong legal-moral presumption in favor of equal treatment of all persons, departures from which must be justified. Moreover, there is a mounting argument that the inherent principle of equal protection is one that mandates equality of *respect* for individuals. See, e.g., Karst (footnote 9 above): "The Equal Citizenship principle [is] the presumptive right 'to be treated by the organized society as a respected, responsible, and participating member.' "[10]

In thinking about whether there are indeed overarching principles (beyond the historical purpose to ban racial discrimination) inherent in equal protection, consider especially the decision in Romer v. Evans (1996; p. 737 below). In Romer, the Court sustained an on-the-face attack on a Colorado constitutional amendment prohibiting all action at any level of state and local government designed to protect homosexuals. The amendment was headed: "No Protected Status Based on Homosexual, Lesbian, or Bisexual Orientation." The majority found that this amendment imposed "a broad and undifferentiated disability on a single named group" that seemed "inexplicable by anything but animus toward the class that it affects." To the majority, the amendment raised "the inevitable inference that the disadvantage imposed [was] born of animosity toward the class of persons affected." The Court held that a state "cannot so deem a class of persons a stranger to its laws." In pursuing underlying values in equal protection litigation and in examining the Romer case in particular, consider whether the Court's approach (which also invoked the deferential, lower tier of equal protection scrutiny in striking down the amendment) reflected a justifiable principle. What is that principle? Prohibiting the creation of a class of "strangers"? "Outcasts"? "Pariahs"? These questions are pursued further in the consideration of Romer, below.

6.   *A note on organization.* The aim of this chapter is to look at the roots, contents, and implications of equal protection to see where we are, how we got here, and where we may be going. A body of law this volatile and diffuse is difficult to organize: one cannot simultaneously bring to bear all of the relevant perspectives—chronological, functional, variations in modes of review, subgroups of substantive doctrine. In pursuing the multiple strands of equal protection, this chapter will proceed as follows: Sec. 2 examines the means-oriented focus of traditional equal protection; it pursues the ingredients of the requisite congruence or fit between classification and purpose in the context of modern economic and social legislation. Sec. 3 turns to the "suspect classifications" branch of heightened scrutiny. It begins with the historically most justified area of strict scrutiny, racial classifications, and then turns to a number of other classifying criteria that have at times triggered (or arguably should trigger) heightened scrutiny—especially the criteria of gender, sexual orientation, alienage, and illegitimacy. Sec. 4 moves from the "suspect classifications" strand of heightened scrutiny to that turning on the presence of "fundamental interests" allegedly drawn from the equal protection clause

[handwritten margin note: means suspect class fundamentalint-]

Westen's would view equality "as a *comparative* claim to receive a particular treatment just because another person or class receives it. The claim to that treatment is not absolute, but relative to whether others receive it.")

10.   See also Baker, "Neutrality, Process, and Rationality: Flawed Interpretations of Equal Protection," 58 Tex.L.Rev. 1029 (1980) ("Society ought to respect the equality of worth of all its members and ought not to condone the subordination of any people"), and O'Fallon, "Adjudication and Contested Concepts: The Case of Equal Protection," 54 N.Y.U.L.Rev. 19 (1979) ("The guarantee of equal protection of the law is best understood in terms of a legal right to equal concern and respect from the legislature"). See generally Lupu, "Untangling the Strands of the Fourteenth Amendment," 77 Mich.L.Rev. 981 (1979).

itself. That section includes both the developments in the relatively well established areas of equal protection ("fundamental rights" law regarding voting, the criminal process, and interstate migration) as well as those spheres where modern efforts to expand the range of fundamental values derivable from equal protection have proven unsuccessful—efforts primarily pertaining to problems of the poor.

SECTION 2. SCRUTINY OF MEANS IN ECONOMIC REGULATIONS: THE RATIONALITY REQUIREMENT

THE RATIONALITY REQUIREMENT: WHEN ARE CLASSIFICATIONS EXCESSIVELY "UNDERINCLUSIVE" OR "OVERINCLUSIVE"?

Introduction. How does one determine whether a classification is "reasonably related" to the purposes of the legislation? In a sense, this ingredient of the equal protection command is an aspect of the broader constitutional requirement that there must be a "rational" connection between legislative means and legitimate ends—a requirement already foreshadowed earlier, in the discussion of due process. (Recall also the very similar requirement—first elaborated in McCulloch, chap. 2 above—that, under the necessary and proper clause, congressional means must have a rational connection to legislative ends.) The added thrust provided by equal protection for that general requirement of "rational" means focuses on legislative *classifications*: statutes are not all-embrace; legislatures characteristically classify; equal protection demands that there be some "rational" connection between classifications and objectives. A minimal "fit" or "congruence" must exist between the classifying means and the legislative ends. But the traditional, "old" equal protection standard does not demand anything approaching a perfect fit: legislatures must often act on the basis of generalizations; perfect congruence would make legislative action impossible and would demand individualized hearings in every case. The deferential old equal protection, then, leaves considerable flexibility to the legislature.

The Court's oft-stated assertion that there *is* a rationality requirement has not gone unchallenged. For the most articulate modern attack on *any* "rationality" review, see Linde, "Due Process of Lawmaking," 55 Neb.L.Rev. 197 (1976). Linde argues that "the dogma that [the Constitution] requires every law to be a rational means to a legislative end [is] not a rational premise for judicial review [and is] even less plausible as a constitutional command to lawmakers." Others, without mounting so basic a challenge to rationality review, assert that the rationality requirement is "largely inconsequential" as a practical matter. See Perry, "Modern Equal Protection," 79 Colum.L.Rev. 1023 (1979). But Linde concedes that his approach "is likely to remain a heresy"; and Perry concedes that "the rationality requirement is not wholly unimportant."[1] The premise of

---

1. See also Michelman, "Politics and Values, or What's Really Wrong with Rationality Review," 13 Creighton L.Rev. 487 (1979); Posner, Economic Analysis of Law (2d ed. 1977); Bennett, " 'Mere' Rationality in [Constitutional Law]," 67 Calif.L.Rev. 1049 (1979); Bice, "Rationality Analysis in Constitutional Law," 65 Minn.L.Rev. 1 (1980); Baker, "Neutrality, Process, and Rationality: Flawed Interpretations of Equal Protection,"

this section is that the rationality requirement is worth exploring at least because the vast majority of Justices have persisted in articulating it for generations. (For an argument that it is a justifiable requirement as well, see Gunther, "Newer Equal Protection.")

The materials in this section involve economic and social legislation that does not evoke the heightened scrutiny associated with "suspect" or near-"suspect" classifications and "fundamental interests." What restraints on classifications-ends relationships should the Court impose in this area? A frequently quoted formulation of the basic standard came in a 1920 decision: "[T]he classification must be reasonable, not arbitrary, and must rest upon some ground of difference having *a fair and substantial relation* to the object of the legislation, so that all persons similarly circumstanced shall be treated alike." (Emphasis added.) F.S. Royster Guano Co. v. Virginia, 253 U.S. 412 (1920). That somewhat demanding standard coexisted, however, with a more deferential-sounding one, one also often cited. That more deferential formulation of equal protection rationality came in Lindsley v. Natural Carbonic Gas Co., 220 U.S. 61 (1911). It included the statement: "When the classification [is] called in question, if any state of facts reasonably can be conceived that would sustain it, the existence of that state of facts at the time the law was enacted must be assumed." In many later cases, from the 1940s through the 1960s, the Court veered toward the more deferential direction and demanded far less than the "fair and substantial relation" formulation seemed to require—although even during that very deferential era, the Court did not wholly abandon articulation of a rationality requirement. See, e.g., Williamson v. Lee Optical Co. (1955; p. 642 below). During the Warren years, there was only one invalidation on the basis of traditional equal protection rationality criteria [Morey v. Doud (1957)], and Morey has been explicitly overruled [New Orleans v. Dukes (1976); p. 649 below]. Yet the Royster formulation, demanding a "fair and substantial relation" between classification and legislative objective, has once again become a recurrent citation by the modern Court. And, at least sporadically, the modern Court has in fact been somewhat less deferential toward state economic legislation than the Warren Court: several decisions have invalidated state laws even while reciting the traditional equal protection criteria. In short, the modern Court has not formally abandoned the traditional equal protection requirement that legislative means must rationally further legitimate legislative ends. Accordingly, some examination of the rationality criteria and their meaning in theory and practice is justified by more than historical reasons. What, then, *is* signified by the old equal protection's demand for some but not perfect congruence between classifications and objectives?

1. *Classifications and adequate congruence: The Tussman-tenBroek analysis.* A classic discussion of the requisite relationship between classifications and legislative objectives is Tussman & tenBroek, "The Equal Protection of the Laws," 37 Calif.L.Rev. 341 (1949). The article is especially useful in illuminating the meaning of the "overinclusive"-"underinclusive" terminology that recurs frequently in the equal protection materials. The following excerpts thus provide useful background.

"The measure of the reasonableness of a classification is the degree of its success in treating similarly those similarly situated. [W]here are we to look for the test of similarity of situation which determines the reasonableness of a classification? The inescapable answer is that we must look beyond the classifi-

58 Tex.L.Rev. 1029 (1980); and Leedes, "The Rationality Requirement of the Equal Protec-   tion Clause," 42 Ohio St.L.J. 639 (1981).

cation to the purpose of the law. A reasonable classification is one which includes all persons who are similarly situated with respect to the purpose of the [law]. The purpose of a law may be either the elimination of a public 'mischief' or the achievement of some positive public good. To simplify the discussion we shall refer to the purpose of a law in terms of the elimination of mischief, since the same argument holds in either case. We shall speak of the defining character or characteristics of the legislative classification as the trait. We can thus speak of the relation of the classification to the purpose of the law as the relation of the Trait to the Mischief. A problem arises at all because the classification in a law usually does not have as its defining Trait the possession of or involvement with the Mischief at which the law aims. [In the usual problem], we are really dealing with the relation of two classes to each other. The first class consists of all individuals possessing the defining Trait; the second class consists of all individuals possessing, or rather, tainted by, the Mischief at which the law aims. The former is the legislative classification; the latter is the class of those similarly situated with respect to the purpose of the law. We shall refer to these two classes as T and M respectively. Now, since the reasonableness of any class T depends entirely upon its relation to a class M, it is obvious that it is impossible to pass judgment on the reasonableness of a classification without taking into consideration, or identifying, the purpose of the [law].

"There are five possible relationships between the class defined by the Trait and the class defined by the Mischief. These relationships can be indicated by the following diagrams:

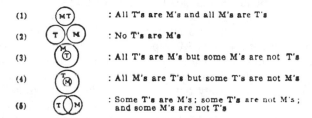

(1) : All T's are M's and all M's are T's

(2) : No T's are M's

(3) : All T's are M's but some M's are not T's

(4) : All M's are T's but some T's are not M's

(5) : Some T's are M's; some T's are not M's; and some M's are not T's

One of these five relationships holds in fact in any case of legislative classification, and we will consider each from the point of view of its 'reasonableness.'

"The first two situations represent respectively the ideal limits of reasonableness and unreasonableness. In the first case, the classification in the law coincides completely with the class of those similarly situated with respect to the purpose of the law. It is perfectly reasonable. In the second case, no member of the class defined in the law is tainted with the mischief at which the law aims. The classification is, therefore, perfectly unreasonable. Classification of the third type may be called 'under-inclusive.' All who are included in the class are tainted with the mischief, but there are others also tainted whom the classification does not include. Since the classification does not include all who are similarly situated with respect to the purpose of the law, there is a prima facie violation of the equal protection requirement of reasonable classification. But the Court has recognized the very real difficulties under which legislatures operate [and] it has refused to strike down indiscriminately all legislation embodying the classificatory inequality here under consideration. In justifying this refusal, the Court has defended under-inclusive classifications on such grounds as: the legislature may attack a general problem in a piecemeal fashion; 'some play must be allowed for the joints of the machine'; '[the] law does all that is needed when it does all that it [can].' The fourth type of classification imposes a burden upon a wider range of individuals than are included in the class of those tainted with the mischief at which the law aims. It can thus be called 'over-inclusive.' [It] is exemplified by the quarantine and the dragnet. The wartime treatment of American citizens of Japanese ancestry is a [striking] instance of the imposition of burdens upon a large class of individuals because some of them were believed to be [disloyal].

"The final situation to be considered is one in which the previously discussed factors of under-inclusiveness and over-inclusiveness are both present. While it may seem paradoxical to assert that a classification can be at once over-inclusive and under-inclusive, many classifications do, in fact, fall into this category, that is, they can be challenged separately on both grounds. For example, in [Hirabayashi v. United States, 320 U.S. 81 (1943)], the classification of 'American citizens of Japanese ancestry' for the purpose of meeting the dangers of sabotage can be challenged both on the grounds that it is under-inclusive, since others—American citizens of German or Italian ancestry—are equally under the strain of divided loyalties, and that it is over-inclusive, since it is not supposed that all American citizens of Japanese ancestry are disloyal. The sustaining of this classification, therefore, requires both the finding of sufficient emergency to justify the imposition of a burden upon a larger class than is believed tainted with the Mischief and the establishment of 'fair reasons' for failure to extend the operation of the law to a wider class of potential saboteurs."[2]

2. *Some preliminary observations on the requirements of congruence.* Consider the congruence demands of the traditional standard as applied in the post-New Deal economic and social regulation cases that follow. To what extent were the classifications involved in the cases "overinclusive" or "underinclusive"? Should they have survived scrutiny under the traditional criteria? Most in fact did survive. Which variety of imperfect classifications, overinclusive or underinclusive ones, most warrant careful scrutiny? Tussman & tenBroek claim there is a stronger prima facie case against overinclusive ones: in an underinclusive classification, they point out, "all who are included in the class are at least tainted by the mischiefs at which the law aims," but overinclusive ones "reach out to the innocent bystander, the hapless victim of circumstance or association." Others (including Justice Jackson in the next case) argue instead that underinclusive classifications present the greater danger of arbitrary government. As Tussman & tenBroek recognized, the Court does not demand perfect congruence; the critical issue in the cases, then, is the degree to which a legislature shall be permitted to generalize or to deal with a problem one step at a time, and thus to fall short of perfect congruence. In most of the cases in this section, the Court deferred widely to legislative discretion. Should the Court have demanded more? Could it have done so without curtailing legislative discretion as to ends? Do value judgments inevitably play a role when courts, in determining whether the rationality standard is met, make

---

2. In 1986, a federal judge vacated Hirabayashi's conviction for failing to register for evacuation to an internment camp, on the ground that, at the original trial, the government had failed to disclose information relevant to the case; but the judge let stand the conviction for curfew violation. 627 F.Supp. 1445 (W.D.Wash.1986). In 1988, Congress implemented the recommendations of the Commission on Wartime Relocation and Internment of Civilians by acknowledging "the fundamental injustice of the evacuation, relocation and internment," and apologizing on behalf of the people of the United States. Reparations were approved, and each living survivor of the internment was to be compensated in an amount approximating $20,000. (For further discussion of the World War II Evacuation and Detention Program, primarily aimed at Japanese–Americans, see the Korematsu case at p. 664 below.)

judgments about what "similarly situated" means and what the "purpose" of the law is?[3]

Railway Express Agency v. New York

336 U.S. 106, 69 S.Ct. 463, 93 L.Ed. 533 (1949).

Justice DOUGLAS delivered the opinion of the Court.

Section 124 of the [New York City Traffic Regulations] provides: "No person shall operate [on] any street an advertising vehicle; provided that nothing herein contained shall prevent the putting of business notices upon business delivery vehicles, so long as such vehicles are engaged in the usual business [of] the owner and not used merely or mainly for advertising.". Appellant is engaged in a nationwide express business. It operates about 1,900 trucks in New York City and sells the space on the exterior sides of these trucks for advertising[, for] the most part unconnected with its own business. It was [convicted]. [The state court] concluded that advertising on [vehicles] constitutes a distraction to vehicle drivers and to pedestrians alike and therefore affects the safety of the public in the use of the streets. We do not sit to weigh evidence on the due process issue in order to determine whether the regulation is sound or appropriate; nor is it our function to pass judgment on its [wisdom].

The question of equal protection of the laws is pressed more strenuously on us. It is pointed out that the regulation draws the line between advertisements of products sold by the owner of the truck and general advertisements. It is argued that unequal treatment on the basis of such a distinction is not justified by the aim and purpose of the regulation. It is said, for example, that one of appellant's trucks carrying the advertisement of a commercial house would not cause any greater distraction of pedestrians and vehicle drivers than if the commercial house carried the same advertisement on its own truck. Yet the regulation allows the latter to do what the former is forbidden from doing. It is therefore contended that the classification which the regulation makes has no relation to the traffic problem since a violation turns not on what kind of advertisements are carried on trucks but on whose trucks they are carried. That, however, is a superficial way of analyzing the problem. [The] local authorities may well have concluded that those who advertise their own wares on their trucks do not present the same traffic problem in view of the nature or extent of the advertising which they use. It would take a degree of omniscience which we lack to say that such is not the case. [We] cannot say that that judgment is not an allowable one. Yet if it is, the classification has relation to the purpose for which it is made and does not contain the kind of discrimination against which [equal protection] affords protection. It is by such practical considerations based on experience rather than by theoretical inconsistencies that the question of equal protection is to be answered. And the fact that New York City sees fit to eliminate from traffic this kind of distraction but does not touch what may be even greater ones in a different category, such as the vivid

---

3. See Bennett, " 'Mere' Rationality in Constitutional Law," 67 Calif.L.Rev. 1049 (1979): "To recognize that rationality is a function of costs, benefits, and alternatives is to recognize that judicial value judgments at some level are unavoidable even when applying [the] most minimal of constitutional standards. [This] means no more than that ascribing irrationality to legislative actions must be a matter of judgment, not science."

displays on Times Square, is immaterial. It is no requirement of equal protection that all evils of the same genus be eradicated or none at [all].

Affirmed. [Justice RUTLEDGE "acquiesced" in the Court's opinion, noting that he was "dubitante" on the equal protection question.]

Justice JACKSON, concurring.

[My] philosophy as to the relative readiness with which we should resort to [the due process and equal protection] clauses is almost diametrically opposed to the philosophy which prevails on this Court. While claims of denial of equal protection are frequently asserted, they are rarely sustained. But the Court frequently uses the due process clause to strike down measures taken by municipalities to deal with activities in their streets and public places which the local authorities consider as creating hazards, annoyances or discomforts to their inhabitants. [The] burden should rest heavily upon one who would persuade us to use the due process clause to strike down a substantive law or ordinance. [Invalidation] of a statute or an ordinance on due process grounds leaves ungoverned and ungovernable conduct which many people find objectionable. Invocation of the equal protection clause, on the other hand, does not disable any governmental body from dealing with the subject at hand. It merely means that the prohibition or regulation must have a broader impact. I regard it as a salutary doctrine that [governments] must exercise their powers so as not to discriminate between their inhabitants except upon some reasonable differentiation fairly related to the object of regulation. This equality is not merely abstract justice. [T]here is no more effective practical guaranty against arbitrary and unreasonable government than to require that the principles of law which officials would impose upon a minority must be imposed generally. Conversely, nothing opens the door to arbitrary action so effectively as to allow those officials to pick and choose only a few to whom they will apply legislation and thus to escape the political retribution that might be visited upon them if larger numbers were [affected].

This case affords an illustration. Even casual observations from the sidewalks of New York will show that an ordinance which would forbid all advertising on vehicles would run into conflict with many interests, including some, if not all, of the great metropolitan newspapers, which use that advertising extensively. Their blandishment of the latest sensations is not less a cause of diverted attention and traffic hazard than the commonplace cigarette advertisement which this truckowner is forbidden to display. But any regulation applicable to all such advertising would require much clearer justification in local conditions to enable its enactment than does some regulation applicable to a few. I do not mention this to criticize the motives of those who enacted this ordinance, but it dramatizes the point that we are much more likely to find arbitrariness in the regulation of the few than of the [many]. In this case, if [New York] should assume that display of any advertising on vehicles tends and intends to distract the attention of persons using the highways and to increase the dangers of its traffic, I should think it fully within its constitutional powers to forbid it all. [Instead, however,] the City seeks to reduce the hazard only by saying that while some may, others may not exhibit such appeals. The same display, for example, advertising cigarettes, which this appellant is forbidden to carry on its trucks, may be carried on the trucks of a cigarette dealer. [The] courts of New York have declared that the sole nature and purpose of the regulation before us is to reduce traffic hazards. There is not even a pretense here that the traffic hazard created by the advertising which is forbidden is in any manner or degree more hazardous than that which is [permitted]. I do not think differences of treatment under law should be approved on classification because of differences unrelated to the legislative purpose. The equal protection clause ceases to assure either equality or protection if it is avoided by any conceivable difference that can be pointed out between those bound and those left free. This Court has often announced the principle that the differentiation must have an appropriate relation to the object of the [legislation].

The question in my mind comes to this. Where individuals contribute to an evil or danger in the same way and to the same degree, may those who do so for hire be prohibited, while those who do so for their own commercial ends but not for hire be allowed to continue? I think the answer has to be that the hireling may be put in a class by himself and may be dealt with differently than those who act on their own. But this is not merely because such a discrimination will enable the lawmaker to diminish the evil. That might be done by many classifications, which I should think wholly unsustainable. It is rather because there is a real difference between doing in self-interest and doing for hire, so that it is one thing to tolerate action from those who act on their own and it is another thing to permit the same action to be promoted for a price. [It] is not difficult to see that, in a day of extravagant advertising[, the] rental of truck space could become an obnoxious enterprise. [In] view of the control I would concede to cities to protect citizens in quiet and orderly use for their proper purposes of the highways and public places, I think the judgment below must be affirmed.

THE WARREN COURT'S APPROACH IN OPERATION

Some introductory questions. In the cases that follow, the Court rejected equal protection challenges to statutes charged with being "underinclusive" protections of a favored group. Were these situations in which Justice Jackson's Railway Express concern should have been heeded? Should the Court have insisted that the regulations "must have a broader impact," to safeguard against arbitrariness? See Klarman, "An Interpretive History of Modern Equal Protection," 70 Mich.L.Rev. 213, 250 (1991). Should the Court have used less imaginativeness to think of conceivable rationales that *might* have influenced a hypothetical legislature? Should it have tested the fit between means and ends on the basis of actual rather than conceivable purposes, and on the basis of demonstrated rather than hypothesized contributions of classifications to purposes?[1]

1. In one sense, the cases in this section are atypical: the Court *did* write an opinion in each of them. In most cases involving economic regulation during the Warren era, by contrast, the challenges were rejected summarily. The Vinson Court of the late 1940s had been as deferential as the Warren Court of the 1950s and 1960s. See, in addition to Railway Express, Daniel v. Family Security Life Insurance Co., 336 U.S. 220 (1949), barring life insurance agencies from operating undertaking businesses and undertakers from serving as life insurance agents, and Kotch v. Board of River Port Pilot Commissioners, 330 U.S. 552 (1947), attacking the administration of Louisiana's pilotage laws on the ground that only relatives and friends of incumbents were granted state certificates. Justice Black's majority opinion in this 5-4 decision relied on the "entirely unique" nature of pilotage "in the light of its history in Louisiana." Justice Rutledge's dissent argued that "[blood was] the crux of selection" and that a standard of "race or consanguinity" was impermissible. See also Goesaert v. Cleary (1948; p. 683 below), a divided Court's rejection of a sex discrimination challenge to a bartender licensing scheme.

1. *Lee Optical.* In WILLIAMSON v. LEE OPTICAL CO., 348 U.S. 483 (1955) (p. 481 above), the challenge to Oklahoma's scheme for the regulation of opticians rested not only on due process but also on equal protection. But the Court, at the height of the deferential stance toward business regulation, rejected the equal protection claim even more summarily than it did the due process one. Justice DOUGLAS stated for a unanimous Court: "[T]he District Court held that it violated [equal protection to] subject opticians to this regulatory system and to exempt [all] sellers of ready-to-wear glasses. The problem of legislative classification is a perennial one, admitting of no doctrinaire definition. Evils in the same field may be of different dimensions and proportions, requiring different remedies. Or so the legislature may think. Or the reform may take one step at a time, addressing itself to the phase of the problem which seems most acute to the legislative mind. The legislature may select one phase of one field and apply a remedy there, neglecting the others. The prohibition of [equal protection] goes no further than invidious discrimination. We cannot say that that point has been reached here. For all this record shows, the ready-to-wear branch of this business may not loom large in Oklahoma or may present problems of regulation distinct from the other branch." Was Justice Douglas's stance even more deferential than the usual rationality standards purportedly governing "old" equal protection scrutiny? Would not adherence to his "one step at a time" approach assure validation of virtually all departures from congruence in the business regulation area?

2. *McGowan and McDonald: The Warren Court's deferential approach at its extreme.* Judicial unwillingness to put any teeth into "old" equal protection standards in the scrutiny of business regulations may have reached its most extreme form in two opinions written by Chief Justice Warren in the 1960s. Do these cases—even more than Lee Optical—reduce scrutiny under the old equal protection to "minimal scrutiny in theory and virtually none in fact"?

a. *McGowan.* In a group of cases in 1961, state Sunday closing laws were sustained against challenges based not only on the religion clauses of the First Amendment but also on equal protection. The Court rejected the latter attack by applying traditional, permissive standards. In McGOWAN v. MARYLAND, 366 U.S. 420 (1961), Chief Justice WARREN spoke for a unanimous Court in rejecting the claim that the exemptions of certain businesses from the Maryland Sunday closing law violated equal protection. One of the provisions, for example, banned the Sunday "sale of all merchandise except the retail sale of tobacco products, confectioneries, milk, bread, fruits, gasoline, greases, drugs and medicines, and newspapers and periodicals." The Chief Justice stated: "The constitutional safeguard is offended only if the classification rests on grounds wholly irrelevant to the achievement of the State's objective. State legislatures are presumed to have acted within their constitutional power despite the fact that, in practice, their laws result in some inequality. A statutory discrimination will not be set aside if any state of facts reasonably may be conceived to justify it. It would seem that a legislature could reasonably find that the Sunday sale of the exempted commodities was necessary either for the health of the populace or for the enhancement of the recreational atmosphere of the day."

b. *McDonald.* Perhaps the most extremely deferential version of traditional equal protection criteria on the Warren Court (and one of the most graphic statements of the sharp difference between the strict scrutiny of the "new" equal protection and the leniency of the "old") came in McDONALD v. BOARD OF ELECTION COMMISSIONERS, 394 U.S. 802 (1969). That was a claim by qualified Cook County, Illinois, voters imprisoned in a county jail while awaiting trial that the state could not deny them absentee ballots when they were provided to other classes of persons—e.g., the physically disabled and those absent from their county of residence for any reason. Chief Justice WARREN's opinion for a unanimous Court first disposed of the claim that this was a case for the Warren Court's new equal protection scrutiny because the "fundamental interest" in voting was involved. Here, the Chief Justice replied, only a right to an absentee ballot, not an impact on "the fundamental right to vote," was at issue; conceivably, there were other opportunities for the challengers to vote. Accordingly, the lower level of the two-tier approach was invoked. The Chief Justice stated the "basic guidelines" governing the "more traditional standards for evaluating" equal protection claims as follows: "The distinctions drawn by a challenged statute must bear some rational relationship to a legitimate state end and will be set aside as violative of [equal protection] only if based on reasons totally unrelated to the pursuit of that goal. Legislatures are presumed to have acted constitutionally even if source materials normally resorted to for ascertaining their grounds for action are otherwise silent, and their statutory classifications will be set aside only if no grounds can be conceived to justify them. With this much discretion, a legislature traditionally has been allowed to take reform 'one step at a time' [Lee Optical]; and a legislature need not run the risk of losing an entire remedial scheme simply because it failed, through inadvertence or otherwise, to cover every evil that might conceivably have been attacked."[2]

3. *The "one step at a time" justification.* Does even a commitment to a deferential stance justify leaning over backwards to quite the degree manifested by Chief Justice Warren's McDonald approach? (a) Need judicial hypothesizing about the requisite relationship go so far as to say that invalidation will result "only if no grounds can be conceived to justify" classifications? (b) Is the "one step at a time" rationale ultimately subversive of *any* real judicial scrutiny under "old" equal protection standards? Some deference to legislative realities is appropriate: legislators may want to experiment, or to respond to immediate needs or political pressures. But judicial blessing of every effort at piecemeal legislation would block all challenges based on underinclusiveness. What limits can and should the Court impose on justifying laws via the "one step at a time" ground? For a valiant effort to articulate curbs on the "one step at a time" rationale, see Note, "Reforming the One Step at a Time Justification in Equal Protection Cases," 90 Yale L.J. 1777 (1981).

POSSIBILITIES OF GREATER SCRUTINY WITHIN THE RATIONALITY FRAMEWORK?

Introduction. As the preceding cases illustrate, at the end of the 1960s the avowed deference of the "old" equal protection was greater than ever. Before turning to the post-Warren Courts' execution of rationality review, three theories that offer potential bases for somewhat greater scrutiny within the framework of rationality standards warrant attention. The first draws on structural considerations pertaining to the Constitution and to representative

2. Chief Justice Warren's justification for the law emphasized the fact that this was "remedial legislation," the result of "a consistent and laudable state policy of adding, over a 50-year period, groups to the absentee coverage as their existence comes to the attention of the legislature." That "Illinois has not gone still further, as perhaps it might," was justified by the "one step at a time" rationale. Can the "remedial" purpose of legislation justify deferential scrutiny even in the context of suspect classifications or fundamental interests? Cf. Katzenbach v. Morgan (1966; p. 998 below.)

government: it suggests heightened judicial concern for minorities with an inadequate say in the governmental process—including, arguably, minorities not entitled to invoke strict scrutiny under the suspect classifications branch of the "new" equal protection. The second theory emphasizes the Constitution's alleged roots in civic republicanism and associated notions of civic virtue and argues that it is impermissible to award opportunities to one group rather than another simply on the basis of raw political power exercising "naked preferences," so that legislation must be justified by public values rather than merely as compromises among private interests. The third position argues that, wherever the rationality standard of the "old" equal protection is appropriate, the Court should engage in more serious, less deferential review in order to assure that the legislative means *genuinely* promote *articulated* governmental purposes.

1. *"Selective intervention" on behalf of minorities (including economic minorities?): The relevance of the Carolene Products footnote.* Justice Douglas, the author of the very deferential opinion in Lee Optical, voted to invalidate several regulatory laws during the three decades beginning with the 1940s. (Recall, e.g., Kotch and Goesaert, above.) Consider the explanation of Justice Douglas's move "from abdication to selective intervention" offered in Karst, "Invidious Discrimination: Justice Douglas and the Return of the 'Natural–Law–Due–Process Formula,'" 16 UCLA L.Rev. 716 (1969). Karst noted that in each case the state was perpetuating "economic advantages for a favored group, at the expense of those who claimed to be relatively disadvantaged. The appeal of such an argument to a Justice with strong egalitarian views is great, great enough in these cases to overcome the inclination to keep the judiciary aloof from decisions about economic regulation." But what about Justice Douglas's opinion in Lee Optical? That, Karst suggests, is distinguishable because there "the losers in the legislature were not permanently disadvantaged minorities. The opticians might well have anticipated new legislative alliances" [though, he concedes in a footnote, "the opticians are still looking for such an alliance"]. In short, "consciously or not," the Douglas record accorded with "a principle of activism in the cause of economic opportunity"—a principle which is "the equal protection analogue of the double standard of judicial review under the due process clauses, enunciated in Justice Stone's footnote 4 [in the Carolene Products case], which made the legitimacy of judicial protection of the losers in the legislative process turn on the losers' long-term chances of becoming winners."

The Carolene Products footnote referred to by Karst (printed at p. 484 above) forms the starting point for most modern structural arguments urging special judicial solicitude for minorities. The third paragraph of that footnote, the "protecting losing minorities" aspect, is of special relevance to equal protection analysis. Recall that Justice Stone suggested a greater basis for judicial scrutiny where there might be "prejudice against discrete and insular minorities"—prejudice which "tends seriously to curtail the operation of those political processes ordinarily to be relied upon to protect minorities." That consideration clearly underlies some of the expansions of strict scrutiny for suspect classifications, considered in sec. 3 below. But can that rationale be applied as well to losing minorities that are not identified by "suspect" criteria—including losing *economic* minorities? Can economic minorities be protected without a return to the interventionism of the Lochner era?[1] The

---

1. Note Karst's comment: "[Perhaps] activism offers no particular risk to a judiciary's independence unless it is directed at the wrong substantive ends." Compare the critical comments by Justice Rehnquist on the "minorities" aspect of the Carolene Products

major modern effort to articulate a theory of judicial review deriving protection of minorities from a "process" rationale akin to the Carolene Products footnote is Ely's 1980 book, Democracy and Distrust. Ely argued, inter alia, for heightened scrutiny in the interest of protecting minorities unable to participate fully in the political process. His "representation-reinforcing," minority-protecting theory emphasizes that "constitutional law appropriately exists for those situations where representative government cannot be trusted." Although Ely does not emphasize economic minorities as beneficiaries of his theory, can it be argued that, by analogy to his approach, the perennially losing opticians in Oklahoma should have received more careful Court scrutiny of their complaint than Lee Optical afforded?

2. *Civic republicanism: Equal protection as a safeguard against "naked preferences."* Consider an alternative view put forth in Sunstein, "Naked Preferences and the Constitution," 84 Colum.L.Rev. 1689 (1984).[2] Sunstein's analysis departs from the process-oriented approach of Ely and argues for substantive restraints on legislation. In his effort to justify a "prohibition of naked preferences," he draws on the asserted tradition of civic republicanism for the notion that governmental action must respond to something other than private interest pressures. Claiming to rely on "the original Madisonian understanding," he insists that the task of legislators "is not to respond to private pressure but instead to select [public] values through deliberation and debate." Accordingly, government action can only be justified on the basis of "some public value" rather than the mere "raw exercise of political power." (He recognizes that this vision is "in considerable tension" with another prominent view of how government does and should operate—i.e., the theory of pluralism and interest-group politics.) Applying his approach to equal protection, he argues: "Although the rationality test is highly deferential, its function is to ensure that classifications rest on something other than a naked preference for one person or group over another. Thus, [in Lee Optical, the] Court upheld deferential treatment of optometrists and opticians on the ground not that [equal protection] tolerated an unprincipled distribution of wealth to one rather than to the other—though there is a plausible argument that such a naked preference was indeed taking place—but that the deferential treatment was a means of protecting consumers. The Court has made clear in rationality cases that the government must be able to invoke some public value that the classification at issue can be said to serve[, thereby] demonstrating that the function of rationality review is to enforce [a] version of the prohibition of

footnote, in objecting to the elevation of alienage to the category of "suspect classifications" triggering strict scrutiny. In his dissent in In re Griffiths (1973; p. 721 below), he stated: "The mere recitation of the words 'insular and discrete minority' is hardly a *constitutional* reason for prohibiting state legislative classifications such as are involved here, and is not necessarily consistent with the theory propounded in that footnote. The approach taken in [these cases] appears to be that whenever the Court feels that a societal group is 'discrete and insular,' it has the constitutional mandate to prohibit legislation that somehow treats the group differently from some other group. Our society [is], to say the least, diverse. It would hardly take

extraordinary ingenuity for a lawyer to find 'insular and discrete' minorities at every turn in the road. Yet, unless the Court can precisely define and constitutionally justify both the terms and analysis it uses, these decisions today stand for the proposition that the Court can choose a 'minority' it 'feels' deserves 'solicitude' and thereafter prohibit the States from classifying that 'minority' differently from the 'majority.' I cannot find [any] constitutional authority for such a 'ward of the Court' approach to equal protection."

2. See also Sunstein, "Public Values, Private Interests, and the Equal Protection Clause," 1982 Sup.Ct.Rev. 127, and Sunstein, "Interest Groups in American Public Law," 38 Stan.L.Rev. 29 (1985).

naked preferences." Can Sunstein's approach be implemented without a return to a variety of ends scrutiny akin to that of the Lochner era? Is his reading of Lee Optical persuasive? Does the civic republicanism position rest on a plausible understanding of American politics, or would it encourage an excessive intrusion of judicial notions of desirable policy into political reality? Compare Posner, "[The] Constitutionality of Preferential Treatment of Racial Minorities," 1974 Sup.Ct.Rev. 1: "The Court's expressed view [is] that the political process is one of honestly attempting to promote efficiency or justice, or some other equally general conception of the public good. [But many] public policies are better explained as the outcome of the pure power struggle—clothed in a rhetoric of public interest that is a mere figleaf—among narrow interest or pressure groups. [The] real 'justification' for most legislation is simply that it is a product of the constitutionally created political process of our society." Cf. Michelman, "Politics and Values, or What's Really Wrong With Rationality Review?," 13 Creighton L.Rev. 487 (1979).

3. *Rationality review "with bite": The "newer equal protection" argument.* A quite different approach is the argument for somewhat intensified scrutiny of means in economic and social regulations set forth in Gunther, "Newer Equal Protection," 86 Harv.L.Rev. 1 (1972). That argument for a "new bite for the old equal protection" suggests that more serious scrutiny under the "mere rationality" standard could be achieved by viewing equal protection "as a means-focused, relatively narrow, preferred ground of decision in a broad range of cases." It would have the Court "less willing to supply justifying rationales by exercising its imagination. It would have the Court assess the means in terms of legislative purposes that have substantial basis in actuality, not merely in conjecture. Moreover, it would have the Justices gauge the reasonableness of questionable means on the basis of materials that are offered to the Court, rather than resorting to rationalizations created by perfunctory judicial hypothesizing." (The "newer equal protection" model was prompted by an unusual phenomenon that first emerged during the 1971 Term: in seven cases during that Term, the Burger Court, in sharp contrast to the Warren Court's pattern, found substantial bases for constitutional challenges even though the traditional, deferential equal protection criteria were recited. See Gunther, "Commentary," 71 Chi.-Kent L. Rev. 813 (1996).[3])

The "newer equal protection" model was not offered to replace strict scrutiny; rather, this means-focused model would impose its constraints on legislative action falling within the old, deferential equal protection tier of scrutiny. (This point warrants emphasis, for it is occasionally misunderstood by

---

3. For a review of some efforts by lower courts to apply the "newer equal protection" model, see, e.g., Comment, " 'Newer' Equal Protection: The Impact of the Means–Focused Model," 23 Buffalo L.Rev. 665 (1974). For a skeptical view of the possibilities of means-oriented rationality review, see, e.g., Note, "Legislative Purpose, Rationality, and Equal Protection," 82 Yale L.J. 123 (1972). See also Justice Rehnquist's dissent in Trimble v. Gordon (1977; p. 726 below), launching an extensive attack on the Court's modern equal protection jurisprudence. He called the Court's "means" scrutiny a "self-imposed" task "stemming not from the Equal Protection Clause but from the Court's insistence on reading so much into it." The basic "purpose" of all legislation was simply "to make the language [in the enacted provision] a part of the law." The Court's approach, he insisted, "expands the normal reading of the word ['purpose'] into something more like motive." In determining how much "imperfection between means and ends is permissible," the Court deemed itself required to "throw into the judicial hopper the whole range of factors which were first thrown into the legislative hopper." That approach rested on a "fundamental flaw": "there is absolutely nothing to be inferred from the fact that we hold judicial commissions that would enable us to answer [better] than the legislators."

judges and commentators (as well as students).) The "newer equal protection" is *not* the same as the "intermediate" scrutiny developed in the modern cases for some quasi-suspect classifications such as gender. The "newer equal protection" theory does not take issue with the heightened scrutiny tiers of "strict" and "intermediate" review. Instead, it is solely addressed to the appropriate intensity of review to be exercised when the lowest tier, that of rationality review, is deemed appropriate. It is in the "mere rationality" cases that the Warren Court virtually abandoned effective scrutiny of any sort. What the "newer equal protection" model asks is that some teeth be put into that lowest level of scrutiny, that it be applied "with bite," focusing on means without second-guessing legislative ends. (Evaluating the importance of the ends is characteristic of all higher levels of scrutiny.) In short, "newer equal protection" seeks to raise slightly the lowest tier of review under the two-or three-tier models; but it does *not* seek to raise the "mere rationality" level appropriate for run-of-the-mill economic regulation cases all the way up to the level of "intermediate" or of "strict" scrutiny. This model was defended not only on the ground that it would take seriously the rationality standard the Court has traditionally stated, but also because it could "improve the quality of the political process—without second-guessing the substantive validity of its results—by encouraging a fuller airing in the political arena of the grounds for legislative action." It argued, for example, that the Court could demand more of the state than it required in Lee Optical. The model is clearly not problem-free. E.g., can it be applied without unduly scrutinizing legislative motivations and the actualities of legislative processes? Would it truly be beneficial to the legislative process? Would it truly encourage "a fuller airing in the political arena of the grounds for legislative action," or would it simply shift the burden of hypothesizing legislative rationales from the Court to counsel defending the challenged legislation? And, although the model purports to be concerned solely with means rather than ends, can it avoid undue intrusion into legislative value choices?

Consider, in examining the materials that follow, the extent to which the modern Court's equal protection decisions in the economic regulation area move in the direction of the Ely "representation-reinforcing," the Sunstein anti-"naked preferences," or the Gunther "newer equal protection" model. With respect to "newer equal protection," a large number of Justices on the Burger Court have indeed spoken of testing legislation by articulated rather than hypothesized purposes, and have scrutinized the empiric underpinnings of the means-ends relationships more closely than the Warren Court had.[4] But

4. For a review of some examples of the modern Court's sporadic emphasis on articulated rather than hypothesized purposes, see Justice Brennan's comment in dissenting in Schlesinger v. Ballard, 419 U.S. 498 (1975) (p. 718 below): "While we have in the past exercised our imaginations to conceive of possible rational justifications for statutory classifications, see [McGowan], we have recently declined to manufacture justifications in order to save an apparently invalid statutory classification. Moreover, we have analyzed asserted governmental interests to determine whether they were in fact the legislative purpose of a statutory classification, Eisenstadt v. Baird [see also Weinberger v. Wiesenfeld (1975; p. 717 below)]; and we have limited our inquiry to the legislature's stated purposes when these purposes are clearly set out in the statute or its legislative history. Johnson v. Robison, 415 U.S. 361 (1974). Never, to my knowledge, have we endeavored to sustain a statute upon a supposition about the legislature's purpose in enacting it when the asserted justification can be shown conclusively *not* to have underlain the classification in any way." See also the formulation in Justice Powell's opinion for the Court in McGinnis v. Royster, 410 U.S. 263 (1973), asking whether the challenged distinction furthered "some legitimate, *articulated* state purpose." Note, too, the extensive debates about the relevance of the legislature's "actu-

resort to techniques akin to ingredients of the "newer equal protection" has been sporadic rather than consistent; and references to articulated purposes and actual contribution of means to ends are in many cases explainable by the fact that the issues arose in situations exerting special pressures toward some heightened scrutiny (e.g., sex discrimination), instead of the "run of the mill" context of economic regulations. Some of the modern decisions that follow involve exercises of heightened scrutiny despite avowals of deferential, rationality standards. Others, by contrast, involve review of economic regulations about as deferential as was common in the Warren era. Although, beginning in the mid–1970s, the Court tended to swerve toward a deferential direction, there are enough later opinions taking judicial scrutiny somewhat more seriously, thus suggesting that the actual content of "rationality" review under equal protection continues in flux.

RATIONALITY REVIEW IN THE POST–WARREN ERA

1. *The early 1970s.* In its early years, the Burger Court repeatedly invalidated laws on equal protection grounds without asserting grounds for heightened scrutiny. Thus, the 7-2 decision in U.S. DEPT. OF AGRICULTURE v. MORENO, 413 U.S. 528 (1973), purporting to apply a rationality standard, struck down a provision of the federal food stamp program for assistance to "households"—households limited to groups of *related* persons. The exclusion of "unrelated persons" was found to be "irrational": it was not only "imprecise"; it was also "wholly without any rational basis." The law recited the congressional purpose as being to "raise levels of nutrition among low-income households" and to increase consumption of food so as to "strengthen our agricultural economy." Justice BRENNAN's majority opinion stated that the statutory exclusion was "clearly irrelevant" to these purposes. He went on to say that the limited legislative history indicated "that the amendment was intended to prevent so-called 'hippies' and 'hippie communes' from participating in the food stamp program." This purpose did not justify the classification, in his view: "For if the constitutional conception of 'equal protection of the laws' means anything, it must at the very least mean that a bare congressional desire to harm a politically unpopular group cannot constitute a *legitimate* governmental interest." [Compare Romer v. Evans (1996; p. 737 below).] In later cases, however, the Court distinguished Moreno and rejected equal protection challenges to the food stamp program. In Lyng v. Castillo, 477 U.S. 635 (1986), the majority found that there was a "rational basis" for a provision that treated "parents, children, and siblings who live together" more favorably than "distant relatives, or groups of unrelated persons, who lived together." And in Lyng v. International Union, Automobile Workers, 485 U.S. 360 (1988), the Court rejected an equal protection attack on a provision withholding benefits from those whose eligibility was a consequence of being on strike. The majority opinion found that the exclusion of strikers was "rationally related to the legitimate governmental objective of avoiding undue favoritism to one side or the other in private labor disputes." Justice Marshall's dissent, joined by Justices Brennan and Blackmun, argued that the anti-striker animus here was

al purpose" in a number of cases of the 1980s—e.g. Fritz, p. 653 below, and Schweiker, p. 657 below. Typically, Justice Brennan contended that actual legislative purpose, not counsel's arguments or judicial hypothesizing, should be determinative, while Justice Rehnquist continued to insist on a much more deferential stance, akin to that of Chief Justice Warren in the McDonald case.

analogous to the anti-hippie animus in Moreno. But in Jimenez v. Weinberger, 417 U.S. 628 (1974), another federal welfare program was struck down in an 8-1 ruling which scrutinized the law a good deal more carefully than the deferential stance dictated by Dandridge v. Williams (1970; p. 912 below) for welfare programs. The majority in Jimenez struck down the provision of the Social Security Act denying disability benefits to some but not all illegitimate children born after the onset of their wage-earner parent's disability. [Note that in both cases grounds for heightened scrutiny arguably lurked in the background. On Moreno, compare Moore v. East Cleveland (1977; p. 584 above); on Jimenez, see sec. 3 below, discussing the heightened scrutiny that *has* been applied to some illegitimacy classifications.]

2. *The late 1970s.* In the late 1970s, the Burger Court seemed most often to retreat to a deferential variety of rationality review akin to that of the Warren era. NEW ORLEANS v. DUKES, 427 U.S. 297 (1976), was a harbinger of that trend. That per curiam opinion overruled Morey v. Doud, 354 U.S. 457 (1957), the only decision between the late 1930s and the 1970s in which the Court had struck down an economic regulation on equal protection grounds.[1] The Court, stating that Morey had "so far depart[ed] from proper equal protection analysis in cases of exclusively economic regulation that it should be, and it is, overruled," sustained a 1972 New Orleans provision which exempted pushcart food vendors who had "continually operated the same business for eight years prior to January 1, 1972" from a prohibition against such vendors in the French Quarter (Vieux Carré). The ordinance was challenged by a vendor barred from continuing his business because he had been in business in the French Quarter for only two years at the time the provision was adopted. The Court emphasized that the grandfather clause was "solely an economic regulation aimed at enhancing the vital role of the French Quarter's tourist-oriented charm in the economy of New Orleans." The Court noted that "rational distinctions [in economic regulations] may be made with substantially less than mathematical exactitude." Pointing to the "analogous situation" in Ferguson v. Skrupa (1963; p. 480 above), the Court rejected the lower court's holding that the grandfather provision "failed even the rationality test" and found instead that "the city's classification rationally furthers the purpose which [the] city had identified as its objective in enacting the provisions, that is, '[preserving] the appearance and custom valued by the Quarter's residents and attractive to tourists.'"

On the same day as Dukes, the Court, in another per curiam opinion, once again applied a very deferential stance in rejecting an equal protection challenge in MASSACHUSETTS BD. OF RETIREMENT v. MURGIA, 427 U.S. 307 (1976). That case sustained a Massachusetts law providing that a uniformed State police officer "shall be retired [upon] his attaining age fifty." After rejecting an argument that age should be viewed as a suspect classification triggering heightened scrutiny (as noted at p. 734 below), the majority applied the "relatively relaxed" rational basis standard: "Perfection in making the necessary classifications is neither possible nor necessary. Such action by a legislature is presumed to be valid. In this case, the [law] clearly meets the requirements of [equal protection], for the State's classification rationally

---

1. In Morey, the Court invalidated an exemption by name of a company from a general regulatory scheme. The Illinois law had imposed financial responsibility requirements on businesses issuing money orders but had explicitly exempted the American Express Company and several others. The 6-3 decision held the exemption unconstitutional. Justice Burton's majority opinion emphasized that the exemption created "a closed class," and that this grant of an economic advantage to a named company bore "no reasonable relation" to the purposes of the law.

furthers the purpose identified by the State: Through mandatory retirement at age 50, the legislature seeks to protect the public by assuring physical preparedness of its uniformed police. Since physical ability generally declines with age, mandatory retirement at 50 serves to remove from police service those whose fitness for uniformed work presumptively has diminished with age. This clearly is rationally related to the State's objective. [That] the State chooses not to determine fitness more precisely through individualized testing after age 50 is not to say that the objective of assuring physical fitness is not rationally furthered by a maximum age limitation. It is only to say [that] the State perhaps has not chosen the best means to accomplish this purpose. But where rationality is the test, a State 'does not violate [equal protection] merely because the classifications made by its laws are imperfect.' " Justice MAR-SHALL, the sole dissenter, launched one of his recurrent attacks on the "rigid two-tier model" of equal protection scrutiny. He argued that the strict scrutiny and mere rationality tiers "simply do not describe the inquiry the Court has undertaken—or should undertake—in equal protection cases. Rather, the inquiry has been much more sophisticated and the Court should admit as much. It has focused upon the character of the classification in question, the relative importance to individuals in the class discriminated against of the governmental benefits that they do not receive, and the state interests asserted in support of the classification." He added: "[However] understandable the Court's hesitancy to invoke strict scrutiny, all remaining legislation should not drop into the bottom tier, and be measured by the mere rationality test." Reiterating his own "flexible," sliding scale, multi-variable equal protection approach, Justice Marshall argued that applying his three critical factors showed that the mandatory retirement law could not stand. He argued moreover, that terminating all officers at 50 seemed "the height of irrationality," especially because the state was already individually testing its police officers for physical fitness.

Although Murgia appeared to some to be a run-of-the-mill case, its highly deferential but bland per curiam opinion in fact masked sharp internal divisions on the Court about the proper intensity of equal protection rationality review. The internal controversy that forms the background of Murgia has been documented by Professor Mark Tushnet in a book review, "Justice Lewis F. Powell and the Jurisprudence of Centrism," 93 Mich.L.Rev. 1854, 1856–1862 (1995). (The documents are preserved in the Thurgood Marshall Papers at the Library of Congress, papers which Tushnet has carefully and productively mined.) Prior to Murgia, the Court had tried several times to reach a consensus on the proper degree of intensity in equal protection review. Each effort proved unsuccessful; the background of Murgia graphically reveals the divisions on the Court. Three-and-a-half years after Gunther's "Newer Equal Protection" article appeared, Justice Brennan produced a draft in Murgia to "reinterpret" the Court's modern rationality cases by articulating a new, more flexible standard. Brennan's standard required that a statutory classification had to rest "upon some ground of difference having a fair and substantial relation to the object of the legislation" (the Royster Guano standard), and also required that the law be sufficiently related to the "state's announced objective." Justice Rehnquist immediately took strong exception to Justice Brennan's approach, insisting that a proper standard should "virtually foreclose judicial invalidation except in the rare, rare case where the legislature has all but run amok." After Justice Brennan circulated his correspondence with Justice Rehnquist to the other Justices, progress on the case came to a halt. By the beginning of April 1976, Tushnet reports, "it seemed that Brennan's opinion might not get a single additional vote." At this point, Justice Powell circulated a draft opinion. In a portion of his draft, Powell cited the Gunther article and endorsed Brennan's view that the Court's application of rationality review had indeed become more flexible. He also cautioned against "imagin[ing] policy where none has been indicated by the legislature." Justice Brennan adopted the Powell opinion, but still could not gain a majority. He then turned over the task of fashioning a majority opinion to Powell, who revised his draft in order to "attain as much unanimity as possible on a general formulation of the rational basis equal protection test." But Justice Rehnquist continued to reject what was now the Powell–Brennan position, and objected that Powell's draft was "really a very significant departure" from prior cases. In a long letter to Powell of May 25, 1976, Justice Rehnquist stated that he had "the most serious reservations about that portion of [Powell's] memorandum which seems to contemplate the bodily assumption into the Equal Protection Clause of Professor Gunther's article." That article, Rehnquist said, "seems to me to be in the area of political science, rather than of constitutional law." Even though Powell continued to redraft his opinion and Rehnquist made an effort at "some accommodating," it soon became clear that "the Court was hopelessly divided on equal protection theory." The per curiam was apparently from Powell's hand. He described his final draft as "about as blandly written as one can write" and designed to leave each of the Justices "free to 'fight again another day.'" Tushnet believes that the Court's "contentious deliberations" in Murgia "helped shape Powell's jurisprudence." When he circulated his final draft, Powell told his colleagues that "my zeal for writing has been so thoroughly dampened by this spring's experience, that it may be sometime before I venture forth again." (For the next few years, he regularly referred to the "struggle" in Murgia.) Ultimately, Tushnet concludes, "Brennan's liberalism [seemed] to Powell more reasonable than Rehnquist's conservatism," and in later cases, he showed "a growing willingness to set aside legislative judgments." Tushnet believes that the Murgia experience showed Powell that, while "it might be relatively easy for an individual Justice like himself to maintain a centrist jurisprudence," it was much more difficult for "the Court as an institution to do so—reasonableness could not always be equated with centrism for the Court as a whole." This background of Murgia may help explain the quite erratic and often divided approaches to rationality review in the ensuing years.

Three years after Murgia, Vance v. Bradley, 440 U.S. 93 (1979), seemed to indicate that the Court had firmly embraced very deferential review. The case rejected an equal protection attack on a federal law requiring Foreign Service personnel to retire at age 60. Although Murgia had foreshadowed the decision, Justice White's majority opinion was noteworthy for illustrating how very little factual data the government needed to provide in order to defend a legislative classification under the rationality standard. He conceded that the classification was "to some extent both under-and over-inclusive," but held that "perfection is by no means required. [In] an equal protection case of this type, [those] challenging the legislative judgment must convince the court that the legislative facts on which the classification is apparently based could not reasonably be conceived to be true by the governmental decisionmaker." Yet only a few weeks after Vance, in NEW YORK CITY TRANSIT AUTH. v. BEAZER, 440 U.S. 568 (1979), statements by several of the Justices indicated that the members of the Burger Court were not so clearly committed after all to as deferential a stance as Justice White's majority opinion in Vance had suggested. Indeed, Justice White himself, the author of Vance, dissented in Beazer. Justice STEVENS's majority opinion in Beazer upheld the exclusion of all methadone users from any Transit Authority (TA) employment, rejecting the lower court's conclusion that, because about 75% of patients who have been on methadone treatment for at least a year were free of illicit drug use and because the exclusion applied to non-safety sensitive jobs, the exclusion had "no rational relation to the demands of the job to be performed." He viewed the exclusionary policy as "supported by the legitimate inference that as long as a treatment program (or other drug use) continues, a degree of uncertainty persists." Justice WHITE's dissent, joined by Justice Marshall, insisted that, given the facts in the record, the Court's result could be reached "only if [equal protection] imposes no real constraint at all in this situation. [The] rule's classification of successfully maintained persons as dispositively different from the general population is left without any justification and, with its irrationality and invidiousness thus uncovered, must fall before the Equal Protection Clause." He commented that the TA had stipulated that one of the reasons for the drug policy was that the TA believed that "an adverse public reaction would result if it were generally known that [TA] employed persons with a prior history of drug abuse, including persons participating in methadone maintenance programs." He found it hard "to reconcile that stipulation of animus against former addicts with our past holdings that 'a bare [desire] to harm a politically unpopular group cannot constitute a *legitimate* governmental interest.' [Moreno, above.]" (Compare a similar emphasis on animus in Romer v. Evans, p. 737 below.)

3. *Rationality review since the 1980s.* The widespread expectation that the Court of the 1980s would return to exercising lowest tier rationality review in a very deferential manner has not been wholly fulfilled. Instead, "old" equal protection review continues in flux, with frequent exercises at the very lenient level but with insistence from a substantial number of Justices in several cases that more serious scrutiny is warranted even in the area of economic and social legislation. (And in one striking case in 1985, Cleburne, p. 728 below, the majority struck down a city's zoning action while explicitly claiming to rely on the deferential rationality standard.) The three cases that follow illustrate the modern pattern: some reiterations of deferential standards, accompanied by recurrent arguments for more serious review. Consider whether these cases suggest a continued potential for putting greater "bite" into rationality review—or whether they simply indicate that the Court is comfortable with using traditional equal protection standards as an occasional, ad hoc interventionist tool. Fritz, the first of the cases, seemed to many to announce a commitment to return to Warren Court deference: it exhibited very lenient scrutiny; and it was a 7-2 decision written by Justice Rehnquist, the Court's most consistent advocate of deferential equal protection review. Yet, only a few months after Fritz, Schweiker v. Wilson demonstrated that Fritz had *not* marked the end of intense division on the Court about putting more "bite" into equal protection. Although the equal protection challenge was rejected in Schweiker, the Court was divided 5-4 instead of 7-2, and the dissent, in a tenor akin to that of rationality review "with bite," was written by Justice Powell, who had silently joined Justice Rehnquist's deferential opinion in Fritz. And in Logan, a majority of Justices actually agreed that the challenged law violated equal protection. (As usual, however, the 1980s also produced a number of cases deferentially rejecting equal protection rationality challenges. See, e.g., G.D. Searle & Co. v. Cohn, 455 U.S. 404 (1982), Exxon Corp. v. Eagerton, 462 U.S. 176 (1983), and Burlington Northern R. Co. v. Ford, 504 U.S. 648 (1992). Even these cases occasionally produced dissents arguing that the challenged classification was irrational, as in Justice Stevens's dissent in the Searle case.) Thus, conflict persists on the Court about a number of recurring issues in rationality review. For example, to what extent should a challenged law be tested by the legislature's actual or articulated purposes rather than by purposes suggested by

counsel, or by conceivable purposes hypothesized by the courts? Should rationality review have *any* "bite"?[2]

U.S. Railroad Retirement Bd. v. Fritz

449 U.S. 166, 101 S.Ct. 453, 66 L.Ed.2d 368 (1980).

Justice REHNQUIST delivered the opinion of the Court.

[Prior to 1974, federal law permitted retired persons who had worked in both railroad and nonrailroad jobs to receive dual benefits, both under social security and the railroad retirement system. The availability of these "windfall" benefits threatened the railroad retirement system with bankruptcy. In 1974, Congress accordingly restructured the railroad retirement system by eliminating future accruals of dual benefits. However, Congress did not make these changes fully retroactive; instead, it included a grandfather provision that expressly preserved windfall benefits for some classes of employees. This case involved the constitutionality of the distinction Congress drew between those employees who could continue to receive dual benefits and those who were denied them. The 1974 law provided that those employees who, as of January 1, 1975, lacked the requisite ten years of railroad employment to qualify for railroad retirement benefits would not receive dual, windfall benefits. However, workers who had already retired and were presently receiving dual benefits would continue to receive them. Workers who had not yet retired but who had qualified for both railroad and social security benefits could receive them only if they (1) had performed some railroad work in 1974; or (2) had a "current connection" with the railroad industry as of December 31, 1974; or (3) had completed 25 years of railroad service as of December 31, 1974. The appellees challenged this system on behalf of the class of unretired railroad workers who would have qualified for dual benefits under the old scheme but would be denied them under the new law because they did not satisfy any of these three criteria. They claimed that depriving one set of unretired workers of dual benefits while continuing them for another who satisfied the criteria denied them equal protection.] The District Court agreed with appellees that a differentiation based solely on whether an employee was "active" in a railroad business as of 1974 was not "rationally related" to the congressional purposes of insuring the solvency of the railroad retirement system and protecting vested benefits. We disagree and reverse.

In [recent] years, [the] Court in cases involving social and economic benefits has consistently refused to invalidate on equal protection grounds legislation which it simply deemed unwise or unartfully drawn. [Applying this principle] to this case, the plain language of [the law] marks the beginning and end of our inquiry.[1] [Congress] determined that some of those who in the past

---

2. Note the reflection of the continuing uncertainties in Justice Powell's dissent from the 5–4 ruling in Schweiker v. Wilson (1981; p. 657 below): "The Court has employed numerous formulations for the 'rational basis' test. Members of the Court continue to hold divergent views on the clarity with which a legislative purpose must appear [Fritz], and about the degree of deference afforded the legislature in suiting means to ends, compare [Lindsley] with [Royster Guano]."

1. This opinion and Justice Brennan's dissent cite a number of equal protection [cases]. The most arrogant legal scholar would not claim that all of these cases applied a uniform or consistent test under the Equal Protection Clause. And realistically speaking, we can be no more certain that this opinion will remain undisturbed than were

received full windfall benefits would not continue to do so. Because Congress could have eliminated windfall benefits for all classes of employees, it is not constitutionally impermissible for Congress to have drawn lines between groups of employees for the purpose of phasing out those benefits. The only remaining question is whether Congress achieved its purpose in a patently arbitrary or irrational way. The classification here is not arbitrary, says appellant, because it is an attempt to protect the relative equities of employees and to provide benefits to career railroad employees.

[Congress] could properly conclude that persons who had actually acquired statutory entitlement to windfall benefits while still employed in the railroad industry had a greater equitable claim to those benefits than the members of appellees' class who were no longer in railroad employment when they became eligible for dual benefits. [Congress] could assume that those who had a current connection with the railroad industry when the Act was passed in 1974, or who returned to the industry before their retirement, were more likely than those who had left the industry prior to 1974 and who never returned, to be among the class of persons who pursue careers in the railroad industry, the class for whom the Railroad Retirement Act was designed. Where, as here, there are plausible reasons for Congress' action, our inquiry is at an end. It is, of course, "constitutionally irrelevant whether this reasoning in fact underlay the legislative decision" [Flemming v. Nestor, 363 U.S. 603 (1960)] because this Court has never insisted that a legislative body articulate its reasons for enacting a statute. This is particularly true where the legislature must necessarily engage in a process of line drawing. [Finally,] we disagree with the District Court's conclusion that Congress was unaware of what it accomplished or that it was misled by the groups that appeared before it. If this test were applied literally to every member of any legislature that ever voted on a law, there would be very few laws which would survive it. The language of the statute is clear, and we have historically assumed that Congress intended what it enacted. To be sure, appellees lost a political battle in which they had a strong interest, but this is neither the first nor the last time that such a result will occur in the [legislative forum].

[Reversed.]

Justice STEVENS, concurring in the judgment.

In my opinion, Justice Brennan's criticism of the Court's approach to this case merits a more thoughtful response than that contained in footnote [1]. Justice Brennan correctly points out that if the analysis of legislative purpose requires only a reading of the statutory language in a disputed provision, and if any "conceivable basis" for a discriminatory classification will repel a constitutional attack on the statute, judicial review will constitute a mere tautological recognition of the fact that Congress did what it intended to do. [When] Congress deprives a small class of persons of vested rights that are protected [for] others who are in a similar though not identical position, I believe the

those who joined the opinion in Lindsley, Royster Guano, or any of the other cases referred to in this opinion and in the dissenting opinion. But like our predecessors and our successors, we are obliged to apply the equal protection component of the Fifth Amendment as we believe the Constitution requires and in so doing we have no hesitation in asserting, contrary to the dissent, that where social or economic regulations are involved, Dandridge v. Williams and Jefferson v. Hackney [both below], together with this case, state the proper application of the test. The comments in the dissenting opinion about the proper cases for which to look for the correct statement of the equal protection rational basis standard, and about which cases limit earlier cases, are just that: comments in a dissenting opinion. [Footnote by Justice Rehnquist.]

Constitution requires something more than merely a "conceivable" or a "plausible" explanation for the unequal treatment. I do not, however, share Justice Brennan's conclusion that every statutory classification must further an objective that can be confidently identified as the "actual purpose" of the legislature. Actual purpose is sometimes unknown. Moreover, undue emphasis on actual motivation may result in identically worded statutes being held valid in one State and invalid in a neighboring State. I therefore believe that we must discover a correlation between the classification and either the actual purpose of the statute or a legitimate purpose that we may reasonably presume to have motivated an impartial legislature. If the adverse impact on the disfavored class is an apparent aim of the legislature, its impartiality would be suspect. If, however, the adverse impact may reasonably be viewed as an acceptable cost of achieving a larger goal, an impartial lawmaker could rationally decide that that cost should be incurred. In this case, however, we need not look beyond the actual purpose of the legislature. [The] congressional purpose to eliminate dual benefits is unquestionably legitimate. [Some] hardship—in the form of frustrated long-term expectations—must inevitably result from any reduction in vested benefits. [A]ny distinction [Congress] chose within the class of vested beneficiaries would involve a difference of degree rather than a difference in entitlement. I am satisfied that a distinction based upon currency of railroad employment represents an impartial method of identifying that sort of difference. Because retirement plans frequently provide greater benefits for recent retirees than for those who retired years ago—and thus give a greater reward for recent service than for past service of equal duration—the basis for the statutory discrimination is supported by relevant precedent. It follows, in my judgment, that the timing of the employees' railroad service is a "reasonable basis" for the classification as that term is used in Lindsley and Dandridge, as well as a "ground of difference having a fair and substantial relation to the object of the legislation" as those words are used in [Royster Guano].

Justice BRENNAN, with whom Justice MARSHALL joins, dissenting.

[The] legal standard applicable to this case is the "rational basis" test. [The] Court today purports to apply this standard, but in actuality fails to scrutinize the challenged classification in the manner established by [our] precedents. [The] mode of analysis employed by the Court [virtually] immunizes social and economic legislative classifications from judicial review. [I. In Johnson v. Robison, 415 U.S. 361 (1974),] eight Members of this Court agreed [on the Royster Guano standard]. [T]he rational basis standard "is not a toothless one" [Mathews v. Lucas, p. 726 below] and will not be satisfied by flimsy or implausible justifications for the legislative classification, proffered after the fact by Government attorneys. See, e.g., [Jimenez; Moreno]. When faced with a challenge to a legislative classification under the rational basis test, the court should ask, first, what the purposes of the statute are, and second, whether the classification is rationally related to achievement of those purposes. II. [A] "principal purpose" of the [Act], as explicitly stated by Congress, was to preserve the vested earned benefits of retirees who had already qualified for them. The classification [here], which deprives some retirees of vested dual benefits that they had earned prior to 1974, directly conflicts with Congress' stated purpose. As such, the classification is not only rationally unrelated to the congressional purpose; it is inimical to it. III. The [Court] avoids the conclusion that [the law] must be invalidated by deviating in three ways from traditional rational basis analysis. First, the Court adopts a tautological approach to statutory [purpose]. Second, it disregards the actual stated purpose of Congress in favor of a justification which was never suggested by any [legislator], and which in fact conflicts with the stated congressional purpose. Third, it upholds the classification without any analysis of its rational relationship to the identified purpose.

A.   The Court states that "the plain language of [the law] marks the beginning and end of our inquiry." This statement is strange indeed, for the "plain language" of the statute can tell us only what the classification is; it can tell us nothing about the purpose of the classification let alone the relationship between the classification and that purpose. Since [the law] deprives appellees of their vested earned dual benefits, the Court apparently assumes that Congress must have *intended* that result. But by presuming purpose from result, the Court reduces analysis to tautology. If that were the extent of our analysis, we would find every statute [perfectly] tailored to achieve its purpose. But equal protection scrutiny under the rational basis test requires the courts first to deduce the independent objectives of the statute, usually from statements of purpose and other evidence in the statute and legislative history, and second to analyze whether the challenged classification rationally furthers achievement of those objectives. The Court's tautological approach will not suffice.

B.   The Court analyzes the rationality of [the law] in terms of a justification suggested by Government attorneys, but never adopted by Congress. The Court states that it is "constitutionally irrelevant whether this reasoning in fact underlay the legislative decision." [But in recent years] this Court has frequently recognized that the actual purposes of Congress, rather than the post hoc justifications offered by Government attorneys, must be the primary basis for analysis under the rational basis test. E.g., [Wiesenfeld; Rodriguez; Murgia; Johnson v. Robison; Califano v. Goldfarb (all noted elsewhere)]. [It] is clear that this Court will no longer sustain a challenged classification under the rational basis test merely because Government attorneys can suggest a "conceivable basis" upon which it might be thought rational. The standard we have applied is properly deferential to the Legislative Branch: where Congress has articulated a legitimate governmental objective, and the challenged classification rationally furthers that objective, we must sustain the provision. In other cases, however, the courts must probe more deeply. Where Congress has expressly stated the purpose of a piece of legislation, but where the challenged classification is either irrelevant to or counter to that purpose, we must view any post hoc justifications proffered by Government attorneys with skepticism. A challenged classification may be sustained only if it is rationally related to achievement of an *actual* legitimate governmental purpose.

The Court argues that Congress chose to discriminate against appellees for reasons of equity, [but] Congress expressed the view that it would be inequitable to deprive any retirees of any portion of the benefits they had been promised and that they had earned under prior law. The Court is unable to cite even one statement in the legislative history by a Representative or Senator that makes the equitable judgment it imputes to Congress. [Congress] asked railroad management and labor representatives to negotiate and submit a bill to restructure the Railroad Retirement [system]. The members of this Joint Labor–Management Negotiating Committee were not appointed by public officials, nor did they represent the interests of the appellee class, who were no longer active railroaders or union members. In an initial proposed restructuring of the system, the Joint Committee devised a means whereby the system's deficit could be completely eliminated without depriving retirees of vested earned benefits. However, labor representatives demanded that benefits be increased for their current members, the cost to be offset by divesting the appellee class of a portion of the benefits they had earned under prior law. [The] Joint Committee negotiators and Railroad Retirement Board members who testified at congressional hearings perpetuated the inaccurate impression that all retirees with earned vested dual benefits under prior law would retain their benefits unchanged. [Of course, misstatements] by witnesses before Congress would not ordinarily lead us to conclude that Congress misapprehended what it was doing. In this instance, however, where complex legislation was drafted by outside parties and Congress relied on them to explain it, where the misstatements are frequent and unrebutted, and where no Member of Congress can be found to have stated the effect of the classification correctly, we are entitled to suspect that Congress may have been misled. [Therefore,] I do not think that this classification was rationally related to an *actual* governmental purpose.

C. The third way in which the Court has deviated from the principles of rational basis scrutiny is its failure to analyze whether the challenged classification is genuinely related to the purpose identified by the Court. Having suggested that "equitable considerations" underlay the challenged classification, [the] Court proceeds to accept that suggestion without further analysis. An unadorned claim of "equitable" considerations is, of course, difficult to assess. It seems to me that before a court may accept a litigant's assertion of "equity," it must inquire what principles of equity or fairness might genuinely support such a judgment. But apparently the Court does not demand such inquiry, for it has failed to address any equitable considerations that might be relevant to the challenged [classification]. [I] conclude that the Government's proffered justification of "equitable considerations" [cannot] be [defended].

SCHWEIKER v. WILSON, 450 U.S. 221 (1981): As noted earlier, Schweiker, only a few months after Fritz, produced a much narrower, 5-4 decision and suggested that the alleged landmark case of Fritz had not, after all, settled the intense debate on the Court about the importance of actual legislative purpose in rationality review. Justice Powell, who had joined the deferential majority opinion in Fritz, now submitted a forceful dissent. He criticized the very deferential rationality cases (e.g., McGowan v. Maryland): "[They] do not describe the importance of actual legislative purpose in our analysis." He argued, moreover, that "post hoc hypotheses about legislative purpose, unsupported by the legislative history," should be received skeptically. His scrutiny accordingly paid considerable attention to "discernable" or "identifiable" legislative purposes. The majority ruling upheld Congress's denial of federal "comfort allowances" to needy aged, blind, and disabled persons confined in public institutions unless the institutions receive federal Medicaid funds. The challengers argued that the scheme bore "no rational relationship to any legitimate objective of the SSI [federal Supplemental Security Income] program." Justice BLACKMUN's majority opinion rejected this challenge:* "[As] long as the classificatory scheme chosen by Congress rationally advances a reasonable and identifiable governmental objective, we must disregard the existence of other methods of allocation that we, as individuals, perhaps would have preferred." He found sufficient indication in the "sparse" legislative record that "the

---

* The challengers also claimed that the classification warranted scrutiny at a level *higher* than that appropriate under rationality review, "because the statute classifies on the basis of mental illness, a factor that greatly resembles other characteristics that this Court has found inherently 'suspect.'" Justice Blackmun found it unnecessary to reach this issue, because he concluded "that this statute does not classify directly on the basis of mental health." This aspect of the case is further discussed below, at p. 728.

decision to incorporate the Medicaid eligibility standards into the SSI scheme must be considered Congress' deliberate, considered choice." He added: "This Court has granted a 'strong presumption of constitutionality' to legislation conferring monetary benefits, because it believes that Congress should have discretion in deciding how to expend necessarily limited resources. Awarding this type of benefit inevitably involves the kind of line-drawing that will leave some comparably needy person outside the favored circle."

Justice POWELL's dissent, joined by Justices Brennan, Marshall and Stevens, countered: "Congress thoughtlessly has applied a statutory classification developed to further legitimate goals of one welfare program [Medicaid] to another welfare program [SSI] serving entirely different needs. The result is an exclusion of wholly dependent people from minimal benefits, serving no government interest. This irrational classification violates [equal protection]." He articulated his approach to rationality review as follows: "[The] question of whether a statutory classification discriminates arbitrarily cannot be divorced from whether it was enacted to serve an identifiable purpose. When a legislative purpose can be suggested only by the ingenuity of a government lawyer litigating the constitutionality of a statute, a reviewing court may be presented not so much with a legislative policy choice as its absence. In my view, the Court should receive with some skepticism post hoc hypotheses about legislative purpose, unsupported by the legislative history.[1] When no indication of legislative purpose appears other than the current position of the Secretary, the Court should require that the classification bear a 'fair and substantial relation' to the asserted purpose. See [Royster Guano]. This marginally more demanding scrutiny indirectly would test the plausibility of the tendered purpose, and preserve equal protection review as something more than 'a mere tautological recognition of the fact that Congress did what it intended to do.' Fritz (Stevens, J., concurring)." Applying this approach to the challenged provision, Justice Powell concluded "that Congress had no rational reason for refusing to pay a comfort allowance to [the challengers], while paying it to numerous otherwise identically situated disabled indigents. This unexplained difference in treatment must have been a legislative oversight."

LOGAN v. ZIMMERMAN BRUSH CO., 455 U.S. 422 (1982): Logan, an unusual case both on its facts and in its manner of disposition, suggested that equal protection rationality review retained bite despite the deferential tone of the Fritz and Schweiker majority opinions. The case involved an Illinois law barring discrimination on the basis of handicap and providing that within 120 days of the filing of a charge of such discrimination, the state agency shall convene a fact finding conference. In the Logan case, the agency inadvertently failed to hold such a hearing within the time limit. The state court found that the 120–day period was mandatory and that the Commission had therefore lost jurisdiction to consider Logan's complaint. Justice BLACKMUN's "opinion of the Court" was devoted entirely to sustaining the challenger's procedural due process attack; that opinion did not mention equal protection. But, in an

---

1. "Some of our cases suggest that the actual purpose of a statute is irrelevant, Flemming v. Nestor, and that the statute must be upheld 'if any state of facts reasonably may be conceived to justify' its discrimination. McGowan v. Maryland. Although these cases preserve an important caution, they do not describe the importance of actual legislative purpose in our analysis. We recognize that a legislative body rarely acts with a single mind and that compromises blur purpose. Therefore, it is appropriate to accord some deference to the executive's view of legislative intent, as similarly we accord deference to the consistent construction of a statute by the administrative agency charged with its enforcement. Ascertainment of actual purpose to the extent feasible, however, remains an essential step in equal protection." [Footnote by Justice Powell.]

unusual move, Justice Blackmun also submitted a separate opinion, joined by Justices Brennan, Marshall and O'Connor, which stated: "Although the Court [in the opinion written by Justice Blackmun himself] considered that it was unnecessary to discuss and dispose of the equal protection claim when the due process issue was being decided in Logan's favor, I regard the equal protection issue as sufficiently important to require comment on my part, particularly inasmuch as a majority of the Members of the Court are favorably inclined toward the claim." Justice Blackmun's separate opinion then explained why the challenged provision did not satisfy the minimum rationality standards of equal protection. (Recall that he had written the deferential majority opinion in Schweiker less than a year earlier.) And, in another separate opinion, Justice Powell, joined by Justice Rehnquist, stated that, even though he could not join Justice Blackmun's concurring opinion, he, too, agreed that the challenged law could not survive even the "minimal standard" of equal protection review. In short, six Justices voted to invalidate the law on "minimum rationality" equal protection grounds. Logan thus is a rare modern example of a case in which a majority agreed that a state law violated equal protection rationality standards.

Justice Blackmun explained his equal protection analysis as follows: "On its face, Logan's equal protection claim is an unconventional one. The [Act] establishes no explicit classifications and does not expressly distinguish between claimants, and the company therefore argues that Logan has no more been deprived of equal protection than anyone would be who is injured by a random act of governmental misconduct. As the [state court] interpreted the statute, however, [it] unambiguously divides claims—and thus, necessarily, claimants—into two discrete groups that are accorded radically disparate treatment. Claims processed within 120 days are given full consideration on the merits. [In] contrast, otherwise identical claims that do not receive a hearing within the statutory period are unceremoniously, and finally, terminated. Because the Illinois court recognized, in so many words, that the [Act] establishes two categories of claims, one may proceed to determine whether the classification drawn by the statute is consistent with the [equal protection]. For over a century, the Court has engaged in a continuing and occasionally almost metaphysical effort to identify the precise nature of [equal protection] guarantees. [Here, Justice Blackmun cited the dissent in Schweiker!] At the minimum level, however, the Court 'consistently has required that legislation classify the persons it affects in a manner rationally related to legitimate governmental objectives.' Schweiker. [The] 'rational-basis standard is "not a toothless one," ' id., quoting Mathews v. Lucas; the classificatory scheme must 'rationally advanc[e] a reasonable and identifiable governmental objective.' Schweiker. I see no need to explore the outer bounds of this test, for I find that the Illinois statute runs afoul of the lowest level of permissible equal protection scrutiny." He continued: "[It] is not enough, under [equal protection], to say that the legislature sought to terminate certain claims and succeeded in doing so, for that is 'a mere tautological recognition of the fact that [the legislature] did what it intended to do.' [Fritz (Stevens, J., concurring in the judgment).] This Court still has an obligation to view the classificatory *system,* in an effort to determine whether the disparate treatment accorded the affected classes is arbitrary. Here, that inquiry yields an affirmative result."

ALLEGHENY PITTSBURGH COAL v. WEBSTER COUNTY, 488 U.S. 336 (1989): In this case, a unanimous Court struck down aspects of the West Virginia property tax system, relying on rational basis review. (Recall the questions raised above about the utility of judicial inquiries into legislative purpose in exercising rational basis review. What light does this case throw on that problem?) The West Virginia Constitution establishes a general principle of uniform taxation so that all property is to be taxed in proportion to its value. For the years beginning in 1975, the County tax assessor valued Allegheny Pittsburgh's real property on the basis of its recent purchase price. Other properties not recently transferred were assessed on the basis of their previous assessments, with minor modifications. The system resulted in gross disparities in the assessed value of comparable properties. Thus, for several years beginning in 1975, the Company was assessed "at roughly 8 to 35 times more than comparable neighboring property, and these discrepancies [continued] for more than ten years." The Court concluded that the assessment system violated equal protection. Chief Justice REHNQUIST's opinion acknowledged that equal protection did not require "immediate general adjustment on the basis of the latest market developments." But the State's argument that the scheme was "rationally related to its purpose of assessing properties at true current value" (because, "when available, it [made] use of exceedingly accurate information about the market value of a property") was not acceptable to the Court, in view of the duration and extent of the disparities here.[1] The Chief Justice emphasized that West Virginia had *not* drawn a distinction similar to that of California, described in footnote 1: "[West Virginia's] Constitution and laws provide that all property [shall] be taxed at a rate uniform throughout the state according to its estimated market value. There is no suggestion [that] the State may have adopted a different system in practice from that specified by statute. [We] have no doubt that [the Company has] suffered [from] 'intentional systematic undervaluation by state officials' of comparable property in Webster County. [The] fairness of one's allocable share of the total property tax burden can only be meaningfully evaluated by comparison with the share of others similarly situated relative to their property holdings. The relative undervaluation of comparable property in Webster County over time therefore denies petitioner the equal protection of law."[2]

Three years later, in NORDLINGER v. HAHN, 505 U.S. 1 (1992), the Court distinguished Allegheny Pittsburgh and upheld California's Proposition

---

1. Chief Justice Rehnquist added in a footnote: "We need not and do not decide today whether Webster County's assessment method would stand on a different footing if it were the law of a State, generally applied, instead of the aberrational enforcement policy it appears to be. [California] has adopted a similar policy [popularly] known as 'Proposition 13,' [which] generally provides that property will be assessed at its 1975–1976 value, and reassessed only when transferred or constructed upon, or, in a limited manner for inflation. The system is grounded on the belief that taxes should be based on the original cost of property and should not tax unrealized paper gains in the value of the property." (The California scheme was sustained in Nordlinger v. Hahn, 505 U.S. 1 (1992), which follows.)

2. West Virginia's system would have survived judicial scrutiny if it had asserted purposes such as California's to justify its differential assessments; the State's failure to do so produced the Court's invalidation. Does this make the Court's ruling a pointless one, because the State could legitimately enact a

system similar in result on the basis of purposes *other* than those before the Court? Or did the Court's ruling, with its emphasis on West Virginia's articulated purpose, serve a useful function? Recall the discussion of the pros and cons of equal protection scrutiny "with bite," earlier in this section. For useful, differing comments on Allegheny Pittsburgh Coal, see Cohen, "State Law in Equality Clothing: A Comment on [Allegheny]," 38 UCLA L.Rev. 87 (1990); Ely, "Another Spin on [Allegheny]," 38 UCLA L.Rev. 107 (1990); and Glennon, "Taxation and Equal Protection," 58 Geo.Wash.L.Rev. 261 (1990). [Cohen comments that Allegheny "seems to apply the Gunther model" and that it "proves Professor Gunther's point that it is possible to conduct a rational basis inquiry 'with bite' if there is a short list of proffered governmental purposes and if the statutory classifications are substantially mismatched to those purposes" (but he concludes that it would be preferable to abandon the "rational basis" standard of review in economic regulation cases).]

13, imposing an acquisition-value taxation system and consequently benefiting longer-term property owners at the expense of newer property owners. Justice BLACKMUN's majority opinion distinguished Allegheny Pittsburgh because of the presence in California of facts justifying the inference that the benefits of an acquisition-value taxation scheme were actually desired. He stated that "the Equal Protection Clause does not demand for purposes of rational-basis review that a legislature or governing decisionmaker actually articulate at any time the purpose or rationale supporting its classification. Fritz. Nevertheless, this Court's review does require that a purpose may conceivably or may reasonably have been the purpose and policy of the relevant governmental decisionmaker. Allegheny Pittsburgh was the rare case where the facts precluded any plausible inference that the reason for the unequal assessment practice was to achieve the benefits of an acquisition-value tax scheme. By contrast, [Proposition 13] was enacted precisely to achieve the benefits of an acquisition-value system." Justice THOMAS concurred in the result, but was unpersuaded that Allegheny Pittsburgh was distinguishable and urged that it be overruled. Justice STEVENS, the sole dissenter, was the only one to propose that the rational basis test be applied with more bite and less deference. He stated: "Similarly situated neighbors have an equal right to share in the benefits of local government. It would obviously be unconstitutional to provide one with more or better fire or police protection than the other; it is just as plainly unconstitutional to require one to pay five times as much in property taxes as the other for the same government services. [The] severe inequalities created by Proposition 13 are arbitrary and unreasonable and do not rationally further a legitimate state interest."

FCC v. BEACH COMMUNICATIONS, INC., 508 U.S. 307 (1993): In this case, decided a year after Nordlinger, Justice THOMAS's majority opinion relied heavily on Fritz in emphasizing an extremely deferential stance. In upholding a distinction among cable facilities in the Cable Communications Policy Act of 1984, he cited Fritz repeatedly and provided the following recapitulation: "[E]qual protection is not a license for courts to judge the wisdom, fairness, or logic of legislative choices. In areas of social and economic policy, a statutory classification that neither proceeds along suspect lines nor infringes fundamental constitutional rights must be upheld against equal protection challenge if there is any reasonably conceivable set of facts that could provide a rational basis for the classification. [This] standard of review is a paradigm of judicial restraint. On rational-basis review, a classification [comes] to us bearing a strong presumption of validity, and those attacking the rationality of the legislative classification have the burden 'to negative every conceivable basis which might support it.' Moreover, because we never require a legislature to articulate its reasons for enacting a statute, it is entirely irrelevant for constitutional purposes whether the conceived reason for the challenged distinction actually motivated the legislature. Thus the absence of 'legislative facts' explaining the distinction 'on the record' has no significance in rational-basis analysis. In other words, a legislative choice is not subject to courtroom fact-finding and may be based on rational speculation unsupported by evidence or empirical data." He added that these limitations on review have "added force" when the legislature is engaged in line-drawing: "[Congress] had to draw the line somewhere. [This] necessity renders the precise coordinates of the resulting legislative judgment virtually unreviewable, since the legislature must be allowed to approach a perceived problem incrementally. [Lee Optical.]" Justice STEVENS, in an opinion concurring solely in the judgment, criticized Justice Thomas's articulation of the proper equal protection standard. Justice Stevens thought it "sweeps too broadly, for it is difficult to imagine a legislative classification that could not be supported by a 'reasonably conceivable state of facts.' Judicial review under the 'conceivable set of facts' test is tantamount to no review at all." Recalling his separate opinion in Fritz, he added: "I continue to believe that when Congress imposes a burden on one group, but leaves unaffected another that is similarly, though not identically, situated, 'the Constitution requires something more than merely a "conceivable" or "plausible" explanation for the unequal treatment.' In my view, when the actual rationale for the legislative classification is unclear, we should inquire whether the classification is rationally related to 'a legitimate purpose that we may *reasonably presume* to have motivated an impartial legislature.' " (Compare, however, the close division on the Court a few weeks after Beach Communications in a 5-4 decision rejecting an equal protection attack on Kentucky laws allowing involuntary commitment of the mentally retarded on the basis of clear and convincing evidence, while requiring a "beyond a reasonable doubt" standard for involuntary commitment grounded on mental illness. Heller v. Doe, 509 U.S. 312 (1993). Justice Kennedy's majority opinion followed the Beach Communications approach. He quoted extensively from that case in ruling that differences in the ease of diagnosis and in the invasiveness of the treatments justified the different standard. In dissent, Justice Souter, joined in part by Justices Stevens, Blackmun and O'Connor, argued that the difference in the burden of proof did not satisfy rational basis standards.)

SECTION 3.   SUSPECT CLASSIFICATIONS AND THE PROBLEMS OF FORBIDDEN DISCRIMINATION

Introduction. We now move from the realm of rationality review to those aspects of equal protection law that may call for heightened scrutiny. This section focuses on the problems of "suspect" and "quasi-suspect" classifications as well as on a range of related problems pertaining to the identification and remedying of forbidden discrimination. Racial discrimination was the major target of the 14th Amendment and thus racial classifications are ordinarily "suspect": this theme is among the few continuously voiced ones in equal protection doctrine. But even racial discrimination still gives rise to differences on a host of questions. This section begins, in sec. 3A, with an examination of classifications disadvantaging racial (and ethnic) minorities (sec. 3A1) and of justifications for invalidating segregation in public facilities, despite the formal equivalence suggested by the "separate but equal" doctrine (sec. 3A2).* The occasions for strict scrutiny of disadvantaging racial classifications, and the meaning of "strict scrutiny," lie at the heart of sec. 3A. Secs. 3B and 3C turn to the question of whether there are classifications beyond race that also trigger heightened scrutiny. Sec. 3B deals with sex discrimination. Gender is considered a "quasi-suspect" classification triggering an "intermediate" level of review. Sec. 3C turns to other classifications (alienage and illegitimacy) which also occasionally elicit heightened scrutiny, and to additional criteria (e.g., disability and sexual orientation) for which claims of more intensive scrutiny have been advanced. This subsection raises a recurrent question: Is it permissible to reason by analogy from the well-established category of disadvantaging

---

* Examination of racial classifications in this opening section is limited to situations where minorities are *disadvantaged*. Examination of the even more controversial constitutional debate about the use of racial factors for "benign" purposes—the problems of "reverse discrimination" and affirmative action—are postponed to sec. 3E.

racial classifications to other classifications which share some, but not all, of the characteristics of race?

The problems raised by the preceding subsections are complex enough. But the final two enter even more difficult and controversial terrain. Sec. 3D deals with the frequently stated requirement that discrimination must be "purposeful" to be actionable under equal protection. If a showing of "purposeful," "intentional" discrimination is indeed necessary, how is it proven? And what is the relevance of discriminatory effects and disadvantaging impacts? The Court often states that impact data are at least usable to prove unconstitutional purpose or motive. Can equal protection also reach situations where governmental action, though not flowing from racial hostility, has the *effect* of producing a disproportionately harmful impact on a minority? (Sec. 3D also deals with the problems of remedying unconstitutional segregation, because the "purpose"-"effect" distinction often arises in that context.) The last section, 3E, considers the controversial problems of "benign" discrimination and affirmative action. What standard of scrutiny should apply to the use of ordinarily suspect racial criteria invoked for the asserted purpose of helping rather than harming disadvantaged groups? What justifications and findings warrant governmental use of affirmative action programs?

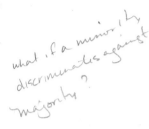

what if a minority discriminates against majority?

A. RACE

1. THE INTENSIVE SCRUTINY OF DISADVANTAGING RACIAL AND ETHNIC CLASSIFICATIONS

1. *The Strauder case.* Seven years after the Slaughter–House Cases (p. 421 above) had emphasized the central anti-racial discrimination concern of the 14th Amendment, the Court applied that theme in STRAUDER v. WEST VIRGINIA, 100 U.S. 303 (1880). Strauder, a black defendant, was convicted of murder by a jury from which blacks had been excluded because of an explicit command of a state law.[1] Strauder unsuccessfully sought to remove his case to a federal court. The Court held that removal should have been granted and found the law unconstitutional. Justice STRONG's majority opinion emphasized that the "common purpose" of the post-Civil War Amendments was the "securing to a race recently emancipated [all] the civil rights the superior race enjoy." He added: "[What is equal protection] but declaring, [in] regard to the colored race, for whose protection the amendment was primarily designed, that no discrimination shall be made against them by law because of their color? [That] the West Virginia statute respecting juries [is] such a discrimination ought not to be doubted. Nor would it be if the persons excluded by it were white men. If in those States where the colored people constitute a majority of the entire population a law should be enacted excluding all white men from jury service, [we] apprehend no one would be heard to claim that it would not be a denial to white men of [equal protection]. Nor if a law should be passed excluding all naturalized Celtic Irishmen, would there be any doubt of its inconsistency with the spirit of the amendment. The very fact that colored people are singled out and expressly denied by a statute all right to participate

---

1. The state law provided: "All white male persons who are twenty-one years of   age and who are citizens of this State shall be liable to serve as [jurors]."

in the administration of the law, as jurors, because of their color, [is] practically a brand upon them, affixed by the law, an assertion of their inferiority, and a stimulant to that race prejudice which is an impediment to securing to individuals of the race that [equal justice]. We do not say [that] a State may not prescribe the qualifications of its jurors, and in so doing make discriminations. It may confine the selection to males, to freeholders, to citizens, to persons within certain ages, or to persons having educational qualifications. We do not believe the 14th Amendment was ever intended to prohibit this. Looking at its history, it is clear it had no such purpose. Its aim was against discrimination because of race or color. [We] are not now called upon to affirm or deny that it had other purposes."[2] [Justices FIELD and CLIFFORD dissented.]

Although Strauder involved discrimination against African Americans (who were the historical focus of the 14th Amendment), the Court has readily found that *all* disadvantaging classifications resting on race and ethnicity are suspect. Indeed, even in Strauder, the first racial discrimination invalidation under the 14th Amendment, the Court mentioned laws directed at "all naturalized Celtic Irishmen" as falling within "the spirit of the amendment." Without much discussion, later Courts have treated discrimination based on national origin (e.g., against Mexican–Americans) or on race generally (e.g., against Asians) the same as discrimination against the black minority.[3]

2. *Race as a "suspect" classification triggering "the most rigid scrutiny": The Korematsu case.* Although, as Strauder illustrates, the Court has long perceived special bite in equal protection when it is used as a weapon against racial discrimination, explicit reference to race as a "suspect" criterion did not come until well into the 20th century, in KOREMATSU v. UNITED STATES, 323 U.S. 214 (1944). Ironically, Korematsu was one of the very rare cases in which a classification based on race *survived* strict scrutiny. The majority sustained a conviction for violating a military order during World War II excluding all persons of Japanese ancestry from designated West Coast areas.[4]

2. Note that in Strauder, the claim of racial discrimination was raised by a black defendant, a member of the excluded class. The law as to challenging discrimination in jury selection has changed since Strauder. For example, in Peters v. Kiff, 407 U.S. 493 (1972), a white defendant successfully challenged a conviction on the ground that blacks had been systematically excluded from jury service. And in Taylor v. Louisiana, 419 U.S. 522 (1975), a male defendant was permitted to object to the exclusion of women. That change in the law stemmed from the change in emphasis regarding the relevant "right" involved: the focus had shifted from an equal protection right to serve on a jury to an aspect of the jury trial guarantee. In Taylor, the Court stated "that the selection of a petit jury from a representative cross section of the community is an essential component of the Sixth Amendment right to a jury trial." (See also J.E.B. v. Alabama ex rel. T.B. (1994); p. 702 below).

3. E.g., Yick Wo v. Hopkins (1886; p. 750 below); Hernandez v. Texas, 347 U.S. 475 (1954). Hernandez struck down discrimi-nation against Mexican–Americans in jury selection. Chief Justice Warren stated that "community prejudices are not static, and from time to time other differences [than 'differences in race and color'] from the community norm may define other groups which need the same protection." [Even Justice Rehnquist, the modern Justice who takes the least interventionist view of equal protection and who is the strongest opponent of the expansion of "suspect classifications" jurisprudence, acknowledged in Trimble v. Gordon (1977; p. 726 below) that classifications based on "national origin, the first cousin of race" (*not* only racial ones) were areas where "the Framers obviously meant [equal protection] to apply."]

4. Soon after the outbreak of war with Japan in 1941, President Roosevelt issued an Executive Order designed to safeguard "against espionage [and] against sabotage" and providing that certain military commanders might designate "military areas" in the United States "from which any or all persons may be excluded, and with respect to which the right of any person to enter, re-

Early in his majority opinion, Justice BLACK stated the governing standard: "[A]ll legal restrictions which curtail the civil rights of a single racial group are immediately suspect. That is not to say that all such restrictions are unconstitutional. It is to say that courts must subject them to the most rigid scrutiny. Pressing public necessity may sometimes justify the existence of such restrictions; racial antagonism never can." But here, the requisite "pressing public necessity" was found. He explained: "Like curfew, exclusion of those of Japanese origin was deemed necessary [by the military authorities] because of the presence of an unascertained number of disloyal members of the group, most of whom we have no doubt were loyal to this country." The military authorities had found "that it was impossible to bring about an immediate segregation of the disloyal from the loyal." The judgment that "exclusion of the whole group [was] a military imperative answers the contention that the exclusion was in the nature of group punishment based on antagonism to those of Japanese origin." In a closing passage, Justice Black reiterated that the Court had not endorsed racial discrimination: "To cast this case into outlines of racial prejudice, without reference to the real military dangers which were presented, merely confuses the issue." Korematsu was excluded, he insisted, "because we are at war with the Japanese Empire, because the properly constituted military authorities feared an invasion of our West Coast and felt constrained to take proper security measures, because they decided that the military urgency of the situation demanded that all citizens of Japanese ancestry be segregated from the West Coast temporarily and finally, because Congress, reposing its confidence in this time of war in our military leaders—as inevitably it must—determined that they should have the power to do just this. There was evidence of disloyalty on the part of some, the military authorities considered that the need for action was great, and time was short. We cannot—by availing ourselves of the calm perspective of hindsight—now say that at that time these actions were unjustified."[5]

main in, or leave shall be subject to whatever restrictions" the "Military Commander may impose in his discretion." The West Coast program established for persons of Japanese ancestry included curfews, detention in relocation centers, and exclusion from the West Coast area. After unanimously upholding the curfew orders in 1943 in Hirabayashi v. United States, the Court in the following year, in Korematsu, sustained the exclusion aspect of the program. (On the partial setting aside of Hirabayashi's conviction decades later, recall p. 638 above.)

5. Note a comment on Korematsu 30 years later, by Justice Douglas, a member of the Korematsu majority. He stated in DeFunis v. Odegaard, (1974; p. 794 below): "It [is] easy in retrospect to denounce what was done, as there actually was no attempted Japanese invasion of our country. [But] those making plans for defense of the Nation had no such knowledge and were planning for the worst." (Justice Douglas was mistaken: an Army historian found that the military authorities did know that there was no threat of invasion in early 1942.) Korematsu (and the evacuation program generally) have elic-

ited extensive criticism. For reasonably contemporaneous comments, see, e.g., Rostow, "The Japanese American Cases—A Disaster," 54 Yale L.J. 489 (1945), and Grodzins, Americans Betrayed: Politics and the Japanese Evacuation (1949). For a thorough modern study, see Irons, Justice at War (1983). Peter Irons's research for this book—and his participation as co-counsel—led to a 1984 District Court judgment vacating Korematsu's conviction. See Korematsu v. United States, 584 F.Supp. 1406 (N.D.Cal.1984). The judgment was vacated because of governmental misconduct regarding the submission of false information to the Supreme Court in the 1940s. Another of Korematsu's co-counsel stated that the 1984 ruling "sucked away the factual underpinnings" of the Court decision. But the Court ruling stays on the books, to be cited either for the "most rigid scrutiny" to be applied to disadvantaging racial classifications—or for the deference to the military in wartime that may, as in Korematsu, satisfy that scrutiny. (See also Personal Justice Denied (1982), the final Report of the Commission on Wartime Relocation and Internment of Civilians. The Commission's Report

Justice MURPHY wrote the strongest dissent—even though he did not invoke the "suspect classification"-"strict scrutiny" test and purported to apply the "reasonableness" standard. He acknowledged that, while "great respect" for military judgment in wartime was "appropriate," "the military claim must subject itself to the judicial process of having its reasonableness determined." He was not persuaded that the deprivation of individual rights here was "reasonably related to a public danger that is so 'immediate, imminent, and impending' as not to admit of delay and not to permit the intervention of ordinary constitutional processes to alleviate the danger." The exclusion order applicable to "all persons of Japanese ancestry" seemed to him "an obvious racial discrimination" and hence a denial of equal protection. He conceded that there was "a very real fear of invasion," and fear of sabotage and espionage, on the West Coast in 1942. But he insisted that "the exclusion, either temporarily or permanently, of all persons with Japanese blood in their veins has [no] reasonable relation" to the "removal of the dangers." He explained: "[T]hat relation is lacking because the exclusion order necessarily must rely for its reasonableness upon the assumption that *all* persons of Japanese ancestry may have a dangerous tendency to commit sabotage and espionage." He found it "difficult to believe that reason, logic or experience could be marshaled in support of such an assumption." He argued that the "forced exclusion was the result in good measure of [an] erroneous assumption of racial guilt rather than bona fide military necessity." The justification for exclusion rested "mainly upon questionable racial and sociological grounds" not charged or proved—"an accumulation of much of the misinformation, half-truths and insinuations that for years have been directed against Japanese Americans by people with racial and economic prejudices—the same people who have been among the foremost advocates of the evacuation. A military judgment based upon such racial and sociological considerations is not entitled to the great weight ordinarily given the judgments based upon strictly military considerations." He accordingly dissented from "this legalization of racism."[6]

In a separate dissent, Justice JACKSON stated that the military orders may or may not have been "expedient military precautions"; but they should not be enforced by civil courts committed to the Constitution. He elaborated: "[A] judicial construction of the due process clause that will sustain this order is a far more subtle blow to liberty than the promulgation of the order itself. A military order, however unconstitutional, is not apt to last longer than the military emergency. [But] once a judicial opinion [rationalizes] the Constitution to show that the Constitution sanctions such an order, the Court for all time has validated the principle of racial discrimination in criminal procedure and of transplanting American citizens. The principle then lies about like a loaded weapon ready for the hand of any authority that can bring forward a plausible claim of an urgent need. [A] military commander may overstep the bounds of

was influential in persuading Congress to enact a 1988 law apologizing for the World War II internment program and providing for reparations.)

6. Justice Murphy noted, too, that "not one person of Japanese ancestry was accused or convicted of espionage or sabotage after Pearl Harbor while they were still free, a fact which is some evidence of the loyalty of the vast majority of these individuals and of the effectiveness of the established methods of combating these evils." He added: "It seems

incredible that under these circumstances it would have been impossible to hold loyalty hearings for the mere 112,000 persons involved—or at least for the 70,000 American citizens." He pointed out that the British government had been able to determine through individualized hearings whether 74,-000 German and Austrian aliens were genuine risks or only "friendly enemies." (The British had accomplished that task in a six month period after the outbreak of war, and only 2,000 were ultimately interned.)

constitutionality, and it is an incident. But if we review and approve, that passing incident becomes a doctrine of the Constitution." Earlier he had noted: "[I]f we cannot confine military expedients by the Constitution, neither would I distort the Constitution to approve all that the military may deem expedient." (Justice ROBERTS also submitted a dissent; Justice FRANKFURTER delivered a concurring opinion.)

Loving v. Virginia

388 U.S. 1, 87 S.Ct. 1817, 18 L.Ed.2d 1010 (1967).

Chief Justice WARREN delivered the opinion of the Court.

This case presents a constitutional question never addressed by this Court: whether a statutory scheme adopted by [Virginia] to prevent marriages between persons solely on the basis of racial classifications violates [the] 14th Amendment. For reasons which seem to us to reflect the central meaning of those constitutional commands, we conclude that these statutes cannot stand. [The appellants, a black woman and a white man, were married in the District of Columbia, returned to Virginia, and were convicted of violating Virginia's ban on miscegenation. The trial judge suspended their one year jail sentences on the condition that they leave the state and not return to Virginia together for 25 years.]

Virginia is now one of 16 States which prohibit and punish marriages on the basis of racial classifications. Penalties for miscegenation arose as an incident to slavery and have been common in Virginia since the colonial period. [T]he State does not contend [that] its powers to regulate marriage are unlimited notwithstanding the commands of the 14th Amendment, [but] argues *state argues* that the meaning of [equal protection] is only that state penal laws containing an interracial element as part of the definition of the offense must apply equally to whites and Negroes in the sense that members of each race are punished to the same degree. Thus, the State contends that, because its miscegenation statutes punish equally both the white and the Negro participants in an interracial marriage, these statutes, despite their reliance on racial classifications, do not constitute an invidious discrimination based upon [race]. Because we reject the notion that the mere "equal application" of a statute containing racial classifications is enough to remove the classifications from the 14th Amendment's proscription of all invidious racial discriminations, we do not accept the State's contention that these statutes should be upheld if there is any possible basis for concluding that they serve a rational purpose. [W]e deal with statutes containing racial classifications, and the fact of equal application does not immunize the statute from the very heavy burden of justification which the 14th Amendment has traditionally required of state statutes drawn according to race.

The State argues that statements [in] Congress about the time of the passage of the 14th Amendment indicate that the Framers did not intend the Amendment to make unconstitutional state miscegenation laws. [W]e have said in connection with a related problem that although these historical sources *original history (1885?)* "cast some light" they are not sufficient to resolve the problem; "[a]t best, they are inconclusive." Brown v. Board of Education [1954; p. 673 below]. We have rejected the proposition that the debates in the Thirty-ninth Congress or in the State legislatures which ratified the 14th Amendment supported the theory [that] the requirement of equal protection of the laws is satisfied by penal laws defining offenses based on racial classifications so long as white and Negro participants in the offense were similarly published. McLaughlin v. Florida [which follows].

[The] State finds support for its "equal application" theory in the decision of the Court in Pace v. Alabama, 106 U.S. 583 (1883). In that case, the Court upheld a conviction under an Alabama statute forbidding adultery or fornication between a white person and a Negro which imposed a greater penalty than that of a statute proscribing similar conduct by members of the same race. The Court reasoned that the statute could not be said to discriminate against Negroes because the punishment for each participant in the offense was the same. However, as recently as the 1964 Term, in rejecting the reasoning of that case, we stated: "Pace represents a limited view of the Equal Protection Clause which has not withstood analysis in the subsequent decisions of this Court." McLaughlin v. Florida. [The] clear and central purpose of the 14th Amendment was to eliminate all official state sources of invidious racial discrimination in the States. [E.g., Slaughter–House Cases; Strauder.] There can be no question but that Virginia's miscegenation statutes rest solely upon distinctions drawn according to race. The statutes proscribe generally accepted conduct if engaged in by members of different races. At the very least, [equal protection] demands that racial classifications, especially suspect in criminal statutes, be subjected to the "most rigid scrutiny" [Korematsu], and, if they are ever to be upheld, they must be shown to be necessary to the accomplishment of some permissible state objective, independent of the racial discrimination which it was the object of the 14th Amendment to eliminate. [There] is patently no legitimate overriding purpose independent of invidious racial discrimination which justifies this classification. The fact that Virginia prohibits only interracial marriages involving white persons demonstrates that the racial classifications must stand on their own justification, as measures designed to maintain White Supremacy.[1] We have consistently denied the constitutionality of measures which restrict the rights of citizens on account of race. There can be no doubt that restricting the freedom to marry solely because of racial classifications violates the central meaning of [equal protection].

Reversed.[2]

Justice STEWART, concurring.

I have previously expressed [in McLaughlin v. Florida] (concurring opinion) the belief that "it is simply not possible for a state law to be valid under our

1. Appellants point out that the State's concern in these statutes, as expressed in the words of the 1924 Act's title, "An Act to Preserve Racial Integrity," extends only to the integrity of the white race. While Virginia prohibits whites from marrying any nonwhite (subject to the exception for the descendants of Pocahontas), Negroes, Orientals, and any other racial class may intermarry without statutory interference. Appellants contend that this distinction renders Virginia's miscegenation statutes arbitrary and unreasonable even assuming the constitutional validity of an official purpose to preserve "racial integrity." We need not reach this contention because we find the racial classifications in these statutes repugnant to the 14th Amendment, even assuming an even-handed state purpose to protect the "integrity" of all races. [Footnote by Chief Justice Warren.]

2. Note that the law struck down in Loving, unlike those in Korematsu and Strauder, did not contain racial classifications explicitly disadvantaging racial minorities. Instead, the Loving law on its face applied equally to blacks and whites. Nevertheless, the Court applied strict scrutiny and struck down the law. Why? Note Palmore v. Sidoti, which follows: "Classifying persons according to their race is more likely to reflect racial prejudice than legitimate public concerns; the race, not the person, dictates the category," (A similar problem is raised by Brown v. Board of Education, p. 673 below, striking down public school racial segregation.)

Constitution which makes the criminality of an act depend upon the race of the actor." Because I adhere to that belief, I concur in the [judgment].

———

McLAUGHLIN v. FLORIDA, 379 U.S. 184 (1964), referred to by Chief Justice Warren as well as Justice Stewart in Loving, invalidated a criminal statute prohibiting cohabitation by interracial married couples. Justice WHITE's majority opinion emphasized: "[We] deal here with a classification based upon the race of the participants, which must be viewed in light of the historical fact that the central purpose of the 14th Amendment was to eliminate racial discrimination emanating from official sources in the States. This strong policy renders racial classifications 'constitutionally suspect' and subject to the 'most rigid scrutiny' [Korematsu], and 'in most circumstances irrelevant' to any constitutionally acceptable legislative purpose [Hirabayashi]. [We] deal here with a racial classification embodied in a criminal statute. [Our] inquiry, therefore, is whether there clearly appears in the relevant materials some overriding statutory purpose requiring the proscription of the specified conduct when engaged in by a white person and a Negro, but not otherwise. Without such justification the racial classification [here] is reduced to an invidious discrimination forbidden by [equal protection]." Compare a statement later in Justice White's opinion: "[A law] which trenches upon the constitutionally protected freedom from invidious official discrimination based on race [bears] a heavy burden of justification [and] will be upheld only if it is necessary, and not merely rationally related, to the accomplishment of a permissible state policy." Is there a significant shift in emphasis in that second passage? The second passage emphasizes means—"necessary" rather than merely rational means—to the accomplishment of a "permissible" state end. The exercises of strict scrutiny in the cases in the rest of this chapter typically insist upon both a "compelling" end and carefully tailored, "necessary" means. Compare Palmore v. Sidoti, which follows.

PALMORE v. SIDOTI, 466 U.S. 429 (1984): This case arose from a custody battle after Palmore and Sidoti (both white) were divorced. Initially, Palmore, the mother, was awarded custody of their three-year-old daughter. When the mother entered a second marriage, to an African American, the state court awarded custody to the father, in "the best interest" of the child. The trial court found that, "despite the strides that had been made in bettering relations between the races in this country, it is inevitable that [the daughter] will, if allowed to remain in the present [situation], suffer from the social stigmatization that is sure to come." The Court unanimously reversed that ruling. Chief Justice BURGER noted that the custody ruling had rested wholly on race, since it was "clear that the outcome would have been different had [Palmore] married a Caucasian male." He proceeded: "A core purpose of the [14th Amendment] was to do away with all governmentally imposed discrimination based on race. Classifying persons according to their race is more likely to reflect racial prejudice than legitimate public concerns; the race, not the person, dictates the category. Such classifications are subject to the most exacting scrutiny; to pass constitutional muster, they must be justified by a compelling governmental interest and must be 'necessary [to] the accomplishment' of its legitimate purpose. [McLaughlin; see Loving.] The goal of granting custody based on the best interests of the child is indisputably a substantial governmental interest for purposes of [equal protection]. It would ignore reality to suggest that racial and ethnic prejudices do not exist or that all manifestations of those prejudices have been eliminated. There is a risk that a child living with a step-parent of a different race may be subject to a variety of pressures and stresses not present if the child were living with parents of the same racial or ethnic origin. The question, however, is whether the reality of private biases and the possible injury they might inflict are permissible considerations for removal of an infant child from the custody of its natural mother. We have little difficulty concluding that they are not. The Constitution cannot control such prejudices but neither can it tolerate them. Private biases may be outside the reach of the law, but the law cannot, directly or indirectly, give them effect. [The] effects of racial prejudice, however real, cannot justify a racial classification removing an infant child from the custody of its natural mother found to be an appropriate person to have such custody." Cf. Note, "Race as a Factor in Custody and Adoption Disputes," 71 Corn.L.Rev. 209 (1985).

———

SCRUTINIZING RACIAL CLASSIFICATIONS: SOME EXAMPLES AND QUESTIONS

"Our Constitution is color-blind," insisted the first Justice Harlan's dissent in Plessy v. Ferguson (p. 671 below). Over the years, some Justices have suggested a per se rule invalidating all governmental distinctions among individuals because of race. And some commentators have argued that such a total ban on racial classifications is the most persuasive justification for a number of Court decisions—e.g., the invalidation of racial segregation in public facilities generally after the 1954 decision in Brown (p. 673 below). But, as the preceding cases illustrate, the Court has not stated so comprehensive a prohibition; rather, disadvantaging racial classifications are ordinarily "suspect," must be subjected to "the most rigid scrutiny," and bear a "very heavy burden of justification." Would a flat rule banning all racial classifications that disadvantage minorities be preferable to the Court's approach? Note Bickel's insistence that all racial discrimination is "illegal, immoral, unconstitutional," in his The Morality of Consent (1975); cf. Greenawalt, "Judicial Scrutiny of 'Benign' Racial Preference in Law School Admissions," 75 Colum.L.Rev. 559 (1975). When—if ever—are or should racial criteria be constitutionally permissible? What justification is strong enough to survive the strict scrutiny avowed by the Court in these cases? Consider the following cases and problems, with special attention to the question of whether they were proper exercises of strict scrutiny. a. In Anderson v. Martin, 375 U.S. 399 (1964), the Court unanimously struck down a state law requiring that every candidate's race appear on the ballots. After rejecting the defense that the requirement was nondiscriminatory because it applied to candidates of all races, Justice Clark's opinion stated: "The vice lies [in] the placing of the power of the State behind a racial classification that induces racial prejudice at the polls." What if it were argued that racial designations helped elect more minority candidates—that, while making most voters more race-conscious and inducing majority race voters to reject minority candidates, it also induced minority voters to vote for more candidates of their own race? b. In per curiam orders in Tancil v. Woolls and Virginia Board of Elections v. Hamm, 379 U.S. 19 (1964), the Court summarily affirmed decisions (a) invalidating laws requiring separate lists of whites and blacks in voting, tax and property records, but (b) sustaining a requirement that every divorce decree indicate the race of the husband and wife. (The trial judge had stated that "the designation of race [may] in certain records serve a useful purpose"—e.g., "for identification or statistical use." He thought that the divorce decree requirement aided "vital statistics.")

c. To what extent can arguments relying on national emergencies or the needs of local order justify racial classifications? Recall Korematsu, above, and note Lee v. Washington, 390 U.S. 333 (1968), approving a federal court order striking down Alabama laws requiring racial segregation in prisons. Noting Alabama's argument that the lower court had made "no allowance for the necessities of prison security and discipline," the Court commented that "we do not so read" the order. A separate concurring notation, by Justices Black, Harlan and Stewart, sought "to make explicit [that] prison authorities have the right, acting in good faith and in particularized circumstances, to take into account racial tensions in maintaining security, discipline, and good order in prisons and jails." May police authorities take race into account in assigning officers to neighborhoods on the basis of the predominant racial composition of the area? d. May a state enact regulations, in the interest of health, based on "special traits" of races, such as alleged susceptibility to particular diseases? If the trait is not possessed by every member of the race, can the regulation be challenged for overinclusiveness? May a state require, for example, that blacks but not whites contemplating marriage be tested for sickle-cell anemia? What about a law requiring persons with a skin pigmentation darker than a certain shade to wear light-colored clothing at night? See Kaplan, "Equal Justice in an Unequal World," 61 Nw.U.L.Rev. 363 (1966), and Dabbs, "Constitutional [Considerations] in Mandatory Sickle Cell Anemia Testing," 7 U.C.D.L.Rev. 509 (1974). Are racial generalizations ever permissible when a minority race is disadvantaged? Or does the "suspectness" of race compel government to act only on an individualized basis and avoid all disadvantaging generalizations? Note the similar problems with respect to gender-based generalizations, below; see especially Manhart (1978; p. 701 below).

---

2. THE UNCONSTITUTIONALITY OF RACIAL SEGREGATION

THE "SEPARATE BUT EQUAL" ERA

1. *The Plessy case.* In PLESSY v. FERGUSON, 163 U.S. 537 (1896), the Court sustained a Louisiana law of 1890 that required "equal but separate accommodations" for "white" and "colored" railroad passengers. (Plessy, the challenger, alleged that he was "seven-eighths Caucasian and one-eighth African blood; that the mixture of colored blood was not discernible in him; and that he was entitled to every right [of] the white race." He was arrested for refusing to leave a seat in a coach for whites.) Justice BROWN's majority opinion, after finding the 13th Amendment inapplicable, stated: "The object of the [14th] Amendment was undoubtedly to enforce the absolute equality of the two races before the law, but in the nature of things it could not have been intended to abolish distinctions based upon color, or to enforce social, as distinguished from political equality, or a commingling of the two races upon terms unsatisfactory to either. Laws [requiring] their separation in places where they are liable to be brought into contact do not necessarily imply the inferiority of either race to the other, and have been generally, if not universally, recognized as within the competency of the state legislatures in the exercise of their police power. The most common instance of this is connected with the establishment of separate schools for white and colored children, which have been [upheld] even by courts of States where the political rights of the colored

race have been longest and most earnestly enforced. [Laws] forbidding the intermarriage of the two races may be said in a technical sense to interfere with the freedom of contract, and yet have been universally recognized as within the police power of the state. [The] distinction between laws interfering with the political equality of the negro and those requiring the separation of the two races in schools, theaters, and railway carriages has been frequently drawn by this Court. [E.g., Strauder.]

"[It is suggested] that the same argument that will justify the state legislature in requiring railways to provide separate accommodations for the two races will also authorize them to require separate cars to be provided for people whose hair is of a certain color, or who are aliens, or who belong to certain nationalities, or to enact laws requiring colored people to walk upon one side of the street, and white people upon the other, or requiring white men's houses to be painted white, and colored men's black, or their vehicles or business signs to be of different colors, upon the theory that one side of the street is as good as the other, or that a house or vehicle of one color is as good as one of another color. The reply to all this is that every exercise of the police power must be reasonable, and extend only to such laws as are enacted in good faith for the promotion of the public good, and not for the annoyance or oppression of a particular class. [In] determining the question of reasonableness, [the legislature] is at liberty to act with reference to the established usages, customs, and traditions of the people, and with a view to the promotion of their comfort, and the preservation of the public peace and good order. Gauged by this standard, we cannot say that [this law] is unreasonable, or more obnoxious to the [14th Amendment] than the [laws] requiring separate schools for colored children, [the] constitutionality of which does not seem to have been [questioned].

"We consider the underlying fallacy of the plaintiff's argument to consist in the assumption that the enforced separation of the two races stamps the colored race with a badge of inferiority. If this be so, it is not by reason of anything found in the act, but solely because the colored race chooses to put that construction upon it. [The argument] assumes that social prejudices may be overcome by legislation, and that equal rights cannot be secured to the negro except by an enforced commingling of the two races. We cannot accept this proposition. If the two races are to meet upon terms of social equality, it must be the result of natural affinities, a mutual appreciation of each other's merits, and a voluntary consent of individuals. [Legislation] is powerless to eradicate racial instincts or to abolish distinctions based upon physical differences, and the attempt to do so can only result in accentuating the difficulties of the present situation. If the civil and political rights of both races be equal, one cannot be inferior to the other civilly or politically. If one race be inferior to the other socially, the [Constitution] cannot put them upon the same plane."

The first Justice HARLAN dissented: "[I] deny that any legislative body or judicial tribunal may have regard to the race of citizens when the civil rights of those citizens are involved. [It] was said in argument that the [law] does not discriminate against either race, but prescribes a rule applicable alike to white and colored citizens. But [every one] knows that [the law] had its origin in the purpose, not so much to exclude white persons from railroad cars occupied by blacks, as to exclude colored people from coaches [assigned] to white persons. [The] fundamental objection, therefore, to the statute is that it interferes with the personal freedom of citizens. The white race deems itself to be the dominant race in this country. And so it is, in prestige, in achievements, in education, in wealth and in power. So, I doubt not, it will continue to be for all time, if it remains true to its great heritage and holds fast to the principles of constitutional liberty. But in view of the Constitution, in the eye of the law, there is in this country no superior, dominant, ruling class of citizens. There is no caste here. Our Constitution is color-blind, and neither knows nor tolerates classes among citizens. [It] is, therefore, to be regretted that this high tribunal [has] reached the conclusion that it is competent for a State to regulate the enjoyment by citizens of their civil rights solely upon the basis of race. In my opinion, the judgment this day rendered will, in time, prove to be quite as pernicious as the decision made [in] the Dred Scott case. [The] present decision [will] encourage the belief that it is possible, by means of state enactments, to defeat the beneficent purposes which the [people] had in view when they adopted the recent amendments of the [Constitution]. Sixty millions of whites are in no danger from the presence here of eight millions of blacks. The destinies of the two races [are] indissolubly linked together, and the interests of both require that the common government of all shall not permit the seeds of race hate to be planted under the sanction of law. What can more certainly arouse race hate, what more certainly create and perpetuate a feeling of distrust between these races, than state enactments, which, in fact, proceed on the ground that colored citizens are so inferior and degraded that they cannot be allowed to sit in public coaches occupied by white citizens? [We] boast of the freedom enjoyed by our people above all other peoples. But it is difficult to reconcile that boast with a state of the law which, practically, puts the brand of servitude and degradation upon a large class of our fellow citizens,—our equals before the law. The thin disguise of 'equal' accommodations [will] not mislead any one, nor atone for the wrong this day done." See generally Lofgren, The Plessy Case: A Legal Historical Interpretation (1987).

2. *The 20th century attack on de jure segregation.* The modern legal attack on officially mandated segregation, led by the NAACP, began with efforts to show that the "separate but equal" doctrine of Plessy was vulnerable in the context of education provided for black students seeking graduate and professional school training. The first in the sequence of modern school segregation cases that culminated in Brown was Missouri ex rel. Gaines v. Canada, 305 U.S. 337 (1938). Gaines, a black applicant, had been refused admission to the University of Missouri Law School because of his race. Missouri's defense to his suit for admission was that, pending the establishment of a black law school in the state, it would pay Gaines's tuition in an out-of-state school. Chief Justice Hughes's majority opinion concluded that the State was obligated to furnish Gaines "within its borders facilities for legal education substantially equal to those which the State there offered for persons of the white race, whether or not other negroes sought the same opportunity." In the absence of such facilities, Gaines was entitled to be admitted to the existing state law school. Subsequent decisions dealing with segregated facilities in graduate and professional education are described in Brown, which follows.[†]

Brown v. Board of Education [Brown I—The Constitutional Ruling]

347 U.S. 483, 74 S.Ct. 686, 98 L.Ed. 873 (1954).

Chief Justice WARREN delivered the opinion of the Court.

[†] For a detailed account of the background and Court consideration of Brown, see Kluger, Simple Justice: The History of Brown v. Board of Education and Black America's Struggle for Equality (1976). See also Tushnet, The NAACP's Legal Strategy Against Segregated Education, 1925–1950 (1987).

These cases come to us from the States of Kansas, South Carolina, Virginia, and Delaware.* [In] each of the cases, minors of the Negro race [seek] the aid of the courts in obtaining admission to the public schools of their community on a nonsegregated basis. In each instance, they had been denied admission to schools attended by white children under laws requiring or permitting segregation according to race. [In most of the cases, the courts below denied relief, relying on] the so-called "separate but equal" doctrine announced by this Court in Plessy.[1] [The] plaintiffs contend that segregated public schools are not "equal" and cannot be made "equal," and that hence they are deprived of the equal protection of the laws. [Argument] was heard in the 1952 Term, and reargument was heard this Term on certain questions propounded by the Court.[2] Reargument was largely devoted to the circumstances surrounding the adoption of the 14th Amendment in 1868. It covered exhaustively consideration of the Amendment in Congress, ratification by the states, then existing practices in racial segregation, and the views of proponents and opponents of the Amendment. This discussion and our own investigation convince us that, although these sources cast some light, it is not enough to resolve the problem with which we are faced. At best, they are inconclusive. The most avid proponents of the post-War Amendments undoubtedly intended them to remove all legal distinctions among "all persons born or naturalized in the United States." Their opponents, just as certainly, were antagonistic to both the letter and the spirit of the Amendments and wished them to have the most limited effect. What others in Congress and the state legislatures had in mind cannot be determined with any degree of certainty.

An additional reason for the inconclusive nature of the Amendment's history, with respect to segregated schools, is the status of public education at that time. In the South, the movement toward free common schools, supported by general taxation, had not yet taken hold. Education of white children was largely in the hands of private groups. Education of Negroes was almost nonexistent, and practically all of the race were illiterate. In fact, any education of Negroes was forbidden by law in some states. Today, in contrast, many Negroes have achieved outstanding success in the arts and sciences as well as in the business and professional world. It is true that public school education [had] advanced further in the North, but the effect of the Amendment on

---

* The cases decided together with Brown v. Board of Education of Topeka were Briggs v. Elliott (South Carolina); Davis v. County School Board of Prince Edward County, Virginia; and Gebhart v. Belton (Delaware). See also Bolling v. Sharpe, the companion case from the District of Columbia, which follows.

1. The exception was the Delaware case, where the highest state court, while adhering to Plessy, ordered that plaintiffs be admitted to the white schools because of their superiority to the black schools.

2. The first three questions propounded by the Court follow: "1. What evidence is there that the Congress which submitted and the State legislatures and conventions which ratified the 14th Amendment contemplated or did not contemplate, understood or did not understand, that it would abolish segregation in public schools? 2. If neither the Congress in submitting nor the States in ratifying the 14th Amendment understood that compliance with it would require the immediate abolition of segregation in public schools, was it nevertheless the understanding of the framers of the Amendment (a) that future Congresses might, in the exercise of their power under section 5 of the Amendment, abolish such segregation, or (b) that it would be within the judicial power, in light of future conditions, to construe the Amendment as abolishing such segregation of its own force? 3. On the assumption that the answers to questions 2(a) and (b) do not dispose of the issue, is it within the judicial power, in construing the Amendment, to abolish segregation in public schools?" [Footnote by Chief Justice Warren.] [Questions 4 and 5 were set for further argument in the Court's disposition of this case. Those questions appear in the footnote to Brown II, below.]

Northern States was generally ignored in the congressional debates. Even in the North, the conditions of public education did not approximate those existing today. The curriculum was usually rudimentary; ungraded schools were common in rural areas; [and] compulsory school attendance was virtually unknown. As a consequence, it is not surprising that there should be so little in the history of the 14th Amendment relating to its intended effect on public education.

In the first cases in this Court construing the 14th Amendment, decided shortly after its adoption, the Court interpreted it as proscribing all state-imposed discriminations against the Negro race.[3] The doctrine of "separate but equal" did not make its appearance in this Court until 1896 in [Plessy], involving not education but transportation. [In] this Court, there have been six cases involving the "separate but equal" doctrine in the field of public education. In Cumming v. Richmond County Board of Education, 175 U.S. 528, and Gong Lum v. Rice, 275 U.S. 78, the validity of the doctrine itself was not challenged.[4] In more recent cases, all on the graduate school level, inequality was found in that specific benefits enjoyed by white students were denied to Negro students of the same educational qualifications. Missouri ex rel. Gaines v. Canada; Sipuel v. Oklahoma, 332 U.S. 631; Sweatt v. Painter, 339 U.S. 629; McLaurin v. Oklahoma State Regents, 339 U.S. 637.[5] In none of these cases was it necessary to reexamine the doctrine to grant relief to the Negro plaintiff. And in [Sweatt], the Court expressly reserved decision on the question whether [Plessy] should be held inapplicable to public education. In the instant cases, that question is directly presented. Here, unlike [Sweatt], there are findings below that the Negro and white schools involved have been equalized or are being equalized, with respect to buildings, curricula, qualifications and salaries

3. Slaughter-House Cases; [Strauder]. [Footnote by Chief Justice Warren.]

4. In the Cumming case, Negro taxpayers [unsuccessfully] sought an injunction requiring the defendant school board to discontinue the operation of a high school for white children until the board resumed operation of a high school for Negro children. Similarly, in the Gong Lum case, the plaintiff, a child of Chinese descent, contended only that state authorities had misapplied the doctrine by classifying him with Negro children and requiring him to attend a Negro school. [Footnote by Chief Justice Warren.]

5. The Sipuel case in 1948 reaffirmed the principles of Gaines, p. 673 above. The Sweatt case in 1950 required the admission of blacks to the University of Texas Law School even though the state had recently established a law school for blacks. Chief Justice Vinson's opinion for the Court found no "substantial equality in the educational opportunities offered white and Negro law students by the State. In terms of number of the faculty, variety of courses and opportunity for specialization, size of the student body, scope of the library, availability of law review and similar activities, the University of Texas Law School is superior. What is more impor-

tant, the University of Texas Law School possesses to a far greater degree those qualities which are incapable of objective measurement but which make for greatness in a law school. Such qualities, to name but a few, include reputation of the faculty, experience of the administration, position and influence of the alumni, standing in the community, traditions and prestige." He added that a law school "cannot be effective in isolation from the individuals and institutions with which the law interacts," and he noted that the newly established black law school "excludes from its student body members of the racial groups which number 85% of the population of the state and include most of the lawyers, witnesses, jurors, judges and other officials with whom petitioner would inevitably be dealing when he becomes a member of the Texas Bar." The McLaurin case in 1950 involved a black student who had been admitted to a state university's graduate program not offered at the state's black school, but had been required to sit in separate sections in or adjoining the classrooms, library and cafeteria facilities. Chief Justice Vinson's opinion found that the restrictions impaired the "ability to study, to engage in discussions and exchange views with other students and, in general, to learn his profession."

of teachers, and other "tangible" factors. Our decision, therefore, cannot turn on merely a comparison of these tangible factors in the Negro and white schools involved in each of the cases. We must look instead to the effect of segregation itself on public education.

In approaching this problem, we cannot turn the clock back to 1868 when the Amendment was adopted, or even to 1896 when Plessy was written. We must consider public education in the light of its full development and its present place in American life throughout the Nation. Only in this way can it be determined if segregation in public schools deprives these plaintiffs of [equal protection]. Today, education is perhaps the most important function of state and local governments. Compulsory school attendance laws and the great expenditures for education both demonstrate our recognition of the importance of education to our democratic society. It is required in the performance of our most basic public responsibilities, even service in the armed forces. It is the very foundation of good citizenship. Today it is a principal instrument in awakening the child to cultural values, in preparing him for later professional training, and in helping him to adjust normally to his environment. In these days, it is doubtful that any child may reasonably be expected to succeed in life if he is denied the opportunity of an education. Such an opportunity, where the state has undertaken to provide it, is a right which must be made available to all on equal terms.

We come then to the question presented: Does segregation of children in public schools solely on the basis of race, even though the physical facilities and other "tangible" factors may be equal, deprive the children of the minority group of equal educational opportunities? We believe that it does. In [Sweatt], this Court relied in large part on "those qualities which are incapable of objective measurement but which make for greatness in a law school." In McLaurin, the Court [again] resorted to intangible considerations: "[the] ability to study, to engage in discussions and exchange views with other students, and, in general, to learn [the] profession." Such considerations apply with added force to children in grade and high schools. To separate them from others of similar age and qualifications solely because of their race generates a feeling of inferiority as to their status in the community that may affect their hearts and minds in a way unlikely ever to be undone. The effect of this separation on their educational opportunities was well stated by a finding in the Kansas case by a court which nevertheless felt compelled to rule against the Negro plaintiffs: "Segregation of white and colored children in public schools has a detrimental effect upon the colored children. The impact is greater when it has the sanction of the law; for the policy of separating the races is usually interpreted as denoting the inferiority of the negro group. A sense of inferiority affects the motivation of a child to learn. Segregation with the sanction of law, therefore, has a tendency to [retard] the educational and mental development of negro children and to deprive them of some of the benefits they would receive in a [racially] integrated school system." Whatever may have been the extent of psychological knowledge at the time of [Plessy], this finding is amply supported by modern authority.[6] Any language in [Plessy] contrary to this finding is rejected.

---

6. K.B. Clark, Effect of Prejudice and Discrimination on Personality Development (Midcentury White House Conference on Children and Youth, 1950); Witmer and Kotinsky, Personality in the Making (1952), c. VI; Deutscher and Chein, The Psychological Effects of Enforced Segregation: A Survey of Social Science Opinion, 26 J. Psychol. 259 (1948); Chein, What are the Psychological Effects of Segregation Under Conditions of Equal Facilities?, 3 Int.J.Opinion and Attitude Res. 229 (1949); Brameld, Educational

We conclude that in the field of public education the doctrine of "separate but equal" has no place. Separate educational facilities are inherently unequal. Therefore, we hold that the plaintiffs and others similarly situated for whom the actions have been brought are, by reason of the segregation complained of, deprived of [equal protection]. This disposition makes unnecessary any discussion whether such segregation also violates [due process]. Because these are class actions, because of the wide applicability of this decision, and because of the great variety of local conditions, the formulation of decrees in these cases presents problems of considerable complexity. On reargument, the consideration of appropriate relief was necessarily subordinated to the primary question—the constitutionality of segregation in public education. We have now announced that such segregation is a denial of [equal protection]. In order that we may have the full assistance of the parties in formulating decrees, the cases will be restored to the docket, and the parties are requested to present further argument on Questions 4 and 5 [see footnote 1 to Brown II, below] previously propounded by the Court for [reargument].

It is so ordered.

BOLLING v. SHARPE, 347 U.S. 497 (1954): In this case, decided on the same day as Brown I, the Court held that racial segregation in the District of Columbia public schools violated the due process clause of the Fifth Amendment. Chief Justice WARREN's opinion stated: "The Fifth Amendment [does] not contain an equal protection clause. [But] the concepts of equal protection and due process, both stemming from our American ideal of fairness, are not mutually exclusive. The 'equal protection of the laws' is a more explicit safeguard of prohibited unfairness than 'due process of law,' and, therefore, we do not imply that the two are always interchangeable phrases. But, as this Court has recognized, discrimination may be so unjustifiable as to be violative of due process. Classifications based solely upon race must be scrutinized with particular care, since they are contrary to our traditions and hence constitutionally suspect. [E.g., Korematsu.] Although the Court has not assumed to define 'liberty' with any great precision, that term is not confined to mere freedom from bodily restraint. Liberty under law extends to the full range of conduct which the individual is free to pursue, and it cannot be restricted except for a proper governmental objective. Segregation in public education is not reasonably related to any proper governmental objective, and thus it imposes on Negro children of the District of Columbia a burden that constitutes an arbitrary deprivation of their liberty in violation of [due process]. In view of our decision that the Constitution prohibits the states from maintaining racially segregated public schools, it would be unthinkable that the same Constitution would impose a lesser duty on the Federal Government." (Is it truly "unthinkable" that the Fifth Amendment imposed a "lesser duty" on the Federal Government than the 14th did on the states?)

Costs, in Discrimination and National Welfare (McIver, ed., 1949), 44–48; Frazier, The Negro in the United States (1949), 674–681. And see generally Myrdal, An American Dilemma (1944). [Footnote by Chief Justice Warren.]

SEGREGATION AND THE BROWN PRINCIPLE

1. *Legally mandated segregation in other public facilities.* Soon after the 1954 decision in Brown, the Court found segregation unconstitutional in other public facilities as well. Despite the Court's emphasis on the school context in Brown, its results in the later cases—all in contexts other than education— were reached in curt per curiam orders, most simply citing Brown.[1] It was not until 1963 that the Court was ready to articulate the import of these per curiam rulings. Johnson v. Virginia, 373 U.S. 61, reversed a contempt conviction for refusal to comply with a state judge's order to move to a section of a courtroom reserved for blacks. Now, the Court was willing to state at last: "[It] is no longer open to question that a State may not constitutionally require segregation of public facilities."

2. *The Brown rationale.* In light of the school segregation opinion and the public facilities cases in note 1, what are the bases and justifications for Brown? What is its scope?[2]

a. *History.* Do the history and "central purpose" of the 14th Amendment justify the decision? Was the Court's treatment of the historical understanding adequate? Consider Bickel's observation that the ban on segregation might well have been an improper implication if the 14th Amendment were a statute, but that "we are dealing with a constitutional amendment, not a statute."[3] He noted that the history of the 14th Amendment "rather clearly" demonstrates "that it was not expected in 1866 to apply to segregation." But his historical survey found "an awareness on the part of [the Framers of the 14th Amendment] that it was *a constitution* they were writing, which led to a choice of language capable of growth," and he concluded that "the record of history, properly understood, left the way open to, in fact invited, a decision based on the moral and material state of the nation in 1954, not 1866." Cf. McConnell, "Originalism and the Desegregation Decision," 81 Va.L.Rev. 947 (1995), and Klarman, "Brown, Originalism and Constitutional Theory," 81 Va.L.Rev. 1881 (1995).

b. *Impact on educational and psychological development.* Was the critical element in Brown the Court's endorsement of the finding that state-imposed

---

1. See, e.g., Mayor of Baltimore v. Dawson, 350 U.S. 877 (1955) (beaches); Gayle v. Browder, 352 U.S. 903 (1956) (buses); Holmes v. Atlanta, 350 U.S. 879 (1955) (golf courses); New Orleans City Park Improvement Association v. Detiege, 358 U.S. 54 (1958) (parks). Cf. Turner v. Memphis, 369 U.S. 350 (1962) (municipal airport restaurant).

2. For a sampling of the extensive commentary generated by Brown, see Wechsler, "Toward Neutral Principles of Constitutional Law," 73 Harv.L.Rev. 1 (1959); Pollak, "Racial Discrimination and Judicial Integrity: A Reply to Professor Wechsler," 108 U.Pa. L.Rev. 1 (1959); C.L. Black, Jr., "The Lawfulness of the Segregation Decisions," 69 Yale L.J. 421 (1960). On the historical data, see Bickel, "The Original Understanding and the Segregation Decision," 69 Harv.L.Rev. 1 (1955). See also the symposia in two volumes of Law & Contemp. Prob., "The Courts, So-

cial Science, and School Desegregation" (1975) and "School Desegregation: Lessons of the First Twenty–Five Years" (1978). For comments on the social science evidence in Brown—footnote 6 in Brown generated considerable controversy about the relevance of these data—, see Cahn, "Jurisprudence," 30 N.Y.U.L.Rev. 150 (1955); K.B. Clark, "The Desegregation Cases," 5 Vill.L.Rev. 224 (1959); and K.B. Clark, "The Social Scientists, the Brown Decision, and Contemporary Confusion," in Argument (Friedman ed. 1969). [See also Stell v. Savannah–Chatham Bd. of Ed., 220 F.Supp. 667 (S.D.Ga.1963), rev'd, 333 F.2d 55 (5th Cir.1964), where the District Judge, after an extensive hearing to survey the social science data nearly a decade after Brown, unsuccessfully tried in effect to "reverse" Brown.]

3. The sources of the comments referred to in this note are cited in footnote 2.

segregation "has a tendency to retard the educational and mental development of Negro children"? Were empirical data central to the Court's holding? The reliance on social science evidence—and the quality of those data, then and now[4]—have been the focus of considerable controversy. See, e.g., Cahn's *Cahn* comment that "I would not have the constitutional rights of Negroes—or of other Americans—rest on any such flimsy foundation as some of the scientific demonstrations in these records. [Behavioral science findings] have an uncertain expectancy of life." Was the central element in the Court's decision the statement that segregation "generates a feeling of inferiority"? What are the critical elements in establishing such a conclusion? Social science data? Judicial notice? History? The intent of the legislators enacting segregation laws? The stereotypical assumption of black inferiority—the assumption which supposedly provided the underpinnings for the general system of segregation? The black community's perception of the stigma imposed by segregation? Note Cahn's emphasis on "the most familiar and universally accepted standards of right and wrong" as demonstrating that "racial segregation under government auspices inevitably inflicts humiliation" and that "official humiliation of innocent, law-abiding citizens is psychologically injurious and morally evil." Can the Court properly rest a decision on "universal" moral standards without added support in empirical data or history?

Compare Professor Black's defense of the "lawfulness" of Brown, empha- *Black* sizing that the Southern cultural tradition during the Jim Crow era makes it clear that "segregation is a massive intentional disadvantaging of the Negro race, as such, by state law." He commented: "[I]f a whole race of people finds itself confined within a system which is set up and continued for the very purpose of keeping it in an inferior station, and if the question is then solemnly propounded whether such a race is being treated 'equally,' I think we ought to exercise one of the sovereign prerogatives of philosophers—that of laughter." And the segregation system, he insisted, clearly met that description. He noted: "Segregation is historically and contemporaneously associated in a functioning complex with practices which are indisputably and grossly discriminatory."[5] Contrast Wechsler's argument: "For me, assuming equal facilities, the question *Wechsler* posed by state-enforced segregation is not one of discrimination at all. Its human and its constitutional dimensions lie entirely elsewhere, in the denial by the state of freedom to associate, a denial that impinges in the same way on any groups or races that may be involved." He asked: "Given a situation where the state must practically choose between denying the association to those individuals who wish it or imposing it on those who would avoid it, is there a basis in neutral principles for holding that the Constitution demands that the claims for

---

4. For a review of the available (and controversial) data, see Goodman, "De Facto School Segregation: A Constitutional and Empirical Analysis," 70 Calif.L.Rev. 275 (1972).

5. Charles Black, who grew up in Texas, added that the "purpose and impact of segregation in the southern regional culture" were "matters of common notoriety, matters not so much for judicial notice as for the background knowledge of educated men who live in the world." Southern segregation at the time of Brown, he emphasized, was not "mutual separation of whites and Negroes," but rather "one in-group enjoying full normal communal life and one out-group that is barred from this life and forced into an inferior life of its own." He concluded that the "regional culture" was properly determinative in Brown: the question was not whether segregation is inevitably discriminatory, but whether "discrimination inheres in that segregation which is imposed by law in the twentieth century in certain specific states in the American Union. And that question has meaning and can find an answer only on the ground of history and of common knowledge about the facts of life."

association should prevail?'' Do Cahn's or Black's arguments answer Wechsler's question?

c. *The scope of the holding.* In view of the emphasis on the impact of segregation on *educational* opportunity in Brown, should the Court have explained more fully the basis for its ultimate general principle "that a State may not constitutionally require segregation of public facilities," rather than resting that development largely on the per curiam orders in note 1, above? Do the considerations articulated in Brown, or other justifications for its result, support a claim that de facto as well as de jure segregation in public schools is unconstitutional? Is the major emphasis in Brown on the existence of *purposeful*, de jure discrimination, or does Brown focus on the *impact* of segregated schools (whether the segregation was "purposeful" or not) in limiting educational opportunity and in generating a sense of inferiority?[6] [Consider the comment in the concurring opinion of Justice Thomas in Jenkins v. Missouri (1995; p. 789 below): "Segregation was not unconstitutional because it might have caused psychological feelings of inferiority. [Psychological] injury is irrelevant to the question whether [state actors] have engaged in intentional discrimination—the critical question for ascertaining violations of [equal protection].'']

———

Brown v. Board of Education [Brown II—The Implementation Decision]

349 U.S. 294, 75 S.Ct. 753, 99 L.Ed. 1083 (1955).

Chief Justice WARREN delivered the opinion of the Court.

These cases were decided on May 17, 1954. The opinions of that date, declaring the fundamental principle that racial discrimination in public education is unconstitutional, are incorporated herein by reference. All provisions of federal, state, or local law requiring or permitting such discrimination must yield to this principle. There remains for consideration the manner in which relief is to be accorded. Because these cases arose under different local conditions and their disposition will involve a variety of local problems, we requested further argument on the question of relief.[1] In view of the nation-wide importance of the decision, we invited the Attorney General of the United States and the Attorneys General of all states requiring or permitting racial

6. The question of the validity of de facto segregation is postponed to sec. 3D below, for consideration with other aspects of the "purpose"-"impact" distinction.

1. Further argument was requested on the following [questions], previously propounded by the Court: "4. Assuming it is decided that segregation in public schools violates the 14th Amendment (*a*) would a decree necessarily follow providing that, within the limits set by normal geographic school districting, Negro children should forthwith be admitted to schools of their choice, or (*b*) may this Court, in the exercise of its equity powers, permit an effective gradual adjustment to be brought about from existing segregated systems to a system not based on color distinctions? 5. On the assumption on which

questions 4(*a*) and (*b*) are based, and assuming further that this Court will exercise its equity powers to the end described in question 4(*b*), (*a*) should this Court formulate detailed decrees in these cases; (*b*) if so, what specific issues should the decrees reach; (*c*) should this Court appoint a special master to hear evidence with a view to recommending specific terms for such decrees; (*d*) should this Court remand to the courts of first instance with directions to frame decrees in these cases, and if so what general directions should the decrees of this Court include and what procedures should the courts of first instance follow in arriving at the specific terms of more detailed decrees?'' [Footnote by Chief Justice Warren.]

discrimination in public education to present their views on that question. The parties, the United States, and [six states] participated [in the argument]. Full implementation of these constitutional principles may require solution of varied local school problems. School authorities have the primary responsibility for elucidating, assessing, and solving these problems; courts will have to consider whether the action of school authorities constitutes good faith implementation of the governing constitutional principles. Because of their proximity to local conditions and the possible need for further hearings, the courts which originally heard these cases can best perform this judicial appraisal. Accordingly, we believe it appropriate to remand the cases to those courts. In fashioning and effectuating the decrees, the courts will be guided by equitable principles. Traditionally, equity has been characterized by a practical flexibility in shaping its remedies and by a facility for adjusting and reconciling public and private needs. These cases call for the exercise of these traditional attributes of equity power. At stake is the personal interest of the plaintiffs in admission to public schools as soon as practicable on a nondiscriminatory basis. To effectuate this interest may call for elimination of a variety of obstacles in making the transition to school systems operated in accordance with the constitutional principles set forth in [Brown I]. Courts of equity may properly take into account the public interest in the elimination of such obstacles in a systematic and effective manner. But it should go without saying that the vitality of these constitutional principles cannot be allowed to yield simply because of disagreement with them.

While giving weight to these public and private considerations, the courts will require that the defendants make a prompt and reasonable start toward full compliance with [Brown I]. Once such a start has been made, the courts may find that additional time is necessary to carry out the ruling in an effective manner. The burden rests upon the defendants to establish that such time is necessary in the public interest and is consistent with good faith compliance at the earliest practicable date. To that end, the courts may consider problems related to administration, arising from the physical condition of the school plant, the school transportation system, personnel, revision of school districts and attendance areas into compact units to achieve a system of determining admission to the public schools on a nonracial basis, and revision of local laws and regulations which may be necessary in solving the foregoing problems. They will also consider the adequacy of any plans the defendants may propose to meet these problems and to effectuate a transition to a racially nondiscriminatory school system. During this period of transition, the courts will retain jurisdiction of these cases. The [cases are accordingly remanded to the lower courts] to take such proceedings and enter such orders and decrees consistent with this opinion as are necessary and proper to admit to public schools on a racially nondiscriminatory basis with all deliberate speed the parties to these [cases]. (As noted earlier, the problems of implementing desegregation since 1955 are considered in sec. 3D below.)

B. GENDER

1. *Introduction: Bases for expanding the categories of "suspect" classifications.* This section and those that follow turn to modern efforts to establish new categories of "suspect" or "quasi-suspect" classifications warranting heightened scrutiny. Three classifications have evoked varying, and often unstable, degrees of heightened scrutiny: gender; alienage; and illegitimacy. (These

developments have been largely products of the post-Warren era.) Still other classifications have been candidates for elevation to more intensive review. In examining the materials that follow, consider especially the extent to which the reasons which justify strict scrutiny of disadvantaging racial classifications are properly applicable to governmental action based on other criteria.

If the history and immediate purpose of the 14th Amendment were all that counted, only racial classifications directed against blacks would be suspect. But, as already noted, the Court has, without much discussion, treated ethnicity like race. Is it possible to generalize more broadly? To what extent can one justify identification of additional classifications warranting heightened scrutiny by extrapolating from the characteristics that have elicited strict scrutiny of racial criteria? Is the critical element the possession of an unalterable trait? A trait distinguishing the possessor from the majority? A trait relied on by the classifier for the purpose—or the effect—of stigmatizing those possessing it? A trait frequently relied upon by the majority to signify its superiority vis-à-vis those possessing the trait? A trait rarely relevant to legitimate governmental objectives yet traditionally used to disadvantage those who possess it? A trait traditionally used and readily usable for "we-they" generalizations as opposed to "they-they" generalizations? The "we-they"/"they-they" labels were originated by Professor Ely in his "The Wages of Crying [Wolf]," 82 Yale L.J. 920 (1973). He suggested special suspicion for classifications in which the decisionmakers (the "we"s) are particularly apt to resort to stereotypes resting on superiority-inferiority judgments when the "we"s resort to classifications disadvantaging the "they"s: "A decision to distinguish blacks from whites (or women from men) will therefore have its roots in a comparison between a 'we' stereotype and a 'they' stereotype, viz. They [blacks or women] are generally inferior to or not so well qualified as *we* [whites or men] are in the following respect(s), which we find sufficient to justify the [classification]." Ely added: "The danger is therefore greater in we-they situations that we will overestimate the validity of the proposed stereotypical classification by seizing upon the positive myths about our own class and the negative myths about theirs [and] too readily assuming that virtually the entire membership of the two classes fit the stereotypes and therefore that not many of 'them' will be unfairly deprived, nor many of 'us' unfairly benefitted, by the proposed classification. In short, I trust your generalizations about the differences between my gang and Wilfred's more than I do your generalizations about the differences between my gang and yours"—i.e., "there is less justification for special scrutiny of 'they-they' generalizations than for 'we-they' generalizations." (Recall the earlier material on Ely's elaboration of this approach in his later writings, especially Democracy and Distrust (1980), urging a "representation-reinforcing," minority-protecting function for judicial review.) What if the classifier relies on a trait which has some but not all of the characteristics that have made race traditionally suspect? Does a partial, incomplete resemblance to racial discrimination justify at least heightened, greater-than-minimal scrutiny? Are varying degrees of scrutiny warranted, depending upon the degree of "suspectness" of the classifying criterion?[1]

---

1. Consider also the passage in Justice Powell's majority opinion in Rodriguez (1973; p. 842 below) characterizing "the traditional indicia of suspectness" as follows: "[The] class [is] saddled with such disabilities, or subjected to such a history of purposeful unequal treatment, or relegated to such a position of political powerlessness as to command extraordinary protection from the majoritarian political process." The reference to "political powerlessness" derives from the last paragraph of the Carolene Products footnote. Should "political powerlessness" alone justify a conclusion of "suspectness"? (Note also the explicit reliance on Stone's footnote in the Court's occasional treatment of alienage as a

2. *The changing attitude toward gender classifications.* While the battle for the ratification of the Equal Rights Amendment was under way in the early 1970s, the Court considered a growing number of cases challenging sex classifications under equal protection. A large number of these challenges succeeded, even though the Court at the outset purported to apply the rationality standard and even though the majority refused to assimilate gender criteria to the fully "suspect" status of racial ones. By the mid–1970s, in Craig v. Boren (1976; p. 686 below), a consensus was reached at last: the majority applied a heightened, intermediate level of scrutiny. Before turning to those modern cases, consider the following samples of sex classifications before the late 1970s. Consider especially the similarities and differences between race and sex discrimination. Consider, too, whether governmental reliance on deprecating stereotypes has become the central focus in the modern cases.

3. *The deferential old equal protection in action.* For the Court's characteristic stance toward sex discrimination claims in an earlier era, see GOESAERT v. CLEARY, 335 U.S. 464 (1948), rejecting an attack on a Michigan law which provided that no woman could obtain a bartender's license unless she was "the wife or daughter of the male owner" of a licensed liquor establishment. (For an even earlier example of the traditional attitude, see Bradwell v. State (1873), noted in Frontiero, p. 684 below.) Justice FRANKFURTER stated: "Michigan could, beyond question, forbid all women from working behind a bar. This is so despite the vast changes in the social and legal position of women. The fact that women may now have achieved the virtues that men have long claimed as their prerogatives and now indulge in vices that men have long practiced, does not preclude the States from drawing a sharp line between the sexes, certainly in such matters as the regulation of the liquor traffic. [The] Constitution does not require legislatures to reflect sociological insight, or shifting social standards, any more than it requires them to keep abreast of the latest scientific standards. [Michigan] evidently believes that the oversight assured through ownership of a bar by a barmaid's husband or father minimizes hazards that may confront a barmaid without such protecting oversight. This Court is certainly not in a position to gainsay such belief by the Michigan legislature. [Since the line drawn] is not without a basis in reason, we cannot give ear to the suggestion that the real impulse behind this legislation was an unchivalrous desire of male bartenders to try to monopolize the calling."[2]

4. *Heightened scrutiny under a deferential, old equal protection guise.* In REED v. REED, 404 U.S. 71 (1971), the appellant's elaborate brief strenuously urged the Court to find sex a suspect classification. The Court declined. Yet the unanimous Court sustained the discrimination claim, while purporting to apply a traditional "rationality" standard. Chief Justice BURGER stated the question as "whether a difference in the sex of competing applicants for letters of

suspect classification. See Graham v. Richardson (1971; p. 720 below)—and note the criticism of that approach in Justice Rehnquist's dissent in In re Griffiths (1973; p. 721 below).) See also Justice Brennan's 1982 effort to restate the rationale for "suspect classifications" analyses, in footnote 2 of his opinion in Plyler v. Doe (p. 850 below).

2. Justice RUTLEDGE, joined by Justices Douglas and Murphy, dissented without challenging the majority's assumptions; instead, he focused on the inadequate fit be-

tween means and ends. The dissenters, like the majority, assumed that "benign," "protective" legislation regarding women was clearly constitutional. (For an explicit modern disapproval of Goesaert, see footnote 4 in Craig v. Boren (1976; p. 686 below).) Recall that, during the Lochner era, one of the few types of laws regulating working conditions readily sustained by the Court was the setting of maximum working hours for women. Muller v. Oregon (1908; p. 470 above) relied on women's alleged dependence and physical weakness to justify such legislation.

administration bears a rational relationship to a state objective that is sought to be advanced by the operation of [the law]." The state courts had sustained a preference for men over women in the appointment of administrators of estates as a rational method "to resolve an issue that would otherwise require a hearing as to the relative merits" of the petitioning relatives. The Court stated: "Clearly the objective of reducing the work load on probate courts by eliminating one class of contests is not without some legitimacy." Nevertheless, there was a denial of equal protection: giving "a mandatory preference to members of either sex over members of the other, merely to accomplish the elimination of hearings on the merits, is to make the very kind of arbitrary legislative choice forbidden by [equal protection]; and whatever may be said as to the positive values of avoiding intrafamily controversy, the choice in this contest may not lawfully be mandated solely on the basis of sex."[3]

5. FRONTIERO v. RICHARDSON, 411 U.S. 677 (1973): Frontiero sustained an equal protection challenge to a federal law affording male members of the armed forces an automatic dependency allowance for their wives but requiring servicewomen to prove that their husbands were dependent. Justice BRENNAN's opinion put forth the most elaborate judicial argument on the books for treating gender as a suspect classification, but he did not get majority support for his analysis. Joined by Justices Douglas, White and Marshall, he concluded that "classifications based upon sex, like [those] upon race, alienage, and national origin, are inherently suspect and must therefore be subjected to close judicial scrutiny." He found implicit support for that position in Reed's "departure from 'traditional' rational-basis analysis." He elaborated:

"[Our] Nation has had a long and unfortunate history of sex discrimination. Traditionally, such discrimination was rationalized by an attitude of 'romantic paternalism' which, in practical effect, put women, not on a pedestal, but in a cage.[1] As a result of notions such as these, our statute books gradually became laden with gross, stereotyped distinctions between the sexes and, indeed, throughout much of the 19th century the position of women in our society was, in many respects, comparable to that of blacks under the pre-Civil War slave codes. Neither slaves nor women could hold office, serve on juries, or bring suit in their own names, and married women traditionally were denied

3. Reed continued to be invoked to invalidate sex classifications in a number of cases after Frontiero, which follows, and before Craig v. Boren (p. 686 below). See, e.g., Stanton v. Stanton, 421 U.S. 7 (1975). In each case, it seemed clear that a challenged statute *would* have survived scrutiny if a truly deferential equal protection approach had been applied and that the reference to Reed in fact signified an unarticulated, heightened (but less than strict) scrutiny. For an early interpretation of Reed, see Gunther, "Newer Equal Protection": "It is difficult to understand [the result in Reed] without an assumption that some special sensitivity to sex as a classifying factor entered into the analysis. [Only] by importing some special suspicion of sex-related means from the new equal protection area can the result be made entirely persuasive. Yet application of new equal protection criteria is precisely what Reed v. Reed purported to avoid."

1. To illustrate the traditional "paternalistic attitude," Justice Brennan quoted from Justice Bradley's concurring opinion in Bradwell v. State, 16 Wall. (83 U.S.) 130 (1873), where the Court sustained a law denying to women the right to practice law: "Man is, or should be, woman's protector and defender. The natural and proper timidity and delicacy which belongs to the female sex evidently unfits it for many of the occupations of civil life. The constitution of the family organization, which is founded in the divine ordinance, as well as in the nature of things, indicates the domestic sphere as that which properly belongs to the domain and functions of womanhood. [The] paramount destiny and mission of woman are to fulfill the noble and benign offices of wife and mother. This is the law of the Creator."

the legal capacity to hold or convey property or to serve as legal guardians of their own children. And although blacks were guaranteed the right to vote in 1870, women were denied even that right [until the] adoption of the 19th Amendment half a century later. It is true, of course, that the position of women in America has improved markedly in recent decades. Nevertheless, it can hardly be doubted that, in part because of the high visibility of the sex characteristic, women still face pervasive, although at times more subtle, discrimination in our educational institutions, in the job market and, perhaps most conspicuously, in the political arena.[2] Moreover, since sex, like race and national origin, is an immutable characteristic, the imposition of special disabilities upon the members of a particular sex because of their sex would seem to violate 'the basic concept of our system that legal burdens should bear some relationship to individual responsibility.' [Weber, an illegitimacy case, p. 726 below.] And what differentiates sex from such nonsuspect statuses as intelligence or physical disability, and aligns it with the recognized suspect criteria, is that the sex characteristic frequently bears no relation to ability to perform or contribute to society. As a result, statutory distinctions between the sexes often have the effect of invidiously relegating the entire class of females to inferior legal status without regard to the actual capabilities of its individual members." Applying the "strict judicial scrutiny" he found appropriate, Justice Brennan found it "clear" that the law was unconstitutional. The Government had relied on promoting "administrative convenience:" "[It] maintains that, as an empirical matter, wives [frequently] are dependent upon their husbands, while husbands rarely are dependent upon their wives. Thus, the Government argues that [Congress] might reasonably have concluded that it would be both cheaper and easier simply conclusively to presume that wives of male members are financially dependent upon their husbands, while burdening female members with the task of establishing dependency in fact. The Government offers no concrete evidence [tending] to support its view that such differential treatment in fact saves the Government any money. [Moreover], any statutory scheme which draws a sharp line between the sexes, *solely* for the purpose of achieving administrative convenience, [violates equal protection]. [Reed.]"

Justice POWELL, joined by Chief Justice Burger and Justice Blackmun, concurred only in the judgment, arguing that it was unnecessary "in this case to characterize sex as a suspect classification" because the case could and should be decided "on the authority of Reed" and "any expansion of its rationale" should be reserved for the future. Moreover, any general categorization of sex classifications as suspect should be postponed because of the pending Equal Rights Amendment ("which if adopted will resolve the substance of this precise question"): "[This] reaching out to pre-empt by judicial action a major

---

2. "It is true, of course, that when viewed in the abstract, women do not constitute a small and powerless minority. Nevertheless, in part because of past discrimination, women are vastly underrepresented in this Nation's decisionmaking [councils]." [Footnote by Justice Brennan.] Compare Ely, Democracy and Distrust (1980), commenting on the relevance of "political powerlessness" to the scrutiny of gender classifications. He suggests that the Court should strike down sex classifications only if they were enacted while women's access to the political process was blocked. But a legislature should then be free to reenact the law: "[In] the event—

unlikely, precisely because access is no longer blocked—that the legislature after such a declaration of unconstitutionality" repassed the same law, it should be sustained: the "fact that due process of lawmaking was denied in 1908 [need not] imply that it was in 1982 as well." He adds: "[If] women don't protect themselves from sex discrimination in the future, it [will be] because for one reason or another—substantive disagreement or more likely the assignment of a low priority to the issue—they don't choose to." But see Note, "Sex Discrimination and [Equal Protection]," 84 Harv.L.Rev. 1499 (1971).

political decision which is currently in process of resolution does not reflect appropriate respect for duly prescribed legislative processes."[3]

Craig v. Boren

429 U.S. 190, 97 S.Ct. 451, 50 L.Ed.2d 397 (1976).

Justice BRENNAN delivered the opinion of the Court.[1]

The interaction of two sections of an Oklahoma statute prohibits the sale of "non-intoxicating" 3.2% beer to males under the age of 21 and to females under the age of 18. The question [is] whether such a gender-based differential constitutes a denial to males 18–20 years of age of [equal protection]. [To] withstand constitutional challenge, previous cases establish that classifications by gender must serve important governmental objectives and must be substantially related to achievement of those objectives. [Reed and subsequent decisions (e.g., Frontiero)] have rejected administrative ease and convenience as sufficiently important objectives to justify gender-based classifications. Reed has also provided the underpinning for decisions that have invalidated statutes employing gender as an inaccurate proxy for other, more germane bases of classification. Hence, "archaic and overbroad" generalizations, Schlesinger v. Ballard [1975; p. 718 below], concerning the financial position of servicewomen, Frontiero, and working women, Weinberger v. Wiesenfeld [1975; p. 717 below], could not justify use of a gender line in determining eligibility for certain governmental entitlements. Similarly, increasingly outdated misconceptions concerning the role of females in the home rather than in the "marketplace and world of ideas" were rejected as loose-fitting characterizations incapable of supporting state statutory schemes that were premised upon their accuracy. In light of the weak congruence between gender and the characteristic or trait that gender purported to represent, it was necessary that the legislatures choose either to realign their substantive laws in a gender-neutral fashion, or to adopt procedures for identifying those instances where the sex-centered generalization actually comported to fact. In this case, too, "Reed, we feel, is controlling." We turn then to the question whether, under Reed, the difference between males and females with respect to the purchase of 3.2% beer warrants the differential in age drawn by the Oklahoma statute. We conclude that it [does not].

We accept for purposes of discussion the District Court's identification of the objective underlying [the law] as the enhancement of traffic safety. [But] appellees' statistics in our view cannot support the conclusion that the gender-based distinction closely serves to achieve that objective and therefore the

3. Justice STEWART, who also concurred solely in the judgment, stated merely that the law worked "an invidious discrimination in violation of the Constitution. [Reed.]" Justice REHNQUIST dissented.

1. This case marks the emergence of a majority consensus on the Court about sex discrimination. Justice Brennan's majority opinion stated the new, "intermediate" scrutiny appropriate for gender classifications in the third sentence of the opinion. Although some of the subsequent cases (e.g., Rostker v. Goldberg, p. 693 below) seemed to cast doubt upon it, the 1982 decision in Hogan (p. 698 below) made clear that intermediate scrutiny, slightly reformulated, retains majority support. See also the formulation in United States v. Virginia (1996; p. 704 below). (The Craig case was also the Court's first occasion to strike down discrimination that was directed against males rather than females. The majority has continued to apply intermediate scrutiny whether the challenger is male or female.)

distinction cannot under Reed withstand equal protection challenge. [Even] were this statistical evidence accepted as accurate, it nevertheless offers only a weak answer to the equal protection question presented here. The most focused and relevant of the statistical surveys, arrests of 18–20–year-olds for alcohol-related driving offenses, exemplifies the ultimate unpersuasiveness of this evidentiary record. Viewed in terms of the correlation between sex and the actual activity that Oklahoma seeks to regulate—driving while under the influence of alcohol—the statistics broadly establish that .18% of females and 2% of males in that age group were arrested for that offense. While such a disparity is not trivial in a statistical sense, it hardly can form the basis for employment of a gender line as a classifying device. Certainly if maleness is to serve as a proxy for drinking and driving, a correlation of 2% must be considered an unduly tenuous "fit." Indeed, prior cases have consistently rejected the use of sex as a decisionmaking factor even though the statutes in question certainly rested on far more predictive empirical relationships than this. Moreover, the statistics exhibit a variety of other shortcomings that seriously impugn their value to equal protection analysis. Setting aside the obvious methodological problems,[2] the surveys do not adequately justify the salient features of Oklahoma's gender-based traffic-safety law. None purports to measure the use and dangerousness of 3.2% beer as opposed to alcohol generally, a detail that is of particular importance since, in light of its low alcohol level, Oklahoma apparently considers the 3.2% beverage to be "nonintoxicating." [There] is no reason to belabor this line of analysis. It is unrealistic to expect either members of the judiciary or state officials to be well versed in the rigors of experimental or statistical technique. But this merely illustrates that proving broad sociological propositions by statistics is a dubious business, and one that inevitably is in tension with the normative philosophy that underlies [equal protection]. Suffice to say that the showing offered by the appellees does not satisfy us that sex represents a legitimate, accurate proxy for the regulation of drinking and driving. In fact, when it is further recognized that Oklahoma's statute prohibits only the selling of 3.2% beer to young males and not their drinking the beverage once acquired (even after purchase by their 18–20–year-old female companions), the relationship between gender and traffic safety becomes far too tenuous to satisfy Reed's requirement that the gender-based difference be substantially related to achievement of the [statutory objective]. [In] sum, the principles embodied in [equal protection] are not to be rendered inapplicable by statistically measured but loose-fitting generalities concerning the drinking tendencies of aggregate groups. We conclude that [this] gender-based differential [is] a denial of [equal protection to males aged 18–20].[3]

Reversed.[4]

Justice POWELL, concurring.

I join the opinion of the Court [but] I do have reservations as to some of the discussion concerning the appropriate standard for equal protection analy-

---

2. The very social stereotypes that find reflection in age differential laws are likely substantially to distort the accuracy of these comparative statistics. Hence "reckless" young men who drink and drive are transformed into arrest statistics, whereas their female counterparts are chivalrously escorted [home]. [Footnote by Justice Brennan.]

3. Insofar as Goesaert v. Cleary may be inconsistent, that decision is [disapproved]. [Footnote by Justice Brennan.]

4. Are gender-based statistical generalizations permissible so long as they are valid rather than stereotypical ones? Note the important discussion of that issue in Manhart (1978; p. 701 below), a case arising under Title VII of the 1964 Civil Rights Act.

sis and the relevance of the statistical evidence. [I] agree that Reed is the most relevant precedent. But I find it unnecessary, in deciding this case, to read that decision as broadly as some of the Court's language may imply. Reed and subsequent cases involving gender-based classifications make clear that the Court subjects such classifications to a more critical examination than is normally applied when "fundamental" constitutional rights and "suspect classes" are not present.* I view this as a relatively easy case. [The] decision [turns] on whether the [state] has adopted a means that bears a "fair and substantial relation" to this objective. Reed. It seems to me that the statistics offered by the [state] do tend generally to support the [classification]. Even so, I am not persuaded that these facts and the inferences fairly drawn from them justify this classification based on a three-year age differential between the sexes, and especially one that is so easily circumvented as to be virtually meaningless. [This] gender-based classification does not bear a fair and substantial relation to the object of the legislation.

Justice STEVENS, concurring.

There is only one Equal Protection Clause. [I] am inclined to believe that what has become known as the two-tiered analysis of equal protection claims does not describe a completely logical method of deciding cases, but rather is a method the Court has employed to explain decisions that actually apply a single standard in a reasonably consistent fashion. I also suspect that a careful explanation of the reasons motivating particular decisions may contribute more to an identification of that standard than an attempt to articulate it in all-encompassing [terms]. In this case, the classification [is] objectionable because it is based on an accident at birth, because it is a mere remnant of the now almost universally rejected tradition of discriminating against males in this age bracket, and because, to the extent it reflects any physical difference between males and females, it is actually perverse.[1] The question then is whether the traffic safety justification put forward by the State is sufficient to make an otherwise offensive classification acceptable. The classification is not totally irrational. For the evidence does indicate that there are more males than females in this age bracket who drive and also more who drink. Nevertheless, [it] is difficult to believe that the statute was actually intended to cope with the problem of traffic safety, since it has only a minimal effect on access to a not-very-intoxicating beverage and does not prohibit its consumption. Moreover, [the] legislation imposes a restraint on [100%] of the males in the class allegedly because about 2% of them have probably violated one or more laws relating to the consumption of alcoholic beverages. It is unlikely that this law will have a significant deterrent effect either on that 2% or on the law-abiding 98%. But even assuming some such slight benefit, it does not seem to me that

---

* As is evident from our opinions, the Court has had difficulty in agreeing upon a standard of equal protection analysis that can be applied consistently to the wide variety of legislative classifications. There are valid reasons for dissatisfaction with the "two-tier" [approach]. Although viewed by many as a result-oriented substitute for more critical analysis, that approach [now] has substantial precedential support. As has been true of Reed and its progeny, our decision today will be viewed by some as a "middle-tier" approach. While I would not endorse that char-acterization and would not welcome a further subdividing of equal protection analysis, candor compels the recognition that the relatively deferential "rational basis" standard of review normally applied takes on a sharper focus when we address a gender-based [classification]. [Footnote by Justice Powell.]

1. Because males are generally heavier than females, they have a greater capacity to consume alcohol without impairing their driving ability than do females. [Footnote by Justice Stevens.]

an insult to all of the young men of the State can be justified by visiting the sins of the 2% on the 98%.[2]

Justice REHNQUIST, dissenting.

The Court's disposition of this case is objectionable on two grounds. First is its conclusion that *men* challenging a gender-based statute which treats them less favorably than women may invoke a more stringent standard of judicial review than pertains to most other types of classifications. Second is the Court's enunciation of this standard, without citation to any source, as being that "classifications by gender must serve *important* governmental objectives and must be *substantially* related to achievement of those objectives." [I] think the [law] challenged here need pass only the "rational basis" equal protection analysis expounded in cases such as [McGowan] and [Lee Optical], and I believe that it is constitutional under that analysis.

I.   [It] is true that a number of our opinions contain broadly phrased dicta implying that the same test should be applied to all classifications based on sex, whether affecting females or males. [E.g., Frontiero; Reed.] However, before today, no decision of this Court has applied an elevated level of scrutiny to invalidate a statutory discrimination harmful to [males]. [There] being no plausible argument that this is a discrimination against females, the Court's reliance on our previous sex-discrimination cases is ill-founded. [The] Court's [standard of review] apparently comes out of thin air. How is this Court to define what objectives are important? How is it to determine whether a particular law is "substantially" related to the achievement of such objective, rather than related in some other way to its achievement? Both of the phrases used are so diaphanous and elastic as to invite subjective judicial preferences or prejudices relating to particular types of legislation, masquerading as judgments whether such legislation is directed at "important" objectives or whether the relationship to those objectives is "substantial" [enough].

II.   The applicable rational basis test is [that described in the passage in McGowan (p. 642 above)]. I believe that [this] more traditional type of scrutiny is appropriate in this case, and I think that the Court would have done well here to heed its own warning that "[i]t is unrealistic to expect [the] judiciary [to] be well versed in the rigors of experimental or statistical technique." [The] Court's criticism of the statistics [conveys] the impression that a legislature in enacting a new law is to be subjected to the judicial equivalent of a doctoral examination in statistics. Legislatures [are] entitled to draw factual conclusions on the basis of the determination of probable cause which an arrest by a police officer normally represents. In this situation, they could reasonably infer that the incidence of drunk driving is a good deal higher than the incidence of arrest. And while [such] statistics may be distorted as a result of stereotyping, the legislature is not required to prove before a court that its statistics are perfect. In any event, if stereotypes are as pervasive as the Court suggests, they may in turn influence the conduct of the men and women in question, and cause the young men to conform to the wild and reckless image which is their stereotype. [Our] only appropriate course is to defer to the reasonable inference supporting the statute—that taken in sufficient quantity this beer has the same effect as any alcoholic beverage. [The statistical] evidence suggests clear differences between the drinking and driving habits of young men and women. Those differences are grounds enough for the State reasonably to conclude that young males pose by far the greater drunk driving hazard, both in terms of sheer

---

2. Justice STEWART, concurring in the judgment, stated that the law "amounts to total irrationality" and to "invidious discrimination. See [Reed]."

numbers and in terms of hazard on a per-driver basis. The gender-based difference in treatment in this case is therefore not [irrational]. [A dissenting notation by Chief Justice BURGER stated that he was "in general agreement" with Justice Rehnquist.]

"REAL" DIFFERENCES OR ARCHAIC GENERALIZATIONS?

1. MICHAEL M. v. SUPERIOR COURT, 450 U.S. 464 (1981): This case upheld California's "statutory rape" law which punished the male, but not the female, participant in sexual intercourse when the female was under 18 and not the male's wife.[1] Justice REHNQUIST's plurality opinion, joined by Chief Justice Burger and Justices Stewart and Powell, stated (five years after Craig v. Boren) that "the Court has had some difficulty in agreeing upon the proper approach and analysis in cases involving challenges to gender-based classifications. [We have held] that the traditional minimum rationality test takes on a somewhat 'sharper focus' when gender-based classifications are challenged. See [Craig; see also Reed]. [Underlying] these decisions is the principle that a legislature may not 'make overbroad generalizations based on sex which are entirely unrelated to any differences between men and women or which demean the ability or social status of the affected class.' But because [equal protection] does not [require] 'things which are different in fact [to] be treated in law as though they were the same,' this Court has consistently upheld statutes where the gender classification is not invidious, but rather realistically reflects the fact that the sexes are not similarly situated in certain circumstances. Parham v. Hughes; Califano v. Webster; Schlesinger v. Ballard; Kahn v. Shevin [all below]. As the Court has stated, a legislature may 'provide for the special problems of women.' Weinberger v. Wiesenfeld."

Applying those principles, Justice Rehnquist sustained the law. He stated: "We are satisfied not only that the prevention of illegitimate pregnancy is at least one of the 'purposes' of the statute, but also that the State has a strong interest in preventing such pregnancy."[2] He continued: "Because virtually all of the significant harmful and inescapably identifiable consequences of teenage pregnancy fall on the young female, a legislature acts well within its authority when it elects to punish only the participant who, by nature, suffers few of the consequences of his conduct. It is hardly unreasonable for a legislature acting to protect minor females to exclude them from punishment. Moreover, the risk of pregnancy itself constitutes a substantial deterrence to young females. No similar natural sanctions deter males. A criminal sanction imposed solely on males thus serves to roughly 'equalize' the deterrents on the sexes. We are

1. The challenger, at the time of the alleged statutory rape, was a seventeen-and-one-half-year-old male who had engaged in intercourse with a sixteen-and-one-half-year-old female.

2. "Although petitioner concedes that the State has a 'compelling' interest in preventing teenage pregnancy, he contends that the 'true' purpose of [the law] is to protect the virtue and chastity of young women. As such, the statute is unjustifiable because it rests on archaic stereotypes. [But the only] question for us [is] whether the legislation violates [equal protection], not whether its

supporters may have endorsed it for reasons no longer generally accepted. Even if the preservation of female chastity were one of the motives of the statute, and even if that motive be impermissible, petitioner's argument must fail because '[i]t is a familiar practice of constitutional law that this Court will not strike down an otherwise constitutional statute on the basis of an allegedly illicit legislative motive.' United States v. O'Brien, 391 U.S. 367 (1968)." [Footnote by Justice Rehnquist.]

unable to accept the contention that the statute is impermissibly underinclusive and must [be] *broadened* so as to hold the female as criminally liable as the male. It is argued that this statute is not *necessary* to deter teenage pregnancy because a gender-neutral statute [would] serve that goal equally well. The relevant inquiry, however, is not whether the statute is drawn as precisely as it might have been, but whether the line chosen by the [State] is within constitutional limitations. In any event, we cannot say that a gender-neutral statute would be as effective as the statute California has chosen to enact. The State persuasively contends that a gender-neutral statute would frustrate its interest in effective enforcement [because] a female is surely less likely to report violations of the statute if she herself would be subject to criminal prosecution. [In] upholding the [law] we also recognize [that] the statute places a burden on males which is not shared by females. But we find nothing to suggest that men, because of past discrimination or peculiar disadvantages, are in need of the special solicitude of the courts. Nor is this a case where the gender classification is made 'solely [for] administrative convenience,' as in [Frontiero], or rests on 'the baggage of sexual stereotypes,' as in Orr v. Orr [p. 717 below]. As we have held, the statute instead reasonably reflects the fact that the consequences of sexual intercourse and pregnancy fall more heavily on the female than on the male."[3]

Justice BRENNAN's dissent, joined by Justices White and Marshall, objected that none of the three opinions comprising the majority "fairly applies the equal protection analysis this Court has so carefully developed since [Craig]." He added that it was "perhaps because the gender classification in California's statutory rape law was initially designed to [further] outmoded sexual stereotypes [regarding the special need to protect young women's chastity], rather than to reduce the incidence of teenage pregnancies, that the State has been unable to demonstrate a substantial relationship between the classification and its newly asserted goal." In arguing that this relationship had not been shown, he rejected, for example, the State's assertion that law enforcement problems created by a gender-neutral statutory rape law would make such a law less effective than a gender-based statute in deterring sexual activity: "Even if fewer persons were prosecuted under the gender-neutral law, as the State suggests, it would still be true that twice as many persons would be *subject* to arrest."

A separate dissent by Justice STEVENS stated that a statute such as this, "applicable to only half of the joint participants in the risk-creating conduct," was impermissible sex discrimination—even though he agreed with the plurality's assumption "that the joint act that this law seeks to prohibit creates a greater risk of harm for the female than for the male." He stated: "The argument that a special need for protection provides a rational explanation for an exemption is one I simply do not comprehend." The fact that a female confronted a greater risk of harm than a male was "a reason for applying the prohibition to her," not for exempting her. "Surely, if we examine the problem from the point of view of society's interest in preventing the risk-creating conduct from occurring at all, it is irrational to exempt 50% of the potential violators." He added: "Finally, even if my logic is faulty and there actually is some speculative basis for treating equally guilty males and females differently, I still believe that any such speculative justification would be outweighed by the paramount interest in even-handed enforcement of the law. A rule that autho-

---

3. Justice STEWART, who joined Justice Rehnquist's opinion, also submitted a separate opinion. Justice BLACKMUN concurred in the judgment, stating that he voted to uphold the gender-based classification on the basis of the Reed and Craig tests.

rizes punishment of only one of two equally guilty wrongdoers violates the essence of the constitutional requirement that the sovereign must govern impartially."

Some comments on "differences" and "formal equality." Michael M. illustrates a recurrent problem in sex discrimination cases: What should be the role of differences between men and women in equal protection analysis? Traditional equal protection principles simply require that those who are similarly situated should be treated alike. Differences in treatment can be justified when they correspond to relevant differences between the sexes. Clearly, there are some "real" differences between men and women—e.g., only women can become pregnant. May legislators invoke such differences in enacting laws? Must they? In cases such as Michael M., some of the Justices seek to determine whether legislative action allegedly relying on "real" differences in fact reflected overbroad, archaic generalizations and stereotypes. What is the ultimate aim of the Court's scrutiny in such cases? Is it to deemphasize the impact of sexual differences in order to achieve a gender-"neutral" society? Should the focus instead be on identifying genuine differences and recognizing to the extent possible the special needs of each gender?

The search for relevant "real" differences between the genders has been controversial. Some critics have argued that the Court's insistence on formal equality—insistence on an essentially gender-blind Constitution—is injurious to women by ignoring important differences between the genders. Similarly, the argument is made that formal equality ultimately holds women to a male standard. The academic literature has become increasingly preoccupied with the battle between a jurisprudence of formal equality—the approach most commonly followed by the Court—and a jurisprudence of differences. Thus, Freedman, "Sex Equality, Sex Differences, and the Supreme Court," 92 Yale L.J. 913 (1983), criticized the dissenters in Michael M. (as well as in Rostker, which follows) for focusing on a means-ends analysis and on "irrationality," rather than on the moral and actual harms of sex discrimination. She argues that the Court should pursue an "explicitly normative theory of sex equality that identifies with some particularity the dynamics and harmful consequences of sexism." And Law, "Rethinking Sex and the Constitution," 132 U.Pa.L.Rev. 955 (1984), argues that sexual equality doctrine must confront squarely the reality of categorical biological differences between men and women. She suggests, for example: "To reconcile the ideal of human equality with the reality of biological difference we must (1) begin to distinguish clearly between laws that classify on the basis of sex and laws that govern reproduction; (2) recognize that laws governing reproduction implicate equality concerns; and (3) establish a test that can determine when laws governing reproduction violate constitutional equality norms." Karst, "Woman's Constitution," 1984 Duke L.J. 447, claims that the "male conception of society underlies the very constitutional doctrine that women seek to use in effecting a reconstructed order of male-female relations." He explores the implications of an alternative constitutional approach, resting on the premise that women as a group "do tend to have a different perception of social relations and a different approach to moral issues," emphasizing the individual "as part of a network of relationships" that finds "security in connection rather than separation and the competitive pursuit of individual power." Consider the validity of these theoretical approaches and their applicability to the problems raised in this group of cases. For useful criticisms of Michael M., see Williams, "The Equality Crisis: Some Reflections on Culture, Courts and Feminism," 7 Women's Rts.L.Rep. 175 (1982), and Olsen, "Statutory Rape: A Feminist Critique of Rights Analysis," 63 Tex.L.Rev. 387 (1984).

2. ROSTKER v. GOLDBERG, 453 U.S. 57 (1981): This 6-3 decision rejected a claim, under the equal protection aspect of Fifth Amendment due process, that the Military Selective Service Act was unconstitutional in "authorizing the President to require the registration of males and not females." Emphasizing that the purpose of draft registration was "to facilitate any eventual conscription," Justice REHNQUIST's majority opinion noted: "The case arises in the context of Congress' authority over national defense and military affairs, and perhaps in no other area has the Court accorded Congress greater deference." He conceded that this did not mean that Congress was "free to disregard the Constitution when it acts in the area of military affairs," but insisted that "the tests and limitations to be applied may differ because of the military context. We of course do not abdicate our ultimate responsibility to decide the constitutional question, but simply recognize that the Constitution itself requires such deference to congressional choice. In deciding the question before us we must be particularly careful not to substitute our judgment of what is desirable for that of Congress, or our own evaluation of evidence for a reasonable evaluation by the Legislative Branch."

Against this background, Justice Rehnquist proceeded to apply "the heightened scrutiny with which we have approached gender-based discrimination, see [Michael M.; Craig; Reed]." He stated: "No one could deny that under the test of [Craig], the Government's interest in raising and supporting armies is an 'important governmental interest.' Congress and its Committees carefully considered and debated two alternative means of furthering that interest: the first was to register only males for potential conscription, and the other was to register both sexes. Congress chose the former alternative. [In] light of the floor debate and the Report of the Senate Armed Services Committee, [it] is apparent that Congress was fully aware [of] the current thinking as to the place of women in the Armed Services. In such a case, we cannot ignore Congress' broad authority [to] raise and support armies." Justice Rehnquist noted that this case was "quite different" from several earlier gender discrimination cases because "Congress did not act 'unthinkingly' or 'reflexively and not for any considered reason.' The question of registering women for the draft not only received considerable national attention [but] also was extensively considered by [Congress]. [This] clearly establishes that the decision to exempt women from registration was not the 'accidental by-product of a traditional way of thinking about females.' " He continued: "Congress determined that any future draft, which would be facilitated by the registration scheme, would be characterized by a need for combat troops. [Since] women are [by statute] excluded from combat, Congress concluded that they would not be needed in the event of a draft, and therefore decided [not to register them]. [This] is not a case of Congress arbitrarily choosing to burden one of two similarly situated [groups]. Men and women, because of the combat restrictions on women, are simply not similarly situated for purposes of a draft or registration for a draft. [The] exemption of women from registration is not only sufficiently but closely related to Congress' purpose in authorizing registration. See [Michael M.; Craig; Reed]. As was the case in Schlesinger v. Ballard [below], 'the gender classification is not invidious, but rather realistically reflects the fact that the sexes are not similarly situated' in this case. The Constitution requires that Congress treat similarly situated persons similarly, not that it engage in gestures of superficial equality.

"In holding the MSSA constitutionally invalid the District Court relied heavily on the President's decision to seek authority to register women and the testimony of members of the Executive Branch and the military in support of that decision. [However,] the President's 'decision to ask for authority to register women is based on equity.' [Congress] was certainly entitled, in the exercise of its constitutional powers to raise and regulate armies and navies, to focus on the question of military need rather than ['equity']. Although the military experts who testified in favor of registering women uniformly opposed the actual drafting of women, there was testimony that in the event of a draft of 650,000 the military could absorb some 80,000 female inductees [to] fill noncombat positions, freeing men to go to the front. In relying on this testimony, [the] District Court palpably exceeded its authority when it ignored Congress' considered response to this line of reasoning. In the first place, assuming that a small number of women could be drafted for noncombat roles, Congress simply did not consider it worth the added burdens of including women in draft and registration plans. [Congress] also concluded that whatever the need for women for noncombat roles during mobilization, whether 80,000 or less, it could be met by volunteers. Most significantly, Congress determined that staffing non-combat positions with women during a mobilization would be positively detrimental to the important goal of military flexibility. [The] District Court was quite wrong in undertaking an independent evaluation of this evidence, rather than adopting an appropriately deferential examination of *Congress'* evaluation of that evidence.''

Justice MARSHALL's dissent, joined by Justice Brennan, stated: ''The Court today places its imprimatur on one of the most potent remaining public expressions of 'ancient canards about the proper role of women.' [Although] the purpose of registration is to assist preparations for drafting civilians into the military, *we are not asked to rule on the constitutionality of a statute governing conscription.* [Consequently,] we are not called upon to decide whether either men or women can be drafted at all, whether they must be drafted in equal numbers, in what order they should be drafted, or once inducted, how they are to be trained for their respective functions. In addition, this case does not involve a challenge to the statutes or policies that prohibit female members of the Armed Forces from serving in combat. It is with this understanding that I turn to the task at hand. [In] my judgment, there simply is no basis for concluding in this case that excluding women from registration is substantially related to the achievement of a concededly important governmental interest in maintaining an effective defense.

''[The Court's analysis] focuses on the wrong question. The relevant inquiry under [Craig] is not whether a *gender-neutral* classification would substantially advance important governmental interests. Rather, the question is whether the gender-based classification is itself substantially related to the achievement of the asserted governmental interest. Thus, the Government's task in this case is to demonstrate that excluding women from registration substantially furthers the goal of preparing for a draft of combat troops. Or, to put it another way, the Government must show that registering women would substantially impede its efforts to prepare for such a draft. Under our precedents, the Government cannot meet this burden without showing that a gender-neutral statute would be a less effective means of attaining this end. [In] this case, the Government makes no claim that preparing for a draft of combat troops cannot be accomplished just as effectively by *registering* both men and women but *drafting* only men if only men turn out to be needed.[1] Nor

1. ''Alternatively, the Government could employ a classification that is related to the statutory objective but is not based on gender, for example, combat eligibility. Under the current scheme, large subgroups of the male population who are ineligible for combat because of physical handicaps or conscientious objector status are nonetheless required to register.'' [Footnote by Justice Marshall.]

can the Government argue that this alternative entails the additional cost and administrative inconvenience of registering women. This Court has repeatedly stated that the administrative convenience of employing a gender classification is not an adequate constitutional justification under the [Craig] test.

"[Both] Congress and the Court have lost sight of the important distinction between *registration* and *conscription*. [The] fact that registration is a first step in the conscription process does not mean that a registration law expressly discriminating between men and women may be justified by a valid conscription program which would, in retrospect, make the current discrimination appear functionally related to the program that emerged. But even addressing the Court's reasoning on its own terms, its analysis is flawed because the entire argument rests on a premise that is demonstrably false. As noted, the majority simply assumes that registration prepares for a draft in which *every* draftee must be available for assignment to combat. But the majority's draft scenario finds no support in [the legislative record]. [Testimony] about personnel requirements in the event of a draft established that women could fill at least 80,000 of the 650,000 positions for which conscripts would be inducted. Thus, with respect to these 80,000 or more positions, the statutes and policies barring women from combat do not provide a reason for distinguishing between male and female potential conscripts; the two groups are, in the majority's parlance, 'similarly situated.' As such, the combat restrictions cannot by themselves supply the constitutionally required justification for the MSSA's gender-based classification. [The] Senate Report concluded [that] drafting *very large numbers* of women' would hinder military flexibility. The discussion does not, however, address the different question whether drafting only a *limited* number of women would similarly impede military flexibility. [The Senate Report establishes] that induction of a large number of men but only a limited number of women [would be] substantially related to important governmental interests. But the discussion and findings in the Senate Report do not enable the Government to carry its burden of demonstrating that *completely* excluding women from the draft by excluding them from registration substantially furthers important governmental objectives." (Justice WHITE also dissented, in an opinion joined by Justice Brennan.)

Note that Rostker, unlike Michael M., does not involve a physical, biological difference between men and women. In Michael M., the majority emphasized that most of the harmful consequences of teenage pregnancy fall on the young female; in Rostker, the majority emphasized that women are ineligible for combat duty. But that "disability" of women was not the product of biological factors but rather the result of a legal construct, the congressionally imposed barrier to women's combat service. And the barrier to combat service was not challenged in the case. Should it have been? Does Rostker suggest basic flaws in the Court's efforts to distinguish "real" differences from overbroad "archaic generalizations"?

3. *Discrimination against fathers (and preference for mothers) of nonmarital children.* The modern Court has repeatedly scrutinized, under the "intermediate" sex discrimination standard, claimed discriminations against fathers of children born outside of marriage. The 5-4 decision in Caban v. Mohammed, 441 U.S. 380 (1979), invalidated a New York law granting the mother but not the father of an illegitimate child the right to block the child's adoption by withholding consent. This provision was challenged by a father who had lived with his children and their mother as a family for several years. Justice Powell's majority opinion concluded that the law was "another example of 'overbroad generalizations' in gender-based classifications" and that "no showing has been made that the [distinction bears] a substantial relationship to the

proclaimed interests of the State in promoting the adoption of illegitimate children." He rejected the argument that the distinction could be justified "by a fundamental difference between maternal and paternal relations," insisting that there was no "universal difference [at] every phase of a child's development," "even if unwed mothers as a class were closer than unwed fathers to their newborn infants." The facts in this case, he added, demonstrated that "an unwed father may have a relationship with his children fully comparable to that of a mother." Justice Stevens's dissent, joined by Chief Justice Burger and Justice Rehnquist, argued that the real differences between the male and female, especially during the child's infancy, were "significant, and that these 'natural differences between unmarried fathers and mothers made it probable that the mother, and not the father or both parents, would have custody of the newborn infant.'" He recognized that the Caban case itself involved the adoption of an older child, but insisted that the "mere fact that an otherwise valid general classification appears arbitrary in an isolated case is not a sufficient reason for invalidating the entire rule." Justice Stewart's separate dissent emphasized that "gender-based classifications are not invariably invalid" and insisted that in many circumstances men and women were not truly "similarly situated": "With respect to a large group of adoptions—those of newborn children and infants—unwed mothers and unwed fathers are simply not similarly situated."

Contrast with Caban a case decided on the same day, Parham v. Hughes, 441 U.S. 347 (1979). In Parham, the Court rejected a sex discrimination attack on a Georgia law denying the father (but not the mother) the right to sue for his nonmarital child's wrongful death. Once again, the Court divided 5-4; but here Justice Powell joined the Caban dissenters to reject the equal protection claim. Although the challenger was the undisputed biological father of the child and had visited him regularly, and had also contributed to his support, the law barred him from bringing the suit because he had not formally legitimated the child. Justice Stewart's plurality opinion (joined by Chief Justice Burger and Justices Rehnquist and Stevens) insisted that the law did not "invidiously discriminate against the [natural father] simply because he was of the male sex." He insisted that mothers and fathers of illegitimate children were not similarly situated because only a father "can by voluntary unilateral action make an illegitimate child legitimate." The statutory classification thus did not "discriminate against fathers as a class but instead distinguishes between fathers who have legitimated their children and those who have not." Thus, there was here no reliance on "overbroad generalizations" and no differential treatment of those similarly situated. Justice White's dissent, joined by Justices Brennan, Marshall and Blackmun, attacked the "startling circularity" in the plurality's argument: "Seemingly, it is irrelevant that as a matter of state law mothers may not legitimate their children, for they are not required to do so in order to maintain a wrongful death action. That only fathers *may* resort to the legitimization process cannot dissolve the sex discrimination in *requiring* them to." (He added in a footnote: "Men and women would therefore not be 'similarly situated.' Under the plurality's bootstrap rationale, a State could require that women, but not men, pass a course to receive a taxi license, simply by limiting admission to the course to women. Men and women would therefore not be 'similarly situated.' Yet requiring a course for women but not for men is quite obviously a classification on the basis of sex.") Thus applying the "intermediate" Craig standard (which the plurality declined to do), Justice White found unjustifiable sex discrimination here. Compare Lehr v. Robertson, 463 U.S. 248 (1983), where the Court upheld a New York provision that denied a natural father, who had never had any substantial relationship with his illegitimate child, a notice or hearing prior to the adoption of his child. Justice Stevens's opinion distinguished Caban because the father had "never established a substantial relationship with his daughter. [If] one parent has an established custodial relationship with a child and the other parent [has] never established a relationship, [equal protection] does not prevent the state from according the two parents different legal rights." Recall that in Caban, Justice Stevens had dissented, dismissing the significance of the fact that in that case there had been a substantial relationship between the natural father and the child. Consider whether the Court's effort to distinguish between "real" differences and "archaic generalizations" in this line of cases serves to strengthen rather than eliminate stereotypes about the roles of each gender.*

4. *More on the problem of sex-specific traits: What constitutes sex discrimination?* In GEDULDIG v. AIELLO, 417 U.S. 484 (1974), the majority held that exclusion of "disability that accompanies normal pregnancy and childbirth" from California's disability insurance system did not constitute "invidious discrimination." Justice STEWART's majority opinion claimed that the challenged classification was not "based upon gender as such" and therefore applied a very deferential standard of review. He argued in a footnote: "The California insurance program does not exclude anyone from benefit eligibility because of gender but merely removes one physical condition—pregnancy—from the list of compensable disabilities. While it is true that only women can become pregnant, it does not follow that every legislative classification concerning pregnancy is a sex-based classification like those considered in Reed and Frontiero. Normal pregnancy is an objectively identifiable physical condition with unique characteristics. Absent a showing that distinctions involving pregnancy are mere pretexts designed to effect an invidious discrimination against the members of one sex or the other, lawmakers are constitutionally free to include or exclude pregnancy from the coverage of legislation such as this on any reasonable basis, just as with respect to any other physical condition. [The] program divides potential recipients into two groups—pregnant women and nonpregnant persons. While the first group is exclusively female, the second includes members of both sexes. The fiscal and actuarial benefits of the program thus accrue to members of both sexes." Moreover, Justice Stewart noted in the text of his opinion: "There is no evidence in the record [that the selection of the risks] work to discriminate against any definable group or class in terms of the aggregate risk protection derived by that group or class from the program. There is no risk from which men are protected and women are not. Likewise, there is no risk from which women are protected and men are not." Justice BRENNAN's dissent, joined by Justices Douglas and Marshall, concluded that there had been sex discrimination in California's "singling out for less favorable treatment a gender-linked disability peculiar to women [even while] men receive full compensation for all disabilities suffered, including those that affect only or primarily their sex, such as prostatectomies, circumcision, hemophilia, and gout. In effect, one set of rules is applied to females and another to males. Such dissimilar treatment of men and women, on the basis of physical characteristics inextricably limited to one sex, inevitably constitutes sex discrimination." And the state's interest in preserving the fiscal integrity of its program could not justify this discrimination.*

---

* Recall also the quite similar questions regarding the rights of a natural father raised in Michael H. (1988; p. 590 above), decided on due process rather than equal protection terms. And note the further pursuit of themes raised by this group of cases and notes in the "modern" sex discrimination cases—e.g., J.E.B., p. 702 below—as well as in the materials on "benign" sex discrimination, at the end of this sec. 3.

SCRUTINY OF GENDER CLASSIFICATIONS ON THE MODERN COURT: REQUIRING AN "EXCEEDINGLY PERSUASIVE JUSTIFICATION"

We now return to the battle over the proper level of judicial scrutiny of gender-based classifications. Should it be strict? Deferential? Intermediate? Craig v. Boren, above, seemed to articulate a consensus that "intermediate" was the proper answer by requiring "important" ends and "substantially related" means. Cases such as Michael M. and Rostker, above, raised concerns that the Court's actual exercise of Craig-level scrutiny was weaker than the Craig standard's words had promised. But the 1982 ruling in Hogan, which follows, provided reassurance by repeating the Craig formulation and applying it with real bite. And Hogan's reiteration of the Craig standard was introduced by the statement that the defenders of a gender-classifying law "must carry the burden of showing an *'exceedingly persuasive justification'* for the classification." Was this italicized phrase truly a mere restatement of Craig, or did it suggest a move toward a level of scrutiny more intensive than "intermediate"? The "exceedingly persuasive" formulation proved central in the 1994 decision in J.E.B. and in the 1996 ruling in U.S. v. Virginia, both in this section. In the Virginia case, Justice Scalia's dissent charged that Justice Ginsburg's resort to that "amorphous" phrase in her majority opinion was in effect an endorsement of strict rather than intermediate scrutiny, thereby "drastically revis[ing] our established standards for reviewing sex-based classifications." Is there merit in his charge? Or did the majority merely apply Craig's intermediate standard with genuine care?

MISSISSIPPI UNIVERSITY FOR WOMEN v. HOGAN, 458 U.S. 718 (1982): This 5-4 decision indicated that a majority of the Court continued to adhere at least to the intermediate level of scrutiny for sex classifications first established in Craig. The ruling sustained a male applicant's challenge to the State's policy of excluding men from the Mississippi University for Women (MUW) School of Nursing. MUW, founded in 1884 (to provide for the "Education of White Girls"), is the oldest state-supported all-female university in the nation. Its School of Nursing was established in 1971. Hogan, a male registered nurse in Columbus, Miss., where MUW is located, was denied admission to the School's baccalaureate program. He was told he could only audit courses and would have to go to one of the State's coeducational nursing schools elsewhere in Mississippi to obtain credits toward a degree. In sustaining Hogan's attack on the School of Nursing's single-sex admissions policy,[1] Justice O'CONNOR's majority opinion applied and restated the Craig standard and

---

* After the constitutional holding in Geduldig, the lower federal courts continued to hold in *statutory* cases (based on Title VII of the 1964 Civil Rights Act) that exclusions of pregnancies from private disability plans were illegal. But the Court put a stop to that trend in General Electric Co. v. Gilbert, 429 U.S. 125 (1976). Although the Court recognized that the statutory ban on sex discrimination has a broader reach than the constitutional one, it closely tracked the Geduldig analysis in the Gilbert case. (The Gilbert ruling was overturned by Congress when it amended Title VII in 1978. See 92 Stat. 2076.)

1. Justice O'Connor repeatedly stated the ruling as a "narrow" one limited to MUW's professional nursing school. But Justice Powell's dissent (noted more fully below) expressed doubt that the majority's analysis could be so limited.

rejected the State's effort to justify its system as "benign" and "compensatory."[2] She sketched the framework for her analysis by stating "several firmly-established principles": "That this statute discriminates against males rather than against females does not exempt it from scrutiny or reduce the standard of review. [Moreover,] the party seeking to uphold a statute that classifies individuals on the basis of their gender must carry the burden of showing an 'exceedingly persuasive justification' for the classification. [Kirchberg v. Feenstra;[3] Feeney (1979; p. 761 below).] The burden is met only by showing that the classification serves 'important governmental objectives and that the discriminatory means employed' are 'substantially related to the achievement of those objectives.' [Although] the test for determining the validity of a gender-based classification is straightforward, it must be applied free of fixed notions concerning the roles and abilities of males and females. Care must be taken in ascertaining whether the statutory objective itself reflects archaic and stereotypic notions. Thus, if the statutory objective is to exclude or 'protect' members of one gender because they are presumed to suffer from an inherent handicap or to be innately inferior, the objective itself is illegitimate. If the State's objective is legitimate and important, we must next determine whether the requisite direct, substantial relationship between objective and means is present. The purpose of requiring that close relationship is to assure that the validity of a classification is determined through reasoned analysis rather than through the mechanical application of traditional, often inaccurate, assumptions about the proper roles of men and women. The need for the requirement is amply revealed by reference to the broad range of statutes already invalidated by this Court, statutes that relied upon the simplistic, outdated assumption that gender could be used as a 'proxy for other, more germane bases of classification' [Craig] to establish a link between objective and classification."

Justice O'Connor found that the MUW scheme could not survive scrutiny under this analysis. She rejected the State's primary justification, that the single-sex admissions policy "compensates for discrimination against women and, therefore, constitutes educational affirmative action." She acknowledged that, in "limited circumstances, a gender-based classification favoring one sex can be justified if it intentionally and directly assists members of the sex that is disproportionately burdened." But such a "benign" justification requires "searching analysis." [E.g., Weinberger v. Wiesenfeld, below.] A state can establish a "compensatory purpose" justification "only if members of the gender benefited by the classification actually suffer a disadvantage related to the classification. [E.g., Califano v. Webster; Schlesinger v. Ballard, below.]" Here, however, the State had made "no showing that women lacked opportunities to obtain training in the field of nursing or to attain positions of leadership in that field when the MUW School of Nursing opened its doors or that women currently are deprived of such opportunities." She noted, for example, that, in 1970, "women earned 94 percent of the nursing baccalaureate degrees conferred in Mississippi and 98.6 percent of the degrees earned nationwide. [Accordingly,] [r]ather than compensate for discriminatory barriers faced by women, MUW's policy of excluding males [tends] to perpetuate the stereotyped view of nursing as an exclusively woman's job. [MUW's] admissions policy lends credibility to the old view that women, not men, should become nurses, and

2. Even though the Court discussed the "benign" justification, the case is noted here rather than with other "benign" sex discrimination cases (in the next group of notes) because of its importance in restating the Craig standard.

3. Kirchberg v. Feenstra, 450 U.S. 455 (1981), struck down a now superseded provision of Louisiana's community property law that gave a husband the unilateral right to dispose of jointly owned community property without his spouse's consent.

makes the assumption that nursing is a field for women a self-fulfilling prophecy. Thus, we conclude that, although the State recited a 'benign, compensatory purpose,' it failed to establish that the alleged objective is the actual purpose underlying the discriminatory classification." Moreover, MUW's policy failed "the second part of the equal protection test, for the State has made no showing that the gender-based classification is substantially and directly related to its proposed compensatory objective. To the contrary, MUW's policy of permitting men to attend classes as auditors fatally undermines its claim that women, at least those in the School of Nursing, are adversely affected by the presence of men. [The] record in this case is flatly inconsistent with the claim that excluding men from the School of Nursing is necessary to reach any of MUW's educational goals. Thus, [we] conclude that the State has fallen far short of establishing the 'exceedingly persuasive justification' needed to sustain the gender-based classification."[4]

Justice POWELL, joined by Justice Rehnquist, submitted the most extensive dissent. He argued that the majority had unduly curtailed valuable diversity in higher education, that the heightened standard of review was inappropriate here, and that "[t]his simply is not a sex discrimination case." In elaborating those conclusions, he objected to the Court's heightened scrutiny of a State's effort "to provide women with a traditionally popular and respected choice of educational environment." He objected to the Court's "legal error" of "applying a heightened equal protection standard, developed in cases of genuine sexual stereotyping, to a narrowly utilized state classification that provides an *additional* choice for women." Moreover, the Mississippi system should survive review even if a heightened standard of scrutiny were applied. Reviewing the history of single-sex education, Justice Powell insisted that the "sexual segregation of students has been a reflection of, rather than an imposition upon, the preference of those subject to the policy." He argued that the heightened standard of review generally applicable to sex discrimination was inappropriate here: "In no previous case have we applied it to invalidate state efforts to *expand* women's choices."[5] He concluded: "[Mississippi's] accommodation [of] student choices is legitimate because it is completely consensual and

4. "Justice Powell's dissent suggests that a second objective is served by the gender-based classification in that Mississippi has elected to provide women a choice of educational environments. Since any gender-based classification provides one class a benefit or choice not available to the other class, however, that argument begs the question. The issue is not whether the benefited class profits from the classification, but whether the State's decision to confer a benefit only upon one class by means of a discriminatory classification is substantially related to achieving a legitimate and substantial goal." [Footnote by Justice O'Connor.] Justice Powell responded to this comment as follows: "This is *not* the issue in this case. Hogan is not complaining about any benefit conferred upon women. Nor is he claiming discrimination because Mississippi offers no all-male college. As his brief states: 'Joe Hogan does not ask to attend an all-male college which offers a Bachelor of Science in nursing; he asks only to attend MUW' and he asks this only for his personal convenience." [The Court also rejected Mississippi's argument that Congress had authorized MUW's single-sex policy. This aspect of the case is considered in chap. 10, at p. 1020 below.]

5. Justice Powell added in a footnote: "Sexual segregation in education differs from the tradition typified by [Plessy v. Ferguson], of 'separate but equal' *racial* segregation. It was characteristic of racial segregation that segregated facilities were offered, not as alternatives to increase the choices available to blacks, but as the *sole* alternative. MUW stands in sharp contrast. Of Mississippi's eight public universities and 16 public junior colleges, only MUW considers sex as a criterion for admission. Women consequently are free to select a coeducational education environment for themselves if they so desire; their attendance at MUW is not a matter of coercion."

is important because it permits students to decide for themselves the type of college education they think will benefit them most. Finally, Mississippi's policy is substantially related to its long-respected objective." Chief Justice BURGER and Justice BLACKMUN submitted separate dissenting notations. [Note the further discussion of single-sex colleges in the Virginia case (1996; p. 704 below).]

A note on the proposed Equal Rights Amendment. The proposed Equal Rights Amendment would have provided that "[e]quality of rights under the law shall not be denied or abridged by the United States or by any State on account of sex" and would have authorized Congress to enact implementing legislation. Although Congress submitted the Amendment to the states early in 1972 and about half the necessary number of states ratified it within a few months, the ratification effort ran into substantial obstacles thereafter. In 1978, Congress extended the period for ratification until 1982. On June 30, 1982, that extension period expired and the proposed amendment accordingly failed of ratification. Thirty-five states had ratified it, but the additional three required states could not be mustered. (Identical amendments have been recurrently introduced in Congress since 1982.) What would have been the impact of the proposed Amendment?[6] Presumably, it would make sex a suspect classification. To what extent would that change the results in the cases considered above? Would it permit laws limited to physical sex differences? Classifications in the interests of privacy? Would it bar all generalizations based on sex—even empirically valid ones? As already noted, the Court has frequently inveighed against differential treatment based on stereotypical, inaccurate generalizations. But what about *valid* generalizations? In LOS ANGELES DEPT. OF WATER & POWER v. MANHART, 435 U.S. 702 (1978), which arose in a statutory rather than a constitutional context, the Court gave its first careful consideration to differential treatment based on an *accurate* generalization—and found that the truth of the generalization did *not* justify different treatment of individuals on the basis of sex. Should the Manhart approach to Title VII govern in constitutional cases as well? Would it if the ERA had been ratified? The generalization in Manhart was that, "[a]s a class, women live longer than men." For that reason, a city pension plan required female employees to make larger contributions than male workers; as a result, female employees received less take-home pay. Justice STEVENS's majority opinion rejected the argument that the differential was defensible because the value of the pension benefits provided to males and females differed. He noted that the generalization here was "unquestionably true" but added: "It is equally true [that] all individuals in the respective classes do not share the characteristic which differentiates the average class representatives." Emphasizing that Title VII barred discrimination against "any *individual*," he concluded that the law barred "treatment of individuals as simply components of a racial, religious, sexual, or national class. [Even] a true generalization about the class is an insufficient reason for disqualifying an individual to whom the generalization does not apply." He added: "Even if the statutory language were less clear, the basic policy of the statute requires that we focus on fairness to individuals rather than fairness to classes. Practices which classify employees in terms of religion, race, or sex tend to preserve traditional assumptions about groups rather than thoughtful scrutiny of individuals."

6. On the impact and desirability of the Amendment, see generally Brown, Emerson, Falk and Freedman, "The Equal Rights Amendment: A Constitutional Basis for Equal Rights for Women," 80 Yale L.J. 871 (1971), and "Equal Rights for Women: A Symposium on the Proposed Constitutional Amendment," 6 Harv.Civ.Rts.-Civ.Libs. L.Rev. 125 (1971).

J.E.B. v. ALABAMA ex rel. T.B., 511 U.S. 127 (1994): In Batson v. Kentucky (1986; p. 750 below), the Court held race-based peremptory challenges unconstitutional. The J.E.B. case eight years later raised a similar question in the context of gender rather than race. The Court held that gender-based peremptory challenges to jurors were also unconstitutional. Alabama sued J.E.B. to establish paternity and award child support on behalf of T.B., the mother of a minor child. The state used most of its peremptory challenges to strike male jurors. (J.E.B., the defendant, in turn used most of his peremptory strikes to remove female jurors, but that issue was not before the Court). As a result, an all-woman jury was empaneled. Justice BLACKMUN's opinion for the Court held that state's gender-based peremptory challenges unconstitutional, explaining: "Under our equal protection jurisprudence, gender-based classifications require 'an exceedingly persuasive justification' in order to survive constitutional scrutiny. [See, e.g., Hogan.] [Far] from proffering an exceptionally persuasive justification for its gender-based peremptory challenges, respondent maintains that its decision to strike virtually all males from the [jury] 'may reasonably have been based upon the perception, supported by history, that men otherwise totally qualified to serve on a jury might be more sympathetic and receptive to the arguments of a man alleged in a paternity action to be the father of an out-of-wedlock child, while women equally qualified to serve on an jury might be more sympathetic and receptive to the arguments of the complaining witness who bore the child.' We shall not accept as a defense to gender-based peremptory challenges 'the very stereotype the law condemns.' [Respondent] offers virtually no support for the conclusion that gender alone is an accurate predictor of jurors' attitudes; yet it urges this Court to condone the same stereotypes that justified the wholesale exclusion of women from juries and the ballot box.[1] [The State] seems to assume that gross generalizations that would be deemed impermissible if made on the basis of race are somehow permissible when made on the basis of gender. [When] state actors exercise peremptory challenges in reliance on gender stereotypes, they ratify and reinforce prejudicial views of the relative abilities of men and women. [The] potential for [public cynicism about jury neutrality] is particularly acute in cases where gender-related issues are prominent, such as cases involving rape, sexual harassment, or paternity. [In] view of these concerns, [equal protection] prohibits discrimination in jury selection on the basis of gender, or on the assumption that an individual will be biased in a particular case for no reason other than the fact that the person happens to be a woman or happens to be a man."

In a concurring opinion, Justice O'CONNOR expressed concern about the continued erosion of the necessarily discretionary and intuitive aspect of peremptory strikes, even though she agreed with the majority with respect to

---

1. "Even if a measure of truth can be found in some of the gender stereotypes used to justify gender-based peremptory challenges, that fact alone cannot support discrimination on the basis of gender in jury selection. We have made abundantly clear in past cases that gender classifications that rest on impermissible stereotypes violate [equal protection] even when some statistical support can be conjured up for the generalization. The generalization advanced by Alabama in support of its asserted right to discriminate on the basis of gender is, at the least, overbroad, and serves only to perpetuate the same 'outmoded notions of the relative capabilities of men and women' that we have invalidated in other contexts. The Equal Protection Clause [acknowledges] that a shred of truth may be contained in some stereotypes, but requires that state actors look beyond the surface before making judgments about people that are likely to stigmatize as well as to perpetuate historical patterns of discrimination." [Footnote by Justice Blackmun.]

peremptory strikes by the government. The importance of her opinion lies mainly in its contrast with Justice Blackmun's on the issue of the relevance of gender to juror attitudes: "We know that like race, gender matters. A plethora of studies make clear that in rape cases, for example, female jurors are somewhat more likely to vote to convict than male jurors. Moreover, although there have been no similarly definitive studies regarding, for example, sexual harassment, child custody, or spousal or child abuse, one need not be a sexist to share the intuition that in certain cases a person's gender and resulting life experience will be relevant to his or her view of the case. [Individuals] are not expected to ignore as jurors what they know as men—or women. Today's decision severely limits a litigant's ability to act on this intuition, for the import of our holding is that any correlation between a juror's gender and attitudes is irrelevant as a matter of constitutional law. But to say that gender makes no difference as a matter of law is not to say that gender makes no difference as a matter of fact. [Today's] decision is a statement that, in an effort to eliminate the potential discriminatory use of the peremptory, gender is now governed by the special rule of relevance formerly reserved for race. Though we gain much from this statement, we cannot ignore what we lose. In extending Batson to gender we have [diminished] the ability of litigants to act on sometimes accurate gender-based assumptions about juror attitudes. These concerns reinforce my conviction that today's decision should be limited to a prohibition on the government's use of gender-based peremptory challenges [because equal protection] prohibits only discrimination by state actors." Justice KENNEDY also issued a concurring opinion, emphasizing that "it is important to recognize that a juror sits not as a representative of a racial or sexual group but as an individual citizen. Nothing would be more pernicious to the jury system than for society to presume that persons of different backgrounds go to the jury room to voice prejudice. [Once] seated, a juror should not give free rein to some racial or gender bias of his or her own."

In a brief dissent, Chief Justice REHNQUIST stated that "the two sexes differ, both biologically and, to a diminishing extent, in experience. It is not merely 'stereotyping' to say that these differences may produce a difference in outlook which is brought into the jury room. Accordingly, use of peremptory challenges on the basis of sex is generally not the sort of derogatory and invidious act which peremptory challenges directed at black jurors may be." In a longer (and more caustic) dissent, Justice SCALIA, joined by Chief Justice Rehnquist and Justice Thomas, remarked: "Today's opinion is an inspiring demonstration of how thoroughly up-to-date and right-thinking we Justices are in matters pertaining to the sexes (or as the Court would have it, genders), and how sternly we disapprove [of] the male chauvinist attitudes of our predecessors. The [Court] stresses the lack of statistical evidence to support the widely held belief that, at least in certain types of cases, a juror's sex has some statistically significant predictive value as to how a juror will behave. This assertion seems to place the Court in opposition to its earlier Sixth Amendment 'fair cross-section' cases. [See Taylor v. Louisiana (1975; p. 664 above).] But times and trends do change, and unisex is unquestionably in fashion. Personally, I am less inclined to demand statistics, and more inclined to credit the perceptions of experienced litigators who have had money on the line. But it does not matter. [Even] if sex was a remarkably good predictor in certain cases, the Court would find its use in peremptories unconstitutional. The core of the Court's reasoning is that peremptory challenges on the basis of any group characteristic subject to heightened scrutiny are inconsistent with the guarantee of [equal protection]. That conclusion can be reached only by focusing unrealistically upon individual exercises of the peremptory challenge, and ignoring the totality of the practice. Since all groups are subject to the peremptory challenge (and will be made the object of it, depending upon the nature of the particular case) it is hard to see how any group is denied equal protection. That explains why peremptory challenges coexisted with the Equal Protection Clause for 120 years. This case is a perfect example of how the system as a whole is even-handed. [For] every man struck by the government, petitioner's own lawyer struck a woman. To say that men were singled out for discriminatory treatment in this process is preposterous. The situation would be different if both sides systematically struck individuals of one group, so that the strikes evinced group-based animus and served as a proxy for segregated venire lists. The pattern here, however, displays not a systemic sex-based animus but each side's desire to get a jury favorably disposed to its case. That is why the Court's characterization of respondent's argument as 'reminiscent of the arguments advanced to justify the total exclusion of women from juries' is patently false. Women were categorically excluded from juries because of doubt that they were competent; women are stricken from juries by peremptory challenge because of doubt that they are well disposed to the striking party's case. There is discrimination and dishonor in the former, and not in the [latter]." (Note the comments on this case in the notes following the next principal case.)

United States v. Virginia

___ U.S. ___, 116 S.Ct. 2264, 135 L.Ed.2d 735 (1996).

Justice GINSBURG delivered the opinion of the Court.

Virginia's public institutions of higher learning include an incomparable military college, Virginia Military Institute (VMI). The United States maintains that the Constitution's equal protection guarantee precludes Virginia from reserving exclusively to men the unique educational opportunities VMI affords. We agree.

I. Founded in 1839, VMI is today the sole single-sex school among Virginia's 15 public institutions of higher learning. VMI's distinctive mission is to produce "citizen-soldiers," men prepared for leadership in civilian life and in military service. VMI pursues this mission through pervasive training of a kind not available anywhere else in Virginia, an "adversative method" [that] constantly endeavors to instill physical and mental discipline in its cadets and impart to them a strong moral code. [Neither] the goal of producing citizen-soldiers nor VMI's implementing methodology is inherently unsuitable to women. And the school's impressive record in producing leaders has made admission desirable to some women. Nevertheless, Virginia has elected to preserve exclusively for men the advantages and opportunities a VMI education affords.

II. From its establishment in 1839, [VMI] has remained financially supported by Virginia. [Today, it] enrolls about 1300 men as cadets. [Its] "adversative, or doubting, model of education" [features] "physical rigor, mental stress, absolute equality of treatment, absence of privacy, minute regulation of behavior, and indoctrination in desirable values." [VMI] cadets live in spartan barracks where surveillance is constant and privacy nonexistent; they wear uniforms, eat together in the mess hall, and regularly participate in drills. Entering students are incessantly exposed to the rat line, "an extreme form of the adversative model," comparable in intensity to Marine Corps boot camp.

Tormenting and punishing, the rat line bonds new cadets to their fellow sufferers and, when they have completed the 7–month experience, to their former [tormentors]. In 1990, prompted by a complaint filed [by] a female high-school student seeking admission to VMI, the United States sued, [alleging] that VMI's exclusively male admission policy violated [equal protection]. The District Court ruled in favor of VMI, [but the Court of Appeals reversed and remanded, suggesting] these options for the State: Admit women to VMI; establish parallel institutions or programs; or abandon state support, leaving VMI free to pursue its policies as a private institution. [In response,] Virginia proposed a parallel program for women: Virginia Women's Institute for Leadership (VWIL). The 4–year, state-sponsored undergraduate program would be located at Mary Baldwin College, a private liberal arts school for women, and would be open, initially, to about 25 to 30 students. Although VWIL would share VMI's mission—to produce "citizen-soldiers"—the VWIL program would differ, as does Mary Baldwin College, from VMI in academic offerings, methods of education, and financial resources. [The] District Court [decided] the plan met the requirements of [equal protection]. [A] divided Court of Appeals [affirmed].

III. The cross-petitions in this case present two ultimate issues. First, does Virginia's exclusion of women from the educational opportunities provided by VMI—extraordinary opportunities for military training and civilian leadership development—deny to women "capable of all of the individual activities required of VMI cadets" the equal protection of the [laws]? Second, if VMI's "unique" situation—as Virginia's sole single-sex public institution of higher education—offends the Constitution's equal protection principle, what is the remedial requirement?

IV. We note, once again, the core instruction of this Court's pathmarking decisions in [J.E.B.] and [Hogan]: Parties who seek to defend gender-based government action must demonstrate an "exceedingly persuasive justification" for that action. Today's skeptical scrutiny of official action denying rights or opportunities based on sex responds to volumes of history. [Since] Reed, the Court has repeatedly recognized that neither federal nor state government acts compatibly with the equal protection principle when a law or official policy denies to women, simply because they are women, full citizenship stature— equal opportunity to aspire, achieve, participate in and contribute to society based on their individual talents and capacities. Without equating gender classifications, for all purposes, to classifications based on race or national origin, the Court, in post-Reed decisions, has carefully inspected official action that closes a door or denies opportunity to women (or to men). To summarize the Court's current directions for cases of official classification based on gender: Focusing on the differential treatment or denial of opportunity for which relief is sought, the reviewing court must determine whether the proffered justification is "exceedingly persuasive." The burden of justification is demanding and it rests entirely on the State. The State must show "at least that the [challenged] classification serves 'important governmental objectives and that the discriminatory means employed' are 'substantially related to the achievement of those objectives.' " The justification must be genuine, not hypothesized or invented post hoc in response to litigation. And it must not rely on overbroad generalizations about the different talents, capacities, or preferences of males and females.

The heightened review standard our precedent establishes does not make sex a proscribed classification. Supposed "inherent differences" are no longer accepted as a ground for race or national origin classifications. Physical differences between men and women, however, are enduring: "The two sexes are not fungible; a community made up exclusively of one [sex] is different from a community composed of both." "Inherent differences" between men and women, we have come to appreciate, remain cause for celebration, but not for denigration of the members of either sex or for artificial constraints on an individual's opportunity.[1] [Such] classifications may not be used, as they once were, to create or perpetuate the legal, social, and economic inferiority of women. Measuring the record in this case against the review standard just described, we conclude that Virginia has shown no "exceedingly persuasive justification" for excluding all women from the citizen-soldier training afforded by VMI. We therefore affirm the Fourth Circuit's initial judgment. [Because] the remedy proffered by Virginia—the Mary Baldwin VWIL program—does not cure the constitutional violation, [we] reverse the Fourth Circuit's final judgment in this case.

V. [Virginia] asserts two justifications in defense of VMI's exclusion of women. First, "[single-sex] education provides important educational benefits," and the option of single-sex education contributes to "diversity in educational approaches." Second, "[the] unique VMI method of character development and leadership training," the school's adversative approach, would have to be modified were VMI to admit women. We consider these [in] turn.

A. Single-sex education affords pedagogical benefits to at least some students, Virginia emphasizes, and that reality is uncontested in this litigation. Similarly, it is not disputed that diversity among public educational institutions can serve the public good. But Virginia has not shown that VMI was established, or has been maintained, with a view to diversifying, by its categorical exclusion of women, educational opportunities within the State. In cases of this genre, our precedent instructs that "benign" justifications proffered in defense of categorical exclusions will not be accepted automatically; a tenable justification must describe actual state purposes, not rationalizations for actions in fact differently grounded. [Neither] recent nor distant history bears out Virginia's alleged pursuit of diversity through single-sex educational options. In 1839, when the State established VMI, a range of educational opportunities for men and women was scarcely contemplated. Higher education at the time was considered dangerous for women; reflecting widely held views about women's proper place, the Nation's first universities and colleges [admitted] only men. VMI was not at all novel in this respect: In admitting no women, VMI followed the lead of the State's flagship school, the University of Virginia, founded in 1819. [Ultimately,] in 1970, [the] University of Virginia introduced coeducation and, in 1972, began to admit women on an equal basis with men. Virginia describes the current absence of public single-sex higher education for women as "an historical anomaly." But the historical record indicates action more deliberate than anomalous: First, protection of women against higher education; next, schools for women far from equal in resources and stature to schools for men; finally, conversion of the separate schools to coeducation. [In] 1990, an official commission [reported]: " 'Because colleges and universities provide opportunities for students to develop values and learn from role

---

1. Several amici have urged that diversity in educational opportunities is an altogether appropriate governmental pursuit and that single-sex schools can contribute importantly to such diversity. Indeed, it is the mission of some single-sex schools "to dissipate, rather than perpetuate, traditional gender classifications." See Brief for Twenty–Six Private Women's [Colleges]. We do not question the State's prerogative evenhandedly to support diverse educational opportunities. We address specifically and only an educational opportunity recognized by the [lower courts] as "unique," an opportunity available only at Virginia's premier military institute, the State's sole single-sex public university or college. [Footnote by Justice Ginsburg.]

models, it is extremely important that they deal with faculty, staff, and students without regard to sex, race, or ethnic origin.' " This statement, the Court of Appeals observed, "is the only explicit one that we have found in the record in which the Commonwealth has expressed itself with respect to gender distinctions." Our 1982 decision in [Hogan] prompted VMI to reexamine its male-only admission policy. Virginia relies on that reexamination as a legitimate basis for maintaining VMI's single-sex character. A Mission Study Committee, appointed by the VMI Board of Visitors, studied the problem from 1983 until 1986 and [counseled] against "change of VMI's status as a single-sex college." Whatever internal purpose the Mission Study Committee served, [we] can hardly extract from that effort any state policy evenhandedly to advance diverse educational options. [In] sum, we find no persuasive evidence in this record that VMI's male-only admission policy "is in furtherance of a state policy of 'diversity.' " [A] purpose genuinely to advance an array of educational options [is] not served by VMI's historic and constant plan—a plan to "afford a unique educational benefit only to males." However "liberally" this plan serves the State's sons, it makes no provision whatever for her daughters. That is not equal protection.

B. Virginia next argues that VMI's adversative method of training provides educational benefits that cannot be made available, unmodified, to women. Alterations to accommodate women would necessarily be [so] "drastic," Virginia asserts, as to transform, indeed "destroy," VMI's program. Neither sex would be favored by the transformation, Virginia maintains: Men would be deprived of the unique opportunity currently available to them; women would not gain that opportunity because their participation would "eliminate the very aspects of [the] program that distinguish [VMI from] other institutions of higher education in Virginia." The District Court forecast from expert witness testimony, and the Court of Appeals accepted, that coeducation would materially affect "at least these three aspects of VMI's program—physical training, the absence of privacy, and the adversative approach." And it is uncontested that women's admission would require accommodations, primarily in arranging housing assignments and physical training programs for female cadets. It is also undisputed, however, that "the VMI methodology could be used to educate women." The District Court even allowed that some women may prefer it to the methodology a women's college might pursue. The parties, furthermore, agree that "some women can meet the physical standards [VMI] now imposes on men." [In] support of its initial judgment for Virginia, [the] District Court made "findings" on "gender-based developmental differences" [that] restate the opinions of Virginia's expert witnesses, opinions about typically male or typically female "tendencies." For example, "males tend to need an atmosphere of adversativeness," while "females tend to thrive in a cooperative atmosphere." [The] United States emphasizes that [we] have cautioned reviewing courts to take a "hard look" at generalizations or "tendencies" of the kind pressed by [Virginia]. State actors controlling gates to opportunity [may] not exclude qualified individuals based on "fixed notions concerning the roles and abilities of males and females."

It may be assumed [that] most women would not choose VMI's adversative method. [However,] it is also probable that "many men would not want to be educated in such an environment." (On that point, even our dissenting colleague might agree.) [The] issue, however, is not whether "women—or men— should be forced to attend VMI" [but] whether the State can constitutionally deny to women who have the will and capacity, the training and attendant opportunities that VMI uniquely affords. The notion that admission of women would downgrade VMI's stature, destroy the adversative system and, with it, even the school, is a judgment hardly proved, a prediction hardly different from other "self-fulfilling prophecies" once routinely used to deny rights or opportunities. When women first sought admission to the bar and access to legal education, concerns of the same order were [expressed]. Medical faculties similarly resisted men and women as partners in the study of medicine. [Surely,] the State's great goal [of producing citizen-soldiers] is not substantially advanced by women's categorical exclusion, in total disregard of their individual merit, from the State's premier "citizen-soldier" corps. Virginia, in sum, "has fallen far short of establishing the 'exceedingly persuasive justification'" that must be the solid base for any gender-defined classification.

VI.   In the second phase of the litigation, Virginia presented its remedial plan—maintain VMI as a male-only college and create VWIL as a separate program for women. [The lower courts approved the plan.] [The] United States challenges this "remedial" ruling as pervasively misguided. A. A remedial decree [must] closely fit the constitutional violation; it must be shaped to place persons unconstitutionally denied an opportunity or advantage in "the position they would have occupied in the absence of [discrimination]." Milliken v. Bradley [1976; p. 783 below.] The constitutional violation in this case is the categorical exclusion of women from an extraordinary educational opportunity afforded men. A proper remedy for an unconstitutional exclusion, we have explained, aims to "eliminate [so far as possible] the discriminatory effects of the past" and to "bar like discrimination in the future." [VWIL] affords women no opportunity to experience the rigorous military training for which VMI is famed. Instead, the VWIL program "deemphasizes" military education, and uses a "cooperative method" of education "which reinforces self-esteem." VWIL students participate in ROTC and a "largely ceremonial" Virginia Corps of Cadets, but Virginia deliberately did not make VWIL a military institute. The VWIL House is not a military-style residence and VWIL students need not live together throughout the 4–year program, eat meals together, or wear uniforms during the school day. VWIL students thus do not experience the "barracks" life "crucial to the VMI experience," the spartan living arrangements designed to foster an "egalitarian ethic." [VWIL] students receive their "leadership training" in seminars [etc.] lacking the "physical rigor, mental stress, [minute] regulation of behavior, and indoctrination in desirable values" made hallmarks of VMI's citizen-soldier training. Kept away from the pressures, hazards, and psychological bonding characteristic of VMI's adversative training, VWIL students will not know the "feeling of tremendous accomplishment" commonly experienced by VMI's successful cadets. Virginia maintains that these methodological differences are "justified pedagogically," based on "important differences between men and women in learning and developmental needs," "psychological and sociological differences" [that] Virginia describes as "real" and "not stereotypes." [Generalizations] about "the way women are," estimates of what is appropriate for most women, no longer justify denying opportunity to women whose talent and capacity place them outside the average description. [In] contrast to the generalizations about women on which Virginia rests, we note again these dispositive realities: VMI's "implementing methodology" is not "inherently unsuitable to women," "some women [do] well under [the] adversative model," "some women, at least, would want to attend [VMI] if they had the opportunity," "some women are capable of all of the individual activities required of VMI cadets," and "can meet the physical standards [VMI] now imposes on men." It is on behalf of these women that the United States has instituted this suit, and it is for them that a remedy must be crafted, a remedy that will end their exclusion from a state-supplied educational opportunity for which they are [fit].

B. In myriad respects other than military training, VWIL does not qualify as VMI's equal. VWIL's student body, faculty, course offerings, and facilities hardly match VMI's. Nor can the VWIL graduate anticipate the benefits associated with VMI's 157–year history, the school's prestige, and its influential alumni network. Virginia, in sum, while maintaining VMI for men only, has failed to provide any "comparable single-gender women's institution." Instead, the Commonwealth has created a VWIL program fairly appraised as a "pale shadow" of VMI in terms of the range of curricular choices and faculty stature, funding, prestige, alumni support and influence. Virginia's VWIL solution is reminiscent [of] Sweatt v. Painter [1950; p. 675 above]. [More] important than the tangible features, the Court emphasized [in Sweatt] are "those qualities which are incapable of objective measurement but which make for greatness" in a school, including "reputation of the faculty, experience of the administration, position and influence of the alumni, standing in the community, traditions and prestige." [In] line with Sweatt, we rule here that Virginia has not shown substantial equality in the separate educational opportunities the State supports at VWIL and VMI. C. [The] Fourth Circuit plainly erred in exposing Virginia's VWIL plan to a deferential analysis, for "all gender-based classifications today" warrant "heightened scrutiny." [J.E.B.] Valuable as VWIL may prove for students who seek the program offered, Virginia's remedy affords no cure at all for the opportunities and advantages withheld from women who want a VMI education and can make the grade. In sum, Virginia's remedy does not match the constitutional violation; the State has shown no "exceedingly persuasive justification" for withholding from women qualified for the experience premier training of the kind VMI affords.

[T]he initial judgment of the Court of Appeals is affirmed [and] the final judgment of the Court of Appeals is reversed. [The case is remanded.] It is so ordered. (Justice THOMAS, whose son was attending VMI, did not participate in this case.)

Chief Justice REHNQUIST, concurring in the judgment.

I. Two decades ago in [Craig], we announced that "to withstand constitutional challenge, [classifications] by gender must serve important governmental objectives and must be substantially related to achievement of those objectives." We have adhered to that standard of scrutiny ever since. While the majority adheres to this test today, it also says that the State must demonstrate an "exceedingly persuasive justification" to support a gender-based classification. It is unfortunate that the Court thereby introduces an element of uncertainty respecting the appropriate test. While terms like "important governmental objective" and "substantially related" are hardly models of precision, they have more content and specificity than does the phrase "exceedingly persuasive justification." That phrase is best confined, as it was first used, as an observation on the difficulty of meeting the applicable test, not as a formulation of the test itself. To avoid introducing potential confusion, I would have adhered more closely to our traditional [standard]. Our cases dealing with gender discrimination also require that the proffered purpose for the challenged law be the actual purpose. It is on this ground that the Court rejects the first of two justifications Virginia [offers]. While I ultimately agree that the State has not carried the day with this justification, I disagree with the Court's method of analyzing the issue.

[Not until Hogan in 1982 was Virginia placed on] on notice that VMI's men-only admissions policy was open to serious question. [Before] this Court, Virginia has sought to justify VMI's single-sex admissions policy primarily on the basis that diversity in education is desirable, and that while most of the public institutions of higher learning in the State are coeducational, there should also be room for single-sex institutions. I agree with the Court that there is scant evidence in the record that this was the real reason that Virginia decided to maintain VMI as men only.* But, unlike the majority, I would consider only evidence that postdates [Hogan], and would draw no negative inferences from the State's actions before that time. [After] Hogan, the State was entitled to reconsider its policy with respect to VMI, and to not have earlier justifications, or lack thereof, held against it. Even if diversity in educational opportunity were the State's actual objective, the State's position would still be problematic. The difficulty with its position is that the diversity benefited only one sex; there was single-sex public education available for men at VMI, but no corresponding single-sex public education available for women. When Hogan placed Virginia on notice that VMI's admissions policy possibly was unconstitutional, VMI could have dealt with the problem by admitting [women]. Was there something else the State could have done to avoid an equal protection violation? I do not think [that] the State's options were as limited as the majority may imply. [Had] Virginia made a genuine effort to devote comparable public resources to a facility for women, and followed through on such a plan, it might well have avoided an equal protection violation. I do not believe the State was faced with the stark choice of either admitting women to VMI [or] abandoning VMI and starting from scratch for both men and [women].

II. The Court defines the constitutional violation in this case as "the categorical exclusion of women from an extraordinary educational opportunity afforded to men." By defining the violation in this way, and by emphasizing that a remedy for a constitutional violation must place the victims of discrimination in " 'the position they would have occupied in the absence of [discrimination],' " the Court necessarily implies that the only adequate remedy would be the admission of women to the all-male institution. [I] would not define the violation in this way; it is not the "exclusion of women" that violates the Equal Protection Clause, but the maintenance of an all-men school without providing any—much less a comparable—institution for women. Accordingly, the remedy should not necessarily require either the admission of women to VMI, or the creation of a VMI clone for women. An adequate remedy [might] be a demonstration by Virginia that its interest in educating men in a single-sex environment is matched by its interest in educating women in a single-sex institution. To demonstrate such, the State does not need to create two institutions with the same number of faculty PhD's, similar SAT scores, or comparable athletic fields. Nor would it necessarily require that the women's institution offer the same curriculum as the [men's]. It would be sufficient [if] the two institutions offered the same quality of education and were of the same overall calibre. [But] the state should avoid assuming demand based on stereotypes; it must not assume a priori, without evidence, that there would be no interest in a

---

* The dissent equates our conclusion that VMI's "asserted interest in promoting diversity" is not " 'genuine,' " with a "charge" that the diversity rationale is "a pretext for discriminating against women." Of course, those are not the same thing. I do not read the Court as saying that the diversity rationale is a pretext for discrimination, and I would not endorse such a proposition. We may find that diversity was not the State's real reason without suggesting, or having to show, that the real reason was "antifeminism." Our cases simply require that the proffered purpose for the challenged gender classification be the actual purpose, although not necessarily recorded. The dissent also says that the interest in diversity is so transparent that having to articulate it is "absurd on its face." Apparently, that rationale was not obvious to the [1980s Committee] which failed to list it among its reasons for maintaining VMI's all-men admission policy. [Footnote by Chief Justice Rehnquist.]

women's school of civil engineering, or in a men's school of nursing. In the end, the women's institution Virginia proposes, VWIL, fails as a remedy, because it is distinctly inferior to the existing men's institution and will continue to be for the foreseeable future. [I] therefore ultimately agree [that] Virginia has not provided an adequate remedy.

Justice SCALIA, dissenting.

Today the Court shuts down an institution that has served the people of [Virginia] with pride and distinction for over a century and a half. To achieve that desired result, it [rejects] the factual findings of two courts below, sweeps aside the precedents of this Court, and ignores the history of our people. As to facts: it explicitly rejects the finding that there exist "gender-based developmental differences" supporting Virginia's restriction of the "adversative" method to only a men's institution, and the finding that the all-male composition of [VMI] is essential to that institution's character. As to precedent: it drastically revises our established standards for reviewing sex-based classifications. And as to history: it counts for nothing the long tradition [of] men's military [colleges]. Much of the Court's opinion is devoted to deprecating the closed-mindedness of our forebears with regard to women's [education]. Closed-minded they were—as every age is, including our [own]. The virtue of a democratic system [is] that it readily enables the people, over time, to be persuaded that what they took for granted is not so, and to change their laws accordingly. That system is destroyed if the smug assurances of each age are removed from the democratic process and written into the Constitution. Since [the Constitution]—the old one—takes no sides in this educational debate, I dissent.

I. I shall devote most of my analysis to evaluating the Court's opinion on the basis of our current equal-protection [jurisprudence]. [I] have no problem with a system of abstract tests such as rational-basis, intermediate, and strict scrutiny (though I think we can do better than applying strict scrutiny and intermediate scrutiny whenever we feel like it). [But] the function of this Court is to preserve our society's values, [not] to revise them; to prevent backsliding from the degree of restriction the Constitution imposed upon democratic government, not to prescribe, on our own authority, progressively higher degrees. [Whatever] abstract tests we may choose to devise, they cannot supersede—and indeed ought to be crafted so as to reflect—those constant and unbroken national traditions that embody the people's understanding of ambiguous constitutional texts. [The] tradition of having government-funded military schools for men is as well rooted in the traditions of this country as the tradition of sending only men into military combat. The people may decide to change the one tradition, like the other, through democratic processes; but the assertion that either tradition has been unconstitutional through the centuries is not law, but politics-smuggled-into-law. And the same applies, more broadly, to single-sex education in general which [is] threatened by today's decision with the cut-off of all state and federal support. Today, however, change is forced upon Virginia, and reversion to single-sex education is prohibited nationwide, not by democratic processes but by order of this Court. Even while bemoaning the sorry, bygone days of "fixed notions" concerning women's education, the Court favors current notions so fixedly that it is willing to write them into the [Constitution] by application of custom-built "tests." This is not the interpretation of a Constitution, but the creation of one.

II. To reject the Court's disposition today, however, it is not necessary to accept my view that the Court's made-up tests cannot displace longstanding national traditions as the primary determinant of what the Constitution means.

It is only necessary to apply honestly the test the Court has been applying to sex-based classifications for the past two decades. [The] United States urged us to hold in this case "that strict scrutiny is the correct constitutional standard for evaluating classifications that deny opportunities to individuals based on their sex." [The Court] effectively accepts [this]. Although the Court in two places recites the test as stated in Hogan, [the] Court never answers the question presented in anything resembling that form. When it engages in analysis, the Court instead prefers the phrase "exceedingly persuasive justification" from Hogan. [But] the Court proceeds to interpret "exceedingly persuasive justification" in a fashion that contradicts the reasoning of Hogan and our other precedents. That is essential to the Court's result, which can only be achieved by establishing that intermediate scrutiny is not survived if there are some women interested in attending VMI, capable of undertaking its activities, and able to meet its physical demands. [Only] the amorphous "exceedingly persuasive justification" phrase, and not the standard elaboration of intermediate scrutiny, can be made to yield this conclusion that VMI's single-sex composition is unconstitutional because there exist several women (or, one would have to conclude under the Court's reasoning, a single woman) willing and able to undertake VMI's program. Intermediate scrutiny has never required a least-restrictive-means analysis, but only a "substantial relation" between the classification and the state interests that it serves. [There] is simply no support in our cases for the notion that a sex-based classification is invalid unless it relates to characteristics that hold true in every instance.

Not content to execute a de facto abandonment of the intermediate [scrutiny test], the Court purports to reserve the question whether, even in principle, a higher standard (i.e., strict scrutiny) should apply. [Some of the Court's] statements are misleading, insofar as they suggest that we have not already categorically *held* strict scrutiny to be inapplicable to sex-based classifications. And the statements are irresponsible, insofar as they are calculated to destabilize current law. Our task is to clarify the law—not to muddy the waters, and not to exact over-compliance by intimidation. [The] Court's intimations are particularly out of place because it is perfectly clear that, if the question of the applicable standard of review for sex-based classifications were to be [reconsidered], the stronger argument would be not for elevating the standard to strict scrutiny, but for reducing it to rational-basis review. The latter certainly has a firmer foundation in our past jurisprudence: Whereas no majority of the Court has ever applied strict scrutiny in a case involving sex-based classifications, we routinely applied rational-basis review until the 1970's. And of course normal, rational-basis review of sex-based classifications would be much more in accord with the genesis of heightened standards of judicial review, the famous footnote in [Carolene Products]. It is hard to consider women a "discrete and insular minority" unable to employ the "political processes ordinarily to be relied upon," when they constitute a majority of the electorate. And the suggestion that they are incapable of exerting that political power smacks of the same paternalism that the Court so roundly condemns. Moreover, a long list of legislation proves the proposition false.

III.   [I] now proceed to describe how the analysis should have been conducted. The question to be answered [is] whether the exclusion of women from VMI is "substantially related to an important governmental objective." A. It is beyond question that Virginia has an important state interest in providing effective college education for its citizens. That single-sex instruction is an approach substantially related to that interest should be evident enough from the long and continuing history in this country of men's and women's colleges. [But] besides its single-sex constitution, VMI is different from other colleges [in employing] a "distinctive educational method." [A] State's decision to maintain within its system one school that provides the adversative method is "substantially related" to its goal of good education. Moreover, it was uncontested that "if the state were to establish a women's VMI-type [i.e., adversative] program, the program would attract an insufficient number of participants to make the program work"; and it was found by the District Court that if Virginia were to include women in VMI, the school "would eventually find it necessary to drop the adversative system altogether." Thus, Virginia's options were an adversative method that excludes women or no adversative method at all. [Virginia's] election to fund one public all-male institution and one on the adversative model—and to concentrate its resources in a single entity that serves both these interests in diversity—is substantially related to the State's important educational interests.

B. The Court today has no adequate response to this clear demonstration of the conclusion produced by application of intermediate scrutiny. Rather, it relies on a series of contentions that are irrelevant or erroneous as a matter of law, foreclosed by the record, [or] both. [The] Court suggests that Virginia's [asserted] interest in promoting diversity of educational options [is] not "genuine," but is a pretext for discriminating against women. [The] relevance of [the 1980s Study Committee] is that its very creation, its sober 3–year study, and the analysis it produced, utterly refute the claim that VMI has elected to maintain its all-male student-body composition for some misogynistic [reason]. Ultimately, in fact, the Court does not deny the evidence supporting [the District Court] findings. It instead makes evident that the parties to this case could have saved themselves a great deal of time, trouble, and expense by omitting a trial. The Court simply dispenses with the evidence submitted at trial—it never says that a single finding of the District Court is clearly erroneous—in favor of the Justices' own view of the world. [The] Court's analysis at least has the benefit of producing foreseeable results. Applied generally, it means that whenever a State's ultimate objective is "great enough to accommodate women" (as it always will be), then the State will be held to have violated [equal protection] if it restricts to men even one means by which it pursues that objective—no matter how few women are interested in pursuing the objective by that means, no matter how much the single-sex program will have to be changed if both sexes are admitted, and no matter how beneficial that program has theretofore been to its participants. [That] VMI would not have to change very much if it were to admit women [is] irrelevant: If VMI's single-sex status is substantially related to the government's important educational objectives, as I have demonstrated above and as the Court refuses to discuss, that concludes the inquiry. There should be no debate in the federal judiciary over "how much" VMI would be required to change if it admitted women and whether that would constitute "too much" change. But if such a debate were relevant, the Court would certainly be on the losing side, [in view of the] findings by two courts below, amply supported by the evidence, and resulting in the conclusion that VMI would be fundamentally altered if it admitted [women]. Finally, the absence of a precise "all-women's analogue" to VMI is irrelevant. In [Hogan], we attached no constitutional significance to the absence of an all-male nursing school. As Virginia notes, if a program restricted to one sex is necessarily unconstitutional unless there is a parallel program restricted to the other sex, "the opinion in Hogan could have ended with its first footnote, which observed that 'Mississippi maintains no other single-sex public university or college.'" [I] have thus far said nothing about VWIL because it is, under our established test, irrelevant, so long as VMI's all-male character is "substantially related" to an important state goal. But VWIL now exists, and the Court's treatment of it shows how far-reaching today's decision is. [Even] though VWIL was carefully designed by professional educators who have tremendous experience in the area, and survived the test of adversarial litigation, the Court simply declares, with no basis in the evidence, that these professionals acted on " 'overbroad' generalizations."

C. A few words are appropriate in response to the concurrence, which finds VMI unconstitutional on a basis that is more moderate than the Court's but only at the expense of being even more implausible. The concurrence [states] that there is "scant evidence in the record" that diversity of educational offering was the real reason for Virginia's maintaining VMI. "Scant" has the advantage of being an imprecise term. I have cited the clearest statements of diversity as a goal for higher education in the [record]. There is no evidence to the contrary, once one rejects (as the concurrence rightly does) the relevance of VMI's founding in days when attitudes towards the education of women were [different].

IV. As is frequently true, the Court's decision today will have consequences that extend far beyond the parties to the case. What I take to be the Court's unease with these consequences, and its resulting unwillingness to acknowledge them, cannot alter the reality. [Under] the constitutional principles announced and applied today, single-sex public education is unconstitutional. By going through the motions of applying a balancing test—asking whether the State has adduced an "exceedingly persuasive justification" for its sex-based classification—the Court creates the illusion that government officials in some future case will have a clear shot at justifying some sort of single-sex public education. Indeed, the Court seeks to create even a greater illusion than that: It purports to have said nothing of relevance to other public schools at all. "We address specifically and only an educational opportunity recognized [as 'unique']." [But] the rationale of today's decision is sweeping: for sex-based classifications, a redefinition of intermediate scrutiny that makes it indistinguishable from strict scrutiny. Indeed, the Court indicates that if any program restricted to one sex is "unique," it must be opened to members of the opposite sex "who have the will and capacity" to participate in it. [T]he single-sex program that will not be capable of being characterized as "unique" [is] nonexistent. [R]egardless of whether the Court's rationale leaves some small amount of room for lawyers to argue, it ensures that single-sex public education is functionally dead. [The] enemies of single-sex education have won; by persuading only seven Justices [that] their view of the world is enshrined in the Constitution, they have effectively imposed that view on all 50 States.

There are few extant single-sex public educational programs. The potential of today's decision for widespread disruption of existing institutions lies in its application to *private* single-sex education. Government support is immensely important to private educational institutions. Charitable status under the tax law is also highly significant for private [colleges,] and it is certainly not beyond the Court that rendered today's decision to hold that a donation to a single-sex college should be deemed contrary to [public policy]. The Court adverts to private single-sex education only briefly, and only to make the assertion that "we address specifically and only an educational opportunity recognized by the District Court and the Court of Appeals as 'unique.' " As I have already remarked, [the Court's] assurance [that this case concerns only a "unique" educational opportunity] assures nothing, unless it is to be taken as a promise that in the future the Court will disclaim the reasoning it has used today to destroy VMI. The Government, in its briefs to this Court, at least purports to address the consequences of its attack on VMI for public support of private single-sex education. It contends that private colleges which are the direct or indirect beneficiaries of government funding are not thereby necessarily converted into state actors to which [equal protection] is then applicable. That is true. It is also virtually meaningless. The issue will be not whether government assistance turns private colleges into state actors, but whether the government itself would be violating the Constitution by providing state support to single-sex colleges. [The] only hope for state-assisted single-sex private schools is that the Court will not apply in the future the principles of law it has applied today. That is a substantial hope, I am happy and ashamed to say. [It] will certainly be possible for this Court to write a future opinion that ignores the broad principles of law set forth today, and that characterizes as utterly dispositive the opinion's perceptions that VMI was a uniquely prestigious all-male institution, conceived in chauvinism, etc., etc. I will not join that [opinion].*

———

Some questions on Hogan, J.E.B., and Virginia. Do Hogan and especially the Virginia case promise a stable standard of scrutiny of gender classifications? Does Virginia, with its emphasis on an "exceedingly persuasive justification," suggest that the intermediate scrutiny of Craig will be applied with heightened intensity in the future? Is Justice Scalia's dissent in Virginia, claiming that the majority had applied strict scrutiny in fact but not in theory, persuasive? Would the Court have been wiser to heed the United States' plea for explicit strict scrutiny? Does the rejection of the VMIL remedy in the Virginia case cast doubt on the constitutionality of all public single-sex colleges? Are single-gender schools still permissible at least at the high school level? In 1977, in Vorchheimer v. School District of Philadelphia, 430 U.S. 703, the Court affirmed (by an equally divided vote) a rejection of an attack on "separate but equal" single-sex public schools. Would such an attack be strengthened as a result of the rulings of the 1980s and 1990s? See Note, "Inner–City Single–Sex Schools: Educational Reform or Invidious Discrimination?," 105 Harv.L.Rev. 1741 (1992). What of sexually segregated athletic programs in public education? Most lower-courts have upheld such programs. See Note, "Boys Muscling in on Girls' Sports," 53 Ohio St.L.J. 891 (1992). Should they be held unconstitutional as reinforcing stereotypes about women athletes? Or are they justified as providing women athletes equal opportunities? The last question relates to the problems of "benign" discrimination, problems that have already surfaced in such cases as Hogan and are pursued in the next sub-section.

Thinking about J.E.B. provides an opportunity to reexamine the earlier materials about the Court's efforts to distinguish between "real" differences and archaic stereotypes. Recall the distinctively different views about the impermissibility of gender-based peremptory challenges in Justice Blackmun's, Justice O'Connor's and Justice Kennedy's opinions in that case. To what extent does each Justice's views reinforce a "jurisprudence of equality," or a "jurisprudence of difference"? Note Justice O'Connor's comment that gender, like race, matters, because studies indicate that in some cases female jurors are more likely to vote a particular way than male jurors. She recognizes that the Court's ruling limits the state's ability to act "on an intuition of gender differences in certain cases, because any correlation between a juror's gender

———

* Immediately after the Court's decision was announced, the Citadel, the only other state-supported military academy in the nation, announced that it would comply with the "letter and spirit" of the Virginia ruling, and that women would be in attendance by August, 1996. VMI, after unsuccessfully exploring the possibility of privatization, also ultimately announced that it would admit women (and did so in late 1996).

and attitudes is irrelevant as a matter of constitutional law." She added: "But to say that gender makes no difference as a matter of law is not to say that gender makes no difference as a matter of fact." Note also Justice Kennedy's insistence on formal equality. Even Justice Blackmun, who argued especially strongly against permitting intuitions based on gender differences to play a role in peremptory challenges, recognized that there was "a measure of truth" in some gender stereotypes. Does J.E.B., then, suggest that government may not recognize that men and women speak with a "different voice" on some issues? See especially the influential book by Carol Gilligan, In a Different Voice (1982), arguing that women typically see the world differently from men, with more concern about caring for others and about relationships. Cf. Frug, "Progressive Feminist Legal Scholarship: Can We Claim 'A Different Voice'?" 15 Harv. Women's L.J. 37 (1992). What would be the constitutional consequences of recognizing gender differences in "voice"? Are there any indications in current gender discrimination doctrine suggesting that government must recognize such differences?

THE BENIGN, COMPENSATORY USE OF GENDER CLASSIFICATIONS

Introduction. As the preceding materials show, the majority of the Court has not treated gender as a "suspect" classification triggering "strict" scrutiny. However, sex classifications clearly disadvantaging women do evoke a heightened, intermediate level of scrutiny. With respect to *benign* sex classifications, the Court, after some initial stumbling, achieved a consensus by the early 1980s: When sex classifications are defended as benign, compensatory aid to women, the Court applies exactly the *same* level of scrutiny as it does to disadvantaging classifications—the level of intermediate scrutiny set forth in Craig, Hogan and, apparently, Virginia. However, the Court insists on considerable proof that the "benign" justification is genuinely rooted in the *actual* legislative purpose. See, e.g., Justice Brennan's frequently cited statement in Weinberger v. Wiesenfeld (1975; p. 717 below): "[T]he mere recitation of a benign, compensatory purpose is not an automatic shield which protects against any inquiry into the actual purposes underlying a statutory scheme." What, if any, lessons for the treatment of benign racial classifications can be drawn from these developments in the sex classification area? See especially the opinions in Bakke and Adarand, sec. 3E below. This group of materials presents an overview of the Court's development of its stance regarding benign gender classifications.

1. *The early approach.* In the modern Court's first encounter with the problem, the majority applied an extremely deferential standard of review. In KAHN v. SHEVIN, 416 U.S. 351 (1974)—decided two years before Craig mandated intermediate scrutiny for sex classifications—Justice DOUGLAS's majority opinion held that a state property tax exemption for widows (but not for widowers) was easily sustainable, because it rested " 'upon some ground of difference having a fair and substantial relation to the subject of the legislation.' Reed." He stated that the state tax law was "reasonably designed to further the state policy of cushioning the financial impact of spousal loss upon the sex for which that loss imposes a disproportionately heavy burden"; thus, laws "designed to rectify the effects of past discrimination against women"

readily passed muster.[1] Justice BRENNAN's dissent, joined by Justice Marshall, urged "close judicial scrutiny" of gender-based classifications, even benign ones. He thought the law served a "compelling governmental interest," but found the statute invalid because it had not resorted to the most narrowly available means. Although "this country's history of pervasive sex discrimination against women" justified "remedial measures to correct the resulting economic imbalances," "less drastic means" were available to achieve that objective, since the property tax exemption was granted to all widows, whatever their financial status: "[The] State could readily narrow the class of beneficiaries to those widows for whom the effects of past economic discrimination against women have been a practical reality." (Justice WHITE also dissented.)

2. *Benignness in alimony laws.* In ORR v. ORR, 440 U.S. 268 (1979), the Court struck down laws which authorized the Alabama courts to impose alimony obligations on husbands but not on wives. Justice BRENNAN's majority opinion, applying the Craig v. Boren standard, found Alabama's scheme unconstitutional. In examining the "benign" justification, he stated that helping needy spouses and "compensating women for past discrimination during marriage" were "legitimate and important" objectives. But the "means" aspect of that test had not been satisfied: "even if sex were a reliable proxy for need, and even if the institution of marriage did discriminate against women, these factors still would not 'adequately justify the salient features of' Alabama's statutory scheme. Under the statute, individualized hearings at which the parties' relative financial circumstances are considered *already* occur. [Since these] hearings can determine which women were in fact discriminated against vis-à-vis their husbands, as well as which family units defied the stereotype and left the husband dependent on the wife, Alabama's alleged compensatory purpose may be effectuated without placing burdens solely on husbands. Progress toward fulfilling such a purpose would not be hampered, and it would cost the State nothing more, if it were to treat men and women equally by making alimony burdens independent of sex." Here, moreover, Alabama's "use of a gender classification actually produces perverse results," by giving "an advantage only to the financially secure wife whose husband is in need." Such a scheme was clearly irrational since nondependent wives are "precisely those who are not 'needy spouses' and who are 'least likely to have been victims [of] discrimination' by the institution of marriage." Finally, Justice Brennan commented generally on the dangers latent in "benign" gender classifications: "[Even] statutes purportedly designed to compensate for and ameliorate the effects of past discrimination must be carefully tailored," since they "carry the inherent risk of reinforcing stereotypes about the 'proper place' of women and their need for special protection."

3. *Benefits programs.* The social security system produced many challenges in the 1970s. Now-Justice Ginsburg was the lead lawyer in most of these; and the plaintiff was a male in many of the cases (as, e.g., in Craig). Thus, WEINBERGER v. WIESENFELD, 420 U.S. 636 (1975), invalidated a Social Security provision applicable when a covered wage earner dies. In the case of a deceased husband and father, benefits were payable both to the widow and to the couple's minor children in her care. But in the case of a deceased

---

1. Note that, before Kahn, Justice Douglas had joined Justice Brennan's opinion in Frontiero (p. 684 above) urging strict scrutiny for sex classifications. His very deferential approach in Kahn suggests that he perceived a sharp difference in the levels of scrutiny for disadvantaging and benign sex classifications. His stance in Kahn is all the more striking because, just one day earlier, he had applied *strict* scrutiny to a "benign" racially preferential law school admissions program in DeFunis (1974; p. 794 below). Were Justice Douglas's positions in DeFunis, Frontiero and Kahn reconcilable?

wife and mother, benefits were payable only to the minor children and not to the widower. The Court sustained the widower's challenge, finding an unjustifiable discrimination against covered female wage earners by affording them less protection for their survivors than that provided for survivors of male wage earners. The Court rejected the effort to defend the classification as a benign one because that had not been the actual purpose of Congress. And CALIFANO v. GOLDFARB, 430 U.S. 199 (1977), set aside a gender-based distinction in a federal benefits program under which survivors' benefits based on the earnings of a deceased husband covered by the Act were payable to his widow, but benefits on the basis of the earnings of a deceased wife were payable to a widower only if he "was receiving at least one-half of his support" from his deceased wife. Justice BRENNAN's plurality opinion found the scheme, "burdening a widower but not a widow with the task of proving dependency upon the deceased spouse," indistinguishable from that struck down in Wiesenfeld. He found the discrimination to be directed against female workers, whose social security taxes produced less protection for their spouses than was produced by the efforts of men. He insisted that Wiesenfeld was inconsistent with Kahn and thought the later, Wiesenfeld analysis should govern. Justice STEVENS's concurrence insisted that the relevant discrimination here was "against surviving male spouses, rather than against deceased female wage earners." Justice REHNQUIST's dissent, joined by Chief Justice Burger and Justices Stewart and Blackmun, argued, inter alia, that the deferential approach of Kahn should be followed with respect to benign sex classifications, that discrimination against men should not be treated as an "invidious discrimination," and that heightened scrutiny of sex distinctions should apply only when they disadvantaged women, because it was women who had "in the past been the victims of unfair treatment."

Contrast SCHLESINGER v. BALLARD, 419 U.S. 498 (1975), rejecting a male officer's attack on sex distinctions in the Navy's promotion system. The system accorded to women officers a 13–year tenure before mandatory discharge for want of promotion; males, by contrast, had to be discharged if they had been twice passed over for promotion, even though they might have had less than 13 years of commissioned service. Justice STEWART's majority opinion purported to apply the deferential rationality standard. Justice BRENNAN's dissent, joined by Justices Douglas and Marshall, insisted that strict scrutiny was applicable, but argued further that the scheme could not even survive rationality review. Justice Stewart insisted that the different treatment of men and women officers reflected "not archaic and overbroad generalizations, but, instead, the demonstrable fact that male and female line officers in the Navy are *not* similarly situated with respect to opportunities for professional service." Justice Brennan's dissent insisted that the majority had conjured up a legislative purpose: "I find nothing in the statutory scheme or the legislative history to support the supposition that Congress intended [to] compensate women for other forms of disadvantage visited upon them by the Navy." CALIFANO v. WEBSTER, 430 U.S. 313 (1977), a per curiam decision, sustained, as a valid benign classification, the Social Security Act's formula for computing old age benefits. Under the challenged statutory formula, a female wage earner could exclude from the computation of her "average monthly wage" three more lower-earning years than a similarly situated male wage earner could exclude. This resulted in a slightly higher "average monthly wage" and a correspondingly higher level of monthly old-age benefits for the retired female wage earner. (In this case, for example, the male challenger was awarded a monthly benefit of $185.70, but a similarly situated female wage earner would have been awarded $240 per month.) In sustaining that scheme, the Court reiterated the Craig standard and stated: "Reduction of the disparity in economic condition between men and women caused by the long history of discrimination against women has been recognized as [an] important governmental objective. Schlesinger v. Ballard; [Kahn]. But 'the mere recitation of a benign, compensatory purpose is not an automatic shield that protects against any inquiry into the actual purposes underlying a legislative scheme.' [Wiesenfeld.] Accordingly, we have rejected attempts to justify gender classifications as compensation for past discrimination against women when the classifications in fact penalized women wage earners, Califano v. Goldfarb; [Wiesenfeld], or when its legislative history revealed that the classification was not enacted as compensation for past discrimination. [Goldfarb; Wiesenfeld.] The statutory scheme involved here is more analogous to those upheld in Kahn and Ballard than to those struck down in Wiesenfeld and Goldfarb. The more favorable treatment of the female wage earner enacted here was not a result of 'archaic and overbroad generalizations' about women or of 'the role-typing society has long imposed' upon women, such as casual assumptions that women are 'the weaker sex' or are more likely to be child-rearers or dependents. Rather, 'the only discernible purpose of [the law's more favorable treatment is] the permissible one of redressing our society's longstanding disparate treatment of women.' The challenged statute operated directly to compensate women for past economic discrimination. [Allowing] women, who as such have been unfairly hindered from earning as much as men, to eliminate additional low-earning years from the calculation of their retirement benefits works directly to remedy some part of the effect of past discrimination. The legislative history [also] reveals that [Congress] purposely enacted the more favorable treatment for female wage earners to compensate for past employment discrimination against women."

4. *Discrimination against whom?* In several of the preceding cases, such as Wiesenfeld and Goldfarb, the Court was in some doubt about whether the alleged discrimination was directed against men or against women. Consider the analysis of that issue in WENGLER v. DRUGGISTS MUTUAL INS. CO., 446 U.S. 142 (1980). There, the Court held that a Missouri workers' compensation law unconstitutionally discriminated "against both men and women" and that this discrimination could not be justified on the ground that it was "benign." The law provided that a widow qualified for death benefits without having to prove actual dependence on her husband's earnings, but that a widower was not entitled to death benefits unless he demonstrated actual dependence on his wife's earnings or mental or physical incapacity to earn wages. Justice WHITE's opinion found that "the statute discriminates against both men and women"—against women because the benefits that the working woman could expect to be paid to a spouse in case of her work-related death were less than those payable to the spouse of the deceased male wage earner, and against men because a widower, unlike a widow, had to prove his incapacity or dependency. He rejected the claim that, regarding women, this was "benign" discrimination and, applying the Craig standard, found that the discriminatory means employed did not substantially serve the statutory end of providing for needy spouses. He also rejected the argument that the discrimination was justified because "most women are dependent on male wage earners and that it is more efficient to presume dependency in the case of women than to engage in case-to-case determination." The burden of making that "benign" justification was not met "simply by noting that in 1925 the state legislature thought widows to be more in need of prompt help than men or that today 'the substantive difference in the economic standing of working men and women justifies the advantage given to widows.' " Justice STEVENS concurred, stating

that "[n]othing has happened since the decision in [Goldfarb] to persuade me that this kind of gender-based classification can simultaneously disfavor the male class and the female class." He agreed, however, that the state had "failed to justify the disparate treatment of persons who have as strong a claim to equal treatment as to similarly situated surviving spouses." The sole dissenter was Justice REHNQUIST, who stated that he continued to believe that Goldfarb was "wrongly decided." (Contrast the treatment of "benign," compensatory racial discriminations, considered in Sec. 3E below.)

C. OTHER CLASSIFICATIONS ARGUABLY WARRANTING HEIGHTENED SCRUTINY

---

1. ALIENAGE

Introduction. We now turn to the question of whether there are classifications beyond those based on race or gender that warrant heightened scrutiny. What criteria are appropriate in evaluating the claims of other groups to heightened scrutiny? Is the appropriate approach assessing the degree to which these groups form analogues to race and gender? We begin this examination by examining the Court's protection of aliens. Alienage is not an "unalterable" trait. Aliens are legitimately excluded from voting, as the Court has always recognized. Does the justification for heightened scrutiny of alienage classifications rest solely, then, on the "political powerlessness" rationale and on the history of discrimination against many groups of aliens? See Graham v. Richardson, below. And if heightened scrutiny for alienage classifications *is* justified, can the "political function" exception be defended (see Foley v. Connelie and Ambach v. Norwick, below)—and how broadly can that exception be read without undermining the generally heightened scrutiny of alienage classifications? In the early 1970s, the Burger Court elevated alienage classifications to the level of "suspect" ones warranting "strict scrutiny" and invalidated state restrictions on aliens in several cases. By the late 1970s, however, the premises for considering alienage as a suspect classification came under increasing questioning, on and off the Court. A number of decisions sustained alienage classifications, state as well as federal ones. The modern Court's developing framework for scrutinizing alienage classifications represented a novel departure in equal protection doctrine: some alienage classifications continued to be subjected to strict scrutiny; but others, pertaining to "governmental functions," were reviewed far more deferentially. This bifurcated scheme raises recurrent questions about the Court's treatment of alienage: Is alienage justifiably a "suspect" classification under the various equal protection rationales for exercising special scrutiny regarding some classifying criteria? Would the Court have been wiser to deal with alienage issues in a different mode—e.g., by treating state alienage classifications not as "suspect" but as warranting special scrutiny because of the predominant federal interest in immigration and because of preemption principles?

1. *The rise of strict scrutiny of alienage classifications.* a. *Graham v. Richardson and welfare benefits.* The Burger Court launched strict scrutiny in the alienage area in GRAHAM v. RICHARDSON, 403 U.S. 365 (1971), holding that states could not deny welfare benefits to aliens. Justice BLACKMUN's

opinion announced: "[The] Court's decisions have established that classifications based on alienage, like those based on nationality or race, are inherently suspect and subject to close judicial scrutiny. Aliens as a class are a prime example of a 'discrete and insular' minority (see [the Carolene Products footnote]) for whom such heightened judicial solicitude is appropriate. Accordingly, it was said in [Takahashi v. Fish & Game Comm'n, 334 U.S. 410 (1948),[1] that] 'the power of a state to apply its laws exclusively to its alien inhabitants as a class is confined within narrow limits.' " He also offered a significant "additional" reason for the invalidation of the restriction: the "area of federal-state relations." Noting that "Congress has not seen fit to impose any burden or restriction on aliens who become indigent after their entry into the United States," he concluded that "state laws that restrict the eligibility of aliens for welfare benefits merely because of their alienage conflict with these overriding national policies in an area constitutionally entrusted to the Federal Government." (Justice HARLAN joined only the federal supremacy portion of Justice Blackmun's opinion.)

b. *Bar admission and public employment.* Two years after Graham, a divided Court applied the strict scrutiny prescribed by Graham to invalidate Connecticut's exclusion of resident aliens from law practice [IN RE GRIFFITHS, 413 U.S. 717 (1973)] and New York's law providing that only American citizens may hold permanent positions in the competitive classified civil service [SUGARMAN v. DOUGALL, 413 U.S. 634 (1973)]. Justice POWELL's majority opinion in Griffiths found none of the asserted state interests sufficiently substantial: neither the "undoubted interest in high professional standards" nor the role of lawyers in protecting clients' interests and serving as "officers of the Court" established that the State "must exclude all aliens from the practice of law." In Dougall, Justice BLACKMUN's majority opinion emphasized that the state barrier did not cover all high policymaking positions but covered a number of menial ones. Accordingly, the restriction had "little, if any, relationship" to the State's "substantial" interest "in having an employee of undivided loyalty." Justice Blackmun added a significant final section to his opinion in Dougall—a section that was to produce major inroads into the constitutional protection of aliens in the late 1970s. He stated that the Court had not held "that a State may not, in an appropriately defined class of positions, require citizenship as a qualification for office. [Such] power inheres in the State by virtue of its obligation [to] 'preserve the basic conception of a political community.' And this power and responsibility of the State applies, not only to the qualifications of voters, but also to persons holding state elective or important non-elective executive, legislative and judicial positions, for officers who participate directly in the formulation, execution, or review of broad public policy perform functions that go to the heart of representative government. [Such] state action [is] not wholly immune from scrutiny under [equal protection]. But our scrutiny will not be so demanding where we deal with matters resting firmly within a State's constitutional prerogatives. This is no more than a recognition of a State's historical power to exclude aliens from participation in its democratic political institutions." Justice REHNQUIST's dissent, applicable to both Griffiths and Dougall, questioned any extension of suspect classification analysis beyond the race area. And, as noted earlier, he objected to the reliance in Graham on the Carolene Products footnote rationale. He also thought any "immutable trait" analysis inapplicable: "[There] is a marked difference be-

---

1. Takahashi held that California's purported ownership of fish in its off-shore waters did not justify denying commercial fishing licenses to aliens. (Takahashi rested largely on preemption, federal supremacy grounds.)

tween a status or condition such as illegitimacy, national origin, or race, which cannot be altered by an individual, and the 'status' of the [challengers here]."

2. *The impairment of strict scrutiny: Deferential review under the "governmental function" exception.* a. *Foley.* In the late 1970s, the Court—drawing on the Dougall exception and reading it broadly—repeatedly relied on it to sustain a number of exclusions of aliens from public employment by exercising deferential review rather than strict scrutiny. The modern trend began with FOLEY v. CONNELIE, 435 U.S. 291 (1978), where Chief Justice BURGER's majority opinion held that New York *could* bar employment of aliens as state troopers. He argued that "to require every statutory exclusion of aliens to clear the high hurdle of 'strict scrutiny' [would] 'obliterate all the distinctions between citizens and aliens, and thus depreciate the historic values of citizenship.' [The] practical consequence [is] that 'our scrutiny will not be so demanding where we deal with matters firmly within a State's constitutional prerogatives.' Dougall. The State need only justify its classification by a showing of some rational relationship between the interests sought to be protected and the limiting qualification." He found that the state police force fell within the Dougall exception: "Police officers in the ranks do not formulate policy, per se, but they are clothed with authority to exercise an almost infinite variety of discretionary powers. [Clearly] the exercise of police authority calls for a very high degree of judgment and discretion." He concluded: "In the enforcement and execution of the laws the police function is one where citizenship bears a rational relationship to the special demands of the particular position."[2]

b. *Ambach.* AMBACH v. NORWICK, 441 U.S. 68 (1979), applied the Dougall exception and Foley to hold that a state may refuse to employ as elementary and secondary school teachers aliens who are eligible for citizenship but who refuse to seek naturalization. Justice POWELL, writing for a 5-4 majority, emphasized that a less demanding scrutiny was required when aliens were excluded from "state functions" that were "bound up with the operation of the State as a governmental entity." He explained: "[The] assumption of [citizenship status] denotes an association with a polity which, in a democratic republic, exercises the powers of governance. [It] is because of this special significance of citizenship that governmental entities [have] wider latitude in limiting the participation of noncitizens." He stressed the importance of public schools in preparing individuals for participation as citizens and in "the preservation of the values on which our society rests," and he noted a teacher's "opportunity to influence the attitudes of students toward government, the political process, and a citizen's social responsibilities." Accordingly, it was "clear that public school teachers come well within the 'governmental function' principle recognized in [Dougall] and Foley."[3]

2. Justice STEWART's concurrence conceded that the judgment was "difficult if not impossible to reconcile" with "the full sweep of the reasoning and authority of some of our past decisions." Nevertheless, he joined the Chief Justice's opinion "because I have become increasingly doubtful about the validity of those decisions (in at least some of which I concurred)." A separate opinion by Justice BLACKMUN, concurring only in the result, agreed that the decision was justified by the Dougall exception. Justice MARSHALL's dissent, joined by Justices Brennan and Stevens, argued that state troopers did not perform functions placing them within the "narrow" Dougall exception. Justice STEVENS, joined by Justice Brennan, also submitted a dissent.

3. Justice BLACKMUN's dissent, joined by Justices Brennan, Marshall and Stevens, stated: "For me, the present case falls on the Dougall–Griffiths [side] of that line, rather than on the narrowly isolated Foley side." Moreover, he differed sharply with the majority's claim that the exclusion here could survive even rationality scrutiny.

c. *Bernal.* BERNAL v. FAINTER, 467 U.S. 216 (1984), identified a limit to the Dougall exception at last: the Court's 8-1 decision found that the exception could not justify the Texas barrier to aliens becoming notaries public. Justice MARSHALL (who had dissented from all applications of the Dougall exception to strict scrutiny) wrote for the majority and applied strict scrutiny. He stated: "We emphasize, as we have in the past, that the political-function exception must be narrowly construed; otherwise the exception will swallow the rule and depreciate the significance that should attach to the designation of a group as a 'discrete and insular' minority for whom heightened judicial solicitude is appropriate." In finding the Dougall exception inapplicable to notaries public, he relied on the fact that their duties, although important, were "essentially clerical and ministerial." In the absence of either policymaking responsibilities or broad discretion of the type exercised by teachers and other public employees, the duties would not be deemed to be within the "governmental function" exception. Justice REHNQUIST was the sole dissenter. (Note that all of the cases in this group of notes involved legally resident aliens. For a case involving undocumented aliens—not legally resident aliens—see Plyler v. Doe (1982; p. 850 below). Plyler held that Texas could not deny free public education to "undocumented" alien children, even though the heightened scrutiny considered in this section applies only to legally resident aliens and even though the Court had earlier held that education was not a fundamental interest. Consideration of Plyler is accordingly postponed to sec. 4, which deals with fundamental interest analysis. In Plyler, the Court explicitly rejected "the claim that 'illegal aliens' are a 'suspect class.'" Noting that "undocumented status is not irrelevant to any proper legislative goal," the Court also pointed out that status was not "an absolutely immutable characteristic since it is the product of conscious, indeed unlawful, action.")

3. *Alienage restrictions and federal preemption: A more appropriate analysis?* Does the Court's oscillating course in alienage cases suggest that its equal protection emphasis is unwise? Note that in some of the preceding cases, principles of federalism and preemption surfaced as alternate grounds of decision. Some commentators have suggested that federalism concerns, not equal protection doctrine, provide the more satisfying explanation of the Court's rulings and the most persuasive basis for future development. Consider especially Note, "The Equal Treatment of Aliens: Preemption or Equal Protection?" 31 Stan.L.Rev. 1069 (1979), arguing that "suspect classifications" analyses "have not provided the Court with an intelligible basis for a review of restrictions based on alienage. Rather, the Court's opinions in this area seem to be following an unarticulated theory of preemption. Ironically, the Court had explicitly constructed much of this framework before its decision in Graham. Fundamental to this theory is the Court's belief that as the federal government, through the immigration scheme, 'invites' resident aliens to enter the country as permanent residents free of restriction—'on an equality of legal privileges with all citizens' [Takahashi]—it is not for the states to alter the terms of immigration with new burdens. Yet the Court appears to reason that since the federal government does not admit resident aliens to the *political* community—admission does not confer citizenship—the states may exclude resident aliens from state [political] functions without offending federal power. [The] Court should recognize that its creation of a suspect classification of alienage has not been a successful experiment and should return to its pre-Graham theory of preemption for the equal treatment of aliens."

For a rare modern Court decision striking down an alienage restriction on federalism-related rather than equal protection grounds, see TOLL v. MORENO, 458 U.S. 1 (1982). The ruling struck down the University of Maryland's policy of granting preferential tuition and fees treatment to students with "in-state" status. "Nonimmigrant aliens" were not eligible for such status even if they were domiciled in Maryland. Justice BRENNAN's opinion relied entirely on federal legislation: "In light of Congress' explicit decision not to bar [such] aliens from acquiring domicile, the State's decision to deny 'in-state' status to [them], *solely* on account of [their] federal immigration status, surely amounts to an ancillary 'burden not contemplated by Congress' in admitting these aliens to the United States. [The] University's policy violates the Supremacy Clause." In the course of his opinion, he stated: "Commentators have noted [that] many of the Court's decisions concerning alienage classifications, such as Takahashi, are better explained in preemption than equal protection terms. Takahashi and Graham stand for the broad principle that 'state regulation not congressionally sanctioned that discriminates against aliens lawfully admitted to the country is impermissible if it imposes additional burdens not contemplated by Congress.' "

4. *Federal restrictions on aliens.* a. *Public employment.* In HAMPTON v. MOW SUN WONG, 426 U.S. 88 (1976), the Court invalidated a Civil Service Commission (CSC) regulation barring resident aliens from employment in the federal competitive civil service—even while recognizing that "overriding national interests may provide a justification for a citizenship requirement in the federal service [though] an identical requirement may not be enforced by a State." Justice STEVENS's opinion found that the national interests offered in defense of the ban either (a) were not properly the concern of the CSC and had not explicitly emanated from Congress or the President, or (b) to the extent that they were within CSC competence, had not been evaluated fully by the CSC. He found it unnecessary to determine the substantive validity of the alien ban under the equal protection component of Fifth Amendment due process and rested instead on the "narrower" ground that "essential procedures" had not been followed—"procedures" involving the source and the deliberativeness of the regulation: "Since these residents were admitted as a result of decisions made by the Congress and the President, [due process] requires that the decision to impose [the] deprivation of an important liberty be made either at a comparable level of government or, if it is to be permitted to be made by the [CSC], that it be justified by reasons which are properly the concern of that agency." And these "structural due process" requirements had not been satisfied here. (Note Justice Stevens's reliance on a similar rationale in his dissent in Fullilove v. Klutznick (1980; p. 812 below).) Justice Stevens explained that when "an overriding national interest" is asserted as a justification for a discriminatory rule which would be barred by equal protection if adopted by a state, "due process requires that there be a legitimate basis for presuming that the [federal] rule was actually intended to serve that interest." Here, there was no basis for such a presumption. He was willing to assume "that if the Congress or the President had expressly imposed the citizenship requirement, it would be justified by the national interest in providing an incentive for aliens to become naturalized, or possibly even as providing the President with an expendable token for treaty negotiating purposes." But those were not interests "which can reasonably be assumed to have influenced the CSC": "we are not willing to presume that the [agency] was deliberately fostering an interest so far removed from [its] normal responsibilities." (In the wake of this decision, President Ford issued an order reviving the bar on aliens in the federal civil service.) Justice REHNQUIST's dissent, joined by Chief Justice Burger and Justices White and Blackmun, charged the majority with enunciating "a novel conception" of procedural due process and evolving from it "a doctrine of delegation of legislative authority which [seems] quite contrary" to the precedents. Though the Court's "innovations" had some appeal in

this case, he thought them "outweighed by the potential mischief which the doctrine bids fair to make in other areas of the law." In his view, the majority "inexplicably melds together the concepts of equal protection, procedural and substantive due process." He argued that the majority had implicitly found "faulty" delegation of power to the CSC. The "overriding national interest" involved here, he insisted, was not any "specific interest in excluding these particular aliens from the civil service, but a general interest in formulating policies toward aliens."

b. *Medical benefits.* In MATHEWS v. DIAZ, 426 U.S. 67 (1976), decided on the same day as Hampton, the Court held that Congress may condition an alien's eligibility for participation in a federal Medicare program on (a) admission for permanent residence and (b) continuous residence in the United States for five years. Justice STEVENS once again wrote the prevailing opinion, but this time for a unanimous Court, applying a deferential standard of review. He reasoned that Congress, under its "broad power over naturalization and immigration," regularly made rules that would be unacceptable if applied to citizens; disparate treatment of aliens and citizens did not demonstrate invidiousness. Turning to the welfare area, he insisted that congressional provision of some benefits to citizens "does not require it to provide like benefits for *all aliens.*" The "real question" was "not whether discrimination between citizens and aliens is permissible" but "whether the statutory discrimination *within* the class of aliens—allowing benefits to some aliens but not to others—" was valid. Justice Stevens's scrutiny was extremely deferential: "The reasons that preclude judicial review of political questions also dictate a narrow standard of review of decisions made by the Congress or the President in the area of immigration and naturalization."

----

2. NONMARITAL CHILDREN

Introduction. The Court's course in reviewing state classifications based on illegitimacy—classifications disadvantaging nonmarital children—has been a wavering one. In no area of classifications triggering occasional heightened scrutiny have the Court's actions been more unpredictable. Does illegitimacy bear sufficient resemblance to race and sex to warrant the heightened scrutiny those classifications have elicited? This section surveys the Court's zigzag course and illustrates the uncertainties in this line of cases. What *is* clear is that, although the Court has never labeled illegitimacy a "suspect" classification, it has in fact exercised a degree of heightened scrutiny in most of the cases and has struck down illegitimacy classifications with some frequency. Only in the late 1980s, in Clark v. Jeter, p. 728 below, did the Court explicitly endorse an intermediate scrutiny standard akin to that in Craig v. Boren, above. In examining these materials, consider whether a coherent approach can indeed be drawn from this erratic pattern.

1. *The origin.* The modern Court's frequent encounters with illegitimacy classifications began in the late Warren years, in LEVY v. LOUISIANA, 391 U.S. 68 (1968), where the Court found a violation of equal protection in a law denying unacknowledged nonmarital children the right to recover for the wrongful death of their mother. The uncertain rationale of the cases is illustrated by this first one in the series: Justice DOUGLAS's majority opinion simultaneously hinted at rationality review and at heightened scrutiny. He stated: "[The] test [is] whether the line drawn is a rational one, [but] we have been extremely sensitive when it comes to basic civil rights and have not hesitated to strike down an invidious classification even though it had history

and tradition on its side. The rights asserted here involve the intimate, familial relationship between a child and his own mother. [Why], in terms of 'equal protection,' should the tortfeasors go free merely because the child is illegitimate? [Illegitimacy] has no relation to the nature of the wrong inflicted on the mother. [It] is invidious to discriminate against [the illegitimate children] when no action, conduct, or demeanor of theirs[1] is possibly relevant to the harm that was done the mother." Justice HARLAN's dissent, joined by Justices Black and Stewart, called the decision a "constitutional curiosit[y]." He insisted that states could properly define eligible plaintiffs in wrongful death laws in terms of "their legal rather than their biological relation to the deceased." Moreover, the law had "obvious justification": to enforce requirements regarding acknowledgment of illegitimate children and to simplify proceedings "by reliance on formal papers."

2. *The wavering aftermath in the early 1970s.* Three years after Levy, Labine v. Vincent, 401 U.S. 532 (1971), indicated to many observers a substantial Court withdrawal from the heightened scrutiny suggested by Levy for state impositions of disadvantages on non-marital children. In Labine, the dissenters in Levy joined with Chief Justice Burger and Justice Blackmun in distinguishing Levy and upholding an intestate succession provision which subordinated the rights of *acknowledged* nonmarital children to those of other relatives of the parent. Justice Black's brief majority opinion found remarkably little federal constitutional basis for review; one passage, indeed, suggested that there might not even be minimum rationality review. But the post-Labine assertions of the demise of Levy proved exaggerated: one year later, in Weber v. Aetna Cas. & Sur. Co., 406 U.S. 164 (1972), Justice Powell's majority opinion followed Levy and distinguished Labine in holding that the claims of dependent unacknowledged non-marital children to death benefits under a workers' compensation law could not be subordinated to the claims of legitimate children.

The wavering course continued in the mid–1970s. Mathews v. Lucas, 427 U.S. 495 (1976), sustained a Social Security Act provision disadvantaging many nonmarital children, explicitly rejected a plea to apply "strict scrutiny," and distinguished all prior rulings invalidating illegitimacy classifications. Justice Blackmun's majority opinion upheld a provision providing benefits for surviving dependent children. For many classes of children—all legitimate ones and some illegitimate ones—dependence was statutorily presumed; but other non-marital children were subjected to an individualized burden of proving dependency. Justice Blackmun rejected the "suspect" label for such classifications and refused to apply formal heightened scrutiny. The Court's "possibly rational," less than "most exacting scrutiny," criterion was readily satisfied here. Though the Court insisted that its level of scrutiny was "not a toothless one," the challengers were required "to demonstrate the insubstantiality" of the means-ends relationship; and here, the statutory scheme reflected "reasonable empirical judgments." Unlike cases such as Weber and Levy, legitimacy here "was simply taken as an indication of dependency," a valid statutory criterion.

3. *The late 1970s.* a. In TRIMBLE v. GORDON, 430 U.S. 762 (1977), the Court continued its uneasy search for an articulable (and consistently applied)

---

1. "We can say with Shakespeare: 'Why bastard, wherefore base? When my dimensions are as well compact, My mind as generous, and my shape as true, As honest madam's issue? Why brand they us With base? with baseness? bastardy? base, base?' King Lear, Act I, Scene 2." [Footnote by Justice Douglas.] [Compare the response in Justice Harlan's dissent: "Supposing that the Bard had any views on the law of legitimacy, they might more easily be discerned from Edmund's character than from the words he utters in defense of the only thing he cares for, himself."]

standard of review of illegitimacy classifications. Trimble made clear that the Court's promise (in Mathews v. Lucas) that scrutiny of illegitimacy classifications would not be "toothless" was not an empty one. The 5-4 decision struck down a provision in the Illinois law governing intestate succession that barred inheritance by nonmarital children from their fathers. Justice POWELL's majority opinion noted that the State had relied in part on its interest in "the promotion of [legitimate] family relationships," but stated that, in a case like this, equal protection "requires more than the mere incantation of a proper state purpose. [Since Labine], we have expressly [rejected] the argument that a State may attempt to influence the actions of men and women by imposing sanctions on the children born of their illegitimate relationships."[2]

b. The heightened scrutiny of Trimble did not produce stability in this area. Indeed, LALLI v. LALLI, 439 U.S. 259 (1978), cast doubt on the continuing vitality of Trimble. The decision upheld a New York law forbidding nonmarital children to inherit from their fathers by intestate succession (even though there was "convincing proof of paternity") unless there was a judicial finding of paternity during the father's lifetime. The Court was sharply divided. Justice POWELL's plurality opinion found that the law was "substantially related" to the important state interests of providing for "the just and orderly disposition of property at death," in light of "the peculiar problems of proof [implicated] in paternal inheritance by illegitimate children." He distinguished Trimble and added: "We do not question that there will be some illegitimate children who would be able to establish their relationship to their deceased fathers without serious disruption of the administration of estates and that, as applied to [them, the law] appears to operate unfairly. But few statutory classifications are entirely free from the criticism that they sometimes produce inequitable results. Our inquiry under [equal protection] does not focus on the abstract 'fairness' of a state law, but on whether the statute's relation to the state interests it is intended to promote is so tenuous that it lacks [rationality]." Justice BRENNAN's dissent argued that New York had available less drastic means of screening out fraudulent claims of paternity.

4. *The 1980s.* Despite the meandering course of decisions in the 1970s, the Court has in fact continued to accord illegitimacy classifications somewhat heightened scrutiny. In Mills v. Habluetzel, 456 U.S. 91 (1982), the Court struck down a Texas law requiring that a paternity suit to identify the natural father of an illegitimate child for the purpose of obtaining child support must be brought before the child is one year old. (Texas imposes no time limit on the right of a *legitimate* child to sue for support.) Justice Rehnquist (who had vehemently opposed any special scrutiny of illegitimacy classifications as recently as Trimble) wrote for the Court in Mills. He stated: "[It] is clear that the support opportunity provided by the State to illegitimate children must be more than illusory. The period for asserting the right to support must be sufficiently long to permit those who normally have an interest in such children to bring an action on their behalf despite the difficult personal, family, and financial circumstances that often surround the birth of a child outside of wedlock." The Court consolidated its Mills approach a year later, in Pickett v. Brown, 462 U.S.

---

2. In a case decided on the same day as Trimble, the Court made clear that deferential rather than heightened scrutiny was appropriate for illegitimacy classifications in the federal immigration context. Fiallo v. Bell, 430 U.S. 787 (1977). (Recall the similarly deferential scrutiny for federal alienage classifications in Mathews v. Diaz (1976; p. 725 above).) Fiallo sustained the narrow definition of the "parent-child" relationship in federal immigration law, which excludes the relationship between an illegitimate child and the natural father from preferred immigration status, even though the relationship between an illegitimate child and the natural mother is included.

1 (1983). It invalidated a Tennessee law that was, for all practical purposes, identical to the Texas one struck down in Mills, except that Tennessee set a two-year rather than a one-year limitation period. Five years later, a unanimous Court at last agreed that an intermediate level of scrutiny *was* appropriate, in CLARK v. JETER, 486 U.S. 456 (1988). Applying Pickett, Justice O'CONNOR's opinion identified the applicable scrutiny as "intermediate" and concluded that Pennsylvania's 6–year statute of limitations for support actions on behalf of nonmarital children did not "withstand heightened scrutiny." She stated that intermediate scrutiny "generally has been applied to discriminatory classifications based on sex or illegitimacy" and that "[t]o withstand an intermediate scrutiny, a statutory classification must be substantially related to an important governmental objective." She insisted that, even if a 6–year period might be reasonable, it was "not substantially related to Pennsylvania's interest in avoiding the litigation of stale or fraudulent claims."

----

3. DISABILITIES: MENTAL RETARDATION; AGE; POVERTY

Mental retardation. Recall that in Schweiker v. Wilson (1981; p. 657 above), a divided Court sustained a provision of a federal welfare program excluding, among others, certain inmates of public mental institutions from "comfort payments." The trial court had struck down the provision after accepting the challengers' claim that the statutory scheme should be "subjected to a heightened standard of review" because the mentally ill "historically have been subjected to purposeful unequal treatment; they have been relegated to a position of political powerlessness; and prejudice against them curtails their participation in the pluralist political system and strips them of political protection against discriminatory legislation." The Court did not reach that issue. Justice Blackmun's majority opinion stated that "we [intimate] no view as to what standard of review applies to legislation expressly classifying the mentally ill as a discrete group." Four years later, the Court confronted the related issue of whether classifications based on mental retardation (rather than mental illness) warrant heightened scrutiny. In the Cleburne case, which follows, the Court rejected the argument that heightened scrutiny was appropriate yet struck down the classification while purporting to apply deferential rationality review. Does Cleburne remind you of the early gender discrimination cases of the 1970s such as Reed v. Reed, p. 683 above, where the Court struck down classifications disadvantaging on the basis of sex even while asserting that it was engaging in deferential review? (Only in later gender discrimination cases did the Court acknowledge that cases such as Reed had in fact applied heightened scrutiny.) Note also Plyler v. Doe (1982; p. 850 below), where the Court explicitly applied heightened scrutiny in a new area, in contrast to its approach in Cleburne.

Cleburne v. Cleburne Living Center, Inc.

473 U.S. 432, 105 S.Ct. 3249, 87 L.Ed.2d 313 (1985).

Justice WHITE delivered the opinion of the Court.

A Texas city denied a special use permit for the operation of a group home for the mentally retarded, acting pursuant to a municipal zoning ordinance requiring permits for such homes. The Court of Appeals for the Fifth Circuit held that mental retardation is a "quasi-suspect" classification and that the ordinance violated [equal protection] because it did not substantially further an important governmental purpose. We hold that a lesser standard of scrutiny is appropriate, but conclude that under that standard the ordinance is invalid as applied in this case.

I. In July, 1980, respondent Jan Hannah purchased a building [in] the city of Cleburne, Texas, with the intention of leasing it to Cleburne Living Centers, Inc. (CLC), for the operation of a group home for the mentally retarded. [After] holding a public hearing on CLC's application, the city council voted three to one to deny a [special use permit]. II. [The] general rule [under equal protection] is that legislation is presumed to be valid and will be sustained if the classification drawn by the statute is rationally related to a legitimate state interest. When social or economic legislation is at issue, [equal protection] allows the states wide [latitude]. The general rule gives way, however, when a statute classifies by race, alienage or national origin. These factors are so seldom relevant to the achievement of any legitimate state interest that laws grounded in such considerations are deemed to reflect prejudice and antipathy—a view that those in the burdened class are not as worthy or deserving as others. For these reasons and because such discrimination is unlikely to be soon rectified by legislative means, these laws are subjected to [strict scrutiny]. Legislative classifications based on gender also call for a heightened standard of review. That factor generally provides no sensible ground for differential treatment. [Because] illegitimacy is beyond the individual's control and bears "no relation to the individual's ability to participate in and contribute to society," official discriminations resting on that characteristic are also subject to somewhat heightened review. We have declined, however, to extend heightened review to differential treatment based on age. [The] lesson of Murgia [p. 649 above and p. 734 below] is that where individuals in the group affected by a law have distinguishing characteristics relevant to interests the state has the authority to implement, the courts have been very reluctant [to] closely scrutinize legislative choices as to whether, how and to what extent those interests should be pursued. In such cases, [equal protection] requires only a rational means to serve a legitimate end.

III. Against this background, we conclude [that] the Court of Appeals erred in holding mental retardation a quasi-suspect [classification]. First, it is undeniable [that] those who are mentally retarded have a reduced ability to cope with and function in the everyday world. Nor are they all cut from the same pattern: [they] range from those whose disability is not immediately evident to those who must be constantly cared for. They are thus different, immutably so, in relevant respects, and the states' interest in dealing with and providing for them is plainly a legitimate one. How this large and diversified group is to be treated under the law is a difficult and often a technical matter, very much a task for legislators guided by qualified professionals and not by the perhaps ill-informed opinions of the judiciary. Heightened scrutiny inevitably involves substantive judgments about legislative decisions, and we doubt that the predicate for such judicial oversight is present where the classification deals with mental retardation. Second, [both] national and state [lawmakers] have been addressing [the] difficulties [of the mentally retarded] in a manner that belies a continuing antipathy or prejudice and a corresponding need for more intrusive oversight by the judiciary. Thus, the federal government has not only outlawed discrimination against the mentally retarded in federally funded programs but it has also provided the retarded with the right to receive "appropriate treatment, services, and habilitation" in a setting that is "least restrictive of [their] personal liberty." [Texas] has similarly enacted [such legislation.] [It] may be, as CLC contends, that legislation designed to benefit, rather than disadvantage, the retarded would generally withstand examination under a test of heightened scrutiny. The relevant inquiry, however, is whether heightened scrutiny is constitutionally mandated in the first instance. Even assuming that many of these laws [would survive scrutiny], merely requiring the legislature to justify its efforts in these terms may lead it to refrain from acting at all. Much recent legislation intended to benefit the retarded also assumes the need for measures that might be perceived to disadvantage them. The Education of the Handicapped Act, for example, requires an "appropriate" education, not one that is equal in all respects to the education of non-retarded children; clearly, admission to a class that exceeded the abilities of a retarded child would not be appropriate. [Given] the wide variation in the abilities and needs of the retarded themselves, governmental bodies must have a certain amount of flexibility and freedom from judicial oversight in shaping and limiting their remedial efforts. Third, the legislative response, which could hardly have occurred and survived without public support, negates any claim that the mentally retarded are politically powerless in the sense that they have no ability to attract the attention of the lawmakers. [Fourth,] if the large and amorphous class of the mentally retarded were deemed quasi-suspect[, it] would be difficult to find a principled way to distinguish a variety of other groups who have perhaps immutable disabilities setting them off from others, who cannot themselves mandate the desired legislative responses, and who can claim some degree of prejudice from at least part of the public at large. One need mention in this respect only the aging, the disabled, the mentally ill, and the infirm. We are reluctant to set out on that course, and we decline to do so.

Doubtless, there have been and there will continue to be instances of discrimination against the retarded that are in fact invidious, and that are properly subject to judicial correction under constitutional norms. But the appropriate method of reaching such instances is not to create a new quasi-suspect classification [but to] look to the likelihood that governmental action premised on a particular classification is valid as a general matter, not merely to the specifics of the case before us. Because mental retardation is a characteristic that the government may legitimately take into account in a wide range of decisions, and because both state and federal governments have recently committed themselves to assisting the retarded, we will not presume that any given legislative action, even one that disadvantages retarded individuals, is rooted in considerations that the Constitution will not tolerate. Our refusal to recognize the retarded as a quasi-suspect class does not leave them entirely unprotected from invidious discrimination. To withstand equal protection review, legislation that distinguishes between the mentally retarded and others must be rationally related to a legitimate governmental purpose. This standard, we believe, affords government the latitude necessary both to pursue policies designed to assist the retarded in realizing their full potential, and to freely and efficiently engage in activities that burden the retarded in what is essentially an incidental manner. The State may not rely on a classification whose relationship to an asserted goal is so attenuated as to render the distinction arbitrary and irrational. See, [e.g., U.S. Dept. of Agriculture v. Moreno (p. 648 above)]. Furthermore, some objectives—such as "a [bare] desire to harm politically unpopular group," [ibid]—are not legitimate state [interests].

IV.   [The] constitutional issue is clearly posed. The City does not require a special use permit in an R–3 zone for apartment houses, multiple dwellings, boarding and lodging houses, fraternity or sorority houses, dormitories, apartment hotels, hospitals, sanitariums, nursing homes for convalescents or the aged (other than for the insane or feeble-minded or alcoholics or drug addicts), private clubs or fraternal orders, and other specified uses. It does, however, insist on a special permit for [the group home here] and it does so [because] it would be a facility for the mentally retarded. May the city require the permit for this facility when other care and multiple dwelling facilities are freely permitted? [In] our view the record does not reveal any rational basis for believing that [the] home would pose any special threat to the city's legitimate [interests].

The District Court found that the City Council's insistence on the permit rested on several factors. First, the Council was concerned with the negative attitude of the majority of property owners located within 200 feet of [the group home], as well as with the fears of elderly residents of the neighborhood. But mere negative attitudes, or fear, unsubstantiated by factors which are properly cognizable in a zoning proceeding, are not permissible bases for treating a home for the mentally retarded differently from apartment houses, multiple dwellings, and the [like]. Second, the Council [was] concerned that the facility was across the street from a junior high school, and feared that the students might harass the occupants of [the] home. But the school itself is attended by about 30 mentally retarded students, and denying a permit based on such vague, undifferentiated fears is again permitting some portion of the community to validate what would otherwise be an equal protection violation. The other objection to the home's location was that it was located on "a five hundred year flood plain." This concern with the possibility of a flood, however, can hardly be based on a distinction between [the] home and, for example, nursing homes, homes for convalescents or the aged, or sanitariums or hospitals, any of which could be located on [the] site without obtaining a special use permit. The same may be said of another concern of the Council—doubts about the legal responsibility for actions which the mentally retarded might take. If there is no concern about legal responsibility with respect to other uses that would be permitted in the area, such as boarding and fraternity houses, it is difficult to believe that the groups of mildly or moderately mentally retarded individuals who would live at [the home] would present any different or special hazard. Fourth, the Council was concerned with the size of the home and the number of people that would occupy it. [But] there would be no restrictions on the number of people who could occupy this home as a boarding house, nursing home, family dwelling, fraternity house, or dormitory. [At] least this record does not clarify [how] the characteristics of the intended occupants of [the] home rationally justify denying to those occupants what would be permitted to groups occupying the same site for different purposes. [The] short of it is that requiring the permit in this case appears to us to rest on an irrational prejudice against the mentally retarded.

[It is so ordered.]

Justice STEVENS, with whom The CHIEF JUSTICE [BURGER] joins, concurring.

The Court of Appeals disposed of this case as if a critical question to be decided were which of three clearly defined standards of equal protection review should be applied to a legislative classification discriminating against the mentally retarded. [But] our cases reflect a continuum of judgmental responses to differing classifications which have been explained in opinions by terms ranging from "strict scrutiny" at one extreme to "rational basis" at the other. I have never been persuaded that these so called "standards" adequately explain the decisional process. Cases involving classifications based on alienage, illegal residency, illegitimacy, gender, age, or—as in this case—mental retardation, do not fit well into sharply defined classifications. [I] have always asked myself whether I could find a "rational basis" for the classification at issue. The term "rational," of course, includes a requirement that an impartial lawmaker could logically believe that the classification would serve a legitimate public purpose that transcends the harm to the members of the disadvantaged class. Thus, the word "rational"—for me at least—includes elements of legitimacy and neutrality that must always characterize the performance of the sovereign's duty to govern impartially. The rational basis test, properly understood, adequately explains why a law that deprives a person of the right to vote because his skin has a different pigmentation than that of other voters violates [equal protection]. [We] do not need to apply a special standard, or to apply "strict scrutiny," or even "heightened scrutiny," to decide such cases. In every equal protection case, we have to ask certain basic questions. What class is harmed by the legislation, and has it been subjected to a "tradition of disfavor" by our laws? What is the public purpose that is being served by the law? What is the characteristic of the disadvantaged class that justifies the disparate treatment? In most cases the answer to these questions will tell us whether the statute has a "rational basis." The answers will result in the virtually automatic invalidation of racial classifications and in the validation of most economic classifications, but they will provide differing results in cases involving classifications based on alienage, gender, or illegitimacy. But that is not because we apply an "intermediate standard of review" in these cases; rather it is because the characteristics of these groups are sometimes relevant and sometimes irrelevant to a valid public purpose, or, more specifically, to the purpose that the challenged laws purportedly intended to serve. Every law that places the mentally retarded in a special class is not presumptively irrational. The differences between mentally retarded persons and those with greater mental capacity are obviously relevant to certain legislative decisions. [Even so,] the Court of Appeals correctly observed [that] the mentally retarded "have been subjected to a history of unfair and often grotesque mistreatment." [The record] convinces me that this permit was required because of the irrational fears of neighboring property owners, rather than for the protection of the mentally retarded persons who would reside in respondent's home.

Justice MARSHALL, with whom Justice BRENNAN and Justice BLACKMUN join, concurring in the judgment in part and dissenting in part.

[The] Court holds the ordinance invalid on rational basis grounds and disclaims that anything special, in the form of heightened scrutiny, is taking place. Yet Cleburne's ordinance surely would be valid under the traditional rational basis test applicable to economic and commercial regulation. In my view, it is important to articulate, as the Court does not, the facts and principles that justify subjecting this zoning ordinance to the searching review—the heightened scrutiny—that actually leads to its [invalidation].

I.   At the outset, [some] curious and paradoxical aspects of the Court's opinion must be noted. [The] Court's heightened scrutiny discussion is [puzzling] given that Cleburne's ordinance is invalidated only after being subjected to precisely the sort of probing inquiry associated with heightened scrutiny. [The] rational basis test invoked today is most assuredly not the rational basis test of [Lee Optical]. [The] Court, for example, concludes that legitimate concerns for fire hazards or the serenity of the neighborhood do not justify singling out respondents to bear the burdens of these concerns, for analogous permitted uses appear to pose similar threats. Yet under the traditional and most minimal version of the rational basis test, "reform may take one step at a time." [Lee Optical.] The "record" is said not to support the ordinance's classifications, but under the traditional standard we do not sift through the record to determine whether policy decisions are squarely supported by a firm factual foundation. Finally, the Court further finds it "difficult to believe" that the retarded present different or special hazards than other groups. In normal circumstances, the burden is not on the legislature to convince the Court that the lines it has drawn are [sensible]. The refusal to acknowledge that something more than minimum rationality review is at work here is, in my view, unfortunate in at least two respects. The suggestion that the traditional rational basis test allows this sort of searching inquiry creates precedent for this Court and lower courts to subject economic and commercial classifications to similar and searching "ordinary" rational basis review—a small and regrettable step back toward the days of [Lochner]. Moreover, by failing to articulate the factors that justify today's "second order" rational basis review, the Court provides no principled foundation for determining when more searching inquiry is to be invoked. [Candor] requires me to acknowledge the particular factors that justify invalidating Cleburne's zoning ordinance under the careful scrutiny it today receives.

II. I have long believed the level of scrutiny employed in an equal protection case should vary with "the constitutional and societal importance of the interest adversely affected and the recognized invidiousness of the basis upon which the particular classification is drawn." [Rodriguez (1973); Marshall, J., dissenting; p. 842 below]. When a zoning ordinance works to exclude the retarded from all residential districts in a community, these two considerations require that the ordinance be convincingly justified as substantially furthering legitimate and important purposes. First, the interest [in] establishing group homes is substantial. [Second,] the mentally retarded have been subject to a "lengthy and tragic history" of segregation and discrimination that can only be called grotesque. [In] light of the importance of the interest at stake and the history of discrimination the retarded have suffered, [equal protection] requires us to do more than review the distinctions drawn by Cleburne's zoning ordinance as if they appeared in a taxing statute or in economic or commercial legislation. The searching scrutiny I would give to restrictions on the ability of the retarded to establish community group homes leads me to conclude that Cleburne's vague generalizations for classifying the "feeble minded" with drug addicts, alcoholics, and the insane, and excluding them where the elderly, the ill, the boarder, and the transient are allowed, are not substantial or important enough to overcome the suspicion that the ordinance rests on impermissible assumptions or outmoded and perhaps invidious [stereotypes].

III. [The] Court downplays the lengthy "history of purposeful unequal treatment" of the retarded by pointing to recent legislative action that is said to "beli[e] a continuing antipathy or prejudice." Building on this point, the Court similarly concludes that the retarded are not "politically powerless" and deserve no greater judicial protection than "any minority" that wins some political battles and loses others. [Once] society begins to recognize certain practices as discriminatory, [the] Court would refrain from approaching such practices with the added skepticism of heightened scrutiny. [But] history makes clear that constitutional principles of equality, like [those] of liberty, property, and due process, evolve over [time]. It is natural that evolving standards of equality come to be embodied in legislation. When that occurs, courts should look to the fact of such change as a source of guidance on evolving principles of [equality]. Moreover, even when judicial action *has* catalyzed legislative change, that change certainly does not eviscerate the underlying constitutional principle. The Court, for example, has never suggested that race-based classifications became any less suspect once extensive legislation had been enacted on the subject. For the retarded, just as for Negroes and women, much has changed in recent years, but much remains the same; outdated statutes are still on the books, and irrational fears or ignorance [continue] to stymie recognition of the dignity and individuality of retarded people. Heightened judicial scrutiny of action appearing to impose unnecessary barriers to the retarded is required in light of increasing recognition that such barriers are inconsistent with evolving principles of [equality]. [The] Court's [claim] that the standard of review must be fixed with reference to the number of classifications to which a characteristic would validly be relevant [is] flawed. [Our] heightened-scrutiny precedents belie the claim that a characteristic must virtually always be irrelevant to warrant heightened scrutiny. [Heightened] but not strict scrutiny is considered appropriate in areas such as gender, illegitimacy, or alienage because the Court views the trait as relevant under some circumstances but not others. [Whenever] evolving principles of equality [require] that certain classifications be viewed as *potentially* discriminatory, and when history reveals systemic unequal treatment, more searching judicial inquiry than minimum rationality becomes [relevant].

IV. In light of the scrutiny that should be applied here, Cleburne's ordinance sweeps too broadly to dispel the suspicion that it rests on a bare desire to treat the retarded as outsiders, pariahs who do not belong in the community. The Court, while disclaiming that special scrutiny is necessary or warranted, reaches the same [conclusion].

Age classifications. Recall the criteria suggested above for according heightened scrutiny to certain classifications.[1] An attempt to establish heightened scrutiny for age classifications failed in MASSACHUSETTS BD. OF RETIREMENT v. MURGIA, 427 U.S. 307 (1976). As noted at p. 649 above, the majority's per curiam opinion applied rationality standards in sustaining a mandatory retirement law for uniformed state police officers. Before applying its deferential criteria, the majority rejected a suspect classification claim: "[The] class of uniformed State Police Officers over 50 [does not] constitute a suspect class for purposes of equal protection analysis. [While] the treatment of the aged in this Nation has not been wholly free of discrimination, such persons, unlike, say, those who have been discriminated against on the basis of race or national origin, have not experienced a 'history of purposeful unequal treatment' or been subjected to unique disabilities on the basis of stereotyped characteristics not truly indicative of their abilities. The class subject to the compulsory retirement feature of the Massachusetts statute consists of uniformed state police officers over the age of 50. It cannot be said to discriminate only against the elderly. Rather, it draws the line at a certain age in middle life. But even old age does not define a 'discrete and insular' group in need of 'extraordinary protection from the majoritarian political process.' Instead, it marks a stage that each of us will reach if we live out our normal span." Justice

---

1. Note also the suggestion in Ely, Democracy and Distrust (1980), that "the doctrine of suspect classifications is a roundabout way of uncovering official attempts to inflict inequality for its own sake—to treat a group worse not in the service of some overriding social goal but largely for the sake of simply disadvantaging its members." Compare a footnote in Justice Marshall's dissent in Cleburne, above: "No single talisman can define those groups likely to be the target of [constitutionally offensive classifications]; experience, not abstract logic, must be the primary guide. The 'political powerlessness' of a group may be relevant, but that factor is neither necessary [e.g., gender] nor sufficient [e.g., minors]. Similarly, immutability [may be] relevant, but many immutable characteristics [e.g., height or blindness], are valid bases [for] classifications under a variety of circumstances."

MARSHALL's dissent, noted in part earlier, observed: "[The] Court is quite right in suggesting that distinctions exist between the elderly and traditional suspect classes such as Negroes, and between the elderly and 'quasi-suspect' classes such as women or illegitimates. [E.g.,] the elderly are not isolated in society, and discrimination against them is not pervasive but is centered primarily in employment. [But the] elderly are undoubtedly discriminated against, and when legislation denies them an important benefit—employment— I conclude that to sustain the legislation [here, the State] must show a reasonably substantial interest and a scheme reasonably closely tailored to achieving that interest."

Poverty and wealth classifications. Dicta by the Warren Court suggested that de jure wealth classifications should trigger strict scrutiny and that even de facto wealth classifications—governmental action that has a differential impact dependent upon economic condition—might have that consequence (even though commentators were skeptical that the Court was in fact prepared to apply such an approach across the board). Burger Court developments made clear that the mere presence of wealth classifications or the mere existence of a disadvantageous impact on the poor does not suffice to evoke heightened review. The Burger Court's attitude is best reflected in Rodriguez (1973; p. 842 below). The most generous Warren Court dicta came in two cases. In Harper v. Virginia Bd. of Elections (1966; p. 858 below), Justice Douglas's majority opinion striking down Virginia's $1.50 poll tax as a precondition for voting stated: "Lines drawn on the basis of wealth or property, like those of race, are traditionally disfavored." Three years later, in McDonald (1969; p. 642 above), Chief Justice Warren stated that "a careful examination on our part is especially warranted where lines are drawn on the basis of wealth or race, two factors which independently render a classification highly suspect and thereby demand a more exacting judicial scrutiny." Yet Harper was a case which also involved the fundamental interest in the franchise. And McDonald in fact applied deferential review.[1] The suspectness of wealth classifications, then, was not clearly established by the Warren Court, though there were many who hoped or feared that it was.

For an examination of the difficulties in considering de facto wealth classifications as suspect, see the comments in Michelman, "Foreword: On Protecting the Poor Through the Fourteenth Amendment," 83 Harv.L.Rev. 7 (1969).[2] He stated that considering wealth a suspect classification is "endemically troublesome as a matter of principle" and added: "The trouble is that, unlike a de facto racial classification which usually must seek its justifications in purposes completely distinct from its race-related impacts, a de facto pecuniary classification typically carries a highly persuasive justification inseparable from the very effect which excites antipathy—i.e., the hard choices it forces

---

1. For a rare pre-Warren Court statement akin to Harper and MacDonald, see Justice Jackson's concurrence in Edwards v. California (1941; p. 336 above), invalidating the California anti-Okie law barring the bringing of nonresident indigents into the state. He remarked that "mere property status, without more," cannot be used to limit the rights of citizens, adding: " 'Indigence' in itself [is] a neutral fact—constitutionally an irrelevance, like race, creed, or color."

2. For elaboration of Michelman's "minimum protection" approach, see the ad-

ditional note on his analysis at p. 911 below, in that part of sec. 4 further examining the arguments for finding a strict scrutiny-triggering interest in "necessities." See also Winter, "Poverty, Economic Equality, and the Equal Protection Clause," 1972 Sup.Ct.Rev. 41; cf. Clune, "The Supreme Court's Treatment of [Wealth Discriminations]," 1975 Sup.Ct.Rev. 289, and Bork, "The Impossibility of Finding Welfare Rights in the Constitution," 1979 Wash.U.L.Q 695.

upon the financially straitened. For the typical form assumed by such a classification is simply the charging of a price, reasonably approximating cost, for some good or service which the complaining person may freely choose to purchase or not to purchase. A de facto pecuniary classification, that is, is usually nothing more or less than the making of a market (e.g., in trial transcripts) or the failure to relieve someone of the vicissitudes of market pricing (e.g., for appellate legal services). [See, e.g., the Griffin and Douglas cases in sec. 4 below, dealing with access to courts as a "fundamental interest."] But the risk of exposure to markets and their 'decisions' is not normally deemed objectionable, to say the least, in our society. Not only do we not inveigh generally against unequal distribution of income or full-cost pricing for most goods. We usually regard it as both the fairest and most efficient arrangement to require each consumer to pay the full market price of what he consumes. [Exceptions], of course, exist. The point is precisely that such 'commodities' as a vote, an effective defense to criminal prosecution, perhaps education, conceivably some others, *are* exceptional, and that the exceptions depend on the special qualities of the excepted commodities. It is uninformative at best, and very likely misleading as well, to defend such exceptional holdings through formulas of disparagement [—invidious or suspect classification; lines drawn on the basis of wealth; discrimination against the indigent—] which apply nonselectively to the pricing practice and refer not at all to any exceptional attributes in the excepted commodities."

That wealth classifications alone (even arguably de jure ones) would not trigger strict scrutiny by the Burger Court first became clear in JAMES v. VALTIERRA, 402 U.S. 137 (1971). There, Justice BLACK's majority opinion rejected an equal protection challenge to a California constitutional requirement that "[n]o low rent housing project shall hereafter be developed [by] any state public body" without prior approval in a local referendum. The provision defined "low rent housing project" as any development "for persons of low income"—"persons or families who lack the amount of income which is necessary [to] enable them, without financial assistance, to live in decent, safe and sanitary dwellings, without overcrowding." He emphasized that the provision did not involve "distinctions based on race," and noted: "Provisions for referendums demonstrate devotion to democracy, not to bias, discrimination, or prejudice." He also rejected the contention that the provision "singled out" advocates of low-income housing by mandating a referendum while many other referenda only take place upon citizen initiative. He replied that "a law making procedure that 'disadvantages' a particular group does not always deny equal protection." The Court should not undertake analysis of a variety of governmental structures to determine which "is likely to 'disadvantage' any of the diverse and shifting groups that make up the American people." Moreover, low-income housing advocates were not in fact singled out: mandatory referenda were required in a variety of areas—e.g., the issuance of long-term local bonds. Justice MARSHALL's dissent, joined by Justices Brennan and Blackmun, insisted that the provision "on its face constitutes invidious discrimination": it was "an explicit classification on the basis of poverty—a suspect classification which demands exacting judicial scrutiny." The majority, he objected, had treated the provision "as if it contained a totally benign, technical economic classification." He insisted that "singling out the poor to bear a burden not placed on any other class of citizens tramples the values the 14th Amendment was designed to protect."[3]

---

3. Note that in Rodriguez (1973; p. 842 below), Justice Powell's majority opinion and Justice Marshall's dissent agreed that wealth was *not* as suspect a classification as race,

4.   SEXUAL ORIENTATION

Romer v. Evans

___ U.S. ___, 116 S.Ct. 1620, 134 L.Ed.2d 855 (1996).

Justice KENNEDY delivered the opinion of the Court.

One century ago, the first Justice Harlan admonished this Court that the Constitution "neither knows nor tolerates classes among citizens." Plessy v. Ferguson (dissenting opinion). Unheeded then, those words now are understood to state a commitment to the law's neutrality where the rights of persons are at stake. The Equal Protection Clause enforces this principle and today requires us to hold invalid a provision of Colorado's Constitution.

I.   [An] amendment to the [Colorado Constitution] adopted in a 1992 statewide referendum [as] "Amendment 2" [stemmed] in large part from ordinances that had been passed in various Colorado municipalities, bann[ing] discrimination in many transactions and activities, including housing, employment, education, public accommodations, and health and welfare services. What gave rise to the statewide controversy was the protection the ordinances afforded to persons discriminated against by reason of their sexual orientation. [Amendment 2], in explicit terms, does more than repeal or rescind these provisions. It prohibits all legislative, executive or judicial action at any level of state or local government designed to protect the named class, a class we shall refer to as homosexual persons or gays and lesbians. The amendment reads: "No Protected Status Based on Homosexual, Lesbian, or Bisexual Orientation. Neither the State of Colorado, through any of its branches or departments, nor any of its agencies, political subdivisions, municipalities or school districts, shall enact, adopt or enforce any statute, regulation, ordinance or policy whereby homosexual, lesbian or bisexual orientation, conduct, practices or relationships shall constitute or otherwise be the basis of or entitle any person or class of persons to have or claim any minority status, quota preferences, protected status or claim of discrimination. This Section of the Constitution shall be in all respects self-executing." [The] State Supreme Court held that Amendment 2 was subject to strict scrutiny [under equal protection] because it infringed the fundamental right of gays and lesbians to participate in the political process. [E.g., Hunter v. Erickson [1969; p. 890 below]; Washington v. School District No. 1 [1982; p. 890 below]]. On remand, the State advanced various arguments in an effort to show that Amendment 2 was narrowly tailored to serve compelling interests, but the trial court found none sufficient. It enjoined enforcement of Amendment 2, and the Supreme Court of Colorado [affirmed]. We granted certiorari and now affirm, [but] on a rationale different from that adopted by the State Supreme Court.

II.   The State's principal argument in defense of Amendment 2 is that it puts gays and lesbians in the same position as all other persons. So, the State says, the measure does no more than deny homosexuals special rights. This reading of the amendment's language is implausible. We rely not upon our own interpretation of the amendment but upon the authoritative construction of Colorado's Supreme Court: ["The] immediate objective of Amendment 2 is, at a minimum, to repeal existing statutes, regulations, ordinances, and policies of

and that in Harris v. McRae, one of the abortion funding cases (1980; p. 551 above), the majority stated that "this Court has held repeatedly that poverty, standing alone, is not a suspect classification." See also Jefferson v. Hackney (1972; p. 754 below).

state and local entities that barred discrimination based on sexual orientation; and various provisions prohibiting discrimination based on sexual orientation at state colleges. The 'ultimate effect' of Amendment 2 is to prohibit any governmental entity from adopting similar, or more protective statutes, regulations, ordinances, or policies in the future unless the state constitution is first amended to permit such measures." Sweeping and comprehensive is the change in legal status effected by this law. So much is evident from the ordinances that the Colorado Supreme Court declared would be void by operation of Amendment 2. Homosexuals, by state decree, are put in a solitary class with respect to transactions and relations in both the private and governmental spheres. The amendment withdraws from homosexuals, but no others, specific legal protection from the injuries caused by discrimination, and it forbids reinstatement of these laws and policies.

The change that Amendment 2 works in the legal status of gays and lesbians in the private sphere is far-reaching, both on its own terms and when considered in light of the structure and operation of modern anti-discrimination laws. [Most] States have chosen to counter discrimination by enacting detailed statutory schemes. Colorado's state and municipal laws typify this emerging tradition of statutory protection and follow a consistent pattern. The laws first enumerate the persons or entities subject to a duty not to discriminate. The list goes well beyond the entities covered by the common law. The Boulder ordinance, for example, has a comprehensive definition of entities deemed places of "public accommodation." They include "any place of business engaged in any sales to the general public and any place that offers services, facilities, privileges, or advantages to the general public or that receives financial support through solicitation of the general public or through governmental subsidy of any kind." [These] statutes and ordinances also depart from the common law by enumerating the groups or persons within their ambit of protection. Enumeration is the essential device used to make the duty not to discriminate concrete and to provide guidance for those who must comply. In following this approach, Colorado's state and local governments have not limited anti-discrimination laws to groups that have so far been given the protection of heightened equal protection scrutiny under our cases. Rather, they set forth an extensive catalogue of traits which cannot be the basis for discrimination, including age, military status, marital status, pregnancy, parenthood, custody of a minor child, political affiliation, physical or mental disability of an individual or of his or her associates—and, in recent times, sexual orientation. Amendment 2 bars homosexuals from securing protection against the injuries that these public-accommodations laws address. That in itself is a severe consequence, but there is more. Amendment 2 [nullifies] specific legal protections for this targeted class in all transactions in housing, sale of real estate, insurance, health and welfare services, private education, and employment.

Not confined to the private sphere, Amendment 2 also operates to repeal and forbid all laws or policies providing specific protection for gays or lesbians from discrimination by every level of Colorado government. The State Supreme Court cited two examples of protections in the governmental sphere that are now rescinded and may not be reintroduced. The first is [the] Colorado Executive Order [which] forbids employment discrimination against " 'all state employees, classified and exempt' on the basis of sexual orientation." Also repealed, and now forbidden, are "various provisions prohibiting discrimination based on sexual orientation at state colleges." The repeal of these measures and the prohibition against their future reenactment demonstrates that Amendment 2 has the same force and effect in Colorado's governmental sector as it does elsewhere and that it applies to policies as well as ordinary legislation.

Amendment 2's reach may not be limited to specific laws passed for the benefit of gays and lesbians. It is a fair, if not necessary, inference from the broad language of the amendment that it deprives gays and lesbians even of the protection of general laws and policies that prohibit arbitrary discrimination in governmental and private settings. See, e.g., [the state law making] agency action subject to judicial review under arbitrary and capricious standard. At some point in the systematic administration of these laws, an official must determine whether homosexuality is an arbitrary and thus forbidden basis for decision. Yet a decision to that effect would itself amount to a policy prohibiting discrimination on the basis of homosexuality, and so would appear to be no more valid under Amendment 2 than the specific prohibitions against discrimination the state court held invalid. If this consequence follows from Amendment 2, as its broad language suggests, it would compound the constitutional difficulties the law creates. The state court did not decide whether the amendment has this effect, however, and neither need we. In the course of rejecting the argument that Amendment 2 is intended to conserve resources to fight discrimination against suspect classes, the Colorado Supreme Court made the limited observation that the amendment is not intended to affect many anti-discrimination laws protecting non-suspect classes. In our view that does not resolve the issue. In any event, even if, as we doubt, homosexuals could find some safe harbor in laws of general application, we cannot accept the view that Amendment 2's prohibition on specific legal protections does no more than deprive homosexuals of special rights. To the contrary, the amendment imposes a special disability upon those persons alone. Homosexuals are forbidden the safeguards that others enjoy or may seek without constraint. They can obtain specific protection against discrimination only by enlisting the citizenry of Colorado to amend the state constitution or perhaps, on the State's view, by trying to pass helpful laws of general applicability. This is so no matter how local or discrete the harm, no matter how public and widespread the injury. We find nothing special in the protections Amendment 2 withholds. These are protections taken for granted by most people either because they already have them or do not need them; these are protections against exclusion from an almost limitless number of transactions and endeavors that constitute ordinary civic life in a free society.

III. [The equal protection guarantee] must co-exist with the practical necessity that most legislation classifies for one purpose or another, with resulting disadvantage to various groups or persons. We have attempted to reconcile the principle with the reality by stating that, if a law neither burdens a fundamental right nor targets a suspect class, we will uphold the legislative classification so long as it bears a rational relation to some legitimate end. Amendment 2 fails, indeed defies, even this conventional inquiry. First, the amendment has the peculiar property of imposing a broad and undifferentiated disability on a single named group, an exceptional and, as we shall explain, invalid form of legislation. Second, its sheer breadth is so discontinuous with the reasons offered for it that the amendment seems inexplicable by anything but animus toward the class that it affects; it lacks a rational relationship to legitimate state interests.

Taking the first point, even in the ordinary equal protection case calling for the most deferential of standards, we insist on knowing the relation between the classification adopted and the object to be attained. The search for the link between classification and objective gives substance to the Equal Protection Clause; it provides guidance and discipline for the legislature, which is entitled to know what sorts of laws it can pass; and it marks the limits of our own authority. In the ordinary case, a law will be sustained if it can be said to advance a legitimate government interest, even if the law seems unwise or works to the disadvantage of a particular group, or if the rationale for it seems tenuous. See [New Orleans v. Dukes; Lee Optical; Railway Express v. New York; Kotch]. The laws challenged in the cases just cited were narrow enough in scope and grounded in a sufficient factual context for us to ascertain that there existed some relation between the classification and the purpose it served. By requiring that the classification bear a rational relationship to an independent and legitimate legislative end, we ensure that classifications are not drawn for the purpose of disadvantaging the group burdened by the law.

Amendment 2 confounds this normal process of judicial review. It is at once too narrow and too broad. It identifies persons by a single trait and then denies them protection across the board. The resulting disqualification of a class of persons from the right to seek specific protection from the law is unprecedented in our jurisprudence. It is not within our constitutional tradition to enact laws of this sort. [Central] both to the idea of the rule of law and to our own Constitution's guarantee of equal protection is the principle that government and each of its parts remain open on impartial terms to all who seek its assistance. [Respect] for this principle explains why laws singling out a certain class of citizens for disfavored legal status or general hardships are rare. A law declaring that in general it shall be more difficult for one group of citizens than for all others to seek aid from the government is itself a denial of equal protection of the laws in the most literal sense. Davis v. Beason, 133 U.S. 333 (1890), not cited by the parties but relied upon by the dissent, is not evidence that Amendment 2 is within our constitutional tradition, and any reliance upon it as authority for sustaining the amendment is misplaced. In Davis the Court approved an Idaho territorial statute denying Mormons, polygamists, and advocates of polygamy the right to vote and to hold office because, as the Court construed the statute, it "simply excludes from the privilege of voting, or of holding any office of honor, trust or profit, those who have been convicted of certain offences, and those who advocate a practical resistance to the laws of the Territory and justify and approve the commission of crimes forbidden by it." To the extent Davis held that persons advocating a certain practice may be denied the right to vote, it is no longer good law. To the extent it held that the groups designated in the statute may be deprived of the right to vote because of their status, its ruling could not stand without surviving strict scrutiny, a most doubtful outcome. To the extent [it] held that a convicted felon may be denied the right to vote, its holding is not implicated by our decision and is unexceptionable.

A second and related point is that laws of the kind now before us raise the inevitable inference that the disadvantage imposed is born of animosity toward the class of persons affected. "[I]f the constitutional conception of 'equal protection of the laws' means anything, it must at the very least mean that a [bare] desire to harm a politically unpopular group cannot constitute a legitimate governmental interest." Dept. of Agriculture v. Moreno [1973; p. 648 above]. Even laws enacted for broad and ambitious purposes often can be explained by reference to legitimate public policies which justify the incidental disadvantages they impose on certain persons. Amendment 2, however, in making a general announcement that gays and lesbians shall not have any particular protections from the law, inflicts on them immediate, continuing, and real injuries that outrun and belie any legitimate justifications that may be claimed for it. We conclude that, in addition to the far-reaching deficiencies of Amendment 2 that we have noted, the principles it offends, in another sense, are conventional and venerable; a law must bear a rational relationship to a legitimate governmental purpose and Amendment 2 does not.

The primary rationale the State offers for Amendment 2 is respect for other citizens' freedom of association, and in particular the liberties of land- lords or employers who have personal or religious objections to homosexuality. Colorado also cites its interest in conserving resources to fight discrimination against other groups. The breadth of the Amendment is so far removed from these particular justifications that we find it impossible to credit them. We cannot say that Amendment 2 is directed to any identifiable legitimate purpose or discrete objective. It is a status-based enactment divorced from any factual context from which we could discern a relationship to legitimate state interests; it is a classification of persons undertaken for its own sake, something [equal protection] does not permit. [We] must conclude that Amendment 2 classifies homosexuals not to further a proper legislative end but to make them unequal to everyone else. This Colorado cannot do. A State cannot so deem a class of persons a stranger to its laws. Amendment 2 violates [equal protection], and the judgment of the Supreme Court of Colorado is affirmed.

It is so ordered.

Justice SCALIA, with whom THE CHIEF JUSTICE [REHNQUIST] and Justice THOMAS join, dissenting.

The Court has mistaken a Kulturkampf for a fit of spite. The constitutional amendment before us here is not the manifestation of a "bare [desire] to harm" homosexuals, but is rather a modest attempt by seemingly tolerant Coloradans to preserve traditional sexual mores against the efforts of a politically powerful minority to revise those mores through use of the laws. That objective, and the means chosen to achieve it, are not only unimpeachable under any constitutional doctrine hitherto pronounced (hence the opinion's heavy reliance upon principles of righteousness rather than judicial holdings); they have been specifically approved by [Congress] and by this Court. In holding that homosexuality cannot be singled out for disfavorable treatment, the Court contradicts a decision, unchallenged here, pronounced only 10 years ago, see Bowers v. Hardwick [p. 593 above], and places the prestige of this institution behind the proposition that opposition to homosexuality is as reprehensible as racial or religious bias. Whether it is or not is *precisely* the cultural debate that gave rise to the Colorado constitutional amendment (and to the preferential laws against which the amendment was directed). Since the Constitution of the United States says nothing about this subject, it is left to be resolved by normal democratic means, including the democratic adoption of provisions in state constitutions. This Court has no business imposing upon all Americans the resolution favored by the elite class from which the Members of this institution are selected, pronouncing that "animosity" toward homosexuality is evil. I vigorously dissent.

I. [In] rejecting the State's arguments that Amendment 2 "puts gays and lesbians in the same position as all other persons," and "does no more than deny homosexuals special rights," the Court considers it unnecessary to decide the validity of the State's argument that Amendment 2 does not deprive homosexuals of the "protection [afforded by] general laws and policies that prohibit arbitrary discrimination in governmental and private settings." I agree that we need not resolve that dispute, because the Supreme Court of Colorado has resolved it for [us]: "[I]t is significant to note that Colorado law currently proscribes discrimination against persons who are not suspect classes, including discrimination based on age; marital or family status; veterans' status; and for any legal, off-duty conduct such as smoking tobacco. *Of course Amendment 2 is not intended to have any effect on this legislation, but seeks only to prevent the adoption of antidiscrimination laws intended to protect gays, lesbians, and bisexuals."* (Emphasis added.) The Court utterly fails to distinguish this portion of the Colorado court's opinion. [The] clear import of the Colorado court's conclusion that it is not affected is that "general laws and policies that prohibit arbitrary discrimination" would continue to prohibit discrimination on the basis of homosexual conduct as well. This analysis, which is fully in accord with (indeed, follows inescapably from) the text of the constitutional provision, lays to rest such [horribles] as the prospect that assaults upon homosexuals could not be prosecuted. The amendment prohibits special treatment of homosexuals, and nothing more. It would not affect, for example, a requirement of state law that pensions be paid to all retiring state employees with a certain length of service; homosexual employees, as well as others, would be entitled to that benefit. But it would prevent the State or any municipality from making death-benefit payments to the "life partner" of a homosexual when it does not make such payments to the long-time roommate of a nonhomosexual employee. [Despite] all of its hand-wringing about the potential effect of Amendment 2 on general antidiscrimination laws, the Court's opinion ultimately does not dispute all this, but assumes it to be true. The only denial of equal treatment it contends homosexuals have suffered is this: They may not obtain *preferential* treatment without amending the state constitution. That is to say, the principle underlying the Court's opinion is that one who is accorded equal treatment under the laws, but cannot as readily as others obtain *preferential* treatment under the laws, has been denied [equal protection]. If merely stating this alleged "equal protection" violation does not suffice to refute it, our constitutional jurisprudence has achieved terminal silliness.

The central thesis of the Court's reasoning is that any group is denied equal protection when, to obtain advantage (or, presumably, to avoid disadvantage), it must have recourse to a more general and hence more difficult level of political decisionmaking than others. The world has never heard of such a principle, which is why the Court's opinion is so long on emotive utterance and so short on relevant legal citation. And it seems to me most unlikely that any multilevel democracy can function under such a principle. For *whenever* a disadvantage is imposed, or conferral of a benefit is prohibited, at one of the higher levels of democratic decisionmaking (i.e., by the state legislature rather than local government, or by the people at large in the state constitution rather than the legislature), the affected group has (under this theory) been denied equal protection. To take the simplest of examples, consider a state law prohibiting the award of municipal contracts to relatives of mayors or city councilmen. Once such a law is passed, the group composed of such relatives must, in order to get the benefit of city contracts, persuade the state legislature—unlike all other citizens, who need only persuade the municipality. It is ridiculous to consider this a denial of equal protection, which is why the Court's theory is unheard-of. The Court might reply that the example I have given is not a denial of equal protection only because the same "rational basis" (avoidance of corruption) which renders constitutional the substantive discrimination against relatives (i.e., the fact that they alone cannot obtain city contracts) also automatically suffices to sustain what might be called the electoral-procedural discrimination against them (i.e., the fact that they must go to the state level to get this changed). This is of course a perfectly reasonable response, and would explain why "electoral-procedural discrimination" has not hitherto been heard of: a law that is valid in its substance is automatically valid in its level of enactment. But the Court cannot afford to make this argument, for as I shall discuss next, there is no doubt of a rational basis for the substance of the prohibition at issue here. The Court's entire novel theory rests upon the proposition that there is something special—something that cannot be justified by normal "rational basis" analysis—in making a disadvantaged group (or a nonpreferred group) resort to a higher decisionmaking level. That proposition finds no support in law or logic.

II. I turn next to whether there was a legitimate rational basis for the substance of the constitutional amendment—for the prohibition of special protection for homosexuals. It is unsurprising that the Court avoids discussion of this question, since the answer is so obviously yes. The case most relevant to the issue before us today is not even mentioned in the Court's opinion: In Bowers v. Hardwick, we held that the Constitution does not prohibit what virtually all States had done from the founding of the Republic until very recent years—making homosexual conduct a crime. That holding is unassailable, except by those who think that the Constitution changes to suit current fashions. But in any event it is a given in the present case: Respondents [did] not urge overruling Bowers. [If] it is constitutionally permissible for a State to make homosexual conduct criminal, surely it is constitutionally permissible for a State to enact other laws merely disfavoring homosexual conduct. [And] a fortiori it is constitutionally permissible for a State to adopt a provision not even disfavoring homosexual conduct, but merely prohibiting all levels of state government from bestowing special protections upon homosexual conduct. Respondents (who, unlike the Court, cannot afford the luxury of ignoring inconvenient precedent) counter Bowers with the argument that a greater-includes-the-lesser rationale cannot justify Amendment 2's application to individuals who do not engage in homosexual acts, but are merely of homosexual "orientation."

[But] assuming that, in Amendment 2, a person of homosexual "orientation" is someone who does not engage in homosexual conduct but merely has a tendency or desire to do so, Bowers still suffices to establish a rational basis for the provision. If it is rational to criminalize the conduct, surely it is rational to deny special favor and protection to those with a self-avowed tendency or desire to engage in the conduct. Indeed, where criminal sanctions are not involved, homosexual "orientation" is an acceptable stand-in for homosexual conduct. A State "does not violate the Equal Protection Clause merely because the classifications made by its laws are imperfect." Just as a policy barring the hiring of methadone users as transit employees does not violate equal protection simply because some methadone users pose no threat to passenger safety, see [Beazer (p. 651 above)], and just as a mandatory retirement age of 50 for police officers does not violate equal protection even though it prematurely ends the careers of many policemen over 50 who still have the capacity to do the job, see [Murgia (p. 649 above)], Amendment 2 is not constitutionally invalid simply because it could have been drawn more precisely so as to withdraw special antidiscrimination protections only from those of homosexual "orientation" who actually engage in homosexual conduct. Moreover, even if the provision regarding homosexual "orientation" were invalid, respondents' challenge to Amendment 2—which is a facial challenge—must fail. It would not be enough for respondents to establish (if they could) that Amendment 2 is unconstitutional as applied to those of homosexual "orientation"; since, under Bowers, Amendment 2 is unquestionably constitutional as applied to those who engage in homosexual conduct, the facial challenge cannot [succeed].

III. [What Colorado] has done is not only unprohibited, but eminently reasonable, with close, congressionally approved precedent in earlier constitutional practice. First, as to its eminent reasonableness. The Court's opinion contains grim, disapproving hints that Coloradans have been guilty of "animus" or "animosity" toward homosexuality, as though that has been established as Unamerican. Of course it is our moral heritage that one should not hate any human being or class of human beings. But I had thought that one could consider certain conduct reprehensible—murder, for example, or polygamy, or cruelty to animals—and could exhibit even "animus" toward such conduct. Surely that is the only sort of "animus" at issue here: moral disapproval of homosexual conduct, the same sort of moral disapproval that produced the centuries-old criminal laws that we held constitutional in Bowers. [But] though Coloradans are, as I say, entitled to be hostile toward homosexual conduct, the fact is that the degree of hostility reflected by Amendment 2 is the smallest conceivable. The Court's portrayal of Coloradans as a society fallen victim to pointless, hate-filled "gay-bashing" is so false as to be comical. Colorado not only is one of the 25 States that have repealed their anti-sodomy laws, but was among the first to do so. But the society that eliminates criminal punishment for homosexual acts does not necessarily abandon the view that homosexuality is morally wrong and socially harmful; often, abolition simply reflects the view that enforcement of such criminal laws involves unseemly intrusion into the intimate lives of citizens.

There is a problem, however, which arises when criminal sanction of homosexuality is eliminated but moral and social disapprobation of homosexuality is meant to be retained. The Court cannot be unaware of that problem; it is evident in many cities of the country, and occasionally bubbles to the surface of the news, in heated political disputes over such matters as the introduction into local schools of books teaching that homosexuality is an optional and fully acceptable "alternate life style." The problem (a problem, that is, for those who wish to retain social disapprobation of homosexuality) is that, because those who engage in homosexual conduct tend to reside in disproportionate numbers in certain communities, have high disposable income, and of course care about homosexual-rights issues much more ardently than the public at large, they possess political power much greater than their numbers, both locally and statewide. Quite understandably, they devote this political power to achieving not merely a grudging social toleration, but full social acceptance, of homosexuality. By the time Coloradans were asked to vote on Amendment 2, their exposure to homosexuals' quest for social endorsement was not limited to newspaper accounts of happenings in places such as New York, Los Angeles, San Francisco, and Key West. Three Colorado cities—Aspen, Boulder, and Denver—had enacted ordinances that listed "sexual orientation" as an impermissible ground for discrimination, equating the moral disapproval of homosexual conduct with racial and religious bigotry. The phenomenon had even appeared statewide: the [Governor] had signed an executive order pronouncing that "in the State of Colorado we recognize the diversity in our pluralistic society and strive to bring an end to discrimination in any form," and directing state agency-heads to "ensure non-discrimination" in hiring and promotion based on, among other things, "sexual orientation." I do not mean to be critical of these legislative successes; homosexuals are as entitled to use the legal system for reinforcement of their moral sentiments as are the rest of society. But they are subject to being countered by lawful, democratic countermeasures as well.

That is where Amendment 2 came in. It sought to counter both the geographic concentration and the disproportionate political power of homosexuals by (1) resolving the controversy at the statewide level, and (2) making the election a single-issue contest for both sides. It put directly, to all the citizens of the State, the question: Should homosexuality be given special protection? They answered no. The Court today asserts that this most democratic of procedures is unconstitutional. Lacking any cases to establish that facially absurd proposition, it simply asserts that it must be unconstitutional, because it has never happened before. [What] the Court says is even demonstrably false at the constitutional level. The Eighteenth Amendment to the Federal Constitution, for example, deprived those who drank alcohol not only of the power to alter the policy of prohibition locally or through state legislation, but even of the power to alter it through state constitutional amendment or federal legislation. The Establishment Clause of the First Amendment prevents theocrats from having their way by converting their fellow citizens at the local, state, or federal statutory level; as does the Republican Form of Government Clause prevent monarchists. But there is a much closer analogy, one that involves precisely the effort by the majority of citizens to preserve its view of sexual morality statewide, against the efforts of a geographically concentrated and politically powerful minority to undermine it. The constitutions of the States of Arizona, Idaho, New Mexico, Oklahoma, and Utah to this day contain provisions stating that polygamy is "forever prohibited." [Polygamists,] and those who have a polygamous "orientation," have been "singled out" by these provisions for much more severe treatment than merely denial of favored status; and that treatment can only be changed by achieving amendment of the state constitutions. The Court's disposition today suggests that these provisions are unconstitutional, and that polygamy must be permitted in these States on a state-legislated, or perhaps even local-option, basis—unless, of course, polygamists for some reason have fewer constitutional rights than homosexuals. [Congress,] by the way, required the inclusion of these antipolygamy provisions in the constitutions of Arizona, New Mexico, Oklahoma, and Utah, as a condition of their admission to statehood. [Thus,] this "singling out" of the sexual practices of a single group for statewide, democratic vote—so utterly alien to our constitutional system, the Court would have us believe—has not only happened, but has received the explicit approval of [Congress]. I cannot say that this Court has explicitly approved any of these state constitutional provisions; but it has approved a territorial statutory provision that went even further, depriving polygamists of the ability even to achieve a constitutional amendment, by depriving them of the power to vote. [Davis v. Beason, 133 U.S. 333 (1890).] [T]he proposition that polygamy can be criminalized, and those engaging in that crime deprived of the vote, remains good law. Beason rejected the argument that "such discrimination is a denial of the equal protection of the laws." This Court cited Beason with approval as recently as 1993, in an opinion authored by the same Justice who writes for the Court today. [Church of Lukumi Babalu Aye (1993; p. 1472 below).] It remains to be explained how [the Idaho law] was not an "impermissible targeting" of polygamists, but (the much more mild) Amendment 2 is an "impermissible targeting" of homosexuals. Has the Court concluded that the perceived social harm of polygamy is a "legitimate concern of government," and the perceived social harm of homosexuality is not?

IV. I strongly suspect that the answer to the last question is yes, which leads me to the last point I wish to make: The Court today [employs] a constitutional theory heretofore unknown to frustrate Colorado's reasonable effort to preserve traditional American moral values. [To] suggest [that] this constitutional amendment springs from nothing more than "a [bare] desire to harm a politically unpopular group" [is] nothing short of insulting. (It is also nothing short of preposterous to call "politically unpopular" a group which enjoys enormous influence in American media and politics, and which, as the trial court here noted, though composing no more than 4% of the population had the support of 46% of the voters on Amendment 2.) When the Court takes sides in the culture wars, it tends to be with the knights rather than the villeins—and more specifically with the Templars, reflecting the views and values of the lawyer class from which the Court's Members are drawn. How that class feels about homosexuality will be evident to anyone who wishes to interview job applicants at virtually any of the Nation's law schools. The interviewer may refuse to offer a job because the applicant is a Republican; because he is an adulterer; because he went to the wrong prep school or belongs to the wrong country club; because he eats snails; because he is a womanizer; because she wears real-animal fur; or even because he hates the Chicago Cubs. But if the interviewer should wish not to be an associate or partner of an applicant because he disapproves of the applicant's homosexuality, *then* he will have violated the pledge which the Association of American Law Schools requires all its member-schools to exact from job interviewers: "assurance of the employer's willingness" to hire homosexuals. This law-school view of what "prejudices" must be stamped out may be contrasted with the more plebeian attitudes that apparently still prevail in [Congress], which has been unresponsive to repeated attempts to extend to homosexuals the protections of federal civil rights [laws]. [Today's] opinion has no foundation in American constitutional law, and barely pretends to. The people of Colorado have adopted an entirely reasonable provision which does not even disfavor homosexuals in any substantive sense, but merely denies them preferential treatment. Amendment 2 is designed to prevent piecemeal deterioration of the sexual morality favored by a majority of Coloradans, and is not only an appropriate means to that legitimate end, but a means that Americans have employed before. Striking it down is an act, not of judicial judgment, but of political will. I dissent.

SOME NOTES AND COMMENTS ON ROMER V. EVANS

1. *The Romer opinions*. Justice Kennedy's majority opinion in Romer contained a number of surprising features. It purported to rely on usually deferential rationality review in striking down Amendment 2. It gave no hint of applying strict scrutiny or even intermediate scrutiny; nor did it explicitly undercut, overrule, or indeed even mention Bowers v. Hardwick. Moreover, the Court explicitly disavowed reliance on the rationale of the Colorado Supreme Court in striking down Amendment 2. (The state court had struck down Amendment 2 as invading the fundamental equal protection right to equal participation in the political process, developed in earlier cases invalidating race-conscious restructurings of the political process such as Hunter v. Erickson (1969; p. 890 below) and Washington v. Seattle School Dist. (1982; p. 890 below).) Can you think of any explanations for these features of the majority opinion? The Romer Court relied instead on an amalgam of alternative arguments. The first was advanced in an amicus brief by a group of law professors (Tribe, Ely, Gunther, Kurland, and Sullivan) claiming that the Colorado provision was a rare example of an on-the-face, literal violation of equal protection by declaring gay persons alone ineligible for protection from discrimination. The second argument was that Amendment 2 could not even survive minimum rationality scrutiny. The claim was that Colorado's justifications of protecting the associational freedom of landlords and employers and of conserving law enforcement resources could not support the over- and under-inclusive means invoked by Amendment 2 and thus revealed that Amendment 2 was solely based on animosity toward gay persons.

Justice Kennedy's opinion, in exercising rationality review, placed great emphasis on the illegitimacy of Colorado's end—essentially, to make homosexuals "unequal to everyone else," an objective he found impermissible because a state "cannot so deem a class of persons a stranger to its laws." In reaching that conclusion, he drew heavily on Moreno, p. 648 above, stating that a bare desire to harm a politically unpopular group "cannot constitute a legitimate governmental interest." Note also Cleburne, above: Cleburne's unusually careful exercise of rationality review ultimately produced the conclusion that the city's behavior rested simply on "an irrational prejudice against the mentally retarded." Consider the analysis of Romer in Sunstein, "Foreword: Leaving Things Undecided," 110 Harv.L.Rev. 4 (1996), putting Romer into the context of "the Moreno-Cleburne–Romer trilogy." He notes that none of these cases established a new "tier of scrutiny," and that all reflected "the possible use of rationality review as a kind of magical trump card, or perhaps joker, hidden in the pack and used on special occasions. In these cases, rationality review, traditionally little more than a rubber stamp, is used to invalidate badly motivated laws without refining a new kind of scrutiny." [Is Romer justifiable as an example of rationality scrutiny "with bite" (or, as some modern commentators would rephrase it, "with teeth")?]

Justice Scalia's dissent has been described as having "not merely a harsh quality but a high degree of sarcasm and contempt." Sunstein, above. Yet, if Justice Scalia's most acerbic passages are put aside, is there logical merit in his views? For example, does he rightly criticize the Court for not mentioning Bowers? Justice Scalia stated: "If it is rational to criminalize the conduct, surely it is rational to deny special favor and protection to those with a self-avowed tendency or desire to engage in the conduct. Indeed, where criminal sanctions are not involved, homosexual 'orientation' is an acceptable stand-in for homosexual conduct." Is that statement justifiable? Was Colorado's Amendment 2 vulnerable because it focused at least in part on status rather than conduct? (Compare Robinson v. California, 370 U.S. 660 (1962), holding that a state may not criminalize a status such as drug addiction.)

2. *Alternative justifications for Romer.* A number of commentators have suggested broader, overarching justifications for the Court's ruling. Sunstein, above, suggests that, despite defects in its technical analysis (e.g., "[p]erhaps the Court should have made clearer that a state may not defend discrimination solely by reference to a desire to discourage, to delegitimate, or not to legitimate homosexuality"), Romer's "inadequate treatment of the technical issue may actually be a virtue. An adequate treatment would have required the Court to write with a breadth and a depth that could not easily have commanded a majority opinion, and that may have foreclosed democratic debate about a series of issues currently engaging the nation and deserving, broadly speaking, a democratic rather than judicial solution." Farber & Sherry, "The Pariah Principle," 13 Constitutional Commentary 257 (1996), defend Romer against its critics by arguing that the ruling was justified because of the principle that "forbids the government from designating any societal group as untouchable, regardless of whether the group in question is generally entitled to some special degree of judicial protection, like blacks, or to no special protection, like left-handers (or, under current doctrine, homosexuals)." They insist that this pariah principle "is firmly rooted in existing constitutional law" and note: "This targeting of homosexuals for who they are [rather than for what they do] is one hallmark of pariah legislation." And Akhil Amar, "Attainder and Amendment 2: Romer's Rightness," 95 Mich.L.Rev. 203 (1996), argues that the text, history, and spirit of the Constitution's Art. I, § 10, Bill of Attainder Clause best justifies the majority ruling. (Farber & Sherry and Amar recognize that there is a close relationship between the pariah and the attainder principles.)

3. *The implications of Romer for other claims involving sexual orientation.* Romer was the first Court ruling protecting homosexuals (and bisexuals) under equal protection. The ruling came after several years of litigation regarding homosexuals' rights in a variety of contexts, and Romer thus raises the question of its significance and meaning in those varied contexts. Much of the litigation has involved the military, whose traditional policy of excluding gays and lesbians has been changed only slightly by recent modifications limiting the extent to which military officials may actively investigate the sexual orientation of members of the service. Many of the lawsuits sought to challenge the basic policy of deeming homosexuality incompatible with military service. An early case was Watkins v. United States Army, 847 F.2d 1329 (9th Cir.1988), vacated and aff'd on other grounds, 875 F.2d 699 (1989) (en banc). In Watkins, a Ninth Circuit panel, by a 2-1 vote, held the Army's barrier to Watkins's service and reenlistment to violate equal protection, stating that "homosexuals constitute [a] suspect class" triggering strict scrutiny. Judge Reinhardt, dissenting, concluded that, in light of Bowers v. Hardwick, the Court was "no longer free" to reach this equal protection conclusion. The full, en banc Ninth Circuit, however, vacated this ruling and decided for Watkins on narrower, estoppel grounds. There have been many more lawsuits since. Note, for example, Cammermeyer v. Aspin, 850 F.Supp. 910 (W.D.Wash.1994), in which the trial judge ordered the Army and the Washington National Guard to reinstate Colonel Margarethe Cammermeyer after having discharged her because she had admitted, in questioning related to a security clearance, that she was a lesbian. The trial judge distinguished conduct from orientation and emphasized that Col. Cammermeyer had done nothing but disclose her orientation, which was "not reliable evidence of her desire or propensity to engage in homosexual conduct." Accordingly, he found the government's policy did not satisfy rationality review. And in Meinhold v. U.S. Dept. of Defense, 34 F.3d 1469 (9th Cir.1994), the Ninth Circuit found that an inference of homosexual conduct could not be drawn in Keith Meinhold's particular case from his statements that he was gay; but the court refused a nationwide injunction because statements by other service members might show a "desire" to engage in prohibited conduct strong enough to support an inference of future homosexual conduct.

The new policy of the United States military, the "don't ask, don't tell" policy now codified in 10 U.S.C. § 654(b), was held unconstitutional under principles of equal protection and free speech in Able v. United States, 880 F.Supp. 968 (E.D.N.Y.1995), but that ruling was overturned in 1996 by the Second Circuit. Other military restrictions on homosexuality have also been sustained. Thus, in Steffan v. Perry, 41 F.3d 677 (D.C.Cir.1994), the majority in an en banc ruling by the Court of Appeals, relying on the rationality standard, upheld the forced resignation of a homosexual midshipman from the U.S. Naval Academy. See also Philips v. Perry, 883 F.Supp. 539 (W.D.Wash.1995), rejecting a free speech challenge to a military discharge. To what extent are future challenges akin to those in the lower federal courts likely to be affected by the decision in Romer v. Evans? Farber & Sherry, note 2 above, do not think that their "pariah principle" would bar current military policy regarding homosexuals. What about a right to same-sex marriage? State courts in Hawaii ruled, in 1993 and 1996 decisions, that the ban on same-sex marriages warranted strict scrutiny as sex discrimination and could not survive that scrutiny. In anticipation of such rulings, Congress enacted the Defense of Marriage Act in order to facilitate the states' denial of recognition of such marriages under the Full Faith and Credit Clause, Art. IV, § 2.

In addition to extensive litigation, there has been a steadily growing flow of literature on the problems raised by sexual orientation questions. For arguments that discrimination against homosexuals warrants heightened scrutiny, see Bernstein, "Power, Prejudice, and the Right to Speak: Litigating 'Outness' Under the Equal Protection Clause," 47 Stan.L.Rev. 269 (1995), Koppelman, "Why Discrimination Against Lesbians and Gay Men is Sex Discrimination," 69 NYU.L.Rev. 197 (1994), and Roberts, "Heightened Scrutiny Under the Equal Protection Clause: A Remedy to Discrimination Based on Sexual Orientation," 42 Drake L.Rev. 485 (1993). See also Epstein, "Caste and the Civil Rights Law: From Jim Crow to Same–Sex Marriages," 92 Mich.L.Rev. 2456 (1994). For an argument that sexual identity is not an immutable trait but is a characteristic created in part through social and political contexts, concluding that the political process cannot systematically silence those challenging heterosexual norms, see Halley, "The Politics of the Closet: Towards Equal Protection for Gay, Lesbian, and Bisexual Identity," 36 UCLA L.Rev. 915 (1989). See generally Sunstein, "Sexual Orientation and the Constitution: A Note on the Relationship Between Due Process and Equal Protection," 55 U.Chi.L.Rev. 1161 (1988), and Sunstein, "Homosexuality and the Constitution," 70 Ind.L.J. 1 (1994); cf. Bradley, "The Right Not to Endorse Gay Rights: A Reply to Sunstein," 70 Ind.L.J. 29 (1994).

D. THE "PURPOSEFUL DISCRIMINATION" REQUIREMENT AND THE "PURPOSE"–"IMPACT" DISTINCTION

---

1. TYPES OF DISCRIMINATION

Introduction. We now turn to the meaning of a principle repeatedly stated by the modern Court: "the invidious quality of a law claimed to be racially discriminatory must ultimately be traced to a racially discriminatory purpose"; governmental action is not unconstitutional "*solely* because it has a racially disproportionate impact." See Washington v. Davis (1976; p. 755 below). The materials in sec. 3D typically involve the racial discrimination context, but the principle has prompted controversy in other areas as well, as in cases claiming sex discrimination. E.g., Feeney (1979; p. 761 below). Sec. 3D1 surveys some of the *types* of unconstitutional purpose. For example, discriminatory purpose may be shown by data regarding the administration of a law, not merely by a disadvantaging racial classification apparent on the face of the law. Moreover, a law neutral in language and application may have been enacted with a purpose or motive to discriminate. All these instances can be viewed as "de jure" discrimination. Sec. 3D1 also begins the exploration of the constitutional validity of so-called "de facto" discrimination—governmental action that is racially neutral in its language, administration and purpose but which has a disadvantaging impact or effect. That exploration provides background for an increasingly central issue in modern discrimination cases, pursued in sec. 3D2: What are the relevant data, and what are the appropriate burdens of proof, in cases in which nonobvious purposeful discrimination is sought to be demonstrated? The "purpose"-"impact" distinction is the pervasive theme of sec. 3D2. Sec. 3D3, finally, deals with a specific area which sheds important light on the "purpose"-"impact" distinction—the problems encountered in the implementation of Brown, the school desegregation decision.

1. *Discrimination in the administration of law.* a. *Yick Wo.* Cases such as Strauder v. West Virginia, p. 663 above, involved explicit disadvantaging racial classifications on the face of the law. Yick Wo is the leading early case illustrating that a facially neutral law may impose purposeful discrimination because of the manner of its administration. A San Francisco ordinance prohibited operating a laundry (except in a brick or stone building) without the consent of the Board of Supervisors. The Board granted permits to operate laundries in wooden buildings to all but one of the non-Chinese applicants, but to none of about 200 Chinese applicants. A Chinese alien who had operated a laundry for many years was refused a permit and imprisoned for illegally operating his laundry. In YICK WO v. HOPKINS, 118 U.S. 356 (1886), the Court, in a habeas corpus proceeding, held the challenger's imprisonment unjustified. Justice MATTHEWS's opinion found discrimination in the *administration* of the law: "[T]he facts shown establish an administration directed so exclusively against a particular class of persons as [to] require the conclusion, that, whatever may have been the intent of the ordinances as adopted, they are applied by the public authorities charged with their administration [with] a mind so unequal and oppressive as to amount to a practical denial by the State of [equal protection]. Though the law itself be fair on its face and impartial in appearance, yet, if it is applied and administered by public authority with an evil eye and an unequal hand, so as practically to make unjust and illegal discriminations between persons in similar circumstances, [the] denial of equal justice is still within the prohibition of the Constitution. The present cases [are] within this class. [While the] consent of the supervisors is withheld from [petitioners] and from two hundred others who have also petitioned, all of whom happen to be Chinese subjects, eighty others, not Chinese subjects, are permitted to carry on the same business under similar conditions. The fact of this discrimination is admitted. No reason for it is shown, and the conclusion cannot be resisted, that no reason for it exists except hostility to the race and nationality to which the petitioners belong, and which in the eye of the law is not justified."

b. *Proof of purposeful discrimination.* Yick Wo illustrates a frequent phenomenon: purposeful, hostile discrimination is inferred from data regarding administration of a facially neutral law. Reliance on statistical data showing a discriminatory pattern of administration has become commonplace in modern cases. Discrimination in jury selection was the earliest area.[1] Soon, the practice

1. See, e.g., Castaneda v. Partida, 430 U.S. 482 (1977), Carter v. Jury Comm'n, 396 U.S. 320 (1970), Hernandez v. Texas, 347 U.S. 475 (1954), and Avery v. Georgia, 345 U.S. 559 (1953). Contrast with these jury cases the divided holding in Swain v. Alabama, 380 U.S. 202 (1965), holding that, without violating equal protection, a prosecutor may use peremptory challenges to strike all blacks from the jury pool in a particular case: "[To] subject the prosecutor's challenge in any particular case to the demands [of equal protection] would entail a radical change in the nature and operation of the challenge," since the "essential nature of the peremptory challenge is that it [is] exercised without a reason stated, without inquiry and without being subject to the court's control." Twenty-one years later, however, this virtual immunization of peremptory challenges from constitutional attack was overruled in BATSON v. KENTUCKY, 476 U.S. 79 (1986), holding that equal protection "forbids the prosecutor to challenge potential jurors solely on account of their race or on the assumption that black jurors as a group will be unable impartially to consider the State's case against a black defendant." Justice POWELL's majority opinion found that "a defendant may make a prima facie showing of purposeful racial discrimination [by] relying solely on the facts concerning [jury] selection *in his case.* [A] consistent pattern of official racial discrimination is not 'a necessary predicate to a violation of [equal protection].' " Justices WHITE, MARSHALL, STEVENS and O'CONNOR submitted concurring opinions. Chief Justice BURGER, joined by Jus-

spread to other fields as well, such as discrimination in voting and employment.[2] The use of statistical and other empirical data allegedly showing purposeful discrimination has become not only an increasingly frequent practice but also an ever more controversial one. The Court's position on what data are relevant (and how much must be shown to prove purposeful discrimination) is a critical issue in equal protection litigation, particularly in view of the modern Court's insistence that mere discriminatory effect does not suffice to show a constitutional violation, but that impact may provide probative data regarding the requisite discriminatory purpose. The cases that follow this group of introductory notes focus on that controversial issue of proof of purposeful discrimination.

2. *Discriminatory motivation.* In a number of modern cases, the Court has spoken at length about the relevance of proof of improper "motive" rather than "purpose." Often, the terms are used interchangeably. Does a focus on "motive" differ from the more common emphasis on discriminatory "purpose"? Typical "purpose" inquiries focus on "objective" empirical data about the administration of law. "Motive" inquiries, at first glance, seem to focus on the subjective state of mind of the defendant. May courts strike down otherwise valid official action because it was adopted for motives of racial hostility? Suppose there is proof of bad motive that contributed to the challenged action, but there is also a showing that the action would have been justifiable on grounds that are constitutionally acceptable. Should courts invalidate in that situation? This problem is explored further in some of the modern cases below. (See especially the first footnote to Arlington Heights (1977; p. 759 below).) Note preliminarily, however, that pleas for judicial scrutiny in this area encounter the Court's inhibitions regarding inquiries into improper motives. See generally Brest, "Palmer v. Thompson: An Approach to the Problem of Unconstitutional Legislative Motive," 1971 Sup.Ct.Rev. 95; Ely, "Legislative and Administrative Motivation in Constitutional Law," 79 Yale L.J. 1205 (1970); and Symposium, "Legislative Motivation," 15 San Diego L.Rev. 925 (1978).

As background for consideration of this problem, consider the 5–4 decision in PALMER v. THOMPSON, 403 U.S. 217 (1971), holding that the city of Jackson, Mississippi, had *not* acted unconstitutionally in closing its public swimming pools after they had been ordered desegregated. Justice BLACK's majority opinion, after noting that there was no "affirmative duty" to operate swimming pools, rejected the argument that the closing was unconstitutional because it "was motivated by a desire to avoid integration." He asserted that "no case in this Court had held that a legislative act may violate equal protection solely because of the motivations of the men who voted for it." Ascertaining motivation was "extremely difficult." Though there was some evidence that the city had acted in part because of "ideological opposition to racial integration," there was also substantial evidence that the city had thought that the pools "could not be operated safely and economically on an

tice Rehnquist, dissented, arguing that "unadulterated equal protection analysis is simply inapplicable to peremptory challenges exercised in any particular case." In another dissent, Justice REHNQUIST, joined by Chief Justice Burger, objected to this restriction on "the historic scope of the peremptory challenge." (Recall the extension of Batson to gender-based peremptory challenges in J.E.B. v. Alabama ex rel. T.B. (1994; p. 702 above).)

2. May the government, in cases claiming violations of equal protection, assert that individual variations in administration of law were not deliberate discriminations? See Snowden v. Hughes, 321 U.S. 1 (1944), stating that "unequal application" of statutes fair on their face is not a violation of equal protection "unless there is shown an element of intentional or purposeful discrimination."

integrated basis." He added that it was "difficult or impossible for any court to determine the 'sole' or 'dominant' motivation behind the choices of a group of legislators. Furthermore, there is an element of futility in a judicial attempt to invalidate a law because of the bad motives of its supporters. If the law is struck down for this reason, rather than because of its facial content or effect, it would presumably be valid as soon as the legislature or relevant governing body repassed it for different reasons." He conceded that there was "language in some of our cases" suggesting "that the motive or purpose behind a law is relevant to its constitutionality." "But," he added, "the focus in those cases was on the actual effect of the enactments, not upon the motivation which led the States to behave as they did," and the record here showed "no state action affecting blacks differently from whites." Justice WHITE's dissent insisted that whites and blacks were not being treated alike when both were denied use of public services: "The fact is that closing the pools is an expression of official policy that Negroes are unfit to associate with whites." He asserted that forbidden "racial motive or animus" was a common focus of judicial inquiry—in the context of federal civil rights legislation, for example. He found that here "desegregation, and desegregation alone," was the cause of the closing. (Can Palmer be squared with the later cases, below, emphasizing the centrality of "discriminatory purpose"? See, e.g., the comments on Palmer in Washington v. Davis, below.)[3]

Compare Gomillion v. Lightfoot, 364 U.S. 339 (1960), finding that an Alabama law redefining the city boundaries of Tuskegee was a device to disenfranchise blacks in violation of the 15th Amendment. The statute, which altered "the shape of Tuskegee from a square to an uncouth twenty-eight-sided figure," was alleged to result in removing from the city "all save only four or five of its 400 Negro voters while not removing a single white voter or resident." Justice Frankfurter's opinion found that, if the allegations were proved, "the conclusion would be irresistible, tantamount for all practical purposes to a mathematical demonstration, that the legislation is solely concerned with segregating white and colored voters by fencing Negro citizens out of town so as to deprive them of their preexisting municipal vote." In Palmer, Justice Black distinguished Gomillion as resting "on the actual effect" of the law, "not upon the motivation" underlying it. But was not the "effect" relevant in Gomillion only because it amounted to a "mathematical demonstration" of discriminatory purpose? Was the real distinction the perception that the proof of improper purpose was clearer in Gomillion than in Palmer?[4]

3. Contrast Griffin v. County School Board of Prince Edward County, 377 U.S. 218 (1964), where the Court found the closing of public schools unconstitutional in one of the counties involved in the first group of school desegregation cases decided together with Brown v. Board of Education. The public school closing scheme included grants of public funds to white children to attend private schools. Justice Black emphasized that "public schools were closed and private schools operated in their place with state and county assistance, for one reason, and one reason only: to ensure [that] white and colored children in Prince Edward County would not, under any circumstances, go to the same school. Whatever nonracial grounds might support a State's allowing a county to abandon public schools, the object must be a constitutional one, and grounds of race and opposition to desegregation do not qualify as constitutional." (In Palmer, Justice Black distinguished Griffin because, "unlike the 'private schools' in [Griffin], there is nothing here to show the city is directly or indirectly involved the funding or operation" of the swimming pools.)

4. Note also Wright v. Rockefeller, 376 U.S. 52 (1964), rejecting a claim that congressional districts in Manhattan were racially gerrymandered: appellants failed to prove that the legislature "was either motivated by racial considerations or in fact drew the districts on racial lines." Note also the later materials on racial impacts and racial pur-

3. *De facto discrimination: Should differential effect be sufficient?* Suppose that no purposeful discrimination appears on the face of a statute or can be inferred from the manner in which it is administered, and that there is insufficient evidence of racially hostile motivation by the lawmakers or administrators. Suppose, moreover, that the challenged action, taken for reasons independent of racial considerations, has a differential impact and disadvantaging effect on racial minorities. Is such action unconstitutional? Is heightened judicial scrutiny of most racially differential impacts justified because they tend to reflect irrational, unconscious racial prejudice?[5] Should mere de facto, adventitious "discrimination" be treated like de jure, purposeful discrimination? By 1980, the answer to the last question was clear: the Court insists on proof of purposeful discrimination to establish a constitutional violation. And that had been clear at least since 1976, when Washington v. Davis, below, was decided. But in the early 1970s, a considerable number of lower courts had assumed that "de facto" discrimination was a constitutional violation. To some extent, this assumption was spurred by the Court's handling of discrimination claims resting on congressional statutes rather than the Constitution.

In a number of cases, the Court held that Congress had validly decided that discriminatory effect is adequate to establish a prima facie statutory claim. Note especially GRIGGS v. DUKE POWER CO., 401 U.S. 424 (1971), a case arising under Title VII, the employment discrimination provision of the Civil Rights Act of 1964. Chief Justice BURGER's opinion for a unanimous Court read the Act as prohibiting an employer from subjecting job applicants to a general intelligence test and from requiring high school diplomas, where the effect was to disadvantage black applicants and where the criteria had not been shown by the employer to predict job performance. He stated that the Act required "the removal of artificial, arbitrary, and unnecessary barriers to employment where the barriers operate invidiously to discriminate on the basis of racial or other impermissible classification. [The Act] proscribes not only overt discrimination but also practices that are fair in form, but discriminatory in operation. [Good] intent or absence of discriminatory intent does not redeem employment procedures or testing mechanisms that operate as 'built-in headwinds' for minority groups and are unrelated to measuring job capability. Congress directed the thrust of the Act to the *consequences* of employment practices, not simply their motivation. More than that, Congress has placed on the employer the burden of showing that any given requirement must have a manifest relationship to the employment in question." (In Griggs, the employer had discriminated openly and purposefully prior to the adoption of the 1964 Act, but that background apparently was not central to the decision. Accordingly, many lower courts read the Act as requiring simply an "effect" showing for a prima facie case, and some applied a similar standard to constitutional claims.)

As Washington v. Davis, below, made clear, while Congress may go a long way toward substituting "effect" for "purpose," a showing of a violation of the

poses, in White v. Regester (1973; p. 873 below) and in the line of cases beginning with Shaw v. Reno (1993; p. 880 below).

5. See generally the arguments in Lawrence, "The Id, the Ego, and Equal Protection: Reckoning With Unconscious Racism," 39 Stan.L.Rev. 317 (1987). Lawrence notes that racism "is a malady that we all share, because we all have been scarred by a common history," and adds that "unconscious prejudice presents [a problem] in that it is not subject to self-correction within the political process. [When] the discriminator is not aware of his prejudice and is convinced that he already walks in the path of righteousness, neither reason nor moral persuasion is likely to succeed. The process defect is all the more intractable, and judicial scrutiny becomes imperative."

Constitution still requires proof that the discrimination was purposeful. That holding was partly foreshadowed by a decision a year after Griggs, in JEFFER-SON v. HACKNEY, 406 U.S. 535 (1972), rejecting a de facto discrimination claim in the welfare benefits context. The case was an attack on a Texas scheme for computing AFDC benefits in allocating the state's fixed amount of welfare money. A lower percentage of "need" was granted to AFDC recipients than to beneficiaries of other categorical assistance programs. One of the grounds for attacking that scheme was that "there is a larger percentage of Negroes and Mexican–Americans in AFDC than in other programs." Justice REHNQUIST's majority opinion was not moved by this "naked statistical argument." He noted that "the number of minority members in all categories is substantial" and added that, "given the heterogeneity of the Nation's population, it would be only an infrequent coincidence that the racial composition of each grant class was identical to that of the others." And he went on to state a broader ground: "The acceptance of appellants' constitutional theory would render suspect each difference in treatment among the grant classes, however lacking in racial motivation and however otherwise rational the treatment might be. Few legislative efforts to deal with the difficult problems posed by current welfare programs could survive such scrutiny, and we do not find it required by the 14th Amendment." [The "purpose-effect" tension permeates this and the following group of cases. Not only the "purpose-effect" dichotomy, but also the "process-result," "individual-group," and, of course, "de jure-de facto" themes reflect variants of that tension. A recurrent underlying question is whether the major focus of equal protection should be on purifying the *processes* of decisionmaking from improper considerations (such as racial hostility or consciousness) or whether it should strive to assure greater equality in *result* and condition. Compare, e.g., Brest, "Foreword: In Defense of the Antidiscrimination Principle," 90 Harv.L.Rev. 1 (1976), with Fiss, "The Fate of an Idea Whose Time Has [Come]," 41 U.Chi.L.Rev. 742 (1974), and Fiss, "Groups and the Equal Protection Clause," 5 Phil. & Pub. Affairs 107 (1976). See also Perry, "The Disproportionate Impact Theory of Racial Discrimination," 125 U.Pa.L.Rev. 540 (1977).]

---

2.   PROVING PURPOSEFUL DISCRIMINATION: THE MODERN COURT'S POSITION

Introduction. The following cases, beginning with Washington v. Davis in 1976, illustrate the modern Court's struggles with the purposeful discrimination requirement. That purposeful discrimination is a necessary basis to demonstrate a constitutional violation was settled fairly readily in Washington v. Davis; but that ruling simply shifted the focus to another battleground. How difficult is the plaintiff's burden of proving purposeful discrimination, and what data are relevant in meeting that burden? And what is the defendant's burden of justification after the plaintiff has established a prima facie case of discrimination? That the Court is indeed divided about these questions is demonstrated by the decisions below.[1] Washington v. Davis reaffirmed that discrimination

---

1. These cases repeatedly raise questions similar to those noted in the text. Consider especially whether the burden of showing purposeful discrimination does and should vary with the type of right asserted. For example, should a purposeful discrimina-tion requirement apply as rigidly when the plaintiff asserts "group rights" (such as representational rights in the governmental structure—e.g., Rogers v. Lodge and Mobile v. Bolden, p. 764 below) as it does in the context of "individual" rights (such as those

could be inferred from effects and contextual data, but its guidelines, and those in Arlington Heights a year later, could not wholly clarify the issue for the entire range of circumstances and for all types of constitutional claims. For example, those cases left room for dispute about the reach of the purposeful discrimination requirement. Do the "purpose" criteria apply only where the underlying claim is an individual one to be free from racial discrimination in such areas as employment and housing? Is it arguable that in other areas (such as jury discrimination or school desegregation or minority representation in the governmental structure), the underlying claim should be seen as one of group representation, with the consequence that a less burdensome "purpose" showing or even a mere "effect" showing might suffice?

Washington v. Davis

426 U.S. 229, 96 S.Ct. 2040, 48 L.Ed.2d 597 (1976).

Justice WHITE delivered the opinion of the Court.

This case involves the validity of a qualifying test administered to applicants for positions as police officers in the District of Columbia Metropolitan Police Department. The test was sustained by the District Court but invalidated by the Court of Appeals. We are in agreement with the District Court and hence reverse the judgment of the Court of Appeals. [The respondents were black applicants for the police force who were rejected for failing to perform satisfactorily on a written test measuring verbal ability, vocabulary, reading and comprehension. [The examination was one generally used throughout the federal service and originally developed by the U.S. Civil Service Commission.] Respondents claimed that the test was racially discriminatory in effect, but did not claim that it constituted "purposeful" discrimination. The District Court found that a higher percentage of blacks than whites had failed the examination and that the test had not been validated to establish its reliability for measuring subsequent job performance. However, the District Court denied relief, finding that the test was reasonably related to the requirements of the police recruit training program and that it was not designed or operated "to discriminate against otherwise qualified blacks." The Court of Appeals followed Griggs, believing that the statutory standards articulated there governed the constitutional issue presented here. The appellate court accordingly found the lack of discriminatory intent regarding the test irrelevant and emphasized its disproportionate impact.] This disproportionate impact, standing alone and without regard to whether it indicated a discriminatory purpose, was held sufficient to establish a constitutional violation, absent proof by petitioners that the test was an adequate measure of job performance in addition to being an indicator of probable success in the training program, a burden which the court ruled petitioners had failed to discharge.

[We] have never held that the constitutional standard for adjudicating claims of invidious racial discrimination is identical to the standards applicable under Title VII, and we decline to do so today. The central purpose of [equal

against racial or sexual discrimination in employment, e.g., Washington v. Davis and Feeney, below)? Or should the plaintiff bear a lesser burden in "group rights" cases? The cases printed in this section 3D2 are not the only ones to raise such issues. Note also the quite lenient application of the purposeful discrimination requirement in the context of school desegregation, in sec. 3D3 below; but see the vote "dilution" cases in sec. 4B below—especially Shaw v. Reno (1993, p. 880 below).

protection is] the prevention of official conduct discriminating on the basis of race. [But] our cases have not embraced the proposition that a law or other official act, without regard to whether it reflects a racially discriminatory purpose, is unconstitutional *solely* because it has a racially disproportionate impact. Almost 100 years ago, [Strauder] established that the exclusion of Negroes from grand and petit juries in criminal proceedings violated [equal protection], but the fact that a particular jury or a series of juries does not statistically reflect the racial composition of the community does not in itself make out an invidious discrimination forbidden by the Clause. [The] school desegregation cases have also adhered to the basic equal protection principle that the invidious quality of a law claimed to be racially discriminatory must ultimately be traced to a racially discriminatory purpose. That there are both predominantly black and predominantly white schools in a community is not alone violative of [equal protection]. The essential element of de jure segregation is "a current condition of segregation resulting from intentional state action. [The] differentiating factor between de jure segregation and so-called de facto segregation [is] *purpose* or *intent* to segregate." [Keyes (p. 776 below).] [See also, in the welfare benefits context, Jefferson v. Hackney (1972; p. 754 above).] This is not to say that the necessary discriminatory racial purpose must be express or appear on the face of the statute, or that a law's disproportionate impact is irrelevant in cases involving Constitution-based claims of racial discrimination. A statute, otherwise neutral on its face, must not be applied so as invidiously to discriminate on the basis of race. [Yick Wo.] It is also clear from the cases dealing with racial discrimination in the selection of juries that the systematic exclusion of Negroes is itself such an "unequal application of the law [as] to show intentional discrimination." A prima facie case of discriminatory purpose may be proved as well by the absence of Negroes on a particular jury combined with the failure of the jury commissioners to be informed of eligible Negro jurors in a community or with racially nonneutral selection procedures. With a prima facie case made out, "the burden of proof shifts to the State to rebut the presumption of unconstitutional action by showing that permissible racially neutral selection criteria and procedures have produced the monochromatic result."

Necessarily, an invidious discriminatory purpose may often be inferred from the totality of the relevant facts, including the fact, if it is true, that the law bears more heavily on one race than another. It is also not infrequently true that the discriminatory impact—in the jury cases for example, the total or seriously disproportionate exclusion of Negroes from jury venires—may for all practical purposes demonstrate unconstitutionality because in various circumstances the discrimination is very difficult to explain on nonracial grounds. Nevertheless, we have not held that a law, neutral on its face and serving ends otherwise within the power of government to pursue, is invalid under [equal protection] simply because it may affect a greater proportion of one race than of another. Disproportionate impact is not irrelevant, but it is not the sole touchstone of an invidious racial discrimination forbidden by the Constitution. Standing alone, it does not trigger the rule that racial classifications are to be subjected to the strictest scrutiny and are justifiable only by the weightiest of considerations.

There are some indications to the contrary in our cases. [See Palmer v. Thompson, above.] [Palmer] warned against grounding decision on legislative purpose or motivation, thereby lending support for the proposition that the operative effect of the law rather than its purpose is the paramount factor. But the holding of the case was that the legitimate purposes of the ordinance—to preserve peace and avoid deficits—were not open to impeachment by evidence that the councilmen were actually motivated by racial considerations. Whatever dicta the opinion may contain, the decision did not involve, much less invalidate, a statute or ordinance having neutral purposes but disproportionate racial consequences. That [Palmer] was not understood to have changed the prevailing rule is apparent from [Keyes].[1] Both before and after [Palmer], however, various Courts of Appeals have held in several contexts, including public employment, that the substantially disproportionate racial impact of a statute or official practice standing alone and without regard to discriminatory purpose, suffices to prove racial discrimination violating [equal protection] absent some justification going substantially beyond what would be necessary to validate most other legislative classifications.[2] The cases impressively demonstrate that there is another side to the issue; but, with all due respect, to the extent that those cases rested on or expressed the view that proof of discriminatory racial purpose is unnecessary in making out an equal protection violation, we are in disagreement. [We] have difficulty understanding how a law establishing a racially neutral qualification for employment is nevertheless racially discriminatory and denies "any person [equal protection]" simply because a greater proportion of Negroes fail to qualify than members of other racial or ethnic groups. Had respondents, along with all others who had failed [the test], whether white or black, brought an action claiming that [it] denied each of them [equal protection] as compared with those who had passed with high enough scores to qualify them as police recruits, it is most unlikely that their challenge would have been sustained. [The test,] which is administered generally to prospective government employees, concededly seeks to ascertain whether those who take it have acquired a particular level of verbal skill; and it is untenable that the Constitution prevents the Government from seeking modestly to upgrade the communicative abilities of its employees rather than to be satisfied with some lower level of competence, particularly where the job requires special ability to communicate orally and in writing. Respondents, as Negroes, could no more successfully claim that the test denied them equal protection than could white applicants who also failed. The conclusion would not be different in the face of proof that more Negroes than whites had been disqualified by [the test]. That other Negroes also failed to score well would, alone, not demonstrate that respondents individually were being denied [equal protection] by the application of an otherwise valid qualifying test being administered to prospective police recruits. Nor on the facts of the case before us would the disproportionate impact of [the test] warrant the conclusion that it is a purposeful device to discriminate against Negroes. [The] test is neutral on its face and rationally may be said to serve a purpose the Government is constitutionally empowered to pursue. Even agreeing with the District Court that the differential racial effect of [the test] called for further inquiry, we think the District Court correctly held that the affirmative efforts of the [Police Department] to recruit black officers, the changing racial composition of the recruit classes and of the force in general, and the relationship of the test to the

other evidence

---

1. To the extent that Palmer suggests a generally applicable proposition that legislative purpose is irrelevant in constitutional adjudication, our prior cases [are] to the [contrary]. [Footnote by Justice White.]

2. At this point, a footnote by Justice White listed—and seemingly repudiated—16 such cases, mainly from the public employment area, but also from such contexts as urban renewal, zoning, public housing, and municipal services. Among the cases he listed with apparent disapproval was the Arlington Heights case, below, a zoning case in which the Court had granted certiorari just a few months earlier. The inclusion of that case prompted Justice Brennan in dissent to question the "propriety" of Justice White's footnote and its "laundry list of lower court decisions."

training program negated any inference that the Department discriminated on the basis of [race].

Under [Title VII], Congress provided that when hiring and promotion practices disqualifying substantially disproportionate numbers of blacks are challenged, discriminatory purpose need not be proved, and that it is an insufficient response to demonstrate some rational basis for the challenged practices. It is necessary, in addition, that they be "validated" in terms of job performance in any one of several [ways]. However this process proceeds, it involves a more probing judicial review of, and less deference to, the seemingly reasonable acts of [administrators] than is appropriate under the Constitution where special racial impact, without discriminatory purpose, is claimed. We are not disposed to adopt this more rigorous standard for the purposes of applying the Fifth and the 14th Amendments in cases such as this. A rule that a statute designed to serve neutral ends is nevertheless invalid, absent compelling justification, if in practice it benefits or burdens one race more than another would be far reaching and would raise serious questions about, and perhaps invalidate, a whole range of tax, welfare, public service, regulatory, and licensing statutes that may be more burdensome to the poor and to the average black than to the more affluent white. [In] our view, extension of the rule beyond those areas where it is already applicable by reason of statute [should] await legislative prescription.[3]

Justice STEVENS, concurring [and joining the Court's opinion].

[The] requirement of purposeful discrimination is a common thread running through the cases summarized [by the Court]. Although it may be proper to use the same language to describe the constitutional claim in each of [the] contexts, the burden of proving a prima facie case may well involve differing evidentiary considerations. The extent of deference that one pays to the trial court's determination of the factual issue [will] vary in different contexts. Frequently the most probative evidence of intent will be objective evidence of what actually happened rather than evidence describing the subjective state of mind of the actor. For normally the actor is presumed to have intended the natural consequences of his deeds. This is particularly true in the case of governmental action which is frequently the product of compromise, of collective decisionmaking, and of mixed motivation. It is unrealistic, on the one hand, to require the victim of alleged discrimination to uncover the actual subjective intent of the decisionmaker or, conversely, to invalidate otherwise legitimate action simply because an improper motive affected the deliberation of a participant in the decisional process. A law conscripting clerics should not be invalidated because an atheist voted for it. My point in making this observation is to suggest that the line between discriminatory purpose and discriminatory impact is not nearly as bright, and perhaps not quite as critical, as the reader of the Court's opinion might assume. I agree, of course, that a constitutional issue does not arise every time some disproportionate impact is shown. On the other hand, when the disproportion is as dramatic as in Gomillion or Yick Wo, it really does not matter whether the standard is phrased in terms of purpose or effect. Therefore, although I accept the statement of the general rule in the Court's opinion, I am not yet prepared to indicate how that standard should be applied in the many cases which have formulated the governing standard in different language. My agreement with the [Court's conclusion] rests on a ground narrower than the Court describes. There are two reasons why I am

3. Justice White also rejected the statutory claim. Justice STEWART joined the constitutional part of Justice White's opinion.

Justice BRENNAN, joined by Justice Marshall, dissented on the statutory issue and did not reach the constitutional claim.

convinced that the challenge to [the test] is insufficient. First, the test serves the neutral and legitimate purpose of requiring all applicants to meet a uniform minimum standard of literacy. Second, the same test is used throughout the federal service. The applicants for employment in the [D.C.] Police Department represent such a small fraction of the total number of persons who have taken the test that their experience is of minimal probative value in assessing the neutrality of the [test].

———

ARLINGTON HEIGHTS v. METROPOLITAN HOUSING CORP., 429 U.S. 252 (1977), reaffirmed the Washington v. Davis principle that "official action will not be held unconstitutional solely because it results in a racially disproportionate impact" and elaborated on the "subjects of proper inquiry" in determining whether an unconstitutional discriminatory purpose exists. The case involved a challenge to a Chicago suburb's refusal to grant a request to rezone certain property from a single-family to a multiple-family classification. A nonprofit developer planned to build federally subsidized townhouse units in the largely white suburb, so that low and moderate income tenants, including members of racial minorities, might live there. Although the lower federal courts found that the suburb's officials were motivated by a concern for the integrity of the zoning plan rather than by racial hostility, the Court of Appeals held the denial of the rezoning request unconstitutional because its "ultimate effect" was racially discriminatory. In reversing that decision, Justice POW-ELL's majority opinion repudiated the Court of Appeals' emphasis on effect rather than purpose, discussed some of the evidentiary data generally relevant to a search for the kind of "discriminatory purpose" required under Washington v. Davis, and found no showing of unconstitutional behavior in the record here. In his discussion of the Davis requirement of "[p]roof of racially discriminatory intent or purpose," he elaborated the ingredients of such an "intent or purpose":

"Davis does not require a plaintiff to prove that the challenged action rested solely on racially discriminatory purposes. Rarely can it be said that a legislature or administrative body operating under a broad mandate made a decision motivated solely by a single concern, or even that a particular purpose was the 'dominant' or 'primary' one." It was enough to show "that a discriminatory purpose has been a motivating factor in the decision."[1] But he made

1. Note a significant footnote added by Justice Powell later in his opinion. He stated: "Proof that the decision by the Village was motivated in part by a racially discriminatory purpose would not necessarily have required invalidation of the challenged decision. Such proof would, however, have shifted to the Village the burden of establishing that the same decision would have resulted even had the impermissible purpose not been considered. If this were established, the complaining party in a case of this kind no longer fairly could attribute the injury complained of to improper consideration of a discriminatory purpose. In such circumstances, there would be no justification for judicial interference with the challenged decision. But in this case respondents failed to make the required threshold showing." [Justice Powell cited the articulation of a similar theme in a First Amendment context in Mt. Healthy City School Dist. Bd. of Educ. v. Doyle, 429 U.S. 274 (1977).] Why should proof of discriminatory purpose *not* produce an immediate invalidation of the law, instead of merely shifting the burden of justification to the government, as Justice Powell states? If the "discriminatory purpose" inquiry is largely designed to cleanse or purify the decisionmaking process, what justifies ever validating a governmental decision once it has been found to have been discriminatorily motivated? See also Hunter v. Underwood (1985; p. 770 below). Arguably, the reason is similar to that often given to

clear that proving such a motivating˙factor would not be easy: "Determining whether invidious discriminatory purpose was a motivating factor demands a sensitive inquiry into such circumstantial and direct evidence of intent as may be available. The impact of the official action [may] provide an important starting point. Sometimes a clear pattern, unexplainable on grounds other than race, emerges from the effect of the state action even when the governing legislation appears neutral on its face. [E.g., Yick Wo; Gomillion.] The evidentiary inquiry is then relatively easy. But such cases are rare. Absent a pattern as stark as that in Gomillion or Yick Wo, impact alone is not determinative, and the Court must look to other evidence. The historical background of the decision is one evidentiary source, particularly if it reveals a series of official actions taken for invidious purposes. The specific sequence of events leading up to the challenged decision also may shed some light on the decisionmaker's purposes. For example, if the property involved here always had been zoned [for multiple-family housing] but suddenly was changed to [a single-family classification] when the town learned of [the developer's] plans to erect integrated housing, we would have a far different case. Departures from the normal procedural sequence also might afford evidence that improper purposes are playing a role. Substantive departures too may be relevant, particularly if the factors usually considered important by the decisionmaker strongly favor a decision contrary to the one reached. The legislative or administrative history may be highly relevant, especially where there are contemporary statements by members of the decisionmaking body, minutes of its meetings, or reports. In some extraordinary instances the members might be called to the stand at trial to testify concerning the purpose of the [official action]."[2] After summarizing those "subjects of proper inquiry," "without purporting to be exhaustive," Justice Powell turned to the record in this case and found (as had the lower courts) no demonstration of a "racially discriminatory intent." Though the refusal to rezone "arguably" bore more heavily on racial minorities, there was "little about the sequence of events leading up to the decision that would spark suspicion." The area in which the tract lay had long been zoned for single family use, and the rezoning request was handled according to the usual procedures. He concluded that the challengers had "simply failed to carry their burden of proving that discriminatory purpose was a motivating factor in the Village's decision. This conclusion ends the constitutional inquiry. The Court of Appeals' further finding that the Village's decision carried a discriminatory

avoid *any* motivation inquiries—the futility of invalidating a law when the lawmakers could enact the very same law if their motives were pure. But would not full adherence to the process-cleansing rationale—the rationale that in part underlies the modern Court's emphasis on "purpose" rather than "effect"—warrant in effect a remand of the issue to the lawmakers for reconsideration on the basis of purely legitimate factors? Some legislators, "after being informed that they initially acted unconstitutionally, may refuse to vote for reenactment. [And] if a statute is invalidated on judicial review, the legislature often will decline or fail to consider a new law. In many situations, therefore, judicial action on the basis of motive results in an effective, not a futile, invalidation." Eisenberg, "Disproportionate Impact and Illicit Motive: Theories of Constitutional Adjudication," 52 N.Y.U. L.Rev. 36 (1977).

2. "This Court has recognized [that] judicial inquiries into legislative or executive motivation represent a substantial intrusion into the workings of other branches of government. Placing a decisionmaker on the stand is therefore 'usually to be [avoided].' " [Footnote by Justice Powell.]

'ultimate effect' is without independent constitutional significance.'"[3]

PERSONNEL ADMINISTRATOR OF MASS. v. FEENEY, 442 U.S. 256 (1979): This decision relied on Davis and Arlington Heights to reject a sex discrimination attack on Massachusetts' law granting "absolute lifetime" preference to veterans for state civil service positions, even though "the preference operates overwhelmingly to the advantage of males." Under the law, "all veterans who qualify for state civil service positions must be considered for appointment ahead of any qualifying nonveterans." (Over 98% of the veterans in Massachusetts were male; only 1.8% were female.) Challenger Helen B. Feeney, who was not a veteran, claimed that the law denied equal protection to women. In rejecting her challenge, Justice STEWART's majority opinion stated that Davis and Arlington Heights "signaled no departure from the settled rule that the 14th Amendment guarantees equal laws, not equal results. [Those principles] apply with equal force to a case involving alleged gender discrimination. When a statute gender-neutral on its face is challenged on the ground that its effects upon women are disproportionately adverse, a two-fold inquiry is thus appropriate. The first question is whether the statutory classification is indeed neutral in the sense that it is not gender-based. If the classification itself, covert or overt, is not based upon gender, the second question is whether the adverse effect reflects invidious gender-based discrimination. In this second inquiry, impact provides an 'important starting point' [Arlington Heights], but purposeful discrimination is 'the condition that offends the Constitution.' "

Engaging in the first step of that inquiry, Justice Stewart noted that Feeney had "acknowledged that state hiring preferences for veterans are not per se invalid, for she has limited her challenge to the absolute lifetime preference." He continued: "The District Court made two central findings that are relevant here: first, that [the law] serves legitimate and worthy purposes; second, that the absolute preference was not established for the purpose of discriminating against women. [Thus,] the distinction between veterans and nonveterans [here] is not a pretext for gender discrimination. [If] the impact of this statute could not be plausibly explained on a neutral ground, impact itself would signal that the real classification made by the law was in fact not neutral. [But this] is not a law that can plausibly be explained only as a gender-based classification. Indeed, it is not a law that can rationally be explained on that ground. Veteran status is not uniquely male. Although few women benefit from the preference, the nonveteran class is not substantially all-female. To the contrary, significant numbers of nonveterans are men, and all nonveterans—male as well as female—are placed at a disadvantage. Too many men are affected by [the law] to permit the inference that the statute is but a pretext for preferring men over women. [The] distinction made by [the law is] quite simply between veterans and nonveterans, not between men and women."

---

3. Three of the Justices disagreed with the majority's handling of the case—Justices MARSHALL, BRENNAN and WHITE (Justice Stevens did not participate in the case). Justice WHITE's dissent objected to the majority's "failure to follow our usual practice in this situation" by remanding for reconsideration in light of Davis. He, the author of Davis, added that he thought it "wholly unnecessary for the Court to embark on a lengthy discussion of the standards for proving the racially discriminatory purpose required by Davis": in light of the lower courts' findings that the suburb's decision rested on legitimate grounds, there was no need "for this Court to list various 'evidentiary sources' or 'subjects of proper inquiry' in determining whether a racially discriminatory purpose existed."

On the second part of the inquiry, Justice Stewart stated: "The dispositive question [is] whether the appellee has shown that a gender-based discriminatory purpose has, at least in some measure, shaped the Massachusetts veterans' preference legislation. [She] points to two basic factors which in her view distinguish [the law] from the neutral rules at issue in [Davis and Arlington Heights]. The first is the nature of the preference, which is said to be demonstrably gender-biased in the sense that it favors a status reserved under federal military policy primarily to men. The second concerns the impact of the absolute lifetime preference upon the employment opportunities of women, an impact claimed to be too inevitable to have been unintended. The appellee contends that these factors, coupled with the fact that the preference itself has little if any relevance to actual job performance, more than suffice [to prove discriminatory intent]. The contention that [the law] is 'inherently non-neutral' or 'gender-biased' presumes that the State, by favoring veterans, intentionally incorporated into its public employment policies the panoply of sex-based and assertedly discriminatory federal laws that have prevented all but a handful of women from becoming veterans. There are two serious difficulties with this argument. First, it is wholly at odds with the District Court's central finding that Massachusetts has not [acted] for the purpose of discriminating against women. Second, it cannot be reconciled with the assumption made by both the appellee and the District Court that a more limited hiring preference for veterans could be sustained. Taken together, these difficulties are fatal. To the extent that the status of veteran is one that few women have been enabled to achieve, every hiring preference for veterans, however modest or extreme, is inherently gender-biased. [Invidious] discrimination does not become less so because the discrimination accomplished is of a lesser magnitude.[1] Discriminatory intent [either] is a factor that has influenced the legislative choice or it is not. The District Court's conclusion that the [law] was not originally enacted or subsequently reaffirmed for the purpose of giving an advantage to males as such necessarily compels the conclusion that the State intended nothing more than to prefer 'veterans.' Given this finding, simple logic suggests that an intent to exclude women from significant public jobs was not at work in this law. To reason that it was [is] merely to restate the fact of impact, not to answer the question of intent.

"To be sure, this case is unusual in that it involves a law that by design is not neutral. The law overtly prefers veterans as such. As opposed to the written test at issue in Davis, it does not purport to define a job related characteristic. To the contrary, it confers upon a specifically described group—perceived to be particularly deserving—a competitive head start. But the District Court found, and the appellee has not disputed, that this legislative choice was legitimate. The basic distinction between veterans and nonveterans having been found not gender-based, and the goals of the preference having been found worthy, [the law] must be analyzed as is any other neutral law that casts a greater burden upon women as a group than upon men as a group. The enlistment policies of the armed services may well have discriminated on the basis of sex. But the history of discrimination against women in the military is not on trial in this case. The appellee's ultimate argument rests upon the presumption, common to the criminal and civil law, that a person intends the natural and foreseeable consequences of his voluntary actions. [It] would [be] disingenuous to say that

---

1. "This is not to say that the degree of impact is irrelevant to the question of intent. But it is to say that a more modest preference, while it might well lessen impact and, as the State argues, might lessen the effec- tiveness of the statute in helping veterans, would not be any more or less 'neutral' in the constitutional sense." [Footnote by Justice Stewart.]

the adverse consequences of this legislation for women were unintended, in the sense that they were not volitional or in the sense that they were not foreseeable. 'Discriminatory purpose,' however, implies more than intent as volition or intent as awareness of consequences. It implies that the decision-maker, in this case a state legislature, selected or reaffirmed a particular course of action at least in part 'because of,' not merely 'in spite of,' its adverse effects upon an identifiable group.[2] Yet nothing in the record demonstrates that this preference for veterans was originally devised or subsequently re-enacted because it would accomplish the collateral goal of keeping women in a stereotypic and predefined place in the Massachusetts Civil Service. [When] the totality of legislative actions establishing and extending the Massachusetts veterans' preference are considered, the law remains what it purports to be: a preference for veterans of either sex over nonveterans of either sex, not for men over women."

Justice STEVENS, joined by Justice White, concurred in the opinion and added: "I confess that I am not at all sure that there is any difference between the two questions [posed]. If a classification is not overtly based on gender, I am inclined to believe the question whether it is covertly gender-based is the same as the question whether its adverse effects 'reflect invidious gender-based discrimination.' However the question is phrased, for me the answer is largely provided by the fact that the number of males disadvantaged by [the law] (1,867,000) is sufficiently large—and sufficiently close to the number of disadvantaged females (2,954,000)—to refute the claim that the rule was intended to benefit males as a class over females as a class." Justice MARSHALL, joined by Justice Brennan, dissented: "In my judgment, [the law] evinces purposeful gender-based discrimination." He elaborated: "To discern the purposes underlying facially neutral policies, this Court [has] considered the degree, inevitability, and foreseeability of any disproportionate impact as well as the alternatives reasonably available. [The] absolute preference formula has rendered desirable state civil service employment an almost exclusively male prerogative. [T]his consequence followed foreseeably, indeed inexorably, from the long history of policies severely limiting women's participation in the military. Although neutral in form, the statute is anything but neutral in application. [Where] the foreseeable impact of a facially neutral policy is so disproportionate, the burden should rest on the State to establish that sex-based considerations played no part in the choice of the particular legislative scheme. Clearly, that burden was not sustained here. The legislative history of the statute reflects the Commonwealth's patent appreciation of the impact the preference system would have on women, and an equally evident desire to mitigate that impact only with respect to certain traditionally female occupations. Until 1971, the statute and implementing [regulations] exempted from operation of the preference any job requisitions 'especially calling for women.' In practice, this exemption, coupled with the absolute preference for veterans, has created a gender-based civil service hierarchy, with women occupying low grade clerical and secretarial jobs

2. "This is not to say that the inevitability or foreseeability of consequences of a neutral rule has no bearing upon the existence of discriminatory intent. Certainly, when the adverse consequences of a law upon an identifiable group are as inevitable as the gender-based consequences of [this law], a strong inference that the adverse effects were desired can reasonably be drawn. But in this inquiry—made as it is under the Constitution—an inference is a working tool, not a synonym for proof. When as here, the impact is essentially an unavoidable consequence of a legislative policy that has in itself always been deemed to be legitimate, and when, as here, the statutory history and all of the available evidence affirmatively demonstrate the opposite, the inference simply fails to ripen into proof." [Footnote by Justice Stewart.]

and men holding more responsible and remunerative positions. Thus, for over 70 years, the Commonwealth has maintained, as an integral part of its veterans' preference system, an exemption relegating female civil service applicants to occupations traditionally filled by women. Such a statutory scheme both reflects and perpetuates precisely the kind of archaic assumptions about women's roles which we have previously held invalid. Particularly when viewed against the range of less discriminatory alternatives available to assist veterans, Massachusetts' choice of a formula that so severely restricts public employment opportunities for women cannot reasonably be thought gender-neutral."[1]

Rogers v. Lodge

458 U.S. 613, 102 S.Ct. 3272, 73 L.Ed.2d 1012 (1982).

Justice WHITE delivered the opinion of the Court.

The issue in this case is whether the at-large system of elections in Burke County, Ga., violates the 14th Amendment rights of Burke County's black citizens. I. Burke County is a large, predominantly rural county located in eastern Georgia. [According] to the 1980 census, Burke County had a total population of 19,349, of whom 10,385, or 53.6%, were black. [W]hites constitute a slight majority of the voting age population. As of 1978, 6,373 persons were registered to vote in Burke County, of whom 38% were black. The Burke County Board of Commissioners governs the county. It was created in 1911 [under state law] and consists of five members elected at large to concurrent 4–year terms by all qualified voters in the county. The county has never been divided into [districts]. In order to be nominated or elected, a candidate must receive a majority of the votes cast in the primary or general election, and a runoff must be held if no candidate receives a majority in the first primary or general election. [There is no residency requirement for candidates.] Each candidate must run for a specific seat on the Board, and a voter may vote only once for any candidate. No Negro has ever been elected to the [Board]. Appellees, eight black citizens, filed this suit in 1976 in [the District Court] on behalf of all black citizens in Burke County. The complaint alleged that the county's system of at-large elections violates appellees' [constitutional] rights [by] diluting the voting power of black citizens. [The] court issued an order [stating] that appellees were entitled to prevail and ordering that Burke County be divided into five districts for purposes of electing County Commissioners. The court later issued detailed findings of fact and conclusions of law in which it stated that while the present method of electing County Commissioners was "racially neutral when adopted, [it] is being *maintained* for invidious purposes" in violation of appellees' 14th and 15th Amendment rights. The Court of Appeals affirmed. It stated that while the proceedings in the District Court took place prior to the decision in Mobile v. Bolden, 446 U.S. 55 (1980) [discussed later in this opinion], the District court correctly anticipated Mobile and required appellees to prove [that] the at-large voting system was maintained for a discriminatory purpose, [that] the District Court's findings were not clearly erroneous, and that its conclusion that the at-large system was maintained for

1. "Only four States afford a preference comparable in scope to that of Massachusetts. Other States and the Federal Government grant point or tie-breaking preferences that do not foreclose opportunities for women." [Footnote by Justice Marshall.]

SECTION 3. SUSPECT CLASSIFICATIONS

invidious purposes was "virtually mandated by the overwhelming proof." [We] affirm.*

II. At-large voting schemes and multimember districts tend to minimize the voting strength of minority groups by permitting the political majority to elect *all* representatives of the district. A distinct minority, whether it be a racial, ethnic, economic, or political group, may be unable to elect any representatives in an at-large election, yet may be able to elect several representatives if the political unit is divided into single-member districts. The minority's voting power in a multimember district is particularly diluted when bloc voting occurs and ballots are cast along strict majority-minority lines. While multimember districts have been challenged for "their winner-take-all aspects, their tendency to submerge minorities and to overrepresent the winning party," Whitcomb v. Chavis [1971; p. 875 below], this Court has repeatedly held that they are not unconstitutional per se. The Court has recognized, however, that multimember districts violate the 14th Amendment if "conceived or operated as purposeful devices to further racial discrimination" by minimizing, canceling out or diluting the voting strength of racial elements in the voting population. Cases charging that multimember districts unconstitutionally dilute the voting strength of racial minorities are thus subject to the standard of proof generally applicable to [equal protection] cases. [Davis and Arlington Heights] made it clear that in order for [equal protection] to be violated, "the invidious quality of a law claimed to be racially discriminatory must ultimately be traced to a racially discriminatory purpose." Neither case involved voting dilution, but in both cases the Court observed that the requirement that racially discriminatory purpose or intent be proved applies to [voting cases]. [Arlington Heights and Davis] both rejected the notion that a law is invalid under [equal protection] simply because it may affect a greater proportion of one race than another. However, both cases recognized that discriminatory intent need not be proved by direct evidence. [Thus] determining the existence of a discriminatory purpose "demands a sensitive inquiry into such circumstantial and direct evidence of intent as may be available."

In Mobile v. Bolden, the Court was called upon to apply these principles to the at-large election system in Mobile, Ala. Mobile is governed by three commissioners who exercise all legislative, executive, and administrative power in the municipality. Each candidate for the City Commission runs for one of three numbered posts in an at-large election and can only be elected by a majority vote. Plaintiffs brought a class action on behalf of all Negro citizens of Mobile alleging that the at-large scheme diluted their voting [strength]. The District Court [ordered] that the commission form of government be replaced by a mayor and a nine-member City Council elected from single-member districts. The Court of Appeals affirmed. This Court reversed. Justice Stewart, writing for himself and three other Justices, noted that to prevail in their contention that the at-large voting system violates [equal protection], plaintiffs had to prove the system was " 'conceived or operated as [a] purposeful devic[e] to further [racial] discrimination.' "[1] [Another] Justice agreed with the stan-

---

* This case is printed here because it (and Mobile v. Bolden, discussed in this opinion) bear on the application of the "purposeful discrimination" "requirement." For further development of claims regarding "vote dilution," see the materials in Sec. 4B (on the fundamental interest in voting), below.

1. With respect to the 15th Amendment, the plurality held that the Amendment prohibits only direct, purposefully discriminatory interference with the freedom of Negroes to vote. [We] express no view on the application of the 15th Amendment to this case. The plurality [in Mobile] noted that plaintiffs' claim under § 2 of the Voting

dard of proof recognized by the plurality. (White, J., dissenting.) The plurality went on to conclude that the District Court had failed to comply with this standard. The District Court had analyzed plaintiffs' claims in light of the standard which had been set forth in Zimmer v. McKeithen, 485 F.2d 1297 (C.A.5 1973). [Zimmer] set out a list of factors[2] gleaned from Whitcomb v. Chavis and White v. Regester [1973; p. 873 below] that a court should consider in assessing the constitutionality of at-large and multimember district voting schemes. [The] plurality in Mobile was of the view that Zimmer was "decided upon the misunderstanding that it is not necessary to show a discriminatory purpose in order to prove a violation of [equal protection]—that proof of a discriminatory effect is sufficient." The plurality observed that while "the presence of the indicia relied on in Zimmer may afford some evidence of a discriminatory purpose," the mere existence of those criteria is not a substitute for a finding of discriminatory purpose. The District Court's standard in Mobile was likewise flawed.

[Because] the District Court in the present case employed the evidentiary factors outlined in Zimmer, it is urged that its judgment is infirm for the same reasons that led to the reversal in Mobile. We do not agree. First, and fundamentally, we are unconvinced that the District Court in this case applied the wrong legal standard. Not only was the District Court's decision rendered a considerable time after [Davis and Arlington Heights], but the trial judge also had the benefit of Nevett v. Sides, 571 F.2d 209 (1978), where the Court of Appeals for the Fifth Circuit assessed the impact of [Davis] and Arlington Heights and held that "a showing of racially motivated discrimination is a necessary element in an equal protection voting dilution claim." [The] District Court referred to Nevett v. Sides and demonstrated its understanding of the controlling standard by observing that a determination of discriminatory intent is "a requisite to a finding of unconstitutional vote dilution" under the 14th and 15th Amendments. Furthermore, while recognizing that the evidentiary factors identified in Zimmer were to be considered, the District Court was aware that it was "not limited in its determination only to the Zimmer factors" but could consider other relevant factors as well. [It] then proceeded to deal with what it considered to be the relevant proof and concluded that the at-large scheme of electing commissioners, "although racially neutral when adopted, is being *maintained* for invidious purposes." That system, "while neutral in origin, [has] been subverted to invidious purposes." For the most part, the District Court dealt with the evidence in terms of the factors set out in Zimmer and its progeny, but as the Court of Appeals stated: "Judge Alaimo employed the constitutionally required standard [and] did not treat the Zimmer criteria as absolute, but rather considered them only to the extent they were relevant to the question of discriminatory intent." Although a tenable argument can be made to the contrary, we are not inclined to disagree with the Court of Appeals' conclusion that the District Court applied the proper legal standard.

Rights Act [added] nothing to their 15th Amendment claim because the "legislative history of § 2 makes clear that it was intended to have an effect no different from that of the 15th Amendment itself." [Footnote by Justice White. See also footnote 4 below.]

2. The primary factors listed in Zimmer include a lack of minority access to the candidate selection process, unresponsiveness of elected officials to minority interests, a tenu-

ous state policy underlying the preference for multimember or at-large districting, and the existence of past discrimination which precludes effective participation in the electoral process. Factors which enhance the proof of voting dilution are the existence of large districts, anti-single-shot voting provisions, and the absence of any provision for at-large candidates to run from geographic sub-districts. [Footnote by Justice White.]

III. A. We are also unconvinced that we should disturb the District Court's finding that the at-large system in Burke County was being maintained for the invidious purpose of diluting the voting strength of the black population. In White v. Regester, we stated that we were not inclined to overturn the District Court's factual findings, "representing as they do a blend of history and an intensely local appraisal of the design and impact of the Bexar County multimember district in the light of past and present reality, political and otherwise." See also Columbus Board of Education v. Penick [(1979; p. 777 below) (Burger, C.J., concurring in judgment)].[3] We are of the view that [the] clearly-erroneous standard [of FRCP 52(a)] applies to the trial court's finding in this case that the at-large system in Burke County is being maintained for discriminatory purposes, as well as to the court's subsidiary findings of fact. The Court of Appeals did not hold any of the District Court's findings of fact to be clearly erroneous, and this Court has frequently noted its reluctance to disturb findings of fact concurred in by two lower courts. We agree with the Court of Appeals that on the record before us, none of the factual findings [is] clearly erroneous.

B. The District Court found that blacks have always made up a substantial majority of the population in Burke County, but that they are a distinct minority of the registered voters. There was also overwhelming evidence of bloc voting along racial lines. Hence, although there had been black candidates, no black had ever been elected to the Burke County Commission. These facts bear heavily on the issue of purposeful discrimination. Voting along racial lines allows those elected to ignore black interests without fear of political consequences, and without bloc voting the minority candidates would not lose elections solely because of their race. Because it is sensible to expect that at least some blacks would have been elected in Burke County, the fact that none [has] ever been elected is important evidence of purposeful exclusion. Under our cases, however, such facts are insufficient in themselves to prove purposeful discrimination absent other evidence such as proof that blacks have less opportunity to participate in the political processes and to elect candidates of their choice. Both the District Court and the Court of Appeals thought the supporting proof in this case was sufficient to support an inference of intentional discrimination. [These] factors were primarily those suggested in [Zimmer]. The District Court began by determining the impact of past discrimination on the ability of blacks to participate effectively in the political process. Past discrimination was found to contribute to low black voter registration because prior to the Voting Rights Act of 1965, blacks had been denied access to the political process by means such as literacy tests, poll taxes, and white primaries. The result was that "Black suffrage in Burke County was virtually nonexistent." Black voter registration in Burke County has increased following the [Act] to the point that some 38% of blacks eligible to vote are registered to do so. On that basis the District Court inferred that "past discrimination has had an adverse effect on black voter registration which lingers to this date." Past discrimination against blacks in education also had the same effect. [The] District Court found further evidence of exclusion from the political process. [E.g., past] discrimination had prevented blacks from effectively participating in Democratic Party affairs and in primary elections. The District Court [concluded] that historical discrimination had restricted the present opportuni-

---

3. The Columbus case, noted at p. 777 below, endorsed a systemwide school desegregation remedy. As in this case, the majority opinion in Columbus was written by Justice White. Note the similarity of his technique in Columbus and in this case (deference to lower court fact findings so long as the Court was generally satisfied that the lower court understood the proper legal standard).

ty of blacks effectively to participate in the political process. Evidence of historical discrimination is relevant to drawing an inference of purposeful discrimination, particularly in cases such as this one where the evidence shows that discriminatory practices were commonly utilized, that they were abandoned when enjoined by courts or made illegal by civil rights legislation, and that they were replaced by laws and practices which, though neutral on their face, serve to maintain the status quo.

Extensive evidence was cited by the District Court to support its finding that elected officials of Burke County have been unresponsive and insensitive to the needs of the black community, which increases the likelihood that the political process was not equally open to blacks. [The] District Court also considered the depressed socioeconomic status of Burke County blacks. [Although] finding that the state policy behind the at-large electoral system in Burke County was "neutral in origin," the District Court concluded that the policy "has been subverted to invidious purposes." As a practical matter, maintenance of the state statute providing for at-large elections in Burke County is determined by Burke County's state representatives, for the legislature defers to their wishes on matters of purely local application. The court found that Burke County's state representatives "have retained a system which has minimized the ability of Burke County Blacks to participate in the political system." The trial court considered, in addition, several factors which this Court has indicated enhance the tendency of multimember districts to minimize the voting strength of racial minorities. It found that the sheer geographic size of the [county] "has made it more difficult for Blacks to get to polling places or to campaign for office." The court also found the requirement that candidates run for specific seats enhances appellees' lack of access because it prevents a cohesive political group from concentrating on a single candidate. [None] of the District Court's findings underlying its ultimate finding of intentional discrimination appears to us to be clearly erroneous; and as we have said, we decline to overturn the essential finding of the District Court, agreed to by the Court of Appeals, that the at-large system in Burke County has been maintained for the purpose of denying blacks equal access to the political processes in the [county]. IV. We also find no reason to overturn the relief ordered by the District Court. Neither the District Court nor the Court of Appeals discerned any special circumstances that would militate against utilizing single-member districts. Where "a constitutional violation has been found, the remedy does not 'exceed' the violation if the remedy is tailored to cure the 'condition that offends the Constitution.' "

[Affirmed.][4]

Justice POWELL, with whom Justice REHNQUIST joins, dissenting.

I. [The lower courts] in this case based their findings of unconstitutional discrimination on the same factors held insufficient in Mobile. Yet the Court

---

4. The Mobile v. Bolden decision led to important legislative consequences. As Justice White noted in Rogers, the Mobile plurality had stated that the claim under § 2 of the Voting Rights Act "added nothing to [the] 15th Amendment claim" because § 2 was "intended to have an effect no different from that of the 15th Amendment itself." Efforts to change the § 2 standard to one of "effect" rather than "purpose" followed soon after the decision in Mobile. The House voted to substitute a "results" test, but the Senate balked. Ultimately, in extending the Voting Rights Act, Congress approved a compromise provision. President Reagan signed the extension on June 29, 1982—two days before Rogers v. Lodge was handed down. (No § 2 claim was involved in Rogers.) [For the terms of the compromise provision (clearly intended to change the interpretation of § 2 set forth in Mobile), see the note in chap. 10, sec. 4 at p. 990 below.]

now finds their conclusion unexceptionable. The Mobile plurality also affirmed that the concept of "intent" was no mere fiction, and held that the District Court had erred in "its failure to identify the state officials whose intent it considered relevant." Although the courts below did not answer that question in this case, the Court today affirms their decision. Whatever the wisdom of Mobile, the Court's opinion cannot be reconciled persuasively with that case. There are some variances in the largely sociological evidence presented in the two cases. But Mobile held that this *kind* of evidence was not enough. Such evidence, we found in Mobile, did not merely fall short, but "fell *far* short of showing that [an at-large electoral scheme was] 'conceived or operated [as a] purposeful devic[e] to further [racial] discrimination.' " Because I believe that Mobile controls this case, I dissent.

II.   The Court's decision today relies heavily on the capacity of the federal district courts—essentially free from any standards propounded by this Court— to determine whether at-large voting systems are "being maintained for the invidious purpose of diluting the voting strength of the black population." Federal courts thus are invited to engage in deeply subjective inquiries into the motivations of local officials in structuring local governments. Inquiries of this kind not only can be "unseemly"; they intrude the federal courts—with only the vaguest constitutional direction—into an area of intensely local and political concern. Emphasizing these considerations, Justice Stevens argues forcefully that the Court's focus of inquiry is seriously mistaken. I agree with much of what he says. As I do not share his views entirely, however, I write separately.

A.   As I understand it, Justice Stevens' critique of the Court's approach rests on three principles with which I am in fundamental agreement. First, it is appropriate to distinguish between "state action that inhibits an individual's right to vote and state action that affects the political strength of various groups." Under this distinction, this case is fundamentally different from cases involving direct barriers to voting. There is no claim here that blacks may not register freely and vote for whom they choose. This case also differs from one-man, one-vote cases [sec. 4A below], in which districting practices make a person's vote less weighty in some districts than in others. Second, I agree with Justice Stevens that vote dilution cases of this kind are difficult if not impossible to distinguish—especially in their remedial aspect—from other actions to redress gerrymanders. Finally, Justice Stevens clearly is correct in arguing that the standard used to identify unlawful racial discrimination in this area should be defined in terms that are judicially manageable and reviewable. In the absence of compelling reasons of both law and fact, the federal judiciary is unwarranted in undertaking to restructure state political systems. This is inherently a political area, where the identification of a seeming violation does not necessarily suggest an enforceable judicial remedy—or at least none short of a system of quotas or group representation. Any such system, of course, would be antithetical to the principles of our democracy.

B.   Justice Stevens would accommodate these principles by holding that subjective intent is irrelevant to the establishment of a case of racial vote dilution under the 14th Amendment. Despite sharing the concerns from which his position is developed, I would not accept this view. "The central purpose of the Equal Protection Clause [is] the prevention of official conduct discriminating on the basis of race." [Davis]. Because I am unwilling to abandon this central principle in cases of this kind, I cannot join Justice Stevens' opinion. Nonetheless, I do agree with him that what he calls "objective" factors should be the focus of inquiry in vote-dilution cases. Unlike the considerations on which the lower courts relied in this case and in Mobile, the factors identified by Justice Stevens as "objective" in fact are direct, reliable, and unambiguous indices of discriminatory *intent*. If we held, as I think we should, that the district courts must place primary reliance on these factors to establish discriminatory intent, we would prevent federal-court inquiries into the *subjective* thought processes of local officials—at least until enough objective evidence had been presented to warrant discovery into subjective motivations in this complex, politically charged area. By prescribing such a rule we would hold federal courts to a standard that was judicially manageable. And we would remain faithful to the central protective purpose of the Equal Protection Clause. In the absence of proof of discrimination by reliance on the kind of objective factors identified by Justice Stevens, I would hold that the factors cited by the Court of Appeals are too attenuated as a matter of law to support an inference of discriminatory intent. I would reverse its judgment on that basis. [The highlights of Justice STEVENS's lengthy dissent are summarized by Justice Powell. Justice Stevens emphasized: "I do not believe that [subjective intent] can [determine] constitutionality. Even if the intent of the political majority were the controlling constitutional consideration, I could not agree that the only political groups that are entitled to protection under the Court's rules are those defined by racial characteristics. [If] the standard [that] the Court applies today extends to all types of minority groups, it is either so broad that virtually every political device is vulnerable or it is so undefined that federal judges can pick and choose almost at will among those that will be upheld and those that will be condemned. [Any] suggestion that political groups in which black leadership predominates are in need of a permanent constitutional shield against the tactics of their political opponents underestimates the resourcefulness, the wisdom, and the demonstrated capacity of such leaders."]

HUNTER v. UNDERWOOD, 471 U.S. 222 (1985), struck down a section of the Alabama Constitution adopted in 1901. The provision disenfranchised all persons convicted of crimes involving "moral turpitude." Underwood, a white person, and Edwards, a black person, were blocked from the voter rolls because each had been convicted of presenting a worthless check. They brought suit claiming that the misdemeanors included within the provision were intentionally adopted to disenfranchise blacks on account of their race. The federal trial court rejected their claim, but the Court of Appeals reversed. Following the approach of Arlington Heights and Mt. Healthy, above, the Court of Appeals, after finding that discriminatory intent was a motivating factor for the provision, concluded that it would not have been enacted in the absence of the racially discriminatory motivation.[1] In affirming that ruling, Justice REHNQUIST's opinion noted that, even though the section "on its face is racially neutral," it clearly had a "racially discriminatory impact," because, as the Court of Appeals had noted, it had "disfranchised [sic] approximately ten times as many blacks as whites." Justice Rehnquist recognized "the difficulties in determining the actual motivations of the various legislators that produced a given decision," but found that the usual difficulties in identifying motivation did "not obtain in this case." He noted that, at the Alabama Constitutional

---

1. In delineating the proper approach under Arlington Heights and Mt. Healthy, the Court of Appeals stated: "To establish a violation of the [14th Amendment] in the face of mixed motives, plaintiffs must prove by a preponderance of the evidence that racial discrimination was a substantial or moti- vating [factor]. They shall then prevail unless the [defendants] prove by a preponderance of the evidence that the same decision would have resulted had the impermissible purpose not been considered." Recall the questions raised about the Mt. Healthy approach in footnote 1 to Arlington Heights, p. 759 above.

Convention of 1901, a "zeal for white supremacy ran rampant." Appellants argued that "the existence of a permissible motive for [the section], namely the disenfranchisement of poor whites, trumps any proof of a parallel impermissible motive." Justice Rehnquist rejected that argument: "Whether or not intentional disenfranchisement of poor whites would qualify as a 'permissible motive,' [it] is clear that where both impermissible racial motivation and racially discriminatory impact are demonstrated, Arlington Heights and Mt. Healthy supply the proper analysis. [An] additional purpose to discriminate against poor whites would not render nugatory the purpose to discriminate against all blacks, and it is beyond peradventure that the latter was a 'but-for' motivation for the enactment of the [section]." The Court also rejected the claim that here there was a "legitimate interest" in denying the franchise to those convicted of crimes involving moral turpitude, pointing out that the 1901 Convention had "selected such crimes as vagrancy, living in adultery, and wife beating that were thought to be more commonly committed by blacks."

Discriminatory purpose and the 13th Amendment. The question of whether the 13th Amendment, like the 14th, includes a purposeful discrimination requirement was raised in MEMPHIS v. GREENE, 451 U.S. 100 (1981), but the majority did not reach that issue. In Greene, black residents sued Memphis because it had closed a street at the border between a white and a black neighborhood. Justice STEVENS's opinion for the Court found that the street closing had only caused "slight inconvenience" to black motorists and was motivated simply by an interest in protecting the tranquility of a residential neighborhood. The "inconvenience" imposed by the City, he concluded, was not "in any sense comparable to the odious practice the 13th Amendment was designed to eradicate" and could not be considered as imposing a stigma amounting to a "badge of slavery." Justice WHITE, who concurred in the judgment, was the only member of the Court to reach the discriminatory purpose question and insisted that "purposeful racial discrimination" was essential to showing a violation of § 1982, the 13th Amendment-implementing law. (Justice MARSHALL's dissent, while purporting not to reach that issue, nevertheless noted that he disagreed with Justice White's position.) The issue left open by most of the Justices in Greene was settled by the Court two years later, in General Building Contractors Ass'n, Inc. v. Pa., 458 U.S. 375 (1982), where the majority (over the dissent of Justices Marshall and Brennan) held that, in an action under § 1981 (another post-Civil War 13th Amendment-implementing law), "proof of discriminatory intent" *is* required; the law does not reach "practices that merely result in a disproportionate impact on a particular class."

————

3. THE DE JURE–DE FACTO DISTINCTION IN THE SCHOOL DESEGREGATION CONTEXT

THE IMPLEMENTATION OF BROWN: FROM DESEGREGATION TO INTEGRATION

1. *Introduction.* We now return to the problem of school desegregation (pursued through Brown II, the 1955 implementation decision, in sec. 3A1 above). The notes that follow consider the aftermath of Brown II. These problems are considered here because they repeatedly raise, in a particular context, the distinction between purposeful discrimination and disadvantaging impacts or effects. Most relevantly, they raise a question similar to that raised

by Rogers v. Lodge, above: even though the Court continues to insist, at least in form, that purposeful, de jure discrimination is essential to establishing an equal protection claim, do its actual practices (e.g., deferring to lower court findings of purposeful discrimination so long as there is some indication that those courts were aware of the purposefulness requirement, as in Rogers v. Lodge above and in the Columbus and Dayton cases below, p. 777 suggest that the Court has in fact gone very far toward substituting an impact, de facto approach in some contexts?

After its promulgation of general guidelines in Brown II, the Court remained silent about implementation for several years. Enforcement of the desegregation requirement was left largely to lower court litigation—and to the political arena. During the early post-Brown years of widespread "massive resistance" in the South, the Court broke its silence only rarely, though firmly: in Cooper v. Aaron (1958; p. 25 above), all of the Justices signed an opinion reaffirming the Brown principle in the face of the official resistance in Little Rock, Arkansas. And in Griffin (1964; p. 752 above), the Court held unconstitutional an effort to avoid desegregation "by a combination of closed public schools and county grants to white children" to attend private schools. During the 1960s (after the doctrine of Brown had been accepted by the other branches of the national government, beginning with the Civil Rights Act of 1964), Court rulings on implementation came with greater frequency, specificity, and urgency. Court actions during the early sixties were limited to invalidations of impermissible student transfer plans and expressions of mounting impatience with the pace of desegregation. E.g., in 1963, the Court unanimously struck down minority-to-majority transfer plans in Goss v. Board of Education, 373 U.S. 683 (1963), holding unconstitutional "transfer plans [based] solely on racial factors which, under their terms, inevitably lead toward segregation of the students by race." But the pace remained slow during most of the sixties: widely used and officially approved "freedom of choice" plans had relatively little impact on the racial composition of schools. The first major reentry by the Court into implementation problems came in 1968, in the Green case (note 1 below), which rejected freedom of choice plans where they failed to produce a "unitary, nonracial system of public education." And beginning with the Swann case in 1971 (p. 775), the Court has repeatedly spoken about remedial requirements in detail.

In all of these cases—even the 1970s ones involving northern communities—the Court has purported to speak solely about remedies for prior *purposeful* discrimination: dismantling the dual school systems established by state-wide de jure segregation in the South; undoing the effects of hostile racial action by local officials in the North. But the Court proved willing to pursue the consequences of past de jure discrimination very far, in time and in impact. And the Court began to place an increasing emphasis on *results* in measuring the success of efforts to eliminate past discrimination. In examining those developments, consider whether the purportedly "remedial" decisions in fact rest on changing perceptions of substantive rights. Do the far-reaching demands for eliminating past discrimination make the distinction between de jure and de facto segregation increasingly unjustifiable, as Justice Powell suggested in his dissent in Keyes, p. 776 below? Or is the continued insistence on finding some formal evidence of past de jure discrimination an indication that condemnation of purposeful discrimination exhausts the command of the 14th Amendment in the school segregation area as in most others?[1]

1. For a useful general survey of the post-Brown developments, see Wilkinson, From Brown to Bakke—The Supreme Court and School Integration: 1954–1978 (1979).

In the 1950s, a lower court, echoing the dominant theme at the time of Brown, stated that the Constitution "does not require integration. It merely forbids [segregation]." Is that still true, in view of the emphasis in Green, below, on producing a "unitary" system? In view of the handling of the purposeful discrimination requirement in the Columbus and Dayton cases, p. 777 below? Note the distinction between "process-oriented" and "result-oriented" antidiscrimination remedies suggested by Owen Fiss: the process orientation "emphasizes the purification of the decisional process," banning decisions based on racial criteria; the result-oriented approach "emphasizes the achievement of certain results"—for example, achieving racial integration rather than merely refraining from racially-based pupil assignments. Do the implementation decisions which follow indicate a shift from process orientation to result orientation? Does the Constitution justify an exclusive emphasis on result, whether or not there was past impurity in the process—the impurity of purposeful discrimination?

2. *"Freedom of choice."* The decision in GREEN v. COUNTY SCHOOL BOARD, 391 U.S. 430 (1968), marked a major turning point in the Court's role in—and requirements for—desegregation. For the first time since Brown II, the Court issued a detailed opinion on the question of remedies. And that opinion, in focusing on the *effects* rather than the purpose and good faith of desegregation efforts, raised important new questions about underlying substantive doctrine as well as the remedies. At the time of Green, freedom of choice plans had become commonplace in the South. School districts argued that good faith plans of that variety, employing no improper pressures on students and parents, adequately complied with the Brown mandate. Opponents of the plans emphasized that desegregation under "freedom of choice" had not significantly changed the racial composition of schools and insisted that the constitutional mandate was not merely the elimination of formal racial barriers but the abolition of racially identifiable schools. Thus, the freedom of choice issue in the context of formerly de jure segregated schools sharply presented the question of whether the 14th Amendment merely required desegregation (the elimination of formal racial barriers) or compelled integration (the creation of racially mixed schools). The Court's answer was clear: its emphasis shifted from "purification of the decisional process" to "achievement of a certain result,"[2] albeit on the theory that achieving results was the only acceptable evidence that the process had been purified.

For critical evaluations of the post-Brown developments, see Graglia, Disaster by Decree—The Supreme Court Decisions on Race and the Schools (1976), and Kurland, "'Brown v. Board of Education Was the Beginning': The School Desegregation Cases in the United States Supreme Court, 1954–1979," 1979 Wash.U.L.Q. 309; cf. Gunther, "Of Rights and Remedies, Legitimacy and Competence," 1979 Wash.U.L.Q. 815. For a survey of the experience in the lower courts in the years immediately after Brown, see McKay, "With All Deliberate Speed," 31 N.Y.U.L.Rev. 991 (1956) and 43 Va.L.Rev. 1205 (1957). For a review of the problems in the years before the Court reentered the picture, see Bickel, "A Decade of School Desegregation," 64 Colum.L.Rev. 193 (1964). For a subsequent evaluation by that observer, see The Supreme Court and the Idea of Progress (1970). See generally Read, "Judicial Evolution of the Law of School Integration Since [Brown]," 39 Law & Contemp.Probs. 7 (1975).

2. The growing emphasis on affirmative obligations to overcome past de jure segregation, on results rather than process, had come somewhat earlier in lower courts and in HEW guidelines issued under the 1964 Civil Rights Act. See, e.g., the extensive discussion of the "duty to desegregate duty to integrate" distinction in United States v. Jefferson County Board of Education, 372 F.2d 836 (5th Cir.1966), and Comment, "The Courts, HEW, and Southern School Desegregation," 77 Yale L.J. 321 (1967).

The Green case involved a small school district with two schools, in a county where about half the population was black and where there was no significant residential segregation. The district had adopted a freedom of choice plan in 1965 to remain eligible for federal financial aid. After three years of operation, no white child had chosen to attend the former black school and about 85% of the black children remained in the all-black school. (Enormous pressure had been put upon black parents who sought to exercise their "freedom of choice.") Under these circumstances, the unanimous Court found the plan to be an inadequate compliance with desegregation requirements. Justice BRENNAN's opinion emphasized that "[r]acial identification of the system's schools" remained "complete" and that "the transition to a unitary, nonracial system of public education was and is the ultimate end to be brought about." He stated: "It is against this background [that] we must measure the effectiveness of respondent School Board's 'freedom-of-choice' plan to achieve that end. The School Board contends that it has fully discharged its obligation by adopting a plan by which every student, regardless of race, may 'freely' choose the school he will attend. The Board attempts to cast the issue in its broadest form by arguing that its 'freedom-of-choice' plan may be faulted only by reading the 14th Amendment as universally requiring 'compulsory integration,' a reading it insists the wording of the Amendment will not support. But [what] is involved here is the question whether the Board has achieved the 'racially nondiscriminatory school system' Brown II held must be effectuated. [School] boards [then] operating state-compelled dual systems [were] clearly charged with the affirmative duty to take whatever steps might be necessary to convert to a unitary system in which racial discrimination would be eliminated root and branch. [It] is relevant that [the Board's] first step did not come [until] 10 years after Brown II directed the making of a 'prompt and reasonable start.' [Such] delays are no longer tolerable. [The] burden on a school board today is to come forward with a plan that promises realistically to work, and promises realistically to work *now*. [There] may well be instances in which [freedom of choice] can serve as an effective device. [But] if there are reasonably available other ways, such for illustration as zoning, promising speedier and more effective conversion to a unitary, nonracial school system, 'freedom of choice' must be held unacceptable." Given the experience here, with a dual system still in existence and the availability of other courses such as zoning, the school officials were required to "fashion steps which promise realistically to convert promptly to a system without a 'white' school and a 'Negro' school, but just schools."[3] In rural and small town areas with no significant residential segregation, the elimination of "freedom of choice" plans and their variants and the adoption of geographic zoning largely eliminated racially identifiable schools. But in large Southern cities with substantial residential segregation— as in the North—geographic zoning alone could not substantially alter the racial composition of schools. In 1971, the Court turned to the problem of metropolitan areas in the South, in Swann, which follows.

---

3. See also Monroe v. Board of Commissioners, 391 U.S. 450 (1968), a companion case to Green, invalidating a "free transfer" plan in a geographically zoned system. Though the plan was not limited to minority-to-majority transfers, it permitted students to return, "at the implicit invitation of the Board," to "the comfortable security of the old, established discriminatory pattern." The Court was unpersuaded by the school officials' argument that without the "free transfer" choice, "white students will flee the school system altogether." (On the problem of "white flight" and resegregation, note, e.g., Bickel, The Supreme Court and the Idea of Progress (1970), and Graglia, Disaster by [Decree] (1976).)

SWANN v. CHARLOTTE–MECKLENBURG BOARD OF EDUCATION, 402 U.S. 1 (1971): By 1971 the Court produced its last major opinion in a Southern desegregation case and spoke in detail about the remedies that were available to assure integration. The case arose in the school district covering the Charlotte, North Carolina, metropolitan area, which had been wholly segregated, de jure, at the time of Brown in 1954. In 1965, the district adopted a court-approved desegregation plan including geographic zoning and free transfers. By 1969, about half of the black students were in formerly white schools, but the remainder attended virtually all-black schools. After Green, the district court ordered the school authorities to prepare a more effective plan. Ultimately, the lower court appointed its own expert and accepted his plan, which involved some redrawing of district lines as well as some busing of elementary school students in both directions. The Court, in a unanimous decision by Chief Justice BURGER, affirmed the district court's order. He emphasized that "[o]nce a right and a violation have been shown, the scope of a district court's equitable powers to remedy past wrongs is broad. [But] it is important to remember that judicial powers may be exercised only on the basis of a constitutional violation." With that background, the Chief Justice turned to the problem areas regarding the central issue in the case, that of student assignments.

Addressing the problem of racial balances or racial quotas, the Court stated: "If we were to read the ruling of the district court to require, as a matter of substantive constitutional right, any particular degree of mixing, that approach would be [disapproved]. The constitutional command to desegregate schools does not mean that every school in every community must always reflect the racial composition of the school system as a whole." But the district court's order was affirmed because here, the use made of mathematical ratios "was no more than a starting point in the process of shaping a remedy, rather than an inflexible requirement. [As] we said in Green, the school authority's remedial plan [is] to be judged by its effectiveness. Awareness of the racial composition of the whole school system is likely to be a useful starting point in shaping a remedy to correct past constitutional violations." For similar reasons, the Court, addressing the question of one-race schools, stated that, although the existence of one-race schools did not demonstrate a constitutional violation, "in a system with a history of segregation the need for remedial criteria of sufficient specificity to assure a school authority's compliance with its constitutional duty warrants a presumption against schools that are substantially disproportionate in their racial composition." In order to produce a unitary system, courts had broad discretion to use "frank—and sometimes drastic—gerrymandering of school districts and attendance zones." And the grouping of schools and the creation of districts that "are neither compact nor contiguous" were permissible remedies. Turning finally to the controversial issue of busing students to schools outside their neighborhoods, the Court, after noting that no rigid guidelines were possible about the scope of permissible transportation, concluded that there was "no basis for holding that the local school authorities may not be required to employ bus transportation as one tool of school desegregation." The Court added, however, that "[a]n objection of transportation of students may have validity when the time or distance of travel is so great as to risk either the health of the children or significantly impinge on the educational process." The Court once again emphasized the flexibility of equitable remedies. The Court ended by noting that, "at some point, school authorities 'should have achieved full compliance with [Brown I].' The systems will then be 'unitary' in the sense required by our [decisions]. It does not follow that the communities served by such systems will remain demographically stable, for in a growing, mobile society, few will do so. Neither school authorities nor district courts are constitutionally required to make year-by-year adjustments of the racial composition of student bodies once the affirmative duty to desegregate has been [accomplished]. and racial discrimination through official action is eliminated from the system. [For an application of the guidelines in this passage to the problem of resegregation (because of population movements) of a previously judicially desegregated school system, see Pasadena City Bd. of Educ. v. Spangler, 427 U.S. 424 (1976), a rare example of a Court holding in the 1970s that a District Judge had imposed excessively harsh intradistrict desegregation remedies.] This does not mean that federal courts are without power to deal with future problems; but in the absence of a showing that either the school authorities or some other agency of the State has deliberately attempted to fix or alter demographic patterns to affect the racial composition of the schools, further intervention by a district court should not be necessary." (In a companion case noted below, the Court held unconstitutional North Carolina's Anti–Busing Law prohibiting school assignments on the basis of race: that purportedly "color blind" directive was found to be an impermissible restraint on the implementation of Brown and Swann, above. North Carolina State Board of Education v. Swann, 402 U.S. 43 (1971).) For contrasting comments on the Swann ruling on busing, compare the praise in Fiss, "The Charlotte–Mecklenburg Case—Its Significance for Northern School Desegregation," 38 U.Chi.L.Rev. 697 (1971), with the doubts expressed in Kaplan, "Segregation Litigation in the Schools—Part II: The General Northern Problem," 58 Nw.U.L.Rev. 157 (1963). Note as well the material on desegregation in the North, in the next group of notes.

DESEGREGATION IN THE NORTH

1. *Broad intradistrict remedies for de jure segregation.* The Denver school case, KEYES v. SCHOOL DISTRICT, 413 U.S. 189 (1973), was the Court's first decision on school desegregation in the North. This ruling came at a time when, as a consequence of the results-oriented emphasis of Green and Swann, the success of desegregation in the formerly de jure segregated South had become considerable, in sharp contrast to the North and the West: a significantly larger percentage of black students in the South were attending majority white schools than in the non-Southern states, were de jure statewide segregation had never been the norm. Justice BRENNAN's majority opinion purported to adhere to the de jure-de facto distinction. (He stated: "We emphasize that the differentiating factor between de jure and so-called de facto segregation [is] *purpose* or *intent* to segregate.") But he set forth criteria that would facilitate a finding of purposeful discrimination in Northern districts that did not have a background of state-mandated segregation; and he announced standards that would permit court orders for districtwide remedies to rest on findings of intentional discrimination in only *part* of the district. The immediate charges of purposeful discrimination were limited to one portion of the citywide Denver school district. The lower court found that the school board (by such techniques as manipulation of attendance zones and schoolsite selection) had "engaged over almost a decade after 1960 in an unconstitutional policy of deliberate racial segregation" with respect to schools in the Park Hill area, and ordered their desegregation. There was also a heavy concentration of black students in the core city area, but the lower court found that the school board had no deliberate segregative policy as to that area and refused to order desegregation there. Justice Brennan's opinion provided guidelines that would permit *district-*

wide desegregation on the basis of the purposeful segregation finding regarding the Park Hill area. He sketched two routes to such a result. First, "where plaintiffs prove that the school authorities have carried out a systematic program of segregation affecting a substantial proportion of the students, schools, teachers and facilities," a finding that the entire district is a dual, segregated one is authorized, absent a showing that the district is divided into clearly unrelated units. And once such a districtwide finding is made, the usual remedies that were developed in the southern context, from Brown II to Swann, are applicable. He explained that "common sense dictates the conclusion that racially inspired school board actions have an impact beyond the particular schools that are the subjects of those actions." Second, even if the areas within a district are treated separately, a showing of intentional segregation in one area may be probative as to intentional segregation in other areas. Accordingly, the finding as to Park Hill was usable in the efforts to prove segregative intent in the core city area. He added: "We have no occasion to consider [here] whether a 'neighborhood school policy' of itself will justify racial or ethnic concentrations in the absence of a finding that school authorities have committed acts constituting de jure segregation."[1]

Justice REHNQUIST was the only member of the Court in total disagreement with the majority. He concluded: "The Court has taken a long leap [in] equating the district-wide consequences of gerrymandering individual attendance zones in a district where separation of the races was never required by law with statutes or ordinances in other jurisdictions which did so require. It then adds to this potpourri a confusing enunciation of evidentiary rules in order to make it more likely that the trial court will on remand reach the result which the Court apparently wants it to reach." He also criticized the "drastic extension" of Brown in Green—an extension which "was barely, if at all, explicated in the latter opinion." He elaborated: "To require that a genuinely 'dual' system be disestablished, in the sense of the assignment of a child to a particular school is not made to depend on his race, is one thing. To require that school boards affirmatively undertake to achieve racial mixing in schools where such mixing is not achieved in sufficient degree by neutrally drawn boundary lines is quite obviously something else." (See also his dissents in the Dayton and Columbus cases, which follow.)

2. *Demonstrating "discriminatory purpose" and imposing intradistrict systemwide remedies in 1979: Reaffirmation of Keys, or drastic expansion?* Despite considerable speculation that the Court would take the occasion to cut back on Keyes, the majority affirmed Court of Appeals decisions mandating broad desegregation remedies in COLUMBUS BOARD OF EDUCATION v. PENICK, 443 U.S. 449 (1979), and DAYTON BOARD OF EDUCATION v. BRINKMAN (Dayton II), 443 U.S. 526 (1979). Justice White's majority opinion showed great deference to the Court of Appeals and rejected the argument that the lower court had misused Keyes. To some of the dissenters, by contrast, the majority's "Delphic" pronouncements marked "a radical new approach to desegregation cases in systems without a history of statutorily mandated

1. An elaborate separate opinion by Justice Powell went considerably further on the issue of rights as well as on remedies. As to the former, he advocated abandonment of the de jure-de facto distinction and urged recognition of a uniform, nationwide right to have local school boards operate "integrated school systems." (See note 3 below.) On the question of remedies, Justice Powell urged greatly reduced use of massive busing as a desegregation tool. In a separate opinion, Justice Douglas agreed with Justice Powell on the issue of rights: he, too, advocated scrapping the de jure-de facto distinction. Chief Justice Burger concurred only in the majority's result. (Justice Rehnquist dissented, as noted below. Justice White did not participate.)

separation of the races." As Justice Rehnquist's dissent in Columbus claimed: "Keyes [is] not overruled, yet [its "essential message" is] ignored." His dissent in Dayton added that the "Court's cascade of presumptions in this case sweeps away the distinction between de facto and de jure segregation." Objecting to the Court's "cavalier treatment of causality," he claimed that the majority's approach "reliev[ed] school desegregation plaintiffs from any showing of a causal nexus between intentional segregative actions and the conditions they seek to remedy." (Justice White denied that charge.)

Justice WHITE's majority opinion in Columbus endorsed the conclusion of the lower federal courts that the school authorities' conduct "not only was animated by an unconstitutional, segregative purpose, but also had current, segregative impact that was sufficiently systemwide to warrant the [system-wide] remedy." Though there had been no statutorily mandated segregation in the 20th century, the trial court found that in 1954, when Brown I was decided, "the Columbus Board was not operating a racially neutral, unitary school system, but was conducting 'an enclave of separate, black schools on the near east side of Columbus' and that '[t]he then-existing racial separation was the direct result of cognitive acts or omissions of those school board members and administrators who had originally intentionally caused and later perpetuated the racial isolation.'" With that finding of de jure segregation in 1954 as the underpinning, Justice White agreed with the lower courts' statement that the Board had, since Brown II, "been under a continuous constitutional obligation to disestablish its dual school system." He emphasized: "[The Board] has pointed to nothing in the record persuading us that at the time of trial the dual school system and its effects had been disestablished." He also approved the District Court's finding that, in the years since 1954, "there had been a series of Board actions and practices[2] that could not 'reasonably be explained without reference to racial concerns' and that 'intentionally aggravated, rather than alleviated,' racial separation in the schools." Justice White rejected the claim that the desegregation decree rested on misapprehension of the controlling law. It was argued, for example, that the courts below had ignored Davis and Arlington Heights by considering the "purposeful discrimination" requirement satisfied "if it were shown that disparate impact would be the natural and foreseeable consequence of the practices and policies of the Board, which, it is said, is nothing more than equating impact with intent, contrary to the controlling precedent." In Justice White's view, however, the trial court had simply "correctly noted that actions having foreseeable and anticipated dispa-rate impact are relevant evidence to prove the ultimate fact, forbidden pur-pose." That approach "stayed well within the requirements of [Davis] and Arlington Heights." Moreover, there had been no "misuse of Keyes": "There was no undue reliance here on the inferences permitted by Keyes, or upon those recognized by Swann. Furthermore, the Board was given ample opportu-nity to counter the evidence of segregative purpose and current, systemwide impact, and the findings of the courts below were against it in both respects."

In the Dayton case, unlike in the Columbus case, the District Court had decided *against* the plaintiffs, finding that they "had failed to prove that acts of intentional segregation over 20 years old had any current incremental segre-gative effects." The Court of Appeals, emphasizing the existence of a dual school system at the time of Brown I, reversed, and ordered a systemwide

---

2. The improper "actions and prac-tices" since 1954 included "the intentionally segregative use of optional attendance zones, discontinuance of attendance areas, and boundary changes; and the selection of sites for new school construction that had the fore-seeable and anticipated effect of maintaining the racial separation of the schools."

remedy. Justice White's opinion stated: "Given intentionally segregated schools in 1954, [the] Court of Appeals was quite right in holding that the Board was thereafter under a continuing duty to eradicate the effects of that system [Columbus] and that the systemwide nature of the violation furnished prima facie proof that current segregation in the Dayton schools was caused at least in part by prior intentionally segregative official acts. Thus, judgment for the plaintiffs was authorized and required absent sufficient countervailing evidence by the defendant school officials. [Keyes; Swann.]" He noted, moreover, that the Dayton Board "had engaged in many post-Brown actions that had the effect of increasing or perpetuating segregation." He added: "The District Court [ignored] this compounding of the original constitutional breach on the ground that there was no direct evidence of continued discriminatory purpose. But the measure of a post-Brown conduct of a school board under an unsatisfied duty to liquidate a dual system is the effectiveness, not the purpose, of the actions in decreasing or increasing the segregation caused by the dual system. As was clearly established in Keyes and Swann, the Board [had] an affirmative responsibility to see that pupil assignment policies and school construction and abandonment practices 'are not used and do not serve to perpetuate or re-establish the dual school system' [Columbus], and the Board has a 'heavy burden' of showing that actions that increased or continued the effects of the dual system serve important and legitimate ends."

Justice STEWART, joined by Chief Justice Burger, concurred in the result in the Columbus case (where the District Court had found for the plaintiffs) but dissented in Dayton. To him, the critical difference was that the Court of Appeals had "ignored the crucial role of the federal district courts in school desegregation litigation." He also disagreed with important elements of the majority's approach, arguing that "the Court has attached far too much importance in each case to the question whether there existed a 'dual school system' in 1954." The Board's duty to desegregate in 1954, he claimed, "does not justify a complete shift of the normal burden of proof" in a 1970s case. In his view, current racial separation in the schools could not be presumed to have been caused by unconstitutional acts committed as long ago as 1954. Turning to the question of the basis for systemwide remedies in post–1954 developments, he concluded that "[t]he plaintiffs in the Columbus case, unlike those in the Dayton case, proved what the Court in Keyes defined as a prima facie case" which the Board had not rebutted. Justice REHNQUIST, joined by Justice Powell, submitted the longest dissent in the Columbus case, and reiterated his views in a brief dissenting statement (again joined by Justice Powell) in Dayton. In Columbus, he claimed that the lower courts had "emasculate[d] the key determinants set down in Keyes": "The lower courts' methodology would all but eliminate the distinction between de facto and de jure segregation and render all school systems captives of a remote and ambiguous past." In exploring the implications of the majority opinions, he offered two suggestions for fathoming them. First, "the Court, possibly chastened by the complexity and emotion that accompanies school desegregation cases, wishes to relegate the determination of a [constitutional violation] in any plan of pupil assignment, and the formulation of a remedy for its violation, to a judgment of a single District Judge," with both "discriminatory purpose" and "systemwide violation" to be treated "as talismanic phrases which, once invoked, warrant only the most superficial scrutiny by appellate courts." The second and only other possible interpretation of the opinions, he insisted, was a "literal reading," and that he found "even more disquieting": "Such a reading would require embracing a novel analytical approach to school segregation in systems without a history of statutorily mandated separation of the races—an approach that would have dramatic consequences for urban school systems in this country." In his view, there were "glaring deficiencies both in the Court's new framework and in its decision to subject [all school systems to a] sweeping racial balance remedy."

Justice Rehnquist attacked the majority's emphasis on 1954 violations to justify current systemwide remedies, insisting that "[a]s a matter of history, case law, or logic, there is nothing to support the novel proposition that the primary inquiry in school desegregation cases involving systems without a history of statutorily mandated racial assignment is what happened in those systems before 1954. As a matter of history, 1954 makes no more sense as a benchmark—indeed it makes *less* sense—than 1968, 1971 or 1973. Perhaps the latter year has the most to commend it, [because] in Keyes this Court first confronted the problem of school segregation in the context of systems without a history of statutorily mandated separation of the races." In Keyes, causality was central: the School Board's past acts were relevant only if "segregation resulting from those actions continues to exist." Justice Rehnquist added: "That inquiry is not central under the approach approved by the Court today. Henceforth, the question is apparently whether pre–1954 acts contributed in some unspecified manner to segregated conditions that existed in 1954. If the answer is yes, then the only question is whether the school board has exploited all integrative opportunities that presented themselves in the subsequent 25 years. If not, a systemwide remedy is in order despite the plaintiff's failure to demonstrate a link between those past acts and current racial imbalance." To him, the majority's analysis of the alleged post–1954 violations underlined its "departure from established doctrines of causation and discriminatory purpose." He commented: "[O]bjective evidence must be carefully analyzed, for it may otherwise reduce the 'discriminatory purpose' requirement to a 'discriminatory impact' test by another name." Claiming that "foreseeability was not one kind of evidence, but the whole ball game" in the District Court's examination of post–1954 actions in the Columbus case, he thought it "somewhat misleading for the Court to refer to these actions as in some sense independent of the constitutional duty it suggests that the Columbus Board assumed in 1954."

In another dissent, Justice POWELL, joined by Justice Rehnquist, found the majority opinions "profoundly disturbing": they seemed "remarkably insensitive to the now widely accepted view that a quarter of a century after [Brown I], the federal judiciary should be limiting rather than expanding the extent to which courts are operating the public school systems of our country." He argued that experience in many cities demonstrated that it was "an illusion" to expect school boards to be "capable of bringing about and maintaining the desired racial balance." He insisted, moreover, that judicial mandates would probably generate "responses that will defeat the integrative purpose of the courts' order": "Parents, unlike school officials, are not bound by these decrees and may frustrate them through the simple expedient of withdrawing their children from a public school system in which they have lost confidence. [W]here inner city populations comprise a large proportion of racial minorities and surrounding suburbs remain white, [the] demonstrated effect of compulsory integration is a substantial exodus of whites from the system." He accordingly urged: "The time has come for a thoughtful re-examination of the proper limits of the role of courts in confronting the intractable problems of public education in our complex society."[3]

3. For a critical comment on the Dayton and Columbus cases, see Kitch, "The Return of Color–Consciousness to the Constitution: Weber, Dayton, and Columbus," 1979

3. *How much vitality does the de jure-de facto distinction retain in school desegregation cases?* In the Northern intradistrict desegregation cases in the preceding notes, the Court has, at least in form, adhered to the "purposeful discrimination" requirement. Yet in Keyes, Columbus, and Dayton, the Court has also been quite lenient in allowing inferences of purposeful discrimination, in much the same way (and by use of very much the same technique of deferring to the "fact findings" of lower federal courts) as it had been in Rogers v. Lodge, above. In examining these Northern school cases, consider whether the Court's guidelines regarding burdens of proof, presumptions, and deference to lower federal courts are consistent with the "purposefulness" criteria articulated in such cases as Davis, Arlington Heights, and Feeney. Is there merit to Justice Rehnquist's dissenting claim in the 1979 cases that the "lower courts' methodology [approved by the Court] would all but eliminate the distinction between de facto and de jure segregation"? Is there justification for applying more lenient standards regarding proof of purposeful discrimination in the school desegregation (and representational) context than in such earlier contexts as employment and zoning?

a. Consider also the partial anticipation (and elaboration) of Justice Rehnquist's 1979 dissents in Justice POWELL's arguments in his separate opinion in the Denver school case, KEYES v. SCHOOL DISTRICT, 413 U.S. 189 (1973) (see p. 776 above). In Keyes, Justice Powell claimed that the modern desegregation cases since Green in 1968 had undercut the justifications for maintaining a constitutional distinction between de jure and de facto school desegregation. Justice Powell stated: "The focus of the school desegregation problem has now shifted from the South to the country as a whole. Unwilling and footdragging as the process was in most places, substantial progress toward achieving integration has been made in Southern States. No comparable progress has been made in many nonsouthern cities, [primarily] because of the de facto/de jure distinction nurtured by the courts and accepted complacently by many of the same voices which denounced the evils of segregated schools in the South. But if our national concern is for those who attend such schools, [we] must recognize that the evil of operating separate schools is no less in Denver than in Atlanta. In my view we should abandon a distinction which long since has outlived its time, and formulate constitutional principles of national rather than merely regional application. [The] doctrine of Brown [did] not retain its original meaning. In a series of decisions extending from 1954 to 1971 the concept of state neutrality was transformed into the present constitutional doctrine requiring affirmative state action to desegregate school systems. The keystone case was Green. [The] language in Green imposing an affirmative duty to convert to a unitary system was appropriate [in the rural setting of that case]. There was, however, reason to question to what extent this duty would apply in the vastly different factual setting of a large city with extensive areas of residential [segregation]. [The] doubt as to whether the affirmative-duty concept would flower into a new constitutional principle of general application was laid to rest by Swann. [Swann] refrained from even considering whether the evolution of constitutional doctrine from Brown I to Green/Swann undercut whatever logic once supported the de facto/de jure distinction. In imposing on metropolitan southern school districts an affirmative duty, entailing large-scale transportation of pupils, to eliminate segregation in the schools, the Court required these districts to alleviate conditions which in large part did *not* result

Sup.Ct.Rev. 1. Kitch argued that the remedies imposed by these cases "focus not on racial discrimination but on redressing racial [imbalance]. They acknowledge that separate but unequal treatment under law is warranted by our history, because they deal with classes of persons and not with individuals." (See also the materials in sec. 3E.)

from historic, state-imposed de jure segregation. Rather, the familiar root cause of segregated schools in *all* the biracial metropolitan areas of our country is essentially the same: one of segregated residential and migratory patterns the impact of which on the racial composition of the schools was often perpetuated and rarely ameliorated by action of public school authorities. This is a national, not a southern, phenomenon. And it is largely unrelated to whether a particular State had or did not have segregative school laws. Whereas Brown I rightly decreed the elimination of state-imposed segregation in that particular section of the country where it did exist, Swann imposed obligations on southern school districts to eliminate conditions which are not regionally unique but are similar both in origin and effect to conditions in the rest of the [country].

"The Court's decision today, while adhering to the de jure/de facto distinction, will require the application of the Green/Swann doctrine of 'affirmative duty' to the Denver School Board despite the absence of any history of state-mandated school segregation. [I] concur in the Court's position that [if] the affirmative-duty doctrine is sound constitutional law for Charlotte, it is equally so for Denver. I would not, however, perpetuate the de jure/de facto distinction nor would I leave to petitioners the initial tortuous effort of identifying 'segregative acts' and deducing 'segregative intent.' I would hold, quite simply, that where segregated public schools exist within a school district to a substantial degree, there is a prima facie case that the duly constituted public authorities, [usually, the school board,] are sufficiently responsible[4] to warrant imposing upon them a nationally applicable burden to demonstrate they nevertheless are operating a genuinely integrated school system. The principal reason for abandonment of the de jure/de facto distinction is that, in view of the evolution of the holding in Brown I into the affirmative-duty doctrine, the distinction no longer can be justified on a principled basis. [And] the facts deemed necessary to establish de jure discrimination present problems of subjective intent which the courts cannot fairly resolve. [In] the evolutionary process since 1954, decisions of this Court have added a significant gloss to [the] original right [in Brown]. Although nowhere expressly articulated in these terms, I would now define it as the right, derived from [equal protection], to expect that once the State has assumed responsibility for education, local school boards will operate *integrated school systems* within their respective districts. This means that school authorities [must] make and implement their customary decisions with a view toward enhancing integrated school opportunities. [A] system would be integrated in accord with constitutional standards if the responsible authorities had taken appropriate steps to (i) integrate faculties and administration; (ii) scrupulously assure equality of facilities, instruction, and curriculum opportunities throughout the district; (iii) utilize their authority to draw attendance zones to promote integration; and (iv) locate new schools, close old ones, and determine the size and grade categories with this same objective in mind. Where school authorities decide to undertake the transportation of students, this also must be with integrative opportunities in mind. [Courts] judging past school board actions with a view to their *general integrative effect* will be best able to assure an absence of [racial] discrimination while avoiding the murky, subjective judgments inherent in the Court's search

---

4. "A prima facie case of constitutional violation exists when segregation is found to a substantial degree in the schools of a particular district. It is recognized, of course, that this term is relative and provides no precise standards. But circumstances, demographic and otherwise, vary from district to district and hard-and-fast rules should not be formulated. The existence of a substantial percentage of schools populated by students from one race only, or predominantly so populated, should trigger the inquiry." [Footnote by Justice Powell.]

for 'segregative intent.' [School board] decisions obviously are not the sole cause of segregated school conditions. But if, after such detailed and complete public supervision, substantial school segregation still persists, the presumption is strong that the school board, by its acts or omissions, is in some part responsible [and] this Court is justified in finding a prima facie case of a constitutional violation. The burden then must fall on the school board to demonstrate it is operating an 'integrated school system.' [In] addition, there are reasons of policy and prudent judicial administration which point strongly toward the adoption of a uniform national rule. [Today's decision,] emphasizing [the] elusive element of segregative intent, will invite numerous desegregation suits in which there can be little hope of uniformity of result. [We] should acknowledge that whenever public school segregation exists to a substantial degree there is prima facie evidence of a constitutional violation by the responsible school board."

b. Justice Powell's argument in Keyes rested largely on the Court's increasing emphasis, since Green, on *results* in cases from southern communities in which formal de jure school segregation once existed—and on the increasingly tenuous search for evidence of deliberate discrimination in the North. (Despite Justice Powell's argument against the de jure-de facto distinction in Keyes, recall that he has been at the forefront in insisting on the "purposeful discrimination" requirement outside the school segregation field.) Despite Justice Powell's conclusions from the ever lighter "purpose" burden in the school desegregation cases, the course of decisions from Green to Columbus and Dayton may simply show, as Justice Rehnquist argues, that the Court has gone too far in imposing affirmative obligations on school authorities. Can it be argued that, for reasons other than Justice Powell's, de facto segregation should be considered a constitutional wrong? To what extent do the factors relied on in Brown I (to demonstrate the harm inherent in school segregation) apply to the de facto situation? Can it be argued that Brown rested as much on the *impact* of segregated schools in diminishing educational opportunities and in fostering feelings of inferiority as on the purpose behind the dual school system? Is the stigma stemming from de facto segregated schools as great as that from de jure segregated schools? Is there similar impairment of educational opportunity? Is condemnation of de facto segregation justified by the purposes of the 14th Amendment? Can de facto school desegregation be considered unconstitutional without undercutting the usual "purposeful discrimination" requirement? Can de facto school segregation be considered unconstitutional without bringing all de facto "discriminations," all differential impacts of governmental action, within the constitutional ban? Can the 14th Amendment be read as safeguarding not only the purity of the process—the elimination of racial hostility from decisionmaking—but also the quality of results, the assurance of equality of condition?[5] Has school segregation law moved steadily, and justifiably, from concern with elimination of racial factors in student assignments to achievement of racial integration as the constitutionally mandated result?

4. *Limits on judicial power to remedy de jure segregation.* a. *Interdistrict remedies.* In 1974, a sharply divided Court addressed the question of the permissible extent of multidistrict remedies for situations in which de jure segregation had been found to exist in only one of the districts. MILLIKEN v.

5. For an extensive examination of developments and problems, see Goodman, "De Facto School Segregation: A Constitutional and Empirical Analysis," 60 Calif.L.Rev. 275 (1972). See also Karst, "Not One Law at Rome and Another at Athens: The Fourteenth Amendment in Nationwide Application," 1972 Wash.U.L.Q. 383.

BRADLEY, 418 U.S. 717 (1974). Milliken reversed lower court orders that had directed interdistrict remedies in the Detroit metropolitan area after a finding of de jure segregation in the city of Detroit. The 5-4 majority concluded "that absent an inter-district violation there is no basis for an inter-district remedy." Milliken marked the limit of the extent to which the Court would back desegregation efforts in Northern metropolitan areas and announced a major obstacle to such efforts. In the Detroit area, the city constituted one school district and there were separate districts for the suburban areas. Blacks were concentrated in the city. The trial court found that there was de jure segregation in the Detroit school system because of acts of state and city officials, and the Court saw no reason to disturb that finding in view of the 1973 standards of Keyes. But the trial court, in fashioning remedies, concluded that desegregation could not be effective if it were limited to the city boundaries and accordingly issued an order including 53 surrounding school districts. In justifying its multidistrict remedy, the lower court pointed not only to the practical obstacles to a narrower order, but also to other considerations: the Detroit district was an agent of the state, and the state had power to prevent segregation there—by changing district boundaries, for example. Moreover, the state had contributed to segregation in the city—e.g., by prohibiting the use of state funds for busing in the city. Concluding that "district lines are simply matters of political convenience and may not be used to deny constitutional rights," the trial judge designated 53 of the 85 suburban school districts and Detroit as the "desegregation area" and, without any finding that there had been de jure segregation in any of the suburban districts, directed the preparation of "an effective desegregation plan" for the entire area. The Court reversed, insisting that the remedy exceeded the scope of the constitutional wrong.

Chief Justice BURGER's majority opinion concluded: "Boundary lines may be bridged where there has been a constitutional violation calling for interdistrict relief, but the notion that school district lines may be casually ignored or treated as a mere administrative convenience is contrary to the history of public education in our country." In delineating the limited circumstances in which interdistrict remedies were permissible, he stated: "Before the boundaries of separate and autonomous school districts may be set aside by consolidating the separate units for remedial purposes or by imposing a cross-district remedy, it must first be shown that there has been a constitutional violation within one district that produces a significant segregative effect in another district. Specifically it must be shown that racially discriminatory acts of the state or local school districts, or of a single school district, have been a substantial cause of inter-district segregation.* Thus an inter-district remedy might be in order where the racially discriminatory acts of one or more school districts caused racial segregation in an adjacent district, or where district lines have been deliberately drawn on the basis of race. [Conversely,] without an inter-district violation and inter-district effect, there is no constitutional wrong calling for an inter-district remedy." He added: "To approve the remedy ordered by the [lower court] would impose on the outlying districts, not shown to have committed any constitutional violation, a wholly impermissible remedy based on a standard not hinted at [in] any holding of this Court." He was not persuaded by the argument that the participation of state officials in maintain-

---

* Is this burden of proof allocation consistent with Keyes? Are there good reasons for different presumptions of segregative effects in intradistrict rather than an interdistrict situation? See generally Sedler, "Metropolitan Desegregation in the Wake of [Milliken]," 1975 Wash.U.L.Q. 535, and Strickman, "School Desegregation at the Crossroads," 70 Nw.U.L.Rev. 725 (1975).

ing de jure segregation in Detroit justified interdistrict relief. Even assuming that there was significant state participation, "established doctrine" required focusing on particular districts. He continued: "The constitutional right of the Negro respondents residing in Detroit is to attend a unitary school system in that district. [The] view of the dissenters, that the existence of a dual system *in Detroit* can be made the basis for a decree requiring cross-district transportation of pupils cannot be supported on the grounds that it represents merely the devising of a suitably flexible remedy for the violation of rights already established by our prior decisions. It can be supported only by drastic expansion of the constitutional right itself, an expansion without any support in [either] principle or precedent."

The most extensive dissent came from Justice MARSHALL, joined by Justices Douglas, Brennan, and White. He found the decision to be "a giant step backwards" and an "emasculation" of equal protection. Justice WHITE's dissent, joined by the other dissenters, stated: "The core of my disagreement is that deliberate acts of segregation and their consequences will go unremedied, not because a remedy will be infeasible or unreasonable in terms of the usual criteria governing school desegregation cases, but because an effective remedy would cause what the Court considers to be undue administrative inconvenience to the State. The result is that [Michigan] has successfully insulated itself from its duty to provide effective desegregation remedies by vesting sufficient power over its public schools in its local school districts." He insisted that the Court had fashioned "out of whole cloth an arbitrary rule that remedies for constitutional violations occurring in a single Michigan school district must stop at the school district line. Apparently, no matter how much less burdensome or more effective [in] many respects, such as transportation, the metropolitan plan might be, the school district line may not be crossed."

Contrast with the disapproval of an interdistrict school desegregation remedy in Milliken the Court's unanimous holding in Hills v. Gautreaux, 425 U.S. 284 (1976), authorizing consideration of a metropolitan area remedy in a housing discrimination case. Justice Stewart's opinion stated: "Nothing in the Milliken decision suggests a per se rule that federal courts lack authority to order parties found to have violated the Constitution to undertake remedial efforts beyond the municipal boundaries of the city where the violation occurred." In Hills, the U.S. Department of Housing and Urban Development (HUD) had violated constitutional and statutory prohibitions of racial discrimination in connection with the selection of sites for public housing in Chicago. (HUD was found to have assisted the Chicago Housing Authority (CHA) in carrying out a racially discriminatory housing program.) The Court found that, in those circumstances, a federal court's remedial order against HUD could properly extend to activities beyond Chicago's city boundaries. The Court rejected both of HUD's major arguments: first, that a metropolitan area order "would constitute the grant of relief incommensurate with the constitutional violation to be repaired"; second, "that a decree regulating HUD's conduct beyond Chicago's boundaries" would unduly interfere with local autonomy. In rejecting HUD's second contention, the Court concluded that "there is no basis for the [claim] that court-ordered metropolitan relief in this case would be impermissible as a matter of law under the Milliken decision. [Here], by contrast, the metropolitan relief order would not consolidate or in any way restructure local units."

b. *Enforcing compliance with court orders: The extent of the federal courts' remedial powers.* In a widely publicized case in 1990, the Court addressed the scope of federal judicial power to enforce compliance with court-ordered remedies for de jure segregation. In MISSOURI v. JENKINS, 495 U.S.

33 (1990), Missouri and the Kansas City, Missouri, School District were found to have operated a segregated school system within the district. Under a desegregation plan approved by the district court, expenditures of over $450 million were necessary. Various state law provisions prevented the school district from raising taxes to finance the 25% share of desegregation costs for which the district court held it liable. The district court thereupon ordered a significant increase in the district's property tax rates, despite the state law limitations. The appellate affirmed the remedy but stated that in the future the lower court should not set the property tax rate itself but should instead authorize the school district to do so and enjoin the operation of state laws standing in the way. The Court overturned the judicial imposition of the tax increase as an abuse of judicial discretion but upheld the power of the trial court to direct the school district to levy its own taxes and to enjoin state laws barring such levies. Justice WHITE's majority opinion found that the district court's order "contravened the principles of [federal/state] comity that must govern the exercise of the [court's] equitable discretion in this area." The trial court should not have ordered the tax increase directly without assuring itself that "no permissible alternative" was available. Here, there was: "the very one outlined by the Court of Appeals[—]it could have authorized or required [the district] to levy property taxes at a rate adequate to fund the desegregation remedy and could have enjoined the operation of state laws that would have prevented [this]. The difference between the two approaches is far more than a matter of form. Authorizing and directing local government institutions to devise and implement remedies not only protects the function of those institutions but, to the extent possible, also places the responsibility for solutions [upon] those who have themselves created the problems." He rejected Missouri's Tenth Amendment argument, noting that the Fourteenth Amendment "permits a federal court to disestablish local government institutions that interfere with its commands." Nor did Article III of the Constitution bar such a district order in a proper case. He concluded that a "local government with taxing authority may be ordered to levy taxes in excess of the limits set by state statute where there is reason based in the Constitution for not observing the statutory limitation. [Where] a particular remedy is required, the State cannot hinder the process by preventing a local government from implementing that remedy." Justice KENNEDY, joined by Chief Justice Rehnquist and Justices O'Connor and Scalia, agreed that the district court had no power to impose a tax directly, but disagreed with respect to the Court of Appeals modification of the remedy. He insisted that this was the equivalent of imposing a tax, and that such action was beyond the Art. III power of the federal courts. He concluded that, "as a prerequisite to considering a taxation order," there must be "a finding that any remedy less costly than the one at issue would so plainly leave the violation unremedied that its implementation would itself be an abuse of discretion." Here, he claimed, there had been no such showing.

c. *Measuring compliance with long-standing decrees: The 1990s Court's unwillingness to support continuing judicial involvement.* As the years pass, and as overt resistance becomes rarer, questions arose about the temporal limits of a desegregation decree. At what point is it possible to say that a decree, originally entered to remedy de jure segregation, is no longer necessary? Recall the Pasadena case (1976; p. 786 above). Does compliance with a decree bring judicial involvement to an end unless there is evidence of new de jure segregation?

i. These questions came to the Court in BOARD OF ED. OF OKLAHOMA CITY v. DOWELL, 498 U.S. 237 (1991). Oklahoma City had at the time of Brown v. Board of Education operated an explicitly segregated school system.

In 1972 the District Court ordered systemwide busing. That plan produced substantial integration in the public schools, and in 1977 the court entered an order terminating the case and ending its jurisdiction, stating: "The School Board, under the oversight of the Court, has operated the Plan properly, and the Court does not foresee that the termination of its jurisdiction will result in the dismantlement of the Plan or any affirmative action by the defendant to undermine the unitary school system so slowly and painfully accomplished over the 16 years during which the cause has been pending before this court." In part because of demographic changes that had "led to greater burdens on young black children," the school board in 1984 reintroduced a neighborhood school system for grades K–4, although allowing any student to transfer from a school in which he or she was in the majority to a school in which he or she would be in the minority. A year later, the challengers argued that the new plan would reinstitute segregation. The District Court refused to reopen the case, but the Court of Appeals reversed, holding that the 1972 decree remained in force and imposed an "affirmative duty [not] to take any action that would impede the process of disestablishing the dual system and its effects." The Supreme Court, however, reversed the Tenth Circuit, with Chief Justice REHNQUIST writing for the majority: "From the very first, federal supervision of local school systems was intended as a temporary measure to remedy past discrimination." Emphasizing that both Brown and Green had stressed the idea of a "transition," the Chief Justice concluded that "injunctions entered in school desegregation cases [are] not intended to operate in perpetuity. [The] legal justification for displacement of local authority by an injunctive decree in a school desegregation case is a violation of the Constitution by the local authorities. Dissolving a desegregation decree after the local authorities have operated in compliance with it for a reasonable period of time recognizes that 'necessary concern for the important values of local control of public school systems' dictates that a federal court's regulatory control of such systems not extend beyond the time required to remedy the effects of past intentional discrimination." The Court acknowledged that a "district court need not accept at face value the profession of a school board which has intentionally discriminated that it will cease to do so in the future." But it noted that the personnel of school boards changes over time, and that "a school board's compliance with previous court orders is obviously relevant" in determining whether to modify or dissolve a desegregation decree. The Court remanded the case for just such a determination of good faith compliance as of 1985. If such good faith compliance were found, and if "the vestiges of past discrimination" had as of that date been eliminated, then the school board could be deemed to have been released from the injunction: "A school district which has been released from an injunction imposing a desegregation plan no longer requires court authorization for the promulgation of policies and rules regulating matters such as assignment of students and the like, but of course remains subject to the mandates of [equal protection]. If the Board was entitled to have the decree terminated as of 1985, the District Court should then evaluate the Board's decision to implement [the neighborhood schools program] under appropriate equal protection principles. [Davis; Arlington Heights.]"

Justice MARSHALL, joined by Justices Blackmun and Stevens, dissented, chastising the majority for suggesting that after 65 years of official segregation, "13 years of desegregation was enough. [I] believe a desegregation decree cannot be lifted so long as conditions likely to inflict the stigmatic injury condemned in Brown I persist and there remain feasible methods of eliminating such conditions. [By] focusing heavily on present and future compliance with [equal protection], the majority's standard ignores how the stigmatic harm identified in Brown I can persist even after the State ceases actively to enforce segregation. [Our] school-desegregation jurisprudence establishes that the *effects* of past discrimination remain chargeable to the school district regardless of its lack of continued enforcement of segregation, and the remedial decree is required until those effects have been finally eliminated. [Our] cases have imposed on school districts an unconditional duty to eliminate *any* condition that perpetuates the message of racial inferiority inherent in the policy of state-sponsored segregation. The racial identifiability of a district's schools is such a condition. [In] a district with a history of state-sponsored school segregation, racial separation, in my view, *remains* inherently unequal."

ii. The Court returned to the issue a year later in FREEMAN v. PITTS, 503 U.S. 467 (1992), and followed Dowell in approving partial withdrawal of judicial supervision of a school system that had long operated under a desegregation order. The school system at issue was the DeKalb County (Georgia) School System, with approximately 73,000 students. The system had entered a consent decree in 1969 and had operated under relatively inactive judicial supervision from that date until 1986, when it moved to dismiss the decree, contending that it had successfully desegregated its school system and replaced a dual school system with a unitary one. The District Court found that although there was considerably greater racial imbalance in the schools than there had been in 1969, this was a function of demographic changes rather than any of the vestiges of a previously dual system. The District Court noted that the existence of effective desegregation for a few years after 1969 was strong evidence of the lack of a connection between the previous segregation and the current racial imbalance. However, although the trial court found that there were no current vestiges of segregation with respect to student assignments and physical facilities, there was as yet no unitary system in the areas of teacher and principal assignments, resource allocation, and some aspects of quality of education. As a result, it withdrew from supervision in the former areas, but refused to dismiss the decree. The Court of Appeals reversed on the issue of the unitary status of the system, holding that only when *all* of the factors specified in Green had been satisfied simultaneously could a school district be considered to have desegregated its system. The Supreme Court, however, with Justice KENNEDY writing for the majority, concluded that the District Court's views about desegregation were substantially correct, approved its incremental approach, and concluded that a partial dismissal of the decree would therefore be appropriate. In holding that, in the course of supervising a desegregation plan, a district court has the authority to relinquish supervision of a school district in incremental stages, the Court stated: "We have said that the [district court's] end purpose must be to remedy the violation and in addition to restore state and local authorities to the control of a school system that is operating in compliance with the Constitution. Partial relinquishment of judicial control, where justified by the facts of the case, can be an important and significant step in fulfilling the district court's duty to return [the] control of schools to local authorities." (Justice BLACKMUN, joined by Justices Stevens and O'Connor, concurred in the judgment, emphasizing that judicial withdrawal from active supervision in some areas did not indicate total withdrawal of jurisdiction. Justice SOUTER also submitted a concurring opinion.)

iii. In UNITED STATES v. FORDICE, 505 U.S. 717 (1992), the Court refused to distinguish universities from primary and secondary schools in holding that the state university system of Mississippi had the same affirmative obligation to dismantle its dual system that primary and secondary school systems had under Green. Writing for the Court, Justice WHITE relied heavily on statistics showing that the state still maintained a system of higher education dominated by racially identifiable institutions. He rejected the state's argument that establishing a true freedom of choice system was sufficient in the higher education context even though not in the primary and secondary school context. He stated: "If the State perpetuates policies and practices traceable to its prior system that continue to have segregative effects—whether by influencing student enrollment decisions or by fostering segregation in other facets of the university system—and such policies are without sound educational justification and can be practicably eliminated, the State has not satisfied its burden of proving that it has dismantled its prior system. Such policies run afoul of [equal protection], even though the State has abolished the legal requirement that whites and blacks be educated separately and has established racially neutral policies not animated by a discriminatory purpose." Justice O'CONNOR concurred, and wrote separately to make clear that even "if the State shows that maintenance of certain remnants of its prior system is essential to accomplish its legitimate goals, then it still must prove that it has counteracted and minimized the segregative impact of such policies to the extent possible." Justice THOMAS also concurred, but noted that in his view there could be a " 'sound educational justification' for maintaining historically black colleges as such. Despite the shameful history of state-enforced segregation, these institutions have survived and flourished. [It] would be ironic, to say the least, if the institutions that sustained blacks during segregation were themselves destroyed in an attempt to combat its vestiges." Justice SCALIA concurred in the judgment in part and dissented in part, objecting to the application of the Green standard to colleges and universities.

iv. In 1995, Missouri v. Jenkins, the Kansas City case, returned to the Supreme Court once more. In MISSOURI v. JENKINS, 115 S.Ct. 2038 (1995), the 5-4 decision of the Court held that a federal court could not order salary increases and remedial education programs on the ground that "student achievement levels were still at or below the national norms at many grade levels." Chief Justice REHNQUIST's majority opinion reiterated that "the nature and scope of the remedy are to be determined by the violation, [which] means that federal-court decrees must directly address and relate to the constitutional violation itself." He noted that, while "a mandate for significant educational improvement, both in teaching and in facilities, may have been justified originally, its indefinite extension is not." He concluded that the lower court's remedy "results in so many imponderables and is so far removed from the task of eliminating the racial identifiability of the [Kansas City] schools that we believe it is beyond the admittedly broad discretion of the District Court." Justice SOUTER, joined by Justices Stevens, Ginsburg, and Breyer, dissented largely because they objected to the Court's taking on issues not properly presented on the record. Justice GINSBURG's separate dissent emphasized the brevity of the remedial period compared to the length and extent of the segregation that had preceded it.

RESTRUCTURING THE POLITICAL PROCESS (AND REPEALING REMEDIES) THAT DISADVANTAGE MINORITIES

Introduction. Although the Court continues to insist that a state is free to repeal antidiscrimination laws and affirmative action programs such as those considered in sec. 3E below, the Court has occasionally barred such action where it involves restructuring of the state's political processes in a way that disadvantages minorities, usually by incorporating the repeals into state constitutional provisions. Recall that in Romer v. Evans (p. 737 above), Colorado's highest court had struck down the state's Amendment 2 by relying on such cases as Hunter v. Erickson and Washington v. Seattle School Dist., both below. The Court, however, explicitly relied on other grounds in holding Amendment 2 unconstitutional. Consider carefully the justifications offered in the Hunter and Seattle School District cases. Are they persuasive? Is the Court of the 1990s likely to endorse such analyses?

HUNTER v. ERICKSON, 393 U.S. 385 (1969), held unconstitutional a city charter amendment adopted by the voters after the Akron City Council had adopted a fair housing ordinance. The charter amendment required that any ordinance regulating real estate transactions "on the basis of race, color, religion, national origin or ancestry must first be approved by a majority" of the voters. Justice WHITE's majority opinion struck down the amendment because it made "an explicitly racial classification" which "obviously made it substantially more difficult to secure enactment of ordinances [covered by the amendment]." Was there truly a "suspect" classification properly triggering strict scrutiny in this case? Justice White conceded that the provision drew "no distinctions among racial and religious groups," but insisted that it did disadvantage "those who would benefit from laws barring [racial and other] discriminations." He added that, although the law "on its face treats Negro and white, Jew and gentile in an identical manner, the reality is that the law's impact falls on the minority. [The state] may no more disadvantage any particular group by making it more difficult to enact legislation in its behalf than it may dilute any person's vote"; the amendment in short placed "special burdens on racial minorities within the governmental process." Justice HARLAN, joined by Justice Stewart, concurred in the ruling, emphasizing that Akron had not "attempted to allocate governmental power on the basis of any general principle," but had instead sought to make it more difficult for minorities to achieve legislation, and therefore had to "bear a far heavier burden of justification, a burden it could not meet." Justice BLACK was the sole dissenter. [Consider whether the Hunter situation truly involved "an explicitly racial classification," or whether it rested on the discriminatory effect of the amendment. If the latter, can Hunter be reconciled with Washington v. Davis?]

Thirteen years later, a 5-4 majority relied heavily on Hunter in WASHINGTON v. SEATTLE SCHOOL DIST., 458 U.S. 457 (1982). The case involved Washington's Initiative 350, adopted soon after the Seattle School Board implemented a mandatory busing plan to reduce de facto school segregation. The Initiative provided (with some exceptions) that "no school board [shall] directly or indirectly require any student to attend a school other than the school which is geographically nearest or next nearest the student's place of residence." (Under one of its exceptions, the Initiative did *not* bar judicial orders requiring mandatory busing in order "to eliminate constitutionally prohibited de jure segregation.") Justice BLACKMUN's majority opinion relied heavily on Hunter. He stated Hunter's central principle as follows: although "the political majority may generally restructure the political process to place obstacles in the path of [anyone] seeking to secure the benefits of governmental action, [a] different analysis is required when the State allocates governmental power non-neutrally, by explicitly using the *racial* nature of a decision to determine the decisionmaking process. State action of this [kind] 'places *special* burdens on racial minorities within the governmental process,' thereby 'making it *more* difficult for certain racial and religious minorities [than for other members of the community] to achieve legislation that is in their interest.' " He concluded: "Initiative 350 must fall because it does 'not attemp[t] to allocate governmental power on the basis of any general principle.' Instead, it uses the racial nature of an issue to define the governmental decisionmaking structure, and thus imposes substantial and unique burdens on racial minorities."[1] Justice Blackmun rejected the argument that the initiative had no racial overtones: "[It] is beyond reasonable dispute [that] the initiative was enacted ' "because of," not merely "in spite of," its adverse effects upon' busing for integration. [Feeney.]" Justice Blackmun emphasized that the practical effect of Initiative 350 was to work a reallocation of power similar to the kind condemned in Hunter. He explained: "Those favoring the elimination of de facto school segregation now must seek relief from the state legislature or from the statewide electorate. Yet authority over all other student assignment decisions, as well as over most other areas of educational policy, remains vested in the local school board. [As] in Hunter, then, the community's political mechanisms are modified to place effective decisionmaking authority over a racial issue at a different level of government." He conceded that "the simple repeal or modification of desegregation or anti-discrimination laws, without more, never has been viewed as embodying a presumptively invalid racial classification." But Initiative 350, he insisted, "works something more than the 'mere repeal' of a desegregation law by the political entity that created it. It burdens all future attempts to integrate Washington schools in districts throughout the State, by lodging decisionmaking authority over the question at a new and remote level of government. [One] group cannot be subjected to a debilitating and often insurmountable disadvantage."[2]

Justice POWELL's dissent, joined by Chief Justice Burger and Justices Rehnquist and O'Connor, objected to "the Court's unprecedented intrusion into the structure of a state government." He emphasized that there was no federal constitutional duty "to adopt mandatory busing [in] the absence of [de jure segregation]." Thus, "a neighborhood school policy and a decision *not* to assign students on the basis of their race does not offend the 14th Amendment." He noted that the school district itself constitutionally could have canceled its integration program at any time, "yet this Court holds that neither the legislature nor the people of Washington could alter what the District had decided. [The Constitution] does not require such a bizarre result." He insisted that Hunter was "simply irrelevant" : The Washington initiative "simply does not place unique political obstacles in the way of racial minorities. In this case, unlike in Hunter, the political system has *not* been redrawn or altered. [Under the Court's] unprecedented theory of a vested constitutional right to local decisionmaking, the State apparently is now forever barred from addressing the perplexing problems of how best to educate fairly *all* children in a multiracial society where, as in this case, the local school board has acted first."

1. Justice Blackmun rejected the dissent's charge that, under the majority's view, "the State's attempt to repeal a desegregation program creates a racial classification, while 'identical action' by the Seattle School Board does not": "It is the State's race-conscious restructuring of its decisionmaking process that is impermissible, not the simple repeal of the Seattle Plan."

2. Justice Blackmun also rejected the argument that Hunter had in effect been overruled. The defenders of the initiative argued that "Hunter applied a simple 'disparate impact' analysis," contrary to the post-Hunter purposeful discrimination approach of Washington v. Davis and Arlington Heights. But this, Justice Blackmun insisted, "misapprehends the basis of the Hunter doctrine": "There is one immediate and crucial difference between Hunter and the [purposeful discrimination cases]": Cases such as Arlington Heights involved facially neutral classifications; the Hunter provision "dealt in explicitly racial terms. [When] the political process or the decisionmaking mechanism used to *address* racially conscious legislation [is] singled out for peculiar and disadvantageous treatment, the governmental action plainly 'rests on "distinctions based on race." ' "

Contrast the Seattle School District case with a companion one, CRAW-FORD v. LOS ANGELES BOARD OF EDUCATION, 458 U.S. 527 (1982). In Crawford, Justice Powell, who had dissented in the Seattle case, wrote for an 8-1 majority in upholding a California constitutional amendment designed to limit the state courts' power to order busing to that exercised by the federal courts. The 1979 amendment provided that state courts could not order mandatory busing unless a federal court would do so to remedy a violation of equal protection. The amendment came in the wake of the California courts' practice of ordering busing to remedy de facto school segregation. In rejecting an equal protection attack on the state constitutional amendment, Justice Powell disagreed with the challengers' claim that (as he phrased it) "once a State chooses to do 'more' than the 14th Amendment requires, it may never recede. We reject an interpretation of the 14th Amendment so destructive of a state's democratic processes and of its ability to experiment." He thought it would be "paradoxical" to conclude that California, by adopting federal equal protection standards that provided for mandatory busing, had thereby violated the 14th Amendment. Justice Powell rejected the challengers' claim that the amendment employed an "explicit racial classification" and imposed a "race-specific" burden on minorities seeking to vindicate state-created rights. The claim was that, by limiting the power of state courts to enforce the state-created right to desegregated schools in de facto segregation situations, Proposition I created a "dual court system" which discriminated on the basis of race. But Justice Powell insisted that Proposition I did *not* "embody a racial classification": "It neither says nor implies that persons are to be treated differently on account of their race. [The] benefit it seeks to confer—neighborhood schooling—is made available regardless of race in the discretion of school boards. Indeed, even if [the amendment] had a racially discriminatory effect, in view of the demographic mix of the [Los Angeles] District, it is not clear which race or races would be affected the most or in what way." (White students were in a minority in the district.) Moreover, "discriminatory purpose" was necessary to show a 14th Amendment violation. He added that "the simple repeal or modification of desegregation or anti-discrimination laws, without more, never has been viewed as embodying a presumptively invalid racial classification."

The challengers' central argument, however, was that the amendment was not a "mere repeal" but rather was invalid under Hunter. Justice Powell replied: "We do not view Hunter as controlling here, nor are we persuaded by [the] characterization of [the amendment] as something more than a mere repeal." It was less than a "repeal" of California's equal protection provision, since the California Constitution still placed upon school boards "a greater duty to desegregate than does the 14th Amendment." He added: "[In short,] having gone beyond the requirements of the Federal Constitution, the State was free to return in part to the standard prevailing generally throughout the United States." Finally, Justice Powell rejected the challengers' claim that the challenged provision, if facially valid, "was nonetheless unconstitutional because enacted with a discriminatory purpose." The state court had found that the voters might have been motivated by the amendment's stated purposes, "chief among them the educational benefits of neighborhood schooling," and that they might also have considered "that the extent of mandatory busing [actually] was aggravating rather than ameliorating the desegregation problem." The state court characterized the challengers' "claim of discriminatory intent on the part of millions of voters as but 'pure speculation.'" Justice Powell saw "no reason to differ with these conclusions," pointing by analogy to the Court's deference to a state court's identification of discriminatory purpose in Reitman v. Mulkey (chap. 10, p. 948, below).[3] Justice MARSHALL, the sole dissenter, insisted at

---

3. A concurring opinion by Justice BLACKMUN, joined by Justice Brennan, em-phasized the "critical distinctions" between this case and the Seattle one. In Crawford, by

length that this case was indistinguishable from the Seattle one. And he insisted that California's provision was even more vulnerable than the Hunter scheme: "Proposition I, by denying full access to the only branch of government [the judiciary] that has been willing to address this issue meaningfully, is far worse for those seeking to vindicate the plainly unpopular cause of racial integration in the public schools than a simple reallocation of an often unavailable and unresponsive legislative process."

Some more questions about the restructuring cases. Was Crawford truly distinguishable from the Seattle case? Was the result in the Seattle case compelled by Hunter? Consider Sunstein's comment, in "Public Values, Private Interest, and the Equal Protection Clause," 1982 Sup.Ct.Rev. 127, suggesting that heightened scrutiny in Hunter was justified "by a suspicion that improper justifications [were] at work," but noting that "arguments against busing are less likely to be animated by racial bias than are arguments against legislation preventing discrimination in housing. Seattle might therefore have been treated differently from Hunter on the ground that invidious motives may well not have been at work." In the Colorado Amendment 2 case, were the arguments based on Hunter and Seattle more persuasive than the rationale the Supreme Court used in Romer v. Evans, above? Similar arguments have been raised in pending litigation challenging California's Proposition 209, adopted by the voters in 1996. Prop. 209 bars not only discrimination against women and minorities but also prohibits "preferences"—e.g., affirmative action programs—based on race or gender. (The central portion of Prop. 209—the California Civil Rights Initiative—provides: "The state shall not discriminate, or grant preferential treatment to, any individual or group on the basis of race, sex, color, ethnicity, or national origin in the operation of public employment, public education, or public contracting.") Are arguments based on Romer v. Evans, Reitman v. Mulkey, Hunter, or the Seattle case likely to be successful in challenging Prop. 209? For an argument that they should be, see Manheim, "Smoke and Mirrors: Providing Only An Illusion of Neutrality, Prop. 209 Violates [Equal Protection]," San Francisco Daily Journal, Dec. 9, 1996, p. 4.

E. THE BENIGN USE OF RACIAL CRITERIA: AFFIRMATIVE ACTION AND RELATED PROGRAMS

Introduction. To what extent may racial classifications be used for "benign" purposes—purposes designed to aid rather than disadvantage minorities? The problems of "benign" or "reverse" discrimination, of affirmative action and preferential programs, are difficult and controversial. The most pervasive problems are: Should the strict scrutiny of racial classifications be relaxed when programs are adopted are employed for the asserted purpose of aiding minorities? What justifications will suffice to permit the benign use of racial criteria? The earlier materials in this section frequently stated that racial classifications are "suspect" and are permissible only for "compelling" justifications. Is benignness of purpose a compelling justification? Or is a level of scrutiny lower than "strictness" appropriate when the objective is benign? When *may* government be color-conscious rather than color-blind? When *must* it be color-conscious? Can courts adequately distinguish between truly benign purposes

contrast to Seattle, there had been no restructuring of the state's decisionmaking process.

and hostile ones masquerading behind a "benign" facade? May benign classifications be used to remedy only the effects of past purposeful state discrimination? Or may they also be used to compensate for past societal injustices? May they be future-oriented? Questions such as these have produced recurrent controversy in the context of benign *racial* classifications. What should be the bearing of the Court's treatment of benign *gender*-based classifications (recall p. 716 above) when the Justices confront benign *racial* programs? Can less-than-strict scrutiny of benign racial classifications be defended on the ground that the 14th Amendment's original purpose was directed at hostile legislation imposing a stigma on the disadvantaged minority? Or does the evolution of equal protection criteria since the 19th century warrant a broader suspicion of *all* racial classifications, benign as well as hostile, so that strict scrutiny is warranted even in the benign context? These problems generated an enormous flood of commentary even before the first major Court consideration of the issues in Bakke in 1978 (p. 795 below). The controversy has continued ever since. Bakke and the later cases air the contending positions at length. These introductory materials are limited to some of the relevant background materials available to the Court when it confronted the Bakke problem.

1. *Color consciousness to remedy purposeful discrimination: The school desegregation context.* As the materials in sec. 3D3 demonstrated, there is at least one area where government need not be color-blind and indeed must be color-conscious. The Court's requirements for eliminating the effects of de jure segregation have increasingly emphasized the *results* of desegregation efforts—results measured by the racial identification of schools. Moreover, in a companion case to Swann, the Court unanimously struck down a state law mandating color-blindness in student assignments as an undue interference with desegregation requirements. North Carolina State Board of Education v. Swann, 402 U.S. 43 (1971). That endorsement of color-consciousness is not limited to the remedying of de jure segregation; race-consciousness is generally permissible to remedy the effects of past purposeful discrimination.

2. *Preferential admissions programs.* Preferential admissions programs in higher education, adopted without specific findings of past purposeful discrimination, began to be challenged in the courts in the early 1970s. The Court avoided decision on a challenge to a law school preferential admissions program in DeFUNIS v. ODEGAARD, 416 U.S. 312 (1974): in a 5-4 decision, the Court dismissed the case as moot on the ground that DeFunis, who had attended the law school while the case was in the courts, was about to graduate. Only Justice DOUGLAS reached the merits. His opinion contained strong passages condemning racial factors in admissions programs but also suggested possible cultural bias in the ordinary admissions criteria and urged that the case be remanded. On the broad constitutional issue, he opposed reliance on racial criteria even for benign purposes and insisted that the 14th Amendment required "the consideration of each application *in a racially neutral way.*" Several years passed before the Court was compelled to reach the merits—and in Bakke, which follows, it divided sharply. In the period between DeFunis and Bakke, the solutions proposed in academic commentary ranged over the entire spectrum.[1] For example, Ely suggested: "When the group that controls the decision making process classifies so as to advantage a minority and disadvantage itself, the reasons for being unusually suspicious, and, consequently,

---

1. See, e.g., Kaplan, "Equal Justice in an Unequal World: Equality for the Negro—The Problem of Special Treatment," 61 Nw. U.L.Rev. 363 (1966); "Developments," 82 Harv.L.Rev. 1065 (1969); Ely, "The Constitutionality of Reverse Racial Discrimination," 41 U.Chi.L.Rev. 723 (1974).

employing a stringent brand of review are lacking." Kaplan argued that "any legal classification by race weakens the government as an educative force"; "[p]reference for Negroes can [be] expected to be a major factor in preventing the education [toward color-blindness] we are trying to bring about through a host of other laws." Others offered a range of intermediate positions between those two polar ones.[2] What justifications should suffice when a preferential program is subjected to a heightened level of scrutiny, whether of the strict or intermediate variety?

3. *Benign programs and objecting members of minority groups.* What if doubts about the benignness of a program arise because of alleged harm to individual members of the supposedly aided minority?[3] One aspect of that problem has arisen in connection with quota and "tipping point" programs designed to promote integrated housing. E.g., may racial exclusion of a black person from a housing project be justified on the ground that the exclusion is pursuant to a quota designed to provide integrated housing for blacks generally? See, e.g., United States v. Starrett City Associates, 840 F.2d 1096 (2d Cir.1988), cert. denied, 488 U.S. 946 (1988).[4] Even if the benign purpose of a program is adequately demonstrated, must it be measured against the costs of the stigma that may be asserted by some members of the benefited group? More generally, may courts view programs that are clearly pro-integration in purpose and effect as "benign" when some segments of the "benefited" minority assert that separation is desirable in the long run or at least temporarily, to develop the group's cohesiveness and pride? Do the school desegregation cases commit the Court to adhering to integration as the only legitimate goal, and to opposing separateness as an ideal, whether it is called "separatism" or "segregation"?

Regents of Univ. of California v. Bakke

438 U.S. 265, 98 S.Ct. 2733, 57 L.Ed.2d 750 (1978).

Justice POWELL announced the judgment of the Court.

This case presents a challenge to the special admissions program of the petitioner, the Medical School of the University of California at Davis, which is designed to assure the admission of a specified number of students from certain minority groups. [The Supreme Court of California held] the special admissions program unlawful, [enjoined] petitioner from considering the race of any applicant, [and ordered Bakke's] admission. For the reasons stated in the following opinion, I believe that so much of the judgment of the California court

---

2. For a sampling of the extensive pre-Bakke commentary on the constitutionality of color conscious admissions programs, see O'Neil, "Preferential Admissions: Equalizing the Access of Minority Groups to Higher Education," 80 Yale L.J. 699 (1971); Graglia, "Special Admission of the 'Culturally Deprived' to Law School," 119 U.Pa.L.Rev. 351 (1970); Bell, "In Defense of Minority [Admissions Programs]," 119 U.Pa.L.Rev. 364 (1970); Sandalow, "Racial Preferences in Higher [Education]," 42 U.Chi.L.Rev. 653 (1975); and Greenawalt, "Judicial Scrutiny of

'Benign' Racial Classifications in Law School Admissions," 75 Colum.L.Rev. 559 (1975).

3. See, e.g., Carter, Reflections of an Affirmative Action Baby (1991).

4. See generally Bittker, "The Case of the Checker–Board [Ordinance]," 71 Yale L.J. 1387 (1962); Navasky, "The Benevolent Housing Quota," 6 Howard L.J. 30 (1960); Ackerman, "Integration for Subsidized Housing and the Question of Racial Occupancy Controls," 26 Stan.L.Rev. 245 (1975); and Note, "Benign Steering and Benign [Quotas]," 93 Harv.L.Rev. 938 (1980).

as holds petitioner's special admissions program unlawful and directs that respondent be admitted to the Medical School must be affirmed. For the reasons expressed in a separate opinion, [Chief Justice Burger and Justices Stewart, Rehnquist and Stevens] concur in this judgment. I also conclude for the reasons stated in the following opinion that the portion of the court's judgment enjoining petitioner from according any consideration to race in its admissions process must be reversed. For reasons expressed in separate opinions, [Justices Brennan, White, Marshall and Blackmun] concur in this judgment.

Affirmed in part and reversed in part.

I.[1] [The Medical School reserved 16 out of 100 places in its entering class for members of minority groups—"Blacks," "Chicanos," "Asians," and "American Indians." A separate committee was established to administer this special admissions program. This admissions procedure was challenged by Allan Bakke, a white applicant who was rejected even though "[i]n both years, applicants were admitted under the special program with grade point averages, MCAT scores, and benchmark scores significantly lower than Bakke's."] Because the special admissions program involved a racial classification, the [California] supreme court held itself bound to apply strict scrutiny. It then turned to the goals the University presented as justifying the special program. Although the court agreed that the goals of integrating the medical profession and increasing the number of physicians willing to serve members of minority groups were compelling state interests, it concluded that the special admissions program was not the least intrusive means of achieving those goals. [The] California court held that [equal protection required] that "no applicant may be rejected because of his race, in favor of another who is less qualified, as measured by standards applied without regard to race."

II.   [Justice Powell first considered Title VI of the Civil Rights Act of 1964.[2]] [We] assume only for the purposes of this case that respondent has a right of action under Title VI. [In] view of the clear legislative intent, Title VI must be held to proscribe only those racial classifications that would violate [equal protection].

III.   A. [The parties] disagree as to the level of judicial scrutiny to be applied to the special admissions program. [En route] to this crucial battle [the] parties fight a sharp preliminary action over the proper characterization of the special admissions program. Petitioner prefers to view it as establishing a "goal" of minority representation in the medical school. Respondent, echoing the courts below, labels it a racial quota. This semantic distinction is beside the point: the special admissions program is undeniably a classification based on race and ethnic background. [W]hite applicants could compete only for 84 seats in the entering class, rather than the 100 open to minority applicants. Whether this limitation is described as a quota or a goal, it is a line drawn on the basis of race and ethnic status. The guarantees of the 14th Amendment extend to persons. [Nevertheless], petitioner argues that the court below erred in applying strict scrutiny [because white males] are not a "discrete and insular minority" requiring extraordinary protection from the majoritarian political

---

1. [Justices Brennan, White, Marshall and Blackmun] join Parts I and V–C of this opinion. [Justice White] also joins Part III–A of this opinion. [Footnote by Justice Powell.]

2. Title VI provides: "No person in the United States shall, on the ground of race, color, or national origin, be excluded from participation in, be denied the benefits of, or be subjected to discrimination under any program or activity receiving Federal financial assistance."

process. [Carolene Products, fn. 4.] [These] characteristics may be relevant in deciding whether or not to add new types of classifications to the list of "suspect" categories or whether a particular classification survives close examination. Racial and ethnic classifications, however, are subject to stringent examination without regard to these additional characteristics. [Hirabayashi; Korematsu.] Racial and ethnic distinctions of any sort are inherently suspect and thus call for the most exacting judicial examination.

B. This perception of racial and ethnic distinctions is rooted in our Nation's constitutional and demographic history. The Court's initial view of the 14th Amendment was that its "one pervading purpose" was "the freedom of the slave race." [Slaughter–House Cases.] [Equal protection], however, was "[v]irtually strangled in its infancy by post-civil-war judicial reactionism." It was relegated to decades of relative desuetude while [due process flourished]. In that cause, the 14th Amendment's "one pervading purpose" was displaced. [But in later decades, as] the Nation filled with the stock of many lands, the reach of the Clause was gradually extended to all ethnic groups seeking protection from official discrimination. [Although] many of the Framers of the 14th Amendment conceived of its primary function as bridging the vast distance between members of the Negro race and the white "majority," the Amendment itself was framed in universal [terms]. Because the landmark decisions in this area [in recent decades] arose in response to the continued exclusion of Negroes from the mainstream of American society, they could be characterized as involving discrimination by the "majority" white race against the Negro minority. But they need not be read as depending upon that characterization for their results. It suffices to say that "[this] Court consistently repudiated '[d]istinctions between citizens solely because of their ancestry' as being 'odious to a free people whose institutions are founded upon the doctrine of equality.' " [Loving v. Virginia.] Petitioner urges us to adopt for the first time a more restrictive view of [equal protection] and hold that discrimination against members of the white "majority" cannot be suspect if its purpose can be characterized as "benign."[3] The clock of our liberties, however, cannot be turned back to 1868. It is far too late to argue that the guarantee of equal protection to *all* persons permits the recognition of special wards entitled to a degree of protection greater than that accorded [others].

Once the artificial line of a "two-class theory" of the 14th Amendment is put aside, the difficulties entailed in varying the level of judicial review according to a perceived "preferred" status of a particular racial or ethnic

---

3. In the view of [Justice Brennan et al.] the pliable notion of "stigma" is the crucial element in analyzing racial classifications. The Equal Protection Clause is not framed in terms of "stigma." Certainly the word has no clearly defined constitutional meaning. It reflects a subjective judgment that is standardless. *All* state-imposed classifications that rearrange burdens and benefits on the basis of race are likely to be viewed with deep resentment by the individuals burdened. The denial to innocent persons of equal rights and opportunities may outrage those so deprived and therefore may be perceived as invidious. These individuals are likely to find little comfort in the notion that the deprivation they are asked to endure is merely the price of membership in the dominant majority and that its imposition is inspired by the supposedly benign purpose of aiding others. One should not lightly dismiss the inherent unfairness of, and the perception of mistreatment that accompanies, a system of allocating benefits and privileges on the basis of skin color and ethnic origin. Moreover, [Justice Brennan et al.] offer no principle for deciding whether preferential classifications reflect a benign remedial purpose or a malevolent stigmatic classification, since they are willing in this case to accept mere post hoc declarations by an isolated state entity—a medical school faculty—unadorned by particularized findings of past discrimination to establish such a remedial purpose. [Footnote by Justice Powell.]

minority are intractable. [The] white "majority" itself is composed of various minority groups, most of which can lay claim to a history of prior discrimination at the hands of the state and private individuals. Not all of these groups can receive preferential treatment and corresponding judicial tolerance of distinctions drawn in terms of race and nationality, for then the only "majority" left would be a new minority of White Anglo–Saxon Protestants. There is no principled basis for deciding which groups would merit "heightened judicial solicitude" and which would not.[4] [Moreover,] there are serious problems of justice connected with the idea of preference itself. First, it may not always be clear that a so-called preference is in fact benign. Courts may be asked to validate burdens imposed upon individual members of particular groups in order to advance the group's general interest. See United Jewish Organizations v. Carey [hereinafter UJO (1977; see fn. 6 below)] [Brennan, J.]. Nothing in the Constitution supports the notion that individuals may be asked to suffer otherwise impermissible burdens in order to enhance the societal standing of their ethnic groups. Second, preferential programs may only reinforce common stereotypes holding that certain groups are unable to achieve success without special protection based on a factor having no relationship to individual worth. Third, there is a measure of inequity in forcing innocent persons in respondent's position to bear the burdens of redressing grievances not of their making. [If] it is the individual who is entitled to judicial protection against classifications based upon his racial or ethnic background because such distinctions impinge upon personal rights, rather than the individual only because of his membership in a particular group, then constitutional standards may be applied consistently. Political judgments regarding the necessity for the particular classification may be weighed in the constitutional balance [Korematsu], but the standard of justification will remain constant. [When classifications] touch upon an individual's race or ethnic background, he is entitled to a judicial determination that the burden he is asked to bear on that basis is precisely tailored to serve a compelling governmental [interest].

C.   Petitioner contends that on several occasions this Court has approved preferential classifications without applying the most exacting scrutiny. [Here,] there was no judicial determination of constitutional violation as a predicate for the formulation of a remedial classification. The employment discrimination cases also do not advance petitioner's cause. For example, in Franks v. Bowman Transportation Co., 424 U.S. 747 (1976), we approved a retroactive award of seniority to a class of Negro truck drivers who had been the victims of

---

4. [Justice Brennan et al.] would require as a justification for a program such as petitioner's only two findings: (i) that there has been some form of discrimination against the preferred minority groups "by society at large" (it being conceded that petitioner had no history of discrimination), and (ii) that "there is reason to believe" that the disparate impact sought to be rectified by the program is the "product" of such discrimination. The breadth of this hypothesis is unprecedented in our constitutional system. The first step is easily taken. No one denies the regrettable fact that there has been societal discrimination in this country against various racial and ethnic groups. The second step, however, involves a speculative leap; but for this discrimination by society at large, Bakke "would have failed to qualify for admission" because Negro applicants—nothing is said about Asians—would have made better scores. Not one word in the record supports this conclusion, and the plurality offers no standard for courts to use in applying such a presumption of causation to other racial or ethnic classifications. This failure is a grave one, since if it may be concluded *on this record* that each of the minority groups preferred by the petitioner's special program is entitled to the benefit of the presumption, it would seem difficult to determine that any of the dozens of minority groups that have suffered "societal discrimination" cannot also claim it, in any area of social intercourse. [Footnote by Justice Powell.]

discrimination—not just by society at large, but by the respondent in that case. While this relief imposed some burdens on other employees, it was held necessary " 'to make [the victims] whole for injuries suffered on account of unlawful employment discrimination.' " [But] we have never approved preferential classifications in the absence of proven constitutional or statutory violations.[5] Nor is petitioner's view as to the applicable standard supported by the fact that gender-based classifications are not subjected to this level of scrutiny. Gender-based distinctions are less likely to create the analytical and practical problems present in preferential programs premised on racial or ethnic criteria. With respect to gender there are only two possible classifications. The incidence of the burdens imposed by preferential classifications is clear. There are no rival groups who can claim that they, too, are entitled to preferential treatment. [More] importantly, the perception of racial classifications as inherently odious stems from a lengthy and tragic history that gender-based classifications do not [share].

[Petitioner also] contends that [UJO] indicates a willingness to approve racial classifications designed to benefit certain minorities, without denominating the classifications as "suspect." [New York] had redrawn its reapportionment plan to meet objections of the Department of Justice under § 5 of the Voting Rights Act of 1965. Specifically, voting districts were redrawn to enhance the electoral power of certain "nonwhite" voters found to have been the victims of unlawful "dilution" under the original reapportionment plan. [UJO] properly is viewed as a case in which the remedy for an administrative finding of discrimination encompassed measures to improve the previously disadvantaged group's ability to participate, without excluding individuals belonging to any other group from enjoyment of the relevant opportunity— meaningful participation in the electoral process.[6] In this case, unlike [UJO],

5. This case does not call into question congressionally authorized administrative actions, such as consent decrees under Title VII or approval of reapportionment plans under § 5 of the Voting Rights Act of 1965. In such cases, there has been detailed legislative consideration of the various indicia of previous constitutional or statutory violations, e.g., South Carolina v. Katzenbach [chap. 10 below], and particular administrative bodies have been charged with monitoring various activities in order to detect such violations and formulate appropriate remedies. Furthermore, we are not here presented with an occasion to review legislation by Congress pursuant to its powers under § 2 of the 13th Amendment and § 5 of the 14th Amendment to remedy the effects of prior discrimination. Katzenbach v. Morgan; Jones v. Alfred H. Mayer Co. [chap. 10 below]. We have previously recognized the special competence of Congress to make findings with respect to the effects of identified past discrimination and its discretionary authority to take appropriate remedial measures. [Footnote by Justice Powell.]

6. As this passage in the text indicates, United Jewish Organizations v. Carey, 430 U.S. 144 (1977) [UJO], gave rise to some

speculation that the Court was willing to apply deferential review to benign racial classifications. In UJO, New York had redrawn districts in Brooklyn in order to maintain black representation in the state legislature, in an attempt to comply with the Voting Rights Act. The redistricting affected an area where about 30,000 Hasidic Jews lived. In order to create substantial non-white majorities in a few districts, New York's revision split the Hasidic community into several districts. The Hasidic Jews attacked the redistricting as unconstitutional racial reapportionment under the 14th and 15th Amendments. In rejecting that challenge, Justice White's opinion (entirely joined by Justice Stevens and partly joined by Justices Brennan, Blackmun and Rehnquist) emphasized two reasons. First, New York had done no more than the Attorney General was authorized to require under the Voting Rights Act. His second, "independent" ground went further: in a portion of the opinion supported only by Justices Stevens and Rehnquist, Justice White gave rise to the speculation about the permissibility of benign racial criteria by stating: "[W]hether or not the plan was authorized [by] the Vot-

there has been no determination by the legislature or a responsible administrative agency that the University engaged in a discriminatory practice requiring remedial efforts. Moreover, the operation of petitioner's special admissions program is quite different from the remedial measures approved [there]. [When] a classification denies an individual opportunities or benefits enjoyed by others solely because of his race or ethnic background, it must be regarded as suspect.

IV. We have held that in "order to justify the use of a suspect classification, a State must show that its purpose or interest is both constitutionally permissible and substantial, and that its use of the classification is 'necessary [to] the accomplishment' of its purpose or the safeguarding of its interest." The special admissions program purports to serve the purposes of: (i) "reducing the historic deficit of traditionally disfavored minorities in medical schools and the medical profession"; (ii) countering the effects of societal discrimination; (iii) increasing the number of physicians who will practice in communities currently underserved; and (iv) obtaining the educational benefits that flow from an ethnically diverse student body. It is necessary to decide which, if any, of these purposes is substantial enough to support the use of a suspect classification. A. If petitioner's purpose is to assure within its student body some specified percentage of a particular group merely because of its race or ethnic origin, such a preferential purpose must be rejected not as insubstantial but as facially invalid. Preferring members of any one group for no reason other than race or ethnic origin is discrimination for its own sake. This the Constitution forbids.

B. The State certainly has a legitimate and substantial interest in ameliorating, or eliminating where feasible, the disabling effects of identified discrimination. [The] school desegregation cases [attest] to the importance of this state goal, [which is] far more focused than the remedying of the effects of "societal discrimination," an amorphous concept of injury that may be ageless in its reach into the past. We have never approved a classification that aids persons perceived as members of relatively victimized groups at the expense of other innocent individuals in the absence of judicial, legislative, or administrative findings of constitutional or statutory violations. After such findings have been made, the governmental interest in preferring members of the injured groups at the expense of others is substantial, since the legal rights of the victims must be vindicated. Without such findings of constitutional or statutory violations,[7] it

ing Rights Act, New York was entitled to consider racial factors in redistricting under the Constitution." He noted that New York's plan "represented no racial slur or stigma with respect to whites or any other race." Although, black representatives were more likely to be elected the redrawn districts, "as long as whites in [Brooklyn], as a group, were provided with fair representation, we cannot conclude that there was a cognizable discrimination against whites." (Justice White paid relatively little attention to the claim that the Hasidic Jews were themselves a "discrete and insular" minority who were being discriminated against by the reapportionment. He noted that the Hasidic Jews had not challenged the lower court's holding that they "had no constitutional right to separate community recognition in reapportionment.") Justice Brennan's concurrence rested solely on the Voting Rights Act but spoke at length about the potential abuses of "benign" racial factors in state action, in a fashion similar to his discussion in his Bakke opinion, below. A separate opinion by Justice Stewart, joined by Justice Powell, concurred in the judgment, finding no "purposeful discrimination." Chief Justice Burger's dissent concluded: "While petitioners may have no constitutional right to remain unified within a single political district, they do have [the] constitutional right not to be carved up so as to create a voting bloc composed of some other ethnic or racial group through [this] kind of racial [gerrymandering]."

7. Mr. Justice Brennan [et al.] misconceive the scope of this Court's holdings under Title VII when they suggest that "disparate impact" alone is sufficient to establish a vio-

cannot be said that the government has any greater interest in helping one individual than in refraining from harming another. Thus, the government has no compelling justification for inflicting such harm. Petitioner does not purport to have made, and is in no position to make, such findings. Its broad mission is education, not the formulation of any legislative policy or the adjudication of particular claims of illegality. [Isolated] segments of our vast governmental structures are not competent to make those decisions, at least in the absence of legislative mandates and legislatively determined criteria. Cf. Hampton v. Mow Sun Wong [p. 724 above]. Hence, the purpose of helping certain groups whom the faculty of the Davis Medical School perceived as victims of "societal discrimination" does not justify a classification that imposes disadvantages upon persons like [respondent]. To hold otherwise would be to convert a remedy heretofore reserved for violations of legal rights into a privilege that all institutions throughout the Nation could grant at their pleasure to whatever groups are perceived as victims of societal discrimination. That is a step we have never approved.

C. Petitioner identifies, as another purpose of its program, improving the delivery of health care services to communities currently underserved. [There] is virtually no evidence in the record indicating that petitioner's special admissions program is either needed or geared to promote that goal. [Petitioner] simply has not carried its burden of demonstrating that it must prefer members of particular ethnic groups over all other individuals in order to promote better health care delivery to deprived citizens. Indeed, petitioner has not shown that its preferential classification is likely to have any significant effect on the problem. D. The fourth goal asserted by petitioner is the attainment of a diverse student body. This clearly is a constitutionally permissible goal for an institution of higher education. Academic freedom, though not a specifically enumerated constitutional right, long has been viewed as a special concern of the First Amendment. The freedom of a university to make its own judgments as to education includes the selection of its student body. [Thus,] in arguing that its universities must be accorded the right to select those students who will contribute the most to the "robust exchange of ideas," petitioner invokes a countervailing constitutional interest, that of the First Amendment[, and] must be viewed as seeking to achieve a goal that is of paramount importance in the fulfillment of its mission. An otherwise qualified medical student with a particular background [may] bring to a professional school of medicine experiences, outlooks and ideas that enrich the training of its student body and better equip its graduates to render with understanding their vital service to humanity. [As] the interest of diversity is compelling in the context of

lation of that statute, and, by analogy, other civil rights measures. That this was not the meaning of Title VII was made quite clear in [Griggs]. [D]isparate impact is a basis for relief under Title VII only if the practice in question is not founded on "business necessity," or lacks "a manifest relationship to the employment in question." Nothing *in this record*—as opposed to some of the general literature cited by Mr. Justice Brennan [et al.]—even remotely suggests that the disparate impact of the general admissions program at Davis Medical School, resulting primarily [from] disparate test scores and grades, [is] without educational justification.

Moreover, the presumption in Griggs—that disparate impact without any showing of business justification established the existence of discrimination in violation of the statute—was based on legislative determinations, wholly absent here, that past discrimination had handicapped various minority groups to such an extent that disparate impact could be traced to identifiable instances of past discrimination. [Thus,] Title VII principles support the proposition that findings of identified discrimination must precede the fashioning of remedial measures embodying racial classifications. [Footnote by Justice Powell.]

a university's admissions program, the question remains whether the program's racial classification is necessary to promote this interest.

V. A. It may be assumed that the reservation of a specified number of seats in each class for individuals from the preferred ethnic groups would contribute to the attainment of considerable ethnic diversity in the student body. But petitioner's argument that this is the only effective means of serving the interest of diversity is seriously flawed. In a most fundamental sense the argument misconceives the nature of the state interest that would justify consideration of race or ethnic background. It is not an interest in simple ethnic diversity, in which a specified percentage of the student body is in effect guaranteed to be members of selected ethnic [groups]. The diversity that furthers a compelling state interest encompasses a far broader array of qualifications and characteristics of which racial or ethnic origin is but a single though important element. Petitioner's special admissions program, focused *solely* on ethnic diversity, would hinder rather than further attainment of genuine [diversity].

The experience of other university admissions programs, which take race into account in achieving the educational diversity valued by the First Amendment, demonstrates that the assignment of a fixed number of places to a minority group is not a necessary means toward that end. An illuminating example is found in the Harvard College program: "In recent years Harvard College has expanded the concept of diversity to include students from disadvantaged economic, racial and ethnic groups. [In] practice, this new definition of diversity has meant that race has been a factor in some admission decisions. When the Committee on Admissions reviews the large middle group of applicants who are 'admissible' and deemed capable of doing good work in their courses, the race of an applicant may tip the balance in his favor just as geographic origin or a life spent on a farm may tip the balance in other candidates' cases. A farm boy from Idaho can bring something to Harvard College that a Bostonian cannot offer. Similarly, a black student can usually bring something that a white person cannot offer. In Harvard college admissions the Committee has not set target-quotas for the number of blacks, or of musicians, football players, physicists or Californians to be admitted in a given year. [But in] choosing among thousands of applicants who are not only 'admissible' academically but have other strong qualities, the Committee, with a number of criteria in mind, pays some attention to distribution among many types and categories of students." In such an admissions program, race or ethnic background may be deemed a "plus" in a particular applicant's file, yet it does not insulate the individual from comparison with all other candidates for the available seats. The file of a particular black applicant may be examined for his potential contribution to diversity without the factor of race being decisive when compared, for example, with that of an applicant identified as an Italian–American if the latter is thought to exhibit qualities more likely to promote beneficial educational pluralism. Such qualities could include exceptional personal talents, unique work or service experience, leadership potential, maturity, demonstrated compassion, a history of overcoming disadvantage, ability to communicate with the poor, or other qualifications deemed important. In short, an admissions program operated in this way is flexible enough to consider all pertinent elements of diversity in light of the particular qualifications of each applicant, and to place them on the same footing for consideration, although not necessarily according them the same weight. [This] kind of program treats each applicant as an individual in the admissions process. [It] has been suggested that an admissions program which considers race only as one factor is simply a subtle and more sophisticated—but no less effective—

means of according racial preference than the Davis program. A facial intent to discriminate, however, is evident in petitioner's preference program and not denied in this case. No such facial infirmity exists in an admissions program where race or ethnic background is simply one element—to be weighed fairly against other elements—in the selection process. [A] Court would not assume that a university, professing to employ a facially nondiscriminatory admissions policy, would operate it as a cover for the functional equivalent of a quota system. In short, good faith would be presumed in the absence of a showing to the contrary in the manner permitted by our cases.[8]

B. In summary, it is evident that the Davis special admissions program involves the use of an explicit racial classification never before countenanced by this Court. [W]hen a State's distribution of benefits or imposition of burdens hinges on the color of a person's skin or ancestry, that individual is entitled to a demonstration that the challenged classification is necessary to promote a substantial state interest. Petitioner has failed to carry this burden. For this reason, that portion of the California court's judgment holding petitioner's special admissions program invalid under the 14th Amendment must be affirmed. C. In enjoining petitioner from ever considering the race of any applicant, however, the courts below failed to recognize that the State has a substantial interest that legitimately may be served by a properly devised admissions program involving the competitive consideration of race and ethnic origin. For this reason, so much of the judgment as enjoins petitioner from any consideration of the race of any applicant must be reversed. VI. With respect to respondent's entitlement to an injunction directing his admission to the Medical School, petitioner has conceded that it could not carry its burden of proving that, but for the existence of its unlawful special admissions program, respondent still would not have been admitted. Hence, respondent is entitled to the injunction, and that portion of the judgment must be affirmed.

Opinion of [Justice BRENNAN, Justice WHITE, Justice MARSHALL, and Justice BLACKMUN], concurring in the judgment in part and dissenting.

[The] difficulty of the issue presented [has] resulted in many opinions, no single one speaking for the Court. But this should not and must not mask the central meaning of today's opinions: Government may take race into account when it acts not to demean or insult any racial group, but to remedy disadvantages cast on minorities by past racial prejudice, at least when appropriate findings have been made by judicial, legislative, or administrative bodies with competence to act in this area. [Since] we conclude that the affirmative admissions program [is] constitutional, we would reverse the judgment below in all [respects].

---

8. Universities [may] make individualized decisions, in which ethnic background plays a part, under a presumption of legality and legitimate educational purpose. So long as the university proceeds on an individualized, case-by-case basis, there is no warrant for judicial interference in the academic process. If an applicant can establish that the institution does not adhere to a policy of individual comparisons, or can show that a systematic exclusion of certain groups results, the presumption of legality might be overcome, creating the necessity of proving legitimate educational purpose. There also are strong policy reasons that correspond to the constitutional distinction between petitioner's preference program and one that assures a measure of competition among all applicants. Petitioner's program will be viewed as inherently unfair by the public generally as well as by [applicants]. Fairness in individual competition for opportunities, especially those provided by the State, is a widely cherished American ethic. Indeed, in a broader sense, an underlying assumption of the rule of law is the worthiness of a system of justice based on fairness to the [individual]. [Footnote by Justice Powell.]

I. [Even] today officially sanctioned discrimination is not a thing of the past. Against this background, claims that law must be "colorblind" or that the datum of race is no longer relevant to public policy must be seen as aspiration rather than as description of reality. [We cannot] let color blindness become myopia which masks the reality that many "created equal" have been treated within our lifetimes as inferior both by the law and by their fellow [citizens]. III. [Unquestionably] a government practice or statute [which] contains "suspect classifications" is to be subjected to "strict scrutiny." [But] whites as a class [do not have] any of the "traditional indicia of [suspectness]." Moreover, [this] is not a case where racial classifications are "irrelevant and therefore prohibited." Nor has anyone suggested that the University's purposes contravene the cardinal principle that racial classifications that stigmatize—because they are drawn on the presumption that one race is inferior to another or because they put the weight of government behind racial hatred and separatism—are invalid without more. On the other hand, the fact that this case does not fit neatly into our prior analytic framework for race cases does not mean that it should be analyzed by applying the very loose rational-basis [standard]. " '[T]he mere recitation of a benign, compensatory purpose is not an automatic shield which protects against any inquiry into the actual purposes underlying a statutory scheme.' " [Webster, quoting Wiesenfeld.] Instead, a number of considerations—developed in gender discrimination cases but which carry even more force when applied to racial classifications—lead us to conclude that racial classifications designed to further remedial purposes "must serve important governmental objectives and must be substantially related to achievement of those objectives." [Craig.]

First, race, like "gender-based classifications, too often [has] been inexcusably utilized to stereotype and stigmatize politically powerless segments of society." While a carefully tailored statute designed to remedy past discrimination could avoid these vices, see, [e.g., Webster; Ballard], we nonetheless have recognized that the line between honest and thoughtful appraisal of the effects of past discrimination and paternalistic stereotyping is not so clear and that a statute based on the latter is patently capable of stigmatizing all women with a badge of inferiority. State programs designed ostensibly to ameliorate the effects of past racial discrimination obviously create the same hazard of stigma, since they may promote racial separatism and reinforce the views of those who believe that members of racial minorities are inherently incapable of succeeding on their own. Second, race, like gender and illegitimacy, is an immutable characteristic which its possessors are powerless to escape or set aside. [Such] divisions are contrary to our deep belief that "legal burdens should bear some relationship to individual responsibility or wrongdoing" and that advancement sanctioned, sponsored, or approved by the State should ideally be based on individual merit or achievement, or at the least on factors within the control of an individual. Because this principle is so deeply rooted it might be supposed that it would be considered in the legislative process and weighed against the benefits of programs preferring individuals because of their race. But this is not necessarily so: The "natural consequence of our governing processes [may well be] that the most 'discrete and insular' of whites [will] be called upon to bear the immediate, direct costs of benign discrimination." UJO (concurring opinion). Moreover, it is clear from our cases that there are limits beyond which majorities may not go when they classify on the basis of immutable characteristics. Thus, even if the concern for individualism is weighed by the political process, that weighing cannot waive the personal rights of individuals under the 14th Amendment. In sum, because of the significant risk that racial classifications established for ostensibly benign purposes can be misused, causing effects not unlike those created by invidious classifications, it is inappropriate to inquire only whether there is any conceivable basis that might sustain such a classification. Instead, to justify such a classification an important and articulated purpose for its use must be shown. In addition, any statute must be stricken that stigmatizes any group or that singles out those least well represented in the political process to bear the brunt of a benign program. Thus our review under the 14th Amendment should be strict—not " 'strict' in theory and fatal in fact," because it is stigma that causes fatality—but strict and searching [nonetheless].

IV. Davis' articulated purpose of remedying the effects of past societal discrimination [is] sufficiently important to justify the use of race-conscious admissions programs where there is a sound basis for concluding that minority underrepresentation is substantial and chronic, and that the handicap of past discrimination is impeding access of minorities to the medical school. A. At least since [Green], it has been clear that a public body which has itself been adjudged to have engaged in racial discrimination cannot bring itself into compliance with [equal protection] simply by ending its unlawful acts and adopting a neutral stance. Three years later, Swann [reiterated] that racially neutral remedies for past discrimination were inadequate where consequences of past discriminatory acts influence or control present decisions. [Moreover,] we stated that school boards, even in the absence of a judicial finding of past discrimination, could voluntarily adopt plans which assigned students with the end of creating racial pluralism by establishing fixed ratios of black and white students in each [school]. Finally, the conclusion that state educational institutions may constitutionally adopt admissions programs designed to avoid exclusion of historically disadvantaged minorities, even when such programs explicitly take race into account, finds direct support in our cases construing congressional legislation designed to overcome the present effects of past discrimination. Congress can and has outlawed actions which have a disproportionately adverse and unjustified impact upon members of racial minorities and has required or authorized race-conscious action to put individuals disadvantaged by such impact in the position they otherwise might have enjoyed. Such relief does not require as a predicate proof that recipients of preferential advancement have been individually discriminated against; it is enough that each recipient is within a general class of persons likely to have been the victims of discrimination. [Indeed,] the requirement of a judicial determination of a constitutional or statutory violation as a predicate for race-conscious remedial actions would be self-defeating. Such a requirement would severely undermine efforts to achieve voluntary compliance with the requirements of [law]. States also may adopt race-conscious programs designed to overcome substantial, chronic minority underrepresentation where there is reason to believe that the evil addressed is a product of past racial [discrimination].[1] [We accordingly] conclude that Davis' goal of admitting minority students disadvantaged by the effects of past discrimination is sufficiently important to justify use of race-conscious admissions criteria.

---

1. [Because] the Regents can exercise plenary legislative and administrative power, it elevates form over substance to insist that Davis could not use race-conscious remedial programs until it had been adjudged in violation of the Constitution or an antidiscrimination statute. For, if [equal protection] required such a violation as a predicate, the Regents could simply have promulgated a regulation prohibiting disparate treatment not justified by the need to admit only qualified students, and could have declared Davis to have been in violation of such a regulation on the basis of the exclusionary effect of the admissions policy applied during the first two years of its operation. [Footnote by Justice Brennan et al.]

B.   Properly construed, therefore, our prior cases unequivocally show that a state government may adopt race-conscious programs if the purpose of such programs is to remove the disparate racial impact its actions might otherwise have and if there is reason to believe that the disparate impact is itself the product of past discrimination, whether its own or that of society at large. There is no question that Davis' program is valid under this test. [Davis] had a sound basis for believing that the problem of underrepresentation of minorities was substantial and chronic and that the problem was attributable to handicaps imposed on minority applicants by past and present racial [discrimination]. Davis clearly could conclude that the serious and persistent underrepresentation of minorities in medicine [is] the result of handicaps under which minority applicants labor as a consequence of a background of deliberate, purposeful discrimination against minorities in education and in society generally, as well as in the medical [profession]. The conclusion is inescapable that applicants to medical school must be few indeed who endured the effects of de jure segregation, the resistance to Brown I, or the equally debilitating pervasive private discrimination fostered by our long history of official discrimination, and yet come to the starting line with an education equal to [whites].

C.   The second prong of our test—whether the Davis program stigmatizes any discrete group or individual and whether race is reasonably used in light of the program's objectives—is clearly satisfied by the Davis [program]. Bakke [was not] in any sense stamped as inferior by the Medical School's [rejection]. Moreover, there is absolutely no basis for concluding that Bakke's rejection [will] affect him throughout his life in the same way as the segregation of the Negro school children in Brown I would have affected them. [This] does not mean that the exclusion of a white resulting from the preferential use of race is not sufficiently serious to require justification; but it does mean that the injury inflicted by such a policy is not distinguishable from disadvantages caused by a wide range of government actions, none of which has ever been thought impermissible for that reason alone. In addition, there is simply no evidence that the Davis program discriminates intentionally or unintentionally against any minority group which it purports to benefit. The program does not establish a quota in the invidious sense of a ceiling on the number of minority applicants to be admitted. Nor can the program reasonably be regarded as stigmatizing the program's beneficiaries or their race as inferior. The Davis program does not simply advance less qualified applicants; rather it compensates applicants, whom it is uncontested are fully qualified to study medicine, for educational disadvantage which it was reasonable to conclude was a product of state-fostered discrimination. Once admitted, these students must satisfy the same degree requirements as regularly admitted students; and their performance is evaluated by the same standards by which regularly admitted students are judged. Under these circumstances, their performance and degrees must be regarded equally with the regularly admitted [students]. Since minority graduates cannot justifiably be regarded as less well qualified than nonminority graduates by virtue of the special admissions program, there is no reasonable basis to conclude that minority graduates [would] be stigmatized as inferior by the existence of such programs.[2] D. We disagree with the lower

---

2.   Consider Nagel, "Equal Treatment and Compensatory Discrimination," 2 Phil. & Pub.Affrs. 348 (1973), suggesting that racially preferential policies "inevitably produce resentment in the better qualified" and "cannot do much for the self-esteem of those who know they have benefited from it [and] may threaten the self-esteem of those in the favored group who would in fact have gained their positions even in the absence of the [policy], but who cannot be sure that they are not among its beneficiaries." Contrast

courts' conclusion that the Davis program's use of race was unreasonable in light of its objectives. [There] are no practical means by which it could achieve its ends in the foreseeable future without the use of race-conscious measures. With respect to any factor (such as poverty or family educational background) that may be used as a substitute for race as an indicator of past discrimination, whites greatly outnumber racial minorities simply because whites make up a far larger percentage of the total population and therefore far outnumber minorities in absolute terms at every socio-economic [level].

E. Finally, Davis' special admissions program cannot be said to violate the Constitution simply because it has set aside a predetermined number of places for qualified minority applicants rather than using minority status as a positive factor to be considered in evaluating the applications of disadvantaged minority applicants. For purposes of constitutional adjudication, there is no difference between the two approaches. In any admissions program which accords special consideration to disadvantaged racial minorities, a determination of the degree of preference to be given is unavoidable, and any given preference that results in the exclusion of a white candidate is no more or less constitutionally acceptable than a program such as that at Davis. Furthermore, the extent of the preference inevitably depends on how many minority applicants the particular school is seeking to admit in any particular year so long as the number of qualified minority applicants exceeds that number. There is no sensible, and certainly no constitutional, distinction between, for example, adding a set number of points to the admissions rating of disadvantaged minority applicants as an expression of the preference with the expectation that this will result in the admission of an approximately determined number of qualified minority applicants and setting a fixed number of places for such applicants as was done here. [That] the Harvard approach does [not] make public the extent of the preference and the precise workings of the system while the Davis program employs a specific, openly stated number, does not condemn the latter plan for purposes of 14th Amendment adjudication. It may be that the Harvard plan is more acceptable to the public than is the Davis "quota." If it is, any State [is] free to adopt it in preference to a less acceptable [alternative]. But there is no basis for preferring a particular preference program simply because in achieving the same goals that [Davis] is pursuing, it proceeds in a manner that is not immediately apparent to the [public].

Justice MARSHALL.

[It] must be remembered that, during most of the past 200 years, the Constitution as interpreted by this Court did not prohibit the most ingenious and pervasive forms of discrimination against the Negro. Now, when a State acts to remedy the effects of that legacy of discrimination, I cannot believe that this same Constitution stands as a barrier. [The] position of the Negro today in America is the tragic but inevitable consequence of centuries of unequal treatment. Measured by any benchmark of comfort or achievement, meaningful equality remains a distant dream for the Negro. [Justice Marshall listed statistics on health, employment, and income.] [I] do not believe that the 14th Amendment requires us to accept that fate. Neither its history nor our past cases lend any support to the conclusion that a University may not remedy the cumulative effects of society's discrimination by giving consideration to race in an effort to increase the number and percentage of Negro doctors. [While] I

O'Neil, "Racial Preference and Higher [Education]," 60 Va.L.Rev. 925 (1974), countering that it would be "perverse [to] strike down on this ground a program which has been sought and extensively utilized by minority applicants themselves. Such a judgment would imply a dangerously gratuitous concern about the welfare of minority groups."

applaud the judgment of the Court that a university may consider race in its admissions process, it is more than a little ironic that, after several hundred years of class-based discrimination against Negroes, the Court is unwilling to hold that a class-based remedy for that discrimination is permissible. In declining to so hold, today's judgment ignores the fact that for several hundred years Negroes have been discriminated against, not as individuals, but rather solely because of the color of their skins. It is unnecessary in 20th century America to have individual Negroes demonstrate that they have been victims of racial discrimination; the racism of our society has been so pervasive that none, regardless of wealth or position, has managed to escape its impact. The experience of Negroes in America has been different in kind, not just in degree, from that of other ethnic groups. [The] dream of America as the great melting pot has not been realized for the Negro; because of his skin color he never even made it into the pot. [Had] the Court been willing in 1896, in [Plessy], to hold that [equal protection] forbids differences in treatment based on race, we would not be faced with this dilemma in 1978. We must remember, however, that the principle that the "Constitution is color-blind" appeared only in the opinion of the lone dissenter. [For] the next 60 years, from Plessy to Brown, ours was a Nation where, *by law,* an individual could be given "special" treatment based on the color of his skin. [I] fear that we have come full circle. After the Civil War our government started several "affirmative action" programs. This Court in the Civil Rights Cases [chap. 10 below] and [Plessy] destroyed the movement toward complete equality. For almost a century no action was taken, and this nonaction was with the tacit approval of the courts. Then we had Brown and the Civil Rights Acts of Congress, followed by numerous affirmative action programs. *Now,* we have this Court again stepping in, this time to stop affirmative action programs of the type used by the University of California.

Justice BLACKMUN.

[I] yield to no one in my earnest hope that the time will come when an "affirmative action" program is unnecessary and is, in truth, only a relic of the past. [At] some time, [the] United States must and will reach a stage of maturity where action along this line is no longer necessary. Then persons will be regarded as persons, and discrimination of the type we address today will be an ugly feature of history that is instructive but that is behind [us]. It is somewhat ironic to have us so deeply disturbed over a program where race is an element of consciousness, and yet to be aware of the fact, as we are, that institutions of higher learning, albeit more on the undergraduate than the graduate level, have given conceded preferences up to a point to those possessed of athletic skills, to the children of alumni, to the affluent who may bestow their largess on the institutions, and to those having connections with celebrities, the famous, and the powerful. [That] the 14th Amendment has expanded beyond its original 1868 [conception] does not mean for me that [it] has broken away from [its] original intended purposes. Those original aims persist. [I] suspect that it would be impossible to arrange an affirmative action program in a racially neutral way and have it successful. To ask that this be so is to demand the impossible. In order to get beyond racism, we must first take account of race. There is no other way. And in order to treat some persons equally, we must treat them differently. We cannot—we dare not—let [equal protection] perpetuate [racial supremacy].

Justice STEVENS, with whom The Chief Justice [BURGER], Justice STEWART, and Justice REHNQUIST join, concurring in the judgment in part and dissenting in part.

[This] is not a class action. [Bakke] challenged petitioner's special admissions program [and the] California Supreme Court upheld his challenge and ordered him admitted. If the state court was correct in its view that the University's special program was illegal, and that Bakke was therefore unlawfully excluded from the medical school because of his race, we should affirm its judgment, regardless of our views about the legality of admissions programs that are not now before the Court. [After construing the state court ruling as containing "no outstanding injunction forbidding any consideration of racial criteria in processing applications," he stated:] It is therefore perfectly clear that the question whether race can ever be used as a factor in an admissions decision is not an issue in this case, and that discussion of that issue is inappropriate. [He proceeded to interpret Title VI as containing a "crystal clear" meaning:] "Race cannot be the basis of excluding anyone from participation in a federally funded program."

———

The vitality of Bakke. Bakke was widely praised as an act of statesmanship and compromise at the time it was decided, but many criticized it as incoherent or at least not resting on clear principle. Do you agree? In the post-Bakke cases that follow, the Court frequently invoked it, especially to justify strict scrutiny of benign racial classifications. In the 1990s, that is especially illustrated by Adarand (p. 830 below), where the Court, if anything, heightened the intensity of its strict scrutiny. Would a program such as that at Davis be sustained by the modern Court? Some would argue that Bakke stands as a solid precedent. See, e.g., Brest & Oshige, "Affirmative Action for Whom?," 47 Stan.L.Rev. 855 (1995), insisting that the "permissibility of using race as an admission criterion continues to be determined by Bakke—particularly Justice Powell's opinion." The Fifth Circuit disagreed, in HOPWOOD v. TEXAS, 78 F.3d 932, cert. denied, 116 S.Ct. 2581 (1996). The majority of the Court of Appeals, in striking down an affirmative action plan at the University of Texas Law School, stated that the Powell view was "not binding precedent," pointed out that it garnered "only his own vote and has never represented the view of a majority of the Court" in any case, and insisted that "recent Supreme Court precedent shows that the diversity interest will not satisfy strict scrutiny," citing such cases as Croson and Adarand, both below. Is the Fifth Circuit's view supported by the cases that follow? Should the Fifth Circuit have paid greater attention to Part V.C. of the Powell opinion, which explicitly endorsed "the competitive consideration of race and ethnic origin" in admissions decisions and which explicitly had the support of a majority of the Court? What significance should be attributed to the denial of certiorari in Hopwood? In a statement accompanying the denial of certiorari, Justice Ginsburg, joined by Justice Souter, noted that the constitutionality of using race or national origin as a factor in admission processes was "an issue of great national importance," but explained her action on the ground that the certiorari petition did not "challenge the lower courts' judgments that the particular admissions procedure used by the University of Texas Law School in 1992 was unconstitutional." [Under that program, minority applicants were evaluated under separate processes and standards from those used to evaluate others. Recall the Davis plan.] Justice Ginsburg stated: "Acknowledging that the 1992 admissions program 'has long since been discontinued and will not be reinstated,' the petitioners do not defend that program in this Court. Instead, petitioners challenge the rationale relied on by the Court of Appeals. '[T]his Court,' however, 'reviews judgments, not opinions.' Accordingly, we must await a final judgment on a program genuinely in controversy before addressing the important question raised in this petition.''

BENIGN USES OF RACIAL CRITERIA IN EMPLOYMENT, CONTRACTING, AND LICENSING PROGRAMS SINCE THE 1980s

1. *Employment discrimination.* Many of the Court's efforts to develop guidelines for assessing affirmative action programs arose in the context of employment discrimination. Typically, the Court was sharply divided in these cases, on such issues as the appropriate standard of review and the identification of state interests and findings that would justify the programs. The most important of the affirmative action employment cases was WYGANT v. JACKSON BOARD OF EDUCATION, 476 U.S. 267 (1986). Justice Powell wrote the plurality opinion, but it was fully joined only by Chief Justice Burger and Justice Rehnquist. The central issue in the case was the constitutionality of a minority preference in teacher lay-offs. The majority judgment was that the layoff provision was unconstitutional, with Justices O'Connor and White, for differing reasons, joining the Powell group to make a 5-4 majority in support of the judgment. The case arose in the following circumstances: After the school board had begun to take "affirmative steps" to hire more minority teachers, faculty layoffs became necessary for fiscal reasons. In 1972, the board and the teachers' union negotiated a collective bargaining agreement which provided that in the future, when layoffs were required, teachers with the most seniority would be retained, "except that at no time will there be a greater percentage of minority personnel laid off than the current percentage of minority personnel employed at the time of the layoff." In consequence, some white teachers were laid off, even though they had more seniority than blacks who were retained. Some of the laid-off teachers brought an action alleging that the layoffs violated their equal protection rights. The District Court dismissed the claim, holding that racial preferences need not be grounded on a finding of past purposeful discrimination, but were permissible as an attempt to remedy societal discrimination by providing "role models" for minority schoolchildren. The Court of Appeals affirmed, but the Supreme Court reversed.

Justice POWELL's plurality opinion applied strict scrutiny, as he had in Bakke. He held that the goal of providing "minority role models" in order to overcome societal discrimination was not "compelling," stating: "This Court never has held that societal discrimination alone is sufficient to justify a racial classification. Rather, the Court has insisted upon some showing of prior discrimination by the governmental unit involved before allowing limited use of racial classifications in order to remedy such discrimination. [The] role model theory employed by the District Court has no logical stopping point. [It] allows the Board to engage in discriminatory hiring and layoff practices long past the point required by any legitimate remedial purpose." Turning to the argument that the layoff provision was justified as a remedy for prior employment discrimination, Justice Powell noted that a public employer "must have sufficient evidence to justify the conclusion that there has been prior discrimination." When such a program is challenged in court, the trial judge must determine "that the employer had a strong basis in evidence for its conclusion that remedial action was necessary." (Justice Powell made clear that the burden was on the challenging parties to *disprove* the existence of the justification for the conclusion that there had been prior discrimination.) But here, there was no need to decide whether the board should be allowed to prove past discrimination, since the layoff provision was not a "necessary" means of achieving even the compelling purpose of remedying such discrimination. Imposing the loss of an existing job imposed too severe a burden on nonminority employees: "While hiring goals impose a diffuse burden, [layoffs] impose the entire burden of achieving racial equality on particular individuals. [That] burden is too intrusive." Accordingly, the layoff plan was "not sufficiently narrowly tailored": "Other, less intrusive means of accomplishing similar purposes—such as the adoption of hiring goals—are available." Justice WHITE's concurrence in the judgment agreed that "[w]hatever the legitimacy of hiring goals or quotas may be, the discharge of white teachers to make room for blacks, none of whom has been shown to be a victim of any racial discrimination, is quite a different matter."

Justice O'CONNOR's concurrence agreed with the plurality's rejection of the "role model" and "societal discrimination" rationales. On the "remedial" justification, however, she insisted that she would not require (and would read the plurality opinion as not requiring) "a contemporaneous antecedent finding of past discrimination by a court or other competent body [as] a constitutional prerequisite to a public employer's voluntary agreement to an affirmative action plan." She elaborated: "A violation of [constitutional] requirements does not arise with the making of a finding; it arises when the wrong is committed. [The] imposition of a requirement that public employers make findings that they have engaged in illegal discrimination before they engage in affirmative action programs would severely undermine public employers' incentive to meet voluntarily their civil rights obligations." Justice MARSHALL's dissent, joined by Justices Brennan and Blackmun, stated: "Because I believe that a public employer, with the full agreement of its employees, should be permitted to preserve the benefits of a legitimate and constitutional affirmative-action hiring plan even while reducing its workforce, I dissent." In a separate dissent, Justices STEVENS argued that there was no need to rely on the remedial rationale to justify the program. Instead, he focused on "whether the Board's action advances the public interest in educating children for the future" and accordingly defended the "role model" justification for the provision: "In the context of public education, it is quite obvious that a school board may reasonably conclude that an integrated faculty will be able to provide benefits to the student body that could not be provided by an all white, or nearly all white, faculty." (Wygant was extensively discussed in Croson, below.)

2. *Some comments.* During the 1980s, as Wygant illustrates, the Court was closely divided in many affirmative action cases arising in the employment discrimination context. However, a few areas of consensus seemed to emerge. For example, voluntary use of race-conscious hiring "goals" by private employers designed to eliminate racial imbalances in traditionally segregated job categories was not unlawful under Title VII. See United Steelworkers v. Weber, 443 U.S. 193 (1979). Furthermore, these measures need not be limited to helping only the actual victims of prior discrimination. However, the Court repeatedly emphasized that race-conscious remedies are constitutionally risky, must be carefully scrutinized, and cannot be accepted as routine. And the Court continued to struggle to find agreement on an appropriate standard of review for such remedies, on what constitutes an adequate predicate for the adoption of benign race-conscious programs, and on what kinds of provisions an affirmative action plan must contain in order to survive judicial scrutiny. In reflecting on employment discrimination cases, consider whether the Court developed a coherent, persuasive approach to affirmative action problems. Are the various holdings in the employment context (often holdings resting in major part on statutory provisions such as Title VII) applicable to the problem of affirmative

action in contracting and licensing cases, cases examined below? Do the latter group of cases show a more successful effort to achieve a consensus about necessary prerequisites for affirmative action programs and about the applicable standard of review? Employment cases such as Wygant repeatedly play a role in the contracting and licensing cases that follow. Is the arguably greater consensus in the contracting and licensing cases likely to yield a broader consensus in the employment context as well?

3. *Contracting and licensing programs.* Since Fullilove in 1980, which follows, the Court has considered a number of federal and local programs granting preferential treatment to racial minorities in the award of public funds or licenses. The cases that follow present a number of recurrent issues, some already raised in Bakke. For example, by what standards should the Court assess the constitutionality of the program? Should different standards apply to state and local rather than federal programs? What is the necessary predicate for the establishment of such programs—e.g., are they justified only to remedy past purposeful discrimination, or may they be invoked as well to remedy historic societal discrimination? In Fullilove, the Court treated a *federal* set-aside program with considerable deference; apparently, the strictest scrutiny was reserved for state and local programs, as the Croson case in 1989 made clear. The Metro Broadcasting case, a year later, upheld race-conscious factors in FCC licensing proceedings, with the majority opinion by Justice Brennan (shortly before his retirement from the Court) explicitly adopting an intermediate scrutiny approach. But in Adarand in 1995, very strict scrutiny reigned even though the set-aside program struck down was that of the federal government. All of these cases are noted or printed below. In examining them, consider: what, in light of the trend of the cases, is the current vitality of Fullilove? Of Metro Broadcasting? Of Croson? Are the mid–1990s Court's mounting limits on race-conscious programs justified?

FULLILOVE v. KLUTZNICK, 448 U.S. 448 (1980): This decision rejected a facial constitutional challenge to a requirement in a congressional spending program that, absent an administrative waiver, 10% of federal funds granted for local public works projects must be used by the state or local grantee to procure services from businesses controlled by members of specified minority groups—Negroes, Spanish-speaking, Orientals, Eskimos and Aleuts.[1] This "minority set-aside" program was challenged on equal protection grounds by nonminority contractors. Although the Court upheld the program's constitutionality, there was no majority opinion: Chief Justice BURGER's opinion announcing the judgment of the Court was joined only by Justices White and Powell. The Chief Justice's opinion contained only passing references to Bakke;

---

1. The 1977 provision originated in an amendment offered on the floor of the House by Rep. Mitchell of Maryland. The sparse 1977 debates on the provision contained no explicit reference to past discrimination in the construction industry. In examining the provision, Chief Justice Burger's plurality opinion commented that its purposes "must be considered against the background of on-going efforts directed toward deliverance of the century-old promise of equality of economic opportunity." He emphasized a 1977 House Committee evaluation of the program. That evaluation included a reference to a 1975 assessment of the program by a House Subcommittee. The 1975 report contained a rare reference to past discrimination in the construction industry, including the statement: "The effects of past inequities stemming from racial prejudice have not remained in the past. The Congress has recognized the reality that past discriminatory practices have, to some degree, adversely affected our present economic system." The Chief Justice concluded: "Against this backdrop of legislative and administrative programs, it is inconceivable that Members of both Houses were not fully aware of the objectives of the MBE provision and of the reasons prompting its enactment."

he concluded: "This opinion does not adopt, either expressly or implicitly, the formulas of analysis articulated in such cases as Bakke. However, our analysis demonstrates that the MBE provision would survive judicial review under either 'test' articulated in the several Bakke [opinions]." Much of his opinion was devoted to surveying the relevant congressional powers under Art. I, § 8, and § 5 of the 14th Amendment (Justice Stewart's dissent criticized this extensive discussion as consisting of "self-evident truisms" not helpful in addressing the central equal protection issue.)

The Chief Justice's opinion went on to emphasize "appropriate deference to the Congress." He elaborated: "Congress, of course, may legislate without compiling the kind of 'record' appropriate with respect to judicial or administrative proceedings. [We] are satisfied that Congress had abundant historical basis from which it could conclude that traditional procurement practices, when applied to minority businesses, could perpetuate the effects of prior discrimination. Accordingly, Congress reasonably determined that the prospective elimination of these barriers to minority firm access to public contracting opportunities generated by the 1977 Act was appropriate to ensure that those businesses were not denied equal opportunity to participate in [federal grants]." In examining the race-conscious means used by Congress, he stated: "[We] are not dealing with a remedial decree of a court but with the legislative authority of Congress. [As] a threshold matter, we reject the contention that in the remedial context the Congress must act in a wholly 'color-blind' fashion. [E.g., Swann; UJO.] It is fundamental that in no organ of government [does] there repose a more comprehensive remedial power than in the [Congress]." He also rejected the charge that the program "impermissibly deprives nonminority businesses of access to at least some portion of the government contracting opportunities generated by the [law]."

Justice POWELL's concurrence joined the Chief Justice's opinion but explicitly claimed to apply the analysis set forth in his Bakke opinion: "Although I would place greater emphasis than The Chief Justice on the need to articulate judicial standards of review in conventional terms, I view his opinion [as] substantially in accord with my own views. [The law] employs a racial classification that is constitutionally prohibited unless it is a necessary means of advancing a compelling governmental interest. [I] believe that [the provision] is justified as a remedy that serves the compelling governmental interest in eradicating the continuing effects of past discrimination identified by Congress." He emphasized that, unlike the Regents in Bakke, Congress was competent to make the past-discrimination findings necessary to sustain the program. Justice MARSHALL, joined by Justices Brennan and Blackmun, concurred in the judgment, stating: "[It] is clear to me that the racial classifications employed [here] are substantially related to the achievement of the important and congressionally articulated goal of remedying the present effects of past racial discrimination. The provision, therefore, passes muster under the equal protection standard I adopted in Bakke. [Doors] that have been shut to Negroes cannot be fully opened without the acceptance of race-conscious remedies. [I] applaud this [result]."

Justice STEWART's dissent, joined by Justice Rehnquist, insisted: "I think today's decision is wrong for the same reason that [Plessy] was wrong. [Equal protection] absolutely prohibits invidious discrimination by government. [Racial] discrimination is by definition invidious discrimination. The rule cannot be any different when the persons injured by a racially biased law are not members of a racial minority. [If] a law is unconstitutional, it is no less unconstitutional just because it is a product of [Congress]. [Today,] the Court [places] its imprimatur on the creation once again by government of privileges based on birth. [By] making race a relevant criterion once again in its own affairs, the Government implicitly teaches the public that the apportionment of rewards and penalties can legitimately be made according to race—rather than according to merit or ability—and that people can, and perhaps should, view themselves and others in terms of their racial characteristics. Notions of 'racial entitlement' will be fostered, and private discrimination will necessarily be encouraged." He apparently opposed *any* racial classifications except those justifiable as remedies for adequately proven past discrimination.

Justice STEVENS's distinctive dissent objected to the lax congressional procedures in arriving at its 10% set-aside figure and in delineating the eligible minority groups. Criticizing "this slapdash statute," he elaborated: "This Act is markedly different from the normal product of the legislative decisionmaking process. The very fact that Congress for the first time in the Nation's history has created a broad legislative classification for entitlement to benefits based solely on racial characteristics identifies a dramatic difference between this Act and the thousands of statutes that preceded it. This dramatic [departure] is not even mentioned in the statement of purpose of the Act or in the reports of [the congressional committees. The floor debate [was] a perfunctory consideration of an unprecedented policy decision of profound constitutional importance to the Nation. [I] see no reason why the character of [congressional] procedures may not be considered relevant to the decision whether the legislative product is [constitutional]. I would hold this statute unconstitutional on a narrower ground [than Justice Stewart's dissent]. It cannot fairly be characterized as a 'narrowly tailored' racial classification because it simply raises too many serious questions that Congress failed to answer or even to address in a responsible way.[1] [When] Congress creates a special preference, or a special disability, for a class of persons, it should identify the characteristic that justifies the special treatment. When the classification is defined in racial terms, I believe that such particular identification is imperative. [Because] it has failed to make that demonstration, it has also failed to discharge its duty to govern impartially embodied in the [Fifth Amendment]." [Recall Justice Steven's somewhat similar approach in Hampton v. Mow Sun Wong (1976; p. 724 above); and compare the evolution of his position in subsequent cases.]

Richmond v. J.A. Croson Co.

488 U.S. 469, 109 S.Ct. 706, 102 L.Ed.2d 854 (1989).

Justice O'CONNOR announced the judgment of the Court and delivered the opinion of the Court with respect to Parts I, III–B, and IV, an opinion with respect to Part II, in which The Chief Justice [REHNQUIST] and Justice WHITE join, and an opinion with respect to Parts III–A and V, in which The Chief Justice [REHNQUIST], Justice WHITE and Justice KENNEDY join.

1. "For example, why were these six racial classifications, and no others, included in the preferred class? Why are aliens excluded from the preference although they are not otherwise ineligible for public contracts? What percentage of Oriental blood or what degree of Spanish-speaking skill is required for membership in the preferred class? How does the legacy of slavery and the history of discrimination against the descendants of its victims support a preference for Spanish-speaking citizens who may be directly competing with black citizens in some overpopulated communities? Why is a preference given only to owners of business enterprises and why is that preference unaccompanied by any requirement concerning the employment of disadvantaged [persons]?" [Footnote by Justice Stevens.]

In this case, we confront once again the tension between [the] guarantee of equal treatment [and] the use of race-based measures to ameliorate the effects of past discrimination on the opportunities enjoyed by members of minority groups in our society. [Relying] largely on our decision in Fullilove, some lower federal courts have applied a similar standard of review in assessing the constitutionality of state and local minority set-aside provisions under [equal protection]. Since our decision [in Wygant], the lower federal courts have attempted to apply its [more restrictive] standard in evaluating the constitutionality of state and local programs which allocate a portion of public contracting opportunities exclusively to minority-owned businesses. We [review] this case to consider the applicability of [Wygant] to a minority set-aside program adopted [by] Richmond, Virginia.[1]

I. [The] Plan was adopted by the Richmond City Council after a public hearing. Seven members of the public spoke to the merits of the ordinance: five were in opposition, two in favor. Proponents of the set-aside provision relied on a study which indicated that, while the general population of Richmond was 50% black, only 0.67% of the city's prime construction contracts had been awarded to minority businesses in the 5–year period from 1978 to 1983. It was also established that a variety of contractors' associations [had] virtually no minority businesses within their membership. The city's legal counsel indicated his view that the ordinance was constitutional under this Court's decision in [Fullilove.] Councilperson Marsh, a proponent of the ordinance, made the following statement: "There is some information, however, that I want to make sure that we put in the record. [I] can say without equivocation, that the general conduct of the construction industry in this area, and the State, and around the nation, is one in which race discrimination and exclusion on the basis of race is widespread." There was no direct evidence of race discrimination on the part of the city in letting contracts or any evidence that the city's prime contractors had discriminated against minority-owned subcontractors. [The case was brought by a contractor whose low bid on a city project was not accepted because of failure to comply with the Plan's requirements. The District Court upheld the Plan, but the Court of Appeals struck it down as violating both prongs of equal protection strict scrutiny.] We affirm.

II. The parties and their supporting amici fight an initial battle over the scope of the city's power to adopt legislation designed to address the effects of past discrimination. Relying on our decision in Wygant, appellee argues that the city must limit any race-based remedial efforts to eradicating the effects of its own prior discrimination. This is essentially the position taken by the [Court of Appeals]. Appellant argues that our decision in Fullilove is controlling, and that as a result the city of Richmond enjoys sweeping legislative power to define and attack the effects of prior discrimination in its local construction industry. We find that neither of these two rather stark alternatives can withstand

1. The Richmond City Council adopted its program in 1983, modeled on the federal one upheld in Fullilove. It required prime contractors on city projects to subcontract at least 30% of the dollar amount of the contract to one or more Minority Business Enterprises (MBEs). Borrowing the definition used by Congress in Fullilove, the Richmond Plan defined an MBE as "[a] business at least [51%] of which is owned and controlled [by] minority group members" and identified eligible minority groups as "Blacks, Spanish-speaking, Orientals, Indians, Eskimos, or Aleuts." There was no geographic limit to the Plan; an otherwise qualified MBE from anywhere in the nation could avail itself of the 30% set-aside. Regulations under the Plan provided that waivers would be granted "in exceptional circumstances," when "every feasible attempt has been made to comply, and it [has been] demonstrated that sufficient, relevant, qualified [MBEs] are unavailable or unwilling to participate in the contract to enable meeting the 30% MBE goal."

analysis. [Appellant relies] heavily on Fullilove for the proposition that a city council, like Congress, need not make specific findings of discrimination to engage in race-conscious relief. Thus, appellant argues "[i]t would be a perversion of federalism to hold that the federal government has a compelling interest in remedying the effects of racial discrimination in its own public works program, but a city government does not." What appellant ignores is that Congress, unlike any State or political subdivision, has a specific constitutional mandate to enforce the dictates of the Fourteenth Amendment. The power to "enforce" may at times also include the power to define situations which *Congress* determines threaten principles of equality and to adopt prophylactic rules to deal with those situations. See [Katzenbach v. Morgan (1961; chap. 10 below).]

[That] Congress may identify and redress the effects of society-wide discrimination does not mean that, a fortiori, the States and their political subdivision are free to decide that such remedies are appropriate. Section 1 of the Fourteenth Amendment is an explicit *constraint* on state power, and the States must undertake any remedial efforts in accordance with that provision. To hold otherwise would be to cede control over the content of [equal protection] to the 50 state legislatures and their myriad political subdivisions. The mere recitation of a benign or compensatory purpose for the use of a racial classification would essentially entitle the States to exercise the full power of Congress under § 5 of the Fourteenth Amendment and insulate any racial classification from judicial scrutiny under § 1. We believe that such a result would be contrary to the intentions of the Framers of the Fourteenth Amendment, who desired to place clear limits on the State's use of race as a criterion for legislative [action]. We do not, as Justice Marshall's dissent suggests, find in § 5 of the Fourteenth Amendment some form of federal pre-emption in matters of race. We simply note what should be apparent to all—§ 1 of the Fourteenth Amendment stemmed from a distrust of state legislative enactments based on race; § 5 [is] " 'a *positive* grant of legislative power' " to Congress. Thus, our treatment of an exercise of congressional power in Fullilove cannot be dispositive here. [It] would seem equally clear, however, that a state or local subdivision (if delegated the authority from the State) has the authority to eradicate the effects of private discrimination within its own legislative jurisdiction. This authority must, of course, be exercised within the constraints of § 1 of the Fourteenth Amendment. Our decision in Wygant is not to the contrary. [As] a matter of state law, [Richmond] has legislative authority over its procurement policies, and can use its spending powers to remedy private discrimination, if it identifies that discrimination with the particularity required by the [Fourteenth Amendment]. Thus, if the city could show that it had essentially become a "passive participant" in a system of racial exclusion practiced by elements of the local construction industry, we think it clear that the city could take affirmative steps to dismantle such a system. It is beyond dispute that any public entity, state or federal, has a compelling interest in assuring that public dollars, drawn from the tax contributions of all citizens, do not serve to finance the evil of private prejudice.

III. A. [The] Richmond Plan denies certain citizens the opportunity to compete for a fixed percentage of public contracts based solely upon their race. To whatever racial group these citizens belong, their "personal rights" to be treated with equal dignity and respect are implicated by a rigid rule erecting race as the sole criterion in an aspect of public decisionmaking. Absent searching judicial inquiry into the justification for such race-based measures, there is simply no way of determining what classifications are "benign" or "remedial" and what classifications are in fact motivated by illegitimate notions of racial inferiority or simple racial politics. Indeed, the purpose of strict scrutiny is to "smoke out" illegitimate uses of race by assuring that the legislative body is pursuing a goal important enough to warrant use of a highly suspect tool. The test also ensures that the means chosen "fit" this compelling goal so closely that there is little or no possibility that the motive for the classification was illegitimate racial prejudice or stereotype. Classifications based on race carry a danger of stigmatic harm. Unless they are strictly reserved for remedial settings, they may in fact promote notions of racial inferiority and lead to a politics of racial hostility. We thus reaffirm the view expressed by the plurality in Wygant that the standard of review under [equal protection] is not dependent on the race of those burdened or benefited by a particular classification. Our continued adherence to the standard of review employed in Wygant does not, as Justice Marshall's dissent suggests, indicate that we view "racial discrimination as largely a phenomenon of the past" or that "government bodies need no longer preoccupy themselves with rectifying racial injustice." [Rather,] our interpretation [stems] from our agreement with the view expressed by Justice Powell in Bakke, that "[t]he guarantee of equal protection cannot mean one thing when applied to one individual and something else when applied to a person of another color." [The] dissent's watered-down version of equal protection review effectively assures that race will always be relevant in American [life]. Even were we to accept a reading of the guarantee of equal protection under which the level of scrutiny varies according to the ability of different groups to defend their interests in the representative process, heightened scrutiny would still be appropriate in the circumstances of this case. One of the central arguments for applying a less exacting standard to "benign" racial classifications is that such measures essentially involve a choice made by dominant racial groups to disadvantage themselves. If one aspect of the judiciary's role under [equal protection] is to protect "discrete and insular minorities" from majoritarian prejudice or indifference, some maintain that these concerns are not implicated when the "white majority" places burdens upon itself. See J. Ely, Democracy and Distrust (1980). In this case, blacks comprise approximately 50% of the population of the city of Richmond. Five of the nine seats on the City Council are held by blacks. The concern that a political majority will more easily act to the disadvantage of a minority based on unwarranted assumptions or incomplete facts would seem to militate for, not against, the application of heightened judicial scrutiny in this [case].

B. [The] District Court found the city council's "findings sufficient to ensure that, in adopting the Plan, it was remedying the present effects of past discrimination in the *construction industry.*" Like the "role model" theory employed in Wygant, a generalized assertion that there has been past discrimination in an entire industry provides no guidance for a legislative body to determine the precise scope of the injury it seeks to remedy. It "has no logical stopping point." Wygant. "Relief" for such an ill-defined wrong could extend until the percentage of public contracts awarded to MBEs in Richmond mirrored the percentage of minorities in the population as a whole. Appellant argues that it is attempting to remedy various forms of past discrimination that are alleged to be responsible for the small number of minority businesses in the local contracting industry. Among these the city cites the exclusion of blacks from skilled construction trade unions and training programs. [The] city also lists a host of nonracial factors which would seem to face a member of any racial group attempting to establish a new business enterprise, such as deficiencies in working capital, inability to meet bonding requirements, unfamiliarity with bidding procedures, and disability caused by an inadequate track record. While there is no doubt that the sorry history of both private and public discrimination in this country has contributed to a lack of opportunities for black entrepreneurs, this observation, standing alone, cannot justify a rigid racial quota in the awarding of public contracts in [Richmond]. It is sheer speculation how many minority firms there would be in Richmond absent past societal discrimination, just as it was sheer speculation how many minority medical students would have been admitted to the medical school at Davis absent past discrimination in educational opportunities. Defining these sorts of injuries as "identified discrimination" would give local governments license to create a patchwork of racial preferences based on statistical generalizations about any particular field of endeavor. These defects are readily apparent in this case. The 30% quota cannot in any realistic sense be tied to any injury suffered by anyone. The District Court relied upon five predicate "facts" in reaching its conclusion that there was an adequate basis for the 30% quota: (1) the ordinance declares itself to be remedial; (2) several proponents of the measure stated their views that there had been past discrimination in the construction industry; (3) minority businesses received .67% of prime contracts from the city while minorities constituted 50% of the city's population; (4) there were very few minority contractors in local and state contractors' associations; and (5) in 1977, Congress made a determination that the effects of past discrimination had stifled minority participation in the construction industry nationally. None of these "findings," singly or together, provide the city of Richmond with a "strong basis in evidence for its conclusion that remedial action was necessary." Wygant. There is nothing approaching a prima facie case of a constitutional or statutory violation by *anyone* in the Richmond construction industry.

The District Court accorded great weight to the fact that the city council designated the Plan as "remedial." But the mere recitation of a "benign" or legitimate purpose for a racial classification is entitled to little or no weight. Racial classifications are suspect, and that means that simple legislative assurances of good intention cannot suffice. The District Court also relied on the highly conclusionary statement of a proponent of the Plan that there was racial discrimination in the construction industry "in this area, and the State, and around the nation." [Such] statements are of little probative value in establishing identified discrimination in the Richmond construction industry. [W]hen a legislative body chooses to employ a suspect classification, it cannot rest upon a generalized assertion as to the classification's relevance to its goals. [The] history of racial classifications in this country suggests that blind judicial deference to legislative or executive pronouncements of necessity has no place in equal protection analysis. See [Korematsu] (Murphy, J., dissenting). Reliance on the disparity between the number of prime contracts awarded to minority firms and the minority population of the city of Richmond is similarly misplaced. [In] this case, the city does not even know how many MBEs in the relevant market are qualified to undertake prime or subcontracting work in public construction projects. Nor does the city know what percentage of total city construction dollars minority firms now receive as subcontractors on prime contracts let by the city. [Without] any information on minority participation in subcontracting, it is quite simply impossible to evaluate overall minority representation in the city's construction expenditures.

The city and the District Court also relied on evidence that MBE membership in local contractors' associations was extremely low. Again, standing alone this evidence is not probative of any discrimination in the local construction industry. There are numerous explanations for this dearth of minority participation, including past societal discrimination in education and economic opportunities as well as both black and white career and entrepreneurial choices.

[For] low minority membership in these associations to be relevant, the city would have to link it to the number of local MBEs eligible for membership. [Finally,] the city and the District Court relied on Congress' finding in connection with the set-aside approved in Fullilove that there had been nationwide discrimination in the construction industry. The probative value of these findings for demonstrating the existence of discrimination in Richmond is extremely limited. [Congress] was exercising its power under [the 14th Amendment] in making a finding that past discrimination would cause federal funds to be distributed in a manner which reinforced prior patterns of discrimination. While the States and their subdivisions may take remedial action when they possess evidence that their own spending practices are exacerbating a pattern of prior discrimination, they must identify that discrimination, public or private, with some specificity before they may use race-conscious relief. Congress has made national findings that there has been societal discrimination in a host of fields. If all a state or local government need do is find a congressional report on the subject to enact a set-aside program, the constraints of [equal protection] will, in effect, have been rendered a nullity. [Justice Marshall] apparently views the requirement that Richmond identify the discrimination it seeks to remedy in its own jurisdiction as a mere administrative headache, an "onerous documentary obligatio[n]." We cannot agree. [The] "evidence" relied upon by the dissent, the history of school desegregation in Richmond and numerous congressional reports, does little to define the scope of any injury to minority contractors in Richmond or the necessary remedy. The factors relied upon by the dissent could justify a preference of any size or duration. Moreover, Justice Marshall's suggestion that findings of discrimination may be "shared" from jurisdiction to jurisdiction in the same manner as information concerning zoning and property values is unprecedented. We have never approved the extrapolation of discrimination in one jurisdiction from the experience of another.

In sum, none of the evidence presented by the city points to any identified discrimination in the Richmond construction industry. We therefore hold that the city has failed to demonstrate a compelling interest in apportioning public contracting opportunities on the basis of race. To accept Richmond's claim that past societal discrimination alone can serve as the basis for rigid racial preferences would be to open the door to competing claims for "remedial relief" for every disadvantaged group. The dream of a Nation of equal citizens in a society where race is irrelevant to personal opportunity and achievement would be lost in a mosaic of shifting preferences based on inherently unmeasurable claims of past wrongs. [See Bakke (Powell, J.).] We think that such a result would be contrary to both the letter and spirit of [equal protection]. The foregoing analysis applies only to the inclusion of blacks within the Richmond set-aside program. There is *absolutely no evidence* of past discrimination against Spanish-speaking, Oriental, Indian, Eskimo, or Aleut persons in any aspect of the Richmond construction industry. [It] may well be that Richmond has never had an Aleut or Eskimo citizen. The random inclusion of racial groups that, as a practical matter, may never have suffered from discrimination in the construction industry in Richmond suggests that perhaps the city's purpose was not in fact to remedy past discrimination. If a 30% set-aside was "narrowly tailored" to compensate black contractors for past discrimination, one may legitimately ask why they are forced to share this "remedial relief" with an Aleut citizen who moves to Richmond tomorrow. The gross overinclusiveness of Richmond's racial preference strongly impugns the city's claim of remedial motivation.

IV.   As noted by the court below, it is almost impossible to assess whether the Richmond Plan is narrowly tailored to remedy prior discrimination since it is not linked to identified discrimination in any way. We limit ourselves to two observations in this regard. First, there does not appear to have been any consideration of the use of race-neutral means to increase minority business participation in city contracting. [If] MBEs disproportionately lack capital or cannot meet bonding requirements, a race-neutral program of city financing for small firms would, a fortiori, lead to greater minority participation. [Second,] the 30% quota cannot be said to be narrowly tailored to any goal, except perhaps outright racial balancing. It rests upon the "completely unrealistic" assumption that minorities will choose a particular trade in lockstep proportion to their representation in the local population. Since the city must already consider bids and waivers on a case-by-case basis, it is difficult to see the need for a rigid numerical quota. [Unlike] the program upheld in Fullilove, the Richmond Plan's waiver system focuses solely on the availability of MBEs; there is no inquiry into whether or not the particular MBE seeking a racial preference has suffered from the effects of past discrimination by the city or prime contractors. Given the existence of an individualized procedure, the city's only interest in maintaining a quota system rather than investigating the need for remedial action in particular cases would seem to be simple administrative convenience. But [this] interest [cannot] justify a rigid line drawn on the basis of a suspect classification. Under Richmond's scheme, a successful black, Hispanic, or Oriental entrepreneur from anywhere in the country enjoys an absolute preference over other citizens based solely on their race. We think it obvious that such a program is not narrowly tailored to remedy the effects of prior discrimination.

V.   Nothing we say today precludes a state or local entity from taking action to rectify the effects of identified discrimination within its jurisdiction. If [Richmond] had evidence before it that nonminority contractors were systematically excluding minority businesses from subcontracting opportunities it could take action to end the discriminatory exclusion. Where there is a significant statistical disparity between the number of qualified minority contractors willing and able to perform a particular service and the number of such contractors actually engaged by the locality or the locality's prime contractors, an inference of discriminatory exclusion could arise. Under such circumstances, the city could act to dismantle the closed business system by taking appropriate measures against those who discriminate on the basis of race or other illegitimate criteria. In the extreme case, some form of narrowly tailored racial preference might be necessary to break down patterns of deliberate exclusion. Nor is the local government powerless to deal with individual instances of racially motivated refusals to employ minority contractors. [Even] in the absence of evidence of discrimination, the city has at its disposal a whole array of race-neutral devices to increase the accessibility of city contracting opportunities to small entrepreneurs of all races. Simplification of bidding procedures, relaxation of bonding requirements, and training and financial aid for disadvantaged entrepreneurs of all races would open the public contracting market to all those who have suffered the effects of past societal discrimination or neglect. [The] city may also act to prohibit discrimination in the provision of credit or bonding by local suppliers and [banks]. In the case at hand, the city has not ascertained how many minority enterprises are present in the local construction market nor the level of their participation in city construction projects. The city points to no evidence that qualified minority contractors have been passed over for city contracts or subcontracts, either as a group or in any individual case. Under such circumstances, it is simply impossible to say that the city has demonstrated "a strong basis in evidence for its conclusion that remedial action was necessary." Wygant. Proper findings in this regard are necessary to define both the scope of the injury and the extent of the remedy necessary to cure its effects. Such findings also serve to assure all citizens that the deviation from the norm of equal treatment of all racial and ethnic groups is a temporary matter, a measure taken in the service of the goal of equality itself. Absent such findings, there is a danger that a racial classification is merely the product of unthinking stereotypes or a form of racial politics. [Because Richmond] has failed to identify the need for remedial action in the awarding of its public construction contracts, its treatment of its citizens on a racial basis violates the dictates of [equal protection].

[Affirmed.]

Justice STEVENS, concurring in part and concurring in the judgment.

[I] do not agree with the premise that seems to underlie today's decision, as well as the decision in Wygant, that a governmental decision that rests on a racial classification is never permissible except as a remedy for a past wrong.[1] I do, however, agree with the Court's explanation of why the Richmond ordinance cannot be justified as a remedy for past discrimination, and therefore joint Parts I, III–B, and IV of its opinion. I write separately to emphasize three aspects of the case that are of special importance to me. First, the city makes no claim that the public interest in the efficient performance of its construction contracts will be served by granting a preference to minority-business enterprises. This case is therefore completely unlike Wygant, in which I thought it quite obvious that the School Board had reasonably concluded that an integrated faculty could provide educational benefits to the entire student body that could not be provided by an all-white, or nearly all-white faculty. [Second,] this litigation involves an attempt by a legislative body, rather than a court, to fashion a remedy for a past wrong. [It] is the judicial system, rather than the legislative process, that is best equipped to identify past wrongdoers and to fashion remedies that will create the conditions that presumably would have existed had no wrong been [committed]. Third, instead of engaging in a debate over the proper standard of review to apply in affirmative-action litigation, I believe it is more constructive to try to identify the characteristics of the advantaged and disadvantaged classes that may justify their disparate treatment. In this case that approach convinces me that, instead of carefully identifying the characteristics of the two classes of contractors that are respectively favored and disfavored by its ordinance, [Richmond] has merely engaged in the type of stereotypical analysis that is a hallmark of violations of [equal protection]. The justification for the ordinance is the fact that in the past white

---

1. In my view the Court's approach to this case gives unwarranted deference to race-based legislative action that purports to serve a purely remedial goal, and overlooks the potential value of race-based determinations that may serve other valid purposes. With regard to the former point: [I] am not prepared to assume that even a more narrowly tailored set-aside program supported by stronger findings would be constitutionally justified. Unless the legislature can identify both the particular victims and the particular perpetrators of past discrimination, [a] remedial justification for race-based legislation will almost certainly sweep too broadly. With

regard to the latter point: I think it unfortunate that the Court in neither Wygant nor this case seems prepared to acknowledge that some race-based policy decisions may serve a legitimate public purpose. I agree, of course, that race is so seldom relevant to legislative decisions on how best to foster the public good that legitimate justifications for race-based legislation will usually not be available. But unlike the Court, I would not totally discount the legitimacy of race-based decisions that may produce tangible and fully justified future benefits. [Footnote by Justice Stevens.]

contractors—and presumably other white citizens in Richmond—have discriminated against black contractors. The class of persons benefited by the ordinance is not, however, limited to victims of such [discrimination]. Indeed, for all the record shows, all of the minority-business enterprises that have benefited from the ordinance may be firms that have prospered notwithstanding the discriminatory conduct that may have harmed other minority firms years ago. Ironically, minority firms that have survived in the competitive struggle, rather than those that have perished, are most likely to benefit from an ordinance of this kind. [The] ordinance is equally vulnerable because of its failure to identify the characteristics of the disadvantaged class of white contractors that justify the disparate treatment. [The] composition of the disadvantaged class of white contractors presumably includes some who have been guilty of unlawful discrimination, some who practiced discrimination before it was forbidden by law, and some who have never discriminated against anyone on the basis of race. Imposing a common burden on such a disparate class merely because each member of the class is of the same race stems from reliance on a stereotype rather than fact or reason.[2] There is a special irony in the stereotypical thinking that prompts legislation of this kind. Although it stigmatizes the disadvantaged class with the unproven charge of past racial discrimination, it actually imposes a greater stigma on its supposed [beneficiaries].

Justice KENNEDY, concurring in part and concurring in the judgment.

I join all but Part II of Justice O'Connor's [opinion]. [The] process by which a law that is an equal protection violation when enacted by a State becomes transformed to an equal protection guarantee when enacted by Congress poses a difficult proposition for me; but it is not before [us]. The moral imperative of racial neutrality is the driving force of [equal protection]. Justice Scalia's opinion underscores that proposition, quite properly in my view. The rule suggested in his opinion, which would strike down all preferences which are not necessary remedies to victims of unlawful discrimination, would serve important structural goals, as it would eliminate the necessity for courts to pass upon each [racial preference]. [Nevertheless,] given that a rule of automatic invalidity for racial preferences in almost every case would be a significant break with our precedents that require a case-by-case test, I am not convinced we need adopt it at this point. On the assumption that it will vindicate the principle of race neutrality found in [equal protection], I accept the less absolute rule contained in Justice O'Connor's opinion, a rule based on the proposition that any racial preference must face the most rigorous scrutiny by the courts. My reasons for doing so are as follows. First, I am confident that, in application, the strict scrutiny standard will operate in a manner generally consistent with the imperative of race [neutrality]. Second, the rule against race-conscious remedies is already less than an absolute one, for that relief may be the only adequate remedy after a judicial determination that a State or its instrumentality has violated [equal protection]. [Third,] the strict scrutiny rule is consistent with our [precedents]. The ordinance before us falls far short of the standard we adopt. [We] are left with an ordinance and a legislative record open to the fair charge that it is not a remedy but is itself a preference which will cause the same corrosive animosities that the Constitution [forbids].

Justice SCALIA, concurring in the judgment.

2. There is, of course, another possibility that should not be overlooked. The ordinance might be nothing more than a form of patronage. But racial patronage, like a racial gerrymander, is no more defensible than political patronage or a political [gerrymander]. [Footnote by Justice Stevens.]

I agree with much of the Court's opinion, and, in particular, with its conclusion that strict scrutiny must be applied to all governmental classification by race, whether or not its asserted purpose is "remedial" or "benign." I do not agree, however, with [the Court's dicta] suggesting [that] state and local governments may in some circumstances discriminate on the basis of race in order (in a broad sense) "to ameliorate the effects of past discrimination." The benign purpose of compensating for social disadvantages, whether they have been acquired by reason of prior discrimination or otherwise, can no more be pursued by the illegitimate means of racial discrimination than can other assertedly benign purposes we have repeatedly rejected. The difficulty of overcoming the effects of past discrimination is as nothing compared with the difficulty of eradicating from our society the source of those effects, which is the tendency—fatal to a nation such as ours—to classify and judge men and women on the basis of their country of origin or the color of their skin. A solution to the first problem that aggravates the second is no solution at all. [At] least where state or local action is at issue, only a social emergency rising to the level of imminent danger to life and limb—for example, a prison race riot, requiring temporary segregation of inmates—can justify an exception to the principle [that] "[o]ur Constitution is [color-blind]." We have in some contexts approved the use of racial classifications by the Federal Government to remedy the effects of past discrimination. I do not believe that we must or should extend those holdings to the States. [A] sound distinction between federal and state (or local) action based on race rests not only upon the substance of the Civil War Amendments, but upon social reality and governmental theory. [The] record shows [that] racial discrimination against any group finds a more ready expression at the state and local than at the federal level. [An] acute awareness of the heightened danger of oppression from political factions in small, rather than large, political units dates to the very beginning of our national history.

[In] my view there is only one circumstance in which the States may act *by race* to "undo the effects of past discrimination": where that is necessary to eliminate their own maintenance of a system of unlawful racial classification. If, for example, a state agency has a discriminatory pay scale compensating black employees in all positions at 20% less than their nonblack counterparts, it may assuredly promulgate an order raising the salaries of "all black employees" by 20%. This distinction explains our school desegregation cases, in which we have made plain that States and localities sometimes have an obligation to adopt race-conscious remedies. [I] agree with the Court's dictum that a fundamental distinction must be drawn between the effects of "societal" discrimination and the effects of "identified" discrimination, and that the situation would be different if Richmond's plan were "tailored" to identify those particular bidders who "suffered from the effects of past discrimination by the city or prime contractors." In my view, however, the reason that would make a difference is not, as the Court states, that it would justify race-conscious action, but rather that it would enable race-neutral remediation. Nothing prevents Richmond from according a contracting preference to identified victims of discrimination. While most of the beneficiaries might be black, neither the beneficiaries nor those disadvantaged by the preference would be identified *on the basis of their race*. In other words, far from justifying racial classification, identification of actual victims of discrimination makes it less supportable than ever, because more obviously unneeded. [When] we depart from this American principle [of color-blindness] we play with fire, and much more than an occasional DeFunis [or] Croson burns.

It is plainly true that in our society blacks have suffered discrimination immeasurably greater than any directed at other racial groups. But those who believe that racial preferences can help to "even the score" display, and reinforce, a manner of thinking by race that was the source of the injustice and that will, if it endures within our society, be the source of more injustice still. The relevant proposition is not that it was blacks, or Jews, or Irish who were discriminated against, but that it was individual men and women, "created equal," who were discriminated against. And the relevant resolve is that that should never happen again. Racial preferences appear to "even the score" (in some small degree) only if one embraces the proposition that our society is appropriately viewed as divided into races, making it right that an injustice rendered in the past to a black man should be compensated for by discriminating against a white. Nothing is worth that embrace. Since blacks have been disproportionately disadvantaged by racial discrimination, any race-neutral remedial program aimed at the disadvantaged *as such* will have a disproportionately beneficial impact on blacks. Only such a program, and not one that operates on the basis of race, is in accord with the letter and the spirit of our Constitution. Since I believe that the appellee here had a constitutional right to have its bid succeed or fail under a decisionmaking process uninfected with racial bias, I concur in the judgment of the Court.

Justice MARSHALL, with whom Justice BRENNAN and Justice BLACKMUN join, dissenting.

It is a welcome symbol of racial progress when the former capital of the Confederacy acts forthrightly to confront the effects of racial discrimination in its midst. In my view, nothing in the Constitution can be construed to prevent [Richmond] from allocating a portion of its contracting dollars for businesses owned or controlled by members of minority groups. Indeed, Richmond's set-aside program is indistinguishable in all meaningful respects from—and in fact was patterned upon—the federal set-aside plan which this Court upheld in [Fullilove]. A majority of this Court holds today, however, that [equal protection] blocks Richmond's initiative. [Today's] decision marks a deliberate and giant step backward in this Court's affirmative action jurisprudence. Cynical of one municipality's attempt to redress the effects of past racial discrimination in a particular industry, the majority launches a grapeshot attack on race-conscious remedies in general. The majority's unnecessary pronouncements will inevitably discourage or prevent governmental entities [from] acting to rectify the scourge of past discrimination. This [is] not the Constitution's command. I. As an initial matter, the majority takes an exceedingly myopic view of the factual predicate on which the Richmond City Council [relied]. The majority's refusal to recognize that Richmond has proven itself no exception to the dismaying pattern of national exclusion which Congress so painstakingly identified infects its entire analysis of this case. [So] long as one views Richmond's local evidence of discrimination against the backdrop of systematic nationwide racial discrimination which Congress had so painstakingly identified in this very industry, this case is readily resolved.

II. [My] view has long been that race-conscious classifications designed to further remedial goals "must serve important governmental objectives and must be substantially related to achievement of those objectives" in order to withstand constitutional scrutiny. Analyzed in terms of this two-prong standard, Richmond's set-aside, like the federal program on which it was modeled, is "plainly constitutional." A.1. [Richmond] has two powerful interests in setting aside a portion of public contracting funds for minority-owned enterprises. The first is the city's interest in eradicating the effects of past racial discrimination. It is far too late in the day to doubt that remedying such discrimination is a compelling, let alone an important, interest. [Richmond] has a second compelling interest in setting aside, where possible, a portion of its contracting dollars. That interest is the prospective one of preventing the city's own spending decisions from reinforcing and perpetuating the exclusionary effects of past discrimination. The majority pays only lip service to this additional governmental interest. [When] government channels all its contracting funds to a white-dominated community of established contractors whose racial homogeneity is the product of private discrimination, it does more than place its imprimatur on the practices which forged and which continue to define that community. It also provides a measurable boost to those economic entities that have thrived within it, while denying important economic benefits to those entities which, but for prior discrimination, might well be better qualified to receive valuable [government contracts].

2. The remaining question with respect to the "governmental interest" prong of equal protection analysis is whether Richmond has proffered satisfactory proof of past racial discrimination to support its twin interests in remediation and in governmental nonperpetuation. [The] varied body of evidence on which Richmond relied provides a "strong," "firm," and "unquestionably legitimate" basis upon which the City Council could determine that the effects of past racial discrimination warranted a remedial and prophylactic governmental response. [Richmond] acted against a backdrop of [federal] studies which demonstrated with such force the nationwide pervasiveness of prior discrimination that Congress presumed that " 'present economic inequities' "in construction contracting resulted from " 'past discriminatory systems.' " [No one] who testified challenged [the] depiction of widespread racial discrimination in area [construction contracting]. [In sum,] to suggest that the facts on which Richmond has relied do not provide a sound basis for its finding of past racial discrimination simply blinks credibility. Richmond's reliance on localized, industry-specific findings is a far cry from the reliance on generalized "societal discrimination" which the majority decries as a basis for remedial action. [The] majority also takes the disingenuous approach of desegregating Richmond's local evidence, attacking it piecemeal, and thereby concluding that no *single* piece of evidence adduced by the city, "standing alone," suffices to prove past discrimination. But items of evidence do not, of course, "stan[d] alone" or exist in alien juxtaposition; they necessarily work together, reinforcing or contradicting each other. [The] majority's perfunctory dismissal of the testimony of Richmond's appointed and elected leaders is also deeply disturbing. [No one,] of course, advocates "blind judicial deference" to the findings of the City Council or the testimony of city leaders. The majority's suggestion that wholesale deference is what Richmond seeks is a classic straw-man argument. [Had] the majority paused for a moment on the facts of the Richmond experience, it would have discovered that the city's leadership is deeply familiar with what racial discrimination is. [When] the legislatures and leaders of cities with histories of pervasive discrimination testify that past discrimination has infected one of their industries, armchair cynicism like that exercised by the majority has no place. [Finally,] I vehemently disagree with the majority's dismissal of the federal findings noted in Fullilove as having "extremely limited" probative value in this case. [No] principle of federalism or of federal [power] forbids a state or local government from drawing upon a nationally relevant historical record prepared by the Federal Government. Of course, Richmond could have built an even more compendious record of past discrimination, one including additional stark statistics and additional individual accounts of past discrimination. But nothing in the Fourteenth Amendment imposes such onerous docu-

mentary obligations upon States and localities once the reality of past discrimination is apparent.

B. In my judgment, Richmond's set-aside plan also comports with the second prong of the equal protection inquiry, for it is substantially related to the interests it seeks to serve in remedying past discrimination and in ensuring that municipal contract procurement does not perpetuate that discrimination. The most striking aspect of the city's ordinance is the similarity it bears to the "appropriately limited" federal set-aside provision upheld in Fullilove. [The] majority takes issue [with] two aspects of Richmond's tailoring: the city's refusal to explore the use of race-neutral measures to increase minority business participation in contracting, and the selection of a 30% set-aside figure. The majority's first criticism is flawed in two respects. First, the majority overlooks the fact that since 1975, Richmond has barred both discrimination by the city in awarding public contracts and discrimination by public contractors [with very limited success]. Second, the majority's suggestion that Richmond should have first undertaken such race-neutral measures as a program of city financing for small firms ignores the fact that such measures, while theoretically appealing, have been discredited by Congress as ineffectual in eradicating the effects of past discrimination in this very industry. [As] for Richmond's 30% target, the majority [ignores] two important facts. First, the set-aside measure affects only 3% of overall city contracting; thus any imprecision in tailoring has far less impact than the majority suggests. But more important, the majority ignores the fact that Richmond's 30% figure was patterned directly on the Fullilove precedent. Congress' 10% figure fell "roughly halfway between the present percentage of minority contractors and the percentage of minority group members in the Nation." [Richmond's] 30% figure similarly falls roughly halfway between the present percentage of Richmond-based minority contractors (almost zero) and the percentage of minorities in Richmond (50%). In faulting Richmond for not presenting a different explanation for its choice of a set-aside figure, the majority honors Fullilove only in the breach.

III. I would ordinarily end my analysis at this point and conclude that Richmond's ordinance satisfies both the governmental interest and substantial relationship prongs of our [equal protection] analysis. However, I am compelled to add more, for the majority has gone beyond the facts of this case to announce a set of principles which unnecessarily restrict the power of governmental entities to take race-conscious measures to redress the effects of prior discrimination. A. Today, for the first time, a majority of this Court has adopted strict scrutiny as its standard of [equal protection] review of race-conscious remedial measures. This is an unwelcome development. A profound difference separates governmental actions that themselves are racist, and governmental actions that seek to remedy the effects of prior racism or to prevent neutral governmental activity from perpetuating the effects of such racism. Racial classifications "drawn on the presumption that one race is inferior to another or because they put the weight of government behind racial hatred and separatism" warrant the strictest judicial scrutiny because of the very irrelevance of these rationales. By contrast, racial classifications drawn for the purpose of remedying the effects of discrimination that itself was race-based have a highly pertinent basis: the tragic and indelible fact that discrimination against blacks and other racial minorities in this Nation has pervaded our Nation's history and continues to scar our society. [In] concluding that remedial classifications warrant no different standard of review under the Constitution than the most brute and repugnant forms of state-sponsored racism, a majority of this Court signals that it regards racial discrimination as largely a phenomenon of the past, and that government bodies need no longer preoccupy themselves with rectifying racial injustice. I, however, do not believe this Nation is anywhere close to eradicating racial discrimination or its vestiges. In constitutionalizing its wishful thinking, the majority today does a grave [disservice].

B. I am also troubled by the majority's assertion that, even if it did not believe generally in strict scrutiny of race-based remedial measures, "the circumstances of this case" require this Court to look upon the Richmond City Council's measure with the strictest scrutiny. The sole such circumstance which the majority cites, however, is the fact that blacks in Richmond are a "dominant racial grou[p]" in the city. [While] I agree that the numerical and political supremacy of a given racial group is a factor bearing upon the level of scrutiny to be applied, this Court has never held that numerical inferiority, standing alone, makes a racial group "suspect" and thus entitled to strict scrutiny review. Rather, we have identified *other* "traditional indicia of suspectness": whether a group has been "saddled with such disabilities, or subjected to such a history of purposeful unequal treatment, or relegated to such a position of political powerlessness as to command extraordinary protection from the majoritarian political process." [Rodriguez, p. 842 below.] It cannot seriously be suggested that nonminorities in Richmond have any "history of purposeful unequal treatment." Nor is there any indication that they have any of the disabilities that have characteristically afflicted those groups this Court has deemed suspect. Indeed, the numerical and political dominance of nonminorities within [Virginia] and the Nation as a whole provide an enormous political check against the "simple racial politics" at the municipal level which the majority fears. In my view, the "circumstances of this case" underscore the importance of *not* subjecting to a strict scrutiny straitjacket the increasing number of cities which have recently come under minority leadership and are eager to rectify, or at least prevent the perpetuation of, past racial discrimination. In many cases, these cities will be the ones with the most in the way of prior discrimination to rectify. [The] majority's view that remedial measures undertaken by municipalities with black leadership must face a stiffer test of [equal protection] scrutiny than remedial measures undertaken by municipalities with white leadership implies a lack of political maturity on the part of this Nation's elected minority officials that is totally unwarranted. Such insulting judgments have no place in constitutional jurisprudence.

C. Today's decision, finally, is particularly noteworthy for the daunting standard it imposes upon States and localities contemplating the use of race-conscious measures to eradicate the present effects of prior discrimination and prevent its perpetuation. [Nothing] in the Constitution or in the prior decisions of this Court supports limiting state authority to confront the effects of past discrimination to those situations in which a prima facie case of a constitutional or statutory violation can be made out. [To] the degree that this parsimonious standard is grounded on a view that either § 1 or § 5 of the Fourteenth Amendment substantially disempowered States and localities from remedying past racial discrimination, the majority is seriously mistaken. With respect, first, to § 5, our precedents have never suggested that this provision [was] meant to pre-empt or limit state police power to undertake race-conscious remedial measures. [As for § 1,] it is too late in the day to assert seriously that [equal protection] prohibits States [from] enacting race-conscious remedies. Our cases [have] demonstrated time and again that race is constitutionally germane, precisely because race remains dismayingly relevant in American life. [The] fact is that Congress' concern in passing the Reconstruction Amendments, and particularly their congressional authorization provisions, was that States would *not* adequately respond to racial violence or discrimination against newly freed slaves. To interpret any aspect of these Amendments as proscribing state remedial responses to these very problems turns the Amendments on their [heads].

IV. The majority today sounds a full-scale retreat from the Court's longstanding solicitude to race-conscious remedial efforts "directed toward deliverance of the century-old promise of equality of economic opportunity." Fullilove. The new and restrictive tests it applies scuttle one city's effort to surmount its discriminatory past, and imperil those of dozens more localities. I, however, profoundly disagree with the cramped vision of [equal protection] which the majority offers today and with its application of that vision to [Richmond's] laudable set-aside [plan].

Justice BLACKMUN, with whom Justice BRENNAN joins, dissenting.

I join Justice Marshall's perceptive and incisive opinion. [I] never thought that I would live to see the day [when] Richmond, Virginia, the cradle of the Old Confederacy, sought on its own, within a narrow confine, to lessen the stark impact of persistent discrimination. [The] Court today regresses. I am confident, however, that, given time, it one day again will do its best to fulfill the great promises of the [Constitution]—a fulfillment that would make this Nation very special.*

———

METRO BROADCASTING, INC. v. FCC, 497 U.S. 547 (1990): This decision upheld two "minority preference policies" of the FCC—the first, a program "awarding an enhancement for minority ownership in comparative proceedings" for new broadcast licenses; the second, a "minority 'distress sale' program," permitting "a limited category of existing radio and television broadcast stations to be transferred only to minority-controlled firms." Justice BRENNAN's majority opinion applied intermediate scrutiny and held that these policies did not violate equal protection principles. He emphasized that the policies were mandated by Congress, and that Fullilove and, in his view, Croson supported his views. He stated: "It is of overriding significance [that] the FCC's minority ownership programs have been specifically approved—indeed, mandated—by Congress. In [Fullilove], Chief Justice Burger [observed that] when a program employing a benign racial classification is adopted by an administrative agency at the explicit direction of Congress, we are 'bound to approach our task with appropriate deference to the [Congress].' [A] majority of

* Did Croson create virtually insuperable obstacles to the creation of affirmative action programs such as set-asides by state or local governments? Controversy over that question broke out soon after the decision. A group of constitutional scholars issued a statement that it would be "irresponsible [to] claim" that Croson cast "doubt on the overall constitutionality of properly constructed race-conscious remedies." The statement encouraged state and local governments to continue their support of affirmative action programs with full vigor. See [Brest, Choper, Ely, Kamisar, Stone, Sunstein, Tribe, et al.], "Constitutional Scholars' Statement on Affirmative Action After [Croson]," 98 Yale L.J. 1711 (1989). Former Solicitor General Fried criticized this statement in "[A] Response to the Scholars' Statement," 99 Yale L.J. 155 (1989), claiming that the statement "adopts the tone at once of Chicken Little and Dr. Pangloss: Something terrible has happened, but it's not so bad after all" and branded it as "misleading insofar as it suggests that no proposition of significance was enunciated." See also "Scholars' Reply to Professor Fried," 99 Yale L.J. 163 (1989), concluding: "We prefer to see Croson as the pragmatic and particularistic opinion that it is." Was Justice O'Connor's scrutiny closer to intermediate than to strict scrutiny? Note the explicitly intermediate standard in Metro Broadcasting, which follows, and contrast the very restrictive strict-scrutiny in Adarand, the next principal case.

the Court in Fullilove did not apply strict scrutiny to the race-based classification at issue. [Three] Members would have upheld benign racial classifications that 'serve important governmental objectives and are substantially related to achievement of those objectives.' [Opinion of Marshall, J.] We apply that standard today. We hold that benign race-conscious measures mandated by Congress—even if those measures are not 'remedial' in the sense of being designed to compensate victims of past governmental or societal discrimination—are constitutionally permissible to the extent that they serve important governmental objectives within the power of Congress and are substantially related to achievement of those objectives. [Our] decision in [Croson] does not prescribe the level of scrutiny to be applied to a benign racial classification employed by Congress. [The] question of congressional action was not before the Court, and so Croson cannot be read to undermine our decision in Fullilove. In fact, much of the language and reasoning in Croson reaffirmed the lesson of Fullilove that race-conscious classifications adopted by Congress to address racial and ethnic discrimination are subject to a different standard than such classifications prescribed by state and local governments. [We] hold that the FCC minority ownership policies pass muster under the test we announce today. First, we find that they serve the important governmental objective of broadcast diversity. Second, we conclude that they are substantially related to the achievement of that objective. [The] interest in enhancing broadcast diversity is, at the very least, an important governmental objective and is therefore a sufficient basis for the Commission's minority ownership policies. Just as a 'diverse student body' contributing to a ' " "robust exchange of ideas" " ' is a 'constitutionally permissible goal' on which a race-conscious university admissions program may be predicated, the diversity of views and information on the airwaves serves important First Amendment values."

Justice Brennan also found that the minority ownership policies were substantially related to the achievement of the government's interest in broadcast diversity. He stated that "we must pay close attention to the expertise of the [FCC] and the factfinding of Congress when analyzing the nexus between minority ownership and programming diversity." He added: "The judgment that there is [such a nexus] does not rest on impermissible stereotyping. [While] we are under no illusion that members of a particular minority group share some cohesive, collective viewpoint, we believe it a legitimate inference for Congress and the Commission to draw that as more minorities gain ownership and policymaking roles in the media, varying perspectives will be more fairly represented on the airwaves. The policies are thus a product of ' "analysis" ' rather than a ' "stereotyped reaction" ' [based on 'habit']." He continued: "Finally, we do not believe that the minority ownership policies at issue impose impermissible burdens on nonminorities. Applicants [for licenses] have no settled expectation that their applications will be granted without consideration of public interest factors such as minority ownership." Justice STEVENS concurred, stating: "Today the Court squarely rejects the proposition that a governmental decision that rests on a racial classification is never permissible except as a remedy for a past wrong. I endorse this focus on the future benefit, rather than the remedial justification, of such decisions. [The] Court demonstrates that this case falls within the extremely narrow category of governmental decisions for which racial or ethnic heritage may provide a rational basis for differential treatment. The public interest in broadcast diversity—like the interest in an integrated police force, diversity in the composition of a public school faculty or diversity in the student body of a professional school—is in my view unquestionably legitimate."

Justice O'CONNOR, joined by Chief Justice Rehnquist and Justices Scalia and Kennedy, dissented, insisting on an across-the-board strict scrutiny standard, for federal as well as state actions. She elaborated: "Congress has considerable latitude [when] it exercises its 'unique remedial powers [under] § 5 of the Fourteenth Amendment' [Croson], but this case does not implicate those powers. [The] Court asserts that Fullilove supports its novel application of intermediate scrutiny to 'benign' race conscious measures adopted by Congress. [Several] reasons defeat this claim. First, Fullilove concerned an exercise of Congress' powers under § 5 of the Fourteenth Amendment. [Second,] Fullilove applies at most only to congressional measures that seek to remedy identified past discrimination. [Finally,] even if Fullilove applied outside a remedial exercise of Congress' § 5 power, it would not support today's adoption of the intermediate standard of review proffered by Justice Marshall but rejected in Fullilove. [Six] Members of the Court rejected intermediate scrutiny in favor of some more stringent form of review. [And,] of course, Fullilove preceded our determination in Croson that strict scrutiny applies to preferences that favor members of minority groups, including challenges considered under the [Fourteenth Amendment]." [Under] the appropriate standard, strict scrutiny, only a compelling interest may support the Government's use of racial classifications. Modern equal protection doctrine has recognized only one such interest: remedying the effects of racial discrimination. The interest in increasing the diversity of broadcast viewpoints is clearly not a compelling interest. It is simply too amorphous, too insubstantial, and too unrelated to any legitimate basis for employing racial classifications. [Our] traditional equal protection doctrine requires, in addition to a compelling state interest, that the Government's chosen means be necessary to accomplish and narrowly tailored to further the asserted interest. [The] chosen means, resting as they do on stereotyping and so indirectly furthering the asserted end, could not plausibly be deemed narrowly tailored. The Court instead finds the racial classifications to be 'substantially related' to achieving the Government's interest, a far less rigorous fit requirement. The FCC's policies fail even this requirement." She concluded: "In sum, the Government has not met its burden even under the Court's test that approves of racial classifications that are substantially related to an important governmental objective. Of course, the programs even more clearly fail the strict scrutiny that should be applied. The Court has determined, in essence, that Congress and all federal agencies are exempted, to some ill-defined but significant degree, from the Constitution's equal protection requirements. This break with our precedents greatly undermines equal protection guarantees, and permits distinctions among citizens based on race and ethnicity which the Constitution clearly forbids." Justice KENNEDY, joined by Justice Scalia, also submitted a separate dissent. He ended with the statement: "I regret that after a century of judicial opinions we interpret the Constitution to do no more than move us from 'separate but equal' to 'unequal but benign.'"

Adarand Constructors, Inc. v. Pena

518 U.S. ___, 115 S.Ct. 2097, 132 L.Ed.2d 158 (1995).

Justice O'CONNOR announced the judgment of the Court and delivered an opinion with respect to Parts I, II, III–A, III–B, III–D, and IV, which is for the Court except insofar as it might be inconsistent with the views expressed in

Justice SCALIA's concurrence, and an opinion with respect to Part III–C in which Justice KENNEDY joins.

Petitioner Adarand Constructors, Inc., claims that the Federal Government's practice of giving general contractors on government projects a financial incentive to hire subcontractors controlled by "socially and economically disadvantaged individuals," and in particular, the Government's use of race-based presumptions in identifying such individuals, violates the equal protection component of the Fifth Amendment's Due Process Clause. The Court of Appeals rejected Adarand's claim. We conclude, however, that courts should analyze cases of this kind under a different standard of review than the one the Court of Appeals applied. We therefore vacate the Court of Appeals' judgment and remand the case for further proceedings.

I. In 1989, the Central Federal Lands Highway Division (CFLHD), which is part of the United States Department of Transportation (DOT), awarded the prime contract for a highway construction project in Colorado to Mountain Gravel & Construction Company. Mountain Gravel then solicited bids from subcontractors for the guardrail portion of the contract. Adarand, a Colorado-based highway construction company specializing in guardrail work, submitted the low bid. Gonzales Construction Company also submitted a bid. The prime contract's terms provide that Mountain Gravel would receive additional compensation if it hired subcontractors certified as small businesses controlled by "socially and economically disadvantaged individuals." Gonzales is certified as such a business; Adarand is not. Mountain Gravel awarded the subcontract to Gonzales, despite Adarand's low bid, and Mountain Gravel's Chief Estimator has submitted an affidavit stating that Mountain Gravel would have accepted Adarand's bid, had it not been for the additional payment it received by hiring Gonzales instead. Federal law requires that a subcontracting clause similar to the one used here must appear in most federal agency contracts, and it also requires the clause to state that "[t]he contractor shall presume that socially and economically disadvantaged individuals include Black Americans, Hispanic Americans, Native Americans, Asian Pacific Americans, and other minorities, or any other individual found to be disadvantaged by the [Small Business] Administration pursuant to section 8(a) of the Small Business Act." Adarand claims that the presumption [discriminates] on the basis of race in violation of the Fifth Amendment obligation not to deny anyone [equal protection].

II. [The Court held that Adarand had standing not only to sue for damages for a contract it had lost in the past, but also to seek forward-looking injunctive and declaratory relief against future use of the subcontracting compensation clause.]

III. The Government urges that "[t]he Subcontracting Compensation Clause program [is] a program based on disadvantage, not on race" and thus that it is subject only to "the most relaxed judicial scrutiny." To the extent that the statutes and regulations involved in this case are race neutral, we agree. The Government concedes, however, that "the race-based rebuttable presumption used in some certification determinations under the Subcontracting Compensation Clause" is subject to some heightened level of scrutiny. The parties disagree as to what that level should be. [Adarand's] claim arises under the Fifth Amendment, which provides that "No person shall . . . be deprived of life, liberty, or property, without due process of law." Although this Court has always understood that Clause to provide [some protection] against arbitrary treatment by the Federal Government, it is not as explicit a guarantee of equal treatment as the Fourteenth Amendment. [Our] cases have accorded varying degrees of significance to the difference in the language of those two Clauses.

We think it necessary to revisit the issue here. A. [The Court reviewed cases involving laws disadvantaging minorities and found that these rulings "did not distinguish between the duties of the States and the Federal Government to avoid racial classifications."] B. [The Court then turned to cases involving the question whether "benign classifications should also be subject to rigid scrutiny."] The Court's failure to produce a majority opinion in Bakke, Fullilove, and Wygant left unresolved the proper analysis for remedial race-based governmental action. [With Croson], the Court finally agreed that the Fourteenth Amendment requires strict scrutiny of all race-based action by state and local governments. But Croson of course had no occasion to declare what standard of review the Fifth Amendment requires for such action taken by the Federal Government. Croson observed simply that the Court's "treatment of an exercise of congressional power in Fullilove cannot be dispositive here," because [the case] did not implicate Congress' broad power under § 5 of the Fourteenth Amendment. [Thus,] some uncertainty persisted with respect to the standard of review for federal racial classifications.

Despite lingering uncertainty in the details, however, the Court's cases through Croson had established three general propositions with respect to governmental racial classifications. First, skepticism: " '[a]ny preference based on racial or ethnic criteria must necessarily receive a most searching examination' " Wygant (plurality opinion of Powell, J.). Second, consistency: "the standard of review under the Equal Protection Clause is not dependent on the race of those burdened or benefited by a particular classification" [Croson], i.e., all racial classifications reviewable under the Equal Protection Clause must be strictly scrutinized. And third, congruence: "[e]qual protection analysis in the Fifth Amendment area is the same as that under the Fourteenth Amendment." Taken together, these three propositions lead to the conclusion that any person, of whatever race, has the right to demand that any governmental actor subject to the Constitution justify any racial classification subjecting that person to unequal treatment under the strictest judicial scrutiny. [A] year later, however, the Court took a surprising turn [in] Metro Broadcasting. [By] adopting intermediate scrutiny as the standard of review for congressionally mandated "benign" racial classifications, Metro Broadcasting departed from prior cases in two significant respects. First, it turned its back on Croson's explanation of why strict scrutiny of all governmental racial classifications is [essential]. We adhere to [the Croson] view today, despite the surface appeal of holding "benign" racial classifications to a lower standard, because "it may not always be clear that a so-called preference is in fact benign" [Bakke (Powell, J.)]. Second, Metro Broadcasting squarely rejected one of the three propositions established by the Court's earlier equal protection cases, namely, congruence between the standards applicable to federal and state racial classifications, and in so doing also undermined the other two—skepticism of all racial classifications, and consistency of treatment irrespective of the race of the burdened or benefited group. Under Metro Broadcasting, certain racial classifications ("benign" ones enacted by the Federal Government) should be treated less skeptically than others; and the race of the benefited group is critical to the determination of which standard of review to apply. Metro Broadcasting was thus a significant departure from much of what had come before it.

The three propositions undermined by Metro Broadcasting all derive from the basic principle that the Fifth and Fourteenth Amendments to the Constitution protect persons, not groups. It follows from that principle that all governmental action based on race [be] subjected to detailed judicial inquiry to ensure that the personal right to equal protection of the laws has not been infringed. These ideas have long been central to this Court's understanding of equal protection, and holding "benign" state and federal racial classifications to different standards does not square with them. [Accordingly,] we hold today that all racial classifications, imposed by whatever federal, state, or local governmental actor, must be analyzed by a reviewing court under strict scrutiny. In other words, such classifications are constitutional only if they are narrowly tailored measures that further compelling governmental interests. To the extent that Metro Broadcasting is inconsistent with that holding, it is [overruled].

Justice Stevens chides us for our "supposed inability to differentiate between 'invidious' and 'benign' discrimination," because it is in his view sufficient that "people understand the difference between good intentions and bad." But [the] point of strict scrutiny is to "differentiate between" permissible and impermissible governmental use of race. And Justice Stevens himself has already explained in his dissent in Fullilove why "good intentions" alone are not enough to sustain a supposedly "benign" [racial classification]. Perhaps it is not the standard of strict scrutiny itself, but our use of the concepts of "consistency" and "congruence" in conjunction with it, that leads Justice Stevens to dissent. According to [him,] our view of consistency "equate[s] remedial preferences with invidious discrimination," and ignores the difference between "an engine of oppression" and an effort "to foster equality in society," or, more colorfully, "between a 'No Trespassing' sign and a welcome mat." It does nothing of the kind. The principle of consistency simply means that whenever the government treats any person unequally because of his or her race, that person has suffered an injury that falls squarely within the language and spirit of the Constitution's guarantee of equal protection. It says nothing about the ultimate validity of any particular law; that determination is the job of the court applying strict scrutiny. The principle of consistency explains the circumstances in which the injury requiring strict scrutiny occurs. The application of strict scrutiny, in turn, determines whether a compelling governmental interest justifies the infliction of that injury. [Requiring] that Congress, like the States, enact racial classifications only when doing so is necessary to further a "compelling interest" does not contravene any principle of appropriate respect for a co-equal Branch of the Government. It is true that various Members of this Court have taken different views of the authority § 5 of the Fourteenth Amendment confers upon Congress to deal with the problem of racial discrimination, and the extent to which courts should defer to Congress' exercise of that authority. We need not, and do not, address these differences today. For now, it is enough to observe that Justice Stevens' suggestion that any Member of this Court has repudiated in this case his or her previously expressed views on the subject is incorrect.

C. [In Sec. III.C., joined only by Justice Kennedy, Justice O'Connor explained why principles of stare decisis did not require adherence to the "untenable" Metro Broadcasting ruling.] D. Our action today makes explicit what Justice Powell thought implicit in the Fullilove lead opinion: federal racial classifications, like those of a State, must serve a compelling governmental interest, and must be narrowly tailored to further that interest. [It] follows that to the extent (if any) that Fullilove held federal racial classifications to be subject to a less rigorous standard, it is no longer controlling. But we need not decide today whether the program upheld in Fullilove would survive strict scrutiny as our more recent cases have defined it. Some have questioned the importance of debating the proper standard of review of race-based legislation. But we agree with Justice Stevens that, "[b]ecause racial characteristics so seldom provide a relevant basis for disparate treatment, and because classifications based on race are potentially so harmful to the entire body politic, it is especially important that the reasons for any such classification be clearly identified and unquestionably legitimate," and that "[r]acial classifications are simply too pernicious to permit any but the most exact connection between justification and classification." Fullilove (dissenting opinion). We think that requiring strict scrutiny is the best way to ensure that courts will consistently give racial classifications that kind of detailed examination, both as to ends and as to means. Korematsu demonstrates vividly that even "the most rigid scrutiny" can sometimes fail to detect an illegitimate racial classification. Any retreat from the most searching judicial inquiry can only increase the risk of another such error occurring in the future. Finally, we wish to dispel the notion that strict scrutiny is "strict in theory, but fatal in fact." The unhappy persistence of both the practice and the lingering effects of racial discrimination against minority groups in this country is an unfortunate reality, and government is not disqualified from acting in response to it. [When] race-based action is necessary to further a compelling interest, such action is within constitutional constraints if it satisfies the "narrow tailoring" test this Court has set out in previous cases.

IV. Because our decision today alters the playing field in some important respects, we think it best to remand the case to the lower courts for further consideration in light of the principles we have announced. The Court of Appeals, following Metro Broadcasting and Fullilove, analyzed the case in terms of intermediate scrutiny [and] did not decide the question whether the interests served by the use of subcontractor compensation clauses are properly described as "compelling." It also did not address the question of narrow tailoring in terms of our strict scrutiny cases, by asking, for example, whether there was "any consideration of the use of race-neutral means to increase minority business participation" in government contracting, Croson, or whether the program was appropriately limited such that it "will not last longer than the discriminatory effects it is designed to eliminate," Fullilove. (Powell, J., concurring). Moreover, unresolved questions remain concerning the details of the complex regulatory regimes implicated by the use of subcontractor compensation clauses. [The] question whether any of the ways in which the Government uses subcontractor compensation clauses can survive strict scrutiny [should] be addressed in the first instance by the lower courts.

[Vacated and remanded.]

Justice SCALIA, concurring in part and concurring in the judgment.

I join the opinion of the Court, except Part III–C, and except insofar as it may be inconsistent with the following: In my view, government can never have a "compelling interest" in discriminating on the basis of race in order to "make up" for past racial discrimination in the opposite direction. Individuals who have been wronged by unlawful racial discrimination should be made whole; but under our Constitution there can be no such thing as either a creditor or a debtor race. That concept is alien to the Constitution's focus upon the individual, and its rejection of dispositions based on [race]. To pursue the concept of racial entitlement—even for the most admirable and benign of purposes—is to reinforce and preserve for future mischief the way of thinking that produced race slavery, race privilege and race hatred. In the eyes of government, we are just one race here. It is American. It is unlikely, if not impossible, that the challenged program would survive under this understanding of strict scrutiny, but I am contented to leave that to be decided on remand.

Justice THOMAS, concurring in part and concurring in the judgment.

I agree with the majority's conclusion that strict scrutiny applies to all government classifications based on race. I write separately, however, to express my disagreement with the premise underlying Justice Stevens' and Justice Ginsburg's dissents: that there is a racial paternalism exception to the principle of equal protection. I believe that there is a "moral [and] constitutional equivalence" between laws designed to subjugate a race and those that distribute benefits on the basis of race in order to foster some current notion of equality. Government cannot make us equal; it can only recognize, respect, and protect us as equal before the law. That these programs may have been motivated, in part, by good intentions cannot provide refuge from the principle that under our Constitution, the government may not make distinctions on the basis of race. As far as the Constitution is concerned, it is irrelevant whether a government's racial classifications are drawn by those who wish to oppress a race or by those who have a sincere desire to help those thought to be disadvantaged. There can be no doubt that the paternalism that appears to lie at the heart of this program is at war with the principle of inherent equality that underlies and infuses our Constitution.

These programs not only raise grave constitutional questions, they also undermine the moral basis of the equal protection principle. Purchased at the price of immeasurable human suffering, the equal protection principle reflects our Nation's understanding that such classifications ultimately have a destructive impact on the individual and our society. [T]here can be no doubt that racial paternalism and its unintended consequences can be as poisonous and pernicious as any other form of discrimination. So-called "benign" discrimination teaches many that because of chronic and apparently immutable handicaps, minorities cannot compete with them without their patronizing indulgence. Inevitably, such programs engender attitudes of superiority or, alternatively, provoke resentment among those who believe that they have been wronged by the government's use of race. These programs stamp minorities with a badge of inferiority and may cause them to develop dependencies or to adopt an attitude that they are "entitled" to preferences. [In] my mind, government-sponsored racial discrimination based on benign prejudice is just as noxious as discrimination inspired by malicious prejudice. In each instance, it is racial discrimination, plain and simple.

Justice STEVENS, with whom Justice GINSBURG joins, dissenting.

Instead of deciding this case in accordance with controlling precedent, the Court today delivers a disconcerting lecture about the evils of governmental racial classifications. For its text the Court has selected three propositions, represented by the words "skepticism," "consistency," and "congruence." I. [The] Court's concept of skepticism is, at least in principle, a good statement of law and of common sense. Undoubtedly, a court should be wary of a governmental decision that relies upon a racial classification. [But,] as the opinions in Fullilove demonstrate, substantial agreement on the standard to be applied in deciding difficult cases does not necessarily lead to agreement on how those cases actually should or will be resolved. In my judgment, because uniform standards are often anything but uniform, we should evaluate the Court's comments on "consistency," "congruence," and stare decisis with the same type of skepticism that the Court advocates for the underlying issue.

II. The Court's concept of "consistency" assumes that there is no significant difference between a decision by the majority to impose a special burden on the members of a minority race and a decision by the majority to provide a benefit to certain members of that minority notwithstanding its incidental burden on some members of the majority. In my opinion that assumption is untenable. There is no moral or constitutional equivalence between a policy that is designed to perpetuate a caste system and one that seeks to eradicate racial subordination. Invidious discrimination is an engine of oppression, subjugating a disfavored group to enhance or maintain the power of the majority. Remedial race-based preferences reflect the opposite impulse: a desire to foster equality in society. No sensible conception of the Government's constitutional obligation to "govern impartially" should ignore this distinction.[1] The consistency that the Court espouses would disregard the difference between a "No Trespassing" sign and a welcome mat. It would treat a Dixiecrat Senator's decision to vote against Thurgood Marshall's confirmation in order to keep African Americans off the Supreme Court as on a par with President Johnson's evaluation of his nominee's race as a positive factor. It would equate a law that made black citizens ineligible for military service with a program aimed at recruiting black soldiers. An attempt by the majority to exclude members of a minority race from a regulated market is fundamentally different from a subsidy that enables a relatively small group of newcomers to enter that market. An interest in "consistency" does not justify treating differences as though they were similarities.

The Court's explanation for treating dissimilar race-based decisions as though they were equally objectionable is a supposed inability to differentiate between "invidious" and "benign" discrimination. But the term "affirmative action" is common and well understood. Its presence in everyday parlance shows that people understand the difference between good intentions and bad. As with any legal concept, some cases may be difficult to classify, but our equal protection jurisprudence has identified a critical difference between state action that imposes burdens on a disfavored few and state action that benefits the few "in spite of" its adverse effects on the many. Indeed, our jurisprudence has made the standard to be applied in cases of invidious discrimination turn on whether the discrimination is "intentional," or whether, by contrast, it merely has a discriminatory "effect." Washington v. Davis. Surely this distinction is at least as subtle, and at least as difficult to apply, as the usually obvious distinction between a measure intended to benefit members of a particular minority race and a measure intended to burden a minority race. A state actor inclined to subvert the Constitution might easily hide bad intentions in the guise of unintended "effects"; but I should think it far more difficult to enact a law intending to preserve the majority's hegemony while casting it plausibly in the guise of affirmative action for minorities. Nothing is inherently wrong with applying a single standard to fundamentally different situations, as long as that standard takes relevant differences into account. For example, if the Court in all equal protection cases were to insist that differential treatment be justified by relevant characteristics of the members of the favored and disfavored classes that provide a legitimate basis for disparate treatment, such a standard would treat dissimilar cases differently while still recognizing that there is, after all, only one Equal Protection Clause. Under such a standard, subsidies for disadvantaged businesses may be constitutional though special taxes on such businesses would be invalid. But a single standard that purports to equate remedial

---

1. As Justice Ginsburg observes, the majority's "flexible" approach to "strict scrutiny" may well take into account differences between benign and invidious programs. [Even] if this is so, however, I think it is unfortunate that the majority insists on applying the label "strict scrutiny" to benign race-based programs. That label has usually been understood to spell the death of any governmental action to which a court may apply it. The Court suggests today that "strict scrutiny" means something different—something less strict—when applied to benign racial classifications. Although I agree that benign programs deserve different treatment than invidious programs, there is a danger that the fatal language of "strict scrutiny" will skew the analysis and place well-crafted benign programs at unnecessary risk. [Footnote by Justice Stevens.]

preferences with invidious discrimination cannot be defended in the name of "equal protection."

Moreover, the Court may find that its new "consistency" approach to race-based classifications is difficult to square with its insistence upon rigidly separate categories for discrimination against different classes of individuals. For example, as the law currently stands, the Court will apply "intermediate scrutiny" to cases of invidious gender discrimination and "strict scrutiny" to cases of invidious race discrimination, while applying the same standard for benign classifications as for invidious ones. If this remains the law, then today's lecture about "consistency" will produce the anomalous result that the Government can more easily enact affirmative-action programs to remedy discrimination against women than it can enact affirmative-action programs to remedy discrimination against African Americans—even though the primary purpose of the Equal Protection Clause was to end discrimination against the former slaves. When a court becomes preoccupied with abstract standards, it risks sacrificing common sense at the altar of formal consistency. As a matter of constitutional and democratic principle, a decision by representatives of the majority to discriminate against the members of a minority race is fundamentally different from those same representatives' decision to impose incidental costs on the majority of their constituents in order to provide a benefit to a disadvantaged minority. [The] former is virtually always repugnant to the principles of a free and democratic society, whereas the latter is, in some circumstances, entirely consistent with the ideal of equality. By insisting on a doctrinaire notion of "consistency" in the standard applicable to all race-based governmental actions, the Court obscures this essential dichotomy.

III. The Court's concept of "congruence" assumes that there is no significant difference between a decision by the Congress of the United States to adopt an affirmative-action program and such a decision by a State or a municipality. [That] assumption [ignores] important practical and legal differences between federal and state or local decisionmakers. These differences have been identified repeatedly and consistently both in opinions of the Court and in separate opinions authored by members of today's majority. [E.g., Metro Broadcasting, Fullilove.] [Moreover,] federal affirmative-action programs represent the will of our entire Nation's elected representatives, whereas a state or local program may have an impact on nonresident entities who played no part in the decision to enact it. Thus, in the state or local context, individuals who were unable to vote for the local representatives who enacted a race-conscious program may nonetheless feel the effects of that program. [Presumably,] the majority is now satisfied that its theory of "congruence" between the substantive rights provided by the Fifth and Fourteenth Amendments disposes of the objection based upon divided constitutional powers. But it is one thing to say (as no one seems to dispute) that the Fifth Amendment encompasses a general guarantee of equal protection as broad as that contained within the Fourteenth Amendment. It is another thing entirely to say that Congress' institutional competence and constitutional authority entitles it to no greater deference when it enacts a program designed to foster equality than the deference due a State legislature. The latter is an extraordinary proposition; and [our] precedents have rejected it explicitly and repeatedly. In my judgment, the Court's novel doctrine of "congruence" is seriously misguided. Congressional deliberations about a matter as important as affirmative action should be accorded far greater deference than those of a State or [municipality].

VI. My skeptical scrutiny of the Court's opinion leaves me in dissent. The majority's concept of "consistency" ignores a difference, fundamental to the idea of equal protection, between oppression and assistance. The majority's concept of "congruence" ignores a difference, fundamental to our constitutional system, between the Federal Government and the States. And the majority's concept of stare decisis ignores the force of binding [precedent]. [Another dissent, by Justice SOUTER, with whom Justice GINSBURG and Justice BREYER joined, is omitted.]

Justice GINSBURG, with whom Justice BREYER joins, dissenting.

[In] view of the attention the political branches are currently giving the matter of affirmative action, I see no compelling cause for the intervention the Court has made in this case. I further agree with Justice Stevens that [large] deference is owed by the Judiciary to "Congress' institutional competence and constitutional authority to overcome historic racial subjugation." I write separately to underscore [the] considerable field of agreement [revealed] in opinions that together speak for a majority of the Court.

I.   [The] divisions in this difficult case should not obscure the Court's recognition of the persistence of racial inequality and a majority's acknowledgment of Congress' authority to act affirmatively, not only to end discrimination, but also to counteract discrimination's lingering effects. Those effects, reflective of a system of racial caste only recently ended, are evident in our workplaces, markets, and neighborhoods. Job applicants with identical resumes, qualifications, and interview styles still experience different receptions, depending on their race. White and African–American consumers still encounter different deals. People of color looking for housing still face discriminatory treatment by landlords, real estate agents, and mortgage lenders. Minority entrepreneurs sometimes fail to gain contracts though they are the low bidders, and they are sometimes refused work even after winning contracts. Bias both conscious and unconscious, reflecting traditional and unexamined habits of thought, keeps up barriers that must come down if equal opportunity and nondiscrimination are ever genuinely to become this country's law and practice. Given this history and its practical consequences, Congress surely can conclude that a carefully designed affirmative action program may help to realize, finally, the "equal protection of the laws" the Fourteenth Amendment has promised since 1868.

II.   The lead opinion uses one term, "strict scrutiny," to describe the standard of judicial review for all governmental classifications by race. But that opinion's elaboration strongly suggests that the strict standard announced is indeed "fatal" for classifications burdening groups that have suffered discrimination in our society. That seems to me, and, I believe, to the Court, the enduring lesson one should draw from Korematsu; for in that case, scrutiny the Court described as "most rigid," nonetheless yielded a pass for an odious, gravely injurious racial classification. A Korematsu-type classification, as I read the opinions in this case, will never again survive scrutiny: such a classification, history and precedent instruct, properly ranks as prohibited. For a classification made to hasten the day when "we are just one race," however, the lead opinion has dispelled the notion that "strict scrutiny" is "fatal in fact." Properly, a majority of the Court calls for review that is searching, in order to ferret out classifications in reality malign, but masquerading as benign. The Court's once lax review of sex-based classifications demonstrates the need for such suspicion. Today's decision thus usefully reiterates that the purpose of strict scrutiny "is precisely to distinguish legitimate from illegitimate uses of race in governmental decisionmaking," "to 'differentiate between' permissible and impermissible governmental use of race," to distinguish " 'between a "No Trespassing" sign and a welcome mat.' " Close review also is in order for this further reason. [As] this very case shows, some members of the historically favored race can be hurt by catch-up mechanisms designed to cope with the lingering effects of entrenched racial subjugation. Court review can ensure that preferences are not so large as to trammel unduly upon the opportunities of others or interfere too harshly with legitimate expectations of persons in once-preferred groups. [While] I would not disturb the programs challenged in this case, and would leave their improvement to the political branches, I see today's decision as one that allows our precedent to evolve, still to be informed by and responsive to changing conditions.*

RACE-CONSCIOUS VOTING DISTRICTS: A TRANSITIONAL NOTE

In a controversial group of cases in the mid–1990s (beginning with Shaw v. Reno and Miller v. Johnson), the Court applied strict scrutiny to the redrawing of congressional districts to achieve a majority in each district of racial groups that otherwise were a minority (commonly called "majority-minority districts"). This race-conscious redistricting was usually a consequence of U.S. Department of Justice pressure under the Voting Rights Act of 1965, which prohibits the use of any electoral practice which "results in a denial or abridgment" of the right to vote on the basis of race or color. The pressure arose because of § 2 and § 5 of the Act: § 2 assures racial minorities an equal opportunity "to participate in the political process and to elect members of their choice," and, as a result of 1982 Amendments to the Act, a violation of § 2 can be demonstrated by discriminatory effects alone (but § 2 purports to reject a right to proportional representation). Moreover, under § 5, covered political jurisdictions must secure preclearance of changes in voting procedures from the federal government. [Recall the initial discussion of these problems in connection with such cases as Rogers v. Lodge (1982; p. 764 above). For the background of the Voting Rights Act, see chap. 10, sec. 4.] These race-conscious redistricting efforts are typically designed to benefit minorities. Although they thus bear some resemblance to the "benign" discrimination cases considered in this section, fuller attention to the Shaw–Miller line of cases is postponed to sec. 4B. The reason for this postponement is that the racial redistricting cases require some understanding of the concepts of outright denials of voting and of "vote dilution," concepts initially developed in the context of the "fundamental" equal protection interest in voting—cases that typically dealt with political rather than racial gerrymandering.

The racial redistricting cases involve, among other issues, the question of whether race-conscious districting affects individual or group rights. (Recall the references to these concepts in the "purposeful discrimination" section of this chapter, sec. 3D above.) In thinking preliminarily about the relevance of the strict scrutiny approach of the modern benign discrimination cases to the voting area, think about whether the rights involved in racial redistricting should be seen as group rather than individual rights. (Note that the preceding benign discrimination cases, from Bakke to Adarand, tended to emphasize

---

* The new Proposed Reforms to Affirmative Action in Procurement (61 Fed.Reg. 26042) (May 23, 1996), issued by the Justice Department, note specifically that they were drafted to comply with Adarand.

individual rights). On this issue, consider also some comments in Justice Souter's dissent in the first of the modern racial redistricting cases, Shaw v. Reno (1993; p. 880 below). He stated: "Until today, the Court has analyzed equal protection claims involving race in electoral districting differently from equal protection claims involving other forms of governmental conduct. [Unlike] other contexts in which we have addressed the State's conscious use of race, see, e.g., [Croson; Wygant], electoral districting calls for decisions that nearly always require some consideration of race for legitimate reasons where there is a racially mixed population. As long as members of racial groups have the commonality of interest implicit in our ability to talk about concepts like 'minority voting strength' and 'dilution of minority votes,' and as long as racial bloc voting takes place, legislators will have to take race into account in order to avoid dilution of minority voting strengths in the districting plans they adopt. [A] second distinction between districting and most other governmental decisions in which race has figured is that those other decisions using racial criteria characteristically occur in circumstances in which the use of race to the advantage of one person is necessarily at the obvious expense of a member of a different race. [In] districting, by contrast [to situations such as Wygant and Croson], the mere placement of an individual in one district instead of another denies no one a right or benefit provided to others. All citizens may register, vote, and be represented. In whatever district, the individual voter has a right to vote in each election. [One's] constitutional rights are not violated merely because a candidate one supports loses the election or because a group (including a racial group) to which one belongs winds up with a representative from outside that group." Are these observations useful and persuasive? Consider, in examining the racial redistricting cases in sec. 4B, whether these observations suggest a major flaw in the majority's strict scrutiny approach in those cases.

SECTION 4.   THE "FUNDAMENTAL INTERESTS" STRAND OF EQUAL PROTECTION STRICT SCRUTINY

Introduction. As noted in sec. 1, the Warren Court's "new" equal protection-strict scrutiny framework contained two major elements: not only the "suspect classifications" theme traced in sec. 3, but also the position that intensive review is warranted whenever governmental action seriously burdens "fundamental rights or interests." This section focuses on that latter strand. The novel aspect of the fundamental interests theme lay in the Warren Court's suggestions that specially protected constitutional rights could be derived directly from the equal protection clause itself. That characteristic should be distinguished from the traditional notion that an equal protection mode of analysis may be applied whenever governmental action discriminatorily burdens a right clearly embodied elsewhere in the Constitution—e.g., the First Amendment. The distinctive feature in most of the fundamental interests cases in *this* section is that the justification for heightened scrutiny purports to stem *entirely* from equal protection itself, *not* from any independent source elsewhere in the Constitution. The Warren Court's derivation of fundamental interests directly from equal protection was a novel departure. Potentially, it promised to raise many of the institutional and interpretive difficulties that marked the history of substantive due process; indeed, the search for "fundamental values" that inhered in this strand of equal protection analysis led some to refer to it as "substantive equal protection." (See Karst & Horowitz, "Reitman v. Mulkey: A

Telophase of Substantive Equal Protection," 1967 Sup.Ct.Rev. 39.) Others commented that the fundamental interests strand of the "new" equal protection was especially attractive to the Warren Court because some Justices were reluctant to cloak their desire to identify new fundamental values in the then-discredited cloak of substantive due process; equal protection, far less identified with much-criticized Lochnerizing, seemed a tempting alternative route.[1] In fact, however, the implementation of fundamental interests-"new" equal protection analysis by the Warren Court was limited to a very few areas. The post-Warren Court has generally adhered to these well-established strands of fundamental interests-"new" equal protection. But the Burger Court refused to expand that analysis into new spheres: "thus far and no further" has been the response to the Warren Court's fundamental interests legacy under equal protection.

This section begins, in sec. 4A, with the 1973 decision in Rodriguez, the decision which most fully and clearly reveals the characteristic post-Warren Court's reluctance to expand fundamental interests-"new" equal protection analysis.[2] Rodriguez is followed by, and should be contrasted with, a later decision, Plyler v. Doe, which, despite the Rodriguez holding that education is not a "fundamental interest," managed to justify heightened scrutiny in striking down the Texas exclusion of illegal "undocumented" alien children from free public education. The focus then shifts to the three strands of fundamental interests—"new" equal protection analysis that became solidly established on the Warren Court and that have been adhered to by subsequent Courts: the fundamental interest in equal access to voting, which has produced not only the removal of a wide range of barriers to the voting booth and the ballot but also the intense modern attention to alleged "dilutions" of voting rights (sec. 4B); access to the judicial process (sec. 4C); and the right of interstate migration, most often impeded by durational residence requirements (sec. 4D). The final group of materials, sec. 4E, returns to one of the themes of Rodriguez by focusing on the most amorphous and controversial aspect of fundamental interests analysis, the unsuccessful effort to derive from equal protection a fundamental interest in such "necessities" as welfare benefits and housing.

---

1. Moreover, the language of equality lent itself more readily to the achievement of the aims of those advocates and judges who sought to find constitutional mandates for affirmative governmental obligations to equalize economic conditions. The legacy of substantive due process was far more associated with an Adam Smith–John Stuart Mill notion of negative restraints on government—a hands-off philosophy rather than one imposing affirmative, egalitarian duties.

2. Rodriguez did not signal abandonment of "fundamental values" modes of adjudication outside the equal protection sphere. Indeed, in 1973, the very year that Rodriguez called a halt to further fundamental value searches under the aegis of equal protection, the Court (in Roe v. Wade) announced its willingness to engage in fundamental value searches under the formerly discredited mode of substantive due process. Rodriguez reflects both the modern Court's unwillingness to find new fundamental interests in the equal protection clause and its readiness to accept the well-established ingredients of fundamental interests-equal protection analysis. Examining Rodriguez at the outset of this section not only provides a useful overview of the modern Court's reluctance to expand, but also focuses special attention on the Court's (occasionally strained) efforts to justify and distinguish the "well-established" fundamental interests in such areas as equal voting rights—areas more fully pursued below.

A. THE MODERN COURT'S GENERAL STANCE: RODRIGUEZ AND PLYLER

San Antonio Independent School Dist. v. Rodriguez

411 U.S. 1, 93 S.Ct. 1278, 36 L.Ed.2d 16 (1973).

[Traditionally, public school education has been financed mainly through property taxes imposed by local school districts. This case involved an attack on the Texas system of financing public education, which relied heavily on local property taxes. The thrust of the attack was that the system violated equal protection because it produced substantial interdistrict disparities in per-pupil expenditures, stemming from the differences in taxable property values among the districts. The challengers in this class action were Mexican–American parents of children in the Edgewood school district in San Antonio, suing on behalf of children of poor families residing in districts having a low property tax base. Although contributions from a statewide "minimum foundation school program" served to reduce interdistrict disparities, district spending continued to vary considerably on the basis of local property wealth.[1] The District Court, exercising strict scrutiny, held that the Texas scheme violated equal protection. The Supreme Court reversed.]

Justice POWELL delivered the opinion of the [Court].

I. [We] must decide, first whether the Texas system of financing public education operates to the disadvantage of some suspect class or impinges upon a fundamental right explicitly or implicitly protected by the Constitution, thereby requiring strict judicial scrutiny. If so, the judgment of the District Court [which had found wealth a "suspect" classification and education a "fundamental interest"] should be affirmed. If not, the Texas scheme must still be examined to determine whether it rationally furthers some legitimate, articulated state purpose and therefore does not constitute an invidious discrimination in violation of [equal protection].

II. [We] find neither the suspect-classification nor the fundamental-interest analysis persuasive. A. The wealth discrimination discovered by the District Court, [and] by several other courts that have recently struck down school financing laws in other States,[2] is quite unlike any of the forms of wealth discrimination heretofore reviewed by this Court. [The] individuals or groups of individuals who constituted the class discriminated against in our prior cases shared two distinguishing characteristics: because of their impecunity they were completely unable to pay for some desired benefit, and as a consequence, they sustained an absolute deprivation of a meaningful opportunity to enjoy

1. For example, a spending comparison between appellees' Edgewood district and the Alamo Heights district—the "most affluent district in the San Antonio area"—indicated "the extent to which substantial disparities exist despite the State's impressive progress in recent years." During the 1967–68 school year, Edgewood had an average assessed property value per pupil of $5960. By taxing itself at a rate of 1.05%—the highest rate in the metropolitan area—the district raised $26 for the education of each child. State and federal support brought Edgewood per pupil

expenditures to $356. By contrast, the affluent Alamo Heights district had a property tax base of more than $49,000 per pupil. By taxing itself at only .85%, it raised $333 per pupil. State and federal support brought Alamo Heights spending to $594 per pupil.

2. Serrano v. Priest, 487 P.2d 1241, 5 Cal.3d 584 (1971); Van Dusartz v. Hatfield, 334 F.Supp. 870 (D.C.Minn.1971); Robinson v. Cahill, 118 N.J.Super. 223, 287 A.2d 187 (1972); Milliken v. Green [Mich.S.Ct.1973]. [Footnote by Justice Powell.]

that benefit.[3] [Even] a cursory examination, however, demonstrates that neither of the two distinguishing characteristics of wealth classifications can be found here. First, [there] is reason to believe that the poorest families are not necessarily clustered in the poorest property districts. [A recent] Connecticut study found that the poor were clustered around commercial and industrial areas—those same areas that provide the most attractive sources of property tax income for school districts. [T]here is no basis on the record [for] assuming that the poorest people [are] concentrated in the poorest districts [in Texas]. [Second], lack of personal resources has not occasioned an absolute deprivation of the desired benefit. The argument here is not that the children [are] receiving no public education; rather, it is that they are receiving a poorer quality education [than] children in districts having more assessable wealth. Apart from the unsettled and disputed question whether the quality of education may be determined by the amount of money expended for it, a sufficient answer to appellees' argument is that, at least where wealth is involved, [equal protection] does not require absolute equality or precisely equal advantages. Nor, indeed, in view of the infinite variables affecting the educational process, can any system assure equal quality of education except in the most relative sense. [For] these two reasons[, the] disadvantaged class is not susceptible of identification in traditional terms.[4] [This] brings us [to] the third way in which the classification scheme might be defined—*district* wealth discrimination. Since the only correlation indicated by the evidence is between district property wealth and expenditures, it may be argued that discrimination might be found without regard to the individual income characteristics of district residents. [However] described, it is clear that appellees' suit asks this Court to extend its most exacting scrutiny to review a system that allegedly discriminates against a large, diverse, and amorphous class, unified only by the common factor of residence in districts that happen to have less taxable wealth than other districts. The system of alleged discrimination and the class it defines have none of the traditional indicia of suspectness: the class is not saddled with such disabilities, or subjected to such a history of purposeful unequal treatment, or relegated to such a position of political powerlessness as to command extraordinary protection from the majoritarian political process. We thus conclude that the Texas system does not operate to the peculiar disadvantage of any suspect class. [Recognizing] that this Court has never heretofore held that wealth discrimination alone provides an adequate basis for invoking strict scrutiny, appellees [also] assert that the State's system impermissibly interferes with the exercise of a "fundamental" right [requiring] the strict standard of judicial [review].

B. In [Brown v. Board of Education], a unanimous Court recognized that "education is perhaps the most important function of state and local governments." [Nothing] this Court holds today in any way detracts from our historic

3. At this point, Justice Powell discussed Griffin v. Illinois, Douglas v. California, Williams v. Illinois, Tate v. Short and Bullock v. Carter, all noted below (mainly in sec. 4C).

4. An educational system might be hypothesized, however, in which the analogy to the wealth discrimination cases would be considerably closer. If elementary and secondary education were made available by the State only to those able to pay a [tuition], there would be a clearly defined class of "poor" people—definable in terms of their inability to pay the prescribed sum—who would be absolutely precluded from receiving an education. That case would present a far more compelling set of circumstances for judicial assistance than the case before us today. [But] Texas [has] provided what it considers to be an adequate base education for all children [and no proof was offered at trial persuasively discrediting the State's assertion]. [Footnote by Justice Powell.] [Cf. Plyler v. Doe, which follows.]

dedication to public education. [But] the importance of a service performed by the State does not determine whether it must be regarded as fundamental for purposes of examination under [equal protection]. [After discussing Shapiro v. Thompson, Lindsey v. Normet, and Dandridge v. Williams (and noting Jefferson v. Hackney and Richardson v. Belcher), all below, Justice Powell continued:] The lesson of these cases [is that it] is not the province of this Court to create substantive constitutional rights in the name of guaranteeing [equal protection]. Thus the key to discovering whether education is "fundamental" is not to be found in comparisons of the relative societal significance of education as opposed to subsistence or housing. Nor is it to be found by weighing whether education is as important as the right to travel. Rather, the answer lies in assessing whether there is a right to education explicitly or implicitly guaranteed by the Constitution. Eisenstadt v. Baird; Dunn v. Blumstein[5]; Police Dept. of Chicago v. Mosley[6]; Skinner v. Oklahoma.[7]] Education, of course, is not among the rights afforded explicit protection under our Federal Constitution. Nor do we find any basis for saying it is implicitly so protected. [It] is appellees' contention, however, that education is distinguishable from other services and benefits provided by the State because it bears a peculiarly close relationship to other rights and liberties accorded protection under the Constitution. Specifically, they insist that education is itself a fundamental personal right because it is essential to the effective exercise of First Amendment freedoms and to intelligent utilization of the right to vote. In asserting a nexus between speech and education, appellees urge that the right to speak is meaningless unless the speaker is capable of articulating his thoughts intelligently and persuasively. The "marketplace of ideas" is an empty forum for those lacking basic communicative tools. [A] similar line of reasoning is pursued with respect to the right to vote.[8] Exercise of the franchise, it is contended, cannot be divorced from the educational foundation of the voter. [We] need not dispute any of these propositions. [Yet] we have never presumed to possess either the ability or the authority to guarantee to the citizenry the most *effective* speech or the most *informed* electoral choice. That these may be desirable goals [is] not to be

---

5. Dunn [p. 863 below] fully canvasses this Court's voting rights cases and explains that "this Court has made clear that a citizen has a *constitutionally protected right* to participate in elections on an equal basis with other citizens in the jurisdiction." [Emphasis supplied.] The constitutional underpinnings of the right to equal treatment in the voting process can no longer be doubted even though, as the Court noted in [Harper], "the right to vote in state elections is nowhere expressly mentioned." [Footnote by Justice Powell.] [Consider this explanation in exploring the voting cases in sec. 4B below. Compare footnote 1 to Justice Stewart's concurrence, below; footnote 2 to Justice Marshall's dissent, below; and footnote 3 in Justice Brennan's opinion in Plyler v. Doe (p. 850 below).]

6. In Mosley [1972; p. 1205 below], the Court struck down a Chicago antipicketing ordinance that exempted labor picketing from its prohibitions. The ordinance was held invalid under [equal protection] after subjecting it to careful scrutiny and finding that the

ordinance was not narrowly drawn. The stricter standard of review was appropriately applied since the ordinance was one "affecting First Amendment interests." [Footnote by Justice Powell.]

7. Skinner [p. 517 above] applied the standard of close scrutiny to a state law permitting forced sterilization of "habitual criminals." Implicit in the Court's opinion is the recognition that the right of procreation is among the rights of personal privacy protected under the Constitution. See [Roe v. Wade]. [Footnote by Justice Powell.]

8. Since the right to vote, per se, is not a constitutionally protected right, we assume that appellees' references to that right are simply shorthand references to the protected right, implicit in our constitutional system, to participate in state elections on an equal basis with other qualified voters whenever the State has adopted an elective process for determining who will represent any segment of the State's population. See n. [4] supra [and sec. 4B below]. [Footnote by Justice Powell.]

doubted. [But] they are not values to be implemented by judicial intrusion into otherwise legitimate state activities.

[Whatever] merit appellees' argument might have if a State's financing system occasioned an absolute denial of educational opportunities to any of its children, that argument provides no basis for finding an interference with fundamental rights where only relative differences in spending levels are involved and where—as is true in the present case—no charge fairly could be made that the system fails to provide each child with an opportunity to acquire the basic minimal skills necessary for the enjoyment of the rights of speech and a full participation in the political process. [Furthermore,] the logical limitations on appellees' nexus theory are difficult to perceive. How, for instance, is education to be distinguished from the significant personal interests in the basics of decent food and shelter? Empirical examination might well buttress an assumption that the ill-fed, ill-clothed, and ill-housed are among the most ineffective participants in the political process and that they derive the least enjoyment from the benefits of the First Amendment. If so, appellees' thesis would cast serious doubt on the authority of Dandridge v. Williams and Lindsey v. Normet [see sec. 4E]. [The] present case, in another basic sense, is significantly different from any of the cases in which [we have] applied strict scrutiny [to] legislation touching upon constitutionally protected rights. Each of our prior cases involved legislation which "deprived," "infringed," or "interfered" with the free exercise of some such fundamental personal right or liberty. A critical distinction between those cases and the one now before us lies in what Texas is endeavoring to do with respect to education. [Every] step leading to the establishment of the system Texas utilizes today [was] implemented in an effort to *extend* [public education]. [We] think it plain that [the] thrust of the Texas system is affirmative and reformatory and, therefore, should be scrutinized under judicial principles sensitive to the nature of the State's efforts and to the rights reserved to the States under the Constitution.

C. [We] need not rest our decision, however, solely on the inappropriateness of the strict scrutiny test. A century [of] adjudication under [equal protection] affirmatively supports the application of the traditional standard of review, which requires only that the State's system be shown to bear some rational relationship to legitimate state purposes. [We] have here nothing less than a direct attack on the way in which Texas has chosen to raise and disburse state and local tax revenues. [A]ppellees would have the Court intrude in an area in which it has traditionally deferred to state legislatures. [Thus] we stand on familiar ground when we continue to acknowledge that the Justices of this Court lack both the expertise and the familiarity with local problems so necessary to the making of wise decisions with respect to the raising and disposition of public revenues. [No] scheme of taxation [has] yet been devised which is free of all discriminatory impact. [And] this case also involves the most persistent and difficult questions of educational policy, another area in which this Court's lack of specialized knowledge and experience counsels against premature interference with the informed judgments made at the state and local levels. Education, perhaps even more than welfare assistance, presents a myriad of "intractable economic, social, and even philosophical problems." [Dandridge v. Williams (1970; p. 912 below).] [In] such circumstances, the judiciary is well advised to refrain from imposing on the States inflexible constitutional restraints that could circumscribe [continued research and experimentation].

III. [The] Texas system of school finance, [w]hile assuring a basic education for every child in the State, [encourages] a large measure of participation in and control of each district's schools at the local level. [Appellees] suggest that local control could be preserved and promoted under other financing systems that resulted in more equality in educational expenditures. While it is no doubt true that reliance on local property taxation for school revenues provides less freedom of choice with respect to expenditures for some districts than for others, the existence of "some inequality" in the manner in which the State's rationale is achieved is not alone a sufficient basis for striking down the entire system. [Nor] must the financing system fail because, as appellees suggest, other methods of satisfying the State's interest, which occasion "less drastic" disparities in expenditures, might be conceived. Only where state action impinges on the exercise of fundamental constitutional rights or liberties must it be found to have chosen the least restrictive alternative. It is also well to remember that even those districts that have reduced ability to make free decisions with respect to how much they spend on education still retain under the present system a large measure of authority as to how available funds will be allocated. They further enjoy the power to make numerous other decisions with respect to the operation of the schools. The people of Texas may be justified in believing [that] along with increased control of the purse strings at the State level will go increased control over local policies. Appellees further urge that the Texas system is unconstitutionally arbitrary because it allows the availability of local taxable resources to turn on "happenstance." [But] any scheme of local taxation—indeed the very existence of identifiable local governmental units—requires the establishment of jurisdictional boundaries that are inevitably arbitrary. It is equally inevitable that some localities are going to be blessed with more taxable assets than others. Nor is local wealth a static quantity. [In] sum, [we] cannot say that [the Texas interdistrict] disparities are the product of a system that is so irrational as to be invidiously discriminatory. [The equal protection standard] is whether the challenged state action rationally furthers a legitimate state purpose or interest. [We] hold that the Texas plan abundantly satisfies this standard.

IV. [A] cautionary postscript seems appropriate. [Affirmance here] would occasion in Texas and elsewhere an unprecedented upheaval in public education. [The] complexity of [the] problems is demonstrated by the lack of consensus with respect to whether it may be said with any assurance that the poor, the racial minorities, or the children in overburdened core-city school districts would be benefitted by abrogation of traditional modes of financing education. [We] hardly need add that this Court's action today is not to be viewed as placing its judicial imprimatur on the status quo. The need is apparent for reform in tax systems which may well have relied too long and too heavily on the local property tax. [But] the ultimate solutions must come from the lawmakers and from the democratic pressures of those who elect them.

Reversed.

Justice STEWART, concurring.

[I] join the opinion [because] I am convinced that any other course would mark an extraordinary departure from principled adjudication under [equal protection]. The uncharted directions of such a departure are suggested, I think, by [Justice Marshall's] imaginative [dissent]. Unlike other provisions of the Constitution, [equal protection] confers no substantive rights and creates no substantive liberties.[1] The function of [equal protection], rather, is simply to

---

1. There is one notable exception to the above statement: It has been established in recent years that [equal protection] confers the substantive right to participate on an equal basis with other qualified voters whenever the State has adopted an electoral process for determining who will represent any segment of the State's population. [But]

measure the validity of *classifications* created by state laws. [Quite] apart from [equal protection], a state law that impinges upon a substantive right or liberty created or conferred by the Constitution is, of course, presumptively invalid, whether or not the law's purpose or effect is to create any classifications. [Numerous] cases in this Court illustrate this principle. In refusing to invalidate the Texas system of financing its public schools, the Court today applies with thoughtfulness and understanding the basic principles [of equal protection].

Justice WHITE, with whom Justice DOUGLAS and Justice BRENNAN join, [dissenting].

[T]his case would be quite different if it were true that the Texas system, while insuring minimum educational expenditures in every district through state funding, extended a meaningful option to all local districts to increase their per-pupil [expenditures]. But for districts with a low per-pupil real estate tax base, [the] Texas system utterly fails to extend a realistic choice to parents because the property tax, which is the only revenue-raising mechanism extended to school districts, is practically and legally unavailable. [Requiring] the State to establish only that unequal treatment is in furtherance of a permissible goal, without also requiring the State to show that the means chosen to effectuate that goal are rationally related to its achievement, makes equal protection analysis no more than an empty [gesture].

Justice MARSHALL, with whom Justice DOUGLAS concurs, [dissenting].

[I] must once more voice my disagreement with the Court's rigidified approach to equal protection analysis. [The] Court apparently seeks to establish today that equal protection cases fall into one of two neat categories which dictate the appropriate standard of review—strict scrutiny or mere rationality. But this Court's [decisions] defy such easy categorization. A principled reading of what this Court has done reveals that it has applied a spectrum of standards in reviewing discrimination allegedly violative of [equal protection]. This spectrum clearly comprehends variations in the degree of care with which the Court will scrutinize particular classifications, depending, I believe, on the constitutional and societal importance of the interest adversely affected and the recognized invidiousness of the basis upon which the particular classification is drawn. [In fact], many of the Court's recent decisions embody the very sort of reasoned approach to [equal protection] for which I previously argued. [See Dandridge v. Williams (1970; p. 912 below).] [I] therefore cannot accept the majority's labored efforts to demonstrate that fundamental interests, which call for [strict scrutiny], encompass only established rights which we are somehow bound to recognize from the text of the Constitution itself. [It] will not do to suggest that the "answer" to whether an interest is fundamental for purposes of equal protection analysis is *always* determined by whether that interest "is a [right] explicitly or implicitly guaranteed by the Constitution." I would like to know where the Constitution guarantees the right to procreate [Skinner v. Oklahoma], or the right to vote in state elections [e.g., Reynolds v. Sims (p. 866 below)],[1] or the right to an appeal from a criminal conviction [e.g., Griffin v.

there is no constitutional right to vote, as [such]. [Footnote by Justice Stewart.] (See sec. 4B below).

1. It is interesting that in its effort to reconcile the state voting rights cases with its theory of fundamentality the majority can muster nothing more than the contention that "[t]he constitutional underpinnings of the right to equal treatment in the voting *process* can no longer be doubted" (emphasis added). If, by this, the Court intends to recognize a substantive constitutional "right to equal treatment in the voting process" independent of [equal protection], the source of

Illinois].[2] These are instances in which, due to the importance of the interests at stake, the Court has displayed a strong concern with the existence of discriminatory state treatment. But the Court has never said or indicated that these are interests which independently enjoy full-blown constitutional [protection].

The majority is, of course, correct when it suggests that the process of determining which interests are fundamental is a difficult one. But I do not think the problem is insurmountable. And I certainly do not accept the view that the process need necessarily degenerate into an unprincipled, subjective "picking-and-choosing" between various interests or that it must involve this Court in creating "substantive constitutional rights in the name of guaranteeing equal protection of the laws." Although not all fundamental interests are constitutionally guaranteed, the determination of which interests are fundamental should be firmly rooted in the text of the Constitution. The task in every case should be to determine the extent to which constitutionally guaranteed rights are dependent on interests not mentioned in the Constitution. As the nexus between the specific constitutional guarantee and the nonconstitutional interest draws closer, the nonconstitutional interest becomes more fundamental and the degree of judicial scrutiny applied when the interest is infringed on a discriminatory basis must be adjusted accordingly. Thus, it cannot be denied that interests such as procreation, the exercise of the state franchise, and access to criminal appellate processes are not fully guaranteed to the citizen by our Constitution. But these interests have nonetheless been afforded special judicial consideration in the face of discrimination because they are, to some extent, interrelated with constitutional guarantees. Procreation is now understood to be important because of its interaction with the established constitutional right of privacy. The exercise of the state franchise is closely tied to basic civil and political rights inherent in the First Amendment. And access to criminal appellate processes enhances the integrity of the range of rights implicit in the [guarantee of due process]. Only if we closely protect the related interests from state discrimination do we ultimately ensure the integrity of the constitutional guarantee itself. This is the real lesson that must be taken from our previous decisions involving interests deemed to be fundamental.

In summary, it seems to me inescapably clear that this Court has consistently adjusted the care with which it will review state discrimination in light of the constitutional significance of the interests affected and the invidiousness of the particular classification. [The] majority suggests, however, that a variable standard of review would give this Court the appearance of a "super-legislature." I cannot agree. Such an approach seems to me a part of the guarantees of our Constitution and of the historic experiences with oppression of and discrimination against discrete, powerless minorities which underlie that document. In truth, the Court itself will be open to the criticism raised by the majority so long as it continues on its present course of effectively selecting in private which cases will be afforded special consideration without acknowl-

such a right is certainly a mystery to me. [Footnote by Justice Marshall—later in his opinion.]

2. It is true that Griffin [also] involved discrimination against indigents, that is, wealth discrimination. But, as the majority points out, [the] Court has never deemed wealth discrimination alone to be sufficient to require strict judicial scrutiny; rather, such review of wealth classifications has been applied only where the discrimination affects an important individual interest, see, e.g., [Harper, below]. Thus, I believe Griffin [can] only be understood as premised on a recognition of the fundamental importance of the criminal appellate process. [Footnote by Justice Marshall—later in his opinion.]

edging the true basis of its action.[3] [It] is true that this Court has never deemed the provision of free public education to be required by the Constitution. [But] education directly affects the ability of a child to exercise his First Amendment [interests]. [Of] particular importance is the relationship between education and the political process and the demonstrated effect of education on the exercise of the franchise by the electorate. [It] is this very sort of intimate relationship between a particular personal interest and specific constitutional guarantees that has heretofore caused the Court to attach special significance, for purposes of equal protection analysis, to individual interests such as procreation and the exercise of the state franchise.[4] [These factors] compel us to recognize the fundamentality of education and to scrutinize with appropriate care the bases for state discrimination affecting equality of educational opportunity in Texas school districts—a conclusion which is only strengthened when we consider the character of the classification in this [case].

[We] are told that in every prior case involving a wealth classification, the members of the disadvantaged class have "shared two distinguishing characteristics: because of their impecunity they were completely unable to pay for some desired benefit, and as a consequence, they sustained an absolute deprivation of a meaningful opportunity to enjoy that benefit." I cannot agree. [Harper, Griffin and Douglas] refute the majority's contention that we have in the past required an absolute deprivation before subjecting wealth classifications to strict scrutiny. [This] is not to say that the form of wealth classification in this case does not differ significantly from those recognized [in previous decisions]. Here, the children [are] being discriminated against not necessarily because of their personal wealth or the wealth of their families, but because of the taxable property wealth of the residents of the district in which they happen to live. The appropriate question, then, is whether the same degree of judicial [scrutiny] that has previously been afforded wealth classifications is warranted here. [That] wealth classifications alone have not necessarily been considered to bear the same high degree of suspectness as have classifications based on, for instance, race or alienage may be explainable on a number of grounds. The "poor" may not be seen as politically powerless as certain discrete and insular minority groups. Personal poverty may entail much the same social stigma as historically attached to certain racial or ethnic groups [but it] is not a permanent disability; its shackles may be escaped. Perhaps, most importantly, though, personal wealth may not necessarily share the general irrelevance as a basis for legislative action that race or nationality is recognized to have. While the "poor" have frequently been a legally disadvantaged group, it cannot be

3. See generally Gunther, ["Newer Equal Protection"]. [Footnote by Justice Marshall.]

4. I believe that the close nexus between education and our established constitutional values with respect to freedom of speech and participation in the political process makes this a different case than our prior decisions concerning discrimination affecting public welfare, see, e.g., [Dandridge v. Williams], or housing, see, e.g., [Lindsey v. Normet]. [See sec. 4E below.] There can be no question that, as the majority suggests, constitutional rights may be less meaningful for someone without enough to eat or without decent housing. But the crucial difference lies in the closeness of the relationship. Whatever the severity of the impact of insufficient food or inadequate housing on a person's life, they have never been considered to bear the same direct and immediate relationship to constitutional concerns for free speech and for our political processes as education has long been recognized to bear. Perhaps the best evidence of this fact is the unique status which has been accorded public education as the single public service nearly unanimously guaranteed in the constitutions of our States. Education, in terms of constitutional values, is much more analogous, in my judgment, to the right to vote in state elections than to public welfare or [public housing]. [Footnote by Justice Marshall.]

ignored that social legislation must frequently take cognizance of the economic status of our citizens. Thus, we have generally gauged the invidiousness of wealth classifications with an awareness of the importance of the interests being affected and the relevance of personal wealth to those interests.

When evaluated with these considerations in mind, it seems to me that discrimination on the basis of group wealth in this case likewise calls for careful judicial scrutiny. First, [local district wealth] bears no relationship whatsoever to the interest of Texas school children in the educational opportunity afforded them [by] Texas. Given the importance of that interest, we must be particularly sensitive to the invidious characteristics of any form of discrimination that is not clearly intended to serve it, as opposed to some other distinct state interest. Discrimination on the basis of group wealth may not, to be sure, reflect the social stigma frequently attached to personal poverty. Nevertheless, insofar as group wealth discrimination involves wealth over which the disadvantaged individual has no significant control, it represents in fact a more serious basis of discrimination than does personal wealth. For such discrimination is no reflection of the individual's characteristics or his abilities. [We] have previously treated discrimination on a basis which the individual cannot control as constitutionally disfavored. Cf. [Weber; Levy, sec. 3C2 above]. [Here], both the nature of the interest and the classification dictate close judicial scrutiny of the purposes which Texas seeks to serve with its present educational financing scheme and of the means it has selected to serve that purpose. [I] need not now decide how I might ultimately strike the balance were we confronted with a situation where the State's sincere concern for local control inevitably produced educational inequality. For on this record, it is apparent that the State's purported concern with local control is offered primarily as an excuse rather than as a justification for interdistrict inequality. [School districts] cannot choose to have the best education in the State by imposing the highest tax rate. Instead, the quality of the educational opportunity offered by any particular district is largely determined by the amount of taxable property located in the district—a factor over which local voters can exercise no [control]. In my judgment, any substantial degree of scrutiny [reveals] that the State has selected means wholly inappropriate to secure its purported interest in assuring its school districts local fiscal control. At the same time, appellees have pointed out a variety of alternative financing schemes which may serve the State's purported interest in local control as well as, if not better than, the present scheme without the current impairment of the educational opportunity of vast numbers of Texas school children. I see no need, however, to explore the practical or constitutional merits of those suggested alternatives at this time for, whatever their positive or negative features, experience with the present financing scheme impugns any suggestion that it constitutes a serious effort to provide local fiscal [control].

Plyler v. Doe

457 U.S. 202, 102 S.Ct. 2382, 72 L.Ed.2d 786 (1982).[1]

Justice BRENNAN delivered the opinion of the Court.

1. Plyler v. Doe was a class action on behalf of certain school-age children of Mexican origin residing in Smith County, Texas, who could not establish that they had been legally admitted into the United States. The suit attacked the exclusion of the children from the public schools of the Tyler Independent School District. Since 1977, the District

The question presented by these cases is whether, consistent with [equal protection], Texas may deny to undocumented school-age children the free public education that it provides to children who are citizens of the United States or legally admitted aliens.

I. Since the late nineteenth century, the United States has restricted immigration into this country. Unsanctioned entry into the United States is a crime, and those who have entered unlawfully are subject to deportation. But despite the existence of these legal restrictions, a substantial number of persons have succeeded in unlawfully entering the United States, and now live within various States, including [Texas]. In May 1975, the Texas legislature [authorized] local school districts to deny enrollment in their public schools to children not "legally admitted" to the [country]. II. The 14th Amendment provides that "No State [shall] deny to *any person within its jurisdiction* the equal protection of the laws." Appellants [argue] that undocumented aliens, because of their immigration status, are not "persons within the jurisdiction" of [Texas], and that they therefore have no right to the equal protection of Texas law. We reject this argument. Aliens, even aliens whose presence [here] is unlawful, have long been recognized as "persons" [under the 14th Amendment]. III. [In] applying [equal protection] to most forms of state action, [we] seek only the assurance that the classification at issue bears some fair relationship to a legitimate public purpose. But we would not be faithful to our obligations [if] we applied so deferential a standard to every classification. [Equal protection] was intended as a restriction on state legislative action inconsistent with elemental constitutional premises. Thus we have treated as presumptively invidious those classifications that disadvantage a "suspect class,"[2] or that impinge upon the exercise of a "fundamental right."[3] With respect to such classifications, it is appropriate to enforce the mandate of equal protection by requiring the State to demonstrate that its classification has been precisely tailored to serve a compelling governmental interest. In addition, we have recognized that certain forms of legislative classification, while not facially invidious, nonetheless give rise to recurring constitutional difficulties; in these limited circumstances we have sought the assurance that the classification

had required "undocumented" children to pay a "full tuition fee" in order to enroll. The lower federal courts held that the exclusion of the children from free public education violated equal protection. The Court affirmed.

2. Several formulations might explain our treatment of certain classifications as "suspect." Some classifications are more likely than others to reflect deep-seated prejudice rather than legislative rationality in pursuit of some legitimate objective. Legislation predicated on such prejudice is easily recognized as incompatible with the constitutional understanding that each person is to be judged individually and is entitled to equal justice under the law. Classifications treated as suspect tend to be irrelevant to any proper legislative goal. Finally, certain groups, indeed largely the same groups, have historically been "relegated to such a position of political powerlessness as to command extraordinary protection from the majoritarian political

process." [Carolene Products.] [Legislation] imposing special disabilities upon groups disfavored by virtue of circumstances beyond their control suggests the kind of "class or caste" treatment that the 14th Amendment was designed to abolish. [Footnote by Justice Brennan.]

3. In determining whether a class-based denial of a particular right is deserving of strict scrutiny under [equal protection], we look to the Constitution to see if the right infringed has its source, explicitly or implicitly, therein. But we have also recognized the fundamentality of participation in state "elections on an equal basis with other citizens in the jurisdiction" even though "the right to vote, per se, is not a constitutionally protected right." With respect to suffrage, we have explained the need for strict scrutiny as arising from the significance of the franchise as the guardian of all rights. [Footnote by Justice Brennan.]

reflects a reasoned judgment [by] inquiring whether it may fairly be viewed as furthering a substantial interest of the State.[4] We turn to a consideration of the standard appropriate for the evaluation of [the Texas law].

A.   Sheer incapability or lax enforcement of the laws barring entry into this country [has] resulted in the creation of a substantial "shadow population" of illegal migrants—numbering in the millions—within our borders. This situation raises the specter of a permanent caste of undocumented resident aliens, encouraged by some to remain here as a source of cheap labor, but nevertheless denied the benefits that our society makes available to citizens and lawful residents. The existence of such an underclass presents most difficult problems for a Nation that prides itself in adherence to principles of equality under law.[5] The children who are plaintiffs in these cases are special members of this underclass. Persuasive arguments support the view that a State may withhold its beneficence from those whose very presence within the United States is the product of their own unlawful conduct. These arguments do not apply with the same force to classifications imposing disabilities on the minor *children* of such illegal entrants. [Their] "parents have the ability to conform their conduct to societal norms," and presumably the ability to remove themselves from the State's jurisdiction; but the children who are plaintiffs in these cases "can affect neither their parents' conduct nor their own status." Trimble v. Gordon. Even if the State found it expedient to control the conduct of adults by acting against their children, legislation directing the onus of a parent's misconduct against his children does not comport with fundamental conceptions of justice. [Weber.] [Trimble and Weber are illegitimacy cases, in sec. 3C2 above.] Of course, undocumented status is not irrelevant to any proper legislative goal. Nor is undocumented status an absolutely immutable characteristic since it is the product of conscious, indeed unlawful, action. But [the Texas law] is directed against children, and imposes its discriminatory burden on the basis of a legal characteristic over which children can have little control. It is thus difficult to conceive of a rational justification for penalizing these children for their presence within the United States. Yet that appears to be precisely the effect of [the law].

Public education is not a "right" granted to individuals by the Constitution. [Rodriguez.] But neither is it merely some governmental "benefit" indistinguishable from other forms of social welfare legislation. Both the importance of education in maintaining our basic institutions, and the lasting impact of its deprivation on the life of the child, mark the distinction. [In] addition, education provides the basic tools by which individuals might lead economically productive lives to the benefit of us all. In sum, education has a fundamental role in maintaining the fabric of our society. We cannot ignore the significant social costs borne by our Nation when select groups are denied the means to absorb the values and skills upon which our social order rests. In addition to the pivotal role of education in sustaining our political and cultural heritage, denial of education to some isolated group of children poses an affront to one of

---

4.   See Craig v. Boren; Lalli v. Lalli [above]. This technique of "intermediate" scrutiny permits us to evaluate the rationality of the legislative judgment with reference to well-settled constitutional [principles]. [Footnote by Justice Brennan.]

5.   We reject the claim that "illegal aliens" are a "suspect class." No case in which we have attempted to define a suspect class has addressed the status of persons unlawfully in our country. Unlike most of the classifications that we have recognized as suspect, entry into this class, by virtue of entry into this country, is the product of voluntary action. Indeed, entry into the class is itself a crime. In addition, it could hardly be suggested that undocumented status is a ["constitutional irrelevancy"]. [Footnote by Justice Brennan.]

the goals of [equal protection]: the abolition of governmental barriers presenting unreasonable obstacles to advancement on the basis of individual merit.
Paradoxically, by depriving the children of any disfavored group of an education, we foreclose the means by which that group might raise the level of
esteem in which it is held by the majority. [Illiteracy] is an enduring disability.
[The] inestimable toll of [the] deprivation [of a basic education] on the social,
economic, intellectual and psychological well-being of the individual, and the
obstacle it poses to individual achievement, makes it most difficult to reconcile
the cost or the principle of a status-based denial of basic education with the
framework of equality embodied in [equal protection].

B.   These well-settled principles allow us to determine the proper level of
deference to be afforded [here]. Undocumented aliens [are not] a suspect class
[and] education [is not] a fundamental [right]. But more is involved in this case
than the abstract question whether [this law] discriminates against a suspect
class, or whether education is a fundamental right. [This law] imposes a
lifetime hardship on a discrete class of children not accountable for their
disabling status. [In] determining the rationality of [this law], we may appropriately take into account its costs to the Nation and to the innocent children who
are its victims. In light of these countervailing costs, the discrimination
contained in [this law] can hardly be considered rational unless it furthers
some substantial goal of the State.

IV.   It is the State's principal argument [that] the undocumented status of
these children *vel non* establishes a sufficient rational basis for denying them
benefits that a State might choose to afford other residents. The State notes
that while other aliens are admitted "on an equality of legal privileges with all
citizens under non-discriminatory laws" [Takahashi], the asserted right of
these children to an education can claim no implicit congressional imprimatur.
Indeed, on the State's view, Congress' apparent disapproval of the presence of
these children [provides] authority for its decision to impose upon them special
disabilities. [But] we are unable to find in the congressional immigration
scheme any statement of policy that might weigh significantly in arriving at an
equal protection balance concerning the State's authority to deprive these
children of an education. [The] States enjoy no power with respect to the
classification of aliens. This power is "committed to the political branches of
the Federal Government." [Although] the States do have some authority to act
with respect to illegal aliens, at least where such action mirrors federal
objectives and furthers a legitimate state [goal], there is no indication that the
disability imposed by the [Texas law] corresponds to any identifiable congressional policy. [To] be sure, [these] children are subject to deportation. But there
is no assurance that a child subject to deportation will ever be deported. [We]
are reluctant to impute to Congress the intention to withhold from these
children, for so long as they are present in this country through no fault of
their own, access to a basic education. In other contexts, undocumented status,
coupled with some articulable federal policy, might enhance State authority
with respect to the treatment of undocumented aliens. But in the area of
special constitutional sensitivity presented by this case, and in the absence of
any contrary indication fairly discernible in the present legislative record, we
perceive no national policy that supports the State in denying these children an
elementary education. [We] therefore turn to the state objectives that are said
to support [the Texas law].

V.   Appellants argue that the classification at issue furthers an interest in
the "preservation of the state's limited resources for the education of its lawful
residents." [But the] State must do more than justify its classification with a
concise expression of an intention to discriminate. [Beyond this,] we discern

three colorable state interests that might support [this law]. First, appellants appear to suggest that the State may seek to protect [itself] from an influx of illegal immigrants. [But there] is no evidence in the record suggesting that illegal entrants impose any significant burden on the State's economy. [We] think it clear that "[c]harging tuition to undocumented children constitutes a ludicrously ineffectual attempt to stem the tide of illegal immigration," at least when compared with the alternative of prohibiting the employment of illegal aliens. Second, [appellants] suggest that undocumented children are appropriately singled out for exclusion because of the special burdens they impose on the State's ability to provide high quality public education. But the record in no way supports the claim that exclusion of undocumented children is likely to improve the overall quality of education in the State. [Of course,] even if improvement in the quality of education were a likely result of barring some *number* of children from the schools of the State, the State must support its selection of *this* group as the appropriate target for exclusion. In terms of educational cost and need, however, undocumented children are "basically indistinguishable" from legally resident alien children. Finally, appellants suggest that undocumented children are appropriately singled out because their unlawful presence within the United States renders them less likely than other children to remain within the boundaries of the State, and to put their education to productive social or political use within the State. Even assuming that such an interest is legitimate, it is an interest that is most difficult to quantify. The State has no assurance that any child, citizen or not, will employ the education provided by the State within the confines of the State's borders. In any event, [many] of the undocumented children disabled by this classification will remain in this country indefinitely, and [some] will become lawful residents or citizens of the United States. It is difficult to understand precisely what the State hopes to achieve by promoting the creation and perpetuation of a subclass of illiterates within our boundaries, surely adding to the problems and costs of unemployment, welfare, and crime. It is thus clear that whatever savings might be achieved by denying these children an education, they are wholly insubstantial in light of the costs involved to these children, the State, and the Nation. VI. If the State is to deny a discrete group of innocent children the free public education that it offers to other children residing within its borders, that denial must be justified by a showing that it furthers some substantial state interest. No such showing was made here.

[Affirmed.]*

Justice BLACKMUN, concurring.

* In a separate notation, Justice MARSHALL stated that he joined the Court's opinion "without in any way retreating from my opinion in [Rodriguez]." He reiterated his belief that the interest in education is "fundamental." He added that the facts here once again demonstrated "the wisdom of rejecting a rigidified approach to equal protection analysis." Does the Plyler result represent the strongest vindication yet of Justice Marshall's long-maintained "sliding scale" position? A number of lower courts, in finding mental illness and mental retardation suspect classifications, relied heavily on Plyler. Recall, too, that a zoning ordinance burdening the mentally retarded was struck down by the Court, in the Cleburne case at p. 728 above, without explicitly applying heightened scrutiny. Thus Cleburne, together with Plyler, lend added support to Justice Marshall's position that the Court's manner of applying its alleged two-or three-tiered scrutiny does not fully reflect what the Court actually does, and that the Court has increasingly resorted to ad hoc interventionism in the face of perceived injustices, despite its protestations that it is applying a carefully structured, predictable scheme of two or three tiers of equal protection review.

I join the opinion and judgment of the Court. Like Justice Powell, I believe that the children involved in this litigation "should not be left on the streets uneducated." I write separately, however, because in my view the nature of the interest at stake is crucial to the proper resolution of this case. [I] joined Justice Powell's opinion [in] Rodriguez, and I continue to believe that it provides the appropriate model for resolving most equal protection disputes. [With] all this said, however, I believe the Court's experience has demonstrated that the Rodriguez formulation does not settle every issue of "fundamental rights" arising under the Equal Protection Clause. Only a pedant would insist that there are *no* meaningful distinctions among the multitude of social and political interests regulated by the States, and Rodriguez does not stand for quite so absolute a proposition. To the contrary, Rodriguez implicitly acknowledged that certain interests, though not constitutionally guaranteed, must be accorded a special place in equal protection analysis. Thus, the Court's decisions long have accorded strict scrutiny to classifications bearing on the right to vote in state elections. [I] believe that accepting the principle of the voting cases [dictates] the outcome [here]. In my view, when the State provides an education to some and denies it to others, it immediately and inevitably creates class distinctions of a type fundamentally inconsistent with [equal protection]. Children denied an education are placed at a permanent and insurmountable competitive disadvantage, for an uneducated child is denied even the opportunity to achieve. And when those children are members of an identifiable group, that group—through the State's action—will have been converted into a discrete underclass. Other benefits provided by the State, such as housing and public assistance, are of course [important]. But classifications involving the complete denial of education are in a sense unique, for they strike at the heart of equal protection values by involving the State in the creation of permanent class distinctions. In a sense, then, denial of an education is the analogue of denial of the right to vote: the former relegates the individual to second-class social status; the latter places him at a permanent political disadvantage. This conclusion is fully consistent with Rodriguez. The Court there reserved judgment on the constitutionality of a state system that "occasioned an absolute denial of educational opportunities to any of its children." [In] contrast to the situation in Rodriguez, it does not take an advanced degree to predict the effects of a complete denial of education upon those children targeted by the State's classification. In such circumstances, the voting decisions suggest that the State must offer something more than a rational basis for its classification. [Given] the extraordinary nature of the interest involved, this makes the classification here fatally [imprecise].

Justice POWELL, concurring.

I join the opinion of the Court, and write separately to emphasize the unique character of the case before us. [I] agree with the Court that their children should not be left on the streets uneducated. Although the analogy is not perfect, our holding today does find support in decisions of this Court with respect to the status of illegitimates. [See Weber.] [Texas] effectively denies to the school age children of illegal aliens the opportunity to attend the free public schools that the State makes available to all residents. They are excluded only because of a status resulting from the violation by parents or guardians of our immigration laws and the fact that they remain in our country unlawfully. The respondent children are innocent in this respect. They can "affect neither their parents' conduct nor their own status." Trimble v. Gordon. Our review in a case such as this is properly heightened. Cf. Craig v. Boren. [These] children [have] been singled out for a lifelong penalty and stigma. A legislative classification that threatens the creation of an underclass of future citizens and

intermediate?

residents cannot be reconciled with one of the fundamental purposes of the 14th Amendment. In these unique circumstances, the Court properly may require that the State's interests be substantial and that the means bear a "fair and substantial relation" to these interests.[1] [The] State's denial of education to these children bears no substantial relation to any substantial state interest. [The] exclusion of [these] children from state-provided education is a type of punitive discrimination based on status that is impermissible under [equal protection].

Chief Justice BURGER, with whom Justice WHITE, Justice REHNQUIST, and Justice O'CONNOR join, dissenting.

Were it our business to set the Nation's social policy, I would agree without hesitation that it is senseless for an enlightened society to deprive any children—including illegal aliens—of an elementary education. [However, we] trespass on the assigned function of the political branches [when] we assume a policymaking role as the Court does today. [The] holding today manifests the justly criticized judicial tendency to attempt speedy and wholesale formulation of "remedies" for the failures—or simply the laggard pace—of the political [processes]. The Court [abuses] the 14th Amendment in an effort to become an omnipotent and omniscient [problem solver]. [The] Court [correctly] rejects any suggestion that illegal aliens are a suspect class or that education is a fundamental right. Yet by patching together bits and pieces of what might be termed quasi-suspect-class and quasi-fundamental-rights analysis, the Court spins out a theory custom-tailored to the facts of these cases. [If] ever a court was guilty of an unabashedly result-oriented approach, this case is a prime example. [Equal protection is] not an all-encompassing "equalizer" designed to eradicate every distinction for which persons are not "responsible." The Court does not [suggest] that appellees' purported lack of culpability for their illegal status prevents them from being deported or otherwise "penalized" under federal law. Yet would deportation be any less a "penalty" than denial of privileges provided to legal residents? The Court's analogy to cases involving discrimination against illegitimate children [is] grossly misleading. The State has not thrust any disabilities upon appellees due to their "status of birth." Rather, appellees' status is predicated upon the circumstances of their concededly illegal presence in this [country]. The second strand of the Court's analysis rests on the premise that, although public education is not a constitutionally-guaranteed right, "neither is it merely some governmental 'benefit' indistinguishable from other forms of social welfare legislation." [This] opaque observation [has] no bearing on the issues at hand. Indeed, it is never made clear what the Court's opinion means on this score. [Is] the Court suggesting that education is more "fundamental" than food, shelter, or medical care? [Equal protection] does not mandate a constitutional hierarchy of governmental [services].

rational basis

Once it is conceded [that] illegal aliens are not a suspect class, and that education is not a fundamental right, our inquiry should focus on and be limited to whether the legislative classification at issue bears a rational relationship to a legitimate state purpose. [It] simply is not "irrational" for a State

---

1. The Chief Justice argues in his [dissent] that this heightened standard of review is inconsistent with the Court's decision in [Rodriguez]. But in Rodriguez no group of children was singled out by the State and then penalized because of their parent's status. [Nor] was any group of children totally deprived of all [education]. If the resident children of illegal aliens were denied welfare assistance, made available by government to all other children who qualify, this also—in my opinion—would be an impermissible penalizing of children because of their parents' status. [Footnote by Justice Powell.]

to conclude that it does not have the same responsibility to provide benefits for persons whose very presence in the State and this country is illegal as it does to provide for persons lawfully present. [It] is significant that the federal government has seen fit to exclude illegal aliens from numerous social welfare [programs]. [These] exclusions [tend] to support the rationality of excluding illegal alien residents of a State from such programs so as to preserve the State's finite revenues for the benefit of lawful [residents]. [The] State may "rationally" choose to take advantage of whatever savings will accrue from limiting access to the tuition-free public schools to its own lawful [residents]. Denying a free education to illegal alien children is not a choice I would make were I a legislator. [But the] fact that there are sound *policy* arguments against the Texas legislature's choice does not render that choice an unconstitutional one. Congress [bears] primary responsibility for addressing the problems occasioned by the millions of illegal aliens flooding across our southern border. [The] solution to this seemingly intractable problem is to defer to the political processes, unpalatable as that may be to some.*

The limits of Plyler. Contrast with Plyler the decision a year later in Martinez v. Bynum, 461 U.S. 321 (1983), rejecting a facial attack on a Texas law authorizing school districts to deny tuition-free education to minors who live apart from their parents and whose presence in the district was "for the primary purpose of attending the public free schools." Justice Powell's majority opinion found this a valid "bona fide residence requirement." Justice Brennan joined the majority in a separate opinion; Justice Marshall was the sole dissenter. Note also Kadrmas v. Dickinson Public Schools, 487 U.S. 450 (1988), a 5-4 decision in which the Court followed the lead of Rodriguez rather than Plyler. The decision upheld a provision under which North Dakota permitted local school boards to assess a user fee for transporting students to and from public schools. Justice O'Connor's majority opinion, relying on Rodriguez, rejected an argument that strict scrutiny should apply on the grounds of wealth discrimination or the presence of a fundamental interest in education. She described Plyler as having applied the intermediate or "heightened" standard of review normally used for classifications based on sex or illegitimacy, but attributed that to the unique circumstances of that case: "Unlike the children in [Plyler], Sarita Kadrmas has not been penalized by the government for illegal conduct by her parents." Justice Marshall, jointed by Justice Brennan, dissented, relying on Plyler, on his Rodriguez dissent, and on the view that classifications based on wealth, especially in the context of education, had "special constitutional significance" and warranted "exacting scrutiny." Justice Stevens, joined by Justice Blackmun, also dissented, claiming that the distinction drawn by the transportation fee could not survive rational basis scrutiny of the variety applied in the Cleburne case, p. 728 above.

---

* Consider the comment on Plyler v. Doe, in Hutchinson, "More Substantive Equal Protection?" 1982 Sup.Ct.Rev. 167: "[Plyler demonstrates] that Rodriguez is now a constitutional relic whose only significance is its holding; as doctrine, it is irrelevant. [Whatev- er] the deficiencies of the old two-tier model, it at least provided some predictability and a common ground of discourse. The new three-tier model promises to be nowhere near as [predictable]." Compare Tushnet, "The Optimist's Tale," 132 U.Pa.L.Rev. 1257 (1984).

B.   DENIAL AND "DILUTION" OF VOTING RIGHTS

Introduction. The 1789 Constitution explicitly left to the states their determination of qualifications of voters for both national and state elections. See, e.g., Art. I, § 2 and Art. II, § 1. A number of constitutional amendments imposed federal limits on state power. See the 14th, 19th, 24th and 26th Amendments. Until the 1960s, the Court typically deferred to states with regard to voter qualifications. But in 1966, in Harper, which follows, and in Reynolds v. Sims (1964; p. 866 below), the Court opened the door to more active supervision of state voting schemes. Equal protection has been the major source of judicial restraints on state authority in this area. Recall the dispute in Rodriguez, above, about the constitutional sources and meaning of the right, a right that a footnote by Justice Powell in that case described as a right "to participate in state elections on an equal basis with other qualified voters." Recall also Justice Stone's footnote 4 in Carolene Products, mentioning "restrictions upon the right to vote" as a specific illustration of restrictions on "political processes." Are there adequate constitutional justifications for the Court's moving beyond specific language in the Constitution to guarantee broad access to the political processes? Ely, in Democracy and Distrust (1980), elaborating upon the theories of the Carolene Products footnote, views "denial of the vote" as "the quintessential stoppage" in the democratic process, justifying active judicial supervision. Do you agree? We begin this examination with outright denials of the right to vote before turning to "dilutions" of the right and denials of ballot access.

---

1.   DENIALS OF THE FRANCHISE

Harper v. Virginia State Board of Elections
383 U.S. 663, 86 S.Ct. 1079, 16 L.Ed.2d 169 (1966).

[Virginia imposed an annual $1.50 poll tax on all residents over 21. The State made payment of the poll taxes a precondition for voting. Appellants' suit to have the poll tax declared unconstitutional was dismissed by a three-judge district court on the authority of Breedlove v. Suttles, 302 U.S. 277 (1937), where the Court had unanimously rejected an equal protection attack on the Georgia poll tax.]

Justice DOUGLAS delivered the opinion of the [Court].

[The] right to vote in state elections is nowhere expressly mentioned [in the Constitution]. It is argued that the right to vote in state elections is implicit, particularly by reason of the First Amendment. [We] do not stop to canvass the relation between voting and political expression. For it is enough to say that once the franchise is granted to the electorate, lines may not be drawn which are inconsistent with [equal protection]. [We] conclude that a State violates [equal protection] whenever it makes the affluence of the voter or payment of any fee an electoral standard. Voter qualifications have no relation to wealth nor to paying or not paying this or any other tax. Our cases demonstrate that [equal protection] restrains the States from fixing voter qualifications which invidiously discriminate. Long ago in [Yick Wo] the Court referred to "the political franchise of voting" as a "fundamental political right, because preservative of all rights." Recently, in Reynolds v. Sims [1964; p. 866 below], we said: "Undoubtedly, the right of suffrage is a fundamental right in a

[free] society. Especially since the right [to vote] in a free and unimpaired manner is preservative of other basic civil and political rights, any alleged infringement of the right of citizens to vote must be carefully and meticulously scrutinized." [It] is argued that a State may exact fees from citizens for many different kinds of licenses; that if it can demand from all an equal fee for a driver's license, it can demand from all an equal poll tax for voting. But we must remember that the interest of the State, when it comes to voting, is limited to the power to fix qualifications. Wealth, like race, creed, or color, is not germane to one's ability to participate intelligently in the electoral process. Lines drawn on the basis of wealth or property, like those of race, are traditionally disfavored. See [e.g., Griffin; Douglas (sec. 4C below)]. To introduce wealth or payment of a fee as a measure of a voter's qualifications is to introduce a capricious or irrelevant factor. [In] this context—that is, as a condition of obtaining a ballot—the requirement of fee paying causes an "invidious" discrimination [that] runs afoul of [equal protection]. [Breedlove v. Suttles sanctioned the use of a poll tax] as "a prerequisite of voting." To that extent [it] is overruled.

We agree, of course, with Mr. Justice Holmes that the Due Process Clause of the 14th Amendment "does not enact Mr. Herbert Spencer's Social Statics" [Lochner]. Likewise, the Equal Protection Clause is not shackled to the political theory of a particular era. In determining what lines are unconstitutionally discriminatory, we have never been confined to historic notions of equality, any more than we have restricted due process to a fixed catalogue of what was at a given time deemed to be the limits of fundamental rights. Notions of what constitutes equal treatment for purposes of [equal protection] *do* change. [Compare Plessy with Brown.] In a recent searching re-examination of [equal protection], we [held] that "the opportunity for equal participation by all voters in the election of state legislators" is required. [Reynolds v. Sims.] We decline to qualify that principle by sustaining this poll tax. Our conclusion [is] founded not on what we think governmental policy should be, but on what [equal protection] requires. We have long been mindful that where fundamental rights and liberties are asserted under [equal protection], classifications which might invade or restrain them must be closely scrutinized and carefully confined. See [e.g., Skinner]. Those principles apply here. For to repeat, wealth or fee paying [has] no relation to voting qualifications; the right to vote is too precious, too fundamental to be so burdened or conditioned.

Reversed.

Justice BLACK [dissenting].

[Poll tax] legislation can "reasonably," "rationally" and without an "invidious" or evil purpose to injure anyone be found to rest on a number of state policies including (1) the State's desire to collect its revenue, and (2) its belief that voters who pay a poll tax will be interested in furthering the State's welfare when they vote. [And] history is on the side of "rationality" of the State's poll tax policy. [Another] reason for my dissent [is] that it seems to be using the old "natural-law-due-process formula" to justify striking down state laws as violations of [equal protection]. There is no more constitutional support for this Court to use [equal protection than to use due process] to write into the Constitution its notions of what it thinks is good governmental [policy].

Justice HARLAN, whom Justice STEWART joins, dissenting.

[The Court uses] captivating phrases, but they are wholly inadequate to satisfy the standard governing adjudication of the equal protection issue: Is there a rational basis for Virginia's poll tax as a voting qualification? I think the answer to that question is undoubtedly "yes." Property qualifications and poll taxes have been a traditional part of our political structure. [It] is certainly a rational argument that payment of some minimal poll tax promotes civic responsibility, weeding out those who do not care enough about public affairs to pay $1.50 or thereabouts a year for the exercise of the franchise. It is also arguable, indeed it was probably accepted as sound political theory by a large percentage of Americans through most of our history, that people with some property have a deeper stake in community affairs, and are consequently more responsible, more educated, more knowledgeable, more worthy of confidence, than those without means, and that the community and Nation would be better managed if the franchise were restricted to such citizens. Property and poll-tax qualifications [are] not in accord with current egalitarian notions of how a modern democracy should be organized. [But] it is all wrong [for] the Court to adopt the political doctrines popularly accepted at a particular moment of our history and to declare all others to be irrational and [invidious]. It was not too long ago that Mr. Justice Holmes felt impelled to remind the Court that [due process] does not enact the laissez-faire theory of society [Lochner]. The times have changed, and perhaps it is appropriate to observe that neither does [equal protection] of that Amendment rigidly impose upon America an ideology of unrestrained [egalitarianism].

The bases and impact of Harper. Harper rested on dual grounds: "fundamental interests" and "suspect classifications" analyses evidently *both* played a role. The former theme has proved the sturdier one, and the focus of this section is on the elaboration of strict scrutiny of laws burdening participation in the electoral process. The "fundamental interest" in voting and the electoral process suggested (somewhat obscurely) by Harper has flourished vigorously since that decision, as the following materials illustrate. (The strict scrutiny of limits on the franchise has not been confined to financial barriers, as the next case, from the close of the Warren era, illustrates.) In examining the materials that follow, consider: What *is* the fundamental interest established by these cases? What *is* the source of the right? Is the fundamental right in these cases derived solely (and legitimately) from equal protection? Are there other possible sources in the Constitution? The "Republican Form of Government" guarantee, Art. IV, § 4, has been held to be nonjusticiable. Would that provision be a more plausible source of the right developed in these cases? Does the right ultimately rest in general structural considerations drawn from the Constitution?

Kramer v. Union Free School District No. 15

395 U.S. 621, 89 S.Ct. 1886, 23 L.Ed.2d 583 (1969).

Chief Justice WARREN delivered the opinion of the Court.

[Sec. 2012 of the New York Education Law] provides that in certain New York school districts residents [may] vote in the school district election only if they (1) own (or lease) taxable real property within the district, or (2) are parents (or have custody of) children enrolled in the local public schools. [The law was unsuccessfully challenged in the lower court by "a bachelor who neither owns nor leases taxable real property": appellant was "a thirty-one-year-old college-educated stockbroker who lives in his parents' home."] [We] must give the statute a close and exacting examination. [Reynolds v. Sims.] This is necessary because statutes distributing the franchise constitute the foundation of our representative society. Any unjustified discrimination in determining who may participate in political affairs or in the selection of public officials undermines the legitimacy of representative government. [Laws] granting the franchise to residents on a selective basis always pose the danger of denying some citizens any effective voice in the governmental affairs which substantially affect their lives. Therefore, if a challenged [law] grants the right to vote to some bona fide residents of requisite age and citizenship and denies the franchise to others, the Court must determine whether the conclusions are necessary to promote a compelling state interest. [Such laws] must be carefully scrutinized by the Court to determine whether each resident citizen has, as far as is possible, an equal voice in the selections. [The] presumption of constitutionality and the approval given "rational" classifications in other types of enactments are based on an assumption that the institutions of state government are structured so as to represent fairly all the people. However, when the challenge to the statute is in effect a challenge of this basic assumption, the assumption can no longer serve as the basis for presuming constitutionality. [The] need for exacting judicial scrutiny of statutes distributing the franchise is undiminished simply because, under a different statutory scheme, the offices subject to election might have been filled through appointment. "[O]nce the franchise is granted to the electorate, lines may not be drawn which are inconsistent with [equal protection]." [Harper.]

We turn therefore to [the] question whether the exclusion is necessary to promote a compelling state interest. [Appellees] argue that the State has a legitimate interest in limiting the franchise in school district elections [to] those "primarily interested in such elections" [and] that the State may reasonably and permissibly conclude that "property taxpayers" [and] parents of the children enrolled in the district's schools are those "primarily interested" in school affairs. [We] need express no opinion as to whether the State in some circumstances might limit the exercise of the franchise to those "primarily interested" or "primarily affected." [For], assuming, arguendo, that New York legitimately might limit the franchise in these school district elections to those "primarily interested in school affairs," close scrutiny of the § 2012 classifications demonstrates that they do not accomplish this purpose with sufficient precision to justify denying appellant the franchise. [§ 2012] does not meet the exacting standard of precision we require of statutes which selectively distribute the franchise. [Its] classifications [permit] inclusion of many persons who have, at best, a remote and indirect interest in school affairs and, on the other hand, exclude others who have a distinct and direct interest in the school meeting [decisions].[1]

Reversed.

Justice STEWART, with whom Justice BLACK and Justice HARLAN join, [dissenting].

[Clearly] a State may reasonably assume that its residents have a greater stake in the outcome of elections held within its boundaries than do other persons [and] that residents, being generally better informed regarding state affairs than are nonresidents, will be more likely [to] vote responsibly. And the

---

1. For example, appellant resides with his parents in the school district, pays state and federal taxes and is interested in and affected by school board decisions; however, he has no vote. On the other hand, an unin-terested unemployed young man who pays no state or federal taxes, but who rents an apartment in the district, can [vote]. [Footnote by Chief Justice Warren.]

same may be said of legislative assumptions regarding the electoral competence of adults and literate persons on the one hand, and of minors and illiterates on the other. [So] long as the classification is rationally related to a permissible legislative end, [there] is no denial of equal protection. Thus judged, the statutory classification involved here seems to me clearly to be valid [and the] Court does not really argue the contrary. [The] Court's asserted justification for applying [its strict] standard cannot withstand analysis. [In] any event, it seems to me that under *any* equal protection standard, short of a doctrinaire insistence that universal suffrage is somehow mandated by the Constitution, the appellant's claim must be [rejected].

ADDITIONAL RESTRICTIONS ON THE FRANCHISE

Introduction. Kramer sought to explain more clearly than Harper had why "equal" participation in the electoral process is a "fundamental interest" triggering equal protection strict scrutiny, even though there is no constitutional "right" to vote. In examining the post-Kramer cases which follow, consider especially what state interests are sufficiently "compelling" to survive strict scrutiny in this area, and what means are sufficiently narrowly tailored. Note that in this area, unlike most other spheres of strict scrutiny, some laws *do* survive judicial review. Does that indicate that a "sliding scale" or "balancing" approach has made significant inroads in the voting rights area?

1.   *Efforts to limit the franchise in the contexts of limited purpose elections and special purpose governmental units.* In CIPRIANO v. HOUMA, 395 U.S. 701 (1969), decided on the same day as Kramer, the unanimous Court invalidated a Louisiana law permitting only property owners to vote in elections regarding the issuance of municipal utility bonds. The Court noted that the bonds were to be paid entirely from the operations of the utilities and not from property taxes. A year later, in PHOENIX v. KOLODZIEJSKI, 399 U.S. 204 (1970), the majority extended Cipriano, holding that the restriction of the franchise to property owners was no more valid in elections on general obligation bonds (which looked largely to property tax revenues for servicing) than in elections on revenue bonds. Justice WHITE's majority opinion concluded that the differences between the interests of property owners and of nonproperty owners were not "sufficiently substantial to justify excluding the latter from the franchise." Three years later, however, the majority found the Kramer–Cipriano–Kolodziejski line of cases inapplicable and sustained an election scheme for a water storage district under which only landowners were permitted to vote and in which votes were proportioned according to the assessed valuation of the land. SALYER LAND CO. v. TULARE LAKE BASIN WATER STORAGE DISTRICT, 410 U.S. 719 (1973). Justice REHNQUIST's majority opinion noted that the district's main purpose was to assure water for farming, and that project costs were assessed upon the land in proportion to benefits received. He found the demanding requirements of such cases as Kramer and Reynolds v. Sims inapplicable to the district "by reason of its special limited purpose and of the disproportionate effect of its activities on landowners as a group." Accordingly, the details of the election scheme were subjected only to the minimal scrutiny, and those details—the exclusion of mere residents and lessees, and weighting the votes according to the value of the land—easily survived that scrutiny. There was a vigorous dissent by Justice DOUGLAS, joined by Justices Brennan and Marshall. He especially objected to voting by the large land-owning corporations which farmed 85% of the land in

the district: "The result is a corporation political kingdom undreamed of by those who wrote our Constitution." See also BALL v. JAMES, 451 U.S. 355 (1981), where a sharply divided Court extended the Salyer exception to the "one person-one vote" rule of Reynolds v. Sims, below, and sustained the constitutionality of a "one acre-one vote" scheme for electing the directors of a large water reclamation district in Arizona. The majority applied the deferential rationality review of Salyer rather than the strict scrutiny of Kramer. In QUINN v. MILLSAP, 491 U.S. 95 (1989), however, a unanimous Court made clear, contrary to the understanding of the Missouri Supreme Court, that Salyer and Ball did *not* mean that equal protection was wholly inapplicable to governmental units lacking general powers. Applying rationality review to a requirement that only property owners could be members of a board of freeholders, which had the power to propose plans of reorganization for local governmental units, the Court found that the requirement served no "defensible" purpose.

2. *Durational residence requirements.* The 6-1 decision in DUNN v. BLUMSTEIN, 405 U.S. 330 (1972), invalidated Tennessee's durational residence requirements for voters. (Tennessee required one year's residence in the state and three months in the county as a condition of voting.) Justice MARSHALL's majority opinion—while recognizing the state's strong interest in limiting voting to residents—held that durational residence requirements were subject to strict scrutiny both because they curtailed the fundamental interest in voting and because they burdened the right to travel.[1] His discussion of the appropriate standard of review afforded him an early opportunity to elaborate the multi-variable, "sliding scale" approach that he was to reiterate frequently. (Recall his Rodriguez dissent, and see Dandridge v. Williams, p. 912 below.) He stated: "[W]hether we look to the benefit withheld by the classification (the opportunity to vote) or the basis for the classification (recent interstate travel), we conclude that the state must show a substantial and compelling reason for imposing durational residence requirements." Such requirements could not stand "unless the State can demonstrate that such laws are '*necessary* to promote a *compelling* government interest.'" This equal protection approach, Justice Marshall explained, was not a "mathematical formula" but rather "a matter of degree: that a heavy burden of justification is on the State, and that the statute will be closely scrutinized in light of its asserted purposes." The "least restrictive means" ingredient of strict scrutiny proved fatal to the Tennessee laws. Tennessee asserted two basic justifications: insuring the "purity of the ballot box" and furthering the goal of having "knowledgeable voters." Neither proved sufficient. With respect to preventing fraud, "30 days appears to be an ample period of [time]—and a year, or three months, too much." (The State closed its registration books 30 days before election.) And with regard to knowledgeability, "the conclusive presumptions of durational residence requirements are much too crude." He added: "By requiring classifications to be tailored to their purpose, we do not secretly require the impossible"; here, the relationship between method and purpose was "simply too attenuated."[2]

---

1. For additional consideration of the right to travel or migrate from state to state (and the invalidation of other durational residence requirements), see sec. 4D below.

2. Chief Justice BURGER was the only dissenter: "Some lines must be drawn. To challenge such lines by the 'compelling state interest' standard is to condemn them all. So far as I am aware, no state law has ever satisfied this seemingly insurmountable standard, and I doubt one ever will." But some challenged laws did survive strict scrutiny in later cases. See, e.g., two decisions in which the Court found 50-day residency require-

3. *Disenfranchisement of felons.* California, like many of the states, disenfranchises convicted felons who have served their sentences and completed their parole. In RICHARDSON v. RAMIREZ, 418 U.S. 24 (1974), the highest state court had struck down that barrier under the assumed compulsion of the higher decree of scrutiny demanded by modern voting cases. But the Court reversed: it found an exception to the usual equal protection standard in the recognition of ex-felons' disenfranchisement in the rarely invoked § 2 of the 14th Amendment. The reduced representation sanction of § 2 is specifically inapplicable to denials of the vote "for participation in rebellion, or other crime." Justice REHNQUIST's majority opinion drew on the language and history of that provision to conclude "that those who framed and adopted the 14th Amendment could not have intended to prohibit outright in § 1 of that Amendment that which was expressly exempted from the lesser sanction of reduced representation imposed by § 2 of the Amendment." He accordingly concluded that "the exclusion of felons from the vote has an affirmative sanction [which] was not present in the case of the other restrictions on the franchise" invalidated in the Harper–Kramer line of cases. Justice MARSHALL, joined by Justice Brennan, dissented on the merits, urging strict scrutiny.

4. *Anti-"raiding" cutoff requirements for voting in primaries: The appropriate level of scrutiny.* The 5-4 decision in ROSARIO v. ROCKEFELLER, 410 U.S. 752 (1973), sustained New York's unusually lengthy enrollment time prerequisite for voting in party primaries. The provisions required voters to register their party affiliations 30 days before a general election in order to be eligible to vote in the following year's party primary. That scheme in effect prevented changes in party affiliation for up to eleven months to retain eligibility to vote in primaries. In rejecting the constitutional attack, Justice STEWART's majority opinion insisted that the challengers' reliance on cases such as Dunn v. Blumstein was not "apposite," since the New York scheme "did not absolutely disenfranchise the class to which the petitioners belong." Rather, it "merely imposed a time deadline." The requirement was not "unreasonably long" and did not unduly burden the exercise of rights of voting and free association. The justifiable purpose of the system was "to inhibit party 'raiding' whereby voters in sympathy with one party designate themselves as voters of another party so as to influence or determine the results of the other party's primary." Justice POWELL's dissent, joined by Justices Douglas, Brennan and Marshall, objected especially to the majority's lack of clarity about applicable standards and insisted that the strict scrutiny of Blumstein was appropriate here. He concluded that the law imposed "substantial and unnecessary restrictions" on voting and associational rights. More than a mere "time deadline" was involved: "Deferment of a right [can] be tantamount to its denial." He added: "The Court's formulation [resembles the] 'rational basis' test." That had been an inappropriate standard since Blumstein; and the "means" requirements of "strict judicial scrutiny" were not met here. Justice Powell's advocacy of a clear-cut strict scrutiny approach soon bore fruit. In KUSPER v. PONTIKES, 414 U.S. 51 (1973), Justice STEWART's majority opinion distinguished Rosario and invalidated an Illinois scheme prohibiting a person from voting in the primary election of a political party "if he has voted in the primary of any other party within the preceding 23 months." The Court

---

ments constitutional. Marston v. Lewis, 410 U.S. 679 (1973); Burns v. Fortson, 410 U.S. 686 (1973). These per curiam decisions accepted the states' judgments that the 50–day period was "necessary" to serve the states' "important interest in accurate voter lists." Justice Marshall's dissents, joined by Justices Douglas and Brennan, insisted that 30 days was sufficient.

emphasized that the provision "substantially restricts an Illinois voter's freedom to change his political party affiliation" and thus significantly encroached upon First Amendment associational freedoms. The Illinois system was found to differ from the New York delayed-enrollment law sustained in Rosario in a number of respects. In New York, disenfranchisement was caused by the voters' own failure to take timely measures to enroll; the Illinois law, by contrast, " 'locks' voters into a preexisting party affiliation from one primary to the next, and the only way to break the 'lock' is to forego voting in *any* primary for a period of almost two years."

Note also the growing role of First Amendment concerns in cases involving intrusions into political party procedures in TASHJIAN v. REPUBLICAN PARTY, 479 U.S. 208 (1986), where the Court struck down a Connecticut law requiring that the voters in any party primary be registered members of that party. The state's Republican Party, which had adopted a party rule permitting independents to vote in its primary, challenged the law. Justice MARSHALL's majority opinion held that the law unconstitutionally interfered with the associational rights of party members to decide for themselves who could vote in their primaries: "The Party's determination of the boundaries of its own association, and of the structure which best allows it to pursue its political goals, is protected by the Constitution." Three years later, in EU v. SAN FRANCISCO COUNTY DEMOCRATIC CENTRAL COMM., 489 U.S. 214 (1989), a unanimous Court relied heavily on Tashjian in striking down several portions of California's election law regulating political parties. One provision barred political parties from endorsing, supporting or opposing "any candidate for nomination by that party for partisan office in the direct primary election." Justice MARSHALL's opinion applied strict scrutiny and held that the bar on candidate endorsements burdened both the speech and associational rights of the parties, and that California's asserted interest in preserving party stability was not "compelling." The Eu case made it especially clear that restrictions on political party organization and procedures are subject to strict scrutiny, and that the triggering fundamental interest involved is the freedom of political association protected by the First Amendment.

---

2. VOTE "DILUTION": THE REAPPORTIONMENT CASES, GERRYMANDERING, AND RACE–CONSCIOUS DISTRICTING

Introduction. Before 1962, legislative districting controversies were thought to be nonjusticiable. The prevailing attitude about the justiciability of districting disputes was reflected in Justice Frankfurter's opinion in COLEGROVE v. GREEN, 328 U.S. 549 (1946). There, the majority refused to reach the merits of a federal court challenge to the congressional districting scheme in Illinois. The challengers contended that the Illinois law delineating congressional districts was unconstitutional because the districts were not approximately equal in population. Justice FRANKFURTER's plurality opinion affirming the dismissal of the complaint stated: "[T]he petitioners ask of this Court what is beyond its competence to grant. [This] controversy concerns matters that bring courts into immediate and active relations with party contests. From the determination of such issues this Court has traditionally remained aloof. [Courts] ought not to enter this political thicket." But in Baker v. Carr (1962;

chap. 1, p. 47 above), the divided Court rejected the claim that equal protection challenges to legislative apportionments were nonjusticiable. Instead, the Court expressed confidence that judicially manageable standards could be formulated. The formulation of standards began two years later, with the "one person-one vote" decision in Reynolds v. Sims, which follows. Did it take the simple-sounding Reynolds "one person-one vote" principle to lay to rest the doubts about the manageability of reapportionment standards? Are Reynolds and its progeny adequately responsive to the values regarding representation that the Court has found in the equal protection clause?[1]

Baker v. Carr had held that the plaintiff's had stated a justiciable cause of action claiming that their equal protection rights had been violated by the apportionment of a Tennessee General Assembly "by virtue of the debasement of their votes." With the one-person-one-vote requirement of Reynolds v. Sims, the Court moved from concern with absolute denials of the franchise as in Harper and Kramer to the question of dilution of voting rights, in view of the Reynolds emphasis on the right of each voter to "an equally effective voice in the election of [members of the] state legislature." Consider the comment by Issacharoff, "Judging Politics: The Elusive Quest for Judicial Review of Political Fairness," 71 Tex.L.Rev. 1643 (1993), that the Court's greatest success in the post-Reynolds cases came in the context of "equal individual access to the political process" and that the "most difficult problem" arose "as individuals claimed rights to effective use of the franchise based on group identities." (See also the same author's "Polarized Voting in the Political Process: The Transformation of Voting Rights Jurisprudence," 90 Mich.L.Rev. 1833 (1992).) To what extent can one trace the problems in the next group of cases (including the race-conscious districting ones) to this changing emphasis from individual to group claims?

Reynolds v. Sims
377 U.S. 533, 84 S.Ct. 1362, 12 L.Ed.2d 506 (1964).

[Within a year of the 1962 ruling in Baker v. Carr, suits challenging state legislative apportionment schemes were instituted in over 30 states. The major decision answering some of the questions left open by Baker came two years later, in Reynolds v. Sims. That case was a challenge to the malapportionment of the Alabama legislature. The challengers claimed discrimination against voters in counties whose populations had grown proportionately far more than others since the 1900 census. The complainants noted that the existing districting scheme was based on the 1900 census, even though the state constitution required legislative representation based on population and decennial reapportionment. The lower federal court found that the old apportionment as well as

---

1. Between Baker v. Carr, and Reynolds v. Sims in 1964, the Court decided two other important cases. Gray v. Sanders, 372 U.S. 368 (1963), struck down Georgia's county unit system in primary elections of state-wide officers. The Court purported not to reach most of the questions left open by Baker v. Carr. The majority insisted that this was "only a voting case" and emphasized that the case had nothing to do "with the composition of the state or federal legisla-

ture." In the second major case, Wesberry v. Sanders, 376 U.S. 1 (1964), the Court held—without reaching the 14th Amendment claims—"that, construed in its historical context, the command of Art. I, § 2, that Representatives be chosen 'by the People of the several States' means that as nearly as practicable one man's vote in a congressional election is to be worth as much as another's." The Court accordingly struck down Georgia's congressional districting statute.

two new ones devised by the legislature violated equal protection. (Chief Justice Warren—a former Governor of California—would claim that, of all the opinions he wrote during his tenure, he was proudest of the opinion which follows.)]

Chief Justice WARREN delivered the opinion of the [Court].

[Gray v. Sanders and Wesberry v. Sanders] are of course not dispositive of or directly controlling [in] these cases involving state legislative apportionment controversies. [But] neither are they wholly inapposite. [Gray] established the basic principle of equality among voters within a State, and held that voters cannot be classified, constitutionally, on the basis of where they live, at least with respect to voting in statewide elections. [And] Wesberry clearly established that the fundamental principle of representative government in this country is one of equal representation for equal numbers of people, without regard to race, sex, economic status, or place of residence within a State. Our problem, then, is to ascertain, in the instant cases, whether there are any constitutionally cognizable principles which would justify departures from the basic standard of equality among voters in the apportionment of seats in state legislatures. [A] predominant consideration in determining whether a State's legislative apportionment scheme constitutes an invidious discrimination violative of rights asserted under [equal protection] is that the rights allegedly impaired are individual and personal in nature. [Undoubtedly,] the right of suffrage is a fundamental matter in a free and democratic society. Especially since the right to exercise the franchise in a free and unimpaired manner is preservative of other basic civil and political rights, any alleged infringement of the right of citizens to vote must be carefully and meticulously [scrutinized].

Legislators represent people, not trees or acres. Legislators are elected by voters, not farms or cities or economic interests. As long as ours is a representative form of government, [the] right to elect legislators in a free and unimpaired fashion is a bedrock of our political system. It could hardly be gainsaid that a constitutional claim had been asserted by an allegation that certain otherwise qualified voters had been entirely prohibited from voting for members of their state legislature. And, if a State should provide that the votes of citizens in one part of the State should be given two times, or five times, or 10 times the weight of votes of citizens in another part of the State, it could hardly be contended that the right to vote of those residing in the disfavored areas had not been effectively diluted. [Of] course, the effect of state legislative districting schemes which give the same number of representatives to unequal numbers of constituents is [identical]. Weighting the votes of citizens differently, by any method or means, merely because of where they happen to reside, hardly seems [justifiable].

Logically, in a society ostensibly grounded on representative government, it would seem reasonable that a majority of the people of a State could elect a majority of that State's legislators. [To] sanction minority control of state legislative bodies would appear to deny majority rights in a way that far surpasses any possible denial of minority rights that might otherwise be thought to result. [And] the concept of equal protection has been traditionally viewed as requiring the uniform treatment of persons standing in the same relation to the governmental action questioned or challenged. With respect to the allocation of legislative representation, all voters, as citizens of a State, stand in the same relation regardless of where they live. Any suggested criteria for the differentiation of citizens are insufficient to justify any discrimination as to the weight of their votes, unless relevant to the permissible purposes of legislative apportionment. Since the achieving of fair and effective representation for all citizens is concededly the basic aim of legislative apportionment, we

---

conclude that [equal protection] guarantees the opportunity for equal participation by all voters in the election of state legislators. Diluting the weight of votes because of place of residence impairs basic constitutional rights under the 14th Amendment just as much as invidious discriminations based upon factors such as race [or] economic status. Our constitutional system amply provides for the protection of minorities by means other than giving them majority control of state legislatures.

[We] are told that the matter of apportioning representation in a state legislature is a complex and many-faceted one. We are advised that States can rationally consider factors other than population. [We] are admonished not to restrict the power of the States to impose differing views as to political philosophy on their citizens. We are cautioned about the dangers of entering into political thickets and mathematical quagmires. Our answer is this: a denial of constitutionally protected rights demands judicial protection; our oath and our office require no less of us. [To] the extent that a citizen's right to vote is debased, he is that much less a citizen. [T]he weight of a citizen's vote cannot be made to depend on where he lives. Population is, of necessity, the starting point for consideration and the controlling criterion for judgment in legislative apportionment controversies. A citizen, a qualified voter, is no more nor no less so because he lives in the city or on the farm. This is the clear and strong command of [equal protection]. [We] hold that, as a basic constitutional standard, [equal protection] requires that the seats in both houses of a bicameral state legislature must be apportioned on a population basis. Simply stated, an individual's right to vote for state legislators is unconstitutionally impaired when its weight is in a substantial fashion diluted when compared with votes of citizens living in other parts of the [State].

[We] find the federal analogy inapposite and irrelevant to state legislative districting schemes. [The] system of representation in the two Houses [of Congress] is one conceived out of compromise and concession indispensable to the establishment of our federal republic [and] is based on the consideration that in establishing our type of federalism a group of formerly independent States bound themselves together under one national government. [Political] subdivisions of States—counties, cities, or whatever—never were and never have been considered as sovereign entities. Rather, they have been traditionally regarded as subordinate governmental instrumentalities created by the [State]. [The] relationship of the States to the Federal Government could hardly be less analogous. [Equal protection] requires that a State make an honest and good faith effort to construct districts, in both houses of its legislature, as nearly of equal population as is practicable. We realize that it is a practical impossibility to arrange legislative districts so that each one has an identical number of residents, or citizens, or voters. Mathematical exactness or precision is hardly a workable constitutional requirement. [So] long as the divergences from a strict population standard are based on legitimate considerations incident to the effectuation of a rational state policy, some deviations from the equal-population principle are constitutionally permissible, [but] neither history alone, nor economic or other sorts of group interests, are permissible factors in attempting to justify disparities from population-based representation. Citizens, not history or economic interests, cast votes. Considerations of area alone provide an insufficient justification for deviations from the equal-population principle. Again, people, not land or trees or pastures, vote. [A] consideration that appears to be of more substance in justifying some deviations from population-based representation in state legislatures is that of insuring some voice to political subdivisions, as political subdivisions. [In] many States much of the legislature's activity involves the enactment of so-called local legislation, directed only to the concerns of particular political subdivisions. And a State may legitimately desire to construct districts along political subdivision lines to deter the possibilities of gerrymandering. [But] if, even as a result of a clearly rational state policy of according some legislative representation to political subdivisions, population is submerged as the controlling consideration, [the] right of all of the State's citizens to cast an effective and adequately weighted vote would be unconstitutionally [impaired].

[Affirmed and remanded.]

[In five companion cases to Reynolds v. Sims, the Court relied on its principles to invalidate apportionment schemes in Colorado, New York, Maryland, Virginia, and Delaware. The Colorado case, LUCAS v. FORTY–FOURTH GEN. ASSEMBLY, 377 U.S. 713, warrants special mention, because the defenders of the districting there argued that it should be sustained because it had been approved by the voters of the state. (The Colorado scheme—relying on the federal analogy in apportioning only one of the two houses on the basis of population—had been approved in 1962 by a statewide referendum. Moreover, the voters had rejected a plan to apportion both houses on the basis of population.) Chief Justice WARREN's opinion concluded that this background did not justify deviation from the Reynolds requirement. He stated: "An individual's constitutionally protected right to cast an equally weighted vote cannot be denied even by a vote of a majority of a State's electorate, if the apportionment scheme adopted by the voters fails to measure up to the requirements of [equal protection]. Manifestly, the fact that an apportionment plan is adopted in a popular referendum is insufficient to sustain its constitutionality or to induce a court of equity to refuse to act. [A] citizen's constitutional rights can hardly be infringed simply because a majority of the people choose that it be. We hold that the fact that a challenged legislative apportionment plan was approved by the electorate is without federal constitutional significance, if the scheme adopted fails to satisfy the basic requirements of [equal protection], as delineated [in Reynolds]."]

Justice HARLAN, dissenting [in all six cases].

The Court's constitutional discussion [is] remarkable [for] its failure to address itself at all to the 14th Amendment as a whole or to the legislative history of the Amendment pertinent to the matter at hand. Stripped of aphorisms, the Court's argument boils down to the assertion that petitioners' right to vote has been invidiously "debased" or "diluted" by systems of apportionment which entitle them to vote for fewer legislators than other voters, an assertion which is tied to [equal protection] only by the constitutionally frail tautology that "equal" means "equal." [The] history of the adoption of the 14th Amendment provides conclusive evidence that neither those who proposed nor those who ratified the Amendment believed that [equal protection] limited the power of the States to apportion their legislatures as they saw fit. Moreover, the history demonstrates that the intention to leave this power undisturbed was deliberate and was widely believed to be essential to the adoption of the Amendment. [See also § 2 of the 14th Amendment. An extensive review of the history is omitted.]

Although [the Court] provides only generalities in elaboration of its main thesis, its opinion nevertheless fully demonstrates how far removed these problems are from fields of judicial competence. [In] one or another of today's opinions, the Court declares it unconstitutional for a State to give consideration to any of the following in establishing legislative districts: (1) history; (2) "economic or other sorts of group interests"; (3) area; (4) geographical considerations; (5) a desire "to insure effective representation for sparsely settled areas''; (6) "availability of access of citizens to their representatives''; (7) theories of bicameralism (except those approved by the Court); (8) occupation; (9) "an attempt to balance urban and rural power''; (10) the preference of a majority of voters in the State. So far as presently appears, the *only* factor which a state may consider, apart from numbers, is political subdivisions. But even "a clearly rational state policy'' recognizing this factor is unconstitutional if "population is submerged as the controlling consideration.'' [I] know of no principle of logic or practical or theoretical politics, still less any constitutional principle, which establishes all or any of these exclusions. [The Court] says only that "legislators represent people, not trees or acres.'' [This] may be conceded. But it is surely equally obvious, and, in the context of elections, more meaningful to note that people are not ciphers and that legislators can represent their electors only by speaking for their interests—economic, social, political—many of which do reflect the place where the electors live. The Court does not establish, or indeed even attempt to make a case for the proposition that conflicting interests within a State can only be adjusted by disregarding them when voters are grouped for purposes of [representation].

Justice STEWART, whom Justice CLARK joins, dissenting [in the Colorado and New York cases].

[My] own understanding of the various theories of representative government is that no one theory has ever commanded unanimous assent. [But] even if it were thought that the rule announced today by the Court is, as a matter of political theory, the most desirable general rule which can be devised, [I] could not join in the fabrication of a constitutional mandate which imports and forever freezes one theory of political thought into our [Constitution]. Representative government is a process of accommodating group interests through democratic institutional arrangements. [Appropriate] legislative apportionment, therefore, should ideally be designed to insure effective representation in the State's legislature, in cooperation with other organs for political power, of the various groups and interests making up the electorate. [Population] factors must often to some degree be subordinated in devising a legislative apportionment plan which is to achieve the important goal of ensuring a fair, effective, and balanced representation of the regional, social, and economic interests within a State. [What] constitutes a rational plan reasonably designed to achieve this objective will vary from State to State, [but] so long as a State's apportionment plan reasonably achieves, in the light of the State's own characteristics, effective and balanced representation of all substantial interests, without sacrificing the principle of effective majority rule, that plan cannot be considered irrational.

[Equal protection] demands but two basic attributes of any plan of state legislative apportionment. First, it demands that, in the light of the State's own characteristics and needs, the plan must be a rational one. Secondly, it demands that the plan must be such as not to permit the systematic frustration of the will of a majority of the electorate of the State. [But,] beyond this, I think there is nothing in the [Constitution] to prevent a State from choosing any electoral legislative structure it thinks best suited to the interests, temper, and customs of its people. In the light of these standards, I turn to the Colorado and New York plans of legislative apportionment. [Applying these standards, Justice Stewart found both plans constitutional. In Colorado, the House was apportioned on a population basis, but the rural areas were significantly overrepresented in the Senate. Nevertheless, the Senate scheme was found permissible because it had been adopted "overwhelmingly" in a 1962 popular referendum. The New York plan assured smaller counties more representation in the Assembly than they would have had under a population-based principle;

New York also limited the representation of the largest counties. This was found justified as a counterbalance to New York City's "concentration of population, homogeneity of interest, and political cohesiveness." Accordingly, Justice Stewart found it "not irrational for the State to be justifiably concerned about such a concentration of political power, and certainly there is nothing in our [Constitution] which prevents a State from reasonably translating such a concern into its [apportionment formula."]*

THE PROGENY OF REYNOLDS v. SIMS: SOME ELABORATIONS OF THE "ONE PERSON–ONE VOTE" THEME

Introduction. Did Reynolds provide a "judicially manageable standard"? Was that standard a justifiable inference from equal protection? Does "one person, one vote" stem persuasively from the equality contemplated in the Equal Protection Clause? Do "vote dilution" claims follow plausibly from "vote denial" cases? Do the "distorting" effects of party cohesion on the equality principle justify or require the Court to limit gerrymandering? (See note 3 below.) Would Justice Stewart's emphasis on "systematic frustration of the majority" have been a preferable, more realistic focus for judicial inquiry? Would it have been a "judicially manageable" standard? Do the emphases on voter equality and majority rule make supermajority requirements impermissible? (See note 4 below.) Questions such as these are suggested by the following sampling of some of the progeny of Reynolds. The widespread reapportionment of state legislatures in the wake of Reynolds did not end the Court's task of elaborating its principles. The materials that follow illustrate some of the difficulties in implementing Reynolds in the more than three decades since that decision.

1. *Application of Reynolds to local government.* AVERY v. MIDLAND COUNTY, 390 U.S. 474 (1968), was the first decision to apply the equal representation requirement to a unit of local government. The case involved a Texas county Commissioners Court—an agency with "general governmental powers." The county had been divided into four districts for purposes of representation on the Commissioners Court. The city of Midland, located in the county, constituted one district, with over 67,000 people; the rural area was divided into three districts, with less than 1,000 people each. Justice WHITE's majority opinion rejected the argument that the Commissioners Court was an administrative rather than a legislative body and concluded "that the Constitution permits no substantial variation from equal population in drawing districts for units of local government having general governmental powers over the entire geographic area served by the body." Whether state power was exercised through the legislature or through local elected officials, equal protection required assurance "that those qualified to vote have the right to an equally

---

* In the wake of Reynolds v. Sims, an intense drive to overturn it by constitutional amendment proved unsuccessful. The implementation of the "one person-one vote" proceeded with remarkable rapidity. By the end of the decade most state legislatures were reapportioned. See McKay, "Reapportionment: Success Story of the Warren Court," 67 Mich.L.Rev. 223 (1968). Was it "a success story"? Early observers were divided about the impact. See generally Reapportionment in the 1970s (Polsby, ed., 1971). For a particularly skeptical view, see Bickel, The Supreme Court and the Idea of Progress (1970). See also Rosenberg, The Hollow Hope (1993). And see McCloskey, "Foreword: The Reapportionment Case," 76 Harv.L.Rev. 54 (1962), and Auerbach, "The Reapportionment Cases: One Person, One Vote—One Vote, One Value," 1964 Sup.Ct.Rev. 1.

effective voice in the election process." A divided Court extended the principles of Avery to a case involving the election of trustees of a junior college district in HADLEY v. JUNIOR COLLEGE DIST., 397 U.S. 50 (1970). The junior college district comprised eight local school districts; the Court found it impermissible to give a district with more than half of the junior college district population the right to elect only half of the trustees. The majority stated the "general rule" as follows: "[W]henever a state or local government decides to select persons by popular election to perform governmental functions, [equal protection] requires that each qualified voter must be given an equal opportunity to participate in that election, and when members of an elected body are chosen from separate districts, each district must be established on a basis which will insure, as far as is practicable, that equal numbers of voters can vote for proportionally equal numbers of officials. It is of course possible that there might be some case in which a State elects certain functionaries whose duties are so far removed from normal governmental activities and so disproportionately affect different groups that a popular election in compliance with [Reynolds] might not be required."

2. *Mathematical inequalities: Permissible deviations from "one person-one vote."* In the years since Reynolds, the Court has adhered rigidly to the maximum possible mathematical equality in districting for congressional elections. But the Court has gradually permitted somewhat greater deviations from equality in state districting, over the dissents of some Justices claiming that the Reynolds principles were being undercut.

a. *Congressional districting.* KIRKPATRICK v. PREISLER, 394 U.S. 526 (1969), drew from the congressional districting principles of Wesberry v. Sanders, above, the requirement "that as nearly as is practicable, one man's vote in a congressional election is to be worth as much as another's." Kirkpatrick rejected a Missouri plan which varied from the "absolute population equality" ideal within a range of 2.8% below and 3.1% above. Justice BRENNAN's majority opinion insisted that variations from absolute equality could not be justified on de minimis grounds, nor by a desire to avoid fragmenting political subdivisions or even to deter political gerrymandering. Instead, states were required to "make a good-faith effort to achieve precise mathematical equality." In 1973, WHITE v. WEISER, 412 U.S. 783, adhered to the "precise equality" approach for congressional districting, even while the Court drifted away from that strictness in a group of state legislative reapportionment cases noted below. The majority insisted that even "small" population variances were impermissible in congressional districting. And in KARCHER v. DAGGETT, 462 U.S. 725 (1983), a 5-4 majority continued to adhere to Kirkpatrick and White in requiring that states, in congressional districting, "come as nearly as practicable to population equality." In the context of a New Jersey apportionment with a maximum variance of approximately 0.7%, Justice BRENNAN's majority opinion maintained the Court's refusal to acknowledge a de minimis exception as long as the state was unable to show why more precise results could not be achieved "using the best available census data." The Court did, however, indicate that certain "consistently applied legislative policies might justify some variance, including, for instance, making districts compact, respecting municipal boundaries, preserving the cores of prior districts, and avoiding contests between incumbent Representatives." Because New Jersey could not make such a showing, even its relatively minor variations were deemed fatal.

b. *State districting.* After rejecting a state's redistricting plan involving substantial variations from population equality in Swann v. Adams, 385 U.S. 440 (1967), the Court in the 1970s began to manifest considerable tolerance toward smaller deviations from the equality ideal. The new trend began in ABATE v. MUNDT, 403 U.S. 182 (1971), where the Court found justification for an 11.9% total deviation from population equality in the apportionment of a county legislature—a larger deviation than those found impermissible in earlier cases. Justice MARSHALL's majority opinion insisted that deviations "must be justified by legitimate state considerations," but found adequate justifications here—including the fact that the local body reflected a "long history of, and perceived need for, close cooperation between the county and its constituent towns." Even greater tolerance was manifested in a leading modern case, a case involving a state legislature—MAHAN v. HOWELL, 410 U.S. 315 (1973). That decision made it clear that a new majority was more receptive to claimed justifications for deviations from equality. Mahan approved a redistricting of the lower house of the Virginia legislature with a maximum variance of 16.4% from population equality. Justice REHNQUIST's majority opinion stated that "more flexibility was constitutionally permissible with respect to state legislative reapportionment than in congressional redistricting," because of the interest in "the normal functioning of state and local governments." Here, the deviations from the equality ideal were justified by "the State's policy of maintaining the integrity of political subdivision lines." The loosening of Court reins on state reapportionment plans became even more manifest a few months later, in two decisions which not only reaffirmed the Mahan receptiveness to a broader range of state justifications, but also found a new category of "minor" deviations in population equality requiring no justifications at all. The cases involved the Connecticut and Texas legislatures. In the Connecticut case, GAFFNEY v. CUMMINGS, 412 U.S. 735 (1973), there was a maximum variation among districts of about 8% and an average deviation of about 2% from the ideal. In the Texas case, WHITE v. REGESTER, 412 U.S. 755 (1973), there was a maximum deviation of 9.9% and an average deviation of less than 2%. Justice WHITE's majority opinion found these to be "relatively minor" population deviations, insufficient to meet the "threshold requirement of proving a prima facie case of invidious discrimination" and accordingly requiring no justifications at all from the states. He distinguished these cases from the "enormous," unjustifiable variations struck down in the "early cases beginning with Reynolds" and from cases such as Mahan, involving deviations "sufficiently large to require justification" but nonetheless justifiable. The Court continued its more relaxed scrutiny of state legislative apportionment in BROWN v. THOMSON, 462 U.S. 835 (1983). Under the general Wyoming reapportionment formula, Niobrara County would have been entitled to no representatives; but, pursuant to a provision of the state constitution, it was allowed one representative, even though the result, in the case of this county, was a disparity of 60% below the mean. Despite this disparity, however, the Court, with Justice POWELL writing for the majority, upheld the apportionment. Relying on Abate and Mahan, Justice Powell determined that the historical adherence to county boundaries in Wyoming justified a disparity of even this magnitude. Compare, however, BOARD OF ESTIMATE v. MORRIS, 489 U.S. 688 (1989), holding that New York City's system for electing its Board of Estimate violated the "one person, one vote" requirement. The Board exercised a wide range of legislative and executive fiscal functions. It consisted of three members elected city-wide plus the elected presidents of each of the City's five boroughs. The population of the boroughs varied widely. This system produced a deviation from population equality that may have been as low as 30.8% and as high as 132%. The Court relied on Reynolds, Abate, and Hadley in striking down this system.

3. *Supermajorities.* West Virginia requires that political subdivisions may not incur bonded indebtedness or exceed constitutional tax rates without the approval of 60% of the voters in a referendum election. A county school bond proposal received only slightly more than 50% of the vote and was therefore defeated. The highest state court found that the 60% requirement violated equal protection because "the votes of those who favored the issuance of the bonds had a proportionately smaller impact on the outcome of the election than the votes of those who opposed issuance of the bonds." The Court reversed in GORDON v. LANCE, 403 U.S. 1 (1971). Chief Justice BURGER, in upholding the supermajority requirement, stated: "Certainly any departure from strict majority rule gives disproportionate power to the minority. But there is nothing in the language of the Constitution, our history or our cases that requires that a majority always prevail on every issue. [The] Constitution itself provides that a simple majority vote is insufficient on some issues. [The] constitutions of many States prohibit or severely limit the power of the legislature to levy new taxes or to create or increase bonded indebtedness, thereby insulating entire areas from majority control. [We] conclude that so long as such provisions do not discriminate [against] any identifiable class they do not violate [equal protection]." In a footnote, he added: "We intimate no view on the constitutionality of a provision requiring unanimity or giving a veto power to a very small group. Nor do we decide whether a State may, consistent with the Constitution, require extraordinary majorities for the election of public officers." See also Lockport v. Citizens for Community Action, 430 U.S. 259 (1977), upholding a concurrent majority requirement for referenda on new county charters. Can Gordon v. Lance be reconciled with Reynolds and its emphasis on political equality? Were not the apportionment plans invalidated in Reynolds attempts to protect minorities? Why were those attempts invalid, while the West Virginia supermajority requirement was valid? Is there adequate explanation in Chief Justice Burger's comment in Gordon v. Lance that, "[u]nlike the restrictions in our previous cases, the West Virginia Constitution singles out no 'discrete and insular minority' for special treatment. The three-fifths requirement applies equally to all bond issues for any purpose, whether for schools, sewers, or highways"?

4. *The initial judicial reluctance to scrutinize political gerrymanders.* The challengers in the 1973 Connecticut case, GAFFNEY v. CUMMINGS, note 2b above, raised a claim going beyond that of population equality: they also argued "that even if acceptable population-wise, the [plan] was invidiously discriminatory because a 'political fairness principle' was followed." The plan was admittedly drawn to create districting "that would achieve a rough approximation of the statewide political strengths of the Democratic and Republican Parties," and the challengers characterized the plan "as nothing less than a gigantic political gerrymander, invidiously discriminatory under the 14th Amendment." In the course of rejecting that claim, Justice WHITE's majority opinion chilled many hopes that political gerrymanders might be subjected to careful judicial scrutiny. He stated that "compactness or attractiveness have never been held to constitute an independent federal constitutional requirement of state legislative districts." And political considerations were permissible: "Politics [is] inseparable from districting and apportionment. [It] is not only obvious, but absolutely unavoidable, that the location and shape of districts may well determine the political complexion of the area. [The] reality is that districting inevitably has and is intended to have substantial political consequences. It may be suggested that those who redistrict and reapportion should work with census, not political, data, and achieve population equality without regard for political impact. But this politically mindless approach may produce, whether intended or not, the most grossly gerrymandered results, and, in any event, it is most unlikely that the political impact of such a plan would

remain undiscovered by the time it was proposed or adopted, in which event the results would be both known and, if not changed, intended." He added: "It is much more plausible to assume that those who redistrict and reapportion work with both political and census data. Within the limits of the population equality standards of [equal protection], they seek, through compromise or otherwise, to achieve the political or other ends of the State, its constituents, and its office-holders. What is done in so arranging for elections, or to achieve political ends or allocate political power, is not wholly exempt from judicial scrutiny under the 14th Amendment. [F]or example, multimember districts may be vulnerable, if racial or political groups have been fenced out of the political process and their voting strength invidiously minimized.[1] Beyond this, we have not ventured far or attempted the impossible task of extirpating politics from what are the essentially political processes of the sovereign States. Even more plainly, judicial interest should be at its lowest ebb when a State purports fairly to allocate political power to the parties in accordance with their voting strength. [We do not] have a constitutional warrant to invalidate a state plan, otherwise within tolerable population limits, because it undertakes, not to minimize or eliminate the political strength of any group or party, but to recognize it and, through districting, provide a rough sort of proportional representation in the legislative halls of the State."[2] The Court's unwillingness to consider purely political gerrymandering as constituting a possible equal protection violation was relaxed somewhat in Davis v. Bandemer, which follows.

Davis v. Bandemer

478 U.S. 109, 106 S.Ct. 2797, 92 L.Ed.2d 85 (1986).

JUSTICE WHITE announced the judgment of the Court and delivered the opinion of the Court as to Part II and an opinion in which JUSTICE BREN-

1. Attacks on multimember districts as tools of racial discrimination have been a prolific source of litigation on the modern Court. The problem has been considered earlier (see sec. 3D2 of this chapter) and is accordingly only briefly reviewed here. In one of the earliest post-Reynolds cases, Burns v. Richardson, 384 U.S. 73 (1966), the Court held that, although multimember rather than single-member districts were permissible, they could be attacked if they were "designed to or would operate to minimize or cancel out the voting strength of racial or political elements of the voting population." See also Fortson v. Dorsey, 379 U.S. 433 (1965). In the early 1970s, the Court began to undertake the task of scrutinizing the purpose and impact of multimember districts. Whitcomb v. Chavis, 403 U.S. 124 (1971), rejected a claim that a multimember district underrepresented minorities, but articulated standards that laid the groundwork for future challenges. These guidelines bore fruit soon after: in White v. Regester, 412 U.S. 755 (1973), the Court for the first time sustained such a claim. (Cf. Connor v. Finch, 431 U.S.

407 (1977), on alleged dilution of black voting strength in single-member districts under a court-ordered redistricting plan.) The most important examinations of constitutional "purposeful discrimination" standards in this area came in Mobile v. Bolden (1980) and Rogers v. Lodge (1982). These cases are fully considered in Rogers v. Lodge at p. 746 above and should be revisited at this point. [On the impact of the Voting Rights Act (including its "effect" rather than "purpose" standards and its easier burdens of proof), see Rome v. United States (1980; chap. 10 below). Note also the powerful presence of the Voting Rights Act in the race-conscious districting cases beginning with Shaw v. Reno, below.]

2. In subsequent years, however, several Justices have written lengthy opinions urging that purely political gerrymandering should be considered violative of equal protection. See, e.g., Justice Stevens's concurrence and Justice Powell's dissent in Karcher v. Daggett (1983; note 2a above). And see especially the next principal case.

NAN, JUSTICE MARSHALL, and JUSTICE BLACKMUN joined as to Parts I,III, and IV.

In this case, we review a judgment [which] sustained an equal protection challenge to Indiana's 1981 state apportionment on the basis that the law unconstitutionally diluted the votes of Indiana Democrats. Although we find such political gerrymandering to be justiciable, we conclude that the District Court applied an insufficiently demanding standard in finding unconstitutional vote dilution. Consequently, we reverse.

I. [The challenged apportionment plan, adopted by the Republican-controlled state legislature in 1981, provided for state senate and house districts of substantially equal population. The Democrats nonetheless claimed that, by using a mix of single and multimembered districts and gerrymandering district lines, the plan substantially understated Democratic voting strength. In elections held under the plan in 1982, the Democrats received 51.9 percent of the total house vote and 53.1 percent of the total senate vote, yet won only forty-three of 100 house seats and only thirteen of twenty-five senate seats. According to Justice Powell's dissent, the districting plan was written by a conference committee of the state legislature with the aid of a private computer firm. All members of the committee were Republicans, and the information fed into the computer primarily concerned the political complexion of the voting precincts. The redistricting process was conducted in secret, and the plan was not revealed until two days before the conclusion of the legislative session; two days later, both houses adopted it.] II. [Justice White held, for the Court, that the political question doctrine did not bar the Court from reaching the merits.]

III.   Having determined that the political gerrymandering claim [is] justiciable, we turn [to] whether the District Court erred in holding that appellees had alleged and proved a violation of [equal protection]. [We agree] with the District Court that in order to succeed the [plaintiffs] were required to prove both intentional discrimination against an identifiable political group and an actual discriminatory effect on that group. See, e.g., [Mobile v. Bolden]. Further, we are confident that if the law challenged here had discriminatory effects on Democrats, this record would support a finding that the discrimination was intentional. Thus, we decline to overturn the District Court's finding of discriminatory intent as clearly erroneous. Indeed, quite aside from the anecdotal evidence, the shape of the House and Senate Districts, and the alleged disregard for political boundaries, we think it most likely that whenever a legislature redistricts, those responsible for the legislation will know the likely political composition of the new districts and will have a prediction as to whether a particular district is a safe one for a Democratic or Republican candidate or is a competitive district that either candidate might win. [As] long as redistricting is done by a legislature, it would not be very difficult to prove that the likely political consequences of the reapportionment were intended. [We] do not accept, however, the District Court's legal and factual bases for concluding that the 1981 Act visited a sufficiently adverse effect on the appellees' constitutionally protected rights to make out a violation of [equal protection]. The District Court held that because any apportionment scheme that purposely prevents proportional representation is unconstitutional, Democratic voters need only show that their proportionate voting influence has been adversely affected. Our cases, however, clearly foreclose any claim that the Constitution requires proportional representation or that legislatures in reapportioning must draw district lines to come as near as possible to allocating seats to the contending parties in proportion to what their anticipated statewide vote will be.

The typical election for legislative seats in the United States is conducted in described geographical districts, with the candidate receiving the most votes in each district winning the seat allocated to that district. If all or most of the districts are competitive—defined by the District Court in this case as districts in which the anticipated split in the party vote is within the range of 45% to 55%—even a narrow statewide preference for either party would produce an overwhelming majority for the winning party in the state legislature. This consequence, however, is inherent in winner-take-all, district-based elections, and we cannot hold that such a reapportionment law would violate [equal protection] because the voters in the losing party do not have representation in the legislature in proportion to the statewide vote received by their party candidates. [This] is true of a racial as well as a political group. It is also true of a statewide claim as well as an individual district claim. To draw district lines to maximize the representation of each major party would require creating as many safe seats for each party as the demographic and predicted political characteristics of the State would permit. This in turn would leave the minority in each safe district without a representative of its choice. We upheld this "political fairness" approach in Gaffney v. Cummings, despite its tendency to deny safe district minorities any realistic chance to elect their own representatives. But Gaffney in no way suggested that the Constitution requires the approach that Connecticut had adopted in that case.

[The] mere fact that a particular apportionment scheme makes it more difficult for a particular group in a particular district to elect the representatives of its choice does not render that scheme constitutionally infirm. This conviction, in turn, stems from a perception that the power to influence the political process is not limited to winning elections. An individual or a group of individuals who votes for a losing candidate is usually deemed to be adequately represented by the winning candidate and to have as much opportunity to influence that candidate as other voters in the district. We cannot presume in such a situation, without actual proof to the contrary, that the candidate elected will entirely ignore the interests of those voters. This is true even in a safe district where the losing group loses election after election. Thus, a group's electoral power is not unconstitutionally diminished by the simple fact of an apportionment scheme that makes winning elections more difficult, and a failure of proportional representation alone does not constitute impermissible discrimination under [equal protection].

As with individual districts, where unconstitutional vote dilution is alleged in the form of statewide political gerrymandering, the mere lack of proportional representation will not be sufficient to prove unconstitutional discrimination. [Unconstitutional] discrimination occurs only when the electoral system is arranged in a manner that will consistently degrade a voter's or a group of voters' influence on the political process as a whole. [An] equal protection violation may be found only where the electoral system substantially disadvantages certain voters in their opportunity to influence the political process effectively. In this context, such a finding of unconstitutionality must be supported by evidence of continued frustration of the will of a majority of the voters or effective denial to a minority of voters of a fair chance to influence the political process. Based on these views, we would reject the District Court's apparent holding that *any* interference with an opportunity to elect a representative of one's choice would be sufficient to allege or make out an equal protection violation, unless justified by some acceptable state interest that the State would be required to demonstrate. In addition to being contrary to the above-described conception of an unconstitutional political gerrymander, such a low threshold for legal action would invite attack on all or almost all reapportionment statutes. District-based elections hardly ever produce a perfect fit between votes and representation. The one-person, one-vcte imperative often mandates departure from this [result]. [Inviting] attack on minor departures from some supposed norm would too much embroil the judiciary in second-guessing what has consistently been referred to as a political task for the legislature, a task that should not be monitored too closely unless the express or tacit goal is to effect its removal from legislative halls. We decline to take a major step toward that end, [so] much at odds with our history and experience.

The District Court's findings do not satisfy this threshold condition to stating and proving a cause of action. In reaching its conclusion, the District Court relied primarily on the results of the 1982 elections. Relying on a single election to prove unconstitutional discrimination is unsatisfactory. The District Court observed, and the parties do not disagree, that Indiana is a swing State. Voters sometimes prefer Democratic candidates, and sometimes Republican. The District Court did not find that because of the 1981 Act the Democrats could not in one of the next few elections secure a sufficient vote to take control of the assembly. Indeed, the District Court declined to hold that the 1982 election results were the predictable consequences of the 1981 Act and express-ly refused to hold that those results were a reliable prediction of [future ones]. [We] recognize that our own view may be difficult of application. Determining when an electoral system has been "arranged in a manner that will consistent-ly degrade a voter's or a group of voters' influence on the political process as a whole" is of necessity a difficult inquiry. Nevertheless, we believe that it recognizes the delicacy of intruding on this most political of legislative func-tions and is at the same time consistent with our prior cases regarding individual multi-member districts, which have formulated a parallel standard. IV. In sum, we hold that political gerrymandering cases are properly justiciable under the Equal Protection Clause. We also conclude, however, that a threshold showing of discriminatory vote dilution is required for a prima facie case of an equal protection violation. In this case, the findings made by the District Court of an adverse effect on the appellees do not surmount the threshold [require-ment].

[Justice O'CONNOR's opinion concurring in the judgment, joined by Chief Justice BURGER and Justice REHNQUIST, insisted that political gerryman-dering poses a nonjusticiable political question. In claiming that there were no judicially manageable standards to resolve the issue, she accused the plurality of moving toward mandating a system of proportional representation for political parties. She acknowledged that "the plurality has qualified its use of a *standard* of proportional representation in a variety of ways so as to avoid a *requirement* of proportional representation. The question is whether these qualifications are likely to be enduring in the face of the tremendous political pressures that courts will confront when called on to decide political gerryman-dering claims. Because the most easily measured indicia of political power relate solely to winning and losing elections, there is a grave risk that the plurality's various attempts to qualify and condition the group right the Court has created will gradually pale in importance. What is likely to remain is a loose form of proportionality, under which *some* deviations from proportionality are permissible, but any significant, persistent deviations from proportionality are suspect."]

JUSTICE POWELL, with whom JUSTICE STEVENS joins, concurring in Part II, and dissenting.

This case presents the question whether a state legislature violates [equal protection] by adopting a redistricting plan designed solely to preserve the power of the dominant political party, when the plan follows the doctrine of "one person, one vote" but ignores all other neutral factors relevant to the fairness of redistricting. [I] agree with the plurality that a partisan political gerrymander violates [equal protection] only on proof of "both intentional discrimination against an identifiable political group and an actual discriminatory effect on that group." [The] plurality argues, however, that appellees failed to establish that their voting strength was diluted statewide despite uncontradicted proof that certain key districts were grotesquely gerrymandered to enhance the election prospects of Republican candidates. [Since] the essence of a gerrymandering claim is that the members of a political party have been denied their right to "fair and effective representation" [Reynolds], I believe that the claim cannot be tested solely by reference to "one person, one vote." Rather, a number of other relevant neutral factors must be [considered].

Gerrymandering is "the deliberate and arbitrary distortion of district boundaries and populations for partisan or personal political purposes." [The] term "gerrymandering," however, is also used loosely to describe the common practice of the party in power to choose the redistricting plan that gives it an advantage at the polls. An intent to discriminate in this sense may be present whenever redistricting occurs. [Consequently,] only a sensitive and searching inquiry can distinguish gerrymandering in the "loose" sense from gerrymandering that amounts to unconstitutional discrimination. Because it is difficult to develop and apply standards that will identify the unconstitutional gerrymander, courts may seek to avoid their responsibility to enforce [equal protection] by finding that a claim of gerrymandering is nonjusticiable. I agree with the plurality that such a course is mistaken. [Moreover,] I am convinced that appropriate judicial standards can and should be developed. Justice Fortas' definition of unconstitutional gerrymandering properly focuses on whether the boundaries of the voting districts have been distorted deliberately and arbitrarily to achieve illegitimate ends. [Kirkpatrick v. Preisler.] Under this definition, the merits of a gerrymandering claim must be determined by reference to the configurations of the districts, the observance of political subdivision lines, and other criteria that have independent relevance to the fairness of [redistricting]. The most important [criteria] are the shapes of voting districts and adherence to established political subdivision boundaries. Other relevant considerations include the nature of the legislative procedures by which the apportionment law was adopted and legislative history reflecting contemporaneous legislative goals. To make out a case of unconstitutional partisan gerrymandering, the plaintiff should be required to offer proof concerning these factors, which bear directly on the fairness of a redistricting plan, as well as evidence concerning population disparities and statistics tending to show vote dilution. No one factor should be [dispositive].[1]

———

Political gerrymandering: Some comments. Was the Court's decision to exercise some scrutiny of political gerrymanders in Davis v. Bandemer—even

---

1. As is evident from the several opinions filed today, there is no "Court" for a standard that properly should be applied in determining whether a challenged redistricting plan is an unconstitutional partisan political gerrymander. The standard proposed by the plurality is explicitly rejected by two Justices, and three Justices also have expressed the view the plurality's standard will "prove unmanageable and arbitrary." (O'Connor, J., joined by Burger, C.J., and Rehnquist, J., concurring in the judgment.) [Footnote by Justice Powell.]

under the quite deferential standard of Justice White's opinion—a wise and justifiable use of judicial resources? See generally Schuck, "The Thickest Thicket: Partisan Gerrymandering and Judicial Regulation of Politics," 87 Colum.L.Rev. 1325 (1987), Lowenstein & Steinberg, "The Quest for Legislative Districting in the Public Interest: Elusive or Illusory?," 33 UCLA L.Rev. 1 (1985), and Shapiro, "Gerrymandering, Unfairness, and the Supreme Court," 33 UCLA L.Rev. 227 (1985). See also Guinier, "Groups, Representation and Race–Conscious Districting: A Case of the Emperor's Clothes," 71 Tex.L.Rev. 1589 (1993). Does Davis v. Bandemer reflect a group rights rather than an individual rights approach? Does it represent a major step toward a right to proportional representation? See Howard & Howard, "The Dilemma of the Voting Rights Act—Recognizing the Emerging Political Equality Norm," 83 Colum.L.Rev. 1615 (1983), Schuck, above, Lowenstein & Steinberg, above, and Note, "The Constitutional Imperative of Proportional Representation," 94 Yale L.J. 163 (1984).

Race-conscious districting. In a footnote in his opinion in Davis v. Bandemer, Justice White stated that, although cases such as Rogers v. Lodge and White v. Regester "involved racial groups, we believe that the principles developed in these cases would apply equally to claims by political groups in individual districts. We note, however, that the elements necessary to a successful vote dilution claim may be more difficult to prove in relation to a claim by a political group. For example, historical patterns of exclusion from the political processes, evidence which would support a vote dilution claim, are in general more likely to be present for a racial group than for a political group." After the decennial census of 1990, population shifts required many states to redistrict. The U.S. Department of Justice, acting pursuant to §§ 2 and 5 of the Voting Rights Act, strongly encouraged the creation of the number of "majority-minority districts"—districts delineated with a majority of racial groups in each district, racial groups that were a minority in the state. The creation of "majority-minority" districts promptly engendered a large number of legal challenges, several of which have reached the Supreme Court. A number of commentators predicted that this legal controversy would develop. See, e.g., Pildes & Niemi, "Expressive Harms, 'Bizarre Districts,' and [Voting Rights]," 92 Mich.L.Rev. 483 (1993), commenting that contemporary voting rights controversies arise from "two alternative conceptions of representative government colliding like tectonic plates. On one side is the long-standing Anglo–American commitment to organize the political representation around geography. On the other side is the increasing power of the [Voting Rights Act], which organizes political representation around the concept of interest." (Other commentators suggested that the creation of "majority-minority" districts in the South was a significant factor in the strong showing of the Republican Party in 1994 elections for the House: by grouping together voters with a traditional Democratic preference, the arguments went, redistricting left open a large number of other districts for Republican victories.) In the line of cases beginning with Shaw v. Reno, below, the Court applied strict scrutiny to the race-conscious districting involved in the creation of "majority-minority" districts. (These cases have already been introduced in connection with sec. 3E of this chapter; but, as indicated there, they are more usefully considered here.)

Shaw v. Reno [Shaw I]
509 U.S. 630, 113 S.Ct. 2816, 125 L.Ed.2d 511 (1993).

Justice O'CONNOR delivered the opinion of the Court.

This case involves two of the most complex and sensitive issues this Court has faced in recent years: the meaning of the constitutional "right" to vote, and the propriety of race-based state legislation designed to benefit members of historically disadvantaged racial minority groups. As a result of the 1990 census, North Carolina became entitled to a twelfth seat in the United States House of Representatives. The General Assembly enacted a reapportionment plan that included one majority-black congressional district. After the Attorney General of the United States objected to the plan pursuant to [§ 5] of the Voting Rights Act, the General Assembly passed new legislation creating a second majority-black district. Appellants allege that the revised plan, which contains district boundary lines of dramatically irregular shape, constitutes an unconstitutional racial gerrymander. The question before us is whether appellants have stated a cognizable claim.

[The] voting age population of North Carolina is approximately 78% white, 20% black, and 1% Native American; the remaining 1% is predominantly Asian. The black population is relatively dispersed; blacks constitute a majority of the general population in only 5 of the State's 100 counties. [The] largest concentrations of black citizens live in the Coastal Plain, primarily in the northern part. The General Assembly's first redistricting plan contained one majority-black district centered in that area of the State. [This district] is somewhat hook shaped. Centered in the northeast portion of the State, it moves southward until it tapers to a narrow band; then, with finger-like extensions, it reaches far into the southern-most part of the State near the South Carolina border. District 1 has been compared to a "Rorschach ink-blot test" and a "bug splattered on a windshield." Wall Street Journal, Feb. 4, 1992. The second majority-black district, District 12, is even more unusually shaped. It is approximately 160 miles long and, for much of its length, no wider than the I–85 corridor. It winds in snake-like fashion through tobacco country, financial centers, and manufacturing areas "until it gobbles in enough enclaves of black neighborhoods." [Of] the 10 counties through which District 12 passes, five are cut into three different districts; even towns are divided. [One] state legislator has remarked that "[i]f you drove down the interstate with both car doors open, you'd kill most of the people in the district."

An understanding of the appellants' claim is critical to our resolution of the case. In their complaint, appellants did not claim that the General Assembly's reapportionment plan unconstitutionally "diluted" white voting strength. They did not even claim to be white. Rather, [they] alleged that the deliberate segregation of voters into separate districts on the basis of race violated their constitutional right to participate in a "color-blind" electoral process. [This] Court never has held that race-conscious state decisionmaking is impermissible in all circumstances. What appellants object to is redistricting legislation that is so extremely irregular on its face that it rationally can be viewed only as an effort to segregate the races for purposes of voting, without regard for traditional districting principles and without sufficiently compelling justification. [We] conclude that appellants have stated a claim upon which relief can be granted under [equal protection].

[Appellants] contend that redistricting legislation that is so bizarre on its face that it is "unexplainable on grounds other than race," demands the same close scrutiny that we give other state laws that classify citizens by race. Our voting rights precedents support that conclusion. [Redistricting] differs from other kinds of state decisionmaking in that the legislature always is aware of race when it draws district lines, just as it is aware of age, economic status, religious and political persuasion, and a variety of other demographic factors. That sort of race consciousness does not lead inevitably to impermissible race discrimination. [When] members of a racial group live together in one community, a reapportionment plan that concentrates members of the group in one district and excludes them from others may reflect wholly legitimate purposes. The district lines may be drawn, for example, to provide for compact districts of contiguous territory, or to maintain the integrity of political subdivisions. The difficulty of proof, of course, does not mean that a racial gerrymander, once established, should receive less scrutiny [than] other state legislation classifying citizens by race. Moreover, it seems clear to us that proof sometimes will not be difficult at all. In some exceptional cases, a reapportionment plan may be so highly irregular that, on its face, it rationally cannot be understood as anything other than an effort to "segregat[e] [voters]" on the basis of race. Gomillion [was] such a case. So, too, would be a case in which a State concentrated a dispersed minority population in a single district by disregarding traditional districting principles such as compactness, contiguity, and respect for political subdivisions. We emphasize that these criteria are important not because they are constitutionally required—they are not—but because they are objective factors that may serve to defeat a claim that a district has been gerrymandered on racial lines.

Put differently, we believe that reapportionment is one area in which appearances do matter. A reapportionment plan that includes in one district individuals who belong to the same race, but who are otherwise widely separated by geographical and political boundaries, and who may have little in common with one another but the color of their skin, bears an uncomfortable resemblance to political apartheid. It reinforces the perception that members of the same racial group—regardless of their age, education, economic status, or the community in which the live—think alike, share the same political interests, and will prefer the same candidates at the polls. We have rejected such perceptions elsewhere as impermissible racial stereotypes. By perpetuating such notions, a racial gerrymander may exacerbate the very patterns of racial bloc voting that majority-minority districting is sometimes said to counteract. The message that such districting sends to elected representatives is equally pernicious. When a district obviously is created solely to effectuate the perceived common interests of one racial group, elected officials are more likely to believe that their primary obligation is to represent only the members of that group, rather than their constituency as a whole. This is altogether antithetical to our system of representative democracy. [For] these reasons, we conclude that a plaintiff challenging a reapportionment statute under [equal protection] may state a claim by alleging that the legislation, though race-neutral on its face, rationally cannot be understood as anything other than an effort to separate voters into different districts on the basis of race, and that the separation lacks sufficient [justification].

Justice Souter apparently believes that racial gerrymandering is harmless unless it dilutes a racial group's voting strength. [But] reapportionment legislation that cannot be understood as anything other than an effort to classify and separate voters by race injures voters in other ways. It reinforces racial stereotypes and threatens to undermine our system of representative democracy by signaling to elected officials that they represent a particular racial group rather than their constituency as a whole. [The dissenters also] suggest that a racial gerrymander of the sort alleged here is functionally equivalent to gerrymanders for nonracial purposes, such as political gerrymanders. [Bandemer.] [But] nothing in our case law compels the conclusion that racial and political gerrymanders are subject to precisely the same constitutional scrutiny. [Finally,] nothing in the Court's highly fractured decision in UJO [1977; p. 799 above]—[which] the dissenters evidently believe controls—forecloses the claim we recognize today. [UJO] set forth a standard under which white voters can establish unconstitutional vote dilution. [Nothing] in the decision precludes white voters (or voters of any other race) from bringing the analytically distinct claim that a reapportionment plan rationally cannot be understood as anything other than an effort to segregate citizens into separate voting districts on the basis of race without sufficient justification [The] appellants here stated such a [claim]. Justice Souter contends that exacting scrutiny of racial gerrymanders under the Fourteenth Amendment is inappropriate because reapportionment "nearly always require[s] some consideration of race for legitimate reasons." [That] racial bloc voting or minority political cohesion may be found to exist in some cases, [however,] is no reason to treat all racial gerrymanders differently from other kinds of racial classification. Justice Souter apparently views racial gerrymandering of the type presented here as a special category of "benign" racial discrimination that should be subject to relaxed judicial review. As we have said, however, the very reason that [equal protection] demands strict scrutiny of all racial classifications is because without it, a court cannot determine whether or not the discrimination truly is "benign." Thus, if appellants' allegations of a racial gerrymander are not contradicted on remand, the District Court must determine whether the reapportionment plan satisfies strict scrutiny.

[The] state appellees suggest that a covered jurisdiction may have a compelling interest in creating majority-minority districts in order to comply with the Voting Rights Act. The States certainly have a very strong interest in complying with federal antidiscrimination laws that are constitutionally valid as interpreted and as applied. But in the context of a Fourteenth Amendment challenge, courts must bear in mind the difference between what the law permits, and what it requires. For example, on remand North Carolina might claim that it adopted the revised plan in order to comply with the "nonretrogression" principle. Under that principle, a proposed voting change cannot be precleared if it will lead to "a retrogression in the position of racial minorities with respect to their effective exercise of the electoral franchise." Beer v. United States, 425 U.S. 130, 141 (1976). In Beer, we held that a reapportionment plan that created one majority-minority district where none existed before passed muster under section 5 because it improved the position of racial minorities. Although the Court concluded that the redistricting scheme at issue in Beer was nonretrogressive, it did not hold that the plan, for that reason, was immune from constitutional challenge. The Court expressly declined to reach that question. [Thus], we do not read Beer or any of our other cases to give covered jurisdictions carte blanche to engage in racial gerrymandering in the name of nonretrogression. [The] state appellees alternatively argue that the General Assembly's plan advanced a compelling interest entirely distinct from the Voting Rights Act. We previously have recognized a significant state interest in eradicating the effects of past racial discrimination. But the State must have a "strong basis in evidence for [concluding] that remedial action [is necessary]." [Croson, quoting Wygant.]

[Racial] classifications of any sort pose the risk of lasting harm to our society. They reinforce the belief, held by too many for too much of our history, that individuals should be judged by the color of their skin. Racial classifications with respect to voting carry particular dangers. Racial gerrymandering, even for remedial purposes, may balkanize us into competing racial factions; it threatens to carry us further from the goal of a political system in which race no longer [matters]. It is for these reasons that race-based districting by our state legislatures demands close judicial scrutiny. [We] hold [that] appellants have stated a claim under [equal protection] by alleging that the North

Carolina General Assembly adopted a reapportionment scheme so irrational on its face that it can be understood only as an effort to segregate voters into separate voting districts because of their race, and that the separation lacks sufficient [justification].

[Reversed and remanded.]

Justice WHITE, with whom Justice BLACKMUN and Justice STEVENS join, dissenting.

The facts of this case mirror those presented in [UJO], where the Court rejected a claim that creation of a majority-minority district violated the Constitution. [Of] particular relevance, five of the Justices reasoned that members of the white majority could not plausibly argue that their influence over the political process had been unfairly canceled. [The] Court today chooses not to overrule, but rather to sidestep, UJO. It does so by glossing over the striking similarities, focusing on surface differences, most notably the (admittedly unusual) shape of the newly created district, and imagining an entirely new cause of action. [The] notion that North Carolina's plan, under which whites remain a voting majority in a disproportionate number of congressional districts, [might] have violated appellants' constitutional rights is both a fiction and a departure from settled equal protection principles. [The] grounds for my disagreement [are] simply stated: Appellants have not presented a cognizable claim, because they have not alleged a cognizable injury. To date, we have held that only two types of state voting practices could give rise to a constitutional claim. The first involves direct and outright deprivation of the right to vote, for example by means of a poll tax or literacy test. Plainly, this variety is not implicated by appellants' allegations. [The] second type of unconstitutional practice is that which "affects the political strength of various groups," Mobile v. Bolden, [1980; discussed in Rogers v. Lodge, p. 764 above], in violation of the Equal Protection Clause. As for this latter category, we have insisted that members of the political or racial group demonstrate that the challenged action have the intent and effect of unduly diminishing their influence on the political process. [The] majority attempts to distinguish UJO by imagining a heretofore unknown type of constitutional claim. [The] logic of its theory appears to be that race-conscious redistricting that "segregates" by drawing odd-shaped lines is qualitatively different from race-conscious redistricting that affects groups in some other way. The distinction is without foundation. The essence of the majority's argument is that UJO dealt with a claim of vote dilution—which required a specific showing of harm—and that cases such as [Gomillion] dealt with claims of racial segregation—which did not. I read these decisions quite differently. [Lacking] support in any of the Court's precedents, the majority's novel type of claim also makes no sense. As I understand the [majority's] theory, a redistricting plan that uses race to "segregate" voters by drawing "uncouth" lines is harmful in a way that a plan that uses race to distribute voters differently is not, for the former "bears an uncomfortable resemblance to political apartheid." The distinction is [untenable]. The other part of the majority's explanation of its holding is related to its simultaneous discomfort and fascination with irregularly shaped districts. Lack of compactness or contiguity, like uncouth district lines, certainly is a helpful indicator that some form of gerrymandering (racial or other) might have taken place. [But] while district irregularities may provide strong indicia of a potential gerrymander, they do no more than that. In particular, they have no bearing on whether the plan ultimately is found to violate the Constitution. Given two districts drawn on similar, race-based grounds, the one does not become more injurious than the other simply by virtue of being snake-like. [By] focusing on looks rather than impact, the majority [in its approach] will unnecessarily hinder to some extent a State's voluntary effort to ensure a modicum of minority representation [where] the minority population is geographically dispersed. [When the] creation of a majority-minority district does not unfairly minimize the voting power of any other group, the Constitution does not justify, much less mandate, such obstruction.

[Although] I disagree [that] appellants' claim is cognizable, the Court's discussion of the level of scrutiny it requires warrants a few comments. I have no doubt that a State's compliance with the Voting Rights Act clearly constitutes a compelling interest. [The] Court [warns] that the State's redistricting effort must be "narrowly tailored" to further its interest in complying with the law. It is evident to me, however, that what North Carolina did was precisely tailored to meet the objection of the Attorney General to its prior plan. Hence, I see no need for a remand at all, even accepting the majority's basic approach. Furthermore, how it intends to manage this standard, I do not know. Is it more "narrowly tailored" to create an irregular majority-minority district as opposed to one that is compact but harms other State interests such as incumbency protection or the representation of rural interests? Of the following two options—creation of two minority influence districts or of a single majority-minority district—is one "narrowly tailored" and the other not? [State] efforts to remedy minority vote dilution are wholly unlike what typically has been labeled "affirmative action." To the extent that no other racial group is injured, remedying a Voting Rights Act violation does not involve preferential treatment. It involves, instead, an attempt to equalize treatment, and to provide minority voters with an effective voice in the political process. [Equal protection] surely, does not stand in the [way].

Justice BLACKMUN, dissenting.

I join Justice White's dissenting opinion. [It] is particularly ironic that the case in which today's majority chooses to abandon settled law and to recognize for the first time this "analytically distinct" constitutional claim, is a challenge by white voters to the plan under which North Carolina has sent black representatives to Congress for the first time since [Reconstruction].

Justice STEVENS, dissenting.

For the reasons stated by Justice White, the decision of the District Court should be affirmed. I add these comments to emphasize that the two critical facts in this case are undisputed: first, the shape of District 12 is so bizarre that it must have been drawn for the purpose of either advantaging or disadvantaging a cognizable group of voters; and, second, regardless of that shape, it was drawn for the purpose of facilitating the election of a second black representative from North Carolina. These unarguable facts, which the Court devotes most of its opinion to proving, give rise to three constitutional questions: Does the Constitution impose a requirement of contiguity or compactness on how the States may draw their electoral districts? Does the Equal Protection Clause prevent a State from drawing district boundaries for the purpose of facilitating the election of a member of an identifiable group of voters? And, finally, if the answer to the second question is generally "No," should it be different when the favored group is defined by race? [The] first question is easy. There is no independent constitutional requirement of compactness or contiguity, and the Court's opinion (despite its many references to the shape of District 12) does not suggest [otherwise]. As for the second question, I believe that [equal protection] is violated when the State creates the kind of uncouth district boundaries seen in Gomillion and this case for the sole purpose of making it more difficult for members of a minority group to win an election. [However, it] is not violated when the majority acts to facilitate the election of a member of a group that lacks such power because it remains underrepresented in the state legislature—whether that group is defined by political affiliation, by common economic interests, or by religious, ethnic, or racial characteristics. The difference between constitutional and unconstitutional gerrymanders has nothing to do with whether they are based on assumptions about the groups they affect, but whether their purpose is to enhance the power of the group in control of the districting process at the expense of any minority group, and thereby to strengthen the unequal distribution of electoral power. When an assumption that people in particular a minority group (whether they are defined by the political party, religion, ethnic group, or race to which they belong) will vote in a particular way is used to *benefit* that group, no constitutional violation occurs. Politicians have always relied on assumptions that people in particular groups are likely to vote in a particular way when they draw new district lines, and I cannot believe that anything in today's opinion will stop them from doing so in the future. Finally, we must ask whether otherwise permissible redistricting to benefit an underrepresented minority group becomes impermissible when the minority group is defined by its race. The Court today answers this question in the affirmative, and its answer is wrong. If it is permissible to draw boundaries to provide adequate representation for rural voters, for union members, for Hasidic Jews, for Polish Americans, or for Republicans, it necessarily follows that it is permissible to do the same thing for members of the very minority group whose history in the United States gave birth to [equal protection]. A contrary conclusion could only be described as [perverse].

Justice SOUTER, dissenting.

[In] my view there is no justification for the Court's decision to depart from our prior decisions by carving out this narrow group of cases for strict scrutiny in place of the review customarily applied in cases dealing with discrimination in electoral districting on the basis of race. [Until] today, the Court has analyzed equal protection claims involving race in electoral districting differently from equal protection claims involving other forms of governmental conduct. [Unlike] other contexts in which we have addressed the State's conscious use of race, electoral districting calls for decisions that nearly always require some consideration of race for legitimate reasons where there is a racially mixed population. As long as members of racial groups have the commonality of interest implicit in our ability to talk about concepts like "minority voting strength," and "dilution of minority votes," and as long as racial bloc voting takes place, legislators will have to take race into account in order to avoid dilution of minority voting strength in the districting plans they adopt. [A] second distinction between districting and most other governmental decisions in which race has figured is that those other decisions using racial criteria characteristically occur in circumstances in which the use of race to the advantage of one person is necessarily at the obvious expense of a member of a different race. Thus, for example, [when] race is used to supplant seniority in layoffs, someone is laid off who would not be otherwise. The same principle pertains in nondistricting aspects of voting law, where race-based discrimination places the disfavored voters at the disadvantage of exclusion from the franchise without any alternative benefit. In districting, by contrast, the mere placement of an individual in one district instead of another denies no one a right or benefit provided to [others].

Our different approaches to equal protection in electoral districting and nondistricting cases reflect these differences. [Because] the legitimate consideration of race in a districting decision is usually inevitable under the Voting Rights Act when communities are racially mixed, however, and because, without more, it does not result in diminished political effectiveness for anyone, we have not taken the approach of applying the usual standard of such heightened "scrutiny" to race-based districting decisions. [If] a cognizable harm like dilution or the abridgment of the right to participate in the electoral process is shown, the districting plan violates the Fourteenth Amendment. If not, it does not. Under this approach, in the absence of an allegation of such cognizable harm, there is no need for further scrutiny because a gerrymandering claim cannot be proven without the element of harm. Nor if dilution is proven is there any need for further constitutional scrutiny; there has never been a suggestion that such use of race could be justified under any type of scrutiny, since the dilution of the right to vote can not be said to serve any legitimate governmental purpose. There is thus no theoretical inconsistency in having two distinct approaches to equal protection analysis, one for cases of electoral districting and one for most other types of state governmental decisions. Nor, because of the distinctions between the two categories, is there any risk that Fourteenth Amendment districting law as such will be taken to imply anything for purposes of general Fourteenth Amendment scrutiny about "benign" racial discrimination, or about group entitlement as distinct from individual protection, or about the appropriateness of strict or other heightened scrutiny. [The] Court offers no adequate justification for treating the narrow category of bizarrely shaped district claims differently from other districting claims. The only justification I can imagine would be the preservation of "sound districting principles," UJO, such as compactness and contiguity. But [such] principles are not constitutionally required, with the consequence that their absence cannot justify the distinct constitutional regime put in place by the Court today. [I] would not respond to the seeming egregiousness of the redistricting now before us by untethering the concept of racial gerrymander in such a case from the concept of harm exemplified by [dilution].

THE AFTERMATH OF SHAW I

1. *Miller v. Johnson.* A significant question remaining open after Shaw I was whether the existence of a bizarrely shaped district was a necessary prerequisite for a finding of unconstitutionality. Two years later, in MILLER v. JOHNSON, 519 U.S. ___, 115 S.Ct. 2475 (1995), the Court answered that question in the negative. As in Shaw, the case concerned a congressional district, in this case the newly created Eleventh District in Georgia. After two previous attempts at congressional redistricting had failed to receive Department of Justice preclearance under the Voting Rights Act, largely for failure to locate certain concentrations of black citizens within a majority-black district and for failure to take the opportunity to create three rather than two majority-black districts, Georgia responded by creating three majority-black districts, including the Eleventh. The Justice Department gave clearance, but suit was filed by white voters in the District, claiming the existence of a racially gerrymandered district. With Justice KENNEDY writing for the majority, the Court held the districting unconstitutional, largely on the authority of Shaw, and confronted directly the question of the relevance of the shape of the District: "The essence of the equal protection claim recognized in Shaw is that the State has used race as a basis for separating voters into districts. Just as the State may not, absent extraordinary justification, segregate citizens on the basis of race in its public parks, buses, golf courses, beaches, and schools, so did we recognize in Shaw that it may not separate its citizens into different voting districts on the basis of race. [Our] observation in Shaw of the consequences of racial stereotyping was not meant to suggest that a district must be bizarre on

its face before there is a constitutional violation. Nor was our conclusion in Shaw that in certain instances a district's appearance [can] give rise to an equal protection claim, a holding that bizarreness was a threshold showing. [Shape] is relevant not because bizarreness is a necessary element of the constitutional wrong or a threshold requirement of proof, but because it may be persuasive circumstantial evidence that race for its own sake, and not other districting principles, was the legislature's dominant and controlling rationale in drawing its district lines. The logical implication [is] that parties may rely on evidence other than bizarreness to establish race-based districting."

Justice Kennedy went on to specify the standard to be applied to make out a claim after Shaw: "Parties alleging that a State has assigned voters on the basis of race are neither confined in their proof to evidence regarding the district's geometry and makeup nor required to make a threshold showing of bizarreness. Although race-based decisionmaking is inherently suspect [Adarand], until a claimant makes a showing sufficient to support that allegation the good faith of a state legislature must be presumed. [Redistricting] legislatures will, for example, almost always be aware of racial demographics, but it does not follow that race predominates in the redistricting process. [The] plaintiff's burden is to show, either through circumstantial evidence of a district's shape and demographics or more direct evidence going to legislative purpose, that race was the predominant factor motivating the legislature's decision to place a significant number of voters within or without a particular district. To make this showing, a plaintiff must prove that the legislature subordinated traditional race-neutral districting principles, including but not limited to compactness, contiguity, respect for political subdivisions or communities defined by actual shared interests, to racial considerations. [Although] by comparison with other districts the geometric shape of the Eleventh District may not seem bizarre on its face, when shape is considered in conjunction with its racial and population densities, [and in conjunction with] evidence showing that the General Assembly was motivated by a predominant, overriding desire to assign black populations to the Eleventh District and thereby permit the creation of a third majority-black district[, Georgia's] congressional redistricting plan cannot be upheld unless it satisfies strict scrutiny, our most rigorous and exacting standard of constitutional review." Finding that standard satisfied neither by Georgia's desire to comply with the views of the Department of Justice, nor by any other interest, the Court upheld the judgment of unconstitutionality.

Justice O'CONNOR issued a brief concurring opinion, explaining the evidentiary importance of "substantial disregard of customary and traditional districting practices." Consequently, she argued, "application of the Court's standard does not throw into doubt the vast majority of the Nation's 435 congressional districts [even] though race may well have been considered in the redistricting process." Justice STEVENS dissented on the grounds that in his view the plaintiffs had no standing to sue, and in addition he, along with Justices Breyer and Souter (in part), joined the dissenting opinion of Justice GINSBURG. Her dissent was based largely on disagreement with what she described as the majority's new "race-as-predominant-factor" standard. She emphasized the history of racial districting to prevent black representation, and noted that "only 14 years ago" the Chairman of the Georgia House Reapportionment Committee had said, "I don't want to draw nigger districts." She also focused on the way in which taking "ethnicity" into account, even as a predominant factor, was very much part of a traditional approach to districting: "Ethnicity itself can tie people together, as volumes of social science literature have documented. [The] creation of ethnic districts reflecting felt identity is not ordinarily viewed as offensive or demeaning to those included in the delineation. [That] ethnicity defines some [voting] groups is a political reality. Until now, no constitutional infirmity has been seen in districting Irish or Italian voters together, for example, so long as the delineation does not abandon traditional apportionment practices. If Chinese–Americans and Russian–Americans may seek and secure group recognition in the delineation of voting districts, then African–Americans should not be dissimilarly treated."

2. *Shaw II*. A year after the decision in Miller, the Court was called upon to decide, after remand, the litigation that had produced Shaw v. Reno (Shaw I). In SHAW v. HUNT (Shaw II), 523 U.S. ___, 116 S.Ct. 1894 (1996), the Court was called upon to decide whether the trial court had correctly determined that, although the North Carolina redistricting plan had been significantly based on race, the justifications were sufficiently compelling to satisfy strict scrutiny. Writing for the Court, Chief Justice REHNQUIST followed Shaw I and Miller in agreeing that strict scrutiny was the appropriate standard, but disagreed that a compelling interest supported the use of race in this case. The Court took issue with the Department of Justice's expansive determination of what was required by sections 2 and 5 of the Voting Rights Act. Since neither the race-based redistricting nor the actual shape of the district were required by the Voting Rights Act, the redistricting could not be said to serve a compelling interest through narrowly tailored means. Thus, the Court "once again" did not reach the question "whether under the proper circumstances compliance with the Voting Rights Act, on its own, could be a compelling state interest." Justice STEVENS, joined (on the merits, but not as to Justice Stevens's objection to the standing of the plaintiffs) by Justices Ginsburg and Breyer, dissented, echoing many of the themes in his dissents in the earlier cases. For Justice Stevens strict scrutiny was inappropriate and, even if were, he would have found it satisfied here: "[S]ome legislators felt that the sorry history of race relations in North Carolina in past decades was a sufficient reason for making it easier for more black leaders to participate in the legislative process and to represent the State in the Congress of the United States. Even if that history does not provide the kind of precise guidance that will justify certain specific affirmative action programs in particular industries, it surely provides an adequate basis for a decision to facilitate the election of representatives of the previously disadvantaged minority.

3. *Bush v. Vera*. On the same day as Shaw II, the Court also decided BUSH v. VERA, 523 U.S. ___, 116 S.Ct. 1941 (1996), presenting many of the same issues in the context of a recent Texas redistricting. Justice O'CONNOR wrote a plurality opinion, representing her views as well as those of Chief Justice Rehnquist and Justice Kennedy. She reiterated that "[s]trict scrutiny does not apply merely because redistricting is performed with consciousness of race. Nor does it apply to all cases of intentional creation of majority-minority districts. [For] strict scrutiny to apply, the plaintiffs must prove that other, legitimate districting principles were 'subordinated' to race. [Miller.] By that, we mean that race must be 'the predominant factor motivating the legislature's [redistricting] decision.' [Miller.]" Applying this standard, especially in light of the evidence that the legislature had focused on race and had "substantially neglected traditional districting criteria such as compactness," Justice O'Connor agreed with the district court that race had been the predominant factor and that strict scrutiny must therefore apply. And in applying strict scrutiny, she concluded, as the Court had in Shaw II, that the racially based districting was not necessary to ameliorate the effects of past discrimination and thus could not satisfy a strict scrutiny standard. In addition to writing a plurality opinion, Justice O'CONNOR wrote her own concurrence, emphasizing that

compliance with the Voting Rights Act might constitute a compelling interest sufficient to withstand strict scrutiny, although that was not a situation presented by this record. Justice KENNEDY also wrote his own concurring opinion, largely to make clear that for him the question of when the creation of a majority-minority district would trigger strict scrutiny was more open than it seemed from the plurality opinion. Justice THOMAS, joined by Justice Scalia, concurred in the judgment, but emphasized that for him strict scrutiny was applicable in any case involving the intentional creation of a majority-minority district, and that race necessarily "predominated" in any case in which a majority-minority district was created because of "racial demographics." Justice STEVENS, joined by Justices Ginsburg and Breyer, dissented, largely to question whether it was plausible for the Court to substitute its judgment for that of political officials about the likelihood of minority candidates prevailing in districts that were not majority-minority: "Perhaps minority candidates, forced to run in majority-white districts, will be able to overcome the long history of stereotyping and discrimination that has heretofore led the vast majority of majority-white districts to reject minority candidates. Perhaps not. I am certain only that bodies of elected federal and state officials are in a far better position than anyone on this Court to assess whether the Nation's long history of discrimination has been overcome, and that nothing in the Constitution requires this unnecessary intrusion into the ability of States to negotiate solutions to political differences while providing long-excluded groups the opportunity to participate effectively in the democratic process." Justice SOUTER, joined by Justices Ginsburg and Breyer, also dissented, in an opinion applicable both to Bush v. Vera and Shaw II. He objected to the entire line of cases starting with Shaw I, finding that they had erected an unworkable and unpredictable standard. The only solutions, he argued, were either to eliminate the use of race entirely, which would be too "revolutionary" and "radical" given existing political realities and districting practices, or to withdraw from the area and "allow for some faith in the political process." He urged the latter course, in part because of Shaw I's proven unworkability and in part because of his view that "racial politics [may] grow wiser as long as minority voters are rescued from submergence."*

---

3. ACCESS TO THE BALLOT: RESTRICTIONS ON CANDIDATES AND PARTIES

Introduction. For nearly 30 years, the Court has reviewed a series of state restrictions on candidates and parties seeking access to the ballot. The cases that follow are of special interest for two reasons. First, they illustrate that, on issues of this sort, the First Amendment, not only equal protection, may be relevant. Second, these cases—although a consequence of the earlier voting rights-strict scrutiny cases in their equal protection aspects—show an especially pervasive degree of instability regarding the appropriate level of scrutiny. Although, throughout the 1970s, the Court continued to apply strict scrutiny at least in form, a number of restrictions were sustained. And by Clements v.

---

* For comments on this line of racial redistricting cases, see, e.g., Karlan, "Still Hazy After All These Years: Voting Rights in the Post–Shaw Era," 26 Cumb. L.Rev. 287 (1995); Karlan, "All Over the [Map]," 1993 Sup.Ct.Rev. 254; Aleinikoff & Issacharoff, "Race and [Redistricting]," 92 Mich.L.Rev. 588 (1993); Issacharoff, "The Constitutional Contours of Race and Politics," 1995 Sup.Ct. Rev. 45, and Guinier, "(E)racing Democracy: The Voting Rights Cases," 108 Harv.L.Rev. 109 (1994).

Fashing in 1982 (note 5 below), the plurality opinion announced that "[n]ot all ballot access restrictions require 'heightened' equal protection scrutiny." Would it make more sense to analyze these cases consistently in First Amendment rather than equal protection terms?

1. *The Williams case.* Beginning with WILLIAMS v. RHODES, 393 U.S. 23 (1968), the Court has had repeated occasion to delineate the states' authority to curtail access to ballots by independent candidates and third parties. In Williams, the Court held that Ohio's election laws created unduly burdensome obstacles to third party candidates seeking a place on presidential ballots. Under the Ohio laws, major parties retained their positions on the ballot simply by obtaining 10% of the votes in the last gubernatorial election. Parties newly seeking access to the presidential election ballot, by contrast, faced greater obstacles: early in the presidential election year, they were required to file petitions signed by 15% of the number of ballots cast in the last gubernatorial election; they had to erect an elaborate party structure; and they had to conduct primaries. Justice BLACK's majority opinion stated that these requirements "made it virtually impossible for a new political party, even though it has hundreds of thousands of members, or an old party, which has a very small number of members," to gain a place on the ballot. As a result, the two established major parties had "a decided advantage over any new parties struggling for existence." He accordingly found strict scrutiny appropriate. Here the state scheme placed "unequal burdens" on "two different, although overlapping, kinds of rights—the right of individuals to associate for the advancement of political beliefs, and the right of qualified voters [to] cast their votes effectively." He concluded that the state had "failed to show any 'compelling interest' which justifie[d] imposing such heavy burdens" on such "precious freedoms." Encouraging a two party system to promote compromise and political stability could not support giving the two major parties a permanent monopoly. And the interest in avoiding run-off elections and preventing voter confusion could not support the crippling restrictions here: those dangers were too remote; and the experience of other states showed that "no more than a handful of parties attempts to qualify for ballot positions even where a very low number of signatures, such as 1% of the electorate, is required."*

2. *Jenness v. Fortson.* Three years after Williams, a unanimous Court found that decision distinguishable in rejecting challenges to Georgia's nominating procedures in JENNESS v. FORTSON, 403 U.S. 431 (1971). Unlike Ohio, Georgia permitted write-in votes and allowed independent candidates to appear on the ballots without third party endorsement if they had filed nominating petitions signed by at least 5% of those eligible to vote in the last election for the office. Petitions could be filed as late as June of the election year, and there were no requirements for establishing an elaborate primary

* There were dissents by Justices STEWART and WHITE and by Chief Justice WARREN. A concurrence by Justice HARLAN stated that he would rest "entirely" on First Amendment associational rights; he rejected reliance on equal protection as "unnecessary." [How far-reaching is the Williams principle? What was the "voting" interest protected? The right to "vote effectively"—i.e., for a particular candidate—rather than simply access to the ballot or equality of votes? Does that suggest a constitutional "right to write-in space," see Note, 83 Harv.L.Rev. 96 (1969)? Cf. Burdick v. Takushi (1992; p. 894 below). Is the basic concern in Williams with *groups* rather than with *individuals?* Should the elaborations of the new principles move in the direction of encouraging third parties, or in the direction of encouraging the major parties to represent divergent viewpoints more effectively? See generally Barton, "The General–Election Ballot: More Nominees or More Representative Nominees?" 22 Stan.L.Rev. 165 (1970); see also Casper, "[Williams v. Rhodes]," 1969 Sup.Ct.Rev. 271.]

election machinery. Justice STEWART found the scheme "vastly different" from that in Williams. The Georgia system did not unduly "freeze the political status quo," and the differing treatment of established large parties and new small parties was justifiable: "There is surely an important state interest in requiring some preliminary showing of a significant modicum of support before printing the name of a political organization and its candidates on the ballot— the interest, if no other, in avoiding confusion, deception, and even frustration of the democratic [process]."

3. *The 1974 decisions.* In STORER v. BROWN, 415 U.S. 724 (1974), and AMERICAN PARTY OF TEXAS v. WHITE, 415 U.S. 767 (1974), the Court reexamined ballot access barriers to independent candidates and small political parties, found them of a magnitude somewhere between Williams v. Rhodes and Jenness v. Fortson, and rejected most of the challenges. The majority acknowledged, however, that a strict scrutiny standard was applicable. In Storer, the Court sustained a California provision denying a ballot position to an independent candidate if he or she had registered with a political party within a year prior to the immediately preceding primary election or had voted in that election. That barrier was not found discriminatory against independents. The one-year disaffiliation provision furthered the state's "compelling" interest in the "stability of its political system." In the Texas case, the Court sustained most of that state's provisions regarding independents and minor parties, but invalidated a provision under which only names of major parties were included on absentee ballots. Justice WHITE's majority opinion noted that the Texas scheme "affords minority political parties a real and substantially equal opportunity for ballot qualification" and found most of the regulations were "valid measures, reasonably taken in pursuit of vital state objectives that cannot be served equally well in significantly less burdensome ways." (See also Illinois State Elections Bd. v. Socialist Workers Party, 440 U.S. 173 (1979), applying strict scrutiny and striking down a state law that had the effect of requiring more signatures to qualify for access to the ballot in Chicago elections than in statewide ones.)

4. *Financial barriers to ballot access.* In BULLOCK v. CARTER, 405 U.S. 134 (1972), and LUBIN v. PANISH, 415 U.S. 709 (1974), the unanimous Court invalidated filing fee requirements for candidates. Chief Justice BURGER wrote the prevailing opinion in each case. Each opinion was marked by some obscurity about the appropriate standard of review: though there were several references to strict scrutiny, there were also invocations of traditional rationality standards. The results, in any event, are clear: the Court is reluctant to sustain financial barriers burdensome not only to voters (as in Harper) but also to candidates. The Texas scheme invalidated in Bullock required candidates for local office to pay fees as high as $8900 to get on the primary ballot. The Chief Justice concluded that the state had not established the "requisite justification" either in its concern about regulating the size of the ballot or in its interest in financing the election. Lubin v. Panish invalidated a California requirement of a fee fixed at a percentage of the salary for the office sought. Petitioner, an indigent, was unable to get on the primary ballot for County Supervisor because he could not pay a filing fee of about $700. The Chief Justice held "that in the absence of reasonable alternative means of valid access, a State may not, consistently with constitutional standards, require from an indigent candidate filing fees he cannot pay."

5. *More deferential scrutiny in ballot access cases: Public officials' candidacies.* In CLEMENTS v. FASHING, 457 U.S. 957 (1982), Justice Rehnquist's plurality opinion announced that "[n]ot all ballot access restrictions require 'heightened' equal protection scrutiny" and sustained two Texas constitutional

provisions limiting a public official's ability to become a candidate for another public office. One provision required certain officeholders to complete their current terms of office before they could be eligible to serve in the state legislature; another, "automatic resignation" provision mandated that, if holders of certain state and county offices whose unexpired term exceeded one year became candidates for any other state or federal office, "such announcement or such candidacy [would] constitute an automatic resignation of the office then held." The "automatic resignation" provision was challenged by four officials whose candidacies for higher judicial office were allegedly inhibited by the state barrier. One of the challengers (a Justice of the Peace) also attacked the state restriction on candidacies for the legislature. In rejecting the equal protection attack, Justice REHNQUIST's plurality opinion (joined by Chief Justice Burger and Justices Powell and O'Connor) began by explaining why the challenged provisions did not "deserve 'scrutiny' more vigorous than that which the traditional [equal protection rationality principles of McDonald and McGowan] would require." He insisted that, in recent years, the Court had departed from "traditional equal protection analysis" only in "two essentially separate, although similar, lines of ballot access cases. One line [involves] classifications based on wealth. [Bullock; Lubin.] The second line [involves] classification schemes that impose burdens on new or small political parties or independent candidates. See, e.g., [Storer; Jenness; Williams v. Rhodes]." He added: "The provisions [challenged here] do not contain any classification that imposes special burdens on minority political parties or independent candidates." In determining whether heightened scrutiny should nevertheless apply, he examined "the nature of the interests that are affected and the extent of the burden these provisions place on candidacy." He limited his examination of the barrier to candidacies for the legislature and solely to the situation of the challenger who was a Justice of the Peace and concluded: "[This] sort of insignificant interference with access to the ballot need only rest on a rational predicate in order to survive a challenge under [equal protection]." And the rationality requirement was readily met here. Justice Rehnquist disposed of the equal protection challenge to the "automatic resignation" provision even more summarily: "The burdens [it] imposes on candidacy are even less [substantial]." In a separate opinion, Justice STEVENS, who also applied a rationality standard, agreed with the rejection of the equal protection claim but gave different reasons for doing so. Justice BRENNAN, joined by Justices Marshall, Blackmun and White, strongly disagreed with Justice Rehnquist's rejection of the equal protection claim. He concluded that the challenged provisions could not "survive even minimal equal protection scrutiny."

6. *A new approach? Emphasizing the First Amendment rather than equal protection in ballot access cases.* Justice STEVENS's majority opinion in ANDERSON v. CELEBREZZE, 460 U.S. 780 (1983), suggested a different methodology for ballot access cases. At issue was an Ohio statute that required independent candidates to file their nominating petitions by late March if they wished to be on the November ballot. John Anderson, independent candidate for President in 1980, challenged the statute on two grounds. First, he claimed that the early filing deadline was an excessive restriction on access to the ballot, one that was not justified by any legitimate state interest. Second, by imposing a filing deadline for independents without requiring comparable action for the nominee of a political party, the statute impermissibly discriminated against independent candidates. The Court upheld Anderson's claim, finding that Ohio's asserted interests in voter education, equal treatment for partisan and independent candidates, and political stability were either illegitimate or too remotely related to the early filing deadline to justify such a

substantial barrier to independent candidates. More important than the particular result, however, were two significant departures in approach from previous ballot access cases. Most noteworthy was the Court's explicit reliance on First Amendment rather than equal protection grounds: "[We] base our conclusions directly on the First and 14th Amendments and do not engage in a separate [equal protection] analysis. We rely [on] the analysis in a number of our prior election [cases]. [These] cases, applying the 'fundamental rights' strand of equal protection analysis, have identified the [First Amendment] rights implicated by restrictions on the eligibility of [candidates]." The Court also made clear that ballot access cases would be decided by an individualized weighing of the various interests involved: "Constitutional challenges to specific provisions of a State's election laws [cannot] be resolved by any 'litmus-paper test' that will separate valid from invalid restrictions. Instead, a court [must] first consider the character and magnitude of the asserted injury to the [First Amendment rights]. It then must identify and evaluate the precise interests put forward by the State as justifications for the burden imposed. [Only] after weighing all these factors is the reviewing court in a position to decide whether the challenged provision is unconstitutional."

7. *Write-in voting.* The focus on the First Amendment was even more apparent in BURDICK v. TAKUSHI, 504 U.S. 428 (1992), in which the Court upheld Hawaii's prohibition on write-in voting. Although Hawaii's election laws satisfied the ballot access requirements of Anderson v. Celebrezze and other cases, the challenger claimed he still had a First Amendment right to write in the candidate of his choice at the election, even if only as a protest, and even if the vote were to be cast for "Donald Duck." In rejecting the claim, Justice WHITE's opinion for the Court first rejected the idea that all restrictions on the right to vote were subject to strict scrutiny: "Election laws will invariably impose some burden on individual voters. [Consequently,] to subject every voting regulation to strict scrutiny and to require that the regulation be narrowly tailored to advance a compelling state interest [would] tie the hands of States seeking to assure that elections are operated equitably and efficiently. [Instead, a] more flexible standard applies. [Anderson.] [Under] this standard, the rigorousness of our inquiry into the propriety of a state election law depends upon the extent to which a challenged regulation burdens First and Fourteenth Amendment rights. [When] those rights are subject to 'severe' restrictions, the regulation must be 'narrowly drawn to advance a state interest of compelling importance.' But when a state election law provision imposes only 'reasonable, nondiscriminatory restrictions' upon the First and Fourteenth Amendment rights of voters, 'the State's important regulatory interests are generally sufficient to justify' the restrictions. [Anderson]." Applying this standard, Justice White found the prohibition on write-in voting constitutionally permissible: "[When] a State's ballot access laws pass constitutional muster, [a] prohibition on write-in voting will be presumptively valid. [In] such situations, the objection [amounts] to nothing more than the insistence that the State record, count, and publish individual protests against the election system or the choices presented on the ballot through the efforts of those who actively participate in the system."

Justice KENNEDY, joined by Justices Blackmun and Stevens, dissented. Noting that "Democratic candidates often run unopposed, especially in state legislative races," he concluded that because the plaintiff "could not write in the name of a candidate he preferred, he had no way to cast a meaningful vote. [The] majority's approval of Hawaii's ban is ironic at a time when the new democracies in foreign countries strive to emerge from an era of sham elections in which the name of the ruling party candidate was the only one on the ballot.

Hawaii does not impose as severe a restriction on the right to vote, but it imposes a restriction that has a haunting similarity in its tendency to exact severe similarities for one who does anything but vote the dominant party ballot." Although Justice Kennedy agreed that there was no independent right to cast a protest vote, and agreed as well with the majority's general standard for ballot access cases, he disagreed with the Court's presumption in favor of the constitutionality of restrictions on write-in voting and offered a more specific application of that standard: a ban on write-in votes is impermissible when it operates as part of a general ballot access mechanism that "deprives some voters of any substantial voice in selecting candidates for the entire range of offices at issue in a particular election."

C. ACCESS TO COURTS

Introduction. In the cases that follow, the Court carefully scrutinizes and frequently invalidates economic barriers impeding access to the criminal and civil processes. What is the proper constitutional basis for this line of cases? The Court has repeatedly divided on the issue of whether procedural due process or equal protection provides the appropriate analytical framework. Justice Harlan was long the leading advocate of the due process approach. The majority has most commonly emphasized the relevance of equal protection; and that strand of the new equal protection has retained vitality on the modern Court. Which provision *does* provide the most appropriate basis for these developments? Does either due process or equal protection provide an adequate basis? The core of procedural due process notions is adequate notice and opportunity to be heard. Do the results in the cases below flow plausibly from these core concepts? In several of the cases, the Court holds that a state may not impose fee requirements and must provide counsel when defendants seek to appeal criminal convictions. Yet the Court continues to maintain that there is no constitutional *right* to appeal a conviction: no such right has been found "fundamental" in the evolution of criminal procedure guarantees. Does a due process right to access and participation nevertheless arise once the state chooses to establish an appellate structure? Do access and participation rights then flow from the "opportunity to be heard" ingredient of due process? Or does equal protection provide a more plausible rationale? Do such economic barriers as fee requirements in filing appeals contravene traditional equal protection standards? Justice Black said in Griffin, which follows, that there is "no rational relationship" between "the ability to pay costs" and "a defendant's guilt or innocence." But are there not other legitimate state objectives to which fee requirements do bear a rational relationship? Since wealth has not been accepted as a suspect classification, something more than the mere existence of economic barriers must be involved to explain the Court interventions. What is that "something more"? Is the stricter scrutiny triggered by the existence of a "fundamental interest" in these cases? Is there a "fundamental interest," for example, in effective participation in the criminal appellate process—even though there is no constitutional "right" to a criminal appeal?[1] What are the plausible limits on the principles implicit in these cases?

1. Recall the effort to explain Griffin, Douglas, and their progeny in the several opinions in the Rodriguez case, above. See generally Goodpaster, "The Integration of Equal Protection, Due Process Standards, and the Indigent's Right of Free Access to the Courts," 56 Iowa L.Rev. 223 (1970), and Michelman, "The Supreme Court and Litigation

GRIFFIN v. ILLINOIS, 351 U.S. 12 (1956): The evolution of the "access to courts" strand of the new equal protection originated in this case. Griffin held that a state must provide a trial transcript or its equivalent to an indigent criminal defendant appealing a conviction on nonfederal grounds. (The state ordinarily required that, in order to obtain review, appellants must furnish transcripts to the appellate court.) The challengers in Griffin attacked the failure to provide them free transcripts and claimed that the resulting "refusal to afford appellate reviews solely because of poverty" was unconstitutional. Justice BLACK's plurality opinion, joined by Chief Justice Warren and Justices Douglas and Clark, stated: "[D]ue process and equal protection both call for procedures in criminal trials which allow no invidious discriminations. [In] criminal trials a State can no more discriminate on account of poverty than on account of religion, race, or color. Plainly the ability to pay costs in advance bears no rational relationship to a defendant's guilt or innocence and could not be used as an excuse to deprive a defendant of a fair trial. [There] is no meaningful distinction between a rule which would deny the poor the right to defend themselves in a trial court and one which effectively denies the poor an adequate appellate review accorded to all who have money enough to pay the costs in advance. It is true that a State is not required by the [Constitution] to provide appellate courts or a right to appellate review at all. See, e.g., McKane v. Durston, 153 U.S. 684 [1894]. But that is not to say that a State that does grant appellate review can do so in a way that discriminates against some convicted defendants on account of their poverty. [All] States now provide some method of appeal from criminal convictions. [To] deny adequate review to the poor means that many of them may lose their life, liberty or property because of unjust convictions which appellate courts would set aside. [There] can be no equal justice where the kind of trial a man gets depends on the amount of money he has. Destitute defendants must be afforded as adequate appellate review as defendants who have money enough to buy transcripts." (Justice FRANKFURTER concurred in the result.)

Justice HARLAN's dissent sketched an approach he elaborated in a number of later cases. He thought the equal protection emphasis misplaced and found no violation of due process. On equal protection, he noted: "All that Illinois has done is to fail to alleviate the consequences of differences in economic circumstances that exist wholly apart from any state action. The Court thus holds that, at least in this area of criminal appeals, [equal protection] imposes on the States an affirmative duty to lift the handicaps flowing from differences in economic circumstances. That holding produces the anomalous result that a constitutional admonition to the States to treat all persons equally means in this instance that Illinois must give to some what it requires others to pay for. [T]he real issue in this case is not whether Illinois *has* discriminated but whether it has a duty *to* discriminate. [T]he issue here is not the typical equal protection question of the reasonableness of a 'classification' on the basis of which the State has imposed legal disabilities, but rather the reasonableness of the State's failure to remove natural disabilities. [I] submit that the basis for that holding is simply an unarticulated conclusion that it violates 'fundamental fairness' for a State which provides for appellate review [not] to see to it that such appeals are in fact available to those it would imprison for serious crimes. That of course is the traditional language of due process." Turning to due process, he asked: "Can it be that, while it was not unconstitutional for Illinois to afford no appeals, its steady progress in increasing the safeguards against erroneous convictions has resulted in a constitution-

Access [Fees]," 1973 Duke L.J. 1153 and 1974 Duke L.J. 527 (emphasizing the "strik- ing resemblances between the interests in voting and in litigating").

al decline?" He insisted that the only due process guarantee was "simply the right not to be denied an appeal for arbitrary or capricious reasons," and "[n]othing of that kind" appeared here. (This early suggestion of the view that equal protection imposes on government "an affirmative duty to lift the handicaps flowing from differences in economic circumstances" (as Justice Harlan charged the majority with implying here) became a central premise of those advocating the expansion of fundamental interests-"new" equal protection analysis into such areas as "necessities" in the late 1960s and early 1970s. See especially sec. 4E below.)

DOUGLAS v. CALIFORNIA, 372 U.S. 353 (1963): This case extended Griffin by holding that a state must appoint counsel for an indigent defendant for "the *first appeal*, granted as a matter of [statutory right], from a criminal conviction." It rejected California's system of appointing counsel only after "an independent investigation of the record" and a determination that "it would be of advantage to the defendant or helpful to the appellate court to have counsel appointed." Justice DOUGLAS's opinion in this 6-3 decision stated that denial of counsel on appeal to an indigent "would seem to be a discrimination at least as invidious as that condemned in Griffin." He elaborated: "We are dealing only with the *first appeal*. [Where] the merits of *the one and only appeal* an indigent has as a right are decided without benefit of counsel, we think an unconstitutional line has been drawn between rich and poor. When an indigent is forced to run this gauntlet of a preliminary showing of merit, the right to appeal does not comport with fair procedure. [The] discrimination is not between 'possibly good and obviously bad cases,' but between cases where the rich man can require the court to listen to argument of counsel before deciding on the merits, but a poor man cannot. There is lacking that equality demanded by the [14th Amendment] where the rich man [enjoys] the benefit of [counsel] while the indigent [is] forced to shift for himself."

Justice HARLAN, joined by Justice Stewart, dissented: "[Equal protection] is not apposite. [This] should be judged solely under [due process]. [As to equal protection, the] States, of course, are prohibited [from] discriminating between 'rich' and 'poor' *as such* in the formulation and application of their laws. But it is a far different thing to suggest that [this] prevents the State from adopting a law of general applicability that may affect the poor more harshly than it does the [rich]. Every financial exaction which the State imposes on a uniform basis is more easily satisfied by the well-to-do than by the indigent. Yet I take it that no one would dispute the constitutional power of the State to levy a uniform sales tax, to charge tuition at a state university, to fix rates for the purchase of water from a municipal corporation, [or] to establish minimum bail for various categories of offenses. [Laws] such as these do not deny equal protection to the less fortunate for one essential reason: [equal protection] does not impose on the States 'an affirmative duty to lift the handicaps flowing from differences in economic circumstances.' To so construe it would be to read into the Constitution a philosophy of leveling that would be foreign to many of our basic concepts of the proper relations between government and society. The State may have a moral obligation to eliminate the evils of poverty, but it is not required by [equal protection] to give to some whatever others can afford. [As to due process,] appellate review is in itself not required by the 14th Amendment [and] thus the question presented is the narrow one whether the State's rules with respect to the appointment of counsel are so arbitrary or unreasonable, *in the context of the particular appellate procedure that it has established,* as to require their invalidation. [What] the Court finds constitutionally offensive here bears a striking resemblance to the rules of this Court and many state courts of last resort on petitions for certiorari or for leave to appeal filed by indigent defendants pro se. The Court distinguishes our review from the present case on the grounds that the California rule relates to 'the *first appeal, granted as a matter of right.*' But I fail to see the significance of this difference. Surely, it cannot be contended that the requirements of fair procedure are exhausted once an indigent has been given one appellate review. [I] cannot agree that the Constitution prohibits a State, in seeking to redress economic imbalances at its bar of justice and to provide indigents with full review, from taking reasonable steps to guard against needless expense. This is all that California has [done]." (Justice CLARK also submitted a dissent.)

ECONOMIC DIFFERENTIATIONS AND THE CRIMINAL PROCESS: THE REACH OF THE GRIFFIN–DOUGLAS PRINCIPLES

1. *Counsel.* ROSS v. MOFFITT, 417 U.S. 600 (1974), refused to extend Douglas to discretionary appeals. Justice REHNQUIST's majority opinion reviewed the Griffin–Douglas line of cases and noted that their "precise rationale" had "never been explicitly stated, some support being derived from [equal protection], and some from [due process]." He added: "Neither clause by itself provides an entirely satisfactory basis for the result reached." Turning to the clauses separately, he disposed of the due process contention in a brief passage. He emphasized the "significant differences between the trial and appellate stages." Defendants were entitled to a trial, but there was no right to an appeal: "Unfairness results only if indigents are singled out by the State and denied meaningful access to the appellate system because of their poverty. That question is more profitably considered under an equal protection analysis." Turning to equal protection, he emphasized that the guarantee "does not require absolute equality" but merely assurance that "indigents have an adequate opportunity to present their claims fairly within the adversarial system." Not providing counsel to assist in seeking discretionary review did not deny indigents "meaningful access" to the highest state court. "[The] fact that a particular service might be of benefit to an indigent defendant does not mean that the service is constitutionally required. The duty of the State under our cases [is] only to assure the indigent defendant an adequate opportunity to present his claims fairly in the context of the State's appellate process." Justice DOUGLAS's dissent, joined by Justices Brennan and Marshall, drew on due process as well as equal protection. Can the Griffin–Douglas principle, developed in the context of expenses on appeals, be extended to the often larger expenditures required to mount a major defense at trial? A defendant who can pay for extensive scientific tests, expert witnesses, and a private investigator, for example, will often be better off than one who cannot afford these. Is the state obligated to minimize the comparative advantage of the well-to-do criminal defendant? See Ake v. Oklahoma, 470 U.S. 68 (1985), in which the Court found a due process right, under certain circumstances, to a state-provided psychiatrist to assist in the preparation and presentation of an insanity defense. Cf. Little v. Streater (1981; p. 901 below) (state-subsidized blood tests afforded to an indigent defendant in a paternity action).

2. *Jail sentences to "work off" fines.* Several Burger Court decisions relied in part on the Griffin–Douglas principles to bar imprisonment for inability to pay fines. For example, in Williams v. Illinois, 399 U.S. 235 (1970), the criminal judgment provided that, if the defendant was in default of payments at the expiration of his sentence, he would remain in jail to "work off" his obligations at the rate of $5 per day. That judgment exposed the indigent appellant to

confinement for 101 days beyond the statutory maximum sentence for the crime. Chief Justice Burger's majority opinion concluded, on the basis of the Griffin equal protection emphasis, "that an indigent criminal defendant may not be imprisoned in default of payment of a fine beyond the maximum authorized by the statute regulating the substantive offense." Justice Harlan concurred in the result.[1]

3. *Noneconomic distinctions and the criminal process.* Does the heightened scrutiny manifested in Griffin, Douglas and their progeny stem from the impact of the challenged state practices on a "fundamental interest"? Is there a "fundamental interest" here analogous to the interest in voting? In the cases in sec. 4B, the presence of the fundamental interest triggered strict scrutiny whether or not economic distinctions were present. The thrust of the Griffin–Douglas principles, by contrast, usually has been more limited. Heightened scrutiny has been exercised only where the interest in access to the criminal process was combined with differential economic impacts. Yet the modern Court has not always treated noneconomic classifications in the criminal area with the extreme deference of the old equal protection. Rather, it has steered a somewhat uncertain course, occasionally invalidating classifications by announcing traditional equal protection standards but applying them "with bite." More commonly, the Court has sustained challenged classifications, yet with occasional restatements of "old" equal protection criteria in the direction of the "newer" equal protection. As suggested earlier, it may be the hovering background presence of a quasi-fundamental interest that induced the Court to voice somewhat more intrusive review criteria in these cases. For an example of an invalidation pursuant to traditional criteria applied "with bite," see Jackson v. Indiana, 406 U.S. 715 (1972), invalidating provisions for the pretrial commitment of incompetent criminal defendants. After 1972, equal protection challenges proved less successful, even though standards somewhat more interventionist than those of the old equal protection have sometimes been voiced. See, e.g., McGinnis v. Royster, 410 U.S. 263 (1973).

ECONOMIC BARRIERS AND CIVIL LITIGATION: THE BASES (AND LIMITS) OF BODDIE

1. *Boddie.* The appellants in BODDIE v. CONNECTICUT, 401 U.S. 371 (1971), were indigent welfare recipients who sought to file divorce actions in the state courts but were unable to pay the required court fees and costs for services of process. (The amount involved was $60.) They claimed that this financial barrier unconstitutionally restricted their access to the courts. Justice HARLAN's majority opinion sustained that claim, relying entirely on due process rather than equal protection. He concluded "that, given the basic position of the marriage relationship in this society's hierarchy of values [on the substantive due process "fundamental" right to marry, recall chap. 8, sec. 3, above] and the concomitant state monopolization of the means for legally dissolving this relationship, due process [prohibits] a State from denying, solely

---

1. See also Tate v. Short, 401 U.S. 395 (1971), where Williams was extended to cover the case of an indigent who was unable to pay fines of $425 for traffic offenses and was ordered to a prison farm for a period to "work off" the fines at $5 a day. In Bearden v. Georgia, 461 U.S. 660 (1983), the Court relied on Williams and Tate to hold that probation may be revoked for nonpayment of a fine only if it is determined that there had been no bona fide efforts to pay, "or that adequate alternative forms of punishment did not exist."

because of inability to pay, access to its courts to individuals who seek judicial dissolution of their marriages." He noted that "this Court has seldom been asked to view access to the courts as an element of due process," but that was because "resort to the courts is not usually the only available, legitimate means of resolving private disputes." Here, however, the claims asserted by would-be plaintiffs were "akin to that of defendants faced with exclusion from the only forum effectively empowered to settle their disputes." Accordingly, the applicable principles were those stated "in our due process decisions that delimit rights of defendants compelled to litigate their differences in the judicial forum." He emphasized one of these "settled principles": "due process requires, at a minimum, that absent a countervailing state interest of overriding significance, persons forced to settle their claims of right and duty through the judicial process must be given a meaningful opportunity to be heard." He concluded with an attempt to limit the scope of the decision: "We do not decide that access for all individuals to the courts is a right that is, in all circumstances, guaranteed [by due process, for] in the case before us this right is the exclusive precondition to the adjustment of the fundamental human relationship. The requirement that these appellants resort to the judicial process is entirely a state-created matter." Justice DOUGLAS's concurring opinion insisted that the equal protection principle of the Griffin line of cases, not due process, was the appropriate ground of decision. Justice BLACK was the only dissenter, emphasizing that his opinion in Griffin did not suggest that its requirements for criminal defendants were applicable to "the quite different field of civil cases."

2. *Kras and Ortwein.* Two months after Boddie, Justice Black, who had dissented there, found broad implications in it. He argued that if Boddie were to continue to be the law, it should be "expanded to all civil cases." Meltzer v. C. Buck LeCraw & Co., 402 U.S. 954 (1971). Lower courts, too, read Boddie broadly. But when the issue of the applicability of Boddie in other civil contexts finally reached the Court, the majority called a halt. Are the distinctions between Boddie and the later cases justifiable?[1] In the first post-Boddie ruling, the Court refused to extend "the principle of Boddie to the no-asset bankruptcy proceeding." UNITED STATES v. KRAS, 409 U.S. 434 (1973). An indigent had challenged the $50 filing fee requirement in voluntary bankruptcy proceedings. Justice BLACKMUN's majority opinion emphasized that Boddie "obviously stopped short of an unlimited rule that an indigent at all times and in all cases has the right to relief without the payment of fees." And the bankruptcy situation was sufficiently distinguishable from divorce: Boddie involved the "fundamental" marital relationship; the interest in discharge in bankruptcy did "not rise to the same constitutional level." Moreover, Boddie had emphasized the "utter exclusiveness" of a court remedy; governmental control over debts is not "nearly so exclusive."[2] In ORTWEIN v. SCHWAB, 410 U.S. 656 (1973), the same 5–4 majority found Kras rather than Boddie applicable in rejecting an attack by indigents on Oregon's $25 filing fee prerequisite to

1. Compare Michelman, "The Supreme Court and Litigation Access Fees [Part I]," 1973 Duke L.J. 1153, with Lupu, "Untangling the Strands of the Fourteenth Amendment," 77 Mich.L.Rev. 981 (1979).

2. Justice STEWART's dissent, joined by Justices Douglas, Brennan, and Marshall, thought the Boddie due process rationale "equally" applicable here. In a separate dissent, Justice MARSHALL went further: "I view [Boddie] as involving the right of access to the courts [and] not just the right to a discharge in bankruptcy. When a person raises a claim of right or entitlement under the laws, the only forum in our legal system empowered to determine that claim is a court." In another dissent, Justice DOUGLAS, joined by Justice Brennan, emphasized that "discrimination based on wealth" is "particularly 'invidious.'"

judicial review of administrative denials of welfare benefits. The Court noted, per curiam, that the interest in welfare payments, like that in a bankruptcy discharge, "has far less constitutional significance than the interest of the Boddie appellants." Moreover, the claim of discrimination against the poor had to fail because welfare payments are "in the area of economics and social welfare" and no suspect classification was involved.

3. *Little.* In the 1980s, however, Boddie was followed and Kras and Ortwein distinguished in the unanimous decision in LITTLE v. STREATER, 452 U.S. 1 (1981), holding that due process entitled an indigent defendant in a paternity action to state-subsidized blood grouping tests. Chief Justice BURG-ER emphasized the unique quality of blood grouping tests as a "source of exculpatory evidence" and "the State's prominent role in litigation." Moreover, paternity proceedings in Connecticut fact had "quasi-criminal" overtones, even though they were characterized as "civil" by the State. Accordingly, "an indigent defendant, who faces the State as an adversary [and] who must overcome the evidentiary burden Connecticut imposes, lacks 'a meaningful opportunity to be heard' [Boddie]." Thus, the "fundamental fairness" require-ment of due process had not been satisfied. According to the Chief Justice, because defendant had "no choice of an alternative forum and his interests, as well as those of the child, are constitutionally significant [because the creation of a parent-child relationship was at stake], this case is comparable to Boddie rather than to Kras and Ortwein." Compare with Little the divided Court's decision on the same day, in Lassiter v. Department of Social Services, 452 U.S. 18 (1981), rejecting the claim of an indigent mother involved in a state court parental status determination proceeding that she was entitled to counsel.

D. DURATIONAL RESIDENCE REQUIREMENTS THAT "PENALIZE" THE RIGHT OF INTERSTATE MIGRATION

Shapiro v. Thompson

394 U.S. 618, 89 S.Ct. 1322, 22 L.Ed.2d 600 (1969).

Justice BRENNAN delivered the opinion of the Court.

[Each of these three appeals is from a federal court decision] holding unconstitutional [Pa., Conn., and D.C. provisions denying] welfare assistance to residents [who] have not resided within their jurisdictions for at least one year immediately preceding their applications for such assistance. We affirm. [There] is no dispute that the effect of the waiting-period requirement [is] to create two classes of needy resident families indistinguishable from each other except that one is composed of residents who have resided a year or more, and the second of residents who have resided less than a year, in the jurisdiction. [The] first class is granted and the second class is denied welfare aid upon which may depend the ability of the families to obtain the very means to subsist—food, shelter, and other necessities of life. We agree [that the laws violate equal protection]. The interests which appellants assert are promoted by the classification either may not constitutionally be promoted by government or are not compelling governmental interests.

Primarily, appellants justify the waiting-period requirement as a protective device to preserve the fiscal integrity of state public assistance programs. [We] do not doubt that the one-year waiting-period device is well suited to discourage the influx of poor families in need of assistance. [But] the purpose of inhibiting migration by needy persons into the State is constitutionally impermissible. This Court long ago recognized that the nature of our Federal Union and our constitutional concepts of personal liberty unite to require that all citizens be free to travel throughout the length and breadth of our land uninhibited by statutes, rules, or regulations which unreasonably burden or restrict this movement. [We] have no occasion to ascribe the source of this right to travel interstate to a particular constitutional provision.[1] [Alternatively,] appellants argue that even if it is impermissible for a State to attempt to deter the entry of all indigents, the challenged classification may be justified as a permissible state attempt to discourage those indigents who would enter the State solely to obtain larger benefits. We observe first that none of the statutes before us is tailored to serve that objective. More fundamentally, a State may no more try to fence out those indigents who seek higher welfare benefits than it may try to fence out indigents generally. [We] do not perceive why a mother who is seeking to make a new life for herself and her children should be regarded as less deserving because she considers, among other factors, the level of a State's public assistance. [Appellants] argue further that the challenged classification may be sustained as an attempt to distinguish between new and old residents on the basis of the contribution they have made to the community through the payment of taxes. [But this] reasoning would logically permit the State to bar new residents from schools, parks, and libraries or deprive them of police and fire protection. Indeed it would permit the State to apportion all benefits and services according to the past tax contributions of its citizens. [Equal protection] prohibits such an apportionment of state services. We recognize that a State has a valid interest in preserving the fiscal integrity of its programs. It may legitimately attempt to limit its expenditures, whether for public assistance, public education, or any other program. But a State may not accomplish such a purpose by invidious distinctions between classes of its citizens. [Similarly, appellants] must do more than show that denying welfare benefits to new residents saves money. The saving of welfare costs cannot justify an otherwise invidious [classification].

Appellants next advance as justification certain administrative and related governmental objectives allegedly served by the waiting-period requirement. [At] the outset, we reject [the] argument that a mere showing of a rational relationship between the waiting period and [the] four admittedly permissible state objectives will suffice, [for] in moving from State to State or to the District of Columbia appellees were exercising a constitutional right, and any classification which serves to penalize the exercise of that right, unless shown to be necessary to promote a *compelling* governmental interest, is unconstitutional. The argument that the waiting-period requirement facilitates budget

---

1. Recall the discussion of the "right to travel interstate" (and the reasons why it can usually be better understood as a right to migrate from state to state) in chap. 5 above. At this point in his Shapiro opinion, Justice Brennan cited a variety of sources for the "right to travel interstate"—the Privileges and Immunities Clause of Art. IV, § 2 (e.g., Corfield v. Coryell), the commerce clause (e.g., Edwards v. California), and the Privileges and Immunities Clause of the 14th Amendment (e.g., Edwards v. California). (See also United States v. Guest, chap. 10, p. 964, below.) Given the uncertain underpinnings of the right of interstate travel, would it be best to rest decisions such as those in this section on the Art. IV, § 2, provision? See the discussion of that provision in chap. 5 above, and in Justice O'Connor's concurrence in Zobel v. Williams, p. 908 below.

predictability is wholly unfounded. The records [are] utterly devoid of evidence [of the use of] the one-year requirement as a means to predict the number of people who will require assistance in the budget year. [The] argument that the waiting period serves as an administratively efficient rule of thumb for determining residency similarly will not withstand scrutiny. [Before] granting an application, the welfare authorities investigate the applicant [and] in the course of the inquiry necessarily learn the facts upon which to determine whether the applicant is a resident. [Similarly,] there is no need for a State to use the one-year waiting period as a safeguard against fraudulent receipt of benefits; for less drastic means are available, and are employed, to minimize that hazard. [And a] state purpose to encourage employment provides no rational basis for imposing a one-year waiting-period restriction on new residents only [because "this logic would also require a similar waiting period for long-term residents of the State"]. We conclude therefore that appellants [do] not use and have no need to use the one-year requirement for the governmental purposes suggested. Thus, even under traditional equal protection tests a classification of welfare applicants according to whether they have lived in the State for one year would seem irrational and unconstitutional. But, [since] the classification here touches on the fundamental right of interstate movement, its constitutionality must be judged by the stricter standard of whether it promotes a *compelling* state interest. Under this standard, the waiting period requirement clearly violates [equal protection].[2]

Affirmed.[3]

Chief Justice WARREN, with whom Mr. Justice BLACK joins, [dissenting, insisting that the central issue was "whether Congress may create minimal

---

2. We imply no view of the validity of waiting-period or residence requirements determining eligibility to vote, eligibility for tuition-free education, to obtain a license to practice a profession, to hunt or fish, and so forth. Such requirements may promote compelling state interests on the one hand, or, on the other, may not be penalties upon the exercise of the constitutional right of interstate travel. [Footnote by Justice Brennan. See the cases that follow.] The Court also rejected the argument that the constitutional challenge "must fail because Congress expressly approved the imposition" of such a requirement as part of the federal-state funded benefit programs. The Court found no such approval and added that, "even if we were to assume, arguendo," that Congress had approved a one-year waiting period, such an approval "would be unconstitutional. Congress may not authorize the States to violate [equal protection]." In reaching this conclusion, Justice Brennan cited Katzenbach v. Morgan (1966; chap. 10 below) and his controversial footnote in that case.

3. Does Shapiro v. Thompson really belong with this fundamental interest-"new" equal protection group of cases? Does it rest on a right derived solely from equal protection? Does it rest on suspect classification

analysis? Or does it simply involve an undue burden on a right protected by parts of the Constitution other than equal protection? Recall that Justice Powell, in Rodriguez, distinguished Shapiro from voting rights and other fundamental rights equal protection cases. Even though Shapiro can be read as resting ultimately on the right of interstate migration, it did encourage assertions of an equal protection fundamental right to "necessities of life." That encouragement came in part from Justice Brennan's passing reference, in the first paragraph of his opinion, to "the very means to subsist—food, shelter, and other necessities of life." It also came in part from the special attention to that passage in Justice Harlan's dissent (which follows), in the course of his general criticism of most of the "new" equal protection methodology. But the Warren Court never specifically held that there was a fundamental equal protection interest in "necessities," any more than it clearly held that wealth was a suspect classification. The failure to develop those Warren Court dicta is traced in sec. 4E below. (Even though Shapiro failed to spur an expansion of welfare and "necessities" rights, it has retained some vitality with respect to its actual holding, regarding the impact of durational residence requirements on the right to travel. See the notes that follow this case.)

residence requirements, not whether the States, acting alone, may do so." He concluded that Congress has this power and had exercised it constitutionally here.]

Justice HARLAN, [dissenting].

In upholding the equal protection argument, the Court has applied an equal protection doctrine of relatively recent vintage: the rule that statutory classifications which either are based upon certain "suspect" criteria or affect "fundamental rights" will be held to deny equal protection unless justified by a "compelling" governmental interest. The "compelling interest" doctrine [constitutes] an increasingly significant exception to the long-established rule that a statute does not deny equal protection if it is rationally related to a legitimate governmental objective. The "compelling interest" doctrine has two branches. The branch which requires that classifications based upon "suspect" criteria be supported by a compelling interest apparently had its genesis in cases involving racial classifications. Today the list [of "suspect" criteria] apparently has been further enlarged to include classifications based upon recent interstate movement, and perhaps those based upon the exercise of *any* constitutional right. [I] think that this branch of the "compelling interest" doctrine is sound when applied to racial classifications [because of the historical purpose of equal protection]. However, I believe that the more recent extensions have been unwise. [I] do not consider wealth a "suspect" statutory criterion. And [when] a classification is based upon the exercise of rights guaranteed against state infringement by [the] Constitution, then there is no need for any resort to [equal protection]; in such instances, this Court may properly and straightforwardly invalidate any undue burden upon those rights under [substantive due process].

The second branch of the "compelling interest" principle is even more troublesome. For it has been held that a statutory classification is subject to the "compelling interest" test if the result of the classification may be to affect a "fundamental right," regardless of the basis of the classification. This rule was foreshadowed in [Skinner] and reemerged in Reynolds v. Sims.[1] It has reappeared today in the Court's cryptic suggestion that the "compelling interest" test is applicable merely because the result of the classification may be to deny the appellees "food, shelter, and other necessities of life," as well as in the Court's statement that "[s]ince the classification here touches on the fundamental right of interstate movement, its constitutionality must be judged by the stricter standard of whether it promotes a *compelling* state interest." I think this branch of the "compelling interest" doctrine particularly unfortunate and unnecessary. It is unfortunate because it creates an exception which threatens to swallow the standard equal protection rule. Virtually every state statute affects important rights. This Court has repeatedly held, for example, that the traditional equal protection standard is applicable to statutory classifications affecting such fundamental matters as the right to pursue a particular occupation, the right to receive greater or smaller wages or to work more or

---

1. Analysis is complicated when the statutory classification is grounded upon the exercise of a "fundamental" right. For then the statute may come within the first branch of the "compelling interest" doctrine because exercise of the right is deemed a "suspect" criterion and also within the second because the statute is considered to affect the right by deterring its exercise. Williams v. Rhodes [p. 891 above] is such a [case]. The present case is another instance, insofar as welfare residence statutes both deter interstate movement and distinguish among welfare applicants on the basis of such movement. Consequently, I have not attempted to specify the branch of the doctrine upon which these decisions rest. [Footnote by Justice Harlan.]

less hours, and the right to inherit property. Rights such as these are in principle indistinguishable from those involved here, and to extend the "compelling interest" rule to all cases in which such rights are affected would go far toward making this Court a "super-legislature." This branch of the doctrine is also unnecessary. When the right affected is one assured by the federal Constitution, any infringement can be dealt with under [due process]. But when a statute affects only matters not mentioned in the [Constitution] and is not arbitrary or irrational, I must reiterate that I know of nothing which entitles this Court to pick out particular human activities, characterize them as "fundamental," and give them added protection under an unusually stringent equal protection test.

[If] the issue is regarded purely as one of equal protection, [this] nonracial classification should be judged by ordinary equal protection standards. [In] light of [the] undeniable relation of residence requirements to valid legislative aims, [I] can find no objection [under equal protection]. The next issue [is] whether a one-year welfare residence requirement amounts to an undue burden upon the right of interstate travel. [I conclude] that the right to travel interstate is a "fundamental" right which [should] be regarded as having its source in [due process]. [The decisive question is] whether the governmental interests served by residence requirements outweigh the burden imposed upon the right to travel. [I] believe that the balance definitely favors constitutionality. [Moreover, to] abolish residence requirements might well discourage highly worthwhile experimentation in the welfare field. Moreover, although [it is argued] that the same objectives could have been achieved by less restrictive means, this is an area in which the judiciary should be especially slow to fetter [legislative] judgment. [Today's decision] reflects to an unusual degree the current notion that this Court possesses a peculiar wisdom all its own whose capacity to lead this Nation out of its present troubles is contained only by the limits of judicial ingenuity in contriving new constitutional principles to meet each problem as it arises. For anyone who, like myself, believes that it is an essential function of this Court to maintain the constitutional divisions between state and federal authority and among the three branches of the Federal Government, today's decision is a step in the wrong direction. This resurgence of the expansive view of "equal protection" carries the seeds of more judicial interference with the state and federal legislative process, much more indeed than does the judicial application of "due process" according to [traditional concepts].

DURATIONAL RESIDENCE REQUIREMENTS

Introduction. Shapiro v. Thompson was an important step in the Warren Court's development of the "fundamental rights and interests" strand of the "new" equal protection in two respects. First, it launched strict scrutiny of durational residence requirements "penalizing" the "right" of interstate mobility. That strand proved a quite sturdy one, and its evolution is traced in this group of notes. Second, Shapiro hinted at an amorphous, new fundamental interest with potentially far-reaching implications in imposing affirmative governmental obligations to redress economic inequalities—the hint Justice Harlan's dissent referred to as the "cryptic suggestion that the 'compelling interest' test is applicable merely because the result of the classification may be to deny appellees food, shelter, and other necessities of life." That strand proved far less sturdy: as Rodriguez confirmed, the Burger Court refused to extend the strict scrutiny of the new equal protection to a broad range of "necessities." (See sec. 4E below.)

Consider, then, the impact of Shapiro on durational residence requirements. Shapiro applies strict scrutiny to "penalties" on the right of interstate travel. (The right of interstate mobility or interstate migration seem more accurate terms.) When are restraints on interstate mobility permissible? And what are the criteria for determining whether a state restriction "penalizes" the constitutional right? For determining whether an asserted state justification is adequately "compelling"? One case considered earlier throws light on the implications of Shapiro. In Dunn v. Blumstein (1972; p. 863 above), the strict scrutiny invalidation of a state one-year residence requirement for voting rested not only on the interference with the "fundamental interest" in participation in the electoral process, but also on the "right" to travel. In Blumstein, Justice Marshall noted that the state sought to avoid "the clear command of Shapiro" by claiming "that durational residence requirements for voting neither seek to nor actually do deter such travel." He insisted that that argument reflected "a fundamental misunderstanding": "Shapiro did not rest upon a finding that denial of welfare actually deterred travel"; rather, it found strict scrutiny triggered by "any classification which serves to *penalize* the exercise" of the right to travel. If the suspiciously viewed residence requirements are those that "serve to *penalize*," and if the notion of "penalty" does not necessarily rest on legislative purpose or effect, how are the occasions for strict scrutiny to be identified? Justice Marshall elaborated on that theme in Maricopa, which follows. Ironically, in the context of distinguishing permissible from impermissible residence requirements as to eligibility for state benefits, the "necessities of life" concept of Shapiro continues to play a role. As Rodriguez and sec. 4E show, "necessities of life" did not become a full-blown new "fundamental interest," as Justice Harlan in Shapiro had feared and as others had hoped. Shapiro's major impact has been confined to the context of residence requirements; but in the evolution of that impact, requirements barring eligibility for "necessities" proved to be particularly vulnerable.

1. *Medical care for indigents.* Justice MARSHALL's majority opinion in MEMORIAL HOSPITAL v. MARICOPA COUNTY, 415 U.S. 250 (1974), reexamined and relied on Shapiro in invalidating an Arizona requirement of a year's residence in a county as a condition to an indigent's receiving free nonemergency hospitalization or medical care. In that reexamination, it emerged that not all residence requirements were impermissible: Shapiro had cautioned that some "waiting periods [may] not be penalties"; in other cases, the Court had sustained durational residence requirements as a condition to lower tuition at state universities. The critical ingredient for triggering strict scrutiny and probable invalidation proved to be the existence of a "penalty"; and whether there was a "penalty" apparently turned largely on whether there was an effect on a "necessity of life"!

Justice Marshall noted that the constitutional right of interstate travel "was involved in only a limited sense in Shapiro." Not mere travel but the right to "migrate with intent to settle and abide" had been central in Shapiro. And though any durational residence requirement "impinges to some extent" on that right, Shapiro had not condemned all such requirements. Instead, it mandated intensive review only when the requirements were "penalties." And whether a durational residence requirement was a "penalty" depended on the impact of the requirement. He acknowledged that the "amount of impact required to give rise to the compelling-state-interest test was not made clear" in Shapiro. Shapiro had suggested two criteria: first, "whether the waiting period would deter migration"; second, "the extent to which the residency requirement served to *penalize* the exercise of the right to travel." In Justice Marshall's view, the second, not the first, criterion was critical. And whether a residence requirement was a "penalty" depended on the nature of the benefits affected: in Shapiro "the Court found denial of the basic 'necessities of life' to be a penalty"; on the other hand, state college tuition differentials between residents and nonresidents had been upheld. Accordingly, "[w]hatever the ultimate parameters of the Shapiro penalty analysis, it is at least clear that medical care is as much 'a basic necessity of life' to an indigent as welfare assistance. And, governmental [benefits] necessary to basic sustenance have often been viewed as being of greater constitutional significance than less essential forms of governmental entitlements." This analysis led to his ultimate conclusion about the appropriate standard of scrutiny: "[The] right of inter-state travel must be seen as insuring new residents the same right to vital government benefits and privileges in the States to which they migrate as are enjoyed by other residents. [Arizona's] durational residency requirement for free medical care penalizes indigents for exercising their right to migrate to and settle in that State. Accordingly, the classification created by the residence requirement, 'unless shown to be necessary to promote a *compelling* interest, is unconstitutional.' Shapiro." Justice Marshall had little difficulty in concluding that the Arizona scheme could not survive the strict scrutiny demanded by that standard: the defenders of the durational residence requirement had not "met their heavy burden of justification, or demonstrated that the State, in pursuing legitimate objectives, has chosen means which do not unnecessarily impinge on constitutionally protected interests."[1]

2. *Divorce laws.* A year later, in rejecting another attack on a residence requirement, Justice Rehnquist wrote for the majority and Justice Marshall was in dissent. In SOSNA v. IOWA, 419 U.S. 393 (1975), the Court upheld a requirement that a party reside in the state for one year before bringing a divorce action against a nonresident. In rejecting the challenge based on the Shapiro-Maricopa line of cases, Justice REHNQUIST noted that most states had "durational residency requirements for divorce" and that the area of domestic relations "has long been regarded as a virtually exclusive province of the States." He found ample justification for the requirement here: "What [the earlier] cases had in common was that the durational residency requirements they struck down were justified on the basis of budgetary or record-keeping considerations which were held insufficient to outweigh the constitutional claims of the individuals. But Iowa's divorce residency requirement is of a different stripe. Appellant was not irretrievably foreclosed from obtaining some part of what she sought, as was the case with the welfare recipients in Shapiro, the voters in Blumstein, or the indigent patient in Maricopa County. [Iowa's] requirement delayed her access to the courts, but, by fulfilling it, a plaintiff could ultimately obtain the same opportunity for adjudication which she asserts ought to be hers at an earlier point in time. Iowa's residency requirement may reasonably be justified on grounds other than purely budgetary considerations or administrative convenience. A decree of divorce is not a matter in which the only interested parties are the State [and] a plaintiff. [Both] spouses are obviously interested [and] a decree of divorce [often includes] provisions [for] custody and support. With consequences of such moment riding on a divorce decree, [Iowa] may insist that one seeking to initiate such a proceeding have

---

1. Justice REHNQUIST was the sole dissenter. However, several other Justices also withheld full support from Justice Marshall's rationale. Chief Justice BURGER and Justice BLACKMUN simply noted their con-currence in the result. And Justice DOUGLAS's concurrence stated that he shared Justice Rehnquist's doubts about "interstate travel per se."

the modicum of attachment to the State required here. Such a requirement additionally furthers the State's parallel interests in both avoiding officious intermeddling in matters in which another State has a paramount interest, and in minimizing the susceptibility of its own divorce decrees to collateral attack. A State such as Iowa may quite reasonably decide that it does not wish to become a divorce mill." Justice MARSHALL, joined by Justice Brennan, dissented, claiming that the majority's approach suggested "a new distaste for the mode of analysis we have applied to this corner of equal protection law." The majority had substituted "an ad hoc balancing test." He was especially critical of the majority's failure to make what "should be the first inquiry: whether the right to obtain a divorce is of sufficient importance that its denial to recent immigrants constitutes a penalty on interstate travel." He added: "In my view, it clearly meets that standard. Accordingly, [I] would scrutinize Iowa's durational residency requirement to determine whether it constitutes a reasonable means of furthering important interests asserted by the State." The majority, by contrast, had not only declined to apply the "compelling interest" test, but had also "conjured up possible justifications for the State's restriction in a manner much more akin to the lenient standard we have in the past applied in analyzing equal protection challenges to business regulations."[2]

ZOBEL v. WILLIAMS, 457 U.S. 55 (1982): In Zobel, the Court held, in an opinion by Chief Justice BURGER, that an Alaska law distributing the income from its natural resources to adult citizens in varying amounts depending on length of residence in the State violated the equal protection rights of newer state citizens. The Chief Justice found that two of Alaska's stated objectives ("creating a financial incentive for individuals to establish and maintain Alaska residence, and assuring prudent management of [its] natural and mineral resources") were "not rationally related to the distinctions Alaska seeks to draw." Most importantly, the Court also held, citing Shapiro v. Thompson, that the objective of rewarding "contributions of various kinds [which] residents have made during their years of residency" was "not a legitimate state purpose. [This] reasoning could open the door to state apportionment of other rights, benefits and services according to length of residency. It would permit the states to divide citizens into expanding numbers of permanent classes. Such a result would be clearly impermissible." Justice BRENNAN's concurrence, joined by Justices Marshall, Blackmun and Powell, joined Chief Justice Burger's opinion but emphasized that Alaska's scheme was "inconsistent with the federal structure" and focused especially on "the Citizenship Clause of the

---

2. What is the constitutional status of other state durational residence requirements in light of Shapiro, Maricopa, and Sosna? All Justices agree that some residence requirements are valid; yet the cases also indicate that others may be vulnerable to constitutional challenge—if they affect "important interests," under Justice Marshall's approach, or if they lack adequate justification, under Justice Rehnquist's analysis. One of the barriers to nonresidents frequently mentioned as permissible is a state tuition preference for local students at state universities. In 1971, a summary affirmance suggested the futility of a Shapiro-based attack

on such a preference scheme: the Court sustained Minnesota's one-year durational residence requirement for receipt of in-state tuition benefits. Starns v. Malkerson, 326 F.Supp. 234, aff'd, 401 U.S. 985 (1971). Yet implementation of such a scheme proved vulnerable via another route, in Vlandis v. Kline, 412 U.S. 441 (1973), which found a reliance on forbidden "irrebuttable presumptions" (see the final subsection of this chapter). For rare modern cases examining right to travel claims in contexts other than durational residence requirements, see Zobel v. Williams, which follows.

Fourteenth Amendment," which "expressly equates citizenship only with simple residence" and "does not provide for, and does not allow for, degrees of citizenship based on length of residence. And [equal protection] would not tolerate such distinctions. In short, as much as the right to travel, equality of citizenship is of the essence in our Republic." He added that "discrimination on the basis of residence must be supported by a valid state interest independent of the discrimination itself. [Length] of residence may, for example, be used to test the bona fides of citizenship—and allegiance and attachment may bear some rational relationship to a very limited number of legitimate state purposes. [E.g., the seven-year residence requirement to run for governor in New Hampshire.] But those instances in which length of residence could provide a legitimate basis for distinguishing one citizen from another are rare."

In an opinion concurring only in the judgment, Justice O'CONNOR advocated a distinctive approach. She argued: "A desire to compensate citizens for their prior contributions is neither inherently invidious nor irrational. Under some circumstances, the objective may be wholly reasonable.[1] Even a generalized desire to reward citizens for past endurance, particularly in a State where years of hardship only recently have produced prosperity, is not innately improper. The difficulty is that plans enacted to further this objective necessarily treat new residents of a State less favorably than the longer-term residents who have past contributions to 'reward.' [Stripped] to its essentials, the plan denies non–Alaskans settling in the State the same privileges afforded longer-term residents. The Privileges and Immunities Clause of Article IV [addresses] just this type of discrimination. [See chap. 5 above.] [The Art. IV] analysis supplies a needed foundation for many of the 'right to travel' claims discussed in the Court's prior opinions. [I believe that application of the Clause] to controversies involving the 'right to travel' would at least begin the task of reuniting this elusive right with the constitutional principles it embodies." She concluded that Alaska's disbursement scheme violated the Clause because there was nothing " 'to indicate that noncitizens constitute a peculiar source of the evil at which the statute is aimed,' " and there was no "substantial relationship between the evil and discrimination practiced against the noncitizens." The two-part test she relied on was taken from Hicklin v. Orbeck (1978; p. 331 above). Justice REHNQUIST's dissent found nothing irrational in Alaska's scheme. He argued that "the illegitimacy of a State's recognizing the past contributions of its citizens has been established by the Court only in certain cases considering an infringement of the right to travel, and the majority rightly declines to apply the strict scrutiny analysis of those right-to-travel cases. The distribution scheme [impedes] no person's right to travel to and settle in Alaska; if anything, the prospect of receiving annual cash dividends would encourage immigration to Alaska. The State's [reward-for-past-contributions] justification cannot, therefore, be dismissed simply by quoting language [from] right-to-travel cases which have no relevance to the question before us. So understood, this [law] clearly passes equal protection muster."[2]

---

1. "A State, for example, might choose to divide its largesse among all persons who previously have contributed their time to volunteer community organizations. [Alternatively,] a State might enact a tax credit for citizens who contribute to the State's ecology by building alternative fuel sources or establishing recycling plants. If the State made this credit retroactive, to benefit those citizens who launched these improvements before they became fashionable, the State once again would be rewarding past contributions. The Court's opinion would dismiss these objectives as wholly illegitimate. I would recognize them as valid goals and inquire only whether their implementation infringed any constitutionally protected interest." [Footnote by Justice O'Connor.]

E.   REFUSALS TO EXPAND FUNDAMENTAL INTERESTS ANALYSIS TO REDRESS OF ECONOMIC INEQUALITIES

Introduction. These materials trace the modern Court developments regarding welfare legislation and "necessities" that anteceded and culminated in Rodriguez: the Court's refusal to fashion equal protection into a broad-ranging tool to redress economic inequalities and impose affirmative obligations on government. As Rodriguez symbolizes, the modern Court has been reluctant to elaborate either strand of the "new" equal protection toward those ends: it has refused to consider wealth or economic status a suspect classification (see sec. 3C3 above); and it has refused to elevate welfare benefits or other "necessities of life" into the realm of fundamental interests. The latter phenomenon is the subject of this subsection. By adopting that stance, the post-Warren Courts have disappointed those who perceived in Warren Court dicta the potential for vast expansion of the new equal protection; but it is not at all clear that the Warren Court itself would have been able to resolve the problems of institutional competence and doctrinal justification such an expansion would entail.[1]

2. The Court relied on Zobel in Williams v. Vermont, 472 U.S. 14 (1985), striking down a Vermont tax scheme that gave a credit against Vermont use taxes for sales or use taxes paid to other states, but only if the purchaser was a Vermont resident at the time the tax was paid to the other state. The parallel with Zobel was even closer in Hooper v. Bernalillo County Assessor, 472 U.S. 612 (1985), striking down on equal protection grounds a New Mexico law granting a special tax exemption to Vietnam veterans who were New Mexico residents before May 8, 1976. Chief Justice Burger's majority opinion distinguished the cases from Shapiro through Maricopa County on the ground that those involved waiting periods, whereas this law, like Alaska's in Zobel, "creates 'fixed, permanent distinctions [between] classes of concededly bona fide residents' based on when they arrived in the State." The Court held that the New Mexico law "suffers from the same constitutional flaw as the Alaska statute in Zobel." A similar statute, but in the civil service context, was before the Court in Attorney General of N.Y. v. Soto–Lopez, 476 U.S. 898 (1986). New York granted a civil service veterans preference, in the form of points added to the scores on civil service examinations, to New York residents, but only to those New Yorkers who were residents at the time they entered military service. Justice Brennan's plurality opinion, joined by Justices Marshall, Blackmun, and Powell, held the act an unconstitutional restriction on the right to travel. Justice

O'Connor, joined by Justices Rehnquist and Stevens, dissented, arguing that there is no "free floating 'right to migrate,' "that Art. IV should provide the basis for the analysis, and that the recognition of state citizens' past sacrifices constituted a "valid state interest" that did not infringe any constitutional right, "including the fundamental right to settle in another State which is protected by [Art. IV]." (On Justice O'Connor's Art. IV rationale, see Bogen, "The Privileges and Immunities Clause of Art. IV," 37 Case W.L.Rev. 794 (1987).)

1. Note the assessment in Gunther, "Newer Equal Protection" (1972): "The list of interests identified as fundamental by the Warren Court was in fact quite modest: voting, criminal appeals and the right of interstate travel were the prime examples. But in the extraordinary amount of commentary that followed, analysts searching for justifications for those enshrinements were understandably tempted to ponder analogous spheres that might similarly qualify. Welfare benefits, exclusionary zoning, municipal services and school financing came to be the most inviting frontiers." See also, e.g., Krislov, "The OEO Lawyers Fail to Constitutionalize a Right to [Welfare]," 58 Minn.L.Rev. 211 (1973), Michelman, "Welfare Rights in a Constitutional Democracy," 1979 Wash. U.L.Q. 659 (compare Bork's comment, "The Impossibility of Finding Welfare Rights in the Constitution," id., at 695), and other sources noted below.

1. *The potentials and problems at the end of the Warren era.* More than any other case, the dicta in Shapiro v. Thompson prompted wide-ranging speculation and advocacy regarding the potential fundamental interest in "necessities" such as welfare aid and housing. What interests might be found to be "fundamental"? What were the limits, in principle and in institutional capabilities, to such an extension of the new equal protection? Much of the commentary supported further expansion.[2] But doubts and reservations were also voiced.[3] Perhaps the most imaginative analysis of "new" equal protection frontiers at the end of the Warren era came in Michelman, "Foreword: On Protecting the Poor Through the [14th Amendment]," 83 Harv.L.Rev. 7 (1969). As noted at p. 735 above, he criticized language suggesting that wealth was a suspect classification on the ground that that was an unacceptable principle in a society generally committed to a market pricing system. But he drew from the fundamental interests analysis a somewhat different approach, arguing that even in a market economy persons were entitled to "minimum protection" against economic deprivations in certain areas. He suggested as an appropriate doctrinal tool to bar certain payment requirements: "It is no justification for deprivation of a fundamental right (i.e., involuntary nonfulfillment of a just want) that the deprivation results from a general practice of requiring persons to pay for what they get." His "minimum protection" approach would emphasize "severe deprivations" rather than "inequalities." It would identify "instances in which persons have important needs or interests which they are prevented from satisfying because of traits or predicaments not adopted by free and proximate choice"; it would then seek to determine which of these instances are intolerable ones by asking which risks of deprivation would be

2. See, e.g., Karst, "Invidious Discrimination: Justice Douglas and the Return of the 'Natural–Law–Due–Process Formula,' "16 U.C.L.A.L.Rev. 716 (1969), suggesting a three-part formulation for identifying whether a classification is an unconstitutional "invidious discrimination": (1) does it "discriminate" against a "disadvantaged group"; (2) does that discrimination relate to an interest that is "basic" or "fundamental" or "critical"; if so, (3) is the state's justification " 'compelling' enough to overcome the presumptive invalidity implied in a phrase like 'strict scrutiny.' " (Compare Justice Marshall's "sliding scale" approach). See also Fallon, "Individual Rights and the Powers of Government," 27 Ga.L.Rev. 343 (1993), and Chemerinsky, "Making the Right Case for Constitutional Entitlements," 44 Mercer L.Rev. 525 (1993).

3. Note, e.g., the comment in "Developments," 82 Harv.L.Rev. 1065 (1969): "[The] suggestion that government has an affirmative duty to raise everyone to a minimum acceptable standard of living has not yet assumed the dignity of a constitutional proposition. Three major reasons for this lack of development may be suggested. The first is the conceptual difficulty of finding support for the proposition in the Constitution. [T]he guarantee of a minimum standard of living appears to be on a completely different level from the guarantee of effectively equal access to the criminal process, to the political process, to education, or even to other state activities. The latter find their sources primarily, if not exclusively, in the state. One seeking income, housing, or a job, on the other hand, is remitted primarily to the private sector for satisfaction of his needs. Second, the practical problems in reallocating resources according to an infinite variety of needs, and in establishing acceptable minimum norms, would be far greater than those which have already attended judicial efforts to impose precise standards of equality on the states. Finally, [legislatures] themselves have taken significant, if as yet small, strides through social security and other welfare measures to provide minimum standards for selected groups of people." See also Cox, "Foreword: Constitutional Adjudication and the Promotion of Human Rights," 80 Harv. L.Rev. 91 (1966), and Sager, "Tight Little Islands: Exclusionary Zoning, Equal Protection, and the Indigent," 21 Stan.L.Rev. 767 (1969); cf. Winter, "Changing Concepts of Equality: From Equality Before the Law to the Welfare State," 1979 Wash.U.L.Q. 741.

consensually deemed unacceptable in a "just society."[4] Michelman recognized that the notion of "minimum protection is more readily assimilated to the due process than to the equal protection clause." Nevertheless, courts might decide to invoke "the verbiage of inequality and discrimination" in developing a "minimum protection" analysis, because, for example, "detecting a failure to provide the required minimum may nonetheless depend in part upon the detection of inequalities; and elimination or reduction of inequality may be entailed in rectifying such a failure, insofar as the just minimum is understood to be a function (in part) of the existing maximum. [W]idening inequalities become increasingly suggestive of failure to furnish the just minimum."[5]

2. *Welfare benefits.* The first indication that the Burger Court would not build on the Shapiro v. Thompson dicta regarding special scrutiny of classifications affecting "necessities" came in DANDRIDGE v. WILLIAMS, 397 U.S. 471 (1970), a decision relied on three years later in Rodriguez. The Court rejected a challenge to Maryland's implementation of the Aid to Families with Dependent Children (AFDC) program, jointly financed by the state and federal governments. Maryland granted most eligible families their "standard of need," but imposed a "maximum grant" limit of $250 per month per family, regardless of the family size or computed standard of need. In rejecting the equal protection attack on that limitation, Justice STEWART's majority opinion stated: "[Here] we deal with state regulation in the social and economic field, [claimed] to violate the 14th Amendment only because the regulation results in some disparity in grants of welfare payments to the largest AFDC families. For this Court to approve the invalidation of state economic or social regulation [here] would be far too reminiscent of an era when the Court thought the 14th Amendment gave it power to strike down state laws 'because they may be unwise, improvident, or out of harmony with a particular school of thought.' [Lee Optical]. That era long ago passed into history. In the area of economics and social welfare, a State does not violate [equal protection] merely because the classifications made by its laws are imperfect. If the classification has some 'reasonable basis,' it does not offend the Constitution. [E.g., McGowan.] To be sure, [the cases] enunciating this fundamental standard under [equal protection] have in the main involved state regulation of business or industry. The administration of public welfare assistance, by contrast, involves the most basic economic needs of impoverished human beings. We recognize the dramatically real factual difference between the cited cases and this one, but we can find no basis for applying a different constitutional standard. It is a standard that has consistently been applied to state legislation restricting the availability of employment opportunities. And it is a standard that is true to the principle that the 14th Amendment gives the federal courts no power to impose upon the States their views of what constitutes wise economic or social policy. [The] intractable economic, social, and even philosophical problems presented by public welfare assistance programs are not the business of this Court. The Constitution may impose certain procedural safeguards upon systems of welfare administration. [See chap. 8, sec. 4.] But the Constitution does not empower

---

4. Cf. Appleton, "Professor Michelman's Quest for a Constitutional Welfare Right," 1979 Wash.U.L.Q. 715. See also Rawls, A Theory of Justice (1971). Professor Rawls's earlier writings heavily influenced Michelman's "just wants" analysis. [But see Nozick, Anarchy, State, and Utopia (1975).]

5. Do the post-Warren Court developments leave any room for adoption of Michel-man's "minimum protection against economic hazards" approach? Note especially the reference in Justice Powell's opinion in Rodriguez to the possibility that "some identifiable quantum of education is a constitutionally protected prerequisite to the meaningful exercise" of other rights. See also Plyler v. Doe (p. 850 above).

this Court to second-guess state officials charged with the difficult responsibility of allocating limited public welfare funds among the myriad of potential recipients." (Justice Stewart readily found a "reasonable basis" for the challenged regulation "in the State's legitimate interest in encouraging employment and in avoiding discrimination between welfare families and the families of the working poor.")

Justice MARSHALL's dissent, joined by Justice Brennan, insisted that the Maryland regulation could not be sustained even under the majority's "reasonableness" test. But he devoted most of his opinion to advocating a stricter standard of review, even while finding the Warren Court's rigid two-tier analysis inappropriate here. (His dissent was the first articulation of his "sliding scale" approach, more fully elaborated in his Rodriguez dissent.) He criticized the majority for "focusing upon the abstract dichotomy between two different approaches to equal protection problems that have been utilized by this Court": "This case simply defies easy characterization in terms of one or the other of these 'tests.' The cases relied on by the Court, in which a 'mere rationality' [rather than 'compelling interest'] test was actually used, are most accurately described as involving the application of equal protection reasoning to the regulation of [business interests]. This case, involving the literally vital interests of a powerless minority—poor families without breadwinners—is far removed from the area of business regulation, as the Court concedes. Why then is the standard used in those cases imposed here? In my view, equal protection analysis of this case is not appreciably advanced by the a priori definition of a 'right,' fundamental or otherwise. Rather, concentration must be placed upon the character of the classification in question, the relative importance to individuals in the class discriminated against of the governmental benefits that they do not receive, and the asserted state interests in support of the classification. [It] is the individual interests here at stake that [most] clearly distinguish this case from the 'business regulation' equal protection cases. AFDC support to needy dependent children provides the stuff that sustains those children's lives: food, clothing, shelter. And this Court has already recognized several times that when a benefit, even a 'gratuitous' benefit, is necessary to sustain life, stricter constitutional standards, both procedural and substantive, are applied to the deprivation of that benefit."[6]

3. *Housing.* An effort to establish a "fundamental interest" in "decent shelter" and "possession of one's home" failed in LINDSEY v. NORMET, 405 U.S. 56 (1972). That 5–2 decision sustained Oregon's summary "forcible entry and wrongful detainer" procedure for the eviction of tenants after alleged nonpayment of rent. Justice WHITE's majority opinion rejected the argument "that a more stringent standard than mere rationality should be applied both to the challenged classification and its stated purpose." One of the rejected contentions was that "the 'need for decent shelter' and the 'right to retain peaceful possession of one's home' are fundamental interests which are particularly important to the poor and which may be trenched upon only after the State demonstrates some superior interest." He replied: "We do not denigrate the importance of decent, safe and sanitary housing. But the Constitution does not provide judicial remedies for every social and economic ill. We are unable to

---

6. The Dandridge rejection of claims that "necessities" are a fundamental interest (and its deferential stance) resurfaced in several other cases between Dandridge and Rodriguez. See, e.g., Richardson v. Belcher, 404 U.S. 78 (1971) (disability benefits), and Jefferson v. Hackney, 406 U.S. 535 (1972) (grant of lower percentage of "need" to AFDC recipients than to beneficiaries of other categorical assistance programs). (In the latter case, Justice Rehnquist's majority opinion also rejected a de facto race discrimination argument, as noted in sec. 3 above.)

perceive in that document any constitutional guarantee of access to dwellings of a particular quality or any recognition of the right of a tenant to occupy the real property of his landlord beyond the term of his lease, without the payment of [rent]. Absent constitutional mandate, the assurance of adequate housing and the definition of landlord-tenant relationships is a legislative not a judicial function." Exercising deferential review, he found no constitutional flaw in the fact that eviction actions "differ substantially from other litigation, where the time between complaint and trial is substantially longer, and where a broader range of issues may be considered." Here, there were "unique factual and legal characteristics of the landlord-tenant relationship that justify special statutory treatment." Accordingly, such features as limiting the issue at trial to that of the tenant's default and barring such defenses as the landlord's failure to maintain the premises were found rational.[7]

DO ANY BASES REMAIN FOR HEIGHTENED SCRUTINY OF WELFARE LAWS?

1. *A review.* The developments traced in the preceding pages apparently dashed all hopes that the modern Court would apply the strict scrutiny of the new equal protection to laws bearing on welfare benefits and other "necessities." Are challenges to such laws accordingly doomed to the very deferential review of the old equal protection? A few bases for more intensive review may remain. First, as Justice Stewart noted in Dandridge, procedural, right-to-hearing claims may succeed in the welfare context as in other areas. Second, the Burger Court occasionally, albeit quite sporadically, has applied rationality review with unusual bite, using analyses akin to the "newer equal protection." (See sec. 2 of this chapter.) And that tendency has sometimes surfaced in the welfare area.[1] Most often, however, the Court has manifested a quite deferential stance.

2. *The brief and troubled life of "irrebuttable presumptions" analysis.* For a brief period in the mid–1970s, the Court opened a route toward heightened scrutiny of legislative classifications via an approach avoiding the language of equal protection. The Court ventured into "irrebuttable presumptions" analysis, purportedly an aspect of procedural due process but in substance similar to very intensive scrutiny of legislative generalizations. In practice, application of the irrebuttable presumptions analysis meant invalidation of the generalization and produced a requirement for individualized hearings. The 1970s manifestation of the irrebuttable presumptions approach was launched by Justice Stewart's majority opinion in Vlandis v. Kline, 412 U.S. 441 (1973), involving tuition preferences for in-state students at a state university. The majority stated: "[S]ince Connecticut purports to be concerned with residency in allocating the

7. One feature of the Oregon system was invalidated, however: a requirement that the tenant desiring to appeal a decision post a bond of twice the rent that would accrue pending decision, with the bond to be forfeited if the tenant lost the appeal. Relying on the Griffin v. Illinois strand of equal protection doctrine, Justice White found that special burden on appeals unjustified by any desire to eliminate frivolous claims. (This aspect of Lindsey was distinguished, however, in Bankers Life & Casualty Co. v. Crenshaw, 486 U.S. 71 (1988).)

1. See, e.g., Jimenez v. Weinberger (1974; p. 649 above), and U.S. Dept. of Agriculture v. Moreno (1973; p. 648 above). Recall, however, Lyng v. Castillo (1986; p. 648 above), applying very deferential review in upholding a distinction between close and distant relatives for purposes of the definition of "household" in the Food Stamp Program.

rates for tuition, [it] is forbidden by [due process] to deny an individual the resident rates on the basis of a permanent and irrebuttable presumption of non-residence, when the presumption is not *necessarily or universally true in fact.* [Due process requires] that the State allow such an individual to present evidence showing that he is a bona fide resident entitled to the in-state rates." [Emphasis added.] The italicized passage was the most extreme statement of the irrebuttable presumptions doctrine, and it was invoked in several cases to strike down legislative generalizations because they were not "universally true in fact."[2] From the outset, most commentators thought the irrebuttable presumptions doctrine puzzling and unjustifiable. The critics argued that the finding of an unconstitutional irrebuttable presumption was essentially the same as holding a classification overbroad under equal protection. The irrebuttable presumptions analysis in effect imposed extraordinarily strict safeguards against "overinclusive" classifications. Under equal protection—even under strict scrutiny—an absolutely perfect fit between classification and purpose is not demanded. But just that seemed to be required by the Vlandis statement that the "presumption" there was "not necessarily or universally true in fact." In short, irrebuttable presumption analysis seemed to be the equivalent of an extremely strict variety of "means" scrutiny.[3]

The irrebuttable presumptions doctrine, never consistently applied during its brief life, was soon abandoned by the Court as a generally acceptable approach.[4] The death blow came in WEINBERGER v. SALFI, 422 U.S. 749 (1975), setting aside a lower court decision that had invalidated on irrebuttable presumptions grounds a duration-of-relationship Social Security eligibility requirement for surviving wives and stepchildren of deceased wage earners. Justice REHNQUIST's majority opinion insisted that the deferential standard of Dandridge was applicable to such claims and distinguished most of the earlier cases on the ground that they involved interests with "constitutionally protected status." To extend the irrebuttable presumptions line of cases to the eligibility requirement here "would turn the doctrine of those cases into a virtual engine of destruction for countless legislative judgments which have heretofore been thought wholly consistent with [the Constitution]." He elaborated: "[If] the Fifth and 14th Amendments permit [the Lee Optical variety of

---

2. See, e.g., Cleveland Bd. of Educ. v. LaFleur, 414 U.S. 632 (1974) (mandatory pregnancy leaves for school teachers); U.S. Department of Agriculture v. Murry, 413 U.S. 508 (1973) (a provision in the federal Food Stamp Act); cf. Stanley v. Illinois, 405 U.S. 645 (1972) (right of father to custody of his illegitimate children); but see Mourning v. Family Publications Serv., Inc., 411 U.S. 356 (1973).

3. See, e.g., Note, "The Irrebuttable Presumption Doctrine in the Supreme Court," 87 Harv.L.Rev. 1534 (1974): "The Court's analysis manifests a misunderstanding of the nature of such presumptions. It has treated them as evidentiary rules involved in the process of fact-finding, failing to recognize that irrebuttable presumptions are nothing more than statutory classifications." The "exacting standard of precision" imposed by this approach "reflects a fundamental confusion between legislative prescription

and adjudicatory application of statutory classifications." The Note called the irrebuttable presumptions analysis a "strange hybrid," "if not simply a confusion," of equal protection and procedural due process scrutiny. See also Note, "Irrebuttable Presumptions: An Illusory Analysis," 27 Stan.L.Rev. 449 (1975), viewing the doctrine as "fundamentally mis conceived," seeing it as "logically equivalent to an equal protection argument," and finding it a "standardless, illusory" approach.

4. The approach may survive for use where there are independent reasons for heightened scrutiny, as when "fundamental interests" are affected. See the discussion in Justice Brennan's majority opinion in Elkins v. Moreno, 435 U.S. 647 (1978), where the Court managed to avoid deciding whether Vlandis should be overruled. But there is no longer basis for claiming that heightened scrutiny can usually be triggered simply by asserting an irrebuttable presumptions claim.

broad] latitude to legislative decisions regulating the private sector of the economy, they surely allow no less latitude in prescribing the conditions upon which funds shall be dispensed from the public treasury. [Under] those standards, the question raised is not whether a statutory provision precisely filters out those, and only those, who are in the factual position which generated the congressional concern reflected in the statute. Such a rule would ban all prophylactic provisions. [Nor] is the question whether the provision filters out a substantial part of the class which caused congressional concern, or whether it filters out more members of the class than non-members. The question is whether Congress [could] rationally have concluded both that a particular limitation [would] protect against [the occurrence of the feared abuse], and that the expense and other difficulties of individual determinations justify the inherent imprecision of a prophylactic rule. We conclude that the duration-of-relationship test meets this constitutional standard. [There is] no basis for our requiring individualized determinations when Congress can rationally conclude not only that generalized rules are appropriate to its purposes and concerns, but also that the difficulties of individual determinations outweigh the marginal increments in the precise effectuation of congressional concern which they might be expected to produce."

CHAPTER 10

The Post-Civil War Amendments and Civil Rights Legislation: Constitutional Restraints on Private Conduct; Congressional Power to Implement the Amendments

INTRODUCTORY OVERVIEW

In the preceding three chapters, the actions challenged on due process and equal protection grounds were clearly actions by an arm of *government;* and the virtually exclusive focus was on the role of the *Court* in elaborating constitutional guarantees. This chapter broadens the focus, adding two significant dimensions. First, the concern here extends beyond limits on *governmental* action to restraints against seemingly *private* conduct. Second, concern here extends beyond the Court's role to that of *Congress* in enforcing and elaborating the provisions of the post-Civil War Amendments.

1. *"State action" limits and private actors.* The first new theme—the applicability of constitutional guarantees to seemingly private conduct—reflects the fact that the 14th and 15th Amendments, like most limits in the Constitution, are addressed to government, not to private behavior. For example, the central prohibitions of § 1 of the 14th Amendment begin with "No State shall." From the beginning, Court interpretations of that Amendment have reiterated "the essential dichotomy set forth in that Amendment between deprivation by the State, subject to scrutiny under its provisions, and private conduct, 'however discriminatory and wrongful,' against which the 14th Amendment offers no shield." But the state-private distinction is deceptively simple. As governmental involvement in the private sector has become more pervasive, traditional notions as to what activity constitutes "state action" have become blurred. Under what circumstances is arguably private behavior subject to such restraints as those in the 14th Amendment? When may a challenger relying on the 14th Amendment insist that the Court impose constitutional restraints on a seemingly "private" actor—or at least require that government withdraw from involvement with "private" actors' conduct? The materials in sec. 2 below pursue such questions.

2. *Congress and the Amendments.* The second theme—the role of Congress—reflects the fact that each of the three post-Civil War amendments grants Congress authority to protect civil rights: the final sections of the 13th, 14th, and 15th Amendments each give "power to enforce" each amendment

"by appropriate legislation." These are of course not the only sources of congressional power to enact civil rights laws: e.g., the commerce power has been invoked on behalf of civil rights. (Recall chap. 3 above.) But the post-Civil War additions, unlike the original grants, were born of a special concern with racial discrimination; and the civil rights powers they confer are potentially the most far-reaching. The scope of these powers is pursued in secs. 3 and 4 below.

3. *Court-Congress interactions.* These two themes, of Court elaboration and congressional power, are combined in this chapter because the evolution of the post-Civil War Amendments has evoked a pattern of institutional interactions unlike those involving Art. I powers. Early congressional action under the post-Civil War Amendments stimulated Court responses that helped inhibit further legislative enforcement; subsequent Court elaborations in turn influenced the modern pattern of more vigorous congressional action. Congress has resorted to these Amendments during only two periods of our history: there was a spurt of activity during the post-Civil War years, and then again in recent decades. For the near-century intervening, the Amendments were effectively in the Court's sole keeping. And the most recent spurt of legislative activity in turn provoked new, broader Court statements of the scope of congressional powers. This historical sequence of Court–Congress interactions yielded the institutional relationships pursued in this chapter.

4. *A note on organization.* To explore these interrelated themes, this chapter is organized to focus on two specific, climactic problems. The first deals with the reach of the Amendments and the state action-private action dichotomy: Does Congress have power to expand the *reach* of the Amendments in order to regulate private rather than governmental invasions of individual rights? That inquiry culminates in the materials in sec. 3 below. The second is the problem of the congressional power to modify the *substantive content* of the Amendments: Is congressional enforcement power limited to providing remedies for substantive rights articulated by the Court, or may it "reinterpret" constitutional rights? That inquiry is pursued in sec. 4 below.

As background, sec. 1 sketches the statutory framework of the post-Civil War laws and their modern counterparts. And as further background—and because of its independent significance as a problem of continuing importance—sec. 2 examines the Court's development of the "state action" concept. Sec. 3 examines the modern efforts to apply the remnants of the post-Civil War laws to private action. That section concludes with the modern varieties of congressional action based on the 14th Amendment, as well as with the rediscovery, in the Jones case, of the 13th Amendment (which is not saddled with a state action limitation) as a far-reaching source of congressional power over private racial discrimination. Sec. 4, finally, focuses on the question of congressional power to provide remedies for, and perhaps to modify, the substantive rights unearthed by the Court in its interpretations. The major context for that examination is voting rights legislation—legislation (beginning in 1965) that went beyond prior, Court-imposed restrictions on voting discrimination in several respects. Are the modern laws "remedial" (providing legislative remedies for judicially identified rights) or "substantive" (resting on a nearly autonomous congressional authority to reinterpret and delineate rights, not merely to provide remedies)? In 1966, Katzenbach v. Morgan (p. 998) suggested a broad legislative power to reinterpret the substantive contours of constitutional rights. Other cases—e.g., Rome v. United States in 1980 (p. 991)—indicate that even if congressional power is viewed as merely "remedial" rather than "substantive," its reach can be great indeed. These materials, then, are not only an essential supplement to an understanding of due process and equal protection guarantees, but also a provocative manifestation of Court–

Congress interactions raising questions reaching back all the way to those considered in connection with Marbury v. Madison—questions about institutional autonomy and ultimate authority in the interpretation of constitutional rights.

SECTION 1.   THE STATUTORY FRAMEWORK

———

THE LAWS OF THE RECONSTRUCTION ERA

Introduction: The historical background and the Slaughter–House Cases. There was an intimate interrelationship among the emancipation of slaves during the Civil War, the adoption of the 13th, 14th, and 15th Amendments, and the enactment of the Civil Rights Acts of 1866, 1870, 1871, and 1875. The central purpose of the Amendments was articulated in the Court's first encounter with them, in 1873. Recall Justice Miller's majority opinion in the Slaughter–House Cases (1873; p. 421 above), stating the "one pervading purpose" underlying all of the Amendments: "[W]e mean the freedom of the slave race, the security and firm establishment of that freedom, and the protection of the newly-made freeman and citizen from the oppressions of those who had formerly exercised unlimited dominion over him."

1. *The 1866 Act.* The 13th Amendment, in 1865, gave constitutional support to the wartime Emancipation Proclamation. Congress, however, considered additional protection of the newly freed black necessary—partly because of the "black codes" enacted in several states, which imposed severe legal restrictions just short of formal slavery. The Civil Rights Act of 1866 sought to end these restrictions. Section 1 stated that all persons born in the United States were "citizens of the United States" and proceeded to list certain rights of "such citizens, of every race and color, without regard to any previous condition of slavery." [See the modern counterparts, 42 U.S.C. §§ 1981, 1982.] That listing of rights was followed by a criminal enforcement provision, § 2. [Its modern counterpart is 18 U.S.C. § 242.] During the debates on the 1866 Act, constitutional doubts were raised about the adequacy of the 13th Amendment to support the constitutionality of the law. These doubts were reflected in President Johnson's veto: "[W]here can we find a Federal prohibition against the power of any State to discriminate [?]" Congress overrode the veto, but the amendment machinery was immediately put in motion. The 14th Amendment—designed in part to validate the 1866 Act—was ratified in 1868.

2. *The 1870 Act.* In 1870, the 15th Amendment was ratified. It prohibits denial of the franchise "on account of race, color, or previous condition of servitude"; unlike § 1 of the 14th Amendment, it explicitly mentions the race/slavery problem that provoked all of the post-Civil War Amendments. Congress promptly passed enforcement legislation. The 1870 Enforcement Act dealt primarily with state denials of voting rights. [See the later federal laws in sec. 4 below.] Sec. 6, however, went further: it provided criminal sanctions for private conspiracies to violate federal rights. [The current version of this criminal provision is 18 U.S.C. § 241.]

3. *The 1871 and 1875 Acts.* In 1871, Congress not only amended the 1870 Act, but also enacted a new law, the Civil Rights Act of 1871. The 1871 Act "to enforce [the] 14th Amendment," known as the Ku Klux Klan Act, was "among the last of the reconstruction legislation to be based on the 'conquered prov-

ince' theory which prevailed in Congress for a period following the Civil War. This statute [established] civil liabilities, together with parallel criminal liabilities.'' Collins v. Hardyman (1951; p. 974 below). The substance of these civil provisions has been preserved. For example, 42 U.S.C. § 1983 creates a cause of action for deprivations, under color of state law, of rights secured by the Constitution and federal laws. And 42 U.S.C. § 1985(3) provides for civil actions for certain private anti-civil rights conspiracies. Finally, the Civil Rights Act of 1875, which contained, inter alia, ''public accommodations'' provisions, is discussed in the 1883 Civil Rights Cases (p. 921 below), holding the provisions unconstitutional.*

THE SURVIVING REMNANTS OF THE POST–CIVIL WAR LAWS: THE MODERN COUNTERPARTS

1. Criminal provisions:

18 U.S.C. § 241 (Derived from § 6 of the 1870 Act): *"Conspiracy against rights. If* two or more persons conspire to injure, oppress, threaten, or intimidate any inhabitant of any State, Territory or District in the free exercise or enjoyment of any right or privilege secured to him by the Constitution or laws of the United States, or because of his having so exercised the same; or

''If two or more persons go in disguise on the highway, or on the premises of another, with intent to prevent or hinder his free exercise or enjoyment of any right or privilege so secured—

''They shall be fined not more than $10,000 or imprisoned not more than ten years, or both; and if death results, they shall be subject to imprisonment for any term of years or for life.''

18 U.S.C. § 242 (Derived from § 2 of the 1866 Act): *"Deprivation of rights under color of law.* Whoever, under color of any law, statute, ordinance, regulation, or custom, willfully subjects any inhabitant of any State, Territory, or District to the deprivation of any rights, privileges, or immunities secured or protected by the [Constitution or laws], or to different punishments, pains, or penalties, on account of such inhabitant being an alien, or by reason of his color, or race, than are prescribed for the punishment of citizens, shall be fined not more than $1,000 or imprisoned not more than one year, or both; and if bodily injury results shall [be] imprisoned not more than ten [years]; and if death results shall be subject to imprisonment for any term of years or for life.''

2. Civil provisions:

42 U.S.C. § 1981 (Derived from the 1866 and 1870 Acts): *"Equal rights under the law.* All persons within the jurisdiction of the United States shall have the same right in every State and Territory to make and enforce contracts, to sue, be parties, give evidence, and to the full and equal benefit of all laws and proceedings for the security of persons and property as is enjoyed by white citizens, and shall be subject to like punishment, pains, penalties, taxes, licenses, and exactions of every kind, and to no other.''

---

* For a review of the post-Civil War laws, and their fate in later decades, see Gressman, "The Unhappy History of Civil Rights Legislation," 50 Mich.L.Rev. 1323 (1952). See also Carr, Federal Protection of Civil Rights (1947). For a useful compilation, see a congressional document, Federal Civil Rights Laws: A Sourcebook (1984).

42 U.S.C. § 1982 (Derived from the 1866 Act): "*Property rights of citizens.* All citizens of the United States shall have the same right, in every State and Territory, as is enjoyed by white citizens thereof to inherit, purchase, lease, sell, hold, and convey real and personal property."

42 U.S.C. § 1983 (Derived from § 1 of the Civil Rights Act of 1871): "*Civil action for deprivation of rights.* Every person who, under color of any statute, ordinance, regulation, custom, or usage, of any State or Territory or the District of Columbia, subjects, or causes to be subjected, any citizen of the United States or other person within the jurisdiction thereof to the deprivation of any rights, privileges or immunities secured by the Constitution and laws, shall be liable to the party injured in an action at law, suit in equity, or other proper proceedings for redress."

42 U.S.C. § 1985(3) (Derived from Civil Rights Act of 1871): "*Conspiracy to interfere with civil rights.* [If] two or more persons in any State or Territory conspire or go in disguise on the highway or on the premises of another, for the purpose of depriving, either directly or indirectly, any person or class of persons of the equal protection of the laws, or of equal privileges and immunities under the laws; [the] party so injured or deprived may have an action for the recovery of damages occasioned by such injury or deprivation, against any one or more of the conspirators."

A brief note on modern civil rights legislation. The modern revival of congressional civil rights activity began with the Civil Rights Act of 1957; that law, like the Civil Rights Act of 1960, was primarily designed to expand remedies against racial discrimination in voting. The Civil Rights Act of 1964— the first comprehensive modern civil rights law—moved substantially beyond the area of voting rights. The 1964 provisions based primarily on Art. I powers of Congress have already been considered, in chap. 3. In addition, the 1964 Act included several provisions primarily rooted in the post-Civil War Amendments. Thus, Titles I and VIII contained new voting rights provisions, and Titles III and IV dealt with desegregation of schools and other public facilities. After the 1965 Voting Rights Act was adopted (see sec. 4 below), Johnson Administration proposals for additional omnibus civil rights laws were repeatedly blocked in the Senate. In 1968, however—after the assassination in April 1968 of Dr. Martin Luther King—new legislation was enacted. (Note especially the 1968 Act's additions of new federal criminal laws dealing with civil rights violence in 18 U.S.C. § 245 (p. ___ below.))

SECTION 2. THE PROBLEM OF STATE ACTION

A. STATE ACTION IN THE 19TH CENTURY: THE COLLAPSE OF EARLY CONGRESSIONAL EFFORTS TO REACH PRIVATE CONDUCT

Civil Rights Cases

109 U.S. 3, 3 S.Ct. 18, 27 L.Ed. 835 (1883).

[Sec. 1 of the Civil Rights Act of 1875 provided: "[A]ll persons within the jurisdiction of the United States shall be entitled to the full and equal enjoyment of the accommodations, advantages, facilities, and privileges of inns, public conveyances on land or water, theatres, and other places of public amusement; subject only to the conditions and limitations established by law, and applicable alike to citizens of every race and color, regardless of any previous condition of servitude." Sec. 2 made violation a misdemeanor and also authorized aggrieved persons to recover $500 "for every such offense." This decision involved five cases, from Kansas, California, Missouri, New York and Tennessee. Four of the cases were criminal indictments; the fifth, an action for the civil penalty. The cases grew out of exclusions of blacks from hotels, theaters and railroads.]

Justice BRADLEY delivered the opinion of the [Court].

Has Congress constitutional power to make such a law? [The] power is sought, first, in the 14th Amendment. [It] is State action of a particular character that is prohibited [by the first section of the 14th Amendment]. Individual invasion of individual rights is not the subject-matter of the amendment. [The] last section of the amendment invests Congress with power to enforce it by appropriate legislation. To enforce what? To enforce the prohibition. To adopt appropriate legislation for correcting the effects of such prohibited State laws and State acts, and thus to render them effectually null, void, and innocuous. This is the legislative power conferred upon Congress, and this is the whole of it. It does not invest Congress with power to legislate upon subjects which are within the domain of State legislation; but to provide modes of relief against State legislation, or State action, of the kind referred to. [But this law] shows that [it] proceeds ex directo to declare that certain acts committed by individuals shall be deemed offences, and shall be prosecuted and punished by proceedings in the [federal courts]. It does not profess to be corrective of any constitutional wrong committed by the States; [it] applies equally to cases arising in States which have the justest laws respecting the personal rights of citizens, and whose authorities are ever ready to enforce such laws, as to those which arise in States that may have violated the prohibition of the amendment. In other words, it steps into the domain of local jurisprudence, and lays down rules for the conduct of individuals in society towards each [other], without referring in any manner to any supposed action of the State or its authorities.

[C]ivil rights, such as are guaranteed by the Constitution against State aggression, cannot be impaired by the wrongful acts of individuals, unsupported by State authority in the shape of laws, customs, or judicial or executive proceedings. The wrongful act of an individual, unsupported by any such authority, is simply a private wrong, or a crime of that individual. [I]f not sanctioned in some way by the State, or not done under State authority, [the injured party's] rights remain in full force, and may presumably be vindicated by resort to the laws of the State for redress. An individual cannot deprive a man of his right to vote, to hold property, to buy and sell, to sue in the courts, or to be a witness or a juror; he may, by force or fraud, interfere with the enjoyment of the right in a particular case; he may commit an assault against the person, or commit murder, or use ruffian violence at the polls, or slander the good name of a fellow citizen; but, unless protected in these wrongful acts by some shield of State law or State authority, he cannot destroy or injure the right; he will only render himself amenable to satisfaction or punishment; and amenable therefor to the laws of the State where the wrongful acts are committed. [The] abrogation and denial of rights, for which the States alone were or could be responsible, was the great seminal and fundamental wrong which was intended to be remedied. And the remedy to be provided must necessarily be predicated upon that wrong. [I]t is clear that the law in question cannot be sustained by any grant of legislative power made to Congress by the

14th Amendment. [Whether] Congress, in the exercise of its power to regulate commerce amongst the several States, might or might not pass a law regulating rights in public conveyances passing from one State to another, [is] a question which is not now before us, as the sections in question are not conceived in any such view.

[Justification for the law is also] sought [in] the 13th Amendment. [Such] legislation may be primary and direct in its character; for the amendment is not a mere prohibition of State laws establishing or upholding slavery, but an absolute declaration that slavery or involuntary servitude shall not exist in any part of the United States. [I]t is assumed, that the power vested in Congress to enforce the article by appropriate legislation, clothes Congress with power to pass all laws necessary and proper for abolishing all badges and incidents of slavery in the United States: and upon this assumption it is claimed, that this is sufficient authority for [enacting this law]; the argument being, that the denial of such equal accommodations and privileges is, in itself, a subjection to a species of servitude within the meaning of the amendment. [W]e are forced to the conclusion that such an act of refusal has nothing to do with slavery or involuntary servitude, and that if it is violative of any right of the party, his redress is to be sought under the laws of the State; or if those laws are adverse to his rights and do not protect him, his remedy will be found in the corrective legislation which Congress has adopted, or may adopt, for counteracting the effect of State laws, or State action, prohibited by the 14th Amendment. It would be running the slavery argument into the ground to make it apply to every act of discrimination which a person may see fit to make as to the guests he will entertain, or as to the people he will take into his coach or cab or car, or admit to his concert or theatre, or deal with in other matters of intercourse or business. Innkeepers and public carriers, by the laws of all the States, so far as we are aware, are bound, to the extent of their facilities, to furnish proper accommodation to all unobjectionable persons who in good faith apply for them. If the laws themselves make any unjust discrimination, amenable to the prohibitions of the 14th Amendment, Congress has full power to afford a remedy under that amendment and in accordance with it.[1] When a man has emerged from slavery, and by the aid of beneficent legislation has shaken off the inseparable concomitants of that state, there must be some stage in the progress of his elevation when he takes the rank of a mere citizen, and ceases to be the special favorite of the [laws]. [The challenged law is unconstitutional.]

So ordered.

Justice HARLAN dissenting.

The opinion in these cases proceeds, it seems to me, upon grounds entirely too narrow and artificial. I cannot resist the conclusion that the substance and spirit of the recent amendments of the Constitution have been sacrificed by a subtle and ingenious verbal criticism. [Was] it the purpose of the [13th Amendment] simply to destroy the institution [of slavery], and then remit the race, theretofore held in bondage, to the several States for such protection, in their civil rights, [as] those States, in their discretion, might choose to provide? [That] there are burdens and disabilities which constitute badges of slavery and servitude, and that the power to enforce by appropriate legislation the 13th

1. Can it be argued that Justice Bradley assumed that state laws would bar racial discrimination in public accommodations? If so, would a state's failure to safeguard against such discrimination constitute "state action" and justify federal corrective remedial legislation? See, e.g., Peters, "Civil Rights and State Non-Action," 34 Notre Dame Law. 303 (1959), and Frank & Munro, "The Original Understanding of 'Equal Protection of the Laws,' "1972 Wash.U.L.Q. 421.

Amendment may be exerted by legislation of a direct and primary character, for the eradication, not simply of the institution, but of its badges and incidents, are propositions which ought to be deemed indisputable. [I] do not contend that the 13th Amendment invests Congress with authority, by legislation, to define and regulate the entire body of the civil rights which citizens enjoy, or may enjoy, in the several States. But I hold that since slavery [was] the moving or principal cause of the adoption of that amendment, and since that institution rested wholly upon the inferiority, as a race, of those held in bondage, their freedom necessarily involved immunity from, and protection against, all discrimination against them, because of their race, in respect of such civil rights as belong to freemen of other races. Congress, therefore, [may] enact laws to protect that people against the deprivation, *because of their race,* of any civil rights granted to other freemen in the same State; and such legislation may be of a direct and primary character operating upon States, their officers and agents, and, also, upon, at least, such individuals and corporations as exercise public functions and wield power and authority under the [State].

It remains now to inquire what are the legal rights of colored persons in respect of the accommodations, privileges and facilities of public conveyances, inns and places of public amusement? *First,* as to public conveyances on land and water. [The] sum of the adjudged cases is that a railroad corporation is a governmental agency, created primarily for public purposes, and subject to be controlled for the public benefit. [Such] being the relations these corporations hold to the public, it would seem that the right of a colored person to use an improved public highway, upon the terms accorded to freemen of other races, is as fundamental [as] are any of the rights which my brethren concede to be so far fundamental as to be deemed the essence of civil [freedom]. *Second,* as to inns. [A] keeper of an inn is in the exercise of a quasi-public employment. [The] public nature of his employment forbids him from discriminating against any person asking admission as a guest on account of the race or color of that person. *Third.* As to places of public amusement. [Within] the meaning of the act of 1875, [they] are such as are established and maintained under direct license of the law. [The] local government granting the license represents [the colored race] as well as all other races within its jurisdiction. A license from the public to establish a place of public amusement, imports, in law, equality of right, at such places, among all the members of that public. [I] am of the opinion that [racial] discrimination practiced by corporations and individuals in the exercise of their public or quasi-public functions is a badge of servitude the imposition of which Congress may prevent under its power, by appropriate legislation, to enforce the [13th Amendment].

[The] assumption that [the 14th] amendment consists wholly of prohibitions upon State laws and State proceedings in hostility to its provisions, is unauthorized by its language. The first clause of the first section [is] of a distinctly affirmative character. [It granted to blacks state as well as national citizenship, and brought them within the protection of the privileges and immunities clause of Art. IV, § 2.] The citizenship thus acquired, by [the colored] race [may] be protected, not alone by the [judiciary], but by congressional legislation of a primary, direct character; this, because the power of Congress is not restricted to the enforcement of prohibitions upon State laws or State action. It is, in terms distinct and positive, to enforce "the *provisions of this article*" of [amendment]—*all* of the provisions—affirmative and prohibitive. But what was secured to colored citizens of the United States—as between them and their respective States—by the national grant to them of State citizenship? With what rights, privileges, or immunities did this grant invest them? There is one, if there be no other—exemption from race discrimination in respect of any civil right belonging to citizens of the white race in the same State.

[But] if it were conceded that the power of Congress could not be brought into activity until the rights specified in the act of 1875 had been abridged or denied by some State law or State action, I maintain that the decision of the court is erroneous. [In] every material sense applicable to the practical enforcement of the 14th Amendment, railroad corporations, keepers of inns, and managers of places of public amusement are agents or instrumentalities of the State, because they are charged with duties to the public, and are amenable, in respect of their duties and functions, to governmental regulation. [I] agree that if one citizen chooses not to hold social intercourse with another, he is not and cannot be made amenable to the [law]. [But the] rights which Congress [endeavored] to secure and protect [here] are legal, not social rights. [Today,] it is the colored race which is denied, by corporations and individuals wielding public authority, rights fundamental in their freedom and citizenship. At some future time, it may be that some other race will fall under the ban of race discrimination. If the constitutional amendments be enforced, according to the intent with which [they] were adopted, there cannot be, in this republic, any class of human beings in practical subjection to another [class].

CRUIKSHANK AND THE LEGACY OF THE CIVIL RIGHTS CASES

1. *Cruikshank, the 14th Amendment limitation to state action—and the recognition of rights against private action outside the 14th Amendment.* UNITED STATES v. CRUIKSHANK, 92 U.S. 542 (1875), involved an indictment under § 6 of the 1870 Act, the predecessor of 18 U.S.C. § 241. Three persons were convicted of participating in a lynching of two blacks. One of the charges was interference with the "right and privilege peaceably to assemble together." The Court held the application of the law unconstitutional. Chief Justice WAITE stated that the indictment would have been adequate if it had charged interference with the right to assemble "for the purpose of petitioning Congress for a redress of grievances," an "attribute of national citizenship"; but the charge was merely a conspiracy "to prevent a meeting for any lawful purpose whatever." Note that even under Cruikshank private misconduct was not wholly outside congressional reach: the opinion recognized that there might be constitutional rights derived from sources not subject to the state action limitation, and that those might accordingly be protected against private as well as state interferences. That distinction—between constitutional rights against the state and constitutional rights not limited by the state action concept—remains an important one in the search for bases of congressional action against private misconduct. As the Guest case (1969; p. 964 below) illustrates, congressional power to reach private conduct under the 14th Amendment still presents substantial difficulties, though the power is not so tightly confined today as it was in the 19th century. That continuing state action difficulty makes the Court's efforts to articulate constitutional rights not based on the 14th and 15th Amendments (and hence not subject to the state action limitation) of special importance.

2. *The legacy of the Civil Rights Cases: A transitional note.* Many of the remaining materials in this chapter explore the contemporary vitality of the Civil Rights Cases. Bear in mind the varied ingredients of the majority's position. *First,* it insisted that the 14th Amendment's self-executing impact did not reach beyond state action to encompass private discrimination as well. The

Court continues to reiterate that position—and continues to cite the Civil Rights Cases for it. Yet notions of what discrimination may fairly be attributed to the state have expanded considerably in recent decades. The ingredients of modern state action concepts—the extent to which the Amendment by its own force *does* reach arguably private action—is the theme of sec. 2B. *Second,* the Civil Rights Cases insisted that congressional enforcement powers under § 5 of the 14th Amendment could not reach beyond the state action limits of § 1 of the Amendment. Modern cases, considered in secs. 3 and 4 below, have taken a more expansive view of congressional powers. *Third,* the majority in the Civil Rights Cases recognized that the 13th Amendment is not limited to state action and extends to private actors as well. But that majority sharply limited congressional enforcement power; it refused to find in § 2 of the 13th Amendment a general congressional power to prohibit private racial discriminations as "badges of servitude." That view has in effect been overruled by the 1968 decision in Jones, p. 978 below.

B. COURT ELABORATIONS OF THE STATE ACTION CONCEPT IN THE 20TH CENTURY

Introduction. Beginning in the 1940s, while congressional power under the 14th Amendment lay dormant (because of political as well as constitutional obstacles), the Court began to expand the boundaries of the state action concept. The results were often clearer than the contents and limits of the principles. In many cases, arguably private conduct was treated as state action; the result was either that the private actor was subjected to constitutional prohibitions or that the state was required to disengage itself from the private activity. What was often obscure was the extent to which additional seemingly private activities could be reached on the basis of those holdings. Yet it seemed all along that the Court's principles were not intended to be limitless. And the modern Court's decisions have made it increasingly clear that a state action limit persists and that not every effort to impose constitutional restraints on arguably private actors will receive judicial support.[1]

Most of the cases from the 1940s to the 1960s involved claims of racial discrimination (and most found the 14th Amendment applicable). Since the rediscovery of the 13th Amendment (which does not have a state action limit) in the late 1960s (and the enactment of modern legislation based on congressional spending and commerce powers), Congress has been able to reach racial discrimination in the private sector without relying on the 14th Amendment.

1. The literature on the state action problem is extensive. See generally Lewis, "The Meaning of State Action," 60 Colum.L.Rev. 1083 (1960); Wechsler, "Toward Neutral Principles of Constitutional Law," 73 Harv.L.Rev. 1 (1959); and Pollak, "Racial Discrimination and Judicial [Integrity]," 108 U.Pa.L.Rev. 1 (1959). See also, e.g., Williams, "The Twilight of State Action," 41 Texas L.Rev. 347 (1963); Van Alstyne & Karst, "State Action," 14 Stan.L.Rev. 3 (1961); Horowitz, "The Misleading Search for ['State Action']," 30 So.Cal.L.Rev. 208 (1957); Henkin, "Shelley v. Kraemer: Notes for a Revised Opinion," 110 U.Pa.L.Rev. 473 (1962); Glennon & Nowak, "A Functional Analysis of [the] 'State Action' Requirement," 1976 Sup. Ct.Rev. 221; and Choper, "Thoughts on State [Action]," 1979 Wash.U.L.Q. 757. For a critical review of the literature as well as of the entire state action concept (urging that it go into "honored retirement as an innocuous truism"), see C.L. Black, Jr., "Foreword: 'State [Action']," 81 Harv.L.Rev. 69 (1967). (Despite that plea for "retirement," the state action concept remains in active service, as the cases of the last two decades, below, illustrate.)

But, as the 1970s cases below illustrate, that development has by no means made state action problems of historical interest only. As the two preceding chapters show, the Court's interpretations of the due process and equal protection clauses have brought a wide range of rights that are not race-related within the 14th Amendment, with resulting efforts to apply those constitutional guarantees to private actors. See, e.g., Jackson (1974; p. 952 below). Since the 1970s, the Court has been far more reluctant to find state action. Consider whether the Court would have been wise and justified to have varied the requirements for finding state action with the type of constitutional claim involved—e.g., by being more willing to find it in racial discrimination cases than in others. (See Justice Marshall's dissent in Jackson, below.)

What must be shown to subject seemingly private actors to the constitutional guarantees ordinarily applicable only to government? The cases of the last five decades present recurrent themes. Note especially the relative emphases on two distinguishable lines of inquiry: first, whether the private actor is sufficiently entangled with, or sufficiently "like," the state to consider the private conduct "state action"; second, whether applicability of constitutional guarantees to the private actor unduly impinges on the private interest in being free to behave in ways constitutionally barred to the state. The second inquiry rests on the assumption that there is a sphere of private behavior in which individuals are free to discriminate. (The terms "discriminate" and "discriminator" are used here as shorthand for the private actor engaging in allegedly unconstitutional behavior, whether it is racially discriminatory or not.) That there are such areas, and that some legitimate freedom in the private sector acts as a limit to expansions of the applicability of 14th Amendment guarantees, is recognized even by those Justices who have advocated the broadest extensions of the state action concept.[2] Freedom of association, rights of privacy, perhaps interests in property, all have some claim to recognition. But what is the relevance of those competing interests to the delineation of the boundaries of the state action concept? Is the individual's freedom of association or of privacy the central ingredient in determining what behavior is not state action for 14th Amendment purposes? Or does the emphasis on individual interests suggest that the support of the "state"—at least in maintaining a legal order—is to be found throughout the entire private sector; that the search for indicia of "state action" is therefore irrelevant; and that the underlying question about the reach of constitutional guarantees is really one of balancing the impact on the aggrieved against the proper area of unrestrained choice and privacy of the discriminator?[3]

Although many of the results in the cases can be explained on such "balancing" grounds, and though explicit consideration of the privacy interests of the discriminator occasionally surfaces in the opinions, most of the cases are preoccupied with the search for adequate elements of the "state." That search for the indicia of state action has followed two distinguishable routes. One may be called the "nexus" approach: it seeks to identify sufficient points of contact between the private actor and the state to justify imposing constitutional

2. See, e.g., Justice Douglas's dissent, joined by Justice Marshall, in the Moose Lodge case in 1972 (p. 947 below): "The associational rights which our system honors permit all white, all black, all brown, and all yellow clubs to be formed. [Government] may not tell a man or woman who his or her associates must be. The individual can be as selective as he desires."

3. See, e.g., Hale, "Force and the [State]," 35 Colum.L.Rev. 149 (1935), Van Alstyne & Karst, footnote 1 above, and Glennon & Nowak, "A Functional Analysis of the Fourteenth Amendment's 'State Action' Requirement," 1976 Sup.Ct.Rev. 221.

restraints on the private actor or commanding state disentanglement. That approach is exemplified by Burton (1961; p. 942 below), which states "that private conduct abridging individual rights does no violence to [equal protection] unless *to some significant extent* the State in any of its manifestations has been found to have become involved in it." (Emphasis added.) That search for "significant" state involvements permeates most of the cases—and raises numerous problems. The Burton approach assumes that a "neutral" state tolerance of private discrimination is permissible. But how much active, affirmative engagement by the state is necessary under that approach? Is it enough that the state "authorizes" the private discrimination? Can authorization be distinguished from mere tolerance, where the state has power to forbid private discrimination and does not exercise that power? When, if ever, is a state prohibited from adhering to "neutrality" (and obliged to take affirmative action to prohibit state behavior from endangering 14th Amendment values)? What varieties of greater active state involvement satisfy the state action requirement? Must the state be shown to approve discrimination? To encourage discrimination? Is it enough that the state confers some benefits on the private discriminator? Must there be special benefits, such as a grant of a monopoly? Is state regulation of the discriminator enough? State licensing? State leasing or sale of property? Is it enough that the state judicial system enforces the private discriminator's wishes, as part of a general system of property and contract law? Questions such as these are characteristic of the "significant state involvements" approach.

The alternative to that "nexus" analysis is the "public function" approach. Instead of searching for formal contacts between the state and the private discriminator, it focuses on the nature of the activity in which the private discriminator engages. Marsh v. Alabama, the company town case which follows, illustrates that approach. Basically, the "public function" analysis treats private enterprises whose "operation is essentially a public function" as sufficiently state-like to be treated as a state for purposes of applying constitutional guarantees. This was one of the earliest, most amorphous, and potentially most far-reaching themes in the expansion of the state action concept, but the cases in recent decades have curtailed it sharply. An examination of the "public function" cases follows, as the first theme in the materials exploring the various strands of state action analysis.

————

THE "PUBLIC FUNCTION" STRAND OF STATE ACTION ANALYSIS

1. *Marsh v. Alabama and modern "public function" analysis.* a. *The decision.* A major source of the view that the private performance of "public functions" can make 14th Amendment restraints applicable was MARSH v. ALABAMA, 326 U.S. 501 (1946).[1] Marsh arose in the context of First Amendment rights and held that a state cannot "impose criminal punishment on a person who undertakes to distribute religious literature on the premises of a company-owned town contrary to the wishes of the town's management." Chickasaw, Alabama, was owned by the Gulf Shipbuilding Corporation. Except for its private ownership, it had "all the characteristics of any other American

1. Recall also the "public function" discussion in Justice Harlan's dissent in the Civil Rights Cases, above, and note the evolution of "public function" analysis in the White Primary Cases, p. 934 below.

town." Marsh, a Jehovah's Witness, was convicted under the state criminal trespass law because she distributed religious literature without permission. Justice BLACK's majority opinion noted that an ordinary town could not have prohibited her activities, in view of the First Amendment. That a corporation owned title to the town could not justify impairing the public's interest "in the functioning of the community in such a manner that the channels of communication remain free." Accordingly, he rejected the argument that "the corporation's right to control the inhabitants of Chickasaw is coextensive with the right of a homeowner to regulate the conduct of his guests." He stated: "Ownership does not always mean absolute dominion. The more an owner, for his advantage, opens up his property for use by the public in general, the more do his rights become circumscribed by the statutory and constitutional rights of those who use it. Thus, the owners of privately held bridges, ferries, turnpikes and railroads may not operate them as freely as a farmer does his farm. Since these facilities are built and operated primarily to benefit the public and *since their operation is essentially a public function,* it is subject to state regulation." (Emphasis added.) Justice Black also noted that many Americans "live in company-owned towns," and that to act "as good citizens, they must be informed." He added: "When we balance the Constitutional rights of owners of property against those of the people to enjoy freedom of press and religion, as we must here, we remain mindful of the fact that the latter occupy a preferred position." He noted, moreover, that "the town and its shopping district are accessible to and freely used by the public in general and there is nothing to distinguish them from any other town and shopping center except the fact that the title to the property belongs to a private corporation." And that property interest could not justify infringement of First Amendment rights: "The 'business block' serves as the community shopping center and is freely accessible and open to the people in the area and those passing through. The managers appointed by the corporation cannot curtail the liberty of press and religion of these people consistently with the purposes of the Constitutional guarantees, and a state statute [which] enforces such action by criminally punishing those who attempt to distribute religious literature clearly violates the [Constitution]."

b. *Some questions.* What satisfied the state action requirement in Marsh? Apparently, the invocation of a state trespass law was not significant to the finding of state action.[2] Rather, Marsh rested largely on the nature of the private activity—the fact that Chickasaw was "a town" which in "its community aspects [did] not differ from other towns" and which therefore exercised a "public function." Is the aim of the "public function" discussion to demonstrate an adequate relationship with the state—i.e., does it rest on an implicit view that the state had "delegated" a nondelegable function to the private entity? Or is the "public function" discussion really a substitute for (rather than part of the search for) formal state involvement? In the latter view, "public function" analysis focuses on a balancing of competing interests—those of the First Amendment claimant and those of the private property owner. Consider the relative emphases on nexus and balancing approaches in the evolution of the public function approach, below.

2. *The refusal to extend Marsh: The modern shopping center cases.* More than 20 years later, the Court returned to the Marsh problem to consider

2. Should that state "nexus" have played a more prominent role? Compare Shelley v. Kraemer (p. 936 below) where, two years later, the Court placed great emphasis on state judicial enforcement of a private restrictive covenant. (Shelley, viewed as a far-reaching and novel approach to state action, barely mentioned Marsh.)

claims that shopping centers, which were replacing downtown business areas throughout the nation, should be subjected to First Amendment constitutional restraints, just as the company town had been in Marsh. In the first of the series of cases, Amalgamated Food Employees Union v. Logan Valley Plaza, Inc., 391 U.S. 308 (1968), that effort succeeded. Justice Marshall's opinion concluded that the shopping center involved in that case was "clearly the functional equivalent to the business district of Chickasaw involved in Marsh." But in 1976, in Hudgens v. NLRB, below, the Court made clear that Logan Valley was no longer the law and that shopping center owners were not engaged in "state action." Between Logan Valley and Hudgens, the 1972 decision in Lloyd Corp. v. Tanner had sought to distinguish Logan Valley; but Hudgens announced that Lloyd had in effect overruled the Logan Valley case. Marsh, it had become clear, would be limited to its immediate context, the company town situation.[3] In Logan Valley, the majority insisted that "the State may not delegate the power, through the use of its trespass laws, wholly to exclude those members of the public wishing to exercise their First Amendment rights," and argued that the shopping center was "unlike a situation involving a person's home," because the shopping center owner could advance "no meaningful claim to protection of a right of privacy." That case involved labor union picketing. Justice Black, the author of Marsh, dissented in Logan Valley, insisting that, under Marsh, private property could be treated as though it were public only "when that property has taken on *all* the attributes of a town." Four years later, in Lloyd Corp. v. Tanner, 407 U.S. 551 (1972), the majority tried to distinguish Logan Valley and permitted a shopping center to exclude anti-war leafleters. Justice Powell's majority opinion stressed that, unlike the Logan Valley picketing, the handbilling "had no relation to any purpose for which the center was [used]." Hudgens v. NLRB, 424 U.S. 507 (1976), brought the short-lived era of treating shopping centers like company towns to an end: Justice Stewart, who had dissented in Lloyd, now announced that Lloyd had in effect overruled Logan Valley. Like Logan Valley, Hudgens arose in the labor picketing context. Justice Powell, who had written Lloyd, agreed with Justice Stewart, stating that, "upon more mature thought," he had concluded that it would have been "wiser" in Lloyd not to have drawn "distinctions based upon rather attenuated factual differences." Justice Marshall, the author of Logan Valley, tried unsuccessfully to preserve Logan Valley by distinguishing Lloyd. His dissent insisted that the majority had taken an "overly formalistic view of the relationship [between] private ownership of property" and the First Amendment.[4]

3. *The reach of the "public function" rationale: The parks context.* Efforts to rely on the "public function" analysis in areas beyond company towns (and, briefly, shopping centers) have encountered considerable difficulties. But the public function theme was relied on as an alternative ground in Justice DOUGLAS's majority opinion in EVANS v. NEWTON, 382 U.S. 296 (1966). That case involved a park created in Macon, Ga., pursuant to a trust established in the 1911 will of Senator Bacon. The trust provided that the park, Baconsfield, be used by whites only. The city originally acted as trustee and

3. This series of company town and shopping center cases is more fully discussed, together with other First Amendment problems, at p. 1292 below.

4. To what extent does the position that prevailed in Lloyd and Hudgens rest on constitutionally protected property rights that are protected not only against Court expansions of state action and free speech principles but also against restrictions by other organs of government, be they Congress, state legislatures, or state courts? That question was considered in PruneYard Shopping Center v. Robins (1980; more fully considered at p. 1366 below).

enforced the racial exclusion, but decided after the racial segregation decisions beginning with Brown that it could no longer participate in discrimination. In the Newton litigation, the state court accepted the city's resignation as trustee and appointed private trustees instead. The Court held that Baconsfield nevertheless could not be operated on a racially restrictive basis. In explaining why the 14th Amendment prohibition continued to apply to the park despite the substitution of private trustees, Justice Douglas relied in part on the ground that, so far as the record showed, "there has been no change in municipal maintenance and concern over this facility." But he suggested a "public function" ground as additional support: "The service rendered even by a private park of this character is municipal in nature. [Golf clubs,] social centers, luncheon clubs, schools such as Tuskegee was at least in origin, and other like organizations in the private sector are often racially oriented. A park, on the other hand, is more like a fire department or police department that traditionally serves the community. Mass recreation through the use of parks is plainly in the public domain; and state courts that aid private parties to perform that public function on a segregated basis implicate the State in conduct proscribed by the 14th Amendment. Like the streets of the company town in [Marsh] [and] the elective process of Terry [p. 935 below], the predominant character and purpose of this park are municipal." Justice HARLAN's dissent, joined by Justice Stewart, vigorously criticized the majority's "vague," "amorphous," and "far-reaching" public function theory. (Justice Rehnquist's opinion for the Court in Flagg Bros. in 1978, at p. 954 below, read Evans v. Newton narrowly and implicitly rejected Justice Douglas's public function argument.)

4. *Public function and private power.* Does the intermittent reliance on the public function analysis rest ultimately on the notion that 14th Amendment restraints become applicable whenever private action has substantial impact on important interests of individuals? How does that "private government" emphasis satisfy the "state action" requirement? Does it rest simply on a balancing of competing interests, with the power and impact of the challenged enterprise playing a large role? Or is the requisite formal state involvement provided by the probability that the "private government" is chartered by the state? (Compare the licensing and regulation cases below.) Is an adequate involvement with the state shown simply by the state's tolerance of the challenged practice? If mere state failure to prohibit suffices, is the approach inconsistent with any genuine effort to preserve a "state action"-"private action" distinction? Would expansion of a "public function" or "private government" approach unduly constitutionalize all operations of "private" groups found subject to the 14th Amendment? Consider the assertion of an "emerging principle" in Berle, "Constitutional Limitations on Corporate Activity—Protection of Personal Rights from Invasion through Economic Power," 100 U.Pa. L.Rev. 933 (1952), suggesting that "principle" to be that a corporation may be "as subject to constitutional limitations as is the state itself." He noted two prerequisites: the "undeniable fact" of the state's action in chartering the corporation, and "the existence of sufficient economic power [to] invade the constitutional rights of the individual to a material degree." To what extent is Berle's "emerging principle" supported by the decisions since his 1952 article?

5. *The modern Court's curtailment of public function analysis: The limitation to powers "exclusively reserved to the State."* Two decisions of the 1970s made it especially clear that the modern Court does not look with favor upon efforts to expand the "public function" analysis launched by Marsh. a. JACKSON v. METROPOLITAN EDISON CO., 419 U.S. 345 (1974) (further noted at p. 952 below), was a suit against a privately owned utility licensed and

regulated by a state public utilities commission. Petitioner sought relief against the company's termination of her electric service for nonpayment. She claimed that the company was bound by the 14th Amendment and that her procedural due process rights had been denied by the failure to give her adequate notice and a hearing. Among the various state action theories she relied on was one urging that "state action is present because respondent provides an essential public service required to be supplied on a reasonably continuous basis by [state law] and hence performs a 'public function.' " Justice REHNQUIST's majority opinion rejected this as well as all other state action claims. As to public function, he stated: "We have, of course, found state action present in the exercise by a private entity of powers traditionally *exclusively reserved to the State*. [Emphasis added. He cited Marsh and the White Primary Cases, below.] If we were dealing with the exercise by [the company] of some power delegated to it by the State which is traditionally associated with sovereignty, such as eminent domain, our case would be quite a different one. [Perhaps] in recognition of the fact that the supplying of utility service is not traditionally the exclusive prerogative of the State, petitioner invites the expansion of a doctrine of this limited line of cases into a broad principle that all businesses 'affected with a public interest' are state actors in all their actions. We decline the invitation for reasons stated long ago in [Nebbia]: '[The] phrase "affected with a public interest" can, in the nature of things, mean no more than that an industry, for adequate reason, is subject to control for the public good.' Doctors, optometrists, lawyers, Metropolitan [the utility here], and Nebbia's upstate New York grocery selling a quart of milk are all in regulated businesses, providing arguably essential goods and services, 'affected with a public interest.' We do not believe that such a status converts their every action, absent more, into that of the State." Justice MARSHALL's dissent announced that the fact that the utility "supplies an essential public service that is in many communities supplied by the government weighs more heavily for me than for the majority. [In] my view, utility service is traditionally identified with the State through universal public regulation or ownership to a degree sufficient to render it a 'public function.' [I agree] that it requires more than a finding that a particular business is 'affected with the public interest' before constitutional burdens can be imposed on that business. But when the activity in question is of such public importance that the State invariably either provides the service itself or permits private companies to act as state surrogates in providing it, much more is involved than just a matter of public interest. In those cases, the State has determined that if private companies wish to enter the field, they will have to surrender many of the prerogatives normally associated with private enterprise and behave in many ways like a governmental body. And when the State's regulatory scheme has gone that far, it seems entirely consistent to impose on the public utility the constitutional burdens normally reserved for the State." (Justice DOUGLAS also dissented.)

b.   Justice REHNQUIST reemphasized the "carefully confined bounds" of the public function doctrine on the modern Court in FLAGG BROS., INC. v. BROOKS, 436 U.S. 149 (1978), holding that a warehouseman's proposed sale of goods entrusted to him for storage to satisfy a warehousemen's lien under the Uniform Commercial Code did not constitute state action.[5] The plaintiff's main

---

5. The claim was that warehousemen's sales pursuant to the UCC were subject to the procedural due process guarantees of the 14th Amendment. The plaintiffs, who sought a hearing on the amount they owed, argued that the UCC procedures would be constitutionally inadequate if the sales were conducted by state officials and that a warehouseman utilizing the UCC *was* engaged in state action. In a series of earlier cases, the Court

claim was that the State had delegated to the warehouseman "a power 'traditionally exclusively reserved to the State.' Jackson. They argued that the resolution of private disputes is a traditional function of civil government." Justice Rehnquist replied that the plaintiffs had "read too much into the language of our previous cases": "While many functions have been traditionally performed by governments, very few have been 'exclusively reserved to the State.'" Reviewing the White Primary Cases (which follow) and Marsh, he elaborated: "These two branches of the public function doctrine have in common the feature of exclusivity. [The] proposed sale by Flagg Brothers [is not (unlike, e.g., Marsh and unlike Terry, below)] the only means of resolving this purely private dispute. [The State's] system of rights and remedies, recognizing the traditional place of private arrangements in ordering relationships in the commercial world, can hardly be said to have delegated to Flagg Brothers an exclusive prerogative of the sovereign.[6] [Creditors] and debtors have had available to them historically a far wider number of choices than has one who would be an elected public official, or a member of Jehovah's Witnesses who wished to distribute literature in Chickasaw, Ala., at the time Marsh was decided. [Even] if we were inclined to extend the sovereign function doctrine outside of its present carefully confined bounds, the field of private commercial transactions would be a particularly inappropriate area into which to expand it. [W]e would be remiss if we did not note that there are a number of state and municipal functions not covered by our election cases nor governed by the reasoning of Marsh which have been administered with a greater degree of exclusivity by States and municipalities than has the function of so-called 'dispute resolution.' Among these are such functions as education, fire and police protection, and tax collection. We express no view as to the extent, if any, to which a city or State might be free to delegate to private parties the performance of such functions and thereby avoid the strictures of the 14th Amendment." (The Court also rejected the claim that the warehouseman's proposed sale constituted state action "because the State has authorized and encouraged it in enacting [the UCC]." The discussion of that claim is noted further below, at p. 954.)

Justice STEVENS's dissent, joined by Justices White and Marshall, responded to the majority's public function analysis as follows: "[The State] has authorized the warehouseman to perform what is clearly a state function. The test of what is a state function for purposes of [due process] has been variously phrased. Most frequently the issue is presented in terms of whether the State has delegated a function traditionally and historically associated with sovereignty. See, e.g., Jackson. [Petitioners argue] that the nonconsensual transfer of property rights is not a traditional function of the sovereign. The overwhelming historical evidence is to the contrary, however, and the Court wisely does not adopt this position. Instead, the Court reasons that state action cannot be found because the State has not delegated to the warehouseman an *exclusive*

---

had held constitutional guarantees regarding minimal hearings applicable to a range of summary creditors' remedies. See, e.g., Sniadach v. Family Finance Corp., 395 U.S. 337 (1969) (garnishment), and Fuentes v. Shevin, 407 U.S. 67 (1972), (repossession), both distinguished by Justice Rehnquist in this case. But note a 1982 creditors' remedies case, Lugar (p. 957 below), where the majority distinguished Flagg Bros. (with Justice Rehnquist among the dissenters).

6. "[It] would intolerably broaden, beyond the scope of any of our previous cases, the notion of state action under the 14th Amendment to hold that the mere existence of a body of property law in a State, whether decisional or statutory, itself amounted to 'state action' even though no state officials or state process were ever involved in enforcing that body of [law]." [Footnote by Justice Rehnquist.]

sovereign function.[7] This distinction, however, is not consistent with our prior decisions on state action; is not even adhered to by the Court in this case; and, most importantly, is inconsistent with the line of cases beginning with Sniadach. [If] it is unconstitutional for a State to allow a private party to exercise a traditional state power because the state supervision of that power is purely mechanical, the State surely cannot immunize its actions from constitutional *scrutiny* by removing even the mechanical supervision. [Whether] termed 'traditional,' 'exclusive,' or 'significant,' the state power to order binding, nonconsensual resolution of a conflict between debtor and creditor is exactly the sort of power with which [due process] is concerned. And the State's delegation of that power to a private party is, accordingly, subject to due process scrutiny."[8]

THE WHITE PRIMARY CASES

The White Primary Cases were a line of decisions culminating in the 1950s; they held that Democratic Party groups in southern one-party states could not exclude African Americans from pre-general election candidate selection processes, despite repeated efforts to eliminate all formal indicia of state involvement in the primary schemes. Although the cases are frequently referred to in discussions of the public function approach, they may represent a distinctive, separable line of development. Arguably, they are explainable on the basis of their special context of voting and elections. Moreover, they may be supportable on the basis of the 15th Amendment and its specific reference to racial discrimination in voting rather than on the 14th Amendment. In addition, the tradition of state regulation of primaries may help explain the White Primary Cases.

The sequence of cases began with Nixon v. Herndon, 273 U.S. 536 (1927), where the exclusion of blacks from Democratic primaries was expressed on the face of a Texas law. That was held to be state racial discrimination in violation of the 14th Amendment. Texas responded by granting the power to prescribe membership qualifications to party executive committees. A resultant racial exclusion was again found unconstitutional under the 14th Amendment, in Nixon v. Condon, 286 U.S. 73 (1932), on the ground that the law had made the committee an agent of the state. This time, Texas enacted no new law. Instead, a third round of racial exclusions stemmed from action of the state party convention. That exclusion survived constitutional attack in Grovey v. Townsend, 295 U.S. 45 (1935): the convention was found to be an organ of a

---

7. "As I understand the Court's notion of 'exclusivity,' the sovereign function here is not exclusive because there may be other state remedies, under different statutes or common-law theories, available to respondents. Even if I were to accept the notion that sovereign functions must be 'exclusive,' the Court's description of exclusivity is incomprehensible. The question is whether a particular action is a uniquely sovereign function, not whether state law forecloses any possibility of recovering for damages for such [activity]." [Footnote by Justice Stevens.]

8. Justice MARSHALL, one of those joining Justice Stevens's dissent, also submitted a separate dissenting opinion. He accused the majority of once again demonstrating "an attitude of callous indifference to the realities of life for the poor," and he objected to the Court's "cavalier treatment of the place of historical factors" in identifying functions "traditionally reserved to the State." [For comments on Flagg Bros., see Brest, "State Action and Liberal [Theory]," 130 U.Pa. L.Rev. 1296 (1982), and Goodman, "Professor Brest on State Action and Liberal [Theory]," 130 U.Pa.L.Rev. 1331 (1982).]

voluntary, private group, not of the state; the state was no longer unconstitutionally involved. But Grovey v. Townsend was overruled nine years later, in SMITH v. ALLWRIGHT, 321 U.S. 649 (1944). While the Nixon cases had relied on the 14th Amendment, Smith found that the white primary established by the state convention violated the 15th Amendment. The Smith Court pointed to an intervening decision, United States v. Classic, 313 U.S. 299 (1941), which had held that Art. I, § 4, authorized congressional control of primaries "where the primary is by law made part of the election machinery." Classic was relevant in Smith, according to Justice REED's majority opinion, "not because exclusion of Negroes from primaries is any more or less state action by reason of the unitary character of the electoral process but because the recognition of the place of the primary in the electoral scheme makes clear that state delegation to a party of the power to fix the qualifications of primary elections is delegation of a state function that may make the party's action the action of the State. [O]ur ruling in Classic as to the unitary character of the electoral process calls for a re-examination as to whether or not the exclusion of Negroes from a Texas party primary was state action." The Court examined the state's laws and concluded: "We think that this statutory system for the selection of party nominees for inclusion on the general election ballot makes the party which is required to follow these legislative directions an agency of the State in so far as it determines the participants in a primary election."[1]

The problem came to the Supreme Court in its most extreme "private" form in TERRY v. ADAMS, 345 U.S. 461 (1953). Terry involved racial exclusion in the "pre-primary" elections of the Jaybird Democratic Association, a "voluntary club" of white Democrats. Candidates who won the Jaybird elections typically ran unopposed in the Democratic primaries. The trial court found a "complete absence" of state involvement in the Jaybirds' operations. The Court nevertheless found the 15th Amendment violated by the exclusion of African American voters from the pre-primary. There was no opinion on which a majority could agree, but only one Justice (Justice MINTON) dissented from the result. Justice BLACK, joined by Justices Douglas and Burton, found that "the combined Jaybird Democratic-general election machinery" was unconstitutional. Though the Amendment "excludes social or business clubs," it includes "any election" in which public officials are elected. Any election machinery with the "purpose or effect" of denying "Negroes on account of their race an effective voice in governmental affairs" was barred: "For a State to permit such a duplication of its election processes" as the Jaybird pre-primary was unconstitutional. In a separate opinion, Justice FRANKFURTER stated that the "vital requirement" was "State responsibility—that somewhere, somehow, to some extent, there be an infusion by conduct by officials [into] any scheme" denying the franchise because of race. Nevertheless, he found a constitutional violation here· he thought that county election officials were in effect "participants in the scheme." They had participated by voting in the primary, and that indicated that they "condone[d]" the effectiveness of the exclusionary pre-primary; the "action and abdication" of state officials had in effect permitted a procedure "which predetermines the legally devised primary." Justice CLARK,

---

1. After Smith v. Allwright, several efforts to preserve "private" white primaries by abandoning much of the state statutory framework of the primary election process were thwarted in the lower courts. Note especially the language in Rice v. Elmore, 165 F.2d 387 (4th Cir.1947), cert. denied, 333 U.S. 875 (1948), where South Carolina had repealed all primary laws. The Court of Appeals concluded: "Having undertaken to perform an important function relating to the exercise of sovereignty by the people, [a political party] may not violate the fundamental principles laid down by the Constitution for its exercise."

joined by Chief Justice Vinson and Justices Reed and Jackson, concurred on the ground that the Jaybirds operated "as an auxiliary of the local Party" and were therefore subject to the principles of Smith v. Allwright. He emphasized the Jaybirds' "decisive power" in the county's electoral process and concluded that "when a state structures its electoral apparatus in a form which devolves upon a political organization the uncontested choice of public officials, that organization itself, in whatever disguise, takes on those attributes of government which draw the Constitution's safeguards into play."

STATE ACTION THROUGH STATE "INVOLVEMENT": THE "NEXUS" STRAND OF STATE ACTION ANALYSIS

Shelley v. Kraemer

334 U.S. 1, 68 S.Ct. 836, 92 L.Ed. 1161 (1948).

[These cases (from Missouri and Michigan) were successful challenges to judicial enforcement of the once widely used practice of restrictive covenants—agreements among property owners to exclude persons of designated races. (For a history of the litigation strategy in the battle against restrictive covenants, see Vose, Caucasians Only: The Supreme Court, the NAACP, and the Restrictive Covenant Cases (1959).) In the Missouri case, for example, a 1911 agreement signed by 30 out of 39 property owners in the area restricted occupancy for 50 years to persons of "the Caucasian race" and excluded "people of the Negro or Mongolian race." The petitioners in these cases were African Americans who had purchased houses from white owners despite the racially restrictive covenants. Respondents, owners of other properties subject to the terms of the covenants, sued to enjoin the black purchasers from occupying the property. The state courts granted the relief.]

Chief Justice VINSON delivered the opinion of the [Court].

Whether the equal protection clause [inhibits] judicial enforcement by state courts of restrictive covenants based on race or color is a question which this Court has not heretofore been called upon to consider. [It] cannot be doubted that among the civil rights intended to be protected from discriminatory state action by the 14th Amendment are the rights to acquire, enjoy, own and dispose of property. Equality in the enjoyment of property rights was regarded by the framers of that Amendment as an essential precondition to the realization of other basic civil rights and liberties which the Amendment was intended to guarantee. Thus, [the present 42 U.S.C. § 1982 (see Jones (1982; p. 978 below))], derived from § 1 of the Civil Rights Act of 1866, which was enacted by Congress while the 14th Amendment was also under consideration, provides: "All citizens of the United States shall have the same right, in every State and Territory, as is enjoyed by white citizens thereof to inherit, purchase, lease, sell, hold, and convey real and personal property." This Court has given specific recognition to the same principle. Buchanan v. Warley, 245 U.S. 60 (1917).[1] It is likewise clear that restrictions on the right of occupancy of the sort sought to be created by the private agreements in these cases could not be squared with

---

1. Buchanan v. Warley held unconstitutional a city ordinance making it unlawful for any "colored person" to occupy a house on a block where the majority of residents were whites.

the requirements of the 14th Amendment if imposed by state statute or local ordinance. [But] the present cases [do] not involve action by state legislatures or city councils. Here the particular patterns of discrimination and the areas in which the restrictions are to operate, are determined, in the first instance, by the terms of agreements among private individuals. Participation of the State consists in the enforcement of the restrictions so defined. The crucial issue [is] whether this distinction removes these cases from [the 14th Amendment].

Since [the] Civil Rights Cases, the principle has become firmly [established] that the action inhibited by the first section of the 14th Amendment is only such action as may fairly be said to be that of the States. That Amendment erects no shield against merely private conduct, however discriminatory or wrongful. We conclude, therefore, that the restrictive agreements standing alone cannot be regarded as violative of any rights guaranteed to petitioners by the 14th Amendment. So long as the purposes of those agreements are effectuated by voluntary adherence to their terms, it would appear clear that there has been no action by the State and the provisions of the Amendment have not been violated. But here there was more. These are cases in which the purposes of the agreements were secured only by judicial enforcement by state courts of the restrictive terms of the agreements. The respondents urge that judicial enforcement of private agreements does not amount to state action; or, in any event, the participation of the State is so attenuated in character as not to amount to state action within the meaning of the 14th Amendment. Finally, it is suggested, even if the States in these cases may be deemed to have acted in the constitutional sense, their action did not deprive petitioners of rights guaranteed by the 14th [Amendment].

That the action of state courts and judicial officers in their official capacities is to be regarded as action of the State within the meaning of the 14th Amendment, is a proposition which has long been established by decisions of this Court. [We] have no doubt that there has been state action in these cases in the full and complete sense of the phrase. The undisputed facts disclose that petitioners were willing purchasers of properties upon which they desired to establish homes. The owners of the properties were willing sellers; and contracts of sale were accordingly consummated. It is clear that but for the active intervention of the state courts, supported by the full panoply of state power, petitioners would have been free to occupy the properties in question without restraint. These are not cases, as has been suggested, in which the States have merely abstained from action, leaving private individuals free to impose such discriminations as they see fit. Rather, these are cases in which the States have made available to such individuals the full coercive power of government to deny to petitioners, on the grounds of race or color, the enjoyment of property rights in premises which petitioners are willing and financially able to acquire and which the grantors are willing to sell. The difference between judicial enforcement and non-enforcement of the restrictive covenants is the difference to petitioners between being denied rights of property available to other members of the community and being accorded full enjoyment of those rights on an equal footing.

The enforcement of the restrictive agreements by the state courts in these cases was directed pursuant to the common-law policy of the States as formulated by those courts in earlier decisions. [The] judicial action in each case bears the clear and unmistakable imprimatur of the State. We have noted that previous decisions of this Court have established the proposition that judicial action is not immunized from the operation of the 14th Amendment simply because it is taken pursuant to the state's common-law policy. Nor is the Amendment ineffective simply because the particular pattern of discrimination, which the State has enforced, was defined initially by the terms of a private agreement. State action, as that phrase is understood for the purposes of the 14th Amendment, refers to exertions of state power in all forms. And when the effect of that action is to deny rights subject to the protection of the 14th Amendment, it is the obligation of this Court to enforce the constitutional commands. We hold that in granting judicial enforcement of the restrictive agreements in these cases, the States have denied petitioners the equal protection of the laws and that, therefore, the action of the state courts cannot stand. [That] discrimination has occurred in these cases is [clear]. Respondents urge, however, that since the state courts stand ready to enforce restrictive covenants excluding white [persons], enforcement of covenants excluding colored persons may not be deemed a denial of equal protection of the laws to the colored persons who are thereby affected. This contention does not bear scrutiny. The parties have directed our attention to no case in which a court, state or federal, has been called upon to enforce a covenant excluding members of the white majority from ownership or occupancy of real property on grounds of race or color. But there are more fundamental considerations. The rights created by the first section of the 14th Amendment are, by its terms, guaranteed to the individual. The rights established are personal rights. It is, therefore, no answer to these petitioners to say that the courts may also be induced to deny white persons rights of ownership and occupancy on grounds of race or color. Equal protection of the laws is not achieved through indiscriminate imposition of [inequalities].

Reversed.[2]

SHELLEY v. KRAEMER: THE APPLICATIONS AND THE SEARCH FOR LIMITS

Introduction. If Shelley had been read at its broadest, a simple citation of the case would have disposed of most subsequent state action cases. Some seemingly "neutral" state nexus with a private actor can almost always be found: at least by way of the usual state law backdrop recognizing exercises of private choices; usually via more concrete state involvement than that. Given the entanglement of private choices with law, a broad application of Shelley might in effect have left no private choices immune from constitutional restraints. But, as the cases that follow illustrate, the Court has rejected so expansive a reading and has taken seriously the Shelley assurance that, despite some of its analysis, a state-private distinction was to be retained. The efforts to find principled limits on the broadest implications of Shelley have produced extensive commentary on and off the Court.

In considering Shelley in light of the subsequent cases, bear in mind some pervasive questions: Is "neutral" judicial enforcement of a covenant a more significant benefit to the private actor than "neutral" provision of police and fire services? Is it as significant a benefit as a grant of governmental funds or monopoly status (considered below)? Denial of "neutral" judicial enforcement

---

2. Justices Reed, Jackson and Rutledge did not participate in the case. [In a companion case to Shelley, Hurd v. Hodge, 334 U.S. 24 (1948), the Court held that the courts in the District of Columbia could not enforce restrictive covenants even though the 14th Amendment is not applicable to the federal government. Chief Justice Vinson stated that such action would deny "rights [protected] by the Civil Rights Act"; moreover, it would be contrary to the public policy of the United States to allow a federal court to enforce an agreement constitutionally unenforceable in state courts. (Recall and compare Bolling v. Sharpe, the companion case to Brown v. Board of Education, p. 677 above.)].

may spur the private actor to resort to self-help. Suppose there is violent resistance to that self-help: may the private property owner call on the police for help? Would that in turn provide the requisite state involvement? Does the Shelley approach give adequate weight to competing interests in privacy, association and property?[1] Over the years, a number of narrower readings of Shelley have been advanced. It has been argued, for example, that Shelley is limited to situations where the state intervention has the effect of blocking a transaction between willing seller and buyer. It has also been urged that Shelley can be explained on the basis of 42 U.S.C. § 1982, cited by the Court. (Cf. Jones, p. 978 below.) Can Shelley also be explained via a "public function" rationale, on the ground that restrictive covenants covering a large area are equivalent to impermissible racial zoning laws?[2] Some applications of Shelley, and some efforts to limit it, follow.

1. *Restrictive covenants and damage actions.* Chief Justice VINSON, who wrote Shelley, dissented five years later when the Court applied it to block enforcement of a restrictive covenant via a damage suit against a co-covenantor. BARROWS v. JACKSON, 346 U.S. 249 (1953). The majority noted that permitting damage judgments would induce prospective sellers either to refuse to sell to non-Caucasians or to "require non-Caucasians to pay a higher price to meet the damages which the seller may incur." The Court said that it "will not permit or require" the state "to coerce respondent to respond in damages for failure to observe a restrictive covenant that this Court would deny [the state] the right to enforce in equity."[3]

2. *Reverter provisions in deeds.* The Court's 5-2 decision in EVANS v. ABNEY, 396 U.S. 435 (1970), demonstrated that Shelley had not barred all state involvement in enforcing private restrictions on property. Senator Bacon's will had conveyed property in trust to Macon, Ga., for use as a park "for white people only." After Evans v. Newton (1966, p. 930 above) had held that the park could not be operated on a racially discriminatory basis, the state court ruled that "Senator Bacon's intention to provide a park for whites only had become impossible to fulfill and that accordingly the trust had failed and the parkland and other trust property had reverted by operation of Georgia law to

---

1. See Henkin, "Shelley v. Kraemer: Notes for a Revised Opinion," 110 U.Pa. L.Rev. 473 (1962): "If the competing claims of liberty and the possibility that they may sometimes prevail are recognized, [Shelley] must be given [a] limited reading." Henkin argues that "there are circumstances where the discriminator can invoke a protected liberty which is not constitutionally inferior to the claim of equal protection. There, the Constitution requires or permits the state to favor the right to discriminate over the victim's claim to equal protection; the state, then, is not in violation of the 14th amendment when it legislates or affords a remedy in support of the discrimination." He suggests as those "special cases" where the discriminator should prevail "those few where the state supports that basic liberty, privacy, autonomy, which outweighs even the equal protection of the laws." Are the only competing interests which limit the application of the Shelley principle those that are themselves of

constitutional dimensions? In other words, is the Shelley principle applicable, and must state action be found, in every situation in which state or federal legislatures have the *power* to outlaw racial discrimination without impinging on constitutional guarantees? Or is Shelley's reach narrower than that?

2. Note Justice Douglas' concurring opinion in Reitman (1967; p. 948 below): "Leaving the zoning function to groups [e.g., real estate brokers] which practice discrimination and are [state-licensed] constitutes state action in the narrowest sense in which Shelley can be construed."

3. Do Shelley and Barrows bar recognition of a restrictive covenant as a defense in actions for damages for breach of contract? See Rice v. Sioux City Memorial Park Cemetery, 245 Iowa 147, 60 N.W.2d 110 (1953), affirmed by an equally divided Court, 348 U.S. 880 (1954), vacated and cert. dismissed as improvidently granted, 349 U.S. 70 (1955).

the heirs of the Senator." The Court, in a majority opinion by Justice BLACK, held that this ruling did not constitute state discrimination under the 14th Amendment: "[A]ny harshness that may have resulted from the State court's decision can be attributed solely to its intention to effectuate as nearly as possible the explicit terms of Senator Bacon's will." He insisted that the situation presented in this case was "easily distinguishable from [Shelley], where we held unconstitutional state judicial action which had affirmatively enforced a private scheme of discrimination against Negroes. Here the effect of the Georgia decision eliminated all discrimination against Negroes in the park by eliminating the park itself, and the termination of the park was a loss shared equally by the white and Negro citizens of Macon." Only Justice BRENNAN's dissent mentioned Shelley: "[Shelley] stands at least for the proposition that where parties of different races are willing to deal with one another a state court cannot keep them from doing so by enforcing a privately authored racial restriction." But he placed greater emphasis on other, related, arguments: "This discriminatory closing is permeated with state action: at the time Senator Bacon wrote his will Georgia statutes expressly authorized and supported the precise kind of discrimination provided for by him; in accepting title to the park, public officials of [Macon] entered into an arrangement vesting in private persons the power to enforce a reversion if the city should ever incur a constitutional obligation to desegregate the park; it is a *public* park that is being closed for a discriminatory reason after having been operated for nearly half a century as a segregated *public* facility. [T]here is state action whenever a State enters into an arrangement which creates a private right to compel or enforce the reversion of a public facility. Whether the right is a possibility of reverter, a right of entry, an executory interest, or a contractual right, it can be created only with the consent of a public body or official."

3. *Other testamentary provisions: The Girard College litigation.* Evans v. Abney dampened the speculation during the preceding two decades about the impact of Shelley on the enforcement of restrictive provisions in wills. For example, there had been doubt about whether a court could enforce a restrictive testamentary provision by cutting off a beneficiary when he or she married someone of another religion or race.[4] In PENNSYLVANIA v. BOARD OF DIRECTORS OF TRUSTS, 353 U.S. 230 (1957), petitioners were denied admission to a school on the basis of race, pursuant to Stephen Girard's will, probated in 1831, setting up a trust for a school solely for "poor white male orphans." The will named the City of Philadelphia as trustee; subsequently, a "Board of Directors of City Trusts," composed of city officials and persons named by local courts, was established to administer the trust and the college. The state court refused to order admission. The Court reversed per curiam: "The Board which operates Girard College is an agency of the State. [Therefore,] even though the Board was acting as trustee, its refusal to admit [petitioners] was discrimination by the State." After that ruling, the state courts substituted private trustees to carry out Girard's will. The Court denied certiorari in 1958. Ten years later, however, the Court of Appeals held that this substitution was unconstitutional state action.[5]

---

4. See Gordon v. Gordon, 332 Mass. 197, 124 N.E.2d 228, cert. denied, 349 U.S. 947 (1955), where the state court enforced such a will and summarily distinguished Shelley and similar cases as involving "quite different considerations from the right to dispose of property by will."

5. Pennsylvania v. Brown, 392 F.2d 120 (3d Cir.1968), cert. denied, 391 U.S. 921 (1968). See generally Clark, "Charitable Trusts, the 14th Amendment, and the Will of Stephen Girard," 66 Yale L.J. 979 (1957). [Does Evans v. Abney, above, cast doubt on

4. *Trespass actions and the sit-in cases.* Does Shelley bar the enforcement of state trespass laws against persons excluded from private property on racial grounds? Is the state's enforcement of the property owner's restrictions sufficient state action to make the 14th Amendment applicable? That was the broadest issue inherent in a number of sit-in convictions of demonstrators who had protested discrimination by restaurants and other businesses prior to the enactment of the public accommodations provisions of the 1964 Civil Rights Act. The broadest reading of Shelley would have covered these cases with ease. Yet, in a series of decisions in the early 1960s, the Court set aside all of the convictions *without* relying on Shelley. The failure to rely on Shelley suggested that more state involvement than even-handed enforcement of private biases was necessary to find unconstitutional state action. For example, in Peterson v. Greenville, 373 U.S. 244 (1963),—one of five sit-in cases reversed at that time— the Court found official segregation policies in the background of the private action and refused to inquire whether the restaurant manager would have excluded the demonstrators had the state been wholly silent: the unconstitutional ingredients "cannot be saved by attempting to separate the mental urges of the discriminators." Justice Harlan's separate opinion asserted that the "ultimate substantive question" was whether "the character of the State's involvement in an arbitrary discrimination is such that it should be held *responsible* for the discrimination." In another sit-in case resting on narrow grounds, Lombard v. Louisiana, 373 U.S. 267 (1963), Justice Douglas argued that state courts cannot "put criminal sanctions behind racial discrimination in public places." He distinguished the restaurant situation from "an intrusion of a man's home or yard or farm or garden," where "the property owner could seek and obtain the aid of the State against the intruder." But the restaurant had "no aura of constitutionally protected privacy about it."

Another group of five sit-in cases reached the Court in 1964. The trespass convictions were once again reversed on narrow grounds; but this time six of the Justices reached the broader issues at last—and divided 3-3. BELL v. MARYLAND, 378 U.S. 226 (1964). None of the opinions took a "simple" view of Shelley. For example, Justice DOUGLAS, joined by Justice Goldberg, reiterated his approach in Lombard and emphasized that restaurant discrimination "did not reflect 'personal' prejudices but business reasons." This was not property associated with privacy interests, but "property that is serving the public." And he argued that Shelley should govern here: "The preferences involved in [Shelley] were far more personal than the motivations of the corporate managers in the present case."[6] Justice BLACK's dissent in Bell, joined by Justices Harlan and White, viewed Shelley and the reach of § 1 of the 14th Amendment more narrowly.[7] Justice Black insisted that § 1 "does not of itself, standing alone, in the absence of some cooperative state action or compulsion, forbid property holders, including restaurant owners, to ban people from entering or remaining upon their premises, even if the owners act out of racial prejudice." He elaborated: "[R]eliance [on Shelley] is misplaced. [The]

the soundness of the most recent decision in the Girard College litigation?]

6. Justice GOLDBERG, joined by Chief Justice Warren and Justice Douglas, also submitted a separate opinion, concluding: "[Under] the Constitution no American can, or should, be denied rights fundamental to freedom and citizenship." Cf. Karst, "Foreword: Equal Citizenship under the 14th Amendment," 91 Harv.L.Rev. 1 (1977).

7. Justice Black's opinion also included an important suggestion of a congressional power to reach further into the private sphere under § 5 of the 14th Amendment than the Court itself could properly go in its interpretations of § 1. He stated that § 1, "unlike [the congressional enforcement power under § 5], is a prohibition against certain conduct only when done by a State." See sec. 3 below.

reason judicial enforcement of the restrictive covenants in Shelley was deemed state action was not merely the fact that a state court had acted, but rather that state enforcement of the covenants had the effect of denying to the parties their federally guaranteed right to own, occupy, enjoy, and use their property without regard to race or color. Thus, the line of cases from [Buchanan v. Warley, the racial zoning ordinance case,] through Shelley establishes these propositions: (1) When an owner of property is willing to sell and a would-be purchaser is willing to buy, then the Civil Rights Act of 1866, which gives all persons the same right to 'inherit, lease, sell, hold and convey' property, prohibits a State [from] preventing the sale on the grounds of the race or color of one of the [parties]. (2) Once a person has become a property owner, then he acquires all the rights that go with ownership. [When] *both* parties are willing parties, then the principles stated in Buchanan and Shelley protect this right. But equally, when one party is unwilling, as when the property owner chooses *not* to sell to a particular person or *not* to admit that person, then [he] is entitled to rely on the guarantee of due process of law [to] protect his free use and enjoyment of property." (Soon after this decision, the Court held in Hamm v. Rock Hill, 379 U.S. 306 (1964), that the enactment of the 1964 Civil Rights Act abated prosecutions against persons who (if the Act had been in force at the time of the sit-in) would have been entitled to service.)

5. *Transitional note.* Recall the questions raised at the beginning of this group of notes about the possible explanations for, and limits upon, the Shelley principle. What are the limits suggested by the materials in these notes? Do the cases below indicate additional limits on broad readings of Shelley and suggest different directions for delineating the scope of the state action concept? The Burton case, which follows, requires state involvement "to some significant extent" to convert private action into unconstitutional discrimination. What constitutes the requisite state involvement? What is the relevance of the use of state property? Of state regulation? Of licensing? Of conferral of other state benefits? Does Reitman, p. 948 below, indicate that state "encouragement" is enough? When does the state "encourage" private discrimination? Is state authorization enough? Can state "authorization" be distinguished from mere failure to prohibit private discrimination when the state has the power to do so?

———

Burton v. Wilmington Parking Authority

365 U.S. 715, 81 S.Ct. 856, 6 L.Ed.2d 45 (1961).

Justice CLARK delivered the opinion of the Court.

In this action for declaratory and injunctive relief it is admitted that the Eagle Coffee Shoppe, Inc., a restaurant located within an off-street automobile parking building in Wilmington, Delaware, has refused to serve appellant food or drink solely because he is a Negro. The parking building is owned and operated by the Wilmington Parking Authority, an agency of the State of Delaware, and the restaurant is the Authority's lessee. [The Supreme Court of Delaware] held that Eagle was acting in "a purely private capacity" under its lease; that its action was not that of the Authority and was not, therefore, state action. [It] also held that under 24 Del.Code § 1501[1] Eagle was a restaurant,

1. The statute provided that: "No keeper of an inn, tavern, hotel, or restaurant, or other place of public entertainment or refreshment of travelers, guests, or customers

not an inn, and that as such it "is not required [under Delaware law] to serve any and all persons entering its place of business." [We conclude] that the exclusion of appellant [was] discriminatory state action. The Authority was created [to] provide adequate parking facilities for the convenience of the public. [Its] first project [was] the erection of a parking facility. [T]he Authority was advised by its retained experts that the anticipated revenue from the parking of cars and proceeds from sale of its bonds would not be sufficient to finance the construction costs of the facility. [To] secure additional capital [the] Authority decided it was necessary to enter long-term leases with responsible tenants for commercial use of some of the space available in the projected "garage building." [In] April 1957 such a private lease, for 20 years, [was] made with [Eagle] for use as a "restaurant." [The lease] contains no requirement that [the] restaurant services be made available to the general public on a nondiscriminatory basis, in spite of the fact that the Authority has power to adopt rules and regulations respecting the use of its facilities. [Upon] completion of the building, the Authority located at appropriate places thereon official signs indicating the public character of the building, and flew from mastheads on the roof both the state and national flags.

[It has always been clear] since the Civil Rights Cases [that] private conduct abridging individual rights does no violence to [equal protection] unless to some significant extent the State in any of its manifestations has been found to have become involved in it. Because the virtue of the right to [equal protection] could only lie in the breadth of its application, its constitutional assurance was reserved in terms whose imprecision was necessary if the right were to be enjoyed in the variety of individual-state relationships which the Amendment was designed to embrace. For the same reason, to fashion and apply a precise formula for recognition of state responsibility under [equal protection] is "an impossible task" which "this Court has never attempted." Only by sifting facts and weighing circumstances can the nonobvious involvement of the State in private conduct be attributed its true significance. [T]he Delaware Supreme Court seems to have placed controlling emphasis on its conclusion that only some 15% of the total cost of the facility was "advanced" from public funds; that the cost of the entire facility was allocated three-fifths to the space for commercial leasing and two-fifths to parking space; that anticipated revenue from parking was only some 30.5% of the total income, the balance of which was expected to be earned by the leasing; [that] the restaurant's main and marked public entrance is on Ninth Street without any public entrance direct from the parking area; and that "the only connection Eagle has with the public facility [is] the furnishing [of] rent which is used by the Authority to defray a portion of the operating expense of an otherwise unprofitable enterprise." While these factual considerations are indeed validly accountable aspects of the [enterprise], we cannot say that they lead inescapably to the conclusion that state action is not present. Their persuasiveness is diminished when evaluated in the context of other [factors]. The land and building were publicly owned. As an entity, the building was dedicated to "public uses" in performance of the Authority's "essential governmental functions." The costs of land acquisition, construction, and maintenance are defrayed entirely from donations by the City of Wilmington, from loans and revenue bonds and from the proceeds of rentals and parking services out of which the loans and bonds were payable. Assuming that the distinction would be significant, cf. Derring-

shall be obliged by law, to furnish entertainment or refreshment to persons whose reception or entertainment by him would be offensive to the major part of his customers, and would injure his [business]." [Footnote by Justice Clark. Cf. the separate opinions, below.]

ton v. Plummer [note 1 below], the commercially leased areas were not surplus state property, but constituted a physically and financially integral and, indeed, indispensable part of the State's plan to operate its project as a self-sustaining unit. [It] cannot be doubted that the peculiar relationship of the restaurant to the parking facility in which it is located confers on each an incidental variety of mutual benefits. [Neither] can it be ignored, especially in view of Eagle's affirmative allegation that for it to serve Negroes would injure its business, that profits earned by discrimination not only contribute to, but are indispensable elements in, the financial success of a governmental agency.

Addition of all these activities, obligations and responsibilities of the Authority, the benefits mutually conferred, together with the obvious fact that the restaurant is operated as an integral part of a public building devoted to a public parking service, indicates that degree of state participation and involvement in discriminatory action which it was the design of the 14th Amendment to condemn. It is irony amounting to grave injustice that in one part of a single building, erected and maintained with public funds by an agency of the State to serve a public purpose, all persons have equal rights, while in another portion, also serving the public, a Negro is a second-class citizen. [In] its lease with Eagle the Authority could have affirmatively required Eagle to discharge the responsibilities under the 14th Amendment imposed upon the private enterprise as a consequence of state participation. But no State may effectively abdicate its responsibilities by either ignoring them or by merely failing to discharge them whatever the motive may be. It is of no consolation to an individual denied [equal protection] that it was done in good faith. [By] its inaction, the Authority, and through it the State, has not only made itself a party to the refusal of service, but has elected to place its power, property and prestige behind the admitted discrimination. The State has so far insinuated itself into a position of interdependence with Eagle that it must be recognized as a joint participant in the challenged activity, which, on that account, cannot be considered to have been so "purely private" as to fall without the scope of the 14th Amendment.

Because readily applicable formulae may not be fashioned, the conclusions drawn [from] this record are by no means declared as universal truths on the basis of which every state leasing agreement is to be tested. Owing to the very "largeness" of government, a multitude of relationships might appear to some to fall within the Amendment's embrace, but that, it must be remembered, can be determined only in the framework of the peculiar facts or circumstances present. Therefore respondents' prophecy of nigh universal application of a constitutional precept so peculiarly dependent for its invocation upon appropriate facts fails to take into account "Differences in circumstances [which] beget appropriate differences in law." [Specifically,] defining the limits of our inquiry, what we hold today is that when a State leases public property in the manner and for the purpose shown to have been the case here, the proscriptions of the 14th Amendment must be complied with by the lessee as certainly as though they were binding covenants written into the agreement [itself].

Reversed and remanded.

Justice STEWART, concurring.

I agree that the judgment must be reversed, but I reach that conclusion by a route much more direct than the one traveled by the Court. In upholding Eagle's right to deny service to the appellant solely because of his race, the [state court] relied upon a [state law] which permits the proprietor of a restaurant to refuse to serve "persons whose reception or entertainment by him would be offensive to the major part of his customers." There is no suggestion in the record that the appellant as an individual was such a person. The [state court] has thus construed this legislative enactment as authorizing discriminatory classification based exclusively on color. Such a law seems to me clearly violative of the [14th Amendment].

Justice HARLAN, whom Justice WHITTAKER joins, dissenting.

The Court's opinion, by a process of first undiscriminatingly throwing together various factual bits and pieces and then undermining the resulting structure by an equally vague disclaimer, seems to me to leave completely at sea just what it is in this record that satisfies the requirement of "state action." I find it unnecessary, however, to inquire into the matter at this stage, for it seems to me apparent [that] the case should first be sent back to the state court for clarification as to the precise basis of its decision. [If Justice Stewart is correct,] I would certainly agree [with his conclusion]. [If], on the other hand, the state court meant no more than that under the statute, as at common law, Eagle was free to serve only those whom it pleased, then, and only then, would the question of "state action" be presented in full-blown [form]. [Justice FRANKFURTER's dissent also urged that the case be sent back to the state court.]

STATE INVOLVEMENT IN PRIVATE ACTION—"TO SOME SIGNIFICANT EXTENT"

Does the Burton majority retreat from the broadest implications of Shelley, by insisting that the state must be involved "to some significant extent" to bring private conduct under the 14th Amendment? Under Burton, it is not enough to find merely *some* nexus between the state and the private discriminator. Does Burton provide adequate guidance for evaluating the "significance" of state involvement? (See Lewis, "Burton v. Wilmington Parking Authority—A Case Without Precedent," 61 Colum.L.Rev. 1458 (1961).) In pursuing the search for indicia of "significant" state involvement, consider the factors appraised in the cases in the following notes.

1. *Leases and sales of public property.* Was the critical factor in Burton the lease of public property? The Burton majority cited Derrington v. Plummer, 240 F.2d 922 (5th Cir.1956), cert. denied, 353 U.S. 924 (1957), where a county had equipped a courthouse basement as a cafeteria and leased it to a private party who refused to serve blacks. The lease required that the cafeteria be open during courthouse hours and that the operator give a discount to county employees. The court held that an injunction against renewal of the lease should be granted: although "a county may in good faith [lawfully] dispose of its surplus property," the property here was not surplus and the purpose of the lease was to furnish service to courthouse users. The court concluded that the county was providing services "through the instrumentality" of the lease and that the lessee accordingly "stands in the place of the County."

2. *Use of public property by private groups.* The question in GILMORE v. MONTGOMERY, 417 U.S. 556 (1974), was the propriety of a federal court injunction barring a city from permitting private segregated school groups and racially discriminatory non-school groups to use its recreational facilities. The Court had little difficulty in sustaining that portion of the injunction that barred *exclusive* temporary use of public recreational facilities by segregated private schools; that clearly interfered with an outstanding federal court school

desegregation order.[1] But the Court had greater difficulty with *nonexclusive* use of recreational facilities by private schools and other segregated groups. Justice BLACKMUN's prevailing opinion remanded that problem for further consideration: "Upon this record, we are unable to draw a conclusion as to whether the use of zoos, museums, parks, and other recreational facilities by private school groups in common with others, and by private nonschool organizations, involves government so directly in the actions of those users as to warrant court intervention on constitutional grounds." The Court emphasized the need for a particularized examination of the circumstances in accordance with the approach of Burton. If the uses could be identified as undermining outstanding desegregation orders for public schools and parks, the case would be relatively easy. But the "problem of private group use is much more complex" if the decision had to turn solely on state action principles. He elaborated: "[The] portion of the District Court's order prohibiting the mere use of such facilities by *any* segregated 'private group, club or organization' is invalid because it was not predicated upon a proper finding of state action. [If,] however, the city or other governmental entity rations otherwise freely accessible recreational facilities, the case for state action will naturally be stronger than if the facilities are simply available to all comers without condition or reservation. Here, for example, petitioners allege that the city engages in scheduling softball games for an all-white church league and provides balls, equipment, fields and lighting. The city's role in that situation would be dangerously close to what was found to exist in Burton."[2]

3. *Governmental involvement through licensing.* Does governmental licensing of a private actor constitute sufficient governmental involvement to warrant the application of constitutional restraints? Does the nature of the licensing scheme make a difference? For example, are licenses that certify qualifications distinguishable from licenses that grant special rights to use scarce resources? In Garner v. Louisiana, 368 U.S. 157 (1961), one of the sit-in cases, Justice Douglas's separate opinion suggested that licensing and regula-

---

1. Does this suggest that a governmental body under a duty to undo the effects of past de jure segregation is less free to make public property available to private discriminatory groups than bodies that have not practiced de jure segregation? Note Norwood v. Harrison, 413 U.S. 455 (1973), holding that Mississippi could not lend textbooks to students in private segregated schools under a long-established program for providing books to all public and private school students. Compare McGlotten v. Connally, 338 F.Supp. 448 (D.D.C.1972), holding that the Government could neither grant tax exemptions nor allow charitable deductions for gifts to discriminating fraternal orders. Though every tax deduction confers benefits, that was not enough to impose constitutional restraints on the beneficiary; here, however, the Government was "sufficiently entwined with private parties" to make the Constitution applicable, in part because of "the aura of government approval inherent in an exempt ruling." See also Green v. Connally, 330 F.Supp. 1150 (D.D.C.), affirmed, 404 U.S. 997 (1971); Bittker & Kaufman, "Taxes and Civil Rights:

'Constitutionalizing' the Internal Revenue Code," 82 Yale L.J. 51 (1972). Note also the ruling, in partial reliance on Green, sustaining the IRS's denial of tax exemptions to racially discriminatory private schools, in Bob Jones University v. United States, 461 U.S. 574 (1983).

2. There were several concurring opinions. Note especially the comments on Burton in Justice WHITE's concurrence, joined by Justice Douglas: "[There] is very plainly state action of some sort involved in the leasing, rental or extending the use of scarce city-owned recreation facilities to [private groups]. The question [is] whether the conceded state action [is] such that the State must be deemed to have denied [equal protection]. [Under Burton,] it is perfectly clear that to violate [equal protection] the State itself need not make, advise or authorize the private decision to discriminate that involves the State in the practice of segregation or would appear to do so in the minds of ordinary citizens."

tion of a restaurant made it a "public facility" and constituted adequate state action. (The majority disposed of the case on narrower grounds.)

a. *Liquor licenses.* The full Court confronted the relevance of licensing in MOOSE LODGE NO. 107 v. IRVIS, 407 U.S. 163 (1972). That 6-3 decision rejected a claim that a private club's racial discrimination was unconstitutional because the club held a state liquor license. In Moose Lodge, the club had refused service in its dining room and bar to a Lodge member's black guest. The lower federal court sustained Irvis's state action claim and declared the Lodge's liquor license invalid. But the Court found that, with one exception, the operation of the state liquor regulation scheme did "not sufficiently implicate the State in the discriminatory guest policies of Moose Lodge so as to make the latter 'State action.' " Justice REHNQUIST, citing Shelley, conceded that "the impetus for the forbidden discrimination need not originate with the State if it is state action that enforces privately originated discrimination." But that did not mean "that discrimination by an otherwise private entity would be violative of [equal protection] if the private entity receives any sort of benefit or service at all from the state, or if it is subject to state regulation in any degree whatever. Since state-furnished services include such necessities of life as electricity, water, and police and fire protection, such a holding would utterly emasculate the distinction between private as distinguished from State conduct." To find unconstitutional state action in situations "where the impetus for the discrimination is private, the State must have 'significantly involved itself with invidious discriminations.' " And he found no such involvement here, emphasizing the distinctions between the Lodge situation and Burton. Here, for example, there was "nothing approaching the symbiotic relationship between lessor and lessee" in Burton. The lower court had emphasized that the liquor regulations were "pervasive." Justice Rehnquist responded: "However detailed this type of regulation may be in some particulars, it cannot be said to in any way foster or encourage racial discrimination." And that conclusion was not undercut by the fact that Pennsylvania limited the number of liquor licenses in each city, since that fell "far short of conferring upon club licensees a monopoly in the dispensing of liquor."

Justice DOUGLAS's dissent explained that he would *not* apply constitutional restrictions to private clubs simply because they had a state license of some kind. He noted that First Amendment and related guarantees create "a zone of privacy"; accordingly, the fact that the Lodge had a racially restrictive policy was "constitutionally irrelevant." Moreover, earlier cases in which he had suggested a state nexus because of licensing (see Garner, above) were inapposite, because a private club "is not in the public domain," and its getting "some kind of permit from the [state] does not make it ipso facto a public [enterprise], any more than the grant to a householder of a permit to operate an incinerator puts the householder in the public domain." But here, there were "special circumstances" distinguishable from the ordinary licensing situation. Here, the State was "putting the weight of its liquor license, concededly a valued and important adjunct to a private club, behind racial discrimination." Here, a group desiring to form a nondiscriminatory club would have to "purchase a license held by an existing club, which can exact a monopoly price for the transfer." And "without a liquor license a fraternal organization would be hard-pressed to survive."[3]

---

3. Justice Marshall joined Justice Douglas's dissent, as well as one by Justice Brennan. Justice BRENNAN stressed the "pervasive regulatory schemes under which the State dictates and continually supervises virtually every detail of the operation of a licensee's business." He thought this state involvement sufficient to fall within the princi-

b. *Broadcast licenses.* In CBS, INC. v. DEMOCRATIC NAT. COMM., 412 U.S. 94 (1973), the majority sustained the FCC's refusal to compel broadcasters to accept editorial advertisements. (The Court's analysis of the First Amendment issues is considered at p. 1453 below.) In the course of the disposition, several of the Justices also addressed the "novel question" whether "the action of a broadcast licensee such as that challenged here is 'governmental action' for purposes of the First Amendment." Chief Justice BURGER concluded "that the policies complained of do not constitute governmental action," but the Chief Justice was joined only by Justices Stewart and Rehnquist in that conclusion.[4] The Chief Justice noted that the FCC had not "fostered the licensee policy challenged here; it [had] simply declined to command particular action because it fell within the area of journalistic discretion." He concluded: "Thus, it cannot be said that the government is a 'partner' to the action of the broadcast licensee complained of here, nor is it engaged in a 'symbiotic relationship' with the licensee, profiting from the invidious discrimination of its proxy. Compare [Moose Lodge] with [Burton]. The First Amendment does not reach acts of private parties in every instance where the Congress or the Commission has merely permitted or failed to prohibit such acts."

c. *Transitional Note: The relevance of governmental licensing, regulation, and benefits.* Reexamine what the relevance of governmental licensing and regulation should be in determining whether constitutional guarantees are applicable to private actors. Should licensing be sufficient only when special benefits, such as monopolies, are conferred? Should regulation or grants of benefits suffice only when the regulation or benefits are immediately relevant to the particular challenged practices of the private actor? (See Powe v. Miles, 407 F.2d 73 (2d Cir.1968): "[The] state must be involved not simply with some activity of the institution [but] with the activity that caused the injury.") The Court reexamined these problems in 1974, in Jackson, p. 952 below. Consideration of that case is postponed until after Reitman, which follows. Reitman considered the problem of state "encouragement" of private discrimination, and raised again an issue first suggested by the separate opinions in Burton: the extent to which state failure to prohibit private discrimination constitutes "authorization."

STATE ACTION THROUGH STATE "ENCOURAGEMENT" AND "AUTHORIZATION"

REITMAN v. MULKEY, 387 U.S. 369 (1967): In 1959 and in 1963, California enacted fair housing laws barring racial discrimination in the sale or rental of private dwellings. In 1964, California voters, acting through the initiative process, adopted Proposition 14, amending the state constitution to

ple banning all state efforts "to authorize, encourage, or otherwise support racial discrimination in a particular facet of life." (Soon after the Irvis decision, Mr. Irvis won his battle on the basis of state law. The Pennsylvania Supreme Court sustained an administrative ruling under the state public accommodations law ordering the Lodge to end its ban on black guests.)

4. Justice BRENNAN's dissent, joined by Justice Marshall, found ample "governmental involvement" to justify application of the First Amendment. He recited the "myriad indicia" of governmental involvement, "including the public nature of the airwaves, the governmentally preferred status of broadcasters, the extensive Government regulation of broadcast programming, and the specific governmental approval of the challenged policy."

prohibit the state from denying "the right of any person [to] decline to sell, lease or rent [real property] to such person or persons as he, in his absolute discretion, chooses." The Mulkeys sued in a state court on the basis of the fair housing laws, claiming that Reitman had refused to rent them an apartment because of their race. They claimed that Proposition 14, which in effect repealed the antidiscrimination laws, violated equal protection, and they prevailed in California's supreme court. (The state court relied on federal precedents, finding, e.g., that the California situation was "undeniably analogous" to the "authorizing" of racial discrimination found by Justice Stewart's concurrence in Burton.) The Court affirmed the state judgment.

Justice WHITE's majority opinion in the 5-4 decision acknowledged that mere repeal of an antidiscrimination law did not establish unconstitutional state action. But the state court here, he claimed, had not "read either our cases or the 14th Amendment as establishing an automatic constitutional barrier to the repeal of an existing [antidiscrimination] law. [Instead, the state court held that] the intent of [Proposition 14] was to authorize private racial discrimination in the housing market, to repeal the [fair housing laws], and to create a constitutional right to discriminate on racial [grounds]. [Moreover,] the court assessed the ultimate impact of [Proposition 14] in the California environment and concluded that [it] would encourage and significantly involve the State in private racial [discrimination]. Private discriminations in housing were now not only free from [fair housing laws] but they also enjoyed a far different status than was true before the passage of those [laws]. The right to discriminate [was] now embodied in the State's basic charter, immune from legislative, executive, or judicial regulation at any level of the state government. Those practicing racial discriminations need no longer rely solely on their personal choice. They could now invoke express constitutional [authority]. [Here] the California court, armed as it was with the knowledge of the facts and circumstances concerning the passage and potential impact of [Proposition 14], and familiar with the milieu in which that provision would operate, has determined that [it] would involve the State in private racial discriminations to an unconstitutional degree. We accept this holding of the California court." Justice White added that none of the Court's precedents "squarely controls the case we now have before us. But they [do] exemplify the necessity for a court to assess the potential impact of official action in determining whether the State has significantly involved itself with invidious discriminations. Here we are dealing with a provision which does not just repeal an existing law forbidding private racial discriminations. [Proposition 14] was intended to authorize, and does authorize, racial discrimination in the housing market. [The state court] believes that [it] will significantly encourage and involve the State in private discriminations. We have been presented with no persuasive considerations indicating that this judgment should be overturned."[1]

1. Justice DOUGLAS joined the Court's opinion but added a comment suggesting that the actions of real estate brokers were akin to zoning and invoking the analogy of the public-function cases. [Recall and compare Hunter v. Erickson (1969; p. 790 above), invalidating an Akron charter amendment requiring that any local ordinance banning racial discrimination in housing must be submitted to a referendum of voters. In Hunter, Justice White found it unnecessary to elaborate on Reitman because in Hunter, unlike Reitman, "there was an explicitly racial classification treating racial housing matters differently from other racial and housing matters." Compare also Romer v. Evans (1996; p. 737 above), where the state court had relied on Hunter in striking down a Colorado constitutional amendment barring laws directed at discrimination against homosexuals; the Court, however, relied on other equal protection principles in reaching the same result.]

Justice HARLAN's dissent, joined by Justices Black, Clark, and Stewart, insisted: "[All] that has happened is that California has effected a pro tanto repeal of its prior statutes forbidding private discrimination. This runs no more afoul of the 14th Amendment than would have California's failure to pass any such antidiscrimination statutes in the first instance. The fact that such repeal was also accompanied by a constitutional prohibition against future enactment of such laws [cannot] affect [the] validity of what California has done. The 14th Amendment does not reach such state constitutional action any more than it does a simple legislative repeal of legislation forbidding private discrimination." He sharply criticized the majority's reliance on the alleged findings of fact by the state court. Here, there were "no disputed issues of fact at all. [The] only 'factual' matter relied on by the [state court] was the context in which Proposition 14 was adopted. [This,] of course, is nothing but a legal conclusion as to federal constitutional law. [I] cannot see that its conclusion is entitled to any special weight in the discharge of our own responsibilities. [It] seems to me manifest that the state court decision rested entirely on what that court conceived to be the compulsion of the 14th Amendment, not on any factfinding by the state courts." More broadly, Justice Harlan objected to the majority's emphasis on the notion that Proposition 14 *encourages* private discrimination": "By focusing on 'encouragement' the Court, I fear, is forging a slippery and unfortunate criterion by which to measure the constitutionality of a statute simply permissive in purpose and effect, and inoffensive on its face. [Here,] we have only the straightforward adoption of a neutral provision restoring to the sphere of free choice [private] behavior within a limited area of the racial problem. The denial of equal protection emerges only from the conclusion [that] the implementation of a new policy of governmental neutrality [has] the effect of lending encouragement to those who wish to discriminate. [This] conclusion appears to me to state only a truism. [A] moment of thought will reveal the far-reaching possibilities of the Court's new doctrine. [Every] act of private discrimination is either forbidden by state law or permitted by it. There can be little doubt that such permissiveness—whether by express constitutional or statutory provision, or implicit in the common law—to some extent 'encourages' those who wish to discriminate to do so. Under this theory 'state action' in the form of laws that do nothing more than passively permit private discrimination could be said to tinge *all* private discrimination with the taint of unconstitutional state encouragement. [I] believe the state action required to bring the 14th Amendment into operation must be affirmative and purposeful, actively fostering discrimination. [I] think that this decision is not only constitutionally unsound, but in its practical potentialities short-sighted. Opponents of state antidiscrimination statutes are now in a position to argue that such legislation should be defeated because, if enacted, it may be [unrepealable]."

State "encouragement." What is the reach of the "encouragement" theme of Reitman? Can a state provision that keeps hands off private discrimination, or "authorizes"—by failing to forbid—private discrimination, be deemed an "encouragement"? Was Proposition 14 truly distinguishable from a mere repeal of an anti-discrimination law? Was there a significant difference here because California did not merely repeal anti-discrimination laws but incorporated that repeal into a constitutional provision? Why should that make a difference? Was the flaw the effect of Proposition 14 in disadvantaging racial minorities, and the lack of the heavy justification required to support such an impact? Would that view be consistent with Washington v. Davis (p. 755 above)? Does Reitman ultimately rest on the notion that a state simply may not "authorize" racial discrimination?

"Authorization" of racial discrimination. Recall the separate opinions in Burton, indicating that a finding of a state "authorization" of private discrimination would be a "more direct," "easy road to decision." Was that truly an easier route? Justice Stewart in Burton was willing to find "authorization." And Justice Harlan in Burton suggested that a finding of "authorization," if the statute could be construed that way, would indeed be a narrower ground. Yet both Justices dissented in Reitman. What kind of "authorization" did they have in mind in Burton? Is "authorization" really any different from failure to prohibit what the state has power to prohibit? Is the "authorization" rationale tantamount to imposing an affirmative duty on the state to prevent private discrimination? Is such "authorization" of unrestrained private choices, by constitutional provision, statute, or common law, "significant involvement" by the state?

Transitional Note. Despite the far-reaching statements about "authorization" and "encouragement" in the cases of the 1960s, the modern Court has refused to apply those concepts broadly. For example, the enforcement of the reverter in the Baconsfield park case, Evans v. Abney, above, could have been considered "authorization" in the sense of some of the earlier cases. And Justice Brennan's dissent in that 1970 case recited "significant" state involvements that were arguably as substantial as those in Burton and Reitman. After Reitman and before Abney, some commentators, noting that no modern Court decision had rejected a racial discrimination claim because of the state action barrier, suggested that the concept was moribund. See e.g., C.L. Black, Jr., "Foreword: 'State Action,' Equal Protection and California's Proposition 14," 81 Harv.L.Rev. 69 (1967). But Abney made it clear that the state action barrier was very much alive. And the more recent decisions, beginning with the Moose Lodge case in 1972 and continuing with the later rulings, below, make it even clearer that the state action barrier remains and indeed has gained new strength.

Reexamine the various, often inchoate, strands that contributed to the expansion of the state action principle through the 1960s in light of the 1974 decision in Jackson, which follows. Note that the rejections of the state action claims in Jackson (and in Flagg Bros. in 1978) occurred in the context of procedural due process assertions, not racial discrimination claims. Should state action criteria be interpreted differently depending on the claims involved? For example, would the public utility in Jackson be subjected to constitutional restraints if it cut off services on racially discriminatory bases? (Note Justice Marshall's dissent in Jackson.) As noted earlier, the Court's unwillingness to intrude further into the private sphere under § 1 of the 14th Amendment may well be related to the growing congressional resort to its power to reach private activities, under the commerce and spending powers and under § 5 of the 14th Amendment. The Court's curtailment of state action coverage may also be related to the newly recognized congressional power to deal with private racial discrimination under § 2 of the 13th Amendment, presumably making the state action analysis unnecessary in the racial discrimination context. However, given the broad range of due process rights now "incorporated" into the 14th Amendment—rights from free speech to procedural due process—the "state action" problem retains vitality, as the next case illustrates. (The scope of congressional enforcement power to move beyond where the Court has gone under the post-Civil War Amendments is the focus of the remaining sections of this chapter. See, e.g., Jones v. Alfred H. Mayer Co. (1968; p. 978 below), analyzed by the lower courts on the basis of 14th

Amendment state action analysis but decided by the Court under the 13th Amendment-based 42 U.S.C. § 1982.)

Jackson v. Metropolitan Edison Co.

419 U.S. 345, 95 S.Ct. 449, 42 L.Ed.2d 477 (1974).

[Petitioner Catherine Jackson brought a federal civil rights action under 42 U.S.C. § 1983 against respondent Metropolitan Edison Co., a private company subject to extensive state regulation because it held a certificate of public convenience from the Pennsylvania Public Utilities Commission (PUC) empowering it to deliver electricity to a specific service area. She sought damages and injunctive relief against the Company for terminating her electric service for alleged nonpayment, claiming that she had not been afforded notice, hearing, and an opportunity to pay any amounts found due. She claimed that under state law she was entitled to reasonably continuous electrical service and that the Company's termination was state action depriving her of property without procedural due process. The lower courts dismissed her complaint.]

Justice REHNQUIST delivered the opinion of the [Court].

[The] mere fact that a business is subject to state regulation does not by itself convert its action into that of the State for purposes of the 14th Amendment. [Moose Lodge.] Nor does the fact that the regulation is extensive and detailed, as in the case of most public utilities, do so. [PUC v. Pollak (1952; discussed below).] It may well be that acts of a heavily regulated utility with at least something of a governmentally protected monopoly will more readily be found to be "state" acts than will the acts of an entity lacking these characteristics. But the inquiry must be whether there is a sufficiently close nexus between the State and the challenged action of the regulated entity so that the action of the latter may be fairly treated as that of the State itself. The true nature of the State's involvement may not be immediately obvious, and detailed inquiry may be required in order to determine whether the test is met. [Burton.] Petitioner advances a series of contentions which, in her view, lead to the conclusion that this case should fall on the Burton side of the line drawn in the Civil Rights Cases, rather than on the Moose Lodge side of that line. We find none of them persuasive. Petitioner first argues that "state action" is present because of the monopoly status allegedly conferred upon [Metropolitan]. As a factual matter, it may well be doubted that the State ever granted or guaranteed Metropolitan a monopoly.[1] But assuming that it had, this fact is not determinative in considering whether Metropolitan's termination of service to petitioner was "state action." In Pollak [below], [we] expressly disclaimed reliance on the monopoly status of the transit authority. Similarly, although certain monopoly aspects were presented in [Moose Lodge], we found that the lodge's action was not subject to the provisions of the 14th Amendment. In each of those cases, there was insufficient relationship between the challenged actions of the entities involved and their monopoly status. There is no indication of any greater connection here. Petitioner next urges that state action is present because respondent provides an essential public service [and] hence

----

1. [Such] public utility companies are natural monopolies created by the economic forces of high threshold capital requirements and virtually unlimited economy of scale. Regulation was superimposed on such natural monopolies as a substitute for competition and not to eliminate [it]. [Footnote by Justice Rehnquist.]

performs a "public function." [The Court rejected that argument. (See p. 931 above.)]

We also reject the notion that Metropolitan's termination is state action because the State "has specifically authorized and approved" the termination practice. In the instant case, Metropolitan filed with the [PUC] a general tariff—a provision of which states Metropolitan's right to terminate service for nonpayment. This provision has appeared in Metropolitan's previously filed tariffs for many years and has never been the subject of a hearing or other scrutiny by the [PUC]. Although the Commission did hold hearings on portions of Metropolitan's general tariff relating to a general rate increase, it never even considered the reinsertion of this provision in the newly filed general [tariff]. The case most heavily relied on by petitioner is [Pollak]. There the Court dealt with the contention that Capital Transit's installation of a piped music system on its buses violated the First Amendment rights of the bus riders. It is not entirely clear whether the Court alternatively held that Capital Transit's action was action of the "State" for First Amendment purposes, or whether it merely assumed arguendo that it was and went on to resolve the First Amendment question adversely to the bus riders. In either event, the nature of the state involvement there was quite different than it is here. The [D.C. PUC], on its own motion, commenced an investigation of the effects of the piped music, and after a full hearing concluded not only that Capital Transit's practices were "not inconsistent with public convenience, comfort, and safety," but that the practice "in fact through the creation of better will among passengers, [tends] to improve the conditions under which the public rides." Here, on the other hand, there was no such imprimatur placed on the practice of Metropolitan about which petitioner complains. The nature of governmental regulation of private utilities is such that a utility may frequently be required by the state regulatory scheme to obtain approval for practices a business regulated in less detail would be free to institute without any approval from a regulatory body. Approval by a state utility commission of such a request from a regulated utility, where the Commission has not put its own weight on the side of the proposed practice by ordering it, does not transmute a practice initiated by the utility and approved by the Commission into "state action." At most, the Commission's failure to overturn this practice amounted to no more than a determination that [the] utility was authorized to employ such a practice if it so desired. Respondent's exercise of the choice allowed by state law, where the initiative comes from it and not from the State, does not make its action in doing so "state action" for purposes of the 14th Amendment. We also find absent in the instant case the symbiotic relationship presented in [Burton]. All of petitioner's arguments taken together show no more than that Metropolitan was a heavily regulated private utility, enjoying at least a partial monopoly in the providing of electrical service within its territory, and that it elected to terminate service to petitioner in a manner which the [PUC] found permissible under state law. Under our decision this is not sufficient to connect the [State] with respondent's action so as to make the latter's conduct attributable to the State for purposes of the 14th [Amendment].

Affirmed.[2]

2. A dissent by Justice DOUGLAS argued, inter alia, that Metropolitan's actions were "sufficiently intertwined with those of the State [to] warrant a holding [of] 'state action.'" He insisted that, under Burton, it was "not enough to examine seriatim each of the factors [and] to dismiss each individually as being insufficient to support a finding of state action. It is the aggregate that is controlling." Here, by contrast, the Court's underlying analysis was "fundamentally sequential rather than cumulative" and there-

Justice MARSHALL, [dissenting].

[Our] state action cases have repeatedly relied on several factors clearly presented by this case: a state-sanctioned monopoly; an extensive pattern of cooperation between the "private" entity and the state; and a service uniquely public in nature. Today the Court takes a major step in repudiating this line of [authority]. When the State confers a monopoly on a group or organization, this Court has held that the organization assumes many of the obligations of the State. Even when the Court has not found state action based solely on the State's conferral of a monopoly, it has suggested that the monopoly factor weighs heavily in determining whether constitutional obligations can be imposed on formally private entities. [The] majority distinguishes [prior] cases with a cryptic assertion that public utility companies are "natural monopolies." The theory behind the distinction appears to be that since the State's purpose in regulating a natural monopoly is not to aid the company but to prevent its charging monopoly prices, the State's involvement is somehow less significant for state action purposes. I cannot agree that so much should turn on so narrow a distinction. [The] difficulty inherent [in] economic analysis counsels against excusing natural monopolies from the reach of state action principles. [The] suggestion that the State would have to "put its own weight on the side of the proposed practice by ordering it" seems to me to mark a sharp departure from our previous state action cases. From the Civil Rights Cases to Moose Lodge, we have consistently indicated that state authorization and approval of "private" conduct would support a finding of state action. [Moreover,] I question the wisdom of giving such short shrift to the extensive interaction between the company and the State, and focusing solely on the extent of state support for the particular activity under challenge. In cases where the State's only significant involvement is through financial support or limited regulation of the private entity, it may be well to inquire whether the State's involvement suggests state approval of the objectionable conduct. But where the State has so thoroughly insinuated itself into the operations of the enterprise, it should not be fatal if the State has not affirmatively sanctioned the particular practice in question. [It also] seems to me in any event that the State *has* given its approval to Metropolitan Edison's termination [procedures]. [What] is perhaps most troubling about the Court's opinion is that it would appear to apply to a broad range of claimed constitutional violations by the company. The Court has not adopted the notion [that] different standards should apply to state action analysis when different constitutional claims are presented. Thus, the majority's analysis would seemingly apply as well to a company that refused to extend service to Negroes, welfare recipients, or any other group that the company preferred, for its own reasons, not to serve. I cannot believe that this Court would hold that the State's involvement with the utility company was not sufficient to impose upon the company an obligation to meet the constitutional mandate of nondiscrimination. Yet nothing in the analysis of the majority opinion suggests [otherwise].

———

FLAGG BROS., INC. v. BROOKS, 436 U.S. 149 (1978): As noted at p. 932 above, this decision reaffirmed the Burger Court majority's determination to view the state action concept narrowly. It held that a warehouseman's sale of

fore constituted "a significant departure"   also submitted a dissent.)
from previous cases. (Justice BRENNAN

bailed goods to satisfy a warehouseman's lien under the UCC was not state action. Most of the opinion, as noted earlier, rejected the "public function" argument. But the Court also rejected the claim that the warehouseman's proposed sale was "properly attributable to the State because the State has authorized and encouraged it in enacting [the UCC]." Justice REHNQUIST's majority opinion responded: "This Court [has] never held that a State's mere acquiescence in a private action converts that action into that of the State. The Court rejected a similar argument in [Jackson]. The clearest demonstration of this distinction appears in [Moose Lodge]. These cases clearly rejected the notion that our prior cases permitted the imposition of 14th Amendment restraints on private action by the simple device of characterizing the State's inaction as 'authorization' or 'encouragement.' It is quite immaterial that the State has embodied its decision not to act in statutory form. If New York had no commercial statutes at all, its courts would still be faced with the decision whether to prohibit or permit the sort of sale threatened here the first time an aggrieved bailor came before them for relief. A judicial decision to deny relief would be no less an 'authorization' or 'encouragement' of that sale than the legislature's decision embodied in this statute. [If] the mere denial of judicial relief is considered sufficient encouragement to make the State responsible for those private acts, all private deprivations of property would be converted into public acts whenever the State, for whatever reason, denies relief sought by the putative property owner. Not only is this notion completely contrary to [the] 'essential dichotomy' between public and private acts, but it has been previously rejected by this Court. [Evans v. Abney.] [New York] is in no way responsible for [the warehouseman's] decision, a decision which the [state] permits but does not compel, to threaten to sell these respondents' belongings."

Justice STEVENS's dissent, joined by Justices White and Marshall, criticized the "permission"-"compulsion" distinction as follows: "Under this approach a State could enact laws authorizing private citizens to use self-help in countless situations without any possibility of federal challenge. A state statute could authorize the warehouseman to retain all proceeds of the lien sale, even if they far exceeded the amount of the alleged debt; it could authorize finance companies to enter private homes to repossess merchandise; or indeed, it could authorize 'any person with sufficient physical power' to acquire and sell the property of his weaker neighbor. An attempt to challenge the validity of any such outrageous statute would be defeated by the reasoning the Court uses today: The Court's rationale would characterize action pursuant to such a statute as purely private action, which the State permits but does not compel. [As] these examples suggest, the [distinction] between 'permission' and 'compulsion' [cannot be the determinative factor] in state-action analysis. [New York,] by enacting [the UCC provision], has acted in the most effective and unambiguous way a State can act. This section specifically authorizes petitioner to sell respondents' possessions; it details the procedures that petitioner must follow; and it grants petitioner the power to convey good title to goods that are now owned by respondents to a third party. While Members of this Court have suggested that statutory authorization alone may be sufficient to establish a state action, it is not necessary to rely on those suggestions in this case because New York has authorized the warehouseman to perform what is clearly a state function."

STATE ACTION DOCTRINE SINCE THE 1980s

In three 1982 cases, the Court returned to the complexities of state action doctrine. In two of the cases, Blum and Rendell–Baker, the majority followed in the footsteps of the modern Court's earlier efforts to circumscribe the scope of the state action concept, and a number of later rulings have continued that trend. E.g., San Fran. Arts & Athletics v. U.S.O.C. (1987; p. 959 below). Thus, Justice Rehnquist, the author of the major narrowing opinions of the prior decade, Jackson and Flagg Bros., was in the majority in Blum and Rendell–Baker, and Justice Marshall dissented. But the third 1982 case, Lugar, produced a strikingly different alignment: Justices Brennan and Marshall were in the majority; Justice Rehnquist was among the dissenters. In examining these cases, consider whether the reformulations in Blum and Rendell–Baker clarify the reach of the modern state action doctrine, and whether Lugar departs from the usual modern approach.

1. *Blum.* In BLUM v. YARETSKY, 457 U.S. 991 (1982), the Court held that certain privately owned nursing homes receiving reimbursements from the state for caring for Medicaid patients were not state actors for purposes of the 14th Amendment claim raised here. A class of Medicaid patients had sued the nursing homes claiming that their procedural due process rights had been violated when they were transferred (by decisions of the physicians and administrators in the nursing homes) from "skilled nursing facilities" to less expensive "health related facilities." The transfer decisions resulted in lower Medicaid benefits for the patients. In turning down the claim that the transfer decision triggered the 14th Amendment's procedural due process requirements, Justice REHNQUIST's majority opinion rejected the argument that the State "affirmatively commands" the transfer. He was "not satisfied that the State is responsible for those decisions"; rather, the decisions ultimately turned "on medical judgments made by private parties according to professional standards that are not established by the State." The mere fact of extensive state regulation of the nursing homes did not trigger 14th Amendment guarantees. Citing Jackson, he stated that "constitutional standards are invoked only when it can be said that the State is *responsible* for the specific conduct of which the plaintiff complains"; here, by contrast, "the complaining party seeks to hold the State liable for the actions of private parties." He added that a state "normally can be held responsible for a private decision only when it has exercised a coercive power or has provided such significant encouragement, either overt or covert, that the choice must in law be deemed to be that of the State. Mere approval of or acquiescence in the initiatives of a private party is not sufficient to justify holding the State [responsible]." Nor was the Burton standard satisfied here simply because the State subsidized the operating and capital costs of the facilities, licensed them, and paid the medical expenses of more than 90% of the patients: "[Privately] owned enterprises providing services that the State would not necessarily provide, even though they are extensively regulated, do not fall within the ambit of Burton." (He also rejected the plaintiffs' "public function" argument.)[1]

2. *Rendell-Baker.* In RENDELL–BAKER v. KOHN, 457 U.S. 830 (1982), the majority, closely tracking Justice Rehnquist's approach in Blum, held that "a private school, whose income is derived primarily from public sources and

---

1. Justice WHITE concurred in the judgment on the basis of an analysis he developed more fully in Lugar, note 3 below. He stated that "respondents must show that the transfer [is] made on the basis of some rule of decision for which the State is responsible." Justice BRENNAN, joined by Justice Marshall, submitted a lengthy dissent, insisting that the majority had departed from Burton, had ignored "the nature of the regulatory framework," and had accordingly failed to perceive "the decisive involvement of the State in the private conduct challenged [here]." He insisted that the "imprint of state power on the private party's actions" was "even more significant" here than in Lugar.

which is regulated by public authorities," could not be considered as engaging in state action when it discharged certain employees. The employees had brought a federal civil rights action claiming that school officials, in firing them from the staff of a small private school for "maladjusted" students, had violated their constitutional rights to free speech and procedural due process. After examining all of the alleged indicia of state action, Chief Justice BURGER's majority opinion concluded that the school's action did not fall within the 14th Amendment. He noted that, even though public funds accounted for almost all of the school's operating budget, it was "not fundamentally different from many private corporations whose business depends primarily on contracts [with] the government. Acts of such private contractors do not become acts of the government by reason of their significant or even total engagement in performing public contracts."[2]

3. *Lugar.* In LUGAR v. EDMONDSON OIL CO., 457 U.S. 922, the third of the 1982 state action trilogy, the majority found the state action requirement satisfied. Lugar was the latest of a long series of cases (from Sniadach in 1969 through Flagg Bros. in 1978) considering procedural due process rights in creditors' summary remedies proceedings. The authors of the majority opinions in Blum and Rendell–Baker were among the dissenters in Lugar. In Lugar, a creditor had, pursuant to a state law, attached the debtor's property in an ex parte proceeding, alleging that the debtor might dispose of the property to defeat creditors. The attachment writ was issued by a state clerk, and the writ was executed by the Sheriff. In a later hearing, a state judge dismissed the attachment. The debtor brought suit against the creditor under § 1983, which authorizes damage actions for deprivation of constitutional rights "under color of any statute [of] any State." Justice WHITE's majority opinion began by holding that if the creditor's conduct was "state action" it also satisfied the statutory "under color of state law" requirement. On the constitutional issue, he stated: "The [central] question is whether, under the facts of this case, [the creditors], who are private parties, may be appropriately characterized as 'state actors.' [We] have consistently held that a private party's joint participation with state officials in the seizure of disputed property is sufficient to characterize that party as a 'state actor' for purposes of the 14th Amendment. [The lower court] erred in holding that in this context 'joint participation' required something more than invoking the aid of state officials to take advantage of state-created attachment procedures. That holding is contrary to the conclusions we have reached as to the applicability of due process standards to such procedures. Whatever may be true in other contexts, this is sufficient when the State has created a system whereby state officials will attach property on the ex parte application of one party to a private dispute."[3]

2. As in Blum, Justice WHITE concurred only in the judgment. Justice MARSHALL's dissent, joined by Justice Brennan, insisted that the State had "delegated to the [school] its statutory duty to educate children with special needs." He relied especially on the "symbiotic relationship" approach of Burton. He also noted that the school was "performing a vital public function." He concluded: "[This] decision [marks] a return to empty formalism in state action doctrine."

3. "Contrary to the suggestion of the dissent, we do not hold today that 'a private party's mere invocation of state legal proce-

dures constitutes 'joint participation' or 'conspiracy' with state [officials]. The holding today [is] limited to the particular context of prejudgment attachment." [Footnote by Justice White.] In finding Flagg Bros. distinguishable, Justice White relied in part on the fact that the creditor's remedy involved in Flagg Bros. (a warehouseman's sale pursuant to a statutory warehouseman's lien) could be exercised without the intervention of a state official, and simply pursuant to state procedures. Here, by contrast, the issuance and execution of the writ of attachment pursuant to the creditor's suit was undertaken by state

Chief Justice BURGER's dissent insisted that the creditor "did no more than invoke a presumptively valid state prejudgment attachment procedure available to all. Relying on a dubious 'but for' analysis, the Court erroneously concludes that the subsequent procedural steps taken by the State in attaching a putative debtor's property in some way transforms [the creditor's] acts into actions of the State. This case is no different from the situation in which a private party commences a lawsuit and secures injunctive relief which, even if temporary, may cause significant injury to the defendant. Invoking a judicial process, of course, implicates the State and its officers but does not transform essentially private conduct into actions of the State." In a longer dissent, Justice POWELL, joined by Justices Rehnquist and O'Connor, stated: "[This] decision is as unprecedented as it is unjust." He insisted that "our cases do not establish that a private party's mere invocation of state legal procedures constitutes 'joint participation.' [Instead,] recent decisions make clear that independent, private decisions made in the context of litigation cannot be said to occur under color of law." He added in a footnote: "The Court avers that its holding 'is limited to the particular context of prejudgment attachment.' However welcome, this limitation lacks a principled basis. It is unclear why a private party engages in state action when filing papers seeking an attachment of property, but not when seeking other relief (e.g., injunction), or when summoning police to investigate a suspected crime."

4. *Tarkanian.* In NCAA v. TARKANIAN, 488 U.S. 179 (1988), the Court was presented with what Justice STEVENS's opinion for a 5-4 majority described as a "mirror image" of a traditional state action case, for the state was involved in committing the final act pursuant to the encouragement of a private party, rather than the other way around. The private party was the National Collegiate Athletic Association (NCAA), which as a result of an investigation had discovered improprieties in the basketball program at the University of Nevada at Las Vegas (UNLV), a state university. Consequently, the NCAA, on threat of imposing even harsher sanctions, urged UNLV that it suspend its successful basketball coach, Jerry Tarkanian, for a two-year period. UNLV complied, and Tarkanian brought suit, claiming, inter alia, that the NCAA had deprived him of due process. At issue was whether the NCAA was to be considered a state actor as a result of its involvement here in essentially compelling the decision of UNLV, which was undoubtedly a state actor. Dismissing easily the claims that the NCAA was itself a state actor by virtue of its performance of a public function, the Court focused on the relationship between the NCAA and UNLV. In so doing Justice Stevens concluded that, unlike the relationship in Burton, here the parties were not in cooperation but were in fact adversaries: "UNLV used its best efforts to retain its winning coach—a goal diametrically opposed to the NCAA's interest in ascertaining the truth of its investigators' reports. [Here, the NCAA] is more correctly characterized as an agent of its remaining members which, as competitors of UNLV, had an interest in the effective and evenhanded enforcement of NCAA's recruitment standards. [Moreover, UNLV] retained the authority to withdraw from the NCAA and establish its own standards. [Neither] UNLV's decision to adopt the NCAA's standards nor its minor role in their formulation is a sufficient reason for concluding that the NCAA was acting under color of Nevada law when it promulgated standards governing athlete recruitment, eligibility, and academic performance. [We] conclude that UNLV has conducted its athletic program under color of the policies adopted by the NCAA, rather

officials. [On the "joint participation" rationale invoked in Lugar, see also United States v. Price (1966; p. 968 below).]

than that those policies were developed and enforced under color of Nevada law." Justice WHITE, joined by Justices Brennan, Marshall, and O'Connor, dissented, concluding that "the NCAA acted jointly with UNLV in suspending Tarkanian." For Justice White, the fact that UNLV had agreed to enforce the NCAA's rules and judgments was more important than the fact that UNLV could have but did not withdraw from that agreement, or that UNLV opposed the sanctions imposed by the NCAA pursuant to that agreement: "The key, [as] with any conspiracy, is that ultimately the parties agreed to take the action. [O]n these facts, the NCAA was 'jointly engaged with [UNLV] officials in the challenged action,' and therefore was a state actor."

5. U.S.O.C. In SAN FRAN. ARTS & ATHLETICS v. U.S.O.C., 483 U.S. 522 (1987), the Court held that the U.S. Olympic Committee was not a "governmental actor." The question arose when the USOC, to which Congress had granted the right to prohibit certain commercial and promotional uses of the word "Olympic," enjoined petitioner from calling its athletic competitions the "Gay Olympic Games." Petitioner claimed that the USOC's action constituted selective, discriminatory enforcement in violation of equal protection. Justice POWELL's majority opinion relied mainly on Rendell–Baker, Blum and Jackson in finding no state action. Justice BRENNAN's dissent, joined by Justice Marshall and "largely" by Justices O'Connor and Blackmun, relied heavily on Burton. He noted, for example: "While in Burton the restaurant was able to pursue a policy of discrimination because the State had failed to impose upon it a policy of non-discrimination, the USOC could pursue its alleged policy of selective enforcement only because Congress *affirmatively* granted it power that it would not otherwise have to control the use of the word 'Olympic.' " (In rejecting this argument, the majority replied, citing Jackson, that petitioner "has failed to demonstrate that the Federal Government can or does exert any influence over the exercise of the USOC's enforcement decisions.")

6. *Edmonson.* In contrast to most of its recent state action decisions (other than, e.g., Lugar, note 3 above), the Court in EDMONSON v. LEES-VILLE CONCRETE CO., 500 U.S. 614 (1991), did find the requisite state action in a decision taken by a non-governmental actor. Holding that use by a private litigant in a civil proceeding of peremptory challenges to exclude jurors on the basis of race constituted state action for Fourteenth Amendment equal protection purposes [recall Batson v. Kentucky (1986; p. 750 above)], Justice KENNEDY's majority opinion for the Court relied heavily on the analytical approach of Lugar. Turning first to the question "whether the claimed constitutional deprivation resulted from the exercise of a right or privilege having its source in state authority," Justice Kennedy found this standard easily satisfied because peremptory challenges in civil litigation were the creatures of "statutory authorization" and because the very idea of a peremptory challenge has "no significance outside a court of law." He then turned to the second part of the "Lugar test, whether a private litigant in all fairness must be deemed a government actor." Recognizing that this is "often a factbound inquiry," Justice Kennedy nevertheless asserted that "our cases disclose certain principles of general application, [including] the extent to which the actor relies on governmental assistance and benefits [Burton]; whether the actor is performing a traditional governmental function [Terry v. Adams; Marsh v. Alabama; U.S.O.C.]; and whether the injury caused is aggravated in a unique way by the incidents of governmental authority [Shelley v. Kraemer]." Applying these principles, the Court relied on the "overt, significant participation of the government" in both the peremptory challenge system and civil litigation generally; on the pervasive statutory regulation of the jury system; and on the active involvement of the judge in voir dire examination of jurors and in

administering the system. It also found the jury system in general and the peremptory challenge system in particular the very embodiment of a traditional governmental function: "The peremptory challenge is used in selecting an entity that is a quintessential governmental body, having no attributes of a private actor. [If] the government confers on a private body the power to choose the government's employees or officials, the private body will be bound by the constitutional mandate of race-neutrality [Tarkanian; Rendell–Baker; Terry]. [Finally,] we note that the injury caused by the discrimination is made more severe because the government permits it to occur within the courthouse itself. [To] permit racial exclusion in this official forum compounds the racial insult inherent in judging a citizen by the color of his or her skin."

Justice O'CONNOR, joined by Chief Justice Rehnquist and Justice Scalia, dissented, maintaining that, in view of Jackson and Blum, it was necessary to show that the government was involved in the specific decision challenged, a showing not made here. She emphasized that "[i]t is the nature of a peremptory that its exercise is left wholly within the discretion of the litigant. [T]he peremptory is, by design, an enclave of private action in a government-managed proceeding." She maintained that the involvement of government in setting up the process of peremptory challenges was "irrelevant to the issue at hand. [All] of this government action [is merely prerequisite to] the use of a peremptory challenge; [it does not constitute] participation *in* the challenge. That these actions may be necessary to a peremptory challenge [no] more makes the challenge state action than the building of roads and provision of public transportation makes state action of riding on a bus." Similarly, she argued, because the choice of whom, if anyone, to strike peremptorily is and always has been a private choice, there was no warrant for concluding that this was a traditional governmental function: "Trials in this country are adversarial proceedings. Attorneys for private litigants do not act on behalf of the government, or even the public as a whole; attorneys represent their clients. [The] actions of a lawyer in a courtroom do not become those of the government by virtue of their location[, even] if those actions are based on race. Racism is a terrible thing. It is irrational, destructive, and mean. [But] not every opprobrious act is a constitutional violation." Justice SCALIA's separate dissent, echoing earlier criticisms of Shelley and Burton, chastised the majority for distorting state action doctrine where race was at issue: "To overhaul the doctrine of state action in this fashion—what a magnificent demonstration of this institution's hostility to race-based judgments, even by private actors! The price of the demonstration is, alas, high, and much of it will be paid by the minority litigants who use our courts." (See also Georgia v. McCollum, 505 U.S. 42 (1992), applying the Edmonson approach to a defendant's use of racially-motivated peremptory challenges in a criminal proceeding.)

7. DeSHANEY v. WINNEBAGO CTY. SOC. SERVS. DEPT., 489 U.S. 189 (1989): Consider this 6-3 decision in light of the earlier cases recurrently raising the question of when a State's *failure* to act triggers 14th Amendment protections (and sometimes the question of when a State is under an affirmative *duty* to act). Petitioner Joshua DeShaney was a boy who was beaten and permanently injured by his father, with whom he lived. When he was one year old, a Wyoming court granted his parents a divorce and awarded custody to his father. Soon after, the father moved to Winnebago County, Wisconsin. Two years later, county social workers received recurrent reports that the father was physically abusing Joshua. The caseworkers noted each of these reports as well as the boy's suspicious injuries, but took no action to remove him from his father's custody. When Joshua was four years old, his father beat him so severely that he suffered permanent brain injuries that left him profoundly

retarded and confined to an institution for life. (The father was subsequently convicted of child abuse.) This action was brought by Joshua and his mother claiming that the *State* had deprived him of his liberty in violation of due process. Chief Justice REHNQUIST's majority opinion rejected that claim: "[Nothing] in the language of the Due Process Clause itself requires the State to protect the life, liberty, and property of its citizens against invasion by private actors. The Clause is phrased as a limitation on the State's power to act, not as a guarantee of certain minimal levels of safety and security. [Its] language cannot fairly be extended to impose an affirmative obligation on the State to ensure that those interests do not come to harm through other means. Nor does history support such an expansive reading of the [text]. Its purpose was to protect the people from the State, not to ensure that the State [protect] them from each other. The Framers were content to leave the extent of governmental obligation in the latter area to the democratic political processes. [Petitioners] contend, however, that even if [due process] imposes no affirmative obligation on the State to provide [adequate] protective services, such a duty may arise out of certain 'special relationships' created or assumed by the State with respect to particular individuals. [They] argue that such a 'special relationship' existed here because the State knew that Joshua faced a special danger of abuse [and] specifically proclaimed, by word and by deed, its intention to protect him against that danger. [Accordingly,] the State acquired an affirmative 'duty,' enforceable through [due process], to do so in a reasonably competent fashion. We reject this argument. It is true that in certain limited circumstances the Constitution imposes upon the State affirmative duties of care and protection with respect to particular individuals. [E.g., Youngberg v. Romeo (1982; p. 600 above).] [But such cases] stand only for the proposition that when the State takes a person into its custody and holds him there against his will, the Constitution imposes upon it a corresponding duty to assume some responsibility for his safety and general well-being. [The] affirmative duty to protect arises not from the State's knowledge of the individual's predicament or from its expressions of intent to help him, but from the limitation which it has imposed on his freedom to act on his own [behalf]. Judges and lawyers, like other humans, are moved by natural sympathy in a case like this to find a way for Joshua and his mother to receive adequate compensation for the grievous harm inflicted upon them. But before yielding to that impulse, it is well to remember once again that the harm was inflicted not by [the State], but by Joshua's father. The most that can be said of the state functionaries in this case is that they stood by and did nothing when suspicious circumstances dictated a more active role for them. In defense of them it must also be said that had they moved too soon to take custody of the son away from the father, they would likely have been met with charges of improperly intruding into the parent-child relationship, charges [also based on due process]."

Justice BRENNAN, joined by Justices Marshall and Blackmun, dissented: "It may well be [that due process] creates no general right to basic governmental services. That, however, is not the question presented here. [I] would focus first on the action that Wisconsin *has* taken with respect to Joshua and children like him, rather than on the actions that the State failed to take." He noted that Shelley and Burton "suggest that a State may be found complicit in an injury even if it did not create the situation that caused the harm." He added: "Through its child-protection program, the State actively intervened in Joshua's life and, by virtue of this intervention, acquired ever more certain knowledge that Joshua was in grave danger. [My] disagreement with the Court arises from its failure to see that inaction can be every bit as abusive of power as action, that oppression can result when a State undertakes a vital duty and then ignores it." Justice BLACKMUN's separate dissent insisted that the facts here involved "not mere passivity, but active state intervention in the life of [Joshua]—intervention that triggered a fundamental duty to aid the boy once the State learned of the severe danger to which he was exposed. The Court fails to recognize this duty because it attempts to draw a sharp and rigid line between action and inaction. But such formalistic reasoning has no place in the interpretation of the broad and stirring Clauses of the 14th Amendment." He ended: "Poor Joshua! [It] is a sad commentary upon American life, and constitutional principles, [that he] now is assigned to live out the remainder of his life profoundly retarded."

SECTION 3. CONGRESSIONAL POWER TO REACH PRIVATE INTERFERENCES WITH CONSTITUTIONAL RIGHTS: MODERN SCOPE AND PROBLEMS

THE INGREDIENTS OF THE PROBLEM: AN INTRODUCTORY SKETCH

To what extent may Congress provide criminal and civil sanctions against private interferences with constitutional rights? The question is complex; the answer, unclear. The question is pursued here by focusing on the background and implications of United States v. Guest (1966; p. 964. Careful examination of these materials suggests answers to some problems and highlights additional ones as yet unresolved. Before doing so, it seems useful to sketch the recurrent clusters of problems presented by cases of this nature, to aid in disentangling the constitutional and statutory issues. At the outset, it should be noted that the central questions are the constitutional and statutory reaches of the modern counterparts of the post-Civil War civil rights laws (see p. 919 above). Recall that those modern counterparts contain both criminal and civil provisions and that they fall into two groups: one reaches only action "under color" of law; the other reaches private conspiracies, without any state nexus requirement on the face of the statutes. Thus, on the criminal side, 18 U.S.C. § 242 covers action "under color" of law, while § 241 is directed at private conspiracies. There is a similar distinction in the major civil provisions: 42 U.S.C. § 1983 is the state action-related statute; § 1985(3) is the civil conspiracy provision. What persons are covered by these provisions? What rights are protected by them? What is the statutory and constitutional reach of the laws? A number of variables require attention in exploring these issues. These introductory notes focus on an intertwined trilogy of concerns: the sources of constitutional rights; vagueness; and statutory construction. This overview of the trilogy is designed to aid understanding of the opinions below. But bear in mind that the trilogy is offered as background and that the primary emphasis here is on the question foreshadowed by the preceding section: the power of Congress to safeguard 14th Amendment rights against interferences by seemingly private actors, either by relying on the Court's interpretations of the state action concept or, more controversially, by invoking a claimed congressional power to reach private actors the Court would not reach on its own.

1. *The sources of constitutional rights.* The most important recurrent theme in analyzing the scope of congressional power to reach private interferences with constitutional rights is the problem of identifying the sources of the

covered rights. Note especially three types of rights, with quite different implications regarding their potential reach to private behavior. *First*, there are the rights presenting problems introduced in sec. 2: due process and equal protection rights under the 14th Amendment, as well as 15th Amendment rights—rights by their terms applicable only to *state* interferences. Under the Court's interpretations of the state action concept, some seemingly private behavior is reachable under the 14th and 15th Amendments. But may Congress go beyond the Court's view of "state action" and reach additional private actors? For example, can the private conspiracies provisions, §§ 241 and 1985(c), be applied to private actors who interfere with 14th Amendment rights? That problem is discussed, but not resolved, in Guest, below. *Second*, the other post-Civil War Amendment, the 13th, is *not* limited to state action; it applies to private interferences generally. And under the Jones case, p. 978 below, Congress, may, under § 2 of that Amendment, deal broadly with private acts of racial discrimination. The 13th Amendment, then, provides an independent constitutional basis for congressional sanctions against private interferences with rights. But its scope is limited by its racial discrimination emphasis; it may not help with non-racial interferences with rights. *Third*, the Court has recognized a number of constitutional rights, based on sources *other* than the post-Civil War Amendments, that are not subject to the state action limitation. Those rights provide additional sources of congressional power to reach private conduct. As the cases below illustrate, the rights involved are largely rights derived from structures and relationships found implicit in the Constitution (recall McCulloch v. Maryland). Note, for example, the reliance on the right to travel in Guest, below.[1]

2. *Specificity and vagueness.* Provisions such as 18 U.S.C. § 242 speak in very general terms: they contain broad references to "rights, privileges, or immunities" under the "Constitution or laws." Even assuming congressional power to reach private interferences with constitutional rights, are those statutory references sufficiently specific to give adequate notice to those subjected to them? To the extent that such phrases appear in criminal provisions, do they risk invalidation for vagueness? That concern may inhibit the Court in searching out new varieties of rights to read into those broadly phrased remnants of the post-Civil War laws. Screws (p. 969) illustrates the Court's difficulties in finding adequate specificity in such broad formulations.

3. *Statutory interpretation.* Another pervasive theme in these materials is that of statutory construction. In construing the general civil rights statutes, what varieties of constitutional rights can be read into such phrases as "rights, privileges, or immunities secured or protected by the Constitution"? Thus, when Congress purports to reach private actors in a statute originally enacted soon after adoption of the 14th Amendment, should the Court read a state action limitation into the statute? Or should the statute be read broadly, in accordance with its apparent terms—thereby including in it constitutional rights *not* subject to the state action limitation (as well as 14th Amendment rights made applicable to private interferences only because of an arguable

---

1. These materials emphasize federal *constitutional* rights. But note that the rights-protecting statutes considered in this section typically speak not only of rights under the Constitution but also of rights under the "laws of the United States." To the extent that Congress acts under powers applica-ble to private individuals—e.g., the commerce and spending powers—Congress may protect the statutory rights it has created against private interferences. Recall, e.g., the public accommodations provisions of the 1964 Civil Rights Act, in chap. 3, and note 18 U.S.C. § 245, p. 972 below.

congressional power to reach beyond Court-announced state action limits)?[2]

A. PRIVATE INTERFERENCES WITH FEDERAL RIGHTS: CRIMINAL SANCTIONS

United States v. Guest

383 U.S. 745, 86 S.Ct. 1170, 16 L.Ed.2d 239 (1966).

Justice STEWART delivered the opinion of the Court.

The six defendants [were indicted] for criminal conspiracy in violation of 18 U.S.C. § 241. [The] indictment alleged a single conspiracy by the defendants to deprive Negro citizens of the free exercise and enjoyment of several specified rights secured by the Constitution and laws of the United States. [The charge involved the killing of Lemuel Penn, a black reserve officer returning from active duty to Washington, D.C. in 1964. The Penn shooting was one of the widely publicized incidents of civil rights violence in the South in the 1960s. The federal indictment was brought after the defendants had been acquitted of murder in a Georgia court.] The defendants [successfully] moved to dismiss the indictment on the ground that it did not charge an offense under the laws of the United States. [We] reverse. [W]e deal here with issues of statutory construction, not with issues of constitutional [power].

II. The second numbered paragraph of the indictment alleged that the defendants conspired to injure, oppress, threaten, and intimidate Negro citizens of the United States in the free exercise and enjoyment of: "The right to the equal utilization, without discrimination upon the basis of race, of public facilities in the vicinity of Athens, Georgia, owned, operated or managed by or on behalf of the State of Georgia or any subdivision thereof." Correctly characterizing this paragraph as embracing rights protected by [equal protection, the] District Court held as a matter of statutory construction that § 241 does not encompass any 14th Amendment rights. [This] was in error, as our opinion in [Price, below,] makes abundantly [clear]. [Unlike] the indictment in Price, [the] indictment in the present case names no person alleged to have acted in any way under the color of state law. The argument is therefore made that, since there exist no [equal protection] rights against wholly private action, the judgment [on] this branch of the case must be affirmed. On its face, the argument is unexceptionable. [Equal protection] speaks to the State or to those acting under the color of its authority. [Since we] deal here only with the bare terms of the [Clause] itself, nothing said in this opinion goes to the question of what kinds of other and broader legislation Congress might constitutionally enact under § 5 of the 14th Amendment to implement [equal protection]. [But here,] the indictment in fact contains an express allegation of state involvement sufficient at least to require the denial of a motion to dismiss. One of the means of accomplishing the object of the conspiracy, according to the indictment, was "By causing the arrest of Negroes by means of false reports that such Negroes

---

2. In the cases of the early 1950s—e.g., the Williams cases. below—the Court supported narrow readings of the statutes, to avoid constitutional doubts. More recent cases, by contrast—e.g., Griffin and Price, below—take a broader view of the meaning of the statutes, in part because of diminished constitutional doubts.

had committed criminal acts." [The] allegation of the extent of official involvement [here] is not clear. [But it] is broad enough to cover a charge of active connivance by agents of the State in the making of the "false reports," or other conduct amounting to official discrimination clearly sufficient to constitute denial of rights protected by [equal protection].

III. The fourth numbered paragraph of the indictment alleged that the defendants conspired to injure, oppress, threaten, and intimidate Negro citizens of the United States in the free exercise and enjoyment of: "The right to travel freely to and from [Georgia] and to use highway facilities and other instrumentalities of interstate commerce within [Georgia]." The District Court was in error in dismissing the indictment as to this paragraph. The constitutional right to travel from one State to another, and necessarily to use the highways and other instrumentalities of interstate commerce in doing so, occupies a position fundamental to the concept of our Federal Union. It is a right that has been firmly established and repeatedly recognized. [See chap. 9 above.] [Although] there have been recurring differences in emphasis within the Court as to the source of the constitutional right of interstate travel, there is no need here to canvass those differences further. All have agreed that the right exists. Its explicit recognition as one of the federal rights protected by what is now 18 U.S.C. § 241 goes back at least as far as 1904. We reaffirm it now.[1] This does not mean, of course, that every criminal conspiracy affecting an individual's right of free interstate passage is within the sanction of § 241. A specific intent to interfere with the federal right must be [proved]. [Screws, below.] Thus, for example, a conspiracy to rob an interstate traveler would not, of itself, violate § 241. But if the predominant purpose of the conspiracy is to impede or prevent the exercise of the right of interstate travel, or to oppress a person because of his exercise of that right, then, whether or not motivated by racial discrimination, the conspiracy becomes a proper object of the federal law under which the indictment in this case was [brought].

Reversed and remanded.

Justice CLARK, with whom Justice BLACK and Justice FORTAS join, concurring.

I join the opinion of the Court in this case, but believe it worthwhile to comment on its Part II. [The] Court's interpretation of the indictment clearly avoids the question whether Congress, by appropriate legislation, has the power to punish private conspiracies that interfere with 14th Amendment [rights]. My Brother Brennan, however, [suggests] that the Court indicates sub silentio that Congress does not have the power to outlaw such conspiracies. Although the Court specifically rejects any such connotation, it is, I believe, both appropriate and necessary under the circumstances here to say that there now can be no doubt that the specific language of § 5 empowers the Congress to enact laws punishing all conspiracies—with or without state action—that interfere with 14th Amendment rights.

Justice HARLAN, concurring in part and dissenting in part.

---

1. As emphasized in [Justice Harlan's] separate opinion, § 241 protects only against interference with rights secured by other federal laws or by the Constitution itself. The right to interstate travel is a right that the Constitution itself guarantees. Although [the cases recognizing that right] in fact involved governmental interference with the right of free interstate travel, their reasoning fully supports the conclusion that the constitutional right of interstate travel is a right secured against interference from any source whatever, whether governmental or private. In this connection, it is important to reiterate that the right to travel freely from State to State finds constitutional protection that is quite independent of the 14th Amendment. [Footnote by Justice Stewart.]

I join [Part II]* of the Court's opinion, but I cannot subscribe to Part III in its full sweep. To the extent that it is there held that § 241 reaches conspiracies, embracing only the action of private persons, [to] interfere with the right of citizens freely to engage in interstate travel, I am constrained to dissent. On the other hand, I agree that § 241 does embrace state interference with such interstate travel, and I therefore consider that this aspect of the indictment is sustainable on the reasoning of Part II of the Court's opinion. [While] past cases do indeed establish that there is a constitutional "right to travel" between States free from unreasonable *governmental* interference, today's decision is the first to hold that such movement is also protected against *private* interference, and depending on the constitutional source of that right, I think it either unwise or impermissible so to read the [Constitution]. I do not gainsay that the immunities and commerce provisions of the Constitution leave the way open for the finding of this "private" constitutional right, since they do not speak solely in terms of governmental action. Nevertheless, I think it wrong to sustain a criminal indictment on such an uncertain ground. To do so subjects § 241 to serious challenge on the score of vagueness and serves in effect to place this Court in the position of making criminal law under the name of constitutional [interpretation].

Justice BRENNAN, with whom The Chief Justice [WARREN] and Justice DOUGLAS join, concurring in part and dissenting in part.

[I] reach the same result as the Court on that branch of the indictment discussed in Part III of its opinion but for other reasons. See footnote [1] infra. And I agree with so much of Part II as construes § 241 to encompass conspiracies to injure, oppress, threaten or intimidate citizens in the free exercise or enjoyment of 14th Amendment rights and holds that, as so construed, § 241 is not void for indefiniteness. [I] do not agree with [that portion] of Part II which holds, as I read the opinion, that a conspiracy to interfere with the exercise of the right to equal utilization of state facilities is not, within the meaning of § 241 [unless] discriminatory conduct by state officers is involved in the alleged conspiracy. [I] believe that § 241 reaches such a private conspiracy, not because the 14th Amendment of its own force prohibits such a conspiracy, but because § 241, as an exercise of congressional power under § 5 of that Amendment, prohibits *all* conspiracies to interfere with the exercise of a "right [secured] by the Constitution." [For] me, the right to use state facilities without discrimination on the basis of race is, within the meaning of § 241, a right created by, arising under and dependent upon the 14th Amendment and hence is a right "secured" by that Amendment. It finds its source in that Amendment. [The] 14th Amendment commands the State to provide the members of all races with equal access to the public facilities it owns or manages, and the right of a citizen to use those facilities without discrimination on the basis of race is a basic corollary of this command. Cf. Brewer v. Hoxie School District No. 46, 238 F.2d 91 (8th Cir.1956) [below]. Whatever may be the status of the right to equal utilization of *privately owned facilities,* it must be emphasized that we are here concerned with the right to equal utilization of *public facilities owned or operated by or on behalf of the [State].*

[My] view as to the scope of § 241 requires that I reach the question of constitutional power—whether § 241 or legislation indubitably designed to punish entirely private conspiracies to interfere with the exercise of 14th

* The action of three of the Justices who join the Court's opinion in nonetheless cursorily pronouncing themselves on the far-reaching constitutional questions deliberately not reached in Part II seems to me, to say the very least, extraordinary. [Footnote by Justice Harlan.]

Amendment rights constitutes a permissible exercise of the power granted to Congress by § 5 of the 14th Amendment. [A] majority of the members of the Court[1] expresses the view today that § 5 empowers Congress to enact laws punishing *all* conspiracies to interfere with the exercise of 14th Amendment rights, whether or not state officers or others acting under the color of state law are implicated in the conspiracy. [§ 5] authorizes Congress to make laws that it concludes are reasonably necessary to protect a right created by and arising under that Amendment; and Congress is thus fully empowered to determine that punishment of private conspiracies interfering with the exercise of such a right is necessary to its full protection. [I] acknowledge that some of the decisions of this Court, most notably an aspect of the Civil Rights Cases, have declared that Congress' power under § 5 is confined to the adoption of "appropriate legislation for correcting the effects [of] prohibited State laws and State [acts]." I do not accept—and a majority of the Court today rejects—this interpretation of § 5. It reduces the legislative power to enforce the provisions of the Amendment to that of the judiciary; and it attributes a far too limited objective to the Amendment's sponsors. Moreover, the language of § 5 of the 14th Amendment and § 2 of the Fifteenth Amendment are virtually the same, and we recently held in South Carolina v. Katzenbach [p. 987 below] that "[t]he basic test to be applied in a case involving § 2 of the Fifteenth Amendment is the same as in all cases concerning the express powers of Congress with relation to the reserved powers of the States." The classic formulation of that test by Chief Justice Marshall in [McCulloch] was there adopted. [It] seems to me that this is also the standard that defines the scope of congressional authority under [§ 5]. Viewed in its proper perspective, [§ 5] appears as a positive grant of legislative power, authorizing Congress to exercise its discretion in fashioning remedies to achieve civil and political equality for all citizens. No one would deny that Congress could enact legisla tion directing state officials to provide Negroes with equal access to state schools, parks and other [state] facilities. [Nor] could it be denied that Congress has the power to punish state officers who [conspire] to threaten, harass and murder Negroes for attempting to use these facilities. And I can find no principle of federalism nor word of the Constitution that denies Congress power to determine that in order adequately to protect the right to equal utilization of state facilities, it is also appropriate to punish other individuals—not state officers themselves and not acting in concert with state officers—who engage in the same brutal conduct for the same misguided purpose. [Section 241] is certainly not model legislation for punishing private conspiracies to interfere with the exercise of the right of equal utilization of state facilities. It deals in only general language [which] plainly brings § 241 close to the danger line of being void for vagueness. But, as the Court holds, a stringent scienter require-ment saves § 241 from condemnation as a criminal statute failing to provide adequate notice of the proscribed conduct. [See Screws, below.] Since this case reaches us on the pleadings, there is no occasion to decide now whether the Government will be able on trial to sustain the burden of proving the requisite specific [intent]. In any event, we may well agree that the necessity to discharge that burden can imperil the effectiveness of § 241 where, as is often the case, the pertinent constitutional right must be implied from a grant of congressional power or a prohibition upon the exercise of governmental power. But since the limitation on the statute's effectiveness derives from Congress' failure to define—with any measure of specificity—the rights encompassed, the

----

1. The majority consists of the Justices joining my Brother Clark's opinion and the Justices joining this [opinion]. [Footnote by Justice Brennan.]

remedy is for Congress to write a law without this [defect]. [See 18 U.S.C. § 245, p. 972 below, enacted two years after this decision.]

––––––––

SOME PROBLEMS OF APPLYING CRIMINAL SANCTIONS TO STATE–INVOLVED DEFENDANTS INTERFERING WITH 14TH AMENDMENT RIGHTS

Introduction. This group of notes focuses on one cluster of problems raised by the Guest case. Note Part II of Justice Stewart's opinion in Guest: that part sustains a portion of the indictment (covering interference with 14th Amendment rights) without reaching the question whether § 5 of the 14th Amendment may reach purely private actors; it does so by finding the allegation "broad enough to cover a charge of active connivance by agents of the State" or "other conduct amounting to official discrimination." Under that theory, "private" defendants may be reached if they are sufficiently involved with state officials. That approach thus relies on the Court's interpretations of § 1 of the 14th Amendment considered in sec. 2 above (e.g., Burton), without asserting any independent congressional power to expand the reach of the 14th Amendment. But even this rationale of reaching private actors because of state "involvement" is not without difficulty, as this group of notes illustrates. There is, first, the problem of *how much* state involvement with the private actors needs to be shown. There is, moreover, the question of construing §§ 241 and 242 as reaching 14th Amendment rights and state-involved private actors. There is, finally, the concern about vagueness problems raised by broad constructions of these general statutes.

1. *The Price case.* UNITED STATES v. PRICE, 383 U.S. 787 (1966), the companion case to Guest, arose out of the widely publicized murder of three civil rights workers near Philadelphia, Mississippi, in 1964. The defendants were three local law enforcement officials and 15 private individuals, all allegedly involved in the killing of civil rights workers Schwerner, Chaney and Goodman. There were two indictments against the 18 defendants: one based on 18 U.S.C. § 242; the other on § 241. The alleged conspiracy involved releasing the victims from jail at night, intercepting and killing them, and disposing of their bodies—all with the purpose to "punish" the victims summarily and thus to deprive them of their 14th Amendment right "not to be summarily punished without [due process of law]." The District Court dismissed most of the charges. The Court reversed all of the dismissals. Justice FORTAS wrote for the Court, stating that the case involved only issues "of construction, not of constitutional power." The first indictment charged, inter alia, substantive violations of 18 U.S.C. § 242 (the "under color" of law provision). The trial court sustained the substantive counts only against the three official defendants; it dismissed those against the private defendants since they were not "officers in fact." The Court reversed. Sec. 242 concededly required that the "person indicted has acted 'under color' of law," and "under color" of law was to be treated "as the same thing as the 'state action' required under the 14th Amendment." But that did not bar reaching private individuals, in view of the Court's interpretations of the state action coverage of the 14th Amendment: "Private persons, jointly engaged with state officials in the prohibited action, are acting 'under color' of law for purposes of the statute. It is enough that [the accused] is a willful participant in joint activity with the State or its agents." Justice Fortas particularly emphasized the relevance of the Burton analysis. Here, he noted, "state officers participated in every phase of the alleged [joint

adventure]: the release from jail, the interception, assault and murder. [Those] who took advantage of participation by state officers in accomplishment of the foul purpose alleged must suffer the consequences of that participation." The second indictment charged all 18 defendants with a conspiracy under 18 U.S.C. § 241, the "private conspiracy" section. Fifteen years earlier, the Court, in one of the Williams cases, below, had left in doubt whether that provision applied to interferences with 14th Amendment rights. But in Price, the Court had no difficulty in holding that § 241 did apply, and that its reach in this context presented no constitutional difficulty because of the presence of state action: "[Section 241] extends to conspiracies otherwise within the scope of the section, participated in by officials alone or in collaboration with private persons."

2. *The Williams cases.* The 1951 Williams cases, referred to in Price, throw light on two problems: first, they provide another example of using Court-developed state action analyses of § 1 of the 14th Amendment to reach private individuals; second, they raise the problem of statutory construction resolved in Price. One of the cases, WILLIAMS v. UNITED STATES, 341 U.S. 97 (1951), was a prosecution under the predecessor of § 242, the "under color" of law provision. Williams, a private detective who had been issued a special police officer's badge, was employed by a lumber company to investigate thefts of its property. Flashing his badge and accompanied by a regular police officer, he beat four suspects until they confessed to the thefts. He was convicted of depriving his victims of the right to be tried by due process of law. The Court affirmed. Justice DOUGLAS's majority opinion concluded that the jury could find that the defendant was "no mere interloper but had a semblance of policeman's power," and that "the manner of his conduct of the interrogations [made] clear that he was asserting the authority granted him and not acting in the role of a private person." In a companion case, UNITED STATES v. WILLIAMS, 341 U.S. 70 (1951), the same defendant, two of his employees who participated in the beatings, and the police officer detailed to assist him, were convicted of conspiracy under the predecessor of § 241, the private conspiracy provision. The Court reversed these convictions; but only eight of the Justices reached the critical issue of statutory construction, and they divided 4-4, leaving the uncertainty that was clarified by the Price case. Justice FRANK-FURTER's opinion, joined by Chief Justice Vinson and Justices Jackson and Minton, argued that § 241 should *not* be read as covering 14th Amendment rights: § 242 was intended to deal fully with conspiracies under color of law (involving 14th Amendment rights); § 241 covered conspiracies by private persons; accordingly, § 241 should be construed as protecting only those rights "which Congress can beyond doubt constitutionally secure against interference by private individuals." The other four Justices—Justice DOUGLAS, joined by Justices Reed, Burton and Clark—took a broader view of § 242, and their view was adopted by the Court in Price. They insisted that § 241, like § 242, was applicable to 14th Amendment rights as well as others.

3. *The Screws case: Vagueness and civil rights laws.* The broad references in 18 U.S.C. §§ 241 and 242 to rights "secured" by the Constitution have stimulated recurrent challenges that the statutes do not give adequate notice of what is prohibited and are therefore void for vagueness. The Court has repeatedly rejected those challenges by reading what Justice Brennan in Guest called "a strict scienter requirement" into the criminal provisions. That reading stems from one of the earliest of the modern cases under the civil rights laws, SCREWS v. UNITED STATES, 325 U.S. 91 (1945). This case involved a "shocking and revolting episode in law enforcement." The defendants were police officers (Screws was a sheriff in Georgia) who arrested the black victim for theft and beat him "with their fists and with a solid-bar blackjack" after he allegedly reached for a gun and used insulting language. The victim was knocked on the ground and beaten until he was unconscious. He died soon

after. "There was evidence that Screws held a grudge against [the victim] and had threatened to 'get' him." The defendants were convicted under 18 U.S.C. § 242 for "willfully" and "under color of law" depriving the victim of his 14th Amendment rights, including "the right not to be deprived of life without due process of law." Justice DOUGLAS's opinion, joined by Chief Justice Stone and Justices Black and Reed, conceded that there would be a serious vagueness problem if "the customary standard of guilt for statutory crimes" were adopted: "If a man intentionally adopts certain conduct in certain circumstances known to him, and that conduct is forbidden by the law under those circumstances, he intentionally breaks the law." Under such a test, "a local law enforcement officer violates [§ 242] if he does an act which some court later holds deprives a person of due process of law." Accordingly state officials would indeed walk on "treacherous ground," given the "character and closeness of decisions of this Court interpreting the due process clause." But he found it possible to read § 242 "more narrowly" to avoid the vagueness difficulty: "[I]f we construe 'willfully' in [§ 242] as connoting a purpose to deprive a person of a specific constitutional right, we would introduce no innovation. [W]here the punishment imposed is only for an act knowingly done with the purpose of doing that which the statute prohibits, the accused cannot be said to suffer from lack of warning or knowledge that the act which he does is a violation of law. [T]he presence of a bad purpose or evil intent alone may not be sufficient. [But] a requirement of a specific intent to deprive a person of a federal right made definite by decision or other rule of law saves the Act from any charge of unconstitutionality on the grounds of [vagueness]. [The] specific intent required by the Act is an intent to deprive a person of a right which has been made specific either by the express terms of the Constitution or laws of the United States or by decisions interpreting them. [Acting "willfully" in the sense in which we use the word means acting] in open defiance or in reckless disregard of a constitutional requirement which has been made specific and definite. [The] fact that the defendants may not have been thinking in constitutional terms is not material where their aim was not to enforce local law but to deprive a citizen of a right and that right was protected by the Constitution. When they so act they at least act in reckless disregard of constitutional prohibitions or guarantees." But in this case, the trial judge had not instructed the jury properly on the question of intent, and the conviction was accordingly reversed.[1]

CONGRESSIONAL POWER TO REACH PRIVATE BEHAVIOR, THE GUEST CASE, AND THE 1968 LAW

1. *Congressional power to reach private actors under § 5 of the 14th Amendment.* Price, Williams and Screws all involved applications of the crimi-

---

1. Justice RUTLEDGE cast the decisive vote to make that disposition possible: though he (like Justice Murphy) considered the trial judge's instructions adequate and thought that the conviction should be affirmed, he noted that the case "cannot have disposition" if each Justice adhered to his belief; he accordingly voted to remand for disposition in accordance with Justice Douglas's views. Justices ROBERTS, FRANKFURTER, and JACKSON dissented, insisting that the "intrinsic vagueness" of the statute "surely cannot be removed by making the statute applicable only where the defendant has the 'requisite bad purpose.' Does that not amount to saying that the black heart of the defendant enables him to know what are the constitutional rights deprivation of which the statute forbids, although we as judges are not able to define their classes or their limits, or, at least, are not prepared to state what they are unless it be to say that [§ 242] protects whatever rights the Constitution protects?" [At the second trial, Screws was acquitted.]

nal sanctions of the civil rights laws to actors reachable under the Court's own interpretations of the state action concept. But Justice Brennan's opinion in Guest (and presumably Justice Clark's comment) suggest that Congress under § 5 of the 14th Amendment may go further in reaching private behavior than the Court would under § 1. How far-reaching is that congressional power? Note that the Brennan and Clark opinions in Guest continue to assume that 14th Amendment rights are rights against the state. Thus, Justice Brennan notes that the 14th Amendment "commands the State to provide the members of all races with equal access" to public facilities. He draws from this obligation a "basic corollary": "the right of a citizen to use those facilities without discrimination on the basis of race." What kinds of private interferences with the relationship between the state and the individual *are* reachable under this view of § 5? Are the private interferences limited to those directly aimed at state officials, in order to hamper them from carrying out their 14th Amendment obligations? Or may Congress also reach private interferences directed against the private citizen who has a "corollary" right against the state? May Congress go even further than that?

The Brennan theory in Guest is most readily applicable where the private interference is directed against the state officials themselves. That was the situation in a case cited by Justice Brennan in Guest, Brewer v. Hoxie School District No. 46, 238 F.2d 91 (8th Cir.1956). Brewer sustained federal power to reach private actors who intimidate state officials in the performance of their 14th Amendment obligations. It upheld an injunction restraining private persons from intimidating school officials who were trying to carry out a plan to desegregate schools. The court noted that the school officials were trying to apply the Constitution as interpreted in Brown and that it followed "as a necessary corollary that they have a federal right to be free from direct and deliberate interference with the performance of the constitutionally imposed duty. The right arises by necessary implication from the imposition of the duty." But Justice Brennan was clearly willing to give that theory a broader reach in Guest: he was prepared to sustain the application of § 241 to a private interference with the private citizen who had a right of access to public facilities. In short, he found power to reach the private actor interfering with the state-victim relationship by intimidations directed not against the state official but against the victim. Under that theory, is it essential that the defendant *intends* to interfere with the victim's access to state facilities? Or is it enough that murder of the victim has the *effect* of interfering with the victim's use of state facilities? Is the theory even more far-reaching than that? *Is* a special relationship between the victim and the state an essential ingredient for invoking § 5? Or may Congress act directly under § 5 to prevent private interferences with access to *private* facilities as well? E.g., may Congress move directly to reach private interferences with access to *private* housing, on the theory that that is appropriate legislation to protect access to *public* housing? The Guest rationale presumably does not go that far. But may justification for such a law be found in either the "remedial" or "substantive" rationales under § 5, considered in sec. 4 below? E.g., is such a power supported by the approach of Katzenbach v. Morgan, p. 998 below—an approach that seemed to give Congress some power to "reinterpret" the content of 14th Amendment guarantees, and perhaps, analogously, some power to redraw the lines between state action and private action under the 14th Amendment?[1]

---

1. See generally Cox, "Foreword: Constitutional Adjudication and the Promotion of Human Rights," 80 Harv.L.Rev. 91 (1966); Feuerstein, "Civil Rights [Crimes]," 19 Vand. L.Rev. 641 (1966); Brest, "The Federal Government's Power to Protect Negroes and Civ-

2. *Criminal sanctions against private conduct: Sources outside the 14th Amendment; Sec. 245 of the 1968 Civil Rights Act.* The Guest case and related materials point to sources of congressional authority beyond 14th Amendment rights. A number of constitutional provisions run against private behavior as well as state conduct. Moreover, private interferences may be reached when Congress establishes new statutory rights under powers that clearly reach private behavior—e.g., the commerce power, used as a basis for the public accommodations provisions of the Civil Rights Act of 1964. Against that background, consider the 1968 provisions affording criminal sanctions against private actors, 18 U.S.C. § 245, which follows. These modern provisions can be viewed as a response to Justice Brennan's suggestion of more specific legislation in Guest. Do the specifications in § 245 cure the vagueness concerns aroused by §§ 241 and 242? What explains the differences in intent requirements for (b)(1) violations and (b)(2) acts? What explains the grouping of § 245(b) into two subsections? What are the sources of the various rights specified? Which are 14th Amendment rights? Which stem from other sources? Does § 245 raise any constitutional questions?[2]

Sec. 245 of the 1968 Act provides, under the heading "Federally protected activities": "[(b)] Whoever, whether or not acting under color of law, by force or threat of force willfully injures, intimidates or interferes with, or attempts to injure, intimidate or interfere with (1) any person because he is or has been, or in order to intimidate such person or any other person or any class of persons from (A) voting or qualifying to vote, qualifying or campaigning as a candidate for elective office, or qualifying or acting as a poll watcher, or any legally authorized election official, in any primary, special, or general election; (B) participating in or enjoying any benefit, service, privilege, program, facility or activity provided or administered by the United States; (C) applying for or enjoying employment, or any perquisite thereof, by any agency of the United States; (D) serving, or attending upon any court of any State in connection with service, as a grand or petit juror in any court of the United States; (E) participating in or enjoying the benefits of any program or activity receiving Federal financial assistance; or (2) any person because of his race, color, religion or national origin and because he is or has been (A) enrolling in or attending any public school or public college; (B) participating in or enjoying any benefit, service, privilege, program, facility or activity provided or administered by any State or subdivision thereof; (C) applying for or enjoying employment, or any perquisite thereof, by any private employer or any agency of any State or subdivision thereof, or joining or using the services or advantages of any labor organization, hiring hall, or employment agency; (D) serving, or attending upon any court of any State in connection with possible service, as a grand or petit juror; (E) traveling in or using any facility of interstate

il Rights Workers Against Privately Inflicted Harm," 1 Harv.C.R.–C.L.L.Rev. 1 (1966); and Note, "Federal Power to Regulate Private [Discrimination]," 74 Colum.L.Rev. 451 (1974).

2. The history of § 245 vividly illustrates interactions between the Court and the other branches. Thus, President Johnson in January 1966 asked for new laws "to try those who murder, attack, or intimidate either civil rights workers or others exercising federal rights." But implementation of that Administration proposal was delayed, in part to await the Court's decisions in Guest and

Price. These cases came down on March 28, 1966. Exactly a month later, the President submitted a special Civil Rights Message to Congress, accompanied by detailed proposals to prescribe "penalties for certain acts of violence or intimidation." The 1966 legislative efforts ended in a Senate filibuster. A slightly revised version of the 1966 proposal was included in the Johnson Administration's 1967 civil rights bill. That bill, as substantially amended, became the Civil Rights Act of 1968, which included § 245.

commerce, or using any vehicle, terminal, or facility of any common carrier by motor, rail, water, or air; (F) enjoying the goods, services, facilities, privileges, advantages, or accommodations of any inn, hotel, motel, or other establishment which provides lodging to transient guests, or of any restaurant, cafeteria, lunchroom, lunch counter, soda fountain, or other facility which serves the public and which is principally engaged in selling food or beverages for consumption on the premises, or of any gasoline station, or of any motion picture house, theater, concert hall, sports arena, stadium, or any other place of exhibition or entertainment which serves the public, or of any other establishment which serves the public and (i) which is located within the premises of any of the aforesaid establishments or within the premises of which is physically located any of the aforesaid establishments, and (ii) which holds itself out as serving patrons of such establishments; or (3) during or incident to a riot or civil disorder, any person engaged in a business in commerce or affecting commerce, including, but not limited to, any person engaged in a business which sells or offers for sale to interstate travelers a substantial portion of the articles, commodities, or services which it sells or where a substantial portion of the articles or commodities which it sells or offers for sale have moved in commerce; or (4) any person because he is or has been, or in order to intimidate such person or any other person or any class of persons from (A) participating, without discrimination on account of race, color, religion or national origin, in any of the benefits or activities described in subparagraphs (1)(A) through (1)(E) or subparagraphs (2)(A) through (2)(F); or (B) affording another person or class of persons opportunity or protection to so participate; or (5) any citizen because he is or has been, or in order to intimidate such citizen or any other citizen from lawfully aiding or encouraging other persons to participate, without discrimination on account of race, color, religion or national origin, in any of the benefits or activities described in subparagraphs (1)(A) through (1)(E) or subparagraphs (2)(A) through (2)(F), or participating lawfully in speech or peaceful assembly opposing any denial of the opportunity to so participate— shall be fined not more than $1,000, or imprisoned not more than one year, or both; and if bodily injury results shall be fined not more than $10,000, or imprisoned not more than ten years, or both; and if death results shall be subject to imprisonment for any term of years or for life. As used in this section, the term 'participating lawfully in speech or peaceful assembly' shall not mean the aiding, abetting, or inciting of other persons to [riot]."

———

B.   PRIVATE INTERFERENCES WITH FEDERAL RIGHTS: CIVIL SANCTIONS

Introduction. As the statutory survey in sec. 1 indicated, several of the laws of the Civil War era afforded civil rather than criminal sanctions; and their modern remnants give rise to problems of statutory scope and constitutional authority analogous to those considered in sec. 3A in connection with the criminal provisions. Thus, 42 U.S.C. § 1983, the civil counterpart of 18 U.S.C. § 242, provides civil remedies for deprivations of rights "under color of law." And 42 U.S.C. § 1985(3) [formerly designated § 1985(c)] grants civil remedies for certain private conspiracies, as 18 U.S.C. § 241 does in the criminal sphere. The notes that follow first consider the more difficult statutory and constitutional problems raised by the civil private conspiracy provision (problems analogous to those raised by Guest) before examining some issues raised by the "under color of law" provision.

1. *Civil remedies against private conspiracies.* a. *The Griffin interpretations of § 1985(c).* In Collins v. Hardyman, 341 U.S. 651 (1951),[1] the Court, beset by constitutional doubts, gave a narrow interpretation to the conspiracy provision in § 1985(c)—the provision granting a civil remedy for conspiracies to deny "the equal protection of the laws, or of equal privileges and immunities under the laws." Collins in effect construed § 1985(c) as reaching only conspiracies under color of state law. Twenty years later, however, in GRIFFIN v. BRECKENRIDGE, 403 U.S. 88 (1971), a unanimous Court discarded that interpretation, found that "many of the constitutional problems" perceived in Collins "simply do not exist," and held § 1985(c) applicable to certain private conspiracies as well. On the congressional power issue, the Court found it unnecessary to reach the 14th Amendment question. Instead, Justice Stewart relied on the power to reach private conduct under the 13th Amendment and in protection of the right of interstate travel.[2] The petitioners in Griffin were African Americans from Mississippi who were passengers in an automobile operated by a Tennesseean in Mississippi, near the Mississippi–Alabama border. They charged that respondents, white Mississippians, had conspired to detain, assault and beat them for the purpose of preventing them and other blacks "from seeking the equal protection of the laws and from enjoying the equal rights, privileges and immunities of citizens," including their rights to free speech, movement, association, assembly, and "their rights not to be enslaved nor deprived of life and liberty other than by due process of law." They claimed that the respondents, mistakenly believing the driver to be a civil rights worker, blocked the car, forced the inhabitants to get out of it, and threatened and clubbed them. The lower federal courts dismissed the complaint on the authority of Collins. Justice STEWART's opinion concluded that, "in the light of the evolution of decisional law," the statute should now be given its "apparent meaning." Not only the text but "companion provisions, and legislative history" pointed "unwaveringly to [§ 1985(c)'s] coverage of private conspiracies." Reading the law to cover private action did not, however, mean that it would apply "to all tortious, conspiratorial interferences with the rights of others." He explained: "The constitutional shoals that would lie in the path of interpreting § 1985(c) as a general federal tort law can be avoided by giving full effect to the congressional purpose—by requiring, as an element of the cause of action," an "invidiously discriminatory motivation." He added: "The language requiring intent to deprive of *equal* protection, or *equal* privileges and immunities, means that there must be some racial, or perhaps otherwise class-based, invidiously discriminatory animus behind the conspirators' action."[3] After finding that petitioners' complaint easily fell within this new construction of

---

1. In Collins, plaintiffs, members of a political club, stated that defendants broke up their meeting (held to adopt a resolution opposing the Marshall Plan) and thus interfered with their rights to petition the national government for redress of grievances and to equal privileges under the laws. There was no allegation that defendants acted under color of law. Justice Jackson's majority opinion insisted that no cause of action under § 1985(c) had been stated. He concluded: "[Such] private discrimination is not inequality before the law unless there is some manipulation of the law or its agencies."

2. Note the parallels in the evolution of the civil and criminal conspiracy provisions:

Collins was decided in the same year as the Williams cases, p. 969 above. In Williams, Justice Frankfurter's opinion had read § 241 narrowly; that statutory interpretation was repudiated in the Price case in 1966. Similarly, Justice Jackson's narrow reading of § 1985(c) in Collins was overturned by Griffin in 1971.

3. Justice Stewart added in a footnote: "We need not decide, given the facts of this case, whether a conspiracy motivated by invidiously discriminatory intent other than racial bias would be actionable under the portion of [the law] before us."

§ 1985(c), Justice Stewart turned to the question of congressional power to reach this private conspiracy. He noted: "That § 1985(c) reaches private conspiracies to deprive others of legal rights can, of itself, cause no doubts of its constitutionality. [Our] inquiry, therefore, need go only to identifying a source of congressional power to reach the private conspiracy alleged by the complaint in this case." He found one adequate constitutional basis in § 2 of the 13th Amendment, concluding "that Congress was wholly within its powers under § 2 of [that] Amendment in creating a statutory cause of action for Negro citizens who have been the victims of conspiratorial, racially discriminatory private action aimed at depriving them of the basic rights that the law secures to all free men." (See Jones, p. 978 below.) He also found an independent basis in "the right of interstate travel," relying, inter alia, on his opinion in Guest. He added that this case did not require "consideration of the scope of the power of Congress under § 5 of the 14th Amendment."

b. *The potential reach of § 1985(3) and the Carpenters case.* What is the constitutionally permissible periphery of 42 U.S.C. § 1985(3)? To what extent may Congress reach "invidiously discriminatory intent other than racial bias"? To what extent may Congress reach private interferences with 14th Amendment rights—an issue not reached in Griffin? For more than a decade after Griffin, the Court had no occasion to engage in a full scale reexamination of § 1985(3). In the meanwhile, lower federal courts divided about its constitutional reach.[4] But in the 1980s, the Court went a long way towards clarifying the scope of the section. UNITED BROTHERHOOD OF CARPENTERS v. SCOTT, 463 U.S. 825 (1983), arose out of a labor dispute that involved a claim that a union had violently interfered with nonunion workers. This, it was alleged, constituted a conspiracy to interfere with nonunion workers' First Amendment rights not to associate with a union. Justice WHITE's majority opinion in the 5-4 ruling found that the claim did not state a cause of action under § 1985(3). He concluded that an alleged conspiracy to infringe First Amendment rights is not a violation of § 1985(3) unless it is proved that "the state is involved in the conspiracy or that the aim of the conspiracy is to influence the activity of the state." Moreover, "the kind of animus that § 1985(3) requires" was not present here. Justice White insisted that Griffin was "not to the contrary": the conspiracy alleged in Griffin was actionable because it involved the right to travel as well as 13th Amendment rights. But "Griffin did not hold that even when the alleged conspiracy is aimed at a right that is by definition a right only against state interference the plaintiff in a § 1985(3) suit nevertheless need not prove that the conspiracy contemplated state involvement of some sort." Justice White next turned to the lower courts' claim that § 1985(3) "not only reaches conspiracies other than those motivated by racial bias but also forbids conspiracies against workers who refuse to join a union." He stated: "We disagree with the latter conclusion and do not affirm the former." Justice White stated: "[It] is a close question whether § 1985(3)

---

4. Thus, in Action v. Gannon, 450 F.2d 1227 (8th Cir.1971), the Eighth Circuit affirmed an injunction enjoining civil rights groups from disrupting services at a Roman Catholic cathedral. Reading Griffin and Guest very broadly, the court insisted that plaintiffs' rights to "the freedom of assembly and worship" were covered by the law and that "Congress was given the power in § 5 [to] enforce the rights guaranteed by the [14th Amendment] against private conspira-

cies." Contrast the Fourth Circuit's decision in Bellamy v. Mason's Stores, Inc., 508 F.2d 504 (4th Cir.1974), insisting (in a case where an employee sued his employer because he had been discharged for membership in the KKK) that the law could not be applied to "persons who conspire without involvement of government to deny another person the right of free association," because the First Amendment limits only the government.

was intended to reach any class-based animus other than animus against Negroes and those who championed their cause, most notably Republicans. [We] find difficult the question whether § 1985(3) provided a remedy for every concerted effort by one political group to nullify the influence of or do other injury to a competing group. [To] accede to that view would go far toward making the federal courts, by virtue of § 1985(3), the monitors of campaign tactics in both state and federal elections, a role that the courts should not be quick to assume." Justice White was more decisive on the issue of the provision's applicability to conspiracies against nonunion workers: "Even if the section must be construed to reach conspiracies aimed at any class or organization on account of its political views, [we] find no convincing support in the legislative history for the proposition that the provision was intended to reach conspiracies motivated by bias towards others on account of their *economic* views, status or activities." Accordingly, he refused to construe the section to "reach conspiracies motivated by economic or commercial animus." Justice BLACKMUN's dissent, joined by Justices Brennan, Marshall and O'Connor, read the legislative history quite differently and found "no basis for the Court's crabbed and uninformed reading of the words of § 1985(3)."

c. *Section 1985(3), abortion, and the Bray case.* In 1993, blockades of abortion clinics served as the arena for the disputes about the ability of the federal civil rights laws to reach private conspiracies. In the wake of repeated obstructions of access to abortion clinics by groups such as Operation Rescue, a group of abortion clinics and supporting organizations brought suit under § 1985(3) seeking a federal court injunction against those who would obstruct access to abortion clinics. The plaintiffs prevailed in the lower federal courts, but in BRAY v. ALEXANDRIA WOMEN'S HEALTH CLINIC, 506 U.S. 263 (1993), the Court reversed, holding that animus towards abortion did not constitute a class-based animus towards women, and thus that the animus required by section 1985(3) was not present. Writing for the majority, Justice SCALIA echoed Carpenters in refusing either to affirm or to reject the suggestion in Griffin that forms of class-based animus other than race-based animus could fall within the domain of section 1985(3). He insisted that § 1985(3) did not include within the notion of a "class" those whose connections lay only in a common "desire to engage in conduct that the section 1985(3) defendant disfavors. [This] definitional ploy would convert the statute into the 'general federal tort law' it was the very purpose of the animus requirement to avoid. ['Women] seeking abortion' is not a qualifying class." Justice Scalia went on to reject the argument that animus towards women seeking abortions constituted animus directed at women in general, even assuming, arguendo, that animus against women was sufficient to make out a § 1985(3) claim. The animus required was "at least a purpose that focuses upon women *by reason of their sex*. [The] record in this case does not indicate that petitioners' demonstrations are motivated by a purpose [directed] specifically to women as a class; to the contrary, the District Court found that petitioners define their 'rescues' not with reference to women, but as physical intervention 'between abortionists and the innocent victims.' [Given] this record, respondents' contention that a class-based animus has been established can be true only if one of two suggested propositions is true: (1) that opposition to abortion can reasonably be presumed to reflect a sex-based intent, or (2) that intent is irrelevant, and a class-based animus can be determined solely by effect. Neither proposition is supportable." Turning to the connection between opposition to abortion and opposition to women as a class, Justice Scalia acknowledged that "[s]ome activities may be such an irrational object of disfavor that, if they are targeted, and if they also happen to be engaged in exclusively or predominantly by a particular class of people, an intent to disfavor that class can readily be presumed. A tax on wearing yarmulkes is a tax on Jews. But opposition to voluntary abortion cannot possibly be considered such an irrational surrogate for opposition to (or paternalism towards) women. Whatever one thinks of abortion, it cannot be denied that there are common and respectable reasons for opposing it, other than hatred of or condescension [toward] (or concerning) women as a class—as is evident from the fact that men and women are on both sides of the issue, just as men and women are on both sides of petitioners' unlawful demonstrations." Moreover, Justice Scalia argued, the right at issue was like the First Amendment right in Carpenters, protected by the Constitution only against state and not private interference. In short, no conspiracy with an intent to interfere with a right protected against private action could be shown. Justice STEVENS, joined by Justice Blackmun, dissented, objecting to the majority's "parsimonious construction" of the statute and claiming that § 1985 covered "a large-scale conspiracy that violates the victims' constitutional rights by overwhelming the local authorities." (Justice O'Connor, joined by Justice Blackmun, also submitted a dissent. Justice Souter dissented in part and Justice Kennedy submitted a separate concurrence.) [A year after Bray, however, a unanimous Court, applying a different statute, upheld the availability of civil remedies against those who would unlawfully obstruct access to abortion clinics. In National Organization For Women, Inc. v. Scheidler, 510 U.S. 249 (1994), the Court held that the civil damages provisions section of the Racketeer Influenced and Corrupt Organizations (RICO) chapter of the Organized Crime Control Act of 1970 could be applied to those who repeatedly and unlawfully blocked access to abortion services. The statute provides remedies against those engaged in a "pattern of racketeering activity." Chief Justice Rehnquist's opinion concluded that the RICO law was not limited to activities that were economically motivated and could be applied as well to those whose unlawful activities were based on ideological motivations. With respect to the specific issue of remedies against those who unlawfully obstruct access to abortion clinics, the Court's decision in Bray has not only been rendered less important by virtue of NOW v. Scheidler, but has also been substantially superseded by the Freedom of Access to Clinic Entrances Act of 1994. The Act rests both on the commerce clause and on § 5 of the 14th Amendment.]

2. *Civil remedies against actions "under color" of state law.* a. 42 U.S.C. § 1983—like its criminal counterpart, 18 U.S.C. § 242—provides remedies against actions "under color" of law. It has given rise to problems similar to those presented by § 242, considered in sec. 3A. A major decision stimulating the widespread modern invocation of § 1983 was Monroe v. Pape, 365 U.S. 167 (1961), permitting a damage action against police officers for unlawful invasion of petitioners' home and for illegal search, seizure and detention. Justice Douglas's majority opinion emphasized that the "specific intent" requirement of Screws for criminal cases was not applicable here: "[§ 1983] should be read against the background of tort liability that makes a man responsible for the natural consequences of his actions." (See generally Klitgaard, "The Civil Rights Acts and Mr. Monroe," 49 Calif.L.Rev. 144 (1961), and Note, "The Proper Scope of the Civil Rights Acts," 66 Harv.L.Rev. 1285 (1953).) Under Monroe, however, local governments were immune from § 1983 actions. That immunity substantially evaporated in light of more recent decisions such as Monell v. Department of Social Services, 436 U.S. 658 (1978), and Owen v. Independence, 445 U.S. 622 (1980). The Court has repeatedly been confronted with problems of defenses (such as "good faith") and implied official immunities (e.g., for judges and legislators) under § 1983. In reading a variety of absolute and qualified defenses into § 1983, the Court has typically relied on

"common-law tradition" and "public policy reasons." Moreover, the readings of § 1983 have been repeatedly influenced by the Court's concern that the provision might turn into a general federal action for all torts committed by state and local officials. (The details of the statutory issues under § 1983 are beyond the scope of this book.)

b. One additional problem under § 1983 warrants mention here—a problem arising from the fact that its language covers not only action "under color" of state law, but refers also to "custom, or usage, of any State." In the Court's first extensive consideration of that phrase, in Adickes v. S.H. Kress & Co., 398 U.S. 144 (1970), Justice Harlan's majority opinion concluded that this "requires state involvement [and] not simply a practice that reflects longstanding social habit." "Custom," he insisted, "must have the force of law by virtue of the persistent practices of state officials." Justice Brennan's dissent argued that "custom" means "custom of the people of a State, not custom of state officials"—"a widespread and longstanding practice," not necessarily "backed by the force of the State."

———

C. Congressional Power to Reach Private Conduct Under the 13th Amendment

———

Jones v. Alfred H. Mayer Co.
392 U.S. 409, 88 S.Ct. 2186, 20 L.Ed.2d 1189 (1968).

Justice STEWART delivered the opinion of the Court.

In this case we are called upon to determine the scope and the constitutionality [of] 42 U.S.C. § 1982.* [P]etitioners filed a complaint [that] respondents had refused to sell them a home [for] the sole reason that petitioner [is] a Negro. Relying in part upon [§ 1982], the petitioners sought injunctive and other relief. [The lower federal courts dismissed the complaint], concluding that § 1982 applies only to state action and does not reach private refusals to sell. [We] reverse. [We] hold that § 1982 bars *all* racial discrimination, private as well as public, in the sale or rental of property, and that the statute, thus construed, is a valid exercise of the power of Congress to enforce the 13th Amendment.[1] At the outset, it is important to make clear precisely what this case does *not* involve. Whatever else it may be, 42 U.S.C. § 1982 is not a comprehensive open housing law, [unlike] the Fair Housing Title (Title VIII) of the Civil Rights Act of 1968.[2] [Thus], although § 1982 contains none of the

---

* As noted above, § 1982 states: "All citizens of the United States shall have the same right, in every State and Territory, as is enjoyed by white citizens thereof to inherit, purchase, lease, sell, hold, and convey real and personal property."

1. Because we have concluded that the discrimination alleged in the petitioners' complaint violated a federal statute that Congress had the power to enact under the 13th Amendment, we find it unnecessary to decide whether that discrimination also violated [equal protection]. [Footnote by Justice Stewart.] [The 14th Amendment state action issue had been the central focus in the lower courts.]

2. Justice Stewart elaborated: "In sharp contrast to Title VIII, [§ 1982] deals only with racial discrimination and does not address itself to discrimination on grounds of religion or national origin. It does not deal specifically with discrimination in the provi-

exemptions that Congress included in the Civil Rights Act of 1968,[3] it would be a serious mistake to suppose that § 1982 in any way diminishes the significance of the law recently enacted by [Congress]. On its face, [§ 1982] appears to prohibit *all* discrimination against Negroes in the sale or rental of property—discrimination by private owners as well as discrimination by public [authorities].[4] Stressing what they consider to be the revolutionary implications of so literal a reading of § 1982, respondents argue that Congress cannot possibly have intended any such result. Our examination of the relevant history, however, persuades us that Congress meant exactly what it said. In its original form, § 1982 was part [of] the Civil Rights Act of 1866. [The Court examined the legislative history at length.] Nor was the scope of the 1866 Act altered when it was re-enacted in 1870, some two years after the ratification of the 14th Amendment. It is quite true that some members of Congress supported the 14th Amendment "in order to eliminate doubt as to the constitutional validity of the Civil Rights Act as applied to the States." But it certainly does not follow that the adoption of the 14th Amendment or the subsequent readoption of the Civil Rights Act were meant somehow to *limit* its application to state action. The legislative history furnishes not the slightest factual basis for any such speculation, and the conditions prevailing in 1870 make it highly [implausible].

The remaining question is whether Congress has power under the Constitution to do what § 1982 purports to do: to prohibit all racial discrimination, private and public, in the sale and rental of property. Our starting point is the 13th Amendment, for it was pursuant to that constitutional provision that Congress originally enacted what is now § 1982. It has never been doubted "[that] the power vested in Congress to enforce the article by appropriate legislation" includes the power to enact laws "direct and primary, operating upon the acts of individuals, whether sanctioned by State legislation or not." [Civil Rights Cases.] Thus, the fact that § 1982 operates upon the unofficial acts of private individuals, whether or not sanctioned by state law, presents no constitutional problem. [The] constitutional question in this case, therefore, comes to this: Does the authority of Congress to enforce the 13th Amendment "by appropriate legislation" include the power to eliminate all racial barriers to the acquisition of real and personal property? We think the answer to that question is plainly yes. "By its own unaided force and effect," the 13th Amendment "abolished slavery, and established universal freedom." [Civil Rights Cases.] Whether or not the Amendment *itself* did any more than that—a question not involved in this case—it is at least clear that the Enabling Clause of that Amendment empowered Congress to do much more. For that clause

sion of services or facilities in connection with the sale or rental of a dwelling. It does not prohibit advertising or other representations that indicate discriminatory preferences. It does not refer explicitly to discrimination in financing arrangements or in the provision of brokerage services. It does not empower a federal administrative agency to assist aggrieved parties. It makes no provision for intervention by the Attorney General. And, although it can be enforced by injunction, it contains no provision expressly authorizing a federal court to order the payment of damages."

3. For an illustration of the exemptions under the Fair Housing Title of the 1968 Act, see § 803(b)(2), making the law inapplicable to "rooms or units in dwellings containing living quarters occupied or intended to be occupied by no more than four families living independently of each other, if the owner actually maintains and occupies one of such living quarters as his residence."

4. Justice Stewart acknowledged that earlier dicta—e.g., Hurd v. Hodge (1948; p. 938 above)—had stated that § 1982 was limited to "governmental action," but emphasized that none of the earlier cases had "presented [the] precise issue for adjudication."

clothed "Congress with power to pass *all laws necessary and proper for abolishing all badges and incidents of slavery in the United States.*" Ibid. (Emphasis added.) [Surely] Congress has the power under the 13th Amendment rationally to determine what are the badges and the incidents of slavery, and the authority to translate that determination into effective legislation. Nor can we say that the determination Congress has made is an irrational one. For this Court recognized long ago that, whatever else they may have encompassed, the badges and incidents of slavery—its "burdens and disabilities"—included restraints upon "those fundamental rights which are the essence of civil freedom, namely, the same right [to] inherit, purchase, lease, sell and convey property, as is enjoyed by white citizens." [Civil Rights Cases.] Just as the Black Codes, enacted after the Civil War to restrict the free exercise of those rights, were substitutes for the slave system, so the exclusion of Negroes from white communities became a substitute for the Black Codes. And when racial discrimination herds men into ghettos and makes their ability to buy property turn on the color of their skin, then it too is a relic of slavery. [At] the very least, the freedom that Congress is empowered to secure under the 13th Amendment includes the freedom to buy whatever a white man can buy, the right to live wherever a white man can live. If Congress cannot say that being a free man means at least this much, then the 13th Amendment made a promise the Nation cannot [keep].

Reversed.[5]

Justice HARLAN, whom Justice WHITE joins, dissenting.

[This decision] appears to me to be most ill-considered and ill-advised. [I] believe that the Court's construction of § 1982 as applying to purely private action is almost surely wrong, and at the least is open to serious doubt. The issue of the constitutionality of § 1982, as construed by the Court, and of liability under the 14th Amendment alone,[1] also present formidable difficulties. Moreover, the political processes of our own era have, since the date of oral argument in this case, given birth to a civil rights statute embodying "fair housing" provisions which would at the end of this year make available to others, though apparently not to the petitioners themselves, the type of relief which the petitioners now seek.[2] It seems to me that this latter factor so diminishes the public importance of this case that by far the wisest course would be [to] dismiss the writ as improvidently granted. [The Court] finds it "plain and unambiguous" [that the language of § 1982] forbids purely private as well as state-authorized discrimination. [I] do not find it so. For me, there is an inherent ambiguity in the term "right," as used in § 1982. The "right" referred to may either be a right to equal status under the law, in which case the statute operates only against state-sanctioned discrimination, or it may be an "absolute" right enforceable against private individuals. To me, the words of the statute, taken alone, suggest the former interpretation, not the latter. [The] Court rests its opinion chiefly upon the legislative history of the Civil Rights

---

5. A concurring opinion by Justice DOUGLAS is omitted.

1. Justice Harlan noted, in a footnote at another point, that the 14th Amendment "state action" argument—not reached by the majority in Jones—had emphasized "the respondents' role as a housing developer who exercised continuing authority over a suburban housing complex with about 1,000 inhabitants."

2. Elsewhere in his opinion, Justice Harlan commented: "In effect, this Court, by its construction of § 1982, has extended the coverage of federal 'fair housing' laws far beyond that which Congress in its wisdom chose to provide in the Civil Rights Act of 1968."

Act of 1866. I shall endeavor to show that those debates do [not] overwhelmingly support the result reached by the Court, and in fact that a contrary conclusion may equally well be drawn. [A discussion of the legislative history is omitted.] [In] holding that the 13th Amendment is sufficient constitutional authority for § 1982 as interpreted, the Court also decides a question of great importance. Even contemporary supporters of the aims of the [1866] Act doubted that those goals could constitutionally be achieved under the 13th Amendment, and this Court has twice expressed similar [doubts].

————

13TH AMENDMENT POWERS AND THE 1866 ACT

1. *The scope of congressional power after the Jones case.* a. How far-reaching is the 13th Amendment power recognized in Jones? Is it an adequate constitutional basis for all conceivable civil rights legislation directed at private conduct? Did it in effect make the public accommodations and employment discrimination provisions of the 1964 Civil Rights Act superfluous? Did it have that effect especially in view of § 1981, another legacy of the Civil Rights Act of 1866?[1] See Runyon v. McCrary (1976; note 2b below).

b. Is there any law against racial discrimination that Congress may not consider a remedy for the "badges of servitude"? May Congress deal with discrimination against groups other than African Americans? See Note, 69 Colum.L.Rev. 1019 (1969), suggesting that the Jones reading indicates that "slavery" now includes "the second class citizenship imposed on members of disparate minority groups. [A] victim's people need not have been enslaved in order to invoke its protection. He need only be suffering today under conditions that could reasonably be called symptoms of a slave society."[2]

c. For an extensive criticism of the Jones majority's reading of history, see Fairman, Reconstruction and Reunion: 1864–1888, Part One (6 History of the Supreme Court of the United States) (1971). (See also Casper, "Jones v.

---

1. As noted above, § 1981 guarantees all persons "the same right [to] make and enforce contracts, to sue, be parties, give evidence, and to the full and equal benefits of all laws and proceedings for the security of persons and property as is enjoyed by white citizens."

2. Cf. Note, "The 'New' 13th [Amendment]," 82 Harv.L.Rev. 1294 (1969), and Calhoun, "The 13th and 14th Amendments: Constitutional Authority for Federal Legislation Against Private Sex Discrimination," 61 Minn.L.Rev. 313 (1977). In McDonald v. Santa Fe Trail Transportation Co., 427 U.S. 273 (1976), the Court implicitly suggested that congressional power under the 13th Amendment can be invoked to curb discrimination against whites. In his majority opinion, Justice Marshall found that § 1981 (as well as the 1964 Civil Rights Act) "affords protection from racial discrimination in private employment to white persons as well as nonwhites." The Court's discussion was limited to statutory issues; the implicit constitutional premise—that the anti-slavery Amendment could benefit races who had never been enslaved— was not discussed by the Justices. Note also Shaare Tefila Congregation v. Cobb, 481 U.S. 615 (1987), and Saint Francis College v. Al-Khazraji, 481 U.S. 604 (1987), companion cases raising the question whether §§ 1981 and 1982, though limited to "racial" discrimination, reached discrimination on the basis of national origin or religion. Looking to the legislative history of the 1866 Act, the Court noted that the concept of "race" as used then was not the same as modern understandings. Accordingly, the Court held unanimously that Jews and Arabs could sue under the sections: "It is evident from the legislative history [that] Jews and Arabs were among the peoples then considered to be distinct races and hence within the protection of the statute. [They] are not foreclosed from stating a cause of action against other members of what today is considered to be part of the Caucasian race."

Mayer: Clio, Bemused and Confused Muse," 1968 Sup.Ct.Rev. 89; compare Kohl, "The Civil Rights Act of 1866, Its Hour Come Round at Last," 55 Va.L.Rev. 272 (1969).) Note Levinson, Book Review, 26 Stan.L.Rev. 461 (1974), concluding that Fairman clearly demonstrates the "slipshod" nature of the majority's historical analysis but adding that its conclusion may nevertheless be warranted, "for the Civil Rights Act of 1866 *did* manifest, however imperfectly and ambivalently, a vision of a new order of freedom for the black man." The real issue, Levinson argues, is not whether the text of the law "dictated" the decision, but "whether the decision was *permitted*." On that issue, the historical background "need not be conclusive regarding its present application." Assuming such open-ended readings are appropriate for constitutional provisions, are they also appropriate for legislative enactments?

2. *Modern interpretations of the 1866 Act.* a. The Court applied the newly discovered 1866 Act—and expanded its broad interpretation—in SULLIVAN v. LITTLE HUNTING PARK, INC., 396 U.S. 229 (1969). There, a residents' association operated a community park and playground facilities. Subject to the board's approval, a member who rented his house could assign his share to his tenant. Sullivan leased his house to Freeman and assigned his membership share to him. The board "refused to approve the assignment, because Freeman was a Negro." Sullivan was expelled for protesting that decision. The Court found that Sullivan and Freeman could sue under § 1982 for damages and injunctive relief. Justice DOUGLAS's majority opinion found the corporation's refusal an interference with the right to "lease" within the terms of the 1866 Act. He rejected the state court's finding that the case involved a private social club: "There was no plan or purpose of exclusiveness. It is open to every white person within the geographic area, there being no selective element other than race." Justice HARLAN's dissent, joined by Chief Justice Burger and Justice White, urged that certiorari be dismissed as improvidently granted because of the "complexities" under the 1866 Act and the existence of the 1968 fair housing law. He noted that the Court had gone beyond the Jones case, above, "(1) by implying a private right to damages for violations of § 1982; (2) by interpreting § 1982 to prohibit a community recreation association from withholding, on the basis of race, approval of an assignment of a membership that was transferred incident to a lease of real property; and (3) by deciding that a white person who is expelled from a recreation association 'for the advocacy of [a Negro's] cause' has 'standing' to maintain an action for relief under § 1982." He commented, moreover: "[Lurking] in the background are grave constitutional issues should § 1982 be extended too far into some types of private discrimination." He cited the Civil Rights Cases. What are those "grave constitutional issues"? Which concerns of the Civil Rights Cases are relevant to 13th Amendment legislation? There is no state action limitation under the 13th Amendment. Is there nevertheless a limitation stemming from the privacy and associational interests of the discriminator? Recall the comments in sec. 2 above, on balancing the competing interests of the discriminator and the victim. Is that variety of balancing relevant to 13th Amendment interpretation? Was there such balancing in Runyon, which follows?

b. In RUNYON v. McCRARY, 427 U.S. 160 (1976), the Court held that § 1981 (derived from the 1866 Act) "prohibits private, commercially operated, nonsectarian schools from denying admission to prospective students because they are Negroes" and that as so applied § 1981 was constitutional. Justice STEWART's majority opinion relied on his approach in Jones for the statutory interpretation, and he found no violation of "constitutionally protected rights of free association and privacy, or a parent's right to direct the education of his children." With respect to freedom of association, he noted that "it may be assumed that parents have a First Amendment right to send their children to educational institutions that promote the belief that racial segregation is desirable, and that the children have an equal right to attend such institutions." But "it does not follow that the *practice* of excluding racial minorities from such institutions is also protected by the same principle." With respect to privacy, he stated that "it does not follow that because government is [largely] precluded from regulating the child-bearing decision, it is similarly restricted [from] regulating the implementation of parental decisions concerning a child's education."[3] Justice WHITE's dissent, joined by Justice Rehnquist, argued that, despite the broad reading of § 1982 in Jones, § 1981 ought not to be given the majority's construction. He argued that the legislative history of § 1981 "confirms that the statute means what it says and no more, i.e., that it outlaws any legal rule disabling any person from making or enforcing a contract, but does not prohibit private racially motivated refusals to contract." The holding, he added, "threatens to embark the judiciary on a treacherous course. [W]hites and blacks will undoubtedly choose to form a variety of associational relationships pursuant to [racially exclusionary contracts]. Social clubs, black and white, and associations designed to further the interests of blacks or whites are but two examples. [As] the associational or contractual relationships become more private, the pressures to hold § 1981 inapplicable to them will increase. Imaginative judicial construction of the word 'contract' is foreseeable; [13th Amendment] limitations on Congress' power to ban 'badges and incidents of slavery' may be discovered; the doctrine of the right to association may be bent to cover a given situation. [Courts] will be called upon to balance sensitive policy considerations against each other, [all] under the guise of 'construing' a statute. This is a task appropriate for the legislature, not for the judiciary." In Patterson v. McLean Credit Union, 491 U.S. 164 (1989), the Court's majority, over vigorous dissents, had requested the parties to address the issue whether Runyon should be overruled. However, the Court unanimously refused to overrule Runyon. Justice White added that he did not "question at this point" the congressional power to ban racial discrimination in private school admission decisions; but "as I see it, Congress has not yet chosen to exercise that power." (In separate concurrences, Justices STEVENS and POWELL indicated that, if the question were a new one, they would agree with Justice White's statutory construction. But they thought the broad Jones view of § 1982 was indistinguishable, and that Jones should not be overruled at this late date.)

c.   Do §§ 1981 and 1982 require a finding of purposeful discrimination to justify recovery? Although that was the question on which certiorari had been granted in Memphis v. Greene (1981; p. 764 above), the majority did not reach the issue. However, Justice White's separate opinion argued that "[p]urposeful racial discrimination" was required under § 1982. (Justice Marshall disagreed.) The issue was in effect settled by the full Court a year later, in General Building Contractors Assn. v. Pennsylvania, 458 U.S. 375 (1982), where Justice Rehnquist's majority opinion held that a suit under § 1981 requires "proof of discriminatory intent" and does not reach "practices that merely result in a disproportionate impact on a particular class." Justice Marshall's dissent,

---

3. In light of the broad readings of §§ 1981 and 1982 by the modern Court, consider the extent to which the revived 1866 laws in effect make unnecessary not only the modern laws against racial discrimination but also the struggles regarding state action theories in the cases in sec. 2 above. See Henkin, "On Drawing Lines," 82 Harv. L.Rev. 63 (1968). Bear in mind, however, that state action analysis remained significant outside the race discrimination area.

joined by Justice Brennan, argued that the majority had "virtually ignore[d] Congress' broad remedial purposes."

SECTION 4. CONGRESSIONAL POWER TO CHANGE THE CONTENT OF CONSTITUTIONAL RIGHTS?—"REMEDIAL" AND "SUBSTANTIVE" POWER UNDER § 5 OF THE 14TH AMENDMENT

———

Introduction. Historically, most of the laws enacted by Congress under its powers to "enforce" the 14th and 15th Amendments were quite narrowly "remedial": Congress simply provided enforcement mechanisms to implement judicially declared rights. For example, the post-Civil War "under color" of law provisions, above, afforded remedies for the deprivation of rights as secured by the Constitution and interpreted by the Court. The Guest case suggested a potentially broader congressional power: the authority to extend the reach of the 14th Amendment to cover some private behavior. But even there, Congress did not purport to modify the substantive *content* of the rights it protected. This section examines congressional authority to go beyond that: not merely to provide sanctions against practices independently held unconstitutional under Court-announced doctrine, but also to determine on its own that certain practices are unlawful even though the Court has not found them unconstitutional.

This novel type of congressional action has arisen largely in the voting rights context. Most of the cases below involve the Voting Rights Act, first adopted in 1965 and extended (and expanded) since. Thus, in South Carolina v. Katzenbach (1966; p. 987 below), the Court sustained a provision, applicable largely to the South, suspending literacy tests—even though the Lassiter case (1959; p. 987 below) had unanimously rejected an on-the-face equal protection attack on literacy tests. Oregon v. Mitchell (1970; p. 1004 below) unanimously sustained the nationwide suspension of literacy tests accomplished by the 1970 Act: this was not seen as a significant extension of the South Carolina case. These laws were sustained on the view that Congress had enacted valid "remedial" legislation—albeit "remedial" actions more far-reaching than the traditional ones. Katzenbach v. Morgan (1966; p. 998 below) upheld another provision of the 1965 Act, barring literacy tests for Puerto Ricans educated in certain Spanish-language schools—even though, in a companion case, Cardona v. Power (1966; p. 1001 below), the Court avoided deciding whether the application of New York's English literacy requirement to those literate in Spanish violated equal protection. Justice Brennan's majority opinion in Morgan contained controversial language indicating that Congress had some power to determine on its own the substantive content of constitutional rights. Morgan, in its passages suggesting that congressional power could be "substantive," not merely "remedial," suggested great judicial deference not only to congressional creation of remedies but also to congressional refashioning of rights.

The "substantive" theory suggested by Morgan has produced extensive commentary on and off the Court. Justice Brennan's opinion sought to limit it to "expansions" of constitutional rights: he insisted in a footnote that Congress could only expand, not "dilute," rights. But others have argued that his rationale for recognizing a congressional "substantive" power can cut both ways; and that, if Congress can in fact dilute Court-delineated rights, Morgan's new congressional authority runs counter to the views of judicial autonomy in Marbury v. Madison. In Oregon v. Mitchell (1970; p. 1004 below), the Morgan rationale did not prove adequate to sustain a congressional effort to lower the minimum voting age in state elections to 18. But a decade after that apparent confinement of Morgan, the Court sustained a far-reaching aspect of the Voting Rights Act in Rome v. United States (1980; p. 991 below). The Rome case held that Congress, acting under its 15th Amendment enforcement power, could constitutionally bar a city from making any governmental changes that were found to be racially discriminatory in effect, even though the city had not engaged in any purposeful discrimination for nearly two decades. But the Court did *not* rely on the novel "substantive" power of Morgan; instead, the Rome decision rested on a broad reading of an expanded "remedial" power. This section focuses on that series of cases and their implications. To what extent does congressional power under the enforcement clauses of the 14th and 15th Amendments extend beyond the providing of sanctions for violations of judicially-declared rights? Can the provisions sustained in the Voting Rights Act cases be justified as merely "remedial," as earlier enactments undoubtedly were? If the "remedial" power is read as broadly as it was in the Rome case, does it make resort to the apparently more controversial "substantive" rationale of Morgan unnecessary? Can Congress, in short, play a powerful role in determining the effective content of constitutional rights by asserting the power to act "remedially"? In what contexts outside of voting rights may Congress invoke the broad powers recognized in the Rome and Morgan cases? In pursuing these questions, this section begins with the background of judicial and congressional action in the voting rights field culminating in the provisions sustained on "remedial" grounds in the cases from South Carolina to Rome.

CONGRESSIONAL PROTECTION OF VOTING RIGHTS: THE BACKGROUND AND THE SOUTH CAROLINA CASE

1. *Chief Justice Warren's summary of the background.* [Prior to the Voting Rights Act of 1965, congressional legislation directed against racial discrimination in voting was quite clearly remedial. Congress merely provided enforcement mechanisms; the rights guaranteed were stated in the very general terms of the Constitution. Delineation of the content of the rights was left to the courts; and implementation was left to litigation resting on the congressionally-prescribed remedies. Frustration with that case-by-case approach led to the enactment of the 1965 Act. Chief Justice WARREN's opinion in SOUTH CAROLINA v. KATZENBACH, 383 U.S. 301 (1966; p. 987 below), contained a summary of the "historical experience" that led Congress to two basic conclusions: "First: Congress felt itself confronted by an insidious and pervasive evil which had been perpetuated in certain parts of our country through unremitting and ingenious defiance of the Constitution. Second: Congress concluded that the unsuccessful remedies which it had prescribed in the past would have to be replaced by sterner and more elaborate measures in order to satisfy the clear commands of the 15th Amendment." Excerpts from the Chief Justice's account of the historical background follow:]

The 15th Amendment [was] ratified in 1870. Promptly thereafter Congress passed the Enforcement Act of 1870, which made it a crime for public officers and private persons to obstruct exercise of the right to vote. [E]nforcement of the laws became spotty and ineffective, and most of their provisions were repealed in 1894. [Meanwhile,] beginning in 1890, [Alabama,] Georgia, Louisiana, Mississippi, North Carolina, South Carolina, and Virginia enacted tests still in use which were specifically designed to prevent Negroes from voting. Typically, they made the ability to read and write a registration qualification. [These] laws were based on the fact that as of 1890 in each of the named States, more than two-thirds of the adult Negroes were illiterate while less than one-quarter of the adult whites were unable to read or write. At the same time, alternate tests were prescribed in all of [the] States to assure that white illiterates would not be deprived of the franchise. These included grandfather clauses, property qualifications, "good character" tests, and the requirement that registrants "understand" or "interpret" certain matter. The course of subsequent 15th Amendment litigation[1] [demonstrates] the variety and persistence of these and similar institutions designed to deprive Negroes of the right to vote. [According to] the evidence in recent Justice Department voting suits, [discriminatory enforcement of voting qualifications] is now the principal method used to bar Negroes from the polls. [White] applicants for registration have often been excused altogether from the literacy and understanding tests or have been given easy versions, have received extensive help from voting officials, and have been registered despite serious errors in their answers. Negroes, on the other hand, have typically been required to pass difficult versions of all the [tests]. The good-morals requirement is so vague and subjective that it has constituted an open invitation to abuse at the hands of voting officials. [In recent years,] Congress has repeatedly tried to cope with the problem by facilitating case-by-case litigation against voting discrimination. The Civil Rights Act of 1957 authorized the Attorney General to seek injunctions against public and private interference with the right to vote on racial grounds. Perfecting amendments in the Civil Rights Act of 1960 permitted the joinder of States as parties defendant, gave the Attorney General access to local voting records, and authorized courts to register voters in areas of systematic discrimination. Title I of the Civil Rights Act of 1964 expedited the hearing of voting cases before three-judge courts and outlawed some of the tactics used to disqualify Negroes from voting in federal elections. [This] legislation has proved ineffective for a number of reasons. Voting suits are unusually onerous to prepare. [Litigation] has been exceedingly slow. [Even when] favorable decisions have finally been obtained, some of the States affected have merely switched to discriminatory devices not covered by the federal decrees or have enacted difficult new tests. [Alternatively,] certain local officials have defied and evaded court orders or have simply closed their registration offices to freeze the voting rolls.

2. *The constitutional status of literacy tests before the 1965 Act.* It was against that background that Congress enacted the Voting Rights Act of 1965 "to rid the country of racial discrimination in voting." One controversial provision of that "complex scheme of stringent remedies aimed at areas where voting discrimination has been most flagrant" suspended literacy tests in covered localities—including many localities where there had been no judicial finding of discriminatory practices. In that sense, Congress moved beyond where the courts had gone. A few years earlier, moreover, the Court had

---

1. The Chief Justice summarized the Court decisions as follows: "Grandfather clauses were invalidated in Guinn v. United States, 238 U.S. 347, and Myers v. Anderson, 238 U.S. 368. Procedural hurdles were struck down in Lane v. Wilson, 307 U.S. 268. The white primary was outlawed in Smith v. Allwright, 321 U.S. 649, and Terry v. Adams, 345 U.S. 461. Improper challenges were nullified in United States v. Thomas, 362 U.S. 58. Racial gerrymandering was forbidden by Gomillion v. Lightfoot, 364 U.S. 339. Finally, discriminatory application of voting tests was condemned in Schnell v. Davis, 336 U.S. 933; Alabama v. United States, 371 U.S. 37; and Louisiana v. United States, 380 U.S. 145."

refused to strike down literacy tests on their face. In LASSITER v. NORTH-AMPTON COUNTY ELECTION BD., 360 U.S. 45 (1959), Justice DOUGLAS, for a unanimous Court, rejected a black citizen's attack on North Carolina's literacy test. The operative part of the state provision stated: "Every person presenting himself for registration shall be able to read and write any section of the [North Carolina] Constitution in the English language." Justice Douglas stated: "The States have long been held to have broad powers to determine the conditions under which the right of suffrage may be exercised, absent of course the discrimination which the Constitution condemns. [Residence] requirements, age, previous criminal record are obvious examples indicating factors which a State may take into consideration in determining the qualifications of voters. The ability to read and write likewise has some relation to standards designed to promote intelligent use of the ballot. Literacy and illiteracy are neutral on race, creed, color, and [sex]. Literacy and intelligence are obviously not synonymous. [Yet] in our society where newspapers, periodicals, books, and other printed matter canvass and debate campaign issues, a State might conclude that only those who are literate should exercise the franchise. [We] do not sit in judgment on the wisdom of [the State's] policy. We cannot say [that] it is not an allowable [one]. Of course a literacy test, fair on its face, may be employed to perpetuate that discrimination which the 15th Amendment was designed to uproot. No such influence is charged here."[2] But Lassiter proved no obstacle to Congress's broad-gauged moves against literacy tests that began 1965.

3. *The South Carolina case.* SOUTH CAROLINA v. KATZENBACH, 383 U.S. 301 (1966), sustained several controversial provisions of the Voting Rights Act of 1965, largely directed at racial discrimination in the South, as a proper exercise of congressional power under § 2 of the 15th Amendment. (Only a brief summary of this case appears here; additional aspects are discussed in the Rome decision, below.) In his general passages, Chief Justice WARREN stated: "Congress may use any rational means to effectuate the constitutional prohibition of racial discrimination in voting. The basic test to be applied [under § 2] is the same as in all cases concerning the express powers of Congress with relation to the reserved powers of the States. [McCulloch.]" He concluded: "[We] reject South Carolina's argument that Congress may appropriately do no more than to forbid violations of the 15th Amendment in general terms—that the task of fashioning specific remedies or of applying them to particular localities must necessarily be left entirely to the courts. Congress is not circumscribed by any such artificial rules." That broad discretion validated the "inventive" use of congressional powers here. Prescribing remedies for voting discrimination "which go into effect without any need for prior adjudication" was "clearly a legitimate response to the problem, for which there is ample precedent under other constitutional provisions. [See McClung; Darby (commerce power cases; in chap. 3 above).]" Congress "had found that case-by-case litigation was inadequate to combat widespread and persistent discrimination in voting"; accordingly, it "might well decide to shift the advantage of time and inertia from the perpetrators of the evil to its victims." And the "specific remedies" in the Act were "appropriate means of combating the evil."

2. Justice Douglas added: "On the other hand, a literacy test may be unconstitutional on its face," and the Court had so ruled. He referred to Davis v. Schnell, 81 F.Supp. 872 (D.Ala.1949), affirmed, 336 U.S. 933 (1949). There, the test was the citizen's ability to "understand and explain" an Article of the U.S. Constitution. It was struck down on its face because the "legislative setting [and] the great discretion it vested in the registrar made it clear that [the] literacy requirement was merely a device to make racial discrimination easy." Justice Douglas added that no such discriminatory inference could be made about the North Carolina test challenged in Lassiter.

Turning to those remedies, the Court focused on the coverage formula for determining the localities in which literacy tests and similar "devices" were to be suspended for a period of five years.[3] The Chief Justice found that the areas covered by the Act "were an appropriate target for the new remedies," noting that the law "intentionally confines these remedies to a small number of States and political subdivisions which in most instances were familiar to Congress by name." He was not persuaded by the argument "that the coverage formula is awkwardly designed in a number of respects and that it disregards various local conditions which have nothing to do with racial discrimination." He replied: "Congress began work with reliable evidence [in judicial proceedings and in findings by the Justice Department and the Civil Rights Commission] of actual voting discrimination in a great majority of the [areas] affected by the new remedies of the Act. The formula eventually evolved to describe these areas was relevant to the problem of voting discrimination, and Congress was therefore entitled to infer a significant danger of the evil in the few remaining States and political subdivisions covered." All of the areas for which there was evidence of actual voting discrimination shared the "two characteristics incorporated by Congress into the coverage formula." The Chief Justice elaborated: "Tests and devices are relevant to voting discrimination because of their long history as a tool for perpetrating the evil; a low voting rate is pertinent for the obvious reason that widespread disenfranchisement must inevitably affect the number of actual voters. Accordingly, the coverage formula is rational in both practice and theory. It was therefore permissible to impose the new remedies on the few remaining States and political subdivisions covered by the formula, at least in the absence of proof that they have been free of substantial voting discrimination in recent years." And it was "irrelevant that the coverage formula excludes certain localities which do not employ voting tests and devices but for which there is evidence of voting discrimination by other means": "Legislation need not deal with all phases of a problem in the same way, so long as the distinctions drawn have some basis in practical experience." Moreover, the existence of the termination procedure was an adequate safeguard against overbreadth of the Act. And South Carolina's argument "that these termination procedures are a nullity because they impose an impossible burden of proof" were not persuasive. The rejection of the constitutional attack on literacy tests in Lassiter did not bar these congressional remedies: Lassiter itself had recognized that literacy tests could be used as discriminatory devices. The record here showed "that in most of the States [covered], various tests and devices have been instituted with the purpose of disenfranchising Negroes, have been framed in such a way as to facilitate this aim, and have been administered in a discriminatory fashion for many years. *Under these circumstances, the 15th Amendment has clearly been violated*." (Emphasis added.) In

---

3. Under this coverage formula, the Act was applicable to any state or political subdivision "for which two findings have been made: (1) the Attorney General has determined that on November 1, 1964, it maintained a 'test or device,' and (2) the Director of the Census has determined that less than 50 percent of its voting-age residents were registered on November 1, 1964, or voted in the presidential election of November, 1964." These findings were not reviewable. Statutory coverage could be terminated if the covered area obtained a declaratory judgment from the District Court for the District of Columbia, "determining that tests and devices have not been used during the preceding five years to abridge the franchise on racial grounds." (See Rome, below.) As a result, a number of areas were promptly brought under the coverage of the Act. (The areas that had been brought under the Act by the time this case reached the Court were the states of South Carolina, Alabama, Alaska, Georgia, Louisiana, Mississippi, and Virginia, 26 counties in North Carolina, three counties in Arizona, one county in Hawaii, and one county in Idaho.)

the covered areas, the Act suspended literacy tests for five years from the last occurrence of substantial voting discrimination. Moreover, § 5 barred any new "standard, practice, or procedure with respect to voting" pending scrutiny by federal authorities to determine whether their use would violate the 15th Amendment.[4] These were found to be "legitimate" remedies, since continuance of the tests "would freeze the effect of past discrimination in favor of unqualified white registrants" and since Congress knew that some of the covered states "had resorted to the extraordinary strategem of contriving new rules of various kinds for the sole purpose of perpetuating voting discrimination in the face of adverse federal court decrees."[5]

4. *The nationwide suspension of literacy tests in the 1970 Act and later extensions of the Voting Rights Act.* The Voting Rights Act Amendments of 1970 not only extended the 1965 Act for five years but added a number of new provisions. In one of the 1970 provisions, Congress suspended the use of literacy tests on a *nationwide* basis, not just in the areas subject to the coverage formula of the 1965 Act. In 1975, the Voting Rights Act was once again amended, and extended for 7 years, until 1982. One of its provisions was to make permanent the nationwide ban on literacy tests. The 1970 Act produced another major Court decision on congressional powers. In Oregon v. Mitchell (1970; p. 1004 below), although the Court divided on all other provisions of the 1970 Act, it was unanimous in one respect: every Justice found the nationwide literacy test suspension constitutional. (See Rome, below.) Some Justices accepted the 1970 extension on the basis of the congressional interest in nationwide uniformity and in "this country's history of discriminatory educational opportunities in both the North and the South." Even Justice Harlan, the member of the Warren Court who took the most restrictive view of congressional powers under the 14th and 15th Amendments, agreed that the expanded reach of the literacy test provision fell within the "remedial" powers of Congress. He explained: "Despite the lack of evidence of specific instances of discriminatory application or effect, Congress could have determined that racial prejudice is prevalent throughout the Nation, and that literacy tests unduly lend themselves to discriminatory application, either conscious or unconscious. The danger of violation of § 1 of the [15th Amendment] was sufficient to authorize the exercise of congressional power under § 2. [While] a less sweeping approach in this delicate area might well have been appropriate, the choice which Congress made was within the range of the reasonable." [Note Justice Harlan's dissent in Morgan (1966; p. 998 below), where he distinguished South Carolina as involving merely "remedial" provisions and claimed that the South

---

4. A partial dissent by Justice BLACK in South Carolina objected to § 5, the prior approval requirement. That remedy, he insisted, utilized means "that conflict with the most basic principles of the Constitution": requiring states "to beg federal authorities to approve their policies [distorts] our constitutional structure." Moreover, the federal approval requirement conflicted with the "Republican Form of Government" guarantee, Art. VI, § 4, since it created the impression that states were "little more than conquered provinces." The impact of § 5 is examined in the Rome case, below. (Other provisions of the Act included authorization for the appointment of federal examiners to list qualified applicants as "eligible voters.") In a ser-

ies of subsequent cases, the majority gave a broad reading to the types of changes subject to the prior approval requirement of § 5. See, e.g., Allen v. State Board of Elections, 393 U.S. 544 (1969), and Beer v. United States, 425 U.S. 130 (1976), further discussed in Rome, below.

5. For an attempt by a county to reinstate a literacy test suspended pursuant to the Act, see Gaston County v. United States, 395 U.S. 285 (1969). Though the Court did not question the county's claim that it had administered its tests in a fair and impartial manner, it rejected the county's reinstatement effort in view of past unequal educational opportunities.

Carolina decision had merely involved "appropriate remedial legislation to cure an established violation of a constitutional command." The "substantive" rather than "remedial" power—relied on, in his view, in the majority opinion in Morgan—by contrast sought to determine "whether there has in fact been an infringement" of equal protection.]

With § 5 of the Voting Rights Act scheduled to expire in August 1982, efforts began in Congress early in 1981 to extend it once again, this time for 10 years. The debate began with consideration of § 5, the "preclearance" provision. But the focus of controversy soon shifted to § 2 and the issue of the appropriate standard of proof for identifying laws that "deny or abridge" the right to vote. The Court's ruling in 1980, in Mobile v. Bolden [discussed in Rogers v. Lodge (1981; p. 764 above)] had determined that § 2 was coextensive with equal protection standards and therefore required proof of discriminatory purpose, not merely discriminatory effects. Civil rights groups, arguing for a "results" standard, maintained that the Court's purposefulness test imposed an unduly burdensome litigation obstacle. Supporters of the Court's decision countered that discrimination, by its very nature, must be intentional and that the "results" standard would eventually lead to the establishment of racial quotas and proportional representation in elections. In November 1981, the House, siding with civil rights advocates, adopted the results standard for § 2 and indefinitely extended § 5's "preclearance" requirement. In the Senate, there was strong opposition to the House's "results" language until Kansas Republican Robert Dole proposed a compromise. The Dole Compromise in effect endorsed judicial attention to "results" as one factor in the consideration of the "totality of circumstances" relevant to a § 2 discrimination claim. However, the Compromise qualified the results standard in order to mollify concerns about racial quotas and proportional representation. The amended version of § 2 resulting from that compromise provides, in § 2(a), that "[n]o voting qualification or prerequisite to voting or standard, practice, or procedure shall be imposed or applied [in] a manner which results in a denial or abridgement of the right [to] vote on account of race or color, or in contravention of the guarantees [provided in subsection (b)]." Sec. 2(b) stated that a violation of § 2(a) is established "if, based on the totality of circumstances, it is shown that the political processes leading to nomination or election [are] not equally open to participation by members of a [protected] class of citizens [in] that its members have less opportunity than other members of the electorate to participate in the political process and to elect representatives of their choice. The extent to which members of a protected class have been elected to office [is] one circumstance which may be considered: *Provided,* That nothing in this section establishes a right to have members of a protected class elected in numbers equal to their proportion in the population." After nearly unanimous approval in both houses, the compromise extension of the Voting Rights Act was signed into law by President Reagan on June, 1982. (For an interpretation of the 1982 extension, see Thornburg v. Gingles, 478 U.S. 30 (1986); recall also the racial redistricting cases in chap. 9, sec. 4.) For a discussion of the underlying principles in conflict during the debate over the modification of § 2, and about the probable consequences of the extension, see Blumstein, "Defining and Proving Race Discrimination: Perspectives on the Purpose vs. Results Approach from the Voting Rights Act," 69 Va.L.Rev. 633 (1983). (Blumstein concluded that the amended § 2 "gives minorities an affirmative entitlement to ballot access but that Congress did not intend the revised [§ 2] to give minorities an affirmative entitlement to proportional representation.") Cf. Howard & Howard, "The Dilemma of the Voting Rights Act—Recognizing the Emerging Political Equality Norm," 83 Colum.L.Rev. 1615 (1983). Is there any doubt about the constitutionality of the amended § 2 under the majority rationale in the Rome case, which follows? Under the analysis of Justice Rehnquist's dissent? Can the § 2 amendment be justified simply under the "remedial" rationale? Or must a justification also draw on the "substantive" rationale of Morgan, below?

5. *Some questions about "remedial" legislation and the "remedial"-"substantive" distinction.* Was the "remedial" power of Congress asserted in the South Carolina case significantly different from that sustained in the earlier, more traditional civil rights laws? Can the exercise of congressional power sustained in South Carolina and Oregon be justified as "remedial," or were those assertions of power in practice indistinguishable from the more controversial "substantive" power suggested in Morgan, below? At the heart of the "remedial" justification for the treatment of literacy provisions in the 1965 and 1970 Acts is the premise that Congress acted on the basis of Court-endorsed rules that discriminatory "tests and devices" *are* unconstitutional. True, Lassiter refused to find literacy tests unconstitutional per se. But Chief Justice Warren did say in the South Carolina case, after examining the evidence before Congress: "Under these circumstances, the Fifteenth Amendment has clearly been violated." Can the South Carolina decision, then, be viewed as an implicit overruling of Lassiter, in view of the new information before Congress? Can a similar rationale support the Oregon expansion of the literacy test ban? The Rome case, which follows, takes an even broader view of the "remedial" powers of Congress. Does Rome make it even more difficult to maintain a practical distinction between the reach of the "remedial" and "substantive" rationales? These questions should be borne in mind when examining Rome; and they will warrant renewed attention after examining the Morgan-related problems printed after Rome. (Rome is printed here, out of chronological sequence, because of the majority's reliance on the remedial rationale. It may be useful to postpone full consideration until after the Morgan and Oregon cases below; the latter decisions antedate Rome.)

Rome v. United States
446 U.S. 156, 100 S.Ct. 1548, 64 L.Ed.2d 119 (1980).

Justice MARSHALL delivered the opinion of the [Court].

At issue in this case is the constitutionality of the Voting Rights Act of 1965 [as amended] and its applicability to electoral changes and annexations made by the city of Rome, Ga. [In 1966, Rome's electoral system changed in several ways, as the result of a state law: e.g., each of the nine members of its city commission would be elected by majority rather than plurality vote, the number of wards would be reduced from nine to three, and each commissioner would henceforth be elected at-large to one of three posts established in each ward. Moreover, the city made a number of annexations to its territory between 1964 and 1975. Because Georgia had been designated a covered jurisdiction under the 1965 Act, the State and its municipalities were required to comply with the preclearance provisions of § 5 of the Act. The Attorney General refused to approve the electoral changes, concluding that in a city such as Rome, with a predominantly white population and a norm of racial bloc voting, the changes would deprive black voters of the opportunity to elect a candidate of their choice. (Under § 5, the Attorney General may approve a change in voting practice only if it "does not have the purpose *and* will not have the effect of denying or abridging the right to vote on account of race or color."

(Emphasis added.) In the Rome case, the Attorney General found no forbidden "purpose" but relied on the "effect" provision.) The Attorney General also refused to preclear 13 of the annexations for purposes of city commission elections, finding that Rome had not carried its burden of proving that these annexations would not dilute the black vote. The city then sought declaratory relief in a three-judge District Court. That court rejected all of the city's challenges, finding that the disapproved changes and annexations, while not adopted for any discriminatory purpose, did have a discriminatory effect. The Supreme Court affirmed.][1]

[II. The city contends that it] may exempt itself from the coverage of the Act. [The city] comes within the preclearance requirement of [§ 4(a)]because it is a political unit in a covered jurisdiction, the State of Georgia. [This section provides] a procedure for exemption from the Act. This so-called "bail out" provision allows a covered jurisdiction to escape the preclearance requirement of § 5 by bringing a declaratory judgment action before [a three-judge court] and proving that no "test or device" has been used in the jurisdiction "during the [17] years preceding the filing of the action for the purpose or with the effect of denying or abridging the right to vote on account of race or color." The District Court refused to allow the city to "bail out" of the Act's coverage, holding that the political units of a covered jurisdiction cannot independently bring a § 4(a) bailout action. We agree. [Under] the plain language of the statute, [any] bailout action to exempt the city must be filed by, and seek to exempt all of, the State of Georgia.

III. The appellants raise [several] issues of law in support of their contention that the Act may not properly be applied to the electoral changes and annexations disapproved by the Attorney General. [A. The city argues] that [§ 5] may not be read as prohibiting voting practices that have only a discriminatory effect. By describing the elements of discriminatory purpose and effect in the conjunctive, Congress plainly intended that a voting practice not be precleared unless *both* discriminatory purpose and effect are absent. Our decisions have consistently interpreted § 5 in this fashion. [The city urges] that we abandon this settled interpretation because in their view § 5, to the extent that it prohibits voting changes that have only a discriminatory effect, is unconstitutional. Because the statutory meaning and congressional intent are plain, [we] reject [the suggestion]. Instead, [we turn to the] constitutional contentions. B. Congress passed the Act under [the 15th Amendment]. [The city claims] that § 1 of the Amendment prohibits only purposeful racial discrimination in voting, and that in enforcing that provision, [Congress] may not prohibit voting practices lacking discriminatory intent even if they are discriminatory in effect. We hold that, even if § 1 of the Amendment prohibits only purposeful discrimination, the prior decisions of this Court foreclose any argument that Congress may not, pursuant to § 2, outlaw voting practices that are discriminatory in effect. The [city is] asking us to do nothing less than overrule our decision in [South Carolina]. [Congress's] authority under § 2 [is] defined in these terms: " 'Whatever legislation is appropriate, that is, adapted to carry out the objects the [Civil War] amendments have in view, [if] not prohibited, is brought within the domain of congressional power.' Ex parte

---

1. On the same day, the Court rejected a *constitutional* attack on the electoral system of Mobile, Ala., in Mobile v. Bolden, discussed in Rogers v. Lodge (1982; p. 764 above). Since the Mobile case did not involve a change of a prior electoral system, it was not subject to § 5 of the Voting Rights Act; the attack rested mainly on the equal protection clause of the 14th Amendment. Four of the Justices in the Mobile majority found that the "purposeful discrimination" standard under the Constitution had not been met; under § 5, by contrast, "effect" *or* "purpose" are decisive.

Virginia [100 U.S. 339 (1880)]." Applying this standard, the Court held that [the challenged provisions, including] the requirement that new voting rules must be precleared and must lack both discriminatory purpose and effect, [were] all appropriate methods for Congress to use to enforce the 15th Amendment. [South Carolina] makes clear that Congress may, under the authority of § 2 of the 15th Amendment, prohibit state action that, though in itself not violative of § 1, perpetuates the effects of past discrimination. Other decisions of this Court also recognize Congress' broad power to enforce the Civil War Amendments. [See Katzenbach v. Morgan and Oregon v. Mitchell, below.] [In] the present case, we hold that the Act's ban on electoral changes that are discriminatory in effect is an appropriate method of promoting the purposes of the 15th Amendment, even if it is assumed that § 1 of the Amendment prohibits only intentional discrimination in voting. Congress could rationally have concluded that, because electoral changes by jurisdictions with a demonstrable history of intentional racial discrimination in voting create the risk of purposeful discrimination, it was proper to prohibit changes that have a discriminatory [impact]. [The city also contends] that, even if the Act and its preclearance requirement were appropriate means of enforcing the 15th Amendment in 1965, they had outlived their usefulness by 1975, when Congress extended the Act for another seven years. We decline this invitation to overrule Congress' judgment that the 1975 extension was warranted. [Congress's] considered determination that at least another seven years of statutory remedies were necessary to counter the perpetuation of 95 years of pervasive voting discrimination is both unsurprising and unassailable. The extension of the Act, then, was plainly [constitutional].

IV. Now that we have reaffirmed our holdings in [South Carolina], we must address [the] contentions that the 1966 electoral changes and the annexations disapproved by the Attorney General do not, in fact, have a discriminatory effect. [We] conclude that the District Court did not clearly err in finding that the city had failed to prove that the 1966 electoral changes would not dilute the effectiveness of the Negro vote in Rome. [The lower court's holding is] consistent with our statement in Beer v. United States [425 U.S. 130 (1976)] that "the purpose of § 5 has always been to insure that no voting procedure changes would be made that would lead to retrogression in the position of racial minorities with respect to their effective exercise of the electoral process." [The] District Court also found that the city had failed to meet its burden of proving that the thirteen disapproved annexations did not dilute the Negro vote in Rome. [This] determination cannot be considered to be clearly erroneous.

[Affirmed.][2]

Justice POWELL, [dissenting].

The Court [holds] that no subdivision may bail out so long as its State remains subject to preclearance. [There is] more involved here than incorrect construction of the statute. The Court's interpretation of § 4(a) renders the

---

2. Justice BLACKMUN, who joined the Court's opinion, submitted a separate statement regarding the affirmance of the lower court's holding regarding the 13 disputed annexations. Justice STEVENS, who also joined the Court's opinion, submitted a separate statement defending (in response to the dissents, below) the statutory and constitutional bases for the Act's "statewide remedy that denies local political units within a covered State the right to 'bail out' separately." With respect to the constitutional issue, he stated: "Congress has the constitutional power to regulate voting practices in Rome, so long as it has the power to regulate such practices in the entire State of Georgia. Since there is no claim that the entire State is entitled to relief from the federal restrictions, Rome's separate claim must fail."

Voting Rights Act unconstitutional as applied to the city of Rome. The preclearance requirement both intrudes on the prerogatives of state and local governments and abridges the voting rights of all citizens in States covered under the Act. Under § 2 of the 15th Amendment Congress may impose such constitutional deprivations only if it is acting to remedy violations of voting rights. See [South Carolina; Morgan (Harlan dissent).] In view of the District Court finding that Rome has not denied [the] voting rights of blacks, the 15th Amendment provides no authority for continuing those deprivations until the entire State of Georgia satisfies the bailout standards of § 4(a).[1]

When this Court first sustained the [1965 Act], it recognized that preclearance under the Act implicates serious federalism concerns. [South Carolina] upheld the imposition of preclearance as a prophylactic measure based on the remedial power of Congress to enforce the 15th Amendment. But the Court emphasized that preclearance, like any remedial device, can be imposed only in response to some harm. [Since] the coverage formula in § 4(b) purported to identify accurately those jurisdictions that had engaged in voting discrimination, the imposition of preclearance was held to be justified "at least in the absence of proof that [the state or local government has] been free of substantial voting discrimination in recent years." [South Carolina] emphasized, however, that a government subjected to preclearance could be relieved of federal oversight if voting discrimination in fact did not continue or materialize during the prescribed period. [As] long as the bailout option is available, there is less cause for concern that the [Act] may overreach congressional powers by imposing preclearance on a nondiscriminating government. Without bailout, the problem of constitutional authority for preclearance becomes acute. The Court today decrees that the citizens of Rome will not have direct control over their city's voting practices until the entire State of Georgia can free itself from the Act's restrictions. Under the current interpretation of the word "State" in § 4(a), Georgia will have to establish not only that it has satisfied the standards in § 4(a), but also that each and every one of its political subdivisions meets those criteria. This outcome makes every city and county in Georgia a hostage to the errors, or even the deliberate intransigence, of a single subdivision.[2] [Today's] ruling [will] seal off the constitutionally necessary safety valve in the [Act]. The preclearance requirement enforces a presumption against voting changes by certain state and local governments. If that presumption is restricted to those governments meeting § 4(b)'s coverage criteria, and if the presumption can be rebutted by a proper showing in a bailout suit, the Act may be seen, as the [South Carolina] Court saw it, as action by Congress at the limit of its authority under the 15th Amendment. But if governments like the city of Rome may not bail out, the statute oversteps those [limits].

Justice REHNQUIST, with whom Justice STEWART joins, [dissenting].

[Rome] is prevented from instituting precisely the type of structural changes which the Court says Mobile may maintain consistently with the Civil War Amendments, [because] Congress has prohibited these changes under the Voting Rights Act as an exercise of its "enforcement" power conferred by those

---

1. In view of the narrower focus of my approach to the statutory and constitutional issues raised in this case, I do not reach the broad analysis offered by Mr. Justice Rehnquist's dissent. [Footnote by Justice Powell.]

2. The Court's position dictates this eccentric result by insisting that subdivisions in covered States can be relieved of preclearance only when their State bails out. In my view this also would cast serious doubt on the Act's constitutionality as applied to any State which could not bail out due to the failings of a single subdivision. A rational approach would treat the states and local governments independently for purposes of [bailout]. [Footnote by Justice Powell.]

Amendments. It is not necessary to hold that Congress is limited to merely providing a forum in which aggrieved plaintiffs may assert rights under the Civil War Amendments in order to disagree with the Court's decision permitting Congress to strait-jacket the city of Rome in this manner. [Congress] is granted only the power to "enforce" by "appropriate" legislation the limitations on state action embodied in those Amendments. While the presumption of constitutionality is due to any act of a coordinate branch of the Federal Government or of one of the States, it is this Court which is ultimately responsible for deciding challenges to the exercise of power by those entities. [Marbury; Nixon.] Today's decision is nothing less than a total abdication of that authority, rather than an exercise of the deference due to a coordinate branch of the [government].[1]

While I agree with [Justice Powell's] conclusion that requiring localities to *submit* to preclearance is a significant intrusion on local autonomy, it is an even greater intrusion on that autonomy to *deny* preclearance sought. There are three theories of congressional enforcement power relevant to this case. First, it is clear that if the proposed changes would violate the Constitution, Congress could certainly prohibit their implementation. It has never been seriously maintained, however, that Congress can do no more than the judiciary to enforce the Amendments' commands. Thus, if the electoral changes in issue do not violate the Constitution, as judicially interpreted, it must be determined whether Congress could nevertheless appropriately prohibit these changes under the other two theories of congressional power. Under the second theory, Congress can act remedially to enforce the judicially established substantive prohibitions of the Amendments. If not properly remedial, the exercise of this power could be sustained only if this Court accepts the premise of the third theory that Congress has the authority under its enforcement powers to determine, without more, that electoral changes with a disparate impact on race violate the Constitution, in which case Congress by a legislative Act could effectively amend the Constitution. I think it is apparent that neither of the first two theories for sustaining the exercise of congressional power support this application of the Voting Rights Act. After our decision in [Mobile], there is little doubt that Rome has not engaged in *constitutionally* prohibited conduct. I also do not believe that prohibition of these changes can genuinely be characterized as a remedial exercise of congressional enforcement powers. Thus, the result of the Court's holding is that Congress effectively has the power to determine for itself that this conduct violates the Constitution. This result violates previously well-established distinctions between the Judicial Branch and the [other Branches].

A. If the enforcement power is construed as a "remedial" grant of authority, it is this Court's duty to ensure that a challenged congressional act does no more than "enforce" the limitations on state power established in the 14th and 15th Amendments. [While the] Amendments prohibit only purposeful discrimination, the decisions of this Court have recognized that in some circumstances, congressional prohibition of state or local action which is not purposefully discriminatory may nevertheless be appropriate remedial legislation under the [Amendments]. See [e.g., Oregon]. Those circumstances, however, are not without judicial limits. These decisions indicate that congressional prohibition of some conduct which may not itself violate the Constitution is

---

1. [The] nature of the enforcement powers conferred by the 14th and 15th Amendments has always been treated as coextensive. For this reason, it is not neces-sary to differentiate between the 14th and 15th Amendment powers for the purposes of this opinion. [Footnote by Justice Rehnquist.]

"appropriate" legislation "to enforce" [the] Amendments if that prohibition is necessary to remedy prior constitutional violations by the governmental unit, or if necessary to effectively prevent purposeful discrimination by a governmental unit. In both circumstances, Congress would still be legislating in response to the incidence of state action violative of [the] Amendments. These precedents are carefully formulated around a historic tenet of the law that in order to invoke a remedy, there must be a wrong—and under a remedial construction of congressional power to enforce [the] Amendments, that wrong must amount to a constitutional violation. Only when the wrong is identified can the appropriateness of the remedy be measured. The Court today identifies the constitutional wrong which was the object of this congressional exercise of power as purposeful discrimination by local governments in structuring their political processes in an effort to reduce black voting strength. The Court goes on to hold that the prohibitions imposed in this case represent an "appropriate" means of preventing such constitutional violations. The Court does not rest this conclusion on any finding that this prohibition is necessary to remedy any prior discrimination by the locality. Rather, the Court reasons that prohibition of changes discriminatory in effect prevent the incidence of changes which are discriminatory in purpose. [What] the Court explicitly ignores is that in this case the city has proven that these changes are not discriminatory in purpose. Neither reason nor precedent support the conclusion that here it is "appropriate" for Congress to attempt to prevent purposeful discrimination by prohibiting conduct which a locality proves is *not* purposeful discrimination. Congress had before it evidence that various governments were enacting [electoral changes] to prevent the participation of blacks in local government by measures other than outright denial of the franchise. Congress could of course remedy and prevent such purposeful discrimination on the part of local governments. And given the difficulties of proving that an [electoral change] has been undertaken for the purpose of discriminating against blacks, Congress could properly conclude that as a remedial matter it was necessary to place the burden of proving lack of discriminatory purpose on the localities. See [South Carolina]. But all of this does not support the conclusion that Congress is acting remedially when it continues the presumption of purposeful discrimination even after the locality has disproved that presumption. Absent other circumstances, it would be a topsy-turvy judicial system which held that electoral changes which have been affirmatively proven to be permissible under the Constitution nonetheless violate the Constitution.

The precedent on which the Court relies simply does not support its remedial characterization. Neither [Oregon] nor [South Carolina] legitimize the use of an irrebuttable presumption that "vote diluting" changes are motivated by a discriminatory animus. The principal electoral practice in issue in those cases was the use of literacy tests. Yet, the Court simply fails to make any inquiry as to whether the particular electoral practices in issue here are encompassed by the "preventive" remedial rationale invoked in South Carolina and Oregon. The rationale does support congressional prohibition of some electoral practices, but simply has no logical application to the "vote-dilution" devices in issue. [In sustaining the nationwide ban of literacy tests in Oregon,] the Court established that under some circumstances, a congressional remedy may be constitutionally overinclusive by prohibiting some state action which might not be purposefully discriminatory. That possibility does not justify the overinclusiveness countenanced by the Court in this case, however. Oregon by no means held that Congress could simply use discriminatory effect as a proxy for discriminatory purpose, as the Court seems to imply. Instead, the Court opinions identified the factors which rendered this prohibition properly remedial. [The] presumption that the literacy tests were either being used to purpose-fully discriminate, or that the disparate effects of those tests were attributable to discrimination in state-administered education, was not very wide of the mark. [Even] if not adopted with a discriminatory purpose, the tests could readily be applied in a discriminatory fashion. Thus a demonstration by the State that it sought to reinstate the tests for legitimate purposes did not eliminate the substantial risk of [discrimination].

Presumptive prohibition of vote diluting procedures is not similarly an "appropriate" means of exacting state compliance with the Civil War Amend-ments. First, these prohibitions are quite unlike the literacy ban, where the disparate effects were traceable to the discrimination of governmental bodies in education even if their present desire to use the tests was legitimate. Any disparate impact associated with the nondiscriminatory electoral changes in issue here results from bloc voting—private rather than governmental discrimi-nation. Nor does the Court invoke this aspect of congressional remedial powers. It is also clear that while most States still utilizing literacy tests may have been doing so to discriminate, a similar generalization could not be made about all government structures which have some disparate impact on black voting strength. At the time Congress passed the Act, one study demonstrated that 60% of all cities nationwide had at-large elections for city officials, for example. This form of government was adopted by many cities throughout this century as a reform measure designed to overcome wide-scale corruption in the ward system of government. [Nor] does the prohibition of all practices with a disparate impact enhance congressional prevention of purposeful discrimina-tion. The changes in issue are not, like literacy tests, though fair on their face, subject to discriminatory application by local authorities. They are either discriminatory from the outset or not. And it is certain that the only constitu-tional wrong implicated—purposeful dilution—can be effectively remedied by prohibiting it where it occurs. For all these reasons, I do not think that the present case is controlled by the result in Oregon. By prohibiting all electoral changes with a disparate impact, Congress has attempted to prevent disparate impacts—not purposeful discrimination. [Unless Congress's "remedial"] pow-ers are to be wholly uncanalized, it cannot be appropriate remedial legislation [to] prohibit Rome from structuring its government in the manner as its population sees fit absent a finding or unrebutted presumption that Rome has, or is, intentionally discriminating against its black citizens. Rome has simply committed no constitutional violations, as this Court has defined them. More is at stake than sophistry at its worst in the Court's conclusion that requiring the local government to structure its political system in a manner that most effectively enhances black political strength serves to remedy or prevent consti-tutional wrongs on the part of the local government. The need to prevent this disparate impact is premised on the assumption that white candidates will not represent black interests, and that States should devise a system encouraging blacks to vote in a bloc for black candidates. The findings in this case alone demonstrate the tenuous nature of these assumptions. The court below ex-pressly found that white officials have ably represented the interests of the black community. Even blacks who testified admitted no dissatisfaction, but expressed only a preference to be represented by officials of their own race. The enforcement provisions of the Civil War Amendments were not premised on the notion that Congress could empower a later generation of blacks to "get even" for wrongs inflicted on their [forebears].

B. [The Court's result] can be sustained only upon the theory that Congress was empowered to determine that structural changes with a disparate impact on a minority group's ability to elect a candidate of their race violates the 14th or 15th Amendments. [Justice Rehnquist's argument that a majority of the Court has never endorsed a "substantive" (rather than "remedial") theory of congressional enforcement powers is printed at p. 1018 below.]

—————

Katzenbach v. Morgan
384 U.S. 641, 86 S.Ct. 1717, 16 L.Ed.2d 828 (1966).

Justice BRENNAN delivered the opinion of the Court.

[Section 4(e)] of the Voting Rights Act of 1965 [provides] that no person who has successfully completed the sixth primary grade in [an accredited school in] Puerto Rico in which the language of instruction was other than English shall be denied the right to vote in any election because of his inability to read or write English. Appellees, registered voters in New York City, brought this suit to challenge the constitutionality of § 4(e) insofar as it pro tanto prohibits the enforcement of the election laws of New York requiring an ability to read and write English. [We hold that] § 4(e) is a proper exercise of the powers granted to Congress by § 5 of the 14th Amendment.

[New York] argues that an exercise of congressional power under § 5 of the 14th Amendment that prohibits the enforcement of a state law can only be sustained if the judicial branch determines that the state law is prohibited by the provisions of the Amendment that Congress sought to enforce. More specifically, [it] urges that § 4(e) cannot be sustained as appropriate legislation to enforce [equal protection] unless the judiciary decides—even with the guidance of a congressional judgment—that the application of the English literacy requirement prohibited by § 4(e) is forbidden by [equal protection] itself. We disagree. Neither the language nor history of § 5 supports such a construction. [A] construction [that] would require a judicial determination that the enforcement of the state law precluded by Congress violated the Amendment, as a condition of sustaining the congressional enactment, [would] confine the legislative power in this context to the insignificant role of abrogating only those state laws that the judicial branch was prepared to adjudge unconstitutional, or of merely informing the judgment of the judiciary by particularizing the "majestic generalities" of § 1 of the Amendment. Thus our task in this case is not to determine whether the New York English literacy requirement as applied [violates equal protection]. Accordingly, our decision in [Lassiter] is inapposite. Lassiter did not present the question before us here: Without regard to whether the judiciary would find that [equal protection] itself nullifies New York's English literacy requirement [as] applied, could Congress prohibit the enforcement of the state law by legislating under § 5 of the 14th Amendment? In answering this question, our task is limited to determining whether such legislation is, as required by § 5, appropriate legislation to enforce [equal protection]. By including § 5 the draftsmen sought to grant to Congress, by a specific provision applicable to the 14th Amendment, the same broad powers expressed in the Necessary and Proper Clause. The classic formulation of the reach of those powers was established [in McCulloch]. [Ex parte Virginia] held that congressional power under § 5 had this same broad scope. Section 2 of the 15th Amendment grants Congress a similar [power]. Correctly viewed, § 5 is a positive grant of legislative power authorizing Congress to exercise its discretion in determining whether and what legislation is needed to secure the guarantees of the 14th Amendment. We therefore proceed to the consideration whether § 4(e) is "appropriate legislation" to enforce [equal protection], that is, under the [McCulloch] standard, whether § 4(e) may be regarded as an enactment to enforce [equal protection], whether it is "plainly adapted to that end" and whether it is not prohibited by but is consistent with "the letter and spirit of the Constitution."[1]

There can be no doubt that § 4(e) may be regarded as an enactment to enforce [equal protection]. [Specifically,] § 4(e) may be viewed as a measure to secure for the Puerto Rican community residing in New York nondiscriminatory treatment by government—both in the imposition of voting qualifications and the provision or administration of governmental services, such as public schools, public housing and law enforcement. Section 4(e) may be readily seen as "plainly adapted" to furthering these aims of [equal protection]. The practical effect of § 4(e) is to prohibit New York from denying the right to vote to large segments of its Puerto Rican community. [This] enhanced political power will be helpful in gaining nondiscriminatory treatment in public services for the entire Puerto Rican community. Section 4(e) thereby enables the Puerto Rican minority better to obtain "perfect equality of civil rights and equal protection of the laws." It was well within congressional authority to say that this need of the Puerto Rican minority for the vote warranted federal intrusion upon any state interests served by the English literacy requirement. It was for Congress, as the branch that made this judgment, to assess and weigh the various conflicting considerations—the risk or pervasiveness of the discrimination in governmental services, the effectiveness of eliminating the state restriction on the right to vote as a means of dealing with the evil, the adequacy or availability of alternative remedies, and the nature and significance of the state interest that would be affected by the nullification of the English literacy requirement as applied to residents who have successfully completed the sixth grade in a Puerto Rican school. It is not for us to review the congressional resolution of these factors. It is enough that we be able to perceive a basis upon which the Congress might resolve the conflict as it did. There plainly was such a basis [here]. Any contrary conclusion would require us to be blind to the realities familiar to the legislators.

The result is no different if we confine our inquiry to the question whether § 4(e) was merely legislation aimed at the elimination of an invidious discrimination in establishing voter qualifications. We are told that New York's English literacy requirement originated in the desire to provide an incentive for non-English speaking immigrants to learn the English language and in order to assure the intelligent exercise of the franchise. Yet Congress might well have questioned, in light of the many exemptions provided, and some evidence suggesting that prejudice played a prominent role in the enactment of the requirement, whether these were actually the interests being served. Congress might have also questioned whether denial of a right deemed so precious and fundamental in our society was a necessary or appropriate means of encouraging persons to learn English, or of furthering the goal of an intelligent exercise of the franchise. Finally, Congress might well have concluded that as a means of furthering the intelligent exercise of the franchise, an ability to read or

---

1. Contrary to the suggestion of the dissent, § 5 does not grant Congress power to exercise discretion in the other direction and to enact "statutes so as in effect to dilute equal protection and due process decisions of this Court." We emphasize that Congress' power under § 5 is limited to adopting measures to enforce the guarantees of the Amendment; § 5 grants Congress no power to restrict, abrogate, or dilute these guaran-

tees. Thus, for example, an enactment authorizing the States to establish racially segregated systems of education would not be—as required by § 5—a measure "to enforce" the Equal Protection Clause since that clause of its own force prohibits such state laws. [Footnote by Justice Brennan. Compare Justice Brennan's footnote [1] in Oregon, which follows, and note the comments on these footnotes in the materials following Oregon.]

understand Spanish is as effective as ability to read English for those to whom Spanish-language newspapers and Spanish-language radio and television programs are available to inform them of election issues and governmental affairs. Since Congress undertook to legislate so as to preclude the enforcement of the state law, and did so in the context of a general appraisal of literacy requirements for voting, to which it brought a specially informed legislative competence, it was Congress' prerogative to weigh these competing considerations. Here again, it is enough that we perceive a basis upon which Congress might predicate a judgment that the application of New York's [requirement] constituted an invidious discrimination in violation of [equal protection].

There remains the question whether the congressional remedies adopted in § 4(e) constitute means which are not prohibited by, but are consistent "with the letter and spirit of the constitution." [Appellees claim that § 4(e)] works an invidious discrimination in violation of the Fifth Amendment by prohibiting the enforcement of the English literacy requirement only for those educated in American-flag schools [in] which the language of instruction was other than English, and not for those educated in schools beyond the territorial limits of the United States in which the language of instruction was also other than English. [This argument] falls on the merits. Section 4(e) does not restrict or deny the franchise but in effect extends the franchise to persons who otherwise would be denied it by state law. Thus we need not decide whether a state literacy law conditioning the right to vote on achieving a certain level of education in an American-flag school [discriminates] invidiously against those educated in non-American-flag schools. We need only decide whether the challenged limitation on the relief effected in § 4(e) was permissible. In deciding that question, the principle that calls for the closest scrutiny of distinctions in laws *denying* fundamental rights [is] inapplicable; for the distinction challenged [here] is presented only as a limitation on a reform measure aimed at eliminating an existing barrier to the exercise of the franchise. Rather, in deciding the constitutional propriety of the limitations in such a reform measure we are guided by the familiar [principle that] "reform may take one step at a time" [Lee Optical]. [The] congressional choice to limit the relief effected in § 4(e) may, for example, reflect Congress' greater familiarity with the quality of instruction in American-flag schools, a recognition of the unique historic relationship between the Congress and the Commonwealth of Puerto Rico, an awareness of the Federal Government's acceptance of the desirability of the use of Spanish as the language of instruction in Commonwealth schools, and the fact that Congress has fostered policies encouraging migration from the Commonwealth to the States. We have no occasion to determine in this case whether such factors would justify a similar distinction embodied in a voting-qualification law that denied the franchise to persons educated in non-American-flag schools. We hold only that the limitation on relief effected in § 4(e) does not constitute a forbidden discrimination since these factors might well have been the basis for the decision of Congress to go "no farther than it [did]."

Reversed.*

Justice HARLAN, whom Justice STEWART joins, dissenting.

Worthy as its purposes may be thought by many, I do not see how § 4(e) can be sustained except at the sacrifice of fundamentals in the American constitutional system—the separation between the legislative and judicial func-

---

* Justice DOUGLAS joined Justice Brennan's opinion except for its last paragraph, reserving judgment on that issue "until such time as it is presented by a member of the class against which that particular discrimination is directed."

tion and the boundaries between federal and state political authority. By the same token I think that the validity of New York's literacy test, a question which the Court considers *only* in the context of the federal statute, must be upheld. It will conduce to analytical clarity if I discuss the second issue first. I. [Applying] the basic equal protection standard, the issue in [CARDONA v. POWER][1] is whether New York has shown that its English-language literacy test is reasonably designed to serve a legitimate state interest. I think that it has. [The] same interests recounted in [Lassiter] indubitably point toward upholding the rationality of the New York voting test. [The] range of material available to a resident of New York literate only in Spanish is much more limited than what is available to an English-speaking resident [and] the business [of] government is conducted in English. [The] ballot [is] likewise in English. It is also true that most candidates [make] their speeches in English. New York may justifiably want its voters to be able to understand candidates directly, rather than through possibly imprecise translations or summaries reported in a limited number of Spanish news media. [Given] the State's legitimate concern with promoting and safeguarding the intelligent use of the ballot, and given also New York's long experience with the process of integrating non-English-speaking residents into the mainstream of American life, I do not see how it can be said that this [requirement] is unconstitutional. I would uphold the validity of the [law], unless the federal statute prevents that result, the question to which I now turn.

II.   [The] pivotal question in [Morgan] is what effect the added factor of a congressional enactment has on the straight equal protection [argument]. The Court declares that [under § 5] the test for judicial review [is] simply one of rationality; that is, in effect, was Congress acting rationally in declaring that the New York statute is irrational? [The] Court has confused the issue of how much enforcement power Congress possesses under § 5 with the distinct issue of what questions are appropriate for congressional determination and what questions are essentially judicial in nature. When recognized state violations of federal constitutional standards have occurred, Congress is of course empowered by § 5 to take appropriate remedial measures to redress and prevent the wrongs. But it is a judicial question whether the condition with which Congress has thus sought to deal is in truth an infringement of the Constitution, something that is the necessary prerequisite to bringing the § 5 power into play at all. [Thus, in South Carolina, we] reviewed first the "voluminous legislative history" as well as judicial precedents supporting the basic congressional finding that the clear commands of the 15th Amendment had been infringed by various state subterfuges [and then] held the remedial steps taken by the legislature under [the 15th] Amendment to be a justifiable exercise of congressional initiative. Section 4(e), however, presents a significantly different

---

1.   CARDONA v. POWER, 384 U.S. 672 (1966), a companion case to Morgan, was an appeal from an unsuccessful state court equal protection challenge to the New York literacy requirement. The plaintiff was a New York resident educated in Puerto Rico who did not allege that she had completed sixth grade education—the minimum under § 4(e). The state courts, prior to the enactment of § 4(e), rejected her equal protection attack. Justice Brennan's majority opinion vacated that judgment and remanded the case: appellant might be covered by § 4(e) and her case "might therefore be moot"; even if she were not so covered, the state court should determine whether "in light of this federal enactment, those applications of the New York English literacy requirement not in terms prohibited by § 4(e) have continuing validity." Justice Douglas, joined by Justice Fortas, reached the merits of the equal protection claim and dissented, arguing that the requirement could not survive the strict scrutiny mandated in voting cases by Harper (chap. 9, p. 858, above).

type of congressional enactment. The question here is not whether the statute is appropriate remedial legislation to cure an established violation of a constitutional command, but whether there has in fact been an infringement of that constitutional command, that is, whether a particular state practice or, as here, a statute is so arbitrary or irrational as to offend [equal protection]. That question is one for the judicial branch ultimately to determine. Were the rule otherwise, Congress would be able to qualify this Court's constitutional decisions under the 14th and 15th Amendments, let alone those under other provisions of the Constitution, by resorting to congressional power under the Necessary and Proper Clause. In view of [Lassiter], I do not think it is open to Congress to limit the effect of that decision as it has undertaken to do by § 4(e). In effect the Court reads § 5 of the 14th Amendment as giving Congress the power to define the *substantive* scope of the Amendment. If that indeed be the true reach of § 5, then I do not see why Congress should not be able as well to exercise its § 5 "discretion" by enacting statutes so as in effect to dilute equal protection and due process decisions of this Court. In all such cases there is room for reasonable men to differ as to whether or not a denial of equal protection or due process has occurred, and the final decision is one of judgment. Until today this judgment has always been one for the judiciary to resolve.

I do not mean to suggest [that] a legislative judgment of the type incorporated in § 4(e) is without any force whatsoever. Decisions on questions of equal protection and due process are based not on abstract logic, but on empirical foundations. To the extent "legislative facts" are relevant to a judicial determination, Congress is well equipped to investigate them, and such determinations are of course entitled to due respect. In [South Carolina], such legislative findings were made to show that racial discrimination in voting was actually occurring. Similarly, in [Heart of Atlanta Motel and McClung (chap. 3 above)], the congressional determination that racial discrimination in a clearly defined group of public accommodations did effectively impede interstate commerce was based on "voluminous testimony" [before Congress] and in the context of which it passed remedial legislation. But no such factual data provide a legislative record supporting § 4(e)[2] by way of showing that Spanish-speaking citizens are fully as capable of making informed decisions in a New York election as are English-speaking citizens. Nor was there any showing whatever to support the Court's alternative argument that § 4(e) should be viewed as but a remedial measure designed to cure or assure against unconstitutional discrimination of other varieties, e.g., in "public schools, public housing and law enforcement." [There] is simply no legislative record supporting such hypothesized discrimination of the sort we have hitherto insisted upon when congressional power is brought to bear on constitutionally reserved state concerns. [Thus], we have here not a matter of giving deference to a congressional estimate, based on its determination of legislative facts, bearing upon the validity *vel non* of a statute, but rather what can at most be called a legislative announcement that Congress believes a state law to entail an unconstitutional deprivation of equal protection. Although this kind of declaration is of course entitled to the most respectful consideration, I do not believe it lessens our responsibility to decide the fundamental issue of whether in fact the state enactment violates federal constitutional rights.

2. There were no committee hearings or reports referring to this section, which was introduced from the floor during debate on the full Voting Rights Act. [Footnote by Justice Harlan.]

In assessing the deference we should give to this kind of congressional expression of policy, it is relevant that the judiciary has always given to congressional enactments a presumption of validity. However, it is also a canon of judicial review that state statutes are given a similar presumption. Whichever way this case is decided, one statute will be rendered inoperative in whole or in part, and although it has been suggested that this Court should give somewhat more deference to Congress than to a state legislature, such a simple weighing of presumptions is hardly a satisfying way of resolving a matter that touches the distribution of state and federal power in an area so sensitive as that of the regulation of the franchise. Rather it should be recognized that while the 14th Amendment is a "brooding omnipresence" over all state legislation, the substantive matters which it touches are all within the primary legislative competence of the States. Federal authority, legislative no less than judicial, does not intrude unless there has been a denial by state action of 14th Amendment limitations. [At least] in the area of primary state concern a state statute that passes constitutional muster under the judicial standard of rationality should not be permitted to be set at naught by a mere contrary congressional pronouncement unsupported by a legislative record justifying that conclusion. [To] hold on this record that § 4(e) overrides the New York literacy requirement seems to me tantamount to allowing the 14th Amendment to swallow the State's constitutionally ordained primary authority in this field. For if Congress by what, as here, amounts to mere ipse dixit can set that otherwise permissible requirement partially at naught I see no reason why it could not also substitute its judgment for that of the States in other fields of their exclusive primary competence [as well].

CONGRESSIONAL POWER AND THE MORGAN CASE

a.   How far-reaching is the § 5 power recognized in Morgan? Though full discussion of the scope of the Morgan rationale is best postponed until after Oregon v. Mitchell, which follows, some preliminary questions are in order here. Is there merit in the following assessment of Morgan in Burt, "Miranda and Title II: A Morganatic Marriage," 1969 Sup.Ct.Rev. 81: "In effect, the Court is saying that—at least in some circumstances—where Congress and the Court disagree about the meaning of the 14th Amendment, the Court will defer to Congress' version. The Court is suggesting that, to some extent at least, § 5 exempts the 14th Amendment from the principle of Court–Congress relationships expressed by Marbury v. Madison, that the judiciary is the final arbiter of the meaning of the Constitution." If so, to what "extent" and under what "circumstances"?

b.   In exploring that question, note that Morgan rests on alternative rationales: First, § 4(e) is a measure to secure for Puerto Ricans in New York nondiscriminatory treatment in the "provision or administration of governmental services." Second, § 4(e) eliminates "an invidious discrimination in establishing voter qualifications." (Under the second theory, the Court permits Congress to find—because the Court perceives "a basis" for the "finding"—that application of New York's English literacy requirement to covered Puerto Ricans itself constitutes "an invidious discrimination in violation of [equal protection].") The second theory seems the more far-reaching. Discrimination against Puerto Ricans in providing public services is clearly unconstitutional under Court-developed interpretations of equal protection; under the first theory, then, Congress can be viewed as implementing judicially-determined constitutional rights. (Even under that theory, Congress is making the factual determination that New York *is* discriminating in public services, and that Puerto Rican voting is an appropriate remedy for such discrimination.) Under the second theory, Congress does more than that. The Court has not held that requiring English literacy tests of Puerto Ricans literate in Spanish is itself unconstitutional discrimination in voting. Under that theory, then, Congress is making the initial determination that an English literacy test in these circumstances is unconstitutional; and the Court readily defers to that determination. Arguably, then, Congress (not the Court) makes a determination about the substantive content of rights under § 1 of the 14th Amendment. Does Morgan, then, recognize a "substantive" power of Congress under § 5 of the 14th Amendment? Is that power distinctively different (and broader than) the expanding "remedial" power considered in the Rome case? Can the congressional determination endorsed in Morgan be justified as resting simply on legislative findings of fact? Or does it involve a resolution of competing values and a delineation of substantive constitutional rights by Congress rather than by the Court? Justice Brennan stated that it "was for Congress" to "assess and weigh the various conflicting considerations," including such considerations as the "significance of the state interest." Did he mean to authorize Congress to make the value choices typically involved in judicial, "strict scrutiny" interpretations of equal protection? Does his justification (that it is "not for us to review the congressional resolution of these factors," so long as the Justices can "perceive a basis upon which the Congress might resolve the conflict as it did") give Congress a general power to resolve the value conflicts in constitutional interpretation with a result different from that the Court might reach—or has reached? May Congress use that rationale to dilute as well as expand constitutional rights? These questions are pursued further in the case that follows.

Oregon v. Mitchell

400 U.S. 112, 91 S.Ct. 260, 27 L.Ed.2d 272 (1970).*

[These cases—in the Court's original jurisdiction—involved constitutional challenges by several states to three provisions of the Voting Rights Act Amendments of 1970. (1) Sec. 302 prohibited denying to any citizen the right to vote in any election "on account of age if such citizen is eighteen years of age or older."[1] By a 5–4 vote, that provision was upheld for federal elections; but

---

* The major constitutional controversy in Oregon v. Mitchell involved the 1970 Act's provision lowering the voting age to 18 in state elections. Enactment came after an extensive constitutional debate in Congress. In Congress, the proponents of the 18–year-old vote provision relied heavily on a statement by Archibald Cox resting on Morgan for the proposition that "Congress has constitutional power to determine what [equal protection] requires," though cautioning that "some constitutional scholars would not share my view. [Possibly,] my reasoning runs the logic of [Morgan] into the ground." Opponents of the lowering of the voting age by statute rather than by constitutional amendment intro-

duced a statement by Louis H. Pollak noting that Morgan "provides the basis for a modestly plausible, but not for an ultimately persuasive, case for the constitutionality of the statute."

1. The congressional findings accompanying § 302 stated that a requirement that a voter be 21 years old "(1) denies and abridges the inherent constitutional rights of citizens eighteen years of age but not yet twenty-one years of age to vote—a particularly unfair treatment of such citizens in view of the national defense responsibilities imposed upon such citizens; (2) has the effect of denying to citizens eighteen years of age [the] due process and equal protection of the laws;

another 5–4 division held the 18–year-old vote provision unconstitutional as applied to state elections.[2] (2) Section 201 expanded the ban on literacy tests in the 1965 Act by making the suspension applicable nationwide. That provision was upheld unanimously, as discussed above. (3) Section 202 prohibited the application of state durational residency requirements in presidential elections and established uniform standards for registration and absentee balloting. It included a provision that voters could register within 30 days of a presidential election. These provisions were sustained by an 8–1 vote, with Justice Harlan the only dissenter. (The portions of the opinions printed here focus on the discussion of the 18–year-old vote provision, because it provided the major test of the scope of the Morgan power.)]

Justice BLACK, announcing the judgments of the Court in an opinion expressing his own view of the [cases].

[T]he responsibility of the States for setting the qualifications of voters in congressional elections [Art. I, § 2] was made subject to the power of Congress to make or alter such regulations if it deemed it advisable to do so [Art. I, § 4]. [I] would hold [that] Congress has ultimate supervisory power over congressional elections. Similarly, it is the prerogative of Congress to oversee the conduct of presidential and vice-presidential elections and to set the qualifications for voters for [them]. On the other hand, [no] function is more essential to the separate and independent existence of the States [than] the power to determine within the limits of the Constitution the qualifications of their own voters for state, county, and municipal [offices]. My Brother Brennan's opinion, if carried to its logical conclusion, would, under the guise of insuring equal protection, blot out all state [power]. [Of course, where] Congress attempts to remedy racial discrimination under its enforcement powers, its authority is enhanced by the avowed intention of the Framers of the 13th, 14th, and 15th Amendments. In enacting the 18–year-old vote provisions [here], Congress made no legislative findings that the 21–year-old vote requirement was used by the States to disenfranchise voters on account of race. I seriously doubt that such a finding, if made, could be supported by substantial evidence. Since Congress has attempted to invade an area preserved to the States by the Constitution without a foundation for enforcing the Civil War Amendments' ban on racial discrimination, I would hold that Congress has exceeded its powers in attempting to lower the voting age in state and local elections. On the other hand, where Congress legislates in a domain not exclusively reserved [to] the States, its enforcement power need not be tied so closely to the goal of eliminating discrimination on account of [race].

Justice BRENNAN, Justice WHITE, and Justice MARSHALL dissent from the judgments insofar as they declare § 302 unconstitutional as applied to state and local elections.

[and] (3) does not bear a reasonable relationship to any compelling State interest."

2. Justices Douglas, Brennan, White and Marshall thought the provision valid as applied to all elections, state as well as federal; Chief Justice Burger and Justices Harlan, Stewart and Blackmun thought the provision exceeded congressional power as applied to any election, federal or state; Justice Black cast the deciding vote—he thought it constitutional as applied to federal elections but not to state elections. The decision was handed down on Dec. 21, 1970. Three months later, on March 23, 1971, Congress submitted the 26th Amendment to the states for ratification. Three months after that, on June 30, 1971, the ratification process was completed. The 26th Amendment provides that the federal and state governments may not deny the vote "on account of age" to citizens "eighteen years of age or older."

[We] believe there is serious question whether a statute [denying the franchise to citizens] between the ages of 18 and 21 [could] withstand present scrutiny under [equal protection]. Regardless of the answer to this question, however, it is clear to us that proper regard for the special function of Congress in making determinations of legislative fact compels this Court to respect those determinations unless they are contradicted by evidence far stronger than anything that has been adduced in these [cases]. A. [W]hen exclusions from the franchise are challenged as violating [equal protection], "the Court must determine whether the exclusions are necessary to promote a compelling state interest." In the present cases, the States justify exclusion of 18- to 21-year-olds from the voting rolls solely on the basis of the States' interests in promoting intelligent and responsible exercise of the franchise. [We must] examine with particular care the asserted connection between age limitations and the admittedly laudable state purpose to further intelligent and responsible voting. [Every State] has concluded [that] citizens 21 years of age and over are capable of responsible and intelligent voting. Accepting this judgment, there remains the question whether citizens 18 to 21 years of age may fairly be said to be less able. State practice itself in other areas casts doubt upon any such proposition. [There is] a nearly unanimous legislative judgment on the part of the States themselves that differences in maturity and intelligence between 18-year-olds and persons over the age of 21 are too trivial to warrant specialized treatment for *any* of the former class in the critically important matter of criminal responsibility. Similarly, every State permits 18-year-olds to marry. [No State] requires attendance at school beyond the age of 18. [T]hat 18-year-olds as a class may be less educated than some of their elders cannot justify restriction of the franchise, for the States themselves have determined that this incremental education is irrelevant to voting qualifications. And finally, we have been cited to no material whatsoever that would support the proposition that intelligence, as opposed to educational attainment, increases between the ages of 18 and 21. [No] State seeking to uphold its denial of the franchise to 18-year-olds has adduced anything beyond the mere difference in age. [As noted,] the relevance of this difference is contradicted by nearly uniform state practice in other areas. But perhaps more important is the uniform experience of those States—Georgia since 1943, and Kentucky since 1955—that have permitted 18-year-olds to vote. [E]very person who spoke to the issue in [Congress] was agreed that 18-year-olds in both States were at least as interested, able, and responsible in voting as were their elders. In short, we are faced with [a] restriction upon the franchise supported only by bare assertions and long practice, in the face of strong indications that the States themselves do not credit the factual propositions upon which the restriction is asserted to rest. But there is no reason for us to decide whether, in a proper case, we would be compelled to hold this restriction a violation of [equal protection]. [For] the question we face today [is] the scope of congressional power under [§ 5].

B.   As we have often indicated, questions of constitutional power frequently turn in the last analysis on questions of fact. This is particularly the case when an assertion of state power is challenged under [equal protection]. When a state legislative classification is subjected to judicial challenge as violating [equal protection], it comes before the courts cloaked by the presumption that the legislature has, as it should, acted within constitutional limitations. [But] this limitation on judicial review of state legislative classifications is a limitation stemming, not from the 14th Amendment itself, but from the nature of judicial review. The nature of the judicial process makes it an inappropriate forum for the determination of complex factual questions of the kind so often involved in constitutional adjudication. Courts, therefore, will overturn a legislative determination of a factual question only if the legislature's finding is so clearly wrong that it may be characterized as "arbitrary," "irrational," or "unreasonable." Limitations stemming from the nature of the judicial process, however, have no application to [Congress]. Should Congress, pursuant to [§ 5], undertake an investigation in order to determine whether the factual basis necessary to support a state legislative discrimination actually exists, it need not stop once it determines that some reasonable men could believe the factual basis exists. Section 5 empowers Congress to make its own determination on the matter. [Morgan.] It should hardly be necessary to add that if the asserted factual basis necessary to support a given state discrimination does not exist, [§ 5] vests Congress with power to remove the discrimination by appropriate means. The scope of our review in such matters has been established by a long line of consistent decisions. "[W]here we find that the legislators, in light of the facts and testimony before them, have a rational basis for finding a chosen regulatory scheme necessary [our] investigation is at an end." [E.g., McClung; Morgan.][1] This scheme is consistent with our prior decisions in related areas. The core of dispute [here] is a conflict between state and federal legislative determinations of the factual issues upon which depends decision of a federal constitutional question—the legitimacy, under [equal protection], of state discrimination against persons between the ages of 18 and 21. Our cases have repeatedly emphasized that, when state and federal claims come into conflict, the primacy of federal power requires that the federal finding of fact control. The Supremacy Clause requires an identical result when the conflict is one of legislative, not judicial, findings. Finally, it is no answer to say that [the law] intrudes upon a domain reserved to the States—the power to set qualifications for voting. It is no longer open to question that the 14th Amendment applies to this, as to any other, exercise of [state power].

C. [A lengthy discussion rejected Justice Harlan's historical argument that the 14th Amendment "was never intended to restrict the authority of the States to allocate their political power as they see fit." It concluded:] We could not accept [Justice Harlan's] thesis even if it were supported by historical evidence far stronger than anything adduced today. But in our view, [his] historical analysis is flawed by his ascription of 20th-century meanings to the words of 19th-century legislators. In consequence, his analysis imposes an artificial simplicity upon a complex era, and presents, as universal, beliefs that were held by merely one of several groups competing for political power. [The] historical record left by the framers of the 14th Amendment, because it is a product of differing and conflicting political pressures and conceptions of federalism, is thus too vague and imprecise to provide us with sure guidance in deciding the pending cases. We must therefore conclude that its framers understood their Amendment to be a broadly worded injunction capable of being interpreted by future generations in accordance with the vision and needs of those generations. We would be remiss in our duty if, in an attempt to find certainty amidst uncertainty, we were to misread the historical record and cease to interpret the Amendment as this Court has always interpreted it. D. There remains only the question whether Congress could rationally have

---

1. As we emphasized in [Morgan], "§ 5 does not grant Congress power [to] enact 'statutes so as in effect to dilute equal protection and due process decisions of this Court.'" As indicated above, a decision of this Court striking down a state statute expresses, among other things, our conclusion that the legislative findings upon which the statute is based are so far wrong as to be unreasonable. Unless Congress were to unearth new evidence in its investigation, its identical findings on the identical issue would be no more reasonable than those of the state legislature. [Footnote by Justice Brennan et al.]

concluded that denial of the franchise to citizens between the ages of 18 and 21 was unnecessary to promote any legitimate interests of the States in assuring intelligent and responsible [voting]. [Congress] had ample evidence upon which it could have based the conclusion that exclusion of citizens 18 to 21 years of age from the franchise is wholly unnecessary to promote any legitimate interest the States may have in assuring intelligent and responsible voting. [Morgan.] If discrimination is unnecessary to promote any legitimate state interest, it is plainly unconstitutional under [equal protection], and Congress has ample power to forbid it under [§ 5].[2]

Justice STEWART, with whom The Chief Justice [BURGER] and Justice BLACKMUN join, concurring in part and dissenting in part.

[Congress] was wholly without constitutional power to alter—for the purpose of *any* elections—the voting age qualifications now determined by the several States. In my view, neither the Morgan case, nor any other case, [establishes] such congressional power, even assuming that all those cases were rightly decided. [To] be sure, recent decisions have established that state action regulating suffrage is not immune from the impact of [equal protection]. But we have been careful in those decisions to note the undoubted power of a State to establish a qualification for voting based on age. Indeed, none of the opinions filed today suggests that the States have anything but a constitutionally unimpeachable interest in establishing some age qualification as such. Yet to test the power to establish an age qualification by the "compelling interest" standard is really to deny a State any choice at all, because no State could demonstrate a "compelling interest" in drawing the line with respect to age at one point rather than another. Obviously, the power to establish an age qualification must carry with it the power to choose 21 as a reasonable voting age, as the vast majority of the States have none.[1] [Morgan] does not hold that Congress has the power to determine what are and what are not "compelling state interests" for equal protection purposes. [Morgan upheld] the statute on two grounds: that Congress could conclude that enhancing the political power of the Puerto Rican community by conferring the right to vote was an appropriate means of remedying discriminatory treatment in public services; and that Congress could conclude that the New York statute was tainted by the impermissible purpose of denying the right to vote to Puerto Ricans, an undoubted invidious discrimination under [equal protection]. Both of these decisional grounds were far-reaching. The Court's opinion made clear that Congress could impose on the States a remedy for the denial of equal protection that elaborated upon the direct command of the Constitution, and that it could override state laws on the ground that they were in fact used as instruments of invidious discrimination even though a court in an individual lawsuit might not have reached that factual conclusion. But it is necessary to go much further to

---

2. Justice DOUGLAS's separate statement insisted that the grant of the franchise to 18–year-olds was valid across the board: "Congress might well conclude that a reduction in the voting age from 21 to 18 was needed in the interest of equal protection. [There] is not a word of limitation in § 5 which would restrict its applicability to matters of race alone."

1. If the Government is correct in its submission that a particular age requirement must meet the "compelling interest" standard, then, of course, a substantial question would exist whether a 21–year-old voter qualification is constitutional even in the absence of congressional action, as my Brothers point out. Yet it is inconceivable to me that this Court would ever hold that the denial of the vote to those between the ages of 18 and 21 constitutes such an invidious discrimination as to be a denial of [equal protection]. The establishment of an age qualification is not state action aimed at any discrete and insular minority. Cf. [Carolene Products, fn. 4]. [Footnote by Justice Stewart.]

sustain § 302. The state laws that it invalidates do not invidiously discriminate against any discrete and insular minority. Unlike the statute considered in Morgan, § 302 is valid only if Congress has the power not only to provide the means of eradicating situations that amount to a violation of [equal protection], but also to determine as a matter of substantive constitutional law what situations fall within the ambit of the clause, and what state interests are "compelling." I concurred in Mr. Justice Harlan's dissent in Morgan. That case, as I now read it, gave congressional power under § 5 the furthest possible legitimate reach. Yet to sustain the constitutionality of § 302 would require an enormous extension of that decision's [rationale].

Justice HARLAN, concurring in part and dissenting in [part].

I think that the history of the 14th Amendment makes it clear beyond any reasonable doubt that no part of the legislation now under review can be upheld as a legitimate exercise of congressional power under that Amendment. [Justice Harlan's extensive examination of the historical data is omitted.*] [I] must confess to complete astonishment at the position of some of my Brethren that the history of [the] Amendment has become irrelevant. [T]he very fact that constitutional amendments were deemed necessary to bring about federal abolition of state restrictions on voting by reason of race, sex, and [the] failure to pay state poll taxes, is itself forceful evidence of the common understanding in 1869, 1919, and 1962, respectively, that the 14th Amendment did not empower Congress to legislate in these respects. It must be recognized, of course, that [the] judiciary has long been entrusted with the task of applying the Constitution in changing circumstances, and as conditions change the Constitution in a sense changes as well. But when the Court disregards the express intent and understanding of the Framers, it has invaded the realm of the political process to which the mending power was committed, and it has violated the constitutional structure which it is its highest duty to protect. As the Court is not justified in substituting its own views of wise policy for the commands of the Constitution, still less is it justified in allowing Congress to disregard those commands as the Court understands them. Although Congress' expression of the view that it does have power to alter state suffrage qualifications is entitled to the most respectful consideration, [this] cannot displace the duty of this Court to make an independent determination whether Congress has exceeded its powers. The reason for this goes beyond Marshall's assertion that: "It is emphatically the province and duty of the judicial department to say what the law is." [Marbury.][1] It inheres in the structure of the constitutional system itself. Congress is subject to none of the institutional restraints imposed on judicial decision-making; it is controlled only by the political process. In Article V, the Framers expressed the view that the political restraints on Congress alone were an insufficient control over the process of constitution making. [To] allow a simple majority of Congress to have final say on matters

---

* Justice Harlan argued that history made it clear that § 1 of the 14th Amendment was not intended to "reach discriminatory voting qualifications." He emphasized § 2 of the 14th Amendment, which provides for sanctions when the right to vote "is denied to any of the male inhabitants of such State, *being twenty-one years of age*, and citizens of the United States." He concluded: "The only sensible explanation of § 2 [is] that the racial voter qualifications it was designed to penalize were understood to be permitted by § 1 of the 14th Amendment." [See also Justice Harlan's dissents in the voting cases in chap. 9.]

1. In fact, however, I do not understand how the doctrine of deference to rational constitutional interpretation by Congress espoused by the majority in [Morgan] is consistent with this statement of Chief Justice Marshall or with our reaffirmation of it in Cooper v. Aaron. [Footnote by Justice Harlan.]

of constitutional interpretation is therefore fundamentally out of keeping with the constitutional structure. Nor is that structure adequately protected by a requirement that the judiciary be able to perceive a basis for the congressional interpretation, the only restriction laid down in [Morgan].

It is suggested that the proper basis for the doctrine enunciated in Morgan lies in the relative factfinding competence of Court, Congress, and state legislatures. [Even] on the assumption that the 14th Amendment does place a limit on the sorts of voter qualifications which a State may adopt, [I do] not see any real force in the reasoning. When my Brothers refer to "complex factual questions," they call to mind disputes about primary, objective facts dealing with such issues as the number of persons between the ages of 18 and 21, the extent of their education, and so forth. [But the] disagreement in these cases revolves around the evaluation [of] largely uncontested factual material. On the assumption that maturity and experience are relevant to intelligent and responsible exercise of the elective franchise, are the immaturity and inexperience of the average 18–, 19–, or 20–year-old sufficiently serious to justify denying such a person a direct voice in decisions affecting his or her life? Whether or not this judgment is characterized as "factual," it calls for striking a balance between incommensurate interests. Where the balance is to be struck depends ultimately on the values and the perspective of the decisionmaker. It is a matter as to which men of good will can and do reasonably differ. I fully agree that judgments of the sort involved here are beyond the institutional competence and constitutional authority of the judiciary. [But] the same reasons which in my view would require the judiciary to sustain a reasonable state resolution of the issue also require Congress to abstain from entering the picture. Judicial deference is based, not on relative factfinding competence, but on due regard for the decision of the body constitutionally appointed to decide. Establishment of voting qualifications is a matter for state legislatures. Assuming any authority at all, only when the Court can say with some confidence that the legislature has demonstrably erred in adjusting the competing interests is it justified in striking down the legislative judgment.

[The] same considerations apply [to] Congress' displacement of state decisions with its own ideas of wise policy. The sole distinction between Congress and the Court in this regard is that Congress presumptively has popular authority for the value judgment it makes. But since the state legislature has a like authority, this distinction between Congress and the judiciary falls short of justifying a congressional veto on the state judgment. The perspectives and values of national legislators on the issue of voting qualifications are likely to differ from those of state legislators, but I see no reason a priori to prefer those of the national figures, whose collective decision, applying nationwide, is necessarily less able to take account of peculiar local conditions. Whether one agrees with this judgment or not, it is the one expressed by the Framers in leaving voter qualifications to the States. The Supremacy Clause does [not] represent a judgment that federal decisions are superior to those of the States whenever the two may differ. To be sure, my colleagues do not expressly say that Congress or this Court is empowered by the Constitution to substitute its own judgment for those of the States. However, before sustaining a state judgment they require a "clear showing that the burden imposed is necessary to protect a compelling and substantial governmental interest."[2] I should think

---

2. It might well be asked why this standard is not equally applicable to the congressional expansion of the franchise before us. Lowering of voter qualifications dilutes the voting power of those who could meet the higher [standard]. [Footnote by Justice Harlan.]

that if [a state voter qualification met that test], no reasonable person would think the qualification undesirable. Equivalently, if my colleagues or a majority of Congress deem a given voting qualification undesirable as a matter of policy, they must consider that the state interests involved are not "compelling" or "substantial" or that they can be adequately protected in other ways. It follows that my colleagues must be prepared to hold invalid as a matter of federal constitutional law all state voting qualifications which they deem unwise, as well as all such qualifications which Congress reasonably deems unwise. For this reason, I find their argument subject to the same objection as if it explicitly acknowledged such a conclusion. It seems to me that the notion of deference to congressional interpretation of the Constitution, which the Court promulgated in Morgan, is directly related to this higher standard of constitutionality which the Court [brought] to fruition in Kramer [chap. 9, p. 860]. When the scope of federal review of state determinations became so broad as to be judicially unmanageable, it was natural for the Court to seek assistance from the national legislature. [In] this area, to rely on Congress would make that body a judge in its own cause. The role of final arbiter belongs to this [Court].

CONGRESSIONAL POWER AFTER THE MORGAN, OREGON, AND ROME CASES

Introduction. The purpose of this group of notes is to explore the reach of the congressional "substantive" or "interpretive" (as distinguished from "remedial") power under the 14th and 15th Amendments—the power suggested by Justice Brennan's opinion for the Court in Morgan and by the opinion signed by Justices Brennan, White and Marshall in Oregon. The central problems are: How far-reaching is that power? Does it risk congressional undercutting of the Court's traditional role in delineating the content of constitutional rights? Can it be invoked to dilute as well as expand constitutional rights? Is it a justifiable power? In exploring the ramifications of this controversial "substantive" power, it is well to bear in mind two additional considerations. First, how well established is the Morgan power that Justice Brennan had so large a hand in formulating? Note 5 below contains the concluding passages from Justice Rehnquist's dissent in the 1980 decision in Rome. Consider his argument there that a "substantive" enforcement power has *not* been embraced by a majority of the Court. Second, is the "substantive" power truly broader than the traditionally less controversial "remedial" power exemplified by the South Carolina case in 1965 and applied quite broadly by the majority in Rome in 1980? Arguably, if the "remedial" power is as broad as Rome suggests, Congress, in many circumstances, may be able to play a very significant role in giving effective content to constitutional rights without any need to resort to the "substantive" power that is the focus of this set of notes.

1. *Some pervasive problems.* What, then, *is* the scope of congressional power to modify the content of constitutional rights? Recall the comments (at p. 1003) about the alternative theories in Morgan. Do both of those theories retain vitality after Oregon? To what extent does the congressional action considered in Oregon rest on Justice Brennan's first theory in Morgan—congressional judgments about remedies that might be appropriate to implement judicially-declared rights? To what extent did the 18–year-old-vote provision need the support of his second theory—congressional determination of the substantive content of constitutional rights? In Morgan, Justice Brennan was ready to validate a congressional determination that the English literacy requirement as

applied to Puerto Ricans was itself unconstitutional under equal protection standards governing voting. In Oregon, does Justice Brennan support a congressional determination that denial of the vote to 18–year-olds itself violates equal protection? Only if such a determination rested on legislative factfinding? Even if it rested on resolution of conflicting "values"? Are equal protection determinations ever wholly "factual," or do they always involve value choices? If Congress is permitted to make determinations that state practices are "unconstitutional," should the Court accord them the deference associated with McCulloch or the even greater deference suggested by the "perceive a basis" test of Morgan? Can such deference be squared with Marbury and Cooper v. Aaron? What principled limits on congressional authority (and judicial deference) are possible? Is congressional modification of constitutional rights permissible only in special circumstances—circumstances taking proper account of congressional competence and judicial authority? Consider the limits on the congressional "substantive" power suggested by Justice Brennan (in note 2 below), as well as the somewhat different ones advanced by several commentators (in note 4 below).

2. *Limiting congressional power to "dilute" constitutional rights: Justice Brennan's footnotes.* a. Can the Court recognize a congressional power in effect to reinterpret constitutional provisions and yet avoid deference to congressional judgments diluting or contracting (rather than expanding) rights? Justice Brennan's footnote [1] in Morgan tried to safeguard against the risk of dilution: Justice Brennan insisted that § 5 "grants Congress no power to restrict, abrogate, or dilute these guarantees." Can that footnote be squared with Justice Brennan's rationale in the Morgan text, deferring to congressional resolution of "the various conflicting considerations" if the Court can "perceive a basis upon which the Congress might resolve the conflict as it did"? What does equal protection prohibit "by its own force"? What does that phrase mean: that the Court has ruled, *and* that no different evaluation of competing considerations is possible? Is that true of the typical due process and equal protection interpretations? In Oregon, the opinion joined by Justice Brennan also contained a footnote [1] that tried to safeguard against uses of the § 5 power to dilute constitutional rights. This footnote purported to reiterate the Morgan footnote's limit on congressional power, but it carried a somewhat different emphasis: it focused on deference to congressional factfinding capacity as the critical element in § 5 power. Was that a retreat from Morgan's deference to congressional resolution of value conflicts? Are findings of fact truly critical in typical equal protection controversies? Note the criticism of Justice Brennan's "modified ratchet theory" in Cohen, "Congressional Power to Interpret Due Process and Equal Protection," 27 Stan.L.Rev. 603 (1975): "This new [Oregon footnote] rationale for the ratchet theory is as unpersuasive as the first [in the Morgan footnote]. If Congress is a more appropriate forum than the courts for determining issues of legislative fact, it is hard to understand why a congressional determination that there exists a sufficient 'factual' basis to [justify] discrimination by the state should, in the absence of new evidence, be entitled to no weight at all." Moreover, Cohen notes that the new footnote in fact recognizes "that the ratchet may be released—that in some cases Congress can turn back the clock on equal protection and due process on the basis of new evidence." Note also Cohen's more general criticism of the Morgan "ratchet theory." He finds two problems: "it does not satisfactorily explain why Congress may move the due process and equal protection handle in only one direction"; and there is "difficulty in determining the direction in which the handle is turning."

b. Even if Justice Brennan's distinction between "dilution" and "expansion" in the Morgan footnote is persuasive, how is it to be applied? Recall the Court's disposition (in the last part of Morgan) of the claim that § 4(e) of the 1965 Act unfairly discriminated against those literate in foreign languages who were not covered by § 4(e). Justice Brennan's scrutiny of that claim was very deferential, supposedly because § 4(e) was viewed as "a reform measure" rather than a restriction on existing rights. Is that "reform" rationale, permitting a legislature to "take one step at a time," persuasive as applied in Morgan?

3. *Potential applications of the Morgan rationale.* a. Would the Morgan rationale justify the anti-busing legislative proposals that followed in the wake of the 1971 Swann decision? President Nixon based his 1972 proposals to limit busing in the desegregation of schools on the ground that the proposed legislation "deals with a remedy and not a right." Is the "remedial" theory of the South Carolina and Rome cases adequate to support anti-busing laws? See Bork, Constitutionality of the President's Busing Proposals (1972). If busing is not viewed as a mere remedy, is congressional action nevertheless supportable on the basis of the "substantive" rationale of Morgan? Suppose Congress were to enact legislation accepting the principle of Brown but determining, after extensive hearings, that busing is an ineffective remedy and that alternative remedies are available and should be used? What other congressional legislation might find support in Morgan? Applying to private conduct all restrictions governing "state action" under § 1 of the 14th Amendment? (See Leedes, "State Action Limitations on Courts and Congressional Power," 60 N.C.L.Rev. 747 (1982).) The civil rights violence provisions of the 1968 Act (p. 972 above)? Prohibitions of de facto segregation in public education? Modifications of the Court's criminal procedure due process decisions (chap. 7 above)? Altering the "one person-one vote" theme of the Court's reapportionment decisions (p. 866 above)? (See also the additional examples noted below.)

b. Can Congress use the Morgan rationale to readjust the balance when constitutional values compete? Are such "balancing" readjustments "expansions" or "dilutions" of constitutional guarantees—or both? For example, may Congress redefine the boundaries between the rights of the free press and the accused? Consider the reliance on the Morgan rationale in an opinion in Welsh v. United States (1970; p. 1468 below). In the Welsh case, Justice White, joined by Chief Justice Burger and Justice Stewart, thought the "religious training and belief" limitation on the conscientious objector exemption in the draft law constitutional on the ground that the Court, by analogy to Morgan, "should respect congressional judgment accommodating the Free Exercise Clause and the power to raise armies." (See also note 3d below.)

c. More than a decade after Morgan, the scope of the legislative power suggested by that ruling attracted an unprecedented degree of interest in Congress. Opponents of various decisions turned to the Morgan rationale in framing legislative responses to the Court rulings. The most controversial proposal was the proposed "Human Life Statute," introduced by Senator Helms and Congressman Hyde. The Helms–Hyde bill was designed to authorize broader state control of abortions or, at least, to express congressional displeasure with the Roe v. Wade decision and to prompt the Court to reconsider it. Sec. 1 of the bill provided: "The Congress finds that present-day scientific evidence indicates a significant likelihood that actual human life exists from conception. The Congress further finds that the fourteenth amendment [was] intended to protect all human beings. Upon the basis of these findings, and in the exercise of the powers of the Congress, including its power under [§ 5], the Congress hereby declares that for the purpose of enforcing the obligation of the States under the fourteenth amendment not to deprive persons of life without due process of law, human life shall be deemed to exist from conception, without regard to race, sex, age, health, defect, or condition of dependency; and for this purpose 'person' shall include all human life as defined herein." The Subcommittee on the Separation of Powers of the Senate Judiciary Committee approved the bill in July, 1981. However, full Senate consideration was postponed because of the position of Senator Hatch, who stated that he had "serious constitutional reservations" about the bill and that he preferred the constitutional amendment route. The proposal was not enacted. Would the proposed "Human Life Statute" have been constitutional? Before approving the proposal, the Senate Subcommittee held extensive hearings on that question. Among the proponents was Stephen H. Galebach, a young Washington lawyer who had advocated such legislation in an article. He argued that the Court's refusal in Roe v. Wade to treat the fetus as a person was merely a decision resting on the incapacity of the judiciary to decide the question of when human life begins, and that, under § 5, Congress was the appropriate body to resolve that question. He relied heavily on Morgan and its progeny, arguing that those decisions made Congress the "co-enforcer of the 14th Amendment." He also claimed that *both* rationales in Morgan permitted Congress to include unborn children within the protections of the 14th Amendment without regard to whether the judiciary would find them to be persons. See Galebach, "A Human Life Statute," Human Life Review 5 (1981) [reprinted in 127 Cong.Rec. S 288]. Contrast Ely & Tribe, "Let There Be Life," The New York Times (March 17, 1981): "Senator Jesse A. Helms wasn't conceived yesterday, and his constitutional advisers undoubtedly have explained to him why an attempt to overrule Roe v. Wade by statute must fail." And note generally Estreicher, "Congressional Power and Constitutional Rights: Reflections on Proposed 'Human Life' Legislation," 68 Va.L.Rev. 333 (1982). Was Galebach's reasoning persuasive? Was his position defensible without repudiating some of the statements in Morgan? Robert H. Bork claimed the proposed law would be unconstitutional because of his view that some of the broad statements regarding congressional power in Morgan were wrong. For a careful review of the arguments for and against the proposal, see Lewis & Rosenberg, "Legal Analysis of Congress' Authority to Enact a Human Life Statute" (Congressional Research Service, The Library of Congress, Feb. 20, 1981).

d. The constitutionality of the Religious Freedom Restoration Act (RFRA) of 1993 has stimulated litigation as well as considerable academic debate. The background of the law is as follows: From the early 1960s to 1990, the Court, in interpreting the Free Exercise of Religion Clause of the First Amendment, purported to follow an approach that required the state to justify any substantial burden on free exercise under a standard akin to strict scrutiny. In 1990, however, in Employment Division v. Smith (p. 1489 below), the Court held the "compelling government interest" test inapplicable to free exercise challenges to neutral, facially nondiscriminatory laws of general applicability (such as Oregon's criminal prohibition on peyote use in the Smith case). Smith, in short, permitted regulation so long as the law was one of general applicability and not motivated by hostility towards religion or toward a particular sect. The 1993 Act was essentially a congressional effort to return the courts to the approach they had taken before Smith. Congress stated its purpose as being "(1) to restore the compelling interest test as set forth [in pre-Smith cases] and to guarantee its application in all cases where free exercise of religion is substantially burdened; and (2) to provide a claim or defense to persons whose religious exercise is substantially burdened by government." To fulfill these purposes, the operative portions of RFRA provided as follows: "(a) In general. Government shall not substantially burden a person's exercise of religion even if the burden results from a rule of general applicability, except as provided in subsection (b) of this section. (b) Exception. Government may substantially burden a person's exercise of religion only if it demonstrates that application of the burden to the person—(1) is in furtherance of a compelling governmental interest; and (2) is the least restrictive means of furthering that compelling governmental interest." Congress thus thought to assure strict scrutiny of all substantial governmental burdens on exercises of religion.

Is RFRA constitutional? A number of lawsuits were brought challenging the Act, mainly on the ground that it exceeded congressional powers under § 5 of the 14th Amendment and that it violated separation of powers principles by interfering with the judicial autonomy guaranteed by Art. III of the Constitution. The district courts divided over the constitutionality of the law, but the courts of appeals typically sustained it. In October 1996, the Court granted review in Flores v. City of Boerne, 877 F.Supp. 355 (W.D.Tex.1995), rev'd, 73 F.3d 1352 (5th Cir.1996). Even though RFRA raised some questions about statutory interpretation, the Court limited its grant of review to arguments about the constitutionality of the Act. The case involved a suit under RFRA by the Roman Catholic Archbishop of San Antonio after the City of Boerne had denied a construction permit for a Catholic church to expand into a historic district. The city's claim that the law was unconstitutional was upheld by the trial court but rejected by the Fifth Circuit. In its petition to the Court, the city asked that Katzenbach v. Morgan be overruled. The Court was expected to decide the case in the Oct. 1996 Term. What rationales can be mustered in support of the Act? Is it within the "remedial" power as articulated in Morgan? Must its defenders resort to the substantive rationale in order to sustain the law? Does it interfere with the role of the courts set forth in Marbury?

For a comprehensive examination of the legal issues, the lower court decisions, and the literature, see Robin Vergeer, "Disposing of the Red Herrings: A Defense of [RFRA]," 69 So.Cal.L.Rev. 589 (1996). For other essays defending RFRA's constitutionality, see, e.g., Laycock, "RFRA, Congress, and the Ratchet," 56 Mont.L.Rev. 145 (1995), Berg, "What Hath Congress Wrought? An Interpretative Guide to [RFRA]," 39 Vill.L.Rev. 1 (1994), Note, "When the Supreme Court Restricts Constitutional Rights, Can Congress Save Us? An Examination of [§ 5 of the 14th Amendment]," 141 U.Pa.L.Rev. 1029 (1993). For writings claiming that RFRA is unconstitutional, see especially Eisgruber & Sager, "Why [RFRA] is Unconstitutional," 69 N.Y.U.L.Rev. 437 (1995). See also Conkle, "[RFRA]: The Constitutional Significance of an Unconstitutional Statute," 56 Mont.L.Rev. 39 (1995), Hamilton, "[RFRA]: Letting the Fox Into the Henhouse Under Cover of [§ 5 of the 14th Amendment]," 16 Cardozo L.Rev. 357 (1995), and Bybee, "Taking Liberties With the First Amendment: Congress, Section 5 and [RFRA]," 48 Vand.L.Rev. 1539 (1995). For additional articles expressing some doubts about RFRA's constitutionality, see Lupu, "Of Time and the [RFRA]," 56 Mont.L.Rev. 171 (1995), and Idleman, "[RFRA]: Pushing the Limits of Legislative Power," 73 Tex.L.Rev. 247 (1994). See generally Lupu, "Statutes Revolving in Constitutional Law Orbits," 79 Va.L.Rev. 1 (1993).

4. *Limits on (and justifications for) congressional power to "interpret" constitutional rights: Some alternative views.* Most commentators on Morgan and Oregon have found Justice Brennan's footnotes unpersuasive efforts to articulate limits on a "substantive" congressional power under § 5 of the 14th Amendment. In addition to Cohen's comments noted earlier, see, e.g., Cox, "Foreword: Constitutional Adjudication and the Promotion of Human Rights," 80 Harv.L.Rev. 91 (1966): "It is hard to see how the Court can persistently give

weight to the congressional judgment in expanding the definition of equal protection in the area of human rights and refuse to give it weight in narrowing the definition where the definition depends upon appraisal of facts. The footnote, therefore, may not be the end of the argument." See also Burt, "Miranda and Title II: A Morganatic Marriage," 1969 Sup.Ct.Rev. 81, suggesting that "the Court was wrong to erect its apparently rigid footnote [1] limitation on § 5 legislation." But those commentators have also tried their hands at justifying a limited congressional authority to determine the content of constitutional rights, and at suggesting safeguards other than those in Justice Brennan's footnotes. Consider the alternative justifications and limits they suggest. Are they persuasive?

a. *"Line-drawing" capacities and congressional power "around the edges" of Court doctrine—consistent with judicial "value preferences."* Burt, after recognizing that the Morgan rationale "to some extent" exempts the 14th Amendment from "the principle of Court–Congress relationships expressed by Marbury," endorses *some* congressional authority, in situations where principled lines to accommodate competing interests are difficult to draw. He notes that "Congress is less burdened by the principled constraints under which courts labor" and suggests that Congress may impose restrictions on states "where the Court does not feel able to do so itself" because of line-drawing difficulties—so long as Congress follows the Court's value preferences rather than imposing its own on the states. Thus, he supports a congressional "revisory authority" that "would be 'around the edges' of the Court's proclaimed doctrine"—i.e., a congressional power to redefine doctrine, but not too much: "As in Morgan, the Court would independently characterize the measure as a 'reform' that it approved or a 'restriction' that it did not." Burt suggests as an example of potential congressional authority the difficulties of delineating the reach of the 14th Amendment to private discrimination: the Court "could not independently proscribe some private discrimination without its proclaimed principle extending to proscribe all discrimination." Congress, by contrast, could "arbitrarily" exempt some private choices, as it did in the Fair Housing Act of 1968. Thus, he endorses a congressional role where "the legislative mechanism is greatly superior to the Court's."[1] Would Burt's approach significantly limit congressional opportunities to resolve conflicts among competing interests in constitutional interpretation? How would the Court determine whether the congressional resolution was in accord with its "value preferences"? E.g., would Burt's approach authorize Congress to "reinterpret" due process by curtailing the situation in which abortions are permissible? Would it

---

1. Note, however, that Burt recognizes the "substantial risk for the Court" in such a view of Morgan: although the Court "retains ample doctrinal handles to disapprove congressional action, nonetheless its presentational rhetoric—that Congress has, to whatever degree, an 'independent' role in interpreting the Constitution—is likely to remove an important restraint on Congress which has, in the past, counseled great wariness in trespassing on the Court's prerogatives." Given that risk, is the "presentational rhetoric" of South Carolina and Rome preferable to that of Morgan? Does the "remedial" (rather than "substantive") rationale of South Carolina and Rome give the Court a better "doctrinal handle" to disapprove con-

gressional actions that a majority of the Justices find unacceptable? See also Monaghan, "Constitutional Common Law," 89 Harv. L.Rev. 1 (1975), Lupu, "Statutes Revolving in Constitutional Orbits," 79 Va.L.Rev. 1 (1993), Gordon, "The Nature and Uses of Congressional Power under Section Five of the 14th Amendment to Overcome Decisions of the Supreme Court," 72 Nw.U.L.Rev. 656 (1977) ("Congress has power to overturn the empirical findings of the Court; but it can do so only as long as it does not infringe on the normative component of the judicial decision"), and Choper, "Congressional Power to Expand Judicial Definitions of the Substantive Terms of the Civil War Amendments," 67 Minn.L.Rev. 299 (1982).

permit Congress to "interpret" due process to ban all state legislation restricting consensual sexual conduct? Would it authorize federal legislation to define the scope of a journalist's privilege in state courts, despite the Court's rejection of such a privilege under the First Amendment in Branzburg (1972; p. 1434 below)? Would his view sustain RFRA (see note 3d above)?

b.   *Fact-finding capacities and the Morgan power.* Rather than endorsing a congressional power to resolve contests among competing interests, so long as they are in accord with the Court's "value preferences," would it be preferable to insist that any congressional power must be justified by its superior fact-finding capacity? The latter emphasis is prominent in Archibald Cox's comments on the § 5 power. In 1966, he drew from the second part of the Morgan rationale "the generalization that Congress, in the field of state activities except as confined by the Bill of Rights, has the power to enact any law which may be viewed as a measure for correction of any condition which Congress might believe involves a denial of equality or other 14th Amendment rights." Cox, "Foreword: Constitutional Adjudication and the Promotion of Human Rights," 80 Harv.L.Rev. 91. In 1971, in "The Role of Congress in Constitutional Determinations," 40 U.Cinn.L.Rev. 199, he argued that "the Morgan decision follows logically from the basic principles determining the respective functions of the legislative and judicial branches outside the field of preferred constitutional rights. Whether a state law denies equal protection depends to a large extent upon the finding and appraisal of the practical importance of relevant facts." He emphasized the "presumption that facts exist which sustain federal legislation" and the "principle of deference to congressional judgment upon questions of proportion and degree, as illustrated by the Due Process and Commerce Clause cases."

Are the actual and potential uses of the Morgan rationale in fact limited to determinations resting on factual grounds? Or may they involve congressional value choices as well? Even if they rest solely on factual bases, why should there be greater deference to congressional rather than to state legislative judgments? (Recall Justice Harlan's dissent in Oregon.) And if there should be greater deference to congressional assessments, should the Court hypothesize facts that might justify congressional resolutions, or should it insist on a factual record in Congress? Was there such a factual record for § 4(e) in the Morgan case? Was there for the provisions involved in Oregon? Arguably, judicial deference should turn on the degree to which the congressional findings truly involve issues of fact, and on the degree to which those factual issues are spelled out in the legislative record. What § 5 legislation would be permissible if Congress's special competence in fact determinations is emphasized? Would it justify "a comprehensive code of criminal procedure applicable to prosecutions in state courts," as Cox suggested in 80 Harv.L.Rev. 91: "Congress would seem to have the power, under the second branch of the Morgan decision, not only to enforce the specifics but also to make its own findings of fact and evaluation of the competing considerations in determining what constitutes due process and what measures are necessary to secure it in practice"?[2]

---

2. See Title II of the Omnibus Crime Control Act of 1968, which included a partial overturning of the Court's required safeguards in the questioning of suspects, established in Miranda v. Arizona, 384 U.S. 436 (1966). The Burt article noted above saw the statute supportable under Morgan because the differences between Miranda and Title II "are limited in scope, and do not entrench upon the basic purposes which the Court was pursuing." Is such legislation nevertheless barred by the anti-"dilution" footnote [1] in Morgan? Could modifications of the Miranda requirements be justified more readily under the "remedial" rationale?

c. *A distinction between "federalism" and "liberty" issues?* William Cohen's search for limits on congressional power under § 5 of the 14th Amendment looks in a different direction. In 27 Stan.L.Rev. 603 (1975), he found Justice Brennan's efforts to articulate limits in Morgan and Oregon unsatisfactory because they gave Congress "an ill-defined power to dilute judicially declared protections of section 1 of the 14th Amendment." Cohen claims that a "viable theory concerning the limits of Congress' enforcement power under [§ 5]—one that realistically assesses the different strengths of Congress and the courts—can be formulated. [The] theory turns partly on considerations of federalism, distinguishing the relative capacity of Congress to draw the lines between national and state power from the courts' sensitivity to the rights of racial, religious, and political minorities." In short, he "distinguishes between congressional competence to make 'liberty' and 'federalism' judgments." Drawing on Wechsler's emphasis on the "political safeguards of federalism" (chap. 2 above), he argues that "a congressional judgment resolving at the national level an issue that could—without constitutional objection—be decided in the same way at the state level, ought normally to be binding on the courts, since Congress presumably reflects a balance between both national and state interests and hence is better able to adjust such conflicts." But a "congressional judgment rejecting a judicial interpretation of the due process or equal protection clauses—an interpretation that had given the individual procedural or substantive protection from state and federal government alike—is entitled to no more deference than the identical decision of the state legislature." Is that approach persuasive? Does it differ functionally from Justice Brennan's "ratchet" theory?[3] Is the "political safeguards" factor the only one that explains judicial deference to congressional judgments when the exercise of Art. I powers allegedly impinges on federalism concerns? Or is there a special breadth to those powers—a breadth not necessarily applicable to congressional "interpretations" of 14th Amendment rights? And even under Art. I powers, does Congress clearly have independent power to determine what is interstate commerce, rather than merely deciding what is appropriate to regulate that commerce?

5. *The state of the Morgan "substantive" rationale in the 1980s.* a. [After all these speculations about congressional "substantive" enforcement power suggested by Morgan, it is useful to consider the actual support for such a power on the modern Court. Justice REHNQUIST addressed that question in the closing passages of his dissent (joined by Justice Stewart) in ROME v. UNITED STATES (1980; p. 941 above). Most of his dissent, printed earlier, argued that the "remedial" power of the South Carolina case could not justify the application of the Voting Rights Act's preclearance provisions to Rome. He then turned to the "substantive" theory (an issue that the majority had not reached in Rome) and argued that it was an untenable theory not supported by a majority of the members of the Court. Do you agree with Justice Rehnquist's reading of the prior cases? (Note especially his view of Morgan in his footnote [4].) He stated:]

The result reached by the Court today can be sustained only upon the theory that Congress was empowered to determine that structural changes with

---

3. Cohen recognizes that the two theories will typically produce the same results: congressional "extensions" of due process and equal protection would usually involve "federalism" decisions; congressional "dilutions" will ordinarily raise "liberty" decisions. But he insists that the outcomes under the two approaches would not always be the same. For a restatement (and slight modification) of Cohen's position, see his later article, "Congressional Power to Validate Unconstitutional State Laws: A Forgotten Solution to an Old Enigma," 35 Stan.L.Rev. 387 (1983).

a disparate impact on a minority group's ability to elect a candidate of their race violate the 14th or 15th Amendments. This construction of the 14th Amendment was rejected in the Civil Rights Cases. The Court emphasized that the power conferred was "remedial" only. [This] interpretation is consonant with the legislative history surrounding the enactment of the Amendment. This construction has never been refuted by a majority of the Members of this Court. Support for this construction in current years has emerged in South Carolina and Oregon.[4] See also opinion of Powell, J., [in Rome]. In South Carolina, the Court observed that Congress could not attack evils not comprehended by the 15th Amendment. In Oregon, five Members of the Court were unwilling to conclude that Congress had the power to determine that establishing the age limitation for voting at 21 denied equal protection to those between the ages of 18 and 20. The opinion of [Justice Stewart] in that case [reaffirmed] that Congress only has the power under the 14th Amendment to "provide the means of eradicating situations that amount to a violation of [equal protection]" but not to "determine as a matter of substantive constitutional law that situations fall within the ambit of the clause." [Justice Harlan,] in a separate opinion, reiterated his belief that it is the duty of the Court, and not the Congress, to determine when States have exceeded constitutional limitations imposed upon their powers. [Cf.] Cooper v. Aaron. [Justice Black] also was unwilling to accept the broad construction of enforcement powers formulated in the opinion of [Justice Brennan,] joined by Justices White and Marshall. The Court today fails to heed this prior precedent. To permit congressional power to prohibit the conduct challenged in this case requires state and local governments to cede far more of their powers to the Federal Government than the Civil War Amendments ever envisioned; and it requires the judiciary to cede far more of its power to interpret and enforce the Constitution than ever envisioned. The intrusion is all the more offensive to our constitutional system when it is recognized that the only values fostered are debatable assumptions about political theory which should properly be left to the local democratic process.

b. A year after his dissent in Rome, Justice Rehnquist found another context in which to touch upon the Morgan power. The case, Pennhurst State School and Hospital v. Halderman, 451 U.S. 1 (1981), involved the interpretation of the Developmentally Disabled Assistance and Bill of Rights Act of 1975. The Act established a federal-state grant program providing financial assistance to programs for the care and treatment of the mentally retarded. The Act's "bill of rights" provision states that mentally retarded persons "have a right to appropriate treatment, services, and habilitation" in "the setting that is least restrictive [of] personal liberty." The Court of Appeals found that Congress had enacted the law "pursuant to both § 5 of the 14th Amendment and the Spending Power," and that the "bill of rights" provision created substantive rights judicially enforceable by private litigants. Justice Rehnquist's majority opinion reversed, holding that the "bill of rights" provision "simply does not

---

4. Explicit support can also be derived from Mr. Justice Harlan's dissenting opinion in [Morgan]. Mr. Justice Harlan clarified the need for the remedial construction of congressional powers. It is also unnecessary, however, to read the majority opinion as establishing the Court's rejection of the remedial construction of the Civil Rights Cases. While [Justice Brennan's] majority opinion did contain language suggesting a rejection of the "remedial" construction of the enforcement powers, the opinion also advanced a remedial rationale which supports the determination reached by the Court. It would be particularly inappropriate to construe [Morgan] as a rejection of the remedial interpretation of congressional powers in view of this Court's subsequent decision in [Oregon]. [Footnote by Justice Rehnquist.]

create substantive rights.'' He accordingly found it unnecessary to address the constitutional issue of whether Congress had the power to impose such affirmative obligations on states. But in the course of ''discerning congressional intent,'' Justice Rehnquist discussed ''the appropriate test for determining when Congress intends to enforce [14th Amendment] guarantees.'' He stated: ''Because [enforcing] legislation imposes congressional policy on a State involuntarily, and because it often intrudes on traditional state authority, we should not quickly attribute to Congress an unstated intent to act under its authority to enforce the Fourteenth Amendment. Our previous cases are wholly consistent with that view, since Congress in those cases expressly articulated its intent to legislate pursuant to § 5. [See, e.g., Morgan.] Those cases, moreover, involved statutes which simply prohibited certain kinds of state conduct. The case for inferring intent is at its weakest where, as here, the rights asserted impose *affirmative* obligations on the States to fund certain services, since we may assume that Congress will not implicitly attempt to impose massive financial obligations on the States.''

c. In EEOC v. Wyoming, 460 U.S. 226 (1983) (chap. 3 above), the Court clarified its position regarding the evidence necessary to show congressional reliance on § 5. (The case involved the application of the federal Age Discrimination in Employment Act to state governments.) Although the Court's disposition of the commerce clause and Tenth Amendment issues made it possible to avoid the § 5 issue, Justice Brennan's majority opinion nevertheless sought to correct what he found to be a significant misconception. The lower court had taken Pennhurst to require of Congress an explicit reliance on § 5 in plain language. In response, Justice Brennan described Pennhurst as containing no such requirement: ''It is in the nature of our review of congressional legislation defended on the basis of Congress's powers under § 5 of the 14th Amendment that we be able to discern some legislative purpose or factual predicate that supports the exercise of that power. That does not mean, however, that Congress need anywhere recite the words 'section 5' or '14th Amendment' or 'equal protection.' [The] rule of statutory construction invoked in Pennhurst was, like all rules of statutory construction, a tool with which to divine the meaning of otherwise ambiguous statutory intent.'' The majority did not deal further with the § 5 question, but Chief Justice Burger's dissent, joined by Justices Powell, Rehnquist, and O'Connor, contended that imposing restrictions on the mandatory retirement laws of the states was beyond Congress's § 5 power. The Chief Justice then outlined the Court's deferential rationality approach to age discrimination claims, as illustrated by Murgia (p. 734 above). He also rejected the argument that this case came within the scope of Morgan: ''Nor can appellant claim that Congress has used the powers we recognized in [Rome; Oregon; Jones; South Carolina; Morgan] to enact legislation that prohibits conduct not in itself unconstitutional because it considered the prohibition necessary to guard against encroachment of guaranteed rights or to rectify past discrimination. There has been no finding [that] the abrogated state law infringed on rights identified by this Court. Nor did Congress use, as it did in [Morgan], its 'specially informed legislative competence' to decide that the state law it invalidated was too intrusive on federal rights to be an appropriate means to achieve the ends sought by the state. [Allowing] Congress to protect constitutional rights statutorily that it has independently defined fundamentally alters our scheme of government.''

d. Note, finally, the potentially important, narrow view of the Morgan power (with heavy reliance on footnote [1] of Justice Brennan's opinion in Morgan) in Justice O'CONNOR's majority opinion in MISSISSIPPI UNIVERSITY FOR WOMEN v. HOGAN (1982; p. 698 above). Justice O'Connor found that a state university had unconstitutionally excluded a male applicant from its women-only School of Nursing. The State offered as an added justification the argument that Congress, in Title IX of the Education Amendments of 1972, had authorized the university's discrimination by exempting from the gender discrimination prohibition of Title IX those undergraduate institutions that traditionally had used single-sex admissions policies. The exemption provision in Title IX, the State argued, was "a congressional limitation upon the broad prohibitions of [equal protection]." Justice O'Connor rejected that claim summarily: Even if the statute were read as attempting to provide a "constitutional exemption, the State's argument would fail." Sec. 5 gave Congress broad power, to be sure; but Congress's power " 'is limited to adopting measures to enforce the guarantees of the Amendment; § 5 grants Congress no power to restrict, abrogate, or dilute these guarantees' [Morgan, quoting Justice Brennan's footnote]. Although we give deference to congressional decisions and classifications, neither Congress nor a State can validate a law that denies the rights guaranteed by the 14th Amendment. The fact that the language of [the exemption provision] applies to the [University] provides the State no solace: '[A] statute apparently governing a dispute cannot be applied by judges, consistently with their obligations, when such an application of the statute would conflict with the Constitution. [Marbury].' "

FREEDOM OF SPEECH—WHY GOVERNMENT RESTRICTS SPEECH—UNPROTECTED AND LESS PROTECTED EXPRESSION

SECTION 1. FREE SPEECH: AN OVERVIEW

Introduction. The history of Supreme Court litigation regarding freedoms of speech and press is brief in years but enormous in volume. The Court's first major encounters with free speech claims did not come until after World War I; yet, in the decades since, claimed infringements of First Amendment rights have become a staple of Court business and a source of frequent controversy. As written, the First Amendment is simple and unqualified: "Congress shall make no law abridging the freedom of speech, or of the press." But there has been a broad consensus that not all expression or communication is included within "the freedom of speech."

Are some types of speech clearly within First Amendment coverage, while others are entitled to less protection, or excluded altogether? What government interests are sufficient to justify lesser or no protection for speech? Chapter 11 explores these questions after this overview. It begins by reviewing the speech that the Court has deemed *not* protected by the First Amendment. Of course, bribery, perjury, and counseling to murder are not considered protected by the First Amendment. Such exclusions are so uncontroversial as to go unlitigated. But the Court has debated extensively whether several other categories of speech should be held outside First Amendment protection: in particular, the categories of incitement, fighting words, libel, obscenity and child pornography. The Court continues to hold such categories unprotected, but the story of Chapter 11 is largely a story of the shrinking of their boundaries to avoid trenching upon speech that is considered clearly within the First Amendment, especially "political" speech and speech critical of governmental policies and officials. The Court has also grappled with the question whether to treat some speech as protected, but not fully protected speech. It has upheld various regulations of sexually explicit but nonobscene speech, and it has treated commercial speech (i.e., advertising) as explicitly enjoying lesser First Amendment protection. Chapter 11 concludes by exploring these "lower value" categories.

Chapter 12 turns from the question of why government regulates speech to the question of how it does so—to the modes or techniques of abridgement, and to their influence on the relevant standard of review. It begins with the crucial distinction between content-based and content-neutral laws. Content-based laws are generally treated as more suspect than content-neutral laws because of judicial concern with discrimination in the regulation of expression. Content-neutral regulations of speech, or of conduct that may amount to speech, are subject to lesser but still heightened scrutiny. Chapter 12 explores the contours of this distinction and the reasons for it. The chapter next examines another, increasingly important distinction in First Amendment law: that between laws enacted or enforced in government's general capacity as sovereign regulator, and regulations that flow from government's role as landlord, educator, employer and patron. In the latter roles, government has been viewed as a hybrid of public actor, bound by First Amendment constraints, and private proprietor at least partially free from them. The public forum, public school, public employment and public subsidy cases are covered in detail, with attention to this public/private distinction. Finally, chapter 12 turns to several procedural doctrines that bar government from regulating speech too soon, too broadly or too unclearly, even if it might permissibly regulate the same speech a different way. Thus, the Court has showed special hostility to prior restraints on speech, and has employed the doctrines of overbreadth and vagueness to invalidate some laws on their face.

Chapter 13, the last of the free expression chapters, turns to several rights ancillary to the right of free speech. It begins with the cases holding that there is a right against compelled speech—that the right to speak entails a right not to speak. It proceeds by examining the right of expressive association held to be implied in the right to speak, and the right against compelled association. It turns next to the right to spend money in connection with political campaigns, a right held implicit in the free speech clause that has generated considerable law and controversy. Finally the chapter concludes with an examination of the constitutional status of the institutional media. One reason for treating the problems of the media separately is the fact that the First Amendment protects not only "the freedom of speech" but also "the freedom of the press." What is the significance of that special mention of the media? Does it entitle the press to preferential rights under the First Amendment?

A. FIRST AMENDMENT HISTORY

In Palko v. Connecticut (p. 435 above), Justice Cardozo characterized protection of speech as a "fundamental" liberty in part because "our history, political and legal," recognized "freedom of thought and speech" as "the indispensable condition of nearly every other form of freedom." Does history in fact support special protection of First Amendment rights? What is the scope of "the freedom of speech" enshrined by the Framers of the Bill of Rights? What evils of pre-Constitution history was the Amendment designed to avert?

1. *Prior restraints.* A prominent technique of restraint in English law after invention of the printing press had been the licensing of printers—the submission of publications to royal officials with the power to give or withhold an imprimatur of approval. John Milton wrote in protest against the practice in Areopagitica—A Speech for the Liberty of Unlicensed Printing (1664). As William Blackstone described the evils of the practice: "[To] subject the press to the restrictive power of a licenser [is] to subject all freedom of sentiment to the prejudices of one man, and make him the arbitrary and infallible judge of all controverted points in learning, religion, and government." 4 Blackstone, Commentaries on the Laws of England *151–52.

Prior restraint through licensing was abandoned in England a century before the adoption of the American Bill of Rights. Nevertheless, a barrier to licensing was at one time viewed as the major thrust of the First Amendment. Blackstone had expressed the view that "[t]he liberty of the press [consists] in laying no *previous* restraints upon publication, and not in freedom from censure for criminal matter when published." Id. Justice Holmes initially embraced the Blackstonian view that freedom of expression was protected solely against prior restraints. See, e.g., Patterson v. Colorado, 205 U.S. 454 (1907) Compare his grudging recognition 12 years later, in Schenck, p. 1036 below, that "[i]t well may be that the prohibition of laws abridging the freedom of speech is not confined to previous restraints, although to prevent them may have been the main purpose."

2. *Seditious libel.* There had been frequent prosecutions in pre-Revolutionary England for seditious libel—"the intentional publication, without lawful excuse or justification, of written blame of any public man, or of the law, or of any institution established by law." The English judges held, on the question of what was "intentional publication," that it was sufficient to show that the defendant had intended to publish writings having a seditious tendency; the Crown did not have to prove that the defendant maliciously intended to cause sedition. Moreover, under English law it was the judge, not the jury, who decided whether the writing had a seditious tendency. See generally Siebert, Freedom of the Press in England, 1476–1776 (1952). In the colonies, by contrast, trials for seditious libel were extremely rare. The best known was the prosecution of John Peter Zenger in New York in 1735. Zenger was tried for criticizing the Governor General of the colony in his weekly publication. The judge refused the pleas of Zenger's counsel that the truth of the alleged libel was an absolute defense and that the jury, not the judge, should decide the issues of seditious tendency and intent. The jury, disregarding the judge's instructions, found Zenger not guilty.

Zechariah Chafee, Jr.'s influential work on free speech argued that the Framers of the First Amendment had more in mind than the banning of the long-gone censorship through licensing: he insisted that they "intended to wipe out the common law of sedition and make further prosecutions for criticism of the government, without any incitement to law-breaking, forever impossible." Chafee, Free Speech in the United States (1941) (revising Freedom of Speech (1920)). Compare, however, Leonard Levy's careful historical study denying that the First Amendment was "intended to wipe out the common law of sedition." Levy, Legacy of Suppression: Freedom of Speech and Press in Early American History (1960). His "revisionist interpretation" claims that 18th century Americans "did not believe in a broad scope for freedom of expression, particularly in the realm of politics." He concludes that "libertarian theory from the time of Milton to the ratification of the First Amendment substantially accepted the right of the state to suppress seditious libel," claims that the First Amendment framers' main concern was with states' rights and the fear of national power rather than with individual liberty, and argues that a "broad libertarian theory of freedom of speech and press did not emerge in the United States" until the Jeffersonian battle against the Sedition Act of 1798. See also Levy, "The Legacy Reexamined," 37 Stan.L.Rev. 767 (1985); Hamburger, "The Development of the Law of Seditious Libel and the Control of the Press," 37 Stan.L.Rev. 661 (1985); Mayton, "Seditious Libel and the Lost Guarantee of a Freedom of Expression," 84 Colum.L.Rev. 91 (1984); Rabban, "An Ahistorical Historian: Leonard Levy on Freedom of Expression in Early American History," 37 Stan. L. Rev. 795 (1986).

The Sedition Act of 1798, enacted by the Federalists because of widespread hostility to ideas stemming from the French Revolution, barred the publication of "false, scandalous, and malicious writing [against] the Government of the United States, or either House of [Congress], or the President, [with] intent to defame [them]; or to bring them [into] contempt or disrepute; or to excite against them [the] hatred of the good people of the United States, or to stir up sedition within the United States. . . ." In order to eliminate the most criticized procedural aspects of English law, the Act provided that truth *would* be a defense, that malicious intent *was* an element of the crime, and that the jury *would* decide such issues as the seditious tendency of the publication. The Act was rigorously enforced, entirely against Jeffersonian Republicans, including their leading newspapers. Although the Supreme Court did not rule on the Act's constitutionality at the time, several lower federal courts, partly manned by Supreme Court Justices riding circuit, upheld it. The Act expired of its own force in March 1801, and the new President, Jefferson, soon pardoned all of those convicted under it. The Act was a major factor in the defeat of the Federalists by the Jeffersonian Republicans in the 1800 election. Levy notes, however, that the Jeffersonians in power "were not much more tolerant of their political critics than the Federalists had been." Levy, Jefferson and Civil Liberties: The Darker Side (1963). On the enforcement of the Act, see Smith, Freedom's Fetters (1956). See also Berns, "Freedom of the Press and the Alien and Sedition Laws: A Reappraisal," 1970 Sup.Ct.Rev. 109.

3. *Later history.* The century after the Sedition Act controversy witnessed efforts to suppress abolitionist literature during the slavery controversy, see Nye, Fettered Freedom: Civil Liberties and the Slavery Controversy, 1830–1860 (rev. ed. 1964), and attempts to suppress seditious publications during the Civil War, see Randall, Constitutional Problems Under Lincoln (rev. ed. 1951). But not until the World War I era did major free speech issues reach the Supreme Court. For exploration of the antecedents of modern free speech jurisprudence in the years before World War I, see Rabban, "The First Amendment in Its Forgotten Years," 90 Yale L.J. 514 (1981); Rabban, "The Free Speech League, the ACLU, and Changing Conceptions of Free Speech in American History," 45 Stan. L. Rev. 47 (1992); Rabban, "The IWW Free Speech Fights and Popular Conceptions of Free Expression Before World War I," 80 Va. L. Rev. 1055 (1994).

B. FIRST AMENDMENT THEORY

Philosophical justifications for the protection of free speech supplement the uncertain light cast by history. Free speech has been thought to serve three principal values: advancing knowledge and "truth" in the "marketplace of ideas," facilitating representative democracy and self-government, and promoting individual autonomy, self-expression and self-fulfillment. See Emerson, The System of Freedom of Expression (1970). These values have animated much of the Court's reasoning in free speech cases, though not always articulately and not always consistently. What is the consequence of one emphasis or another for the implementation of First Amendment values in the decisions that follow?

1. *Truth.* The classic statements of the value of speech in the search for truth are those of John Milton and John Stuart Mill. John Milton wrote in 1644, protesting a licensing scheme for books: "And though all the winds of doctrine were let loose to play upon the earth, so Truth be in the field, we do injuriously, by licensing and prohibiting, to misdoubt her strength. Let her and Falsehood grapple; who ever knew Truth put to the worst, in a free and open encounter?" Milton, Areopagitica—A Speech for the Liberty of Unlicensed Printing (1644). John Stuart Mill's classic libertarian argument came two centuries after Milton's, in On Liberty (1859). Mill's central argument was that the suppression of opinion is wrong, whether or not the opinion is true: if it is true, society is denied the truth; if it is false, society is denied the fuller understanding of truth which comes from its conflict with error; and when the received opinion is part truth and part error, society can know the whole truth only by allowing the airing of competing views.

As Mill summarized his argument in chapter II of On Liberty: "First, if any opinion is compelled to silence, that opinion may, for aught we can certainly know, be true. To deny this is to assume our own infallibility. Secondly, though the silenced opinion be in error, it may, and very commonly does, contain a portion of the truth; and since the general or prevailing opinion on any subject is rarely or never the whole truth, it is only by the collision of adverse opinions that the remainder of the truth has any chance of being supplied. Thirdly, even if the received opinion be not only true, but the whole truth; unless it is suffered to be, and actually is, vigorously and earnestly contested, it will, by most of those who receive it, be held in the manner of a prejudice, with little comprehension or feeling of its rational grounds. And not only this, but, fourthly, the meaning of the doctrine itself will be in danger of being lost, or enfeebled."

Justice Brandeis echoed these truth-based rationales for speech protection in his concurrence in Whitney v. California (1927; p. 1054 below): "freedom to think as you will and to speak as you think are means indispensable to the discovery and spread of political truth." Justice Holmes did too in his dissent in Abrams v. United States (1919; p. 1040 below): "[W]hen men have realized that time has upset many fighting faiths, they may come to believe even more than they believe the very foundations of their own conduct that the ultimate good desired is better reached by free trade in ideas—that the best test of truth is the power of the thought to get itself accepted in the competition of the market and that truth is the only ground upon which their wishes safely can be carried out. That at any rate is the theory of our constitution." Is there reason to expect truth to emerge through the self-regulating operation of a free "marketplace of ideas"? Any more than to expect the commercial marketplace always to be efficient or just? Justice Holmes would have allowed government considerable latitude to regulate the commercial marketplace. Recall Chapter 8. Why would he tie government's hands and insist on laissez-faire when it comes to the marketplace of ideas?

A number of commentators have criticized the "marketplace" rationale on the ground that its assumptions do not fit the realities of contemporary society. See e.g., Barron, "Access to the Press—A New First Amendment Right," 80 Harv.L.Rev. 1641 (1967) (arguing that the notion of a "self-operating marketplace of ideas [has] long ceased to exist" and insisting that a "realistic view of the first amendment requires recognition that a right of expression is somewhat thin if it can be exercised only at the sufferance of the managers of mass communications"); Baker, "Scope of the First Amendment Freedom of Speech," 25 UCLA L.Rev. 964 (1978) (arguing that "the hope that the marketplace leads to truth [is] implausible" and that "the marketplace of ideas appears improperly biased in favor of presently dominant groups"); Wellington, "On Freedom of Expression," 88 Yale L.J. 1105 (1979) ("In the long run, true ideas do tend to drive out false ones. The problem is that the short run may be very long."); Ingber, "The Marketplace of Ideas: A Legitimizing Myth," 1984 Duke L.J. 1 (noting that, in economic markets, government regulation is needed "to correct failures in the economic market caused by real world conditions," and suggesting that regulation might be needed to correct "communicative market failures" as well). Note also Herbert Marcuse's assertion that, "[u]nder the rule of monopolistic media—themselves the mere instruments of economic and political power—a mentality is created for which right and wrong, true and false are predefined wherever they affect the vital interests of the society." See Marcuse, "Repressive Tolerance," in Robert Wolff et al., A Critique of Pure Tolerance 95 (1965). See also Powe, "Mass Speech and the Newer First Amendment," 1982 Sup.Ct.Rev. 243.

2. *Self-government.* Some emphasize that speech is essential to representative government. Alexander Meiklejohn argued that "public" speech—speech on public issues affecting "self-government"—must be wholly immune from regulation, while "private" speech is entitled to less complete protection. See Meiklejohn, Free Speech and Its Relation to Self–Government (1948). He analogized public speech to a town meeting in which all viewpoints should be presented in order to arrive at wise public policy. Zechariah Chafee, Jr. criticized Meiklejohn for taking too narrow a view of the First Amendment, finding it "shocking" that he would apparently omit to protect art and literature. See Chafee, "Book Review," 62 Harv.L.Rev. 891 (1949). Meiklejohn replied that art, literature, philosophy and the sciences should indeed be included in the First Amendment, as they help "voters acquire the intelligence, integrity, sensitivity, and generous devotion to the general welfare that, in theory, casting a ballot is assumed to express." Meiklejohn, "The First Amendment Is an Absolute," 1961 Sup.Ct.Rev. 245. Former judge Robert Bork disagreed with Meiklejohn's concession: many activities beyond art and literature inform voting, but if there is not to be "an analogical stampede, the protection of the first amendment must be cut off when it reaches the outer limits of political speech." Bork, "Neutral Principles and Some First Amendment Problems," 47 Ind.L.J. 1 (1971). For contemporary argument that the First Amendment is principally about political deliberation, see Sunstein, "Free Speech Now," 59 U. Chi. L. Rev. 255 (1992); Sunstein, Democracy and the Problem of Free Speech (1993). See also BeVier, "The First Amendment and Political Speech: An Inquiry Into the Substance and Limits of Principle," 30 Stan.L.Rev. 299 (1978).

Various justices have emphasized the political function of free speech. For example, Justice Brennan, in New York Times Co. v. Sullivan (1964; p. 1094 below), invoked "a profound national commitment to the principle that debate on public issues should be uninhibited, robust, and wide-open, and that it may well include vehement, caustic, and sometimes unpleasantly sharp attacks on government and public officials." And Justice Black, in Mills v. Alabama, 384 U.S. 214 (1966), stated that "there is practically universal agreement that a major purpose of [the First Amendment] was to protect the free discussion of governmental affairs."

Free speech in the political conception arguably serves at least four different functions. First, as Meiklejohn's town meeting analogy suggests, broad debate informs and improves the making of public policy. Second, free speech prevents government from entrenching itself indefinitely—it keeps clear the "channels of political change." Ely, Democracy and Distrust (1980). Third, free speech prevents government abuse of power. See Blasi, "The Checking Value in First Amendment Theory," 1977A.B.F. Res. J. 521 (emphasizing "the value that free speech, a free press, and free assembly can serve in checking the abuse of power by public officials," and arguing that "the role of the ordinary citizen is not so much to contribute on a continuing basis to the formation of public policy as to retain a veto power to be employed when the decisions of officials pass certain bounds"). Fourth, free speech promotes political stability by providing a safety valve for dissent. As Justice Brandeis cautioned in his Whitney concurrence, "Those who won our independence [knew] that fear breeds repression; that repression breeds hate; that hate menaces stable government [and] that the path of safety lies in the opportunity to discuss freely supposed grievances and proposed remedies." See also Emerson, The System of Freedom of Expression (1970) (arguing that freedom of expression "provides a framework in which the conflict necessary to the progress of a society can take place without destroying the society").

If the principal purpose of speech is to further democracy, may government intervene in the marketplace of ideas in order to improve the deliberative quality of the discussion? For arguments along these lines, see Sunstein, supra; Fiss, "Free Speech and Social Structure," 71 Iowa L. Rev. 1405 (1986). Robert Post criticizes such "collectivist" political speech theories for assuming that there is some proper conception of good political discourse that stands outside of political debate itself. See Post, Constitutional Domains: Democracy, Community, Management (1995), chap. 7.

3. *Autonomy.* A third rationale for protecting speech emphasizes the values of individual liberty, autonomy, and self-fulfillment. Unlike the truth and self-government theories, which view speech as instrumental to desired social consequences, autonomy theories emphasize the intrinsic worth of speech to individual speakers and listeners. Justice Brandeis echoed this theme too in his Whitney concurrence, suggesting that "[t]hose who won our independence believed that the final end of the State was to make men free to develop their faculties; [they] valued liberty both as an end and as a means." An emphasis on individual self-realization readily extends First Amendment protection beyond the political realm to art, literature and even entertainment and advertising. See Redish, "The Value of Free Speech," 130 U.Pa.L.Rev. 591 (1982) (arguing that democratic self-government is not an end in itself but a means to "the much broader value of individual self-realization," and thus that the First Amendment is "much broader than Bork or Meiklejohn would have it").

Some autonomy-based theories of free speech emphasize the affirmative value of speech in the development of rational human capacities. See Baker, Human Liberty and Freedom of Speech (1989); Richards, "Free Speech and Obscenity Law: Toward a Moral Theory of the First Amendment," 123 U.Pa. L.Rev. 45 (1974); Baker, "Scope of the First Amendment Freedom of Speech," 25 UCLA L.Rev. 964 (1978). Others emphasize the obverse: the inconsistency of censorship with human autonomy, and the impropriety of paternalism as a ground for interference with speech. See Strauss, "Persuasion, Autonomy, and Freedom of Expression," 91 Colum. L. Rev. 334 (1991) (arguing that a central principle of the First Amendment is that government may not stop speech for reason of its power to persuade the listener, and that "[v]iolating the persuasion principle is wrong for some of the reasons that lies [are] wrong: both involve a denial of autonomy in the sense that they interfere with a person's control over her own reasoning processes"). See also Scanlon, "A Theory of Freedom of Expression," 1 Phil. & Pub.Aff. 204 (1972) ("an autonomous person cannot accept without independent consideration the judgment of others as to what he should believe or what he should do," including the judgment of the state expressed through the suppression of dissent); but see Scanlon, "Freedom of Expression and Categories of Expression," 40 U.Pitt.L.Rev. 519 (1979) (retreating from autonomy-centered view of speech).

Autonomy theories of speech have been criticized as being too broad. See Bork, supra (arguing that self-fulfillment is not a principle that can "distinguish speech from any other human activity," for "an individual may develop his faculties or derive pleasure from trading on the stock market [or] engaging in sexual activities," and there is no neutral way to rank speech ahead of these alternative forms of "personal gratification").

4. *Negative theories.* Some theories of speech protection focus less on the affirmative instrumental or intrinsic value of speech than on the special reasons to distrust government in the realm of speech regulation. Frederick Schauer thus defends free speech on the basis of an "argument from governmental incompetence"—an emphasis on "a distrust of the ability of govern-

ment to make the necessary distinctions, a distrust of governmental determinations of truth and falsity." Schauer, Free Speech: A Philosophical Enquiry (1982). Schauer states: "Even if there is nothing especially good about speech compared to other conduct, the state may have less ability to regulate speech than it has to regulate other forms of conduct, or the attempt to regulate speech may entail special harms or special dangers not present in regulation of other conduct. [Throughout] history the process of regulating speech has been marked with what we now see to be fairly plain errors"—including "the banning of numerous admittedly great works of art because someone thought them obscene." He adds that "acts of suppression that have been proved erroneous seem to represent a disproportionate percentage of the governmental mistakes of the past. [Experience] arguably shows that governments are particularly bad at censorship." He concludes: "Freedom of speech is based in large part on a distrust of the ability of government to make the necessary distinctions, a distrust of governmental determinations of truth and falsity, an appreciation of the fallibility of political leaders, and of somewhat deeper distrust of governmental power in a more general sense." See also Schauer, "The Second–Best First Amendment," 31 Wm. & Mary L. Rev. 1 (1989).

For a related argument that free speech doctrine should assume government is prone to pathological reactions to speech, see Blasi "The Pathological Perspective and the First Amendment," 85 Colum.L.Rev. 449 (1985) (arguing that "the overriding objective at all times should be to equip the first amendment to do maximum service in those historical periods when intolerance of unorthodox ideas is most prevalent. [The] first amendment, in other words, should be targeted for the worst of times."). For criticisms of Blasi, see Redish, "The Role of Pathology in First Amendment Theory: A Skeptical Examination," 38 Case W.Res.L.Rev. 618 (1988); Christie, "Why the First Amendment Should Not Be Interpreted From the Pathological [Perspective]," 1986 Duke L.J. 683.

Why might government regulation of speech be more suspect than governmental regulation of other activities? With respect to political speech, the answer is easy: the incumbent regime will be biased in its own favor against dissidents and challengers. Can this argument be broadened to reach cultural or social dissent as well? See Justice Jackson's opinion in the second flag salute case, West Va. Bd. of Educ. v. Barnette (1943; p. 1362 below): "If there is any fixed star in our constitutional constellation, it is that no official, high or petty, can prescribe what shall be orthodox in politics, nationalism, religion, or other matters of opinion or force citizens to confess by word or act their faith therein."

5. *Eclectic theories*. Are these varying rationales better considered jointly than separately? The Court itself relies upon an amalgam of the above theories. Some commentators argue that any adequate protection of free speech must rely upon "several strands of theory in order to protect a rich variety of expressional modes." Tribe, American Constitutional Law 789 (2d Ed.1988). See also Bloustein, "The Origin, Validity, and Interrelationships of the Political Values Served by Freedom of Expression," 33 Rutgers L.Rev. 372 (1981); Shiffrin, "The First Amendment and Economic Regulation: Away From a General Theory of the First Amendment," 78 Nw.U.L.Rev. 1212 (1983).

C. FIRST AMENDMENT JURISPRUDENCE

Assuming that freedom of expression warrants protection because of its values to society and the individual, what is the appropriate judicial responsibility for protecting it? Should speech have a preferred position in the Constitution, and thus receive greater protection from regulation than other activities? The Court has long shown special judicial solicitude for free speech, meaning that governmental action directed at expression must satisfy a greater burden of justification than governmental action directed at most other forms of behavior. What justifies this special protection of freedom of expression? Assuming that speech is to be specially protected, what judicial techniques best implement that protection? Should protection be absolute? If not, are exceptions to protection better made through categorization of types of speech as more or less valuable and of types of regulation as more or less permissible? Or is it better to uphold a speech regulation only by explicit balancing of speech values against countervailing governmental interests? Do categories reflect implicit balancing in any event?

1. *Justifying special protection for speech.* Since the New Deal, the Court has deferred to government in the economic sphere, upholding a wide range of regulation against equal protection and substantive due process challenge. Recall Chapter 8. In speech cases, by contrast, the Court treats speech as enjoying strong presumptive protection, and frequently intervenes to strike down government regulation. Thus, the Court has declined to read the Fourteenth Amendment as mandating laissez-faire in economic markets. But it has read the First Amendment to require a considerable amount of laissez-faire in the marketplace of ideas. Justice Holmes himself expressed both positions: in his dissent in Lochner v. New York (1905; p. 460 above), he wrote that labor regulation is permissible because the liberty clause "does not enact Mr. Herbert Spencer's Social Statics," nor does it "embody a particular economic theory" of free trade. But in his dissent in Abrams v. United States (1919; p. 1040 below), he argued that regulation of dissident speech is impermissible because the free speech clause recognizes that "the ultimate good desired is better reached by free trade in ideas—that the best test of truth is the power of the thought to get itself accepted in the competition of the market."

What explains this asymmetrical approach? One of the most influential statements of the modern Court's double standard occurs in footnote 4 in Justice Stone's opinion in United States v. Carolene Products Co. (1938; p. 478 above). Stone spoke of a "narrower scope for operation of the presumption of constitutionality when legislation appears on its face to be within a specific prohibition of the Constitution, such as those of the first ten amendments, which are deemed equally specific when held to be embraced within the 14th." Are First Amendment rights truly more "specific" than, for example, the contracts clause and other protections of "property"? He also suggested, more tentatively, a "more exacting judicial scrutiny" of legislation restricting the "political processes," listing "restraints upon the dissemination of information" among his examples. But the Court's special solicitude has extended well beyond political speech.

Does the explanation lie instead in the difference in the practical functions of speech and economic transactions? Justice Frankfurter—though he objected to the view that free speech was entitled to a "preferred position" and was often willing to defer to government speech regulation himself—suggested as much in explicating Holmes' asymmetrical opinions: "The ideas now governing the constitutional protection of freedom of speech derive essentially from the opinions of Mr. Justice Holmes, [who] seldom felt justified in opposing his own opinion to economic views which the legislature embodied in law. But since he also realized that the progress of civilization is to a considerable extent the displacement of error which once held sway as official truth by beliefs which in turn have yielded to other beliefs, for him the right to search for truth was of a different order than some transient economic dogma. And without freedom of expression, thought becomes checked and atrophied. Therefore, in considering what interests are so fundamental as to be enshrined in the Due Process Clause, those liberties of the individual which history has attested as the indispensable conditions of an open as against a closed society come to this Court with a momentum for respect lacking when appeal is made to liberties which derive merely from shifting economic arrangements." Kovacs v. Cooper, 336 U.S. 77 (1949) (Frankfurter, J., concurring).

Might it be argued that economic markets and the marketplace of ideas should be treated the same? Arguments for symmetry have been made from both directions. For an overview of these arguments, see Sullivan, "Free Speech and Unfree Markets," 42 UCLA L. Rev. 949 (1995). Some have suggested that constitutional guarantees should be rigorously enforced against regulation of both speech and economic markets. See, e.g., R.H. Coase, "The Economics of the First Amendment: The Market for Goods and the Market for Ideas," 64 Am. Econ. Rev. Proc. 384 (1974); Epstein, "Property, Speech, and the Politics of Distrust," 59 U. Chi. L. Rev. 41 (1992). For a reply to Epstein, see Michelman, "Liberties, Fair Values, and Constitutional Method," 59 U. Chi. L. Rev. 91 (1992). For criticism of the export of market metaphors to the area of speech, see Radin, Market Rhetoric and Reality: Commodification in Words and the World (1996). Others have suggested a symmetrical move in the opposite direction: that there should be no more presumptive protection for speech against government regulation than for economic activities. On this view, there are imperfections in the marketplace of ideas, just as there are in the economic marketplace. If speech has negative external effects, if some persons or entities have monopoly power over speech, or if the distribution of speech is skewed by unequal speaking power, say these commentators, then regulation may be justified in the interest of speech itself just as regulation in the economic markets is sometimes justified in the interest of efficiency or distribution. For variations on such views, see Sunstein, Democracy and the Problem of Free Speech (1993); Schauer, "Uncoupling Free Speech," 64 U. Colo. L. Rev. 935 (1993); Balkin, "Some Realism About Pluralism: Legal Realist Approaches to the First Amendment," 1990 Duke L. J. 375. Neither of these arguments for symmetry has made headway with the contemporary Supreme Court, which continues to accord heightened protection to speech.

2. *Absolutes versus balancing.* An important debate in First Amendment adjudication in the 1960s was over whether First Amendment rights are "absolute" or subject to the "balancing" of competing interests. Justice Black was the principal advocate of the former position. Justice Black wrote, "I do not subscribe to ['the doctrine that permits constitutionally protected rights to be "balanced" away when a majority of the Court thinks that a State might have interest sufficient to justify abridgment of those freedoms'] for I believe that the First Amendment's unequivocal command that there shall be no abridgment of the rights of free speech and assembly shows that the men who drafted our Bill of Rights did all the 'balancing' that was to be [done]. [I] fear that the creation of 'tests' by which speech is left unprotected under certain circumstances is a standing invitation to abridge [it]." Konigsberg v. State Bar of California, 366 U.S. 36 (1961) (Black, J., dissenting). See also Black, "The Bill of Rights," 35 N.Y.U.L.Rev. 865 (1960), and Black, A Constitutional Faith (1968).

Justices Frankfurter and Harlan rejected Black's approach and advocated explicit balancing instead. For example, Justice Harlan wrote for the majority in Konigsberg, supra, which upheld a denial of bar admission to an applicant who had refused to answer questions about Communist Party membership, as follows: "[W]e reject the view that freedom of speech and association [are] 'absolutes,' not only in the undoubted sense that where the constitutional protection exists it must prevail, but also in the sense that the scope of that protection must be gathered solely from a literal reading of the First Amendment. Throughout its history this Court has consistently recognized [that] constitutionally protected freedom of speech is narrower than an unlimited license to talk. [When] constitutional protections are asserted against the exercise of valid governmental powers a reconciliation must be effected, and that perforce requires an appropriate weighing of the respective interests involved." Similarly, Justice Frankfurter defended balancing: "Absolute rules would inevitably lead to absolute exceptions, and such exceptions would eventually corrode the rules. The demands of free speech in a democratic society as well as [countervailing governmental interests] are better served by candid and informed weighing of the competing interests, within the confines of the judicial process, than by announcing dogmas too inflexible for the non-Euclidean problems to be solved." Dennis v. United States (1951; p. 1061 below).

There may be somewhat less to the "absolutes"-"balancing" debate than meets the eye. See, e.g., Kalven, "Upon Rereading Mr. Justice Black on the First Amendment," 14 U.C.L.A.L.Rev. 428 (1967) (commenting that the "absolutes"-"balancing" controversy "seems to me on the whole to have been an unfortunate, misleading, and unnecessary one"). Justice Black, for example, did not support every freedom of expression claim. Justice Harlan's "balancing," on the other hand, was not necessarily deferential. In one of the flag burning cases, Street v. New York, p. 1220 below, for example, he wrote the majority opinion sustaining the First Amendment challenge while Justice Black dissented on the ground that the prosecution was not for "spoken words," but for speech "used as an integral part of conduct" in burning the flag in public. Similarly, in Cohen v. California (1971; p. 1081 below), the "Fuck the Draft" case, Justice Harlan's statement for the majority was one of the most speech-protective (albeit largely "balancing" in approach), while Justice Black was once again in dissent.

The relative merits of absolute and balancing approaches were explored in an extended debate between Laurent Frantz and Wallace Mendelson. Frantz favored rules and argued that balancing would tend inevitably to be too deferential to government judgments or to the prejudices of the predominant political culture, and would provide inadequate guidance to decisionmakers. See Frantz, "The First Amendment in the Balance," 71 Yale L.J. 1424 (1962); Frantz, "Is the First Amendment Law? A Reply to Professor Mendelson," 51 Cal. L. Rev. 729 (1963). See also Ely, "Flag Desecration: A Case Study in the Roles of Categorization and Balancing in First Amendment Analysis," 88 Harv. L. Rev. 1482 (1975) ("[W]here messages are proscribed because they are dangerous, balancing tests inevitably become intertwined with the ideological predispositions of those doing the balancing—or if not that, at least with the relative confidence or paranoia of the age in which they are doing it."). Mendelson, in contrast, favored balancing: "Balancing seems to me the essence of the judicial process—the nexus between abstract law and concrete [life]. Surely the choice is simply this: shall the balancing be done 'intuitively' or rationally; covertly or out in the open?" Mendelson, "The First Amendment and the Judicial Process: A Reply to Mr. Frantz," 17 Vand.L.Rev. 479 (1964). For a discussion of "First Amendment balancing in the Harlan manner," see Gunther, "In Search of Judicial Quality on a Changing Court: The Case of Justice Powell," 24 Stan.L.Rev. 1001 (1972).

3. *Categorization versus balancing.* Even if it is conceded that the First Amendment is *not* absolute, a pervasive question of judicial methodology remains: should any reduced protection for speech be analyzed in terms of

"categorization" or of "balancing"? Categorization strives for "bright line" rules. One kind of categorization distinguishes what expression is within the First Amendment from that which is outside: for example "political" speech is "in," "fighting words" or "obscenity" are "out." See Chapter 11. A related kind does not result in total exclusion from First Amendment coverage, but rather classifies some types of speech as less valuable than "core" speech in order to require lesser justification from the government to permit restrictions. (A different kind of categorization distinguishes among kinds of government regulation of speech: for example, between "content-based" and "content-neutral" laws, or between laws in "public forums" and "nonpublic forums." See Chapter 12.) Categorization of speech as protected or unprotected forecloses balancing of interests in a particular case. It sorts cases into those presumptively won either by government or by the speaker. Balancing, in contrast, could go either way. See generally, Sullivan, "The Supreme Court: 1991 Term—Foreword: The Justices of Rules and Standards," 106 Harv. L. Rev. 22 (1992); Sullivan, "Post-Liberal Judging: The Roles of Categorization and Balancing," 63 U. Colo. L. Rev. 293 (1992).

Categorization of types of speech finds certain varieties of speech unprotected on a wholesale basis because the claim simply does not belong in the First Amendment ballpark—either because some "utterances are no essential part of any exposition of ideas, and are of such slight social value as a step to truth," or because, as is often suggested implicitly, there are such powerful state interests justifying restrictions that the type of expression can be wholly excluded from "the freedom of speech." Chaplinsky v. New Hampshire (1942; p. 1077 below). See generally, on this "two-level" theory of speech, Kalven, "The Metaphysics of the Law of Obscenity," 1960 Sup.Ct.Rev. 1. The balancing approach, by contrast, asserts that a very broad range of expression is presumptively within the First Amendment and can be found unprotected only after the restrictions are shown to be outweighed by the governmental interest in a particular case. A balancing approach, in short, permits judicial evaluations only on the state interest side of the balance, and would not shortcut the balancing process by encouraging judicial evaluations on the First Amendment side, excluding certain varieties of speech from protection at the threshold, on a wholesale basis

Again, there may be more to the categorization-balancing debate than meets the eye. Balancing can function effectively as a rule if it is given a sufficiently speech-protective form. When regulations are subject to strict judicial scrutiny, which requires both a showing of "compelling" state ends and the unavailability of less restrictive means, the government virtually always loses and the speaker virtually always wins. Strict scrutiny thus functions more like categorization than balancing. Likewise, minimum rationality review amounts in practice to a category in the government's favor. True balancing continues to operate only when the Court applies intermediate scrutiny to speech. Conversely, categorization itself can reflect a prior or implicit balancing process. Melville Nimmer argued that the Court's categories sometimes emerge from "definitional balancing," which is a "third approach which avoids the all or nothing implications of absolutism versus ad hoc balancing." Thus, if the Court holds, for example, that knowingly or recklessly false and defamatory statements of fact are unprotected by the First Amendment, it "must have implicitly [referred] to certain competing policy considerations." Thus definitional balancing generates per se rules or categories for future cases in which the balance is certain to come out the same way. Nimmer, "The Right to Speak from Time to Time: First Amendment Theory Applied to Libel and Misapplied to Privacy," 56 Cal. L. Rev. 935 (1968).

Categorization has the attraction of clarity and of providing guidance to judges and other government officials. Categorization is also defended as a welcome recognition of the diversity of the types of speech, and a welcome alternative to the excessive flexibility of balancing: by avoiding the assessment of every allegedly protected speech manifestation against all relevant state interests, the argument goes, manipulative, result-oriented uses of balancing are sharply curtailed. Finally, categorization might be speech-protective after all. A unitary theory of the First Amendment that would extend similar strong protection to all varieties of communication might ultimately dilute First Amendment protections, because some types of speech will inevitably receive less protection, with the result that even the protection of core, political speech will suffer. "It is inconceivable that we will ignore such well-established governmental concerns as safety, reputation, protection against fraud, and protection of children. [Certain] state interests are inevitably going to be recognized, and the alternatives then are diluting those tests that are valuable precisely because of their strength, or formulating new tests and categories that leave existing standards strong within their narrower range. [A] narrow but strong First Amendment, with its strong principle universally available for all speech covered by the First Amendment, has much to be said for it. First Amendment protection can be like an oil spill, thinning out as it broadens." Schauer, "Codifying the First Amendment: New York v. Ferber," 1982 Sup. Ct. Rev. 285. See also Sunstein, Democracy and the Problem of Free Speech (1993).

But categorization also may cast entire classes of speech outside the First Amendment on a wholesale basis, without adequate examination of the bases for the conclusion. It may also, in its striving for general and bright-line rules, unduly slight the distinctions among types of speech within the category and the differences in contexts (and competing state interests) that particular examples of excluded speech may in fact present. Finally, variation in the levels of protection for speech may result ultimately in a myriad, increasingly ad hoc range of First Amendment rules and an excessive codification harmful to long range protection of First Amendment values.

For additional comments on categorization generally, see, e.g., Schauer, "Categories and the First Amendment: A Play in Three Acts," 34 Vand.L.Rev. 265 (1981); Schauer, "Speech and 'Speech'—Obscenity and 'Obscenity': An Exercise in the Interpretation of Constitutional Language," 67 Geo.L.J. 899 (1979); Scanlon, "Freedom of Expression and Categories of Expression," 40 U.Pitt.L.Rev. 519 (1979); and Ely "Flag Desecration: A Case Study in the Roles of Categorization and Balancing in First Amendment Analysis," 88 Harv.L.Rev. 1482 (1975). For additional comments on balancing generally, see Aleinikoff, "Constitutional Law in the Age of Balancing," 96 Yale L.J. 943 (1987).

SECTION 2.   INCITEMENT

A.   THE WORLD WAR I CASES: "CLEAR AND PRESENT DANGER"

Introduction. Should the First Amendment protect incitement to violation of law? Consider John Stuart Mill, writing in On Liberty: "No one pretends that actions should be as free as opinions. On the contrary, even opinions lose immunity, when the circumstances in which they are expressed are such as to constitute their expression a positive instigation to some mischievous act. An opinion that corn-dealers are starvers of the poor, or that private property is robbery, ought to be unmolested when simply circulated through the press, but may justly incur punishment when delivered orally to an excited mob assembled before the house of a corn-dealer, or when handed about among the same mob in the form of a placard. Acts of whatever kind, which, without justifiable cause, do harm to others, may be, and in the more important cases absolutely require to be, controlled by the unfavorable sentiments, and, when needful, by the active interference of mankind. The liberty of the individual must be thus far limited; he must not make himself a nuisance to other people." The Court has grappled mightily with the question how to draw the line between "opinion" and "instigation."

Indeed, the Court's first significant encounter with the problem of articulating the scope of constitutionally protected freedom of speech came in a series of cases involving agitation against the war and the draft during World War I. Typically in these cases, the speaker presented claims at the core of First Amendment concerns: expression critical of government policies. The government asserted especially strong interests for restraining speech: protecting governmental operations, even assuring the survival of government. Moreover, the government's restrictions often resembled the traditional curbs on seditious libel.

The "clear and present danger" test, first set forth by Justice Holmes in Schenck, has been hailed as an approach to the problem of subversive advocacy that avoids extremes. At one extreme, it can be argued that restriction on speech, at least political speech, is *never* legitimate—that punishment must be limited to illegal action, even if the speech directly "incites" that action. Holmes rejected that "perfect immunity" for speech. At the other extreme, it has been argued that "[t]here [should] be no constitutional protection for any speech advocating the violation of law." Bork, "Neutral Principles and Some First Amendment Problems," 47 Ind. L. J. 1 (1971). Holmes likewise rejected that approach; "clear and present danger" purports to draw the line somewhere in between. But Holmes also rejected a far more restrictive intermediate solution: the "bad tendency" test widely applied by the lower courts at the time, which held that "any tendency in speech to produce bad acts, no matter how remote, would suffice to validate a repressive statute." Chafee, Book Review, 62 Harv.L.Rev. 891 (1949). "Clear and present danger" leans more strongly toward protection of speech than does "bad tendency."

The cases that developed the "clear and present danger" test arose under section 3 of Title I of the 1917 Espionage Act. (The Abrams case involved 1918 amendments to the law.) The 1917 Act, while largely directed at espionage and disclosure of military secrets, also created three new offenses: "[1] Whoever, when the United States is at war, shall willfully make or convey false reports or false statements with intent to interfere with the operation or success of the military or naval forces of the United States or to promote the success of its enemies, and [2] whoever, when the United States is at war, shall willfully cause or attempt to cause insubordination, disloyalty, mutiny, or refusal of duty, in the military or naval forces of the United States, or [3] shall willfully obstruct the recruiting or enlistment service of the United States, to the injury of the service or of the United States, shall be punished by a fine of not more than $10,000 or imprisonment for not more than twenty years, or both." Although very few cases under the 1917 and 1918 laws reached the Supreme Court, there were over 2,000 convictions in the lower federal courts.

What is the meaning of "clear and present danger" as used in the following cases? Does the scope of permissible government justification for regulating subversive advocacy vary over time? The Schenck case gave birth to the language; but Schenck was followed within a week by two other Holmes decisions, Frohwerk and Debs, which purported to follow Schenck. Later in the same year came Holmes' dissent in Abrams. Did the Abrams dissent simply apply the Schenck standard, or did it reinterpret "clear and present danger"? Does the test undervalue legitimate state interests for curtailing speech? Or does it permit too much incursion on speech, amounting to a shield too likely to collapse under stress? District Judge Learned Hand's opinion in Masses is reprinted to promote critical examination of the Schenck–Abrams criterion. Does Hand's analysis, dealing with the same World War I statute about two years before Schenck, suggest a useful alternative to that of Holmes?

Schenck v. United States

249 U.S. 47, 39 S.Ct. 247, 63 L.Ed. 470 (1919).

Justice HOLMES delivered the opinion of the Court.

This is an indictment in three counts. The first charges a conspiracy to violate the Espionage Act of June 15, 1917, by causing and attempting to cause insubordination, & c., in the military and naval forces of the United States, and to obstruct the recruiting and enlistment service of the United States, when the United States was at war with the German Empire, to-wit, that the defendants wilfully conspired to have printed and circulated to men who had been called and accepted for military service [a document] alleged to be calculated to cause such insubordination and obstruction. [The] second count alleges a conspiracy to commit an offence against the United States, to-wit, to use the mails for the transmission of matter declared to be non-mailable by [the 1917 Espionage Act], to-wit, the above mentioned document. [The] third count charges an unlawful use of the mails for the transmission of the same matter. [The] defendants were found guilty on all the counts. They set up the First Amendment to the Constitution, [and] bringing the case here on that ground have argued some other points [also].

The document in question upon its first printed side recited the first section of the 13th Amendment, said that the idea embodied in it was violated by the Conscription Act and that a conscript is little better than a convict. In impassioned language it intimated that conscription was despotism in its worst form and a monstrous wrong against humanity in the interest of Wall Street's chosen few. It said "Do not submit to intimidation," but in form at least confined itself to peaceful measures such as a petition for the repeal of the act. The other and later printed side of the sheet was headed "Assert Your Rights." It stated reasons for alleging that any one violated the Constitution when he refused to recognize "your right to assert your opposition to the draft," and went on, "If you do not assert and support your rights, you are helping to deny or disparage rights which it is the solemn duty of all citizens and residents of the United States to retain." It described the arguments on the other side as coming from cunning politicians and a mercenary capitalist press, and even silent consent to the conscription law as helping to support an infamous conspiracy. It denied the power to send our citizens away to foreign shores to shoot up the people of other lands, and added that words could not express the condemnation such cold-blooded ruthlessness deserves, & c., & c., winding up, "You must do your share to maintain, support and uphold the rights of the people of this country." Of course the document would not have been sent unless it had been intended to have some effect, and we do not see what effect it could be expected to have upon persons subject to the draft except to influence them to obstruct the carrying of it out. The defendants do not deny that the jury might find against them on [this].

But it is said, suppose that that was the tendency of this circular, it is protected by the [First Amendment]. Two of the strongest expressions are said to be quoted respectively from well-known public men. It well may be that the prohibition of laws abridging the freedom of speech is not confined to previous restraints, although to prevent them may have been the main purpose, as intimated in Patterson v. Colorado, 205 U.S. 454 [1907]. We admit that in many places and in ordinary times the defendants in saying all that was said in the circular would have been within their constitutional rights. But the character of every act depends upon the circumstances in which it is done. The most stringent protection of free speech would not protect a man in falsely shouting fire in a theatre and causing a panic. [The] question in every case is whether the words used are used in such circumstances and are of such a nature as to create a clear and present danger that they will bring about the substantive evils that Congress has a right to prevent. It is a question of proximity and degree. When a nation is at war many things that might be said in time of peace are such a hindrance to its effort that their utterance will not be endured so long as men fight, and that no Court could regard them as protected by any constitutional right. It seems to be admitted that if an actual obstruction of the recruiting service were proved, liability for words that produced that effect might be enforced. [The 1917 law] punishes conspiracies to obstruct as well as actual obstruction. If the act (speaking, or circulating a paper), its tendency and the intent with which it is done are the same, we perceive no ground for saying that success alone warrants making the act a [crime].[1]

Judgments affirmed.

FROHWERK v. UNITED STATES, 249 U.S. 204 (1919): In this case and in Debs, which follows (both decided a week after Schenck), Justice Holmes once again spoke for the Court in affirming convictions under the 1917 Act. Consider what light these cases throw on the meaning of the clear and present danger standard he had stated in Schenck. In Frohwerk, Justice Holmes stated: "This is an indictment in thirteen counts." The first alleges a conspiracy between [Frohwerk] and one Carl Gleeser, they then being engaged in the preparation and publication of a newspaper, the Missouri Staats Zeitung, to violate the [1917 Act]. It alleges as overt acts the preparation and circulation of twelve articles, & c. in the said newspaper at different dates from July 6, 1917, to December 7 of the same year. The other counts allege attempts to cause disloyalty, mutiny and refusal of duty in the military and naval forces of the United States, by the same publications, each count being confined to the

1. Holmes here appeared to be analogizing the clear and present danger test to criminal attempt law, which he had helped to develop while sitting on the Massachusetts Supreme Judicial Court. See, e.g., Commonwealth v. Peaslee, 59 N.E. 55 (Mass.1901) (Holmes, J.): "The question on the evidence [is] whether the defendant's acts come near enough to the accomplishment of the substantive offense to be punishable. [It] is a question of degree. [The] degree of proximity held sufficient may vary with [circumstances]."

publication of a single date. [A motion to dismiss based on the First Amendment was overruled.] Frohwerk was found [guilty and sentenced to a fine and to ten years imprisonment on each count, with the imprisonment on the substantive counts to run concurrently with that on the conspiracy charge.]

"[With regard to the constitutional argument] we think it necessary to add to what has been said in [Schenck] only that the First Amendment while prohibiting legislation against free speech as such cannot have been, and obviously was not, intended to give immunity for every possible use of language. [We] venture to believe that neither Hamilton nor Madison, nor any other competent person then or later, ever supposed that to make criminal the counselling of a murder within the jurisdiction of Congress would be an unconstitutional interference with free speech. [We] have decided in [Schenck] that a person may be convicted of a conspiracy to obstruct recruiting by words of persuasion. [S]o far as the language of the articles goes there is not much to choose between expressions to be found in them and those before us in [Schenck]. The first begins by declaring it a monumental and inexcusable mistake to send our soldiers to France, says that it comes no doubt from the great trusts, and later that it appears to be outright murder without serving anything practical; speaks of the unconquerable spirit and undiminished strength of the German nation, and characterizes its own discourse as words of warning to the American people. [In the second article, after] deploring 'the draft riots in Oklahoma and elsewhere' in language that might be taken to convey an innuendo of a different sort, it is said that the previous talk about legal remedies is all very well for those who are past the draft age and have no boys to be [drafted]. Who then, it is asked, will pronounce a verdict of guilty upon him if he stops reasoning and follows the first impulse of nature: self-preservation; and further, whether, while technically he is wrong in his resistance, he is not more sinned against than sinning; and yet again whether the guilt of those who voted the unnatural sacrifice is not greater than the wrong of those who now seek to escape by ill-advised resistance. [There] is much more to the general effect that we are in the wrong and are giving false and hypocritical reasons for our course, but the foregoing is enough to indicate the kind of matter with which we have to deal.

"It may be that all this might be said or written even in time of war in circumstances that would not make it a crime. We do not lose our right to condemn either measures or men because the Country is at war. It does not appear that there was any special effort to reach men who were subject to the draft, and if the evidence should show that the defendant was a poor man, turning out copy for Gleeser, his employer, at less than a day laborer's pay, for Gleeser to use or reject as he saw fit, in a newspaper of small circulation, there would be a natural inclination to test every question of law to be found in the record very thoroughly before upholding the very severe penalty imposed. But [on this] record it is impossible to say that it might not have been found that the circulation of the paper was in quarters where a little breath would be enough to kindle a flame and that the fact was known and relied upon by those who sent the paper out. [When] we consider that we do not know how strong the Government's evidence may have been we find ourselves unable to say that the articles could not furnish a basis for a conviction upon the first count at least."

DEBS v. UNITED STATES, 249 U.S. 211 (1919): In this companion case to Frohwerk, the defendant was Eugene V. Debs, the long-time leader and frequent presidential candidate of the Socialist party. In 1912, Debs had gotten over 900,000 votes, nearly 6% of the total. In 1920 (while Debs was in jail because of the conviction affirmed in this case) he again received over 900,000 votes, 3.4% of the total vote. Debs did not serve the full ten-year term to which he was sentenced: in 1921, he was released, on order of President Harding. The Court considered two counts of the indictment. The first alleged that, in June 1918, Debs had "caused and incited and attempted to cause and incite insubordination, disloyalty, mutiny and refusal of duty in the [armed] forces" and "with intent so to do delivered, to an assembly of people, a public speech." The second alleged that he "obstructed and attempted to obstruct the recruiting and enlistment service" of the U.S. and "to that end and with that intent delivered the same speech." In affirming the conviction, Justice HOLMES wrote:

"The main theme of the speech [delivered at the state convention of the Ohio Socialist Party] was socialism, its growth, and a prophecy of its ultimate success. With that we have nothing to do, but if a part or the manifest intent of the more general utterances was to encourage those present to obstruct the recruiting service and if in passages such encouragement was directly given, the immunity of the general theme may not be enough to protect the speech. The speaker began by saying that he had just returned from a visit to the workhouse in the neighborhood where three of their most loyal comrades were paying the penalty for their devotion to the working class—[persons] who had been convicted of aiding and abetting another in failing to register for the draft. He said that he had to be prudent and might not be able to say all that he thought, thus intimating to his hearers that they might infer that he meant more, but he did say that those persons were paying the penalty for standing erect and for seeking to pave the way to better conditions for all mankind. Later he added further eulogies and said that he was proud of them. [There] followed personal experiences and illustrations of the growth of socialism, a glorification of minorities, and a prophecy of the success of the international socialist crusade, with the interjection that 'you need to know that you are fit for something better than slavery and cannon fodder.' The rest of the discourse had only the indirect though not necessarily ineffective bearing on the offences alleged that is to be found in the usual contrasts between capitalists and laboring men, sneers at the advice to cultivate war gardens, attribution to plutocrats of the high price of coal, & c. [The] defendant addressed the jury himself, and while contending that his speech did not warrant the charges said 'I have been accused of obstructing the war. I admit it. Gentlemen, I abhor war. I would oppose the war if I stood alone.' The statement was not necessary to warrant the jury in finding that one purpose of the speech, whether incidental or not does not matter, was to oppose not only war in general but this war, and that the opposition was so expressed that its natural and intended effect would be to obstruct recruiting. If that was intended and if, in all the circumstances, that would be its probable effect, it would not be protected by reason of its being part of a general program and expressions of a general and conscientious belief.

"[The chief defense is] that based upon the First Amendment, [disposed of in Schenck]. There was introduced [in evidence] an 'Anti-war Proclamation and Program' adopted at St. Louis in April, 1917, coupled with testimony that about an hour before his speech the defendant had stated that he approved of that platform in spirit and in substance. [Counsel] argued against its admissibility, at some length. This document contained the usual suggestion that capitalism was the cause of the war and that our entrance into it 'was instigated by the predatory capitalists in the United States.' [Its] first recommendation was, 'continuous, active, and public opposition to the war, through demonstrations, mass petitions, and all other means within our power.' Evidence that the defendant accepted this view and this declaration of his duties at the time that he made his speech is evidence that if in that speech he used words tending to obstruct the recruiting service he meant that they should have that effect. [We] should add that the jury were most carefully instructed that they could not find the defendant guilty for advocacy of any of his opinions unless the words used had as their natural tendency and reasonably probable effect to obstruct the recruiting service, & c., and unless the defendant had the specific intent to do so in his mind. Without going into further particulars we are of opinion that the verdict on the fourth count, for obstructing and attempting to obstruct the recruiting service of the United States, must be sustained. Therefore it is less important to consider whether that upon the third count, for causing and attempting to cause insubordination, & c., in the military and naval forces, is equally impregnable. The jury were instructed that for the purposes of the statute the persons designated by the Act of May 18, 1917, registered and enrolled under it, and thus subject to be called into the active service, were a part of the military forces of the United States. The Government presents a strong argument from the history of the statutes that the instruction was correct and in accordance with established legislative usage. We see no sufficient reason for differing from the [conclusion]."

Abrams v. United States

250 U.S. 616, 40 S.Ct. 17, 63 L.Ed. 1173 (1919).

[After seizing power during the Russian Revolution of 1917, the revolutionary government signed a peace treaty with Germany. The overthrown Czarist government of Russia had been an ally of the United States in the war against Germany. In 1918, the United States sent military forces to cities in the northern part of the Soviet Union. The Abrams defendants, who were all Russian immigrants and, according to their own testimony, "revolutionists" and "anarchists," perceived the American military expedition as an attempt to "crush the Russian revolution." They wrote and distributed thousands of circulars on New York City streets advocating a general strike and appealing to workers in ammunitions factories to stop producing weapons to be used against the Russian revolutionaries. They were convicted under 1918 amendments to the Espionage Act that prohibited urging any curtailment of production of materials necessary to the prosecution of the war against Germany with intent to hinder its prosecution. Specifically, they were found guilty of having "intended to incite, provoke and encourage resistance to the United States" during World War I, and of conspiring "to urge, incite and advocate curtailment of production [of] ordnance and ammunition, necessary [to] the prosecution of the war."

[The Court sustained the convictions, rejecting the constitutional attack summarily on the basis of Schenck and finding the proof sufficient to sustain the charges. Justice CLARKE's majority opinion stated: "It will not do to say [that] the only intent of these defendants was to prevent injury to the Russian cause. Men must be held to have intended, and to be accountable for, the effects which their acts were likely to produce. Even if their primary purpose and intent was to aid the cause of the Russian Revolution, the plan of action which they adopted necessarily involved, before it could be realized, defeat of the war program of the United States, for the obvious effect of this appeal, if it should become effective, as they hoped it might, would be to persuade persons of character such as those whom they regarded themselves as addressing not to aid government loans and not to work in ammunition factories where their work would produce 'bullets, bayonets, cannon' and other munitions of war, the use of which would cause the 'murder' of Germans and [Russians]. [The] interpretation we have put upon these articles circulated in the greatest port of our land, from which great numbers of soldiers were at the time taking ship daily, and in which great quantities of war supplies of every kind were at the time being manufactured for transportation overseas, is [the] fair interpretation of [them]. [The writings] sufficiently show, that while the immediate occasion for this particular outbreak of lawlessness, on the part of the defendant alien anarchists, may have been resentment caused by our Government sending troops into Russia as a strategic operation against the Germans on the eastern battle front, yet the plain purpose of their propaganda was to excite, at the supreme crisis of the war, disaffection, sedition, riots, and, as they hoped, revolution, in this country for the purpose of embarrassing and if possible defeating the military plans of the Government in Europe."]

Justice HOLMES, joined by Justice Brandeis, dissenting.

This indictment is founded wholly upon the publication of two leaflets which I shall describe in a moment. [There were four counts; the majority found sufficient evidence to justify conviction under the third and fourth.] The third count alleges a conspiracy to encourage resistance to the United States in the [war with Germany] and to attempt to effectuate the purpose by publishing the [two] leaflets. The fourth count lays a conspiracy to incite curtailment of production of things necessary to the prosecution of the war and to attempt to accomplish it by publishing the second [leaflet]. The first of these leaflets says that the President's cowardly silence about the intervention in Russia reveals the hypocrisy of the plutocratic gang in Washington. It intimates that "German militarism combined with allied capitalism to crush the Russian revolution"— goes on that the tyrants of the world fight each other until they see a common enemy—working class enlightenment, when they combine to crush it; and that now militarism and capitalism combined, though not openly, to crush the Russian revolution. It says that there is only one enemy of the workers of the world and that is capitalism; that it is a crime for workers of America, & c., to fight the workers' republic of Russia, and ends "Awake! Awake, you Workers of the World! Revolutionists." A note adds "It is absurd to call us pro-German. We hate and despise German militarism more than do you hypocritical tyrants. We have more reasons for denouncing German militarism than has the coward of the White House."

The other leaflet, headed "Workers Wake Up," with abusive language says that America together with the Allies will march for Russia to help the Czecho–Slovaks in their struggle against the Bolsheviki, and that this time the hypocrites shall not fool the Russian emigrants and friends of Russia in America. It tells the Russian emigrants that they now must spit in the face of the false military propaganda by which their sympathy and help to the prosecution of the war have been called forth and says that with the money they have lent or are going to lend "they will make bullets not only for the Germans but also for the Workers Soviets of Russia," and further, "Workers in the ammunition factories, you are producing bullets, bayonets, cannon, to murder not only the Germans, but also your dearest, best, who are in Russia and are fighting for freedom." It then appeals to the same Russian emigrants at some length not to consent to the "inquisitionary expedition to Russia," and says that the destruction of the Russian revolution is "the politics of the march to Russia." The leaflet winds up by saying "Workers, our reply to this barbaric intervention has to be a general strike!," and after a few words on the spirit of revolution, exhortations not to be afraid, and some usual tall talk ends "Woe unto those who will be in the way of progress. Let solidarity live! The Rebels."

[With regard to the fourth count] it seems too plain to be denied that the suggestion to workers in the ammunition factories that they are producing bullets to murder their dearest, and the further advocacy of a general strike, both in the second leaflet, do urge curtailment of production of things necessary to the prosecution of the war within the meaning of [the 1918 amendments of the] Act of 1917. But to make the conduct criminal that statute requires that it should be "with intent by such curtailment to cripple or hinder the United States in the prosecution of the war [with Germany]." It seems to me that no such intent is proved. I am aware of course that the word intent as vaguely used in ordinary legal discussion means no more than knowledge at the time of the act that the consequences said to be intended will ensue. Even less than that will satisfy the general principle of civil and criminal liability. But, when words are used exactly, a deed is not done with intent to produce a consequence unless that consequence is the aim of the deed. It may be obvious, and obvious to the actor, that the consequence will follow, and he may be liable for it even if he regrets it, but he does not do the act with intent to produce it unless the aim to produce it is the proximate motive of the specific act, although there may be some deeper motive behind. It seems to me that this statute must be taken to use its words in a strict and accurate sense. They would be absurd in any other. A patriot might think that we were wasting money on aeroplanes, or making more cannon of a certain kind than we needed, and might advocate curtailment with success, yet even if it turned out that the curtailment hindered and was thought by other minds to have been obviously likely to hinder the United States in the prosecution of the war, no one would hold such conduct a crime. I admit that my illustration does not answer all that might be said but it is enough to show what I think and to let me pass to a more important aspect of the case. I refer to the [First Amendment].

I never have seen any reason to doubt that the questions of law that alone were before this Court in the cases of [Schenck, Frohwerk, and Debs] were rightly decided. I do not doubt for a moment that by the same reasoning that would justify punishing persuasion to murder, the United States constitutionally may punish speech that produces or is intended to produce a clear and imminent danger that it will bring about forthwith certain substantive evils that the United States constitutionally may seek to prevent. The power undoubtedly is greater in time of war than in time of peace because war opens dangers that do not exist at other times. But as against dangers peculiar to war, as against others, the principle of the right to free speech is always the same. It is only the present danger of immediate evil or an intent to bring it about that warrants Congress in setting a limit to the expression of opinion where private rights are not concerned. Congress certainly cannot forbid all effort to change the mind of the country. Now nobody can suppose that the surreptitious publishing of a silly leaflet by an unknown man, without more, would present any immediate danger that its opinions would hinder the success of the government arms or have any appreciable tendency to do so. Publishing those opinions for the very purpose of obstructing, however, might indicate a greater danger and at any rate would have the quality of an attempt. So I assume that the second leaflet if published for the purposes alleged in the fourth count might be punishable. [But] I do not see how anyone can find the intent required by the statute in any of the defendants' words. The second leaflet is the only one that affords even a foundation for the charge, and there, without invoking the hatred of German militarism expressed in the former one, it is evident from the beginning to the end that the only object of the paper is to help Russia and stop American intervention there against the popular government—not to impede the United States in the war that it was carrying on. To say that two phrases taken literally might import a suggestion of conduct that would have interference with the war as an indirect and probably undesired effect seems to me by no means enough to show an attempt to produce that effect.

In this case sentences of twenty years imprisonment have been imposed for the publishing of two leaflets that I believe the defendants had as much right to publish as the Government has to publish the Constitution of the United States now vainly invoked by them. Even if I am technically wrong and enough can be squeezed from these poor and puny anonymities to turn the color of legal litmus paper; I will add, even if what I think the necessary intent were shown; the most nominal punishment seems to me all that possibly could be inflicted, unless the defendants are to be made to suffer not for what the indictment alleges but for the creed that they avow—a creed that I believe to be the creed of ignorance and immaturity when honestly held, as I see no reason to doubt that it was held here, but which, although made the subject of examination at the trial, no one has a right even to consider in dealing with the charges before the Court.

Persecution for the expression of opinions seems to me perfectly logical. If you have no doubt of your premises or your power and want a certain result with all your heart you naturally express your wishes in law and sweep away all opposition. To allow opposition by speech seems to indicate that you think the speech impotent, as when a man says that he has squared the circle, or that you do not care whole-heartedly for the result, or that you doubt either your power or your premises. But when men have realized that time has upset many fighting faiths, they may come to believe even more than they believe the very foundations of their own conduct that the ultimate good desired is better reached by free trade in ideas—that the best test of truth is the power of the thought to get itself accepted in the competition of the market, and that truth is the only ground upon which their wishes safely can be carried out. That at any rate is the theory of our Constitution. It is an experiment, as all life is an experiment. Every year if not every day we have to wager our salvation upon some prophecy based upon imperfect knowledge. While that experiment is part of our system I think that we should be eternally vigilant against attempts to check the expression of opinions that we loathe and believe to be fraught with death, unless they so imminently threaten immediate interference with the lawful and pressing purposes of the law that an immediate check is required to save the country. I wholly disagree with the argument of the Government that the First Amendment left the common law as to seditious libel in force. History seems to me against the notion. I had conceived that the United States through many years had shown its repentance for the Sedition Act of 1798, by repaying fines that it imposed. Only the emergency that makes it immediately dangerous to leave the correction of evil counsels to time warrants making any exception to the sweeping command, "Congress shall make no [law] abridging the freedom of speech." Of course I am speaking only of expressions of opinion and exhortations, which were all that were uttered here, but I regret that I cannot put into more impressive words my belief that in their conviction upon this indictment the defendants were deprived of their rights under the [Constitution].[2]

***

2. Soon after Abrams, Justice Holmes also joined in dissents from other decisions affirming convictions under the 1917 Act. See Pierce v. United States, 252 U.S. 239 (1920), and Schaefer v. United States, 251 U.S. 466 (1920).

SUBVERSIVE ADVOCACY FROM SCHENCK TO ABRAMS

1. *Comparing the Schenck–Frohwerk–Debs approach.* Which evaluation of the evidence in Abams seems closer to the approach of Schenck–Frohwerk–Debs: the majority's or the dissent's? Clear and present danger supposedly assures special attention to the time dimension: speech may not be curtailed until there is an immediate risk of an evil; speech with a remote tendency to cause danger cannot be curtailed. But did Holmes' Schenck opinion truly reject a "bad tendency" criterion and replace it with one of "clear and present" immediacy? Note the reference to "the act, [its] tendency and the intent" at the end of the opinion. What is the relevance of "intent" to immediate risk of harm? "Tendency"? Is the "shouting fire" analogy apt? To political speech? Are truth and falsity relevant? What if the speaker believes that there is a fire? Was Holmes' approach in Frohwerk more protective of speech than the "bad tendency" test? The Frohwerk opinion refers to "language that might be taken to convey an innuendo of a different sort," and to "a little breath" that might "kindle a flame." Did Holmes persuasively demonstrate the "clear and present danger" of Debs' speech? Did he deprecate the "general theme" unduly? Did he unduly emphasize what "his hearers [might] infer"? Was a "natural tendency and reasonably probable effect" enough to send Debs to jail? Should the speech of a national candidate for President be treated the same as a cry of "fire" in a crowded theater?

2. *The evolution of Holmes' Abrams dissent.* The Abrams dissent, with its infusion of a genuine immediacy element, arguably made the clear and present danger test more speech-protective than did Schenck–Frohwerk–Debs. Did Justice Holmes change his mind about free speech in the period between the Schenck trilogy of cases in the spring of 1919 and the Abrams dissent in the fall of that year? Some of Justice Holmes' correspondence suggests as much. Gerald Gunther concludes "that Holmes was [at the time of Schenck] quite insensitive to any claim for special judicial protection of free speech; that the Schenck standard was not truly speech-protective; and that it was not until the fall of 1919, with his famous dissent in [Abrams], that Holmes put some teeth into the clear and present danger formula, at least partly as a result of probing criticism by acquaintances such as Learned Hand." Gunther, "Learned Hand and the Origins of Modern First Amendment Doctrine: Some Fragments of History," 27 Stan.L.Rev. 719 (1975); see also Gunther, Learned Hand: the Man and the Judge 161–70 (1994). In the summer of 1918, for example, Holmes, in a letter to Hand, espoused the "natural right" to silence "the other fellow when he disagrees": free speech, he insisted, "stands no differently than freedom from vaccination"—a freedom that the state could legitimately curtail, as demonstrated in Jacobson v. Massachusetts, 197 U.S. 11 (1905), a decision consistent with Justice Holmes' generally deferential due process philosophy. In 1918, Holmes seemed impervious to Hand's arguments that the "natural right" to silence dissenters must be curbed by the law in the interests of democratic presuppositions and the search for truth.

Debs provoked criticism of Holmes both by Hand in correspondence and by Ernst Freund in an article in The New Republic. Freund wrote that "to be permitted to agitate at your own peril, subject to a jury's guessing at motive, tendency and possible effect, makes the right of free speech a precarious gift." Freund, "The Debs Case and Freedom of Speech," The New Republic, May 3, 1919, reprinted at 40 U. Chi. L. Rev. 239 (1973). And in the spring of 1919, Hand insisted to Holmes that liability for speech should not rest on guesses about the future impact of the words (the central theme of clear and present danger): "in nature the causal sequence is perfect, but responsibility does not go pari passu"; the legal responsibility of the speaker should not turn "upon reasonable forecast." Instead, Hand argued, the punishability of speech should begin only "when the words [are] directly an incitement." But, once again, Holmes was impervious to the criticism. Holmes began his letter in response to Hand's critique of the Debs approach, "I don't quite get your point." And Hand wrote to Freund, "I have so far been unable to make [Holmes] see that he and we have any real differences." The Abrams dissent may have indicated some eventual responsiveness on Holmes' part to these criticisms. The correspondence is recounted in Gunther, Learned Hand: the Man and the Judge, at 164–66.[3] For further argument that Holmes' attitude toward free speech did shift significantly in 1919, see White, "Justice Holmes and the Modernization of Free Speech Jurisprudence: The Human Dimension," 80 Cal. L. Rev. 391 (1992).

For the contrary view that Holmes' views were consistent but that he was simply "biding his time until the Court should have before it a conviction so clearly wrong as to let him speak out his deepest thoughts about the First Amendment," see Chafee, Free Speech in the United States 86 (1941). For further argument that Holmes' views did not undergo a conversion, see Novick, Honorable Justice: the Life of Oliver Wendell Holmes 473–74 (1989); Novick, "The Unrevised Holmes and Freedom of Expression," 1991 Sup. Ct. Rev. 303.

3. *The impact of the Abrams dissent.* The Abrams dissent emphasizes immediacy more than its predecessors. Does it concentrate adequately on immediate proximity of speech to danger? Note the comment about a "silly leaflet" that would not present "any immediate danger" *or* "have any appreciable tendency to do so." Is "tendency" enough? Note also the reference to "the present danger of immediate evil" *or* "an intent to bring it about." Should "intent" be enough? Are "tendency" and "intent" reliable indicia of immediacy of danger? Is Holmes' approach applicable only in contexts (as with the 1917 Act) where the law is mainly directed at an evil other than speech (e.g., obstruction of military recruiting), and where speech is evidence of the risk of that evil? Or is it also useful when the legislature proscribes speech directly? Does Holmes accept the legislative statement of the evil? Must speech create immediate risk of causing the legislatively determined evil—e.g., interference with recruiting? Or does the Court define the evil? Note the reference to "an immediate [check] required to save the country," in Holmes' last paragraph. Is Holmes concerned with the gravity of the evil? Do immediacy requirements vary with gravity?

4. *An alternative approach: Learned Hand and the Masses case.* Two years before the issue reached the Court in Schenck, the problem of interpreting the Espionage Act of 1917 arose in a case before Learned Hand, then a District Judge for the Southern District of New York. Hand's opinion in Masses

---

3. For further discussion of Holmes' apparent shift from a more restrictive to a more libertarian view, see Ragan, "Justice Oliver Wendell Holmes, Jr., Zechariah Chafee, Jr., and the Clear and Present Danger Test for Free Speech: The First Year, 1919," 58 J.Am. Hist. 24 (1971); Kalven, "Professor Ernst Freund and Debs v. United States," 40 U.Chi.L.Rev. 235 (1973); Ginsburg, "Afterword to Ernst Freund and the First Amendment Tradition," 40 U.Chi.L.Rev. 243 (1973); Cover, "The Left, the Right and the First Amendment: 1918–1928," 40 Md.L.Rev. 349 (1981); Rabban, "The Emergence of Modern First Amendment Doctrine," 50 U.Chi.L.Rev. 1205 (1983); Bogen, "The Free Speech Metamorphosis of Mr. Justice Holmes," 11 Hofstra L.Rev. 97 (1982); O'Fallon & Rogat, "Mr. Justice Holmes: A Dissenting Opinion," 36 Stan.L.Rev. 1349 (1984); Baker, The Justice From Beacon Hill (1991). For criticism of the Abrams dissent as too permissive, see Wigmore, "Abrams v. United States: Freedom of Speech and Freedom of Thuggery in War–Time and Peace–Time," 14 Ill. L. Rev. 539 (1920).

plainly reveals considerable solicitude for speech, but it does so without mentioning clear and present danger. Although the opinion was technically only an interpretation of the Act, Hand's private correspondence makes clear that it was designed as a carefully considered alternative to the prevalent constitutional analyses of free speech issues. See Gunther, Learned Hand: the Man and the Judge, at 151–61, 168–69. Consider the advantages and disadvantages of Hand's approach in the World War I context. How would Schenck, Debs, or Abrams have gone under that standard? Would Hand's approach have avoided some of the difficulties of the clear and present danger test?

Masses Publishing Co. v. Patten

244 Fed. 535 (S.D.N.Y.1917).

LEARNED HAND, District Judge. The plaintiff applies for a preliminary injunction against the postmaster of New York to forbid his refusal to accept its magazine in the mails under the following circumstances: The plaintiff is a publishing company in the city of New York engaged in the production of a monthly revolutionary journal called "The Masses," containing both text and cartoons. [In] July, 1917, the postmaster of New York, acting upon the direction of the Postmaster General, advised the plaintiff that the August [issue] to which he had had access would be denied the mails under the Espionage Act of June 15, 1917. [T]he defendant, while objecting generally that the whole purport of the [issue] was in violation of the law, since it tended to produce a violation of the law, to encourage the enemies of the United States, and to hamper the government in the conduct of the war, specified four cartoons and four pieces of text as especially falling within [the 1917 Act]. [In] this case there is no dispute of fact which the plaintiff can successfully challenge except the meaning of the words and pictures in the magazine. As to these the query must be: What is the extreme latitude of the interpretation which must be placed upon them, and whether that extremity certainly falls outside any of the provisions of the [1917 Act]. Unless this be true, the decision of the postmaster must stand. It will be necessary, first, to interpret the law, and, next, the words and pictures. [N]o question arises touching the war powers of Congress. [Here] is presented solely the question of how far Congress after much discussion has up to the present time seen fit to exercise a power which may extend to measures not yet even considered, but necessary to the existence of the state as [such].

Coming to the act itself, [I] turn directly to section 3 of title 1, which the plaintiff is said to violate. That section contains three provisions. The first is, in substance, that no one shall make any false statements with intent to interfere with the operation or success of the military or naval forces of the United States or to promote the success of its enemies. The defendant says that the cartoons and text of the magazine, constituting, as they certainly do, a virulent attack upon the war, [may] interfere with the success of the military forces of the United States. That such utterances may have the effect so ascribed to them is unhappily true. [Dissension] within a country is a high source of comfort and assistance to its [enemies]. All this, however, is beside the question whether such an attack is a willfully false statement. That phrase properly includes only a statement of fact which the utterer knows to be false, and it cannot be maintained that any of these statements are of fact, or that the plaintiff believes them to be false. They are all within the range of opinion and of criticism; they are all certainly believed to be true by the utterer. As such they fall within the scope of that right to criticise either by temperate reasoning, or by immoderate and indecent invective, which is normally the privilege of the individual in countries dependent upon the free expression of opinion as the ultimate source of authority. The argument may be trivial in substance, and violent and perverse in manner, but so long as it is confined to abuse of existing policies or laws, it is impossible to class it as a false statement of facts of the kind here in question. To modify this provision, so clearly intended to prevent the spreading of false rumors which may embarrass the military, into the prohibition of any kind of propaganda, honest or vicious, is to disregard the meaning of the language, established by legal construction and common use, and to raise it into a means of suppressing intemperate and inflammatory public discussion, which was surely not its purpose.

The next phrase relied upon is that which forbids any one from willfully causing insubordination, disloyalty, mutiny, or refusal of duty in the military or naval forces of the United States. The defendant's position is that to arouse discontent and disaffection among the people with the prosecution of the war and with the draft tends to promote a mutinous and insubordinate temper among the troops. This, too, is true; men who become satisfied that they are engaged in an enterprise dictated by the unconscionable selfishness of the rich, and effectuated by a tyrannous disregard for the will of those who must suffer and die, will be more prone to insubordination than those who have faith in the cause and acquiesce in the means. Yet to interpret the word "cause" so broadly would, as before, involve necessarily as a consequence the suppression of all hostile criticism, and of all opinion except what encouraged and supported the existing policies, or which fell within the range of temperate argument. It would contradict the normal assumption of democratic government that the suppression of hostile criticism does not turn upon the justice of its substance or the decency and propriety of its temper. Assuming that the power to repress such opinion may rest in Congress in the throes of a struggle for the very existence of the state, its exercise is so contrary to the use and wont of our people that only the clearest expression of such a power justifies the conclusion that it was intended.

The defendant's position, therefore, in so far as it involves the suppression of the free utterance of abuse and criticism of the existing law, or of the policies of the war, is not, in my judgment, supported by the language of the statute. Yet there has always been a recognized limit to such expressions, incident indeed to the existence of any compulsive power of the state itself. One may not counsel or advise others to violate the law as it stands. Words are not only the keys of persuasion, but the triggers of action, and those which have no purport but to counsel the violation of law cannot by any latitude of interpretation be a part of that public opinion which is the final source of government in a democratic state. The defendant asserts not only that the magazine indirectly through its propaganda leads to a disintegration of loyalty and a disobedience of law, but that in addition it counsels and advises resistance to existing law, especially to the draft. The consideration of this aspect of the case more properly arises under the third phrase of section 3, which forbids any willful obstruction of the recruiting or enlistment service of the United States, but, as the defendant urges that the magazine falls within each phrase, it is as well to take it up now. To counsel or advise a man to an act is to urge upon him either that it is his interest or his duty to do it. While, of course, this may be accomplished as well by indirection as expressly, since words carry the meaning that they impart, the definition is exhaustive, I think, and I shall use it. Political agitation, by the passions it arouses or the convictions it engenders, may in fact stimulate men to the violation of law. Detestation of existing policies is easily transformed into forcible resistance of the authority which puts them in execution, and it would be folly to disregard the causal relation between the two. Yet to assimilate agitation, legitimate as such, with direct incitement to violent resistance, is to disregard the tolerance of all methods of political agitation which in normal times is a safeguard of free government. The distinction is not a scholastic subterfuge, but a hard-bought acquisition in the fight for freedom, and the purpose to disregard it must be evident when the power exists. If one stops short of urging upon others that it is their duty or their interest to resist the law, it seems to me one should not be held to have attempted to cause its violation. If that be not the test, I can see no escape from the conclusion that under this section every political agitation which can be shown to be apt to create a seditious temper is illegal. I am confident that by such language Congress had no such revolutionary purpose in view.

It seems to me, however, quite plain that none of the language and none of the cartoons in this paper can be thought directly to counsel or advise insubordination or mutiny, without a violation of their meaning quite beyond any tolerable understanding. I come, therefore, to the third phrase of the section, which forbids any one from willfully obstructing the recruiting or enlistment service of the United States. [Here] again, [since] the question is of the expression of opinion, I construe the sentence, so far as it restrains public utterance, as I have construed the other two, and as therefore limited to the direct advocacy of resistance to the recruiting and enlistment service. If so, the inquiry is narrowed to the question whether any of the challenged matter may be said to advocate resistance to the draft, taking the meaning of the words with the utmost latitude which they can bear. As to the cartoons it seems to me quite clear that they do not fall within such a test. Certainly the nearest is that entitled "Conscription," and the most that can be said of that is that it may breed such animosity to the draft as will promote resistance and strengthen the determination of those disposed to be recalcitrant. There is no intimation that, however hateful the draft may be, one is in duty bound to resist it, certainly none that such resistance is to one's [interest].

The text offers more embarrassment. The poem to Emma Goldman and Alexander Berkman, at most, goes no further than to say that they are martyrs in the cause of love among nations. Such a sentiment holds them up to admiration, and hence their conduct to possible emulation. [The] paragraphs upon conscientious objectors are of the same kind. [It] is plain enough that the paper has the fullest sympathy for these people, that it admires their courage, and that it presumptively approves their conduct. [Moreover], these passages [occur] in a magazine which attacks with the utmost violence the draft and the war. That such comments have a tendency to arouse emulation in others is clear enough but that they counsel others to follow these examples is not so plain. Literally at least they do not, and while, as I have said, the words are to be taken, not literally, but according to their full import, the literal meaning is the starting point for interpretation. One may admire and approve the course of a hero without feeling any duty to follow him. There is not the least implied intimation in these words that others are under a duty to follow. The most that can be said is that, if others do follow, they will get the same admiration and the same approval. Now, there is surely an appreciable distance between esteem and emulation; and unless there is here some advocacy of such emulation, I cannot see how the passages can be said to fall within [the law]. The question before me is quite the same as what would arise upon a motion to dismiss an indictment at the close of the proof: Could any reasonable man say, not that the indirect result of the language might be to arouse a seditious disposition, for that would not be enough, but that the language directly advocated resistance to the draft? I cannot think that upon such language any verdict would [stand].[1]

COMPARING THE HOLMES AND HAND APPROACHES

1. *The strengths and weaknesses of Hand's "incitement" approach.* Is the Masses "incitement" standard distinctively different from "clear and present danger"? Hand's test focused less on forecasts about the likelihood that the speech would produce danger (e.g., draft obstruction) and focused more on the speaker's words. Does the shift in focus from proximity of danger to content of speech promote greater protection of speech? How would Eugene Debs have fared under the Masses approach? Arguably, courts are more competent to use traditional judicial tools to scrutinize words for evidence of incitement than they are to assess risks and hazard guesses about the possible future impact of words in complex contexts. Can it also be argued that Masses articulates speech values more effectively than Schenck and even Abrams?

But Hand's Masses approach may have had weaknesses as well as strengths. How would it deal with the indirect but purposeful incitement of Marc Anthony's oration over the body of Caesar? How would it deal with the problem of the harmless inciter, the speaker explicitly urging law violation but with little realistic hope of success? Should even express incitement sometimes be protected? See Scanlon, "A Theory of Freedom of Expression," 1 Phil. & Pub.Aff. 204 (1972) (arguing that speech may not be restricted on the ground that it will lead listeners to believe "subsequent harmful acts [to] be worth performing"); Perry, "Freedom of Expression: an Essay on Theory and Doctrine," 78 Nw.U.L.Rev. 1137 (1983) ("Advocacy of any course of action, lawful or unlawful, consists in part of information and ideas that facilitate the pursuit and achievement of a better understanding of reality.").

2. *The differences between Hand and Holmes: Some historical data.* Learned Hand's correspondence reveals that he perceived a considerable difference between his Masses approach and Holmes' clear and present danger test, even as refined in the Abrams dissent, which he welcomed. In a series of letters from 1919 to 1921 to Professor Zechariah Chafee, Jr., the period's most prominent commentator on First Amendment problems, Hand elaborated the differences between the Masses analysis and the alternatives. See Gunther, Learned Hand: the Man and the Judge 167–70 (1994). As Hand wrote to Chafee, soon after Abrams: "I do not altogether like the way Justice Holmes put the limitation. I myself think it is a little more manageable and quite adequate a distinction to say that there is an absolute and objective test to language. [I] still prefer that which I attempted to state in my first 'Masses' opinion, rather than to say that the connection between the words used and the evil aimed at should be 'immediate and direct.' "He elaborated later: "I prefer a

---

1. District Judge Hand's decision granting the preliminary injunction was reversed on appeal. Masses Publishing Co. v. Patten, 246 Fed. 24 (2d Cir.1917). The Circuit Court not only emphasized the broad administrative discretion of the Postmaster General, but also disagreed with Hand's incitement test: "This court does not agree that such is the law. If the natural and reasonable effect of what is said is to encourage resistance to a law, and the words are used in an endeavor to persuade to resistance, it is immaterial that the duty to resist is not mentioned, or the interest of the persons addressed in resistance is not suggested." As Hand wrote in one of his letters, his opinion "seemed to meet with practically no professional approval whatever." Gunther, Learned Hand: the Man and the Judge, at 160.

test based upon the nature of the utterance itself. If, taken in its setting, the effect upon the hearers is only to counsel them to violate the law, it is unconditionally illegal. [As] to other utterances, it appears to me that regardless of their tendency they should be permitted."

Hand's major objection to formulations such as "clear and present danger" or "natural and reasonable tendency" was that they were too slippery in "practical administration": "I think it is precisely at those times when alone the freedom of speech becomes important as an institution, that the protection of a jury on such an issue is illusory." And, as he said in another letter, "I am not wholly in love with Holmesy's test and the reason is this. Once you admit that the matter is one of degree, [you] give to Tomdickandharry, D.J., so much latitude that the jig is at once up. [Even] the Nine Elder Statesmen have not shown themselves wholly immune from the 'herd instinct' and what seem 'immediate and direct' to-day may seem very remote next year even though the circumstances surrounding the utterance be unchanged. I own I should prefer a qualitative formula, hard, conventional, difficult to evade." See generally Gunther, "Learned Hand and the Origins of Modern First Amendment Doctrine: Some Fragments of History," 27 Stan. L. Rev. 719 (1975).

B.   THE "RED SCARE" CASES

In the wake of World War I and the Russian Revolution, the United States entered the "Red Scare" era, a period of feverish anti-radicalism that lasted from the 1920s to the 1930s. In addition to mass deportations of aliens by the federal government, two thirds of the states enacted laws prohibiting the advocacy of criminal anarchy and criminal syndicalism. Soon, such laws came before the Court in the following cases.

Gitlow v. New York

268 U.S. 652, 45 S.Ct. 625, 69 L.Ed. 1138 (1925).

Justice SANFORD delivered the opinion of the Court.

Benjamin Gitlow was indicted [and convicted] for the statutory crime of criminal anarchy. New York Penal Law, §§ 160, 161.[1] [The] contention here is that the statute, by its terms and as applied in this case, is repugnant to the

---

1. The New York statute (enacted well before the Red Scare, in 1902, after the assassination of President McKinley) provided:

"§ 160. *Criminal anarchy defined.* Criminal anarchy is the doctrine that organized government should be overthrown by force or violence, or by assassination of the executive head or of any of the executive officials of government, or by any unlawful means. The advocacy of such doctrine either by word of mouth or writing is a felony.

"§ 161. *Advocacy of criminal anarchy.* Any person who:

"1. By word of mouth or writing advocates, advises or teaches the duty, necessity or propriety of overthrowing or overturning organized government by force or violence, or by assassination of the executive head or of any of the executive officials of government, or by any unlawful means; or,

"2. Prints, publishes, edits, issues or knowingly circulates, sells, distributes or publicly displays any book, paper, document, or written or printed matter in any form, containing or advocating, advising or teaching the doctrine that organized government should be overthrown by force, violence or any unlawful [means],

"Is guilty of a [felony]."

due process clause of the [14th Amendment]. The indictment was in two counts. The first charged that the defendant had advocated, advised and taught the duty, necessity and propriety of overthrowing and overturning organized government by force, violence and unlawful means, by certain writings therein set forth entitled "The Left Wing Manifesto"; the second that he had printed, published and knowingly circulated and distributed a certain paper called "The Revolutionary Age," containing the writings set forth in the [first count].

The defendant is a member of the Left Wing Section of the Socialist Party, a dissenting branch or faction of that party formed [in 1919] in opposition to its dominant policy of "moderate Socialism." The conference elected a National Council, of which the defendant was a member, and left to it the adoption of a "Manifesto." This was published in The Revolutionary Age, the official organ of the Left Wing. The defendant was on the board of managers of the paper and was its business manager. He arranged for the printing [and publication of 16,000 copies of the first issue of the paper, which contained the Left Wing Manifesto]. It was admitted that the defendant signed a card subscribing to the Manifesto and Program of the [Left Wing]. There was no evidence of any effect resulting from the publication and circulation of the Manifesto. [The Manifesto] condemned the dominant "moderate Socialism" for its recognition of the necessity of the democratic parliamentary state [and] advocated [the] necessity of accomplishing the "Communist Revolution" by a militant and "revolutionary Socialism," based on "the class struggle" and mobilizing the "power of the proletariat in action," through mass industrial revolts developing into mass political strikes and "revolutionary mass action," for the purpose of conquering and destroying the parliamentary state and establishing in its place, through a "revolutionary dictatorship of the proletariat," the system of [Communist Socialism].

The court [charged] the jury, in substance, that they must determine what was the intent, purpose and fair meaning of the Manifesto; [that] a mere statement or analysis of social and economic facts and historical incidents, in the nature of an essay, accompanied by prophecy as to the future course of events, but with no teaching, advice or advocacy of action, would not constitute the advocacy, advice or teaching of a doctrine for the overthrow of government within the meaning of the statute; that a mere statement that unlawful acts might accomplish such a purpose would be insufficient, unless there was a teaching, advising and advocacy of employing such unlawful acts for the purpose of overthrowing [government]. The defendant's counsel submitted two requests to charge which embodied in substance the statement that to constitute criminal anarchy within the meaning of the statute it was necessary that the language used or published should advocate, teach or advise the duty, necessity or propriety of doing "some definite or immediate act or acts" of force, violence or unlawfulness directed toward the overthrowing of organized government. These were [denied]. [The] sole contention here [is] that as there was no evidence of any concrete result flowing from the publication of the Manifesto or of circumstances showing the likelihood of such result, the statute as construed and [applied] penalizes the mere utterance, as such, of "doctrine" having no quality of incitement, without regard either to the circumstances of its utterance or to the likelihood of unlawful consequences; [and thus] contravenes [due process].

The statute does not penalize the utterance or publication of abstract "doctrine" or academic discussion having no quality of incitement to any concrete action. It is not aimed against mere historical or philosophical essays. It does not restrain the advocacy of changes in the form of government by constitutional and lawful means. What it prohibits is language advocating, advising or teaching the overthrow of organized government by unlawful means. These words imply urging to [action]. The Manifesto, plainly, is neither the statement of abstract doctrine [nor] mere prediction that industrial disturbances and revolutionary mass strikes will result spontaneously in an inevitable process of evolution in the economic system. It advocates and urges in fervent language mass action which shall progressively foment industrial disturbances and through political mass strikes and revolutionary mass action overthrow and destroy organized parliamentary government. It concludes with a call to action in these words: "The proletarian revolution and the Communist reconstruction of society—*the struggle for these*—is now indispensable. [The] Communist International calls the proletariat of the world to the final struggle!" This is not the expression of philosophical abstraction, the mere prediction of future events; it is the language of direct incitement. The means advocated for bringing about the destruction of organized parliamentary government, namely, mass industrial revolts usurping the functions of municipal government, political mass strikes directed against the parliamentary state, and revolutionary mass action for its final destruction, necessarily imply the use of force and violence, and in their essential nature are inherently unlawful in a constitutional government of law and order. That the jury were warranted in finding that the Manifesto advocated not merely the abstract doctrine of overthrowing organized government by force, violence and unlawful means, but action to that end, is clear.

For present purposes we may and do assume that freedom of speech and of the press—which are protected by the First Amendment from abridgment by Congress—are among the fundamental personal rights and "liberties" protected by the due process clause of the 14th Amendment from impairment by the States.[2] [It] is a fundamental principle, long established, that the freedom of speech and of the press which is secured by the Constitution, does not confer an absolute right to speak or publish, without responsibility, whatever one may choose. [A] State may punish utterances endangering the foundations of organized government and threatening its overthrow by unlawful means. [In] short this freedom does not deprive a State of the primary and essential right of [self preservation]. By enacting the present statute the State has determined, through its legislative body, that utterances advocating the overthrow of organized government by force, violence and unlawful means, are so inimical to the general welfare and involve such danger of substantive evil that they may be penalized in the exercise of its police power. That determination must be given great weight. Every presumption is to be indulged in favor of the validity of the statute. Mugler v. Kansas [p. 459 above]. That utterances inciting to the overthrow of organized government by unlawful means, present a sufficient danger of substantive evil to bring their punishment within the range of legislative discretion, is clear. Such utterances, by their very nature, involve danger to the public peace and to the security of the State. They threaten breaches of the peace and ultimate revolution. And the immediate danger is none the less real and substantial, because the effect of a given utterance cannot be accurately foreseen. The State cannot reasonably be required to measure the danger from every such utterance in the nice balance of a jeweler's scale. A single revolutionary spark may kindle a fire that, smouldering for a time, may burst into a sweeping and destructive conflagration. It cannot be said that the State is acting arbitrarily or unreasonably when in the exercise of its judgment as to the measures necessary to protect the public peace and safety, it

2. This dictum was the Court's first indication that First Amendment guarantees are "incorporated" in the 14th Amendment.

seeks to extinguish the spark without waiting until it has enkindled the flame or blazed into the conflagration. It cannot reasonably be required to defer the adoption of measures for its own peace and safety until the revolutionary utterances lead to actual disturbances of the public peace or imminent and immediate danger of its own destruction; but it may, in the exercise of its judgment, suppress the threatened danger in its incipiency. [We] cannot hold that the present statute is an arbitrary or unreasonable exercise of the police power of the State unwarrantably infringing the freedom of speech or press; and we must and do sustain its constitutionality.

This being so it may be applied to every utterance—not too trivial to be beneath the notice of the law—which is of such a character and used with such intent and purpose as to bring it within the prohibition of the statute. [In] other words, when the legislative body has determined generally, in the constitutional exercise of its discretion, that utterances of a certain kind involve such danger of substantive evil that they may be punished, the question whether any specific utterance coming within the prohibited class is likely, in and of itself, to bring about the substantive evil, is not open to consideration. It is sufficient that the statute itself be constitutional and that the use of the language comes within its prohibition. It is clear that the question in such cases is entirely different from that involved in those cases where the statute merely prohibits certain acts involving the danger of substantive evil, without any reference to language itself, and it is sought to apply its provisions to language used by the defendant for the purpose of bringing about the prohibited results. There, if it be contended that the statute cannot be applied to the language used by the defendant because of its protection by the freedom of speech or press, it must necessarily be found, as an original question, without any previous determination by the legislative body whether the specific language used involved such likelihood of bringing about the substantive evil as to deprive it of the constitutional protection. In such cases it has been held that the general provisions of the statute may be constitutionally applied to the specific utterance of the defendant if its natural tendency and probable effect was to bring about the substantive evil which the legislative body might prevent. [Schenck; Debs.] And the ["clear and present danger" passage in Schenck]—upon which great reliance is placed in the defendant's argument— was manifestly intended, as shown by the context, to apply only in cases of this class, and has no application to those like the present, where the legislative body itself has previously determined the danger of substantive evil arising from utterances of a specified character. [It] was not necessary, within the meaning of the statute, that the defendant should have advocated "some definite or immediate act or acts" of force, violence or unlawfulness. It was sufficient if such acts were advocated in general terms; and it was not essential that their immediate execution should have been advocated. Nor was it necessary that the language should have been "reasonably and ordinarily calculated to incite certain persons" to acts of force, violence or unlawfulness. The advocacy need not be addressed to specific persons. Thus, the publication and circulation of a newspaper article may be an encouragement or endeavor to persuade to murder, although not addressed to any person in [particular].

Affirmed.

Justice HOLMES, dissenting.

[Justice] Brandeis and I are of opinion that this judgment should be reversed. The general principle of free speech, it seems to me, must be taken to be included in the 14th Amendment, in view of the scope that has been given to the word "liberty" as there used, although perhaps it may be accepted with a somewhat larger latitude of interpretation than is allowed to Congress by the sweeping language that governs or ought to govern the laws of the United States. If I am right, then I think that the criterion sanctioned by the full Court in [Schenck] applies. [It] is true that in my opinion this criterion was departed from in [Abrams], but the convictions that I expressed in that case are too deep for it to be possible for me as yet to believe that it [has] settled the law. If what I think the correct test is applied, it is manifest that there was no present danger of an attempt to overthrow the government by force on the part of the admittedly small minority who shared the defendant's views. It is said that this manifesto was more than a theory, that it was an incitement. Every idea is an incitement. It offers itself for belief and if believed it is acted on unless some other belief outweighs it or some failure of energy stifles the movement at its birth. The only difference between the expression of an opinion and an incitement in the narrower sense is the speaker's enthusiasm for the result. Eloquence may set fire to reason. But whatever may be thought of the redundant discourse before us it had no chance of starting a present conflagration. If in the long run the beliefs expressed in proletarian dictatorship are destined to be accepted by the dominant forces of the community, the only meaning of free speech is that they should be given their chance and have their way. If the publication of this document had been laid as an attempt to induce an uprising against government at once and not at some indefinite time in the future it would have presented a different question. The object would have been one with which the law might deal, subject to the doubt whether there was any danger that the publication could produce any result, or in other words, whether it was not futile and too remote from possible consequences. But the indictment alleges the publication and nothing more.

Whitney v. California

274 U.S. 357, 47 S.Ct. 641, 71 L.Ed. 1095 (1927).

Justice SANFORD delivered the opinion of the Court.

[Anita Whitney was convicted under the Criminal Syndicalism Act of California, enacted in 1919.[1] The charge was that she "did [organize] and assist in organizing, and was, is, and knowingly became a member of an organization [organized] to advocate, teach, aid and abet criminal syndicalism." She had attended the 1919 national convention of the Socialist Party as a delegate from the Oakland branch. The convention split between the "radicals" and the old-line democratic Socialists. The "radicals"—including Whitney—went to another hall and formed the Communist Labor Party [CLP], adopting a platform similar to the Left Wing Manifesto involved in Gitlow. Later in 1919, she was a branch delegate to a convention called to organize a California unit of the CLP. As a member of that convention's resolutions committee, she supported a

---

1. The pertinent provisions of the Act stated:

"Section 1. The term 'criminal syndicalism' as used in this act is hereby defined as any doctrine or precept advocating, teaching or aiding and abetting the commission of crime, sabotage, [or] unlawful acts of force and violence or unlawful methods of terrorism as a means of accomplishing a change in industrial ownership or control, or effecting any political change.

"Sec. 2. Any person who: ... [4.] Organizes or assists in organizing, or is or knowingly becomes a member of, any organization, society, group or assemblage of persons organized or assembled to advocate, teach or aid and abet [criminal syndicalism];

"Is guilty of a [felony]."

moderate resolution proposing the achievement of the CLP's goals through traditional political processes. The proposed resolution was defeated on the floor and a more militant program was adopted. Whitney remained a member of the Party and testified at the trial "that it was not her intention that the [CLP] of California should be an instrument of terrorism or violence."]

While it is not denied that the evidence warranted the jury in finding that the defendant became a member of and assisted in organizing the [CLP] of California, and that this was organized to [advocate] criminal syndicalism as defined by the Act, it is urged that the Act, as here construed and applied, deprived the defendant of her liberty without due process of law. [The] argument is, in effect, that the character of the state organization could not be forecast when she attended the convention; that she had no purpose of helping to create an instrument of terrorism and violence; that she "took part in formulating and presenting to the convention a resolution which, if adopted, would have committed the new organization to a legitimate policy of political reform by the use of the ballot"; that it was not until after the majority of the convention turned out to be "contrary-minded, and other less temperate policies prevailed" that the convention could have taken on the character of criminal syndicalism; and that as this was done over her protest, her mere presence in the convention, however violent the opinions expressed therein, could not thereby become a crime. This contention, while advanced in the form of a constitutional objection to the Act, is in effect nothing more than an effort to review the weight of the evidence for the purpose of showing that the defendant did not join and assist in organizing the [CLP] with a knowledge of its unlawful character and purpose. This question, which is foreclosed by the verdict of the jury, [is] one of fact merely which is not open to review in this Court, involving as it does no constitutional question [whatever].

[The Act] as applied in this case [is not] repugnant to the due process clause as a restraint of the rights of free speech, assembly, and association. That [a state] may punish those who abuse [freedom of speech] by utterances inimical to the public welfare, tending to incite to crime, disturb the public peace, or endanger the foundations of organized government and threaten its overthrow by unlawful means, is not open to question. [Gitlow.] [The legislative] determination must be given great weight. [The] essence of the offense [is] the combining with others in an association for the accomplishment of the desired ends through the advocacy and use of criminal and unlawful methods. It partakes of the nature of a criminal conspiracy. [That] such [united] action involves even greater danger to the public peace and security than the isolated utterances and acts of individuals, is clear. We cannot hold that, as here applied, the Act is an unreasonable or arbitrary exercise of the police power of the State, unwarrantably infringing any right of free speech, assembly or association, or that those persons are protected from punishment by [due process] who abuse such rights by joining and furthering an organization thus menacing the peace and welfare of the [State].

Affirmed.

Justice BRANDEIS, joined by Justice HOLMES, concurring.

The felony which the statute created is a crime very unlike the old felony of conspiracy or the old misdemeanor of unlawful assembly. The mere act of assisting in forming a society for teaching syndicalism, of becoming a member of it, or of assembling with others for that purpose is given the dynamic quality of crime. There is guilt although the society may not contemplate immediate promulgation of the doctrine. Thus the accused is to be punished, not for attempt, incitement or conspiracy, but for a step in preparation, which, if it threatens the public order at all, does so only remotely. The novelty in the prohibition introduced is that the statute aims, not at the practice of criminal syndicalism, nor even directly at the preaching of it, but at association with those who propose to preach it.

Despite arguments to the contrary which had seemed to me persuasive, it is settled that the due process clause of the 14th Amendment applies to matters of substantive law as well as to matters of procedure. Thus all fundamental rights comprised within the term liberty are protected by the [Constitution] from invasion by the States. The right of free speech, the right to teach and the right of assembly are, of course, fundamental rights. These may not be denied or abridged. But, although the rights of free speech and assembly are fundamental, they are not in their nature absolute. Their exercise is subject to restriction, if the particular restriction proposed is required in order to protect the State from destruction or from serious injury, political, economic or moral. That the necessity which is essential to a valid restriction does not exist unless speech would produce, or is intended to produce, a clear and imminent danger of some substantive evil which the State constitutionally may seek to prevent has been settled. See [Schenck].

It is said to be the function of the legislature to determine whether at a particular time and under the particular circumstances the formation of, or assembly with, a society organized to advocate criminal syndicalism constitutes a clear and present danger of substantive evil; and that by enacting the law here in question the legislature of California determined that question in the affirmative. Compare [Gitlow]. The legislature must obviously decide, in the first instance, whether a danger exists which calls for a particular protective measure. But where a statute is valid only in case certain conditions exist, the enactment of the statute cannot alone establish the facts which are essential to its validity. Prohibitory legislation has repeatedly been held invalid because unnecessary, where the denial of liberty involved was that of engaging in a particular business. The power of the courts to strike down an offending law is no less when the interests involved are not property rights, but the fundamental personal rights of free speech and assembly.

This Court has not yet fixed the standard by which to determine when a danger shall be deemed clear; how remote the danger may be and yet be deemed present; and what degree of evil shall be deemed sufficiently substantial to justify resort to abridgment of free speech and assembly as the means of protection. To reach sound conclusions on these matters, we must bear in mind why a State is, ordinarily, denied the power to prohibit dissemination of social, economic and political doctrine which a vast majority of its citizens believes to be false and fraught with evil consequence.

Those who won our independence believed that the final end of the State was to make men free to develop their faculties; and that in its government the deliberative forces should prevail over the arbitrary. They valued liberty both as an end and as a means. They believed liberty to be the secret of happiness and courage to be the secret of liberty. They believed that freedom to think as you will and to speak as you think are means indispensable to the discovery and spread of political truth; that without free speech and assembly discussion would be futile; that with them, discussion affords ordinarily adequate protection against the dissemination of noxious doctrine; that the greatest menace to freedom is an inert people; that public discussion is a political duty; and that this should be a fundamental principle of the American government. They recognized the risks to which all human institutions are subject. But they knew that order cannot be secured merely through fear of punishment for its infraction; that it is hazardous to discourage thought, hope and imagination; that fear breeds repression; that repression breeds hate; that hate menaces stable government; that the path of safety lies in the opportunity to discuss freely supposed grievances and proposed remedies; and that the fitting remedy for evil counsels is good ones. Believing in the power of reason as applied through public discussion, they eschewed silence coerced by law—the argument of force in its worst form. Recognizing the occasional tyrannies of governing majorities, they amended the Constitution so that free speech and assembly should be guaranteed.

Fear of serious injury cannot alone justify suppression of free speech and assembly. Men feared witches and burned women. It is the function of speech to free men from the bondage of irrational fears. To justify suppression of free speech there must be reasonable ground to fear that serious evil will result if free speech is practiced. There must be reasonable ground to believe that the danger apprehended is imminent. There must be reasonable ground to believe that the evil to be prevented is a serious one. Every denunciation of existing law tends in some measure to increase the probability that there will be violation of it. Condonation of a breach enhances the probability. Expressions of approval add to the probability. Propagation of the criminal state of mind by teaching syndicalism increases it. Advocacy of law-breaking heightens it still further. But even advocacy of violation, however reprehensible morally, is not a justification for denying free speech where the advocacy falls short of incitement and there is nothing to indicate that the advocacy would be immediately acted on. The wide difference between advocacy and incitement, between preparation and attempt, between assembling and conspiracy, must be borne in mind. In order to support a finding of clear and present danger it must be shown either that immediate serious violence was to be expected or was advocated, or that the past conduct furnished reason to believe that such advocacy was then contemplated.

Those who won our independence by revolution were not cowards. They did not fear political change. They did not exalt order at the cost of liberty. To courageous, self-reliant men, with confidence in the power of free and fearless reasoning applied through the processes of popular government, no danger flowing from speech can be deemed clear and present, unless the incidence of the evil apprehended is so imminent that it may befall before there is opportunity for full discussion. If there be time to expose through discussion the falsehood and fallacies, to avert the evil by the processes of education, the remedy to be applied is more speech, not enforced silence. Only an emergency can justify repression. Such must be the rule if authority is to be reconciled with freedom. Such, in my opinion, is the command of the Constitution. It is therefore always open to Americans to challenge a law abridging free speech and assembly by showing that there was no emergency justifying it.

Moreover, even imminent danger cannot justify resort to prohibition of these functions essential to effective democracy, unless the evil apprehended is relatively serious. Prohibition of free speech and assembly is a measure so stringent that it would be inappropriate as the means for averting a relatively trivial harm to society. A police measure may be unconstitutional merely because the remedy, although effective as a means of protection, is unduly harsh or oppressive. Thus, a State might, in the exercise of its police power, make any trespass upon the land of another a crime, regardless of the results or of the intent or purpose of the trespasser. It might, also, punish an attempt, a conspiracy, or an incitement to commit the trespass. But it is hardly conceivable that this Court would hold constitutional a statute which punished as a felony the mere voluntary assembly with a society formed to teach that pedestrians had the moral right to cross unenclosed, unposted, waste lands and to advocate their doing so, even if there was imminent danger that advocacy would lead to a trespass. The fact that speech is likely to result in some violence or in destruction of property is not enough to justify its suppression. There must be the probability of serious injury to the State. Among free men, the deterrents ordinarily to be applied to prevent crime are education and punishment for violations of the law, not abridgment of the rights of free speech and assembly.

[The California] legislative declaration [stating that the Act was "necessary to the immediate preservation of the public peace and safety," because many people were going "from place to place in this state" advocating criminal syndicalism] satisfies the requirement of the constitution of the State concerning emergency legislation. [But] it does not preclude enquiry into the question whether, at the time and under the circumstances, the conditions existed which are essential to validity under the Federal Constitution. As a statute, even if not void on its face, may be challenged because invalid as applied, the result of such an inquiry may depend upon the specific facts of the particular case. Whenever the fundamental rights of free speech and assembly are alleged to have been invaded, it must remain open to a defendant to present the issue whether there actually did exist at the time a clear danger; whether the danger, if any, was imminent; and whether the evil apprehended was one so substantial as to justify the stringent restriction interposed by the legislature. The legislative [declaration] creates merely a rebuttable presumption that these conditions have been satisfied.

Whether in 1919, when Miss Whitney did the things complained of, there was in California such clear and present danger of serious evil, might have been made the important issue in the case. She might have required that the issue be determined either by the court or the jury. She claimed below that the statute as applied to her violated the [Constitution]; but she did not claim that it was void because there was no clear and present danger of serious evil, nor did she request that the existence of these conditions of a valid measure thus restricting the rights of free speech and assembly be passed upon by the court or a jury. On the other hand, there was evidence on which the court or jury might have found that such danger existed. I am unable to assent to the suggestion in the opinion of the Court that assembling with a political party, formed to advocate the desirability of a proletarian revolution by mass action at some date necessarily far in the future, is not a right within the protection of the 14th Amendment. In the present case, however, there was other testimony which tended to establish the existence of a conspiracy, on the part of members of the International Workers of the World, to commit present serious crimes; and likewise to show that such a conspiracy would be furthered by the activity of the society of which Miss Whitney was a member. Under these circumstances the judgment of the state court cannot be disturbed. Our power of review in this case [from a state court] is limited [to] the particular claims duly made below, and denied. [We] lack here the power occasionally exercised on review of judgments of lower federal courts to correct in criminal cases vital errors, although the objection was not taken in the trial court. Because we may not enquire into the errors now alleged, I concur in affirming the judgment of the state court.

––––––––

THE GITLOW–WHITNEY PROBLEM

1. *Legislative presumptions of harm from speech.* In Gitlow and Whitney, unlike the Schenck trilogy and Abrams, the Court was faced with a prior legislative declaration that certain classes of speech caused an intolerable risk of serious harm. Was the Gitlow majority correct in saying that the "clear and present danger" standard was inapplicable in such cases? Arguably, the clear and present danger test made it inherently difficult for judges to confront and set aside a legislative judgment that a particular variety of speech is dangerous. The clear and present danger test puts great emphasis on context and guesses about future harm; to the extent that this involves an empirical judgment, judges may feel particularly incompetent to second-guess legislative judgments. Recall that, in his dissents from Court invalidations of state economic regulations on substantive due process grounds, Holmes repeatedly urged deference to legislative judgments, in cases beginning with Lochner. What explains his abandonment of such deference here? Should it matter that the Gitlow law was enacted in 1902, long before the evolution of the post-World War I radicalism that gave rise to the Gitlow prosecution? In contrast, Whitney involved prosecution for 1919 behavior under a 1919 law. On these questions, see Rogat, "Mr. Justice Holmes, Some Modern Views—The Judge as Spectator," 31 U.Chi. L.Rev. 213 (1964), and Linde, "'Clear and Present Danger' Reexamined: Dissonance in the Brandenburg Concerto," 22 Stan.L.Rev. 1163 (1970).

2. *An alternative approach: the Masses test.* Would adoption of the Masses "incitement" test have alleviated the judicial difficulty in Gitlow and Whitney? By emphasizing what speech is protected (and the speaker's words rather than guesses about future harms), would courts have been in a better position to protect speech without direct confrontations with legislative judgments that particular types of speech present a "clear and present danger" of an especially grave evil?

3. *Comparing the Holmes and Brandeis approaches.* Was Brandeis more successful than Holmes in confronting the Gitlow–Whitney problem? In what respects do Brandeis' justifications for the clear and present danger test differ from Holmes'? Brandeis, like Holmes, was extremely deferential to legislative judgments underlying economic regulations during the Lochner era. Note how his Whitney concurrence sidesteps direct confrontation with the California legislature by considering Whitney's challenge to the law only "as applied." Might Brandeis have justified lessened deference to the legislature here by emphasizing that the legislators, by curtailing expressions of speech and opinions, had undercut the basis for the usual reliance on the processes of representation? Recall the Carolene Products footnote, above. Note also that Brandeis' version adds an additional variable to the "immediacy of harm" emphasis of Holmes: Brandeis also speaks of the "gravity of the evil." Brandeis' concurrence also relied in part on the freedom of association implied in the First Amendment. See p. 1374 below. On the Whitney litigation and the Brandeis opinion, see Blasi, "The First Amendment and the Ideal of Civic Courage: The Brandeis Opinion in Whitney v. California," 29 Wm. & Mary L.Rev. 653 (1988). On Holmes' and Brandeis' approaches, see Lahav, "Holmes and Brandeis: Libertarian and Republican Justifications for Free Speech," 4 J. Law & Pol. 451 (1987).

4. *Retreat from Gitlow–Whitney: Fiske, DeJonge and Herndon.* In the decade following Whitney, the Court for the first time overturned convictions involving subversive advocacy and the right of association. Although First Amendment claimants prevailed, not all these holdings rested on First Amendment grounds. In FISKE v. KANSAS, 274 U.S. 380 (1927), decided the same

day as Whitney, the Court held unconstitutional an application of the Kansas version of criminal syndicalism legislation to a defendant who had solicited new members for a branch of the Industrial Workers of the World (IWW). The only trial evidence of IWW doctrine was the preamble to its constitution, containing such statements as: "Between [the working and employing] classes a struggle must go on until the workers of the World organize as a class, take possession of the earth, and the machinery of production and abolish the wage system." Justice SANFORD, for a unanimous Court, found this language insufficient to establish "that the organization in which he secured members advocated any crime, violence or other unlawful acts or methods as a means of effecting industrial or political changes or revolution." Arguably, Fiske rested not on First Amendment but rather on procedural due process grounds: the impermissibility of drawing conclusory inferences from inadequate factual bases.

In DE JONGE v. OREGON, 299 U.S. 353 (1937), the Court did reverse a conviction solely on substantive First Amendment grounds. DeJonge was charged under Oregon's criminal syndicalism law with participating in a meeting called by the Communist Party The Court unanimously held that such participation alone could not make out a crime. Chief Justice HUGHES stated: "[The] right of peaceable assembly is a right cognate to those of free speech and free press and is equally fundamental. [It] follows [that] peaceable assembly for lawful discussion cannot be made a crime. The question, if the rights of free speech and peaceable assembly are to be preserved, is not as to the auspices under which the meeting is held but as to its purpose; not as to the relations of the speakers, but whether their utterances transcend the bounds of the freedom of speech which the Constitution protects."

In HERNDON v. LOWRY, 301 U.S. 242 (1937), Herndon, a black organizer for the Communist party in the South, was convicted of an "attempt to incite insurrection" under a Georgia law prohibiting "any combined resistance to the lawful authority of the State, with intent to the denial thereof, when the same is manifested or intended to be manifested by acts of violence." The conviction rested on documents in Herndon's possession urging party members to vote for black self-determination. In overturning that conviction by a vote of 5–4, the Court rested in part on First Amendment grounds. Justice ROBERTS' majority opinion emphasized that there was no evidence that Herndon had ever advocated "forcible subversion" nor incited anyone to imminent insurrection, and suggested that all he had done on the facts was to advocate "an ultimate ideal." In "these circumstances, to make membership in the party and solicitation of members for that party a criminal offense, punishable by death, in the discretion of a jury, is an unwarranted invasion of the right of freedom of speech." Justice Roberts also rested in part on grounds of vagueness: the law did not furnish "a sufficiently ascertainable standard of guilt," and thus permitted a jury to function as "a dragnet which may enmesh anyone who agitates for a change of government if a jury can be persuaded that he ought to have foreseen his words would have some effect in the future conduct of others."

C.   THE SMITH ACT PROSECUTIONS

After World War II, fears mounted of threats to national security posed by the Soviet Union and China, and anti-communist sentiment generated a number of restrictions on subversive speech. Former State Department official Alger Hiss was convicted of perjury in connection with a congressional inquiry into his alleged spying activities for the Soviet Union. Senator Joseph McCarthy conducted a series of hearings accusing government officials of communist activities. Against this backdrop, the national leaders of the Communist Party were prosecuted under the Smith Act of 1940, a federal law quite similar to the New York criminal anarchy statute sustained in Gitlow. When the first group of defendants brought their appeals to the Court, in the 1951 Dennis case below, they relied extensively on the clear and present danger test, which during the 1930s and 1940s had "emerged as the applicable standard not only for the kinds of issues with respect to which it originated but also for a wide variety of other First Amendment problems." Greenawalt, "Speech and Crime," 1980 A.B.F. Res. J. 647. The opinions in Dennis reexamine that standard at length.

————

Dennis v. United States

341 U.S. 494, 71 S.Ct. 857, 95 L.Ed. 1137 (1951).

Chief Justice VINSON announced the judgment of the Court and an opinion in which Justices REED, BURTON and MINTON join.

Petitioners were indicted in July, 1948, for violation of the conspiracy provisions of the Smith Act during the period of April, 1945, to July, 1948,[1] [and convicted after jury trial. The] indictment charged the petitioners with wilfully and knowingly conspiring (1) to organize as the Communist Party of the United States of America a society, group and assembly of persons who teach and advocate the overthrow and destruction of the Government of the United States by force and violence, and (2) knowingly and wilfully to advocate and teach the duty and necessity of overthrowing and destroying the Government of the United States by force and [violence]. The trial of the case extended over nine months, [resulting] in a record of 16,000 pages. Our limited grant of the writ of certiorari has removed from our consideration any question as to the sufficiency of the [evidence]. [T]he Court of Appeals held that the record supports the following broad conclusion: [that] the Communist Party is a highly disciplined organization, adept at infiltration into strategic positions, use of aliases, and double-meaning language; that the Party is rigidly controlled; that Communists, unlike other political parties, tolerate no dissension from the policy laid down by the guiding forces; [that] the literature of the Party and the statements and activities of its leaders, petitioners here, advocate, and the general goal of the Party was, during the period in question, to achieve a successful overthrow of the existing order by force and [violence].

1. Sections 2 and 3 of the Smith Act provided as follows:

"Sec. 2. (a) It shall be unlawful for any person—

"(1) to knowingly or willfully advocate, abet, advise, or teach the duty, necessity, desirability, or propriety of overthrowing or destroying any government in the United States by force or violence, or by the assassination of any officer of any such [government];

"(3) to organize or help to organize any society, group, or assembly of persons who teach, advocate, or encourage the overthrow or destruction of any government in the United States by force or violence; or to be or become a member of, or affiliate with, any such society, group, or assembly of persons, knowing the purposes [thereof].

"Sec. 3. It shall be unlawful for any person to attempt to commit, or to conspire to commit, any of the acts prohibited [by] this title."

[No] one could conceive that it is not within the power of Congress to prohibit acts intended to overthrow the Government by force and violence. The question with which we are concerned here is not whether Congress has such *power,* but whether the *means* which it has employed conflict with [the] Constitution. [Petitioners attack] the statute on the grounds that by its terms it prohibits academic discussion of the merits of Marxism–Leninism, that it stifles ideas and is contrary to all concepts of a free speech and a free press. [The] very language of the Smith Act negates [this] interpretation. [The Act] is directed at advocacy, not discussion. Thus, the trial judge properly charged the jury that they could not convict if they found that petitioners did "no more than pursue peaceful studies and discussions or teaching and advocacy in the realm of ideas." [But the application of the Act] in this case has resulted in convictions for the teaching and advocacy of the overthrow of the Government by force and violence, which, even though coupled with the intent to accomplish that overthrow, contains an element of speech. For this reason, we must pay special heed to the demands of the First Amendment marking out the boundaries of speech.

[Although] no case subsequent to Whitney and Gitlow has expressly overruled the majority opinions in those cases, there is little doubt that subsequent opinions have inclined toward the Holmes–Brandeis rationale. [In] this case we are [therefore] squarely presented with the application of the "clear and present danger" test, and must decide what that phrase imports. [Overthrow] of the Government by force and violence is certainly a substantial enough interest for the Government to limit speech. [If], then, this interest may be protected, the literal problem which is presented is what has been meant by the use of the phrase ["clear and present danger"]. Obviously, the words cannot mean that before the Government may act, it must wait until the putsch is about to be executed, the plans have been laid and the signal is awaited. If Government is aware that a group aiming at its overthrow is attempting to indoctrinate its members and to commit them to a course whereby they will strike when the leaders feel the circumstances permit, action by the Government is required. The argument that there is no need for Government to concern itself, for Government is strong, it possesses ample powers to put down a rebellion, it may defeat the revolution with ease needs no answer. For that is not the question. Certainly an attempt to overthrow the Government by force, even though doomed from the outset because of inadequate numbers or power of the revolutionists, is a sufficient evil for Congress to prevent. The damage which such attempts create both physically and politically to a nation makes it impossible to measure the validity in terms of the probability of success, or the immediacy of a successful attempt. [We] must therefore reject the contention that success or probability of success is the criterion.

The situation with which Justices Holmes and Brandeis were concerned in Gitlow was a comparatively isolated event, bearing little relation in their minds to any substantial threat to the safety of the community. [They] were not confronted with any situation comparable to the instant one—the development of an apparatus designed and dedicated to the overthrow of the Government, in the context of world crisis after crisis. Chief Judge Learned Hand, writing for the majority [of the Second Circuit] below, interpreted the phrase as follows: "In each case [courts] must ask whether the gravity of the 'evil,' discounted by its improbability, justifies such invasion of free speech as is necessary to avoid the danger." We adopt this statement of the rule. As articulated by Chief Judge Hand, it is as succinct and inclusive as any other we might devise at this [time]. Likewise, we are in accord with the court below, which affirmed the trial court's finding that the requisite danger existed. The mere fact that from the period 1945 to 1948 petitioners' activities did not result in an attempt to overthrow the Government by force and violence is of course no answer to the fact that there was a group that was ready to make the attempt. The formation by petitioners of such a highly organized conspiracy, with rigidly disciplined members subject to call when the leaders, these petitioners, felt that the time had come for action, coupled with the inflammable nature of world conditions, similar uprisings in other countries, and the touch-and-go nature of our relations with countries with whom petitioners were in the very least ideologically attuned, convince us that their convictions were justified on this score. And this analysis disposes of the contention that a conspiracy to advocate, as distinguished from the advocacy itself, cannot be constitutionally restrained, because it comprises only the preparation. It is the existence of the conspiracy which creates the danger. [If] the ingredients of the reaction are present, we cannot bind the Government to wait until the catalyst is added.

[Petitioners] intended to overthrow the Government of the United States as speedily as the circumstances would permit. Their conspiracy to organize the Communist Party and to teach and advocate the overthrow of the [Government] by force and violence created a "clear and present danger" of an attempt to overthrow the Government by force and [violence].

Affirmed.

Justice FRANKFURTER, concurring in affirmance of the judgment.

[The] historic antecedents of the First Amendment preclude the notion that its purpose was to give unqualified immunity to every expression that touched on matters within the range of political interest. [Absolute] rules would inevitably lead to absolute exceptions, and such exceptions would eventually corrode the rules. The demands of free speech in a democratic society as well as the interest in national security are better served by candid and informed weighing of the competing interests, within the confines of the judicial process, than by announcing dogmas too inflexible for the non-Euclidean problems to be solved. But how are competing interests to be assessed? Since they are not subject to quantitative ascertainment, the issue necessarily resolves itself into asking, who is to make the adjustments?—who is to balance[?] Full responsibility for the choice cannot be given to the courts. Courts are not representative bodies. [Their] judgment is best informed, and therefore most dependable, within narrow limits. Their essential quality is detachment, founded on independence. History teaches that the independence of the judiciary is jeopardized when courts become embroiled in the passions of the day and assume primary responsibility in choosing between competing political, economic and social pressures. Primary responsibility for adjusting the interests which compete in the situation before us of necessity belongs to the Congress. [We] are to set aside the judgment [of legislators] only if there is no reasonable basis for [it].

[These] general considerations underlie decision of the case before us. On the one hand is the interest in security. The Communist Party was not designed by these defendants as an ordinary political party. For the circumstances of its organization, its aims and methods, and the relation of the defendants to its organization and aims we are concluded by the jury's verdict. [In] finding that the defendants violated [the statute,] we may not treat as established fact that the Communist Party in this country is of significant size, well-organized, well-disciplined, conditioned to embark on unlawful activity when given the command. But in determining whether application of the statute to the defendants is within the constitutional powers of Congress, we are not limited to the facts found by the jury. We must view such a question in the light of whatever is relevant to a legislative judgment. We may take judicial notice that the Communist doctrines which these defendants have conspired to advocate are in the ascendency in powerful nations who cannot be acquitted of unfriendliness to the institutions of this country. We may take account of evidence brought forward at this trial and elsewhere, much of which has long been common knowledge. In sum, it would amply justify a legislature in concluding that recruitment of additional members for the Party would create a substantial danger to national security.

On the other hand is the interest in free speech. The right to exert all governmental powers in aid of maintaining our institutions and resisting their physical overthrow does not include intolerance of opinions and speech that cannot do harm although opposed and perhaps alien to dominant, traditional opinion. [And a] public interest is not wanting in granting freedom to speak their minds even to those who advocate the overthrow of the Government by force. For, as the evidence in this case abundantly illustrates, coupled with such advocacy is criticism of defects in our society. [Moreover, suppressing] advocates of overthrow inevitably will also silence critics who do not advocate overthrow but fear that their criticism may be so construed. [It] is self-delusion to think that we can punish [the defendants] for their advocacy without adding to the risks run by loyal citizens who honestly believe in some of the reforms these defendants advance. It is a sobering fact that in sustaining the convictions before us we can hardly escape restriction on the interchange of [ideas].

[But it] is not for us to decide how we would adjust the clash of interests which this case presents were the primary responsibility for reconciling it ours. Congress has determined that the danger created by advocacy of overthrow justifies the ensuing restriction on freedom of speech. [To] make validity of legislation depend on judicial reading of events still in the womb of time—a forecast, that is, of the outcome of forces at best appreciated only with knowledge of the topmost secrets of nations—is to charge the judiciary with duties beyond its [equipment].

Justice JACKSON, concurring.

[The] "clear and present danger" test was an innovation by [Justice] Holmes in [Schenck, refined] in later cases, all arising before the era of World War II revealed the subtlety and efficacy of modernized revolutionary techniques used by totalitarian parties. [I] would save it, unmodified, for application as a "rule of reason" in the kind of case for which it was devised. When the issue is criminality of a hotheaded speech on a street corner, or circulation of a few incendiary pamphlets, or parading by some zealots behind a red flag, or refusal of a handful of school children to salute our flag, it is not beyond the capacity of the judicial process to gather, comprehend, and weigh the necessary materials for decision whether it is a clear and present danger of substantive evil or a harmless letting off of steam. It is not a prophecy, for the danger in such cases has matured by the time of trial or it was never present. The test applies and has meaning where a conviction is sought to be based on a speech or writing which does not directly or explicitly advocate a crime but to which such tendency is sought to be attributed by construction or by implication from external circumstances. The formula in such cases favors freedoms that are vital to our society, and, even if sometimes applied too generously, the consequences cannot be grave.

[I] think reason is lacking for applying that test to this case. If we must decide that this Act and its application are constitutional only if we are convinced that petitioner's conduct creates a "clear and present danger" of violent overthrow, we must appraise imponderables, including international and national phenomena which baffle the best informed foreign offices and our most experienced politicians. [No] doctrine can be sound whose application requires us to make a prophecy of that sort in the guise of a legal decision. The judicial process simply is not adequate to a trial of such far-flung issues. The answers given would reflect our own political predilections and nothing more. The authors of the clear and present danger test never applied it to a case like this, nor would I. If applied as it is proposed here, it means that the Communist plotting is protected during its period of incubation; its preliminary stages of organization and preparation are immune from the law; the Government can move only after imminent action is manifest, when it would, of course, be too [late].

Justice BLACK, dissenting.

[The] only way to affirm these convictions is to repudiate directly or indirectly the established "clear and present danger" rule. This the Court does in a way which greatly restricts the protections afforded by the First Amendment. [I] cannot agree that the First Amendment permits us to sustain laws suppressing freedom of speech and press on the basis of Congress' or our own notions of mere "reasonableness." [The] Amendment as so construed is not likely to protect any but those "safe" or orthodox views which rarely need its protection. I must also express my objection to the holding [because] it sanctions the determination of a crucial issue of fact by the judge rather than by the [jury]. Public opinion being what it now is, few will protest the conviction of these Communist petitioners. There is hope, however, that in calmer times, when present pressures, passions and fears subside, this or some later Court will restore the First Amendment liberties to the high preferred place where they belong in a free society.

Justice DOUGLAS, dissenting.

If this were a case where those who claimed protection under the First Amendment were teaching the techniques of sabotage, the assassination of the President, the filching of documents from public files, the planting of bombs, the art of street warfare, and the like, I would have no doubts. The freedom to speak is not absolute; the teaching of methods of terror and other seditious conduct should be beyond the pale along with obscenity and immorality. This case was argued as if those were the facts. The argument imported much seditious conduct into the record. That is easy and it has popular appeal, for the activities of Communists in plotting and scheming against the free world are common knowledge. But the fact is that no such evidence was introduced at the trial. There is a statute which makes a seditious conspiracy unlawful. Petitioners, however, were not charged with a "conspiracy to overthrow" the Government. They were charged with a conspiracy to form a party and groups and assemblies of people who teach and advocate the overthrow of our Government by force or violence and with a conspiracy to advocate and teach its overthrow by force and violence. It may well be that indoctrination in the techniques of terror to destroy the Government would be indictable under either statute. But the teaching which is condemned here is of a different character.

So far as the present record is concerned, what petitioners did was to organize people to teach and themselves teach the Marxist–Leninist doctrine contained chiefly in four books: Foundations of Leninism by Stalin (1924), The Communist Manifesto by Marx and Engels (1848), State and Revolution by Lenin (1917), History of the Communist Party of the Soviet Union (B) (1939). Those books are to Soviet Communism what Mein Kampf was to Nazism. If they are understood, the ugliness of Communism is revealed, its deceit and cunning are exposed, the nature of its activities becomes apparent, and the chances of its success less likely. That is not, of course, the reason why petitioners chose these books for their classrooms. They are fervent Communists to whom these volumes are gospel. They preached the creed with the hope that some day it would be acted upon. The opinion of the Court does not outlaw these texts nor condemn them to the fire, as the Communists do literature offensive to their creed. But if the books themselves are not outlawed, if they can lawfully remain on library shelves, by what reasoning does their use in a classroom become a crime? [The] Act, as construed, requires the element of intent—that those who teach the creed believe in it. The crime then depends not on what is taught but on who the teacher is. That is to make freedom of speech turn not on *what is said,* but on the *intent* with which it is said. Once we start down that road we enter territory dangerous to the liberties of every [citizen].

There comes a time when even speech loses its constitutional immunity. Speech innocuous one year may at another time fan such destructive flames that it must be halted in the interests of the safety of the Republic. That is the meaning of the clear and present danger test. When conditions are so critical that there will be no time to avoid the evil that the speech threatens, it is time to call a halt. Otherwise, free speech which is the strength of the Nation will be the cause of its destruction. Yet free speech is the rule, not the exception. The restraint to be constitutional must be based on more than fear, on more than passionate opposition against the speech, on more than a revolted dislike for its contents. There must be some immediate injury to society that is likely if speech is [allowed].

[If] we are to take judicial notice of the threat of Communists within the nation, it should not be difficult to conclude that *as a political party* they are of little consequence. [Communism] in the world scene is no bogeyman; but Communism as a political faction or party in this country plainly is. Communism has been so thoroughly exposed in this country that it has been crippled as a political force. Free speech has destroyed it as an effective political party. [How] it can be said that there is a clear and present danger that this advocacy will succeed is, therefore, a mystery. [I]n America [Communists] are miserable merchants of unwanted ideas; their wares remain unsold. [But] the mere statement of the opposing views indicates how important it is that we know the facts before we act. Neither prejudice nor hate nor senseless fear should be the basis of this solemn act. Free speech [should] not be sacrificed on anything less than plain and objective proof of danger that the evil advocated is [imminent].

[Justice CLARK did not participate in the decision.]

"CLEAR AND PRESENT DANGER" AFTER DENNIS

1. *The Dennis formulation.* Did Dennis ignore clear and present danger? Distort clear and present danger? Or fall prey to the inherent weaknesses of clear and present danger? What, if anything, did the Holmes standard say about the Dennis problem? What "substantive evil" was relevant? Actual overthrow? Risk of overthrow? Conspiracy to overthrow? Conspiracy to advocate overthrow? Was a greater emphasis on immediacy in Dennis compelled by the earlier cases? Did Dennis consider risks more remote than the Abrams dissent would permit? Than the Whitney concurrence? What degree of deference to the legislative judgment was appropriate in Dennis? Should the legislative judgment have been assessed in terms of the 1940 circumstances, when the

Smith Act became law? The circumstances in 1948, when the Dennis indictment was brought? Should the Court have insisted on greater record evidence of the 1948 situation? Should it have ignored the world situation? See Linde, " 'Clear and Present Danger' Reexamined: Dissonance in the Brandenburg Concerto," 22 Stan.L.Rev. 1163 (1970) (arguing that, in view of the interval of more than a decade between the enactment of the Smith Act and the Dennis decision, it was effectively impossible to point to any particular "legislative judgment that would deserve deference for its assessment of the danger from revolutionary speech"). For the view that the Dennis formulation is a "powerful formula" for resolving a variety of speech issues, see Van Alstyne, "A Graphic Review of the Free Speech Clause," 70 Calif.L.Rev. 107, 128 (1982).

2. *Clear and present danger and Learned Hand.* In Dennis, the Court adopted the clear and present danger formulation set forth by Chief Judge Learned Hand in the decision of the court of appeals for the Second Circuit affirming the convictions below. How could Hand, the author of the Masses opinion, have adopted the clear and present danger test he had long criticized, and interpreted it in a relatively speech-restrictive way? The answer, suggests Gerald Gunther, is that he was "a judge of a lower court who took seriously his obligation to follow Supreme Court precedents," and that his Masses test had sunk "into oblivion in the years between World War I and World War II," while the Supreme Court "had adhered to and struggled to clarify its 'clear and present danger' test." Gunther, Learned Hand: the Man and the Judge 600 (1994). Privately, Hand said at the time that he would still have preferred to rely on the Masses test, id. at 604, and that he personally would never have prosecuted the Communist leaders, for " '[t]he blood of martyrs is the seed of the church,' " id. at 603.

In his last years, Judge Hand repudiated the view that rights such as speech should receive special judicial protection, suggesting that he viewed the Bill of Rights primarily as merely "admonitory or hortatory, not definite enough to be guides on concrete occasions." Hand, The Bill of Rights (1958); see also Hand, "Chief Justice Stone's Concept of the Judicial Function," in The Spirit of Liberty (3d ed. Dilliard 1960).

3. *Free speech theory and the advocacy of totalitarian government.* Dennis, even more sharply than the earlier subversive speech cases, raises the question why the First Amendment should protect those who, were they in power, would deny free speech rights to others. Some have argued it should not: "Speech advocating violent overthrow [of government is] not 'political speech' as that term must be defined by a Madisonian system of government [because] it violates constitutional truths about processes and because it is not aimed at a new definition of political truth by a legislative majority. Violent overthrow of government breaks the premises of our system concerning the ways in which truth is defined, and yet those premises are the only reasons for protecting political speech." Bork, "Neutral Principles and Some First Amendment Problems," 47 Ind.L.J. 1 (1971). See also Auerbach, "The Communist Control Act of 1954: A Proposed Legal–Political Theory of Free Speech," 23 U.Chi.L.Rev. 173 (1956) (arguing that "in suppressing totalitarian movements a democratic society is not acting to protect the status quo, but the very same interests which freedom of speech itself seeks to secure—the possibility of peaceful progress under freedom. [One] type of constitutional change in the constitutional system is excluded—'a change which would endanger its democratic character.' This [is] the basic postulate which should control [the] interpretation of the [First Amendment].").

For arguments to the contrary, finding First Amendment value in protecting radically subversive speech, see Emerson, The System of Freedom of Expression (1970) (arguing that "democratic society should tolerate opinion which attacks the fundamental institutions of democracy for much the same reasons that it tolerates other opinion," and that "suppression of any group in a society destroys the atmosphere of freedom essential to the life and progress of a healthy community. [It] is not possible for a society to practice both freedom of expression and suppression of expression at the same time."); Meiklejohn, Free Speech and Its Relation to Self–Government 48 (1948) (arguing that the First Amendment "means that certain substantive evils which, in principle, Congress has a right to prevent, must be endured if the only way of avoiding them is by the abridging of that freedom of speech upon which the entire structure of our free institutions rests"); Smith, "Radically Subversive Speech and the Authority of Law," 94 Mich. L. Rev. 348 (1995) (arguing that radically subversive speech is valuable because a democracy, unlike an authoritarian regime, requires recognition of the possibility that the existing state might be illegitimate).

4. *Retreat from Dennis: Yates, Scales and Noto.* After Dennis, the Government brought Smith Act cases against over 120 Communists who were "lower echelon" rather than "first string" leaders. By the time the cases reached the Supreme Court, McCarthy had died and anti-communist fervor had somewhat abated. In YATES v. UNITED STATES, 354 U.S. 298 (1957), the Court set aside the convictions of 14 defendants. Justice HARLAN's majority opinion found that the trial court's instructions to the jury gave inadequate guidance on the distinction between advocacy of abstract doctrine and advocacy of action: "[We] are [faced] with the question whether the Smith Act prohibits advocacy and teaching of forcible overthrow as an abstract principle, divorced from any effort to instigate action to that end, so long as such advocacy or teaching is engaged in with evil intent. We hold that it does not. The distinction between advocacy of abstract doctrine and advocacy directed at promoting unlawful action is one that has been consistently recognized in the opinions of this Court. [We] need not, however, decide the issue before us in terms of constitutional compulsion, for our first duty is to construe this statute. In doing so we should not assume that Congress chose to disregard a constitutional danger zone so clearly [marked]. [Mere] doctrinal justification of forcible overthrow, [even] though uttered with the hope that it may ultimately lead to violent revolution, is too remote from concrete action to be regarded as the kind of indoctrination preparatory to action which was condemned in Dennis. [Dennis was] not concerned with a conspiracy to engage at some future time in seditious advocacy, but rather with a conspiracy to advocate presently the taking of forcible action in the future. [The] essential distinction is that those to whom the advocacy is addressed must be urged to *do* something, now or in the future, rather than merely to *believe* in [something]."

After Yates, the government increasingly resorted to use of the membership clause of the Smith Act, which made it a felony knowingly to become or be a member of any organization that advocates the overthrow of the Government of the United States by force or violence. In SCALES v. UNITED STATES, 367 U.S. 203 (1961), the Court affirmed a conviction under the clause, but Justice HARLAN's majority opinion construed the statute to require "specific intent" and "active" rather than merely "nominal" membership: "[The] clause does not make criminal all association with an organization which has been shown to engage in illegal advocacy. There must be clear proof that a defendant 'specifically intend[s] to accomplish [the aims of the organization] by resort to violence.' Thus the member for whom the organization is a vehicle for the advancement of legitimate aims and policies does not fall within the ban of the statute: he lacks the requisite specific intent 'to bring about the overthrow of the government as speedily as circumstances would permit.' Such a person may be foolish, deluded, or perhaps merely optimistic, but he is not by this statute made a criminal." Justice Harlan found the evidence below sufficient to sustain the conviction under the statute as so construed: "[T]his evidence sufficed to make a case for the jury on the issue of illegal Party advocacy. Dennis and Yates have definitely laid at rest any doubt that present advocacy of *future* action for violent overthrow satisfies statutory and constitutional requirements equally with advocacy of *immediate* action to that end. Hence this record cannot be considered deficient because it contains no evidence of advocacy for immediate overthrow. [The] evidence amply showed that Party leaders were continuously preaching during the indictment period the inevitability of eventual forcible overthrow [and the jury] was entitled to infer from this systematic preaching that [the]doctrine of violent revolution [was] put forward as a guide to future action." Justices Black, Douglas and Brennan dissented. Justice Douglas stated: "The case is not saved by showing that petitioner was an active member. None of the activity constitutes a crime. [Not] one single illegal act is charged to petitioner."

Scales was the last defendant convicted under the Smith Act. In another Smith Act membership clause case, decided as a companion case to Scales, the Court reversed a conviction because "the evidence of illegal Party advocacy was insufficient." NOTO v. UNITED STATES, 367 U.S. 290 (1961). With Justice HARLAN once again writing for the Court, the opinion noted that the evidence of "advocacy of action" was "sparse indeed," was not "broadly based" geographically, and "lacked the compelling quality which in Scales was supplied by the petitioner's own utterances and systematic course of conduct as a high Party official." He added: "It need hardly be said that it is upon the particular evidence in a particular record that a particular defendant must be judged, and not upon the evidence in some other record or upon what may be supposed to be the tenets of the [Party]." Here, the record "bears much of the infirmity that we found in the Yates record."

5. *The impact of Yates, Scales and Noto.* Were Yates, Scales and Noto truly restatements of Dennis? Or does the emphasis in Yates, Scales, and Noto on the distinction between advocacy of abstract doctrine and advocacy of action, and on the need for close scrutiny of the evidence, mark a significant shift in emphasis? Can Justice Harlan's opinions be viewed as the beginning of a "long-delayed vindication of Masses"? Consider Gunther's comment: "[Harlan] reinvigorated free speech protection in the post-Dennis years by exhibiting the best qualities of judicial craftsmanship so long associated with Learned Hand. Harlan found a way to curtail prosecutions under the Smith Act even though the constitutionality of the Act had been sustained in Dennis. He did it by invoking techniques very similar to those applied by Hand in Masses to the World War I Espionage Act: he read the statute in terms of constitutional presuppositions; and he strove to find standards 'manageable' by judges and capable of curbing jury discretion. He insisted on strict statutory standards of proof emphasizing the actual speech of the defendants—a variation on the 'hard,' 'objective,' words-oriented focus of Masses. Harlan claimed to be interpreting Dennis. In fact, Yates and Scales represented doctrinal evolution in a new direction, a direction in the Masses tradition." Gunther, "Learned Hand and the Origins of Modern First Amendment Doctrine," 27 Stan. L. Rev. 719 (1975).

6. *Other federal anti-Communist legislation of the 1950s.* The Subversive Activities Control Act of 1950 was an intricate scheme for registration and

disclosure to be administered by the Subversive Activities Control Board (SACB). In its first encounter with the statute, a divided Court sustained the basic legislative scheme and upheld a SACB order requiring the Communist Party to register with the Attorney General as a "Communist-action organization." COMMUNIST PARTY v. SACB, 367 U.S. 1 (1961). Justice FRANK-FURTER wrote for the Court that freedom of speech and of association did not prevent Congress "from requiring the registration and filing of information, including membership lists, by organizations substantially dominated or controlled by the foreign powers controlling the world Communist movement." The SACB order requiring the Communist Party to register was never implemented, however, as both the Party and several members successfully argued that registration would violate the privilege against self-incrimination because it could be used as a basis for prosecution under the Smith Act and other laws. See Communist Party v. United States, 331 F.2d 807 (D.C.Cir.1963), cert. denied, 377 U.S. 968 (1964); Albertson v. SACB, 332 F.2d 317 (D.C.Cir.1964), reversed, 382 U.S. 70 (1965).

The 1950 Act provided for various sanctions consequent upon a registration order. The Court struck down several of these sanctions. In APTHEKER v. SECRETARY OF STATE, 378 U.S. 500 (1964), the Court held "unconstitutional on its face" a provision providing for passport denials to members of the Communist Party because it "too broadly and indiscriminately restricts the right to travel and thereby abridges the liberty guaranteed by the Fifth Amendment." In UNITED STATES v. ROBEL, 389 U.S. 258 (1967), the Court likewise invalidated, as an infringement of the First Amendment right of association, a provision for denial of employment in any defense facility to members of the Communist Party. Both Aptheker and Robel emphasized the "overbreadth" of the provisions: they swept in both protected and unprotected speech or association. After this and other extensive litigation, the SACB was disbanded.

The Communist Control Act of 1954 likewise proved ineffectual. It provided that "the Communist Party should be outlawed," and that the Party was "not entitled to any of the rights, privileges, and immunities attendant upon legal bodies created under [the] laws of the United States or [any] subdivision thereof." In the only case involving the 1954 Act to reach the Court, the Justices construed the provision narrowly in order to avoid constitutional issues. Communist Party v. Catherwood, 367 U.S. 389 (1961).

The federal government also made efforts to stop the ingress of foreign communist doctrine. In LAMONT v. POSTMASTER GENERAL, 381 U.S. 301 (1965), the Court invalidated a 1962 law under which the Post Office screened foreign unsealed mail, detained "communist political propaganda," and notified the addressee that the mail would be destroyed unless the addressee requested delivery by returning a reply card. Justice Douglas' majority opinion relied on a First Amendment right to "receive information and ideas" and noted that the reply card requirement was "almost certain to have a deterrent effect" and imposed an impermissible affirmative obligation on the addressee. But see Kleindienst v. Mandel, 408 U.S. 753 (1972) (upholding a provision of the 1950 Act making foreign Communists ineligible to receive visas).

7. *Vietnam era cases.* Issues parallel to those in the World War I Espionage Act cases arose in connection with opposition to United States policy in the Vietnam war. In BOND v. FLOYD, 385 U.S. 116 (1966), the Court held that the First Amendment barred Georgia from refusing to seat Julian Bond, a duly elected representative, in the state legislature. The State's justification was that Bond could not conscientiously take the required oath to "support the

Constitution of this State and of the United States" in light of statements he had made or subscribed to that were critical of the draft and of Vietnam policy. Bond was an official of the Student Nonviolent Coordinating Committee (SNCC), which issued a statement that "We are in sympathy with, and support, the men in this country who are unwilling to respond to a military draft." Chief Justice WARREN's opinion for a unanimous Court held that Bond could not have been constitutionally convicted for counseling, aiding, or abetting the refusal or evasion of draft registration. The SNCC statement alone "cannot be interpreted as a call to unlawful refusal to be drafted." Nor could Bond's own statement that he admired the courage of people who burned their draft cards. "No useful purpose would be served by discussing the many decisions of this Court which establish that Bond could not have been convicted for these statements consistently with the First Amendment." And Bond's position as an elected legislator did not change the situation: "[W]hile the State has an interest in requiring its legislators to swear to a belief in constitutional processes of government, surely the oath gives it no interest in limiting its legislators' capacity to discuss their views of local or national policy."

In WATTS v. UNITED STATES, 394 U.S. 705 (1969), the Court reversed, per curiam, a conviction under a 1917 law making it a felony "knowingly and willfully" to make "any threat to take the life" of the President. Petitioner had said at a public rally: "Now I have already received my draft classification as 1–A and I have got to report for my physical this Monday coming. I am not going. If they ever make me carry a rifle, the first man I want to get in my sights is L.B.J. They are not going to make me kill my black brothers." The opinion stated: "What is a threat must be distinguished from what is constitutionally protected speech. [We] do not believe that the kind of political hyperbole indulged in by petitioner fits within that statutory term. [We] agree with petitioner that his only offense [was] 'a kind of very crude offensive method of stating a political opposition to the President.' Taken in context, and regarding the expressly conditional nature of the statement and the reaction of the listeners [laughter], we do not see how it could be interpreted otherwise." Why does Watts assume that true threats may be punished? Because they constitute clear and present danger? Because there is an overriding national interest in protecting the President from threats as well as from actual harm? Because threats against the President are not valuable "speech"?

D. THE MODERN INCITEMENT TEST

Brandenburg v. Ohio

395 U.S. 444, 89 S.Ct. 1827, 23 L.Ed.2d 430 (1969).

PER CURIAM.

The appellant, a leader of a Ku Klux Klan group, was convicted under the Ohio Criminal Syndicalism statute for "advocat[ing] the duty, necessity, or propriety of crime, sabotage, violence, or unlawful methods of terrorism as a means of accomplishing industrial or political reform" and for "voluntarily assembl[ing] with any society, group, or assemblage of persons formed to teach or advocate the doctrines of criminal syndicalism." He was fined $1,000 and sentenced to one to 10 years' imprisonment.

The record shows that a man, identified at trial as the appellant, telephoned an announcer-reporter on the staff of a Cincinnati television station and invited him to come to a Ku Klux Klan "rally" to be held at a [farm]. With the cooperation of the organizers, the reporter and a cameraman attended the meeting and filmed the events. Portions of the films were later broadcast on the local station and on a national network. The prosecution's case rested on the films and on testimony identifying the appellant as the person who communicated with the reporter and who spoke at the [rally]. One film showed 12 hooded figures, some of whom carried firearms. They were gathered around a large wooden cross, which they burned. No one was present other than the participants and the newsmen who made the film. Most of the words uttered during the scene were incomprehensible when the film was projected, but scattered phrases could be understood that were derogatory of Negroes and, in one instance, of Jews.[1] Another scene on the same film showed the appellant, in Klan regalia, making a speech. The speech, in full, was as follows: "This is an organizers' meeting. We have had quite a few members here today which are—we have hundreds, hundreds of members throughout [Ohio]. I can quote from a newspaper clipping from the Columbus, Ohio Dispatch, five weeks ago Sunday morning. The Klan has more members in [Ohio] than does any other organization. We're not a revengent organization, but if our President, our Congress, our Supreme Court, continues to suppress the white, Caucasian race, it's possible that there might have to be some revengeance taken. We are marching on Congress July the Fourth, four hundred thousand strong. From there we are dividing into two groups, one group to march on St. Augustine, Florida, the other group to march into Mississippi. Thank you." The second film showed six hooded figures one of whom, later identified as the appellant, repeated a speech very similar to that recorded on the first film. The reference to the possibility of "revengeance" was omitted, and one sentence was added: "Personally, I believe the nigger should be returned to Africa, the Jew returned to Israel." Though some of the figures in the films carried weapons, the speaker did not.

The Ohio [law] was enacted in 1919. From 1917 to 1920, identical or quite similar laws were adopted by 20 States and two territories. [In 1927,] this Court sustained the constitutionality of California's Criminal Syndicalism Act, the text of which is quite similar to that of the laws of Ohio. [Whitney.] The Court upheld the statute on the ground that, without more, "advocating" violent means to effect political and economic change involves such danger to the security of the State that the State may outlaw it. Cf. [Fiske v. Kansas]. But Whitney has been thoroughly discredited by later decisions. See [Dennis]. These later decisions have fashioned the principle that the constitutional guarantees of free speech and free press do not permit a State to forbid or proscribe advocacy of the use of force or of law violation except where such advocacy is directed to inciting or producing imminent lawless action and is

---

1. The significant portions that could be understood were:

"How far is the nigger going to—yeah."

"This is what we are going to do to the niggers."

"A dirty nigger."

"Send the Jews back to Israel."

"Let's give them back to the dark garden."

"Save America."

"Let's go back to constitutional betterment."

"Bury the niggers."

"We intend to do our part."

"Give us our state rights."

"Freedom for the whites."

"Nigger will have to fight for every inch he gets from now on." [Footnote by the Court.]

likely to incite or produce such action.[2] As we said in [Noto], "the mere abstract teaching [of] the moral propriety or even moral necessity for a resort to force and violence, is not the same as preparing a group for violent action and steeling it to such action." See also [Herndon v. Lowry]. A statute which fails to draw this distinction impermissibly intrudes upon the freedoms guaranteed by the First and 14th Amendments. It sweeps within its condemnation speech which our Constitution has immunized from governmental control. Cf. [Yates; De Jonge].

Measured by this test, Ohio's [law] cannot be sustained. The Act punishes persons who "advocate or teach the duty, necessity, or propriety" of violence "as a means of accomplishing industrial or political reform"; or who publish or circulate or display any book or paper containing such advocacy; or who "justify" the commission of violent acts "with intent to exemplify, spread or advocate the propriety of the doctrines of criminal syndicalism"; or who "voluntarily assemble" with a group formed "to teach or advocate the doctrines of criminal syndicalism." Neither the indictment nor the trial judge's instructions to the jury in any way refined the statute's bald definition of the crime in terms of mere advocacy not distinguished from incitement to imminent lawless action. Accordingly, we are here confronted with a statute which, by its own words and as applied, purports to punish mere advocacy and to forbid, on pain of criminal punishment, assembly with others merely to advocate the described type of action.[3] Such a statute falls within the condemnation of the First and 14th Amendments. The contrary teaching of [Whitney] cannot be supported, and that decision is therefore overruled.

Reversed.

Justice BLACK, concurring.

I agree with [Justice Douglas] that the "clear and present danger" doctrine should have no place in the interpretation of the First Amendment. I join the Court's opinion, which, as I understand it, simply cites [Dennis] but does not indicate any agreement [with] the "clear and present danger" doctrine on which Dennis purported to rely.

Justice DOUGLAS, concurring.

[Though] I doubt if the 'clear and present danger' test is congenial to the First Amendment in time of a declared war, I am certain it is not reconcilable with the First Amendment in days of peace. [I] see no place in the regime of the First Amendment for any 'clear and present danger' test, whether strict and tight as some would make it, or free-wheeling as the Court in Dennis rephrased it. When one reads the opinions closely and sees when and how the 'clear and present danger' test has been applied, great misgivings are aroused. First, the threats were often loud but always puny and made serious only by judges so wedded to the status quo that critical analysis made them nervous. Second, the

2. It was on the theory that the Smith Act embodied such a principle and that it had been applied only in conformity with it that this Court sustained the Act's constitutionality. [Dennis.] That this was the basis for Dennis was emphasized in [Yates], in which the Court overturned convictions for advocacy of the forcible overthrow of the Government under the Smith Act, because the trial judge's instructions had allowed conviction for mere advocacy, unrelated to its tendency to produce forcible action. [Footnote by the Court.]

3. Statutes affecting the right of assembly, like those touching on freedom of speech, must observe the established distinctions between mere advocacy and incitement to imminent lawless action, for as Chief Justice Hughes wrote in [De Jonge]: "The right of peaceable assembly is a right cognate to those of free speech and free press and is equally fundamental." [Footnote by the Court.]

test was so twisted and perverted in Dennis as to make the trial of those teachers of Marxism an all-out political trial which was part and parcel of the cold war that has eroded substantial parts of the First Amendment. [The] line between what is permissible and not subject to control and what may be made impermissible and subject to regulation is the line between ideas and overt acts. The example usually given by those who would punish speech is the case of one who falsely shouts fire in a crowded theatre. This is, however, a classic case where speech is brigaded with action.

THE IMPACT OF BRANDENBURG

1. *The best of Hand and Holmes?* To what extent does the Brandenburg standard change rather than restate First Amendment doctrine? Can Brandenburg be viewed as combining the most protective ingredients of Hand's incitement emphasis in Masses with the most useful elements of Holmes' clear and present danger heritage? Can Brandenburg be viewed as building on Yates and Scales to produce the Court's most speech-protective standard in this context? Consider the following comment: "The incitement emphasis is Hand's; the reference to 'imminent' reflects a limited influence of Holmes, combined with later experience; and 'the likely to incite or produce such action' addition in the Brandenburg standard is the only reference to the need to guess about future consequences of speech, so central to the Schenck approach. Under Brandenburg, probability of harm is no longer the central criterion for speech limitations. The inciting language of the speaker—the Hand focus on 'objective' words—is the major consideration. And punishment of the harmless inciter is prevented by the Schenck-derived requirement of a likelihood of dangerous consequences." Gunther, "Learned Hand and the Origins of Modern First Amendment Doctrine," 27 Stan. L. Rev. 719 (1975).

2. *Later applications of Brandenburg.* The Brandenburg standard was the primary ground for reversal of a disorderly conduct conviction in HESS v. INDIANA, 414 U.S. 105 (1973). After a campus anti-war demonstration during which there had been arrests, over 100 demonstrators blocked the street until they were moved to the curb by the police. Hess, standing off the street, said: "We'll take the fucking street later (or again)." The state court relied primarily on a finding that this statement was "intended to incite further lawless action on the part of the crowd in the vicinity of appellant and was likely to produce such action." The Court summarily reversed: "At best, [the] statement could be taken as counsel for present moderation; at worst, it amounted to nothing more than advocacy of illegal action at some indefinite future time." The Court added that "since there was no evidence, or rational inference from the import of the language, that his words were intended to produce, and likely to produce, *imminent* disorder, those words could not be punished by the State on the ground that they had 'a tendency to lead to violence.' "

In NAACP v. CLAIBORNE HARDWARE CO., 458 U.S. 886 (1982) the Court set aside, on First Amendment grounds, a large damage award against alleged participants in an economic boycott by black citizens of white merchants in a Mississippi county. The boycott sought to secure compliance with a list of demands for racial justice. One of the defendants was Charles Evers, the Field Secretary of the NAACP, who took a leading role in the boycott. One of the arguments advanced to defend the imposition of liability on Evers was that "a finding that his public speeches were likely to incite lawless action could justify holding him liable for unlawful conduct that in fact followed within a reasonable period." In one speech, Evers had stated that boycott violators would be "disciplined" by their own people. Justice STEVENS' opinion rejected the incitement rationale for imposing liability on Evers:

"While many of the comments in Evers' speeches might have contemplated 'discipline' in the permissible form of social ostracism, it cannot be denied that references [e.g.] to the possibility that necks would be [broken] implicitly conveyed a sterner message. In the passionate atmosphere in which the speeches were delivered, they might have been understood as inviting an unlawful form of discipline or, at least, as intending to create a fear of violence whether or not improper discipline was specifically intended. [This] Court has made clear, however, that mere *advocacy* of the use of force or violence does not remove speech from the protection of the First Amendment. [The] emotionally charged rhetoric of Charles Evers' speeches did not transcend the bounds of protected speech set forth in Brandenburg. The lengthy addresses generally contained an impassioned plea for black citizens to unify, to support and respect each other, and to realize the political and economic power available to them. In the course of those pleas, strong language was used. If that language had been followed by acts of violence, a substantial question would be presented whether Evers could be held liable for the consequences of that unlawful conduct. In this case, however, [almost all] acts of violence identified in 1966 occurred weeks or months after the April 1, 1966 speech; the chancellor made no finding of any violence after the challenged 1969 speech. [When an advocate's] appeals do not incite lawless action, they must be regarded as protected speech."

3. *The scope of Brandenburg.* The "incitement" and "advocacy" language of Brandenburg describes speech that in some way *urges* people to action. Does Brandenburg apply as well to the communication of *information* that may lead to criminal acts, such as instructions for manufacturing illegal drugs, a manual on how to be a "hit man," plans for the security system at Fort Knox, or information allegedly endangering national security because it relates to the construction of illegal (in private hands) bombs or weapons? Do the dangers involved in the dissemination of this type of information fit the Brandenburg model? Does the relevance of Brandenburg turn at least on the presence of some "political" component in the information? Is the incitement deemed punishable by Brandenburg limited to face-to-face encounters? Can lawless action be directed over television, radio, cable or the internet? Does use of such communications media preclude a finding of imminence?

Does Brandenburg have any application to speech facilitating purely private, interpersonal crimes, apart from any ideological context? Consider the definition of criminal solicitation in the ALI Model Penal Code, § 5.02(1): "A person is guilty of solicitation to commit a crime if with the purpose of promoting or facilitating its commission he commands, encourages, or requests another person to engage in specific conduct which would constitute such crime or an attempt to commit such crime or which would establish his complicity in its commission or attempted commission." See also the definitions of attempt and conspiracy in Model Penal Code §§ 5.01(1)(c) and 5.03(1). See generally Greenawalt, "Speech and Crime," 1980 A.B.F.Res.J. 645.

4. *Deference to legislative determinations of the dangerousness of speech.* Note that Brandenburg, in overruling Whitney, rejected the notion that a legislature may conclusively presume an entire category of speech dangerous without regard to individual context and circumstances. Compare LANDMARK COMMUNICATIONS, INC. v. VIRGINIA, 435 U.S. 829 (1978), which held that a criminal statute barring accurate disclosure of information about confidential proceedings before a Judicial Inquiry Commission could not constitutionally be applied to "third persons who are strangers to the inquiry, including news

media." Chief Justice BURGER's opinion rejected the state court's reliance on the legislature's explicit finding "that a clear and present danger to the orderly administration of justice would be created by divulgence of the confidential proceedings of the Commission": "Deference to a legislative finding cannot limit judicial inquiry when First Amendment rights are at stake. [A legislative declaration] does not preclude [judicial] enquiry into the question whether, at the time and under the circumstances, the conditions existed which are essential to validity under the [Constitution]. Were it otherwise, the scope of freedom of speech and of the press would be subject to legislative definition and the function of the First Amendment as a check on legislative power would be nullified."

SECTION 3. FIGHTING WORDS AND HOSTILE AUDIENCES

Introduction. Like the cases just covered in section 1, the cases that follow involve the problem of speech that induces violence or potential violence on the part of listeners. But here the violence or is directed against the speaker rather than undertaken in sympathy with the speaker's cause. The typical claim is that a speaker's provocative message so outrages the audience that some listeners are likely to resort to violence in response. The state seeks to stop the speaker in order to promote the interest in assuring order and avoiding violence. The problem has arisen both in the context of one-on-one encounters between individuals, which has given rise to the doctrine of "fighting words," and in the context of encounters between speakers and hostile audiences, which has given rise to judicial concern over the problem of the "heckler's veto."

Does the apprehension of hostile listener reaction justify restricting the speaker? Should speakers be punished for provoking listeners to punch or want to punch them in the nose? Only if the speaker uses extremely provocative words? Even if the audience is very easily provoked? Does the First Amendment impose an obligation on the government to protect the speaker from the violent listener or the angry crowd? Or may government stop the speaker, simply by showing that his words created an immediate danger of disorder? Would recognition of that justification legitimate a "heckler's veto"? Assuming that law enforcement's capacity to prevent violent listener reaction will never be perfect, must society tolerate occasional brawls as a price of free speech?

———

A. FIGHTING WORDS

———

Contrast the outcomes in the following pair of cases, each involving a proselytizing Jehovah's Witness who caused offense and anger in an audience on the public streets.

1. *The Cantwell decision.* Jesse Cantwell, a Jehovah's Witness, was arrested while proselytizing on the streets of New Haven, Connecticut, and convicted of the common law offense of inciting a breach of the peace. In CANTWELL v. CONNECTICUT, 310 U.S. 296 (1940), the Court, invalidated the conviction. Justice ROBERTS wrote for the Court: "[We] must determine whether the alleged protection of the State's interest [in 'peace and good order'] has been pressed, in this instance, to a point where it has come into fatal collision with the overriding interest [in the First Amendment] protected by the federal compact. [No] one would have the hardihood to suggest that the principle of freedom of speech sanctions incitement to riot or that religious

liberty connotes the privilege to exhort others to physical attack upon those belonging to another sect. When clear and present danger of riot, disorder, interference with traffic upon the public streets, or other immediate threat to public safety, peace, or order appears, the power of the State to prevent or punish is obvious. Equally obvious is it that a State may not unduly suppress free communication of views, religious or other, under the guise of conserving desirable conditions.

"[Having] these considerations in mind, we note that Jesse Cantwell, on April 26, 1938, was upon a public street, where he had a right to be, and where he had a right peacefully to impart his views to others. There is no showing that his deportment was noisy, truculent, overbearing or offensive. [It] is not claimed that he intended to insult or affront the hearers by playing the record. It is plain that he wished only to interest them in his propaganda. The sound of the phonograph is not shown to have disturbed residents of the street, to have drawn a crowd, or to have impeded traffic. Thus far he had invaded no right or interest of the public or of the men accosted.

"The record played by Cantwell embodies a general attack on all organized religious systems as instruments of Satan and injurious to man; it then singles out the Roman Catholic Church for strictures couched in terms which naturally would offend not only persons of that persuasion, but all others who respect the honestly held religious faith of their fellows. The hearers were in fact highly offended. One of them said he felt like hitting Cantwell and the other that he was tempted to throw Cantwell off the street. The one who testified he felt like hitting Cantwell said, in answer to the question 'Did you do anything else or have any other reaction?' 'No, sir, because he said he would take the victrola and he went.' The other witness testified that he told Cantwell he had better get off the street before something happened to him and that was the end of the matter as Cantwell picked up his books and walked up the street. Cantwell's conduct, in the view of the court below, considered apart from the effect of his communication upon his hearers, did not amount to a breach of the peace. One may, however, be guilty of the offense if he commit acts or make statements likely to provoke violence and disturbance of good order, even though no such eventuality be intended. [But in practically all such cases], the provocative language which was held to amount to a breach of the peace consisted of profane, indecent, or abusive remarks directed to the person of the hearer. Resort to epithets or personal abuse is not in any proper sense communication of information or opinion safeguarded by the [Constitution].

"We find in the instant case no assault or threatening of bodily harm, no truculent bearing, no intentional discourtesy, no personal abuse. On the contrary, we find only an effort to persuade a willing listener to buy a book or to contribute money in the interest of what Cantwell, however misguided others may think him, conceived to be true religion. [Although] the contents of the record not unnaturally aroused animosity, we think that, in the absence of a statute narrowly drawn to define and punish specific conduct as constituting a clear and present danger to a substantial interest of the State, the petitioner's communication, considered in the light of the constitutional guarantees, raised no such clear and present menace to public peace and order as to render him liable to conviction of the common law offense [in question]."

2. *The Chaplinsky decision.* The brief opinion in CHAPLINSKY v. NEW HAMPSHIRE, 315 U.S. 568 (1942), in contrast, unanimously upheld a conviction under a state law stating that no person "shall address any offensive, derisive or annoying word to any other person who is lawfully in any street or other public place, nor call him by any offensive or derisive name." The state

court interpreted the law to ban words that "men of common intelligence would understand would be words likely to cause an average addressee to fight"—"face-to-face words plainly likely to cause a breach of the peace by the addressee, words whose speaking constitute a breach of the peace by the speaker." Chaplinsky, a Jehovah's Witness engaged in distributing literature on the streets of Rochester, New Hampshire, had allegedly attracted a "restless" crowd by denouncing all religion as a "racket." When a disturbance broke out, a police officer escorted Chaplinsky away. The police officer and Chaplinsky encountered the City Marshal. Chaplinsky claimed that he asked the Marshal to arrest the ones responsible for the disturbance. The Marshal insisted that he merely told Chaplinsky that the crowd had gotten restless. In the ensuing argument between Chaplinsky and the City Marshal, Chaplinsky called the Marshal a "God damned racketeer" and "a damned Fascist" (and added that "the whole government of Rochester are Fascists or agents of Fascists"). The conviction was based on using these words to the Marshal.

Justice MURPHY's opinion found it obvious that "the appellations 'damned racketeer' and 'damned Fascist' are epithets likely to provoke the average person to retaliation, and thereby cause a breach of the peace." In his most important passage, Justice Murphy stated more generally: "[It] is well understood that the right of free speech is not absolute at all times and under all circumstances. There are certain well-defined and narrowly limited classes of speech, the prevention and punishment of which have never been thought to raise any Constitutional problem. These include the lewd and obscene, the profane, the libelous, and the insulting or 'fighting' words—those which by their very utterance inflict injury or tend to incite an immediate breach of the peace. It has been well observed that such utterances are no essential part of any exposition of ideas, and are of such slight social value as a step to truth that any benefit that may be derived from them is clearly outweighed by the social interest in order and morality. 'Resort to epithets or personal abuse is not in any proper sense communication of information or opinion safeguarded by the [Constitution].' Cantwell."

3. *The Court's methodology in excluding "fighting words" from First Amendment protection.* The Chaplinsky opinion has elements of both categorization and balancing. In describing "fighting words" as one of the "classes of speech, the prevention and punishment of which have never been thought to raise any Constitutional problem," it categorizes such speech as wholly outside of First Amendment coverage. But Justice Murphy also engages in balancing: he attaches a low value to the speech claiming protection ("no essential part of any exposition of ideas"; "slight social value as a step to truth"), and measures that weak variety of "speech" against the competing state interests ("any benefit that may be derived [is] clearly outweighed by the social interest in order and morality"). Such balancing takes place, however, not case by case, but rather at the general, wholesale or definitional level, producing a total exclusion of a class of speech from First Amendment coverage and avoiding any more particularized inquiry.

4. *The contemporary vitality of the "fighting words" exception.* The Court has never overruled Chaplinsky's holding that "fighting words" are excluded from free speech protection, but it has not sustained a conviction on the basis of the fighting words doctrine since Chaplinsky. Does this mean that the fighting words doctrine is "nothing more than a quaint remnant of an earlier morality that has no place in a democratic society dedicated to the principle of free expression"? Gard, "Fighting Words as Free Speech," 58 Wash. U.L.Q. 531, 535–36 (1980). For a contrary view, see Greenawalt, "Insults and Epithets, Are They Protected Speech?" 42 Rutgers L. Rev. 287 (1990) (arguing that

fighting words should not be protected because they are intended to inflict harm rather than communicate ideas).

In GOODING v. WILSON, 405 U.S. 518 (1972), the Court reversed a conviction under a Georgia statute providing that any person "who shall, without provocation, use to or of [another], opprobrious words or abusive language, tending to cause a breach of the peace," was guilty of a misdemeanor. Anti-war picketers at an Army building refused a police request to stop blocking access to inductees. In the ensuing scuffle, appellee said to a police officer, "White son of a bitch, I'll kill you," "You son of a bitch, I'll choke you to death," and "You son of a bitch, if you ever put your hands on me again, I'll cut you all to pieces." Justice BRENNAN's majority opinion found that statute void on its face because it swept in protected speech ranging beyond the "fighting words" punishable under Chaplinsky. Justice Brennan replied: "We have [made] our own examination of the Georgia cases [and conclude that] Georgia appellate decisions have not construed [the statute] to be limited in application, as in Chaplinsky, to words that 'have a direct tendency to cause acts of violence by the person to whom, individually, the remark is addressed.' "

In ROSENFELD v. NEW JERSEY, LEWIS v. NEW ORLEANS, and BROWN v. OKLAHOMA, reported at 408 U.S. 901, 913, and 914 (1972), the majority summarily vacated three convictions for use of offensive language and remanded for reconsideration in light of Gooding. Rosenfeld had addressed a school board meeting attended by about 150 people, including about 40 children, and had "used the adjective 'm[other] f[ucking]' on four occasions, to describe the teachers, the school board, the town and his own country." He was convicted under a "disorderly person" statute prohibiting "indecent" and "offensive" language in public places and interpreted to cover words "of such a nature as to be likely to incite the hearer to an immediate breach of the peace or to be likely, in the light of the gender and age of the listener and the setting of the utterance, to affect the sensibilities of a hearer." Lewis had addressed police officers who were arresting her son as "g[od] d[amn] m[other] f[uckers]." She was convicted under a breach of the peace statute prohibiting anyone from wantonly cursing, reviling, or using "obscene or opprobrious language" toward a police officer on duty. Brown, in a meeting at a university chapel, had referred to some policemen as "m[other] f[ucking] fascist pig cops" and to a particular policeman as that "black m[other] f[ucking] pig." He was convicted under a statute barring "any obscene or lascivious language or word in any public place, or in the presence of females."

Chief Justice BURGER and Justices Blackmun and Rehnquist dissented in all three cases and Justice Powell dissented in Rosenfeld. Chief Justice Burger stated: "When we undermine the general belief that the law will give protection against fighting words and profane and abusive language such as the utterances involved in these cases, we take steps to return to the law of the jungle." In a case like Rosenfeld, there might not be instantaneous retaliation, but it was imaginable that "some justifiably outraged parent whose family were exposed to the foul mouthings of the speaker would 'meet him outside' [and] resort to the 19th Century's vigorous modes of dealing with such people." Justice REHNQUIST insisted that Lewis' words were "fighting words," and that the words in the other two cases were "lewd and obscene" and "profane" in the Chaplinsky sense.

Should it matter that Lewis, like Chaplinsky, addressed her epithets to a law enforcement officer? Should a speaker be freer to insult such an officer than to insult an "average addressee"? Consider Justice Powell's concurrence in Lewis: while assuming that Lewis' epithet would amount to proscribable fighting words if addressed to the average citizen, he noted that "the situation may be different where such words are addressed to a police officers trained to exercise a higher degree of restraint than the average citizen."

5. *The limitation of the "fighting words" exception to words that "tend to incite an immediate breach of the peace."* Justice Murphy's opinion in Chaplinsky defined fighting words as *either* those "which by their very utterance inflict injury" *or* those which "tend to incite an immediate breach of the peace." He also suggested that their suppression was justified by the social interest in "order *and* morality." Later cases, however, have focused only on the breach-of-peace and order rationales. As John Ely put it, later cases made clear that the "fighting words" exception "was no longer to be understood as a euphemism for controversial or dirty talk but was to require instead a quite unambiguous invitation to a brawl." Ely, Democracy and Distrust 114 (1980). Later cases have also tended to limit fighting words to those directed face-to-face to an individual, rather than generally at a group. See Terminiello v. Chicago, p. 1085 below, which reversed the breach-of-peace conviction of a speaker who had condemned an angry crowd outside the auditorium as "snakes," "slimy snakes," "slimy scum."

For example, in TEXAS v. JOHNSON, 491 U.S. 397 (1989), the Court invalidated on free speech grounds the conviction of a political protestor who burned an American flag. The statute under which he was convicted prohibited desecration of a flag in a manner the defendant "knows will seriously offend one or more persons likely to observe or discover [such] action." The Court rejected the government's argument that Johnson's conduct fell within the exception for fighting words as defined in Chaplinsky. Justice BRENNAN wrote for the Court: "No reasonable onlooker would have regarded Johnson's generalized expression of dissatisfaction with the policies of the Federal Government as a direct personal insult or an invitation to exchange fisticuffs. We thus conclude that the State's interest in maintaining order is not implicated on these facts."

Has the Court erred since Chaplinsky by failing to reiterate that words may be proscribed if they "by their very utterance inflict injury"? Does the "fighting words" exception as narrowed to words that cause breaches of the peace give too much protection to listeners who respond to provocation by fighting? Does it wrongly reinforce the macho code of barroom brawls? Does it give too little protection to those who respond to insulting epithets by flight rather than fight? Does it permit greater insult to be leveled at the average woman than the average man? Or is the determination of what words would cause the "average addressee to fight" an objective and gender-neutral one? Would it be constitutional to outlaw "street harassment," defined as occurring when a man addresses to a woman in a public place unwelcome "references to male or female genitalia or to female body parts or to sexual activities, solicitation of sex, [or] similar words that by their very utterance inflict injury or naturally tend to provoke violent resentment, even if the woman did not herself react with violence"? See Bowman, "Street Harassment and the Informal Ghettoization of Women," 106 Harv. L. Rev. 517, 575 (1993).

The limits of Chaplinsky became especially clear with the Court's 1971 decision in Cohen v. California, a decision reversing the breach-of-the-peace conviction of a war protestor who wore in public a jacket emblazoned "Fuck the Draft." First, Chaplinsky had included "the lewd" and "the profane" as categories of speech not entitled to First Amendment protection. Cohen made clear, however, that profanity was at least sometimes protected speech, as did Rosenfeld, Lewis, and Brown a year later. Second, Cohen reiterated that the fighting words exception is limited to statements "directed to the person of the hearer," not addressed generally to the world at large. Third, Cohen undermined the notion that there is any unprotected category of "words that by their very utterance inflict injury." It emphasized the emotive power of words and suggested that preventing psychic offense was not, at least in this case, a sufficient justification for punishing speech.

————

Cohen v. California

403 U.S. 15, 91 S.Ct. 1780, 29 L.Ed.2d 284 (1971).

Justice HARLAN delivered the opinion of the Court.

This case may seem at first blush too inconsequential to find its way into our books, but the issue it presents is of no small constitutional significance. [Cohen] was convicted [of violating a California law] which prohibits "maliciously and willfully disturb[ing] the peace or quiet of any neighborhood or person [by] offensive conduct." He was given 30 days' imprisonment. The facts upon which his conviction rests are detailed in the opinion of the [state court] "On April 26, 1968, the defendant was observed in the Los Angeles County Courthouse in the corridor outside [of] the Municipal Court wearing a jacket bearing the words 'Fuck the Draft.' [There] were women and children present in the corridor. The defendant was arrested. The defendant testified that he wore the jacket as a means of informing the public of the depth of his feelings against the Vietnam War and the draft. The defendant did not engage in, nor threaten to engage in, nor did anyone as the result of his conduct in fact commit or threaten to commit any act of violence." In affirming the conviction the [state court] held that "offensive conduct" means "behavior which has a tendency to provoke *others* to acts of violence or to in turn disturb the peace," and that the State had proved this element because, on the facts of this case, "[i]t was certainly reasonably foreseeable that such conduct might cause others to rise up to commit a violent act against the person of the defendant or attempt to forceably remove his jacket." [We reverse.]

I. In order to lay hands on the precise issue which this case involves, it is useful first to canvass various matters which this record does *not* present. The conviction quite clearly rests upon the asserted offensiveness of the *words* Cohen used to convey his message to the public. The only "conduct" which the State sought to punish is the fact of communication. Thus, we deal here with a conviction resting solely upon "speech," not upon any separately identifiable conduct which allegedly was intended by Cohen to be perceived by others as expressive of particular views but which, on its face, does not necessarily convey any message and hence arguably could be regulated without effectively repressing Cohen's ability to express himself. Cf. [United States v. O'Brien]. Further, the State certainly lacks power to punish Cohen for the underlying content of the message the inscription conveyed. At least so long as there is no showing of an intent to incite disobedience to or disruption of the draft, Cohen [could not] be punished for asserting the evident position on the inutility or immorality of the draft his jacket reflected. [Yates.] [Cohen's] conviction, then, rests squarely upon his exercise of the "freedom of speech" [and] can be justified, if at all, only as a valid regulation of the manner in which he exercised that freedom, not as a permissible prohibition on the substantive message it conveys. This does not end the inquiry, of course, for the [First Amendment has] never been thought to give absolute protection to every individual to speak whenever or wherever he pleases, or to use any form of address in any circumstances that he chooses. In this vein, too, however, we think it important to note that several issues typically associated with such problems are not presented here.

In the first place, Cohen was tried under a statute applicable throughout the entire State. Any attempt to support this conviction on the ground that the statute seeks to preserve an appropriately decorous atmosphere in the courthouse where Cohen was arrested must fail in the absence of any language in the statute that would have put appellant on notice that certain kinds of otherwise permissible speech or conduct would nevertheless [not] be tolerated in certain places. No fair reading of the phrase "offensive conduct" can be said sufficiently to inform the ordinary person that distinctions between certain locations are thereby created.

In the second place, as it comes to us, this case cannot be said to fall within those relatively few categories of instances where prior decisions have established the power of government to deal more comprehensively with certain forms of individual expression simply upon a showing that such a form was employed. This is not, for example, an obscenity case. Whatever else may be necessary to give rise to the States' broader power to prohibit obscene expression, such expression must be, in some significant way, erotic. [Roth.] It cannot plausibly be maintained that this vulgar allusion to the [draft] would conjure up such psychic stimulation in anyone likely to be confronted with Cohen's crudely defaced jacket.

This Court has also held that the States are free to ban the simple use, without a demonstration of additional justifying circumstances, of so-called "fighting words," those personally abusive epithets which, when addressed to the ordinary citizen, are, as a matter of common knowledge, inherently likely to provoke violent reaction. [Chaplinsky.] While the four-letter word displayed by Cohen in relation to the draft is not uncommonly employed in a personally provocative fashion, in this instance it was clearly not "directed to the person of the hearer." No individual actually or likely to be present could reasonably have regarded the words on appellant's jacket as a direct personal insult. Nor do we have here an instance of the exercise of the State's police power to prevent a speaker from intentionally provoking a given group to hostile reaction. Cf. [Feiner; below]. There is, as noted above, no showing that anyone who saw Cohen was in fact violently aroused or that [Cohen] intended such a result.

Finally, [much] has been made of the claim that Cohen's distasteful mode of expression was thrust upon unwilling or unsuspecting viewers, and that the State might therefore legitimately act as it did in order to protect the sensitive from otherwise unavoidable exposure to appellant's crude form of protest. Of course, the mere presumed presence of unwilling listeners or viewers does not serve automatically to justify curtailing all speech capable of giving offense. While this Court has recognized that government may properly act in many situations to prohibit intrusion into the privacy of the home of unwelcome views and ideas which cannot be totally banned from the public dialogue, we have at the same time consistently stressed that "we are often 'captives' outside the sanctuary of the home and subject to objectionable speech." [Rowan, p. 1169 below.] The ability of government, consonant with the Constitution, to shut off discourse solely to protect others from hearing it is, in other words, dependent upon a showing that substantial privacy interests are being invaded in an essentially intolerable manner. Any broader view of this authority would effectively empower a majority to silence dissidents simply as a matter of personal predilections.

In this regard, persons confronted with Cohen's jacket were in a quite different posture than, say, those subjected to the raucous emissions of sound trucks blaring outside their residences. Those in the Los Angeles courthouse could effectively avoid further bombardment of their sensibilities simply by averting their eyes. And, while it may be that one has a more substantial claim to a recognizable privacy interest when walking through a courthouse corridor than, for example, strolling through Central Park, surely it is nothing like the interest in being free from unwanted expression in the confines of one's own home. Given the subtlety and complexity of the factors involved, if Cohen's "speech" was otherwise entitled to constitutional protection, we do not think the fact that some unwilling "listeners" in a public building may have been briefly exposed to it can serve to justify this breach of the peace conviction where, as here, there was no evidence that persons powerless to avoid appellant's conduct did in fact object to it, and where [the statute] evinces no concern [with] the special plight of the captive auditor, but, instead, indiscriminately sweeps within its prohibitions all "offensive conduct" that disturbs "any neighborhood or person."

II. Against this background, the issue flushed by this case stands out in bold relief. It is whether California can excise, as "offensive conduct," one particular scurrilous epithet from the public discourse, either upon the theory of the court below that its use is inherently likely to cause violent reaction or upon a more general assertion that the States, acting as guardians of public morality, may properly remove this offensive word from the public vocabulary. The rationale of the California court is plainly untenable. At most it reflects an "undifferentiated fear or apprehension of disturbance [which] is not enough to overcome the right to freedom of expression." [Tinker, p. 1293 below.] We have been shown no evidence that substantial numbers of citizens are standing ready to strike out physically at whoever may assault their sensibilities with execrations like that uttered by Cohen. There may be some persons about with such lawless and violent proclivities, but that is an insufficient base upon which to erect, consistently with constitutional values, a governmental power to force persons who wish to ventilate their dissident views into avoiding particular forms of expression. The argument amounts to little more than the self-defeating proposition that to avoid physical censorship of one who has not sought to provoke such a response by a hypothetical coterie of the violent and lawless, the States may more appropriately effectuate that censorship themselves.

Admittedly, it is not so obvious that the [First Amendment] must be taken to disable the States from punishing public utterance of this unseemly expletive in order to maintain what they regard as a suitable level of discourse within the body politic. We think, however, that examination and reflection will reveal the shortcomings of a contrary viewpoint. At the outset, we cannot overemphasize that, in our judgment, most situations where the State has a justifiable interest in regulating speech will fall within one or more of the various established exceptions, discussed above but not applicable here, to the usual rule that governmental bodies may not prescribe the form or content of individual expression. Equally important to our conclusion is the constitutional backdrop against which our decision must be made. The constitutional right of free expression is powerful medicine in a society as diverse and populous as ours. It is designed and intended to remove governmental restraints from the arena of public discussion, putting the decision as to what views shall be voiced largely into the hands of each of us, in the hope that use of such freedom will ultimately produce a more capable citizenry and more perfect polity and in the belief that no other approach would comport with the premise of individual dignity and choice upon which our political system rests. See [Whitney concurrence].

To many, the immediate consequence of this freedom may often appear to be only verbal tumult, discord, and even offensive utterance. These are, however, within established limits, in truth necessary side effects of the broader enduring values which the process of open debate permits us to achieve. That the air may at times seem filled with verbal cacophony is, in this sense, not a sign of weakness but of strength. We cannot lose sight of the fact that, in what otherwise might seem a trifling and annoying instance of individual distasteful abuse of a privilege, these fundamental societal values are truly [implicated].

Against this perception of the constitutional policies involved, we discern certain more particularized considerations that peculiarly call for reversal of this conviction. First, the principle contended for by the State seems inherently boundless. How is one to distinguish this from any other offensive word? Surely the State has no right to cleanse public debate to the point where it is grammatically palatable to the most squeamish among us. Yet no readily ascertainable general principle exists for stopping short of that result were we to affirm the judgment below. For, while the particular four-letter word being litigated here is perhaps more distasteful than most others of its genre, it is nevertheless often true that one man's vulgarity is another's lyric. Indeed, we think it is largely because governmental officials cannot make principled distinctions in this area that the Constitution leaves matters of taste and style so largely to the individual.

Additionally, we cannot overlook the fact, because it is well illustrated by the episode involved here, that much linguistic expression serves a dual communicative function: it conveys not only ideas capable of relatively precise, detached explication, but otherwise inexpressible emotions as well. In fact, words are often chosen as much for their emotive as their cognitive force. We cannot sanction the view that the Constitution, while solicitous of the cognitive content of individual speech, has little or no regard for that emotive function which, practically speaking, may often be the more important element of the overall message sought to be [communicated]. Finally, and in the same vein, we cannot indulge the facile assumption that one can forbid particular words without also running a substantial risk of suppressing ideas in the process. Indeed, governments might soon seize upon the censorship of particular words as a convenient guise for banning the expression of unpopular views. [It] is, in sum, our judgment that, absent a more particularized and compelling reason for its actions, the State may not, consistently with the [First Amendment], make the simple public display here involved of this single four-letter expletive a [criminal offense].

Reversed.

Justice BLACKMUN, with whom Chief Justice [BURGER] and Justice BLACK join.

I dissent, and I do so for two reasons: 1. Cohen's absurd and immature antic, in my view, was mainly conduct and little speech. Further, the case appears to me to be well within the sphere of [Chaplinsky]. As a consequence, this Court's agonizing over First Amendment values seems misplaced and unnecessary. [Justice White dissented on other grounds.]

The Court's methodology in Cohen. Some commentators view Cohen as abandoning the categorization approach employed in Chaplinsky in favor of a balancing approach that seeks to identify the First Amendment values inherent in the communication and to articulate and evaluate the state interests allegedly justifying restraint. For the view that Cohen is a model speech-protective balancing opinion, see Gunther, "[The] Case of Justice Powell," 24 Stan.L.Rev. 1001 (1972); Rutzick, "Offensive Language and The Evolution of First Amendment Protection," 9 Harv.C.R.–C.L.Rev. 1 (1974) (noting that the "reformulated balancing model enunciated by the Court in Cohen and Gooding is substantially more sensitive to the demands of free speech than was the original Chaplinsky model" because it "recognizes the social value in the communication of emotions" and gives "some weight to personal value in the act of expression itself"). See also Farber, "Civilizing Public Discourse: [The] Enduring Significance of Cohen v. California," 1980 Duke L.J. 283; Cohen, "A Look Back at Cohen v. California," 34 UCLA L.Rev. 1595 (1987). Other commentators see Cohen in part as a speech-protective use of the categorization approach. See Ely, "Flag Desecration: A Case Study in the Roles of Categorization and Balancing in First Amendment Analysis," 88 Harv.L.Rev. 1482 (1975) ("in Cohen, [the] Court employed [the] categorization approach it had adopted in Brandenburg," for, with "little trace of balancing," it limited the unprotected category of "fighting words" to "an unambiguous invitation to a brawl"). For criticism of Cohen, see Bickel, The Morality of Consent (1975) (arguing that the "speech" involved in Cohen "constitutes an assault"), Berns, The First Amendment and the Future of American Democracy (1976) (arguing that "not all speech contributes to a 'more perfect polity,'" and that "protecting the conventions of decency" should be permissible), and Cox, The Role of the Supreme Court in American Government (1976) ("extending the protection of the First Amendment to sheer vulgarity, useful only in its ability to shock, [may] give the vulgarities an imprimatur which contributes to the lowering of public discourse").

B. HOSTILE AUDIENCES

The hostile audience cases that follow are similar to the fighting words cases in that they involve speech that provokes unsympathetic listeners to violence or threats of violence. But they differ in two respects. First, fighting words are treated as offensive because of the form their message takes; Chaplinsky would not likely have been convicted if he had said, "with all due respect, I find the incumbent government less than honorable." Hostile audience cases arise when an audience is provoked either by the form of the message or by the message itself. Second, and in part because it is not the form of speech that is pivotal, the hostile audience decisions have addressed the problem through balancing rather than categorization.

Do the "heckler's veto" cases that follow give adequate weight to the First Amendment interests of the abrasive speaker in the public forum, or do they give undue weight to audience reactions as justifications for curtailment of speech? Does the First Amendment impose responsibility on the state to restrain the hostile audience, or does the speaker bear the risk of having his provocative words stopped by the hecklers' response? By what standards can the competing interests best be reconciled? By what mechanisms? Subsequent punishment? Permit systems? Protective custody but not punishment of the speaker in violent situations?

1. *Terminiello and "provocative" speech which "invites dispute."* In TERMINIELLO v. CHICAGO, 337 U.S. 1 (1949), the Court reversed the breach of

the peace conviction of an abrasive speaker, but on the basis of an improper charge to the jury and without directly reaching the "hostile audience" issue. The speaker viciously denounced various political and racial groups; outside the auditorium, an angry crowd gathered; the speaker then condemned the crowd as "snakes," "slimy scum," etc. After the disturbance, he was convicted under a breach of the peace statute construed by the trial judge to include speech which "stirs the public to anger, invites dispute, brings about a condition of unrest, or creates a disturbance." Justice DOUGLAS' majority opinion found that standard unconstitutional: "[A] function of free speech under our system of government is to invite dispute. It may indeed best serve its high purpose when it induces a condition of unrest, creates dissatisfaction with conditions as they are, or even stirs people to anger. Speech is often provocative and challenging. It may strike at prejudices and preconceptions and have profound unsettling effects as it presses for acceptance of an idea. That is why freedom of speech, though not absolute [Chaplinsky], is nevertheless protected against censorship or punishment, unless shown likely to produce a clear and present danger of a serious substantive evil that rises far above public inconvenience, annoyance, or unrest."

2. *The Feiner problem: Focus on protected words or on audience context?* To what extent should protection of speech turn on the response of the particular audience? To what extent should it turn on the words and content of the speech? Can the Court delineate the protected area by stating, e.g., that words short of "fighting words" are protected, no matter what their probable impact? Or must the boundaries of protection depend on the context and environment?

————

Feiner v. New York

340 U.S. 315, 71 S.Ct. 303, 95 L.Ed. 295 (1951).

[Feiner's disorderly conduct conviction stemmed from the following circumstances: In March 1949, Feiner addressed a crowd of 75 to 80 persons, black and white, on a street corner in a predominantly black residential section of Syracuse, N.Y. Soon after he began, two policemen, summoned by a telephone complaint, arrived to investigate. They found the crowd filling the sidewalk and spreading into the street. In the course of Feiner's speech urging his listeners to attend a meeting of the Young Progressives of America at a hotel that evening, he protested the cancellation of a permit to hold the meeting in a public school and made derogatory remarks about President Truman and the Mayor of Syracuse (calling them both "bums") and about the American Legion ("a Nazi Gestapo"). He also said: "The Negroes don't have equal rights; they should rise up in arms and fight for them." Feiner's statements, delivered in a "loud, highpitched voice," "stirred up a little excitement," and there was "some pushing, shoving and milling around" in the crowd. After Feiner had been speaking about 20 minutes, one of the onlookers said to the arresting policeman: "If you don't get that son of a bitch off, I will go over and get him off there myself." The policeman finally "stepped in to prevent it resulting in a fight." After Feiner ignored two police requests to stop speaking, he was arrested. The specifications underlying the disorderly conduct charge included the following: "By ignoring and refusing to heed and obey reasonable police orders issued [to] regulate and control said crowd and to prevent a breach [of] the peace and to prevent injuries to pedestrians attempting to use said walk."]

Chief Justice VINSON delivered the opinion of the Court.

We are not faced here with blind condonation by a state court of arbitrary police action. [The state courts] found that the officers in making the arrest were motivated solely by a proper concern for the preservation of order and protection of the general welfare, and that there was no evidence which could lend color to a claim that the acts of the police were a cover for suppression of petitioner's views and opinions. Petitioner was thus neither arrested nor convicted for the making or the content of his speech. Rather, it was the reaction which it actually engendered. [Cantwell.] [This] Court respects [the] interests of the community in maintaining peace and order on its streets. [We] cannot say that the preservation of that interest here encroaches on the constitutional rights of this petitioner.

We are well aware that the ordinary murmurings and objections of a hostile audience cannot be allowed to silence a speaker, and are also mindful of the possible danger of giving overzealous police officials complete discretion to break up otherwise lawful public meetings. [But] we are not faced here with such a situation. It is one thing to say that the police cannot be used as an instrument for the suppression of unpopular views, and another to say that, when as here the speaker passes the bounds of argument or persuasion and undertakes incitement to riot, they are powerless to prevent a breach of the peace. Nor in this case can we condemn the considered judgment of three New York courts approving the means which the police, faced with a crisis, used in the exercise of their power and duty to preserve peace and order. The findings [below] as to [the] imminence of greater disorder coupled with petitioner's deliberate defiance of the police officers convince us that we should not reverse this conviction in the name of free speech.

Affirmed.

Justice BLACK, dissenting.

The record before us convinces me that petitioner, a young college student, has been sentenced to the penitentiary for the unpopular views he expressed on matters of public interest while lawfully making a street-corner speech. [It] seems far-fetched to suggest that the "facts" show any imminent threat of riot or uncontrollable disorder. [Nor] does one isolated threat to assault the speaker forebode disorder. [Moreover], assuming that the "facts" did indicate a critical situation, I reject the implication of the Court's opinion that the police had no obligation to protect petitioner's constitutional right to talk. The police of course have power to prevent breaches of the peace. But if, in the name of preserving order, they ever can interfere with a lawful public speaker, they first must make all reasonable efforts to protect him. Here the policemen did not even pretend to try to protect petitioner. According to the officers' testimony, the crowd was restless but there is no showing of any attempt to quiet it; pedestrians were forced to walk into the street, but there was no effort to clear a path on the sidewalk; one person threatened to assault petitioner but the officers did nothing to discourage this when even a word might have sufficed. Their duty was to protect petitioner's right to talk, even to the extent of arresting the man who threatened to interfere. Instead, they shirked that duty and acted only to suppress the right to speak.

Finally, I cannot agree with the Court's statement that petitioner's disregard of the policeman's unexplained request amounted to such "deliberate defiance" as would justify an arrest or conviction for disorderly conduct. On the contrary, I think that the policeman's action was a "deliberate defiance" of ordinary official duty as well as of the constitutional right of free speech. For at least where time allows, courtesy and explanation of commands are basic elements of good official conduct in a democratic society. [Today's] holding means that as a practical matter, minority speakers can be silenced in any city.

[Concurring opinion of Justice Frankfurter and dissenting opinion of Justice Douglas, joined by Justice Minton, omitted.]

DISTINGUISHING FEINER IN LATER CASES

1. *Street Demonstrations.*   Contrast the holding in Feiner with the holdings of several later cases involving street demonstrations that attracted hostile crowds. In EDWARDS v. SOUTH CAROLINA, 372 U.S. 229 (1963), the Court reversed breach of peace convictions of 187 black student demonstrators who had walked along the South Carolina State House grounds to protest against racial discrimination. They carried placards with such messages as "Down with segregation." After a large crowd of onlookers gathered, they were ordered to disperse within 15 minutes; when they did not do so, they were arrested. The Court, in an opinion by Justice STEWART, held that "South Carolina infringed the petitioners' constitutionally protected rights." He added: "The 14th Amendment does not permit a State to make criminal the peaceful expression of unpopular views. [Terminiello.]" He noted that there had been no violence by the demonstrators or the onlookers; that there was no evidence of "fighting words"; and that the circumstances were "a far cry from the situation" in Feiner. Justice CLARK's lone dissent viewed the record differently. To him, there was a "much greater danger of riot and disorder" here than in Feiner. "[This] was by no means the passive demonstration which this Court relates. [It] is my belief that anyone conversant with the almost spontaneous combustion in some Southern communities in such a situation will agree that the City Manager's action may well have averted a major catastrophe."

Why was the protest march in Edwards "a far cry" from Feiner? Because here there was "peaceful expression of unpopular views" rather than "incitement to riot"? Does the difference lie in the fact that the onlookers in Edwards in fact remained peaceful and that ample police were at hand? What if there had been some disorder? Would the speech still have been protected because most onlookers in most cities would remain peaceful? Should the focus be on the reasonable audience's reaction, or on the actual audience's response? Would an outbreak of disorder simply show police failure to protect "peaceful" speech?

In COX v. LOUISIANA, 379 U.S. 536 (1965), the Court likewise invalidated a breach of peace conviction of a civil rights demonstrator who had attracted the attention of a hostile crowd. The case arose from the following circumstances: In December, 1961, 23 students from a black college were arrested in Baton Rouge, Louisiana, for picketing stores that maintained segregated lunch counters. The students were placed in a jail on the third floor of a local courthouse. The next day, appellant, Cox, an ordained minister, led about 2,000 students in a peaceful march toward the courthouse in order to protest the jailing. As Cox, at the head of the group, approached the vicinity of the courthouse, he was met by the police chief, who, according to Cox, permitted the demonstration but insisted that it must be confined to the west side of the street, across from the courthouse. The students lined up on the sidewalk 101 feet from the courthouse steps. They were about five deep and spread almost the entire length of the block. About 100 to 300 whites gathered on the opposite sidewalk. About 75 policemen were stationed on the street between the two groups. Some demonstrators carried picket signs advocating boycotts of "unfair" stores and the group sang songs and hymns, including "We Shall Overcome" and "God Bless America." The jailed students, out of sight of the demonstrators, responded by singing, and this in turn was greeted by cheers from the demonstrators. Cox gave a speech protesting the "illegal arrest" of the jailed students and urged the demonstrators to sit at segregated lunch counters. This evoked some "muttering" and "grumbling" from the white onlookers across the street. The sheriff viewed Cox's appeal to sit in at lunch counters as "inflammatory" and ordered the demonstration "broken up immediately." When the demonstrators did not disperse, policemen exploded tear gas shells. The demonstrators ran away. The next day, Cox was arrested and charged with several offenses.

Justice GOLDBERG, writing for the Court, invalidated Cox's conviction for "disturbing the peace" by congregating with others on a public street and failing to disperse when ordered to do so by a law enforcement officer: "It is clear to us that on the facts of this case, which are strikingly similar to those present in [Edwards], Louisiana infringed appellant's rights of free speech and free assembly by convicting him under this statute. [Our] independent examination of the [record] shows no conduct which the State had a right to prohibit as a breach of the peace. [The State argues] that while the demonstrators started out to be orderly, the loud cheering and clapping by the students in response to the singing from the jail converted the peaceful assembly into a riotous one. The record, however, does not support this assertion. [Our] conclusion that the entire meeting from the beginning until its dispersal by tear gas was orderly and not riotous is confirmed by a film of the events. [The] State contends that the conviction should be sustained because of fear expressed [that] 'violence was about to erupt' because of the demonstration. [But] the students themselves were not violent and threatened no violence. [There] is no indication [that] any member of the white group threatened violence. And [the] policemen [could] have handled the crowd. This situation, like that in Edwards, is 'a far cry from the situation in [Feiner].' Nor is there any evidence here of ['fighting words']."

In GREGORY v. CHICAGO, 394 U.S. 111 (1969), 85 demonstrators had "marched in a peaceful and orderly procession from city hall to the mayor's residence to press their claims for desegregation of the public schools," accompanied by about 100 police. The number of bystanders increased to over 1,000, and "the onlookers became unruly," shouting various threats and racial epithets at the demonstrators. Chicago police, "to prevent what they regarded as an impending civil disorder," demanded that the demonstrators disperse. When they refused to do so, they were arrested for disorderly conduct. Chief Justice WARREN's very brief opinion justifying the Court's reversal of the convictions asserted that this was "a simple case": as in Edwards, petitioners' peaceful conduct was activity protected by the First Amendment. Nor could the conviction rest on refusal to follow the dispersal request: petitioners were convicted for the demonstration, "not for a refusal to obey a police officer." Justice BLACK, joined by Justice Douglas, concurred but noted "that when groups with diametrically opposed, deep-seated views are permitted to air their emotional grievances, side by side, on city streets, tranquility and order cannot be maintained even by the joint efforts of the finest and best officers and of those who desire to be the most law-abiding protestors of their grievances."

2. *Permit requirements as an alternative approach.* Would a prior permit scheme be a more speech-protective mechanism to deal with the hostile audience problem than the use of on-the-spot police discretion? See generally Blasi, "Prior Restraints on Demonstrations," 68 Mich.L.Rev. 1481 (1970).

In KUNZ v. NEW YORK, 340 U.S. 290 (1951), decided the same day as Feiner, the Court reversed a conviction for violating a New York City ordinance which prohibited public worship meetings in the street "without first obtaining a permit" from the police commissioner. The ordinance also made it unlawful "to ridicule or denounce any form of religious belief" or to "expound atheism or agnosticism [in] any street." Kunz, a Baptist minister, was convicted for holding a meeting in 1948 without a permit. Two years earlier, he had obtained a permit, but that had been revoked in the same year after an administrative hearing: there had been complaints that Kunz had engaged in "scurrilous attacks on Catholics and Jews," and the revocation was based on "evidence that he had ridiculed and denounced other religious beliefs in his meetings." Kunz's application for permits in 1947 and 1948 were "disapproved," without stated reasons. Chief Justice VINSON's majority opinion condemned the permit system as involving impermissibly standardless discretion: "Disapproval of the 1948 permit application by the police commissioner was justified by the New York courts on the ground that a permit had previously been revoked 'for good reasons.' It is noteworthy that there is no mention in the ordinance of reasons for which such a permit application can be refused. [We] have here, then, an ordinance which gives an administrative official discretionary power to control in advance the right of citizens to speak on religious matters on the streets of New York. As such, the ordinance is clearly invalid as a prior restraint on the exercise of First Amendment rights."

Justice JACKSON dissented: "[It] seems hypercritical to strike down local laws on their faces for want of standards when we have no standards. [I]f the Court conceives, as Feiner indicates, that upon uttering insulting, provocative or inciting words the policeman on the beat may stop the meeting, then its assurance of free speech in this decision is 'a promise to the ear to be broken to the hope,' if the patrolman on the beat happens to have prejudices of his own. [It] seems to me that this [permit] procedure better protects freedom of speech than to let everyone speak without leave, but subject to surveillance and to being ordered to stop in the discretion of the police."

3. *Permit fees.* Should it be permissible to deny a permit for a meeting or parade because of anticipated fears of violence and hostile audience reactions? If not, may government charge demonstrators a fee based on such anticipated reactions? In FORSYTH COUNTY, GEORGIA v. NATIONALIST MOVEMENT, 505 U.S. 123 (1992), the Court invalidated a county ordinance requiring demonstrators on public property to pay a fee of up to $1000 a day to cover any public cost that "exceeds the usual and normal cost of law enforcement." The county administrator was authorized to vary the fee depending on "the expense incident ... to the maintenance of public order." The ordinance was passed in response to 1987 civil rights marches in Forsyth County, which had billed itself as "the whitest county in America." After a march by a group of 90 civil rights demonstrators was forced to halt by a crowd of 400 counter-demonstrators, a second march was held in which 20,000 civil rights demonstrators, including several senators and an assistant attorney general, marched successfully past a crowd of 1000 counter-demonstrators, who in turn were contained by 3000 state and local police and national guardsmen. The cost of police protection on that occasion was $670,000. This case arose when a group called the Nationalist Movement proposed to demonstrate in opposition to the federal holiday commemorating the birthday of Martin Luther King, Jr., and was assessed a $100 fee by the county.

The Court, in an opinion by Justice BLACKMUN, held the ordinance facially invalid, reasoning that it left impermissibly standardless discretion in the hands of the county administrator. "There are no articulated standards either in the ordinance or in the county's established practice. The administrator is not required to rely on any objective factors. He need not provide any explanation for his decision, and that decision is unreviewable. Nothing in the law or its application prevents the official from encouraging some views and discouraging others through the arbitrary application of fees. The First Amendment prohibits the vesting of such unbridled discretion in a government official." Justice Blackmun also noted that imposing such a fee legitimated a heckler's veto: "The fee assessed will depend on the administrator's measure of the amount of hostility likely to be created by the speech based on its content. Those wishing to express views unpopular with bottle-throwers, for example, may have to pay more for their permit. [Speech] cannot be financially burdened, any more than it can be punished or banned, simply because it might offend a hostile mob." Nor could the ordinance be saved by the $1000 fee cap, for "a tax based on the content of speech does not become more constitutional because it is a small tax." Chief Justice REHNQUIST, joined by Justices White, Scalia and Thomas, dissented.

Forsyth County suggests that the public should bear the cost of protecting a speaker who is likely to provoke a hostile audience (although it does not rule out the permissibility of a flat user fee for speech in public spaces without regard to whether the audience is likely to be hostile). Is this the proper allocation of the cost, as the public is broadly speaking the beneficiary of free speech? If so, should there be a government-funded victims compensation fund to compensate bystanders injured in a riot caused by a speaker? See generally Schauer, "Uncoupling Free Speech," 93 Colum. L. Rev. 1321 (1992).

4. *The right to heckle.* What about the First Amendment interests of the heckler? See In re Kay, 1 Cal.3d 930, 83 Cal.Rptr. 686, 464 P.2d 142 (1970), setting aside a conviction for disturbing a lawful meeting. A small part of a large crowd at a Fourth of July celebration "engaged in rhythmical clapping and some shouting for about five or ten minutes. This demonstration did not affect the program"—the speaker finished his speech despite the protest. The California Supreme Court opinion commented: "Audience activities, such as heckling, interrupting, harsh questioning, and booing, even though they may be impolite and discourteous, can nonetheless advance the goals of the First Amendment." To construe the law within constitutional limits, the Court interpreted it to require "that the defendant substantially impaired the conduct of the meeting by intentionally committing acts in violation of implicit customs or usages or of explicit rules for governance of the meeting, of which he knew, or as a reasonable man should have known."

SECTION 4. INJURY TO REPUTATION AND SENSIBILITY

Introduction. In 1942, the Court in Chaplinsky readily categorized libel with other types of speech properly cast outside the First Amendment. Ten years later, in Beauharnais, which follows, the Court followed that lead in the group libel context. But in the 1960s, beginning with New York Times v. Sullivan, the Court retreated from the peremptory categorical exclusion of libel and, ever since, has exercised more careful First Amendment scrutiny. This section examines some of the highlights of this development. It does not cover suits for injuries to reputation (and to privacy) in detail; that is left to courses in torts and media law. The focus here is on the Court's methodology in bringing these areas into the First Amendment ballpark, and on the bearing of the Court's analyses on other First Amendment problems.

———

A. BEAUHARNAIS AND GROUP LIBEL

———

1. *The Beauharnais case.* The 5–4 decision in BEAUHARNAIS v. ILLINOIS, 343 U.S. 250 (1952), sustained an Illinois criminal group libel law prohibiting the publishing, selling, or exhibiting in any public place of any publication which "portrays depravity, criminality, unchastity, or lack of virtue of a class of citizens, of any race, color, creed or religion, [or which] exposes the citizens of any race, color, creed or religion to contempt, derision, or obloquy, or which is productive of breach of the peace or riots." Beauharnais, president of the White Circle League, had organized the circulation of a leaflet setting forth a petition calling on Chicago officials "to halt the further encroachment, harassment and invasion of white people, their property, neighborhoods and persons, by the Negro." The leaflet called on Chicago's white people to unite and warned that if "persuasion and the need to prevent the white race from becoming mongrelized by the negro will not unite us, then the [aggressions], rapes, robberies, knives, guns and marijuana of the negro surely will." The trial court refused to give a "clear and present danger" charge requested by petitioner.

Justice FRANKFURTER's majority opinion, after quoting Justice Murphy's Chaplinsky passage about unprotected classes of speech, stated: "No one will gainsay that it is libelous falsely to charge another with being a rapist, robber, carrier of knives and guns, and user of marijuana. The precise question before us, then, is whether [the 14th Amendment] prevents a State from punishing such libels—as criminal libel has been defined, limited and constitutionally recognized time out of mind—directed at designated collectivities and flagrantly disseminated. [If] an utterance directed at an individual may be the object of criminal sanctions, we cannot deny to a State power to punish the same utterance directed at a defined group, unless we can say that this is a wilful and purposeless restriction unrelated to the peace and well-being of the State.

"Illinois [could conclude, from the State's own experience,] that wilful purveyors of falsehood concerning racial and religious groups promote strife and tend powerfully to obstruct the manifold adjustments required for free, ordered life in a metropolitan, polyglot community. From the murder of the abolitionist Lovejoy in 1837 to the Cicero riots of 1951, Illinois has been the scene of exacerbated tension between races, often flaring into violence and destruction. In many of these outbreaks, utterances of the character here in question, so the Illinois legislature could conclude, played a significant part. [In] the face of this history and its frequent obligato of extreme racial and religious propaganda, we would deny experience to say that the Illinois legislature was without reason in seeking ways to curb false or malicious defamation of racial and religious groups, made in public places and by means calculated to have a powerful emotional impact on those to whom it was presented. [It] may be argued, and weightily, that this legislation will not help matters. [But it] is not within our competence to confirm or deny claims of social scientists as to the dependence of the individual on the position of his racial or religious group in the community. [W]e are precluded from saying that speech concededly punishable when immediately directed at individuals cannot be outlawed if directed at groups with whose position and esteem in society the affiliated individual may be inextricably involved. [Libelous] utterances not being within the area of constitutionally protected speech, it is unnecessary, either for us or for the State courts, to consider the issues behind the phrase 'clear and present danger.' [We] find no warrant in the Constitution for denying to Illinois the power to pass the law here under attack."

There were dissenting opinions by Justices Black, Douglas, Reed and Jackson. Justice BLACK, joined by Justice Douglas, wrote: "[Reliance upon the 'group libel law'] label may make the Court's holding more palatable for those who sustain it, but the sugar-coating does not make the censorship less deadly. However tagged, the Illinois law is not that criminal libel which has been 'defined, limited and constitutionally recognized time out of mind.' For as 'constitutionally recognized' that crime has provided for punishment of false, malicious, scurrilous charges against individuals, not against huge groups. This limited scope of the law of criminal libel [has] confined state punishment of speech and expression to the narrowest of areas involving nothing more than purely private feuds. Every expansion of the law of criminal libel so as to punish discussion of matters of public concern means a corresponding invasion of the area dedicated to free expression by the First Amendment." He concluded: "I think the [First Amendment] 'absolutely' forbids such laws without any 'ifs' or 'buts' or 'whereases.' [If] there be minority groups who hail this holding as their victory, they might consider the possible relevancy of this ancient remark: 'Another such victory and I am undone.'"

2. *Debate over Beauharnais.* Was Beauharnais correct to subordinate "individualistic liberalism" to prevention of the social harms of group libels? See Riesman, "Democracy and Defamation: Control of Group Libel," 42 Colum.L.Rev. 727 (1942), cited by both majority and minority. Or are group libel laws, as Justice Black suggested, likely to curtail valuable discussion and hurt the very minority groups they seek to protect? See Tanenhaus, "Group Libel," 35 Cornell L.Q. 261 (1950); Beth, "Group Libel and Free Speech," 39 Minn. L.Rev. 167 (1955).

3. *The vitality of Beauharnais.* Have the First Amendment developments of recent decades drained Beauharnais of all vitality? Some of the measures adopted by Skokie, Illinois, in the late 1970s to block planned demonstrations by American neo-Nazis relied on the approach sustained in Beauharnais. As noted in the fuller treatment of the Skokie controversy at p. 1112 below, state and lower federal courts struck down all of the ordinances designed to block the Nazi marchers, including one that prohibited the "dissemination of any materials within [Skokie] which [intentionally] promotes and incites hatred against persons by reasons of their race, national origin, or religion." Most of the judges found Beauharnais no longer controlling. The Seventh Circuit, for example, stated: "It may be questioned, after cases such as Cohen v. California, Gooding v. Wilson, and Brandenburg v. Ohio, whether the *tendency to induce violence* approach sanctioned implicitly in Beauharnais would pass constitutional muster today." Collin v. Smith, 578 F.2d 1197 (7th Cir.1978). But note Justice Blackmun's dissent, joined by Justice Rehnquist, from a denial of a stay of the Court of Appeals order: "Beauharnais has never been overruled or formally limited in any way." Smith v. Collin, 436 U.S. 953 (1978). For examples of later efforts to resuscitate and extend the reasoning of Beauhar-

nais, see the materials below on hate speech and the regulation of pornography as the subordination of women.

———

B. LIBEL

———

New York Times Co. v. Sullivan

376 U.S. 254, 84 S.Ct. 710, 11 L.Ed.2d 686 (1964).

Justice BRENNAN delivered the opinion of the Court.

We are required in this case to determine for the first time the extent to which the constitutional protections for speech and press limit a State's power to award damages in a libel action brought by a public official against critics of his official conduct. [This libel action stemmed from a paid, full-page, fundraising advertisement in the New York Times in March 1960 by the Committee to Defend Martin Luther King and the Struggle for Freedom in the South. The ad, headed "Heed Their Rising Voices," charged the existence of "an unprecedented wave of terror" against blacks engaged in nonviolent demonstrations in the South. Sullivan, the Montgomery, Ala., police commissioner, sued the Times and several black clergymen who had signed the ad. Sullivan objected especially to the claim that "truckloads of police armed with shotguns and teargas ringed the Alabama State College Campus" in Montgomery and that Dr. King had been assaulted and arrested seven times. Sullivan's witnesses testified that they took the charges to implicate Sullivan, and that he did not participate in the events regarding Dr. King. Sullivan offered no proof that he had suffered actual pecuniary loss. He recovered a judgment for $500,000 under Alabama libel law. The judgment was based on several inaccurate statements in the ad—e.g., the statement that Dr. King had been arrested seven times: in fact he had been arrested four times. The Court rejected the argument that First Amendment guarantees were inapplicable because the statements were published as part of a "paid 'commercial' " ad and concluded: "We hold that the rule of law applied by the Alabama courts is constitutionally deficient for failure to provide the safeguards for freedom of speech and of the press that are required by the [First Amendment] in a libel action brought by a public official against critics of his official conduct. We further hold that under the proper safeguards the evidence presented in this case is constitutionally insufficient to support the judgment." In explaining that conclusion, Justice Brennan stated:]

Under Alabama law, [a] publication is "libelous per se" if the words "tend to injure a person [in] his reputation" or to "bring [him] into public contempt." [Once] "libel per se" has been established, the defendant has no defense as to stated facts unless he can persuade the jury that they were true in all their particulars. [Unless] he can discharge the burden of proving truth, general damages are presumed, and may be awarded without proof of pecuniary injury. The question before us is whether this rule of liability, as applied to an action brought by a public official against critics of his official conduct, abridges the freedom of speech and of the [press].

Respondent [and] the Alabama courts [rely heavily] on statements of this Court to the effect that the Constitution does not protect libelous publications. Those statements do not foreclose our inquiry here. None of the cases sustained the use of libel laws to impose sanctions upon expression critical of the official conduct of public officials. [Like] insurrection, contempt, advocacy of unlawful acts, breach of the peace, obscenity, solicitation of legal business, and the various other formulae for the repression of expression that have been challenged in this Court, libel can claim no talismanic immunity from constitutional limitations. It must be measured by standards that satisfy the [First Amendment].

[W]e consider this case against the background of a profound national commitment to the principle that debate on public issues should be uninhibited, robust, and wide-open, and that it may well include vehement, caustic, and sometimes unpleasantly sharp attacks on government and public officials. [See Terminiello, DeJonge.] The present advertisement, as an expression of grievance and protest on one of the major public issues of our time, would seem clearly to qualify for the constitutional protection. The question is whether it forfeits that protection by the falsity of some of its factual statements and by its alleged defamation of respondent. Authoritative interpretations of the First Amendment guarantees have consistently refused to recognize an exception for any test of truth—whether administered by judges, juries, or administrative officials—and especially not one that puts the burden of proving truth on the speaker. "The constitutional protection does not turn upon the truth, popularity, or social utility of the ideas and beliefs which are offered." [NAACP v. Button, p. 1383 below.] [E]rroneous statement is inevitable in free debate and [must] be protected if the freedoms of expression are to have the "breathing space" that they "need [to] survive" [ibid]. [Injury] to official reputation affords no more warrant for repressing speech that would otherwise be free than does factual error. [If] judges are to be treated as "men of fortitude, able to thrive in a hardy climate," surely the same must be true of other government officials, such as elected city commissioners. Criticism of their official conduct does not lose its constitutional protection merely because it is effective criticism and hence diminishes their official reputations.

If neither factual error nor defamatory content suffices to remove the constitutional shield from criticism of official conduct, the combination of the two elements is no less inadequate. This is the lesson to be drawn from the great controversy over the Sedition Act of 1798, which first crystallized a national awareness of the central meaning of the First Amendment. [Although] the Sedition Act was never tested in this Court, the attack upon its validity has carried the day in the court of history. Fines levied in its prosecution were repaid by Act of Congress on the ground that it was unconstitutional. [President Jefferson] pardoned those who had been convicted and sentenced under the Act and remitted their fines. [Its] invalidity [has] also been assumed by Justices of this Court. [These] views reflect a broad consensus that the Act, because of the restraint it imposed upon criticism of government and public officials, was inconsistent with the [First Amendment].

What a State may not constitutionally bring about by means of a criminal statute is likewise beyond the reach of its civil law of libel. The fear of damage awards under a rule such as that invoked by the Alabama courts here may be markedly more inhibiting than the fear of prosecution under a criminal statute. [The] judgment awarded in this case—without the need for any proof of actual pecuniary loss—was [1,000] times greater than that provided by the Sedition Act. And since there is no double jeopardy limitation applicable to civil lawsuits, this is not the only judgment that may be awarded against petitioners for the same publication. Whether or not a newspaper can survive a succession of such judgments, the pall of fear and timidity imposed upon those who would give voice to public criticism is an atmosphere in which the First Amendment freedoms cannot [survive].

The state rule of law is not saved by its allowance of the defense of truth. A defense for erroneous statements honestly made is no less essential here than was the requirement of proof of guilty knowledge which [we have] held indispensable to a valid conviction of a bookseller for possessing obscene writings for sale. [A] rule compelling the critic of official conduct to guarantee the truth of all his factual assertions—and to do so on pain of libel judgments virtually unlimited in amount—leads to a comparable "self-censorship." Allowance of the defense of truth, with the burden of proving it on the defendant, does not mean that only false speech will be deterred.[1] [Under] such a rule, would-be critics of official conduct may be deterred from voicing their criticism, even though it is believed to be true and even though it is in fact true, because of doubt whether it can be proved in court or fear of the expense of having to do so. They tend to make only statements which "steer far wider of the unlawful zone." The rule thus dampens the vigor and limits the variety of public debate. It is inconsistent with the [First Amendment].

The constitutional guarantees require, we think, a federal rule that prohibits a public official from recovering damages for a defamatory falsehood relating to his official conduct unless he proves that the statement was made with "actual malice"—that is, with knowledge that it was false or with reckless disregard of whether it was false or not.[2] [We] consider that the proof presented to show actual malice lacks the convincing clarity which the constitutional standard demands, and hence that it would not constitutionally sustain the judgment for respondent under the proper rule of law. [E.g., we] think the evidence against the Times supports at most a finding of negligence in failing to discover the misstatements, and is constitutionally insufficient to show the recklessness that is required for a finding of actual malice. We also think the evidence was constitutionally defective in another respect: it was incapable of supporting the jury's finding that the allegedly libelous statements were made "of and concerning" respondent. [There] was no reference to respondent in the advertisement, either by name or official position. [As the highest state court made clear, reliance was placed solely] on the bare fact of respondent's official position. [This] has disquieting implications for criticism of governmental conduct. [It raises] the possibility that a good-faith critic of government will be penalized for his criticism [and] strikes at the very center of the constitutionally protected area of free expression. We hold that such a proposition may not constitutionally be utilized to establish that an otherwise impersonal attack on governmental operations was a libel of an official responsible for those operations. Since it was relied on exclusively, [the] evidence was constitutionally insufficient to support a finding that the statements referred to [respondent].

Reversed and remanded.

1. Even a false statement may be deemed to make a valuable contribution to public debate, since it brings about "the clearer perception and livelier impression of truth, produced by its collision with error." Mill, On Liberty; see also Milton, Areopagitica. [Footnote by Justice Brennan.]

2. We have no occasion here to determine how far down into the lower ranks of government employees the "public official" designation would extend for purposes of this rule, or otherwise to specify categories of persons who would or would not be included. [Nor] need we here determine the boundaries of the "official conduct" [concept]. [Relocated footnote by Justice Brennan.]

Justice BLACK, with whom Justice DOUGLAS joins (concurring).

[I] base my vote to reverse on the belief that the First and 14th Amendments not merely "delimit" a State's power to award damages to "public officials against critics of their official conduct" but completely prohibit a State from exercising such a [power]. "Malice," even as defined by the Court, is an elusive, abstract concept, hard to prove and hard to disprove. The requirement that malice be proved provides at best an evanescent protection for the right critically to discuss public affairs. [Therefore], I vote to reverse exclusively on the ground that the [defendants] had an absolute, unconditional constitutional right to publish in the Times advertisement their criticisms of the Montgomery agencies and [officials]. [In another concurrence, Justice GOLDBERG, joined by Justice Douglas, stated that the Constitution afforded "an absolute, unconditional privilege to criticize official conduct" of public officials, but did not protect "defamatory statements directed against the private conduct of a public official or private citizen."]

THE MEANING OF NEW YORK TIMES

1. *The immediate impact of the decision.* By saving the New York Times and other newspapers from potentially crippling damage judgments, the New York Times decision arguably made possible important coverage of and advertisement by the civil rights movement in the South at a time of crucial activity against racial segregation. For an account of the events leading up to the decision and the stakes involved, see Anthony Lewis, Make No Law (1991).

2. *The First Amendment interest in false statements of fact.* What is the First Amendment value in the false statements of fact inherent in defamatory statements? Did New York Times overrule the Chaplinsky dictum that libel was a category of speech wholly outside First Amendment protection? Justice Brennan, relying on John Stuart Mill, suggested in New York Times that "[e]ven a false statement may be deemed to make a valuable contribution to public [debate]." But a decade later, Justice Powell wrote for the Court in Gertz v. Welch that, although "[u]nder the First Amendment there is no such thing as a false idea, [there] is no constitutional value in false statements of fact."

Is the better view of New York Times not that it held libel intrinsically valuable, but that it held the protection of negligent libels instrumentally necessary to afford adequate "breathing room" for truth? Consider Justice Powell's acknowledgement in Gertz that "some falsehood" needs to be protected "in order to protect speech that matters." On this view, New York Times continued to treat some libel as wholly unprotected; it simply limited that category to knowingly or recklessly false statements. Consider Justice Brennan's statement two years after New York Times, in Garrison v. Louisiana, 379 U.S. 64 (1964), which extended the New York Times principle to state *criminal* libel cases: "Although honest utterance, even if inaccurate, may further the fruitful exercise of the right of free speech, it does not follow that the lie, knowingly and deliberately published about a public official, should enjoy a like immunity. [For] the use of the known lie as a tool is at once at odds with the premises of democratic government and with the orderly manner in which economic, social, or political change is to be effected. Calculated falsehood falls into that class of utterances [which are excluded under Chaplinsky]. Hence the knowingly false statement and the false statement made with reckless disregard of the truth do not enjoy constitutional protection."

Note that, despite Justice Powell's statement that "there is no such thing as a false idea," the Court has rejected the idea that the First Amendment requires any separate threshold inquiry into whether an allegedly defamatory statement is one of fact of opinion. See Milkovich v. Lorain Journal Co., 497 U.S. 1 (1990). Writing for the Court, Chief Justice Rehnquist explained that any statement that "does not contain a provably false factual connotation will receive full constitutional protection," but that a false statement of fact gains no constitutional immunity if the speaker simply adds "the words 'I think.'"

3. *The Court's methodology in New York Times.* Soon after the New York Times decision, Harry Kalven reported that Alexander Meiklejohn viewed it as "'an occasion for dancing in the streets.'" Kalven, "The New York Times Case: A Note on 'The Central Meaning of the First Amendment,'" 1964 Sup.Ct.Rev. 191. In their view, the "central meaning of the [First] Amendment is that seditious libel cannot be made the subject of government sanction," and New York Times got that principle "right side up for the first time." Kalven added "that the effect of the Times opinion," by effectively guaranteeing freedom to criticize the government, "is necessarily to discard or diminish in importance the clear-and-present danger test, the balancing formula, [and] the two-level speech theory of Beauharnais."

Did the Times opinion truly eschew balancing? True, there was no "ad hoc balancing": no resort to the view "that the court, in each case, balance the individual and social interest in freedom of expression against the social interest sought by the regulation." Emerson, "Toward a General Theory of the First Amendment," 72 Yale L.J. 877 (1963). But as Kalven himself recognized, there was, "of course, a sense in which the Court did indulge in balancing. It did not go the whole way and give an absolute privilege to the 'citizen-critic'"; it did balance "two obvious conflicting interests." As Melville Nimmer described New York Times, it was a case of "definitional balancing": the derivation, through a balancing process, of a series of categorical rules for differing problems of free speech. Nimmer, "The Right to Speak from Times to [Time]," 56 Calif.L.Rev. 935 (1968). On this view, a category of unprotected speech simply represents a per se rule for an implicit balancing that would always come out the same way if engaged in case by case. For a critical analysis of definitional balancing, see Aleinikoff, "Constitutional Law in the Age of Balancing," 96 Yale L.J. 943 (1987).

4. *Criticism of New York Times.* There have been recurrent attacks on New York Times on the ground that it gives inadequate protection to the reputation interests of defamation plaintiffs. See, e.g., Nagel, "How Useful is Judicial Review in Free Speech Cases?," 69 Cornell L. Rev. 302 (1984); Monaghan, "Of 'Liberty' and 'Property,'" 62 Cornell L. Rev. 405 (1977). For a critical analysis of the reputation interest, see Post, "The Social Foundations of Defamation Law: Reputation and the Constitution," 74 Calif.L.Rev. 691 (1986).

There have also been mounting complaints from the other side: that the principles of accommodation give inadequate protection to defamation defendants. These critics have complained of the ease with which defamation cases under the New York Times standard can get to a jury, the increasingly large verdicts against defendants, and the "chilling effects" caused by the litigation burdens and legal fees even in cases where defendants ultimately prevail on appeal. See, e.g., Anderson, "Libel and Press Self–Censorship," 53 Tex.L.Rev. 422 (1975); Lewis, "New York Times v. Sullivan [Reconsidered]," 83 Colum.L.Rev. 602 (1983); Symposium, "Defamation and the First Amendment: New Perspectives," 25 Wm. & Mary L.Rev. 743 (1984); Smolla, "[The] Rejuvenation of the American Law of Libel," 132 U. Pa. L. Rev. 1 (1984); LeBel,

"Reforming the Tort of Defamation [Within] the Current Constitutional Framework," 66 Neb.L.Rev. 249 (1987).

Would any alternative approach better reconcile the competing interests in speech and reputation? Consider Justice White's argument in dissent in Dun & Bradstreet v. Greenmoss Builders, p. 1103 below, that the "necessary breathing room for speakers can be ensured by limitations on recoverable damages; it does not also require depriving many public figures of any room to vindicate their reputations sullied by false statements of fact." For the view that a return to the common law of defamation, with strict liability but relatively low damage awards, would be preferable, see Epstein, "Was New York Times v. Sullivan Wrong?," 53 U.Chi.L.Rev. 782 (1986). For the proposal that plaintiffs ought to be able to obtain a declaration of falsity (requiring no showing of fault and including no damage awards) as an alternative to libel suits, see Leval, "The No–Money, No–Fault Libel Suit: Keeping Sullivan in Its Proper Place," 101 Harv.L.Rev. 1287 (1988); and Franklin, "A Declaratory Judgment Alternative to Current Libel Law," 74 Calif.L.Rev. 809 (1986).

5. *Procedural developments after New York Times.* The Court has given plaintiffs one significant procedural victory since New York Times: In Herbert v. Lando, 441 U.S. 153 (1979), the Court rejected a television producer's claim to a broad First Amendment-based editorial privilege that would have precluded questions in pretrial discovery proceedings pertaining to his liability under the Times "actual malice" standard. Lando leaves members of the press open to wide-ranging inquiries on the issue of whether they were guilty of knowing or reckless falsity, and thus to the costs of defending against extensive discovery. Although the press vehemently criticized that ruling, none of the Justices was prepared to uphold all of the broad media claims; even Justices Marshall and Brennan were only willing to grant a limited privilege.

Most other procedural rulings in this area since New York Times, however, have benefited defendants: In Philadelphia Newspapers, Inc. v. Hepps, 475 U.S. 767 (1986), the Court held, by a 5–4 vote, that the plaintiff was required to bear the burden of proof in establishing the allegedly defamatory statement in cases governed by New York Times or Gertz (see below), as those decisions had displaced the common law rule presuming falsity. New York Times itself required that evidence of actual malice be clear and convincing; a preponderance of evidence was not enough. Anderson v. Liberty Lobby, Inc., 477 U.S. 242 (1986), required lower courts to inquire into the convincing clarity of actual malice evidence at the summary judgment stage. And in Bose Corp. v. Consumers Union, 466 U.S. 485 (1984), the Court held that appellate courts "must exercise independent judgment and determine [de novo] whether the record establishes actual malice with convincing clarity," rather than review the judgment below only for clear error. See generally Matheson, "Procedure in Public Person Defamation Cases: The Impact of the First Amendment," 66 Tex. L. Rev. 215 (1987).

EXTENSION OF NEW YORK TIMES TO OTHER SETTINGS

The Court has considered three variables in deciding how far to extend New York Times' substantive limits on liability to other settings: (1) the identity of the plaintiff (public official, public figure or private figure), (2) the identity of the defendant (media or non-media), and (3) the nature of the issue discussed (matter of public or private concern). It has also considered whether to vary the available remedies in various settings.

With respect to substantive limits on liability, the Court has most often emphasized the status of the plaintiff. The "actual malice" requirement, which originated in a case involving a public official, has been extended to "public figures" (see Butts and Walker below), but not in identical form to "private figures" (see Gertz below). While, typically, defendants in the Court's cases have been media defendants, a majority of the Court has concluded that the principles of liability should be the same for media and non-media defendants alike (see Dun & Bradstreet below). For an argument in favor of that result, see Shiffrin, "Defamatory Non–Media Speech and First Amendment Methodology," 25 UCLA L.Rev. 915 (1978). As to the nature of the issue involved, the Court has relaxed the New York Times standard for liability, although not for presumed or punitive damages, in suits by private figures alleging defamation on matters of public concern (see Gertz below), but has held that standard altogether inapplicable in suits by private figures alleging defamation on matters of private concern (see Dun & Bradstreet below). The Court has also varied the permissible bases of damages in these different settings (see Gertz, Dun & Bradstreet below). Do the rules that have evolved in the following cases strike a proper balance between First Amendment values and the interest in protecting individual reputations?

1.   *Public figures.* In CURTIS PUBLISHING CO. v. BUTTS and ASSOCI-ATED PRESS v. WALKER, decided together at 388 U.S. 130 (1967), the Court applied the New York Times rule to libel actions "instituted by persons who are not public officials, but who are 'public figures' and involved in issues in which the public has a justified and important interest." Butts grew out of a Saturday Evening Post article which claimed that the University of Georgia athletic director (and former football coach) had fixed a football game. In Walker, a retired general challenged an AP report that he had led a violent crowd in opposition to the enforcement of a desegregation decree at the University of Mississippi. The Court was sharply divided in its reasoning: Four of the Justices (Harlan, Clark, Stewart and Fortas) opposed extending the New York Times rule; three (Chief Justice Warren, and Justices Brennan and White) urged application of New York Times to public figures; the remaining two (Black and Douglas) urged a broader press immunity, as they had in New York Times. But the result was that the New York Times rule was extended to "public figures" cases.

In announcing the view that became the Court position, Chief Justice WARREN stated that "differentiation between 'public figures' and 'public officials' and adoption of separate standards of proof for each have no basis in law, logic, or First Amendment policy. Increasingly in this country, the distinctions between governmental and private sectors are blurred. [It] is plain that although they are not subject to the restraints of the political process, 'public figures,' like 'public officials,' often play an influential role in ordering society. And surely as a class these 'public figures' have as ready access as 'public officials' to mass media, [both] to influence policy and to counter criticism of their views and activities. Our citizenry has a legitimate and substantial interest in the conduct of such persons, and freedom of the press to engage in uninhibited debate about their involvement in public issues and events is as crucial as it is in the case of 'public officials.' "

In announcing the position of the four Justices who opposed extension of the New York Times rule, Justice HARLAN examined the similarities and differences between "public officials" and other "public figures," agreed that "public figures" actions "cannot be left entirely to state libel laws," but insisted that "the rigorous federal requirements of New York Times are not the only appropriate accommodation of the conflicting interests at stake." He concluded: "We [would] hold that a 'public figure' who is not a public official may also recover damages for a defamatory falsehood whose substance makes substantial danger to reputation apparent, on a showing of highly unreasonable conduct constituting an extreme departure from the standards of investigation and reporting ordinarily adhered to by responsible publishers."

In later cases, however, the Court has construed the "public figure" category quite narrowly. In Gertz, below, for example, the Court found that a lawyer who had "long been active in community and professional affairs," and was "well-known in some circles," was nonetheless a private figure because "he had achieved no general fame or notoriety in the community [or] pervasive involvement in the affairs of society." In Time, Inc. v. Firestone, 424 U.S. 448 (1976), the Court held that a wealthy divorcee whose divorce was mischaracterized in Time was not a public figure because she had not assumed "any role of especial prominence in the affairs of society, other than perhaps Palm Beach society." In Hutchinson v. Proxmire, 443 U.S. 111 (1979), the Court held that a scientist whose federally funded research on monkey behavior had been characterized by the defendant Senator as an egregious example of wasteful government spending was not a public figure, as he had not "thrust himself or his views into public controversy to influence others." And in Wolston v. Reader's Digest Ass'n, Inc., 443 U.S. 157 (1979), the Court held that Wolston's brief stint in the public eye in 1958, after a criminal contempt conviction for failure to appear before a grand jury investigating Soviet espionage, did not make him a public figure for purposes of a 1974 allegation that he was a "Soviet agent." The majority emphasized that Wolston had not "voluntarily thrust" or "injected" himself into the controversy.

2. *Private figures.* After extending the New York Times standard to "public figures," the divided Court's balancing approach encountered new challenges when publishers claimed First Amendment defenses to defamation suits by *private* individuals. At first, in the 1971 Rosenbloom decision, Justice Brennan's plurality opinion extended New York Times to a "private" plaintiff's action claiming defamation in a report "about the individual's involvement in an event of public or general interest." But in Gertz, Justice Powell spoke for a majority holding that state libel law could impose liability in suits by private individuals "on a less demanding showing" than that required by New York Times "so long as [states] do not impose liability without fault," though it imposed some restrictions on damages in the absence of actual malice.

ROSENBLOOM v. METROMEDIA, INC., 403 U.S. 29 (1971), arose from a libel action by a distributor of nudist magazines, based on radio reports about police action against his allegedly obscene books, about his lawsuit, and about police interference with his business. Some of the news reports referred to "girlie book peddlers" and the "smut literature racket." Justice BRENNAN's plurality opinion, joined by Chief Justice Burger and Justice Blackmun, argued that the critical criterion should be the *subject matter* of the allegedly defamatory report rather than the status of the plaintiff. He insisted that experience since New York Times had "disclosed the artificiality, in terms of the public's interest, of a simple distinction between 'public' and 'private' individuals" and concluded: "If a matter is a subject of public or general interest, it cannot suddenly become less so merely because a private individual is involved, or because in some sense the individual did not 'voluntarily' choose to become involved. The public's primary interest is in the event; the public focus is on the conduct of the participant and the content, effect, and significance of the conduct, not the participant's prior anonymity or notoriety. [We] honor the commitment to robust debate on public issues [by] extending constitutional protection to all discussion and communication involving matters of public or general concern without regard to whether the persons involved are famous or anonymous."

In GERTZ v. ROBERT WELCH, INC., 418 U.S. 323 (1974), however, the Court abandoned Rosenbloom and held that a private person should be able to recover without meeting the New York Times standard. The decision arose in a libel action by Elmer Gertz, a Chicago lawyer, against the publisher of "American Opinion," an "outlet for the views of the John Birch Society." Gertz had been retained by a victim's family in a civil suit against a Chicago policeman who had been convicted of murder. The magazine charged Gertz with being an architect of the "frame-up" of the policeman in the murder trial and called Gertz, inter alia, a "Communist-fronter." The Court found that Gertz was not a "public figure." Justice POWELL's majority opinion stated the new standard of liability for private libel actions as follows: "We hold that, so long as they do not impose liability without fault, the States may define for themselves the appropriate standard of liability for a publisher or broadcaster of defamatory falsehoods injurious to a private individual. This approach provides a more equitable boundary between the competing concerns involved here. It recognizes the strength of the legitimate state interest in compensating private individuals for wrongful injury to reputation, yet shields the press and broadcast media from the rigors of strict liability for defamation. At least this conclusion obtains where, as here, the substance of the defamatory statement 'makes substantial danger to reputation apparent.' Our inquiry would involve [different] considerations [if] a State purported to condition civil liability on a factual misstatement whose content did not warn a reasonably prudent editor or broadcaster of its defamatory potential." Regarding the new constitutional restraints on damage awards, Justice Powell announced that states may ordinarily go no further "than compensation for actual injury": "[W]e hold that the States may not permit recovery of presumed or punitive damages, at least when liability is not based on a showing of knowledge of falsity or reckless disregard for the truth."

Justice Powell explained that the state interest in compensating injuries to private individuals was stronger than in the case of "public figures," and that distinction made a less demanding standard of liability appropriate here. Public figures could use the remedy of "self-help" more effectively because of their "significantly greater access" to the media. Private persons, by contrast, were "more vulnerable to injury." Moreover, there was "a compelling normative consideration" for a stronger defamation remedy by private persons: unlike public figures, they had not "voluntarily exposed themselves to increased risk of injury from defamatory falsehoods concerning them." In short, "private individuals are not only more vulnerable to injury than public officials and public figures; they are also more deserving of recovery." The Rosenbloom plurality rule had abridged the legitimate state concern with private plaintiffs' injuries "to a degree that we find unacceptable." Moreover, Rosenbloom had unwisely imposed the task on judges of deciding "on an ad hoc basis which publications address issues of 'general or public interest' and which do not." Accordingly, the new Gertz rule, leaving states free to impose any standard of liability short of "liability without fault" in private person cases, seemed preferable.

In explaining the conclusion that "the private defamation plaintiff who establishes liability under a less demanding standard than that stated by New York Times may recover only such damages as are sufficient to compensate him for actual injury," Justice Powell stated: "Like the doctrine of presumed damages, jury discretion to award punitive damages unnecessarily exacerbates the danger of media self-censorship." He noted, however, that "actual injury" is "not limited to out-of-pocket loss": "Indeed, the more customary types of actual harm inflicted by defamatory falsehood included impairment of reputation and standing in the community, personal humiliation, and mental anguish and suffering." [Justice Blackmun, a member of the Rosenbloom plurality, wrote that he thought the Rosenbloom rule more logical than the new approach, but had decided to vote with Justice Powell "to create a majority": "A definitive ruling [is] paramount."]

Justice BRENNAN's dissent was the only opinion in Gertz to adhere fully to the Rosenbloom plurality approach. He insisted that the claim that public figures had greater access to the media to clear their names was unrealistic: "In the vast majority of libels involving public officials or public figures, the ability to respond through the media will depend on the same complex factor on which the ability of a private individual depends: the unpredictable event of the media's continuing interest in the story." Moreover, "the idea that certain 'public' figures have voluntarily exposed their entire lives to public inspection, while private individuals have kept theirs carefully shrouded from public view is, at best, a legal fiction." The new rule, he argued, denied "free expression its needed 'breathing space.' "Widespread adoption of a reasonable care standard in private defamations—"the probable result of today's decision"—will "lead to self-censorship."

Justice WHITE's lengthy dissent argued that even the Gertz protection of the media went too far: "I fail to see how the quality or quantity of public debate will be promoted by further emasculation of state libel laws [protecting non-public persons] for the benefit of the news media." He argued that traditional libel laws should be permitted to stand, particularly in view of "the increasingly prominent role [and power of the] mass media." He conceded that the New York Times rule itself was justifiable because "seditious libel—criticism of government and public officials—falls beyond the police power of the State." But traditional standards of liability and the authorization of punitive as well as general damages should be permitted to stand when private citizens were defamed. He argued that experience showed "that some publications are so inherently capable of injury, and actual injury so difficult to prove, that the risk of falsehood should be borne by the publisher, not the victim." [Justice DOUGLAS' dissent came from the opposite direction: he continued to insist that the First Amendment barred all libel suits "for public discussion of public issues." Chief Justice BURGER also submitted a dissent.]

3. *Speech on matters of private concern.* In DUN & BRADSTREET, INC. v. GREENMOSS BUILDERS, 472 U.S. 749 (1985), the alleged defamation involved a private credit report given by Dun & Bradstreet to a bank regarding Greenmoss, a construction contractor. The report erroneously claimed that Greenmoss had filed for voluntary bankruptcy. A Vermont jury, instructed that it need not consider "actual malice," returned a verdict for the builder and awarded $50,000 in compensatory and $300,000 in punitive damages. The Vermont Supreme Court found the Gertz standard inapplicable, holding that the operations of credit reporting agencies were not the type of activities encompassed by New York Times and its progeny. A divided Supreme Court affirmed this holding, but not on the ground that nonmedia defendants were excluded from New York Times. Rather, a majority of the Court—Justice White in concurrence plus the four dissenters—found no relevant distinction between the institutional media and other forms of communication. The plurality declined to reach any such distinction, emphasizing a different distinction between speech on matters of public and private concern.

Justice POWELL, writing for himself and Justices Rehnquist and O'Connor, began with the proposition that "not all speech is of equal First Amendment importance." He relied on a distinction that had surfaced in other modern First Amendment cases (e.g., Connick v. Myers [1983; p. 1304 below]) between speech "on matters of public concern" and speech "on matters of purely private concern" far from the core of the First Amendment. "[In] light of the reduced constitutional value of speech involving no matters of public concern, we hold that the state interest adequately supports awards of presumed and punitive damages—even absent a showing of 'actual malice.' " Applying this approach, Justice Powell found that credit reports such as the one at issue here—involving nothing that "concerns a public matter"—were outside the Gertz principles. The credit report, he wrote, contained "speech solely in the individual interest of the speaker and its specific business audience. [Moreover,] since the credit report was made available to only five subscribers, who, under the terms of the subscription agreement, could not disseminate it further, it cannot be said that the report involves any 'strong interest in the free flow of commercial information.' "

Chief Justice BURGER and Justice WHITE separately concurred in the judgment, each urging that Gertz itself be overruled. Justice White also urged that the entire constitutionalization of the law of defamation, going back to New York Times, be reevaluated: "I remain convinced that Gertz was erroneously decided. I have also become convinced that the Court struck an improvident balance in [New York Times]. In a country like ours, [adequate] information about their government is of transcendent importance [to the people]. That flow of intelligence deserves full First Amendment protection. Criticism and assessment of the performance of public officials and of government in general are not subject to penalties imposed by law. But these First Amendment values are not at all served by circulating false statements of fact about public officials. On the contrary, erroneous information frustrates these values. They are even more disserved when the statements falsely impugn the honesty of those men and women and hence lessen the confidence in government. [It] is difficult to argue that the United States did not have a free and vigorous press before the rule in New York Times was announced."

Justice BRENNAN, joined by Justices Marshall, Blackmun and Stevens, dissented. He rejected the claim that the relevant distinction was between the media and other forms of communication. But rejecting the media/nonmedia distinction did not for the dissenters compel the conclusion reached by the Court. Rather, Justice Brennan objected to the distinction between matters of public and private concern. And even if there were such a distinction, he viewed Justice Powell's delineation as "impoverished": "[This] Court has consistently rejected the argument that speech is entitled to diminished First Amendment protection simply because it concerns economic matters. [Even] if the subject matter of credit reporting were properly considered [as] purely a matter of private discourse, this speech would fall well within the range of valuable expression for which the First Amendment demands protection. Much expression that does not directly involve public issues receives significant protection."

4. *Defamation law: a summary.* Justice O'Connor's 1986 majority opinion in Philadelphia Newspapers, Inc. v. Hepps, usefully summarized the state of the law after Dun & Bradstreet: "One can discern [two] forces that may reshape the common-law landscape to conform to the First Amendment. The first is whether the plaintiff is a public official or figure, or is instead a private figure. The second is whether the speech at issue is of public concern. When the speech is of public concern and the plaintiff is a public official or public figure, the Constitution clearly requires the plaintiff to surmount a much higher

barrier before recovering damages from a media defendant than is raised by the common law. When the speech is of public concern but the plaintiff is a private figure, as in Gertz, the Constitution still supplants the standards of the common law, but the constitutional requirements are, in at least some of their range, less forbidding than when the plaintiff is a public figure and the speech is of public concern. When the speech is of exclusively private concern and the plaintiff is a private figure, as in Dun & Bradstreet, the constitutional requirements do not necessarily force any change in at least some of the features of the common-law landscape.''

————

C.   NON-DEFAMATION TORTS

————

1. *Intentional infliction of emotional distress.*   The tort of intentional infliction of emotional distress may be pressed against private individuals even when the sole source of the distress is a speech act. But Chief Justice REHNQUIST's opinion for a unanimous Court in HUSTLER MAGAZINE v. FALWELL, 485 U.S. 46 (1988), held that a public figure offended by an ''outrageous'' magazine parody could not recover for the tort of intentional infliction of emotional distress without a showing of the ''actual malice'' required by New York Times. The case involved a suit by Jerry Falwell, a nationally known minister and commentator on politics and public affairs, seeking damages against the magazine for invasion of privacy, libel, and intentional infliction of emotional distress. The jury found for Falwell only on the last claim. The basis of the suit was a Hustler ''parody'' of an advertisement for Campari Liqueur entitled ''Jerry Falwell Talks About His First Time.'' The parody was modeled after actual Campari ads that included interviews with various celebrities about their ''first times.'' Although it was clear by the end of each interview that this meant the first time they had sampled Campari, the ads clearly played on the sexual double entendre of the general subject of ''first times.'' Copying the form and layout of these Campari ads, Hustler chose Falwell as a featured celebrity and printed an alleged ''interview'' with him in which he states that his ''first time'' was during a drunken incestuous rendezvous with his mother in an outhouse. The parody suggested that Falwell was a hypocrite who preached only when he was drunk. In small print at the bottom of the page, the ad contained the disclaimer, ''Ad parody—not to be taken seriously.'' The magazine's table of contents also listed the ad as ''Fiction; Ad and Personality Parody.''

In deciding against Falwell, the Court stated: ''This case presents us with a novel [question]. We must decide whether a public figure may recover damages for emotional harm caused by the publication of an ad parody offensive to him, and doubtless gross and repugnant in the eyes of most. Respondent would have us find that a State's interest in protecting public figures from emotional distress is sufficient to deny First Amendment protection to speech that is patently offensive and is intended to inflict emotional injury, even when that speech could not reasonably have been interpreted as stating actual facts about the public figure involved. This we decline to do.

''[The] sort of robust political debate encouraged by the First Amendment is bound to produce speech that is critical of those who hold public office or those public figures who are 'intimately involved in the resolution of important public [questions].' Such criticism, inevitably, will not always be reasoned or moderate; public figures as well as public officials will be subject to 'vehement, caustic, and sometimes unpleasantly sharp attacks.' [In Falwell's view,] so long as the utterance was intended to inflict emotional distress, was outrageous, and did in fact inflict serious emotional distress, it is of no constitutional import whether the statement was a fact or an opinion, or whether it was true or false. It is the intent to cause injury that is the gravamen of the tort, and the State's interest in preventing emotional harm simply outweighs whatever interest a speaker may have in speech of this type.

"Generally speaking the law does not regard the intent to inflict emotional distress as one which should receive much solicitude, and it is quite understandable that most if not all jurisdictions have chosen to make it civilly culpable where the conduct in question is sufficiently 'outrageous.' But in the world of debate about public affairs, many things done with motives that are less than admirable are protected by the First Amendment. In Garrison v. Louisiana, we held that even when a speaker or writer is motivated by hatred or ill-will his expression was protected by the First Amendment. [Thus,] while such a bad motive may be deemed controlling for purposes of tort liability in other areas of the law, we think the First Amendment prohibits such a result in the area of public debate about public figures.

"Were we to hold otherwise, there can be little doubt that political cartoonists and satirists would be subjected to damages awards without any showing that their work falsely defamed its subject. [The] appeal of the political cartoon or caricature is often based on exploration of unfortunate physical traits or politically embarrassing events—an exploration often calculated to injure the feelings of the subject of the portrayal. The art of the cartoonist is often not reasoned or even-handed, but slashing and one-sided. [But from] the viewpoint of history it is clear that our political discourse would have been considerably poorer without [cartoonists]. [Falwell] contends, however, that the caricature in question here was so 'outrageous' as to distinguish it from more traditional political cartoons. There is no doubt that the caricature of [Falwell] and his mother published in Hustler is at best a distant cousin of [traditional] political cartoons, [and] a rather poor relation at that. If it were possible by laying down a principled standard to separate the one from the other, public discourse would probably suffer little or no harm. But we doubt that there is any such standard, and we are quite sure that the pejorative description 'outrageous' does not supply one. 'Outrageousness' in the area of political and social discourse has an inherent subjectiveness about it which would allow a jury to impose liability on the basis of the jurors' tastes or views, or perhaps on the basis of their dislike of a particular expression. An 'outrageousness' standard thus runs afoul of our longstanding refusal to allow damages to be awarded because the speech in question may have an adverse emotional impact on the audience. Admittedly, these oft-repeated First Amendment principles, like other principles, are subject to limitations. [Pacifica, p. 1164 below; Chaplinsky.] [But] the sort of expression involved in this case does not seem to us to be governed by any exception to the general First Amendment principles stated above.

"We conclude that public figures and public officials may not recover for the tort of intentional infliction of emotional distress by reason of publications such as the one here at issue without showing in addition that the publication contains a false statement of fact which was made with 'actual malice,' i.e., with knowledge that the statement was false or with reckless disregard as to whether or not it was true. This is not merely a 'blind application' of the New York Times standard, it reflects our considered judgment that such a standard is necessary to give adequate 'breathing space' to the freedoms protected by the First Amendment." Justice WHITE concurred, but stated that New York

Times had "little to do with this case, for here the jury found that the ad contained no assertion of fact."

For the view that Hustler treats the realm of protected speech as one in which the ordinary norms of community life are suspended in order to ensure that no one community norm becomes entrenched, see Post, "The Constitutional Concept of Public Discourse: Outrageous Opinion, Democratic Deliberation, and Hustler Magazine v. Falwell," 103 Harv.L.Rev. 603 (1990).

2. *Invasion of privacy.* States have recognized various privacy torts since publication of the much-discussed article by Warren and Brandeis, "The Right to Privacy," 4 Harv.L.Rev. 193 (1890). Four distinct types of privacy invasion have emerged: intrusion into the plaintiff's private affairs, public disclosure of nonnewsworthy facts the plaintiff would have preferred to keep secret, publicity placing the plaintiff in a false light, and appropriation of the plaintiff's name or likeness. See Prosser, "Privacy," 48 Calif.L.Rev. 383 (1960). See also Kennedy & Alderman, The Right of Privacy (1996). Some degree of privacy is arguably necessary to human dignity and individuality. See Edelman, "Free Press v. Privacy: Haunted by the Ghost of Justice Black," 68 Tex. L. Rev. 1195 (1990). Preserving privacy, however, by definition often impedes the free flow of information. For criticism of privacy torts on free speech grounds, see Kalven, "Privacy in Tort Law—Were Warren and Brandeis Wrong?," 31 Law & Contemp. Prob. 326 (1966); Zimmerman, "Requiem for a Heavyweight: a Farewell to Warren and Brandeis's Privacy Tort," 68 Cornell L. Rev. 291 (1983); Posner, "The Right to Privacy," 12 Ga. L. Rev. 393 (1978). Should the First Amendment be read to limit the reach of privacy torts? The Supreme Court has reached this question only with respect to "false light" invasion of privacy claims, claims against disclosure of facts already in the public record, and appropriation claims. It has yet to confront a case involving public disclosure of truly private facts.

3. *"False light" invasion of privacy.* In "false light" privacy cases, the claim is that the disclosure not only invaded privacy but was also false—though not necessarily injurious to reputation, the gist of defamation actions. The decision in TIME, INC. v. HILL, 385 U.S. 374 (1967), focused primarily on "false light" privacy actions, and the decision by a divided Court was that the New York Times standard should be applicable to such actions. The Hill suit arose from the following circumstances: In 1952, the Hill family had been held hostage by three escaped convicts for 19 hours but was released unharmed. Three years later, a play portrayed the incident as involving considerable violence, though in fact there had been none. Life magazine's story on the play posed the actors in the original Hill home and indicated that the play accurately portrayed the actual incident. The original incident had been widely reported, but the Hills had tried to stay out of the public eye thereafter. Though the Life magazine report that was the subject of the action did not substantially damage the Hills' reputation—they were portrayed as courageous—they ultimately recovered a $30,000 judgment under New York law.

The Hill suit was based on a New York "right of privacy" statute prohibiting anyone from using "for advertising purposes, or for the purposes of trade, the name, portrait or picture of any living person without having first obtained the written consent of such person." Under the statute, truth was a defense in actions "based upon newsworthy people or events," but a "newsworthy person" could recover when he or she was the subject of a "fictitious" report—a report involving "material and substantial falsification." Justice BRENNAN's opinion for the Court concluded that "the constitutional protections for speech and press preclude the application of the New York statute to redress false reports of matters of public interest in the absence of proof that the defendant published the report with knowledge of its falsity or in reckless disregard of the truth." Moreover, Justice Brennan went on to indicate, in a much-debated dictum, that "newsworthiness" would offer similar protection even in a "true" privacy action.

Does the Hill principle, announced in 1967, survive the Court's 1974 retreat in Gertz from Justice Brennan's position that the New York Times principle applies to all "newsworthy" matters? Does Hill move well beyond the seditious libel-political speech emphasis that was seen as the "central meaning" of the First Amendment in New York Times? Nimmer criticized the Court for failing to "pierce the superficial similarity between false light invasion of privacy and defamation" and urged that disclosure of nondefamatory matters interfering with privacy not be afforded First Amendment protection. He noted, for example, that, unlike "injury arising from defamation, 'more speech' is irrelevant in mitigating the injury due to an invasion of privacy." See Nimmer, "The Right to Speak From Times to Time: First Amendment Theory Applied to Libel and Misapplied to Privacy," 56 Calif.L.Rev. 935 (1968). Or, on the other hand, is New York Times even more obviously applicable in the nondefamation setting because only true speech is involved, not false statements of fact? See Kalven, "The Reasonable Man and the First Amendment: Hill, Butts, and Walker," 1967 Sup.Ct.Rev. 267, suggesting that "the logic of New York Times and Hill taken together grants the press some measure of constitutional protection for anything the press thinks is a matter of public interest."

4. *Disclosure of rape victims' names.* In COX BROADCASTING CORP. v. COHN, 420 U.S. 469 (1975), a father had sued because of the broadcasting of the fact that his daughter had been a rape victim. Barring liability, the Court relied especially on "the public interest in a vigorous press." The decision did not reach the question of whether Hill and its dictum had survived Gertz. The Court held merely that civil liability in a "true" privacy action could not be imposed upon a broadcaster for accurately publishing information released to the public in official court records. Justice WHITE's opinion for the Court commented: "In this sphere of collision between claims of privacy and those of the free press, the interests on both sides are plainly rooted in the traditions and significant concerns of our society." But he found it unnecessary to decide "the broader question whether truthful publication may ever be subjected to civil or criminal liability," or "whether the State may ever define and protect an area of privacy free from unwanted publicity in the press." However, he recognized the "impressive credentials for a right of privacy" and claimed that earlier cases had "carefully left open the question" whether the Constitution requires "that truth be recognized as a defense in a defamation action brought by a private person," as well as "the question whether truthful publication of very private matters unrelated to public affairs could be constitutionally proscribed."

Cox Broadcasting's prohibition on the restriction of lawfully obtained truthful information, including the identities of juveniles and victims of sexual offenses, has been applied in a number of subsequent cases. For example, in FLORIDA STAR v. B.J.F., 491 U.S. 524 (1989), a newspaper had published the name of a victim of a sexual offense, a name obtained from a police report made available in the police department's press room. Justice Marshall's majority opinion overturned a judgment based on a state law barring the publication of the names of such victims. Although again declining "to hold broadly that truthful publication may never be punished consistent with the First Amendment," Justice Marshall found the law unacceptable. Justice Scalia concurred in part and in the judgment. Justice White, the author of Cox Broadcasting, dissented, joined by Chief Justice Rehnquist and Justice O'Connor, distinguishing Cox as involving judicial records. He also raised doubts about the entire line of privacy cases beginning with Time, Inc. v. Hill. Questioning whether privacy was being unduly sacrificed in all of them, he observed that "[t]oday, we have hit the bottom of the slippery slope. I would find a place to draw the line higher on the hillside: a spot high enough to protect B.J.F.'s desire for privacy and peace-of-mind in the wake of a horrible personal tragedy."

5. *Appropriation torts.* In ZACCHINI v. SCRIPPS–HOWARD BROADCASTING CO., 433 U.S. 562 (1977), the suit was based on the plaintiff's "right of publicity" rather than any interest in privacy or in reputation. The Court distinguished Time and held that the First Amendment does not "immunize the media [from liability for damages] when they broadcast a performer's entire act without his consent." Zacchini performed a "human cannonball" act in which he was shot from a cannon into a net some 200 feet away. The defendant filmed Zacchini's performance at a county fair and showed the entire 15–second act on a television news program. In allowing recovery, Justice White emphasized that the Court in Hill "was aware that it was adjudicating a 'false light' privacy case, [not] a case involving 'intrusion' "or "private details" about a nonnewsworthy person. And neither did Hill involve a claim of a "right of publicity" as here; this kind of claim was a "discrete kind of 'appropriation.' "Unlike "false light" cases designed to protect the interest in reputation, suits such as this one rested on the state interest "in protecting the proprietary interest of the individual in his act in part to encourage such entertainment," an interest "closely analogous to those of patent and copyright law." Moreover, a "right of publicity" case did not significantly intrude on dissemination of information to the public: "the only question is who gets to do the publishing." Accordingly, Justice White found the performer's claim a strong one, and the media arguments weak. Justice Powell, joined by Justices Brennan and Marshall, dissented.

Issues similar to those in Zacchini are presented by the inherent tensions between copyright law and First Amendment principles. See Harper & Row v. Nation Enterprises, 471 U.S. 539 (1985), where The Nation magazine published an article containing 300 to 400 words from former President Ford's yet-to-be published memoirs. Justice O'Connor's majority opinion rejected the argument that the "fair use" defense under the copyright laws had to be interpreted in light of the First Amendment when the words of an important public figure were involved. She stated that, in view of the First Amendment protections already embodied in copyright law, and the latitude the fair use defense traditionally afforded to scholarship and comment, there was no warrant for expanding the doctrine of fair use to create what amounted to a public figure exception to copyright. Justice Brennan, joined by Justices White and Marshall, dissented.

D. HATE SPEECH

---

1. *Arguments for regulation of hate speech.* During recent years, there has been extensive debate about the extent to which the First Amendment bars efforts to curb speech perceived as harmful and offensive to racial or religious minorities or other historically disempowered groups, apart from the tendency

of that speech to incite immediate violence. Arguments that such hate speech regulation should be permissible have drawn on several strands in existing First Amendment law, and on the countervailing interest in equality enshrined in the equal protection clause. See generally Matsuda et al., Words that Wound: Critical Race Theory, Assaultive Speech, and the First Amendment (1993).

a. Some have argued that hate speech should be proscribable as *group libel*. In Beauharnais v. Illinois, p. 1092 above, the Court found no First Amendment bar against a law prohibiting "expos[ure of] the citizens of any race, color, creed or religion to contempt, derision, or obloquy," reasoning that libel, whether individual or group, lies outside the First Amendment altogether. Beauharnais has never been overruled. But later decisions have unsettled its foundations. New York Times v. Sullivan and its progeny have assumed that libel is unprotected only to the extent it amounts to a provably false statement of fact, which would appear to exclude libel claims against the mere expression of racist views. Further, New York Times limited libel actions against government officials to speech that is "of and concerning" an individual in particular, not directed against a government in general. That holding arguably further undermines the notion that group libel is unprotected, although it might be countered that a verbal attack on a group of private individuals on the basis of their race is a far cry from seditious libel, and thus implicates lesser First Amendment concern.

b. Some have argued that hate speech should be proscribable as *fighting words* under the original definition set forth in Chaplinsky, which included words that "by their very utterance inflict injury" in addition to words that tend to incite immediate breaches of the peace. On this view, racist or other bigoted epithets should be no more protected when they cause fright or flight than when they cause fights, for in either case they are "no essential part of any exposition of ideas." But this strand of the fighting words doctrine has unraveled since Chaplinsky, as the Court has tended to limit fighting words to those that cause a face-to-face provocation to a brawl. For an argument that this strand of Chaplinsky is still extant or worth reviving, see Grey, "Responding to Abusive Speech on Campus: A Model Statute," Reconstruction, Winter 1990, at 50, 53 (arguing that fighting words, properly understood, are "essentially equivalent to words that would justify imposition of tort liability for intentional infliction of emotional distress"); Grey, "Civil Rights vs. Civil Liberties: The Case of Discriminatory Verbal Harassment," 8 Soc. Phil. & Pol. 81 (1991).

c. Some have argued that racist and other bigoted insults should be carved out as a *new category* of unprotected speech, apart from any analogy to group libel or fighting words. On this view, the unprotected categories enumerated in Chaplinsky did not constitute a closed set, but may be extended to any speech that is "of such slight social value as a step to truth that any benefit that may be derived from them is clearly outweighed by [social interests.]" For an early proposal of a new tort cause of action against racial insults, see Delgado, "Words that Wound: a Tort Action for Racial Insults, Epithets, and Name–Calling," 17 Harv. C.R. & C.L. Rev. 133 (1982). For an argument that "[r]acist speech is best treated as a *sui generis* category, presenting an idea so historically untenable, so dangerous, and so tied to perpetuation of violence and degradation [that] it is properly treated as outside the realm of protected discourse, see Matsuda, "Public Response to Racist Speech: Considering the Victim's Story," 87 Mich.L.Rev. 2320 (1989).

d. Some have argued that even if racist and other bigoted speech is otherwise understood as within the realm of First Amendment protection, any speech interest is trumped by the countervailing constitutional interest in *equality*. On this view, a compelling interest in eradicating racial hierarchy justifies the elimination of targeted expressions of race hatred, just as it justifies certain racial and other group preferences or affirmative action in education and employment. See Lawrence, "If He Hollers Let Him Go: Regulating Racist Speech on Campus," 1990 Duke L. J. 431 (arguing that the First Amendment should permit the regulation of "face-to-face racial vilification"). Lawrence draws heavily on Brown v. Board of Education, which he reads to have prohibited racial segregation "because of the message [it] conveys—the message that black children are an untouchable caste, unfit to be educated with white children." In his view, Brown is a precedent for holding that the expression of an idea must yield to the requirements of equal protection.

2. *Arguments against regulation of hate speech.* Arguments against hate speech regulations question both their constitutionality and their efficacy. a. The *constitutional* arguments emphasize that cases since Chaplinsky have undermined the notion that words can be regulated based on their content in order to limit their emotive or psychic impact or their tendency to arouse anger or alarm, and suggest that hate speech regulations are unduly paternalistic. See, e.g., Strossen, "Regulating Racist Speech on Campus: A Modest Proposal?" 1990 Duke L.J. 484 (arguing that proposals such as Lawrence's "would endanger fundamental free speech values," "violate the cardinal principles that speech restrictions must be content-and viewpoint-neutral," and go well beyond the narrow bounds the Court has imposed on the "fighting words" doctrine); Fried, "A New First Amendment Jurisprudence: A Threat to Liberty," 59 U. Chi. L. Rev. 225 (1992) (assailing "those who promulgate these regulations [for] assign[ing] to themselves the authority to determine which ideas are false and which false ideas people may not express as they choose"); Weinstein, "A Constitutional Roadmap to the Regulation of Campus Hate Speech," 38 Wayne L.Rev. 163 (1991) (condemning as "thought control" the purpose "to combat racism by preventing its contagion from infecting the hearts and minds of a new generation of potential racists and sexists").

b. The arguments from from *inefficacy* stress that hate speech regulations, on their own terms, are likely to be futile or counter-productive. For example, Strossen argues that, because racial insults and epithets "constitute only a small fraction of all racist speech," eliminating them "would not effectively address the underlying problem of racism itself, of which racist speech is a symptom." On this view, an articulate diatribe about racial inferiority, which is clearly not proscribable as hate speech, might well be more hurtful to an individual and contribute more to the social construction of racism than do vulgar racial epithets, which are disfavored under conventional social norms and thus more easily discounted or ignored. See Henry Louis Gates, Jr., "Let Them Talk," The New Republic, Sept. 20, 1993, at 37. Kenneth Karst argues that "for women and for the members of racial and ethnic minorities a first amendment doctrine that offers less protection to 'low value' speech is not just unhelpful; it is dangerous." He suggests that while subordination is accomplished in part by speech, a subordinated group's "escape from subordinate status is accomplished primarily though persuasion," and that "precisely because an important part of a group's subordination consists in silencing, their emancipation requires a generously defined freedom of expression." Karst, "Boundaries and Reasons: Freedom of Expression and the Subordination of Groups," 1990 Ill.L.Rev. 95. For an argument that grassroots organization of minority voices is preferable to top-down disciplinary solutions to racist speech, see Calleros, "Paternalism, Counter–Speech, and Campus Hate–Speech [Codes]," 27 Ariz. St. L.J. 1249 (1995). For a reply to these various inefficacy arguments, see Delgado & Yun, " 'The Speech We Hate': First Amendment Totalism, The ACLU and the Principle of Dialogic Politics," 27 Ariz. St. L. J. 1281 (1995).

The clash between these arguments percolated in the lower courts in two contexts prior to the Court's decisions in R.A.V. v. St. Paul and Wisconsin v. Mitchell, below, which effectively precluded, at least for now, most regulation of racist or other group-directed hate speech: first, the enactment of laws to restrain a proposed neo-Nazi demonstration in the predominantly Jewish village of Skokie, Illinois, and second, the enactment of assorted hate speech regulations on university campuses.

3. *Restraining Nazi demonstrations: the Skokie controversy.* In the late 1970s, plans by American Nazis to hold marches and meetings in Illinois spurred a range of efforts by local governments to block the demonstrations and prompted the courts to reexamine the procedural and substantive principles governing freedom of expression. Ultimately, all local efforts to stop the Nazis were struck down by the state and lower federal courts. What was the proper resolution of the constitutional disputes engendered by the Nazis' plans? Could any other measures of control have withstood First Amendment attack?

Most of the Nazi plans focused on a proposed march in Skokie, Illinois, a community with a large Jewish population, including many survivors of Nazi persecutions. In the first round of the Skokie efforts to stop the demonstration, a state trial court issued an *injunction* prohibiting the National Socialist Party from engaging in a number of activities in the town—e.g., "parading in the uniform" of the Party; "displaying the swastika"; and "[d]istributing pamphlets [that] incite or promote hatred against persons of Jewish faith or ancestry or hatred against any person of any faith or ancestry, race or religion." The Illinois appellate courts refused to stay the injunction pending appeal, and the Illinois Supreme Court denied a petition for direct expedited appeal to that court. The Party then sought a stay in the U.S. Supreme Court. The Court treated the stay petition as a petition for certiorari, granted the writ, and summarily reversed the highest state court's denial of the stay. In its 5–4 per curiam disposition in NATIONAL SOCIALIST PARTY v. SKOKIE, 432 U.S. 43 (1977), the Court emphasized the need for "strict procedural safeguards" in the First Amendment area, including immediate appellate review. In response to that ruling, the Illinois courts ultimately set aside the preliminary injunction that had barred the Nazis' march. In the first instance, the intermediate appellate court modified the injunction, leaving in effect only a provision enjoining the defendants from "displaying the swastika" during the march. 366 N.E.2d 347. Thereafter, the Illinois Supreme Court held that the entire injunction, including the swastika provision, was unconstitutional. 373 N.E.2d 21. The majority concluded, "albeit reluctantly," that "the display of the swastika cannot be enjoined under the fighting-words exception to free speech, nor can anticipation of a hostile audience justify the prior restraint. Furthermore, Cohen and Erznoznik direct the citizens of Skokie that it is their burden to avoid the offensive symbol if they can do so without unreasonable inconvenience."

By the time the injunction dispute ended, a second round of efforts to block the Nazi demonstration had gotten under way. In May 1977, Skokie enacted three *ordinances* to prohibit demonstrations such as the one the Nazis contemplated. The first established a comprehensive permit system for parades and public assemblies, requiring permit applicants to obtain $300,000 in public liability insurance and $50,000 in property damage insurance. The second prohibited the "dissemination of any materials within [Skokie] which [intentionally] promotes and incites hatred against persons by reason of their race, national origin, or religion." (Compare the Illinois group libel law sustained by the Court in 1952, in Beauharnais v. Illinois, p. 1092 above.) The third ordinance prohibited public demonstrations by members of political parties while wearing "military-style" uniforms.

Represented by a Jewish ACLU attorney, the National Socialist Party of America and its leader at that time, Frank Collin, brought a federal court action to challenge the Skokie ordinances on First Amendment grounds. In Collin v. Smith, 447 F.Supp. 676 (1978), the District Court held the ordinances unconstitutional, commenting that "it is better to allow those who preach racial hate to expend their venom in rhetoric rather than to be panicked into embarking on the dangerous course of permitting the government to decide what its citizens may say and hear." The Court of Appeals affirmed that decision in almost all respects. In invalidating the ban on dissemination of materials promoting and inciting hatred, the majority found Beauharnais not controlling: "It may be questioned, after cases such as Cohen v. California, Gooding v. Wilson, and Brandenburg v. Ohio, whether the *tendency to induce violence* approach sanctioned implicitly in Beauharnais would pass constitutional muster today." Collin v. Smith, 578 F.2d 1197 (7th Cir., 1978). With the Nazi demonstration scheduled for June 25, 1978, Skokie sought a Supreme Court stay of the Court of Appeals ruling, pending review. On June 12, 1978, however, the Supreme Court denied the stay. Justice Blackmun, joined by Justice Rehnquist, dissented from that order, stating that the Court of Appeals decision "is in some tension with this Court's decision, 25 years ago, in Beauharnais," and noting that "Beauharnais has never been overruled or formally limited in any way." Smith v. Collin, 436 U.S. 953.

With all legal obstacles to the Skokie march removed by the Court's denial of the stay, Collin cancelled the planned demonstration three days before it was to take place. Relying on the rulings in the Skokie litigation, the Nazis had obtained a federal court order setting aside the Chicago Park District's $60,000 liability insurance requirement which had previously blocked Nazi demonstrations in city parks there. Collin explained that the aim of the Nazis' Skokie efforts had been "pure agitation to restore our right to free speech." He stated that "he had used the threat of the Skokie march to win the right to rally in [Chicago]." No serious violence occurred when about 25 Nazis held a rally in a Chicago park on July 9, 1978.

The final scene in the Skokie drama took place in October, 1978, when the Court declined to review the Seventh Circuit decision invalidating the Skokie ordinances. SMITH v. COLLIN, 439 U.S. 916. Justice BLACKMUN, joined by Justice White, dissented, urging that certiorari be granted "in order to resolve any possible conflict that may exist between the ruling of the Seventh Circuit here and Beauharnais." He added: "I also feel that the present case affords the Court an opportunity to consider whether, in the context of the facts that this record appears to present, there is no limit whatsoever to the exercise of free speech. There indeed may be no such limit, but when citizens assert, not casually but with deep conviction, that the proposed demonstration is scheduled at a place and in a manner that is taunting and overwhelmingly offensive to the citizens of that place, that assertion, uncomfortable though it may be for judges, deserves to be examined. It just might fall into the same category as one's 'right' to cry 'fire' in a crowded theater, for 'the character of every act depends upon the circumstances in which it is done.' Schenck."

For the view that permitting the Nazi march served the value of mastering pervasive social tendencies toward intolerance, and that it makes sense to carve out free speech as an arena of "extraordinary self-restraint" in order to promote self-restraint in other arenas, see Bollinger, The Tolerant Society: Freedom of Speech and Extremist Speech in America (1986).

4. *Regulating racist and other bigoted speech on campus.* Beginning in the late 1980s, a number of colleges and universities around the nation, responding to reports of racial incidents on campuses, considered or adopted regulations to curb hate speech—speech expressing hatred or bias toward members of racial, religious, or other groups. These regulations provoked extensive debates on the campuses, in the media, and in the academic literature about the permissibility under the First Amendment of such rules.

In April 1988, for example, the University of Michigan adopted a regulation subjecting individuals to discipline for "[any] behavior, verbal or physical, that stigmatizes or victimizes an individual on the basis of race, ethnicity, religion, sex, sexual orientation, creed, national origin, ancestry, age, marital status, handicap or Viet–Nam era veteran status" which "has the purpose or reasonably foreseeable effect of interfering with an individual's academic efforts, employment, participation in University sponsored extra-curricular activities or personal safety." A federal district court held the regulation unconstitutional under the First Amendment as overbroad and impermissibly vague. Doe v. University of Mich., 721 F.Supp. 852 (E.D.Mich.1989).

In March 1989, Stanford University considered a proposal to regulate "epithets and other forms of expression that by accepted community standards stigmatize, victimize or pejoratively characterize persons or groups on the basis of personal or cultural differences." It drew pointed opposition, including objections by one of the co-authors that such restrictions were "incompatible with the mission and meaning of a university" and inconsistent with the broad protection afforded by the First Amendment to offensive speech. See Gunther, "Good Speech, Bad Speech—Should Universities Restrict Expression That is Racist or Otherwise Denigrating? No," 42 Stanford Lawyer 7 (Spring 1990). The proposed regulations were withdrawn in the face of such criticism, and in October 1989, a different, far more limited and speech-protective regulation, drafted by Stanford law professor Thomas Grey, was proposed. It was adopted in June 1990. This new addition to Stanford's "fundamental standard" of conduct for members of the university community focused on "discriminatory harassment": "Speech or other expression constitutes harassment by personal vilification if it: (a) is intended to insult or stigmatize an individual or small group of individuals on the basis of their sex, race, color, handicap, religion, sexual orientation, or national and ethnic origin; and (b) is addressed directly to the individual or individuals whom it insults or stigmatizes; and (c) makes use of insulting or 'fighting' words or non-verbal symbols. In [this context], insulting or 'fighting' words or non-verbal symbols are [those] 'which by their very utterance inflict injury or tend to incite to an immediate breach of the peace,' and which are commonly understood to convey direct and visceral hatred or contempt for human beings on the basis of their sex, race, color, handicap, religion, sexual orientation, or national and ethnic origin."

In 1995, a California state court struck down the Stanford standard under a California statute providing that a private university may not impose limitations speech that would violate the First Amendment if imposed by a public university. The decision, Corry v. Stanford, No. 740309 (Cal. Super. Ct. Santa Clara Co. Feb. 27, 1995), held that the Stanford standard was overbroad under Chaplinsky because it reached insults that did not threaten to provoke immediate violence, and was impermissibly content-discriminatory under R.A.V. v. St. Paul, below, because it focused on bigoted insults while leaving other insults alone. After reading R.A.V., consider whether this decision was correct, or whether the Stanford standard arguably fit within any of the exceptions outlined by Justice Scalia. For an account of the history of the Stanford standard by its author, and an argument for its constitutionality even in the wake of R.A.V., see Grey, "How to Write a Speech Code Without Really Trying: Reflections on the Stanford Experience," 29 U.C. Davis L. Rev. 891 (1996).

————

R.A.V. v. City of St. Paul

505 U.S. 377, 112 S.Ct. 2538, 120 L.Ed.2d 305 (1992)

Justice SCALIA delivered the opinion of the Court.

In the predawn hours of June 21, 1990, petitioner and several other teenagers allegedly assembled a crudely-made cross by taping together broken chair legs. They then allegedly burned the cross inside the fenced yard of a black family that lived across the street from the house where petitioner was staying. Although this conduct could have been punished under any of a number of laws [including laws against terroristic threats, arson, and criminal damage to property], one of the two provisions under which [St. Paul] chose to charge petitioner (then a juvenile) was the St. Paul Bias–Motivated Crime Ordinance which provides:

> "Whoever places on public or private property a symbol, object, appellation, characterization or graffiti, including, but not limited to, a burning cross or Nazi swastika, which one knows or has reasonable grounds to know arouses anger, alarm or resentment in others on the basis of race, color, creed, religion or gender commits disorderly conduct and shall be guilty of a misdemeanor."

Petitioner moved to dismiss this count on the ground that the St. Paul ordinance was substantially overbroad and impermissibly content-based and therefore facially invalid under the First Amendment. The trial court granted this motion, but the Minnesota Supreme Court reversed.

I. [Assuming,] arguendo, that all of the expression reached by the ordinance is proscribable under the "fighting words" doctrine, we nonetheless conclude that the ordinance is facially unconstitutional in that it prohibits otherwise permitted speech solely on the basis of the subjects the speech addresses. The First Amendment generally prevents government from proscribing speech, or even expressive conduct, because of disapproval of the ideas expressed. Content-based regulations are presumptively invalid. From 1791 to the present, however, our society, like other free but civilized societies, has permitted restrictions upon the content of speech in a few limited areas, which are "of such slight social value as a step to truth that any benefit that may be derived from them is clearly outweighed by the social interest in order and morality." Chaplinsky. [Our] decisions since the 1960's have narrowed the scope of the traditional categorical exceptions for defamation and for obscenity, but a limited categorical approach has remained an important part of our First Amendment jurisprudence.

We have sometimes said that these categories of expression are "not within the area of constitutionally protected speech," or that the "protection of the First Amendment does not extend" to them. Such statements must be taken in context, however. [What] they mean is that these areas of speech can, consistently with the First Amendment, be regulated because of their constitutionally proscribable content (obscenity, defamation, etc.)—not that they are categories of speech entirely invisible to the Constitution, so that they may be made the vehicles for content discrimination unrelated to their distinctively proscribable content. Thus, the government may proscribe libel; but it may not make the further content discrimination of proscribing only libel critical of the government. [Nor could a] city council [enact] an ordinance prohibiting only those legally obscene works that contain criticism of the city government or, indeed, that do not include endorsement of the city government. Such a simplistic, all-or-nothing-at-all approach to First Amendment protection is at odds with common sense and with our jurisprudence as well.

The proposition that a particular instance of speech can be proscribable on the basis of one feature (e.g., obscenity) but not on the basis of another (e.g., opposition to the city government) is commonplace, and has found application in many contexts. We have long held, for example, that nonverbal expressive activity can be banned because of the action it entails, but not because of the ideas it expresses—so that burning a flag in violation of an ordinance against outdoor fires could be punishable, whereas burning a flag in violation of an ordinance against dishonoring the flag is not.

[Thus], the exclusion of "fighting words" from the scope of the First Amendment simply means that, for purposes of that Amendment, the unprotected features of the words are, despite their verbal character, essentially a "nonspeech" element of communication. Fighting words are thus analogous to a noisy sound truck: [both] can be used to convey an idea; but neither has, in and of itself, a claim upon the First Amendment. As with the sound truck, however, so also with fighting words: The government may not regulate use based on hostility—or favoritism—towards the underlying message expressed.

The concurrences describe us as setting forth a new First Amendment principle that prohibition of constitutionally proscribable speech cannot be "underinclusive" [so that] "a government must either proscribe all speech or no speech at all." That easy target is of the concurrences' own invention. In our view, the First Amendment imposes not an "underinclusiveness" limitation but a "content discrimination" limitation upon a State's prohibition of proscribable speech. There is no problem whatever, for example, with a State's prohibiting obscenity (and other forms of proscribable expression) only in certain media or markets, for although that prohibition would be "underinclusive," it would not discriminate on the basis of content.

Even the prohibition against content discrimination that we assert the First Amendment requires is not absolute. [When] the basis for the content discrimination consists entirely of the very reason the entire class of speech at issue is proscribable, no significant danger of idea or viewpoint discrimination exists. [Thus, a state] might choose to prohibit only that obscenity which is the most patently offensive in its prurience—i.e., that which involves the most lascivious displays of sexual activity. But it may not prohibit, for example, only that obscenity which includes offensive political messages. And the Federal Government can criminalize only those threats of violence that are directed against the President, since the reasons why threats of violence are outside the First Amendment (protecting individuals from the fear of violence, from the disruption that fear engenders, and from the possibility that the threatened violence will occur) have special force when applied to the person of the President. But the Federal Government may not criminalize only those threats against the President that mention his policy on aid to inner cities. [And a state] may choose to regulate price advertising in one industry but not in others, because the risk of fraud [is] in its view greater there. But a State may not prohibit only that commercial advertising that depicts men in a demeaning fashion.

Another valid basis for according differential treatment to even a content-defined subclass of proscribable speech is that the subclass happens to be associated with particular "secondary effects" of the speech, so that the regulation is "justified without reference to the content of the ... speech," Renton v. Playtime Theatres, Inc. [p. 1162 below]. A State could, for example, permit all obscene live performances except those involving minors. Moreover, since words can in some circumstances violate laws directed not against speech but against conduct (a law against treason, for example, is violated by telling the enemy the nation's defense secrets), a particular content-based subcategory of a proscribable class of speech can be swept up incidentally within the reach of a statute directed at conduct rather than speech. Thus, for example, sexually derogatory "fighting words," among other words, may produce a violation of Title VII's general prohibition against sexual discrimination in employment practices. Where the government does not target conduct on the basis of its expressive content, acts are not shielded from regulation merely because they express a discriminatory idea or philosophy. [Finally,] it may not even be necessary to identify any particular "neutral" basis, so long as the nature of the content discrimination is such that there is no realistic possibility that official suppression of ideas is afoot. (We cannot think of any First Amendment interest that would stand in the way of a State's prohibiting only those obscene motion pictures with blue-eyed actresses.)

II.   Applying these principles to the St. Paul ordinance, we conclude that, even as narrowly construed by the Minnesota Supreme Court [to apply only to] "fighting words," the remaining, unmodified terms make clear that the ordinance applies only to "fighting words" that insult, or provoke violence, "on the basis of race, color, creed, religion or gender." Displays containing abusive invective, no matter how vicious or severe, are permissible unless they are addressed to one of the specified disfavored topics. Those who wish to use "fighting words" in connection with other ideas—to express hostility, for example, on the basis of political affiliation, union membership, or homosexuality—are not covered. The First Amendment does not permit St. Paul to impose special prohibitions on those speakers who express views on disfavored subjects.

In its practical operation, moreover, the ordinance goes even beyond mere content discrimination, to actual viewpoint discrimination. Displays containing some words—odious racial epithets, for example—would be prohibited to proponents of all views. But "fighting words" that do not themselves invoke race, color, creed, religion, or gender—aspersions upon a person's mother, for example—would seemingly be usable ad libitum in the placards of those arguing in favor of racial, color, etc. tolerance and equality, but could not be used by that speaker's opponents. One could hold up a sign saying, for example, that all "anti-Catholic bigots" are misbegotten; but not that all "papists" are, for that would insult and provoke violence "on the basis of religion." St. Paul has no such authority to license one side of a debate to fight freestyle, while requiring the other to follow Marquis of Queensbury Rules.

[Justice STEVENS] suggests that [the ordinance is directed] not to speech of a particular content, but to particular "injuries" that are "qualitatively different" from other injuries. This is word-play. What makes the anger, fear, sense of dishonor, etc. produced by violation of this ordinance distinct from the anger, fear, sense of dishonor, etc. produced by other fighting words is nothing other than the fact that it is caused by a distinctive idea, conveyed by a distinctive message.

[The] content-based discrimination reflected in the St. Paul ordinance comes within neither any of the specific exceptions to the First Amendment prohibition we discussed earlier, nor within a more general exception for content discrimination that does not threaten censorship of ideas. It assuredly does not fall within the exception for content discrimination based on the very reasons why the particular class of speech at issue (here, fighting words) is proscribable. [St. Paul] has not singled out an especially offensive mode of expression—it has not, for example, selected for prohibition only those fighting words that communicate ideas in a threatening (as opposed to a merely obnoxious) manner. Rather, it has proscribed fighting words of whatever manner that communicate messages of racial, gender, or religious intolerance. [Nor does it aim] only at the "secondary effects" of the speech. [As] we said in Boos v. Barry [p. 1208 below], "listeners' reactions to speech are not the type of 'secondary effects' we referred to in Renton."

Finally, St. Paul [argues] that, even if the ordinance regulates expression based on hostility towards its protected ideological content, this discrimination is nonetheless justified because it is narrowly tailored to serve compelling state interests [in protecting the] rights of members of groups that have historically been subjected to discrimination, including the right of such group members to live in peace where they wish. We do not doubt that these interests are compelling, and that the ordinance can be said to promote them. [The] dispositive question in this case, [however,] is whether content discrimination is reasonably necessary to achieve St. Paul's compelling interests; it plainly is not. An ordinance not limited to the favored topics, for example, would have precisely the same beneficial effect. In fact the only interest distinctively served by the content limitation is that of displaying the city council's special hostility towards the particular biases thus singled out. That is precisely what the First Amendment forbids. The politicians of St. Paul are entitled to express that hostility—but not through the means of imposing unique limitations upon speakers who (however benightedly) disagree.

Let there be no mistake about our belief that burning a cross in someone's front yard is reprehensible. But St. Paul has sufficient means at its disposal to prevent such behavior without adding the First Amendment to the fire.

[Reversed.]

Justice WHITE, with whom Justice BLACKMUN and Justice O'CONNOR join, and with whom Justice STEVENS joins except as to Part I(A), concurring in the judgment.

I agree with the majority that the judgment of the Minnesota Supreme Court should be reversed. However, our agreement ends there. This case could easily be decided within the contours of established First Amendment law by holding, as petitioner argues, that the St. Paul ordinance is fatally overbroad because it criminalizes not only unprotected expression but expression protected by the First Amendment. [Instead,] the majority casts aside long-established First Amendment doctrine [and] adopts an untried theory. This is hardly a judicious way of proceeding, and the Court's reasoning in reaching its result is transparently wrong.

I. A. This Court's decisions have plainly stated that expression falling within certain limited categories so lacks the values the First Amendment was designed to protect that the Constitution affords no protection to that expression. Chaplinsky. [Thus,] this Court has long held certain discrete categories of expression [e.g.,child pornography, obscenity and most libel] to be proscribable on the basis of their content. All of these categories are content based. But the Court has held that First Amendment does not apply to them because their expressive content is worthless or of de minimis value to society. [This] categorical approach has provided a principled and narrowly focused means for distinguishing between expression that the government may regulate freely and that which it may regulate on the basis of content only upon a showing of compelling need.

[Nevertheless,] the majority holds that the First Amendment protects those narrow categories of expression long held to be undeserving of First Amendment protection—at least to the extent that lawmakers may not regulate some fighting words more strictly than others because of their content. The Court announces that such content-based distinctions violate the First Amendment because "the government may not regulate use based on hostility—or favoritism—towards the underlying message expressed." Should the government want to criminalize certain fighting words, the Court now requires it to criminalize all fighting words.

To borrow a phrase, "Such a simplistic, all-or-nothing-at-all approach to First Amendment protection is at odds with common sense and with our jurisprudence as well." It is inconsistent to hold that the government may proscribe an entire category of speech because the content of that speech is evil, but that the government may not treat a subset of that category differently without violating the First Amendment; the content of the subset is by definition worthless and undeserving of constitutional protection. [A] ban on all fighting words or on a subset of the fighting words category would restrict only the social evil of hate speech, without creating the danger of driving viewpoints from the marketplace. [By] characterizing fighting words as a form of "debate," the majority legitimates hate speech as a form of public discussion. [Furthermore, by] placing fighting words, which the Court has long held to be valueless, on at least equal constitutional footing with political discourse and other forms of speech that we have deemed to have the greatest social value, the majority devalues the latter category.

B. In a second break with precedent, the Court refuses to sustain the ordinance even though it would survive under the strict scrutiny applicable to other protected expression. [The] Court expressly concedes that [the government interest in ensuring the rights of members of groups that have historically been subject to discrimination] is compelling and is promoted by the ordinance, [but holds that such a law]could never pass constitutional muster if [its object] could be accomplished by banning a wider category of speech. This appears to be a general renunciation of strict scrutiny review, a fundamental tool of First Amendment analysis.

C. The Court has patched up its argument with an apparently nonexhaustive list of ad hoc exceptions, in what can be viewed either as an attempt to confine the effects of its decision to the facts of this case, or as an effort to anticipate some of the questions that will arise from its radical revision of First Amendment law. [For example,] Title VII makes it unlawful to discriminate "because of [an] individual's race, color, religion, sex, or national origin," and the regulations covering hostile workplace claims forbid "sexual harassment," which includes "unwelcome sexual advances, requests for sexual favors, and other verbal or physical conduct of a sexual nature" which creates "an intimidating, hostile, or offensive working environment." [Hence,] the majority's second exception, which the Court indicates would insulate a Title VII hostile work environment claim from an underinclusiveness challenge because "sexually derogatory 'fighting words' ... may produce a violation of Title VII's general prohibition against sexual discrimination in employment practices." [But if] the relationship between the broader statute and specific regulation is sufficient to bring the Title VII regulation within [this exception], then all St. Paul need do to bring its ordinance within [it] is to add some prefatory language concerning discrimination generally.

II.   Although I disagree with the Court's analysis, I do agree with its conclusion: The St. Paul ordinance is unconstitutional. However, I would decide the case on overbreadth grounds. [Although] the ordinance as construed reaches categories of speech that are constitutionally unprotected, it also criminalizes a substantial amount of expression that—however repugnant—is shielded by the First Amendment. [I] understand the [Minnesota Supreme Court] to have ruled that St. Paul may constitutionally prohibit expression that "by its very utterance" causes "anger, alarm or resentment." Our fighting words cases have made clear, however, that such generalized reactions are not sufficient to strip expression of its constitutional protection. The mere fact that expressive activity causes hurt feelings, offense, or resentment does not render the expression unprotected. The ordinance is therefore fatally overbroad and invalid on its face.

Justice BLACKMUN, concurring in the judgment.

I regret what the Court has done in this case. [I] fear that the Court has been distracted from its proper mission by the temptation to decide the issue over "politically correct speech" and "cultural diversity," neither of which is presented here. [I] see no First Amendment values that are compromised by a law that prohibits hoodlums from driving minorities out of their homes by burning crosses on their lawns, but I see great harm in preventing the people of Saint Paul from specifically punishing the race-based fighting words that so prejudice their community. I concur in the judgment, however, because I agree with Justice WHITE that this particular ordinance reaches beyond fighting words to speech protected by the First Amendment.

Justice STEVENS, with whom Justice WHITE and Justice BLACKMUN join as to Part I, concurring in the judgment.

[While] I agree that the St. Paul ordinance is unconstitutionally overbroad for the reasons stated in Part II of Justice WHITE's opinion, I write separately to suggest how the allure of absolute principles has skewed the analysis of both the majority and concurring opinions.

I.   [The] Court today revises the categorical approach [articulated in Chaplinsky]. It is not, the Court rules, that certain "categories" of expression are "unprotected," but rather that certain "elements" of expression are wholly "proscribable." To the Court, an expressive act, like a chemical compound, consists of more than one element. Although the act may be regulated because it contains a proscribable element, it may not be regulated on the basis of another (nonproscribable) element it also contains. [I] am, however, even more troubled by the second step of the Court's analysis—namely, its conclusion that the St. Paul ordinance is an unconstitutional content-based regulation of speech. Drawing on broadly worded dicta, the Court establishes a near-absolute ban on content-based regulations of expression and holds that the First Amendment prohibits the regulation of fighting words by subject matter. [This] aspect of the Court's ruling fundamentally misunderstands the role and constitutional status of content-based regulations on speech.

[Although] the Court has, on occasion, declared that content-based regulations of speech are "never permitted," Mosley, such claims are overstated. [In] broadest terms, our entire First Amendment jurisprudence creates a regime based on the content of speech. The scope of the First Amendment is determined by the content of expressive activity: Although the First Amendment broadly protects "speech," it does not protect [e.g., price-fixing, threats, or antitrust conspiracies]. Likewise, whether speech falls within one of the categories of "unprotected" or "proscribable" expression is determined, in part, by its content. Whether a magazine is obscene, a gesture a fighting word, or a photograph child pornography is determined, in part, by its content. Even within categories of protected expression, the First Amendment status of speech is fixed by its content. [The] level of protection given to [allegedly libelous] speech depends upon its subject matter: speech about public officials or matters of public concern receives greater protection than speech about other topics. It can, therefore, scarcely be said that the regulation of expressive activity cannot be predicated on its content: much of our First Amendment jurisprudence is premised on the assumption that content makes a difference. Consistent with this general premise, we have frequently upheld content-based regulations of speech.

[The] Court today goes beyond even the overstatement in Mosley and applies the prohibition on content-based regulation to speech that the Court had until today considered wholly "unprotected" by the First Amendment—namely, fighting words. This new absolutism in the prohibition of content-based regulations severely contorts the fabric of settled First Amendment law. Our First Amendment decisions have created a rough hierarchy in the constitutional protection of speech. Core political speech occupies the highest, most protected position; commercial speech and nonobscene, sexually explicit speech are regarded as a sort of second-class expression; obscenity and fighting words receive the least protection of all. Assuming that the Court is correct that this last class of speech is not wholly "unprotected," it certainly does not follow that fighting words and obscenity receive the same sort of protection afforded core political speech. Yet in ruling that proscribable speech cannot be regulated based on subject matter, the Court does just that. Perversely, this gives fighting words greater protection than is afforded commercial speech. If Congress can prohibit false advertising directed at airline passengers without also prohibiting false advertising directed at bus passengers and if a city can prohibit political advertisements in its buses while allowing other advertisements, it is ironic to hold that a city cannot regulate fighting words based on "race, color, creed, religion or gender" while leaving unregulated fighting words based on "union membership or homosexuality."

[Perhaps] because the Court recognizes these perversities, it quickly offers some ad hoc limitations on its newly extended prohibition on content-based regulations. [For example, the Court concedes that] "the Federal Government can criminalize only those physical threats that are directed against the President." [Precisely] this same reasoning, however, compels the conclusion that St. Paul's ordinance is constitutional. Just as Congress may determine that threats against the President entail more severe consequences than other threats, so [St. Paul] may determine that threats based on the target's race, religion, or gender cause more severe harm to both the target and to society than other threats.

II.   Although I agree with much of Justice WHITE's analysis, I do not join Part I–A of his opinion because I have reservations about the "categorical approach" to the First Amendment. Admittedly, the categorical approach to the First Amendment has some appeal: either expression is protected or it is not—the categories create safe harbors for governments and speakers alike. But this approach sacrifices subtlety for clarity and is, I am convinced, ultimately unsound. As an initial matter, the concept of "categories" fits poorly with the complex reality of expression. Few dividing lines in First Amendment law are straight and unwavering, and efforts at categorization inevitably give rise only to fuzzy boundaries. [Moreover,] the categorical approach does not take seriously the importance of context. The meaning of any expression and the legitimacy of its regulation can only be determined in context. Whether, for example, a picture or a sentence is obscene cannot be judged in the abstract, but rather only in the context of its setting, its use, and its audience.

Perhaps sensing the limits of such an all-or-nothing approach, the Court has applied its analysis less categorically than its doctrinal statements suggest. The Court has recognized intermediate categories of speech (for example, for indecent nonobscene speech and commercial speech) and geographic categories of speech (public fora, limited public fora, nonpublic fora) entitled to varying levels of protection. The Court has also stringently delimited the categories of unprotected speech. While we once declared that "libelous utterances [are] not . . . within the area of constitutionally protected speech," Beauharnais, our rulings in New York Times Co. v. Sullivan [and progeny] have substantially qualified this broad claim. Similarly, we have consistently construed the "fighting words" exception set forth in Chaplinsky narrowly. [In] short, the history of the categorical approach is largely the history of narrowing the categories of unprotected speech. This evolution, I believe, indicates that the categorical approach is unworkable and the quest for absolute categories of "protected" and "unprotected" speech ultimately futile.

III. As the foregoing suggests, I disagree with both the Court's and part of Justice WHITE's analysis of the constitutionality St. Paul ordinance. Unlike the Court, I do not believe that all content-based regulations are equally infirm and presumptively invalid; unlike Justice WHITE, I do not believe that fighting words are wholly unprotected by the First Amendment. To the contrary, I believe our decisions establish a more complex and subtle analysis, one that considers the content and context of the regulated speech, and the nature and scope of the restriction on speech. Applying this analysis and assuming arguendo (as the Court does) that the St. Paul ordinance is not overbroad, I conclude that such a selective, subject-matter regulation on proscribable speech is constitutional.

[Looking] to the content and character of the regulated activity, two things are clear. First, by hypothesis the ordinance bars only low-value speech, namely, fighting words. [Second,] the ordinance regulates "expressive conduct [rather] than . . . the written or spoken word." Looking to the context of the regulated activity, it is again significant that the statute (by hypothesis) regulates only fighting words. [By] hypothesis, then, the St. Paul ordinance restricts speech in confrontational and potentially violent situations. The case at hand is illustrative. The cross-burning in this case—directed as it was to a single African–American family trapped in their home—was nothing more than a crude form of physical intimidation. That this cross-burning sends a message of racial hostility does not automatically endow it with complete constitutional protection.

[The] St. Paul ordinance regulates speech not on the basis of its subject matter or the viewpoint expressed, but rather on the basis of the harm the speech causes. [Contrary] to the Court's suggestion, the ordinance regulates only a subcategory of expression that causes injuries based on "race, color, creed, religion or gender," not a subcategory that involves discussions that concern those characteristics. [Moreover,] even if the St. Paul ordinance did regulate fighting words based on its subject matter, such a regulation would, in my opinion, be constitutional. [As] we have long recognized, subject-matter regulations generally do not raise the same concerns of government censorship and the distortion of public discourse presented by viewpoint regulations.

Contrary to the suggestion of the majority, the St. Paul ordinance does not regulate expression based on viewpoint. The Court contends that the ordinance requires proponents of racial intolerance to "follow the Marquis of Queensbury Rules" while allowing advocates of racial tolerance to "fight freestyle." The law does no such thing. [The] response to a sign saying that "all [religious] bigots are misbegotten" is a sign saying that "all advocates of religious tolerance are misbegotten." Assuming such signs could be fighting words (which seems to me extremely unlikely), neither sign would be banned by the ordinance for the attacks were not "based on ... religion" but rather on one's beliefs about tolerance. Conversely (and again assuming such signs are fighting words), just as the ordinance would prohibit a Muslim from hoisting a sign claiming that all Catholics were misbegotten, so the ordinance would bar a Catholic from hoisting a similar sign attacking Muslims. The St. Paul ordinance is evenhanded. In a battle between advocates of tolerance and advocates of intolerance, the ordinance does not prevent either side from hurling fighting words at the other on the basis of their conflicting ideas, but it does bar both sides from hurling such words on the basis of the target's "race, color, creed, religion or gender." To extend the Court's pugilistic metaphor, the St. Paul ordinance simply bans punches "below the belt"—by either party. It does not, therefore, favor one side of any debate.

Finally, it is noteworthy that the St. Paul ordinance is, as construed by the Court today, quite narrow. The St. Paul ordinance does not ban all "hate speech," nor does it ban, say, all cross-burnings or all swastika displays. [Petitioner] is free to burn a cross to announce a rally or to express his views about racial supremacy, he may do so on private property or public land, at day or at night, so long as the burning is not so threatening and so directed at an individual as to "by its very [execution] inflict injury." Taken together, these several considerations persuade me that the St. Paul ordinance is not an unconstitutional content-based regulation of speech. Thus, were the ordinance not overbroad, I would vote to uphold it.

THE IMPLICATIONS OF R.A.V.

1. *Distinguishing the regulation of hate speech from the regulation of hate crimes.* One term after R.A.V., the Court confronted a First Amendment challenge to a state law enhancing the sentence for bias-motivated assault. Two state supreme courts—Wisconsin and Ohio—had reasoned that aggravating the penalty for racially motivated hate crimes violated the principle of viewpoint neutrality set forth in R.A.V. Just as government may not selectively regulate unprotected speech such as fighting words on the basis of the viewpoint of the speaker, these state courts reasoned, so government may not regulate conduct based solely on the viewpoint of an actor. For an articulation of this position, see Gellman, "Sticks and Stones Can Put You in Jail, But Can Words Increase Your Sentence?," 39 U.C.L.A. L.Rev. 333 (1991).

In WISCONSIN v. MITCHELL, 508 U.S. 476 (1993), the Supreme Court unanimously rejected that argument, drawing a sharp distinction between the regulation of speech and conduct. The effect of Mitchell was to limit the holding of R.A.V. to viewpoint-selective laws aimed expressly at otherwise unprotected words or symbols. Chief Justice REHNQUIST delivered the opinion of the Court: "On the evening of October 7, 1989, a group of young black men and boys, including Mitchell, gathered at an apartment complex in Kenosha, Wisconsin. Several members of the group discussed a scene from the motion picture 'Mississippi Burning,' in which a white man beat a young black boy who was praying. The group moved outside and Mitchell asked them: 'Do you all feel hyped up to move on some white people?' Shortly thereafter, a young white boy approached the group on the opposite side of the street where they were standing. As the boy walked by, Mitchell said: 'You all want to fuck somebody up? There goes a white boy; go get him.' Mitchell counted to three and pointed in the boy's direction. The group ran towards the boy, beat him severely, and stole his tennis shoes. The boy was rendered unconscious and remained in a coma for four days.

"After a jury trial in the Circuit Court for Kenosha County, Mitchell was convicted of aggravated battery. That offense ordinarily carries a maximum sentence of two years' imprisonment. But because the jury found that Mitchell had intentionally selected his victim because of the boy's race, the maximum sentence for Mitchell's offense was increased to seven years under [a Wisconsin] provision [that] enhances the maximum penalty for an offense whenever the defendant 'intentionally selects the person against whom the crime ... is committed ... because of the race, religion, color, disability, sexual orientation, national origin or ancestry of that person....' The Circuit Court sentenced Mitchell to four years' imprisonment for the aggravated battery. Mitchell [appealed] his conviction and sentence, [and] the Wisconsin Supreme Court [relying on R.A.V., held] that the statute 'violates the First Amendment directly by punishing what the legislature has deemed to be offensive thought.' [We] reverse.

"[Mitchell] argues that the Wisconsin penalty-enhancement statute is invalid because it punishes the defendant's discriminatory motive, or reason, for acting. But [a defendant's motive for committing an offense is traditionally a factor considered by a judge at sentencing, and] motive plays the same role under the Wisconsin statute as it does under federal and state antidiscrimination laws, which we have previously upheld against constitutional challenge. Title VII, for example, makes it unlawful for an employer to discriminate against an employee 'because of such individual's race, color, religion, sex, or national origin.' [In] R.A.V. v. St. Paul, we cited Title VII [as] an example of a permissible content-neutral regulation of conduct.

"Nothing in our decision last Term in R.A.V. compels a different result here. [W]hereas the ordinance struck down in R.A.V. was explicitly directed at expression (i.e., "speech" or "messages"), the statute in this case is aimed at conduct unprotected by the First Amendment. Moreover, the Wisconsin statute singles out for enhancement bias-inspired conduct because this conduct is thought to inflict greater individual and societal harm. For example, according to the State and its amici, bias-motivated crimes are more likely to provoke retaliatory crimes, inflict distinct emotional harms on their victims, and incite community unrest. The State's desire to redress these perceived harms provides an adequate explanation for its penalty-enhancement provision over and above mere disagreement with offenders' beliefs or biases. As Blackstone said long ago, 'it is but reasonable that among crimes of different natures those should be most severely punished, which are the most destructive of the public safety and happiness.' 4 W. Blackstone, Commentaries * 16. [Reversed.]"

2. *The limits of the distinction between R.A.V. and Mitchell.* Mitchell permitted the state to enhance punishment for a crime motivated by the victim's race. In so doing, the Court focused heavily on the material consequences of such conduct: it assumed that such violence has greater in terrorem and incendiary effects on society than ordinary violence. What if the state instead enhanced punishment for a crime "motivated by the defendant's beliefs

about race," or by "the defendant's attempt to communicate a racist message"? Such crimes might have similar effects to those described in Mitchell. But for the view that such laws might violate the First Amendment, even though Mitchell was correctly decided, see Tribe, "The Mystery of Motive, Private and [Public]," 1993 Sup. Ct. Rev. 1.

3. *Hostile environment sexual or racial harassment.* Federal civil rights statutes barring employment discrimination have been construed to bar sexual or racial harassment in the workplace, including by the creation of a racially or sexually hostile environment that adversely affects working conditions. After R.A.V. and Mitchell, are such laws constitutional? For the argument that such laws raise serious First Amendment questions, see Browne, "Title VII as Censorship: Hostile-Environment Harassment and the First Amendment," 52 Ohio State L. J. 481 (1991); Volokh, "Freedom of Speech and Workplace Harassment," 39 U.C.L.A. L. Rev. 1791 (1992). For a defense based partly on the notion that employees in the workplace context are effectively a captive audience, see Fallon, "Sexual Harassment, Content–Neutrality, and the First Amendment Dog That Didn't Bark," 1994 S. Ct. Rev. 1. See also Strossen, "Regulating Workplace Sexual Harassment and Upholding the First Amendment—Avoiding a Collision," 37 Vill. L. Rev. 757 (1992).

SECTION 5. SEXUALLY EXPLICIT EXPRESSION

Introduction. Recall that in Chaplinsky, p. 1077 above, the Court categorized "obscenity," like libel and fighting words, as expression outside of First Amendment protection, because it is "of such slight social value as a step to truth that any benefit that may be derived from [it] is outweighed by the social interest in order and morality." The Court has continued to regard obscenity as an unprotected category of speech, although it has struggled mightily with the question of how to define that category—how to delineate the area excluded from constitutional protection so that properly protected speech would not also be curtailed. The Court has added an additional category of sexually explicit speech to the Chaplinsky list by holding that child pornography is unprotected speech. If speech is sexually explicit but is not obscene and does not constitute child pornography, it is within the realm of First Amendment protection, but the Court has wrestled with the question whether it should occupy a subordinate position as "lower value" speech. A majority of the Court has never agreed with the creation of such a formal low-value category for sexually explicit speech, but the Court has nonetheless upheld a number of restrictions on such speech through balancing analysis. These developments are examined in turn in this section.

What justifications might there be for restraining sexually explicit speech? To safeguard against the violent or anti-social conduct that it might cause (under clear and present danger? under an incitement test?)? To avoid the "corrupting" of individual morals and character by the "sin of obscenity"— whether or not improper behavior results? To protect the sensibilities of the audience by safeguarding against the risk of shock from offensive sexual materials? To protect children against exposure to sexual materials, because of the greater susceptibility of the immature to their harmful effects? To protect society's moral standards against erosion? To preserve or improve the quality of life or the tone of the community? To promote equality values barring sex discrimination, by curbing materials that contribute to the subordination of women and by banning stimuli that may encourage sexual harassment?

Questions such as these assume that obscenity may belong in the First Amendment ballpark, thus triggering a requirement of some justification. But are sexually explicit materials properly considered a variety of "speech"? Are they more aptly described as aids to sexual arousal or sexual activity itself? Do they communicate ideas and appeal to the intellectual process, or do they simply induce a purely physical effect ? Which if any of the values underlying First Amendment protection (surveyed above in sec. 1) justify the imposition of First Amendment scrutiny here ? The arguments from self-government and democracy seem largely directed at political speech. The arguments from the marketplace of ideas and the search for truth are broader and seem to include scientific debate as well. But do they also extend to artistic and literary communication? Note that the Court's definitions of obscenity in the cases that follow protect materials of certain "literary, artistic, political, or scientific value" and that the obscenity category typically focuses on hard-core pornography. Can such materials nevertheless claim First Amendment protection? Do they serve the autonomy, self-realization rationale for protecting speech?

The Court's first direct encounter with the constitutionality of obscenity control took place fifteen years after Chaplinsky, in Roth, which follows. The Warren Court's attempt to define unprotected obscenity in Roth spawned a tortuous period of divided rulings, until a new definition of obscenity was agreed upon in 1973 by the Burger Court in Miller and Paris Adult, below. The Miller test continues to define unprotected obscenity today. Materials on child pornography, pornography as the subordination of women, and the regulation of sexually explicit speech follow the account of these developments in obscenity law.

A. OBSCENITY

Roth v. United States
Alberts v. California

354 U.S. 476, 77 S.Ct. 1304, 1 L.Ed.2d 1498 (1957).

[In these cases, the Court sustained the validity of federal and state obscenity laws without reaching the question of whether any particular materials to which the laws were applied were obscene. Roth, a New York publisher and seller, was convicted of mailing obscene advertising and an obscene book in violation of a federal statute barring the mailing of "obscenity." Alberts, engaged in the mail order business, was convicted under a California law for "lewdly keeping for sale obscene and indecent books" and "publishing an obscene advertisement of them."]

Justice BRENNAN delivered the opinion of the Court.

The dispositive question is whether obscenity is utterance within the area of protected speech and press. Although this is the first time the question has been squarely presented [here], expressions found in numerous opinions indicate that this Court has always assumed that obscenity is not protected by the freedoms of speech and press. In light [of] history, it is apparent that the unconditional phrasing of the First Amendment was not intended to protect every utterance. [T]here is sufficiently contemporaneous evidence to show that obscenity [like libel, see Beauharnais] was outside the protection intended for speech and [press]. All ideas having even the slightest redeeming social importance—unorthodox ideas, controversial ideas, even ideas hateful to the prevailing climate of opinion—have the full protection of the guaranties, unless excludable because they encroach upon the limited area of more important interests. But implicit in the history of the First Amendment is the rejection of obscenity as utterly without redeeming social importance. This rejection for that reason is mirrored in the universal judgment that obscenity should be restrained, reflected in the international agreement of over 50 nations, in the obscenity laws of all of the 48 States, and in the 20 obscenity laws enacted by the Congress from 1842 to 1956. This is the same judgment expressed [in Chaplinsky]. [We] hold that obscenity is not within the area of constitutionally protected speech or press.

It is strenuously urged that these obscenity statutes offend the constitutional guaranties because they punish incitation to impure sexual *thoughts,* not shown to be related to any overt antisocial conduct which is or may be incited in the persons stimulated to such *thoughts.* [It] is insisted that the constitutional guaranties are violated because convictions may be had without proof either that obscene material will perceptibly create a clear and present danger of antisocial conduct, or will probably induce its recipients to such conduct. But, in light of our holding that obscenity is not protected speech, the complete answer to this argument is [in Beauharnais].

However, sex and obscenity are not synonymous. Obscene material is material which deals with sex in a manner appealing to prurient interest.[3] The portrayal of sex, e.g., in art, literature and scientific works, is not itself sufficient reason to deny material the constitutional protection of freedom of speech and press. Sex, a great and mysterious motive force in human life, has indisputably been a subject of absorbing interest to mankind through the ages; it is one of the vital problems of human interest and public [concern]. The fundamental freedoms of speech and press [are] indispensable to [our free society's] continued growth. [It] is therefore vital that the standards for judging obscenity safeguard the protection of freedom of speech and press for material which does not treat sex in a manner appealing to prurient interest.

The early leading standard of obscenity allowed material to be judged merely by the effect of an isolated excerpt upon particularly susceptible persons. Regina v. Hicklin, [1868] L.R. 3 Q.B. 360 [which defined obscenity as material tending "to deprave and corrupt those whose minds are open to such immoral influences"]. Some American courts adopted this standard but later decisions have rejected it and substituted this test: whether to the average person, applying contemporary community standards, the dominant theme of the material taken as a whole appeals to prurient interest. The Hicklin test,

3. I.e., material having a tendency to excite lustful thoughts. Webster's New International Dictionary (Unabridged, 2d ed., 1949) defines *prurient,* in pertinent part, as follows: "Itching; longing; uneasy with desire or longing; of persons, having itching, morbid, or lascivious longings; of desire, curiosity or propensity, lewd."

[We] perceive no significant difference between the meaning of obscenity developed in the case law and the definition of the A.L.I., Model Penal Code (Tent.Draft No. 6, 1957): "[A] thing is obscene if, considered as a whole, its predominant appeal is to prurient interest, i.e., a shameful or morbid interest in nudity, sex, or excretion, and if it goes substantially beyond customary limits of candor in description or representation of such matters." [Footnote by the Court.]

judging obscenity by the effect of isolated passages upon the most susceptible persons, might well encompass material legitimately treating with sex, and so it must be rejected as unconstitutionally restrictive of the freedoms of speech and press. On the other hand, the substituted standard provides safeguards adequate to withstand the charge of constitutional infirmity. Both trial courts below sufficiently followed the proper [standard]. [W]e hold that these statutes, applied according to the proper standard for judging obscenity, do not offend constitutional safeguards against convictions based upon protected material, or fail to give men in acting adequate notice of what is [prohibited].

Affirmed.

[Chief Justice WARREN concurred in the result, stating that the defendants were "engaged in the commercial exploitation of the morbid and shameful craving for materials with prurient effect. I believe that [government] can constitutionally punish such conduct. That is all [we] need to decide." Justice HARLAN, concurred in the result in Alberts, reasoning that the states have broad latitude under their police powers to regulate obscenity: "[It] is not irrational, in our present state of knowledge, to consider that pornography can induce a type of sexual conduct which a State may deem obnoxious to the moral fabric of society. [E]ven assuming that pornography cannot be deemed ever to [cause] criminal sexual conduct, [the] State can reasonably draw the inference that over a long period of time the indiscriminate dissemination of materials, the essential character of which is to degrade sex, will have an eroding effect on moral standards." But Justice Harlan dissented in Roth, concluding that the federal interest in regulating obscenity was much more "attenuated," and that under the postal power Congress could regulate only "hard-core" pornography. Justice DOUGLAS, joined by Justice BLACK, dissented: "When we sustain these convictions, we make the legality of a publication turn on the purity of thought which a book or tract instills in the mind of the reader. I do not think we can approve that standard and be faithful to the command of the First Amendment. [I] reject too the implication that problems of freedom of speech and of the press are to be resolved by weighing against the values of free expression, the judgment of the Court that a particular form of that expression has 'no redeeming social importance.' I would give the broad sweep of the First Amendment full support. I have the same confidence in the ability of our people to reject noxious literature as I have in their capacity to sort out the true from the false in theology, economics, politics, or any other field."]

THE STRUGGLE TO DEFINE OBSCENITY BETWEEN ROTH AND MILLER

1. *Overview.* Dissenting in Paris Adult Theatre I v. Slaton, 413 U.S. 49, 73 (1973), Justice Brennan summarized the tortured course of obscenity law in the period between Roth and Miller: "[Our] efforts to implement [the Roth] approach demonstrate that agreement on the existence of something called 'obscenity' is still a long and painful step from agreement on a workable definition of the term. [To] be sure, five members of the Court did agree in Roth that obscenity could be determined by asking 'whether to the average person, applying contemporary community standards, the dominant theme of the material taken as a whole appeals to prurient interest.' [But by] 1967 the following views had emerged: [Justices] Black and Douglas consistently maintained that government is wholly powerless to regulate any sexually oriented matter on the ground of its obscenity. [Justice] Harlan [believed] that the

Federal Government [could] control the distribution of 'hard core' pornography, while the States [could ban] 'any material which, taken as a whole, has been reasonably found in state judicial proceedings to treat with sex in a fundamentally offensive manner, under rationally established criteria for judging such material.' Jacobellis v. Ohio, [378 U.S. 184 (1964)]. [Justice] Stewart regarded 'hard core' pornography as the limit of both federal and state power. See, e.g., Ginzburg v. United States, 383 U.S. 463 (1966) (dissenting opinion); [Jacobellis] (concurring opinion. [Justice Stewart's concurrence in Jacobellis said of 'hard-core pornography': 'I shall not today attempt further to define the kinds of material I understand to be embraced within that shorthand description; and perhaps I could never succeed in intelligibly doing so. But I know it when I see it, and the motion picture involved in this case is not that.']).

"The view that, [in this period] enjoyed the most, but not majority, support was an interpretation of Roth adopted by [Chief Justice Warren and Justices Fortas and Brennan] in Memoirs v. Massachusetts, 383 U.S. 413 (1966). We expressed the view that Federal or State Governments could control the distribution of material where 'three [elements] coalesce: it must be established that (a) the dominant theme of the material taken as a whole appeals to a prurient interest in sex; (b) the material is patently offensive because it affronts contemporary community standards relating to the description or representation of sexual matters; and (c) the material is utterly without redeeming social value.' Even this formulation, however, concealed differences of opinion.[1] Moreover, it did not provide a definition covering all situations.[2] Nor, finally, did it ever command a majority of the [Court].

"In the face of this divergence of opinion the Court began the practice in Redrup v. New York, 386 U.S. 767 (1967), of per curiam reversals of convictions for the dissemination of materials that at least five members of the Court, applying their separate tests, deemed not to be obscene. [The] Redrup approach [resolves] cases as between the parties, but offers only the most obscure guidance to legislation, adjudication by other courts, and primary conduct. By disposing of cases through summary reversal or denial of certiorari we have deliberately and effectively obscured the rationale underlying the decisions. It comes as no surprise that judicial attempts to follow our lead conscientiously have often ended in hopeless [confusion]."

2. *Kingsley Pictures and sexual immorality.* Most obscenity rulings in this period, treating obscenity as simply wholly outside the First Amendment, were conspicuously silent about the interests thought to justify control of expression pertaining to sex. One case in the post-Roth years—though not dealing directly with an "obscenity" law—spoke more explicitly about such justifications. KINGSLEY INT'L PICTURES CORP. v. REGENTS, 360 U.S. 684 (1959), invalidated a New York motion picture licensing law. The law banned any "immoral" film, defined as a film that "portrays acts of sexual immorality [or] which expressly or impliedly presents such acts as desirable, acceptable, or proper patterns of behavior." The state denied a license to the film "Lady Chatterley's Lover" under this law because "its subject matter is adultery

1. In supporting this statement, Justice Brennan noted: "Compare Jacobellis v. Ohio, supra, at 192–195 (Brennan, J., joined by Goldberg, J.) (community standards national), with id., at 200–201 (Warren, C.J., joined by Clark, J., dissenting) (community standards local)."

2. In supporting this comment, Justice Brennan stated: "See Mishkin v. New York, 383 U.S. 502 (1966) (prurient appeal defined in terms of a deviant sexual group); Ginzburg v. United States, supra ('pandering' probative evidence of obscenity in close cases). See also Ginsberg v. New York, 390 U.S. 629 (1968) (obscenity for juveniles)."

presented as being right and desirable for certain people under certain circumstances." The Court reversed. Justice STEWART's opinion emphasized that "sexual immorality" under the New York scheme was "entirely different from" concepts like "obscenity" or "pornography," and that New York had not claimed that "the film would itself operate as an incitement to illegal action." He concluded that the state had prevented the exhibition of the film "because that picture advocates an idea—that adultery under certain circumstances may be proper behavior. Yet the First Amendment's basic guarantee is of freedom to advocate ideas. The State, quite simply, has thus struck at the very heart of constitutionally protected liberty. [The constitutional] guarantee is not confined to the expression of ideas that are conventional or shared by a majority. It protects advocacy of the opinion that adultery may sometimes be proper, no less than advocacy of socialism or the single tax."

3. *Stanley and possession of obscene materials.* In STANLEY v. GEORGIA, 394 U.S. 557 (1969), the Court reversed a conviction for knowing "possession of obscene matter," holding that the First Amendment prohibits "making the private possession of obscene material a crime." Justice MARSHALL's opinion, in striking contrast to the approach of the earlier obscenity cases, systematically canvassed the asserted state justifications. In Stanley, a search of a home for bookmaking evidence had uncovered obscene films. Georgia defended its law on the basis of Roth and with the argument: "If the State can protect the body of the citizen, may it [not] protect his mind?" Justice Marshall replied: "[The constitutional] right to receive information and ideas, regardless of their social worth, [is] fundamental to our free society. Moreover, in the context of this case—a prosecution for mere possession [in] the privacy of a person's own home—that right takes on an added dimension. For also fundamental is the right to be free, except in very limited circumstances, from unwanted governmental intrusions into one's privacy. [W]e think that mere categorization of these films as 'obscene' is insufficient justification for such a drastic invasion of personal liberties guaranteed by the [First Amendment]. Whatever may be the justifications for other statutes regulating obscenity, we do not think they reach into the privacy of one's own home. If the First Amendment means anything, it means that a State has no business telling a man, sitting alone in his own house, what books he may read or what films he may watch.

"[Y]et in the face of these traditional notions of individual liberty, Georgia asserts the right to protect the individual's mind from the effects of obscenity. We are not certain that this argument amounts to anything more than the assertion that the State has the right to control the moral content of a person's thoughts.[3] To some, this may be a noble purpose, but it is wholly inconsistent with the philosophy of the First Amendment. [Kingsley Pictures.] Whatever the power of the state to control public dissemination of ideas inimical to the public morality, it cannot constitutionally premise legislation on the desirability of controlling a person's private thoughts. Perhaps recognizing this, Georgia asserts that exposure to obscenity may lead to deviant sexual behavior or crimes of sexual violence. [Given] the present state of knowledge, the State may

---

3. " 'Communities believe, and act on the belief, that obscenity is immoral, is wrong for the individual, and has no place in a decent society. They believe, too, that adults as well as children are corruptible in morals and character, and that obscenity is a source of corruption that should be eliminated. Obscenity is not suppressed primarily for the protection of others. Much of it is suppressed for the purity of the community and for the salvation and welfare of the "consumer." Obscenity, at bottom, is not crime. Obscenity is sin.' Henkin, Morals and the Constitution: The Sin of Obscenity, 63 Colum.L.Rev. 391, 395 (1963)." [Footnote by Justice Marshall.]

no more prohibit mere possession of [obscenity] on the ground that it may lead to antisocial conduct than it may prohibit possession of chemistry books on the ground that they may lead to the manufacture of homemade spirits. It is true that in Roth this Court rejected the necessity of proving that exposure to obscene material would create a clear and present danger of antisocial [conduct]. But that case dealt with public distribution of obscene materials and such distribution is subject to different objections. For example, there is always the danger that obscene material might fall into the hands of children or that it might intrude upon the sensibilities or privacy of the general public. No such dangers are present in this case. Finally, we are faced with the argument that prohibition of possession of [obscenity] is a necessary incident to statutory schemes prohibiting distribution. That argument is based on alleged difficulties of proving an intent to distribute or in producing evidence of actual distribution. We are not convinced that such difficulties exist, but even if they did we do not think that they would justify infringement of the individual's right to read or observe what he pleases. Because that right is so fundamental to our scheme of individual liberty, its restriction may not be justified by the need to ease the administration of otherwise valid criminal laws." [Justice STEWART, joined by Justices Brennan and White, concurred only in the result, solely on the ground that the films were seized in violation of the Fourth Amendment. Justice Brennan later, in his Paris Adult dissent, said he was "now inclined to agree" with much of the principal Stanley opinion.]

4. *Reidel: Roth survives Stanley.* Two years after Stanley, the Court made clear that Stanley was not a basis for questioning the validity of obscenity *distribution* laws. In UNITED STATES v. REIDEL, 402 U.S. 351 (1971), a federal district court had relied on Stanley to dismiss an indictment under the federal law prohibiting the mailing of obscene materials—the law involved in Roth. The lower court had reasoned that "if a person has the right to receive and possess this material, then someone must have the right to deliver it to him," and had concluded that the federal prohibition could not be applied "where obscene material is not directed at children, or it is not directed at an unwilling public, where the material such as this case is solicited by adults." Justice WHITE's majority opinion gave short shrift to that argument: "To extrapolate from Stanley's right to have and peruse obscene material in the privacy of his own home a First Amendment right in Reidel to sell it to him would effectively scuttle Roth, the precise result that the Stanley opinion abjured." As the Reidel Court read Stanley, its "focus" was "on freedom of mind and thought and on the privacy of one's home." Reidel could not claim infringement of those rights; commerce implicates no privacy interests. "Roth has squarely placed obscenity and its distribution outside the reach of the First Amendment and they remain there today. Stanley did not overrule [Roth]."

Justice MARSHALL's separate opinion in Reidel disagreed strongly with Justice White's narrow reading of Stanley. He insisted that "Stanley turned on an assessment of which state interests may legitimately underpin governmental action." Stanley merely approved "regulatory action taken to protect children and unwilling adults from exposure to materials deemed to be obscene." But Stanley, he maintained, made an "assessment of state interests" approach appropriate for distribution cases as well. Applying that approach, Justice Marshall concurred in Reidel. Mail distribution "poses the danger that obscenity will be sent to children"; though Reidel himself planned to sell only to adults who requested his materials, "the sole safeguard designed to prevent the receipt of his merchandise by minors was his requirement that buyers declare their age." He accordingly concluded "that distributors of purportedly obscene merchandise may be required to take more stringent steps to guard against possible receipt by minors."

5. *The 1970 Obscenity Commission Report.* The U.S. Commission on Obscenity and Pornography was established by Congress in 1967. Its Report, submitted in 1970, rested in part on empirical studies of the impact of sexual literature. It concluded, for example, that patterns of sexual behavior were "not altered substantially by exposure to erotica"; that the available data did not demonstrate that "erotic material is a significant cause of sex crime"; and that exposure to erotica has "little or no effect" on attitudes regarding sexuality or sexual morality. The Commission majority's legislative recommendations included one urging that laws "prohibiting the sale, exhibition, or distribution of sexual materials to consenting adults should be repealed." The Commission also recommended the adoption of state laws "prohibiting the commercial distribution or display for sale of certain sexual materials to young persons," as well as laws "prohibiting public displays of sexually explicit pictorial materials."

For criticism of the 1970 Report, see Sunderland, Obscenity: The Court, the Congress and the President's Commission (1975) (noting that "the complexities and subtleties of human sexuality within society are extremely difficult to duplicate in the laboratory," and that the Commission neglected "indirect effects" such as "the influence exerted on attitudes by public law, qua law," and "the long-term effects of pornography"). See also Clor, "Science, Eros and [the Law]," 10 Duq.L.Rev. 63 (1971) (emphasizing the "limitations of behavioral social science as a resolver of controversial questions in public policy," and suggesting that "it will be unfortunate if people conclude that the obscenity problem has now been resolved because now, at last, we have the *scientific facts*").

6. *The Burger Court's new judicial definition of obscenity.* In two decisions decided together in 1973, the Court attempted a new definition and clarification of what constitutes unprotected obscenity. The result was effectively to get the Court out of the business of "Redruping," or case by case review, and to shift the burden of obscenity determinations to the state and local courts.

Miller v. California

413 U.S. 15, 93 S.Ct. 2607, 37 L.Ed.2d 419 (1973).

[As Chief Justice Burger described the facts, Miller had "conducted a mass mailing campaign to advertise the sale of illustrated books, euphemistically called 'adult' material. [H]e was convicted of violating California Penal Code § 311.2(a), a misdemeanor, by knowingly distributing obscene matter [by causing] five unsolicited advertising brochures to be sent through the mail. [While] the brochures contain some descriptive printed material, primarily they consist of pictures and drawings very explicitly depicting men and women in groups of two or more engaging in a variety of sexual activities with genitals often prominently displayed."]

Chief Justice BURGER delivered the opinion of the Court.

This is one of a group of "obscenity-pornography" cases being reviewed [in] a re-examination of standards enunciated in earlier cases involving what [Justice] Harlan called "the intractable obscenity problem." [This] case involves the application of a State's criminal obscenity statute to a situation in which sexually explicit materials have been thrust by aggressive sales action upon unwilling recipients who had in no way indicated any desire to receive such materials. This Court has recognized that the States have a legitimate interest in prohibiting dissemination or exhibition of obscene material when the mode of dissemination carries with it a significant danger of offending the sensibilities of unwilling recipients or of exposure to juveniles. [Stanley.] It is in this context that we are called on to define the standards which must be used to identify obscene material that a State may regulate.

Obscene material is unprotected by the First Amendment. [Roth.] [However, state] statutes designed to regulate obscene materials must be carefully limited. As a result, we now confine the permissible scope of such regulation to works which depict or describe sexual conduct. That conduct must be specifically defined by the applicable state law, as written or authoritatively construed. [The] basic guidelines for the trier of fact must be: (a) whether "the average person, applying contemporary community standards" would find that the work, taken as a whole, appeals to the prurient interest [Roth], (b) whether the work depicts or describes, in a patently offensive way, sexual conduct specifically defined by the applicable state law, and (c) whether the work, taken as a whole, lacks serious literary, artistic, political, or scientific value. We do not adopt as a constitutional standard the *"utterly* without redeeming social value" test of [Memoirs]. If a state law that regulates obscene material is thus limited, as written or construed, [First Amendment values] are adequately protected by the ultimate power of appellate courts to conduct an independent review of constitutional claims when necessary.

We emphasize that it is not our function to propose regulatory schemes for the States. [It] is possible, however, to give a few plain examples of what a state statute could define for regulation under [part] (b) of the standard announced in this opinion: (a) Patently offensive representations or descriptions of ultimate sexual acts, normal or perverted, actual or simulated. (b) Patently offensive representations or descriptions of masturbation, excretory functions, and lewd exhibition of the genitals.

Sex and nudity may not be exploited without limit by films or pictures exhibited or sold in places of public accommodation any more than live sex and nudity can be exhibited or sold without limit in such public places. At a minimum, prurient, patently offensive depiction or description of sexual conduct must have serious literary, artistic, political, or scientific value to merit First Amendment protection. For example, medical books [necessarily] use graphic illustrations and descriptions of human anatomy. In resolving the inevitably sensitive questions of fact and law, we must continue to rely on the jury system, accompanied by the safeguards that judges, rules of evidence, presumption of innocence and other protective features provide, as we do with [other] offenses against society and its individual members.

[Justice] Brennan, author of the opinions of the Court, or the plurality opinions, in [Roth, Jacobellis, Ginzburg, Mishkin, and Memoirs], has abandoned his former position and now maintains that no formulation of this Court, the Congress, or the States can adequately distinguish obscene material unprotected by the First Amendment from protected expression. [Paris, below.] Paradoxically, [he] indicates that suppression of unprotected obscene material is permissible to avoid exposure to unconsenting adults, as in this case, and to juveniles, although he gives no indication of how the division between protected and nonprotected materials may be drawn with greater precision for these purposes than for regulation of commercial exposure to consenting adults only.

Nor does he indicate where in the Constitution he finds the authority to distinguish between a willing "adult" one month past the state law age of majority and a willing "juvenile" one month younger.

Under the holdings announced today, no one will be subject to prosecution for the sale or exposure of obscene materials unless these materials depict or describe patently offensive "hard core" sexual conduct specifically defined by the regulating state law, as written or construed. We are satisfied that these specific prerequisites will provide fair notice to a dealer in such materials that his public and commercial activities may bring prosecution. If the inability to define regulated materials with ultimate, god-like precision altogether removes the power of the States or the Congress to regulate, then "hard core" pornography may be exposed without limit to the juvenile, the passerby, and the consenting adult alike, as, indeed, Mr. Justice Douglas contends. [In] this belief, however, [he] now stands alone. [Today,] for the first time since [Roth], a majority of this Court has agreed on concrete guidelines to isolate "hard core" pornography from expression protected by the First Amendment. Now we may abandon the casual practice of [Redrup] and attempt to provide positive guidance to the federal and state courts [alike].

Under a National Constitution, fundamental First Amendment limitations on the powers of the States do not vary from community to community, but this does not mean that there are, or should or can be, fixed, uniform national standards of precisely what appeals to the "prurient interest" or is "patently offensive." These are essentially questions of fact, and our nation is simply too big and too diverse for this Court to reasonably expect that such standards could be articulated for all 50 States in a single formulation, even assuming the prerequisite consensus exists. [It] is neither realistic nor constitutionally sound to read the First Amendment as requiring that the people of Maine or Mississippi accept public depiction of conduct found tolerable in Las Vegas, or New York City. [People] in different States vary in their tastes and attitudes, and this diversity is not to be strangled by the absolutism of imposed uniformity. [We] hold that the requirement that the jury evaluate the materials with reference to "contemporary standards of the State of California" [is] constitutionally adequate.

The dissenting Justices sound the alarm of repression. But, in our view, to equate the free and robust exchange of ideas and political debate with commercial exploitation of obscene material demeans the grand conception of the First Amendment and its high purposes in the historic struggle for freedom. [The] First Amendment protects works which, taken as a whole, have serious literary, artistic, political, or scientific value, regardless of whether the government or a majority of the people approve of the ideas these works represent. [But] the public portrayal of hard core sexual conduct for its own sake, and for the ensuing commercial gain, is a different matter. There is no evidence, empirical or historical, that the stern 19th century American censorship of public distribution and display of material relating to sex in any way limited or affected expression of serious literary, artistic, political, or scientific ideas. [We] do not see the harsh hand of censorship of ideas [and] "repression" of political liberty lurking in every state regulation of commercial exploitation of human interest in sex. [In] sum, we (a) reaffirm the Roth holding that obscene material is not protected by the First Amendment; (b) hold that such material can be regulated by the States, subject to the specific safeguards enunciated above, without a showing that the material is "*utterly* without redeeming social value"; and (c) hold that obscenity is to be determined by applying "contemporary community standards," [not "national standards"].

Vacated and remanded.

Justice DOUGLAS, [dissenting].

[Until] a civil proceeding has placed a tract beyond the pale, no criminal prosecution should be sustained. For no more vivid illustration of vague and uncertain laws could be designed than those we have fashioned. [If] a specific book [has] in a civil proceeding been condemned as obscene [and] thereafter a person publishes [it], then a vague law has been made specific. There would remain the underlying question whether the First Amendment allows an implied exception in the case of obscenity. I do not think it does and my views on the issue have been stated over and over again. But at least a criminal prosecution brought at that juncture would not violate [the] void-for-vagueness test. No such protective procedure has been designed by California in this case. Obscenity—which even we cannot define with precision—is a hodge-podge. To send men to jail for violating standards they cannot understand, construe, and apply is a monstrous thing to do in a Nation dedicated to fair trials and due process.

Justice BRENNAN, with whom Justices STEWART and MARSHALL join, dissenting.

In my dissent in [Paris, below], I noted that I had no occasion to consider the extent of state power to regulate the distribution of sexually oriented material to juveniles or the offensive exposure of such material to unconsenting adults. [I] need not now decide whether a statute might be drawn to impose, within the requirements of the First Amendment, criminal penalties for the precise conduct at issue here [—mailing unsolicited brochures]. For it is clear that under my dissent in [Paris], the statute [here] is unconstitutionally overbroad, and therefore invalid on its [face].

Paris Adult Theatre I v. Slaton

413 U.S. 49, 93 S.Ct. 2628, 37 L.Ed.2d 446 (1973).

[This case arose from a Georgia civil proceeding to enjoin the showing of two allegedly obscene films at two "adult" theaters. At a trial before a judge, the evidence consisted primarily of the films and of photographs of the entrance to the theaters. As described by Chief Justice Burger, these photographs "show a conventional, inoffensive theatre entrance, without any pictures, but with signs indicating that the theatres exhibit 'Atlanta's Finest Mature Feature Films.' On the door itself is a sign saying: 'Adult Theatre—You must be 21 and able to prove it. If viewing the nude body offends you, Please Do Not Enter.' "(Two state investigators who saw the films testified that the signs did not indicate "the full nature of what was shown. In particular, nothing indicated that the films depicted—as they did—scenes of simulated fellatio, cunnilingus, and group sex intercourse.") The trial judge dismissed the complaint. He held the showing of obscene films permissible where there was "requisite notice to the public" and "reasonable protection against the exposure of these films to minors." The Georgia Supreme Court reversed. The Supreme Court vacated and remanded for reconsideration in light of Miller, but noted that "nothing precludes the State of Georgia from the regulation of the allegedly obscene material exhibited in Paris Adult Theatre I provided that the applicable Georgia law, as written or authoritatively interpreted by the Georgia courts, meets the First Amendment standards set forth in Miller."]

Chief Justice BURGER delivered the opinion of the [Court].

We categorically disapprove the theory [that] obscene, pornographic films acquire constitutional immunity from state regulation simply because they are exhibited for consenting adults only. [Although] we have often pointedly recognized the high importance of the state interest in regulating the exposure of obscene materials to juveniles and unconsenting adults, this Court has never declared these to be the only legitimate state interests permitting regulation of obscene material. [In] particular, we hold that there are legitimate state interests at stake in stemming the tide of commercialized obscenity, even assuming it is feasible to enforce effective safeguards against exposure to juveniles and to passersby.[1] [These] include the interest of the public in the quality of life and the total community environment, the tone of commerce in the great city centers, and, possibly, the public safety itself. The Hill–Link Minority Report of the Commission on Obscenity and Pornography [1970] indicates that there is at least an arguable correlation between obscene materi-al and crime. Quite apart from sex crimes, however, there remains one problem of large proportions aptly described by Professor Bickel: "It concerns the tone of the society, the mode, or to use terms that have perhaps greater currency, the style and quality of life, now and in the future. A man may be entitled to read an obscene book in his room, or expose himself indecently there. [We] should protect his privacy. But if he demands a right to obtain the books and pictures he wants in the market, and to foregather in public places—discreet, if you will, but accessible to all—with others who share his tastes, *then to grant him his right is to affect the world about the rest of us, and to impinge on other privacies.* Even supposing that each of us can, if he wishes, effectively avert the eye and stop the ear (which, in truth, we cannot), what is commonly read and seen and heard and done intrudes upon us all, want it or not." 22 The Public Interest 25–26 (Winter, 1971). (Emphasis added.) As [Chief] Justice Warren stated, there is a "right of the Nation and of the States to maintain a decent society" [Jacobellis dissent].

But, it is argued, there is no scientific data which conclusively demonstrate that exposure to obscene materials adversely affects men and women or their society. It is [urged] that, absent such a demonstration, any kind of state regulation is "impermissible." We reject this argument. It is not for us to resolve empirical uncertainties underlying state legislation, save in the excep-tional case where that legislation plainly impinges upon rights protected by the Constitution itself. [Although] there is no conclusive proof of a connection between antisocial behavior and obscene material, the legislature of Georgia could quite reasonably determine that such a connection does or might exist. In deciding Roth, this Court implicitly accepted that a legislature could legitimate-ly act on such a conclusion to protect *"the social interest in order and morality."*

From the beginning of civilized societies, legislators and judges have acted on various unprovable assumptions. [If] we accept the unprovable assumption that a complete education requires certain books and the well nigh universal belief that good books, plays, and art lift the spirit, improve the mind, enrich the human personality and develop character, can we then say that a state

---

1. It is conceivable that an "adult" the-atre can—if it really insists—prevent the ex-posure of its obscene wares to juveniles. An "adult" bookstore, dealing in obscene books, magazines, and pictures, cannot realistically make this claim. [The] legitimate interest in preventing exposure of juveniles to obscene materials cannot be fully served by simply barring juveniles from the immediate physi-cal premises of "adult" bookstores, when there is a flourishing "outside business" in these materials. [Footnote by the Court.]

legislature may not act on the corollary assumption that commerce in obscene books, or public exhibitions focused on obscene conduct, have a tendency to exert a corrupting and debasing impact leading to antisocial behavior? [The sum of experience] affords an ample basis for legislatures to conclude that a sensitive, key relationship of human existence, central to family life, community welfare, and the development of human personality, can be debased and distorted by crass commercial exploitation of sex. Nothing in the Constitution prohibits a State from reaching such a conclusion and acting on it legislatively simply because there is no conclusive evidence or empirical [data].

It is asserted, however, that standards for evaluating state commercial regulations are inapposite in the present context, as state regulation of access by consenting adults to obscene material violates the constitutionally protected right to privacy enjoyed by petitioners' customers. [I]t is unavailing to compare a theater open to the public for a fee, with the private home of [Stanley] and the marital bedroom of [Griswold]. [Nothing] in this Court's decisions intimates that there is any "fundamental" privacy right "implicit in the concept of ordered liberty" to watch obscene movies in places of public accommodation. [The] idea of a "privacy" right and a place of public accommodation are, in this context, mutually exclusive. Conduct or depictions of conduct that the state police power can prohibit on a public street do not become automatically protected by the Constitution merely because the conduct is moved to a bar or a "live" theatre stage, any more than a "live" performance of a man and woman locked in a sexual embrace at high noon in Times Square is protected by the Constitution because they simultaneously engage in a valid political dialogue. [We also] reject the claim that [Georgia] is here attempting to control the minds or thoughts of those who patronize theaters. [Where] communication of ideas, protected by the First Amendment, is not involved, or the particular privacy of the home protected by Stanley, or any of the other "areas or zones" of constitutionally protected privacy, the mere fact that, as a consequence, some human "utterances" or "thoughts" may be incidentally affected does not bar the State from acting to protect legitimate state interests. Cf. [Roth; Beauharnais]. [Finally, for] us to say that our Constitution incorporates the proposition that conduct involving consenting adults only is always beyond state regulation, is a step we are unable to take. [W]e hold that the States have a legitimate interest in regulating commerce in obscene material and in regulating exhibition of obscene material in places of public accommodation, including so-called "adult" theaters from which minors are [excluded].

Vacated and remanded.

Justice BRENNAN, with whom Justices STEWART and MARSHALL join, dissenting.

[I] am convinced that the approach initiated 16 years ago in [Roth], and culminating in the Court's decision today, cannot bring stability to this area of the law without jeopardizing fundamental First Amendment values, and I have concluded that the time has come to make a significant departure from that approach. [The] essence of our problem in the obscenity area is that we have been unable to provide "sensitive tools" to separate obscenity from other sexually oriented but constitutionally protected speech, so that efforts to suppress the former do not spill over into the suppression of the latter. [I] am reluctantly forced to the conclusion that none of the available formulas, including the one announced today, can reduce the vagueness [of] our obscenity standards to a tolerable level. The vagueness of the standards in the obscenity area produces a number of separate problems, [including a] lack of fair notice, [a] chill on protected expression, and [a severe] stress [on] the state and federal judicial machinery. [These problems] persuade me that a significant change in direction is urgently required. I turn, therefore, to the alternatives that are now open.

1. The approach requiring the smallest deviation from our present course would be to draw a new line between protected and unprotected speech, still permitting the States to suppress all material on the unprotected side of the line. In my view, clarity cannot be obtained pursuant to this approach except by drawing a line that resolves all doubt in favor of state [power]. We could hold, for example, that any depiction or description of human sexual organs [is] outside the protection of the First Amendment. [That] formula would [reduce the vagueness problems. But it] would be appallingly [overbroad].

2. The alternative adopted by the Court today [adopts] a restatement of the Roth–Memoirs definition of obscenity. [In] my view, the restatement leaves unresolved the very difficulties that compel our rejection of the underlying Roth approach, while at the same time contributing substantial difficulties of its own. [T]he Court today permits suppression if the government can prove that the materials lack "*serious* literary, artistic, political or scientific value." But [Roth] held that certain expression is obscene, and thus outside the protection of the First Amendment, precisely *because* it lacks even the slightest redeeming social value. The Court's approach necessarily assumes that some works will be deemed obscene—even though they clearly have *some* social value—because the State was able to prove that the value, measured by some unspecified standard, was not sufficiently "serious" to warrant constitutional protection. That result [is] nothing less than a rejection of the fundamental First Amendment premises and rationale of the Roth opinion and an invitation to widespread suppression of sexually oriented speech.

3. [I] have also considered the possibility of reducing our own role, and the role of appellate courts generally, in determining whether particular matter is obscene. Thus, [we] might adopt the position that where a lower federal or state court has conscientiously applied the constitutional standard, its finding of obscenity will be no more vulnerable to reversal by this Court than any finding of fact. [But] it is implicit in [Redrup] that the First Amendment requires an independent review by appellate courts of the constitutional fact of obscenity. [In any event, while this approach would mitigate institutional stress,] it would neither offer nor produce any cure for the other vices of vagueness. [Plainly], the institutional gain would be more than offset by the unprecedented infringement of First Amendment rights.

4. Finally, I have considered the view, urged so forcefully since 1957 by our Brothers Black and Douglas, that the First Amendment bars the suppression of any sexually oriented expression. [But that would strip] the States of power to an extent that cannot be justified by the commands of the Constitution, at least so long as there is available an alternative approach that strikes a better balance between the guarantee of free expression and the States' legitimate interests.

[Given the] inevitable side-effects of state efforts to suppress what is assumed to be *unprotected* speech, we must scrutinize with care the state interest that is asserted to justify the suppression. For in the absence of some very substantial interest in suppressing such speech, we can hardly condone the ill-effects that seem to flow inevitably from the [effort]. Because we assumed—incorrectly, as experience has proven—that obscenity could be separated from other sexually oriented expression without significant costs, [we] had no occasion in Roth to prove the asserted state interest in curtailing unprotected, sexually oriented speech. Yet, as we have increasingly come to appreciate the vagueness of the concept of obscenity, we have begun to recognize and articulate the state interests at stake. [The] opinions in Redrup and [Stanley] reflected our emerging view that the state interests in protecting children and in protecting unconsenting adults may stand on a different footing from the other asserted state interests. It may well be, as one commentator has argued, that "exposure to [erotic material] is for some persons an intense emotional experience. A communication of this nature, imposed upon a person contrary to his wishes, has all the characteristics of a physical assault. [It] constitutes an invasion of his privacy."[1] But cf. [Cohen]. Similarly, if children are "not possessed of that full capacity for individual choice which is the presupposition of First Amendment guarantees," [the] State may have a substantial interest in precluding the flow of obscene materials even to consenting juveniles. [But whatever the strength of those interests, they] cannot be asserted in defense of the holding of the Georgia Supreme Court. [The justification here] must be found [in] some independent interest in regulating the reading and viewing habits of consenting adults.

[Of course, a State need not] remain utterly indifferent to—and take no action bearing on—the morality of the community. The traditional description of state police power does embrace the regulation of morals as well as health, safety, and general welfare of the citizenry. And much legislation—compulsory public education laws, civil rights laws, even the abolition of capital punishment—is grounded, at least in part, on a concern with the morality of the community. But the State's interest in regulating morality by suppressing obscenity, while often asserted, remains essentially unfocused and ill-defined. And, since the attempt to curtail unprotected speech necessarily spills over into the area of protected speech, the effort to serve this speculative interest through the suppression of obscene material must tread heavily on rights protected by the First Amendment.

[In] short, while I cannot say that the interests of the State—apart from the question of juveniles and unconsenting adults—are trivial or nonexistent, I am compelled to conclude that these interests cannot justify the substantial damage to constitutional rights and to this Nation's judicial machinery that inevitably results from state efforts to bar the distribution even of unprotected material to consenting adults. I would hold, therefore, that at least in the absence of distribution to juveniles or obtrusive exposure to unconsenting adults, the [First Amendment prohibits governments] from attempting wholly to suppress sexually oriented materials on the basis of their allegedly "obscene" contents. Nothing in this approach precludes [governments] from taking action to serve what may be strong and legitimate interests through regulation of the manner of distribution of sexually oriented material. [I] do not pretend to have found a complete and infallible [answer]. Difficult questions must still be faced, notably in the areas of distribution to juveniles and offensive exposure to unconsenting adults. Whatever the extent of state power to regulate in those areas, it should be clear that the view I espouse today would introduce a large measure of clarity to this troubled area, would reduce the institutional pressure on this Court and the rest of the State and Federal Judiciary, and would guarantee fuller freedom of expression while leaving room for the protection of

---

1. T. Emerson, The System of Freedom of Expression 496 (1970). [Footnote by Justice Brennan.]

legitimate governmental [interests].[2]

OBSCENITY LAW AFTER MILLER AND PARIS

1. *Justifications for obscenity regulation.* What government interests do the preceding cases suggest are served by suppressing obscene speech? Consider the following: a. *Debasement of individual character.* The Hicklin test held the harm of obscenity to be the "depravity and corruption" it induced in the mind of its consumer. This frankly paternalistic rationale seeks to protect the consumer from his own worst impulses. See Henkin, "Morals and the Constitution: The Sin of Obscenity," 63 Colum.L.Rev. 391 (1963). But this rationale was undermined by Stanley, which held that the choice to consume obscene materials was up to the consumer, at least in his own home. The opinions in Miller and Paris make little reference to this rationale; Chief Justice Burger mentions the "corrupting and debasing impact" of obscenity only insofar as it leads to "antisocial behavior."

b. *Offense to unwilling onlookers.* Exposure to obscenity can be shocking to the sensibilities of many adults, who would not willingly view it. Children are presumed incapable of consenting to such exposure. All the justices appear to agree that obscenity may be regulated to prevent unwilling exposure to these audiences. Even Justice Brennan, dissenting in Paris, notes that he might uphold laws aimed at "distribution to juveniles or obtrusive exposure to unconsenting adults." Should this narrow range of state interests be the only ones tolerable in the obscenity sphere, as Justice Brennan suggested? Or do even these interests clash with the Court's approach in Cohen v. California, which read the First Amendment to require that those offended by Cohen's jacket should simply avert their eyes?

c. *Inducement of criminal conduct.* Justice Harlan, concurring in Alberts, observed that obscenity might well induce "criminal sexual conduct," and Chief Justice Burger, writing for the Court in Paris, noted that there is "at least an arguable correlation between obscene material and [sex] crimes." This rationale supposes that readers and viewers of obscene materials will be induced to imitate their depictions of adultery, fornication, prostitution, sexual assault, rape, oral or anal sex, bestiality or other activities made criminal by many states. But note the absence in this reasoning of any requirement of tight causation or "clear and present danger" that these results will follow from

---

2. Justice Douglas also dissented. In three additional decisions handed down together with Miller and Paris, the Court, with the same 5-to-4 division, sustained obscenity controls in other contexts. In United States v. Twelve 200–Foot Reels, 413 U.S. 123 (1973), the majority held that federal laws could be applied to prevent the importation of obscene material for private use. In United States v. Orito, 413 U.S. 139 (1973), the Court sustained the federal ban on interstate transportation of obscene materials as applied to transport for private use. Do these decisions leave anything in Stanley intact? And in Kaplan v. California, 413 U.S. 115 (1973), the majority upheld the application of a state obscenity law to a book without pictorial contents.

Contrast State v. Henry, 78 Or.App. 392, 717 P.2d 189 (1986), rejecting the Roth–Paris line of reasoning and holding that criminal obscenity prosecution, not being an historically well-established exception to free speech principles, violated the free speech guarantee of the Oregon Constitution. See also Hawaii v. Kam, 69 Hawaii 483, 748 P.2d 372 (1988), holding that the Hawaii Constitution's right of privacy required striking down laws prohibiting the sale of obscene material.

obscenity consumption, or of intent on the part of the obscenity disseminator to bring them about. In this respect, Miller and Paris differ quite markedly from Brandenburg in the incitement context.

d. *Eroding moral standards.* Justice Harlan also noted in Alberts that obscenity can have "an eroding effect on moral standards," and Chief Justice Burger in Paris notes that "crass commercial exploitation of sex" can undermine "a sensitive, key relationship of human existence, central to family life." May government suppress speech to uphold a particular moral view of sex, in particular that it is appropriately practiced only in private and in heterosexual monogamous marriages? For the view that it may not, see Lockhart & McClure, "Literature, the Law of Obscenity, and the Constitution," 38 Minn. L. Rev. 295 (1954). Kingsley Pictures at least somewhat undermines this rationale for regulating obscenity, by holding that speech may not be suppressed on the ground that it expresses immoral ideas. Can the interest in public morality be accepted as a justification to bar obscenity without undercutting Justice Harlan's protective approach to offensive speech in Cohen?

e. *Harming the social fabric.* Writing for the Court in Paris Adult, Chief Justice Burger notes that commercial distribution of obscenity causes harm to "the quality of life and the total community environment" even if it is consumed only by willing adults. Quoting Bickel, he takes a communitarian rather than an individualist view of speech: "'what is commonly read and seen and heard and done intrudes upon us all, want it or not.'" On this view, the Stanleys of the world are never truly home alone consuming pornography in a purely self-regarding way. Obscenity distribution and consumption affects even non-observing bystanders. Is this view consistent with the rhetoric of the "marketplace of ideas"? Contrast this view with the highly individualistic and relativistic approach the Court took to offensive speech in Cohen and Hustler.

2. *The value of obscenity as "speech"?* Given the tensions between these government interests and other areas of First Amendment law, is the assertedly low value of sexually explicit materials doing most of the work in the Court's obscenity cases? Chaplinsky spoke of unprotected speech as that which has so little value as a step to truth that it is "clearly outweighed" by social interests. If obscenity is sufficiently low-value speech, then even vague or problematic social interests might be sufficient to justify its regulation. What features of obscenity might render it of low value?

a. *Non-political.* Are art and literature subordinate to political speech? If so, then perhaps obscenity is unprotected because non-political. But if that is so, "the novel, the poem, the painting, the drama, or the piece of sculpture" would likewise be unprotected. Kalven, "The Metaphysics of the Law of Obscenity," 1960 Sup.Ct.Rev. 1 The self-expression or autonomy rationale certainly brings literature and art within the First Amendment. But even Alexander Meiklejohn, a strong defender of the political conception of the First Amendment, eventually viewed literature and art as part of political discourse broadly construed: they educate voters and so give them "the knowledge, intelligence, sensitivity to human values [and] capacity for sane and objective judgment which, so far as possible, a ballot should express." Meiklejohn, "The First Amendment Is an Absolute," 1961 Sup.Ct.Rev. 245. For an exploration of the values of artistic expression, see Nahmod, "Artistic Expression and Aesthetic Theory: The Beautiful, The Sublime and the First Amendment," 1987 Wis.L.Rev. 221.

b. *Non-cognitive.* Is obscenity more like conduct than speech because it bypasses the brain for the groin? Frederick Schauer, for example, argues that the First Amendment should be read to protect speech that appeals to cognitive and emotive processes. In contrast, hard-core pornography is "designed to produce a purely physical effect": "The concept fundamental to the Miller test is that material appealing to the prurient interest *is* sex, and not merely describing or advocating sex. Material that appeals to the prurient interest is material that turns you on. Period." Schauer,"Speech and 'Speech'—Obscenity and 'Obscenity': An Exercise in the Interpretation of Constitutional Language," 67 Geo.L.J. 899 (1979). See also Sunstein, "Words, Conduct, Caste," 60 U. Chi. L. Rev. 795 (1993) ("Many forms of pornography are not an appeal to the exchange of ideas, political or otherwise; they operate as masturbatory aids and do not qualify for top-tier First Amendment protection"). Might such a view undermine protection for other speech that operates in both rational and irrational ways?

c. *Not susceptible to counterspeech.* The premise of much speech protection is that more speech is a better remedy than state suppression. Can anyone really talk back to obscene materials? Or do they act by an insidious conditioning mechanism that undermines the possibility of counterspeech? Consider Clor, Obscenity and Public Morality (1969): Obscene materials "do not make arguments which are to be met by intelligent defense," but rather have an effect upon "a delicate network of moral and aesthetic feelings, sensibilities, [and] tastes." Thus those "whose sensibilities are frequently assaulted by prurient and lurid impressions may become desensitized." Might the same argument apply to other areas of speech, such as commercial or political advertising?

3. *Critiques of obscenity law after Miller.* In addition to questioning the above justifications, critics of Miller have suggested that it privileges one conception of sex over others in violation of the usual First Amendment norm of viewpoint neutrality. On this view, Miller in effect permits government to punish sexual dissent. For example, see Richards, "Free Speech and Obscenity Law: Toward a Moral Theory of the First Amendment," 123 U.Pa.L.Rev. 45 (1974) (arguing that pornography can be seen to embody the "idea of [sexuality] as a profound and shattering ecstasy," or "a view of sensual delight in the erotic celebration of the body," in opposition to more repressive "Victorian" or "Catholic" views); Gey, "The Apologetics of Suppression: The Regulation of Pornography as Act and Idea," 86 Mich.L.Rev. 1564 (1988) (arguing that "the suppression of pornography [permits] the state [to] certify and enforce a moral code that reinforces and justifies the political status quo"). See generally Cole, "Playing by Pornography's Rules: The Regulation of Sexual Expression," 143 U. Pa. L. Rev. 111 (1994).

4. *Post-Miller decisions.* Although the number of obscenity cases decided by the Court has diminished dramatically since the 1973 rulings, the Miller–Paris standards have not wholly extricated the Court from the unwelcome task of case-by-case review in obscenity cases. In JENKINS v. GEORGIA, 418 U.S. 153 (1974), for example, the Court unanimously reversed a state conviction for showing the film "Carnal Knowledge." The state court had mistakenly assumed that, under the new standards, a jury verdict virtually precluded further review regarding most elements of obscenity. Justice REHNQUIST countered: "Even though questions of appeal to the 'prurient interest' or of patent offensiveness are 'essentially questions of fact,' it would be a serious misreading of Miller to conclude that juries have unbridled discretion in determining what is 'patently offensive.' [While the Miller illustrations] did not purport to be an exhaustive catalog of what juries might find patently offensive, [they were] certainly intended to fix substantive constitutional limitations [on] the type of material subject to such a determination." He concluded that, under Miller, "Carnal Knowledge" "could not be found to depict sexual conduct in a patently

offensive way. [While] the subject matter of the picture is, in a broader sense, sex, and there are scenes in which sexual conduct including 'ultimate sexual acts' is to be understood to be taking place, the camera does not focus on the bodies of the actors at such time. There is no exhibition whatever of the actors' genitals, lewd or otherwise, during these scenes. There are occasional scenes of nudity, but nudity alone is not enough to make material legally obscene under the Miller standards." The Court relied in part on the fact that the film starred prominent actors (including Jack Nicholson) and had been nominated for Academy Awards. Jenkins thus implicitly concluded that the obscenity laws could not be easily extended to "mainstream" materials, regardless of local views. Justice BRENNAN, joined by Justices Stewart and Marshall, and Justice DOUGLAS concurred separately in the result.

5. *Community standards.* Whose standards are to govern in determination of "prurient interest," "patent offensiveness," and "serious literary, artistic, political or scientific value": those of the locality, the state or the nation? Chief Justice Burger wrote in Miller that the "people of Maine or Mississippi" need not tolerate depictions that might be "tolerable in Las Vegas, or New York City." In HAMLING v. UNITED STATES, 418 U.S. 87 (1974), the Court opted for local rather than statewide or national standards in federal obscenity prosecutions and rejected the argument that application of local standards would unduly inhibit producers of materials for a national market. The Hamling ruling was again by a 5-to-4 vote. (In Jenkins, the Court had similarly refused to require that statewide standards be applied in state prosecutions, even though a statewide standard had been used in Miller.) And in SMITH v. UNITED STATES, 431 U.S. 291 (1977), the majority held that determination of local "community standards" in federal obscenity prosecutions was for the jury, even where the defendant had mailed the allegedly obscene materials solely intrastate, in a state which had no law prohibiting sales to adults. Justice BLACKMUN's majority opinion concluded that state law, although relevant, "is not conclusive as to the issue of contemporary community standards for appeal to the prurient interest and patent offensiveness." Justice STEVENS dissented: "The question of offensiveness to community standards, whether national or local, is not one that the average juror can be expected to answer with evenhanded consistency. [In] the final analysis, the guilt or innocence of a criminal defendant in an obscenity trial is determined primarily by individual jurors' subjective reactions to the materials in question rather than by the predictable application of rules of law. As [Justice] Harlan noted: '[It is] often true that one man's vulgarity is another's lyric [and that is why] the Constitution leaves matters of taste and style [to] the individual' [Cohen]."

Smith also made clear, however, that the "literary, artistic, political, or scientific value" factor of the Miller test was *not* to be measured by local community standards. This point was elaborated in POPE v. ILLINOIS, 481 U.S. 497 (1987), where Justice WHITE's majority opinion stated: "Just as the ideas a work represents need not obtain majority approval to merit protection, neither [does] the value of the work vary from community to community based on the degree of local acceptance it has won. The proper inquiry is not whether an ordinary member of any given community would find serious [value] in allegedly obscene material, but whether a reasonable person would find such value in the material, taken as a whole." Justice SCALIA's concurrence argued that it was "quite impossible" to come to an objective assessment of (at least) literary or artistic value: "Just as there is no use arguing about taste, there is no use litigating about it." He suggested "the need for reexamination of Miller," but offered no alternative to it. Justice STEVENS' dissent, joined by

Justice Marshall, attacked the majority's "reasonable person" standard, insisting that "communicative material of this sort is entitled to the protection of the First Amendment if *some reasonable persons* could consider it as having serious [value]."

6. *Serious value.* Is "serious value" a magic bullet that allows mainstream publishers and producers to escape obscenity charges, confining the practical reach of Miller to hard-core pornography? Publishers have often called expert witnesses to testify to serious artistic value in obscenity trials. See generally de Grazia, Girls Lean Back Everywhere (1992). Similar testimony was offered in two prominent obscenity trials in the early 1990s. An art gallery and its directors were tried in Cincinnati for obscenity violations as a result of displaying an exhibit of photographs by Robert Mapplethorpe containing explicit depictions of homoerotic and sadomasochistic activities. The curator of the exhibit testified to the artistic value of the photographs. Asked repeatedly by prosecutors whether she would describe particular photographs as depicting male genitalia, she demurred, answering that she saw instead, for example, examples of "classical line and form." The Cincinnati jury found the defendants not guilty. Expert testimony on the antecedents of rap in early African–American oral traditions was less successful in averting an obscenity conviction in Broward County, Florida, for sellers of the sexually graphic recording "As Nasty As They Wanna Be" by the rap group 2 Live Crew. A federal trial judge in Fort Lauderdale found the album obscene in a civil proceeding, concluding that music could be legally obscene. The judgment was reversed by the Court of Appeals. Luke Records, Inc. v. Navarro, 960 F.2d 134 (11th Cir.1992). Does such expert testimony take an unduly formalist view of art, underestimating its controversial moral and political content? See Adler, Note, "Post–Modern Art and the Death of Obscenity Law," 99 Yale L.J. 1359 (1990).

7. *The Attorney General's Commission on Pornography, 1986.* Sixteen years after the 1970 Commission's Report, a new Commission, appointed by Attorney General Edwin Meese, concluded that some forms of obscenity *could* cause violent antisocial conduct. In assessing the effects of sexually explicit materials, the new Commission emphasized distinctions among the content of such materials, distinguishing between (a) materials portraying sexual violence; (b) materials that contained no explicit violence but were plainly degrading, usually to women; and (c) materials, that, while sexually explicit, contained neither violence nor degradation.

With respect to sexually violent materials, the Commission concluded that the "scientific findings and ultimate conclusions of the 1970 Commission are least reliable for today, [because] material of this variety was largely absent from that Commission's inquiries. [The] research [shows] a causal relationship between exposure to [sexually violent material] and aggressive behavior towards women." The Commission relied not solely on "experimental evidence" but also on "clinical evidence" and on "less scientific evidence [as well as] our own common sense." Turning to materials containing no violence but depicting women "as existing solely for the sexual satisfaction of [men]," the Commission found the evidence "more tentative" but inclined somewhat in the same direction as with sexually violent material. But with regard to material containing neither violence nor degradation, "we are on the current state of the evidence persuaded that material of this type does not bear a causal relationship to rape or other acts of sexual violence."

With respect to the framing and enforcement of legal restraints, the Commission found that the type of material currently designated as legally obscene was properly considered outside the coverage of the First Amendment.

But its recommendations about law enforcement started with the assumption that the constitutional permissibility of regulation did not address the advisability of regulation. It rejected all proposals for expanding the scope of existing obscenity laws, recommended that enforcement of existing obscenity laws take into account as priorities the subdivisions recommended by the Commission, and urged that enforcement of existing obscenity laws against sexually violent materials be increased substantially. It divided on the issue whether there should be any enforcement at all regarding materials neither violent nor degrading. Noting that the category of sexually violent material is dominated by material "unquestionably protected by the First Amendment," the Commission nevertheless urged enforcement of existing laws with respect to the segment of that material that was legally obscene, even though such regulation "would likely address little more than the tip of the iceberg." In reaching this conclusion, the Commission emphasized that "law serves an important symbolic function [even through] strikingly underinclusive regulation. Conversely, we are aware of the message conveyed by repeal or non-enforcement of existing laws with respect to certain kinds of materials. [We] are unwilling to have the law send out the wrong signal." The Commission's report prompted immediate controversy and considerable criticism.

For further discussion of the "causation" problem, see Schauer (a member of the Commission), "Causation Theory and the Causes of Sexual Violence," 1987 A.B.F.Res.J. 737 (noting that "the claim of [the Report], put accurately, is that sexually violent material, some but not much of which happens to be sexually explicit and some but even less of which is legally obscene, bears a causal relationship, taken probabilistically, to the incidence of sexual violence," and arguing that, since the causal relationship is independent of sexual explicitness, government regulation under existing First Amendment doctrine is both "strikingly underinclusive" and "a false cut at the problem"). For criticism of the Commission's Report, see Hawkins & Zimring, Pornography in a Free Society (1988).

B. CHILD PORNOGRAPHY

---

1. *The Ferber case.* In NEW YORK v. FERBER, 458 U.S. 747 (1982), the Court unanimously rejected a First Amendment attack on a New York law designed to deal with the problem of child pornography. The law prohibited the distribution of material depicting children engaged in sexual conduct; it did not require that the material be legally obscene. Ferber, the owner of a bookstore specializing in sexually oriented products, was convicted under § 263.15 of the New York Penal Law for selling two films devoted almost exclusively to depicting young boys masturbating. The provision stated: "A person is guilty of promoting a sexual performance by a child when, knowing the character and content thereof, he produces, directs or promotes any performance which includes sexual conduct by a child less than sixteen years of age." Another section of the law defined "sexual conduct" as "actual or simulated sexual intercourse, deviate sexual intercourse, sexual bestiality, masturbation, sadomasochistic abuse, or lewd exhibition of the genitals." The Court found Ferber's conviction constitutional.

In upholding the law, Justice WHITE, who wrote the majority opinion, echoed the Chaplinsky approach by "classifying child pornography as a category of material outside the protection of the First Amendment." Justice White noted that this case was the Court's "first examination of a statute directed at and limited to depictions of sexual activity involving children.[1] We believe our inquiry should begin with the question of whether a State has somewhat more freedom in proscribing works which portray sexual acts or lewd exhibitions of genitalia by children [than in regulating obscenity]." In his view the 1973 Miller obscenity standard did not delineate the extent of state power over child pornography. The portions of his opinion explaining why states have "greater leeway" over child pornography stated:

"*First*. It is evident [that] a state's interest in 'safeguarding the physical and psychological well being of a minor' is 'compelling.' The prevention of sexual exploitation and abuse of children constitutes a government objective of surpassing importance. [The] legislative judgment [is] that the use of children as subjects of pornographic materials is harmful to the physiological, emotional, and mental health of the [child].

"*Second*. The distribution of photographs and films depicting sexual activity by juveniles is intrinsically related to the sexual abuse of children in at least two ways. First, the materials produced are a permanent record of the children's participation and the harm to the child is exacerbated by their circulation. Second, the distribution network for child pornography must be closed if the production of material which requires the sexual exploitation of children is to be effectively controlled. [Ferber argues] that it is enough for the State to prohibit the distribution of materials that are legally obscene under the Miller test. While some States may find that this approach properly accommodates [their interests], it does not follow that the First Amendment prohibits a State from going further. The Miller [standard] does not reflect the State's particular and more compelling interest in prosecuting those who promote the sexual exploitation of children. [E.g.,] a work which, taken on the whole, contains serious literary, artistic, political, or scientific value may nevertheless embody the hardest core of child pornography. 'It is irrelevant to the child [who has been abused] whether or not the material has a literary, artistic, political, or [social value].'

"*Third*. The advertising and selling of child pornography provides an economic motive for and is thus an integral part of the production of such materials, an activity illegal throughout the nation. 'It rarely has been suggested that the constitutional freedom for speech and press extends its immunity to speech or writing used as an integral part of conduct in violation of a valid criminal statute.' We note that were the statutes outlawing the employment of children in these films and photographs fully effective, and the constitutionality of these laws have not been questioned, the First Amendment implications

1. Justice White had noted earlier that, "[i]n recent years, the exploitive use of children in the production of pornography has become a serious national problem." The federal government and 47 states had enacted statutes "specifically directed at the production of child pornography." At least half of these did not require "that the materials produced be legally obscene." Moreover, 35 states and Congress had passed legislation prohibiting the distribution of such materials. Twenty of these states prohibited the distribution of material depicting children engaged in sexual conduct without requiring that the material be legally obscene. New York was one of these 20 states. (The laws in the other 15 states, as well as the federal law, prohibited the dissemination of such material only if it was obscene.)

would be no greater than that presented by laws against distribution: enforceable production laws would leave no child pornography to be marketed.

"*Fourth.* The value of permitting live performances and photographic reproductions of children engaged in lewd sexual conduct is exceedingly modest, if not de minimis. We consider it unlikely that visual depictions of children performing sexual acts or lewdly exhibiting their genitals would often constitute an important and necessary part of a literary performance or scientific or educational work. [If] it were necessary for literary or artistic value, a person over the statutory age who perhaps looked younger could be utilized. Simulation outside of the prohibition of the statute could provide another alternative. Nor is there any question here of censoring a particular literary theme or portrayal of sexual activity. The First Amendment interest is limited to that of rendering the portrayal somewhat more 'realistic' by utilizing or photographing children.

"*Fifth.* Recognizing and classifying child pornography as a category of material outside the protection of the First Amendment is not incompatible with our earlier decisions. [See American Mini Theatres and, e.g., Chaplinsky; Beauharnais.] [Thus], it is not rare that a content-based classification of speech has been accepted because it may be appropriately generalized that within the confines of the given classification, the evil to be restricted so overwhelmingly outweighs the expressive interests, if any, at stake, that no process of case-by-case adjudication is [required].

"There are, of course, limits on the category of child pornography which, like obscenity, is unprotected by the First Amendment. As with all legislation in this sensitive area, the conduct to be prohibited must be adequately defined by the applicable state law, as written or authoritatively construed. [The] test for child pornography is separate from the obscenity standard enunciated in Miller, but may be compared to it for purpose of clarity. The Miller formulation is adjusted in the following respects: A trier of fact need not find that the material appeals to the prurient interest of the average person; it is not required that sexual conduct portrayed be done so in a patently offensive manner; and the material at issue need not be considered as a whole.

"[The law's] prohibition incorporates a definition of sexual conduct that comports with the above-stated principles. [We] hold that § 263.15 sufficiently describes a category of material the production and distribution of which is not entitled to First Amendment protection. It is therefore clear that there is nothing unconstitutionally 'underinclusive' about a statute that singles out this category of material for proscription. It also follows that the State is not barred by the First Amendment from prohibiting the distribution of unprotected materials produced outside the State."

Justice O'CONNOR, while joining Justice White's opinion, also submitted a separate concurrence. She emphasized that the Court had not held that "New York must except 'material with serious literary, scientific or educational value' from its statute. The Court merely holds that, even if the First Amendment shelters such material, New York's current statute is not sufficiently overbroad to support [Ferber's] facial attack." She went on to suggest that the compelling state interests involved here "might in fact permit New York to ban knowing distribution of works depicting minors engaged in explicit sexual conduct, regardless of the social value of the depictions. For example, a 12–year-old child photographed while masturbating surely suffers the same psychological harm whether the community labels the photograph 'edifying' or 'tasteless.' The audience's appreciation of the depiction is simply irrelevant to New York's asserted interest in protecting children from psychological, emotional, and mental harm."

Justice BRENNAN, joined by Justice Marshall, submitted an opinion concurring in the judgment. He stated that he agreed "with much of what is said in the Court's opinion" but insisted that application of a law such as New York's to "depictions of children that in themselves do have serious literary, artistic, scientific or medical value, would violate the First Amendment." He explained that "the limited classes of speech, the suppression of which does not raise serious First Amendment concerns, have two attributes": they are "of exceedingly 'slight social value,'" and the state has a compelling interest in their regulation. See [Chaplinsky]." But the "First Amendment value of depictions of children that are in themselves serious contributions to art, literature or science, is, by definition, simply not 'de minimis.' At the same time, the State's interest in suppression of such materials is likely to be far less compelling. For the Court's assumption of harm to the child [lacks] much of its force where the depiction is a serious contribution to art or science. [In] short, it is inconceivable how a depiction of a child that is itself a serious contribution to the world of art or literature or science can be deemed 'material outside the protection of the First Amendment.'" Justice Stevens submitted a separate opinion concurring only in the judgment and Justice Blackmun simply noted his concurrence in the result.

2. *The Court's methodology in Ferber.* On its face, the majority's analysis suggests that Ferber is a rare modern case in the tradition of the Chaplinsky exclusionary categorization approach: the majority simply casts outside the First Amendment the entire class of child pornography, even though the class concededly includes materials not "obscene." But that technique produces vastly more discussion in this case than it had in Chaplinsky, and the Court also draws on a variety of other First Amendment techniques. In contrast to the Chaplinsky approach, the majority speaks at length not only about the limited social value of the communication involved but also, and most notably, about the state interests justifying restraint. So seen, Ferber contains earmarks of the "definitional balancing" technique involved in New York Times v. Sullivan, in the sense that that case held "malicious" defamation of public officials unprotected. See Schauer, "Codifying the First Amendment: New York v. Ferber," 1982 Sup.Ct.Rev. 285 (noting that "Ferber can be viewed as partially relying on [a] 'covered but outweighed' path to nonprotection" and adds that defamation cases provide one of the closest parallels to the Ferber methodology). Note too that Justice White, in examining the First Amendment side of the balance, finds the value of child pornography "exceedingly modest, if not de minimis" by stating that child pornography does not constitute "an important and necessary part of a literary performance or scientific or educational work." Does that mark a departure from prior analyses? Does a work have to be "necessary" to literary expression to qualify for First Amendment protection?

3. *Possession of child pornography.* In OSBORNE v. OHIO, 495 U.S. 103 (1990), Stanley v. Georgia was held inapplicable to child pornography, with the effect of allowing the mere possession of child pornography to be made unlawful. Justice WHITE's majority opinion concluded that the same interests in eliminating the entire chain of distribution that justified the result in Ferber also justified eliminating the demand by criminalizing possession of child pornography. The Court also rejected Osborne's overbreadth challenge to the Ohio law. Although the law on its face barred the possession of "nude" photographs and although simple depictions of nudity cannot be proscribed, Justice White relied on the fact that the state courts had limited the reach of

the law to cases in which "such nudity constitutes a lewd exhibition or involves a graphic focus on the genitals, and where the person depicted is neither the child nor the ward of the person charged." Because of the lack of instructions on lewdness at trial, however, the conviction was reversed on due process grounds and remanded for a new trial. Justice BRENNAN, joined by Justices Marshall and Stevens, dissented, emphasizing the statute's overbreadth and believing that the narrowing state court construction was an insufficient guarantee that the law would not be applied to material as innocuous as the "well-known commercial advertisement for a suntan lotion show[ing] a dog pulling the bottom half of a young girl's bikini." The dissent also objected to the failure to extend Stanley to child pornography.

———

C. PORNOGRAPHY AS SUBORDINATION OF WOMEN

———

1. *Feminist anti-pornography theory.* Beginning in the 1980's, opponents of sexually explicit materials advocated a novel theory for restrictive legislation that treated pornography as a civil rights violation on the ground that it constitutes sex discrimination, or the subordination of women to men. The argument was reflected in a model ordinance drafted in 1983 by two feminist theorists, Catharine MacKinnon and Andrea Dworkin, for the city of Minneapolis.

MacKinnon and Dworkin argued that pornography posed a problem not of immorality but of power: "Pornography sexualizes rape, battery, sexual harassment, prostitution, and child sexual abuse. [More] generally, it eroticizes the dominance and submission that is the dynamic common to them all. It makes hierachy sexy." MacKinnon, "Pornography, Civil Rights, and Speech," 20 Harv.C.R.–C.L.L.Rev. 1 (1985). "Pornography, unlike obscenity, is a discrete, identifiable system of sexual exploitation that hurts women as a class by creating inequality and abuse." Dworkin, "Against the Male Flood: Censorship, Pornography, and Equality," 8 Harv. Women's L.J. 1 (1985). See also MacKinnon, Only Words (1993); MacKinnon, "Not A Moral Issue," 2 Yale L. & Pol.Rev. 321 (1984); and MacKinnon, Feminism Unmodified: Discourses on Life and Law (1987) ("While defenders of pornography argue that allowing all speech, including pornography, frees the mind to fulfill itself, pornography freely enslaves women's minds and bodies.").

Note that the MacKinnon–Dworkin argument, like Justice Burger's argument for the majority in Paris Adult Theatre, views sexual speech as shaping the community rather than as merely gratifying individual consumers. But Justice Burger treated obscenity as a minority practice deviating from governing norms of privacy and monogamous heterosexual marriage, while MacKinnon and Dworkin view pornography as the expression of existing majority practice.

2. *Feminist arguments against pornography regulation.* Many feminists opposed the MacKinnon–Dworkin argument: "[F]or many women (perhaps most), pornography is primarily victimizing, threatening and oppressive, [but] for others, [it] is on occasion liberating and transformative, [a] healthy attack on a stifling and oppressive societal denial of female sexuality," and a defiance of oppression by "marital, familial, productive, and reproductive values." West, "The Feminist–Conservative Anti–Pornography [Alliance]," 1987 A.B.F.Res.J.

681. "By defining sexually explicit images of women as subordinating and degrading to them, the [MacKinnon-Dworkin] ordinance reinforces the stereotypical view that 'good' women do not seek and enjoy sex [and] perpetuates a stereotype of women as helpless victims, incapable of consent, and in need of protection." Hunter & Law, "Brief Amici Curiae of Feminist Anti–Censorship Task Force," 21 U. Mich. J. L. Ref. 69 (1987–88). See also, Strossen, Defending Pornography: Free Speech, Sex, and the Fight for Women's Rights (1995); Meyer, "Sex, Sin, and Women's Liberation: Against Porn-Suppression," 72 Tex. L. Rev. 1097 (1994).

3. *Gay pornography.* Does the MacKinnon–Dworkin argument apply to pornography depicting gay or lesbian sex? How can such pornography subordinate women? For an argument that gay male pornography both liberates and helps build community among gay men and that feminist antipornography arguments should not apply to it, see Sherman, "Love Speech: The Social Utility of Pornography," 47 Stan. L. Rev. 661 (1995).

4. *The invalidation of the MacKinnon–Dworkin ordinance.* The MacKinnon–Dworkin ordinance was adopted by the Minneapolis City Council at the end of 1983, but vetoed by the city's mayor on the ground that the "remedy sought [is] neither appropriate nor enforceable within our cherished tradition and constitutionally protected right of free speech." It was enacted in revised form, however, by Indianapolis in 1984. The doctrinal arguments made to defend the ordinance rested heavily upon Beauharnais and Ferber, above, as well as upon American Mini Theatres and Pacifica, below. Proponents also argued that promoting civil rights and equality, itself a constitutional value under the 14th Amendment, provides a "compelling" interest outweighing any First Amendment interest at stake.

The Indianapolis ordinance was struck down by U.S. District Judge Sarah Evans Barker as overbroad, sweeping in protected speech as well as unprotected obscenity. The Court of Appeals affirmed that judgment, but on the different First Amendment ground that the ordinance aimed impermissibly at viewpoint. The Supreme Court summarily affirmed the Seventh Circuit's decision. Chief Justice Burger and Justices Rehnquist and O'Connor dissented, urging that the case be set for oral argument.

Is the decision that follows correctly decided? For a negative answer, see Sunstein, "Pornography and the First Amendment," 1986 Duke L.J. 589 (1986), arguing that antipornography legislation is "directed at harm rather than at viewpoint" and that because of its "focus on harm, antipornography legislation [does] not pose the dangers associated with viewpoint-based restrictions." For a contrary view, see Tribe, American Constitutional Law 925 (2d ed. 1988): "*[a]ll* viewpoint-based regulations are targeted at some supposed harm, whether it be linked to an unsettling ideology like Communism [or] to socially shunned practices like adultery." Noting that government may outlaw incitements of sexual violence against women, as it may other incitements of crimes, Tribe adds that it is "altogether different, and far more constitutionally tenuous, for a government to outlaw [the] incitement of violence against women *only* when such incitement is caused by words or pictures that express a particular point of view: that women are meant for domination. The analogue would be a ban on anti-capitalist speeches that incite robbery, leaving other equally effective incitements to robbery unprohibited." Sunstein replies that the First Amendment permits a variety of nonneutral speech regulations to prevent serious harms: for example, employers may be banned during unionization periods from engaging in anti-union speech. In such cases, he argues, "the partisanship of the regulation is not apparent because there is so firm a consensus on the presence of real-world harms that the objection from neutrality does not even register." He urges the same view of antipornography regulations given pornography's harms. For further commentary, see Stone, "Anti–Pornography Legislation As Viewpoint Discrimination," 9 Harv.J.L. & Pub.Pol. 701 (1986), Kagan, "Regulation of Hate Speech and Pornography After R.A.V." 60 U. Chi. L. Rev. 873 (1993).

American Booksellers Ass'n v. Hudnut

771 F.2d 323 (7th Cir.1985); aff'd mem., 475 U.S. 1001 (1986).

EASTERBROOK, Circuit Judge [for the Court of Appeals].

Indianapolis enacted an ordinance defining "pornography" as a practice that discriminates against women. [The] City's definition of "pornography" is considerably different from "obscenity," [which] is not protected by the [First Amendment].

"Pornography" under the ordinance is "the graphic sexually explicit subordination of women, whether in pictures or in words, that also includes one or more of the following: (1) Women are presented as sexual objects who enjoy pain or humiliation; or (2) Women are presented as sexual objects who experience sexual pleasure in being raped; or (3) Women are presented as sexual objects tied up or cut up or mutilated or bruised or physically hurt, or as dismembered or truncated or fragmented or severed into body parts; or (4) Women are presented as being penetrated by objects or animals; or (5) Women are presented in scenarios of degradation, injury, abasement, torture, shown as filthy or inferior, bleeding, bruised, or hurt in a context that makes these conditions sexual; or (6) Women are presented as sexual objects for domination, conquest, violation, exploitation, possession, or use, or through postures or positions of servility or submission or display."

The statute provides that the "use of men, children, or transsexuals in the place of women in [provisions] (1) through (6) above shall also constitute pornography under this section." The ordinance as passed in April 1984 defined "sexually explicit" to mean actual or simulated intercourse or the uncovered exhibition of the genitals, buttocks or anus. An amendment in June 1984 deleted this provision, leaving the term undefined.

The Indianapolis ordinance [unlike the obscenity standard] does not refer to the prurient interest, to offensiveness, or to the standards of the community. It demands attention to particular depictions, not to the work judged as a whole. It is irrelevant under the ordinance whether the work has literary, artistic, political, or scientific value. The City and many amici point to these omissions as virtues. They maintain that pornography influences attitudes, and the statute is a way to alter the socialization of men and women rather than to vindicate community standards of offensiveness. And as one of the principal drafters of the ordinance has asserted, "if a woman is subjected, why should it matter that the work has other value?" [MacKinnon, "Pornography, Civil Rights, and Speech," above.] [Those] supporting the ordinance say that it will play an important role in reducing the tendency of men to view women as sexual objects, a tendency that leads to both unacceptable attitudes and discrimination in the workplace and violence away from it. Those opposing the ordinance point out that much radical feminist literature is explicit and depicts women in ways forbidden by the ordinance and that the ordinance would reopen old battles.

[We] do not try to balance the arguments for and against [the ordinance]. The ordinance discriminates on the ground of the content of the speech. Speech treating women in the approved way—in sexual encounters "premised on equality"—is lawful no matter how sexually explicit. Speech treating women in the disapproved way—as submissive in matters sexual or as enjoying humiliation—is unlawful no matter how significant the literary, artistic, or political qualities of the work taken as a whole. The state may not ordain preferred viewpoints in this way. The Constitution forbids the state to declare one perspective right and silence opponents. The ordinance contains four prohibitions. People may not "traffic" in pornography, "coerce" others into performing in pornographic works, or "force" pornography on anyone. Anyone injured by someone who has seen or read pornography has a right of action against the maker or seller. [For] purposes of all four offenses, it is generally "[not] a defense that the respondent did not know or intend that the materials were [pornography]." But the ordinance provides that damages are unavailable in trafficking cases unless the complainant proves "that the respondent knew or had reason to know that the materials were pornography." [Moreover, it] is a complete defense to a trafficking case that all of the materials in question were pornography only by virtue of category (6) of the definition of [pornography]. The district court held the ordinance [unconstitutional].

Under the First Amendment the government must leave to the people the evaluation of ideas. Bold or subtle, an idea is as powerful as the audience allows it to be. A belief may be pernicious—the beliefs of Nazis led to the death of millions, those of the Klan to the repression of millions. A pernicious belief may prevail. Totalitarian governments today rule much of the planet, practicing suppression of billions and spreading dogma that may enslave others. One of the things that separates our society from theirs is our absolute right to propagate opinions that the government finds wrong or even hateful. The ideas of the Klan may be propagated. [Brandenburg]. Communists may speak freely and run for office. [DeJonge]. The Nazi Party may march through a city with a large Jewish population. [Collin v. Smith]. People may teach religions that others despise. People may seek to repeal laws guaranteeing equal opportunity in employment or to revoke the constitutional amendments granting the vote to blacks and women. They may do this because "above all else, the First Amendment means that government has no power to restrict expression because of its message [or] its [ideas]." [Police Department v. Mosley, p. 1205 below.]

Under the ordinance graphic sexually explicit speech is "pornography" or not depending on the perspective the author adopts. Speech that "subordinates" women and [even] simply presents women in "positions of servility or submission or display" is forbidden, no matter how great the literary or political value of the work taken as a whole. Speech that portrays women in positions of equality is lawful, no matter how graphic the sexual content. This is thought control. It establishes an "approved" view of women, of how they may react to sexual encounters, of how the sexes may relate to each other. Those who espouse the approved view may use sexual images; those who do not, may not.

Indianapolis justifies the ordinance on the ground that pornography affects thoughts. Men who see women depicted as subordinate are more likely to treat them so. Pornography is an aspect of dominance. It does not persuade people so much as change them. It works by socializing, by establishing the expected and the permissible. In this view pornography is not an idea; pornography is the injury. There is much to this perspective. Beliefs are also facts. People often act in accordance with the images and patterns they find around them. [People] taught from birth that black people are fit only for slavery rarely rebelled against that creed; beliefs coupled with the self-interest of the masters established a social structure that inflicted great harm while enduring for centuries. Words and images act at the level of the subconscious before they persuade at the level of the conscious. Even the truth has little chance unless a statement fits within the framework of beliefs that may never have been subjected to rational study.

Therefore we accept the premises of this legislation. Depictions of subordination tend to perpetuate subordination. The subordinate status of women in turn leads to affront and lower pay at work, insult and injury at home, battery and rape on the streets.[1] In the language of the legislature, "[p]ornography is central in creating and maintaining sex as a basis of discrimination. Pornography is a systematic practice of exploitation and subordination based on sex which differentially harms women. The bigotry and contempt it produces, with the acts of aggression it fosters, harm women's opportunities for equality and rights [of all kinds]."

Yet this simply demonstrates the power of pornography as speech. All of these unhappy effects depend on mental intermediation. Pornography affects how people see the world, their fellows, and social relations. If pornography is what pornography does, so is other speech. Hitler's orations affected how some Germans saw Jews. Communism is a world view, not simply a Manifesto by Marx and Engels or a set of speeches. The Alien and Sedition Acts [rested] on a sincerely held belief that disrespect for the government leads to social collapse and revolution—a belief with support in the history of many nations. Most governments of the world act on this empirical regularity, suppressing critical speech. In the United States, however, the strength of the support for this belief is irrelevant. Seditious libel is protected speech unless the danger is not only grave but also imminent.

Racial bigotry, anti-semitism, violence on television, reporters' biases— these and many more influence the culture and shape our socialization. None is directly answerable by more speech, unless that speech too finds its place in the popular culture. Yet all is protected as speech, however insidious. Any other answer leaves the government in control of all of the institutions of culture, the great censor and director of which thoughts are good for us. Sexual responses often are unthinking responses, and the association of sexual arousal with the subordination of women therefore may have a substantial effect. But almost all cultural stimuli provoke unconscious responses. Religious ceremonies condition their participants. Teachers convey messages by selecting what not to [cover]. People may be conditioned in subtle ways. If the fact that speech plays a role in a process of conditioning were enough to permit governmental regulation, that would be the end of freedom of speech.

It is possible to interpret the claim that the pornography is the harm in a different way. Indianapolis emphasizes the injury that models in pornographic films and pictures may suffer. The record contains materials depicting sexual torture, penetration of women by red-hot irons and the like. These concerns have nothing to do with written materials subject to the statute, and physical injury can occur with or without the "subordination" of women. [A] state may make injury in the course of producing a film unlawful independent of the

---

1. [In] saying that we accept the finding that pornography as the ordinance defines it leads to unhappy consequences, we mean only that there is evidence to this effect, that this evidence is consistent with much human experience, and that as judges we must accept the legislative resolution of such disputed empirical [questions]. [Footnote by Judge Easterbrook.]

viewpoint expressed in the film. The more immediate point, however, is that the image of pain is not necessarily pain. [The film] Body Double is sexually explicit and a murder occurs—yet no one believes that the actress suffered pain or died. [No one] believes that [Jane Fonda in Barbarella] was actually tortured to make the film. In Carnal Knowledge a woman grovels to please the sexual whims of a character played by Jack Nicholson; no one believes that there was a real sexual submission, and the Supreme Court held the film protected by the First Amendment. And this works both ways. The description of women's sexual domination of men in Lysistrata was not real dominance. Depictions may affect slavery, war, or sexual roles, but a book about slavery is not itself slavery, or a book about death by poison a murder.

Much of Indianapolis's argument rests on the belief that when speech is "unanswerable," and the metaphor that there is a "marketplace of ideas" does not apply, the First Amendment does not apply either. The metaphor is honored; Milton's Aeropagitica and Mill's On Liberty defend freedom of speech on the ground that the truth will prevail, and many of the most important cases under the First Amendment recite this position. The Framers undoubtedly believed it. As a general matter it is true. But the Constitution does not make the dominance of truth a necessary condition of freedom of speech. To say that it does would be to confuse an outcome of free speech with a necessary condition for the application of the amendment. A power to limit speech on the ground that truth has not yet prevailed and is not likely to prevail implies the power to declare truth. At some point the government must be able to say (as Indianapolis has said): "We know what the truth is, yet a free exchange of speech has not driven out falsity, so that we must now prohibit falsity." If the government may declare the truth, why wait for the failure of speech? Under the First Amendment, however, there is no such thing as a false idea [Gertz], so the government may not restrict speech on the ground that in a free exchange truth is not yet dominant. At any time, some speech is ahead in the game; the more numerous speakers prevail. Supporters of minority candidates may be forever "excluded" from the political process because their candidates never win, because few people believe their positions. This does not mean that freedom of speech has failed.

We come, finally, to the argument that pornography is "low value" speech, that it is enough like obscenity that Indianapolis may prohibit it. Some cases hold that speech far removed from politics and other subjects at the core of the Framers' concerns may be subjected to special regulation. E.g., [Pacifica (p. 1164 below); American Mini Theaters (p. 1159 below); Chaplinsky]. These cases do not sustain statutes that select among viewpoints, however. [At] all events, "pornography" is not low value speech within the meaning of these cases. Indianapolis seeks to prohibit certain speech because it believes [it] influences social relations and politics on a grand scale, that it controls attitudes at home and in the legislature. This precludes a characterization of the speech as low value. True, pornography and obscenity have sex in common. But Indianapolis left out of its definition any reference to literary, artistic, political, or scientific value. The ordinance applies to graphic sexually explicit subordination in works great and small.[2] The Court sometimes balances the value of speech against the

---

2. Indianapolis briefly argues that [Beauharnais], which allowed a state to penalize "group libel," supports the ordinance. In Collin v. Smith [p. 1113 above], we concluded that cases such as New York Times v. Sullivan had so washed away the foundations of Beauharnais that it could not be considered authoritative. If we are wrong in this, however, the case still does not support the ordinance. It is not clear that depicting women as subordinate in sexually explicit ways, even combined with a depiction of pleasure in

costs of its restriction, but it does this by category of speech and not by the content of particular works. [Indianapolis] has created an approved point of view and so loses the support of these cases.

Any rationale we could imagine in support of this ordinance could not be limited to sex discrimination. Free speech has been on balance an ally of those seeking change. Governments that want stasis start by restricting speech. [Change] in any complex system ultimately depends on the ability of outsiders to challenge accepted views and the reigning institutions. Without a strong guarantee of freedom of speech, there is no effective right to challenge what is. [The] definition of "pornography" is unconstitutional. No construction or excision of particular terms could save [it].

Affirmed.

D. SEXUALLY EXPLICIT BUT NON-OBSCENE EXPRESSION

Introduction. The Court has considered a number of free speech challenges to laws regulating sexual expression that falls short of any of the definitions of obscenity considered above. In these cases, the Court has wrestled with the question whether such speech ought to be understood to occupy a subordinate position under the First Amendment, even if it does not comprise a wholly unprotected category of speech. Justice Stevens has been a leading advocate of such a "lower value" approach: for example, in American Mini Theatres, below, he suggested that "few of us would march our sons and daughters off to war to preserve the citizen's right to see 'Specified Sexual Activities' exhibited in the theaters of our choice." In several plurality opinions, Justice Stevens has supported content regulation of sexually offensive displays and speech under an approach that falls short of categorical exclusion of that type of communication from the First Amendment, but that treats such expression as less valuable than core, political speech and accordingly more readily restrainable.

By and large, however, that view has not prevailed on the Court, at least not explicitly. The Court invalidated a ban on the display of nudity in drive-in theaters in Erznoznik, below, an effective ban on nude dancing in Schad, below, and a ban on "dial-a-porn" telephone services in Sable, below. In each of these decisions, the Court proceeded from the assumption that indecent or sexually explicit speech that does not amount to obscenity is protected speech and that severe restrictions or total bans of such speech will be strictly reviewed.

On the other hand, the Court has upheld a number of restrictions on sexually explicit but non-obscene expression. As one commentator put it, restrictions on sexual expression "will be permitted so long as those restrictions do not have the effect of a de facto prohibition on dissemination." Schauer, "Categories and the First Amendment," 34 Vand.L.Rev. 265 (1981). Instead of categorizing such speech as lower-value for all purposes, the Court has balanced

---

rape, would fit within the definition of a group libel. The well received film Swept Away used explicit sex, plus taking pleasure in rape, to make a political statement, not to defame. Work must be an insult or slur for its own sake to come within the ambit of Beauharnais, and a work need not be scurrilous at all to be "pornography" under the ordinance. [Footnote by Judge Easterbrook.]

the burden on such speech against the relevant state interests. It has upheld, for example, what Laurence Tribe calls "erogenous zoning" laws: laws that disperse or concentrate establishments that specialize in materials of specified sexual content. Tribe, American Constitutional Law 934 (2d ed. 1988). See American Mini Theatres, Renton, below. The Court has also upheld less than total restrictions of sexually explicit speech on the broadcasting and cable media, reasoning that special features of these media give government a greater interest in regulating sexual expression there than in other settings. See Pacifica, Denver Area Telcom, below.

Would similar restrictions be tolerated if applied to speech of specified political content? May speech of specified political content be channeled to another time or place so long as it is not totally banned? By deferring to content-specific regulations of sexual expression in these circumstances, has the Court implicitly, if not explicitly, treated sexually explicit speech as a subordinate species? Did Justice Stevens lose the battle but win the war? In examining these materials that follow, consider whether it is better to embrace openly Justice Stevens' "lower value" methodology, which treats the First Amendment as covering widely differing varieties of speech that must be aligned in a hierarchy with differing degrees of protection, or to maintain a unitary approach to the value of speech. Can the "lower value" approach be defended as enabling the Justices to deal sensibly with relatively insignificant speech without risking dilution of the protection for "political" expression at the core of the First Amendment? Or does the "lower value" approach show the weakness of judicial efforts to check majoritarian repression, by defining speech as "less valuable" in exactly those situations where it most sharply attacks majoritarian values? Do the cases suggest that, even under a unitary approach, a low valuation of sexual speech will merely appear anyway in a different guise?

NUDITY BANS

1. *Nudity on drive-in movie screens.* In ERZNOZNIK v. JACKSONVILLE, 422 U.S. 205 (1975), the Court sustained a challenge to the facial validity of an ordinance prohibiting drive-in movie theaters with screens visible from public streets from showing films containing nudity. The ordinance prohibited exhibitions of "the human male or female bare buttocks, human female bare breasts, or human bare pubic areas." Concededly, the ban applied to nonobscene films. The city's major defense was that "it may protect its citizens against unwilling exposure to materials that may be offensive." In rejecting that claim, Justice POWELL's majority opinion developed an approach similar to that articulated by Justice Harlan in Cohen. He stated:

"This Court has considered analogous issues—pitting the First Amendment rights of speakers against the privacy rights of those who may be unwilling viewers or auditors—in a variety of contexts. Such cases demand delicate balancing. [Although] each case ultimately must depend on its own specific facts, some general principles have emerged. A State or municipality may protect individual privacy by enacting reasonable time, place, and manner regulations applicable to all speech irrespective of content. But when the government, acting as censor, undertakes selectively to shield the public from some kinds of speech on the ground that they are more offensive than others, the First Amendment strictly limits its power. See, e.g., [Mosley, p. 1205 below]. Such selective restrictions have been upheld only when the speaker intrudes on the privacy of the home or the degree of captivity makes it impractical for the unwilling viewer or auditor to avoid exposure. The plain, if at times disquieting, truth is that in our pluralistic society, [with] constantly proliferating new and ingenious forms of expression, 'we are inescapably captive audiences for many purposes.' [Rowan.] Much that we encounter offends our esthetic, if not our political and moral, sensibilities. Nevertheless, the Constitution does not permit government to decide which types of otherwise protected speech are sufficiently offensive to require protection for the unwilling listener or viewer. Rather, absent the narrow circumstances described above, the burden normally falls upon the viewer to 'avoid further bombardment of [his] sensibilities simply by averting [his] eyes.' [Cohen.]

"The Jacksonville ordinance discriminates among movies solely on the basis of content. Its effect is to deter drive-in theaters from showing movies containing any nudity, however innocent or even educational. This discrimination cannot be justified as a means of preventing significant intrusions on privacy. The ordinance seeks only to keep these films from being seen from public streets and places where the offended viewer readily can avert his eyes. In short, the screen of a drive-in theater is not 'so obtrusive as to make it impossible for an unwilling individual to avoid exposure to it.' [Redrup.] Thus, we conclude that the limited privacy interest of persons on the public streets cannot justify this censorship of otherwise protected speech on the basis of its content."

Justice Powell also rejected two other proffered justifications. With respect to the claim that the ordinance was intended to regulate expression accessible to minors, he found the law "overbroad in its proscription." He noted that it was not limited to sexually explicit nudity and applied to all films "containing *any* uncovered buttocks or breasts, irrespective of context or pervasiveness." That would bar films "containing a picture of a baby's buttocks, the nude body of a war victim, or scenes from a culture in which nudity is indigenous." Justice Powell commented: "Clearly all nudity cannot be deemed obscene even as to minors." The city also defended the ordinance as a traffic regulation, claiming that "nudity on a drive-in movie screen distracts passing motorists, thus slowing the flow of traffic and increasing the likelihood of accidents." Noting that nothing in the record indicated that the law was in fact aimed at traffic regulation, Justice Powell commented: "[E]ven if this were the purpose of the ordinance, it nonetheless would be invalid. By singling out movies containing even the most fleeting and innocent glimpses of nudity the legislative classification is strikingly underinclusive. There is no reason to think that a wide variety of other scenes in the customary screen diet [would] be any less distracting to the passing motorist. [Even] a traffic regulation cannot discriminate on the basis of content unless there are clear reasons for the distinctions."

Chief Justice BURGER's dissent, joined by Justice Rehnquist, accused the majority of taking a "rigidly simplistic approach" and concluded that the ordinance was "narrowly drawn to regulate only certain unique public exhibitions of nudity; it would be absurd to suggest that it operates to suppress expression of *ideas*." He elaborated: "Whatever validity the notion that passersby may protect their sensibilities by averting their eyes may have when applied to words printed on an individual's jacket, see [Cohen], it distorts reality to apply that notion to the outsize screen of a drive-in movie theater. Such screens [are] designed to [attract and hold] the attention of all observers. [It is] not unreasonable for lawmakers to believe that public nudity on a giant screen [may] have a tendency to divert attention from [the driver's] task and cause accidents. [Moreover,] those persons who legitimately desire to [view the films] are not foreclosed from doing so. [The films] may be exhibited [in] indoor theaters [and in any] drive-in movie theater [with a] screen [shielded] from public view. Thus, [the ordinance is] not a restriction on any 'message.' [The] First Amendment interests involved in this case are trivial at best." Justice WHITE submitted a separate dissent. There was also a concurring opinion by Justice DOUGLAS.

2. *Live nude dancing.* Six years later, even after the Court upheld a zoning ordinance directed at adult theaters, see American Mini Theatres, below, SCHAD v. MOUNT EPHRAIM, 452 U.S. 61 (1981), reiterated that a total ban on displays of nudity is impermissible. The challenge was brought by the operators of a store selling "adult" materials who had added a coin-operated mechanism permitting customers to watch a live, nude dancer performing behind a glass panel. The ordinance of the Borough of Mt. Ephraim, N.J., described the "permitted uses" in the small community's commercial zone and barred all other uses. As construed by the state courts, the ban covered all "live entertainment." Justice WHITE's majority opinion stated: "By excluding live entertainment throughout [the] Borough, [the ordinance] prohibits a wide range of expression that has long been held to be within the protections of the [First Amendment]. Entertainment, as well as political and ideological speech, is protected. [Nor] may an entertainment program be prohibited solely because it displays the nude human figure. 'Nudity alone' does not place otherwise protected material outside the mantle of the First Amendment. [When] a zoning law infringes upon a protected liberty, it must be narrowly drawn and must further a sufficiently substantial government.

"[In] this case, however, Mount Ephraim has not adequately justified its substantial restriction of protected activity. [The] Borough has presented no evidence, and it is not immediately apparent as a matter of experience, that live entertainment poses problems [more] significant than those associated with various permitted uses; nor does it appear that the Borough's zoning authority has arrived at a defensible conclusion that unusual problems are presented by live entertainment. [Mount] Ephraim asserts that it could have chosen to eliminate all commercial uses within its boundaries. Yet we must assess the exclusion of live entertainment in light of the commercial uses Mount Ephraim allows, not in light of what the Borough might have done.[4] [The] Borough [contends] that live entertainment in general and nude dancing in particular are amply available in close-by areas outside the limits of the Borough. [But] there is no evidence in this record to support the proposition that the kind of entertainment appellants wish to provide is available in reasonably nearby [areas]."

Chief Justice BURGER, joined by Justice Rehnquist, dissented: "[Even] assuming that the 'expression' manifested in the nude dancing that is involved here is somehow protected speech under the First Amendment, [Mt. Ephraim] is entitled to regulate it. [The] zoning ordinance imposes a minimal intrusion on genuine rights of expression; only by contortions of logic can it be made [otherwise]. [To] invoke the First Amendment to protect the activity involved in this case trivializes and demeans that great Amendment."

For another decision on the constitutionality of a ban on public nudity as applied to nude dancing, see Barnes v. Glen Theatre, Inc., p. 1231 below.

---

4. "Thus, our decision today does not establish that every unit of local government entrusted with zoning responsibilities must provide a commercial zone in which live entertainment is permitted." [Footnote by Justice White.]

"EROGENOUS ZONING"

1. *Low value speech?* In YOUNG v. AMERICAN MINI THEATRES, 427 U.S. 50 (1976), the Court upheld portions of a Detroit "Anti–Skid Row Ordinance" that differentiated between motion picture theaters that exhibited sexually explicit "adult movies" and those that showed other fare. The Court rejected the claim that the statutory classification was unconstitutional because it was based on the content of communication protected by the First Amendment. The Detroit ordinance required dispersal of "adult" theaters and bookstores—e.g., it stated that an "adult" theater may not be located within 1,000 feet of any two other "regulated uses" (such as bars, billiard halls, hotels and cabarets) or within 500 feet of a residential area. Theaters are classified as "adult" on the basis of the character of the motion pictures they exhibit. If a theater presented "material distinguished or characterized by emphasis on matters depicting, describing or relating to 'specified sexual activities' or 'specified anatomical areas,' "[5] it was an "adult" establishment. The impact of the classification was to channel the display of the sexually explicit (but not necessarily obscene) materials into limited portions of the city, not to ban the display from the city entirely. The ordinance was challenged by the operators of two adult motion picture theaters located within 1,000 feet of two other "regulated uses." The city argued that the ordinance was a zoning law needed because the location of several "regulated uses" in the same neighborhood tended to attract undesirable transients, adversely affected property values, and caused an increase in crime.

In his plurality opinion, Justice STEVENS identified the communication here as being of lower value than core, political speech: "A remark attributed to Voltaire characterizes our zealous adherence to the principle that the Government may not tell the citizen what he may or may not say. Referring to a suggestion that the violent overthrow of tyranny might be legitimate, he said: 'I disapprove of what you say, but I will defend to the death your right to say it.' The essence of that comment has been repeated time after time in our decisions invalidating attempts [to] impose selective controls upon the dissemination of ideas. [Some of our statements], read literally and without regard for the facts of the case in which [they were] made, would absolutely preclude any regulation of expressive activity predicated in whole or in part on the content of the communication. [But under our decisions the] question whether speech is, or is not, protected by the First Amendment often depends on the content of the speech. [e.g., incitement, fighting words, private-figures defamation, and obscenity.] [The Detroit ordinances draw a line] on the basis of content without violating the Government's paramount obligation of neutrality in its regulation of protected communication. For the regulation of the places where sexually explicit films may be exhibited is unaffected by whatever social, political, or philosophical message the film may be intended to communicate; whether the motion picture ridicules or characterizes one point of view or another, the effect of the ordinances is exactly the same.

5. The ordinance defined these terms as follows: "Specified Sexual Activities" were defined as: "1. Human Genitals in a state of sexual stimulation or arousal; 2. Acts of human masturbation, sexual intercourse or sodomy; 3. Fondling or other erotic touching of human genitals, pubic region, buttock or female breast."

"Specified Anatomical Areas" were defined as: "1. Less than completely and opaquely covered: (a) human genitals, pubic region, (b) buttock, and (c) female breast below a point immediately above the top of the areola; and 2. Human male genitals in a discernibly turgid state, even if completely and opaquely covered."

"Moreover, even though we recognize that the First Amendment will not tolerate the total suppression of erotic materials that have some arguably artistic value, it is manifest that society's interest in protecting this type of expression is of a wholly different, and lesser, magnitude than the interest in untrammeled political debate that inspired Voltaire's immortal comment. Whether political oratory or philosophical discussion moves us to applaud or to despise what is said, every schoolchild can understand why our duty to defend the right to speak remains the same. But few of us would march our sons and daughters off to war to preserve the citizen's right to see 'Specified Sexual Activities' exhibited in the theaters of our choice. Even though the First Amendment protects communication in this area from total suppression, we hold that the State may legitimately use the content of these materials as the basis for placing them in a different classification from other motion pictures.

"The remaining question is whether the line drawn by these ordinances is justified by the city's interest in preserving the character of its neighborhoods. [The] record discloses a factual basis for the [Council's] conclusion that this kind of restriction will have the desired effect.[6] It is not our function to appraise the wisdom of its decision to require adult theaters to be separated rather than concentrated in the same areas. In either event, the city's interest in attempting to preserve the quality of urban life is one that must be accorded high respect. Moreover, the city must be allowed a reasonable opportunity to experiment with solutions to admittedly serious problems. Since what is ultimately at stake is nothing more than a limitation on the place where adult films may be exhibited,[7] even though the determination of whether a particular film fits that characterization turns on the nature of its content, we conclude that the city's interest in the present and future character of its neighborhoods adequately supports its classification of [motion pictures]."

Justice POWELL, whose vote was necessary to produce the 5–4 majority, concurred only in the judgment and in portions of the plurality opinion: "[My] approach to the resolution of this case is sufficiently different [from Justice Stevens'] to prompt me to write separately.[1] I view the case as presenting an example of innovative land-use regulation, implicating First Amendment concerns only incidentally and to a limited [extent]. [This zoning] situation is not analogous [to] any other prior case. The unique situation presented by this ordinance calls [for] a careful inquiry into the competing concerns of the State and the interests protected by the guaranty of free expression. Because a substantial burden rests upon the State when it would limit in any way First

---

6. "The Common Council's determination was that a concentration of 'adult' movie theaters causes the area to deteriorate and become a focus of crime, effects which are not attributable to theaters showing other types of films. It is this secondary effect which this zoning ordinance attempts to avoid, not the dissemination of 'offensive' speech. In contrast, in Erznoznik, the justifications offered by the city rested primarily on the city's interest in protecting its citizens from exposure to unwanted, 'offensive' speech. The only secondary effect relied on to support that ordinance was the impact on traffic—an effect which might be caused by a distracting open-air movie even if it did not exhibit nudity." [Footnote by Justice Stevens.]

7. "The situation would be quite different if the ordinance had the effect of suppressing, or greatly restricting access to, lawful speech. Here, however, the District Court [found]: 'There are myriad locations in the City of Detroit which must be over 1,000 feet from existing regulated establishments. This burden on First Amendment rights is [slight].' " [Footnote by Justice Stevens.]

1. "I do not think we need reach, nor am I inclined to agree with, the [holding] that nonobscene, erotic materials may be treated differently under First Amendment principles from other forms of protected [expression]." [Footnote by Justice Powell.]

Amendment rights, it is necessary to identify with specificity the nature of the infringement in each [case].

"The inquiry for First Amendment purposes [looks] only to the effect of this ordinance upon freedom of expression. This prompts essentially two inquiries: (i) does the ordinance impose any content limitation on the creators of adult movies or their ability to make them available to whom they desire, and (ii) does it restrict in any significant way the viewing of these movies by those who desire to see them? On the record in this case, these inquiries must be answered in the negative. At most the impact of the ordinance on these interests is incidental and minimal. [The] ordinance is addressed only to the places at which this type of expression may be presented, a restriction that does not interfere with content. Nor is there any significant overall curtailment of adult movie presentations, or the opportunity for a message to reach an audience. [In] these circumstances, it is appropriate to analyze the permissibility of Detroit's action under the four-part test of United States v. O'Brien [p. 1213 below]. Under that test, a governmental regulation is sufficiently justified, despite its incidental impact upon First Amendment interests, 'if it is within the constitutional power of the Government; if it furthers an important or substantial governmental interest; if the governmental interest is unrelated to the suppression of free expression; and if the incidental restriction [on] First Amendment freedoms is no greater than is essential to the furtherance of that interest.' [There is] no question that the Ordinance was within the power of the Detroit Common Council to enact. Nor is there doubt that the interests furthered by this Ordinance are both important and substantial. The third and fourth tests of O'Brien also are met on this record. It is clear [that] Detroit has not embarked on an effort to suppress free expression. The Ordinance was already in existence, and its purposes clearly set out, for a full decade before adult establishments were brought under it. When this occurred, it is clear [that] the governmental interest prompting the inclusion in the ordinance of adult establishments was wholly unrelated to any suppression of free expression.[2] Nor is there reason to question that the degree of incidental encroachment upon such expression was the minimum necessary to further the purpose of the [ordinance].[3]

"The dissent perceives support for its position in [Erznoznik]. I believe this perception is a clouded one. [T]he ordinance in Erznoznik was a misconceived attempt directly to regulate content of expression. The Detroit zoning ordinance, in contrast, affects expression only incidentally and in furtherance of governmental interests wholly unrelated to the regulation of expression. [Although] courts must be alert to the possibility of direct rather than incidental effects of zoning on expression, and especially to the possibility of pretextual use of the power to zone as a means of suppressing expression, it is clear that this is not such a case."

---

2. "[The Council] simply acted to protect the economic integrity of large areas of its city against the effects of a predictable interaction between a concentration of certain businesses and the responses of people in the area. If it had been concerned with restricting the message purveyed by adult theaters, it would have tried to close them or restrict their number rather than circumscribe their choice as to location." [Footnote by Justice Powell.]

3. "In my view [the] dissent misconceives the issue in this case by insisting that it involves an impermissible time, place and manner restriction based on the content of expression. It involves nothing of the kind. We have here merely a decision by the city to treat certain movie theaters differently because they have markedly different effects upon their [surroundings]." [Footnote by Justice Powell.]

Justice STEWART, joined by Justices Brennan, Marshall and Blackmun, dissented: "[This] case does not involve a simple zoning ordinance, or a content-neutral time, place, and manner restriction, or a regulation of obscene expression or other speech that is entitled to less than the full protection of the First Amendment. The kind of expression at issue here is no doubt objectionable to some, but that fact does not diminish its protected status any more than did the particular content of the 'offensive' expression in [Erznoznik or Cohen]. What this case does involve is the constitutional permissibility of selective interference with protected speech whose content is thought to produce distasteful effects. It is elementary that a prime function of the First Amendment is to guard against just such interference. By refusing to invalidate Detroit's ordinance the Court rides roughshod over cardinal principles of First Amendment law, which require that time, place and manner regulations that affect protected expression be content-neutral except in the limited context of a captive or juvenile audience. In place of these principles the Court invokes a concept wholly alien to the First Amendment. [The Court] stands 'Voltaire's immortal comment' on its head. For if the guarantees of the First Amendment were reserved for expression that more than a 'few of us' would take up arms to defend, then the right of free expression would be defined and circumscribed by current popular [opinion].

"The fact that the 'offensive' speech here may not address 'important' topics—'ideas of social and political significance,' in the Court's terminology—does not mean that it is less worthy of constitutional protection [e.g., Cohen]. Moreover, in the absence of a judicial determination of obscenity, it is by no means clear that the speech is not 'important' even on the Court's terms. I can only interpret today's decision as an aberration. The Court is undoubtedly sympathetic, as am I, to the well-intentioned efforts of Detroit to 'clean up' its streets and prevent the proliferation of 'skid rows.' But it is in those instances where protected speech grates most unpleasantly against the sensibilities that judicial vigilance must be at its height. [The] factual parallels between [Erznoznik] and this [case] are [striking]. The Court must never forget that the consequences of rigorously enforcing the guarantees of the First Amendment are frequently unpleasant. Much speech that seems to be of little or no value will enter the marketplace of ideas, threatening the quality of our social discourse and, more generally, the serenity of our lives. But that is the price to be paid for constitutional freedom."

2. *"Secondary effects."* A decade later, the Court again upheld an "erogenous zoning" law, embracing Justice Powell's balancing approach in American Mini Theatres rather than Justice Stevens' low-value approach. Unlike the Detroit ordinance at issue in Mini Theatres, the zoning ordinance at issue in RENTON v. PLAYTIME THEATRES, INC., 475 U.S. 41 (1986), attempted to regulate the location of adult theaters by concentrating them rather than by dispersing them. The ordinance provided that such establishments "may not be located within 1,000 feet of any residential zone, single-or multiple-family dwelling, church, park, or school." Justice REHNQUIST's majority opinion found the ordinance consistent with the First Amendment: "The ordinance is [properly] analyzed as a form of time, place, and manner regulation. [This type of regulation is explored in chap. 12, sec. 2, below.] [Describing] the ordinance as a time, place, and manner regulation is, of course, only the first step in our inquiry. This Court has long held that regulations enacted for the purpose of restraining speech on the basis of its content presumptively violate the First Amendment. On the other hand, so-called 'content-neutral' time, place, and manner regulations are acceptable so long as they are designed to serve a

substantial governmental interest and do not unreasonably limit alternative avenues of communication.

"[At] first glance, the Renton ordinance, like the ordinance in American Mini Theatres, does not appear to fit neatly into either the 'content-based' or the 'content-neutral' category. To be sure, the ordinance treats theaters that specialize in adult films differently from other kinds of theaters. Nevertheless, [the] Renton ordinance is aimed not at the *content* of the films shown at 'adult motion picture theatres,' but rather at the *secondary effects* of such theaters on the surrounding community. [The] District Court's finding as to 'predominate' intent [is] more than adequate to establish that the city's pursuit of its zoning interests here was unrelated to the suppression of free expression. The ordinance by its terms is designed to prevent crime, protect the city's retail trade, maintain property values, and generally 'protec[t] and preserv[e] the quality of [the city's] neighborhoods, commercial districts, and the quality of urban life,' not to suppress the expression of unpopular views." Justice Rehnquist found that these interests were "substantial," that the experience of other cities had proven such a zoning approach effective, and that the availability of 520 acres, "more than five percent of the entire land area of Renton," furnished "reasonable alternative avenues of communication." Although most of this land was available only at economically prohibitive prices, the Court did not find this relevant: "That respondents must fend for themselves in the real estate market, on an equal footing with other prospective purchasers and lessees, does not give rise to a First Amendment violation. [Nothing in the] First Amendment compels the Government to ensure that adult theaters, or any other kinds of speech-related businesses for that matter, will be able to obtain sites at bargain prices." Notably, Justice STEVENS simply signed onto Justice Rehnquist's opinion (recall his footnote in Mini Theatres referring to "secondary effects").

Justice BRENNAN, joined by Justice Marshall, dissented: "Renton was interested not in controlling the 'secondary effects' associated with adult businesses, but in discriminating against adult theaters based on the content of the films they exhibit." He added that, even "assuming that the ordinance should be treated like a content-neutral time, place, and manner restriction, I would still find it unconstitutional [, because] it does not provide for reasonable alternative avenues of communication" and because it was not narrowly tailored to serve a significant governmental interest. Moreover, he rejected the Court's conclusion that Renton was entitled to rely for its findings on the experiences of other cities, arguing that this type of evidence was inadequate to justify regulation where First Amendment interests were at stake, and too likely to conceal a true motive of hostility to the particular views expressed by the communication.

Is the "secondary effects" reasoning of Renton confined to laws regulating sexually explicit materials? If so, is that because, as Justice Stevens insisted all along, they involve a "lower value" kind of speech? Consider the implications of the distinction between content regulation and secondary effects regulation as it might pertain to "full value" communication. May a city, in order to preserve tranquility in the park, restrict all "inflammatory" speeches, regardless of the point of view expressed? May a state, in order to prevent bodily injury, restrict all discussions of violence? May a city bar all political rallies to prevent the accumulation of litter? Are these content regulations or secondary effects regulations? Are not most content regulations premised ultimately on "secondary effects" of the communication? For a case setting forth limits to the "secondary effects" reasoning of Renton, see Boos v. Barry, p. 1208 below.

————

INDECENCY BANS ON THE COMMUNICATIONS MEDIA

The Court has considered several restrictions on sexually explicit but not obscene communications over various communications media. These decisions follow a pattern similar to that in the zoning cases: outright bans are invalidated but some partial regulations are upheld. In the decisions that follow, note that Justice Stevens' theory that indecent speech should explicitly be assigned low First Amendment value again falls short of capturing a majority of the Court.

FCC v. Pacifica Foundation

438 U.S. 726, 98 S.Ct. 3026, 57 L.Ed.2d 1073 (1978).

[This decision held that the Federal Communications Commission has power to regulate radio broadcasts that are indecent but not obscene. It arose from the following circumstances: In a mid-afternoon weekday broadcast, respondent's New York radio station aired a 12–minute monologue called "Filthy Words" by George Carlin, a satiric humorist. The monologue, recorded before a live audience that frequently interrupted with laughter, began by referring to Carlin's thoughts about "the words you couldn't say on the public, ah, airwaves, um, the ones you definitely wouldn't say, ever," especially the "original" seven dirty words: "shit, piss, fuck, cunt, cocksucker, motherfucker, and tits." Carlin repeated these words in a variety of colloquialisms. The monologue was aired as part of a program on contemporary attitudes toward the use of language. Immediately before the broadcast, the station had advised listeners that it would include "sensitive language which might be regarded as offensive to some."

[The FCC received a complaint from a man who stated that he had heard the broadcast while driving with his young son. In response, the FCC issued a Declaratory Order granting the complaint and holding that Pacifica "could have been the subject of administrative sanctions." However, the FCC did not impose formal sanctions; instead, it stated that the Order would be "associated with the station's license file, and in the event that subsequent complaints are received, the [FCC] will then decide whether it should utilize any of the available sanctions it has been granted by Congress." The FCC explained that Carlin's "patently offensive," though *not* obscene, language should be regulated by principles analogous to those found in the law of nuisance where the "law generally speaks to *channeling* behavior more than actually prohibiting it." Later, the FCC explained that its regulation of certain words depicting sexual and excretory activity was designed to channel them "to times of day when children most likely would not be exposed." The Court of Appeals overturned the FCC Order. The Court reversed, sustaining the FCC's action by a vote of 5–4.

[Justice STEVENS, writing for the majority, found that the governing statute's prohibition of "censorship" by the FCC did not limit the Commission's authority to impose sanctions "on licensees who engage in obscene, indecent, or profane broadcasting," found Carlin's monologue "indecent" within the meaning of the statute, and rejected Pacifica's argument that "indecent" broadcasts should be limited to those that were "obscene." He also wrote for the majority in part IV(C) of his opinion, below, noting the special problems of the broadcast medium. But in part IV(B) of his opinion, below, Justice Stevens wrote only for himself, Chief Justice Burger and Justice Rehnquist.]

IV(B). When the issue is narrowed to the facts of this case, the question is whether the First Amendment denies government any power to restrict the public broadcast of indecent language in any circumstances. For if the government has any such power, this was an appropriate occasion for its exercise. The words of the Carlin monologue are unquestionably "speech" within the meaning of the First Amendment. It is equally clear that the [FCC's] objections to the broadcast were based in part on its content. The order must therefore fall if, as Pacifica argues, the First Amendment prohibits all governmental regulation that depends on the content of speech. Our past cases demonstrate, however, that no such absolute rule is mandated by the Constitution. [See, e.g., the cases on "fighting words," obscenity, libel, and commercial speech, as well as Mini Theatres.]

The question in this case is whether a broadcast of patently offensive words dealing with sex and excretion may be regulated because of its content. [T]he fact that society may find speech offensive is not a sufficient reason for suppressing it. Indeed, if it is the speaker's opinion that gives offense, that consequence is a reason for according it constitutional protection. [If] there were any reason to believe that the Commission's characterization of the Carlin monologue as offensive could be traced to its political content—or even to the fact that it satirized contemporary attitudes about four letter words[1]—First Amendment protection might be required. But that is simply not this case. These words offend for the same reasons that obscenity offends. Their place in the hierarchy of First Amendment values was aptly sketched by Mr. Justice Murphy [in Chaplinsky].

Although these words ordinarily lack literary, political, or scientific value, they are not entirely outside the protection of the First Amendment. Some uses of even the most offensive words are unquestionably protected. [E.g., Hess v. Indiana.] Indeed, we may assume, arguendo, that this monologue would be protected in other contexts. Nonetheless, the constitutional protection accorded to a communication containing such patently offensive sexual and excretory language need not be the same in every context. It is a characteristic of speech such as this that both its capacity to offend and its "social value" [Chaplinsky] [vary] with the circumstances. Words that are commonplace in one setting are shocking in another. To paraphrase [Justice] Harlan, one occasion's lyric is another's vulgarity. Cf. [Cohen]. In this case it is undisputed that the content of Pacifica's broadcast was "vulgar," "offensive," and "shocking." Because content of that character is not entitled to absolute constitutional protection under all circumstances, we must consider its context in order to determine whether the Commission's action was constitutionally permissible.

IV(C). We have long recognized that each medium of expression presents special First Amendment problems. And of all forms of communication, it is broadcasting that has received the most limited First Amendment protection.

---

1. The monologue does present a point of view; it attempts to show that the words it uses are "harmless" and that our attitudes toward them are "essentially silly." The Commission objects, not to this point of view, but to the way in which it is expressed. The belief that these words are harmless does not necessarily confer a First Amendment privilege to use them while proselytizing, just as the conviction that obscenity is harmless does not license one to communicate that conviction by the indiscriminate distribution of an obscene leaflet. [Footnote by Justice Stevens.]

[The] reasons for these distinctions are complex, but two have relevance to the present case. First, the broadcast media have established a uniquely pervasive presence in the lives of all Americans. Patently offensive, indecent material presented over the airwaves confronts the citizen, not only in public, but also in the privacy of the home, where the individual's right to be let alone plainly outweighs the First Amendment rights of an intruder. [Rowan, p. 1169 below.] Because the broadcast audience is constantly tuning in and out, prior warnings cannot completely protect the listener or viewer from unexpected program content. To say that one may avoid further offense by turning off the radio when he hears indecent language is like saying that the remedy for an assault is to run away after the first blow. One may hang up on an indecent phone call, but that option does not give the caller a constitutional immunity or avoid a harm that has already taken place.[2]

Second, broadcasting is uniquely accessible to children, even those too young to read. Although Cohen's written message might have been incomprehensible to a first grader, Pacifica's broadcast could have enlarged a child's vocabulary in an instant. Other forms of offensive expression may be withheld from the young without restricting the expression at its source. Bookstores and motion picture theaters, for example, may be prohibited from making indecent material available to children. [Ginsberg v. New York]. The ease with which children may obtain access to broadcast material, coupled with the concerns recognized in Ginsberg, amply justify special treatment of indecent broadcasting.

It is appropriate [to] emphasize the narrowness of our holding. This case does not involve a two-way radio conversation between a cab driver and a dispatcher, or a telecast of an Elizabethan comedy. We have not decided that an occasional expletive in either setting would justify any sanction or, indeed, that this broadcast would justify a criminal prosecution. The [FCC's] decision rested entirely on a nuisance rationale under which context is all-important. The concept requires consideration of a host of variables. The time of day was emphasized by the [FCC]. The content of the program in which the language is used will also affect the composition of the audience, and differences between radio, television, and perhaps closed-circuit transmissions, may also be relevant. As [Justice] Sutherland wrote, a "nuisance may be merely a right thing in the wrong place—like a pig in the parlor instead of the barnyard." Euclid v. Ambler Realty Co. We simply hold that when the Commission finds that a pig has entered the parlor, the exercise of its regulatory power does not depend on proof that the pig is obscene.

Reversed.

[Justice POWELL, joined by Justice BLACKMUN, wrote a separate concurrence, declining to join part IV(B) of Justice Stevens' opinion:]

[T]he Commission sought to "channel" the monologue to hours when the fewest unsupervised children would be exposed to it. [This] consideration provides strong support for the Commission's holding. The Court has recognized society's right to "adopt more stringent controls on communicative materials available to youths than on those available to adults." [The] Commission properly held that [the] language involved in this case is as potentially degrading and harmful to children as representations of many erotic acts. In most instances, the dissemination of this kind of speech to children may be

2. Outside the home, the balance between the offensive speaker and the unwilling audience may sometimes tip in favor of the speaker, requiring the offended listener to turn away. See [Erznoznik and Cohen]. [Footnote by Justice Stevens.]

limited without also limiting willing adults' access to it. [The] difficulty is that such a physical separation of the audience cannot be accomplished in the broadcast media. During most of the broadcast hours [the] broadcaster cannot reach willing adults without also reaching children. This [is] one of the distinctions between the broadcast and other media. [The] Commission was entitled to give substantial weight to this [difference].

A second difference [is] that broadcasting [comes] directly into the home, the one place where people ordinarily have the right not to be assaulted by uninvited and offensive sights and sounds. Although the First Amendment may require unwilling adults to absorb the first blow of offensive but protected speech when they are in public before they turn away, a different order of values obtains in the home. [This] is not to say, however, that the Commission has an unrestricted license to decide what speech, protected in other media, may be banned from the airwaves in order to protect unwilling adults from momentary exposure to it in their homes. Making the sensitive judgments required in these cases is not easy. But this responsibility has been reposed initially in the Commission, and its judgment is entitled to respect. [It] is said that this ruling will have the effect of "reduc[ing] the adult population [to hearing] only what is fit for children." [Butler v. Michigan, 352 U.S. 380 (1957)]. This argument is not without force. [But the] Commission's holding does not prevent willing adults from purchasing Carlin's record, from attending his performances, or indeed, from reading the transcript reprinted as an appendix to the Court's opinion. On its face, it does not prevent respondent from broadcasting the monologue during late evening hours. [On] the facts of this case, the Commission's order did not violate respondent's First Amendment rights.

[I] do not join Part IV(B), however, because I do not subscribe to the theory that the Justices of this Court are free generally to decide on the basis of its content which speech protected by the First Amendment is most "valuable" and hence deserving of the most protection, and which is less "valuable" and hence deserving of less protection. In my view, the result in this case does not turn on whether Carlin's monologue, viewed as a whole, or the words that comprise it, have more or less "value" than a candidate's campaign speech. This is a judgment for each person to make, not one for the judges to impose upon him. The result turns instead on the unique characteristics of the broadcast media, combined with society's right to protect its children from speech generally agreed to be inappropriate for their years, and with the interest of unwilling adults in not being assaulted by such offensive speech in their homes. Moreover, I doubt whether today's decision will prevent any adult who wishes to receive Carlin's message in Carlin's own words from doing so, and from making for himself a value judgment as to the merit of the message and words.

Justice BRENNAN, with whom Justice MARSHALL joins, dissenting:

For the second time in two years, see [American Mini Theatres], the Court refuses to embrace the notion, completely antithetical to basic First Amendment values, that the degree of protection the First Amendment affords protected speech varies with the social value ascribed to that speech by five Members of this Court. [Despite] our unanimous agreement that the Carlin monologue is protected speech, a majority of the Court [finds] that, on the facts of this case, the FCC is not constitutionally barred from imposing sanctions on Pacifica for its airing of the Carlin monologue. This majority apparently believes that the FCC's disapproval of Pacifica's afternoon broadcast of Carlin's "Dirty Words" recording is a permissible time, place, and manner [regulation].

"The ability of government, consonant with the Constitution, to shut off discourse solely to protect others from hearing it [is] dependent upon a showing that substantial privacy interests are being invaded in an essentially intolerable manner." [Cohen.] [But an] individual's actions in switching on and listening to communications transmitted over the public airways and directed to the public at large do not implicate fundamental privacy interests, even when engaged in within the home. Instead, [these] actions are more properly viewed as a decision to take part, if only as a listener, in an ongoing public discourse [through] communication he voluntarily admits into his home. [Moreover,] the very fact that those interests are threatened only by a radio broadcast precludes any intolerable invasion of privacy; for unlike other intrusive modes of communication, such as sound trucks, "[t]he radio can be turned off"—and with a minimum of effort. Whatever the minimal discomfort suffered by a listener who inadvertently tunes into a program he finds offensive during the brief interval before he can simply extend his arm and switch stations, [it] is surely worth the candle to preserve the broadcaster's right to send, and the right of those interested to receive, a message entitled to full First Amendment protection. To reach a contrary balance [is] clearly, to follow [Justice] Stevens' reliance on animal metaphors, "to burn the house to roast the pig."

[The] government unquestionably has a special interest in the well-being of children. [But here] the Court, for the first time, allows the government to prevent minors from gaining access to materials that are not obscene, and are therefore protected, as to them. [This] result violates [the] principle of Butler v. Michigan [that government may not] "reduce the adult population [to] reading only what is fit for children." [Taken] to their logical extreme, the [majority's] rationales would support the cleansing of public radio of any "four-letter words" whatsoever, regardless of their context. The rationales could justify the banning from radio of a myriad of literary works, novels, poems, and plays by the likes of Shakespeare, Joyce, Hemingway, Ben Jonson, Henry Fielding, Robert Burns, and Chaucer; they could support the suppression of a good deal of political speech, such as the Nixon tapes; and they could even provide the basis for imposing sanctions for the broadcast of certain portions of the Bible. [I] would place the responsibility and the right to weed worthless and offensive communications from the public airways where it belongs and where, until today, it resided: in a public free to choose those communications worthy of its attention from a marketplace unsullied by the censor's hand.

[It is no answer to suggest that] "[t]here are few, if any, thoughts that cannot be expressed by the use of less offensive language." [For a] given word may have a unique capacity to capsule an idea, evoke an emotion, or conjure up an image. [Cohen] [Nor is it sufficient to suggest alternatives to hearing the broadcast, such as buying Carlin's record, for] in many cases, the medium may well be the message. [There] runs throughout the opinions of my Brothers Powell and Stevens [a] depressing inability to appreciate that in our land of cultural pluralism, there are many who think, act, and talk differently from the Members of this Court, and who do not share their fragile sensibilities. [Today's] decision will thus have its greatest impact [on] persons who do not share the Court's view as to which words or expressions are acceptable and who, for a variety of reasons, including a conscious desire to flout majoritarian conventions, express themselves using words that may be regarded as offensive by those from different socio-economic backgrounds. [The Court] confirm[s] Carlin's prescience as a social commentator by the result it reaches today.

[Justice STEWART, joined by Justices Brennan, White and Marshall, dissented on the ground that the constitutional questions in the case could be avoided by holding that Congress intended, by using the word "indecent," "to prohibit nothing more than obscene speech."]

THE LIMITS OF PACIFICA

1. *Captive audiences: Pacifica's privacy invasion rationale.* Recall that in Cohen, Justice Harlan's opinion rejected any "captive audience" rationale for restricting Cohen's speech. He reasoned that, in the public square, government may not shield listeners from offensive speech—they must simply avert their eyes and ears. But, as Pacifica and Denver Area illustrate, the Court *has* allowed government to rely upon such "captive audience" rationales when applied to the home. Pacifica relied upon ROWAN v. U.S. POST OFFICE DEPARTMENT, 397 U.S. 728 (1970), which upheld against First Amendment challenge a federal law permitting recipients of a "pandering advertisement" that offered for sale "matter which the addressee in his sole discretion believes to be erotically arousing or sexually provocative" to request a post office order requiring the mailer to remove his or her name from his mailing list and to stop all future mailings. The law was enacted in response to concern "with use of mail facilities to distribute unsolicited advertisements that recipients found to be offensive because of their lewd and salacious character." A mail order business claimed that the federal law violated its right to communicate.

Chief Justice BURGER's opinion found the constitutional challenge unpersuasive: "[T]he right of every person 'to be let alone' must be placed in the scales with the right of others to communicate. In today's complex society we are inescapably captive audiences for many purposes, but a sufficient measure of individual autonomy must survive to permit every householder to exercise control over unwanted mail. [Weighing] the highly important right to communicate [against] the very basic right to be free from sights, sounds and tangible matter we do not want, it seems to us that a mailer's right to communicate must stop at the mailbox of an unreceptive addressee. [In] effect the power of a householder under the statute is unlimited; he may prohibit the mailing of a dry goods catalog because he objects to the contents—or indeed the text of the language touting the merchandise. Congress provided the sweeping power not only to protect privacy but to avoid possible constitutional questions that might arise from vesting the power to make any discretionary evaluation of the material in a governmental official." The Chief Justice added: "If this prohibition operates to impede the flow of even valid ideas, the answer is that no one has a right to press even 'good' ideas on an unwilling recipient. That we are often 'captives' outside the sanctuary of the home and subject to objectionable speech and other sound does not mean we must be captives everywhere."

Was the law in Pacifica truly parallel to the law upheld in Rowan? Does it matter who controls the right to opt out: government or the householder? Consider the development of the so-called "V-chip" for television. Such a device would enable parents to block selected channels or shows based on their violent content. Would a law mandating that television sets contain V-chips provide a closer analogy to Rowan than did the law in Pacifica? What if the V-chip screened out only programs rated excessively violent by a government official?

Does the "captive audience" rationale for broadcasting or cable restrictions extend beyond sexually explicit speech? Consider the following comment: "It is no wonder that Julian Bond [then a civil rights activist] is outraged about the FCC's doing nothing to stop an announcer on a radio station in the South who frequently uses the word 'nigger.' Bond argued that if the FCC can stop people who use four-letter words that are offensive [under Pacifica], they surely ought to stop someone who uses a word that is offensive to half the audience in the South." Gunther, "The Highest Court, The Toughest Issues," Stanford Magazine, Fall–Winter 1978, 34 (criticizing Pacifica). Would the FCC action Bond suggested be constitutional? Could government ban, on grounds of offensiveness or harm to children, the broadcast of political advertisements for an anti-abortion candidate that contained photographs of aborted fetuses? See Levi, "The FCC, Indecency, and Anti-Abortion Political Advertising," III Villanova Sports & Ent. L. J. 85 (1996).

The Court limited Rowan's "captive audience" rationale in CONSOLIDATED EDISON [Con Ed] v. PUBLIC SERVICE COMM'N [PSC], 447 U.S. 530 (1980), which invalidated an order of the New York PSC prohibiting the inclusion in monthly electric bills of inserts that discussed controversial issues of public policy. The PSC order had barred "utilities from using bill inserts to discuss political matters, including the desirability of future development of nuclear power." The highest state court had sustained the order as protecting the privacy of the utility's customers, reasoning that they "have no choice whether to receive the insert and the views expressed in the insert may inflame their sensibilities." The Court reversed. Justice POWELL's majority opinion explained: "Even if a short exposure to Consolidated Edison's views may offend the sensibilities of some consumers, [they may] escape exposure to objectionable material simply by transferring the bill insert from envelope to wastebasket." Justice STEVENS concurred in the judgment, reiterating his "lower value speech" theory of American Mini Theatres and Pacifica, but limiting it to cases of offensiveness that is "independent[] of the message the speaker intends to convey."

Does the Con Ed principle apply only to political speech? Or does it extend to sexual materials? In BOLGER v. YOUNGS DRUG PRODUCTS CORP., 463 U.S. 60 (1983), the Court invalidated a federal law barring the mailing of unsolicited advertisements for contraceptive products, especially condoms. One of the proffered justifications was to protect recipients from offense. The Court rejected that argument. Writing for the Court, Justice MARSHALL observed: "[We] have never held that [government] can shut off the flow of mailings to protect those recipients who might potentially be offended. The First Amendment 'does not permit the government to prohibit speech as intrusive unless the "captive" audience cannot avoid objectionable speech.' [The] 'short, regular, journey from mail box to trash can [is] an acceptable burden [so] far as the Constitution is concerned." Any interest in protecting children's sensibilities, he suggested, could be adequately served by parental self-help: "We can reasonably assume that parents already exercise substantial control over the disposition of mail once it enters their mailbox. [And parents] must already cope with a multitude of external stimuli that color their children's perception of sensitive subjects." The advertisements were "entirely suitable for adults. [The] level of discourse reaching a mailbox cannot be limited to that which would be suitable for a sandbox." Pacifica was distinguished on the ground that the receipt of mail is "far less intrusive and uncontrollable" than are radio and television broadcasts.

Justice REHNQUIST, joined by Justice O'Connor, concurred in the judgment. He noted the substantial governmental interest in preventing intrusion into the home, but argued that the statute here imposed an unduly large restriction in view of the extent of the intrusion. Justice STEVENS, also concurring in the judgment, took issue with the majority's "virtually complete rejection of offensiveness as a possibly legitimate justification for the suppression of speech." But he found the statute nonetheless objectionable because it prohibits "ideas, not style": by limiting information about contraception but not conception, it excluded "one advocate from a forum to which adversaries have unlimited access."

How far beyond the home does the "captive audience" rationale extend? To the sidewalks outside? See Frisby, p. 1261 below. To a hospital or clinic? See Madsen, p. 1263 below. To a municipal bus? See Lehman, p. 1272 below.

2. *Total indecency bans.* Although Pacifica allowed some regulation of material that was "indecent" but not legally obscene, a unanimous Court placed sharp limits on such regulation in SABLE COMMUNICATIONS, INC. v. FCC, 492 U.S. 115 (1989). At issue was congressional control of "sexually-oriented pre-recorded telephone messages" ("dial-a-porn" services), available on a pay-per-message basis by a telephone call initiated by the listener. In 1988, Congress amended the Communications Act of 1934 to target such services, criminally prohibiting telephone messages that were either obscene or indecent. But the Court, in an opinion by Justice WHITE, struck down the indecency component of the law. He reiterated existing doctrine in concluding that "[s]exual expression which is indecent but not obscene is protected by the First Amendment." The question was thus whether the nature of dial-a-porn services was such as to justify restrictions on such protected material. Justice White rejected the government's argument that Pacifica was controlling, noting both that Pacifica did not deal with a total ban and that there was a "manifest" difference between a radio show that can "intrude on the privacy of the home without prior warning as to program content" and a medium that requires a presumably aware listener "to take steps to receive the communication. [Placing] a telephone call is not the same as turning on a radio and being taken by surprise by an indecent message."

The Government did not claim that it could have restricted indecent materials if the audience were limited to adults, but argued that keeping children from using such services was a sufficiently compelling interest that it justified the total prohibition. Although Justice White acknowledged the importance of the interest in protecting children, he found this prohibition insufficiently narrowly tailored, in light of the availability of numerous technological alternatives, such as credit card payments, access codes, and scrambling options. Although a limited number of children might be able to circumvent these barriers, the prohibition had "the invalid effect or limiting the content of adult telephone conversations to that which is suitable for children to hear." Justice SCALIA concurred, commenting on the value judgments implicit in the "narrow tailoring" requirement, and leaving open the possibility that, with better evidence than was presented here on the "infeasibility of alternative means to [provide] adequate protection of minors," a restriction on telephonic communication of indecent material might be upheld. He added that, "while we hold that the Constitution prevents Congress from banning indecent speech in this fashion, we do not hold that the Constitution requires public utilities to carry it." Justice BRENNAN, joined by Justices Marshall and Stevens, concurred with respect to the indecency aspect of the Court's holding, but dissented from the conclusion that obscene communications could be restricted.

3. *Authorizing cable operators to regulate indecent programming.* In light of Sable, Congress could not simply ban indecent programming on cable television. But may it authorize cable operators to decline to show such programming on stations where they would not ordinarily have editorial discretion? That was the question that reached the Court in DENVER AREA EDUCATIONAL TELECOMMUNICATIONS CONSORTIUM v. FCC, 524 U.S. ___, 116 S.Ct. 2374 (1996). In that decision, a plurality led by Justice Breyer in

part applied the reasoning of the majority in Pacifica to the medium of cable television. The case involved a challenge by cable programmers and viewers to three provisions of the Cable Television Consumer Protection and Competition Act of 1992. Parts of the law applied to "leased access channels," which are channels that federal law requires cable operators to reserve for commercial use by cable programmers who are unaffiliated with the operator. Other parts applied to "public access channels," which are channels that federal law permits municipalities to reserve for their own public, educational, or educational use as a condition of granting a cable franchise, and which municipalities have historically so reserved. Cable operators are normally denied any editorial discretion on leased or public access channels.

Section 10(a) of the Act authorized "a cable operator to enforce prospectively a written and published policy of prohibiting programming that the cable operator reasonably believes describes or depicts sexual or excretory activities or organs in a patently offensive manner as measured by contemporary community standards." Section 10(b) imposed a blocking requirement on any indecent leased access programming the cable operator opted to show: such material had to be segregated "on a single channel" and blocked, for example by scrambling, "unless the subscriber requests access to such channel in writing." Section 10(c) authorized the FCC to promulgate regulations permitting cable operators to prohibit "obscene material, sexually explicit conduct, or material soliciting or promoting unlawful conduct," and the FCC defined "sexually explicit conduct" under section 10(c) in much the same language as 10(a).

The Court upheld section 10(a) but struck down sections 10(b) and 10(c). It divided into three camps on the reasoning. Justice KENNEDY, joined in a partial concurrence and partial dissent by Justice Ginsburg, would have struck down all three provisions. Justice Kennedy reiterated that indecent but nonobscene programming is protected speech. He rejected the government's argument that Pacifica had established a generally lower standard of review for regulations of indecent speech: "Other than the few categories of expression which can be proscribed, we have been reluctant to mark off new categories of speech for diminished constitutional protection. Our hesitancy reflects skepticism about the possibility of courts' drawing principled distinctions to use in judging governmental restrictions on speech and ideas, [Cohen,] a concern heightened here by the inextricability of indecency from expression. [In] artistic or political settings, indecency may have strong communicative content, protesting conventional norms or giving an edge to a work by conveying 'otherwise inexpressible emotions.' In scientific programs, the more graphic the depiction (even if to the point of offensiveness), the more accurate and comprehensive the portrayal of the truth may be. Indecency often is inseparable from the ideas and viewpoints conveyed, or separable only with loss of truth or expressive power."

Accordingly, Justice Kennedy would have subjected the Act's content-based regulation of indecent programming to strict scrutiny under Sable and would have found that it "cannot survive this exacting review. However compelling Congress' interest in shielding children from indecent programming, the provisions in this case are not drawn with enough care to withstand scrutiny under our precedents. [First,] to the extent some operators may allow indecent programming, children in localities those operators serve will be left unprotected. Partial service of a compelling interest is not narrow tailoring. [Second,] to the extent cable operators prohibit indecent programming on access channels, not only children but adults will be deprived of it. The Government may not 'reduce the adult population ... to [viewing] only what is fit for children.' Butler." Finally, he reasoned that the provision would function more like the ban struck down in Sable than the channeling permitted in Pacifica: "The plurality ignores a key difference of this case from Pacifica. There, the broadcaster wanted to air the speech in question; here, the cable operator does not. So the safe harbor of late-night programming permitted by the FCC in Pacifica would likely promote speech, whereas suppression will follow [here]."

A second camp of justices would have upheld all three provisions. Justice THOMAS, joined by Chief Justice Rehnquist and Justice Scalia in a partial dissent and partial concurrence, viewed sections 10(a) and 10(c) as simply restoring some measure of editorial discretion to cable operators that was rightfully theirs in the first place. "[T]he author of a book [has] no right to have the book sold in a particular bookstore without the store owner's consent." Likewise, "a programmer is protected in searching for an outlet for cable programming, but has no free-standing First Amendment right to have that programming transmitted." It is normally up to the cable operator to pick and choose what to show. Leased and public access requirements deprive cable operators of that discretion, and, in Justice Thomas's view, Congress should be free to give it back, even if only partially. In Justice Thomas's view, Sable had no bearing in this setting; he recalled Justice Scalia's admonition in Sable that, while Congress may not ban indecency, " 'we do not hold that the Constitution requires public utilities to carry it.' " Justice Thomas would have subjected section 10(b) to strict scrutiny as a content-based burden on the free speech rights of viewers and programmers, but found that standard met because the provision was narrowly tailored to a "compelling interest in protecting the physical and psychological well-being of minors" that could not be served effectively by such alternatives as lockboxes, which would require constant parental monitoring.

The plurality opinion of Justice BREYER, which controlled the outcome, steered between the poles marked out by Justices Kennedy and Thomas. Justice Breyer began by rejecting any conventional standard of First Amendment scrutiny in favor of explicit balancing. He noted the rapid "changes taking place in the law, the technology, and the industrial structure related to telecommunications." Thus, "no definitive choice among competing analogies (broadcast, common carrier, bookstore) allows us to declare a rigid single standard, good for now and for all future media and purposes."

With respect to section 10(a), Justice Breyer wrote that "the importance of the interests at stake here—protecting children from exposure to patently offensive depictions of sex; the accommodation of the interests of programmers in maintaining access channels and of cable operators in editing the contents of their channels; the similarity of the problem and its solution to those at issue in Pacifica; and the flexibility inherent in an approach that permits private cable operators to make editorial decisions, lead us to conclude that 10(a) is a sufficiently tailored response to an extraordinarily important problem." Justice Breyer relied heavily on Pacifica for support: cablecasting, like radio broadcasting, he wrote, is highly accessible to children, pervasive, and likely to confront citizens in the privacy of their homes without prior warning. Moreover, "the permissive nature of 10(a) means that it likely restricts speech less than, not more than, the ban at issue in Pacifica." In any event, adult viewers could still receive indecent programming through other means such as videotape or direct broadcast satellite. Justice Breyer also distinguished Sable: "The ban at issue in Sable [was] not only a total governmentally imposed ban on a category of communications, but also involved a communications medium, telephone service, that was significantly less likely to expose children to the banned material, was less intrusive, and allowed for significantly more control over what comes into the home than either broadcasting or the cable transmission system before us."

In contrast, Justice Breyer found section 10(b) insufficiently narrowly tailored to the government's compelling interest in protecting children from indecent programming. The block-and-segregate requirement was mandatory, not permissive, and the government had available less restrictive alternatives, such as permitting cable subscribers to opt out of receiving indecent programming (rather than being blocked and thus made to opt in), or permitting parents to selectively block undesired content within the household by use of "lockboxes," "V-chips" or similar devices that enable owners to block out unwanted channels or shows. Finally, Justice Breyer found section 10(c) unconstitutional even though, like 10(a), it was permissive. The countervailing first amendment interests of cable operators were weaker with respect to public access channels than leased access channels, he suggested, because cable operators never had any discretion over channels that local governments reserved. Moreover, municipal authorities supervise public access programming, providing a "locally accountable body capable of addressing the problem, should it arise, of patently offensive programming broadcast to children" on such channels. Thus an additional "cable operator's veto" was unnecessary. Finally, he noted, there was little showing that indecent programming was much of a problem on public access channels.

Justice STEVENS wrote separately to note that he viewed section 10(c) as more restrictive than 10(a) because it allowed cable operators to restrict speech municipal authorities would have permitted; Justice O'CONNOR wrote separately to argue that both these sections were merely permissive and thus constitutional because more like channeling than a total ban; and Justice SOUTER wrote separately to defend Justice Breyer's flexible, evolutionary approach against charges by Justices Kennedy and Thomas that it amounted to lawless ad hoc balancing. The upshot was that the Court upheld section 10(a) by a vote of 7–2 (with Justices Breyer, Stevens, Souter, and O'Connor plus Chief Justice Rehnquist and Justices Scalia and Thomas in the majority), struck down section 10(b) by a vote of 6–3 (with Justices Breyer, Stevens, Souter, and O'Connor plus Justices Kennedy and Ginsburg in the majority), and struck down section 10(c) by a vote of 5–4 (with only Justices Breyer, Stevens, and Souter plus Justices Kennedy and Ginsburg in the majority).

4. *Indecency on the Internet.* Does the government's ability to regulate indecent speech extend to the new medium of the internet? The internet is a worldwide network of linked computers across which individual users can transmit information and images. Unlike broadcasting and cable, the internet has no central source of programming, and users have access to a much greater variety of offerings. In AMERICAN CIVIL LIBERTIES UNION v. RENO, 929 F.Supp. 824 (E.D.Pa.1996), a three-judge district court struck down two provisions of the Communications Decency Act of 1996, including one that made it a crime to use an "interactive computer service" to send or "display in a manner available" to a person under the age of 18 "any comment, request, suggestion, proposal, image, or other communication that, in context, depicts or describes, in terms patently offensive as measured by contemporary community standards, sexual or excretory activities or organs." The court held that the law unconstitutionally denied adults access to fully protected speech and was not narrowly tailored to protecting children. The court declined to extend the rationale of Pacifica from broadcasting to the internet. One judge depicted the internet as "a never-ending worldwide conversation," and a "far more speech-enhancing medium than print, the village green or the mails." Two of the judges also found the indecency provisions impermissibly vague.

SECTION 6. COMMERCIAL SPEECH

Introduction. This section considers one last category of speech—commercial advertising, or speech that merely proposes a commercial transaction—that, because of its content, was once treated as wholly outside the First Amendment. Since 1976, commercial speech has been held to be protected, but not fully protected speech. It thus operates as a category of "lower value" speech not entitled to the high degree of protection afforded to "core" speech. A number of justices have questioned this categorization approach, urging that commercial speech instead be protected just like other speech unless it poses distinctively commercial harms, such as the danger of deception or over-reaching. Their approach would substitute balancing for categorization. But they have not yet commanded a majority of the Court. Thus, commercial speech continues to stand as the lone formal exception to the two-level approach to speech set forth in Chaplinsky: unlike incitement, fighting words, malicious libel, obscenity, or child pornography, it enjoys First Amendment protection, but not as much First Amendment protection as other speech.

Before 1976, the Court assumed that most types of commercial speech fell wholly outside the First Amendment. The leading case was decided soon after the classic exclusionary categorization case, Chaplinsky. In VALENTINE v. CHRESTENSEN, 316 U.S. 52 (1942)—a ruling Justice Douglas was later to call "casual, almost offhand"—the Court stated that the First Amendment imposed no "restraint on government as respects purely commercial advertising." Valentine sustained a ban on distribution of a handbill advertisement soliciting customers to pay admission to tour a privately owned submarine. The entrepreneur in Valentine printed his advertising message on one side of the circular; on the other side, he published a protest against the city's denial of permission to use a municipal pier for his exhibit. The Court viewed the ban as a regulation of business activity rather than protected political speech and considered the political protest as merely an attempt to evade the city regulation forbidding distribution of advertisements in the streets. similar to that governing restrictions on protected speech.

The Valentine approach did not mean that First Amendment protection was barred simply because the speaker had a commercial motive. Recall that New York Times v. Sullivan rejected the argument that the First Amendment did not apply to a "paid 'commercial' advertisement": "That the Times was paid for publishing the advertisement is as immaterial [as] is the fact that newspapers and books are sold." Moreover, movies and books have long enjoyed First Amendment protections even though they are produced and distributed for profit. Nevertheless, the commercial-noncommercial distinction played a significant role in the cases after Valentine.[1] In the early 1970s, moreover, the Court gave more weight to Valentine's commercial speech doctrine than it had in years. For example, the 5-to-4 decision in PITTSBURGH PRESS CO. v. PITTSBURGH HUMAN RELATIONS COMM'N, 413 U.S. 376 (1973), upheld a

---

1. Compare Martin v. Struthers (1943; p. 1240 below), barring the application of a city ordinance prohibiting uninvited door-to-door solicitors for Jehovah's Witnesses, with Breard v. Alexandria (1951; p. 290 below), sustaining a conviction of magazine subscription solicitors (and emphasizing the householders' interests in privacy and repose).

sex discrimination ordinance prohibiting newspapers from listing employment advertisements in gender-designated columns. Justice Powell's majority opinion found that the advertisements resembled the "Chrestensen rather than the [New York Times] advertisement. None expresses a position on whether, as a matter of social policy, certain positions ought to be filled by members of one or the other sex, nor does any of them criticize [the sex discrimination ordinance]. Each is no more than a proposal of possible employment. The advertisements are thus classic examples of commercial speech [not protected by the First Amendment]." But shortly after that indication of vigor in the Valentine doctrine, the Court changed course.

The new trend began with BIGELOW v. VIRGINIA, 421 U.S. 809 (1975), which held that Virginia could not criminalize advertisement in Virginia newspapers of the availability of abortions in New York. It flourished a year later in Virginia Pharmacy, which follows. According to the Court in Virginia Pharmacy, "the notion of unprotected 'commercial speech' all but passed from the scene" in Bigelow. That was an overstatement of the impression at the time Bigelow was decided, as Bigelow had arisen in the special setting of abortion, an independently constitutionally protected activity. But Virginia Pharmacy spoke far more broadly and made it clear that the commercial speech exception had indeed shrunk drastically. Virginia Pharmacy in turn spawned a series of cases, below, in which the Court has struggled to delineate the contours of permissible restrictions on commercial advertising.

From the beginning of the Court's modern ventures into this area, it has been clear that commercial advertising does not enjoy as much constitutional protection as most types of speech, although it is no longer wholly excluded from First Amendment coverage. With respect to commercial speech (as with the indecent words and displays that are considered "less valuable speech" under Justice Stevens' position in some of the preceding cases), the Court has found the First Amendment interests weaker and the case for state restraints stronger than in other areas of speech. Was inclusion of commercial advertising within the First Amendment a mistake? Should it be excluded from the First Amendment in light of the underlying purposes of the constitutional concern with "speech"? Would total exclusion of commercial speech encourage a return to wholesale exclusionary categorization in other areas of speech in the Chaplinsky manner? Does treatment of commercial advertising as a less valuable variety of speech produce even greater risks to the First Amendment than total exclusion would, by increasing the legitimacy of a methodology allocating differing and often lower weights to particular types of speech on the First Amendment balancing scale?

Virginia Pharmacy Board v. Virginia Citizens Consumer Council

425 U.S. 748, 96 S.Ct. 1817, 48 L.Ed.2d 346 (1976).

Justice BLACKMUN delivered the opinion of the [Court].

[A Virginia law provided that pharmacists were guilty of "unprofessional conduct" if they advertised the prices of prescription drugs. Since only pharmacists were authorized to dispense such drugs, the law effectively prevented the dissemination of prescription drug price information in the State. About 95% of all prescription drugs were prepared by pharmaceutical manufacturers rather than by the pharmacists themselves. The Court affirmed a lower court's invalidation of the law on First Amendment grounds. Justice Blackmun began by noting that the challenge to the law came not from a pharmacist but from prescription drug consumers who claimed that the First Amendment entitled them to drug price information. He commented: "Certainly that information may be of value. Drug prices [in the state] strikingly vary from outlet to outlet even within the same locality." He found that the audience for drug price information could assert a First Amendment interest: "[W]here a speaker exists [as here], the protection afforded [by the First Amendment] is to the communication, to its source and to its recipients both. [If] there is a right to advertise, there is a reciprocal right to receive the advertising, and it may be asserted by [the consumers here]." He continued:]

IV. The appellants contend that the advertisement of prescription drug prices is outside the protection of the First Amendment because it is "commercial speech." There can be no question that in past decisions the Court has given some indication that commercial speech is unprotected. [Last] Term, in [Bigelow], the notion of unprotected "commercial speech" all but passed from the scene. We reversed a conviction for violation of a Virginia statute that made the circulation of any publication to encourage or promote the processing of an abortion in Virginia a misdemeanor. The defendant had published in his newspaper the availability of abortions in New York. We rejected the contention that the publication was unprotected because it was commercial. [Some] fragment of hope for the continuing validity of a "commercial speech" exception arguably might have persisted because of the subject matter of the advertisement in Bigelow. We noted that [the] advertisement "did more than simply propose a commercial transaction. It contained factual material of clear 'public interest.'" And, of course, the advertisement related to activity with which, at least in some respects, the State could not interfere. [Here,] in contrast, the question whether there is a First Amendment exception for "commercial speech" is squarely before us. Our pharmacist does not wish to editorialize on any subject, cultural, philosophical, or political. He does not wish to report any particularly newsworthy fact, or to make generalized observations even about commercial matters. The "idea" he wishes to communicate is simply this: "I will sell you the X prescription drug at the Y price." Our question, then, is whether this communication is wholly outside the protection of the First Amendment.

V. [It] is clear [that] speech does not lose its First Amendment protection because money is spent to project it, as in a paid [advertisement]. [E.g., New York Times.] [Our] question is whether speech which does "no more than propose a commercial transaction" is so removed from any "exposition of ideas" [Chaplinsky] and from "truth, science, morality, and arts in general, in its diffusion of liberal sentiments on the administration of Government" [Roth] that it lacks all protection. Our answer is that it is not. Focusing first on the individual parties to the transaction that is proposed in the commercial advertisement, we may assume that the advertiser's interest is a purely economic one. That hardly disqualifies him for protection under the First Amendment. The interests of the contestants in a labor dispute are primarily economic, but it has long been settled that both the employee and the employer are protected by the First Amendment where they express themselves on the merits of the dispute in order to influence its outcome. [As] to the particular consumer's interest in the free flow of commercial information, that interest may be as keen, if not keener by far, than his interest in the day's most urgent political debate. [Those] whom the suppression of prescription drug price information hits the hardest are the poor, the sick, and particularly the aged. [When] drug prices vary as strikingly as they do, information as to who is charging what becomes more than a convenience. It could mean the alleviation of physical pain or the enjoyment of basic necessities.

Generalizing, society also may have a strong interest in the free flow of commercial information. Even an individual advertisement, though entirely "commercial," may be of general public interest. The facts of decided cases furnish illustrations: [e.g.,] advertisements stating that referral services for legal abortions are available [and] that a manufacturer of artificial furs promotes his product as an alternative to the extinction by his competitors of fur-bearing mammals. [Obviously], not all commercial messages contain the same or even a very great public interest element. There are few to which such an element, however, could not be added. Our pharmacist, for example, could cast himself as a commentator on store-to-store disparities in drug prices, giving his own and those of a competitor as proof. We see little point in requiring him to do so, and little difference if he does not.

Moreover, there is another consideration that suggests that no line between publicly "interesting" or "important" commercial advertising and the opposite kind could ever be drawn. Advertising, however tasteless and excessive it sometimes may seem, is nonetheless dissemination of information as to who is producing and selling what product, for what reason, and at what price. So long as we preserve a predominantly free enterprise economy, the allocation of our resources in large measure will be made through numerous private economic decisions. It is a matter of public interest that those decisions, in the aggregate, be intelligent and well informed. To this end, the free flow of commercial information is indispensable. And if it is indispensable to the proper allocation of resources in a free enterprise system, it is also indispensable to the formation of intelligent opinions as to how that system ought to be regulated or altered. Therefore, even if the First Amendment were thought to be primarily an instrument to enlighten public decisionmaking in a democracy, we could not say that the free flow of information does not serve that goal.

Arrayed against these substantial individual and societal interests are a number of justifications for the advertising ban. These have to do principally with maintaining a high degree of professionalism on the part of licensed pharmacists. Indisputably, the State has a strong interest in maintaining that professionalism. [Price] advertising, it is argued, will place in jeopardy the pharmacist's expertise and, with it, the customer's health. It is claimed that the aggressive price competition that will result from unlimited advertising will make it impossible for the pharmacist to supply professional services in the compounding, handling, and dispensing of prescription drugs. [The] strength of these proffered justifications is greatly undermined by the fact that high professional standards, to a substantial extent, are guaranteed by the close regulation to which pharmacists in Virginia are subject. [At] the same time, we cannot discount the Board's justifications entirely. The Court regarded justifications of this type sufficient to sustain the advertising bans challenged on due process and equal protection grounds [in several cases].[1]

The challenge now made, however, is based on the First Amendment. This casts the Board's justifications in a different light, for on close inspection it is seen that the State's protectiveness of its citizens rests in large measure on the advantages of their being kept in ignorance. The advertising ban does not

1. Justice Blackmun cited several modern economic regulation, deferential review cases (see chap. 8 above): Head v. New Mexico Board, 374 U.S. 424 (1963) (optometrists' services); Williamson v. Lee Optical Co., 348 U.S. 483 (1955) (eyeglass frames; p. 481 above); and Semler v. Oregon State Board of Dental Examiners, 294 U.S. 608 (1935) (dentists' services).

directly affect professional standards one way or the other. It affects them only through the reactions it is assumed people will have to the free flow of drug price information. [It] appears to be feared that if the pharmacist who wishes to provide low cost, and assertedly low quality, services is permitted to advertise, he will be taken up on his offer by too many unwitting customers. They will choose the low-cost, low-quality service and drive the "professional" pharmacist out of business. They will [destroy] the pharmacist-customer relationship. [There] is, of course, an alternative to this highly paternalistic approach. That alternative is to assume that this information is not in itself harmful, that people will perceive their own best interests if only they are well enough informed, and that the best means to that end is to open the channels of communication rather than to close them. If they are truly open, nothing prevents the "professional" pharmacist from marketing his own assertedly superior product, and contrasting it with that of the low-cost, high-volume prescription drug retailer. But the choice among these alternative approaches is not ours to make or the Virginia General Assembly's. It is precisely this kind of choice, between the dangers of suppressing information, and the dangers of its misuse if it is freely available, that the First Amendment makes for us. Virginia is free to require whatever professional standards it wishes of its pharmacists. [But] it may not do so by keeping the public in ignorance of the entirely lawful terms that competing pharmacists are [offering].

VI.   In concluding that commercial speech, like other varieties, is protected, we of course do not hold that it can never be regulated in any way. Some forms of commercial speech regulation are surely permissible. We mention a few only to make clear that they are not before us and therefore are not foreclosed by this case. [There] is no claim, for example, that the prohibition on prescription drug price advertising is a mere time, place, and manner restriction. We have often approved restrictions of that kind provided that they are justified without reference to the content of the regulated speech, that they serve a significant governmental interest, and that in so doing they leave open ample alternative channels for communication of the information. [But this law] singles out speech of a particular content and seeks to prevent its dissemination completely. Nor is there any claim that prescription drug price advertisements are forbidden because they are false or misleading in any way. Untruthful speech, commercial or otherwise, has never been protected for its own sake. [E.g., Gertz.] Obviously, much commercial speech is not provably false, or even wholly false, but only deceptive or misleading. We foresee no obstacle to a State's dealing effectively with this problem.[2] The First Amend-

---

2. In concluding that commercial speech enjoys First Amendment protection, we have not held that it is wholly undifferentiable from other forms. There are common-sense differences between speech that does "no more than propose a commercial transaction" and other varieties. Even if the differences do not justify the conclusion that commercial speech is valueless, and thus subject to complete suppression by the State, they nonetheless suggest that a different degree of protection is necessary to insure that the flow of truthful and legitimate commercial information is unimpaired. The truth of commercial speech, for example, may be more easily verifiable by its disseminator than, let us say, news reporting or political commentary, in that ordinarily the advertiser seeks to disseminate information about a specific product or service that he himself provides and presumably knows more about than anyone else. Also, commercial speech may be more durable than other kinds. Since advertising is the sine qua non of commercial profits, there is little likelihood of its being chilled by proper regulation and foregone entirely.

Attributes such as these, the greater objectivity and hardiness of commercial speech, may make it less necessary to tolerate inaccurate statements for fear of silencing the speaker. They may also make it appropriate to require that a commercial message appear in such a form, or include such additional

ment, as we construe it today, does not prohibit the State from insuring that the stream of commercial information flows cleanly as well as freely. Also, there is no claim that the transactions proposed in the forbidden advertisements are themselves illegal in any way. [Cf., e.g., Pittsburgh Press.] Finally, the special problems of the electronic broadcast media are likewise not in this case. What is at issue is whether a State may completely suppress the dissemination of concededly truthful information about entirely lawful activity, fearful of that information's effect upon its disseminators and its recipients. Reserving other questions[3] we conclude that the answer to this one is in the negative.

Affirmed.[4]

Justice REHNQUIST, dissenting.

The logical consequences of the Court's decision in this case, a decision which elevates commercial intercourse between a seller hawking his wares and a buyer seeking to strike a bargain to the same plane as has been previously reserved for the free marketplace of ideas, are far reaching indeed. Under the Court's opinion the way will be open not only for dissemination of price information but for active promotion of prescription drugs, liquor, cigarettes and other products the use of which it has previously been thought desirable to discourage. Now, however, such promotion is protected by the First Amendment so long as it is not misleading or does not promote an illegal product or [enterprise].

The Court speaks of the consumer's interest in the free flow of commercial [information]. It goes on to observe that "society also may have a strong interest in the free flow of commercial information." [But these interests] should presumptively be the concern of the [Virginia Legislature]. The Court speaks of the importance in a "predominantly free enterprise economy" of intelligent and well-informed decisions as to allocation of resources. While there is again much to be said for [this] as a matter of desirable public policy, there is certainly nothing in the [Constitution] which requires [Virginia] to hew to the teachings of Adam Smith in its legislative decisions regulating the pharmacy profession. E.g., [Nebbia, chap. 8 above]. [I]f the sole limitation on permissible state proscription of advertising is that it may not be false or misleading, surely the difference between pharmacists' advertising and lawyers' and doctors' advertising can be only one of degree and not of [kind].

The Court insists that the rule it lays down is consistent even with the view that the First Amendment is "primarily an instrument to enlighten public decisionmaking in a democracy." I had understood this view to relate to public decisionmaking as to political, social, and other public issues, rather than the

information, warnings and disclaimers as are necessary to prevent its being deceptive. They also make inapplicable the prohibition against [prior restraints]. [Footnote by Justice Blackmun.]

3. We stress that we have considered in this case the regulation of commercial advertising by pharmacists. Although we express no opinion as to other professions, the distinctions, historical and functional, between professions, may require consideration of quite different factors. Physicians and lawyers, for example, do not dispense standardized products; they render professional *services* of almost infinite variety and nature,

with the consequent enhanced possibility for confusion and deception if they were to undertake certain kinds of advertising. [Footnote by Justice Blackmun. (Note the cases which follow, involving regulations of other professions, including lawyers.)]

4. Chief Justice Burger's concurrence emphasized the reservation in footnote [3] of the opinion regarding advertising by physicians and lawyers. Justice Stewart, concurring, wrote separately to explain "why I think today's decision does not preclude [regulation of false or deceptive advertising]." Justice Stevens did not participate.

decision of a particular individual as to whether to purchase one or another kind of shampoo. It is undoubtedly arguable that many people in the country regard the choice of shampoo as just as important as who may be elected to local, state, or national political office, but that does not automatically bring information about competing shampoos within the protection of the First Amendment. It is one thing to say that the line between strictly ideological and political commentaries and other kinds of commentary is difficult to [draw]. But it is another thing to say that because that line is difficult to draw, we will stand at the other end of the [spectrum].

In the case of "our" hypothetical pharmacist, he may now presumably advertise not only the prices of prescription drugs, but may attempt to energetically promote their sale so long as he does so truthfully. Quite consistently with Virginia law requiring prescription drugs to be available only through a physician, "our" pharmacist might run any of the following representative advertisements in a local newspaper: "Pain getting you down? Insist that your physician prescribe Demerol. You pay a little more than for aspirin, but you get a lot more relief." "Can't shake the flu? Get a prescription for tetracycline from your doctor today." "Don't spend another sleepless night. Ask your doctor to prescribe Seconal without delay." Unless the State can show that these advertisements are either actually untruthful or misleading, it presumably is not free to restrict in any way commercial efforts on the part of those who profit from the sale of prescription drugs to put them in the widest possible circulation. But such a line simply makes no allowance whatever for what appears to have been a considered legislative judgment in most States that while prescription drugs are a necessary and vital part of medical care and treatment, there are sufficient dangers attending their widespread use that they simply may not be promoted in the same manner as hair creams, deodorants, and toothpaste. The very real dangers that general advertising for such drugs might create in terms of encouraging, even though not sanctioning, illicit use of them by individuals for whom they have not been prescribed, or by generating patient pressure upon physicians to prescribe them, are simply not dealt with in the Court's [opinion].

This case presents a fairly typical First Amendment problem—that of balancing interests in individual free speech against public welfare determinations embodied in a legislative enactment. [Here] the rights of the appellees seem to me to be marginal at best. There is no ideological content to the information which they seek and it is freely available to them—they may even publish it if they so desire. [On] the other hand, the societal interest against the promotion of drug use for every ill, real or imaginary, seems to me extremely strong. I do not believe that the First Amendment mandates the Court's "open door policy" toward such commercial advertising.

COMMERCIAL SPEECH AND FIRST AMENDMENT THEORY

1. *Advertising as "speech."* Is commercial speech "speech" or merely an aspect of the conduct of commercial sales? For an argument that advertising is merely a first step in contracts or exchanges that are fully regulable, see Farber, "Commercial Speech and First Amendment Theory," 74 Nw. L. Rev. 372 (1979). See also Posner, "Free Speech in an Economic Perspective," 20 Suffolk L. Rev. 1 (1986) (suggesting that unlike most speech, which will be underproduced because speakers cannot fully capture its benefits once it is disseminated, the benefits of commercial speech "are more readily captured by

its producer through sale of the underlying product," reducing the need for free speech protection); Cass, "Commercial Speech, Constitutionalism, Collective Choice," 56 U. Cin. L. Rev. 1317 (1988).

2. *Advertising and the rationales for freedom of speech.* Recall the varying rationales for protecting expression under the First Amendment. Does speech that does "no more than propose a commercial transaction" warrant protection under any of these rationales? Does commercial advertising contribute to better decisionmaking in a representative form of government (recall the Meiklejohn rationale)? Is it a part of the free marketplace of ideas (recall the Holmes rationale)? Is protection of advertising justifiable only under an individual self-realization, autonomy rationale? If the primary purpose of commercial advertising is to contribute to a more efficient operation of the free *economic* market, is that a quality relevant to First Amendment theory? Can protection of the economic market under the First Amendment be reconciled with the modern Court's "hands-off" attitude in economic regulation cases (recall chap. 8)? Consider the following comments in light of Virginia Board:

a. *Self-government.* Justice Rehnquist dissented from Virginia Pharmacy and progeny on the ground that "in a democracy, the economic is subordinate to the political." Central Hudson, below. On this view, advertising is subordinate to expressions of political ideology and dissent, for it does not inform public deliberation or contribute to representative government. For elaborations of this critique of protection for commercial speech, see Jackson & Jeffries, "Commercial Speech: Economic Due Process and the First Amendment," 65 Va.L.Rev. 1 (1979); Sunstein, Democracy and the Problem of Free Speech 130–44 (1993). In Virginia Pharmacy, Justice Blackmun answers such arguments by suggesting that "public decisionmaking" should be viewed broadly, and that the free flow of commercial information contributes to that process by making the "numerous private economic decisions" that drive our "free enterprise economy" more "intelligent and well informed." Jackson & Jeffries reply: this is "a non sequitur. [In] terms of relevance to political decisionmaking, advertising is neither more nor less significant than a host of other market activities that legislatures concededly may regulate." For a contrary view, see Shiffrin, "The First Amendment and Economic Regulation: Away from a General Theory of the First Amendment," 78 Nw.U. L. Rev. 1213 (1983).

b. *Truth.* The Millian notion that the unregulated clash of individual expression will produce truth in the long run might seem unrelated to pitches for sales for short-run profit. But Justice Blackmun's opinion likens the clash between advertisers to other clashes of opinion: if the discount drug retailer advertises his low prices, "nothing prevents the 'professional' pharmacist from marketing his own assertedly superior product." Individuals, he suggests, may be relied on to choose between them. See Coase, "Advertising and Free Speech," 6 J. Legal Studies 1 (1977) (arguing for parallel treatment of markets and the marketplace of ideas). Jackson & Jeffries, supra, argue that this argument confuses economic values—"the opportunity of the individual producer or consumer to maximize his own economic utility" and "the aggregate economic efficiency of a free market economy"—with free speech values, effectively resurrecting Lochner under the guise of the First Amendment.

c. *Autonomy.* Some proponents of autonomy as a central value underlying the free speech clause reject protection for commercial speech because it is generally engaged in by corporations, which lack a human personality or capacity for self-fulfillment. See Jackson & Jeffries, supra ("[w]hatever else it may mean, the concept of a first amendment right of speaker autonomy in matters of belief and expression stops short of a seller hawking his wares");

Baker, Human Liberty and Freedom of Speech 194–224 (1989); Baker,"Commercial [Speech]," 62 Iowa L.Rev. 1 (1976) ("commercial speech is not a manifestation of individual freedom or choice," and "lacks the crucial connections with individual liberty and self-realization which exist for speech generally"); Baker, "Turner Broadcasting: Content–Based Regulation of Persons and Presses," 1994 S. Ct. Rev. 57.

Justice Blackmun's opinion suggests, however, that it is not the speaker's but rather the *listener*'s autonomy that matters here: the alternative to "paternalistic" speech regulation is to assume that *consumers* "will perceive their own best interests if only they are well enough informed." For the view that such listener autonomy is a central free speech value that helps justify protection of commercial speech, see Strauss, "Persuasion, Autonomy and Freedom of Expression," 91 Colum. L. Rev. 334 (1991); Neuborne, "The First Amendment and Government Regulation of Capital Markets," 55 Brooklyn L. Rev. 5 (1989); Redish, "The First Amendment in the Marketplace: Commercial Speech and the Values of Free Expression," 39 Geo. Wash. L. Rev. 429 (1971) (choosing among "the relative merits of competing products" promotes "the intangible goal of rational self-fulfullment"). But are consumers truly choosing freely when they respond to advertising? Is not a goal of advertising to create demands and alter tastes? Might the listener's autonomy be impaired by lack of relevant information or by addiction to a product? See Fallon, "Two Senses of Autonomy," 46 Stan. L. Rev. 875 (1994); Law, "Addiction, Autonomy and Advertising," 77 Iowa L. Rev. 909 (1992) (arguing that advertising for psychoactive products that cause physiological dependence may be regulated).

d. *Negative First Amendment theory.* Some theories rely less on the affirmative values of free speech than on the premise that there is special reason to distrust government when it regulates speech. For example, incumbents have an incentive to suppress challengers and dissidents. But is there any reason to fear that government will suppress commercial speech for ideologically partisan reasons? See Scanlon, "Freedom of Expression and Categories of Expression," 40 Pitt. L. Rev. 519 (1979) (arguing that commercial speech should not get full protection because government is less partisan in the competition between firms than in the struggle between political views). What if government is captured by powerful private interest groups, such as the pharmacy profession in Virginia Pharmacy? If bias against a competitor of a such a group justifies First Amendment protection of the competitor's advertising, should it also justify protection of the competitor's production and sales under the equal protection or due process clauses? See Jackson & Jeffries, supra ("Exactly the same values that are impaired by Virginia's ban against drug price advertising are also invaded by [most] other instances of governmental regulation of the economy.").

3. *"Commonsense differences" between commercial and other speech.* In dictum in Virginia Pharmacy, the Court set forth three important limitations on protection for commercial speech: free speech protection does not extend to (1) advertisements for illegal transactions, or (2) factually false or misleading advertisements, and commercial speech does not enjoy (3) special procedural protections such as the ban on prior restraint (or, as the Court later made clear, in Bates, below, overbreadth doctrine). Justice Blackmun explained this "different degree of protection" by reference to two "commonsense differences": that commercial speech is hardier than other speech because profit-driven, and more objectively verifiable than other speech. Are these distinctions persuasive? Consider the following comments:

a. *Hardiness.* "It might just as easily be said that we need not fear that commercial magazines and newspapers will cease publication for fear of governmental regulation, because they are in business for profit." Redish, "The Value of Free Speech," 130 U. Pa. L. Rev. 591 (1982). "[O]ther interests can be just as strong as economics, sometimes stronger. [Speech] backed by religious feeling can persist in extraordinarily hostile climates; [a]rtistic impulses can also cause expression to persist in the face of hostile government regulation." Kozinski & Banner, "Who's Afraid of Commercial Speech?," 76 Va. L. Rev. 627 (1990).

b. *Verifiability.* "[T]he seller can check his facts more easily than can a third party. However so can certain politicians who make false and deceptive political statements regarding facts within their knowledge." Alexander, "Speech in the Local [Marketplace]," 14 San Diego L. Rev. 357 (1977). "It is certainly easier to determine the truth of the claim 'Cucumbers cost sixty-nine cents' than the claim 'Republicans will govern more effectively.' But not all commercial speech is so objective. What about the statement 'America is turning 7–Up'?" Kozinski & Banner, supra. "[M]uch scientific speech can easily be labeled true or false, but we would be shocked at the suggestion that it is therefore entitled to a lesser degree of protection." Id.

4. *Defining commercial speech.* Virginia Board defined commercial speech as that which "does no more than propose a commercial transaction," and made clear that it did *not* include all speech produced for profit. Later in Central Hudson, below, the Court referred to commercial speech as "expression related solely to the economic interests of the speaker and its audience." Justice Stevens, in concurrence, objected that such a definition "is unquestionably too broad." Later decisions would appear to agree with him. It is settled that corporate speech can amount to political or other fully protected speech, even when engaged in out of commercial self-interest. A corporation, for example, enjoys full First Amendment protection when it advocates its business interests in a political referendum campaign. See First National Bank v. Bellotti, p. 1413 below. The fact of economic motivation does not automatically ratchet down the level of scrutiny. Thus the definition of commercial speech would appear to be the narrower one set forth in Virginia Board.

What if an advertisement contains a mixture of promotional and informational content? In BOLGER v. YOUNGS DRUG PRODUCTS CORP., 463 U.S. 60 (1983), the Court invalidated a federal statute prohibiting the mailing of unsolicited advertisements for contraceptives. At issue were a "drug store flyer" as well as two informational pamphlets, "Condoms and Human Sexuality" and "Plain Talk about Venereal Disease." One of the informational pamphlets repeatedly referred to Youngs' products by name, and the other emphasized generic descriptions of condoms, a product in which Youngs had a leading market position. At the outset, Justice MARSHALL's opinion for the Court reasoned that the materials amounted to commercial rather than fully protected speech: "The mailings constitute commercial speech notwithstanding the fact that they contain discussions of important public issues such as venereal disease and family planning. A company has the full panoply of protections available [for] its direct comments on public issues, so there is no reason for providing similar constitutional protection when such statements are made in the context of commercial transactions. [We] conclude [that] all of the mailings in this case are entitled to the qualified but nonetheless substantial protection accorded to commercial speech."

Similarly, in BOARD OF TRUSTEES, STATE UNIV. OF NEW YORK v. FOX, 492 U.S. 469 (1989), the Court held that promotional speeches at student-run "Tupperware parties" were properly considered commercial speech even though, in addition to making sales pitches for tupperware products, "[t]hey also touch[ed] on other subjects, [such] as how to be financially responsible and how to run an efficient home." Justice SCALIA, writing for the Court, rejected the sellers' argument that "pure speech and commercial speech [were] 'inextricably intertwined' and that the entirety must therefore be classified as noncommercial." He noted that "there is nothing whatever 'inextricable' about the noncommercial aspects of these presentations. No law of man or of nature makes it impossible to sell housewares without teaching home economics, or to teach home economics without selling housewares. [Including] these home economics elements no more converted [the sellers'] presentations into educational speech, than opening sales presentations with a prayer or a Pledge of Allegiance would convert them into religious or political speech. [Advertising] which 'links a product to a current public debate' is not thereby entitled to the constitutional protection afforded noncommercial speech. [Bolger, Central Hudson]."

COMMERCIAL SPEECH AFTER VIRGINIA PHARMACY

1. *Real estate "For Sale" signs as protected speech.* In LINMARK ASSOCIATES, INC. v. WILLINGBORO, 431 U.S. 85 (1977), the Court relied in part on Virginia Pharmacy to strike down an ordinance prohibiting the posting of real estate "For Sale" and "Sold" signs. The town's objective was to stem the flight of white homeowners from a racially integrated community through "panic selling." Justice MARSHALL wrote for the Court: "The [town here, like the State in Virginia Pharmacy,] acted to prevent its residents from obtaining certain information. That information [is] of vital interest to Willingboro residents, since it may bear on one of the most important decisions they have a right to make: where to live and raise their families. The [town] has sought to restrict the free flow of this data because it fears that otherwise, homeowners will make decisions inimical to what the [town] views as the homeowners' self-interest and the corporate interest of the township: they will choose to leave town. The [town's] concern, then, was not with any commercial aspect of 'For Sale' signs—with offerors communicating offers to offerees—but with the substance of the information communicated to Willingboro citizens. If dissemination of this information can be restricted, then every locality in the country can suppress any facts that reflect poorly on the locality, so long as a plausible claim can be made that disclosure would cause the recipients of the information to act 'irrationally.' Virginia Pharmacy denies government such sweeping powers [to deny its citizens] information that is neither false nor misleading."

2. *Contraceptive advertising.* The Court relied on Virginia Pharmacy in CAREY v. POPULATION SERVICES INT'L, 431 U.S. 678 (1977), which invalidated a New York ban on the advertising or display of nonprescription contraceptives. Justice Brennan noted that here, as in Virginia Pharmacy, there were "substantial individual and societal interests in the free flow of commercial information," and, as in Bigelow, the information suppressed "related to activity with which, at least in some respects, the State could not interfere." For another decision invalidating a contraceptive advertising ban, see Bolger v. Youngs Drugs Products Corp., p. 1170 above.

3. *Regulating the legal profession and other professions.* Virginia Pharmacy had left some doubt about whether it would apply to commercial communications by lawyers. But the Court soon made it clear that the Virginia Pharmacy principles would apply to lawyers' advertising as well. The course of decisions

began with the 5–4 ruling in BATES v. STATE BAR OF ARIZONA, 433 U.S. 350 (1977), holding that states could not prohibit lawyers from price advertising of "routine legal services." Justice BLACKMUN's majority opinion noted that the case did not involve advertising relating to the "*quality* of legal services" or to "in-person solicitation of clients." He rejected a variety of justifications for the restraint, including "adverse effect on professionalism" and the claim that attorney advertising was "inherently misleading." The major dissent was by Justice Powell, joined by Justice Stewart, who claimed that the decision would "effect profound changes in the practice of law" and who argued that the majority had given inadequate weight to "the two fundamental ways in which the advertising of professional services [differs] from that of tangible products: the vastly increased potential for deception and the enhanced difficulty of effective regulation in the public interest."

A year later, two cases involving lawyers' solicitation of clients came to the Court. In these cases, the distinction between commercial and non-commercial speech proved critical. In OHRALIK v. OHIO STATE BAR ASSOCIATION, 436 U.S. 447 (1978), involving "classic examples of 'ambulance chasing,'" the Court sustained a lawyer's suspension from law practice for violating anti-solicitation rules. The case involved an attorney who solicited contingent fee employment from accident victims. Justice POWELL's majority opinion stated that "the State may proscribe in-person solicitation for pecuniary gain under circumstances likely to result in adverse consequences" without a showing of actual harm and with some leeway for prophylactic rules. But in IN RE PRIMUS, 436 U.S. 412 (1978), the Court set aside disciplinary action in a case involving an attorney who did volunteer work for the ACLU. She had been reprimanded for writing a letter asking a woman who had been sterilized whether she wanted to become a plaintiff in a lawsuit against a doctor who had allegedly participated in a program of sterilizing pregnant mothers as a condition of continued receipt of Medicaid benefits. Justice Powell's majority opinion there emphasized that the attorney's letter fell within "the generous zone of First Amendment protection reserved for associational freedoms" [see NAACP v. Button (p. 1383 below)] and concluded that a state may not punish a lawyer "who, seeking to further political and ideological goals through associational activity, including litigation, advises a lay person of her legal rights and discloses in a subsequent letter that free legal assistance is available from a nonprofit organization." Accordingly, more "exacting" scrutiny was justified in Primus than in Ohralik: in the "political expression or association" context of Primus, the First Amendment required a showing that the attorney's solicitation had "in fact" produced harm, a showing not made here. Justice REHNQUIST's dissent insisted that there was "no principled distinction" between the cases and suggested that the majority had developed "a jurisprudence of epithets and slogans [in] which 'ambulance chasers' suffer one fate and 'civil liberties lawyers' another."

Bates and its progeny were explored and applied in a number of cases over the ensuing decade. IN RE R.M.J., 455 U.S. 191 (1982), held unconstitutional a range of Missouri restrictions on lawyer advertising. The restrictions limited such advertising to certain categories of information and, in some instances, to certain specified language. Justice POWELL's opinion for a unanimous Court sustained all of the First Amendment challenges, emphasizing that the advertisements were not actually or inherently "misleading," and that regulations of potentially misleading advertisement must be "narrowly drawn."

In ZAUDERER v. OFFICE OF DISCIPLINARY COUNSEL, 471 U.S. 626 (1985), an Ohio attorney had been reprimanded for advertising his availability to represent women who had suffered injuries in connection with the use of the

Dalkon Shield intrauterine device. The ad contained a line drawing of the device and stated: "If there is no recovery, no legal fees are owed by our clients." The State objected in part because the ad solicited clients with respect to a specific legal problem and contained an illustration. Justice WHITE's opinion for the Court struck down the restriction on illustrations: "[W]e are unsure that the State's desire that attorneys maintain their dignity in their communications with the public is an interest substantial enough to justify the abridgment of their First Amendment rights. [The] mere possibility that some members of the population might find advertising embarrassing or offensive cannot justify suppressing it." He also rejected Ohio's attempt to forbid solicitation regarding specific legal problems, rejecting in the process the State's attempt to apply Ohralik to large-scale advertising. He noted that the "advertisement—and print advertising generally—poses much less risk of over-reaching or undue influence."

The Zauderer ruling in turn provided a major basis for the Court's decision in SHAPERO v. KENTUCKY BAR ASS'N, 486 U.S. 466 (1988), striking down a flat ban on direct-mail solicitation by lawyers that was "targeted" to specific recipients known to need legal services of a particular kind. Kentucky, while finding the solicitation here neither false nor misleading, nevertheless claimed that it was needed to prevent potential clients from feeling "overwhelmed." Justice BRENNAN's majority opinion found this justification insufficient to satisfy either Zauderer or Central Hudson, below. Moreover, he distinguished Ohralik as dealing with the special dangers of face-to-face solicitation and found the flat ban too broad a remedy for a mere possibility of abuse: "The State can regulate [any] abuses and minimize mistakes through far less restrictive and more precise means." Justice O'CONNOR's dissent, joined by Chief Justice Rehnquist and Justice Scalia, expressed some doubts about the Court's entire venture in the commercial speech area, but focused her objections on the application of the commercial speech principles to regulation of attorney advertising. She commented that Bates had "proved to be problematic in its application" and urged that the Court "return to the States the legislative function that has so inappropriately been taken away from them in the context of attorney advertising."

Two years later, PEEL v. ATTORNEY REGISTRATION AND DISCIPLINARY COMM'N OF ILL., 496 U.S. 91 (1990), followed both Zauderer and Shapero in invalidating a disciplinary sanction for an attorney's representation on his letterhead that he was "certified as a civil trial specialist by the National Board of Trial Advocacy." Justice STEVENS' plurality opinion concluded that truthful representation of certification by a legitimate organization with "rigorous requirements" could not be deemed misleading under the First Amendment just because some readers might think the organization was governmentally affiliated.

The Court later took a similarly skeptical approach to state regulation of solicitation and advertising by certified public accountants. In EDENFIELD v. FANE, 507 U.S. 761 (1993), the Court struck down a Florida rule prohibiting certified public accountants from engaging in "direct, in-person, uninvited solicitation." Writing for the Court, Justice KENNEDY found substantial the state's asserted interests in protecting potential clients against fraud, over-reaching and invasions of privacy, and in protecting CPAs against compromising their professional independence. But he found that the state had failed to show by adequate studies or anecdotal evidence that its rule directly and materially advanced these interests. Finally, Justice Kennedy distinguished the ban on face-to-face solicitation by lawyers upheld in Ohralik, reasoning that, "[u]nlike a lawyer, a CPA is not 'a professional trained in the art of persuasion,' " and that "[t]he typical client of a CPA is far less susceptible to manipulation than the young accident victim in Ohralik." Justice O'CONNOR was the lone dissenter: "In my view, the States have [broad] authority to prohibit commercial speech that, albeit not directly harmful to the listener, is inconsistent with the speaker's membership in a learned profession and therefore damaging to the profession and society at large. [I] see no constitutional difference between a rule prohibiting in-person solicitation by attorneys, and a rule prohibiting in-person solicitation by [CPAs]." In IBANEZ v. FLORIDA BOARD OF ACCOUNTANCY, 512 U.S. 136 (1994), the Court held that it was not "inherently misleading for an attorney to advertise truthfully in the yellow pages or on business cards that she was also a certified public accountant."

The Court, however, remains willing to uphold some restrictions on lawyer advertising. In FLORIDA BAR v. WENT FOR IT, INC., 518 U.S. __, 115 S.Ct. 2371 (1995), the Court upheld, by a vote of 5–4, a Florida Bar rule prohibiting personal injury lawyers from sending targeted direct-mail solicitations to victims and their relatives for 30 days following an accident or disaster, and from receiving referrals from anyone who made such a contact. A lawyer and a referral service challenged the law under the free speech clause and obtained summary judgment in the lower courts. The Supreme Court reversed. Justice O'CONNOR, writing for the Court, held that the bar rule served substantial state interests in "protecting the privacy and tranquility of personal injury victims and their loved ones against intrusive, unsolicited contact by lawyers," and in "protecting the flagging reputations of Florida lawyers by preventing them from engaging in conduct that, the Bar maintains, 'is universally regarded as deplorable and beneath common decency because of its intrusion upon the special vulnerability and private grief of victims or their families.' " The state, she found, had also demonstrated that the law directly advanced this interest by submitting a 106–page report of survey data on the privacy and reputational harms of direct-mail solicitation. Finally, Justice O'Connor noted, the rule was narrowly tailored because "limited to a brief period" during which there are "many other ways for injured Floridians to learn about the availability of legal representation." For example, "Florida permits lawyers to advertise on primetime television and radio as well as in newspapers and other media. They may rent space on billboards. They may send untargeted letters to the general population, or to discrete segments thereof. There are, of course, pages upon pages devoted to lawyers in the Yellow Pages of Florida telephone directories. These listings are organized alphabetically and by area of specialty. The palliative devised by the Bar to address [the substantial] harms [of targeted direct-mail solicitations] is narrow both in scope and in duration. The Constitution, in our view, requires nothing more."

Justice KENNEDY wrote a pointed dissent, joined by Justices Stevens, Souter and Ginsburg: "I take it to be uncontroverted that when an accident results in death or injury, it is often urgent at once to investigate the occurrence, identify witnesses, and preserve evidence. Vital interests in speech and expression are, therefore, at stake when by law an attorney cannot direct a letter to the victim or the family explaining this simple fact and offering competent legal assistance. Meanwhile, represented and better informed parties, or parties who have been solicited in ways more sophisticated and indirect, may be at work. Indeed, these parties, either themselves or by their attorneys, investigators, and adjusters, are free to contact the unrepresented persons to gather evidence or offer settlement. This scheme makes little sense."

Justice Kennedy found that the bar rule did not serve substantial state interests. The state's asserted privacy interest "is that victims or their families will be offended by receiving a solicitation during their grief and trauma. But we do not allow restrictions on speech to be justified on the ground that the expression might offend the listener. The occupants of a household receiving mailings are not a captive audience, [and all] the recipient of objectionable mailings need do is to take 'the "short, though regular, journey from mail box to trash can." ' Bolger. [And] to the extent the bar seeks to protect lawyers' reputations by preventing them from engaging in speech some deem offensive, the State is doing nothing more [than] manipulating the public's opinion by suppressing speech that informs us how the legal system works. This, of course, is censorship pure and simple." Even if these interests were substantial, wrote Justice Kennedy, the bar rule had not been shown to directly and materially advance them. The 106–page study submitted by the Florida Bar was "noteworthy for its incompetence. [Our] cases require something more than a few pages of self-serving and unsupported statements by the State." Finally, he argued, the bar rule "prohibits far more speech than necessary to serve the purported state interest. [The] accident victims who are prejudiced to vindicate the State's purported desire for more dignity in the legal profession will be the very persons who most need legal advice, for they are the victims who, because they lack education, linguistic ability, or familiarity with the legal system, are unable to seek out legal services. [The] Court's opinion [bears] the hallmark of a censor. [I] dissent."

WHAT STANDARD OF SCRUTINY FOR COMMERCIAL SPEECH?

Having found commercial speech to be protected by the First Amendment, but not to the same extent as other speech, the Court settled on an intermediate standard of scrutiny reminiscent of the standard the Court applies to content-neutral regulations of conduct or the time, place and manner of speech. See Ch. 12. According to the Central Hudson decision, which follows, government may justify a regulation of truthful and nonmisleading advertising of lawful transactions only if it "directly advances" a "substantial" government interest by means that are "not more extensive than necessary." Does this standard dilute normal First Amendment protections? Do the cases that follow Central Hudson adhere to this standard or alter it? In which direction?

Central Hudson Gas v. Public Service Comm'n

447 U.S. 557, 100 S.Ct. 2343, 65 L.Ed.2d 341 (1980).

[The New York Public Service Commission (PSC) prohibited electrical utilities from engaging in promotional advertising designed to stimulate demand for electricity. The ban continued a policy begun at a time of severe fuel shortage, even though the shortage had eased. The PSC permitted "institutional and informational" advertising not intended to promote sales. The Court invalidated the promotional advertising restriction.]

[Justice] POWELL delivered the opinion of the Court.

The Commission's order restricts only commercial speech, that is, expression related solely to the economic interests of the speaker and its audience. [In previous] commercial speech cases, a four-part analysis has developed. At the outset, we must determine whether the expression is protected by the First Amendment. For commercial speech to come within that provision, it at least must concern lawful activity and not be misleading. Next, we ask whether the asserted governmental interest is substantial. If both inquiries yield positive answers, we must determine whether the regulation directly advances the governmental interest asserted, and whether it is not more extensive than is necessary to serve that interest.

[The] Commission does not claim that the expression at issue either is inaccurate or relates to unlawful activity. [The] Commission [argues that] the State's interest in conserving energy is sufficient to support suppression of advertising designed to increase consumption of electricity. In view of our country's dependence on energy resources beyond our control, no one can doubt the importance of energy conservation. Plainly, therefore, the state interest asserted is substantial. [Moreover,] the State's interest in energy conservation is directly advanced by the Commission order at issue here. There is an immediate connection between advertising and demand for electricity. Central Hudson would not contest the advertising ban unless it believed that promotion would increase its sales. Thus, we find a direct link between the state interest in conservation and the Commission's order.

[The] critical inquiry in this case [is] whether the Commission's complete suppression of speech ordinarily protected by the First Amendment is no more extensive than necessary to further the State's interest in energy conservation. The Commission's order reaches all promotional advertising, regardless of the impact of the touted service on overall energy use. [The] Commission's order prevents appellant from promoting electric services [such as the "heat pump" and the use of electric heat as a "backup" to solar and other heat sources] that would reduce energy use by diverting demand from less efficient sources, or that would consume roughly the same amount of energy as do alternative sources. In neither situation would the utility's advertising endanger conservation or mislead the public. To the extent that the Commission's order suppresses speech that in no way impairs the State's interest in energy conservation, the Commission's order violates the [First Amendment]. The Commission also has not demonstrated that its interest in conservation cannot be protected adequately by more limited regulation of appellant's commercial expression. To further its policy of conservation, the Commission could attempt to restrict the format and content of Central Hudson's advertising. It might, for example, require that the advertisements include information about the relative efficiency and expense of the offered service. In the absence of a showing that more limited speech regulation would be ineffective, we cannot approve the complete suppression of Central Hudson's [advertising].

Reversed.

Justice BLACKMUN, with whom Justice BRENNAN joins, concurring.

[I] concur only in the Court's judgment, [because] I believe the test now evolved and applied by the Court is not consistent with our prior cases and does not provide adequate protection for truthful, nonmisleading, noncoercive commercial speech. I agree with the Court that [its] level of intermediate scrutiny is appropriate for a restraint on commercial speech designed to protect consumers from misleading or coercive speech, or a regulation related to the time, place, or manner of commercial speech. I do not agree, however, that the Court's four-part test is the proper one to be applied when a State seeks to suppress information about a product in order to manipulate a private economic decision that the State cannot or has not regulated or outlawed directly. [I] disagree with the Court [when] it says that suppression of speech may be a permissible means to achieve [energy conservation]. [I] seriously doubt whether suppression of information concerning the availability and price of a legally offered product is ever a permissible way for the State to "dampen" demand for or use of the product. Even though "commercial" speech is involved, such a regulatory measure strikes at the heart of the First Amendment. This is because it is a covert attempt by the State to manipulate the choices of its citizens, not by persuasion or direct regulation, but by depriving the public of the information needed to make a free choice.

Justice STEVENS, with whom Justice BRENNAN joins, concurring [in the judgment].

This case involves a governmental regulation that completely bans promotional advertising by an electric utility. This ban encompasses a great deal more than mere proposals to engage in certain kinds of commercial transactions. It prohibits all advocacy of the immediate or future use of electricity. It curtails expression by an informed and interested group of persons of their point of view on questions relating to the production and consumption of electrical energy—questions frequently discussed and debated by our political leaders. [I] concur in the result because I do not consider this to be a "commercial speech" case. Accordingly, I see no need to decide whether the Court's four-part analysis adequately protects commercial speech—as properly defined—in the face of a blanket ban of the sort involved in this case.

Justice REHNQUIST [dissenting].

The Court's analysis [is] wrong in several respects. Initially, I disagree with the Court's conclusion that the speech of a state-created monopoly, which is the subject of a comprehensive regulatory scheme, is entitled to protection under the First Amendment. [The] extensive regulations governing decisionmaking by public utilities suggest that for purposes of First Amendment analysis, a utility is far closer to a state-controlled enterprise than is an ordinary corporation.[1] Accordingly, I think a State has broad discretion in determining the statements that a utility may make in that such statements emanate from the entity created by the State to provide important and unique public services. [I] also think New York's ban on such advertising falls within the scope of permissible state regulation of an economic activity by an entity that could not exist in corporate form, say nothing of enjoy monopoly status, were it not for the laws of New York.

[The] Court's decision today fails to give due deference to [the] subordinate position of commercial speech. [The] test adopted by the [Court] elevates the protection accorded commercial speech that falls within the scope of the First Amendment to a level that is virtually indistinguishable from that of noncommercial speech. I think [that] by labeling economic regulation of business conduct as a restraint on "free speech," [the Court has] gone far to resurrect the discredited doctrine of cases such as [Lochner]. [Identification] of speech that falls within [the First Amendment's] protection is not aided by the metaphorical reference to a "marketplace of ideas." There is no reason for believing that the marketplace of ideas is free from market imperfections any more than there is to believe that the invisible hand will always lead to optimum economic decisions in the commercial market. [Even] if I were to agree that commercial speech is entitled to some First Amendment protection, I would hold here that the State's decision to ban promotional advertising, in

---

1.   Compare Justice Rehnquist's majority opinion in Jackson v. Metropolitan Edison Co. (1974; chap. 10, p. 952 above), holding that a public utility's termination of service is not "state action" and is therefore not subject to Fourteenth Amendment restrictions.

light of the substantial state interest at stake, [is] constitutionally [permissible].

The plethora of opinions filed in this case highlights the doctrinal difficulties that emerge from this Court's decisions granting First Amendment protection to commercial speech. [I] remain of the view that the Court unleashed a Pandora's box when it "elevated" commercial speech to the level of traditional political speech by according it First Amendment protection. [The] notion that more speech is the remedy to expose falsehood and fallacies is wholly out of place in the commercial [bazaar]. [In] a democracy, the economic is subordinate to the [political].

[The] final part of the Court's [test] leaves room for so many hypothetical "better" ways that any ingenious lawyer will surely seize on one of them to secure the invalidation of what the state agency actually did. [It] is in my view inappropriate for the Court to invalidate the State's ban on commercial advertising here based on its speculation that in some cases the advertising may result in a net savings in electrical energy [use].

―――――

COMMERCIAL SPEECH REGULATION AFTER CENTRAL HUDSON

1. *Commercial speech and "least restrictive alternative" analysis.* Central Hudson stated that commercial speech regulations must be "no more extensive than necessary" to serve a substantial government interest. In BOARD OF TRUSTEES, STATE UNIV. OF NEW YORK. v. FOX, 492 U.S. 469 (1989), the Court explicitly clarified that this did *not* mean that government must employ the "least restrictive alternative." The case involved a regulation by the University restricting the operation of commercial enterprises on its campuses. The effect of the regulation was to bar a company from selling its housewares in dormitories through the use of "Tupperware parties." Justice SCALIA's majority opinion rejected the constitutional challenge. He first concluded that the speech involved was commercial, and that the Central Hudson analysis was applicable. Turning to that analysis, he noted that the speech proposed a lawful transaction and was not misleading. He found the state interests in promoting an educational rather than a commercial atmosphere on campuses, insuring the security of students, and preventing their exploitation were sufficiently substantial to satisfy that prong of the Central Hudson test.

Accordingly, the case turned on the fit between these ends and the means employed to achieve them. Justice Scalia acknowledged that the Court's own prior statements in Central Hudson and in cases such as Zauderer, above, supported the impression that the use of the word "necessary" in Central Hudson could be read as incorporating a "least restrictive alternative" requirement. Nevertheless, he rejected such a reading. He drew on McCulloch v. Maryland in noting that the word "necessary" sometimes has a looser rather than a more restrictive meaning and concluded: "Whatever the conflicting tenor of our prior dicta may be, we now focus upon this specific issue for the first time, and conclude that the reason of the matter requires something short of a least-restrictive-means standard. [What] our decisions require is a 'fit between the legislature's ends and the means chosen to accomplish those ends,'—a fit that is not necessarily perfect, but reasonable; that represents not necessarily the single best disposition but one whose scope is 'in proportion to the interest served'; that employs not necessarily the least restrictive means but [a] means narrowly tailored to achieve the desired objective. Within those bounds we leave it to governmental decisionmakers to judge what manner of regulation may best be employed."

Justice Scalia rejected the argument that this standard was as permissive as minimal rational basis scrutiny in equal protection law. He explained: "There it suffices the law could be thought to further a legitimate governmental goal, without reference to whether it does so at inordinate cost. Here we require the government goal to be substantial, and the cost to be carefully calculated. Moreover, since the state bears the burden of justifying its restrictions, [it] must affirmatively establish the reasonable fit we require. By declining to impose, in addition, a least-restrictive-means requirement, we take account of the difficulty of establishing with precision the point at which restrictions become more extensive than their objective requires, and provide the legislative and executive branches needed leeway in a field (commercial speech) 'traditionally subject to governmental [regulation].' "[2]

2. *Billboards and newsracks: may commercial speech be treated differently?* In METROMEDIA, INC. v. SAN DIEGO, 453 U.S. 490 (1981), the Court struck down an ordinance regulating the placement of *non*-commercial billboards, but made clear that portions of the ordinance banning offsite commercial billboards would be permissible. Applying the Central Hudson test, Justice WHITE's plurality opinion found that the ban on commercial billboards satisfied its first, second, and fourth criteria, but found more problematic the question of whether such a ban "directly advanced" the acknowledged governmental interests "in traffic safety and the appearance of the city." Finding no ulterior motives, the plurality reviewed deferentially the determinations made by San Diego, especially those relating to traffic safety, and suggested that the ban on commercial billboards satisfied all aspects of the Central Hudson test. Because the dissenting opinions of Chief Justice BURGER and Justices REHNQUIST and STEVENS would have upheld the restriction in its entirety, a majority of the Court agreed that restrictions of *commercial* billboards for both aesthetic and traffic safety reasons satisfy the Central Hudson standard.

In CITY OF CINCINNATI v. DISCOVERY NETWORK, INC., 507 U.S. 410 (1993), however, the Court held that commercial speech may not be treated differently from non-commercial speech for aesthetic or safety purposes in the absence of distinctively commercial harm. Cincinnati barred respondents from placing 62 newsracks on public property to dispense free advertisements for adult education classes and real estate sales, treating such materials as "commercial handbills" whose distribution on public property was prohibited. But the city permitted the placement on public property of between 1500 and 2000 newsracks distributing general circulation newspapers. The city defended the selective commercial newsrack ban as "motivated by its interest in the safety and attractive appearance of its streets and sidewalks" and as justified by the lower value of commercial speech. The Court invalidated the ban.

Justice STEVENS, writing for the Court, found there to be an insufficiently "reasonable fit" between the selective exclusion and the city's asserted ends under the standards set forth in Central Hudson and Fox: "The city argues that there is a close fit between its ban on newsracks dispensing 'commercial handbills' and its interest in safety and esthetics because every decrease in the number of such dispensing devices necessarily effects an increase in safety and

---

2. Note that the Court has similarly rejected the use of least-restrictive-means in assessing the validity of content-neutral time, place, and manner restrictions. The requirement of "narrow tailoring" of means to significant governmental ends in that context has not been read as requiring least restrictive alternative. See, e.g., Ward v. Rock Against Racism, 491 U.S. 781 (1989; p. 1260 below).

an improvement in the attractiveness of the cityscape. In the city's view, the prohibition is thus entirely related to its legitimate interests in safety and esthetics. We accept the validity of the city's proposition, but consider it an insufficient justification for the discrimination against respondents' use of newsracks that are no more harmful than the permitted newsracks, and have only a minimal impact on the overall number of newsracks on the city's sidewalks. The major premise supporting the city's argument is the proposition that commercial speech has only a low value. Based on that premise, the city contends that the fact that assertedly more valuable publications are allowed to use newsracks does not undermine its judgment that its esthetic and safety interests are stronger than the interest in allowing commercial speakers to have similar access to the reading public. We cannot agree. In our view, the city's argument attaches more importance to the distinction between commercial and noncommercial speech than our cases warrant and seriously underestimates the value of commercial speech.

"[In] this case, the distinction bears no relationship whatsoever to the particular interests that the city has asserted. It is therefore an impermissible means of responding to the city's admittedly legitimate interests. [The] city has asserted an interest in esthetics, but respondent publishers' newsracks are no greater an eyesore than the newsracks permitted to remain on Cincinnati's sidewalks. Each newsrack, whether containing 'newspapers' or 'commercial handbills,' is equally unattractive. [The] city's primary concern [is] with the aggregate number of newsracks on its streets. On that score, however, all newsracks, regardless of whether they contain commercial or noncommercial publications, are equally at fault. [Cincinnati] has not asserted an interest in preventing commercial harms by regulating the information distributed by respondent publishers' newsracks. [In] the absence of some basis for distinguishing between 'newspapers' and 'commercial handbills' that is relevant to an interest asserted by the city, we are unwilling to recognize Cincinnati's bare assertion that the 'low value' of commercial speech is a sufficient justification for its selective and categorical ban on newsracks dispensing 'commercial handbills.' "

Justice Stevens purported to distinguish rather than overrule Metromedia: while "seven Justices in the Metromedia case were of the view that San Diego could completely ban offsite commercial billboards for reasons unrelated to the content of those billboards, [those] seven Justices did not say that San Diego could distinguish between commercial and noncommercial offsite billboards that cause the same esthetic and safety concerns. That question was not presented in Metromedia."

Justice BLACKMUN concurred but reiterated the view he expressed in his Central Hudson concurrence that truthful, nonmisleading advertisement of lawful activity ought to be treated the same as fully protected speech. Chief Justice REHNQUIST, joined by Justices White and Thomas, dissented. Presuming that a flat ban on the placement of newsracks on public property would be constitutional, the Chief Justice reasoned that "if (as I am certain) Cincinnati may regulate newsracks that disseminate commercial speech based on the interests it has asserted, I am at a loss as to why its scheme is unconstitutional because it does not also regulate newsracks that disseminate noncommercial speech. One would have thought that the city, perhaps even following the teachings of our commercial speech jurisprudence, could have decided to place the burden of its regulatory scheme on less protected speech (i.e., commercial handbills) without running afoul of the First Amendment. Today's decision, though, places the city in the position of having to decide between restricting more speech—fully protected speech—and allowing the proliferation of newsracks on its street corners to continue unabated. It scarcely seems logical that the First Amendment compels such a result."

3. *The rise and fall of the "vice" exception: restrictions on advertising harmful products and services.* Central Hudson makes clear that the limited protection of commercial advertising does not extend to advertising of illegal activity. But what of restrictions on the advertising of products or services that are not unlawful but are widely viewed as harmful, such as cigarettes, alcohol, and gambling? In POSADAS DE PUERTO RICO ASSOCS. v. TOURISM COMPANY OF PUERTO RICO, 478 U.S. 328 (1986), the Court upheld, by a vote of 5–4, a Puerto Rico law prohibiting gambling casinos from advertising their facilities to residents of Puerto Rico.

Justice REHNQUIST's majority opinion stated: "The particular kind of commercial speech at issue here [concerns] a lawful activity and is not misleading or fraudulent, at least in the abstract. We must therefore proceed to the three remaining steps of the Central Hudson analysis. [The] first [involves] an assessment of the strength of the government's interest in restricting the speech. The interest at stake in this case [is] the reduction of demand for casino gambling by the residents of Puerto Rico." Justice Rehnquist found that the legislative determination that excess gambling would impair the health, safety, and welfare of Puerto Rico residents, "some of the very same concerns [that] have motivated the vast majority of the 50 States to prohibit casino gambling," were sufficient to qualify as a "substantial" governmental interest. Turning to the remaining steps of the Central Hudson analysis, Justice Rehnquist noted that the law directly advanced the government's asserted interest: "[Puerto Rico] obviously believed [that] advertising of casino gambling aimed at [its residents] would serve to increase the demand for the product advertised. We think the legislature's belief is [reasonable]." Finally, he found the law "no more extensive than necessary to serve the government's interest," noting that the law had been construed to permit advertising of casino gambling aimed at tourists, and rejecting the challengers' argument that Puerto Rico ought employ "a 'counterspeech' policy" as a less restrictive means.

The challengers also claimed that the law was unconstitutional because of such rulings as Carey and Bigelow, which dealt with contraceptive and abortion advertising. Justice Rehnquist rejected this argument, noting that those cases dealt with constitutionally protected activities that could not have been prohibited by the State. Puerto Rico, however, could have banned gambling entirely: "[T]he greater power to completely ban casino gambling necessarily includes the lesser power to ban advertising of casino gambling, and Carey and Bigelow are hence inapposite. [It] is precisely because the government could have enacted a wholesale prohibition of the underlying conduct that it is permissible for the government to take the less intrusive step of allowing the conduct, but reducing the demand through restrictions on advertising. It would surely be a Pyrrhic victory for casino owners [to] gain recognition of a First Amendment right to advertise their casinos to the residents of Puerto Rico, only to thereby force the legislature into banning casino gambling by residents altogether. It would just as surely be a strange constitutional doctrine which would concede to the legislature the authority to totally ban a product or activity, but deny to the legislature the authority to forbid the stimulation of demand for the product or activity."

Justice BRENNAN, joined by Justices Marshall and Blackmun, dissented, arguing that regulation of commercial speech "in order to deprive consumers of accurate information concerning lawful activity" ought to receive "strict judicial scrutiny." He went on to argue that, even under the more relaxed standard set forth in Central Hudson, the regulation should fall: "While tipping its hat to these standards, the Court does little more than defer to what it perceives to be the determination by Puerto Rico's legislature that [the ban] is reasonable." He was especially skeptical about Puerto Rico's claim that increasing demand for gambling by local residents would cause real or substantial harms: "Puerto Rico has legalized gambling casinos, and permits its residents to patronize them. Thus, the Puerto Rico Legislature has determined that permitting residents to engage in casino gambling will not produce the 'serious harmful effects' that have led a majority of States to ban such activity. Residents of Puerto Rico are also permitted to engage in a variety of other gambling activities—including horse racing, 'picas,' cockfighting, and the Puerto Rico lottery—all of which are allowed to advertise freely to residents. Indeed, it is surely not farfetched to suppose that the legislature chose to restrict casino advertising not because of the 'evils' of casino gambling, but because it preferred that Puerto Ricans spend their gambling dollars on the Puerto Rico lottery." Justice STEVENS, joined by Justices Marshall and Blackmun, also dissented, emphasizing that the law effectively discriminated among speakers based on their intended audience: the regulation "applies one standard to the New York Times and another to the San Juan Star."

The Court's deferential approach to the regulation of gambling advertising in Poadas led many observers to conclude that there was an implicit "vice" exception to the protection of commercial speech. The Court reinforced such an impression in UNITED STATES v. EDGE BROADCASTING CO., 509 U.S. 418 (1993), which upheld a federal statute prohibiting the broadcast of lottery advertisements except by stations licensed to states that conduct lotteries. Edge Broadcasting operated a radio station in North Carolina, a nonlottery state, but over 90% of its listeners were in neighboring Virginia, a lottery state. North Carolina listeners could also hear a number of Virginia radio stations that broadcast lottery ads. The Court rejected Edge's claim that it had a First Amendment right to broadcast advertisements for the Virginia lottery. Justice WHITE wrote the opinion for the Court. Upholding the law both on its face and as applied to Edge, he wrote: "We have no doubt that the statutes directly advanced the governmental interest at stake in this case. [Instead] of favoring either the lottery or the nonlottery State, Congress opted to support the antigambling policy of a State like North Carolina by forbidding stations in such a State from airing lottery advertising. At the same time it sought not to unduly interfere with the policy of a lottery sponsoring State such as Virginia. [This] congressional policy of balancing the interests of lottery and nonlottery States is the substantial governmental interest that satisfies Central Hudson. [It] is also the interest that is directly served by applying the statutory restriction to all stations in North Carolina." He noted that here, "as in Posadas de Puerto Rico, the Government obviously legislated on the premise that the advertising of gambling serves to increase the demand for the advertised product. See also Central Hudson. Congress clearly was entitled to determine that broadcast of promotional advertising of lotteries undermines North Carolina's policy against gambling, even if the North Carolina audience is not wholly unaware of the lottery's existence."

Justice STEVENS, joined by Justice Blackmun, dissented: "I would hold that suppressing truthful advertising regarding a neighboring State's lottery, an activity which is, of course, perfectly legal, is a patently unconstitutional means of effectuating the Government's asserted interest in protecting the policies of nonlottery States. Indeed, I had thought that we had so held [in Bigelow, which] held that a State 'may not, under the guise of exercising internal police powers, bar a citizen of another State from disseminating information about an activity that is legal in that State.' [Unless] justified by a truly substantial governmental interest, this extreme, and extremely paternalistic, measure surely cannot withstand scrutiny under the First Amendment."

But in RUBIN v. COORS BREWING CO., 514 U.S. 476 (1995), and 44 Liquormart, Inc. v. Rhode Island, which follows, the Court decisively rejected any notion that there is a "vice" exception to the protection of commercial speech. In Coors, the Court unanimously invalidated a provision of the federal Alcohol Administration Act that prohibited beer labels from displaying alcohol content. The government defended the provision as necessary to preventing "strength wars" among brewers who would seek to compete in the marketplace based on the potency of their beer. Justice THOMAS wrote the opinion of the Court. At the outset, he rejected the government's suggestion "that legislatures have broader latitude to regulate speech that promotes socially harmful activities, such as alcohol consumption, than they have to regulate other types of speech." Rather, he wrote, the Central Hudson test applied to commercial advertising of vice and other activities alike. Applying that test, he found that the government had asserted "a significant interest in protecting the health, safety, and welfare of its citizens by preventing brewers from competing on the basis of alcohol strength, which could lead to greater alcoholism and its attendant social costs."

But Justice Thomas found that the provision did not directly advance that interest, "given the overall irrationality of the Government's regulatory scheme. While the laws governing labeling prohibit the disclosure of alcohol content unless required by state law, federal regulations [prohibit disclosure of alcohol content in] beer advertising [only] in States that affirmatively prohibit [it]. As only 18 States at best prohibit disclosure of content in advertisements, brewers remain free to disclose alcohol content in advertisements, but not on labels, in much of the country. The failure to prohibit the disclosure of alcohol content in advertising, which would seem to constitute a more influential weapon in any strength war than labels, makes no rational sense if the government's true aim is to suppress strength wars. [Additionally, while the act] bans the disclosure of alcohol content on beer labels, it allows the exact opposite in the case of wines and spirits. Thus, distilled spirits may contain statements of alcohol content, and such disclosures are required for wines with more than 14 percent alcohol. If combatting strength wars were the goal, we would assume that Congress would regulate disclosure of alcohol content for the strongest beverages as well as for the weakest ones. Further, the Government permits brewers to signal high alcohol content through use of the term 'malt liquor.' [One] would think that if the Government sought to suppress strength wars by prohibiting numerical disclosures of alcohol content, it also would preclude brewers from indicating higher alcohol beverages by using descriptive terms. [The] irrationality of this unique and puzzling regulatory framework ensures that the labeling ban will fail to achieve [its asserted] end."

Finally, Justice Thomas concluded, the ban was "more extensive than necessary" because the government had alternative options, "such as directly limiting the alcohol content of beers, prohibiting marketing efforts emphasizing high alcohol strength (which is apparently the policy in some other Western nations), or limiting the labeling ban only to malt liquors, [all] of which could advance the Government's asserted interest in a manner less intrusive to respondent's First Amendment rights." Justice STEVENS concurred in the judgment but would not have applied the Central Hudson test: "I think respondent has a constitutional right to give the public accurate information about the alcoholic content of the malt beverages that it produces. I see no reason why the fact that such information is disseminated on the labels of respondent's products should diminish that constitutional protection. On the contrary, the statute at issue here should be subjected to the same stringent review as any other content-based abridgment of protected speech."

---

44 Liquormart, Inc. v. Rhode Island

521 U.S. ___, 116 S.Ct. 1495, 134 L.Ed.2d 711 (1996).

[Rhode Island law prohibited advertisement of the price of alcoholic beverages "in any manner whatsoever," except by tags or signs inside liquor stores. The state courts had several times upheld the law against First Amendment challenge, finding that the law reasonably served the state goal of promoting "temperance." Two high-volume discount liquor retailers challenged the law under the free speech clause in federal court. The Rhode Island Liquor Stores Association intervened on behalf of the state. The district court invalidated the law, finding "that Rhode Island's off-premises liquor price advertising ban has no significant impact on levels of alcohol consumption in Rhode Island." The court of appeals reversed, finding "inherent merit" in Rhode Island's argument that competitive price advertising would lower prices and that lower prices would produce more sales, increasing the consumption of alcohol.

[The Supreme Court unanimously reversed, invalidating the Rhode Island law. But it divided into several camps on the reasoning. Justice Stevens announced the judgment of the Court and wrote a plurality opinion joined at different points by Justices Kennedy, Souter, Thomas and Ginsburg. Joined by Justices Kennedy and Ginsburg only, he wrote that bars against "dissemination of truthful, nonmisleading commercial messages for reasons unrelated to the preservation of a fair bargaining process" should receive strict scrutiny, which the Rhode Island law failed. In the alternative, Justice Stevens wrote, joined on this point by Justices Kennedy, Souter and Ginsburg, the Rhode Island law in any event failed the Central Hudson test. Justice Thomas concurred but would have held that a ban on truthful price information is per se illegitimate. Justice O'Connor, joined by Chief Justice Rehnquist and Justices Souter and Breyer, concurred in the judgment, reasoning simply that the Rhode Island law failed the Central Hudson test. Justice Scalia concurred in the judgment.]

Justice STEVENS [joined by Justices KENNEDY and GINSBURG].

[Not] all commercial speech regulations are subject to a similar form of constitutional review. [When] a State regulates commercial messages to protect consumers from misleading, deceptive, or aggressive sales practices, or requires the disclosure of beneficial consumer information, the purpose of its regulation is consistent with the reasons for according [less than full] constitutional protection to commercial speech and therefore justifies less than strict review. However, when a State entirely prohibits the dissemination of truthful, nonmisleading commercial messages for reasons unrelated to the preservation of a fair bargaining process, there is far less reason to depart from the rigorous review that the First Amendment generally demands. [Complete] speech bans, unlike content-neutral restrictions on the time, place, or manner of expression, are particularly dangerous because they all but foreclose alternative means of disseminating certain information.

[The] special dangers that attend complete bans on truthful, nonmisleading commercial speech cannot be explained away by appeals to the "commonsense distinctions" that exist between commercial and noncommercial speech. [It] is the State's interest in protecting consumers from "commercial harms" [such as deception and overreaching] that provides "the typical reason why commercial speech can be subject to greater governmental regulation than noncommercial speech." Discovery Network. Yet bans that target truthful, nonmisleading commercial messages rarely protect consumers from such harms. Instead, [bans] against truthful, nonmisleading commercial speech [usually] rest solely on the offensive assumption that the public will respond "irrationally" to the truth. Linmark. The First Amendment directs us to be especially skeptical of regulations that seek to keep people in the dark for what the government perceives to be their own good. That teaching applies equally to state attempts to deprive consumers of accurate information about their chosen products.

Justice STEVENS [joined by Justices KENNEDY, SOUTER and GINSBURG].

The State argues that the price advertising prohibition should [be] upheld because it directly advances the State's substantial interest in promoting temperance, and because it is no more extensive than necessary. Central Hudson. [The] State bears the burden of showing not merely that its regulation will advance its interest, but also that it will do so "to a material degree." Edenfield. We can agree that common sense supports the conclusion that a prohibition against price advertising [will] tend to mitigate competition and maintain prices at a higher level than would prevail in a completely free market. [We] can even agree [that] demand, and hence consumption throughout the market, is somewhat lower whenever a higher, noncompetitive price level prevails. However, [we] cannot agree [that] the price advertising ban will significantly advance the State's interest in promoting temperance. [The] State has presented no evidence to suggest that its speech prohibition will significantly reduce market-wide consumption. Indeed, the District Court's considered and uncontradicted finding on this point is directly to the contrary. [In] addition, [the] State has not identified what price level would lead to a significant reduction in alcohol consumption, nor has it identified the amount that it believes prices would decrease without the ban. Thus, [any] connection between the ban and a significant change in alcohol consumption would be purely fortuitous. [Any] conclusion that elimination of the ban would significantly increase alcohol consumption would [rest on] "speculation or conjecture."

[The] State also cannot satisfy the requirement that its restriction on speech be no more extensive than necessary. It is perfectly obvious that alternative forms of regulation that would not involve any restriction on speech would be more likely to achieve the State's goal of promoting temperance. [Higher] prices can be maintained either by direct regulation or by increased taxation. Per capita purchases could be limited as is the case with prescription drugs. Even educational campaigns focused on the problems of excessive, or even moderate, drinking might prove to be more effective. As a result, even under the less than strict standard that generally applies in commercial speech cases, the State has failed to establish a "reasonable fit" between its abridgment of speech and its temperance goal. Fox, Coors, Linmark. It necessarily follows that the price advertising ban cannot survive the more stringent constitutional review that Central Hudson itself concluded was appropriate for the complete suppression of truthful, nonmisleading commercial speech.

Justice STEVENS [joined by Justices KENNEDY, THOMAS, and GINSBURG].

[Relying] on the Central Hudson analysis set forth in Posadas and Edge Broadcasting, Rhode Island [argues] that, because expert opinions as to the effectiveness of the price advertising ban "go both ways," the Court of Appeals correctly concluded that the ban constituted a "reasonable choice" by the legislature. [The] reasoning in Posadas does support the State's argument, but, on reflection, we are now persuaded that Posadas [clearly] erred in concluding that it was "up to the legislature" to choose suppression over a less speech-restrictive policy. The Posadas majority's conclusion on that point cannot be reconciled with the unbroken line of prior cases striking down similarly broad regulations on truthful, nonmisleading advertising when non-speech-related alternatives were available. [We] also cannot accept the State's [contention that it may ban liquor price advertising because it may ban the sale of alcoholic beverages outright. Such] "greater-includes-the-lesser" reasoning, [which was] endorsed toward the end of the majority's opinion in Posadas, [is] inconsistent with both logic and well-settled doctrine. [Contrary] to the assumption made in Posadas, we think it quite clear that banning speech may sometimes prove far more intrusive than banning conduct. [Finally,] we find unpersuasive the State's contention that, under Posadas and Edge, the price advertising ban should be upheld because it targets commercial speech that pertains to a "vice" activity. [Our] decision last Term striking down an alcohol-related advertising restriction effectively rejected the very contention respondents now make. See Coors Brewing. Moreover, the scope of any "vice" exception to the protection afforded by the First Amendment would be difficult, if not impossible, to define.

Justice SCALIA, concurring in part and concurring in the judgment.

[The] briefs and arguments of the parties in the present case provide no illumination on [state legislative practices toward advertising regulation at the time the First and Fourteenth Amendments were adopted.] [Since] I do not believe we have before us the wherewithal to declare Central Hudson wrong—or at least the wherewithal to say what ought to replace it—I must resolve this case in accord with our existing jurisprudence, which all except Justice Thomas agree would prohibit the challenged regulation. I am not disposed to develop new law, or reinforce old, on this issue, and accordingly I merely concur in the judgment of the Court.

Justice THOMAS, concurring in part and concurring in the judgment.

In cases such as this, in which the government's asserted interest is to keep legal users of a product or service ignorant in order to manipulate their choices in the marketplace, the balancing test adopted in Central Hudson should not be applied, in my view. Rather, such an "interest" is per se illegitimate and can no more justify regulation of "commercial" speech than it can justify regulation of "noncommercial" speech. [Where,] as here, the asserted interest is one that is to be achieved through keeping would-be recipients of the speech in the dark, [a]pplication of the advancement-of-state-interest prong of Central Hudson makes little sense. [Faulting] the State for failing to show that its price advertising ban decreases alcohol consumption "significantly," as Justice Stevens does, seems to imply that if the State had been more successful at keeping consumers ignorant and thereby decreasing their consumption, then the restriction might have been upheld. This contradicts Virginia Pharmacy Board's rationale for protecting "commercial" speech in the first instance.

[In] their application of [Central Hudson,] both Justice Stevens and Justice O'Connor hold that because the State can ban the sale of lower priced alcohol altogether by instituting minimum prices or levying taxes, it cannot ban advertising regarding lower priced liquor. [Their] opinions would appear to commit the courts to striking down restrictions on speech whenever a direct regulation (i.e., a regulation involving no restriction on speech regarding lawful activity at all) would be an equally effective method of dampening demand by legal users. But it would seem that directly banning a product (or rationing it, taxing it, controlling its price, or otherwise restricting its sale in specific ways) would virtually always be at least as effective in discouraging consumption as merely restricting advertising regarding the product would be, and thus virtually all restrictions with such a purpose would fail the fourth prong of the Central Hudson test. [I] welcome this outcome; but, rather than "applying" the fourth prong of Central Hudson to reach the inevitable result that all or most such advertising restrictions must be struck down, I would adhere to the doctrine adopted in Virginia Pharmacy Board, and in Justice Blackmun's Central Hudson concurrence, that all attempts to dissuade legal choices by citizens by keeping them ignorant are impermissible.

Justice O'CONNOR, with whom Chief Justice REHNQUIST and Justices SOUTER and BREYER join, concurring in the judgment.

[I] agree with the Court that Rhode Island's price-advertising ban is invalid. I would resolve this case more narrowly, however, by applying our established Central Hudson test to determine whether this commercial-speech regulation survives First Amendment scrutiny. Under that test, [our] conclusion is plain: Rhode Island's regulation fails First Amendment scrutiny. Both parties agree that the first two prongs of the Central Hudson test are met. Even if we assume arguendo that Rhode Island's regulation also satisfies the requirement that it directly advance the governmental interest, Rhode Island's regulation fails the final prong; that is, its ban is more extensive than necessary to serve the State's interest.

Rhode Island offers [one] justification for its ban on price advertising[: to] keep alcohol prices high as a way to keep consumption low. By preventing sellers from informing customers of prices, the regulation prevents competition from driving prices down and requires consumers to spend more time to find the best price for alcohol. The higher cost of obtaining alcohol, Rhode Island argues, will lead to reduced consumption. The fit between Rhode Island's method and this particular goal is not reasonable. [The] State has other methods at its disposal [that] would more directly accomplish this stated goal without intruding on sellers' ability to provide truthful, nonmisleading information to customers. [A sales] tax, for example, is not normally very difficult to administer and would have a far more certain and direct effect on prices, without any restriction on speech. The principal opinion suggests further alternatives, such as limiting per capita purchases or conducting an educational campaign about the dangers of alcohol consumption. The ready availability of such alternatives—at least some of which would far more effectively achieve Rhode Island's only professed goal, at comparatively small additional administrative cost—demonstrates that the fit between ends and means is not narrowly tailored. [Because] Rhode Island's regulation fails even the less stringent standard set out in Central Hudson, nothing here requires adoption of a new analysis for the evaluation of commercial speech regulation.

COMMERCIAL SPEECH REGULATION AFTER LIQUORMART

1. *What standard of scrutiny?* A number of justices have advocated full strict scrutiny for at least some regulations of commercial speech: Justices Brennan, Marshall, Blackmun and Stevens did so in pre-Liquormart concurrences or dissents, and Justices Stevens, Kennedy, Ginsburg and Thomas did so in Liquormart. But never have five of them sat on the Court at the same time or on on the same case. Thus, while the plurality in Liquormart questions the

wisdom of the Central Hudson test, a majority (those joining Justice O'Connor's concurrence plus Justice Scalia, concurring in the result) declines to alter or abandon it. Thus, even after Liquormart, Central Hudson remains the governing test for reviewing commercial speech regulations.

But what does Central Hudson mean after Liquormart? Arguably, the stringency of a standard of review depends more on its application than its verbal formulation: it is a function of the factors that must be examined, the strength of the state justifications required, and the rigor with which an appellate court will in fact examine legislative or lower court determinations with respect to those justifications. Does Liquormart subject the Rhode Island regulation to the practical equivalent of strict scrutiny? Is its emphasis on the availability of less restrictive regulatory alternatives such as price floors and taxes consistent with the holding in Fox that the government need not employ the least restrictive alternative? Is Justice Thomas correct to predict that, after Liquormart, no ban on truthful price advertising may be upheld? Even if that is so, does the stringent application of Central Hudson in Liquormart have any application beyond the context of a total ban on truthful price data? For discussion of such questions, see Sullivan, "Cheap Spirits, Cigarettes and Free Speech," 1996 Sup. Ct. Rev. 123.

2. *Paternalism and commercial speech.* The opinions of Justices Stevens and Thomas in Liquormart emphasize the illegitimacy of any government interest in keeping consumers ignorant of truthful and nonmisleading commercial information. Tracking the reasoning of Virginia Pharmacy, they suggest that government may not suppress truthful price data out of fear that consumers will act on it in ways that are harmful to their self-interest. How far does this anti-paternalism rationale extend? May the state ban tobacco ads that depict smokers as rugged and healthy or as socially and financially successful, on the ground that such positive images of smoking will induce consumers to act against their own self-interest in health? For an argument that such regulation should be permissible, see Blasi & Monaghan, "The First Amendment and Cigarette Advertising," 250 JAMA 502 (1986). For an argument that such regulation is unconstitutional, see Redish, "Tobacco Advertising and the First Amendment," 81 Iowa L. Rev. 589 (1996).

CHAPTER 12

FREEDOM OF SPEECH—HOW GOVERNMENT RESTRICTS SPEECH— MODES OF ABRIDGMENT AND STANDARDS OF REVIEW

———

Chapter 11 explored the distinction between protected and unprotected or less protected forms of expression. In Chapter 12, the focus shifts from the nature of the speech involved to the nature of the government regulation. Section 1 examines a second key distinction: that between regulations that aim at the content of speech and regulations that aim at some other, content-neutral interest, such as peace and quiet, the orderly movement of crowds, the aesthetic attractiveness of public spaces, or the economic competitiveness of an industry. Outside the area of unprotected categories of speech, the Court has scrutinized content-based distinctions more carefully than those it considers content-neutral, although it still subjects most content-neutral regulations of speech or symbolic conduct to heightened rather than minimum rationality review. Section 2 turns to the problem of speech-restrictive laws that the government enacts or enforces in its capacity as proprietor, educator, employer or patron. The discussion there begins with the law governing public forums and ends with the problem of unconstitutional conditions. Finally, Section 3 turns to a set of doctrines—the doctrines of overbreadth, vagueness and prior restraint—that bar government from restricting speech too broadly, too unclearly or too soon, even if it could restrict the same speech under a law that was written differently.

SECTION 1. THE DISTINCTION BETWEEN CONTENT-BASED AND CONTENT-NEUTRAL REGULATIONS

———

Introduction. Suppose that a municipality enacted laws prohibiting the construction or maintenance, even on private property, of:

1. any billboard supporting a Republican candidate
2. any political billboard
3. any political message on a billboard owned by a Republican
4. any billboard tending to arouse political anger or hostility
5. any billboard
6. any structure, except a building, exceeding 12 feet in height

7. any message on a billboard during the three weeks preceding a general election

8. any billboard in any area zoned for residential use

9. any billboard larger than 12 by 40 feet

Every one of these laws equally would prohibit a Republican proprietor from erecting, in a residential neighborhood, a 20–by–50–foot billboard urging election of a Republican candidate in a close race in the weeks just before the election. Yet while each of these laws would have the identical effect on such proposed speech, the Court would scrutinize them quite differently. Which of these laws appear content-neutral? Which ones appear content-based? Which ones, if any, do not appear to aim at speech at all? Are some of these laws more troubling than others under First Amendment principles? Which ones? Why? These questions are explored in the following materials.

A. CONTENT-BASED RESTRICTIONS

The Court has increasingly treated the distinction between content-based and content-neutral regulations as a crucial one in First Amendment law. The Court has considered several distinct types of content-based regulation, which are worth disentangling at the outset:

1. *Viewpoint restrictions.* The Court generally treats restriction of the expression of a particular point of view as the paradigm violation of the First Amendment. Several of the decisions already explored in Chapter 11 are illustrative. For example, Kingsley Int'l Pictures Corp. v. Regents (1959; p. 1129 above) held that a state may not deny a license to a film "because that picture advocates an idea—that adultery under certain circumstances may be proper behavior. [The] First Amendment's basic guarantee is of freedom to advocate ideas." Brandenburg v. Ohio (1969; p. 1071 above) made clear that, in the absence of incitement to imminent lawless action, the "mere advocacy" of violent overthrow of democracy or capitalism could not be made a crime. Justice Scalia's opinion for the Court in R.A.V. v. St. Paul (1992; p. 1115 above), the cross-burning case, suggested that the St. Paul ordinance prohibiting symbols that tend to arouse racial anger or alarm was invalid in part as "viewpoint discrimination" because it prohibited fighting words by bigots but not against them: "St. Paul has no [authority] to license one side of a debate to fight freestyle, while requiring the other to follow Marquis of Queensbury rules." And Judge Easterbrook's decision in American Booksellers Ass'n v. Hudnut (1985; p. 1151 above) invalidated the feminist anti-pornography ordinance as "thought control" because "speech that 'subordinates' women [is] forbidden" while speech "that portrays women in positions of equality is lawful, no matter how graphic the sexual content."

2. *Subject matter restrictions.* Is content discrimination suspect in the absence of viewpoint discrimination? What if government eliminates expression on an entire topic? Should banning all political billboards be treated as strictly as banning Republican billboards? The Court has generally scrutinized subject matter restrictions strictly. Recall that Justice Scalia's opinion for the Court subjected the St. Paul ordinance in R.A.V. to strict scrutiny not only because it involved viewpoint discrimination but also because it forbade only those fight-

ing words that were "addressed to one of the specified disfavored topics" of race, color, creed, religion or gender. Recall too the Court's invalidation of a ban on the display of all nudity on drive-in theater screens in Erznoznik v. Jacksonville (1975; p. 1156 above). Consider the following cases involving other restrictions on the subject matter of speech.

In POLICE DEPT. v. MOSLEY, 408 U.S. 92 (1972), the Court invalidated a Chicago disorderly conduct ordinance which barred picketing within 150 feet of a school while the school was in session, but exempted "peaceful picketing of any school involved in a labor dispute." Mosley had conducted a solitary picket outside a Chicago high school, carrying a sign saying "Jones High School practices black discrimination." Justice MARSHALL's opinion for the Court found the law's "selective exclusion [of speech] from a public place" unconstitutional. He stated: "The central problem with Chicago's ordinance is that it describes the permissible picketing in terms of its subject matter. [The] operative distinction is the message on a picket sign. [Above] all else, the First Amendment means that government has no power to restrict expression because of its message, its ideas, its subject matter, or its content. To permit the continued building of our politics and culture, and to assure self-fulfillment for each individual, our people are guaranteed the right to express any thought, free from government censorship. The essence of this forbidden censorship is content control. [Necessarily], then, under [equal protection], not to mention the First Amendment itself, government may not grant the use of a forum to people whose views it finds acceptable, but deny use to those wishing to express less favored or more controversial views. And it may not select which issues are worth discussing or debating in public facilities. There is an 'equality of status in the field of ideas,' and government must afford all points of view an equal opportunity to be heard."

Justice Marshall noted that "reasonable 'time, place and manner' regulations of picketing may be necessary to further significant governmental interests." But this was not a time, place, and manner regulation, as it defined the prohibited speech "in terms of subject matter," which was "never permitted." He rejected the argument that preventing school disruption justified the ordinance: "If peaceful labor picketing is permitted, there is no justification for prohibiting all nonlabor picketing, both peaceful and nonpeaceful. 'Peaceful' nonlabor picketing [is] obviously no more disruptive than 'peaceful' labor picketing. But Chicago's ordinance permits the latter and prohibits the former." Moreover, he rejected the argument that a city could prohibit all nonlabor picketing "because, as a class, nonlabor picketing is more prone to produce violence than labor picketing": "Predictions about imminent disruption from picketing involve judgments appropriately made on an individualized basis, not by means of broad classifications, especially those based on subject matter."

Technically, Justice Marshall rested the Mosley judgment on the equal protection clause of the Fourteenth Amendment. But he noted: "Of course, the equal protection claim in this case is closely intertwined with First Amendment interests: the Chicago ordinance affects picketing, which is expressive conduct; moreover, it does so by classifications formulated in terms of the subject of the picketing." Later cases have assimilated the Mosley holding into First Amendment analysis.

In CAREY v. BROWN, 447 U.S. 455 (1980), the Court found another picketing restriction unconstitutional under Mosley. The case involved a peaceful picket outside the mayor's home advocating racial integration of the schools through busing. The picketers were convicted under a state law that generally barred picketing outside residences or dwellings, but exempted "the peaceful picketing of a place of employment involved in a labor dispute." Justice BRENNAN, writing for the majority, held that the law impermissibly "accords preferential treatment to the expression of views on one particular subject; information about labor disputes may be freely disseminated, but discussion of all other issues is restricted." It was thus "constitutionally indistinguishable" from Mosley. Justice REHNQUIST, joined by Chief Justice Burger and Justice Blackmun, dissented, arguing that the basis for distinction in the law was "not content, [but] rather the character of the residence sought to be picketed."

SIMON & SCHUSTER, INC. v. MEMBERS OF NEW YORK STATE CRIME VICTIMS BOARD, 502 U.S. 105 (1991), involved a challenge to New York's "Son of Sam" law, enacted to prevent a serial murderer and other criminals from profiting at the expense of their victims from books about their crimes. The law required payment to the Crime Victims Board of any proceeds due to a person accused of, convicted of, or admitting to a crime, for the production of a book or other work describing the crime. The Board was to place these funds in escrow for five years so that they would be available to satisfy any damage judgments that victims of the defendant's crimes might obtain. The law was challenged by the publisher of a book entitled "Wiseguy: Life in a Mafia Family." A principal source for the book was a former organized crime operative, Henry Hill, who, in exchange for compensation, had recounted his participation in various robberies, extortions, drug dealing and frauds. New York sought payment from the publisher and the publisher challenged the statute under the First Amendment. The Court unanimously invalidated the statute. Justice O'CONNOR, writing for the Court, stated: "[T]he Government's ability to impose content-based burdens on speech raises the specter that the Government may effectively drive certain ideas or viewpoints from the marketplace. The Son of Sam law is a such a content-based statute. It singles out income derived from expressive activity for a burden the State places on no other income, and it is directed only at works with a specified content. Whether the First Amendment 'speaker' is considered to be Henry Hill, whose income the statute places in escrow because of the story he has told, or Simon & Schuster, which can publish books about crime with the assistance of only those criminals willing to forgo remuneration for at least five years, the statute plainly imposes a financial disincentive only on speech of a particular content."

Because the statute was content-based, Justice O'Connor subjected it to strict scrutiny, and found it not narrowly tailored to the state's "undisputed compelling interest in ensuring that criminals do not profit from their crimes." She found that the State had not shown "any greater interest in compensating victims from the proceeds of such 'storytelling' than from any of the criminal's other assets." She also found the law "significantly overinclusive" as it would potentially sweep in "such works as The Autobiography of Malcolm X, which describes crimes committed by the civil rights leader before he became a public figure; Civil Disobedience, in which Thoreau acknowledges his refusal to pay taxes and recalls his experience in jail; and even the Confessions of Saint Augustine, in which the author laments 'my past foulness and the carnal corruptions of my soul,' one instance of which involved the theft of pears from a neighboring vineyard." Justice KENNEDY, concurring in the judgment, would not have applied strict scrutiny but would have found the law invalid per se: "Here a law is directed to speech alone where the speech in question is not obscene, not defamatory, not words tantamount to an act otherwise criminal, not an impairment of some other constitutional right, not an incitement to lawless action, and not calculated or likely to bring about imminent harm the State has the substantive power to prevent. No further inquiry is necessary to reject the State's argument that the statute should be upheld. [The] New York statute amounts to raw censorship based on content. [That] ought to end the matter.''

Could the defect of the laws struck down in Mosley and Carey be cured by an ordinance barring *all* picketing outside a school or home? Would such a law be less restrictive of speech? How? Could New York pass a new law requiring the escrow of *all* proceeds from crime and apply it to Henry Hill's book proceeds? What is the difference between that law and the law struck down in Simon & Schuster? The above cases indicate that the Court will accord subject matter restrictions strict scrutiny, which is almost always fatal. But as the next case suggests, there might be occasional exceptions.

In BURSON v. FREEMAN, 504 U.S. 191 (1992), the Court upheld against First Amendment challenge a state law prohibiting the solicitation of votes, the display of political posters or signs, and the distribution of political campaign materials within 100 feet of the entrance to a polling place. Justice BLACK-MUN announced the judgment of the Court and wrote for a plurality joined by Chief Justice Rehnquist and Justices White and Kennedy: "This Court has held that the First Amendment's hostility to content-based regulation extends not only to a restriction on a particular viewpoint, but also to a prohibition of public discussion of an entire topic. [As] a facially content-based restriction on political speech in a public forum, [the ban on campaign materials] must be subjected to exacting scrutiny. Tennessee asserts [that] its regulation protect[s] the right of its citizens to vote freely for the candidates of their choice [and] protects the right to vote in an election conducted with integrity and reliability. [These interests] obviously are compelling ones. [To] survive strict scrutiny, however, a State must do more than assert a compelling state interest—it must demonstrate that its law is necessary to serve the asserted interest. [An] examination of the evolution of election reform, both in this country and abroad, demonstrates the necessity of restricted areas in or around polling places. [That history] reveals a persistent battle against two evils: voter intimidation and election fraud. After an unsuccessful experiment with an unofficial ballot system, all 50 States, together with numerous other Western democracies, settled on the same solution: a secret ballot secured in part by a restricted zone around the voting compartments. [It] is the rare case in which we have held that a law survives strict scrutiny. This, however, is such a rare case. [The] State [has] asserted that the exercise of free speech rights conflicts with another fundamental right, the right to cast a ballot in an election free from the taint of intimidation and fraud. A long history, a substantial consensus, and simple common sense show that some restricted zone around polling places is necessary to protect that fundamental right. Given the conflict between these two rights, we hold that requiring solicitors to stand 100 feet from the entrances to polling places does not constitute an unconstitutional compromise.''

Justice KENNEDY wrote a separate concurrence, stating that, despite the preference he expressed in Simon & Schuster for a per se rule against rather than strict scrutiny of content discrimination, "there is a narrow area in which the First Amendment permits freedom of expression to yield to the extent necessary for the accommodation of another constitutional right. That principle can apply here without danger that the general rule permitting no content restriction will be engulfed by the analysis.'' Justice SCALIA concurred in the judgment, finding that the vicinity of the polling place was not a traditional public forum and therefore that viewpoint neutrality was all that was required. (Nonpublic forum cases are discussed at p. 1267 below). Justice STEVENS dissented, joined by Justices O'Connor and Souter: "Tennessee's statutory 'campaign-free zone' raises constitutional concerns of the first magnitude. The statute directly regulates political expression and thus implicates a core concern of the First Amendment. Moreover, it targets only a specific subject matter (campaign speech) and a defined class of speakers (campaign workers) and thus regulates expression based on its content. [Within] the zone, [the law] silences all campaign-related expression, but allows expression on any other subject: religious, artistic, commercial speech, even political debate and solicitation concerning issues or candidates not on the day's ballot. [This] discriminatory feature of the statute severely undercuts the credibility of its purported law-and-order justification. Tennessee's content-based discrimination is particularly problematic because such a regulation will inevitably favor certain groups of candidates. [Candidates] with fewer resources, candidates for lower visibility offices, and 'grassroots' candidates benefit disproportionately from last-minute campaigning near the polling place." Accordingly, the dissenters concluded, the law could not survive the applicable strict scrutiny.

3. *Speaker restrictions.* Would Mosley and Carey have come out any differently if the law had limited the antipicketing exception to "unions" rather than speech concerning a labor dispute? Would the "Son of Sam" law have fared better if it had escrowed all proceeds of "memoirs by criminal defendants"? A speaker's identity can sometimes function as a proxy for viewpoint or subject matter. When it does, the Court typically applies the same strict scrutiny to speaker-based restrictions as it applies to other content restrictions.

Speaker restrictions, however, are not always considered the practical equivalent of content restrictions. For example, the Court has treated as content-neutral, because based on status rather than content, a tax benefit for veterans' groups alone, see Regan v. Taxation with Representation (1983; p. 1319 below); a rule requiring cable operators to carry the programs of over-the-air broadcasters, but not other video programmers, see Turner Broadcasting v. FCC (1994; p. 1369 below); an injunction against protesters outside an abortion clinic, see Madsen v. Women's Health Center (1994; p. 1263 below); a policy permitting charitable but not advocacy organizations to solicit funds from federal office workers, see Cornelius v. NAACP (1985, p. 1279 below); and a grant of access to public teachers' mailboxes for the incumbent union but not its rival, see Perry Ed. Ass'n v. Perry Local Educators' Ass'n (1983, p. 1277 below).

4. *Communicative impact on the audience.* Laws barring speech that is deemed likely to cause a certain response in the audience based on its content are typically viewed as skeptically as direct content restrictions. Recall, for example, Forsyth Co. v. Nationalist Movement (1992; p. 1090 above), which invalidated a scheme calibrating the price of a parade permit to the expected hostility of the audience response. Likewise, Cohen v. California (1971; p. 1081) held that a breach-of-peace law could not be applied in order to prevent audience offense. And R.A.V. v. St. Paul (1992; p. 1115) found content-based a ban on symbols that caused racial anger or alarm. Consider also in this connection the following case:

In BOOS v. BARRY, 485 U.S. 312 (1988), the Court struck down a provision of the District of Columbia Code prohibiting display within 500 feet of a foreign embassy of any sign tending to bring that foreign government into "public odium" or "public disrepute." Writing for the Court, Justice O'CONNOR concluded that, although the provision was not viewpoint-based, it was content-based, because "the government has determined that an entire category of speech—[displays] critical of foreign governments—is not to be permitted." It was accordingly subject to "exacting scrutiny," which it failed because it was not "narrowly tailored" to any interest in "protecting the dignity of foreign diplomatic personnel"; such an interest could be served by the "less restrictive alternative" of prohibiting the intimidation, coercion, threatening, or harassment of foreign officials. Speaking only for herself and Justices Stevens and Scalia, Justice O'Connor distinguished Renton v. Playtime Theatres (1986, p. 1162 above), which had upheld a zoning ordinance as aimed only at the "secondary effects" of adult theaters: "Listeners' reactions to speech are not the type of 'secondary effects' we referred to in Renton. To take an example factually close to Renton, if the ordinance there was justified by the city's desire to prevent the psychological damage it felt was associated with viewing adult movies, then analysis of the measure as a content-based statute would have been appropriate. The hypothetical regulation targets the direct impact of a particular category of speech, not a secondary feature that happens to be associated with that type of speech."

Justice BRENNAN, in a concurring opinion joined by Justice Marshall, agreed that the ordinance was content-based but objected to any implication that content-based regulations could ever be subject to "secondary effects" analysis outside the area of sexually explicit speech: "[S]econdary effects [analysis] offer[s] countless excuses for content-based suppression of political speech. No doubt a plausible argument could be made that the political gatherings of some parties are more likely than others to attract large crowds causing congestion, that picketing for certain causes is more likely than other picketing to cause visual clutter, or that speakers delivering a particular message are more likely than others to attract an unruly audience. Our traditional analysis rejects such a priori categorical judgments based on the content of speech. [Mosley.]" Chief Justice REHNQUIST, joined in his partial dissent by Justices White and Blackmun, would have upheld the regulation. The Court, however, unanimously upheld another challenged provision prohibiting any congregation of three or more persons within 500 feet of a foreign embassy, finding this provision content-neutral and not unduly restrictive.

Might it be argued that all content-based laws are in a sense aimed at the communicative impact of expression, and presumptively invalid for that reason? In that case, laws aimed at audience response are just examples of the general category. See Ely, "Flag Desecration: A Case Study in the Roles of Categorization and Balancing in First Amendment Analysis," 88 Harv. L. Rev. 1482 (1975); Ely, Democracy and Distrust 110–116 (1980); Tribe, American Constitutional Law, chap. 12 (2d ed. 1988) (suggesting that any law "aimed at the communicative impact of an act" receives strict scrutiny while those "aimed at the noncommunicative impact of an act" are invalidated only if they "unduly constrict the flow of information and ideas"). But see Stone, "Content Regulation and the First Amendment," 25 Wm. & Mary L.Rev. 189 (1983) (arguing that the concern with the content basis of laws is broader than a concern with communicative impact).

5. *Content-neutral laws.* Two types of content-neutral laws have come before the Court on free speech challenge. One type of content-neutral law, instead of focusing specifically on expression, is aimed at a wider range of behavior and has only an "incidental" impact on speech. A First Amendment challenge typically arises against such a law when the violator seeks to engage in an instance of expressive or symbolic conduct. This type of challenge is reviewed below in the materials on United States v. O'Brien (1968; p. 1213 below) and Arcara v. Cloud Books (1986; p. 1218 below). A second type of content-neutral law aims at expression, but for reasons unrelated to its content. For example, a law limiting the decibel level of amplified sound or an injunction keeping protestors a certain distance from an abortion clinic entrance aim at

interests in tranquility and orderly movement that have nothing to do with the communicative impact of the speech. "Time, place and manner" regulations of speech in the public forum represent the largest single example of this type of content-neutral law. The Court's treatment of these regulations is explored below at p. 1244.

The contemporary standard of review for content-neutral regulations, as opposed to those that are content-based, is a form of intermediate scrutiny: government can justify content-neutral regulations of speech, or of conduct that might amount to speech, only if it can show that they are closely tailored to serve a "substantial" or "significant" governmental interest. The interest need not be compelling, and the means/ends fit need not be perfect; the state is not obliged to exhaust less restrictive alternatives before it may enact or enforce a content-neutral law. The Court has used some different language in setting forth the standards of review applicable to O'Brien-type restrictions on symbolic conduct on the one hand and time, place and manner regulations of speech on the other. In particular, it has set forth in the time, place and manner context a seemingly additional requirement that a law leave open "ample alternative channels of communication." But the Court has insisted that the O'Brien test "is little if any, different from the standard applied to time, place, and manner restrictions." Clark v. Community for Creative Non–Violence, 468 U.S. 288 (1984). Thus the O'Brien and time, place and manner standards are now used relatively interchangeably. Should they be?

6. *Reasons for differential treatment of content-based and content-neutral laws.* What First Amendment considerations warrant requiring high standards of justification for content-based regulations, yet less intensive scrutiny of content-neutral ones? Consider the following possibilities:

a. *Purpose.* Are content-based laws more likely than content-neutral laws to reflect governmental disapproval of the ideas expressed? Government bias in favor of its own viewpoint? Government paternalism toward the listener? Are these improper motivations for a law? For an argument that such concerns with illicit motivation partially explain special scrutiny of content-based laws, see Stone, "Content Regulation and the First Amendment," 25 Wm. & Mary L.Rev. 189 (1983). If the content basis of a law is merely evidentiary of the true problem of illegitimate motive, should content-neutral laws be invalidated whenever such an impermissible purpose can be smoked out? If so, should there be a unitary standard of scrutiny?

b. *Effect.* Are content-based laws more likely than content-neutral laws to distort the dialogue that would otherwise take place? Stone, supra, argues as much: "Any law that substantially prevents the communication of a particular idea, viewpoint, or item of information violates the first amendment except, perhaps, in the most extraordinary of circumstances. This is so, not because such a law restricts 'a lot' of speech, but because by effectively excising a specific message from public debate, it mutilates 'the thinking process of the community.'" Do all content-based laws cause such distortion? A law that bars political billboards, for example, has no effect on political leaflets. And yet the presumption against content-based laws extends even to such partial regulations. Should the Court give more consideration to the extent of a content-based law? Moreover, what is the status quo from which "distortion" should be measured? See Baker, "Turner Broadcasting: Content–Based Regulation of Persons and Presses," 1994 Sup. Ct. Rev. 57 ("There is no 'natural' version of public dialogue that the First Amendment could prohibit the government from distorting," given government's existing role in shaping the debate); Sunstein, Democracy and the Problem of Free Speech (1994).

If effect on speech is the problem, might not a content-neutral law do more substantial damage than a content-based law to the permissible quantity, and effective exercise, of speech? For example, judicial invalidation of content-based restrictions might create an incentive for flat bans rather than partial prohibitions, despite their greater impact on the total quantity and diversity of speech. See Redish, "The Content Distinction in First Amendment Analysis," 34 Stan.L.Rev. 113 (1981) ("While governmental attempts to regulate the content of expression undoubtedly deserve strict judicial review, it does not logically follow that equally serious threats to first amendment freedoms cannot derive from restrictions imposed to regulate expression in a manner unrelated to content. [Whatever] rationale one adopts for the constitutional protection of speech, the goals behind that rationale are undermined by *any* limitation on expression, content-based or not.").

c. *Political safeguards*. Are content-neutral laws less likely to require judicial intervention because the political process itself will help protect unpopular speakers against such laws? Consider the case of Lady Godiva, who allegedly rode naked on horseback to Coventry Market to protest an excessive tax. A law prohibiting "nude tax protests" is likely to evince hostility to Lady Godiva's ideas. A law prohibiting "public nudity" generally, in contrast, is less likely to have been passed out of similar hostility. Lady Godiva need not fight passage of such a law by herself; nude sunbathers and commercial purveyors of nude entertainment will be her political allies. Might the impact of this type of content-neutral law on nonspeech interests make it less likely that they will be passed at all? Would the same argument apply to a content-neutral time, place or manner regulation of speech?

For further commentary on the content-based/content-neutral distinction, see Williams, "Content Discrimination and the First Amendment," 139 U. Pa. L. Rev. 615 (1991); Stephan, "The First Amendment and Content Discrimination," 68 Va.L.Rev. 203 (1982); Farber, "Content Regulation and the First Amendment: A Revisionist View," 68 Geo.L.J. 727 (1980); Emerson, "First Amendment Doctrine and the Burger Court," 68 Calif.L.Rev. 422 (1980); Stone, "Restrictions of Speech Because of Its Content: the Peculiar Case of Subject Matter Restrictions," 46 U.Chi. L. Rev. 81 (1976); Karst, "Equality as a Central Principle in the First Amendment," 43 U.Chi.L.Rev. 20 (1975).

7. *Total medium bans*. Is a government ban on resort to a particular medium or format of expression more like a content-based or a content-neutral law? Such laws involve discrimination on neither the basis of viewpoint nor subject matter, yet do single out for special treatment activities of First Amendment concern. Consider the following pairs of regulations: A prohibition on all bookstores in a certain area; and a prohibition on all commercial establishments in a certain area, implicitly including bookstores. A prohibition on parades, designed to prevent obstruction of traffic; and a prohibition on obstructing traffic, which is applied evenhandedly to trucks that take excessively long to make a delivery, to people who park illegally in intersections, and to organizers of parades. A prohibition on soundtrucks designed to prevent excess noise; and a prohibition on making excess noise, applied to motorcycles, jackhammers, and soundtrucks. A prohibition on billboards; and a prohibition on all structures higher than a certain height and thus implicitly prohibiting billboards along with other structures. Is the first example in each of these pairs more troublesome than the second? Why? Does it have something to do with testing the legitimacy and sincerity of the motives of the regulators?

Total medium bans have posed difficult questions for the Court that are explored in a number of cases below. The Court struck down various total medium bans in cases of the 1930s and 1940s, focusing on their negative effects on the distribution of speech. See, e.g., the invalidation of a total ban on handbills in Schneider v. State (1939; p. 1239 below); and the invalidation of a ban on door-to-door canvassing in Martin v. Struthers (1943; p. 1240 below). These cases in effect treated medium bans as just as suspect under the First Amendment as discrimination against particular ideas. Why? Because a ban on a particular format might have a major effect on the quantity of communication? Because restriction of an entire format might discriminate in effect against those groups who are financially unable to resort to more conventional (and more expensive) means of communication, such as newspapers and the broadcasting media? Modern cases have tended to emphasize the theme of discrimination rather distribution, with the result that a number of total medium bans have been upheld under less intense scrutiny than content-based distinctions receive. See, e.g., the ban on posting signs on public property sustained in City Council v. Taxpayers for Vincent (1984; p. 1249 below); and the ban on camping in a public park sustained against demonstrators seeking to dramatize the plight of the homeless in Clark v. Community for Creative Non–Violence (1984; p. 1254 below). Is it tenable to see discrimination as the First Amendment's *only* concern? The Court made clear that it will still invalidate some total medium bans on the ground that they suppress too much speech, without regard to whether they do so selectively, in City of Ladue v. Gilleo (1994; p. 1243 below), which involved a ban on residential signs.

B.   CONTENT-NEUTRAL LAWS AND SYMBOLIC CONDUCT

Introduction. What if critics of public policies seek to express their views through symbolic *behavior* rather than words: e.g., by burning a draft card or by mutilating or burning the flag? Can such critics claim as much protection as would be afforded if the criticism had been expressed through the more traditional modes—through the spoken or printed word? As is already clear from R.A.V. v. St. Paul (1992; p. 1115 above), the cross-burning case, the Court recognizes symbolic conduct as constitutionally protected "speech." Indeed, as early as 1931, in Stromberg v. California, 283 U.S. 359, the Court held unconstitutional a state prohibition on displaying a red flag "as a sign, symbol or emblem of opposition to organized government," stating that the law curtailed "the opportunity for free political discussion." Barnettc v. West Va. Bd. of Ed. (1943; p. 1362 below) held that public school children could not be compelled to salute the flag in violation of their religious scruples. And the prevailing opinion in Brown v. Louisiana (1966; p. 1268 below), protecting a public library sit-in, emphasized that First Amendment rights "are not confined to verbal expression" and "embrace appropriate types of action." See also Tinker v. Des Moines School District (1969; p. 1293 below) (black armbands as symbolic war protest); Hurley v. Irish–American Gay, Lesbian and Bisexual Group of Boston, (1995; p. 1371 below) (parade as "a form of expression, not just motion").

In cases such as Stromberg and R.A.V., the challenged law was aimed expressly at symbolic conduct for reason of its symbolism and communicative impact. May a critic claim First Amendment immunity from a governmental restraint that is not so aimed but that happens to hit his "speech"? The following cases raise the question whether an assertedly content-neutral law that has the effect of prohibiting symbolic conduct should be treated as content-neutral in fact, and even if so, whether a person engaged in symbolic conduct in violation of that law should nonetheless be exempted from it.

United States v. O'Brien

391 U.S. 367, 88 S.Ct. 1673, 20 L.Ed.2d 672 (1968).

Chief Justice WARREN delivered the opinion of the Court.

On the morning of March 31, 1966, David Paul O'Brien and three companions burned their Selective Service registration certificates on the steps of the South Boston Courthouse. A sizable crowd, including several [FBI agents], witnessed the event. Immediately after the burning, [O'Brien] stated [that] he had burned his registration certificate because of his beliefs, knowing that he was violating federal law. [For this act, O'Brien was convicted. He stated] to the jury that he burned the certificate publicly to influence others to adopt his antiwar beliefs, as he put it, "so that other people would reevaluate their positions with Selective Service, with the armed forces, and reevaluate their place in the culture of today, to hopefully consider my position."

The indictment upon which he was tried charged that he "willfully and knowingly did mutilate, destroy, and change by burning [his] Registration Certificate" in violation of [§ 462(b)(3) of the Universal Military Training and Service Act (UMTSA) of 1948], amended by Congress in 1965 (adding the words italicized below), so that at the time O'Brien burned his certificate an offense was committed by any person "who forges, alters, *knowingly destroys, knowingly mutilates,* or in any manner changes any such certificate." (Italics supplied.) [The Court of Appeals] held the 1965 Amendment unconstitutional as a law abridging freedom of speech. At the time the Amendment was enacted, a regulation of the Selective Service System required registrants to keep their registration certificates in their "personal possession at all times." Wilful violations of regulations promulgated pursuant to [UMTSA] were made criminal by statute. The Court of Appeals, therefore, was of the opinion that conduct punishable under the 1965 Amendment was already punishable under the nonpossession regulation, and consequently that the Amendment served no valid purpose; further, that in light of the prior regulation, the Amendment must have been "directed at public as distinguished from private destruction." On this basis, the court concluded that the 1965 Amendment ran afoul of the First Amendment by singling out persons engaged in protests for special treatment. [We] hold that the 1965 Amendment is constitutional both as enacted and [as applied].

When a male reaches the age of 18, he is required by the [Act] to register with a local draft board. He is assigned a Selective Service number, and within five days he is issued a registration certificate. Subsequently, [he] is assigned a classification denoting his eligibility for induction. [Both] the registration and classification certificates bear notices that the registrant must notify his local board [of] every change in address, physical condition, [etc.]. [The] 1965 Amendment plainly does not abridge free speech on its face. [On its face, it] deals with conduct having no connection with speech. [It] does not distinguish between public and private destruction,[1] and it does not punish only destruc-

---

1. Compare the comment in the opinion of the Court of Appeals, 376 F.2d at 541: "We would be closing our eyes [if] we did not see on the face of the amendment that it was

tion engaged in for the purpose of expressing views. [Cf. Stromberg.] A law prohibiting destruction of Selective Service certificates no more abridges free speech on its face than a motor vehicle law prohibiting the destruction of drivers' licenses, or a tax law prohibiting the destruction of books and records.

[O'Brien nonetheless] first argues that the 1965 Amendment is unconstitutional as applied to him because his act of burning his registration certificate was protected "symbolic speech" within the First Amendment. His argument is that the freedom of expression which the First Amendment guarantees includes all modes of "communication of ideas by conduct," and that his conduct is within this definition because he did it in "demonstration against the war and against the draft." We cannot accept the view that an apparently limitless variety of conduct can be labeled "speech" whenever the person engaging in the conduct intends thereby to express an idea. However, even on the assumption that the alleged communicative element in O'Brien's conduct is sufficient to bring into play the First Amendment, it does not necessarily follow that the destruction of a registration certificate is constitutionally protected activity. This Court has held that when "speech" and "non-speech" elements are combined in the same course of conduct, a sufficiently important governmental interest in regulating the nonspeech element can justify incidental limitations on First Amendment freedoms. To characterize the quality of the governmental interest which must appear, the Court has employed a variety of descriptive terms: compelling; substantial; subordinating; paramount; cogent; strong. *[We] think it clear that a government regulation is sufficiently justified if it is within the constitutional power of the Government; if it furthers an important or substantial governmental interest; if the governmental interest is unrelated to the suppression of free expression; and if the incidental restriction on alleged First Amendment freedoms is no greater than is essential to the furtherance of that interest* [emphasis added]. We find that the 1965 Amendment [meets] all of these requirements, and consequently that O'Brien can be constitutionally convicted for violating it. [Pursuant to its power] to classify and conscript manpower for military service, [Congress] may establish a system of registration [and] may require such individuals within reason to cooperate in the registration system. The issuance of certificates indicating the registration and eligibility classification of individuals is a legitimate and substantial administrative aid in the functioning of this system. And legislation to insure the continuing availability of issued certificates serves a legitimate and substantial purpose in the system's administration.

O'Brien's argument to the contrary is necessarily premised upon his unrealistic characterization of Selective Service certificates. He essentially adopts the position that such certificates are so many pieces of paper designed to notify registrants of their registration or classification, to be retained or tossed in the wastebasket according to the convenience or taste of the registrant. [However, the registration and classification certificates serve] purposes in addition to initial notification. Many of these purposes would be defeated by the certificates' destruction or mutilation. Among these are [proving that the individual has registered for the draft, facilitating communication between registrants and local boards, demonstrating availability for induction in times of national crisis, and reminding registrants to notify local boards of changes in status]. The many functions performed by Selective Service certificates estab-

precisely directed at public as distinguished from private destruction. [In] singling out persons engaging in protest for special treat- ment the amendment strikes at the very core of what the First Amendment protects."

lish beyond doubt that Congress has a legitimate and substantial interest in preventing their wanton and unrestrained destruction and assuring their continuing availability by punishing people who knowingly and wilfully destroy or mutilate them. And we are unpersuaded that the pre-existence of the nonpossession regulations in any way negates this interest. In the absence of a question as to multiple punishment, it has never been suggested that there is anything improper in Congress' providing alternative statutory avenues of prosecution to assure the effective protection of one and the same [interest].

Equally important, a comparison of the regulations with the 1965 Amendment indicates that they protect overlapping but not identical governmental interests, and that they reach somewhat different classes of wrongdoers. The gravamen of the offense defined by the statute is the deliberate rendering of certificates unavailable for the various purposes which they may serve. Whether registrants keep their certificates in their personal possession at all times, as required by the regulations, is of no particular concern under the 1965 Amendment, as long as they do not mutilate or destroy the certificates so as to render them unavailable. [And] the 1965 Amendment [is] concerned with abuses involving *any* issued Selective Service certificates, not only with the registrant's own certificates. [We] think it apparent that the continuing availability to each registrant of his Selective Service certificates substantially furthers the smooth and proper functioning of the system that Congress has established to raise [armies].

It is equally clear that the 1965 Amendment specifically protects this substantial governmental interest. We perceive no alternative means that would more precisely and narrowly assure the continuing availability of issued Selective Service certificates than a law which prohibits their wilful mutilation or destruction. [Moreover,] both the governmental interest and the operation of the 1965 Amendment are limited to the noncommunicative aspect of O'Brien's conduct. The governmental interest and the scope of the 1965 Amendment are limited to preventing harm to the smooth and efficient functioning of the Selective Service System. When O'Brien deliberately rendered unavailable his registration certificate, he wilfully frustrated this governmental interest. For this noncommunicative impact of his conduct, and for nothing else, he was convicted. The case [is] therefore unlike one where the alleged governmental interest in regulating conduct arises in some measure because the communication allegedly integral to the conduct is itself thought to be harmful. In Stromberg [the 1931 "red flag" case], for example, the statute was aimed at suppressing communication [and therefore] could not be sustained as a regulation of noncommunicative conduct. [We] find that because of the Government's substantial interest in assuring the continuing availability of issued Selective Service certificates, because amended § 462(b) is an appropriately narrow means of protecting this interest and condemns only the independent noncommunicative impact of conduct within its reach, and because the noncommunicative impact of O'Brien's act of burning his registration certificate frustrated the Government's interest, a sufficient governmental interest has been shown to justify O'Brien's conviction.

O'Brien finally argues that the 1965 Amendment is unconstitutional as enacted because what he calls the "purpose" of Congress was "to suppress freedom of speech." We reject this argument because under settled principles the purpose of Congress, as O'Brien uses that term, is not a basis for declaring this legislation unconstitutional. It is a familiar principle of constitutional law that this Court will not strike down an otherwise constitutional statute on the basis of an alleged illicit legislative motive. [Inquiries] into congressional motives or purposes are a hazardous matter. When the issue is simply the interpretation of legislation, the Court will look to statements by legislators for guidance as to the purpose of the legislature, because the benefit to sound decision-making in this circumstance is thought sufficient to risk the possibility of misreading Congress' purpose. It is entirely a different matter when we are asked to void a statute that is, under well-settled criteria, constitutional on its face, on the basis of what fewer than a handful of Congressmen said about it. What motivates one legislator to make a speech about a statute is not necessarily what motivates scores of others to enact it, and the stakes are sufficiently high for us to eschew guesswork. We decline to void essentially on the ground that it is unwise legislation which Congress has the undoubted power to enact and which could be reenacted in its exact form if the same or another legislator made a "wiser" speech about it.

Reversed.[2]

―――――

THE SIGNIFICANCE OF O'BRIEN

1. *Expression and action.* Chief Justice Warren assumed arguendo that O'Brien's act was symbolic conduct without deciding as much. In so doing, he cautioned that conduct does not become speech "whenever the person engaging in the conduct intends thereby to express an idea." Was he too "cavalier" toward O'Brien's symbolic speech claim? See Alfange, "Free Speech and Symbolic Conduct: The Draft–Card Burning Case," 1968 Sup.Ct.Rev. 1. Warren feared that an "apparently limitless variety of conduct" might be labeled "speech." Is that fear of such a "slippery slope" justified, or are there principled ways of distinguishing action from speech? See Emerson, The System of Freedom of Expression (1970) (arguing that "[t]o some extent expression and action are always mingled; [the] guiding principle must be to determine which element is predominant. [It] seems quite clear that the predominant element in [the burning of a draft card] is expression (opposition to the draft) rather than action (destruction of a piece of cardboard"). But see Ely, "Flag Desecration: A Case Study in the Roles of Categorization and Balancing in First Amendment Analysis," 88 Harv. L. Rev. 1482 (1975) ("[B]urning a draft card to express opposition to the draft is an undifferentiated whole, 100% action and 100% expression. [Attempts] to determine which element 'predominates' will therefore inevitably degenerate into question-begging judgments about whether the activity should be protected."); Henkin, "Foreword: On Drawing Lines," 82 Harv.L.Rev. 63 (1968) ("A constitutional distinction between speech and conduct is specious. [The] meaningful constitutional distinction is not between speech and conduct, but between conduct that speaks, communicates, and other kinds of conduct."). See also Velvel, "Freedom of Speech and the Draft Card Burning Cases," 16 U.Kan.L.Rev. 149 (1968)

2. A concurring notation by Justice HARLAN stated: "I wish to make explicit my understanding that [the Court's criteria do] not foreclose consideration of First Amendment claims in those rare instances when an 'incidental' restriction upon expression, imposed by a regulation which furthers an 'important or substantial' governmental interest and satisfies the Court's other criteria, in practice has the effect of entirely preventing a 'speaker' from reaching a significant audience with whom he could not otherwise lawfully communicate. This is not such a case, since O'Brien manifestly could have conveyed his message in many ways other than by burning his draft card." Justice DOUGLAS dissented, urging reargument on "the question of the constitutionality of a peacetime draft," but stated the next year in Brandenburg v. Ohio, p. 1071 above, that O'Brien's conviction was inconsistent with the First Amendment.

(arguing that draft-card burning was an especially effective means of protesting the war because it attracted media attention); Nimmer, "The Meaning of Symbolic Speech Under the First Amendment," 21 UCLA L.Rev. 29 (1973) (suggesting that symbolic conduct requires an audience—i.e., both a "communicator and a communicatee") ; Baker, "Scope of the First Amendment Freedom of Speech," 25 UCLA L.Rev. 964 (1978).

2. *Legislative motivation.* Should the Court have gone the other way in O'Brien because "the 'purpose' of Congress was 'to suppress freedom of speech' "? See Alfange, supra (suggesting that the legislative history of the 1965 amendment shows with "indisputable clarity" that "the intent of [members of Congress] was purely and simply to put a stop to this particular form of antiwar protest, which they deemed extraordinarily contemptible and vicious— even treasonous—at a time when American troops were engaged in combat"). Chief Justice Warren rejected summarily any inquiry into congressional motive, and noted that the most provocative statements by members of Congress were offset by the more authoritative committee reports: while the reports "make clear a concern with the 'defiant' destruction [of draft cards] and with 'open' encouragement to others to destroy their cards, both reports also indicate that this concern stems from an apprehension that unrestrained destruction of cards would disrupt the smooth functioning of the Selective Service System."

Clearly, the Court frequently does inquire into the motivation of executive and administrative decisions. Recall, e.g., the Mt. Healthy case, discussed in connection with Arlington Heights, p. 759 above, and the Yick Wo case, p. 750 above. Yet, as in O'Brien, the Court is sometimes reluctant to inquire into *legislative* motivation. Among the reasons for that inhibition are the difficulty of ascertaining "real" motivation in a multi-member body, the inappropriateness of questioning the integrity of a coordinate branch, and the futility of striking down a law that could be reenacted after an assertion of legitimate motives. But doesn't the distinction between content-based and content-neutral laws require some inquiry into legislative ends? Must that inquiry be into objective purpose rather than subjective motive? On the problem of motivation inquiries, see generally Ely, "Legislative and Administrative Motivation in Constitutional Law," 79 Yale L.J. 1205 (1970); Brest, "Palmer v. Thompson: An Approach to the Problem of Unconstitutional Legislative Motive," 1971 Sup.Ct.Rev. 95; and Symposium, "Legislative Motivation," 15 San Diego L.Rev. 925 (1978).

3. *The O'Brien test and the content-based/content-neutral distinction.* O'Brien set forth a test that has since become canonical in the review of content-neutral laws: they must "further an important or substantial governmental interest" and involve an "incidental restriction on alleged First Amendment freedoms [that] is no greater than is essential to the furtherance of that interest." The latter part of the test has been modified in later cases to make clear that, while a content-neutral law must be closely tailored to its ends, the government need *not* employ the least restrictive alternative. See Ward v. Rock Against Racism (1989; p. 1260 below). O'Brien also set forth an influential definition for distinguishing content-based from content-neutral laws: for a law to be treated as content-neutral, the governmental interest behind the law must be "unrelated to the suppression of free expression." Thus the third of the four factors listed in the O'Brien test italicized above actually performs a critical switching function at the threshold: in situations where the state interest *is* "related to the suppression of free expression," strict scrutiny is required *unless* the speech is in an unprotected category; but where the state interest is *unrelated* to the suppression of free expression, balancing (albeit reasonably strong balancing) is the appropriate response. See Ely, "Flag

Desecration: A Case Study in the Roles of Categorization and Balancing in First Amendment Analysis," 88 Harv. L. Rev. 1482 (1975).

How can a court tell whether a law is or is not "related to the suppression of free expression"? As Ely explains, "restrictions on free expression are seldom defended on the ground that the state simply didn't like what the defendant was saying: reference will generally be made to some danger beyond the message, such as the danger of riot, unlawful action, or violent overthrow of the government. The constitutional reference must therefore be not to the ultimate interest to which the state points, for that will always be unrelated to expression, but rather to the causal connection the state asserts. If, for example, the state asserts an interest in discouraging riots, the Court should ask why that interest is implicated in the case at bar. If the answer is, as in such cases it will likely have to be, that the danger of riot was created by what the defendant was saying, the state's interest is not unrelated to the suppression of free expression, and the inhibition should be upheld only in the event the expression falls within one of the few unprotected categories." Ely, supra.

How speech-protective was the application of the O'Brien test in O'Brien itself? Ely suggests that the supposedly "substantial" governmental interests identified by the Court were in fact merely "plausible but little more." And the "no greater restriction than essential" criterion was weakly applied: the Court essentially deferred to the government without serious inquiry whether alternative means would serve the government's interest nearly as efficiently at much less cost to speech. See Ely, supra.

4. *"Incidental" restrictions on expression.* In O'Brien, the Court formulated its less-than-strict scrutiny approach to deal with what it called "incidental limitations on First Amendment freedoms." Was the effect of the law on O'Brien's speech merely "incidental"? Or did the law forbid precisely the action O'Brien engaged in as speech? Should the central question be what was aimed at, as O'Brien suggests, or rather what was hit? See generally Stone, "Content–Neutral Restrictions," 54 U.Chi.L.Rev. 46 (1987).

Should all "incidental" restrictions on speech receive the heightened First Amendment scrutiny required by the O'Brien test? Do some laws have an impact on speech only as a mere byproduct or side effect? A "no parking" zone might preclude one from using a car covered with bumper stickers as a mobile billboard parked before a desired audience. A "no speeding" law might prevent a newscaster from reaching the studio in time to announce the news. Should such laws be subject to any First Amendment review when applied in such circumstances, or need they only satisfy the requirements of minimum rationality? Consider ARCARA v. CLOUD BOOKS, INC., 478 U.S. 697 (1986), which involved a New York law defining places of prostitution, assignation, and lewdness as public health nuisances and providing for the closure of any building found to be such a nuisance. In Arcara, an investigation of an "adult" bookstore found that sexual acts and solicitations to perform sexual acts were occurring on the premises. As a result, the store was ordered closed as a nuisance. The bookstore claimed that this had the effect of preventing the sale of books and other materials that were presumptively protected by the First Amendment. The highest state court, applying the O'Brien test, found that the closure order incidentally burdened speech and that it was unnecessarily broad to achieve its purpose, since an injunction against the illegal activity could achieve the same effect.

The Court reversed that judgment, upholding the closure remedy and holding that it did not warrant even the less stringent scrutiny of the O'Brien standard. Chief Justice BURGER's majority opinion explained that, "unlike the symbolic draft card burning in O'Brien, the sexual activity carried on [here] manifests absolutely no element of protected expression." He continued: "Nor does the distinction drawn by the [law] inevitably single out bookstores or others engaged in First Amendment protected activities for the imposition of its burden. [If] the city imposed closure penalties for demonstrated Fire Code violations or health hazards from inadequate sewage treatment, the First Amendment would not aid the owner of premises who had knowingly allowed such violations to persist." Nor was Chief Justice Burger impressed by the argument that the closure burdened bookselling activities: "The severity of this burden is dubious at best, and is mitigated by the fact that respondents remain free to sell the same materials at another location. In any event, this argument proves too much, since every civil and criminal remedy imposes some conceivable burden on First Amendment protected activities." He added: "[W]e have not traditionally subjected every criminal or civil sanction [to] 'least restrictive means' scrutiny simply because each particular remedy will have some effect [on] First Amendment activities. [Rather,] we have subjected such restrictions to scrutiny only where it was conduct with a significant expressive element that drew the legal remedy in the first place, as in O'Brien, or where a statute based on a nonexpressive activity has the inevitable effect of singling out those engaged in expressive activity, as in Minneapolis Star [1983; p. 1440 below.] This case involves neither situation, and we conclude the First Amendment is not implicated by the enforcement of the public health regulation of general application against the physical premises in which respondents happen to sell books." Justice O'CONNOR's concurrence, joined by Justice Stevens, emphasized that there had been no evidence that the use of a generally applicable regulatory statute was merely a "pretext" for closing down a bookstore.

Justice BLACKMUN, joined by Justices Brennan and Marshall, dissented, arguing: "Until today, this Court has never suggested that a State may suppress speech as much as it likes, without justification, so long as it does so through generally applicable regulations that have 'nothing to do with any expressive conduct.' [When] a State directly and substantially impairs First Amendment activities, such as by shutting down a bookstore, I believe that the state must show, at a minimum, that it has chosen the least restrictive means of pursuing its legitimate objectives. [Petitioner] has not demonstrated that a less restrictive remedy would be inadequate to abate the nuisance. [Because the law] is not narrowly tailored to further the asserted governmental interest, it is unconstitutional as applied."

Was the majority's refusal to apply any First Amendment scrutiny in Arcara justifiable under O'Brien or under general First Amendment principles? Would the opposite result have extended the First Amendment to virtually every law? See Alexander, "Trouble on Track Two: Incidental Regulations of Speech and Free Speech Theory," 44 Hastings L.J. 921 (1993) (arguing that virtually every law, even a marginal tax rate, may be said to have some "incidental" effect on speech, and thus questioning First Amendment review of content-neutral regulation); see also Dorf, "Incidental Burdens on Fundamental Rights," 109 Harv. L. Rev. 1175 (1996).

―――――

FLAG DESECRATION

May government bar the burning, mutilation, or physical misuse of the United States flag? The Court considered a series of challenges to efforts to curb such symbolic protests beginning in 1969, but did not squarely reach the central constitutional issue until the flag-burning cases of 1989 and 1990. Is flag desecration "speech" entitled to strong First Amendment protection? What state interests underlie the efforts to protect the flag? Can any of them be described as content-neutral? If not, can any of them be described as compelling?

In STREET v. NEW YORK, 394 U.S. 576 (1969), the Court, in a 5–4 decision, overturned a conviction under a New York law that made it a crime "publicly [to] mutilate, deface, defile, or defy, trample upon, or cast contempt upon either by words or act [any flag of the United States]." Street had burned a flag on a street corner after hearing that civil rights leader James Meredith had been shot by a sniper in Mississippi. He had said to the crowd that gathered, "We don't need no damn flag," and when a police officer stopped and confronted him, he had replied: "Yes, that is my flag; I burned it. If they let that happen to Meredith we don't need an American flag." The Court did not reach the question whether it was constitutional to ban flag burning as a means of political protest, finding instead that, on the record below, the law had been unconstitutionally applied to permit punishment of Street "merely for speaking defiant or contemptuous words about the American flag." Justice HARLAN's majority opinion noted that Street's words had not constituted incitement or fighting words, reiterated that "public expression of ideas may not be prohibited merely because the ideas are themselves offensive to some of their hearers," and held that the conviction could not be justified "on the theory that by making [his] remarks about the flag appellant failed to show the respect for our national symbol which may properly be demanded of every citizen," for the flag-salute cases (see Barnette, p. 1362 below) had established "the freedom to express publicly one's opinions about our flag, including those opinions which are defiant or contemptuous." Chief Justice WARREN and Justices BLACK, WHITE and FORTAS dissented, each arguing that Street had been punished for his act, not his words, and that the state had constitutional authority to protect the flag from acts of desecration.

In SMITH v. GOGUEN, 415 U.S. 566 (1974), the Court, in a 6-to-3 decision, reversed a appellee's conviction, under a Massachusetts law making it a a crime to "publicly mutilate, trample upon, deface or treat contemptuously the flag of the United States," for wearing a small United States flag sewn to the seat of his trousers. Justice POWELL's majority opinion found it unnecessary to reach a variety of First Amendment claims and rested instead on "the due process doctrine of vagueness." Though appellee's behavior seemed to reflect "immaturity" and "silly conduct," Justice Powell observed that "casual treatment of the flag in many contexts has become a widespread contemporary phenomenon." Here, the statutory language "fails to draw reasonably clear lines between the kinds of nonceremonial treatment (of the flag) that are criminal and those that are not." Fair notice standards were not met, given "today's tendencies to treat the flag unceremoniously." Justice Powell emphasized: "Statutory language of such standardless sweep allows policemen, prosecutors, and juries to pursue their personal predilections." Justice WHITE disagreed with the majority's reasoning, though not its result. He defended the constitutionality of flag mutilation laws, but objected to the conviction for being contemptuous of the flag: "To convict on this basis is not to protect the physical integrity or to protect against acts interfering with the proper use of the flag, but to punish for communicating ideas about the flag unacceptable to the controlling majority." Justice REHNQUIST, joined by Chief Justice Burger, dissented at length, describing the flag as a "unique physical object" and emphasizing the strong state interest in protecting "the physical integrity of a unique national symbol." There was also a dissent by Justice Blackmun, joined by Chief Justice Burger.

And in SPENCE v. WASHINGTON, 418 U.S. 405 (1974), the Court, per curiam, overturned a conviction under a Washington statute prohibiting "improper use" of the flag, including the display of any flag to which a "word, figure, mark, picture, design, drawing or advertisement" had been attached. Spence had displayed a United States flag, which he owned, outside the window of his apartment with a large peace symbol made of removable tape affixed to both sides. He testified that he had done so as a protest against the invasion of Cambodia and the killings at Kent State University. The Court found Spence's "pointed expression of anguish [about] the then current domestic and foreign affairs of his government" to be speech within the meaning of the First Amendment: "An intent to convey a particularized message was present, and in the surrounding circumstances the likelihood was great that the message would be understood by those who viewed it." The Court was willing to assume arguendo that the state's asserted interest in "preserving the national flag as an unalloyed symbol of our country" was valid even though it noted that such an interest was "directly related to expression." But it nonetheless found the statute "unconstitutional as applied to appellant's activity. There was no risk that appellant's acts would mislead viewers into assuming that the Government endorsed his viewpoint. To the contrary, he was plainly and peacefully protesting the fact that it did not." Justice REHNQUIST, joined by Chief Justice Burger and Justice White, dissented: "The true nature of the State's interest in this case is not only one of preserving 'the physical integrity of the flag,' but also one of preserving the flag as 'an important symbol of nationhood and unity.' [It] is the character, not the cloth, of the flag which the State seeks to protect. [The statute] withdraws a unique national symbol from the roster of materials that may be used as a background for communications. [I] do not believe the Constitution prohibits Washington from making that decision."

Does Spence helpfully delineate the contours of protected symbolic conduct? Note the Court's emphasis on two factors: the speaker's intent; and the context indicating that the message would be understood by the audience. Is that a useful approach? Is it adequate? Does it risk the slippery slope Chief Justice Warren feared in O'Brien? What about conduct more ambiguous than that in Spence? See Note, "First Amendment Protection of Ambiguous Conduct," 84 Colum.L.Rev. 467 (1984). For criticism of the Spence standard, see Post, "Recuperating First Amendment Doctrine," 47 Stan. L. Rev. 1249 (1995).

Is there any governmental interest in the flag that is "unrelated to the suppression of free expression" within the meaning of O'Brien? See Ely, "Flag Desecration: A Case Study in the Roles of Categorization and Balancing in First Amendment Analysis," 88 Harv. L. Rev. 1482 (1975) (suggesting that flag misuse laws "do not single out certain messages for proscription," but *do* single out one set of messages, namely the set of messages conveyed by the American flag, for protection," and that "[o]rthodoxy of thought can be fostered not simply by placing unusual restrictions on 'deviant' expression but also by granting unusual protection to expression that is officially acceptable"). Consider the flag-burning cases of 1989 and 1990, which follow.

Texas v. Johnson

491 U.S. 397, 109 S.Ct. 2533, 105 L.Ed.2d 342 (1989).

Justice BRENNAN delivered the opinion of the Court.

After publicly burning an American flag as a means of political protest, Gregory Lee Johnson was convicted of desecrating a flag in violation of Texas law. This case presents the question whether his conviction is consistent with the First Amendment. We hold that it is not.

I. While the Republican National Convention was taking place in Dallas in 1984, [Johnson] participated in a political demonstration dubbed the "Republican War Chest Tour." [The] purpose of this event was to protest the policies of the Reagan administration and of certain Dallas-based corporations. The demonstrators marched through the Dallas streets, chanting political slogans and stopping at several corporate locations to stage "die-ins" intended to dramatize the consequences of nuclear war. On several occasions they spray-painted the walls of buildings and overturned potted plants, but Johnson himself took no part in such activities. He did, however, accept an American flag handed to him by a fellow protestor who had taken it from a flag pole outside one of the targeted buildings. The demonstration ended in front of Dallas City Hall, where Johnson unfurled the American flag, doused it with kerosene, and set it on fire. While the flag burned, the protestors chanted, "America, the red, white, and blue, we spit on you." After the demonstrators dispersed, a witness to the flag-burning collected the flag's remains and buried them in his backyard. No one was physically injured or threatened with injury, though several witnesses testified that they had been seriously offended by the flag-burning. Of the approximately 100 demonstrators, Johnson alone was charged with a crime. The only criminal offense with which he was charged was the desecration of a venerated object.[1] [He] was convicted, sentenced to one year in prison, and fined $2,000. [The] Texas Court of Criminal Appeals [overturned the conviction. We] affirm.

II. Johnson was convicted of flag desecration for burning the flag rather than for uttering insulting words. This fact somewhat complicates our consideration of his conviction under the First Amendment. We must first determine whether Johnson's burning of the flag constituted expressive conduct, permitting him to invoke the [First Amendment]. [Spence.] If his conduct was expressive, we next decide whether the State's regulation is related to the suppression of free expression. [O'Brien.] If the State's regulation is not related to expression, then the less stringent standard we announced in [O'Brien] for regulations of noncommunicative conduct controls. If it is, then we are outside of O'Brien's test, and we must ask whether this interest justifies Johnson's conviction under a more demanding standard.[2] [Spence.] A third possibility is that the State's asserted interest is simply not implicated on these facts, and in that event the interest drops out of the picture.

The First Amendment literally forbids the abridgement only of "speech," but we have long recognized that its protection does not end at the spoken or written word. [In] deciding whether particular conduct possesses sufficient

1. Tex. Penal Code Ann. section 42.09 (1989) [provided]: "Section 42.09. Desecration of Venerated Object. (a) A person commits an offense if he intentionally or knowingly desecrates: (1) a public monument; (2) a place of worship or burial; or (3) a state or national flag. (b) For purposes of this section, 'desecrate' means deface, damage, or otherwise physically mistreat in a way that the actor knows will seriously offend one or more persons likely to observe or discover his action." [Footnote by Justice Brennan.]

2. Although Johnson has raised a facial challenge to [the law], we choose to resolve this case on the basis of his ["as applied" claim]. Because the prosecution of a person who had not engaged in expressive conduct would pose a different case, and because we are capable of disposing of this case on narrower grounds, we address only Johnson's claim that [the law] as applied to political expression like his violates the First Amendment. [Footnote by Justice Brennan.]

communicative elements to bring the First Amendment into play, we have asked whether "[a]n intent to convey a particularized message was present, and (whether) the likelihood was great that the message would be understood by those who viewed it." [Spence.] [Especially] pertinent to this case are our decisions recognizing the communicative nature of conduct relating to flags. Attaching a peace sign to the flag, Spence; saluting the flag [Barnette (1943); p. 1362 below]; and displaying a red flag, Stromberg, we have held, all may find shelter under the First Amendment. That we have had little difficulty identifying an expressive element in conduct relating to flags should not be surprising. The very purpose of a national flag is to serve as a symbol of our country. [Pregnant] with expressive content, the flag as readily signifies this Nation as does the combination of letters found in "America." [Texas] conceded for purposes of its oral argument in this case that Johnson's conduct was expressive conduct. [Johnson] burned an American flag as part—indeed, as the culmination—of a political demonstration that coincided with the convening of the Republican Party and its renomination of Ronald Reagan for President. The expressive, overtly political nature of this conduct was both intentional and overwhelmingly apparent [and thus implicates] the First Amendment.

III.   The Government generally has a freer hand in restricting expressive conduct than it has in restricting the written or spoken word. It may not, however, proscribe particular conduct because it has expressive elements. [It] is [not] simply the verbal or nonverbal nature of the expression, but the governmental interest at stake, that helps to determine whether a restriction on that expression is valid. Thus, [we] have limited the applicability of O'Brien's relatively lenient standard to those cases in which "the governmental interest is unrelated to the suppression of free expression." [In] order to decide whether O'Brien's test applies here, therefore, we must decide whether Texas has asserted an interest in support of Johnson's conviction that is unrelated to the suppression of expression. If we find that an interest asserted by the State is simply not implicated on the facts before us, we need not ask whether O'Brien's test applies. The State offers two separate interests to justify this conviction: preventing breaches of the peace, and preserving the flag as a symbol of nationhood and national unity. We hold that the first interest is not implicated on this record and that the second is related to the suppression of expression.

A.   Texas claims that its interest in preventing breaches of the peace justifies Johnson's conviction for flag desecration. However, no disturbance of the peace actually occurred or threatened to occur because of Johnson's burning of the flag. [The] only evidence offered [at trial] to show the reaction to Johnson's actions was the testimony of several persons who had been seriously offended by the flag-burning. The State's position, therefore, amounts to a claim that an audience that takes serious offense at particular expression is necessarily likely to disturb the peace and that the expression may be prohibited on this basis. Our precedents do not countenance such a presumption. On the contrary, they recognize that a principal "function of free speech under our system of government is to invite [dispute]." [Terminiello.] [We] have not permitted the Government to assume that every expression of a provocative idea will incite a riot, but have instead required careful consideration of the actual circumstances surrounding such [expression]. [Brandenburg.] To accept Texas' arguments that it need only demonstrate "the potential for a breach of the peace," and that every flag-burning necessarily possesses that potential, would be to eviscerate our holding in Brandenburg. This we decline to do.

Nor does Johnson's expressive conduct fall within that small class of "fighting words" that are "likely to provoke the average person to retaliation, and thereby cause a breach of the peace." [Chaplinsky.] No reasonable onlooker would have regarded Johnson's generalized expression of dissatisfaction with the policies of the Federal Government as a direct personal insult or an invitation to exchange fisticuffs. We thus conclude that the State's interest in maintaining order is not implicated on these [facts].

B.   The State also asserts an interest in preserving the flag as a symbol of nationhood and national unity. [We are persuaded, as we were in Spence,] that this interest is related to expression in the case of Johnson's burning of the flag. The State, apparently, is concerned that such conduct will lead people to believe either that the flag does not stand for nationhood and national unity, but instead reflects other, less positive concepts, or that the concepts reflected in the flag do not in fact exist, that is, we do not enjoy unity as a Nation. These concerns blossom only when a person's treatment of the flag communicates some message, and thus are related "to the suppression of free expression" within the meaning of O'Brien. We are thus outside of O'Brien's test altogether.

IV.   It remains to consider whether the State's interest in preserving the flag as a symbol of nationhood and national unity justifies Johnson's conviction. [Johnson] was not [prosecuted] for the expression of just any idea; he was prosecuted for his expression of dissatisfaction with the policies of this country, expression situated at the core of our First Amendment values. Moreover, Johnson was prosecuted because he knew that his politically charged expression would cause "serious offense." If he had burned the flag as a means of disposing of it because it was dirty or torn, he would not have been convicted of flag desecration under this Texas law: federal law designates burning as the preferred means of disposition of a flag "when it is in such condition that it is no longer a fitting emblem for display," and Texas has no quarrel with this means of disposal. The Texas law is thus not aimed at protecting the physical integrity of the flag in all circumstances, but is designed instead to protect it only against impairments that would cause serious offense to others. Texas concedes as [much]. Whether Johnson's treatment of the flag violated Texas law thus depended on the likely communicative impact of his expressive conduct. [This] restriction on Johnson's expression is content-based. [Johnson's] political expression was restricted because of the content of the message he conveyed. We must therefore subject the State's asserted interest in preserving the special symbolic character of the flag to "the most exacting scrutiny." [Boos.]

Texas argues that its interest in preserving the flag as a symbol of nationhood and national unity survives this close analysis. [The] State's argument is not that it has an interest simply in maintaining the flag as a symbol of *something,* no matter what it symbolizes. [Rather,] the State's claim is that it has an interest in preserving the flag as a symbol of *nationhood* and *national unity,* a symbol with a determinate range of meanings. According to Texas, if one physically treats the flag in a way that would tend to cast doubt on either the idea that nationhood and national unity are the flag's referents or that national unity actually exists, the message conveyed thereby is a harmful one and therefore may be prohibited.

If there is a bedrock principle underlying the First Amendment, it is that the Government may not prohibit the expression of an idea simply because society finds the idea itself offensive or disagreeable. [We] have not recognized an exception to this principle even where our flag has been involved. [Street; Spence.] [Nothing] in our precedents suggests that a State may foster its own view of the flag by prohibiting expressive conduct relating to it. To bring its argument outside our precedents, Texas attempts to convince us that even if its interest in preserving the flag's symbolic role does not allow it to prohibit words or some expressive conduct critical of the flag, it does permit it to forbid the outright destruction of the flag. [Texas'] focus on the precise nature of Johnson's expression [misses] the point of our prior decisions: their enduring lesson, that the Government may not prohibit expression simply because it disagrees with its message, is not dependent on the particular mode in which one chooses to express an idea. If we were to hold that a State may forbid flag-burning wherever it is likely to endanger the flag's symbolic role, but allow it wherever burning a flag promotes that role—as where, for example, a person ceremoniously burns a dirty flag—we would be saying that when it comes to impairing the flag's physical integrity, the flag itself may be used as a symbol [only] in one direction. We would be permitting a State to "prescribe what shall be orthodox" by saying that one may burn the flag to convey one's attitude toward it and its referents only if one does not endanger the flag's representation of nationhood and national unity.

We never before have held that the Government may ensure that a symbol be used to express only one view of that symbol or its referents. Indeed, in Schacht v. United States [398 U.S. 58 (1970)], we invalidated a federal statute permitting an actor portraying a member of one of our armed forces to "'wear the uniform of that armed force if the portrayal does not tend to discredit that armed force.'" This proviso, we held, "which leaves Americans free to praise the war in Vietnam but can send persons like Schacht to prison for opposing it, cannot survive in a country which has the First Amendment." We perceive no basis on which to hold that the principle underlying our decision in Schacht does not apply to this case. To conclude that the Government may permit designated symbols to be used to communicate only a limited set of messages would be to enter territory having no discernible or defensible boundaries. Could the Government, on this theory, prohibit the burning of state flags? Of copies of the Presidential seal? Of the Constitution? In evaluating these choices under the First Amendment, how would we decide which symbols were sufficiently special to warrant this unique status? To do so, we would be forced to consult our own political preferences, and impose them on the citizenry, in the very way that the First Amendment forbids us to do.

There is, moreover, no indication—either in the text of the Constitution or in our cases interpreting it—that a separate juridical category exists for the American flag alone. [The] First Amendment does not guarantee that other concepts virtually sacred to our Nation as a whole—such as the principle that discrimination on the basis of race [is] odious and destructive—will go unquestioned in the marketplace of ideas. [Brandenburg.] We decline, therefore, to create for the flag an exception to the joust of principles protected by the First Amendment. It is not the State's ends, but its means, to which we object. It cannot be gainsaid that there is a special place reserved for the flag in this Nation, and thus we do not doubt that the Government has a legitimate interest in making efforts to "preserv[e] the national flag as an unalloyed symbol of our country." [Spence.] [To] say that the Government has an interest in encouraging proper treatment of the flag, however, is not to say that it may criminally punish a person for burning a flag as a means of political protest.

[We] are fortified in today's conclusion by our conviction that forbidding criminal punishment for conduct such as Johnson's will not endanger the special role played by our flag or the feelings it inspires. To paraphrase Justice Holmes, we submit that nobody can suppose that this one gesture of an unknown man will change our Nation's attitude towards its flag. [Abrams.] [We] are tempted to say, in fact, that the flag's deservedly cherished place in our community will be strengthened, not weakened, by our holding today. Our decision is a reaffirmation of the principles of freedom and inclusiveness that the flag best reflects, and of the conviction that our toleration of criticism such as Johnson's is a sign and source of our strength. [It] is the Nation's resilience, not its rigidity, that Texas sees reflected in the flag—and it is that resilience that we reassert today. The way to preserve the flag's special role is not to punish those who feel differently about these matters. It is to persuade them that they are wrong. [Precisely] because it is our flag that is involved, one's response to the flag-burner may exploit the uniquely persuasive power of the flag itself. We can imagine no more appropriate response to burning a flag than waving one's own, no better way to counter a flag-burner's message than by saluting the flag that burns, no surer means of preserving the dignity even of the flag that burned than by—as one witness here did—according its remains a respectful burial. We do not consecrate the flag by punishing its desecration, for in doing so we dilute the freedom that this cherished emblem represents.

[Affirmed.]³

Chief Justice REHNQUIST, with whom Justice WHITE and Justice O'CONNOR join, dissenting.

In holding this Texas statute unconstitutional, the Court ignores Justice Holmes' familiar aphorism that "a page of history is worth a volume of logic." For more than 200 years, the American flag has occupied a unique position as the symbol of our Nation, a uniqueness that justifies a governmental prohibition against flag burning in the way [Johnson] did here.¹

[The] American flag, [throughout] more than 200 years of our history, has come to be the visible symbol embodying our Nation. It does not represent the views of any particular political party, and it does not represent any particular political philosophy. The flag is not simply another "idea" or "point of view" competing for recognition in the marketplace of ideas. Millions [of] Americans regard it with an almost mystical reverence regardless of what sort of social, political, or philosophical beliefs they may have. I cannot agree that the First Amendment invalidates the Act of Congress, and the laws of 48 of the 50 States, which make criminal the public burning of the flag.

[But] the Court insists that the [Texas law infringes on] Johnson's freedom of expression. Such freedom, of course, is not absolute. [Here] it may [well] be said that the public burning of the American flag by Johnson was no essential part of any exposition of ideas [Chaplinsky], and at the same time it had a tendency to incite a breach of the peace. [The] Court could not, and did not, say that Chaplinsky's utterances were not expressive phrases—they clearly and succinctly conveyed an extremely low opinion of the addressee. The same may be said of Johnson's public burning of the flag in this case; it obviously did

---

3. Justice KENNEDY, who joined Justice Brennan's opinion to make the 5–to–4 majority here, added a concurrence noting: "Sometimes we must make decisions we do not like. We make them because they are right, right in the sense that the law and the Constitution [compel] the result." He added: "I do not believe the Constitution gives us the right to rule as the [dissenters] urge, however painful this judgment is to announce. [It] is poignant but fundamental that the flag protects those who hold it in contempt. [Johnson's] acts were speech. [So] I agree with the Court that he must go free."

1. At this point, Chief Justice Rehnquist devoted a substantial number of pages to a review of the importance of the flag in American history and literature. He quoted from the poetry of Ralph Waldo Emerson and from Francis Scott Key's "Star–Bangled Banner." Moreover, he printed the full text of John Greenleaf Whittier's "Barbara Fritchie" (including the line "'Shoot if you must, This old grey head, But spare your country's flag,' She said").

convey Johnson's bitter dislike of his country. But his act, like Chaplinsky's provocative words, conveyed nothing that could not have been [conveyed] just as forcefully in a dozen different ways. As with "fighting words," so with flag burning, for purposes of the [First Amendment].

[Flag burning] is the equivalent of an inarticulate grunt or roar that [is] most likely to be indulged in not to express any particular idea, but to antagonize others. [The] Texas statute deprived Johnson of only one rather inarticulate symbolic form of protest—a form of protest that was profoundly offensive to many—and left him with a full panoply of other symbols and every conceivable form of verbal expression to express his deep disapproval of national policy. Thus, in no way can it be said that Texas is punishing him because his hearers [were] profoundly opposed to the message that he sought to convey. Such opposition is no proper basis for restricting speech or expression under the First Amendment. It was Johnson's use of this particular symbol, and not the idea that he sought to [convey], for which he was punished. Our prior cases dealing with flag desecration statutes have left open the question that the Court resolves today. [E.g., Street; Spence.]

The Court concludes its opinion with a regrettably patronizing civics lecture, presumably addressed [in part] to the Members of both Houses of Congress [and] the members of the 48 state legislatures that enacted prohibitions against flag burning. [The] Court's role as the final expositor of the Constitution is well established, but its role as a platonic guardian admonishing those responsible to public opinion as if they were truant school children has no similar place in our system of government. [Surely] one of the high purposes of a democratic society is to legislate against conduct that is regarded as evil and profoundly offensive to the majority of people—whether it be murder, embezzlement, pollution, or flag burning. [Uncritical] extension of constitutional protection to the burning of the flag risks the frustration of the very purpose for which organized governments are instituted. The Court decides that the American flag is just another symbol, about which not only must opinions pro and con be tolerated, but for which the most minimal public respect may not be enjoined. The government may conscript men into the Armed Forces where they [may] die for the flag, but the government may not prohibit the public burning of the banner under which they fight. I would uphold the Texas statute as applied in this case.

Justice STEVENS, dissenting.

[A] country's flag is a symbol of more than "nationhood and national unity." [It is also] a symbol of freedom, of equal opportunity, of religious tolerance, and of goodwill for other peoples who share our aspirations. [The] value of the flag as a symbol cannot be measured. Even so, I have no doubt that the interest in preserving that value for the future is both significant and legitimate. [The] content of respondent's message has no relevance whatsoever to the case. [Moreover, the] case has nothing to do with "disagreeable ideas." It involves disagreeable conduct that, in my opinion, diminishes the value of an important national asset. The Court is therefore quite wrong in blandly asserting that respondent "was prosecuted for his expression of dissatisfaction with the policies of this [country]." Respondent was prosecuted because of the method he chose to express his dissatisfaction with those policies. Had he chosen to spray paint [his] message of dissatisfaction on the facade of the Lincoln Memorial, there would be no question about the power of the Government to prohibit his means of expression. [Though] the asset at stake in this case is intangible, given its unique value, the same interest supports a prohibition on the desecration of the American flag.[1]

THE AFTERMATH OF TEXAS v. JOHNSON

1. *Congressional response to Johnson.* The decision in Johnson elicited considerable public criticism. Soon after the decision, and after outraged floor speeches, the House and Senate passed, by overwhelming votes, resolutions disagreeing with the ruling and pledging to seek means to restore penalties for "such reprehensible conduct." In short order, the battle lines were drawn between those in Congress who wanted the Constitution amended to permit restraints on flag desecration and those who supported new legislation rather than a constitutional amendment. President Bush strongly supported the amendment approach, and many of those who agreed with him believed that any new federal law would meet the same fate in the Court as did the Texas law in Johnson. But others (including many liberal Democrats) believed that a carefully drawn statute might be upheld, and that this would forestall the pressure for a constitutional amendment. Several constitutional scholars, including Laurence Tribe, Rex Lee and Geoffrey Stone, testified before Congress that a flag-burning statute might be drafted so as to pass constitutional muster. For a summary of these arguments, see Stone, "Flag Burning and the Constitution," 75 Iowa L.Rev. 111 (1989). The statutory strategy prevailed, and the Flag Protection Act of 1989 was adopted by overwhelming majorities in each House. The bill became law without the President's signature. The new law was immediately and publicly violated in order to challenge its constitutionality. The result was the 1990 Eichman case, which follows.

UNITED STATES v. EICHMAN, 496 U.S. 310 (1990), a year after Johnson, struck down the 1989 law, once again in a 5-to-4 decision. The Flag Protection Act of 1989 provided in relevant part: "(a)(1) Whoever knowingly mutilates, defaces, physically defiles, burns, maintains on the floor or ground, or tramples upon any flag of the United States shall be [fined] or imprisoned for not more than one year or both. (2) This subsection does not prohibit any conduct consisting of the disposal of the flag when it has become worn or soiled." The Eichman case stemmed from two prosecutions, one in Washington, D.C., the other in Seattle. In each case, the trial courts dismissed the charges on the ground that the Act was unconstitutional.

1. The Court suggests that a prohibition against flag desecration is not content-neutral because this form of symbolic speech is only used by persons who are critical of the flag or the ideas it represents. In making this suggestion the Court does not pause to consider the far-reaching consequences of its introduction of disparate impact analysis into our First Amendment jurisprudence. It seems obvious that a prohibition against the desecration of a gravesite is content-neutral even if it denies some protesters the right to make a symbolic statement by extinguishing the flame in Arlington Cemetery where John F. Kennedy is buried while permitting others to salute the flame by bowing their heads. Few would doubt that a protester who extinguishes the flame has desecrated the gravesite, regardless of whether he prefaces that act with a speech explaining that his purpose is to express deep admiration or unmitigated scorn for the late President. Likewise, few would claim that the protester who bows his head has desecrated the gravesite, even if he makes clear that his purpose is to show disrespect. In such a case, as in a flag burning case, the prohibition against desecration has absolutely nothing to do with the content of the message that the symbolic speech is intended to convey. [Footnote by Justice Stevens.]

The Government conceded in Eichman that the flag-burning here constituted expressive conduct, but asked the Court to reconsider its rejection in Johnson of the claim that flag burning, like obscenity or "fighting words," was not protected by the First Amendment. Justice BRENNAN's majority opinion replied: "This we decline to do." That left only the question of whether the Flag Protection Act was "sufficiently distinct" from the Texas law in Johnson to be enforceable here. The Government argued that, unlike the law in Johnson, the new federal law did not "target expressive conduct on the basis of the content of its message," that the federal law was designed to safeguard "the physical integrity of the flag under all circumstances," and that it proscribed "conduct (other than disposal) that damages or mistreats a flag, without regard to the actor's motive, his intended message, or the likely effects of his conduct on onlookers." In rejecting that effort, Justice Brennan stated:

"Although [the Act] contains no explicit content-based limitation, [it] is nevertheless clear that the Government's asserted *interest* is 'related to the suppression of free expression,' Johnson, and concerned with the content of such expression. The Government's interest in protecting the 'physical integrity' of a privately owned flag rests upon a perceived need to preserve the flag's status as a symbol of our Nation and certain national ideals. But the mere destruction or disfigurement of a particular physical manifestation of the symbol, without more, does not diminish or otherwise affect the symbol itself in any way. For example, the secret destruction of a flag in one's own basement would not threaten the flag's recognized meaning. Rather, the Government's desire to preserve the flag as a symbol for certain national ideals is implicated 'only when a person's treatment of the flag communicates [a] message' to others that is inconsistent with those ideals.

"Moreover, the precise language of the Act's prohibitions confirms Congress' interest in the communicative impact of flag destruction. The Act criminalizes the conduct of anyone who 'knowingly mutilates, defaces, physically defiles, burns, maintains on the floor or ground, or tramples upon any flag.' Each of the specified terms—with the possible exception of 'burns'—unmistakably connotes disrespectful treatment of the flag and suggests a focus on those acts likely to damage the flag's symbolic value.

"Although Congress cast the Flag Protection Act in somewhat broader terms than the Texas statute at issue in Johnson, the Act still suffers from the same fundamental flaw: it suppresses expression out of concern for its likely communicative impact. Despite the Act's wider scope, its restriction on expression cannot be 'justified without reference to the content of the regulated speech.' The Act therefore must be subjected to 'the most exacting scrutiny,' and for the reasons stated in Johnson, the Government's interest cannot justify its infringement on First Amendment rights. We decline the Government's invitation to reassess this conclusion in light of Congress' recent recognition of a purported 'national consensus' favoring a prohibition on flag-burning. Even assuming such a consensus exists, any suggestion that the Government's interest in suppressing speech becomes more weighty as popular opposition to that speech grows is foreign to the First Amendment.

"Government may create national symbols, promote them, and encourage their respectful treatment. But the [Act] goes well beyond this by criminally proscribing expressive conduct because of its likely communicative impact. We are aware that desecration of the flag is deeply offensive to many. But the same might be said, for example, of virulent ethnic and religious epithets, see [Terminiello], vulgar repudiations of the draft, see [Cohen], and scurrilous caricatures, see [Hustler]. 'If there is a bedrock principle underlying the First

Amendment, it is that the Government may not prohibit the expression of an idea simply because society finds the idea itself offensive or disagreeable.' Johnson. Punishing desecration of the flag dilutes the very freedom that makes this emblem so revered, and worth revering."

Justice STEVENS' dissent, joined by Chief Justice Rehnquist and Justices White and O'Connor, developed the argument in his Johnson dissent: "[C]ertain methods of expression may be prohibited if (a) the prohibition is supported by a legitimate societal interest that is unrelated to suppression of the ideas the speaker desires to express; (b) the prohibition does not entail any interference with the speaker's freedom to express these ideas by other means; and (c) the interest in allowing the speaker complete freedom of choice of alternative methods of expression is less important than the societal interest supporting the prohibition." He thought that all of these criteria were satisfied here. He emphasized that the Government may "protect the symbolic value of this flag without regard to the specific content of the flag burners' speech. The prosecution in this case does not depend upon the object of the defendants' protest."

3. *Statute versus amendment.* Which would have had more effect on free speech law: the Flag Protection Act if it had been upheld, or a constitutional amendment providing that "Congress and the States shall have power to prohibit the physical desecration of the flag of the United States"? The assumption of many of the reluctant backers of the Flag Protection Act in Congress was that the constitutional amendment would be by far the greater evil. Such an amendment would, for the first time, have amended an original provision of the Bill of Rights. It would also have been only the fifth constitutional amendment to overrule a decision of the Supreme Court. For the contrary argument that a constitutional amendment would have done *less* harm to the fabric of First Amendment doctrine than would a new flag desecration law upheld by the Court, see Michelman, "Saving Old Glory: On Constitutional Iconography," 42 Stan.L.Rev. 1337 (1990).

The decision in Eichman spurred a renewed campaign for a constitutional amendment, but the proposed amendment that reached the floor of both Houses in 1990 fell 34 votes short of the required two-thirds majority in the House and nine votes short in the Senate. A 1995 version of the proposed amendment fared better, passing by a vote of 312–120 in the House but falling three votes short in the Senate, which voted for the amendment 63–46. Renewed proposals for a flag desecration amendment continue to circulate in the 105th Congress.

————

NUDE DANCING

Recall that the Court invalidated a citywide ban on nude entertainment in Schad v. Mt. Ephraim (1981; p. 1158 above) but upheld zoning regulations concentrating or dispersing adult entertainment establishments in Young v. American Mini Theatres (1976; p. 1159 above) and Renton v. Playtime Theatres (1986; p. 1162 above). A 1991 challenge to a ban on public nudity as applied to nude dancing elicited sharp disagreement among the Justices over the applicable standard of review: the plurality found the law content-neutral and reviewed its application under the O'Brien test; Justice Scalia found it content-neutral but subject to more deferential review; and the dissent found it content-based because aimed at communicative impact.

The challenge in BARNES v. GLEN THEATRE, INC., 501 U.S. 560 (1991), was brought by the Kitty Kat Lounge, a bar featuring women "go-go" dancers; by Glen Theatre, Inc., operator of an adult bookstore featuring women dancing behind glass panels for the entertainment of customers in a coin-operated booth; and by individual dancers working at these establishments. They objected to an Indiana public indecency statute that provided, in relevant part, that "[a] person who knowingly or intentionally, in a public place, [appears] in a state of nudity [commits] public indecency, a [misdemeanor]," and that " '[n]udity' means the showing of the human male or female genitals, pubic area, or buttocks with less than a fully opaque covering [or] the showing of the female breast with less than a fully opaque covering of any part of the nipple." The Indiana courts had interpreted the statute to apply to public accommodations such as respondents' businesses, and to require that dancers at such establishments wear "pasties and G-strings." The respondents claimed that the statute violated the First Amendment as applied to prevent them from exhibiting totally nude dancing. The Court, by a vote of 5–4, held that "the Indiana statutory requirement that the dancers in the establishments involved in this case must wear pasties and G-strings does not violate the First Amendment." The majority vote depended upon three separate opinions.

Chief Justice REHNQUIST, joined by Justices O'Connor and Kennedy, first conceded that "nude dancing of the kind sought to be performed here is expressive conduct within the outer perimeters of the First Amendment, though we view it as only marginally so." He then proceeded to apply the O'Brien test, on the reasoning that the Indiana statute was content-neutral and had only an incidental effect on expression: "Indiana, of course, has not banned nude dancing as such, but has proscribed public nudity across the board." He continued: "Applying the four-part O'Brien test, [we] find that Indiana's public indecency statute is justified despite its incidental limitations on some expressive activity. The public indecency statute is clearly within the constitutional power of the State and furthers substantial governmental interests. It is impossible to discern, other than from the text of the statute, exactly what governmental interest the Indiana legislators had in mind when they enacted this statute, for Indiana does not record legislative history, and the State's highest court has not shed additional light on the statute's purpose. Nonetheless, the statute's purpose of protecting societal order and morality is clear from its text and history. Public indecency statutes of this sort are of ancient origin and presently exist in at least 47 States. Public indecency, including nudity, was a criminal offense at common law. [Public] nudity was considered an act malum in se. Public indecency statutes such as the one before us reflect moral disapproval of people appearing in the nude among strangers in public places. [This] and other public indecency statutes were designed to protect morals and public order. The traditional police power of the States is defined as the authority to provide for the public health, safety, and morals, and we have upheld such a basis for legislation. [Paris Adult, Hardwick.]

"[This] interest is unrelated to the suppression of free expression. Some may view restricting nudity on moral grounds as necessarily related to expression. We disagree. It can be argued, of course, that almost limitless types of conduct—including appearing in the nude in public—are 'expressive,' and in one sense of the word this is true. People who go about in the nude in public may be expressing something about themselves by so doing. But the court rejected this expansive notion of 'expressive conduct' in O'Brien, saying: 'We cannot accept the view that an apparently limitless variety of conduct can be labeled "speech" whenever the person engaging in the conduct intends thereby to express an idea.' [Respondents] contend that even though prohibiting nudity in public generally may not be related to suppressing expression, prohibiting the performance of nude dancing is related to expression because the State seeks to prevent its erotic message. [But] we do not think that when Indiana applies its statute to the nude dancing in these nightclubs it is proscribing nudity because of the erotic message conveyed by the dancers. Presumably numerous other erotic performances are presented at these establishments and similar clubs without any interference from the State, so long as the performers wear a scant amount of clothing. Likewise, the requirement that the dancers don pasties and G-strings does not deprive the dance of whatever erotic message it conveys; it simply makes the message slightly less graphic. The perceived evil that Indiana seeks to address is not erotic dancing, but public nudity. The appearance of people of all shapes, sizes and ages in the nude at a beach, for example, would convey little if any erotic message, yet the State still seeks to prevent it. Public nudity is the evil the State seeks to prevent, whether or not it is combined with expressive activity."

Justice SCALIA filed an opinion concurring only in the judgment: "I agree that the judgment of the Court of Appeals must be reversed. In my view, however, the challenged regulation must be upheld, not because it survives some lower level of First Amendment scrutiny, but because, as a general law regulating conduct and not specifically directed at expression, it is not subject to First Amendment scrutiny at all. [Indiana's] statute is in the line of a long tradition of laws against public nudity, which have never been thought to run afoul of traditional understanding of 'the freedom of speech.' Public indecency—including public nudity—has long been an offense at common law. Indiana's first public nudity statute predated by many years the appearance of nude barroom dancing. It was general in scope, directed all public nudity, and not just at public nude expression; and all succeeding statutes, down to the present one, have been the same. Were it the case that Indiana in practice targeted only expressive nudity, while turning a blind eye to nude beaches and unclothed purveyors of hot dogs and machine tools, it might be said that what posed as a regulation of conduct in general was in reality a regulation of only communicative conduct. Respondents have adduced no evidence of that. Indiana officials have brought many public indecency prosecutions for activities having no communicative element.

"[The] dissent confidently asserts that the purpose of restricting nudity in public places in general is to protect nonconsenting parties from offense; and argues that since only consenting, admission-paying patrons see respondents dance, that purpose cannot apply and the only remaining purpose must relate to the communicative elements of the performance. Perhaps the dissenters believe that 'offense to others' ought to be the only reason for restricting nudity in public places generally, but there is no basis for thinking that our society has ever shared that Thoreauvian 'you-may-do-what-you-like-so-long-as-it-does-not-injure-someone-else' beau ideal—much less for thinking that it was written into the Constitution. The purpose of Indiana's nudity law would be violated, I think, if 60,000 fully consenting adults crowded into the Hoosier Dome to display their genitals to one another, even if there were not an offended innocent in the crowd. Our society prohibits, and all human societies have prohibited, certain activities not because they harm others but because they are considered, in the traditional phrase, 'contra bonos mores,' i.e., immoral. In American society, such prohibitions have included, for example, sadomasochism, cockfighting, bestiality, suicide, drug use, prostitution, and sodomy. [The] Constitution does not prohibit [such laws] simply because they regulate 'morality.' [See Hardwick, Paris Adult.] The purpose of the Indiana statute, as both its text and the manner of its enforcement demonstrate, is to enforce the traditional moral belief that people should not expose their private parts indiscriminately, regardless of whether those who see them are disedified. Since that is so, the dissent has no basis for positing that, where only thoroughly edified adults are present, the purpose must be repression of communication.

"Since the Indiana regulation is a general law not specifically targeted at expressive conduct, its application to such conduct does not in my view implicate the First Amendment. [V]irtually every law restricts conduct, and virtually any prohibited conduct can be performed for an expressive purpose—if only expressive of the fact that the actor disagrees with the prohibition. It cannot reasonably be demanded, therefore, that every restriction of expression incidentally produced by a general law regulating conduct pass normal First Amendment scrutiny, or even [the O'Brien test.] Nor do our holdings require such justification: We have never invalidated the application of a general law simply because the conduct that it reached was being engaged in for expressive purposes and the government could not demonstrate a sufficiently important state interest. [We should adopt here explicitly the regime we] explicitly adopted [in] another First Amendment context: that of free exercise. In Employment Div., Dept. of Human Resources of Ore. v. Smith [1990; p. 1489 below], we held that general laws not specifically targeted at religious practices did not require heightened First Amendment scrutiny even though they diminished some people's ability to practice their religion. [There] is even greater reason to apply this approach to the regulation of expressive conduct. Relatively few can plausibly assert that their illegal conduct is being engaged in for religious reasons; but almost anyone can violate almost any law as a means of expression. In the one case, as in the other, if the law is not directed against the protected value (religion or expression) the law must be obeyed."

Justice SOUTER also filed an opinion concurring only in the judgment: He agreed with Chief Justice Rehnquist that O'Brien was the appropriate test, but did not find it satisfied by the state interest in order and morality. Instead he found the Indiana law, like the law upheld in Renton v. Playtime Theatres (1986; p. 1162 above), justified as preventing "secondary effects" of nude dancing: "[The state] assert[s] that the statute is applied to nude dancing because such dancing 'encourages prostitution, increases sexual assaults, and attracts other criminal activity.' This asserted justification for the statute may not be ignored merely because it is unclear to what extent this purpose motivated the Indiana Legislature in enacting the statute. Our appropriate focus is not an empirical enquiry into the actual intent of the enacting legislature, but rather the existence or not of a current governmental interest in the service of which the challenged application of the statute may be constitutional. [In] my view, the interest asserted by petitioners [is] sufficient under O'Brien to justify the State's enforcement of the statute against the type of adult entertainment at issue here.

"[This] interest [is] 'unrelated to the suppression of free expression.' [To] say that pernicious secondary effects are associated with nude dancing establishments is not necessarily to say that such effects result from the persuasive effect of the expression inherent in nude dancing. It is to say, rather, only that the effects are correlated with the existence of establishments offering such dancing, without deciding what the precise causes of the correlation actually are. It is possible, for example, that the higher incidence of prostitution and sexual assault in the vicinity of adult entertainment locations results from the concentration of crowds of men predisposed to such activities, or from the simple viewing of nude bodies regardless of whether those bodies are engaged in expression or not. In neither case would the chain of causation run through the persuasive effect of the expressive component of nude dancing. [Finally,] the restriction [is] no greater than essential to further the governmental interest. [Pasties] and a G-string moderate the expression to some degree, to be sure, but only to a degree. Dropping the final stitch is prohibited, but the limitation is minor when measured against the dancer's remaining capacity and opportunity to express the erotic message. ''

Justice WHITE dissented, joined by Justices Marshall, Blackmun and Stevens. The dissenters found the O'Brien standard inapplicable because the law, in their view, was aimed here at the communicative impact of nude dancing: "The purpose of forbidding people from appearing nude in parks, beaches, hot dog stands, and like public places is to protect others from offense. But that could not possibly be the purpose of preventing nude dancing in theaters and barrooms since the viewers are exclusively consenting adults who pay money to see these dances. The purpose of the proscription in these contexts is to protect the viewers from what the State believes is the harmful message that nude dancing communicates. [The] emotional or erotic impact of the dance is intensified by the nudity of the performers. [The] sight of a fully clothed, or even a partially clothed, dancer generally will have a far different impact on a spectator than that of a nude dancer, even if the same dance is performed. The nudity is itself an expressive component of the dance, not merely incidental 'conduct.'

"[This] being the case, it cannot be that the statutory prohibition is unrelated to expressive conduct. Since the State permits the dancers to perform if they wear pasties and G-strings but forbids nude dancing, it is precisely because of the distinctive, expressive content of the nude dancing performances at issue in this case that the State seeks to apply the statutory prohibition. It is only because nude dancing performances may generate emotions and feelings of eroticism and sensuality among the spectators that the State seeks to regulate such expressive activity, apparently on the assumption that creating or emphasizing such thoughts and ideas in the minds of the spectators may lead to increased prostitution and the degradation of women. But generating thoughts, ideas, and emotions is the essence of communication. [Thus] the level of First Amendment protection to be accorded the performances at issue here [should be the] 'exacting scrutiny' [required in Texas v. Johnson.] [Our] cases require us to affirm absent a compelling state interest supporting the statute. [Even] if there were compelling interests, the Indiana statute is not narrowly drawn.''

For further exploration of the issues in Barnes, see the opinions of Judges Posner (concurring) and Easterbrook (dissenting) in the decision in Court of Appeals for the Seventh Circuit holding the application of the law unconstitutional below. Miller v. City of South Bend, 904 F.2d 1081 (1990) (en banc). See also Blasi, "Six Conservatives in Search of the First Amendment: the Revealing Case of Nude Dancing," 33 Wm. & Mary L. Rev. 611 (1992).

SECTION 2. GOVERNMENT'S POWER TO LIMIT SPEECH IN ITS CAPACITY AS PROPRIETOR, EDUCATOR, EMPLOYER AND PATRON

A. SPEECH IN PUBLIC FORUMS AND OTHER GOVERNMENT PROPERTY

Introduction. To what extent may government regulate those who want to march in city streets or speak in parks to publicize their views? To what extent does concern with such values as order, quiet, traffic control and audience sensibilities justify curbs on expression in these contexts? Restraints on speech in public places in the interest of local tranquility did not reach the Court until the late 1930s. But since then, these problems have produced a constant flow of litigation as a variety of minorities have sought to use streets, parks, and other public places to publicize their causes, change views and win adherents. Many early cases were stimulated by the "robust evangelism" of the Jehovah's Witnesses. During the fifties, as Harry Kalven remarked, "the story of the streets became a bit quaint." But by the sixties, with the rise of the civil rights and anti-war movements, it became clear "that the story [was] not over." Kalven, "The Concept of the Public Forum: Cox v. Louisiana," 1965 Sup.Ct. Rev. 1. In this era, the proselytizing of the single evangelist selling magazines, ringing doorbells, and speaking at street corners, gave way to a different kind of public speech: sizeable parades in streets, vigils in parks, protest meetings outside public buildings.

What legal analyses are appropriate in evaluating the claims of those who seek access to public places to air their views? Does the First Amendment guarantee speakers access to the public forum or merely assure them equal access if public spaces are opened to speech at all? Recall the decisions above in Police Dept. v. Mosley (1972; p. 1208 above) and Boos v. Barry (1988; p. 1208 above), illustrating that the Court will readily strike down content-based speech restrictions in the public forum. Should it strike down some content-neutral "time, place, and manner" restrictions as well? May government prohibit noisy parades in residential areas late at night or mass gatherings on heavily travelled streets during rush hour? How far may it go in advancing interests in public safety and order, aesthetic attractiveness, or tranquility, privacy and repose? Furthermore, should speech in all public places be treated alike? The streets and parks have been treated as the quintessential public forum. Might some other public places—the Senate gallery? courtrooms? libraries? jails? transportation facilities?—be so specialized in their function as to justify total exclusion of public speakers? These questions are explored in the materials that follow.

———

EARLY PUBLIC FORUM CASES

1. *The First Amendment "right" to a public forum.* Is government free to exclude any speech it wishes from public places because it "owns" them? Is government in this context equivalent to a private proprietor? This was the view articulated by Justice Holmes when he was a state court judge. In MASSACHUSETTS v. DAVIS, 162 Mass. 510, 39 N.E. 113 (1895), aff'd, 167 U.S. 43 (1897), the Massachusetts Supreme Judicial Court upheld the conviction of a preacher for speaking on Boston Common without a required permit from the mayor. Justice HOLMES wrote: "For the legislature absolutely or conditionally to forbid public speaking in a highway or public park is no more an infringement of the rights of a member of the public than for the owner of a private house to forbid it in his house." The Court affirmed, reasoning—at a time before the First Amendment had been held to apply against the states— that "the right to absolutely exclude all right to use, necessarily includes the authority to determine under what circumstances such use may be availed of, as the greater power contains the lesser."

The later Court has not embraced that view. Since the 1930s, the Court has imposed limits on the speech restrictions government may impose on speech in the "public forum." The origin of the right to speak in a public forum is often traced to a dictum in Justice ROBERTS' opinion in HAGUE v. CIO, 307 U.S. 496 (1939): "Wherever the title of streets and parks may rest they have immemorially been held in trust for the use of the public and, time out of mind, have been used for purposes of assembly, communicating thoughts between citizens, and discussing public questions. Such use of the streets and public places has, from ancient times, been a part of the privileges, immunities, rights and liberties of citizens. The privilege [to] use the streets and parks for communication of views on national questions may be regulated in the interest of all; [but] it must not, in the guise of regulation, be abridged or denied." In answer to Justice Holmes' suggestion that a city is the equivalent of a private proprietor possessing a right to exclude, Justice Roberts suggested that the public has "a kind of First–Amendment easement" of access to the streets and parks for purposes of speech. Kalven, "The Concept of the Public Forum: Cox v. Louisiana," 1965 Sup. Ct. Rev. 1; see Stone, "Fora Americana: Speech in Public Places," 1974 Sup. Ct. Rev. 233.

2. *Guaranteed access versus equal access: is the issue distribution or discrimination?* Does the First Amendment mandate some guaranteed minimum access to the public forum? Or does it merely require that, if the public forum is opened to speech, it is opened on an evenhanded basis? Both answers appear in different strands of the early cases concerning public forums. One strand suggests that government *must* make some public places available for the expression of ideas. This strand treats the streets and parks as important to the distribution of speech. Just as handbilling is the "poor man's printing press," so streets and parks have special importance for those who cannot afford to resort to other means of communication. On this view, access to the public forum operates as a compelled subsidy for speech that otherwise might not be heard. Another strand in the early public forum cases focuses on discrimination rather than distribution. On this view, government's obligation is merely to provide *equal* access to public places if if permits access for speech at all. On this view, the danger is not that there will be too little speech, but that the government will pick and choose among speakers in a biased way. Might the two different approaches point to different outcomes in some cases? How would each approach treat a law banning "radical demonstrations in the park"? How would each approach treat a law banning "all demonstrations in the park"?

For an endorsement of the broader, guaranteed-access view, see Kalven, "The Concept of the Public Forum: Cox v. Louisiana," 1965 Sup.Ct.Rev. 1 ("[I]n an open democratic society the streets, the parks, and other public places are an important facility for public discussion and political process. They are in brief a public forum that the citizen can commandeer."). For a critical reexamination of Kalven's position, see Post, "Between Governance and Management: The History and Theory of the Public Forum," 34 UCLA L.Rev. 1713 (1987) (suggesting that government is subject to greater First Amendment restraints when it acts to govern the general public than when it acts in a "managerial" capacity toward its own institutions). For further discussion of the public forum, see Stone, "Fora Americana: Speech in Public Places," 1974 Sup. Ct. Rev. 233; Cass, "First Amendment Access to Government Facilities," 65 Va.L.Rev. 1287 (1979); Goldberger, "Judicial Scrutiny in Public Forum Cases: Misplaced Trust in the Judgment of Public Officials," 32 Buffalo L.Rev. 175 (1983); Farber & Nowak, "The Misleading Nature of Public Forum Analysis:

Content and Context in First Amendment Adjudication," 70 Va.L.Rev. 1219 (1984).

3. *Early cases: standardless licensing and the problem of discrimination.* Several of the Court's early public forum decisions invalidated standardless licensing schemes for conferring too much discretion on public officials to discriminate on the basis of content in regulating access to the public forum. These cases give more support to the equal-access than the guaranteed-access approach. For example, in Lovell v. Griffin, (1938; p. 1340 below), the Court invalidated a conviction for leafleting without a license from the city manager on the ground that the licensing scheme vested unfettered discretion in the city manager. HAGUE v. CIO, the 1939 case containing Justice Roberts' famous dictum above, relied on Lovell in holding a Jersey City, N.J., ordinance "void upon its face" because access to streets and parks required a permit, and the standards of the ordinance governing issuance of the permit did not adequately curb the possible use of discretion. Thus, a permit could be refused on the "mere opinion [of the head of the police] that such refusal will prevent 'riots, disturbances or disorderly assemblage.' It can thus [be] made the instrument of arbitrary suppression of free expression of views on [national affairs]." That risked "uncontrolled official suppression." And in Cantwell v. Connecticut (1940; p. 1076 above), the Court invalidated a law requiring official approval for the solicitation of contributions to "religious causes."

And in SAIA v. NEW YORK, 334 U.S. 558 (1948), the Court's 5–4 decision held invalid a Lockport, N.Y., ordinance prohibiting the use of amplification devices without the permission of the police chief. Relying on Lovell, Hague, and Cantwell, Justice DOUGLAS' majority opinion found the ordinance unconstitutional "on its face" for establishing a standardless "previous restraint" on free speech. He stated: "Loud-speakers are today indispensable instruments of effective public speech. The sound truck has become an accepted method of political campaigning. It is the way people are reached. [This] ordinance would be a dangerous weapon if it were allowed to get a hold on our public life. Noise can be regulated by regulating decibels. The hours and place of public discussion can be controlled. But to allow the police to bar the use of loud-speakers because their use can be abused is like barring radio receivers because they too make a noise. [Any] abuses which loud-speakers create can be controlled by narrowly drawn statutes. When a city allows an official to ban them in his uncontrolled discretion, it sanctions a device for suppression of free communication of ideas. In this case a permit is denied because some persons were said to have found the sound annoying. In the next one a permit may be denied because some people find the ideas annoying. Annoyance at ideas can be cloaked in annoyance at sound. The power of censorship inherent in this type of ordinance reveals its vice." Justice FRANKFURTER dissented, joined by Justices Reed and Burton, arguing that "no arbitrary action or discrimination" had been shown, and that loudspeakers were instruments of "aural aggression" that could intrude into "cherished privacy: [Surely] there is not a constitutional right to force unwilling people to listen." Justice Jackson also dissented.

For later analogues to these early cases emphasizing the dangers of abuse of official discretion over speech, and thus the equal-access rather than the guaranteed-access approach, see, e.g., STAUB v. BAXLEY, 355 U.S. 313 (1958) (striking down on its face an ordinance prohibiting the solicitation of membership in dues-paying organizations without a permit from city officials, and holding that First Amendment freedoms may not be made "contingent upon the uncontrolled will of an official"); HYNES v. MAYOR OF ORADELL, 425 U.S. 610 (1976) (invalidating as vague an ordinance requiring advance notice to police in writing by "any person desiring to canvass, solicit or call from house to house [for] a recognized charitable [or] political campaign or cause," holding that such an ordinance suffered "from the vice condemned in [Lovell, Cantwell, and Staub]"); LAKEWOOD v. PLAIN DEALER PUBLISHING CO., 486 U.S. 750 (1988)(see p. 1340 below) (invalidating a city ordinance requiring a permit from the mayor in order to place newsracks on public property, holding that it conferred impermissibly "unbridled discretion").

In contrast to these standardless licensing schemes, permit requirements for speech in the public forum have been upheld when they contain some objective criteria that curtail the possibility of discrimination against disfavored content. In COX v. NEW HAMPSHIRE, 312 U.S. 569 (1941), a unanimous Court affirmed the convictions of several Jehovah's Witnesses for violating a state law prohibiting a "parade or procession" upon a public street without first obtaining a permit from local authorities and paying a license fee of not more than three hundred dollars a day. The defendants had marched on busy city sidewalks carrying signs bearing such slogans as "Religion is a Snare and a Racket" and "Serve God and Christ the King." They did not apply for a permit and none was issued.

Writing for the Court, Chief Justice HUGHES stated: "The authority of a municipality to impose regulations in order to assure the safety and convenience of the people in the use of public highways has never been regarded as inconsistent with civil liberties. [The] control of travel on the streets of cities is the most familiar illustration of this recognition of social need. Where a restriction of the use of highways in that relation is designed to promote the public convenience in the interest of all, it cannot be disregarded by the attempted exercise of some civil right which in other circumstances would be entitled to protection. One would not be justified in ignoring the familiar red traffic light because he thought it his religious duty to disobey the municipal [command]. As regulation of the use of the streets for parades and processions is a traditional exercise of control by local government, the question in a particular case is whether that control is exerted so as not to deny or unwarrantedly abridge the right of assembly and the opportunities for the communication of thought and the discussion of public questions immemorially associated with resort to public places.

"In the instant case, we are aided by the opinion of the Supreme Court of the State, [which] defined the limitations of the authority conferred for the granting of licenses. [T]he state court considered and defined the duty of the licensing authority and the rights of the appellants to a license for their parade, with regard only to considerations of time, place and manner so as to conserve the public convenience. The obvious advantage of requiring application for a permit [was] giving the public authorities notice in advance so as to afford opportunity for proper policing. [Moreover,] the license served 'to prevent confusion by overlapping parades, [to] secure convenient use of the streets by other travelers, and to minimize the risk of disorder.' [The] court held that the licensing board was not vested with arbitrary power or an unfettered discretion; that its discretion must be exercised with 'uniformity of method of treatment upon the facts of each application, free from improper or inappropriate considerations and from unfair discrimination'; that a 'systematic, consistent and just order of treatment, with reference to the convenience of public use of the highways, is the statutory mandate.' [If] a municipality has authority to control the use of its public streets for parades or processions, as it undoubtedly has, it cannot be denied authority to give consideration, without unfair discrimination, to time, place and manner in relation to the other proper uses of the streets. We find it impossible to say that the limited authority conferred by the licensing provisions of the statute in question as thus construed by the state court contravened any constitutional right.[1] [There] is no evidence that the statute has been administered otherwise than in the fair and non-discriminatory manner which the state court has construed it to [require]."

Consider the following comment: "Of course, Cox v. New Hampshire did no more than to give a general standard for accommodation of the conflicting interests. It did not tell whether certain congested areas or certain times of the day might not always be held unavailable for parading, nor whether the size of some crowds might always be too large. But it seems [to] symbolize the ideal of Robert's Rules of Order for use of the public forum of the streets." Kalven, "The Concept of the Public Forum: Cox v. Louisiana," 1965 Sup.Ct.Rev. 1. But see Baker, "Unreasoned Reasonableness: Mandatory Parade Permits and Time, Place, and Manner Restrictions," 32 Hastings L. J. 711 (1981) (emphasizing the harms of licensing schemes: the loss of "'spontaneous' demonstrations," the requirement that protestors "bow to the very authorities" they may be criticizing, and the creation of opportunities for subtle official "harassment").

4. *Early cases: total medium bans and the problem of distribution.* May government deny access to the public forum for an entire medium of speech, so long as it does so even-handedly? Is such a total medium ban an impermissible interference with free speech even when the risks of abuse of discretion are absent? In SCHNEIDER v. STATE, 308 U.S. 147 (1939), the Court invalidated the ordinances of four different New Jersey communities forbidding distribution of leaflets. The cities' central defense was that flat bans were necessary to prevent littering. Justice ROBERTS, writing for the Court, replied: "Municipal authorities [have] a duty to keep their communities' streets open for movement of people and [property]. So long as legislation to this end does not abridge the constitutional liberty of one rightfully upon the street to import information through speech or the distribution of literature, it may lawfully regulate the conduct of those using the streets. For example, [the] guarantee of freedom of speech or of the press [does not] deprive a municipality of power to enact regulations against throwing literature broadcast in the streets. [This] Court has characterized the freedom of speech and freedom of press as fundamental personal rights and liberties. [Mere] legislative preferences or beliefs respecting matters of public convenience may well support regulation directed at other personal activities, but be insufficient to justify such as diminishes the exercise of rights so vital to the maintenance of democratic institutions. And so, as cases arise, the delicate and difficult task falls upon the courts to weigh the circum-

1. The Court also sustained the license fee requirement, noting that it was "not a revenue tax, but one to meet the expense incident to the administration of the Act," and thus constitutional. Should municipalities be permitted to impose fees—even very large fees—so long as they are designed to defray the cost of policing? Could such a scheme be attacked as imposing an undue financial burden on the exercise of a constitutional right? See generally Blasi, "Prior Restraints on Demonstrations," 68 Mich.L.Rev. 1481 (1970). See also Goldberger, "A Reconsideration of Cox v. New Hampshire: Can Demonstrators be Required to Pay the Costs of Using America's Public Forums?," 62 Tex. L.Rev. 403 (1983) (arguing that a "proper

distribution of costs" would allocate "the costs generated by speech activities to the society as a whole"); Neisser, "Charging for Free Speech: User Fees and Insurance in the Marketplace of Ideas," 74 Geo.L.J. 257 (1985). The Court has never invalidated a content-neutral user fee. Recall, however, the Court's invalidation in Forsyth Co. v. Nationalist Movement (1992; p. 1090 above) of a user fee to be calculated according to the anticipated hostility of the audience. Are other advance payment conditions—e.g., insurance requirements—vulnerable to a First Amendment attack? Recall the litigation pertaining to the planned Nazi demonstrations in Skokie and Chicago in the late 1970s, p. 1112 above.

stances and to appraise the substantiality of the reasons advanced in support of the regulation of the free enjoyment of the rights.

"[Although] the alleged offenders were not charged with themselves scattering paper in the streets, their convictions were sustained upon the theory that distribution by them encouraged or resulted in such littering. We are of opinion that the purpose to keep the streets clean [is] insufficient to justify an ordinance which prohibits a person rightfully on a public street from handing literature to one willing to receive it. Any burden imposed upon the city authorities in cleaning and caring for the streets as an indirect consequence of such distribution results from the constitutional protection of the freedom of speech and press. This constitutional protection does not deprive a city of all power to prevent street littering. There are obvious methods of preventing littering. Amongst these is the punishment of those who actually throw papers on the street. [It] is suggested that the [ordinance is] valid because [its] operation is limited to streets and alleys and leaves persons free to distribute printed matter in other places. [But the] streets are natural and proper places for the dissemination of information and opinion; and one is not to have the exercise of his liberty of expression in appropriate places abridged on the plea that it may be exercised in some other place."

Note that Schneider accepted that a city's interest in preventing littering and keeping its streets clean is a legitimate and content-neutral local interest, and that distributing leaflets creates a risk of littering. Yet the Court struck down the ban, by applying a variety of strict scrutiny. Invalidating the leaflet ban might impose greater cost on the city in cleaning the streets; yet that was a cost that had to be borne because of the First Amendment. And antilitter laws were available as a less restrictive means. As Kalven stated in "The Concept of the Public Forum," supra: "Leaflet distribution in public places [is] a method of communication that carries as an inextricable and expected consequence substantial littering of the [streets]. It is also a method of communication of some annoyance to a majority of people so [addressed]. Yet the constitutional balance in Schneider was struck emphatically in favor of keeping the public forum open for this mode of communication. [The] operative theory of the Court, at least for the leaflet situation, is that, although it is a method of communication that interferes with the public use of the streets, the right to the streets as a public forum is such that leaflet distribution cannot be prohibited and can be regulated only for weighty reasons." Kalven concluded that Schneider strengthened the case for an assured minimum access right to the streets as a public forum.

Like the decision in Schneider invalidating a flat ban on leafleting, the decision in MARTIN v. STRUTHERS, 319 U.S. 141 (1943), invalidated an ordinance prohibiting a medium of communication: here, the distribution of handbills to residences by ringing doorbells or otherwise summoning residents to the door. The City of Struthers, an Ohio industrial community, argued that the law was necessary to protect residents from annoyance and crime; and it emphasized that many of the residents worked night shifts and slept days, making them especially vulnerable to "casual bell pushers" disrupting their sleep. The ordinance was challenged by a Jehovah's Witness who had gone door-to-door to distribute leaflets advertising a religious meeting. Justice BLACK, writing for the Court, stated: "While door to door distributors of literature may be either a nuisance or a blind for criminal activities, they may also be useful members of society engaged in the dissemination of ideas in accordance with the best tradition of free discussion. The widespread use of this method of communication by many groups espousing various causes attests its major importance. [Door-to-door] distribution of circulars is essential to the poorly financed causes of little people. Freedom to distribute information to every citizen whenever he desires to receive it is so clearly vital to the preservation of a free society that, putting aside reasonable police and health regulations of time and manner of distribution, it must be fully preserved." Justice Black noted that it would be permissible to make it an offense "for any person to ring the bell of a householder who has appropriately indicated that he is unwilling to be disturbed. [Because the] dangers of distribution [such as annoyance and crime] can so easily be controlled by traditional legal methods, leaving to each householder the full right to decide whether he will receive strangers as visitors, [the] stringent prohibition [here] can serve no purpose but that forbidden by the Constitution, the naked restriction of the dissemination of ideas."

Compare with the decisions in Schneider and Martin the decision in KOVACS v. COOPER, 336 U.S. 77 (1949), which upheld a Trenton, N.J., ordinance designed to regulate loudspeakers. Kovacs was convicted of violating a ban on "any device known as a sound truck, loud speaker or sound amplifier [which] emits therefrom loud and raucous noises and is attached to and upon any vehicle operated or standing [upon] streets or public places." Justice REED's plurality opinion was joined only by Chief Justice Vinson and Justice Burton. He indicated that absolute prohibition of loudspeakers would probably be unconstitutional but found that the ordinance was valid because, as construed by the state court, it applied only to loudspeakers emitting "loud and raucous" noises. He explained: "City streets are recognized as a normal place for the exchange of ideas by speech or paper. But this does not mean the freedom is beyond all control. We think it is a permissible exercise of legislative discretion to bar sound trucks with broadcasts of public interest, amplified to a loud and raucous volume, from the public ways of municipalities. On the business streets, [such] distractions would be dangerous to traffic at all hours useful for the dissemination of information, and in the residential thoroughfares the quiet and tranquility so desirable for city dwellers would likewise be at the mercy of advocates of particular religious, social or political persuasions. We cannot believe that rights of free speech compel a municipality to allow such mechanical voice amplification on any of its streets. [The] preferred position of freedom of speech [does] not require legislators to be insensible to claims by citizens to comfort and convenience. [That] more people may be more easily and cheaply reached by sound trucks [is] not enough to call forth constitutional protection for what those charged with public welfare reasonably think is a nuisance when easy means of publicity are open. [We] think that the need for reasonable protection in the homes or business houses from the distracting noises of vehicles equipped with such sound amplifying devices justifies the ordinance."

Justice JACKSON concurred in the result even though, unlike Justice Reed, he viewed the ordinance as a flat ban on loudspeakers. He thought the prohibition was justified because loudspeakers conflict "with quiet enjoyment of home and park": loudspeaker regulations were permissible so long as they did not seek "to censor the contents." He agreed with the Kovacs dissenters' position that it was a repudiation of Saia, above. Saia, he noted, "struck down a more moderate exercise of the state's police power" than the one sustained here. In another opinion concurring in the result, Justice FRANKFURTER also sustained the ordinance as a flat ban, in accordance with his Saia dissent. He emphasized that, so long as a city does not seek to censor or discriminate among ideas, "it is not for us to supervise the limits the legislature may impose in safeguarding the steadily narrowing opportunities for serenity and reflection."

Justice BLACK, joined by Justices Douglas and Rutledge, dissented: "The appellant was neither charged with nor convicted of operating a sound truck that emitted 'loud and raucous noises.' The charge [was] that he violated the city ordinance 'in that he [used] a device known as a sound truck.' [This] ordinance wholly bars the use of all loud speakers mounted upon any vehicle in any of the city's public streets. In my view this repudiation of [Saia] makes a dangerous and unjustifiable breach in the constitutional barriers designed to insure freedom of expression. Ideas and beliefs are today chiefly disseminated to the masses of people through the press, radio, moving pictures, and public address systems. [The] basic premise of the First Amendment is that all present instruments of communication, as well as others that inventive genius may bring into being, shall be free from governmental censorship or prohibition. Laws which hamper the free use of some instruments of communication thereby favor competing channels. [Thus,] laws like [this] can give an overpowering influence to views of owners of legally favored instruments of communication.

"There are many people who have ideas that they wish to disseminate but who do not have enough money to own or control publishing plants, newspapers, radios, moving picture studios, or chains of show places. Yet everybody knows the vast reaches of these powerful channels of communication which from the very nature of our economic system must be under the control and guidance of comparatively few people. [It] is no reflection on the value of preserving freedom for dissemination of the ideas of publishers of newspapers [etc.] to believe that transmission of ideas through public speaking is also essential. [Criticism] of governmental action [should] not be limited to criticisms by press, radio, and moving pictures. [And] it is an obvious fact that public speaking today without sound amplifiers is a wholly inadequate way to reach the people on a large scale. Consequently, to tip the scales against transmission of ideas through public speaking [is] to deprive the people of a large part of the basic advantages of the receipt of ideas that the First Amendment was designed to protect.

"There is no more reason that I can see for wholly prohibiting one useful instrument of communication than another. If Trenton can completely bar the streets to the advantageous use of loud speakers, all cities can do the same. In that event preference in the dissemination of ideas is given those who can obtain the support of newspapers [etc.] or those who have money enough to buy advertising from newspapers [etc.]. This Court should no more permit this invidious prohibition against the dissemination of ideas by speaking than it would permit a complete blackout of the press, the radio, or moving pictures. [I] am aware that the 'blare' of this new method of carrying ideas is susceptible of abuse. [But] ordinances can be drawn which adequately protect a community [without] absolutely denying to the community's citizens all information that may be disseminated or received through this new avenue for trade in ideas. [A] city ordinance that reasonably restricts the volume of sound, or the hours during which an amplifier may be used, does not [infringe] free speech. [But this] ordinance [is] an absolute prohibition of all uses of an amplifier on any of the streets of Trenton at any time." Justice Murphy also dissented.

Would a flat ban on all sound trucks be constitutional? Should it be? Did the various opinions in Kovacs settle the issue? Are the access claims of loudspeaker users entitled to special weight because of the importance of sound trucks (like leaflets) as a form of "poor man's printing press"? Is a ban on loudspeakers justifiable because of a legislative judgment that the particular method of communication is obnoxious? Would a specific ban on all speeches or marches in residential neighborhoods be similarly supportable on grounds of deference to legislative judgment? A ban on all street demonstrations? Would it depend on the available alternative communication channels?

In the decades following these cases, the reasoning of Schneider, Martin and the Kovacs dissenters was rarely used to invalidate content-neutral regulations of speakers' access to public spaces. The Court extended the antidiscrimination principle of the standardless licensing decisions to invalidate nearly every content-based regulation in the public forum. Recall Police Dept. v. Mosley (1972; p. 1205 above) and Carey v. Brown (1980; p. 1205 above); but see Burson v. Freeman (1992; p. 1207 above). But the Court upheld several regulations that challengers sought to characterize as total medium bans, characterizing them instead as "time, place and manner" regulations that were to be upheld so long as the government could show they were closely tailored to a significant governmental interest. (This modern "time, place and manner" test is elaborated below at p. 1244.) See, e.g., Heffron v. ISKCON (1981; p. 1245 below); City Council v. Taxpayers for Vincent (1984; p. 1249 below). The distributive strand of the Schneider line of cases stayed partially alive in the Court's admonition that time, place and manner laws must also leave open "ample alternative channels of communication." But such a requirement was less protective of speakers than Justice Roberts' approach in Schneider, which had suggested that "one is not to have the exercise of his liberty of expression in appropriate places abridged on the plea that it may be exercised in some other place."

Schneider and its progeny were never overruled, however, and in 1994, the Rehnquist Court dramatically resurrected them in a decision demonstrating that the presumption against total medium bans is, at least in some circumstances, still alive. In CITY OF LADUE v. GILLEO, 512 U.S. 43 (1994), the Court unanimously invalidated an ordinance of the City of Ladue, a residential suburb of St. Louis, Missouri, that banned the posting of most signs in order to minimize visual clutter. The ordinance provided for ten exceptions, including signs identifying a home or business, for-sale signs, and on-site signs advertising gasoline. Gilleo challenged the ordinance because it barred her from placing an an 8.5-by 11-inch sign in the second story window of her home stating, "For Peace in the Gulf." The district court and the court of appeals invalidated the ordinance on the ground that the selective exemptions rendered it impermissibly content-based. Justice STEVENS wrote for the Court affirming the judgment, but on an expressly different ground. He held that, even assuming that the ordinance and the exemptions were content-neutral, the ordinance banned "too much" speech: "In examining the propriety of Ladue's near-total prohibition of residential signs, we will assume, arguendo, the validity of the City's submission that the various exemptions are free of impermissible content or viewpoint discrimination [because the distinctions are drawn to distinguish signs that are likely to cause more visual clutter from those that are not. Nevertheless,] Ladue has almost completely foreclosed a venerable means of communication that is both unique and important. [Often] placed on lawns or in windows, residential signs play an important part in political campaigns, during which they are displayed to signal the resident's support for particular candidates, parties, or causes. [Our] prior decisions have voiced particular concern with laws that foreclose an entire medium of expression. [Lovell, Martin, Schneider.] Although prohibitions foreclosing entire media may be completely free of content or viewpoint discrimination, the danger they pose to the freedom of speech is readily apparent—by eliminating a common means of speaking, such measures can suppress too much speech.

"Ladue contends, however, that its ordinance is a mere regulation of the 'time, place, or manner' of speech because residents remain free to convey their desired messages by other means, such as hand-held signs, 'letters, handbills, flyers, telephone calls, newspaper advertisements, bumper stickers, speeches, and neighborhood or community meetings.' [We] are not persuaded that adequate substitutes exist for the important medium of speech that Ladue has closed off. Displaying a sign from one's own residence often carries a message quite distinct from placing the same sign someplace else, or conveying the same text or picture by other means. Precisely because of their location, such signs provide information about the identity of the 'speaker.' [Residential] signs are an unusually cheap and convenient form of communication. Especially for persons of modest means or limited mobility, a yard or window sign may have no practical substitute.

"[A] special respect for individual liberty in the home has long been part of our culture and our law; that principle has special resonance when the government seeks to constrain a person's ability to speak there. Most Americans would be understandably dismayed, given that tradition, to learn that it was illegal to display from their window an 8–by 11–inch sign expressing their political views. Whereas the government's need to mediate among various competing uses, including expressive ones, for public streets and facilities is constant and unavoidable, see [Cox v. New Hampshire], its need to regulate temperate speech from the home is surely much less pressing. Our decision that Ladue's ban on almost all residential signs violates the First Amendment by no means leaves the City powerless to address the ills that may be associated with residential signs. We are confident that more temperate measures could in large part satisfy Ladue's stated regulatory needs without harm to the First Amendment rights of its citizens." Justice O'Connor wrote a separate concurrence suggesting that the Court should have decided first whether the ordinance was content-based.

Did the sign ban struck down in Ladue differ in any material respect from the medium bans at issue in Schneider, Martin and Kovacs? How important was it to the holding in Ladue that the ban regulated the use of one's own private home? Should it have mattered whether or not Gilleo herself was advancing "the poorly financed causes of little people"? See generally Stone, "Content-Neutral Restrictions," 54 U. Chi. L. Rev. 46 (1987).

————

THE MODERN "TIME, PLACE AND MANNER" TEST

Introduction. Recall that in Cox v. New Hampshire, Chief Justice Hughes wrote that a government faced with public access claims by speakers is entitled to "give consideration, without unfair discrimination, to time, place and manner in relation to the other proper uses of the streets." What government interests justify such time, place and manner regulations in the traditional public forum of the streets and parks? How closely must such regulations fit those asserted interests? Should courts defer to legislative and executive judgments on the management of public forums? Or should they scrutinize them independently to make sure government has not, "in the guise of regulation," suppressed too much speech? Should the Court's only concern be content neutrality, or does an emphasis on discrimination or the lack of it obscure underlying problems with the degree of access speakers enjoy? Consider the following decisions elaborating the standard of review for time, place and manner regulations, organized by reference to the asserted government interest.

———

PUBLIC ORDER AND SAFETY

In COX v. LOUISIANA, 379 U.S. 536 (1965), the Court invalidated a breach of peace conviction arising from a civil rights demonstration near a courthouse. That part of the decision, and the factual circumstances of the case, are described above at p. 1088. In the same decision, the Court also overturned Cox's conviction under a Louisiana law prohibiting the obstruction of "the free, convenient and normal use of any public sidewalk, street, [or] other passageway [by] impeding, hindering, stifling, retarding or restraining traffic or passage thereon." Justice GOLDBERG wrote for the Court: "The rights of free speech and assembly, while fundamental in our democratic society, still do not mean that everyone with opinions or beliefs to express may address a group at any public place and at any time. The constitutional guarantee of liberty implies the existence of an organized society maintaining public order, without which liberty itself would be lost in the excesses of anarchy. The control of travel on the streets is a clear example of governmental responsibility to insure this necessary order. A restriction in that relation, designed to promote the public convenience in the interest of all, and not susceptible to abuses of discriminatory application, cannot be disregarded by the attempted exercise of some civil right which, in other circumstances, would be entitled to protection. One would not be justified in ignoring the familiar red light because this was thought to be a means of social protest. Nor could one, contrary to traffic regulations, insist upon a street meeting in the middle of Times Square at the rush hour as a form of freedom of [speech]. Governmental authorities have the duty and responsibility to keep their streets open and available for movement.

"[But we] have no occasion in this case to consider the constitutionality of the uniform, consistent, and nondiscriminatory application of a statute forbidding all access to streets and other public facilities for parades and meetings. Although the statute here involved on its face precludes all street assemblies and parades, it has not been so [applied]. City officials [indicated] that certain meetings and parades are permitted in Baton Rouge, even though they have the effect of obstructing traffic, provided prior approval is obtained. [The] statute itself provides no standards for the determination of local officials as to which assemblies to permit or which to prohibit. [It] appears that the authorities in Baton Rouge permit or prohibit parades or street meetings in their completely uncontrolled discretion. [The] pervasive restraint on freedom of discussion by the practice of the authorities under the statute is not any less effective than a statute expressly permitting such selective [enforcement]. [Such] broad discretion in a public official [permits] the official to act as a censor."

Compare the Court's decision upholding as a permissible time, place and manner regulation the "booth rule" restricting literature distribution and solicitation of funds at the Minnesota State Fair in HEFFRON v. INTERNATIONAL SOCIETY FOR KRISHNA CONSCIOUSNESS (ISKCON), 452 U.S. 640 (1981). Minnesota State Fair Rule 6.05 prohibited the sale or distribution of any merchandise, including printed or written material, except from booths rented to all applicants in a nondiscriminatory manner on a first-come, first-served basis. The rule was challenged by ISKCON, a religious society espousing the views of the Krishna religion. ISKCON asserted that the Rule suppressed the practice of Sankirtan, a religious ritual that enjoins its members to go into public places to distribute or sell religious literature and to solicit donations for the support of the Krishna religion. The highest state court struck down the rule, but Justice WHITE's majority opinion found the restriction permissible. He explained: "[The] First Amendment does not guarantee the right to communicate one's views at all times and places or in any manner that may be desired. [See Cox v. Louisiana.] [T]he activities of ISKCON, like those of others protected by the First Amendment, are subject to reasonable time, place, and manner restrictions. [Cox v. New Hampshire.] We have often approved restrictions of that kind provided that they are justified without reference to the content of the regulated speech, that they serve a significant governmental interest, and that in doing so they leave open ample alternative channels for communication of the information." Under that standard, the Court held the booth rule valid.

Justice White found Rule 6.05 clearly content-neutral, for it applied "even-handedly to all who wish to distribute and sell written materials or to solicit funds. [Nor] does Rule 6.05 suffer from the more covert forms of discrimination that may result when arbitrary discretion is vested in some governmental authority. The method of allocating space is a straightforward first-come, first-served system." Moreover, it served a "significant governmental interest"— "the need to maintain the orderly movement of the crowd given the large number of exhibitors and persons attending the Fair." (The Fair had an average daily attendance of over 100,000.) "[I]t is clear that a State's interest in protecting the 'safety and convenience' of persons using a public forum is a valid governmental objective. [And the] flow of the crowd and demands of safety are more pressing in the context of the Fair [than in the typical city street or park]."

Turning to the fit between the booth rule and this end, Justice White rejected the state court's reasoning that an exemption for the Hare Krishna devotees alone would not defeat the state's interest: "[The] justification for the Rule should not be measured by the disorder that would result from granting an exemption solely to ISKCON. [If the Rule cannot be applied to ISKCON], it is no more valid with respect to the [other] organizations that have rented booths at the Fair. [Intercepting] fair patrons as they move about, [as ISKCON wishes to do], and if success is achieved, stopping them momentarily or for longer periods as money is given or exchanged for literature [could lead to] widespread disorder at the fairgrounds. [Obviously], there would be a much larger threat to the State's interest in crowd control if all other religious, nonreligious, and noncommercial organizations could likewise move freely about the fairgrounds distributing and selling literature and soliciting funds at will." He added: "For similar reasons, we cannot agree with the [state court that the Rule] is an unnecessary regulation because the State could avoid the threat [posed] by ISKCON by less restrictive means, such as penalizing disorder or disruption, limiting the number of solicitors, or putting more narrowly drawn restrictions on the location and movement of [solicitors] and [distributors]," since "it is quite improbable that [such] alternative means [would] deal adequately with the [problem]."

Justice White found as well that "alternative forums for the expression [exist] despite the effects of the Rule": "[The] Rule does not prevent ISKCON from practicing Sankirtan anywhere outside the fairgrounds. [It] does not exclude ISKCON from the fairgrounds, nor does it deny that organization the right to conduct any desired activity at some point within the forum. Its members may mingle with the crowd and orally propagate their views [and] may also arrange for a booth and distribute and sell literature and solicit funds from that location on the fairgrounds itself. [Considering] the limited functions of the Fair and the [confined] area within which it operates, we are unwilling to say that [the Rule] does not provide ISKCON and other organizations with an adequate means to sell and solicit on the fairgrounds."

Four Justices were in partial dissent. Justice BRENNAN, joined by Justices Marshall and Stevens, agreed that the limitation of literature sales and funds solicitation to fixed booths was justified, not as a crowd control measure but as an "antifraud measure." But they found the ban on distribution of literature outside of booths "an overly intrusive means of achieving the State's interest in crowd control." Justice Brennan stated his general approach as follows:

"[Once] a governmental regulation is shown to impinge upon basic First Amendment rights, the burden falls on the government to show the validity of its asserted interest and the absence of less intrusive alternatives. See, e.g., [Schneider]. The challenged 'regulation must be narrowly tailored to further the State's legitimate interest.' [The Rule] does not meet this test. [Significantly], each and every fairgoer, whether political candidate, concerned citizen, or member of a religious group, is free to give speeches, engage in face-to-face advocacy, campaign, or proselytize. No restrictions are placed on any fairgoer's right to speak at any time, at any place, or to any person. [Because of the Rule], however, as soon as a proselytizing member of ISKCON hands out a free copy of the Bhagavad–Gita to an interested listener, or a political candidate distributes his campaign brochure to a potential voter, he becomes subject to arrest and removal from the fairgrounds. This constitutes a significant restriction on First Amendment rights.

"In support of its crowd control justification, the State contends that if fairgoers are permitted to distribute literature, large crowds will gather, blocking traffic lanes and causing safety problems. [But] the State has failed to provide any support for these assertions. Relying on a general, speculative fear of disorder, the [State] has placed a significant restriction on respondents' ability to exercise core First Amendment rights. This restriction is not narrowly drawn to advance the State's interests, and for that reason is unconstitutional. [If] the State had a reasonable concern that distribution in certain parts of the fairgrounds—for example, entrances and exits—would cause disorder, it could have drafted its rule to prohibit distribution of literature at those points. If the State felt it necessary to limit the number of persons distributing an organization's literature, it could, within reason, have done that as well. It had no right, however, to ban all distribution of literature outside the booths." Justice Blackmun also concurred in part and dissented in part, favoring the same result as Justice Brennan.

Should the booth rule have been viewed as a total medium ban akin to the bans on distributing literature struck down in Schneider and Martin? Distribution was prohibited in the open thoroughfares of the fair and confined to the "private" space of rented booths. Should there have been any concern that the rule would have content-differential effects, disadvantaging unpopular speakers who need to approach their audience because their audience is unlikely to come to them? ISKCON ventured such an argument, but Justice White replied: "The argument is interesting but has little force. [A preference for listener-initiated exchanges over those originating with the speaker] is inherent in the determination to confine exhibitors to fixed locations, it applies to all exhibitors alike, and it does not invalidate the Rule as a reasonable time, place, and manner regulation."

AESTHETICS

May government limit speech in order to protect the attractive appearance or ambience of its public spaces, even without regard to concerns of public safety? May it prevent visual or aural "pollution"? Is securing beautiful or tranquil surroundings enough of a reason to limit speech? Is there a danger that assertion of such amorphous, intangible interests might conceal improper hostility to the regulated speech? The Court has recognized government aesthetic interests as substantial or significant in a number of cases.

In METROMEDIA, INC. v. SAN DIEGO, 453 U.S. 490 (1981), for example, the Court reviewed a free speech challenge to a San Diego ordinance regulating billboard displays in order "to eliminate hazards to pedestrians and motorists brought about by distracting sign displays" and "to preserve and improve the appearance of the City." Recall that the Court upheld part of the ordinance restricting commercial billboard displays, see p. 1193 above. While the Court struck down the part of a San Diego ordinance restricting noncommercial billboard displays, the opinions of a majority of the Court—the four members of the plurality plus the three dissenters—indicated considerable general willingness to defer to the government's aesthetic interests.

The plurality opinion of Justice WHITE, joined by Justices Stewart, Marshall and Powell, acknowledged the problems billboards pose "for land-use planning and development," but found San Diego's ordinance impermissibly content-based because it provided a number of exceptions, including exceptions for on-site commercial signs, government signs, temporary political campaign signs, for-sale and for-lease signs, religious symbols, signs telling the time and temperature, historical commemorative plaques, and signs within shopping malls: "[Billboards] combine communicative and noncommunicative aspects. [The] government has legitimate interests in controlling the noncommunicative aspects of the medium, but [the First Amendment forecloses] a similar interest in controlling the communicative aspects." The plurality found that the exceptions unconstitutionally distinguished among subject matters. The exceptions for commercial billboards inverted the usual First Amendment hierarchy "by affording a greater degree of protection to commercial than to noncommercial speech." And "[w]ith respect to noncommercial speech, the city may not choose the appropriate subjects for public discourse. Because some noncommercial messages may be conveyed on billboards throughout the commercial and industrial zones, San Diego must similarly allow billboards conveying other noncommercial messages throughout those zones."

Justice BRENNAN, joined by Justice Blackmun, concurred in the judgment, focusing not on any discrimination in the ordinance but rather on its distributive aspects. Justice Brennan argued that "the *practical* effect of the San Diego ordinance is to eliminate the billboard as an effective medium of communication. [Instead] of relying on the exceptions to the ban to invalidate the ordinance, I would apply the tests [developed] to analyze content-neutral prohibitions of particular media of communication. [Schad, Schneider, Martin.]" Under such a standard, he argued, the city must show "that a sufficiently substantial governmental interest is directly furthered by the total ban, and that any more narrowly drawn restriction, i.e., anything less than a total ban, would promote less well the achievement of that goal." He found the ban unjustified under that standard. He found the evidentiary support for the traffic safety claims weak, and he was especially skeptical of the asserted aesthetic interests: "[A] billboard is not necessarily inconsistent with oil storage tanks, blighted areas, or strip development. Of course, it is not for a court to impose its own notion of beauty on San Diego. But before deferring to a city's judgment, a court must be convinced that the city is seriously and comprehensively addressing aesthetic concerns with respect to its environment." (In comparing Justice White's and Justice Brennan's opinions, recall the discussion above of the discrimination and distribution—or equal-access and guaranteed-access—strands in the early public forum cases. For an example of a later case adopting Justice Brennan's rather than Justice White's approach in Metromedia, see Ladue v. Gilleo, 1994, p. 1243 above, involving a ban on residential signs.)

Chief Justice BURGER, Justice REHNQUIST, and Justice STEVENS each filed a separate dissent. The Chief Justice chided the plurality for undervaluing the importance of local control over local problems. Because ample alternative channels of communications were available, he would not hold the First Amendment to bar San Diego's justifiable and reasonable effort to do something about "what it perceives—and what it has a right to perceive—as ugly and dangerous eyesores thrust upon its citizens." Justice Stevens' dissent disagreed that completely effective alternative channels of communication were available. But he did not see the diminution of communications opportunities as fatal: "The essential concern embodied in the First Amendment is that government not impose its viewpoint on the public or select the topics on which public debate is permissible," and no viewpoint discrimination was presented. Justice Stevens emphasized that a government interest "in securing beautiful surroundings" may sometimes outweigh interests in "uninhibited expression by means of words and pictures in public places." He noted that "some total prohibitions may be permissible. It seems to be accepted by all that a zoning regulation excluding billboards from residential neighborhoods is justified by the interest in maintaining pleasant surroundings and enhancing property values." He argued that the same concerns should legitimate a billboard ban in industrial zones. Justice Rehnquist largely agreed with the other dissents.

The Court in Metromedia did not reach the question of the permissibility of a total, content-neutral, prohibition of billboards. But the various opinions alluded to such a flat ban in dicta. Justice White, the author of the Metromedia plurality opinion, observed several years later: "A majority of this Court found [in Metromedia] that [aesthetic] considerations *would* be sufficient to justify a content-neutral ban on all outdoor advertising signs, notwithstanding the extent to which such signs convey First Amendment protected messages." Lakewood v. Plain Dealer Publishing Co., 486 U.S. 750, 783 (1988) (White, J., dissenting) (citing the plurality opinion and the dissenting opinions of Burger, C.J. and Rehnquist and Stevens, JJ.) (emphasis added). Consider in light of Metromedia the following cases involving a ban on the placement of political signs on utility poles and crosswires, and a ban on overnight camping in a public park as applied to anti homelessness demonstrators.

Members of City Council v. Taxpayers for Vincent
466 U.S. 789, 104 S.Ct. 2118, 80 L.Ed.2d 772 (1984).

Justice STEVENS delivered the opinion of the Court.

Section 28.04 of the Los Angeles Municipal Code prohibits the posting of signs on public property. The question presented is whether that prohibition abridges appellees' freedom of speech within the meaning of the First Amendment. [In March 1979, Roland Vincent was a candidate for the Los Angeles City Council. Taxpayers for Vincent, a group of his supporters, arranged for the production and posting of signs with Vincent's name on them. They attached the signs to utility poles at various locations by draping them over the cross-arms which support the poles and stapling the cardboard together at the bottom. The signs read: "Roland Vincent—City Council." Acting under § 28.04, city employees removed all posters attached to utility poles, including Vincent's signs. Most of the signs that were removed were commercial ones, but 48 out of more than 1200 signs removed from public property during the first week of March were "Vincent" signs. This suit challenged the constitutionality of the ordinance. The trial court dismissed the case, but the Court of Appeals reversed. After rejecting an overbreadth challenge, the Supreme Court turned to the "as applied" attack:]

The ordinance prohibits appellees from communicating with the public in a certain manner, and presumably diminishes the total quantity of their communication in the City. [But it] has been clear since this Court's earliest decisions [that] the state may sometimes curtail speech when necessary to advance a significant and legitimate state interest. [The] First Amendment forbids the government from regulating speech in ways that favor some viewpoints or ideas at the expense of [others]. That general rule has no application to this case. For there is not even a hint of bias or censorship in the City's enactment or enforcement of this ordinance.

In [O'Brien] the Court set forth the appropriate [four-step] framework for reviewing a viewpoint neutral regulation of this kind. [In] this case, [Taxpayers] do not dispute that it is within the constitutional power of the City to attempt to improve its appearance, or that this interest is basically unrelated to the suppression of ideas. Therefore the critical inquiries are whether that interest is sufficiently substantial to justify the effect of the ordinance on appellees' expression, and whether that effect is no greater than necessary to accomplish the City's purpose.

[Metromedia] dealt with San Diego's prohibition of certain forms of outdoor billboards. There the Court considered the city's interest in avoiding visual clutter, and seven Justices explicitly concluded that this interest was sufficient to justify a prohibition of billboards. [We] reaffirm the conclusion of the majority in Metromedia. The problem addressed by this ordinance—the visual assault on the citizens of Los Angeles presented by an accumulation of signs posted on public property—constitutes a significant substantive evil within the City's power to prohibit. We turn to the question whether the scope of the restriction on appellees' expressive activity is substantially broader than necessary to protect the City's interest in eliminating visual clutter. The incidental restriction on expression which results from the City's attempt to accomplish such a purpose is considered justified as a reasonable regulation of the time, place, or manner of expression if it is narrowly tailored to serve that interest. [By] banning these signs, the City did no more than eliminate the exact source of the evil it sought to remedy.

It is true that the esthetic interest in preventing the kind of litter that may result from the distribution of leaflets on the public streets and sidewalks cannot support a prophylactic prohibition against the citizens' exercise of that method of expressing his views. In Schneider v. State [1939; p. 1239 above] the Court held that ordinances that absolutely prohibited handbilling on the streets were invalid. The Court explained that cities could adequately protect the esthetic interest in avoiding litter without abridging protected expression merely by penalizing those who actually litter. Taxpayers contend that their interest in supporting Vincent's political campaign, which affords them a constitutional right to distribute [leaflets] on the public streets of Los Angeles, provides equal support for their asserted right to post temporary signs on objects adjacent to the streets and sidewalks. They argue that the mere fact that their temporary signs "add somewhat" to the city's visual clutter is entitled to no more weight than the temporary unsightliness of discarded handbills and the additional street cleaning burden that were insufficient to justify the ordinances reviewed in Schneider.

The rationale of Schneider is inapposite in the context of the instant case. There, individual citizens were actively exercising their right to communicate directly with potential recipients of their message. The conduct continued only while the speakers or distributors remained on the scene. In this case, appellees posted dozens of temporary signs throughout an area where they would remain unattended until removed. As the Court expressly noted in Schneider, the First Amendment does not "deprive a municipality of power to enact regulations against throwing literature broadcast in the [streets]." A distributor of leaflets has no right simply to scatter his pamphlets in the air—or to toss large quantities of paper from the window of a tall building or a low flying airplane. Characterizing such an activity as a separate means of communication does not diminish the state's power to condemn it as a public nuisance. [With] respect to signs posted by appellees, [it] is the tangible medium of expressing the message that has the adverse impact on the appearance of the landscape. In Schneider, an anti-littering statute could have addressed the substantive evil without prohibiting expressive activity, whereas application of the prophylactic rule actually employed gratuitously infringed upon the right of an individual to communicate directly with a willing listener. Here, the substantive evil—visual blight—is not merely a possible by-product of the activity, but is created by the medium of expression itself. In contrast to Schneider, therefore, the application of [the] ordinance in this case responds precisely to the substantive problem which legitimately concerns the City. The ordinance curtails no more speech than is necessary to accomplish its purpose.

[The challengers argue] that a prohibition against the [posting of signs on public property] cannot be justified on esthetic grounds if it fails to apply to all equally unattractive signs [including those on private property.] [But the] private citizen's interest in controlling the use of his own property justifies the disparate treatment. Moreover, by not extending the ban to all locations, a significant opportunity to communicate by means of temporary signs is preserved, and private property owners' esthetic concerns will keep the posting of signs on their property within reasonable bounds. Even if some visual blight remains, a partial, content-neutral ban may nevertheless enhance the City's appearance.

[A] a restriction on expressive activity may be invalid if the remaining modes of communication are inadequate. [E.g., Heffron.] The Los Angeles ordinance does not affect any individual's freedom to exercise the right to speak and to distribute literature in the same place where the posting of signs on public property is prohibited. To the extent that the posting of signs on public property has advantages over these forms of expression, there is no reason to believe that these same advantages cannot be obtained through other means. To the contrary, the findings [indicate] that there are ample alternative modes of communication in Los Angeles. Notwithstanding appellees' general assertions [concerning] the utility of political posters, nothing in the findings indicates that the posting of political posters on public property is a uniquely valuable or important mode of communication, or that appellees' ability to communicate effectively is threatened by ever-increasing restrictions on expression.

Appellees suggest that the public property covered by the ordinance is [a] "public forum." [Appellees'] reliance on the public forum doctrine is misplaced. They fail to demonstrate the existence of a traditional right of access respecting such items as utility poles for purposes of their communication comparable to that recognized for public streets and parks, and it is clear that "the First Amendment does not guarantee access to government property simply because it is owned or controlled by the government." [Greenburgh, p. 1276 below.] Rather, the "existence of a right of access to public property and the standard by which limitations upon such a right must be evaluated differ depending on the character of the property at issue." [Perry, p. 1277 below.] Lampposts can of course be used as signposts, but the mere fact that government property can be used as a vehicle for communication does not mean that the Constitution requires such uses to be permitted.[1] Public property which is not by tradition or designation a forum for public communication may be reserved by the state "for its intended purposes, communicative or otherwise, as long as the regulation on speech is reasonable and not an effort to suppress expression merely because public officials oppose the speaker's view." [Perry.] Given our analysis of the legitimate interest served by the ordinance, its viewpoint neutrality, and the availability of alternative channels of communication, the ordinance is certainly constitutional as applied to appellees under this standard.

Finally, [Taxpayers] argue that Los Angeles could have written an ordinance that would have had a less severe effect on expressive activity such as theirs, by permitting the posting of any kind of sign at any time on some types of public property, or by making a variety of other more specific exceptions to the ordinance: for signs carrying certain types of messages (such as political campaign signs), for signs posted during specific time periods (perhaps during political campaigns), for particular locations (perhaps for areas already cluttered by an excessive number of signs on adjacent private property), or for signs meeting design specifications (such as size or color). Plausible public policy arguments might well be made in support of any such exception, but it by no means follows that it is therefore constitutionally mandated, nor is it clear that some of the suggested exceptions would even be constitutionally permissible. For example, even though political speech is entitled to the fullest possible measure of constitutional protection, there are a host of other communications that command the same respect. An assertion that "Jesus Saves," that "Abortion is Murder," that every woman has the "Right to Choose," or that "Alcohol Kills," may have a claim to a constitutional exemption from the ordinance that is just as strong as "[Roland] Vincent—City Council." To create an exception for appellees' political speech and not these other types of speech might create a risk of engaging in constitutionally forbidden content discrimination. [Carey; Mosley.] Moreover, the volume of permissible postings under such a mandated exemption might so limit the ordinance's effect as to defeat its aim of combatting visual blight. Any constitutionally mandated exception to the City's total prohibition against temporary signs on public property would necessarily rest on a judicial determination [that] the City's interests in esthetics are not sufficiently important to justify the prohibition in that

---

1. Any tangible property owned by the government could be used to communicate—bumper stickers may be placed on official automobiles—and yet appellees could not seriously claim the right to attach "Taxpayer for Vincent" bumper stickers to City-owned automobiles. At some point, the government's relationship to things under its dominion and control is virtually identical to a private owner's property interest in the same kinds of things, and in such circumstances, the State, "no less than a private owner of property, has power to preserve the property under its control for the use to which it is lawfully dedicated." [Adderley; p. 1269 below.] [Footnote by Justice Stevens.]

category. But [there is] no basis for questioning the substantiality of the esthetic interest [or] for believing that a uniquely important form of communication has been abridged for the categories of expression engaged in by [the challengers]. Therefore, we accept the City's position that it may decide that the esthetic interest in avoiding "visual clutter" justifies a removal of signs creating or increasing that clutter. [We] hold that on this record [the] interests are sufficiently substantial to justify this content neutral, impartially administered [prohibition].

[Reversed.]

Justice BRENNAN, with whom Justice MARSHALL and Justice BLACK-MUN join, dissenting.

[Because] the Court's lenient approach towards the restriction of speech for reasons of aesthetics [here and in Metromedia] threatens seriously to undermine the protections of the First Amendment, I dissent. [In my view, Los Angeles] has not shown that its interest in eliminating "visual clutter" justifies its restriction of appellees' ability to communicate with the local electorate. [In] deciding this First Amendment question, the critical importance of the posting of signs as a means of communication must not be overlooked. Use of this medium of communication is particularly valuable in part because it entails a relatively small expense in reaching a wide audience, allows flexibility in accommodating various formats, typographies, and graphics, and conveys its message in a manner that is easily read and understood by its reader or viewer. There may be alternative channels of communication, but the prevalence of a large number of signs in Los Angeles is a strong indication that, for many speakers, those alternatives are far less satisfactory. [There] is no proof [e.g.] that a sufficient number of private parties would allow the posting of signs on their property. A speaker with a message that is generally unpopular or simply unpopular among property owners is hardly likely to get his message across if forced to rely on this medium. [Similarly], the adequacy of distributing handbills is dubious, [for] a message on a sign will typically reach far more people than one on a handbill. [Because] the City has completely banned the use of this particular medium of communication, and because, given the circumstances, there are no equivalent alternative media that provide an adequate substitute, the Court must examine with particular care the justifications that the City proffers for its ban.

[If a] restriction is content-neutral, the court's task is to determine (1) whether the governmental objective advanced by the restriction is substantial, and (2) whether the restriction imposed on speech is no greater than is essential to further that objective. Unless both conditions are met the restriction must be invalidated. [I suggested] in Metromedia [that] courts should exercise special care in addressing these questions when a purely aesthetic objective is asserted to justify a restriction of speech. [I] adhere to that view. [A]esthetic interests are easy for a city to assert and difficult for a court to evaluate. [The] source of those difficulties is the unavoidable subjectivity of aesthetic judgments. As a consequence, [laws] defended on aesthetic grounds raise problems for judicial review that are not presented by laws defended on more objective grounds—such as national security, public health, or public safety. [E.g.,] a reviewing court faces substantial difficulties determining whether the actual objective is related to the suppression of speech. The asserted interest in aesthetics may be only a facade for content-based suppression. [Thus, the real] objective might simply be the elimination of the messages typically carried by the signs. [The] City might easily mask [such an] objective [by] declaring that signs constitute visual clutter.

[Similarly,] when a total ban is justified solely in terms of aesthetics, the means inquiry necessary to evaluate the constitutionality of the ban may be impeded by deliberate or unintended government manipulation. [Once] the government has identified a substantial aesthetic objective and has selected a preferred means of achieving its objective, it will be possible for the government to correct any mismatch between means and ends by redefining the ends to conform with the means. [When] a court reviews a restriction of speech imposed in order to promote an aesthetic objective, there is a significant possibility that the court will be able to do little more than pay lip service to the First Amendment inquiry into the availability of less restrictive alternatives.

The fact that there are difficulties inherent in judicial review of aesthetics-based restrictions of speech does not imply that government may not engage in such activities. [But] because the implementation of these functions creates special dangers to our First Amendment freedoms, there is a need for more stringent judicial scrutiny than the Court seems willing to exercise. In cases like this, where a total ban is imposed on a particularly valuable method of communication, a court should require the government to provide tangible proof of the legitimacy and substantiality of its aesthetic objective. [Statements] of aesthetic objectives should be accepted as substantial and unrelated to the suppression of speech only if the government demonstrates that it is pursuing an identified objective seriously and comprehensively and in ways that are unrelated to the restriction of speech. [In] this case, however, there is no indication that the City has addressed its visual clutter problem in any way other than by prohibiting the posting of signs—throughout the City and without regard to the density of their presence. Therefore, I would hold that the prohibition violates appellees' First Amendment rights.

[A] more limited approach to the visual clutter problem, however, might well pass constitutional muster. I have no doubt, [for example,] that signs posted on public property in certain areas—including, perhaps, parts of Los Angeles—could contribute to the type of eyesore that a city would genuinely have a substantial interest in eliminating. These areas might include parts of the City that are particularly pristine, reserved for certain uses, designated to reflect certain themes, or so blighted that broad gauged renovation is necessary. Presumably, in these types of areas the City would also regulate the aesthetic environment in ways other than the banning of temporary signs. [Similarly,] Los Angeles might be able to attack its visual clutter problem in more areas of the City by reducing the stringency of the ban, perhaps by regulating the density of temporary signs, and coupling that approach with additional measures designed to reduce other forms of visual clutter. In [this] case, I believe that Los Angeles' total ban sweeps so broadly and trenches so completely on appellees' use of an important medium of political expression that it must be struck down as violative of the [First Amendment].

Clark v. Community for Creative Non–Violence

468 U.S. 288, 104 S.Ct. 3065, 82 L.Ed.2d 221 (1984).

Justice WHITE delivered the opinion of the Court.

The issue in this case is whether a National Park Service regulation prohibiting camping in certain parks violates the First Amendment when applied to prohibit demonstrators from sleeping in Lafayette Park and the Mall in connection with a demonstration intended to call attention to the plight of the homeless. We hold that it does [not].

I. The Interior Department, through the National Park Service, is charged with responsibility for the [management] of the National Parks and is authorized to promulgate rules and regulations for the use of the parks in accordance with the purposes for which they were established. The network of National Parks includes the National Memorial-core parks [Lafayette Park and the Mall].[1] Under the regulations involved in this case, camping in National Parks is permitted only in campgrounds designated for that purpose. No such campgrounds have ever been designated in Lafayette Park or the Mall.[2] [Demonstrations] for the airing of views or grievances are permitted in the Memorial-core parks, but for the most part only by Park Service permits. Temporary structures may be erected for demonstration purposes but may not be used for camping.[3]

In 1982, the Park Service issued a renewable permit to respondent Community for Creative Non–Violence (CCNV) to conduct a wintertime demonstration in Lafayette Park and the Mall for the purpose of demonstrating the plight of the homeless. The permit authorized the erection of two symbolic tent [cities]. The Park Service, however, [denied] CCNV's request that demonstrators be permitted to sleep in the symbolic tents. CCNV and several individuals then filed an action to prevent the application of the anti-camping regulations to the proposed [demonstration].[4]

II. We need not differ with the view of the Court of Appeals that overnight sleeping in connection with the demonstration is expressive conduct protected to some extent by the First Amendment. We assume for present purposes, but do not decide, that such is the case, cf. [O'Brien], but this assumption only begins the inquiry. Expression, whether oral or written or symbolized by conduct, is subject to reasonable time, place, and manner restrictions. We have often noted that restrictions of this kind are valid provided that they are justified without reference to the content of the regulated speech, that they are narrowly tailored to serve a significant governmental interest, and that they leave open ample alternative channels for communication of the information. It is also true that a message may be delivered by conduct that is intended to be communicative and that, in context, would reasonably be understood by the viewer to be communicative. [Spence.] Symbolic expression of this kind may be forbidden or regulated if the conduct

---

1. Lafayette Park is a seven-acre square located across Pennsylvania Avenue from the White House. The Mall is a stretch of land running westward from the Capitol to the Lincoln Memorial some two miles away. (It includes the Washington Monument as well as a series of pools, trees, lawns, and other greenery.) Both park areas are visited by "vast numbers of visitors."

2. The regulation defined "camping" as "the use of park land for living accommodation purposes such as sleeping activities, or making preparations to sleep." Under the regulations, these activities "constitute camping when it reasonably appears [that] the participants [are] in fact using the area as a living accommodation regardless of the intent of the participants or the nature of

any other activities in which they may also be engaging."

3. The regulations state: "In connection with permitted demonstrations or special events, temporary structures may be erected for the purpose of symbolizing a message or meeting logistical needs such as [first aid facilities]. Temporary structures may not be used outside designated camping areas for [camping activities]."

4. The District Court had granted summary judgment for the Park Service. The Court of Appeals had reversed by a vote of 6–5 in an en banc decision, finding the regulations invalid as applied. (The eleven judges produced six opinions.) See 703 F.2d 586.

itself may constitutionally be regulated, if the regulation is narrowly drawn to further a substantial governmental interest, and if the interest is unrelated to the suppression of free speech. [O'Brien.]

The United States submits [that] the regulation forbidding sleeping is defensible either as a time, place, or manner restriction or as a regulation of symbolic conduct. We [agree]. [The regulations,] including the ban on sleeping, are clearly limitations on the manner in which the demonstration could be carried out. That sleeping, like the symbolic tents themselves, may be expressive and part of the message delivered by the demonstration does not make the ban any less a limitation on the manner of demonstrating, for reasonable time, place, and manner regulations normally have the purpose and direct effect of limiting expression but are nevertheless valid. Neither does the fact that sleeping, arguendo, may be expressive conduct, rather than oral or written expression, render the sleeping prohibition any less a time, place, or manner regulation. [We] have very little trouble concluding that the Park Service may prohibit overnight sleeping in the parks involved here.

The requirement that the regulation be content neutral is clearly satisfied. [It] is not disputed here that the prohibition on camping, and on sleeping specifically, is content neutral and is not being applied because of disagreement with the message presented. Neither was the regulation faulted, nor could it be, on the ground that without overnight sleeping the plight of the homeless could not be communicated in other ways. The regulation otherwise left the demonstration intact, with its symbolic city, signs, and the presence of those who were willing to take their turns in a day-and-night vigil. Respondents do not suggest that there was, or is, any barrier to delivering to the media, or to the public by other means, the intended message concerning the plight of the homeless. It is also apparent to us that the regulation narrowly focuses on the Government's substantial interest in maintaining the parks in the heart of our capital in an attractive and intact condition, readily available to the millions of people who wish to [enjoy them]. To permit camping [would] be totally inimical to these [purposes].

[It] is evident from our cases that the validity of this regulation need not be judged solely by reference to the demonstration at hand. [Heffron.] Absent the prohibition on sleeping, there would be other groups who would demand permission to deliver an asserted message by camping in Lafayette Park. Some of them would surely have as credible a claim in this regard as does CCNV, and the denial of permits to still others would present difficult problems for the Park Service. With the prohibition, however, [at] least some around-the-clock demonstrations lasting for days on end will not materialize, others will be limited in size and duration, and the purposes of the regulation will thus be materially served. Perhaps these purposes would be more effectively and not so clumsily achieved by preventing tents and 24–hour vigils entirely in the core areas. But the Park Service's decision to permit non-sleeping demonstrations does not, in our view, impugn the camping prohibition as a valuable, but perhaps imperfect, protection to the parks. If the Government has a legitimate interest in ensuring that the National Parks are adequately protected, which we think it has, and if the parks would be more exposed to harm without the sleeping prohibition than with it, the ban is safe from invalidation under the First Amendment as a reasonable regulation on the manner in which a demonstration may be carried out. As in [Taxpayers for Vincent], the regulation "responds precisely to the substantive problems which legitimately concern the [Government]."

[The] foregoing analysis demonstrates that the Park Service regulation is sustainable under the four-factor standard of [O'Brien] for validating a regulation of expressive conduct, which, in the last analysis is little, if any, different from the standard applied to time, place, and manner restrictions.[5] No one contends that aside from its impact on speech a rule against camping or overnight sleeping in public parks is beyond the constitutional power of the Government to enforce. And [there] is a substantial government interest in conserving park property, an interest that is plainly served by, and requires for its implementation, measures such as the proscription of sleeping that are designed to limit the wear and tear on park properties. That interest is unrelated to suppression of expression.

We are unmoved by [view] that the challenged regulation is unnecessary, and hence invalid, because there are less speech-restrictive alternatives that could have satisfied the government interest in preserving park lands. There is no gainsaying that preventing overnight sleeping will avoid a measure of actual or threatened damage to Lafayette Park and the Mall. The Court of Appeals' suggestions that the Park Service minimize the possible injury by reducing the size, duration, or frequency of demonstrations would still curtail the total allowable expression in which demonstrators could engage, whether by sleeping or otherwise, and these suggestions represent no more than a disagreement with the Park Service over how much protection the core parks require or how an acceptable level of preservation is to be attained. We do not believe, however, that either [O'Brien] or the time, place, and manner decisions assign to the judiciary the authority to replace the Park Service as the manager of the Nation's parks or endow the judiciary with the competence to judge how much protection of park lands is wise and how that level of conservation is to be attained.

[Reversed.] [Chief Justice Burger filed a separate concurrence suggesting that the activity here was more "conduct" than speech.]

Justice MARSHALL, with whom Justice BRENNAN joins, dissenting.

I. [The] proper starting point for analysis [is] a recognition that the activity in which respondents seek to engage [is] symbolic speech protected by the First Amendment. The majority [so] assumes, without deciding. [This] case requires a closer look at the nature of the expressive conduct at issue and the context in which that conduct would be displayed. [Missing] from the majority's description is any inkling that Lafayette Park and the Mall have served as the sites for some of the most rousing political demonstrations in the Nation's history. [The] primary purpose for making *sleep* an integral part of the demonstration was "to re-enact the central reality of homelessness" and to impress upon public consciousness, in as dramatic a way as possible, that

---

5. Reasonable time, place, and manner restrictions are valid even though they directly limit oral or written expression. It would be odd to insist on a higher standard for limitations aimed at regulable conduct and having only an incidental impact on speech. Thus, if the time, place, and manner restriction on expressive sleeping, if that is what is involved in this case, sufficiently and narrowly serves a substantial enough governmental interest to escape First Amendment condemnation, it is untenable to invalidate it under O'Brien on the ground that the governmental interest is insufficient to warrant the intrusion on First Amendment concerns or that there is an inadequate nexus between the regulation and the interest sought to be served. We note that only recently, in a case dealing with the regulation of signs, the Court framed the issue under O'Brien and then based a crucial part of its analysis on the time, place, and manner cases. [Taxpayers for Vincent.] [Footnote by Justice White.]

homelessness is a widespread problem, often ignored, that confronts its victims with life-threatening [deprivations].

In a long line of cases, this Court has afforded First Amendment protection to expressive conduct that qualifies as symbolic speech. In light of the surrounding context, respondents' proposed activity meets the qualifications. The Court has previously acknowledged the importance of context in determining whether an act can properly be denominated as "speech" for First Amendment purposes and has provided guidance concerning the way in which courts should "read" a context in making this determination. The leading case is [Spence], where this Court [looked] first to the intent of the speaker and second to the perception of the audience. Here respondents clearly intended to protest the reality of homelessness by sleeping outdoors in the winter in the near vicinity of the [White House]. Nor can there be any doubt that in the surrounding circumstances the likelihood was great that the political significance of sleeping in the parks would be understood by those who viewed it. [This] likelihood stems from the remarkably apt fit between the activity in which respondents seek to engage and the social problems they seek to highlight. [It] is true that we all go to sleep as part of our daily regimen and that, for the most part, sleep represents a physical necessity and not a vehicle for expression. But these characteristics need not prevent an activity that is normally devoid of expressive purpose from being used as a novel mode of communication.

[The] Government contends that a forseeable difficulty of administration counsels against recognizing sleep as a mode of expression protected by the First Amendment. The predicament the Government envisions can be termed "the imposter problem": the problem of distinguishing bona fide protesters from imposters [without] inquiring into the sincerity of demonstrators [in a way that] would necessarily be content-sensitive. I find this argument unpersuasive. [The] administrative difficulty the Government envisions is now nothing more than a vague apprehension. [The Government also] contends that the Spence approach is overinclusive because "[actions] such as assassination of political figures and the bombing of government buildings can fairly be characterized as intended to convey a message that is readily perceived by the public." [The answer to the] Government's argument [is that, even if] an act is defined as speech, it must still be balanced against countervailing government interests. The balancing which the First Amendment requires would doom any argument seeking to protect anti-social acts such as assassination or destruction of government property from government interference because compelling interests would outweigh the expressive value of such conduct.

II.   Although sleep in the context of this case is symbolic speech protected by the First Amendment, it is nonetheless subject to reasonable time, place, and manner restrictions. I agree with the standard enunciated by the majority.[1] I conclude, however, that the regulations at issue [here], as applied to respondents, fail to satisfy this standard. [The] majority cites no evidence indicating that sleeping engaged in as symbolic speech will cause *substantial* wear and tear on park property. Furthermore, the Government's application of the sleeping ban in the circumstances of this case is strikingly underinclusive. The majority acknowledges that a proper time, place, and manner restriction must be "narrowly tailored." Here, however, the tailoring requirement is virtually forsaken inasmuch as the Government offers no justification for applying its absolute ban on sleeping yet is willing to allow respondents to engage in

---

1. I also agree with the majority that no substantial difference distinguishes the test applicable to time, place, and manner restrictions and the test articulated in United States v. O'Brien. [Footnote by Justice Marshall.]

activities—such as feigned sleeping—that is no less burdensome. In short, there are no substantial governmental interests advanced by the Government's regulations as applied to respondents. All that the Court's decision advances are the prerogatives of a bureaucracy that over the years has shown an implacable hostility towards citizens' exercise of First Amendment rights.

III. [In] this case, as in some others involving time, place, and manner restrictions, the Court has dramatically lowered its scrutiny of governmental regulations once it has determined that such regulations are content neutral. The result has been the creation of a two-tiered approach to First Amendment cases: while regulations that turn on the content of the expression are subjected to a strict form of judicial review [unless they involve standardless licensing], regulations that are aimed at matters other than expression receive only a minimal level of scrutiny. [By] narrowly limiting its concern to whether a given regulation creates a content-based distinction, the Court has seemingly overlooked the fact that content-neutral restrictions are also capable of unnecessarily restricting protected expressive activity. To be sure, the general prohibition against content-based regulations is an essential tool of First Amendment analysis. [Mosley.] The Court, however, has transformed the ban against content-distinctions from a floor that offers all persons at least equal liberty under the First Amendment into a ceiling that restricts persons to the protection of First Amendment equality—but nothing more.[2] The consistent imposition of silence upon all may fulfill the dictates of an even-handed content-neutrality. But it offends our "profound national commitment to the principle that debate on public issues should be uninhibited, robust, and wide-open." [New York Times v. Sullivan.]

[Moreover,] this case reveals a mistaken assumption regarding the motives and behavior of government officials who create and administer content-neutral regulations. The Court's salutary skepticism of governmental decisionmaking in First Amendment matters suddenly dissipates once it determines that a restriction is not content-based. The Court evidently assumes that the balance struck by officials is deserving of deference so long as it does not appear to be tainted by content discrimination. What the Court fails to recognize is that public officials have strong incentives to overregulate even in the absence of an intent to censor particular views. This incentive stems from the fact that of the two groups whose interests officials must accommodate—on the one hand, the interests of the general public and on the other, the interests of those who seek to use a particular forum for First Amendment activity—the political power of the former is likely to be far greater than that of the latter. [In light of government officials' greater] sensitivity to regulatory as opposed to First Amendment interests, [facial] viewpoint-neutrality is no shield against unneces-

2. Furthermore, a content-neutral regulation does not necessarily fall with random or equal force upon different groups or different points of view. A content-neutral regulation that restricts an inexpensive mode of communication will fall most heavily upon relatively poor speakers and the points of view that such speakers typically espouse. See, e.g., [Taxpayers for Vincent]. This sort of latent inequality is very much in evidence in this case, for respondents lack the financial means necessary to buy access to more conventional modes of persuasion.

A disquieting feature about the disposition of this case is that it lends credence to the charge that judicial administration of the First Amendment, in conjunction with a social order marked by large disparities in wealth and other sources of power, tends systematically to discriminate against efforts by the relatively disadvantaged to convey their political ideas. In the past, this Court has taken such considerations into account in adjudicating the First Amendment rights of those among us who are financially deprived. See, e.g., [Martin v. Struthers.] [Footnote by Justice Marshall.]

sary restrictions on unpopular ideas or modes of expression, and [here] the Court [should have] subject[ed] the Government's restrictive policy to something more than minimal [scrutiny].

––––––

TRANQUILITY, PRIVACY AND REPOSE

1. *Noise regulations.* Recall that, in Kovacs v. Cooper (1949; p. 1241 above), the Court upheld a ban on "loud and raucous" sound trucks. In WARD v. ROCK AGAINST RACISM, 491 U.S. 781 (1989), the Court rejected a First Amendment challenge to New York City's regulation mandating the use of city-provided sound systems and technicians to control the volume of concerts at the Bandshell in Central Park. The regulation was challenged by a group that claimed that the inability to use its own equipment and technicians in a concert in a public forum interfered with its free expression rights. There was a consensus on the Court that the case involved a "public forum," that the City's interest in limiting excessive noise was substantial, and that the regulation was "content-neutral."

The central dispute accordingly turned on how strictly to interpret the "narrowly tailored means" requirement. Recall that O'Brien had suggested that content-neutral restrictions are valid "if the incidental restriction on alleged First Amendment freedoms is no greater than is essential to the furtherance of that interest." The Court of Appeals in Ward had read O'Brien to require the "least intrusive means" and found that the city had not shown that it lacked other, less restrictive means of regulating concert volume. Justice KENNEDY, writing for the Court, explicitly repudiated this view: "the Court of Appeals erred in requiring the city to prove that this regulation was the least intrusive means." Justice Kennedy noted that, in CCNV, the Court had rephrased O'Brien's requirement to demand only means that are "narrowly drawn" to further a substantial governmental interest, and had announced that this "narrowly drawn" means requirement was the same as the "narrowly tailored" requirement for time, place, and manner regulations of the public forum. Here, he found that the regulation satisfied this test; it was "narrowly tailored to serve a significant governmental interest," and the lower court should not have "sift[ed] through all the available or imagined" alternative means. "[O]ur cases quite clearly hold that restrictions on the time, place, or manner of protected speech are not invalid 'simply because there is some imaginable alternative that might be less burdensome on speech.'

"[Lest] any confusion on the point remain, we reaffirm today that a regulation of the time, place, or manner of protected speech must be narrowly tailored to serve the government's legitimate content-neutral interests but that it need not be the least-restrictive or least-intrusive means of doing so. Rather, [narrow] tailoring is satisfied 'so long as [the] regulation promotes a substantial government interest that would be achieved less effectively absent the regulation.' [Albertini; p. 1276 below.] [To] be sure, this standard does not mean that a time, place, or manner regulation may burden substantially more speech than is necessary to further the government's legitimate interests. [So] long as the means chosen are not substantially broader than necessary to achieve the government's interest, however, the regulation will not be invalid simply because a court concludes that the government's interest could be adequately served by some less-speech-restrictive alternative." Applying this deferential standard, and finding that the regulation left open "ample alternative channels of communication," he concluded that it was "a reasonable regulation of the place and manner of expression." Justice Blackmun concurred in the result.

Justice MARSHALL, joined by Justices Brennan and Stevens, dissented at length, contending that a "least-restrictive-alternative" analysis was built into the "narrowly tailored" requirement. To hold otherwise, he said, was a "serious distortion of the narrow tailoring requirement. [By] holding that the guidelines are valid time, place, and manner restrictions, notwithstanding the availability of less intrusive but effective means of controlling volume, the majority deprives the narrow tailoring requirement of all meaning." Justice Marshall elaborated: "Until today, a key safeguard of free speech has been government's obligation to adopt the least intrusive restriction necessary to achieve its goals. [The] majority replaces constitutional scrutiny with mandatory deference. [Under the majority's view, it will be enough] that the challenged regulation advances the government's interest only in the slightest, for any differential burden on speech that results does not enter the calculus. Despite its protestations to the contrary, the majority thus has abandoned the requirement that restrictions on speech be narrowly tailored in any ordinary use of the phrase. Indeed, after today's decision, a city could claim that bans on handbill distribution or on door-to-door solicitation are the most effective means of avoiding littering and [fraud]. Logically extended, the majority's analysis would permit such far reaching restrictions on speech. [In effect, the majority] instructs courts to refrain from examining how much speech may be restricted to serve an asserted interest and how that level of restriction is to be achieved. If a court cannot engage in such inquiries, I am at a loss to understand how a court can ascertain whether the government has adopted a regulation that burdens substantially more speech than is necessary."

2. *Protecting "captive audiences."* Recall that in Cohen v. California (p. 1081 above), the Court held that audiences must simply avert their eyes and ears when they encounter speech that offends them in open public spaces; government may not protect them in advance. The Court likewise held in Consolidated Edison Co. v. PSC and Bolger v. Youngs Drug Products (p. 1170 above), that audiences offended by mail they receive must simply make the "short, regular, journey from mail box to trash can." But the Court held in Rowan v. Post Office (p. 1169 above) that an offended recipient may request that his or her name be removed from mailing lists, and held in FCC v. Pacifica (p. 1164 above) that the federal government may bar indecent radio broadcasts during daytime hours to prevent assault on unwilling listeners who are "captive" in their homes. Are there other contexts in which the Court will permit government to protect the sensibilities of a "captive audience," even from speech upon the public streets and sidewalks? Consider the following cases, which involved targeted residential picketing and abortion clinic protests.

a. *Targeted residential picketing.* Recall that in Carey v. Brown (1980; p. 1205 above), the Court invalidated a law banning all residential picketing except labor picketing, but did not reach the question of the validity of a law "barring all residential picketing regardless of its subject matter." Justice Brennan's majority opinion stated: "We are not to be understood to imply [that] residential picketing is beyond the reach of uniform and nondiscriminatory regulation. For the right to communicate is not limitless. [The] State's interest in protecting the well-being, tranquility, and privacy of the home is certainly of the highest order in a free and civilized society." In FRISBY v. SCHULTZ, 487 U.S. 474 (1988), the Court narrowly construed and sustained a flat ban on what it called "focused picketing" of a particular residence. A group ranging from 11 to over 40 people, all opposed to abortions, picketed, on six occasions within one month, the residence of a doctor who performed abortions.

The picketing was orderly and peaceful. Thereafter, the town (a residential suburb of Milwaukee with a population of about 4300) enacted a flat ban on all residential picketing, barring picketing "on or about the residence [of] any individual." The lower courts enjoined the ordinance, but the Court upheld it. As construed by the Court, the ordinance did not prohibit all residential picketing but only residential picketing that focused on and took place in front of a particular residence.

Justice O'CONNOR's majority opinion in the 6–3 ruling noted that "a public street does not lose its status as a traditional public forum simply because it runs through a residential neighborhood," but nevertheless concluded that the ordinance was valid because it was content-neutral, was "narrowly tailored to serve a significant government interest," and left open "ample alternative channels of communication." Justice O'Connor found the latter requirement "readily" satisfied here, in light of the narrow construction she invoked: the ordinance left protesters free to march through the neighborhood, so long as they did not focus on a particular residence; moreover, they were left free to proselytize door-to-door, and to distribute literature. In addition, there was a "significant government interest": "the protection of residential privacy." She noted that earlier decisions had held that "individuals are not required to welcome unwanted speech into their own homes," citing Pacifica and Kovacs, and added: "There simply is no right to force speech into the home of an unwilling listener."

Turning to the means/end fit, Justice O'Connor found the ordinance "narrowly tailored to protect only unwilling recipients of the communications. [A] complete ban can be narrowly tailored, but only if each activity within the proscription's scope is an appropriately targeted evil. [Taxpayers for Vincent]." She elaborated: "The type of focused picketing [here] is fundamentally different from more generally directed means of communication, that may not be completely banned in residential areas. See, e.g., [Schneider ; Martin .] [Here the] picketing is narrowly directed at the household, not the public. The type of picketers banned by the [ordinance] generally do not seek to disseminate a message to the general public, but to intrude upon the targeted resident, and to do so in an especially offensive way. Moreover, even if some such picketers have a broader communicative purpose, their activity nonetheless inherently and offensively intrudes on residential privacy. The devastating effect of targeted picketing on the quiet enjoyment of the home is beyond doubt. [Even] a solitary picket can invade residential privacy. [The] offensive and disturbing nature of the form of the communication banned by [the] ordinance thus can scarcely be questioned. [The] First Amendment permits the government to prohibit offensive speech as intrusive when the 'captive' audience cannot avoid the objectionable speech. [Con Ed, Bolger.] The target of the focused picketing banned [here] is just such a 'captive.' The resident is figuratively, and perhaps literally, trapped within the home, and because of the unique and subtle impact of such picketing is left with no ready means of avoiding the unwanted speech. Thus, the 'evil' of targeted residential picketing [is] 'created by the medium of expression itself.' [Taxpayers for Vincent.] Accordingly, [this] ordinance's complete ban of that particular medium of expression is narrowly tailored." She thus rejected the facial challenge to the ordinance.

Justice BRENNAN's dissent, joined by Justice Marshall, accepted that the majority had set forth the appropriate legal test, but argued that the ordinance banned "significantly more speech than is necessary to achieve the government's substantial and legitimate goal." In explaining why the ordinance was not "narrowly tailored," he acknowledged that there were clearly "many aspects of residential picketing that, if unregulated, might easily become intrusive or unduly coercive." Some of these aspects were illustrated here: the trial court had found that the protesters had, for example, warned young children not to go near the house because the physician was a "baby killer," had repeatedly trespassed on her property, and had at least once blocked the exits to her home. Such "intrusive and coercive abuses" could clearly be regulated: "Thus, for example, the government could constitutionally regulate the number of residential picketers, the hours during which a residential picket may take place, or the noise level of such a picket, [to] neutralize the intrusive or unduly coercive aspects of picketing around the home. But to say that picketing may be substantially regulated is not to say that it may be prohibited in its entirety. Once size, time, volume, and the like have been controlled to ensure that the picket is no longer intrusive or coercive, only the speech itself remains, conveyed perhaps by a lone, silent individual, walking back and forth with a sign. Such speech, which no longer implicates the heightened governmental interest in residential privacy, is nevertheless banned by [the ordinance]. Therefore, [it] is not narrowly tailored."

In a separate dissent, Justice STEVENS stated: "[Under this ordinance,] it is unlawful for a fifth-grader to carry [a sign saying 'Get Well Charlie—our Team Needs You'] in front of a residence for the period of time necessary to convey its friendly message to its intended audience. [My] hunch is that the town will probably not enforce its ban against friendly, innocuous, or even brief unfriendly picketing, and that the Court may be right in concluding that its legitimate sweep makes its overbreadth insubstantial. But [the] scope of the ordinance gives the town officials far too much discretion in making enforcement decisions; while [we] await further developments, potential picketers must act at their peril."

b. *Abortion clinic protests.* In MADSEN v. WOMEN'S HEALTH CENTER, INC., 512 U.S. 753 (1994), the Court in part upheld and in part struck down a Florida state court injunction that limited the activities of antiabortion protestors on the public streets outside an abortion clinic. The injunction was aimed largely at protecting the privacy and repose of women seeking to enter and use the abortion clinic's facilities. Chief Justice REHNQUIST, writing for the Court, first found that the injunction was not content-or viewpoint-based simply because it restricted only the speech of antiabortion protesters: "To accept petitioners' claim would be to classify virtually every injunction as content or viewpoint based. An injunction, by its very nature, applies only to a particular group (or individuals) and regulates the activities, and perhaps the speech, of that group." The injunction had been issued because the protestors had violated a previous narrower injunction against blocking clinic access. "[In] determining content neutrality [we] look to governmental purpose as the primary consideration. Here, the state court imposed restrictions on petitioners [because] they repeatedly violated the court's original order. That petitioners all share the same viewpoint regarding abortion does not in itself demonstrate that some invidious content-or viewpoint-based purpose motivated the issuance of the order. It suggests only that those in the group whose conduct violated the court's order happen to share the same opinion regarding abortions being performed at the clinic."

Having found the injunction content-neutral, Chief Justice Rehnquist nonetheless held that the Ward time, place, and manner test must be applied with special stringency in the context of an injunction, as opposed to a general statute, because "[i]njunctions [carry] greater risks of censorship and discriminatory application than do general ordinances. [When] evaluating a content-neutral injunction, we [must ask] whether the challenged provisions of the injunction burden no more speech than necessary to serve a significant government interest." The majority opinion agreed with the Florida Supreme Court that the injunction served a number of "significant government interests": interests "[in] protecting a woman's freedom to seek lawful medical or counseling services in connection with her pregnancy, [in] ensuring the public safety and order, in promoting the free flow of traffic on public streets and sidewalks, [in] protecting the property rights of all its citizens [and in vindicating] the State's strong interest in residential privacy [Frisby], applied by analogy to medical privacy. The [state] court observed that while targeted picketing of the home threatens the psychological well-being of the 'captive' resident, targeted picketing of a hospital or clinic threatens not only the psychological, but the physical well-being of the patient held 'captive' by medical circumstance. We agree [that] the combination of these governmental interests is quite sufficient to justify an appropriately tailored injunction to protect them."

Chief Justice Rehnquist then considered whether each challenged provision of the injunction met the heightened narrow tailoring requirement he had set forth. He upheld the injunction's requirement of a "36-foot buffer zone" around the front of the clinic in which the protestors were barred from "congregating, picketing, patrolling, [or] demonstrating." He emphasized the need for "some deference" to the state court's findings "even under our heightened review": "The state court seems to have had few other options to protect access given the narrow confines around the clinic. The state court was convinced that allowing the petitioners to remain on the clinic's sidewalk and driveway was not a viable option in view of the failure of the first injunction to protect access. And allowing the petitioners to stand in the middle of [the adjacent street] would obviously block vehicular traffic. [Protesters] standing across the narrow street from the clinic can still be seen and heard from the clinic parking lots. On balance, we hold that the 36-foot buffer zone around the clinic entrances and driveway burdens no more speech than necessary to accomplish the governmental interest at stake." He held, however, that the 36-foot buffer zone was invalid as applied to the private property along the side and back of the clinic, as there had been no showing that such speech interfered with clinic access.

He next turned to a portion of the injunction restraining the petitioners from "singing, chanting, whistling, shouting, yelling, use of bullhorns, auto horns, sound amplification equipment or other sounds or images observable to or within earshot of the patients inside the clinic" during the hours of 7:30 a.m. through noon on Mondays through Saturdays. He upheld the provision restricting high noise levels, noting that "[n]oise control is particularly important around hospitals and medical facilities during surgery and recovery periods": "We hold that the limited noise restrictions imposed by the state court order burden no more speech than necessary to ensure the health and well-being of the patients at the clinic. The First Amendment does not demand that patients at a medical facility undertake Herculean efforts to escape the cacophony of political protests." But, he held, "[t]he same cannot be said for the 'images observable' provision. [This] broad prohibition [burdens] more speech than necessary to achieve the purpose of limiting threats to clinic patients or their families. [Even] if the blanket ban on 'images observable' was intended to reduce the level of anxiety and hypertension suffered by the patients inside the clinic, it would still fail. The only plausible reason a patient would be bothered by 'images observable' inside the clinic would be if the patient found the expression contained in such images disagreeable. But it is much easier for the clinic to pull its curtains than for a patient to stop up her ears, and no more is required to avoid seeing placards through the windows of the clinic. This provision of the injunction violates the First Amendment."

Chief Justice Rehnquist's majority opinion next invalidated a provision of the state court order requiring that the protestors "refrain from physically approaching any person seeking services of the clinic 'unless such person indicates a desire to communicate' in an area within 300 feet of the clinic. The state court was attempting to prevent clinic patients and staff from being 'stalked' or 'shadowed' by the petitioners as they approached the clinic. But it is difficult, indeed, to justify a prohibition on all uninvited approaches of persons seeking the services of the clinic, regardless of how peaceful the contact may be, without burdening more speech than necessary to prevent intimidation and to ensure access to the clinic. Absent evidence that the protesters' speech is independently proscribable (i.e., 'fighting words' or threats), or is so infused with violence as to be indistinguishable from a threat of physical harm, this provision cannot stand."

Finally, the majority opinion invalidated the injunction's prohibition against picketing, demonstrating, or using sound amplification equipment within 300 feet of the residences of clinic staff: "[T]he 300–foot zone around the residences in this case is much larger than the zone provided for in the ordinance which we approved in Frisby. The ordinance at issue there [was] limited to 'focused picketing taking place solely in front of a particular residence.' By contrast, the 300–foot zone would ban 'general marching through residential neighborhoods, or even walking a route in front of an entire block of houses.' [Frisby.] The record before us does not contain sufficient justification for this broad a ban on picketing; it appears that a limitation on the time, duration of picketing, and number of pickets outside a smaller zone could have accomplished the desired result.

"[In] sum, we uphold the noise restrictions and the 36–foot buffer zone around the clinic entrances and driveway because they burden no more speech than necessary to eliminate the unlawful conduct targeted by the state court's injunction. We strike down as unconstitutional the 36–foot buffer zone as applied to the private property to the north and west of the clinic, the 'images observable' provision, the 300–foot no-approach zone around the clinic, and the 300–foot buffer zone around the residences, because these provisions sweep more broadly than necessary to accomplish the permissible goals of the injunction."

Justice STEVENS concurred in part and dissented in part. Unlike the majority, he would have subjected the injunction to more deferential scrutiny, not more stringent scrutiny, than a comparable statute, because an injunction is limited "solely to an individual or a limited group of individuals, who, by engaging in illegal conduct, have been judicially deprived of some liberty." Under that more lenient standard, he would have upheld the 300–foot no-approach zone around the clinic, but would not have reached the question whether the other restrictions were permissible time, place or manner regulations because he viewed the question as not technically presented by the cert. petition. Justice Souter also wrote a separate concurrence.

Justice SCALIA, joined by Justices Kennedy and Thomas, concurred in the portions of the majority opinion striking down portions of the injunction, but dissented sharply from the portions upholding the 36–foot buffer zone and the noise prohibition: "[The majority's] appearance of moderation and Solomonic wisdom [is] deceptive." Describing at length a videotape from the record, he concluded that it showed "that a great many forms of expression and conduct occurred in the vicinity of the clinic. These include singing, chanting, praying, shouting, the playing of music both from the clinic and from handheld boom boxes, speeches, peaceful picketing, communication of familiar political messages, handbilling, persuasive speech directed at opposing groups on the issue of abortion, efforts to persuade individuals not to have abortions, personal testimony, interviews with the press, and media efforts to report on the protest. What the videotape, the rest of the record, and the trial court's findings do not contain is any suggestion of violence near the clinic, nor do they establish any attempt to prevent entry or exit."

Justice Scalia disagreed with the majority's standard of review. He derided the new standard of "intermediate-intermediate scrutiny" as manufactured "for this abortion-related case." He argued instead that restrictions upon speech imposed by injunction generally are "at least as deserving of strict scrutiny as a statutory, content-based restriction," because injunctions likewise lend themselves "to the targeted suppression of particular ideas." He also argued that the particular injunction here was content-based, because it reached all those "acting in concert or participation" with the protestors rather than merely those who had violated the previous order; it thus was, in his view, "tailored to restrain persons distinguished, not by proscribable conduct, but by proscribable views." He found that all the provisions of the injunction failed strict scrutiny, and even failed the majority's test, given the lack of tailoring between the injunction under review and any violation by all of the protestors of the previous injunction or other Florida law. He concluded that, "since in this case a general regulation establishing time, place, and manner restrictions for all citizens is not at issue, these petitioners have a right, not merely to demonstrate and protest at some reasonably effective place, but to demonstrate and protest where they want to and where all other Floridians can, namely, right there on the public sidewalk in front of the clinic. 'One is not to have the exercise of his liberty of expression in appropriate places abridged on the plea that it may be exercised in some other place.' [Schneider.] [What] we have decided seems to be, and will be reported by the media as, an abortion case. But it will go down in the lawbooks, it will be cited, as a free-speech injunction case—and the damage its novel principles produce will be considerable."

IS A TIME, PLACE OR MANNER REGULATION EVER INVALID?

The preceding cases suggest that Harry Kalven's strong view of First Amendment access rights to the streets and parks, defeatable only on a showing of strong countervailing state interests, generally has not prevailed. Scrutiny in recent time, place and manner cases has most commonly been quite deferential on the substantiality of the state's interests, as well as the relationship of the means chosen to the implementation of those interests. The Court's implementation of the requirement that a regulation be "narrowly drawn to further a substantial governmental interest"—a requirement common to both symbolic expression claims and time, place, and manner restrictions—does not involve strict scrutiny, nor serious inquiry into the availability of "less restrictive means" to implement the governmental interest. Can First Amendment claimants ever prevail under such review? Is time place and manner review heightened in theory but toothless in fact?

The Supreme Court does occasionally invalidate a challenged time, place or manner restriction. A leading example is UNITED STATES v. GRACE, 461 U.S. 171 (1983). In Grace, the challengers attacked a provision of 40 U.S.C. § 13k which prohibited the "display [of] any flag, banner, or device designed or adapted to bring into public notice any party, organization, or movement" in the U.S. Supreme Court building and on its grounds. One of the challengers sought to distribute to passers-by on the sidewalk leaflets concerning the removal of unfit judges from the bench. The other, Mary Grace, sought to display on the sidewalk a two-and-a-half by four foot sign on which was inscribed verbatim the text of the First Amendment. The Court held the prohibition invalid as applied to the the public sidewalks surrounding the Court building.

Justice WHITE stated: "The sidewalks comprising the outer boundaries of the Court grounds are indistinguishable from any other sidewalks in Washington, D.C., and we can discern no reason why they should be treated any differently. Sidewalks, of course, are among those areas of public property that traditionally have been held open to the public for expressive activities and are clearly within those areas of public property that may be considered, generally without further inquiry, to be public forum property. [There is] no separation, no fence, and no indication whatever to persons stepping from the street to the curb and sidewalks that serve as the perimeter of the Court grounds that they have entered some special type of enclave. [Traditional] public forum property occupies a special position in terms of First Amendment protection and will not lose its historically recognized character for the reason that it abuts government property that has been dedicated to a use other than as a forum for public expression."

Justice White rejected the Government's argument that the ban could be justified as "a reasonable time, place, and manner restriction" on public forum property. He found no sufficient connection with any of the asserted state interests to warrant the restriction. He questioned whether the ban substantially served the purpose of maintaining proper order and decorum within the Court grounds. He also rejected the Government's claim that the restraint was needed lest it *"appear* to the public that the Supreme Court is subject to outside influence or that picketing or marching, singly or in groups, is an acceptable or proper way of appealing to or influencing the Supreme Court": "[We] seriously doubt that the public would draw a different inference from a lone picketer carrying a sign on the sidewalks around the building than it would from a similar picket on the sidewalks across the street." In a separate opinion, Justice MARSHALL argued that the ban should be found "unconstitutional on its face": "[Since] the continuing existence of the statute will inevitably have a chilling effect on freedom of expression, there is no virtue in deciding its constitutionality on a piecemeal basis."

In addition to producing the occasional Supreme Court decision such as Grace, time, place and manner review, even under the relatively deferential Ward/CCNV standard, frequently produces judgments of invalidity in the lower federal courts. Arguably, by requiring governments to adduce some empirical evidence that the harms they seek to avoid are material, and that the means they have chosen are superior to obvious alternatives, the test continues to serve a protective First Amendment purpose. Minimal rationality review, in contrast, does not require such a showing of actual purpose or empirically sound means/end fit, but may be satisfied entirely by conjectural justifications arrived at ex post. And the need to satisfy heightened scrutiny in the event of a challenge might in some settings discourage a government from imposing time, place and manner restrictions in the first place.

SPEAKER ACCESS TO PUBLIC PLACES OTHER THAN STREETS AND PARKS

Introduction. In Hague v. CIO, Justice Roberts, in speaking of public places which have "immemorially" and "time out of mind" been used for "discussing public questions," mentioned only "streets and parks." And most of the preceding materials involved access to and regulation of streets and parks. What of other public places? In a series of modern cases, the Court has confronted claims of speakers seeking access to such nontraditional forums as libraries, jail environs, buses, military installations, mailboxes and federal charitable campaigns. Should an assured minimum-access claim be recognized in these contexts as well? At least an equal-access claim?

The cases that follow consider two different approaches to these questions. One approach, typical in earlier cases such as Brown, Adderley and Grayned, asks with respect to any public property whether the proposed speech is compatible or not with its other principal uses. On this approach, speech restrictions might theoretically be invalidated in any public space, depending on its particular characteristics. See Stone, "Fora Americana: Speech in Public Places," 1974 Sup.Ct.Rev. 233 (noting that the incompatibility approach turns on functional considerations that bring "streets, parks, public libraries, and other publicly owned places [all] under the same roof"). The second approach, typical of later cases and summarized below in Perry Ed. Ass'n v. Perry Local Educators' Ass'n (1983; p. 1277), instead uses the characteristics of public property as a ground to classify it in advance as a "public forum," a "designated public forum," or a "nonpublic forum," with different rules applying to each category.

As you read the following materials, consider which approach seems more helpful. How do the governing criteria vary between these approaches? What is the role in each of tradition or custom? What is the role in each of the contemporary function of the property? What is the role in each of the compatibility of expressive activities with other uses of the property? The availability to the First Amendment claimant of alternative forums for expression? The relationship between the subject matter of the protest and the nontraditional forum of protest?

LIBRARIES, JAILS AND SCHOOLS

1. *Libraries.* BROWN v. LOUISIANA, 383 U.S. 131 (1966), arose from events at a segregated regional public library in Louisiana in 1964. Five young black men entered the reading room and one of them, Brown, asked branch assistant Reeves for a book. Reeves told Brown that she did not have the book but would request it from the state library and would notify him upon receipt. When Reeves asked the young black men to leave, they refused. Instead, Brown, in protest against the library's "whites only" policy, sat down and the others stood near him. There was no noise or boisterous talking. After about 10 minutes, the sheriff arrived and asked the men to leave; when they did not, he arrested them. Brown and his companions were convicted under Louisiana's breach of the peace statute.

The sharply divided 5–4 decision reversed the convictions. Justice FORTAS' plurality opinion, joined only by Chief Justice Warren and Justice Douglas, stated at the outset that there was no evidence that petitioners had violated the law—"no disorder, no intent to provoke a breach of the peace and no circumstances indicating that a breach might be occasioned by petitioners' actions." But he did not rest exclusively on this due process ground. He added: "We are here dealing with an aspect of a basic constitutional right—the right [of] speech and of assembly, and freedom to petition the Government for a redress of grievances. [These] rights are not confined to verbal expression. They embrace appropriate types of action which certainly include the right in a peaceable and orderly manner to protest by silent and reproachful presence, in a place where the protestant has every right to be, the unconstitutional segregation of public facilities. Accordingly, even if the accused action were within the scope of the [law], [we] would have to hold that the statute cannot constitutionally be applied to punish petitioners' actions in the circumstances of this case. The statute was deliberately and purposefully applied solely to terminate the reasonable, orderly, and limited exercise of the right to protest the unconstitutional segregation of a public facility. Interference with this right, so exercised, by state action is intolerable under our Constitution. [Fortunately], the circumstances here were such that no claim can be made that use of the library by others was disturbed by the demonstration. [Were] it otherwise, a factor not present in this case would have to be considered." Justices BRENNAN and WHITE each concurred in the judgment. Justice White found that petitioners' actions did not "depart significantly from what normal library use would contemplate."

Justice BLACK dissented, joined by Justices Clark, Harlan and Stewart: "[I]t is incomprehensible to me that a State must measure disturbances in its libraries and on the streets with identical standards. [A] tiny parish branch library, staffed by two women, is not a department store [nor] a bus terminal [nor] a public thoroughfare as in Edwards and Cox v. Louisiana." He continued: "[The plurality's] conclusion that the statute was unconstitutionally applied because it interfered with the petitioners' so-called protest establishes a completely new constitutional doctrine. [The First Amendment] does not guarantee to any person the right to use someone else's property, even that owned by government and dedicated to other purposes, as a stage to express dissident ideas. The novel constitutional doctrine of the prevailing opinion [exalts] the power of private nongovernmental groups to determine what use shall be made of governmental property over the power of the elected governmental officials."

Consider the comment in Kalven, "Upon Rereading Mr. Justice Black on the First Amendment," 14 U.C.L.A.L.Rev. 428 (1967): "[I]t remains something of a puzzle how Justice Black, who has been so sympathetic to the 'poor man's printing press' and so tolerant of noise in Kovacs, the intrusion in [Martin v. Struthers], the anonymity in [Talley v. California], can be so impatient with this kind of communication. It is as though his strategy of protecting all speech just because it was something other than conduct traps him when he is confronted by conduct which is symbolic."

2. *Jails.* In ADDERLEY v. FLORIDA, 385 U.S. 39 (1966), in contrast, the Court upheld the convictions of 32 students at Florida A. & M. University in Tallahassee for "trespass with a malicious and mischievous intent" upon the premises of the county jail. They had gone to the jail to protest the arrests of other students the day before and to demonstrate against racial segregation. They did not leave at the county sheriff's request. They did move back from the jail entrance but remained in a driveway normally used by the sheriff's department to transport prisoners to and from the courts several blocks away and by commercial vehicles.

Justice BLACK, writing for the Court, rejected the students' claim that their convictions violated their First Amendment rights. "The sheriff, as jail custodian, had power [to] direct that this large crowd of people get off the grounds. There is not a shred of evidence in this record that this power was exercised [because] the sheriff objected to what was being sung or said by the demonstrators or because he disagreed with the objectives of their protest. The record reveals that he objected only to their presence on that part of the jail grounds reserved for jail uses. There is no evidence at all that on any other occasion had similarly large groups of the public been permitted to gather on this portion of the jail grounds for any purpose. Nothing in the [Constitution] prevents Florida from even-handed enforcement of its general trespass statute against those refusing to obey the sheriff's order to remove themselves from what amounted to the curtilage of the jailhouse. The State, no less than a private owner of property, has power to preserve the property under its control for the use to which it is lawfully dedicated. For this reason there is no merit to the petitioners' argument that they had a constitutional right to stay on the property, over the jail custodian's objections, because this 'area chosen for the peaceful civil rights demonstration was not only "reasonable" but also particularly appropriate.' Such an argument has as its major unarticulated premise the assumption that people who want to propagandize protests or views have a constitutional right to do so whenever and however and wherever they please. [We reject] that concept. The [Constitution] does not forbid a State to control the use of its own property for its own lawful nondiscriminatory purpose."

Justice DOUGLAS dissented, joined by Chief Justice Warren and Justices Brennan and Fortas: "[T]he Court errs in treating the case as if it were an ordinary trespass case or an ordinary picketing case. The jailhouse, like an executive mansion, a legislative chamber, a courthouse, or the statehouse itself [Edwards], is one of the seats of government, whether it be the Tower of London, the Bastille, or a small county jail. And when it houses political prisoners or those whom many think are unjustly held, it is an obvious center for protest. The right to petition for the redress of grievances has an ancient history and is not limited to writing a letter or sending a telegram to a congressman; it is not confined to appearing before the local city council, or writing letters to the President or Governor or Mayor. Conventional methods of petitioning may be, and often have been, shut off to large groups of our citizens. Legislators may turn deaf ears; formal complaints may be routed endlessly through a bureaucratic maze; courts may let the wheels of justice grind very slowly. Those who do not control television and radio, those who cannot afford to advertise in newspapers or circulate elaborate pamphlets may have only a more limited type of access to public officials. Their methods should not be condemned as tactics of obstruction and harassment as long as the assembly and petition are peaceable, as these were.

"There is no question that petitioners had as their purpose a protest against the arrest of Florida A. & M. students for trying to integrate public theatres. [There] was no violence; no threat of violence; no attempted jail break; no storming of a prison; no plan or plot to do anything but protest. The evidence is uncontradicted that the petitioners' conduct did not upset the jailhouse routine. [There] was no shoving, no pushing, no disorder or threat of riot. It is said that some of the group blocked part of the driveway leading to the jail entrance. [But] whenever the students were requested to move they did so. If there was congestion, the solution was a further request to move to lawns or parking areas, not complete ejection and arrest.

"[We] do violence to the First Amendment when we permit this 'petition for redress of grievances' to be turned into a trespass action. [Only] the sheriff's fiat transformed lawful conduct into an unlawful trespass. To say that a private owner could have done the same if the rally had taken place on private property is to speak of a different case, as an assembly and a petition for redress of grievances run to government, not to private proprietors. The Court forgets that prior to this day our decisions have drastically limited the application of state statutes inhibiting the right to go peacefully on public property to exercise First Amendment rights [quoting Hague v. CIO]. [There] may be some public places which are so clearly committed to other purposes that their use for the airing of grievances is anomalous. There may be some instances in which assemblies and [petitions] are not consistent with other necessary purposes of public property. A noisy meeting may be out of keeping with the serenity of the statehouse or the quiet of the courthouse. No one, for example, would suggest that the Senate gallery is the proper place for a vociferous protest rally. And in other cases it may be necessary to adjust the right to [petition] to the other interest inhering in the uses to which the public property is normally put. But this is quite different from saying that all public places are off limits to people with grievances. And it is farther yet from saying that the 'custodian' of the public property in his discretion can decide when public places shall be used for the communication of ideas."

Does Justice Black in Adderley retreat all the way to Justice Holmes' analogy between the state and the private property owner in Massachusetts v. Davis, p. 1235) above? Would Justice Black sustain a blanket prohibition of the use of streets and parks for meetings and parades? Or are his broad comments applicable only to such nontraditional forums as jailhouse driveways? Does the holding in Adderley reject any assured access claim beyond the traditional public forum of the streets and parks? Or is there access to nontraditional forums so long as there is no showing of substantial disruption of or interference with the functioning of their primary uses? Is that the message of the Brown case? Can a claim to a nontraditional public forum be adequately analyzed without inquiries as to the availability of adequate alternative forums in which the speaker may reach the desired audience? Should the public forum claimant be required to demonstrate his special interest in the particular location? Was there special justification for the protest near the jailhouse in Adderley? As much as with the library protest in Brown?

3. *Schools*. In GRAYNED v. ROCKFORD, 408 U.S. 104 (1972), the Court sustained an ordinance barring a demonstration near a school. Grayned had participated in a demonstration in front of a high school protesting black underrepresentation in activities at the school. The Court affirmed a conviction under an "antinoise" ordinance stating that no person on grounds "adjacent to any [school] building" in which a class is in session "shall willfully make or assist in the making of any noise or diversion which disturbs or tends to disturb the peace or good order of such school session." Justice MARSHALL's majority opinion emphasized that it was "the nature of a place, 'the pattern of its normal activities,'" which determines the reasonableness of "time, place and manner" restrictions: "The crucial question is whether the manner of expression is basically incompatible with the normal activity of a particular place at a particular time."

Here, he found the restraint appropriate to the school environment: "Although a silent vigil may not unduly interfere with a public library [Brown], making a speech in the reading room almost certainly would. That same speech should be perfectly appropriate in a park. [Our] cases make clear that in assessing the reasonableness of a regulation, we must weigh heavily the fact that communication is involved [Schneider; Hague]; the regulation must be narrowly tailored to further the State's legitimate interest. Access to the 'streets, sidewalks, parks, and other similar public places [for] the purpose of exercising [First Amendment rights] cannot constitutionally be denied broadly.' In light of these general principles, we do not think that Rockford's ordinance is an unconstitutional regulation of activity around a school. [The] public sidewalk adjacent to school grounds may not be declared off-limits for expressive activity by members of the public. [But] expressive activity may be prohibited if it 'materially disrupts classwork or involves substantial disorder or invasion of the rights of others.' [Tinker; p. 1293 below.] We would be ignoring reality if we did not recognize that the public schools [are] often the focus of significant grievances. [But] schools could hardly tolerate boisterous demonstrators who drown out classroom conversation, make studying impossible, block entrances, or incite children to leave the schoolhouse. [The ordinance] is narrowly tailored to further Rockford's compelling interest in having an undisrupted school session conducive to the students' learning, and does not unnecessarily interfere with First Amendment rights.''

BUSES, THEATERS, AND MILITARY BASES

Several decisions in the mid–1970s began to foreshadow the Court's later categorizing approach to public property. 1. *Public transportation.* In LEHMAN v. SHAKER HEIGHTS, 418 U.S. 298 (1974), the Court upheld a city rule against political advertising on city-owned buses. The city allowed commercial advertising on the buses. A candidate for state assembly who sought unsuccessfully to buy space for campaign advertisements challenged the rule. The Court rejected the challenge in a 5–4 decision. Justice BLACKMUN wrote a plurality opinion joined by Chief Justice Burger and Justices White and Rehnquist: "[It] is urged that the car cards here constitute a public forum protected by the First Amendment, and that there is a guarantee of nondiscriminatory access to such publicly owned and controlled areas of communication 'regardless of the primary purpose for which the area is dedicated.' We disagree. [This situation is] different from the traditional settings where First Amendment values inalterably prevail. Although [our cases have] been jealous to preserve access to public places for purposes of free speech, the nature of the forum and the conflicting interests involved have remained important in determining the degree of protection afforded. [Here], we have no open spaces, no meeting hall, park, street corner, or other public thoroughfare. Instead, the city is engaged in commerce. [The] car card space, although incidental to the provision of public transportation, is a part of the commercial venture. In much the same way that a newspaper or periodical, or even a radio or television station, need not accept every proffer of advertising from the general public, a city transit system has discretion to develop and make reasonable choices concerning the type of advertising that may be displayed in its [vehicles].''

Justice Blackmun found that the city's distinction between commercial and political advertising was not "arbitrary, capricious, or invidious": "Here, the city has decided that '[p]urveyors of goods and services saleable in commerce may purchase advertising space on an equal basis, whether they be house builders or butchers.' This decision is little different from deciding to impose a 10–, 25–, or 35–cent fare, or from changing schedules or the location of bus stops. Revenue earned from long-term commercial advertising could be jeopardized by a requirement that short-term candidacy or issue-oriented advertisements be displayed on car cards. Users would be subjected to the blare of political propaganda. There could be lurking doubts about favoritism, and sticky administrative problems might arise in parceling out limited space to eager politicians. In these circumstances, the managerial decision to limit car card space to innocuous and less controversial commercial and service oriented advertising does not rise to the dignity of a First Amendment violation. Were we to hold to the contrary, display cases in public hospitals, libraries, office buildings, military compounds, and other public facilities immediately would become Hyde Parks open to every would-be pamphleteer and politician. This the Constitution does not require. No First Amendment forum is here to be found.''

Justice DOUGLAS, whose vote was needed to forge a majority, concurred in the judgment, emphasizing that transit users were a "captive audience" whom the city could constitutionally protect: "[A] streetcar or bus is plainly not a park or sidewalk or other meeting place for discussion. [It] is only a way to get to work or back home. The fact that it is owned and operated by the city does not without more make it a forum. [If] we are to turn a bus or street car into either a newspaper or a park, we take great liberties with people who because of necessity become commuters and at the same time captive viewers or listeners." Justice Douglas cited his dissent in Public Utilities Comm'n v. Pollak, 343 U.S. 451 (1952), in which the Court had rejected a claim that the use of radio receivers on city buses violated listeners' First Amendment rights; there, Justice Douglas had stated that "the man on the streetcar has no choice but to sit and listen, or perhaps to sit and to try *not* to listen."

Justice BRENNAN dissented, joined by Justices Stewart, Marshall and Powell: "[The] city created a forum for the dissemination of information and expression of ideas when it accepted and displayed commercial and public service advertisements on its rapid transit vehicles. Having opened a forum for communication, the city is barred by the [First Amendment] from discriminating among forum users solely on the basis of message content."

What if the transit system had excluded *all* advertising, commercial as well as noncommercial? Is a city bus an "anomalous" place for messages? Note that the government property involved here (bus advertising) and in the next note (municipal theater) is property designed for communicative purposes, in contrast to the primary *non*communicative purposes of the public property involved in such contexts as jails. Should that make a difference in the analysis? Even assuming the city could bar all messages on city buses, why could it discriminate against political speech? Doesn't such a subject matter distinction run afoul of Mosley? Is an exception to the Mosley principle justified because the city is running the bus as a business? See generally Wells & Hellerstein, "The Governmental–Proprietary Distinction in Consitutional Law," 66 Va. L. Rev. 1073 (1980) (suggesting that government's "quasi-business interest may adequately support regulation that a court might strike down if applied to the public at large"). Finally, should members of the "captive audience" on the bus have been required, like Cohen's audience, simply to avert their eyes?

2. *Municipal theaters.* Contrast Justice Blackmun's reluctance to recognize a public forum claim in Lehman with his majority opinion less than a year later in SOUTHEASTERN PROMOTIONS, LTD. v. CONRAD, 420 U.S. 546 (1975). There, the Court found that the challenger's First Amendment rights were violated when the municipal board managing city theaters in Chattanooga refused permission to present "the controversial rock musical 'Hair.'" The refusal was based on the ground that the production would not be "in the best interest of the community." Although the alleged obscenity of "Hair" had been the major issue in the lower courts, Justice Blackmun did not reach that question. Instead, he found that the refusal constituted a prior restraint imposed without affording the "rigorous procedural safeguards" required by Freedman v. Maryland, p. 1342 below.

In the course of reaching that conclusion, Justice Blackmun commented that the municipal theaters were "public forums designed for and dedicated to expressive activities. [Petitioner] was not seeking to use a facility primarily serving a competing use. [E.g., Adderley; Brown.] Nor was rejection of the application based on any regulation of time, place, or manner related to the nature of the facility or applications from other users. [E.g., Cox v. New Hampshire.] No rights of individuals in surrounding areas were violated by noise or any other aspect of the production. [Kovacs v. Cooper.] There was no captive audience. See [Lehman; Pollak]. Whether the petitioner might have used some other, privately owned, theater in the city for the production is of no consequence. [That] alone would not justify an otherwise impermissible prior restraint. [Schneider.]"

Justice DOUGLAS, in a concurring opinion, thought the majority's holding did not go far enough: in his view, no prior screening process of any sort was permissible. And he added: "A municipal theater is no less a forum for the expression of ideas than is a public park, or a sidewalk." A dissent by Justice WHITE, joined by Chief Justice Burger, concluded that, whether or not "Hair" was obscene, the city "could constitutionally forbid exhibition of the musical for children" and could "reserve its auditorium for productions suitable for exhibition to all the citizens of the city, adults and children alike." Another dissent, by Justice REHNQUIST, argued that a public auditorium should not be equated with public streets and parks. He feared that the majority had given "no constitutionally permissible role in the way of selection to the municipal authorities" and asked: "May a municipal theater devote an entire season to Shakespeare, or is it required to book any potential producer on a first-come, first-served basis?" He concluded that a city policy not to show attractions "of the kind that would offend any substantial number of potential theater goers" was not "arbitrary or unreasonable." He added: "A municipal theater may not be run by municipal authorities as if it were a private theater, free to judge on a content basis alone which play it wished to have performed and which it did not. But, just as surely, that element of it which is 'theater' ought to be accorded some constitutional recognition along with that element of it which is 'municipal.'"

3. *Military bases.* To what extent may a First Amendment claimant gain access to a military base that has been opened up to the general public for some purposes? The per curiam decision in Flower v. United States, 407 U.S. 197 (1972), suggested that military bases might be treated as nontraditional public forums. There, the 7–to–2 decision reversed a conviction for distributing peace leaflets on a street within the boundaries of an Army base in San Antonio: "Whatever power the authorities may have to restrict general access to a military facility, here the fort commander chose not to exclude the public from the street where petitioner was arrested." But when the Court confronted the issue more fully four years later, in GREER v. SPOCK, 424 U.S. 828 (1976), the majority interpreted Flower narrowly.

The decision upheld two regulations at Fort Dix, a large Army post in rural New Jersey, that barred political activities on the base: the first prohibited, inter alia, speeches and demonstrations of a partisan political nature; the second, distribution of literature without prior approval of the base commander. Justice STEWART's majority opinion emphasized that the business of a base such as Fort Dix was "to train soldiers, not to provide a public forum," and rejected any claim to a generalized constitutional right to "make political speeches or distribute leaflets" there. He observed that in Spock, unlike in Flower, the military authorities had never "abandoned any claim of special interest" in regulating political activities. Noting "the special constitutional function of the military in our national life," he stated: "The notion that federal military reservations, like municipal streets and parks, have traditionally served as a place for free public assembly and communication of thoughts by private citizens [is] historically and constitutionally false." After using these broad grounds to reject the "on the face" challenges, the majority turned down the "as applied" attacks with similar deference and brevity. With respect to the ban on speeches and demonstrations, Justice Stewart noted that the regulation had been applied evenhandedly rather than discriminatorily, in accordance with a policy of "keeping official military activities there wholly free of entanglement with partisan political campaigns of any kind"—a policy "wholly consistent with the American constitutional tradition of a politically neutral military establishment under civilian control." And with respect to the prior approval requirement for the distribution of literature, he noted that it did not authorize bans on "conventional political campaign literature," but only prohibitions of literature constituting "a clear danger to [military] loyalty, discipline, or morale." And since the challengers had not submitted any material for approval, they could not claim that that regulation had been arbitrarily applied.

Justice POWELL's concurrence viewed the central question as "whether the manner of expression is basically incompatible with the normal activity of a particular place at a particular time." Here, it was significant that access was sought to an "enclave of [the military] system that stands apart from and outside of many of the rules that govern ordinary civilian life in our country." In that context, "our inquiry is not limited to claims that the exercise of First Amendment rights is disruptive of base activity. We also must consider functional and symbolic incompatibility with the 'specialized society separate from civilian society' that has its home on the base." Using that framework, Justice Powell found the ban on political meetings justified by "the legitimate interests of the public in maintaining the reality and appearance of the political neutrality of the Armed Services," interests which "outweigh [those] of political candidates and their servicemen audience in the availability of a military base for campaign activities." The requirement of prior approval to distribute literature, in his view, was justified not by the public interest in military neutrality, but rather by "the unique need of the military to 'insist upon a respect for duty and a discipline without counterpart in civilian life.'"

Justice BRENNAN's lengthy dissent, joined by Justice Marshall, argued that the challengers should be permitted to speak at Fort Dix even if the military installation was not a "public forum." "[The] determination that a locale is a 'public forum' has never been erected as an absolute prerequisite to all forms of demonstrative First Amendment activity. [Because] the permissibility of a certain form of public expression at a given locale may differ depending on whether it is asked if the locale is a public forum or if the form of expression is compatible with the activities occurring at the locale, it becomes apparent that there is need for a flexible approach. Otherwise, with the rigid characterization of a given locale as not a public forum, there is the danger that certain forms of public speech at the locale may be suppressed, even though they are basically compatible with the activities otherwise occurring at the locale."

Applying his more flexible test, Justice Brennan concluded that leaflet distribution should be permitted "in those streets and lots unrestricted to civilian traffic," since those areas did not "differ in their nature and use from city streets and lots where open speech long has been protected." Political rallies posed more difficulty because of the "potential for disruption even in unrestricted areas," but not so much as "significantly to impair training or defense, thereby requiring its prohibition." Justice Brennan further argued that the ban was not necessary for military neutrality because no one would associate the speakers' causes with the military, and that allowing speech in unrestricted areas might even enhance neutrality because the military itself is "highly susceptible to politicization," and its isolated members would benefit from "the moderating influence of other ideas." "It borders on casuistry to contend that by evenhandedly permitting public expression to occur in unrestricted portions of a military installation, the military will be viewed as sanctioning the causes there espoused. [In view of the challengers'] willingness to submit to reasonable regulation as to time, place, and manner, it hardly may be argued that Fort Dix's purpose was threatened here."

The Court reaffirmed its view of the special nature of military bases in UNITED STATES v. ALBERTINI, 472 U.S. 675 (1985). That case upheld the exclusion of an individual from Hickam Air Force Base in Hawaii after he had previously been barred for prior unlawful conduct. He sought to enter the base in order to engage in peaceful expressive activity during Hickam's annual open house, when the general public was allowed to enter. Justice O'Connor's majority opinion emphasized that Hickam had not become a public forum merely because the general public had been invited on that day and relied in part on O'Brien in sustaining Albertini's conviction for reentering the base after he had been barred. See also Brown v. Glines, 444 U.S. 348 (1980). Are these military bases cases explainable on the basis of the Court's typical extraordinary deference to military judgments in a range of constitutional contexts? Recall, e.g., Rostker v. Goldberg (sex discrimination; p. 693 above); see also Goldman v. Weinberger (freedom of religion; p. 1485 below).

THE MODERN TRICHOTOMY OF TRADITIONAL, DESIGNATED AND NONPUBLIC FORUMS

1. *Mailboxes.* In U.S. POSTAL SERVICE v. COUNCIL OF GREEN-BURGH CIVIC ASSNS., 453 U.S. 114 (1981), the Court rejected a First Amendment challenge to a federal law, 18 U.S.C. §1725, that prohibited the deposit of unstamped "mailable matter" in home letter boxes approved by the Postal Service. It was challenged by a group of civic associations who asserted that the ban on their delivering messages to local residents by placing unstamped notices and pamphlets in the letter boxes of private homes unduly inhibited their communications with the residents. Justice REHNQUIST, writing for the Court, found the First Amendment challenge without merit. Finding that a letter box "is not traditionally [a] 'public forum,'" he found it unnecessary to apply the principles governing time, place, and manner restrictions on the use of public forums: "property owned or controlled by the government which is *not* a public forum may be subject to a prohibition of speech, leafleting, picketing, or other forms of communication without running afoul of the First Amendment [so long as the government] act[s] reasonably in imposing such restrictions, and the prohibition [is] content-neutral. §1725 is both a reasonable and content-neutral regulation."

In rejecting the "public forum" claim, Justice Rehnquist noted that a "letterbox provided by a postal customer which meets the Postal Service's specifications [becomes] part of the [Service's] nationwide system for the receipt and delivery of mail. [In] effect, the postal customer, although he pays for the physical components of the 'authorized depository,' agrees to abide by the Postal Service's regulations in exchange for the Postal Service agreeing to deliver and pick up his mail. [A] letter box, once designated an 'authorized depository,' does not [undergo] a transformation into a 'public forum' of some limited nature to which the First Amendment guarantees access to all comers. There is neither historical nor constitutional support for the characterization of a letter box as a public forum. [It] is difficult to conceive of any reason why this Court should treat a letter box differently for First Amendment access purposes than it has in the past treated the military base in [Greer], the jail [in

Adderley], or the advertising space [in] city rapid transit cars in [Lehman]. In all these cases, this Court recognized that the First Amendment does not guarantee access to property simply because it is owned or controlled by the government. [Since] a letter box is not traditionally such a 'public forum,' [traditional time, place and manner] analysis [is] unnecessary. To be sure, if a governmental regulation is based on the content of the speech or the message, that action must be scrutinized more carefully. [But] in this case there simply is no question that §1725 does not regulate speech on the basis of content."

Justice BRENNAN, concurring in the judgment, insisted that a letter box *is* a public forum, but that the law was a reasonable time, place, and manner regulation. He noted that the restraint was "content-neutral" and that it advanced "a significant governmental interest—preventing loss of mail revenues." Moreover, there were "ample alternative channels for communication"—e.g., placing circulars under doors or attaching them to doorknobs. But he objected to the majority's methodology: "The Court declines to analyze §1725 as a time, place, and manner restriction. Instead, it concludes that a letterbox is not a public forum. [I] believe that [this] ignores the proper method of analysis. '[The] crucial question is whether the manner of expression is basically incompatible with the normal activity of a particular place at a particular time.' [Grayned.] [I] believe that the mere deposit of mailable matter without postage is not 'basically incompatible' with the 'normal activity' for which a letter box is [used]. On the contrary, the mails and the letter box are specifically used for the communication of information and ideas, and thus surely constitute a public forum appropriate for the exercise of First Amendment rights subject to reasonable time, place, and manner [restrictions]."

Justice MARSHALL dissented: "First, I disagree with the Court's assumption that if no public forum is involved, the only First Amendment challenges to be considered are whether the regulation is content-based and reasonable. Even if the Postal Service were not a public forum, [the] statute advanced in its aid is a law challenged as an abridgment of free expression. [The] question, then, is whether this statute burdens any First Amendment rights enjoyed by appellees. If so, it must be determined whether this burden is justified by a significant governmental interest substantially advanced by the statute." The Postal Service could not meet this standard, he argued, because "the statute's asserted purposes easily could be advanced by less intrusive alternatives, such as a nondiscriminatory permit requirement for depositing unstamped circulars in letter boxes." In any event, he argued, given "its pervasive and traditional use as purveyor of written communication, the Postal Service [may] properly be viewed as a [public forum]. For the Postal Service's very purpose is to facilitate communication, which surely differentiates it from the military bases, jails, and mass transportation discussed in cases relied on by the Court." Justice STEVENS, in a separate dissent, agreed with Justice Marshall's result, but on the different ground that letter boxes are private property and the law "interferes with the owner's receipt of information that he may want to receive" without adequate justification.

2.   *Teachers' mailboxes.* In PERRY EDUCATION ASSN. v. PERRY LOCAL EDUCATORS' ASSN., 460 U.S. 37 (1983), the Court upheld a provision of a collective bargaining contract restricting access to the interschool mail system and teacher mailboxes in the Perry Township schools to the incumbent union, the Perry Education Association (PEA). Similar access was denied to the Perry Local Educators' Association (PLEA), a rival teacher group. The Court rejected PLEA's First Amendment challenge. Justice WHITE, writing for the Court, acknowledged that the policy implicated the First Amendment. But, he wrote, "[t]he existence of a right of access to public property and the standard by

which limitations upon such a right must be evaluated differ depending on the character of the property at issue:

"In places which by long tradition or by government fiat have been devoted to assembly and debate, the rights of the state to limit expressive activity are sharply circumscribed. At one end of the spectrum are [streets and parks. Hague v. CIO.] In these quintessential public forums, the government may not prohibit all communicative activity. For the state to enforce a content-based exclusion it must show that its regulation is necessary to serve a compelling state interest and that it is narrowly drawn to achieve that end. The state may also enforce regulations of the time, place, and manner of expression which are content-neutral, are narrowly tailored to serve a significant government interest, and leave open ample alternative channels of communication.

"A second category consists of public property which the state has opened for use by the public as a place for expressive activity. The Constitution forbids a state to enforce certain exclusions from a forum generally open to the public even if it was not required to create the forum in the first place. [E.g., Southeastern Promotions.] Although a state is not required to indefinitely retain the open character of the facility, as long as it does so it is bound by the same standards as apply to the traditional public forum.

"Public property which is not by tradition or designation a forum for public communication is governed by different standards. [Greenburgh.] [In] addition to time, place, and manner regulations, the state may reserve the forum for its intended purposes, communicative or otherwise, as long as the regulation on speech is reasonable and not an effort to suppress expression merely because public officials oppose the speaker's view. '[The] State, no less than a private owner of property, has power to preserve the property under its control for the use to which it is lawfully dedicated.' [Greenburgh; Greer; Adderley.]

"The school mail facilities at issue here fall within this third category [of nonpublic forums]. [The] interschool mail system is not a traditional public forum. [On] this point the parties agree. [The] internal mail system [is] not held open to the general public. It is instead PLEA's position that the school mail facilities have become a 'limited public forum' from which it may not be excluded because of the periodic use of the system by private non-school connected groups, and PLEA's own unrestricted access to the system prior to PEA's certification as exclusive representative. Neither of these arguments is persuasive. [The] schools do allow some outside organizations such as the YMCA, Cub Scouts, and other civic and church organizations to use the facilities. This type of selective access does not transform government property into a public forum. [Greer; Lehman.] Moreover, even if we assume that by granting access to [some groups], the school district has created a "limited" public forum, the constitutional right of access would in any event extend only to other entities of similar character. While the school mail facilities thus might be a forum generally open for use [by] other organizations that engage in activities of interest and educational relevance to students, they would not as a consequence be open to an organization such as PLEA, which is concerned with the terms and conditions of teacher employment.

"[Nor does the] access policy adopted by the Perry schools favor[] a particular viewpoint, that of the PEA, on labor relations, [in which case it would] be strictly scrutinized regardless of whether a public forum is involved. There is [no] indication that the school board intended to discourage one viewpoint and advance another. We believe it is more accurate to characterize the access policy as based on the *status* of the respective unions rather than their views. Implicit in the concept of the nonpublic forum is the right to make distinctions in access on the basis of subject matter and speaker identity. These distinctions may be impermissible in a public forum but are inherent and inescapable in the process of limiting a nonpublic forum to activities compatible with the intended purpose of the property. The touchstone for evaluating these distinctions is whether they are reasonable in light of the purpose which the forum at issue serves.

"The differential access provided PEA and PLEA is reasonable because it is wholly consistent with the district's legitimate interest in 'preserv[ing] the property [for] the use to which it is lawfully dedicated.' [Greenburgh.] Use of school mail facilities enables PEA to perform effectively its obligations as exclusive representative of *all* Perry Township teachers. Conversely, PLEA does not have any official responsibility in connection with the school district and need not be entitled to the same rights of access to school mailboxes. [Moreover], exclusion of the rival union may reasonably be considered a means of insuring labor-peace within the [schools]. Finally, the reasonableness of the limitations on PLEA's access to the school mail system is also supported by the substantial alternative channels that remain open for union-teacher communication to take place. These means range from bulletin boards to meeting facilities to the United States mail. During election periods, PLEA is assured of equal access to all modes of communication. [On] government property that has not been made a public forum, not all speech is equally situated, and the state may draw distinctions which relate to the special purpose for which the property is used. [For] a school mail facility, the difference in status between the exclusive bargaining representative and its rival is such a distinction."

Justice BRENNAN dissented, joined by Justices Marshall, Powell, and Stevens: "[Because] the exclusive access provision in the collective bargaining agreement amounts to viewpoint discrimination that infringes the respondents' First Amendment rights and fails to advance any substantial state interest, I dissent. [According] to the Court, the petitioner's status as the exclusive bargaining representative provides a reasonable basis for the exclusive access policy. The Court fundamentally misperceives the essence of the respondents' claims. [This] case does not involve an 'absolute access' claim. It involves an 'equal access' claim. As such it does not turn on whether the internal school mail system is a 'public forum.' In focusing on the public forum issue, the Court disregards the First Amendment's central proscription against censorship, in the form of viewpoint discrimination, in any forum, public or nonpublic. [Addressing] the question of viewpoint discrimination directly, free of the Court's irrelevant public forum analysis, it is clear that the exclusive access policy discriminates on the basis of viewpoint. [The] only reason for [PEA] to seek an exclusive access policy is to deny its rivals access to an effective channel of communication. No other group is explicitly denied access to the mail system. In fact, [many] other groups have been granted access to the system. [The] board has agreed to amplify the speech of [PEA], while repressing the speech of [PLEA] based on [PLEA's] point of view. This sort of discrimination amounts to censorship and infringes the First Amendment rights of the respondents [without] further[ing] any substantial state interest."

3. *Charitable campaigns in federal offices.* CORNELIUS v. NAACP LEGAL DEFENSE AND ED. FUND, 473 U.S. 788 (1985), was a 4–3 decision (Justices Marshall and Powell did not participate) that upheld the exclusion of political and advocacy groups from the Combined Federal Campaign (CFC), an annual charitable fundraising drive conducted in federal offices during working hours mainly through the voluntary efforts of federal employees. The Court upheld an Executive Order limiting the organizations that could participate in

CFC to voluntary, tax-exempt, nonprofit charitable agencies that provide direct health and welfare services to individuals; the Order expressly excluded legal defense and political advocacy groups. Justice O'CONNOR's plurality opinion, following the tripartite classification of fora articulated in Perry, found the CFC (not the federal workplace generally) the relevant forum and held that it was a "nonpublic forum," not a "traditional" public forum or a "public forum created by government designation": "[The] government does not create a public forum by inaction or by permitting limited discourse, but only by intentionally opening a non-traditional forum for public discourse. [Perry.] Accordingly, the Court has looked to the policy and practice of the government to ascertain whether it intended to designate a place not traditionally open to assembly and debate as a public forum. The Court has also examined the nature of the property and its compatibility with expressive activity to discern the government's intent. [Not] every instrumentality used for communication, however, is a traditional public forum or a public forum by designation. [Greenburgh.] [We] will not find that a public forum has been created in the face of clear evidence of a contrary intent, nor will we infer that the government intended to create a public forum when the nature of the property is inconsistent with expressive activity."

Here, she was not persuaded that the CFC was a "designated" public forum: "The government's consistent policy has been to limit participation in the CFC to 'appropriate' voluntary agencies. [Such] selective access, unsupported by evidence of a purposeful designation for public use, does not create a public forum. [Greer v. Spock.] Nor does the history of the CFC support a finding that the Government was motivated by an affirmative desire to provide an open forum for charitable solicitation in the federal workplace. [The] historical background indicates that the Campaign was designed to minimize the disruption to the workplace that had resulted from unlimited ad hoc solicitation activities by *lessening* the amount of expressive activity occurring on federal property. [Moreover,] the nature of the Government property involved strengthens the conclusion that the CFC is a nonpublic forum. The federal workplace, like any place of employment, exists to accomplish the business of the employer. [It] follows that the Government has the right to exercise control over access to the federal workplace in order to avoid interruptions to the performance of the duties of its employees."

Having determined that the CFC was a "nonpublic forum," Justice O'Connor held the exclusion to merely a standard of reasonableness: "Control over access to a nonpublic forum can be based on subject matter and speaker identity so long as the distinctions drawn are reasonable in light of the purpose served by the forum and are viewpoint neutral. [Perry.] Although a speaker may be excluded from a nonpublic forum if he wishes to address a topic not encompassed within the purpose of the forum [Lehman] or if he is not a member of the class of speakers for whose especial benefit the forum was created [Perry], the government violates the First Amendment when it denies access to a speaker solely to suppress the point of view he espouses on an otherwise includible subject." She emphasized: "The Government's decision to restrict access to a nonpublic forum need only be *reasonable;* it need not be the most reasonable or the only reasonable limitation. In contrast to a public forum, a finding of strict incompatibility between the nature of the speech or the identity of the speaker and the functioning of the nonpublic forum is not mandated. [Cf. Perry; Lehman.] [Nor] is there a requirement that the restriction be narrowly tailored or that the Government's interest be compelling. The First Amendment does not demand unrestricted access to a nonpublic forum merely because use of that forum may be the most efficient means of delivering the speaker's message [Greenburgh.] Here, as in [Perry], the speakers have access to alternative channels, including direct mail and in-person solicitation outside the workplace." Here, "the President could reasonably conclude" that "a dollar directly spent on providing food or shelter to the needy is more beneficial than a dollar spent on litigation that might or might not result in aid to the needy," that the participation of legal defense and political advocacy groups would generate controversy and thus "be detrimental to the Campaign and disruptive of the federal workplace," and that the exclusion of legal defense and political advocacy groups would "avoid the reality and the appearance of government favoritism or entanglement with particular viewpoints."[1]

Justice BLACKMUN dissented, joined by Justice Brennan. He objected to the majority's holding that, "when the Government acts as the holder of public property other than streets, parks, and similar places, the Government may do whatever it reasonably intends to do, so long as it does not intend to suppress a particular viewpoint." He argued that the CFC was a limited public forum, and that the government's exclusion of "speech that would be compatible with the intended uses of the property" triggered a demand for a "compelling governmental interest." Applying this analysis here, he concluded that the asserted justifications "neither reserve the CFC for expressive activity compatible with the property nor serve any other compelling governmental interest." Moreover, he argued that the challenged exclusions were "blatantly viewpoint-based" because "Government employees may hear only from those charities that think that charitable goals can best be achieved within the confines of existing social policy and the status quo." Justice STEVENS also submitted a dissent, arguing that the case could be disposed of without using "multitiered analysis" to label the forum, simply on the ground of viewpoint discrimination.

4. *Post Office sidewalks.* Usually, streets and sidewalks are public forums on which speech restrictions demand a strong justification. But UNITED STATES v. KOKINDA, 497 U.S. 720 (1990), indicated that use of an area that *seems* to be a sidewalk does not necessarily assure the most careful scrutiny. The Court upheld a Postal Service prohibition of "soliciting" contributions on postal premises. The regulation was applied to soliciting by volunteers for the National Democratic Policy Committee who had set up a table on the sidewalk near the entrance of the Bowie, Maryland, post office in order to collect contributions. As described by the lower court, the post office was a "freestanding" building, with its own sidewalk and parking lot. It was located on a major highway. "A sidewalk runs along the edge of the highway, separating the post office property from the street. To enter the post office, cars enter a driveway that traverses the public sidewalk and enter a parking lot that surrounds the post office building. Another sidewalk runs adjacent to the building itself, separating the parking lot from the building. Postal patrons must use [this] sidewalk to enter the post office. The sidewalk belongs to the post office and is used for no other purpose."

Justice O'CONNOR's plurality opinion, joined by Chief Justice Rehnquist and Justices White and Scalia, began by concluding that the postal "sidewalk" was not the kind of sidewalk that constituted a traditional public forum. Instead, she found that the postal sidewalk was a nonpublic forum and that the postal regulation was constitutional because viewpoint-neutral and reasonable

---

1. Justice O'Connor did acknowledge that "the purported concern to avoid controversy excited by particular groups may conceal a bias against the viewpoint advanced by the excluded speakers." Accordingly, she re- manded the case for determination "whether the exclusion of respondents was impermissibly motivated by a desire to suppress a particular point of view."

as applied: "Respondents contend that although the sidewalk is on postal service property, because it is not distinguishable from the municipal sidewalk across the parking lot from the post office's entrance, it must be a traditional public forum and therefore subject to strict scrutiny. This argument is unpersuasive. [The] postal sidewalk at issue does not have the characteristics of public sidewalks traditionally open to expressive activity. The municipal sidewalk that runs parallel to the road in this case is a public passageway. The Postal Service's sidewalk is not such a thoroughfare. Rather, it leads only from the parking area to the front door of the post office." Although the postal entryways are open to the public, "that fact alone does not establish that such areas must be treated as traditional public fora." She noted that the Postal Service had not "expressly dedicated its sidewalks to any expressive activity." Instead, the sidewalk was "expressly dedicated to only one means of free communication: the posting of public notices on designated bulletin boards. [To] be sure, individuals and groups have been permitted to leaflet, speak, and picket on postal premises, [but] a practice of allowing some speech activities on public postal property [does] not add up to the dedication of postal property to speech activities. [Cornelius.]"

In finding the restriction "reasonable," Justice O'Connor emphasized what she called "a long-settled principle" that "governmental actions are subject to a lower level of First Amendment scrutiny" when the government is not acting "as lawmaker [but] rather as proprietor." She emphasized that Congress had wanted the Postal Service "to be run more like a business" than had its predecessor, the Post Office Department. Noting that regulation must merely be "reasonable" when Government acts in a proprietary capacity [Lehman], she found that "it is reasonable to restrict access [to] solicitation, because solicitation is inherently disruptive of the Postal Service's business." The plurality also found no impermissible content discrimination in singling out solicitation for special treatment. She claimed that it was "anomalous that the Service's allowance of some avenues of speech would be relied upon as evidence that is impermissibly suppressing other speech. If anything, the Service's generous accommodation of some types of speech testifies to its willingness to provide as broad a forum as possible, consistent with its postal mission."

Significantly, however, the "reasonableness" standard did not attract a majority of the Court. Justice KENNEDY, who had joined the Court after Cornelius, concurred only in the judgment and specifically distanced himself from the plurality's approach. He suggested that the walkway surrounding a post office "may be an appropriate place for the exercise of vital rights of expression. As society becomes more insular in character, it becomes essential to protect public places where traditional modes of speech [can] take place." However, he found it unnecessary to determine whether the sidewalk was a public or nonpublic forum, because in his view "the postal regulation [meets] the traditional standards we have applied to time, place, and manner restrictions of protected expression," citing Clark and Ward. "Given the Postal Service's past experience with expressive activity on its property, I cannot reject its judgment that in-person solicitation deserves different treatment from alternative forms of solicitation and expression."

Justice BRENNAN, joined by Justices Marshall and Stevens and in part by Justice Blackmun, dissented, criticizing the plurality's distinction between types of sidewalks: "[The plurality] insists, with logic that is both strained and formalistic, that the specific sidewalk at issue is not a public forum. This conclusion is unsupportable. [It] is only common sense that a public sidewalk adjacent to a public building to which citizens are freely admitted is a natural location for speech to occur. [It] is irrelevant that [this] sidewalk [may] have been constructed only to provide access to the [post office]. Public sidewalks, parks, and streets have been reserved for public use as forums for speech even though government has not constructed them for expressive purposes. Parks are usually constructed to beautify a city and to provide opportunities for recreation, rather than to afford a forum for soapbox orators or leafleteers; streets are built to facilitate transportation, not to enable protestors to conduct marches; and sidewalks are created with pedestrians in mind, not solicitors. [That] the walkway at issue is a sidewalk open and accessible to the general public is alone sufficient to identify it as a public forum. [Whatever] the proper application of public forum doctrine to novel situations [such as those in Cornelius and Perry], we ought not unreflectively transfer principles [developed] in those specialized and difficult contexts to traditional forums such as streets, sidewalks, and parks."

Justice Brennan added: "Even if I did not believe that the postal sidewalk is a 'traditional' public forum, I would find that it is a 'limited-purpose' forum from which respondents may not be excluded absent a showing of a compelling interest to which any exclusion is narrowly tailored." He insisted that the regulation could not pass muster under that requirement or the standard applicable to time, place, and manner regulations. In his view the regulation as applied "prohibits all solicitation anywhere on postal service property. It sweeps an entire category of expressive activity off a public forum solely in the interest of administrative convenience. It does not attempt to limit nondisruptive solicitation to a time, place, and manner consistent with post office operations; and it does not require that evidence of disruption be shown." He added: "Even if I did not believe that [this] sidewalk was a public forum, I nevertheless could not agree [that] the postal regulation [is] reasonable. [The] Postal Service does not subject to the same categorical prohibition many other types of speech presenting the same risk of disruption as solicitation, such as soapbox oratory, pamphleteering, [or] even flag-burning. [This] inconsistent treatment renders the prohibition on solicitation unreasonable." He added: "[The] Service could quite easily design [rules] governing solicitation that would [fall] far short of a total ban—[e.g.,] reasonable restrictions on the size and placement of tables [or] on solicitation during peak postal hours. [Although] the Government would not be required to choose the least restrictive alternatives [if this were a nonpublic forum], these other approaches [are] so obvious that the no-solicitation regulation can scarcely be considered [reasonable]."

5. *Airport terminals.* Shifting majorities in INTERNATIONAL SOCIETY FOR KRISHNA CONSCIOUSNESS, INC. [ISKCON] v. LEE, 505 U.S. 672 (1992) and its companion case, LEE v. ISKCON, 505 U.S. 830 (1992), upheld a ban on the solicitation of money in a public airport terminal, but struck down a ban on the sale or distribution of literature. The Port Authority that operates the three major airports in the New York metropolitan area had promulgated rules restricting such activities to sidewalks outside the airports' terminals. The Court considered a challenge by ISKCON to these rules. The multiple opinions produced three holdings.

First, by a vote of 5–4, the Court found airport terminals to be *nonpublic forums.* Chief Justice REHNQUIST, writing for the Court on this point, stated that, "given the lateness with which the modern air terminal has made its appearance, it hardly qualifies for the description of having 'immemorially ... time out of mind' been held in the public trust and used for purposes of expressive activity. [Hague.] [Nor] can we say that [airport] terminals generally have been intentionally opened by their operators to [expressive] activity; the frequent and continuing litigation evidencing the operators' objections belies any such claim. [Airports] are commercial establishments funded by users fees and designed to make a regulated profit," and their purpose is "the facilitation of passenger air travel, not the promotion of expression." Accordingly, "[t]he restrictions here challenged [need] only satisfy a requirement of reasonableness. [Kokinda, Cornelius.]"

Justice KENNEDY's partial concurrence disagreed that airports were nonpublic forums, and was joined on this point by Justices Blackmun, Stevens and Souter: "Our public forum doctrine ought not to be a jurisprudence of categories rather than ideas or convert what was once an analysis protective of expression into one which grants the government authority to restrict speech by fiat." Justice Kennedy's opinion noted the importance of public forums to democracy: "At the heart of our jurisprudence lies the principle that in a free nation citizens must have the right to gather and speak with other persons in public places." He also objected to the majority's deference to the airport authorities' managerial role: "The Court [reintroduces] today into our First Amendment law a strict doctrinal line between the proprietary and regulatory functions of government which I thought had been abandoned long ago. [Compare Davis with Hague; Schneider; Grayned.] [But a] fundamental tenet of our Constitution is that the government is subject to constraints which private persons are not." Finally, he charged that "[t]he Court's analysis rests on an inaccurate view of history. The notion that traditional public forums are property which have public discourse as their principal purpose is a most doubtful fiction. The types of property that we have recognized as the quintessential public forums are streets, parks, and sidewalks. It would seem apparent that the principal purpose of streets and sidewalks, like airports, is to facilitate transportation, not public discourse. [Similarly], the purpose for the creation of public parks may be as much for beauty and open space as for discourse. Thus under the Court's analysis, even the quintessential public forums would appear to lack the necessary elements of what the Court defines as a public forum."

Justice Kennedy urged an alternative approach: "In my view the policies underlying the doctrine cannot be given effect unless we recognize that open, public spaces and thoroughfares which are suitable for discourse may be public forums, whatever their historical pedigree and without concern for a precise classification of the property. [Without] this recognition our forum doctrine retains no relevance in times of fast-changing technology and increasing insularity. In a country where most citizens travel by automobile, and parks all too often become locales for crime rather than social intercourse, our failure to recognize the possibility that new types of government property may be appropriate forums for speech will lead to a serious curtailment of our expressive activity. One of the places left in our mobile society that is suitable for discourse is a metropolitan airport. [If] the objective, physical characteristics of the property at issue and the actual public access and uses which have been permitted by the government indicate that expressive activity would be appropriate and compatible with those uses, the property is a public forum.

"[Under] this analysis, it is evident that the public spaces of the Port Authority's airports are public forums. [First, there are] physical similarities between the Port Authority's airports and public streets. [Airports have] broad, public thoroughfares full of people and lined with stores and other commercial activities. [Second,] the airport areas involved here are open to the public without restriction. [Third,] and perhaps most important, [when] adequate time, place, and manner regulations are in place, expressive activity is quite compatible with the uses of major airports."

Justice SOUTER, joined by Justices Blackmun and Stevens, filed a separate partial concurrence and partial dissent agreeing with Justice Kennedy that airport terminals should be analyzed as public forums: "To treat the class of such forums as closed by their description as 'traditional,' taking that word merely as a charter for examining the history of the particular public property claimed as a forum, has no warrant in a Constitution whose values are not to be left behind in the city streets that are no longer the only focus of our community life. If that were the line of our direction, we might as well abandon the public forum doctrine altogether."

The Court, second, upheld the *solicitation ban* by a vote of 6–3. Chief Justice REHNQUIST again wrote for the Court on this point: "We have on many prior occasions noted the disruptive effect that solicitation may have on business. 'Solicitation requires action by those who would respond: The individual solicited must decide whether or not to contribute (which itself might involve reading the solicitor's literature or hearing his pitch), and then, having decided to do so, reach for a wallet, search it for money, write a check, or produce a credit card.' [Kokinda; see Heffron.] Passengers who wish to avoid the solicitor may have to alter their path, slowing both themselves and those around them. The result is that the normal flow of traffic is impeded. This is especially so in an airport, where [delays] may be particularly costly. [In] addition, face-to-face solicitation presents risks of duress that are an appropriate target of regulation. The skillful, and unprincipled, solicitor can target the most vulnerable, including those accompanying children or those suffering physical impairment and who cannot easily avoid the solicitation. The unsavory solicitor can also commit fraud through concealment of his affiliation or through deliberate efforts to shortchange those who agree to purchase. Compounding this problem is the fact that, in an airport, the targets of such activity frequently are on tight schedules. This in turn makes such visitors unlikely to stop and formally complain to airport authorities. As a result, the airport faces considerable difficulty in achieving its legitimate interest in monitoring solicitation activity to assure that travelers are not interfered with unduly.

"The Port Authority has concluded that its interest in monitoring the activities can best be accomplished by limiting solicitation and distribution to the sidewalk areas outside the terminals. This sidewalk area is frequented by an overwhelming percentage of airport users. Thus the resulting access of those who would solicit the general public is quite complete. In turn we think it would be odd to conclude that the Port Authority's terminal regulation is unreasonable despite the Port Authority having otherwise assured access to an area universally traveled. The inconveniences to passengers and the burdens on Port Authority officials flowing from solicitation activity may seem small, but viewed against the fact that 'pedestrian congestion is one of the greatest problems facing the three terminals,' the Port Authority could reasonably worry that even such incremental effects would prove quite disruptive. Moreover, 'the justification for the Rule should not be measured by the disorder that would result from granting an exemption solely to ISKCON.' [Heffron.] For if petitioner is given access, so too must other groups. [We] conclude that the solicitation ban is reasonable."

Justice O'CONNOR, who had joined the majority in finding airports to be nonpublic forums, concurred in the holding that the solicitation ban was constitutional, but wrote separately to emphasize that the fact that "airports are not public fora [does] not mean that the government can restrict speech in whatever way it likes." In her view, some inquiry into a nonpublic forum's "characteristic nature and function" was still required. Even taking into account that an airport is "multipurpose," operating more like "a shopping mall" than like a jail, mailbox, or post office sidewalk, however, she found that "the ban on solicitation is reasonable. Face-to-face solicitation is incompatible with the airport's functioning in a way that the other, permitted activities are not. '[As] residents of metropolitan areas know from daily experience, confrontation by a person asking for money disrupts passage and is more intrusive and intimidating than an encounter with a person giving out information.' [Kokinda.] The record in this case confirms that the problems of congestion and fraud that we have identified with solicitation in other contexts have also proved true in the airports' experience."

Justice KENNEDY provided a sixth vote to uphold the solicitation ban, finding that, even though in his view an airport was a public forum, the solicitation ban satisfied the appropriately heightened scrutiny: "The regulation may be upheld as either a reasonable time, place, and manner restriction, or as a regulation directed at the nonspeech element of expressive conduct. The two standards have considerable overlap in a case like this one. [Solicitation] is a form of protected speech. If the Port Authority's solicitation regulation prohibited all speech which requested the contribution of funds, I would conclude that it was a direct, content-based restriction of speech in clear violation of the First Amendment. The Authority's regulation does not prohibit all solicitation, however; it prohibits the 'solicitation and receipt of funds.' I do not understand this regulation to prohibit all speech that solicits funds. [The] regulation permits expression that solicits funds, but limits the manner of that expression to forms other than the immediate receipt of money.

"So viewed, [the] Port Authority's rule survives our test for speech restrictions in the public forum. In-person solicitation of funds, when combined with immediate receipt of that money, creates a risk of fraud and duress which is well recognized, and which is different in kind from other forms of expression or conduct. [Because] the Port Authority's solicitation ban is directed at these abusive practices and not at any particular message, idea, or form of speech, the regulation is a content-neutral rule serving a significant government interest. [The] regulation does not burden any broader category of speech or expressive conduct than is the source of the evil sought to be avoided. [And] the Port Authority has left open ample alternative channels for the communication of the message which is an aspect of solicitation. [Requests] for money continue to be permitted, and in the course of requesting money solicitors may explain their cause, or the purposes of their organization, without violating the regulation. It is only if the solicitor accepts immediate payment that a violation occurs. Thus the solicitor can continue to disseminate his message, for example by distributing preaddressed envelopes in which potential contributors may mail their donations."

Justice SOUTER, joined by Justices Blackmun and Stevens, dissented from the judgment upholding the solicitation ban, finding the ban not narrowly tailored to preventing coercion because, "[w]hile a solicitor can be insistent, a pedestrian on the street or airport concourse can simply walk away or walk on," and finding it not narrowly tailored to preventing fraud because the Port Authority had available less restrictive alternatives such as prohibiting fraudulent misrepresentations directly and imposing disclosure requirements on solicitors.

In its third holding, by a vote of 5–4, the Court invalidated the *ban on sale or distribution of literature* in the airport terminals. Justice KENNEDY concurred in the judgment on this issue, joined by Justices Blackmun, Stevens and Souter: "[A] grant of plenary power allows the government to tilt the dialogue heard by the public, to exclude many, more marginal voices. [We] have long recognized that the right to distribute flyers and literature lies at the heart of the liberties guaranteed by the Speech and Press Clauses of the First Amendment. [Schneider.] The Port Authority's rule, which prohibits almost all such activity, is among the most restrictive possible of those liberties. [I] have no difficulty deciding the regulation cannot survive the [stringent] rules applicable to regulations in public forums. The regulation is not drawn in narrow terms and it does not leave open ample alternative channels for communication. The Port Authority's concerns with the problem of congestion can be addressed through narrow restrictions on the time and place of expressive activity." Justice O'CONNOR, concurring in the judgment, provided the fifth vote to invalidate the distribution ban. She stated that the distribution ban was impermissible even under the lenient "reasonableness" test she and the majority viewed as applicable to nonpublic forums: "While the difficulties posed by solicitation in a nonpublic forum are sufficiently obvious that its regulation may 'ring of common-sense,' the same is not necessarily true of leafletting. '[The] distribution of literature does not require that the recipient stop in order to receive the message the speaker wishes to convey; instead the recipient is free to read the message at a later time.'"

Chief Justice REHNQUIST, joined by Justices White, Scalia and Thomas, dissented from the judgment invalidating the distribution ban: "Leafletting presents risks of congestion similar to those posed by solicitation. The weary, harried, or hurried traveler may have no less desire and need to avoid the delays generated by having literature foisted upon him than he does to avoid delays from a financial solicitation. [Moreover,] those who accept material may often simply drop it on the floor once out of the leafletter's range, creating an eyesore, a safety hazard, and additional clean-up work for airport staff." Thus, he concluded that "the distribution ban, no less than the solicitation ban, is reasonable."

6. *The Court's trichotomy of public places.* Is categorizing public places into "traditional, quintessential" public forums, "limited" or "designated" public forums, and "nonpublic" forums a helpful approach? There has been considerable criticism of the Court's tripartite classification scheme. See, e.g., Farber & Nowak, "The Misleading Nature of Public Forum Analysis: Content and Context in First Amendment Adjudication," 70 Va.L.Rev. 1219 (1984) ("classification of public places as various types of forums has only confused judicial opinions by diverting attention from the real First Amendment [issues]—the First Amendment values and governmental interests involved in the case"); Tribe, Constitutional Choices (1985) (criticizing Perry as avoiding "a rigorous analysis of the viewpoint discrimination issue by focusing on the public forum analysis"). For the contrary view, see BeVier, "Rehabilitating Public Forum Doctrine: In Defense of Categories," 1993 Sup. Ct. Rev. 79 (arguing that the central function of the First Amendment is to prevent government distortion of public dialogue, not to enhance the amount of speech, and that "[t]he role of categorical analysis in public forum jurisprudence is to generalize about the kinds of places where denials of access tend systematically to trigger well-founded concerns about deliberate governmental abuse and distortion").

7. *The special problem of solicitation.* Is solicitation of funds speech protected by the First Amendment? The Court has held as much in invalidating various restrictions on solicitation. See, e.g., Murdock v. Pennsylvania, 319 U.S. 105 (1943) (flat tax); Hynes v. Mayor of Oradell, 425 U.S. 610 (1976) (licensing requirement); Schaumburg v. Citizens for Better Environment, 444 U.S. 620 (1980) (overhead limit). In Schaumburg, the Court stated that "charitable appeals for funds [involve] a variety of speech interests—communication of information, the dissemination and propagation of views and ideas, and the

advocacy of causes—that are within the protection of the First Amendment." But in Kokinda and ISKCON, the Court readily deferred to government bans on solicitation on public property, suggesting that solicitation causes unique harms. These cases emphasize that solicitation poses greater risk to crowd control than other modes of expression because those solicited must stop and reach for money. They also suggest that solicitation raises a danger of fraud that will be difficult to police except by a prophylactic ban.

Are these problems unique to the settings of "nonpublic forums" such as airports and post office sidewalks? Could a city ban solicitation on all streets and sidewalks? Recall that the Court upheld a solicitation ban throughout the open thoroughfares of the Minnesota State Fair in Heffron v. ISKCON (1981; p. 1245 above), relying on conventional time, place and manner analysis. Is the solicitation ban in Heffron distinguishable from a city-wide solicitation ban because a fair is more enclosed than city streets? Because a citywide ban is broader? Or do the special problems of solicitation emphasized by the Justices in Heffron, Kokinda and ISKCON suggest that even a citywide ban on in-person solicitation on the streets might be upheld?

Consider in light of these questions the issue of whether begging in public places implicates the First Amendment. Does begging communicate information or advocate a cause? Is it distinguishable for First Amendment purposes from commercial sales? On commercial solicitation, see Breard v. Alexandria, 341 U.S. 622 (1951) (upholding an ordinance barring door-to-door solicitation for magazine subscriptions without the prior consent of the homeowners). Even if it is protected expression, does begging trigger government interests similar to those found sufficient in Kokinda and ISKCON? For the view that begging is protected speech and that most restrictions on it are unconstitutional, see Hershkoff & Cohen, "Begging to Differ: The First Amendment and the Right to Beg," 104 Harv. L. Rev. 896 (1991). For an argument for government leeway to regulate the public location of begging, see Ellickson, "Controlling Chronic Misconduct in City Spaces: Of Panhandlers, Skid Rows, and Public Space Zoning," 105 Yale L.J. 1165 (1996).

Note that ISKCON, while upholding the airport solicitation ban, invalidated a ban on the *sale* or distribution of literature at airports. Is the sale of literature more like the distribution of leaflets or the solicitation of funds? If sales of charitable literature are allowed in a public place, must sales of other items be granted equal access? What about sales of other expressive items, such as commemorative key rings or message-bearing T-shirts? Would a ban on all peddling in public streets implicate the First Amendment as applied to such sales? Can government draw any lines short of a flat ban without discriminating impermissibly on the basis of the expressive content of the merchandise? Justice Kennedy, who along with Justice O'Connor was one of only two justices to vote for both results in ISKCON, stated in his partial concurrence: "Much of what I have said about the solicitation of funds may seem to apply to the sale of literature, but the differences between the two activities are of sufficient significance to require they be distinguished for constitutional purposes. [The] danger of a fraud arising from such sales is much more limited than from pure solicitation, because in the case of a sale the nature of the exchange tends to be clearer to both parties. [And] the flat ban on sales of literature leaves open fewer alternative channels of communication [as] sales of literature must be completed in one transaction to be workable."

RELIGIOUS SPEECH ON PUBLIC PROPERTY

The exclusion of religious expression from public spaces would appear to be content discrimination that would normally be impermissible in a traditional or designated public forum, or viewpoint discrimination that would be impermissible even in a nonpublic forum. But is such exclusion dictated by the countervailing constitutional command of the establishment clause of the First Amendment? Establishment principles are explored at length in Chapter 14 below. As interpreted by the modern Court, the establishment clause prohibits government from establishing religion not only through coercion but also through symbolic endorsement or financial support. Government bodies have sometimes read the clause to require it to exclude religious speech from forums it has otherwise opened to expression. When these cases have come before the Court, it has consistently held that the free speech clause forbids such discrimination, and that the establishment clause does not require it. Consider the following decisions.

WIDMAR v. VINCENT, 454 U.S. 263 (1981): In this case, the Court exercised the strict scrutiny it typically applies to content-based exclusions from public places. It held that a state university that makes its facilities generally available for the activities of registered student groups may not constitutionally bar a group desiring to use the facilities for religious worship and discussion. The case arose when the University of Missouri at Kansas City, relying on its policy of prohibiting the use of its facilities "for purposes of religious worship or religious teaching," barred a student religious group from meeting anywhere on its grounds. The Court rejected the University's argument that its interest in promoting the separation of church and state was adequate to survive strict scrutiny. (The Court's discussion of the establishment clause issue is noted at p. 1543 below.)

In explaining the application of free speech principles here, Justice POWELL's majority opinion stated: "Through its policy of accommodating their meetings, the University has created a forum generally open for use by student groups. Having done so, the University has assumed an obligation to justify its discriminations and exclusions under applicable constitutional norms. The Constitution forbids a State to enforce certain exclusions from a forum generally open to the public, even if it was not required to create the forum in the first place. The University's institutional mission, which it describes as providing a *secular* education' to its students, does not exempt its actions from constitutional scrutiny. With respect to persons entitled to be there, our cases leave no doubt that the First Amendment rights of speech and association extend to the campuses of state universities. Here the [University] has discriminated against student groups and speakers based on their desire to use a generally open forum to engage in religious worship and discussion. These are forms of speech and association protected by the First Amendment. In order to justify discriminatory exclusion from a public forum based on the religious content of a group's intended speech, the University must therefore satisfy the standard of review appropriate to content-based exclusions. It must show that its regulation is necessary to serve a compelling state interest and that it is narrowly drawn to achieve that end. See [Carey.]" Finding that there would be no establishment clause violation if the university granted access to religious student groups, Justice Powell found no compelling state interest in their exclusion.

In an opinion concurring only in the judgment, Justice STEVENS took issue with the majority's approach: "In my opinion, the use of the terms 'compelling state interest' and 'public forum' to analyze the question presented in this case may needlessly undermine the academic freedom of public universities." He elaborated: "Because every university's resources are limited, an educational institution must routinely make decisions concerning the use of the time and space that is available for extracurricular activities. In my judgment, it is both necessary and appropriate for those decisions to evaluate the content of a proposed student activity. I should think it obvious, for example, that if two groups of 25 students requested the use of a room at a particular time—one to view Mickey Mouse cartoons and the other to rehearse an amateur performance of Hamlet—the First Amendment would not require that the room be reserved for the group that submitted its application first. [Judgments] of this kind should be made by academicians, not by federal judges, and their standards for decision should not be encumbered with ambiguous phrases like 'compelling state interest.' Thus, I do not subscribe to the view that a public university has no greater interest in the content of student activities than the police chief has in the content of a soap box oration on Capitol Hill. A university legitimately may regard some subjects as more relevant to its educational mission than others.

"But the university, like the police officer, may not allow its agreement or disagreement with the viewpoint of a particular speaker to determine whether access to a forum will be granted. If a state university is to deny recognition to a student organization—or is to give it a lesser right to use school facilities than other student groups—it must have a valid reason for doing so." Despite his different approach, Justice Stevens found the University decision unjustified. He explained: "It seems apparent that the policy under attack would allow groups of young philosophers to meet to discuss their skepticism that a Supreme Being exists, or a group of political scientists to meet to debate the accuracy of the view that religion is the 'opium of the people.' If school facilities may be used to discuss anti-clerical doctrine, it seems to me that comparable use by a group desiring to express a belief in God must also be permitted. The fact that their expression of faith includes ceremonial conduct is not, in my opinion, a sufficient reason for suppressing their discussion entirely."

Justice WHITE, the sole dissenter, disagreed with the majority's Establishment Clause and free speech analysis. He objected to the argument that, "because religious worship uses speech, it is protected by the Free Speech Clause of the First Amendment." He added: "This case involves religious worship only; the fact that that worship is accomplished through speech does not add anything to [the challengers'] argument. That argument must rely upon the claim that the state's action impermissibly interferes with the free exercise of respondents' religious practices. Although this is a close question, I conclude that it does not."

LAMB'S CHAPEL v. CENTER MORICHES UNION FREE SCHOOL DIST., 508 U.S. 384 (1993): This case involved a free speech challenge to a local school district policy that permitted public school facilities to be used after school hours for social, civic, and recreational purposes and by political organizations, but provided that "the school premises shall not be used by any group for religious purposes." The school district twice denied permission to Lamb's Chapel, a local evangelical organization, to show a six-part film series featuring a psychologist who would argue in favor of "Christian family values instilled at an early stage." The district gave as its reason that the series appeared "church related."

The Court unanimously held the district's rule unconstitutional as applied to the Lamb's Chapel film series. Justice WHITE wrote for the Court: "There is no question that the District, like the private owner of property, may legally preserve the property under its control for the use to which it is dedicated. It is also common ground that the District need not have permitted after-hours use of its property for any [expressive] uses." The Church had argued that the schools had been opened after hours to such a wide variety of speech that the district's program should be analyzed as a designated public forum. Justice White declined to reach that issue, holding that, even assuming that the after-hours program was *not* a traditional or designated public forum, the exclusion of the Lamb's Chapel series amounted to impermissible viewpoint discrimination:

"That all religions and all uses for religious purposes are treated alike under [the rule] does not answer the critical question whether it discriminates on the basis of viewpoint to permit school property to be used for the presentation of all views about family issues and child-rearing except those dealing with the subject matter from a religious standpoint. There is no suggestion [that] a lecture or film about child-rearing and family values would not be a use for social or civic purposes otherwise permitted. [Nor] is there any indication [that] the application to exhibit the particular film involved here [would] have been denied for any reason other than [its] religious perspective. In our view, denial on that basis was plainly invalid under [Cornelius:] 'although a speaker may be excluded from a nonpublic forum if he wishes to address a topic not encompassed within the purpose of the forum . . . or if he is not a member of the class of speakers for whose special benefit the forum was created . . . the government violates the First Amendment when it denies access to a speaker solely to suppress the point of view he espouses on an otherwise includible subject.' "

As in Widmar, the Court rejected the government's Establishment Clause defense (see p. 1543 below). For a later decision relying heavily on Lamb's Chapel, see Rosenberger v. Rector and Visitors of the University of Virginia, ___ U.S. ___, 115 S.Ct. 2510 (1995), which held that a public university may not deny funds to an evangelical student magazine under a policy subsidizing a variety of student magazines but expressly excluding "religious activities." The case is considered at p. 1324 below in connection with other cases involving free speech challenges to selective subsidies.

CAPITOL SQUARE REVIEW BOARD v. PINETTE, ___ U.S. ___, 115 S.Ct. 2440 (1995): In this case the Court invalidated the denial of permission to the Ku Klux Klan to erect a large Latin cross on Capitol Square, a 10–acre, state-owned plaza surrounding the Statehouse in Columbus, Ohio. The Square was designated a public forum by state law, and several unattended displays had been permitted there. The Court assumed that the Board had denied permission solely on the ground of the cross's religious content and that such a ground for exclusion would violate the free speech clause unless required by the establishment clause, which the Court held it was not. (For the establishment clause aspects of the ruling, see p. 1528 below). Justice SCALIA's plurality opinion stated: "Respondents' religious display in Capitol Square was private expression. Our precedent establishes that private religious speech, far from being a First Amendment orphan, is as fully protected under the Free Speech Clause as secular private expression. Indeed, in Anglo–American history, at least, government suppression of speech has so commonly been directed precisely at religious speech that a free-speech clause without religion would be Hamlet without the prince. [Heffron, Widmar.] It is undeniable, of course, that speech which is constitutionally protected against state suppression is not thereby accorded a guaranteed forum on all property owned by the State. [But] Capitol Square [is] a traditional public forum. Petitioners do not claim that their denial of respondents' application was based upon a content-neutral time, place, or manner restriction. To the contrary, they concede—indeed it is the essence of their case—that the Board rejected the display precisely because its content was religious." The rest of the plurality and the concurring opinions went on to reject the argument that this exclusion was required by the establishment clause.

———

FIRST AMENDMENT ACCESS RIGHTS TO PRIVATE PROPERTY?

Introduction. The preceding materials focused on claimed rights of access to *public* property. Do the principles of those cases aid in developing claims of access to *private* property as well? Is there a "private forum" counterpart to the public forum? In Marsh v. Alabama, 326 U.S. 501 (1946) (p. 928 above), the Court initiated the "public function" state action theory by holding that Jehovah's Witnesses could claim a constitutional right of access to distribute religious literature in a company-owned town. Does such a principle extend to shopping centers? Are shopping centers the modern functional equivalent of the public square?

1. *Logan Valley.* In 1968, the 5–4 decision in AMALGAMATED FOOD EMPLOYEES v. LOGAN VALLEY PLAZA, 391 U.S. 308, relied in part on Marsh to hold that a state trespass law could not be applied to enjoin peaceful union picketing of a supermarket in a privately owned shopping center. Justice MARSHALL's majority opinion found that the ban on picketing could not be justified on the ground that picketing constituted an unconsented invasion of private property rights: "The shopping center here is clearly the functional equivalent of the business district of Chickasaw involved in Marsh. [We] see no reason why access to a business district in a company town for the purpose of exercising First Amendment rights should be constitutionally required, while access for the same purpose to property functioning as a business district should be limited simply because the property surrounding the 'business district' is not under the same ownership." Accordingly, Justice Marshall applied public forum principles: "The essence of [such cases as Lovell, Hague, and Schneider] is that streets, sidewalks, parks, and other similar public places are so historically associated with the exercise of First Amendment rights that access to them for the purpose of exercising such rights cannot constitutionally be denied broadly and absolutely. [Here] it is perfectly clear that a prohibition against trespass on the mall operates to bar all speech within the shopping center to which respondents object." Thus, here, as in Marsh, the State could not "delegate the power, through the use of its trespass laws, wholly to exclude those members of the public wishing to exercise their First Amendment rights on the premises in a manner and for a purpose generally consonant with the use to which the property is actually put."

2. *Lloyd.* The Logan Valley decision was "distinguished" four years later, in the 5–4 decision in LLOYD CORP. v. TANNER, 407 U.S. 551 (1972). In Lloyd, the lower federal courts had relied on Marsh and Logan Valley in holding unconstitutional the application to anti-war leafleteers of a shopping center ban on the distribution of handbills. The Court reversed, finding the facts in its earlier cases "significantly different." Justice POWELL emphasized that in Logan Valley the First Amendment activity—union picketing of a store—"was related to the shopping center's operations" and the store was "in the center of a large private enclave with the consequence that no other reasonable opportunities" to convey the picketers' message existed. Here, by contrast, the handbilling "had no relation to any purpose for which the center was built and being used" and alternative means of communication were

available. He noted, moreover, that "[a]lthough accommodations between [speech and property values] are sometimes necessary, and the courts properly have shown a special solicitude for the [First Amendment], this Court has never held that a trespasser or an uninvited guest may exercise general rights of free speech on property privately owned."

Justice MARSHALL's dissent, joined by Justices Douglas, Brennan and Stewart, objected to the majority's departure from Logan Valley. He emphasized the "tremendous need" of the handbillers to have access to the private shopping center: "For many persons who do not have easy access to television, radio, the major newspapers, and the other forms of mass media, the only way they can express themselves to a broad range of citizens on issues of general public concern is to picket, or to handbill, or to utilize other free or relatively inexpensive means of communication. The only hope that these people have to be able to communicate effectively is to be permitted to speak in those areas in which most of their fellow citizens can be found. One such area is the business district of a city or town or its functional equivalent."

3. *Hudgens.* Even though Lloyd had purported to distinguish Logan Valley, HUDGENS v. NLRB, 424 U.S. 507 (1976), announced that Lloyd had in effect overruled Logan Valley. Hudgens involved labor picketing of a store in a private shopping center. The picketers were employees of a warehouse maintained by the store owner at a location outside of the shopping center. Justice STEWART's majority opinion concluded that "the constitutional guarantee of free expression has no part to play in a case such as this. [If] the respondent in the Lloyd case did not have a First Amendment right to enter that shopping center to distribute handbills concerning Vietnam, then the respondents in the present case did not have a First Amendment right to enter this shopping center for the purpose of advertising their strike." Justices Marshall and Brennan dissented. On labor speech and the First Amendment generally, see Pope, "The Three–Systems Ladder of First Amendment Values: Two Rungs and a Black Hole," 11 Hast. Con.L.Q. 189 (1984).

B. SPEECH IN PUBLIC SCHOOLS

Introduction. Unlike streets and parks and other public "forums," public education is a context in which speech is highly controlled. The classroom is a place of structured dialogue bounded by teacher authority and rules of decorum, and the curriculum itself prescribes which ideas are to be studied and discussed. On the other hand, not every aspect of school is curricular. Students socialize outside of class, in the hallways, cafeterias or playing fields. And students might engage in silent demonstrative conduct even while in class. Does the First Amendment protect student speech in these noncurricular contexts? What should the standard of review be for a restriction on student speech? Should school authorities be given more authority to curtail disruption, or nip it in the bud, than the police enjoy with respect to speakers in the public square? Only in curricular settings or in noncurricular settings too? The following cases explore these questions.

In TINKER v. DES MOINES INDEPENDENT COMMUNITY SCHOOL DISTRICT, 393 U.S. 503 (1969), the Court held that a public school could not discipline two high school students and one junior high school student for wearing black armbands to school to publicize their objections to the Vietnam war. They were asked to remove their armbands and refused. In accordance with a school policy adopted two days earlier in anticipation of such a protest, the students were suspended until they were ready to return without the armbands. The lower federal court refused to enjoin the disciplinary action.

In reversing, Justice FORTAS' majority opinion stated that "First Amendment rights, applied in light of the special characteristics of the school environment, are available to teachers and students. It can hardly be argued that either students or teachers shed their constitutional rights to freedom of speech or expression at the schoolhouse gate. [The] problem here involves direct, primary First Amendment rights akin to 'pure speech.' The school officials banned and sought to punish petitioners for a silent, passive expression of opinion, unaccompanied by any disorder or disturbance on the part of petitioners. There is here no evidence whatever of petitioners' interference, actual or nascent, with the schools' work or of collision with the rights of other students to be secure and to be let alone. Accordingly, this case does not concern speech or action that intrudes upon the work of the schools or the rights of other students.

"[In] our system, undifferentiated fear or apprehension of disturbance is not enough to overcome the right to freedom of expression. [In] order for the State [to] justify prohibition of a particular expression of opinion, it must be able to show that its action was caused by something more than a mere desire to avoid the discomfort and unpleasantness that always accompany an unpopular viewpoint. [Here, there was no] evidence that the school authorities had reason to anticipate that the wearing of the armbands would substantially interfere with the work of the school or impinge upon the rights of other students. On the contrary, the action of the school authorities appears to have been based upon an urgent wish to avoid the controversy which might result from the expression, even by the silent symbol of armbands, of opposition to this Nation's part in the conflagration in Vietnam.

"It is also relevant that the school authorities did not purport to prohibit the wearing of all symbols of political or controversial significance. The record shows that students in some of the schools wore buttons relating to national political campaigns, and some even wore the Iron Cross, traditionally a symbol of Nazism. The order prohibiting the wearing of armbands did not extend to these. Instead, a particular symbol [was] singled out for prohibition. [In] our system, state-operated schools may not be enclaves of totalitarianism. School officials do not possess absolute authority over their students. Students in school as well as out of school [are] possessed of fundamental rights which the State must respect, just as they themselves must respect their obligations to the State. In our system, students may not be regarded as closed-circuit recipients of only that which the State chooses to communicate. They may not be confined to the expression of those sentiments that are officially approved.

"[This] principle [is] not confined to the supervised and ordained discussion which takes place in the classroom. The principal use to which the schools are dedicated is to accommodate students during prescribed hours for the purpose of certain types of activities. Among those activities is personal intercommunication among the students. [A] student's rights, therefore, do not embrace merely the classroom hours. When he is in the cafeteria, or on the playing field, or on the campus during the authorized hours, he may express his opinions, even on controversial subjects like the conflict in Vietnam, if he does so without 'materially and substantially interfer[ing] with the requirements of appropriate discipline in the operation of the school' and without colliding with the rights of others. [This standard was quoted from Burnside v. Byars, 363 F.2d 744 (5th Cir.1966) (holding school could not ban "freedom buttons").] But conduct by the student, in class or out of it, which for any reason—whether it stems from time, place, or type of behavior—materially disrupts classwork or involves substantial disorder or invasion of the rights of others is, of course, not immunized by the constitutional guarantee of freedom of speech."

A caustic dissent by Justice BLACK charged the majority with taking over from school officials "the power to control pupils." He objected to any view that "students and teachers may use the schools at their whim as a platform for the exercise of free speech—'symbolic' or 'pure.' [I] have never believed that any person has a right to give speeches or engage in demonstrations where he pleases and when he pleases." He argued, moreover, that "the record overwhelmingly shows that the [wearing of the] armbands did exactly what [the school officials] foresaw it would, that is, took the students' minds off their classwork and diverted them to thoughts about the highly emotional subject of the Vietnam war. [One] does not need to be a prophet or the son of a prophet to know that after the Court's holding today some students [will] be ready, able, and willing to defy their teachers on practically all orders. This is the more unfortunate for the schools since groups of students all over the land are already running loose, conducting break-ins, sit-ins, lie-ins, and smash-ins." Justice HARLAN also dissented, conceding that the First Amendment applied in school but arguing that impermissible viewpoint discrimination had not been demonstrated.

After Tinker, could a public school prohibit students from wearing all buttons or insignia on their clothing? All "political" buttons or insignia? Could it require students to wear prescribed uniforms? Could it ban the wearing of "gang colors" to prevent outbreaks of violence? Could it stop male students from wearing T-shirts bearing sexist slogans in order to boost female students' self-esteem and academic performance? Could it bar *teachers* from wearing black armbands?

In BOARD OF EDUCATION v. PICO, 457 U.S. 853 (1982), the Court confronted the problem of school authorities' removal of books from school libraries. Members of the school board of Island Trees, New York, obtained from a conservative parents' organization a list of books described as "objectionable" or "improper fare for school students." They found nine of these books in the high school library, including Slaughter House Five, by Kurt Vonnegut, Jr.; The Naked Ape, by Desmond Morris; Down These Mean Streets, by Piri Thomas; Best Short Stories of Negro Writers, edited by Langston Hughes; Go Ask Alice, of anonymous authorship; Laughing Boy, by Oliver LaFarge; Black Boy, by Richard Wright; A Hero Ain't Nothin' But A Sandwich, by Alice Childress; and Soul On Ice, by Eldridge Cleaver. The board ordered all the books except Slaughter House Five removed, condemning them as "anti-American, anti-Christian, anti-Semitic, and just plain filthy." They disregarded the recommendation of a staff/parent committee that several more of the books should be retained. The Court held that summary judgment should not have been granted below to the school board, because there remained a genuine issue of material fact: namely, whether the book removal was ideologically or pedagogically motivated.

Justice BRENNAN's plurality opinion was joined by Justices Marshall, Stevens and (in large part) Blackmun. Justice Brennan noted at the outset that the case did not raise the "difficult" issue of limits upon the school board's discretion "to prescribe the curricula of the Island Trees schools. On the contrary, the only books at issue in this case are *library* books, books that by their nature are optional rather than required reading. Our adjudication of the present case thus does not intrude into the classroom, or into the compulsory courses taught there." While acknowledging the role of the public schools in " 'inculcating fundamental values necessary to the maintenance of a democratic political system,' " Justice Brennan held that "the First Amendment rights of students may be directly and sharply implicated by the removal of books from the shelves of a school library. [In] a variety of contexts 'the Constitution protects the right to receive information and ideas.' Stanley v. Georgia. This right is an inherent corollary of the rights of free speech and press that are explicitly guaranteed by the Constitution. [The school board members] emphasize the inculcative function of secondary education, and argue that they must be allowed *unfettered* discretion to 'transmit community values' through [the] schools. But that sweeping claim overlooks the unique role of the school library. It appears from the record that use of the Island Trees school libraries is completely voluntary on the part of students. Their selection of books from these libraries is entirely a matter of free choice; the libraries afford them an opportunity at self-education and individual enrichment that is wholly optional. Petitioners might well defend their claim of absolute discretion in matters of *curriculum* by reliance upon their duty to inculcate community values. But we think that petitioners' reliance upon that duty is misplaced where, as here, they attempt to extend their claim of absolute discretion beyond the compulsory environment of the classroom, into the school library and the regime of voluntary inquiry that there holds sway.

"In rejecting petitioners' claim of absolute discretion to remove books from their school libraries, we do not deny that local school boards have a substantial legitimate role to play in the determination of school library content. [We hold only] that [such] discretion may not be exercised in a narrowly partisan or political manner. If a Democratic school board, motivated by party affiliation, ordered the removal of all books written by or in favor of Republicans, few would doubt that the order violated the constitutional rights of the students denied access to those books. The same conclusion would surely apply if an all-white school board, motivated by racial animus, decided to remove all books authored by blacks or advocating racial equality and integration. Our Constitution does not permit the official suppression of *ideas*. Thus whether petitioners' removal of books from their school libraries denied respondents their First Amendment rights depends upon the motivation behind petitioners' actions. If petitioners *intended* by their removal decision to deny respondents access to ideas with which petitioners disagreed, and if this intent was the decisive factor in petitioners' decision,[1] then petitioners have exercised their discretion in violation of the Constitution. [On] the other hand, [an] unconstitutional motivation would *not* be demonstrated if it were shown that petitioners had decided to remove the books at issue because those books were pervasively vulgar [or] was [otherwise] based solely upon the 'educational suitability' of the books.

"[Nothing] in our decision today affects in any way the discretion of a local school board to choose books to *add* to the libraries of their schools. Because we are concerned in this case with the suppression of ideas, our holding today affects only the discretion to *remove* books. In brief, we hold that local school boards may not remove books from school library shelves simply because they dislike the ideas contained in those books and seek by their removal to 'prescribe what shall be orthodox in politics, nationalism, religion, or other

---

1. By "decisive factor" we mean a "substantial factor" in the absence of which the opposite decision would have been reached. See Mt. Healthy City Board of Ed. v. Doyle, 429 U.S. 274 (1977). [Footnote by Justice Brennan.]

matters of opinion.' [Barnette.] Such purposes stand inescapably condemned by our precedents." Because the key question of intent was disputed in the record, the Court remanded for trial. (The case was abandoned after remand and there was no further hearing on the merits.)

Justice BLACKMUN, concurring in part and concurring in the judgment, disagreed with the plurality's emphasis on the right to receive information: "[T]he State may not suppress exposure to ideas—for the sole *purpose* of suppressing exposure to those ideas—absent sufficiently compelling reasons. [This] principle necessarily applies in at least a limited way to public education. [In] my view, then, the principle involved here is both narrower and more basic than the 'right to receive information' identified by the plurality. I do not suggest that the State has any affirmative obligation to provide students with information or ideas, something that may well be associated with a 'right to receive.' " Justice WHITE, casting the crucial fifth vote, concurred only in the judgment, expressing no view on the constitutional merits. He suggested that the case should have been decided narrowly under routine summary judgment law, thus avoiding "a dissertation on the extent to which the First Amendment limits the discretion of the school board to remove books from the school library."

Chief Justice BURGER dissented, joined by Justices Powell, Rehnquist, and O'Connor. He argued that the schools' role in inculcating fundamental values necessitated "content-based decisions about the appropriateness of retaining materials in the school library and curriculum." Such decisions "express the views of their community; they may err, of course, and the voters may remove them." He concluded by "categorically" rejecting the "notion that the Constitution dictates that judges, rather than parents, teachers, and local school boards, must determine how the standards of morality and vulgarity are to be treated in the classroom."

Justice REHNQUIST dissented, joined Chief Justice Burger and Justice Powell. He urged that the Court "candidly recogniz[e] that the role of government as sovereign is subject to more stringent limitations than is the role of government as employer, property owner, or [educator]": "[Had] petitioners been the members of a town council, I suppose all would agree that [ordinarily] they could not have prohibited the sale of these books by private booksellers within the municipality. But we have also recognized that the government may act in other capacities than as sovereign, and when it does the First Amendment may speak with a different voice. When it acts as an educator, at least at the elementary and secondary school level, the government is engaged in inculcating social values and knowledge in relatively impressionable young people. Obviously there are innumerable decisions to be made as to what courses should be taught, what books should be purchased, or what teachers should be employed. In every one of these areas the members of a school board will act on the basis of their own personal or moral values, will attempt to mirror those of the community, or will abdicate the making of such decisions to so-called 'experts.' [In] the very course of administering the many-faceted operations of a school district, the mere decision to purchase some books will necessarily preclude the possibility of purchasing others. The decision to teach a particular subject may preclude the possibility of teaching another subject. A decision to replace a teacher because of ineffectiveness may by implication be seen as a disparagement of the subject matter taught. In each of these instances, however, the book or the exposure to the subject matter may be acquired elsewhere. The managers of the school district are not proscribing it as to the citizenry in general, but are simply determining that it will not be included in the curriculum or school library. In short, actions by the government as educator do not raise the same First Amendment concerns as actions by the government as sovereign.

"[Despite] Justice Brennan's suggestion to the contrary, this Court has never held that the First Amendment grants junior high school and high school students a right of access to certain information in school. It is true that the Court has recognized a limited version of that right in other settings, [but] not one of these cases concerned or even purported to discuss elementary or secondary educational institutions. [The] idea [that] students have a right of access, *in the school,* to information other than that thought by their educators to be necessary is contrary to the very nature of an inculcative education. Education consists of the selective presentation and explanation of ideas. The effective acquisition of knowledge depends upon an orderly exposure to relevant information. [Determining] what information *not* to present to the students is often as important as identifying relevant material. [The] libraries of such schools serve as supplements to this inculcative role. Unlike university or public libraries, elementary and secondary school libraries are not designed for free-wheeling inquiry; they are tailored, as the public school curriculum is tailored, to the teaching of basic skills and ideas. [Finally,] the most obvious reason that petitioners' removal of the books did not violate respondents' right to receive information is the ready availability of the books [elsewhere]. The government as educator does not seek to reach beyond the confines of the school. Indeed, following the removal from the school library of the books at issue in this case, the local public library put all nine books on display [and they were] fully accessible to any inquisitive student."

Justice Rehnquist concluded by suggesting that Justice Brennan's distinctions between book acquisition and removal and between good and bad motives were incoherent in relation to the asserted right to receive ideas: "[If] Justice Brennan truly has found a 'right to receive ideas, [the] distinction between acquisition and removal makes little sense. The failure of a library to acquire a book denies access to its contents just as effectively as does the removal of the book from the library's shelf. [If] 'suppression of ideas' is to be the talisman, one would think that a school board's public announcement of its refusal to acquire certain books would have every bit as much impact on public attention as would an equally publicized decision to remove the books. And yet only the latter action would violate the First Amendment under Justice Brennan's analysis. [Moreover,] bad motives and good motives alike deny access to the books removed. If [there truly is] a constitutional right to receive information, it is difficult to see why the reason for the denial makes any difference. Of course Justice Brennan's view is that intent matters because the First Amendment does not tolerate an officially prescribed orthodoxy. But this reasoning mixes First Amendment apples and oranges. The right to receive information differs from the right to be free from an officially prescribed orthodoxy. Not every educational denial of access to information casts a pall of orthodoxy over the [classroom]." He accordingly found the school board's decision "sufficiently related to 'educational suitability' to pass muster under the First Amendment." Justices Powell and O'Connor also filed separate dissents.

Parent-initiated book removal from school curricula and libraries continues to be a frequently litigated issue in the lower courts. Does Pico give adequate guidance? Consider the following comment: "[I]f school boards know that the courts will sometimes get involved, even if only in extreme cases, and [therefore] restrain themselves accordingly, Pico may serve as an effective constitutional limit, even if that limit is poorly defined and mostly symbolic and self-enforced." Yudof, "Library Book Selection and the Public Schools: The Quest for the Archimedean Point," 59 Ind.L.J. 527 (1984).

Pico identified a school library as lying somewhere between the prescribed curriculum and the realm in which students are free, as public citizens, to engage in voluntary expression and inquiry. Do First Amendment interests attenuate, and government interests increase, as student speech moves closer to the curriculum? Consider the following cases involving speech at a mandatory school assembly and production of a school newspaper in connection with a journalism class.

In BETHEL SCHOOL DIST. NO. 403 v. FRASER, 478 U.S. 675 (1986), the Court held that the First Amendment did not prevent a school district "from disciplining a high school student for giving a lewd speech at a [school] assembly." Fraser, in nominating a fellow student for student elective office before a high school assembly of approximately 600 students, delivered a speech containing sexual innuendo.[2] During the speech, some students hooted, yelled, and made gestures simulating the sexual activities alluded to in the speech; others appeared bewildered and embarrassed. The school disciplined Fraser under its disruptive-conduct rule by suspending him for two days. He brought an action claiming a violation of his First Amendment rights. The District Court sustained his claim and the Court of Appeals, relying upon Tinker, affirmed. The Court reversed by a vote of 7–2.

Chief Justice BURGER's majority opinion chastised the lower court for ignoring the "marked distinction between the political 'message' of the armbands in Tinker and the sexual content of [Fraser's] speech" here and pointed out that Tinker had emphasized that the armbands worn there did not intrude upon the work of the schools. He pointed out that the "undoubted freedom to advocate unpopular and controversial views in schools and classrooms must be balanced against the society's countervailing interest in teaching students the boundaries of socially appropriate behavior." He added that the inculcation of fundamental societal values was truly the "work of the schools." Accordingly, the school district had acted legitimately in "imposing sanctions upon Fraser in response to his offensively lewd and indecent speech": "Unlike the sanctions imposed [in] Tinker, the penalties imposed [here] were unrelated to any political viewpoint. The First Amendment does not prevent the school officials from determining that to permit a vulgar and lewd speech such as [Fraser's] would undermine the school's basic educational mission. A high school assembly [is] no place for a sexually explicit monologue directed towards an unsuspecting audience of teenage students. Accordingly, it was perfectly appropriate for the school to disassociate itself to make the point to the pupils that vulgar speech and lewd conduct is wholly inconsistent with the 'fundamental values' of public school education."

In an opinion concurring in the judgment, Justice BRENNAN agreed that the school officials' action was not unconstitutional "under the circumstances of this case," but emphasized that Fraser would have been protected had he given the same speech outside of the school environment and might well even have been protected "had he given it in school but under different circumstances, where the school's legitimate interests in teaching and maintaining civil public discourse were less weighty." Justice MARSHALL agreed with

2. Fraser's speech had included the following passage: "I know a man who is firm— he's firm in his pants, he's firm in his shirt, his character is firm—but most [of] all, his belief in you, the students of Bethel, is firm. Jeff Kuhlman is a man who takes his point and pounds it in. If necessary, he'll take an issue and nail it to the wall. He doesn't attack things in spurts—he drives hard, pushing and pushing until finally—he succeeds. Jeff is a man who will go to the very end—even the climax, for each and every one of you."

Justice Brennan's principles but dissented, relying on the fact that the school board "had not demonstrated any disruption of the educational process." Justice STEVENS also submitted a dissent, arguing that Fraser did not have adequate "reason to anticipate punitive consequences" from his speeches.

HAZELWOOD SCHOOL DISTRICT v. KUHLMEIER, 484 U.S. 260 (1988), examined the extent to which educators may exercise editorial control over the contents of a high school newspaper produced as part of a school journalism class and funded by the school. The 6–3 decision upheld a high school principal's deletion of two stories from the school newspaper. One story described three students' experiences with pregnancy; the other discussed the impact of parents' divorce on students at the school. At the outset, Justice WHITE's majority opinion found that the newspaper was not a public forum, either traditionally or by "designation." "Accordingly, school officials were entitled to regulate the contents of [the newspaper] in any reasonable manner. It is this standard, rather than our decision in Tinker, that governs this case." He proceeded:

"The question whether the First Amendment requires a school to tolerate particular student speech—the question that we addressed in Tinker—is different from the question whether the First Amendment requires a school affirmatively to promote particular student speech. The former question addresses educators, ability to silence a student's personal expression that happens to occur on the school premises. The latter question concerns educators' authority over school-sponsored publications, theatrical productions, and other expressive activities that students, parents, and members of the public might reasonably perceive to bear the imprimatur of the school. These activities may fairly be characterized as part of the school curriculum, whether or not they occur in a traditional classroom setting, so long as they are supervised by faculty members and designed to impart particular knowledge or skills to student participants and audiences.

"Educators are entitled to exercise greater control over this second form of student expression to assure that participants learn whatever lessons the activity is designed to teach, that readers or listeners are not exposed to material that may be inappropriate for their level of maturity, and that the views of the individual speaker are not erroneously attributed to the school. Hence, a school may in its capacity as publisher of a school newspaper or producer of a school play 'disassociate itself,' Fraser, [from] speech that is, for example, ungrammatical, poorly written, inadequately researched, biased or prejudiced, vulgar or profane, or unsuitable for immature audiences.[1] A school must be able to set high standards for the student speech that is disseminated under its auspices [and] may refuse to disseminate student speech that does not meet those standards. In addition, a school must be able to take into account the emotional maturity of the intended audience in determining whether to disseminate student speech on potentially sensitive [topics]. [Accordingly,] we conclude that the standard articulated in Tinker for determining when a school may punish student expression need not also be the standard for determining when a school may refuse to lend its name and resources to the dissemination of student expression. Instead, we hold that educators do not offend the First

1. The dissent perceives no difference between the First Amendment analysis applied in Tinker and that applied in Fraser. We disagree. The decision in Fraser rested on the 'vulgar,' 'lewd,' and 'plainly offensive' character of a speech delivered at an official school assembly rather than on any propensity of the speech to 'materially disrupt[ ]classwork or involve[ ]substantial disorder or invasion of the rights of others.' [Footnote by Justice White.]

Amendment by exercising editorial control over the style and content of student speech in school-sponsored expressive activities so long as their actions are reasonably related to legitimate pedagogical concerns. This standard is consistent with our oft-expressed view that the education of the Nation's youth is primarily the responsibility of parents, teachers, and state and local school officials, and not of federal judges. It is only when the decision to censor a school-sponsored publication, theatrical production, or other vehicle of student expression has no valid educational purpose that the First Amendment [requires] judicial intervention to protect students' constitutional rights."

Applying this standard, Justice White held that the principal's deletion of the pregnancy story was "reasonable" because, even though the students mentioned had consented and fictitious names had been used, it was possible that "the students' anonymity was not adequately protected," so that there was a reasonable fear that "the article violated whatever pledge of anonymity had been given to the pregnant students." Moreover, since the article contained discussion of sexual histories and students' use of birth control, it was not unreasonable "for the principal to have concluded that such frank talk was inappropriate in a school-sponsored publication distributed to 14–year-old freshmen and presumably taken home to be read by students' even younger brothers and sisters." Similarly, the deletion of the divorce story was reasonable because a student quoted by name in the article made comments sharply critical of her father, so that the principal could have concluded "that an individual publicly identified as an inattentive parent [was] entitled to an opportunity to defend himself as a matter of journalistic fairness."

Justice BRENNAN's dissent, joined by Justices Marshall and Blackmun, argued that Tinker was controlling and that, under Tinker's standard, there was no valid basis for deleting the stories. In his view, the principal had "violated the First Amendment's prohibitions against censorship of any student expression that neither disrupts classwork nor invades the rights of others, and against any censorship that is not narrowly tailored to serve its purpose." He elaborated: "If mere incompatibility with the school's pedagogical message were a constitutionally sufficient justification for the suppression of student speech, school officials [could convert] our public schools into 'enclaves of totalitarianism' that 'strangle the free mind at its source.' The First Amendment permits no such blanket censorship authority." The Tinker test, he insisted, was adequate to resolve the issue here. After applying it in Fraser, the Court had avoided it here by distinguishing between personal and school-sponsored speech, a distinction unsupported by the precedents. The Court's opinion, he concluded, "denudes high school students of much of the First Amendment protection that Tinker itself prescribed. [The] young men and women of Hazelwood East expected a civics lesson, but not the one the Court teaches them today."

After Hazelwood, could the school restrain publication of the same stories if printed in an "underground" student newspaper funded through private advertisements and sales? Even if distributed on school property? Do Fraser and Hazelwood have any application to a public university setting? For commentary, see Hafen, "Hazelwood School District and the Role of First Amendment Institutions," 1988 Duke L.J. 685 (arguing that Hazelwood indicates that Fraser was "an important transitional case that signalled the Court's [recognition] that broad interpretations of Tinker [had] reduced schools' institutional authority in ways that undermined their educational effectiveness"); Diamond, "The First Amendment and Public Schools: the Case Against Judicial Intervention," 59 Tex. L. Rev. 477 (1981); Wright,"The Constitution on Campus," 22 Vand. L. Rev. 1027 (1969).

Note that Fraser and Hazelwood emphasize the government's interest in removing its apparent imprimatur of approval from lewd or controversial speech. Does this interest in disassociation suggest that government, not the student, will be perceived as the speaker here? Implicit in this view is that government *as speaker* is not constrained by the First Amendment in the same way as it is constrained as sovereign. Do these suggestions in Fraser and Hazelwood vindicate Justice Rehnquist's dissent in Pico? Might government distort public dialogue even in its role as speaker or editor? For commentary on the issue of government speech, see, e.g., Yudof, When Government Speaks: Politics, Law, and Government Expression in America (1983); Kamenshine, "The First Amendment's Implied Political Establishment Clause," 67 Calif.L.Rev. 1104 (1979); Shiffrin, "Government Speech," 27 U.C.L.A.L.Rev. 565 (1980); Ziegler, "Government Speech and the Constitution: The Limits of Official Partisanship," 21 B.C.L.Rev. 578 (1980).

C. SPEECH AND ASSOCIATION BY PUBLIC EMPLOYEES AND CONTRACTORS

Introduction. To what extent does the First Amendment limit governmental power to regulate the behavior of its employees or contractors? Does the government's status as employer or contractor justify regulations and disqualifications because of political expression or association? Is ideological conformity sometimes a bona fide occupational qualification? Does it matter if the expression or association takes place on or off the job?

The questions would not have been viewed as substantial constitutional ones if Justice HOLMES' views as a state court judge had prevailed. In 1892, he said: "The petitioner may have a constitutional right to talk politics, but he has no constitutional right to be a policeman. There are few employments for hire in which the servant does not agree to suspend his constitutional right of free speech, as well of idleness, by the implied terms of his contract. The servant cannot complain, as he takes the employment on the terms which are offered him." McAULIFFE v. MAYOR OF NEW BEDFORD, 155 Mass. 216, 29 N.E. 517 (1892). But the Holmes position has not prevailed: it has long been recognized that, even though there is no "right" to public employment or to a contract, some constitutional restrictions apply when government attempts to discharge employees or contractors for reason of their exercise of constitutionally protected liberties. Why should this be? Because the public sector has grown enormously in relation to the private sector in the twentieth century? Because losing one's job can be as coercive as a criminal fine? Because constitutional rights are inalienable through bargaining with the government? See generally Van Alstyne, "The Demise of the Right–Privilege Distinction in Constitutional Law," 81 Harv.L.Rev. 1439 (1968); Kreimer, "Allocational Sanctions: the Problem of Negative Rights in a Positive State," 132 U. Pa. L. Rev. 1293 (1984); Epstein, "Foreword: Unconstitutional Conditions, State Power and the Limits of Consent," 102 Harv. L. Rev. 4 (1988); Sullivan, "Unconstitutional Conditions," 102 Harv. L. Rev. 1413 (1989).

The decisions that follow first explore the question of whether government may discharge or otherwise sanction an employee for statements or other expressive activity. Two types of issues should be distinguished here. The first is the extent to which an employee's First Amendment speech rights *as a citizen* may be restricted because of the government's interest in regulating public employment. The second concerns the public employee's free speech rights *as an employee*. The focus next shifts to the question whether hiring and firing decisions may be based on party affiliation—i.e., whether a patronage system violates employee rights of political association. Finally, the materials consider whether rights of speech or association enjoyed by public employees should also extend to independent contractors with the government.

———

PUBLIC EMPLOYEE SPEECH

In PICKERING v. BOARD OF EDUCATION, 391 U.S. 563 (1968), the Court held that a public school teacher could not constitutionally be dismissed from his job for writing a letter to a newspaper criticizing the school board's handling of revenue measures for the schools and its allocation of financial resources between the schools' educational and athletic programs. Justice MARSHALL's majority opinion "unequivocally" rejected the proposition that "teachers may constitutionally be compelled to relinquish the First Amendment rights they would otherwise enjoy as citizens to comment on matters of public interest in connection with the operation of the public schools in which they work." He relied heavily on decisions from the 1950s and 1960s invalidating efforts to require public employees, especially teachers, to disclose their associations and swear loyalty oaths to the state. (These cases are noted below at p. 1390.) But he also noted that "the State has interests as an employer in regulating the speech of its employees that differ significantly from those it possesses in connection with regulation of the speech of the citizenry in general. The problem in any case is to arrive at a balance between the interests of the teacher, as a citizen, in commenting upon matters of public concern and the interest of the State, as an employer, in promoting the efficiency of the public services it performs through its employees."

In the circumstances of the case, Justice Marshall found that the government interests did not outweigh Pickering's speech rights: "[T]he question whether a school system requires additional funds is a matter of legitimate public concern on which the judgment of the school administration, including the School Board, cannot, in a society that leaves such questions to popular vote, be taken as conclusive. On such a question free and open debate is vital to informed decision-making by the electorate. Teachers are, as a class, the members of a community most likely to have informed and definite opinions as to how funds allotted to the operation of the schools should be spent. Accordingly, it is essential that they be able to speak out freely on such questions without fear of retaliatory dismissal. [Pickering's statements were] critical of his ultimate employer but [had not been shown] to have in any way either impeded the teacher's proper performance of his daily duties in the classroom or to have interfered with the regular operation of the schools generally. In these circumstances we conclude that the interest of the school administration in limiting teachers' opportunities to contribute to public debate is not significantly greater than its interest in limiting a similar contribution by any member of the general public." Accordingly, absent any malicious libel of the school board actionable under the New York Times standard, Pickering could not be dismissed.

See also Givhan v. Western Line Consolidated School District, 439 U.S. 410 (1979), extending the Pickering principle to a teacher's dismissal for statements criticizing the school's allegedly racially discriminatory policies in a series of *private* encounters with a school principal. For commentary, see Schauer, " 'Private' Speech and the 'Private' Forum," 1979 Sup. Ct. Rev. 217. Contrast with Pickering and Givhan the Court's decision in the following case involving speech by an assistant district attorney critical of her supervisors.

———

Connick v. Myers

461 U.S. 138, 103 S.Ct. 1684, 75 L.Ed.2d 708 (1983).

[The case arose in the following circumstances: Sheila Myers, an Assistant District Attorney in New Orleans, was informed by her boss, long-time New Orleans D.A. Harry Connick, Sr., that she would be transferred to prosecute cases in a different section of the criminal court. Myers strongly opposed the transfer and expressed her view to several supervisors, including Connick. When one supervisor told that her concerns were not shared by others in the office, she told him she would do some research and prepared a questionnaire soliciting the views of her fellow staff members concerning office transfer policy, office morale, the need for a grievance committee, the level of confidence in supervisors, and whether employees felt pressured to work in political campaigns. She distributed the questionnaire to 15 assistant district attorneys. One of Connick's first assistants told Connick that Myers was creating a "mini-insurrection" within the office. Connick promptly told Myers that she was being terminated because of her refusal to accept the transfer and because her distribution of the questionnaire was an act of insubordination. Myers claimed that her termination violated the free speech clause, and the district court and court of appeals below agreed, relying on Pickering. The Court reversed by a vote of 5–4.]

Justice WHITE delivered the opinion of the Court.

[It has long] been settled that a state cannot condition public employment on a basis that infringes the employee's constitutionally protected interest in freedom of expression. [Pickering.] [But the lower courts misapplied Pickering] in striking the balance for respondent. [Connick] contends at the outset that no balancing of interests is required in this case because Myers' questionnaire concerned only internal office matters and that such speech is not upon a matter of "public concern," as the term was used in Pickering. Although we do not agree that Myers' communication in this case was wholly without First Amendment protection, there is much force to Connick's submission. The repeated emphasis in Pickering on the right of a public employee "as a citizen, in commenting upon matters of public concern," was not accidental. This language [reflects] both the historical evolvement of the rights of public employees, and the common sense realization that government offices could not function if every employment decision became a constitutional matter. [Pickering], its antecedents and progeny, lead us to conclude that if Myers' questionnaire cannot be fairly characterized as constituting speech on a matter of public concern, it is unnecessary for us to scrutinize the reasons for her discharge. When employee expression cannot be fairly considered as relating to any matter of political, social, or other concern to the community, government officials should enjoy wide latitude in managing their offices, without intrusive oversight by the judiciary in the name of the [First Amendment].

We do not suggest, however, that Myers' speech, even if not touching upon a matter of public concern, is totally beyond the protection of the First

Amendment. [We] in no sense suggest that speech on private matters falls into one of the narrow and well-defined classes of expression which carries so little social value, such as obscenity, that the state can prohibit and punish such expression by all persons in its jurisdiction. For example, an employee's false criticism of his employer on grounds not of public concern may be cause for his discharge but would be entitled to the same protection in a libel action accorded an identical statement made by a man on the street. We hold only that when a public employee speaks not as a citizen upon matters of public concern, but instead as an employee upon matters only of personal interest, absent the most unusual circumstances, a federal court is not the appropriate forum in which to review the wisdom of a personnel decision taken by a public agency allegedly in reaction to the employee's behavior. Our responsibility is to ensure that citizens are not deprived of fundamental rights by virtue of working for the government; this does not require a grant of immunity for employee grievances not afforded by the First Amendment to those who do not work for the state.

Whether an employee's speech addresses a matter of public concern must be determined by the content, form, and context of a given statement, as revealed by the whole record. In this case, with but one exception, the questions posed by Myers to her coworkers do not fall under the rubric of matters of "public concern." We view the questions pertaining to the confidence and trust that Myers' coworkers possess in various supervisors, the level of office morale, and the need for a grievance committee as mere extensions of Myers' dispute over her transfer to another section of the criminal court. Unlike the dissent, we do not believe these questions are of public import in evaluating the performance of the District Attorney as an elected official. Myers did not seek to inform the public that the District Attorney's office was not discharging its governmental responsibilities in the investigation and prosecution of criminal cases. Nor did Myers seek to bring to light [wrongdoing] or breach of public trust on the part of Connick and others. Indeed, the questionnaire, if released to the public, would convey no information at all other than the fact that a single employee is upset with the status quo. While discipline and morale in the workplace are related to an agency's efficient performance of its duties, the focus of Myers' questions is not to evaluate the performance of the office but rather to gather ammunition for another round of controversy with her superiors. These questions reflect one employee's dissatisfaction with a transfer and an attempt to turn that displeasure into a cause célèbre. To presume that all matters which transpire within a government office are of public concern would mean that virtually every remark—and certainly every criticism directed at a public official—would plant the seed of a constitutional case. [The] First Amendment does not require a public office to be run as a roundtable for employee complaints over internal office affairs.

One question in Myers' questionnaire, however, does touch upon a matter of public concern. Question 11 inquires if assistant district attorneys "ever feel pressured to work in political campaigns on behalf of office supported candidates." We have recently noted that official pressure upon employees to work for political candidates not of the worker's own choice constitutes a coercion of belief in violation of fundamental constitutional rights. [Branti; Elrod, p. 1312 below.] In addition, there is a demonstrated interest in this country that government service should depend upon meritorious performance rather than political service. [E.g., Letter Carriers, p. 1312 below.] Given this history, we believe it apparent that the issue of whether assistant district attorneys are pressured to work in political campaigns is a matter of interest to the community upon which it is essential that public employees be able to speak out freely without fear of retaliatory dismissal.

Because one of the questions in Myers' survey touched upon a matter of public concern, and contributed to her discharge, we must determine whether Connick was justified in discharging Myers. Here the District Court again erred in imposing an unduly onerous burden on the state to justify Myers' discharge. The District Court viewed the issue of whether Myers' speech was upon a matter of "public concern" as a threshold inquiry, after which it became the government's burden to "clearly demonstrate" that the speech involved "substantially interfered" with official responsibilities. Yet Pickering unmistakably states [that] the state's burden in justifying a particular discharge varies depending upon the nature of the employee's expression. Although such particularized balancing is difficult, the courts must reach the most appropriate possible balance of the competing interests.

The Pickering balance requires full consideration of the government's interest in the effective and efficient fulfillment of its responsibilities to the public. [Connick's] judgment [was] that Myers' questionnaire was an act of insubordination which interfered with working relationships. When close working relationships are essential to fulfilling public responsibilities, a wide degree of deference to the employer's judgment is appropriate. Furthermore, we do not see the necessity for an employer to allow events to unfold to the extent that the disruption of the office and the destruction of working relationships is manifest before taking action. We caution that a stronger showing may be necessary if the employee's speech more substantially involved matters of public concern. [Also] relevant is the manner, time, and place in which the questionnaire was distributed. [The] fact that Myers, unlike Pickering, exercised her rights to speech at the office supports Connick's fears that the functioning of his office was endangered.

Finally, the context in which the dispute arose is also significant. This is not a case where an employee, out of purely academic interest, circulated a questionnaire so as to obtain useful research. [When] employee speech concerning office policy arises from an employment dispute concerning the very application of that policy to the speaker, additional weight must be given to the supervisor's view that the employee has threatened the authority of the employer to run the office. Although we accept the District Court's factual finding that Myers' reluctance to accede to the transfer order was not a sufficient cause in itself for her dismissal, [this] does not render irrelevant the fact that the questionnaire emerged after a persistent dispute between Myers and Connick and his deputies over office transfer policy.

Myers' questionnaire touched upon matters of public concern in only a most limited sense; her survey, in our view, is most accurately characterized as an employee grievance concerning internal office policy. The limited First Amendment interest involved here does not require that Connick tolerate action which he reasonably believed would disrupt the office, undermine his authority, and destroy close working relationships. Myers' discharge therefore did not offend the First Amendment. [Although] today the balance is struck for the government, this is no defeat for the First Amendment. For it would indeed be a Pyrrhic victory for the great principles of free expression if the Amendment's safeguarding of a public employee's right, as a citizen, to participate in discussions concerning public affairs were confused with the attempt to constitutionalize the employee grievance that we see presented [here].

[Reversed.]

Justice BRENNAN, with whom Justice MARSHALL, Justice BLACKMUN, and Justice STEVENS join, dissenting.

[Speech] about "the manner in which government is operated or should be operated" is an essential part of the communications necessary for self-governance the protection of which was a central purpose of the First Amendment. Because the questionnaire addressed such matters and its distribution did not adversely affect the operations of the [Office] or interfere with Myers' working relationship with her fellow employees, I dissent.

[The] Court distorts the balancing analysis required under Pickering by suggesting that one factor, the context in which a statement is made, is to be weighed *twice*—first in determining whether an employee's speech addresses a matter of public concern and then in deciding whether the statement adversely affected the government's interest as an employer. [Moreover,] in concluding that the effect of respondent's personnel policies on employee morale and the work performance of the District Attorney's Office is not a matter of public concern, the Court impermissibly narrows the class of subjects on which public employees may speak out without fear of retaliatory dismissal.

[The Court] suggests that there are two classes of speech of public concern: statements "of public import" because of their content, form and context, and statements that, by virtue of their subject matter, are "inherently of public concern." In my view, however, whether a particular statement by a public employee is addressed to a subject of public concern does not depend on where it was said or why. The First Amendment affords special protection to speech that may inform public debate about how our society is to be governed—regardless of whether it actually becomes the subject of a public controversy.

[The] Court's adoption of a [narrower] conception of what subjects are of public concern seems prompted by its fears that a broader view "would mean that [every] criticism directed at a public official [would] plant the seed of a constitutional case." Obviously, not every remark directed at a public official by a public employee is protected by the First Amendment.[1] [The] proper means to ensure that the courts are not swamped with routine employee grievances mischaracterized as First Amendment cases is not to restrict artificially the concept of "public concern," but to require that adequate weight be given to the public's important interests in the efficient performance of governmental functions and in preserving employee discipline and harmony sufficient to achieve that end.

Although the Court finds most of Myers' questionnaire unrelated to matters of public interest, it does hold that one question—asking whether Assistants felt pressured to work in political campaigns on behalf of office-supported candidates—addressed a matter of public importance and concern. The Court also recognizes that this determination of public interest must weigh heavily in the balancing of competing interests required by Pickering. Having gone that far however, the Court misapplies the Pickering test and holds—against our previous authorities—that a public employer's mere apprehension that speech will be disruptive justifies suppression of that speech when all the objective evidence suggests that those fears are essentially [unfounded]. Such extreme deference to the employer's judgment is not appropriate when public employees voice critical views concerning the operations of the agency for which they work. [In] order to protect public employees' First Amendment right to

---

1. Perhaps the simplest example of a statement by a public employee that would not be protected by the First Amendment would be answering "No" to a request that the employee perform a lawful task within the scope of his duties. Although such a re-fusal is "speech," which implicates First Amendment interests, it is also insubordination, and as such it may serve as the basis for a lawful dismissal. [Footnote by Justice Brennan.]

voice critical views on issues of public importance, the courts must make their own appraisal of the effects of the speech [in question].

The Court's decision today inevitably will deter public employees from making critical statements about the manner in which government agencies are operated for fear that doing so will provoke their dismissal. As a result, the public will be deprived of valuable information with which to evaluate the performance of elected officials. Because protecting the dissemination of such information is an essential function of the First Amendment, I dissent.

———

RANKIN v. McPHERSON, 483 U.S. 378 (1987): This case, like Connick, involved the distinction between employee speech related to a matter of public concern and speech not so related. The Court held by a vote of 5–4 that a clerical employee in a county constable's office could not be discharged for remarking, after hearing of the attempted assassination of President Reagan in 1981, "If they go for him again, I hope they get him." Justice MARSHALL's majority opinion held that the remark constituted speech on a matter of public concern and that the firing violated the First Amendment. He noted that the remark was made in the course of a conversation addressing the policies of the Reagan Administration and added that the "inappropriate or controversial character of a statement is irrelevant to the question whether it deals with a matter of public concern." Having determined that the remark in the context in which it was made did involve a matter of public concern, Justice Marshall balanced the employee's speech interest against the State's interest in the "effective functioning" of government under the Pickering test. He noted that the State "bears a burden of justifying the discharge on legitimate grounds" and commented that the State's interest in content-related sanctions was minimal where the employee "serves no confidential, policymaking, or public contact role." He concluded that there had been no showing that McPherson's statement had interfered with the effective functioning of the office, nor that it was made in a context where it could bring discredit upon the office, and thus that her discharge violated the First Amendment. Justice POWELL concurred, emphasizing that this case involved only "a single, offhand comment" directed to "a co-worker who happened also to be her boyfriend" in a private conversation that was unforeseeably overheard by another coworker.

Justice SCALIA, joined by Chief Justice Rehnquist and Justices White and O'Connor, dissented. He insisted that "no law enforcement agency is required by the First Amendment to permit one of its employees to 'ride with the cops and cheer for the robbers.'" After disagreeing with the majority's conclusion that this was speech on a matter of public concern, he argued that the employee's statement was, because of the unprotected nature of actual threats, "so near the category of completely unprotected speech" that it could not "fairly be viewed as lying within the 'heart' of the First Amendment's protection." Finding the State's interest in not having such statements made by its employees quite reasonable, he also objected to the Court's distinction between policymaking and nonpolicymaking employees: "Nonpolicymaking employees [can] hurt working relationships and undermine public confidence in an organization every bit as much as policy making employees. I, for one, do not look forward to the new First Amendment world the Court creates, in which nonpolicymaking employees of the [EEOC] must be permitted to make remarks on the job approving of racial discrimination, nonpolicymaking employees of the Selective Service System to advocate noncompliance with the draft laws, [and] nonpolicymaking constable's deputies to express approval for the assassination of the President.''

After Connick, who is to determine whether an employee's speech is on a matter of public or private concern: the employer or a court or jury adjudicating the First Amendment claim? What if there is a factual dispute about what was actually said? In WATERS v. CHURCHILL, 511 U.S. 661 (1994), a plurality opinion by Justice O'CONNOR ruled that a public employer does not violate the First Amendment if it fires an employee for what the employer reasonably believed was speech on a matter of private concern, even if that belief turns out to have been mistaken. Justice SCALIA concurred but argued that the employer ought not be liable unless it had purposely retaliated against an employee for speech on a matter of public concern. Justice STEVENS' dissent argued that an employer ought be absolutely liable if the speech for which the employee was fired was on a matter of public concern, regardless of the employer's state of mind.

What is the scope of public employee speech on a matter of "public concern" under Pickering? Is such speech limited to criticism of governmental policy, as was involved in the letter to the editor in Pickering or in the political hyperbole in McPherson? And how severe must the financial penalty be to trigger First Amendment scrutiny? Must one lose one's job or will a lesser burden suffice? The Court took a broad view of the answers to both questions in UNITED STATES v. NATIONAL TREASURY EMPLOYEES UNION, 513 U.S. 454 (1995). The case involved a challenge to section 501 (b) of the Ethics in Government Act, as amended in 1989 and 1991 to bar a wide range of officers and employees of the federal government from receiving payment of any honorarium "for an appearance, speech or article (including a series of appearances, speeches, or articles if the subject matter is directly related to the individual's official duties or the payment is made because of the individual's status with the Government)." The honorarium ban was challenged by a class of executive branch employees below grade GS–16. Among the class were a mail handler who had given lectures on the Quaker religion, an aerospace engineer who had lectured on black history, a microbiologist at the Food and Drug Administration who had reviewed dance performances, and a tax examiner who wrote articles about the environment.

Justice STEVENS wrote for the Court invalidating the ban: "Federal employees who write for publication in their spare time have made significant contributions to the marketplace of ideas. They include literary giants like Nathaniel Hawthorne and Herman Melville, who were employed by the Customs Service; Walt Whitman, who worked for the Departments of Justice and Interior; and Bret Harte, an employee of the mint. Respondents have yet to make comparable contributions to American culture, but they share with these great artists important characteristics that are relevant to the issue we confront." Justice Stevens found the case governed by Pickering rather than Connick: "Respondents' expressive activities in this case fall within the protected category of citizen comment on matters of public concern rather than employee comment on matters related to personal status in the workplace. The speeches and articles for which they received compensation in the past were addressed to a public audience, were made outside the workplace, and involved content largely unrelated to their government employment." And he found that the government's "prohibition on compensation unquestionably imposes a significant burden on expressive activity. See [Simon & Schuster.][1]"

1. This proposition is self-evident even to those who do not fully accept Samuel Johnson's cynical comment: " 'No man but a blockhead ever wrote, except for money.' " J.

Turning to the government's asserted justifications, Justice Stevens stated: "The Government's underlying concern is that federal officers not misuse or appear to misuse power by accepting compensation for their unofficial and nonpolitical writing and speaking activities. This interest is undeniably powerful, but the Government cites no evidence of misconduct related to honoraria in the vast rank and file of federal employees below grade GS–16. [Congress] reasonably could assume that payments of honoraria to [its own Members,] judges or high-ranking officials in the Executive Branch might generate [an] appearance of improper influence. Congress could not, however, reasonably extend that assumption to all federal employees below Grade GS–16, an immense class of workers with negligible power to confer favors on those who might pay to hear them speak or to read their articles."

Justice Stevens also found the necessity of the total ban to "operational efficiency" called into "serious doubt" by the fact that honoraria were banned for "a *series* of appearances, speeches, or articles" only if "the subject matter is directly related to the individual's official duties or the payment is made because of the individual's status with the Government." He explained: "Congress' decision to provide a total exemption for all unrelated series of speeches undermines application of the ban to individual speeches and articles with no nexus to Government employment. Absent such a nexus, no corrupt bargain or even appearance of impropriety appears likely. The Government's only argument against a general nexus limitation is that a wholesale prophylactic rule is easier to enforce than one that requires individual nexus determinations. The nexus limitation for series, however, unambiguously reflects a congressional judgment that agency ethics officials [can] enforce the statute when it includes a nexus test. A blanket burden on the speech of nearly 1.7 million federal employees requires a much stronger justification than the Government's dubious claim of administrative convenience. [Such] anomalies in the text of the statute and regulations underscore our conclusion: the speculative benefits the honoraria ban may provide the Government are not sufficient to justify this crudely crafted burden on respondents' freedom to engage in expressive activities. Section 501(b) violates the First Amendment."

Justice Stevens, for the Court, held that the appropriate remedy was facial invalidation of the statutory provision. Justice O'CONNOR concurred in the judgment in part and dissented in part, arguing that facial invalidation was excessive and that the Court should have invalidated the provision only to the extent it was applied without a nexus provision.

Chief Justice REHNQUIST, joined by Justices Scalia and Thomas, dissented: "The ban neither prohibits anyone from speaking or writing, nor does it penalize anyone who speaks or writes; the only stricture effected by the statute is a denial of compensation. [Unlike] the law at issue in Simon & Schuster, the honoraria ban is neither content nor viewpoint based. As a result, the ban does not raise the specter of Government control over the marketplace of ideas. To the extent that the honoraria ban implicates First Amendment concerns, the proper standard of review is found in our cases dealing with the Government's ability to regulate the First Amendment activities of its employees.

"[Applying] these standards to the honoraria ban, I cannot say that the balance that Congress has struck between its interests and the interests of its employees to receive compensation for their First Amendment expression is

Boswell, Life of Samuel Johnson LL.D. 302
(R. Hutchins ed. 1952). [Footnote by Justice
Stevens.]

unreasonable. The Court largely ignores the Government's foremost interest—prevention of impropriety and the appearance of impropriety—by focusing solely on the burdens of the statute as applied to several carefully selected Executive Branch employees whose situations present the application of the statute where the Government's interests are at their lowest ebb [but who] by no means represent the breadth of the class. [Nor is it necessarily true that] federal employees below grade GS–16 have negligible power to confer favors on those who might pay to hear them speak or to read their articles. [Tax] examiners, bank examiners, enforcement officials, or any number of federal employees have substantial power to confer favors even though their compensation level is below Grade GS–16. [The] Government's related concern regarding the difficulties that would attach in administering a case-by-case analysis of the propriety of particular honoraria also supports the honoraria ban's validity. [Congress] reasonably determined that the prior ethics regime, which required these case-by-case determinations, was inadequate.

"[Unlike] our prototypical application of Pickering which normally involves a response to the content of employee speech, the honoraria ban prohibits no speech and is unrelated to the message or the viewpoint expressed by the government employee. Because there is only a limited burden on respondents' First Amendment rights, Congress reasonably could have determined that its paramount interests in preventing impropriety and the appearance of impropriety in its work force justified the honoraria ban." Chief Justice Rehnquist also objected to the remedy: "One would expect the Court to hold the statute inapplicable on First Amendment grounds to persons such as the postal worker who lectures on the Quaker religion, and others of similar ilk. But the Court, [in] what may fairly be described as an O. Henry ending, holds the statute inapplicable to the entire class before the Court."

————

PUBLIC EMPLOYEE PARTY AFFILIATION

Introduction. Since the rise of political parties in the early days of the republic, elected officials have engaged in the practice of political patronage: rewarding one's political friends with jobs in or contracts with the government, and declining so to reward one's political enemies. Various statutory devices have been employed over time to check this "spoils system," including state and federal bribery and extortion laws, and the use of merit examinations and civil service protection for rank and file government employees. Another device is the federal Hatch Act and the state mini-Hatch acts, which prohibit active political campaigning by public employees. The decisions that follow rejected challenges to these laws brought by public employees who claimed that they had a free speech right to electioneer. The decisions noted after the Hatch Act cases review First Amendment challenges by public employees from the other side of the patronage coin: claims by discharged or demoted public officials that they have been turned out by the victorious party solely because of their different party affiliation in violation of their rights of free political association. The right of association is explored in greater depth in Chapter 13.

1. *Prohibitions of political activities by public employees: the Hatch Act cases.* In UNITED PUBLIC WORKERS v. MITCHELL, 330 U.S. 75 (1947), the Court sustained the constitutionality of § 9(a) of the Hatch Act of 1940, prohibiting federal employees in the executive branch from taking "any active part in political management or in political campaigns." The Court held that "Congress may regulate the political conduct of government employees 'within

reasonable limits,' even though the regulation trenches to some extent upon unfettered political action." Justice Black dissented: "It would hardly seem to be imperative to muzzle millions of citizens because some of them, if left their constitutional freedoms, might corrupt the political process." He suggested that the law actually harmed "the body politic" by "depriving it of the political participation and interest of such a large segment of our citizens."

A second major challenge to the Act was brought in the 1970s. But it also failed: in UNITED STATES CIVIL SERVICE COMM'N v. NATIONAL ASS'N OF LETTER CARRIERS, 413 U.S. 548 (1973), the Court rejected an on-the-face, overbreadth attack on § 9(a) and "unhesitatingly reaffirm[ed]" Mitchell: "Neither the right to associate nor the right to participate in political activities is absolute. [P]lainly identifiable acts of political management and political campaigning may constitutionally be prohibited on the part of federal employees." Justice WHITE's majority opinion deferred to the congressional judgment that "partisan political activities by federal employees must be limited if the Government is to operate effectively and fairly, elections are to play their proper part in representative government, and employees themselves are to be sufficiently free from improper influences." He noted that the restrictions were "not aimed at particular parties, groups or points of view, but apply equally to all [covered] partisan activities. [Nor] do they seek to control political opinions or beliefs, or to interfere with or influence anyone's vote at the polls." Applying the Pickering balancing test, he found three government interests substantial enough to outweigh the free speech claims of public employees: ensuring that public employees "administer the law in accordance with the will of Congress, rather than [with the] will of a political party," preventing the use of government workers "to build a powerful, invincible, and perhaps corrupt political machine," and ensuring "that Government employees [are] free from pressure [to] vote in a certain way or perform political chores in order to curry favor with their superiors rather than to act out of their own beliefs."

Justice DOUGLAS, joined by Justices Brennan and Marshall, dissented: "[No] one could object if employees were barred form using office time to engage in outside activities whether political or otherwise. But it is of no concern of Government what an employee does in his spare time, [unless] what he does impairs efficiency or other facets of the merits of his job."

2. *Patronage dismissals of public employees.* In several decisions, the Court has sharply curtailed governmental power to penalize public employees on party allegiance grounds. The process began with ELROD v. BURNS, 427 U.S. 347 (1976), a 5–3 decision holding that the newly elected Democratic Sheriff of Cook County, Illinois, could not discharge several Republican employees—three process servers and a juvenile court bailiff and security guard. Justice BRENNAN's plurality opinion, joined by Justices White and Marshall, held that "[t]he cost of the practice of patronage is the restraint it places on freedoms of belief and association. [An] individual who is a member of the out-party maintains affiliation with his own party at the risk of losing his job." He went on to reject three government interests asserted in defense of patronage practices. He doubted that it served "the need to insure effective government and the efficiency of public employees," which could be safeguarded by discharge for good cause, and argued that the lack of an efficiency justification distinguished the case from Mitchell and Letter Carriers. He also denied that wholesale patronage is necessary "for political loyalty" and implementation of the electorate's policy choices; this interest, he argued, could be served by "[l]imiting patronage dismissals to policymaking positions." And he found that patronage was not necessary to the "preservation of the two-party system," which had already survived the inroads made by civil service merit systems.

Justice STEWART's concurrence, joined by Justice Blackmun, concluded more narrowly that "a nonpolicymaking, nonconfidential government employee [cannot be discharged] from a job that he is satisfactorily performing upon the sole ground of his political beliefs." Justice POWELL, joined by Chief Justice Burger and Justice Rehnquist, dissented, finding strong government interests served by patronage: "[Patronage] hiring practices have contributed to American democracy by stimulating political activity and by strengthening parties. [Patronage] hiring practices also enable party organizations to persist and function at the local level. [In] the dull periods between elections, [precinct] organizations must be maintained; new voters registered; and minor political 'chores' performed for citizens. [It] is naive to think that these types of political activities are motivated at these levels by some academic interest in 'democracy.' [As] every politician knows, the hope of some reward generates a major portion of the local political activity supporting parties." The dissenters found these state interests sufficient to outweigh the limited First Amendment interest in avoiding "the coercion on associational choices that may be created by one's desire [to]obtain [government] employment."

Four years later in BRANTI v. FINKEL, 445 U.S. 507 (1980), the Court reconsidered patronage systems and expanded the immunity of public employees from patronage dismissals, but left the contours of the broadened constitutional protections somewhat unclear. The new governing rule in Branti invoked criteria differing from Elrod: "the ultimate inquiry is not whether the label 'policymaker' or 'confidential' fits a particular position; rather, the question is whether the hiring authority can demonstrate that party affiliation is an appropriate requirement for the effective performance of the public office involved."[2]

In Branti, two Republican assistant county public defenders successfully challenged their dismissal by the newly-named Democratic head of the public defender's office. Justice STEVENS' majority opinion concluded, under his newly formulated standard, that "it is manifest that the continued employment of an assistant public defender cannot properly be conditioned upon his allegiance to the political party in control of the county government." He noted that any policymaking in a public defender's office related to the needs of individual clients, not to any partisan political interests, and that the assistant public defenders' access to confidential information arising out of attorney-client relationships had no bearing on party concerns. Accordingly, "it would undermine, rather than promote, the effective performance of an assistant public defender's office to make his tenure dependent on his allegiance to the dominant political party." He conceded that "party affiliation may be an acceptable requirement for some types of government employment," but insisted that the "policymaking or confidential position" criterion did not adequately delineate the proper use of party considerations. He explained: "Under some circumstances, a position may be appropriately considered political even though it is neither confidential nor policymaking in character." (He gave as an example the use of local election judges of different parties to supervise elections at the precinct level.) He added: "It is equally clear that party affiliation is not necessarily relevant to every policymaking or confidential

---

2. Justice Stevens, the author of the new standard in Branti, had not participated in Elrod. Justice Stewart, the author of the concurring opinion in Elrod, dissented in Branti on the ground that the positions involved here were not "nonconfidential" ones. But Justice Blackmun, who had joined Justice Stewart's concurrence in Elrod, was with the majority in Branti. Moreover, Chief Justice Burger, among the dissenters in Elrod, also joined the Branti majority. Justice Powell elaborated his dissenting views in Elrod in a strong dissent in Branti, joined by Justice Rehnquist and, in part, Justice Stewart.

position." (In illustrating that statement he noted that a "policymaking" football coach could not be discharged on party affiliation grounds, but that the position of a speechwriting assistant to a governor could properly involve party allegiance if it was to be performed "effectively.") Justice Stevens expressly declined to decide whether a prosecutor, like a public defender, was protected from dismissal on grounds of political party affiliation or loyalty.

Justice POWELL, in the major dissent, objected to the majority's new, "substantially expanded standard for determining which governmental employees may be retained or dismissed on the basis of political affiliation," which he feared would create "vast uncertainty." He noted, for example, that "it would be difficult to say [under the new standard] that 'partisan' concerns properly are relevant to the performance of the duties of a United States Attorney." As in his Elrod dissent, he emphasized that patronage appointments "helped build stable political parties" and that political parties served "a variety of substantial governmental interests." They helped candidates "to muster donations of time and money necessary to capture the attention of the electorate" and thus contribute to the democratic process; moreover, they "aid effective governance after election campaigns end." The majority's approach, he argued, imposed "unnecessary constraints upon the ability of responsible officials to govern effectively and to carry out new policies." Moreover, the "breakdown of party discipline that handicaps elected officials also limits the ability of the electorate to choose wisely among candidates." He concluded: "In sum, the effect of the Court's decision will be to decrease the accountability and denigrate the role of our national political parties."

In Elrod and Branti, then, the First Amendment was held to prohibit patronage dismissals of public employees unless the government could demonstrate that party affiliation was an appropriate requirement for the position involved. Ten years after Branti, the Court confronted the question whether the First Amendment also barred patronage practices other than dismissals. In RUTAN v. REPUBLICAN PARTY OF ILLINOIS, 497 U.S. 62 (1990), a divided Court extended Elrod and Branti to decisions about hiring, promotion, transfer, and recalls after layoffs. The case arose from Illinois Republican Governor James Thompson's institution of a hiring freeze, exceptions to which depended on permissions from his office. The challengers claimed that his office operated as a "patronage machine," and that they were denied promotions, transfers and recalls because they lacked Republican credentials. None of these decisions, Justice BRENNAN's majority opinion held, could constitutionally be based on party affiliation and support. Even without being discharged, he found, "[e]mployees who find themselves in dead-end positions due to their political backgrounds [will] feel a significant obligation to support political positions held by their superiors, and to refrain from acting on the political views they actually hold." He held that employees need not show that their treatment amounts to a constructive discharge in order to prevail in their First Amendment claims. Patronage practices even short of dismissal or its equivalent, he held, must be "narrowly tailored to further vital government interests." Justice STEVENS concurred separately.

Justice SCALIA vigorously dissented, joined by Chief Justice Rehnquist and Justice Kennedy and, in part, by Justice O'Connor. Justice Scalia insisted that "Elrod and Branti should be overruled, rather than merely not extended." In his extensive attack on Elrod and Branti, he emphasized the difference in the constitutional restrictions "upon the government in its capacity as lawmaker, i.e., as the regulator of private conduct" and "the restrictions [upon] the government in its capacity as employer." Thus, private citizens "cannot be punished for speech of merely private concern, but government employees can be fired without reason" [Connick v. Myers], and private citizens "cannot be punished for partisan political activity, but [public] employees can be dismissed and otherwise punished for that reason" [Mitchell; Letter Carriers]. He added, in a section of the dissent not joined by Justice O'Connor: "The provisions of the Bill of Rights were designed to restrain transient majorities from impairing long-recognized personal liberties. They did not create by implication novel individual rights overturning accepted political norms. Thus, when a practice not expressly prohibited by the text of the Bill of Rights bears the endorsement of a long tradition of open, widespread, and unchallenged use that dates back to the beginning of the Republic, we have no proper basis for striking it down. Such a venerable and accepted tradition is not to be laid on the examining table and scrutinized for its conformity to some abstract principle of First–Amendment adjudication devised by this Court."

Justice Scalia further objected to the majority's use of a "strict-scrutiny standard." Reiterating that speech restrictions on public employees "are not judged by the test applicable to similar restrictions on speech by non-employees," he noted that the Mitchell case had applied a lenient test of whether the practice could be "reasonably deemed" to further a legitimate goal. He argued that patronage practices satisfied even a less deferential "general 'balancing' test: can the governmental advantages of this employment practice reasonably be deemed to outweigh its 'coercive' effects?" Reiterating Justice Powell's arguments in defense of patronage in his Elrod dissent, Justice Scalia noted that "patronage stabilizes political parties and prevents excessive political fragmentation," both strong governmental interests. He added to Justice Powell's list an additional interest served by patronage: "Patronage, moreover, has been a powerful means of achieving the social and political integration of excluded groups. ['Every] ethnic group that has achieved political power in American cities has used the bureaucracy to provide jobs in return for political support.'" He conceded that "the patronage system entails some constraint upon the expression of views [and] considerable constraint upon the employee's right to associate with the other party." But he denied that patronage really involved "coercion" at all and insisted it did not represent "a significant impairment of free speech or free association."

In Elrod, Branti, and Rutan, there were speech interests on both sides. If the out-party employees' free speech and association claims are rejected, they are given an incentive to tailor their views and allegiance to the other party against their true beliefs. If those claims are sustained, however, the expressive and associational rights of members of the in-party are arguably diminished. Moreover, constraints on patronage might even diminish the quantity of political speech on the whole by inhibiting party activism. Did the Court undervalue the interests of the in-party in these cases? Did it undervalue the contributions of patronage to political expression?

Note that the standard of scrutiny in the patronage cases is stricter than the Pickering balancing test. Pickering permits the government to win if it can demonstrate an interest in efficiency in a particular case. Elrod, Branti and Rutan, in contrast, presume as a general matter that party affiliation is not a justifiable basis for government employment decisions unless the government can demonstrate narrow tailoring to vital "interests." Is it odd to give less constitutional protection in this context to speech, which is an enumerated right, than to association, which is not? Is there a possibility for confusion in applying the two standards if a fact situation involves retaliation for a mixture of both speech and party affiliation?

SPEECH AND PARTY AFFILIATION OF INDEPENDENT CONTRACTORS

Should the protections granted to public employees in the Pickering and Elrod lines of cases extend to independent contractors with government? On the one hand, contractors might appear less vulnerable to government coercion of belief and association than employees are, as they are less dependent on government work and more likely as a practical matter to support both parties. On the other hand, treating contractors differently from employees might encourage government simply to manipulate job titles and work arrangements so as to increase its power to enforce ideological and partisan fealty. The issue divided the lower courts until settled by the following decisions.

In BOARD OF COMMISSIONERS, WABAUNSEE CO. v. UMBEHR, ___ U.S. ___, 116 S.Ct. 2342 (1996), a case involving an outspoken trash hauler, the Court extended to independent contractors the protections of the Pickering line of cases, and in O'HARE TRUCK SERVICE, INC. v. CITY OF NORTHLAKE, ___ U.S. ___, 116 S.Ct. 2353 (1996), a case involving a politically recalcitrant tow truck operator, the Court extended to independent contractors the protections of the Elrod line of cases.

Umbehr had a contract to haul trash for Wabuansee County, Kansas. While under contract, he was an outspoken critic of the three-member governing body of the County. Umbehr spoke at the Board's meetings, and wrote critical letters and editorials in local newspapers regarding the County's landfill user rates, the Board's meeting practices, and the County's alleged mismanagement of taxpayers' money. The county terminated his contract and Umbehr filed a First Amendment complaint. The Court, by a vote of 7–2, affirmed the court of appeals' reversal of a summary judgment for the county.

Justice O'CONNOR wrote for the Court in Umbehr. She reviewed the possible distinctions between public employees and contractors and found them no basis for a departure from the Pickering balancing test: "[I]ndependent contractors work at a greater remove from government officials than do most government employees. [The] Board argues that the lack of day-to-day control accentuates the government's need to have the work done by someone it trusts. [Umbehr,] on the other hand, argues that the government interests in maintaining harmonious working environments and relationships recognized in our government employee cases are attenuated where the contractor does not work at the government's workplace and does not interact daily with government officers and employees. He also points out that to the extent that he is publicly perceived as an independent contractor, any government concern that his political statements will be confused with the government's political positions is mitigated. The Board [retorts] that the cost of fending off litigation, and the potential for government contracting practices to ossify into prophylactic rules to avoid potential litigation and liability, outweigh the interests of independent contractors, who are typically less financially dependent on their government contracts than are government employees. Each of these arguments for and against the imposition of liability has some force. But all of them can be accommodated by applying our existing framework for government employee cases to independent contracts. We [see] no reason to believe that proper application of the Pickering balancing test cannot accommodate the differences between employees and independent contractors." She emphasized that because the case applied only to a terminations, "we need not address the possibility of suits by bidders or applicants for new government contracts."

In O'Hare, a tow truck operator who had been on the city's rotation list was removed from the list after its owner, John Gratzianna, refused political support and campaign contributions to the mayor and supported the mayor's opponent in the election. Without deciding the case on the merits, the Court held that O'Hare had stated a First Amendment claim. Justice KENNEDY wrote for the Court, which again voted 7–2: "There is no doubt that if Gratzianna had been a public employee whose job was to perform tow truck operations, the city could not have discharged him for refusing to contribute to [the mayor's] campaign or for supporting his opponent. [We] cannot accept the proposition [that] those who perform the government's work outside the formal employment relationship are subject to what we conclude is the direct and specific abridgment of First Amendment rights described in this complaint. [We] see no reason [why] the constitutional claim here should turn on the distinction [between employees and contractors,] which is, in the main, a creature of the common law of agency and torts. Recognizing the distinction in these circumstances would invite manipulation by government, which could avoid constitutional liability simply by attaching different labels to particular jobs."

Justice Kennedy was not convinced that patronage practices are less coercive of independent contractors than employees: "[Perhaps] some contractors are so independent from government support that the threat of losing business would be ineffective to coerce them to abandon political activities. The same might be true of certain public employees, however; they, too, might find work elsewhere if they lose their government jobs. If results were to turn on these sorts of distinctions, courts would have to inquire into the extent to which the government dominates various job markets as employer or as contractor. We have been, and we remain, unwilling to send courts down that path. [Nor are we willing to assume that most independent contractors are] 'political hermaphrodites,' who find it in their self-interest to stay on good terms with both major political parties and so are not at great risk of retaliation for political association." He concluded: "The absolute right to enforce a patronage scheme, insisted upon by respondents as a means of retaining control over independent contractors, [has] not been shown to be a necessary part of a legitimate political system in all instances. [We] decline to draw a line excluding independent contractors from the First Amendment safeguards of political association afforded to employees."

Justice SCALIA, joined by Justice Thomas, filed a vigorous dissent from both Umbehr and O'Hare. He first expressed astonishment that in O'Hare, despite the addition of Justice Thomas (who opposes the Elrod line) to the Court and the fact that all four Rutan dissenters remained on the Court, the Court had not only declined to overrule Elrod and Branti, but had "extended [them] far beyond Rutan to the massive field of all government contracting." He reiterated that patronage is a longstanding American tradition, and, noting elaborate state and federal laws governing procurement practices, suggested that any answer to its disadvantages in the contracting context must come from the political process and not the Court. He insisted that political favoritism is an inevitable feature of government: "Government favors those who agree with its political views, and disfavors those who disagree, every day—in where it builds its public works, in the kinds of taxes it imposes and collects, in its regulatory prescriptions, in the design of its grant and benefit programs—in a million ways, including the letting of contracts for government business." And he argued that, even if Elrod and Branti had made any sense, there was no reason to extend them to contractors: "If it is to be possible to dig in our cleats at some point on this [slippery] slope—before we end up holding that the First Amendment requires the City of Chicago to have as few potholes in Republican wards (if any) as in Democratic ones—would not the most defensible point of termination for this indefensible exercise be public employment? A public employee is always an individual, and a public employee below the highest political level (which is exempt from Elrod) is virtually always an individual who is not rich; the termination or denial of a public job is the termination or denial of a livelihood. A public contractor, on the other hand, is usually a corporation; and the contract it loses is rarely its entire business, or even an indispensable part of its entire business."

Suppose that a government contracts out the job of providing security services at a public housing project, and later finds out that the contractor is affiliated with a party that preaches racial supremacy. After O'Hare, may the government terminate the contract?

————

D. SPEECH SUBSIDIZED BY PUBLIC FUNDS

————

The principle that governmental benefits may not be conditioned on relinquishing First Amendment rights has not been limited to employment. In SPEISER v. RANDALL, 357 U.S. 513 (1958), for example, the Court overturned a California requirement that property tax exemptions for veterans would be available only to those who would declare that they did not advocate the forcible overthrow of the government. Rejecting California's claim that it could condition the award of a "privilege" or "bounty," Justice Brennan's opinion for the Court noted that "to deny an exemption to claimants who engage in certain forms of speech is in effect to penalize them for such speech." The principle has been extended to a variety of government benefits, including both tax benefits and direct grants.

Why should government be constrained not to make speech or silence a condition of a benefit, when it is free not to confer the benefit at all? After all, government is not constitutionally required affirmatively to subsidize the exercise of constitutional rights. This is the conundrum of all so-called "unconstitutional conditions" cases. Unconstitutional conditions problems arise when government offers a benefit on condition that the recipient perform or forego an activity that is generally constitutionally protected from government interference. Such problems have given rise to voluminous commentary. See generally Hale, "Unconstitutional Conditions and Constitutional Rights," 35 Colum. L. Rev. 321 (1935); Van Alstyne, "The Demise of the Right–Privilege Distinction in Constitutional Law," 81 Harv.L.Rev. 1439 (1968); Kreimer, "Allocational Sanctions: the Problem of Negative Rights in a Positive State," 132 U. Pa. L. Rev. 1293 (1984); Epstein, "Foreword: Unconstitutional Conditions, State Power and the Limits of Consent," 102 Harv. L. Rev. 4 (1988); Sullivan, "Unconstitutional Conditions," 102 Harv. L. Rev. 1413 (1989).

In the speech context, the Court has attempted to resolve the conundrum by distinguishing denials of benefits that operate as "penalties" on speech from those that operate as mere "nonsubsidies." Under this distinction, government may not use the leverage of a subsidy to induce recipients to refrain from speech they would otherwise engage in with their own resources, but it may refrain from paying for speech with which it disagrees. This distinction is structurally parallel to the distinctions the Court has drawn in the preceding contexts of public space, public education and public employment. In those contexts, the Court similarly distinguished public forums from nonpublic forums, noncurricular from curricular aspects of public schools, and public employee speech as a citizen on matters of public concern from employee speech on internal matters of labor grievance. In the first category of each pair, the Court views the government as constrained by the First Amendment in much the same manner as if it were regulating the general citizenry, and employs strict or intermediate scrutiny. In the second category of each pair, the Court defers to government with only minimal scrutiny, viewing it as having far more constitutional leeway in its capacity as manager, educator, or boss than it does in its capacity as sovereign regulator. The following pair of cases illustrate the distinction between nonsubsidies and funding penalties on speech.

In REGAN v. TAXATION WITH REPRESENTATION OF WASHING-TON, 461 U.S. 540 (1983), the Court unanimously upheld against First Amendment challenge a provision of the Internal Revenue Code barring a nonprofit organization that engages in lobbying from receiving tax-deductible contributions. There is no doubt that lobbying, or attempting to influence legislation, is a protected First Amendment activity. The issue in the case was whether lobbying organizations were entitled to the same tax benefits as nonprofit organizations that do not lobby. The Code provides for tax exemptions to two kinds of nonprofit organization: section 501(c)(3) organizations may not lobby, but taxpayers who contribute to them are permitted to deduct the amount of their contributions on their federal income tax returns; section 501(c)(4) organizations are free to lobby, but contributions to 501(c)(4) organizations are not tax-deductible to the contributor. Taxation With Representation (TWR) challenged the prohibition against substantial lobbying in section 501(c)(3) because it wanted to use tax-deductible contributions to support its substantial lobbying activities.

Justice REHNQUIST, writing for the Court, accepted that tax-deductibility of contributions to contributors represented a substantial benefit to TWR: "Both tax exemptions and tax deductibility are a form of subsidy that is administered through the tax system. A tax exemption has much the same effect as a cash grant to the organization of the amount of tax it would have to pay on its income. Deductible contributions are similar to cash grants of the amount of a portion of the individual's contributions. The system Congress has enacted provides this kind of subsidy [in the form of tax exemptions] to nonprofit civic welfare organizations generally, and an additional subsidy [in the form of tax deductibility to contributors] to those charitable organizations that do not engage in substantial lobbying. In short, Congress chose not to subsidize lobbying as extensively as it chose to subsidize other activities that nonprofit organizations undertake to promote the public welfare." But Justice Rehnquist rejected the argument that denial of the benefit of tax deductibility violated TWR's First Amendment rights: "TWR is certainly correct when it states that we have held that the government may not deny a benefit to a person because he exercises a constitutional right. But TWR is just as certainly incorrect when it claims that this case fits the [Speiser] model. The Code does not deny TWR the right to receive deductible contributions to support its nonlobbying activity, nor does it deny TWR any independent benefit on account of its intention to lobby. Congress has merely refused to pay for the lobbying out of public moneys. This Court has never held that Congress must grant a benefit such as TWR claims here to a person who wishes to exercise a constitutional right. [Congress] is not required by the First Amendment to subsidize lobbying."

Justice Rehnquist, quoting Speiser, noted that "[t]he case would be different if Congress were to discriminate invidiously in its subsidies in such a way as to ' "[aim] at the suppression of dangerous ideas." ' " But he held that an exception allowing veterans' organizations to receive tax-deductible contributions even if they lobbied did not constitute content discrimination in violation of this principle. He pointed out that the exemption was based on status, not content: "Veterans have 'been obliged to drop their own affairs to take up the burdens of the nation,' [and our] country has a longstanding policy of compensating veterans for their past contributions by providing them with numerous advantages." In the absence of any viewpoint discrimination, Justice Rehnquist held applicable only a minimal standard of review: "It is not irrational for Congress to decide that tax-exempt charities such as TWR should not further benefit at the expense of taxpayers at large by obtaining a further subsidy for lobbying."

Justice BLACKMUN, joined by Justices Brennan and Marshall, concurred but emphasized that "[t]he constitutional defect that would inhere in 501(c)(3) alone is avoided by 501(c)(4)," for TWR could simply use its existing 501(c)(3) organization for its nonlobbying activities while establishing a 501(c)(4) affiliate to pursue its goals through lobbying. Thus, in the concurring justices' view, "[a] 501(c)(3) organization's right to speak is not infringed, because it is free to make known its views on legislation through its 501(c)(4) affiliate without losing tax benefits for its nonlobbying activities."

Contrast with TWR the Court's holding in FCC v. LEAGUE OF WOMEN VOTERS [LWV], 468 U.S. 364 (1984). The Public Broadcasting Act of 1967 established the Corporation for Public Broadcasting (CPB), a nonprofit corporation, to disburse federal funds to noncommercial television and radio stations in support of station operations and educational programming. In LWV, the Court invalidated, by a vote of 5–4, a provision of the Act forbidding any "noncommercial educational broadcasting station which receives a grant from the Corporation" to "engage in editorializing." Justice BRENNAN, writing for the majority, found the no-editorializing condition to be a penalty on public broadcasters' protected speech, not a mere nonsubsidy of speech as in TWR: "In this case, [unlike] the situation faced by the charitable organization in [TWR], a noncommercial educational station that receives only 1% of its overall income from CPB grants is barred absolutely from all editorializing. Therefore, in contrast to the appellee in Taxation With Representation, such a station is not able to segregate its activities according to the source of its funding. The station has no way of limiting the use of its federal funds to all noneditorializing activities, and, more importantly, it is barred from using even wholly private funds to finance its editorial activity." He noted that the case would be different if Congress permitted "public broadcasting stations, [like] the charitable organization in [TWR, which could lobby through a 501(c)(4) affiliate], to make known its views on matters of public importance through [a] nonfederally funded, editorializing affiliate without losing federal grants for its noneditorializing broadcast activities."

Having found the editorial ban a penalty on public broadcasters' speech, he also found it impermissibly content-based, even under the less stringent review applicable to broadcasters than other speakers: "Because broadcast regulation involves unique considerations [such as spectrum scarcity], our cases have not followed precisely the same approach that we have applied to other media and have never gone so far as to demand that such regulations serve 'compelling' governmental interests. [But], as our cases attest, [restrictions on broadcaster speech] have been upheld only when we were satisfied that the restriction is narrowly tailored to further a substantial governmental interest, such as ensuring adequate and balanced coverage of public issues." [See Red Lion v. FCC, 1969, p. 1450 below.] Under this intermediate standard of scrutiny, he found the government's justifications for the editorial ban inadequate: it was not closely tailored to the goal of protecting public broadcasters from "being coerced, as a result of federal financing, into becoming vehicles for Government propagandizing or the objects of governmental influence," and was far too broad to serve any goal of preventing public broadcasting stations "from becoming convenient targets for capture by private interest groups wishing to express their own partisan viewpoints."

Justice REHNQUIST, joined by Chief Justice Burger and Justice White, argued that TWR ought to have been controlling and the restriction found a permissible nonsubsidy of speech. He wrote that the majority had presented "a scenario in which the Government appears as the 'Big Bad Wolf,' and appellee Pacifica as 'Little Red Riding Hood.' In the Court's scenario, the Big Bad Wolf cruelly forbids Little Red Riding Hood to take to her grandmother some of the food that she is carrying in her basket. [A] truer picture of the litigants, [would show] that some of the food in the basket was given to Little Red Riding Hood by the Big Bad Wolf himself, and that the Big Bad Wolf had told Little Red Riding Hood in advance that if she accepted his food she would have to abide by his conditions. Congress, in enacting [the editorial ban], has simply determined that public funds shall not be used to subsidize noncommercial, educational broadcasting stations which engage in 'editorializing.' " Nor did Justice Rehnquist find any problem in the ban's extension to private as well as public sources of funds: "Given the impossibility of compartmentalizing programming expenses in any meaningful way, it seems clear to me that the only effective means for preventing the use of public moneys to subsidize the airing of management's views is for Congress to ban a subsidized station from all on-the-air editorializing." He therefore rejected the majority's application of intermediate scrutiny: "[W]hen the Government is simply exercising its power to allocate its own public funds, we need only find that the condition imposed has a rational relationship to Congress' purpose in providing the subsidy and that it is not primarily 'aimed at the suppression of dangerous ideas.' " Here, he found, the condition was both rational and viewpoint-neutral: "[I]t is plainly rational for Congress to have determined that taxpayer moneys should not be used to subsidize management's views. [Furthermore,] Congress' prohibition is strictly neutral. In no sense can it be said that Congress has prohibited only editorial views of one particular ideological bent." Justice STEVENS also dissented, finding the ban viewpoint-neutral and justified by "the overriding interest in forestalling the creation of propaganda organs for the Government."

In RUST v. SULLIVAN, 500 U.S. 173 (1991), the Court found a speech-restrictive condition on funds more analogous to the one upheld in TWR than the one struck down in LWV. In Rust, the Court upheld Health and Human Services Department regulations forbidding projects receiving federal family planning funds under Title X of the Public Health Service Act from counseling or referring women for abortion and from encouraging, promoting or advocating abortion. If the funding recipient engaged in either of these activities, they had to be "physically and financially separate" from the recipient's Title X project. The regulations permitted Title X projects to provide pregnant women with information about childbirth and prenatal care, but advised them to tell any pregnant woman who inquired about abortion that the project does not consider abortion an "appropriate method of family planning." Doctors and Title X grantees challenged the regulations under under the First Amendment as well as the right of privacy implicit in the Fifth Amendment's due process clause. The Court rejected both challenges. (For the portions of the decision rejecting the Fifth Amendment challenge, see p. 553 above.)

The challengers argued that the regulations impermissibly discriminated on the basis of viewpoint because they prohibited discussion of abortion while requiring doctors or counselors to provide information about continuing a pregnancy to term. They relied on the Court's previous statements that, even in the provision of subsidies, government may not "aim at the suppression of dangerous ideas." Chief Justice REHNQUIST, writing for the majority in the 5–4 decision, rejected this argument: "The Government can, without violating the Constitution, selectively fund a program to encourage certain activities it believes to be in the public interest, without at the same time funding an alternative program which seeks to deal with the problem in another way. In so doing, the Government has not discriminated on the basis of viewpoint; it has merely chosen to fund one activity to the exclusion of the other. [This] is not a case of the Government 'suppressing a dangerous idea,' but of a prohibition on a project grantee or its employees from engaging in activities outside of the project's scope. To hold that the Government unconstitutionally discriminates on the basis of viewpoint when it chooses to fund a program dedicated to advance certain permissible goals, because the program in advancing those goals necessarily discourages alternative goals, would render numerous Government programs constitutionally suspect. [When] Congress established a National Endowment for Democracy to encourage other countries to adopt democratic principles, it was not constitutionally required to fund a program to encourage competing lines of political philosophy such as communism and fascism. [Within] far broader limits than petitioners are willing to concede, when the government appropriates public funds to establish a program it is entitled to define the limits of that program."

The challengers also argued that the regulations impermissibly conditioned the receipt of Title X funding on the relinquishment of their right to engage in abortion advocacy and counseling with their own funds. Chief Justice Rehnquist rejected this argument too: "[H]ere the Government is not denying a benefit to anyone, but is instead simply insisting that public funds be spent for the purposes for which they were authorized. The Secretary's regulations do not force the Title X grantee to give up abortion-related speech; they merely require that the grantee keep such activities separate and distinct from Title X activities. Title X expressly distinguishes between a Title X grantee and a Title X project. The grantee, which normally is a health care organization, may receive funds from a variety of sources for a variety of purposes. The grantee receives Title X funds, however, for the specific and limited purpose of establishing and operating a Title X project. The regulations govern the scope of the Title X project's activities, and leave the grantee unfettered in its other activities. [In] contrast, our 'unconstitutional conditions' cases involve situations in which the Government has placed a condition on the recipient of the subsidy rather than on a particular program or service, thus effectively prohibiting the recipient from engaging in the protected conduct outside the scope of the federally funded program. [See FCC v. LWV.]" He found it irrelevant that Title X required all Title X projects to raise private matching funds, and that the abortion counseling and advocacy restrictions extended to those funds: "The recipient is in no way compelled to operate a Title X project; to avoid the force of the regulations, it can simply decline the subsidy. [Potential] grant recipients can choose between accepting Title X funds—subject to the Government's conditions that they provide matching funds and forgo abortion counseling and referral in the Title X project—or declining the subsidy and financing their own unsubsidized program. We have never held that the Government violates the First Amendment simply by offering that choice."

Chief Justice Rehnquist cautioned that "[t]his is not to suggest that funding by the Government, even when coupled with the freedom of the fund recipients to speak outside the scope of the Government-funded project, is invariably sufficient to justify Government control over the content of expression." He cited as examples cases upholding speech rights in traditional public forums and academic freedom at public universities. But he found no infringement of any analogous traditional doctor-patient relationship: "Nothing in [the regulations] requires a doctor to represent as his own any opinion that he does not in fact hold. Nor is the doctor-patient relationship established by the Title X program sufficiently all encompassing so as to justify an expectation on the part of the patient of comprehensive medical advice."

Justice BLACKMUN dissented, joined by Justices Marshall and Stevens: "Until today, the Court never has upheld viewpoint-based suppression of speech simply because that suppression was a condition upon the acceptance of public funds. Whatever may be the Government's power to condition the receipt of its largess upon the relinquishment of constitutional rights, it surely does not extend to a condition that suppresses the recipient's cherished freedom of speech based solely upon the content or viewpoint of that speech. [Speiser.] It cannot seriously be disputed that the counseling and referral provisions at issue in the present cases constitute content-based regulation of speech. Title X grantees may provide counseling and referral regarding any of a wide range of family planning and other topics, save abortion. The regulations are also clearly viewpoint based. While suppressing speech favorable to abortion with one hand, the Secretary compels antiabortion speech with the other." Justice Blackmun contended that this viewpoint discrimination distinguished the regulations from those upheld in TWR. He also disagreed with Chief Justice Rehnquist that they constituted mere earmarking of funds to the limited purpose of preconception family planning advice: "[The] majority's claim that the regulations merely limit a Title X project's speech to preventive or preconceptional services rings hollow in light of the broad range of nonpreventive services that the regulations authorize Title X projects to provide [including referral for prenatal or adoption services, physical examinations, and treatment of gynecological problems and sexually transmitted diseases]." He concluded that the regulations should receive and be struck down under strict scrutiny. Justice O'Connor also dissented solely on the ground that the regulations exceeded HHS's statutory authority.

After Rust, could government constitutionally condition disbursement of federal Medicaid or Medicare funds to doctors upon their agreement to refrain from prescribing certain especially expensive drugs or courses of treatment? Could it condition federal grants for medical research on researchers' agreement not to publish any results not precleared by the government? Could it condition the disbursement to individual artists of grants from the National Endowment for the Arts upon the artists' agreement not to create any art during the grant period that is "indecent, i.e., patently offensive by contemporary community standards"? Could Congress cure any problem with such a condition by reauthorizing the Endowment with a statutory purpose of supporting "excellent art that meets commonly held standards of decency"? Would a restriction of funding to "excellent" art be an unconstitutional condition? A restriction of grants to "landscapes"? For commentary on such questions, see Fiss, "State Activism and State Censorship," 100 Yale L.J. 2087 (1991); Cole, "Beyond Unconstitutional Conditions: Charting Spheres of Neutrality in Government–Funded Speech," 67 N.Y.U. L. Rev. 675 (1992); Sabrin, "Thinking About Content: Can It Play an Appropriate Role in Government Funding of the Arts?," 102 Yale L. J. 1209 (1993); Post, "Subsidized Speech," 106 Yale L.J. 151 (1996); Redish & Kessler, "Government Subsidies and Free Expression," 80 Minn. L. Rev. 543 (1995). For commentary on Rust, see Roberts, "Rust v. Sullivan and the Control of Knowledge," 61 Geo. Wash. L. Rev. 587 (1993).

The TWR and Rust decisions both stated in dictum that subsidies may not be made selectively so as to "aim at the suppression of dangerous ideas." In ROSENBERGER v. RECTOR AND VISITORS OF THE UNIVERSITY OF VIRGINIA, ___ U.S. ___, 115 S.Ct. 2510 (1995), the Court invalidated a funding limitation as viewpoint discrimination. The case arose from a program at the University of Virginia in which mandatory student fees were used to pay the costs of extracurricular activities, including the costs of printing various student-edited publications. The University refused to pay the printing costs of "Wide Awake," a publication of a student group dedicated to advancing "the Christian perspective," under guidelines prohibiting the use of the activities fees for any "religious activity," defined as any activity that "primarily promotes or manifests a particular belief in or about a deity or an ultimate reality." Leaders of the student group claimed that this denial of funding violated their right of free speech. The University argued that it was a permissible nonsubsidy, and that in any event the establishment clause compelled the group's exclusion from the funding program. The Court held, by a vote of 5–4, that Wide Awake's exclusion was forbidden by the free speech clause and was not required by the establishment clause. (For the Court' establishment clause ruling in Rosenberger, see p. 1546 below.)

Justice KENNEDY, writing for the Court, found the funding restriction to constitute discrimination on the basis of viewpoint, not subject matter. He analogized the University's action to the school district's exclusion of a religious film series from after-hours use of public school facilities that was invalidated by the Court in Lamb's Chapel v. Center Moriches School Dist. (1993; p. 1290 above): "[W]e have observed a distinction between, on the one hand, content discrimination, which may be permissible if it preserves the purposes of [a] limited forum, and, on the other hand, viewpoint discrimination, which is presumed impermissible when directed against speech otherwise within the forum's limitations. The [Student Activities Fund (SAF)] is a forum more in a metaphysical than in a spatial or geographic sense, but the same principles are applicable. [It] is [something] of an understatement to speak of religious thought and discussion as just a viewpoint, as distinct from a comprehensive body of thought. The nature of our origins and destiny and their dependence upon the existence of a divine being have been subjects of philosophic inquiry throughout human history. We conclude, nonetheless, that here, as in Lamb's Chapel, viewpoint discrimination is the proper way to interpret the University's objections to Wide Awake. By the very terms of the SAF prohibition, the University does not exclude religion as a subject matter but selects for disfavored treatment those student journalistic efforts with religious editorial viewpoints. Religion may be a vast area of inquiry, but it also provides, as it did here, a specific premise, a perspective, a standpoint from which a variety of subjects may be discussed and considered. The prohibited perspective, not the general subject matter, resulted in the refusal to make third-party payments, for the subjects discussed were otherwise within the approved category of publications."

The University, relying on TWR and Rust, argued that "content-based funding decisions are both inevitable and lawful." Justice Kennedy found TWR inapposite because it involved no viewpoint discrimination, and Rust inapposite because it, in effect, involved government speech: "[In Rust,] the government did not create a program to encourage private speech but instead used private speakers to transmit specific information pertaining to its own program. We recognized that when the government appropriates public funds to promote a particular policy of its own it is entitled to say what it wishes. When the government disburses public funds to private entities to convey a governmental message, it may take legitimate and appropriate steps to ensure that its message is neither garbled nor distorted by the grantee. It does not follow, however, [that] viewpoint-based restrictions are proper when the University does not itself speak or subsidize transmittal of a message it favors but instead expends funds to encourage a diversity of views from private speakers. [The] distinction between the University's own favored message and the private speech of students is evident in the case before us. [The] University declares that the student groups eligible for SAF support are not the University's agents, are not subject to its control, and are not its responsibility. Having offered to pay the third-party contractors on behalf of private speakers who convey their own messages, the University may not silence the expression of selected viewpoints."

Justice SOUTER dissented, joined by Justices Stevens, Ginsburg and Breyer: "There is no viewpoint discrimination in the University's application of its Guidelines to deny funding to Wide Awake. [If] the Guidelines were written or applied so as to limit only [Christian] advocacy and no other evangelical efforts that might compete with it, the discrimination would be based on viewpoint. But that is not what the regulation authorizes; it applies to Muslim and Jewish and Buddhist advocacy as well as to Christian. And since it limits funding to activities promoting or manifesting a particular belief not only 'in' but 'about' a deity or ultimate reality, it applies to agnostics and atheists as well as it does to deists and theists. The Guidelines, and their application to Wide Awake, thus do not skew debate by funding one position but not its competitors. As understood by their application to Wide Awake, they simply deny funding for hortatory speech that 'primarily promotes or manifests' any view on the merits of religion; they deny funding for the entire subject matter of religious apologetics." He distinguished Lamb's Chapel as a case in which antireligious perspectives were permitted and only religious perspectives were excluded.

Why did Justice Kennedy in Rosenberger distinguish Rust as a case about government speech, rather than simply a case that, like TWR, did not involve viewpoint discrimination? Did he mean to suggest that some viewpoint discrimination in government subsidies *is* allowed? When government is itself the speaker, it might be argued, viewpoint discrimination is inevitable. A government-sponsored drug treatment program, for example, need not give equal time to a campaign to legalize marijuana. But if government gave out grants for private research "on optimal drug policy," could it rescind the money from a researcher whose data led him to conclude that marijuana should be legalized? Assuming that the NEA could not deny a grant to an artist who intends to paint excellent but "unpatriotic" pictures of the flag, may the Post Office reject his work in commissioning the next national postage stamp?

SECTION 3. IMPERMISSIBLE FORMS OF SPEECH-RESTRICTIVE LAW: OVERBREADTH, VAGUENESS AND PRIOR RESTRAINT

This section turns to a last set of doctrines limiting how government may regulate speech: the doctrines of overbreadth, vagueness and prior restraint. The flaw in laws invalidated on these grounds is procedural: government went about things the wrong way even if the speaker might constitutionally be restricted if government went about it in a different way. An overbroad law sweeps in too much speech, a vague law is unclear about what speech it sweeps in, and a prior restraint is premature even if publication might be subsequently punished. These doctrines are accordingly of particular usefulness to a speaker whose own speech might not be protected under the First Amendment under a differently drawn law.

————

A.   OVERBREADTH

————

Introduction. The modern Court has repeatedly invoked the principle that "a governmental purpose to control or prevent activities constitutionally subject [to] regulation may not be achieved by *means which sweep unnecessarily broadly and thereby invade the area of protected freedoms.*" NAACP v. Alabama (1964; p. 1376 below) (emphasis added.). Thus, even if speech is proscribable by a properly drawn law, a speaker may be able to invalidate a law that is overly broad.

For example, recall the case of GOODING v. WILSON (1972; p. 1079 above), in which the Court invalidated a conviction of an antiwar demonstrator at an induction center who in a scuffle with police said such things as "White son of a bitch, I'll kill you." He was convicted under a Georgia statute prohibiting the use of "opprobrious words or abusive language, tending to cause a breach of the peace." The Court, per Justice Brennan, held that the law swept in too much protected speech along with fighting words proscribable under Chaplinsky: "[It] matters not that the words appellee used might have been constitutionally prohibited under a narrowly and precisely drawn statute. At least when statutes regulate or proscribe speech and when 'no readily apparent construction suggests itself as a vehicle for rehabilitating the statutes in a single prosecution,' [the] transcendent value to all society of constitutionally protected expression is deemed to justify allowing 'attacks on overly broad statutes with no requirement that the person making the attack demonstrate that his own conduct could not be regulated by a statute drawn with the requisite narrow specificity.' [Dombrowski v. Pfister, 380 U.S. 479 (1965).]" Unlike the New Hampshire courts in Chaplinsky, Justice Brennan found, the Georgia courts in Gooding v. Wilson had failed to narrowly construe the opprobrious-words statute to limit its reach to fighting words. Accordingly, the Court voided the statute on its face.

For an example of similar overbreadth reasoning, recall Justice White's concurrence in R.A.V. v. City of St. Paul (1992; p. 1115 above), finding that a law barring racist symbols causing anger or alarm was overbroad because not limited to fighting words. For other examples of overbreadth determinations covered in earlier sections, see Erznoznik v. Jacksonville (1975; p. 1156 above) (ban on nudity in drive-in movies); Schad v. Mt. Ephraim (1981; p. 1158 above) (ban on live entertainment).

1. *The distinctive features of overbreadth.* Overbreadth analysis is an exception to two traditional rules of constitutional litigation. First, it results in the invalidation of a law "on its face" rather than "as applied" to a particular speaker. Ordinarily, a particular litigant claims that a statute is unconstitutional as applied to him or her; if the litigant prevails, the courts carve away the unconstitutional aspects of the law by invalidating its improper applications on a case-by-case basis. If a law restricting speech is invalidated as applied to a protected speaker, it is held inapplicable to that speaker, and thus, in effect, judicially trimmed down. Overbreadth analysis, in contrast, does not reach the

question whether the *challenger's* speech is constitutionally protected; instead it strikes down the statute entirely, because it might be applied to others not before the Court whose activities are constitutionally protected. When invalidated for overbreadth, a law is not narrowed, but rather becomes wholly unenforceable until a legislature rewrites it or a properly authorized court construes it more narrowly.

Second, overbreadth is an exception to the usual rules of standing. Ordinarily, challengers to a law are not permitted to raise the rights of third parties and can only assert their own interests. See generally Note, "Standing to Assert Constitutional Jus Tertii," 88 Harv.L.Rev. 423 (1974). In overbreadth analysis, challengers *are* in effect permitted to raise the rights of third parties. But see Monaghan, "Overbreadth," 1981 Sup. Ct. Rev. 1 (arguing that overbreadth involves first-party, not third-party standing, because the litigant's own conduct may only be regulated by a valid rule of law); Monaghan, "Third–Party Standing," 84 Colum. L. Rev. 277 (1984).

The factor that motivates courts to depart from these normal adjudicatory rules is the concern with the deterrent or "chilling" effect of the overbroad statute on third parties not courageous enough to bring suit. The Court assumes that an overbroad law's very existence may cause others not before the court to refrain from constitutionally protected speech or expression. An overbreadth ruling is designed to remove that deterrent effect on the speech of those third parties. As Justice Brennan wrote in Gooding, invalidation for overbreadth is "necessary because persons whose expression is constitutionally protected may well refrain from exercising their rights for fear of criminal sanctions provided by a statute susceptible of application to protected expression." See generally Note, "The Chilling Effect in Constitutional Law," 69 Colum.L.Rev. 808 (1969); Note, "The First Amendment Overbreadth Doctrine," 83 Harv.L.Rev. 844 (1970); Sedler, "The Assertion of Constitutional Jus Tertii: A Substantive Approach," 70 Calif.L.Rev. 1308 (1982); Redish, "The Warren Court, the Burger Court, and the First Amendment Overbreadth Doctrine," 78 Nw. L. Rev. 1031 (1983); Fallon, "Making Sense of Overbreadth," 100 Yale L.J. 853 (1991). An additional reason to contain overbroad statutes, like vague statutes, is to curb "their potential for selective enforcement" at the discretion of law enforcement officials. See Karst, "Equality as a Central Principle in the First Amendment," 43 U. Chi. L. Rev. 20 (1975).

2. *The attractiveness of overbreadth analysis.* Overbreadth analysis has been especially attractive to some Justices because it gives the appearance of judicial modesty. Rather than rewriting a law, it purports to leave alternatives open to the legislature. By holding out the prospect that narrower means may be available to achieve legislative objectives, it conveys the appearance of intervening in legislative policy choices far more marginally than outright "balancing" would. See, e.g., United States v. Robel (1967; p. 1070 above), which invalidated as overbroad a federal law making it a crime for members of Communist organizations to be employed in a defense facility, because it swept in passive and active members alike. Chief Justice Warren's opinion disavowed any substantive "balancing": "[We] have confined our analysis to whether Congress has adopted a constitutional means in achieving its concededly legitimate [goal]. In making this determination we have found it necessary to measure the validity of the means [against] both the goal [and] the First Amendment. But we have in no way 'balanced' those respective interests. We have ruled only that the Constitution requires that the conflict between congressional power and individual rights be accommodated by legislation drawn more narrowly to avoid the conflict."

Is this appearance of judicial modesty deceptive? For an argument that Robel engaged in implicit balancing despite its disavowal, see Gunther, "Reflections on [Robel]," 20 Stan.L.Rev. 1140 (1968). Arguably, overbreadth analysis cannot altogether avoid substantive judgments. In order to decide that a law sweeps in protected as well as unprotected expression, a judgment of overbreadth necessarily must delineate some contours of protected expression. To strike down an excessively broad "means" because it impinges on an "area of protected freedom" presupposes, after all, at least an implicit judgment about what the contours of that "area" are.

A second attraction of overbreadth analysis in the context of state laws is an apparent respect for the values of federalism. In the case of state legislation, only the state courts have authority to construe the statute; the federal courts, including the Supreme Court, may construe federal statutes but must abide by state court construction of state laws. Thus a federal court lacks authority to issue a narrowing construction of an overbroad state law. For a federal court in effect to rewrite a state statute by narrowing it arguably would amount to a quasi-legislative intrusion upon state policymaking prerogatives. Thus a judgment of facial invalidation of an overbroad state statute appears to defer to the state's policymaking role. But is facial invalidation truly a less intrusive exercise of federal judicial power than a narrowing construction would be?

3. *Criticisms of overbreadth analysis.* Overbreadth analysis has elicited a number of criticisms, beginning in the Warren Court era. One set of criticisms relates to its departure from usual case and controversy requirements. First, it has been criticized for allowing the Court to act "as if it had a roving commission" to cure unconstitutional provisions. Cox, The Warren Court (1968); see Younger v. Harris, 401 U.S. 37 (1971) (Black, J.) (noting that the federal judicial power to resolve "concrete disputes [does] not amount to an unlimited power to survey the statute books and pass judgment on laws before the courts are called upon to enforce them"). Second, it has been criticized for permitting decisions outside of concrete factual settings and in sterile, abstract contexts. See Bickel, The Least Dangerous Branch (1962). Third, it has been criticized as too speculative. It allows a court to invalidate a law so long as it can hypothesize some impermissible application in circumstances not before it. See, e.g., Gooding v. Wilson, supra (Burger, C.J., dissenting) (criticizing overbreadth for resting on "some insubstantial or imagined potential for occasional and isolated applications that go beyond constitutional bounds"); Younger, supra ("[T]he existence of a 'chilling effect' even in the area of First Amendment rights has never been considered a sufficient basis, in and of itself, for prohibiting state action.").

A second set of criticisms of overbreadth relates to its consequences. Typically, overbreadth analysis assumes that the challenger's behavior is not protected by the First Amendment and is reachable by the state under a more "narrowly drawn" law. Thus the doctrine permits an individual whose own First Amendment rights have not been violated to enjoy a free ride unless and until the appropriate legislature or court redraws the statute. This may well undermine important state interest in the meantime. And there may be various practical obstacles to prompt redrafting by the relevant policymaking bodies. Moreover, it may appear perverse for an unprotected speaker to wield a more powerful weapon against a law than a protected speaker can, since the protected speaker is more likely to be confined to an "as applied" analysis.

4. *Limits on overbreadth analysis: the requirement of "substantial" overbreadth.* The above criticisms bore fruit in 1973, when the Court required that overbreadth must be "substantial" before facial invalidation is appropriate and

suggested that overbreadth analysis was less applicable when the challenged statute affected "conduct" rather than "speech." In BROADRICK v. OKLA-HOMA, 413 U.S. 601 (1973), Justice White—who had dissented from some earlier overbreadth invalidations—wrote for the majority, and Justice Brennan—who had written some of the major overbreadth opinions of the Warren era—wrote for most of the dissenters. Broadrick arose from a challenge to § 818 of Oklahoma's Merit System Act restricting political activities by classified civil servants. Among the challenged provisions of this mini-Hatch Act was one prohibiting employees from "tak[ing] part in the management or affairs of any political party or in any political campaign, except to exercise his right as a citizen privately to express his opinion and to cast his vote." Other provisions more specifically prohibited soliciting for campaign contributions. Appellants, who had campaigned for a superior, challenged § 818 on vagueness and overbreadth grounds. The Court's 5–4 decision rejected those challenges. Justice WHITE's majority opinion devoted most of its focus to overbreadth:

"Appellants assert that § 818 has been construed as applying to such allegedly protected political expression as the wearing of political buttons or the displaying of bumper stickers. But appellants did not engage in any such activity. They are charged with actively engaging in partisan political activities—including the solicitation of money—among their co-workers for the benefit of their superior. Appellants concede [that] § 818 would be constitutional as applied to this type of conduct. [See the Hatch Act cases, p. 1311 above.] They nevertheless maintain that the statute is overbroad and purports to reach protected, as well as unprotected conduct, and must therefore be struck down on its face and held to be incapable of any constitutional application. We do not believe that the overbreadth doctrine may appropriately be invoked in this manner here."

Justice White then proceeded to justify and delineate a "substantial overbreadth" approach: "Embedded in the traditional rules governing constitutional adjudication is the principle that a person to whom a statute may constitutionally be applied will not be heard to challenge that statute on the ground that it may conceivably be applied unconstitutionally to others, in other situations not before the Court. [This principle reflects] the conviction [that] our constitutional courts are not roving commissions assigned to pass judgment on the validity of the Nation's laws. [In] the past, the Court has recognized some limited exceptions to these principles, but only because of the most 'weighty countervailing policies.' [One such exception] has been carved out in the area of the First Amendment. It has long been recognized that the First Amendment needs breathing space and that statutes attempting to restrict or burden the exercise of First Amendment rights must be narrowly drawn and represent a considered legislative judgment that a particular mode of expression has to give way to other compelling needs of society. As a corollary, the Court has altered its traditional rules of standing to permit [litigants] in the First Amendment area to challenge a statute not because their own rights of free expression are violated, but because of a judicial prediction or assumption that the statute's very existence may cause others not before the court to refrain from constitutionally protected speech or expression.

"Such claims of facial overbreadth have been entertained in cases involving statutes which, by their terms, seek to regulate 'only spoken words.' [Gooding v. Wilson.] In such cases, it has been the judgment of this Court that the possible harm to society in permitting some unprotected speech to go unpunished is outweighed by the possibility that protected speech of others may be muted and perceived grievances left to fester because of the possible inhibitory effects of overly broad statutes. Overbreadth attacks have also been allowed where the Court thought rights of association were ensnared in statutes which, by their broad sweep, might result in burdening innocent associations. [See, e.g., Robel; Aptheker.]

"[The] consequence of our departure from traditional rules of standing in the First Amendment area is that any enforcement of a statute thus placed at issue is totally forbidden until and unless a limiting construction or partial invalidation so narrows it as to remove the seeming threat or deterrence to constitutionally protected expression. Application of the overbreadth doctrine in this manner is, manifestly, strong medicine. It has been employed by the Court sparingly and only as a last resort. Facial overbreadth has not been invoked when a limiting construction has been or could be placed on the challenged statute. See [e.g., Cox v. New Hampshire]. Equally important, overbreadth claims, if entertained at all, have been curtailed when invoked against ordinary criminal laws that are sought to be applied to protected conduct.

"It remains a 'matter of no little difficulty' to determine when a law may properly be held void on its face and when 'such summary action' is inappropriate. [But] the plain import of our cases is, at the very least, that facial overbreadth adjudication is an exception to our traditional rules of practice and that its function, a limited one at the outset, attenuates as the otherwise unprotected behavior that it forbids the State to sanction moves from 'pure speech' towards conduct and that conduct—even if expressive—falls within the scope of otherwise valid criminal [laws]. Although such laws, if too broadly worded, may deter protected speech to some unknown extent, there comes a point where that effect—at best a prediction—cannot, with confidence, justify invalidating a statute on its face and so prohibiting a State from enforcing the statute against conduct that is admittedly within its power to proscribe. [To] put the matter another way, particularly where conduct and not merely speech is involved, we believe that the overbreadth of a statute must not only be real, but substantial as well, judged in relation to the statute's plainly legitimate sweep. It is our view that § 818 is not substantially overbroad and that whatever overbreadth may exist should be cured through case-by-case analysis of the fact situations to which its sanctions, assertedly, may not be applied.

"Unlike ordinary breach-of-the-peace statutes or other broad regulatory acts, § 818 is directed, by its terms, at political expression which if engaged in by private persons would plainly be protected by the [First Amendment]. But at the same time, § 818 is not a censorial statute, directed at particular groups or viewpoints. The statute, rather, seeks to regulate political activity in an even-handed and neutral manner. As indicated, such statutes have in the past been subject to a less exacting overbreadth scrutiny. Moreover, the fact remains that § 818 regulates a substantial spectrum of conduct that is as manifestly subject to state regulation as the public peace or criminal trespass. Without question, the conduct appellants have been charged with falls squarely within those proscriptions. Appellants assert that § 818 goes much farther. [They point to] interpretive rules purporting to restrict such allegedly protected activities as the wearing of political buttons or the use of bumper stickers. It may be that such restrictions are impermissible and that § 818 may be susceptible of some other improper applications. But, as presently construed, we do not believe that § 818 must be discarded in toto because some persons' arguably protected conduct may or may not be caught or chilled by the statute. Section 818 is not substantially overbroad and is not, therefore, unconstitutional on its face."

The major dissent was by Justice BRENNAN, joined by Justices Stewart and Marshall. (Justice Douglas dissented separately.) Justice Brennan thought the decision a "wholly unjustified retreat from fundamental and previously well-established" principles. The majority had conceded the possibility of some "improper applications", and "that assumption requires a finding that the statute is unconstitutional on its face."

Justice Brennan objected to the majority's "substantial overbreadth" approach: "In the first place, the Court makes no effort to define what it means by 'substantial overbreadth.' We have never held that a statute should be held invalid on its face merely because it is possible to conceive of a single impermissible application, and in that sense a requirement of substantial overbreadth is already implicit in the doctrine. [Whether] the Court means to require some different or greater showing of substantiality is left obscure by today's opinion, in large part because the Court makes no effort to explain why the overbreadth of the Oklahoma Act, while real, is somehow not quite substantial. [More] fundamentally, the Court offers no rationale to explain its conclusion that, for purposes of overbreadth analysis, deterrence of conduct should be viewed differently from deterrence of speech, even where both are equally protected by the [First Amendment]. At this stage, it is obviously difficult to estimate the probable impact of today's decision. If the requirement of 'substantial' overbreadth is construed to mean only that facial review is inappropriate where the likelihood of an impermissible application of the statute is too small to generate a 'chilling effect' on protected speech or conduct, then the impact is likely to be small. On the other hand, if today's decision necessitates the drawing of artificial distinctions between protected speech and protected conduct, and if the 'chill' on protected conduct is rarely, if ever, found sufficient to require the facial invalidation of an overbroad statute, then the effect could be very grave indeed."

What is the definition of "substantial" overbreadth? How great a ratio of protected to unprotected speech must be covered to qualify? In City Council v. Taxpayers for Vincent (1984; p. 1249 above), Justice Stevens' majority opinion stated: "The concept of 'substantial overbreadth' is not readily reduced to an exact definition. It is clear, however, that the mere fact that one can conceive of some impermissible applications of a statute is not sufficient to render it susceptible to an overbreadth challenge. On the contrary, [there] must be a realistic danger that the statute itself will significantly compromise recognized First Amendment protections of parties not before the Court for it to be facially challenged on overbreadth grounds." For discussion, see Fallon, "Making Sense of Overbreadth," 100 Yale L.J. 853 (1991).

Applying Broadrick, the Court found no substantial overbreadth in the New York child pornography law at issue in NEW YORK v. FERBER (1982; p. 1145 above). The claim there was that the New York law was "unconstitutionally overbroad because it would forbid the distribution of material with serious literary, scientific or educational value or material which does not threaten the harms sought to be combatted by the State." Justice WHITE wrote for the Court: "We consider this the paradigmatic case of a state statute whose legitimate reach dwarfs its arguably impermissible applications. [While] the reach of the statute is directed at the hard core of child pornography, the [highest New York court] was understandably concerned that some protected expression, ranging from medical textbooks to pictorials in National Geographic, would fall prey to the statute. How often, if ever, it may be necessary to employ children to engage in conduct clearly within the reach of the [law] in order to produce educational, medical or artistic works cannot be known with certainty. Yet we seriously doubt [that] these arguably impermissible applications of the statute amount to more than a tiny fraction of the materials within the statute's reach. [Under] these circumstances, [the law] is 'not substantially overbroad and whatever overbreadth exists should be cured through case-by-case analysis of the fact situations to which its sanctions, assertedly, may not be applied.' [Broadrick.]"

In an opinion concurring in the judgment, Justice STEVENS objected to the majority's quantitative approach. He stated: "My reasons for avoiding overbreadth analysis in this case are more qualitative than quantitative. When we follow our traditional practice of adjudicating difficult and novel constitutional questions only in concrete factual situations, the adjudications tend to be crafted with greater wisdom. Hypothetical rulings are inherently treacherous and prone to lead us into unforeseen errors; they are qualitatively less reliable than the products of case-by-case adjudication. [Moreover,] generally marginal speech does not warrant the extraordinary protection afforded by the overbreadth doctrine."

5. *Limits on overbreadth analysis: requiring that a statute be incapable of a narrowing construction.* In BROCKETT v. SPOKANE ARCADES, INC., 472 U.S. 491 (1985), the Court held that appeals to the "prurient interest" under the Miller test for obscenity did not encompass "material that provoked only normal, healthy social desires," but was limited to materials appealing to a "shameful or morbid interest" in sex. It thus held a Washington obscenity law unconstitutional because it defined "prurient interest" as "that which incites lasciviousness or lust," a definition broad enough to encompass "normal" as well as "shameful" sexual responses. But despite this apparent overbreadth finding, the Court declined to permit an individual whose own rights were violated under the statute to invalidate the law on its face, limiting the challenger to an "as applied" challenge. Justice WHITE, writing for a 6–2 majority, explained: "[An] individual whose own speech [may] validly be prohibited [is] permitted to challenge a statute on its face because it also threatens others not before the court. [But where, as here,] the parties challenging the statute are those who desire to engage in protected speech that the overbroad statute purports to punish, [there is] no want of a proper party to challenge the [law and it] may forthwith be declared invalid to the extent it reaches too far, but otherwise left intact." Justice Brennan, joined by Justice Marshall, dissented, insisting that the law was "substantially overbroad and therefore invalid on its face."

When is such partial validation appropriate? In Brockett, the United States Supreme Court could not issue a narrowing construction of the state statute; only the state courts could. But the Court in effect decided that a narrowing construction was readily available to the state courts, as the improper portion of the obscenity definition was easily severable from the rest. Its invalidation of the law as applied in effect cued the state courts as to how to rewrite the law. On the relationship between overbreadth and severability, see Dorf, "Facial Challenges to State and Federal Statutes," 46 Stan. L. Rev. 235 (1994).

In Brockett, the state's otherwise constitutional obscenity statute could be "trimmed of unconstitutional branches," but the Court continues to employ facial invalidation when a statute is "rotten at its very root." Tribe, American Constitutional Law 1029 (2d ed. 1988). For example, the Court has invalidated facially several laws designed to limit charitable solicitation to organizations with low overhead expenses. The 8–1 decision in SCHAUMBURG v. CITIZENS FOR BETTER ENVIRONMENT, 444 U.S. 620 (1980), struck down as overbroad an ordinance barring door-to-door and on-street solicitations of contributions by charitable organizations that did not use at least 75% of their receipts for "charitable purposes." "Charitable purposes" were defined to exclude solicitation expenses. Because of that 75% rule, Citizens for a Better Environment (CBE), an environmental group, was denied permission to solicit contributions in Schaumburg, a suburb of Chicago. CBE challenged the law as a violation of free speech protections.

Justice WHITE's majority opinion found that CBE was entitled to a "judgment of facial invalidity if the ordinance purported to prohibit canvassing by a substantial category of charities to which the 75–percent limitation could not be applied consistently with the [First Amendment], even if there was no demonstration that CBE itself was one of these organizations." The organizations to whom the 75% rule could not be applied were found to be those whose "primary purpose is not to provide money or services for the poor, the needy or other worthy objects of charity, but to gather and disseminate information about and advocate positions on matters of public concern." Typically, these organizations use paid employees not only to solicit funds but also to gather information and advocate positions and thus "would necessarily spend more than 25% of their budgets on salaries and administrative expenses [but] would be completely barred from solicitation in [Schaumburg]." As to such organizations, the ordinance constituted "a direct and substantial limitation of protected activity that cannot be sustained unless it serves a sufficiently strong, subordinating interest that the Village is entitled to protect." Here, Justice White concluded, "the Village's proffered justifications are inadequate."

The Court found that the asserted interests "in protecting the public from fraud, crime and undue annoyance" were "indeed substantial," but were "only peripherally promoted by the 75–percent requirement and could be sufficiently served by measures less destructive of First Amendment interests." With respect to the prevention of fraud, the Court found the 75% rule not a justifiable device for distinguishing charitable from commercial enterprises: organizations primarily engaged in research, advocacy or publication that use their own paid staffs to carry out these functions could not be labeled as presumptively "fraudulent" or as using the "charitable" label as a cloak for profit making. Under the First Amendment, Schaumburg had to employ more precise measures to separate genuine charitable organizations from profitmaking ones—e.g., by prohibiting fraudulent misrepresentations or by requiring financial disclosures. Nor was the Court able to "perceive any substantial relationship" between the 75% rule and the interests in the protection of safety and residential privacy. Organizations devoting more than 25% of their funds to administrative expenses were no more likely "to employ solicitors who would be a threat to public safety than are other charitable organizations." And "householders are equally disturbed by solicitation on behalf of organizations satisfying the 75–percent requirement as they are by solicitation on behalf of other organizations. The 75–percent requirement protects privacy only by reducing the total number of solicitors." Moreover, "[other] provisions of the ordinance, [such as those] permitting homeowners to bar solicitors from their property by posting signs, [suggest] the availability of less intrusive and more effective measures to protect privacy. See [Rowan; Martin]."

In short, the flaw in the statute in Schaumburg was "not simply that it includes within its sweep some impermissible applications, but that in all its applications it operates on a fundamentally mistaken premise that high solicitation costs are an accurate measure of fraud." There was no obvious way for such a statute to be narrowed to a "core of easily identifiable and constitutionally proscribable conduct." In the absence of any conceivable available narrowing construction, facial invalidation was the chosen remedy. In this setting, unlike Brockett, partial invalidation was not an available option.

In SECRETARY OF STATE v. JOSEPH H. MUNSON CO., 467 U.S. 947 (1984), the Court extended Schaumburg to strike down a similar restriction on charitable solicitations despite its provision for a waiver if a charitable organization could demonstrate that the overhead limit "would effectively prevent [it] from raising contributions." The law was challenged by a professional fundraiser who claimed primarily the First Amendment rights of his customers, who were not parties to the action. But the Court, in an opinion by Justice BLACKMUN, found these factors insufficient to distinguish Schaumburg, as the possibility of gaining an exemption was inadequate to prevent the inhibition of protected solicitation.[1]

In Munson, Justice Blackmun distinguished the claim at issue from the type of overbreadth claim in which the challenger's own conduct is unprotected, but the challenge is permitted in order to protect the First Amendment rights of third parties not before the Court. In Schaumburg, he suggested, the term " 'overbreadth' [was] used to describe a challenge to a statute that in *all its applications* directly restricts protected First Amendment activity and does not employ means narrowly tailored to serve a compelling governmental interest (emphasis added)."

Is the latter type of case truly an "overbreadth" case? In Justice Blackmun's interpretation of Schaumburg in Munson, the overhead limit was void "in all its applications" because it drew the wrong sort of line—it used high overhead as a proxy for fraud when such a financial structure might have indicated instead the organization's devotion to education and advocacy. Thus there was no issue whether the overbreadth was substantial or insubstantial in Broadrick's terms; the ratio of impermissible to permissible applications was infinite. Are Schaumburg and Munson simply determinations on the merits that the law amounted to impermissible speaker-based discrimination with content-differential effects? See Monaghan, supra (arguing that "overbreadth determinations are simply determinations on the merits of the litigant's substantive constitutional claim"). Recall that the Court frequently invalidates speech-restrictive statutes on their face without any consideration of their overbreadth. See, e.g., Justice Scalia's majority opinion, as opposed to Justice White's concurrence, in R.A.V. v. St. Paul above. Is overbreadth analysis better reserved for laws that have some constitutional applications?

6. *Overbreadth and due process.* What is the effect of a narrowing change in the challenged state law after an overbreadth lawsuit is brought? Ordinarily, an authoritative narrowing construction of an overbroad statute can blunt the effectiveness of an overbreadth attack. The effect of subsequent changes in state law came before the Court in two cases, in 1989 and 1990. The net result of the cases was that a legislative change after the lawsuit was brought could not eliminate an overbreadth challenge, but a *judicial* narrowing of an otherwise overbroad law was effective to eliminate the overbreadth concern.

In MASSACHUSETTS v. OAKES, 491 U.S. 576 (1989), a law that prohibited the taking of nude and similar photographs of those under the age of 18 was challenged by a man who had been convicted for taking "sexually provocative" photographs of "his partially nude and physically mature 14–year–old stepdaughter." After the highest state court had struck down the law as substan-

---

1. For the most recent in the Schaumburg line of cases, see Riley v. National Federation of the Blind, 487 U.S. 781 (1988), striking down a range of licensing, disclosure, and presumptive fee limitations on professional fundraisers. Justice Brennan's prevailing opinion found this regulatory scheme insufficiently different from those at issue in Schaumburg and Munson to survive First Amendment scrutiny. Justices Scalia and Stevens concurred in part; Chief Justice Rehnquist, joined by Justice O'Connor, dissented.

tially overbroad, the legislature amended the law to add a "lascivious intent" requirement. As a result, four Justices (Justice O'Connor, joined by Chief Justice Rehnquist and Justices White and Kennedy) refused to reach the overbreadth challenge, insisting that the overbreadth doctrine did not apply to laws no longer in force: "Because it has been repealed, the former version of [the law] cannot chill protected expression in the future." A majority, however, disagreed: Justice SCALIA, joined on this issue by Justices Blackmun, Brennan, Marshall and Stevens, rejected the argument that an amendment could foreclose an overbreadth challenge. He explained: "It seems to me strange judicial theory that a conviction initially invalid can be resuscitated by postconviction alteration of the statute under which it was obtained. The overbreadth doctrine serves to protect constitutionally legitimate speech not merely ex post, but also ex ante, that is, when the legislature is contemplating what sort of statute to enact. If the promulgation of overbroad laws was cost free, as the plurality's new doctrine would make it—that is, if no conviction of constitutionally proscribable conduct would be lost, so long as the offending statute was narrowed before the final appeal—then legislatures would have significantly reduced incentive to stay within constitutional bounds in the first place. [In consequence,] a substantial amount of legitimate speech would be 'chilled' as a consequence of the rule the plurality would adopt." (However, Justice Scalia, joined by Justice Blackmun, found the law not substantially overbroad; only Justice Brennan, joined by Justices Marshall and Stevens, would have struck it down on overbreadth grounds.)

In OSBORNE v. OHIO, 495 U.S. 103 (1990), another child pornography case, Justice WHITE's majority opinion found that a *judicial* narrowing of an otherwise overbroad law *did* end the overbreadth concern. He explained: "Legislators who know they can cure their own mistakes by amendment without significant cost may not be as careful to avoid drafting overbroad statutes as they might otherwise be. But a similar effect will not be likely if a judicial construction of a statute to eliminate overbreadth is allowed to be applied in the case before the Court. This is so primarily because the legislatures cannot be sure that the statute, when examined by a court, will be saved by a narrowing construction rather than invalidated for overbreadth." Accordingly, the statute as construed could be applied "to conduct occurring prior to the construction, provided such application affords fair warning for the defendant." Here, the Court found such "fair warning" yet nevertheless held the conviction violative of due process because the jury had not been instructed in accordance with the highest state court's subsequent narrowing construction. Do the differing results in these two cases make sense?

7. *The Court's continued reliance on overbreadth invalidation.* Two 1987 cases illustrated not only that overbreadth analysis has clearly survived Broadrick, but that overbreadth can be a useful technique for fashioning some agreement among Justices who would otherwise disagree about the First Amendment protection of the particular conduct involved in a case. By relying on overbreadth, potential applications of the law that most Justices would agree would be unconstitutional provide a way of turning a hard case on the facts into one that, as decided, seems substantially easier. In HOUSTON v. HILL, 482 U.S. 451 (1987), for example, overbreadth analysis enabled the Court to achieve some degree of agreement where the particular facts were substantially more problematic under the First Amendment than was the statute involved. The case arose from an incident in which Hill, a founding member of the Gay Political Caucus, observed a friend intentionally stopping traffic on a busy street, evidently to enable a vehicle to enter traffic. Two Houston police officers, one of them named Kelley, approached the friend and

began speaking with him. Soon after, Hill began shouting to the officers "in an admitted attempt to divert Kelley's attention from [the friend]. Hill first shouted 'why don't you pick on somebody your own size?' After [Officer Kelley] responded '[A]re you interrupting me in my official capacity of a Houston police officer?' Hill then shouted 'Yes, why don't you pick on somebody my size?'" Hill was arrested under a section of the municipal code for "wilfully or intentionally interrupt[ing] a city policeman [by] verbal challenge during an investigation." After Hill was acquitted in a local court, he brought suit to challenge the law, under which he had been arrested several times and which he was likely to encounter again. The text of the section provided that it was "unlawful for any person to assault, strike or in any manner oppose, molest, abuse or interrupt any policeman in the execution of his duty, or any person summoned to aid in making the arrest."

Justice BRENNAN's majority opinion found the provision overbroad under the Broadrick line of cases. Noting that the provisions dealing with assaulting and striking had been preempted by state law, he found that "the enforceable portion of the ordinance deals not with core criminal conduct, but with speech." He stated that the freedom "verbally to oppose or challenge police action without thereby risking arrest is one of the principal characteristics by which we distinguish a free nation from a police state" and found the ordinance "not narrowly tailored to prohibit only disorderly conduct or fighting words." He added: "Although we appreciate the difficulties of drafting precise laws, we have repeatedly invalidated laws that provide the police with unfettered discretion to arrest individuals for words or conduct that annoy or offend them." He noted, too, that the ordinance was "much more sweeping than [that] struck down in Lewis v. New Orleans [1972; p. 1079 above]." He concluded: "The Constitution does not allow such speech to be made a crime." A partial concurrence by Justice POWELL, joined by Justices O'Connor and Scalia, agreed with the overbreadth judgment, but not with its reasoning. He insisted that the view "that the ordinance 'deals not with core criminal conduct, but with speech' [draws] a distinction where none exists." He emphasized, moreover, that there was "no doubt that a municipality constitutionally may punish an individual who chooses to stand near a police officer and persistently attempts to engage the officer in conversation while the officer is directing traffic at a busy intersection." Nevertheless, he concluded that, in the absence of an authoritative limiting construction of the ordinance, it vested excessive discretion in police officers to act against protected speech and was thus unconstitutional.

Overbreadth was also the tool for fashioning agreement in BOARD OF AIRPORT COMMISSIONERS v. JEWS FOR JESUS, 482 U.S. 569 (1987), decided on the same day as the Houston case. At issue was the Board's resolution providing that "if any individual and/or entity seeks to engage in First Amendment activities within the Central Terminal Area at Los Angeles International Airport, said individual and/or entity shall be deemed to be acting in contravention of the stated policy" of the Board. Respondents, who were prevented from distributing religious literature on a pedestrian walkway in the airport, brought an action challenging the resolution. Justice O'CONNOR's opinion relied exclusively on the spectacular overbreadth of the resolution and thus was able to avoid the difficult issues of the constitutionally protected nature of the respondents' behavior and of the then-unsettled "public forum status" of an airport terminal. Speaking for a unanimous Court, she concluded that the resolution was overbroad and hence facially void: "On its face, the resolution [reaches] the universe of expressive activity [and prohibits] all protected expression." She noted that it reached "even talking and reading, or the wearing of campaign buttons or symbolic clothing. Under such a sweeping ban, virtually every individual who enters [the airport] may be found to violate the resolution by engaging in some 'First Amendment activit[y].' We think it obvious that such a ban cannot be justified [because] no conceivable governmental interest would justify such an absolute prohibition on speech."

8. *"Less restrictive means" analysis and its relation to overbreadth.* Overbreadth cases typically emphasize the availability of more carefully tailored, narrower means to achieve legislative ends. "Less restrictive means" analysis, however, is not limited to the overbreadth context. For example, the strict scrutiny applied to content-based laws requires carefully tailored means to "compelling" ends. Does this suggest that overbreadth is simply one application of strict scrutiny? See Monaghan, supra.

B. VAGUENESS

An "overbreadth" challenge should not be confused with one based on "vagueness," though a challenger will often assert both grounds of invalidity. An unconstitutionally vague statute, like an overbroad one, creates risks of a "chilling effect" upon protected speech and produces rulings of facial invalidity. But a statute can be quite specific—i.e., *not* "vague"—and yet be overbroad. Consider a law forbidding "the display of a nude human body on a motion picture screen." A statute can also be vague but not overbroad. Consider a law forbidding "all unprotected speech."

The concept of vagueness under the First Amendment draws on the procedural due process requirement of adequate notice, under which a law must convey "sufficiently definite warning as to the proscribed conduct when measured by common understanding and practices." Jordan v. DeGeorge, 341 U.S. 223 (1951). A law will be void on its face for vagueness if persons "of common intelligence must necessarily guess at its meaning and differ as to its application." Connally v. General Construction Co. 269 U.S. 385 (1926). One of the purposes of this requirement is to ensure fair notice to the defendant. But the ban on vagueness protects not only liberty, but also equality and the separation of executive from legislative power through the prevention of selective enforcement. See Smith v. Goguen (1974; p. 1220 above): "[We] have recognized [that] the more important aspect of the vagueness doctrine 'is not actual notice, but the other principal element of the doctrine—the requirement that "legislatures [set] reasonably clear guidelines for law enforcement officials and triers of fact in order to prevent arbitrary and discriminatory enforcement." ' " See also Kolender v. Lawson, 461 U.S. 352 (1983) (striking down on vagueness grounds a California law "that requires persons who loiter or wander on the streets to provide a 'credible and reliable' identification and to account for their presence when requested by a peace officer"); Papachristou v. Jacksonville, 405 U.S. 156 (1972) (unanimously invalidating as vague a vagrancy ordinance directed at "rogues and vagabonds, or dissolute persons who go about begging," "common drunkards," "common night walkers," "habitual loafers," and "persons wandering or strolling around from place to place without any lawful purpose or object"). See generally Amsterdam, "The Void-for-Vagueness Doctrine in the Supreme Court," 109 U.Pa.L.Rev. 67 (1960);

Jeffries, "Legality, Vagueness and the Construction of Statutes," 71 Va. L. Rev. 189 (1985).

But a finding of First Amendment vagueness has greater bite than a finding of due process vagueness: Vagueness challenges in the First Amendment context, like overbreadth challenges, typically produce facial invalidations, while statutes found vague as a matter of due process typically are invalidated "as applied" to a particular defendant. Why might this be? Does it follow from a special concern about the "chilling effect" of vague statutes on protected speech? As Justice Powell wrote in Smith v. Goguen, supra, "Where a statute's literal scope, unaided by a narrowing state court interpretation, is capable of reaching expression sheltered by the First Amendment, the [vagueness] doctrine demands a greater degree of specificity than in other contexts." And as the Court stated in Baggett v. Bullitt, 377 U.S. 360 (1964), which invalidated a loyalty oath for teachers, vague statutes cause citizens to " 'steer far wider of the unlawful zone' [than] if the boundaries of the forbidden areas were clearly marked," causing them to "restrict[] their conduct to that which is unquestionably safe. Free speech may not be so inhibited."

For an example of a decision finding a law impermissibly vague under the First Amendment, as well as overbroad, consider COATES v. CINCINNATI, 402 U.S. 611 (1971): An ordinance made it illegal for "three or more persons to assemble [on] any of the sidewalks [and] there conduct themselves in a manner annoying to persons passing by." Justice STEWART's opinion found the ordinance "unconstitutionally vague because it subjects the exercise of the right of assembly to an unascertainable standard, and unconstitutionally broad because it authorizes the punishment of constitutionally protected conduct." On the vagueness point, he stated that the "annoying" criterion meant that "no standard of conduct is specified at all." With respect to overbreadth, he emphasized that the right of assembly could not be restricted "simply because its exercise may be 'annoying' to some people." Such a prohibition "contains an obvious invitation to discriminatory enforcement against those whose association together is 'annoying' because their ideas, their lifestyle or their physical appearance is resented by the majority of their fellow citizens." The majority analyzed the ordinance in Coates "on the face" rather than "as applied." It was able to state all of the facts known to the Court in a portion of a single sentence: the record "tells us no more than that [Coates] was a student involved in a demonstration and the other appellants were pickets involved in a labor dispute." To the four dissenters, that lack of record data was a major factor counseling against a ruling of unconstitutionality. Justice White's dissent argued the law was not vague on its face and added: "Even accepting the overbreadth doctrine with respect to statutes clearly reaching speech, the Cincinnati ordinance does not purport to bar or regulate speech as such."

For an example of a decision rejecting a First Amendment vagueness challenge, recall Grayned v. Rockford (1972; p. 1271 below), where Justice Marshall's opinion found an anti-noise ordinance applicable to places adjacent to school buildings not vague because the state courts were likely to interpret the law "to prohibit only actual or imminent interference with the 'peace or good order' of the school. "Justice Marshall argued that the ordinance was distinguishable from the ordinance in Coates or general breach of the peace ordinances because it was "written specifically for the school context, where the prohibited disturbances are easily measured by their impact on the normal activities of the school."

Does vagueness, like overbreadth, permit a speaker third-party standing to represent the rights of others not before the Court? It is clear that a litigant may invalidate a law on its face if it is vague in all its possible applications. For example, the Court held in Coates that "no standard of conduct is specified at all." Such a statute has no core of proscribable speech to which it might constitutionally be applied. But what if a litigant's own conduct was unquestionably within the core of the statute's permissible application, and he or she seeks to invalidate the law because it might be vague to others? See Smith v. Goguen, supra (White, J., concurring) (arguing that anyone of "reasonable comprehension" should have "realize[d] that sewing a flag on the seat of his pants is contemptuous of the flag"); Young v. American Mini Theatres (1976; p. 1159 above) (rejecting a vagueness challenge because zoning law was "unquestionably applicable" to the challengers' speech and the Court was "not persuaded" that the law would have a significant chilling effect on other protected speakers).

C. PRIOR RESTRAINT

Introduction. The Court has frequently reiterated that prior restraint is especially disfavored under the First Amendment: "Any system of prior restraints of expression comes to this Court bearing a heavy presumption against its constitutional validity." Bantam Books, Inc. v. Sullivan, 372 U.S. 58 (1963). That theme has strong historical roots. As noted above in Chapter 11, the licensing system for English presses against which Milton protested played a central role in the development of free speech theories. Blackstone, indeed, argued that prior restraint was the *only* evil to be guarded against, and that subsequent punishment was permissible; and Holmes initially embraced that idea and abandoned it only grudgingly in Schenck. But the question whether there is contemporary justification for greater suspicion of prior restraint than of subsequent punishment is more controversial. The prior restraint concept, like the overbreadth and vagueness doctrines, focuses on the constitutional *means* of restricting speech. Thus, a prior restraint may be struck down even though the particular expression involved could validly be restricted through subsequent criminal punishment or civil liability. In examining these materials, consider especially whether the special hostility to prior restraint is justified, either as a theoretical or a practical matter.

LICENSING

1. The concern with administrative discretion. What's wrong with licensing? What are the evils of a system that requires preclearance of speech by an official censor? Recall the cases involving standardless licensing of speech in the public forum, noted at p. 1237 above. Those cases found standardless licensing schemes to confer excessive discretion on public officials, creating the risk of selective and content-discriminatory enforcement. Because of concern with the risks of abuse of discretionary authority, laws granting excessive discretion have been invalidated on their face, apart from any showing that, as applied, the discretion was in fact unconstitutionally abused and without any showing by the challenger that specific protected speech was curtailed. The following case provides a classic illustration:

In LOVELL v. GRIFFIN, 303 U.S. 444 (1938), the Court invalidated a conviction under an ordinance of the city of Griffin, Georgia, prohibiting the distribution of "circulars, handbooks, advertising, or literature of any kind" within the city "without first obtaining written permission from the City Manager." Alma Lovell, a Jehovah's Witness, distributed religious tracts without applying for a permit. She challenged her conviction on free press and free exercise of religion grounds. Chief Justice HUGHES' opinion for a unanimous Court, in reversing her conviction, stated: "The ordinance is not limited to 'literature' that is obscene or offensive to public morals or that advocates unlawful conduct. [It] embraces 'literature' in the widest sense. The ordinance is comprehensive with respect to the method of distribution. There is thus no restriction in its application with respect to time or place. It is not limited to ways which might be regarded as inconsistent with the maintenance of public order or as involving disorderly conduct, the molestation of the inhabitants, or the misuse or littering of the streets. The ordinance prohibits the distribution of literature of any kind at any time, at any place, and in any manner without a permit from the City Manager.

"We think that the ordinance is invalid on its face. Whatever the motive which induced its adoption, its character is such that it strikes at the very foundation of the freedom of the press by subjecting it to license and censorship. The struggle for the freedom of the press was primarily directed against the power of the licensor. [The] liberty of the press became initially a right to publish '*without* a license what formerly could be published only *with* one.' While this freedom from previous restraint upon publication cannot be regarded as exhausting the guaranty of liberty, the prevention of that restraint was a leading purpose in the adoption of the [First Amendment]. As the ordinance is void on its face, it was not necessary for appellant to seek a permit under it. She was entitled to contest its validity in answer to the charge against [her]."

The reasons for *facially* invalidating licensing laws that grant excessive administrative discretion, as opposed to allowing licensees to challenge abuses of discretion case by case, were elaborated in the 4–3 decision (Chief Justice Rehnquist and Justice Kennedy did not participate) in LAKEWOOD v. PLAIN DEALER PUBLISHING CO., 486 U.S. 750 (1988). At issue was a local ordinance restricting the placement of newspaper vending racks on public property. Newsracks could be placed on public property only upon an application for and receipt of an annual permit that could be denied for a number of specified reasons including "other terms and conditions deemed necessary and reasonable by the Mayor." Justice BRENNAN's opinion for the Court allowed a facial challenge to the ordinance: "[W]e have [identified] two major First Amendment risks associated with unbridled licensing schemes: self-censorship by speakers in order to avoid being denied a license to speak; and the difficulty of effectively detecting, reviewing, and correcting content-based censorship 'as applied' without standards by which to measure the licensor's action. It is when statutes threaten these risks to a significant degree that courts must entertain an immediate facial attack on the law. Therefore, a facial challenge lies whenever a licensing law gives a government official or agency substantial power to discriminate based on the content or viewpoint of speech by suppressing disfavored speech or disliked speakers."

The Court went on to find these criteria for facial challenges satisfied here: "[The City's scheme is] the sort of system in which an individual must apply for multiple licenses over time, or periodically renew a license. [In addition,] the licensing system [is directed] narrowly and specifically at expression or conduct commonly associated with expression: the circulation of newspapers. Such a framework [establishes] an official charged particularly with reviewing speech, or conduct commonly associated with it, breeding an 'expertise' tending to favor censorship over speech. [Because] of these features in the regulatory system [here], we think that a facial challenge is appropriate, and that standards controlling the Mayor's discretion must be required. Of course, the City may require periodic licensing, and may even have special licensing procedures for conduct commonly associated with expression; but the Constitution requires that [it] establish neutral criteria to insure that the licensing decision is not based on the content or viewpoint of the speech being considered. In contrast to the type of law [here], laws of general application that are not aimed at conduct commonly associated with [expression] carry with them little danger of censorship. For example, a law requiring building permits is rarely effective as a means of censorship. [Such] laws provide too blunt a censorship instrument to warrant judicial intervention prior to an allegation of actual misuse.''

Having decided to entertain the facial challenge, the Court had little difficulty in holding the standardless ordinance unconstitutional: "The City asks us to presume that the Mayor will deny a permit application only for reasons related to the health, safety, or welfare of Lakewood [citizens]. This presumes the Mayor will act in good faith and adhere to standards absent from the statute's face. But this is the very presumption that the doctrine forbidding unbridled discretion disallows. The doctrine requires that the limits that the City claims are implicit in its law be made explicit by textual incorporation, binding judicial or administrative construction, or well-established practice. This Court will not write nonbinding limits into a silent state statute.''

Justice WHITE, joined by Justices Stevens and O'Connor, dissented. He viewed facial challenges as the exception and not the rule, and an exception that in past cases had been allowed only in those circumstances in which the relevant conduct could not have been prohibited entirely. But where there is no such absolute right to engage in the relevant conduct, he argued, a scheme allowing that conduct under some circumstances but not others should be actionable only if and when it is actually applied in an unconstitutional manner: "[T]he [Lovell] lines of cases would be applicable here if the [City] sought to license the distribution of all newspapers in the City, or if it required licenses for all stores which sold newspapers. These are obviously newspaper circulation activities which a municipality cannot prohibit and therefore, any licensing scheme of this scope would have to pass muster under the [Lovell] doctrine. But—and this is critical—Lakewood has not cast so wide a net. Instead, it has sought to license only the placement of newsracks [on] City property. As I read our precedents, the [Lovell] line of cases is applicable here only if the Plain Dealer has a constitutional right to distribute its papers by means of dispensing devices or newsboxes, affixed to the public sidewalks. I am not convinced that this is the case. [Where] an activity that could be forbidden altogether (without running afoul of the First Amendment) is subjected to a local license requirement, the mere presence of administrative discretion in the licensing scheme will not render it invalid per se. In such a case—which does not involve the exercise of First Amendment protected freedoms—the [Lovell] doctrine does not apply, and our usual rules concerning the permissibility of discretionary local licensing laws (and facial challenges to those laws) must prevail. [The] Court mentions the risk of censorship, the ever-present danger of censorship, and the power of prior restraint to justify the result. Yet these fears and concerns have little to do with this case, which involves the efforts of Ohio's largest newspaper to place a handful of newsboxes in a few locations in a small suburban community. [It] is hard to see how the Court's concerns have any applicability here.''

2. *Procedural safeguards.* The flaws of a licensing scheme may be correct ed as a substantive matter by the provision of objective standards for the licensor to administer. See Cox v.New Hampshire (1941; p. 1238 above). Should procedural safeguards also be required to check abuses of administrative discretion? Some decades ago, the Court's special suspicion of excessive discretion by administrators had especially frequent airings in the context of motion picture licensing, under censorship schemes then widely in use. Beginning with Joseph Burstyn, Inc. v. Wilson, 343 U.S. 495 (1952), the Court scrutinized the statutory standards in film licensing schemes with special care, to avoid abuse of administrative discretion. The Court declined to impose a ban on all prior restraints of films, see Times Film Corp. v. Chicago, 365 U.S. 43 (1961), but repeatedly invalidated particular laws because they lacked adequate specificity, see, e.g., Burstyn (invalidating a ban on a movie as "sacrilegious"). But in the Freedman case in 1965, the Court announced "procedural safeguards designed to obviate the dangers of a censorship system"—safeguards which have proven important in the protection of First Amendment interests in contexts well beyond the obscenity area.

FREEDMAN v. MARYLAND, 380 U.S. 51 (1965), was a successful constitutional attack on the procedural aspects of a Maryland motion picture censorship law. The challenger exhibited a movie without first submitting the picture to the state censorship board. He was convicted for failure to submit the film for licensing (even though the State conceded that the movie would have been licensed if it had been properly submitted). He argued that the censorship scheme was an invalid prior restraint. He focused particularly on the procedure for an initial decision by the censorship board which, without any judicial participation, effectively barred exhibition of any disapproved film unless and until the exhibitor undertook a time-consuming appeal to the state courts in order to get the censorship agency's decision reversed. The statute did not impose a time limit for completion of judicial review. The Court, in an opinion by Justice BRENNAN, found the statutory procedure, especially its long time delays for the review process, unconstitutional. Noting that "[risk] of delay is built into the Maryland procedure," Justice Brennan stressed the "heavy presumption" against the validity of prior restraints, noted that a state "is not free to adopt whatever procedures it pleases for dealing with obscenity [without] regard to the possible consequences for constitutionally protected speech," and added: "The administration of a censorship system for motion pictures presents peculiar dangers to constitutionally protected speech. Unlike a prosecution for obscenity, a censorship proceeding puts the initial burden on the exhibitor or distributor. Because the censor's business is to censor, there inheres the danger that he may well be less responsive than a court [to] the constitutionally protected interests in free expression. And if it is made unduly onerous, by reason of delay or otherwise, to seek judicial review, the censor's determination may in practice be final."

The Court proceeded to identify several constitutionally mandated safeguards: "[W]e hold that a noncriminal process which requires the prior submission of a film to a censor avoids constitutional infirmity only if it takes place under procedural safeguards designed to obviate the dangers of a censorship system. First, the burden of proving that the film is unprotected expression must rest on the censor. As we said in Speiser v. Randall, 'Where the transcendent value of speech is involved, due process certainly requires [that] the State bear the burden of persuasion to show that the appellants engaged in criminal speech.' Second, while the State may require advance submission of all films, in order to proceed effectively to bar all showings of unprotected films, the requirement cannot be administered in a manner which would lend an effect of finality to the censor's determination whether a film constitutes protected expression. [Because] only a judicial determination in an adversary proceeding ensures the necessary sensitivity to freedom of expression, only a procedure requiring a judicial determination suffices to impose a valid final restraint. To this end, the exhibitor must be assured [that] the censor will, within a specified brief period, either issue a license or go to court to restrain showing the film. Any restraint imposed in advance of a final judicial determination on the merits must similarly be limited to preservation of the status quo for the shortest fixed period compatible with sound judicial resolution. Moreover, we are well aware that, even after expiration of a temporary restraint, an administrative refusal to license [may] have a discouraging effect on the exhibitor. Therefore, the procedure must also assure a prompt final judicial decision, to minimize the deterrent effect of an interim and possibly erroneous denial of a license. It is readily apparent that the Maryland procedural scheme does not satisfy these criteria [and it therefore constitutes] an invalid previous restraint." A concurring statement by Justice DOUGLAS, joined by Justice Black, stated: "I do not believe any form of censorship—no matter how speedy or prolonged it may be—is permissible."

The Freedman standards were relied on in Justice O'Connor's plurality opinion in FW/PBS, INC. v. DALLAS, 493 U.S. 215 (1990). The case held that an ordinance requiring the licensing of sexually oriented businesses was an unconstitutional prior restraint in violation of Freedman because there was no "effective limitation on the time within which the licensor's decision must be made" and because the ordinance failed to provide "an avenue for a prompt judicial review." But Justice O'Connor also held that Freedman's requirement that the licensor bear the burden of going to court and the burden of proof was inapplicable where there was no "direct censorship of particular expressive material." Since the licensing board evaluated the business and not each film or book, it was not "passing judgment on the content of any protected speech" and thus a truncated version of the Freedman requirements was sufficient. Justice White (joined by Chief Justice Rehnquist) and Justice Scalia would have upheld the scheme without applying any of the Freedman requirements.

On special procedural safeguards in the First Amendment context generally, see Monaghan, "First Amendment 'Due Process,' "83 Harv.L.Rev. 518 (1970); Bogen, "First Amendment Ancillary Doctrines," 37 Md.L.Rev. 679 (1978).

3. *Standing to challenge licensing schemes.* The Court allowed both Lovell and Freedman to challenge the licensing scheme at issue on its face, without their having applied for and been refused a license. As the Court explained in Lovell: "As the ordinance is void on its face, it was not necessary for appellant to seek a permit under it. She was entitled to contest its validity in answer to the charge against [her]." See also Shuttlesworth v. Birmingham, 394 U.S. 147 (1969) (invalidating on its face, as conferring "virtually unbridled and absolute power," a parade permit ordinance authorizing the city commission to deny a permit if "in its judgment the public welfare, peace, safety, health, decency, good order, morals, or convenience require" as much, at the behest of a civil rights marcher who had not sought or obtained a permit).

Thus speakers need not challenge the denial of permission in advance—or even to seek permission—where the claim is that the law is unconstitutional *on its face.* But if the challenge is that a valid permit law is unconstitutionally *applied*, the challengers may not go ahead and hold their meeting or parade if they want to preserve their constitutional defenses. In POULOS v. NEW HAMPSHIRE, 345 U.S. 395 (1953), for example, a conviction for holding a meeting in a park without a required permit was sustained without considering the argument that the denial had been arbitrary, because the speakers had not gone to court to challenge the denial of the permission. In Poulos, unlike Lovell, the law requiring a permit was valid on its face; it was the administrative denial of the permit that was claimed to be unconstitutional. Justice REED was unpersuaded by the defendant's objection that "his right to preach may be postponed until a case, possibly after years, reaches this Court for final adjudication of constitutional rights": "Delay is unfortunate, but the expense and annoyance of litigation is a price citizens must pay for life in an orderly society where the rights of the First Amendment have a real and abiding meaning." Has such delay been curtailed as a result of the "careful procedural provisions"—including time requirements—required by Freedman?

4. *Does the prior restraint-subsequent punishment distinction make sense?* What reason is there for special hostility to prior restraint as distinguished from subsequent punishment? Consider the following arguments that prior restraints are worse than subsequent punishments: (1) It is easier for an official to restrict speech "by a simple stroke of the pen" than by the more cumbersome apparatus of subsequent punishment and thus prior restraint is likely to restrict more speech. (2) Censors will have an professional bias in favor of censorship, and thus will systematically overvalue government interests and undervalue speech. (3) Censors operate more informally than judges and so afford less procedural safeguards to speakers. (4) Speech suppressed in advance never reaches the marketplace of ideas at all. (5) When speech is suppressed in advance, there is no empirical evidence from which to measure its alleged likely harms; subsequent punishment will thus afford more protection to speech whose bark is worse than its bite. See Emerson, "The Doctrine of Prior Restraint," 20 Law & Contemp. Probs. 648 (1955).

Some of these asserted justifications go to the timing of the restraint. Are such justifications coherent? Doesn't the threat of subsequent punishment, if it is effective, have an equally deterrent effect on speech? Consider the following comment: "The doctrine of prior restraint focuses on the largely irrelevant *timing* of the restraint, to the detriment of attention to those flaws that are the actual source of the objection. It is the identity and discretion of the restrainers and not the timing of the restraint that is important." Schauer, Free Speech: A Philosophical Enquiry 152 (1982). Other justifications above concern the institutional features of administrative licensing schemes. Are such problems cured by the substantive safeguards of objective standards and the procedural safeguards of Freedman? Do they exist at all when the prior restraint is issued not by an executive official but by a judge? Consider the following comment: the only legitimate basis for hostility to interim prior restraints is that "they authorize abridgment of expression prior to a full and fair determination of the constitutionally protected nature of the expression by an independent judicial forum." Redish "The Proper Role of the Prior Restraint Doctrine in First Amendment Theory," 70 Va.L.Rev. 53 (1984).

In KINGSLEY BOOKS, INC. v. BROWN, 354 U.S. 436 (1957), the Court itself suggested that prior restraints—at least in a scheme with clear standards and speedy judicial hearings—are *not* inevitably more harmful to speech than subsequent punishments. That 5–4 decision sustained a New York procedure, § 22–a, which authorized an injunction to prevent the sale and distribution of allegedly obscene printed matter pending an expedited trial. Kingsley consented to an injunction pendente lite and, after trial, his books were found obscene, their further distribution was enjoined, and they were ordered destroyed. Kingsley did not challenge the finding of obscenity, but objected to the injunction as a prior restraint. In sustaining the procedure, Justice FRANK-FURTER's opinion stated:

"The phrase 'prior restraint' is not a self-wielding sword. Nor can it serve as a talismanic test. [One] would be bold to assert that the in terrorem effect of [criminal sanctions] less restrains booksellers in the period before the law strikes than does § 22–a. Instead of requiring the bookseller to dread that the offer for sale of a book may, without prior warning, subject him to a criminal prosecution, [the] civil procedure assures him that such consequences cannot follow unless he ignores a court order specifically directed to him for a prompt and carefully circumscribed determination of the issue of obscenity. Until then, he may keep the book for sale and sell it on his own judgment rather than steer 'nervously among the treacherous shoals.'

"[Criminal] enforcement and the proceeding under § 22–a interfere with a book's solicitation of the public precisely at the same stage. In each situation the law moves after publication; the book need not in either case have yet passed into the hands of the public. [In] each case the bookseller is put on notice by the complaint that sale of the publication charged with obscenity in the period before trial may subject him to penal consequences. In the one case he may suffer fine and imprisonment for violation of the criminal statute, in the other, for disobedience of the temporary injunction. The bookseller may of course stand his ground and confidently believe that in any judicial proceeding the book could not be condemned as obscene, but both modes of procedure provide an effective deterrent against distribution prior to adjudication of the book's content—the threat of subsequent penalization."

For further commentary on the distinction between prior restraints and subsequent punishments, see Blasi, "Prior Restraints on Demonstrations," 68 Mich.L.Rev. 1481 (1970); Barnett, "The Puzzle of Prior Restraint," 29 Stan. L.Rev. 539 (1977); Fiss, The Civil Rights Injunction (1978); Blasi, "Toward a Theory of Prior Restraint: The Central Linkage," 66 Minn.L.Rev. 11 (1981); Mayton, "Toward a Theory of First Amendment Process: Injunctions of Speech, Subsequent Punishment, and the Costs of the Prior Restraint Doctrine," 67 Cornell L.Rev. 245 (1982); Jeffries, "Rethinking Prior Restraint," 92 Yale L.J. 409 (1983); and Scordato, "Distinction Without a Difference: A Reappraisal of the Doctrine of Prior Restraint," 68 N.C.L.Rev. 1 (1989).

INJUNCTIONS

Near v. Minnesota

283 U.S. 697, 51 S.Ct. 625, 75 L.Ed. 1357 (1931).

Chief Justice HUGHES delivered the opinion of the [Court].

[A Minnesota law authorized abatement, as a public nuisance, of a "malicious, scandalous and defamatory newspaper, or other periodical." Pursuant to that law, a local prosecutor sought to abate publication of "The Saturday Press." The Press had published articles charging in substance "that a Jewish gangster was in control of gambling, bootlegging and racketeering in Minneapolis, and that law enforcing officers and agencies were not energetically performing their duties." The Press especially targeted the chief of police, who was charged with several loosely-defined offenses, e.g., "illicit relations with gangsters [and] participation in graft." A state court order "abated" the Press and perpetually enjoined the defendants from publishing or circulating "any publication whatsoever which is a malicious, scandalous or defamatory newspaper." In setting aside this state injunction, the Court noted that the law was "unusual if not unique," reminded that "the liberty of the press, and of speech," was protected by the 14th Amendment, and stated:]

[The] object of the statute is not punishment, in the ordinary sense, but suppression of the offending newspaper. [The] reason for the enactment [is] that prosecutions to enforce penal statutes for libel do not result in "efficient repression or suppression of the evils of scandal." [The] operation and effect of the statute [is] that public authorities may bring the owner or publisher of a newspaper or periodical before a judge upon a charge of conducting a business of publishing scandalous and defamatory matter [and] unless the owner or publisher is able [to prove] that the charges are true and are published with good motives and for justifiable ends, his newspaper or periodical is suppressed and further publication is made punishable as a contempt. This is of the essence of censorship.

The question is whether a statute authorizing such proceedings [is] consistent with the conception of the liberty of the press as historically conceived and guaranteed. In determining the extent of the constitutional protection, it has been generally, if not universally, considered that it is the chief purpose of the guaranty to prevent previous restraints upon publication. The struggle in England, directed against the legislative power of the licenser, resulted in renunciation of the censorship of the press. The liberty deemed to be established was thus described by Blackstone: "The liberty of the press is indeed essential to the nature of a free state; but this consists in laying no *previous* restraints upon publications, and not in freedom from censure for criminal matter when [published]." [The] criticism upon Blackstone's statement has not been because immunity from previous restraint upon publication has not been regarded as deserving of special emphasis, but chiefly because that immunity cannot be deemed to exhaust the conception of the liberty guaranteed by state and federal [constitutions].

[The] protection even as to previous restraint is not absolutely unlimited. But the limitation has been recognized only in exceptional cases. [No] one would question but that a government might prevent actual obstruction to its recruiting service or the publication of the sailing dates of transports or the number and location of troops. On similar grounds, the primary requirements of decency may be enforced against obscene publications. The security of the community life may be protected against incitements to acts of violence and the overthrow by force of orderly government. These limitations are not applicable [here].

The fact that for approximately [150] years there has been almost an entire absence of attempts to impose previous restraints upon publications relating to the malfeasance of public officers is significant of the deep-seated conviction that such restraints would violate constitutional right. Public officers, whose character and conduct remain open to debate and free discussion in the press, find their remedies for false accusations in actions under libel laws providing for redress and punishment, and not in proceedings to restrain the publication of newspapers and periodicals. [The] fact that the liberty of the press may be abused by miscreant purveyors of scandal does not make any the less necessary the immunity of the press from previous restraint in dealing with official misconduct. Subsequent punishment for such abuses as may exist is the appropriate remedy, consistent with constitutional privilege.

The statute in question cannot be justified by reason of the fact that the publisher is permitted to show, before injunction issues, that the matter published is true and is published with good motives and for justifiable ends. If such a statute [is] valid, it would be equally permissible for the legislature to provide that at any time the publisher of any newspaper could be brought before a court, or even an administrative officer, and required to produce proof of the truth of his publication, or of what he intended to publish and of his motives, or stand enjoined. If this can be done, the legislature may provide the machinery for determining in the complete exercise of its discretion what are justifiable ends and restrain publication accordingly. And it would be but a step to a complete system of censorship. [We] hold the statute, so far as it authorized the proceedings in this action, [to] be an infringement of the liberty of the press guaranteed by the [14th Amendment].

Judgment reversed.

Justice BUTLER joined by Justices Van DEVANTER, McREYNOLDS and SUTHERLAND, dissenting.

[T]he *previous restraint* referred to by [Blackstone] subjected the press to the arbitrary will of an administrative officer. [The] Minnesota statute does not operate as a *previous* restraint on publication within the proper meaning of that phrase. It does not authorize administrative control in advance such as was formerly exercised by the licensers and censors but prescribes a remedy to be enforced by a suit in equity. In this case there was previous publication made in the course of the business of regularly producing malicious, scandalous and defamatory periodicals. The business and publications unquestionably constitute an abuse of the right of free press. [There] is no question of the power of the State to denounce such transgressions. The restraint authorized is only in respect of continuing to do what has been duly adjudged to constitute a nuisance. [It] is fanciful to suggest similarity between the granting or enforcement of the decree authorized by this statute to prevent *further* publication of malicious, scandalous and defamatory articles and the *previous restraint* upon the press by licensers as referred to by Blackstone and described in the history of the times to which he [alludes]. It is well known [that] existing libel laws are inadequate effectively to suppress evils resulting from the kind of [publications] that are shown in this case. The doctrine [of this ruling] exposes the peace and good order of every community and the business and private affairs of every individual to the constant and protracted false and malicious assaults of any insolvent publisher who may have purpose and sufficient capacity to contrive and put into effect a scheme or program for oppression, blackmail or extortion.[1]

Why should an injunction ever be considered a prior restraint? A judicial determination lacks the institutional features that make administrative censorship particularly suspect: it is formal rather than informal, a judge is not in the business of censorship, and it requires some consideration of evidence rather than a mere stroke of the pen. See Redish, "The Proper Role of the Prior Restraint Doctrine in First Amendment Theory," 70 Va.L.Rev. 53 (1984) (suggesting that permanent injunctions issued after trial are far less problematic than nonjudicial administrative licensing schemes, with preliminary injunc-

1. For a vivid depiction of the background of Near v. Minnesota, see Friendly, Minnesota Rag: The Dramatic Story of the Landmark Supreme Court Case That Gave New Meaning to Freedom of the Press (1981).

tions and temporary restraining orders falling in between). Yet the Court in Near and later cases has extended the presumption against prior restraint in the licensing context to judicial restraints as well. For the view that Near was not really about the procedural problem of prior restraint, but rather the substantive problem of seditious libel, see Jeffries, "Rethinking Prior Restraint," 92 Yale L.J. 409 (1983).

A frequent explanation for the extension of prior restraint doctrine to injunctions stems from the "collateral bar rule": the rule that an injunction must be obeyed until lifted, and that if it is violated, its unconstitutionality is no defense to a finding of contempt. Perhaps the most famous application of the rule arose in connection with a Good Friday civil rights protest march in Birmingham in 1963, led by several black ministers, including the Rev. Martin Luther King, Jr. The marchers challenged a Birmingham parade permit ordinance that was ultimately found to be unconstitutional. They marched in the face of an ex parte injunction directing compliance with the ordinance without challenging the injunction in court before marching. Indeed, they openly flouted the injunction because they considered it "raw tyranny." In WALKER v. BIRMINGHAM, 388 U.S. 307 (1967), the Court held, by a vote of 5–4, that they could not defend against contempt charges by asserting the unconstitutionality of the ordinance or the injunction. Justice STEWART, writing for the Court, concluded: "This Court cannot hold that the petitioners were constitutionally free to ignore all the procedures of the law and carry their battle to the streets." The Alabama courts had justifiably relied on the general rule that court orders must be obeyed until "reversed for error by orderly review." Justice BRENNAN's dissent, joined by Chief Justice Warren and Justices Douglas and Fortas, insisted that the Court had elevated a "rule of judicial administration above the right of free expression."

Note that the Court in Walker suggested that the case might have come out differently if the injunction had been "transparently invalid." Does this afford some greater latitude to disobey injunctions? Recall that Lovell, Freedman and Shuttlesworth were permitted to disobey permit schemes found by the Court to be facially unconstitutional. Why should those bound by an injunction be more restricted? See generally Blasi, "Prior Restraints on Demonstrations," 68 Mich. L. Rev. 1482 (1970).

Moreover, the Court has mitigated the effect of Walker by imposing procedural safeguards limiting the power of courts to issue speech-restrictive injunctions. For example, in CARROLL v. PRESIDENT & COMM'RS OF PRINCESS ANNE, 393 U.S. 175 (1968), the Court found unconstitutional the ex parte procedure followed in issuing a 10–day temporary restraining order against holding a public rally. Petitioners had held a meeting at which they made "aggressively and militantly racist" speeches to a crowd of both whites and blacks. They announced that they would resume the rally the following night. Before then, local officials obtained the order restraining petitioners and their "white supremacist" National States Rights Party from holding meetings "which will tend to disturb and endanger the citizens of the County." There was no notice to petitioners prior to the issuance of the order. The rally was cancelled and petitioners (rather than ignoring the injunction as in Walker) challenged the injunction in court. Justice FORTAS' opinion for the Court found no adequate justification for the ex parte nature of the proceedings. In the rare situations where prior restraints were permissible, "the Court has insisted upon careful procedural provisions." [Freedman.] "There is a place in our jurisprudence for ex parte issuance, without notice, of temporary restraining orders of short duration; but there is no place within the area of basic freedoms guaranteed by the First Amendment for such orders where no showing is made that it is impossible to serve or to notify the opposing parties and to give them an opportunity to participate." Here, procedural care was even more important than in the obscenity context of Freedman: "The present case involves a rally and 'political' speech in which the element of timeliness may be important." Without an adversary hearing, there was "insufficient assurance of the balanced analysis and careful conclusions which are essential in the area of First Amendment adjudication."

––––––––

PRIOR RESTRAINT AND NATIONAL SECURITY

Recall that in Near, the Court cautioned that the presumption against prior restraint is not absolute: "No one would question but that a government might prevent actual obstruction to its recruiting service or the publication of the sailing dates of transports or the number and location of troops." When, if ever, are concerns of national security sufficient to justify a prior restraint? The following cases explore this question.

––––––––

New York Times Co. v. United States [the Pentagon Papers Case]

403 U.S. 713, 91 S.Ct. 2140, 29 L.Ed.2d 822 (1971).

PER CURIAM.

We granted certiorari in these cases in which the United States seeks to enjoin the New York Times and the Washington Post from publishing the contents of a classified study entitled "History of U.S. Decision–Making Process on Viet Nam Policy."[1]

"Any system of prior restraints of expression comes to this Court bearing a heavy presumption against its constitutional validity." [Bantam Books; see Near.] The Government "thus carries a heavy burden of showing justification for the enforcement of such a restraint." The [District Court] in the New York Times case and the [District Court] and the [Court of Appeals] in the Washington Post case held that the Government had not met that burden. We agree. The judgment of the Court of Appeals for the District of Columbia Circuit is

––––––––

1. Portions of that secret Defense Department study (popularly known as the "Pentagon Papers") were published by The New York Times (beginning June 13, 1971) and the Washington Post (on June 18, 1971). The top-secret study reviewed in considerable detail the formulation of American policy toward Indochina, including military operations and diplomatic negotiations. The newspapers obtained this study from Daniel Ellsberg, a former Pentagon official. The government actions to restrain further publication made their way through two district courts and two courts of appeals between June 15 and June 23. The Government claimed that publication would interfere with national security and would undermine the ability to conduct diplomatic negotiations, produce the death of military personnel, and prolong the war. On June 25, the Supreme Court granted certiorari in the Times and Post cases. The cases were argued on June 26 and the decision was issued on June 30, 1971. Restraining orders remained in effect while the decision was pending. (Four Justices—Black, Douglas, Brennan and Marshall—dissented from the decision to grant certiorari and urged summary action instead, stating that they "would not continue the restraint" on the newspapers.)

therefore affirmed. The order of the Court of Appeals for the Second Circuit is reversed and the case is remanded with directions to enter a judgment affirming the judgment of the District Court. [The] stays entered June 25, 1971, by the Court are vacated. The mandates shall issue forthwith.

So ordered.

Justice BLACK, with whom Justice DOUGLAS joins, concurring.

[I] believe that every moment's continuance of the injunctions against these newspapers amounts to a flagrant, indefensible, and continuing violation of the First Amendment. Furthermore, after oral arguments, I agree completely [with] my Brothers Douglas and Brennan. In my view it is unfortunate that some of my Brethren are apparently willing to hold that the publication of news may sometimes be enjoined. Such a holding would make a shambles of the First Amendment. [The] press was protected [by the First Amendment] so that it could bare the secrets of government and inform the people. Only a free and unrestrained press can effectively expose deception in government. [To] find that the President has "inherent power" to halt the publication of news by resort to the courts would wipe out the First Amendment. [The] word "security" is a broad, vague generality whose contours should not be invoked to abrogate the fundamental law embodied in the [First Amendment].

Justice DOUGLAS, with whom Justice BLACK joins, [concurring].

[The First Amendment] leaves [no] room for governmental restraint on the press. There is, moreover, no statute barring the publication by the press of the material which the Times and Post seek to use. [18 U.S.C. § 793(e), prohibiting "communication" of information relating to the national defense that could be used to the injury of the United States, does not apply to publication.] [I]t is apparent that Congress was capable of and did distinguish between publishing and communication in the various sections of the Espionage Act.[2] So any power that the Government possesses must come from its "inherent power." The power to wage war is "the power to wage war successfully." But the war power stems from a declaration of war. The Constitution by Article I, § 8, gives Congress, not the President, power "to declare War." Nowhere are presidential wars authorized.

[These] disclosures[3] may have a serious impact. But that is no basis for sanctioning a previous restraint on the press. [Near.] [The] Government says that it has inherent powers to go into court and obtain an injunction to protect [national] security. [Near] repudiated that expansive doctrine in no uncertain terms. The dominant purpose of the First Amendment was to prohibit the widespread practice of governmental suppression of embarrassing information. [A] debate of large proportions goes on in the Nation over our posture in Vietnam. The debate antedated the disclosure of the contents of the present documents. The latter are highly relevant to the debate in progress. Secrecy in

2. Justice Douglas added: "The other evidence that § 793 does not apply to the press is a rejected version of § 793. That version read: 'During any national emergency, [the] President may [prohibit] the publishing or communicating of [any] information relating to the national defense which, in his judgment, is of such character that it is or might be useful to the enemy.' During the [1917] debates in the Senate the First Amendment was specifically cited and that provision was defeated."

3. There are numerous sets of this material in existence and they apparently are not under any controlled custody. Moreover, the President has sent a set to the Congress. We start then with a case where there already is rather wide distribution of the material that is destined for publicity, not secrecy. I have gone over the material listed in the in camera brief of the United States. It is all history, not future events. None of it is more recent than 1968. [Footnote by Justice Douglas.]

government is fundamentally anti-democratic, perpetuating bureaucratic errors. Open debate and discussion of public issues are vital to our national health. [The] stays in these cases that have been in effect for more than a week constitute a flouting of the principles of the [First Amendment].

Justice BRENNAN, [concurring].

The error that has pervaded these cases from the outset was the granting of any injunctive relief whatsoever, interim or otherwise. The entire thrust of the Government's claim throughout these cases has been that publication of the material sought to be enjoined "could," or "might," or "may" prejudice the national interest in various ways. But the First Amendment tolerates absolutely no prior judicial restraints of the press predicated upon surmise or conjecture that untoward consequences may result.[1] Our cases, it is true, have indicated that there is a single, extremely narrow class of cases in which the First Amendment's ban on prior judicial restraint may be overridden. Our cases have thus far indicated that such cases may arise only when the Nation "is at war" [Schenck], during which times "no one would question but that a government might prevent actual obstruction to its recruiting service or the publication of the sailing dates of transports or the number and location of troops." [Near.] Even if the present world situation were assumed to be tantamount to a time of war, or if the power of presently available armaments would justify even in peacetime the suppression of information that would set in motion a nuclear holocaust,[2] in neither of these actions has the Government presented or even alleged that publication of items from or based upon the material at issue would cause the happening of an event of that nature. "The chief purpose of [the First Amendment's] guarantee [is] to prevent previous restraints upon publication." [Near.] Thus, only governmental allegation and proof that publication must inevitably, directly and immediately cause the occurrence of an event kindred to imperiling the safety of a transport already at sea can support even the issuance of an interim restraining order. [Unless] and until the Government has clearly made out its case, the First Amendment commands that no injunction may issue.

Justice STEWART, with whom Justice WHITE joins, concurring.

[The] only effective restraint upon executive policy and power in the areas of national defense and international affairs may lie in an enlightened citizenry. [For] this reason, it is perhaps here that a press that is alert, aware, and free most vitally serves the basic purpose of the First Amendment. [Yet] it is elementary that the successful conduct of international diplomacy and the maintenance of an effective national defense require both confidentiality and secrecy. [I] think there can be but one answer to this dilemma, if dilemma it be. The responsibility must be where the power is. [The] Executive must have the largely unshared duty to determine and preserve the degree of internal security necessary to exercise [its] power successfully. [It] is the constitutional duty of the Executive—as a matter of sovereign prerogative and not as a matter of law as the courts know law—through the promulgation and enforcement of executive regulations to protect the confidentiality necessary to carry out its respon-

---

1. Freedman v. Maryland and similar cases regarding temporary restraints of allegedly obscene materials are not in point. For those cases rest upon the proposition that "obscenity is not protected by the freedoms of speech and press." Here there is no question but that the material sought to be suppressed is within the protection of the First Amendment; the only question is whether, notwithstanding that fact, its publication may be enjoined for a time because of the presence of an overwhelming [national interest]. [Footnote by Justice Brennan.]

2. See the Progressive case, which follows.

sibilities in the fields of international relations and national defense. This is not to say that Congress and the courts have no role to play. Undoubtedly Congress has the power to enact specific and appropriate criminal laws to protect government property and preserve government secrets. [But] in the cases before us we are asked neither to construe specific regulations nor to apply specific laws. We are asked, instead, to perform a function that the Constitution gave to the Executive, not the Judiciary. We are asked, quite simply, to prevent the publication by two newspapers of material that the Executive Branch insists should not, in the national interest, be published. I am convinced that the Executive is correct with respect to some of the documents involved. But I cannot say that disclosure of any of them will surely result in direct, immediate, and irreparable damage to our Nation or its people. That being so, there can under the First Amendment be but one judicial resolution of the issues before us. I join the judgments of the Court.

Justice WHITE, with whom Justice STEWART joins, concurring.

I concur in today's judgments, but only because of the concededly extraordinary protection against prior restraints enjoyed by the press under our constitutional system. I do not say that in no circumstances would the First Amendment permit an injunction against publishing information about government plans or operations. Nor, after examining the materials the Government characterizes as the most sensitive and destructive, can I deny that revelation of these documents will do substantial damage to public interests. Indeed, I am confident that their disclosure will have that result. But I nevertheless agree that the United States has not satisfied the very heavy burden which it must meet to warrant an injunction against publication in these cases, at least in the absence of express and appropriately limited congressional authorization for prior restraints in circumstances such as these.

The Government's position is simply stated: The responsibility of the Executive for the conduct of the foreign affairs and for the security of the Nation is so basic that the President is entitled to an injunction against publication of a newspaper story whenever he can convince a court that the information to be revealed threatens "grave and irreparable" injury to the public interest; and the injunction should issue whether or not the material to be published is classified, whether or not publication would be lawful under relevant criminal statutes enacted by Congress and regardless of the circumstances by which the newspaper came into possession of the information. At least in the absence of legislation by Congress, based on its own investigations and findings, I am quite unable to agree that the inherent powers of the Executive and the courts reach so far as to authorize remedies having such sweeping potential for inhibiting publications by the press. [To] sustain the Government in these cases would start the courts down a long and hazardous road that I am not willing to travel, at least without congressional guidance and direction.

[Prior] restraints require an unusually heavy justification under the First Amendment; but failure by the Government to justify prior restraints does not measure its constitutional entitlement to a conviction for criminal publication. That the Government mistakenly chose to proceed by injunction does not mean that it could not successfully proceed in another way. [Justice White discussed a number of "potentially relevant" criminal provisions.] It is thus clear that Congress has addressed itself to the problems of protecting the security of the country and the national defense from unauthorized disclosure of potentially damaging information. Cf. [the Steel Seizure Case, p. 356 above]. It has not, however, authorized the injunctive remedy against threatened publication. It has apparently been satisfied to rely on criminal sanctions and their deterrent effect on the responsible as well as the irresponsible press. I am not, of course, saying that either of these newspapers has yet committed a crime or that either would commit a crime if they published all the material now in their possession. That matter must await resolution in the context of a criminal proceeding if one is [instituted].[3]

Justice MARSHALL, [concurring].

[I] believe the ultimate issue in this case [is] whether this Court or the Congress has the power to make law. [I]n some situations it may be that under whatever inherent powers the [Executive may have], there is a basis for the invocation of the equity jurisdiction of this Court as an aid to prevent the publication of material damaging to "national security," however that term may be defined. It would, however, be utterly inconsistent with the concept of separation of powers for this Court to use its power of contempt to prevent behavior that Congress has specifically declined to prohibit. There would be a similar damage to the basic concept of these co-equal branches of Government if when the [executive] had adequate authority granted by Congress to protect "national security" it can choose instead to invoke the contempt power of a court to enjoin the threatened conduct. [In] these cases we are not faced with a situation where Congress has failed to provide the Executive with broad power to protect the Nation from disclosure of damaging state secrets. [See the power to "classify" secret materials in 18 U.S.C. Chap. 37, Espionage and Censorship.] [It] is plain that Congress has specifically refused to grant the authority the Government seeks from this Court. [It] is not for this Court to fling itself into every breach perceived by some Government [official].

Justice HARLAN, with whom Chief Justice BURGER and Justice BLACKMUN join, dissenting.

[I] consider that the Court has been almost irresponsibly feverish in dealing with these cases. [The] frenzied train of events [see footnote 1 to this case] took place in the name of the presumption against prior restraints created by the First Amendment. Due regard for the extraordinarily important and difficult questions involved in these litigations should have led the Court to shun [its] precipitate timetable. In order to decide the merits of these cases properly, some or all of the following questions should have been [faced].[1]

---

3. On July 1, 1971—the day after the decision in this case—Attorney General Mitchell commented that the Justice Department "will prosecute all those who have violated federal criminal laws in connection with this matter" and added: "A review of the Court's opinions indicates that there is nothing in them to affect the situation." Daniel Ellsberg and Anthony Russo were subsequently indicted by a grand jury in Los Angeles under provisions of federal espionage, theft and conspiracy laws. (Another federal grand jury, in Boston, investigated the involvement of newspapers and reporters.) On May 11, 1973, District Judge Byrne dismissed the Ellsberg–Russo indictment and granted a mistrial because the "totality of the circumstances" of improper government conduct "offends 'a sense of justice.' "

1. The questions posed by Justice Harlan were as follows:

1. Whether the Attorney General is authorized to bring these suits in the name of the United States. Compare [In re Debs, 158 U.S. 564 (1895)] with [the Steel Seizure Case]. This question involves as well the construction and validity of a singularly opaque statute—the Espionage Act, 18 U.S.C. § 793(e).

2. Whether the First Amendment permits the federal courts to enjoin publication of stories which would present a serious threat to national security. See [Near] (dictum).

3. Whether the threat to publish highly secret documents is of itself a sufficient implication of national security to justify an

These are difficult questions of fact, of law, and of judgment; the potential consequences of erroneous decision are enormous. The time which has been available [has] been wholly inadequate for giving these cases the kind of consideration they deserve. It is a reflection on the stability of the judicial process that these great issues [should] have been decided under the pressures engendered by the torrent of publicity that has attended these litigations from their inception.

Forced as I am to reach the merits of these cases, I dissent from the opinion and judgments of the Court. Within the severe limitations imposed by the time constraints under which I have been required to operate, I can only state my reasons in telescoped form. [It] is plain to me that the scope of the judicial function in passing upon the activities of the Executive Branch of the Government in the field of foreign affairs is very narrowly restricted. This view is, I think, dictated by the concept of separation of powers upon which our constitutional system rests. [I] agree that, in performance of its duty to protect the values of the First Amendment against political pressures, the judiciary must review the initial Executive determination to the point of satisfying itself that the subject matter of the dispute does lie within the proper compass of the President's foreign relations power. [Moreover], the judiciary may properly insist that the determination that disclosure of the subject matter would irreparably impair the national security be made by the head of the Executive Department concerned [after] actual personal consideration by that officer. [But] in my judgment the judiciary may not properly go beyond these two inquiries and redetermine for itself the probable impact of disclosure on the national security. "[T]he very nature of executive decisions as to foreign policy is political, not judicial. Such decisions are wholly confided by our Constitution to the political departments. They are delicate, complex, and involve large elements of prophecy. They are and should be undertaken only by those directly responsible to the people whose welfare they advance or imperil. They are decisions of a kind for which the Judiciary has neither aptitude, facilities nor responsibility and which has long been held to belong in the domain of political power not subject to judicial intrusion or inquiry." Chicago & Southern Air Lines v. Waterman Steamship Corp., 333 U.S. 103, 111 (1948) (Jackson, J.).

Even if there is some room for the judiciary to override the executive determination, it is plain that the scope of review must be exceedingly narrow. I can see no indication in the opinions of [the lower courts] in the Post litigation that the conclusions of the Executive were given even the deference owing to an administrative agency, much less that owing to a co-equal branch

injunction on the theory that regardless of the contents of the documents harm enough results simply from the demonstration of such a breach of secrecy.

4. Whether the unauthorized disclosure of any of these particular documents would seriously impair the national security.

5. What weight should be given to the opinion of high officers in the Executive Branch of the Government with respect to questions 3 and 4.

6. Whether the newspapers are entitled to retain and use the documents notwithstanding the seemingly uncontested facts that the documents, or the originals of which they are duplicates, were purloined from the Government's possession and that the newspapers received them with knowledge that they had been feloniously acquired.

7. Whether the threatened harm to the national security or the Government's possessory interest in the documents justifies the issuance of an injunction against publication in light of—a. The strong First Amendment policy against prior restraints on publication; b. The doctrine against enjoining conduct in violation of criminal statutes; and c. The extent to which the materials at issue have apparently already been otherwise disseminated.

of the Government operating within the field of its constitutional prerogative. [Pending] further hearings in each case conducted under the appropriate ground rules, I would continue the restraints on publication. I cannot believe that the doctrine prohibiting prior restraints reaches to the point of preventing courts from maintaining the status quo long enough to act responsibly in matters of such national importance as those involved here.

Justice BLACKMUN.

I join Justice Harlan in his dissent. [The] First Amendment, after all, is only one part of an entire Constitution. [See, e.g., the Executive's power in Art. II.] First Amendment absolutism has never commanded a majority of this Court. [E.g., Near; Schenck.] What is needed here is a weighing, upon properly developed standards, of the broad right of the press to print and of the very narrow right of the Government to prevent. Such standards are not yet developed. The parties here are in disagreement as to what those standards should be. But even the newspapers concede that there are situations where restraint is in order and is constitutional. [I] therefore would remand these cases to be developed expeditiously, of course, but on a schedule permitting [orderly presentation of evidence]. [I] add one final comment. [Judge Wilkey], dissenting in the District of Columbia case, [concluded] that there were a number of examples of documents that, [if] published, "could clearly result in great harm to the nation," and he defined "harm" to mean "the death of soldiers, the destruction of alliances, the greatly increased difficulty of negotiation with our enemies, the inability of our diplomats to negotiate." [I] share his concern. I hope that damage has not already been done. If, however, damage has been done, and if, with the Court's action today, these newspapers proceed to publish the critical documents and there results therefrom "the death of soldiers, the destruction of alliances, the greatly increased difficulty of negotiation with our enemies, the inability of our diplomats to negotiate," to which list I might add the factors of prolongation of the war and of further delay in the freeing of United States prisoners, then the Nation's people will know where the responsibility for these sad consequences rests.

[Chief Justice BURGER's dissent stated that he agreed "generally" with Justices Harlan and Blackmun, but that he was "not prepared to reach the merits." He urged that the temporary restraining orders be extended pending a full trial on the merits. He commented that the cases had been "conducted in unseemly haste" and that "we literally do not know what we are acting on."]

Were the principles of Near and the Pentagon Papers case properly applied in UNITED STATES v. PROGRESSIVE, INC., 467 F.Supp. 990 (W.D.Wis. 1979)? There, the District Court issued an order enjoining The Progressive, a monthly magazine, from publishing technical material on hydrogen bomb design in an article entitled "The H–Bomb Secret: How We Got It, Why We're Telling It." The author and publisher claimed that the article merely synthesized information available in public documents, insisting that the article would contribute to informed opinion about nuclear weapons and would benefit the nation by demonstrating that open debate was preferable to "an oppressive and ineffective system of secrecy and classification." In issuing the temporary injunction, the District Judge distinguished the Pentagon Papers case on three grounds: (1) the documents there had contained only "historical data"; (2) the Government there had not proved that publication affected the national security; and (3) the Government there had failed to establish a statutory basis for injunctive relief.[1]

Although the Government conceded that at least some of the information in the article had been declassified or was in the public domain, it argued that the interest in "national security" permitted it to bar publication of information "originating in the public domain, if when drawn together, synthesized and collated, such information acquires the character of presenting immediate, direct and irreparable harm to the interests of the United States." It submitted affidavits from Cabinet members asserting that publication would increase the risk of thermonuclear proliferation. The District Judge accepted the Government's key claims. He noted that the article "contains concepts that are not found in the public realm, concepts that are vital to the operation of the bomb." Moreover, despite the prior declassification of some of the materials in the article, he found that "the danger lies in the exposition of certain concepts never heretofore disclosed in conjunction with one another." Though the District Judge conceded that the article probably did not "provide a 'do-it-yourself' guide for the hydrogen bomb," he noted that the article "could possibly provide sufficient information to allow a medium size nation to move faster in developing a hydrogen weapon."

In justifying "the first instance of prior restraint against a publication in this fashion in the history of this country," the District Judge explained: "A mistake in ruling against The Progressive [will] curtail defendants' First Amendment rights in a drastic and substantial fashion. [But a] mistake in ruling against the United States could pave the way for thermonuclear annihilation for us all. In that event, our right to life is extinguished and the right to publish becomes moot." He concluded: "Because of this 'disparity of risk,' because the government has met its heavy burden of showing justification for the imposition of a prior restraint, [and] because the Court is unconvinced that suppression of the objected-to technical portions of the [article] would in any plausible fashion impede the defendants in their laudable crusade to stimulate public knowledge of nuclear armament and bring about enlightened debate on national policy questions, the Court finds that the objected-to portions of the article fall within the narrow area recognized by the Court in Near v. Minnesota in which a prior restraint on publication is appropriate."[2] He added: "In view of the showing of harm made by the United States, a preliminary injunction would be warranted even in the absence of statutory authorization

---

1. For statutory support, the District Court relied primarily upon the Atomic Energy Act of 1954, which imposes sanctions on anyone who "communicates, transmits, or discloses [restricted data] with reason to believe such data will be utilized to injure the United States or to secure an advantage to any foreign nation." 42 U.S.C. § 2274(b). The Act also authorizes the Government to seek injunctive relief, 42 U.S.C. § 2280. The trial court ruled that the statute and its definition of "restricted data"—including "all data concerning design, manufacture, or utilization of atomic weapons"—were neither vague nor overbroad "[a]s applied to this case" and that the prohibition against one who "communicates" extended to publication in a magazine.

2. In arguing that the Near exception applied, the District Judge pointed to the "troop movements" reference there and added: "Times have changed significantly since 1931 when Near was decided. Now war by foot soldiers has been replaced in large part by war by machines and bombs. No longer need there be any advance warning or any preparation time before a nuclear war could be commenced. In light of these factors, this court concludes that publication of the technical information of the hydrogen bomb contained in the article is analogous to publication of troop movements or locations in time of war and falls within the extremely narrow exception to the rule against prior restraint."

because of the existence of the likelihood of direct, immediate and irreparable injury to our nation and its people. New York Times (Justice Stewart)."[3]

Even if it may not restrain the press, may the government seek civil and criminal remedies against former employees who publish secret information? Dicta in the Pentagon Papers Case suggested as much. May the government impose employment sanctions as well? Obviously it may fire or demote an employee who divulges secrets. The question of further remedies against a former government employee who had agreed not to disclose confidential government information without authorization came before the Court in SNEPP v. UNITED STATES, 444 U.S. 507 (1980). Snepp, a former CIA employee, had agreed not to divulge classified information without authorization and not to publish any information relating to the Agency without prepublication clearance. Without submitting his manuscript for clearance, he published a book about CIA activities in Viet Nam. (The Government did not claim that the book contained classified data.) The Court of Appeals held that Snepp could be subjected to punitive damages, but refused to impress a constructive trust on his profits from the book. The Supreme Court's per curiam reversal, without argument, held that punitive damages were an inappropriate and inadequate remedy and instead imposed a constructive trust on Snepp's profits. The majority's only mention of the First Amendment came in a footnote insisting that "this Court's cases make clear that—even in the absence of an express agreement—the CIA could have acted to protect substantial government interests by imposing reasonable restrictions on employee activities that in other contexts might be protected by the First Amendment. The Government has a compelling interest in protecting both the secrecy of information important to our national security and the appearance of confidentiality so essential to the effective operation of our foreign intelligence service. The agreement that Snepp signed is a reasonable means for protecting this vital interest." A dissent by Justice STEVENS, joined by Justices Brennan and Marshall, objected not only to the Court's extraordinary procedure (deciding without argument an issue raised only in the Government's conditional cross-petition for certiorari, filed to bring the entire case up in the event the Court granted Snepp's certiorari petition) but also to the Court's fashioning of a "drastic new remedy [to] enforce a species of prior restraint on a citizen's right to criticize his government."

For commentary on New York Times and related problems, see, e.g., Symposium, "National Security and the First Amendment," 26 Wm. & Mary L.Rev. 715 (1985), and Cox, "Foreword: Freedom of Expression in the Burger Court," 94 Harv.L.Rev. 1 (1980). For commentary on Snepp, see Easterbrook, "Insider Trading, Secret Agents, Evidentiary Privileges, and the Production of Information," 1981 Sup. Ct. Rev. 309; Medow, "The First Amendment and the Secrecy State," 130 U. Pa.L. Rev. 775 (1982); Sunstein, "Government Control of Information," 74 Calif. L. Rev. 889 (1986).

PRIOR RESTRAINT AND FAIR TRIAL

In NEBRASKA PRESS ASS'N v. STUART, 427 U.S. 539 (1976), the Court for the first time considered the permissibility of a prior restraint on the press

---

3. The Government's proceedings against the "Progressive" were abandoned before full appellate proceedings and a hearing regarding a permanent injunction could take place, because similar information pertaining to nuclear weapons was published independently by others while the litigation was under way.

imposed in the interest of protecting a criminal defendant's right to a fair trial before an impartial jury. The Court reemphasized the high constitutional barriers to prior restraints and held the challenged pretrial restraint unconstitutional. There were several opinions in support of that judgment. Although the majority opinion by Chief Justice Burger was a narrow one limited to the facts of this case, the several concurring opinions indicated that most of the Justices were even more reluctant than the Chief Justice to sustain "gag orders" in the interest of fair trials.

The state court order, issued in anticipation of a trial in a widely publicized mass murder case, prohibited publication or broadcasting of the accused's confessions or admissions, and of any other facts "strongly implicative" of the accused. In his majority opinion, Chief Justice BURGER found that "the showing before the state court" did not justify the order. Though the Chief Justice rejected the priority, "in all circumstances," of the "right to publish" over the "right of an accused," he found a common thread in the prior decisions such as Near and Pentagon Papers: "[P]rior restraints [are] the most serious and least tolerable infringement on First Amendment rights. A criminal penalty or [a defamation judgment] is subject to the whole panoply of protections afforded by deferring the impact of the judgment until all avenues of appellate review have been exhausted. [A] prior restraint [has] an immediate and irreversible sanction. If it can be said that a threat of criminal or civil sanctions after publication 'chills' speech, prior restraint 'freezes' it at least for the time." Moreover, "the protection against prior restraints should have particular force as applied to reporting of criminal proceedings." He cautioned that the First Amendment's "extraordinary protections" imposed special fiduciary duties on editors and publishers—duties "not always observed." Despite this admonition, however, he indicated that courts could do little to enforce that "fiduciary duty": "[T]he barriers to prior restraint remain high."

Turning to a scrutiny of the justifications for the "gag order," Chief Justice Burger drew on Judge Learned Hand's formulation in the Dennis case (p. 1061 above): "We turn now to the record in this case to determine whether, as Learned Hand put it, 'the gravity of the "evil" discounted by its improbability, justified such invasion of free speech as is necessary to avoid the danger.' To do so, we must examine the evidence before the trial judge when the order was entered to determine (a) the nature and extent of pretrial news coverage; (b) whether other measures would be likely to mitigate the effects of unrestrained pretrial publicity; (c) how effectively a restraining order would operate to prevent the threatened danger. The precise terms of the restraining order are also important. We must then consider whether the record supports the entry of a prior restraint on publication, one of the most extraordinary remedies known to our jurisprudence." In applying this analysis, the Chief Justice noted that, though the trial judge could reasonably conclude, "based on common human experience, that publicity might impair" the defendant's rights, his conclusion about the impact of publicity on prospective jurors "was of necessity speculative." Moreover, he concluded that the record could not support a finding that alternative measures to curb the impact of media publicity would not have been effective. He noted several possible alternatives: change of venue; postponement of the trial; careful questioning of jurors; jury instructions; sequestration of jurors; and curbing statements by the contending lawyers, the police, and witnesses. [See Sheppard v. Maxwell, 384 U.S. 333 (1966).] The Chief Justice also questioned the efficacy of any restraint of the media, in view, e.g., of the likelihood of rumors in a sensational case. Turning to the terms of the order, he especially objected to the ban on reporting "implicative" information as "too vague and too broad." He concluded that, though there was no doubt about "the gravity of the evil pretrial publicity can work, [the] probability that it would do so here was not demonstrated with the degree of certainty our cases on prior restraint require."

Justices POWELL and WHITE, while joining the majority opinion, submitted brief concurring statements of their own. Justice Powell emphasized "the unique burden" on a proponent of prior restraint on pretrial publicity. Justice White's statement indicated his "grave doubt [whether] orders with respect to the press such as were entered in this case would ever be justifiable."

In an opinion concurring only in the judgment, Justice BRENNAN, joined by Justices Stewart and Marshall, urged an absolute ban on prior restraints issued in the interest of a fair trial: "I would hold [that] resort to prior restraints on the freedom of the press is a constitutionally impermissible method for enforcing [the right to a fair trial]; judges have at their disposal a broad spectrum of devices for ensuring that fundamental fairness is accorded the accused without necessitating so drastic an incursion on the equally fundamental and salutary constitutional mandate that discussion of public affairs in a free society cannot depend on the preliminary grade of judicial censors." He emphasized that "[c]ommentary and reporting on the criminal justice system is at the core of First Amendment values." Though he recognized pretrial publicity could "destroy the fairness of a criminal trial," he viewed the bar on prior restraints on the press as applicable "no matter how shabby the means by which the information is obtained." He added in a footnote that this did "not necessarily immunize [the press] from civil liability for libel or invasion of privacy or from criminal liability for transgressions of general criminal laws during the course of obtaining that information."

Justice Brennan stressed that, under Near and its progeny, exceptions to the ban on prior restraints were confined to "exceptional cases." He insisted that the narrow national security exception recognized in dicta in Near and Pentagon Papers did not mean, as the highest state court had assumed in this case, "that prior restraints can be justified on an ad hoc balancing approach that concludes that the 'presumption' must be overcome in light of some perceived 'justification.'" Rather, "prior restraints even within a recognized exception to the rule against prior restraints will be extremely difficult to justify; but as an initial matter, the purpose for which a prior restraint is sought to be imposed 'must fit within one of the narrowly defined exceptions to the prohibition against prior restraints.'" And there was no justification here for creating "a new, potentially pervasive exception [for fair trial purposes] to this settled rule of virtually blanket prohibition of prior restraints." He added that "speculative deprivation of an accused's Sixth Amendment right to an impartial jury [is not] comparable to the damage to the Nation or its people that Near and New York Times would have found sufficient to justify a prior restraint on reporting."

In another separate opinion concurring in the judgment, Justice STEVENS stated that he subscribed to "most" of Justice Brennan's opinion, but pointed out some problems he was not yet ready to resolve: "Whether the same absolute protection would apply no matter how shabby or illegal the means by which the information is obtained, no matter how serious an intrusion on privacy might be involved, no matter how demonstrably false the information might be, no matter how prejudicial it might be to the interests of innocent persons, and no matter how perverse the motivation for publishing it, is a question I would not answer without further argument."

Does the Court's special hostility to prior restraint in Nebraska Press underestimate the damage that might be done by other methods of restricting pretrial reporting? Does that emphasis implicitly open the door to other sanctions that may threaten free speech and press to a similar degree, such as subsequent punishment of reporters and orders excluding the press and public from hearings? See Barnett, "The Puzzle of Prior Restraint," 29 Stan.L.Rev. 539 (1977). Barnett suggests that "single-minded application of the prior restraint doctrine" as in Nebraska Press "can warp the law by diminishing the protection afforded against restrictions on speech that do not carry the label 'prior restraint'—though they may be no less suppressive in fact—and by diminishing the force of other protective doctrines even in 'prior restraint' cases. More generally, it can confuse first amendment analysis by diverting attention from other doctrinal considerations that may be more apt, such as the substantive dimensions of protected speech." The issue of closing criminal proceedings to the press and public was not before the Court in Nebraska Press, but reached the Court three years later, when a divided Court rejected a constitutional attack on an order closing pretrial hearings. See the Gannett case, p. 1425 below.

CHAPTER 13

RIGHTS ANCILLARY TO FREEDOM OF SPEECH

Introduction. The Supreme Court has interpreted the right of free speech to entail several associated rights: the right *not* to speak, the right to associate with others for expressive purposes (and *not* to associate), and the right to facilitate speech through the expenditure of money in connection with political campaigns. None of these ancillary rights is separately enumerated in the First Amendment, except to the extent that the right of association derives in part from "the right of the people peaceably to assemble, and to petition the Government for a redress of grievances." The right to "freedom of the press," in contrast, is separately enumerated. These ancillary rights are examined in this chapter in turn. Section 1 examines claims that the government may not force one to speak or to serve as a mouthpiece or platform for the speech of others. Section 2 considers what regulations restricting group activities or compelling disclosure about them might violate the First Amendment right of association, or the right against compelled association. Section 3 deals with efforts to regulate the use of money in political campaigns. The "speech" involved here is manifested in funds directed to the support of candidates and causes; the typical regulatory interests asserted are those in assuring the integrity and openness of the electoral process and in equalizing the relative financial ability of persons and groups to influence the outcome of elections. Section 4 surveys a series of problems involving the institutional media, considers whether the media are entitled to special protection because "the press" is separately mentioned in the text of the First Amendment, and examines the Court's different treatment of the print and broadcasting media.

SECTION 1.   COMPELLED SPEECH: THE RIGHT *NOT* TO SPEAK

Does the right to speak free of government interference entail a right to be free of government compulsion to speak? May government use citizens as mouthpieces for official orthodoxy? May government compel citizens to serve as vehicles for favored expression even if the speech so favored does not express the government's point of view? Any particular point of view? May government compel citizens to provide access to their property for the speech of others? Does it matter whether that property ordinarily has an expressive function? Does it matter why government has sought to compel such access? Does it matter to whom bystanders are likely to attribute the content of the required speech? The following cases examine these questions.

A.   COMPELLED INDIVIDUAL SPEECH

1. *Citizens as mouthpieces.* In several cases in the 1940s, members of Jehovah's Witnesses attacked public school regulations requiring students to

salute the flag and recite the pledge of allegiance. The challengers claimed that their participation in the exercises amounted to the worship of "graven images" in a manner "forbidden by command of scripture," and thus that the state's requirements violated their rights to the free exercise of religion and to freedom of speech. In the first case, MINERSVILLE SCHOOL DIST. v. GOBITIS, 310 U.S. 586 (1940), the Court sustained the flag salute requirement, finding no grounds for a free exercise exemption. But the Court overruled Gobitis only three years later in WEST VIRGINIA STATE BD. OF EDUC. v. BARNETTE, 319 U.S. 624 (1943). Justice JACKSON wrote for the Court in Barnette, finding that the rights of free speech and free worship precluded the state from making the flag salute and pledge compulsory:

"[T]he compulsory flag salute and pledge requires affirmation of a belief and an attitude of mind. It is not clear whether the regulation contemplates that pupils forego any contrary convictions of their own and become unwilling converts to the prescribed ceremony or whether it will be acceptable if they simulate assent by words without belief and by a gesture barren of meaning. [Either way,] the power of compulsion is invoked without any allegation that remaining passive during a flag salute ritual creates a clear and present danger that would justify an effort even to muffle expression. To sustain the compulsory flag salute we are required to say that a Bill of Rights which guards the individual's right to speak his own mind, left it open to public authorities to compel him to utter what is not in his mind."

Having found that the compulsory flag salute implicated freedom of speech, Justice Jackson rejected the argument, relied upon in Gobitis, that the matter should be left to the legislature: "The very purpose of the Bill of Rights was to withdraw certain subjects from the vicissitudes of political controversy, to place them beyond the reach of majorities and officials and to establish them as legal principles to be applied by the courts. One's right to life, liberty, and property, to free speech, a free press, freedom of worship and assembly, and other fundamental rights may not be submitted to vote; they depend on the outcome of no elections. [First Amendment rights] are susceptible of restriction only to prevent grave and immediate danger to interests which the State may lawfully protect."

Finally, he rejected the adequacy of the state's justification that the flag salute promoted national unity: "National unity as an end which officials may foster by persuasion and example is not in question. The problem is whether under our Constitution compulsion as here employed is a permissible means for its achievement. Struggles to coerce uniformity of sentiment in support of some end thought essential to their time and country have been waged by many good as well as by evil men. [Ultimate] futility of such attempts to compel coherence is the lesson of every such effort from the Roman drive to stamp out Christianity as a disturber of its pagan unity, the Inquisition, as a means to religious and dynastic unity, the Siberian exiles as a means to Russian unity, down to the fast failing efforts of our present totalitarian enemies. Those who begin coercive elimination of dissent soon find themselves exterminating dissenters. Compulsory unification of opinion achieves only the unanimity of the graveyard. It seems trite but necessary to say that the First Amendment to our Constitution was designed to avoid these ends by avoiding these beginnings."

He concluded: "[W]e apply the limitations of the Constitution with no fear that freedom to be intellectually and spiritually diverse or even contrary will disintegrate the social organization. To believe that patriotism will not flourish if patriotic ceremonies are voluntary and spontaneous instead of a compulsory routine is to make an unflattering estimate of the appeal of our institutions to free minds. We can have intellectual individualism and the rich cultural diversities that we owe to exceptional minds only at the price of occasional eccentricity and abnormal attitudes. When they are so harmless to others or to the State as those we deal with here, the price is not too great. But freedom to differ is not limited to things that do not matter much. That would be a mere shadow of freedom. The test of its substance is the right to differ as to things that touch the heart of the existing order. If there is any fixed star in our constitutional constellation, it is that no official, high or petty, can prescribe what shall be orthodox in politics, nationalism, religion, or other matters of opinion or force citizens to confess by word or act their faith therein."

Justice BLACK, joined by Justice Douglas, submitted a "statement of reasons for our change of view" since Gobitis. Justice FRANKFURTER's lengthy dissent stated: "One who belongs to the most vilified and persecuted minority in history is not likely to be insensible to the freedoms guaranteed by our Constitution. [But] as a member of this Court I am not justified in writing my private notions of policy into the Constitution. [Of course] patriotism cannot be enforced by the flag salute. But neither can the liberal spirit be enforced by judicial invalidation of illiberal legislation." Justices Roberts and Reed joined Justice Frankfurter in adhering to Gobitis.

2. *Citizens as mobile billboards.* The Court relied heavily on Barnette in WOOLEY v. MAYNARD, 430 U.S. 705 (1977). The case involved a New Hampshire law requiring most automobiles to bear license plates carrying the state motto, "Live Free or Die." Challengers were a married couple, members of Jehovah's Witnesses, who found the motto repugnant to their moral, religious and political beliefs and who covered up the motto on their license plate, a misdemeanor. Chief Justice BURGER's majority opinion stated: "Here, as in Barnette, we are faced with a state measure which forces an individual as part of his daily life—indeed constantly while his automobile is in public view— to be an instrument for fostering public adherence to an ideological point of view he finds unacceptable. In doing so, the State 'invades the sphere of intellect and spirit which it is the purpose of the First Amendment [to] reserve from all official control.' [Barnette.] New Hampshire's statute in effect requires that appellees use their private property as a 'mobile billboard' for the State's ideological message—or suffer a penalty," and this burden was not justified by any sufficiently weighty state interest. Chief Justice Burger emphasized that First Amendment freedom of thought "includes both the right to speak freely and the right to refrain from speaking at all"; both rights are "complementary components of a broader concept of 'individual freedom of mind.' "

Was the Court correct to analogize the license plate in Wooley to the flag salute in Barnette? Was there a comparable degree of government ventriloquy involved? To whom would passing motorists likely attribute the license plate motto: Maynard or New Hampshire? What is the remedy here: allowing Maynard to cover up the motto? To request a mottoless license plate? Do such remedies themselves involve compelled speech?

3. *Compelled disclosure of speaker identity.* In TALLEY v. CALIFORNIA, 362 U.S. 60 (1960), the Court, by a vote of 6–3, invalidated a Los Angeles ordinance that prohibited the distribution of any handbill in the city unless it had printed on it the name and address of the person who prepared, distributed, or sponsored it. The ordinance was challenged by distributors of unsigned handbills urging readers to boycott certain Los Angeles merchants who were allegedly engaging in racially discriminatory employment practices. Holding the

ordinance "void on its face," the Court noted that the identification requirement would tend to restrict freedom of expression. Writing for the Court,
Justice Black noted that "persecuted groups and sects from time to time
throughout history have been able to criticize oppressive practices and laws
either anonymously or not at all." The Court rejected the argument that the
law was a justifiable "way to identify those responsible for fraud, false advertising and libel," stating that "the ordinance is in no manner so limited."

In McINTYRE v. OHIO ELECTIONS COMMISSION, __ U.S. __, 115
S.Ct. 1511 (1995), the Court, by a vote of 7–2, invalidated an Ohio election law
that, like the law of virtually every state, prohibited the circulation of anonymous leaflets in connection with political campaigns. The law provided: "No
person shall write, print, post, or distribute [any] general publication [designed]
to promote the nomination or election or defeat of a candidate, or to promote
the adoption or defeat of any issue [unless] there appears on such [publication]
in a conspicuous place [the] name and residence or business address of [the]
person who issues [it]." Margaret McIntyre was fined $100 by the Commission
for circulating leaflets opposing a school tax referendum that were either
unsigned or signed only "Concerned Parents and Taxpayers."

Justice STEVENS, writing for the Court, reaffirmed Talley and held that
"an author's decision to remain anonymous, like other decisions concerning
omissions or additions to the content of a publication, is an aspect of the
freedom of speech protected by the First Amendment." He noted that "[g]reat
works of literature have frequently been produced by authors writing under
assumed names," including those written under such pseudonyms as Mark
Twain, O. Henry, Voltaire, George Sand, and George Eliot. He noted further
that "the Court's reasoning [in Talley] embraced a respected tradition of
anonymity in the advocacy of political causes," including the Federalist Papers,
written under the pseudonym "Publius," and the papers of the Anti–Federalists, written under such pseudonyms as "Cato," "Brutus," and "the Federal
Farmer."

Justice Stevens held the Ohio anonymity requirement invalid even though
it was narrower than the blanket ban on anonymous handbilling struck down
in Talley. First, he held strict scrutiny to be the appropriate standard: "When a
law burdens core political speech, we apply 'exacting scrutiny,' and we uphold
the restriction only if it is narrowly tailored to serve an overriding state
interest." Next, he found Ohio's proffered interests in increasing voter information and preventing fraud insufficient to satisfy such scrutiny: "[Ohio's] interest in providing voters with additional relevant information does not justify a
state requirement that a writer make statements or disclosures she would
otherwise omit." And while the state had an undoubtedly legitimate interest in
preventing the dissemination of false factual statements in election campaigns,
he wrote, "we are not persuaded that they justify [the anonymity ban's]
extremely broad prohibition," which "encompasses documents that are not
even arguably false or misleading." He suggested that Ohio's direct regulation
of falsity in other detailed provisions of its election code was a less restrictive
alternative. Finally, he distinguished mandatory disclosure of political expenditures, which the Court had upheld in Buckley v. Valeo (1976; p. 1400 below), as
"a far cry from compelled self-identification on all election-related writings. A
written election-related document—particularly a leaflet—is often a personally
crafted statement of a political viewpoint [and] identification of the author
against her will is particularly intrusive [because] it reveals unmistakably the
content of her thoughts on a controversial issue."

Justice Stevens concluded: "Under our Constitution, anonymous pamphleteering is not a pernicious, fraudulent practice, but an honorable tradition of advocacy and of dissent. Anonymity is a shield from the tyranny of the majority. [Mill, On Liberty.] It thus exemplifies the purpose behind [the] First Amendment: [to] protect unpopular individuals from retaliation—and their ideas from suppression—at the hand of an intolerant society." Justice GINSBURG concurred separately, emphasizing that, in another setting, "a State's interest in protecting an election process 'might justify a more limited identification requirement.'"

Justice THOMAS concurred in the judgment, but argued that the interpretation of the free speech and press clauses should be determined by reference to "their original meaning," not by the broader principles employed by the majority. Under such an originalist approach, he found McIntyre's leaflets protected by the First Amendment: "There is little doubt that the Framers engaged in anonymous political writing. The essays in the Federalist Papers, published under the pseudonym of 'Publius,' are only the most famous example of the outpouring of anonymous political writing that occurred during the ratification of the Constitution. Of course, the simple fact that the Framers engaged in certain conduct does not necessarily prove that they forbade its prohibition by the government. In this case, however, the historical evidence indicates that Founding-era Americans opposed attempts to require that anonymous authors reveal their identities on the ground that forced disclosure violated the 'freedom of the press.' For example, the earliest and most famous American experience with freedom of the press, the 1735 Zenger trial, [involved] a printer, John Peter Zenger, who refused to reveal the anonymous authors of published attacks on the Crown governor of New York. When the governor and his council could not discover the identity of the authors, they prosecuted Zenger himself for seditious libel. Although the case set the colonies afire for its example of a jury refusing to convict a defendant of seditious libel against Crown authorities, it also signified at an early moment the extent to which anonymity and the freedom of the press were intertwined in the early American mind." He cited as another example the successful Anti–Federalist attack on Federalist editors' policy of refusing to publish anonymous works, which in his view indicated that "both Anti–Federalists and Federalists believed that the freedom of the press included the right to publish without revealing the author's name." He concluded: "While [I] am loath to overturn a century of practice shared by almost all of the States, I believe the historical evidence from the framing outweighs recent tradition."

Justice SCALIA dissented, arguing that, to the contrary, the nearly uniform tradition among the states over the last century trumped the ambiguous textual and historical claims for anonymous leafletting. He objected that the majority had invalidated "a species of protection for the election process that exists, in a variety of forms, in every State except California, and that has a pedigree dating back to the end of the 19th century. Preferring the views of the English utilitarian philosopher John Stuart Mill to the considered judgment of the American people's elected representatives from coast to coast, the Court discovers a hitherto unknown right-to-be-unknown while engaging in electoral politics." He disagreed with Justice Thomas about the inference to be drawn from the history of anonymous pamphleteering: "to prove that anonymous electioneering was used frequently is not to establish that it is a constitutional right." He would have deferred therefore, to the states' longstanding tradition disfavoring anonymity in connection with elections: "Where the meaning of a constitutional text (such as 'the freedom of speech') is unclear, the widespread and long-accepted practices of the American people are the best indication of what fundamental beliefs it was intended to enshrine." Justice Scalia also viewed anonymity more skeptically than the majority, noting that it might well "facilitate[] wrong by eliminating accountability." He would have recognized an "exemption from otherwise valid disclosure requirements," if at all, only "on the part of someone who could show a 'reasonable probability' that the compelled disclosure would result in 'threats, harassment, or reprisals from either Government officials or private parties.'"

B. COMPELLED ACCESS FOR THE SPEECH OF OTHERS

---

1. *Compelled rights of reply.* May government compel the press to furnish free coverage of replies by those it has attacked? Two decisions came to opposite answers for the electronic and print media. In RED LION BROAD-CASTING CO. v. FCC, 395 U.S. 367 (1969), reviewed below at p. ___, the Court upheld against First Amendment challenge the FCC's "fairness doctrine," which required broadcast stations to provide free reply time for individuals subjected to personal attack on the air. The Court relied heavily on the scarcity of the broadcast spectrum as a justification for imposing forced access rights on unwilling media.

In contrast, in MIAMI HERALD PUB. CO. v. TORNILLO, 418 U.S. 241 (1974), the Court held unconstitutional Florida's "right of reply" law, which granted political candidates a right to equal space to reply to criticism and attacks on their record by a newspaper. The state court had sustained the law because it furthered the "broad societal interest in the free flow of informa-tion." Chief Justice BURGER's opinion concluded, however, that the law violated the First Amendment rights of the newspaper by forcing it to publish undesired speech: "[Government] compulsion to publish that which '[newspa-per editors believe] should not be published' is unconstitutional. A responsible press is an undoubtedly desirable goal, but press responsibility is not mandated by the Constitution and like many other virtues it cannot be legislated." The fact that the newspaper was not being prevented from giving its own views did not help the defenders of the law: "The Florida statute exacts a penalty on the basis of the content of a newspaper. [Faced] with the penalties that would accrue to any newspaper that published news or commentary arguably within the reach of the right-of-access statute, editors might well conclude that the safe course is to avoid controversy. [Government]-enforced right of access inescapably 'dampens the vigor and limits the variety of public debate.'" And even if there were no such consequences to the law, it would nevertheless be invalid "because of its intrusion into the function of editors": "A newspaper is more than a passive receptacle or conduit for news, comment, and advertising. The choice of material to go into a newspaper, and the decisions made as to limitations on the size and content of the paper, and treatment of public issues and public officials—whether fair or unfair—constitute the exercise of editorial control and judgment."

2. *Compelled access by speakers to private property.* In PRUNEYARD SHOPPING CENTER v. ROBINS, 447 U.S. 74 (1980), a shopping center, in accordance with its nondiscriminatory policy of barring all expressive activity not directly related to its commercial purposes, had excluded several high school students who sought to solicit signatures for a petition protesting a UN

resolution against Zionism. California's highest court interpreted its *state* constitution to guarantee such speakers access to a privately owned shopping center, even though the Supreme Court had rejected such an access right as a matter of federal First Amendment law (see pp. 1292 above). PruneYard argued that that interpretation violated its own free speech rights. The Court unanimously rejected that argument.

Justice REHNQUIST's opinion for the Court concluded that "state constitutional provisions which permit individuals to exercise free speech and petition rights on the property of a privately owned shopping center to which the public is invited" do not violate the shopping center owner's "First Amendment right not to be forced by the State to use his property as a forum for the speech of others." Although there might be circumstances in which a State could not require an individual "to participate in the dissemination of an ideological message by displaying it on his private property," this was not such a case. Since PruneYard was open to the public, the views expressed in passing out pamphlets or seeking signatures "will not likely be identified with those of the owner." Moreover, "no specific message is dictated by the State to be displayed," so that there was "no danger of governmental discrimination for or against a particular message." And PruneYard could "expressly disavow any connection with a message by simply posting signs in the area where the speakers or handbillers stand." The majority opinion thus found both Wooley and Barnette distinguishable.

Justice POWELL's partial concurrence, joined by Justice White, cautioned that the decision did not constitute "blanket approval for state efforts to transform privately owned commercial property into public forums." He explained that, "even when no particular message is mandated by the State, First Amendment interests are affected by state action that forces a property owner to admit third-party speakers." He noted that "customers might well conclude that the messages reflect the view of the proprietor." Moreover, there might be valid First Amendment objections when speakers sought use of the premises "as a platform for views that [the owner] finds morally repugnant": "To require the owner to specify the particular ideas he finds objectionable enough to compel a response would force him to relinquish his 'freedom to maintain his own beliefs without public disclosure.' Thus, the right to control one's own speech may be burdened impermissibly even when listeners will not assume that the messages expressed on private property are those of the owner." But he found that, "[o]n the record before us, I cannot say that customers of this vast center would be likely to assume that appellees' limited speech activity expressed the views of the PruneYard or of its owner," nor that the owner had any strong ideological disagreement with anything the students or other groups were likely to say. Justices White, Marshall and Blackmun also submitted separate concurrences.

A compelled access issue again came before the Court in PACIFIC GAS & ELEC. CO. [PG&E] v. PUBLIC UTIL. COMM'N [PUC], 475 U.S. 1 (1986). In upholding a First Amendment claim against state-compelled access, the Court relied on Tornillo and distinguished PruneYard. The case involved a newsletter distributed by PG&E to its customers in the monthly billing envelope. The Commission found that the "extra space" in billing envelopes (i.e., the difference between the maximum weight mailable with a postage stamp and the weight of the monthly bill and any required legal notices) belonged to the ratepayers. The PUC held that PG&E had to allow a private advocacy group called Toward Utility Rate Normalization (TURN), which was typically opposed to PG&E in ratemaking proceedings and elsewhere, to use the extra space four times a year to communicate with PG&E customers. PG&E, a privately owned utility, claimed that requiring it "to include in its billing envelope speech of a third party with which the utility disagrees" violated its First Amendment rights.

The Court sustained this First Amendment claim. Justice POWELL's plurality opinion, joined only by Chief Justice Burger and Justices Brennan and O'Connor, relied heavily on Tornillo in overturning this state-imposed access: "Compelled access like that ordered in this case both penalizes the expression of particular points of view and forces speakers to alter their speech to conform with an agenda they do not set. These impermissible effects are not remedied by the Commission's definition of the relevant property rights. [The] concerns that caused us to invalidate the compelled access rule in Tornillo apply to appellant as well as to the institutional press. [Just] as the State is not free to 'tell a newspaper in advance what it can print and what it cannot,' [the] State is not free either to restrict appellant's speech to certain topics or views or to force appellant to respond to views that others may hold. [Under] Tornillo a forced access rule that would accomplish these purposes indirectly is similarly forbidden. [PruneYard] is not to the contrary. [Notably] absent [there] was any concern that access to this area might affect the shopping center owner's exercise of his own right to speak: the owner did not even allege that he objected to the content of the pamphlets; nor was the access right content-based. PruneYard thus does not undercut the proposition that forced associations that burden protected speech are impermissible."

Justice Powell emphasized that the Commission's order did not "simply award access to the public at large; rather, it discriminates on the basis of the viewpoints of the selected speakers." Among the acknowledged purposes of the access order was the aim "to assist groups [that] challenged [PG&E] in the Commission's ratemaking proceedings in raising funds. [Access] to the envelopes thus is not content-neutral. [Because] access is awarded only to those who disagree with [PG&E's] views and who are hostile to [its] interests, [PG&E] must contend with the fact that whenever it speaks out on a given issue, it may be forced [to] help disseminate hostile views. [PG&E] 'might well conclude' that, under these circumstances, 'the safe course is to avoid controversy,' thereby reducing the free flow of information and ideas that the First Amendment seeks to promote. Appellant does not [have] the right to be free from vigorous debate. But it *does* have the right to be free from government restrictions that abridge its own rights in order to 'enhance the relative voice' of its opponents. [In addition to constituting an impermissible content regulation by favoring some groups rather than others, the] Commission's access order also impermissibly requires appellant to associate with speech with which appellant may disagree. [For] corporations as for individuals, the choice to speak includes within it the choice of what not to say. [Were] the government freely able to compel corporate speakers to propound political messages with which they disagree, this protection [of corporate speech] would be empty, for the government could require speakers to affirm in one breath that which they deny in the next."

Justice MARSHALL concurred only in the judgment, emphasizing two distinctions between this case and PruneYard: PG&E had "issued no invitation to the general public to use its billing envelope for speech or for any other purpose," and the state here had deprived PG&E of control over "the space in [its billing] envelope that [it] would otherwise use for its own speech." Chief Justice Burger, while joining Justice Powell's opinion, submitted a separate concurrence as well.

Justice REHNQUIST, joined by Justices White and Stevens, dissented, emphasizing PG&E's status as a corporation and regulated public utility: "This Court has recognized that natural persons enjoy negative free speech rights because of their interest in self-expression; an individual's right not to speak or to associate with the speech of others is a component of the broader constitutional interest of natural persons in freedom of conscience. [Extension] of the individual freedom of conscience decisions to business corporations strains the rationale of those cases beyond the breaking point. To ascribe to such artificial entities an 'intellect' or 'mind' for freedom of conscience purposes is to confuse metaphor with reality." Even if such a right extended to the institutional media, he argued, it ought not extend to other businesses: "Corporations generally have not played the historic role of newspapers as conveyers of individual ideas and opinion." The dissenters also distinguished Tornillo on the ground that the likelihood of deterrence of speech by PG&E was minimal.

Justice STEVENS added in a separate dissent: "I assume that the plurality would not object to a utility commission rule dictating the format of the bill, even as to required warnings and the type size of various provisos and disclaimers [and] would permit the Commission to require the utility to disseminate legal notices of public hearings and ratemaking proceedings written by it. [Given] that the Commission can require the utility to make certain statements and to carry the Commission's own messages to its customers, it seems but a small step to acknowledge that the Commission can also require the utility to act as the conduit for a public interest group's message that bears a close relationship to the purpose of the billing envelope. An analog to this requirement appears in securities law: the Securities and Exchange Commission requires the incumbent board of directors to transmit proposals of dissident shareholders which it opposes. Presumably the plurality does not doubt the constitutionality of the SEC's requirement under the First Amendment." Justice Blackmun did not participate in the case.

Should a corporation such as PG&E have a right against compelled speech? A right of free speech at all? Justice Rehnquist's dissent in PG&E notwithstanding, the Court has held that they do. See First National Bank v. Bellotti, p. 1413 below. Is such protection justified? If corporations lack autonomy comparable to that of individuals, what theory of free speech calls for their protection? Is corporate speech instrumentally valuable in ventilating important ideas, even if it is not intrinsically valuable to any human agent? But if corporations lack autonomy rights, what purpose is served in protecting them against compelled speech? For critical assessments of corporate speech rights, see Bezanson, "Institutional Speech," 80 Iowa L. Rev. 735 (1995); Baker, "Turner Broadcasting: Content–Based Regulation of Persons and Presses," 1994 Sup. Ct. Rev. 57.

In TURNER BROADCASTING SYSTEM, INC. v. FCC, 512 U.S. 622 (1994)(Turner I), the Court considered a claim that compelled access for broadcasters to cable television transmission violates the First Amendment. In Turner, the Court rejected cable operators' argument that sections 4 and 5 of the Cable Television Consumer Protection and Competition Act of 1992, which require cable operators to carry the signals of a specified number of local broadcast television stations, were subject to strict scrutiny under the Court's compelled-speech precedents. Congress enacted the "must-carry" provisions out of concern that "the physical characteristics of cable transmission, compounded by the increasing concentration of economic power in the cable industry, are endangering the ability of over-the-air broadcast television stations to compete for a viewing audience and thus for necessary operating revenues." Cable operators, relying upon Tornillo and PG&E, argued that the must-carry rules interfered with their editorial discretion and forced them to carry unwanted speech in violation of their First Amendment rights.

Justice KENNEDY, writing for the Court, began by acknowledging that "[a]t the heart of the First Amendment lies the principle that each person should decide for him or herself the ideas and beliefs deserving of expression, consideration, and adherence," and that "[g]overnment action [that] requires the utterance of a particular message favored by the Government contravenes this essential right." But he found that the must-carry rules did not fall within this core principle because they were content-neutral rather than content-based: "the must-carry rules, on their face, impose burdens and confer benefits without reference to the content of speech. Although the provisions interfere with cable operators' editorial discretion by compelling them to offer carriage to a certain minimum number of broadcast stations, [the] number of channels a cable operator must set aside depends only on the operator's channel capacity, [not] the programming it offers to subscribers." He also rejected the cable operators' argument that "Congress' purpose in enacting [must-carry] was to promote speech of a favored content": "Our review of the Act and its various findings persuades us that Congress' overriding objective in enacting must-carry was not to favor programming of a particular subject matter, viewpoint, or format, but rather to preserve access to free television programming for the 40 percent of Americans without cable. [This] overriding congressional purpose is unrelated to the content of expression disseminated by cable and broadcast speakers." Thus, Justice Kennedy concluded, the must-carry rules, unlike those at issue in Tornillo and PG&E, involved no content-based trigger or penalty. Also unlike the rules in Tornillo and PG&E, must-carry would not "force cable operators to alter their own messages to respond to the broadcast programming they are required to carry. Given cable's long history of serving as a conduit for broadcast signals, there appears little risk that cable viewers would assume that the broadcast stations carried on a cable system convey ideas or messages endorsed by the cable operator."

Having found the compelled access here content-neutral, Justice Kennedy concluded that the appropriate standard of scrutiny was not strict scrutiny as in Tornillo or PG&E, but rather the intermediate scrutiny set forth in United States v. O'Brien and Ward v. Rock Against Racism. He concluded that the must-carry provisions served three important interests unrelated to the suppression of free expression: "(1) preserving the benefits of free, over-the-air local broadcast television, (2) promoting the widespread dissemination of information from a multiplicity of sources, and (3) promoting fair competition in the market for television programming." But, joined on this point only by Chief Justice Rehnquist and Justices Blackmun and Souter, he found the congressional record and the record on summary judgment below insufficient to demonstrate that must-carry was narrowly tailored to those interests. Accordingly, this plurality concluded that the case should be remanded for development of a more thorough factual record concerning the harms broadcasters would suffer without must-carry and the harms cable would suffer with it.

Justice STEVENS provided a fifth vote for this disposition, even though, in his separate opinion concurring in part and in the judgment, he stated that he would have preferred to affirm the summary judgment below for the government. In Justice Stevens' view, "[a]n industry need not be in its death throes before Congress may act to protect it from economic harm threatened by a monopoly," and thus, without further findings, the record demonstrated a sufficiently close fit between the must-carry rules and the harms they were designed to avert. But he voted with the plurality to avoid the possibility that "no disposition of this appeal would command the support of a majority of this Court." Justice Blackmun also filed a concurrence.

Justice O'CONNOR, joined by Justices Scalia and Ginsburg and in part by Justice Thomas, dissented in part, arguing that the must-carry rules amounted to impermissibly content-based compelled speech: "[L]ooking at the statute at issue, I cannot avoid the conclusion that its preference for broadcasters over cable programmers is justified with reference to content"—for example, by Congress's advertence to the desirable diversity and local affairs focus of broadcast programming. She continued: "[M]y conclusion that the must-carry rules are content based leads me to conclude that they are an impermissible restraint on the cable operators' editorial discretion as well as on the cable programmers' speech. For reasons related to the content of speech, the rules restrict the ability of cable operators to put on the programming they prefer, and require them to include programming they would rather avoid. This, it seems to me, puts this case squarely within the rule of [PG&E and Tornillo.]" Justice GINSBURG also filed a separate partial dissent agreeing that the must-carry rules reflected a content preference and thus required strict scrutiny.

The remand in Turner I led to 18 months of additional factfinding, after which the district court granted summary judgment for the Government and other appellees, concluding that the expanded record contained substantial evidence supporting Congress' predictive judgment that the must-carry provisions furthered important governmental interests in preserving cable carriage of local broadcast stations, and were narrowly tailored to promote those interests. In TURNER BROADCASTING SYSTEM, INC. v. FCC, ___ U.S. ___, 117 S.Ct. 1174 (1997) (Turner II), the Court affirmed by a vote of 5–4. Justice KENNEDY again wrote for the Court. Reiterating the standard of review set forth in Turner I, he emphasized the need for deference to Congress: "This is not a case in which we are called upon to give our best judgment as to the likely economic consequences of certain financial arrangements or business structures, or to assess competing economic theories and predictive judgments, as we would in a case arising, say, under the antitrust laws. [The] issue before us is whether, given conflicting views of the probable development of the television industry, Congress had substantial evidence for making the judgment that it did. We need not put our imprimatur on Congress' economic theory in order to validate the reasonableness of its judgment. [We] cannot displace Congress' judgment respecting content-neutral regulations with our own, so long as its policy is grounded on reasonable factual findings supported by evidence that is substantial for a legislative determination." Under this approach, Justice Kennedy found, after an exhaustive review of the factual contentions in the case, that the must-carry requirements were substantially related to important government interests in competition and diversity in video programming. Justice BREYER, who had replaced Justice BLACKMUN, who voted with the majority in Turner I, joined the majority, but concurred separately to note the presence of "important First Amendment interests on both sides of the equation," and to say that he found persuasive the diversity rationale but not the competition rationale. Justice O'CONNOR wrote an extended dissent, joined by all the other dissenters in Turner I. She criticized the majority for applying an "inappropriately lenient level of scrutiny" and "exhibiting an extraordinary and unwarranted deference for congressional judgments," and found even on the new record that "the statute is not narrowly tailored to serve a substantial interest in preventing anticompetitive conduct."

3. *Compelled access to a parade.* HURLEY v. IRISH–AMERICAN GAY, LESBIAN AND BISEXUAL GROUP OF BOSTON [GLIB], ___ U.S. ___, 115 S.Ct. 2338 (1995), held that a privately organized St. Patrick's Day parade need

not include, against the organizers' will, a self-proclaimed gay contingent among its marchers. Massachusetts state antidiscrimination law forbids discrimination on the basis of, inter alia, sexual orientation in the admission or treatment of any person in a place of public accommodation. The state courts found the annual Boston St. Patrick's Day parade to be a public accommodation, found GLIB's exclusion from the parade to be based on sexual orientation, and ordered GLIB admitted to the parade. John J. "Wacko" Hurley and other members of the South Boston Allied War Veterans Council, the private organization that customarily organized the parade, protested this forced inclusion as a violation of their First Amendment rights, and the Court sustained their claim.

Justice SOUTER wrote for a unanimous Court: "The issue in this case is whether Massachusetts may require private citizens who organize a parade to include among the marchers a group imparting a message the organizers do not wish to convey. We hold that such a mandate violates the First Amendment. [We] use the word 'parade' to indicate marchers who are making some sort of collective point, not just to each other but to bystanders along the way. [Parades] are [a] form of expression, not just motion. [The] protected expression that inheres in a parade is not limited to its banners and songs, [but extends to its] 'symbolism.' [A] narrow, succinctly articulable message is not a condition of constitutional protection, which if confined to expressions conveying a 'particularized message,' would never reach the unquestionably shielded painting of Jackson Pollock, music of Arnold Schonberg, or Jabberwocky verse of Lewis Carroll. [The] South Boston celebration is [expressive:] Spectators line the streets; people march in costumes and uniforms, carrying flags and banners with all sorts of messages (e.g., 'England get out of Ireland,' 'Say no to drugs'); marching bands and pipers play, floats are pulled along, and the whole show is broadcast over Boston television. To be sure, [the Council] is rather lenient in admitting participants. But a private speaker does not forfeit constitutional protection simply by combining multifarious voices, or by failing to edit their themes to isolate an exact message as the exclusive subject matter of the speech. [The] presentation of an edited compilation of speech generated by other persons is a staple of most newspapers' opinion pages, which, of course, fall squarely within the core of First Amendment security [Tornillo], [and the] selection of contingents to make a parade is entitled to similar protection.

"Respondents' participation as a unit in the parade was equally expressive. GLIB was formed for the very purpose of marching in it, as the trial court found, in order to celebrate its members' identity as openly gay, lesbian, and bisexual descendants of the Irish immigrants, to show that there are such individuals in the community, and to support the like men and women who sought to march in the New York [St. Patrick's Day] parade. [M]embers of GLIB [the previous year] marched behind a shamrock-strewn banner with the simple inscription 'Irish American Gay, Lesbian and Bisexual Group of Boston.' GLIB understandably seeks to communicate its ideas as part of the existing parade, rather than staging one of its own.

"[Hurley and the Council] disclaim any intent to exclude homosexuals as such, and no individual member of GLIB claims to have been excluded from parading as a member of any group that the Council has approved to march. Instead, the disagreement goes to the admission of GLIB as its own parade unit carrying its own banner. Since every participating unit affects the message conveyed by the private organizers, the state courts' application of the statute produced an order essentially requiring petitioners to alter the expressive content of their parade. [The] state courts' application of the statute had the effect of declaring the sponsors' speech itself to be the public accommodation.

Under this approach any contingent of protected individuals with a message would have the right to participate in petitioners' speech, so that the communication produced by the private organizers would be shaped by all those protected by the law who wished to join in with some expressive demonstration of their own. But this use of the State's power violates the fundamental rule of protection under the First Amendment, that a speaker has the autonomy to choose the content of his own message.

"[The Council's] claim to the benefit of this principle of autonomy to control one's own speech is as sound as the South Boston parade is expressive. [The] Council clearly decided to exclude a message it did not like from the communication it chose to make, and that is enough to invoke its right as a private speaker to shape its expression by speaking on one subject while remaining silent on another. The message it disfavored is not difficult to identify. Although GLIB's point (like the Council's) is not wholly articulate, a contingent marching behind the organization's banner would at least bear witness to the fact that some Irish are gay, lesbian, or bisexual, and the presence of the organized marchers would suggest their view that people of their sexual orientations have as much claim to unqualified social acceptance as heterosexuals and indeed as members of parade units organized around other identifying characteristics. The parade's organizers may not believe these facts about Irish sexuality to be so, or they may object to unqualified social acceptance of gays and lesbians or have some other reason for wishing to keep GLIB's message out of the parade. But whatever the reason, it boils down to the choice of a speaker not to propound a particular point of view, and that choice is presumed to lie beyond the government's power to control."

Justice Souter rejected GLIB's attempt to analogize the case to Turner Broadcasting, finding that a parade, unlike a cable system, is a not mere "conduit" that is unlikely to be identified with the speech it carries: "[T]his metaphor is not apt here, because GLIB's participation would likely be perceived as having resulted from the Council's customary determination about a unit admitted to the parade, that its message was worthy of presentation and quite possibly of support as well. [Unlike the individual, unrelated programs on cable, the] parade's overall message is distilled from the individual presentations along the way, and each unit's expression is perceived by spectators as part of the whole." Nor, he found, did the St. Patrick's Day parade present any problem, as cable had in Turner, of a "monopolistic opportunity to shut out some speakers": "Considering that GLIB presumably would have had a fair shot (under neutral criteria developed by the city) at obtaining a parade permit of its own, respondents have not shown that petitioners enjoy the capacity to 'silence the voice of competing speakers,' as cable operators do with respect to program providers who wish to reach subscribers." Justice Souter likewise rejected GLIB's attempt to analogize the case to PruneYard, noting that there, "the proprietors were running 'a business establishment that is open to the public to come and go as they please,' that the solicitations would 'not likely be identified with those of the owner,' and that the proprietors could 'expressly disavow any connection with the message by simply posting signs in the area where the speakers or handbillers stand' "—all conditions absent in a moving, expressive parade, where "[d]isclaimers would be quite curious."

Suppose the parade had been run by the City of Boston rather than the South Boston Allied War Veterans Council. Would GLIB's exclusion have been forbidden by the First Amendment? Would such a parade have amounted to a public forum? A limited public forum? Or not a public forum at all? If the federal government sponsored a parade for military veterans, would it be obliged to include a contingent of avowedly gay former service members? Even if it maintained a policy of excluding homosexuals from the military? Recall the materials in chapter 11, section 2A.

4. *The Court's methodology in compelled speech cases.* Note that the question whether government has compelled a speaker to utter or to be associated with undesired speech is a threshold question. If a law does not compel speech, as the Court found the California constitutional provision upheld in PruneYard did not, then no First Amendment scrutiny is required; rationality review is sufficient. If a law *does* compel speech, then it is analyzed just as a law forbidding speech would be analyzed. Thus, if a law compels speech of a particular content, as did the laws in Barnette, Wooley, and McIntyre, or compels counterspeech in response to speech of particular content, as did the laws in Tornillo and PG&E, it is treated as content-based and receives strict scrutiny. But if a law compels speech for reasons unrelated to content, as did the must-carry rules in Turner as the majority read them, then, at most, intermediate scrutiny under O'Brien and Ward is required.

5. *Constitutional compelled speech.* Federal and state regulatory schemes compel a great deal of speech. Recall Justice Stevens' example, in dissent in PG&E, of the SEC requirement that certain materials, including dissident stockholders' proposals, be included in the proxy statements of publicly traded corporations. Consider also the requirement that the Surgeon General's official warnings on the dangers of tobacco be affixed to cigarette packages, and the Food and Drug Administration's many requirements that food content or drug warnings be disclosed on food and drug labels. Most of these regulatory requirements have never been the subject of any serious First Amendment challenge. What explains this seeming deference to compelled speech in the regulatory context? The fact that the speakers in this setting are corporations, which lack freedom of conscience? Recall Justice Rehnquist's dissent in PG&E. The fact that speech in connection with sales of securities and consumer products is commercial speech, whose regulation is subject generally to more deferential review? Recall that in dictum in Virginia Board of Pharmacy (1976; p. 1176 above), the Court suggested that it may be "appropriate to require that a commercial message appear in such a form, or include such additional information, warnings and disclaimers as are necessary to prevent its being deceptive." Or are such regulations best understood as infringing speech rights, but justified nonetheless by the government's compelling interest in protecting health and safety?

SECTION 2.   FREEDOM OF ASSOCIATION

Introduction. This section focuses on the concept of freedom of association, a concept which has surfaced occasionally in cases considered earlier. As early as De Jonge v. Oregon (1937; p. 1060 above), the Court relied on the First Amendment reference to "the right of the people peaceably to assemble" in invalidating a conviction. In NAACP v. Alabama, the 1958 decision that follows, the Court identified an independent constitutional "right of association" and began to develop that right vigorously. The right to associate reflects the notion that individual rights of expression can be made more effectual by collective action. As the Court later summarized in Roberts v. United States Jaycees (1984; p. 1399 below): "An individual's freedom to speak, worship, and to petition the Government for the redress of grievances could not be vigorously protected from interference by the State unless a correlative freedom to engage in group effort toward those ends were not also guaranteed." The Court has tended to view the right of association as dependent on underlying individual rights of expression; there is no right of association in the abstract. See Dallas v. Stanglin, 490 U.S. 19 (1989) (rejecting a freedom of association claim against a Dallas ordinance barring social dancing between teenagers and adults, stating "we do not think the Constitution recognizes a generalized right of 'social association' that includes chance encounters in dance halls").

The Court has reviewed several types of government infringement of the right of expressive association protected by the First Amendment. Most directly, government might simply outlaw an organization or membership in it. The Court has limited such direct restrictions in cases discussed earlier. Recall, for example, that in Scales and Noto (1957; p. 1068 above), the Court held that mere membership in the Communist Party was insufficient for conviction unless the organization actively advocated lawless action and the individual member knowingly and actively sought to advance that end. Likewise, recall that the Court in Brandenburg (1969; p. 1071 above), overruling Whitney, held that one may not be punished simply for assembling with an organization that advocates violent political or industrial reform.

The materials that follow explore several additional government techniques sometimes held to infringe associational liberty. First, government might seek to monitor or intimidate an association by requiring either that the group or an individual member of a group disclose information about group membership in violation of what the Court in NAACP v. Alabama called the right to "privacy in group association." See section 2A below. Second, government might restrict activities centrally linked to the purpose of an association, such as meetings or litigation or boycott activities. See section 2B below. Third, government might deny governmental benefits or privileges to members of certain associations. Recall that in the Elrod line of cases (pp. 1312 above), the Court held that most public jobs may not be conditioned on membership in the victorious political party. Before that, the Court considered a number of denials of government privileges to members of "subversive" organizations. See section 2C below.

The Court has also held that the right to associate entails a right not to associate, comparable to the right not to speak. It has therefore, for example, invalidated certain compulsory fees exacted from unwilling group members and reviewed laws requiring groups to include unwanted members. See section 2D below. These various techniques of interference with associational freedom are examined in turn in the materials that follow.

A. COMPELLED DISCLOSURE OF MEMBERSHIP

A series of cases in the late 1950s and early 1960s reviewed efforts to inhibit the activities of the National Association for the Advancement of Colored People (NAACP) by requiring disclosure of its membership lists in various contexts. In addition to the cases that follow, see Bates v. Little Rock, 361 U.S. 516 (1960), invalidating a requirement that membership lists be disclosed in connection with an occupational license tax, and Louisiana ex rel Gremillion v. NAACP, 366 U.S. 293 (1961), restraining enforcement of a statute requiring nonprofit organizations to file membership lists. On these and related cases generally, see Kalven, The Negro and the First Amendment (1965). Note that associational liberty issues are raised when government seeks information not only about an organization's members, but also about an individual's associational activities and beliefs. Typically, the governmental demands are challenged because they allegedly "chill" the exercise of First Amendment freedoms.

NAACP v. Alabama

357 U.S. 449, 78 S.Ct. 1163, 2 L.Ed.2d 1488 (1958).

[In this case, the Court held unconstitutional Alabama's demand that the NAACP reveal the names and addresses of all of its Alabama members and agents. The State's demand was made in the course of an injunction action brought in 1956 to stop the NAACP from conducting activities in Alabama, on the ground that it had failed to comply with the requirement that foreign corporations qualify before "doing business" in the State. The NAACP, a New York membership corporation, operated in Alabama largely through local affiliates that were unincorporated associations. It considered itself exempt from the State's foreign corporation registration law. While the injunction action was pending, the State moved for the production of a large number of the NAACP's records. The NAACP "produced substantially all the data called for [except] its membership lists, as to which it contended that Alabama could not constitutionally compel disclosure." The trial court adjudged the NAACP in contempt and imposed a $100,000 fine.]

Justice HARLAN delivered the opinion of the Court.

Effective advocacy of both public and private points of view, particularly controversial ones, is undeniably enhanced by group association, as this Court has [recognized] by remarking upon the close nexus between the freedoms of speech and assembly. [E.g., De Jonge.] It is beyond debate that freedom to engage in association for the advancement of beliefs and ideas is an inseparable aspect of the "liberty" assured by the Due Process Clause of the 14th Amendment, which embraces freedom of speech. Of course, it is immaterial whether the beliefs sought to be advanced by association pertain to political, economic, religious or cultural matters, and state action which may have the effect of curtailing the freedom to associate is subject to the closest scrutiny. The fact that Alabama [has] taken no direct action [to] restrict the right of petitioner's members to associate freely does not end inquiry into the effect of the production order. [I]n the domain of these indispensable liberties, whether of speech, press, or association, the decisions of this Court recognize that abridgment of such rights, even though unintended, may inevitably follow from varied forms of governmental [action]. It is hardly a novel perception that compelled disclosure of affiliation with groups engaged in advocacy may constitute [an effective] restraint on freedom of association. [There is a] vital relationship between freedom to associate and privacy in one's associations. [Inviolability] of privacy in group association may in many circumstances be indispensable to preservation of freedom of association, particularly where a group espouses dissident [beliefs].

We think that the production order [must] be regarded as entailing the likelihood of a substantial restraint upon the exercise by petitioner's members of their right to freedom of association. Petitioner has made an uncontroverted showing that on past occasions revelation of the identity of its rank-and-file members has exposed these members to economic reprisal, loss of employment, threat of physical coercion, and other manifestations of public hostility. Under these circumstances, we think it apparent that compelled disclosure of petitioner's Alabama membership is likely to affect adversely the ability of petitioner and its members to pursue their collective effort to foster beliefs which they admittedly have the right to advocate, in that it may induce members to withdraw from the Association and dissuade others from joining it because of fear of exposure of their beliefs shown through their associations and of the consequences of this [exposure].

We turn to the [question] whether Alabama has demonstrated an interest in obtaining the disclosures it seeks from petitioner which is sufficient to justify the deterrent effect which we have concluded these disclosures may well have on the free exercise [of] constitutionally protected right of association. [Such a] "subordinating interest of the State must be compelling." It is important to bear in mind that petitioner asserts no right to absolute immunity from state investigation. [Petitioner] has not objected to divulging the identity of its members who are employed by or hold official positions with it. It has urged the rights solely of its ordinary rank-and-file [members]. Whether there was "justification" in this instance turns solely on the substantiality of Alabama's interest in obtaining the membership lists. [The] exclusive purpose [claimed] was to determine whether petitioner was conducting intrastate business in violation of the Alabama foreign corporation registration statute. [W]e are unable to perceive that the disclosure of the names of petitioner's rank-and-file members has a substantial bearing on the state interest. [W]hatever interest the State may have in obtaining names of ordinary members has not been shown to be sufficient to overcome petitioner's constitutional objections to the production order.[1] [W]e conclude that Alabama has fallen short of showing a controlling justification for the deterrent effect on the free enjoyment of the right to associate which disclosure of membership lists is likely to [have].

Reversed.

––––––––

Shelton v. Tucker

364 U.S. 479, 81 S.Ct. 247, 5 L.Ed.2d 231 (1960).

[This case held unconstitutional an Arkansas statute—Act 10—which required every teacher, as a condition of employment in a state-supported school or college, to file "annually an affidavit listing without limitation every organization to which he has belonged or regularly contributed within the preceding five years." Shelton, who had taught in the Little Rock schools for 25 years, refused to file an affidavit, and his contract was not renewed. In the trial court, the evidence showed that he was not a member of any organization advocating the overthrow of the Government but that he was a member of the NAACP. The trial court upheld Act 10, finding that the information sought was "relevant."]

1. Justice Harlan distinguished BRYANT v. ZIMMERMAN, 278 U.S. 63 (1926), where the Court had upheld a New York law requiring disclosure of membership lists of any organization requiring an oath as a condition of membership. That law had been challenged by a member of the Ku Klux Klan. One of the distinctions noted by Justice Harlan was that Bryant had rested on "the peculiar character of the Klan's activities, involving acts of unlawful intimidation and violence." Moreover, the KKK, unlike the NAACP here, had refused to give the state "*any* information as to its local activities."

Justice STEWART delivered the opinion of the [Court].

It is urged [that] Act 10 deprives teachers in Arkansas of their rights to personal, associational, and academic liberty. [I]n considering this contention, we deal with two basic postulates. *First.* There can be no doubt of the right of a state to investigate the competence and fitness of those whom it hires to teach in its schools. [Here], there can be no question of the relevance of a state's inquiry into the fitness and competence of its teachers. *Second.* [To] compel a teacher to disclose his every associational tie is to impair that teacher's right of free association. [Such] interference with personal freedom is conspicuously accented when the teacher serves at the absolute will of those to whom the disclosure must be made. [The] statute does not provide that the information it requires be kept confidential. [The] record contains evidence to indicate that fear of public disclosure is neither theoretical nor groundless. Even if there were no disclosure to the general public, the pressure upon a teacher to avoid any ties which might displease those who control his professional destiny would be constant and heavy. [The] vigilant protection of constitutional freedoms is nowhere more vital than in the community of American [schools].

The question to be decided here is not whether the State [can] ask certain of its teachers about all their organizational relationships. It is not whether the State can ask all of its teachers about certain of their associational ties. It is not whether teachers can be asked how many organizations they belong to, or how much time they spend in organizational activity. The question is whether the State can ask every one of its teachers to disclose every single organization with which he has been associated over a five-year period. The scope of the inquiry required by Act 10 is completely unlimited. [The Act] requires a teacher [to] list, without number, every conceivable kind of associational tie—social, professional, political, avocational, or religious. Many such relationships could have no possible bearing upon the teacher's occupational competence or fitness. [This] Court has held that, even though the governmental purpose be legitimate and substantial, that purpose cannot be pursued by means that broadly stifle fundamental personal liberties when the end can be more narrowly achieved. The breadth of legislative abridgment must be viewed in the light of less drastic means for achieving the same basic purpose. [The] unlimited and indiscriminate sweep of the statute now before us brings it within the ban of our prior cases. The statute's comprehensive interference with associational freedom goes far beyond what might be justified in the exercise of the State's legitimate inquiry into the fitness and competency of its teachers.

Reversed.

Justice FRANKFURTER, joined by Justices Clark, Harlan, and Whittaker, dissenting.

[The] Court strikes down [the law] on the ground that "many such relationships could have no possible bearing upon the teacher's occupational competence or fitness." [But] presumably, a teacher may have so many divers associations, so many divers commitments, that they consume his time and energy and interest at the expense of his work or even of his professional dedication. [A] school board is entitled to inquire whether any of its teachers has placed himself, or is placing himself, in a condition where his work may suffer. [A] teacher's answers to the questions which Arkansas asks, moreover, may serve the purpose of making known to school authorities persons who come into contact with the teacher in all of the phases of his activity in the community, and who can be questioned, if need be, concerning the teacher's conduct in matters which this Court can certainly not now say are lacking in any pertinence to professional fitness. [The selection of teachers] is an intricate affair [and] if it is to be informed, it must be based upon a comprehensive range of information. I am unable to say [that] Arkansas could not reasonably find that the information which the statute requires [is] germane to that selection. [Of course,] if the information gathered [is] used to further a scheme of terminating the employment of teachers solely because of their membership in unpopular organizations, that use will run afoul of the Fourteenth Amendment. It will be time enough, if such use is made, to hold the application of the [law] unconstitutional.

Gibson v. Florida Legislative Investigation Comm.

372 U.S. 539, 83 S.Ct. 889, 9 L.Ed.2d 929 (1963).

Justice GOLDBERG delivered the opinion of the Court.

This case is the culmination of protracted litigation involving legislative investigating committees of the State of Florida and the Miami branch of the [NAACP]. [In 1957, an earlier legislative committee had sought the entire membership list of the local NAACP branch. Florida's highest court barred that request but stated that the committee could compel the custodian of the records to bring them to committee hearings and to refer to them to determine whether specific individuals, identified as or suspected of being Communists, were NAACP members. The respondent Committee here was established in 1959 to resume the investigation. Gibson, the President of the Miami branch, was ordered to bring the records pertaining to the identity of members of and contributors to the Miami and state NAACP organizations. Gibson, relying on the First Amendment, did not bring the records but told the Committee that he would answer questions concerning membership in the NAACP on the basis of his personal knowledge. He was given the names and shown photographs of 14 persons previously identified as being involved in Communist or Communist-front affairs. Gibson said that he could associate none of them with the NAACP. For his failure to produce the records, a state court found him in contempt and sentenced him to six months' imprisonment and a $1200 fine.]

[It] is an essential prerequisite to the validity of an investigation which intrudes into the area of constitutionally protected rights of speech, press, association and petition that the State convincingly show a substantial relation between the information sought and a subject of overriding and compelling state interest. Absent such a ["nexus"], the Committee has not "demonstrated so cogent an interest in obtaining and making public" the membership information sought [as] to "justify the substantial abridgment of associational freedom which such disclosures will effect." [Bates v. Little Rock.]

[The] Committee contends that [e.g., Uphaus and Barenblatt] compel a result here upholding the legislative right of inquiry.[1] In [those cases], however,

---

1. The Court here referred to two cases involving Cold War era legislative investigations into internal "subversion." In BARENBLATT v. UNITED STATES, 360 U.S. 109 (1959), the Court rejected the First Amendment claim of a witness who had been held in contempt of Congress for refusing to answer several questions concerning his membership in the Communist Party. Justice HARLAN, writing for the 5–4 majority, held that Congress "has wide power to legislate in the field of Communist activity in this country, and to conduct appropriate investigations in aid thereof," and that this valid legislative purpose outweighed Barenblatt's First Amendment interest in refusing to testify. Justice BLACK, joined by Chief Justice Warren and Justice Douglas, dissented on the ground that

it was a refusal to answer a question or questions concerning the witness' *own* past or present membership *in the Communist Party* which supported his conviction. It is apparent that [the] result in those cases were founded on the holding that the Communist Party is not an ordinary or legitimate political party [and] that, because of its particular nature, membership therein is *itself* a permissible subject of regulation and legislative scrutiny. [Here,] however, it is not alleged Communists [who are] the witnesses before the Committee and it is not discovery of their membership in that party which is the object of the challenged inquiries. Rather, it is the NAACP itself which is the subject of the investigation, and it is its local president [who was] held in contempt. [There] is no suggestion that the Miami branch of the NAACP or the national organization with which it is affiliated was, or is, itself a subversive organization [or that their] activities or policies [were] either Communist dominated or influenced. In fact, this very record indicates that the association was and is against communism and has voluntarily taken steps to keep Communists from being [members]. [Compelling] such an organization [to] disclose its membership presents [a] question wholly different from compelling the Communist Party to disclose its own membership.

[The] record in this case is insufficient to show a substantial connection between the Miami branch of the NAACP and Communist *activities* which [is] an essential prerequisite to demonstrating the immediate, substantial, and subordinating state interest necessary to sustain its right of inquiry into the membership lists. [There] is here merely indirect, less than unequivocal, and mostly hearsay testimony that in years past some 14 people who were asserted to be, or to have been, Communists or members of Communist front or "affiliated organizations" attended occasional meetings of the Miami branch of the NAACP "and/or" were members of that branch, which had a total membership of about 1,000. [The] strong associational interest in maintaining the privacy of membership lists of groups engaged in the constitutionally protected free trade in ideas and beliefs may not be substantially infringed upon such a

the committee was not acting in aid of a legitimate legislative function: "I think Barenblatt's conviction violates the Constitution because the chief aim, purpose and practice of the House Un–American Activities Committee, as disclosed by its many reports, is to try witnesses and punish them because they are or have been Communists or because they refuse to admit or deny Communist affiliations. The punishment imposed is generally punishment by humiliation and public shame." Justice BRENNAN agreed in a separate dissent: "[N]o purpose for the investigation of Barenblatt is revealed by the record except exposure purely for the sake of exposure."

In UPHAUS v. WYMAN, 360 U.S. 72 (1959), decided the same day as Barenblatt, the Court similarly upheld a conviction for contempt of a state legislative process. Uphaus refused to produce a list of all guests who had attended a summer camp conducted in New Hampshire by World Fellowship, Inc., of which he was executive director. Justice CLARK's majority opinion rejected Uphaus' First Amendment claim, noting that

here the New Hampshire Attorney General, acting as a one-man legislative committee investigating subversion, "had valid reason to believe that the speakers and guests at World Fellowship might be subversive persons within the meaning of the New Hampshire Act." He added that "exposure—in the sense of disclosure—is an inescapable incident of an investigation" such as this, and that "the governmental interest in self-preservation is sufficiently compelling to subordinate the interest in associational privacy." Justice BRENNAN, joined by Chief Justice Warren and Justices Black and Douglas, dissented, insisting that the record showed "that the investigatory objective was the impermissible one of exposure for exposure's sake." He could find "no serious and substantial relationship between the furnishing [of] further minutiae about what was going on at the [camp] and the process of legislation. [We] must demand some initial showing by the state sufficient to counter balance the interest in privacy. [The State] has made no such showing here."

slender showing. [While,] of course, all legitimate organizations are the beneficiaries of these protections, they are all the more essential here, where the challenged privacy is that of persons espousing beliefs already unpopular with their neighbors and the deterrent and "chilling" effect on the free exercise of constitutionally enshrined rights of free speech, expression, and association is consequently the more immediate and substantial.

Reversed.

Justice HARLAN, whom Justices CLARK, STEWART, and WHITE join, [dissenting].

[Until] today, I had never supposed that any of our decisions [could] possibly be taken as suggesting any difference in the degree [of] investigatory interest as between Communist infiltration *of* organizations and Communist activity *by* organizations. See, e.g., [Barenblatt]. [The "nexus" here was sufficient] unless "nexus" requires an investigating agency to prove in advance the very things it is trying to find out. [I] also find it difficult to see how this case really presents any serious question as to interference with freedom of association. Given the willingness of the petitioner to testify from recollection as to individual memberships in the local branch of the NAACP, the germaneness of the membership records to the subject matter of the Committee's investigation, and the limited purpose for which their use was sought—as an aid to refreshing the witness' recollection, involving their divulgence only to the petitioner himself—this case of course bears no resemblance whatever to [NAACP v. Alabama] or [Bates], [where] the State had sought general divulgence of local NAACP membership lists without any showing of a justifying state interest.

COMPELLED DISCLOSURE OF POLITICAL CAMPAIGN CONTRIBUTIONS

In BUCKLEY v. VALEO, 424 U.S. 1 (1976), which is covered in greater detail at p. 1400 below, the Court rejected challenges to the disclosure provisions of the Federal Election Campaign Act. The Act required that every political candidate and "political committee" maintain records of the name and address of every person contributing more than $10 in a calendar year and his or her occupation and principal place of business if his contribution exceeded $100, to make such records available for inspection by the Federal Election Commission (FEC), and to file quarterly reports with the FEC disclosing the source of every contribution exceeding $100.

The per curiam opinion stated: "We long have recognized that significant encroachments on First Amendment rights of the sort that compelled disclosure imposes cannot be justified by a mere showing of some legitimate governmental interest. Since [NAACP v. Alabama] we have required that the subordinating interests of the State must survive exacting scrutiny. We also have insisted that there be a 'substantial relation' [Gibson] between the governmental interest and the information required to be disclosed. This type of scrutiny is necessary even if any deterrent effect on the exercise of First Amendment rights arises, not through direct government action, but indirectly as an unintended but inevitable result of the government's conduct in requiring disclosure. [NAACP v. Alabama.]

"Appellees argue that the disclosure requirements of the Act differ significantly from those at issue in Alabama and its progeny because the Act only requires disclosure of the names of contributors and does not compel political organizations to submit the names of their members. [T]he invasion of privacy of belief may be as great when the information sought concerns the giving and spending of money as when it concerns the joining of [organizations]. The strict test established by Alabama is necessary because compelled disclosure has the potential for substantially infringing the exercise of First Amendment rights. But we have acknowledged that there are governmental interests sufficiently important to outweigh the possibility of infringement.

"[The] governmental interests sought to be vindicated by the disclosure requirements are of this magnitude. They fall into three categories. First, disclosure provides the electorate with information 'as to where political campaign money comes [from]' in order to aid the voters in evaluating those who seek Federal office. [Second], disclosure requirements deter actual corruption and avoid the appearance of corruption by exposing large [contributions] to the light of publicity. [Third, such] requirements are an essential means of gathering the data necessary to detect violations of the contribution limitations. [Thus, the] disclosure requirements [directly] serve substantial governmental interests. [It] is undoubtedly true that public disclosure of contributions [will] deter some individuals who otherwise might contribute. In some instances, disclosure may even expose contributors to harassment or retaliation. These are not insignificant burdens on individual rights, and they must be weighed carefully against the interests which Congress has sought to promote by this legislation. [But we agree] that disclosure requirements—certainly in most applications—appear to be the least restrictive means of curbing the evils of campaign ignorance and corruption that Congress found to exist."

The Court also rejected the claim that the disclosure requirements were invalid as applied to minor parties: "[NAACP v. Alabama] is inapposite where, as here, any serious infringement on First Amendment rights brought about by the compelled disclosure of contributors is highly speculative. It is true that the governmental interest in disclosure is diminished when the contribution in question is made to a minor party with little chance of winning an election. [We] are not unmindful that the damage done by disclosure to [the] minor parties [could] be significant. [In] some instances fears of reprisal may deter contributions to the point where the movement cannot survive. [There] could well be a case [where] the threat to the exercise of First Amendment rights is so serious and the state interest furthered by disclosure so insubstantial that the Act's requirements cannot be constitutionally applied. But no appellant in this case has tendered record evidence of [that] sort. [On] this record, the substantial public interest in disclosure identified by the legislative history of this Act outweighs the harm generally alleged. [In any particular case,] [m]inor parties must be allowed sufficient flexibility in the proof of injury to assure a fair consideration of their claim. The evidence offered need show only a reasonable probability that the compelled disclosure of a party's contributors' names will subject them to threats, harassment or reprisals from either government officials or private parties."

Chief Justice BURGER dissented from this portion of Buckley: "[Secrecy] and privacy as to political preferences and convictions are fundamental in a free society. [I] suggest the Court has failed to give the traditional standing to some of the First Amendment values at stake here. Specifically, it has failed to confine the particular exercise of governmental power within limits reasonably required. [Shelton v. Tucker.] [It] seems to me that the threshold limits fixed at $10 and $100 for anonymous contributions are constitutionally impermissible on their face. [To] argue that a 1976 contribution of $10 or $100 entails a risk of corruption or its appearance is simply too extravagant to be maintained. [There] is, in short, no relation whatever between the means used and the legitimate goal of ventilating possible undue influence. Congress has used a shotgun to kill wrens as well as hawks.

"In saying that the lines drawn by Congress are 'not wholly without rationality,' the Court [makes an] abrupt departure from traditional standards; [surely] a greater burden rests on Congress than merely to avoid 'irrationality' when regulating in the core area of the First Amendment. Even taking the Court at its word, the particular dollar amounts fixed by Congress that must be reported to the Commission fall short of meeting the test of rationality when measured by the goals sought to be achieved. Finally, no legitimate public interest has been shown in forcing the disclosure of modest contributions that are the prime support of new, unpopular or unfashionable political causes. There is no realistic possibility that such modest donations will have a corrupting influence, especially on parties that enjoy only 'minor' status. Major parties would not notice them; minor parties need [them]. Flushing out the names of supporters of minority parties will plainly have a deterrent effect on potential [contributors]."

The possibility held out by Buckley—that certain minor parties might, on a proper showing, obtain exemptions from compelled disclosures—was realized in BROWN v. SOCIALIST WORKERS '74 CAMPAIGN COMMITTEE, 459 U.S. 87 (1982). In an opinion by Justice MARSHALL, the Court held, unanimously on this point, that the Socialist Workers Party in Ohio had made a sufficient showing of a "reasonable probability of threats, harassment, or reprisals" so that it could not constitutionally be compelled to disclose information concerning campaign contributions. The Court noted that the Party was "a minor political party which historically has been the object of harassment by government officials and private parties." (The Court also held, over the dissents of Justices O'Connor, Rehnquist, and Stevens, that the same showing also exempted the Party from compelled disclosure of campaign *disbursements*.)

B. RESTRICTIONS ON ORGANIZATIONAL ACTIVITY

The Court has invalidated various direct restraints on characteristic associational activity. For example, in Healy v. James, 408 U.S. 169 (1972), the Court invalidated efforts by Central Connecticut State College to prevent a local chapter of Students for a Democratic Society (SDS) from holding meetings or otherwise organizing on campus, at least in the absence of any demonstrated actual misconduct. More controversial has been the constitutionality of restrictions on such organizational activity as conducting political litigation or boycotts.

LITIGATION

NAACP v. Button
371 U.S. 415, 83 S.Ct. 328, 9 L.Ed.2d 405 (1963).

[This case held unconstitutional a Virginia prohibition of "the improper solicitation of any legal or professional business" as applied to NAACP litigation activities. The Virginia Conference of the NAACP had financed litigation aimed at ending racial segregation of the Virginia public schools. In this litigation, cases were typically not initiated by aggrieved persons applying to the Conference for assistance. Instead, a local NAACP branch usually invited a member of the Conference legal staff to explain to a meeting of parents and children the legal steps necessary to achieve desegregation. The staff member would bring printed forms authorizing NAACP attorneys, rather than any particular lawyer, to represent the signers in desegregation suits.

[Virginia had long banned the solicitation of legal business in the form of "running" or "capping." Before 1956, there was no attempt to apply those regulations to curb the NAACP's activities in sponsoring litigation directed at racial segregation. But in 1956, the laws were amended by adding a Chapter 33 to include, in the definition of "runner" or "capper," an agent for any organization which "employs, retains or compensates" any lawyer "in connection with any judicial proceeding in which it has no pecuniary right or liability." Virginia's highest court held that the NAACP's Virginia activities violated Chapter 33.]

Justice BRENNAN delivered the opinion of the Court.

[We] hold that the activities of the NAACP, its affiliates and legal staff shown on this record are modes of expression and association protected by the [First Amendment] which Virginia may not prohibit [as] improper solicitation of legal business. [We reject] the contention that "solicitation" is wholly outside the area of freedoms protected by the First Amendment. [Abstract] discussion is not the only species of communication which the Constitution protects; the First Amendment also protects vigorous advocacy, certainly of lawful ends, against governmental intrusion. [In] the context of NAACP objectives, litigation is not a technique of resolving private differences; it is a means for [achieving] equality of treatment for the members of the Negro community. [It] is thus a form of political expression. Groups which find themselves unable to achieve their objectives through the ballot frequently turn to the courts. [And] litigation may well be the sole practicable avenue open to a minority to petition for redress of grievances. [There] is no longer any doubt that the [First Amendment protects] certain forms of orderly group activity. Thus we have affirmed the right "to engage in association for the advancement of beliefs and ideas." NAACP v. Alabama. [The] NAACP is not a conventional political party, but [for the group] it assists, [association] for litigation may be the most effective form of [political association].

[Under Chapter 33,] a person who advises another that his legal rights have been infringed and refers him to a particular attorney or group of attorneys [for] assistance has committed a [crime]. There thus inheres in the statute the gravest danger of smothering all discussion looking to the eventual institution of litigation on behalf of the rights of members of an unpopular minority. [Such] a vague and broad statute lends itself to selective enforcement against unpopular causes. We cannot close our eyes to the fact that the militant Negro civil rights movement has engendered the intense resentment and opposition of the politically dominant white community of Virginia; litigation assisted by the NAACP has been bitterly fought. In such circumstances a statute broadly curtailing group activity leading to litigation may easily become a weapon of oppression, however evenhanded its terms appear. Its mere existence could well freeze out of existence all such activity on behalf of the civil rights of Negro citizens. [We] have consistently held that only a compelling state interest in the regulation of a subject within [a state's power] can justify limiting First Amendment freedoms. [However] valid may be Virginia's interest in regulating the traditionally illegal practices of barratry, maintenance and champerty, that interest does not justify the prohibition of the NAACP activities disclosed by this record.

[Objection] to the intervention of a lay intermediary [in the regulation of law practice usually derive] from the element of pecuniary gain. [But here] no monetary stakes are involved, and so there is no danger that the attorney will [subvert] the paramount interests of his client to enrich himself or an outside sponsor. And the aims and interests of NAACP have not been shown to conflict with those of its members and nonmember Negro litigants. [Resort] to the courts to seek vindication of constitutional rights is a different matter from the oppressive, malicious, or avaricious use of the legal process for purely private gain. Lawsuits attacking racial discrimination, at least in Virginia, are neither very profitable nor very [popular]. We conclude that [the] State has failed to advance any substantial regulatory interest in the form of substantive evils flowing from petitioner's activities, which can justify the broad prohibitions which it has imposed. [Because] our disposition is rested on the First Amendment, [we] do not reach the considerations of race or racial discrimination which are the predicate of petitioner's challenge to the statute under [equal protection].

Reversed. [Justice DOUGLAS filed a concurring opinion emphasizing the law's racially discriminatory purpose, and Justice WHITE concurred in the judgment stating that he would support a more narrowly drawn law.]

Justice HARLAN, with whom Justices CLARK and STEWART join, [dissenting].

[Justice Harlan's dissent conceded that the First Amendment protects the "right to join together for purposes of obtaining judicial redress." But he noted that "as we move away from speech alone and into the sphere of conduct—even conduct associated with speech or resulting from it—the area of legitimate governmental interest expands." Thus, he found that "litigation, whether or not associated with the attempt to vindicate constitutional rights, is *conduct*. It is speech *plus*. Although the State surely may not broadly prohibit individuals with a common interest from joining together to petition a court for redress of their grievances, it is equally certain that the State may impose reasonable regulations limiting the permissible form of litigation and the manner of legal representation within its borders." He found the regulations here reasonable under that standard:]

The interest which Virginia has here asserted is that of maintaining high professional standards among those who practice law within its borders. [Although] these professional standards may have been born in a desire to curb malice and self-aggrandizement by those who would use clients and the courts for their own pecuniary ends, they have acquired a far broader significance during their long development. [A] State's felt need for regulation of professional conduct may reasonably extend beyond mere "ambulance chasing." [Running] perhaps even deeper is the desire of the profession, of courts, and of legislatures to prevent any interference with the uniquely personal relationship between lawyer and client and to maintain untrammeled by outside influences the responsibility which the lawyer owes to the courts he serves. [The] important function of organizations like petitioner in vindicating constitutional rights [is] not substantially impaired by this statute. [This enactment], contrary to the majority's suggestion, [does not] prevent petitioner from recommending the services of attorneys who are not subject to its directions and control. [It] prevents only the solicitation of business for attorneys subject to petitioner's control, and as so limited, should be sustained.

———

A year after Button, in BROTHERHOOD OF RAILROAD TRAINMEN v. VIRGINIA, 377 U.S. 1 (1964), the Court extended its holding outside the area of litigation involving constitutional rights. The union advised its members to obtain legal advice before making settlements of their personal injury claims, and recommended particular attorneys. The result of its plan was "to channel legal employment to the particular lawyers approved by the Brotherhood." A Virginia court issued an injunction against the union for solicitation and unauthorized practice of law. Justice BLACK's majority opinion concluded that the injunction violated the First Amendment: "The State can no more keep these workers from using their cooperative plan to advise one another than it could use more direct means to bar them from resorting to the courts to vindicate their legal rights." As in the Button case, "the State again has failed to show any appreciable public interest in preventing the Brotherhood from carrying out its plan to recommend the lawyers it selects to represent injured workers. [The] Constitution protects the associational rights of the members of the union precisely as it does those of the NAACP." Justice CLARK's dissent, joined by Justice Harlan, objected that "[p]ersonal injury litigation is not a form of political expression, but rather a procedure for the settlement of damage claims," and thus that Button was distinguishable.

The Button and Trainmen cases in turn provided the basis for setting aside a state order against another variety of allegedly unauthorized practice of law by a union in UNITED MINE WORKERS v. ILLINOIS STATE BAR ASS'N, 389 U.S. 217 (1967). The union had employed a salaried attorney to assist its members with workmen's compensation claims. Justice BLACK's majority opinion concluded that the state order "substantially impairs the associational rights of the Mine Workers and is not needed to protect the State's interest in high standards of legal ethics." Justice HARLAN dissented. And the Court relied on the Button, Trainmen, and United Mine Workers cases in UNITED TRANSPORTATION UNION v. STATE BAR OF MICHIGAN, 401 U.S. 576 (1971), setting aside a broad state court injunction against a union's plan purportedly designed to protect union members from excessive fees by incompetent attorneys in FELA actions. Justice BLACK, writing for the Court, emphasized "the basic right to group legal action, a right first asserted in this Court by an association of Negroes seeking the protection of freedoms guaranteed by the Constitution." He added: "The common thread running through our decisions in NAACP v. Button, Trainmen, and United Mine Workers is that collective activity undertaken to obtain meaningful access to the courts is a fundamental right within the protection of the First Amendment. [That] right would be a hollow promise if courts could deny associations of workers or others the means of enabling their members to meet the costs of legal representation." Justices Harlan, White and Blackmun dissented in part.

Were the associational rights concerns protected in the NAACP context of Button equally applicable in the union cases that followed? Would a distinction between "personal injury litigation" and "civil rights litigation" itself have been constitutional? Recall that in Ohralik (p. 1186 above), the right of commercial free speech did not bar regulation of in-person solicitation of clients; but in Primus, the companion case, the Court relied on the Button legacy to protect an ACLU lawyer against solicitation charges for seeking a client to bring a suit against alleged compulsory sterilization. Should the Court have inquired further into (and explicitly relied upon) the State's motives in Button? May reluctance to identify improper motives in cases such as Button have led the Court to give inadequate weight in other cases to "purer" state concerns regarding professional ethics and conflicts of interest?

BOYCOTTS

Does the right of association extend to collective efforts to induce employers or merchants to change their policies? Does it extend to picketing or other forms of boycott? The Court has reviewed a number of disputes over labor picketing. In Thornhill v. Alabama, 310 U.S. 88 (1940), the Court held unconstitutional a statute that had been applied to ban all picketing. In Giboney v. Empire Storage & Ice Co., 336 U.S. 490 (1949), however, the Court upheld an injunction barring, as a conspiracy in restraint of trade, a union picket against a wholesale dealer to induce it to refrain from selling to nonunion peddlers. The Court unanimously rejected the argument that the injunction was "an unconstitutional abridgement of free speech because the picketers were attempting peacefully to publicize truthful facts about a labor dispute." Later decisions "established a broad field in which a State, in enforcing some public policy, [could] constitutionally enjoin peaceful picketing in preventing effectuation of that policy." International Brotherhood of Teamsters v. Vogt, Inc., 354 U.S. 284 (1957).

Does the state's power to regulate economic boycotts extend to a boycott motivated by political purposes? This question came before the Court in NAACP v. CLAIBORNE HARDWARE CO., 458 U.S. 886 (1982). The case involved an NAACP boycott of white merchants by black citizens in Claiborne County, Mississippi. The boycott, begun in 1966, sought to induce white civic and business leaders to comply with a long list of black citizens' demands for equality and racial justice. The boycott was conducted by largely peaceful means, but it included some incidents of violence as well. In a civil action brought by some of the merchants to recover economic losses allegedly caused by the boycott, a state trial court imposed a judgment for over $1,250,000 on a large group of defendants (including the NAACP). The Mississippi Supreme Court, although not accepting all of the lower court's theories, upheld the judgment of liability on the basis of the common law tort of malicious interference with plaintiffs' businesses. The court found the boycott unlawful because, in its view, the defendants had agreed to use and did use force, violence, and intimidation to coerce nonparticipating blacks to join the boycott, and remanded for a recomputation of damages.

Without dissent (Justice Rehnquist concurred only in the result and Justice Marshall did not participate), the United States Supreme Court reversed, holding "that the nonviolent elements of petitioners' activities are entitled to the protection of the First Amendment" and that, "[w]hile the State legitimately may impose damages for the consequences of violent conduct, it may not award compensation for the consequences of nonviolent, protected activity."

Justice STEVENS, writing for the Court, began by explaining why "the nonviolent elements of petitioners' activities" were entitled to First Amendment protection. He noted that the boycott "took many forms": "The boycott was supported by speeches and nonviolent picketing. Participants repeatedly encouraged others to join in its cause. Each of these elements of the boycott is a form of speech or conduct that is ordinarily entitled to protection under the

[First] Amendment. [In] addition, [the names] of boycott violators were read aloud at meetings [and] published in a local black newspaper. Petitioners admittedly sought to persuade others to join the boycott through social pressure and the 'threat' of social ostracism. Speech does not lose its protected character, however, simply because it may embarrass others or coerce them into action." He also noted that "[t]he right to associate does not lose all constitutional protection merely because some members of the group may have participated in conduct or advocated doctrine that itself is not protected. [De Jonge.]"

True, the "presence of protected activity [did] not end the relevant constitutional inquiry": "Governmental regulation that has an incidental effect on First Amendment freedoms may be justified in certain narrowly defined instances. [O'Brien.] A nonviolent and totally voluntary boycott may have a disruptive effect on local economic conditions. This Court has recognized the strong governmental interest in certain forms of economic regulation, even though such regulation may have an incidental effect on rights of speech and association. The right of business entities to 'associate' to suppress competition may be curtailed. Unfair trade practices may be restricted. Secondary boycotts and picketing by labor unions may be prohibited." But, Justice Stevens added, "[w]hile States have broad power to regulate economic activity, we do not find a comparable right to prohibit peaceful political activity such as that found in the boycott in this case. This Court has recognized that expression on public issues 'has always rested on the highest rung of the hierarchy of First Amendment values.' "

Applying these principles, Justice Stevens suggested that the purpose of affecting governmental action was protected by the First Amendment even if there was also an anti-competitive effect: "[A] major purpose of the boycott in this case was to influence governmental action. [The] petitioners certainly foresaw—and directly intended—that the merchants would sustain economic injury as a result of their campaign. [However], the purpose of petitioners' campaign was not to destroy legitimate competition. [The] right of the State to regulate economic activity could not justify a complete prohibition against a nonviolent, politically-motivated boycott designed to force governmental and economic change and to effectuate rights guaranteed by the Constitution itself."

He continued: "[The] fact that such activity is constitutionally protected [imposes] a special obligation on this Court to examine critically the basis on which liability was imposed." Clearly, there were unprotected aspects of the boycott: "The First Amendment does not protect violence. [There] is no question that acts of violence occurred. No federal rule of law restricts a State from imposing tort liability for business losses that are caused by violence and by threats of violence. When such conduct occurs in the context of a constitutionally protected activity, however, 'precision of regulation' is demanded. [NAACP v. Button.] Specifically, the presence of activity protected by the First Amendment imposes restraints on the grounds that may give rise to damage liability and on the persons who may be held accountable for those damages." One such restraint was that petitioners could not be held liable for *all* damages "resulting from the boycott"; "[o]nly those losses proximately caused by unlawful conduct may be recovered."

A second restraint concerned who may be named as a defendant: "The First Amendment [restricts] the ability of the State to impose liability on an individual solely because of his association with another. [See, e.g., Scales; Noto.] Civil liability may not be imposed merely because an individual belonged to a group, some members of which committed acts of violence. For liability to be imposed by reason of association alone, it is necessary to establish that the group itself possessed unlawful goals and that the individual held a specific intent to further those illegal aims. 'In this sensitive field, the State may not employ "means that broadly stifle fundamental personal liberties when the end can be more narrowly achieved." Shelton v. Tucker.' " With respect to most of the petitioners, the record failed to show an adequate basis to sustain the judgments against them. Mere participation in the local meetings of the NAACP was "an insufficient predicate on which to impose liability." That would "not even constitute 'guilt by association,' since there is no evidence that the association possessed unlawful aims. Rather, liability could only be imposed on a 'guilt *for* association' theory. Neither is permissible under the First Amendment." Nor could NAACP liability be predicated on any allegedly unlawful conduct by NAACP leader and boycott organizer Charles Evers: "To impose liability without a finding that the NAACP authorized—either actually or apparently—or ratified unlawful conduct would impermissibly burden the rights of political association that are protected by the First Amendment." (For the portion of the decision finding that Evers' speech did not constitute unlawful incitement, see p. 1074 above.)

Justice Stevens concluded: "The taint of violence colored the conduct of some of the petitioners. They, of course, may be held liable for the consequences of their violent deeds. The burden of demonstrating that it colored the entire collective effort, however, is not satisfied by evidence that violence occurred or even that violence contributed to the success of the boycott. A massive and prolonged effort to change the social, political, and economic structure of a local environment cannot be characterized as a violent conspiracy simply by reference to the ephemeral consequences of relatively few violent acts. Such a characterization must be supported by findings that adequately disclose the evidentiary basis for concluding that specific parties agreed to use unlawful means, that carefully identify the impact of such unlawful conduct, and that recognize the importance of avoiding the imposition of punishment for constitutionally protected activity. The burden of demonstrating that fear rather than protected conduct was the dominant force in the movement is heavy. [The] findings of [the trial court] are constitutionally insufficient to support the judgment that all petitioners are liable for all losses resulting from the boycott."

Does NAACP v. Claiborne Hardware have any application to an economically motivated boycott? In INTERNATIONAL LONGSHOREMEN'S ASS'N v. ALLIED INTERNATIONAL, INC., 456 U.S. 212 (1982), decided shortly before Claiborne, the Court rejected a First Amendment claim by a union that refused to unload cargoes shipped from the Soviet Union, as a protest against the Soviet invasion of Afghanistan. The unanimous Court found the protest to be an illegal secondary boycott under federal labor law and rejected the claim that the boycott "was not a labor dispute [but] a political dispute." The Court noted that "conduct designed not to communicate but to coerce merits [little] consideration under the First Amendment." Does Claiborne overrule Longshoremen's? If not, is the distinction between "political" and "economic" purposes justifiable under the First Amendment? For later rulings declining to apply NAACP v. Claiborne Hardware to boycotts stemming from economic rather than political purposes, see Allied Tube & Conduit Corp. v. Indian Head, Inc., 486 U.S. 492 (1988), and FTC v. Superior Court Trial Lawyers Ass'n, 493 U.S. 411 (1990).

C. DENIAL OF GOVERNMENT BENEFITS BECAUSE OF ASSOCIATION

———

Even if government may not outlaw an association, force disclosure of its membership, or restrict its central activities, may it nonetheless use associational ties as a ground for disqualification from government benefits such as jobs and licenses? May it condition such benefits on oaths of loyalty or disavowal of disfavored associations? These questions have been much litigated before the Court.

The Court has several times relied upon the prohibition on bills of attainder to hold that associational ties may not be the basis for denying a position of public trust. Soon after the Civil War, the Court struck down, as bills of attainder, loyalty oaths directed at former supporters of the Confederacy. See Cummings v. Missouri, 4 Wall. (71 U.S.) 277 (1867) (invalidating denial of the right to preach to those who did not disavow Confederate sympathy), and Ex parte Garland, 4 Wall. (71 U.S.) 333 (1867) (invalidating denial of the right to practice law in federal courts to those who did not disavow Confederate sympathy). The Court has relied on the bill of attainder ban in only one modern case: United States v. Brown, 381 U.S. 437 (1965), holding unconstitutional a federal law making it a crime for a member of the Communist Party to serve as an officer or an employee of a labor union. Chief Justice Warren's majority opinion emphasized that it was not necessary that a bill of attainder name the parties to be punished. He viewed the prohibition "as an implementation of the separation of powers, a general safeguard against legislative exercise of the judicial function, or more simply—trial by legislature."

Far more commonly, however, the issue has arisen in connection with First Amendment claims. Such claims typically assert either that membership in an organization is not in itself a sufficient ground to deny a public privilege, or that refusal to discuss or disavow membership is not such a ground. The following materials briefly trace the history of the Court's disposition of such claims.

1. *The Cold War period.* During the Cold War era that followed World War II, loyalty-security programs proliferated at all levels of government and in the private sector. These programs aimed to prevent Communists and other "subversives" from occupying sensitive government or industrial positions. See generally Note, "Developments in the Law—the National Security Interest and Civil Liberties," 85 Harv. L. Rev. 1130 (1972); Brown, Loyalty and Security: Employment Tests in the United States (1958); Gellhorn, Individual Freedom and Governmental Restraints (1956).

The Court initially sustained various loyalty programs against constitutional challenge. For example, Adler v. Board of Education, 342 U.S. 485 (1952), upheld a New York law barring from a position as a public school teacher anyone who knowingly became a member of any organization that advocated the violent overthrow of government. In Garner v. Los Angeles Bd. of Public Works, 341 U.S. 716 (1951), the Court upheld a requirement that each city employee take an oath that, within the past five years, he or she had not advocated the overthrow of government by force or violence or belonged to any organization advocating such overthrow, and that the employee disclose whether he or she was or ever had been a Communist Party member. Such requirements were deemed relevant to fitness for the job. The only limitation the Court imposed was a requirement of *knowing* membership. In Wieman v. Updegraff, 344 U.S. 183 (1952), a unanimous Court struck down, on due process grounds, an Oklahoma loyalty oath requiring employees to state that they were not and had not for five years been affiliated with any organization that had been deemed a "Communist front or subversive organization." The Court distinguished Garner and Adler on the ground that, under the Oklahoma law, it did not matter "whether association existed innocently or knowingly."

During this period, the Court likewise generally rejected the constitutional claims of state employees and licensees who had been dismissed for refusing to answer questions relating to subversion. The Court accepted that penalties for the mere fact of political belief or association would violate First Amendment rights, but found that lack of cooperation with a proper inquiry was a proper ground for dismissal. Thus, in Slochower v. Board of Higher Educ., 350 U.S. 551 (1956), the Court held unconstitutional the dismissal of a New York City college professor merely for invoking the self-incrimination privilege in refusing to answer an inquiry into his past Communist activities. But in Lerner v. Casey, 357 U.S. 468 (1958), the Court sustained the discharge of a subway conductor who had refused to answer on self-incrimination grounds his employer's questions about his Communist Party association. Justice Harlan for the majority insisted that Lerner "had been discharged neither because of any inference of Communist Party membership [nor] because of the assertion of [a] constitutional protection, but rather because of the doubt created as to his 'reliability' by his refusal to answer a relevant question put by his employer. [It] was this lack of candor [which was decisive]."[1]

During these years, the Court also considered a number of cases involving refusals to answer subversion-related questions in the course of bar admission proceedings. In its first encounters with the problem, in 1957, the Court held on due process grounds that a state could not refuse to admit applicants to the bar on the basis of mere membership in the Communist party. Schware v. Board of Bar Examiners, 353 U.S. 232 (1957); Konigsberg v. State Bar, 353 U.S. 252 (1957). But when the Konigsberg case returned to the Court four years later, the Court upheld the denial of admission on the ground that the applicant had refused, on First Amendment grounds, to answer questions about his political associations and beliefs. KONIGSBERG v. STATE BAR OF CALIFORNIA [Konigsberg II], 366 U.S. 36 (1961). Justice HARLAN, writing for the 5–4 majority, once again emphasized the distinction between refusals to answer relevant questions and substantive grounds for denials of a license. Thus, a state could deny admission for refusing to answer even if affirmative answers would not by themselves have justified exclusion. In response to Konigsberg's claim that questions about his Communist Party membership "unconstitutionally impinged upon rights of free speech and association," Justice Harlan replied: "[We] regard the State's interest in having lawyers who are devoted to the law in its broader sense, [including] its procedures for orderly change, as clearly sufficient to outweigh the minimal effect upon free association occasioned by compulsory disclosure in the circumstances here presented."

Justice BLACK's dissent, joined by Chief Justice Warren and Justice Douglas, insisted that Konigsberg had in fact been rejected because the Committee suspected that he had once been a Communist Party member. He

---

1. Note that, at the time these cases were decided, the Fifth Amendment was not yet applicable to the states. The Fifth Amendment self-incrimination privilege was first held applicable to the states in Malloy v. Hogan, 378 U.S. 1 (1964). Decisions such as Lerner did not survive this development; later cases invalidated the loss of public benefits on account of the invocation of Fifth Amendment rights. See Spevack v. Klein, 385 U.S. 511 (1967); Garrity v. New Jersey, 385 U.S. 493 (1967); Gardner v. Broderick, 392 U.S. 273 (1968); Lefkowitz v. Turley, 414 U.S. 70 (1973).

argued, moreover, that the majority's result was indefensible even if its balancing approach were justifiable: "It seems plain to me that the inevitable effect of the majority's decision is to condone a practice that will have a substantial deterrent effect upon the associations entered into by anyone who may want to become a lawyer in California"; accordingly, the impact on First Amendment rights could not be dismissed as "minimal." Justice Brennan also dissented.

In a companion case to Konigsberg II, In re Anastaplo, 366 U.S. 82 (1961), the Court upheld Illinois' refusal to admit a bar applicant who had not been a member of the Communist party, but who declined to answer all questions and defended on historical and ideological grounds his abstract belief in the "right of revolution."

2. *The Warren Court.* By the late 1960s, it became clear that the grounds for disqualification from public employment and public "privileges" had shrunk considerably and, in the subversion area, had become essentially synonymous with the grounds for criminal punishment developed in the Scales–Yates–Brandenburg line of cases discussed in chapter 11. Moreover, it had become clear that the scope of inquiry, which had been much broader than the scope of disqualifying criteria in the 1950s, no longer extended much beyond the scope of permissible grounds for disqualification. The 1958 decision in NAACP v. Alabama proved a critical turning point in bringing about this more speech-protective approach, although the Court also employed several techniques other than the strict scrutiny used in that decision.

For example, in the 1960s, the Warren Court struck down several state-imposed loyalty oaths on "void-for-vagueness" grounds. In CRAMP v. BOARD OF PUBLIC INSTRUCTION, 368 U.S. 278 (1961), the Court invalidated a Florida law requiring public employees to swear that they had never "knowingly lent their aid, support, advice, counsel or influence to the Communist Party." Even though the state court had construed the law to include "the element of scienter," Justice STEWART emphasized its "extraordinary ambiguity" and found it "completely lacking [in] terms susceptible of objective measurement." He added that the "vice of unconstitutional vagueness [was] further aggravated [because the law] operates to inhibit the exercise of individual freedoms affirmatively protected by the Constitution." Similarly, in BAGGETT v. BULLITT, 377 U.S. 360 (1964), the Court, in partial reliance on Cramp, invalidated two state loyalty oath requirements, including one obligating state employees to swear that they were not members of a "subversive organization." The majority found the requirements "invalid on their face because their language is unduly vague, uncertain and broad."

Recall too the Court's holding on overbreadth grounds that mere membership in the Communist party was insufficient to justify denial of a passport, Aptheker v. Secretary of State (1964; p. 1070 above), or a job in a defense facility, United States v. Robel (1967; p. 1070 above). The Court more directly repudiated its 1950s approach in the following cases, which extended the Yates–Scales–Noto approach to the employment and licensing context. Note that these cases, like the Pickering and Speiser lines of cases explored above, see pp. 1303, 1318, reject the view that a government job or benefit is a mere "privilege" that may be denied or conditioned any way the government sees fit.

Elfbrandt v. Russell

384 U.S. 11, 86 S.Ct. 1238, 16 L.Ed.2d 321 (1966).

Justice DOUGLAS delivered the opinion of the Court.

This [case] involves questions concerning the constitutionality of an Arizona Act requiring an oath [to support the federal and state Constitutions] from state employees. [The] Legislature put a gloss on the oath by subjecting to a prosecution for perjury and for discharge from public office anyone who took the oath and who "knowingly and wilfully becomes or remains a member of the communist party of the United States or [other subversive organizations]." Petitioner, a teacher and a Quaker, decided she could not in good conscience take the oath, not knowing what it meant and not having any chance to get a hearing at which its precise scope and meaning could be determined.

We recognized in [Scales, p. 1068 above] [that] a "blanket prohibition of association with a group having both legal and illegal aims" would pose "a real danger that legitimate political expression or association would be impaired." [Any] lingering doubt that proscription of mere knowing membership, without any showing of "specific intent," would run afoul of the Constitution was set at rest by our decision in [Aptheker, p. 1070 above]. [The passport law there] covered membership which was not accompanied by a specific intent to further the unlawful aims of the organization, and we held it unconstitutional. The oath and accompanying statutory gloss challenged here suffer from an identical constitutional infirmity. One who subscribes to this Arizona oath and who is, or thereafter becomes, a knowing member of an organization which has as "one of its purposes" the violent overthrow of the government, is subject to immediate discharge and criminal penalties. Nothing in the oath, the statutory gloss, or the construction of the oath and statutes given by the Arizona Supreme Court purports to exclude association by one who does not subscribe to the organization's unlawful ends. [Thus,] the "hazard of being prosecuted for knowing but guiltless behavior" is a reality. People often label as "communist" ideas which they oppose; and they make up our juries.

[Those] who join an organization but do not share its unlawful purposes and who do not participate in its unlawful activities surely pose no threat, either as citizens or as public employees. Laws such as this which are not restricted in scope to those who join with the "specific intent" to further illegal action impose, in effect, a conclusive presumption that the member shares the unlawful aims of the organization. [This] Act threatens the cherished freedom of association protected by the First Amendment. [A] statute touching those protected rights must be "narrowly drawn." [Legitimate] legislative goals "cannot be pursued by means that broadly stifle fundamental personal liberties when the end can be more narrowly achieved." [Shelton v. Tucker.] [A] law which applies to membership without the "specific intent" to further the illegal aims of the organization infringes unnecessarily on protected freedoms. It rests on the doctrine of "guilt by association" which has no place here. Such a law cannot stand.

Reversed.

Justice WHITE, with whom Justices CLARK, HARLAN and STEWART join, dissenting.

According to unequivocal prior holdings of this Court, a state is entitled to condition public employment upon its employees abstaining from knowing membership in the Communist Party and other organizations advocating the violent overthrow of the government which employs them; the state is constitutionally authorized to inquire into such affiliations and it may discharge those who refuse to affirm or deny them. [E.g., Garner; Adler; Lerner; Wieman; Slochower.] The Court does not mention or purport to overrule these cases. [If] the State is entitled to condition employment on the absence of knowing membership, and if an employee obtains employment by falsifying his present qualifications, there is no sound constitutional reason for denying the State the power to treat such false swearing as perjury. [If] a government may remove from office and criminally punish its employees who engaged in certain political activities [see the Hatch Act cases, p. 1311 above], it is unsound to hold that it may not, on pain of criminal penalties, prevent its employees from affiliating with the Communist Party or other organizations prepared to employ violent means to overthrow constitutional government. Our Constitution does not require this kind of protection for the secret proselyting of government employees into the Communist Party.

Keyishian v. Board of Regents

385 U.S. 589, 87 S.Ct. 675, 17 L.Ed.2d 629 (1967).

Justice BRENNAN delivered the opinion of the Court.

As faculty members of the State University, [appellants'] continued employment was conditioned upon their compliance with a New York plan [which] the State utilizes to prevent the appointment or retention of "subversive" persons in state employment. [Each appellant] refused to sign, as regulations then in effect required, [a] certificate that he was not a Communist, and that if he had ever been a Communist, he had communicated that fact to the President of the State University. [Each] was notified that his failure to sign the certificate would require his dismissal. [A lower federal court rejected appellants' constitutional challenges.] We reverse.

[The New York law] requires removal for "treasonable or seditious" utterances or acts. [But the] teacher cannot know the extent, if any, to which a "seditious" utterance must transcend mere statement about abstract doctrine, the extent to which it must be intended to and tend to indoctrinate or incite to action in furtherance of the defined doctrine. The crucial consideration is that no teacher can know just where the line is drawn between "seditious" and nonseditious utterances and acts. [The] standards of permissible statutory vagueness are strict in the area of free expression. New York's complicated and intricate scheme plainly violates this standard. [The] danger of chilling effect upon the exercise of vital First Amendment rights must be guarded against by sensitive tools which clearly inform teachers what is being proscribed. [The] regulatory maze [here] has the quality of "extraordinary ambiguity" found to be fatal to the oaths considered in Cramp and [Baggett]. [We] therefore hold that [several provisions are] unconstitutional [for vagueness].

Appellants have also challenged the constitutionality of the discrete provisions [which] make Communist Party membership, as such, prima facie evidence of disqualification. [These provisions were upheld] in Adler. [But] constitutional doctrine which has emerged since that decision has rejected its [premise] that public employment, including academic employment, may be conditioned upon the surrender of constitutional rights which could not be abridged by direct government action. [Mere] Party membership, even with knowledge of the Party's unlawful goals, can not suffice to justify criminal punishment, see [Scales, Noto, Yates]; nor may it warrant a finding of moral unfitness justifying disbarment. [Schware.] [Elfbrandt] and Aptheker state the governing standard: legislation which sanctions membership unaccompanied by specific intent to further the unlawful goals of the organization or which is not active membership violates constitutional limitations.

Measured against this standard, [these provisions] sweep overbroadly into association which may not be proscribed. The presumption of disqualification arising from proof of mere membership [cannot be rebutted by] proof of nonactive membership or a showing of the absence of intent to further unlawful aims. [Thus, the provisions] suffer from impermissible "overbreadth." They seek to bar employment both for association which legitimately may be proscribed and for association which may not be proscribed consistently with First Amendment rights. Where statutes have an overbroad sweep, just as where they are vague, "the hazard of loss of substantial impairment of those precious rights may be critical," [since] those covered by the statute are bound to limit their behavior to that which is unquestionably safe. [Shelton v. Tucker.] We therefore hold [the relevant provisions] invalid insofar as they proscribe mere knowing membership without any showing of specific intent to further the unlawful aims of the [Communist Party].

Reversed and remanded.

Justice CLARK, with whom Justices HARLAN, STEWART and WHITE join, [dissenting].

[In] view of [the] long list of decisions covering over 15 years of this Court's history, in which no opinion of this Court even questioned the validity of the Adler line of cases, it is strange to me that the Court now finds that "the constitutional doctrine which has emerged since [has] rejected [Adler's] major premise." With due respect, as I read them, our cases have done no such [thing]. The majority says that the [New York] Law is bad because it has an "overbroad sweep." I regret to say [that] the majority has by its broadside swept away one of our most precious rights, namely, the right of self-preservation.

LOYALTY REQUIREMENTS AND THE MODERN COURT

1. *Loyalty oaths.* In COLE v. RICHARDSON, 405 U.S. 676 (1972), the Court, by a vote of 4–3, upheld a two-part loyalty oath required of all Massachusetts public employees. The first part (an "affirmative" oath) required a promise to "uphold and defend the federal and state constitutions"; the second (a "negative" oath typically disclaiming forbidden beliefs and associations) required a promise to "oppose the overthrow of the [government] by force, violence or by any illegal or unconstitutional method." The Court read the "oppose the overthrow" clause as imposing no significantly greater obligation than the "uphold and defend" provision and accordingly concluded that both parts of the oath were constitutional. Chief Justice BURGER summarized the prior oath cases as follows: government may not condition employment on taking an oath "relating to political beliefs. [Nor] may employment be conditioned on an oath that one has not engaged, or will not engage, in protected speech activities such as the following: criticizing institutions of government; discussing political doctrine that approves the overthrow of certain forms of government; and supporting candidates for political office. Employment may not be conditioned on an oath denying past, or abjuring future, associational activities within constitutional protection; such protected activities include membership in organizations having illegal purposes unless one knows of the

purpose and shares a specific intent to promote the illegal purpose." And there had been special concern with vagueness in the oath cases "because uncertainty as to an oath's meaning may deter individuals from engaging in constitutionally protected activity conceivably within the scope of the oath." He found none of these problems implicated by the oath in Cole. Justice DOUGLAS' dissent, in contrast, found that the "oppose" clause made advocacy of overthrow, protected by cases such as Brandenburg, "a possible offense." Justice MARSHALL's dissent, joined by Justice Brennan, found the "oppose" clause "not only vague, but also overbroad."

2. *Bar admission cases.* In three 5–4 decisions in 1971, the Court returned to the problem of the state's power to inquire about subversive associations in the course of determining the moral fitness of applicants for admission to the bar. In two of the cases, Baird and Stolar, the petitioner prevailed; in the third, Wadmond, the constitutional challenge failed.

In BAIRD v. STATE BAR OF ARIZONA, 401 U.S. 1 (1971), the Court invalidated a denial of admission to the bar that was based on the applicant's refusal to answer the question whether she had ever been a member of the Communist Party or any organization "that advocates overthrow of the United States Government by force or violence." Justice BLACK's plurality opinion, joined by Justices Douglas, Brennan and Marshall, reiterated that the First Amendment's "protection of association prohibits a State from excluding a person from a profession or punishing him solely because he is a member of a particular political organization" and that "[w]hen a State seeks to inquire about an individual's beliefs and associations, a heavy burden lies upon it to show that the inquiry is necessary to protect a legitimate state interest. Of course Arizona has a legitimate interest in determining whether petitioner has the qualities of character and the professional competence requisite to the practice of law. But here petitioner has already supplied the Committee with extensive personal and professional information to assist its determination. [A] State may not inquire about a man's views or associations solely for the purpose of withholding a right or benefit because of what he believes." Justice STEWART concurred in the judgment, reasoning that Arizona had failed to confine its inquiry to *knowing* membership in subversive organizations. Justice BLACKMUN, joined by Chief Justice Burger and Justices Harlan and White, found Baird's refusal "reminiscent of the obstructionist tactics condemned in Konigsberg," and found Arizona's question legitimately "directed not at mere belief but at advocacy and at the call to violent action and force in pursuit of that advocacy."

In APPLICATION OF STOLAR, 401 U.S. 23 (1971), the Court, with the same lineup of Justices as in Baird, invalidated Ohio's refusal of bar admission to an applicant who refused to answer questions about membership in "any organization which advocates the overthrow of the government of the United States by force," and about all other organizations of which he had been a member. The plurality opinion by Justice BLACK, joined by Justices Douglas, Brennan and Marshall, concluded that requests for general lists of organizational memberships were "impermissible in light of the First Amendment [under Shelton v. Tucker]." The question about subversive organization membership was impermissible as well because the First Amendment barred the State "from penalizing a man solely because he is a member of a particular organization." Justice STEWART again cast the decisive concurring vote. Justice BLACKMUN, for the same dissenters as in Baird, found the subversive organization question permissible, even if the general organizational questions were invalid under Shelton v. Tucker.

In LAW STUDENTS CIVIL RIGHTS RESEARCH COUNCIL v. WAD-MOND, 401 U.S. 154 (1971), however, the Court went the other way. This challenge did not arise from a refusal to admit a particular bar applicant, but was "a broad attack, primarily on First Amendment vagueness and over-breadth grounds," on New York's bar admission screening system, brought by individuals and organizations representing a class of law students and gradu-ates planning to practice law in New York. Justice STEWART, whose concur-rences had been decisive in sustaining the constitutional challenges in Baird and Stolar, now joined the dissenters in those cases and wrote the opinion for the Court rejecting the constitutional attack. The Court held that New York could constitutionally ask a two-tier question asking first, whether the appli-cant had been a member of any organization he or she knew advocated the overthrow of government by force or violence, and second, if the first answer was affirmative, whether the applicant had the "specific intent to further the aims of such organization." Justice Stewart wrote that the question was "precisely tailored to conform to the relevant decisions of this Court." He added: "[We] are not persuaded that careful administration of such a system as New York's need result in chilling effects upon the exercise of constitutional freedoms." Justice BLACK dissented, joined by Justice Douglas, and Justice MARSHALL dissented, joined by Justice Brennan.

Is the upshot of these three cases that bar authorities may inquire into an applicant's knowing membership in the Communist Party with the specific intent to advance its ends, and refuse bar admission to one who refuses to cooperate with such a properly narrowed inquiry, but may not refuse admission to one who refuses to answer a question that may disadvantage him or her on the basis of organizational affiliation alone? On moral character requirements for bar admission generally, see Rhode, "Moral Character as a Professional Credential," 94 Yale L.J. 491 (1985).

D. THE RIGHT *NOT* TO ASSOCIATE

---

1. *Compulsory fees.* Soon after NAACP v. Alabama launched the modern elaboration of a "right of association," claims were made that there was a similar right *not* to associate. Typically, the claims came from individuals who objected to compulsory contributions to organizations—e.g., employees subject to union shop agreements and lawyers attacking dues requirements under integrated bar systems. For more than a decade, the Court managed to avoid the central constitutional issues in cases raising such First Amendment claims. See Railway Employees' Dept. v. Hanson, 351 U.S. 225 (1956); International Ass'n of Machinists v. Street, 367 U.S. 740 (1961); Lathrop v. Donohue, 367 U.S. 820 (1961); Brotherhood of Railway Clerks v. Allen, 373 U.S. 113 (1963).

Finally, in ABOOD v. DETROIT BOARD OF EDUC., 431 U.S. 209 (1977), the Court confronted the constitutional claim in the context of public employ-ees' unions. Abood involved public sector employees who were subject to an agency shop agreement adopted by a school board and a union pursuant to state law. Under the agreement, every nonunion employee was required to pay to the union "a service fee equal in amount to union dues" as a condition of employment. That scheme was challenged by dissenting employees who object-ed to having to pay fees for (1) "collective bargaining in the public sector" and

(2) "ideological union expenditures not directly related to collective bargaining." Justice STEWART's majority opinion recognized a right to "refus[e] to associate" and rejected the first challenge but sustained the second.

In upholding the exaction of compulsory fees for collective bargaining expenses, Justice Stewart relied in part on earlier cases that had upheld, largely on statutory grounds, the exaction of compulsory dues in the private sector. He found that in the public sector, as in the private sector, the interests in the operation of a collective bargaining system, in assuring labor peace, and in avoiding the risk of "free riders" overcame the objectors' First Amendment interests "in not being compelled to contribute to the costs of exclusive union representation." Justice Stewart concluded, however, that the First Amendment barred requiring dissidents to contribute financially to the support of an ideological cause they found objectionable. He relied on Elrod v. Burns (1976; p. 1312 above), which held that the First Amendment bars a state "from compelling an individual [to] associate with a political party as a condition of retaining public employment." Likewise, a public employee may not be required "to contribute to the support of an ideological cause he may oppose as a condition of holding a job as a public school teacher." The union was free to advance "ideological causes not germane to its duties as collective-bargaining representative," but it had to finance such expenditures with dues only from "employees who do not object to advancing those ideas and who are not coerced into doing so against their will by the threat of loss of governmental employment." He accordingly remanded for development of remedies to prevent "compulsory subsidization of ideological activities by employees who object thereto without restricting the union's ability to require every employee to contribute to the cost of collective-bargaining activities."

Justice POWELL, joined by Chief Justice Burger and Justice Blackmun, concurred in the judgment, arguing that "compelling a government employee to give financial support to a union in the public sector—regardless of the uses to which the union puts the contribution—impinges seriously upon interests in free speech and association protected by the First Amendment," and that the burden should have rested with the State to come forward and demonstrate, as to each union expenditure for which it would exact support from minority employees, that the "compelled contribution is necessary to serve overriding governmental objectives." He objected to the majority's placement of the burden on the dissenting employee to come forward and identify his disagreement in order to obtain a rebate from the union.

For later elaboration of the line between expenditures that may be funded with compulsory fees and those that are not sufficiently related to an organization's core mission to justify their being imposed on dissenters, see Ellis v. Railway Clerks, 466 U.S. 435 (1984) (permitting compelled contributions to be used for union conventions, publications and social activities); Keller v. State Bar of California, 496 U.S. 1 (1990) (restricting use of compulsory state bar dues to expenditures for regulating the legal profession or improving the quality of legal services, and suggesting that expenditures "to endorse or advance a gun control or nuclear weapons freeze initiative" would be impermissible); Lehnert v. Ferris Faculty Ass'n, 500 U.S. 507 (1991) (holding that union may not use compulsory dues for political purposes unrelated to contract negotiations). For discussion of the procedures necessary for protecting the rights of dissenters, see Chicago Teachers Union v. Hudson, 475 U.S. 292 (1986). For commentary, see Cantor, "Forced Payments to Service Institutions and Constitutional Interests in Ideological Non–Association," 36 Rutgers L. Rev. 3 (1984).

Should taxpayers have an Abood right to a rebate pro rata of the amount of their taxes used by government to further ideological causes with which they disagree? If not, what distinguishes taxes from compulsory union or bar dues? Should students at a public university have an Abood right to a rebate of the amount of their compulsory student activities fee used to finance publications or other speech activities to which they have an ideological objection? Recall Rosenberger (p. 1324 above).

2. *Compulsory membership.* In ROBERTS v. UNITED STATES JAYCEES, 468 U.S. 609 (1984), the Court rejected an all-male organization's claim that a state antidiscrimination law infringed its freedom of association by requiring it to admit women. At issue was a Minnesota statute prohibiting sex discrimination in a "place of public accommodation." The law had been applied to the Jaycees, or Junior Chamber of Commerce, a national civic organization which restricted full voting membership to men between the ages of 18 and 35. The Jaycees argued that this restriction on their membership policies interfered with their members' freedom of association.

Justice BRENNAN's opinion for the Court first rejected any claim on the Jaycees' part to a right of intimate association rooted in the liberty clause of the fourteenth amendment, given its large and relatively unselective composition. He then proceeded to consider the Jaycees' claim to a right of association protected by the First Amendment. Because the Jaycees engaged in various civic, educational, and related activities, the Court found expressive associational rights "plainly implicated in this case": "There can be no clearer example of an intrusion into the internal structure or affairs of an association than a regulation that forces the group to accept members it does not desire. Such a regulation may impair the ability of the original members to express only those views that brought them together. Freedom of association therefore plainly presupposes a freedom not to associate. Abood." But Justice Brennan did not find that right dispositive here: "The right to associate for expressive purposes is [not] absolute. Infringements on that right may be justified by regulations adopted to serve compelling state interests, unrelated to the suppression of ideas, that cannot be achieved through means significantly less restrictive of associational freedoms." Justice Brennan found this standard satisfied here: "We are persuaded that Minnesota's compelling interest in eradicating discrimination against its female citizens justifies the impact that application of the statute to the Jaycees may have on the male members' associational freedoms."

Crucially, Justice Brennan found the state antidiscrimination law content-neutral both on its face and as applied: "[T]he Minnesota Act does not aim at the suppression of speech, does not distinguish between prohibited and permitted activity on the basis of viewpoint, and does not license enforcement authorities to administer the statute on the basis of such constitutionally impermissible criteria, [nor was it] applied in this case for the purpose of hampering the organization's ability to express its views." Any restriction on associational liberty was merely incidental to Minnesota's interest in preventing sex discrimination. Nor was there any indication that the law imposed "any serious burden on the male members' freedom of expressive association": "The Act requires no change in the Jaycees' creed of promoting the interests of young men, and it imposes no restrictions on the organization's ability to exclude individuals with ideologies or philosophies different from those of its existing members. [Because] Jaycees already invites women to share the group's views and philosophy and to participate in much of its training and community activities, [any] claim that admission of women as full voting members will impair a symbolic message conveyed by the very fact that women are not permitted to vote is attenuated at best." In the absence of a showing far more substantial than that attempted here, "we decline to indulge in the sexual stereotyping that underlies appellee's contention that, by allowing women to vote, application of the Minnesota Act will change the content or impact of an organization's speech."

Justice O'CONNOR's concurring opinion drew a distinction between rights of commercial association and rights of expressive association. As to the former, state regulation should be "readily permit[ted]," but there remained "the ideal of complete protection for purely expressive association." Because the Jaycees, in her view, were primarily commercial, she concurred in rejecting the associational challenge. Justice Rehnquist concurred only in the judgment.

After Jaycees, may the Male Supremacist Society of Minnesota exclude women? May the Feminist Separatist Organization exclude men? May the Ku Klux Klan exclude black members? May the NAACP exclude members of the Ku Klux Klan? May the Boston St. Patrick's Day Parade exclude gay men and lesbians? Recall Hurley (p. 1371 above). See generally Linder, "Freedom of Association after [Roberts]," 82 Mich.L.Rev. 1878 (1984).

The Court unanimously followed Roberts in BOARD OF DIRECTORS OF ROTARY INTERNATIONAL v. ROTARY CLUB, 481 U.S. 537 (1987). The Court held that application of a California antidiscrimination law that barred exclusion of women from local Rotary clubs did not deny either freedom of intimate, private association or freedom of expressive association. (In a footnote, however, the Court noted that "we have no occasion [to] consider the extent to which the First Amendment protects the right of individuals to associate in the many clubs and other entities with selective membership that are found throughout the country. Whether the 'zone of privacy' established by the First Amendment extends to a particular [club] requires a careful inquiry into the objective characteristics of the particular relationships at issue.") A year later, in NEW YORK STATE CLUB ASS'N v. CITY OF NEW YORK, 487 U.S. 1 (1988), the Court unanimously upheld against facial First Amendment challenge a law prohibiting racial, religious, or sex discrimination in any institution, club, or place of accommodation that has more than 400 members, provides regular meal service, and "regularly receives payment from [nonmembers] for facilities and services for the furtherance of trade or business." Justice WHITE's opinion stated that it was "conceivable [that] an association might be able to show that it is organized for specific expressive purposes and that it will not be able to advocate its desired viewpoints nearly as effectively if it cannot confine its membership. [Here,] however, it seems sensible enough to believe that many of the large clubs covered by the [law] are not of this kind." Note also the cursory rejection of a law firm's freedom of association claim in a Title VII sex discrimination case, in Hishon v. King & Spalding, 467 U.S. 69 (1984).

SECTION 3.   MONEY AND POLITICAL CAMPAIGNS

Buckley v. Valeo

424 U.S. 1, 96 S.Ct. 612, 46 L.Ed.2d 659 (1976).

PER CURIAM.[1]

---

1. The Court of Appeals had sustained almost all provisions of the complex Act. Only   Justices Brennan, Stewart, and Powell joined all portions of the per curiam opinion revers-

These appeals present constitutional challenges to the key provisions of the Federal Election Campaign Act of 1971 [FECA]and related provisions [as] amended in 1974. [The challenged laws] in broad terms [provide]: (a) individual political contributions are limited to $1,000 to any single candidate per election with an overall annual limitation of $25,000 by any contributor; independent expenditures by individuals and groups "relative to a clearly identified candidate" are limited to $1,000 a year; campaign spending by candidates for various federal offices and spending for national conventions by political parties are subject to prescribed limits; (b) contributions and expenditures above certain threshold levels must [be] publicly disclosed; (c) a system for public funding of Presidential campaign activities is established; [and] (d) a Federal Election Commission is established to administer [the Act].

[The majority summarized its conclusions as follows: "[W]e sustain the individual contribution limits, the disclosure and reporting provisions, and the public financing scheme. We conclude, however, that the limitations on campaign expenditures, on independent expenditures, [and] on expenditures by a candidate from his personal funds are constitutionally infirm." Moreover, the composition of the Federal Election Commission was held unconstitutional. The excerpts that follow focus on the contribution and expenditure provisions. For the holding on the composition of the FEC, see p. 390 above. For the holding on the disclosure provisions, see p. 1381 above.]

I. *Contribution and Expenditure Limitations.*

[A.] *General Principles.* The Act's contribution and expenditure limitations operate in an area of the most fundamental First Amendment activities. Discussion of public issues and debate on the qualifications of candidates are integral to the operation of the system of government established by our Constitution. [In] upholding the constitutional validity of the Act's contribution and expenditure provisions on the ground that those provisions should be viewed as regulating conduct not speech, the Court of Appeals relied upon United States v. O'Brien. [We] cannot share the view that the present Act's contribution and expenditure limitations are comparable to the restrictions on conduct upheld in O'Brien. The expenditure of money simply cannot be equated with such conduct as destruction of a draft card. Some forms of communication made possible by the giving and spending of money involve speech alone, some involve conduct primarily, and some involve a combination of the two. Yet, this Court has never suggested that the dependence of a communication on the expenditure of money operates itself to introduce a nonspeech element or to reduce the exacting scrutiny required by the [First Amendment].

Even if the categorization of the expenditure of money as conduct were accepted, the limitations challenged here would not meet the O'Brien test because the governmental interests advanced in support of the Act involve "suppressing communication." The interests served by the Act include restricting the voices of people and interest groups who have money to spend and reducing the overall scope of federal election campaigns. Although the Act does not focus on the ideas expressed by persons or groups subjected to its regulations, it is aimed in part at equalizing the relative ability of all voters to affect electoral outcomes by placing a ceiling on expenditures for political expression

ing the Court of Appeals judgment in part. There were separate opinions by Chief Justice Burger and Justices White, Marshall, Blackmun and Rehnquist, all joining the opinion in part and dissenting in part, though in differing respects. Justice Stevens did not participate. Excerpts from the separate opinions are printed below.

by citizens and groups. Unlike [the situation in O'Brien], it is beyond dispute that the interest in regulating the alleged "conduct" of giving or spending money "arises in some measure because the communication allegedly integral to the conduct is itself thought to be harmful." Nor can the Act's contribution and expenditure limitations be sustained [by] reference to the constitutional principles reflected in such decisions as [Kovacs v. Cooper.] [The] critical difference between this case and those time, place and manner cases is that the present Act's contribution and expenditure limitations impose direct quantity restrictions on political communication and association [in] addition to any reasonable time, place, and manner regulations otherwise imposed.[2]

A restriction on the amount of money a person or group can spend on political communication during a campaign necessarily reduces the quantity of expression by restricting the number of issues discussed, the depth of their exploration, and the size of the audience reached.[3] This is because virtually every means of communicating ideas in today's mass society requires the expenditure of money. [The] expenditure limitations contained in the Act represent substantial rather than merely theoretical restraints on the quantity and diversity of political speech. [E.g., the] $1,000 ceiling on spending "relative to a clearly identified candidate" would appear to exclude all citizens and groups except candidates, political parties and the institutional press from any significant use of the most effective means of [communication].

By contrast with a limitation upon expenditures for political expression, a limitation upon the amount that any one person or group may contribute [entails] only a marginal restriction upon the contributor's ability to engage in free communication. A contribution serves as a general expression of support for the candidate and his views, but does not communicate the underlying basis for the support. [At most,] the size of the contribution provides a very rough index of the intensity of the contributor's support for the candidate. A limitation on [contributions] thus involves little direct restraint [on] political communication, for it permits the symbolic expression of support evidenced by a contribution but does not in any way infringe the contributor's freedom to discuss candidates and issues. While contributions may result in political expression if spent by a candidate or an association to present views to the voters, the transformation of contributions into political debate involves speech by someone other than the contributor.

Given the important role of contributions in financing political campaigns, contribution restrictions could have a severe impact on political dialogue if the limitations prevented candidates and political committees from amassing the resources necessary for effective advocacy. There is no indication, however, that the contribution limitations imposed by the Act would have any dramatic adverse effect on the funding of campaigns and political associations.[4] The

---

2. The nongovernmental appellees argue that just as the decibels emitted by a sound truck can be regulated consistent with the First Amendment, Kovacs, the Act may restrict the volume of dollars in political campaigns without impermissibly restricting freedom of speech. This comparison underscores a fundamental misconception. The decibel restriction upheld in Kovacs limited the *manner* of operating a sound truck but not the *extent* of its proper use. By contrast, the Act's dollar ceilings restrict the extent of the rea-

sonable use of virtually every means of communicating information. [Footnote by the Court.]

3. Being free to engage in unlimited political expression subject to a ceiling on expenditures is like being free to drive an automobile as far and as often as one desires on a single tank of gasoline. [Footnote by the Court.]

4. Statistical findings agreed to by the parties reveal that approximately 5.1% of the $73,483,613 raised by the 1161 candidates for

overall effect of the Act's contribution ceilings is merely to require candidates and political committees to raise funds from a greater number of persons and to compel people who would otherwise contribute amounts greater than the statutory limits to expend such funds on direct political expression, rather than to reduce the total amount of money potentially available to promote political expression. The Act's contribution and expenditure limitations also impinge on protected associational freedoms. [In] sum, although the Act's contribution and expenditure limitations both implicate fundamental First Amendment interests, its expenditure ceilings impose significantly more severe restrictions on protected freedoms of political expression and association than do its limitations on financial contributions.

B. *Contribution Limitations.* [T]he primary First Amendment problem raised by the Act's contribution limitations is their restriction of one aspect of the contributor's freedom of political association. [G]overnmental "action which may have the effect of curtailing the freedom to associate is subject to the closest scrutiny." [NAACP v. Alabama.] Yet, [e]ven a " 'significant interference' with protected rights of political association" may be sustained if the State demonstrates a sufficiently important interest and employs means closely drawn to avoid unnecessary abridgment of associational [freedoms].

It is unnecessary to look beyond the Act's primary purpose—to limit the actuality and appearance of corruption resulting from large individual financial contributions—in order to find a constitutionally sufficient justification for the $1,000 contribution limitation. [To] the extent that large contributions are given to secure political quid pro quos from current and potential officeholders, the integrity of our system of representative democracy is undermined. [The] deeply disturbing examples surfacing after the 1972 election demonstrate that the problem is not an illusory one. [Of] almost equal concern [is] the impact of the appearance of corruption stemming from public awareness of the opportunities for abuse inherent in a regime of large individual financial contributions. [Appellants] contend that the contribution limitations must be invalidated because bribery laws and narrowly-drawn disclosure requirements constitute a less restrictive means of dealing with "proven and suspected quid pro quo arrangements." But laws making criminal the giving and taking of bribes deal with only the most blatant and specific attempts of those with money to influence governmental action. And [Congress] was surely entitled to conclude that disclosure was only a partial measure, and that contribution ceilings were a necessary legislative concomitant to deal with the reality or appearance of [corruption].

[Appellants also argue] that the contribution limitations work [an] invidious discrimination between incumbents and [challengers] [5] There is [no] evidence to support the claim that the contribution limitations in themselves

---

Congress in 1974 was obtained in amounts in excess of [$1,000]. [Footnote by the Court.]

5. In this discussion, we address only the argument that the contribution limitations alone impermissibly discriminate against nonincumbents. We do not address the more serious argument that these limitations, in combination with the limitation on expenditures, [invidiously] discriminate against major-party challengers and minor-party candidates. [The] appearance of fairness [may] not reflect political reality. [It] is axiomatic that an incumbent usually begins the race with significant advantages. [In some circumstances] the overall effect of the contribution and expenditure limitations [could] foreclose any fair opportunity of a successful challenge. However, since we decide [below] that the ceilings on [expenditures] are unconstitutional, [we] need not express any opinion with regard to the alleged invidious discrimination resulting from the full sweep of the legislation as enacted. [Footnote by the Court.]

discriminate against major-party challengers to incumbents. The charge of discrimination against minor-party and independent candidates is more troubling, but the record provides no basis for concluding that the Act invidiously disadvantages such candidates. [T]he restriction would appear to benefit minor-party and independent candidates relative to their major-party opponents because major-party candidates receive far more money in large contributions. Although there is some force to appellants' response that minor-party candidates are primarily concerned with their ability to amass the resources necessary to reach the electorate rather than with their funding position relative to their major-party opponents, [we] conclude that the impact of the Act's $1,000 contribution limitation on major-party challengers and on minor-party candidates does not render the provision unconstitutional on its face.

[The Court also rejected similar challenges to the $5000 limit on contributions to candidates by "political committees," the limits on volunteers' incidental expenses, and the $25,000 limit on total contributions by an individual during a calendar year.]

C. *Expenditure Limitations.* The Act's expenditure ceilings impose direct and substantial restraints on the quantity of political speech. [It] is clear that a primary effect of these expenditure limitations is to restrict the quantity of campaign [speech]. [While neutral] as to the ideas expressed, [the restrictions] limit political expression "at the core of our electoral process and of the First Amendment [freedoms]."

1. *The $1,000 limitation on expenditures "relative to a clearly identified candidate."* Section 608(e)(1) provides that "[n]o person may make any expenditure [relative] to a clearly identified candidate during a calendar year [which] exceeds $1,000." [Appellants claim] that the provision is unconstitutionally vague. [Unconstitutional vagueness] can be avoided only by reading § 608(e)(1) as limited to communications that include explicit words of advocacy of election or defeat of a candidate. [We] turn then to the basic First Amendment question—whether § 608(e)(1), even as thus narrowly and explicitly construed, impermissibly burdens the constitutional right of free expression. [T]he constitutionality of § 608(e)(1) turns on whether the governmental interests advanced in its support satisfy the exacting scrutiny applicable to limitations on core First Amendment rights of political expression.

We find that the governmental interest in preventing corruption and the appearance of corruption is inadequate to justify § 608(e)(1)'s ceiling on independent expenditures. First, [the section] prevents only some large expenditures. So long as persons and groups eschew expenditures that in express terms advocate the election or defeat of a clearly identified candidate, they are free to spend as much as they want to promote the candidate and his views. [It] would naively underestimate the ingenuity and resourcefulness of persons and groups desiring to buy influence to believe that they would have much difficulty devising expenditures that skirted the restriction on express advocacy of election or defeat but nevertheless benefited the candidate's campaign. [Second, the] parties defending § 608(e)(1) contend that it is necessary to prevent would-be contributors from avoiding the contribution limitations by the simple expedient of paying directly for media advertisements or for other portions of the candidate's campaign activities. [But] controlled or coordinated expenditures are treated as contributions rather than expenditures under the Act [and are restricted by the valid § 608(b)]. By contrast, § 608(e)(1) limits expenditures for express advocacy of candidates made totally independently of the candidate and his campaign. Unlike contributions, such independent expenditures may well provide little assistance to the candidate's campaign and indeed may prove counterproductive. The absence of prearrangement and coordination of an expenditure with the candidate or his agent not only undermines the value of the expenditure to the candidate, but also alleviates the danger that expenditures will be given as a quid pro quo for improper commitments from the candidate. [While] the independent expenditure ceiling thus fails to serve any substantial governmental interest in stemming the reality or appearance of corruption in the electoral process, it heavily burdens core First Amendment expression.

It is argued, however, that the ancillary governmental interest in equalizing the relative ability of individuals and groups to influence the outcome of elections serves to justify [this expenditure limitation]. But the concept that government may restrict the speech of some elements of our society in order to enhance the relative voice of others is wholly foreign to the First Amendment, which was designed "to secure 'the widest possible dissemination of information from diverse and antagonistic sources,'" and "'to assure unfettered interchange of ideas.'" [The] First Amendment's protection against governmental abridgment of free expression cannot properly be made to depend on a person's financial ability to engage in public discussion. The Court's decisions in Mills v. Alabama, 384 U.S. 214 (1966), and in Tornillo [1974; p. 1366 above] held that legislative restrictions on advocacy of the election or defeat of political candidates are wholly at odds with the guarantees of the First Amendment. In Mills, the Court addressed the question whether "a State [can] make it a crime for the editor of a daily newspaper to write and publish an editorial *on election day* urging people to vote a certain way on issues submitted to them." We held that "no test of reasonableness could save [such] a state law from invalidation as a violation of the First Amendment." Yet the prohibition on election day editorials invalidated in Mills is clearly a lesser intrusion on constitutional freedom than a $1,000 limitation on the amount of money any person or association can spend *during an entire election year* in advocating the election or defeat of a candidate for public office. [The] legislative restraint [invalidated] in Tornillo [also] pales in comparison to the limitations imposed by § 608(e)(1). [We] conclude that § 608(e)(1)'s independent expenditure limitation is unconstitutional under the First Amendment.

2. *Limitation on expenditures by candidates from personal or family resources.* The Act also sets limits on expenditures by a candidate "from his personal funds, or the personal funds of his immediate family, in connection with his campaigns during any calendar year." § 608(a)(1). [The] ceiling on personal expenditures by a candidate in furtherance of his own [candidacy] clearly and directly interferes with constitutionally protected freedoms. [The] interest in equalizing the relative financial resources of candidates competing for elective office [is] clearly not sufficient to justify the provision's infringement of fundamental First Amendment rights. First, the limitation may fail to promote financial equality among candidates. A candidate who spends less of his personal resources on his campaign may nonetheless outspend his rival as a result of more successful fundraising efforts. Indeed, a candidate's personal wealth may impede his efforts to persuade others that he needs their financial contributions or volunteer efforts to conduct an effective campaign. Second, and more fundamentally, the First Amendment simply cannot tolerate § 608(a)'s restriction upon the freedom of a candidate to speak [on] behalf of his own [candidacy].

3. *Limitations on campaign expenditures.* Section 608(c) of the Act places limitations on overall campaign expenditures by candidates seeking nomination for election and election to federal office. [Presidential] candidates may spend $10,000,000 in seeking nomination for office and an additional $20,000,000 in

the general election campaign. [Senate campaign expenditures are limited to] the greater of eight cents multiplied by the voting-age population or $100,000 [in the primary], and in the general election the limit is increased to 12 cents multiplied by the voting-age population or $150,000. The Act imposes blanket $70,000 limitations on both primary campaigns and general election campaigns for the House of Representatives. [These limits are subject to adjustments for inflation.]

[No] governmental interest that has been suggested is sufficient to justify [these restrictions] on the quantity of political expression. [The] interest in alleviating the corrupting influence of large contributions is served by [the] contributions limitations and disclosure provisions. [The] interest in equalizing the financial resources of candidates [is not a convincing justification] for restricting the scope of federal election campaigns. [The] campaign expenditure ceilings appear to be designed primarily to serve the governmental interests in reducing the allegedly skyrocketing costs of political campaigns. [But the] First Amendment denies government the power to determine that spending to promote one's political views is wasteful, excessive, or unwise. In the free society ordained by our Constitution it is not the government but the people— individually as citizens and candidates and collectively as associations and political committees—who must retain control over the quantity and range of debate on public issues in a political campaign. [W]e hold that § 608(c) is constitutionally invalid.

In sum, the [contribution limits] are constitutionally valid. These limitations along with the disclosure provisions, constitute the Act's primary weapons against the reality or appearance of improper influence stemming from the dependence of candidates on large campaign contributions. The contribution ceilings thus serve the basic governmental interest in safeguarding the integrity of the electoral process without directly impinging upon the rights of individual citizens and candidates to engage in political debate and discussion. By contrast, the First Amendment requires the invalidation of the Act's independent expenditure ceiling, its limitation on a candidate's expenditures from his own personal funds, and its ceilings on overall campaign expenditures. These provisions place substantial and direct restrictions on the ability of [candidates] to engage in protected political expression, restrictions that the First Amendment cannot [tolerate].

III. *Public Financing of Presidential Election Campaigns*

[Portions of the Act codified at Subtitle H of the Internal Revenue Code provided for a Presidential Election Campaign Fund, financed by taxpayer checkoff on tax returns, that would provide for up to $20 million (indexed for inflation) to finance presidential campaigns by major parties (those that had received more than 25 per cent of the popular vote in the preceding presidential election). It also provided for funding for minor-party campaigns (those receiving 5 to 25 per cent of the vote in the previous election) and new-party campaigns (those receiving less than 5 per cent in the current election) proportional to their share of the vote. Public subsidies for party nominating conventions and matching funds for primary campaigns were also provided. As a condition of receiving a public subsidy, major-party candidates were required to limit their campaign expenditures to the amount of the subsidy and to forego all private contributions except to the extent that the fund was insufficient to provide the full entitlement. Minor-party candidates similarly had to limit their campaign expenditures to the amount of the major-party entitlement and forego private contributions except to the extent needed to make up the difference between that amount and their public funding grant. The Court rejected Spending Clause and equal protection challenges to the funding provisions. In response to the First Amendment challenge, it held:]

Subtitle H is a congressional effort, not to abridge, restrict, or censor speech, but rather to use public money to facilitate and enlarge public discussion and participation in the electoral process, goals vital to a self-governing people. Thus, Subtitle H furthers, not abridges, pertinent First Amendment values.

[In a footnote earlier in the opinion, the Court summarized its holding on the public funding conditions as follows: "For the reasons discussed in Part III, Congress may engage in public financing of election campaigns and may condition acceptance of public funds on an agreement by the candidate to abide by specified expenditure limitations. Just as a candidate may voluntarily limit the size of the contributions he chooses to accept, he may decide to forego private fundraising and accept public funding."]

Affirmed in part and reversed in part.

Chief Justice BURGER, concurring in part and dissenting [in part].

Contribution and expenditure limits. I agree fully with that part of the Court's opinion that holds unconstitutional the limitations the Act puts on campaign expenditures. [Yet] when it approves similarly stringent limitations on contributions, the Court ignores the reasons it finds so persuasive in the context of expenditures. For me contributions and expenditures are two sides of the same First Amendment [coin]. [Limiting] contributions, as a practical matter, will limit expenditures and will put an effective ceiling on the amount of political activity [that] Government will permit to take place. [The] Court's attempt to distinguish the communication inherent in political *contributions* from the speech aspects of political *expenditures* simply will not wash. We do little but engage in word games unless we recognize that people—candidates and contributors—spend money on political activity because they wish to communicate ideas, and their constitutional interest in doing so is precisely the same whether they or someone else utter the words. [It] is not simply speculation to think that the limitations on contributions will foreclose some candidacies.[1] The limitations will also alter the nature of some electoral contests drastically. At any rate, the contribution limits are a far more severe restriction on First Amendment activity than the sort of "chilling" legislation for which the Court has shown such extraordinary concern in the past. If such restraints can be justified at all, they must be justified by the very strongest of [state interests].

Justice WHITE, concurring in part and dissenting [in part].

I dissent [from] the Court's view that the expenditure limitations [violate] the First Amendment. [This] case depends on whether the nonspeech interests of the Federal Government in regulating the use of money in political campaigns are sufficiently urgent to justify the incidental effects that the limitations visit upon the First Amendment interests of candidates and their supporters. [This] is essentially the question the Court asks and answers in the affirmative with respect to the limitations on contributions. [The] Court thus accepts the congressional judgment that the evils of unlimited contributions are sufficiently threatening to warrant restriction regardless of the impact of the

---

1. Candidates who must raise large initial contributions in order to appeal for more funds to a broader audience will be handicapped. It is not enough to say that the contribution ceilings "merely require candi- dates [to] raise funds from a greater number of persons," where the limitations will effectively prevent candidates without substantial personal resources from doing just that. [Footnote by Chief Justice Burger.]

limits on the contributor's opportunity for effective speech and in turn on the total volume of the candidate's political communications by reason of his inability to accept large sums from those willing to give. The congressional judgment, which I would also accept, was that other steps must be taken to counter the corrosive effects of money in federal election campaigns. One of these steps is § 608(e) [the expenditure limits]. [The] Court strikes down [this] provision, strangely enough claiming more insight as to what may improperly influence candidates than is possessed by the majority of Congress that passed this Bill and the President who signed it. [It] would make little sense to me, and apparently made none to Congress, to limit the amounts an individual may give to a candidate or spend with his approval but fail to limit the amounts that could be spent on his behalf. Yet the Court permits the former while striking down the latter [limitation]. I would take the word of those who know—that limiting independent expenditures is essential to prevent transparent and widespread evasion of the contribution limits.

[The] Court also rejects Congress' judgment manifested in § 608(c) that the federal interest in limiting total campaign expenditures by individual candidates justifies the incidental effect on their opportunity for effective political speech. I disagree both with the Court's assessment of the impact on speech and with its narrow view of the values the limitations will serve. [As] an initial matter, the argument that money is speech and that limiting the flow of money to the speaker violates the First Amendment proves entirely too much. Compulsory bargaining [has] increased the labor costs of those who publish newspapers, which are in turn an important factor in the recent disappearance of many daily papers. [Justice White also referred to tax, antitrust, and price control legislation.] But it has not been suggested, nor could it be successfully, that these laws, and many others, are invalid because they siphon [off] large sums that would otherwise be available for communicative activities. In any [event], money is not always equivalent to or used for speech, even in the context of political campaigns. [The] judgment of Congress was that reasonably effective campaigns could be conducted within the limits established by the Act and that the communicative efforts of these campaigns would not seriously suffer. [There] is no sound basis for invalidating the expenditure limitations, so long as the purposes they serve are legitimate and sufficiently substantial, which in my view they are.

[Expenditure] ceilings reinforce the contribution limits and help eradicate the hazard of corruption. [Moreover,] the corrupt use of money by candidates is as much to be feared as the corrosive influence of large contributions. [I] have little doubt in addition that limiting the total that can be spent will ease the candidate's understandable obsession with fundraising, and so free him and his staff to communicate in more places and ways unconnected with the fundraising function. [It] is also important to restore and maintain public confidence in federal elections. It is critical to obviate or dispel the impression that federal elections are purely and simply a function of money, that federal offices are bought and sold or that political races are reserved for those who have the facility—and the stomach—for doing whatever it takes to bring together those interests, groups, and individuals that can raise or contribute large fortunes in order to prevail at the polls. The ceiling on candidate expenditures represents the considered judgment of Congress that elections are to be decided among candidates none of whom has an overpowering advantage by reason of a huge campaign war chest. [This] seems an acceptable purpose and the means chosen a common sense way to achieve [it].

I also disagree with the Court's judgment that § 608(a), which limits the amount of money that a candidate or his family may spend on his campaign, violates the Constitution. [By] limiting the importance of personal wealth, § 608(a) helps to assure that only individuals with a modicum of support from others will be viable candidates. This in turn would tend to discourage any notion that the outcome of elections is primarily a function of money. Similarly, § 608(a) tends to equalize access to the political arena, encouraging the less wealthy [to] run for political office. As with the campaign expenditure limits, Congress was entitled to determine that personal wealth ought to play a less important role in political campaigns than it has in the past. Nothing in the First Amendment stands in the way of that [determination].

[In a separate opinion, Justice BLACKMUN dissented from the upholding of the contribution restrictions. He found no "principled constitutional distinction" between limits on contributions and limits on expenditures.

[In another separate opinion, Justice MARSHALL dissented from the invalidation of the limits on the amount a candidate may spend from his own funds. He emphasized the governmental interest "in promoting the reality and appearance of equal access to the political arena," insisting that even if the wealthy candidate's initial advantage can be overcome, "the perception that personal wealth wins elections may not only discourage potential candidates without significant personal wealth [but] also undermine public confidence in the integrity of the electoral process." (He noted: "In the Nation's seven largest States in 1970, 11 of the 15 major senatorial candidates were millionaires. The four who were not millionaires lost their bid for election.") He added that the concern about the appearance that only the wealthy can become candidates was heightened by the impact of the contribution limits sustained by the Court: "Large contributions are the less wealthy candidate's only hope of countering the wealthy candidate's immediate access to substantial sums of money. [Regardless] of whether the goal of equalizing access would justify a legislative limit on personal candidate expenditures standing by itself, I think it clear that goal justifies [the limits here] when they are considered in conjunction with the remainder of the Act."

[Finally, Chief Justice BURGER and Justice REHNQUIST dissented from the upholding of the public financing provisions. Justice Rehnquist argued that Congress had "enshrined the Republican and Democratic parties in a permanently preferred position."]

THE PROBLEMS AND PROGENY OF BUCKLEY

1. *The Court's methodology in Buckley.* The Court assumed that FECA implicated the First Amendment. What was the speech involved? Is writing a check speech? Is writing a check facilitative of speech? Would price ceilings on book sales implicate the First Amendment? Moreover, what level of scrutiny did the Court apply in Buckley? Why was any heightened scrutiny appropriate? Because the Act covered political speech at the core of the First Amendment? Because the Act decreased the quantity of speech? Don't all content-neutral regulations decrease the quantity of speech? Why should the quantity restriction here receive stricter scrutiny? Finally, the Court applied a lower degree of scrutiny to the contribution limits than to the expenditure limits, enabling it to uphold the contribution limits as preventing corruption or the appearance of corruption. Do contributions implicate a lesser First Amendment interest than independent expenditures? Do congressional judgments warrant greater deference with respect to contribution limits than to expenditure limits? For

commentary on such questions, see Polsby, "Buckley v. Valeo: The Special Nature of Political Speech," 1976 Sup.Ct.Rev. 1.

2. *Equalization of speaking power.* The Court rejected as illegitimate the asserted governmental interest "in equalizing the relative ability of individuals and groups to influence the outcome of elections," finding such an interest "wholly foreign to the First Amendment." Did the Court give adequate weight to the interest in equality as a justification for expenditure limits? Should the Court have taken more seriously the claims that financing limits "enhance" the electoral process in order to correct perceived "distortions" in the free market of ideas? Were there speech interests on both sides? Consider the following comments:

a. "We do not think of 'one person one vote' as an example of reducing the speech of some to enhance the relative speech of others. [Why should] superior spending power [be] rightfully mine [if] superior voting power is not [?]" Strauss, "Corruption, Equality, and Campaign Finance," 94 Colum. L. Rev. 1369 (1994).

b. "[In the political process,] ideas and candidates [should] prevail because of their inherent worth, not because [one or the other] side puts on a more elaborate show of support." Wright, "Politics and the Constitution: Is Money Speech?," 85 Yale L.J. 1001 (1976). See also Wright, "Money and the Pollution of Politics: Is the First Amendment an Obstacle to Political Equality?" 82 Colum.L.Rev. 609 (1982).

c. "[Buckley, like Lochner, rests on] a decision to take the market status quo as just and prepolitical, and to use that decision to invalidate democratic efforts at reform." Sunstein, "Free Speech Now," 59 U. Chi. L. Rev. 255 (1992).

d. "[W]hen wealth is unfairly distributed and money dominates politics, then, though individual citizens may be equal in their vote and their freedom to hear the candidates they wish to hear, they are not equal in their own ability to command the attention of others for their own candidates, interests, and convictions. [But] democracy [supposes] that citizens are equals not only as judges but as participants as well." Dworkin, "The Curse of American Politics," N.Y. Rev. of Books, Oct. 17, 1996.

e. "[In a fair constitutional democracy,] each eligible voter should receive the same amount of financial resources for the purpose of participating in electoral politics." Foley, "Equal–Dollars–Per–Voter: A Constitutional Principle of Campaign Finance," 94 Colum. L. Rev. 1204 (1994).

How effectively could campaign finance restrictions advance the goal of equality among speakers in political campaigns, assuming such a goal were permissible? Is wealth only one basis for political inequality? Would finance reform leave untouched inequality among candidates and their campaigns based on fame, incumbency, and experience in the political arena? Based on the time their supporters were willing to donate to their campaigns? See BeVier, "Campaign Finance Reform: Specious Arguments, Intractable Dilemmas," 94 Colum. L.Rev. 1258 (1994); see also BeVier, "Money and Politics: A Perspective on the First Amendment and Campaign Finance Reform," 73 Calif.L.Rev. 1045 (1985).

3. *Public funding of political campaigns.* Buckley upheld public subsidies for presidential elections conditioned on expenditure limits that would be unconstitutional if imposed directly. Could Congress constitutionally extend public funding with similar conditions to congressional elections? To be constitutional under Buckley, any subsidy scheme would have to be voluntary. Would

that undercut its effectiveness? Would it be sufficient to offer subsidies in kind, such as free air time for candidates on the broadcast media, exacted from broadcasters as a condition of their public license? For arguments in favor of public funding, see Raskin & Bonifaz, "The Constitutional Imperative and Practical Superiority of Democratically Financed Elections," 94 Colum. L. Rev. 1160 (1994); see also Powe, "Mass Speech and the Newer First Amendment," 1982 Sup. Ct. Rev. 243.

4. *Other government interests in campaign finance limits*. Buckley found the government interest in avoidance of corruption or the appearance of corruption sufficient to justify contribution limits. Are there any other government interests that might suffice to justify campaign finance reform? Might spending limits reduce the diversion of candidates' time to fund-raising, increase the responsiveness of elected officials to their constituencies rather than "special interests," or improve the quality of debate by shifting candidates' energies away from expensive but uninformative ads? Does any of these justifications itself raise First Amendment problems? For commentary on government interests other than the avoidance of corruption, see Blasi, "Free Speech and the Widening Gyre of Fund–Raising: Why Campaign Spending Limits May Not Violate the First Amendment After All," 94 Colum. L. Rev. 1281 (1994); Sorauf, "Politics, Experience, and the First Amendment: The Case of American Campaign Finance," 94 Colum. L. Rev. 1348 (1994).

5. *Post-Buckley decisions: political action committees*. The FECA recognized the existence of "multicandidate political action committees [PACs]," defined as any political committee "which has received contributions from more than 50 persons [and] has made contributions to 5 or more candidates for Federal Office." Post–Buckley decisions on finance limitations directed at PACs have tracked the distinction between contributions and expenditures set forth in Buckley. Thus, in CALIFORNIA MEDICAL ASSN. [CMA] v. FEC, 453 U.S. 182 (1981), the Court upheld a provision of the law limiting individuals and unincorporated associations to contributions of no more than $5,000 per year to any multicandidate political committee. Justice MARSHALL's plurality opinion, joined by Justices Brennan, White, and Stevens, stated: "Nothing in [the challenged provision] limits the amount CMA or any of its members may independently expend in order to advocate political views; rather the statute restrains only the amount that [an individual or association] may contribute to [a political action committee]." Finding this to be a contribution rather than an expenditure limitation, and relying on Buckley, the Court found that such contributions were not entitled to "full First Amendment protection." Moreover, Justice Marshall rejected the claim that because the contributions here, unlike those in Buckley, flowed "to a political committee, rather than to a candidate," the provision did not "further the governmental interest in preventing the actual or apparent corruption of the political process." He argued that the provision was necessary to "prevent circumvention of the varied limitations on contributions [upheld] in Buckley," since the $1,000 limit on contributions to a particular candidate and the $25,000 limit on total annual contributions to all candidates could be "easily evaded" if unlimited contributions to political actions committees were permitted.

In a separate opinion, Justice BLACKMUN agreed with the plurality's result but not its reasoning. He stated that he did not agree that "the First Amendment test to be applied to contribution limitations is different from the test applicable to expenditure limitations." Both types of limits were permissible "if the State demonstrates a sufficiently important interest and employs means closely drawn to avoid unnecessary abridgement of associational freedoms." Under this standard, he thought the provision a constitutional means of "preventing evasion of the limitations on contributions" sustained in Buckley. Justice STEWART, joined by Chief Justice Burger and Justices Powell and Rehnquist, dissented on jurisdictional grounds.

In FEC v. NATIONAL CONSERVATIVE PAC, 470 U.S. 480 (1985), by contrast, the Court held unconstitutional a provision of the federal Act prohibiting PACs from spending more than $1,000 on behalf of a presidential candidate who elects to receive public financing under the Act. Relying heavily on Buckley's invalidation of expenditure limits, Justice REHNQUIST's majority opinion held that this spending limit also violated the First Amendment. He emphasized that the expenditures at issue here produced "speech at the core of the First Amendment." Since the Court had found in Buckley that limits on individual independent expenditures uncoordinated with the candidate or his campaign could not be justified in the interest of safeguarding against corruption or the appearance of corruption, there were similar reasons for finding the limits on spending by political committees "constitutionally infirm."

Justice WHITE, joined by Justices Brennan and Marshall, dissented, relying heavily on the views he had expressed in Buckley. He noted that the majority was "concerned with the interests of the PAC's contributors" and insisted that the contributors to the PAC were not "engaging in speech to any greater extent than [those] who contribute directly to political campaigns. Buckley explicitly distinguished between [using] one's own money to express one's views, [and] giving money to someone else in the expectation that that person will use the money to express views with which one is in agreement." This case, he argued, fell "within the latter category." Like the contribution limits upheld in Buckley, the challenged provision here did not "in any way infringe the contributor's freedom to discuss candidates and issues." Accordingly, Buckley should mean that this provision was constitutional. Justice MARSHALL submitted a separate dissent, stating: "Although I joined the portion of the Buckley per curiam that distinguished contributions from independent expenditures for First Amendment purposes, I now believe that the distinction has no constitutional significance. [In] both cases the regulation is of the same form: It concerns the amount of money that can be spent for political activity. [I] have come to believe that the limitations on independent expenditures challenged in [Buckley] and here are justified by the congressional interests in promoting 'the reality and appearance of equal access to the political arena,' and in eliminating political corruption and the appearance of such corruption."

6. *Post-Buckley decisions: political parties.* In COLORADO REPUBLICAN FEDERAL CAMPAIGN COMMITTEE v. FEC, ___ U.S. ___, 116 S.Ct. 2309 (1996), the Court held that political parties, like individuals, candidates, and PACs, have a First Amendment right to make unlimited independent expenditures. At issue was a provision of FECA imposing dollar limits upon political party "expenditures in connection with the general election campaign of a [congressional] candidate." The Colorado Republican party ran radio advertisements attacking the presumptive Democratic candidate for Senate before any Republican nominee had been selected. The Democrats and the FEC successfully charged the Colorado Republicans with violating FECA by exceeding the party expenditure limit.

Justice BREYER, joined in a plurality opinion by Justices O'Connor and Souter, held that "the First Amendment prohibits the application of this provision to the kind of expenditure at issue here—an expenditure that the political party has made independently, without coordination with any candidate." He reasoned that "independent expression of a political party's views is 'core' First Amendment activity no less than is the independent expression of individuals, candidates, or other political committees. [We] therefore believe that this Court's prior case law controls the outcome here. We do not see how a Constitution that grants to individuals, candidates, and ordinary political committees the right to make unlimited independent expenditures could deny the same right to political parties." The plurality rejected the government's view that party expenditures on behalf of a candidate's election should be conclusively presumed to be coordinated with the candidate's campaign and thus treated as "contributions" regulable under Buckley. But in light of its finding that the ads in this case had in fact been independent of any candidate's campaign, the plurality declined to reach the question whether the First Amendment forbids congressional efforts to limit expenditures that were in fact coordinated rather than independent.

Justice KENNEDY, joined by Chief Justice Rehnquist and Justice Scalia, concurred in the judgment and dissented in part. He would have gone further and invalidated the party expenditure limits on their face, whether applied to coordinated or independent expenditures by a party: "The central holding in [Buckley] is that spending money on one's own speech must be permitted, and this is what political parties do when they make the expenditures FECA restricts. [Political] parties have a unique role in [public debate]; they exist to advance their members' shared political beliefs. [Having] identified its members, however, a party can give effect to their views only by selecting and supporting candidates, [who] are necessary to make the party's message known and effective, and vice versa. It makes no sense, therefore, to ask, as FECA does [in the provision not reached by the plurality], whether a party's spending is made 'in cooperation, consultation, or concert with' its candidate. The answer in most cases will be yes, but that provides more, not less, justification for holding unconstitutional the statute's attempt to control this type of party spending, which bears little resemblance to the contributions discussed in Buckley."

Justice THOMAS, joined by Chief Justice Rehnquist and Justice Scalia in a concurrence in the judgment and partial dissent, also would have invalidated the party spending limits on their face: "As applied in the specific context of campaign funding by political parties, the anti-corruption rationale [set forth in Buckley] loses its force. What could it mean for a party to 'corrupt' its candidate or to exercise 'coercive' influence over him? The very aim of a political party is to influence its candidate's stance on issues and, if the candidate takes office or is reelected, his votes. When political parties achieve that aim, [that] is not corruption; that is successful advocacy of ideas in the political marketplace and representative government in a party system." Speaking only for himself, Justice THOMAS would have gone even further and jettisoned the expenditure-contribution distinction altogether: "A contribution is simply an indirect expenditure; though contributions and expenditures may [differ] in form, they do not differ in substance."

Justice STEVENS, joined by Justice Ginsburg, dissented, arguing that the party expenditure limits were constitutional as to both independent and coordinated expenditures because they served important interests both in avoiding corruption and in "leveling the electoral playing field by constraining the cost of federal campaigns."

7. *Post-Buckley decisions: corporations and political campaigns.* The Court has considered various claims that election regulations unduly limited corporate political speech. In FIRST NATIONAL BANK OF BOSTON v. BELLOTTI, 435 U.S. 765 (1978), the Court, by a vote of 5–4, invalidated a Massachusetts statute prohibiting any corporation from making contributions

or expenditures "for the purpose [of] influencing or affecting the vote on any questions submitted to the voters, other than one materially affecting any of the property, business or assets of the corporation." The law further specified that "[n]o question submitted to the voters solely concerning the taxation of the income, property, or transactions of individuals shall be deemed materially to affect the property, business or assets of the corporation." The challengers in this case (banks and business corporations) were prevented from spending money to oppose a proposed state constitutional amendment to authorize a graduated individual income tax. The state court upheld the statute, holding that the First Amendment rights of a corporation were limited to issues that materially affect its business, property, or assets.

The Supreme Court reversed, with Justice POWELL writing the majority opinion. To begin inquiry with the extent of corporate free speech rights (as the state court had done), he wrote, was to pose "the wrong question": "The proper question [is] not whether corporations 'have' First Amendment rights and, if so, whether they are coextensive with those of natural persons. Instead, the question must be whether [the law] abridges expression that the First Amendment was meant to protect. We hold that it does." In explaining why substantial First Amendment interests were implicated, Justice Powell noted that the expression the challengers wanted to engage in—publicizing their views on a proposed constitutional amendment—lay "at the heart of the First Amendment's protection": "It is the type of speech indispensable to decision-making in a democracy. [The] inherent worth of the speech in terms of its capacity for informing the public does not depend on the identity of its [source]." The Constitution and the case law accordingly did not support "the proposition that speech that otherwise would be within the protection of the First Amendment loses that protection simply because its source is a corporation that cannot prove, to the satisfaction of a court, a material effect on its business or property."

Having found the First Amendment implicated, Justice Powell found that the law was content-based and thus required strict scrutiny: "In the realm of protected speech, the legislature is constitutionally disqualified from dictating the subjects about which persons may speak and the speakers who may address a public issue. [Mosley.] If a legislature may direct business corporations to 'stick to business,' it also may limit other corporations—religious, charitable, or civic—to their respective 'business' when addressing the public. Such power in government to channel the expression of views is unacceptable under the First Amendment. Especially where, as here, the legislature's suppression of speech suggests an attempt to give one side of a debatable public question an advantage in expressing its views to the people, the First Amendment is plainly offended."

Under strict scrutiny, Justice Powell found, the law could not survive because it prohibited "protected speech in a manner unjustified by a compelling state interest." The state asserted, first, an interest "in sustaining the active role of the individual citizen in the electoral process and thereby preventing diminution of the citizen's confidence in government." Justice Powell did not find this interest "implicated in this case": he concluded that "there had been no showing that the relative voice of corporations has been overwhelming or even significant in influencing referenda in Massachusetts, or that there has been any threat to the confidence of the citizenry in government." Moreover, he found that the risk of actual or apparent corruption recognized in cases involving candidate elections "simply is not present in a popular vote on a public issue." The "State's paternalism evidenced by this statute" was inconsistent with the First Amendment's emphasis on the people's right to hear.

The state also asserted a second interest in "protecting the rights of shareholders whose views differ from those expressed by management on behalf of the corporation." Justice Powell also rejected this justification, finding that the statute poorly fit it: the statute was underinclusive in that it permitted corporations to lobby for legislation and contribute to candidates, and overinclusive in that it forbade them from spending on referenda even if the shareholders unanimously agreed on their position. Moreover, "The fact that a particular kind of ballot question has been singled out for special treatment undermines the likelihood of a genuine state interest in protecting shareholders. It suggests instead that the legislature may have been concerned with silencing corporations on a particular subject." Justice Powell also questioned the strength of the state interest in protecting shareholders from compulsory support of objectionable causes, noting that "no shareholder has been 'compelled' to contribute anything, [for] the shareholder invests in a corporation of his own volition and is free to withdraw his investment at any time and for any reason."

In a lengthy dissent, Justice WHITE, joined by Justices Brennan and Marshall, insisted that the majority's "fundamental error" was "its failure to realize that the state regulatory interests [are] themselves derived from the First Amendment"—primarily, the value of promoting the free marketplace of ideas by preventing corporate domination. Although Justice White conceded that corporate speech was within the First Amendment, he insisted that corporate speech was "subject to restrictions which individual expression is not." He noted that corporate communications do not further a "principal function of the First Amendment, the use of communication as a means of self-expression, self-realization and self-fulfillment." He added: "Ideas which are not a product of individual choice are entitled to less First Amendment protection." Moreover, "the restriction of corporate speech concerned with political matters impinges much less severely upon the availability of ideas to the general public than do restrictions upon individual speech."

Justice White argued further that the "governmental interest in regulating corporate political communications [raises] considerations which differ significantly from those governing the regulation of individual speech. [T]he special status of corporations has placed them in a position to control vast amounts of economic power which may, if not regulated, dominate not only the economy but also the very heart of our democracy, the electoral process. Although [Buckley] provides support for the position that the desire to equalize the financial resources available to candidates does not justify the limitation upon the expression of support which a restriction upon individual contributions entails, the interest of [the states] which have restricted corporate political activity is quite different. It is not one of equalizing the resources of opposing candidates or opposing positions but rather of preventing institutions which have been permitted to amass wealth as a result of special advantages extended by the State for certain economic purposes from using that wealth to acquire an unfair advantage in the political process. [The] State need not permit its own creation to consume it." Moreover, Justice White found compelling the state's additional interest in "assuring that shareholders are not compelled to support and financially further beliefs with which they disagree."

A separate dissent by Justice REHNQUIST concluded "that the 14th Amendment does not require a State to endow a business corporation with the power of political speech." He emphasized that corporations were created by the state and were limited to rights explicitly or implicitly guaranteed as part of the state-granted charter. He insisted that it could not be readily concluded that "the right of political expression is [necessary] to carry out the functions of a corporation organized for commercial purposes." He explained: "[The] States might reasonably feel that the corporation would use its economic power to obtain further benefits beyond those already bestowed." And he emphasized: "I can see no basis for concluding that the liberty of a corporation to engage in political activity with regard to matters having no material effect on its business is necessarily incidental to the purposes for which the Commonwealth permitted these corporations to be organized." Accordingly, the Massachusetts law provided "at least as much protection as the 14th Amendment requires." He noted that he would uphold the law even if the legislature's actual motive had been to "muzzle corporations on [the tax] issue" in order to increase the chances that the referendum would pass.

In FEC v. NATIONAL RIGHT TO WORK COMMITTEE [NRWC], 459 U.S. 197 (1982), the Court distinguished Bellotti in upholding a restriction on a nonprofit corporation's ability to raise funds for contributions to candidate elections. Federal election law prohibits corporations and labor unions from making contributions or expenditures in connection with federal elections. A section of the 1971 FECA, however, permits some participation by unions and corporations in the federal electoral process by allowing these organizations to establish and pay the expenses of "separate segregated funds" which may be used to support candidates during federal elections. Just as for-profit corporations must limit solicitations to stockholders and executive and administrative personnel, a corporation without capital stock may solicit contributions to a fund it has established only from "members" of the corporation. The FEC found NRWC in violation of the provision because it sent out a mass mailing soliciting contributions from nonmembers. The Court upheld this application of the law against First Amendment challenge, holding that NRWC's associational rights were overborne by governmental interests in "ensur[ing] that substantial aggregations of wealth amassed by the special advantages which go with the corporate form of organization [are] not be converted into political 'war chests' which could be used to incur political debts from legislators who are aided by the contributions, [and] protect[ing] the individuals who have paid money into a corporation or union for purposes other than the support of candidates from having that money used to support political candidates to whom they may be opposed."

In FEC v. MASSACHUSETTS CITIZENS FOR LIFE, INC. [MCFL], 479 U.S. 238 (1986), the Court held that, although a requirement that independent campaign expenditures on behalf of candidates be made out of a segregated fund was constitutionally permissible with respect to ordinary profit-making corporations, the provision violated the First Amendment as applied to those corporations that were, like MCFL,"more akin to voluntary political associations than business firms." Justice BRENNAN's opinion held that the First Amendment barred restrictions on the use by such a corporation of its general funds to support candidates for office, in this case by a pro-life organization. He found the financial segregation requirement, "while [not] an absolute restriction on speech, a substantial one." He distinguished FRWC as a case about candidate contributions, not independent expenditures. He found no anticorruption interest relevant to MCFL's expenditures and found no interest in protecting contributors from the diversion of their funds to causes they do not support: "individuals who contribute to [MCFL] are fully aware of its political purposes, and in fact contribute precisely because they support those purposes." Accordingly, MCFL could not constitutionally be subjected to the segregated fund requirement of the federal Act. Chief Justice REHNQUIST, joined by Justices White, Blackmun, and Stevens, dissented.

Four years later however, in AUSTIN v. MICHIGAN CHAMBER OF COMMERCE, 494 U.S. 652 (1990), the Court *upheld* a Michigan restriction on corporate independent campaign expenditures that was substantially identical to the federal restriction upheld in FEC v. MCFL. The Michigan law in Austin barred corporations from using corporate treasury funds for independent expenditures regarding political candidates, but allowed such corporate spending from segregated funds used solely for political purposes. In sustaining the ban, Justice MARSHALL's majority opinion emphasized the "unique legal and economic characteristics of corporations" that enable them "to use 'resources amassed in the economic marketplace' to obtain 'an unfair advantage in the political marketplace.' " He elaborated that "the political advantage of corporations is unfair because '[t]he resources in the treasury of a business corporation [are] not an indication of popular support for the corporation's political ideas. They reflect instead the economically motivated decisions of investors and customers. The availability of these resources may make a corporation a formidable political presence, even though the power of the corporation may be no reflection of the power of its ideas.'" He held that the state had "articulated a sufficiently compelling rationale" for its restrictions on spending since the law was designed to deal with "the corrosive and distorting effects of immense aggregations of wealth that are accumulated with the help of the corporate form and that have little or no correlation to the public's support for the corporation's political ideas."

He also held that the law was "sufficiently narrowly tailored to achieve its goal" because it was "precisely targeted to eliminate the distortion caused by corporate spending while also allowing corporations to express their political views [through] separate segregated funds." He noted that, because persons contributing to such segregated funds understood that their money would be used solely for political purposes, "the speech generated accurately reflects contributors' support for the corporation's political views." He added: "We emphasize that the mere fact that corporations may accumulate large amounts of wealth is not the justification for [the law]; rather, the unique state-conferred corporate structure that facilitates the amassing of large treasuries warrants the limit on independent expenditures."

Having concluded that the law itself was constitutional, Justice Marshall went on to hold it permissibly applied to the Michigan Chamber of Commerce. Unlike MCFL, the Michigan group "was involved in a wide range of activities other than political activity" and "had a large number of members many of whom might not share the Chamber's political goals." He distinguished MCFL on the ground that it, unlike the Michigan group, "was formed for the express purpose of promoting political ideas, [could not] engage in business activities," and was independent from the influence of business corporations. (Justice Marshall also rejected the claim that Michigan's exemption for labor unions and "media" corporations violated equal protection.)

Justice SCALIA dissented: " 'Attention all citizens. To assure the fairness of elections by preventing disproportionate expression of the views of any single powerful group, your Government has decided that the following associations of persons shall be prohibited from speaking or writing in support of any candidate:—' In permitting Michigan to make private corporations the first object of this Orwellian announcement, the Court today endorses the principle that too much speech is an evil that the democratic majority can proscribe. I dissent because that principle is contrary to our case law and incompatible with the absolute central truth of the First Amendment: that government cannot be trusted to assure, through censorship, the 'fairness' of political debate." Justice Scalia rejected the majority's view that the corporate form conferred advantages so different in kind from other state benefits as to justify a restriction on political speech. He viewed much of the majority opinion as an attempt to overrule or undercut Buckley's rejection of restrictions on political activity purely because of the resources available to a speaker. He also objected strongly to the majority's "cavalier treatment of the narrow tailoring requirement," urging the Court to uphold, as it had in most other areas, "[t]he principle [that] the mere potential harm does not justify a restriction on speech."

In another dissent, Justice KENNEDY, joined by Justices O'Connor and Scalia, objected that the majority had upheld "a direct restriction on the independent expenditure of funds for political speech for the first time in its history." He argued further that the Court's own distinction between the Michigan Chamber and MCFL was itself a "value-laden, content-based speech suppression that permits some nonprofit corporate groups but not others to engage in political speech." He found the Michigan law unable to survive "exacting First Amendment scrutiny": "[In] Buckley and Bellotti, [we] rejected the argument that the expenditure of money to increase the quantity of political speech somehow fosters corruption. The key to the majority's reasoning appears to be that because some corporate speakers are well-supported, [government] may ban all corporate speech to ensure that it will not dominate political debate. The argument is flawed in at least two respects. First, the statute is overinclusive because it covers all groups which use the corporate form, including all nonprofit corporations. Second, it assumes that the government has a legitimate interest in equalizing the relative influence of speakers. [Similar arguments were] rejected in Bellotti."

Does Austin overrule Buckley or Bellotti? Does Justice Marshall persuasively distinguish the government rationale upheld in Austin from the equalization rationale found impermissible in Buckley? If a corporation may make unlimited expenditures on referendum campaigns under Bellotti, why can its independent expenditures in support of political candidates be regulated under Austin? Does corporate spending with respect to candidate elections implicate a compelling government interest even if that spending is not coordinated with the candidate? What, exactly, is that interest? Why was it not implicated by the corporate spending in Bellotti? Note that Justice White, dissenting in Bellotti, suggested that that decision cast doubt on a range of state and federal election laws restricting corporate political expenditures. Does Austin lift that cloud? For commentary on the issues raised by Austin, see Brudney, "Association, Advocacy and the First Amendment," 4 Wm. & Mary Bill of Rts. J. 3 (1995); Fisch, "Frankenstein's Monster Hits the Campaign Trail: an Approach to Regulation of Corporate Political Expenditures," 32 Wm. & Mary L. Rev. 587 (1991); Lowenstein, "A Patternless Mosaic: Campaign Finance and the First Amendment after Austin," 21 Cap. U. L. Rev. 381 (1992).

8. *Post-Buckley decisions: referenda.* Recall that, in Bellotti, the Court found little state interest in regulating the financing of campaigns concerning a referendum. Are the concerns about the role of money in representative elections generally absent in the context of direct democracy? In CITIZENS AGAINST RENT CONTROL [CARC] v. BERKELEY, 454 U.S. 290 (1981), the Court invalidated a Berkeley, California, ordinance imposing a $250 limit on personal contributions to committees formed to support or oppose ballot measures. Chief Justice BURGER's opinion for the Court found the limit on contributions an unconstitutional interference with "rights of association" and "individual and collective rights of expression." Although Buckley had sustained limits on contributions in candidate elections, the Chief Justice insisted that "Buckley does not support limitations on contributions to committees formed to favor or oppose *ballot measures.*" He pointed out, moreover, that

Bellotti had relied on Buckley "to strike down state legislative limits on advocacy relating to ballot measures." He rejected the City's effort to distinguish those cases on the ground that the Berkeley limit was "necessary as a prophylactic measure to make known the identity of supporters and opponents of ballot measures." He found that interest "insubstantial" in this case because the disclosure provisions of the ordinance assured that the identities of contributors would be known. Moreover, there was no evidence that the limit was necessary to preserve voters' confidence in the initiative process. Justices Rehnquist, Marshall, Blackmun and O'Connor all filed concurring statements.

The sole dissenter, Justice WHITE, reiterated his dissenting positions in Buckley and Bellotti. He insisted, moreover, that the Berkeley limit was "a less encompassing regulation of campaign activity" than those involved in the earlier cases and that the challenged ordinance was "tailored to the odd measurements of Buckley and Bellotti." For example, Berkeley had followed those decisions by regulating "contributions but not expenditures" and by limiting personal but not corporate spending. He commented: "[The] result here illustrates that the Buckley framework is most problematical and strengthens my belief that there is a proper role for carefully drafted limitations on expenditures."

In MEYER v. GRANT, 486 U.S. 414 (1988), a unanimous Court struck down a Colorado law prohibiting the payment of people circulating petitions in connection with a voter initiative. Justice STEVENS' opinion for the Court stressed that this restriction "involves a limitation on political expression subject to exacting scrutiny. Buckley. [The] refusal to permit appellees to pay petition circulators restricts political expression in two ways. First, it limits the number of voices who will convey appellees' message and the hours they can speak and, therefore, limits the size of the audience they can reach. Second, it makes it less likely that appellees will garner the number of signatures necessary to place the matter on the ballot, thus limiting their ability to make the matter the focus of statewide discussion. [That] appellees remain free to employ other means to disseminate their ideas does not take their speech through petition circulators outside the bounds of First Amendment protection. Colorado's prohibition of paid petition circulators restricts access to the most effective, fundamental, and perhaps economical avenue of political discourse, direct one-on-one communication. That it leaves open 'more burdensome' avenues of communication, does not relieve its burden on First Amendment expression. The First Amendment protects appellees' right not only to advocate their cause but also to select what they believe to be the most effective means for so doing. [We] are not persuaded by the State's argument that the prohibition is justified by its interest in making sure that an initiative has sufficient grass roots support to be placed on the ballot, or by its interest in protecting the integrity of the initiative process."

9. *The limits of Buckley's anticorruption rationale: candidates' promises in election campaigns.* In BROWN v. HARTLAGE, 456 U.S. 45 (1982), petitioner, a candidate for a county office, had made a campaign promise that, if elected, he would lower his salary "to a more realistic level." Shortly after making the statement, he learned that it arguably violated the Kentucky Corrupt Practices Act, which prohibited candidates from offering material benefits to voters in consideration for their votes. The candidate retracted the statement and was elected. Thereafter, a suit was brought to set aside his election because of his "illegal" promise. The state court granted the relief, finding the candidate's promise to be "an attempt to buy votes or to bribe the voters." In reversing that judgment, Justice BRENNAN's opinion applied strict scrutiny and addressed three possible justifications for the law: "first, as a

prohibition on buying votes; second, as facilitating the candidacy of persons lacking independent wealth; and third, as an application of the State's interests [with] respect to factual misstatements." He found none of these justifications adequate under the First Amendment.

He emphasized that "there are constitutional limits on the State's power to prohibit candidates from making promises in the course of an election campaign," because such promises "enhance the accountability of government officials" and "assist the voters in predicting the effect of their vote." Here, the candidate had not offered "the voters a payment from his personal funds"; all he had done was to declare an intention "to exercise the fiscal powers of government office," with the benefit extending "beyond those voters who cast their ballots for [him], to all taxpayers and citizens." Thus, like a "promise to lower taxes [or] to increase taxes in order to provide some group with a desired public [service]," the promise here could not "be deemed beyond the reach of the First Amendment, or considered as inviting the kind of corrupt arrangement the appearance of which a State may have a compelling interest in avoiding. See [Buckley]."

SECTION 4.   FREEDOM OF THE PRESS

Introduction. The First Amendment protects not only "the freedom of speech" but also freedom "of the press." Does that specific reference to the "press" entitle the media to special constitutional protection? Or are press claims more properly analyzed as an aspect of the general freedom of expression guaranteed by the "speech" clause? This section focuses on the constitutional protection of the press. This introduction probes whether the press merits protections more extensive than those generally available to disseminators of information and opinion. The section then turns to several functional problems that have given rise to recurrent litigation regarding the contours of press protections. May government compel journalists to divulge information they possess, in aid of such state interests as criminal law enforcement? Does the press enjoy a constitutional right of access to such places as jails and courtrooms in order to obtain newsworthy information? Are the media exempt from tax laws, regulations or civil liability that extend to others? Does it matter whether these laws single out the "press" for special treatment or treat it the same as everyone else? Finally, the Court has read the First Amendment to confer lesser protection on broadcasters than on the print media. Why should this be so? Is such differential treatment still warranted? How should it bear on new media such as cable television and the Internet?

1. *The press as a "fourth branch" of government.* Does the press clause simply reiterate the speech clause or does it provide some protection to the institutional media beyond that enjoyed by other speakers? The most prominent advocate of special significance for the press clause was Justice Stewart. He argued that "the Free Press guarantee is, in essence, a *structural* provision of the Constitution. [It] extends protection to an institution. The publishing business [is] the only organized private business that is given explicit constitutional protection. [If] the Free Press guarantee meant no more than freedom of expression, it would be a constitutional redundancy. [It] is [a] mistake to suppose that the only purpose of the constitutional guarantee of a free press is to insure that a newspaper will serve as a neutral forum for debate, a 'market

place for ideas,' a kind of Hyde Park Corner for the community. A related theory sees the press as a neutral conduit of information between the people and their elected leaders. These theories, in my view, again give insufficient weight to the institutional autonomy of the press that it was the purpose of the Constitution to guarantee." Justice Stewart also noted that the system of separation of powers "deliberately created an internally competitive system" and argued that the "primary purpose [of the Press Clause was to] create a fourth institution outside the Government as an additional check on the three official branches. [The] relevant metaphor [is that] of the Fourth Estate." In his view, then, the First Amendment protected "the institutional autonomy of the press." Stewart, "Or of the Press," 26 Hast.L.J. 631 (1975).

2. *The press as just another speaker.* For an argument contrary to Justice Stewart's, consider dictum in Chief Justice BURGER's concurring opinion in FIRST NATIONAL BANK OF BOSTON v. BELLOTTI, 435 U.S. 765 (1978): "Because the First Amendment was meant to guarantee freedom to express and to communicate ideas, I can see no difference between the right of those who seek to disseminate ideas by way of a newspaper and those who give lectures or speeches that seek to enlarge the audience by publication and wide dissemination." He explained: "I perceive two fundamental difficulties with a narrow reading of the Press Clause. First although certainty on this point is not possible, the history of the Clause does not suggest that the authors contemplated a 'special' or 'institutional' privilege.[1] [Indeed] most pre-First Amendment commentators 'who employed the term "freedom of speech" with great frequency used it synonymously with freedom of the press.'[2] Those interpreting the Press Clause as extending protection only to, or creating a special role for, the 'institutional press' must either (a) assert such an intention on the part of the Framers for which no supporting evidence is available; (b) argue that events after 1791 somehow operated to 'constitutionalize' this interpretation; or (c) candidly acknowledging the absence of historical support, suggest that the intent of the Framers is not important today.

"To conclude that the Framers did not intend to limit the freedom of the press to one select group is not necessarily to suggest that the Press Clause is redundant. The Speech Clause standing alone may be viewed as a protection of the liberty to express ideas and beliefs, while the Press Clause focuses specifically on the liberty to disseminate expression broadly and 'comprehends every sort of publication which affords a vehicle of information and opinion.' Lovell v. Griffin. Yet there is no fundamental distinction between expression and dissemination. The liberty encompassed by the Press Clause, although complementary to and a natural extension of Speech Clause liberty, merited special mention simply because it had been more often the object of official restraints. [The] second fundamental difficulty with interpreting the Press Clause as conferring special status on a limited group is one of definition. The very task of including some entities within the 'institutional press' while excluding others, whether undertaken by legislature, court or administrative agency, is reminiscent of the

---

1. The Chief Justice cited Lange, "The Speech and Press Clauses," 23 U.C.L.A.L.Rev. 77 (1975) (rejecting arguments for special protection for the press, suggesting that it would water down general protection for speech and necessitate content-based distinctions). Compare Bezanson, "The New Free Press Guarantee," 63 Va.L.Rev. 731 (1977) (arguing that the "independence" of the press justifies special protection); Anderson, "The Origins of the Press Clause," 30 UCLA L.Rev. 455 (1983) (arguing that the press clause historically had meaning independent of the speech clause).

2. The Chief Justice was quoting from Levy, Legacy of Suppression: Freedom of Speech and Press in Early American History (1963).

abhorred licensing system of Tudor and Stuart England—a system the First Amendment was intended to ban from this country. Further, the officials undertaking that task would be required to distinguish the protected from the unprotected on the basis of such variables as content of expression, frequency or fervor of expression, or ownership of the technological means of dissemination. Yet nothing in this Court's opinions supports such a confining approach to the scope of Press Clause protection.[3] [In short], the First Amendment does not 'belong' to any definable category of persons or entities: it belongs to all who exercise its freedoms."

Chief Justice Burger's disinclination to rest media protections on the Press Clause has been the typical position of the Court. Most press claims have been adjudicated by analysis of the Speech Clause and of general principles of freedom of expression. Would it be preferable to rest any "special status" rights of the press on further elaboration of the Press Clause, or does the press receive adequate protection under the Court's readings of the Speech Clause and the First Amendment generally? Consider these questions in reviewing the materials that follow.

A.   PRESS ACCESS TO NEWSWORTHY GOVERNMENTAL INFORMATION

Introduction. Does the First Amendment entitle the press to obtain information the government seeks to withhold? On the view that the press has special institutional responsibility as a watchdog of government, such access rights would appear indispensable. But claims of a special press right of access in general have not fared well—even with Justice Stewart, the leading advocate of the "fourth branch" theory—as the following cases demonstrate. In 1980, however, a 7–1 majority endorsed an access claim to criminal trials, in the Richmond Newspapers case. What is the proper scope of that newly recognized access? For commentary on press rights of access in order to obtain government information, see BeVier, "An Informed Public, An Informing Press: The Search for a Constitutional Principle," 68 Calif.L.Rev. 482 (1980) (arguing that courts may recognize press rights to publish and disseminate information without also recognizing a right of access to government information) ; Baker, "Press Rights and Government Power to Structure the Press," 34 U.Miami L.Rev. 819 (1980) (noting a distinction between "offensive" and "defensive" press claims and suggesting that defensive rights of the press against government intrusions are more persuasive than offensive, right-of-access claims); Dyk, "Newsgathering, Press Access, and the First Amendment," 44 Stan. L. Rev. 927 (1992) (arguing for heightened press access to check government).

---

3. "Near v. Minnesota, which examined the meaning of freedom of the press, did not involve a traditional institutionalized newspaper but rather an occasional publication (nine issues) more nearly approximating the product of a pamphleteer than the traditional newspaper." [Footnote by Chief Justice Burger.]

PRESS ACCESS TO JAILS

1. *Pell and Saxbe.* The Court first confronted press demands for access to jails in companion cases, PELL v. PROCUNIER, 417 U.S. 817 (1974), and SAXBE v. WASHINGTON POST CO., 417 U.S. 843 (1974). In Pell, the majority rejected an attack on a California rule providing that "press and other media interviews with specific individual inmates will not be permitted." And in Saxbe, the Court turned back a challenge to a very similar Federal Bureau of Prisons prohibition of press interviews of individually designated prisoners in most federal prisons. Justice STEWART delivered the majority opinion in each case. Central to his rejection of the journalists' claim was his assertion that, although the First Amendment bars "government from interfering in any way with the free press," it does not "require government to accord the press special access to information not shared by members of the public generally." He explained: "It is one thing to say that a journalist is free to seek out sources of information not available to members of the general public, that he is entitled to some constitutional protection of the confidentiality of such sources, cf. [Branzburg], and that government cannot restrain the publication of news emanating from such sources. Cf. [Pentagon Papers]. It is quite another thing to suggest that the Constitution imposes upon government the affirmative duty to make available to journalists sources of information not available to members of the public generally."

Justice POWELL found that approach unduly simplistic. He concluded in Pell that an absolute ban on interviews "impermissibly restrains the ability of the press to perform its constitutionally established function of informing the people on the conduct of their government." Elaborating that position in Saxbe in a lengthy dissent joined by Justices Brennan and Marshall, he stated: "I cannot follow the Court in concluding that *any* governmental restriction on press access to information, so long as it is nondiscriminatory, falls outside the purview of First Amendment concern. [It] goes too far to suggest that the government must justify under the stringent standards of First Amendment review every regulation that might affect in some tangential way the availability of information to the news media. But to my mind it is equally impermissible to conclude that no governmental inhibition of press access to newsworthy information warrants constitutional scrutiny. At some point official restraints on access to news sources, even though not directed solely at the press, may so undermine the function of the First Amendment that it is both appropriate and necessary to require the Government to justify such regulations in terms more compelling than discretionary authority and administrative convenience." He argued that "this sweeping prohibition of prisoner-press interviews substantially impairs a core value of the First Amendment." He noted that freedom of speech protects two kinds of interests, individual and societal. Here, the "societal function" of "preserving free public discussion of governmental affairs" was critical. He emphasized: "In seeking out the news the press [acts] as an agent of the public at large. [The] underlying right is the right of the public generally. The press is the necessary representative of the public's interest in this context and the instrumentality which effects the public's right."

In a separate dissent, Justice DOUGLAS, joined by Justices Brennan and Marshall, similarly rested on the right "of the people": "the public's interest in being informed about prisons [is] paramount." Accordingly, the interview bans were "an unconstitutional infringement on the public's right to know protected by the free press guarantee of the First Amendment."

2. *The KQED case.* Press access claims similar to those rejected in Pell and Saxbe resurfaced four years later. But in HOUCHINS v. KQED, INC., 438

U.S. 1 (1978), the 7–person Court, in an unusual division, sustained a portion of the claim of access to jails. The case arose from an action filed by San Francisco public television station KQED, which sought to gain access to a county jail to investigate allegedly shocking conditions. After the suit was filed, Sheriff Houchins modified his "no-access" policy of barring the general public and the media from Santa Rita and launched a monthly tour program limited to groups of 25 persons. Those on the tour were not permitted to take photographs or interview inmates. The lower court awarded KQED preliminary relief, giving the news media access to the jail "at reasonable times and hours" and authorizing inmate interviews and the use of photographic and sound equipment.

The Court, dividing 3–1–3 (Justices Marshall and Blackmun did not participate in the case), held the order proper in part. Chief Justice BURGER's opinion viewed the case as governed by Pell and Saxbe and found no basis for judicial relief: "[Until] the political branches decree otherwise, [the media have] no right of special access to the [jail] different from or greater than that accorded the public generally." He explained that Branzburg's "dictum, that 'news gathering is not without its First Amendment protections,' in no sense implied a constitutional right of access to news sources. [There] is an undoubted right to gather news 'from any source by means within the law,' but that affords no basis for the claim that the First Amendment compels others— private persons or governments—to supply information."

Justice STEVENS' dissent, joined by Justices Brennan and Powell, insisted that Pell was distinguishable because in Pell there had been "substantial press and public access" to the jail: there, the rejected media claim asserted the additional right "to interview specifically designated inmates"; but the Pell ruling was no basis for upholding the general "no access" policy that prevailed at the jail at the time the suit was filed. He asserted that "the Court has never intimated that a nondiscriminatory policy of excluding entirely both the public and the press from access to information about prison conditions would avoid constitutional scrutiny. Indeed, Pell itself strongly suggests the contrary." He stated that "the probable existence of a constitutional violation rested upon the special importance of allowing a democratic community access to knowledge about how its servants were treating [prisoners]." He added: "[E]ven though the Constitution provides the press with no greater right of access to information than that possessed by the public at large, a preliminary injunction is not invalid simply because it awards special relief to a successful litigant which is a representative of the press." In elaborating the constitutional premises for that decision, he put special emphasis on the belief that "information-gathering is entitled to some measure of constitutional protection." KQED, accordingly, should prevail in his view not because of any special press privilege but as an advocate of "the public's right to be informed."

Justice STEWART's decisive concurrence agreed with the Chief Justice's basic premises that the press had no special access rights, but differed in applying those principles here: "Whereas [Chief Justice Burger] appears to view 'equal access' as meaning access that is identical in all respects, I believe that the concept of equal access must be accorded more flexibility in order to accommodate the practical distinctions between the press and the general public." That "practical accommodations" approach permitted him to find a basis for limited relief for KQED. Emphasizing the "critical role played by the press in American society," he explained: "[T]erms of access that are reasonably imposed on individual members of the public may, if they impede effective reporting without sufficient justification, be unreasonable as applied to journalists who are there to convey to the general public what the visitors see."

Accordingly, the First Amendment "required the Sheriff to give members of the press *effective* access" to all areas open to the public. Simply permitting reporters to sign up for the monthly tours "on the same terms as the public" was inadequate "as a matter of constitutional law." Accordingly, the trial court's order permitting press access "on a more flexible and frequent basis than scheduled monthly tours" was justified in order "to keep the public informed," as was the order permitting the media to bring cameras and recording equipment into the jail. (However, Justice Stewart found the preliminary injunction overbroad in authorizing press access to areas of the jail closed to the public and in permitting interviews of randomly encountered inmates. Those aspects of the injunction "gave the press access to areas and sources of information from which persons on the public tours had been excluded, and thus enlarged the scope of what [was] opened to public view.")

PRESS ACCESS TO JUDICIAL PROCEEDINGS

1. *Pretrial hearings.* In GANNETT CO. v. DePASQUALE, 443 U.S. 368 (1979), a divided Court rejected a newspaper publisher's attack on an order barring the public, including the press, from a pretrial hearing on suppression of evidence in a murder case. The prevailing opinion held that the press and the public had no independent constitutional right to insist upon access to such pretrial proceedings when the accused, the prosecutor, and the trial judge all had agreed to close the hearing in order to assure a fair trial. Although the Justices focused primarily on the Sixth Amendment provision that, in "all criminal prosecutions, the accused shall enjoy the right to [a] public trial," some comments on First Amendment issues surfaced in most of the opinions. All of the Justices agreed that the problem here was distinguishable from that in Nebraska Press (p. 1357 above), since the issue here was "not one of prior restraint on the press but, rather, one of *access* to a judicial proceeding."

Justice STEWART, writing for the Court, accepted that the Sixth Amendment's public trial guarantee reflected the public as well as the defendant's interest, but held that "our adversary system of criminal justice is premised upon the proposition that the public interest is fully protected by the participants of the litigation," who had agreed to the closure order here. He found nothing in the structure, text or history of the Sixth Amendment to support "any correlative right in members of the public to insist upon a public trial." He found it unnecessary to decide whether there was any First Amendment right to attend criminal trials: "[E]ven assuming, arguendo, that the [First Amendment] may guarantee such access in some situations, a question we do not decide, this putative right was given all appropriate deference by the [trial judge] in the present case."[1]

Justice POWELL's concurring opinion considered the First Amendment issue more fully and concluded, relying on his approach in Saxbe: "Because of the importance of the public's having accurate information concerning the

---

1. In finding that "appropriate deference," he noted that none of the spectators in the courtroom, including Gannett's reporter, had objected when the defendants made their closure motion; that counsel for Gannett was nevertheless given a later opportunity to object to closure; that the trial judge had acknowledged a First Amendment access interest, but had concluded that it was outweighed by the defendants' right to a fair trial in this case; and that denial of access here was in any event "not absolute but only temporary," since the lower court made available a transcript of the suppression hearing after the alleged danger of prejudice had dissipated.

operation of its criminal justice system, I would hold explicitly that petitioner's reporter had an interest protected by the [First Amendment] in being present at the pretrial suppression hearing." But he suggested that a closure motion would be appropriate if "a fair trial for the defendant is likely to be jeopardized by publicity." Applying this standard, Justice Powell found that the First Amendment right of access had been "adequately respected" by the trial judge in this case. Justice REHNQUIST's concurring opinion took a narrower view of the First Amendment. He stated: "Despite the Court's seeming reservation of the [question], it is clear that this Court repeatedly has held that there is no First Amendment right of access in the public or the press to judicial or other governmental proceedings." In his view, the Court had "emphatically" rejected Justice Powell's view "that the First Amendment is some sort of constitutional 'sunshine law' that requires notice, an opportunity to be heard and substantial reasons before a governmental proceeding may be closed to the public and press."

Justice BLACKMUN's partial dissent, joined by Justices Brennan, White and Marshall, derived a public right of access from the Sixth Amendment and argued that states could not exclude the public "from a proceeding within the ambit of the Sixth Amendment's guarantee without affording full and fair consideration to the public's interest in maintaining an open proceeding." Emphasizing the "societal interest in the public trial that exists separately from, and at times in opposition to, the interests of the accused," he argued that a court may not give effect to "an accused's attempt to waive his public trial right" in all circumstances: "[The] public trial interest cannot adequately be protected by the prosecutor and judge in conjunction, or connivance, with the defendant." Justice Blackmun recognized, however, that "the publication of information learned in an open proceeding may harm irreparably, under certain circumstances, the ability of the defendant to obtain a fair trial," and suggested that "limited exceptions to the principle of publicity" would be acceptable if "necessary" in such cases.

2. *Criminal trials.* A year after Gannett, the 7–1 decision in RICHMOND NEWSPAPERS, INC. v. VIRGINIA, 448 U.S. 555 (1980), held that, "[a]bsent an overriding interest articulated in findings, the trial of a criminal case must be open to the public." Chief Justice BURGER's opinion announcing the judgment (joined by Justices White and Stevens) stated that the "narrow question" was "whether the right of the public and press to attend criminal trials is guaranteed under [the] Constitution," a question not reached in Gannett. After reviewing the historical practice of having trials "open to all who cared to observe," he concluded that, when the Constitution was adopted, "criminal trials both here and in England had long been presumptively open." He noted the "nexus between openness, fairness, and the perception of fairness" and commented: "To work effectively, it is important that society's criminal process 'satisfy the appearance of justice,' and the appearance of justice can best be provided by allowing people to observe it." Although attendance at trials "is no longer a wide-spread pastime," that merely validated "the media claim of functioning as surrogates for the public" in the modern context. The "unbroken, uncontradicted history" supported his conclusion that "a presumption of openness inheres in the very nature of a criminal trial under our system of justice."

Turning to the constitutional sources for an access claim not explicitly guaranteed, he concluded that "the right to attend criminal trials is implicit in the guarantees of the First Amendment." In reaching that conclusion, he discussed the interrelationship of several provisions of the First Amendment, and the relevance of the Ninth Amendment as well. The First Amendment protections of speech, press, and the right to assemble "share a common core purpose of assuring freedom of communication on matters relating to the functioning of government. Plainly it would be difficult to single out any aspect of government of higher concern and importance to the people than the manner in which criminal trials are conducted." Accordingly, the First Amendment could be read "as protecting the right of everyone to attend trials so as to give meaning to those explicit guarantees"; thus, "the First Amendment guarantees of speech and press, standing alone, prohibit government from summarily closing courtroom doors." He distinguished Pell and Saxbe as involving "penal institutions which, by definition [and tradition], are not 'open' or public places."

The Chief Justice conceded that the Constitution did not spell out a "right of the public to attend trials." But he noted that this had not "precluded recognition of important rights not enumerated": "Notwithstanding the appropriate caution against reading into the Constitution rights not explicitly defined, the Court has acknowledged that certain unarticulated rights are implicit in enumerated guarantees. For example, the rights of association and of privacy [as well as] the right to travel appear nowhere in the Constitution or Bill of Rights. Yet these important but unarticulated rights have nonetheless been found to share constitutional protection in common with explicit guarantees." He also noted that the Ninth Amendment had been adopted "to allay the fears of those who were concerned that expressing certain guarantees could be read as excluding others." In short, "fundamental rights, even though not expressly guaranteed, have been recognized by the Court as indispensable to the enjoyment of rights explicitly defined," and "the right to attend criminal trials" could accordingly be found "implicit in the guarantees of the First Amendment."

On the facts of the case, Chief Justice Burger found no "overriding interest articulated in findings" for closing the criminal trial here. The defendant had requested the closure; the prosecution had not objected. The trial judge made no findings to support closure, nor any inquiry "as to whether alternative solutions would have met the need to ensure fairness," such as witnesses' exclusion from the courtroom or their sequestration during the trial. He cautioned: "We have no occasion here to define the circumstances in which all or parts of a criminal trial may be closed to the [public]." A trial judge could impose "reasonable limitations on access to a trial" in the interests of the fair administration of justice. Moreover, "since courtrooms have limited capacity, there may be occasions when not every person who wishes to attend can be accommodated. In such situations, reasonable restrictions on general access are traditionally imposed, including preferential seating for media representatives."

In a brief separate statement Justice WHITE, who joined the Chief Justice's opinion, noted that this decision would have been unnecessary if the majority had adopted the dissent's Sixth Amendment position in Gannett. Justice STEVENS, who joined the Chief Justice's opinion, also submitted a separate concurrence viewing the Court as recognizing for the first time a broad First Amendment right of access to "newsworthy matter": "the First Amendment protects the public and the press from abridgment of their rights of access to information about the operation of their government, including the Judicial Branch; given the total absence of any record justification for the closure order entered in this case, that order violated the First Amendment."

In an opinion concurring in the judgment, Justice BRENNAN, joined by Justice Marshall, stated: "Because I believe that the First Amendment [secures a] public right of access [to trial proceedings], I agree with those of my

Brethren who hold that, without more, agreement of the trial judge and the parties cannot constitutionally close a trial to the public." Justice Brennan relied in part on his "Address," 32 Rutgers L.Rev. 173 (1979), arguing that "the First Amendment embodies more than a commitment to free expression and communicative interchange for their own sakes; it has a *structural* role to play in securing and fostering our republican system of self-government. Implicit in this structural role is not only 'the principle that debate on public issues should be uninhibited, robust, and wide open,' but the antecedent assumption that valuable public debate [must] be informed. The structural model links the First Amendment to that process of communication necessary for a democracy to survive, and thus entails solicitude not only for communication itself, but for the indispensable conditions of meaningful communication."

Applying this approach, he found, perusing materials similar to those relied on by the Chief Justice, that, "[a]s a matter of law and virtually immemorial custom, public trials have been the essentially unwavering rule in ancestral England and in our own Nation." Moreover, publicity served several "particular purposes" of the judicial process. He noted, for example, that "judges are not mere umpires, but, in their own sphere, lawmakers—a coordinate branch of *government*. [Thus,] so far as the trial is the mechanism for judicial factfinding, as well as the initial forum for legal decisionmaking, it is a genuine governmental proceeding. It follows that the conduct of the trial is preeminently a matter of public interest. [Popular] attendance at trials, in sum, substantially furthers the particular public purposes of that critical judicial proceeding. In that sense, public access is an indispensable element of the trial process itself." He concluded: "What countervailing interest might be sufficiently compelling to reverse this presumption of openness need not concern us now, for the statute at stake here authorizes trial closures at the unfettered discretion of the judge and parties."

A separate opinion by Justice STEWART concurring in the judgment emphasized that Gannett had left open the First Amendment issues reached here and concluded: "Whatever the ultimate answer to [the First Amendment] question may be with respect to pretrial suppression hearings in criminal cases, the [First Amendment] clearly give[s] the press and the public a right of access to trials themselves, civil as well as criminal. [With] us, a trial is by very definition a proceeding open to the press and to the public. [Even] more than city streets, sidewalks, and parks as areas of traditional First Amendment activity, a trial courtroom is a place where representatives of the press and of the public are not only free to be, but where their presence serves to assure the integrity of what goes on." He added, however, that the access right was not "absolute": "[Much] more than a city street, a trial courtroom must be a quiet and orderly place. Moreover, every courtroom has a finite physical capacity, and there may be occasions when not all who wish to attend a trial may do so. And while there exist many alternative ways to satisfy the constitutional demands of a fair trial, those demands may also sometimes justify limitations upon the unrestricted presence of spectators in the courtroom." Here, reversal was in order because "the trial judge appears to have given no recognition to the right of representatives of the press and members of the public to be present at [the] murder trial."

In still another opinion concurring in the judgment, Justice BLACKMUN reiterated his Sixth Amendment position in Gannett and went beyond: "[W]ith the Sixth Amendment set to one side in this case, I am driven to conclude, as a secondary position, that the First Amendment must provide some measure of protection for public access to the trial. [It] is clear and obvious to me, on the approach the Court has chosen to take, that, by closing this criminal trial, the trial judge abridged [the] First Amendment interests of the public."

Justice REHNQUIST, the sole dissenter, adhered to his position in Gannett and found nothing in the First, Sixth, or Ninth Amendments, or in any other constitutional provision, to prohibit what the state trial judge had done in this case.

What is the scope of Richmond Newspapers? Was it the watershed that Justice Stevens depicted? To what extent should it extend beyond criminal trials to other governmental information and proceedings? For comments on the implications of Richmond Newspapers, see, e.g., Cox, "Freedom of Expression in the Burger Court," 94 Harv.L.Rev. 1 (1980), and Lewis, "A Public Right to Know About Public Institutions: The First Amendment as Sword," 1980 Sup.Ct.Rev. 1 (arguing that Richmond Newspapers "put to rest [the] claim that the Press Clause [gives journalists] a distinct and preferred status. As a practical matter it has not been a winning argument anyway. [Most] future cases seeking access to government information will probably be brought by press organizations, but they will be based on the rights of the public.").

3. *The scope of Richmond Newspapers.* In GLOBE NEWSPAPER CO. v. SUPERIOR COURT, 457 U.S. 596 (1982), the Court concluded that the First Amendment had been violated by a Massachusetts law which had been construed to *require* the exclusion of the press and the general public from the courtroom during the testimony of a minor who had allegedly been a victim of a sex offense. The case arose when the Boston Globe unsuccessfully sought access to a state court trial where the defendant had been charged with the rape of three girls who were minors. In upholding the State's mandatory closure rule, the highest state court had distinguished Richmond Newspapers by emphasizing "at least one notable exception" to the tradition of "openness" in criminal trials: "cases involving sexual assault." The mandatory closure law accordingly operated "in an area of traditional sensitivity to the needs of victims."

Justice BRENNAN, writing for the majority, found the law invalid under the principles of Richmond Newspapers. In his view, Richmond Newspapers "firmly established for the first time that the press and general public have a constitutional right of access to criminal trials," even though no such right was "explicitly mentioned [in] the First Amendment." Protecting "the free discussion of governmental affairs" was a major purpose of the Amendment; offering such protection served "to ensure that the individual citizen can effectively participate in and contribute to our republican system of self-government." A "right of access to *criminal trials*" was properly afforded by the First Amendment because "the criminal trial historically has been open to the press and general public" and because "the right of access to criminal trials plays a particularly significant role in the functioning of the judicial process and the government as a whole." This constitutional right of access, though not "absolute," was entitled to protection unless the State showed "that the denial [of access] is necessitated by a compelling governmental interest, and is narrowly tailored to serve that interest." Massachusetts' defense of its law could not survive that strict scrutiny.

Justice Brennan conceded that the first of the two interests put forth by the state—protecting the physical and psychological well-being of minor victims of sex crimes from further trauma and embarrassment—was "a compelling one." But the closure law was not "a narrowly tailored means of accommodating the State's asserted interest: That interest could be served just as well by requiring the trial court to determine on a case-by-case basis whether the State's legitimate concern for the well-being of the minor victim necessitates closure." Nor could the closure law be sustained on the basis of the State's second asserted interest—"the encouragement of minor victims of sex crimes to come forward and provide accurate testimony." In rejecting that argument, Justice Brennan stated: "Not only is the claim speculative in empirical terms, but it is also open to serious question as a matter of logic and common sense. [Even if the law] effectively advanced the State's interest, it is doubtful that the interest would be sufficient to overcome the constitutional attack, for that same interest could be relied on to support an array of mandatory-closure rules designed to encourage victims to come forward: Surely it cannot be suggested that minor victims of sex crimes are the *only* crime victims who, because of publicity, [are] reluctant to come forward and testify."

Justice O'CONNOR concurred only in the judgment. She stated that she did not interpret Richmond Newspapers "to shelter every right that is 'necessary to the enjoyment of other First Amendment rights.' Instead, Richmond Newspapers rests upon our long history of open criminal trials and the special value, for both public and accused, of that openness. [Thus] I interpret neither Richmond Newspapers nor [today's decision] to carry any implications outside the context of criminal trials."

Chief Justice BURGER, joined by Justice Rehnquist, dissented, objecting to the Court's "expansive interpretation" of Richmond Newspapers and "its cavalier rejection of the serious interests supporting Massachusetts' mandatory closure rule." He claimed that Richmond Newspapers had *not* established "a First Amendment right of access to all aspects of all criminal trials under all circumstances." Although that case had emphasized the traditional openness of criminal trials in general, there was "clearly a long history of exclusion of the public from trials involving sexual assaults, particularly those against minors. [It] would misrepresent the historical record to state that there is an 'unbroken, uncontradicted history' of open proceedings in cases involving the sexual abuse of minors"; and such a specific "history of openness" was necessary to invoke Richmond Newspapers.

The Chief Justice also found the majority's "wooden application" of strict scrutiny "inappropriate." He emphasized: "Neither the purpose of the law nor its effect is primarily to deny the press or public access to information; the verbatim transcript is made available to the public and the media and may be used without limit. We therefore need only examine whether the restrictions imposed are reasonable and whether the interests of the [State] override the very limited incidental effects of the law on First Amendment rights." To him, it seemed "beyond doubt, considering the minimal impact of the law on First Amendment rights and the overriding weight of the [State's] interest in protecting child rape victims, that the Massachusetts law is not unconstitutional." Moreover, there was adequate justification for making the law mandatory rather than discretionary: "[V]ictims and their families are entitled to assurance [of] protection. The legislature did not act irrationally in deciding not to leave the closure determination to the idiosyncracies of individual judges subject to the pressures available to the media."

In another broad interpretation of Richmond Newspapers, the Court in PRESS–ENTERPRISE CO. v. SUPERIOR COURT, 464 U.S. 501 (1984), held Richmond Newspapers applicable to voir dire examination of prospective jurors in a criminal trial—in this instance, a trial involving charges of rape and murder of a teenage girl. Chief Justice BURGER's opinion for the Court rejected a generalized interest in protecting the privacy of prospective jurors, relying extensively on history to show that public jury selection has long been an integral part of public trials. As in both Richmond Newspapers and Globe, however, the Court did not hold the right of public access to this facet of a trial to be absolute: "The presumption of openness may be overcome only by an overriding interest based on findings that closure is essential to preserve higher values and is narrowly tailored to serve that interest. The interest is to be articulated along with findings specific enough that a reviewing court can determine whether the closure order was properly entered." The Chief Justice found this standard unmet in this case, especially in light of the trial court's failure to consider alternatives to closure to protect the privacy of prospective jurors. And he suggested a specific alternative: "The jury selection process may, in some circumstances, give rise to a compelling interest of a prospective juror when interrogation touches on deeply personal [matters]. For example a prospective juror might privately inform the judge that she, or a member of her family, had been raped but had declined to seek prosecution because of the embarrassment and emotional trauma from the very disclosure of the [episode]. By requiring the prospective juror to make an affirmative request, the trial judge can ensure that there is in fact a valid basis for a belief that disclosure infringes a significant interest in privacy."

Richmond Newspapers was extended even further in another Press–Enterprise case two years later, PRESS–ENTERPRISE CO. v. SUPERIOR COURT, 478 U.S. 1 (1986) (Press–Enterprise II). Relying entirely on the First Amendment, the Court held that a newspaper had a right of access to the transcripts of a preliminary hearing in a criminal case, despite the objections of the trial judge, the prosecutor and the defendant, all of whom believed that pre-trial publicity would jeopardize the defendant's right to a fair trial. Writing for the Court, Chief Justice BURGER refused to view the right of access and the right to a fair trial as necessarily in tension. Although the defendant clearly had a right to a fair trial, "one of the important means of assuring a fair trial is that the process be open to neutral observers." He went on to conclude that the preliminary hearing in a criminal case should be treated as a trial for First Amendment access purposes: "[T]he First Amendment question cannot be resolved solely on the label we give the event, i.e., 'trial' or otherwise, particularly where the preliminary hearing functions much like a full scale trial." Because of a tradition of access to preliminary hearings of the type at issue here and because public access plays a positive and important role in the functioning of the process (since "the preliminary hearing is often the final and most important step in the criminal proceeding"), there was a presumptive First Amendment right of access here. It followed that access could not be denied in the absence of specific findings that there was a substantial probability of injury to the accused's right to a fair trial and that there were no reasonable alternatives to closure adequate to protect the defendant's rights: "The First Amendment right of access cannot be overcome by the conclusory assertion that publicity might deprive the defendant of [a fair trial]." Justice STEVENS, joined in part by Justice Rehnquist, dissented: "[The] freedom to obtain information that the Government has a legitimate interest in not disclosing [is] far narrower than the freedom to disseminate information. [In] this case, the risk of prejudice to the defendant's right to a fair trial is perfectly obvious," and "that risk is far more significant than the countervailing interest in publishing the transcript of the preliminary hearing sooner rather than later. [I] fear that today's decision will simply further unsettle the law in this area."

4. *Press interference with judicial proceedings.* Is the government interest in the administration of justice ever sufficient to justify punishing publication, as opposed to excluding the press from judicial proceedings? In LANDMARK COMMUNICATIONS, INC. v. VIRGINIA, 435 U.S. 829 (1978), the Court

invalidated the conviction of a newspaper publisher for printing an accurate report of a pending inquiry by the Virginia Judicial Inquiry and Review Commission that had identified the state judge under investigation. A state law deemed information before the Commission confidential and made disclosure a crime. Chief Justice BURGER, writing for the Court, noted that the information published lay near "the core of the First Amendment" and that the "interests advanced by the imposition of criminal sanctions [were] insufficient to justify the actual and potential encroachments on freedom of speech and of the press." Noting that the operation of judicial inquiry commissions, like the operation of the judicial system itself, was a matter of public interest, he insisted that the State's "legitimate" interests were not "sufficient to justify the subsequent punishment of speech at issue here." The asserted interests were promoting efficient Commission proceedings, protecting the reputation of Virginia's judges, and maintaining the institutional integrity of its courts. In the course of his discussion, the Chief Justice commented that "injury to official reputation is an insufficient reason 'for repressing speech that would otherwise be free.'"

In Landmark, the Court relied heavily a line of cases involving the application of contempt sanctions to publications, even though the state sanctions in Landmark rested on a legislative finding of clear and present danger rather than on the inherent contempt power of the courts. That line of cases began with BRIDGES v. CALIFORNIA, 314 U.S. 252 (1941), which reversed contempt convictions in two companion cases. In the first, a newspaper, the Los Angeles Times, was found guilty of contempt for publishing editorials about the pending sentencing of two union members who had previously been convicted of assaulting non-union workers. One editorial, for example, criticized the defendants as "thugs" and "gorillas," urged the judge to sentence them to San Quentin, and stated that the judge would "make a serious mistake if he grants probation." In the second, union leader Harry Bridges—while a motion for a new trial in a labor dispute was pending—had caused the newspaper publication of his telegram to the Secretary of Labor threatening a strike if the "outrageous" court decision were enforced. The newspaper and Bridges were convicted of contempt. The lower courts had rested their contempt findings on the "tendency" of the publications to interfere with the "orderly administration of justice." Justice Black's majority opinion in the 5–4 decision concluded that punishment was permissible only where there was a clear and present danger that justice would be obstructed, and described the clear and present danger standard as "a working principle that the substantive evil must be extremely serious and the degree of imminence extremely high before utterances can be punished." Justice Frankfurter's dissent stated: "A trial is not 'a free trade in ideas.'"

In PENNEKAMP v. FLORIDA, 328 U.S. 331 (1946), the Court reaffirmed that the "essential right of the courts to be free of intimidation and coercion [is] consonant with a recognition that freedom of the press must be allowed in the broadest scope compatible with the supremacy of order." In Pennekamp v. Florida, a newspaper involved in an anti-vice crusade published editorials and a cartoon implying that the judges were using legal technicalities to hinder the prosecution of several rape and gambling cases. The newspaper and its associate editor, Pennekamp, were held in contempt and fined by a Florida court. As in Bridges, the Court applied the clear and present danger test and reversed. In CRAIG v. HARNEY, 331 U.S. 367 (1947), the Court held that to warrant a sanction, "[t]he fires which [the expression] kindles must constitute an imminent, not merely a likely, threat to the administration of justice. The danger must not be remote or even probable; it must immediately imperil." Craig v.

Harney reversed contempt convictions of a newspaper editor who, in an effort to influence an elected lay judge on a pending motion for a new trial in a private lawsuit, published inaccurate reports and unfair criticisms of the judge's action in directing a verdict for a landlord. Justice Douglas' majority opinion commented: "[T]he law of contempt is not made for the protection of judges who may be sensitive to the winds of public opinion. Judges are supposed to be men of fortitude, able to thrive in a hardy climate." One of the dissenters, Justice Jackson, retorted: "From our sheltered position, fortified by life tenure, [it] is easy to say that this local judge ought to have shown more fortitude in the face of criticism. [Of] course, the blasts of these little papers in this small community do not jolt us, but I am not so confident that we would be indifferent if a news monopoly in our entire jurisdiction should perpetrate this kind of an attack on us."

And in WOOD v. GEORGIA, 370 U.S. 375 (1962), the Court invalidated a contempt citation against an elected sheriff in Bibb County, Georgia, who publicly criticized judges who had ordered a grand jury investigation into black voting practices, charging them with an attempt to intimidate black voters and analogizing them to the Ku Klux Klan. Chief Justice WARREN, writing for the Court, held that the state's showing had fallen far short of meeting the clear and present danger standard: "The type of 'danger' evidenced by the record is precisely one of the types of activity envisioned by the [framers of the First Amendment]. Men are entitled to speak as they please on matters vital to them; errors in judgment or unsubstantiated opinions may be exposed, of course, but not through punishment for contempt for the expression. [In] the absence of some other showing of a substantive evil actually designed to impede the course of justice, [his] utterances are entitled to be protected." Justice HARLAN, joined by Justice Clark, dissented, distinguishing Bridges, Pennekamp and Harney on the ground that here the speaker was an elected official and his intended audience a jury rather than a presumably hardier judge. (Note, however, that in Cox v. Louisiana, 379 U.S. 559 (1965) (Cox II), the Court found the Bridges line of cases and the clear and present danger test inapplicable to regulation of a crowd demonstrating outside a courthouse. In this context, the Court gave greater deference to the government interest in protecting judges from intimidation or the appearance of intimidation. The Grace case, p. 1266 above, striking down a ban on signs on the Supreme Court sidewalks, suggests that this reasoning has been limited.)

In Landmark, Chief Justice Burger found the state courts' efforts to distinguish the Bridges line of cases "unpersuasive" and added: "The threat to the administration of justice posed by the speech and publications in Bridges [et al.] was, if anything, more direct and substantial than the threat posed by Landmark's article."

B. GOVERNMENTAL DEMANDS FOR INFORMATION FROM THE PRESS

Introduction. Recall the discussion of the strong presumption against prior restraint in Chapter 12C above. Restraints against publication are not the only sanctions that may confront the press because of information in its possession. The materials that follow arise from situations in which government, typically in the interest of law enforcement, demands that journalists disclose information they have obtained in the course of their newsgathering activities. Can the First Amendment be read to grant to journalists a special immunity from governmental inquiries? The Branzburg case raises that question in the context of grand jury investigations. The Zurcher case involves a claimed press privilege against newsroom searches based on ex parte warrants.

Branzburg v. Hayes

408 U.S. 665, 92 S.Ct. 2646, 33 L.Ed.2d 626 (1972).

[This decision rejected the claims of three journalists: Branzburg, Pappas, and Caldwell. Branzburg, a Louisville reporter, had written articles about drug activities he had observed. He declined to testify before a state grand jury, refusing to identify the persons he had seen possessing marijuana or making hashish. Pappas, a Massachusetts television reporter covering a "civil disorder," was allowed to remain in Black Panther headquarters for several hours on the condition that he disclose nothing. He broadcast no report and refused to tell a grand jury about what had taken place inside the headquarters. Caldwell was a New York Times reporter who had written articles about the Black Panthers after interviewing their leaders. He refused to appear before a federal grand jury investigating "possible violations of a number of criminal statutes" (including those protecting the President against assassination). The trial court issued a protective order stating that he was not required to reveal confidential information unless the government showed "a compelling national interest" in his testimony "which cannot be served by any alternative means." Caldwell thought that limited privilege inadequate, refused to appear, and was sentenced for contempt. Caldwell's conviction was set aside by the Court of Appeals. The Branzburg and Pappas convictions were affirmed by state courts. The reporters sought a conditional privilege that would have barred their mandatory appearance before the grand jury unless the government could demonstrate that they possessed information relevant to a crime and that the information they possessed was unavailable from other sources.]

Opinion of the Court [by Justice WHITE].

The issue in these cases is whether requiring newsmen to appear and testify before state or federal grand juries abridges the freedom of speech and press guaranteed by the First Amendment. We hold that it does not.

[The journalists] press First Amendment claims that may be simply put: that to gather news it is often necessary to agree either not to identify the source of information published or to publish only part of the facts revealed, or both; that if the reporter is nevertheless forced to reveal these confidences to a grand jury, the source so identified and other confidential sources of other reporters will be measurably deterred from furnishing publishable information, all to the detriment of the free flow of information protected by the First Amendment.

[News] gathering [qualifies] for First Amendment protection; without some protection for seeking out the news, freedom of the press could be eviscerated. But these cases involve no intrusions upon speech or assembly, [and] no penalty, civil or criminal, related to the content of published material, is at issue here. The use of confidential sources by the press is not forbidden or restricted. [No] attempt is made to require the press to publish its sources of information or indiscriminately to disclose them on request. The sole issue [is] the obligation of reporters to respond to grand jury subpoenas as other citizens do and to answer questions relevant to an investigation into the commission of crime. [The Constitution does not protect] the average citizen from disclosing to a grand jury information that he has received in confidence. The claim is, however, that reporters are [exempt].

[The] great weight of authority is that newsmen are not exempt from the normal duty of appearing before a grand jury and answering questions relevant to a criminal [investigation]. The prevailing constitutional view of the newsman's privilege is very much rooted in the ancient role of the grand jury. [I]ts investigative powers are necessarily broad. [The] longstanding principle that "the public has a right to every man's evidence," except for those persons protected by a constitutional, common law, or statutory privilege, is particularly applicable to grand jury proceedings. A [minority] of States have provided newsmen a statutory privilege of varying breadth; [none] has been provided by federal statute.

[We] are asked to [interpret] the First Amendment to grant newsmen a testimonial privilege that other citizens do not enjoy. This we decline to do. [On] the records now before us, we perceive no basis for holding that the public interest in law enforcement and in ensuring effective grand jury proceedings is insufficient to override the consequential, but uncertain, burden on news gathering which is said to result from insisting that reporters, like other citizens, respond to relevant questions put to them in the course of a valid grand jury investigation or criminal trial. This conclusion [does not] threaten the vast bulk of confidential relationships between reporters and their sources. [Only] where news sources themselves are implicated in crime or possess information relevant to the grand jury's task need they or the reporter be concerned about grand jury subpoenas. Nothing before us indicates that a large number or percentage of *all* confidential news sources fall into either category and would in any way be deterred by our [holding].

There remain those situations where a source is not engaged in criminal conduct but has information suggesting illegal conduct by others. Newsmen frequently receive information from such sources pursuant to a tacit or express agreement to withhold the source's name and suppress any information that the source wishes not published. [The] argument that the flow of news will be diminished by compelling reporters to aid the grand jury in a criminal investigation is not irrational, nor are the records before us silent on the matter. But we remain unclear how often and to what extent informers are actually deterred from furnishing information when newsmen are forced to testify before a grand jury. [The] evidence fails to demonstrate that there would be a significant constriction of the flow of news to the public if this Court reaffirms the prior common-law and constitutional rule regarding the testimonial obligations of newsmen. Estimates of the inhibiting effect of such subpoenas on the willingness of informants to make disclosures to newsmen are widely divergent and to a great extent speculative. It would be difficult to canvass the views of the informants themselves; surveys of reporters on this topic are chiefly opinions of predicted informant behavior and must be viewed in the light of the professional self-interest of the interviewees. [Accepting] the fact, however, that an undetermined number of informants not themselves implicated in crime will nevertheless [refuse] to talk to newsmen if they fear identification by a reporter in an official investigation, we cannot accept the argument that the public interest in possible future news about crime from undisclosed, unverified sources must take precedence over the public interest in pursuing and prosecuting those crimes reported to the press by informants and in thus deterring the commission of such crimes in the [future].

We are admonished that refusal to provide a First Amendment reporter's privilege will undermine the freedom of the press to collect and disseminate news. But this is not the lesson history teaches us. [From] the beginning of our country the press has operated without constitutional protection for press informants, and the press has flourished. [It] is said that currently press subpoenas have multiplied, that mutual distrust and tension between press and officialdom have increased, that reporting styles have changed, and that there is now more need for confidential sources. [These] developments, even if true, are treacherous grounds for a far-reaching interpretation of the [First Amendment].

[The] requirements of those cases [e.g., NAACP v. Alabama] which hold that a State's interest must be "compelling" or "paramount" to justify even an indirect burden on First Amendment rights, are also met here. As we have indicated, the investigation of crime by the grand jury implements a fundamental governmental role of securing the safety of the person and property of the [citizen]. If the test is that the government "convincingly show a substantial relation between the information sought and a subject of overriding and compelling state interest" [Gibson], it is quite apparent (1) that the State has the necessary interests in extirpating the traffic in illegal drugs, in forestalling assassination attempts on the President, and in preventing the community from being disrupted by violent disorders endangering both persons and property; and (2) that, based on the stories Branzburg and Caldwell wrote and Pappas' admitted conduct, the grand jury called these reporters as they would others—because it was likely that they could supply information to help the government determine whether illegal conduct had occurred and, if it had, whether there was sufficient evidence to return an indictment.

We are unwilling to embark the judiciary on [the] administration of a constitutional newsman's privilege[, which] would present practical and conceptual difficulties of a high order. Sooner or later, it would be necessary to define those categories of newsmen who qualified for the privilege, a questionable procedure in light of the traditional doctrine that liberty of the press is the right of the lonely pamphleteer [just] as much as of the large metropolitan publisher who utilizes the latest photocomposition methods. [Almost] any author may quite accurately assert that he is contributing to the flow of information to the public, that he relies on confidential sources of information, and that these sources will be silenced if he is forced to make disclosures before a grand jury. [In] each instance where a reporter is subpoenaed to testify, the courts would also be embroiled in preliminary factual and legal determinations with respect to whether the proper predicate had been laid for the reporter's appearance. [In] the end, by considering whether enforcement of a particular law served a "compelling" governmental interest, the courts would be inextricably involved in distinguishing between the value of enforcing different criminal laws. [At] the federal level, Congress has freedom to determine whether a statutory newsman's privilege is necessary and desirable and to fashion standards and rules as narrow or broad as deemed necessary [and], equally important, to re-fashion those rules as experience from time to time may dictate. There is also merit in leaving state legislatures free, within First Amendment limits, to fashion their own standards. [In addition], there is much force in the pragmatic view that the press has at its disposal powerful mechanisms of communication and is far from helpless to protect itself from harassment or substantial [harm].

[Finally,] news gathering is not without its First Amendment protections, and grand jury investigations, if instituted or conducted other than in good faith, would pose wholly different issues for resolution under the First Amendment. Official harassment of the press undertaken not for purposes of law enforcement but to disrupt a reporter's relationship with his news sources would have no justification. Grand juries are subject to judicial control and subpoenas to motions to quash. We do not expect courts will forget that grand juries must operate within the limits of the First Amendment as well as the Fifth.

So ordered.

Justice POWELL, concurring in the opinion of the Court.

I add this brief statement to emphasize what seems to me to be the limited nature of the Court's holding. The Court does not hold that newsmen, subpoenaed to testify before a grand jury, are without constitutional rights with respect to the gathering of news or in safeguarding their sources. [As] indicated in the concluding portion of the opinion, the Court states that no harassment of newsmen will be tolerated. If a newsman believes that the grand jury investigation is not being conducted in good faith he is not without remedy. Indeed, if the newsman is called upon to give information bearing only a remote and tenuous relationship to the subject of the investigation, or if he has some other reason to believe that his testimony implicates confidential source relationships without a legitimate need of law enforcement, he will have access to the Court on a motion to quash and an appropriate protective order may be entered. The asserted claim to privilege should be judged on its facts by the striking of a proper balance between freedom of the press and the obligation of all citizens to give relevant testimony with respect to criminal conduct. The balance of these vital constitutional and societal interests on a case-by-case basis accords with the tried and traditional way of adjudicating such questions. In short, the courts will be available to newsmen under circumstances where legitimate First Amendment interests require protection.

Justice STEWART, with whom Justices BRENNAN and MARSHALL join, dissenting.

The Court's crabbed view of the First Amendment reflects a disturbing insensitivity to the critical role of an independent press in our society. [While] Justice Powell's enigmatic concurring opinion gives some hope of a more flexible view in the future, the Court in these cases holds that a newsman has no First Amendment right to protect his sources when called before a grand jury. The Court thus invites state and federal authorities to undermine the historic independence of the press by attempting to annex the journalistic profession as an investigative arm of [government].

The reporter's constitutional right to a confidential relationship with his source stems from the broad societal interest in a full and free flow of information to the public. It is this basic concern that underlies the Constitution's protection of a free press. [A] corollary of the right to publish must be the right to gather news. [This right] implies, in turn, a right to a confidential relationship between a reporter and his source. [This] follows as a matter of simple logic once three factual predicates are recognized: (1) newsmen require informants to gather news; (2) confidentiality [is] essential to the creation and maintenance of a news-gathering relationship with informants; and (3) the existence of an unbridled subpoena power [will] either deter sources from divulging information or deter reporters from gathering and publishing information. After today's decision, the potential [source must] choose between risking exposure by giving information or avoiding the risk by remaining [silent].

The impairment of the flow of news cannot, of course, be proved with scientific precision, as the Court seems to demand. [But] we have never before demanded that First Amendment rights rest on elaborate empirical studies demonstrating beyond any conceivable doubt that deterrent effects [exist]. Rather, on the basis of common sense and available information, we have asked, often implicitly, (1) whether there was a rational connection between the cause (the governmental action) and the effect (the deterrence or impairment of First Amendment activity) and (2) whether the effect would occur with some regularity, i.e., would not be de minimis. And in making this determination, we have shown a special solicitude towards the "indispensable liberties" protected by the First Amendment. [Once] this threshold inquiry has been satisfied, we have then examined the competing interests in determining whether there is an unconstitutional infringement of First Amendment freedoms. [E.g., NAACP v. Alabama.] Surely the analogous claim of deterrence here is as securely grounded in evidence and common sense as the claims in [earlier cases], although the Court calls the claim "speculative." [To] require any greater burden of proof is to shirk our duty to protect values securely embedded in the Constitution. [We] cannot escape the conclusion that when neither the reporter nor his source can rely on the shield of confidentiality against unrestrained use of the grand jury's subpoena power, valuable information will not be published and the public dialogue will inevitably be impoverished.

[As our cases hold with respect to witnesses called before legislative investigations, I would hold that,] when a reporter is asked to appear before a grand jury and reveal confidences, [the] government must (1) show that there is probable cause to believe that the newsman has information which is clearly relevant to a specific probable violation of law; (2) demonstrate that the information sought cannot be obtained by alternative means less destructive of First Amendment rights; and (3) demonstrate a compelling and overriding interest in the information. [Both] the "probable cause" and "alternative means" requirements [would] serve the vital function of mediating between the public interest in the administration of justice and the constitutional protection of the full flow of information. These requirements would avoid a direct conflict between these competing concerns, and they would generally provide adequate protection for newsmen. No doubt the courts would be required to make some delicate judgments in working out this accommodation. But that, after all, is the function of courts of law. Better such judgments, however difficult, than the simplistic and stultifying absolutism adopted by the Court in denying any force to the First Amendment in these cases.

Justice DOUGLAS, dissenting.

[There] is no 'compelling need' that can be shown which qualifies the reporter's immunity from appearing or testifying before a grand jury, unless the reporter himself is implicated in a crime. His immunity in my view [is] quite complete.

JOURNALISTIC PRIVILEGE AFTER BRANZBURG

1. *The judicial and legislative response to Branzburg.* Most lower court judges have followed the tenor of Justice Powell's more speech-protective concurrence in Branzburg rather than the White opinion. This has contributed to the fact that, according to most studies, not nearly as many journalists have been compelled to give grand jury testimony in the wake of Branzburg as had been predicted at the time of the decision. See Murasky, "The Journalist's

Privilege: Branzburg and Its Aftermath," 52 Tex.L.Rev. 829 (1974). For a skeptical assessment of the chilling effect arguments in Branzburg, see Lewis, "A Preferred Position for Journalism?," 7 Hofstra L.Rev. 595 (1979): "My guess is that most confidential sources talk to the press for their own compelling reasons of conscience or ideology or personal animus—and will continue to do so even if an occasional case demonstrates that reporters may come under legal pressure to name their sources."

In response to Branzburg, numerous bills to establish a journalists' privilege were introduced in state legislatures and in Congress. While absolute immunity proposals did not fare well, over half the states have enacted press "shield" laws providing at least a qualified privilege against revelation of journalists' sources. See Sack, "Reflections on the Wrong Question: Special Constitutional Privilege for the Institutional Press," 7 Hofstra L.Rev. 629 (1979).

2. *Searches of newsrooms pursuant to ex parte warrants.* The Court once more rejected a press claim for special protection from law enforcement demands for information in ZURCHER v. STANFORD DAILY, 436 U.S. 547 (1978). In that case, the Court upheld an ex parte warrant authorizing a search of a campus newspaper office for photographs of a violent demonstration.[1] The police obtained an ex parte warrant for a search of the Daily's offices for pictures and negatives that might help them to identify the demonstrators. The Daily's civil suit claimed that the police decision to engage in a search rather than proceed by subpoena violated the First Amendment. In rejecting the claim, Justice WHITE's majority opinion emphasized the Fourth Amendment rather than the First. His opinion in Zurcher was as skeptical as that in Branzburg about press allegations of chilling effects and risks to confidential sources. His reasoning contained only one sentence suggesting that First Amendment considerations be taken into account in applying Fourth Amendment search warrant criteria in the media context: "[Prior cases insist] that courts apply the warrant requirements with particular exactitude when First Amendment interests would be endangered by the search."

As in Branzburg, Justice POWELL's concurrence built upon a passing remark in the prevailing opinion and elaborated the relevance of First Amendment concerns, stating: "This is not to say that a warrant which would be sufficient to support the search of an apartment or an automobile necessarily would be reasonable in supporting the search of a newspaper office. [While] there is no justification for the establishment of a separate Fourth Amendment procedure for the press, a magistrate asked to issue a warrant for the search of press offices can and should take cognizance of the independent values protected by the First Amendment—such as those highlighted by Mr. Justice Stewart—when he weighs such factors." And he added in a footnote that his separate opinion here, like that in Branzburg, could be read as supporting the view "that under the warrant requirement of the Fourth Amendment, the magistrate should consider the values of a free press as well as the societal interests in enforcing the criminal law." Justice STEWART's dissent argued that warrants to search newspaper offices should issue only when a magistrate

---

1. The division on the Court was strikingly similar to that in Branzburg. Justice Powell once again supplied the critical vote for the majority with a separate concurrence putting a more speech-protective gloss on Justice White's opinion; Justice Stewart once again dissented on First Amendment grounds, this time joined only by Justice Marshall. (Justice Brennan did not participate in the case.) Justice Stevens, who had replaced Justice Douglas since Branzburg, submitted a separate dissent, based on the Fourth Amendment.

finds probable cause to believe that it would be impractical to obtain the evidence by a subpoena. He emphasized that subpoena applications permit the press to obtain an adversary hearing prior to producing the information, by making a motion to quash; ex parte warrants, by contrast, provide "no opportunity to challenge the necessity for the search until after it has occurred and the constitutional protection of the newspaper has been irretrievably invaded."

As a result of legislative efforts that began in the wake of the Stanford Daily decision, Congress adopted the Privacy Protection Act in 1980. 42 U.S.C. § 2000aa. The Act requires state and federal law enforcement officers to use subpoena procedures to obtain documents from persons engaged in the communications industry. Search warrants are permitted only in exceptional circumstances, such as when there is a fear that the needed materials would be destroyed.

C. LAWS DISCRIMINATING AGAINST THE PRESS

Minneapolis Star & Tribune Co. v. Minnesota Comm'r of Revenue

460 U.S. 575, 103 S.Ct. 1365, 75 L.Ed.2d 295 (1983).

Justice O'CONNOR delivered the opinion of the Court.

This case presents the question of a State's power to impose a special tax on the press and, by enacting exemptions, to limit its effect to only a few newspapers.

I. Since 1967, Minnesota has imposed a sales tax on most sales of goods. In general, the tax applies only to retail sales. [As] part of this general system of taxation and in support of the sales tax, Minnesota also enacted a tax on the "privilege of using, storing or consuming in Minnesota tangible personal property." This use tax applies to any nonexempt tangible personal property unless the sales tax was paid on the sales price. Like the classic use tax, this use tax protects the State's sales tax by eliminating the residents' incentive to travel to States with lower sales taxes to buy goods rather than buying them in Minnesota.

The appellant [is] the publisher of a morning [and] an evening newspaper (until 1982) in Minneapolis. From 1967 until 1971, it enjoyed an exemption from the sales and use tax provided by Minnesota for periodic publications. In 1971, however, while leaving the exemption from the sales tax in place, the legislature amended the scheme to impose a "use tax" on the cost of paper and ink products consumed in the production of a publication. Ink and paper used in publications became the only items subject to the use tax that were components of goods to be sold at retail. In 1974, the legislature again amended the statute, this time to exempt the first $100,000 worth of ink and paper consumed by a publication in any calendar year, in effect giving each publication an annual tax credit of $4,000. Publications remained exempt from the sales tax. After the enactment of the $100,000 exemption, 11 publishers, producing 14 of the 388 paid circulation newspapers in the State, incurred a tax liability in 1974. [Appellant] was one of the 11, and, of the $893,355 collected, it paid $608,634, or roughly two-thirds of the total revenue raised by the tax. In 1975, 13 publishers, producing 16 out of 374 paid circulation papers, paid a tax. That year, [appellant] again bore roughly two-thirds of the total receipts from the use tax on ink and paper. [Appellant] instituted this action to seek a refund of the use taxes it paid from January 1, 1974 to May 31, 1975. [The] Minnesota Supreme Court upheld the [tax]. [The Court held that this taxing system violated appellant's First Amendment rights.]

II.   Star Tribune argues that we must strike this tax on the authority of Grosjean v. American Press Co., 297 U.S. 233 (1936). Although there are similarities, [we] agree with the State that Grosjean is not controlling. In Grosjean, [Louisiana] imposed a license tax of 2% of the gross receipts from the sale of advertising on all newspapers with a weekly circulation above 20,000. Out of at least 124 publishers in the State, only 13 were subject to the tax. After noting that the tax was "single in kind" and that keying the tax to circulation curtailed the flow of information, this Court held the tax invalid as an abridgment of the freedom of the press. [The argument of the publishers] emphasized the events leading up to the tax and the contemporary political climate in Louisiana. All but one of the large papers subject to the tax had "ganged up" on Senator Huey Long, and a circular distributed by Long and the governor to each member of the state legislature described "lying newspapers" as conducting "a vicious campaign" and the tax as "a tax on lying." [Although] the Court's opinion did not describe this history, it stated, "[The tax] is bad because, in the light of its history and of its present setting, it is seen to be a deliberate and calculated device in the guise of a tax to limit the circulation of information," an explanation that suggests that the motivation of the legislature may have been significant. Our subsequent cases have not been consistent in their reading of Grosjean on this point. [We] think that the result in Grosjean may have been attributable in part to the perception on the part of the Court that the state imposed the tax with an intent to penalize a selected group of newspapers. In the case currently before us, however, there is no legislative history and no indication, apart from the structure of the tax itself, of any impermissible or censorial motive on the part of the legislature. We cannot resolve the case by simple citation to Grosjean. Instead, we must analyze the problem anew under the general principles of the First Amendment.

III.   Clearly, the First Amendment does not prohibit all regulation of the press. It is beyond dispute that [government] can subject newspapers to generally applicable economic regulations without creating constitutional problems. Minnesota, however, has not chosen to apply its general sales and use tax to newspapers. Instead, it has created a special tax that applies only to certain publications protected by the First Amendment. Although the State argues now that the tax on paper and ink is part of the general scheme of taxation, the use tax provision is facially discriminatory, singling out publications for treatment that [is] unique in Minnesota tax law.

[By] creating this special use tax, [Minnesota] has singled out the press for special treatment. We then must determine whether the First Amendment permits such special taxation. A tax that burdens rights protected by the First Amendment cannot stand unless the burden is necessary to achieve an overriding governmental interest.

[There] is substantial evidence that differential taxation of the press would have troubled the Framers of the First Amendment. [The] fears of the [Framers] were well-founded. A power to tax differentially, as opposed to a power to tax generally, gives a government a powerful weapon against the taxpayer selected. When the State imposes a generally applicable tax, there is little cause for concern. We need not fear that a government will destroy a selected group of taxpayers by burdensome taxation if it must impose the same burden on the rest of its constituency. When the State singles out the press, though, the political constraints that prevent a legislature from passing crippling taxes of general applicability are weakened, and the threat of burdensome taxes becomes acute. That threat can operate as effectively as a censor to check critical comment by the press, undercutting the basic assumption of our political system that the press will often serve as an important restraint on government. [Differential] treatment, unless justified by some special characteristic of the press, suggests that the goal of the regulation is not unrelated to suppression of expression, and such a goal is presumptively unconstitutional. Differential taxation of the press, then, places such a burden on the interests protected by the First Amendment that we cannot countenance such treatment unless the State asserts a counterbalancing interest of compelling importance that it cannot achieve without differential taxation.

IV. The main interest asserted by Minnesota in this case is the raising of revenue. [Standing alone], however, it cannot justify the special treatment of the press, for an alternative means of achieving the same interest without raising concerns under the First Amendment is clearly available: the State could raise the revenue by taxing businesses generally, avoiding the censorial threat implicit in a tax that singles out the press. Addressing the concern with differential treatment, Minnesota invites us to look beyond the form of the tax to its substance. The tax is, according to the State, merely a substitute for the sales tax, which, as a generally applicable tax, would be constitutional as applied to the press. There are two fatal flaws in this reasoning. First, the State has offered no explanation of why it chose to use a substitute for the sales tax rather than the sales tax itself. [Further,] even assuming that the legislature did have valid reasons for substituting another tax for the sales tax, we are not persuaded that this tax does serve as a substitute. The State asserts that this scheme actually *favors* the press over other businesses, because the same rate of tax is applied, but, for the press, the rate applies to the cost of components rather than to the sales price. We would be hesitant to fashion a rule that automatically allowed the State to single out the press for a different method of taxation as long as the effective burden was no different from that on other taxpayers or the burden on the press was lighter than that on other businesses. One reason for this reluctance is that the very selection of the press for special treatment threatens the press not only with the current *differential* treatment, but with the possibility of subsequent differentially *more burdensome* treatment. Thus, even without actually imposing an extra burden on the press, the government might be able to achieve censorial effects, for "[t]he threat of sanctions may deter [the] exercise of [First Amendment] rights almost as potently as the actual application of sanctions." NAACP v. Button.

A second reason to avoid the proposed rule is that courts as institutions are poorly equipped to evaluate with precision the relative burdens of various methods of taxation. The complexities of factual economic proof always present a certain potential for error, and courts have little familiarity with the process of evaluating the relative economic burden of taxes. In sum, the possibility of error inherent in the proposed rule poses too great a threat to concerns at the heart of the First Amendment, and we cannot tolerate that possibility.[1]

1. If a State employed the same *method* of taxation but applied a lower *rate* to the press, so that there could be no doubt that the legislature was not singling out the press to bear a more burdensome tax, we would, of course, be in a position to evaluate the rela-

Minnesota, therefore, has offered no adequate justification for the special treatment of newspapers.

V. Minnesota's ink and paper tax violates the First Amendment not only because it singles out the press, but also because it targets a small group of newspapers. The effect of the $100,000 exemption [is] that only a handful of publishers pay any tax at [all]. The State explains this exemption as part of a policy favoring an "equitable" tax system, although there are no comparable exemptions for small enterprises outside the press. [Whatever] the motive of the legislature in this case, we think that recognizing a power in the State not only to single out the press but also to tailor the tax so that it singles out a few members of the press presents such a potential for abuse that no interest suggested by Minnesota can justify the [scheme].

VI. We need not and do not impugn the motives of the Minnesota legislature in passing the ink and paper tax. Illicit legislative intent is not the sine qua non of a violation of the First Amendment. We have long recognized that even regulations aimed at proper governmental concerns can restrict unduly the exercise of rights protected by the First Amendment. A tax that singles out the press [places] a heavy burden on the State to justify its action. Since Minnesota has offered no satisfactory justification for its tax on the use of ink and paper, the tax violates the First Amendment.

[Reversed.]

Justice REHNQUIST, dissenting.

Today we learn from the Court that a State runs afoul of the First Amendment [where] the State structures its taxing system to the advantage of newspapers. [The Court recognizes that Minnesota] could avoid constitutional problems by imposing on newspapers the 4% sales tax that it imposes on other retailers. Rather than impose such a tax, however, the Minnesota legislature decided to provide newspapers with an exemption from the sales tax and impose a 4% use tax on ink and paper; thus, while both taxes are part of one [system], newspapers are classified differently within that system. The problem the Court finds too difficult to deal with is whether this difference in treatment results in a significant burden on newspapers. [Had] a 4% sales tax been imposed, the Minneapolis Star & Tribune would have been liable for $1,859,950 in 1974. The same "complexities of factual economic proof" can be analyzed for 1975. [Had] the sales tax been imposed, as the Court agrees would have been permissible, the Minneapolis Star & Tribune's liability for 1974 and 1975 would have been $3,685,092. The record further indicates that the Minneapolis Star & Tribune paid $608,634 in use taxes in 1974 and $636,113 in 1975—a total liability of $1,244,747. We need no expert testimony from modern day Euclids or Einsteins to determine that the $1,224,747 paid in use taxes is significantly less burdensome than the $3,685,092 that could have been levied by a sales tax. A fortiori, the Minnesota taxing scheme which singles out newspapers for "different treatment" has benefited, not burdened, the "freedom of speech, [and] of the press."

[No] First Amendment issue is raised unless First Amendment rights have been [infringed]. [The] State is required to show that its taxing scheme is

tive burdens. And, given the clarity of the relative burdens, as well as the rule that differential methods of taxation are not automatically permissible if less burdensome, a lower tax rate for the press would not raise the threat that the legislature might later impose an extra burden that would escape detection by the courts. Thus, our decision does not, as the dissent suggests, require Minnesota to impose a greater tax burden on publications. [Footnote by Justice O'Connor.]

rational. But in this case that showing can be made easily. [So] long as the State can find another way to collect revenue from the newspapers, imposing a sales tax on newspapers would be to no one's advantage; not the newspaper and its distributors who would have to collect the tax, not the State who would have to enforce collection, and not the consumer who would have to pay for the paper in odd amounts. The reasonable alternative Minnesota chose was to impose the use tax on ink and paper.

[The] Court finds in very summary fashion that the exemption newspapers receive for the first $100,000 of ink and paper used also violates the [First Amendment]. I cannot agree. [The] exemption is in effect a $4,000 credit which benefits all newspapers. Minneapolis Star & Tribune was benefited to the amount of $16,000 in the two years in question; $4,000 each year for its morning paper and $4,000 each year for its evening paper. Absent any improper motive on the part of the Minnesota legislature in drawing the limits of this exemption, it cannot be construed as violating the First Amendment. [There] is no reason to conclude that the State, in drafting the $4,000 credit, acted other than reasonably and rationally to fit its sales and use tax scheme to its own local needs and usages. To collect from newspapers their fair share of taxes under the sales and use tax scheme and at the same time avoid abridging the freedoms of speech and press, the Court holds today that Minnesota must subject newspapers to millions of additional dollars in sales tax liability. Certainly this is a hollow victory for the newspapers and I seriously doubt the Court's conclusion that this result would have been intended by the ["Framers of the First Amendment"]. [Justice White concurred in part and dissented in part; Justice Blackmun joined the majority opinion except for one footnote.]

———————

THE IMPLICATIONS AND LIMITS OF MINNEAPOLIS STAR

1. *Is the press special?* The Court in Minneapolis Star emphasizes the dangers involved in singling out "the press" for special regulatory treatment. Yet, as the preceding materials in this section illustrate, the Court typically has refused to recognize claims of the press to special protection beyond that available to anyone who exercises First Amendment rights by communicating information and opinion. Is the Court's focus on "the press" in Minneapolis Star therefore superfluous? Is it inconsistent with prior decisions? Or does this case suggest that in some areas the press *will* receive more protection than other claimants under the First Amendment?

If the latter reading is unwarranted and there remains nothing constitutionally special about the press, what was the Court's ground for employing strict scrutiny in Minneapolis Star? That singling out the press presumptively risks content discrimination, as exemplified by the overt bias of Huey Long in Grosjean? Does Minneapolis Star suggest that certain subjects—e.g., criticism of government in a broad sense—will receive special protection? Does Minneapolis Star treat the press as an especially highly protected format of communication? Should it be permissible, by analogy, for zoning regulations to single out bookstores or billboards for special treatment?

2. *Slippery slopes.* Although couched in different terms, Justice Rehnquist's objections to the majority's creation of a prophylactic rule to safeguard the press against future abuses of the taxing power raise the perennial problem of the use and misuse of "slippery slope" arguments. The same argument appears in numerous guises, including the search for a "stopping point," the fear of "a foot in the door," the question of "Where do you draw the line?," and

the wariness of abuse of power. Perhaps the most noteworthy characterization is Justice Stewart's use of an Arabian proverb in his dissent in Pittsburgh Press Co. v. Human Relations Commission (1973; p. 1168 above): "The camel's nose is in the tent." But regardless of how phrased, the point is the same—if we permit this seemingly innocuous exercise of a power, we are on a slippery slope leading inevitably to much more dangerous exercises of that same power. See generally Schauer, "Slippery Slopes," 99 Harv.L.Rev. 361 (1985).

The contrast between the majority and Justice Rehnquist's dissent makes Minneapolis Star an appropriate vehicle for reconsidering under what circumstances, if any, a currently innocuous exercise of power should be precluded for fear that it will lead to a far less innocuous abuse. Is Court review of every abuse likely? Will such review be timely? If the Court cannot check every abuse, can lower courts serve that function? Can nonjudicial bodies be trusted to follow the spirit as well as the letter of constitutional decisions? But does eagerness to decide cases on the basis of where a currently innocuous policy might lead fly in the face of the Court's reluctance to decide anything other than the case before it? Is a slippery slope argument a variant of an advisory opinion, in the sense that the basis for the decision is a hypothetical scenario that may never occur? Could we not prevent all abuses of power by granting no power whatsoever?

3. *Antimedia, intramedium and intermedia discrimination.* In ARKANSAS WRITERS' PROJECT, INC. v. RAGLAND, 481 U.S. 221 (1987), the Court relied on Minneapolis Star in striking down an Arkansas sales tax scheme that exempted newspapers and "religious, professional, trade and sports journals" but not other types of magazines. Part V of Justice O'Connor's opinion in Minneapolis had relied on the existence of discrimination *within* the class of publications, as opposed to distinctions between newspapers and other commodities. This more overt form of content discrimination was the basis for the Court's decision in Ragland. Justice MARSHALL found that the Arkansas exemption not only resembled the $100,000 exemption in Minneapolis Star, but also was even more troublesome because "a magazine's tax status depends entirely on its *content.*" He noted that this type of content-based regulation "does not evade the strictures of the First Amendment merely because it does not burden the expression of particular *views* by specific magazines." Justice SCALIA, joined by Chief Justice Rehnquist, dissented, for reasons paralleling those articulated in Justice Rehnquist's dissent in Minneapolis Star. He argued as well that the selective tax exemption should not be subject to strict scrutiny because it amounted to a subsidy that infringed no one's rights. He commented: "Are government research grant programs or the funding activities of the Corporation for Public Broadcasting subject to strict scrutiny because they provide money for the [study] of some subjects but not others? Because there is no principled basis to distinguish the subsidization of speech in [such an area]—which we would surely uphold—from the subsidization that we strike down here, our decision today places the granting or denial of protection within our own idiosyncratic discretion."

Contrast with Arkansas Writers' Project the decision in LEATHERS v. MEDLOCK, 499 U.S. 439 (1991), upholding a selective sales tax exemption scheme. Arkansas imposed a sales tax on most goods and services, including cable television, but exempted newspapers, magazines and direct satellite broadcast services. Cable operators and subscribers challenged the selective exemption under the First Amendment. The Court rejected the challenge. Justice O'CONNOR, writing for the Court, found Arkansas' tax scheme distinguishable from the ones struck down in Minneapolis Star and Ragland: "[Those] cases demonstrate that differential taxation of First Amendment speakers is constitutionally suspect when it threatens to suppress the expression of particular ideas or viewpoints. Absent a compelling justification, the government may not exercise its taxing power to single out the press. [A] tax is also suspect if it targets a small group of speakers. [Finally,] for reasons that are obvious, a tax will trigger heightened scrutiny under the First Amendment if it discriminates on the basis of the content of taxpayer speech.

"The Arkansas tax at issue here presents none of these types of discrimination. The Arkansas sales tax is a tax of general applicability. It applies to receipts from the sale of all tangible personal property and a broad range of services, unless within a group of specific exemptions. [The] tax does not single out the press. [Furthermore,] there is no indication in this case that Arkansas has targeted cable television in a purposeful attempt to interfere with its First Amendment activities. [Unlike] the taxes involved in Grosjean and Minneapolis Star, the Arkansas tax has not selected a narrow group to bear fully the burden of the tax. The danger from a tax scheme that targets a small number of speakers is the danger of censorship; a tax on a small number of speakers runs the risk of affecting only a limited range of views. The risk is similar to that from content-based regulation: It will distort the market for ideas. [There] is no comparable danger from a tax on the services provided by a large number of cable operators offering a wide variety of programming throughout the State. [This] is not a tax structure that resembles a penalty for particular speakers or particular ideas." Finally, Justice O'Connor rejected cable's argument that the "intermedia discrimination" effected by the tax scheme was impermissible: "Regan v. Taxation with Representation stands for the proposition that a tax scheme that discriminates among speakers does not implicate the First Amendment unless it discriminates on the basis of ideas."

Justice MARSHALL dissented, joined by Justice Blackmun. He would have found that the intermedia discrimination here triggered strict scrutiny no less than the intramedium discrimination struck down in Minneapolis Star and Ragland: "Because cable competes with members of the print and electronic media in the larger information market, the power to discriminate between these media triggers the central concern underlying the nondiscrimination principle: the risk of covert censorship. [By] imposing tax burdens that disadvantage one information medium relative to another, the State can favor those media that it likes and punish those that it dislikes. [We] have previously recognized that differential taxation within an information medium distorts the marketplace of ideas by imposing on some speakers costs not borne by their competitors. Differential taxation across different media likewise 'limits the circulation of information to which the public is entitled,' where, as here, the relevant media compete in the same information market."

In TURNER BROADCASTING v. FCC, 512 U.S. 622 (1994)(Turner I), see p. 1369 above, which held that requirements that cable operators carry broadcast signals were subject only to the level of scrutiny appropriate to content-neutral regulations, the Court found no impermissible discrimination against cable operators or programmers. First, it rejected the cable operators' argument "that strict scrutiny applies because the must-carry provisions single out certain members of the press—here, cable operators—for disfavored treatment." Justice KENNEDY wrote for the Court: "Regulations that discriminate among media, or among different speakers within a single medium, often present serious First Amendment concerns. [Minneapolis Star, Arkansas Writers' Project.] It would be error to conclude, however, that the First Amendment mandates strict scrutiny for any speech regulation that applies to one medium (or a subset thereof) but not others. [Leathers.] As Leathers illustrates, the fact that a law singles out a certain medium, or even the press as a whole, 'is insufficient by itself to raise First Amendment concerns.' The taxes invalidated in Minneapolis Star and Arkansas Writers' Project [targeted] a small number of speakers, and thus threatened to 'distort the market for ideas.' But such heightened scrutiny is unwarranted when the differential treatment is 'justified by some special characteristic of' the particular medium being regulated. The must-carry provisions [are] justified by special characteristics of the cable medium: the bottleneck monopoly power exercised by cable operators and the dangers this power poses to the viability of broadcast television. Appellants do not argue, nor does it appear, that other media [that] transmit video programming such as [satellite] are subject to bottleneck monopoly control, or pose a demonstrable threat to the survival of broadcast television. It should come as no surprise, then, that Congress decided to impose the must-carry obligations upon cable operators only. [Moreover,] the regulations are broad-based, applying to almost all cable systems in the country, rather than just a select few. As a result, the provisions do not pose the same dangers of suppression and manipulation that were posed by the more narrowly targeted regulations in Minneapolis Star and Arkansas Writers' Project [and thus] do not call for strict scrutiny."

Second, the Court likewise rejected cable *programmers'* argument that strict scrutiny was called for "because the must-carry provisions favor one set of speakers (broadcast programmers) over another (cable programmers). [Not] all speaker-partial laws are presumed invalid. Rather, [speaker-based] laws demand strict scrutiny when they reflect the Government's preference for the substance of what the favored speakers have to say (or aversion to what the disfavored speakers have to say). [Congress] granted must-carry privileges to broadcast stations on the belief that the broadcast television industry is in economic peril due to the physical characteristics of cable transmission and the economic incentives facing the cable industry. Thus, the fact that the provisions benefit broadcasters and not cable programmers does not call for strict scrutiny under our precedents."

4. *Laws of general applicability.* In COHEN v. COWLES MEDIA CO., 501 U.S. 663 (1991), the Court held that the First Amendment did not bar an action in state court for promissory estoppel against a newspaper that breached its promise of confidentiality to a source. Dan Cohen, who worked for the Republican candidate for governor in the 1982 election, leaked to the Minneapolis Star and another paper documents indicating that a Democratic candidate for lieutenant governor had had two criminal charges brought against her. The papers promised him confidentiality, but later made the editorial judgment to identify him as the source in their stories. He was fired by his employer as a result. Cohen sued the papers for breach of contract and fraud and won $200,000 in compensatory and $500,000 in punitive damages from a jury. The Minnesota Supreme Court found the fraud and contract theories untenable but held that the compensatory damages judgment could be sustained on a promissory estoppel theory, except that it would violate the newspapers' First Amendment rights. The Supreme Court reversed and remanded, finding no First Amendment bar to a promissory estoppel action.

Justice WHITE wrote for the Court: "Respondents [rely on a line of cases holding] that 'if a newspaper lawfully obtains truthful information about a matter of public significance then state officials may not constitutionally punish publication of the information, absent a need to further a state interest of the highest order.' [E.g., Landmark, Fla. Star.] [This] case, however, is not controlled by this line of cases but, rather, by the equally well-established line of decisions holding that generally applicable laws do not offend the First Amendment simply because their enforcement against the press has incidental effects on its ability to gather and report the news. As the cases relied on by respondents recognize, the truthful information sought to be published must have been lawfully acquired. The press may not with impunity break and enter an office or dwelling to gather news. Neither does the First Amendment relieve a newspaper reporter of the obligation shared by all citizens to respond to a grand jury subpoena and answer questions relevant to a criminal investigation, even though the reporter might be required to reveal a confidential source. [Branzburg.] The press, like others interested in publishing, may not publish copyrighted material without obeying the copyright laws. [Zacchini.] Similarly, the media must obey the National Labor Relations Act, Associated Press v. NLRB, 301 U.S. 103 (1937), and the Fair Labor Standards Act, Oklahoma Press Publishing Co. v. Walling, 327 U.S. 186 (1946); may not restrain trade in violation of the antitrust laws, Associated Press v. United States, 326 U.S. 1 (1945); Citizen Publishing Co. v. United States, 394 U.S. 131 (1969); and must pay non-discriminatory taxes, [Murdock; Minneapolis Star.] Accordingly, enforcement of such general laws against the press is not subject to stricter scrutiny than would be applied to enforcement against other persons or organizations.

"There can be little doubt that the Minnesota doctrine of promissory estoppel is a law of general applicability. It does not target or single out the press. Rather, [the] doctrine is generally applicable to the daily transactions of all the citizens of Minnesota. The First Amendment does not forbid its application to the press. [Respondents] and amici argue that permitting Cohen to maintain a cause of action for promissory estoppel will inhibit truthful reporting because news organizations will have legal incentives not to disclose a confidential source's identity even when that person's identity is itself newsworthy. [But] if this is the case, it is no more than the incidental, and constitutionally insignificant, consequence of applying to the press a generally applicable law that requires those who make certain kinds of promises to keep them."

Justice BLACKMUN, joined by Justices Marshall and Souter, dissented. He regarded the lawsuit as penalizing the content of the newspapers' speech and thus as controlled by such cases as Hustler v. Falwell (p. 1105 above): "There, we found that the use of a claim of intentional infliction of emotional distress to impose liability for the publication of a satirical critique violated the First Amendment. There was no doubt that Virginia's tort of intentional infliction of emotional distress was 'a law of general applicability' unrelated to the suppression of speech. Nonetheless, a unanimous Court found that, when used to penalize the expression of opinion, the law was subject to the strictures of the First Amendment. [As] in Hustler, the operation of Minnesota's doctrine of promissory estoppel in this case cannot be said to have a merely 'incidental' burden on speech; the publication of important political speech is the claimed violation. Thus, as in Hustler, the law may not be enforced to punish the expression of truthful information or opinion."

Justice SOUTER, joined by Justices Marshall, Blackmun and O'Connor, also dissented, finding that, even if the promissory estoppel law did have general applicability, "it [is still] necessary to articulate, measure, and compare the competing interests involved [to] determine the legitimacy of burdening constitutional interests." He emphasized the "importance of the information to public discourse," and argued that "[t]he importance of this public interest is integral to the balance that should be struck in this case. There can be no doubt that the fact of Cohen's identity expanded the universe of information relevant to the choice faced by Minnesota voters in that State's 1982 gubernatorial election, the publication of which was thus of the sort quintessentially subject to strict First Amendment. The propriety of his leak to respondents could be taken to reflect on his character, which in turn could be taken to reflect on the character of the candidate who had retained him as an adviser. An election could turn on just such a factor; if it should, I am ready to assume that it would be to the greater public good, at least over the long run."

Was the newspapers' argument in Cowles Media consistent with the journalists' argument in Branzburg? In Branzburg, the press claimed that any pressure to reveal the names of confidential sources would dry up those sources, reducing the flow of information to the public. In Cowles, the press claimed that it had a First Amendment right to reveal its sources' names, and that this revelation would serve the interest in ensuring the flow of information to the public—an argument Justice Souter endorsed in his dissent. How can both these arguments hold simultaneously? For exploration of the issues raised in Cowles, see Levi, "Dangerous Liaisons: Seduction and Betrayal in Confidential Press–Source Relations," 43 Rutgers L. Rev. 609 (1991).

D. DIFFERENTIAL REGULATION OF THE BROADCAST MEDIA

Introduction. To what extent are constitutional restrictions on regulation of the print media applicable to the broadcast media? To what extent may broadcasters be treated differently? That issue has arisen in materials covered earlier. Recall, e.g., the Pacifica case (1978; p. 1164 above), justifying regulation of an indecent radio broadcast on the ground that broadcasting is uniquely intrusive into the home and accessible to children. Recall also the emphasis on the unique nature of broadcasting in Red Lion (1969; p. 1366 above), in which the Court permitted government to enforce rights of access to broadcasting based on the scarcity of the over-the-air spectrum.

In both Pacifica and Red Lion, the Court upheld restrictions upon broadcasters that would have been impermissible if imposed on those seeking to communicate by print or the non-broadcast spoken word. For example, the Court held, in contrast to Pacifica, that offended audiences must simply avert their eyes or ears if they saw Cohen's jacket at a courthouse or received Bolger Drug Products' condom advertisements in the mail. And the Court held, in contrast to Red Lion, that a governmentally imposed right of access violated the First Amendment rights of the Miami Herald newspaper in Tornillo (1974; p. 1366 above). In contrast, the Court was willing to allow government to impose greater access obligations on the broadcast media, rejecting First Amendment challenges beginning with Red Lion, below.

To understand the cases that follow, it is helpful to consider briefly the background of broadcast regulation. As the Court recounted in Red Lion: "Before 1927, the allocation of frequencies was left entirely to the private sector, and the result was chaos. It quickly became apparent that broadcast frequencies constituted a scarce resource whose use could be regulated and rationalized only by the Government. Without government control, the medium would be of little use because of the cacophony of competing voices, none of which could be clearly and predictably heard." Accordingly, Congress enacted the Radio Act of 1927 and the Communications Act of 1934. As the Court recounted in Turner Broadcasting: "In the Communications Act of 1934, Congress created a system of free broadcast service and directed that communications facilities be licensed across the country in a 'fair, efficient, and equitable' manner. Congress designed this system of allocation to afford each community of appreciable size an over-the-air source of information and an outlet for exchange on matters of local concern. [It] has long been a basic tenet of national communications policy that 'the widest possible dissemination of information from diverse and antagonistic sources is essential to the welfare of the public.'" The 1934 Act created the Federal Communications Commission (FCC) and authorized it to confer licenses on broadcasters and to regulate the broadcast spectrum "as public convenience, interest, or necessity requires." Licenses provide for use but not ownership of a portion of the broadcast spectrum. The Court upheld broadcast licensing in National Broadcasting Co. v. United States, 319 U.S. 190 (1943). For an overview of the tension between broadcasting law and ordinary free speech principles, see Weinberg, "Broadcasting and Speech," 81 Calif. L. Rev. 1101 (1993). For commentary critical of broadcast licensing in particular, see Coase, "The Federal Communications Commission," 2 J. L. & Econ. 1 (1959); Spitzer, "The Constitutionality of Licensing Broadcasters," 64 N.Y.U. L Rev. 990 (1989). On the law of broadcasting generally, see Carter, Franklin & Wright, The First Amendment and the Fifth Estate—Regulation of Electronic Mass Media (1989).

SCARCITY, ACCESS AND THE BROADCASTING MEDIA

1. *Right-of-reply obligations on the broadcasting media.* May government safeguard individual reputations by requiring a broadcaster to afford reply time to the target of an attack? When government has sought to vindicate the interest in private reputation by authorizing defamation actions, the Court has sharply curtailed suits against the press. But when the FCC sought to provide rights of access for individuals attacked on the air and imposed requirements that radio and television stations give reply time, the Court sustained the regulations against the claim that they violated the First Amendment rights of the broadcaster. May government regulate the media with the aim of improving the marketplace of ideas?

RED LION BROADCASTING CO. v. FCC, 395 U.S. 367 (1969), rejected broadcasters' First Amendment challenge to the FCC "fairness doctrine," which required licensed broadcast stations to present discussion of public issues, to assure fair coverage for each side, and to provide free reply time in response to certain personal attacks and political editorials. In sustaining those regulations in Red Lion, Justice WHITE's opinion for a unanimous Court reasoned that restricting the editorial discretion of the broadcasting media would "enhance rather than abridge the freedoms of speech and press." He emphasized the "scarcity of broadcast frequencies, the Government's role in allocating those frequencies, and the legitimate claims of those unable without governmental assistance to gain access to those frequencies for expression of their views." He began from the supposition that "differences in the characteristics of news media justify differences in the First Amendment standards applied to them. Just as the Government may limit the use of sound amplifying equipment potentially so noisy that it drowns out civilized private speech, so may the Government limit the use of broadcast equipment." He continued:

"Where there are substantially more individuals who want to broadcast than there are frequencies to allocate, it is idle to posit an unabridgeable First Amendment right to broadcast comparable to the right of every individual to speak, write, or publish. If 100 persons want broadcast licenses but there are only 10 frequencies to allocate, all of them may have the same 'right' to a license; but if there is to be any effective communication by radio, only a few can be licensed and the rest must be barred from the airwaves. It would be strange if the First Amendment, aimed at protecting and furthering communications, prevented the Government from making radio communication possible by requiring licenses to broadcast and by limiting the number of licenses so as not to overcrowd the spectrum.

"[A] license permits broadcasting, but the licensee has no constitutional right to be the one who holds the license or to monopolize a radio frequency to the exclusion of his fellow citizens. There is nothing in the First Amendment which prevents the Government from requiring a licensee to share his frequency with others and to conduct himself as a proxy or fiduciary with obligations to present those views and voices which are representative of his community and which would otherwise, by necessity, be barred from the airwaves. [It] is the right of the viewers and listeners, not the right of the broadcasters, which is paramount. It is the purpose of the First Amendment to preserve an uninhibited marketplace of ideas in which truth will ultimately prevail, rather than to countenance monopolization of that market, whether it be by the Government itself or a private licensee. [It]is the right of the public to receive suitable access to social, political, esthetic, moral, and other ideas and experiences which is crucial here.

"[We cannot] say that it is inconsistent with the First Amendment goal of producing an informed public capable of conducting its own affairs to require a broadcaster to permit answers to personal attacks occurring in the course of discussing controversial issues, or to require that the political opponents of those endorsed by the station be given a chance to communicate with the public. Otherwise, station owners and a few networks would have unfettered power to make time available only to the highest bidders, to communicate only their own views on public issues, people and candidates, and to permit on the air only those with whom they agreed. There is no sanctuary in the First Amendment for unlimited private censorship operating in a medium not open to all.

"It is strenuously argued, however, that if political editorials or personal attacks will trigger an obligation in broadcasters to afford the opportunity for expression to speakers who need not pay for time and whose views are unpalatable to the licensees, then broadcasters will be irresistibly forced to self-censorship and their coverage of controversial public issues will be eliminated or at least rendered wholly ineffective. Such a result would indeed be a serious matter, for should licensees actually eliminate their coverage of controversial issues, the purposes of the doctrine would be stifled. [At] this point, however, as the Federal Communications Commission has indicated, that possibility is at best speculative.

"[It] does not violate the First Amendment to treat licensees given the privilege of using scarce radio frequencies as proxies for the entire community, obligated to give suitable time and attention to matters of great public concern. To condition the granting or renewal of licenses on a willingness to present representative community views on controversial issues is consistent with the ends and purposes of those constitutional provisions forbidding the abridgment of freedom of speech and freedom of the press. In view of the scarcity of broadcast frequencies, the Government's role in allocating those frequencies, and the legitimate claims of those unable without governmental assistance to gain access to those frequencies for expression of their views, we hold the regulations and ruling at issue here are both authorized by statute and constitutional."

Justice White noted in a footnote: "We need not deal with the argument that even if there is no longer a technological scarcity of frequencies limiting the number of broadcasters, there nevertheless is an economic scarcity in the sense that the Commission could or does limit entry to the broadcasting market on economic grounds and license no more stations than the market will support. [A] related argument, which we also put aside, is that quite apart from scarcity of frequencies, technological or economic, Congress does not abridge freedom of speech or press by legislation directly or indirectly multiplying the voices and views presented to the public through timesharing, fairness doctrines, or other devices which limit or dissipate the power of those who sit astride the channels of communication with the general public."

For commentary on the problems raised by Red Lion, see, e.g., Bollinger, "Freedom of the Press and Public Access: Toward a Theory of Partial Regulation of the Mass Media," 75 Mich.L.Rev. 1 (1976); Van Alstyne, "The Mobius Strip of the First Amendment: Perspectives on Red Lion," 29 S.C.L.Rev. 539 (1978); and Krattenmaker & Powe, "The Fairness Doctrine Today: A Constitutional Curiosity and An Impossible Dream," 1985 Duke L.J. 151. On the fairness doctrine generally, see Schmidt, Freedom of the Press vs. Public Access (1976), and Friendly, The Good Guys, The Bad Guys and the First Amendment (1976). See also Powe, "Or of The [Broadcast] Press," 55 Tex.L.Rev. 39 (1976).

2. *The limits of Red Lion: technological versus economic scarcity.* Note that the Red Lion opinion emphasized technological scarcity and expressly declined to reach the broader argument that government may compel access or otherwise regulate speech in order to solve problems of economic scarcity. In Tornillo, Chief Justice BURGER reviewed and rejected, with respect to the print press, arguments for "an enforceable right of access to the press" and the concomitant claim "that Government has an obligation to ensure that a wide variety of views reach the public." Access advocates emphasized the concentration of power in the newspaper business and the shrinking number of newspapers, noted the disappearance of real opportunity to form competing newspapers by dissidents, and accordingly urged "that the only effective way to insure fairness and accuracy" is "for government to take affirmative action." But the Court in Tornillo was not persuaded: "However much validity may be found in these arguments, at each point the implementation of a remedy such as an enforceable right of access necessarily calls for some mechanism, either governmental or consensual. If it is governmental coercion, this at once brings about a confrontation with the [First Amendment]." For the position of "access advocates," see Barron, "Access to the Press—A New First Amendment Right," 80 Harv.L.Rev. 1641 (1967), and Lange, "The Role of the Access Doctrine in the Regulation of the Mass Media," 52 N.Car.L.Rev. 1 (1973). For reflections on Tornillo, see Powe, "Tornillo," 1987 Sup.Ct.Rev. 345; Schmidt, Freedom of Press vs. Public Access (1976). For a later effort to generalize the holding of Red Lion to broader settings, see Fiss, "Free Speech and Social Structure," 71 Iowa L. Rev. 1405 (1986).

3. *Repeal of the fairness doctrine.* The fairness doctrine, despite its validation in Red Lion, was subject to considerable criticism. Broadcasters resisted being treated less protectively than other media. Some observers charged that the doctrine perversely made television and radio blander rather than more diverse because it gave stations an incentive to avoid controversial editorials and pointed attacks. Others criticized it as unadministrable. Above all it was criticized for obsolescence: the expanded capacity of the electromagnetic

spectrum and the growth of programming competition from cable and satellite diminished the "scarcity" rationale.

In August 1987, the FCC repealed the fairness doctrine, after an extensive administrative proceeding noting the rise of competition in information services markets and finding that the doctrine "chilled" the First Amendment rights of broadcasters. See Syracuse Peace Council, 2 FCC Rec. 5043 (1987); FCC, Fairness Doctrine Obligations of Broadcast Licensees, 102 F.C.C.2d 143 (1985). In announcing the repeal, then-FCC chairman Mark Fowler stated: "The First Amendment does not guarantee a fair press, only a free press."

4. *A constitutional right of access to the broadcasting media for editorial advertisements?* Red Lion held that the First Amendment permitted access obligations to be imposed on broadcasters. But does the First Amendment compel such access? The Court answered this question in the negative three years after Red Lion in COLUMBIA BROADCASTING, INC. v. DEMOCRATIC NATIONAL COMM., 412 U.S. 94 (1973). The CBS case originated with complaints filed before the FCC in 1970 by the Democratic National Committee and an anti-war group challenging certain broadcasters' policies of refusing all editorial advertisements. The FCC sustained the broadcasters' position, but the Court of Appeals reversed, holding that "a flat ban on paid public issue announcements is in violation of the First Amendment, at least when other sorts of paid announcements are accepted." The Supreme Court held that, even assuming the broadcasters' refusal amounted to state action, broadcasters were not constitutionally required to accept such advertisements.

Chief Justice BURGER's opinion for the Court rejected the argument that a broad right of access could be drawn from the Red Lion ruling. Instead, he emphasized the statutory indications "that Congress intended to permit private broadcasting to develop with the widest journalistic freedom consistent with its public obligations." He emphasized that even broadcasters have substantial editorial discretion, and concluded: "To agree that debate on public issues should be 'robust, and wide-open' does not mean that we should exchange 'public trustee' broadcasting, with all its limitations, for a system of self-appointed editorial commentators." The Chief Justice cautioned against constitutionally mandating an extension of the fairness doctrine: "The Commission's responsibilities under a right-of-access system would tend to draw it into a continuing case-by-case determination of who should be heard and when." Moreover, he noted "the reality that in a very real sense listeners and viewers constitute a 'captive audience.' "

Justice DOUGLAS' concurrence took a far firmer constitutional position on the side of the broadcasters: "My conclusion is that TV and radio stand in the same protected position under the First Amendment as do newspapers and magazines." The Red Lion case, in which he had not participated, curtailed broadcasters' rights unduly, he insisted, since "the First Amendment puts beyond the reach of government federal regulation of news agencies save only business or financial practices which do not involve First Amendment rights." Justice BRENNAN's extensive dissent, joined by Justice Marshall, concluded, in "balancing" the competing interests, that the broadcasters' "absolute ban on editorial advertising" could "serve only to inhibit, rather than to further" robust public debate. He insisted that the fairness doctrine was "insufficient" to provide that kind of debate. He noted not only the interests of broadcasters and of the listening and viewing public, "but also the independent First Amendment interest of groups and individuals in effective self-expression." Drawing on access principles developed in the public forum context, he commented: "[F]reedom of speech does not exist in the abstract. On the contrary, the right to speak can flourish only if it is allowed to operate in an effective forum—whether it be a public park, a schoolroom, a town meeting hall, a soapbox, or a radio and television frequency. For in the absence of an effective means of communication, the right to speak would ring hollow indeed." Accordingly, "in light of the current dominance of the electronic media as the most effective means of reaching the public, any policy that *absolutely* denies citizens access to the airwaves" was unjustifiable.

5. *A statutory right of access to the broadcasting media for candidates seeking federal elective office.* Sec. 312(a)(7) of the Communications Act of 1934, as added by the Federal Election Campaign Act of 1971, authorizes the FCC to revoke a broadcaster's license "for willful or repeated failure to allow reasonable access to or to permit purchase of reasonable amounts of time for the use of a broadcasting station by a legally qualified candidate for Federal elective office on behalf of his candidacy." The 6–3 decision in CBS, INC. v. FCC, 453 U.S. 367 (1981), found that this provision created a major new statutory right of access—a right that enlarged the political broadcasting responsibilities of licensees. The Court also held that the FCC's interpretation and application of the provision did not violate broadcasters' First Amendment rights. The controversy originated in October 1979, when the Carter–Mondale Presidential Committee asked each of the three major television networks to sell the Committee a half-hour of early December 1979 air time. The Committee sought to broadcast a documentary on the record of the Carter Administration, to augment President Carter's planned announcement of his candidacy for re-election. All three networks denied the request, relying on their across-the-board rules about political broadcasts. The Committee filed a complaint, and the FCC ruled that the networks' reasons were "deficient" under the FCC's interpretation of the statute. The FCC concluded that the networks had violated the law by failing to provide "reasonable access." Chief Justice BURGER—who had emphasized "the widest journalistic freedom" for broadcasters in CBS v. DNC, above—wrote the majority opinion. Justice WHITE's dissent, joined by Justices Rehnquist and Stevens, strongly disagreed with the Chief Justice's broad reading of the law and with the Court's endorsement of the FCC standards and their application.

Can CBS v. DNC and CBS v. FCC be reconciled? Are broadcasters better viewed as conduits for speech or as speakers and editors in their own right? Are they both? Do the two CBS decisions simply reflect consistent judicial deference to the expertise of the FCC?

6. *The standard of review in broadcasting cases.* Recall that the Court, in FCC v. LEAGUE OF WOMEN VOTERS, 468 U.S. 364 (1984), invalidated 47 U.S.C. § 399, which prohibited "editorializing" by noncommercial educational broadcasting stations receiving public funds from the Corporation for Public Broadcasting. The Court found the law to be content-based, but nonetheless held that the special features of broadcasting dictated applying a standard lower than strict scrutiny. Justice BRENNAN, writing for the Court, stated that regulation of the content of broadcasting would be upheld "only when we [are] satisfied that the restriction is narrowly tailored to further a substantial governmental interest, such as ensuring adequate and balanced coverage of public issues." Because the restriction on expression of editorial opinion was found to lie "at the heart of First Amendment protection," the Court applied its standard carefully and found the government's justifications insufficient to justify the restriction. For a fuller account of the opinions, see p. 1320 above. Is a different standard of review warranted for broadcasting than for other media?

NEW MEDIA: CABLE TELEVISION AND THE INTERNET

How should the Court treat regulation of newly emerging media such as cable television and the worldwide web of linked computers known as the Internet, or cyberspace? Are traditional First Amendment principles applicable? Or are new principles needed to suit new technologies? For commentary, see Bhagwat, "Of Markets and Media: The First Amendment, the New Mass Media, and the Political Components of Culture," 74 N. Car. L Rev. 141 (1995); Symposium, "Emerging Media Technology and the First Amendment," 104 Yale L. J. 1611 (1995).

1. *Cable television and the First Amendment.* Cable television transmits video signals over fiberoptic wire rather than over the electromagnetic spectrum. Originally a device to route television to areas with poor over-the-air reception, it has expanded dramatically and today is the source of television transmission for over 60% of American homes with television sets. The First Amendment status of cable was long unsettled. The cable industry argued against application of Red Lion or any other lesser standard of protection, reasoning that technological scarcity is not an issue on cable systems. On the other hand, cable is in part a vehicle for broadcasting transmission, and cable systems depend on the grant of municipal franchises, including rights-of-way over streets and utility poles. Government has sometimes taken the position that cable is more like broadcasting than like print media by virtue of these facts, and therefore more regulable.

The Supreme Court put to rest this debate in TURNER BROADCASTING v. FCC, 512 U.S. 622 (1994)(Turner I), see p. 1369 above. In the course of rejecting the cable industry's argument for strict scrutiny of the requirement that it carry certain broadcast signals, the Court rejected any argument for applying Red Lion or extending it by analogy to the cable context. Justice KENNEDY wrote for the Court: "There can be no disagreement on an initial premise: Cable programmers and cable operators engage in and transmit speech, and they are entitled to the protection of the speech and press provisions of the First Amendment. [Leathers.] Through 'original programming or by exercising editorial discretion over which stations or programs to include in its repertoire,' cable programmers and operators 'seek to communicate messages on a wide variety of topics and in a wide variety of formats.' Los Angeles v. Preferred Communications, Inc., 476 U.S. 488 (1986). [The] Government [contends] that regulation of cable television should be analyzed under the same First Amendment standard that applies to regulation of broadcast television. It is true that our cases have permitted more intrusive regulation of broadcast speakers than of speakers in other media. Compare [Red Lion with Tornillo.] But the rationale for applying a less rigorous standard of First Amendment scrutiny to broadcast regulation, whatever its validity in the cases elaborating it, does not apply in the context of cable regulation.

"The justification for our distinct approach to broadcast regulation rests upon the unique physical limitations of the broadcast medium. As a general matter, there are more would-be broadcasters than frequencies available in the electromagnetic spectrum. And if two broadcasters were to attempt to transmit over the same frequency in the same locale, they would interfere with one another's signals, so that neither could be heard at all. The scarcity of broadcast frequencies thus required the establishment of some regulatory mechanism to divide the electromagnetic spectrum and assign specific frequencies to particular broadcasters. In addition, the inherent physical limitation on the number of speakers who may use the broadcast medium has been thought to require some adjustment in traditional First Amendment analysis to permit the Government to place limited content restraints, and impose certain affirmative obligations, on broadcast licensees

"[Although] courts and commentators have criticized the scarcity rationale since its inception, we have declined to question its continuing validity as support for our broadcast jurisprudence, and see no reason to do so here. The broadcast cases are inapposite in the present context because cable television does not suffer from the inherent limitations that characterize the broadcast medium. Indeed, given the rapid advances in fiber optics and digital compression technology, soon there may be no practical limitation on the number of speakers who may use the cable medium. Nor is there any danger of physical interference between two cable speakers attempting to share the same channel. In light of these fundamental technological differences between broadcast and cable transmission, application of the more relaxed standard of scrutiny adopted in Red Lion and the other broadcast cases is inapt when determining the First Amendment validity of cable regulation.

"[Although] the Government acknowledges the substantial technological differences between broadcast and cable, it advances a second argument for application of the Red Lion framework to cable regulation. It asserts that the foundation of our broadcast jurisprudence is not the physical limitations of the electromagnetic spectrum, but rather the 'market dysfunction' that characterizes the broadcast market. Because the cable market is beset by a similar dysfunction, the Government maintains, the Red Lion standard of review should also apply to cable. While we agree that the cable market suffers certain structural impediments, the Government's argument is flawed in two respects. First, as discussed above, the special physical characteristics of broadcast transmission, not the economic characteristics of the broadcast market, are what underlies our broadcast jurisprudence. Second, the mere assertion of dysfunction or failure in a speech market, without more, is not sufficient to shield a speech regulation from the First Amendment standards applicable to nonbroadcast media. See, e.g., [Austin, MCFL, Tornillo.]"

Accordingly, Justice Kennedy proceeded to use ordinary First Amendment principles—in particular, the distinction between content-based and content-neutral laws—to analyze the must-carry rules. He did, however, find cable's particular characteristics relevant in applying those principles, and thus found cable's "chokehold" monopoly relevant to the determination that the must-carry rules were content-neutral: "When an individual subscribes to cable, the physical connection between the television set and the cable network gives the cable operator bottleneck, or gatekeeper, control over most (if not all) of the television programming that is channeled into the subscriber's home. Hence, simply by virtue of its ownership of the essential pathway for cable speech, a cable operator can prevent its subscribers from obtaining access to programming it chooses to exclude. A cable operator, unlike speakers in other media, can thus silence the voice of competing speakers with a mere flick of the switch. The potential for abuse of this private power over a central avenue of communication cannot be overlooked. The First Amendment's command that government not impede the freedom of speech does not disable the government from taking steps to ensure that private interests not restrict, through physical control of a critical pathway of communication, the free flow of information and ideas."

In DENVER AREA EDUCATIONAL TELECOMMUNICATIONS CONSORTIUM v. FCC, ___ U.S. ___ , 116 S.Ct. 2374 (1996), see p. 1171 above, the plurality opinion expressly declined to decide whether cable is more analogous to print or to broadcasting. As Justice BREYER explained for the plurality in declining to analogize cable either to a common carrier or to a bookstore: "Both categorical approaches suffer from the same flaws: they import law developed in very different contexts into a new and changing environment, and they lack the flexibility necessary to allow government to respond to very serious practical problems without sacrificing the free exchange of ideas the First Amendment is designed to protect." Justice SOUTER elaborated in concurrence: "All of the relevant characteristics of cable are presently in a state of technological and regulatory flux. [Thus] we should be shy about saying the final word today about what will be accepted as reasonable tomorrow." Justice THOMAS, joined by Chief Justice Rehnquist and Justice Scalia in partial dissent, found the plurality's approach unsatisfactory and would have preferred to state directly that cable's First Amendment protection was equivalent to that of the print press: "Our First Amendment distinctions between media, dubious from their infancy, placed cable in a doctrinal wasteland in which regulators and cable operators alike could not be sure whether cable was entitled to the substantial First Amendment protections afforded the print media or was subject to the more onerous obligations shouldered by the broadcast media. Over time, however, we have drawn closer to recognizing that cable operators should enjoy the same First Amendment rights as the nonbroadcast media. [In] Turner, we stated expressly what we had implied in Leathers: The Red Lion standard does not apply to cable television. [In] Turner, by adopting much of the print paradigm, and by rejecting Red Lion, we adopted with it a considerable body of precedent that governs the respective First Amendment rights of competing speakers. In Red Lion, we had legitimized consideration of the public interest and emphasized the rights of viewers, at least in the abstract. Under that view, 'it is the right of the viewers and listeners, not the right of the broadcasters, which is paramount.' After Turner, however, that view can no longer be given any credence in the cable context. It is the operator's right that is preeminent."

Municipal governments have typically exacted from cable operators the requirement that they dedicate one or more channels to the government as public access channels to be used for public, educational or governmental purposes. Federal legislation governing the cable industry has explicitly permitted such arrangements, and has additionally required that cable operators dedicate a certain number of "leased access" channels for programming from sources unaffiliated with them. Does compulsion to provide public access and leased access channels raise any serious First Amendment issue? Although this issue was not directly in issue in Denver Area, Justice Thomas' opinion questioned the constitutionality of requiring public access and leased access channels in the first place: "There is no getting around the fact that leased and public access are a type of forced speech. Though the constitutionality of leased and public access channels is not directly at issue in these cases, the position adopted by the Court in Turner ineluctably leads to the conclusion that the federal access requirements are subject to some form of heightened scrutiny. Following Turner, some commentators have questioned the constitutionality of leased and public access. Such questions are not at issue here." But he argued that even if such access were assumed to be constitutional, cable programmers and viewers had no First Amendment right to insist that any particular programming be shown.

If public access channels are constitutionally created, then do they function as public forums? Justice KENNEDY's opinion in Denver Area took such a view, and thus concluded that government could not authorize content-based discrimination on such channels: "Public access channels meet the definition of a public forum. We have recognized two kinds of public forums. The first and most familiar are traditional public forums, like streets, sidewalks, and parks, which by custom have long been open for public assembly and discourse. 'The second category of public property is the designated public forum, whether of a limited or unlimited character—property that the State has opened for expressive activity by part or all of the public.' Public access channels fall in the second category. Required by the franchise authority as a condition of the franchise and open to all comers, they are a designated public forum of unlimited character. The House Report for the 1984 Cable Act [characterized] public access channels as 'the video equivalent of the speaker's soapbox or the electronic parallel to the printed leaflet. They provide groups and individuals who generally have not had access to the electronic media with the opportunity to become sources of information in the electronic marketplace of ideas.' "

On this view, must a public access channel permit a program by a racist speaker whose speech does not rise to the level of Brandenburg incitement? An indecent program that is not obscene or otherwise proscribed by law? Note Justice Thomas' reply to Justice Kennedy in Denver Area: "Public access channels are [not] public fora. [Cable] systems are not public property. Cable systems are privately owned and privately managed, and [no] case [holds] that government may designate private property a public forum [absent] at least some formal easement or other property interest."

2. *The Internet and the First Amendment.* The Internet began as a government defense project in 1969 and developed into a decentralized global network for communicating information. The Internet is not a physical entity, but rather a vast network of interconnected computers which allows nearly instantaneous worldwide transmission of data between linked individuals and organizations. Individuals can access the Internet through a variety of means including non-profit organizations such as university networks and on-line service providers who provide Internet access for a monthly fee.

The rapid expansion of the Internet presents numerous questions about the parameters of free speech protection and the proper extent of government regulation and control. Proponents of regulation cite the potential for uncontrolled dissemination of pornography, rampant copyright infringement, and the proliferation of harassment and unwanted invasions of privacy. Critics of regulatory frameworks argue that the legislative and judicial response cannot keep pace with the growth of technology; thus, the market should be allowed to develop technological solutions to these problems on its own.

The term "Internet" encompasses several different modes of communication: e-mail (one-to-one or one-to-several electronic messaging), listserv (one-to-many messaging), usenet (newsgroups), telnet (remote computer utilization), real time "chat" functions, and the worldwide web. All of these areas have different technological qualities. Any regulatory scheme or constitutional framework may need to take account of these technological differences in fashioning appropriate boundaries for speech protection. For instance, the expansion and increasing popularity of newsgroups, bulletin boards, and web pages essentially allows individuals to be their own content publishers. An important threshold issue is how to characterize the nature of the speech that occurs in these mediums. A single web page can contain commercial advertisements, political speech, and obscene material. The information can either be embedded into the web page itself, or it can take the form of links to other web pages.

Postings to computer bulletin boards can also present difficult issues about the responsibility for the content of the postings if found to be libelous or defamatory. Should the service providers who maintain the bulletin boards be considered conduits for the distribution of information or publishers with editorial control? In Cubby, Inc. v. CompuServe, Inc., 776 F.Supp. 135

(S.D.N.Y.1991), the court drew an analogy between CompuServe's "electronic library" and a bookstore, calling both passive distributors who could not be held liable for libelous or defamatory material in their "stores" if the material was provided by third parties and CompuServe neither knew nor had reason to know of the defamatory content. On the other hand, the court in Stratton Oakmont, Inc. v. Prodigy Services Co., 1995 WL 323710 (N.Y.Sup.1995), found Prodigy liable for defamatory statements made by subscribers on Moneytalk, one of its monitored bulletin boards. Prodigy, which bills itself as a family-oriented on-line provider, was analogized to a publisher of a newspaper (Tornillo), and with an increase in editorial control over the content of the bulletin boards, the court held, comes an increase in liability for defamatory or libelous statements made by subscribers since the content is monitored and regulated by Prodigy employees.

A related issue is the location of liability for harassment through threatening postings either to newsgroups or directly to personal e-mail accounts. See United States v. Baker, 890 F.Supp. 1375 (E.D.Mich.1995), on the question of whether a university should be liable for sexual threats and harassing speech perpetrated by a student over its computer network. Does the fact that members of the university community have access to e-mail and campus newsgroups as part of the educational mission of the university alter the level of administrative responsibility (and hence liability) for objectionable conduct perpetuated over the network? Is it constitutionally permissible for a university to restrict students' access to protected material, for example, by prohibiting students from downloading indecent material?

In the first major test of government regulation of speech on the Internet, a three-judge court struck down a federal law, the Communications Decency Act, which makes it a crime to use any "interactive computer service" to send or "display in a manner available to" a person under age 18 any material that describes sexual or excretory activities or organs "in terms patently offensive as measured by contemporary community standards"—unless one makes "reasonable efforts" to prevent access by under–18–year–olds. ACLU v. Reno, 929 F.Supp. 824 (E.D.Pa.1996). One of the judges concurring in that result characterized the Internet as "the most participatory marketplace of mass speech that this country—and indeed the world—has yet seen," and noted the "democratizing" effects of instantaneous global communication. Who should bear the burden of preventing minors' access to indecent materials on the Internet? Their parents or teachers through the use of filtering technology that enables one to opt out of exposure to certain messages? Or the disseminators of the material, through the use of access technology that requires one to prove adult identity in order to opt in? Recall earlier discussions of indecent or offensive mailings and broadcasts.

The issue of transmission of obscene as well as indecent material over the Internet is complicated by its technological mechanics. In order to create a communications network that could withstand a nuclear attack, the government created a packet-based system for sending messages. A message sent from an individual in San Francisco to an individual in Little Rock is broken up into packets which may be routed through different servers in various locations across the country before they reach their final destination and are reassembled into their original form. In the context of a transmission of sexually explicit material, the data could pass through some jurisdictions where it would be considered obscene and some where it would be considered indecent, but not obscene. How should a court determine the proper forum for evaluating whether a particular transmission is obscene? At the point of origin (the server where the information is stored)? At various points along the message route? At the point where the user downloads the material? See United States v. Thomas, 74 F.3d 701 (6th Cir.1996), cert. denied, 117 S.Ct. 74 (1996). Whose community standards should be used in evaluating whether a transmission is obscene? The community of Internet users? The community where the download occurs? Where the upload occurs? Who will be ultimately liable for the transmission? The individuals who upload the material onto a web site or newsgroup, the individuals who download the material onto their individual hard drives, or the Internet service providers through whose servers and networks these transmissions take place?

Should questions about speech on the Internet be resolved by finding the most appropriate analogies between existing law on the protection of speech rights and the characteristics of this new medium? For instance, are bulletin boards more like bookstores or newspapers? Are Internet service providers more like common carriers or do they have some responsibility to regulate the content that passes through their networks? Are on-line service providers more like distributors of information provided by third parties or publishers of content? Is the Internet a pervasive and invasive medium like broadcasting (Pacifica) and cable (Denver Area Telecom) where content is pushed into the eyes and ears of viewers? Or is the Internet best understood as more of a "pull" technology where participants must venture out and subscribe to newsgroups and mailing lists, download data from remote sites, and type in web addresses in order to view particular pages? If this pull interpretation prevails, regulation of speech on the Internet may require the development of entirely new analogies and constitutional frameworks. On the other hand, if the Internet comes to be dominated by "push" technologies, which allow subscribers to request and receive custom content, analogies to broadcast and cable may appear more applicable. Push services go to favorite web sites, automatically download data, send updates, and push the data directly onto the subscriber's hard drive, thereby alleviating the need for subscribers to venture out onto the web in order to pull the data themselves. The opposite of surfing the web, these push technologies allow companies to become personal broadcasters. Push technologies and the availability of access to the web through television further complicate the search for parallels to prior methods of constitutional analysis. Just as web pages and bulletin boards give everyone the opportunity to be a publisher, so push technologies promise everyone the opportunity to be his or her own broadcaster. Does this vast communication potential demand the imposition of a regulatory scheme to prevent abuses or does it represent the ultimate free marketplace of ideas where speech can best be countered by more speech?

CHAPTER 14

THE RELIGION CLAUSES: FREE EXERCISE AND ESTABLISHMENT

Introduction. The First Amendment provides that "Congress shall make no law respecting an establishment of religion, or prohibiting the free exercise thereof." The two clauses have given rise to separate bodies of case law. But this should not obscure the fact that the two clauses are interrelated. They protect overlapping values, but they often exert conflicting pressures. Consider the common practice of exempting church property from taxation. Does the benefit conveyed by government to religion via that exemption constitute an "establishment"? Would the "free exercise" of religion be unduly burdened if church property were not exempted from taxation? Articulating satisfactory criteria to accommodate the sometimes conflicting emanations of the two religion clauses is a recurrent challenge in this chapter.

After an introductory overview in Section 1 that considers the original history of the religion clauses and the problem of defining religion, Section 2 examines ways in which government may be said to abridge the free exercise of religion. The most direct way is by deliberately prohibiting or disadvantaging a religious sect or its central practices. While such laws are rare in contemporary society, the Court has subjected them to strictest scrutiny. A harder case is presented when religious objections are raised to the application of general regulations. For example, may the Amish claim constitutional exemption from compulsory education laws? Such claims raise one of the tensions arising from the coexistence of the two religion clauses: If a state *must* grant an exemption because of the "free exercise" command, is it thereby granting a preference to religion in violation of the "establishment" provision? The Court has held free exercise to require some religious exemptions from generally applicable laws, but has narrowed the scope of such compelled exemptions in recent cases. Congress sought to reverse that trend in by providing for statutory religious exemption claims under the Religious Freedom Restoration Act of 1993.

Section 3 focuses on three establishment clause issues: the use or apparent endorsement of religious teachings or symbols by governmental bodies; the rendering of government financial aid to activities conducted by religious organizations; and the grant by government of exemptions from general laws or other accommodation of religion. The third issue is related to the question of compelled exemptions under the free exercise clause: it asks whether government is *permitted* to exempt religiously motivated practices from general laws, even if it is not compelled to do so. The principal tension in the establishment clause cases is among conceptions of government neutrality under the establishment clause: Does it require a "wall of separation" between church and state? Does it require formal neutrality, whereby government never adverts to religion, for advantage or for disadvantage? Or does it require simply that government treat religious organizations and activities equally, including them in any benefit schemes generally enjoyed by others?

SECTION 1: AN OVERVIEW OF THE RELIGION CLAUSES

1. *History of the religion clauses.* a. *The dominant view: voluntarism and separatism.* An influential view of the history of the religion clauses was set forth by Justice Black, writing for the Court in EVERSON v. BOARD OF EDUCATION, 330 U.S. 1 (1947). That decision, explored further below at p. 1532, held that a state may, consistent with the establishment clause, pay to bus children to and from parochial school. But before reaching that conclusion, Justice Black reviewed historical evidence suggesting that the framers favored, in Jefferson's words, "a wall of separation between church and state":

"A large proportion of the early settlers of this country came here from Europe to escape the bondage of laws which compelled them to support and attend government-favored churches. The centuries immediately before and contemporaneous with the colonization of America had been filled with turmoil, civil strife, and persecutions generated in large part by established sects determined to maintain their absolute political and religious supremacy. With the power of government supporting them, at various times and places, Catholics had persecuted Protestants, Protestants had persecuted Catholics, Protestant sects had persecuted other Protestant sects, Catholics of one shade of belief had persecuted [other Catholics], and all of these had from time to time persecuted Jews. In efforts to force loyalty to whatever religious group happened to be on top and in league with the government of a particular time and place, men and women had been fined, cast in jail, cruelly tortured, and [killed].

"These practices of the old world were transplanted and began to thrive in the soil of the new America. The very charters granted by the English Crown to the individuals and companies designated to make the laws which would control the destinies of the colonials authorized these individuals and companies to erect religious establishments which all, whether believers or nonbelievers, would be required to support and attend. [These] practices became so commonplace as to shock the freedom-loving colonials into a feeling of abhorrence. The imposition of taxes to pay ministers' salaries and to build and maintain churches and church property aroused their indignation. It was these feelings which found expression in the First Amendment. [Virginia provided] able leadership for the movement. The people there, as elsewhere, reached the conviction that individual religious liberty could be achieved best under a government which was stripped of all power to tax, to support, or otherwise to assist any or all religions, or to interfere with the beliefs of any religious individual or group.

"The movement toward this end reached its dramatic climax in Virginia in 1785–86 when the Virginia legislative body was about to renew Virginia's tax levy for the support of the established church. Thomas Jefferson and James Madison led the fight against this tax. Madison wrote his great Memorial and Remonstrance against the law. In it, he eloquently argued that a true religion did not need the support of law; that no person, either believer or non-believer, should be taxed to support a religious institution of any kind; that the best interest of a society required that the minds of men always be wholly free; and that cruel persecutions were the inevitable result of government-established religions. Madison's Remonstrance received strong support throughout Virginia, and [when] the proposed tax measure [came up] for consideration [it] not only died in committee, but the Assembly enacted the famous 'Virginia Bill for Religious Liberty' originally written by Thomas Jefferson.

"The preamble to that Bill stated [that] 'Almighty God hath created the mind free; that all attempts to influence it by temporal punishments or burthens, or by civil incapacitations, tend only to beget habits of hypocrisy and meanness, and are a departure from the plan of the Holy author of our religion, who being Lord both of body and mind, yet chose not to propagate it by coercions on either . . .; that to compel a man to furnish contributions of money for the propagation of opinions which he disbelieves, is sinful and tyrannical; that even the forcing him to support this or that teacher of his own religious persuasion, is depriving him of the comfortable liberty of giving his contributions to the particular pastor, whose morals he would make his [pattern].' The statute itself enacted 'That no man shall be compelled to frequent or support any religious worship, place or ministry whatsoever, nor shall be enforced, restrained, molested, or burthened in his body or goods, nor shall otherwise suffer on account of his religious opinions or [belief].' This Court has previously recognized that the provisions of the First Amendment, in the drafting and adoption of which Madison and Jefferson played such leading roles, had the same objective and were intended to provide the same protection against governmental intrusion on religious liberty as the Virginia statute."

Four justices joined a dissent by Justice RUTLEDGE, disagreeing with the result but agreeing with Justice Black about the history. Justice Rutledge's dissent likewise put heavy emphasis on Madison's Remonstrance: "As the Remonstrance discloses throughout, Madison opposed every form and degree of official relation between religion and civil authority. For him religion was a wholly private matter beyond the scope of civil power either to restrain or to support. Denial or abridgment of religious freedom was a violation of rights both of conscience and of natural equality. State aid was no less obnoxious or destructive to freedom and to religion itself than other forms of state interference. 'Establishment' and 'free exercise' were correlative and coextensive ideas, representing only different facets of the single great and fundamental freedom. The Remonstrance, following the Virginia statute's example, referred to the history of religious conflicts and the effects of all sorts of establishments, current and historical, to suppress religion's free exercise. With Jefferson, Madison believed that to tolerate any fragment of establishment would be by so much to perpetuate restraint upon that freedom. Hence he sought to tear out the institution not partially but root and branch, and to bar its return forever."

Consider the following comment on the Black and Rutledge opinions: "What emerges from the Court's examination of history is a pair of fundamental principles [animating] the first amendment: voluntarism and separatism. [Voluntarism means] that the advancement of a church would come only from the voluntary support of its followers and not from the political support of the state. [Separatism means] that both religion and government function best if each remains independent of the other." Tribe, American Constitutional Law § 14–3 (2d ed. 1988). See also Van Alstyne, "Trends in the Supreme Court: Mr. Jefferson's Crumbling Wall—A Comment on Lynch v. Donnelly," 1984 Duke L.J. 770 ("Voluntarism [was] the principle of personal choice. Separatism was the principle of non-entanglement.").

b. *A minority view: nonpreferentialism.* The historical account set forth in Everson by Justices Black and Rutledge has been relied upon as authoritative in many later decisions. But some dispute that account of the history of the religion clauses. One leading revisionist account suggests that the First Amendment was intended merely to prevent "the establishment of a national church or religion, or the giving of any religious sect or denomination a preferred status," Cord, Separation of Church and State: Historical Fact and Current

Fiction (1982). On this view, government might support religion in general so long is it does not prefer one religion over another.

Several Justices have found the nonpreferentialist view persuasive, though it has never come close to commanding a majority of the Court. For example, in WALLACE v. JAFFREE, 472 U.S. 38 (1985), which invalidated under the establishment clause several Alabama statutes permitting silent prayer or meditation in public schools, Justice REHNQUIST wrote a dissent taking issue with the "wall of separation" metaphor. He read the history to indicate that Madison did not embrace a strict separationist view of the religion clauses at the time the religion clauses were framed. He emphasized that Madison originally proposed constitutional language barring the establishment of a *"national* religion" and argued that this proposal "obviously does not conform to the 'wall of separation' between church and State idea which latter-day commentators have ascribed to him." Justice Rehnquist concluded: "It seems indisputable from [glimpses] of Madison's thinking, as reflected by actions on the floor of the House in 1789, that he saw the Amendment as designed to prohibit the establishment of a national religion, and perhaps to prevent discrimination among sects. He did not see it as requiring neutrality on the part of government between religion and irreligion. Thus the Court's opinion in Everson—while correct in bracketing Madison and Jefferson together in their exertions in their home State leading to the enactment of the Virginia Statute of Religious Liberty—is totally incorrect in suggesting that Madison carried these views onto the floor of the United States House of Representatives when he proposed the language which would ultimately become the Bill of Rights." Justice Rehnquist also noted that the First Congress had provided for financial aid to sectarian schools in the Northwest Territory and for a presidential proclamation and prayer on the Thanksgiving holiday.

Similarly, in ROSENBERGER v. RECTOR, ___ U.S. ___, 115 S.Ct. 2510 (1995), a decision holding that the establishment clause did not bar Virginia from including a religious magazine among the student activities it subsidized, Justice THOMAS found "much to commend" in the view that "the Framers saw the Establishment Clause simply as a prohibition on governmental preferences for some religious faiths over others." He emphasized that the Virginia assessment that Madison opposed in the Remonstrance was a "Bill Establishing a Provision for Teachers of the Christian Religion." Thus, in Justice Thomas' view, "Madison's objection to the assessment bill did not rest on the premise that religious entities may never participate on equal terms in neutral government programs. [Rather, according] to Madison, the Virginia assessment was flawed because it 'violated that equality which ought to be the basis of every law.' [The] bill singled out religious entities for special benefits. [The] funding provided by the Virginia assessment was to be extended only to Christian sects, and the Remonstrance seized on this defect: 'Who does not see that the same authority which can establish Christianity, in exclusion of all other Religions, may establish with the same ease any particular sect of Christians, in exclusion of all other Sects.'" Justice Thomas also cited Justice Rehnquist's Jaffree dissent for evidence of Madison's nonpreferentialism in the House debates on the First Amendment, and cited "historical examples of [public] funding [of religion] that date back to the time of the founding. To take but one famous example, both Houses of the First Congress elected chaplains, [Congress] enacted legislation providing for an annual salary of $500 to be paid out of the Treasury, [and] Madison himself was a member of the committee that recommended the chaplain system in the House."

c.   *Reply to the minority view.* In several opinions, Justice SOUTER has sought to refute the nonpreferentialist arguments made by Justices Rehnquist and Thomas, relying in part upon Laycock, " 'Nonpreferential' Aid to Religion: A False Claim About Original Intent," 27 Wm. & Mary L. Rev. 875 (1986). In his concurrence in LEE v. WEISMAN, 505 U.S. 577 (1992), a case invalidating recitation of a prayer at a middle-school graduation ceremony, Justice SOUTER wrote: "Some have read[] the Establishment Clause to permit 'nonpreferential' state promotion of religion. While a case has been made for this position, [I] find in the history of the Clause's textual development a more powerful argument supporting the Court's jurisprudence following Everson. When James Madison arrived at the First Congress with a series of proposals to amend the National Constitution, one of the provisions read that 'the civil rights of none shall be abridged on account of religious belief or worship, nor shall any national religion be established, nor shall the full and equal rights of conscience be in any manner, or on any pretext, infringed.' Madison's language did not last long. It was [changed] to read that 'no religion shall be established by law, nor shall the equal rights of conscience be infringed' [and then] 'Congress shall make no laws touching religion, or infringing the rights of conscience' [and then] 'Congress shall make no law establishing Religion, or prohibiting the free exercise thereof, nor shall the rights of conscience be infringed.' [The] House [thus] rejected [a] version [that] arguably ensured only that 'no religion' enjoyed an official preference over others, and deliberately chose instead a prohibition extending to laws establishing 'religion' in general.

"[The] Senate's treatment of this House proposal, and the House's response to the Senate, confirm that the Framers meant the Establishment Clause's prohibition to encompass nonpreferential aid to religion. In September 1789, the Senate considered a number of provisions that would have permitted such aid, and ultimately it adopted one [that provided]: 'Congress shall make no law establishing articles of faith or a mode of worship, or prohibiting the free exercise of religion.' The Senate sent this proposal to the House along with its versions of the other constitutional amendments proposed.

"Though it accepted much of the Senate's work on the Bill of Rights, the House rejected the Senate's version of the Establishment Clause and called for a joint conference committee, to which the Senate agreed. The House conferees ultimately won out, persuading the Senate to accept this as the final text of the Religion Clauses: 'Congress shall make no law respecting an establishment of religion, or prohibiting the free exercise thereof.' What is remarkable is that, unlike the earliest House drafts or the final Senate proposal, the prevailing language is not limited to laws respecting an establishment of 'a religion,' 'a national religion,' 'one religious sect,' or specific 'articles of faith.' The Framers repeatedly considered and deliberately rejected such narrow language and instead extended their prohibition to state support for 'religion' in general."

In light of this history, Justice Souter concluded that the nonpreferentialist view could be correct only if " 'the Framers were extraordinarily bad drafters.' " He also rejected a nonpreferentialist interpretation of the Virginia assessment controversy: "The Virginia Statute for Religious Freedom, written by Jefferson and sponsored by Madison, captured the separationist response to [measures providing state support for religion.] Condemning all establishments, however nonpreferentialist, the Statute broadly guaranteed that 'no man shall be compelled to frequent or support any religious worship, place, or ministry whatsoever,' including his own." And he dismissed post-ratification evidence of the founding generation's tolerance of public support of religion: "Although evidence of historical practice can indeed furnish valuable aid in the interpretation of contemporary language, [such acts] prove only that public officials, no matter when they serve, can turn a blind eye to constitutional principle."

In ROSENBERGER v. RECTOR, Justice SOUTER dissented, and likewise reiterated Everson's view of the history. He specifically took issue with Justice Thomas's interpretation of the Virginia assessment controversy: "[It is not] fair to argue that Madison opposed the bill only because it treated religious groups unequally. [Madison] strongly inveighed against the proposed aid for religion for a host of reasons [and] many of those reasons would have applied whether or not the state aid was being distributed equally among sects, and whether or not the aid was going to those sects in the context of an evenhanded government program: [e.g.,] 'In matters of Religion, no man's right is abridged by the institution of Civil Society, and ... Religion is wholly exempt from its cognizance'; ['State] support of religion is a contradiction to the Christian Religion itself; for every page of it disavows a dependence on the powers of this world'; ['Experience] witnesseth that ecclesiastical establishments, instead of maintaining the purity and efficacy of Religion, have had a contrary operation.' [Madison's] Remonstrance did not argue for a bill distributing aid to all sects and religions on an equal basis, and the outgrowth of the Remonstrance and the defeat of the Virginia assessment was not such a bill; rather, it was the Virginia Bill for Establishing Religious Freedom, which [proscribed] the use of tax dollars for religious purposes."

d. *The relevance of original history.* Are the above debates about the original meaning of the religion clauses relevant to their contemporary interpretation? Consider Justice Brennan's concurrence in Abington School Dist. v. Schempp, 374 U.S. 203 (1963), which struck down the practice of Bible-reading in public schools: "A too literal quest for the advice of the Founding Fathers [seems] to me futile and misdirected. [The] historical record is at best ambiguous, and statements can readily be found to support either side of the proposition." Moreover, he added, "Our religious composition makes us a vastly more diverse people than were our forefathers. They knew differences chiefly among Protestant sects. Today the Nation is far more heterogenous religiously."

2. *The incorporation of the religion clauses against the states.* Free exercise of religion, like freedom of speech, is easily understood as the type of "liberty" that might be encompassed by the Fourteenth Amendment and thus applied to the states. The establishment clause presents a more difficult case for incorporation. At the time the First Amendment was adopted, several states, unlike Virginia, had officially established churches. One of the motivations of the establishment clause was arguably to bar Congress from interfering with state establishments. Thus Cord, supra, argues that the First Amendment was meant to "safeguard the right of freedom of conscience in religious beliefs against invasion solely by the national government [but] to allow the states, unimpeded, to deal with religious establishments and aid to religious institutions as they saw fit." See also Howe, The Garden and the Wilderness (1965).

Nonetheless, the Court, beginning with Everson, has assumed that the establishment clause was incorporated into the Fourteenth Amendment and was therefore applicable to the states—without serious discussion of the federalism problem, or the additional textual difficulty of using the "liberty" of the 14th Amendment as the incorporation route. Justice Brennan sought to fill these gaps in his concurrence in Schempp, supra: "It has been suggested, with some support in history, that [incorporation of the establishment clause] is conceptually impossible because the Framers meant the [clause] also to foreclose any attempt by Congress to disestablish the existing official state churches. [But] the last of the formal state establishments was dissolved more than three decades before the Fourteenth Amendment was ratified, and thus the problem of protecting official state churches from federal encroachments could hardly have been any concern of those who framed the post-Civil War Amendments.

"[It] has also been suggested that the 'liberty' guaranteed by the 14th Amendment logically cannot absorb the Establishment Clause because that clause is not one of the provisions of the Bill of Rights which in terms protects a 'freedom' of the individual. The fallacy in this contention [is] that it underestimates the role of the Establishment Clause as a coguarantor, with the Free Exercise Clause, of religious liberty. The Framers did not entrust the liberty of religious beliefs to either clause alone."

3. *Reconciling the religion clauses.* Some commentators have suggested that the two religion clauses can be harmonized by recognizing that "establishment" and "free exercise" serve a single value—protecting the individual's freedom of religious belief and practices, with "free exercise" barring the curbing of that freedom through penalties and "establishment" barring inhibitions on individual choice that arise from governmental aid to religion. Yet viewing the clauses as protecting that single goal does not eliminate the potential tensions. If either the anti-penalties or anti-rewards theme is taken as an absolute, the competing theme will be unduly denigrated: if all penalties are barred, undue benefit to religion may result; if all benefits are barred, undue burdens on religion may be the consequence. Identifying a single "freedom" value, then, does not eliminate the need for accommodation.

Would "neutrality" be a better reconciling theme? Can the religion clauses be read as making the Constitution "religion-blind"? Philip Kurland proposed as the unifying principle that "the freedom and separation clauses should be read as a single precept that government cannot utilize religion as a standard for action or inaction because these clauses prohibit classification in terms of religion either to confer a benefit or to impose a burden." Kurland, "Of Church and State and the Supreme Court," 29 U.Chi.L.Rev. 1 (1961). This view would limit government to secular criteria and would forbid any deliberate accommodation of religion. The Court has never embraced such a strict "neutrality" approach, as the materials below demonstrate. For critical commentary on Kurland's position, see Choper, "The Religion Clauses of the First Amendment: Reconciling the Conflict," 41 U.Pitt.L.Rev. 673 (1980); Pfeffer, "Religion–Blind Government," 15 Stan.L.Rev. 389 (1963).

As another possibility, consider the view that the two clauses might be reconciled by a broad view of permissible accommodation. On this view, free exercise compels some accommodation of religion, establishment forbids other accommodation of religion, and between these two areas lies a broad zone where religious accommodation by government is neither forbidden nor required. This was the view expressed by Justice HARLAN in dissent from SHERBERT v. VERNER, 374 U.S. 398 (1963), which held that free exercise compelled the grant of unemployment benefits to a person who lost her job because she observed Saturday as her sabbath. Justice Harlan expressly noted his disagreement with Kurland that all religious accommodations were forbidden. He viewed a religious exemption from the definition of voluntary unemployment as constitutionally permissible but not compelled: "[There] is, I believe, enough flexibility in the Constitution to permit a legislative judgment accommodating an unemployment compensation law to the exercise of religious beliefs such as appellant's. [But] I cannot subscribe to the conclusion that the State is constitutionally compelled to carve out an exception to its general rule of eligibility in the present case. Those situations in which the Constitution may require special treatment on account of religion are, in my view, few and far between."

4. *The definition of "religion."* How should religion be distinguished from secular moral or philosophical beliefs? From matters of mere personal preference? How should religious organizations be distinguished from other nongovernmental associations commanding significant loyalty and adherence? These questions can be important in delimiting the scope of religious exemptions or in identifying when government benefits constitute establishments.

The Court considered the scope of a statutory definition of "religion" in a series of cases arising in the Vietnam era under draft laws that provided for a conscientious objector exemption. Section 6(j) of the Universal Military Training and Service Act of 1948 exempted from combatant military service those persons who were conscientiously opposed to participation in "war in any form" by reason of their "religious training and belief." The latter phrase was defined by the law as a "belief in a relation to a Supreme Being involving duties superior to those arising from any human relation, but [not including] essentially political, sociological, or philosophical views or a merely personal moral code." (A 1967 amendment deleted the statutory reference to a "belief in a relation to a Supreme Being.")

In UNITED STATES v. SEEGER, 380 U.S. 163 (1965), the Court interpreted the statutory term "religion" very broadly. Seeger stated on his selective service form that he preferred to leave the question about his belief in a Supreme Being "open" and that he believed in "goodness and virtue for their own sakes" and had "a religious faith in a purely ethical creed [without] belief in God, except in the remotest sense." Justice CLARK's opinion for the Court found Seeger entitled to the exemption: "[The] test of belief 'in a relation to a Supreme Being' is whether a given belief that is sincere and meaningful occupies a place in the life of its possessor parallel to that filled by the orthodox belief in God of one who clearly qualifies for the exemption. Where such beliefs have parallel positions in the lives of their respective holders we cannot say that one is 'in a relation to a Supreme Being' and the other is not." Justice Clark emphasized "the richness and variety of spiritual life in our country" and noted the writings of modern theologians, whose definitions of God differed from traditional theism. In a concurring opinion, Justice DOUGLAS stated that he "would have difficulties" if he "read the statute differently" from the Court: "For then those who embraced one religious faith rather than another would be subject to penalties; and that kind of discrimination, as we held in [Sherbert], would violate the Free Exercise Clause [and] would also result in a denial of equal protection by preferring some religions over others."

In WELSH v. UNITED STATES, 398 U.S. 333 (1970), Justice BLACK's plurality opinion, joined by Justices Douglas, Brennan and Marshall, found an exemption appropriate even though Welsh had struck the word "religious" on his application: "[V]ery few registrants are fully aware of the broad scope of the word 'religious' as used in § 6(j)." Moreover, Welsh's claim was not barred by the exclusion in § 6(j) of those persons with "essentially political, sociological, or philosophical views or a merely personal moral code." That language, Justice Black concluded, should not be read "to exclude those who hold strong beliefs about our domestic and foreign affairs or even those whose conscientious objection to participation in all wars is founded to a substantial extent upon considerations of public policy. The two groups of registrants that obviously do fall within these exclusions from the exemption are those whose beliefs are not deeply held and those whose objection to war does not rest at all upon moral, ethical, or religious principle but instead rests solely upon considerations of policy, pragmatism, or expediency." Justice HARLAN, concurring in the result, found that § 6(j) must be read as limited to "those opposed to war in general because of theistic beliefs" but that, so read, was unconstitutional: Congress "cannot draw the line between theistic or nontheistic religious beliefs on the one hand and secular beliefs on the other. Any such distinctions are not, in my view, compatible with the Establishment Clause." He concluded that the Court, rather than nullifying the exemption entirely, should extend its coverage to those who, like Welsh, had been unconstitutionally excluded. Justice WHITE's dissent concluded that, whether or not Seeger was an accurate reflection of legislative intent, he could not join a "construction of § 6(j) extending draft exemption to those who disclaim religious objections to war and whose views about war represent a purely personal code arising not from religious training and belief as the statute requires but from readings in philosophy, history, and sociology." And he would have found that the "religious training and belief" requirement did not violate the establishment clause even were it not required by the free exercise clause: "It is very likely that § 6(j) is a recognition by Congress of free exercise values. [That] judgment is entitled to respect."

The 8–1 decision in GILLETTE v. UNITED STATES, 401 U.S. 437 (1971), held that Congress could constitutionally refuse to exempt those who did not oppose all wars but only particular conflicts. One such selective objector, for example, claimed that it was his duty as a faithful Catholic to discriminate between "just" and "unjust" wars, and to refuse participation in the latter. Justice MARSHALL's majority opinion read the statute to require that "conscientious scruples relating to war and military service must amount to conscientious opposition to participating personally in any war and all war." He found the exemption constitutional as so construed. While "the Establishment Clause forbids subtle departures from neutrality, 'religious gerrymanders,' as well as obvious abuses, [still,] a claimant alleging 'gerrymander' must be able to show the absence of a neutral, secular basis for the lines government has drawn." And that showing had not been made here: "We conclude not only that the affirmative purposes underlying § 6(j) [such as the government's interest in "fairness"] are neutral and secular, but also that valid neutral reasons exist for limiting the exemption to objectors to all war, and that the section therefore cannot be said to reflect a religious preference." He also found the government's interest sufficient to justify any burden on selective objectors' rights of free exercise. Justice DOUGLAS dissented, emphasizing the "implied First Amendment right" of "conscience" and arguing that the law worked "an invidious discrimination in favor of religious persons and against others with like scruples."

What distinguishes a religious pacifist from a pacifist whose beliefs rest only on "essentially political, sociological, or philosophical views or a merely personal moral code"? A belief in a "supreme being"? Why should that matter? Because it suggests a source of countervailing sovereignty to that of the state? A belief in a transcendent reality? A belief that one's activity will have consequences beyond one's lifetime? Participation in rituals such as prayer? Adherence to a sacred text? The fact that one is born into a religious "way of life" rather than acquiring it through individual choice? Doesn't that leave out converts to a faith? A belief that not all questions in the universe can be answered through human rationality? Why should that matter? Because it disables the religionist from participating fully in rationalist political debate? Is a religious exemption a kind of compensation for the disadvantage religious arguments suffer in secular politics? Is any of these features common to all religions?

For commentary on the definition of religion, see, e.g, Choper, "Defining 'Religion' in the First Amendment," 1982 U.Ill.L.Rev. 579 (confining the definition of religious belief to that necessarily involving fear of "extratemporal consequences"); Freeman, "The Misguided Search for the Constitutional Definition of Religion," 71 Geo. L.J. 1519 (1983) (arguing for defining religion by analogy); Greenawalt, "Religion as a Concept in Constitutional Law," 72 Cal.L.Rev. 753 (1984) (same); Note, "Toward a Constitutional Definition of Religion," 91 Harv.L.Rev. 1056 (1978).

Assuming that it is possible to define religion at all, should it be defined the same way for free exercise and establishment purposes? Consider the argument that religion should be defined broadly for free exercise but narrowly for establishment clause purposes. See Tribe, American Constitutional Law § 14–6 (1st ed. 1978). Such an approach would allow broad religious exemptions, but would not jeopardize every government action that reflects some arguably religious precept. Thus, for example, Mr. Seeger might receive his draft exemption on the ground that his pacifist beliefs were adequately "religious" for that purpose, but then teach his beliefs in a public school classroom without running afoul of the establishment clause. But a dual definition of religion "presents a number of problems, most importantly the first amendment's text." Tribe, American Constitutional Law § 14–6 (2d ed. 1988) (retreating from his earlier approach). As Justice Rutledge wrote in his Everson dissent, " 'Religion' appears only once in the Amendment. But the word governs two prohibitions and governs them alike. It does not have two meanings." Might the Seeger problem above be solved not by defining "religion" narrowly for establishment clause purposes, but rather by defining narrowly what constitutes an "establishment"?

5. *The limits of judicial inquiry into religious content.* Why insist on an objective definition of religion? Why not allow religion to be subjectively defined by its adherents? One danger is that such a definition might invite fraud, and create the problem of religious "impostors." It might also expand the definition of religion so greatly that courts would respond by curtailing the substantive scope of free exercise protection. On the other hand, secular inquiry into the truth or falsity of religious beliefs would appear to be a core violation of free exercise. The Court tried to steer between these difficulties in UNITED STATES v. BALLARD, 322 U.S. 78 (1944). The defendants in Ballard were indicted under the federal mail fraud laws. They had solicited funds for the "I Am" movement. Among their representations were the claims that they had been selected as "divine messengers" to communicate the message of the "alleged divine entity, Saint Germain" and that they had, "by reason of supernatural attainments, the power to heal persons of ailments and diseases." Justice DOUGLAS' majority opinion stated that the First Amendment barred submission to the jury of "the truth or verity of respondents' religious doctrines or beliefs," though it did not bar submission to the jury of the question whether the defendants sincerely believed their representations. He commented: "Men may believe what they cannot prove. They may not be put to the proof of their religious doctrines or beliefs. [The] miracles of the New Testament, the Divinity of Christ, life after death, the power of prayer are deep in the religious convictions of many. If one could be sent to jail because a jury in a hostile environment found those teachings false, little indeed would be left of religious freedom."

Is the Court's resolution of the difficulty here satisfactory? Can a jury find that defendants knew that their representations were false *without* inquiring into the truth or falsity of the underlying beliefs? Justice JACKSON, dissenting, expressed doubt whether the "sincerity" of beliefs can be examined without treading on the forbidden area of their content: "I do not see how we can separate an issue as to what is believed from considerations as to what is believable." Chief Justice Stone also dissented, joined by Justices Roberts and Frankfurter.

Another source of controversy regarding judicial power to decide questions of religious doctrine has been the recurrent effort to draw courts into disputes arising from church schisms. The normal rule is that courts should try to stay out of internal church disputes. But "marginal judicial involvement" is permissible, so long as the courts do not decide church property disputes by "resolving underlying controversies [of] religious doctrine." The Court has said that courts may apply "[n]eutral principles of law, developed for use in all property disputes," in adjudicating church property controversies, but that the religion clauses preclude determining matters "at the very core of a religion—the interpretation of particular church doctrines and the importance of those doctrines to religion." See Presbyterian Church v. Hull Church, 393 U.S. 440 (1969). The Court has been sharply divided over the application of these guidelines. See, e.g., Jones v. Wolf, 443 U.S. 595 (1979).

SECTION 2. THE FREE EXERCISE OF RELIGION

Introduction. To some extent, claims based on the free exercise of religion overlap with free speech claims. For example, recall the free speech objections raised by members of Jehovah's Witnesses in cases such as Cantwell v. Connecticut, Lovell v. Griffin, Martin v. Struthers, and Wooley v. Maynard. But the "free exercise" guarantee raises distinctive problems. *First*, "exercise" implies more than belief or expression; it often implies conduct or action. In many of the cases that follow, the free exercise claimant argues that a general law resting on state interests not related to religion either interferes with behavior dictated by religious belief or compels conduct forbidden by religious belief. Should government have more leeway to regulate conduct than belief? *Second*, the establishment clause has no parallel in the speech clause. In the religion context, however, it places limits on how far either legislatures or courts can go in exempting religious believers from general regulations, or otherwise accommodating free exercise values. The free exercise cases that follow look first at the question whether government may deliberately disadvantage religion or a particular religion, and second at whether religious practitioners are entitled to exemptions from generally applicable laws that conflict with dictates of their faith.

A. LAWS DISCRIMINATING AGAINST RELIGION

Free exercise clearly bars outlawing or compelling *belief* in a particular religious faith. As Chief Justice Burger stated in McDaniel v. Paty, see below, "The Free Exercise Clause categorically prohibits government from regulating, prohibiting, or rewarding religious beliefs as such." Perhaps because this principle is so basic, free exercise controversies over such attempts at thought control are rare. In TORCASO v. WATKINS, 367 U.S. 488 (1961), the Court struck down a Maryland requirement that all holders of public office declare their belief in the existence of God. The decision stated: "Neither the State nor the Federal Government can constitutionally force a person 'to profess a belief or disbelief in any religion,'" nor could they "aid those religions based on a belief in the existence of God as against those religions founded on different beliefs." Torcaso rested principally on the free exercise clause, but also noted by way of analogy the religious test clause of Article VI: "[N]o religious Test shall ever be required as a Qualification to any Office or public Trust under the United States."

In McDANIEL v. PATY, 435 U.S. 618 (1978), the Court invalidated, under the free exercise clause, a Tennessee provision disqualifying clergy from being legislators or constitutional convention delegates. (Tennessee was the last state to retain the disqualification, once commonplace in state laws.) Chief Justice BURGER's plurality opinion, joined by Justices Powell, Rehnquist and Stevens, found the absolute bar on interference with religious *beliefs* inapplicable, because the state barrier referred to "*status* [as] 'minister' or 'priest'" and ministerial status was "defined in terms of conduct and activity rather [than] belief." The plurality nonetheless applied strict scrutiny to the disqualification's burden on religious practice, and found the State's "preventing-establishment-of-religion" rationale inadequate to support the ban: "[T]he American experience provides no persuasive support for the fear that clergymen in public office will be less careful of anti-establishment interests or less faithful to their oaths of civil office than their unordained counterparts." Separate concurrences by Justice BRENNAN, joined by Justice Marshall, and by Justice STEWART found that the disqualification did directly burden religious belief and thus was absolutely prohibited under Torcaso, without any further balancing. Justice Brennan wrote: "Clearly freedom of belief protected by the Free Exercise Clause embraces freedom to profess or practice that belief, even including doing so to earn a livelihood." Justice Stewart wrote: "The disability imposed on McDaniel, like the one imposed on Torcaso, implicates the 'freedom to believe' more than the less absolute 'freedom to act.'" (Note that both Torcaso and McDaniel rejected the government's argument that a public job or office is a mere "privilege" to which the state may attach conditions that would otherwise violate the First Amendment. Recall the Pickering and Speiser lines of cases covered in Chapter 12.)

Free exercise challenges arise more commonly when laws regulate religious practice or conduct. While previous eras have witnessed various forms of overt discrimination against disfavored religions, modern legislation rarely evinces outright hostility to particular religions or religious practices. Like overt racial bigotry, overt religious prejudice rarely appears on the face of contemporary laws. The Court has proved willing, however, to look behind the face of a statute to discern religiously discriminatory purpose, as illustrated in the Lukumi case, which follows. In Lukumi, the Court unanimously invalidated a city ordinance prohibiting the ritual slaughter of animals, finding that the law, while apparently neutral on its face, actually was targeted against practitioners of the Santeria faith and thus violated the free exercise clause.

Church of the Lukumi Babalu Aye v. City of Hialeah

508 U.S. 520, 113 S.Ct. 2217, 124 L.Ed.2d 472 (1993).

Justice KENNEDY delivered the opinion of the Court, except as to Part II–A–2.

[This] case involves practices of the Santeria religion, which originated in the nineteenth century. When hundreds of thousands of members of the Yoruba people were brought as slaves from eastern Africa to Cuba, their traditional African religion absorbed significant elements of Roman Catholicism. The resulting syncretion, or fusion, is Santeria, "the way of the saints." The Cuban Yoruba express their devotion to spirits, called orishas. [The] Santeria faith teaches that every individual has a destiny from God, a destiny fulfilled with the aid and energy of the orishas. The basis of the Santeria religion is the nurture of a personal relation with the orishas, and one of the principal forms of devotion is an animal sacrifice. [According] to Santeria teaching, the orishas are powerful but not immortal. They depend for survival on the sacrifice. Sacrifices are performed at birth, marriage, and death rites, for the cure of the sick, for the initiation of new members and priests, and during an annual celebration. Animals sacrificed in Santeria rituals include chickens, pigeons, doves, ducks, guinea pigs, goats, sheep, and turtles. The animals are killed by the cutting of the carotid arteries in the neck. The sacrificed animal is cooked and eaten, except after healing and death rituals. Santeria adherents faced widespread persecution in Cuba, so the religion and its rituals were practiced in secret. The open practice of Santeria and its rites remains infrequent.

[The Church's] announcement of plans to open a Santeria church in Hialeah prompted the city council to hold an emergency public session on June 9, 1987. [The] city council adopted Resolution 87–66, which noted the "concern" expressed by residents of the city "that certain religions may propose to engage in practices which are inconsistent with public morals, peace or safety," and declared that "the City reiterates its commitment to a prohibition against any and all acts of any and all religious groups which are inconsistent with public morals, peace or safety." [In] September 1987, the city council adopted three substantive ordinances addressing the issue of religious animal sacrifice. Ordinance 87–52 defined "sacrifice" as "to unnecessarily kill, torment, torture, or mutilate an animal in a public or private ritual or ceremony not for the primary purpose of food consumption," and prohibited owning or possessing an animal "intending to use such animal for food purposes." It restricted application of this prohibition, however, to any individual or group that "kills, slaughters or sacrifices animals for any type of ritual, regardless of whether or not the flesh or blood of the animal is to be consumed." The ordinance contained an exemption for slaughtering by "licensed establishments" of animals "specifically raised for food purposes." [Ordinance] 87–71 [defined] sacrifice as had Ordinance 87–52, and then provided that "it shall be unlawful for any person, persons, corporations or associations to sacrifice any animal within the corporate limits of the City of Hialeah, Florida." The final Ordinance, 87–72, defined "slaughter" as "the killing of animals for food" and prohibited slaughter outside of areas zoned for slaughterhouse use. The ordinance provided an exemption, however, for the slaughter or processing for sale of "small numbers of hogs and/or cattle per week in accordance with an exemption provided by state law." All ordinances and resolutions passed the city council by unanimous vote. Violations [were] punishable by fines not exceeding $500 or imprisonment not exceeding 60 days, or both.

[At] a minimum, the protections of the Free Exercise Clause pertain if the law at issue discriminates against some or all religious beliefs or regulates or prohibits conduct because it is undertaken for religious reasons. Indeed, it was "historical instances of religious persecution and intolerance that gave concern to those who drafted the Free Exercise Clause." These principles, though not often at issue in our Free Exercise Clause cases, have played a role in some. [See, e.g, McDaniel v. Paty.]

[If] the object of a law is to infringe upon or restrict practices because of their religious motivation, the law is not neutral; and it is invalid unless it is justified by a compelling interest and is narrowly tailored to advance that interest. To determine the object of a law, we must begin with its text, for the minimum requirement of neutrality is that a law not discriminate on its face. [Petitioners] contend that three of the ordinances fail this test of facial neutrality because they use the words "sacrifice" and "ritual," words with strong religious connotations. We agree that these words are consistent with the claim of facial discrimination, but the argument is not conclusive. The words "sacrifice" and "ritual" have a religious origin, but current use admits also of secular meanings. [But] facial neutrality is not determinative. [The] Free Exercise Clause protects against governmental hostility which is masked, as well as overt.

[The] record in this case compels the conclusion that suppression of the central element of the Santeria worship service was the object of the ordinances. [The June 9 resolution aimed at] "certain religions" [and] it cannot be maintained that city officials had in mind a religion other than Santeria. It is [also] a necessary conclusion that almost the only conduct subject to Ordinances 87–40, 87–52, and 87–71 is the religious exercise of Santeria church members. [Ordinance] 87–71 excludes almost all killings of animals except for religious sacrifice, and the primary purpose requirement narrows the proscribed category even further, in particular by exempting Kosher slaughter. Operating in similar fashion is Ordinance 87–52, which prohibits the "possession, sacrifice, or slaughter" of an animal with the "intent to use such animal for food purposes" [but exempts] "any licensed [food] establishment" with regard to "any animals which are specifically raised for food purposes," if the activity is permitted by zoning and other laws. This exception, too, seems intended to cover Kosher slaughter. [Ordinance] 87–40 incorporates the Florida animal cruelty statute. Its prohibition is broad on its face, punishing "whoever ... unnecessarily ... kills any animal." The city claims that this ordinance is the epitome of a neutral prohibition. [But the city] deem[s] [k]illings for religious reasons [unnecessary but] deems hunting, slaughter of animals for food, eradication of insects and pests, and euthanasia as necessary. [The city's] application of the ordinance's test of necessity devalues religious reasons for killing by judging them to be of lesser import than nonreligious reasons. Thus, religious practice is being singled out for discriminatory treatment.

[The] legitimate governmental interests in protecting the public health and preventing cruelty to animals could be addressed by restrictions stopping far short of a flat prohibition of all Santeria sacrificial practice. [Counsel] for the city conceded at oral argument that, under the ordinances, Santeria sacrifices would be illegal even if they occurred in licensed, inspected, and zoned slaughterhouses. [With] regard to the city's interest in ensuring the adequate care of animals, regulation of conditions and treatment, regardless of why an animal is kept, is the logical response to the city's concern, not a prohibition on possession for the purpose of sacrifice.

[In part II–A–2 of Justice Kennedy's opinion, which was joined only by Justices Stevens, Blackmun and O'Connor, he added: "In determining if the object of a law is a neutral one under the Free Exercise Clause, we can also find guidance in our equal protection cases. [Here], as in equal protection cases, we may determine the city council's object from both direct and circumstantial evidence. [Arlington Heights.] [The] minutes and taped excerpts of the June 9 session, both of which are in the record, evidence significant hostility exhibited by residents, members of the city council, and other city officials toward the Santeria religion and its practice of animal sacrifice. The public crowd that attended the June 9 meetings interrupted statements by council members critical of Santeria with cheers and the brief comments of [the Church's leader] with taunts. When [a council member supporting the ordinances] stated that in prerevolution Cuba 'people were put in jail for practicing this religion,' the audience applauded. [One council member said that the] 'Bible says we are allowed to sacrifice an animal for consumption,' [and] continued, 'but for any other purposes, I don't believe that the Bible allows that.' [The] chaplain of the Hialeah Police Department told the city council that Santeria was a sin, 'foolishness,' 'an abomination to the Lord,' and the worship of 'demons.' [This] history discloses the object of the ordinances to target animal sacrifice by Santeria worshippers because of its religious motivation." Resuming his opinion for the Court, Justice Kennedy continued:]

In sum, [the] ordinances had as their object the suppression of religion. The pattern we have recited discloses animosity to Santeria adherents and their religious practices; the ordinances by their own terms target this religious exercise; the texts of the ordinances were gerrymandered with care to proscribe religious killings of animals but to exclude almost all secular killings; and the ordinances suppress much more religious conduct than is necessary in order to achieve the legitimate ends asserted in their defense.

[A] law burdening religious practice that is not neutral or not of general application must undergo the most rigorous of scrutiny. [It] follows from what we have already said that these ordinances cannot withstand this scrutiny. First, even were the governmental interests compelling, [all] four ordinances are overbroad or underinclusive. [The] absence of narrow tailoring suffices to establish the invalidity of the ordinances. [Moreover,] [w]here government restricts only conduct protected by the First Amendment and fails to enact feasible measures to restrict other conduct producing substantial harm or alleged harm of the same sort, the interest given in justification of the restriction is not compelling.

[Reversed.]

Justice SCALIA, joined by Chief Justice REHNQUIST, concurring in part and concurring the in the judgment.

I do not join [part II–A–2] because it departs from the opinion's general focus on the object of the laws at issue to consider the subjective motivation of the lawmakers, i.e., whether the Hialeah City Council actually intended to disfavor the religion of Santeria. [But] it is virtually impossible to determine the singular "motive" of a collective legislative body, and this Court has a long tradition of refraining from such inquiries. [The] First Amendment does not refer to the purposes for which legislators enact laws, but to the effects of the laws enacted: "Congress shall make no law ... prohibiting the free exercise [of religion].... " This does not put us in the business of invalidating laws by reason of the evil motives of their authors. Had the Hialeah City Council set out resolutely to suppress the practices of Santeria, but ineptly adopted ordinances that failed to do so, I do not see how those laws could be said to "prohibit the free exercise" of religion. Nor, in my view, does it matter that a legislature consists entirely of the pure-hearted, if the law it enacts in fact singles out a religious practice for special burdens. Had the ordinances here been passed with no motive on the part of any councilman except the ardent desire to prevent cruelty to animals (as might in fact have been the case), they would nonetheless be invalid.

[Justice SOUTER filed an opinion concurring in part and in the judgment and Justice BLACKMUN, joined by Justice O'Connor, filed an opinion concurring in the judgment. Both these opinions found this an easy case for invalidation, reasoning that, in Justice Souter's words, Hialeah had enacted "a rare example of a law actually aimed at suppressing religious exercise," and that such a law is nearly always invalid. Justices Souter and Blackmun declined to join all of Justice Kennedy's opinion, however, because it referred in dictum to aspects of the test set forth in Employment Division v. Smith, see p. 1489 below, that they found objectionable.]

LUKUMI AND RELIGIOUS GERRYMANDERS

Justice Kennedy called the law in Lukumi a "religious gerrymander"—that is, "an impermissible attempt to target petitioners and their religious practices." Hialeah's law was struck down under the Free Exercise clause. But the Court has also struck down "religious gerrymanders" under the Establishment Clause. For example, in LARSON v. VALENTE, 456 U.S. 228 (1982), the Court struck down a Minnesota law imposing registration and reporting requirements for charitable solicitations and excepting some, but not all, religious organizations from the law. The requirements applied only to religious organizations that solicit more than 50% of their funds from nonmembers. The Court found that this scheme violated the "clearest command of the Establishment Clause": "one religious denomination cannot be officially preferred over another." The law was challenged by the Unification Church, which consists of followers of Rev. Sun Myung Moon, on the ground that it preferred traditional over untraditional religions.

In invalidating the 50% rule, Justice BRENNAN's majority opinion applied strict scrutiny and found the law not closely tailored to any government interest in preventing fraudulent or abusive solicitation practices. He emphasized Minnesota's "*selective* legislative imposition of burdens and advantages upon particular denominations," noting that "the provision was drafted with the explicit intention of including particular religious denominations and excluding others. One state senator observed that other lawmakers seemed to have a religious animus toward groups that were included, stating, " 'I'm not sure why we're so hot to regulate the Moonies anyway.' " By contrast, an earlier version of the law was eliminated when "the legislators perceived that [it] would bring a Roman Catholic Archdiocese within the Act." Justice Brennan found that the 50% rule's capacity "—indeed, its express design—to burden or favor selected religious denominations led the Minnesota Legislature to discuss the characteristics of various sects with a view towards 'religious gerrymandering.' "

Note that Larson, like Lukumi, looked behind the facial neutrality of the law to discern a religiously discriminatory purpose. Why was Larson litigated under the establishment rather than the free exercise clause? Because its selective favoritism toward mainstream religions was more apparent than its selective burdens on unorthodox ones? Because the selective burdens did not fall upon practices central to the free exercise of the Unification faith? Was animal sacrifice more central to Santeria practitioners than solicitation was to Unification Church members? Is solicitation an aspect of the free exercise of religion at all? Should prosecutors, juries and judges be entrusted with deciding such questions?

Conversely, why was Lukumi litigated as a free exercise rather than an establishment case? Justice Kennedy noted several times Hialeah's careful exemption of the kosher slaughter practices used by Orthodox Jews. Did such exemptions create religious favoritism in violation of the establishment clause? Justice Kennedy expressly declined to reach that issue in Lukumi: "We need not discuss whether [the] differential treatment of two religions is itself an independent constitutional violation. Cf. Larson v. Valente. It suffices to recite this feature of the law as support for our conclusion that Santeria alone was the exclusive legislative concern." Does it seem implausible to imagine that Hialeah had "established" Orthodox Judaism, itself a minority faith? The Court has suggested that religious favoritism might violate the establishment clause whether it favors mainstream or minority faiths. See the Kiryas Joel case, p. 1551 below.

————

B. NEUTRAL LAWS ADVERSELY AFFECTING RELIGION: ARE RELIGIOUS EXEMPTIONS CONSTITUTIONALLY COMPELLED?

————

The religiously discriminatory law in Lukumi was unusual. Free exercise claims are more commonly raised against facially neutral laws that are not targeted at a religious practice, but which have a disproportionately adverse impact on religious practitioners. Such laws might either require conduct that is incompatible with religious practice or forbid conduct that is religiously required. The free exercise claimant typically seeks exemption from, not invalidation of the law.

The Court's first major decision on free exercise exemptions was REYNOLDS v. UNITED STATES, 98 U.S. 145 (1878), which upheld application of a federal law making bigamy a crime in the territories to a Mormon claiming that polygamy was his religious duty. As Chief Justice WAITE read the First Amendment, "Congress was deprived of all legislative power over mere opinion, but was left free to reach actions which were in violation of social duties or subversive of good order." He reviewed the traditional condemnation of multiple marriages in modern western society, and cited studies suggesting that "polygamy leads to the patriarchal principle, which, when applied to large communities, fetters the people in stationary despotism, while that principle cannot long exist in connection with monogamy." He concluded: "Laws are made for the government of actions, and while they cannot interfere with mere religious belief and opinions, they may with practices. Suppose one believed that human sacrifices were a necessary part of religious worship, would it be seriously contended that the civil government under which he lived could not interfere to prevent a sacrifice? Or if a wife religiously believed it was her duty to burn herself upon the funeral pile of her dead husband, would it be beyond the power of the civil government to prevent her carrying her belief into practice? So here, as a law of the organization of society under the exclusive dominion of the United States, it is provided that plural marriages shall not be allowed. Can a man excuse his practices to the contrary because of his religious belief? To permit this would be to make the professed doctrines of religious belief superior to the law of the land, and in effect to permit every citizen to become a law unto himself. Government could exist only in name under such circumstances."

CANTWELL v. CONNECTICUT, 310 U.S. 296 (1940), see p. 1076 above, modified Reynolds' belief-action distinction somewhat, suggesting that religious conduct was not wholly outside the protection of the free exercise clause, even if it was subject to greater regulation than belief. Justice ROBERTS wrote: "[Free exercise] embraces two concepts,—freedom to believe and freedom to act. The first is absolute, but in the nature of things, the second cannot be. [In] every case the power to regulate must be so exercised as not, in attaining a permissible end, unduly to infringe the protected freedom." Still, the Court continued to uphold regulations of conduct that adversely affected religionists. For example, PRINCE v. MASSACHUSETTS, 321 U.S. 158 (1944), upheld a law making it a crime for a child under 18 to sell any newspapers, periodicals or merchandise in public places even as applied to a child of Jehovah's Witnesses, whose faith viewed it as a religious duty to perform such work.

And in BRAUNFELD v. BROWN, 366 U.S. 599 (1961), the Court rejected a free exercise challenge to a Pennsylvania Sunday closing law. The challengers were Orthodox Jews whose religion required that they close their stores on Saturdays. They alleged that the Sunday closing laws would place them at such a severe competitive disadvantage as to force them out of business. Chief Justice WARREN's plurality opinion, joined by Justices Black, Clark and Whittaker, rejected the free exercise challenge. Citing Reynolds and Cantwell, he emphasized that, unlike the freedom to hold religious beliefs and opinions, the "freedom to act, even when the action is in accord with one's religious convictions, is not totally free from legislative restrictions." He added that the law here did not "make criminal the holding of any religious belief or opinion, nor force anyone to embrace any religious belief. [It simply made] the practice of their religious beliefs more expensive. To strike down [legislation] which imposes only an indirect burden on the exercise of religion, i.e., legislation which does not make unlawful the religious practice itself, would radically restrict the operating latitude of the [legislature]. We are a cosmopolitan nation made up of people of almost every conceivable religious preference. [Consequently,] it cannot be expected, much less required, that legislators enact no law regulating conduct that may in some way result in an economic disadvantage to some religious sects and not to others because of the special practices of the various religions. [If] the State regulates conduct by enacting a general law within its power, the purpose and effect of which is to advance the State's secular goals, the statute is valid despite its indirect burden on religious observance unless the State may accomplish its purpose by means which do not impose such a burden.

"As we pointed out in [McGowan v. Maryland, 1961; p. 1519 below, rejecting an establishment clause challenge to Sunday closing laws], we cannot find a State without power to provide a weekly respite from all labor and, at the same time, to set one day of the week apart from the others as a day of rest, repose, recreation and tranquility. [To] permit the exemption [sought by the challengers] might well undermine the State's goal of providing a day that, as best possible, eliminates the atmosphere of commercial noise and activity. [E]nforcement problems would be more difficult [and Saturday observers] might well [receive] an economic advantage over their competitors who must remain closed on that day. [Competitors might] assert that they have religious convictions which compel them to close their businesses on what had formerly been their least profitable day. This might make necessary a state-conducted inquiry into the sincerity of the individual's religious beliefs, a practice which a State might believe would itself run afoul of the spirit of constitutionally protected religious guarantees." Justice Frankfurter, joined by Justice Harlan, also rejected the free exercise claim in a separate opinion.

Justice BRENNAN's dissent argued that the law violated the free exercise clause because it "put an individual to a choice between his business and his religion." He argued that the state's interest was "the mere convenience of having everyone rest on the same day. It is to defend this interest that the Court holds that a State need not follow the alternative route of granting an exemption for those who in good faith observe a day of rest other than Sunday. [The Court] conjures up several difficulties with such a system which seem to me more fanciful than real. [The] Court [has] exalted administrative convenience to a constitutional level high enough to justify making one religion economically disadvantageous." Justices Stewart and Douglas also dissented.

Compare with the decision in Braunfeld the Court's decision in the following case, which held that a state must pay unemployment benefits to a Saturday sabbatarian.

———

Sherbert v. Verner

374 U.S. 398, 83 S.Ct. 1790, 10 L.Ed.2d 965 (1963).

Justice BRENNAN delivered the opinion of the [Court].

[Appellant, a Seventh-day Adventist, was discharged by her employer "because she would not work on Saturday, the Sabbath Day of her faith." She was unable to obtain other employment because she would not take Saturday work. Her claim for South Carolina state unemployment compensation was denied because the state compensation law barred benefits to workers who failed, without good cause, to accept "suitable work when offered." The highest state court sustained the denial of benefits.]

[If the state decision is to stand] it must be either because her disqualification as a beneficiary represents no infringement by the State of her constitutional rights of free exercise; or because any incidental burden on the free exercise of appellant's religion may be justified by a "compelling state interest in the regulation of a subject within the State's constitutional power to regulate." NAACP v. Button [p. 1383 above]. We turn first to the question whether the disqualification for benefits imposes any burden on the free exercise of appellant's religion. We think it is clear that it does. In a sense the consequences of such a disqualification to religious principles and practices may be only an indirect result of welfare legislation within the State's general competence to enact; it is true that no criminal sanctions directly compel appellant to work a six-day week. But this is only the beginning, not the end, of our inquiry. [Here] not only is it apparent that appellant's declared ineligibility for benefits solely derives from the practice of her religion, but the pressure upon her to forego that practice is unmistakable. The ruling forces her to choose between following the precepts of her religion and forfeiting benefits, on the one hand, and abandoning one of the precepts of her religion in order to accept work, on the other hand. Governmental imposition of such a choice puts the same kind of burden upon the free exercise of religion as would a fine imposed against appellant for her Saturday worship.

[We] must next consider whether some compelling state interest [justifies] the substantial infringement of appellant's First Amendment right. [The] appellees suggest no more than a possibility that the filing of fraudulent claims by unscrupulous claimants feigning religious objections to Saturday work might not only dilute the unemployment compensation fund but also hinder the scheduling by employers of necessary Saturday work. [But] no such objection appears to have been made before the [state courts, and] there is no proof whatever to warrant such fears of malingering or deceit. [Even if] there were such risks, it would plainly be incumbent upon the appellees to demonstrate that no alternative forms of regulation would combat such abuses without infringing First Amendment rights. In these respects, then, the state interest asserted in the present case is wholly dissimilar to the interests which were found to justify the less direct burden upon religious practices in [Braunfeld]. [That statute was] saved by a countervailing factor which finds no equivalent in the instant case—a strong state interest in providing one uniform day of rest for all workers. That secular objective could be achieved, the Court found, only by declaring Sunday to be that day of rest. [Here] no such justifications underlie the determination of the state court that appellant's religion makes her ineligible to receive [benefits].

In holding as we do, plainly we are not fostering the "establishment" of the Seventh-day Adventist religion in South Carolina, for the extension of unemployment benefits to Sabbatarians in common with Sunday worshippers reflects nothing more than the governmental obligation of neutrality in the face of religious differences, and does not represent that involvement of religious with secular institutions which it is the object of the Establishment Clause to forestall. [Schempp.] [Nor] do we, by our decision today, declare the existence of a constitutional right to unemployment benefits on the part of all persons whose religious convictions are the cause of their unemployment. This is not a case in which an employee's religious convictions serve to make him a nonproductive member of society. [Our] holding today is only that South Carolina may not constitutionally apply the eligibility provisions so as to constrain a worker to abandon his religious convictions respecting the [day of rest].

[Reversed and remanded.] [Justice Douglas filed a concurrence.]

Justice STEWART, concurring in the result.

[I] think that the guarantee of religious liberty embodied in the Free Exercise Clause affirmatively requires government to create an atmosphere of hospitality and accommodation to individual belief or disbelief. [Yet] in cases decided under the Establishment Clause the Court [has] decreed that government must blind itself to the differing religious beliefs and traditions of the people. With all respect, I think it is the Court's duty to face up to the dilemma posed by the conflict between the [religion clauses].

[I] cannot agree that today's decision can stand consistently with [Braunfeld]. The Court says that there was a "less direct burden upon religious practices" in that case than in this. With all respect, I think the Court is mistaken simply as a matter of fact. The Braunfeld case involved a *criminal* statute [and a drastic impact on the challenger's business]. The impact upon the appellant's religious freedom in the present case is considerably less onerous [than in Braunfeld]. Even upon the unlikely assumption that the appellant could not find suitable non-Saturday employment, the appellant at the worst would be denied a maximum of 22 weeks of compensation payments. I agree with the Court that the possibility of that denial is enough to infringe upon the appellant's constitutional right to the free exercise of her religion. But it is clear to me that in order to reach this conclusion the Court must explicitly reject the reasoning of [Braunfeld]. I think [Braunfeld] was wrongly decided and should be overruled, and accordingly I concur in the result [here].

Justice HARLAN, whom Justice WHITE joins, dissenting.

[In] no proper sense can it be said that the State discriminated against the appellant on the basis of her religious beliefs or that she was denied benefits *because* she was a Seventh-day Adventist. She was denied benefits just as any other claimant would be denied benefits who was not "available for work" for personal reasons. With this background, this Court's decision comes into clearer focus. What the Court is holding is that if the State chooses to condition unemployment compensation on the applicant's availability for work, it is constitutionally compelled to *carve out an exception*—and to provide benefits—for those whose unavailability is due to their religious convictions. Such a holding has particular significance in two respects.

First, despite the Court's protestations to the contrary, the decision necessarily overrules [Braunfeld]. Clearly, any differences between this case and Braunfeld cut against the present appellant. *Second,* the implications of the present decision are far more troublesome than its apparently narrow dimensions would indicate at first glance. [The meaning of the holding is that the State] must *single out* for financial assistance those whose behavior is religiously motivated, even though it denies such assistance to others whose identical behavior [is] not religiously motivated. It has been suggested that such singling out of religious conduct for special treatment may violate the constitutional limitations on state action. See Kurland, "Of Church and State and the Supreme Court," 29 U.Chi.L.Rev. 1 (1961). My own view, however, is that at least under the circumstances of this case it would be a permissible accommodation of religion for the State, if it *chose* to do so, to create an exception to its eligibility requirements for persons like the appellant. The constitutional obligation of "neutrality" is not so narrow a channel that the slightest deviation from an absolutely straight course leads to condemnation. [There is] enough flexibility in the Constitution to permit a legislative judgment accommodating an unemployment compensation law to the exercise of religious beliefs such as appellant's. [I] cannot subscribe to the conclusion that the State is constitutionally *compelled* to carve out an exception to its general rule of eligibility in the present case. Those situations in which the Constitution may require special treatment on account of religion are, in my view, few and far between. [Such] compulsion in the present case is particularly inappropriate in light of the indirect, remote, and insubstantial effect of the decision below on the exercise of appellant's religion and in light of the direct financial assistance to religion that today's decision [requires].

FREE EXERCISE EXEMPTIONS FROM SHERBERT TO SMITH

In the wake of Sherbert, religious objectors to general regulations repeatedly came to the Court, invoking Sherbert's strict scrutiny in claiming constitutionally mandated exemptions. Although the Court typically adhered to the Sherbert analysis in form, it quite frequently rejected the religious objectors' claims in fact. The major cases in which the free exercise claims succeeded were a number of decisions in the unemployment compensation context of Sherbert (note 1, below), and a ruling in the education setting, Wisconsin v. Yoder (note 2, below). In other cases, the Court, despite frequent lip service to Sherbert's strict scrutiny standard, in fact exercised a quite deferential variety of review and accordingly refused to carve out exemptions from general regulations.

1. *Unemployment compensation cases after Sherbert.* THOMAS v. RE-VIEW BOARD, 450 U.S. 707 (1981), a case factually very close to Sherbert, relied on it to strike down Indiana's denial of unemployment compensation to a Jehovah's Witness who quit his job in a munitions factory because of his religious objections to war. A state court upheld the denial of compensation,

because the law denied compensation to all employees who voluntarily left employment for personal reasons without good cause. Chief Justice Burger's majority opinion, however, found the coercive impact here "indistinguishable from Sherbert" and rejected an argument that the grant of benefits to the employee would violate the Establishment Clause. Justice Rehnquist was the sole dissenter, insisting that majority had read free exercise "too broadly" and had failed "to squarely acknowledge that such a reading conflicts with many of our Establishment Clause cases." He urged that Sherbert be overruled. HOBBIE v. UNEMPLOYMENT APPEALS COMM'N, 480 U.S. 136 (1987), likewise followed Sherbert in upholding the unemployment compensation claim of an employee whose religious beliefs had changed during the course of her employment. And in FRAZEE v. ILLINOIS EMPLOYMENT SECURITY DEPT., 489 U.S. 829 (1989), Sherbert, Thomas, and Hobbie were applied to an applicant whose refusal to accept employment that required that he work on Sunday was not based on his membership in "an established sect or church," but only on his claim that "as a Christian, he could not work on the 'Lord's Day.' " Justice White's opinion for a unanimous Court found Frazee's lack of membership in a particular sect irrelevant, since there was no question that his belief was both sincere and religious in nature.

2. *Compulsory education laws.* In WISCONSIN v. YODER, 406 U.S. 205 (1972), Yoder, a member of the Old Order Amish, was convicted and fined $5 for refusing to send his 15–year-old daughter to school after she had completed the eighth grade, in violation of Wisconsin's requirement of school attendance until age sixteen. The Amish object to high school education because of their "fundamental belief that salvation requires life in a church community separate and apart from the world and worldly influence." They believe that high school exposes their children to worldly influence and emphasizes "intellectual and scientific accomplishments, self-distinction, competitiveness, worldly success, and social life with other students." The Amish society, by contrast, emphasizes "informal learning-through-doing" and "wisdom, rather than technical knowledge; community welfare, rather than competition; and separation [from] contemporary worldly society." Attendance at school through the eighth grade is acceptable to the Amish because it "prepares children to read the Bible [and] to be good farmers and citizens," and because such education does not "significantly expose their children to worldly values." The Wisconsin Supreme Court overturned Yoder's conviction because it violated the free exercise clause. The Court affirmed, with six Justices joining the majority opinion and only one Justice dissenting in part.

Chief Justice BURGER's majority opinion insisted that "a State's interest in universal education" must be balanced "when it impinges on fundamental rights and interests." The State could not prevail unless it showed that its requirement did not "deny the free exercise of religious beliefs" and that there was "a state interest of sufficient magnitude to override the [free exercise claim]." And "only those interests of the highest order and those not otherwise served can overbalance legitimate claims of free exercise. [E.g., Sherbert.]" Applying this analysis, the Chief Justice began by asking whether the Amish claim was "rooted in religious belief." (The sincerity of the Amish was conceded.) "Thus, if the Amish asserted their claims because of their subjective evaluation and rejection of the contemporary secular values accepted by the majority, much as Thoreau rejected the social values of his time and isolated himself at Walden Pond, their claims would not rest on a religious basis. Thoreau's choice was philosophical and personal rather than religious, and such belief does not rise to the demands of the Religion Clauses." But the Amish way of life, the Chief Justice found, was "not merely a matter of personal preference, but one of deep religious conviction, shared by an organized group, and intimately related to daily living." Compulsory school-attendance laws required the Amish "to perform acts undeniably at odds with fundamental tenets of their religious beliefs" and carried with them "a very real threat of undermining the Amish community and religious practice."

Chief Justice Burger proceeded to reject the State's attempted reliance on the "belief"-"action" distinction: "in this context belief and action cannot be neatly confined in logic-tight compartments." Nor could the case be disposed of because the law was facially nondiscriminatory, for such a regulation might nevertheless "offend the constitutional requirement for governmental neutrality if it unduly burdens the free exercise of religion. [E.g., Sherbert.]" Accordingly exercising the heightened scrutiny demanded by this case as well as Sherbert, the Court examined the interests asserted by the State. Chief Justice Burger noted the State's claim that "some degree of education is necessary to prepare citizens to participate [effectively] in our open political system [and] to be self-reliant and self-sufficient participants in society," but replied that an additional one or two years of formal high school would do "little to serve those interests."

Turning to the State's argument that the Amish position fostered "ignorance," the Chief Justice replied that "the Amish community has been a highly successful social unit within our society, even if apart from the conventional 'mainstream.' Its members are productive and very law-abiding members of society." The State also argued that children "may choose to leave the Amish community, and that if this occurs they will be ill-equipped for life." The Chief Justice found this argument "highly speculative": "There is nothing in this record to suggest that the Amish qualities of reliability, self-reliance and dedication to work would fail to find ready markets in today's society." Accordingly, the State's interest here "emerges as somewhat less substantial than requiring such attendance for children generally." The Court added that it was "not dealing with a way of life and mode of education by a group claiming to have recently discovered some 'progressive' [process] for rearing children for modern life." In view of the long history of the Amish as a "successful and self-sufficient segment of American society" and their showing of "the adequacy of their alternative mode of continuing informal vocational education in terms of precisely those overall interests that the State advances," a showing that "probably few other religious groups or sects could make, and weighing the minimal difference between what the State would require and what the Amish already accept, it was incumbent on the State to show with more particularity how its admittedly strong interest in compulsory education would be adversely affected by granting an exemption to the Amish. [Sherbert.]" The Court dismissed in a footnote the claim that a mandatory exemption for the Amish would violate the establishment clause: "Accommodating the religious beliefs of the Amish can hardly be characterized as sponsorship or active involvement."

Justice DOUGLAS dissented in part, emphasizing the potential conflict of interest between Amish parents and their children. He insisted that the free exercise rights of Amish children had to be reached here. Some Amish children might want to attend high school in order to be able to choose whether to adhere or break with the Amish tradition. (The majority opinion, as well as the concurring notations by Justices Stewart and White, insisted that this issue was not presented by the record.) Justice Douglas also objected to the majority's emphasis on the "law and order record" of the Amish, finding it "quite irrelevant." He disagreed with the majority's view that Thoreau's "philosophical and personal" position fell outside of the Religion Clauses, insisting that this was contrary to the implications of the rulings in Seeger and Welsh, p. 1468 above.

3. *Denials of free exercise claims between Sherbert and Smith.* Even though Sherbert and Yoder held that the free exercise clause mandated exemptions from government regulations in certain circumstances, a much larger number of cases during this period rejected such claims. The heightened scrutiny announced by such decisions as Sherbert and Yoder proved quite deferential in fact.

a. UNITED STATES v. LEE, 455 U.S. 252 (1982): Lee, a member of the Old Order Amish, employed several Amish to work on his farm and in his carpentry shop. He objected, on religious grounds, to paying the social security tax for his employees, arguing that "the Amish believe it sinful not to provide for their own elderly." Chief Justice BURGER's majority opinion found Yoder distinguishable and rejected Lee's claim. The Chief Justice conceded that "there is a conflict between the Amish faith and the obligations imposed by the social security system" and accepted that heightened scrutiny was appropriate. In nevertheless upholding application of the tax law to Lee, he noted that "the State may justify a limitation on religious liberty by showing that it is essential to accomplish an overriding governmental interest"; here, mandatory participation in the social security system was indispensable to the fiscal vitality of the system. The Chief Justice distinguished Yoder on the ground that here "it would be difficult to accommodate the comprehensive social security system with myriad exceptions flowing from a wide variety of religious beliefs." He also noted that there was "no principled way" to distinguish between general taxes and social security taxes, so that, if Lee's claim were granted, a religious opponent to war "would have a similarly valid claim to be exempt from paying [a] percentage of the income tax." "The tax system could not function if denominations were allowed to challenge [it] because tax payments were spent in a manner that violates their religious beliefs."

In a separate opinion concurring only in the judgment, Justice STEVENS criticized the majority for imposing upon the Government "a heavy burden of justifying the application of neutral general laws [to] individual conscientious objectors. In my opinion, it is the objector who must shoulder the burden of demonstrating that there is a unique reason for allowing him a special exemption from a valid law of general applicability." The Amish ought to prevail under strict scrutiny, which he opposed, because an exemption to them would be costless to the government: "[T]he nonpayment of these taxes by the Amish would be more than offset by the elimination of their right to collect benefits. [Since] the Amish have demonstrated their capacity to care for their own, the social cost of eliminating this relatively small group of dedicated believers would be minimal." Nor was there a great risk of myriad similar claims: "[T]he Amish claim applies only to a small religious community within an established welfare system of its own." Nevertheless, he agreed with the majority's result because of the difficulties involved in processing claims to religious exemption from taxes.

b. BOB JONES UNIVERSITY v. UNITED STATES, 461 U.S. 574 (1983): This decision rejected a free exercise challenge to IRS denials of tax-exempt status to two educational institutions that practiced racial discrimination in accordance with the religious beliefs upon which they were founded. The IRS claimed that the schools were disqualified as "charities" because their racial policies were "contrary to settled public policy." After finding that the IRS policy was authorized by Congress, Chief Justice BURGER's opinion for the Court rejected the free exercise claim despite formal application of strict scrutiny. Under the Lee standard that "[t]he state may justify a limitation on religious liberty by showing that it is essential to accomplish an overriding governmental interest," the Court found the governmental interest in eradicating racial discrimination in education sufficiently "compelling."

c. GOLDMAN v. WEINBERGER, 475 U.S. 503 (1986): In rejecting a free exercise challenge in this case, involving military service, the Court abandoned any reliance on heightened scrutiny and instead adopted an openly deferential approach. Goldman was an Orthodox Jew, a clinical psychologist in the Air Force, who was disciplined for wearing a yarmulke in violation of uniform dress regulations barring the wearing of headgear indoors. He sought an exemption from the Air Force regulation under the strict scrutiny standard of Sherbert. Justice REHNQUIST's majority opinion answered: "Our review of military regulations challenged on First Amendment grounds is far more deferential than constitutional review of similar [regulations] designed for civilian society. The military need not encourage debate or tolerate protest to the extent that such tolerance is required of the civilian state by the First Amendment; to accomplish its mission the military must foster instinctive obedience, unity, commitment, and esprit de corps." Accordingly, "when evaluating whether military needs justify a particular restriction on religiously motivated conduct, courts must give great deference to the professional judgment of military authorities concerning the relative importance of a particular military interest." In this case, the military judgment was that "the traditional outfitting of personnel in standardized uniforms encourages the subordination of personal preferences and identities in favor of the overall group mission. [The] First Amendment does not require the military to accommodate such practices as the wearing of [the yarmulke] in the face of its view that they would detract from the uniformity sought by the dress regulations." The regulations could constitutionally be applied "even though their effect is to restrict the wearing of the headgear required [by] religious beliefs."

In a concurring opinion, Justice STEVENS, joined by Justices White and Powell, admitted that Goldman presented "an especially attractive case for an exception" but worried about the application of such an exemption to members of other religious groups who wished to wear, e.g., turbans and dreadlocks. He accordingly insisted on testing the validity of the regulation "as it applied to all service personnel who have sincere religious beliefs." The interest in uniformity was important because it was an interest "in uniform treatment for the members of all religious faiths"; yet the "very strength of [Captain Goldman's] claim creates the danger that a similar claim on behalf of a Sikh or a Rastafarian might readily be dismissed as 'so extreme, so unusual, or so faddish an image that public confidence in his ability to perform his duties will be destroyed.' If exceptions from dress code regulations are to be granted, [inevitably] the decisionmaker's evaluation of the character and the sincerity of the requester's faith—as well as the probable reaction of the majority to the favored treatment of a member of that faith—will play a critical part in the decision. [Yet the] Air Force has no business drawing distinctions between such persons when it is enforcing commands of universal application."

Justice BRENNAN's dissent, joined by Justice Marshall, attacked the majority's "subrational-basis standard—absolute, uncritical 'deference to the professional judgment of military authorities.'" He insisted that even a deferential standard of review "need not, and should not, mean that the Court must credit arguments that defy common sense" and urged a stricter standard: "When a military service burdens the free exercise rights of its members in the name of necessity, it must provide, [at] a minimum, a *credible* explanation of how the contested practice is likely to interfere with the proffered military interest. Unabashed ipse dixit cannot outweigh a constitutional right." He rejected as "totally implausible" the claim that the "group identity of the Air Force would be threatened" by the wearing of yarmulkes. In response to the Government's fear of "a classic parade of horribles, the specter of a brightly-colored, 'rag-tag band of soldiers,'" he stated: "Although turbans, saffron robes, and dreadlocks are not before us [and] must each be evaluated against the reasons a service branch offers for prohibiting personnel from wearing them while in uniform, a reviewing court could legitimately give deference to dress and grooming rules that have a *reasoned* basis in, for example, functional utility, health and safety considerations, and the goal of a polished, professional appearance. It is the lack of any reasoned basis for prohibiting yarmulkes that is so striking here."

Justice BLACKMUN's dissent stated that the Air Force was justified in considering "the cumulative costs of accommodating constitutionally indistinguishable requests for religious exemptions" and also shared Justice Stevens' concern about discriminating in favor of mainstream religions. He nevertheless joined the dissenters because the "Air Force simply has not shown any reason to fear that a significant number of enlisted [people] would request religious exemptions that could not be denied on neutral grounds such as safety, let alone that granting these requests would noticeably impair the overall image of the service." Justice O'CONNOR's dissent, joined by Justice Marshall, found "two consistent themes" in the precedents: "First, when the government attempts to deny a free exercise claim, it must show that an unusually important interest is at stake, whether that interest is denominated 'compelling,' 'of the highest order,' or 'overriding.' [She relied on the varying formulations in Sherbert, Yoder, and Lee.] Second, the government must show that granting the requested exemption will do substantial harm to that interest, whether by showing that the means adopted is the 'least restrictive' or 'essential,' or that the interest will not 'otherwise be served.' These two requirements are entirely sensible [and there is no reason why they] should not apply in the military, as well as the civilian, context." Applying these standards here, she stated that she "would require the Government to accommodate the sincere religious belief of Captain Goldman."[1]

d.   O'LONE v. ESTATE OF SHABAZZ, 482 U.S. 342 (1987), presented a free exercise claim in another special institutional context. The setting there was a prison rather than the military. The Court once again rejected the claim in a very deferential opinion. Members of the Islamic faith challenged prison regulations relating to time and places of work which had the effect of preventing them from attending Jumu'ah, a Friday midday service. Chief Justice REHNQUIST's majority opinion applied a "reasonableness" standard that specifically rejected the view that prison officials have the burden of disproving "the availability of alternatives." Justice Brennan, joined by Justices Marshall, Blackmun, and Stevens, dissented.

e.   BOWEN v. ROY, 476 U.S. 693 (1986): The Court by a vote of 8–1 rejected a free exercise challenge to a requirement in the federal AFDC and Food Stamp programs that applicants for welfare benefits be identified by social security numbers. The challengers claimed that assignment of a number for their two-year-old daughter, Little Bird of the Snow, would violate their religious beliefs because it would "rob the spirit" of the child. Chief Justice

---

1. After Goldman, Congress enacted Public Law 100–180, permitting members of military to "wear an item of religious apparel while wearing the uniform," unless "the wearing of the item would interfere with the performance [of] military duties [or] the item of apparel is not neat and conservative."

BURGER's majority opinion rejected the claim regarding the *government*'s use of the number by distinguishing free exercise claims with respect to personal conduct from such claims with respect to the government's conduct: "Never to our knowledge has the Court interpreted the First Amendment to require the Government *itself* to behave in ways that the individual believes will further his or her spiritual development. [Free exercise] does not afford an individual a right to dictate the conduct of the Government's internal procedures."

The Court did not rule definitively on the requirement that the *applicant* furnish a social security number as a condition of receiving aid, but five justices indicated that they thought that free exercise warranted an exception here. Chief Justice BURGER, writing on this issue only for himself and Justices Powell and Rehnquist, would have rejected both aspects of the free exercise claim, asserting that scrutiny should be more deferential in the case of a condition on benefits than in the case of "governmental action [that] criminalizes religiously inspired activity or inescapably compels conduct that some find objectionable for religious reasons." Justice WHITE's brief dissent apparently would have granted both aspects of the free exercise claim, finding that the case was controlled by Sherbert and Thomas. Justice O'CONNOR, joined by Justices Brennan and Marshall, disputed Chief Justice Burger's distinction between "conditions" and "compulsion," arguing that the fact that the "underlying dispute involves an award of benefits rather than an exaction of penalties does not grant the Government license to apply a different version of the Constitution." Applying heightened scrutiny, she would have exempted Roy from providing the number. Justices BLACKMUN and STEVENS filed separate partial concurrences, agreeing that free exercise did not bar the government's own use of the social security number, but claiming that the record was insufficient to allow consideration of the claims with respect to Roy's furnishing the number. However, Justice Blackmun appended to his concurrence a comment that, if forced to reach the latter issue, he would agree with Justice O'Connor's position. Given Justice Blackmun's comment, and the view of the four dissenters, there was apparently a majority on the Court to uphold a free exercise claim regarding the furnishing of the number.

f. LYNG v. NORTHWEST INDIAN CEMETERY PROTECTIVE ASS'N, 485 U.S. 439 (1988): This was an unsuccessful free exercise challenge to the U.S. Forest Service's plan to build a road through and permit timber harvesting in an area of national forest traditionally used by several Indian tribes as sacred areas for religious rituals. In a 5–3 decision, the Court rejected the free exercise claim. Justice O'CONNOR's majority opinion acknowledged that the challengers' beliefs were "sincere" and that "the Government's proposed actions [would] have severe adverse effects on the practice of their religion," but insisted that the burden was not sufficiently great to trigger any form of heightened scrutiny. Accordingly, the Government did not have to meet a "compelling interest" standard of justification for the project. Relying heavily on Bowen v. Roy, above, she stated: "The building of a road or the harvesting of timber on publicly owned land cannot meaningfully be distinguished from the use of a Social Security number in Roy. In both cases, the challenged Government action would interfere significantly with private persons' ability to pursue spiritual fulfillment according to their own religious beliefs. In neither case, however, would the affected individuals be coerced by the Government's action into violating their religious beliefs; nor would either governmental action penalize the religious activity by denying any person an equal share of the rights, benefits, and privileges enjoyed by other citizens." She acknowledged that "indirect coercion or penalties on the free exercise of religion, not just outright prohibitions, are subject to scrutiny under the First Amendment.

[But] this does not and cannot imply that incidental effects of governmental programs, which may make it more difficult to practice certain religions but which have no tendency to coerce individuals into acting contrary to their religious beliefs, require government to bring forward a compelling justification for otherwise lawful actions. The crucial word in the constitutional text is 'prohibit.' "

Justice O'Connor went on to rely heavily on the possibility that many similar claims might impair the operation of government: "[Government] simply could not operate if it were required to satisfy every citizen's religious needs and desires. [The] First Amendment must apply to all citizens alike, and it can give to none of them a veto of public programs that do not prohibit the free exercise of religion. The Constitution does not, and courts cannot, offer to reconcile the various competing demands on Government, many of them rooted in sincere religious belief, that inevitably arise in so diverse a society as ours. That task [is] for the legislatures and other institutions." Thus, though the Government could not forbid the Indian challengers from visiting the area, these rights "do not divest the Government of its right to use what is, after all, *its* land."

Justice BRENNAN, joined by Justices Marshall and Blackmun, dissented. He objected to the majority's limitation of free exercise claims to cases of direct or indirect "coercion": "The constitutional guarantee [draws] no such fine distinctions between types of restraints on religious exercise, but rather is directed against any form of governmental action that frustrates or inhibits religious practice. [I] cannot accept the Court's premise that the form of the Government's restraint on religious practice, rather than its effect, controls our constitutional analysis. [Ultimately,] the Court's coercion test turns on a distinction between governmental actions that compel affirmative conduct inconsistent with religious belief, and those governmental actions that prevent conduct consistent with religious belief. [Such] a distinction is without constitutional significance. The crucial word in the constitutional text, as the Court itself acknowledges, is 'prohibit,' a comprehensive term that in no way suggests that the intended protection is aimed only at governmental actions that coerce affirmative conduct." He accordingly insisted that the Sherbert "compelling interest" standard was appropriate here.

4. *The Court's methodology in the era between Sherbert and Smith.* In the preceding cases, the Court used three techniques to distinguish Sherbert and Yoder. In some cases, it found an overriding government interest in uniformity, for example in the administration of the tax laws. In others, it found that free exercise interests were attenuated and government interests paramount in specialized environments such as prisons and the military. And in others, it applied a narrow definition of what constitutes a burden on religious practice, rejecting free exercise claims seeking to alter "internal" government operations such as the use of social security numbers and the development of federal property.

Can these findings be reconciled with Sherbert and Yoder? In particular, can the narrow definition of burdens on free exercise set forth in Roy and Lyng be reconciled with Sherbert? Didn't Sherbert itself compel a change in "internal government operations," and in the use of government "property"? Can government actions even with respect to its own "internal" operations have negative external effects on religious practitioners? See Williams & Williams, "Volitionalism and Religious Liberty," 76 Cornell L. Rev. 769 (1991) (arguing that the Court undervalues the beliefs of "nonvolitionalist" religions, i.e., those that believe that negative religious consequences can attach even to events over which the religious adherent exercised no personal control). Should the fact that the government had a monopoly over use of a unique worship site have mattered in Lyng? Could the Native American worshippers in Lyng themselves have asserted a countervailing property right? See Lupu, "Where Rights Begin: the Problem of Burdens on the Free Exercise of Religion," 102 Harv. L. Rev. 933 (1988) (arguing that government actions that are comparable to harms actionable at common law should count as burdens on religion, and that in Lyng, the government interfered, in effect, with a prescriptive easement of access to the worship site). In reading the 1990 Smith case, which follows, consider whether the pattern of decisions after Sherbert and Yoder justified abandoning strict scrutiny of most neutral government regulations challenged as violations of free exercise.

Employment Division, Dept. of Human Resources v. Smith

494 U.S. 872, 110 S.Ct. 1595, 108 L.Ed.2d 876 (1990).

Justice SCALIA delivered the opinion of the Court.

This case requires us to decide whether the Free Exercise Clause [permits] Oregon to include religiously inspired peyote use within the reach of its general criminal prohibition on use of that drug, and thus permits the State to deny unemployment benefits to persons dismissed from their jobs because of such religiously inspired use.

I.   Oregon law prohibits the knowing or intentional possession of a "controlled substance," [including] the drug peyote, a hallucinogen derived from [a plant]. Respondents Alfred Smith and Galen Black were fired from their jobs with a private drug rehabilitation organization because they ingested peyote for sacramental purposes at a ceremony of the Native American Church, of which both are members. When respondents applied to petitioner Employment Division for unemployment compensation, they were determined to be ineligible for benefits because they had been discharged for work-related "misconduct". [The Oregon Supreme Court, after a first round of litigation that went up to the Supreme Court, found on remand that respondents' peyote use fell within the prohibition of Oregon's criminal laws, that those laws made no exception for sacramental use of the drug, but that that the ban on sacramental peyote use was invalid under the free exercise clause. Thus, the state court ruled, Oregon could not deny unemployment benefits for engaging in conduct that was constitutionally protected. The Court again granted certiorari.]

II.   Respondents' claim for relief rests on our decisions in Sherbert, Thomas, and Hobbie, in which we held that a State could not condition the availability of unemployment insurance on an individual's willingness to forgo conduct required by his religion. As we observed in Smith I, however, the conduct at issue in those cases was not prohibited by law. [Now that it is clear] that Oregon does prohibit the religious use of peyote, we proceed to consider whether that prohibition is permissible under the Free Exercise Clause.

A.   [The] free exercise of religion means, first and foremost, the right to believe and profess whatever religious doctrine one desires. [But] the "exercise of religion" often involves not only belief and profession but the performance of (or abstention from) physical acts: assembling with others for a worship service, participating in sacramental use of bread and wine, proselytizing, abstaining from certain foods or certain modes of transportation. It would be true, we think (though no case of ours has involved the point), that a state would be "prohibiting the free exercise [of religion]" if it sought to ban such acts or abstentions only when they are engaged in for religious reasons, or only because of the religious belief that they display. It would doubtless be unconstitutional, for example, to ban the casting of "statues that are to be used for worship purposes," or to prohibit bowing down before a golden calf.

Respondents in the present case, however, seek to carry the meaning of "prohibiting the free exercise [of religion]" one large step further. They contend that their religious motivation for using peyote places them beyond the reach of a criminal law that is not specifically directed at their religious practice, and that is concededly constitutional as applied to those who use the drug for other reasons. They assert, in other words, that "prohibiting the free exercise [of religion]" includes requiring any individual to observe a generally applicable law that requires (or forbids) the performance of an act that his religious belief forbids (or requires). As a textual matter, we do not think the words must be given that meaning. It is no more necessary to regard the collection of a general tax, for example, as "prohibiting the free exercise [of religion]" by those citizens who believe support of organized government to be sinful, than it is to regard the same tax as "abridging the freedom [of] the press" of those publishing companies that must pay the tax as a condition of staying in business. It is a permissible reading of the text, in the one case as in the other, to say that if prohibiting the exercise of religion (or burdening the activity of printing) is not the object of the tax but merely the incidental effect of a generally applicable and otherwise valid provision, the First Amendment has not been offended.

Our decisions reveal that the latter reading is the correct one. We have never held that an individual's religious beliefs excuse him from compliance with an otherwise valid law prohibiting conduct that the State is free to regulate. On the contrary, the record of more than a century of our free exercise jurisprudence contradicts that proposition. [We] first had occasion to assert that principle in [Reynolds], where we rejected the claim that criminal laws against polygamy could not be constitutionally applied to those whose religion commanded the practice. [Subsequent] decisions have consistently held that the right of free exercise does not relieve an individual of the obligation to comply with a "valid and neutral law of general applicability on the ground that the law proscribes (or prescribes) conduct that his religion prescribes (or proscribes)." United States v. Lee (Stevens, J., concurring in judgment). [See also Prince; Braunfeld; Gillette.]

The only decisions in which we have held that the First Amendment bars application of a neutral, generally applicable law to religiously motivated action have involved not the Free Exercise Clause alone, but the Free Exercise Clause in conjunction with other constitutional protections, such as freedom of speech and of the press, see [Cantwell; Murdock]; or the right of parents, acknowledged in Pierce v. Society of Sisters, to direct the education of their children, see Wisconsin v. Yoder. Some of our cases prohibiting compelled expression, decided exclusively upon free speech grounds, have also involved freedom of religion [see Wooley v. Maynard; Barnette.]

[The] present case does not present such a hybrid situation, but a free exercise claim unconnected with any communicative activity or parental right. Respondents urge us to hold, quite simply, that when otherwise prohibitable conduct is accompanied by religious convictions, not only the convictions but the conduct itself must be free from governmental regulation. We have never held that, and decline to do so now. There being no contention that Oregon's drug law represents an attempt to regulate religious beliefs, the communication of religious beliefs, or the raising of one's children in those beliefs, the rule to which we have adhered ever since Reynolds plainly controls.

B. [Respondents] argue that even though exemption from generally applicable criminal laws need not automatically be extended to religiously motivated actors, at least the claim for a religious exemption must be evaluated under the balancing test set forth in Sherbert. Under the Sherbert test, governmental actions that substantially burden a religious practice must be justified by a compelling governmental interest. [We] have never invalidated any governmental action on the basis of the Sherbert test except the denial of unemployment compensation. Although we have sometimes purported to apply the Sherbert test in contexts other than that, we have always found the test satisfied [United States v. Lee; Gillette v. United States]. In recent years we have abstained from applying the Sherbert test (outside the unemployment compensation field) at all. [Roy; Lyng; Goldman; O'Lone.]

Even if we were inclined to breathe into Sherbert some life beyond the unemployment compensation field, we would not apply it to require exemptions from a generally applicable criminal law. The Sherbert test, it must be recalled, was developed in a context that lent itself to individualized governmental assessment of the reasons for the relevant conduct. As a plurality of the Court noted in Roy, a distinctive feature of unemployment compensation programs is that their eligibility criteria invite consideration of the particular circumstances behind an applicant's unemployment. [Our] decisions in the unemployment cases stand for the proposition that where the State has in place a system of individual exemptions, it may not refuse to extend that system to cases of "religious hardship" without compelling reason.

Whether or not the decisions are that limited, they at least have nothing to do with an across-the-board criminal prohibition on a particular form of conduct. [Although] we have sometimes used the Sherbert test to analyze free exercise challenges to such laws, we have never applied the test to invalidate one. We conclude today that the sounder approach, and the approach in accord with the vast majority of our precedents, is to hold the test inapplicable to such challenges. The government's ability to enforce generally applicable prohibitions of socially harmful conduct, like its ability to carry out other aspects of public policy, "cannot depend on measuring the effects of a governmental action on a religious objector's spiritual development." [Lyng.] To make an individual's obligation to obey such a law contingent upon the law's coincidence with his religious beliefs, except where the State's interest is "compelling"— permitting him, by virtue of his beliefs, "to become a law unto himself," Reynolds—contradicts both constitutional tradition and common sense.

The "compelling government interest" requirement seems benign, because it is familiar from other fields. But using it as the standard that must be met before the government may accord different treatment on the basis of race, or before the government may regulate the content of speech, is not remotely comparable to using it for the purpose asserted here. What it produces in those other fields—equality of treatment, and an unrestricted flow of contending speech—are constitutional norms; what it would produce here—a private right to ignore generally applicable laws—is a constitutional anomaly.[2]

---

2. [Just] as we subject to the most exacting scrutiny laws that make classifications based on race or on the content of speech, so too we strictly scrutinize governmental classifications based on religion. But we have held that race-neutral laws that have the *effect* of disproportionately disadvantaging a particular racial group do not thereby become sub-

Nor is it possible to limit the impact of respondents' proposal by requiring a "compelling state interest" only when the conduct prohibited is "central" to the individual's religion. Cf. [Lyng (Brennan, J., dissenting).] It is no more appropriate for judges to determine the "centrality" of religious beliefs before applying a "compelling interest" test in the free exercise field, than it would be for them to determine the "importance" of ideas before applying the "compelling interest" test in the free speech field. What principle of law or logic can be brought to bear to contradict a believer's assertion that a particular act is "central" to his personal faith? Judging the centrality of different religious practices is akin to the unacceptable "business of evaluating the relative merits of differing religious claims." United States v. Lee (Stevens, J., concurring). [Repeatedly] and in many different contexts, we have warned that courts must not presume to determine the place of a particular belief in a religion or the plausibility of a religious claim. [E.g., Thomas; Ballard.]

If the "compelling interest" test is to be applied at all, then, it must be applied across the board to all actions thought to be religiously commanded. Moreover, if "compelling interest" really means what it says (and watering it down here would subvert its rigor in the other fields where it is applied), many laws will not meet the test. Any society adopting such a system would be courting anarchy, but that danger increases in direct proportion to the society's diversity of religious beliefs, and its determination to coerce or suppress none of them. Precisely because [we] value and protect [religious] divergence, we cannot afford the luxury of deeming *presumptively invalid,* as applied to the religious objector, every regulation of conduct that does not protect an interest of the highest order. The rule respondents favor would open the prospect of constitutionally required religious exemptions from civic obligations of almost every conceivable kind—ranging from compulsory military service [e.g., Gillette] to the payment of taxes [United States v. Lee] to health and safety regulation such as manslaughter and child neglect laws, compulsory vaccination laws, drug laws, and traffic laws; to social welfare legislation such as minimum wage laws, child labor laws, animal cruelty laws, environmental protection laws, and laws providing for equality of opportunity for the races [Bob Jones University]. The First Amendment's protection of religious liberty does not require this.

Values that are protected against government interference through enshrinement in the Bill of Rights are not thereby banished from the political process. Just as a society that believes in the negative protection accorded to the press by the First Amendment is likely to enact laws that affirmatively foster the dissemination of the printed word, so also a society that believes in the negative protection accorded to religious belief can be expected to be solicitous of that value in its legislation as well. It is therefore not surprising that a number of States have made an exception to their drug laws for sacramental peyote use. But to say that a nondiscriminatory religious-practice exemption is permitted, or even that it is desirable, is not to say that it is constitutionally required, and that the appropriate occasions for its creation can be discerned by the courts. It may fairly be said that leaving accommodation to

ject to compelling-interest analysis under the Equal Protection Clause, see Washington v. Davis; and we have held that generally applicable laws unconcerned with regulating speech that have the *effect* of interfering with speech do not thereby become subject to compelling-interest analysis under the First Amendment, see Citizen Publishing Co. v. United States, 394 U.S. 131 (1969) (antitrust laws). Our conclusion that generally applicable, religion-neutral laws that have the effect of burdening a particular religious practice need not be justified by a compelling governmental interest is the only approach compatible with these precedents. [Footnote by Justice Scalia.]

the political process will place at a relative disadvantage those religious practices that are not widely engaged in; but that unavoidable consequence of democratic government must be preferred to a system in which each conscience is a law unto itself or in which judges weigh the social importance of all laws against the centrality of all religious beliefs.

[Reversed.]

Justice O'CONNOR, concurring in the judgment [joined by Justices BRENNAN, MARSHALL, and BLACKMUN as to Parts I and II of the opinion, but not as to the judgment.]

Although I agree with the result the Court reaches, [I] cannot join its opinion. In my view, today's holding dramatically departs from well-settled First Amendment jurisprudence, appears unnecessary to resolve the question presented, and is incompatible with our Nation's fundamental commitment to individual religious [liberty].

II. A. The Court today [interprets] the [Free Exercise] Clause to permit the government to prohibit, without justification, conduct mandated by an individual's religious beliefs, so long as that prohibition is generally applicable. But a law that prohibits certain conduct—conduct that happens to be an act of worship for someone—manifestly does prohibit that person's free exercise of his religion. A person who is barred from engaging in religiously motivated conduct is barred from freely exercising his religion. [The] First Amendment [does] not distinguish between laws that are generally applicable and laws that target particular religious practices. Indeed, few States would be so naive as to enact a law directly prohibiting or burdening a religious practice as such.

[To] say that a person's right to free exercise has been burdened, of course, does not mean that he has an absolute right to engage in the conduct. Under our established First Amendment jurisprudence, we have recognized that the freedom to act, unlike the freedom to believe, cannot be absolute. Instead, we have respected both the First Amendment's express textual mandate and the governmental interest in regulation of conduct by requiring the Government to justify any substantial burden on religiously motivated conduct by a compelling state interest and by means narrowly tailored to achieve that interest.

[The] Court attempts to support its narrow reading of the Clause by claiming that "[w]e have never held that an individual's religious beliefs excuse him from compliance with an otherwise valid law prohibiting conduct that the State is free to regulate." But as the Court later notes, as it must, in cases such as Cantwell and Yoder we have in fact interpreted the Free Exercise Clause to forbid application of a generally applicable prohibition to religiously motivated conduct. [The] Court endeavors to escape from our decisions in Cantwell and Yoder by labeling them "hybrid" decisions, but there is no denying that both cases expressly relied on the Free Exercise Clause, and that we have consistently regarded those cases as part of the mainstream of our free exercise jurisprudence. Moreover, in each of the other cases cited by the Court to support its categorical rule, we rejected the particular constitutional claims before us only after carefully weighing the competing interests. [Prince; Braunfeld; Gillette; Lee.] That we rejected the free exercise claims in those cases hardly calls into question the applicability of First Amendment doctrine in the first place. Indeed, it is surely unusual to judge the vitality of a constitutional doctrine by looking to the win-loss record of the plaintiffs who happen to come before us.

B. [In] my view, [the] essence of a free exercise claim is relief from a burden imposed by government on religious practices or beliefs, whether the burden is imposed directly through laws that prohibit or compel specific religious practices, or indirectly through laws that, in effect, make abandonment of one's own religion or conformity to the religious beliefs of others the price of an equal place in the civil community. [A] State that makes criminal an individual's religiously motivated conduct burdens that individual's free exercise of religion in the severest manner possible,. [I] would have thought it beyond argument that such laws implicate free exercise concerns. Indeed, we have never distinguished between cases in which a State conditions receipt of a benefit on conduct prohibited by religious beliefs and cases in which a State affirmatively prohibits such conduct. The Sherbert compelling interest test applies in both kinds of cases. [E.g., Lee; Gillette; Yoder.]

[Legislatures], of course, have always been "left free to reach actions which were in violation of social duties or subversive of good order." [Reynolds.] [But once] it has been shown that a government regulation or criminal prohibition burdens the free exercise of religion, we have consistently asked the Government to demonstrate that unbending application of its regulation to the religious objector "is essential to accomplish an overriding governmental interest" [Lee] or represents "the least restrictive means of achieving some compelling state interest" [Thomas]. To me, the sounder approach—the approach more consistent with our role as judges to decide each case on its individual merits—is to apply this test in each case to determine whether the burden on the specific plaintiffs before us is constitutionally significant and whether the particular criminal interest asserted by the State before us is compelling.

[The] Court today gives no convincing reason to depart from settled First Amendment jurisprudence. There is nothing talismanic about neutral laws of general applicability or general criminal prohibitions, for laws neutral toward religion can coerce a person to violate his religious conscience or intrude upon his religious duties just as effectively as laws aimed at religion. [A] law that makes criminal such an activity therefore triggers constitutional concern—and heightened judicial scrutiny—even if it does not target the particular religious conduct at issue. Our free speech cases similarly recognize that neutral regulations that affect free speech values are subject to a balancing, rather than categorical, approach. See e.g., [O'Brien (1968; p.___ above)]. [The] Court's parade of horribles not only fails as a reason for discarding the compelling interest test, it instead demonstrates just the opposite: that courts have been quite capable of applying our free exercise jurisprudence to strike sensible balances between religious liberty and competing state interests.

Finally, the Court today suggests that the disfavoring of minority religions is an "unavoidable consequence" under our system of government and that accommodation of such religions must be left to the political process. In my view, however, the First Amendment was enacted precisely to protect the rights of those whose religious practices are not shared by the majority and may be viewed with hostility. The history of our free exercise doctrine amply demonstrates the harsh impact majoritarian rule has had on unpopular or emerging religious groups such as the Jehovah's Witnesses and the Amish. [The] compelling interest test reflects the First Amendment's mandate of preserving religious liberty to the fullest extent possible in a pluralistic society. For the Court to deem this command a "luxury" is to denigrate "[t]he very purpose of a Bill of Rights."

III.   The Court's holding today not only misreads settled First Amendment precedent; it appears to be unnecessary to this case. I would reach the same result applying our established free exercise jurisprudence. [In Part III, Justice O'Connor, writing only for herself, found that Oregon had "a compelling interest in prohibiting the possession of peyote by its citizens." The critical question thus was "whether exempting respondents from the State's general criminal prohibition 'will unduly interfere with fulfillment of the governmental interest.' [Lee.]" She concluded: "Although the question is [close,] uniform application of Oregon's criminal prohibition is 'essential to accomplish' its overriding interest in 'preventing the physical harm' " caused by drug use. She rejected the argument that any incompatibility between the general law and an exemption was "belied by the fact that the Federal Government and several States provide exemptions for the religious use of peyote," finding that such other exemptions did not mean that Oregon was "*required*" to grant an exemption by the First Amendment. She added moreover, that the constitutionality of applying Oregon's general criminal prohibition "cannot, and should not turn on the centrality of the particular religious practice at issue."]

Justice BLACKMUN, with whom Justices BRENNAN and MARSHALL join, dissenting.

[I] agree with Justice O'Connor's analysis of the applicable free exercise doctrine, and I join parts I and II of her opinion. As she points out, "the critical question in this case is whether exempting respondents from the State's general criminal prohibition 'will unduly interfere with fulfillment of the governmental interest.' " I do disagree, however, with her specific answer to that question.

I. In weighing respondents' clear interest in the free exercise of their religion against Oregon's asserted interest in enforcing its drug laws, it is important to articulate in precise terms the state interest involved. It is not the State's broad interest in fighting the critical "war on drugs" that must be weighed against respondents' claim, but the State's narrow interest in refusing to make an exception for the religious, ceremonial use of peyote. [E.g., Thomas; Yoder.] Failure to reduce the competing interests to the same plane of generality tends to distort the weighing process in the State's favor.

[Oregon] has never sought to prosecute respondents, and does not claim that it has made significant enforcement efforts against other religious users of peyote. The State's asserted interest thus amounts only to the symbolic preservation of an unenforced prohibition. [But] a government interest in ["symbolism"] cannot suffice to abrogate the constitutional rights of individuals. [The] State proclaims an interest in protecting the health and safety of its citizens from the dangers of unlawful drugs. It offers, however, no evidence that the religious use of peyote has ever harmed anyone. [The] carefully circumscribed ritual context in which respondents used peyote is far removed from the irresponsible and unrestricted recreational use of unlawful [drugs]. [Moreover,] just as in Yoder, the values and interests of those seeking a religious exemption in this case are congruent, to a great degree, with those the State seeks to promote through its drug laws. Not only does the Church's doctrine forbid nonreligious use of peyote; it also generally advocates self-reliance, familial responsibility, and abstinence from alcohol.

[Finally,] the State argues that granting an exception for religious peyote use would erode its interest in the uniform, fair, and certain enforcement of its drug laws. The State fears that, if it grants an exemption for religious peyote use, a flood of other claims to religious exemptions will follow. It would then be placed in a dilemma, it says, between allowing a patchwork of exemptions that would hinder its law enforcement efforts, and risking a violation of the Establishment Clause by arbitrarily limiting its religious exemptions. [The] State's apprehension of a flood of other religious claims is purely speculative. Almost half the States, and the Federal Government, have maintained an exemption for religious peyote use for many years, and apparently have not found themselves overwhelmed by claims to other religious exemptions. Allowing [such an] exemption [would] not necessarily oblige the State to grant a similar exemption to other religious groups. The unusual circumstances that make the religious use of peyote compatible with the State's interests in health and safety and in preventing drug trafficking would not apply to other religious claims. Some religions, for example, might not restrict drug use to a limited ceremonial context, as does the Native American Church. Some religious claims involve drugs such as marijuana and heroin, in which there is significant illegal traffic, [so] that it would be difficult to grant a religious exemption without seriously compromising law enforcement efforts. That the State might grant an exemption for religious peyote use, but deny other religious claims arising in different circumstances, would not violate the Establishment Clause. Though the State must treat all religions equally, and not favor one over another, this obligation is fulfilled by the uniform application of the "compelling interest" *test* to all free exercise claims, not by reaching uniform *results* as to all claims.

III.   [Finally], although I agree with Justice O'Connor that courts should refrain from delving into questions of whether, as a matter of religious doctrine, a particular practice is "central" to the religion, I do not think this means that the courts must turn a blind eye to the severe impact of a State's restrictions on the adherents of a minority religion. Respondents believe, and their sincerity has *never* been at issue, that the peyote plant embodies their deity, and eating it is an act of worship and communion. Without peyote, they could not enact the essential ritual of their religion. [This] potentially devastating impact must be viewed in light of the federal policy—reached in reaction to many years of religious persecution and intolerance—of protecting the religious freedom of Native Americans. See American Indian Religious Freedom Act, 42 U.S.C. § 1996 ("it shall be the policy of the United States to protect and preserve for American Indians their inherent right of freedom to believe, express, and exercise the traditional religions . . ., including but not limited to access to sites, use and possession of sacred objects, and the freedom to worship through ceremonials and traditional rites"). [The] American Indian Religious Freedom Act, in itself, may not create rights enforceable against government action restricting religious freedom, but this Court must scrupulously apply its free exercise analysis to the religious claims of Native Americans, however unorthodox they may be. Otherwise, both the First Amendment and the stated policy of Congress will offer to Native Americans merely an unfulfilled and hollow promise. [I] dissent.

SMITH AND RELIGIOUS EXEMPTIONS

1. *The history of religious exemptions.* The opinions in Smith allude to the text of the First Amendment and the Court's free exercise precedents, but do not discuss whether the framers might have viewed some religious exemptions as mandatory. In "The Origins and Historical Understanding of Free Exercise of Religion," 103 Harv.L.Rev. 1409 (1990), Michael McConnell traced the historical origins of the free exercise clause, noted that pressure for the free exercise clause came from the evangelical religious movements of the colonial and founding periods, and argued that evangelicals viewed the constitutional guarantee of free exercise as protecting their right actively to fulfill religious obligations without state interference. He concluded that an interpretation of free exercise to mandate religious exemptions was both within the contemplation of the Framers and consistent with then-popular views about religious

liberty and limited government. While he conceded that "exemptions were not common enough to compel the inference that the term 'free exercise of religion' necessarily included an enforceable right to exemption," he concluded nonetheless that "the modern doctrine of free exercise exemptions [before Smith] is more consistent with the original understanding than is a position that leads only to the facial neutrality of legislation." In "Free Exercise Revisionism and the Smith Decision," 57 U.Chi.L.Rev. 1109 (1990), McConnell criticized the Court for failing to undertake in Smith "even a cursory inquiry into the history of the clause." For an alternative view of the same history, see Hamburger, "A Constitutional Right of Religious Exemption: An Historical Perspective," 60 Geo. Wash. L. Rev. 915 (1992).

2. *The political theory of religious exemptions.* Recall footnote 4 of Carolene Products, which favored judicial intervention where the political process is unlikely to protect "discrete and insular" minorities. Are religious practitioners in need of such protection? Mainstream sects are likely to be able to obtain many exemptions through the political process. Sacramental wine used in Catholic and some Protestant ceremonies, for example, was exempted by statute from Prohibition. Recall too the legislative exemption of the Catholic church from the solicitation restrictions in Larson v. Valente, p. 1476 above. Note that none of the claims for judicial free exercise exemptions above were made by members of the largest Christian denominations.

But are members of minority faiths similarly able to protect their religious practices through the political process? Should the Court presume minority religionists, like racial minorities and political dissenters, in need of judicial protection from majority prejudice? Justices Scalia and O'Connor answered this question quite differently in Smith. Justice O'Connor viewed religious minorities as politically powerless and thus in need of judicial solicitude: "[T]he First Amendment was enacted precisely to protect the rights of those whose religious practices are not shared by the majority and may be viewed with hostility. The history of our free exercise doctrine amply demonstrates the harsh impact majoritarian rule has had on unpopular or emerging religious groups." Justice Scalia, in contrast, noted that "a number of States have made an exception to their drug laws for sacramental peyote use," suggesting that even minority faiths may obtain legislative exemptions without resort to the courts. He conceded that "leaving accommodation to the political process will place at a relative disadvantage those religious practices that are not widely engaged in," but viewed that as an "unavoidable consequence of democratic government." Which of these views is more persuasive? Which one is borne out by the passage of RFRA, below?

Should religious exemptions be required to compensate for a structural disadvantage the religious suffer in politics—namely, that the establishment clause disables them from using religious arguments as a basis for legislation? For such an argument, see Greene, "The Political Balance of the Religion Clauses," 102 Yale L.J. 1611 (1993). Is religious argument truly excluded from political debate? For expansive views of its permissibility, see Carter, The Culture of Disbelief: How American Law and Politics Trivialize Religious Devotion (1993); Perry, Love and Power: The Role of Religion and Morality in American Politics (1991); Perry, "Religious Arguments in Public Political Debate," 29 Loyola L. Rev. 1421 (1996). For a more cautiously approving view, see Greenawalt, Religious Convictions and Political Choice (1988); Greenawalt, "Religious Expression in the Public Square," 29 Loyola L. Rev. 1411 (1996). For arguments for greater restraint on religious participation in politics because the establishment clause forbids translation of religious commitments into public policy, see Teitel, "A Critique of Religion as Politics in the Public

Sphere," 78 Cornell L. Rev. 747 (1993); Audi, "The Separation of Church and State and the Obligations of Citizenship," 18 Phil. & Pub. Affairs 259 (1989).

Consider the following observations on this issue by Justice Scalia in his dissent in Edwards v. Aguillard (1987; p. 1515 below): "[T]he purpose forbidden by Lemon is the purpose to 'advance religion.' Our cases in no way imply that the Establishment Clause forbids legislators merely to act upon their religious convictions. We surely would not strike down a law providing money to feed the hungry or shelter the homeless if it could be demonstrated that, but for the religious beliefs of the legislators, the funds would not have been approved. Also, political activism by the religiously motivated is part of our heritage. [We] do not presume that the sole purpose of a law is to advance religion merely because it was supported strongly by organized religions or by adherents of particular faiths. To do so would deprive religious men and women of their right to participate in the political process. [Such] religious activism [resulted, for example,] in the abolition of slavery. Similarly, we will not presume that a law's purpose is to advance religion merely because it 'happens to coincide or harmonize with the tenets of some or all religions,' Harris v. McRae [rejecting establishment clause challenge to restrictions on abortion funding.]"

3. *Smith and constitutional jurisprudence.* Justice Scalia's opinion for the Court in Smith reflects a strong mistrust of judicial balancing. Indeed, in a footnote, he suggested that "it is horrible to contemplate that federal judges will regularly balance against the importance of general laws the significance of religious practice." He found any judicial inquiry into the significance or "centrality" of a religious practice offensive to free exercise. For elaboration of Justice Scalia's general antipathy toward balancing, see Scalia, "The Rule of Law as a Law of Rules," 56 U.Chi.L.Rev. 1175 (1989). How warranted is Justice Scalia's concern that balancing in the free exercise area will invite subjective or arbitrary judicial discretion? See Marshall, "In Defense of Smith and Free Exercise Revisionism," 58 U. Chi. L. Rev. 1109 (1990) ("exemption analysis threatens free exercise values because it requires courts to consider the legitimacy of the religious claim"). But see McConnell, "Free Exercise Revisionism," supra: "Why is the Free Exercise Clause a particular target? [Unless] Smith is the harbinger of a wholesale retreat from judicial discretion across the range of constitutional law, there should be some explanation of why the problem in this field is more acute than it is elsewhere."

Justice O'Connor, in contrast, endorsed a "balancing, rather than categorical, approach," and argued that courts had adequately protected state interests even though they engaged in balancing under Sherbert, Yoder and their progeny. She favored continued case-by-case determination of "whether the burden on the specific plaintiffs before us is constitutionally significant and whether the particular criminal interest asserted by the State before us is compelling." She denied any need to inquire into the centrality of religious practices. But can the Court determine whether a burden is "constitutionally significant" without making such a centrality inquiry? Is there a danger that courts making such an inquiry will exhibit unconscious bias, viewing minority religions through the lens of mainstream practices? For arguments in favor of judicial balancing in free exercise cases during the pre-Smith era, see Gianella, "The Religious Liberty Guarantee," 80 Harv. L. Rev. 1381 (1967); Marcus, "[Applying] Standards Under the Free Exercise Clause," 1973 Duke L. J. 1217.

Was Smith consistent with the doctrine of stare decisis? Note that Justice Scalia sought to distinguish rather than overrule prior cases inconsistent with the deferential rule embraced in Smith. Are these distinctions persuasive? See McConnell, "Free Exercise Revisionism," supra (arguing that the Court's distinction of Yoder and the unemployment compensation cases "appears to have one function only: to enable the Court to reach the conclusion it desired in Smith without openly overruling any prior decisions"). Would candid overrule have been preferable? Did the pre-Smith decisions themselves lack candor? Did Smith simply state the rule immanent in the earlier decisions? Note Justice O'Connor's objection to "judg[ing] the vitality of a constitutional doctrine by looking to the win-loss record of the plaintiffs who happen to come before us."

4. *Religious exemptions and anarchy.* Justice Scalia warned in Smith that to grant widespread judicial exemptions in response to free exercise claims "would be courting anarchy," and held that the Court's new rationality test "must be preferred to a system in which each conscience is a law unto itself." How severe is the threat of anarchy as a practical matter? Does Justice Scalia overestimate the practical dangers of religious deviance from conventional norms? Would Mormon polygamy undermine the institution of monogamous marriage elsewhere in the society? Would Native American peyote ingestion threaten the war on drugs? Justice Blackmun's dissent in Smith viewed a peyote exception as largely self-limiting. Was his argument persuasive?

Is the threat to the rule of law greater if a religious practice threatens physical harm to its practitioners? Recall the dictum in Reynolds suggesting that human sacrifice could hardly be countenanced even if mandated by a religion. Is this so even if the participants were adult volunteers? May adults forego medical treatment barred by their religion? May they withhold such treatment from their children? Is there an argument that the threat to the rule of law is minimal in these cases because such practices are unlikely to be widely imitated?

What if the religious practice has significant external effects on the community? Should religious organizations be allowed to pay workers in their commercial enterprises less than the minimum wage because they work for spiritual reasons? What if this gives the religious enterprises a competitive advantage over other businesses? See Tony & Susan Alamo Foundation v. Secretary of Labor, 471 U.S. 290 (1985) (rejecting a free exercise challenge to the application of the minimum wage, overtime, and recordkeeping requirements of the Fair Labor Standards Act). Does the case against exemption increase with the size, and therefore, the "market power" of the religion? Would such an approach require the Roman Catholic church to admit women as priests in order to combat gender discrimination?

For discussion of these and related issues, see McConnell, "Religious Freedom at a Crossroads," 59 U. Chi. L. Rev. 115 (1992); and Sullivan, "Religion and Liberal Democracy," 59 U. Chi. L. Rev. 195 (1992).

5. *The aftermath of Smith: The Religious Freedom Restoration Act of 1993.* After the Court issued the Smith decision and denied rehearing, a broad coalition of religious groups began working on legislation that would contain its effects by restoring a range of religious exemptions. The coalition attracted strong bipartisan support in Congress, and in 1993, the Congress overwhelmingly passed and the President signed the Religious Freedom Restoration Act (RFRA), 42 U.S.C. §§ 2000bb et seq. The Act contained formal findings that "laws 'neutral' toward religion may burden religious exercise without compelling justification," and that Smith had "virtually eliminated the requirement that the government justify burdens on religious exercise imposed by laws neutral toward religion." The Act identified as one of its purposes "to restore the compelling interest test as set forth in [Sherbert] and [Yoder]."

The operative provisions of the Act, 42 U.S.C. §§ 2000bb–1, provide: "(a) Government shall not substantially burden a person's exercise of religion even if the burden results from a rule of general applicability, except as provided in subsection (b) of this section. (b) Government may substantially burden a person's exercise of religion only if it demonstrates that application of the burden to the person (1) is in furtherance of a compelling governmental interest; and (2) is the least restrictive means of furthering that compelling governmental interest."

Did Congress have the authority to enact RFRA under section 5 of the 14th Amendment? See the materials on Katzenbach v. Morgan (1966; p. 998 above). Does RFRA violate the separation of powers by permitting Congress to overrule a Supreme Court constitutional precedent by statute rather than constitutional amendment? Recall Marbury v. Madison. Does RFRA violate the establishment clause by giving benefits to religion that are not required by the free exercise clause as the Court construed the latter clause in Smith? See p. 1548 below. For debate on whether RFRA is constitutional, see Laycock, "The Religious Freedom Restoration Act," 1993 B.Y.U. L. Rev. 221; Laycock & Thomas, "Interpreting the Religious Freedom Restoration Act," 73 Tex. L. Rev. 209 (1994); Idleman, "The Religious Freedom Restoration Act: Pushing the Limits of Legislative Power," 73 Tex. L. Rev. 247 (1994); Eisgruber & Sager, "Why the Religious Freedom Restoration Act Is Unconstitutional," 69 N.Y.U. L. Rev. 437 (1994); Marshall, "The Religious Freedom Restoration Act: Establishment, Equal Protection and Free Speech Concerns," 56 Mont.L.Rev. 227 (1995); Lupu, "Of Time and the RFRA: a Lawyer's Guide to the Religious Freedom Restoration Act," 56 Mont.L.Rev. 171 (1995).

Assuming RFRA was constitutionally enacted, how should it be interpreted? Does the "substantial burden" test track the holdings of the pre-Smith cases? Will application of this threshold requirement limit the range of RFRA's application? Does the "compelling interest" test apply to all religious exemption claims, or only to those to which pre-Smith decisions applied it? Does the requirement that government demonstrate the necessity of application of the burden "to the person" preclude inquiry into whether *other* exemptions in the aggregate will undermine the effectiveness of the law? Recall Justice Steven's concern in Goldman that an exception for Jewish yarmulkes would lead to exceptions for Sikh turbans and Rastafarian dreadlocks. Will RFRA give greater protection to religionists on balance than the pre-Smith cases?

SECTION 3.   THE ESTABLISHMENT CLAUSE

Introduction. All interpretations of the establishment clause agree that it prohibits the creation of an official church. Thus, requiring oaths of fidelity to a faith or tithes or other financial support for a church would be paradigmatic violations of the clause. There, however, agreement ends. Modern debates over the scope of the establishment clause have centered on what the clause might prohibit beyond official oaths or tithes. Does the establishment clause bar official sponsorship of religious tenets or symbols, even if no citizen is coerced to support them? Should psychological "coercion" count? Is government "endorsement" of religion troubling even in the absence of coercion? Must religious entities be excluded from all forms of public financial support? May they be included on an equal footing with other recipients of government largesse? Or should there be an absolute bar on government aid to religious evangelism? The cases that follow explore these questions. Section A explores cases involving claims that government has impermissibly sponsored religious doctrines or symbols. Section B asks when, if ever, government financial aid to religion might be permissible. And section C considers possible establishment clause objections to government's deliberate efforts to accommodate religion, for example by legislative exemptions from general laws.

At the outset, it must be noted that the Court set forth an influential test for establishment clause violations in LEMON v. KURTZMAN, 403 U.S. 602 (1971), that is often referred to in the materials that follow. Lemon struck down certain types of financial aid to public schools, a topic covered below. Summarizing past decisions, Lemon held that a statute must meet three criteria in order to withstand establishment clause attack: "First, the statute must have a secular legislative purpose; second, its principal or primary effect must be one that neither advances nor inhibits religion; finally, the statute must not foster 'an excessive government entanglement with religion.'"

The Lemon test has been sharply criticized, and several Justices have called for its express repudiation. The principal criticisms are: (1) that the "purpose" requirement, taken literally, would invalidate all deliberate government accommodation of religion, even though such accommodation is sometimes required by the free exercise clause, and has sometimes been held permissible under the establishment clause even if not constitutionally compelled; (2) that legislative "purpose" is in any case difficult to ascertain in a multi-member body, and (3) that the "entanglement" prong contradicts the previous two—*some* administrative "entanglement" is essential to ensure that government aid does not excessively promote religious purposes. Faced with these criticisms, the Court has not formally renounced the Lemon test, but has relied on it less and less in recent cases. The Court's decisions over the last decade increasingly employ entirely different sets of analytical devices for distinguishing establishments. How would you characterize the Court's implicit replacements for the Lemon test? How do they differ from Lemon? Are they an improvement?

———

A. ENSHRINING OFFICIAL BELIEFS

———

"RELEASED TIME" PROGRAMS IN PUBLIC SCHOOLS

The Court subjected itself to charges of inconsistency in its initial encounters with problems involving alleged governmental support for religious themes. In McCOLLUM v. BOARD OF EDUCATION, 333 U.S. 203 (1948), the Court struck down a school board's practice of permitting students to attend sectarian classes held in the public schools during school hours by parochial school instructors. Justice Black's majority opinion found two problems: first, public school buildings were used for the purpose of providing religious education, and second, the program afforded "sectarian groups an invaluable aid in that it help[ed] to provide pupils for their religious classes through use of the state's compulsory public school machinery." Just four years later, however, the Court held in Zorach, which follows, that releasing children during school hours to attend sectarian classes *outside* the public school did *not* violate the establishment clause. Is the challenged program in Zorach sufficiently unlike that in McCollum to warrant a different result? Or did Zorach implicitly overrule McCollum?

Zorach v. Clauson

343 U.S. 306, 72 S.Ct. 679, 96 L.Ed. 954 (1952).

Justice DOUGLAS delivered the opinion of the Court.

New York City has a program which permits its public schools to release students during the school day so that they may leave the school buildings and school grounds and go to religious centers for religious instruction or devotional exercises. A student is released on written request of his parents. Those not released stay in the classrooms. The churches make weekly reports to the schools, sending a list of children who have been released from public school but who have not reported for religious instruction. This "released time" program involves neither religious instruction in public school classrooms nor the expenditure of public funds. All costs, including the application blanks, are paid by the religious organizations.

[Appellants, taxpayers and residents whose children attend public schools, challenge the law], contending it is in essence not different from the one involved in [McCollum]. Their [argument] reduces itself to this: the weight and influence of the school is put behind a program for religious instruction; public school teachers police it, keeping tab on students who are released; the classroom activities come to a halt while the students who are released for religious instruction are on leave; the school is a crutch on which the churches are leaning for support in their religious training; without the cooperation of the schools this "released time" program, like the one in [McCollum], would be futile and ineffective. [The highest state court sustained the law.]

[No] one is forced to go to the religious classroom and no religious exercise or instruction is brought to the classrooms of the public schools. A student need not take religious instruction. He is left to his own desires as to the manner or time of his religious devotions, if any. There is a suggestion that the system involves the use of coercion to get public school students into religious classrooms. There is no evidence in the record before us that supports that conclusion. [If] in fact coercion were used, if it were established that any one or more teachers were using their office to persuade or force students to take the religious instruction, a wholly different case would be presented. [Hence] we put aside that claim of coercion both as respects the "free exercise" of religion and "an establishment of religion."

Moreover, apart from that claim of coercion, we do not see how New York by this type of "released time" program has made a law respecting an establishment of [religion]. There cannot be the slightest doubt that the First Amendment reflects the philosophy that Church and State should be [separated]. The First Amendment, however, does not say that in every and all respects there shall be a separation of Church and State. Rather, it studiously defines the manner, the specific ways, in which there shall be no concert or union or dependency one on the other. That is the common sense of the matter. Otherwise the state and religion would be aliens to each other—hostile, suspicious, and even unfriendly. Churches could not be required to pay even property taxes. Municipalities would not be permitted to render police or fire protection to religious groups. Policemen who helped parishioners into their places of worship would violate the Constitution. Prayers in our legislative halls; the appeals to the Almighty in the messages of the Chief Executive; the proclamations making Thanksgiving Day a holiday; "so help me God" in our courtroom oaths—these and all other references to the Almighty that run through our laws, our public rituals, our ceremonies would be flouting the First Amendment. A fastidious atheist or agnostic could even object to the supplication with which the Court opens each session: "God save the United States and this Honorable Court." We would have to press the concept of separation of Church and State to these extremes to condemn the present law on constitutional grounds. [We] are a religious people whose institutions presuppose a Supreme Being. We guarantee the freedom to worship as one chooses. We make room for as wide a variety of beliefs and creeds as the spiritual needs of man deem necessary. We sponsor an attitude on the part of government that shows no partiality to any one group and that lets each flourish according to the zeal of its adherents and the appeal of its dogma. When the state encourages religious instruction or cooperates with religious authorities by adjusting the schedule of public events to sectarian needs, it follows the best of our traditions. For it then respects the religious nature of our people and accommodates the public service to their spiritual needs. To hold that it may not would be to find in the Constitution a requirement that the government show a callous indifference to religious groups. That would be preferring those who believe in no religion over those who do believe. [Government] may not coerce anyone to attend church, to observe a religious holiday, or to take religious instruction. But it can close its doors or suspend its operations as to those who want to repair to their religious sanctuary for worship or instruction. No more than that is undertaken here. [The] constitutional standard is the separation of Church and State. The problem [is] one of degree.

In the McCollum case the classrooms were used for religious instruction and the force of the public school was used to promote that instruction. Here, [the] public schools do no more than accommodate their schedules to a program of outside religious instructions. We follow [McCollum]. But we cannot expand it to cover the present released time program unless separation of Church and State means that public institutions can make no adjustments of their schedules to accommodate the religious needs of the people. We cannot read into the Bill of Rights such a philosophy of hostility to religion.

Affirmed.

Justice BLACK, [dissenting].

[Here as in McCollum], the school authorities release some of the children on the condition that they attend the religious classes, get reports on whether they attend, and hold the other children in the school building until the religious hour is over. As we attempted to make categorically clear, the McCollum decision would have been the same if the religious classes had not been held in the school buildings. [New York] is manipulating its compulsory education laws to help religious sects get pupils. This is not separation but combination of [Church and State].

Justice JACKSON, dissenting.

This released time program is founded upon a use of the State's power of coercion, which, for me, determines its unconstitutionality. Stripped to its essentials, the plan has two stages, first, that the State compel each student to yield a large part of his time for public secular education and, second, that some of it be "released" to him on condition that he devote it to sectarian religious purposes. [If] public education were taking so much of the pupils' time as to injure the public or the students' welfare by encroaching upon their religious opportunity, simply shortening everyone's school day would facilitate voluntary and optional attendance at Church classes. But that suggestion is rejected upon the ground that if they are made free many students will not go to the Church. Hence, they must be deprived of freedom for this period, with Church attendance put to them as one of the two permissible ways of using it. .The distinction attempted between [McCollum] and this is trivial, almost to the point of cynicism. [The] wall which the Court was professing to erect between Church and State has become even more warped and twisted than I expected. Today's judgment will be more interesting to students of psychology and of the judicial processes than to students of constitutional law. [Justice Frankfurter agreed with Justice Jackson and also filed a separate dissent.]

THE SCHOOL PRAYER CASES

1. *Teacher-led prayers, Bible readings, and moments of silence.* The Court has consistently struck down school prayer initiated by school officials as a violation of the establishment clause. The Court's first encounter with the problem came in ENGEL v. VITALE, 370 U.S. 421 (1962). There, the New York Board of Regents had prepared a "non-denominational" prayer for use in the public schools, which read: "Almighty God, we acknowledge our dependence upon Thee, and we beg Thy blessings upon us, our parents, our teachers and our Country." A local school board directed that the prayer be recited daily by each class. That practice was challenged by parents of a number of students who claimed that it was "contrary to the beliefs, religions, or religious practices of both themselves and their children." The highest state court upheld the practice, so long as the schools did not compel any student to join in the prayer over a parent's objection. Justice BLACK's majority opinion held the practice "wholly inconsistent with the Establishment Clause." The practice was clearly "a religious activity" and the establishment clause "must at least mean that [it] is no part of the business of government to compose official prayers for any group of the American people to recite as a part of a religious program carried on by government."

Justice Black added: "Neither the fact that the prayer may be denominationally neutral, nor the fact that its observance on the part of the students is voluntary, can serve to free it from the limitations of the Establishment Clause, as it might from the Free Exercise [Clause]. Although these two clauses may in certain instances overlap, they forbid two quite different kinds of governmental encroachment upon religious freedom. The Establishment Clause, unlike the Free Exercise Clause, does not depend upon any showing of direct governmental compulsion and is violated by the enactment of laws which establish an official religion whether those laws operate directly to coerce nonobserving individuals or not. This is not to say, of course, that laws officially prescribing a particular form of religious worship do not involve coercion of such individuals. When the power, prestige and financial support of government is placed behind a particular religious belief, the indirect coercive pressure upon religious minorities to conform to the prevailing officially approved religion is plain. But the purposes underlying the Establishment Clause go much further than that. [Its] most immediate purpose rested on the belief that a union of government and religion tends to destroy government and to degrade religion. [Another] purpose [rested upon] an awareness of the historical fact that governmentally established religions and religious persecutions go hand in hand."

Justice STEWART's dissent relied on Zorach in concluding that New York's practice merely recognized "the deeply entrenched and highly cherished

spiritual traditions of our Nation"—and that the references to religion and to
God in such practices as congressional prayers and official oaths was similarly
justified. Justice Douglas concurred separately; Justices Frankfurter and White
did not participate.

One year after Engel, the Court extended the principles of that case beyond
state-composed prayers. ABINGTON SCHOOL DIST. v. SCHEMPP, 374 U.S.
203 (1963), held that the establishment clause prohibits state laws and practices "requiring the selection and reading at the opening of the school day of
verses from the Holy Bible and the recitation of the Lord's Prayer by the
students in unison." The Pennsylvania law in Schempp provided: "At least ten
verses from the Holy Bible shall be read, without comment, at the opening of
each public school on each school day. Any child shall be excused from such
Bible reading, or attending such Bible reading, upon the written request of his
parent or guardian." The Schempp family, members of the Unitarian Church,
successfully challenged high school opening exercises involving the recitation of
the Lord's Prayer as well as the reading of the Bible verses.

Justice CLARK's opinion for the Court stated: "The wholesome 'neutrality'
of which this Court's cases speak [stems] from a recognition of the teachings of
history that powerful sects or groups might bring about a fusion of governmental and religious functions or a concert or dependency of one upon the other to
the end that official support of the State or Federal Government would be
placed behind the tenets of one or of all orthodoxies. This the Establishment
Clause prohibits. [The] test may be stated as follows: what are the purpose and
the primary effect of the enactment? If either is the advancement or inhibition
of religion then the enactment exceeds the scope of legislative power as
circumscribed by the Constitution." Applying those principles (which foreshadowed the Lemon test), Justice Clark noted that "it is no defense to urge that
the religious practices here may be relatively minor encroachments on the First
Amendment. The breach of neutrality that is today a trickling stream may all
too soon become a raging torrent." He pointed out that the decision did not bar
the "study of the Bible or of religion, when presented objectively as part of a
secular program of education." But that was not the case here: these were
"religious exercises, required by the State in violation of the command of the
First Amendment that the Government maintain strict neutrality, neither
aiding nor opposing religion." Justices Douglas, Goldberg and Brennan filed
separate concurrences.

Justice STEWART, the sole dissenter, insisted that "religion and government must necessarily interact in countless ways" and that "there are areas in
which a doctrinaire reading of the Establishment Clause leads to irreconcilable
conflict with the Free Exercise Clause." He elaborated: "The dangers both to
government and to religion inherent in official support of instruction in the
tenets of various religious sects [see McCollum] are absent in the present cases,
which involve only a reading from the Bible unaccompanied by comments
which might otherwise constitute instruction. [In] the absence of coercion upon
those who do not wish to [participate], such provisions cannot [be] held to
represent the type of support of religion barred by the [Establishment Clause].
[W]hether [the exercises] are constitutionally invalid [turns] on the question of
coercion. [Certain] types of exercises would present situations in which no
possibility of coercion on the part of secular officials could be claimed to exist.
[But] a law which provided for religious exercises during the school day and
which contained no excusal provision would obviously be unconstitutionally
coercive upon those who did not wish to participate. And even under a law
containing an excusal provision, if the exercises were held during the school
day, and no equally desirable alternative were provided by the school authori-

ties, the likelihood that children might be under at least some psychological compulsion to participate would be great. In a case such as the latter, however, I think we would err if we *assumed* such coercion in the absence of any evidence. Viewed in this light, it seems to be clear that the [record here is] wholly inadequate to support an informed or responsible decision."

The issue of school prayer returned to the Court in WALLACE v. JAFFREE, 472 U.S. 38 (1985). The decision struck down an Alabama law authorizing schools to set aside one minute at the start of each day "for meditation or voluntary prayer." The statute was an amendment of an earlier law which had authorized a one-minute period of silence in all public schools merely "for meditation." Justice STEVENS' opinion for the Court stated that "the individual freedom of conscience protected by the First Amendment embraces the right to select any religious faith or none at all." He found that the law "was not motivated by any clearly secular purpose," thus violating the Lemon test. He noted that the state legislator sponsoring the amendment had said that it was an "effort to return voluntary prayer" to the public schools. He elaborated: "The legislative intent to return prayer to the public schools is, of course, quite different from merely protecting every student's right to engage in voluntary prayer during an appropriate moment of silence during the school day." The earlier law "already protected that right, containing nothing that prevented any student from engaging in voluntary prayer during a silent minute of meditation." Hence, the amendment to that law must have been enacted "to convey a message of State endorsement and promotion of prayer. [The] addition of 'or voluntary prayer' indicates that the State intended to characterize prayer as a favored practice. Such an endorsement is not consistent with the established principle that the Government must pursue a course of complete neutrality toward religion."

Justice O'CONNOR concurred in the result. She did not view all moment-of-silence requirements as unconstitutional. She suggested that the crucial question was whether the state had endorsed religion. "By mandating a moment of silence, the State does not necessarily endorse any activity that might occur during the period," nor "encourage[] prayer over other specified alternatives." But in this case, "the purpose and likely effect" of the Alabama amendment was "to endorse and sponsor voluntary prayer in the public schools." Here the state had "conveyed or attempted to convey the message that children should use the moment of silence for prayer." Chief Justice Burger and Justices White and Rehnquist dissented.

2. *School prayer and "coercion."* Do the school prayer cases, like the released-time cases above, turn on the principle that coercion into a profession of belief violates the establishment clause, and the assumption that the public school setting is inherently coercive? What makes the school setting coercive? The fact that attendance is compulsory? The psychological immaturity of children, and their lack of fully developed faculties of resistance and consent? See Stone, "In Opposition to the School Prayer Amendment," 50 U. Chi. L. Rev. 823 (1983) (noting that children are especially vulnerable to peer pressure).

Why should coercion be a prerequisite to a finding of establishment? The free exercise clause already prohibits coercion into faith or out of it. As Justice Clark noted in Schempp, "the Free Exercise Clause [recognizes] the right of every person to freely choose his own [religious] course, free of any compulsion from the state." Would limiting establishment to cases of "coercion" make the establishment clause mere surplusage, redundant of the free exercise clause? What else beyond coercion might the establishment clause prohibit? One possibility is religious incentives or inducements that fall short of coercion. See, e.g., Choper, "Religion in the Schools," 47 Minn.L.Rev. 329 (1963) (arguing that the establishment clause is violated in public schools when the state engages in "solely religious activity that is likely to result in (1) compromising the student's religious or conscientious beliefs or (2) influencing the student's freedom of religious or conscientious choice"). Why should it not be enough that the school practices are "solely religious"? Why should it also be necessary to demonstrate impact on student beliefs or choice? Another possibility is suggested by Justice O'Connor's Jaffree concurrence: she argues that the state may not "endorse" religion. Does endorsement cover a broader range of cases than coercion? Why should government have to refrain from religious speech or symbolism if it is not coercing or influencing a citizen to change his or her faith? Justice O'Connor suggested in Jaffree, citing her concurrence in Lynch v. Donnelly (1984; p. 1521 below), that endorsement sends a message of symbolic civic excommunication to nonmembers of the endorsed faith. Why should such a message constitute establishment in the absence of a showing that religious beliefs will be altered as a result?

Consider which principle, coercion or endorsement, animates the various opinions in the following case, which invalidated an official prayer at a middle school graduation ceremony.

Lee v. Weisman

505 U.S. 577; 112 S. Ct. 2649; 120 L.Ed.2d 467 (1992).

[The principal of a Providence middle school invited a rabbi to deliver prayers at the school's graduation ceremony, pursuant to the school district's longstanding custom of inviting members of the clergy for this purpose. The principal advised the rabbi that his prayers should be nonsectarian. The rabbi's invocation read: "God of the Free, Hope of the Brave: For the legacy of America where diversity is celebrated and the rights of minorities are protected, we thank You. May these young men and women grow up to enrich it. For the liberty of America, we thank You. May these new graduates grow up to guard it. For the political process of America in which all its citizens may participate, for its court system where all may seek justice we thank You. May those we honor this morning always turn to it in trust. For the destiny of America we thank You. May the graduates of Nathan Bishop Middle School so live that they might help to share it. May our aspirations for our country and for these young people, who are our hope for the future, be richly fulfilled. AMEN." The rabbi's benediction read: "O God, we are grateful to You for having endowed us with the capacity for learning which we have celebrated on this joyous commencement. Happy families give thanks for seeing their children achieve an important milestone. Send Your blessings upon the teachers and administrators who helped prepare them. The graduates now need strength and guidance for the future, help them to understand that we are not complete with academic knowledge alone. We must each strive to fulfill what You require of us all: To do justly, to love mercy, to walk humbly. We give thanks to You, Lord, for keeping us alive, sustaining us and allowing us to reach this special, happy occasion. AMEN." Deborah Weisman, a student at the school, raised an establishment clause challenge to the practice of prayer at the district's graduation ceremonies.]

Justice KENNEDY delivered the opinion of the Court.

These dominant facts mark and control the confines of our decision: State officials direct the performance of a formal religious exercise at promotional and graduation ceremonies for secondary schools. Even for those students who object to the religious exercise, their attendance and participation in the state-sponsored religious activity are in a fair and real sense obligatory, though the school district does not require attendance as a condition for receipt of the diploma. [The] controlling precedents as they relate to prayer and religious exercise in primary and secondary public schools compel the holding here that the policy of the city of Providence is an unconstitutional one. [It] is beyond dispute that, at a minimum, the Constitution guarantees that government may not coerce anyone to support or participate in religion or its exercise. [The] State's involvement in the school prayers challenged today violates these central principles.

[We] are asked to recognize the existence of a practice of nonsectarian prayer, prayer within the embrace of what is known as the Judeo–Christian tradition, prayer which is more acceptable than one which, for example, makes explicit references to the God of Israel, or to Jesus Christ, or to a patron saint. [But] though the First Amendment does not allow the government to stifle prayers which aspire to [a civic religion], neither does it permit the government to undertake that task for itself. The First Amendment's Religion Clauses mean that religious beliefs and religious expression are too precious to be either proscribed or prescribed by the State. The design of the Constitution is that preservation and transmission of religious beliefs and worship is a responsibility and a choice committed to the private sphere, which itself is promised freedom to pursue that mission. [The] suggestion that government may establish an official or civic religion as a means of avoiding the establishment of a religion with more specific creeds strikes us as a contradiction that cannot be accepted.

The degree of school involvement here made it clear that the graduation prayers bore the imprint of the State and thus put school-age children who objected in an untenable position. [As] we have observed before, there are heightened concerns with protecting freedom of conscience from subtle coercive pressure in the elementary and secondary public schools. Our decisions in [Engel and Schempp] recognize, among other things, that prayer exercises in public schools carry a particular risk of indirect coercion. [What] to most believers may seem nothing more than a reasonable request that the nonbeliever respect their religious practices, in a school context may appear to the nonbeliever or dissenter to be an attempt to employ the machinery of the State to enforce a religious orthodoxy.

We need not look beyond the circumstances of this case to see the phenomenon at work. The undeniable fact is that the school district's supervision and control of a high school graduation ceremony places public pressure, as well as peer pressure, on attending students to stand as a group or, at least, maintain respectful silence during the Invocation and Benediction. This pressure, though subtle and indirect, can be as real as any overt compulsion. Of course, in our culture standing or remaining silent can signify adherence to a view or simple respect for the views of others. And no doubt some persons who have no desire to join a prayer have little objection to standing as a sign of respect for those who do. But for the dissenter of high school age, who has a reasonable perception that she is being forced by the State to pray in a manner her conscience will not allow, the injury is no less real. There can be no doubt that for many, if not most, of the students at the graduation, the act of standing or remaining silent was an expression of participation in the Rabbi's prayer. That was the very point of the religious exercise. It is of little comfort to a dissenter, then, to be told that for her the act of standing or remaining in silence signifies mere respect, rather than participation. What matters is that, given our social conventions, a reasonable dissenter in this milieu could believe that the group exercise signified her own participation or approval of it.

Finding no violation under these circumstances would place objectors in the dilemma of participating, with all that implies, or protesting. We do not address whether that choice is acceptable if the affected citizens are mature adults, but we think the State may not, consistent with the Establishment Clause, place primary and secondary school children in this position. Research in psychology supports the common assumption that adolescents are often susceptible to pressure from their peers towards conformity, and that the influence is strongest in matters of social convention. To recognize that the choice imposed by the State constitutes an unacceptable constraint only acknowledges that the government may no more use social pressure to enforce orthodoxy than it may use more direct means.

[Although] attendance at graduation [ceremonies] is voluntary, [the argument] that the option of not attending the graduation excuses any inducement or coercion in the ceremony itself [lacks] all persuasion. Law reaches past formalism. And to say a teenage student has a real choice not to attend her high school graduation is formalistic in the extreme. [Everyone] knows that in our society and in our culture high school graduation is one of life's most significant occasions. A school rule which excuses attendance is beside the point. Attendance may not be required by official decree, yet it is apparent that a student is not free to absent herself from the graduation exercise in any real sense of the term "voluntary," for absence would require forfeiture of those intangible benefits which have motivated the student through youth and all her high school years.

[The government argues] that the prayers are an essential part of these ceremonies because for many persons an occasion of this significance lacks meaning if there is no recognition, however brief, that human achievements cannot be understood apart from their spiritual essence. [But this]fails to acknowledge that what for many of Deborah's classmates and their parents was a spiritual imperative was for [her] religious conformance compelled by the State. [The] Constitution forbids the State to exact religious conformity from a student as the price of attending her own high school graduation. [To] say that a student must remain apart from the ceremony at the opening invocation and closing benediction is to risk compelling conformity in an environment analogous to the classroom setting, where we have said the risk of compulsion is especially high.

[We] do not hold that every state action implicating religion is invalid if one or a few citizens find it offensive. People may take offense at all manner of religious as well as nonreligious messages, but offense alone does not in every case show a violation. We know too that sometimes to endure social isolation or even anger may be the price of conscience or nonconformity. But, by any reading of our cases, the conformity required of the student in this case was too high an exaction to withstand the test of the Establishment Clause. The prayer exercises in this case are especially improper because the State has in every practical sense compelled attendance and participation in an explicit religious exercise at an event of singular importance to every student, one the objecting student had no real alternative to avoid. [No] holding by this Court suggests that a school can persuade or compel a student to participate in a religious exercise. That is being done here, and it is forbidden by the Establishment Clause.

[Affirmed.]

Justice BLACKMUN, with whom Justices STEVENS and O'CONNOR join, concurring.

[The] Court holds that the graduation prayer is unconstitutional because the State "in effect required participation in a religious exercise." Although our precedents make clear that proof of government coercion is not necessary to prove an Establishment Clause violation, it is sufficient. Government pressure to participate in a religious activity is an obvious indication that the government is endorsing or promoting religion.

But it is not enough that the government restrain from compelling religious practices: it must not engage in them either. The Court repeatedly has recognized that a violation of the Establishment Clause is not predicated on coercion. The Establishment Clause proscribes public schools from "conveying or attempting to convey a message that religion or a particular religious belief is favored or preferred," even if the schools do not actually "impose pressure upon a student to participate in a religious activity." [There] is no doubt that attempts to aid religion through government coercion jeopardize freedom of conscience. Even subtle pressure diminishes the right of each individual to choose voluntarily what to believe. [Our] decisions have gone beyond prohibiting coercion, however, because the Court has recognized that "the fullest possible scope of religious liberty" entails more than freedom from coercion. [The] mixing of government and religion can be a threat to free government, even if no one is forced to participate. When the government puts its imprimatur on a particular religion, it conveys a message of exclusion to all those who do not adhere to the favored beliefs. A government cannot be premised on the belief that all persons are created equal when it asserts that God prefers some.

[We] have believed that religious freedom cannot exist in the absence of a free democratic government, and that such a government cannot endure when there is fusion between religion and the political regime. We have believed that religious freedom cannot thrive in the absence of a vibrant religious community and that such a community cannot prosper when it is bound to the secular. And we have believed that these were the animating principles behind the adoption of the Establishment Clause. To that end, our cases have prohibited government endorsement of religion, its sponsorship, and active involvement in religion, whether or not citizens were coerced to conform.

Justice SOUTER, with whom Justices STEVENS and O'CONNOR join, concurring.

[Petitioners] rest most of their argument on a theory that [the] Establishment Clause [does] not forbid the state to sponsor affirmations of religious belief that coerce neither support for religion nor participation in religious observance. I appreciate the force of some of the arguments supporting a "coercion" analysis of the Clause. [See] McConnell, "Coercion: The Lost Element of Establishment," 27 Wm. & Mary L. Rev. 933 (1986). But we could not adopt that reading without abandoning our settled law, a course that, in my view, the text of the Clause would not readily permit. Nor does the extratextual evidence of original meaning stand so unequivocally at odds with the textual premise inherent in existing precedent that we should fundamentally reconsider our course.

Over the years, this Court has declared the invalidity of many noncoercive state laws and practices conveying a message of religious endorsement. [For example,] in Wallace v. Jaffree, we struck down a state law requiring a moment of silence in public classrooms not because the statute coerced students to participate in prayer (for it did not), but because the manner of its enactment "conveyed a message of state approval of prayer activities in the public schools." [Our] precedents [cannot] support the position that a showing of coercion is necessary to a successful Establishment Clause claim.

[While] petitioners insist that the prohibition extends only to the "coercive" features and incidents of establishment, they cannot easily square that claim with the constitutional text. The First Amendment forbids not just laws "respecting an establishment of religion," but also those "prohibiting the free exercise thereof." Yet laws that coerce nonadherents to "support or participate in any religion or its exercise," would virtually by definition violate their right to religious free exercise. Thus, a literal application of the coercion test would render the Establishment Clause a virtual nullity. [Without] compelling evidence to the contrary, we should presume that the Framers meant the Clause to stand for something more than petitioners attribute to it.

Petitioners argue from the political setting in which the Establishment Clause was framed, and from the Framers' own political practices following ratification, that government may constitutionally endorse religion so long as it does not coerce religious conformity. [They contend, for example,] that because the early Presidents included religious messages in their inaugural and Thanksgiving Day addresses, the Framers could not have meant the Establishment Clause to forbid noncoercive state endorsement of religion. [But Jefferson] steadfastly refused to issue Thanksgiving proclamations of any kind, in part because he thought they violated the Religion Clauses. [He] accordingly construed the Establishment Clause to forbid not simply state coercion, but also state endorsement, of religious belief and observance. [During] his first three years in office, James Madison also refused to call for days of thanksgiving and prayer, though later, amid the political turmoil of the War of 1812, he did so on four separate occasions. Upon retirement, in an essay condemning as an unconstitutional "establishment" the use of public money to support congressional and military chaplains, he concluded that "religious proclamations by the Executive recommending thanksgivings & fasts are shoots from the same root with the legislative acts reviewed." [To] be sure, the leaders of the young Republic engaged in some of the practices that separationists like Jefferson and Madison criticized. The First Congress did hire institutional chaplains, and Presidents Washington and Adams unapologetically marked days of "public thanksgiving and prayer." [Yet this proves] at worst that [the framers,] like other politicians, could raise constitutional ideals one day and turn their backs on them the next.

[Petitioners] argu[e] that graduation prayers are no different from presidential religious proclamations and similar official "acknowledgments" of religion in public life. But religious invocations in Thanksgiving Day addresses and the like, rarely noticed, ignored without effort, conveyed over an impersonal medium, and directed at no one in particular, inhabit a pallid zone worlds apart from official prayers delivered to a captive audience of public school students and their families. [When] public school officials, armed with the State's authority, convey an endorsement of religion to their students, they strike near the core of the Establishment Clause. However "ceremonial" their messages may be, they are flatly unconstitutional.

Justice SCALIA, with whom Chief Justice REHNQUIST and Justices WHITE and THOMAS join, dissenting.

[In] holding that the Establishment Clause prohibits invocations and benedictions at public-school graduation ceremonies, the Court—with nary a mention that it is doing so—lays waste a tradition that is as old as public-school graduation ceremonies themselves, and that is a component of an even more longstanding American tradition of nonsectarian prayer to God at public celebrations generally. As its instrument of destruction, the bulldozer of its social engineering, the Court invents a boundless, and boundlessly manipulable, test of psychological coercion.

[From] our Nation's origin, prayer has been a prominent part of governmental ceremonies and proclamations. The Declaration of Independence, the document marking our birth as a separate people, "appealed to the Supreme Judge of the world for the rectitude of our intentions" and avowed "a firm reliance on the protection of divine Providence." In his first inaugural address, after swearing his oath of office on a Bible, George Washington deliberately made a prayer a part of his first official act as President, [offering] "fervent supplications to that Almighty Being who rules over the universe." [Such] supplications have been a characteristic feature of inaugural addresses ever since. [Our] national celebration of Thanksgiving likewise dates back to President Washington. [This] tradition of Thanksgiving Proclamations—with their religious theme of prayerful gratitude to God—has been adhered to by almost every President. The other two branches of the Federal Government also have a long-established practice of prayer at public events. [Congressional] sessions have opened with a chaplain's prayer ever since the First Congress. And this Court's own sessions have opened with the invocation "God save the United States and this Honorable Court" since the days of Chief Justice Marshall.

[The] Court presumably would separate graduation invocations and benedictions from other instances of public "preservation and transmission of religious beliefs" on the ground that they involve "psychological coercion." [But a] few citations of "research in psychology" that have no particular bearing upon the precise issue here cannot disguise the fact that the Court has gone beyond the realm where judges know what they are doing. The Court's argument that state officials have "coerced" students to take part in the invocation and benediction at graduation ceremonies is, not to put too fine a point on it, incoherent.

[The] Court's notion that a student who simply sits in "respectful silence" during the invocation and benediction (when all others are standing) has somehow joined—or would somehow be perceived as having joined—in the prayers is nothing short of ludicrous. [Surely] "our social conventions" have not coarsened to the point that anyone who does not stand on his chair and shout obscenities can reasonably be deemed to have assented to everything said in his presence. [But] let us assume the very worst, that the nonparticipating graduate is "subtly coerced" ... to stand! Even that [does] not remotely establish a "participation" (or an "appearance of participation") in a religious exercise. [It is] a permissible inference that one who is standing is doing so simply out of respect for the prayers of others that are in progress.

[The] deeper flaw in the Court's opinion does not lie in its wrong answer to the question whether there was state-induced "peer-pressure" coercion; it lies, rather, in the Court's making violation of the Establishment Clause hinge on such a precious question. The coercion that was a hallmark of historical establishments of religion was coercion of religious orthodoxy and of financial support by force of law and threat of penalty. Typically, attendance at the state church was required; only clergy of the official church could lawfully perform sacraments; and dissenters, if tolerated, faced an array of civil disabilities. [Thus,] while I have no quarrel with the Court's general proposition that the Establishment Clause "guarantees that government may not coerce anyone to support or participate in religion or its exercise," I see no warrant for expanding the concept of coercion beyond acts backed by threat of penalty—a brand of coercion that, happily, is readily discernible to those of us who have made a career of reading the disciples of Blackstone rather than of Freud. The Framers were indeed opposed to coercion of religious worship by the National Government; but, as their own sponsorship of nonsectarian prayer in public events demonstrates, they understood that "speech is not coercive; the listener may do as he likes."

The Court relies on our "school prayer" cases, [Engel and Schempp.] But whatever the merit of those cases, they do not support, much less compel, the Court's psycho-journey. [School] instruction is not a public ceremony. [And] we have made clear our understanding that school prayer occurs within a framework in which legal coercion to attend school (i. e., coercion under threat of penalty) provides the ultimate backdrop. [Finally,] our school-prayer cases turn in part on the fact that the classroom is inherently an instructional setting, and daily prayer there—where parents are not present to counter "the students' emulation of teachers as role models and the children's susceptibility to peer pressure," might be thought to raise special concerns regarding state interference with the liberty of parents to direct the religious upbringing of their children. [Voluntary] prayer at graduation—a one-time ceremony at which parents, friends and relatives are present—can hardly be thought to raise the same concerns.

[Given] the odd basis for the Court's decision, invocations and benedictions will be able to be given at public-school graduations next June, as they have for the past century and a half, so long as school authorities make clear that anyone who abstains from screaming in protest does not necessarily participate in the prayers. All that is seemingly needed is an announcement, or perhaps a written insertion at the beginning of the graduation Program, to the effect that, while all are asked to rise for the invocation and benediction, none is compelled to join in them, nor will be assumed, by rising, to have done so. That obvious fact recited, the graduates and their parents may proceed to thank God, as Americans have always done, for the blessings He has generously bestowed on them and on their country. [The] founders of our Republic knew the fearsome potential of sectarian religious belief to generate civil dissension and civil strife. And they also knew that nothing, absolutely nothing, is so inclined to foster among religious believers of various faiths a toleration—no, an affection—for one another than voluntarily joining in prayer together, to the God whom they all worship and seek. [To] deprive our society of that important unifying mechanism, in order to spare the nonbeliever what seems to me the minimal inconvenience of standing or even sitting in respectful nonparticipation, is as senseless in policy as it is unsupported in law.

RELIGION IN THE PUBLIC SCHOOL CURRICULUM

1. *The Ten Commandments.* In STONE v. GRAHAM, 449 U.S. 39 (1980), the Court held unconstitutional a Kentucky law that required the posting of a copy of the Ten Commandments, purchased with private contributions, in public school classrooms. In sustaining the law, the state trial court had emphasized that the law's "avowed purpose" was "secular and not religious." The Court reversed summarily, without hearing argument on the merits. The majority's per curiam opinion concluded that the law had "no secular legislative purpose," even though it required that each display of the Ten Commandments have a notation in small print stating: "The secular application of the

Ten Commandments is clearly seen in its adoption as the fundamental legal code of Western Civilization and the Common Law of the United States." The majority viewed the predominant purpose of the posting requirement as "plainly religious," since the Ten Commandments are "undeniably a sacred text in the Jewish and Christian faiths." Even though some of the Commandments address secular matters, "the first part of the Commandments concerns the religious duties of believers."

Justice Rehnquist's dissent insisted that the Court's ruling was "without precedent in Establishment Clause jurisprudence." He noted: "The fact that the asserted secular purpose may overlap what some may see as a religious objective does not render [the law] unconstitutional." Justice Stewart also dissented on the merits; Chief Justice Burger and Justice Blackmun objected to the summary disposition, arguing that the case should have been given plenary consideration.

2. *Teaching evolution and creationism.* In EPPERSON v. ARKANSAS, 393 U.S. 97 (1968), the Court invalidated the Arkansas version of the Tennessee "anti-evolution" law that gained national notoriety in the Scopes "monkey law" trial in 1927. The Court found the law to be in conflict with the establishment clause mandate of "neutrality." The Arkansas law prohibited teachers in state schools from teaching "the theory or doctrine that mankind ascended or descended from a lower order of animals." The highest state court had expressed "no opinion" on "whether the Act prohibits any explanation of the theory of evolution or merely prohibits teaching that the theory is true." On either interpretation, Justice FORTAS' majority opinion concluded, the law could not stand: "The overriding fact is that Arkansas' law selects from the body of knowledge a particular segment which it proscribes for the sole reason that it is deemed to conflict with a particular religious doctrine; that is, with a particular interpretation of the Book of Genesis by a particular religious group." The Court found it unnecessary to rely on broad academic freedom principles because of the availability of the "narrower terms" of the First Amendment's religion provisions: "The State's undoubted right to prescribe the curriculum for its public schools" did not include the right to bar "the teaching of a scientific theory or doctrine where that prohibition is based upon reasons that violate the First Amendment." Here, given the history of the Arkansas law, "fundamentalist sectarian conviction was and is the law's reason for existence." This plainly was not the required religious neutrality: "Arkansas did not seek to excise from the curricula of its schools and universities all discussion of the origin of man. The law's effort was confined to an attempt to blot out a particular theory because of its supposed conflict with the Biblical account, literally read."

In separate opinions, Justices BLACK and STEWART explained that they concurred solely on the ground of vagueness. Justice Black criticized the majority for reaching out to "troublesome" First Amendment questions. He noted, for example, that "a state law prohibiting all teaching of human development or biology is constitutionally quite different from a law that compels a teacher to teach as true only one theory of a given doctrine" and he stated that he was not ready to hold "that a person hired to teach schoolchildren takes with him into the classroom a constitutional right to teach sociological, economic, political, or religious subjects that the school's managers do not want discussed." He questioned, moreover, whether the majority's view achieved "religious neutrality": If some considered evolution anti-religious, was the state constitutionally bound to permit teaching of anti-religious doctrine? Did the Court's holding infringe "the religious freedom of those who consider evolution an anti-religious doctrine?" Since there was no indication that the "literal Biblical doctrine" of evolution was taught, could not the removal of the subject of evolution be justified as leaving the State "in a neutral position toward these supposedly competing religious and anti-religious doctrines?" Justice Black also objected that "it is simply too difficult to determine what [a legislature's] motives were."

Edwards v. Aguillard

482 U.S. 578, 107 S.Ct. 2573, 96 L.Ed.2d 510 (1987).

Justice BRENNAN delivered the opinion of the Court.

The question for decision is whether Louisiana's "Balanced Treatment for Creation–Science and Evolution–Science in Public School Instruction" Act (Creationism Act) is facially invalid as violative of the Establishment Clause. The Creationism Act forbids the teaching of the theory of evolution in public schools unless accompanied by instruction in "creation science." No school is required to teach evolution or creation science. If either is taught, however, the other must also be taught. The theories of evolution and creation science are statutorily defined as "the scientific evidences for (creation or evolution) and inferences from those scientific evidences." Appellees, who include parents of children attending Louisiana public schools, Louisiana teachers, and religious leaders, challenged the constitutionality of the Act. [The] District Court [granted summary judgment to appellees, holding] that the Creationism Act violated the Establishment Clause either because it prohibited the teaching of evolution or because it required the teaching of creation science with the purpose of advancing a particular religious doctrine. The Court of Appeals affirmed. [We affirm.]

[The] Court has been particularly vigilant in monitoring compliance with the Establishment Clause in elementary and secondary schools. [Families] entrust public schools with the education of their children, but condition their trust on the understanding that the classroom will not purposely be used to advance religious views that may conflict with the private beliefs of the student and his or her family. Students in such institutions are impressionable and their attendance is involuntary. The State exerts great authority and coercive power through mandatory attendance requirements, and because of the students' emulation of teachers as role models and the children's susceptibility to peer pressure.

Lemon's first prong focuses on the purpose that animated adoption of the Act. [In] this case, appellants have identified no clear secular purpose for the Louisiana Act. True, the Act's stated purpose is to protect academic freedom. This phrase might, in common parlance, be understood as referring to enhancing the freedom of teachers to teach what they will. The Court of Appeals, however, correctly concluded that the Act was not designed to further that goal. [Even] if "academic freedom" is read to mean "teaching all of the evidence" with respect to the origin of human beings, the Act does not further this purpose. The goal of providing a more comprehensive science curriculum is not furthered either by outlawing the teaching of evolution or by requiring the teaching of creation science.

While the Court is normally deferential to a State's articulation of a secular purpose, it is required that the statement of such purpose be sincere and not a sham. It is [clear] that requiring schools to teach creation science with evolution does not advance academic freedom. The Act does not grant teachers a flexibility that they did not already possess to supplant the present science curriculum with a presentation of theories, besides evolution, about the origin of life. [Furthermore,] the goal of basic "fairness" is hardly furthered by the Act's discriminatory preference for the teaching of creation science and against the teaching of evolution. While requiring that curriculum guides be developed for creation science, the Act says nothing of comparable guides for evolution. Similarly, research services are supplied for creation science but not for evolution. Only "creation scientists" can serve on the panel that supplies the resource services. The Act forbids school boards to discriminate against anyone who "chooses to be a creation-scientist" or to teach "creationism," but fails to protect those who choose to teach evolution or any other non-creation science theory, or who refuse to teach creation science. [Moreover,] the Act fails even to ensure that creation science will be taught, but instead requires the teaching of this theory only when the theory of evolution is taught. Thus we agree with the Court of Appeals' conclusion that the Act does not serve to protect academic freedom, but has a distinctly different purpose of discrediting "evolution by counterbalancing its teaching at every turn with the teaching of creationism. . . ."

[We] need not be blind in this case to the legislature's preeminent religious purpose in enacting this statute. There is a historic and contemporaneous link between the teachings of certain religious denominations and the teaching of evolution. It was this link that concerned the Court in [Epperson, above]. [The] same historic and contemporaneous antagonisms between the teachings of certain religious denominations and the teaching of evolution are present in this case. The preeminent purpose of the Louisiana legislature was clearly to advance the religious viewpoint that a supernatural being created humankind. The term "creation science" was defined as embracing this particular religious doctrine by those responsible for the passage of the Creationism Act. Senator Keith's leading expert on creation science, Edward Boudreaux, testified at the legislative hearings that the theory of creation science included belief in the existence of a supernatural creator.

[Furthermore,] it is not happenstance that the legislature required the teaching of a theory that coincided with this religious view. The legislative history documents that the Act's primary purpose was to change the science curriculum of public schools in order to provide persuasive advantage to a particular religious doctrine that rejects the factual basis of evolution in its entirety. The sponsor of the Creationism Act, Senator Keith, explained during the legislative hearings that his disdain for the theory of evolution resulted from [his] own religious beliefs. [The] state senator repeatedly stated that scientific evidence supporting his religious views should be included in the public school curriculum to redress the fact that the theory of evolution incidentally coincided with what he characterized as religious beliefs antithetical to his own. The legislation therefore sought to alter the science curriculum to reflect endorsement of a religious view that is antagonistic to the theory of evolution. In this case, the purpose of the Creationism Act was to restructure the science curriculum to conform with a particular religious viewpoint. Out of many possible science subjects taught in the public schools, the legislature chose to affect the teaching of the one scientific theory that historically has been opposed by certain religious sects. As in Epperson, the legislature passed the Act to give preference to those religious groups which have as one of their tenets the creation of humankind by a divine creator.

[Because] the primary purpose of the Creationism Act is to advance a particular religious belief, the Act endorses religion in violation of the First Amendment. We do not imply that a legislature could never require that scientific critiques of prevailing scientific theories be taught. [Teaching] a variety of scientific theories about the origins of humankind to schoolchildren might be validly done with the clear secular intent of enhancing the effectiveness of science instruction. But because the primary purpose of the Creationism Act is to endorse a particular religious doctrine, the Act furthers religion in violation of the Establishment Clause.

[Affirmed.]

Justice POWELL, with whom Justice O'CONNOR joins, concurring.

I write separately to note certain aspects of the legislative history, and to emphasize that nothing in the Court's opinion diminishes the traditionally broad discretion accorded state and local school officials in the selection of the public school curriculum. [A] religious purpose alone is not enough to invalidate an act of a state legislature. The religious purpose must predominate. [Here,] it is clear that religious belief is the Balanced Treatment's Act's "reason for existence." [Whatever] the academic merit of particular subjects or theories, the Establishment Clause limits the discretion of state officials to pick and choose among them for the purpose of promoting a particular religious belief. The language of the statute and its legislative history convince me that the Louisiana legislature exercised its discretion for this purpose in this [case]. [Justice White concurred in the judgment, finding no reason to overturn the summary judgment below.]

Justice SCALIA, with whom Chief Justice REHNQUIST joins, dissenting.

[There] is ample evidence that the majority is wrong in holding that the Balanced Treatment Act is without secular purpose. [Senator] Keith and his witnesses testified essentially: (1) [There] are two and only two scientific explanations for the beginning of life—evolution and creation [science]. (2) The body of scientific evidence supporting creation science is as strong as that supporting evolution. In fact, it may be [stronger]. (3) Creation science is educationally valuable. Students exposed to it better understand the current state of scientific evidence about the origin of [life]. (4) Although creation science is educationally valuable and strictly scientific, it is now being censored from or misrepresented in the [public schools]. (5) The censorship of creation science [has] harmful effects. [E.g., it] deprives students of knowledge of one of the two scientific explanations for the origin of life and leads them to believe that evolution is proven [fact]. [We] have no way of knowing, of course, how many legislators believed the testimony of Senator Keith and his witnesses. But in the absence of evidence to the contrary, we have to assume that many of them [did].

[Moreover, the] Louisiana Legislature explicitly set forth its secular purpose ("protecting academic freedom") in the very text of the Act. [If] one adopts the obviously intended meaning of the statutory terms "academic freedom," there is no basis whatever for concluding that the purpose they express is a "sham." [The] legislative history gives ample evidence of the sincerity of the Balanced Treatment Act's articulated purpose. Witness after witness urged the legislators to support the Act so that students would not be "indoctrinated" but would instead be free to decide for themselves, based upon a fair presentation of the scientific evidence, about the origin of life. [It] is undoubtedly true that what prompted the Legislature to direct its attention to the misrepresentation of evolution in the schools (rather than the inaccurate presentation of other topics) was its awareness of the tension between evolution and the religious beliefs of many children. But [a] valid secular purpose is not rendered impermissible simply because its pursuit is prompted by concern for religious [sensitivities].

[Criticizing the Court's inquiry into legislative motivation under the Lemon "purpose" test, Justice Scalia continued:] [W]hile it is possible to discern the objective "purpose" of a statute (i. e., the public good at which its provisions appear to be directed), or even the formal motivation for a statute where that is explicitly set forth (as it was, to no avail, here), discerning the subjective motivation of those enacting the statute is, to be honest, almost always an impossible task. The number of possible motivations, to begin with, is not binary, or indeed even finite. In the present case, for example, a particular legislator need not have voted for the Act either because he wanted to foster religion or because he wanted to improve education. He may have thought the bill would provide jobs for his district, or may have wanted to make amends with a faction of his party he had alienated on another vote, or he may have been a close friend of the bill's sponsor, or he may have been repaying a favor he owed the Majority Leader, or he may have hoped the Governor would appreciate his vote and make a fundraising appearance for him, or he may have been pressured to vote for a bill he disliked by a wealthy contributor or by a flood of constituent mail, or he may have been seeking favorable publicity, or he may have been reluctant to hurt the feelings of a loyal staff member who worked on the bill, or he may have been settling an old score with a legislator who opposed the bill, or he may have been mad at his wife who opposed the bill, or he may have been intoxicated and utterly unmotivated when the vote was called, or he may have accidentally voted "yes" instead of "no," or, of course, he may have had (and very likely did have) a combination of some of the above and many other motivations. To look for the sole purpose of even a single legislator is probably to look for something that does not exist.

Putting that problem aside, however, where ought we to look for the individual legislator's purpose? We cannot of course assume that every member present (if, as is unlikely, we know who or even how many they were) agreed with the motivation expressed in a particular legislator's preenactment floor or committee statement. Quite obviously, "what motivates one legislator to make a speech about a statute is not necessarily what motivates scores of others to enact it." Can we assume, then, that they all agree with the motivation expressed in the staff-prepared committee reports they might have read—even though we are unwilling to assume that they agreed with the motivation expressed in the very statute that they voted for? Should we consider postenactment floor statements? Or postenactment testimony from legislators, obtained expressly for the lawsuit? Should we consider media reports on the realities of the legislative bargaining? All of these sources, of course, are eminently manipulable. Legislative histories can be contrived and sanitized, favorable media coverage orchestrated, and postenactment recollections conveniently distorted. Perhaps most valuable of all would be more objective indications—for example, evidence regarding the individual legislators' religious affiliations. And if that, why not evidence regarding the fervor or tepidity of their beliefs?

Having achieved, through these simple means, an assessment of what individual legislators intended, we must still confront the question (yet to be addressed in any of our cases) how many of them must have the invalidating intent. If a state senate approves a bill by vote of 26 to 25, and only one of the 26 intended solely to advance religion, is the law unconstitutional? What if 13 of the 26 had that intent? What if 3 of the 26 had the impermissible intent, but 3 of the 25 voting against the bill were motivated by religious hostility or were simply attempting to "balance" the votes of their impermissibly motivated colleagues? Or is it possible that the intent of the bill's sponsor is alone enough to invalidate it—on a theory, perhaps, that even though everyone else's intent was pure, what they produced was the fruit of a forbidden tree? Because there are no good answers to these questions, this Court has recognized from Chief Justice Marshall, see Fletcher v. Peck, to Chief Justice Warren, United States v. O'Brien, that determining the subjective intent of legislators is a perilous enterprise.

Given the many hazards involved in assessing the subjective intent of governmental decisionmakers, the first prong of Lemon is defensible, I think, only if the text of the Establishment Clause demands it. That is surely not the case. [In] the past we have attempted to justify our embarrassing Establishment Clause jurisprudence on the ground that it "sacrifices clarity and predictability for flexibility." [I] think it time that we sacrifice some "flexibility" for "clarity and predictability." Abandoning Lemon's purpose test—a test which exacerbates the tension between the Free Exercise and Establishment Clauses, has no basis in the language or history of the amendment, and, as today's decision shows, has wonderfully flexible consequences—would be a good place to start.

RELIGIOUS SYMBOLISM OUTSIDE THE SCHOOL CONTEXT

Outside the context of the public schools, the Court has been more tolerant of governmental sponsorship of religious symbolism. No justice has seriously questioned, for example, the permissibility of the motto "In God We Trust" on the national currency, or the recitation of the phrase "one nation under God" in the Pledge of Allegiance. What explains this deferential view? That these practices have lost their religious significance over time? That they merely commemorate historical fact about the piety of the founding generation? That the non-believing observer can readily ignore them? What is the Court's basis for rejecting most establishment clause challenges in the following cases?

1. *Sunday closing laws.* McGOWAN v. MARYLAND, 366 U.S. 420 (1961), was one of four companion cases in which the Court rejected claims that Sunday Closing Laws violated the religion clauses. Chief Justice WARREN wrote the majority opinions. He noted in McGowan that there is "no dispute that the original laws which dealt with Sunday labor were motivated by religious forces." But he concluded: "In light of the evolution of our Sunday Closing Laws through the centuries, and of their more or less recent emphasis upon secular considerations, it is not difficult to discern that as presently written and administered, most of them, at least, are of a secular rather than of a religious character, and that presently they bear no relationship to establishment of religion as those words are used in the [Constitution]. The present purpose and effect of most of them is to provide a uniform day of rest for all citizens; the fact that this day is Sunday, a day of particular significance for the dominant Christian sects, does not bar the State from achieving its secular [goals]. Sunday is a day apart from all others. The cause is irrelevant; the fact exists."

2. *Legislative prayer.* In MARSH v. CHAMBERS, 463 U.S. 783 (1983), the Court upheld "the Nebraska Legislature's practice of opening each legislative day with a prayer by a chaplain paid by the State." Chief Justice BURGER's majority opinion relied largely on history to sustain the practice despite the fact that the position of chaplain had been held for 16 years by a Presbyterian, that the chaplain was paid at public expense, and that all of the prayers were "in the Judeo–Christian tradition." This was the first case since Lemon in 1971 that did not apply the three-pronged test. Instead, the majority looked at the

specific features of the challenged practice in light of a long history of acceptance of legislative and other official prayers. The majority concluded: "Weighed against the historical background, [the allegedly vulnerable] factors do not serve to invalidate Nebraska's practice."

The Chief Justice viewed prayer in this context as "unique" in its historical roots: "The opening of sessions of legislative and other deliberative public bodies with prayer is deeply embedded in the history and tradition of this country. From colonial times through the founding of the Republic and ever since, the practice of legislative prayer has coexisted with the principles of disestablishment and religious freedom. In the very courtrooms in which the United States District Judge and later three Circuit Judges heard and decided this case, the proceedings opened with an announcement that concluded, 'God save the United States and this Honorable Court.' The same invocation occurs at all sessions of this Court. [Although] prayers were not offered during the Constitutional Convention, the First Congress, as one of its early items of business, adopted the policy of selecting a chaplain to open each session with prayer. [On] April 25, 1789, the Senate elected its first chaplain; the House followed suit on May 1, 1789. A statute providing for the payment of these chaplains was enacted into law on September 22, 1789. [In] light of the unambiguous and unbroken history of more than 200 years, there can be no doubt that the practice of opening legislative sessions with a prayer has become part of the fabric of our society. [It] is simply a tolerable acknowledgment of beliefs widely held among the people of this country."

Justice BRENNAN, joined by Justice Marshall, filed a lengthy dissent: "Legislative prayer clearly violates the principles of neutrality and separation that are embedded within the Establishment Clause. It is contrary to the fundamental message of Engel and Schempp. It intrudes on the right to conscience by forcing some legislators either to participate in a 'prayer opportunity,' with which they are in basic disagreement, or to make their disagreement a matter of public comment by declining to participate. It forces all residents of the State to support a religious exercise that may be contrary to their own beliefs. It requires the State to commit itself on fundamental theological issues. It has the potential for degrading religion by allowing a religious call to worship to be intermeshed with a secular call to order. And it injects religion into the political sphere by creating the potential that each and every selection of a chaplain, or consideration of a particular prayer, or even reconsideration of the practice itself, will provoke a political battle along religious lines and ultimately alienate some religiously identified group of citizens." Under the Lemon test, he argued, the practice could not be sustained, since the purpose and effect were "clearly religious" and there was also excessive political entanglement.

Justice STEVENS also dissented: "In a democratically elected legislature, the religious beliefs of the chaplain tend to reflect the faith of the majority of the lawmakers' constituents. Prayers may be said by a Catholic priest in the Massachusetts Legislature and by a Presbyterian minister in the Nebraska Legislature, but I would not expect to find a Jehovah's Witness or a disciple of Mary Baker Eddy or the Reverend Moon serving as the official chaplain in any state legislature. Regardless of the motivation of the majority that exercises the power to appoint the chaplain, it seems plain to me that the designation of a member of one religious faith to serve as the sole official chaplain of a state legislature for a period of 16 years constitutes the preference of one faith over another in violation of the Establishment Clause of the First Amendment."

3. *Public religious displays.* Clearly, it would violate the establishment clause for government to place a Latin cross on the dome of the state capitol.

Such symbolism would clearly constitute religious "endorsement." Even under a narrow nonpreferentialist view, government is barred from the symbolic union of a church and the state. The establishment clause, at a minimum, prohibits theocracy. But may a government place, or permit others to place, elsewhere on public property a display depicting the birth of Christ at Christmas or a menorah commemorating the Jewish feast of Chanukah? Does such a display implicate the establishment clause to the same extent as the cross on the capitol? Will its predominant meaning appear religious? Regardless of the surrounding context? What if private parties finance the display? Will such a display likely be attributed to the government? The following cases consider the constitutionality of such public displays.

Lynch v. Donnelly

465 U.S. 668, 104 S.Ct. 1355, 79 L.Ed.2d 604 (1984).

Chief Justice BURGER delivered the opinion of the Court.

[Each] year, in cooperation with the downtown retail merchants' association, the City of Pawtucket, Rhode Island, erects a Christmas display as part of its observance of the Christmas holiday season. The display is situated in a park owned by a nonprofit organization and located in the heart of the shopping district. The display is essentially like those to be found in hundreds of towns or cities across the Nation—often on public grounds—during the Christmas season. The Pawtucket display comprises many of the figures and decorations traditionally associated with Christmas, including, among other things, a Santa Claus house, reindeer pulling Santa's sleigh, candy-striped poles, a Christmas tree, carolers, cutout figures representing such characters as a clown, an elephant, and a teddy bear, hundreds of colored lights, a large banner that reads "SEASONS GREETINGS," and the crèche at issue here. All components of this display are owned by the City. The crèche, which has been included in the display for 40 or more years, consists of the traditional figures, including the Infant Jesus, Mary and Joseph, angels, shepherds, kings, and animals, all ranging in height from 5″ to 5′. In 1973, when the present crèche was acquired, it cost the City $1365; it now is valued at $200. The erection and dismantling of the crèche costs the City about $20 per year; nominal expenses are incurred in lighting the crèche. No money has been expended on its maintenance for the past 10 years. The District Court held that the City's inclusion of the crèche in the display violates the Establishment Clause. [A] divided panel of the [First] Circuit affirmed. [We] reverse.

[There] is an unbroken history of official acknowledgment by all three branches of government of the role of religion in American life from at least 1789. [Our] history is replete with official references to the value and invocation of Divine guidance in deliberations and pronouncements of the Founding Fathers and contemporary leaders. [Long] before Independence, a day of Thanksgiving was celebrated as a religious holiday to give thanks for the bounties of Nature as gifts from God. [Executive Orders] and other official announcements of Presidents and of the Congress have proclaimed both Christmas and Thanksgiving National Holidays in religious terms. [Thus,] it is clear that Government has long recognized—indeed it has subsidized—holidays with religious significance. Other examples of reference to our religious heritage are found in the statutorily prescribed national motto "In God We Trust," which Congress and the President mandated for our currency, and in the language "One nation under God," as part of the Pledge of Allegiance to the [American flag]. [One] cannot look at even this brief resume without finding that our history is pervaded by expressions of religious beliefs such as are found in Zorach. Equally pervasive is the evidence of accommodation of all faiths and all forms of religious expression, and hostility toward [none].

This history may help explain why the Court consistently has declined to take a rigid, absolutist view of the Establishment Clause. [In] our modern, complex society, whose traditions and constitutional underpinnings rest on and encourage diversity and pluralism in all areas, an absolutist approach in applying the Establishment Clause is simplistic and has been uniformly reject-ed by the Court. Rather than mechanically invalidating all governmental conduct or statutes that confer benefits or give special recognition to religion in general or to one faith—as an absolutist approach would dictate—the Court has scrutinized challenged legislation or official conduct to determine whether, in reality, it establishes a religion or religious faith, or tends to do so. In each case, the inquiry calls for line drawing; no fixed, per se rule can be framed. [In] the line-drawing process we have often found it useful to inquire whether the challenged law or conduct has a secular purpose, whether its principal or primary effect is to advance or inhibit religion, and whether it creates an excessive entanglement of government with religion. [Lemon.] But, we have repeatedly emphasized our unwillingness to be confined to any single test or criterion in this sensitive area.

[In] this case, the focus of our inquiry must be on the crèche in the context of the Christmas season. [Viewed in this context,] there is insufficient evidence to establish that the inclusion of the crèche is a purposeful or surreptitious effort to express some kind of subtle governmental advocacy of a particular religious message. In a pluralistic society a variety of motives and purposes are implicated. [The] crèche in the display depicts the historical origins of this traditional event long recognized as a National Holiday. [The] display is sponsored by the City to celebrate the Holiday and to depict the origins of that Holiday. These are legitimate secular purposes.

[The] District Court found that the primary effect of including the crèche is to confer a substantial and impermissible benefit on religion in general and on the Christian faith in particular. [But we] are unable to discern a greater aid to religion deriving from inclusion of the crèche than from [endorsements] previ-ously held not violative of the Establishment Clause [e.g., in McGowan, Zorach, and Marsh.] The dissent asserts that some observers may perceive that the City has aligned itself with the Christian faith by including a Christian symbol in its display and that this serves to advance religion. We can assume, arguendo, that the display advances religion in a sense; but our precedents plainly contemplate that on occasion some advancement of religion will result from governmental action. [Here,] whatever benefit to one faith or religion or to all religions, is indirect, remote and incidental; display of the crèche is no more an advance-ment or endorsement of religion than the Congressional and Executive recogni-tion of the origins of the Holiday itself as "Christ's Mass," or the exhibition of literally hundreds of religious paintings in governmentally supported [muse-ums].

[To] forbid the use of this one passive symbol—the crèche—at the very time people are taking note of the season with Christmas hymns and carols in public schools and other public places [would] be a stilted over-reaction con-trary to our history and to our holdings. If the presence of the crèche in this display violates the Establishment Clause, a host of other forms of taking official note of Christmas, and of our religious heritage, are equally offensive to the Constitution. The Court has acknowledged that the "fears and political problems" that gave rise to the Religion Clauses in the 18th century are of far less concern today. [Everson.] We are unable to perceive the Archbishop of Canterbury, the Vicar of Rome, or other powerful religious leaders behind every public acknowledgment of the religious heritage long officially recognized by the three constitutional branches of government. Any notion that these symbols pose a real danger of establishment of a state church is farfetched indeed.

[Reversed.]

Justice O'CONNOR, concurring.

I concur in the opinion of the Court. I write separately to suggest a clarification of our Establishment Clause doctrine. The suggested approach leads to the same result in this case as that taken by the Court, and the Court's opinion, as I read it, is consistent with my analysis.

The Establishment Clause prohibits government from making adherence to a religion relevant in any way to a person's standing in the political community. Government can run afoul of that prohibition in two principal ways. One is excessive entanglement with religious institutions, which may interfere with the independence of the institutions, give the institutions access to government or governmental powers not fully shared by nonadherents of the religion, and foster the creation of political constituencies defined along religious lines. The second and more direct infringement is government endorsement or disapproval of religion. Endorsement sends a message to nonadherents that they are outsiders, not full members of the political community, and an accompanying message to adherents that they are insiders, favored members of the political community. Disapproval sends the opposite message.

[The] central issue in this case is whether Pawtucket has endorsed Christianity by its display of the crèche. To answer that question, we must examine both what Pawtucket intended to communicate in displaying the crèche and what message the City's display actually conveyed. The purpose and effect prongs of the Lemon test represent these two aspects of the meaning of the City's action. [The] proper inquiry under the purpose prong of Lemon, I submit, is whether the government intends to convey a message of endorsement or disapproval of religion. Applying that formulation to this case, I would find that Pawtucket did not intend to convey any message of endorsement of Christianity or disapproval of nonChristian religions. The evident purpose of including the crèche in the larger display was not promotion of the religious content of the crèche but celebration of the public holiday through its traditional symbols. Celebration of public holidays, which have cultural significance even if they also have religious aspects, is a legitimate secular [purpose].

[The] effect prong of the Lemon test [requires] that a government practice not have the effect of communicating a message of government endorsement or disapproval of religion. It is only practices having that effect, whether intentionally or unintentionally, that make religion relevant, in reality or public perception, to status in the political community. Pawtucket's display of its crèche, I believe, does not communicate a message that the government intends to endorse the Christian beliefs represented by the crèche. Although the religious and indeed sectarian significance of the crèche [is] not neutralized by the setting, the overall holiday setting changes what viewers may fairly understand to be the purpose of the display—as a typical museum setting, though not neutralizing the religious content of a religious painting, negates any message of endorsement of that content. The display celebrates a public holiday, and no one contends that declaration of that holiday is understood to be an endorsement of religion. The holiday itself has very strong secular components and traditions. Government celebration of the holiday [generally] is not understood to endorse the religious content of the holiday. [The] crèche is a traditional symbol of the holiday that is very commonly displayed along with purely secular symbols, as it was in Pawtucket.

These features combine to make the government's display of the crèche in this particular physical setting no more an endorsement of religion than such governmental "acknowledgments" of religion as [printing] "In God We Trust," on coins, and opening court sessions with "God save the United States and this honorable court." Those government acknowledgments of religion serve, in the only ways reasonably possible in our culture, the legitimate secular purposes of solemnizing public occasions, expressing confidence in the future, and encouraging the recognition of what is worthy of appreciation in society. For that reason, and because of their history and ubiquity, those practices are not understood as conveying government approval of particular religious beliefs. The display of the crèche likewise [cannot] fairly be understood to convey a message of government endorsement of [religion].

Justice BRENNAN, with whom Justices MARSHALL, BLACKMUN and STEVENS join, dissenting.

[In] my view, Pawtucket's maintenance and display at public expense of a symbol as distinctively sectarian as a crèche simply cannot be squared with our prior cases. [The] City's inclusion of the crèche in its Christmas display simply does not reflect a "clearly secular purpose." [The] nativity scene, unlike every other element of the Hodgson Park display, reflects a sectarian exclusivity that the avowed purposes of celebrating the holiday season and promoting retail commerce simply do not encompass. [The] inclusion of a distinctively religious element like the crèche [demonstrates] that a narrower sectarian purpose lay behind the decision to include a nativity scene.

[The] "primary effect" of including a nativity scene in the City's display [is] to place the government's imprimatur of approval on the particular religious beliefs exemplified by the crèche. [The] effect on minority religious groups, as well as on those who may reject all religion, is to convey the message that their views are not similarly worthy of public recognition nor entitled to public support. [Finally], it is evident that Pawtucket's inclusion of a crèche [does] pose a significant threat of fostering "excessive entanglement."

[The] Court, by focusing on the holiday "context" in which the nativity scene appeared, seeks to explain away the clear religious import of the crèche. [It] blinks reality to claim, as the Court does, that by including such a distinctively religious object as the crèche in its Christmas display, Pawtucket has done no more than made use of a "traditional" symbol of the holiday, and has thereby purged the crèche of its religious content and conferred only an "incidental and indirect" benefit on religion. [Even] in the context of Pawtucket's seasonal celebration, the crèche retains a specifically Christian religious meaning. [It] is the chief symbol of the characteristically Christian belief that a divine Savior was brought into the world and that the purpose of this miraculous birth was to illuminate a path toward salvation and redemption. For Christians, that path is exclusive, precious and holy. But for those who do not share these beliefs, the symbolic re-enactment of the birth of a divine being who has been miraculously incarnated as a man stands as a dramatic reminder of their differences with Christian faith. [To] be so excluded on religious grounds by one's elected government is an insult and an injury that, until today, could not be countenanced by the Establishment Clause.

[The] Court apparently believes that once it finds that the designation of Christmas as a public holiday is constitutionally acceptable, it is then free to conclude that virtually every form of governmental association with the celebration of the holiday is also constitutional. The vice of this dangerously superficial argument is that it overlooks the fact that the Christmas holiday in our national culture contains both secular and sectarian elements. To say that government may recognize the holiday's traditional, secular elements of gift giving, public festivities and community spirit, does not mean that government may indiscriminately embrace the distinctively sectarian aspects of the holiday.

When government decides to recognize Christmas day as a public holiday, it does no more than accommodate the calendar of public activities to the plain fact that many Americans will expect on that day to spend time visiting with their families, attending religious services, and perhaps enjoying some respite from pre-holiday activities. The Free Exercise Clause, of course, does not necessarily compel the government to provide this accommodation, but neither is the Establishment Clause offended by such a step. Cf. [Zorach]. [If] public officials go further and participate in the *secular* celebration of Christmas—by, for example, decorating public places with such secular images as wreaths, garlands or Santa Claus figures—they move closer to the limits of their constitutional power but nevertheless remain within the boundaries set by the Establishment Clause. But when those officials participate in or appear to endorse the distinctively religious elements of this otherwise secular event, they encroach upon First Amendment freedoms. For it is at that point that the government brings to the forefront the theological content of the holiday, and places the prestige, power and financial support of a civil authority in the service of a particular faith.

The inclusion of a crèche in Pawtucket's otherwise secular celebration of Christmas clearly violates these principles. Unlike such secular figures as Santa Claus, reindeer and carolers, a nativity scene represents far more than a mere "traditional" symbol of Christmas. The essence of the crèche's symbolic purpose and effect is to prompt the observer to experience a sense of simple awe and wonder appropriate to the contemplation of one of the central elements of Christian dogma—that God sent His son into the world to be a Messiah. Contrary to the Court's suggestion, the crèche is far from a mere representation of a "particular historic religious event." It is, instead, best understood as a mystical re-creation of an event that lies at the heart of Christian faith. To suggest, as the Court does, that such a symbol is merely "traditional" and therefore no different from Santa's house or reindeer is not only offensive to those for whom the crèche has profound significance, but insulting to those who insist for religious or personal reasons that the story of Christ is in no sense a part of "history" nor an unavoidable element of our national ["heritage"].

[The] Court has never comprehensively addressed the extent to which government may acknowledge religion by, for example, incorporating religious references into public ceremonies [, and] I do not presume to offer a comprehensive approach. Nevertheless, [at] least three principles—tracing the narrow channels which government acknowledgments must follow to satisfy the Establishment Clause—may be identified. First, although the government may not be compelled to do so by the Free Exercise Clause, it may, consistently with the Establishment Clause, act to accommodate to some extent the opportunities of individuals to practice their religion. [That] principle would justify government's decision to declare December 25th a public holiday. Second, our cases recognize that while a particular governmental practice may have derived from religious motivations and retain certain religious connotations, it is nonetheless permissible for the government to pursue the practice when it is continued today solely for secular reasons. [McGowan.] Thanksgiving Day, in my view, fits easily within this principle.

Finally, we have noted that government cannot be completely prohibited from recognizing in its public actions the religious beliefs and practices of the American people as an aspect of our national history and culture. While I remain uncertain about these questions, I would suggest that such practices as the designation of "In God We Trust" as our national motto [and] the references to God contained in the Pledge of Allegiance can best be understood [as] a form of "ceremonial deism," protected from Establishment Clause scrutiny chiefly because they have lost through rote repetition any significant religious content. Moreover, these references are uniquely suited to serve such wholly secular purposes as solemnizing public occasions, or inspiring commitment to meet some national challenge in a manner that simply could not be fully served in our culture if government were limited to purely non-religious phrases. The practices by which the government has long acknowledged religion are therefore probably necessary to serve certain secular functions, and that necessity, coupled with their long history, gives those practices an essentially secular meaning. The crèche fits none of these categories. [By] insisting that such a distinctively sectarian message is merely an unobjectionable part of our "religious heritage," the Court takes a long step backwards to the days when Justice Brewer could arrogantly declare for the Court that "this is a Christian nation." Church of Holy Trinity v. United States, 143 U.S. 457 (1892). Those days, I had thought, were forever put behind us by the Court's decision in [Engel], in which we rejected a similar argument [in defense of the Regents' Prayer].

The American historical experience concerning the public celebration of Christmas, if carefully examined, provides no support for the Court's decision. [Attention] to the details of history should not blind us to the cardinal purposes of the Establishment Clause, nor limit our central inquiry in these cases— whether the challenged practices "threaten those consequences which the Framers deeply feared." [The] intent of the Framers with respect to the public display of nativity scenes is virtually impossible to discern primarily because the widespread celebration of Christmas did not emerge in its present form until well into the [nineteenth century]. [There] is no evidence whatsoever that the Framers would have expressly approved a Federal celebration of the Christmas holiday including public displays of a nativity scene.

[Pawtucket's] action should be recognized for what it is: a coercive, though perhaps small, step toward establishing the sectarian preferences of the majority at the expense of the minority, accomplished by placing public facilities and funds in support of the religious symbolism and theological tidings that the crèche [conveys].

Justice BLACKMUN, joined by Justice STEVENS, dissenting.

The crèche has been relegated to the role of a neutral harbinger of the holiday season, useful for commercial purposes, but devoid of any inherent meaning and incapable of enhancing the religious tenor of a display of which it is an integral part. The city has its victory—but it is a Pyrrhic one indeed. The import of [the decision] is to encourage use of the crèche in a municipally sponsored display, a setting where Christians feel constrained in acknowledging its symbolic meaning and non-Christians feel alienated by its presence. Surely, this is a misuse of a sacred symbol.

In ALLEGHENY COUNTY v. AMERICAN CIVIL LIBERTIES UNION [ACLU], 492 U.S. 573 (1989), a majority of the Court held unconstitutional a freestanding display of a nativity scene on the main staircase of a county courthouse. Unlike the display in the Lynch case, the crèche belonged to a Catholic organization and was not surrounded by figures of Santa Claus or other Christmas decorations. But a different majority in the same case upheld the display of a Jewish Chanukah menorah placed next to a Christmas tree and a sign saying "Salute to Liberty" in the City–County Building, a block away from the courthouse. The menorah was owned by a Jewish group, but stored, erected, and removed annually by the city.

In the course of reaching these holdings, the Court, by a 5–4 majority, adopted Justice O'Connor's "no endorsement" analysis as a general approach to establishment clause adjudication. Justice BLACKMUN, joined by Justices Brennan, Marshall, O'Connor and Stevens, noted: "In recent years, we have paid particularly close attention to whether the challenged governmental practice either has the purpose or effect of 'endorsing' religion. [Of course,] the word 'endorsement' is not self-defining. [But whether] the key word is 'endorsement,' 'favoritism,' or 'promotion,' the essential principle remains the same. The Establishment Clause, at the very least, prohibits government from appearing to take a position on questions of religious belief or from 'making adherence to a religion relevant in any way to a person's standing in the political community.' [Lynch (O'Connor, J., concurring).]"

Justice KENNEDY, joined by Chief Justice Rehnquist and Justices White and Scalia, rejected the majority's "endorsement" analysis, viewing it as reflecting "an unjustified hostility toward religion." The dissent argued for a narrower test of establishment: "government may not coerce anyone to support or participate in any religion or its exercise; and it may not, in the guise of avoiding hostility or callous indifference, give direct benefits to religion in such a degree that it in fact 'establishes a [state] religion or religious faith, or tends to do so.' [Lynch.] [But] non-coercive government action within the realm of flexible accommodation or passive acknowledgement of existing symbols does not violate the Establishment Clause unless it benefits religion in a way more direct and more substantial than practices that are accepted in our national heritage." He also objected that Justice O'Connor's endorsement test disregarded history: "Few of our traditional practices recognizing the part religion plays in our society [such as Thanksgiving Proclamations and legislative prayer] can withstand scrutiny under a faithful application of this formula." Finally, he argued, the "endorsement" approach was "unworkable in practice": it "threatens to trivialize constitutional adjudication [by embracing] a jurisprudence of minutiae" governing the detailed context of governmental displays.

Justice O'CONNOR, joined by Justices Brennan and Stevens, defended the endorsement test against Justice Kennedy's attack and criticized his proposed narrower test: "An Establishment Clause standard that prohibits only 'coercive' practices or overt efforts at government proselytization, but fails to take account of the numerous more subtle ways that government can show favoritism to particular beliefs or convey a message of disapproval to others, would not, in my view, adequately protect the religious liberty or respect the religious diversity of the members of our pluralistic political community. Thus, this Court has never relied on coercion alone as the touchstone of Establishment Clause analysis. To require a showing of coercion, even indirect coercion, as an essential element of an Establishment Clause violation would make the Free Exercise Clause a redundancy."

A 5–4 majority of the Court likewise found the crèche display here unconstitutional. Justice BLACKMUN, joined by Justices Brennan, Marshall, O'Connor and Stevens, noted that "here, unlike in Lynch, nothing in the context of the display detracts from the crèche's religious message." Lynch, for example, was accompanied by Santa's house, reindeer, and a wishing well; here, the crèche "stands alone." The crèche conveyed an essentially religious message and constituted an endorsement of Christian doctrine. Justice KENNEDY, joined by Chief Justice Rehnquist and Justices White and Scalia, dissented from this holding. In his view, the crèche display was a permissible, noncoercive accommodation of religious faith: "The crèche [is a] purely passive symbol[] of [a] religious holiday. Passersby who disagree with [its] message are free to ignore [it], or even to turn their backs, just as they are free to do so when they disagree with any other form of government speech." Justice Kennedy conceded that "[s]ymbolic recognition or accommodation of religious faith may violate the Clause in an extreme case, [such as] the permanent erection o f a large Latin cross on the roof of city hall." But the crèche here, in his view, represented no similar "effort to proselytize on behalf of a particular religion."

By a vote of 6–3, however, the Court upheld the display of the menorah. Justice BLACKMUN, writing here only for himself, found that the menorah, while "a religious symbol," conveyed a message that was "not exclusively religious." He emphasized that it stood next to a Christmas tree and a sign saluting liberty and thus had "an 'overall holiday setting' that represents both Christmas and Chanukah—two holidays, not one." He acknowledged that a simultaneous endorsement of Judaism and Christianity would still violate the establishment clause, but insisted that government may acknowledge both Christmas and Chanukah as secular holidays. Moreover, he argued, "the relevant question [is] whether the combined display of the tree, the sign, and the menorah has the effect of endorsing both Christian and Jewish faiths, or rather simply recognizes that both Christmas and Chanukah are part of the same winter-holiday season, which has attained a secular status in our society. [The] latter seems far more plausible and is also in line with Lynch." Justice O'CONNOR agreed that the menorah display was constitutional but criticized Justice Blackmun for obscuring the religious nature of the menorah and the holiday of Chanukah. She added: "One need not characterize Chanukah as a 'secular holiday' or strain to argue that the menorah has a 'secular dimension' in order to conclude that [the] display does not convey a message of endorsement of Judaism or of religion in general." She concluded that the joint display as a whole "conveyed a message of pluralism and freedom of belief during the holiday season" and was therefore permissible.

Justice BRENNAN, joined by Justices Marshall and Stevens, dissented with respect to the menorah, finding that it was "indisputably a religious symbol, used ritually in a celebration that has deep religious significance." He concluded that government may not "promote pluralism by sponsoring or condoning displays having strong religious associations on its property." Justice STEVENS, joined by Justices Brennan and Marshall, also dissented with respect to the menorah, arguing that the establishment clause "should be construed to create a strong presumption against the display of religious symbols on public property. There is always a risk that such symbols will offend nonmembers of the faith being advertised as well as adherents who consider the particular advertisement disrespectful."

In CAPITOL SQUARE REVIEW BOARD v. PINETTE, ___ U.S. ___, 115 S.Ct. 2440 (1995), the Court held that the free speech clause compelled the city of Columbus, Ohio, to permit the Ku Klux Klan to erect a large unattended Latin cross on a public square adjacent to the Statehouse, and that the establishment clause did not forbid it. Having found that the free speech clause otherwise barred content-based discrimination against the cross, the Court held, by a vote of 7–2, that permitting the cross equal access to public property along with other unattended private symbols would not, as the city argued, violate the establishment clause, even assuming that the Klan cross was an entirely religious and not political symbol (Justice Thomas alone would have treated it as the latter). The Court was divided on the appropriate establishment clause analysis, but there were still five votes—those of the concurring and dissenting justices—for applying the "endorsement" test.

While Justice SCALIA wrote for seven Justices on the result, he wrote only for a four-Justice plurality in his reasoning. Joined by the Chief Justice and Justices Kennedy and Thomas, he acknowledged that the endorsement test had been applied in previous cases but would not have applied it here. He would have paid no attention to what any observer would have thought, reasonably or otherwise, about whether the Christian symbolism of the Klan cross ought to be attributed to the city government of Columbus: "Petitioners argue [that], because an observer might mistake private expression for officially endorsed religious expression, [permitting the cross would violate the establishment clause.] [Petitioners] rely heavily on Allegheny County and Lynch, but each is easily distinguished. In Allegheny County we held that the display of a privately-sponsored creche on the 'Grand Staircase' of the Allegheny County Courthouse violated the Establishment Clause. That staircase was not, however, open to all on an equal basis, so the County was favoring sectarian religious expression. [In] Lynch we held that a city's display of a creche did not violate the Establishment Clause because, in context, the display did not endorse religion. [The] case neither holds nor even remotely assumes that the government's neutral treatment of private religious expression can be unconstitutional. [What] distinguishes Allegheny County and [Lynch] is the difference between government speech and private speech. Petitioners assert, in effect, that that distinction disappears when the private speech is conducted too close to the symbols of government [and thus] private speech can be mistaken for government speech. That proposition cannot be accepted, at least where, as here, the government has not fostered or encouraged the mistake. [It] has radical implications for our public policy to suggest that neutral laws are invalid whenever hypothetical observers may—even reasonably—confuse an incidental benefit to religion with state endorsement." The plurality would have adopted instead a per se rule: "Religious expression cannot violate the Establishment Clause where it (1) is purely private and (2) occurs in a traditional or designated public forum, publicly announced and open to all on equal terms."

Justice O'CONNOR wrote a concurrence joined by Justices Souter and Breyer, and Justice SOUTER wrote a concurrence joined by Justices O'Connor and Breyer. The three concurring Justices expressly reaffirmed Justice O'Connor's endorsement test. Justice O'Connor wrote: "I part company with the plurality on a fundamental point: I disagree that 'it has radical implications for our public policy to suggest that neutral laws are invalid whenever hypothetical observers may—even reasonably—confuse an incidental benefit to religion with State endorsement.' On the contrary, when the reasonable observer would view a government practice as endorsing religion, I believe that it is our duty to hold the practice invalid. The plurality today takes an exceedingly narrow view of the Establishment Clause that is out of step both with the Court's prior cases and with well-established notions of what the Constitution requires. The Clause is more than a negative prohibition against certain narrowly defined forms of government favoritism; it also imposes affirmative obligations that may require a State, in some situations, to take steps to avoid being perceived as supporting or endorsing a private religious message."

The concurring justices would have required Columbus to exclude the cross from the public square if they had thought its message would be attributed to the city, but they did not view such attribution as likely in the circumstances of this case. Justice O'Connor emphasized that the cross was in the public square rather than upon a government building: "In this case, I believe, the reasonable observer would view the Klan's cross display fully aware that Capitol Square is a public space in which a multiplicity of groups, both secular and religious, engage in expressive conduct [and] able to read and understand an adequate disclaimer. [On] the facts of this case, therefore, I conclude that the reasonable observer would not interpret the State's tolerance of the Klan's private religious display in Capitol Square as an endorsement of religion." Justice Souter stressed that the city could easily have required the Klan to affix a sign to the cross disclaiming any government endorsement of the Christian faith.

Justices STEVENS and GINSBURG each filed a dissent. Justice Stevens wrote that "the Constitution generally forbids the placement of a symbol of a religious character in, on, or before a seat of government." In his view, "the Establishment Clause prohibits government from allowing, and thus endorsing, unattended displays that take a position on a religious issue. If the State allows such stationary displays in front of its seat of government, viewers will reasonably assume that it approves of them. [A] reasonable observer would likely infer endorsement from the location of the cross erected by the Klan in this case. Even if the disclaimer at the foot of the cross (which stated that the cross was placed there by a private organization) were legible, that inference would remain, because a property owner's decision to allow a third party to place a sign on her property conveys the same message of endorsement as if she had erected it herself." Justice Ginsburg emphasized that the disclaimer here was inadequate, deferring the question whether a disclaimer could ever dispel the establishment clause problem

Does the Lemon test have any continuing utility in the religious symbolism cases? Or would it be fair to say that the Court has adopted a different three-part test: coercion and endorsement are impermissible under the establishment clause, but mere acknowledgment of religion is not? On this analysis, the school cases are treated as instances of coercion, even if it means stretching that concept quite far to embrace even psychological coercion. The crèche in Allegheny is invalidated as endorsement. But Sunday closings, legislative prayer, and crèches or menorahs in secularized contexts each count as mere government acknowledgments of religion, comparable to religious allusions in holiday proclamations, on the currency, in the pledge of allegiance, and in the art on the walls of public museums. Are such holdings sufficiently respectful toward religion? See Kurland, "The Religion Clauses and the Burger Court," 34 Cath.U.L.Rev. 1 (1984) (arguing that the Court's treatment of the crèche in Lynch "further detracts from the religious significance of the Christmas holiday, [which] every year [pays] more homage to Mammon than to God").

Can the endorsement test be objectively administered, or will it always tend to be administered from the perspective of members of majority faiths? See Van Alstyne, "Trends in the Supreme Court: Mr. Jefferson's Crumbling Wall—A Comment on [Lynch]," 1984 Duke L.J. 770 (suggesting that Lynch reflected "religious ethnocentrism"); Tushnet, "The Constitution of Religion," 18 Conn.L.Rev. 701 (1986) (noting that "judges will always be broadly representative of the general population, and will be susceptible to all the distortions of interpretation that membership in the majority entails"). Can the endorsement test be consistently administered? Why is a creche less of an endorsement when surrounded by reindeer and talking wishing wells than when it is standing alone? For commentary favorable toward the endorsement test, see

Beschle, "The Conservative as Liberal: The Religion Clauses, Liberal Neutrality, and the Approach of Justice O'Connor," 62 Notre Dame L.Rev. 151 (1987); Marshall, "'We Know It When We See It': The Supreme Court and Establishment," 59 S.Cal.L.Rev. 495 (1986); Comment, "Lemon [Reconstituted]," 1986 B.Y.U.L.Rev. 465; and "Developments in the Law—Religion and the State," 100 Harv.L.Rev. 1606 (1987). For commentary critical of the test, see Smith, "Symbols, Perceptions, and Doctrinal Illusions: Establishment Neutrality and the 'No Endorsement' Test," 86 Mich.L.Rev. 266 (1987).

Note that the Capitol Square case, as the plurality saw it, was not about *government* religious speech at all, whether mere acknowledgment or otherwise. In the plurality's view, the ground for validation here was that the government would simply be treating private religious speakers equally with other speakers if it admitted them to the public square. For cases employing similar "religious equality" reasoning, see the discussion of Widmar and Rosenberger at pp. 1543–46 below.

B. FINANCIAL AID TO RELIGIOUS INSTITUTIONS

Introduction. The Court did not become fully engaged in deciding issues of financial assistance to religious institutions until the late 1940s. Earlier encounters with the problem were inconclusive. Thus, Bradfield v. Roberts, 175 U.S. 291 (1899)—the Court's first decision in the area—sustained a federal appropriation for the construction of a public ward to be administered as part of a hospital under control of sisters of the Roman Catholic church; but the Court in Bradfield did not reach the issue of whether aid to religious institutions is permissible, because it held that the hospital was not a religious body. See also Reuben Quick Bear v. Leupp, 210 U.S. 50 (1908) (upholding federal disbursement to Catholic schools of funds held in trust for education of Sioux Indians). Several decades later, the issue of aid to religious institutions produced the Court's first full-scale examination of constitutional guidelines, in Everson v. Board of Education, below.

In considering Everson, note the Court's recognition of the tension between anti-establishment and free exercise values. Note also that the aid challenged in that case—provision of free school bus access to parochial school students—was aid directed to individuals (as distinguished from direct aid to the parochial institutions themselves). Since Everson, the Court has often accorded great weight to the identity of the immediate recipient of aid in determining whether an aid program violates the establishment clause. Finally, note the efforts by both the majority and the dissent to classify the aid program in Everson. The majority likens the program to the provision of fire, police, and sanitation services to parochial schools. The dissent, on the other hand, rejects this comparison and instead analogizes the Everson aid program to the provision of "textbooks, of school lunches, of athletic equipment, [and] of writing and other materials." Which attempts at classification are more persuasive? Would some type of "bright line" rule be preferable in this area, or should the Court adopt a balancing test similar to the one developed in other First Amendment areas?

EVERSON: "NO TAX LARGE OR SMALL"

Everson v. Board of Education

330 U.S. 1, 67 S.Ct. 504, 91 L.Ed. 711 (1947).

Justice BLACK delivered the opinion of the [Court].

[A New Jersey statute authorized school districts to make rules and contracts to transport children to and from school, "including the transportation of school children to and from school other than a public school, except such school as is operated for profit." Pursuant to that law, a local school board adopted a resolution authorizing reimbursement to parents for money spent to transport their children on public buses. A local taxpayer challenged those payments going to parents of Roman Catholic parochial school students. The highest state court denied relief.]

The only contention here is that the state statute and the resolution, insofar as they authorized reimbursement to parents of children attending parochial schools, violate the Federal Constitution [including by] forc[ing] inhabitants to pay taxes to help support and maintain schools which are dedicated to, and which regularly teach, the Catholic Faith. This is alleged to be a use of state power to support church schools contrary to the prohibition of the First Amendment which the 14th Amendment made applicable to the states.

[Whether this law] is one respecting an "establishment of religion" requires an understanding of the meaning of that language, particularly with respect to the imposition of [taxes]. [We think it appropriate] to review the background and environment of the period in which that constitutional language was fashioned and adopted. [For this portion of the opinion, see p. 1462 above.]

[The] "establishment of religion" clause of the First Amendment means at least this: Neither a state nor the Federal Government can set up a church. Neither can pass laws which aid one religion, aid all religions, or prefer one religion over another. Neither can force nor influence a person to go to or to remain away from church against his will or force him to profess a belief or disbelief in any religion. No person can be punished for entertaining or professing religious beliefs or disbeliefs, for church attendance or non-attendance. No tax in any amount, large or small, can be levied to support any religious activities or institutions, whatever they may be called, or whatever form they may adopt to teach or practice religion. Neither a state nor the Federal Government can, openly or secretly, participate in the affairs of any religious organizations or groups and vice versa. In the words of Jefferson, the clause against establishment of religion by law was intended to erect "a wall of separation between church and State."

We must [not strike down the New Jersey law] if it is within the State's constitutional power even though it approaches the verge of that power. New Jersey cannot consistently with the establishment clause of the First Amendment contribute tax-raised funds to the support of an institution which teaches the tenets and faith of any church. On the other hand, other language of the amendment commands that New Jersey cannot hamper its citizens in the free exercise of their own religion. Consequently, it cannot exclude individual Catholics, Lutherans, Mohammedans, Baptists, Jews, Methodists, Non-believers, Presbyterians, or the members of any other faith, *because of their faith, or lack of it,* from receiving the benefits of public welfare legislation. While we do not mean to intimate that a state could not provide transportation only to children attending public schools, we must be careful, in protecting the citizens of New Jersey against state-established churches, to be sure that we do not inadvertently prohibit New Jersey from extending its general state law benefits to all its citizens without regard to their religious belief.

Measured by these standards, we cannot say that the First Amendment prohibits New Jersey from spending tax-raised funds to pay the bus fares of parochial school pupils as a part of a general program under which it pays the fares of pupils attending public and other schools. It is undoubtedly true that children are helped to get to church schools. There is even a possibility that some of the children might not be sent to the church schools if the parents were compelled to pay their children's bus fares out of their own pockets when transportation to a public school would have been paid for by the State. [Similarly,] parents might be reluctant to permit their children to attend schools which the state had cut off from such general government services as ordinary police and fire protection, connections for sewage disposal, public highways and sidewalks. Of course, cutting off church schools from these services, so separate and so indisputably marked off from the religious function, would make it far more difficult for the schools to operate. But such is obviously not the purpose of the First Amendment. That Amendment requires the state to be a neutral in its relations with groups of religious believers and non-believers; it does not require the state to be their adversary. State power is no more to be used so as to handicap religions than it is to favor them.

This Court has said that parents may, in the discharge of their duty under state compulsory education laws, send their children to a religious rather than a public school if the school meets the secular educational requirements which the state has power to impose. See Pierce v. Society of Sisters (1925; p. 517 above). It appears that these parochial schools meet New Jersey's requirements. The State contributes no money to the schools. It does not support them. Its legislation, as applied, does no more than provide a general program to help parents get their children, regardless of their religion, safely and expeditiously to and from accredited schools.

The First Amendment has erected a wall between church and state. That wall must be kept high and impregnable. We could not approve the slightest breach. New Jersey has not breached it here.

Affirmed.

Justice JACKSON, joined by Justice FRANKFURTER, dissenting.

[The] Court's opinion marshals every argument in favor of state aid and puts the case in its most favorable light, but much of its reasoning confirms my conclusions that there are no good grounds upon which to support the present legislation. In fact, the undertones of the opinion, advocating complete and uncompromising separation of Church from State, seem utterly discordant with its conclusion yielding support to their commingling in educational matters.

Justice RUTLEDGE, joined by Justices FRANKFURTER, JACKSON and BURTON, dissenting.

The Amendment's purpose was [to] create a complete and permanent separation of the spheres of religious activity and civil authority by comprehensively forbidding every form of public aid or support for religion. [Justice Rutledge provided an extensive review of history; see p. 1463 above.] Does New Jersey's action furnish support for religion by use of the taxing power? Certainly it does, if the test remains undiluted as Jefferson and Madison made it, that money taken by taxation from one is not to be used or given to support another's religious training or belief, or indeed one's own. [T]he prohibition is [absolute].

Two great drives are constantly in motion to abridge, in the name of education, the complete division of religion and civil authority which our forefathers made. One is to introduce religious education and observances into the public schools. The other, to obtain public funds for the aid and support of various private religious schools. [Both] avenues were closed by the Constitution. Neither should be opened by this Court. The matter is not one of quantity, to be measured by the amount of money expended. Now as in Madison's day it is one of principle, to keep separate [spheres] as the First Amendment drew them, to prevent the first experiment upon our [liberties].

AID TO PAROCHIAL EDUCATION SINCE EVERSON

1. *The "wall of separation."* In establishment clause cases in the years immediately following Everson, the Court repeatedly cited the "wall of separation" metaphor approvingly. Later Courts however, have been less enthusiastic about the metaphor. In his 1971 majority opinion in Lemon v. Kurtzman, for example, Chief Justice Burger commented: "[We] must recognize that the line of separation, far from being a 'wall,' is a blurred, indistinct, and variable barrier depending on all the circumstances of a particular relationship." And in Lynch v. Donnelly (1984; p. 1521 above), Chief Justice Burger's opinion of the Court called the "wall of separation" metaphor "a useful figure of speech," but went on to say that "the metaphor itself is not a wholly accurate description of the practical aspects of the relationship that in fact exists between church and state."

2. *Forms of aid: texts, tests, teachers, teaching aids and tuition.* Everson held, on the one hand, that "[n]o tax in any amount, large or small, can be levied to support any religious activities or institutions," and, on the other hand, that the establishment clause does not bar the extension of "general state law benefits to all its citizens without regard to their religious belief." The Court was silent on the issue of aid to parochial education for two decades after Everson. But it returned to the issue in Board of Education v. Allen, 392 U.S. 236 (1968), holding that a state may lend books on secular subjects to parochial school students without violating the establishment clause. In Lemon v. Kurtzman, 403 U.S. 602 (1971), better known for its restatement of the three-pronged establishment clause test, the Court concluded that the state's reimbursement of non-public schools for the cost of teachers' salaries, textbooks, and instructional materials, and its payment of a salary supplement to teachers in nonpublic schools, resulted in excessive entanglement of church and state.

The Court's decisions involving aid to parochial education after Allen and Lemon were far from consistent. In Meek v. Pittenger, 421 U.S. 349 (1975), and Wolman v. Walter, 433 U.S. 229 (1977), for example, the Court held that states cannot constitutionally lend instructional materials such as maps, magazines, transparencies, tape recorders, and laboratory equipment to parochial school students, despite its holding in Allen that lending *books* to such students is permissible. Wolman also held that states cannot provide transportation for parochial school students to take field trips, despite its holding in Everson that states *can* provide such students with transportation to and from school. In Levitt v. Committee for Public Education, 413 U.S. 472 (1973), the Court held that states may not reimburse parochial schools for the cost of administering tests that are state-required but teacher-prepared. In Committee for Public Education v. Regan, 444 U.S. 646 (1980), however, the Court held that states *may* subsidize parochial schools for the expense of administering state-prepared examinations. And in Mueller v. Allen (1983; below), the Court upheld a form of financial aid to parents of parochial school students (tax deductions) despite its rejection of a similar type of aid (tuition rebates and tax deductions) in Committee for Public Education v. Nyquist, 413 U.S. 756 (1973). For an attempt to find coherence in the parochial education cases, see Tribe, American Constitutional Law 1219–21 (2d ed. 1988).

In attempting to reconcile these decisions, the Court has relied upon several distinctions. First, it has looked at the breadth of the statutory class of beneficiaries: the broader the class, the more likely the Court is to uphold the statute. Is a distinction on the basis of breadth of statutory class a tenable one? The Court has upheld statutes that provide aid to private school students, as opposed to *all* students, on several occasions, presumably because the public school students were already receiving the aid in question. If this reasoning is extended, however, does it not suggest that financial aid to parochial school students is permissible, so long as the statutory class includes all private school students? If this is the case, does the breadth-of-statutory-classification distinction require anything more than that parochial school students not receive benefits that students in other schools do not receive?

A second distinction upon which the Court has repeatedly relied is based upon the identity of the initial recipient of the aid. The Court has been far more receptive to programs that channel aid to parochial school students and their parents than it has been to programs that give aid directly to parochial schools. Is this distinction a helpful one? Does it not ignore the economic reality that parochial schools benefit whenever parents of parochial school students benefit? (Recall Everson.) In considering Mueller, which follows, note the Court's reliance upon the two distinctions just noted. Is the Court's reasoning persuasive? Or is the dissent's claim that this case is indistinguishable from Nyquist closer to the mark?

———

Mueller v. Allen

463 U.S. 388, 103 S.Ct. 3062, 77 L.Ed.2d 721 (1983).

Justice REHNQUIST delivered the opinion of the Court.

Minnesota allows taxpayers, in computing their state income tax, to deduct certain expenses incurred in providing for the education of their children. The [Court of Appeals] held that the Establishment Clause [was] not offended by this arrangement. We now affirm.

[Minnesota's income tax law permits its taxpayers to deduct from gross income actual expenses incurred for "tuition, textbooks and transportation" for the education of their dependents attending elementary or secondary schools. (The deduction is available for expenses incurred in sending children to public as well as nonpublic schools.) The deduction is limited to $500 per child in primary school and $700 per child in secondary school. About 820,000 children attend Minnesota public schools and about 91,000 attend nonpublic schools; about 95% of the latter group attend sectarian schools.]

One fixed principle in this field is our consistent rejection of the argument that "any program which in some manner aids an institution with a religious affiliation" violates the Establishment Clause. For example, it is now well-established that a state may reimburse parents for expenses incurred in transporting their children to school [Everson], and that it may loan secular textbooks to all school-children within the state. [Allen.] Notwithstanding the repeated approval given programs such as those in Allen and Everson, our decisions also have struck down arrangements resembling, in many respects, these forms of assistance. See, e.g., [Lemon; Levitt; Meek; Wolman .] In this case we are asked to decide whether Minnesota's tax deduction bears greater resemblance to those types of assistance to parochial schools we have approved, or to those we have struck down. Petitioners place particular reliance on our decision in [Nyquist], where we held invalid a New York statute providing public funds for the maintenance and repair of the physical facilities of private schools and granting thinly disguised "tax benefits," actually amounting to tuition grants, to the parents of children attending private schools. [We] conclude that [the provision here] bears less resemblance to the arrangement struck down in Nyquist than it does to assistance programs upheld in our prior decisions and those discussed with approval in Nyquist.

The general nature of our inquiry in this area has been guided, since [Lemon], by the "three-part" test laid out in that case. [While] this principle is well settled, our cases have also emphasized that it provides 'no more than [a] helpful signpost' in dealing with establishment clause challenges. With this caveat in mind, we turn to the specific challenges raised [here] under the Lemon framework. Little time need be spent on the question of whether the Minnesota tax deduction has a secular purpose. Under our prior decisions, governmental assistance programs have consistently survived this inquiry even when they have run afoul of other aspects of the Lemon framework. This reflects, at least in part, our reluctance to attribute unconstitutional motives to the states, particularly when a plausible secular purpose for the state's program may be discerned from the face of the statute. A state's decision to defray the cost of educational expenses incurred by parents—regardless of the type of schools their children attend—evidences a purpose that is both secular and understandable. An educated populace is essential to the political and economic health of any community, and a state's efforts to assist parents in meeting the rising cost of educational expenses plainly serves this secular purpose of ensuring that the state's citizenry is well-educated. Similarly, Minnesota, like other states, could conclude that there is a strong public interest in assuring the continued financial health of private schools, both sectarian and non-sectarian. By educating a substantial number of students such schools relieve public schools of a correspondingly great burden—to the benefit of all taxpayers. In addition, private schools may serve as a benchmark for [public schools]. All these justifications are [sufficient] to satisfy the secular purpose inquiry of Lemon.

We turn therefore to the more difficult but related question whether the Minnesota statute has "the primary effect of advancing the sectarian aims of the nonpublic schools." In concluding that it does not, we find several features of the Minnesota tax deduction particularly significant. First, an essential feature of Minnesota's arrangement is the fact that [the provision] is only one among many deductions [available] under the Minnesota tax laws. Our decisions consistently have recognized that traditionally "[l]egislatures have especially broad latitude in creating classifications and distinctions in tax statutes." [The] Minnesota legislature's judgment that a deduction for educational expenses fairly equalizes the tax burden of its citizens and encourages desirable expenditures for educational purposes is entitled to substantial deference.[1] Other characteristics of [the provision] argue equally strongly for the provision's constitutionality. Most importantly, the deduction is available for educational expenses incurred by *all* parents, including those whose children attend public schools and those whose children attend non-sectarian private schools or sectarian private [schools]: "the provision of benefits to so broad a spectrum of groups is an important index of secular effect."

In this respect, as well as others, this case is vitally different from the scheme struck down in Nyquist. There, public assistance amounting to tuition grants was provided only to parents of children in *nonpublic* schools. [Unlike] the assistance at issue in Nyquist, [the Minnesota law] permits *all* parents— whether their children attend public school or private—to deduct their childrens' educational expenses. [As our] decisions indicate, a program [that] neutrally provides state assistance to a broad spectrum of citizens is not readily subject to challenge under the Establishment Clause. We also agree [that], by channeling whatever assistance it may provide to parochial schools through individual parents, Minnesota has reduced the Establishment Clause objections to which its action is subject. It is true, of course, that financial assistance provided to parents ultimately has an economic effect comparable to that of aid given directly to the schools attended by their children. It is also true, however, that under Minnesota's arrangement public funds become available only as a result of numerous, private choices of individual parents of school-age children. For these reasons, we recognized in Nyquist that the means by which state assistance flows to private schools is of some importance. [It] is noteworthy that all but one of our recent cases invalidating state aid to parochial schools [the exception was Nyquist] have involved the direct transmission of assistance from the state to the schools themselves. [Where], as here, aid to parochial schools is available only as a result of decisions of individual parents no "imprimatur of State approval" can be deemed to have been conferred on any particular religion, or on religion generally.

We find it useful [to] compare the attenuated financial benefits flowing to parochial schools from the [provision here] to the evils against which the Establishment Clause was designed to protect. These dangers are well-described by our statement that "what is at stake as a matter of policy [in establishment clause cases] is preventing that kind and degree of government involvement in religious life that, as history teaches us, is apt to lead to strife and frequently strain a political system to the breaking point." [Nyquist.] It is important, however, to "keep these issues in perspective": "At this point in the 20th century we are quite far removed from the dangers that prompted the Framers to [adopt the establishment clause]. The risk of significant religious or denominational control over our democratic processes—or even of deep political division along religious lines—is remote, and when viewed against the positive contributions of sectarian schools, [any] such risk seems entirely tolerable in

---

1. Our decision in Nyquist is not to the contrary on this point. We expressed considerable doubt there that the "tax benefits" provided by New York law properly could be regarded as parts of a genuine system of tax laws. [Indeed], the question whether a program having the elements of a "genuine tax deduction" would be constitutionally acceptable was expressly reserved in Nyquist. While the economic consequences of the program in Nyquist and that in this case may be difficult to distinguish, we have recognized on other occasions that "the form of the [state's assistance to parochial schools must be examined] for the light that it casts on the substance." [Lemon.] The fact that the Minnesota plan embodies a "genuine tax deduction" is thus of some relevance, especially given the traditional rule of deference accorded legislative classifications in tax statutes. [Footnote by Justice Rehnquist.]

light of the continuing oversight of this Court." Wolman [separate opinion by Powell, J.]. The Establishment Clause of course extends beyond prohibition of a state church or payment of state funds to one or more churches. We do not think, however, that its prohibition extends to the type of tax deduction established by Minnesota. The historic purposes of the clause simply do not encompass the sort of attenuated financial benefit, ultimately controlled by the private choices of individual parents, that eventually flows to parochial schools from the neutrally available tax benefit at issue in this case.

Petitioners argue that, notwithstanding [its facial neutrality], in application the statute primarily benefits religious institutions. Petitioners rely [on] a statistical analysis of the type of persons claiming the tax deduction. They contend that most parents of public school children incur no tuition expenses, and that other expenses deductible under [the provision] are negligible in value; moreover, they claim that 96% of the children in private schools in 1978–1979 attended religiously-affiliated institutions. Because of all this, they reason, the bulk of deductions taken [will] be claimed by parents of children in sectarian schools. Respondents reply that petitioners have failed to consider the impact of deductions for items such as transportation, summer school tuition, tuition paid by parents whose children attended schools outside the school districts in which they resided, rental or purchase costs for a variety of equipment, and tuition for certain types of instruction not ordinarily provided in public schools.

We need not consider these contentions in detail. We would be loath to adopt a rule grounding the constitutionality of a facially neutral law on annual reports reciting the extent to which various classes of private citizens claimed benefits under the law. Such an approach would scarcely provide the certainty that this field stands in need of, nor can we perceive principled standards by which such statistical evidence might be evaluated. Moreover, the fact that private persons fail in a particular year to claim the tax relief to which they are entitled—under a facially neutral statute—should be of little importance in determining the constitutionality of the statute permitting such relief.

Finally, private educational institutions, and parents paying for their children to attend these schools, make special contributions to the areas in which they operate. [If] parents of children in private schools choose to take especial advantage of the relief provided by [the law], it is no doubt due to the fact that they bear a particularly great financial burden in educating their children. More fundamentally, whatever unequal effect may be attributed to the statutory classification can fairly be regarded as a rough return for the benefits [provided] to the state and all taxpayers by parents sending their children to parochial schools. In the light of all this, we believe it wiser to decline to engage in the type of empirical inquiry into those persons benefited by state law which petitioners urge.[2] Thus, we hold that the Minnesota tax

---

2. Our conclusion is unaffected by the fact that [the provision] permits deductions for amounts spent for textbooks and transportation as well as tuition. In [Everson], we approved a statute reimbursing parents of *all* schoolchildren for the costs of transporting their children to school. Doing so by means of a deduction rather than a direct grant, only serves to make the state's action less objectionable. Likewise, in [Allen], we approved state loans of textbooks to *all* schoolchildren; although we disapproved in [Meek and Wolman] direct loans of instructional materials to sectarian schools, we do not find those cases controlling. First, they involved assistance provided to the schools themselves, rather than tax benefits directed to individual parents. Moreover, we think that state assistance for the rental of calculators, ice skates, tennis shoes, and the like, scarcely poses the type of dangers against which the

deduction for educational expenses satisfies the primary effect inquiry of our Establishment Clause cases.

Turning to the third part of the Lemon inquiry, we have no difficulty in concluding that the Minnesota statute does not "excessively entangle" the state in religion. The only plausible source of the "comprehensive, discriminating, and continuing state surveillance" necessary to run afoul of this standard would lie in the fact that state officials must determine whether particular textbooks qualify for a deduction. In making this decision, state officials must disallow deductions taken from "instructional books and materials used in the teaching of religious tenets, doctrines or worship, the purpose of which is to inculcate such tenets, doctrines or worship." Making decisions such as this does not differ substantially from making the types of decisions approved in earlier opinions of this Court. [See, e.g., Allen.][3]

[Affirmed.]

Justice MARSHALL, with whom Justices BRENNAN, BLACKMUN and STEVENS join, dissenting.

The Establishment Clause [prohibits] a State from subsidizing religious education, whether it does so directly or indirectly. In my view, this principle of neutrality forbids [any] tax benefit, including the tax deduction at issue here, which subsidizes tuition payments to sectarian schools. I also believe that the Establishment Clause prohibits the tax deductions that Minnesota authorizes for the cost of books and other instructional materials used for sectarian purposes.

I. [The] Minnesota tax statute violates the Establishment Clause for precisely the same reason as the statute struck down in Nyquist: it has a direct and immediate effect of advancing religion.

A. "[A]id to the educational function of [parochial] schools [necessarily] results in aid to the sectarian enterprise as a whole" because "[t]he very purpose of those schools is to provide an integrated secular and religious education." [Meek.] For this reason, aid to sectarian schools must be restricted to ensure that it may not be used to further the religious mission of those schools. Indirect assistance in the form of financial aid to parents for tuition payments is [impermissible] because it is not "subject [to] restrictions" which "'guarantee the separation between secular and religious educational functions [and] ensure that State financial aid supports only the former.'" [Nyquist, quoting Lemon.] By ensuring that parents will be reimbursed for tuition payments they make, the Minnesota statute requires that taxpayers in general pay for the cost of parochial education and extends a financial "incentive to parents to send their children to sectarian schools." Nyquist. [That] parents receive a reduction of their tax liability, rather than a direct reimbursement, is of no greater significance here than it was in Nyquist. [It] is equally irrelevant

Establishment Clause was intended to guard. [Footnote by Justice Rehnquist.]

3. No party to this litigation has urged that the Minnesota plan is invalid because it runs afoul of the rather elusive inquiry, subsumed under the third part of the Lemon test, whether the Minnesota statute partakes of the "divisive political potential" condemned in Lemon. The argument is advanced, however, by [amicus]. The Court's language in [Lemon] respecting political divi-

siveness was made in the context of Pennsylvania and Rhode Island statutes which provided for either direct payments of, or reimbursement of, a proportion of teachers' salaries in parochial schools. We think, in the light of the treatment in [later] cases, the language must be regarded as confined to cases where direct financial subsidies are paid to parochial schools or to teachers in parochial schools. [Footnote by Justice Rehnquist.]

whether a reduction in taxes takes the form of a tax "credit," a tax "modification," or a tax "deduction." What is of controlling significance is not the form but the "substantive impact" of the [financial aid].

B. 1. [The] majority first attempts to distinguish Nyquist on the ground that Minnesota makes all parents [eligible,] whereas the New York law allowed a deduction only for parents whose children attended nonpublic schools. [That] the Minnesota statute makes some small benefit available to all parents cannot alter the fact that the most substantial benefit provided by the statute is available only to those parents who send their children to schools that charge tuition. It is simply undeniable that the single largest expense that may be deducted under the Minnesota statute is tuition. The statute is little more than a subsidy of tuition masquerading as a subsidy of general educational expenses. The other deductible expenses are de minimis in comparison to tuition expenses.

[The] bulk of the tax benefits afforded by the Minnesota scheme are enjoyed by parents of parochial school children not because parents of public school children fail to claim deductions to which they are entitled, but because the latter are simply *unable* to claim the largest tax deduction that Minnesota authorizes. [Parents] who send their children to free public schools are simply ineligible to obtain the full benefit of the deduction except in the unlikely event that they buy $700 worth of pencils, notebooks, and bus rides for their school-age children. Yet parents who pay at least $700 in tuition to nonpublic, sectarian schools can claim the full deduction even if they incur no other educational expenses. That this deduction has a primary effect of promoting religion can easily be determined without any resort to the type of "statistical evidence" that the majority fears would lead to constitutional uncertainty. [In] this case, it is undisputed that well over 90% of the children attending tuition-charging schools in Minnesota are enrolled in sectarian schools. History and experience likewise instruct us that any generally available financial assistance for elementary and secondary school tuition expenses mainly will further religious education because the majority of the schools which charge tuition are sectarian. Because Minnesota, like every other State, is committed to providing free public education, tax assistance for tuition payments inevitably redounds to the benefit of nonpublic, sectarian schools and parents who send their children to those schools.

2. The majority also asserts that the Minnesota statute is distinguishable from the statute struck down in Nyquist in another respect: the tax benefit available under Minnesota law is a "genuine tax deduction," whereas the New York law provided a benefit which, while nominally a deduction, also had features of a "tax credit." [This] is a distinction without a difference. Our prior decisions have rejected the relevance of the majority's formalistic distinction between tax deductions and the tax benefit at issue in [Nyquist].

III. [The] lines drawn in Nyquist were drawn on a reasoned basis with appropriate regard for the principles of neutrality embodied by the Establishment Clause. I do not believe that the same can be said of the lines drawn by the majority today. For the first time, the Court has upheld financial support for religious schools without any reason at all to assume that the support will be restricted to the secular functions of those schools and will not be used to support religious instruction. This result is flatly at odds with the fundamental principle that a State may provide no financial support whatsoever to promote [religion]. I dissent.

GRAND RAPIDS SCHOOL DISTRICT v. BALL, 473 U.S. 373 (1985), and AGUILAR v. FELTON, 473 U.S. 402 (1985): The Grand Rapids case struck down two programs, the Shared Time and Community Education Programs of the city. Under the former, public school teachers offered supplementary classes such as remedial reading in parochial school classrooms. In the second program, parochial school employees received additional pay from the public school system to conduct "community education" classes such as arts and crafts after school hours in the parochial school buildings. In respect to the latter program, Justice BRENNAN's majority opinion was concerned that "the religious message [the teachers] are expected to convey during the regular schoolday will infuse the supposedly secular classes they teach after school." With respect to the former, he relied on Meek v. Pittenger and noted: "Teachers in [a religious] atmosphere may well subtly (or overtly) conform their instruction to the environment in which they teach, while students will perceive the instruction in the context of the dominantly religious message of the institution, thus reinforcing the indoctrinating effect." He added: "Government promotes religion as effectively when it fosters a close identification of its powers with those of any—or all—religious denominations as when it attempts to inculcate specific religious doctrines. [This] effect—the symbolic union of government and religion in one sectarian enterprise—is an impermissible effect under the Establishment Clause."

The Aguilar case involved a federally funded New York program quite similar to the Grand Rapids Shared Time Program. New York provided services to educationally deprived children living in low-income areas with federal financial assistance under Title I of the Elementary and Secondary School Act of 1965. It allowed public school teachers to go to parochial schools to teach math and reading and provide guidance counseling. New York tried to make its program constitutional by purging classrooms of religious symbols during the public school teachers' visits, and monitoring the program to ensure its separation from the larger program of religious inculcation in the surrounding parochial school. But Justice BRENNAN, once again writing for the Court, found that this supervisory system itself resulted in "the excessive entanglement of church and state." He suggested that "ongoing inspection" of religious schools by "agents of the state" to "ensure the absence of a religious message" offended the religion clauses. Justice POWELL, concurring in both the Aguilar and Grand Rapids cases, found that the risk of entanglement was compounded by "the additional risk of political divisiveness." He insisted that there was "a considerable risk of continuing political strife over the propriety of direct aid to religious schools and the proper allocation of limited governmental resources." He noted, however, that if Congress "could fashion a program of evenhanded financial assistance to both public and private schools that could be administered, without governmental supervision in the private schools, so as to prevent the diversion of the aid from secular purposes, we would be presented with a different question."

Chief Justice BURGER and Justices WHITE and REHNQUIST each filed brief dissents. Justice Rehnquist noted that the Court had taken "advantage of the 'Catch-22' paradox of its own creation, whereby aid must be supervised to ensure no entanglement but the supervision itself is held to cause an entanglement." Justice O'CONNOR's dissent in Aguilar, like those of Justices Rehnquist and White, explained her disagreements with much of the Court's establishment clause doctrine for reasons similar to those set forth in the separate opinions by Justices O'Connor, White and Rehnquist in Wallace v. Jaffree (1985; p. 1506 above).

Can Grand Rapids and Aguilar be reconciled with Mueller? Do they not involve aid programs directed at a general class of beneficiaries that just happens to include parochial school students? Does the physical presence of public employees on parochial school premises distinguish the cases? Is there special reason for concern here about political "divisiveness"? As Justice Powell's concurrence suggests, members of the Court have sometimes expressed concern about political as well as administrative entanglement between church and state. In Lemon, the Court stated: "Ordinarily political debate and division, however vigorous or even partisan, are normal and healthy manifestations of our democratic system of government, but political division along religious lines was one of the principal evils against which the First Amendment was intended to protect." Why is political divisiveness over matters of religion more threatening than ordinary political divisiveness? Can religious factions be expected to behave differently than social or economic factions? In Lynch, Chief Justice Burger cautioned not to place too much emphasis on divisiveness inquiries, noting that "this Court has not held that political divisiveness alone can serve to invalidate otherwise permissible conduct."

3. *Aid to higher education: is a different standard appropriate?* The majority of the Court has typically found fewer establishment clause barriers to financial aid to colleges than to elementary and secondary schools. Although the Court has applied the three-part test developed in the elementary and secondary school context ("purpose," "effect," and "entanglement"), the Justices have found it more readily satisfied in higher education cases and have been less prone to find excessive "entanglement" in state supervision schemes. The distinction between the levels of education was first articulated in Chief Justice BURGER's plurality opinion in TILTON v. RICHARDSON, 403 U.S. 672 (1971): "There are generally significant differences between the religious aspects of church-related institutions of higher learning and parochial elementary and secondary schools. [C]ollege students are less impressionable and less susceptible to religious indoctrination. [Furthermore], by their very nature, college and postgraduate courses tend to limit the opportunities for sectarian influence by virtue of their own internal disciplines. [Since] religious indoctrination is not a substantial purpose [of] these church-related colleges, [there] is less likelihood than in primary and secondary schools that religion will permeate the area of secular education. This reduces the risk that government aid will in fact serve to support religious activities. Correspondingly the necessity for intensive government surveillance is diminished and the resulting entanglements between government and religion lessened. Such inspection as may be necessary to ascertain that the facilities are devoted to secular education is minimal."

Tilton upheld federal construction grants to church-related colleges. The funds had to be used for facilities devoted exclusively to secular educational purposes. The pattern of Tilton was followed two years later in Hunt v. McNair, 413 U.S. 734 (1973), where a divided Court sustained a construction aid program using state-issued revenue bonds to permit colleges to borrow funds at low interest. In ROEMER v. MARYLAND PUBLIC WORKS BD., 426 U.S. 736 (1976), the majority went a step further: it approved annual noncategorical grants to eligible private colleges, including some church-related ones, subject only to the restriction that the funds not be used for "sectarian purposes." Justice BLACKMUN's plurality opinion conceded that the "entanglement" problem (arising from the supervision needed to assure that funds were used only for secular purposes) was more serious in the context of annual grants than with "one-time" aid. He nevertheless found the program permissible.

FROM SEPARATION TO ASSIMILATION ON FINANCIAL AID

If Everson articulated, at least in theory, a separationist view of church and state, Mueller v. Allen articulated an alternative view that might be labeled assimilationist. In a strict separationist view, no financial benefit "large or small" could flow from government to religious institutions. In the most expansive assimilationist view, religious individuals or institutions may receive unlimited government financial aid so long as they do so on the same terms as other comparable beneficiaries. This approach would conceive neutrality under the establishment clause as requiring equal access for religion, not a wall of separation between church and state. On this view, exclusion of religious participants from the programs of the welfare state may discourage religious choices people would have made in the absence of the state or its programs. Which view of the religion clauses is more persuasive? More administrable? For elaboration of the assimilationist approach and its premises, see McConnell, "Religious Freedom at a Crossroads," 59 U. Chi. L. Rev. 115 (1992); see also Laycock, "Formal, Substantive, and Disaggregated Neutrality Toward Religion," 39 DePaul L. Rev. 993 (1990) (endorsing "substantive neutrality" toward religion that "[n]either encourages or discourages religious belief or disbelief, practice or nonpractice"). For a critique, see Sullivan, "Religion and Liberal Democracy," 59 U.Chi. L. Rev. 195 (1992).

The Court has never embraced completely the separationist view, as the holding, as opposed to the rhetoric, of Everson itself demonstrated. Indeed, a pre-Mueller precursor of the assimilationist view may be found in WALZ v. TAX COMM'N, 397 U.S. 664 (1970), which upheld a state tax exemption for "real or personal property used exclusively for religious, educational or charitable purposes." Writing for the Court, Chief Justice Burger noted that the tax exemption conferred "indirect economic benefit" upon churches, but emphasized that the state had "granted exemption to all houses of religious worship within a broad class of property owned by nonprofit, quasi-public corporations which include hospitals, libraries, playgrounds, scientific, professional, historical and patriotic groups." Likewise, in another pre-Mueller case, WIDMAR v. VINCENT, 454 U.S. 263 (1981), the Court struck down a state university's ban on the use of its facilities for prayer and religious discussion by student groups. In reaching that conclusion, the Court rejected the university's claim that permitting use of the university forum by the student groups would have violated the establishment clause. Justice POWELL's majority opinion found that an "equal access" policy would not violate the establishment clause. In applying the "effect" part of the Lemon test, he insisted that any aid to religious groups from a policy of "nondiscrimination against religious speech" would be only "incidental," because "an open forum in a public university does not confer any imprimatur of State approval on religious sects or practices" and the forum "was available to a broad class of non-religious as well as religious speakers": "The provision of benefits to so broad a spectrum of groups is an important index of secular effect." For a holding very similar to Widmar's, see Lamb's Chapel v. Center Moriches Union Free School Dist., 508 U.S. 384 (1993) (allowing inclusion of religious film in after-hour series at a public school).

On the other hand, the Court has not committed itself to wholesale assimilationism, even after Mueller. For example, it remains concerned about the symbolism of having public employees on parochial school premises, or directing a government check to a church rather than to individual parents of parochial school children. These symbolic harms would be irrelevant under the view that substantive equality of treatment is all that matters. But the Court has clearly been moving in the direction of the assimilationist view. See Lupu, "The Lingering Death of Separationism," 62 Geo. Wash. L. Rev. 230 (1994). Consider the Court's extension of the assimilationist approach in the following cases:

WITTERS v. WASHINGTON DEPT. OF SERVICES FOR BLIND, 474 U.S. 481 (1986), held that the "effect" prong of the Lemon test was not violated by a law authorizing payment to a visually handicapped person for vocational rehabilitation services, where the recipient sought to use the funds to pay his tuition at a Christian college in order to prepare himself a career as a "pastor, missionary, or youth director." The Court was unanimous in supporting that result. Justice MARSHALL's opinion emphasized that the aid program provided "no financial incentive for students to undertake sectarian education" and did not "tend to provide greater or broader benefits for recipients who apply their aid to religious education." Moreover, there was no showing that any "significant portion of the aid expended under the Washington program as a whole will end up flowing to religious education." Justice Marshall's reliance on the small quantity of aid that found its way into religious education, however, did not seem to represent the views of the majority. Concurring opinions by Justices WHITE, POWELL (joined by Chief Justice Burger and Justice Rehnquist) and O'CONNOR all emphasized their reliance on Mueller v. Allen, above. Justice Powell criticized the Court for not relying directly on that case. He insisted that Mueller meant that "state programs that are wholly neutral in offering educational assistance to a class defined without reference to religion do not violate the [effect] part of the [Lemon] test, because any aid to religion results from the private choices of individual beneficiaries."

BOWEN v. KENDRICK, 487 U.S. 589 (1988): This was a challenge to the Adolescent Family Life Act of 1982, which authorizes the federal grants to public and nonpublic organizations, including organizations with ties to religious denominations, for counseling services and research "in the area of premarital adolescent sexual relations and pregnancy." Some of the grants, the Court noted, went "to various organizations that were affiliated with religious denominations and that had corporate requirements that the organizations abide by religious doctrines." The Court, in a majority opinion by Chief Justice REHNQUIST, rejected an on-the-face attack on the Act and remanded the as-applied challenge for further proceedings.

Applying the three-part Lemon standard, the Court held that the Act on its face did not violate the establishment clause. As to the first prong of Lemon, the Court had no difficulty in concluding that the problem of teenage pregnancy constituted a valid secular purpose. With respect to the "effect" prong, the Court found the issue somewhat more difficult. There were two problems. The first was the specific mention of religious organizations in the law itself. But since various institutions in the public and private sector were also mentioned, the Court found that any effect of advancing religion was "incidental and remote." Second, the law permits "religious institutions to participate as recipients of federal funds." But again Justice Rehnquist found this permissible: "[This] Court has never held that religious institutions are disabled by the First Amendment from participating in publicly sponsored social welfare programs." Moreover, "nothing on the face of the [law] indicates that a significant proportion of the federal funds will be disbursed to 'pervasively sectarian' institutions," and thus this case was distinguishable from the Grand Rapids case and more closely resembled Tilton and Roemer. The Court also rejected a claim that the Act necessarily advanced religion because religiously affiliated grantees provided the counseling services: although the establishment clause bars government-financed indoctrination into "the beliefs of a particular religious faith," the Court insisted that when aid goes to religiously affiliated institutions that are not "pervasively sectarian," it would not "presume that [it will] be used in a way that would have the primary effect of advancing religion." Finally, the Court did not find a violation of the "excessive entanglement" prong of Lemon, concluding that there was no reason to fear that the monitoring involved here would "cause government to intrude unduly into the day-to-day operations of the religiously affiliated [grantees]." In remanding the as-applied challenge to the trial court, the Court suggested that the validity of the law as applied would turn on such issues as the "pervasive sectarian" nature of the grantees and whether any of the aid was used to finance "specifically religious activit[ies] in an otherwise substantially secular setting."

Justice O'CONNOR's concurrence emphasized that the majority opinion should not read as tolerating "the kind of improper administration that seems to have occurred [here]." She insisted that "*any* use of public funds to promote religious doctrines" was unconstitutional and that "*extensive* violations—if they can be proved in this case—will be highly relevant in shaping an appropriate remedy that ends such abuses." Justice KENNEDY, joined by Justice Scalia, also submitted a concurrence, arguing that a finding that funds went to a pervasively sectarian institution would still not be a sufficient condition for unconstitutionality, but only a preliminary step in determining the way federal funds were used: "The question in an as-applied challenge is not whether the entity is of a religious character, but how it spends its grant."

Justice BLACKMUN, joined by Justices Brennan, Marshall and Stevens, dissented, insisting the law was unconstitutional under the "effect" prong of Lemon. He would have found the law invalid on its face, because the involvement of religious organizations in teaching and counseling create an unacceptable risk that the message would in fact be religious. Although the Court had "recognized that the Constitution does not prohibit the government from supporting secular social-welfare services solely because they are provided by a religiously affiliated organization," he argued, there is "a very real and important difference between running a soup kitchen or a hospital, and counseling pregnant teenagers on how to make the difficult decisions facing them. The risk of advancing religion at public expense, and of creating an appearance that the government is endorsing the medium and the message, is much greater when the religious organization is directly engaged in pedagogy, with the express intent of shaping belief and changing behavior, than when it is neutrally dispensing medication, food, or shelter."

In ZOBREST v. CATALINA FOOTHILLS SCHOOL DIST., 509 U.S. 1 (1993), the Court, relying on Mueller and Witters, held that the provision of a publicly funded sign-language interpreter to a deaf student in a parochial school classroom did not violate the establishment clause. The Individuals with Disabilities Education Act and its state equivalent provided for funding such interpreters for hearing-impaired students generally. Writing for the Court, Chief Justice REHNQUIST held that the establishment clause did not mandate exclusion from such funding of an otherwise eligible student attending parochial school: "[W]e have consistently held that government programs that neutrally provide benefits to a broad class of citizens defined without reference to religion are not readily subject to an Establishment Clause challenge just because sectarian institutions may also receive an attenuated financial bene-fit." He emphasized that the Act did not distinguish between public and parochial schools, and found that it thus "creates no financial incentive for parents to choose a sectarian school." He rejected the argument that the establishment clause absolutely barred the presence of a public employee on parochial school premises. And he found no danger that the sign-language interpreter would personally assist in religious instruction: "Nothing in this record suggests that a sign-language interpreter would do more than accurately interpret whatever material is presented to the class as a whole." He conclud-ed: "[Zobrest's] parents have chosen of their own free will to place him in a pervasively sectarian environment. The sign-language interpreter they have requested will neither add to nor subtract from that environment, and hence the provision of such assistance is not barred by the Establishment Clause."

Justice BLACKMUN, joined by Justice Souter, dissented, objecting that "[u]ntil now, the Court never has authorized a public employee to participate directly in religious indoctrination. Yet that is the consequence of today's decision." Justice O'Connor, joined by Justice Stevens also dissented, on statutory grounds.

Recall that in ROSENBERGER v. RECTOR AND VISITORS OF THE UNIV. OF VIRGINIA, ___ U.S. ___, 115 S.Ct. 2510 (1995), , see p. 1324 above, the Court held that the free speech clause required inclusion of an otherwise eligible student-edited evangelical Christian magazine called "Wide Awake" in a student activities program funded with mandatory student fees. The Court rejected the University's defense that such inclusion would violate the estab-lishment clause. Justice KENNEDY, writing for the Court, found the establish-ment clause issue similar to that in Widmar: "The governmental program here is neutral toward religion. There is no suggestion that the University created it to advance religion or adopted some ingenious device with the purpose of aiding a religious cause. The object of the [funding program] is to open a forum for speech and to support various student enterprises, including the publication of newspapers, in recognition of the diversity and creativity of student life. [The] neutrality of the program distinguishes the student fees from a tax levied for the direct support of a church or group of churches.

"Government neutrality is apparent [also because the] University has taken pains to disassociate itself from the private speech involved in this case. [There] is no real likelihood that the speech in question is being either endorsed or coerced by the State. [We] do not confront a case where, even under a neutral program that includes nonsectarian recipients, the government is making direct money payments to an institution or group that is engaged in religious activity. [It is undisputed] that no public funds flow directly to [the Christian magazine's] coffers.

"It does not violate the Establishment Clause for a public university to grant access to its facilities on a religion-neutral basis to a wide spectrum of student groups, including groups which use meeting rooms for sectarian activities, accompanied by some devotional exercises. See [Widmar, Lamb's Chapel.] [A] public university may maintain its own computer facility and give student groups access to that facility, including the use of the printers, on a religion neutral, say first-come-first-served, basis. [There] is no difference in logic or principle, and no difference of constitutional significance, between a school using its funds to operate a facility to which students have access, and a school paying a third-party contractor to operate the facility on its behalf. [Any] benefit to religion is incidental to the government's provision of secular services for secular purposes on a religion-neutral basis. [By] paying outside printers, the University in fact attains a further degree of separation from the student publication, for it avoids the duties of supervision, escapes the costs of upkeep, repair, and replacement attributable to student use, and has a clear record of costs. [Moreover,] the student publication is not a religious institution. [It] is instead a publication involved in a pure forum for the expression of ideas.''

Justice O'CONNOR wrote a concurrence, noting that ''particular features of the University's program—such as the explicit disclaimer, the disbursement of funds directly to third-party vendors, the vigorous nature of the forum at issue, and the possibility for objecting students to opt out—convince me that providing such assistance in this case would not carry the danger of impermissible use of public funds to endorse Wide Awake's religious message.'' Justice THOMAS likewise concurred, emphasizing the historical pedigree of tax exemptions for religious institutions and arguing that the direct subsidy here posed no greater establishment clause problem: ''The historical evidence of government support for religious entities through property tax exemptions is [overwhelming]. [Walz.] [This] tradition puts to rest the notion that the Establishment Clause bars monetary aid to religious groups even when the aid is equally available to other groups. A tax exemption in many cases is economically and functionally indistinguishable from a direct monetary subsidy. In one instance, the government relieves religious entities (along with others) of a generally applicable tax; in the other, it relieves religious entities (along with others) of some or all of the burden of that tax by returning it in the form of a cash subsidy. Whether the benefit is provided at the front or back end of the taxation process, the financial aid to religious groups is undeniable. The analysis under the Establishment Clause must also be the same.''

Justice SOUTER, joined by Justices Stevens, Ginsburg and Breyer, dissented, arguing that funding Wide Awake would violate the establishment clause because it would employ ''public funds for the direct subsidization of preaching the word. [If] the Clause was meant to accomplish nothing else, it was meant to bar this use of public money.'' He criticized the majority for ''blanch[ing] the patently and frankly evangelistic character of the magazine.'' He also found it no defense that the ''University's funding scheme is 'neutral,' in the formal sense that it makes funds available on an evenhanded basis to secular and sectarian applicants alike'': ''Evenhandedness as one element of a permissibly attenuated benefit is, of course, a far cry from evenhandedness as a sufficient condition of constitutionality for direct financial support of religious proselytization, and our cases have unsurprisingly repudiated any such attempt to cut the Establishment Clause down to a mere prohibition against unequal direct aid.'' He distinguished other cases permitting the inclusion of religious beneficiaries in funding programs: ''Witters, Mueller, and Zobrest [explicitly] distinguished the indirect aid in issue from contrasting examples in the line of cases striking down direct aid, and each thereby expressly preserved the core constitutional principle that direct aid to religion is impermissible.'' He found unconvincing the argument that payment to the third-party printer broke the chain of direct aid: ''If this indeed were a critical distinction, the Constitution would permit a State to pay all the bills of any religious institution.'' He also found unconvincing the argument that the mandatory student fee somehow differed for establishment clause purposes from a general tax: ''[O]ur cases on direct government aid have frequently spoken in terms in no way limited to tax revenues.'' He concluded: ''The Court is ordering an instrumentality of the State to support religious evangelism with direct funding. This is a flat violation of the Establishment Clause.''

C. LEGISLATIVE ACCOMMODATIONS OF RELIGION

———

Introduction. How much leeway should government have to "accommodate" free exercise concerns, when the free exercise clause does not compel such accommodation? Statutory accommodations in the interest of free exercise values present recurrent problems of tension between the goals of the free exercise and establishment clauses. Statutory exemptions are widespread in legislation in such areas as social security and labor. Recall that, in Sherbert, Justice Harlan's dissent argued that legislators have broad discretion to promote free exercise values by enacting statutory accommodations. By what standards should statutory accommodations of religious practices be judged? Might some legislative accommodations amount to the impermissible establishment of religion? The following cases explore this question.

1. *Accommodation versus delegation.* One clear limit on religious accommodation is that government may not, consistent with the establishment clause, delegate to a religious entity the power to exercise civic authority. LARKIN v. GRENDEL'S DEN, INC., 459 U.S. 116 (1982), struck down a Massachusetts law that gave churches and schools the power to veto the issuance of liquor licenses to restaurants within 500 feet of the church or school buildings. By a vote of 8–1, the Court balked at the notion that governmental authority could so be conferred on religious organizations. Chief Justice BURGER's majority opinion conceded a church's "valid interest in being insulated from certain kinds of commercial establishments, including those dispensing liquor," but concluded that the delegation of a veto power to churches had the effect of "advancing religion," impermissible under the Lemon standards. He added that "the mere appearance of a joint exercise of legislative authority by Church and State provides a significant symbolic benefit to religion in the minds of some." Moreover, turning to the "entanglement" prong of the Lemon test, he found that the law "enmeshes churches in the exercise of substantial governmental powers contrary to our consistent interpretation of the Establishment Clause." Justice REHNQUIST, the sole dissenter, argued that because the state could have banned all liquor establishments within 500 feet of a church, the Constitution did not prevent the state from electing a less drastic alternative of allowing each church to decide whether it wished to be "unmolested by activities at a neighboring bar."

2. *Permissible statutory accommodations and their limits.* Title VII of the Civil Rights Act of 1964, which forbids employment discrimination on the basis of, inter alia, race, gender or religion, requires employers to make reasonable accommodations to the religious practices of employees. (For an interpretation of the statutory "reasonable accommodation" requirement, see Trans World Airlines v. Hardison, 432 U.S. 63 (1977).) The Court has never questioned the permissibility of that accommodation provision. But ESTATE OF THORNTON v. CALDOR, INC., 472 U.S. 703 (1985), struck down a Connecticut law providing: "No person who states that a particular day of the week is observed as his Sabbath may be required to work on such day. An employee's refusal to work on his Sabbath shall not constitute grounds for his dismissal." The law was the result of a substantial revision of the State's Sunday closing laws; under the revision, many businesses were allowed to remain open on Sundays. Chief Justice BURGER's opinion for the Court held that this mandatory, absolute deference to the Sabbath observer constituted an impermissible establishment of religion because the statute clearly advanced "a particular religious

practice." Justice O'CONNOR, joined by Justice Marshall, filed a concurring opinion in which she sought to distinguish the exception here from that in Title VII. To her, the crucial distinctions were the exclusive religious orientation and absolute character of the Connecticut law: "[A] statute outlawing employment discrimination based on race, color, religion, sex, or national origin has the valid secular purpose of assuring employment opportunity to all groups in our pluralistic society. Since Title VII calls for reasonable rather than absolute accommodation and extends that requirement to all religious beliefs rather than protecting only the Sabbath observance, I believe an objective observer would perceive it as an anti-discrimination law rather than an endorsement of religion or a particular religious provision."

In CORPORATION OF PRESIDING BISHOP v. AMOS, 483 U.S. 327 (1987), the Court upheld a different provision of Title VII, this one accommodating religious employers rather than employees. Title VII generally prohibits discrimination in employment on the basis of religion, but exempts religious organizations. The exemption, 42 U.S.C. § 702, provides that the antidiscrimination provision "shall not apply [to] a religious corporation [with] respect to the employment of individuals of a particular religion to perform work connected with a carrying on by such corporation [of] its activities." An employee of the Mormon Church who had been discharged from his job as a janitor at a gymnasium run by the Church for failing to qualify as a church member claimed that his firing on the basis of religion violated the Act. The Church claimed that its action was permitted by the exemption in § 702. The employee in turn claimed that if § 702 were "construed to allow religious employers to discriminate on religious grounds in hiring for nonreligious jobs," it violated the establishment clause.

Without dissent, the Court rejected the establishment clause attack on § 702. Justice WHITE's opinion defended the constitutionality of the general principle underlying the exemption: "We find unpersuasive the District Court's reliance on the fact that [§ 702] singles out religious entities for a benefit. Although the Court has given weight to this consideration in its past decisions [e.g., Mueller; Nyquist, above], it has never indicated that statutes that give special consideration to religious groups are per se invalid. That would run contrary to the teaching of our cases that there is ample room for accommodation of religion under the Establishment Clause. Where [government] acts with the proper purpose of lifting a regulation that burdens the exercise of religion, we see no reason to require that the exemption come packaged with benefits to secular entities." Justice White insisted that the exemption was "in no way questionable under the Lemon analysis." Under its "purpose" prong, the law need not be "unrelated to religion"; rather, "Lemon's 'purpose' requirement aims at preventing the [governmental] decisionmaker [from] abandoning neutrality and acting with the intent of promoting a particular point of view in religious matters." Nor did the exemption violate the "effect" prong: "A law is not unconstitutional simply because it *allows* churches to advance religion. [For] a law to have forbidden 'effects,' [it] must be fair to say that the *government itself* has advanced religion through its own activities and influence." Justice BRENNAN, joined by Justice Marshall, concurred in the judgment. He emphasized that "religious organizations have an interest in autonomy in ordering their internal affairs" and must be free to discriminate on a religious basis with respect to religious activities. He was willing to uphold the extension of the exemption to nonreligious activities because distinguishing religious from nonreligious activities would necessitate "ongoing government entanglement in religious affairs," which in turn would have a chilling effect on free exercise. Justice O'CONNOR also concurred only in the judgment, empha-

sizing her "endorsement" approach set forth in Lynch v. Donnelly. She urged
the Court to recognize that laws such as this *do* advance religion, but that the
Constitution permits such advancement unless the government's purpose was
to endorse religion and "the statute actually conveys a message of endorsement." Justice BLACKMUN also concurred in the judgment, indicating substantial agreement with Justice O'Connor's opinion.

Two years later, however, in TEXAS MONTHLY, INC. v. BULLOCK, 489
U.S. 1 (1989), the Court refused to accept an "accommodation" argument in
the context of a tax exemption available only to religious publications. The
decision struck down a Texas law exempting from the sales tax "[p]eriodicals
that are published or distributed by a religious faith and that consist wholly of
writings promulgating the teaching of the faith and books that consist wholly of
writings sacred to a religious faith." Justice BRENNAN's plurality opinion,
joined by Justices Marshall and Stevens, held that the statute violated the
establishment clause, relying heavily on the fact that the exemption was not
available to any similarly situated nonreligious publication. He thus distinguished such cases as Mueller and Widmar, for in each of these the benefit to
religious organizations was one also available to secular organizations: "In all
of these cases, [we] emphasized that the benefits derived by religious organizations flow to a large number of nonreligious groups as well. Indeed were those
benefits confined to religious organizations, they could not have appeared other
than as state sponsorship of religion. [How] expansive the class of exempt
organizations or activities must be to withstand constitutional assault depends
upon the State's secular aim in granting a tax exemption." For example, if the
State chose "to subsidize, by means of a tax exemption, all groups that
contributed to the community's cultural, intellectual, and moral betterment,
than the exemption for religious publications could be retained." The plurality
distinguished the Amos case on the ground that there, but not here, granting
the exemption "prevented potentially serious encroachments on protected
religious freedoms," since in most cases the payment of a sales tax would not
violate the religious tenets of a religious organization.

Justice BLACKMUN, joined by Justice O'Connor, concurred in the judgment. He stressed the inevitable tension between free exercise and establishment clause values and insisted that the plurality had gone too far in preferring
the latter over the former. He therefore would hold only that "a tax exemption
limited to the sale of religious literature by religious organizations violates the
Establishment Clause." The exemption here constituted a "preferential support
for the communication of religious messages. Although some forms of accommodating religion are constitutionally permissible, this one surely is not." Justice
White also concurred in the judgment.

Justice SCALIA, joined by Chief Justice Rehnquist and Justice Kennedy,
dissented. He argued that the decision would invalidate many religiously
targeted tax exemptions, e.g., for church-owned residences for members of the
clergy, motor vehicles owned by religious organizations, and meals served at
church functions. He relied heavily on Walz, arguing that its sustaining of a tax
exemption for religious property did not depend on the availability of a similar
exemption for property owned by nonreligious charitable organizations. More
broadly, he rejected the conclusion in both the plurality and the concurring
opinions that "no law is constitutional whose 'benefits [are] confined to
religious organizations' except, of course, those laws that are unconstitutional
unless they contain benefits confined to religious organizations. Our jurisprudence affords no support for this unlikely proposition." He added that the
Court had "often made clear that '[t]he limits of permissible state accommodation of religion are by no means coextensive with a noninterference mandated

by the Free Exercise Clause.' " Although it was "not always easy to determine when accommodation slides over into promotion, and neutrality into favoritism," the "withholding of a tax upon the dissemination of religious materials is not even a close case." He argued that where an exemption "comes so close to being a constitutionally required accommodation, there is no doubt that it is at least a permissible one."

Three years after Widmar, Congress enacted the Equal Access Act of 1984, 28 U.S.C. § 4071. The Act extended the access rights recognized for university students in Widmar to secondary school students. The Act provided, inter alia: "It shall be unlawful for any public secondary school which receives Federal financial assistance and which has a limited open forum to deny equal access [to] any students who wish to conduct a meeting within that limited open forum on the basis of the religious, political, philosophical or other content of the speech at such meetings." The Senate Report accompanying the bill contained a finding that high school students are capable of understanding the difference between student-initiated religious speech and state-sponsored religious activity. In BOARD OF EDUCATION v. MERGENS, 496 U.S. 226 (1990), the Court interpreted the Act broadly and rejected the argument that the law violated the establishment clause by mandating school sponsorship of religious organizations. The Court held that the school officials' denial of a request for formation of a student Christian club violated the Act and that the application of the law here did not violate the establishment clause. There was no majority opinion on the establishment clause analysis. Justice O'CONNOR's plurality opinion, joined by Chief Justice Rehnquist and Justices White and Blackmun, found that requiring the school to recognize the religious club did not violate the three-pronged Lemon test. On the "effect" issue, she stated: "Because the Act on its face grants equal access to both secular and religious speech, we think it clear that the Act's purpose was not to 'endorse or disapprove of religion,' Wallace v. Jaffree (quoting Lynch v. Donnelly, O'Connor, J., concurring). [There] is a crucial difference between *government* speech endorsing religion, which the Establishment Clause forbids, and *private* speech endorsing religion, which the Free Speech and Free Exercise Clauses protect. We think that secondary school students are mature enough and are likely to understand that a school does not endorse or support student speech that it merely permits on a nondiscriminatory basis."

Justice KENNEDY, joined by Justice Scalia, concurred only in the judgment on the establishment clause issue. He rejected Justice O'Connor's endorsement test and argued instead that the establishment clause is violated only where government either gives such direct benefits to a religion that it has the effect or tendency of establishing a state religion, or "coerce[s] any student to participate in a religious activity." He found no such "coercion" here. Justice MARSHALL's concurrence in the judgment, joined by Justice Brennan, emphasized that the Act as applied could be sustained only if a school took special steps to disassociate itself from religious speech and "to avoid appearing to endorse [a religious group's] goals." He insisted that the plurality approach dismissed "too lightly the distinctive pressures created by [the school's] highly structured environment." Justice STEVENS, the sole dissenter, relied solely on statutory grounds, arguing that the Act's requirements were triggered only if other "controversial or partisan" groups were granted access, which was not the case here.

3. *Accommodation and religious gerrymandering.* May a legislature accommodate a religious community by allowing to isolate itself in its own governmental district? The Court answered that question negatively in BOARD OF EDUC. OF KIRYAS JOEL v. GRUMET, 512 U.S. 687 (1994). The case

involved a community of highly religious Jews, the Satmar Hasidim. Most children in the community attended religious schools, but in order to receive the benefits of federal and state funds for special education, schoolchildren with special needs were sent to public schools in the surrounding county. (They were unable to receive public special education in annexes to local religious schools because of the holding in Aguilar v. Felton, p. 1541 above.) In light of ridicule and other inconveniences suffered by the Satmar children under this practice, the community sought to create its own village public school district in order to avoid the need for its special-needs children to attend county public schools. The legislature and Governor of New York agreed. By a vote of 6–3, the Court invalidated the special law creating the new school district.

Justice SOUTER, writing for the Court, found the law carving out the separate school district to serve the Satmar community to violate the establishment clause under Larkin v. Grendel's Den, which "teaches that a State may not delegate its civic authority to a group chosen according to a religious criterion. [It] is [not] dispositive that the recipients of state power in this case are a group of religious individuals united by common doctrine, not the group's leaders or officers. Although some school district franchise is common to all voters, the State's manipulation of the franchise for this district limited it to Satmars, giving the sect exclusive control of the political subdivision. In the circumstances of this case, the difference between thus vesting state power in the members of a religious group as such instead of the officers of its sectarian organization is one of form, not substance. [If] New York were to delegate civic authority to 'the Grand Rebbe,' Larkin would obviously require invalidation (even though under McDaniel the Grand Rebbe may run for, and serve on his local school board), and the same is true if New York delegates political authority by reference to religious belief. [There is a difference] between a government's purposeful delegation on the basis of religion and a delegation on principles neutral to religion, to individuals whose religious identities are incidental to their receipt of civic authority." He looked behind the facial neutrality of the state law to find a legislative history indicating the state's intent to draw "boundary lines of the school district that divide residents according to religious affiliation."

Justice O'CONNOR concurred in part and in the judgment, emphasizing the particularity of the accommodation here: "Accommodations may [justify] treating those who share [a deeply held] belief differently; but they do not justify discriminations based on sect. A state law prohibiting the consumption of alcohol may exempt sacramental wines, but it may not exempt sacramental wine used by Catholics but not by Jews." She argued that a more generally drafted statute might survive establishment clause challenge: "A district created under a generally applicable scheme would be acceptable even though it coincides with a village which was consciously created by its voters as an enclave for their religious group." Justice KENNEDY concurred in the judgment, objecting to New York's "religious gerrymandering," which drew "political boundaries on the basis of religion."

Justice SCALIA, joined by Chief Justice Rehnquist and Justice Thomas, dissented: "The Court today finds that the Powers That Be, up in Albany, have conspired to effect an establishment of the Satmar Hasidim. I do not know who would be more surprised at this discovery: the Founders of our Nation or Grand Rebbe Joel Teitelbaum, founder of the Satmar. The Grand Rebbe would be astounded to learn that after escaping brutal persecution and coming to America with the modest hope of religious toleration for their ascetic form of Judaism, the Satmar had become so powerful, so closely allied with Mammon, as to have become an 'establishment' of the Empire State. And the Founding

Fathers would be astonished to find that the Establishment Clause—which they designed 'to insure that no one powerful sect or combination of sects could use political or governmental power to punish dissenters,' has been employed to prohibit characteristically and admirably American accommodation of the religious practices (or more precisely, cultural peculiarities) of a tiny minority sect." He distinguished Larkin v. Grendel's Den on the ground that here there was no delegation to a religious entity, and emphasized the facial neutrality of the law. He found no basis for finding a religious preference here, nor for presuming that New York would not be "as accommodating toward other religions (presumably those less powerful than the Satmar Hasidim) in the future."

APPENDIX A

THE CONSTITUTION OF THE UNITED STATES OF AMERICA

We the People of the United States, in Order to form a more perfect Union, establish Justice, insure domestic Tranquility, provide for the common defence, promote the general Welfare, and secure the Blessings of Liberty to ourselves and our Posterity, do ordain and establish this Constitution for the United States of America.

ARTICLE I. *Legislative*

SECTION 1. All legislative Powers herein granted shall be vested in a Congress of the United States, which shall consist of a Senate and House of Representatives. *Congress*

SECTION 2. The House of Representatives shall be composed of Members chosen every second Year by the People of the several States, and the Electors in each State shall have the Qualifications requisite for Electors of the most numerous Branch of the State Legislature. *House*

No Person shall be a Representative who shall not have attained to the Age of twenty five Years, and been seven Years a Citizen of the United States, and who shall not, when elected, be an Inhabitant of that State in which he shall be chosen.

Representatives and direct Taxes shall be apportioned among the several States which may be included within this Union, according to their respective Numbers, which shall be determined by adding to the whole Number of free Persons, including those bound to Service for a Term of Years, and excluding Indians not taxed, three fifths of all other Persons. The actual Enumeration shall be made within three Years after the first Meeting of the Congress of the United States, and within every subsequent Term of ten Years, in such Manner as they shall by Law direct. The Number of Representatives shall not exceed one for every thirty Thousand, but each State shall have at Least one Representative; and until such enumeration shall be made, the State of New Hampshire shall be entitled to chuse three, Massachusetts eight, Rhode Island and Providence Plantations one, Connecticut five, New–York six, New Jersey four, Pennsylvania eight, Delaware one, Maryland six, Virginia ten, North Carolina five, South Carolina five, and Georgia three.

When vacancies happen in the Representation from any State, the Executive Authority thereof shall issue Writs of Election to fill such Vacancies.

The House of Representatives shall chuse their Speaker and other Officers; and shall have the sole Power of Impeachment.

SECTION 3. The Senate of the United States shall be composed of two Senators from each State, chosen by the Legislature thereof, for six Years; and each Senator shall have one Vote. *Senate*

Immediately after they shall be assembled in Consequence of the first Election, they shall be divided as equally as may be into three Classes. The Seats of the Senators of the first Class shall be vacated at the Expiration of the second Year, of the second Class at the Expiration of the fourth Year, and of the third Class at the Expiration of the sixth Year, so that one third may be chosen every second Year; and if Vacancies happen by Resignation, or otherwise, during the Recess of the Legislature of any State, the Executive thereof may make temporary Appointments until the next Meeting of the Legislature, which shall then fill such Vacancies.

No Person shall be a Senator who shall not have attained to the Age of thirty Years, and been nine Years a Citizen of the United States, and who shall not, when elected, be an Inhabitant of that State for which he shall be chosen.

The Vice President of the United States shall be President of the Senate, but shall have no Vote, unless they be equally divided.

The Senate shall chuse their other Officers, and also a President pro tempore, in the Absence of the Vice President, or when he shall exercise the Office of President of the United States.

The Senate shall have the sole Power to try all Impeachments. When sitting for that Purpose, they shall be on Oath or Affirmation. When the President of the United States is tried the Chief Justice shall preside: And no Person shall be convicted without the Concurrence of two thirds of the Members present.

Judgment in Cases of Impeachment shall not extend further than to removal from Office, and disqualification to hold and enjoy any Office of honor, Trust or Profit under the United States: but the Party convicted shall nevertheless be liable and subject to Indictment, Trial, Judgment and Punishment, according to Law.

SECTION 4. The Times, Places and Manner of holding Elections for Senators and Representatives, shall be prescribed in each State by the Legislature thereof; but the Congress may at any time by Law make or alter such Regulations, except as to the Places of chusing Senators.

The Congress shall assemble at least once in every Year, and such Meeting shall be on the first Monday in December, unless they shall by Law appoint a different Day.

SECTION 5. Each House shall be the Judge of the Elections, Returns and Qualifications of its own Members, and a Majority of each shall constitute a Quorum to do Business; but a smaller Number may adjourn from day to day, and may be authorized to compel the Attendance of absent Members, in such Manner, and under such Penalties as each House may provide.

Each House may determine the Rules of its Proceedings, punish its Members for disorderly Behaviour, and, with the Concurrence of two thirds, expel a Member.

Each House shall keep a Journal of its Proceedings, and from time to time publish the same, excepting such Parts as may in their Judgment require Secrecy; and the Yeas and Nays of the Members of either House on any question shall, at the Desire of one fifth of those Present, be entered on the Journal.

Neither House, during the Session of Congress, shall, without the Consent of the other, adjourn for more than three days, nor to any other Place than that in which the two Houses shall be sitting.

SECTION 6. The Senators and Representatives shall receive a Compensation for their Services, to be ascertained by Law, and paid out of the Treasury of the United States. They shall in all Cases, except Treason, Felony and Breach of the Peace, be privileged from Arrest during their Attendance at the Session of their respective Houses, and in going to and returning from the same; and for any Speech or Debate in either House, they shall not be questioned in any other Place.

No Senator or Representative shall, during the Time for which he was elected, be appointed to any civil Office under the Authority of the United States, which shall have been created, or the Emoluments whereof shall have been encreased during such time; and no Person holding any Office under the United States, shall be a Member of either House during his Continuance in Office.

SECTION 7. All Bills for raising Revenue shall originate in the House of Representatives; but the Senate may propose or concur with amendments as on other Bills.

Every Bill which shall have passed the House of Representatives and the Senate, shall, before it become a Law, be presented to the President of the United States; If he approve he shall sign it, but if not he shall return it, with his Objections to that House in which it shall have originated, who shall enter the Objections at large on their Journal, and proceed to reconsider it. If after such Reconsideration two thirds of that House shall agree to pass the Bill, it shall be sent, together with the Objections, to the other House, by which it shall likewise be reconsidered, and if approved by two thirds of that House, it shall become a Law. But in all such Cases the Votes of both Houses shall be determined by Yeas and Nays, and the Names of the Persons voting for and against the Bill shall be entered on the Journal of each House respectively. If any Bill shall not be returned by the President within ten Days (Sunday excepted) after it shall have been presented to him, the Same shall be a Law, in like Manner as if he had signed it, unless the Congress by their Adjournment prevent its Return, in which Case it shall not be a Law.

Every Order, Resolution, or Vote to which the Concurrence of the Senate and House of Representatives may be necessary (except on a question of Adjournment) shall be presented to the President of the United States; and before the Same shall take Effect, shall be approved by him, or being disapproved by him, shall be repassed by two thirds of the Senate and House of Representatives, according to the Rules and Limitations prescribed in the Case of a Bill.

SECTION 8. The Congress shall have Power To lay and collect Taxes, Duties, Imposts and Excises, to pay the Debts and provide for the common Defence and general Welfare of the United States; but all Duties, Imposts and Excises shall be uniform throughout the United States;

To borrow Money on the credit of the United States;

To regulate Commerce with foreign Nations, and among the several States, and with the Indian Tribes;

To establish an uniform Rule of Naturalization, and uniform Laws on the subject of Bankruptcies throughout the United States;

To coin Money, regulate the Value thereof, and of foreign Coin, and fix the Standard of Weights and Measures;

To provide for the Punishment of counterfeiting the Securities and current Coin of the United States;

To establish Post Offices and post Roads;

To promote the Progress of Science and useful Arts, by securing for limited Times to Authors and Inventors the exclusive Right to their respective Writings and Discoveries;

To constitute Tribunals inferior to the supreme Court;

To define and punish Piracies and Felonies committed on the high Seas, and Offences against the Law of Nations;

To declare War, grant Letters of Marque and Reprisal, and make Rules concerning Captures on Land and Water;

To raise and support Armies, but no Appropriation of Money to that Use shall be for a longer Term than two Years;

To provide and maintain a Navy;

To make Rules for the Government and Regulation of the land and naval Forces;

To provide for calling forth the Militia to execute the Laws of the Union, suppress Insurrections and repel Invasions;

To provide for organizing, arming, and disciplining, the Militia, and for governing such Part of them as may be employed in the Service of the United States, reserving to the States respectively, the Appointment of the Officers, and the Authority of training the Militia according to the discipline prescribed by Congress;

To exercise exclusive Legislation in all Cases whatsoever, over such District (not exceeding ten Miles square) as may, by Cession of particular States, and the Acceptance of Congress, become the Seat of the Government of the United States, and to exercise like Authority over all Places purchased by the Consent of the Legislature of the State in which the Same shall be, for the Erection of Forts, Magazines, Arsenals, dock-Yards, and other needful Buildings;—And

To make all Laws which shall be necessary and proper for carrying into Execution the foregoing Powers, and all other Powers vested by this Constitution in the Government of the United States, or in any Department or Officer thereof.

SECTION 9. The Migration or Importation of such Persons as any of the States now existing shall think proper to admit, shall not be prohibited by the Congress prior to the Year one thousand eight hundred and eight, but a Tax or duty may be imposed on such Importation, not exceeding ten dollars for each Person.

The Privilege of the Writ of Habeas Corpus shall not be suspended, unless when in Cases of Rebellion or Invasion the public Safety may require it.

No Bill of Attainder or ex post facto Law shall be passed.

No Capitation, or other direct, Tax shall be laid, unless in Proportion to the Census or Enumeration herein before directed to be taken.

No Tax or Duty shall be laid on Articles exported from any State.

No Preference shall be given by any Regulation of Commerce or Revenue to the Ports of one State over those of another; nor shall Vessels bound to, or from, one State, be obliged to enter, clear or pay Duties in another.

No Money shall be drawn from the Treasury, but in Consequence of Appropriations made by Law; and a regular Statement and Account of the

Receipts and Expenditures of all public Money shall be published from time to time.

No Title of Nobility shall be granted by the United States: And no Person holding any Office of Profit or Trust under them, shall, without the Consent of the Congress, accept of any present, Emolument, Office, or Title, of any kind whatever, from any King, Prince or foreign State.

SECTION 10. No State shall enter into any Treaty, Alliance, or Confederation; grant Letters of Marque and Reprisal; coin Money; emit Bills of Credit; make any Thing but gold and silver Coin a Tender in Payment of Debts; pass any Bill of Attainder, ex post facto Law, or Law impairing the Obligation of Contracts, or grant any Title of Nobility.

No State shall, without the Consent of the Congress, lay any Imposts or Duties on Imports or Exports, except what may be absolutely necessary for executing its inspection Laws: and the net Produce of all Duties and Imposts, laid by any State on Imports or Exports, shall be for the Use of the Treasury of the United States; and all such Laws shall be subject to the Revision and Controul of the Congress.

No State shall, without the Consent of Congress, lay any Duty of Tonnage, keep Troops, or Ships of War in time of Peace, enter into any Agreement or Compact with another State, or with a foreign Power, or engage in War, unless actually invaded, or in such imminent Danger as will not admit of delay.

ARTICLE II.

SECTION 1. The executive Power shall be vested in a President of the United States of America. He shall hold his Office during the Term of four Years, and, together with the Vice President, chosen for the same Term, be elected, as follows

Each State shall appoint, in such Manner as the Legislature thereof may direct, a Number of Electors, equal to the whole Number of Senators and Representatives to which the State may be entitled in the Congress: but no Senator or Representative, or Person holding an Office of Trust or Profit under the United States, shall be appointed an Elector.

The Electors shall meet in their respective States, and vote by Ballot for two Persons, of whom one at least shall not be an Inhabitant of the same State with themselves. And they shall make a List of all the Persons voted for, and of the Number of Votes for each; which List they shall sign and certify, and transmit sealed to the Seat of the Government of the United States, directed to the President of the Senate. The President of the Senate shall, in the Presence of the Senate and House of Representatives, open all the Certificates, and the Votes shall then be counted. The Person having the greatest Number of Votes shall be the President, if such Number be a Majority of the whole Number of Electors appointed; and if there be more than one who have such Majority, and have an equal Number of Votes, then the House of Representatives shall immediately chuse by Ballot one of them for President; and if no Person have a Majority, then from the five highest on the List the said House shall in like Manner chuse the President. But in chusing the President, the Votes shall be taken by States, the Representation from each State having one Vote; a quorum for this Purpose shall consist of a Member or Members from two thirds of the States, and a Majority of all the States shall be necessary to a Choice. In every Case, after the Choice of the President, the Person having the greatest Number of Votes of the Electors shall be the Vice President. But if there should

A-5

remain two or more who have equal Votes, the Senate shall chuse from them by Ballot the Vice President.

The Congress may determine the Time of chusing the Electors, and the Day on which they shall give their Votes; which Day shall be the same throughout the United States.

No Person except a natural born Citizen, or a Citizen of the United States, at the time of the Adoption of this Constitution, shall be eligible to the Office of President; neither shall any Person be eligible to that Office who shall not have attained to the Age of thirty five Years, and been fourteen Years a Resident within the United States.

In Case of the Removal of the President from Office, or of his Death, Resignation, or Inability to discharge the Powers and Duties of the said Office, the Same shall devolve on the Vice President, and the Congress may by Law provide for the Case of Removal, Death, Resignation or Inability, both of the President and Vice President, declaring what Officer shall then act as President, and such Officer shall act accordingly, until the Disability be removed, or a President shall be elected.

The President shall, at stated Times, receive for his Services, a Compensation, which shall neither be encreased nor diminished during the Period for which he shall have been elected, and he shall not receive within that Period any other Emolument from the United States, or any of them.

Before he enter on the Execution of his Office, he shall take the following Oath or Affirmation:—"I do solemnly swear (or affirm) that I will faithfully execute the Office of President of the United States, and will to the best of my Ability, preserve, protect and defend the Constitution of the United States."

SECTION 2. The President shall be Commander in Chief of the Army and Navy of the United States, and of the Militia of the several States, when called into the actual Service of the United States; he may require the Opinion, in writing, of the principal Officer in each of the executive Departments, upon any Subject relating to the Duties of their respective Offices, and he shall have Power to grant Reprieves and Pardons for Offences against the United States, except in Cases of Impeachment.

He shall have Power, by and with the Advice and Consent of the Senate, to make Treaties, provided two thirds of the Senators present concur; and he shall nominate, and by and with the Advice and Consent of the Senate, shall appoint Ambassadors, other public Ministers and Consuls, Judges of the supreme Court, and all other Officers of the United States, whose Appointments are not herein otherwise provided for, and which shall be established by Law: but the Congress may by Law vest the Appointment of such inferior Officers, as they think proper, in the President alone, in the Courts of Law, or in the Heads of Departments.

The President shall have Power to fill up all Vacancies that may happen during the Recess of the Senate, by granting Commissions which shall expire at the End of their next Session.

SECTION 3. He shall from time to time give to the Congress Information of the State of the Union, and recommend to their Consideration such Measures as he shall judge necessary and expedient; he may, on extraordinary Occasions, convene both Houses, or either of them, and in Case of Disagreement between them, with Respect to the Time of Adjournment, he may adjourn them to such Time as he shall think proper; he shall receive Ambassadors and other public Ministers; he shall take Care that the Laws be faithfully executed, and shall Commission all the Officers of the United States.

SECTION 4. The President, Vice President and all Civil Officers of the United States, shall be removed from Office on Impeachment for, and Conviction of, Treason, Bribery, or other high Crimes and Misdemeanors.

ARTICLE III. *Judicial*

SECTION 1. The judicial Power of the United States, shall be vested in one supreme Court, and in such inferior Courts as the Congress may from time to time ordain and establish. The Judges, both of the supreme and inferior Courts, shall hold their Offices during good Behaviour, and shall, at stated Times, receive for their Services, a Compensation, which shall not be diminished during their Continuance in Office.

SECTION 2. The judicial Power shall extend to all Cases, in Law and Equity, arising under this Constitution, the Laws of the United States, and Treaties made, or which shall be made, under their Authority;—to all Cases affecting Ambassadors, other public Ministers and Consuls;—to all Cases of admiralty and maritime Jurisdiction;—to Controversies to which the United States shall be a Party;—to Controversies between two or more States;—between a State and Citizens of another State;—between Citizens of different States;—between Citizens of the same State claiming Lands under Grants of different States, and between a State, or the Citizens thereof, and foreign States, Citizens or Subjects.

In all Cases affecting Ambassadors, other public Ministers and Consuls, and those in which a State shall be Party, the Supreme Court shall have original Jurisdiction. In all the other Cases before mentioned, the supreme Court shall have appellate Jurisdiction, both as to Law and Fact, with such Exceptions, and under such Regulations as the Congress shall make.

The Trial of all Crimes, except in Cases of Impeachment, shall be by Jury; and such Trial shall be held in the State where the said Crimes shall have been committed; but when not committed within any State, the Trial shall be at such Place or Places as the Congress may by Law have directed.

SECTION 3. Treason against the United States, shall consist only in levying War against them, or in adhering to their Enemies, giving them Aid and Comfort. No Person shall be convicted of Treason unless on the Testimony of two Witnesses to the same overt Act, or on Confession in open Court.

The Congress shall have Power to declare the Punishment of Treason, but no Attainder of Treason shall work Corruption of Blood, or Forfeiture except during the Life of the Person attainted.

ARTICLE IV. *Full Faith Credit*

SECTION 1. Full Faith and Credit shall be given in each State to the public Acts, Records, and judicial Proceedings of every other State. And the Congress may by general Laws prescribe the Manner in which such Acts, Records and Proceedings shall be proved, and the Effect thereof.

SECTION 2. The Citizens of each State shall be entitled to all Privileges and Immunities of Citizens in the several States.

A Person charged in any State with Treason, Felony, or other Crime, who shall flee from Justice, and be found in another State, shall on Demand of the executive Authority of the State from which he fled, be delivered up, to be removed to the State having Jurisdiction of the Crime.

No Person held to Service or Labour in one State, under the Laws thereof, escaping into another, shall, in Consequence of any Law or Regulation therein, be discharged from such Service or Labour, but shall be delivered up on Claim of the Party to whom such Service or Labour may be due.

SECTION 3. New States may be admitted by the Congress into this Union; but no new State shall be formed or erected within the Jurisdiction of any other State; nor any State be formed by the Junction of two or more States, or Parts of States, without the Consent of the Legislatures of the States concerned as well as of the Congress.

The Congress shall have Power to dispose of and make all needful Rules and Regulations respecting the Territory or other Property belonging to the United States; and nothing in this Constitution shall be so construed as to Prejudice any Claims of the United States, or of any particular State.

SECTION 4. The United States shall guarantee to every State in this Union a Republican Form of Government, and shall protect each of them against Invasion; and on Application of the Legislature, or of the Executive (when the Legislature cannot be convened) against domestic Violence.

ARTICLE V. Amendments

The Congress, whenever two thirds of both Houses shall deem it necessary, shall propose Amendments to this Constitution, or, on the Application of the Legislatures of two thirds of the several States, shall call a Convention for proposing Amendments, which, in either Case, shall be valid to all Intents and Purposes, as Part of this Constitution, when ratified by the Legislatures of three fourths of the several States, or by Conventions in three fourths thereof, as the one or the other Mode of Ratification may be proposed by the Congress; Provided that no Amendment which may be made prior to the Year One thousand eight hundred and eight shall in any Manner affect the first and fourth Clauses in the Ninth Section of the first Article; and that no State, without its Consent, shall be deprived of its equal Suffrage in the Senate.

ARTICLE VI. Supreme law

All Debts contracted and Engagements entered into, before the Adoption of this Constitution, shall be as valid against the United States under this Constitution, as under the Confederation.

This Constitution, and the Laws of the United States which shall be made in Pursuance thereof; and all Treaties made, or which shall be made, under the Authority of the United States, shall be the supreme Law of the Land; and the Judges in every State shall be bound thereby, any Thing in the Constitution or Laws of any State to the Contrary notwithstanding.

The Senators and Representatives before mentioned, and the Members of the several State Legislatures, and all executive and judicial Officers, both of the United States and of the several States, shall be bound by Oath or Affirmation, to support this Constitution; but no religious Test shall ever be required as a Qualification to any Office or public Trust under the United States.

ARTICLE VII. Ratification

The Ratification of the Conventions of nine States, shall be sufficient for the Establishment of this Constitution between the States so ratifying the Same.

* * *

ARTICLES IN ADDITION TO, AND AMENDMENT OF, THE CONSTITUTION OF THE UNITED STATES OF AMERICA, PROPOSED BY CONGRESS, AND RATIFIED BY THE SEVERAL STATES, PURSUANT TO THE FIFTH ARTICLE OF THE ORIGINAL CONSTITUTION.

AMENDMENT I [1791].

Congress shall make no law respecting an establishment of religion, or prohibiting the free exercise thereof; or abridging the freedom of speech, or of the press; or the right of the people peaceably to assemble, and to petition the Government for a redress of grievances.

AMENDMENT II [1791].

A well regulated Militia, being necessary to the security of a free State, the right of the people to keep and bear Arms, shall not be infringed.

AMENDMENT III [1791].

No Soldier shall, in time of peace be quartered in any house, without the consent of the Owner, nor in time of war, but in a manner to be prescribed by law.

AMENDMENT IV [1791].

The right of the people to be secure in their persons, houses, papers, and effects, against unreasonable searches and seizures, shall not be violated, and no Warrants shall issue, but upon probable cause, supported by Oath or affirmation, and particularly describing the place to be searched, and the persons or things to be seized.

AMENDMENT V [1791].

No person shall be held to answer for a capital, or otherwise infamous crime, unless on a presentment or indictment of a Grand Jury, except in cases arising in the land or naval forces, or in the Militia, when in actual service in time of War or public danger; nor shall any person be subject for the same offence to be twice put in jeopardy of life or limb; nor shall be compelled in any criminal case to be a witness against himself, nor be deprived of life, liberty, or property, without due process of law; nor shall private property be taken for public use, without just compensation.

Due Process

AMENDMENT VI [1791].

In all criminal prosecutions, the accused shall enjoy the right to a speedy and public trial, by an impartial jury of the State and district wherein the crime shall have been committed, which district shall have been previously ascertained by law, and to be informed of the nature and cause of the accusation; to be confronted with the witnesses against him; to have compulsory process for obtaining Witnesses in his favor, and to have the Assistance of Counsel for his defence.

AMENDMENT VII [1791].

In Suits at common law, where the value in controversy shall exceed twenty dollars, the right of trial by jury shall be preserved, and no fact tried by a jury, shall be otherwise re-examined in any Court of the United States, than according to the rules of the common law.

AMENDMENT VIII [1791].

Excessive bail shall not be required, nor excessive fines imposed, nor cruel and unusual punishments inflicted.

AMENDMENT IX [1791].

The enumeration in the Constitution, of certain rights, shall not be construed to deny or disparage others retained by the people.

AMENDMENT X [1791].

The powers not delegated to the United States by the Constitution, nor prohibited by it to the States, are reserved to the States respectively, or to the people.

AMENDMENT XI [1798].

The Judicial power of the United States shall not be construed to extend to any suit in law or equity, commenced or prosecuted against one of the United States by Citizens of another State, or by Citizens or Subjects of any Foreign State.

AMENDMENT XII [1804].

The Electors shall meet in their respective states and vote by ballot for President and Vice–President, one of whom, at least, shall not be an inhabitant of the same state with themselves; they shall name in their ballots the person voted for as President, and in distinct ballots the person voted for as Vice–President, and they shall make distinct lists of all persons voted for as President, and of all persons voted for as Vice–President, and of the number of votes for each, which lists they shall sign and certify, and transmit sealed to the seat of the government of the United States, directed to the President of the Senate;—The President of the Senate shall, in the presence of the Senate and House of Representatives, open all the certificates and the votes shall then be counted;—The person having the greatest number of votes for President, shall be the President, if such number be a majority of the whole number of Electors appointed; and if no person have such majority, then from the persons having the highest numbers not exceeding three on the list of those voted for as President, the House of Representatives shall choose immediately, by ballot, the President. But in choosing the President, the votes shall be taken by states, the representation from each state having one vote; a quorum for this purpose shall consist of a member or members from two-thirds of the states, and a majority of all the states shall be necessary to a choice. And if the House of Representatives shall not choose a President whenever the right of choice shall devolve upon them, before the fourth day of March next following, then the Vice–President shall act as President, as in the case of the death or other constitutional disability of the President—The person having the greatest number of votes as Vice–President, shall be the Vice–President, if such number be a majority of the whole number of Electors appointed, and if no person have a majority, then from the two highest numbers on the list, the Senate shall choose the Vice–President; a quorum for the purpose shall consist of two-thirds of the whole number of Senators, and a majority of the whole number shall be necessary to a choice. But no person constitutionally ineligible to the office of President shall be eligible to that of Vice–President of the United States.

AMENDMENT XIII [1865].

SECTION 1. Neither slavery nor involuntary servitude, except as a punishment for crime whereof the party shall have been duly convicted, shall exist within the United States, or any place subject to their jurisdiction.

SECTION 2. Congress shall have power to enforce this article by appropriate legislation.

AMENDMENT XIV [1868].

SECTION 1. All persons born or naturalized in the United States and subject to the jurisdiction thereof, are citizens of the United States and of the State wherein they reside. No State shall make or enforce any law which shall abridge the privileges or immunities of citizens of the United States; nor shall any State deprive any person of life, liberty, or property, without due process of law; nor deny to any person within its jurisdiction the equal protection of the laws.

SECTION 2. Representatives shall be apportioned among the several States according to their respective numbers, counting the whole number of persons in each State, excluding Indians not taxed. But when the right to vote at any election for the choice of electors for President and Vice President of the United States, Representatives in Congress, the Executive and Judicial officers of a State, or the members of the Legislature thereof, is denied to any of the male inhabitants of such State, being twenty-one years of age, and citizens of the United States, or in any way abridged, except for participation in rebellion, or other crime, the basis of representation therein shall be reduced in the proportion which the number of such male citizens shall bear to the whole number of male citizens twenty-one years of age in such State.

SECTION 3. No person shall be a Senator or Representative in Congress, or elector of President and Vice President, or hold any office, civil or military, under the United States, or under any State, who, having previously taken an oath, as a member of Congress, or as an officer of the United States, or as a member of any State legislature, or as an executive or judicial officer of any State, to support the Constitution of the United States, shall have engaged in insurrection or rebellion against the same, or given aid or comfort to the enemies thereof. But Congress may by a vote of two-thirds of each House, remove such disability.

SECTION 4. The validity of the public debt of the United States, authorized by law, including debts incurred for payment of pensions and bounties for services in suppressing insurrection or rebellion, shall not be questioned. But neither the United States nor any State shall assume or pay any debt or obligation incurred in aid of insurrection or rebellion against the United States, or any claim for the loss or emancipation of any slave; but all such debts, obligations and claims shall be held illegal and void.

SECTION 5. The Congress shall have power to enforce, by appropriate legislation, the provisions of this article.

AMENDMENT XV [1870].

SECTION 1. The right of citizens of the United States to vote shall not be denied or abridged by the United States or by any State on account of race, color, or previous condition of servitude.

SECTION 2. The Congress shall have power to enforce this article by appropriate legislation.

AMENDMENT XVI [1913].

The Congress shall have power to lay and collect taxes on incomes, from whatever source derived, without apportionment among the several States, and without regard to any census or enumeration.

AMENDMENT XVII [1913].

The Senate of the United States shall be composed of two Senators from each State, elected by the people thereof, for six years; and each Senator shall have one vote. The electors in each State shall have the qualifications requisite for electors of the most numerous branch of the State legislatures.

When vacancies happen in the representation of any State in the Senate, the executive authority of such State shall issue writs of election to fill such vacancies: *Provided,* That the legislature of any State may empower the executive thereof to make temporary appointments until the people fill the vacancies by election as the legislature may direct.

This amendment shall not be so construed as to affect the election or term of any Senator chosen before it becomes valid as part of the Constitution.

AMENDMENT XVIII [1919].

SECTION 1. After one year from the ratification of this article the manufacture, sale, or transportation of intoxicating liquors within, the importation thereof into, or the exportation thereof from the United States and all territory subject to the jurisdiction thereof for beverage purposes is hereby prohibited.

SECTION 2. The Congress and the several States shall have concurrent power to enforce this article by appropriate legislation.

SECTION 3. This article shall be inoperative unless it shall have been ratified as an amendment to the Constitution by the legislatures of the several States, as provided in the Constitution, within seven years from the date of the submission hereof to the States by the Congress.

AMENDMENT XIX [1920].

The right of citizens of the United States to vote shall not be denied or abridged by the United States or by any State on account of sex.

Congress shall have power to enforce this article by appropriate legislation.

AMENDMENT XX [1933].

SECTION 1. The terms of the President and Vice President shall end at noon on the 20th day of January, and the terms of Senators and Representatives at noon on the 3d day of January, of the years in which such terms would have ended if this article had not been ratified; and the terms of their successors shall then begin.

SECTION 2. The Congress shall assemble at least once in every year, and such meeting shall begin at noon on the 3d day of January, unless they shall by law appoint a different day.

SECTION 3. If, at the time fixed for the beginning of the term of the President, the President elect shall have died, the Vice President elect shall become President. If a President shall not have been chosen before the time fixed for the beginning of his term, or if the President elect shall have failed to qualify, then the Vice President elect shall act as President until a President shall have qualified; and the Congress may by law provide for the case wherein neither a President elect nor a Vice President elect shall have qualified, declaring who shall then act as President, or the manner in which one who is to act shall be selected, and such person shall act accordingly until a President or Vice President shall have qualified.

SECTION 4. The Congress may by law provide for the case of the death of any of the persons from whom the House of Representatives may choose a President whenever the right of choice shall have devolved upon them, and for the case of the death of any of the persons from whom the Senate may choose a Vice President whenever the right of choice shall have devolved upon them.

SECTION 5. Sections 1 and 2 shall take effect on the 15th day of October following the ratification of this article.

SECTION 6. This article shall be inoperative unless it shall have been ratified as an amendment to the Constitution by the legislatures of three-fourths of the several States within seven years from the date of its submission.

AMENDMENT XXI [1933].

SECTION 1. The eighteenth article of amendment to the Constitution of the United States is hereby repealed.

SECTION 2. The transportation or importation into any State, Territory, or possession of the United States for delivery or use therein of intoxicating liquors, in violation of the laws thereof, is hereby prohibited.

SECTION 3. This article shall be inoperative unless it shall have been ratified as an amendment to the Constitution by conventions in the several States, as provided in the Constitution, within seven years from the date of the submission hereof to the States by the Congress.

AMENDMENT XXII [1951].

SECTION 1. No person shall be elected to the office of the President more than twice, and no person who has held the office of President, or acted as President, for more than two years of a term to which some other person was elected President shall be elected to the office of the President more than once. But this Article shall not apply to any person holding the office of President when this Article was proposed by the Congress, and shall not prevent any person who may be holding the office of President, or acting as President, during the term within which this Article becomes operative from holding the office of President or acting as President during the remainder of such term.

SECTION 2. This article shall be inoperative unless it shall have been ratified as an amendment to the Constitution by the legislatures of three-fourths of the several States within seven years from the date of its submission to the States by the Congress.

AMENDMENT XXIII [1961].

SECTION 1. The District constituting the seat of Government of the United States shall appoint in such manner as the Congress may direct:

A number of electors of President and Vice President equal to the whole number of Senators and Representatives in Congress to which the District would be entitled if it were a State, but in no event more than the least populous State; they shall be in addition to those appointed by the States, but they shall be considered, for the purposes of the election of President and Vice President, to be electors appointed by a State; and they shall meet in the District and perform such duties as provided by the twelfth article of amendment.

SECTION 2. The Congress shall have power to enforce this article by appropriate legislation.

AMENDMENT XXIV [1964].

SECTION 1. The right of citizens of the United States to vote in any primary or other election for President or Vice President, for electors for President or Vice President, or for Senator or Representative in Congress, shall not be denied or abridged by the United States or any State by reason of failure to pay any poll tax or other tax.

SECTION 2. The Congress shall have power to enforce this article by appropriate legislation.

AMENDMENT XXV [1967].

SECTION 1. In case of the removal of the President from office or of his death or resignation, the Vice President shall become President.

SECTION 2. Whenever there is a vacancy in the office of the Vice President, the President shall nominate a Vice President who shall take office upon confirmation by a majority vote of both Houses of Congress.

SECTION 3. Whenever the President transmits to the President pro tempore of the Senate and the Speaker of the House of Representatives his written declaration that he is unable to discharge the powers and duties of his office, and until he transmits to them a written declaration to the contrary, such powers and duties shall be discharged by the Vice President as Acting President.

SECTION 4. Whenever the Vice President and a majority of either the principal officers of the executive departments or of such other body as Congress may by law provide, transmit to the President pro tempore of the Senate and the Speaker of the House of Representatives their written declaration that the President is unable to discharge the powers and duties of his office, the Vice President shall immediately assume the powers and duties of the office as Acting President.

Thereafter, when the President transmits to the President pro tempore of the Senate and the Speaker of the House of Representatives his written declaration that no inability exists, he shall resume the powers and duties of his office unless the Vice President and a majority of either the principal officers of the executive department or of such other body as Congress may by law provide, transmit within four days to the President pro tempore of the Senate and the Speaker of the House of Representatives their written declaration that the President is unable to discharge the powers and duties of his office. Thereupon Congress shall decide the issue, assembling within forty-eight hours for that purpose if not in session. If the Congress, within twenty-one days after receipt of the latter written declaration, or, if Congress is not in session, within twenty-one days after Congress is required to assemble, determines by two-thirds vote of both Houses that the President is unable to discharge the powers and duties of his office, the Vice President shall continue to discharge the same as Acting President; otherwise, the President shall resume the powers and duties of his office.

AMENDMENT XXVI [1971].

SECTION 1. The right of citizens of the United States, who are eighteen years of age or older, to vote shall not be denied or abridged by the United States or by any State on account of age.

SECTION 2. The Congress shall have power to enforce this article by appropriate legislation.

AMENDMENT XXVII [1992].

No law varying the compensation for the services of the Senators and Representatives shall take effect until an election of Representatives shall have intervened.*

* The 27th amendment was proposed by James Madison in 1789 as part of the same package as the Bill of Rights. It was approved by the first Congress in the same year, and by 1792 six states had ratified it. A seventh joined in 1873, but then nothing happened until 1978, when the movement to ratify the amendment was reinvigorated. The eighth ratification occurred in 1978, and another 32 states joined by May 12, 1992. Although a sufficient number of states had thus seemingly ratified the amendment, several members of Congress expressed concern about the noncontemporaneous nature of the ratification, citing, inter alia, Coleman v. Miller (1939; p. 48 above). Resolutions were proposed to consider whether the ratification of the proposed amendment was valid, and both the House and Senate Judiciary Committees scheduled hearings on the matter. On May 13, 1992, however, the Archivist of the United States, announced that he would certify the adoption of the amendment. On May 14, 1992, House Speaker Thomas Foley backed away from a planned challenge to the validity of the amendment and agreed that it was now to be considered part of the Constitution. Many ascribed his decision to political considerations, claiming that Foley believed that the American electorate was unlikely to support an expensive constitutional challenge to preserve the possibility of congressional pay raises, in a year which had already seen extensive scandals in the House bank and post office.

*

Table of Justices

Two sets of dates are given for each Justice, indicating his entire life as well as his years on the Supreme Court; but only the term of office is indicated for each President. The Presidents who made no appointments to the Supreme Court are not included in the table. They were Presidents William H. Harrison (Mar.–Apr. 1841), Zachary Taylor (1849–50), Andrew Johnson (1865–1869), and Jimmy Carter (1977–1981).

The symbol * and the figure (1) designate the Chief Justices. The other figures trace lines of succession in filling vacancies among the Associate Justices. For example, by following the figure (2) it can be seen that Justice Rutledge was succeeded by Justice Thomas Johnson, he by Justice Paterson, he in turn by Justice Livingston, etc.[1]

Appointed by President Washington, Federalist from
Virginia (1789–1797)

* (1) Jay, John (1745–1829). Fed. from N.Y. (1789–1795). Resigned.
  (2) Rutledge, John (1739–1800). Fed. from S.C. (1789–1791). Resigned without ever sitting.
  (3) Cushing, William (1732–1810). Fed. from Mass. (1789–1810). Died.
  (4) Wilson, James (1724–1798). Fed. from Pa. (1789–1798). Died.
  (5) Blair, John (1732–1800). Fed. from Va. (1789–1796). Resigned.
  (6) Iredell, James (1750–1799). Fed. from N.C. (1790–1799). Died.
  (2) Johnson, Thomas (1732–1819). Fed. from Md. (1791–1793). Resigned.
  (2) Paterson, William (1745–1806). Fed. from N.J. (1793–1806). Died.
* (1) Rutledge, John (1739–1800). Fed. from S.C. (1795). [Unconfirmed recess appointment.]
  (5) Chase, Samuel (1741–1811). Fed. from Md. (1796–1811). Died.
* (1) Ellsworth, Oliver (1745–1807). Fed. from Conn. (1796–1800). Resigned.

Appointed by President John Adams, Federalist from
Massachusetts (1797–1801)

  (4) Washington, Bushrod (1762–1829). Fed. from Pa. and Va. (1798–1829). Died.
  (6) Moore, Alfred (1755–1810). Fed. from N.C. (1799–1804). Resigned.
* (1) Marshall, John (1755–1835). Fed. from Va. (1801–1835). Died.

---

1. The initial version of this table was prepared by Professor Margaret Spahr, Hunter College of the City University of New York. [For biographical sketches of most of the Justices, see the four-volume collection, The Justices of the United States Supreme Court 1789–1969: Their Lives and Major Opinions (Friedman & Israel, eds., 1969).]

Appointed by President Jefferson, Republican from Virginia (1801–1809)

(6) Johnson, William (1771–1834). Rep. from S.C. (1804–1834). Died.
(2) Livingston, [Henry] Brockholst (1757–1823). Rep. from N.Y. (1806–1823). Died.
(7) Todd, Thomas (1765–1826). Rep. from Ky. (1807–1826). Died.

Appointed by President Madison, Republican from Virginia (1809–1817)

(5) Duvall, Gabriel (1752–1844). Rep. from Md. (1811–1835). Resigned.
(3) Story, Joseph (1779–1845). Rep. from Mass. (1811–1845). Died.

Appointed by President Monroe, Republican from Virginia (1817–1825)

(2) Thompson, Smith (1768–1843). Rep. from N.Y. (1823–1843). Died.

Appointed by President John Quincy Adams, Republican from Massachusetts (1825–1829)

(7) Trimble, Robert (1777–1828). Rep. from Ky. (1826–1828). Died.

Appointed by President Jackson, Democrat from Tennessee (1829–1837)

(7) McLean, John (1785–1861). Dem. (later Rep.) from Ohio (1829–1861). Died.
(4) Baldwin, Henry (1780–1844). Dem. from Pa. (1830–1844). Died.
(6) Wayne, James M. (1790–1867). Dem. from Ga. (1835–1867). Died.
* (1) Taney, Roger B. (1777–1864). Dem. from Md. (1836–1864). Died.
(5) Barbour, Philip P. (1783–1841). Dem. from Va. (1836–1841). Died.

Appointed by President Van Buren, Democrat from New York (1837–1841)

(8) Catron, John (1778–1865). Dem. from Tenn. (1837–1865). Died.
(9) McKinley, John (1780–1852). Dem. from Ky. (1837–1852). Died.
(5) Daniel, Peter V. (1784–1860). Dem. from Va. (1841–1860). Died.

Appointed by President Tyler, Whig from Virginia (1841–1845)

(2) Nelson, Samuel (1792–1873). Dem. from N.Y. (1845–1872). Resigned.

Appointed by President Polk, Democrat from Tennessee (1845–1849)

(3) Woodbury, Levi (1789–1851). Dem. from N.H. (1845–1851). Died.

(4) Grier, Robert C. (1794–1870). Dem. from Pa. (1846–1870). Resigned.

Appointed by President Fillmore, Whig from
New York (1850–1853)

(3) Curtis, Benjamin R. (1809–1874). Whig from Mass. (1851–1857). Resigned.

Appointed by President Pierce, Democrat from
New Hampshire (1853–1857)

(9) Campbell, John A. (1811–1889). Dem. from Ala. (1853–1861). Resigned.

Appointed by President Buchanan, Democrat from
Pennsylvania (1857–1861)

(3) Clifford, Nathan (1803–1881). Dem. from Me. (1858–1881). Died.

Appointed by President Lincoln, Republican from
Illinois (1861–1865)

(7) Swayne, Noah H. (1804–1884). Rep. from Ohio (1862–1881). Resigned.
(5) Miller, Samuel F. (1816–1890). Rep. from Iowa (1862–1890). Died.
(9) Davis, David (1815–1886). Rep. (later Dem.) from Ill. (1862–1877). Resigned.
(10) Field, Stephen J. (1816–1899). Dem. from Cal. (1863–1897). Resigned.
* (1) Chase, Salmon P. (1808–1873). Rep. from Ohio (1864–1873). Died.

Appointed by President Grant, Republican from
Illinois (1869–1877)

(4) Strong, William (1808–1895). Rep. from Pa. (1870–1880). Resigned.
(6) Bradley, Joseph P. (1803–1892). Rep. from N.J. (1870–1892). Died.
(2) Hunt, Ward (1810–1886). Rep. from N.Y. (1872–1882). Resigned.
* (1) Waite, Morrison (1816–1888). Rep. from Ohio (1874–1888). Died.

Appointed by President Hayes, Republican from
Ohio (1877–1881)

(9) Harlan, John Marshall (1833–1911). Rep. from Ky. (1877–1911). Died.
(4) Woods, William B. (1824–1887). Rep. from Ga. (1880–1887). Died.

Appointed by President Garfield, Republican from
Ohio (Mar.–Sept. 1881)

(7) Matthews, Stanley (1824–1889). Rep. from Ohio (1881–1889). Died.

B-3

*Appointed by President Arthur, Republican from
New York (1881–1885)*

(3) Gray, Horace (1828–1902). Rep. from Mass. (1881–1902). Died.
(2) Blatchford, Samuel (1820–1893). Rep. from N.Y. (1882–1893). Died.

*Appointed by President Cleveland, Democrat from
New York (1885–1889)*

(4) Lamar, Lucius Q.C. (1825–1893). Dem. from Miss. (1888–1893). Died.
* (1) Fuller, Melville W. (1833–1910). Dem. from Ill. (1888–1910). Died.

*Appointed by President Harrison, Republican from
Indiana (1889–1893)*

(7) Brewer, David J. (1837–1910). Rep. from Kansas (1889–1910). Died.
(5) Brown, Henry B. (1836–1913). Rep. from Mich. (1890–1906). Resigned.
(6) Shiras, George (1832–1924). Rep. from Pa. (1892–1903). Resigned.
(4) Jackson, Howell E. (1832–1895). Dem. from Tenn. (1893–1895). Died.

*Appointed by President Cleveland, Democrat from
New York (1893–1897)*

(2) White, Edward D. (1845–1921). Dem. from La. (1894–1910). Promoted to
chief justiceship.
(4) Peckham, Rufus W. (1838–1909). Dem. from N.Y. (1895–1909). Died.

*Appointed by President McKinley, Republican from
Ohio (1897–1901)*

(10) or (8) McKenna, Joseph (1843–1926). Rep. from Cal. (1898–1925).
Resigned.

*Appointed by President Theodore Roosevelt, Republican from
New York (1901–1909)*

(3) Holmes, Oliver Wendell (1841–1935). Rep. from Mass. (1902–1932). Resigned.
(6) Day, William R. (1849–1923). Rep. from Ohio (1903–1922). Resigned.
(5) Moody, William H. (1853–1917). Rep. from Mass. (1906–1910). Resigned.

*Appointed by President Taft, Republican from
Ohio (1909–1913)*

(4) Lurton, Horace H. (1844–1914). Dem. from Tenn. (1909–1914). Died.
(7) Hughes, Charles E. (1862–1948). Rep. from N.Y. (1910–1916). Resigned.
* (1) White, Edward D. (1845–1921). Promoted from associate justiceship.
(1910–1921). Died.
(2) Van Devanter, Willis (1859–1941). Rep. from Wyo. (1910–1937). Retired.
(5) Lamar, Joseph R. (1857–1916). Dem. from Ga. (1910–1916). Died.
(9) Pitney, Mahlon (1858–1924). Rep. from N.J. (1912–1922). Retired.

Appointed by President Wilson, Democrat from
New Jersey (1913–1921)

(4) McReynolds, James C. (1862–1946). Dem. from Tenn. (1914–1941). Retired.
(5) Brandeis, Louis D. (1856–1941). Dem. from Mass. (1916–1939). Retired.
(7) Clarke, John H. (1857–1945). Dem. from Ohio (1916–1922). Resigned.

Appointed by President Harding, Republican from
Ohio (1921–1923)

* (1) Taft, William H. (1857–1930). Rep. from Conn. (1921–1930). Resigned.
(7) Sutherland, George (1862–1942). Rep. from Utah (1922–1938). Retired.
(6) Butler, Pierce (1866–1939). Dem. from Minn. (1922–1939). Died.
(9) Sanford, Edward T. (1865–1930). Rep. from Tenn. (1923–1930). Died.

Appointed by President Coolidge, Republican from
Massachusetts (1923–1929)

(8) Stone, Harlan F. (1872–1946). Rep. from N.Y. (1925–1941). Promoted to chief justiceship.

Appointed by President Hoover, Republican from
California (1929–1933)

* (1) Hughes, Charles E. (1862–1948). Rep. from N.Y. (1930–1941). Retired.
(9) Roberts, Owen J. (1875–1955). Rep. from Pa. (1930–1945). Resigned.
(3) Cardozo, Benjamin N. (1870–1938). Dem. from N.Y. (1932–1938). Died.

Appointed by President Franklin D. Roosevelt, Democrat from
New York (1933–1945)

(2) Black, Hugo, L. (1886–1971). Dem. from Ala. (1937–1971). Retired.
(7) Reed, Stanley F. (1884–1980). Dem. from Ky. (1938–1957). Retired.
(3) Frankfurter, Felix (1882–1965). Ind. from Mass. (1939–1962). Retired.
(5) Douglas, William O. (1898–1980). Dem. from Conn. and Wash. (1939–1975). Retired.
(6) Murphy, Frank (1893–1949). Dem. from Mich. (1940–1949). Died.
(4) Byrnes, James F. (1879–1972). Dem. from S.C. (1941–1942). Resigned.
* (1) Stone, Harlan F. (1872–1946). Promoted from associate justiceship (1941–1946). Died.
(8) Jackson, Robert H. (1892–1954). Dem. from N.Y. (1941–1954). Died.
(4) Rutledge, Wiley B. (1894–1949). Dem. from Ia. (1943–1949). Died.

Appointed by President Truman, Democrat from
Missouri (1945–1953)

(9) Burton, Harold H. (1888–1964). Rep. from Ohio (1945–1958). Retired.
* (1) Vinson, Fred M. (1890–1953). Dem. from Kentucky (1946–1953). Died.
(6) Clark, Tom C. (1899–1977). Dem. from Texas (1949–1967). Retired.
(4) Minton, Sherman (1890–1965). Dem. from Indiana (1949–1956). Retired.

Appointed by President Eisenhower, Republican from
New York (1953–1961)

* (1) Warren, Earl (1891–1974). Rep. from Cal. (1953–1969). Retired.
  (8) Harlan, John Marshall (1899–1971). Rep. from New York (1955–1971). Retired.
  (4) Brennan, William J., Jr., (1906–____). Dem. from New Jersey (1956–1990). Retired.
  (7) Whittaker, Charles E. (1901–1973). Rep. from Missouri (1957–1962). Retired.
  (9) Stewart, Potter (1915–1985). Rep. from Ohio (1958–1981). Retired.

Appointed by President Kennedy, Democrat from
Massachusetts (1961–1963)

  (7) White, Byron R. (1917–____). Dem. from Colorado (1962–1993). Retired.
  (3) Goldberg, Arthur J. (1908–1990). Dem. from Illinois (1962–1965). Resigned.

Appointed by President Lyndon B. Johnson, Democrat from
Texas (1963–1969)

  (3) Fortas, Abe (1910–1982). Dem. from Tenn. (1965–1969). Resigned.
  (6) Marshall, Thurgood (1908–1993). Dem. from N.Y. (1967–1991). Retired.

Appointed by President Nixon, Republican from
California (1969–1974)

* (1) Burger, Warren E. (1907–1995). Rep. from Minn. and Va. (1969–1986). Resigned.
  (3) Blackmun, Harry A. (1908–____). Rep. from Minn. (1970–1994). Retired.
  (2) Powell, Lewis F., Jr., (1907–____). Dem. from Va. (1972–1987). Retired.[1]
  (8) Rehnquist, William H. (1924–____). Rep. from Ariz. (1972–1986). Promoted to chief justiceship.

Appointed by President Ford, Republican from
Michigan (1974–1977)

  (5) Stevens, John Paul (1920–____). Rep. from Ill. (1975–____).

---

1. On June 26, 1987, Justice Powell, citing reasons of health and age, announced his retirement from the Supreme Court. On July 1, 1987, President Reagan nominated Judge Robert H. Bork of the United States Court of Appeals for the District of Columbia to fill the seat vacated by Justice Powell. The Senate Judiciary Committee began hearings on the Bork nomination September 15, 1987, and took twelve days of testimony. On October 6, 1987, the Judiciary Committee voted 9–5 to send Bork's name to the Senate floor with a recommendation that it be rejected. On October 23, 1987, after 23 hours of floor debate, the Senate formally rejected the nomination by a vote of 42–58. In February 1988, Justice Kennedy was confirmed for the seat vacated by Justice Powell.

Appointed by President Reagan, Republican from
California (1981–1989)

(9) O'Connor, Sandra Day (1930–___). Rep. from Ariz. (1981–___).

*(1) Rehnquist, William H. (1924–___). Promoted from associate justiceship. (1986–___).

(8) Scalia, Antonin E. (1936–___). Rep. from District of Columbia (1986–___).

(2) Kennedy, Anthony M. (1936–___). Rep. from California (1988–___).

Appointed by President Bush, Republican from
Texas (1989–1993)

(4) Souter, David H. (1939–___). Rep. from New Hampshire (1990–___).

(6) Thomas, Clarence (1948–___). Rep. from Ga. (1992–___).

Appointed by President Clinton, Democrat from
Arkansas (1993–___)

(7) Ginsburg, Ruth Bader (1933–___). Dem. from New York (1993–___).

(3) Breyer, Stephen G. (1938–___). Dem. from Mass. (1994–___).

*

INDEX

References are to Pages.

ABORTION
Court decisions, 530 et seq.
Political responses, 545 et seq.

ADEQUATE STATE GROUNDS, 69–74.

ADVISORY OPINIONS, 28–29.

AFFIRMATIVE ACTION
Race, 793 et seq.
Repealing remedies, 789 et seq.

AGRICULTURE
National regulation, 189, 235.

ALIENS
National regulation, 724 et seq.
State regulation, 720 et seq.

AMENDMENTS TO CONSTITUTION
Abortion proposal, 545.
Amendment process, 250.
Bricker proposal, 254.

APPEALS
Indigents' rights, 896 et seq.

APPORTIONMENT
Reapportionment, see Reapportionment

ARMED FORCES
Congressional control, 371 et seq.
Presidential authority, 371 et seq.

ARTICLES OF CONFEDERATION, 99.

ASSEMBLY, RIGHT OF
See Freedom of Expression.

ASSOCIATION, RIGHT OF
See Freedom of Expression.

AUTONOMY
Coordinate branches, 20, 23.
Personal, 527 et seq.
State, 206 et seq.

"BADGES OF SERVITUDE"
Congressional power, 978 et seq.
Thirteenth Amendment, 420 et seq., 978 et seq.

BANK OF THE UNITED STATES
Constitutionality, 89 et seq.
History, 98 et seq.

BAR ADMISSIONS
State control, 1391 et seq., 1396 et seq.

"BENIGN" CLASSIFICATIONS, 793 et seq.

BILL OF RIGHTS
Federal government, 418 et seq.
States, applicability and "incorporation," 432 et seq.

BIRTH CONTROL, 518 et seq.

BUSING
Court decisions, 775 et seq.
State action, 792.

CAROLENE PRODUCTS FOOTNOTE, 484.

CASE OR CONTROVERSY, 28 et seq.

CENSORSHIP
See Freedom of Expression.

CERTIORARI
Rules, 68 et seq.

CHILD LABOR
Commerce power, 173, 191.
Taxing power, 229.

CHURCH AND STATE, 1461 et seq., 1500 et seq.
See also Establishment of Religion.

CITIZENSHIP
See Privileges and Immunities.

CIVIL RIGHTS LAWS
Civil provisions, 920 et seq.
Congressional power, 962 et seq.
Criminal provisions, 920.
Early laws (post—Civil War), 920 et seq.
Modern laws, 921, 972.
Private interference, 962 et seq.

CIVIL WAR AMENDMENTS, 420 et seq.

"CLEAR AND PRESENT DANGER"
See Freedom of Expression.

COMMERCE
See Interstate Commerce.

COMPACTS
Interstate, 353.

CONGRESS
Consent to state laws, 300 et seq.
Control of federal courts, 74 et seq.
Legislative immunity, 413.
Preemption, 337 et seq.
Regulatory powers, 89 et seq.
Term limits, state regulation, 115 et seq.

CONTINGENCIES
Impact on justiciability, 44–45.

CONTRACEPTION, 518 et seq.

CONTRACT, LIBERTY OF, 454 et seq.

CONTRACTS CLAUSE
Contemporary dimensions, 510 et seq.
Nineteenth Century, 505 et seq.

COUNSEL
Indigents, 897 et seq.
Right in criminal cases, 443.

"COURT–PACKING PLAN", 183.

DEATH
Right to die, 602 et seq.

DELEGATION OF LEGISLATIVE POWERS, 399 et seq.

DISCRIMINATION
Affirmative action, 793 et seq.
Age, 734 et seq.
Aliens, 720 et seq.
Criminal and civil process, 896 et seq.
Economic regulation, 635 et seq.
Employment, 810 et seq.
Homosexuality, 737 et seq.
Local regulation of commerce, 281 et seq.
Mental retardation, 728 et seq.
Nonmarital children, 725 et seq.
Poverty, 735 et seq.
"Purposeful discrimination," 749 et seq.
Racial, 201 et seq., 663 et seq.
Repealing remedies, 789 et seq.
Sex, 681 et seq.
Sexual orientation, 737 et seq.
Speech, 1203 et seq.
State regulation of commerce, 271 et seq.
Voting, 839 et seq., 858 et seq.

"DOUBLE STANDARD"
Due process, 482 et seq., 529 et seq.
Equal protection, 628 et seq.

DUE PROCESS OF LAW
Civil liberties, 1022 et seq.
Civil proceedings, 615 et seq.
Congressional power to enforce and modify, 984 et seq.
Criminal law administration, 432 et seq.
Economic regulation, 454 et seq.
Fourteenth Amendment standards, 432 et seq.
Mentally retarded, 600.

DUE PROCESS OF LAW—Cont'd
Procedural, 432 et seq., 615 et seq.
Substantive, 453 et seq., 516 et seq.

ECONOMIC REGULATION
Affirmative action, 812 et seq.
National, 89 et seq.
State, 258 et seq., 453 et seq., 635 et seq.

EDUCATION
Gun-free zones, 142 et seq.
Race, preferential admissions, 794 et seq.
Racial segregation, 673 et seq.
Religion, 1482 et seq., 1513 et seq., 1532 et seq.
Sex discrimination, 704 et seq.

ELECTIONS
See Voting.

ELEVENTH AMENDMENT, 225 et seq.

EMINENT DOMAIN, 486 et seq.

EQUAL PROTECTION
Affirmative action, 793 et seq.
Aliens, 720 et seq.
Congressional power to enforce and modify, 984 et seq.
Criminal and civil process, 896 et seq.
Economic regulation, 635 et seq.
Homosexuality, 737 et seq.
Mental retardation, 728 et seq.
"New," 630 et seq.
"Newer," 632, 646.
Nonmarital children, 725 et seq.
"Old," 629 et seq.
Overview, 628 et seq.
Poverty, 735 et seq.
Racial discrimination, 663 et seq.
Sex, 681 et seq.
Sexual orientation, 737 et seq.
Voting, 858 et seq.

ESTABLISHMENT OF RELIGION
Bus transportation, 1532 et seq.
Financial aid, 1482 et seq., 1513 et seq., 1532 et seq.
History, 1462 et seq.
Released time, 1501 et seq.
School prayers, 1464 et seq., 1504 et seq.
Sunday closing laws, 1478 et seq., 1519.

EXECUTIVE AGREEMENTS, 365 et seq.

EXECUTIVE POWERS
Domestic, 355 et seq.

EXTRADITION
Interstate obligation, 353.

FAMILY RELATIONS, 516 et seq.

FEDERAL OFFICEHOLDERS
Term limits, state regulation, 115 et.

FIREARMS
Congressional regulation, 142 et seq.

FISCAL POWERS OF CONGRESS, 89 et seq., 228 et seq.

FOREIGN AFFAIRS
Congressional power, 256 et seq.

FREEDOM OF EXPRESSION
See also Establishment of Religion.
Access to information, 1422 et seq.
Access to media, 1366 et seq., 1450 et seq.
Access to private property, 1261 et seq., 1366 et seq.
Access to public property, 1234 et seq.
Advocacy of illegal acts, 1034 et seq.
Association, 1374 et seq.
Balancing, 1031 et seq.
Bar admissions, 1391 et seq., 1396 et seq.
Cable television, 1455 et seq.
Categorization, 1075 et seq.
Censorship, 1023–1024 et seq.
"Clear and present danger," 1035 et seq.
Commercial speech, 1175 et seq.
Compelled speech, 1363 et seq.
Content-based restrictions, 1204 et seq.
Content-neutral restrictions, 1209 et seq.
Demands for information, 1375 et seq.
Demonstrations and mass protests, 1261 et seq.
Fighting words, 1076 et seq.
Flag desecration, 1219.
General theories and values, 1025 et seq.
Government employees, 1303 et seq., 1390 et seq.
Hate speech, 1109 et seq.
History, 1025 et seq.
Hostile audiences, 1085 et seq.
Immorality, 1155 et seq.
Incitement, 1034 et seq., 1046 et seq., 1071 et seq.
Indecency, 1155 et seq.
Interference with courts, 1266 et seq.
Internet, 1455.
Labor picketing, 1387 et seq.
Leafletting, 1237 et seq.
Libel, 1092 et seq.
Licensing, 1339 et seq.
Loudspeakers, 1237, 1241 et seq.
Loyalty oaths, 1390 et seq.
Media, 1164 et seq., 1345 et seq., 1420 et seq.
Noise regulations, 1260 et seq.
Non-defamation torts, 1105 et seq.
Nude dancing, 1230 et seq.
Obscenity, 1026 et seq.
Offensive speakers, 1155 et seq., 1164 et seq.
Overbreadth, 1326 et seq., 1392 et seq.
Permit requirements, 1237 et seq.
Political campaigns, 1381 et seq., 1400 et seq., 1454.
"Preferred position," 1029 et seq.
Prior restraints, 1023–1024 et seq., 1392 et seq.
Private property, 1261 et seq., 1366 et seq.
Promoting litigation, 1383 et seq.
Public forum, 1234 et seq.
Public or private figures, 1100.
Public order and safety, 1245 et seq.
Sensitive audiences, 1140 et seq.

FREEDOM OF EXPRESSION—Cont'd
"Speech-conduct" distinction, 1268 et seq.
Subversive advocacy, 1034 et seq.
Symbolic expression, 1212 et seq.
Syndicalism laws, 1050 et seq.
"Time, place and manner", 1244 et seq.
Visual pollution, 1254 et seq.

FREEDOM OF INTERSTATE MIGRA-TION, 335 et seq.

FREEDOM OF PRESS, 1420 et seq.

FREEDOM OF RELIGION
See also Establishment Clause
Clothing, 1485.
Compulsory education, 1482 et seq.
Conscientious objectors, 1469 et seq.
Curriculum, 1513 et seq.
Discriminatory laws, 1472 et seq.
Displays, 1520.
Disproportionate impact, 1477 et seq.
Drug use, 1489 et seq.
Employment and, 1479 et seq., 1484 et seq.
Establishment Clause and, 1500 et seq.
Flag salute, 1362.
Free exercise, 1471 et seq.
Freedom to act, 1478.
History, 1461 et seq.
Legislative accommodation, 1548 et seq.
Legislative prayer, 1519 et seq.
Legislators, 1472.
Marriage, 1477.
Public schools, 1501 et seq.
Religion, defined, 1468 et seq.
Religious exemptions, 1496 et seq.
Sacred grounds, 1487–1488.
School admission denials, 1484.
Subsidized activities, 1464 et seq.
Sunday closing laws, 1478 et seq.
Symbolism, 1519 et seq.
Taxation and, 1532.
Unemployment compensation, 1479 et seq.

FREEDOM TO TRAVEL, 335 et seq., 901 et seq.

"FUNDAMENTAL RIGHTS AND INTER-ESTS"
Due process, 454 et seq.
Equal protection, 840 et seq.

GENDER–BASED CLASSIFICATIONS
See Sex Discrimination.

GENERAL WELFARE CLAUSE
Spending, 235 et seq.
Taxing, 228 et seq.

GERRYMANDERING
See Legislative Districting.

GRANTS–IN–AID, 244 et seq.

GROUP LIBEL, 1092 et seq.

GUN–FREE SCHOOL ZONES ACT
Congressional regulation, 142 et seq.

HATE CRIMES, 1123 et seq.

HATE SPEECH, 1109 et seq.

HEARING, RIGHT TO, 615 et seq.

HIGHWAYS
State regulation, 299 et seq.

HOMOSEXUALITY, 593 et seq., 737 et seq.

ILLEGITIMACY
See Nonmarital Children.

IMPEACHMENT
Judicial review, 54 et seq.
Process, 411 et seq.

IMPLIED POWERS
Constitutionality, 89 et seq.
History, 98 et seq.

IMPOUNDMENT, 383 et seq.

INDIAN TRIBES
State autonomy, 225 et seq.

INDIGENTS
Appeals, 896 et seq.
Counsel, 897 et seq.
Equal protection, 896 et seq.

INJUNCTIONS
See Courts.

INSURANCE
State regulation, 346.

INTERGOVERNMENTAL IMMUNITIES
Regulation, 206 et seq., 352 et seq.
Taxation, 351 et seq.

INTERMEDIATE SCRUTINY, 686 et seq.

INTERSTATE COMMERCE
Congressional regulation,
    "Affecting commerce" rationale, 198 et
        seq.
    Agriculture, 189, 235.
    Antitrust, 163.
    Child labor, 173, 191.
    Content-based boundaries, 148.
    Crime, 196 et seq.
    Current of commerce, 168.
    Firearms, 142 et seq.
    Groundwork, 159 et seq.
    History, 141 et seq.
    Labor standards, 178, 180, 191.
    Mining, 180.
    Police regulations, 169 et seq.
    Preemption, 337 et seq.
    Production, 189 et seq., 191 et seq.
    Prohibition technique, 169 et seq., 191 et
        seq.
    Racial discrimination, 201 et seq.
    Radioactive waste disposal, 213.
    Railroads, 166 et seq.
    Rational basis test, 155 et seq.
    Regulation of local because of effect on
        interstate, 166 et seq., 189 et seq.
    Substantial effect test, 151 et seq.

INTERSTATE COMMERCE—Cont'd
Local regulation,
    Milk industry, 281 et seq.
    Solid waste, 284 et seq.
State regulation,
    Business entry, 317 et seq.
    Exports, 291 et seq.
    Groundwork, 261 et seq.
    Highways, 299 et seq., 305.
    Milk industry, 287 et seq., 315 et seq.
    Motor vehicles, 298 et seq.
    Natural resources, 295 et seq.
    Railroads, 300 et seq.
State taxation, 350.

INTERSTATE OBLIGATIONS
Compacts, 353.
Privileges and immunities, 328 et seq.
Rendition, 353.

INVESTIGATIONS
Grand juries, 1434 et seq.

IRREBUTTABLE PRESUMPTIONS, 914
et seq.

JENNER–BUTLER BILL, 83.

JUDICIAL CODE
Civil rights, 919 et seq.
Federal court structure, 65 et seq.

JUDICIAL REVIEW
Antecedents, 14.
Authoritativeness, 20 et seq.
Hamilton's justification, 6.
Legitimacy, 13 et seq.
Marshall's justification, 2 et seq.

JUDICIARY ACT OF 1789
Section 13, p. 7.
Section 25, p. 67.

JURISDICTION, CONGRESSIONAL, CONTROL OF
Lower federal courts, 84.
Statutory framework, 65 et seq.
Supreme Court, 74 et seq.

JUSTICIABILITY, 45 et seq.
Impeachment, 54 et seq.

LABOR RELATIONS
National power, 185.
State power, 480.

LEGISLATIVE DISTRICTING
Justiciability, 47.

LEGISLATIVE VETO, 375 et seq.

LEGISLATORS
Motives, 755 et seq., 1213 et seq.
Obligation to consider constitutionality, 20 et
    seq.

LIBEL, 1024–1025, 1092 et seq.

LITERACY TESTS
Legislation, 984 et seq.

LOYALTY OATHS
See Freedom of Expression.

MANUFACTURING
National power, 164 et seq., 189 et seq.

MARRIAGE, 587 et seq.
Religion, 1477

MENTAL RETARDATION
Discrimination, 728 et seq.

MILITARY
Education, sex discrimination, 704 et seq.
Presidential and congressional power, 371 et seq.

MILK REGULATION BY LOCALITIES
Commerce barriers, 281 et seq.

MILK REGULATION BY STATES
Commerce barriers, 287 et seq., 315 et seq.
Due process barriers, 474 et seq.

MINING
National power, 180.

MISCEGENATION, 667.

MOOTNESS, 44.

MOTION PICTURES
State regulation, 1135 et seq.

"NATURAL LAW"
Due process adjudication, 453 et seq., 516 et seq.
Due process antecedents, 454 et seq.
Equal protection, 840 et seq.

NATURAL RESOURCES
State control, 295 et seq.

NECESSARY AND PROPER CLAUSE, 98 et seq.

"NECESSITIES"
Equal protection, 901 et seq.

NEW DEAL LEGISLATION, 176 et seq.

NEWS MEDIA
Access by, 1422 et seq.
Access to, 1366 et seq., 1450 et seq.
Sanctions against, 1349 et seq.

NINTH AMENDMENT, 518 et seq.

NONMARITAL CHILDREN
Discrimination, 725 et seq.

NOTICE AND HEARING, 433, 615 et seq.

NULLIFICATION, 64 et seq.

OBSCENITY, 1026 et seq.

OCCUPATION OF THE FIELD
See Preemption.

OVERBREADTH, 1326 et seq., 1392 et seq.

PAROCHIAL SCHOOLS, AID TO, 1482 et seq., 1513 et seq., 1532 et seq.

POLITICAL PARTIES
Access to ballot, 890 et seq.

POLITICAL PARTIES—Cont'd
White primaries, 934 et seq.

POLITICAL QUESTIONS
Justiciability, 45 et seq.
Textually demonstrable commitments, 54 et seq.

POLL TAXES, 858.

PORNOGRAPHY, 1026 et seq., 1145 et seq.

PRAYERS IN PUBLIC SCHOOLS, 1464 et seq., 1504 et seq.

PREEMPTION, 337 et seq.

"PREFERRED FREEDOMS", 1029 et seq.

PRESIDENCY
Amenability to judicial process, 404 et seq.
Domestic affairs, 355 et seq.
Executive privilege, 404 et seq.

PRESS
See Freedom of Press; News Media.

PRIOR RESTRAINTS
See Freedom of Expression.

PRIVACY
Government protection, 1107 et seq.
Individual rights, 527 et seq.

PRIVILEGES AND IMMUNITIES.
National citizenship, 429 et seq.
State citizenship, 328 et seq.

PROTECTIONISM
See Discrimination.

"PURPOSEFUL DISCRIMINATION", 749 et seq.

RACIAL DISCRIMINATION, 663 et seq.
Affirmative action, 793 et seq.
Interstate commerce, 201 et seq.

RADIOACTIVE WASTE
Disposal, commerce power, 213.

RAILROADS
National regulation, 166 et seq.
State regulation, 300 et seq.

RATIONALITY REVIEW, 460, 635 et seq.

REAPPORTIONMENT, 865 et seq.
Justiciability, 47.
Racial redistricting, 839 et seq.

RELEASED TIME, 1501 et seq.

RELIGION
See Establishment of Religion; Freedom of Religion.

RIPENESS, 44–45.

SCHOOLS
See Education.

SEGREGATION, RACIAL
De facto, 781.

SEGREGATION, RACIAL—Cont'd
De jure-de facto distinction, 776 et seq.
Public facilities, 667 et seq.
Remedies, 771 et seq.
Schools, 667 et seq.

SEPARATION OF POWERS, 354 et seq.

SEX DISCRIMINATION
Education, 704 et seq.
Equal protection, 681 et seq.
Equal Rights Amendment, 701.
Pornography as subordination, 1149 et seq.

SEXUAL ORIENTATION, 737 et seq.

SLAVERY, 420 et seq., 978 et seq.

SOLID WASTE
Local discrimination, 284 et seq.

SPEECH, FREEDOM OF
See Freedom of Expression.

SPENDING POWER,@ 235 et seq.

STANDING TO SUE
Associations, 33 et seq.
Congressional control, 37 et seq.
Federal courts, 30.
Taxpayers' actions, 37 et seq.

"STATE ACTION"
Fourteenth Amendment, 921 et seq.
    Authorization, 948 et seq.
    Encouragement, 948 et seq.
    Involvement, 942 et seq.
    Nexus theory, 936 et seq.
    Public function theory, 928 et seq.

STATE AUTONOMY, 206 et seq.

STRICT SCRUTINY
Due process, 516 et seq.
Equal protection, 663 et seq.

SUNDAY CLOSING LAWS, 1478 et seq.

SUPREME COURT AUTHORITY
Congressional control, 74 et seq.
Rules, 68 et seq.
State court decisions,
    Adequate state grounds, 69 et seq.
    Authority to review, 60.
    State resistance, 64 et seq.
    Statutory basis, 66 et seq.
Workload, 69 et seq.

SUSPECT CLASSIFICATIONS
See Equal Protection.

SYMBOLIC SPEECH
See Freedom of Expression.

TAXATION
National,
    Regulatory impacts, 228 et seq.
    State immunities, 351 et seq.
State,
    Commerce, 350.
    Federal immunities, 89 et seq., 351 et seq.
    Use taxes, 288.

TAXPAYERS' SUITS, 37 et seq.

TENTH AMENDMENT
Commerce power, 207 et seq.
Congressional term limits, 127–128.

TERM LIMITS
Congressional representatives, state regulation, 115 et seq.

THIRTEENTH AMENDMENT, 420 et seq., 978 et seq.

TREATIES
Basis for legislation, 252 et seq.
Executive agreements, 365 et seq.
Limitations on, 254 et seq.

UNCONSTITUTIONALITY
Effect of ruling, 6.

VAGUENESS, 1023–1024 et seq., 1392.

VOTING
Congressional power, 985 et seq.
Equal protection scrutiny, 858 et seq.
First Amendment, 880 et seq.
Reapportionment, 865 et seq.
    Racial redistricting, 839 et seq.
Term limits, state regulation, 115 et seq.

WAGE REGULATION
National, 191.
State, 472.

WAR POWERS
Congressional control of executive authority, 371 et seq.
Economic regulation, 250 et seq.

WASTE DISPOSAL
Commerce power, 213.

WELFARE LEGISLATION
Conditions, 244 et seq.
Equal protection scrutiny, 901 et seq.

WOMEN
Autonomy, 530 et seq.
Discrimination, 681 et seq.

WORKING CONDITIONS
National regulation, 173, 191 et seq.
State regulation, 460.

ZONING, 486 et seq.
Standing to sue, 30 et seq.

†

1-56662-453-3